MEDIEVAL SCANDINAVIA

Garland Encyclopedias of the Middle Ages (Vol. 1)
Garland Reference Library of the Humanities (Vol. 934)

MEDIEVAL SCANDINAVIA

AN ENCYCLOPEDIA

PHILLIP PULSIANO
Editor

KIRSTEN WOLF
Co-editor

Paul Acker
Associate Editor

Donald K. Fry
Associate Editor

ADVISERS

Knut Helle
Universitetet i Bergen

Göran Hallberg
Dialekt-och Orntnamnsarkivet i Lund

Vésteinn Ólason
Háskóli Íslands

James E. Knirk
Universitetet i Oslo

David M. Wilson
British Museum

Garland Publishing, Inc.
New York & London 1993

Library of Congress Cataloging–in–Publication Data

Medieval Scandinavia: an encyclopedia/Phillip Pulsiano, editor;
    Kirsten Wolf, co-editor; Paul Acker, associate editor, Donald K. Fry,
    associate editor; advisers, Knut Helle . . . [et al.].
    p. cm. — (Garland reference library of the humanities; vol. 934. Garland encyclopedias of the Middle Ages;
    v. 1)
    Includes index.
    ISBN 0-8240-4787-7
    1. Scandinavia–Civilization–encyclopedias. 2. Northmen–Encyclopedias.
I. Pulsiano, Phillip, 1955–. II. Wolf, Kirsten, 1959– . III. Series: Garland reference library of the humanities.
Garland encyclopedias of the Middle Ages; v. 1.

DL30. M43 1993
948'.02'03—dc20
                                                92–19300
                                              CIP

Printed on acid-free, 250-year-life paper
Manufactured in the United States of America

CONTENTS

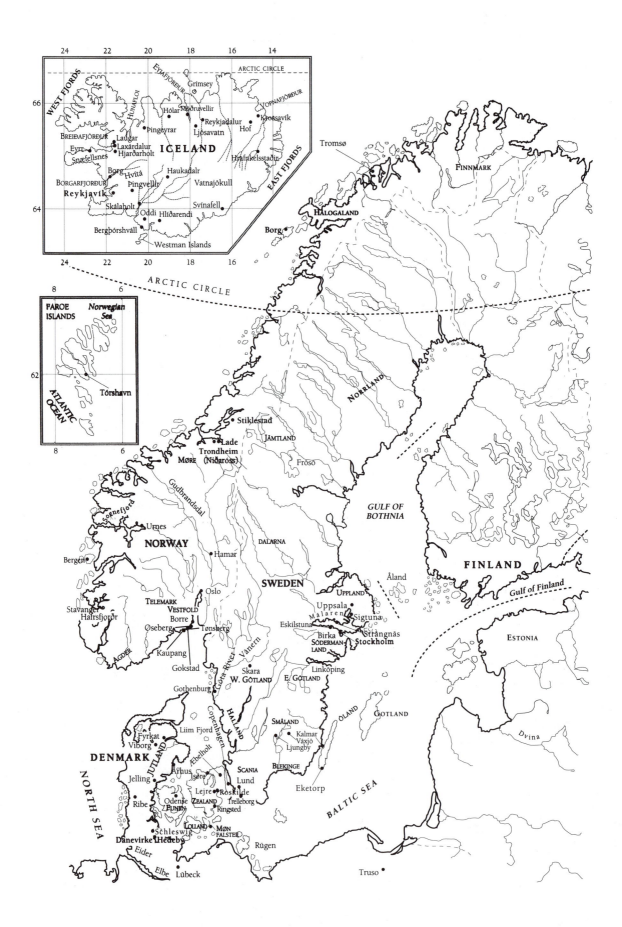

ICELAND

ARCTIC CIRCLE

WEST FJORDS
EYJAFJÖRÐUR
Grímsey
VOPNAFJÖRÐUR
HÚNAFLÓI
Hólar Möðruvellir
Reykjadalur
Krossavík
BREIÐAFJÖRÐUR
Laugar
Þingeyrar
Ljósavatn
Hof
Laxárdalur
Eyrr
Hjarðarholt
Snæfellsnes
Hrafnkelsstaðir
Borg Hvítá
Haukadalr
Vatnajökull
Pingvellir
Skálaholt
Svínafell
Oddi Hlíðarendi
Bergþórshváll
Westman Islands
Reykjavík

FAROE ISLANDS
Norwegian Sea
Tórshavn
ATLANTIC OCEAN

EAST FJORDS

Tromsø

FINNMARK

HÁLOGALAND

Borg

NORRLAND

Stiklestad

JÄMTLAND

Lade
Trondheim (Niðaróss)
MØRE
Frösö

GULF OF BOTHNIA

Gudbrandsdal

Sognefjord
Urnes

NORWAY

Bergen
Hamar
DALARNA

FINLAND

Gulf of Finland

Oslo

SWEDEN

UPPLAND
Åland
Uppsala
Målaren
Sigtuna
Eskilstuna
Strängnäs
Birka
Stockholm
SÖDERMAN-
LAND

ESTONIA

TELEMARK
VESTFOLD
Borre
Oseberg
Tønsberg
Kaupang
Gokstad
AGDER
Stavanger
Hafrsfjorð

Skara
Linköping
W. GÖTLAND
E. GÖTLAND

Dvina

Gothenburg
Göta River
Vänern

GOTLAND

ÖLAND

SMÅLAND
Kalmar
Växjö
Ljungby

Copenhagen
HALLAND

Liim Fjord
Fyrkat
Viborg

BLEKINGE
Eketorp

DENMARK
JUTLAND
Ebelholt
Århus
Isøre
SCANIA
Lund
Jelling
Lejre Roskilde
Trelleborg
Odense
ZEALAND
Ribe
FUNEN
Ringsted
BALTIC SEA

NORTH SEA
LOLLAND
MØN
FALSTER
Schleswig
Danevirke Hedeby
Rügen
Eider
Elbe Lübeck
Truso

PREFACE

Medieval Scandinavia: An Encyclopedia offers students who lack command of the various Scandinavian languages a basic tool for the study of medieval Scandinavia, or more precisely, *Norden* (comprising Denmark, Finland, Iceland, Norway, and Sweden) from roughly the Migration Period to the Reformation. As the twenty-one volumes of the *Kulturhistorisk Leksikon for nordisk middelalder* attest, the subject is both complex and vast. We thus make no claims to completeness, but strove to present a balanced, informative, and up-to-date reference work. While the volume is directed toward students, we hope that scholars too will find the work a useful tool, one that offers not only a synthesis of current scholarship, but new views on a variety of subjects.

The volume was begun in 1985, and its initial scope and design were markedly different from the final product; it was, in all, to be a much slimmer volume—roughly one quarter the size of the present work. The volume grew as our own understanding of the complexity of the task matured. Yet, from early on in the project, we stayed firm in our belief that the reader would best be served by generally lengthier entries rather than by a proliferation of brief entries; breadth without depth seemed a compromise ill-suited to the needs of our intended readers. Although this decision meant that fewer entries would be included, we believe that the reader, especially students at various levels of skill, will come away from the volume better informed and with a clearer sense of direction in pursuing further a given topic. The decision to expand the scope of the volume while maintaining a balance among its entries posed numerous obstacles, not the least of which was locating contributors for the growing variety of topics. As our list of entries grew along with the number of contributors to the volume (of which there are over 250), earlier estimates for the work's completion were set aside; further delays were caused by aging computing equipment. More decisive were the delays caused by the necessity of checking bibliographical citations, which, as one would expect, are extensive in such a work.

Entries within the volume are arranged alphabetically as follows: a, b, c, d, ð, e, f, g, h, i, j, k, l, m, n, o, p, q, r, s, t, þ, u, ü, v, w, x, y, z, ä, æ, ö, ø, œ, ǫ, å. No distinction is made between short and long vowels in alphabetization. Icelandic conventions are adhered to in the treatment of Icelandic personal names as headwords and within the bibliographies. Thus, a reader would look under Bragi Boddason, not under Boddason, Bragi, for the entry on this particular skaldic poet. Entries range in length from *ca.* 150 words to *ca.* 5,000 words.

Each entry is accompanied by a bibliography. While readers unfamiliar with the Scandinavian languages and with German may express frustration at the inclusion of foreign titles, the editors nevertheless remained conscious of their needs while seeking to avoid misrepresenting scholarship by restricting bibliographies to works written in English. Encyclopedias often contain bibliographies that are highly abbreviated, thus requiring a reader to turn continuously to the prefatory list of abbreviations; and even with this aid, bibliographical entries are often so severely clipped as to lead the reader into confusion. We have brought some relief to the reader by spelling out bibliographical citations in full, including, for books, series titles, editors (where appropriate), and publishers. For articles, pagination and volume numbers are supplied. We use only one abbreviation in the bibliographies, since the work is commonly cited: *KLNM = Kulturhistorisk Leksikon for nordisk middelalder.* Bibliographies are divided into a number of sections: Editions (Ed.), Lexicographical aids (Lex.), Bibliographies (Bib.), Translations (Tr.), and Literature (Lit.). Some bibliographies contain subsections, which we have indicated in boldface. Cross-references to other entries within the volume appear at the end of an entry and are complemented by an index appearing at the end of the volume. Additional cross-references as headwords appear throughout the volume. The cross-references to other entries or headwords within the volume are uncomplicated and should present no problems for the reader. Where appropriate, by-names and foreign terms are translated parenthetically within the entry.

Although the editors played a very active, at times perhaps overbearing role in the execution of their tasks, the entries nonetheless reflect the scholarship and views of the individual writers. While contributors were free to choose their own method and focus, the particular views of an author are generally set within a balanced critical context. Thus, readers can expect to find in these pages traces of critical debate upon a variety of issues as well as a synthesis of scholarship. Entries range from detailed discussions of, for example, individual works, artifacts, and historical figures to broad surveys of a variety of subjects, such as genres, historical movements, art, and, broader still, particular countries.

We would like to thank the Fulbright Foundation for a collaborative research grant for 1985–86, which allowed for two of the editors to conduct preliminary research in Iceland on the project. Jakob Benediktsson graciously discussed with us his own experiences as one of the editors of the *Kulturhistorisk Leksikon for nordisk middelalder;* his advice and wit were welcome antidotes to the difficulties such a project as this one posed. We are grateful for the courtesy shown to us by the staff of the Stofnun Árna Magnússonar á Íslandi in according us a place in the institute in 1985–86, and to Helgi Þorláksson in particular for drafting an initial list of entry-titles for the historical items in this volume. Knut Helle has been a wellspring of sound advice and did much to identify contributors to the project. The editor and co-editor also wish to express their thanks to Richard Perkins and Peter Foote for an invitation to discuss the project at University College London in 1987 and to Anthony Faulkes for extending his hospitality to them at the University of Birmingham. Mary Ellen Faturri worked as a research assistant on the project in 1989–90, and René Luthe picked up the banner in 1990–91; both provided valuable assistance in searching out bibliographical references. Mary Quilter, formerly of the interlibrary-loan office at Falvey Memorial Library, Villanova University, was enormously helpful in securing items for the volume. Villanova University was especially supportive throughout this project, providing support services, research assistants, leave of absence in 1985–86, and a Summer Faculty Research Assistantship in 1985. Sincere thanks are also due to Gary Kuris of Garland Publishing for his support and patience and for his careful reading of the manuscript in its final stages, to Chuck Bartelt, who moved the volume through the press, and to Jón Skaptason for his assistance with computer problems at various times throughout the project. We are also grateful to Mary Catherine Staples for her help with certain technical terms. Finally, we would like to thank the contributors for their willingness to write for the volume and for their patience over the years it has taken to prepare this work.

It is difficult to detail the various duties of each of the editors, since overlap is inevitable in a project of this sort. While the task of editing the entries fell to each editor, Donald K. Fry was responsible, in the main, for matters of style, and Paul Acker, who worked with the editor and, later, with Kirsten Wolf on developing the initial list of entries, devoted much of his attention to bibliographical matters in the early and middle stages of the project. Kirsten Wolf's broad knowledge of Old Norse, her attention to detail, and her bibliographical work brought decided focus to the editing of the entries. She was also responsible for the bulk of the translations of the entries, for which she has this editor's deepest gratitude. For the editor's part, after the many years of daily work on this project, he wishes only to say *jucundi acti labores. Deo gratias!*

Phillip Pulsiano

CONTRIBUTORS

Paul Acker
St. Louis University
St. Louis, Missouri

   Alvíssmál
   Valla-Ljóts saga

Björn Ambrosiani
Riksantikvarieämbetet
Statens Historiska Museum
Stockholm, Sweden

   Birka

Frederic Amory
University of San Francisco
San Francisco, California

   Kennings
   Sólarljóð

Mikael Andersen
Skanderborg, Denmark

   Tools and Utensils
   Transport

+Philip N. Anderson
Portland, Oregon

   Guðrúnarhvǫt
   Lokasenna
   Oddrúnargrátr

Árni Björnsson
Þjóðminjasafn Íslands
Reykjavík, Iceland

   Laurentius saga biskups

Ásdís Egilsdóttir
Háskóli Íslands
Reykjavík, Iceland

   Biskupa sögur

Reidar Astås
Eik lærerhøgskole
Tønsberg, Norway

   Leiðarvísan
   Óláfr, St.
   Style: West Norse

Sverre Bagge
Universitetet i Bergen
Bergen, Norway

   Education
   Hirð
   Oratio contra clerum Norvegiae

Søren Balle
Aarhus Universitet
Århus, Denmark

   Aggesen, Sven
   Encomium Emmae reginae
   Harald Gormsson (Bluetooth)
   Knud (Cnut) the Great
   Margrethe I
   Valdemar

Jørgen H. P. Barfod
Lyngby, Denmark

   Warfare

Geraldine Barnes
University of Sydney
New South Wales, Australia

   Elis saga ok Rósamundu
   Erex saga
   Ívens saga
   Parcevals saga
   Riddarasögur (Translated)

Michael P. Barnes
University College London
London, England

   Language

Marcel M. H. Bax
Rijksuniversiteit Groningen
Groningen, Netherlands

   Hárbarðsljóð
   Senna–Mannjafnaðr

Otto B. Bekken
Agder distrikthøgskole
Kristiansand, Norway

   Algorismus

Ole Jørgen Benedictow
Universitetet i Oslo
Oslo, Norway

   Demography
   Family Structure
   Plague

John Bergsagel
Københavns Universitet
Copenhagen, Denmark

Music and Musical Instruments

Paul Bibire
Cambridge University
Cambridge, England

Hungrvaka
Magnúss saga helga eyjajarls
Páls saga biskups
Þorláks saga helga

Ingmar Billberg
Malmö Museer
Malmö, Sweden

Settlement, Rural

Alan Binns
Stiftung Louisenlund
Dannewerk, Germany

Navigation
Ships and Shipbuilding

Bjarni Einarsson
Stofnun Árna Magnússonar á Íslandi
Reykjavík, Iceland

Ágrip af Nóregs konunga sǫgum
Egill Skalla-Grímsson
Egils saga Skalla-Grímssonar
Fagrskinna
Gunnlaugs saga ormstungu
Íslendingadrápa
Skáldasǫgur

Benjamin Blaney
Mississippi State University
Mississippi State, Mississippi

Berserkr

Charlotte Blindheim
Universitetet i Oslo
Oslo, Norway

Borre
Kaupang

Alan Boucher
Cambridge, England

Einars þáttr Skúlasonar

Régis Boyer
Université de Paris-Sorbonne
Paris, France

Alcuin: De virtutibus et vitiis
Drauma-Jóns saga
Flóres saga konungs ok sona hans
Gregory, St.: Dialogues
Hrings saga ok Tryggva
Svarfdœla saga
Þórðar saga hreðu

S. A. J. Bradley
University of York
York, England

Mandevilles Rejse

Peter Buchholz
University of South Africa
Pretoria, South Africa

Religion, Pagan Scandinavian

Jesse L. Byock
University of California, Los Angeles
Los Angeles, California

Alþingi
Bóndi
Goði
Hólmganga
Outlawry

Olav Bø
Universitetet i Oslo
Oslo, Norway

Ballads: Norway

Calum Campbell
Edinburgh, Scotland

Áns saga bogsveigis

Birte Carlé
Odense Universitet
Odense, Denmark

Flóres saga ok Blankiflúr

Helen Carron
University College London
London, England

Dunstanus saga
Ísleifs þáttr biskups
Játvarðar saga

Martin Chase, S.J.
John Carroll University
Cleveland, Ohio

Christian Poetry: West Norse
Einarr Skúlason

Michael Chesnutt
Københavns Universitet
Copenhagen, Denmark

Folklore
Helga þáttr ok Úlfs
Orkneyinga saga

Arne Emil Christensen
Universitetet i Oslo
Oslo, Norway

Gokstad
Oseberg

Eric Christiansen
New College, Oxford
Oxford, England

Saxo Grammaticus

Marit Christoffersen
Agder distriktshøgskole
Kristiansand, Norway

Algorismus

Marlene Ciklamini
Rutgers University
New Brunswick, New Jersey

Ásmundar saga kappabana
Gísls þáttr Illugasonar
Ketils saga hœngs
Sturla Þórðarson

Carol J. Clover
University of California, Berkeley
Berkeley, California

Hallfreðar saga
Kormáks saga
Þorsteins saga hvíta

Margaret Clunies Ross
University of Sydney
New South Wales, Australia

Bragi Boddason
Eilífr Goðrúnarson
Encyclopedic Literature
Fornafn
Heiti
Þjóðólfr of Hvin
Úlfr Uggason

David W. Colbert
Seattle, Washington

Ballads: Introduction
Ballads: Denmark

Robert Cook
Háskóli Íslands
Reykjavík, Iceland

Grettis saga
Kirialax saga
Klári (Clári) saga
Rémundar saga keisarasonar
Vápnfirðinga saga

Margaret Cormack
Smith College
Northampton, Massachusetts

Theodoricus: Historia de
antiquitate regum
Norwagiensium

Edward J. Cowan
University of Guelph
Guelph, Ontario, Canada

Orkney, Norse in
Scotland, Norse in

Barbara E. Crawford
University of St. Andrews
St. Andrews, Scotland

Caithness

Göran Dahlbäck
Stockholms Universitet
Stockholm, Sweden

Sweden

Troels Dahlerup
Aarhus Universitet
Århus, Denmark

Church Organization and Function:
Denmark

Helen Damico
University of New Mexico
Albuquerque, New Mexico

Sǫrla þáttr
Women in Eddic Poetry

Tommy Danielsson
Ludvika, Sweden

Hrafns þáttr Guðrúnarsonar
Jǫkuls þáttr Búasonar
Kjalnesinga saga
Odds þáttr Ófeigssonar
Sneglu-Halla þáttr
Þorgríms þáttr Hallasonar
Þorsteins þáttr sǫgufróða
Þorvarðar þáttr krákunefs

Dafney Davidson
New York, New York

Hákon góði ("the good") Haraldsson
Hákon jarl ("earl") Sigurðarson

Hans Jacob Debes
Fróðskaparsetur Føroya
Tórshavn, Faroe Islands

Faroe Islands

Peter Dinzelbacher
Salzburg, Austria

Ansgar, St.
Draumkvæde
Visionary Literature

M. J. Driscoll
Oxford, England

Ectors saga ok kappa hans
Gibbons saga
Love Poetry: West Norse
Mírmanns saga
Nitida saga
Sálus saga ok Nikanors
Sigurðar saga fóts ok Ásmundar
húnakongs
Sigurðar saga turnara
Sigurðar saga þǫgla
Vilhjálms saga sjóðs

Sten Ebbesen
Københavns Universitet
Copenhagen, Denmark

Boethius de Dacia
Johannes de Dacia
Martinus de Dacia
Sunesen, Anders

Einar G. Pétursson
Stofnun Árna Magnússonar á Íslandi
Reykjavík, Iceland

Codex Regius

Randi Eldevik
Oklahoma State University
Stillwater, Oklahoma

Trójumanna saga

D. A. H. Evans
University College
Dublin, Ireland

Hávamál
Hugsvinnsmál
Viktors saga ok Blávus

Jonathan D. M. Evans
University of Georgia
Athens, Georgia

Friðþjófs saga ins frœkna
Hrólfs saga kraka
Sǫrla saga sterka

Anthony Faulkes
University of Birmingham
Birmingham, England

Harðar saga
Outlaw Sagas
Snorra Edda

Gillian Fellows-Jensen
Københavns Universitet
Copenhagen, Denmark

Hemings þáttr Áslákssonar
Place-names

Ole Fenger
Aarhus Universitet
Århus, Denmark

Laws: Denmark
Social Structure

Edward G. Fichtner
Queens College, City University of New York
Flushing, New York

Auðunar þáttr vestfirzka
Þorsteins þáttr stangarhǫggs

Bjarne Fidjestøl
Universitetet i Bergen
Bergen, Norway

Bjarni Kolbeinsson
Gamli kanóki
Skaldic Verse
Þorbjǫrn hornklofi

†R. G. Finch
University of Glasgow
Glasgow, Scotland

Atlakviða
Atlamál
Þiðreks saga af Bern
Volsung-Niflung Cycle
Vǫlsunga saga

Alison Finlay
Birkbeck College, University of
London
London, England

Bjarnar saga Hítdœlakappa
Brandkrossa þáttr
Droplaugarsona saga
Fljótsdœla saga

Hans Fix
Ernst-Moritz-Arndt-Universität
Greifswald, Germany

Grágás
Jónsbók
Laws: Iceland

Stephen E. Flowers
Austin, Texas

Magic

Peter Foote
University College London
London, England

Conversion
Færeyinga saga
Jóns saga ens helga

Britta Olrik Frederiksen
Københavns Universitet
Copenhagen, Denmark

Bible, East Norse: Denmark
Dyrerim, De gamle danske
Prayer Books: East Norse

Karsten Friis-Jensen
Københavns Universitet
Copenhagen, Denmark

Latin Language and Literature

Birgitta Fritz
Svenskt Diplomatarium, Riksarkivet
Stockholm, Sweden

Royal Administration and
Finances: Sweden

Donald K. Fry
Poynter Institute for Media Studies
St. Petersburg, Florida

Bede

Signe Horn Fuglesang
Universitetet i Oslo
Oslo, Norway

Iconography
Viking Art

Kari Ellen Gade
Indiana University
Bloomington, Indiana

Crime and Punishment
Háttalykill
Þórðr Kolbeinsson

Jürg Glauser
Universität Tübingen
Tübingen, Germany

Ála flekks saga
Bærings saga
Dámusta saga
Dínus saga drambláta
Lygisaga
Magús saga jarls
Sigrgarðs saga frœkna
Sigrgarðs saga ok Valbrands
Supernatural Beings: Draugr,
Aptrganga
Þjalar-Jóns saga
Valdimars saga
Vilmundar saga viðutan

Robert Glendinning
University of Manitoba
Winnipeg, Manitoba, Canada

Guðrúnarkviða I–III

James Graham-Campbell
University College London
London, England

Hoards

Kaaren Grimstad
University of Minnesota
Minneapolis, Minnesota

Elucidarius
Reginsmál and Fáfnismál

Otto Gschwantler
Universität Wien
Vienna, Austria

Hamðismál in fornu
Hymiskviða

Gunnar Harðarson
Reykjavík, Iceland

Hauksbók

Aaron Gurevich
Academija Nauk SSSR
Moscow, (former) U.S.S.R.

Hyndluljóð
Land Tenure and Inheritance

R. A. Hall
York Archaeological Trust
York, England

Five Boroughs
York

Peter Hallberg
Göteborgs Universitet
Gothenburg, Sweden

Eddic Poetry
Sturlunga saga

Joseph Harris
Harvard University
Cambridge, Massachusetts

Grottasǫngr
Gull-Ásu-Þórðar saga
Sigrdrífumál
Þorleifs þáttr jarlsskálds
Þorsteins þáttr Austfirðings

Richard L. Harris
University of Saskatchewan
Saskatoon, Saskatchewan, Canada

Grípisspá
Hjálmþés saga

Kirsten Hastrup
Københavns Universitet
Copenhagen, Denmark

Calendar and Time-reckoning
Cosmography

Einar Haugen
Harvard University
Cambridge, Massachusetts

Dialects

Odd Einar Haugen
Universitetet i Bergen
Bergen, Norway

Nicodemus, Gospel of

Fredrik J. Heinemann
Universität-Gesamthochschule Essen
Essen, Germany

Baldrs draumar

Anne Heinrichs
Freie Universität Berlin
Berlin, Germany

Krákumál
Óláfs saga helga
Reykdœla saga (ok Víga-Skútu)

Wilhelm Heizmann
Universität Göttingen
Göttingen, Germany

Flóamanna saga
Maríu saga

Helgi Þorláksson
Stofnun Árna Magnússonar á Íslandi
Reykjavík, Iceland

Sturlung Age

Knut Helle
Universitetet i Bergen
Bergen, Norway

Norway
Royal Administration and Finances:
  Norway
Towns

Joyce Hill
University of Leeds
Leeds, England

Leiðarvísir
Tristrams saga ok Ísoddar

Thomas D. Hill
Cornell University
Ithaca, New York

Lilja
Rígsþula

Tage Hind
Københavns Universitet
Copenhagen, Denmark

Drama

Marta Hoffmann
Oslo, Norway

Clothmaking

Gösta Holm
Lunds Universitet
Lund, Sweden

Annals: Sweden
Eufemiavisorna
Knittel(vers)
Konung Alexander
Love Poetry: East Norse
Sju vise mästare
Swedish Literature, Miscellaneous

Poul Holm
Fiskeri- og Søfartsmuseet
Esbjerg, Denmark

Ireland, Norse in

†Ludvig Holm-Olsen
Universitetet i Bergen
Bergen, Norway

Konungs skuggsjá
Sverris saga

Elisabeth M. C. van Houts
Newnham College
Cambridge University
Cambridge, England

Norman Literature, Scandinavian
  Influence on
William of Jumièges: Gesta
  Normannorum ducum

Frank Hugus
University of Massachusetts
Amherst, Massachusetts

Blómstrvallasaga

J. R. Hunter
University of Bradford
Bradford, England

Glass

Kai Hørby
Københavns Universitet
Copenhagen, Denmark

Denmark
Royal Administration and Finances:
  Denmark

Lanae H. Isaacson
Stanford University
Stanford, California

Ballads: Faroes

Grethe Jacobsen
Copenhagen, Denmark

Crafts
Guilds
Pregnancy and Childbirth

Jakob Benediktsson
Reykjavík, Iceland

Annals: Iceland (and Norway)
Íslendingabók
Landnámabók
Rómverja saga
Veraldar saga

Alfred Jakobsen
Universitetet i Trondheim
Dragvoll, Norway

Ásbjarnar þáttr selsbana
Eirspennill
Geographical Literature
Jóns þáttr biskups Halldórssonar
Thomas saga erkibiskups
Þrymskviða

Sven-Bertil Jansson
Svenskt visarkiv
Stockholm, Sweden

Ballads: Sweden
Chronicles, Rhymed
Schacktavelslek

Henry A. Jefferies
Luton, England

Cogadh Gaedhel re Galaibh

†Helle Jensen
Københavns Universitet
Copenhagen, Denmark

Eiríks saga víðfǫrla

Judith Jesch
University of Nottingham
Nottingham, England

Hrómundar saga Gripssonar
Illuga saga Griðarfóstra

Jenny Jochens
Towson State University
Towson, Maryland

Coronation
Marriage and Divorce
Succession

Hilding Johansson
Lunds Universitet
Lund, Sweden

Liturgy and Liturgical Texts

Jón Hnefill Aðalsteinsson
Háskóli Íslands
Reykjavík, Iceland

Riddles

Jón Viðar Sigurðsson
Universitetet i Bergen
Bergen, Norway

Hákon Hákonarson
Magnús Hákonarson
Óláfr Tryggvason
Stiklestad, Battle of

Bengt R. Jonsson
Svenskt visarkiv
Stockholm, Sweden

Love Poetry: East Norse

Peter A. Jorgensen
University of Georgia
Athens, Georgia

Exempla
Gríms saga loðinkinna
Hálfdanar saga Brǫnufóstra
Rímur

Marianne E. Kalinke
University of Illinois, Urbana-Champaign
Urbana, Illinois

Jarlmanns saga ok Hermanns
Old Norse–Icelandic Literature,
  Foreign Influence on
Riddarasögur (Indigenous)

Allan Karker
Aarhus Universitet
Århus, Denmark

Jon Præst
Numerals

Lennart Karlsson
Statens Historiska Museum
Stockholm, Sweden

Ironwork
Wood Carving: Denmark and Sweden

Ruth Mazo Karras
University of Pennsylvania
Philadelphia, Pennsylvania

Haraldr harðráði ("hard-ruler")
  Sigurðarson
Haraldr hárfagri ("fair-hair")
  Hálfdanarson
Slavery

I. J. Kirby
University of Lausanne
Lausanne, Switzerland

Bible: West Norse
Christian Prose: West Norse
Stjórn

Anne Kjellberg
Kunstindustrimuseet i Oslo
Oslo, Norway

Textiles, Furnishing

Heinz Klingenberg
Albert-Ludwigs-Universität
Freiburg im Breisgau, Germany

Helgi Poems

James E. Knirk
Universitetet i Oslo
Oslo, Norway

Konungasögur
Runes and Runic Inscriptions:
  Introduction
Runes and Runic Inscriptions:
  Norway

Kolbrún Haraldsdóttir
Universität Erlangen-Nürnberg
Erlangen, Germany

Flateyjarbók

John Kousgård Sørensen
Københavns Universitet
Copenhagen, Denmark

Land Registers
Personal Names

Henry Kratz
University of Tennessee
Knoxville, Tennessee

Hrafnkels saga Freysgoða
Rök Stone
Saints' Lives: Iceland and Norway

Riti Kroesen
Leiden, Netherlands

Gísla saga Súrssonar
Ǫrvar-Odds saga

Sigurd Kværndrup
Skælskør Folkehøjskole
Skælskør, Denmark

Harpestreng, Henrik
Profectio Danorum in Hierosolymam
Saints' Lives: Denmark

Øivind Larsen
Universitetet i Oslo
Oslo, Norway

Medicine and Medical Treatment

Anna Larsson
Uppsala, Sweden

Vadstena Language

Christer Laurén
Vasa Universitet
Vasa, Finland

Bible, East Norse: Sweden

Hans-Emil Lidén
Universitetet i Bergen
Bergen, Norway

Architecture
Churches, Stone
Stave Church
Temples, Heathen

Niels-Knud Liebgott
Nationalmuseet
Copenhagen, Denmark

  Martyrologies
  Pottery
  Reliquaries

Fritze Lindahl
Nationalmuseet
Copenhagen, Denmark

  Jewelry

Thomas Lindkvist
Uppsala Universitet
Uppsala, Sweden

  Feudal Influences and Tendencies

John Lindow
University of California, Berkeley
Berkeley, California

  Brands þáttr ǫrva
  Freyr and Freyja
  Halldórs þáttr Snorrasonar
  Hreiðars þáttr heimska
  Mythology
  Stúfs þáttr
  Þáttr
  Ǫlkofra þáttr

Jonna Louis-Jensen
Københavns Universitet
Copenhagen, Denmark

  Breta sǫgur
  Hulda-Hrokkinskinna
  Morkinskinna

Niels Lund
Københavns Universitet
Copenhagen, Denmark

  Gorm
  Sven Haraldsson (Forkbeard)
  Viking Age

Ellen Marie Magerøy
Riksantikvaren
Oslo, Norway

  Carving: Bone, Horn, and Walrus
    Tusk
  Wood Carving: Norway
  Wood Carving: Iceland

Hallvard Magerøy
Universitetet i Oslo
Oslo, Norway

  Bandamanna saga
  Bǫglunga sǫgur
  Diplomatics
  Ljósvetninga saga
  Political Literature

Magnús Stefánsson
Universitetet i Bergen
Bergen, Norway

  Church Organization and Function:
    Norway
    Iceland

Mary Malcolm
The British Council
Dubai, United Arab Emirates

  Bjǫrn Arngeirsson Hítdœlakappi
  Commemorative Poetry
  Þórarinn loftunga

Rikke Malmros
Aarhus Universitet
Århus, Denmark

  Ágrip af sǫgu Danakonunga
  Knýtlinga saga
  Leiðangr

Sue M. Margeson
Castle Museum
Norwich, England

  Manx Crosses

Margrét Eggertsdóttir
Reykjavík, Iceland

  Finnboga saga ramma
  Gull-Þóris saga
  Gunnars saga Keldugnúpsfífls

Edith Marold
Christian-Albrechts-Universität
Kiel, Germany

  Einarr Helgason skálaglamm
  Eiríksmál
  Eyvindr Finnsson skáldaspillir
  Merlínusspá

Jeffrey A. Mazo
Ilford, England

  Grímnismál
  Vafþrúðnismál

Bernadine McCreesh
Université du Québec à Chicoutimi
Chicoutimi, Quebec, Canada

  Eyrbyggja saga
  Hávarðar saga Ísfirðings

David McDougall
University of Toronto
Toronto, Ontario, Canada

  Homilies (West Norse)

John S. McKinnell
University of Durham
Durham, England

  Vatnshyrna
  Víga-Glúmr Eyjólfsson
  Víga-Glúms saga
  Vǫluspá

Rory McTurk
University of Leeds
Leeds, England

  Kingship
  Ragnars saga loðbrókar

W. I. Miller
University of Michigan
Ann Arbor, Michigan

  Hœnsa-Þóris saga

Stephen Mitchell
Harvard University
Cambridge, Massachusetts

  Fornaldarsögur
  Guta saga
  Óðinn
  Skírnismál

Lennart Moberg
Uppsala, Sweden

  Konungastyrelsen

Bridget Morris
University of Hull
Hull, England

  Birgitta, St.
  Christian Poetry: East Norse
  Christian Prose: East Norse
  Saints' Lives: Sweden
  Vadstena

C. D. Morris
University of Glasgow
Glasgow, England

Birsay

Arthur D. Mosher
University of South Carolina
Columbia, South Carolina

Baldr

Lotte Motz
Oxford, England

Supernatural Beings: Elves, Dwarfs,
and Giants
Svipdagsmál
Vǫlundr

Michael Müller-Wille
Christian-Albrechts-Universität Kiel
Kiel, Germany

Burial Mounds and Practices
Graves
Hedeby

Else Mundal
Universitetet i Oslo
Oslo, Norway

Bookprose/Freeprose Theory
Supernatural Beings: Fylgja
Supernatural Beings: Norns
Women in Sagas

Bjørn Myhre
Universitetet i Oslo
Oslo, Norway

Houses, Rural

Janken Myrdal
Stockholms Universitet
Stockholm, Sweden

Agriculture

Hans-Peter Naumann
Universität Zürich
Zürich, Switzerland

Bósa saga (Herrauðs saga ok Bósa)
Gǫngu-Hrólfs saga
Hálfdanar saga Eysteinssonar
Hrólfs saga Gautrekssonar
Supernatural Beings: Dísir

Arnved Nedkvitne
Universitetet i Bergen
Bergen, Norway

Fishing, Whaling, and Seal Hunting
Hunting
Trade

Anna Nilsén
Uppsala Universitet
Uppsala, Sweden

Painting

Margareta Nockert
Statens Historiska Museer
Stockholm, Sweden

Fashions

Tore Nyberg
Odense Universitet
Odense, Denmark

Adam of Bremen
Erik, St.
Knud (Cnut), St.
Monasticism

Eva Odelman
Riksarkivet
Stockholm, Sweden

Petrus de Dacia

Astrid E. J. Ogilvie
Climatic Research Unit
University of East Anglia
Norwich, England

Climate

Tove Hovn Ohlsson
Helsingborg, Sweden

Tiódels saga

Ólafía Einarsdóttir
Københavns Universitet
Copenhagen, Denmark

Magnúss saga lagabœtis
Sverrir Sigurðarson

Ólafur Halldórsson
Stofnun Árna Magnússonar á Íslandi
Reykjavík, Iceland

Einars þáttr Sokkasonar
Flríssbók
Greenland, Norse in
Jómsvíkinga saga
Óláfs saga Tryggvasonar

Jens E. Olesen
Odense, Denmark

Council of the Realm

Tineke Padmos
Rijksuniversiteit Groningen
Groningen, Netherlands

Hárbarðsljóð
Senna–Mannjafnaðr

Richard Perkins
University College London
London, England

Arabic Sources for Scandinavia(ns)

Russell Poole
Massey University
Palmerston North, New Zealand

Darraðarljóð
Gunnlaugr ormstunga
Lausavísur
Liðsmannaflokkr
Óttarr svarti
Sighvatr Þórðarson

John Porter
University of London
London, England

Arons saga Hjǫrleifssonar

Rosemary Power
Belfast, Northern Ireland

Helga þáttr Þórissonar
Þorsteins þáttr bæjarmagns

Knud Prange
Brønshøj, Denmark

Seals (Sigilla)

Omeljan Pritsak
Harvard University
Cambridge, Massachusetts

Hervarar saga ok Heiðreks konungs
Hlǫðskviða
Rūs'
Varangians

Lise Præstgaard Andersen
Odense Universitet
Odense, Denmark

Maiden Warriors
Partalopa saga

Phillip Pulsiano
Villanova University
Villanova, Pennsylvania

Bárðar saga Snæfellsáss
Bevis saga
England, Norse in
Old English Literature, Norse
  Influence on
Stamford Bridge, Battle of

Fabrizio D. Raschellà
Università degli Studi della Tuscia
Viterbo, Italy

Glossography
Grammatical Treatises

Gad Rausing
Lunds Universitet
Lund, Sweden

Ynglinga saga

Magnus Rindal
Universitetet i Oslo
Oslo, Norway

Barlaams ok Josaphats saga
Laws: Norway

Jannie Roed
University College London
London, England

Þinga saga

Else Roesdahl
Aarhus Universitet
Århus, Denmark

Danevirke
Fortification
Fortresses, Trelleborg
Jelling

Elizabeth Rowe
Stanford University
Stanford, California

Króka-Refs saga
Þorsteins draumr Síðu-Hallssonar
Þorsteins saga Síðu-Hallssonar
Víglundar saga

Geoffrey Russom
Brown University
Providence, Rhode Island

Eddic Meters
Íþróttir

Christopher Sanders
Ordbog over det norrøne prosasprog
Københavns Universitet
Copenhagen, Denmark

Strengleikar

Gudmund Sandvik
Universitetet i Oslo
Oslo, Norway

Þing

Carlo Santini
Università di Perugia
Perugia, Italy

Historia Norwegiae

Paul Schach
University of Nebraska
Lincoln, Nebraska

Fóstbrœðra saga
Gunnars saga Þiðrandabana
Hákonar saga gamla Hákonarsonar
Hákonar saga Ívarssonar
Heiðarvíga saga
Saga

Erik Schia
Oldsaksamlingen
Utgravningskontoret for Oslo
Oslo, Norway

Houses, Urban

Jens Peter Schjødt
Aarhus Universitet
Århus, Denmark

Loki
Þórr

Herman Schück
Stockholms Universitet
Stockholm, Sweden

Chancery
Chronicles: Sweden
Royal Assemblies

Hubert Seelow
Universität Erlangen-Nürnberg
Erlangen, Germany

Hálfs saga ok Hálfsrekka

Rudolf Simek
Universität Wien
Vienna, Austria

Cosmology
Egils saga einhenda ok Ásmundar
  berserkjabana
Encyclopedic Literature
Mǫttuls saga
Samsons saga fagra
Þorsteins saga Víkingssonar

Jeffrey L. Singman
Middle English Dictionary
University of Michigan
Ann Arbor, Michigan

Bjǫrn Breiðvíkingakappi
Þórarinn svarti

Elsa Sjöholm
Stockholms Universitet
Stockholm, Sweden

Laws: Sweden

Kolbjørn Skaare
Universitetet i Oslo
Oslo, Norway

Coins and Mints

Bi Skaarup
Københavns Bymuseum
Copenhagen, Denmark

Diet and Nutrition

Tryggve Sköld
Umeå Universitet
Umeå, Sweden

Lapland

Inge Skovgaard-Petersen
Københavns Universitet
Copenhagen, Denmark

Annals: Denmark
Bjarkamál
Brávallaþula
Chronicles: Denmark
Divine Heroes, Native

Povl Skårup
Aarhus Universitet
Århus, Denmark

Karlamagnús saga

Brian Smith
Shetland Archives
Lerwick, Shetland

Shetland, Norse in

Bergljot Solberg
Universitetet i Bergen
Bergen, Norway

Weapons

C. M. Sperberg-McQueen
University of Illinois at Chicago
Chicago, Illinois

Sigurðarkviða in skamma
Sigurðarkviðu, Brot af

Håkon Stang
Universitetet i Oslo
Oslo, Norway

Russia, Norse in

Stefán Karlsson
Stofnun Árna Magnússonar á Íslandi
Reykjavík, Iceland

Guðmundar sögur biskups
Hauksbók
Möðruvallabók

Marie Stoklund
Nationalmuseet
Copenhagen, Denmark

Runes and Runic Inscriptions:
Denmark

Sandra Straubhaar
Michigan State University
East Lansing, Michigan

Skáldkonur

Folke Ström
Göteborgs Universitet
Gothenburg, Sweden

Hallfreðr Óttarsson
Kormákr Ǫgmundarson

Svavar Sigmundsson
Háskóli Íslands
Reykjavík, Iceland

Prayer Books: Iceland and Norway

Lars Svensson
Svenska Akademiens Ordboksredaktion
Lund, Sweden

Alphabet
Palaeography

Sverrir Tómasson
Stofnun Árna Magnússonar á Íslandi
Reykjavík, Iceland

Laxdœla saga
Tristrams saga ok Ísǫndar

Elisabeth Svärdström
Bromma, Sweden

Runes and Runic Inscriptions:
Sweden

Paul Beekman Taylor
Université de Genève
Geneva, Switzerland

Vǫlundarkviða

Börje Tjäder
Uppsala, Sweden

Old Swedish Legendary

Richard F. Tomasson
University of New Mexico
Albuquerque, New Mexico

Settlement, Age of

G. A. van der Toorn-Piebenga
Rijksuniversiteit Groningen
Groningen, Netherlands

Miracles, Collections of

Anne Trygstad
Bozeman, Montana

Järsta Stone

John Tucker
University of Victoria
Victoria, British Columbia, Canada

Plácítus saga and drápa

Þorleifur Hauksson
Uppsala Universitet
Uppsala, Sweden

Árna saga biskups

Erik Ulsig
Aarhus Universitet
Århus, Denmark

Landownership

Jouko Vahtola
University of Oulu
Oulu, Finland

Finland

Paula Vermeyden
Universiteit van Amsterdam
Amsterdam, Netherlands

Gautreks saga

Vésteinn Ólason
Háskóli Íslands
Reykjavík, Iceland

Ballads: Iceland
Íslendingasögur
Njáls saga
Vatnsdœla saga

+Erik Wahlgren
San Diego, California

America, Norse in
Kensington Stone
"Maine Coin"
Viking Hoaxes
Vinland Map
Vinland Sagas

Birgitta Linderoth Wallace
Canadian Parks Service
Halifax, Nova Scotia, Canada

L'Anse aux Meadows

Diana Edwards Whaley
University of Newcastle upon Tyne
Newcastle upon Tyne, England

Árnórr Þórðarson jarlaskáld
Heimskringla
Skáld
Skaldic Meters
Snorri Sturluson
Sæmundr Sigfússon inn fróði

Kirsten Williams
University College London
London, England

Dudo of St.-Quentin: De moribus et
    actis primorum normanniæ ducum

David M. Wilson
British Museum
London, England

Man, Isle of

William Winter
Western New Mexico University
Silver City, New Mexico

Hanseatic League

Kirsten Wolf
University of Manitoba
Winnipeg, Manitoba, Canada

Alexanders saga
Amicus and Amileus
Gyðinga saga
Jóns saga leiksveins
Legenda
Melkólfs saga ok Salomons konungs
Pamphilus ok Galathea
Physiologus
Postola sögur
Reykjahólabók
Skarðsbók
Skjǫldunga saga
Visio Tnugdali
Yngvars saga víðfǫrla

Lars Wollin
Uppsala Universitet
Uppsala, Sweden

Style: East Norse

Stefanie Würth
Universität München
Munich, Germany

Helreið Brynhildar
Hrómundar þáttr hálta
Nornagests þáttr
Þorvalds þáttr tasalda
Qgmundar þáttr dytts ok Gunnars
    helmings

Hugo Yrwing
Lund, Sweden

Gotland

Horst Zettel
Friedrich-Alexander-Universität
Erlangen, Germany

France, Norse in
Germany, Norse in

Otto J. Zitzelsberger
Rutgers University
Newark, New Jersey

Adonias saga
Flóvents saga Frakkakonungs
Konráðs saga keisarasonar
Sturlaugs saga starfsama

Adam of Bremen, known solely by his work *Gesta Hammaburgensis ecclesiae pontificum*, was presumably a canon from a cathedral school in Bavaria or Franconia (Bamberg?). He arrived in Bremen 1066/7 at the request of Archbishop Adalbert of Hamburg-Bremen (1043–1072) and became the archbishop's "expert" in missionary matters. After extensive studies in his new field, he wrote the *Descriptio insularum aquilonis*, which forms the fourth book of his *Gesta*. The first three books contain the story of the archbishops, beginning, after an introduction on the Saxons, with the first three bishops of Bremen (–845) (Book 1:11–23). Adam deals extensively with Ansgar (d. 865), the monk of Corvey and missionary of Scandinavia, thereby reproducing the general outlook of Rimbert's *Vita Anskarii* in making Ansgar archbishop of Hamburg in 832, having him succeed to the vacant bishopric of Bremen in 847 (1:15–34). For the period *ca.* 950 to Alebrand (d. 1043) (1:35–63, 2:1–82), Adam had access to sources in the cathedral archive of Bremen concerning ecclesiastical matters, such as lists of suffragan bishops consecrated. But he stresses as a most valuable informant the Danish king Sven Estridsen (1047–1074/5), whom he visited in Denmark probably around 1068/9. Missionary bishops returning to Bremen with reports also afforded valuable information. In Book 3:1–71 (3:72–78 is a transitional passage to the *Descriptio*), Adam, in a grandiose way, creates a portrait of the tragic decline of Archbishop Adalbert and his betrayal, yet faithfulness toward the religious duties of his office. Adam wants to prove that whatever Adalbert did wrong, he never forgot his task to care for the Scandinavian mission, and, therefore, that the archbishopric is indispensable for the spread of the Gospel to Scandinavia.

Book 4:1–9 describes the Danes, 4:21–30 the Swedes (*sueones* or *suedi*); between them, a passage on the Baltic Sea with its islands and shores has been inserted (4:11–20), followed by a section on the Norwegians (4:31–34) and the islands of the "Ocean" (4:35–44). Adam shows particular interest in formulating a measured judgment of the non-Christian habits of the Scandinavian, Slavic, and Baltic peoples, but he also stresses their vices, thereby demonstrating that conversion is necessary. His famous description of the pagan temple of the *sueones*, *Ubsola*, incorporates material from myth, and could be a literary fiction to enhance the urgency of missionary efforts. Especially in Books 1–3, Adam displays his classical reading; the influence of Cicero,

Sallust, Vergil, Lucan, Terence, Horace, Ovid, Persius, Statius, and Juvenal is clearly discernible (Piltz). The geographical information on Scandinavia is valuable, since in most cases it is the earliest we have. But it rests upon hearsay, except for parts concerning the Danish islands, which Adam may have visited himself. Adalbert died before the *Gesta* was finished, and the work was dedicated to his successor Liemar. Adam is believed to have lived into the 1080s, since he seems to have been the author of many of the added *scholia*. The MS tradition begins around 1100 with part of Book 2, and has been divided into three branches: the A group (most original), the B (Danish), and the C (German) MS (Schmeidler).

Ed.: Migne, J.-P., ed. *Mag. Adami. Gesta Hammaburgensis Ecclesiæ Pontificum. Patrologiae Cursus Completus, Series Latina*. Paris: Garnier, 1884, vol. 146, cols. 451–662; Schmeidler, Bernhard, ed. *Magistri Adami Bremensis Gesta Hammaburgensis Ecclesiae Pontificum*. Monumenta Germaniae Historica, Scriptores rerum Germanicarum in usum scholarum, 2. Hannover and Leipzig: Bibliopolii Hahniani, 1917; Christensen, C. A., ed. *Adamus Bremensis Gesta Hammaburgensis Ecclesiae Pontificum. Codex Havniensis. Published in photolithography with preface by C. A. Christensen*. Copenhagen: Rosenkilde & Bagger, 1948. **Tr.**: Adam of Bremen. *History of the Archbishops of Hamburg-Bremen*. Trans. Francis J. Tschan. Records of Civilization: Sources and Studies. New York: Columbia University Press, 1959. **Bib.**: Tschan, pp. 230–8 [see above]; Kristensen, pp. 213–6 [see below]; Hallencrevtz, Carl Fredrik, *et al.*, pp. 409–21 [see below]. **Lit.**: Kristensen, Anne K. G. *Studien zur Adam von Bremen Überlieferung: Die Wiener Handschrift, Erstredaktion oder später verkürzte Fassung?* Skrifter udgivet af det Historiske Institut ved Københavns Universitet, 5. Copenhagen: Københavns Universitet, Historisk Institut, 1975; Hallencreutz, Carl Fredrik, *et al.*, eds. *Adam av Bremen. Historien om Hamburgstiftet och dess biskopar*. Trans. Emanuel Svenberg. Stockholm: Proprius, 1984 [pp. 295–407 comprise the following articles: Nyberg, Tore. "Stad, skrift och stift. Några historiska inledningsfrågor," pp. 295–339; Piltz, Anders. "Adam, bibeln och auctores. En studie i litterär teknik," pp. 340–53; Hallencreutz, Carl Fredrik, "Adam, Sverige och trosskiftet. Det missionsvetenskapliga perspektivet," pp. 354–78; Johannesson, Kurt. "Adam och hednatemplet i Uppsala," pp. 379–407]; Hallencreutz, Carl Fredrik. *Adam Bremensis and Sueonia: A Fresh Look at Gesta Hammaburgensis Ecclesiae Pontificum*. Acta Universitatis Upsaliensis C: Organisation och historia, 47. Uppsala: Almqvist & Wiksell, 1984; Nyberg, Tore. *Die Kirche in Skandinavien.*

Mitteleuropäischer und englischer Einfluss im 11. und 12. Jahrhundert. Beiträge zur Geschichte und Quellenkunde des Mittelalters, 10. Sigmaringen: Thorbecke, 1986, esp. pp. 24–35; Nyberg, Tore. "Adam av Bremen och terminologi." *Fornvännen* 82 (1987), 115–26.

Tore Nyberg

[See also: Church Organization and Function; Conversion]

Adonias saga

Adonias saga ("The Saga of Adonias"), an indigenous Icelandic *riddarasaga* from the late 14th century, is extant in forty-five MS copies, eight of which are vellums that all show lacunae or are otherwise defective. Of these, the oldest is probably AM 567 VI b 4to, a single-leaf fragment from about 1400; all the remaining vellums evidently were written at various times later in the 15th century. AM 593 4to, uniquely among the preserved vellums, contains a prologue as well as a pious conclusion given by the copyist in a set of three rhyming couplets. The only edition, admittedly a "provisional" one, so far printed of *Adonias saga* is based on this MS, and it is from the text given there that the following summary is made.

In the prologue, the copyist complains discursively about the amassing of worldly goods and about pride and avarice. The following chapter details the division of the world by the sons of Noah.

The saga proper begins in the next chapter. King Marsilius of Syria is told by his wife, Queen Semerana from India, who is versed in astrology, that in a year's time the stars will be especially propitious for the childless couple to conceive a child who eventually will rule the realm, and also that his own life will be short. Constancius, a powerful, sinister duke, overhears the conversation, and on the specified day he has Marsilius forcibly taken into a building where he is locked in a bedchamber with Remedia, the duke's daughter. Smitten by her beauty, Marsilius deflowers the reluctant maiden, who then informs him that baleful things lie in store for him. At the same time, the duke, unrecognized by the king's wife, impregnates her. After Marsilius is taken back to his court, he is silent about what has happened. Semerana gives birth to a son who is named Constantinus, while Remedia secretly bears a son named Adonias. At a banquet at which the infant Constantinus is brought forward, Marsilius, unable to control his rage, calls the lad a whoreson and also insults Constancius. After lunging at the latter with his sword, the blustering Marsilius is killed by Constancius, who soon thereafter ascends the throne.

Adonias is reared in seclusion by his mother until, out of increasing fear that Constancius will kill them both, she entrusts him to the safekeeping of King Lodovikus of Spain, whom she subsequently marries. Adonias and Constantinus grow up apace in their respective lands with neither having an equal in physical or mental prowess. Each is dubbed a knight and given a castle with a retinue. But while Constantinus stays at home because his father does not wish him to take part in an offensive against Lodovikus, Adonias shows more initiative. On learning that Syrian forces are approaching Spain, he gathers a large force of giant warriors with whose aid the invaders are repelled. After a long series of military actions, Adonias and Constantinus finally meet face-to-face in single combat. Constantinus is vanquished, but his life is spared by Adonias, who takes him into his retinue. Another lengthy string of offensives and counter-offensives follows, which at the end results in victory for the Spanish forces and ignominious death for Constancius. The saga concludes with the marriage of Adonias to Albaria, daughter of Emperor Teodosius of Italy.

Adonias saga, which runs to seventy-one chapters, is unnecessarily prolonged by its unrelenting account of large-scale military preparations and actions as well as duels and other single encounters. It is also overloaded with the stock banquets, hunting scenes, and hyperbole associated with the genre to which it belongs. Attention is given to descriptions of crude violence and horror for their own sake, as when Constancius is systematically tortured, maimed, and mutilated before at length being hanged, and when defeated and disgraced combatants bow to the victors and beg for decapitation. Thematically, the saga focuses on the struggle between the *falskonungr*, the evil usurper of a throne, who vainly attempts to thwart fate through deception and the use of brute force, and the rightful, foreordained claimant and his trusty helpers. The presentation of parallel pairs of simultaneous occurrences, *e.g.*, defloration of Remedia and seduction of Semarana, birth of Constantinus and birth of Adonias, does more than point up the role of chance in human affairs. In *Adonias saga*, it is a structural device that provides a contrasting double perspective. In the later action as the narrative shifts in place but not in time from one encampment to another, the parallels serve to reduce somewhat the unrelieved monotony of an otherwise strictly linear plot.

Ed.: Widding, Ole, ed. "Om Rævestreger. Et kapitel i Adonius saga." *Opuscula* 1. Bibliotheca Arnamagnæana, 20. Copenhagen: Munksgaard, 1960, pp. 331–4; Loth, Agnete, ed. "Adonias saga." In *Late Medieval Icelandic Romances.* 5 vols. Editiones Arnamagnæanæ, ser. B, vols. 20–4. Copenhagen: Munksgaard, 1962–65, vol. 3, pp. 67–230 [with English résumé translated by Gillian Fellows Jensen]. **Lit.**: Loth, Agnete. "To blade af Adonias saga." *Opuscula* 3. Bibliotheca Arnamagnæana, 29. Copenhagen: Munksgaard, 1967, pp. 194–7 [MS discussion]; Sverrir Tómasson, "The 'fræðisaga' of Adonias." In *Structure and Meaning in Old Norse Literature: New Approaches to Textual Analysis and Literary Criticism.* Ed. John Lindow *et al.* Viking Collection, 3. Odense: Odense University Press, 1986, pp. 378–93.

Otto J. Zitzelsberger

[See also: *Riddarasögur*]

Aggesen, Sven

Aggesen, Sven, is known as the author of the *Brevis historia*, a history of Denmark, ending at 1185. Born about 1140–1150, Sven was a Danish nobleman, the contemporary of Saxo Grammaticus, whom he described as his "contubernalis" ("comrade"). Sven belonged to the Thrugotsen family, which had produced men in high positions, such as the brothers Archbishop Asser of Lund, Bishop Sven of Viborg, and Christian, whose son Eskil became archbishop of Lund (1138–1177) and whose other son Agge was Sven's father. Perhaps both Sven and Saxo were the king's men, perhaps not, as "contubernalis" may only signify that they were in some sense "colleagues" as writers. Sven may have studied in France, judging from his knowledge of the school of Bernard of Chartres (d. ca. 1126). Like Saxo, Sven gave an account of the law of the *hird*, the *Lex castrensis* or *Vederlov*, of which a third contemporary Danish version exists (and perhaps a now-lost fourth, somewhat longer Danish version existed). These three versions are related in some way, although not in the sequence of clauses or in exact wording. They may rest on a common oral tradition, or just be recording the same facts, or they may be interdependent as written sources (Saxo never copies any text word for word). Many of the possible combinations of the three MSS into a stemma giving the line of descent have been tried;

ultimate proof remains lacking. The reliability of the information supplied—e.g., whether this law really goes back to Knud (Cnut) the Great and his hirð, the Þingaliðd—is in question.

Both the *Lex castrensis* and the *Brevis historia* are found together in two MS traditions, designated A and S. These are quite dissimilar (Gertz 1915, 1917). S is a heavily adapted version from the late 13th century, copied from a now-lost MS by Stephen Hansen Stephanius for his 1642 edition (*Suenonis Aggonis filii . . . quæ extant Opuscula* [Sorø, 1642]). MS A (AM 33 4to) had been owned by Claus Christoffersen Lyschander (1558–1624), who was educated as a theologian and became royal historiographer. Probably around 1570, he copied it from a now-lost medieval MS whose many abbreviations and conventional signs he did not understand; so MS A is entirely unintelligible. MS A was reconstructed by Gertz in 1915 as the version X. Sometimes the S version gives the clue to the correct solution in the reconstruction of A; in other cases, the X text rests entirely on Gertz's skill and ingenuity. The two versions S and A (X) differ in the arrangement of the parts; in S, the *Lex* is placed at the end, but in A (X), at the beginning. In X, the introduction to the *Lex* mentions the author's plan to make a genealogy of the Danish kings, but the Lyschander copy only has a short introduction to a genealogy that itself is missing; S has a genealogy, but apparently a different one, based on Saxo. Probably, the *Lex* was written first, around 1178–1185, and the *Brevis historia* shortly after 1185, perhaps with a *Genealogia* written in between.

Ed.: Gertz, M. Cl., ed. *En ny Text af Sven Aggesøns Værker genvunden paa Grundlag af Codex Arnæmagnæanus 33, 4°*. Copenhagen: Gyldendal, 1915 [edition of X with explanation of the reconstruction procedures]; Gertz, M. Cl., ed. "Svenonis Aggonis Filii Opuscula Historica. I. Lex Castrensis. II. Brevis Historia Regum Dacie. III. Series et Genealogiæ Regum Danorum." In his *Scriptores Minores Historiæ Danicæ Medii Ævi*. Selskabet for Udgivelse af Kilder til dansk Historie. Copenhagen: Gad, 1917, vol. 1, pp. 55–156 [parallel edition of X and S; note that S, too, is reconstructed to medieval spelling]. **Tr.**: Gertz, M. Cl., trans. *Sven Aggesøns historiske Skrifter, oversatte efter den paa Grundlag af Codex Arnæmagnæanus 33, 4° restituerede nye Text*. Selskabet for historiske Kildeskrifters Oversættelse. Copenhagen: Schønberg, 1916–17 [Danish translation of X, with an introduction]; Olrik, Jørgen, trans. *Krøniker fra Valdemarstiden*. Selskabet for historiske Kildeskrifters Oversættelse. Copenhagen: Schønberg, 1900–01, pp. 23–116 [Danish translation of S]; Christiansen, Eric, trans. *The Works of Sven Aggesen* [forthcoming Viking Society for Northern Research, Text Series]. **Lit.**: Bolin, Sture. *Om Nordens äldsta historieforskning. Studier över dess metodik och källvärde*. Lunds Universitets årsskrift, N.F. Avd. 1, 27.3. Lund: Ohlsson, 1931, pp. 41–53; Christensen, Aksel E. *Danmarks historie. 1: Tiden indtil 1340*. Copenhagen: Gyldendal, 1977, pp. 358–60, 370–2, 515–79 [with extensive bibliography, esp. to the *Vederlov*]; Christensen, Karsten. *Om overleveringen af Sven Aggesens værker*. Skrifter udgivet af Det historiske institut ved Københavns Universitet, 10. Copenhagen: Den danske historiske forening, 1978 [with extensive references]; Kristensen, Anne K. G. *Danmarks ældste Annalistik. Studier over lundensisk Annalskrivning i 12. og 13. Århundrede*. Skrifter udgivet af Det historiske institut ved Københavns Universitet, 3. Copenhagen: Gyldendal, 1969 [links with Danish annals; with English summary]; Riis, Thomas. *Les institutions politiques centrales du Danemark 1100–1332*. Odense University Studies in History and Social Sciences, 46. Odense: Odense University Press, 1977, pp. 31–47 [about the *Vederlov*]; Weibull, Curt. "Vem var Saxo? Ett diskussionsinlägg." *Historisk tidskrift* (Denmark) 78.1 (1978), 87–96 [German summary]; Weibull, Curt. "Ny och äldre historieskrivning om Danmark under tidlig medeltid." *Historisk tidskrift* (Denmark) 86.1 (1986), 1–25.

Søren Balle

[**See also:** Chronicles; *Hirð*; Saxo Grammaticus]

Agriculture. Barley was the most commonly grown grain in Sweden and Denmark. Rye had an early breakthrough in Finland about 1000–1200. In eastern Sweden and also in parts of Denmark at that time, the cultivation of rye spread more generally in the late Middle Ages and in the 16th century. In Norway, oats were extensively cultivated, together with barley, probably already in the high Middle Ages.

Animal husbandry occupied a strong position in northern Sweden, Finland, and Norway. These regions concentrated on dairy farming, with cows as the most important animal, although goats were also used as milk-producing animals. Even in the woodlands in southern Sweden, northern Scania, and the heaths of Jutland, livestock breeding dominated, although in a more diverse form. Besides milk cows, sheep were also bred in some regions, providing wool and meat. Pigs were raised for their meat. In the late Middle Ages and to a growing extent in the 16th century, oxen were exported in oxen-drives from Denmark and southern Sweden to distant towns and markets.

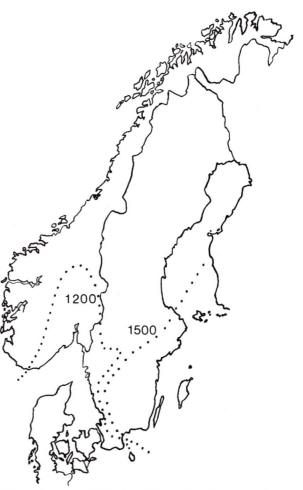

1. Approximate spread of the plow with a mold board *ca.* 1200 and 1500.

In Iceland, grain cultivation disappeared during the late Middle Ages, but animal husbandry had always dominated. From the 15th century, sheep raising expanded at the expense of cattle breeding.

From the middle of the 16th century, it is possible to make fairly accurate estimates of the average farm size in different regions of Scandinavia. Tithe registers are preserved on a larger scale than from the preceding centuries. In addition, wealth taxes were imposed in Sweden/Finland in 1571, and in Denmark in 1564, and the registers have been preserved for most of Sweden/Finland and from two counties in Denmark. From these registers, we can deduce that in the woodlands of northern Scandinavia a normal household had about two draught animals (horses) and four to six cows, with a grain harvest of about 10–20 hectoliters. In the plains of central and southern Scandinavia, a normal household with agricultural production had a stock of about three to six draught animals (oxen and horses) and two to four cows, with a grain harvest of about 20–40 hectoliters. From the late Middle Ages, we have a couple of inventories and some tithe registers that seem to indicate that the average farm at that time was about the same size as the later farms. It is not possible to obtain any more exact information for the preceding centuries.

The earliest certain yield calculations can be made for half a dozen estates in eastern Sweden and in one similar case from Denmark from accounts preserved from the 15th and early 16th century. A normal yield/seed ratio was about 1:3. This ratio is rather low, but not much lower than in other parts of western Europe at this time.

Agriculture must be seen as a system. The work cycle in grain growing spans at least a year from the preparations for the production up to the final product. This work cycle includes several stages, directly or indirectly related to each other. This means that the development of a given implement can be understood only in relation to other implements and techniques. There is also interaction between grain growing and livestock breeding, the animals consuming products from the fields and delivering draft power and manure.

In the Roman Iron Age, roughly the first part of the first millennium A.D., iron was used in Scandinavia to a much lesser extent than in the Roman Empire. The only agricultural tools for which iron was used were small sickles and scythes.

About the middle of the first millennium A.D., the consumption and production of iron quickly grew. The scythes became longer, which meant a much higher productivity in haymaking, since every man could cut more. Equally important was the introduction of iron shares for the ard, a plow without moldboard, dominating Scandinavia at that time. The sickles also became longer and more effective. This greater use of iron was a common development for most of Scandinavia.

The high Middle Ages must be described region by region. In Finland, a new type of slash-and-burn agriculture was introduced in about the 13th century. Instead of cutting deciduous wood to burn, coniferous wood, such as spruce, was cut. This change implied planning over several years, because the spruce had to be left to dry for at least one or two years, compared with hardwood trees, which could be burned the same year they were cut. Since most parts of Finland were covered by coniferous wood, especially spruce, this new method allowed a large extension of the area usable for agricultural production and provided the foundation for a fast-growing population.

Associated with this new type of "swidden" agriculture were several other changes. Rye was replacing barley as the most important grain. The rye mostly used was of a special kind well adapted to swidden agriculture. It had a very coarse straw, but gave high yields. This change was associated with the introduction of a new and better type of sickle, the bow sickle, thus allowing the rye straw to be more easily cut than with the older angled sickle.

The most important implement was the ard, or plow, and even here new technology followed. Use of the *sokha*, an ard with two shares, spread in the eastern parts of Finland. This type of ard suited slash-and-burn culture, where the ground often remained uncleared of stones and tree trunks. Perhaps a simple type of harrow, the twig harrow, was introduced at the same time.

This development can be described as a complex of new agricultural techniques, and it spread to Finland from northern Russia in about the 12th century. This technological complex also played a great role in the rapid colonization of northern Russia. Together with the changes in corn growing, a special type of flail was probably also introduced, facilitating the threshing of a growing grain production.

In Sweden, a new technological complex was introduced about 1000–1200, but with a different content. Even here, the clearing of new land was essential. The ironshod spade did not exist in Sweden or in Scandinavia before 1000, but it then spread generally. This tool facilitated clearing, but was also crucial for the making of ditches. The laws from the 13th century show that ditches had great importance, especially in the eastern parts of Sweden. Archaeological remains indicate that ditches were not introduced on a larger scale until after around 1000. Ditching of the arable lands made it possible to cultivate rather humid soils.

Ard shares were made considerably longer. In the early Middle Ages up to the Viking Age, iron shares had a length of about 10 cm.; in the high Middle Ages, they were normally 20–30 cm. long. This lengthening allowed improved cultivation of the soil and was probably associated with the general introduction of the two-field system in eastern Sweden. In the early Middle Ages, the arable land was planted every year, followed by a long period of fallow. There was no need for tilling the fallow every year as in the two-field system. That greater parts of the arable land were laid fallow and broken every year implied a need for a more effective tilling implement. In southern Scandinavia, we find the plow with a moldboard as the new implement.

Connected with this Swedish shift in soil-tilling technique was the development of improved techniques of grain processing. The flail came more generally into use, replacing the earlier threshing stick. Furthermore, the watermill, and in the 14th century the windmill, was introduced and replaced the handmill, which allowed a dramatic growth of productivity in milling.

In Denmark, the changes were as great as in the northern parts of Scandinavia, but shared more similarities with changes in the rest of western Europe. A strong resemblance was that the introduction of the plow played a major role. The plow spread from the south to the whole of Denmark, including Scania, about 1000–1200 and also spread to western Sweden (Västergötland) and southern Norway during this period. This development meant that tilling was improved. The ridging of fields to counteract moisture was also introduced, and facilitated the introduction of a more developed system of crop rotations. The two-field system spread, and the three-field system also came into use together with an increase in rye cultivation. Another resemblance between Denmark and other parts of western Europe was the reclaiming of arable land from the sea, with dikes built in the fenlands of southwestern Jutland.

The harrow probably belongs to the technological system shift in Scandinavia. In the early Middle Ages, the soil was most likely prepared with earth rakes after the fields had been plowed. The iron-shod spade, the watermill, and presumably also the flail were introduced in Denmark about 1000–1200.

The technological development in Norway is less well known, but seems to have been mainly similar to the change in the rest of Scandinavia, with the introduction of iron-shod spades, longer ard shares, and, in the south, the plow, connected with an extended land reclamation.

There is a less dramatic change in the late Middle Ages. During the 15th century, the plow spread in a second wave of extension to central and northern Sweden and probably also to central Norway. In Finland and eastern Sweden, the ard and the sokha still dominated until the 18th and 19th centuries.

Another common change in the late Middle Ages was a more extensive use of iron. For example, harrows with iron teeth were introduced around 1500, but wood harrows were used along with the iron harrows until the 19th century.

From the 13th century at the latest, the bow sickle gradually spread in Denmark and large parts of Sweden, replacing the angled sickle. This change eventually became associated with the expanding cultivation of rye as a winter crop in these regions during the Middle Ages. A winter crop had coarser straw than a spring crop. Barley and oats were always sown as a spring crop.

In livestock breeding, technical equipment had less importance than in grain growing, except in haymaking. The cattle shed was introduced in most of Scandinavia 500 B.C.–A.D. 500, and therefore haymaking was essential during the Middle Ages.

The development of the scythe in the early Middle Ages was connected with the strong position of livestock breeding at that time. But the technical advances in grain growing led to its increased importance over haymaking or livestock breeding, which had no comparable innovations.

The agrarian crises of the 14th and 15th centuries turned many farms into meadows or pastures. This shift resulted in a relatively stronger position for animal husbandry. In this period, there was probably a change of scythe types in Sweden and Denmark, when the still-used type with a long handle was introduced.

In the high Middle Ages, and certainly also before that, cattle were herded by adult herdsmen. But after the Middle Ages, children and women normally herded the cattle in Norway and Sweden. The first evidence of cattle being tended by women or children comes from the 15th century, and perhaps this change is related to the agrarian crises of the late Middle Ages, with the period's shortage of manpower and growing importance of cattle breeding.

Technology and society, however, cannot be seen in isolation from each other. The technological leap forward about 1000–1200, which has been called the agricultural revolution of the Middle Ages, was contemporary in western Europe and Scandinavia, but it took a rather different form in each region. These differing technological systems suggest that external causes, such as social and economic change, played a decisive role in their development. At the same time, technological change in general, which brought about an increase in the clearing of land and richer crop yields, provided the basis for economic and social changes, such as the founding of towns and the building of castles.

Bib.: Myrdal, Janken. "Medeltidens jordbruk." *Rig* 65 (1983), 17–21 [with an index to articles about agriculture in *KLNM*]. **Lit.**: Steensberg, Axel. *Ancient Harvesting Implements: A Study in Archaeology and Human Geography.* Nationalmuseets skrifter, Arkæologisk-Historisk række, 1. Copenhagen: Gyldendal, 1943; Vilkuna, Kustaa. "Die Pfluggeräte Finnlands." *Studia Fennica* 16 (1971), 5–178; Sølvberg, Ingvild Øye. *Driftsmåter i vestnorsk jordbruk ca. 600–1350.* Bergen: Universitetsforlaget, 1976; Lerche, Grith, and Axel Steensberg. *Agricultural Tools and Field Shapes.* Copenhagen: National Museum of Denmark, 1980; Gissel, Svend, *et al. Desertion and Land Colonization in the Nordic Countries c. 1300–1600.* Stockholm: Almqvist & Wiksell, 1981; Myrdal, Janken. *Medeltidens åkerbruk: Agrarteknik i Sverige ca 1000 till 1520.* Nordiska museets handlingar, 105. Stockholm: Nordiska museet, 1985; Bjørn, Claus, ed. *Det danske landbrugs historie.* Det danske landbrugs historie, 1. Copenhagen: Gad, 1988.

Janken Myrdal

Ágrip af Nóregs konunga sǫgum

Ágrip af Nóregs konunga sǫgum ("Summary of the Sagas of the Kings of Norway") is a late title (17th century) for the oldest preserved history of the kings of Norway in the Old Norse vernacular. *Ágrip* means "summary"; this designation is, however, not really appropriate, even though the work is much shorter than other sagas of the Norwegian kings. Many of its stories are detailed and even verbose. Its proportion is imperfect, and important events may be treated summarily, while minor episodes may receive a substantial presentation.

Ágrip is preserved in only one MS, AM 325 II 4to (Copenhagen), which appears to be an Icelandic copy of a Norwegian original, though hardly the author's own MS. Probably written in the first half of the 13th century, it now contains twenty-four leaves but was originally considerably longer. The first leaf has been cut away as has one leaf later in the text, and a gathering of most likely eight leaves at the end and probably an additional four leaves at another place have been lost. The sagas seem to have begun with Hálfdan svarti ("the black"), the father of Haraldr hárfagri ("fair-hair"), and it now ends in the mid-12th century. The original saga is assumed to have come to an end in 1177, like *Fagrskinna* and *Heimskringla*, which, in view of the probable age of *Ágrip*, assumes that its author knew that *Sverris saga* was being written. The original *Ágrip* may have been composed as early as the last decade of the 12th century, and most likely in Niðaróss (Trondheim). It is reasonable to assume that the author made use of oral traditions about the kings, but it is obvious that he also employed written sources, chiefly the *Historia de antiquitate regum Norwagiensium* by Theodoricus Monachus, probably written shortly before 1188, and the *Historia Norwegiae*, which is difficult to date precisely, so that an unknown common source cannot be excluded. *Ágrip*'s author may also have used a saga about Hákon Aðalsteinsfóstri ("Æthelstan's foster-son"), and most likely lost historical works by the Icelanders Ari Þorgilsson and Sæmundr Sigfússon. Many passages are close translations of the Latin works, but the sources are also used freely with many additions that are not found in comparable sources.

Ágrip is a patriotic Norwegian work. The vocabulary and the style of this saga are unlike the ordinary Icelandic sagas of the 13th century. *Ágrip* was used extensively by the authors of *Fagrskinna*, *Heimskringla*, and *Morkinskinna*. They presumably had access to a better text than the surviving one, which has many faults and omissions that can be attributed to a sloppy copyist.

Ed.: Dahlerup, Verner, ed. *Ágrip af Noregs konunga sögum*. Samfund til udgivelse af gammel nordisk litteratur, 2. Copenhagen: Møller, 1880 [diplomatic edition]; Finnur Jónsson, ed. *Ágrip af Nóregs konunga sǫgum*. Altnordische Saga-Bibliothek, 18. Halle: Niemeyer, 1929; Indrebø, Gustav, ed. *Ágrip, ei liti norsk kongesoge*. Norrøne bokverk, 32. Oslo: Det norske samlaget, 1936 [with modern Norwegian translation]; Bjarni Einarsson, ed. *Ágrip af Nóregskonunga sǫgum; Fagrskinna—Nóregs konunga tal*. Íslenzk fornrit, 29. Reykjavik: Hið íslenzka fornritafélag, 1984. **Lit.**: Storm, Gustav. "Norske Historieskrivere paa Kong Sverres Tid." *Aarbøger for nordisk Oldkyndighed og Historie* (1871), 410–31; Koht, Halvdan. "Sagaernes opfatning av vår gamle historie." *Historisk tidsskrift* (Norway) 5th ser., 2 (1914), 379–420; rpt. in his *Innhogg og utsyn i norsk historie*. Kristiania [Oslo]: Aschehoug, 1921, pp. 76–91; Indrebø, Gustav. "Aagrip." *Edda* 17 (1922), 18–65; Paasche, Fredrik. "Tendens og syn i kongesagaen." *Edda* 17 (1922), 1–17; rpt. in *Rikssamling og kristendom*. Ed. Andreas Holmsen and Jarle Simensen. Norske historikere i utvalg, 1. Oslo: Universitetsforlaget, 1967, pp. 56–75; Berntsen, Toralf. *Fra sagn til saga. Studier i kongesagaen*. Kristiania [Oslo]: Gyldendal, 1923, pp. 23–94; Finnur Jónsson. "Ágrip." *Aarbøger for nordisk Oldkyndighed og Historie* 3rd ser., 18 (1928), 261–317; Bjarni Aðalbjarnarson. *Om de norske kongers sagaer*. Skrifter utg. av Det Norske Videnskaps-Akademi i Oslo, II. Hist.-filos. klasse, 1936, 4. Oslo: Dybwad, 1937, pp. 1–54; Ellehøj, Svend. *Studier over den ældste norrøne historieskrivning*. Bibliotheca Arnamagnæana, 26. Copenhagen: Munksgaard, 1965, pp. 197–276; Ulset, Tor. *Det genetiske forholdet mellom Ágrip, Historia Norwegiæ og Historia de antiquitate regum Norwagiensium: En analyse med utgangspunkt i oversettelseteknikk samt en diskusjon omkring begrepet "latinisme" i samband med norrøne tekster*. Oslo: Novus, 1983.

Bjarni Einarsson

[**See also**: *Fagrskinna*; *Heimskringla*; *Historia Norwegiae*; *Konungasögur*; *Morkinskinna*; *Sverris saga*; Sæmundr Sigfússon inn fróði; Theodoricus: *Historia de antiquitate regum Norwagiensium*]

Ágrip af sǫgu Danakonunga

("Summary of the History of the Kings of Denmark") is a brief chronicle about the Danish kings from Sigurðr hringr ("ring") to Valdemar sejr ("the victorious"; d. 1241). It is introduced by a genealogical table for the Danish-born queen of Norway, Magnús lagabœtir's ("law-mender") wife, Ingeborg (d. 1287), and was composed in her honor. The text is preserved in one copy made for Árni Magnússon from a lost parchment codex, which also contained *Sverris saga*. Storm, who edited the chronicle under the title *En oldnorsk Saga om Danekongerne* ("An Old Norwegian Saga About the Danish Kings," 1878), maintained that it was based on *Heimskringla* and that the language was Old Norwegian. Bjarni Guðnason (1982), who coined the title *Ágrip af sǫgu Danakonunga*, points out that *Knýtlinga saga* was also used and that *Ágrip* may have been written by an Icelander, perhaps Sturla Þórðarson (d. 1284). The Norse material often has factual or verbal agreement with *Heimskringla* or *Knýtlinga saga*; the compendium must have used them both or had sources in common with them. Up to and including Erik Ejegod ("ever-good"; d. 1104), *Ágrip* does not contain more than what may be attributed to the lost **Konunga ævi* ("Life-history of Kings") by Ari fróði ("the learned") Þorgilsson. There follows some Norse information that goes back to the now-lost **Hryggjarstykki* by Eiríkr Oddsson and his continuator. After this material comes a catalogue of Danish kings; the Old Danish rather than Old Norse forms of names indicate, as Storm pointed out, that *Ágrip* used a Danish and not a Norse source. The same catalogue was used by *Knýtlinga saga*, where, however, the names are presented in Old Norse. *Ágrip* reveals independent knowledge of Adam of Bremen's *Gesta Hammaburgensis ecclesiae pontificum*. A large part of *Ágrip* consists of short notes typical of 13th-century Danish historiography of the chapter of Lund (*e.g.*, *Annales Lundenses* and *Annales Ryenses*, *Vetus chronica Sialandiae*, *Series ac brevior historia regum Danie*, and the chronicle *Reges Danorum*). *Ágrip* may have been composed 1261–1287 by a Norwegian or Icelandic scribe during a stay in Lund, where its material, Norse, Danish, and Bremensian, was present and known to Danish historiographers.

Ed.: Storm, Gustav, ed. *En oldnorsk Saga om Danekongerne*. Forhandlinger i Videnskabs-Selskabet i Christiania, 1878, no. 6. Christiania [Oslo]: Dybwad, 1879, pp. 6.1–6.15 [critical edition with parallels from Danish annals]; Bjarni Guðnason, ed. *Danakonunga sǫgur*. Íslenzk fornrit, 35. Reykjavik: Hið íslenzka fornritafélag, 1982, pp. 323–36 [normalized edition with commentaries in modern Icelandic].

Rikke Malmros

[**See also**: Adam of Bremen; Annals; Chronicles; *Heimskringla*; *Íslendingabók*; *Knýtlinga saga*; Sturla Þórðarson]

Ála flekks saga

("The Saga of Spotted Áli") is an anonymous Icelandic *riddarasaga* or *fornaldarsaga*, composed probably around or shortly before 1400 (perhaps in Oddi in South Iceland). The saga survives in more than thirty-five MSS; the oldest (AM 589e 4to) is dated to the second half of the 15th century. Between the 17th and the 19th century, three cycles of *Rímur af Ála flekki* were composed based on the material of the saga.

King Richard of England exposes his newborn son. The child is, however, found by an old couple, who raise him and name him Áli flekkr because of a birthmark on his right cheek. At the age of eight, he is taken into the king's household, but the wicked maid Blátǫnn binds Áli by a spell and sends him to the troll-woman Nótt. Áli escapes and comes to Tartaríá, where he marries the maiden-king Þorbjǫrg. Áli is then transformed by Blátǫnn's brother Glóðarauga into a werewolf and causes much damage in his father's kingdom. Áli is finally caught, but his foster-mother recognizes him, and Áli takes off his wolfskin. In a dream, Nótt flogs Áli; he wakes up seriously wounded and travels to India, where he is healed of his wounds by Nótt's brothers. Eventually, Áli returns and becomes king of England.

In spite of the dominance of the (probably Celtic) magic-spell motif (*álǫg*, Irish *geis*), the saga is not a translation of a foreign story but an Icelandic text based on themes and narrative patterns of various older sagas. Like other *riddarasögur*, *Ála flekks saga* is difficult to classify. On the basis of its motifs and the structure of its contents and narrative, it can be grouped with both the original *riddarasögur* and the *fornaldarsögur*. Few texts demonstrate as much as *Ála flekks saga* the tendency in late-medieval Icelandic sagas to merge several mutually related literary traditions. Fairy-tale elements are found in the exposure motif, the magic spell, and the werewolf theme; the last two elements are probably due to Irish influence. The account of Áli's first spell resembles a wicked-stepmother fairy tale. The battle scenes and the maiden-king theme belong to the *riddarasaga* tradition. Apart from a number of motif-parallels with *Íslendingasögur* (*e.g.*, *Finnboga saga*, *Gunnlaugs saga*: exposure of a child), *Ála flekks* saga also shares characteristics with a number of *fornaldarsǫgur*, such as *Hrólfs saga kraka* and *Hálfdanar saga Brǫnufóstra*, which contains an episode in the hall of the troll-woman, and which is further related to *Ála flekks saga* through a genealogical connection. Some MSS of *Hálfdanar saga* state that Hálfdan was Áli's grandfather (likewise *Bósa saga* and *Vilmundar saga viðutan*).

The narrative style of *Ála flekks saga* is simple and popular. It exhibits few of the stylistic traits found in *riddarasǫgur*. Accordingly, the saga has been called "the most Icelandic *lygisaga*."

Ed.: Lagerholm, Åke, ed. *Drei Lygisǫgur. Egils saga einhenda ok Ásmundar berserkjabana. Ála flekks saga. Flóres saga konungs ok sona hans*. Altnordische Saga-Bibliothek, 17. Halle: Niemeyer, 1927, pp. 84–120 [German introduction, pp. lii–lxxi]; Bjarni Vilhjálmsson, ed. *Riddarasǫgur*. 6 vols. Reykjavik: Íslendingasagnaútgáfan; Haukadalsútgáfan, 1949–54, vol. 5, pp. 123–60. **Bib.**: Kalinke, Marianne E., and P. M. Mitchell. *Bibliography of Old Norse–Icelandic Romances*. Islandica, 44. Ithaca and London: Cornell University Press, 1985, pp. 19–21; Finnur Sigmundsson. *Rímnatal*. 2 vols. Reykjavik: Rímnafélagið, 1966, vol. 1, pp. 13–15. **Lit.**: Finnur Jónsson. *Den oldnorske og oldislandske Litteraturs Historie*. 3 vols. 2nd ed. Copenhagen: Gad, 1920–24, vol. 3, pp. 109–10; Schlauch, Margaret. *Romance in Iceland*. Princeton: Princeton University Press; New York: American–Scandinavian Foundation; London: Allen & Unwin, 1934; rpt. New York: Russell & Russell, 1973; Stefán Einarsson. "Heimili (skólar) fornaldarsagna og riddarasagna." *Skírnir* 140 (1966), 272; Jorgensen, Peter A. "Literarisch verwandte Stellen in verschiedenen Fornaldarsagas." In *Fourth International Saga Conference*. Munich: Institut für Nordische Philologie der Universität München, 1979, 17 pp. [photocopies of papers distributed to participants]; Buchholz, Peter. *Vorzeitkunde. Mündliches Erzählen und Überliefern im mittelalterlichen Skandinavien nach dem Zeugnis von Fornaldarsaga und eddischer Dichtung*. Skandinavistische Studien, 13. Neumünster: Wachholtz, 1980; Nahl, Astrid van. *Originale Riddarasǫgur als Teil altnordischer Sagaliteratur*. Texte und Untersuchungen zur Germanistik und Skandinavistik, 3. Frankfurt am Main and Bern: Lang, 1981; Glauser, Jürg. *Isländische Märchensagas. Studien zur Prosaliteratur im spätmittelalterlichen Island*. Beiträge zur nordischen Philologie, 12. Basel and Frankfurt am Main: Helbing & Lichtenhahn, 1983; Kalinke, Marianne. "Norse Romance (*Riddarasǫgur*)." In *Old Norse–Icelandic Literature: A Critical Guide*. Ed. Carol J. Clover and John Lindow. Islandica, 45. Ithaca and London: Cornell University Press, 1985, pp. 316–63; Kalinke, Marianne E. "The Misogamous Maiden Kings of Icelandic Romance." *Scripta Islandica* 37 (1986), 47–71; Gísli Sigurðsson. *Gaelic Influence in Iceland. Historical and Literary Contacts: A Survey of Research*. Studia Islandica, 46. Reykjavik: Menningarsjóður, 1988, pp. 66–7.

Jürg Glauser

[**See also:** *Bósa saga ok Herrauðs*; *Finnboga saga ramma*; *Fornaldarsǫgur*; *Gunnlaugs saga ormstungu*; *Hálfdanar saga Brǫnufóstra*; *Hrólfs saga kraka*; *Lygisaga*; Old Norse–Icelandic Literature, Foreign Influence on; *Riddarasǫgur*; *Vilmundar saga viðutan*]

Alcuin: De virtutibus et vitiis ("On Virtues and Vices")

is one of the minor Latin works of Albinus Flaccus, an Anglo-Saxon Benedictine monk and theologian (b. *ca.* 735, d. 804 in Tours). Probably the chief cleric of his time, Alcuin took upon himself, by order of Charlemagne, to restore the intellectual life of the West. He became the head of the cathedral school in York (778) and of the court school in Aachen (782), and finally, abbot of Saint-Martin-de-Tours (796). *De virtutibus et vitiis* deals with moral theology, one of Alcuin's specialties. It was translated in Norway by the end of the 12th century. It survives in the Old Norwegian *Homilíubók* (AM 619 4to, *ca.* 1200), where it acts as a kind of introduction to the homilies. Fragments exist in three Icelandic MSS from the 15th century, all of which go back to a lost original. In addition, extracts from it appear in the Old Norwegian *Landslǫg*, as well as in the Old Icelandic legal text *Jónsbók* (end of the 13th century). The popularity of Alcuin's work shows that the Benedictine influence was strong in Norway during the missionary period.

Ed.: Unger, Carl R., ed. *Gammel norsk homiliebog. (codex Arn. Magn. 619 qv.)*. Norsk oldskriftselskabs samlinger, 1.5 Christiania [Oslo]: Brøgger & Christie, 1862–64; Flom, George T., ed. *Codex AM 619 quarto. Old Norwegian Book of Homilies. . . .* University of Illinois Studies in Language and Literature, 14, no. 4. Urbana: University of Illinois Press, 1929; Indrebø, Gustav, ed. *Gamal norsk homiliebok. cod. AM. 619 4°*. Norsk historisk kjeldeskrift-institutt, Skrifter, 54. Oslo: Dybwad, 1931; rpt. Oslo: Universitetsforlaget, 1966; Knudsen, Trygve, ed. *Gammelnorsk homiliebok etter AM 619 qv*. Corpus Codicorum Norvegicorum Medii Aevi, Series in Quarto, 1. Oslo: Selskapet til utgivelse av gamle norske håndskrifter, 1952 [facsimile]; Widding, Ole, ed. *Alkuin: De virtutibus et vitiis i norsk-islandsk overlevering*. Editiones Arnamagnæanæ, ser. A, vol. 4. Copenhagen: Munksgaard, 1960 [with Latin text]. **Lit.**: Widding, O. "Alcuin and the Icelandic Law-Books." *Saga-Book of the Viking Society* 14 (1953–57), 291–5.

Régis Boyer

[**See also:** Bible; Homilies (West Norse); *Jónsbók*; Laws]

Alexanders saga

("Alexander's Saga") is a prose translation of *Alexandreis*, a Latin epic about the life and career of Alexander the Great. The Latin poem was written in dactylic hexameters by Galterus de Castellione (*ca.* 1180), based primarily on Quintus Curtius Rufus's *Historia Alexandri magni*.

Alexanders saga survives in five medieval Icelandic MSS. The chief MS, AM 519a 4to from about 1280, is incomplete, with two leaves lost. A fragment of *Alexanders saga* is found in AM 655 XXIX 4to. The saga also appears in AM 226 fol., Stock. Perg. 4to no. 24, and AM 225 fol. (a copy of AM 226 fol.); these MSS have a shortened text and contain a translation of an additional work, the *Epistola Alexandri ad Aristotelem*. In Stock. Perg. 4to no. 24, the *Epistola* comes immediately after the saga, while in AM 226 fol. (and AM 225 fol.), it is incorporated into the saga. Finally, the saga is found in a large number of late MSS, only one of which, Stock. Papp. fol. no. 1, has textual significance. For a detailed discussion of the MSS, see Jón Helgason (1966).

The translation is characterized by its beautiful language, and the condensed style of the poem is often expanded to give a more diffuse narrative. While Galterus expects his readers to be familiar with Middle Eastern topography, classical mythology, and the story of Alexander the Great in general, the translator finds it necessary to add explanations. Where rhetorical exclamations occur or where Galterus's opinion is clearly stated, the translator frequently adds that these passages are not his own but those of Galterus. The translation fluctuates between very accurate rendering and paraphrase. The expression is almost always idiomatic, with occasional Latinisms. Both alliteration and rhyme are used now and again. The ten books of the poem are not all equally and thoroughly translated. Book 1 is abridged, mainly by the omission of two long passages. Books 2–6 are translated with the greatest fullness; from Book 7 on, there is a notable tendency to abbreviate.

At the end of *Alexanders saga* in AM 226 fol. and Stock. Perg. 4to no. 24 (but not in AM 519a 4to), a note says that Bishop Brandr Jónsson translated the saga from Latin into Norse. The same is said in all the MSS of *Gyðinga saga* that preserve the epilogue, except for DKNVSB 41 8vo, Lbs. 714 8vo, and Lbs. 4270 4to. According to *Gyðinga saga*, Brandr Jónsson translated both sagas: ". . . but it was translated into Norse by the priest Brandr Jónsson, who was later bishop of Hólar, and [Brandr] then [translated] Alexander the Great at the command of the honorable lord King Magnús, son of King Hákon the Old." It seems natural to take the appended phrase, "at the command of . . . King Magnús, son of King Hákon the Old," as applying to both sagas. Since it is known that Brandr Jónsson was in Norway 1262–1263, the translations were probably made during this year.

Some scholars have maintained that *Alexanders saga* is superior to *Gyðinga saga* in style and thus that the translations are not the work of the same man. In such a comparison, however, the differing nature of the originals must also be taken into account. The source for *Alexanders saga* has an extensive and colorful vocabulary and contains many emotive passages and pieces of rhetoric; it is thus only natural that a translation of this work would have a much more flexible and imaginative use of language than that of the more chronicle-like source texts of *Gyðinga saga*. The possibility that the same man was responsible for both translations cannot be excluded, therefore, on stylistic grounds alone.

Ed.: Unger, C. R., ed. *Alexanders saga: Norsk Bearbeidelse fra trettende Aarhundrede af Philip Gautiers latinske Digt Alexandreis*. Christiania [Oslo]: Feilberg og Landmark, 1848; [Finnur Jónsson, ed.] *Alexanders saga: Islandsk Oversættelse ved Brandr Jónsson (Biskop til Holar 1263–64)*. Udgiven af Kommissionen for det Arnamagnæanske Legat. Copenhagen: Gyldendal, 1925; Halldór Kiljan Laxness, ed. *Alexandreis það er Alexanders saga mikla*. Reykjavik: Heimskringla; Copenhagen: Munksgaard, 1945; Jón Helgason, ed. *Alexanders saga: The Arna-Magnæan Manuscript 519a, 4to*. Manuscripta Islandica, 7. Copenhagen: Munksgaard, 1966. Skårup, Povl. "Bréf Alexandri Magni. Den norrøne oversættelse af Epistola Alexandri Magni ad Aristotelem, udgivet sammen med forlægget." *Opuscula* 9. Bibliotheca Arnamagnæana, 39. Copenhagen: Reitzel, 1991, pp. 19–99. **Bib.**: Kalinke, Marianne E., and P. M. Mitchell. *Bibliography of Old Norse–Icelandic Romances*. Islandica, 44. Ithaca: Cornell University Press, 1985, pp. 21–2. **Lit.**: Widding, Ole. "Það finnur hver sem um er hugað." *Skírnir* 134 (1960), 61–73; Einar Ól. Sveinsson. "Athugasemdir um Alexanderssögu og Gyðingasögu." *Skírnir* 135 (1961), 237–47; Einar Ól. Sveinsson. "*Alexandreis* et *La saga d'Alexandre*." In *Rencontres et courants littéraires franco-scandinaves. Actes du 7ᵉ Congrès International d'Histoire des Littératures Scandinaves (Paris 7–12 juillet 1968)*. Paris: Lettres Modernes, Minard, 1972, pp. 11–40; Lönnroth, Lars. *Njáls saga: A Critical Introduction*. Berkeley and Los Angeles: University of California Press, 1976; Hallberg, Peter. "Några språkdrag i Alexanders saga och Gyðinga saga—med en utblick på Stjórn." In *Sjötíu ritgerðir helgaðar Jakobi Benediktssyni 20. júlí 1977*. 2 vols. Ed. Einar G. Pétursson and Jónas Kristjánsson. Reykjavik: Stofnun Árna Magnússonar, 1977, vol. 1, pp. 234–50; Wolf, Kirsten. "Gyðinga saga, Alexanders saga, and Bishop Brandr Jónsson." *Scandinavian Studies* 60 (1988), 371–400; Wolf, Kirsten. "On the Authorship of *Hrafnkels saga*." *Arkiv för nordisk filologi* 106 (1991), 104–24.

Kirsten Wolf

[**See also**: *Gyðinga saga*; Old Norse–Icelandic Literature, Foreign Influence on]

Algorismus is the only known medieval Scandinavian treatise giving the principles of the Hindu-Arabic place-value numeral system, and instructions on how to calculate using this system. The complete text is found in several Old Norse MSS: AM 544 4to (fols. 90r–93r), AM 685d 4to (fols. 24r–29r), and GkS 1812 4to (fols. 13v–16v), whereas AM 736 III 4to contains only a fragment. AM 544 4to forms part of *Hauksbók*, named after the Icelandic lawman Haukr Erlendsson. He probably compiled and maybe even edited some of the texts while staying mostly in Norway from 1301 until he died in 1334. *Algorismus* is considered to have been written by Haukr's "first Icelandic secretary" sometime during the period when Haukr was domiciled in Norway, while the other versions are supposed to be younger.

The treatise is named after the most famous mathematician in Baghdad about A.D. 825, Muḥammad Ibn Mūsā al-Khwārizmī. His name was latinized to "Algorizmi," the origin of the title *Algorismus* as well as the word "algorithm."

How the Hindu-Arabic numerals initially came to Europe is a debated question. We know, however, that al-Khwārizmī's treatise on the Hindu art of reckoning was translated into Latin in Spain during the 12th century. This version laid the foundation for a series of texts. About 1300, the two most influential works of this kind were Alexander de Villa Dei's *Carmen de Algorismo* and Johannis de Sacrobosco's *Tractatus de arte numerandi* (also called *Algorismus vulgaris* and *De algorismo*). Both these works must have been known to the Old Norse translator, as well as fragments from the Greek mathematical traditions, probably transmitted via Boethius.

The most important source for the Old Norse *Algorismus* is the *Carmen de Algorismo*, which shows a high degree of correspondence on central points. As in the *Carmen*, we find seven different branches of reckoning: *viðrlagning* (addition), *afdráttr* (subtraction), *tvífaldan* (duplication), *helmingaskipti* (mediation), *margfaldan* (multiplication), *skipting* (division), and "*taka rót undan*" ("to take the root of," a branch that describes how to calculate square and also cube roots).

Sacrobosco gives nine different branches. In his work, as in the older tradition, the zero is not regarded as a numeral, as opposed to the *Carmen* and to *Algorismus*. Although admitting that the zero is special in some respects, both treat it as a numeral. *Carmen* and *Algorismus* state as a fact the Hindu origin of our numerals; in *Tractatus de arte numerandi*, the art of reckoning is ascribed to "an Arabic philosopher called Algus." Sacrobosco provides several fanciful etymologies for the term "algorismus."

One common trait in all these three works is the total lack of calculation by fractions, except for a comment in *Algorismus* about a certain mark signifying one half, while al-Khwārizmī presents several such calculations. The three works also introduce terms for the different numeral positions. The translator of Algorismus calls every number less than ten a "finger" (*fingr*, Latin *digitus*), every number corresponding to an amount of tens a "joint" (*liðr*, Latin *articulus*), and a number that consists of both, a "composite number" (*samsætt tala*; Latin *compositus*).

Unlike all its known sources, *Algorismus* ends with a section on God's creation of proportional relations among the four elements, an idea that probably goes back to Plato's *Timaeus*. The very last sentence of the text promises a figure called the "perfect cube." Unfortunately, this figure is lacking in all the MSS.

The great advantages of the Hindu-Arabic place-value notational system were not readily recognized in medieval European society, the competing system being the Roman numerals with their simple rules of addition and subtraction. Despite the invention of printing in Europe and the wider diffusion of algoristic texts, the superiority of the system of calculation represented by *Algorismus* was not universally recognized until about 1600.

Ed.: Munch, P. A., ed. and trans. "Algorismus, eller Anviisning til at kende og anvende de saakaldte arabiske Tal, efter Hr. Hauk Erlendssøns Codex meddelt og ledsaget med Oversættelse." *Annaler for nordisk Oldkyndighed og Historie* (1848), 353–75; Eiríkur Jónsson and Finnur Jónsson, eds. *Hauksbók udgiven efter de Arnamagnæanske håndskrifter no. 371, 544 og 675, 4° samt forskellige papirshåndskrifter af det kongelige nordiske Oldskrift-selskab.* Copenhagen: Thiele, 1892–96; Jón Helgason, ed. *Hauksbók. The Arna-Magnæan Manuscripts 371, 4°, 544, 4°, and 675, 4°.* Manuscripta Islandica, 5. Copenhagen: Munksgaard, 1960 [facsimile]. **Lit.**: Halliwell, James Orchard. *Rara mathematica.* London: Parker, 1841; rpt. Hildesheim and New York: Olm, 1977; Smith, David Eugene, and Louis Charles Karpinski. *The Hindu-Arabic Numerals.* Boston and London: Ginn, 1911; Benedict, Suzan Rose. *A Comparative Study of the Early Treatises Introducing into Europe the Hindu Art of Reckoning.* Concord: Rumford, 1916; Vogel, Kurt. *Mohammed ibn Musa Alchwarizmi's Algorismus: Das früheste Lehrbuch zum Rechnen mit indischen Ziffern.* Aalen: Zeller, 1963; Bekken, Otto B., and Marit Christoffersen. *Algorismus i Hauksbók i europeisk perspektiv.* Kristiansand: Agder distriktshøgskole, 1985.

Otto B. Bekken and Marit Christoffersen

[**See also:** *Hauksbók*; Numerals]

Alphabet. Latin script came to Scandinavia along with Christianity via the Continent (Germany) and England. Denmark received the art of writing mainly from Germany, although some letters (*y*, perhaps also *æ* and *ø*) suggest Anglo-Saxon insular influence. A typical feature of Danish script is that insular *f* (ꝼ) is lacking, and that *th* is used for the voiceless dental fricative, and occasionally for its voiced counterpart. The thorn sign (þ) never achieved currency in Danish script, although it does occur in some law texts, following Swedish or Norwegian models. It is used virtually throughout *Skånelagen* (SKB B 76), from the early 14th century, and sporadically in some MSS from Zealand, the youngest from the start of the 15th century. As in contemporary German script, *w* occurs initially and after consonants in Danish texts. Crossed *l* and *n* (*ƚ*, *ꞥ*) are used to indicate palatalization in a few MSS (*e.g.*, SKB B 74). Slashed *ø* replaces the earlier *œ*; in the 16th century, this sound is represented by *o* with a superscript dot or stroke. The letter *æ* is written as a ligature of *a* and *e*; the sound could previously be denoted by hooked *ę* (*e-caudata*), or hooked *æ* (*ǽ*) adopted from Carolingian script. The crossed vowels *u*, *v*, *y* (*ʉ*, *ꝟ*, *ɏ*) for front-mutated *u* are peculiar to Danish script. The rounded vowel that developed out of long *a* was written *aa*, a practice that survived until the present century, when it was replaced by *a* with a superscript *o* (*å*).

Sweden, like Denmark, received the art of writing largely from Germany. The oldest MSS in Swedish, however, show West Norse influence, including insular features that reached Sweden via Norway. For example, in the fragment of the older *Västgötalagen* (SKB B 193), we find the runic character *þ*, *ð*, insular *ꝼ*, *ø*, *æ*, *y*, the ligature of *s* and *k* (ꝁ), and the runic character ᛘ for *maþär* 'man.' Soon afterward, however, Swedish loses insular *ꝼ*, *ð*, and the ligature ꝁ. In the later Middle Ages (*ca.* 1370–1526), *þ* is replaced by *th* initially and *dh* medially and finally. As in Denmark, the predominant script in 15th-century books and documents is Gothic hybrid. Typical features of this style are that *a* has a single chamber (like the cursive form); that the stems of *f* and tall *s* (ſ) project below the line; that *b*, *d*, and sometimes *l* have loops; that *k* has a raised loop; and that final *m* and *n* often have the last minim prolonged. At the time of the Reformation, Swedish differed from Danish script in replacing the medieval forms *aᵉ* and *oᵉ* (orginally *a* and *o* with superscript *e*) with the German *ä* and *ö*. In addition, Swedish acquired a new letter with the substitution of *å* for *aa*.

Icelandic script has a dual origin: continental Caroline minuscule and insular English script (partly transmitted via Norway). From English or Norwegian writing came the runic character *þ*, which in the oldest MSS appears in all positions in the word. Some of the oldest texts have a *w* similar to that used in England and Norway. Norwegian influence in the 13th century led to the adoption of more insular letters, *ð*, ꝼ, ƿ. Following East Norse usage, *ð* became more common than *þ* in medial and final positions. Around the middle of the 14th century, Icelanders ceased to write *ð* (although the sound was retained); they used *d* instead, and continued to do so until some time into the 19th century. Insular *v* is rare after 1350. Insular *ꝼ*, which was introduced in the 13th century, did not disappear from cursive script until the 18th century, surviving a little longer in book script. After 1800, this character was used only for calligraphic purposes. Vowel signs in medieval Icelandic are used as in contemporary Norwegian. One difference is that *ǫ*, the sign for back-mutated *a*, is more common in Iceland than in Norway. This sound probably developed early into a mid-rounded front vowel; it was replaced by *ö* in the 16th century. Otherwise, the modern Icelandic alphabet is virtually identical to that used in Old Icelandic.

Norway was the part of Scandinavia where insular script was most prominent. In the oldest, particularly East Norwegian, texts (*ca.* 1150–1225), we find the insular letters *þ*, *ð*, long *r* (ꞃ), *ꝼ*, *v*, *æ*, and English usages like *u* for *y*, *eo* for *ø*, the use of the nasal bar for *m*, and more rarely for *n*. West Norwegian MSS also have insular letters, although less frequently. The period had no specific documentary script. During the period 1225–1300, the insular letters *f* and *v* are in full use, *ð* is increasingly being replaced at the end of the period by round *d* (ꝺ), several letters change their shape, and cursive script starts to appear in diplomas by the end of the period. In the Gothic period (*ca.* 1300–1550), cursive script also becomes standard in books, the insular letters disappear, and the Danish alphabet is introduced at the end of the Middle Ages. Norwegian writing came under the influence of Danish in the 16th century. As in the other Nordic countries, neo-Gothic script prevailed from the Reformation until the 1870s. Latin style was used for texts in Latin or Romance languages.

On the Faroes, the Norwegian alphabet was used in the Middle Ages, later to be replaced by Danish script. In 1846, a new alphabet with a standard orthography was created by Dean V. U. Hammershaimb. It was based on normalized Old Icelandic, from which *ð* (but not *þ*) was adopted, although it is now silent. The orthography is largely etymological. The only medieval linguistic monuments that survive are a few parchment letters from around 1400, but no MS books.

Lit.: Hægstad, Marius. "Nordische (altnordische) Schrift." In *Reallexikon der germanischen Altertumskunde.* Ed. Johannes Hoops. Strassburg: Trübner, 1915–16, vol. 3, pp. 331–41; Brøndum-Nielsen, Johannes.

"Den nordiska—västnordiska och danska —skriften." In *Svend Dahls bibliotekshandbok*. Ed. Samuel E. Bring. Uppsala and Stockholm: Almqvist & Wiksell, 1924, vol. 1, pp. 75–106; Jansson, Sam. "Svenskt skrivskick under medeltiden och fram till våra dagar." In *Svend Dahls bibliotekshandbok*, vol. 1, pp. 107–26; Spehr, Harald. *Der Ursprung der isländischen Schrift und ihre Weiterbildung bis zur Mitte des XIII. Jahrhunderts*. Halle: Niemeyer, 1929; Nielsen, Lauritz. *Danmarks middelalderlige Haandskrifter*. Copenhagen: Gyldendal, 1937; Kroman, Erik. "Dansk palæografi." In *Palæografi. A. Danmark og Sverige*. Nordisk kultur, 28:A. Ed. Johannes Brøndum-Nielsen. Stockholm: Bonnier; Oslo: Aschehoug; Copenhagen: Schultz, 1944, pp. 36–81; Jansson, Sam. "Svensk paleografi." In *Palæografi*, pp. 82–130; Björn Þórólfsson. "Nokkur orð um íslenzkt skrifletur." In *Landsbókasafn Íslands. Árbók 1948–1949* (1950), 116–52; Seip, Didrik Arup. *Palæografi. B. Norge og Island*. Nordisk kultur, 28:B. Ed. Johannes Brøndum-Nielsen. Stockholm: Bonnier; Oslo: Aschehoug; Copenhagen: Schultz, 1954; Jansson, Sam. "Latinska alfabetets utveckling i medeltida svensk brevskrift. De enskilda bokstavernas historia." *Acta Philologica Scandinavica* 22 (1954), 81–148; Hreinn Benediktsson. *Early Icelandic Script as Illustrated in Vernacular Texts from the Twelfth and Thirteenth Centuries*. Icelandic Manuscripts, Series in Folio, 2. Reykjavik: Manuscript Institute of Iceland, 1965; Svensson, Lars. *Nordisk paleografi. Handbok med transkriberade och kommenterade skriftprov*. Lundastudier i nordisk språkvetenskap, ser. A, no. 28. Lund: Studentlitteratur, 1974.

Lars Svensson

[**See also:** Palaeography; Runes and Runic Inscriptions]

Alþingi ("the Althing") was the national legislative and judicial assembly of medieval Iceland. The "thing," or voting assembly of freemen, was a governing institution widely used by the Germanic peoples. At the beginning of the Viking Age, there were many thing-assemblies throughout Scandinavia, and Norse settlers frequently established things abroad. The Icelandic *Alþingi* was unusual, however, in that it united all regions of an entire country under a common legal and judicial system, without depending upon the executive power of a monarch or regional rulers.

The *Alþingi* was established around 930, but little is known about its specific organization during the earliest decades, because *Grágás* and the sagas generally portray the assembly as it was after the constitutional reforms of the mid-960s. The *Alþingi* met for two weeks every summer at Þingvǫllr on the Øxará (Axe River) in southwestern Iceland, a site easily accessible from most of the island. The convening of the *Alþingi* before 999 cannot be precisely dated, but in that year the opening day was set as the Thursday after the first ten weeks of the summer, that is, between June 18 and 24.

The site of the *Alþingi* was hallowed, and the proceedings were set in motion by the *allsherjargoði*, a man distinguished as the holder of the *goðorð* established by Þorsteinn Ingólfsson, a leader instrumental in the founding of the *Alþingi* and a son of Iceland's first settler. A truce was observed during the session, and all freemen, except those under sentence of outlawry, could attend. The lawspeaker (*lǫgsǫgumaðr*) presided over the *Alþingi* and made the practical arrangements. Either he or the *allsherjargoði* closed the meeting. The *Alþingi* officially ended with a ceremony called *vápnatak* (weapon taking), when men struck their weapons together, presumably signifying agreement with the work accomplished during the assembly. Although weapons were banned at *Alþingi* meetings in 1154, the available evidence suggests that the new ruling was soon ignored.

Along with the lawspeaker, the island's chieftains or *goðar* (sing. *goði*) were required by law to attend the *Alþingi*. Each *goði* could demand that every ninth *þingfararkaupsbóndi* ("thing-tax-paying-farmer") among his thingmen accompany him, and he levied a thing-attendance tax called *þingfararkaup* on those *þingfararkaupsbœndr* who did not attend. The funds so collected were used to offset the travel expenses of those followers who accompanied their *goðar* to the *Alþingi*. Chieftains embroiled in feuds or contentious lawsuits could bring larger followings with them. Attendance at the *Alþingi* was not limited to participants in politics, disputes, and legal cases. The assembly drew craftsmen, ale brewers, vendors, and peddlers from all over the island, and sometimes from foreign lands. It was a lively scene, marked by buying and selling, exchange of news and gossip, courtship, and the making and breaking of friendships and alliances. At times, emissaries from foreign lands attended, as well as Icelanders recently returned from abroad.

Þingvǫllr is a site of great beauty, as well as a natural amphitheater. The heart of the assembly was a small hill with grassy slopes and with a rock outcropping called the "Lǫgberg" (Law Rock). A massive rock cliff stands behind the Lǫgberg, and the voice of the speaker standing at the Law Rock can be heard at a distance. The *Alþingi* sessions were held in open air. Although the setting was not urban, the annual meeting was an impressive gathering that fulfilled many functions of a national capital and contributed significantly to the island's unity. With wood given by St. Óláfr of Norway, a church was built at Þingvǫllr a few decades after the conversion, and there is some evidence that a second church was later erected. Except for these and a local farmstead, Þingvǫllr had no permanent, year-round buildings. Most of those attending the assembly pitched tents, but leaders were obliged to maintain turf booths (*búðir*, sing. *búð*) for themselves and their most important followers. Booths were roofed with homespun cloth when the *Alþingi* was in session; some were quite large and were maintained on the same site from year to year. Ale brewers, craftsmen, and merchants also had their own booths.

The legislative council (*lǫgrétta*), Iceland's supreme legislative authority, met on the Neðri-vellir (Lower Fields). Its voting members were the *goðar* and later also included the two bishops of Iceland. Each *goði* brought with him two advisers who were not permitted to vote. One adviser sat in front of his *goði*, and the other behind him. The bishops were not permitted to bring advisers. There were probably three concentric circles of wooden benches, with the chieftains sitting in the middle ring. The *lǫgrétta* reviewed existing laws, made new ones, and granted exemptions from the law. It also had the power to make treaties, representing Iceland in its few dealings with foreign lands.

The *lǫgsǫgumaðr* served as the chairman of the *lǫgrétta*. Elected by the *goðar* for a three-year term, he was annually required to recite one-third of the laws at the *Lǫgberg*. In this way, the entire body of law was proclaimed over a three-year cycle. Each chieftain was required to attend this recitation or to send his two *lǫgrétta* advisers as stand-ins. Other interested persons could attend and participate in the ensuing discussion. In the 12th century, when literacy became widespread and lawbooks became available, the practice of reciting the laws from memory ended.

The *Alþingi*, as first established, seems to have had a judicial function, but again the sources are vague. A central problem that arose is, however, clear. In the period immediately following the founding of the *Alþingi*, the only way to try a case of manslaughter was to take the suit to the assembly in the region where the killing had occurred. This arrangement proved inadequate to cope with the feuds between opponents living in different districts, and efforts to solve this and related problems led to the constitutional reforms of the mid-960s.

The reforms gave Iceland an extensive system of regional and national courts. As part of the new arrangements, the country was divided into four geographical quarters. Three local assembly districts were established in three of the quarters, but the North, due to topography and the dispersion of its population, requested four, and this request was granted. In each local district, a springtime assembly (várþing) was held. Some of these local assemblies are known to have predated the reforms, while others may have been newly formed. Four new law courts were established at the Alþingi to provide a more impartial setting than at the district courts. Called fjórðungsdómar, these new "quarter courts" of the Alþingi were named for the island's four geographical quarters and were referred to as the Court of the North Quarter, South Quarter, and so on. Cases were brought to the court of the quarter in which the defendant lived.

The quarter courts functioned both as courts of first instance and as courts of appeal for cases not settled at the várþing. Holders of the thirty-six "full" or original chieftaincies (goðorð that predated the reforms) appointed the judges for these courts. Although each court was named for a specific quarter, the judges were selected on an island-wide basis. A party to a lawsuit could challenge any judge whose impartiality was in question. A decision in the fjórðungsdómr had to be nearly unanimous.

About 1005, a court of appeals, the fimtardómr or fifth court, was created at the Alþingi to handle cases deadlocked in the quarter courts. Here, verdicts were decided by a simple majority. After Christianity took hold, a priests' court (prestadómr) was also established. Like the quarter courts and the fifth court, it sat before a panel of judges composed of farmers. These additions completed the court system at the Alþingi as it existed in the Free State period.

From the 9th to the 13th century, Iceland maintained its independence, with the Alþingi as a public arena for resolving disputes and regulating power. In the 13th century, the importance of the Alþingi diminished as the power of a group referred to in modern studies as the stórgoðar (literally "big chieftains") grew, and the disruptions of the Sturlung period became more frequent. When Iceland succumbed to Norwegian power in 1262–1264, the independence of the Alþingi was severely curtailed. The Norwegian Crown abolished the old chieftaincies. New royal officials, frequently Icelanders, then dominated the assembly. In 1271, with the introduction of a new Norwegian-inspired law code, the Alþingi relinquished its role as a general assembly. With few exceptions, it met for only three to four days each year, and for the most part booths were no longer maintained. The Alþingi became a representative body functioning somewhat like a Norwegian lagting, with proceedings devoted largely to judicial matters. Under the Norwegians, and later under the Danes, the assembly also served as the usual forum for promulgating official acts. The Alþingi continued to meet at Þingvǫllr until 1798, when it was disbanded, only to be revived in 1845 in a changed form in Reykjavík.

Lit.: Foote, Peter, and David M. Wilson. The Viking Achievement: The Society and Culture of Early Medieval Scandinavia. London: Sidgwick & Jackson, 1970; Jón Jóhannesson. A History of the Old Icelandic Commonwealth: Íslendinga saga. Trans. Haraldur Bessason. University of Manitoba Icelandic Studies, 2. Winnipeg: University of Manitoba Press, 1974; Hastrup, Kirsten. Culture and History in Medieval Iceland: An Anthropological Analysis of Structure and Change. Oxford: Clarendon, 1985; Byock, Jesse L. "Governmental Order in Early Medieval Iceland." Viator 17 (1986), 19–34; Björn Thorsteinsson. Thingvellir: Iceland's National Shrine. Trans. Peter Foote. Reykjavik: Örn og Örlygur, 1987; Byock, Jesse L. Medieval Iceland: Society, Sagas, and Power. Berkeley, Los Angeles, and London: University of California Press, 1988.

Jesse L. Byock

[See also: Bóndi; Goði; Grágás; Iceland; Laws; Sturlung Age]

Alvíssmál ("The Lay of Alvíss") is the last of the wisdom poems preserved in the Codex Regius of the Poetic Edda. Two stanzas are also preserved in MSS of the Snorra Edda, where they are quoted (under the title Alsvinnsmál) to illustrate poetic terms for wind and night. The poem is usually classed among the later eddic poems, composed perhaps in the early 13th century.

Alvíssmál takes the form of a poetic dialogue, in ljóðaháttr meter, between Þórr and a dwarf, Alvíss ("all-wise"). The first eight stanzas and the final stanza constitute a narrative frame. Alvíss is about to carry off Þórr's daughter, apparently with the gods' consent. Þórr claims that only he has the right to give away his daughter; he will do so only if the dwarf can tell him all he wants to know from each of the world's regions. At this point, the wisdom section of the poem begins. In a series of thirteen questions and answers, Þórr asks for the names of such things as heaven and earth, the sun and moon; Alvíss tells him what they are called by men, gods, giants, dwarfs, elves, and denizens of hell. In the final stanza, Þórr says he has never seen such wisdom, but that too much talk has trapped the dwarf: he has been caught above ground after daybreak, and "now sun shines in the hall." Apparently, this means that Alvíss, who lives "beneath the earth under a stone," himself turns to stone when struck by sunlight. Such a final transformation occurs more explicitly in the heroic eddic poem Helgakviða Hjǫrvarðssonar (sts. 12–30), in which a giantess turns to stone at daybreak, having been delayed by the taunts and questions of Atli and Helgi.

Among eddic wisdom poems, Alvíssmál bears some comparison with Vafþrúðnismál, in which Óðinn questions a giant about mythological lore. Indeed, many scholars have sometimes thought that Óðinn, who often quested after wisdom, would have made a more appropriate main figure in Alvíssmál than Þórr, who elsewhere is treated as a comic dupe of clever giants. But Þórr does not really match wits with the dwarf; he only questions him as a diversionary tactic. Alvíss knows all things; Þórr need only know one thing, the dwarf's vulnerability to sunlight, which Alvíss overlooks. Þórr thus exemplifies the advice given in the wisdom poem Hávamál (sts. 54–56) that one should be "moderately wise" rather than "all-wise." Þórr also fits the frame story of Alvíssmál in that here, as in Þrymskviða, he must stop an otherworldly creature from marrying a goddess.

Some scholars have seen the wisdom section of the poem as reflecting either an old belief in separate languages for the gods and men, or a system of taboo words such as were still used by Shetland fishermen in the recent past. Others have seen the wisdom section as a versified handbook of poetic terms, similar in spirit to Snorri's Edda. Further, this section has attracted attention as one of the most rigorously schematic or formulaic of all eddic compositions.

A few details suggest that the poet attempted to integrate the wisdom section and the narrative frame. Þórr asks Alvíss for the terms for "night" but not for "day," as if to avoid reminding the dwarf of his vulnerability to daylight. Þórr asks thirteen questions, which may reflect a familiar superstition; certainly the thirteenth and final stanza proves unlucky for the dwarf. Alvíss tells Þórr that dwarfs call the sun "Dvalins leika" ("Dvalinn's plaything"). Dvalinn, a dwarf whose name probably means "the delayed one," was presumably also delayed past sunrise. This allusion to Dvalinn may then foreshadow the demise of Alvíss at the end of the poem.

Ed.: Finnur Jónsson, ed. *Edda Snorra Sturlusonar*. Copenhagen: Gyldendal, 1931; Neckel, Gustav, ed. *Edda. Die Lieder des Codex Regius nebst verwandten Denkmälern. I: Text.* 5th ed. rev. Hans Kuhn. Heidelberg: Winter, 1983. **Tr.**: Hollander, Lee M., trans. *The Poetic Edda: Translated with an Introduction and Explanatory Notes.* 2nd rev. ed. Austin: University of Texas Press, 1962; rpt. 1988; Terry, Patricia, trans. *Poems of the Vikings: The Elder Edda.* Indianapolis: Bobbs-Merrill, 1969; Faulkes, Anthony, trans. *Snorri Sturluson. Edda.* London and Melbourne: Dent, 1987. **Lit.**: Güntert, Hermann. *Vor der Sprache der Götter und Geister: Bedeutungsgeschichtliche Untersuchungen zur homerischen und eddischen Göttersprache.* Halle: Niemeyer, 1921; Klingenberg, Heinz. "*Alvíssmál*: Das Lied vom überweisen Zwerg." *Germanisch-romanische Monatsschrift* 48 (1967), 113–42; Watkins, Calvert. "Language of Gods and Language of Men: Remarks on Some Indo-European Metalinguistic Traditions." In *Myth and Law Among the Indo-Europeans: Studies in Indo-European Comparative Mythology.* Ed. Jaan Puhvel. Berkeley: University of California Press, 1970, pp. 1–17; Moberg, Lennart. "The Language of Alvíssmál." *Saga-Book of the Viking Society* 18 (1973), 299–323.

Paul Acker

[**See also:** *Codex Regius*; Eddic Meters; Eddic Poetry; *Hávamál*; Helgi Poems; *Snorra Edda*; *Þrymskviða*; *Vafþrúðnismál*]

America, Norse in. The earliest seemingly reliable, if fragmentary, descriptions of any part of North America and its inhabitants were a by-product of the discovery and colonization of coastal Greenland by Icelanders. The chance discovery of American shores by Bjarni Herjólfsson, and the subsequent expeditions by Leifr Eiríksson, the latter's brother Þorvaldr, and their kinsman by marriage Þorfinnr Þórðarson Karlsefni, are variously narrated in the two so-called "Vinland sagas." Through these partly contradictory and fictional but in many ways realistic Icelandic prose narratives emerges the picture of a sparsely inhabited and almost endless territory that grew more attractive as the explorers and would-be settlers proceeded southward. Pasturage for dairy cattle, forest trees for ship building and house timbers, an abundance of fish and game, wild berries in profusion, along with the possibilities of agriculture, were powerful initial inducements to attempted colonization. There is no record of the diseases that afflicted later European settlers; the Norse tenure many have been too short for that. Collision with the indigenous population, probably the Beothuk and related tribes, appears to have put an end to these early efforts in the south. Norse efforts at trading with the natives soon degenerated into open combat.

Bjarni's landfall, followed by his cruise northward along the American coastline, is believed to have taken place in 986. Leifr's subsequent year-long expedition may have occurred shortly before the year 1000. A few years later, Karlsefni's attempt at settling in the New World filled a three-year period of adventure, internal dissension, and general frustration that put an end to prospects of Norse occupation in any area resembling what Leifr, allegedly on the basis of a discovery of grapevines and grapes, had termed "Vínland." This failure did not, however, inhibit the Norse Greenlanders from repeated, if chiefly unreported, utilization of the timber resources available on Canadian shores. The fetching of such timber went on for centuries, probably past the year 1347, when a voyage to Markland ("Forest Land") by a small Greenland ship was last reported in Icelandic annals.

The major factor involved in these visits to the American mainland and/or its offshore islands was the state of affairs in Greenland itself, where, beginning in 986, a modest Norse civilization was conducted for something like 500 years until its presumed extinction, under circumstances never fully explained, in the late 15th century. What we can glean concerning Greenland conditions derives not merely from the Vinland sagas but also from incidental accounts in other *Íslendingasögur* whose principal focus is Iceland. More precise knowledge is afforded by archaeology. Hundreds of structures and entire farmsteads in Greenland, largely clustered in the so-called Eastern (Southern) and Western (Northern) Settlements have now been excavated and analyzed. As many as 4,000 Scandinavians may at one time have been resident in Greenland, with fishing, sealing, and whaling as supplements to the dairy farming that was their main staple. A small rune stone, probably dating from around 1333, was found in 1824 on the island of Kingiktorsoak north of Upernavik. Set in one of a group of three cairns of Norse type, it is accepted as reliable evidence of medieval Norse penetration of the Arctic. It now appears that northerly travels on both sides of Davis Strait by huntsmen and adventurers must have led to the frequent contact with the natives of the Dorset and Thule cultures, who, irrespective of tribe, were referred to by the Norsemen as *skrælingar* 'wretches.' Conducted with due caution on both sides, such contacts would have led to trade. Of principal interest to the whites was the acquisition of pelts and the ivory of walrus and narwhal. Ivory was not only carved by Eskimo and Norse craftsmen, but also used by the latter to pay tithes to the Church, and in quantities impressive enough to support the notion of considerable trade between the two races.

Recent warming of the Arctic and sub-Arctic climate has led to the discovery of numerous articles of Norse manufacture at Eskimo dwelling sites on the Arctic mainland and neighboring islands. The exact significance of terminal location for easily portable objects is not easily determined, although trade, pillage, and the careless dropping or discarding of artifacts during camping or travel are among the obvious explanations. Items have been picked up from the east and west coasts of Ellesmere Island, which faces northern Greenland across Kane Basin. Most are from the vicinity of Bache Peninsula, especially from winter houses of the Thule culture on Knud Peninsula and Skraeling Island. The artifacts include ship nails, pieces of woolen cloth, fragments of smelted iron and copper, bits of chain mail, blades, and a carpenter's plane. A European figurine of wood was found on Baffin Island, a bronze bowl on Devon Island, and part of a merchant's scale on the Cumberland Peninsula. All of the foregoing test as medieval.

The claim of Norse origin for structures in the Ungave Bay region has not been sustained, and the only confirmed early Norse habitation site is at L'Anse-aux-Meadows, near the shallow Épaves Bay, northern Newfoundland. Here H. and A.-S. Ingstad have uncovered a number of structures, including turf-built houses, workshops, smithy, bath-house, charcoal kiln, as well as small artifacts. These finds include a spindle whorl of soapstone, a needle bone of quartzite, jasper and iron pyrites for striking fire, badly corroded iron rivets, scattered nails, scraps of worked wood including a ship's rib, slag, and incinerated animal bones. All criteria support an approximate date of 1000. No region of grapevines, L'Anse-aux-Meadows probably served for a few short years as a boat repair station for expeditions into the St. Lawrence Valley. H. Ingstad considers it the site of Leifr Eiríksson's houses. Now restored, the L'Anse-aux-Meadows cluster is maintained as a public exhibit by Parks Canada.

Despite the recent discovery of smelted iron pieces at Silimiut on the west coast of Hudson Bay, popular theories regarding early Norse pushes into the Dakotas or Minnesota are supported neither by archaeological evidence nor by historical probabilty.

Lit.: Olesen, Tryggvi J. *Early Voyages and Northern Approaches 1000–1632.* The Canadian Centenary Series. London and New York: Oxford University Press, 1964; Pohl, Frederick J. *The Viking Settlements of North America.* New York: Potter, 1972; Lee, Thomas E. "The Norse Presence in Arctic Ungava." *American-Scandinavian Review* 61.3 (September 1973), 242–57; Ingstad, Anne-Stine. *The Discovery of a Norse Settlement in America: Excavations at L'Anse aux Meadows, Newfoundland.* Oslo: Universitetsforlaget, 1977; McGovern, Thomas H. "The Vinland Adventure: A North Atlantic Perspective." *North American Archaeologist* 2 (1980), 285–308; Schledermann, Peter. "Eskimo and Viking Finds in the High Arctic." *National Geographic* 159. 5 (May 1981), 575–601; Gorelic, Eleanor, ed. *Vikings in the West.* Chicago: Archaeological Institute of America, 1982 [articles by G. Jones, T. H. McGovern, H. Ingstad, A.-S. Ingstad, R. McGhee, and B. L. Wallace]; McGhee, Robert. "Contact Between Native North Americans and the Medieval Norse: A Review of the Evidence." *American Antiquity* 49.1 (1984), 4–26; Ingstad, Helge. *The Norse Discovery of America. 2. The Historical Background and the Evidence of the Norse Settlement Discovered in Newfoundland.* Oslo: Norwegian University Press, 1985; Jones, Gwyn. *The Norse Atlantic Saga: Being the Norse Voyage of Discovery and Settlement to Iceland, Greenland, and North America.* 2nd. ed. Oxford: Oxford University Press, 1986; Wahlgren, Erik. *The Vikings and America.* Ancient Peoples and Places, 102. London and New York: Thames & Hudson, 1986.

†**Erik Wahlgren**

[See also: Greenland, Norse in; Kensington Stone; L'Anse aux Meadows; "Maine Coin"; Viking Hoaxes; Vinland Map; Vinland Sagas]

Amicus and Amileus is a tale about the self-sacrificing friendship between two knights, Amicus and Amileus, contrasting their mutual loyalty with a number of betrayals of the trust and obligations of love by other characters. The numerous translations of the tale into almost all European languages attest to its popularity. The interest in the tale is further indicated by the fact that it was repeatedly adapted into different narrative forms, such as miracle play, exemplum, prose tale, and ballad.

Traditionally, all versions of the Amicus and Amileus tale are assigned to one of two categories: romance or hagiography. The romantic group adds new elements; the theme is an exposition of the virtues of the two friends, who are so dear to God that miracles are worked on their behalf, and so zealous in the cause of the Church that they are rewarded with martyrdom (Leach 1937: ix).

A comparison of the oldest extant version of the tale, that of Radulfus Tortarius in verse from about 1090, with the younger versions, *e.g.*, the *Vita Amici et Amelii* from the 12th century, in which the two friends are clearly presented as saints, reveals that originally the tale lacked the hagiographic character of the later versions, *i.e.*, the romantic versions represent more nearly the original form of the tale, which is thought to have come into existence, probably as a *chanson de geste*, in southern France in the 11th century.

The East Norse versions of the tale can undisputably be classified as belonging to the hagiographic group. The Old Swedish version, "Aff Amelio oc Amico," is found in *Sjælinna thröst* from about 1420. The work is essentially an exposition of the Ten Commandments and is based chiefly on the Low German *Der große Seelentrost*; the story of Amicus and Amileus is found in connection with the Eighth Commandment. Although much material is drawn from the *Seelentrost*, which for this section is based on Vincent of Beauvais's *Speculum historiale*, the Old Swedish version is primarily a translation of the *Vita* from the 12th century. The exact source of a Latin verse summarizing the content of the legend that is appended to the Swedish story remains obscure. The Danish version, "Af amicus oc amelius," is found in *Siæla tröst*, extant in two fragments from about 1425. The work is a translation from the original of the Swedish *Siælinna thröst*; the Amicus and Amileus legend contains the same Latin verse at the end of the story.

The story appears in West Norse as a short, incomplete saga and a long, elaborate cycle of *rímur*. The two West Norse versions have generally been classified as hagiographies, but they contain features so characteristic of romance that they both, in particular the saga, may be better labeled as romance (Hume 1970: 80). *Amícus saga ok Amilíus* was probably translated during the later years of the reign of Hákon V (1299–1319). According to Hamer (1985), the narrative technique suggests that the translation was originally made in Norway. According to Kölbing (1877), the saga may share a common source with Vincent of Beauvais's *Speculum historiale* (itself an abridged version of the story a few removes from the *Vita*); Leach implies that the saga descends directly from the *Speculum historiale*. The saga is found in one MS only, Stock. Perg. 4to no. 6 (fols. 1–3r) from the 14th century, which is defective at the beginning because of a lacuna before fol. 1. The so-called *Rímur af Amíkus og Amilíus* in AM 609c 4to from the 17th century are not based on the story in the *Speculum historiale*, nor on the Icelandic rendering of it, but stem ultimately from a Latin *vita* of the type edited by Kölbing (1884: xcvii–cx).

Ed.: Liffman, J. W., and George Stephens, eds. *Herr Ivan Lejon-Riddaren, en svensk rimmad dikt ifrån 1300–talet, tillhörande sagokretsen om Konung Arthus och hans runda bord. Efter gamla handskrifter.* Samlinger utgivna av Svenska fornskrift-sällskapet, ser. 2:2–4. Stockholm: Norstedt, 1845–49, pp. cxxix–cxxx; Kölbing, Eugen, ed. "Bruchstück einer Amícus ok Amilíus saga." *Germania* 19 [N.S. 7] (1874), 184–9; Kölbing, Eugen, ed. *Elis saga ok Rosamundu. Mit Einleitung, deutscher Übersetzung und Anmerkungen zum ersten Mal herausgegeben.* Heilbronn: Henninger, 1881; rpt. Wiesbaden: Lindig, 1981, p. ix, n. 1; Kölbing, Eugen, ed. *Amis and Amiloun. Zugleich mit der altfranzösichen Quelle. Nebst einer Beilage: Amícus ok Amilíus Rímur.* Altenglische Bibliothek, 2. Heilbronn: Henninger, 1884, pp. 189–229, 251–3; Nielsen, Niels, ed. *Sjælens trøst ("Siæla trøst").* Udgivet for Universitets-Jubilæets danske Samfund. Copenhagen: Schultz, 1937–52, pp. 73–88; Henning, Sam, ed. *Siælinna thröst. Första delin aff the bokinne som kallas siællina thröst. Efter cod. Holm*

A 108 (f.d. cod. Ångsö). Samlingar utgivna av Svenska fornskrift-
sällskapet, 59. Uppsala: Almqvist & Wiksell, 1954, pp. 331–45; Slay,
Desmond, ed. *Romances. Perg. 4:o nr. 6 in the Royal Library, Stockholm.*
Early Icelandic Manuscripts in Facsimile, 10. Copenhagen: Rosenkilde
& Bagger, 1972. **Bib.**: Widding, Ole, *et al.* "The Lives of the Saints in
Old Norse Prose: A Handlist." *Mediaeval Studies* 25 (1963), 294–337,
esp. 299; Kalinke, Marianne E., and P. M. Mitchell. *Bibliography of Old
Norse–Icelandic Romances.* Islandica, 44. Ithaca and London: Cornell
University Press, 1985, pp. 23–4. **Lit.**: Kölbing, Eugen. "Zur
Ueberlieferung der Sage von Amicus und Amelius." *Beiträge zur
Geschichte der deutschen Sprache und Literatur* 4 (1877), 271–314;
Heller, Bernard. "L'épée symbole et gardienne de chasteté." *Romania* 36
(1907), 36–49; 37 (1908), 162–3; Krappe, A. H. "The Legend of
Amicus and Amelius." *Modern Language Review* 18 (1923), 152–61;
Björn K. Þórólfsson. *Rímur fyrir 1600.* Safn Fræðafjelagsins um Ísland
og Íslendinga, 9. Copenhagen: Møller, 1934, pp. 481–2; Leach, Mac
Edward, ed. *Amis and Amiloun.* Early English Text Society, o.s. 203.
London: Oxford University Press, 1937; Thorén, Ivar. *Studier över
Själens trøst. Bidrag til kännedomen om den litterära verksamheten i
1400–talets Vadstena.* Uppsala: Almqvist & Wiksell, 1942, pp. 84–6,
143–4; Hume, Kathryn. "Structure and Perspective. Romance and
Hagiographic Features in the Amicus and Amelius Story." *Journal of
English and Germanic Philology* 69 (1970), 89–107; Hamer, Andrew.
"Translation and Adaptation in *Amícus ok Amílíus saga.*" In *Sources and
Relations: Studies in Honour of J. E. Cross. Leeds Studies in English* n. s.
16 (1985), 246–58.

Kirsten Wolf

[**See also**: Old Norse–Icelandic Literature, Foreign Influence on]

Amícus saga ok Amílíus *see* Amicus and Amileus

Anders Sunesen *see* Sunesen, Anders

Annals

1. DENMARK. For a long time, it was a common belief that
every medieval monastery kept annals year by year, independent
of other written source material. A hundred years of study has
completely overthrown this theory. In spite of the fact that the
period of annal writing lasted from approximately 1130 to 1400,
with an aftermath of learned compilations from the 16th century,
the number of genuine annals is no more than seventeen. Since
about seventy medieval monasteries can be placed on the map in
Denmark, it is clear that not all of them produced annals, taking
into account that some may be lost. The remaining annals show
much interdependence, so few entries can be considered firsthand
information.

Most of the Danish annals belonging to the period up to the
middle of the 13th century were written at the archiepiscopal see
at Lund. The earliest ones are the so-called "Colbaz annals." After
a preface on the history of the world, they cover the years 1130 to
1177. At that time, they were transferred to Pomerania, where
they were continued in the Cistercian monastery of Colbaz. The
original version is now preserved in the university library of
Marburg. Basically, these annals are an Easter table with interlinear and marginal additions, all with considerable confusion among
the entries. Perhaps a copy of the Colbaz annals was made before
they were removed from Lund, which would explain curious similarities between these annals and Danish annals from the beginning of the 13th century.

One of the Danish annals is *Valdemarárbogen* ("The Annals
of Valdemar," king of Denmark, 1202–1241). This book seems to

have been written in the royal chancellery, since it shows special
interest in dynastic events and wars, and since a copy of it is found
in the *Valdemars jordebog* ("Valdemar's Land Register") containing lists of royal incomes during the 13th century. These annals
cover the years 1130 to 1219, after which they suddenly stop, thus
providing a *terminus ad quem* for their composition.

During the following decades, the Valdemar annals were used
alongside the tradition from Lund for annals from Næstved and
Sorø. The middle of the 13th century saw the appearance of two
new Lund annals. One of them, which treats the period 1074–
1255, is the only one to include entries for 1074–1130. Its sources
are the *Necrologium Lundense* and the *Roskilde Chronicle*
(*Roskildekrøniken*). The annals from 1074 to 1255 are known
only in a Danish translation from about 1400. The other set of
annals from Lund is an elaborate piece of work, covering the time
from the Creation until the year 1267. The oldest MS dates from
about 1300, and is part of a collection kept in the German town
of Erfurt. The earliest part of these annals is based on Isidore of
Seville's *Etymologiarum* (5:39; *ca.* A.D. 600), on Bede's *Historia
ecclesiastica* (731) and *Chronica maiora* (725), and on various
other chronicles. At the entry for the year 767, Danish material
begins with the *Lejre Chronicle* (*Lejrekrøniken*) and excerpts from
Adam of Bremen. From 1074 onward, the text shows heavy
exploitation of the predecessors from Lund and the Valdemar
annals.

The combination of chronicle with annal is characteristic of
the annals written down about 1300 and during the first half of
the 14th century. These writings include Danish legendary history
from Saxo's *Gesta Danorum*, supplemented by legends, probably
of recent invention.

About the year 1300, the center of annal writing seems to
have shifted from Lund to Sorø. *Vetus chronica Sialandiae* ("The
Old Chronicle of Zealand") was written in Sorø. The *Annals of Ryd*
(*Rydårbogen*) are based upon Sorø history writing, and the *Jutish
Chronicle* (*Jyske krønike*) depends on the Ryd annals as well as on
materials from Sorø. Finally, there is the *Younger Zealand Chronicle*
(*Den yngre Sjællandske krønike*), which includes the *Older Zealand
Chronicle* (*Den ældre Sjællandske krønike*).

The *Annals of Ryd* were written in the Cistercian monastery
of Ryd at the fjord of Flensburg. Three versions are known, all
beginning with a legendary history, but each with a different closing year. One of them, in Latin, stops at 1288. It seems to have
been written during the second half of the 13th century. The oldest MS of this work from about 1300 is kept in the Stadtsbibliothek
of Hamburg. Of the two versions in Danish, one stops in 1226, the
other in 1314. The *Annals of Ryd* offer rather personal impressions, and are strongly biased against the Teutons.

A complete, abbreviated version of Saxo's work constitutes
the first half of the *Jutish Chronicle.* The second half comprises
annals covering the time from about 1190 to 1340, most detailed
for the last twenty years, but still without coherence and causality.
Events taking place in Jutland receive particular stress during the
period when Denmark was dissolved into several mortgaged crown
lands. This chronicle was widely known in Denmark, Sweden,
and northern Germany, as may be seen from several 15th-century
MSS as well as two printed versions in Low German from the 16th
century.

A little younger than the *Jutish Chronicle* is a *Zealandic
Chronicle*, the last part of which contains entries up to the year
1282. The *Younger Zealandic Chronicle* covers 1308 to 1363, and
is assumed to be the work of three authors. No MSS survive, and

the texts of the *Older* as well as the *Younger Zealandic Chronicle* are extant only in print from 1695. The latter is considered the peak of Danish annal writing: the entries are strictly chronological, but rich in detail and with strongly expressed opinions about King Valdemar IV (1340–1374). This work was the culmination of Danish annals in their medieval form.

Ed.: Jørgensen, Ellen, ed. *Annales Danici Medii Ævi*. Copenhagen: Gad, 1920; Kroman, Erik, ed. *Corpus Codicum Danicorum Medii Ævi*. 5. *Annales*. Copenhagen: Munksgaard, 1965; Kroman, Erik, ed. *Danmarks middelalderlige annaler*. Copenhagen: Selskabet for udgivelse af kilder til dansk historie, 1980 [texts in Latin and Old Danish]. **Lit.**: Kristensen, Anne K. G. *Danmarks ældste annalistik. Studier over lundensisk Annalskrivning. i 12. og 13. Århundrede*. Skrifter udgivet af Det historiske institut ved Københavns Universitet, 3. Copenhagen: Gyldendal, 1969 [English summary]; Christiansen, Tage E. "Bo Falk eller Mogens Jensen? Yngre Sjællandske Krønikes forfatter." *Historisk tidsskrift* (Denmark) 84 (1984), 1–22 [English summary].

Inge Skovgaard-Petersen

[See also: Adam of Bremen; Chronicles; Land Registers; Monasticism; Saxo Grammaticus]

2. ICELAND (AND NORWAY). The medieval Icelandic annals can be divided into three groups (using Storm's numbering):

(a) The oldest annals: (I) *Resensannáll* (*Annales Reseniani*), (II) *Forni annáll* (*Annales vetustissimi*), (III) *Høyers annáll*, and the oldest part of (IV) *Konungsannáll* (*Annales regii*). These four annals were written down at the end of the 13th and the beginning of the 14th century. Annals II and IV are preserved in vellum MSS. I exists in an accurate copy made by Árni Magnússon, and III in a copy from about 1600. Annal I ends in 1295, II in 1314, and III in 1310; the oldest hand in IV ends in 1306, while the younger hands continue until 1341. Annals I–III are very closely related until about 1280; IV also has most of the same material, but is much fuller in the 12th and 13th centuries. All are derived from a common tradition, which must have had its beginning around 1280, although IV seems to have made use of another source.

(b) Annals written at the end of the 14th century: (V) *Skálholtsannáll*, (VI) a fragment of another annal from Skálholt, (VII) *Lǫgmannsannáll* (with the continuation, *Nýi annáll*), and (IX) *Flateyjarannáll*. With the exception of *Nýi annáll*, they are preserved in vellum MSS, all more or less defective, apart from IX. Until about 1300, these annals are based on annals related to I–III and/or IV, and for the 14th century are partly related. None of them goes farther than the year 1394, except for *Nýi annáll*, which continues VII until 1430 and was originally in the same codex, although now existing only in copies. *Nýi annáll* is an independent work written in Skálholt, while VII originates in the northern part of the country, compiled by the priest Einarr Hafliðason (d. 1393), mostly written down by himself.

(c) Two annals written in the 16th century with the use of lost medieval annals: (VIII) *Gottskálksannáll*, written by the priest Gottskálk Jónsson (d. 1590), preserved in the author's autograph. It goes to 1578, but until 1394 copies a lost annal; for the 15th century, it has only scattered entries, but is fuller in the 16th century. (X) *Oddaverja annáll* is a chronicle-like compilation from the end of the 16th century, which, along with numerous other sources, uses both VII (including *Nýi annáll*) and a lost annal related to IV.

All the oldest annals and most of the later ones contain a brief annal extract about foreign events from the birth of Christ (IV and IX from Caesar). In IV, these entries are in Latin, in the others mainly in Icelandic. In I–III, they are concerned primarily with the names of emperors and popes, containing among other items a complete list of popes. The foreign material is drawn from medieval chronicles and annals, probably through intermediaries. Much of the older material is found in Ekkehard of Aura; parallels are also found in Peter Comestor's *Historia scholastica* and in Vincent of Beauvais's *Speculum historiale*, as well as in Danish and Swedish annals. The Icelandic *Veraldar saga* is used in V and VII. Annal IV, and thereafter IX, are introduced with a survey of the first ages.

The Icelandic annals have a common chronological system based on the Easter cycle; individual years are indicated by Dominical letters and Lunar letters ("prikstafir") according to the system used in the Icelandic Easter tables. Years are normally added every tenth and twentieth year.

The Icelandic and Norse material derives primarily from Icelandic historical works. For the oldest period, *Íslendingabók* is the main source; later sources include *Hungrvaka* and the Icelandic *biskupa sögur*, *Íslendinga saga* and other sagas included in the Sturlunga collection, *Heimskringla*, *Knýtlinga saga*, *Hákonar saga Hákonarsonar*, *Magnúss saga lagabœtis*, and various *Íslendingasögur*.

Storm (1888) and Finnur Jónsson (1920–24) argued that no annals had been written before the MS tradition from which I–IV derive. The assertion was called into question by Beckman (1912), who demonstrated that certain annal entries from the 12th century (*e.g.*, on solar eclipses) had to be based on contemporary records; these entries could originally have been inserted into the Easter tables. Hermann Pálsson (1965, 1970) has argued that much of the material found in IV and not in I–III in the 12th and 13th centuries must originate in the monastery at Þingeyrar. Jónas Kristjánsson (1980) has examined Beckman's theories and established the influence of the archiepiscopal see in Lund in the first half of the 12th century, where the recording of Danish annals began at exactly the same time. A large number of entries from the 12th and 13th centuries cannot be derived from known historical works or sagas.

Ólafía Einarsdóttir (1964, 1965, 1967) has supported the theories of Storm and Finnur Jónsson, asserting that until the end of the 13th century the Icelandic annals appropriated their material from known historical works and sagas. Her opinions have been criticized by several scholars (Axelson 1968; Þorleifur Hauksson 1972; Jónas Kristjánsson 1980).

Several scholars have associated the annal tradition with Sturla Þórðarson (d. 1284) or his nearest circle. This ascription seems likely, even though convincing arguments are lacking. The composition of the MS in which Annal I is found could suggest that it was undertaken by a man with comprehensive historical interests (see Storm's edition, p. iv).

The Icelandic annals are very important historical sources, but the analysis of their interrelationships and their relation to the various sources is far from complete.

Ed.: Storm, Gustav, ed. *Islandske Annaler indtil 1578*. Christiania [Oslo]: Grøndahl, 1888; rpt. Norsk historisk kjeldeskrift-institutt, 1977; Buergel-Goodwin, Heinrich, ed. *Konungs annáll*. "*Annales Islandorum regii*." *Isländska handskriften No. 2087 4to i den gamla samlingen på det stora Kungliga Biblioteket i Köpenhamn i* diplomatarisk avtryck. Uppsala: Berling, 1906; Hannes Þorsteinsson, ed. "Nýi annáll." In *Annálar 1400–1800* 1. Reykjavik: Hið íslenzka bókmenntafélag, 1922–27, pp. 1–27. **Lit.**: Buergel-Goodwin, Heinrich. *Konungsannáll. "Annales Islandorum regii." Beschreibung der Handschrift, Laut- und Formenlehre, als Einleitung zu einem diplomatarischen Abdruck des Cod. reg. 2087, 4to, Gamle Samling der Kgl. Bibliotek zu Kopenhagen.* Munich: Oldenbourg, 1904; Kålund, Kr., and N. Beckman, eds. *Alfræði íslenzk. Islandsk encyclopædisk litteratur.* 3 vols. Copenhagen: Møller, 1908–18, vol. 2, pp. cxxiii–cxxxiii; Beckman, Natanael. "Annalstudier." *Studier i nordisk filologi* 3.4 (1912), 1–12; Beckman, Natanael. "Quellen und Quellenwert der isländischen Annalen." In *Xenia Lidéniana. Festskrift tillägnad professor Evald Lidén på hans femtio årsdag den 3 oktober 1912.* Stockholm: Norstedt, 1912, pp. 16–39; Finnur Jónsson. *Den oldnorske og oldislandske Litteraturs Historie.* 2nd ed. 3 vols. Copenhagen: Gad, 1920–24, vol. 3, pp. 68–76; Axelson, Sven. *Sverige i utländsk annalistik, 900–1400, med särskild hänsyn till de isländska annalerna.* Stockholm: Akademisk avhandling—Stockholms högskola, 1955. Ólafía Einarsdóttir. *Studier i kronologisk metode i tidlig islandsk historieskrivning.* Bibliotheca Historica Lundensis, 13. Stockholm: Natur och kultur, 1964, pp. 293–326; Ólafía Einarsdóttir, "Sverige i islandsk annalistik 1190–1270." *Scandia* (1965), 331–44; Ólafía Einarsdóttir. "Hvornår forfattedes sagaen om Magnus lagabøter." *Historisk tidsskrift* (Norway) 46 (1967), 59–67; Ólafía Einarsdóttir. "Om de to håndskrifter af Sturlunga saga." *Arkiv för nordisk filologi* 83 (1968), 44–80; Axelson, Sven. "Sverige i isländsk annalistik 1190–1270. Ett genmäle." *Historisk tidsskrift* (Norway) 47 (1968), 133–43; Hermann Pálsson. *Eftir þjóðveldið: heimildir annála um íslenzka sögu 1263–98.* Reykjavik: Heimskringla, 1965; Hermann Pálsson. *Tólfta öldin: Þættir um menn og málefni.* Reykjavik: Jón Helgason, 1970; Þorleifur Hauksson, ed. *Árna saga biskups.* Reykjavik: Stofnun Árna Magnússonar, 1972, pp. lxii–xcix; Jón Helgason. "Tólf annálagreinar frá myrkum árum." In *Sjötíu ritgerðir helgaðar Jakobi Benediktssyni 20 júlí 1977.* 2 vols. Ed. Einar G. Pétursson and Jónas Kristjánsson. Reykjavik: Stofnun Árna Magnússonar, 1977, vol. 2, pp. 399–418; Jónas Kristjánsson. "Annálar og Íslendingasögur." *Gripla* 4 (1980), 295–319.

Jakob Benediktsson

[**See also:** *Biskupa sögur; Hákonar saga gamla Hákonarsonar; Heimskringla; Hungrvaka; Íslendingabók; Íslendingasögur; Knýtlinga saga; Magnúss saga lagabœtis;* Sturla Þórðarson; *Sturlunga saga; Veraldar saga*]

3. SWEDEN. Swedish annals are short notices in Latin concerning historical events chronologically arranged, year by year. The custom of writing annals was brought to Sweden from Denmark by monks in connection with the expansion of monasticism. The oldest parts of the first Swedish annals are not much more than copies of Danish ones. Nine annals are preserved in Sweden, along with a number of more fragmentary ones. They may be divided into two groups, an older one consisting of three annals wholly or partially written shortly after their last events (with the end years 1263, 1288, and 1336, respectively), and a younger group produced in the 15th century or later. Most of the MSS are copies of the common type; four annals, however, are preserved in MSS where different hands have succeeded each other. A document of the last kind is Cod. Ups. C 70, which includes the oldest Swedish annal, covering the period 916 (the year when Denmark is said to have been christianized) to 1263. The original of the Danish part of the annal was probably written in a Dominican convent or at the archiepiscopal see in Lund; a copy of it is sup-

posed to have been brought by a Black Friar to a Dominican monastery in Sweden, perhaps Skänninge in Östergötland. Another of the oldest annals, which covers the period 1160–1320 plus a solitary notice for 1336, is preserved in Cod. Ups. C 92, together with a table of popes and a table of kings.

The relationship among the different annals has been the subject of much discussion. All are compilations, and there are many common notices. A firm chronological framework is constructed by use of lists of bishops, popes, and kings. Some data have been taken from calendars, chronological records, necrologia, and obituaries, especially those kept in monasteries (*e.g.*, Skänninge, Stockholm) and cathedral chapters (esp. Uppsala).

The annals play an important role for our knowledge of Sweden's medieval history; they have been extensively used by historians from the 16th century (Ericus Olai) up to the present.

The authors of the medieval rhymed chronicles benefited from annals. Ingvar Anderson (1928), for instance, found that the author of the *Erikskrönikan* had made use of certain annals, both for the chronological order and for many historical details.

As a rule, the individual notices for a given year have no mutual connection. The entries for the year 1275 (Cod. Holm D 4), for example, read as follows: *Bellum fuit in Hofwum, Eodem anno obiit domicellus Ericus* ("There was a battle at Hova. The same year Prince Erik died"). But exceptions may be found, such as the following notices for the year 1344 (in Cod. Ups. DG 26:12): *Mortuus est dominus Wlpho Gudmari maritus beatæ Birgittæ, Eodem avtem anno primum factæ sunt revelationes eidem beatæ Birgittæ* ("Ulf Gudmarsson, the husband of St. Birgitta, died. The same year the holy Birgitta had her first revelations").

Ed.: Paulsson, Göte, ed. *Annales suecici medii ævi. Svensk medeltidsannalistik.* Bibliotheca historica Lundensis, 32. Lund: Gleerup, 1974; Fant, Ericus Michael, ed. *Scriptores rerum Svecicarum medii ævi.* 3 vols. Uppsala: Zeipel & Palmblad, 1818–76 [a much-used edition that is now out of date, the editorial principles being unsatisfactory]. **Lit.**: Andersson, Ingvar. *Källstudier till Sveriges historia 1230–1436.* Lund: Lindström, 1928 [esp. pp. 1–3, 20–43, 55–100]; Bolin, Sture. *Om Nordens äldsta historieforskning. Studier över dess metodik och källvärde.* Lunds Universitets årsskrift, N.F., avd. 1, Band 27.3. Lund: Ohlsson, 1931; Engström, Sten. "Om tillkomsten av den s.k. Chronologia anonymi." In *Kungl. humanistiska vetenskapssamfundet i Uppsala. Årsbok 1963–64.* Stockholm and Wiesbaden: Almqvist & Wiksell; Harrassowitz, 1966, pp. 1–80 [German summary, pp. 68–78].

Gösta Holm

Áns saga bogsveigis ("The Saga of Án Bow-bender") belongs to a group of *fornaldarsögur* known as *Hrafnistumanna sögur* ("sagas of the men of Hrafnista"), which also include *Ketils saga hœngs, Gríms saga loðinkinna,* and *Qrvar-Odds saga.*

The oldest extant recension of *Áns saga bogsveigis* is preserved in MS AM 343a 4to from the early 15th century. Orthographical variations in the text suggest that the scribe had access to two earlier MSS. The saga exists in some form in forty-six paper MSS of later date. In addition, there exist eight fits of *rímur*, composed in the beginning of the 15th century and based on an earlier version of the saga.

The narrative is reminiscent of the style of many *Íslendingasögur*, but in terms of content the saga is a typical *fornaldarsaga*. Án is a stock figure, the youth with no skill or promise, ridiculously dressed in tatters, despised and insulted.

His enormous strength is a secret, since he takes no part in manly sports, and his ultimate success is a surprise only to the other actors in his story. As a youth, he meets a dwarf, Litr, who gives him a great bow and some arrows in the tradition of the *Gusisnautar* ("gifts of Gusir"), the arrow that Qrvar-Oddr took from Gusir, king of the Finns. When he is grown up, Án has his brother Þórir take him to the court of the bad King Ingjaldr, where he receives the name "bogsveigr" ("bow-bender") after a silly trick he performs to attract the attention of the warriors. Án is outlawed for killing the king's two half-brothers by shooting magnificently, but illegally, from hiding. He flees the king's vengeance, but has started a lifetime feud, which is eventually ended when he has his revenge on the king through his son Þórir háleggr ("long-leg").

Ed.: Rafn, C. C., ed. *Fornaldar sögur Nordrlanda*. 3 vols. Copenhagen: Popp, 1829–30, vol. 2, pp. 323–62; Ólafur Halldórsson, ed. *Áns rímur bogsveigis*. Íslenzkar miðaldarímur, 2. Reykjavik: Stofnun Árna Magnússonar, 1973; Campbell, Calum, ed. *Áns saga bogsveigis* [in preparation: Editiones Arnamagnæanæ]. **Lit.**: Kölbing, Eugen. *Beiträge zur vergleichenden Geschichte der romantischen Poesie und Prosa des Mittelalters*. Breslau: Koshher, 1876; Läffler, Leopold F. *En kärleksvisa i Áns saga bogsvegis*. Svenska Litteratursällskapet i Finland, 103.1. Helsingfors: [s.n.], 1912; Reuschel, Helga. *Untersuchungen über Stoff und Stil der Fornaldarsaga*. Buhl-Badan: Konkordia, 1933; Schlauch, Margaret. *Romance in Iceland*. Princeton: Princeton University Press; New York: American-Scandinavian Foundation; London: Allen & Unwin, 1934; rpt. New York: Russell & Russell, 1973; Stefán Einarsson. *A History of Icelandic Literature*. New York: Johns Hopkins University Press; American-Scandinavian Foundation, 1957; Hughes, S. F. D. "The Literary Antecedents of *Áns saga bogsveigis*." *Mediaeval Scandinavia* 9 (1976), 196–235.

Calum Campbell

[**See also:** *Fornaldarsögur*; *Gríms saga loðinkinna*; *Ketils saga hœngs*; *Rímur*; *Qrvar-Odds saga*]

Ansgar, St., also known as the "Apostle of the North," was born in Picardy around 801 and died in Bremen on February 3, 865, the date of his feast day. He was educated at the Benedictine monastery at Corbie, and in 822 was sent as a teacher to the monastery of Corvey in Westphalia. When King Harald Klak of Denmark converted to Christianity in 826 at the court of Emperor Louis the Pious, Ansgar was recommended by Archbishop Ebo of Reims and Abbot Wala of Corvey to undertake missionary activity in Denmark. After the expulsion of Harald from the country, Ansgar traveled to Sweden, where King Björn permitted him to found the first church in Scandinavia at Björkö. In 831, Ansgar was consecrated first bishop of Hamburg, and in 832 was named by Pope Gregory IV as papal legate for the Scandiavian and Slavonic mission. Ansgar entrusted the mission of Sweden to Gausbert, and focused his attention on converting Denmark. In 834, through the patronage of Emperor Louis, the monastery of Turnhout, Flanders, was assigned to Ansgar as a training center and source of revenue for the Scandinavian mission. But in 845, the Christian mission suffered a severe setback when the Vikings plundered Hamburg. In 847, Ansgar was appointed to the see of Bremen, which was united with Hamburg in 847/8, and he began his missionary efforts anew. He succeeded in founding churches in Schleswig, Ribe, and Sigtuna.

Ansgar probably wrote many volumes, including extracts from devotional texts and perhaps also a booklet on his visions by which the whole of his life was guided. But only one letter, some prayers (*pigmentum*), and a life of St. Willehad are preserved. The main source about Ansgar's life is Rimbert's *Vita Anskarii*, which contains much valuable information on the history of the Catholic mission in early-medieval Scandinavia.

Lit.: Rimbert. *Vita Anskarii*. *Scriptores rerum Germanicarum* 55. Ed. G. Waitz. Hannover: Bibliopoli Hahniani, 1884; Robinson, Charles H., trans. *Anskar, the Apostle of the North, 801–865: Translated from the Vita Anskarii by Bishop Rimbert, His Fellow Missionary and Successor*. London: Society for the Propagation of the Gospel in Foreign Parts, 1921; Allmang, G. "Anschaire." In *Dictionnaire d'histoire et de géographie ecclésiastiques* 3. Ed. Mgr. Alfred Baudrillart. Paris: Letouzey et Ané, 1924, cols. 435–41; Oppenheim, Philippus. *Der heilige Ansgar und die Anfänge des Christentums in den nordischen Ländern: Ein Lebens- und Zeitbild*. Munich: Heuber, 1931; Oppermann, C. J. A. *The English Missionaries in Sweden and Finland*. London: Society for Promoting Christian Knowledge; New York: Macmillan, 1937; Weibull, L. "Ansgarius." *Scandia* 14 (1941), 186–99; "St. Anskar." In *Butler's Lives of the Saints* 1. Rev. ed. Herbert Thurston, S.J., and Donald Attwater. New York: Kenedy, 1956, pp. 242–3; Hilpisch, St. "Ansgar." In *Lexikon für Theologie und Kirche* 1. Ed. Josef Höfler and Karl Rahner. Freiburg im Breisgau: Herder, 1957, cols. 597–8; Maarschallkerweerd, Pancrazi. "Anscario." In *Bibliotheca Sanctorum* 1. Rome: Città Nuova, 1961, cols. 1337–9; Mehnert, Gottfried. *Ansgar, Apostel des Nordens*. Kiel: Lutherische Verlagsgesellschaft, 1964; Dörres, Hermann, and Georg Kretschmar. *Ansgar: Seine Bedeutung für die Mission*. Hamburg: Velmede, 1965; Schultz, S. A. "Ansgar, St." In *New Catholic Encyclopedia* 1. New York etc.: McGraw-Hill, 1967, p. 586; Lammers, W. "Ansgar." In *Lexikon des Mittelalters* 1. Munich and Zurich: Artemis, 1980, cols. 690–1; Hallencreutz, Carl. F. "Missionary Spirituality—the Case of Ansgar." *Studia Theologica* 36 (1982), 105–18.

Peter Dinzelbacher

[**See also:** Conversion]

Arabic Sources for Scandinavia(ns).

The age of Islamic expansion (7th and 8th centuries) resulted in the spread of Arabic-speaking and Islamic peoples over an area stretching from the Atlantic to the borders of China, from the Sahara and Sind to northern Spain, the Caucasus, the Caspian and Aral seas. The Viking Age (9th–11th centuries) finds the Scandinavians or people of Scandinavian background in places as far east or south as the Volga, the Caspian and Black Sea area, Baghdad, Spain, the Mediterranean, and North Africa. Later, Scandinavians traveled to the Holy Land as crusaders and pilgrims. There was, then, considerable scope for direct contact between Scandinavians on the one hand, and Islamic/Arabic-speaking peoples on the other; and information about the former and their homelands naturally also reached the latter indirectly. The "Golden Age" of Arabic literature (750–1055) corresponds relatively closely with the Viking Age, and the authors of the Arabic "Silver Age" (1055–1258) also sometimes offer information about Scandinavia and Scandinavians. Arabic sources refer to Scandinavians mainly under two names: *ar-Rūs* (also: *ar-Rūsīya*), particularly those in Russia and easterly areas; and *al-Majūs*, used particularly in Andalusian or North African sources and/or of Vikings in the west. Other names for Scandinavia(ns) also appear, *e.g.*, *Warank* (*cf.* Old Norse *væringjar*) and *al-Urmān* (*cf.* Latin *Nordmanni, etc.*).

It is primarily the works of Arabic-writing geographers, historians, and travelers that are of interest in this context. Perhaps the oldest notice appears in a work (essentially a list of post-routes) compiled by Ibn Khurradādhbih (ca. 825–912), which tells how the Rūs merchants carry their wares (furs, swords) along the Russian rivers to the Black Sea and the Caspian; often they travel the length of the Caspian to Jurjān and thence by camel to Baghdad. The historian al-Yaʿqūbī (d. ca. 890s) is the first to tell of Viking activity in Spain and makes a positive identification between ar-Rūs and al-Majūs. Of several later Arabic historians who also tell of the various Viking attacks on Spain during the 9th and 10th centuries, Ibn al-Qūṭīya (d. 977) gives an especially detailed account of the Majūs attack on Seville in 844. Ibn Rusta's geography (written ca. 903–913) contains a quite detailed ethnographical account of the Rūs, perhaps those from Novgorod. It mentions, for example, their attacks on the "Slavs" (aṣ-aqāliba), their slaves, their many towns, their physical appearance, clothes, system of arbitration, duels, medicine men, sacrifices, and burial customs (cremation and suttee). Undoubtedly, the most sensational source in this context is Ibn Faḍlān's firsthand account of an embassy sent by the caliph in Baghdad to the Bulgars on the Volga in the early 920s. Ibn Faḍlān gives an eyewitness description of the Rūs merchants he encountered on the Volga and the ship-burial cremation of one of their chieftains with the concomitant sacrifice of one of his slave girls. He also gives secondhand information about the Rūs king and his lifestyle Al-Masʿūdī (d. 956), one of the most important figures of medieval Arabic letters, mentions both the Rūs and the Majūs as well as northernmost Europe in his works. He tells, e.g., of Rūs mercenaries in Byzantine service and of an ill-fated Rūs expedition to the Caspian in 912. Rūs activity on the Caspian is also mentioned by the historian (Ibn) Miskawayh (d. 1030). He describes in detail how the Rūs occupied the town of Bardhaʿa (Azerbaijan) in 943, but were eventually forced to withdraw by disease and by the local Muslim ruler. Al-Idrīsī's Kitāb Rujār ("Book of Roger"), written for Roger II of Sicily (completed 1154), describes a Ptolemaic world map. This map covered Iceland, the Faroes, and the rest of Scandinavia, and featured various Scandinavian towns (e.g., Oslo, Sigtuna). The account by Ibn Diḥya (d. 1235) of a handsome Andalusian poet al-Ghazāl's (fl. 9th century) diplomatic mission to a country of the Majūs in the north should be treated with extreme circumspection as a historical source. Al-Qazwīnī's (d. 1283) geography contains descriptions of, inter alia, Norse whaling off Ireland and probably (on information derived from a 10th-century Spanish Jewish traveler, Ibrāhīm ibn Yaʿqūb aṭ-Ṭurṭūshī) the Danish Viking Age town of Schleswig. The greatest historian of medieval Islam, Ibn Khaldūn (d. 1406), also mentions the Rūs and interestingly dates a Majūs attack on Nakūr in present-day Morocco as early as about 760. He, as well as previous writers (most notably Ibn al-Athīr [d. 1233]), refers to the crusader attack on Sidon of 1110, in which the Norwegian king Sigurðr Jórsalafari ("crusader") took part.

Ed.: There are at least fifty medieval writers in Arabic whose works are relevant under the present heading. Extracts from precisely fifty authors were published with introductions and notes by Seippel, Alexander. Rerum Normannicarum fontes Arabici. Oslo: Brøgger, 1896–1928. Seippel's excerpts are translated into Norwegian with useful introductions, notes, and bibliography by Birkeland, Harris. Nordens historie i middelalderen etter harabiske kilder. Oslo: Dybwad, 1954. But a large number of Seippel's extracts have, of course, been reedited since 1896. For new editions, translations, studies, etc., see: The Encyclopaedia of Islam. Leiden: Brill, 1913–38, but more particu-

larly: The Encyclopaedia of Islam: New Edition. Leiden: Brill, 1954–[in progress], under individual authors. Both editions of The Encyclopaedia also contain articles on general topics (e.g., [1st ed.]: Rūs; [2nd ed.]: Djughrāfiyā; al-Madjūs). Bib.: A fairly recent summary bibliography of the subject is Wikander, Stig. "Bibliographia normanno-orientalis." Bibliography of Old Norse–Icelandic Studies (1974), 7–16. Lit.: Background to individual authors and topics: Ibn Khurradādhbih: Hrbek, Ivan. "The Russians in Baghdād in the 9th Century." Archiv orientální 36 (1968), 563–6. Arabic sources for the Vikings in Spain and North Africa: Jón Stefánsson. "The Vikings in Spain. From Arabic (Moorish) and Spanish Sources." Saga-Book of the Viking Club 6 (1908–09), 31–46; Melvinger, Arne. Les premières incursions des Vikings en Occident d'après les sources arabes. Uppsala: Almqvist & Wiksell, 1955. Ibn Fadlān: The literature is extensive. There is an edition and German translation with detailed commentary and notes by Togan, A. Zeki Validi. Ibn Fadlān's Reisebericht. Leipzig: Deuʿsche Morgenländische Gesellschaft, 1939; rpt. Nendeln: Kraus, 1966. A Swedish translation is in Wikander, Stig. Araber vikingar väringar. Norrtälje: Svenska Humanistiska Förbundet, 1978, pp. 31–75. A useful starting point is Smyser, H. M. "Ibn Fadlān's account of the Rūs with some commentary and some allusions to Beowulf." In Franciplegius: Medieval and Linguistic Studies in Honor of Francis Peabody Magoun, Jr. Ed. Jess B. Bessinger, Jr., and Robert P. Creed. New York: New York University Press; London: Allen and Unwin, 1965, pp. 92–119. Al-Masʿūdī: Dunlop, D. M. The History of the Jewish Khazars. Princeton Oriental Studies, 16. Princeton: Princeton University Press, 1954; Shboul, Ahmad M. H. Al-Masʿūdī & His World: A Muslim Humanist and His Interest in Non-Muslims. London: Ithaca, 1979. (Ibn) Miskawayh: Margoliouth, D. S. "The Russian Seizure of Bardhaʿah in 943 A.D." Bulletin of the School of Oriental Studies, London Institution 1.2 (1918), 82–95. Ibn Diḥya's account of al-Ghazāl: The Encyclopaedia of Islam. 2nd ed., s.v. al-Ghazāl; El-Hajji, Abdurrahman Ali. Andalusian Diplomatic Relations with Western Europe During the Umayyad Period (A.H. 138–366/A.D. 755–976). An Historical Survey. Beirut: Dar al-Irshad, 1970, pp. 166–203. Aṭ-Ṭurṭūshī: El-Hajji, Andalusian Diplomatic Relations, pp. 228–71. Al-Idrīsī: Tuulio (Tallgren), O. J. Du nouveau sur Idrīsī. Studia Orientalia, 6.3. Helsinki: Societas Orientalis Fennica, 1936. Ibn Khaldūn's account of the Majūs attack on Nakūr: Melvinger, Arne. Les premières incursions des Vikings, pp. 129 ff.

Richard Perkins

Architecture. By and large, Scandinavia, comprising Denmark, Sweden, Norway, and Finland, remained a wood-building area throughout the Middle Ages. Only churches and the most important castles and palaces for the king, the bishops, and, in the late Middle Ages, the nobility, were built in stone. In Finland, Sweden, and Norway, the majority of the churches were built in wood. Wood also remained the building material as far as vernacular architecture is concerned. Only toward the end of the Middle Ages did stone buildings appear in the towns, especially in Stockholm and Malmö. A survey of architectural developments may be divided into three parts: churches (discussed in separate entries), castles and palaces, and vernacular buildings.

Castles and palaces. Broadly speaking, the evolution of military architecture in Scandinavia in the Middle Ages followed the general European pattern. As early as the 11th century, fortifications of the motte type, earthen mounds crowned by wooden towers and surrounded by ditches and palisades, must have existed in Denmark, Sweden, and Norway (Oslo). The first Danish stone constructions, dating from the 12th century, were freestanding, mostly circular, towers, probably surrounded by palisades or even walls (Søborg I and Bastrup at Zealand). Square towers (*kastalar*) were built in Sweden (Stockholm, Kalmar, Borgholm), Gotland, and Finland. Besides the tower castle, curtain-wall castles also occur from around the middle of the 12th century, *e.g.*, Søborg II with a *palatium* and a chapel situated within the precincts. Søborg was obviously modeled on the 11th-century *pfalz* (imperial palace) in Goslar, Germany. Bishop Absalon's castle in Copenhagen, founded in 1167, had an almost circular shape, while in Norway King Sverrir Sigurðarson built strongholds surrounded by stone enclosures of a more irregular form in Trondheim and Bergen toward the end of the 12th century.

More regular curtain-wall castles, often with small towers (*tourelles*) at the corners of the *enceinte*, appear in Denmark from the first half of the 13th century (*e.g.*, Nyborg, Funen, Dragsholm, Zealand, and Hammershus, Bornholm). In Sweden, the old tower castle in Stockholm remained the core of a new, four-sided construction built around 1250, parts of which are still preserved. Other castles of similar type were Örebro, Nyköping, and Västerås, together with Ragnhildsholmen, Akershus, and Båhus, Norway. In Finland, a series of castles, including Åbo, Tavastehus, and Viborg, were founded in the second half of the 13th century. Åbo and Tavastehus were regular curtain-wall castles, while Viborg started out as a tower castle surrounded by a wall. Besides castles proper, so-called "defense churches" (two-storied churches, or churches built with towers for defense) were built in Scandinavia in the 12th century, especially at Bornholm, Öland, and around Kalmar.

The early castles in Scandinavia were built solely for warfare. The living quarters were usually rather small and coarse. Around 1250, the Norwegian King Håkon Håkonarson built a remarkable palace in Bergen. Although it was surrounded by curtain walls with two gate towers, it was primarily designed as a residence for the king. The precinct contained two large halls, one of which, Håkonshallen, is still standing. It is a three-storied building, including cellarage in the basement, probably living rooms on the first floor, and a large banqueting hall (37 by 16.4 m.) in the uppermost story. The details are Early Gothic and show influence from England. A little later (*ca.* 1270), a massive tower building containing living quarters and a private chapel for the king was built by Håkon's successor Magnús. This tower forms the core of the Rosenkrantz tower from 1563–1565.

In Scandinavia in the 14th century, castles and city walls with projecting towers were built to cover the length of the walls between them. The city wall surrounding Visby in Gotland from around 1280 is the first, and in fact a unique example of this kind of fortification in Scandinavia as far as city walls are concerned. Kalmar castle was built with four round protruding corner towers from 1275–1300. Vordingborg, with its famous "Gåsetårn" still standing, and Kalundborg are Danish examples from around 1350 contemporary with Tønsberghus in Norway, while Raseborg in Finland is a little later (1380).

Influence from the Baltic area, where the Teutonic Knights developed special types of castles, letting regular square walls merge with four building ranges around an open courtyard, can be traced in some of the Scandinavian castles built or rebuilt in the 14th century, *e.g.*, Åbo and Tavastehus in Finland, Stegeholm in Sweden, Visborg in Gotland, and "Krogen," later replaced by Kronborg castle, in Denmark. Besides these new types of castles, older types persisted. Tower castles (keeps or donjons) were still erected, but usually with larger and better living quarters intended for permanent living than the older towers. Danish examples are the Korsør

tower, Gurre in Zealand; and Kärnan near Helsingborg, now Sweden. A late example is Gjorslev castle, Zealand, built around 1400 by the bishop of Roskilde on a cruciform plan with a massive tower over the crossing.

Fortified manorhouses are known in Scandinavia from around 1400 onward. Good examples still preserved are Vik's house in Uppland and Glimmingehus in Scania (1499). Even the Rosenkrantz tower in Bergen, built by Scottish craftsmen as late as in 1562–1565, must be said to represent a late-medieval type of building.

Around 1500, castles with gun towers appear in Scandinavia. Steinvikholm, Trøndelag, Norway (1525–1527), is a good example. It has a fairly regular trapezoid plan with two diagonally placed projecting round towers modeled on castles built by the Teutonic Knights in the Baltic area (Riga). Another castle of this kind is the mighty Olofsborg in the eastern part of Finland.

Vernacular architecture. Four different building techniques were in vernacular use in Scandinavia in the Middle Ages: corner timbering (*i.e.*, walls of horizontal logs notched together in the corners), stave building (frame building with vertical planking), frame building with horizontal planking, and half timbering. Corner timbering was widely used within the Scandinavian pine-forest area, while the frame-building techniques, including half timbering, were mostly used in the southern and western areas, where oak was the dominant tree. In Norway, however, the stave building technique with pine as building material, reached a peak of perfection in the stave churches. Buildings in frame construction with horizontal planking are also occasionally found along the coast where wood was sparse.

The longhouse (*hall, skåle, sal*) was a frame building, often with a series of internal posts supporting the roof. Usually it was divided into areas or quarters for both men and cattle with communication between the areas. The type goes back to prehistoric times, but it seems to have been in use, especially in Denmark and along the coast and in the mountain areas of Norway, in the Middle Ages as well.

Within the pine areas of Finland, Sweden, and Norway, the *gård* (farmstead) seems to have consisted of a series of relatively small timber buildings, each built for a special purpose and placed independent of each other, either within the frame of a rectangle, or in Norway more at random. Besides buildings for cattle and for crops, the buildings were *stove* ("dwelling-house"), *eldhus* ("firehouse"), *bur* (storage house, usually one-storied), and *loft* (storage house, usually two-storied). Similar types of buildings were also used in towns. The ground plan of the *stove* may differ, but the two- or three-room plan was most common, especially in Norway.

Lit.: (a) **Military architecture**: Frølén, H. *Nordens befästa rundkyrkor.* Stockholm: [n.p.], 1911; Fischer, Gerhard, and Dorethea Fischer. *Norske kongeborger.* 2 vols. Oslo: Gyldendal, 1951–54; Tuulse, Armin, et al. "Borg." *KLNM* 2 (1957), 119–38; Tuulse, Armin. *Burgen des Abendlandes.* Trans. Gerhard Eimer. Vienna: Schroll, 1958; Stiesdal, H. "Types of Public and Private Fortifications in Denmark." In *Danish Medieval History, New Currents.* Ed. Niels Skyum-Nielsen and Niels Lund. Copenhagen: Museum Tusculanum, 1981, pp. 207–20. (b) **Vernacular architecture**: Erixon, Sigurd E., ed. *Byggnadskultur.* Nordisk kultur, 17. Stockholm: Bonnier; Oslo: Aschehoug; Copenhagen: Schultz, 1953; Erixon, Sigurd E., ed. *Landbrug og bebyggelse.* Nordisk kultur, 13. Stockholm: Bonnier; Oslo: Aschehoug; Copenhagen: Schultz, 1956; Steensberg, Axel. "Bindingsværk." *KLNM* 1 (1956), 546–54;

Steensberg, Axel. "Bulhus." *KLNM* 2 (1957), 348–60; Itkonen, T. I., and Allan Karker. "Bur." *KLNM* 2 (1957), 366–8; Stigum, Hilmar, *et al.* "Eldhus." *KLNM* 3 (1958), 555–61; Steensberg, Axel, *et al.* "Gård." *KLNM* 5 (1960), 618–35; Homman, Olle, *et al.* "Knuttimring." *KLNM* 8 (1963), 603–15; Horskjær, Erik, and Charlotte Blindheim. "Langhus." *KLNM* 10 (1965), 313–6; Homman, Olle, *et al.* "Loft." *KLNM* 10 (1965), 669–78; Berg, Arne, *et al.* "Stavbygning." *KLNM* 17 (1972), 84–95; Berg, Arne, *et al.* "Stove." *KLNM* 17 (1972), 242–53; Stoklund, Bjarne, and Niilo Valonen. "Stuehus." *KLNM* 17 (1972), 342–8; Myhre, Bjørn, *et al.*, eds. *Vestnorsk byggeskikk gjennom to tusen år: tradisjon og forandring fra romertid til det 19. århundre.* Arkeologisk Museum i Stavanger, Skrifter 7. Stavanger: Arkeologisk Museum i Stavanger, 1981.

Hans Emil-Lidén

[See also: Churches, Stone; Fortification; Fortresses, Trelleborg; Houses; Stave Church]

Arinbjarnarkviða *see* Egill Skalla-Grímsson

Árna saga biskups

Árna saga biskups ("The Saga of Bishop Árni") is one of the Icelandic *biskupa sögur*, and narrates the life of Árni Þorláksson, bishop in Skálholt 1271–1298. The saga is preserved in forty MSS and MS fragments, including two parchment fragments from the 14th century, i.e., two leaves in AM 220 VI fol. and three leaves from the so-called *Reykjarfjarðarbók* (R) of *Sturlunga saga*, AM 122b fol. All known versions of the saga are derived from the latter MS mainly through two copies (*B, J) made in the 17th century.

Árna saga is both a political document and a traditional biography, following the hero's life in strict chronological order. His youth is described briefly, apart from some minor incidents showing his piety or forwarding his elevation. Once Árni has been consecrated bishop at age thirty-four, the author concentrates on his role in the disputes between the Church and the leading laymen, especially over property donated to the churches, but owned and administered from the beginning by powerful families. The consolidation of ecclesiastical and secular power was the period's most important political issue, after Iceland had come under the Norwegian throne. The saga's meticulous account of this protracted struggle is therefore an invaluable source of Icelandic history for the years 1270–1290. *Árna saga* abounds with references to letters and documents; sixty-eight written sources are directly quoted, and more than twenty others are mentioned. The author goes so far as to reconstruct the speeches of the bishop and his antagonists in a true classical tradition. The access to written sources locates the author in Skálholt and in Bishop Árni's immediate surroundings. As a chronological source, the author used a chronicle closely related to the *Annales regii*.

The *terminus post quem* for the writing of the saga is fairly well defined. It was written after Árni Helgason, Árni Þorláksson's nephew, succeeded him to the bishop's office (1304–1320). For the *terminus ante quem*, we have to rely on indirect evidence. Various points in the saga indicate that Árni Helgason was alive when it was written, and that the great struggle between bishop and laymen was still fresh in the author's memory. Árni Helgason himself seems to be the informant for a few incidents. The saga was written most likely in Skálholt during Árni Helgason's term in office, either by Árni himself or under his auspices.

In its preserved form, the narrative ends in 1290, seven years before the church farm dispute was settled. Scholars have dis-agreed as to whether the saga originally extended up to Árni's death or whether it went any farther than 1290. This question is difficult to decide, but certain facts can be mentioned: *Árna saga* was placed at the end of MS R. The copy of R that is thought to be the oldest, J, has one short additional chapter, which is a digression from the main subject and does not form a convincing conclusion. Still, there is no reason to consider this chapter a later addition. Material that could be derived from the saga looms large in chronicles of the period 1290–1297. But the settlement of the church farm dispute, which took place in Norway in 1297, is nowhere mentioned in the chronicles. We may thus suppose that something was lost from the end of the saga, and that the saga never extended to the settlement of the church farm dispute and the death of Bishop Árni.

Ed.: [Jón Sigurðsson and Guðbrandur Vigfússon, eds.] *Biskupa sögur.* 2 vols. Copenhagen: Møller, 1858–78, vol. 1, pp. 679–786; Þorleifur Hauksson, ed. *Árna saga biskups.* Reykjavik: Stofnun Árna Magnússonar, 1972. **Bib.**: Halldór Hermannsson. *Bibliography of the Icelandic Sagas and Minor Tales.* Islandica, 1. Ithaca: Cornell University Library, 1908, p. 1; Halldór Hermannsson. *The Sagas of the Icelanders (Íslendinga sögur): A Supplement to Bibliography of the Icelandic Sagas and Minor Tales.* Islandica, 24. Ithaca: Cornell University Press; London: Oxford University Press, 1935, p. 15; Jóhann S. Hannesson. *The Sagas of the Icelanders (Íslendingasögur): A Supplement to Islandica I and XXIV.* Islandica, 38. Ithaca: Cornell University Press, 1957, p. 15. **Lit.**: Finnur Jónsson. *Den oldnorske og oldislandske Litteraturs Historie.* 2nd ed. 3 vols. Copenhagen: Gad, 1920–24, vol. 3, pp. 62–3; Magnús Már Lárusson. "Árna saga biskups." *KLNM* 1 (1956), 251; Jón Jóhannesson. *A History of the Old Icelandic Commonwealth. Íslendinga saga.* Trans. Haraldur Bessason. University of Manitoba Icelandic Studies, 2. Winnipeg: University of Manitoba Press, 1974; Magnús Stefánsson. "Frá goðakirkju til biskupskirkju." In *Saga Íslands.* Ed. Sigurður Líndal. Reykjavik: Hið íslenska bókmentafélag, 1978, vol. 3, pp. 111–226; Foote, Peter. "Bischofssaga (*Biskupa sögur*)." In *Reallexikon der Germanischen Altertumskunde.* Berlin and New York: de Gruyter, 1978, vol. 3, p. 42; Bekker-Nielsen, Hans. "Árna saga biskups." In *Dictionary of the Middle Ages.* Ed. Joseph R. Strayer. New York: Scribner, 1982–89, vol. 1, p. 537.

Þorleifur Hauksson

[See also: *Biskupa sögur*; *Jónsbók*]

Arnórr Þórðarson jarlaskáld

Arnórr Þórðarson jarlaskáld (after 1010–after 1073). The son of the skald Þórðr Kolbeinsson, Arnórr grew up at Hítarnes, West Iceland. In early adulthood, he sailed to Norway (and possibly Denmark) as a merchant and skald, making an exuberant appearance before Magnús Ólafsson góði ("good") and Haraldr Sigurðarson (later harðráði, "hard ruler"). His nickname, "earls' skald," celebrates his service of the earls of Orkney, Rǫgnvaldr Brúsason (d. *ca.* 1045), to whom he was related by marriage, and Þorfinnr Sigurðarson (d. *ca.* 1065). His (now vestigial) memorial poems for Icelanders who died around 1055 and around 1073 might suggest that he resettled in Iceland in later life.

Arnórr's verse survives in 581 and one-half lines of fragmentary quotations in vellum MSS of the late 13th to 15th centuries and in 17th- or 18th-century paper copies. The chief sources are *Flateyjarbók* (108 half-strophes), *Hrokkinskinna* (83), *Hulda* (68), *Morkinskinna* (33), and MSS of *Heimskringla* (41), *Orkneyinga saga* (38), *Snorra Edda* (18 and 3 couplets), *Fagrskinna* (16), and Snorri Sturluson's separate *Ólafs saga helga* (15).

Arnórr's poetry richly exploits skaldic tradition with motifs of weapons flying, carrion beasts scavenging, or ships being launched; a great variety of *heiti*, including nine for "sword"; and some 150 kennings, from the obvious *Áleifs sonr* to the esoteric *erfiði Austra* ("burden of [the dwarf] Austri" = "sky"). He also employs more unusual items, including images of sparks flying from weapons and horns sounding, and several rare and unique words. Fleeting allusions to the gods Óðinn, Njǫrðr, or Baldr, to valkyries, or to pagan creation myths, belong, like those to such legendary heroes as the Burgundian Gjúki, purely to the level of diction. The numerous Christian references, including one to God and St. Michael judging mankind, seem by contrast substantial and sincere. The poetry is by skaldic standards moderately ornate in diction and word order, rather than extremely artificial. There are verbal resemblances to lines by the 11th-century skalds Hallfreðr vandræðaskáld ("the troublesome skald"), Sighvatr Þórðarson, and Þjóðólfr Arnórsson. The *hrynhent* poems by Markús Skeggjason (*ca.* 1104) and Sturla Þórðarson (*ca.* 1262) echo Arnórr.

Four main poems can be reconstructed from the fragments, all panegyrics on contemporary Norse rulers and all in the *dróttkvætt* meter except *Hrynhenda*, which is the first surviving panegyric in *hrynhent*. *Hrynhenda* (*ca.* 1045) begins with fleeting references to Arnórr's own trading voyages, but mainly concerns Magnús Óláfsson: his boyhood journey out of exile in Russia, conquest of Norway, triumphant voyage to Denmark, suppression of Wends at Jóm (Jomne) and Hlýrskógsheiðr (Lyrskovsheden), and ousting of Sven Estridsen from Denmark, especially at Helganes (Helgenæs). The only major poem by Arnórr to address directly a living hero, *Hrynhenda* is distinguished by extravagant praise (in apostrophes and second-person verbs) and seafaring descriptions both precise and imaginative. Named for its novel meter, *Hrynhenda* has a strongly trochaic pulse and relatively straightforward word order.

Magnússdrápa (*ca.* 1046/7) covers much the same events, but offers more factual detail and close-up battle description, including macabre images of the wolf scavenging on the battlefield.

Þorfinnsdrápa (*ca.* 1065) commemorates Þorfinnr Sigurðarson's victories against the Scots at Dýrnes (Deerness) and Torfnes (Tarbatness), defeat of his nephew Rǫgnvaldr off Rauðabjǫrg (Roberry), and raiding at Vatnsfjǫrðr (Loch Vatten) in the Hebrides and in England. It has an unusually personal tone of lament, and Arnórr recalls winter drinking scenes and his own presence at Vatnsfjǫrðr and (reluctantly) at Rauðabjǫrg. Battle descriptions are enlivened by short clauses focusing on graphic details and sharpened by specification of place, time, and numbers of ships. The general praise includes the *impossibilia* topos, "the sun will turn black, the earth sink in the sea, and the sky be rent before a ruler finer than Þorfinnr will be born in the isles," which echoes *Vǫluspá* or a common source.

Haraldsdrápa (*ca.* 1066, called simply an *erfidrápa* 'memorial poem' for Haraldr in the MSS) covers Haraldr Sigurðarson's later career: his struggle for Denmark against Sven Estridsen (especially a raid on Fjón [Funen] and victory at the Niz [Nis/Nissan] estuary), home policy (suppression of an Upland rebellion), and attempted conquest of England (victory near York, defeat and death in the unnamed battle of Stamford Bridge). There is one personal prayer for Haraldr, but otherwise the treatment is distant and vague, padded out by generalized praise and heroic clichés. Here, Arnórr uses interesting compound adjectives, but fewer and plainer kennings than elsewhere.

Ed.: Finnur Jónsson, ed. *Den norsk-islandske skjaldedigtning.* Vols. 1A–2A (tekst efter håndskrifterne) and 1B–2B (rettet tekst). Copenhagen and Christiania [Oslo]: Gyldendal, 1912–15; rpt. Rosenkilde & Bagger, 1967 (A) and 1973 (B), vol. 1A, pp. 332–54 [diplomatic text]; vol. 1B, pp. 305–27 [edited text]; Turville-Petre, E. O. G. *Scaldic Poetry.* Oxford: Clarendon, 1976, pp. 93–7; Edwards, Diana. "The Poetry of Arnórr jarlaskáld: An Edition and Study." Diss. Oxford University, 1980 [published version forthcoming]. **Bib.**: Hollander, Lee M. *A Bibliography of Skaldic Studies.* Copenhagen: Munksgaard, 1958, pp. 65–6 [supplement forthcoming by Paul Bibire *et al.*]. **Lit.**: Hollander, Lee M. "Arnórr Thórdarson jarlaskáld and His Poem *Hrynhent.*" *Scandinavian Studies* 17 (1942), 99–109; Edwards, Diana. "Christian and Pagan References in Eleventh-century Norse Poetry: The Case of Arnórr jarlaskáld." *Saga-Book of the Viking Society* 21.1–2 (1982–83), 34–53; Edwards, Diana C. "Clause Arrangement in Skaldic Poetry." *Arkiv för nordisk filologi* 98 (1983), 123–75, esp. 149–75; Fidjestøl, Bjarne. "Arnórr Þórðarson: Skald of the Orkney Jarls." In *The Northern and Western Isles in the Viking World: Survival, Continuity and Change.* Ed. Alexander Fenton and Hermann Pálsson. Edinburgh: Donald, 1984, pp. 239–57.

Diana Edwards Whaley

[**See also:** Christian Poetry, West Norse; *Fagrskinna*; *Flateyjarbók*; Hallfreðr Óttarsson; *Heimskringla*; *Heiti*; *Hulda-Hrokkinskinna*; Kennings; *Lausavísur*; *Morkinskinna*; *Óláfs saga helga*; *Orkneyinga saga*; Sighvatr Þórðarson; *Skáld*; Skaldic Meters; Skaldic Verse; *Snorra Edda*; Sturla Þórðarson; Þórðr Kolbeinsson]

Arons saga Hjǫrleifssonar

("The Saga of Aron Hjǫrleifsson") tells the story of Aron Hjǫrleifsson (1199–1255), a vigorous young warrior whose family loyalties led him to become an adherent of Bishop Guðmundr Arason in his conflict with Sighvatr Sturluson and his sons Tumi and Sturla. Aron played a leading part in the killing of Tumi at Hólar in February 1222, and was seriously wounded in the reprisal raid on Grímsey that Sighvatr and Sturla mounted in April that year. Aron was then outlawed, spending the next four years evading Sturla's pursuits, and narrowly avoiding death on several occasions. In 1226, he escaped to Norway and set out on a pilgrimage to Jerusalem. On his return, he joined the household of King Hákon Hákonarson in Bergen, enjoying royal honor and patronage, and finally reconciling with Sturla's brother Þórðr.

Because of its connection with the Sturlungs, *Arons saga* is usually printed as an appendix to *Sturlunga saga*, though there is no MS connection. The text of the saga has to be reconstructed from an early 15th-century vellum fragment (AM 551d δ 4to), from 17th-century paper copies (AM 212 fol. and AM 426 fol.), and from *Guðmundar saga biskups* in *Codex Resenianus* (AM 399 4to).

The unknown author's generously partial treatment of the bishop suggests that the saga might have been composed in the context of the campaign for Guðmundr's canonization, toward the middle of the 14th century. This dating would also fit with the use of extracts from two poems by the priest Þormóðr Óláfsson, who was alive in 1338 and is credited with a verse in praise of Gunnarr of Hlíðarendi in the *Kálfalækjarbók* MS (AM 133 fol.) of *Njáls saga* from about 1350.

The question of the saga's sources is made more complicated and more interesting by the existence of Sturla Þórðarson's earlier and complementary treatment of Aron's exploits in *Íslendinga saga*.

The accounts differ in various respects: they each contain some material not in the other; they offer divergent information on the same events; and their emphases and interpretations do not always agree. Sturla's account is more sober in tone, as befits the historian. He tends to be more logical and probably more accurate, and to present Aron in a less heroic light than the biographer, whose urgently special pleading involves a glorification of his hero and an attendant blackening of his enemies. At the same time, the two accounts are remarkably similar in some places, even showing close verbal agreement, and there is clearly some connection between them. A tentative conclusion would be that both authors had access to common written sources, bréf 'documents' rather than sǫgur 'stories, accounts.' For the Norwegian episodes, it seems likely that the biographer relied on oral sources.

In his vivid handling of dramatic action, his detailing of the tensions of heroic conflict and the frustration and danger of outlawry, and in his grasp of the connection between personal and political concerns, the author measures up to the model of the classic Íslendingasögur. In his clerical persuasiveness, however, he lacks their rigorous objectivity.

Ed.: Jón Jóhannesson, et al., eds. *Sturlunga saga.* 2 vols. Reykjavik: Sturlunguútgáfan, 1946, vol. 2, pp. 237–78. **Tr.**: Porter, John, trans. *Aron's Saga.* London: Pirate, 1975. **Lit.**: Björn Magnússon Ólsen. "Um Sturlungu." *Safn til sögu Íslands og íslenzkra bókmennta* 3 (1902), 193–510 [see esp. "Um afstöðu Íslendinga sögu og Aróns sögu," pp. 254–72]; Hermann Pálsson. "Athugasemd um Arons sögu." *Saga* 3 (1960–63), 299–303; Glendinning, Robert. "*Arons saga* and *Íslendingasaga*: A Problem in Parallel Transmission." *Scandinavian Studies* 41 (1969), 41–51; Porter, John. "Some Aspects of *Arons saga Hjörleifssonar.*" *Saga-Book of the Viking Society* 18.1 (1970–71), 136–66; Stefán Karlsson. "En konjektur til Áróns saga." *Opuscula* 5. Bibliotheca Arnamagnæana, 31. Copenhagen: Munksgaard, 1975, pp. 412–4.

John Porter

[**See also**: *Guðmundar sögur biskups*; *Njáls saga*; Sturla Þórðarson; Sturlung Age; *Sturlunga saga*]

Art *see* **Viking Art**

Ásbjarnar þáttr selsbana ("The Tale of Ásbjǫrn Seal-slayer"), which appears in Snorri's saga of St. Óláfr, stands as one of the high points of his narrative art. Crop failure in Hálogaland forces Ásbjǫrn Sigurðarson from Þrándarnes to travel south to his maternal uncle Erlingr Skjálgsson at Jaðarr in search of grain supplies. On his way back, he is robbed of his cargo and insulted by the king's steward, Þórir selr ("seal") of Kǫrmt. In a subsequent revenge action, Ásbjǫrn kills Þórir in the presence of the king. Erlingr Skjálgsson's intervention averts the execution of the death sentence, but Ásbjǫrn must promise to take over the duties of the slain steward. His paternal uncle, Þórir hundr ("dog") of Bjarkey, persuades him to break his promise, and Ásbjǫrn is then killed by the royal envoy Ásmundr Grankelsson.

The episode is closely integrated into the story line of the saga, revealing some of the reasons why two of the most powerful men in the country, Erlingr Skjálgsson and Þórir hundr, became Óláfr's bitter enemies. While demonstrating royal power at its peak, the killing of Ásbjǫrn also anticipates the king's decline and fall.

Apart from its inclusion in Snorri, the first part of the episode is extant in somewhat inferior artistic form in the so-called *Oldest Saga of St. Óláfr.* The complete story is found in the *Legendary Saga*

of St. Óláfr; its opening episode reproduces almost verbatim the extant part of the *Oldest Saga.* It is reasonable to assume, therefore, that the whole episode in the *Legendary Saga* stems (via intermediaries?) from the *Oldest Saga.*

In Snorri, the episode is more than twice as long as in the *Legendary Saga*, which is more interested in the conflict between Erlingr and the king. Note the concluding words: "From these sorts of things one can observe something about the dealings between King Óláfr and Erlingr. They had many other dealings with each other." The opening and conclusion of the story are no doubt a condensed version of a longer story. Practically all the material dealing with Þórir hundr has been omitted. Comparative study of the two episodes suggests that they derive from a lost older exemplar, a written saga set in Hálogaland, in which Þórir hundr is one of the principal actors.

Ed.: Storm, Gustav, ed. *Otte brudstykker af den ældste saga om Olav den hellige.* Christiania [Oslo]: Grøndahl, 1893 [the *Oldest Saga*]; Johnsen, Oscar Albert, ed. *Olafs saga hins helga. Efter pergamenthaandskrift i Uppsala Universitets Bibliotek, Delagardieske samling nr. 8 II.* Det norske historiske kildeskriftfonds skrifter, 19. Kristiania [Oslo]: Dybwad, 1922; [the *Legendary Saga*]; Bjarni Aðalbjarnarson, ed. Snorri Sturluson. *Heimskringla.* 3 vols. Íslenzk fornrit, 26–8. Reykjavik: Hið íslenzka fornritafélag, 1941–51, vol. 2, pp. 194–213 [Snorri's version]; Guðni Jónsson, ed. "Brot úr elztu sögu Óláfs helga." In *Konunga sögur.* 3 vols. Reykjavik: Íslendingasagnaútgáfan, 1957, vol. 1 [the *Oldest Saga*]; Heinrichs, Anne, et al., eds. *Olafs saga hins helga. Die "Legendarische Saga" über Olaf den Heiligen (Hs. Delagard. Saml. nr. 8 II).* Heidelberg: Winter, 1982, pp. 108–14 [the *Legendary Saga*, with German translation]. **Tr.**: Snorri Sturluson. *Heimskringla: History of the Kings of Norway.* Trans. Lee M. Hollander. Austin: University of Texas Press, 1964, pp. 377–93 [Snorri's version]. **Lit.**: Storm, Gustav. *Snorre Sturlasöns Historieskrivning, kritisk Undersögelse.* Copenhagen: Luno, 1873, pp. 80ff.; Berntsen, Toralf. *Fra sagn til saga. Studier i Kongesagaen.* Christiania [Oslo]: Gyldendal, 1923, p. 139; Schreiner, Johan. *Saga og oldfunn. Studier til Norges eldste historie.* Oslo: Dybwad, 1927, pp. 106, 159; Munch, Johan Storm. "Tore Hund og hans rike." *Håløygminne* (1969), 494; Sogge, Ingebjørg. *Vegar til eit bilete. Snorri Sturluson og Tore Hund.* Nordisk Institutt. Universitet i Trondheim. Skrifter, 1. Trondheim: Tapir, 1976, pp. 50ff.; Jakobsen, Alfred. "Omkring Selsbane-tåtten." In *Festskrift til Ludvig Holm-Olsen på hans 70–årsdag den 9. juni 1984.* Ed. Bjarne Fidjestøl et al. Øvre Ervik: Alvheim & Eide, 1984, pp. 175–84; Jakobsen, Alfred. "Njáls saga og Selsbane-tåtten." *Arkiv för nordisk filologi* 99 (1984), 126–30.

Alfred Jakobsen

[**See also**: *Óláfs saga helga*; *Þáttr*]

Ásmundar saga kappabana ("The Saga of Ásmundr the Champion-slayer") is a *fornaldarsaga*. The main MSS are SKB 7 4to of the early 14th century and AM 586 4to of the 15th century.

The saga revolves around the notion that fate shapes events. The workings of fate begin and end with stock characters and traditional motifs. King Buðli of Sweden is a tyrannical and covetous king. Despite warnings, he forces two supernatural smiths to forge a pair of magical swords. He then spoils the swords in capricious trials of the iron's strength and resiliency, and commands that they be reforged. In an imprecisely worded curse, the second smith vows that his sword will be the death of the king's grandsons. Ch. 1 ends with the king sinking the sword into the sea, in a futile attempt to avert the curse.

King Buðli's only daughter is the mother of the saga's champions. Hildibrandr is her son by her first marriage and is fostered by the king of the Huns. Then, in a remarriage to a champion of the Danish king who has conquered the country, she gives birth to Ásmundr. Hildibrandr develops into a renowned warrior and avenges the slaying of Buðli by killing the king of the Danes.

Ásmundr, meanwhile, has fallen in love with the daughter of the king of the Danes, who assumes the role of a vengeful deity of fate. By realistic and supernatural means, she contrives the combat of the stepbrothers. Hildibrandr realizes whom he has to confront. Ásmundr, despite numerous allusions and hints, remains oblivious and kills Hildibrandr in the second act of blood revenge. Thus Hildibrandr dies, the victim of Ásmundr's lady love.

Ásmundar saga kappabana's mood is not tragic, merely pseudo-heroic. Accordingly, the nontragic slaying of Hildibrandr is staged just prior to Ásmundr's wedding. With this celebration, fate and the saga have run their course.

Despite its ostensibly tragic theme, the reluctant slaying of a close kinsman in a duel, the saga is entertaining. Its fairy-tale setting initiates a swiftly moving plot that features lively dialogue and some carefully structured scenes.

Criticism of the saga has focused less on its literary qualities than on the few narrative elements that are relics of the heroic age. These include the saga's main theme; the thematic relationship to the *Hildebrandslied*, the sole, fragmentary, Old High German heroic lay, in which a father is forced by fate to kill his son, and a related heroic tale in Saxo's *Gesta Danorum* (Book 7:IX:2–X:1); the name Hildibrandr; and the elegiac eddic verses commemorating the death of Hildibrandr.

Ed.: Rafn, C. C., ed. *Fornaldar sögur Nordrlanda*. 3 vols. Copenhagen: Popp, 1829–30, vol. 2, pp. 337–54; Detter, Ferdinand, ed. *Zwei Fornaldarsögur (Hrólfssaga Gautrekssonar und Ásmundarsaga kappabana) nach Cod. Holm. 7, 4to*. Halle: Niemeyer, 1891; Guðni Jónsson, ed. *Fornaldar sögur Norðurlanda*. 4 vols. Akureyri: Íslendingasagnaútgáfan, 1954, vol. 1, pp. 383–408; Olrik, Jørgen, and H. Ræder, eds. *Saxonis Gesta Danorum*. Copenhagen: Levin & Munksgaard, 1931. **Tr.**: Ellis Davidson, Hilda, ed., and Peter Fisher, trans. *Saxo Grammaticus. The History of the Danes. Books I–IX*. 2 vols. Cambridge: Brewer; Totowa: Rowman and Littlefield, 1979–80, vol. 1, pp. 220–5; vol. 2, pp. 116–9. **Lit.**: Halvorsen, E. F. *On the Sources of the Ásmundarsaga kappabana*. Studia Norvegica, 5. Oslo: Aschehoug, 1951; Ciklamini, Marlene. "The Combat Between Two Half-Brothers: A Literary Study of the Motif in *Ásmundar saga kappabana* and *Saxonis Gesta Danorum*." *Neophilologus* 50 (1966), 269–79, 370–79.

Marlene Ciklamini

[**See also:** *Fornaldarsögur, Saxo Grammaticus*]

Atlakviða ("The Lay of Atli") is one of the earliest heroic lays of the *Poetic Edda*. It was probably composed around 900 by Þorbjǫrn hornklofi ("horn-clawed"), author of *Hrafnsmál*, or perhaps slightly earlier if Þorbjǫrn was merely influenced by it, and not actually its author. *Atlakviða* is preserved in the *Codex Regius*, where it is described as originating in Greenland. However, Greenland was not settled until about 985, and a Norwegian provenance is likely.

The lay tells how Atli, lord of the Huns, invites the Burgundian rulers, the Niflungs Gunnarr and Hǫgni, to visit him and to accept wealth and costly gifts. Gunnarr asks his brother Hǫgni for advice, suggesting that they are as wealthy as Atli himself. Hǫgni indicates a ring entwined with a hair from a wolf sent by Atli's queen, their sister Guðrún, interpreting it as a warning of treachery. Gunnarr accepts the invitation in a mood of heroic defiance. They ride to Atli's court, extensions

and after a further warning by Guðrún, Gunnarr is seized without resistance, and Hǫgni is eventually overpowered. Gunnarr is offered his life in return for the Niflung treasure, but he insists on first holding Hǫgni's bloody heart in his hand. The heart of the cowardly Hjalli is brought to him, but Gunnarr sees through the deception. When Hǫgni's heart is finally cut out and shown to him, he exults that now he alone knowns where the treasure lies hidden; never will he reveal his secret. Gunnarr is thrown into a snake pit, where, bravely playing a harp, he meets his end. Guðrún avenges her brothers on Atli by giving him the hearts of their two sons to eat, and then stabbing him. She sets fire to the royal hall, and perishes in the flames.

Gunnarr has to accept Atli's invitation or be labeled a coward for avoiding the associated treachery and danger. Gottzmann proposes a more complex motivation, based on the assumption that Atli's offer of gifts implies a demand that Gunnarr submit to Atli's overlordship.

Atlakviða provides the earliest version of the legend dealing with the Burgundian rulers at Atli's court and with Guðrún's vengeance. In its original form, it can be thought of as an early Norse redaction of a West Germanic, possibly a specifically High German, tradition deriving from Burgundian heroic legend, inhering in the historical interaction of Burgundians and Huns in the 5th century. Some argue for a Low German exemplar, and others for the transmission to Scandinavia of continental heroic Germanic material, including *Atlakviða*, through lost Gothic lays via the Baltic area, without any West Germanic mediation. The Norse poem may have been influenced by *Hamðismál*.

The style and meter of *Atlakviða* present something of a mosaic, so much so that multiple authorship by as many as four poets has been suggested. The use together of both *fornyrðislag* and *málaháttr* meter along with quite startling stylistic variations do not inevitably lead to that conclusion.

Largely as the result of the vagaries of oral and written transmission, *Atlakviða* in its extant form contains obscurities and other defects, yet it remains an effective and vigorous statement of heroism triumphant in defeat and of implacable vengeance. *Atlamál* provides an essentially later and very different treatment of the same legend.

Ed.: Dronke, Ursula, ed. and trans. *The Poetic Edda. 1. Heroic Poems*. Oxford: Clarendon, 1969. **Lit.**: Petsch, Robert. "Gunnar im Schlangenturm." *Beiträge zur Geschichte der deutschen Sprache und Literatur* 41 (1916), 171–9; Genzmer, Felix. "Der Dichter der Atlakviða." *Arkiv för nordisk filologi* 42 (1926), 97–134; Reichardt, Konstantin. "Der Dichter der Atlakviða." *Arkiv för nordisk filologi* 42 (1926), 323–6; Singer, Samuel. "Gunnar im Schlangenturm." *Zeitschrift für Volkskunde* 39 (1929), 69–71; Eis, Gerhard. "Die Hortforderung." *Germanisch-romanische Monatsschrift*, n.s. 38 (1957), 209–23; Dronke, Ursula. "The Lay of Attila." *Saga-Book of the Viking Society* 16 (1963), 1–21; Eis, Gerhard. "Das alte Atlilied." *Germanisch-romanische Monatsschrift*, n.s. 15 (1965), 430–4; Andersson, Theodore M. "An Alemannic 'Atlakviða.'" In *Studies for Einar Haugen: Presented by Friends and Colleagues*. Ed. Evelyn Scherabon Firchow *et al*. Janua Linguarum, Series Maior, 59. The Hague and Paris: Mouton, 1972, pp. 31–45; Gottzmann, Carola L. *Das alte Atlilied: Untersuchungen der Gestaltungsprinzipien seiner Handlungsstruktur*. Germanische Bibliothek, 3. Heidelberg: Winter, 1973; Finch, R. G. "*Atlakviða, Atlamál*, and *Vǫlsunga Saga: A Study in Combination and Integration.*" In *Specvlvm Norroenvm: Norse Studies in Memory of Gabriel Turville-Petre.* Ed. Ursula Dronke *et al.* Odense: Odense University Press, 1981, pp. 123–38; Hallberg, Peter. "Elements of Imagery in the *Edda.*" In *Edda: A Collection of Essays.* Ed. Robert J. Glendinning and Haraldur Bessason. University of Manitoba Icelandic Studies, 4. Winnipeg: University of Manitoba Press, 1983, pp. 47–85.

†R. G. Finch

[See also: *Atlamál*; *Codex Regius*; Eddic Meters; Eddic Poetry; Þorbjǫrn hornklofi]

Atlamál ("The Lay of Atli"), of unknown authorship, dates from no earlier than the 12th century, and is one of the youngest poems in the *Poetic Edda.* It is preserved in the *Codex Regius* as "the Greenlandic *Atlamál*," although internal evidence for a Greenlandic provenance is hardly compelling. Even so, there are factors, as Dronke points out, such as the harsh atmosphere of the poem, the nature of its violence and cruelty, and the nonaristocratic milieu of its action, that make the Greenlandic ascription credible.

Atlamál tells how Atli invites his brothers-in-law, the Niflungs Gunnarr and Hǫgni, to visit him. Guðrún, Atli's wife, sends a warning, cut in runes, of his treacherous intent, but Vingi, Atli's messenger, distorts them. Hǫgni's wife discerns their true meaning, but neither this, nor her ill-omened dreams, nor those of Gunnarr's wife, affect the decision to accept. After a sea voyage, they arrive at Atli's farm, where Vingi, seemingly conscience-stricken, warns them. They kill him. Atli and his men attack, Guðrún fighting on her brothers' side. Gunnarr and Hǫgni are overpowered. Bitter recriminations between Atli and Guðrún reveal the misery of their life together. To increase Guðrún's grief, Atli orders that Hǫgni's heart be cut out, that Gunnarr be hanged, and that serpents be brought. Hǫgni dies courageously, rejecting the cowardly Hjalli as a substitute. Gunnarr plays a harp with his toes until he succumbs to the serpents. Further recriminations between Atli and Guðrún make Guðrún's affection for her slain brother manifest. Feigning meekness, Guðrún lulls Atli into a false sense of security, and avenges her brothers by giving him the blood of the sons she bore him to drink as wine in goblets fashioned from their skulls. Hǫgni's son Hniflungr and Guðrún both stab Atli. Before Atli dies, there are again recriminations, Guðrún mentioning her attachment to her first husband, Sigurðr. Guðrún makes an unsuccessful attempt at suicide.

This essentially late version of the legend lacks any reference to Burgundians and Huns, the action having been transferred from royal courts to a farming community in an attempt at modernization that also includes the substitution of a runic message for a ring entwined with a wolf's hair. The sea voyage may reflect a motif earlier than the land journey of *Atlakviða.* The Niflungs' treasure is not mentioned, the motivation for Atli's treachery seems to be sheer malice, and the attempted substitution of Hjalli for Hǫgni is ill-founded. References to Guðrún's first son show the poet's acquaintance with the wider ramifications of the developing legend cycle.

Atlamál is written in *málaháttr* meter, and influenced in some respects by the style of the prose sagas. The grandeur of *Atlakviða* is largely replaced by sentimental and elegiac passages, the heroic spirit by simple heroics. Fantastic and grotesque elements are exaggerated, *e.g.,* Atli is also served with his sons' blood, and Gunnarr plays the harp with his toes.

The poet was almost certainly acquainted with *Atlakviða* and with *Hrafnsmál*, and perhaps influenced by a lost poem. The name "Limfjǫrðr" (Liim Fjord) in stanza 4 suggests that he utilized a Danish source, possibly in ballad form, itself drawing on German tradition.

Ed.: Dronke, Ursula, ed. and trans. *The Poetic Edda. 1. Heroic Poems.* Oxford: Clarendon, 1969. **Lit.**: Petsch, Robert. "Gunnar im Schlangenturm." *Beiträge zur Geschichte der deutschen Sprache und Literatur* 41 (1916), 171–9; Singer, Samuel. "Gunnar im Schlangenturm." *Zeitschrift für Volkskunde* 39 (1929), 69–71; Mohr, Wolfgang. "Entstehung und Heimat der jüngeren Edda-lieder südgermanischen Stoffes." *Zeitschrift für deutsches Altertum und deutsche Literatur* 75 (1938), 217–80; Mohr, Wolfgang. "Wortschatz und Motive der jüngeren Edda-lieder südgermanischen Stoffes." *Zeitschrift für deutsches Altertum und deutsche Literatur* 76 (1939), 149–217; Finch, R. G. "*Atlakviða, Atlamál*, and *Vǫlsunga Saga*: A Study in Combination and Integration." In *Specvlvm Norroenvm: Norse Studies in Memory of Gabriel Turvile-Petre.* Ed. Ursula Dronke *et al.* Odense: Odense University Press, 1981, pp. 123–38; Andersson, Theodore M. "Did the Poet of *Atlamál* Know *Atlaqviða*?" In *Edda: A Collection of Essays.* Ed. Robert J. Glendinning and Haraldur Bessason. University of Manitoba Icelandic Studies, 4. Winnipeg: University of Manitoba Press, 1983, pp. 243–57.

†R. G. Finch

[See also: *Atlakviða*; *Codex Regius*; Eddic Meters; Eddic Poetry]

Auðunar þáttr vestfirzka ("The Tale of Auðunn of the West Fjords"), one of the many shorter prose narratives known as *þættir* (sing. *þáttr*), tells of a young man from the western fjords of Iceland who undertakes a journey to Greenland. There he acquires a great (polar?) bear, which he resolves to take to Denmark to present to King Sven. In passing through Norway, he encounters King Haraldr, who tries to persuade him to part with the bear. Auðunn refuses, yet Haraldr grudgingly allows him and the bear to proceed to Denmark.

Impoverished and hungry, Auðunn must beg for sustenance for himself and the bear. In Denmark, Aki, King Sven's steward, agrees to furnish the necessary provisions, but requires in return a half-interest in the bear. When Auðunn finally comes into the king's presence, he explains that he wants to give the bear to the king, but cannot because half of it now belongs to Aki. Sven accepts Auðunn's gift, and offers him the hospitality of his court. He punishes Aki for his greed by banishing him from the country.

Later, Auðunn discloses to the king his desire to make a pilgrimage to Rome. King Sven reluctantly grants him leave to go, but asks him to return to Denmark after completing his pilgrimage. Auðunn returns so sick and emaciated that the king at first hardly recognizes him, but when he does, the king welcomes him to his court. Later, when Auðunn asks leave to return to Iceland, the king accedes, bestowing a number of gifts upon him. On passing through Norway, King Haraldr questions him closely about his treatment at the hands of King Sven. Auðunn describes Sven's magnanimity, gifts are exchanged, and the king allows Auðunn to return unhindered to Iceland. The story closes with a brief reference to Þorsteinn Gyðuson, one of Auðunn's descendants.

Like many Icelandic stories, *Auðunar þáttr vestfirzka* may have a historical basis, since the Þorsteinn Gyðuson mentioned at the end is known to have died in the year 1190. On the other hand, the events in it bear a strong resemblance to many European folktales (Stefán Einarsson 1939). The interpretation of the story is made somewhat more difficult by the MS tradition. The versions in the three main MSS, represented by the letters M, F, and A, are in general agreement as to the main events of the story, but each includes some details not mentioned in the others. The twelve later MSS play no role in establishing the text.

From the beginning, the story has been read as a study of character and conduct. Thorlacius (1818), who translated it into Latin, saw it as a model of behavior for king and subject. Taylor (1947–8) regarded it as a study of character. Harris (1976) stressed the interplay of structure and content. Fichtner (1979) viewed it from an anthropological perspective as an account of a young man's initiation into adulthood, specifically into the adult custom of gift giving. Each of these interpretations illuminates a different facet of this appealing story of a young man who makes his way with courage and dignity through the hazardous world of medieval Scandinavia.

Ed.: Guðbrandr Vigfusson and C. R. Unger, eds. *Flateyjarbók: En Samling af norske Konge-Sagaer med indskudte mindre Fortællinger om Begivenheder i og undenfor Norge samt Annaler.* 3 vols. Christiania [Oslo]: Malling, 1860–68, vol. 3, pp. 410–15 [diplomatic transcription of MS F, GkS 1005 fol., called the "Flateyjarbók"]; Finnur Jónsson, ed. *Morkinskinna.* Samfund til udgivelse af gammel nordisk litteratur, 32. Copenhagen: Jørgensen, 1932, pp. 180–7 [diplomatic transcription of MS M, GkS 1009 fol., called the "Morkinskinna"]; Björn K. Þórólfsson and Guðni Jónsson, eds. *Vestfirðinga sǫgur.* Íslenzk fornrit, 6. Reykjavik: Hið íslenzka fornritafélag, 1943, pp. 359–68 [normalized edition of MS M]. **Tr.**: Thorlacius, Birger, trans. *Solennia academica ad celebrandum diem . . . Frederico Sexto . . . de Auduno . . . islandice et latine. . . .* Copenhagen: Schultz, 1818 [edition and Latin translation prepared for the fiftieth birthday of King Frederik VI of Denmark from a source close to A]; Mitchell, Philip M., trans. "Authun and His Bear." In *A Pageant of Old Scandinavia.* Ed. Henry Goddard Leach. Princeton: Princeton University Press; New York: American-Scandinavian Foundation, 1946, pp. 202–8 [based on MS M]; Jones, Gwyn, trans. "Authun and the Bear." In *Eirik the Red and Other Icelandic Sagas.* The World's Classics, 582. London: Oxford University Press, 1961, pp. 163–70 [based on MS M]; Hermann Pálsson, trans. "Audun's Story." In *Hrafnkel's Saga and Other Icelandic Stories.* Harmondsworth: Penguin, 1971, pp. 121–8 [based on MS F]. **Lit.**: Stefán Einarsson. "Ævintýriatvik í Auðunar þætti vestfirzka." *Skírnir* 113 (1939), 161–71; Taylor, Arnold R. "Auðunn and the Bear." *Saga-Book of the Viking Society* 13 (1947–48), 78–96 [with translation]; Harris, Joseph C. "Theme and Genre in Some *Íslendinga þættir.*" *Scandinavian Studies* 48 (1976), 1–28; Fichtner, Edward G. "Gift Exchange and Invitation in the *Auðunar þáttr vestfirzka.*" *Scandinavian Studies* 51 (1979), 249–72.

Edward G. Fichtner

[**See also:** Folklore; *Þáttr*]

Austrfararvísur *see* Sighvatr Þórðarson

Baldr, according to the *Prose* or *Snorra Edda*, was the son of Óðinn (st. 22), husband of Nanna, and father of Forseti (st. 32). The skaldic poet Þjóðólfr of Hvin speaks of Þórr as Baldr's brother in his *Haustlǫng* (st. 17); *Vǫluspá* (st. 33) and *Lokasenna* (st. 28) seem to indicate that Frigg is Baldr's mother. The story of Baldr's death and the gods' failure to accomplish his return from Hel provide the pivotal catastrophe in the preparation for Ragnarǫk in both *Snorra Edda* (chs. 49–50) and *Vǫluspá* (sts. 31–33) (see Ciklamini 1978: 57). Other sources for Baldr include *Baldrs draumar*, where Óðinn learns from the *vǫlva* ("prophetess") that Baldr has had bad dreams about his impending death; the Old High German *Second Merseburg Charm*, in which the magician Óðinn heals the hoof of Phol, Baldr's horse, the injury also being prophetic of some future harm to come to Baldr; *Hyndluljóð* (st. 29), where mention is made of revenge on Hǫðr as Baldr's murderer; *Eiríksmál* (st. 3), which prophesies Baldr's return to the new world after Ragnarǫk. Quite another story emerges in Saxo's *Gesta Danorum*, where Baldr becomes a heroic semideity who is killed in his quest for the woman he loves (Book 3). Here, Baldr is stripped of all mythological significance.

Schier summarizes four suggested etymologies for Baldr's name: (1) **bhel* 'white, shining,' indicating his possible function as a sun-deity; (2) Old English *bealder* 'lord, prince,' interpreted as a projection of the characteristics of Christ onto Baldr; (3) Old Norse *baldr*, Old High German *bald* 'bold, brave,' referring to strength or warlike qualities; and (4) **bhel* 'sprout, germinate, bud,' indicating his function as a vegetation or fertility god. Some scholars have thus interpreted the Baldr story as the essential narrative in a Scandinavian fertility cult or as a cyclical myth of the seasons (see Kroes 1951, Schneider 1947).

Snorra Edda provides the longest version of the story of Baldr's death, similar to that of *Vǫluspá*, but the numerous details and the arrangement of events have resulted in scholarly skepticism about its value in the reconstruction of pre-Christian Germanic mythology. Because Baldr had dreams portending injury, the Æsir extracted oaths from everything in the universe not to harm him. The mistletoe is overlooked because Frigg thought it too small to do Baldr harm. The gods then make sport by throwing things at Baldr as he stands in the ring, since nothing can harm him. Loki, however, goes to Frigg disguised as an old woman, and tricks her into telling him the secret of the mistletoe. He quickly brings it to the ring and places it in blind Hǫðr's hand, encouraging him to do honor to Baldr as the others are. Hǫðr's throw kills Baldr. Although all the gods mourn, Óðinn knows best what harm the Æsir have suffered through Baldr's death. Hermóðr rides to Hel on Óðinn's horse Sleipnir to see what ransom she will accept for Baldr. In the meantime, Baldr's body is burned on his ship, along with that of his wife Nanna, who has died of grief. An extended narration of the funeral procession follows. Hermóðr tells Hel of the great mourning among the Æsir, but she responds that everything in the world must prove its love for Baldr by weeping for him. The Æsir then send messengers out who convince everything to weep, except the giantess Þǫkk, who refuses. So Baldr remains in Hel. Because the Æsir suspect that the giantess is really Loki in disguise, they search, but Loki hides in a mountain, occasionally turning himself into a salmon. The gods pursue him and Þórr catches him by the tail. Loki is chained to three rocks with the entrails of one of his sons; poison from a serpent drips in his face. Loki's wife holds a bowl under the serpent's mouth, but when she goes to empty it, Loki cries out in such pain that the earth quakes. He must remain bound until Ragnarǫk.

This story, Þórr's visit to Útgarða-Loki, and Þórr's fishing expedition are the three longest narratives of *Snorra Edda*. The lack of clear support in the eddic poems for many of the details and the sequence of events has led critics to attribute much of Snorri's account to the influence of Christianity (see Bugge 1899, Frazer 1919). But in recent years, archaeology and comparative mythology have argued for the antiquity of many of the details of the myth (see Hauck 1970, Dumézil 1948). Particularly, Hauck's successful interpretation of three distinctive amulet types of the 3rd and 4th centuries demonstrates that many motifs, such as Loki's disguise as an old woman, originate in pre-Christian Scandinavia. Dieterle's (1986) taxonomic investigation of the underlying structure in Snorri's account also provides a convincing demonstration of Loki's original role in the myth. The Christian influence in Snorri's narration may then be a matter of style rather than substance, *i.e.*, the author organized the elements of the myth in a way that profoundly reminds the Christian reader of the Crucifixion, while remaining faithful to the mythological tradition (see Turville-Petre 1964, Mosher 1983).

Ed.: Finnur Jónsson, ed. *Den norsk-islandske skjaldedigtning.* Vols. 1A–2A (tekst efter håndskrifterne) and 1B–2B (rettet tekst). Copenhagen and Christiania [Oslo]: Gyldendal, 1912–15; rpt. Rosenkilde & Bagger, 1967(A) and 1973(B); Steinmeyer, Elias von, ed. *Die kleineren althochdeutschen Sprachdenkmäler.* Berlin: Weidmann, 1916; rpt. 1963; Olrik, Jørgen, and H. Ræder, eds. *Saxonis Gesta Danorum.* Copenhagen: Levin & Munksgaard, 1931; Snorri Sturluson. *Edda.* Ed. Anne Holtsmark and Jón Helgason. 2nd ed. Copenhagen: Gad, 1950; rpt. Munksgaard, 1968; Neckel, Gustav, ed. *Edda: Die Lieder des Codex Regius nebst verwandten Denkmälern. I: Text.* 5th ed. rev. Hans Kuhn. Heidelberg: Winter, 1983. **Tr.**: Bellows, Henry Adams, trans. *The Poetic Edda: Translated from the Icelandic with an Introduction and Notes.* New York: American-Scandinavian Foundation, 1923; rpt. New York: Biblo and Tannen, 1969; Brodeur, Arthur Gilchrist, trans. *The Prose Edda by Snorri Sturluson.* New York: American-Scandinavian Foundation, 1929; rpt. 1960; Ellis Davidson, Hilda, ed., and Peter Fisher, trans. *Saxo Grammaticus. The History of the Danes. Books I–IX.* 2 vols. Cambridge: Brewer; Totowa: Rowman and Littlefield, 1979–80; Faulkes, Anthony, trans. *Snorri Sturluson. Edda.* Everyman Classics. London and Melbourne: Dent, 1987. **Lit.**: Bugge, Sophus. *The Home of the Eddic Poems.* Trans. William Henry Schofield. London: Nutt, 1899; Frazer, J. G. *Baldr the Beautiful. The Golden Bough 7.* 3rd ed. London: Macmillan, 1919; Schneider, Hermann. "Beiträge zur Geschichte der nordischen Götterdichtung." *Beiträge zur Geschichte der deutschen Sprache und Literatur* 69 (1947), 301–50; Dumézil, Georges. *Loki.* Paris: Maisonneuve, 1948; Kroes, H. W. J. "Die Balderüberlieferungen und der zweite Merseburger Zauberspruch." *Neophilologus* 35 (1951), 201–13; Vries, Jan de. *Altgermanische Religionsgeschichte.* 2 vols. Grundriss der germanischen Philologie, 12. 2nd ed. Berlin: de Gruyter, 1956–57; Turville-Petre, E. O. G. *Myth and Religion of the North: The Religion of Ancient Scandinavia.* New York: Holt, Rinehart and Winston, 1964; rpt. Westport: Greenwood, 1975; Ellis Davidson, H. R. *Gods and Myths of Northern Europe.* Harmondsworth: Penguin, 1964; Hauck, Karl. *Goldbrakteaten aus Sievern.* Munich: Fink, 1970, pp. 184–8; Schier, K. "Baldr." In *Reallexikon der germanischen Altertumskunde.* Rev. ed. Berlin: de Gruyter, 1973– ; Ciklamini, Marlene. *Snorri Sturluson.* Twayne's World Authors Series, 493. Boston: Twayne, 1978; Mosher, Arthur D. "The Story of Baldr's Death: The Inadequacy of Myth in the Light of Christian Faith." *Scandinavian Studies* 55 (1983), 305–15; Dieterle, Richard L. "The Song of Baldr." *Scandinavian Studies* 58 (1986), 285–307.

Arthur D. Mosher

[**See also:** *Baldrs draumar*; *Eiríksmál*; *Hyndluljóð*; *Loki*; Mythology; *Óðinn*; *Saxo Grammaticus*; *Snorra Edda*; *Þjóðólfr of Hvin*; *Vǫluspá*]

Baldrs draumar ("Baldr's Dreams"), also called *Vegtamskviða* ("The Lay of Vegtamr"), is an anonymous eddic poem traditionally ascribed to the late 12th century and preserved in a 14th-century MS (AM 748 I 4to). The poem relates Óðinn's ride on his eight-legged horse Sleipnir to Niflhel, the abode of the dead, after the gods and goddesses had met to discuss Baldr's threatening dreams. Óðinn first encounters a hellhound. Then, using necromancy, he raises a long-dead sibyl (*vǫlva*) from her grave and compels her to answer three questions: for whom is the hall of Hel so lavishly decorated? (answer: for Baldr, signifying his imminent death); who will kill Baldr? (answer: Hǫðr); and who will avenge Baldr? (answer: Váli, Baldr's half-brother, the son of Óðinn and the giantess Rindr). A fourth question reveals Óðinn's true identity (he has called himself *Vegtamr* 'travel-tame'), and provokes the sibyl's angry and ironic demand that he ride home proudly, to return only at Ragnarǫk ("the doom of the gods").

Among the other Scandinavian sources that shed light on this incident, Snorri Sturluson's *Edda* provides the fullest account of the Baldr myth. Baldr is praised by all as the best of the gods. He is also the wisest, the most excellent of speech, and the most merciful; but none of his judgments are ever fulfilled (ch. 22). His death occurs in chapter 49. Alarmed by his dreams, the gods attempt to avert disaster by having his mother, Frigg, take an oath from all creatures, animate and inanimate, not to harm Baldr. Only the mistletoe, considered too young, is exempted. In disguise, the evil Loki discovers from Frigg the lethal character of the mistletoe. During a game in which the gods pelt the apparently invulnerable Baldr with deadly objects, Loki persuades the blind Hǫðr to throw a stalk of mistletoe at Baldr and guides his aim. Struck dead, Baldr is laid to rest on a ship with great pomp and sorrow. Meanwhile, Hermóðr (a brother of Baldr) rides Sleipnir to Hel and negotiates Baldr's return, with the condition that all creatures, the quick and the dead, must weep at his death. All comply save the giantess Þǫkk (Snorri implies she is Loki in yet another disguise); consequently, Baldr must remain in Hel.

Other eddic poems confirm the traditional nature of Snorri's account without adding anything significant (see *Vǫluspá* sts. 31–35, *Skírnismál* sts. 21–22, *Lokasenna* st. 28, and *Hyndluljóð* st. 29). The eddic poem *Vafþrúðnismál* resembles *Baldrs draumar* in its question-and-answer structure that ends with Óðinn's revealing his identity by posing a riddle to which only he can know the answer: "What did Óðinn whisper into Baldr's ear before he was laid on his funeral pyre?" In addition, *Þrymskviða* shares with *Baldrs draumar* three lines (in sts. 14 and 1, respectively), and *Helgakviða Hundingsbana II* st. 44 is reminiscent of *Baldrs draumar* st. 5. Literary borrowing cannot be ruled out, but is an unlikely, certainly unnecessary, notion, given the formulaic character of the poetry. Finally, Saxo Grammaticus (Book 3 of his *Gesta Danorum*) offers a euhemerized version of the Baldr story.

Despite the insights gained by comparison with other sources of the Baldr myth, the ending of the poem remains obscure. How Óðinn's fourth question ("Who are the maidens who weep so passionately, who throw their kerchiefs in the air?") betrays his identity has never been convincingly explained. Indeed, the significance of the maidens and the act they perform is unclear. The parallel with *Vafþrúðnismál* shows how Óðinn could reveal his identity with an unaswerable question, but does not clarify why he should want to do so here. Perhaps, as some commentators have observed, the poem has been garbled in transmission; nevertheless, it reads as a unified, if problematical, work.

Ed.: Sijmons, B., and Hugo Gering, eds. *Die Lieder der Edda.* 3 vols. Germanistische Handbibliothek, 7/1–5. Halle: Waisenhaus, 1903–31 [most valuable for its *Kommentar*]; Boer, Richard C, ed. *Die Edda mit historish-critischem Commentar.* 2 vols. Haarlem: Tjeenk Willink, 1922 [most valuable for its *Commentar* (vol. 2)]; Neckel, Gustav, ed. *Edda: Die Lieder des Codex Regius nebst verwandten Denkmälern. I. Text.* 5th ed. rev. Hans Kuhn. Heidelberg: Winter, 1983. **Tr.**: Bellows, Henry Adams, trans. *The Poetic Edda: Translated from the Icelandic with an Introduction and Notes.* New York: American-Scandinavian Foundation, 1923; rpt. Biblo and Tannen, 1969; Hollander, Lee M., trans. *The Poetic Edda: Translated with an Introduction and Explanatory Notes.* 2nd rev. ed. Austin: University of Texas Press, 1962; rpt. 1988; Taylor, Paul B., and W. H. Auden, trans. *The Elder Edda: A Selection.*

London: Faber and Faber, 1969; rpt. in their *Norse Poems*. London: Athlone, 1986. **Lit**.: Allén, Sture. "Baldrs draumar 14 och Guðrúnarkviða II, 9—två samhöriga eddaställen." *Arkiv för nordisk filologi* 76 (1961), 74–95 [compares sts. 14 and 9 and offers translations]; Schröder, Franz Rolf. "Die eddischen 'Baldrs Träume.'" *Germanisch-Romanische Monatsschrift*, N.F. 14 (1964), 329–37 [thinks little of the poem, but indispensable for its discussion of the work's context]; Turville-Petre, E. O. G. *Myth and Religion of the North: The Religion of Ancient Scandinavia*. New York: Holt, Rinehart and Winston, 1964; rpt. Westport: Greenwood, 1975 [the most complete discussion in English of the Baldr myth and other questions of Norse mythology and religion]; Fleck, Jere. "Drei Vorschläge zu *Baldrs draumar*." *Arkiv för nordisk filologi* 84 (1969), 19–37 [provocative but not entirely persuasive]; Lindow, John. "*Baldrs draumar*." In *Dictionary of the Middle Ages*. Ed. Joseph R. Strayer. New York: Scribner, 1982–89, vol. 2, pp. 56–7; Heinemann, Fredrik J. "*Ealuscerwen-Meoduscerwen*, the Cup of Death, and *Baldrs Draumar*." *Studia Neophilologica* 55 (1983), 3–10.

Fredrik J. Heinemann

[See also: Baldr; Eddic Meters; Eddic Poetry; Helgi Poems; *Hyndluljóð*; *Lokasenna*; Saxo Grammaticus; *Skírnismál*; *Snorra Edda*; *Þrymskviða*; *Vafþrúðnismál*; *Vǫluspá*]

Ballads

1. INTRODUCTION. Folksong fragments in medieval MSS are few, but they suffice to prove that the style of the Scandinavian ballad has a medieval origin. The style defines the genre, justifies its name, and readily distinguishes it from other folksong genres in the same postmedieval sources: ballads in broadside, literary, or international (particularly German) style, or lyrics. The style of the ballad has more than preserved the identity of the genre; it is the means by which this kind of folksong has thrived longest in an oral tradition. This is achieved by simplicity in oral presentation; ballads keep to a narrow range of stanzaic forms with refrains, a formulaic diction, and a "balladic" narrative technique that makes heavy use of type scenes and commonplaces for presenting stereotyped kinds of action. The complete dominance of narrative commonplaces over ornamental formulas reflects the recreation of the ballad in performance by memory rather than by improvisation, although creative singers seem to have improvised on their own the version that then remained as their "own." The narrative employs the objective, "behavioristic" narration and scenic structure familiar from saga style, but each scene is typically articulated as situation, confrontation, action or alarm, and reaction. Many of these narrative bits are presented in stanzaic commonplaces, of which there are hundreds.

Because of the dearth of medieval evidence, the origin and early history of the genre remains largely conjectural. German origin proved unlikely when the heroic ballads were shown to be West Nordic; yet the theory has been revived as a market-singer and broadside theory formed by analogy with 19th-century data. Against this background, a coherent explanation of ballad style within the context of medieval European song upholds what has been the consensus: that the Scandinavian genre developed out of Old French folksong sometime in the 13th century. The genre's stanzaic forms are all present in the *ronde*, the song to which the *carole* was danced, which existed in the French tradition from the 13th century. The dance is first reliably witnessed in Scandinavia from the mid-13th century, in Denmark and Sweden in a courtly setting. Both Faroese practice and the ballad refrains seem to in-

dicate occasional dancing. The *ronde* texts are, moreover, formulaic type scenes similar to the stanzaic commonplaces, which are so characteristic of the Scandinavian genre that they can be recognized when they occur, often rather awkwardly, in a Swedish romance translation from 1303. Another ballad type reproduces that of the *chanson de toile* (or *d'histoire*), and several ballads (Jonsson *et al.* 1978 = TSB D 23–24) are to all intents surviving *chansons de toile* in such a way as to exploit their narrative possibilities, for instance by resinging as ballads the sort of bridal-quest tales related by Saxo (*e.g.*, TSB D 44–56 "Knight comes just in time to rescue his beloved from a forced marriage"). Like the *chansons de toile*, true-love ballads explore the ethical consequences of love in an artistic kin society, but in greater detail.

The (idealized) mimetic portrayal of the rural aristocacy has given us the term *riddervise* (ballad of chivalry or knightly ballad, TSB D 1–440). Its predominant theme is love (TSB D 1–268), but it also treats ethical themes involving questions of justice and various forms of honor: chastity, kinship, and fealty. Its two keynotes are truth and honor (*tro og ære*). The group is finally elaborated by international epic and folktale motifs in the novelistic ballads (*romanviser*, TSB D 380–440). Many historical ballads (TSB C 1–41), like the Danish royal-wedding ballads, have assimilated historical events to these traditional ballad themes; the Swedish abduction ballads (*klosterrovsvisor*) develop the elopements of the bridal-quest ballads, and can probably be dated to the 14th century. There are, in addition, a few semiliterary chronicle ballads. In certain of the ballads of the supernatural (TSB A 1–75), the element of faery (*e.g.*, runic spells) is a palpable symbol for erotic power. This deeper look into human nature may have prompted, perhaps among the humbler classes, a departure from an aristocratic social sphere into the deep psychic space of the fairy tales of transformation and the folklore of supernatural beings, a symbolic vehicle for unconscious experience that even today has the power to charm. The religious ballads (*legendeviser*, TSB B 1–37) are largely resung religious legends or late international ballads. In the peasant environment of the jocular ballads (*skæmteviser*, TSB F 1–77), all norms, and the ballad themes with them, are turned bottoms up; love becomes sex, chastity turns into lust, and so on. The heroic ballads (*kæmpeviser*) subordinate love, justice, and honor to the heroic mettle, displayed in the troll ballads (*troldviser*, TSB E 113–167) through encounters with supernatural beings, and in the ballads of champions (TSB E 1–112) through the adventures and conflicts of prodigious warriors. Many represent heroic, marvelous, and romantic sagas resung as ballads, and their multiepisodic narratives owe much to saga narrative art. The Faroese long heroic ballads (*kvæðir*) are perhaps best characterized as a genre as *rímur* resung by a preliterate society, sometime before 1425 (the date of Claudius Clavus's Greenland stanza [see below]), in the style of the knightly ballads in Icelandic tradition.

Ballads are "folk"-songs in the same sense that they exist within an oral community, including the only marginally literate "aristocratic folk." Medieval evidence cannot determine the social context of the ballad, although its dance situation is somewhat better in evidence as a courtly than as a popular entertainment. Internal evidence, however, argues for an aristocratic milieu as the only plausible context for the mimetic portrayal of medieval rural aristocracy and the thematic role of kin society in the knightly ballads, just as the fantastic scene of the heroic ballads (and of knightly ballads of Icelandic origin) has its natural origin in a free peasant society.

To judge from the wealth of postmedieval texts, ballads have flourished in inverse proportion to the vernacular literary output during the Middle Ages. While literate Iceland was busy translating and adapting the French romances, Latinate Denmark was adapting French folksongs, just as the preliterate Faroes later adapted the *rímur*. Denmark is clearly the center for the knightly ballad, just as the Faroes are for the heroic ballad; thus, 208 knightly ballads occur only in Denmark, and 104 heroic ballads only in the Faroes. By the 19th century, ballads were centered in traditional communities that remained relatively isolated, geographically and socially, from the effects of literacy. Yet these centers were not isolated from one another, because ballads were often fetched by one center from another. Ballads from the Vedel-Syv volume (see below) were sung in Norway and the Faroes in the literary language (Danish), while those from oral tradition were gradually assimilated into the borrowing dialect. Much of the seemingly archaic ballad diction could be a result of incomplete assimilation, preserved in tradition as a poetic jargon. Despite regional dialect differences and thematic preferences, the Scandinavian ballad area, like the genre itself, is an interrelated whole, quite distinct from German on the south, Finnish on the east, and Scots to the west.

Most collectors, like their informants, have been musically illiterate, and melodies were collected even later and more sporadically than texts. Yet even recent ballad melodies can have such archaic traits as modal and pentatonic tonality, or make use of formulaic intonations. The melody tends to remain subordinate to the narrative, asserting itself only in the lyrical refrain.

The Faroese ballads function as dance songs, which were presumably more widespread at one time. A letter from 1538 places a ballad stanza at an aristocratic wedding feast, and later in the century we hear of ballads from the serving men's quarters (*borgestueviser*). Only in the Faroese (and Manø) dance did ballads retain a communal function. As individual solo song, from which come most recordings, the medieval ballad had to compete at a disadvantage with the subjective, sentimental, and sensational broadside ballad.

Catalogue: Jonsson, Bengt R., et al., eds. *The Types of the Scandinavian Medieval Ballad: A Descriptive Catalogue*. Instituttet for sammenlignende kulturforskning, ser. B, vol. 59; Skrifter utgivna av Svenskt visarkiv, 5. Stockholm: Svenskt visarkiv; Bergen, and Tromsø: Universitetsforlaget, 1978 [abbreviated TSB]. **Tr.**: Rossel, Sven H., trans. *Scandinavian Ballads*. Wisconsin Introductions to Scandinavia, 2.2. Madison: University of Wisconsin, Department of Scandinavian Studies, 1982. **Bib.**: Holtzapfel, Otto. *Bibliographie zur mittelalterlichen skandinavischen Volksballade*. NIF Publications, 4. Turku: Nordic Institute of Folklore, 1975. **Lit.**: Steenstrup, Johannes C. H. R. *The Medieval Popular Ballad*. Trans. Edward Godfrey Cox. Boston: Ginn, 1914; rpt. Seattle: University of Washington Press, 1968 [rpt. includes bibliographic essay by Karl-Ivar Hildeman]; Hustvedt, Sigurd Bernhard. *Ballad Criticism in Scandinavia and Great Britain During the Eighteenth Century*. New York: American-Scandinavian Foundation, 1916; Hustvedt, Sigurd Bernhard. *Ballad Books and Ballad Men*. Cambridge: Harvard University Press, 1930; Olrik, Axel. *Nordens trylleviser*. Copenhagen: Schultz, 1934; Frandsen, Ernst. *Folkevisen*. Århus: Universitetsforlaget; Copenhagen: Levin & Munksgaard, 1935; Grüner-Nielsen, Hakon. *De færøske Kvadmelodiers Tonalitet i Middelalderen belyst gennem Nutidsoverleveringen*. Færoensia, 1. Copenhagen: Munksgaard, 1945 [English summary, pp. 69–79]; Dal, Erik. *Nordisk folkeviseforskning siden 1800: Omrids af text- og melodistudiets historie og problemer især i Danmark*. Universitets-Jubilæets danske Samfund, 376.

Copenhagen: Schultz, 1956 [English summary, pp. 410–30]; Jørgensen, Jens Anker. *Jorden og slægten: En indføring i folkevisens univers*. Copenhagen: Forlaget Fremad, 1976; Piø, Iørn. "On Reading Orally-Performed Ballads: The Medieval Ballads of Denmark." In *Oral Tradition—Literary Tradition: A Symposium*. Ed. Hans Bekker-Nielsen et al. Odense: Odense University Press, 1977, pp. 69–82; Holtzapfel, Otto, et al., eds. *The European Medieval Ballad: A Symposium*. Odense: Odense University Press, 1978; Holtzapfel, Otto. *Det balladeske: Fortællemåden i den ældre episke folkevise*. Odense: Odense Universitetsforlag, 1980 [English summary, pp. 102–7]; Andersen, Lise Præstgaard. "The Development of the Genres: The Danish Ballad." *Sumlen* (1981), 25–35; Bø, Gudleiv. "Synspunkter på folkevisa som kunst." *Tradisjon* 11 (1981), 33–43 [English summary, p. 44]; Colbert, David. *The Birth of the Ballad: The Scandinavian Medieval Genre*. Stockholm: Svenskt Visarkiv, 1989.

David Colbert

2. DENMARK. Denmark's preeminence among ballad communities is the result of its many aristocratic songbooks. Of its 569 medieval ballad types, only 230 occur in recent tradition, whereas 475 were written down before 1700. Beginning in 1553 with the *Heart Book*, four spontaneous courtly garlands included medieval ballads among many love lyrics and other newfangled songs. By the 1580s, antiquarian interest had inspired two large collections, mostly of ballads, by the historian Anders Sørensen Vedel and by the Norwegian Margrete Lange. Vedel published a book of 100 ballads in 1591, which prompted a ballad revival among the ladies of the landed gentry, from whom we have eighteen major MSS by 1660. After this date, the aristocratic MSS began to stagnate, while the peasant songbooks that succeeded them rarely include more than a single medieval ballad. Yet this same period brought a boom in the market for broadside prints, among which ballads were the steady sellers, as was Peder Syv's 1695 revision of Vedel's edition with an additional 100 ballads. This authoritative edition long hampered the further collection of texts in Denmark, but an augmented reissue in 1814 by Rasmus Byerup offered over 100 melodies, where only eight had previously been noted. Text collection began again in earnest only after Svend Grundtvig's appeal for fresh versions in 1844 in connection with his mammoth edition *Danmarks gamle Folkeviser* ("The Ancient Folksongs of Denmark," abbreviated "DgF"), begun in 1853. His correspondents sent him the bulk of the material now known from Zealand, Funen, and South Jutland. But from 1868 on, the richest harvest was coaxed from the rural proletariat of central Jutland, especially in the Hammerum district around Herning, by Evald Tang Kristensen. By the turn of the century, texts from popular tradition outnumbered those from aristocratic MSS, although representing fewer ballad types. In his edition, Grundtvig launched the principle of printing every text in full, reflecting the authenticity of versions in oral tradition; however, hypothetical archetypes reconstructed on various principles remained the goal for most popular editions until the 1960s.

The masters of ballad tradition have been the womenfolk. The many true-love ballads and resolute heroines in aristocratic tradition certainly reflect their role, and three-fourths of recent informants knowing more than two ballads are women.

The gulf between an early aristocratic and a late popular tradition is probably more apparent than real. Vedel especially must have gathered many of his texts from the "common man," to whom he acknowledges a debt for heroic ballads. A text of "Lave Stisøn og fru Eline" (TSB D 229), gathered locally in eastern Scania about 1600, demonstrates both the terser style, and the heightened drama this style made possible, within the popular tradition of the Renaissance. Many "medieval" ballads are newer songs in old ballad style, for instance, an aristocratic jewel-like "Torbens datter og hendes faderbane" (TSB D 332), or a highly popular international ballad like "Redselille og Medelvold" (TSB D 288). Nevertheless, when compared with the aristocratic songbooks, texts from popular tradition are typically briefer, usually with the dramatic tension relaxed in favor of a more lyrical style. By weakening the scenic structure and using repetition of commonplaces, the social scene becomes more abstract and less mimetic. In short, the characteristic Scandinavian knightly ballad is assimilated here, both in style and content, to the international ballads that figure so prominently in popular tradition.

Both the scenic, formulaic aristocratic style and the terser popular style were probably medieval. Claudius Clavus's Greenland stanza (1425–1450) and the simplified cast of characters that it implies reappear about 1700 in a short heroic ballad (TSB E 90) from popular tradition in Småland, while the seven-stanza fragment of "Ridderen i hjorteham" (TSB A 43) from about 1500 is wholly in the style of the aristocratic songbooks. Which of these two styles is the earlier has often been debated, and can be answered only by a theory of generic origin. The aristocratic MSS leave at least an initial presumption that the marginally literate aristocracy of Denmark, and particularly its womenfolk, were the prime movers of the Scandinavian genre, in particular the knightly ballad, from its inferred origin in the 13th century to the close of aristocratic oligarchy in 1660. Subsequently left to popular tradition alone, the ballad tended to lose much of its Nordic character in favor of a more lyrical, abstract, and universal international material and style.

Ed.: *Danmarks gamle Folkeviser*. Ed. S. H. Grundtvig (vols. 1–5), Axel Olrik and Hakon Grüner-Nielsen (vols. 6–9), H. Grüner-Nielsen *et al.* (vol. 10), Hjalmar Thuren *et al.* (vol. 11), Sven H. Rossel *et al.* (vol. 12). Copenhagen: Samfundet til den danske Literaturs Fremme, 1853–1976; vols 1–10 (ed. Erik Dal) rpt. Copenhagen: Universitets-Jubilæets danske Samfund, 1966–76; Kristensen, Evald Tang, ed. *Et hundrede gamle danske Skjæmteviser*. Århus: [n.p.], 1901. Tr.: Grüner-Nielsen, Hakon, ed. *Danske Skæmteviser*. Copenhagen: Luno, 1927–28; Olrik, Axel, and Ida Falbe-Hanse, eds. *A Book of Danish Ballads*. Trans. E. M. Smith-Dampier. Princeton: Princeton University Press; New York: American-Scandinavian Foundation, 1939; Dal, Erik. *Danish Ballads and Folk Songs*. Trans. Henry Meyer. Copenhagen: Rosenkilde & Bagger; New York: American-Scandinavian Foundation, 1967. Bib.: Holzapfel, Otto. *Bibliographie zur mittelalderlichen skandinavischen Volksballade*. NIF Publications, 4. Turku: Nordic Institute of Folklore, 1975. Lit.: Dal, Erik. *Nordisk folkeviseforskning siden 1800: Omrids af text- og melodistudiets historie og problemer især i Danmark*. Copenhagen: Schultz, 1956 [English summary, pp. 410–30]; Piø, Iørn. "On Reading Orally-Performed Ballads: The Medieval Ballads of Denmark." In *Oral Tradition—Literary Tradition: A Symposium*. Ed. Hans Bekker-Nielsen *et al.* Odense: Odense University Press, 1977, pp. 69–82; Holzapfel, Otto. *Det balladeske: Fortællemåden i den ældre episke folkevise*. Odense: Odense Universitetsforlag, 1980 [English summary, pp. 102–7]; Andersen, Lise Præstgaard. "The Development of the Genres: The Danish Ballad." *Sumlen* (1981), 25–35; Andersen, Flemming G., *et al. The Ballad as Narrative*. Odense: Odense University Press, 1982; Piø, Iørn. *Nye veje til Folkevisen. Studier i Danmarks gamle Folkeviser*. Copenhagen: Gyldendal, 1985 [English summary, pp. 327–34]; Piø, Iørn. "'Ebbe Skammelsøn' (DgF 354): A Sixteenth-Century Broadside Ballad." In *Narrative Folksong. New Directions: Essays in Appreciation of W. Edson Richmond*. Ed. Carol L. Edwards and Kathleen E. B. Manley. Boulder: Westview, 1985, pp. 18–57.

David Colbert

3. FAROES. The Faroe Islands offer a treasure trove for ballad research. Scholars interested in ballads as literary history, records of style, and performed songs will find exceptional research opportunities in the Faroes. Faroese ballads also offer insight into the common Scandinavian past underlying them. In modern Faroese society, ballads serve as reminders of a past heritage and also offer a sense of individual and collective identity. Faroese ballads have played a role in the islands' transition from Danish-dominated outpost to modern society.

For centuries, Faroese ballads continued to be sung and danced, but remained uncollected. In 1639, the Danish scholar Ole Worm published several Faroese ballads. The Romantic Movement in Denmark led to the publication of Faroese ballads that were still being performed. The first significant collection of Faroese ballads was that of Jens Christian Svabo. Svabo classified songs into *Kvæðir* (heroic ballads), *Rímur* (epic ballads), and *Taattir* (satirical ballads). The Danish pastor H. C. Lyngby followed Svabo's lead with his publication of heroic ballads concerning Sigurðr Fáfnisbani ("Fáfnir's killer"). The Faroese then began collecting ballads actively, often drawing on their own repertoires. Faroese editions stimulated active performance among the Faroese.

Scholarly interest in Faroese ballads continued with the editions of Venceslaus Ulricus Hammershaimb, principally known as a student of West Scandinavian languages. The Danish ballad scholar Svend Grundtvig and a colleague, J. Bloch, compiled a diplomatic edition of Faroese ballads, *Føroya Kvæði: Corpus Carminum Færoensium*. The work consists of sixteen volumes, indices, and 234 ballad types, and provides an introduction to Faroese tradition. Later works of the musicologist Hjalmar Thuren complement Grundtvig's edition by focusing on dance and melody.

Faroese *kvæðir* (sing. *kvæði*) are well represented within the corpus; multiepisodic songs called *tættir* (sing. *táttur*) form cycles of *kvæðir*. The *kvæðir* reflect medieval traditions of such champions as Sigurðr, Charlemagne, and Roland. After 1600, Danish heroic ballads became part of Faroese culture, often displacing *kvæði*. In addition to *kvæði* and Danish ballads, the Faroese corpus contains distinct epic songs, the *rímur* (sing. *ríma*), and *taattir*, still sung very occasionally. The ballad community now selects songs from a limited number of *kvæðir* and *taattir*.

The multiepisodic Faroese ballads stand in contrast to East Nordic monoepisodic ballads. Within the "cantos" (*tættir*) of the *kvæðir* are many dramatic events that the "supra" hero of the *kvædir* binds together, as individual *tættir* weave from scene to scene. The tendency of the Faroese ballad to employ multiepisodic themes has led to ballads of greater length, often several hundred stanzas.

The *kvæðir* exhibit the same basic stanzaic forms as those of Danish *kæmpeviser* (heroic ballads). Ballad stanzas comprise either two end-rhyming lines, or four lines with end-rhyme on alternating lines. In addition, the Faroese ballads employ refrains that are often elaborate, reflecting the role of the chorus and the song's intricate melody. In two-line verses, the refrain either interweaves between strophic lines, *tvíflættað* (Hammershaimb LIII), or appends to each stanza, as in four-line ballad strophes.

The Faroe Islands reflect the wider Scandinavian tradition of dancing to ballads. The traditions of evening-long dancing to the *kvæðir*, of a *kvæðakempa* ("lead singer") who leads the way, and of extended celebration, are admittedly on the wane. However, ballads are still sung and danced, for, like the quintessentially Faroese *grindadráp* ("pilot-whale hunt"), heroic ballads communicate Faroese identity to the Faroese, and to others. The ballads also give singers a chance to perform, win renown, and communicate key Faroese traditions and values.

The Faroese *kvæðakempa* is the central figure in performance; as such, he prides himself on a distinctive repertoire, the result of many performances. Each singer's songs vary, yet certain traditional themes recur. The *kvæðakempa* "owns" the ballads of his repertoire, jealously guarding them and singing them sparingly. Such *kvæðakempar* as Hans Johannessen or Jens and Albert Djurhuus of Sandur have enriched common Faroese traditions. Their role as traditional performers still commands much community respect.

Modern ballad researchers have drawn attention to another performance context involving the Faroese ballad, namely the *kvøldseta*, a family singing activity that represents a ballad setting removed from communal celebration.

With its close connection to dance and legendary past, the Faroese *kvæði* enjoys a unique place. Not only does the ballad symbolize Faroese and common Scandinavian medieval tradition, the *kvæði* also constitutes an important foundation for national identity and for a modern society's self-esteem.

Ed.: Svabo, Jens Christian, ed. *Svabos Kvart*. MS Gl. Kgl. Saml. 2894, 1781–82; Johannes Klemmentsen, ed. *Sandoyarbók*. Tórshavn: [n.p.], 1821; Lyngby, H. C., ed. *Færøiske qvæder om Sigurd Fofnersbane og hans Æt*. Randers: Elmenhoff, 1822; Schrøter, J. H., ed. *Sange fra Oldtiden betræffende danske Tildragelser. . . .* Copenhagen: [n.p.], 1825; Hammershaimb, V. U., ed. *Færøiske Kvæder*. 2 vols. Nordiske oldskrifter udgivne af det Nordiske literatur-samfund, 12, 20. Copenhagen: Berling, 1851–55; Hammershaimb, V. U., ed. *Færøsk anthologi. Tekst samt historisk og grammatisk indledning.* Copenhagen: Möller, 1891; Matras, Christian, and Napoleon Djurhuus, eds. *Føroya kvæði: Corpus carminum Færoensium* 1–. Copenhagen: Universitets-Jubilæets danske Samfund, 1941–. **Tr.**: Smith-Dampier, E. M., trans. *Sigurd the Dragon-Slayer: A Faroese Ballad-Cycle*. Oxford: Blackwell, 1934; rpt. New York: Kraus, 1969. **Lit.**: Thuren, Hjalmar. *Dans og kvaddigtning paa Færøerne*. Copenhagen: Høst, 1901; Thuren, Hjalmar. *Folkesangen paa Færøerne*. Copenhagen: Høst, 1908; Matras, Christian. "Folkedigtning." In *Færøerne*. Dansk-Færøsk Samfund, 2. Copenhagen: Dansk-Færøsk Samfund, 1958, pp. 83–99; Svabo, Jens Christian. *Indberetninger fra en Reise i Færøe 1781 og 1782*. Copenhagen: Selskabet til Udgivelse af Færøske Kildeskrifter og Studier, 1959; Nolsøe, Mortan. "Some Problems Concerning the Development of the Faroese Heroic Ballad." *Jahrbuch für Volksliedforschung* 17 (1972), 87–93; Conroy, Patricia L. "Faroese Ballads and Oral-Formulaic Composition." Diss. University of California, Berkeley, 1974; Hughes, S. F. D. "'Völsunga rímur' and 'Sjúrðar kvæði': Romance and Ballad, Ballad and Dance." In *Ballads and Ballad Research: Selected Papers of the International Conference on Nordic and Anglo-American Ballad Research. University of Washington, Seattle, May 2–6, 1977*. Ed. Patricia Conroy. Seattle: University of Washington Press, 1978, pp. 37–45; Conroy, Patricia L. "Creativity in Oral Transmission: An Example from Faroese Ballad Tradition." *Arv* 35 (1979), 25–48; Conroy, Patricia. "Ballad Composition in Faroese Heroic Tradition: The Case of 'Hermilds kvæði.'" *Fróðskaparrit* 27 (1979), 75–101; Conroy, Patricia. "Oral Composition in Faroese Ballads." *Jahrbuch für Volksliedforschung* 25 (1980), 34–50; Andreassen, Eydun. "Folkekulturen i nasjonalromantisk og nasjonalistisk tolkning." *Tradisjon* 10 (1980), 65–73; Wylie, Jonathan, and David Margolin. *The Ring of Dancers: Images of Faroese Culture*. Philadelphia: University of Pennsylvania Press, 1981; Honko, Lauri. "Folktradition och identitet." In *Folktradition och regional identitet i Norden*. Ed. Aili Nenola-Kallio. NIF Publications, 12. Åbo: Nordiska Institutet för Folkdiktning, 1982, pp. 11–24; West, John F. *The History of the Faroe Islands, 1709–1816. 1: 1709–1723*. Copenhagen: Reitzel, 1985; Joensen, Jóan Pauli. *Fra bonde til fisker: Studier i overgangen fra bondesamfund til fiskersamfund på Færøerne*. Annales Societatis Scientiarum Færoensis (Fróðskaparrit). Supplementum 13. Tórshavn: Føroya Fornminnissavn, 1987.

Lanae H. Isaacson

4. ICELAND. The standard edition counts 110 ballad types, but some twenty of these are either fragments of only one stanza or likely to be late and literary ballad imitations. Collection began in the 17th century and was done systematically in the middle of the 19th century, when the tradition was already declining. Ballads of chivalry are by far the largest group, and even the smaller groups of supernatural and legendary ballads often have a chivalric setting. Erotic themes dominate all these groups of ballads. Passionate love is a favored subject, as well as the hatred arising from frustrated love or enforced sexual union. Erotic themes also abound, although treated in a lighter vein, in a handful of jocular ballads that demonstrate human weakness and folly. The smallest group is heroic or champion ballads, their function being fulfilled instead by *rímur*.

Most Icelandic ballad types are known elsewhere, and were not composed originally in Iceland. Icelandic ballads follow the same metrical patterns as ballads in Scandinavia, and always seem to have been sung. Only a few melodies have been preserved.

Communal dancing was practiced in Iceland in the Middle Ages and down to about 1700. Dance gatherings are described in some sources, and ballads were probably one of the several kinds of poetry sung to the dance.

It is impossible to know the origins of all ballads preserved in Iceland, but the largest group that can be traced seems to have come to the country through Norway, in some cases possibly the Faroes, before the mid-16th century. Ballads no doubt became known in Iceland soon after they first appeared in Norway. A somewhat smaller group shows closest kinship to Danish tradition and seems to have arrived later. A dozen or so types appear to be indigenous. They are composed mostly in quatrains and sometimes without refrain, and are generally in a more traditional Icelandic style and a more regular meter than the rest.

The transference of a ballad to Iceland usually involved a shortening or trimming of the stories, seldom compensated for by new material. Sometimes this brevity resulted in a clumsy or incoherent text, but in other cases the trimming enhanced the poetic effect of the ballad's swift narration. In the context of Icelandic poetry, the ballad is a thing apart: it uses free rhythms and abstains from alliteration, besides taking a number of liberties with grammar and conventional usage. When the liberties taken are moderate, they add to the charm and exotic flavor of the ballads, where not only language but also human emotions have a freer play than is common in Icelandic poetry from the period. These characteristics may have helped the ballad to survive in surroundings that were not altogether favorable.

Ed.: Jón Helgason, ed. *Íslenzk fornkvæði: Islandske folkeviser.* 8 vols. Editiones Arnamagnæanæ, ser. B, vols. 10–17. Copenhagen: Munksgaard, 1962–70 (vols. 1–7); Copenhagen: Reitzel, 1981 (vol. 8) [philological edition of all available texts arranged by sources]; Vésteinn Ólason and Hreinn Steingrímsson, eds. *Sagnadansar.* Reykjavik: Rannsóknastofnun í bókmenntafræði and Menningarsjóður, 1979 [popular edition of selected texts of each type and the melodies that have been recorded]. **Lit.**: Vésteinn Ólason. *The Traditional Ballads of Iceland.* Reykjavik: Stofnun Árna Magnússonar, 1982.

Vésteinn Ólason

5. NORWAY. We have little direct evidence for Norwegian ballads from the Middle Ages. But that such ballads were well known is attested by postmedieval ballads and certain linguistic features of Middle Norwegian. Before the middle of the 19th century, no organized collecting of ballads took place. In contrast to Denmark and Sweden, where the aristocracy committed them to writing up to the 16th century, it may be an advantage that the oral tradition was not collected before a more scholarly methodology had emerged. The late recording of the Norwegian ballads, therefore, both shows the continuing strength of the ballad tradition and allows a glimpse of the earlier tradition as it existed in text and melody.

The first large edition appeared in 1853 (Landstad), and in 1858 a specimen of a scholarly edition appeared (Bugge). The collections gradually became large, and scholarly investigation increased, especially by the philologist Bugge. Liestøl's dissertation from 1915 about the connection between Norwegian ballads and Norse literature was a very important addition to ballad research. Liestøl demonstrated that the large group of ballads about trolls and giants was largely of Norwegian or Norwegian-Faroese origin. This opinion has prevailed, so that one can speak of West and East Scandinavian ballad composition. Most of the famous Scandinavian ballads treating subjects from the age of chivalry and many of a historical content belong to the East Scandinavian group. Such ballads are also found in Norwegian ballad tradition, but most often as loans from the neighboring countries. Linguistic similarity made it easy for the ballads to wander from one Scandinavian country to another. That the wandering resulted in extensive variants is evident. Another group of ballads tells of human beings meeting supernatural forces, as they are known from popular belief. This group contains relatively many ballads that must be of Norwegian origin. Norwegian tradition is rich in popular beliefs and ideas that could lend subjects for composition. The natural-mythical ballads are therefore an important group within the Norwegian ballads.

We also have a number of legendary ballads. In this group is found *Draumkvæde*, a visionary poem that is unique in Scandinavian ballad tradition. We have more than 100 recordings of the poem, most of them fragmentary. The first scholars tried to find direct models in Irish-Scottish visions from the early Middle Ages. But, in light of the poem's distinct Catholic allusions, later scholars reexamined the dating of the poem, and it is now believed that it was composed relatively soon after the Reformation in 1537. Much of the content is visionary, and some of it is derived from mythological conceptions and from popular beliefs.

The Norwegian ballad tradition is not as rich as the Danish and Swedish; around 200 types are known. One reason for this lack is the late collection, but we have evidence of many ballads that have been lost.

Much the same can be said about the melodies. There are known tunes for most of the ballads, but it often happens that the same melody is used for several ballads. As in the other Scandinavian countries, the chain dance disappeared, probably as early as the 17th century. We must go to the Faroe Islands to find the chain dance in an unbroken tradition.

Formally, the Norwegian ballads are very similar to the ones found in other Scandinavian countries and in Great Britain. The refrain is often unknown, partly because it was not so important when the chain dance disappeared. The rhyme forms seldom show a full rhyme, because of the linguistic change from Middle Norwegian to the more recent dialect forms. Most of the Norwegian ballads are written down in a central area in South Norway, Telemark.

Ballads from Denmark and Sweden have also received dialect forms in the Norwegian tradition.

Ed.: Landstad, M. B. *Norske Folkeviser.* Christiania [Oslo]: Tønsberg, 1853; rpt. Oslo: Universitetsforlaget, 1968; Bugge, Sophus, ed. *Gamle norske Folkeviser.* Christiania [Oslo]: Feilberg & Landmark, 1858; rpt. Oslo, Bergen, and Tromsø: Universitetsforlaget, 1971; Liestøl, Knut, and Moltke Moe, eds. *Norske folkevisor.* 3 vols. Kristiania [Oslo]: Dybwad, 1920–24; rev. ed. Olav Bø. Oslo: Det norske Samlaget, 1977; Blom, Ådel Gjøstein, and Olav Bø, eds. *Norske balladar i oppskrifter frå 1800-talet.* Oslo: Det norske Samlaget, 1973; Blom, Ådel Gjøstein, ed. *Norske mellomalderballadar. 1: Legendeviser.* Instituttet for sammenlignende kulturforskning, ser. B, vol. 66. Oslo, Bergen, and Tromsø: Universitetsforlaget, 1982. **Bib.**: Blom, Ådel Gjøstein. ["Introduction"]. In *Norske mellomalderballadar.* **Lit.**: **(a) Draumkvæde**: Moe, Moltke. "Middelalderens visionsdigtning." In *Moltke Moes samlede skrifter.* 3 vols. Ed. Knut Liestøl. Instituttet for sammenlignende kulturforskning, ser. B, 1, 6, 9. Oslo: Aschehoug, 1925–27, vol. 3, pp. 199–247 [English summary]; Liestøl, Knut. "Draumkvæde. A Norwegian Visionary Poem from the Middle Ages." *Studia Norvegica* 1 (1946), 2–144; Strömbäck, Dag. "Om Draumkvædet och dess källor." *Arv* 2 (1946), 35–70; Hildeman, Karl Ivar. "I marginalen till Draumkvædet." In his *Medeltid på vers.* Stockholm: Almqvist & Wiksell, 1958; Barnes, Michael, ed. *Draumkvæde: An Edition and Study.* Studia Norvegica, 16. Oslo, Bergen, and Tromsø: Universitetsforlaget, 1974; Bø, Olav. "Draumkvedet —Kenntnisse und Vermutungen." *Norveg* 17 (1975), 155–72; **(b) General literature**: Christophersen, H. P. *The Early History of Ballad-Literature, with Special Reference to English and Scandinavian Ballads.* Cambridge: Cambridge University Press, 1942; Liestøl, Knut. "Scottish and Norwegian Ballads." *Studia Norvegica* 1.1 (1946), 3–16; Liestøl, Knut. "Den skotske ballade Sir Patrick Spens." *Arv* 4 (1948), pp. 28–49; Dal, Erik. *Nordisk folkeviseforskning siden 1800: Omrids af text- og melodistudiets historie og problemer især i Danmark.* Universitets-Jubilæets danske Samfund, 376. Copenhagen: Schultz, 1956; Dal, Erik. "Scandinavian Ballad Research Today." *Scandinavica* 1 (1962), 15–6; Grambo, Ronald. "Folkloristic Research in Norway 1945–1976." *Norveg* 20 (1977), 221–86; Holzapfel, Otto, *et al.*, eds. *The European Medieval Ballad. A Symposium.* Odense: Odense University Press, 1978; Bø, Olav. "'Margjit og Targjei Risvollo': The Classic Triangle in a Norwegian Ballad." In *Narrative Folksong. New Directions: Essays in Appreciation of W. Edson Richmond.* Ed. Carol L. Edwards and Kathleen E. B. Manley. Boulder: Westview, 1985, pp. 284–303.

Olav Bø

6. SWEDEN. According to the type-catalogue of the Scandinavian medieval ballad, 260 ballad types are represented in Swedish tradition. Most of them belong to the common ballad stock of Scandinavia, yet thirty-four are exclusively Swedish. Although there is evidence that ballads existed in Sweden as early as the beginning of the 14th century, the oldest known record is found in a MS

from about 1550: a fragment of "Sankt Göran och draken" (TSB B 10). Remarkably enough, it is preserved with a fragmentary tune; only four other ballad tunes have been recorded in Sweden before 1800. The most important old ballad text sources are the song MSS kept by men and women of the nobility in the 16th and 17th centuries, the oldest of which is that of Harald Olufsson (ca. 1570–1590) in the Royal Library of Stockholm. In the 17th century, for antiquarian reasons, collecting folklore was carried out on the initiative of the Swedish government. Thus, at the end of the century, several ballad texts were recorded, especially in Västergötland, now preserved in MS Vs 20 in the Royal Library. Also of great importance is the collection of Petter Rudebeck from Småland (ca. 1690–1700).

Influenced by German and English romanticism, a group of young Swedes in the 1810s began collecting folksongs, mostly ballads. Great collections were brought together by Rääf, Wallman, Afzelius, and others. Together with the poet and historian Geijer in 1814–1818, Afzelius published the first edition of Swedish ballads, *Svenska folkvisor*. Twenty years later, Arwidsson began publishing *Svenska fornsånger* (1834–42), where texts from the 16th- and 17th-century MSS were edited together with the recordings made by Rääf and others. Important collections in the 19th century also were made by Hyltén-Cavallius, Dybeck, Djurklou, Säve, Wiede, Ericsson, Wigström, and in Swedish Finland by Wefvar. In the first decades of the 20th century, Andersson, Dahlström, and Forslin continued the collecting work in Finland. The Swedish ballads of Finland were edited in 1934 by Andersson (and Forslin). Since the 1950s, most valuable material has been tape-recorded, especially in provinces far from Stockholm, such as Bohuslän, Dalsland, Blekinge, Jämtland, and the Swedish-speaking archipelago of Finland.

Some of the ballad types can be studied in a great number of variants, such as the ballads of the supernatural "De två systrarna" (TSB A 38), "Näcken bortför jungfrun" (TSB A 481), the legendary ballads "Sankte Staffan" (TSB B 8), "Liten Karin" (TSB B 141), the ballads of chivalry "Kärestans död" (TSB D 280), "Herr Peders sjöresa" (TSB D 361), "Liten båtsman" (TSB D 3991), and some jocular ballads, such as "Bonden och kråkan" (TSB F 58). Several ballad types have survived up to the present times because they were repeatedly printed in broadsheets, or because they were elements in popular culture, like "Sankte Staffan." On the other hand, several ballad types are preserved only in one or two variants recorded in the 16th or 17th century. The historical ballads are known only in a very few variants, and from the last 100 years only in a couple of trivial fragments.

How the ballad genre was introduced in Sweden remains an unsolved problem. It is usually maintained that the ballad reached Sweden from Denmark some decades after its introduction there, probably in the second half of the 13th century. Although there is no hard evidence, in Sweden the ballads may also have once been sung by people while dancing, although they were only recorded in solo performance.

According to an opinion now often disputed, the ballads were created by the nobility and long cherished only by the upper classes. But the preserved material shows that in Sweden they were orally transmitted by the peasantry at least from the 17th century. The oldest known informant is a peasant woman from Västergötland, Ingierd Gunnarsdotter, born 1601/2. From the modern ballad material (19th and 20th centuries), it is obvious that ballads during the last 200 years were popular in all strata of society. The majority of informants mentioned for the Swedish material are women. Ballads about the unlucky fate of women, such as the legendary songs "Herr Peder och Kerstin" (TSB B 20), "Maria Magdalena" (TSB B 16), and "Liten Karin," seem to have been especially appreciated by the female sex. Inversely, more men than women sang the ballads "Sankte Staffan" and "Jungfru Maria och Jesus" (TSB B 4), which were performed in popular settings where for the most part only men participated.

Ed.: Geijer, E. G., and A. A. Afzelius, eds. *Svenska folkvisor från forntiden*. 3 vols. Stockholm: Häggström, 1814–18; enlarged edition: Bergström, Richard, and Leonard Höijer, eds. 3 vols. Stockholm: Häggström, 1880; new edition with music commentaries: Sahlgren, Jöran, ed. 4 vols. Uppsala: Kungl. Gustav Adolfs akademien, 1957–60; Arwidsson, A. I., ed. *Svenska fornsånger. En samling af kämpa-visor, folk-visor, lekar och dansar, samt barn- och vallsånger*. 3 vols. Stockholm: Norstedt, 1834–42; Andersson, Otto, ed. *Folkevisor. 1. Den äldre folkvisan*. Finlands svenska folkdiktning, 5.1. Skrifter utgivna av Svenska Litteratursällskapet i Finland, 246. Helsinki: [n.p.], 1934; Jonsson, Bengt R., ed. *Svenska medeltidsballader. Ett urval*. Stockholm: Natur och Kultur, 1962; Jonsson, Bengt R. et al., eds. *Sveriges Medeltida Ballader*. Utgivna av Svenskt visarkiv. Stockholm: Almqvist & Wiksell, 1983 (vol. 1), 1986 (vol. 2), 1990 (vol. 3) [vols. 4–9 to be published; standard edition of Swedish ballads]. **Lit.**: Ek, Sverker. *Den svenska folkvisan*. Stockholm: Natur och Kultur, 1924; Ek, Sverker. *Studier till den svenska folkvisans historia*. Göteborgs Högskolas Årsskrift, 37.1. Gothenburg: Wettergren & Kerber, 1931; Hildeman, Karl-Ivar. *Politiska visor från Sveriges senmedeltid*. Stockholm: Geber, 1950; Hildeman, Karl-Ivar. *Medeltid på vers*. Skrifter utgivna av Svenskt visarkiv, 1. Stockholm: Almqvist & Wiksell, 1958; Arnberg, Matts, ed. *Den medeltida balladen. En orientering och kommentarer till Sveriges Radios inspelningar*. Stockholm: Sveriges Radio, 1962; Hildeman, Karl-Ivar. "Ballad och vislyrik." In *Ny illustrerad svensk litteraturhistoria*. Ed. E. N. Tigerstedt. 2nd ed. Stockholm: Natur och Kultur, 1967, vol. 1, pp. 226–77; Jonsson, Bengt R. *Svensk balladtradition, 1. Källor och balladtyper*. Svenskt visarkivs handlingar, 1. Stockholm: Svenskt visarkiv, 1967; Lönnroth, Lars. *Den dubbla scenen. Muntlig diktning från Eddan till ABBA*. Stockholm: Prisma, 1978, pp. 81–111; Hildeman, Karl-Ivar. *Tillbaka till balladen. Uppsatser och essayer*. Skrifter utgivna av Svenskt visarkiv, 9. Stockholm: Svenskt visarkiv, 1985.

Sven-Bertil Jansson

[**See also:** *Draumkvæde*; Folklore; Love Poetry; *Rímur*]

Bandamanna saga ("The Saga of the Confederates") is one of the shorter *Íslendingasögur*. Oddr, son of the poor but wise farmer Ófeigr Skíðason, leaves home in defiance of his father. He first tries his hand at fishing, but soon becomes a rich merchant, trading with foreign countries and owning his own ocean-going ships. Finally, he buys the large estate of Melr in Miðfjǫrðr in northern Iceland and becomes a chieftain (*goði*) in the district. But before leaving for another voyage, he hands over the control of both estate and chieftaincy to a man whom he prizes far too highly, the energetic but treacherous Óspakr Glúmsson. When Oddr returns home from his journey, he has to force Óspakr to give back the farm and the chieftaincy. Óspakr takes revenge by stealing sheep and killing Oddr's kinsman and best friend, Váli. Oddr prosecutes Óspakr for the crime. But when his case comes before the judges in the *þing*, Oddr nearly loses because of a minor error in procedure. Then Oddr's old father, Ófeigr, who is well acquainted with the law, suddenly turns up in court. He pleads the case for his son, and saves the day. By means of cunning persuasion and illegal gifts of money to the judges, Ófeigr gets them to declare Óspakr an outlaw. Eight other chiefs envy Oddr and would like his riches. They band together into a confederation and prosecute Oddr for offering illegal bribes. The case is heard in the *þing* the following year. But on this occasion, too, Ófeigr manages to use bribery and cunning to overcome the confederation of chiefs. To crown his victory, Oddr receives the hand of the daughter of the most noble and likable of the chiefs who had sworn against him, and father and son become friends.

Bandamanna saga is one of the greatest works of art in the saga literature. Ófeigr is one of the many outstanding old men described in this literature, equal to Egill Skalla-Grímsson and Njáll Þorgeirsson. The main part of the saga, and the most original part, deals with the proceedings in court, where Ófeigr's astonishing knowledge of his fellow men, his cynicism, and his fantastic eloquence overcome the most insurmountable obstacles and turn imminent tragedy into a happy ending. Such pure comedy is very rare in the *Íslendingasögur*. Also unusual is the date of these events, the middle of the 11th century, somewhat later than the period when most of the *Íslendingasögur* take place. Unusual, too, is the social satire and the sharp stabs at the chieftains as a class. *Bandamanna saga* is a work of fiction. But the author's main characters are persons who really lived at the time he is writing about, and the environment is typically Icelandic. *Bandamanna saga* was probably written during the latter half of the 13th century. As in the case of all the *Íslendingasögur*, the author is unknown. The main text of *Bandamanna saga* is found in the vellum codex *Möðruvallabók*, from the middle of the 14th century. There is a shortened version of the saga in a MS, *Konungsbók*, from the 15th century. In this more recent version, much of the artistic value of the saga is lost. But it contains certain details that seem to be more original than the account of the same in *Möðruvallabók*.

Ed.: Guðni Jónsson, ed. *Grettis saga Ásmundarsonar.* Íslenzk fornrit, 7. Reykjavik: Hið íslenzka fornritafélag, 1936; Magerøy, Hallvard, ed. *Bandamanna saga.* Samfund til udgivelse af gammel nordisk litteratur, 67.1. Copenhagen: Jørgensen, 1956; Samfund til udgivelse af gammel nordisk litteratur, 67.2. Copenhagen: Andelsbogtrykkeriet i Odense, 1976 [diplomatic edition of both versions of the saga]; Magerøy, Hallvard, ed. *Bandamanna saga.* London: Viking Society for Northern Research; Oslo: Dreyer, 1981 [main version, in normalized language, with glossary by Peter Foote]. **Tr.**: Hermann Pálsson, trans. *The Confederates & Hen-Thorir.* Edinburgh: Southside, 1975, pp. 43–90 [main version]. **Lit.**: Magerøy, Hallvard. *Studiar i Bandamanna saga.* Bibliotheca Arnamagnæana, 18. Copenhagen: Munksgaard, 1957; Lindow, John. "A Mythic Model in *Bandamanna saga* and Its Significance." *Michigan Germanic Studies* 3 (1977), 1–12; Sverrir Tómasson. "Bandamanna saga og áheyrendur á 14. og 15. öld." *Skírnir* 151 (1977), 97–117; Clover, Carol J. "The Germanic Context of the Unferþ Episode." *Speculum* 55 (1980), 444–68 [discusses the central flyting motif of *Bandamanna saga* within a broader literary context].

Hallvard Magerøy

[See also: *Íslendingasögur, Möðruvallabók*]

Bárðar saga Snæfellsáss ("The Saga of Bárðr Snæfell-god"), a late 13th- or early 14th-century "postclassical" *Íslendingasaga*, is preserved in five vellum fragments and twenty-two paper copies.

The earliest MSS, with the possible exception of AM 564a 4to (late 14th or early 15th century), date from the 15th century (AM 489 4to, AM 162h fol., AM 471 4to, and AM 551a 4to). Among the paper MSS, the most important are AM 158 fol. and AM 486 4to; Guðbrandr Vigfússon takes the latter to be a copy of AM 564a 4to while it was still whole.

Finnur Jónsson suggests that the author of the saga was also the author of *Víglundar saga*, based on a reference to Bárðr in *Víglundar saga* and a reference to Víglundr in *Bárðar saga*. This evidence is slim, making the case for common authorship tenuous. Finnur Jónsson suggests further that the second part of the saga, which he takes to be a tasteless appendage, was written by a different author. Yet none of the older MSS (AM 489 4to and AM 162h fol., which cover the point of division) divide the saga into two parts. The question of whether *Bárðar saga* is one or two sagas is a major issue in the interpretation of the theme of the work. The first part of the saga tells of Bárðr Dumbsson, who, upon dreaming about King Haraldr Hálfdanarson and the coming to the throne of King Óláfr Tryggvason, leaves Norway to explore and settle parts of Iceland. No sooner has he established himself than his daughter Helga disappears, and Bárðr, unable to contain his grief, severs himself from society. Yet he inexplicably reappears throughout the saga to aid his friends when they are in need, becoming in effect a *bjargvættr* ("guardian spirit") like his father, Dumbr, and gaining the nickname "Snæfellsáss" ("Snæfell-" after Snæfellsnes, the western peninsula that forms the setting for most of the story, and *áss* 'god'). The second part tells of the adventures of Bárðr's son Gestr, who travels to Norway and enters the service of King Óláfr Tryggvason. One evening the revenant King Ragnarr appears at court offering the treasures stored in his barrow "to the man who dares get them from me." Gestr accepts the challenge and, accompanied by twenty men and the priest Jósteinn, journeys to the barrow. In the ensuing struggle with Ragnarr, Gestr calls on Bárðr for help, but for the first time, Bárðr's powers fail him. Gestr then calls on Óláfr, and vows to accept Christianity if he is saved, which he is. The night following Gestr's baptism, Bárðr returns as an avenging spirit: the next day Gestr's eyes burst, and he dies in the gown of his baptism.

Bárðar saga draws upon a wide range of folklore motifs and incorporates material from a variety of sources, most notably *Landnámabók*. Readers of Old English will discover parallels between *Beowulf*'s descent into Grendel's lair and Gestr's descent into Ragnarr's barrow. So too, the entrance of Ragnarr into Óláfr's court resembles the entrance of the Green Knight in *Sir Gawain and the Green Knight*. The similarities, however, are only suggestive at best. *Bárðar saga* is a fast-paced, absorbing story marked by characteristically dry and sometimes grim humor and by careful attention to descriptive detail.

Ed.: Guðbrandr Vigfússon, ed. *Bárðarsaga Snæfellsáss, Víglundarsaga, Þórðarsaga, Draumavitranir, Völsaþáttr.* Nordiske Oldskrifter, 27. Copenhagen: Det nordiske Literatur-Samfund; Berling, 1860; Finnur Jónsson, ed. *Den norsk-islandske skjaldedigtning.* Vols. 1A-2A (tekst efter håndskrifterne) and 1B-2B (rettet tekst). Copenhagen and Christiania [Oslo]: Gyldendal, 1912–15; rpt. Copenhagen: Rosenkilde & Bagger, 1967 (A) and 1973 (B), vol. 1B, pp. 449–51 [poetry only]; Jón Skaptason and Phillip Pulsiano, eds. and trans. *Bárðar saga.* Garland Library of Medieval Literature, 8A. New York and London: Garland, 1984 [with facing-page English translation]; Þórhallur Vilmundarson and Bjarni Vilhjálmsson, eds. *Harðar saga.* Íslenzk fornrit,

13. Reykjavik: Hið íslenzka fornritafélag, 1991, pp. 99–172. **Lit.**: Gotzen, Joseph. *Über die Bárðar saga Snæfellsáss.* Diss. Friedrich-Wilhelms-Universität. Berlin: Ebering, 1903 [informative but dated]; Finnur Jónsson. *Den oldnorske og oldislandske Litteraturs Historie.* 3 vols. 2nd ed. Copenhagen: Gad, 1920–23, vol. 3, pp. 81–2; Ellis, Hilda R. "Fostering by Giants in Old Norse Saga Literature." *Medium Ævum* 10 (1941), 70–85; Kuhn, Hans. "Bárðr Snæfellsáss." *Science in Iceland* 1 (1968), 50–4; Schach, Paul. "The Theme of the Reluctant Christian in the Icelandic Sagas." *Journal of English and Germanic Philology* 81 (1982), 186–203; Motz, Lotte. "Gods and Demons of the Wilderness: A Study in Norse Tradition." *Arkiv för nordisk filologi* 99 (1984), 175–87; Kress, Helga. "Fyrir dyrum fóstru. Textafræðingar og konan í textanum út frá vísu eftir Helgu Bárðardóttur í Bárðar sögu Snæfellsáss." *Tímarit Háskóla Íslands* 4 (1989), 133–44.

Phillip Pulsiano

[**See also:** *Íslendingasögur; Landnámabók; Víglundar saga*]

Barlaams ok Josaphats saga

Barlaams ok Josaphats saga ("The Saga of Barlaam and Josaphat") is a religious tale based upon legends of the life of Buddha. It probably originated in Central Asia, dating back to the 6th century, and is later found in both Christian and non-Christian versions. The original author is unknown. The tale was translated from Georgian into Greek, and from Greek into Latin in the 11th and 12th centuries. From the latter version, the tale was translated into most European vernaculars, among them Norwegian, Icelandic, and Swedish.

According to the saga of Guðmundr Arason, bishop of Hólar, the Old Norwegian translation of *Barlaams ok Josaphats saga* must have been undertaken by King Hákon ungi ("the young"; cf. *Biskupa sögur* 2, p. 54). Hákon ungi must have been the son of Hákon Hákonarson. He was born in 1232, appointed king in 1240, and died in 1257. Whether Hákon performed the actual translation personally or had it translated by others cannot be determined.

The Old Norwegian translation is preserved in three medieval MSS and thirteen fragments. The Norwegian MS, Stock. Perg. fol. 6, is the oldest, dating from about 1275. Stock. 6 is the basis of the editions of Keyser and Unger (1851) and Rindal (1980 and 1981). This version is based primarily on the Latin translation from the 12th century, but the author must also have utilized other sources, notably the *Speculum historiale, Stjórn,* and various legends of saints. The Old Norwegian translation is rendered in a particular type of prose style known as "florid style." The Icelandic version is preserved in MS Stock. Perg. fol. 3, published by Loth (1969). She contends that the Icelandic magnate Björn Þorleifsson (*ca.* 1470–1550) both translated the tale and wrote MS Stock. 3 personally. The main source of this MS is a German legendary *Passional* or *Der heiligen Leben.* The Icelandic version is much shorter than its Norwegian counterpart, being completely independent of the latter.

There are also two Swedish versions extant, the older being found in the *Old Swedish Legendary* from the end of the 13th century (edited by Stephens 1847 and 1858) and based on the *Legenda aurea.* The younger was probably translated by Olaus Gunnari about 1440 (edited by Klemming 1887–89). The main source of the later version is the *Speculum historiale,* but there is evidence that MS Stock. 6 was also used.

The Old Norwegian translation relates the story of Josaphat, the Indian prince, and the Christian hermit Barlaam. At Josaphat's birth, it is prophesied that he will become a Christian. His father tries to isolate him from Christian influence and from all evils of this world. Despite these precautions, Josaphat discovers the existence of suffering, evil, and death. Barlaam then comes to him in disguise and converts him to Christianity by learned conversations and parables. Josaphat is baptized, and later manages to convert his father to the new faith. Subsequently, he succeeds his father on the throne, and has his realm convert to Christianity. Then he relinquishes his kingship and goes out into the desert to look for Barlaam. They meet, and live together as hermits until their death.

The tale is essentially an encomium on Christianity, martyrdom, and hermit life, with the lessons to be learned made explicit in classical dialogue form.

Ed.: Stephens, George, ed. *Ett forn–svenskt legendarium.* 2 vols. Samlingar utgifna af Svenska fornskrift-sällskapet, 7.1–2. Stockholm: Norstedt, 1847–58; Keyser, R., and C. R. Unger, eds. *Barlaams ok Josaphats saga.* Christiania [Oslo]: Feilberg & Landmark, 1851; Klemming, G. E., ed. *Prosadikter från Sveriges medeltid.* Samlingar utgifna af Svenska fornskrift-sällskapet, 91, 96–7. Stockholm: Norstedt, 1887–89; Loth, Agnete, ed. *Reykjahólabók. Islandske helgenlegender.* 2 vols. Editiones Arnamagnæanæ, ser. A, vols. 15–6. Copenhagen: Munksgaard, 1969–70, vol. 1; Rindal, Magnus, ed. *Barlaams ok Josaphats saga. Manuscript no. 6 fol. in the Royal Library, Stockholm and the Norwegian Fragments.* Corpus Codicum Norvegicorum Medii Aevi, Quarto Serie, 6. Oslo: Society for Publication of Old Norwegian Manuscripts, 1980 [facsimile]; Rindal, Magnus, ed. *Barlaams ok Josaphats saga.* Norrøne tekster, nr. 4. Oslo: Norsk historisk kjeldeskrift-institutt, 1981. **Tr.**: No translations of the Scandinavian versions; for the Greek text, see: Woodward, G. R., and H. Mattingly, eds. and trans. *Barlaam and Ioasaph.* Loeb Classical Library, 34. London: Heinemann, 1914; rpt. 1967. **Lit.**: [Jón Sigurðsson and Guðbrandur Vigfússon, eds.] *Biskupa sögur.* 2 vols. Copenhagen: Møller, 1858–78; Peri (Pflaum), Hiram. *Der Religionsdisput der Barlaam-Legende, ein Motiv abendländischer Dichtung.* Acta Salamanticensia. Filosofía y letras, 14.3. Salamanca: Universidad de Salamanca, 1959; Haugen, Odd Einar. "Om tidsforholdet mellom *Stjórn* og *Barlaams ok Josaphats saga.*" *Maal og minne* (1983), 18–28.

Magnus Rindal

[**See also:** *Old Swedish Legendary, Reykjahólabók;* Saints' Lives; *Stjórn*]

Bede

Bede. Medieval Scandinavian writers knew the Venerable Bede (673–735), the premier historian, scientist, and theologian of Anglo-Saxon England, mostly as a scholar of chronology. *Landnámabók* begins: "In the book *De Ratione Temporum* [*Aldarfarsbók*] which the Venerable Bede composed, there is mention of an island which is called Thule, of which books record that it lies six days' sail north of Britain. There, said he, there came no day in winter, and no night in summer when the day is at its longest. . . . Now according to what is written, Bede the priest died 735 years after the Incarnation of our Lord, and more than a hundred years before Iceland was settled by Norse men" (Jones 1986: 156). Bede's chronology influenced the Icelandic Easter tables, and the Dionysian dating from the birth of Christ used by Ari Þorgilsson in his *Íslendingabók.* The Icelandic annals use Bede's chronology and mention him often, recording his death under 735: "Andlát Beda prests." The *Gottskálks annáll* lists 722 as the composition date of Bede's *Martyrology* and *Kalendarium.* The *Oddaverja annáll* for 870 repeats Bede's Thule reference, noting that he died 121 years earlier, or in 749(!). Benedikz comments that the annalists "rested

. . . firmly on his authority, even if they got his obit anything up to five or ten years out and were often none too sure of what he actually said in his treatise on chronology" (1976: 338–9).

Benedikz (1976: 340) speculates that Ari and the early Icelandic historians knew Bede's *Historia ecclesiastica*. Saxo Grammaticus refers to it in Book 1 of his *Gesta Danorum*, as does the *Rhymed Chronicle*, which calls Bede "the honest man," or "Venerable." The story of the inspired poet Hallbjǫrn in *Þorleifs þáttr jarlsskálds* may derive from Bede's story of Cædmon in *Historia ecclesiastica* 4:24, although Jónas Kristjánsson (1956: c, 213–29) attributes it to the miracle story of Bede's unfinished tomb inscription.

Scandinavian homilists drew extensively on Bede's sermons, genuine and spurious. For example, a sermon for the Feast of All Saints (*á allra heilagra messu*) survives in the *Icelandic Homily Book* (*ca.* 1200), SKB 15 4to, and in the *Norwegian Homily Book* (after 1200), AM 619 4to; both stem directly from Bede's (spurious) homily 3.71: "Legimus in ecclesiasticis historiis" (Migne 1862: vol. 94, cols. 452–5).

AM 764 4to, a 14th-century miscellany, contains on fol. 36r a short paraphrase of chs. 38–39 of Bede's *Vita Cuthberti*, and a short life of Bede, including the miraculous angel finishing his tomb inscription and blind Bede preaching to the stones (Turville-Petre 1959: 106–8). *Maríu saga* (ch. 61) contains Hermann of Tournai's story of the canons of Laon, which includes this remark about Bede's supposed tomb: "At Wilton, in Somerset, they were shown the grave of the Venerable Bede, beside whom rested a famous poetess, Murier" (Turville-Petre 1959: 110, Unger 1871: 639–54, from Migne 1862: vol. 156, cols. 961 ff.). MS E of this work, Stock. Perg. 4to no. 1, from the first half of the 15th century, "digresses, and gives an account of Bede's life and work, together with three reasons why he was called *venerabilis* and not *sanctus*" (Turville-Petre 1959: 120).

This evidence and many smaller instances suggest that medieval Scandinavians revered Bede for his reputation but had limited direct contact with his works.

Ed.: Migne, J.-P., ed. *Patrologiae Cursus Completus, Series Latina*. Paris: Garnier, 1862, vol. 94, cols. 452–5, vol. 156, cols. 961 ff.; Unger, C. R., ed. *Maríu Saga. Legender om Jomfru Maria og hendes Jertegn*. 2 vols. Christiania [Oslo]: Brögger & Christie, 1871, pp. 650–2; Wisén, Theodor, ed. *Homiliu-bók. Isländska homilier efter en handskrift från tolfte århundradet*. Lund: Gleerup, 1872, p. 39; Gudbrand Vigfusson, ed., and George W. Dasent, trans., *Icelandic Sagas and Other Historical Documents Relating to the Settlements and Descents of the Northmen on the British Isles*. 4 vols. Rolls Series, 88. London: Eyre & Spottiswoode, 1887–94; rpt. [Millwood]: Kraus, 1964, vol. 2, pp. 433–4 [Bede's life in AM 764 4to]; Storm, Gustav, ed. *Islandske Annaler indtil 1578*. Christiania [Oslo]: Grøndahl, 1888; rpt. Norsk historisk kjeldeskrift-institutt, 1977, pp. 310, 448, and under years 731, 732, 735, and 870; Finnur Jónsson, ed. *Landnámabók. I–III. Hauksbók. Sturlubók. Melabók*. Udgiven af det Kongelige nordiske Oldskrift-selskab. Copenhagen: Gyldendal, 1900; Indrebø, Gustav, ed. *Gamal norsk homiliebok. cod. AM 619 4°* Norsk historisk kjeldeskrift-institutt, Skrifter, 54. Oslo: Dybwad, 1931; rpt. Oslo: Universitetsforlaget, 1966, pp. 143 ff.; Olrik, Jørgen, and H. Ræder, eds. *Saxonis Gesta Danorum*. Copenhagen: Levin & Munksgaard, 1931, p. 10 [Vol. 2. *Indicem Verborum Continens*, by Franz Blatt. Copenhagen: Levin & Munksgaard, 1957]; Colgrave, Bertram, ed. and trans. *Two Lives of Saint Cuthbert*. Cambridge: Cambridge University Press, 1940, pp. 142–307, chs. 38–9 on pp. 280–5; Jones, Charles W., ed. *Bedae Opera de Temporibus*.

Cambridge: Medieval Academy of America, 1943, p. 239 [*De temporum ratione*, ch. 31], pp. 297–8 [*De temporibus liber*, ch. 7]; Jónas Kristjánsson, ed. *Eyfirðinga sǫgur*. Íslenzk fornrit, 9. Reykjavik: Hið íslenzka fornritafélag, 1956 [*Þorleifs þáttr jarlsskálds*]; Jakob Benediktsson, ed. *Íslendingabók. Landnámabók*. Íslenzk fornrit, 1. Reykjavik: Hið íslenzka fornritafélag, 1968, pp. xxii–xxiv; Colgrave, Bertram, and R. A. B. Mynors, eds. and trans. *Bede's Ecclesiastical History of the English People*. Oxford: Clarendon, 1964, pp. 114–5 [translates Sturla version]. **Lit.**: Kålund, Kr., and N. Beckman, eds. *Alfræði Íslenzk. Islandsk encyclopædisk litteratur*. 3 vols. Samfund til udgivelse af gammel nordisk litteratur, 37, 41, 45. Copenhagen: Møller, 1908–18, vol. 2, pp. x, 70–1; vol. 3, p. 52 ff.; Turville-Petre, G. *Origins of Icelandic Literature*. Oxford: Clarendon, 1953, pp. 114–20; Lukman, Niels. "Beda." *KLNM* 1 (1956), 396–8; Turville-Petre, Gabriel. "Legends of England in Icelandic Manuscripts." In *The Anglo-Saxons: Studies in Some Aspects of Their History and Culture Presented to Bruce Dickins*. Ed. Peter Clemoes. London: Bowes & Bowes, 1959, pp. 104–21; rpt. in his *Nine Norse Studies*. London: Viking Society for Northern Research, 1972, pp. 59–78; Jones, Gwyn. *The Norse Atlantic Saga: Being the Norse Voyages of Discovery and Settlement to Iceland, Greenland, and North America*. Rev. ed. Oxford: Oxford University Press, 1986. Ellehøj, Svend. *Studier over den ældste norrøne historieskrivning*. Bibliotheca Arnamagnæana, 26. Copenhagen: Munksgaard, 1965, pp. 66–8, 76–80; Benedikz, Benedikt S. "Bede in the Uttermost North." In *Famulus Christi*. Ed. Gerald Bonner. London: SPCK, 1976, pp. 334–41; Fell, Christine E. "Anglo-Saxon Saints in Old Norse Sources and Vice Versa." In *Proceedings of the Eighth Viking Congress Aarhus 24–31 August 1977*. Ed. Hans Bekker-Nielsen et al. Odense: Odense University Press, 1981, pp. 95–106 [esp. pp. 97–100].

Donald K. Fry

Berserkr. The stereotypical *berserkr* of the sagas is a ferocious warrior. When he goes into battle or is otherwise denied what he wishes, he falls into an ecstatic battle fury (*berserksgangr*) in which, as Snorri states, "they were as mad as dogs or wolves, bit into their shields, and were as strong as bears or bulls. They killed men, and neither fire nor iron affected them" (*Ynglinga saga*, ch. 6). This figure occurs most often in the role of unwelcome suitor, where he challenges a man (usually either very old or very young) to a duel for the man's property, wife, and/or daughter. A hero, usually a visitor in the home of the challenged man, replaces his host in the duel, slays the *berserkr*, and thus wins for himself fame, fortune, and often also a wife.

Such stereotyped berserks generally occur in pairs or groups of twelve. If there are two, they are brothers (e.g., *Eyrbyggja saga*, ch. 25); if there are twelve, they generally form a band of outlaws (e.g., *Grettis saga*, ch. 19) or an elite band of troops acting as a king's bodyguard (e.g., *Hrólfs saga kraka*, ch. 24). The earliest recorded use of the term *berserkr*, in Þorbjǫrn hornklofi's ("horn-clawed") poem *Haraldskvæði*, refers to King Haraldr hárfagri ("fair-hair") Hálfdanarson's elite troop of *berserkir*, although without specifying the exact number. Þorbjǫrn equates King Haraldr's *berserkir* with the *Úlfheðnar* (literally "wolf-skins") as the berserks fought in the battle of Hafrsfjǫrðr in the late 9th century. The figure of the *berserkr* and the *Úlfheðinn* must be older than the 9th century, however. The German cognate name *Wolfhetan* and numerous variants are known from the 9th, even possibly the 8th, century. Moreover, graphic representations of *Úlfheðnar* or *berserkir* are known from the 6th and 7th centuries in both Scandinavia and Germany. A bronze matrix found in Torslunda in

Öland depicts a figure dressed in an animal's skin, complete with animal's head and mask yet with clearly human arms and legs, carrying a sword and a spear, and accompanying a one-eyed dancing figure (Óðinn or one of his worshipers). Similar figures have been found in Germany at Obrigheim and Gutenstein. This widespread distribution would seem to indicate a Germanic origin for the berserkr/Úlfheðinn figure.

Two etymologies for berserkr have been proposed. The first derives from the adjective berr 'bare' plus serkr 'shirt,' indicating "one who fights without protective armor," a meaning that was endorsed by Snorri Sturluson. This interpretation is possible, but is more likely a folk etymology based on the language of the 13th century. According to the second and more likely etymology, berserkr is derived from *berr or *beri 'bear' plus serkr, indicating "one dressed in a bear's skin," and thus parallel to Úlfheðinn 'wolfskin.' The existence of such Old Norse forms as bersi/bessi 'bear, little bear' and bera 'female bear,' and such compounds as berharðr 'bold as a bear' and berfjall 'bear hide' are ample evidence for assuming the earlier existence of *berr or *beri.

The cultic origin of the berserkr and his role in the initiation rituals of the Germanic Männerbünde (secret male societies) have been demonstrated in the works of a number of scholars. By the 13th century, however, the berserkr had become a purely literary figure. This older and more positive view of the berserkr and his relationship with the belief in shape shifting are reflected in several sagas where the hero himself shows berserkr or berserkr-like qualities. In Egils saga Skalla-Grímssonar, for example, Egill's grandfather Úlfr is known as Kveld-Úlfr ("evening wolf"), because he takes on the shape of a wolf at night (ch. 1). Later, he has an attack of berserk fury during a fight with King Haraldr's men. After the fury has passed, he is so exhausted that he never recovers, and he dies on the way to Iceland. His son Skalla-Grímr similarly rages against Egill and a playmate, and Egill is saved only by the quick thinking of a self-sacrificing maid.

Vǫlsunga saga also reflects this older belief when Sigmundr and his son/nephew Sinfjǫtli put on wolfskins and become wolves for a period of time (ch. 8). The Icelandic lawbook Grágás specifically outlaws the practice of berserksgangr.

Most sagas, however, know only the stereotyped berserkr. He becomes the foil for Christian missionaries who slay berserkir, thus convincing the heathen of Christ's superiority (Njáls saga, ch. 103; Kristni saga, ch. 2; Vatnsdœla saga, ch. 46). Especially in the late fornaldarsǫgur, the berserkr becomes a magician or just one more fabulous monster among the other exotica (see, e.g., the character Qgmundr in Qrvar-Odds saga or the brothers Gautan and Ógautan in Þorsteins saga Víkingssonar).

Lit.: Güntert, Hermann. Über altisländische Berserkergeschichten. Beilage zum Jahresbericht des Heidelberger Gymnasiums. Heidelberg: Hörning, 1912; Dehmer, Heinz. Primitives Erzählungsgut in den Íslendinga-Sögur. Von deutscher Poeterey, 2. Leipzig: Weber, 1927; Weiser, Lilly. Altgermanische Jünglingsweihen und Männerbünde: Ein Beitrag zur deutschen und nordischen Altertums- und Volkskunde. Bausteine zur Volkskunde und Religionswissenschaft, 1. Bühl: Konkordia, 1927; Noreen, Erik. "Ordet bärsärk." Arkiv för nordisk filologi 48 (1932), 242–54; Reuschel, Helga. Untersuchungen über Stoff und Stil der Fornaldarsaga. Bausteine zur Volkskunde und Religionswissenschaft, 7. Bühl: Konkordia, 1933; Höfler, Otto. Kultische Geheimbünde der Germanen. Frankfurt am Main: Diesterweg, 1934; Schlauch, Margaret. Romance in Iceland. Princeton: Princeton University Press; New York: American-Scandinavian Foundation; London: Allen & Unwin, 1934; rpt. New York: Russell & Russell, 1973; Danielli, Mary. "Initiation Ceremonial from Old Norse Literature." Folklore 56 (1945), 229–45; Eliade, Mircea. The Myth of the Eternal Return. Trans. Willard R. Trask. New York: Pantheon, 1954; rpt. as Cosmos and History: The Myth of the Eternal Return. New York: Harper & Row, 1959; Eliade, Mircea. Birth and Rebirth: The Religious Meanings of Initiation in Human Culture. Trans. Willard R. Trask. New York: Harper & Row, 1958; rpt. as Rites and Symbols of Initiation: The Mysteries of Birth and Rebirth. New York: Harper & Row, 1965; See, Klaus von. "Berserker." Zeitschrift für deutsche Wortforschung 17 (1961), 129–35; rpt. as "Exkurs zum Haraldskvæði: Berserker" in his Edda, Saga, Skaldendichtung: Aufsätze zur skandinavischen Literatur des Mittelalters. Heidelberg: Winter, 1981, pp. 311–7; Vries, Jan de. Altnordisches etymologisches Wörterbuch. 2nd ed. Leiden: Brill, 1962; Eliade, Mircea. Shamanism: Archaic Techniques of Ecstasy. Trans. Willard R. Trask. Bollingen Series, 76. Princeton: Princeton University Press, 1964; rpt. 1974; Beck, Heinrich. Das Ebersignum im Germanischen: Ein Beitrag zur germanischen Tier-Symbolik. Quellen und Forschungen zur Sprach- und Kulturgeschichte der germanischen Völker, N.S. 16. Berlin: de Gruyter, 1965; Ciklamini, Marlene. "The Literary Mold of the hólmgǫngumaðr." Scandinavian Studies 37 (1965), 117–38; Boberg, Inger M. Motif-Index of Early Icelandic Literature. Bibliotheca Arnamagnæana, 27. Copenhagen: Munksgaard, 1966 [esp. motif no. 610.3 and subsections and no. F 1041.8.6]; Sieg, Gerd. "Die Zweikämpfe der Isländersagas." Zeitschrift für deutsches Altertum und deutsche Literatur 95 (1966), 1–27; Müller, Günter. "Zum Namen Wolfhetan und seinen Verwandten." Frühmittelalterliche Studien 1 (1967), 200–12; Beck, Heinrich. "Die Stanzen von Torslunda und die literarische Überlieferung." Frühmittelalterliche Studien 2 (1968), 237–50; Bruce-Mitford, R. L. S. "Fresh Observations on the Torslunda Plates." Frühmittelalterliche Studien 2 (1968), 233–6; Holtsmark, Anne. "On the Werewolf Motif in Egil's saga Skalla-Grímssonar." Scientia Islandica/Science in Iceland 1 (1968), 7–9; Kuhn, Hans. "Kämpen und Berserker." Frühmittelalterliche Studien 2 (1968), 218–27 [trans. and rev. of his "Kappar og berserkir." Skírnir 123 (1949), 98–113; rpt. in his Kleine Schriften. Berlin: de Gruyter, 1971, vol. 2, pp. 521–31]; Müller, Günter. "Germanische Tiersymbolik und Namengebung." Frühmittelalterliche Studien 2 (1968), 202–17; Arent, A. Margaret. "The Heroic Pattern: Old Germanic Helmets, Beowulf, and Grettis saga." In Old Norse Literature and Mythology: A Symposium. Ed. Edgar C. Polomé. Austin: University of Texas Press, 1969, pp. 130–99; Dumézil, Georges. The Destiny of the Warrior. Trans. Alf Hiltebeitel. Chicago: University of Chicago Press, 1970; Blaney, Benjamin. "The berserkr: His Origin and Development in Old Norse Literature." Diss. University of Colorado, 1972; Grimstad, Kaaren. "A Comic Role of the Viking in the Family Sagas." In Studies for Einar Haugen: Presented by Friends and Colleagues. Ed. Evelyn Scherabon et al. Janua Linguarum, Series Maior, 59. The Hague and Paris: Mouton, 1972, pp. 243–52; Zitzelsberger, Otto. "The berserkir in the fornaldarsǫgur." In Fourth International Saga Conference. Munich: Institut für nordische Philologie der Universität München, 1979, 13 pp. [papers distributed to participants]; Davidson, Hilda R. E. "Shape-Changing in Old Norse Sagas." In Animals in Folklore. Ed. Joshua R. Porter and William M. S. Russell. Cambridge: Brewer; Totowa: Rowman and Littlefield, 1978, pp. 126–42; Beard, D. J. "The Berserkr in Icelandic Literature." In Approaches to Oral Literature. Ed. Robin Thelwall. Ulster: New University of Ulster, 1978, pp. 99–114; Blaney, Benjamin. "The Berserk Suitor: The Literary Application of a Stereotyped Theme." Scandinavian Studies 54 (1982), 279–94.

Benjamin Blaney

Bersǫglisvísur see **Sighvatr Þórðarson**

Bevers saga see **Bevis saga**

Bevis saga ("Bevis's Saga") is a 13th-century *riddarasaga* translated from a lost version of the Anglo-Norman *Boeve de Haumtone*. The saga survives in two nearly complete texts, Stock. Perg. fol. no. 7 (late 15th century) and Perg. 4to no. 6 (*ca.* 1400); in two fragments, AM 567 II 4to (14th century) and AM 567 VII 4to (*ca.* 1400); and in a copy made in 1690, Papp. fol. no. 46, of the version in the now-lost 14th-century compilation known as *Ormsbók*. The saga also exists in a number of late paper copies.

The text of the saga contained in Perg. 4to no. 6 begins with the marriage of the aging and childless Earl Guion of Hamtun to the daughter of the king of Scotland, although she has been promised to the emperor of Germany. They have a son, Bevis, but in her growing unhappiness in the marriage, Bevis's mother arranges for Guion to be killed by the emperor. Bevis discovers the crime and accuses his mother, who then orders his death. Ignoring the advice of his knight Sabaoth to flee the country, Bevis kills the emperor, but is then sold by his mother to seamen, who take him to Egypt and to King Erminrikr. The king promises Bevis his daughter Josvena if he will agree to convert to Christianity. Bevis initially refuses, but later, after Josvena declares her love for him, he recants. He then kisses the king's daughter, but is afterward falsely accused by two knights of having had intercourse with her. Bevis is then sent to King Brandemon, where he is held prisoner in a pit for seven years. Josvena, meanwhile, is promised to King Ivorius of Munbrak. Bevis escapes, finds Josvena, and together they flee. After giving birth to two sons, Josvena is kidnaped by Eskopart, a giant whose life Bevis had earlier spared. Seven years pass before Bevis and Josvena are reunited. Bevis then learns that Ivorius had mounted an attack upon Erminrikr; he amasses an army and puts Ivorius to flight. Bevis and Ivorius meet again later in single combat, and again Bevis is successful in routing Ivorius's troops. Soon after, Bevis hears that the King of England has attacked Sabaoth's lands. The king, daunted by Bevis's large army, seeks peace. Bevis then sails to Flanders, Rome, Jerusalem, and, finally, Munbrak, where he finds Josvena grievously ill. Sick from grief, Bevis lies by her side, and they both die.

Like its Anglo-Norman source, *Bevis saga* is a sprawling, adventure-filled narrative, replete with betrayals, abductions, battles, intrigues, and frustrated romance, yet underscored by a Christian tone. Apart from the Old Norse and Anglo-Norman tellings, this popular romance appears in verse and prose in Italian, Welsh, English, and Netherlandic versions.

Ed.: Cederschiöld, Gustaf, ed. *Fornsögur Suðrlanda. Magus saga jarls, Konraðs saga, Bærings saga, Flovents saga, Bevers saga. Med inledning.* Lund: Berling, 1884, pp. 209–67. Bib.: Kalinke, Marianne E., and P. M. Mitchell. *Bibliography of Old Norse–Icelandic Romances.* Islandica, 44. Ithaca and London: Cornell University Press, 1985, pp. 26–7. Lit.: Kölbing, Eugen. "Studien zur Bevis saga." *Beiträge zur Geschichte der deutschen Sprache und Literatur* 19 (1894), 1–130; Sanders, Christopher. "The Order of Knights in *Ormsbók*." *Opuscula* 7. Bibliotheca Arnamagnæana, 34. Copenhagen: Reitzel, 1979, pp. 140–56; Skårup, Povl. "Er Bevers saga og Olif & Landres oversat fra engelsk?" *Gripla* 4 (1980), 65–75.

Phillip Pulsiano

[See also: *Riddarasögur*]

Bible

1. EAST NORSE: DENMARK. Examples of Old Danish biblical translations are late and scarce in comparison with those in other Nordic languages. The reason may not only be that much material has been lost, but also that the Bible was not translated until late because those able to read and write also knew Latin.

Biblical translation proper is found in only one MS, Thott 8 fol., the provenance of which is unknown, but which has been dated by means of its watermarks to around 1475–1490; it is written in three hands. It contains a fragment of a translation of the Vulgate, which may never have been completed, from Genesis 2:9 to 2 Kings 23:18 inclusive, along with a number of primarily narrative additions. Its linguistic form shows both East and West Danish features. The translation bears witness to the use of a glossary (*Catholicon*) and is done throughout according to the *verbum de verbo* principle, but with such clumsy results that the choice of this method has been ascribed to inexperience or pedagogical aims rather than the common reasons: a respect for the sacred text and a humanistic endeavor to imitate Latin. The mixed language and the errors that are not mistranslations suggest that the MS is a copy (of a not much older original). However, since some of the errors may be interpreted as errors in hearing, it has also been suggested that this MS may have been written at the dictation of the translator, or someone working from a rough draft of the translation.

The other material comprises chiefly Bible texts used for devotion or liturgy. A number of psalms, which were an important part of the hours, were translated in the prayer books, among them the seven penitential psalms, which are also found in the miscellanies AM 76 8vo (from *ca.* 1450–1500) and Stock. A 29 (from *ca.* 1450). The Gospel and Epistle texts for the Sundays of the ecclesiastical year are found in two collections of sermons translated from Swedish (Upps. C 56, from *ca.* 1450, and GkS 1390 4to, dated to the 15th century) and in Christiern Pedersen's *Jærtegnspostil*, printed in 1515 and 1518 in Paris and Leipzig. The Gospel and Epistle translations are paraphrastic; moreover, the Danish reviser of the sermons in Upps. C 56 approached a popular narrative style. There is a paraphrase in a legendary style of Matthew 26–27 in a collection of legends (in Stock. K 4, from *ca.* 1450). In very free renderings of various kinds, there are sections of the apocryphal gospels on Mary's childhood and Assumption (in Stock. K 4 and *Jesu Barndoms Bog*, printed in 1508), on Jesus's childhood (in the same works) and his descent into Hell (in Stock. *A 115 from *ca.* 1325), and on Pilate (in *Sjælens Trøst*). Finally, many biblical quotations are found scattered in sermons and other religious literature; whether they are momentary creations or excerpted from elsewhere is unknown.

Direct traces of the Danish Bible translations of the Middle Ages are hardly to be found in the translations of the Reformation period (*e.g.*, the New Testament in 1524 and 1529, and the entire Bible in 1550); but with the Reformation, there is no thorough change in the form of the biblical language.

Ed.: Molbech, Christian, ed. *Den ældste danske Bibel-Oversættelse eller det gamle Testamentes otte første Bøger, fordanskede efter Vulgata.* Copenhagen: Seidelin, 1828 [with glossary]; Brandt, C. J., and R. Th. Fenger, eds. *Christiern Pedersens Danske Skrifter* 1 and 2. Copenhagen: Gyldendal, 1850 and 1851; Brandt, C. J., ed. *De hellige Kvinder, en Legende-Samling.* Dansk Klosterlæsning, 1.2. Copenhagen: Gad, 1859 [ed. from Stock. K 4]; Klemming, G. E., ed. *Svenska medeltids-postillor.* 3 vols. Samlingar utgifna af Svenska fornskrift-sällskapet, 101–2. Stockholm: Norstedt, 1893 [ed. from Uppsala C 56]; Jacobsen, J. P., and R. Paulli, eds. *Danske folkebøger fra 16. og 17. Århundrede* 1. Copenhagen: Gyldendal, 1915 [*Jesu Barndoms Bog*]; Kristensen, Marius, ed. *En klosterbog fra middelalderens slutning (AM 76,8°)*.

Samfund til udgivelse af gammel nordisk litteratur, 54. Copenhagen: Jørgensen, 1933; Nielsen, Karl Martin, ed. *Middelalderens danske bønnebøger.* 5 vols. Copenhagen: Gyldendal, 1945–82 [with survey of the biblical material in the prayer books, vol. 5, pp. 83–4, 128 ff.]; Brøndum-Nielsen, Johs., ed. *Et gammeldansk Digt om Christi Opstandelse efter Fragment Stockh. A115 (c. 1325).* Det Kongelige Danske Videnskabernes Selskab, A 115 (c. 1325) Historisk-filologiske Meddelelser, vol. 35, nr. 1. Copenhagen: Munksgaard, 1955; *Gammeldansk Bibeloversættelse. Den utrykte del.* 4 vols. Copenhagen: Det danske Sprog- og Litteraturselskab, 1968–69 [duplicated for use by Ordbog over det ældre danske Sprog; complements Molbech's ed. of 1828]; Ejder, Bertil, ed. *Svenska Medeltidspostillor.* Samlingar utgivna av Svenska fornskrift-sällskapet, 253. Lund: Blom, 1983 [ed. of GkS 1390 4to]. **Bib.**: Johansson, Hilding-Jarl Gallén. "Bibelöversättning." *KLNM* 1 (1956), 519–20. **Lit.**: Haastrup, Niels. "Omkring den ældste danske Bibeloversættelse." *Selskab for nordisk Filologi. Årsberetning for 1963–1964* (1965), 5–7; Haastrup, Niels. *Infinitiv + skullende. Skolegrammatiske studier i den ældste danske Bibeloversættelse.* Copenhagen: Akademisk Forlag, 1968 [German summary]; Diderichsen, Paul. *Dansk prosahistorie.* Copenhagen: Gyldendal, 1968, vol. 1.1, pp. 107–45; Ejder, Bertil. *Det bibliska materialet i de östnordiska postillorna på folkspråken.* Samlingar utgivna av Svenska fornskrift-sällskapet, 250. Lund: Kungliga biblioteket; Blom, 1976.

Britta Olrik Frederiksen

SWEDEN. King Magnus Eriksson (1316–1374) and St. Birgitta (1302 [1303?]–1373) both appear to have possessed a large Swedish Bible. The king's book is called "unus grossus liber biblie in swenico." Their Bible is considered to have been the paraphrastic translation of the Pentateuch, probably from the first half of the 14th century. This paraphrase is preserved in two copies, one from the beginning of the 15th century, the other from the beginning of the 16th. The person who undertook the Pentateuch paraphrase used as one of his sources the Norwegian Bible translation from the 13th century, upon which the Bible text in *Stjórn* is also based. Approximately three-fifths of the whole text, about 500 printed pages, is occupied by the translation itself; the rest consists of theological exposition associated with the Pentateuch.

The dialect of the author is apparently that of Västergötland, but he remains unidentified. St. Birgitta's confessor is usually mentioned as a possible author. The style is simple and beautiful, and has been compared, for example, with that of the provincial laws.

Very few of the books of the Bible have been preserved in Old Swedish translation. An abridged translation of the Acts of the Apostles is preserved in a copy from around 1385; the apocryphal Gospel of Nicodemus belongs to the first half of the 15th century.

The other extant translations of the books of the Bible are considered to have been undertaken by the Brigettine brothers Nicolaus Ragvaldi from Vadstena and Jöns Budde from Nådendal at the end of the 15th century. The Old Swedish biblical translations are thus usually associated with St. Birgitta and the Brigettine Order. Nicolaus translated the Book of Joshua and the Book of Judges; Judith, Esther, Ruth, and the Books of the Maccabees were, according to the testimony of the preserved copy (1484), translated by Jöns Budde. The Apocalypse is found in an anonymous translation in the same MS as the translations by Jöns Budde. A linguistic examination reveals that the Apocalypse was translated probably by Jöns Budde, and that it is older than his other Bible translations.

There must have existed translations of the Gospels, which were read frequently, of the other books of the New Testament,

and of the Psalter, since the books of the Old Testament, which are less frequently read, were also found in translations. But one can also see the Book of Judges as a natural continuation of the Pentateuch. The Gospel of Nicodemus describes the death of Jesus, and the Acts of the Apostles give an account of the oldest history of the Church, and the Books of the Maccabees are about religious heroes. The books of Judith, Esther, and Ruth were probably considered suitable reading for the Brigettine sisters. Finally, the Apocalypse may have suited the literary taste of the Middle Ages. Thus, one does not necessarily have to presuppose lost translations in order to understand the selection.

In addition, there are translations of Bible texts in other preserved Old Swedish literature. A MS of the *Skänninge Legendary* contains the first chapter of the Gospel according to Luke, and many psalms form part of the Old Swedish translation of *Virgin Mary's Hours*, printed in 1525. The Old Swedish collections of sermons contain the text of the Gospels for all the Sundays and festivals of the ecclesiastical year.

The medieval sermon contained many biblical quotations beyond the texts of the individual days; they also contained a great number of quotations from other sources. But a translation from the Latin was possibly made on that occasion. The question whether the large number of relatively long quotations go back to now-lost Swedish translations of the books of the Bible remains open.

The biblical translations of the Reformation, the New Testament in 1526, and the entire Bible in 1541, may linguistically be connected to the medieval biblical quotations. The Pentateuch paraphrase may have had a stylistically favorable influence on the reformers.

Ed.: Klemming, G. E., ed. *Svenska medeltidens bibelarbeten.* 2 vols. Samlingar utgifna af Svenska fornskrift-sällskapet, 9. Stockholm: Norstedt, 1848–55 ["De fem Moseböckerna," vol. 1, pp. 151–425; "Josua bok," vol. 2, pp. 1–66; "Domareboken," pp. 67–141; "Judiths bok," pp. 143–75; "Esthers bok," pp. 177–204; "Ruths bok," pp. 205–14; "Machabeernes böcker," pp. 215–328; "Johannis uppenbarelse," pp. 329–69; "Nicodemi evangelium," pp. 371–411]; Klemming, G. E., ed. *Klosterläsning.* Samlingar utgifna af Svenska fornskrift-sällskapet, 22. Stockholm: Norstedt, 1877–78 ["Apostlagärningar," pp. 129–78; "Nicodemi evangelium," pp. 375–419]; Geete, Robert, ed. *Jungfru Marie Psaltare (Rosenkrans) af Alanus de Rupe.* Skrifter utgifna af Svenska fornskrift-sällskapet, 159–61. Stockholm: Almqvist & Wiksell, 1923–25; Stephens, George, ed. *Ett forn svenskt legendarium.* 2 vols. Samlingar utgivna av Svenska fornskrift–sällskapet, 7.1–2. Stockholm: Norstedt, 1947–58. **Lit.**: Linton, O. "Medeltida bibeltolkning." *Uppsala Universitets Årsskrift* 11.6 (1941), 1–25; Ahlbäck, O. "Jöns Buddes språk och landsmansskap." *Studier i nordisk filologi* 40–41.1 (1952), 1–152; Thorell, Olof. *Fem Moseböcker på fornsvenska enligt Cod. Holm. A 1.* Samlingar utgivna av Svenska fornskrift-sällskapet, 212. Uppsala: Almqvist & Wiksell, 1959; Lindblad, Gustaf. "Ett språkligt grundmönster i Nya Testamentet 1526." *Nysvenska studier* 51 (1971), 5.57; Ejder, Bertil. *Det bibliska materialet i de östnordiska postillorna på folkspråken.* Samlingar utgivna av Svenska fornskrift–sällskapet, 250. Stockholm: Kungliga biblioteket; Blom, 1976.

Christer Laurén

2. WEST NORSE. It is not known for certain, and probably never will be, whether the entire Bible was translated into Old Norse; but the evidence is largely against it. The published lists of book collections in medieval libraries in Norway and Iceland seldom make reference to the possession of a complete Bible; and

most of those that are mentioned were probably Latin bibles. In the countries of western Europe that principally influenced Norway and Iceland in the medieval period, a complete Bible in the vernacular is a late phenomenon; in France and Germany, the first ones date from the end of the 13th century, while the first complete English Bible appeared a century later. Not until the 16th century do the first vernacular bibles appear in Norway and Iceland; in the MS collections in Copenhagen, Reykjavik, and elsewhere, there is no evidence of a medieval translation.

On the other hand, it has long been known that certain parts of the Bible were translated into Old Norse; and it is very probable that other parts were also. In the countries of western Europe, the parts of the Bible most commonly translated at an early date were the historical books of the Old Testament and Apocrypha, the Psalter, and the Gospels, either individually or in the form of a gospel harmony, principally Tatian's *Diatessaron*. This is largely the picture that has emerged in the West Norse area. The compilation known as *Stjórn* comprises substantial fragments of three separate versions of part, or the whole, of Jewish history from the Creation to the Exile (Genesis–Exodus 18; Exodus 19–Deuteronomy; Joshua–2 Kings). Brandr Jónsson, bishop of Hólar (d. 1264), is credited with the translation of the Maccabean materials that form part of the so-called *Gyðinga saga*. In certain MSS, notably AM 226 fol., these translations are included with *Rómverja saga* and *Alexanders saga* in a Bible-based world history up to the time of Christ. The recent publication of a substantial part of an Icelandic text of the Book of Psalms, copied by a 16th-century hand into a 13th-century Latin Psalter to function as a gloss but taken from a translation that is almost certainly pre-Reformation, establishes beyond reasonable doubt that the Psalter was translated in the medieval period. This assertion is borne out by the frequent mention of psalters in the medieval book collections, some of which may well have been Norse. And the remarkable similarity between certain quotations from the Gospels in Grímr Hólmsteinsson's 13th-century life of John the Baptist and Oddur Gottskálksson's 16th-century translation of the New Testament makes it virtually certain that Grímr was making use of a Norse translation of the Gospels, even though no such translation is known at the present day. It is impossible to say for certain how early translations of parts of the Bible into Old Norse began to be made; but the importance of such books as history, and for liturgical and evangelical purposes, suggests an early date, perhaps even in the 11th century.

Apart from translations proper, the Bible is represented in Old Norse by a multitude of quotations, some short, some long, some close to the Bible text, some in the form of reference, incorporated into other works, and principally in the religious prose that has survived from the medieval period. The shorter saga of the apostle Paul (ed. Unger 1874: 216–36) is little more than an adaptation of the events of Paul's life as recorded in the Acts of the Apostles, and the lives of other apostles also incorporate substantial passages from this source. On the other hand, many works of religious prose are taken directly from a Latin work, and the Bible quotations are merely translated *ad hoc* from the original; this is the case, for instance, with Alcuin's treatise *De virtutibus et vitiis* and the *Elucidarius* of Honorius Augustodunensis. Only very occasionally does it seem probable that the Norse writer was using a Norse text of parts of the scriptures, although this is true of Grímr Hólmsteinsson and probably the author of *Konungs skuggsjá*, who seems almost certain to have known the 13th-century translation of the books of the Kings. Otherwise, it is probable that the Vulgate text of the Bible was used for quotations, though there is some evidence that texts of the Old Latin Bible were also known and used. On occasion, it can be shown that the Latin text was the ultimate rather than the immediate source of a given quotation. Evidence has been traced of the use of Tatian's *Diatessaron* in the homilies, as well as use of the individual Gospels, and of the psalter version of the Psalms of David as well as the Vulgate text; the Bible text used by Comestor in his *Historia scholastica* is the direct source of many quotations, while the source of the Bel and the Dragon story as found in *Hauksbók* is Ælfric's Old English homily "De falsis diis." The liturgy of the Church is also a common direct source of material ultimately biblical: the Lord's Prayer, the Ten Commandments, the Hail Mary, and common bidding prayers (such as that which goes back to Ezekiel 33:11), and exhortations for the offertory (Tobit 4, 7, and 8) are cases in point. The use made of the Bible, directly or indirectly, in Old Norse literature is substantial and on the whole impressively accurate.

Ed.: Unger, C. R., ed. *Stjórn: Gammelnorsk bibelhistorie fra verdens skabelse til det babyloniske fangenskab*. Christiania [Oslo]: Feilberg & Landmark, 1862; Unger, C. R., ed. *Postola sögur. Legendariske fortællinger om apostlernes liv deres kamp for kristendommens udbredelse samt deres martyrdød*. Christiania [Oslo]: Bentzen, 1874; Guðmundur Þorláksson, ed. *Gyðinga saga. En bearbejdelse fra midten af det 13. årh. ved Brandr Jónsson*. Samfund til udgivelse af gammel nordisk litteratur, 6. Copenhagen: Møller, 1881; Sigurður Nordal, ed. *Hið Nýa Testament 1540. Oddr Gottskálksson's Translation of the New Testament*. Monumenta Typographica Islandica, 1. Copenhagen: Levin & Munksgaard, 1933; Uecker, Heiko, ed. *Der Wiener Psalter: Cod. Vind. 2713*. Editiones Arnamagnæanæ, ser. B, vol. 27. Copenhagen: Reitzel, 1980. **Lit.**: Guðbrandur Vigfússon. "Um Stjórn." *Ný félagsrit* 23 (1863), 132–51; Storm, Gustav. "De norsk-islandske Bibeloversættelser fra 13de og 14de Aarhundrede og Biskop Brandr Jónsson." *Arkiv för nordisk filologi* 3 (1886), 244–56; Einar Ól. Sveinsson. "Athugasemdir um Stjórn." In *Studia Centenalia in Honorem Memoriae Benedikts S. Þórarinsson*. Ed. B. S. Benedikz. Reykjavik: Ísafold, 1961, pp. 17–32; Selma Jónsdóttir. *Lýsingar í Stjórnarhandriti: AM 227 fol*. Reykjavik: Almenna bókafélagið, 1971; Hallberg, Peter. "Some Observations on the Language of *Dunstanus saga*, with an Appendix on the Bible Compilation *Stjórn*." *Saga-Book of the Viking Society* 18 (1973), 324–53; Hofmann, Dietrich. "Die Königsspiegel-Zitate in der Stiórn: Ihre Bedeutung für die Entstehungs- und Textgeschichte beider Werke." *Skandinavistik* 3 (1973), 1–40; Bagge, Sverre. "Forholdet mellom Kongespeilet og Stjórn." *Arkiv för nordisk filologi* 89 (1974), 163–202; Kirby, I. J. *Biblical Quotation in Old Icelandic–Norwegian Religious Literature*. 2 vols. Reykjavik: Stofnun Árna Magnússonar, 1976–80; Hallberg, Peter. "Några språkdrag i Alexanders saga och Gyðinga saga—med en utblick på Stjórn." In *Sjötíu ritgerðir helgaðar Jakobi Benediktssyni 20. júlí 1977*. 2 vols. Ed. Einar G. Pétursson and Jónas Kristjánsson. Reykjavik: Stofnun Árna Magnússonar, 1977, vol. 1, pp. 234–50; Haugen, Odd Einar. "Om tidsforholdet mellom *Stjórn* og *Barlaams ok Josaphats saga*." *Maal og minne* (1983), 18–28; Jakob Benediktsson. "Stjórn og Nikulás saga." *Gripla* 6 (1984), 7–11; Kirby, I. J. *Bible Translation in Old Norse*. Université de Lausanne, Publications de la Faculté des Lettres, 27. Geneva: Droz, 1986; Astås, Reidar. *Et bibelverk fra middelalderen: Studier i Stjórn*. 2 vols. Oslo: Novus, 1987; Wolf, Kirsten. "Brandr Jónsson and *Stjórn*." *Scandinavian Studies* 62 (1990), 163–88; Wolf, Kirsten. "Peter Comestor's *Historia Scholastica* in Old Norse Translation." *Amsterdamer Beiträge zur älteren Germanistik* 33 (1991), 149–66.

I. J. Kirby

[See also: Alcuin: *De virtutibus et vitiis*; *Alexanders saga*; Birgitta, St.; Christian Poetry; Christian Prose; *Elucidarius*; *Gyðinga saga*; *Hauksbók*; Homilies (West Norse); *Nicodemus, Gospel of*; *Postola sögur*; *Rómverja saga*; Saints' Lives; *Stjórn*]

Birgitta, St. (St. Bridget of Sweden; 1302 [1303?]–1373), was a Swedish saint and mystic and founder of the Brigettine Order. Born in Finsta, Uppland, she was the daughter of *lagman* ("lawman") Birger Persson, and, on her mother's side, was related to the royal house of Sweden. At age fourteen, she married Ulf Gudmarsson, who became a knight and *lagman* in the province of Närke. There were eight children of the marriage; the best known was the second-eldest daughter, St. Katarina, who became the first abbess (although never consecrated) of the monastic foundation at Vadstena in Östergötland. Ulf died in 1344, and shortly afterward Birgitta received her "vision of calling." She renounced her worldly possessions, and took up residence near the Cistercian monastery of Alvastra in Östergötland.

Here, she received some of her most important visions, including the revelation of the Rule for a new monastic order. She was supported by spiritual counselors and confessors, including Mathias, canon of Linköping, Sweden's foremost theologian of the time, and two clerics with the name Petrus Olofsson, who were authors of the *Vita*, the earliest biography of the saint. In 1349, Birgitta was instructed in a vision to go to Rome, and she arrived there in time for the holy year of Jubilee in 1350. She remained in Rome with a small following of Swedes for the rest of her life, and never returned to her native country. In Rome, she was involved in seeking papal authorization for her new order, which was granted in 1370. But it was not until 1419 that the order was formally constituted by Pope Martin V. Birgitta made occasional visits abroad, to Cyprus and Sicily. In 1372, she traveled to the Holy Land, where she received an important cycle of visions relating to the nativity and life of Christ. Toward the end of her life, she made the acquaintance of Alphonso of Pecha, formerly bishop of Jaén; he edited and published her collected revelations and promoted her case for canonization. After her death on July 23, 1373, her relics were translated to Vadstena. She was canonized in 1391, and her official feast day today is July 23.

Altogether, Birgitta received some 700 visions, many of which were extremely influential long after her death. They vary considerably in length, and cover an enormous range of material, from questions of theology, to descriptions of heaven and hell, to judgment scenes of church and political magnates, to highly personalized messages intended for her intimate circle of followers, and to a monastic rule and instructions for life. Nearly all of the recorded visions are occasional pieces, and rarely do they contain circumstantial details. Birgitta's revelations came to her in different ways: she would appear as one half-dead, or she would experience God through her senses, or feel Him as a palpable movement in her breast; or she would simply become rapt in ecstatic prayer. When she was roused from a vision, she wrote it down immediately in her native tongue, and her confessors translated it into Latin. During her lifetime, her revelations remained as private documents. The canonization edition consists of eight books, the last of which contains revelations concerning kings and church leaders that are of political interest and relevance, and other works, such as the *Regula salvatoris* and the *Sermo angelicus*, which is a collection of daily readings to be used during the night office at the monastery.

St. Birgitta's spirituality is characterized by a strong interest in the humanity of Christ, who is perceived as a crusading knight impatiently waiting to do justice. She also identifies closely with the Virgin, who is the central devotional figure in the Brigettine Order. Her Marian revelations were popular throughout Europe during the 15th century. Her legal background is reflected in another cycle of visions that involve judgment scenes of the souls of the departed. Another characteristic is the practical interest she takes in temporal matters. Hers is a missionary mysticism, and she is intent upon regeneration and reform. Like the Old Testament prophets, she puts special emphasis on God's severe judgment of the wicked, and she strives to save human souls, to renovate the Church militant, and to raise the degenerate moral standards she observes all around her, among clergy and laypeople alike. The monastic order she founded is a testimony to her lasting influence not only in Sweden, but also throughout Europe.

Ed.: *Revelationes S. Birgitte*. Lübeck: Ghotan, 1492 [*editio princeps*]; Collijn, Isak, ed. *Acta et processus canonizacionis beate Birgitte, efter cod. A14 Holm., cod. Ottob. lat. 90, o. cod. Harl. 612, med inledning, person- och ortregister*. Samlingar utgivna av Svenska fornskrift-sällskapet, ser. 2. Latinska skrifter, 1. Uppsala: Almqvist & Wiksell, 1924–31; Collijn, Isak, ed. *Birgerus Gregorii. Legenda sancte Birgitte*. Samlingar utgivna av Svenska fornskrift–sällskapet, ser. 2, Latinska skrifter, 4. Uppsala: Almqvist & Wiksell, 1946; Undhagen, Carl-Gustaf, ed. *Birger Gregerssons Birgitta-officium*. Samlingar utgivna av Svenska fornskrift-sällskapet, ser 2, Latinska skrifter, 6. Uppsala: Almqvist & Wiksell, 1960; Bergh, Birger, ed. *Den heliga Birgittas Revelaciones: Book VII*. Samlingar utgivna av Svenska fornskrift-sällskapet, ser. 2, Latinska skrifter, 7.7. Uppsala: Almqvist & Wiksell, 1967; Bergh, Birger, ed. *Sancta Birgitta. Revelaciones: Book V: Liber questionum*. Samlingar utgivna av Svenska fornskrift–sällskapet, ser. 2, Latinska skrifter, 7.5. Uppsala: Almqvist & Wiksell, 1971; Eklund, Sten, ed. *Sancta Birgitta. Opera minora. II. Sermo Angelicus*. Samlingar utgivna av Svenska fornskrift–sällskapet, ser. 2, Latinska skrifter 8.2. Uppsala: Almqvist & Wiksell, 1972; Eklund, Sten, ed. *Sancta Birgitta. Opera minora. I. Regula Salvatoris*. Samlingar utgivna av Svenska fornskrift–sällskapet, ser. 2, Latinska skrifter, 8.1. Uppsala: Almqvist & Wiksell, 1975; Undhagen, Carl-Gustaf, ed. *Sancta Birgitta. Revelaciones. Book I, with Magister Mathias' Prologue*. Samlingar utgivna av Svenska fornskrift–sällskapet, ser. 2, Latinska skrifter, 7.1. Uppsala: Almqvist & Wiksell, 1978; Morris, Bridget, ed. *Book V of St. Birgitta's Uppenbarelser. Edited from MS Cod. Ups. C61*. Samlingar utgivna av Svenska fornskrift–sällskapet, 80. Lund: Blom, 1991. **Lit.**: Westman, K. B. *Birgitta-studier*. Uppsala: Akademiska boktryckeriet; Berling, 1911 [published also as *Uppsala universitets årsskrift 1 (1911)*]; Kraft, Salomon. *Textstudier till Birgittas revelationer*. Kyrkohistorisk årsskrift, 29. Uppsala: Almqvist & Wiksell, 1929; Vernet, F. "Brigitte de Suède." In *Dictionnaire de spiritualité ascétique et mystique*. Ed. Marcel Viller, S. J. Paris: Beauchesne, 1937, vol. 1, cols. 1943–58; Brilioth, Yngve. *Svenska kyrkans historia. Den senare medeltiden 1274–1521*. Uppsala: Almqvist & Wiksell, 1941; Jørgensen, Johannes. *St. Bridget of Sweden*. 2 vols. Trans. Ingeborg Lund. London: Longmans, 1954; Colledge, Eric. "*Epistola solitarii ad reges*: Alphonse of Pecha as Organizer of Birgittine and Urbanist Propaganda." *Mediaeval Studies* 18 (1956), 19–49; Nyberg, Tore. *Birgittinische Klostergründungen des Mittelalters*. Bibliotheca historica Lundensis, 15. Lund: Gleerup, 1965; Ekwall, Sara. *Vår äldsta Birgittabiografi och dennas viktigaste varianter*. Kungl. vitterhets historie och antikvitets akademiens handlingar, hist. ser., 12. Stockholm: Kungl. vitterhets historie och antikvitets akademien, 1965; Montag, Ulrich. *Das Werk der heiligen Birgitta von Schweden in oberdeutscher Überlieferung. Texte und Untersuchungen*. Münchener Texte und Untersuchungen zur deutschen Literatur des Mittelalters, 18. Munich:

Beck, 1968; Klockars, Birgit. *Birgitta och böckerna. En undersökning av den heliga Birgittas källor.* Kungl. vitterhets historie och antikvitets akademiens handlingar, hist. ser., 11. Stockholm: Kungl. vitterhets historie och antikvitets akademien, 1966; Kilström, Bengt Ingmar. *Bibliographia Birgittina. Skrifter av och om den heliga Birgitta samt om birgittinska kloster och birgittinskt fromhetsliv, i urval.* Strängnäs: Societatis Sanctae Birgittae, 1973; Stolpe, Sven. *Birgitta i Sverige.* Stockholm: Askild & Karnekull, 1973; Stolpe, Sven. *Birgitta i Rom.* Stockholm: Askild & Karnekull, 1973; Rossing, Anna. *Studier i den heliga Birgittas spiritualitet.* Akademisk avhandling för filosofie, doktorsexamen, Litteraturvetenskapliga institutionen. Stockholm: Stockholms Universitet, 1986.

Bridget Morris

[**See also:** Bible; Christian Prose; Iconography; Liturgy and Liturgical Texts; Monasticism; Saints' Lives; Vadstena; Visionary Literature]

Birka. Rimbert's *Vita Anskarii* (ca. 870) and Adam of Bremen's *Gesta Hammaburgensis ecclesiae pontificum* (ca. 1075) mention many places in Scandinavia, including Birka, the town of the Svear and the most important harbor of the Baltic. It was abandoned before 1000, but even in the Middle Ages was identified with the island of Björkö in Lake Mälaren, about 30 km. west of Stockholm.

This island of about 1,500 m. in width contains an occupation deposit ("Black Earth") about 13 hectares in extent and up to 2 m. deep, a town rampart, a fortress, and 2,000–3,000 burial mounds. The bays around the shore shelter harbors and stone jetties, which, because of the land elevation, now lie about 5 m. above sea level.

In 1871–1895, the Swedish naturalist Hjalmar Stolpe excavated about 4,500 sq. m. of the occupation deposit and about 1,100 burials. The Black Earth contained large quantities of refuse, including tens of thousands of animal and bird bones, many hundreds of bone ice skates, combs, bone pins, metal objects, and pottery. Tools, molds, and crucibles show that industrial processes had been carried on.

The burials indicate a native and a foreign tradition. The "native" consists of cremation layers under mounds and occasionally boat-shaped stone settings or triangular stone settings with concave sides. The "foreign burials," inhumations in coffins and chamber graves, were confined to areas on the edge of the town. These graves are probably of foreign merchants, craftsmen, and their families, either Christian or Muslim, who came from East and West. They may also have been the graves of Scandinavians newly converted to Christianity.

The inhumation burials contained many well-preserved details of clothing and equipment that, although belonging to foreigners, provide information about Viking Age chronology, culture, and customs of dress. The graves also contained much imported jewelry, glass and bronze vessels, weapons, pottery, and so on (see particularly Birka II). The finds are stored in Statens Historiska Museum, Stockholm.

Most research into Birka has concentrated on the grave goods that have been published in *Birka I* and *II*:1–3 and elsewhere (Arbman 1937, Geijer 1938, Selling 1955, Gräslund 1980, K. Ambrosiani 1981, Jansson 1985, Duczko 1985, Ericson 1987).

A trench dug through one of the jetties in the Black Earth in 1969–1971 revealed stratigraphy useful for Birka's chronology, but much remains to be done. Stolpe's discoveries must be studied

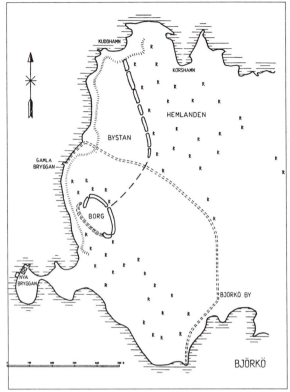

2. Björkö

and trial excavations made to establish the town plan and its stratigraphy, and to answer questions about visible earthworks.

The finds from Birka date from the Viking Age. The site was settled by around 800 and was abandoned in the 970s, when a large hoard of Arab coins and silver rings was deposited. Birka was permanently occupied, averaging 700–1,000 inhabitants. *Vita Anskarii* mentions a reeve and a "thing," a king living nearby, and Christians before Ansgar's mission. The mission had little success outside the town. The earliest Swedish town law is the "Bjärköarätt," perhaps deriving from Birka.

Birka played an important part in the hinterland of the Mälaren. In exchange for simple manufactured and imported products, its inhabitants acquired such necessities as provisions, fuel, hay, and raw materials that could not be produced on the small island. Its situation on the route from the iron- and fur-producing forests of northern Scandinavia was also important. Raw materials were transported to the town in winter and exported overseas in summer. The many luxury articles found in the Birka graves illustrate surplus from this trade.

Birka also had a significant role in Viking Age trade between East and West, probably largely in the form of valuable, easily portable commodities, such as silver, silk, swords, and slaves.

Ed.: Schmeidler, Bernhard, ed. *Magistri Adami Bremensis Gesta Hammaburgensis Ecclesiae Pontificum.* Monumenta Germaniae Historica, Scriptores rerum Germanicarum in usum scholarum, 2. Hannover and Leipzig: Bibliopolii Hahniani, 1917; Rimbert. "Angars liv." In *Boken om Ansgar.* Trans. Eva Odelman. Stockholm: Proprius, 1986. **Lit.**: Arbman, Holger. *Schweden und das karolingische Reich.*

Studien zu den Handelsverbindungen des 9. Jahrhunderts. Kungl. vitterhets historie och antikvitets akademiens handlingar, 43. Stockholm: Kungl. vitterhets historie och antikvitets akademien; Wahlström & Widstrand, 1937; Arbman, Holger, and Greta Arwidsson, eds. *Birka.* Stockholm: Kungl. vitterhets historie och antikvitets akademien; Almqvist & Wiksell, 1938–89; Geijer, Agnes. *Die Textilfunde aus den Gräbern* [*Birka* 3]. Stockholm: Kungl. vitterhets historie och antikvitets akademien, 1938; Selling, Dagmar. *Wikingerzeitliche und frühmittelalterliche Keramik in Schweden.* Stockholm: Petterson, 1955; Ambrosiani, Björn, *et al. Birka. Svarta Jordens Hamnområde.* Arkeologisk undersökning 1970–1971. Riksantikvarieämbetet Rapport C 1, 1973. Stockholm: [s.n.], 1973; Hägg, Inga. *Kvinnodräkten i Birka: Livplaggens rekonstruktion på grundval av det arkeologiska materialet.* Uppsala: Institut för arkeologi, 1974. Gräslund, Ann-Sofie. *The Burial Customs: A Study of the Graves on Björkö* [*Birka* 4]. Stockholm: Kungl. vitterhets historie och antikvitets akademien, 1980 [monograph]; Ambrosiani, Kristina. *Viking Age Combs, Comb Making and Comb Makers in the Light of the Finds from Birka and Ribe.* Stockholm Studies in Archaeology 2 (1981) [monograph]; Ambrosiani, Björn. "Specialization and Urbanization in the Mälaren Valley—a Question of Maturity." In *Society and Trade in the Baltic During the Viking Age.* Acta Visbyensia, 7. Visby: Gotlands Fornsal, 1985; Duczko, Wladyslaw. *The Filigree and Granulation Work of the Viking Period: An Analysis of the Material from Björkö.* [*Birka* 5]. Stockholm: Kungl. vitterhets historie och antikvitets akademien, 1985 [monograph]; Jansson, Ingmar. *Ovala spännbucklor: en studie av vikingatida standardsmycken med utgångspunkt från Björköfynden.* Aun 7 (1985) [monograph]; Ericson, Per. *Osteology of the Eider.* Statens Historiska Museum Studies, 5. Stockholm: Statens Historiska Museum, 1987; Ambrosiani, Björn. *Birka on the Island of Björkö. Cultural Monuments in Sweden.* Stockholm: Riksantikvarieämbetet, 1988.

Björn Ambrosiani

[**See also:** Burial Mounds and Burial Practices; Iconography; Sweden]

Birsay has been described as "one of the most numinous of Scotland's archaeological sites," and it has received considerable attention, both historical and archaeological, over the years. Mentioned in *Orkneyinga saga* especially in relation to the building of a minster dedicated to Christ by Earl Þorfinnr, it has a rich history stretching both forward and backward. The site of both a Norse minster and palace, it was later the location of the Stewart Earl's palace, and had formerly also been a major cultural center of the Pictish period. Iron Age remains are also located here, and a particularly significant Early Prehistoric midden site, economically at a stage anterior to Skara Brae, yet chronologically later, is found on the extremity of the Point of Buckquoy.

Work since about 1970 has widened the perspective. Debate has occurred on the location of both the Norse palace and, more particularly, the minster, with alternatives promulgated for both the Village area ("Palace" or "Place") near St. Magnus Parish Church, and for the Brough of Birsay, a tidal island at the northwest extremity of the Bay of Birsay. Recent archaeological investigation has identified two major mound sites, multiperiod in date, to the south of the Village. Saevar Howe was originally examined in the 19th century, when a cemetery of long-cists and artifacts including an iron bell were found and identified as pre-Viking. These cists are now clearly Christian Norse in date, and succeed settlements of both the Viking and Pictish periods. Similarly, at Beachview, buildings and midden deposits indicate a Late Viking

settlement overlying a long archaeological sequence. To the north of the Village, on the coastal margins of the Point of Buckquoy, a number of Pictish and Viking sites have been identified and partially examined. These sites include Pictish-period burial cairns, Viking cist graves, Norse settlement debris, and remains of both Viking farmstead buildings and Pictish buildings, essentially cellular in form. It has been postulated that the artifactual material from one of these sites in particular indicates a degree of cultural interaction, if not integration, that suggests an absence of violence in the relations between native Picts and incoming Vikings.

Although this interpretation is still controversial, many of the same artifactual forms can also be identified in the assemblages from the long-running excavations on the Brough of Birsay. Here, surrounding a small stone chapel, dated variously to the 11th and 12th centuries, is a small Christian graveyard, with two levels of graves, Pictish and Norse. The latter presumably date from the 11th century onward, but there is no sign of pagans here before this date. Indeed, a series of Norse buildings, of various dates but presumably all part of the farmstead, appear to respect the lines of the churchyard, although much clearance and reconstruction have taken place on the site. An earlier chapel and churchyard have been identified, below the later structures and graves. Artifacts from older excavations and both buildings and artifacts from recent works indicate a flourishing Pictish-period community, displaced in the Viking period. Debate continues as to whether this evidence should be interpreted in terms of a "Celtic" monastery. Recent survey and excavation work has also extended the area on this island known to have been occupied in the Viking period.

The buildings on the Brough of Birsay also clearly include finely built structures, which have therefore been identified with the Earls. Similarly, the fine craftsmanship of the chapel and buildings to the north of it have encouraged identification with the Cathedral and Bishop's Palace. However, the dedication to St. Peter and architectural details have been seen by others as inimical to this association. Recent excavations beneath the Parish Church have provided tantalizing but inconclusive evidence of a finely built earlier structure, possibly of 11th- or 12th-century date. But, whatever the original disposition of Þorfinnr's minster, it cannot be denied that the whole area of Birsay was a, and at times *the*, major center of political and ecclesiastical power in the Orkney Earldom, with an influence stretching far beyond the immediate area.

Lit.: Curle, Cecil L. *Pictish and Norse Finds from the Brough of Birsay 1934–1974.* Society of Antiquaries of Scotland, Monograph Series, 1. Edinburgh: Society of Antiquaries of Scotland, 1982; *Birsay: A Centre of Political and Ecclesiastical Power.* Orkney Heritage 2 (1983) [entire issue devoted to Birsay]; Morris, Christopher D. "Viking Orkney: A Survey." In *The Prehistory of Orkney.* Ed. Colin Renfrew. Edinburgh: Edinburgh University Press, 1985, pp. 210–42; Ritchie, Anne. "Orkney in the Pictish Kingdom." In *The Prehistory of Orkney,* pp. 183–207; Hunter, John R. *Rescue Excavations on the Brough of Birsay 1974–1982.* Society of Antiquaries of Scotland, Monograph Series, 4. Edinburgh: Society of Antiquaries of Scotland, 1986; Crawford, Barbara E. *Scandinavian Scotland.* Scotland in the Early Middle Ages, 2. Leicester: Leicester University Press, 1987; Christopher D. Morris. *The Birsay Bay Project. 1. Brough Road Excavations 1976–1982.* University of Durham, Department of Archaeology, Monograph Series, 1. Durham: University of Durham Press, 1989.

Christopher D. Morris

[**See also:** *Orkneyinga saga;* Scotland, Norse in]

Bishops' Sagas *see* Biskupa sögur

Biskupa sögur ("Bishops' Sagas") tell of Icelandic bishops from the 11th to the 14th centuries. They were written down from around 1200 until the middle of the 14th century. Many of them were composed by contemporaries of the bishops, and some of the authors, who were all educated as clerics, are known. In addition, short biographies of the last Catholic bishops were written in the 16th and 17th centuries.

The sagas that are normally considered as belonging to the bishops' sagas are: (1) *Sagas of the bishops of Skálholt. Hungrvaka* contains short biographies of the first five bishops of Skálholt, *i.e.*, Ísleifr Gizurarson, Gizurr Ísleifsson, Þorlákr Rúnólfsson, Magnús Einarsson, and Klœngr Þorsteinsson, covering the period from 1056 (the establishment of the episcopal see in Skálholt) to 1176 (the death of Klœngr Þorsteinsson). The saga of Þorlákr Þórhallsson (d. 1193), *Þorláks saga helga*, is the life of the first Icelandic saint. It exists in three redactions; the two youngest are more detailed and fuller than the oldest. The youngest versions tell of Þorlákr's headstrong disputes with the chieftains, especially Jón Loptsson, over the administration of churches and their properties, and over the moral standards of both clergymen and laymen. Jón Loptsson's mistress, Ragnheiðr, was none other than Þorlákr's sister (*cf. Oddaverja þáttr*). In the oldest version, these disputes are only briefly mentioned. In addition, fragments of two different lives of Þorlákr in Latin are extant. *Páls saga* is the biography of Þorlákr's successor in the episcopal see, Páll Jónsson (d. 1211). *Þorláks saga, Hungrvaka*, and *Páls saga* are sometimes considered to have been written by the same author. Some scholars have asserted with more certainty that *Hungrvaka* and *Páls saga* are by the same author. In any case, it seems certain that the intention was to write a continuous history of the episcopal see of Skálholt, a kind of "gesta episcoporum," which was begun when a bishop of Skálholt became a saint. Much emphasis is placed upon the welfare of the Church, its growth, and prosperity in these three sagas. The youngest saga about a Skálholt bishop is the saga of Árni Þorláksson (d. 1298), *Árna saga biskups*. It was composed around 1300, and its author is possibly the bishop's successor and relative, Árni Helgason (d. 1320).

(2) *Sagas of the bishops of Hólar.* The life of Jón Ǫgmundarson (d. 1121), *Jóns saga helga*, was originally written in Latin by the monk Gunnlaugr Leifsson (d. 1218/9), but the saga is preserved only in Icelandic in three versions. There is a considerable difference in style among the three versions. Bergr Sokkason (d. 1345) has been suggested as the author of one of them. The oldest saga of Guðmundr Arason (d. 1237), the so-called *Prestssaga* ("priest's saga"), was written shortly after his death, but was not completed. Its author is possibly Abbot Lambkárr Þorgilsson (d. 1249). Later, four different Guðmundr sagas were written in the period 1315–1360. The author of the youngest saga was Arngrímr Brandsson (d. 1361), and it is possible that Bergr Sokkason wrote the oldest. The saga of Laurentius Kálfsson (d. 1331), *Laurentius saga Kálfssonar*, is the youngest of the actual *biskupa sögur*. It was written by Einarr Hafliðason (d. 1393).

In addition, two *þættir* have been regarded as belonging to the *biskupa sögur*: *Ísleifs þáttr biskups* and *Jóns þáttr Halldórssonar*, both treating bishops of Skálholt. *Ísleifs þáttr* is preserved in *Ólafs saga helga* in *Flateyjarbók* (end of the 14th century) and also independently in a 15th-century MS. *Jóns þáttr Halldórssonar* tells in exempla-style of some events in the life of this Dominican. The *þáttr* was composed shortly after Jón Halldórsson's death (1399).

Moreover, Ari Þorgilsson's *Íslendingabók* and *Kristni saga* also tell of the bishops. In *Íslendingabók* (1122–1133), there is a list of names of foreign bishops, after which the work tells of the first two Icelandic bishops, in particular of Gizurr Ísleifsson. *Kristni saga* (13th century) describes the introduction of Christianity and, like Ari, gives a brief description of the bishops.

In some of the *biskupa sögur*, in the Latin fragments and the oldest version of *Þorláks saga, Hungrvaka, Páls saga, Jóns saga helga*, and in *Prestssaga Guðmundar Arasonar*, the "computatio Gerlandi" is used, *i.e.*, the years are seven years less than in the normal Christian calendar. All the *biskupa sögur* that are preserved in their entirety are in Icelandic. Lives about the saints Þorlákr and Jón were written in Latin, and a Latin *Guðmundar saga* was also composed. One of the reasons for writing these sagas in Latin may have been to obtain the pope's acceptance of the holy men. This acceptance was, however, not given in the Middle Ages; the Icelandic saint-bishops were not canonized. On the basis of the Latin life, liturgical texts were composed for use on the saints' feast days.

The earliest critical work on the *biskupa sögur* is the preface to the first edition of *biskupa sögur* as a corpus (1858–1878), with main interest on dating and authorship. Sigurður Nordal (1933, 1953) first drew the literary-historical connections between the composition of *biskupa sögur* of the northern and southern parts of Iceland. His ideas about the origin and development of the *biskupa sögur* agree with his theories about the three "schools" of Icelandic saga composition. Thus, he considered the *biskupa sögur* of the southern school to have been composed under the influence of the artistic clerical school of the north, with *Jóns saga helga* as the model for *Þorláks saga helga*. Bjarni Aðalbjarnarson (1958), however, was the first to take the Latin fragments into consideration and to draw attention to the fact that since St. Þorlákr was the country's first saint, his life should be regarded as the oldest *biskupa saga*.

Scholars now agree that *Þorláks saga* is the oldest *biskupa saga*, since the origin of the genre can be traced to the important historical event when Þorlákr Þórhallsson, bishop of Skálholt, became the country's first saint. He was declared a saint at the *Alþingi* in 1198, and elevated in the same year. A year after Þorlákr's consecration as a saint, Páll Jónsson read at the *Alþingi* some of the saint's miracles, which form the core of the oldest extant book of miracles. Along with the book of miracles, the oldest preserved works about Þorlákr are some Latin fragments from two different lives and also a number of *lectiones*. One Latin fragment of *Þorláks saga* reveals that there was an introduction about Þorlákr's predecessors in the episcopal see, and might thus be the first sign of the composition of a "gesta episcoporum." It is possible that an account of Þorlákr's elevation along with his miracles was written in Latin, and that the description of the events found in one of the Latin *lectiones* may be based on such a work.

The *biskupa sögur* are often divided into two categories: saints' lives and historical works. But despite the different aims of the composition of the sagas, it is risky to draw such a decisive distinction between them. The sagas of the holy men were written first and foremost as hagiography. These sagas are, however, also church-historical sources, although in a somewhat different way. *Þorláks saga* has, for example, been considered a trustworthy source, because it is written so shortly after Þorlákr's death. Many of the sagas in the latter category, which normally are considered historical works, *i.e.*, *Hungrvaka, Páls saga*, and *Laurentius saga*, are nonetheless influenced in style, structure, and ideology by saints' lives. It is important to bear this influence in mind when their value as sources is evaluated. But *biskupa sögur* are nonetheless significant sources. In many respects, they form the basic source of Icelandic church history and also the history of the people, because the bishops took some part in the secular administration. *Hungrvaka*'s words about Bishop Gizurr give some idea of the high esteem in which the bishops were held: "He received high rank and so much honor already early in his episcopate, that every man would sit and stand as he requested, young and old, wealthy and poor, women and men, and it was correct to say that he was both king and bishop over the country while he lived." The sagas are no less important as sources of knowledge about the educational standards of their authors and their audience. Their literary importance naturally varies, and they seem hardly as attractive as the *Íslendingasögur* and the *konungasögur* at first sight. Since the oldest *biskupa sögur* can be dated to about 1200, they play an important role in the evolution of Icelandic saga writing. Their importance is not least due to the fact that they are contemporary sagas. The miracles that follow the sagas of the saint-bishops give a unique insight into the daily life of the time. As such, they are an invaluable addition to the picture that their secular parallels, *e.g.*, *Sturlunga saga*, give of the life and mentality of the people in Iceland in the Middle Ages.

Ed.: [Jón Sigurðsson and Guðbrandur Vigfússon, eds.] *Biskupa sögur*. 2 vols. Copenhagen: Møller, 1858–78; Kålund, Kristian, ed. *Sturlunga saga*. 2 vols. Copenhagen and Kristiania [Oslo]: Gyldendal, 1906–11; Jón Helgason, ed. *Byskupa sǫgur* 1. Det kongelige nordiske oldskriftselskab. Copenhagen: Munksgaard, 1938 [*Hungrvaka*, *Byskupa ættir*, *Ísleifs þáttr*]; Jón Jóhannesson et al., eds. *Sturlunga saga*. 2 vols.. Reykjavik: Sturlunguútgáfan, 1946; Guðni Jónsson, ed. *Byskupa sögur*. 3 vols. Akureyri: Íslendingasagnaútgáfan; Haukadalsútgáfan, 1948; Jón Helgason, ed. *Byskupa sǫgur. MS Perg. fol. No. 5 in the Royal Library of Stockholm*. Corpus Codicum Islandicorum Medii Aevi, 19. Copenhagen: Munksgaard, 1950 [facsimile]; Stefán Karlsson, ed. *Sagas of Icelandic Bishops: Fragments of Eight Manuscripts*. Early Icelandic Manuscripts in Facsimile, 7. Copenhagen: Rosenkilde & Bagger, 1967 [facsimile of AM 219 fol., AM 220 fols. I–VI, AM 221 fol.]; Árni Björnsson, ed. *Laurentius saga biskups*. Reykjavik: Ísafold, 1969; Þorleifur Hauksson, ed. *Árna saga biskups*. Reykjavik: Stofnun Árna Magnússonar, 1972; Jón Helgason, ed. *Byskupa sǫgur 2*. Editiones Arnamagnæanæ, ser. A, vol. 13.2. Copenhagen: Reitzel, 1978 [*Þorláks saga*, *Páls saga*]; Stefán Karlsson, ed. *Guðmundar sögur biskups I: Ævi Guðmundar biskups, Guðmundar saga A*. Editiones Arnamagnæanæ, ser. B, vol. 6. Copenhagen: Reitzel, 1983; Ásdís Egilsdóttir, ed. *Þorláks saga helga*. Reykjavik: Þorlákssjóður, 1989. **Tr.**: Leith, Disney, trans. *Stories of the Bishops of Iceland*. London: Masters, 1895; Gudbrand Vigfusson and F. York Powell, eds. and trans. *Origines Islandicae: A Collection of the More Important Sagas and Other Native Writings Relating to the Settlement and Early History of Iceland*. 2 vols. Oxford: Clarendon, 1905; rpt. Millwood: Kraus, 1976; Turville-Petre, G., and E. S. Olszewska, trans. *The Life of Gudmund the Good, Bishop of Holar*. London: Viking Society for Northern Research, 1942; Wolf, Kirsten. "A Translation of the Latin Fragments Containing the Life and Miracles of St. Þorlákr along with a Collection of *Lectiones* for Recitation on His Feast-days." *Proceedings of the PMR Conference* 14 (1989), 261–76. **Bib.**: Samuelson, David Robert. "The Operation of the Bishop's Legend in Early Medieval England and Iceland." Diss. University of Michigan, 1977; Koppenberg, Peter. *Hagiographische Studien zu den Biskupa Sögur: Unter besonderer Berücksichtigung der Jóns saga helga*. Scandia, Wissenschaftliche Reihe, 1. Bochum: Scandia, 1980. **Lit.**: Sigurður Nordal, ed. *Egils saga Skalla-Grímssonar*. Íslenzk fornrit, 2. Reykjavik: Hið íslenzka fornritafélag, 1933, p. lxvii; Sigurður Nordal.

"Sagalitteraturen." In *Litteraturhistorie: Norge og Island*. Nordisk kultur, 8:B. Stockholm: Bonnier; Oslo: Aschehoug; Copenhagen: Schultz, 1953, pp. 180–273 [see esp. pp. 212–4]; Turville-Petre, G. *Origins of Icelandic Literature*. Oxford: Clarendon, 1953; Bjarni Aðalbjarnarson. "Bemerkninger om de eldste islandske bispesagaer." *Studia Islandica*, 17. Reykjavik: Heimspekideild Háskóla Íslands; Menningarsjóður, 1958, pp. 27–37; Stancliffe, Clare. *St. Martin and His Hagiographer: History and Miracle in Sulpicius Severus*. Oxford Historical Monographs. Oxford: Clarendon, 1983.

Ásdís Egilsdóttir

[**See also:** *Árna saga biskups*; Conversion; *Flateyjarbók*; *Guðmundar sögur biskups*; *Hungrvaka*; *Ísleifs þáttr biskups*; *Íslendingabók*; *Jóns saga ens helga*; *Jóns þáttr biskups Halldórssonar*; *Laurentius saga biskups*; *Ólafs saga helga*; *Páls saga biskups*; Saints' Lives; *Þorláks saga helga*]

Bjarkamál ("The Lay of Bjarki") is a Latin poem of 298 hexameters appearing near the end of Book 2 of Saxo Grammaticus's *Gesta Danorum*. Saxo tells that he had completed the poem on the basis of small vernacular strophes. Short quotations from **Bjarkamál in fornu* ("The Ancient *Bjarkamál*") or **Húskarlahvǫt* ("The Incitement of the Housecarls"; *Ólafs saga helga*, ch. 208) are found in Snorri Sturluson's *Edda* and in his *Heimskringla*.

The poem takes the form of a dialogue between two housecarls of King Rollo (Hrólfr kraki). During the last fight of the Danish king, the two housecarls incite each other to fight a Swedish army clandestinely attacking the royal residence at Lejre. In the course of their dialogue, they hear that the king has fallen; now his men must avenge him in return for the golden rings he had presented them. During the battle, the warrior Biarco (Bjarki) suspects Óðinn's presence, and he utters a threat to the god. He orders Hialto (Hjalti) to fight on until both of them lie dead beside their king, as noble warriors should. Before and after the poem, Saxo tells in prose about the antecedents and the consequences of the battle. In broad outline, the story agrees with the last part of *Hrólfs saga kraka* (ca. 1400); at least this part must have had an original older than Saxo. Whether it was written down, we do not know, nor if it was Icelandic or Danish.

The poem as presented in *Gesta Danorum* has formerly been considered a Latin translation of a Nordic original. But according to Friis-Jensen (1987), Saxo has the full responsibility for its style, meter, and most of the content. Stephanius, in his 1645 edition of Saxo's Danish history, identified numerous quotations from classical and medieval authors. Among the latter, Galterus de Castellione's *Alexandreis* from 1182 marks a *terminus a quo* for Saxo's work. At the same time, the *Alexandreis* emphasizes that fame after death is ensured by beautiful poetry. Saxo mentions this thought several times, as well as other ideas common to the two authors, *e.g.*, the fidelity expected of the housecarls and the nobility of the warriors.

The classical ideals are of no less importance for *Bjarkamál*. Friis-Jensen (1987) calls the poem a small-scale Latin epic emulating Book 2 of Vergil's *Aeneid*. For instance, the battle is fought in the middle of the night, and the darkness is suddenly ruptured by the flaming town or castle in both poems. No other description of the fall of Lejre refers to this fire. In that way, Saxo made Lejre parallel to Troy.

Galterus's *Alexandreis* was translated into Icelandic (*Alexanders saga*) in the mid-13th century by Bishop Brandr Jónsson.

Perhaps this text was the source of the quotation from "Master Galterus" in *Hrólfs saga kraka*.

Ed.: Stephanius, Stephan Johannis, ed. *Historicam Danicam Saxonis Grammatici*. Sorö: Crusius, 1645. Stephanius, Stephan Johannis. *Notae uberiores in Historiam Danicam Saxonis Grammatici*. Ed. H. D. Schepelern. Copenhagen: Museum Tusculanum, 1978 [facsimile of notes from 1645 ed.; English introduction]; Olrik, Jørgen, and H. Ræder, eds. *Saxonis Gesta Danorum*. Copenhagen: Levin & Munksgaard, 1931. **Tr**.: Ellis Davidson, Hilda, ed., and Peter Fisher, trans. *Saxo Grammaticus. The History of the Danes. Books I–IX*. 2 vols. Cambridge: Brewer; Totowa: Rowman and Littlefield, 1979–80 [with commentary by Hilda Ellis Davidson]. **Lit**.: Olrik, Axel. *The Heroic Legends of Denmark*. Trans. Lee M. Hollander. New York: American-Scandinavian Foundation, 1919; rpt. Millwood: Kraus, 1976; Finnur Jónsson. *Den oldnorske og oldislandske Litteraturs Historie*. 3 vols. 2nd ed. Copenhagen: Gad, 1920–24, vol. 2; Friis-Jensen, Karsten. *Saxo Grammaticus as Latin Poet: Studies in the Verse Passages of the Gesta Danorum*. Analecta Romana Instituti Danici, Supplementum, 14. Rome: Bretschneider, 1987.

Inge Skovgaard-Petersen

[**See also**: *Alexanders saga*; *Fóstbrœðra saga*; *Hrólfs saga kraka*; Saxo Grammaticus]

Bjarnar saga Hítdœlakappa

Bjarnar saga Hítdœlakappa ("The Saga of Bjǫrn Hítdœlir-champion") belongs to a group of *skáldasögur* sharing essentially the same narrative. In common with two of these (*Kormáks saga* and *Hallfreðar saga*), *Bjarnar saga* is considered to be among the earliest *Íslendingasögur*, as its loose construction and unsophisticated style suggest. Together with the later *Gunnlaugs saga*, these sagas each relate a poet's lifelong love for a woman who becomes another man's wife. In *Bjarnar saga* and *Gunnlaugs saga*, the husband is himself a poet and poetic rivalry is an important theme. Bjarni Einarsson's attempt (1961) to derive this narrative from the European Tristan romance, through the medium of *Kormáks saga*, is unconvincing; the diverse use of narrative motifs suggests more complex relationships, involving extensive preliterary interchange of verses and anecdotal material among various traditions.

While Bjǫrn Arngeirsson Hítdœlakappi is virtually unknown outside the saga, his adversary Þórðr Kolbeinsson is a well-known court poet. The saga presents Þórðr unambiguously as a villain, maintaining throughout his obsessive aggression toward Bjǫrn despite his own physical cowardice. He treacherously marries Bjǫrn's betrothed wife, Oddný, persuading her by a lie about Bjǫrn's death. After several adventures abroad (most, including the duel in Russia by which he wins the title "kappi" and the sword Mæringr, patently fictional), the hero returns to Iceland, where a feud arises during his disastrous winter sojourn in Þórðr's household, in the course of which, the saga implies, he and Oddný become adulterous lovers.

Poetic rivalry achieves prominence as the feud begins with an exchange of libelous attacks, or *níð*. Most explicitly, Bjǫrn carves an effigy depicting Þórðr in a pose suggesting a homosexual act, symbolically attributing to Þórðr both cowardice and the sexual humiliation represented by Bjǫrn's appropriation of his wife. But *níð* also permeates the saga's structure through a pattern of verbal exchanges in which taunting verses, often in symmetrical pairs, are quoted or alluded to. Reminiscences of the poet's ancient role as practitioner of *níð*, with its essentially erotic symbolism, may

account for the association of love with poets in these *skáldasögur*, although only in *Bjarnar saga* is *níð* so prominent.

The feud modulates into a more conventional series of armed attacks on the hero, at first instigated indirectly and then personally led by Þórðr. After winning the friendship of the influential Þorsteinn Kuggason, an interlude that Sigurður Nordal (1938) probably wrongly believed to be based on a lost **Þorsteins saga Kuggasonar*, Bjǫrn dies in a heroic last stand, alone and almost unarmed against twenty-four attackers. The narrative abounds with archetypal motifs, such as the hero's prophetic dreams, the failure of his borrowed sword, and the recognition by Kolli, ostensibly the son of Þórðr, that he is attacking his true father.

Bjarnar saga was probably written before 1230 in Hítardalr in western Iceland, where its action takes place. The author may have belonged to the Þingeyrar monastery, but attempts to discern traces of clerical style have been inconclusive. Some hagiographical leanings are revealed in the hero's devotion to St. Óláfr, his building of a church, and his composing a *drápa* in honor of St. Thomas the Apostle.

The saga is poorly preserved in late, incomplete paper MSS, the best being a 17th-century copy of a 14th-century vellum, of which a fragment survives. Modern editors substitute for the lost beginning an extract from an extended version of Snorri Sturluson's life of St. Óláfr, which includes a summary, probably closely based on *Bjarnar saga*, of the hero's early life and adventures abroad. A second, shorter lacuna is irrecoverable. Poor preservation may explain the saga's relative neglect, despite its considerable literary merit and influence on later sagas: *Gunnlaugs saga*, *Þorsteins saga hvíta*, and, most notably, *Laxdœla saga* and the account given in *Eyrbyggja saga* of another poet and lover, Bjǫrn Breiðvíkingakappi, to whom are attributed three of the same verses in variant forms, probably as a result of confusion between the poets' traditions before either saga was written.

Ed.: Boer, R. C., ed. *Bjarnar saga Hítdælakappa*. Halle: Niemeyer, 1893; Sigurður Nordal and Guðni Jónsson, eds. *Borgfirðinga sögur*. Íslenzk fornrit, 3. Reykjavik: Hið íslenzka fornritafélag, 1938 [*Bjarnar saga* pp. 111–211; Sigurður Nordal's introduction pp. lviii–xcvii]; Simon, John L. C., ed. "A Critical Edition of *Bjarnar saga Hítdœlakappa*." Diss. University of London, 1966 [includes translation]. **Tr**.: Bachman, W. Bryant, Jr., trans. *Four Old Icelandic Sagas and Other Tales*. Lanham: University Press of America, 1985, pp. 151–222. **Bib**.: Halldór Hermannsson. *Bibliography of the Icelandic Sagas and Minor Tales*. Islandica, 1. Ithaca: Cornell University Library, 1908, pp. 5–6; rpt. New York: Kraus, 1966; Halldór Hermannsson. *The Sagas of Icelanders (Íslendinga sögur): A Supplement to Bibliography of the Icelandic Sagas and Minor Tales*. Islandica, 24. Ithaca: Cornell University Press; London: Oxford University Press, 1935, p. 17; Jóhann S. Hannesson. *The Sagas of Icelanders (Íslendinga sögur): A Supplement to Islandica I and XXIV*. Islandica, 38. Ithaca: Cornell University Press, 1957, pp. 19–20. **Lit**.: Vogt, W. H. "Die Bjarnar saga hítdœlakappa. Lausavísur, frásagnir, saga." *Arkiv för nordisk filologi* 37 (1921), 27–79; Guelpa, Patrick. "Le concept de níð à partir de *Bjarnar saga Hítdælakappi*." *Études germaniques* 38 (1983), 442–53; Bjarni Einarsson. *Skáldasögur: Um uppruna og eðli ástaskáldasagnanna fornu*. Reykjavik: Menningarsjóður, 1961 [English summary]; Ström, Folke. *Níð, ergi and Old Norse Moral Attitudes*. Dorothea Coke Memorial Lecture. London: Viking Society for Northern Research, 1973; Dronke, Ursula. "The Poet's Persona in the Skalds' Sagas." *Parergon* 22 (1978), 23–8; Dronke, Ursula. "*Sem jarla forðum*. The influence of *Rígsþula* on two saga-episodes." In *Specvlvm Norroenum: Studies in Memory of Gabriel*

Turville-Petre. Ed. Ursula Dronke *et al.* Odense: Odense University Press, 1981, pp. 56–72; Jesch, Judith. "Two Lost Sagas." *Saga-Book of the Viking Society* 21 (1982–83), 1–14.

Alison Finlay

[See also: Bjǫrn Arngeirsson Hítdœlakappi; *Eyrbyggja saga; Gunnlaugs saga ormstungu; Hallfreðar saga; Íslendingasögur, Kormáks saga; Laxdœla saga; Skáldasögur,* Þórðr Kolbeinsson; *Þorsteins saga hvíta*]

Bjarni Kolbeinsson was the son of the well-known Norwegian Orkneyian chief Kolbeinn hrúga ("heap") and a great-grand-daughter of Páll Þorsteinsson, earl of the Orkneys. Bjarni thus came of a mighty family in the Isles, as *Orkneyinga saga* states, and he was a close friend of Earl Haraldr Maddaðarson (*Orkneyinga saga,* ch. 109). From 1188 until his death (September 15, 1223), he was bishop of the Orkneys. As such, he initiated the canonization of Earl Rǫgnvaldr Kali Kolsson, and while he was in office an important part of the St. Magnus cathedral in Kirkwall was erected. Bjarni is mentioned five times as a participant in diplomatic missions or political assemblies in Norway (1194, 1208, 1210, 1218, 1223). He is also known to have had friends among the Icelandic aristocrats of his day (Hrafn Sveinbjarnarson, Sæmundr Jónsson).

At the end of the *Snorra Edda* in GkS 2367 4to are preserved forty stanzas of a poem called *Jómsvíkingadrápa,* together with thirty stanzas of an unnamed poem, most commonly called *Málsháttakvæði.* The *stef* ("refrain") stanza of this last poem is also quoted anonymously in *Flateyjarbók.* In *Snorra Edda,* no author is given for either poem, but in *Óláfs saga Tryggvasonar en mesta,* where eighteen stanzas of *Jómsvíkingadrápa* are preserved (five of which are not in the *Snorra Edda*), they are assigned to "Bjarni byskup." *Jómsvíkingasaga* in MS AM 510 4to also contains an allusion to the *drápa* that "Bjarni biskup . . . orti um Jómsvíkinga." Möbius conjectured that both *Jómsvíkingadrápa* and *Málshattakvæði,* quoted in GkS 2367 4to, are by the same skald.

Jómsvíkingadrápa is a regularly built *drápa* with *stef* in stanzas 15, 19, 23, 27, 31, and 35. Untypically, the *stef* occupies lines 1, 4, 5, and 8 of each *stef* stanza. If the *slœmr* ("slim end"; the last subdivision of a poem) originally had the same length as the *inngangr* ("introduction"), as was generally the case, the poem would have been fifty stanzas long, five stanzas now being lost. The *drápa* is composed in the meter *munnvǫrp,* which is a simplified *dróttkvætt* meter, without *hendingar* in the odd lines and with *skothendingar* instead of *aðalhendingar* in the even lines.

The poem tells part of the story of the Jomsvikings, and seems to refer to oral tradition in numerous phrases such as *frák* ("I heard"), *frágum vér* ("we heard"), and *segja menn* ("men say"). The poem probably was composed in the same period as the written sagas about the Jomvikings, and it seems to have been influenced by them or by traditions used by them, *e.g.,* in the mention of the skalds Vigfúss and Hǫvarðr (st. 34). On the other hand, the poem differs from the prose tradition, *e.g.,* in the prominence given to the Norwegian chieftain Ármóðr, forefather of the well-known Arnmœðlingar (sts. 21, 29). The main subject of the poem is the Jomsvikings' attack on Norway and the battle against Earl Hákon in Hjǫrungavágr (Sunnmøre). In particular, it concentrates on Vagn Ákason, who, despite the Jomsvikings' military defeat, succeeded in realizing his vow to marry Ingibjǫrg, the daughter of the Norwegian chief Þorkell leira ("loam-field").

The *stef* in this poem on Viking warfare and love contains a complaint in which the poet gives vent to his grief that the wife of a nobleman causes him sorrow. This *stef* seems to be a model for the stereotypical introductory stanzas with an erotic content called *mansǫngr,* found in the later Icelandic *rímur,* a word that occurs nowhere in skaldic poetry, except in *Jómsvíkingadrápa,* where it is said that Vagn Ákason "spoke *mansǫngr* on" Ingibjǫrg, and in *Málsháttakvæði. Jómsvíkingadrápa* probably marks a turning point in the history of skaldic verse, as it is the first poem by a historically well-known poet, who chooses as his subject old lore, hence the skald's own denomination *sǫgukvæði,* and treats it in a lighthearted, ironic manner. In his introduction to the poem, the skald alludes to his unhappy love, and he parodies common skaldic introductions: "I call nobody to listen to my poem. . . . I have not learned poetry under hanged men. . . . I present a *sǫgukvæði* to people who are not listening." It may be significant that the skald is a compatriot of Rǫgnvaldr Kali, who half a century earlier had introduced troubadour influences into skaldic poetry after his visit to Narbonne, where he was accompanied by Bjarni's predecessor as bishop, Vilhjálmr. Moreover, Rǫgnvaldr was a coauthor of *Háttalykill,* which also tells *forn frœði* ("old lore"). The Orkney islands seem to have been a center for the flourishing of *sǫgukvæði* around 1200.

Although Bjarni's authorship of *Málsháttakvæði* cannot be proven, some similarities between this proverb poem and *Jómsvíkingadrápa* are worth mentioning: a light tone of irony, numerous allusions to real and heroic history, and a concentration on erotic motives (Möbius 1874, Holtsmark 1937). Several scholars remain skeptical about Bjarni's authorship, however, and take *Málsháttakvæði* to be an imitation of Bjarni's poem (de Vries 1941–42), which may be considerably later (Hermann Pálsson 1984). Bjarni has also been mentioned, with little real evidence, as the possible author of some *þulur* preserved in the *Snorra Edda* (Bugge).

Ed.: Möbius, Theodor. "Malshatta-kvæði." *Zeitschrift für deutsche Philologie. Ergänzungsband* (1874), 3–74, 615–6 [edition and commentary]; Petersens, Carl af, ed. *Jómsvíkinga saga (efter Cod. AM. 510, 4:to) samt Jómsvíkinga drápa.* Lund: Gleerup, 1879 [diplomatic and critical editions of *Jómsvíkingadrápa* with commentary, pp. 104–33]; Finnur Jónsson, ed. *Den norsk-islandske skjaldedigtning.* Vols. 1A-2A (tekst efter håndskrifterne) and 1B-2B (rettet tekst). Copenhagen and Christiania [Oslo]: Gyldendal, 1912–15; rpt. Copenhagen: Rosenkilde & Bagger, 1967 (A) and 1973 (B), Vol. 2A, pp. 1–10, 129–36; vol. 2B, pp. 1–10, 138–45 [standard edition]. **Lit.**: Bugge, Sophus. "Biskop Bjarne Kolbeinssøn og Snorres Edda." *Annaler for nordisk Oldkyndighed og Historie* (1875), 209–46 [on *þulur*]; Jón Stefánsson. "Bjarne Kolbeinsson, the Skald, Bishop of Orkney, 1188–1223." *Orkney and Shetland Miscellany* 1 (1907), 43–7; Holtsmark, Anne. "Bjarne Kolbeinsson og hans forfatterskap." *Edda* 37 (1937), 1–17; Vries, Jan de. *Altnordische Literaturgeschichte.* 2 vols. Grundriss der germanischen Philologie, 15–6. Berlin: de Gruyter, 1941–42; rpt. 1964–67; Lindow, John. "Narrative and the Nature of Skaldic Poetry." *Arkiv för nordisk filologi* 92 (1981), 94–121; Hermann Pálsson. "A Florilegium in Norse from Medieval Orkney." In *The Northern and Western Isles in the Viking World: Survival, Continuity and Change.* Ed. Alexander Fenton and Hermann Pálsson. Edinburgh: Donald, 1984, pp. 258–64.

Bjarne Fidjestøl

[See also: Commemorative Poetry; *Flateyjarbók;* Folklore; *Háttalykill; Jómsvíkinga saga;* Love Poetry; *Óláfs saga Tryggvasonar; Orkneyinga saga; Skáld;* Skaldic Meters; Skaldic Verse; *Snorra Edda*]

Bjǫrn Arngeirsson Hítdœlakappi ("champion of the people of Hítardalr") is known principally as the protagonist of *Bjarnar saga Hítdœlakappi*, written possibly by or under the auspices of one or more of Bjǫrn's descendants in the Hítardalr region of western Iceland (Sigurður Nordal 1938: xc–xcv).

Traditionally accepted as a more or less faithful record of oral traditions that attached themselves to poetry probably composed by Bjǫrn himself (d. *ca.* 1204), *Bjarnar saga* characterizes Bjǫrn as a valiant and respected champion who becomes embroiled in a bitter, frequently petty, and to him ultimately fatal conflict with a fellow skald, Þórðr Kolbeinsson. Recently, however, the biographical truth of this picture has been questioned, most seriously by Bjarni Einarsson (1961), who nevertheless accepts Bjǫrn Ásgeirsson as a historical personage. Bjǫrn's reputation as a skald depends largely on *Bjarnar saga*. Outside the saga, two *vísuorð* of his incompletely preserved fifteenth *lausavísa* are cited in the *Third Grammatical Treatise* by Ólafr hvítaskáld ("white skald") Þórðarson (d. 1259). Unlike his saga rival, Þórðr Kolbeinsson, Bjǫrn is not mentioned in the list of poets entitled *Skáldatal*. Although the saga describes Bjǫrn's visits to several foreign courts, we have no record of any court poetry, extant or otherwise, anywhere attributed to him. *Bjarnar saga* does, however, refer to two lost poems by Bjǫrn: a *drápa* to the apostle Thomas (ch. 19); and *Eykyndilsvísur* ("Isle-candle Vísur," ch. 23), in Oddný's honor. Bjǫrn's extant corpus, recorded in Bjarnar saga, comprises three *runhent* strophes of *Grámagaflím* ("Lump-sucker Satire"), and twenty-four *lausavísur*, one (st. 4) in *fornyrðislag* meter, the remainder in *dróttkvætt* meter (stanza numbers refer to Finnur Jónsson's 1912 numeration). With few exceptions (notably those that refer least directly to Þórðr), the vehemence of the feelings expressed in these strophes is more impressive than their artistry or dignity. Some (particularly *Grámagaflím*) are coarse, and many are abusive. Only stanzas 1, 2, and 13 could possibly be described as love poetry, despite the saga's love interest.

In spite of Bjarni Einarsson's (1961) attempts to prove otherwise, a number of stanzas have apparently been inappropriately or incompletely assimilated into the saga (*e.g.*, sts. 1, 9, 11, 13), which suggests that they were borrowed rather than created by the saga writer, and so predate the extant prose account. Removed from their prose context, many stanzas do seem to offer independent testimony to much of the saga's material. But this assessment is not tantamount to accepting that any stanzas were composed during Bjǫrn's lifetime, much less by Bjǫrn himself. Stanzas in oral circulation may have become attached to those traditions concerning Bjǫrn that they seemed or were adapted to fit (variant forms of *lausavísur* 1, 10, and 19 are apparently attributed to Bjǫrn Breiðvíkingakappi in *Eyrbyggja saga*, ch. 40). All in all, we are best advised to think in terms of oral traditions surrounding Bjǫrn Ásgeirsson that incorporate poetry probably about, and possibly by, the subject himself.

Ed.: Finnur Jonsson, ed. *Den norsk-islandske skjaldedigtning*. Vols. 1A-2A (tekst efter håndskrifterne) and 1B-2B (rettet tekst). Copenhagen and Christiania [Oslo]: Gyldendal, 1912–15; rpt. Copenhagen: Rosenkilde & Bagger, 1967 (A) and 1973 (B), Vol. 1A, pp. 300–5, 1B, pp. 276–83; Sigurður Nordal and Guðni Jónsson, eds. *Borgfirðinga sǫgur*. Íslensk fornrit, 3. Reykjavik: Hið íslenzka fornritafélag, 1938 [Sigurður Nordal's introduction to *Bjarnar saga* details earlier editions and scholarship]; Kock, Ernst A., ed. *Den norsk-isländska skaldediktningen*. 2 vols. Lund: Gleerup, 1946–50, vol. 1, pp. 141–5;

Simon, John L. C., ed. "A Critical Edition of *Bjarnar saga Hítdœlakappi*." Diss. University of London, 1966. **Tr.**: Gudbrand Vigfusson and F. York Powell, eds. *Corpus Poeticum Boreale: The Poetry of the Old Northern Tongue from the Earliest Times to the Thirteenth Century*. Oxford: Clarendon, 1883; rpt. New York: Russell and Russell, 1965, vol. 2, pp. 108–9 [*Grámagaflím* and *lausavísa* 15]; Turville-Petre, E. O. G. *Scaldic Poetry*. Oxford: Clarendon, 1976, pp. 87–90 [translations of *Grámagaflím* and *lausavísur* 14 and 22]; Frank, Roberta. *Old Norse Court Poetry: The Dróttkvætt Stanza*. Islandica, 42. Ithaca and London: Cornell University Press, 1978, pp. 161–2, 172–4 [translations of *lausavísur* 2 and 19]. **Bib.**: Halldór Hermannsson. *Bibliography of the Icelandic Sagas and Minor Tales*. Islandica, 1. Ithaca: Cornell University Library, 1908; rpt. New York: Kraus, 1966, pp. 5–6; Halldór Hermannsson. *The Sagas of Icelanders (Íslendinga sǫgur): A Supplement to Bibliography of the Icelandic Sagas and Minor Tales*. Islandica, 24. Ithaca: Cornell University Press, 1935, p. 17; Hollander, Lee M. *A Bibliography of Skaldic Studies*. Copenhagen: Munksgaard, 1958. **Lit.**: Bjarni Einarsson. *Skáldasögur: Um uppruna og eðli ástaskáldasagnanna fornu*. Reykjavik: Menningarsjóður, 1961 [English summary]; Bjarni Einarsson. "The Lovesick Skald: A Reply to Theodore M. Andersson (*Mediaeval Scandinavia* 1969)." *Mediaeval Scandinavia* 4 (1971), 21–41; Marold, Edith. "The Presentation of the Skalds in *Íslendingasögur*." In *Alþjóðlegt fornsagnaþing, Reykjavík 2.-8. ágúst 1973: Fyrirlestrar*. 2 vols. Reykjavik, 1973, vol. 2, 19 pp. [mimeographed]; Poole, Russell. "Some *lausavísur* Reconnected." In *Alþjóðlegt fornsagnaþing*, vol. 2, 15 pp. [mimeographed]; Simon, John L. "Some Aspects of the Verses in Bjarnar saga." *Parergon* 22 (1978), 39; Dronke, Ursula. "*Sem jarla forðum*: The Influence of *Rígsþula* on Two Saga Episodes." In *Specvlvm Norroenvm: Norse Studies in Memory of Gabriel Turville-Petre*. Ed. Ursula Dronke *et al*. Odense: Odense University Press, 1981, pp. 56–72; Harris, Joseph. "Satire and the Heroic Life: Two Studies (*Helgakviða Hundingsbana I*, 18 and Bjǫrn Hítdœlakappi's *Grámagaflím*)." In *Oral Traditional Literature: A Festschrift for Albert Bates Lord*. Ed. John Miles Foley. Columbus: Slavica, 1981, pp. 322–40; Perkins, Richard. "Rowing Chants and the Origins of *dróttkvæðr háttr*." *Saga-Book of the Viking Society* 21 (1984–85), 155–221 [with particular reference to *lausavísa* 1].

Mary Malcolm

[**See also**: *Bjarnar saga Hítdœlakappa*; *Lausavísur*; *Skáld*; Skaldic Meters; Skaldic Verse]

Bjǫrn Breiðvíkingakappi ("champion of the people of Breiðavík"), one of the few love poets of the *Íslendingasögur*, is identified in *Eyrbyggja saga* as the son of Ásbrandr of Kambr, living on Snæfellsnes in western Iceland at the end of the 10th century. The story recounts his adulterous relationship with Þuríðr Barkardóttir, half-sister of Snorri goði ("the priest"). In the saga, Bjǫrn leaves Iceland to become a Viking adventurer, while Þuríðr gives birth to a boy, Kjartan, hinted to be Bjǫrn's son. Bjǫrn later returns to Iceland, where he sees Kjartan and comments on the boy's paternity in two cryptic *dróttkvætt* stanzas. Bjǫrn is, however, obliged to leave Iceland permanently, faced with the animosity of Þuríðr's powerful half-brother. Many years later, Icelandic traders en route for Ireland are blown off course, and discover a mysterious land where the local chieftain turns out to be Bjǫrn.

In all, the saga attributes seven stanzas to Bjǫrn. The authenticity of these stanzas, and even the authenticity of Bjǫrn himself, are not wholly certain. There are suspicious similarities between Bjǫrn and his namesake Bjǫrn Hítdœlakappi ("champion of the people of Hítardalr"), the hero of *Bjarnar saga*. The story of Bjǫrn's illicit love for Þuríðr parallels in many respects Bjǫrn Hítdœlakappi's love for Oddný eykyndill ("isle-candle"). Verses 28 and 29 attributed to Bjǫrn in *Eyrbyggja saga* resemble verses 12 and 1 in *Bjarnar saga*, while verses 27 in *Eyrbyggja saga* and 29 in *Bjarnar saga* are so similar that they have generally been regarded as two versions of the same stanza. Bjǫrn himself is not found in any source outside of *Eyrbyggja saga*, although his father Ásbrandr, his sister Þuríðr, his brother Arnbjǫrn sterki ("the strong"), his paramour Þuríðr, and her husband Þóroddr are all found in *Landnámabók*, in which Kjartan also figures, but as the legitimate son of Þóroddr and Þuríðr. These facts, combined with the evident literary creativity of the author of *Eyrbyggja saga*, make it quite likely that the story of Bjǫrn Breiðvíkingakappi has been assimilated to Bjǫrn Hítdœlakappi's, if indeed the former ever even existed.

If Bjǫrn did exist, he was unusual among contemporary skalds. Five of the stanzas attributed to Bjǫrn deal in some way with love, a rare theme in Viking Age verse. Whether genuinely from the Viking Age or not, stanza 24 remains one of the most admired examples of love poetry in Old Icelandic, comparable in sentiment and theme to the continental *alba*, or dawn song:

> Guls mundum vit vilja
> viðar ok blás i miðli
> (grand fæk af stoð stundum
> stengs) þenna dag lengstan,
> alls í aptan, þella,
> ek tegumk sjalfr at drekka
> opt horfinnar erfi
> armlinns, gleði minnar.

[We two would wish this day to be the longest between the golden forest and the dark (?); I sometimes get pain from the prop of the ribbon, for this evening, tree of arm-serpent, I shall make myself ready to drink to the memory of my joy which has often passed. (Turville-Petre 1976: 64)]

Stanza 30 is in the rare meter known as *hálfhneppt*, of which the earliest other example, aside from one attributed spuriously to Haraldr hárfagri ("fair-hair") Hálfdanarson, occurs in a verse by Óttarr svarti ("the black"), from about 1018, some twenty years later than the supposed date for Bjǫrn's stanza.

Ed.: Finnur Jónsson, ed. *Den norsk-islandske skjaldedigtning*. Vols. 1A-2A (tekst efter håndskrifterne) and 1B-2B (rettet tekst). Copenhagen and Christiania [Oslo]: Gyldendal, 1912–15; rpt. Copenhagen: Rosenkilde & Bagger, 1967 (A) and 1973 (B), Vol. 1A, pp. 133–4; vol. 1B, pp. 125–6. **Lit.**: Kock, Ernst A. *Notationes Norrœnæ. Anteckningar till Edda och skaldediktning*. Lunds Universitets Årskrift, n.s., sec. 1. Lund: Gleerup, 1923–41, vol. 3, pp. 7, 70–2 [entire work published in 27 parts]; Bjarni Einarsson. *Skáldasögur. Um uppruna og eðli ástaskáldasagnanna fornu*. Reykjavík: Menningarsjóður, 1961 [English summary]; Vries, Jan de. *Altnordische Literaturgeschichte*. 2 vols. Grundriss der germanischen Philologie, 15–6. Berlin: de Gruyter, 1941–42; rpt. 1964–67, vol. 1, pp. 195–7; Einar Ól. Sveinsson. "Eyrbyggja sagas kilder." *Scripta Islandica* 19 (1968), 3–18; Andersson, Theodore M. "Skalds and Troubadours." *Mediaeval Scandinavia* 2 (1969), 7–41; Bjarni Einarsson. "The Lovesick Skald: A Reply to Theodore M. Andersson (*Mediaeval Scandinavia* 1969)." *Mediaeval Scandinavia* 4 (1971), 21–41; Bjarni Einarsson. "On the Role of Verse in Saga-Literature." *Mediaeval Scandinavia* 7 (1974), 118–25; Turville-Petre, E. O. G. *Scaldic Poetry*. Oxford: Clarendon, 1976; Frank, Roberta. *Old Norse Court Poetry: The Dróttkvætt Stanza*. Islandica, 42. Ithaca and London: Cornell University Press, 1978; Dronke, Ursula. "Sem jarla *forðum*: The Influence of *Rígsþula* on Two Saga Episodes." In *Specvlvm Norroenvm: Norse Studies in Memory of Gabriel Turville-Petre*. Ed. Ursula Dronke *et al.* Odense: Odense University Press, 1981, pp. 56–72.

Jeffrey L. Singman

[**See also:** *Bjarnar saga Hítdœlakappa*; *Eyrbyggja saga*; *Landnámabók*; Love Poetry; *Óttarr svarti*; *Skáld*; Skaldic Meters; Skaldic Verse]

Blómstrvallasaga ("The Saga of Blómstrvǫllr") is an anonymous Icelandic prose romance composed before 1500. The earliest and most important of its thirty-three exclusively paper MSS originated in Iceland in the mid-16th century. The latest MSS (of virtually no textual value) were copied in Iceland during the first decades of the 20th century.

A relatively brief work, *Blómstrvallasaga* is nonetheless a fine example of the genre known either as *riddarasaga* or *lygisaga*. Such sagas were modeled both on foreign sources, especially French, and on the native *fornaldarsögur*. They enjoyed widespread popularity in Iceland from the mid-13th century through the Reformation.

Blómstrvallasaga is a frame narrative centered primarily on the exploits of two brothers, Etgarð and Áki, who are violently separated from one another at an early age. Etgarð is carried off to the lair of a dragon, which he kills; he gathers gold, silver, and armor, and rides to the country of Kazdidonia and becomes its king. Áki is befriended by a giantess, with whom he lives after having slain her father and mother. After many years, the two brothers make their respective ways to the fabled African paradise of Blómstrvǫllr ("plain of flowers"). Neither recognizes the other, and they duel for supremacy of the kingdom. Prevented from killing each other only through the intervention of mutual friends, they are reunited, and each brother recounts his *ævisaga* ("life story"). The saga ends with a magnificent wedding feast of the brothers and other worthies of Blómstrvǫllr.

The unknown author of this romance borrowed copiously from other sagas, most notably the later Icelandic redactions of *Þiðreks saga af Bern* (early 14th century). This saga provided names of characters (Etgarð, Áki, Samson) and of locations (Fricilia, Lyravald, Húnaland, Salerni), and motifs (the abducting dragon, armed attack in the forest). From the longer version of *Qrvar-Odds saga* (late 14th or early 15th century), the author appropriated the "finngalkn" ("centaur") episode and the love-of-a-giantess motif. Minor borrowings are posited from *Alexanders saga* (mid-13th century) and possibly *Parcevals saga* (mid-13th century) as well. *Hákonar saga Hákonarsonar* (mid-13th century) supplied the author with most of the material in the prologue to *Blómstrvallasaga*. In addition, *Blómstrvallasaga* shows many themes and motifs that appear in the majority of the native *riddarasögur*: combat for a princess, pitched battle against heathen Saracens, various magic objects, an exotic (non-Scandinavian) setting, a wealth of fabulous monsters, unwanted suitors, the telling of the *ævisaga*, and the traditional happy ending.

Ed.: Möbius, Theodor, ed. *Blómstrvallasaga*. Leipzig: Breitkopf & Hærtel, 1855; Hugus, Frank, ed. "*Blómstrvalla saga*: A Critical Edition of an Original Icelandic Romance." Diss. University of Chicago, 1972. **Lit.**: Hugus, Frank. "*Blómstrvallasaga* and *Þiðriks saga af Bern*." *Scandinavian Studies* 46 (1974), 151–68; Hugus, Frank. "Some Notes on the Sources of Blómstrvallasaga." *Opuscula* 5. Bibliotheca Arnamagnæana, 31. Copenhagen: Munksgaard, 1975, pp. 335–42.

Frank Hugus

[**See also:** *Alexanders saga; Fomaldarsögur; Hákonar saga gamla Hákonarsonar; Lygisaga; Parcevals saga; Riddarasögur; Þiðreks saga af Bem; Qrvar-Odds saga*]

Boethius de Dacia was a Danish philosopher active at the University of Paris in the 1270s. "Boethius" is a latinization of the Nordic name "Bo." Because of a misinterpretation of the epithet "de Dacia/Dacus" = "from Denmark," some scholars have called him "Boethius of Sweden." Nothing is known about Boethius's life except that he was a master of arts, the author of some thirty learned works (ten preserved), and with Siger of Brabant became one of the main targets of the condemnation issued by the bishop of Paris in 1277. He may at some later time have become a Dominican. Boethius was an important linguistic theoretician who contributed to the development of the theory of "modi significandi." The theory distinguishes between a word's lexical meaning (the thing it signifies) and its secondary semantic components (the ways in which it signifies the thing, "modi significandi"). Grammaticality depends exclusively on concord of "modi significandi." The "modi significandi" were supposed to be linguistic universals, although not having the same sort of morphological expression in all languages. The "modi significandi" reflect ways of understanding ("modi intelligendi") common to all humankind, and they in turn are based on real features of things ("modi essendi"). Boethius is best known for his theory of knowledge and science, which makes each science an autonomous system into which it is impossible to incorporate nonscientific facts known only through revelation. Thus, Christian beliefs about a temporal beginning of the world, about the existence of a first pair of human beings, or about the resurrection and the ultimate good of the individual are true, but it would be an error to try to assign them a place in scientific theories.

Ed.: *Boethii Daci Opera* = Corpus Philosophorum Danicorum Medii Aevi [CPhD], 4–9. The Danish Society of Language and Literature. Copenhagen: Gad, 1969–; contents of individual volumes: Pinborg, Joannes, and Henricus Roos, eds. *Modi significandi sive Quaestiones super Priscianum minorem.* CPhD, 4.1–2, 1969; Sajó, Géza, ed. *Quaestiones de generatione et corruptione—Quaestiones super libros Physicorum.* CPhD, 5.1–2, 1972–74; Green-Pedersen, N.J., *et al.,* eds. *Topica—Opuscula.* CPhD, 6.1–2, 1976 [*Opuscula* = *De aeternitate mundi, De summo bono, De somniis*]; Fioravanti, Gianfranco, ed. *Quaestiones super IVm Meteorlogicorum.* CPhD, 8, 1979; Ebbesen, S. *Sophismata.* CPhD, 9 [forthcoming]. **Tr.:** McDermott, A. Charlene Senape, trans. *Godfrey of Fontaine's Abridgement of Boethius of Dacia's Modi significandi sive Quaestiones super Priscianum maiorem.* History of Linguistic Science, ser. 3; Studies in the History of Linguistics, 22. Amsterdam: Benjamin, 1980; Wippel, John F., trans. *Boethius of Dacia: On the Supreme Good, On the Eternity of the World, On Dreams.* Mediaeval Sources in Translation, 30. Toronto: Pontifical Institute of Mediaeval Studies; Leiden: Brill, 1987. **Bib.:** Pinborg, Jan. "Zur Philosophie des Boethius de Dacia. Ein Ueberblick." *Studia Mediewistyczne* 15 (1974), 165–85; rpt. in Pinborg, Jan. *Medieval Semantics, Selected Studies on Medieval Logic and Grammar.* Ed. Sten Ebbesen. London: Variorum, 1984; Green-Pedersen, N. J., in CPhD, 6.2, 1976 [see above]; Wippel, J. F. *Boethius de Dacia* [see above]. **Lit.:** Jensen, Søren Skovgaard. "On the National Origin of the Philosopher

Boetius de Dacia." *Classica et Mediaevalia* 24 (1963), 232–41; Pinborg, Jan. *Die Entwicklung der Sprachtheorie im Mittelalter.* Beiträge zur Geschichte der Philosophie und Theologie des Mittelalters, Texte und Untersuchungen, 42.2. Münster: Aschendorff; Copenhagen: Frost-Hansen, 1967; Pinborg, Jan. "Zur Philosophie" [see above].

Sten Ebbesen

Bondakonst *see* Swedish Literature, Miscellaneous

Bóndi (pl. *bœndr,* also *búi, bóandi,* and *búandi*) was a term widely used throughout the Scandinavian cultural area to denote a free farmer. Specific rights and privileges varied from place to place. In medieval Iceland, a *bóndi* was usually the head of a household. The word derives from the verb *búa,* meaning "to prepare" or "to fix one's abode." According to the eddic poem *Rígsþula,* the social classes in Old Scandinavia descended from the god Rígr, or Heimdallr. One of his offspring was Karl, a freeholding farmer. Karl and his children represent the freeholding class. One of Karl's sons was named Bóndi.

In medieval Iceland, everyone was required by law to be domiciled in the household of a *bóndi.* A household legally existed wherever an individual, a farmer, often referred to as a *húsbóndi,* owned either land or milking stock. The term *bóndi* thus applied to both landowners and tenant farmers. Among the tenant farmers were householders who sometimes rented sizable parcels of land. If a renter, called a *leiglendingr, leiguliði,* or *landseti,* possessed sufficient milking stock or fishing equipment, he enjoyed the full rights of freemen. A renter whose wealth was insufficient had his rights curtailed, especially those allowing full participation as juror or judge in court proceedings. The law further distinguishes *bœndr* from two categories of freemen who had no land and insufficient stock: laborers (*griðmenn*) and cottagers (*búðsetumenn*). Both groups were banned from serving on several types of *kviðir* (sing. *kviðr*), the juries and panels of judges so important to Icelandic legal and political life. *Leysingjar* (sing. *leysingi*), or freedmen, were another category of farmers. A *leysingi* who owned or rented sufficient property to form a household was called a *bóndi.* During his lifetime, however, a *leysingi* remained connected with, and at times dependent upon, the manumitter, who retained inheritance rights if his former slave died without an heir. The connection was broken in the second generation, and the offspring of freedmen assumed the rights that accrued to their property status.

Farmers who owned a legislated minimum of property (the value of a cow, a boat, a horse, or a net for each member of the household) were called *þingfararkaupsbœndr,* or "thing-tax-paying farmers." These *bœndr* were required to pay the thing-attendance tax, or *þingfararkaup.* This large group of substantial householders enjoyed full rights under the law. They were eligible to participate, not only in local assemblies, but also in all judicial and legislative proceedings open to farmers at the *Alþingi.* Only those who qualified to pay *þingfararkaup* were allowed to serve on a *búakviðr,* a jury or panel of five or nine neighbors who handed down verdicts on questions of fact. *Þingfararkaupsbœndr* were also responsible for specific public duties: to contribute to the upkeep of the poor (*manneldi*), to assist in beaching ships (*skipsdráttr*), and after 1096, to tithe. *Íslendingabók* reports that, around the year 1000, the number of *bœndr* eligible to pay *þingfararkaup* stood at 4,560. The *þingfararkaupsbœndr* and their households thus made up a very large part of the population. *Þingfararkaupsbœndr* were not separated into groups or classes by formal legal distinctions, although the sagas reveal marked differences in wealth and prestige among farmers. The *goðar* (sing. *goði*), or chieftains, legally belonged to this broad group; and in the sagas it is often difficult to determine whether a *bóndi* was also a *goði*. The legal distinction between *goðar* and *bœndr* is minimized in the laws, which set the same compensation for injury, six marks (48 legal ounces), for all freemen, including *goðar*.

Landnámabók tells us that women settlers had the right to claim land, and the sagas give numerous examples of women functioning as heads of households. Women householders, nevertheless, cannot be counted as full *þingfararkaupsbœndr* because of their exclusion from many aspects of the judicial process. *Eyrbyggja saga* tells us that after the late 10th century women were denied the right to lead a prosecution for manslaughter. *Grágás*, in its written 13th-century form, specifies that a woman was excluded from becoming a judge or serving as a member of a *kviðr*, and in most instances was barred from acting as a witness. Such restrictions may have applied in the earlier period as well.

Bœndr were required by law to declare themselves "in thing with" (*í þing með*) a *goði*, and, at least in theory, a *bóndi* was free to choose his chieftain. Apparently, some farmers chose not to join any chieftain's following. As followers of a chieftain, farmers were known as *þingmenn* (sing. *þingmaðr*), and in this capacity they assumed certain duties. They had to accompany their chieftain to the *várþing*, the local springtime assembly. A chieftain could also require a ninth of his followers to accompany him to the *Alþingi*. In addition to serving on *kviðr*, *bœndr* also composed the panels of judges in courts at the local assembly as well as in the quarter courts and the fifth court at the *Alþingi*. Judges had to be free males at least twelve years old, have a fixed domicile, and be responsible for their oaths and commitments.

The thing-attendance tax was one of the few imposts a chieftain could legally demand from his thingmen, and was paid by those propertied farmers who did not attend the *Alþingi*. The funds so collected were used by the chieftain to defray travel expenses for those thingmen who did accompany him to the national assembly. The tax does not seem to have been large enough to place an undue burden on farmers. In levying it, as in making other demands, the *goðar* were solicitous of the farmers' wishes, because the bond between chieftains and their *þingmenn* was voluntary during much of the Free State's history, and could be terminated at will by either party. Legally, *bœndr* were permitted to change chieftains as frequently as once a year.

The status of farmers as free agents was probably reinforced by the *hreppar* (sing. *hreppr*), local communal units that provided fire and livestock insurance, and administered poor relief. A *hreppr* included a minimum of twenty *þingfararkaupsbœndr*, and was independent of the *goðar* and later of parish arrangements. The *hreppar* were self-governing, but precisely how they functioned is unclear. Also obscure is when and how they came into being, although Iceland seems to have been divided into *hreppar* as early as the 900s, *i.e.*, before the introduction of Christianity. The law stipulated that a *hreppsóknarmaðr*, the major official of a *hreppr*, be a landowner. A renter (*leiglendingr*) could, however, be elected as *hreppsóknarmaðr* if the landholders chose to waive the property requirement.

Lit.: Gunnar Karlsson. "Goðar og bændur." *Saga* 10 (1972), 5–57; Jón Jóhannesson. *A History of the Old Icelandic Commonwealth: Íslendinga saga.* Trans. Haraldur Bessason. University of Manitoba Icelandic Studies, 2. Winnipeg: University of Manitoba Press, 1974; Hastrup, Kirsten. *Culture and History in Medieval Iceland: An Anthropological Analysis of Structure and Change.* Oxford: Clarendon, 1985; Byock, Jesse L. "Governmental Order in Early Medieval Iceland." *Viator* 17 (1986), 19–34; Byock, Jesse L. *Medieval Iceland: Society, Sagas, and Power.* Berkeley, Los Angeles, and London: University of California Press, 1988.

Jesse L. Byock

[See also: *Alþingi*; *Eyrbyggja saga*; Family Structure; *Goði*; *Grágás*; Iceland; *Íslendingabók*; *Landnámabók*; *Rígsþula*]

Bookprose/Freeprose Theory

Bookprose/Freeprose Theory. The two terms were first used by Heusler in his 1914 book *Die Anfänge der isländischen Saga* to designate two different theories about how the sagas were created. Heusler used the term "freeprose" to designate the older theory that sagas were created in oral tradition. He used the term "bookprose" to designate a new theory, for which the leading spokesman was the founder of the so-called "Icelandic school," Björn Magnússon Ólsen. According to this theory, there were no oral sagas, only disconnected oral traditions, which an author drew upon in composing a written saga. At the earliest stages of saga research, scholars held that all kinds of sagas were created in the oral tradition. In Heusler's time, the old theory that written sagas were something very close to a copy of the oral sagas was modified in several ways.

Heusler, who favored freeprose, emphasized that the theory was relevant only in connection with the genres *Íslendingasögur*, *konungasögur*, and *fornaldarsögur*. But in all these genres, there were sagas that should be regarded as works by individual authors. None of the *konungasögur* fully reflected the old oral form; only minor parts of some *konungasögur* could be regarded as freeprose. Among the *fornaldarsögur*, only those based on written sources, such as *Vǫlsunga saga*, were to be regarded as bookprose; for the rest, Heusler assumed an underlying oral saga. The question was most complicated concerning the *Íslendingasögur*, which were at the center of the discussion.

Heusler thought that many sagas lay between the typical freeprose saga based on an oral saga and the typical bookprose saga based to some extent on oral tradition but the work of an individual author.

While favoring freeprose, Heusler was free to regard individual sagas as bookprose. Concerning the larger *Íslendingasögur*, Heusler, like many of his predecessors, considered the contribution of an individual author extensive. The freeprose theory, as Heusler defined it, claimed that a saga writer might have recorded an oral saga, but he might also make changes in areas beyond the saga teller's competence concerning structure, style, language, and use of sources.

A scholar favoring bookprose, on the other hand, could never hold a freeprose view on any saga, since the bookprose theory denied the possibility of an oral saga. While the two theories could come very close to each other, the fundamental difference concerned the matter of sources for the written saga. According to the bookprose theory, the main sources were oral prose tradition, poetic tradition, and written sources. According to the freeprose theory, the main source for a freeprose saga was an oral saga, but the saga writer could use as secondary sources all the material that the bookprose theory regarded as main sources.

According to the freeprose theory, the distinctive saga style was formed at the oral stage, while the bookprose theorists were more inclined to regard this style as literary. Heusler and Liestøl believed that the parallel passages, even long ones like those in *Ljósvetninga saga*, were oral variants, and a proof of the existence of oral sagas. In the view of the bookprose school, parallel passages, at least the longer ones, resulted from literary or scribal variation. In this discussion, the bookprose theorists gained the upper hand. In accordance with their theories, they preferred the word "author"; the freeprose scholars preferred the phrase "saga writer" to designate the person who had written the sagas.

Since a freeprose scholar could hold a bookprose view of individual sagas, since not a whole genre of the sagas in question could be defined as freeprose or bookprose according to the freeprose theory, and since many *Íslendingasögur* in Heusler's opinion were neither freeprose nor bookprose sagas, but rather something in between, these terms (especially "freeprose" and "freeprosaist") proved inexact and unfit for a scientific discussion. But Heusler also used the terms in a different way: "freeprose" to designate what in each saga could be defined as the result of oral creation, and "bookprose" to designate what in each saga could be defined as the result of an individual author's work. But few later scholars followed him in the use of this more precise definition.

The problem of historical truth was not part of the bookprose/freeprose theories as Heusler defined them. But since there was a logical connection and since many of the freeprose advocates, among them Liestøl, Heusler's successor on the freeprose front, were interested in the question of the sagas' historical truth, the two problems were soon mingled. In the polemics between freeprosaists and bookprosaists, the latter under the leadership of the scholars in the Icelandic school, among whom Sigurður Nordal took the leading position after Björn Magnússon Ólsen, freeprose was very often defined as a theory that presupposed an oral saga very much like the written saga behind almost every *Íslendingasaga*, a theory that gave the author no credit; and a very naive belief in the sagas' historical truth was made part of the freeprose theory.

The same confusion of ideas did not take place with the bookprose theory. Among the supporters of this theory, there have been scholars who looked upon the oral tradition as a very important source for the author, and scholars who did not pay much attention to oral tradition, holding the opinion that it had little or no influence on the author's final result. This radical form of the bookprose theory is sometimes called the "fiction theory."

Lit.: Heusler, Andreas. *Die Anfänge der isländischen Saga*. Abhandlungen der königlich preussischen Akademie der Wissenchaften, Jahrgang 1913, phil.-hist. Classe, 9. Berlin: Reimer, 1914; Liestøl, Knut. *Upphavet til den islendske ættesaga*. Instituttet for sammenlignende kulturforskning. Serie A: Forelesninger. Oslo: Aschehoug, 1929 [English translation by Jayne, A. G. *The Origin of the Icelandic Family Sagas*. Cambridge: Harvard University Press, 1930]; Sigurður Nordal. *The Historical Element in the Icelandic Family Sagas*. Glasgow University Publications, The W. P. Ker Memorial Lectures, 15. Glasgow: Jackson, 1957; Hofmann, Dietrich. "Die mündliche Vorstufe der altnordischen Prosaerzählkunst." *Annales Universitatis Saraviensis* 10 (1961), 163–78; Andersson, Theodore M. "The Doctrine of Oral Tradition in the Chanson de Geste and Saga." *Scandinavian Studies* 34 (1962), 219–36; Andersson, Theodore M. *The Problem of Icelandic Saga Origins: A Historical Survey*. Yale Germanic Studies, 1. New Haven and London: Yale University Press, 1964; Andersson, Theodore M. "The Textual Evidence for an Oral Family Saga." *Arkiv för nordisk filologi* 81 (1966), 1–23; Mundal, Else. *Sagadebatt*. Oslo, Bergen, and Tromsø: Universitetsforlaget, 1977.

Else Mundal

Borre (Old Norse Borró) was a necropolis on the Oslofjord, Vestfold, Norway, for Norwegian members of the Swedish dynasty of Ynglings.

Ynglingatal (st. 32) mentions a Hálfdan, son of Eysteinn, who was buried "á Borrói." Tradition from the 1820s (possibly earlier) linked this reference to the county of Borre in northern Vestfold. Here on the shoreline of the Oslofjord, in front of the medieval church of Borre, a group of nine large barrows, two large cairns, and twenty-three smaller mounds were discovered in 1852. Originally, there must have been more barrows, destroyed by the farming of the land. Today, the group consists of five barrows, two cairns, and the smaller mounds. The largest of the barrows measures about 50 m. x 7–8 m. In 1852, a magnificent ship burial came to light in one of the large barrows. Unfortunately, we do not know which mound, for the "excavation" was done during sandmining on the spot. An archaeologist was called in at the very last moment. Only a small part of the grave goods was rescued. The most precious item preserved is remnants of a claw beaker, rare in Norwegian contexts, but common in Swedish chieftain's graves. There are also at least four pairs of stirrups, parts of a beautifully decorated bridle, and a series of decorated gilt bronze mountings for at least one harness. Skeletons of horses were also found.

The bridle and the harness mountings are decorated in a pattern different from that on the Oseberg carvings, but very similar to some of the bronze mountings from the Gokstad ship. These mountings had given name to a specific stylistic group, the "Borre style" of ornament. The new and most characteristic element in the Borre style is the "ring-chain," a ribbon pattern consisting of twisted double ribbons, ending in *en face* animal heads. Animal heads seen *en profile* were also used by the metalworkers of the Borre style. They also applied "gripping beasts" adapted from the Oseberg style of ornament. A certain "hatching" of the ornaments shows that filigree work should be seen behind the ornaments in the Borre style group. The style became very popular and is found on metalwork all over Scandinavia. It is also found on the monumental stones on the Isle of Man. The Vikings brought it with them to the colonies in eastern Europe. The Borre style was already developed in the 9th century (Wilson 1970) and remained in use in the 10th century, partly parallel with the Jelling style.

It may be safely supposed that a chieftain and his warriors were buried in the ship, of which nothing is left. According to the report, it was smaller than the Oseberg and Gokstad ships (17–21 m.), but of the same construction. It seems reasonable to believe that the other large barrows contained ship(?) burials of the same high standard, but this guess has not been confirmed by excavations. The very monumentality of these large barrows links them to people belonging to the highest level of society, as in the Oseberg and Gokstad finds not far from Borre.

The 1852 grave cannot be dated earlier than about A.D. 900, contemporary with the Gokstad grave. In 1921, the better part of the smaller mounds was excavated. Nothing was found except some rivets, dated to the Viking Age. The shoreline tells us that all barrows, large and small, must belong to this period. All in all, it seems reasonable to connect the Borre find with the Vestfold branch of the Yngling dynasty (Brøgger 1916), which has long been regarded as the cradle of early Norwegian history. King Haraldr hárfagri ("fair-hair") Hálfdanarson belonged to this dynasty. He set out to conquer and unite all Norway into one realm, probably from Vestfold.

Snorri based his *Ynglinga saga* on *Ynglingatal*, a laudatory poem about persons living long before the poem was composed (*ca.* 890). The proof of its reliability should obviously be based on archaeological data. In 1987, a new research project started, applying modern archaeological surveying methods. It aims to collect as much information as possible about the original landscape, the construction and dating of the barrows, traces of grave robbing, possible traces of buildings (the royal farm?), and traces of possible harbors, without large-scale excavations, at least in the initial stage. The results of the 1988 campaign were promising, but so far nothing has been published (communication by Bjørn Myhre).

Lit.: Brøgger, A. W. *Borrefundet og Vestfoldkongernes Graver.* Videnskapets Skrifter. II. Hist.-filos. Klasse. No. 1. Kristiania [Oslo]: Dybwad, 1916; Blindheim, Charlotte. "Det gåtefyllte Borre. Noen jubileumsrefleksjoner om feltet og funnet." In *Nasjonalparken i Borre. Jubileumsskrift ved et 50-års minne 1932–1982.* Borre: [n.p.], 1982, pp. 13–7; Sawyer, P. H. *Kings and Vikings. Scandinavia and Europe. AD 700–1100.* London and New York: Methuen, 1982; Blindheim, Charlotte. "Introduction." *Proceedings of the Tenth Viking Congress.* Ed. James E. Knirk. Universitetets Oldsaksamlings Skrifter, ny rekke, 9. Oslo: Universitetets Oldsaksamling, 1987, pp. 27–42; **(a) Borre style**: Foote, Peter, and David M. Wilson. *The Viking Achievement: The Society and Culture of Early Medieval Scandinavia.* London: Sidgwick & Jackson, 1970; rev. ed. 1979; Graham-Campbell, James. *The Viking World.* London: Lincoln, 1980, pp. 140–1; Graham-Campbell, James, and Dafydd Kidd. *The Vikings.* London: British Museum, 1980, pp. 158–9.

Charlotte Blindheim

[**See also:** Þjóðólfr of Hvin; Viking Art; *Ynglinga saga*]

Bósa saga (Herrauðs saga ok Bósa)

Bósa saga (Herrauðs saga ok Bósa) ("The Saga of Bósi" or "The Saga of Herrauðr and Bósi"), an anonymous *fornaldarsaga* composed sometime before 1350, is extant in two independent recensions. An older form is found in vellum MSS from the 15th century (AM 586 4to, AM 343a 4to, AM 510 4to, AM 577 4to). A later, different, and much expanded form is found in paper MSS from the 17th and 18th centuries. The anonymous *Bósa rímur*, composed around 1500, is based on the older recension. The rich and complicated textual history shows that the material was popular in Iceland until recent times.

The saga treats two different heroes: the undaunted Viking son Bósi and the knightly Prince Herrauðr. When King Hringr of Östergötland wants to hang the two blood-brothers for manslaughter, Busla, Bósi's foster-mother, forces the king to yield through her magical runic saying (*Buslubœn*). In repentance, both must get the *gammsegg*, a kind of dragon's egg, from Bjarmaland.

On the journey, Bósi seduces a farmer's daughter and receives information from her about the *gammsegg*. They steal the egg from the temple of the heathen god Jómali. At the same time, they release Princess Hleiðr, who was intended for human sacrifice, and Herrauðr becomes engaged to her in a courtly fashion.

After their return, the blood-brothers participate in the famous Brávalla battle. In the meantime, Hringr is killed, and Hleiðr is kidnaped.

The brothers pursue the abductors and arrive at the right moment at Hleiðr's party, in which they participate as musicians without being recognized. They manage to bring back the bride, who is smuggled out of the party hall in a harp box. Earlier, the sexual athlete Bósi again had seduced a farmer's daughter, a narrative sequence that is repeated until he finds a wife and forces the princess Edda to marry him.

In a fantastic naval battle, in which monsters attack from both sides, the blood-brothers conquer the enemy, and the couples are finally united in a double party. In the meantime, a young dragon has hatched the *gammsegg*, which Herrauðr gives to his little daughter. Of her later suitors, only the one who can conquer the serpent may approach her. This is the Danish dragonslayer Ragnarr loðbrók.

The saga is the prototype of the fairy-tale-like bridal-quest narrative. The triple kidnaping of the princess contrasts with the sexual scenes with the farmer's daughter. It is not the invention of the author, but rather the prose paraphrase of a widespread type of erotic popular song. In addition, the author uses Oberon motifs, as in the Old French *Huon de Bordeaux* and the Middle High German *König Rother*.

The knowledge of the mythical Brávalla battle and the Jómali temple, which is also mentioned in *Óláfs saga helga*, has its origin in Norse tradition. The concluding genealogical literary play shows the connection with *Ragnars saga loðbrókar*. With the *Buslubœn* curse, formulas in eddic verse are preserved. The narrative perspective emphasizes the activities of the nasty, violent, but witty farmer's son Bósi and not the aristocrat. The sarcastic humor and the burlesque scenes have contributed to the long-lasting popularity of the often-told and well-composed saga.

Ed.: Rafn, C. C., ed. *Fornaldar Sögur Nordrlanda.* 3 vols. Copenhagen: Popp, 1829–30, vol. 3; Jiriczek, Otto Luitpold, ed. *Die Bósa-saga in zwei Fassungen nebst Proben aus den Bósa-rímur.* Strassburg: Trübner, 1893; Jiriczek, Otto Luitpold, ed. *Die Bósa-rímur.* Germanistische Abhandlungen, 10. Breslau: Koebner, 1894; rpt. Hildesheim and New York: Olm, 1977; Ólafur Halldórsson, ed. *Bósa rímur.* Íslenzkar miðaldarímur, 3. Reykjavik: Stofnun Árna Magnússonar, 1974. **Tr.**: Hermann Pálsson and Paul Edwards, trans. *Seven Viking Romances.* Harmondsworth: Penguin, 1985. **Lit.**: Nerman, Birger. "Bósasagen." In *Studier i Sväriges Hedna Litteratur.* Uppsala: Appelberg, 1913, pp. 184–202; Schröder, Franz Rolf. "Motivwanderungen im Mittelalter." *Germanisch-romanische Monatsschrift* 16 (1928), 7–13; Krappe, Alexander H. "La source de la Saga af Herrauði ok Bósa." *Neuphilologische Mitteilungen* 29 (1928), 250–6; Briem, O. B. "Germanische und russische Heldendichtung (nebst Bemerkungen zur Bósasage)." *Germanisch-romanische Monatsschrift* 17 (1929), 341–55; Hermann Pálsson and Paul Edwards. *Legendary Fiction in Medieval Iceland.* Studia Islandica, 30. Reykjavik: Heimspekideild Háskola Íslands; Menningarsjóður, 1971; Naumann, Hans-Peter. "Die Abenteuersaga. Zu einer Spätform altisländischer Erzählkunst." *Skandinavistik* 8 (1978), 41–55; Thompson, Clairborne W. "The Runes in Bósa saga ok Herrauðs." *Scandinavian Studies* 50 (1978), 50–6; Naumann, Hans-Peter. "Erzählstrategien in der Fornaldarsaga: Die Prüfungen des Helden." In *Akten der Fünften Arbeitstagung der Skandinavisten des deutschen Sprachgebiets.* Ed. H. Uecker. St. Augustin: Kretschmer, 1983, pp. 131–42.

Hans-Peter Naumann

[**See also:** *Fornaldarsögur*; *Óláfs saga helga*; *Ragnars saga loðbrókar*; *Rímur*]

Bragi Boddason (the Old), a Norwegian poet probably of the second half of the 9th century, is generally reckoned to be the earliest skald whose compositions have been preserved, although in fragmentary form. Details of his life are tentative, and several semimythological stories exist, linking him in one case with ancestors of settlers in Iceland (*Landnámabók*, S112, H86, M30; *Hálfs saga ok Hálfsrekka*, ch. 11; *Geirmundar þáttr heljarskinns*, ch. 2). *Skáldatal*, an Icelandic catalogue of poets and their patrons, names him as a court poet of Ragnarr loðbrók ("hairy-breeches"), Eysteinn beli ("belly"), and Bjǫrn at Haugi (*Edda Snorra Sturlusonar*, ch. 3, pp. 251–69). Snorri Sturluson also connected Bragi with Ragnarr loðbrók and attributed two groups of stanzas to a *Ragnarsdrápa*, a *drápa* or sequence of stanzas with a refrain, in honor of Ragnarr. Snorri quotes these stanzas in chs. 52 and 62 of *Skáldskaparmál* (Finnur Jónsson 1931: 134, 155; Faulkes 1987: 106, 123–4). Although Ragnarr was a hero of the Danes, recent scholarship indicates the probability of a Norwegian origin for this legendary Viking (Smyth 1977).

Bragi's *Ragnarsdrápa* is thought to have been a shield poem, which gave verbal representation to a set of pictures and mythological subjects painted on a leather-covered shield that the poet had received from his patron. The resulting poem was the skald's counter-gift to his lord. A similar context underlies Þjóðólfr of Hvin's *Haustlǫng*. In 1860, Gísli Brynjúlfsson proposed that such shields were divided into four fields and hence had four poetic subjects. Subsequent editorial arrangement of the hypothetical *Ragnarsdrápa* has followed this view, even though Snorri clearly admits only the stanzas mentioned above (3–7 and 8–12 in Finnur Jónsson's *Skjaldedigtning*) as part of this *drápa*. Following Finnur Jónsson's arrangement, *Ragnarsdrápa*'s four subjects were the encounter between the heroes Hamðir and Sǫrli and the Gothic tyrant Jǫrmunrekkr (Ermanaric), also subject of the eddic poem *Hamðismál* (sts. 3–7); Hildr's incitement to battle of her father, Hǫgni, and her abductor, Heðinn (8–12); how Gefjon and her giant oxen won land from the Swedish king Gylfi (13); and a version of the god Þórr's fishing expedition to catch the World Serpent (14–19). Convention has also allocated to the *drápa* two half-stanza introductory verses, in the second of which the poet thanks the "son of Sigurðr" (Ragnarr's father is said to have been Sigurðr hringr ["ring"]) for the shield (1–2), and finishes off the *drápa* with a half-stanza (20) on the metamorphosis of the giant Þjazi's eyes into a pair of stars. Hence the *Ragnarsdrápa* we read in the standard editions is a scholarly reconstruction for which there is only partial authority in the work in which its component verses are to be found, Snorri Sturluson's *Edda* (ca. 1225).

Other medieval texts in which stanzas attributed to Bragi occur are MSS F (*Codex Frisianus*, AM 45 fol.), J (*Jǫfraskinna*, AM 38 fol.), and K (AM 35 fol.) of *Heimskringla* (*Ynglinga saga*, ch. 5) for *Ragnarsdrápa* 13; the *Fourth Grammatical Treatise* (Ólsen 1884: 129) for *Ragnarsdrápa* 3; MSS of *Landnámabók*, *Hálfs saga* and *Geirmundar þáttr* (for details see paragraph 1) for a *lausavísa* on the twins Geirmundr and Hámundr heljarskinn.

Ed.: Björn Magnússon Ólsen, ed. *Den Tredje og Fjærde Grammatiske Afhandling i Snorres Edda Tilligemed de Grammatiske Afhandlingers Prolog og To Andre Tillæg*. Samfund til udgivelse af gammel nordisk litteratur, 12. Islands grammatiske litteratur i middelalderen 2. Copenhagen: Knudtzon, 1884 [for *Ragnarsdrápa* 3]; Finnur Jónsson, ed. *Den norsk-islandske skjaldedigtning*. Vols. 1A-2A (tekst efter håndskrifterne) and 1B–2B (rettet tekst). Copenhagen and Christiania [Oslo]: Gyldendal, 1912–15; rpt. Copenhagen: Rosenkilde & Bagger, 1967 (A) and 1973 (B); Finnur Jónsson, ed. *Edda Snorra Sturlusonar*. Copenhagen: Gyldendal, 1931; Jón Jóhannesson et al., eds. *Sturlunga saga*. 2 vols. Reykjavik: Sturlunguútgáfan, 1946 [for *Geirmundar þáttr heljarskinns*, vol. 1, pp. 5–11]; Bjarni Aðalbjarnarson, ed. *Heimskringla*. 3 vols. Íslenzk fornrit, 26–8. Reykjavik: Hið íslenzka fornritafélag, 1941–51 [*Ragnarsdrápa* 13, vol. 1, p. 21]; Jakob Benediktsson, ed. *Íslendingabók. Landnámabók*. Íslenzk fornrit, 1. Reykjavik: Hið íslenzka fornritafélag, 1968 [for *lausavísa* on Geirmundr and Hámundr heljarskinn, p. 151]; Dronke, Ursula, ed. and trans. *The Poetic Edda. 1. Heroic Poems*. Oxford: Clarendon, 1969 [for *Ragnaradrápa* 3–6 and *Hamðismál*, pp. 204–14]; Clunies Ross, Margaret. "An Edition of the *Ragnarsdrápa* of Bragi Boddason." Diss. Oxford University, 1973; Turville-Petre, E. O. G. *Scaldic Poetry*. Oxford: Clarendon, 1976; Frank, Roberta. *Old Norse Court Poetry: The Dróttkvætt Stanza*. Islandica, 42. Ithaca and London: Cornell University Press, 1978; Seelow, Hubert, ed. *Hálfs saga ok Hálfsrekka*. Reykjavik: Stofnun Árna Magnússonar, 1981 [for *lausavísa* on Geirmundr and Hámundr heljarskinn]. **Tr.**: Hollander, Lee M. *The Skalds: A Selection of Their Poems, With Introductions and Notes*. New York: American-Scandinavian Foundation, 1945; rpt. Ann Arbor: University of Michigan Press, 1968 [Bragi Boddason, pp. 25–37]; Faulkes, Anthony, trans. *Snorri Sturluson. Edda*. Everyman Classics. London and Melbourne: Dent, 1987 [Bragi's verses pp. 7, 69, 72–4, 89, 95, 99, 105–6, 120, 123–4, 132, 142; see also Index of Names, p. 224]. **Bib.**: Hollander, Lee M. *A Bibliography of Skaldic Studies*. Copenhagen: Munksgaard, 1958; Bekker-Nielsen, Hans. *Old Norse–Icelandic Studies: A Select Bibliography*. Toronto Medieval Bibliographies, 1. Toronto: University of Toronto Press, 1967. **Lit.**: Gísli Brynjúlfsson. "Brage den Gamles Kvad om Ragnar Lodbrogs Skjold." *Aarbøger for nordisk Oldkyndighed og Historie* (1860), 3–13; Reichhardt, Konstantin. *Studien zu den Skalden des 9. und 10. Jahrhunderts*. Palaestra, 159. Leipzig: Mayer & Müller, 1928; Finnur Jónsson. "Brage skjald." *Acta Philologica Scandinavica* 5 (1930–31), 237–86; Vogt, W. H. "Bragis schild." *Acta Philologica Scandinavica* 5 (1930–31), 1–28; Jón Jóhannesson. *Gerðir Landnámabókar*. Reykjavik: Félagsprentsmiðjan, 1941, pp. 165–70; Lie, Hallvard. "Skaldestil-studier." *Maal og minne* (1952), 1–92; rpt. *Om Sagakunst og Skaldskap. Utvalgte Avhandlinger*. Øvre Ervik: Alvheim & Eide, 1982, pp. 109–200; Lie, Hallvard. "Billedbeskrivende dikt." *KLNM* 1 (1956), 542–5; Lie, Hallvard. "*Natur*" og "*unatur*" i skaldekunsten. Avhandlinger utg. av Det norske Videnskaps-Akademie i Oslo, 2. Hist.-filos. Kl. No. 1. Oslo: Aschehoug, 1957; rpt. *Om Sagakunst og Skaldskap*, pp. 201–315; Almqvist, Bo. *Norrön niddiktning. Traditionshistoriska studier i versmagi. 1. Nid mot furstar*. Nordiska texter och undersökningar, 21. Uppsala: Almqvist & Wiksell, 1965, pp. 28–34 [for analysis of exchange between Bragi and a troll-woman, as reported in *Snorra Edda*, in tradition of Icelandic ákvæðaskáld to whom supernatural powers were attributed]; Lie, Hallvard. "*Ragnarsdrápa*." *KLNM* 13 (1968), 647–9; Clunies Ross, Margaret. "Hildr's Ring: A Problem in the *Ragnarsdrápa*, Strophes 8–12." *Mediaeval Scandinavia* 6 (1973), 75–92; Lindow, John. "The Two Skaldic Stanzas in Gylfaginning: Notes on Sources and Text History." *Arkiv för nordisk filologi* 92 (1977), 106–24 [on Bragi's Gefjon stanza]; Smyth, Alfred P. *Scandinavian Kings in the British Isles, 850–80*. Oxford: Oxford University Press, 1977; Clunies Ross, Margaret. "The Myth of Gefjon and Gylfi and Its Function in *Snorra Edda* and *Heimskringla*." *Arkiv för nordisk filologi* 93 (1978), 149–65; Clunies Ross, Margaret. "Style and Authorial Presence in Skaldic Mythological Poetry." *Saga-Book of the Viking Society* 20 (1981), 276–304; Lindow, John. "Narrative and the Nature of Skaldic Poetry." *Arkiv för nordisk filologi* 97 (1982), 94–121;

Kuhn, Hans. *Das Dróttkvætt*. Heidelberg: Winter, 1983 [esp. pp. 275–9]; Marold, Edith. *Kenningkunst. Ein Beitrag zu einer Poetik der Skaldendichtung*. Berlin and New York: de Gruyter, 1983 [esp. pp. 67–114]; Sørensen, Preben Meulengracht. "Thor's Fishing Expedition." In *Words and Objects: Towards a Dialogue Between Archaeology and History of Religion*. Ed. Gro Steinsland. The Institute for Comparative Research in Human Culture, B.71. Oslo: Norwegian University Press; Oxford and New York: Oxford University Press, 1986, pp. 257–78.

Margaret Clunies Ross

[**See also:** Iconography; *Skáld; Lausavísur;* Skaldic Meters; Skaldic Verse; *Snorra Edda*]

Brandkrossa þáttr

Brandkrossa þáttr ("The Tale of Brandkrossi") is not a self-contained narrative, but was devised, probably late in the 13th century, as an amplifying prologue to *Droplaugarsona saga*, which is referred to in the *þáttr* as *Helganna saga*. It provides more detail, sometimes in contradiction to the saga's own account, of the antecedents of the main characters of *Droplaugarsona saga*. The first section traces Helgi Ásbjarnarson's descent from his grandfather, the hero of *Hrafnkels saga*; but this saga was clearly unknown to the author of the *þáttr*, whose source was some version of *Landnámabók*. An outline of Helgi's character and early life culminates in his acquisition of a farm at Oddsstaðir. The displaced former occupant sacrifices a bull to Freyr, ritually cursing his supplanter, an incident possibly deriving from a comparable event in *Víga-Glúms saga*.

The second, more fantastic section, by the author's own admission entertaining rather than factual, turns abruptly to an anecdote involving Grímr, maternal ancestor of the sons of Droplaug. Grímr possesses a remarkable ox, Brandkrossi, after which are named both the *þáttr* itself and, the author fancifully claims, the two bays in eastern Iceland called "Krossavík." One day, Brandkrossi is seized by an inexplicable frenzy and disappears, swimming far out to sea. Distressed by his loss, Grímr visits Norway and encounters the half-giant Geitir, whose daughter he marries. In Geitir's cave dwelling, the ox reappears, and, in the form of a hide stuffed with meal, is bestowed on Grímr by Geitir, who confesses to having caused its mysterious frenzy in order to summon it over the sea.

The *þáttr* survives in paper MSS no older than the 17th century, all derived from a single lost MS. Since the *þáttr* is unlikely to have existed independently of *Droplaugarsona saga*, this lost MS was probably that from which a single leaf survives, recording a fragment of the saga (AM 162c fol.). Other literary relationships of the *þáttr* are obscure. Despite the preoccupation with superstition and ritual, the style is literary. Two incidents invite comparison with *Víga-Glúms saga* and *Eyrbyggja saga*, but no clear influence can be shown. It is likely that the *þáttr* was known to the author of *Hrafnkels saga*, but its influence on the saga, if any, was slight.

Ed.: Jón Jóhannesson, ed. *Austfirðinga sǫgur*. Íslenzk fornrit, 11. Reykjavik: Hið íslenzka fornritafélag, 1950 [*Brandkrossa þáttr* is edited pp. 183–91; introduction, pp. 82–6]. **Tr.**: Gudbrand Vigfusson and F. York Powell, eds. and trans. *Origines Islandicae: A Collection of the More Important Sagas and Other Native Writings Relating to the Settlement and Early History of Iceland*. 2 vols. Oxford: Clarendon, 1905; rpt. Millwood: Kraus, 1976, vol. 2, pp. 533–6 [entitled *Helganna saga* I; ch. 1 only].

Alison Finlay

[**See also:** *Droplaugarsona saga; Eyrbyggja saga; Hrafnkels saga Freysgoða; Landnámabók; Þáttr, Víga-Glúms saga*]

Brands þáttr ǫrva

Brands þáttr ǫrva ("The Tale of Brandr the Generous"), well known as a short tale of high stylistic value, is found in *Morkinskinna* and *Hulda-Hrokkinskinna*, in versions that differ only slightly. The Icelander Brandr inn ǫrvi ("the generous") arrives in Niðaróss (Trondheim) on a trading voyage. His friend, the poet Þjóðólfr, boasts to King Haraldr harðráði ("hard-ruler") Sigurðarson of Brandr's generosity and suggests that no man would be more fitting a choice if Iceland were to have a king. Haraldr sends Þjóðólfr to ask Brandr to give him first his cloak, then his ax chased with gold, and finally his precious tunic. Brandr complies wordlessly with all three requests, but tears an arm from the tunic. The king responds: "This man is both wise and noble. It is clear to me why he has torn off the arm; it seems to him that I have only one arm, and that one only to receive, but never to give. Bring him to me." The king rewards Brandr, "and this was done," the text ends, "to test him." *Brands þáttr* is virtually a paradigm of the *utanferðar þáttr*, a short narrative about an Icelander's journey to Norway, encounter with the king, successful outcome of that encounter with concomitant reward, and (in this case implicit) journey back to Iceland. As is made explicit, the encounter takes the form of testing by the king, and here the testing is tripled. Tests and tripling connect the text directly with the realm of folktale, and further connection might be found in the rewards the king gives to Brandr. However, the *þáttr* lacks the advance in social status of the protagonist common to *þættir* and folktales, perhaps because the author begins by identifying Brandr's generosity and kingly potential. It is easy to suspect that this departure from the generic norm was brought about by the use of the text to explain Brandr's nickname, "the generous."

Ed.: Einar Ól. Sveinsson and Matthías Þórðarson, eds. *Eyrbyggja saga*. Íslenzk fornrit, 4. Reykjavik: Hið íslenzka fornritafélag, 1935, pp. 187–91. **Tr.**: Leach, Henry Goddard, ed. and trans. *A Pageant of Old Scandinavia*. Princeton: Princeton University Press; New York: American-Scandinavian Foundation, 1946, pp. 201–2; Boucher, Alan, trans. *A Tale of Icelanders*. Reykjavik: Iceland Review, 1980, pp. 68–9.

John Lindow

[**See also:** *Hulda-Hrokkinskinna; Morkinskinna; Þáttr*]

Brávallaþula

Brávallaþula ("The Metrical Name List of Brávellir [Bråvalla]") tells of the legendary battle of Brávellir, where Harald Wartooth (Hilditǫnn) lost his life to his nephew Sigurðr hringr ("ring"), king of the Swedes. The *þula* is known from Saxo's translation into Latin in *Gesta Danorum*. Here, Saxo enumerates the champions (some 160 are named), and their nicknames and places of origin are often added. The same list is given, although in shorter form, in the so-called *Sǫgubrot* preserved in an Icelandic MS of about 1300 (AM 1e β 1 fol.).

The origin of the *þula* is disputed. Some scholars argue that the work displays traces of Norwegian or Telemarkian patriotism, while others, on the basis of linguistic analyses, maintain that the work originated more specifically in southeastern Norway, where Saxo and the author of *Sǫgubrot* had models available in MSS written in that region. However, recent scholarship has demonstrated the unreliability of these claims, since knowledge of early Norwegian dialects is defective. From the perspective of literary history, the þula fits easily into an Icelandic setting, where such metrical name lists flourished in the 12th century, and it is to this period that we can assign the Brávallaþula.

The differences between the two versions lie in the description of the battle and its antecedents and in the enumeration of the chieftains. If we follow Saxo's story, Óðinn, who impersonates Brun(i), Harald's servant, sows strife between Harald and his nephew. Harald is now blind, but still able to fight, and the two armies meet at Brávellir. Starkad is on the side of the Swedes, and it was said to be in his verses that the story of the battle was recorded. Multitudes fall on either side, and, in the end, Harald learns that the Swedish army is deployed in a wedge formation like his own. Only Óðinn could have taught them this formation, and Harald knows now that the god has turned against him. Óðinn, who is now acting as Harald's charioteer under the name of Brúni, batters the king to death with his own club. His nephew gives him a magnificent funeral, which is fully described by Saxo and in Sǫgubrot. Contrary to Saxo, Sǫgubrot does not mention any divine intervention in the battle: Harald is killed by a certain Brúni, but his identification with Óðinn is not noted. Whereas Saxo names Icelanders on both sides, none are named in Sǫgubrot; generally, there are fewer names in the latter text. The description of the combat also differs. In Saxo, one duel follows the next, whereas in Sǫgubrot, the fighting is more complicated. Minor distinctions can be observed in the descriptions of Harald's funeral. In both versions, Sigurðr asks the chieftains to present the deceased king with costly objects so that he can enter Valhǫll in style. In Sǫgubrot, Harald is buried in a mound at the battle field, but in Saxo he is cremated and his urn brought to Lejre.

The differences between the two texts suggests that Saxo expanded the mythological element of the poem, introducing the Brávellir theme as part of his overall plan for Book 8. In this book, several episodes resemble the Ragnarǫk myth; one story is reminiscent of the Fimbul winters, another of the wolf Fenrir. The myth also depicts a great combat in which the gods and the einherjar (fallen warriors in Valhǫll) meet. In having the names contained in Brávallaþula reflect those of men and women who appear in the first ten books of Gesta Danorum, Saxo is able to spread the combatants over several hundreds of years and superimpose the great battle of the Ragnarǫk myth upon ordinary chronology. The battle at Brávellir thus becomes a turning point in history when paganism is ended and Christianity introduced.

Both national and historical considerations can explain why Sǫgubrot does not mention the Icelanders. The whole story is meant to have taken place in the old days, i.e., before Iceland was inhabited, so it stands to reason that no Icelander could participate in the Brávellir battle. Rationalism can explain Óðinn's subdued role.

Ed.: Petersens, Carl af, and Emil Olsen, eds. Sǫgur Danakonunga. Sǫgubrot af fornkonungum; Knytlinga saga. Samfund til udgivelse af gammel nordisk litteratur, 46. Copenhagen: Ohlsson, 1919–25; Olrik, Jørgen, and H. Ræder, eds. Saxonis Gesta Danorum. Vol. 1. Copenhagen: Levin & Munksgaard, 1931. Vol. 2. Indicem Verborum Continens, by Franz Blatt. Copenhagen: Levin & Munkgaard, 1957. Tr.: Ellis Davidson, Hilda, ed., and Fisher, Peter, trans. Saxo Grammaticus. The History of the Danes. Books I–IX. 2 vols. Cambridge: Brewer; Totowa: Rowman and Littlefield, 1979–80. Lit.: Olrik, Axel. "Brávallakvadets

Kæmperække." Arkiv för nordisk filologi 10 (1894), 223–87; Olrik, Axel. The Heroic Legends of Denmark. Trans. Lee M. Hollander. New York: American-Scandinavian Foundation, 1919; rpt. Millwood: Kraus, 1976; Seip, Didrik Arup. Norsk språkhistorie til omkring 1370. 2 vols. 2nd ed. Oslo: Aschehoug, 1955; Bjarni Guðnason. "Um Brávallaþulu." Skírnir 32 (1958), pp. 82–128; Bjarni Guðnason. Um Skjöldungasǫgu. Reykjavík: Menningarsjóður, 1963; Bjarni Guðnason, ed. Danakonunga sǫgur. Íslenzk fornrit, 35. Reykjavík: Hið íslenzka fornritafélag, 1982; Skovgaard-Petersen, Inge. Da Tidernes Herre var nær. Studier i Saxos historiesyn. Copenhagen: Den danske historiske forening, 1987.

Inge Skovgaard-Petersen

[See also: Divine Heroes, Native; Saxo Grammaticus]

Breta sǫgur ("The Sagas of the British") is the title, as transmitted in Hauksbók and AM 573 4to, of an Old Norse rendering of Geoffrey of Monmouth's Historia regum Britanniae (ca. 1136), with additions from other sources. The text of Breta sǫgur is poorly preserved. In the MSS, it is linked with the β-version of Trójumanna saga, and, like the latter text, it is extant in both a shorter and a longer redaction, the shorter of which is found only in Hauksbók and in transcriptions of this MS. Haukr Erlendsson copied the Trójumanna saga and Breta sǫgur portions of Hauksbók between 1302 and 1310 and, as he did with other texts that he copied, considerably shortened them. The Hauksbók redaction of Breta sǫgur contains a large number of mistakes, some of which probably result from being condensed. The abridgment is especially pronounced toward the end, which is all the more unfortunate since Hauksbók is the only extant MS of Breta sǫgur to contain the last chapters of the work. Furthermore, the text of Hauksbók is difficult to read in many places, partly because of wear and tear, and partly because of 17th-century attempts to touch up the worn passages.

The longer redaction is represented by two MSS, both defective: AM 573 4to (14th century) and Stock. Papp. fol. no. 58, a 17th-century copy of the lost "Ormr Snorrason's book" (14th century). The text in AM 573 4to has several lacunae and ends defectively within Valvers þáttr, which in this MS follows the account of King Arthur's death (Historia, Book 11). The text of Stock. Papp. fol. no. 58 breaks off in Historia, Book 5. A badly mutilated and partly illegible fragment of an otherwise lost 14th-century MS of Breta sǫgur was discovered in the binding of an Icelandic MS in Trinity College, Dublin, in 1968. The text of this fragment (as yet unpublished) is fuller than that of AM 573 4to, which seems to indicate that both of the preserved redactions go back to an abridged version of the original translation; Stock. Papp. fol. no. 58 does not cover the relevant part of the narrative.

The first chapters of the saga, which summarize the story of Aeneas and Turnus, are directly or indirectly derived from Vergil's Aeneid, and continue the tale as told in the concluding chapters of the β-version of Trójumanna saga. Two items are found only in the Hauksbók redaction: the poem Merlínusspá and a short catalogue listing the West Saxon kings from Caedwalla to Æthelstan. This regnal list, of uncertain provenance, is surely a later addition to the original translation of Geoffrey's Historia. Merlínusspá is a free metrical rendering of Geoffrey's Prophetiae Merlini. Written sometime before the Historia, the Prophetiae were later inserted into Geoffrey's work as part of Book 7. The MSS of Breta sǫgur ascribe the poem to the Icelandic monk Gunnlaugr Leifsson of Þingeyrar (d. 1218 or 1219). Some scholars have assumed that

Gunnlaugr Leifsson's *Merlínusspá* opened the way for a translation of Geoffrey's *Historia* in Iceland at the beginning of the 13th century. Chiefly on the basis of stylistic arguments, however, Halvorsen feels inclined to count *Breta sǫgur* and *Trójumanna saga* (*i.e.*, the β-version) among the pseudo-historical works that were translated at the behest of King Hákon Hákonarson of Norway (1217–1263).

Ed.: Jón Sigurðsson, ed. "Trójumanna saga ok Breta sǫgur." *Annaler for nordisk Oldkyndighed og Historie* (1848), 3–215, (1849), 3–145 [the *Hauksbók* text with selected variants from the longer redaction, accompanied by a Danish translation]; Eiríkur Jónsson and Finnur Jónsson, eds. *Hauksbók udgiven efter de Arnamagnæanske håndskrifter no. 371, 544 og 675, 4° samt forskellige papirshåndskrifter af det kongelige nordiske Oldskrift-selskab*. Copenhagen: Thiele, 1892–96; Faral, E., ed. *La légende arthurienne. Études et documents*. Paris: Champion, 1929; Griscom, A., ed. *The Historia Regum Britanniae of Geoffrey of Monmouth*. London: Longmans, Green, 1929; Hammer, Jacob, ed. *Geoffrey of Monmouth. Historia Regum Britanniae. A Variant Version Edited from Manuscripts*. Cambridge: Medieval Academy of America, 1951; Jón Helgason, ed. *Hauksbók: The Arna-Magnæan Manuscripts 371, 4to, 544, 4to and 675, 4to*. Manuscripta Islandica, 5. Copenhagen: Munksgaard, 1960; Wright, Neil, ed. *The Historia Regum Britannie of Geoffrey of Monmouth. 1: Bern, Burgerbibliothek, MS 568; 2: The First Variant Version: A Critical Edition*. Cambridge: Brewer, 1985, 1988 [to be continued]; a critical edition of *Breta sǫgur* will appear in Editiones Arnamagnæanæ, ser. A, vol. 10. **Lit.**: Hamel, A. G. van. "The Old-Norse Version of the Historia Regum Britanniæ and the Text of Geoffrey of Monmouth." *Études celtiques* 1 (1936), 197–247; J. S. Eysteinsson. "The Relationship of *Merlínusspá* and Geoffrey of Monmouth's *Historia*." *Saga-Book of the Viking Society* 14 (1953–57), 95–112; Halvorsen, E. F. *The Norse Version of the Chanson de Roland*. Bibliotheca Arnamagnæana, 19. Copenhagen: Munksgaard, 1959; Halvorsen, E. F. "Breta sǫgur." *KLNM* 2 (1957), 220–3; Jakob Benediktsson. "Merlínusspá." *KLNM* 11 (1966), 556–7; Springborg, Peter. "Nyt og gammelt fra Snæfjallaströnd." In *Afmælisrit Jóns Helgasonar. 30. júní 1969*. Ed. Jakob Benediktsson *et al.* Reykjavik: Heimskringla, 1969, pp. 288–327 [on the fragment of *Breta sǫgur* in Trinity College, Dublin, see pp. 297–8]; Stefán Karlsson. "Aldur Hauksbókar." *Fróðskaparrit* 13 (1964), 114–21.

Jonna Louis-Jensen

[**See also:** *Grípisspá*; *Hauksbók*; *Merlínusspá*; *Trójumanna saga*]

Brunkebergsvisan *see* **Swedish Literature, Miscellaneous**

Brynhildr *see* **Vǫlsung-Niflung Cycle**

Burial Mounds and Burial Practices. In some areas of northern Europe from the Early Bronze Age to the Viking Age, burials were covered with mounds. Two kinds of mounds may be distinguished on the basis of the materials used in their construction: first, those exclusively made of stone (called "cairns" after the Celtic word for megalithic stone monuments; the Norwegian and Swedish term is *röse*); second, those built of earth, turf, and stones (called "mounds" or "barrows"; Danish *høj*, Norwegian *haug*, Swedish *hög*). Generally, these cairns and mounds/barrows have a domed profile (Fig. 3), but there are stone settings that may be filled with stones or earth and turf, and that show a flat profile. These cairn- or mound-like stone settings are known from many

Late Iron Age cemeteries in Scandinavia in different forms: circular, triangular, square, rectangular, ship-formed, or triangular with concave sides; they are often raised up without any covering (Fig. 3). Cemeteries with Viking Age mounds, cairns, and stone settings are preserved in many parts of Scandinavia, especially in central Sweden (Mälaren area), where in view of their topographical connection with medieval villages they are called "village grave fields" (Swedish *bygravfält*). The cemeteries of the Early Iron Age (Pre-Roman, Roman Iron Age, Migration Period) are characterized by stone settings with low or flat profiles, varying forms (circular, rectangular, square, triangular), and upright stones (Fig. 4); they contain cremation burials (deposits on ground surface, in pits and urns), mostly with few grave goods. From the Migration Period on, mounds with domed profiles become predominant, and are accompanied by stone settings of varying forms (circular, triangular, square, and ship-formed; Fig. 4). Cremation burials, mostly deposits on the surface, are common. Some inhumation graves occur in the Migration and Vendel periods; their number increases in the Viking Age, especially in the late phase. The grave goods of the Late Iron Age are far richer and more differentiated than in the Early Iron Age, and include costume, multiple grave goods, and animals.

Excellent examples of Viking Age mounds can be found at the grave fields of Birka (Björkö), where 465 mounds with cremation burials and 176 mounds with inhumation graves have been excavated. The mounds are usually of a more or less regular circular outline. The diameter of the circular mounds with cremation burials varies from 1.8 m. to 16.8 m., with the large majority between 3 m. and 6 m. The height varies from 0.15 m. to 1.95 m., mostly between 0.30 m. and 0.90 m. The mounds with inhumation burials have diameters from 3 m. to 14 m.; the mounds with chamber graves tend to be larger (5–14 m.).

A small group of Viking Age mounds can be classified as "great mounds" (Swedish *storhögar*, Norwegian *storhauger*) or "king" or "royal mounds" (Swedish *kungshögar*, Norwegian *kongshauger*), which are characterized by their monumental size. Notable examples are the two "royal" mounds at Jelling, with a diameter of about 70 m. and a height of about 11 m., the northern one with a large chamber grave, and the mounds of Gokstad and Oseberg, Vestfold, southern Norway, with a diameter of about 45 m., a height of 5–6 m., and containing ship burials. Generally, large mounds are defined as being more than 20–25 m. in diameter. In Sweden, most of the mounds are distributed in the Mälaren area and adjoining regions, where excavations have brought to light burials from the Migration Period and Late Iron Age. The best-known mounds are those from Gamla ("Old") Uppsala, containing richly equipped cremation burials from the 6th century. Another example dating to the Migration Period is the grave field with large mounds from Högom, Medelpad, in northern Sweden. Many large mounds are registered in southern, western, and middle Norway. In Vestlandet (northern Rogaland, Hordaland, Sogn and Fjordane, and Møre and Romsdal), about 300 mounds are known with a diameter of more than 22 m. and a volume of more than 400 cubic m. (height 2.2 m. and more). Only one third of these mounds have been excavated, mostly partially. About 50 percent of these belong to the Early Iron Age (Pre-Roman Iron Age to Migration Period), 25 percent to the Late Iron Age (Merovingian times and Viking Age), and the rest to the Iron Age and Bronze Age. Without question, the burials in large mounds generally represent members of leading "aristocratic" and "royal" families; they are interpreted as visible signs of consolidated power and territorial claim. Additionally, they functioned as religious, juridical, and political centers (*cf.* Old Uppsala in the Viking Age and large mounds from the Migration Period).

Attempts have been made to differentiate the grave mounds and grave furnishings on the basis of regional archaeological data and to offer a sociological interpretation by connecting the archaeological sources with historically known groups of a stratified society (Norwegian *lagdelt samfunn*). Scholars have attempted, for instance, to assign the standard accoutrements of 10th-century warrior burials (often with horses) in the Old Danish realm with the group of *hempægi* ("home-companion"), *þegn*, and *dregn* (both terms denote dependence on or sworn loyalty to the king) of the written sources (runic inscriptions) who were active in royal service. On the other hand, there are burials without any grave goods, but that are closely connected with rich burials, and that are often interpreted as burials of slaves. The interpretation of Viking graves is complicated by religious ambivalence or change from heathendom to Christianity. As several studies of the last years show, a complex pattern is emerging, where religious, social, economic and other factors must be taken into consideration.

Bib.: Lindqvist, Sune. "Hauglegging" *KLNM* 6 (1961), 246–50. **Lit.:** **(a) Denmark/Schleswig-Holstein:** Brøndsted, Johannes. "Danish Inhumation Graves of the Viking Age." *Acta Archaeologica* 7 (1936), 81–228; Ramskou, Thorkild. "Viking Age Cremation Graves in Denmark." *Acta Archaeologica* 21 (1950), 137–82; Voss, Fridtjof, *et al.* "Das Höftland von Langballigau an der Flensburger Förde. Die Oberflächenformen. Das jüngereisenzeitliche Gräberfeld. Die Vegetation der Mündungsniederung." *Offa* 30 (1973), 60–132; Randsborg, Klavs. *The Viking Age in Denmark: The Formation of a State.* London: Duckworth, 1980, pp. 121–35; Krogh, Knud. "The Royal Viking-Age Monuments at Jelling in the Light of the Recent Archaeological Excavations: A Preliminary Report." *Acta Archaeologica* 53 (1982), 183–216; Roesdahl, Else. "10. århundredes overklassegrave og 'staten' o. 950." In *Fra stamme til stat. Symposium på Sostrup Kloster 23.–25. maj 1984.* Højbjerg: Mortensen, 1984, pp. 109–14; Andersen, Hans Hellmuth. "Vorchristliche Königsgräber in Dänemark und ihre Hintergründe—Versuch einer Synthese." *Germania* 65 (1987), 159–73; Müller-Wille, Michael. *Das wikingerzeitliche Gräberfeld von Thumby-Bienebek (Kr. Rendsburg-Eckernförde).* Teil 2. Offa-Bücher, 62. Neumünster: Wachholtz, 1987, pp. 69–90. **(b) Iceland:** Kristján Eldjárn. *Kuml og haugfé úr heiðnum sið á Íslandi.* Akureyri: Bókaútgáfan Norðri, 1956. **(c) Norway:** Brøgger, Anton Wilhelm. *Borrefundet og Vestfoldkongenes graver.* Videnskapsselskapets Skrifter, II. Hist.-Filos. Klasse, 1916. Kristiania [Oslo]: Dybwad, 1916; Brøgger, Anton Wilhelm.

GROUPS	FREE OF EARTH	COVERED WITH TURF	EXCLUSIVELY STONE (Examples)
TYPES — Profile Domed	Cairn	Mound Barrow	Upright stone / Unfilled stone-setting
TYPES — Profile Flat	Stone setting (cairn-like)	Stone setting	Stone circle
Form / **VARIATIONS**	○ ▽ □ ( ) △	○ ▽ □ ( ) △	⁰⁰⁰ ⊞ ⊞ ○○○
	Circular / Triangular / Square / Rectangular / Ship-formed / Triangular with concave sides	Circular / Triangular / Square / Rectangular / Ship-formed / Triangular with concave sides	Circular / Square / Rectangular / Ship-formed
Special terms (sw)	Långröse / Treudd	Långhög / Treudd	Domarring / Skepps-sättning

3.

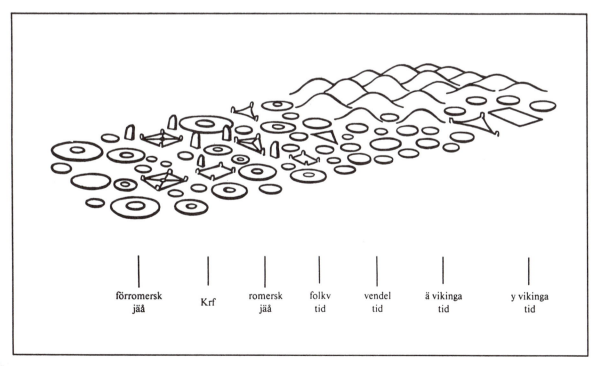

förromersk jää | Krf | romersk jää | folkv tid | vendel tid | ä vikinga tid | y vikinga tid

4.

"Gullalder." *Viking* 1 (1937), 137–95; Grieg, Sigurd. "Raknehaugen." *Viking* 5 (1941), 1–28; Brøgger, Anton Wilhelm. "Oseberg-graven—Haugbrottet." *Viking* 9 (1945), 1–44; Ringstad, Bjørn. *Vestlandets største gravminner. Et forsøk på lokalisering av forhistoriske maktsentra.* Avhandling for magistergraden i arkeologi. Bergen: Universitetet i Bergen, 1987. **(d) Sweden**: Hyenstrand, Åke. *Arkeologisk regionindelning av Sverige.* Stockholm: Riksantikvarieämbetet, 1979; Hyenstrand, Åke. *Ancient Monuments and Prehistoric Society.* Stockholm: Central Board of National Antiquities, 1979; Gräslund, Anne-Sofie. *Birka IV. The Burial Customs: A Study of the Graves on Björkö.* Stockholm: Almqvist & Wiksell, 1980; Hyenstrand, Åke. *Excavations at Helgö VI: The Mälaren Area.* Stockholm: Almqvist & Wiksell, 1981; Wijkander, Keith. *Kungshögar och sockenbildning. Studier i Södermanlands administrativa indelning under vikingatid och tidig medeltid.* Sörmländska handlingar, 39. Nyköping: Södermanlands museum, 1983; Bennett, Agneta. *Graven religiös och social symbol. Strukturer i folkvandringstidens gravskick i Mälarområdet.* Theses and Papers in North-European Archaeology, 18. Stockholm: Institute of Archaeology at the University of Stockholm, 1987.

Michael Müller-Wille

[See also: Graves; Religion, Pagan Scandinavian]

Bærings saga ("The Saga of Bæringr") is an anonymous Icelandic *riddarasaga* probably from the beginning of the 14th century, the date of the oldest MS, AM 580 4to. The saga is extant in more than fifty-five MSS and in different redactions. Between the 16th and the 19th centuries, six *rímur*-cycles were composed based on the material of the saga, as was also the short *Berrings vísa* (CCF 42) composed in the Faroe Islands in the 19th century.

The saga can be summarized as follows: The knight Heinrekr takes possession of the royal throne in Saxonland. Meanwhile, in England, Bæringr is trained to become a brave knight. At the age of twenty-three, he attempts to recapture his father's kingdom, but his fleet sinks. While in France, Bæringr gains the friendship of the king of Constantinople; he becomes engaged to the king's sister Vindemia, and returns to Saxonland. On his journey, Bæringr defeats a number of adversaries and rejects gentle ladies, who fall in love with him because of his good looks. With God's help, he finally defeats the sorcerer Heinrekr in a great battle. Bæringr marries Vindemia and becomes the emperor of the Roman Empire.

Of the stories composed in Iceland around 1300 and based on material from older texts, *Bærings saga* is considered among the oldest. It draws on motifs found in *Rémundar saga keisarasonar* (the series of battles and journeys), *Mírmanns saga* (the chaste, Christian knight), *Ívens saga* (the easily consoled widow), and *Þiðreks saga* (for its North German roots). It is possible that certain features of the conflict as described in the saga may go back to historical events in North Germany.

As in *Sigrgarðs saga ok Valbrands* and *Adonias saga*, the plot of *Bærings saga* develops as a consequence of the initial villainy (usurpation and murder, flight, exile) in a series of conflicts and flights until the victory and the final progress at the end. Two elements of the saga are particularly noteworthy. First, because of the physical attraction of the knight, the conflicts with the adversaries are not limited to the male sex only, but also include love intrigues (the "Potiphar" motif). Second, the text, unlike other sagas, merges the plot involving the courtly milieu with a Christian moral attitude. Occasional proverbs and, in particular, the distinctive expression of the narrator emphasize and elucidate the thematic and ideological structure of the saga: in the character of the hero Bæringr, superior to all heathens, Christian chivalry is effectively glorified, and its superiority as a belief system establishing guidelines of moral conduct is firmly demonstrated.

Ed.: Cederschiöld, Gustaf, ed. "Bærings saga." In *Fornsögur Suðrlanda. Magus saga jarls, Konraðs saga, Bærings saga, Flovents saga, Bevers saga. Med inledning.* Lund: Berling, 1884, pp. 85–123 [detailed retelling in German, pp. clxxv–clxxxv; introduction in Swedish, pp. clxxxvi–cxcii]; Matras, Christian, and Napoleon Djurhuus, eds. "Berrings vísa." In *Føroya kvæði. Corpus carminum Færoensium* 1–. Copenhagen: Universitets-Jubilæets danske Samfund, 1941–, vol. 2, no. 42, pp. 105–7. **Bib.**: Finnur Sigmundsson. *Rímnatal.* 2 vols. Reykjavik: Rímnafélagið, 1966, vol. 1, pp. 95–8; Kalinke, Marianne E., and P. M. Mitchell. *Bibliography of Old Norse–Icelandic Romances.* Islandica, 44. Ithaca and London: Cornell University Press, 1985. **Lit.**: Leach, Henry Goddard. *Angevin Britain and Scandinavia.* Harvard Studies in Comparative Literature, 6. Cambridge: Harvard University Press; London: Milford; Oxford: Oxford University Press, 1921; rpt. Millwood: Kraus, 1975; Finnur Jónsson. *Den oldnorske og oldislandske Litteraturs Historie.* 3 vols. 2nd ed. Copenhagen: Gad, 1924, vol. 3, p. 104; Schlauch, Margaret. *Romance in Iceland.* Princeton: Princeton University Press; New York: American-Scandinavian Foundation; London: Allen & Unwin, 1934; rpt. New York: Russell and Russell, 1973; Björn K. Þórólfsson. *Rímur fyrir 1600.* Safn Fræðafjelagsins um Ísland og Íslendinga, 9. Copenhagen: Møller, 1934, pp. 412–3; Vries, Jan de. *Altnordische Literaturgeschichte.* 2 vols. Grundriss der germanischen Philologie, 15–16. Berlin: de Gruyter, 1941–42; rpt. 1964–67, vol. 2, p. 535; Togeby, Knud. "L'influence de la littérature française sur les littératures scandinaves au moyen âge." In *Généralités.* Ed. Hans Ulrich Gumbrecht. Grundriss der romanischen Literaturen des Mittelalters, 1. Heidelberg: Winter, 1972, pp. 333–95, esp. 379; Halvorsen, E. F. "Bærings saga." *KLNM* 21 (1977), 132–3; Kalinke, Marianne E. *King Arthur North-by-Northwest: The matière de Bretagne in Old Norse–Icelandic Romances.* Bibliotheca Arnamagnæana, 37. Copenhagen: Reitzel, 1981; Nahl, Astrid van. *Originale Riddarasögur als Teil altnordischer Sagaliteratur.* Texte und Untersuchungen zur Germanistik und Skandinavistik, 3. Frankfurt am Main and Bern: Lang, 1981; Glauser, Jürg. *Isländische Märchensagas. Studien zur Prosaliteratur im spätmittelalterlichen Island.* Beiträge zur nordischen Philologie, 12. Basel and Frankfurt am Main: Helbing & Lichtenhahn, 1983; Kalinke, Marianne. "Norse Romance (*Riddarasögur*)." In *Old Norse–Icelandic Literature: A Critical Guide.* Ed. Carol J. Clover and John Lindow. Islandica, 45. Ithaca and London: Cornell University Press, 1985, pp. 316–63; Hermann Pálsson. "The Use of Latin Proverbs and Sententiae in the Riddarasögur." In *Les Sagas de Chevaliers (Riddarasögur). Actes de la Ve Conférence Internationale sur les Sagas . . . (Toulon. Juillet 1982).* Ed. Régis Boyer. Civilisations, 10. Paris: Presses de l'Université de Paris-Sorbonne, 1985, pp. 385–91; Hermann Pálsson. *Áhrif Hugsvinnsmála á aðrar fornbókmenntir.* Studia Islandica, 43. Reykjavik: Menningarsjóður, 1985; Jochens, Jenny M. "Consent in Marriage: Old Norse Law, Life, and Literature." *Scandinavian Studies* 58 (1986), 142–76.

Jürg Glauser

[See also: *Adonias saga; Ívens saga; Mírmanns saga; Rémundar saga keisarasonar; Riddarasögur; Rímur; Sigrgarðs saga ok Valbrands; Þiðreks saga af Bern*]

Bǫglunga sǫgur ("Sagas of the Baglar"), one of the *konungasögur*, is the most important source for Norwegian history 1202–1217. During this period, political power in Norway was divided between two factions, the Birkibeinar ("birch-legs"), with their center in central Norway (Þrœndalǫg), and the Baglar (from *bagall*, *i.e.*, Crosier), who usually controlled southeastern Norway. The saga deals with three Birkibeinar kings, Hákon Sverrisson (r. 1202–1203), Guttormr Sigurðarson (r. 1204), and Ingi Bárðarson (r. 1204–1217), and three Baglar kings, Ingi Magnússon (r. 1196–1202), Erlingr steinveggr ("stonewall"; r. 1204–1207), and Philippús Símonarson (r. 1207–1217). It consists primarily of the historical reporting of military and political events, and is based on information from participants in the activities. Detailed accounts of the constant battles between the two parties comprise the first part of the saga (1202–1209); a truce in the fall of 1208 puts a stop to the hostilities. The rest of the saga relates more episodically political events and court intrigues in the Birkibeinar empire, but also includes passages concerning the Baglar.

Bǫglunga sǫgur is a direct continuation of *Sverris saga*, although it does not attain the earlier work's status as literature. The Birkibeinar kings receive a continuous presentation of their reigns, but the reigns of the first and last Baglar kings are only fragmentarily presented. Both of the Birkibeinar kings who died as grown men receive honorable necrologies, in accordance with European literary tradition, whereas none of the Baglar kings receives a necrology. It appears, then, that *Bǫglunga sǫgur* was conceived as a work where the Birkibeinar kings were the central characters.

Nowhere is *Bǫglunga sǫgur* transmitted in its original and complete form. There are two main redactions, one longer one, which covers the entire period 1202–1217, and one shorter one, covering only the years 1202–1210. Four parchment fragments of the longer version are preserved, but this version is most completely preserved in a translation from Old Norse into Danish by the Norwegian priest Peder Claussøn Friis (d. 1614) and printed in Copenhagen by the Danish scholar Ole Worm in 1633. The shorter version is preserved in two large Icelandic vellums containing collections of *konungasǫgur*, *Eirspennill* and *Skálholtsbók yngsta*, and a parchment fragment.

Bǫglunga sǫgur most likely was written in stages, like *Sverris saga*. The fuller initial part was probably composed around 1210, whereas the final part seems to have been written very shortly after Ingi Bárðarson's death in 1217. Both parts were most likely written by one or more Icelanders. The scholarly consensus has been that the shorter version is more original; however, the shorter version must have come about by a revision of the initial part of the longer version. Some of the events in *Bǫglunga sǫgur* are also presented in other Old Norse sources, especially in the beginning of *Hákonar saga Hákonarsonar*.

Ed.: Rafn, C. C. *et al.*, eds. *Fornmanna sǫgur*. 12 vols. Copenhagen: Popp, 1828–46, vol. 9, pp. 1–228 [includes all texts of the longer version and the *Eirspennill* text of the shorter version, with variants; *Eirspennill*, pp. 439–70; *Skálholtsbók yngsta*, pp. 255–91]; Magerøy, Hallvard, ed. *Soga om birkebeinar og baglar Bǫglunga sǫgur*. Norsk Historisk Kjeldeskrift-Institutt, Norrøne tekster, 5. Oslo: Kjeldeskriftfondet; Solum, 1988. **Lit.**: Helle, Knut. *Omkring Bǫglungasǫgur*. Universitetet i Bergen, Årbok 1958, Historisk-Antikvarisk rekke Nr. 7. Bergen: Grieg, 1959; Jensen, Helle. "Fragmenter af et kongesagahåndskrift fra det 13. århundrede." *Opuscula* 6. Bibliotheca Arnamagnæana, 33. Copenhagen: Reitzel, 1979, pp. 24–73 [includes an edition of the oldest fragment of the longer version]; Jónas Kristjánsson. *Eddas and Sagas: Iceland's Medieval Literature*. Trans. Peter Foote. Reykjavik: Hið íslenska bókmenntafélag, 1988, p. 154; Magerøy, Hallvard. "Litterære drag i Bǫglunga sǫgur." In *Festskrift til Finn Hødnebø 29. desember 1989*. Ed. Bjørn Eithun *et al.* Oslo: Novus, 1989, pp. 196–209.

Hallvard Magerøy

[**See also:** *Eirspennill*; *Hákonar saga gamla Hákonarsonar*; *Konungasǫgur*; Political Literature; *Sverris saga*]

Caithness, the most northeasterly province of mainland Scotland, was more heavily settled by Vikings than any other part of the mainland. The Old Norse name *Katanes* ("The headland of the tribe of Cats") incorporates the name of one of the seven provinces of the Picts, which originally covered the area north of the Oykell River (Dornoch Firth). The name "Caithness" may have been applied first by the Norse to Duncansby Head, but was extended in its application to the northern half of the former Pictish province as Scandinavian settlement spread south. The southern half of the province came to be called "Sutherland" (*Suðrland*), and even in the later Middle Ages Sutherland and Caithness were referred to as "the two provinces of the Caithness-men." Both the earldom and bishopric of Caithness covered the entire area north of the Oykell River, although the earls lost control of Sutherland in the 13th century.

The date at which Norse settlement occurred in Caithness is not clearly specified in any historical or saga source. It can be assumed to be later than in the islands, and likely to have followed the successful campaigns of Sigurðr inn ríki ("the mighty") Eysteinsson, earl of Orkney, and Þorsteinn rauði ("the red") Ólafsson in the late 9th century. Strong saga tradition recorded their conquest of Caithness and Sutherland to the banks of the Oykell. Archaeological evidence broadly supports a 10th-century settlement period: the pagan graves are nearly all clustered close to the northern and eastern coastal zone and in southeast Sutherland, and none of them suggests an early Viking date. The distribution of Norse place-names provides a much more complete picture of the total settlement by settlers of Norse speech. These place-names suggest that there was an obliteration of older place-names in the low-lying arable lands of northeast Caithness. As the terrain becomes higher to the south and west, Celtic place-names appear in increasing numbers, and at the 400-m. contour line Norse place-names fade out. Such a demarcation zone between the two languages may suggest a situation of confrontation between the two cultures. The Celtic place-names are not, however, pre-Norse but of a later Gaelic type, which suggests a spread of Gaelic speakers into the totally Norse-speaking province later in the Middle Ages. Elsewhere in Caithness, Norse place-names are scattered along the coastal zone and up river valleys, heavily intermixed with Celtic names. These are areas where the Gaelic language was spoken until comparatively recently.

Despite the early conquests of Sigurðr and Þorsteinn, the earls of Orkney had a long battle to assure themselves of political control in Caithness. Their protagonists were native "kings of Scots" (so-called in *Orkneyinga saga* and *Njáls saga*) and are thought to have been rulers of the province of Moray, south and west of Inverness. One of them is likely to have been the famous MacBeth. This struggle continued through the late 10th century and the first half of the 11th. During this period, the earls are said to have received support for their claim to authority in Caithness from the southern line of kings in Scotland, whose assertion of hegemony to the whole of Scotland was challenged by the Moray dynasty. The marriage of Earl Sigurðr digri ("the stout") Hlǫðvisson (*ca.* 985–1014) to a daughter of Malcolm II of Scotland is strong evidence for the alliance of Norse earls and south Scottish royal dynasty. This alliance inevitably led to the situation of the earls submitting to the kings of Scotland and eventually being in the position of vassals who held their earldom by royal grant. Þorfinnr Sigurðarson's close relationship with his grandfather Malcolm II strengthened Scottish control in Caithness, and he is said to have been given Caithness and Sutherland along with the title of earl by the king, who appointed counselors to govern the land with him. Formal acknowledgment that Caithness and Sutherland and other parts of the Scottish littoral settled by Scandinavian-speaking colonists were in fact part of the kingdom of Scotland was made in 1098, when King Magnús berfœttr ("bare-leg") Ólafsson of Norway agreed in a treaty with the king of Scots that only the offshore islands came under Magnús's rule.

Formal subjection to Scottish overlordship did not mean that the kings immediately had direct authority in Caithness. In all political and social respects, Caithness was a part of the Scandinavian North until the 13th century and closely tied to the islands across the Pentland Firth. It formed one half of the joint earldom of Orkney-Caithness until the late 14th century, and when the islands were divided among joint heirs Caithness seems usually to have been attached to the southeast portion of Orkney. The earls' administration and defensive system was established throughout Caithness and Sutherland following the recorded incidence of the territorial divisions of ouncelands and pennylands, which were to become the basis of the payments of *skattr* (tax). The earls had various administrative centers and residences: in the 11th century, Earl Þorfinnr resided at Duncansby; an important earldom castle

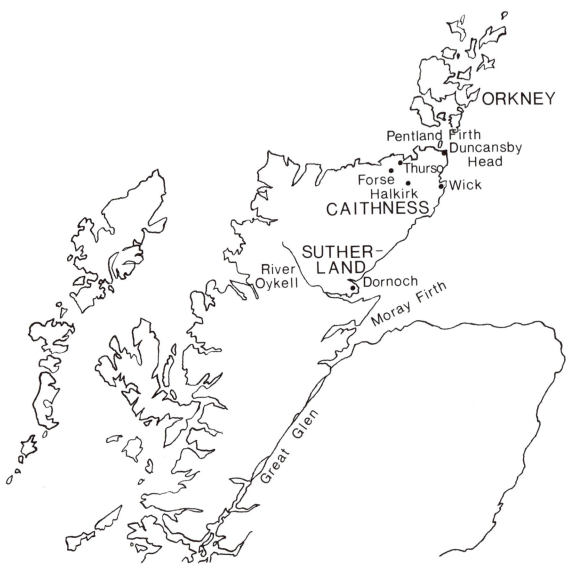

5. Caithness

at Thurso was first recorded in 1154; and Murkle, east of Thurso, was also a residence. But Brawl near Halkirk was perhaps the most important comital seat in the later Middle Ages.

The 12th-century section of *Orkneyinga saga* and the shorter *Haralds saga Maddaðarsonar* give much information about the contemporary situation in Caithness. In fact, the saga writer's knowledge of Caithness, both its geography and genealogies, is so specific as to suggest that he stayed there for a time with some branch of the family of Sveinn Ásleifarson. Several stirring events took place in Caithness during this period: the murder of Earl Rǫgnvaldr Kali Kolsson at Forsie in 1158; the battle of Earl Haraldr Maddaðarson with the claimant Haraldr ungi ("the young") Eiríksson near Wick in 1198, showing how important retention of control of Caithness was for an earl's power.

Another marked feature of the history of Caithness in the 12th and early 13th centuries is the situation of permanent tension between earls and bishops. This tension resulted from the appointment of Scottish bishops as part of the Scottish Crown's determination to draw the area more firmly under its own control. It is more than likely that prior to the appointment of Bishop Andrew (1147/51) the area had lain within the jurisdiction of the bishops of Orkney, who cannot have welcomed this development, nor did the earl, who frequently exercised some control over the appointment of Orkney bishops at this time. The tension that erupted between Earl Haraldr and Bishop John (1187/9–1202) and Earl Jón Haraldsson and Bishop Adam (1213–1222) was primarily over financial matters, and in the latter case over the question of tithes, which were increased perhaps to put them in line with Scottish practice. The maiming of Bishop John and the murder of Bishop Adam that followed provided the Scottish kings with the opportunity to exercise financial and judicial control over the earls and their earldom. But the power of the earls was most particularly curbed by the establishment of a feudal power center in Sutherland, which was detached from the earldom of Caithness and made into a separate earldom for a vassal of the king. At the same time, the bishop moved his see to Dornoch in Sutherland and had a cathedral built there well away from the dangers of residence in the Scandinavian North. By the time of Hákon Hákonarson's expedition to Scotland in 1263, Caithness had been securely turned into an integral part of the medieval Scottish kingdom.

Ed.: Fordun, Johannes de. *Chronica gentis Scotorum*. Ed. William F. Skene. Edinburgh: Edmonston and Douglas, 1871–72; Johnston, A. W., and A. Johnston. *Diplomatarium Katanense et Sutherlandense: Caithness and Sutherland Records*. Viking Club. Old-Lore Series, 10. London: Viking Society for Northern Research, 1909. **Tr.**: Taylor, Alexander Burt, trans. *The Orkneyinga Saga*. Edinburgh: Oliver and Boyd, 1938; Hermann Pálsson and Paul Edwards, trans. *Orkneyinga Saga: The History of the Earls of Orkney*. Harmondsworth: Penguin, 1981. **Lit.**: Calder, James T. *Sketch of the Civil and Traditional History of Caithness from the Tenth Century*. Wick: Rae, 1887; rpt. 1971; Gray, James. *Sutherland and Caithness in Saga-Time*. Edinburgh: Oliver and Boyd, 1922; Crawford, Barbara E. "Peter's Pence in Scotland." In *The Scottish Tradition: Essays in Honour of Ronald Gordon Cant*. Ed. G. W. S. Barrow. St. Andrews University Publications, 60. Edinburgh: Scottish Academic Press; London: Chatto & Windus, 1974, pp. 14–22; Crawford, Barbara E. "The Earldom of Caithness and the Kingdom of Scotland, 1150–1266." *Northern Scotland* 2.2 (1976–77), 97–117; rpt. with some additions in *Essays on the Nobility of Medieval Scotland*. Ed. K. J. Stringer. Edinburgh: Donald, 1985, pp. 25–43; Chesnutt, Michael. "*Haralds Saga Maddaðarsonar*." In *Specvlvm Norroenvm: Norse Studies in Memory of Gabriel Turville-Petre*. Ed. Ursula Dronke *et al.* Odense: Odense University Press, 1981, pp. 33–55; Cowan, Edward J. "Caithness in the Sagas." In *Caithness: A Cultural Crossroads*. Ed. John R. Baldwin. Edinburgh: Scottish Society for Northern Studies, 1982, pp. 75–85; Nicolaisen, William F. H. "Scandinavians and Celts in Caithness: The Place-Name Evidence." In *Caithness: A Cultural Crossroads*, pp. 75–85; Waugh, Doreen J. "Caithness Place-Names." *Nomina* 8 (1984), 15–28; Waugh, Doreen J. "A Detailed Account of Some Caithness Place-Names." *Scottish Language* 4 (1985), 37–90; Crawford, Barbara E. "The Making of a Frontier: The Firthlands from the Ninth to the Twelfth Centuries." In *Firthlands of Ross and Sutherland*. Ed. John R. Baldwin. Edinburgh: Scottish Centre for Northern Studies, University of Edinburgh, 1986, pp. 33–46; Batey, Colleen E. *Freswick Links, Caithness. A Re-appraisal of the Late Norse Site in Its Context*. 2 vols. British Archaeological Reports, British Series, 179.i–ii. Oxford: B.A.R, 1987; Batey, Colleen E. "Viking and Late Norse Caithness: The Archaeological Evidence." In *Proceedings of the Tenth Viking Congress*. Ed. James E. Knirk. Universitetets Oldsaksamlings Skrifter, ny rekke, 9. Oslo: Universitetets Oldsaksamling, 1987, pp. 131–48; Waugh, Doreen J. "The Place-Names of Canisbay, Caithness." *Northern Scotland* 7.2 (1987), 99–111; Macgregor, Lindsay J., and Barbara E. Crawford, eds. *Ouncelands and Pennylands: The Proceedings of a Day Conference Held in the Centre for Advanced Historical Studies, St. Andrews on 23 February 1985*. St. John's House Paper, 3. St. Andrews: St. John's House, University of St. Andrews, 1987; Crawford, Barbara E. *Scandinavian Scotland*. Scotland in the Early Middle Ages, 2. Studies in the Early History of Britain. Leicester: Leicester University Press, 1987.

Barbara E. Crawford

[**See also**: *Orkneyinga saga*; Scotland, Norse in]

Calendar and Time Reckoning. The sun year played an important part in the conception of time in medieval Scandinavia. There was a time of light and a time of darkness, and both summer and winter solstices were ritually marked. But the year was also a framework of social activities, and we would be wrong in assuming that the year was just time.

The old Nordic concept of the year was *ár*. As a time indicator, it comprised the solar year, but, like many other key concepts in the semantic field of temporal and spatial categories, it had multiple reference. First and foremost, *ár* was a qualitative rather than quantitative entity, concerning the content and the yield of the year as much as its length. *Ár* meant "fertility" and "abundance" and was related to the cycle of farming life. The best wishes for one another and for society was *ár og friðr*, "abundance and peace." Apart from meaning "peace," *friðr* also denoted kinship, friendship, and love. The yield of the year was not only a question of the harvest but also the ability to harvest in the proper and peaceful country of friends. This required a law. The law was decided at the *þing*, or people's assembly. The *þing* was not just a place, but also a time of the year. It was the time when news and goods were exchanged, and when the calendar for next year was determined.

As a time indicator, the half-year was of equal importance. It would be wrong to say that the year was divided into two. Rather, summer and winter made up the year. If we regard the year from the point of view of the yield, the summer was production time, and winter consumption time.

The transition from summer to winter and vice versa was socially marked. Even today, the Icelanders celebrate the first summer day (sometime in April), and in Norway the 14th of April is still called *sommermål* 'summer measure.' The passage of time implied recurrent leaps from one qualitative state to another.

The dual nature of the year can be read directly from the old month names. In the summer half-year, beginning mid-April, most months were named after economic activities. During winter, from mid-October, most months had noneconomic names. In summer, there was a "sowing month," a "sheep month," and a "hay month," for instance. At the point of intersection between summer and winter, there was a "slaughtering month" in the pastoral areas of Iceland, Norway, and Sweden, while the agricultural country of Denmark had a "seeds month." In winter, there was a "*yule* month," and months like *þorri* (*Torre* or *Torsmåned*), *gói* (*Gjö* or *Gøjemåned*), and "single month." The point is that these months hardly were months in our sense of the term. Rather, they indicated seasons of particular activities. In summer, most activities were connected to production. In winter, various rituals had more significance than economics. *Þorri* and *gói* are of obscure origin, and may derive from a prehistoric calendar. There were sacrifices connected with them, and even today a *þorrablót*, literally "sacrifice," is the name of a popular, revitalized feast in Iceland held in February. The *yule* month is the time of the ancient celebration of winter solstice, conflated with the Christian Christmas in the Middle Ages.

Like the solar year, the day was also marked by a cyclical character. It comprised a time of light and a time of darkness. Thus, the day was defined by the visible movements of the sun, directly acknowledged in its name, *sólarhringr*, or "sun-ring." Apart from being divided into day and night, the *sólarhringr* was divided into eight parts, named by the cardinal directions. Each eighth had a name, which either referred to a physical fact, like *miðdegi* 'midday,' or a meal, like *dag-mál* and *nátt-mál* ("day-" and "night-meal"). Meal, or *mál*, also meant measure, and clearly activities like eating were measures of the time of the day.

From a modern point of view, neither the months nor the meals were precise indicators of time. Yet in the medieval Nordic perspective, they were by no means imprecise. Hay month occurred when time was ripe for the harvest; and *dag-mál* happened when the first meal of the day was taken. Thus, time reckoning was generally connected to social activities rather than to abstract notions of time. When the Julian calendar was introduced in the wake of Christianity, attempts were made to calibrate the two scales, but in popular usage the old names of months, days, and meals persisted.

An example of calibration was found in the *rímstaf* 'rhyme-stave,' a calendar stave known also from southern parts of Europe, but assuming a separate Nordic identity. The stave had a summer side and a winter side, upon which both the old feasts and the new Christian holidays were marked by various symbols. It was in use among Scandinavian peasants until the 17th century, and is the oldest known example of an abstract measuring of time that was truly popular.

Generally, in medieval Scandinavia time was measured from the ego standing at the center of its own world. Time of the day was measured either by the position of the sun on the horizon or by the meal one was to have. Time of the year was measured according to social activities, as defined by people. The scale was qualitative rather than quantitative. This distinction also obtained for the prevailing concepts of history, where the Christian intervention of an absolute chronological scale only very slowly replaced the relative scale of qualitatively defined time spaces that made up the popular notions of history.

Lit.: Nilsson, Martin P. *Primitive Time-Reckoning*. Lund: Gleerup, 1920; Beckman, N. "Isländsk och medeltida skandinavisk tideräkning." In *Tidsregning*. Ed. Martin Nilsson. Nordisk kultur, 21. Stockholm: Bonnier; Oslo: Aschehoug; Copenhagen: Schultz, 1934, pp. 5–76; Hastrup, Kirsten. *Culture and History in Medieval Iceland: An Anthropological Analysis of Structure and Change*. Oxford: Clarendon, 1985.

Kirsten Hastrup

Carving: Bone, Horn, and Walrus Tusk.

Carved objects in bone, horn, and walrus tusk are known from the Viking Age and the Christian Middle Ages. Walrus ivory was a very valuable material that became particularly prevalent after the Norse colonization of Greenland from the end of the 10th century onward. Whalebone was most suitable when the carver needed larger slabs. Animal horn was used throughout the Middle Ages, especially for drinking vessels, which might also be decorated with carving. To some extent, carvings may have been inspired by ivory carvings from more southern areas, but the expensive ivory of the African elephant was late in coming to the Nordic countries, and was little used.

In contrast to the art of wood carving, carving in bone, horn, and tusk was restricted to small objects by the limited size of the material. But the same four categories of carving are found: incised work, relief, openwork, and sculpture in the round. Our knowledge of this art is based on a limited number of objects and on information from written sources. Many of the objects, however, are difficult to date.

1. NORWAY. The decorated objects in bone known from the early Viking Age, combs and other items from the 9th and 10th centuries, have a simple, incised ornamentation of circles, dots, and lined borders. Animal heads also occur. Similarly, the decorative styles of the late Viking Age also appear on small objects in bone. The decoration may consist of plaited ribbons and animal ornamentation. But only a few objects preserved are of certain Norwegian origin.

There is rather more Norwegian material from the Christian Middle Ages, although the majority of these objects are doubtless lost. Almost without exception, the most representative carvings (of walrus ivory) are now found in museums outside Norway. On stylistic grounds, these objects have been assigned to Norway and the North Sea area. These pieces include objects for ecclesiastical purposes and the treasures of affluent people, suitable as gifts between kings and other prominent persons. It is probable that alongside these rich examples there always existed less luxurious objects with simpler decoration.

The form of many of these objects is adapted to the natural shape of the walrus tusk. They are long and slender pieces, either straight or curved, and tapering at one end. They were hollowed out and, among other things, have been used as bugles or reliquaries. The outside may be chamfered in different ways, making them, for example, octagonal in cross-section. The carved ornamentation in relief that decorates the outside of the older pieces in particular has a dense, intricate pattern. On some of the objects, it is possible to recognize the figure-of-eights and animal figures marking the latest period style (Urnes style) of the Viking Age, while the dragon wings, vines, and lions are distinctive of the Romanesque style, in particular as expressed on the portals of Norwegian stave churches. Some of the carvings even show the characteristic pattern known from many of the church portals of a foliate scroll emerging from the mouth of a beast and following an undulating path, with spirally coiled lateral branches inhabited by four-legged animals and winged dragons in complicated interlacing.

Some objects seem to point to workshops in the city of Niðaróss (Trondheim), since the motifs and the style of the ornamentation are similar to the stone carver's art as expressed there in the 12th century. This ornamentation includes scrolls intertwined with small lions and beasts. Examples include the head of a staff, possibly an abbot's staff (Tau cross), and a bugle. The head of the staff (Fig. 6), dated to the end of the 12th century, is said to have been found on the island of Munkholmen, near Trondheim, the earlier site of a Benedictine abbey (Niðarholmr). The frisky lions prancing among the spirals have a strange, caricature-like appearance. According to the collector, the bugle (Fig. 7) was one of the treasures of the church of Sainte-Chapelle in Paris. A runic inscription, dated to the 13th century, confirms the Nordic origin. This piece may have been a gift from a Norwegian to a French king. It is uncertain, however, whether the carving and the runes have a Norwegian or Icelandic origin.

The head of a crozier (Fig. 8) has been found in Garðar on Greenland, in the grave of Jón smyrill ("merlin"), who was bishop there from 1188 to his death in 1209. The actual crook ends in a large tuft of lobed leaves, a motif commonly found in the carving on Norwegian stave churches. The rest of the ornamentation consists of simple geometrical patterns. In addition to Niðaróss in Norway, Greenland and Iceland have been suggested as countries of origin.

Views also differ concerning the origin of a large number of chessmen in walrus ivory, found on the island of Lewis in the Hebrides (Figs. 9a and 9b). The different categories of figures,

6. Head of a staff made of walrus tusk, probably end of the 12th century. From the isle of Munkholmen, near Trondheim. National Museum, Copenhagen.

7. Bugle (?) of walrus tusk; 13th century. Said to have belonged to Sainte-Chapelle, Paris. Museo Nazionale di Firenze.

8. Head of crozier, walrus tusk; end of 12th century. From Garðar, Greenland. National Museum, Copenhagen (after the exhibition catalogue, "Norwegian Medieval Art Abroad" [Oslo: University Museum of National Antiquities, 1972]).

9. Two of the chessmen from the Isle of Lewis, Hebrides. King and Bishop with decorated chairbacks. British Museum, London.

10. The head of Bishop Páll's (d. 1211) crozier, found in his grave. National Museum of Iceland, Reykjavík. Photo: Gísli Gestsson.

11. Pax from Breiðabólstaður church, Iceland; probably carved in the 15th century. National Museum of Iceland, Reykjavík. Photo: Gísli Gestsson.

12. Detail of an Icelandic drinking horn, showing St. Nicholas. Private collection, Norway. Photo: E.M. Magerøy.

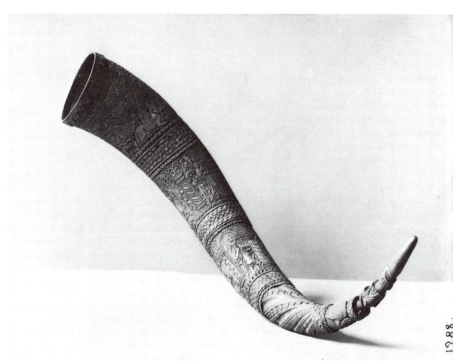

13. "The Trinity Horn" from Iceland; first half of the 16th century. Staatliche Kunstsammlungen, Dresden. Photo: The Oslo Museum of Applied Art (Teigen, 1930).

kings, queens, bishops, knights, and soldiers (castles), are easily recognizable by their clothing; the pawns are octagonal, with a rounded top. The figures seem to be more typically Norwegian than English. This opinion applies in particular to the ornamentation (foliate scrolls and animals) on some of the chairbacks of the sitting figures. There are similarities with the wood carving from the stave churches and with the stone carving on the older parts of the cathedral in Trondheim (1150s). The figures must have been carved in the second half of the 12th century, or a little later.

Walrus ivory was also used for lidded boxes. Three such boxes with carving in relief are thought to have a Norwegian origin. They show human figures and beasts entwined in foliage richly supplied with rows of beads and bunches of grapes. Their style places these carvings at the transition into the Gothic period.

Crucifixes made from walrus tusk are also known, although only fragments remain. The style of a torso of Christ crowned with thorns, found buried in the ground in Trondheim, is English-influenced Early Gothic. Of greater repute is the much discussed "Bitter Christ," a torso of Christ from a crucifix, a work of high quality. Recent studies have shown, however, that this work may well have an English origin.

A bugle shows Gothic influence, and has been linked to Erik of Pomerania because his Norwegian coat-of-arms is carved in one of the three blazons. The other two blazons are empty, and were possibly intended to hold his Danish and Swedish coats-of-arms. He was chosen in 1389 as king of Norway, and of Sweden and Denmark in 1396. The ornamentation has been carved with a minute exactness of detail, but the motifs include foliate decoration in Romanesque style.

A much discussed diptych of walrus ivory, bone, and wood is known as "Christian I's portable altar," although it has not been possible to establish that it ever belonged to this monarch, king of Denmark and Norway 1448/50–1481. This carving is considered to be of Norwegian workmanship from the 14th century. It consists of small plates of walrus tusk, framed in the same material. The two wings did not belong together originally, however, and the outer frame of oak is secondary. All the plates are carved in relief, with representations of figures in Gothic-type frames of different patterns. The one wing, depicting scenes from the life of St. Ólafr, with female saints and Christian symbols on the surrounding frame, seems somewhat older than the other wing because of the Romanesque details in the ornamentation, among other reasons. This wing, at least, may possibly have an Icelandic origin. The other wing depicts scenes from the life of the Virgin Mary. Both the figures and the ornamented frame reflect a purer High Gothic style.

A splendid work in walrus ivory is the head of a crozier known as the Digby crozier after its English owner. It is of Romanesque type, with rich Gothic and Romanesque foliage, both in relief on the shaft and as openwork branches extending from the main spiral. At the center of the vegetation, we find two figures, on the one side of the crozier a bishop in vestments, and on the other side a king with a crown, orb, and long-handled axe, undoubtedly St. Ólafr. For stylistic and iconographical reasons, this work is assumed to have a Norwegian origin and to be an archbishop's crozier from Niðaróss. The main indication that the staff originated in Norway at the end of the 14th century is the mixture of older and newer styles.

A small box made from elephant ivory, with lid and gilded silver mountings, is said to have been presented, together with its content of relics, to the cathedral of Lund by Bishop Aslak Bolt of Bergen sometime before 1430. The box is hollowed out of one piece of ivory, but the outside surface is octagonal. Each of the eight sides contains two standing figures in relief on a crosshatched background: Christ and the twelve apostles, the Virgin Mary and Child, and John the Baptist and St. Anthony. The style is Late Gothic, of North German character, and the box is thought to have been carved in Bergen, where the German influence was especially strong in the late Middle Ages.

Most Norwegian drinking horns preserved from the Middle Ages belong to the goldsmith's art, since most of the various kinds of ornamentation are found on the metal mountings, while the horns themselves are smooth and unornamented. The known carvings are relatively late, and almost all have a simple, incised ornamentation that classifies them as folk art. They were, in fact, carved in Norwegian rural districts, and the style of the carving is retarded, making it difficult to establish if the horns are actually from the Middle Ages. The ornamentation is dominated by the Romanesque twining stems and leaves.

2. ICELAND. In Iceland, excavations have brought to light some bone combs dating from the 10th and 11th centuries and ornamented with incised lines. An example of sculpture in the round is a statuette in whalebone of a sitting, male figure. This sculpture was found in a grave from the 10th century, together with pieces for a game and a die. The statuette may have been the "king" in a board game.

We know the name of a female Icelandic carver from Christian times, the priest's wife Margrét in haga ("the skillful"), who did work for Páll Jónsson, bishop of Skálholt from 1195 until his death in 1211. His biography, *Páls saga biskups*, written shortly after his death, says that Margrét was the most skillful carver in the whole of Iceland. Specially mentioned examples are a particularly fine crozier of walrus tusk presented to the archbishop of Niðaróss, and a splendid altar frontal obviously designed to be made in gold, silver, and walrus tusk. Nothing has been preserved, however, that can be said with certainty to come from her hands. Of particular interest in this connection is the head in walrus tusk of Bishop Páll's crozier, found in his grave (Fig. 10). The volute ends in an animal head (dragon or lion?) gaping above a small figure of a lion carved in relief on the staff itself. Several small lions in relief are carved on a raised belt farther down the staff.

Croziers of walrus tusk are also mentioned in written sources referring to Iceland's other bishopric, Hólar, but only from the 14th century.

Paxes (*tabulae pacis*) of different materials were commonly used in Icelandic churches from the middle of the 14th century onward. Several known examples are of whalebone, with religious motifs carved in relief. A particularly large and elaborate tablet survives from Breiðabólstaður church in Fljótshlíð in southern Iceland. The tablet (Fig. 11), which is composed of several plates like the diptych linked to Christian I (see above under NORWAY), seems to have its roots in the same tradition as the "St. Ólafr wing" of the diptych, but the work is simpler and less detailed. The tablet was probably carved in the 15th century. There are only four plates, with narrative scenes under tripartite arches: the Annunciation, the Nativity, the Road to Calvary, and the Resurrection. The smaller, dividing plates carry pictures of Christ on the Cross and Christ as the Savior of the World.

The Icelandic drinking horns are of particular interest. At least ten of the thirty-three horns known today from the period

1400–1650 have carving from the Middle Ages.

Characteristic of this carving is the division into zones or belts, as found on many South European, more or less typical Byzantine, elephant ivories ("oliphants") from the early Middle Ages. The different zones containing representations of figures are separated by belts of ornamentation. The figures are often placed in chains of rings or scrolls, sometimes under arches supported by columns. Several of the horns are twisted toward the narrow end.

Most of the carving of the figures, ornamentation, and inscriptions is in low relief. The figures are biblical characters or male or female saints (Fig. 12), and the inscriptions contain prayers to God and to the saints. In the Middle Ages, ceremonial drinking was essential in religious gatherings, and there is no doubt that the horns were used for "commemorative drinking," where people toasted the Trinity, the Virgin Mary, the apostles, and the saints.

Icelandic handicraft was marked by conservatism. The human figures on the horns reflect a range of styles, Early, High, and Late Gothic. The most ancient motifs reflect the Romanesque style. The last applies especially to "a dragon devouring a human being" and "a human being in combat with an animal" carved in the round on some of the tips of the horns, as well as fabulous creatures in relief. The ornamentation shows a strong tendency to keep to one of the distinctive types of Romanesque plant ornamentation found in Europe and to ancient motifs of interlaced ribbons. The inscriptions are sometimes decorative, like the ornamentation, and many are interlaced with ribbons. The most commonly used script developed from the Gothic minuscules.

Some of the horns are of normal size and must have come from inland cows or oxen, but some are very large and may have been imported from the Continent. The largest known Icelandic drinking horn, called the "Trinity Horn" from its principal motif, is about 86 cm. long and may be an aurochs horn (Fig. 13). It has a great wealth of carved motifs, probably dating from the first half of the 16th century. The main source of inspiration is found in books of hours and liturgical books printed in Paris around 1500. This horn must be one of the latest from the Middle Ages. Many of the horns from after 1550 are also marked by the medieval tradition, as the carvers kept mainly to ancient motifs and features of style.

Lit.: (a) Norway: Madden, Frederic. "Historical Remarks on the Introduction of the Game of Chess into Europe, and on the Ancient Chessmen Discovered in the Isle of Lewis." *Archaeologica* 24 (1832), 203–91; Mackeprang, M. "Det saakaldte Christian I.s Rejsealter." *Aarbøger for nordisk Oldkyndighed og Historie* 16 (1926), 77–98; Kielland, Thor. "Sculpture sur os norvégienne et islandaise depuis l'antiquité jusqu'aux temps modernes." *Acta Archaeologica* 1 (1930), 111–20; *Norrøn beinskurd. Benskulptur og hornarbeider i Norge og på Island ca. 500–1850.* Oslo: Kunstindustrimuseet i Oslo, 1930 [exhibition catalogue]; Rydbeck, Monica. "Medeltida elfenbensskulpturer i Lunds universitets historiska museum." *Meddelanden från Lunds universitets historiska museum 1930/31* (1931), 91–104, esp. p. 98; Berg, Knut. "Fra museer og samlinger III. Digby-staven. Norsk benskurd fra middelalderen?" *Kunst og Kultur* 40 (1957), 217–30 [includes illustrations]; Grieg, Sigurd. "Tre norske drikkehorn fra middelalderen." *Viking. Tidsskrift for norrøn arkeologi* 23 (1959), 87–109 [no summary, but illustrations]; Lasko, P. E. "A Romanesque Ivory Carving." *British Museum Quarterly* 23 (1960), 12–16 + pl.; Philippowich, Eugen V. *Elfenbein. Ein Handbuch für Sammler und Liebhaber.* Braunschweig: Klinkhardt & Biermann, 1961, pp. 95–9; Blindheim, Martin. "En romansk Kristus-figur av hvalross-tann." *Årbok 1968–69,* Kunstindustrimuseet i Oslo (1969), 22–32 [English summary];

Beckwith, John. *Ivory Carvings in Early Medieval England.* London: Miller & Medcalf, 1972, pp. 158–62; Blindheim, Martin, ed. *Norge 872–1972: Norwegian Medieval Art Abroad.* Oslo: University Museum of National Antiquities, 1972 [exhibition catalogue]; Blindheim, Martin. "Scandinavian Art and Its Relations to European Art Around 1200." In *The Year 1200: A Symposium.* New York: Metropolitan Museum of Art, 1975, pp. 434–5 + pl.; Christiansen, Tage E. "Ivories: Authenticity and Relationships." *Acta Archaeologica* 46 (1975), 119–33, esp. pp. 123–33: "The New York Cross and the Oslo Christ." (b) Iceland: *Norrøn beinskurd. Benskulptur og hornarbeider i Norge og på Island ca. 500–1850.* Oslo: Kunstindustrimuseet i Oslo, 1930 [exhibition catalogue]; Kristján Eldjárn. *Kuml og haugfé úr heiðnum sið á Íslandi.* Reykjavik: Bókaútgáfan Norðri, 1956, Fig. 156 [index to text and list of illustrations in English]; Kristján Eldjárn. *Ancient Icelandic Art.* Munich: Reich, 1957 [esp. illustration nos. 1 and 23 with texts]; Philippowich, Eugen V. *Elfenbein,* pp. 117–8 [see above]; Kristján Eldjárn. *Hundrað ár í Þjóðminjasafni.* Reykjavik: Menningarsjóður, 1962 [illustration nos. 1 and 21]; Magerøy, Ellen Marie. "Utskårne drikkehorn fra Island." *By og bygd. Norsk Folkemuseums årbok.* Oslo: Norsk Folkemuseum, 1970, pp. 67–96 [English summary]; Kristján Eldjárn. "Beinspjald með helgum sögum." In *Afmælisrit til Steingríms J. Þorsteinssonar.* Ed. Aðalgeir Kristjánsson et al. Reykjavik: Leiftur, 1971, pp. 97–112 [English summary]; Magerøy, Ellen Marie. "Margrét in haga." In *Kvinnenes kulturhistorie. Fra antikken til år 1800.* Ed. Kari Vogt et al. Oslo: Universitetsforlaget, 1985, vol. 1, pp. 147–8 [bibliography p. 326]; Magerøy, Ellen Marie. *Islandske drikkehorn med middelalderskurd.* The Ása G. Wright Memorial Lectures, 7. Reykjavik: National Museum of Iceland, 1987 [English summary].

Ellen Marie Magerøy

[See also: Iconography; Viking Art; Wood Carving]

Chancery. Because of their firm organization and continuity, episcopal seats and cathedrals have been models for lay society, and often placed their resources at the disposal of royal power. Letters providing donations, granting privileges, and so on, written in the king's name for the benefit of spiritual institutions, were often composed on the initiative of the recipient.

The king's and the nation's chancery took place within the framework of *capella regis,* the clerics who acted as servants to the king. Chancery varies in its forms during the period and is difficult to follow without thorough investigation.

In Denmark, the activity of the chancery can be observed from the beginning of the 12th century. Chancellorship came into existence in the latter part of the 12th century, based probably on a German model. During the 13th century, the chancellor was an important adviser, for a long time a bishop and later, during the ecclesiastical controversy, a learned cleric. Apart from that pattern, the organization appears to have been vague. After a period of decline, a new chancellorship came into existence at the end of the 14th century held by the bishop of Roskilde, soon becoming an honorary position (*summus cancellarius*). A *justitiarius,* a secular man, who gradually came to be called the chancellor of the kingdom, had the reponsibility for written judgments. The current chancery was administered through a royal chancellor and his assistants, clerics with spiritual sinecures. From around 1510, we know of an instruction for the chancery, which at that time had been moved to the castle in Copenhagen, where a royal archive was established.

In Norway, chancery appears around the middle of the 12th century. One hundred years later, it was highly developed within the framework of the *hirð.* A *capella regis* was organized with papal approval. It was exempted from episcopal jurisdiction and comprised fourteen churches throughout the kingdom, especially the Apostles' Church in Bergen and Mary's Church in Oslo. As a part of the displacement of the government work from Bergen to Oslo, the chancellorship of 1314 combined with the provostship in Mary's Church. That the chancellor and the scribe signed outgoing letters makes it possible to follow closely the activities, which were performed with striking continuity by a small number of clerics. From the end of the 14th century, when the government work was moved to Denmark, the establishment changed character. Except for Erik of Pomerania's time, when the bishop of Oslo was the chancellor, the work was conducted by the provost of Mary's Church, but corresponded more to the Danish *justitiarius*.

In Sweden in the beginning of the 13th century, bishops occasionally carried the title of chancellor, but this designation must probably be taken as an indication of the extent to which the weak royal power was dependent on the support of the Church in the performance of written activity. Royal chancery does not take firm shape until 1278, when a royal position as dean of the cathedral of Linköping was established. During the following half-century, the chancellorship united with this position. Around the middle of the 14th century, Magnus Eriksson created with papal assistance a *capella regis* modeled on that in his Norwegian kingdom: he could have at his disposal bursaries for his clerics, and the chancellorship was held by a dean. After declining, chancery almost ended during the time of Margrethe and Erik of Pomerania, when the government work was moved to Denmark. During the revolt of the 1430s, Bishop Thomas Simonsson in Strängnäs played an important role in the national council (*riksråd*). He administered a new great seal and guarded the kingdom's documents. His successors from the 1470s also had the duty of keeping the register of the kingdom and were called "chancellor of the realm," receiving a small fief in compensation. The domestic leaders, whether they were kings or regents, had their own organization of clerics, connected to themselves but often supported through ecclesiastical charges. The chancery in the service of the kingdom took place through collaboration among the regent, the archbishop in Uppsala, and the bishop in Strängnäs.

Lit.: Christensen, William. *Dansk Statsforvaltning i det 15. Århundrede.* Copenhagen: Gad, 1903 [with a review by Erik Arup in *Historisk tidsskrift* (Denmark) 7.4 (1902–04), 529–58]; Agerholt, Johan. "Gamal brevskipnad." In *Meddelelser fra det Norske Riksarkiv* 3. Kristiania [Oslo]: Gundersen, 1933, pp. 395–813; Jörgensen, Poul Johs. *Dansk Retshistorie. Retskildernes og Forfatningsrettens Historie indtil sidste Halvdel af det 17. Århundrede.* Copenhagen: Gad, 1947; Sjödin, Lars. "Urkundsstilar från 1300–talets mitt." In *Archivistica et mediaevistica Ernesto Nygren oblata.* Stockholm: Norstedt, 1956, pp. 366–407; Schück, Herman. *Ecclesia Lincopensis. Studier om Linköpingskyrkan under medeltiden och Gustav Vasa.* Stockholm Studies in History, 4. Stockholm: Almqvist & Wiksell, 1959; Schück, Herman. "Kansler och capella regis under folkungatiden." *Historisk tidskrift* (Sweden) 83 (1963), 133–87; Carlsson, Gottfrid, et al. "Kansler." *KLNM* 8 (1963), 232–9; Carlsson, Gottfrid, et al. "Kansli." *KLNM* 8 (1963), 239–43; Hamre, Lars, et al. "Kapellgeistlighet." *KLNM* 8 (1963), 256–64; Skyum Nielsen, Niels. "Den danske konges kancelli i 1250'erne." In *Festskrift til Astrid Friis.* Ed. Svend Ellehøj et al. Copenhagen: Rosenkilde & Bagger, 1963, pp. 225–45; Skyum Nielsen, Niels. "Kanslere og skrivere i Danmark 1250–1282." In *Middelalderstudier. tilegnede Aksel E. Christensen på tresårdagen 11. September 1966.* Ed. Tage E. Christiansen et al. Copenhagen: Munksgaard, 1966, pp. 141–84; Schück, Herman.

Rikets brev och register: Arkivbildande, kansliväsen och tradition inom den medeltida svenska statsmakten. Skrifter utgivna av Svenska Riksarkivet, 4. Stockholm: Liber, 1976; Bagge, Sverre. *Den kongelige kapellgeistlighet 1150–1319.* Bergen: Universitetsforlaget, 1976; Blom, Grethe Authén. "Tønsbergkanselliet 1355–1365." In *Festskrift til Alfred Jakobsen.* Ed. Jan Ragnar Hagland et al. Trondheim: Tapir, 1987, pp. 12–24.

Herman Schück

[**See also:** Diplomatics; Royal Adminstration and Finances]

Childbirth *see* Pregnancy and Childbirth

Christian Poetry

1. EAST NORSE: SWEDEN. The earliest poetry comprises the rhymed Offices in Latin, which became popular in the 13th century, and are based largely on established European liturgical models. The earliest extant Offices honor the local saints Botvid, Sigfrid, Erik, and Henrik. The first named Office writer was Brynolf Algotsson, bishop of Skara 1278–1317. Four Offices are attributed to him (but see Milveden 1972): two in honor of the Swedish saints Helena of Skövde and Eskil to be used on their feast days, one to the Blessed Virgin, and one celebrating the donation to Brynolf by the Norwegian king Håkon Magnússon of the relic of a thorn from the Crown of Thorns at Lödöse in 1304. Nikolaus Hermansson, bishop of Linköping 1374–1391, is another acclaimed author of Offices, the most famous of which is an Office in honor of his close friend St. Birgitta, composed sometime before her canonization in 1391, perhaps in connection with the official consecration of Vadstena monastery in 1384. The Office, which makes constant use of Birgitta's revelations to illustrate her life, was widely used in the dioceses of Linköping (and thus at Vadstena), Skara, and Åbo. The alliterating opening lines of the antiphon for the first vespers are among the most celebrated lines of medieval Swedish poetry:

> Rosa rorans bonitatem
> stella stillans claritatem.
> Birgitta, vas gratiae,
> rora celi pietatem,
> stilla vite puritatem
> in vallem miseriae.
> [Rose, distilling dew of goodness/ Star, pouring out
> brightness./ Birgitta, vessel of grace,/ Bedew the piety of
> heaven,/ Pour purity of Life,/ Into the vale of tears.]

Nikolaus also wrote Offices in honor of St. Anne, whose cult was strong during the 14th century, and St. Ansgar, who enjoyed a revival of interest in the liturgy during the later Middle Ages. According to the documents relating to his canonization, Nikolaus is also the author of the two first nocturnes and six antiphons and responses of an Office in honor of St. Erik.

Another Office praising St. Birgitta was written by Birger Gregersson, archbishop of Uppsala 1367–1383, and is known by the words of its opening antiphon "Birgitte matris inclite." A carefully composed work that makes elegant use of cursus, it was used in the dioceses of Uppsala, Strängnäs, and Västerås, and also in Brigettine daughter-houses abroad. It gives details of her childhood, travels abroad, and miracles. Birger is also author of an t>fot

RISIAPETY**73

Office to St. Botvid. At least four Offices were written in the 15th century by the Vadstena monk Johan Benekinsson (d. 1461), although only one survives, praising St. Birgitta's daughter, Katarina Ulfsdotter.

Other works composed by medieval ecclesiastics are preserved, in some cases in modified form, in the collection *Piae cantiones ecclesiasticae et scholasticae veterum episcoporum* published by Jakob Fenno in Åbo in 1582.

Several poems in the vernacular survive, most of which are translations or adaptations of foreign material (ed. Klemming 1881–82). The majority are poems and prayers addressed to Christ and the major saints, but there are a small number of rhymed meditations about the Virgin Mary, biblical stories in verse, and an exposition on the Ten Commandments attributed to Bishop Henrick Tidemanni (d. 1500). *Den vises sten*, which survives in MS Cod. Ups. C 391, written at Vadstena around 1379, consists of twelve verses and tells of a precious stone with healing powers, which is guarded by a wise man. Poetic renderings of the popular didactic work *Kroppens och själens träta* ("Debate of the Body and Soul") exist in Swedish and Danish versions; and *En syndares omvändelse* ("The Conversion of a Sinner"), which tells in *knittelvers* of the salvation of a sinner Vratislaus, is the first known drama in Swedish.

DENMARK. Rhymed Offices in Latin include celebrations of Kjeld of Viborg, Knud (Cnut) Lavard, St. Knud, and Thøger of Vestervig. About 1196–1206, Anders Sunesen, archbishop of Lund, composed his *Hexaemeron*, an exegetical account of the creation, comprising twelve books in 8,040 hexameters. With the growth of the cult of the Virgin toward the end of the Middle Ages, a large number of hymns and sequences about her were produced; many of them are contained in prayer books, and some include musical notation. In Latin, for instance, Jacobus Nicholai wrote a *Salutacio beate Marie virginis gloriose* (MS SKB A 39, late 14th century); and in the 15th century, there are additional hymns and sequences. There are extant translations into Danish of some of the popular Marian sequences, such as one on the seven joys of the Virgin (*Gaude virgo, mater Christi*, translated first into Swedish and then into Danish), and the Franciscan sequence *Stabat mater*. Several macaronic poems also survive. Two vernacular poets are known by name: Per Ræf Lille, who is thought to have composed five lengthy Marian poems contained in MS AM 76 8vo ("En klosterbog" ["A Monastic Book"], ca. 1470–1500; the MS also contains a litany poem in twelve verses); and Herr Michael, priest at St. Alban's Church at Odense, who wrote a poetic version of Alanus de Rupe's meditation on the rosary entitled *En skøn udlægning af den salige jomfru Marias rosenkrans* ("A Glorious Exposition of the Blessed Virgin Mary's Rosary") in 1496, just after the founding of a Rosicrucian brotherhood in Odense. He is also the author of a poetic collection about the creation, *Om tingenes skabelse* ("On the Creation of Things"), and an account of the stages in human life, *Om menneskets levned* ("On the Life of Man"). All three works were printed in Copenhagen in 1514–1515.

Apart from the Marian poetry, a small but significant amount of poetry exists in the vernacular. Within the general tradition of the ballad, there is a distinct group, the legendary ballads; circulated in Sweden as well as Denmark, these contain stories from the life of Christ, saints' legends, and visionary tales. From the early 14th century, there is a fragment of a rhymed version of the Gospel of Nicodemus (*Gammeldansk digt*; SKB A 115, ca. 1325). *Gamle Sang, som haffue varit brugt i Paffuedommet*, which was compiled by Hans Thomesen in 1569, contains five medieval hymns

in Danish, the most celebrated of which is the *dagvise* that opens with the words *Den signede dag som wi nu see*. The earliest known copy of this hymn is in Swedish (MS Cod. Ups. C 4, ca. 1450), and contains five of the nine verses that survive in two 16th-century versions in Danish. Whether the poem is originally Swedish or Danish is an open question. Other didactic poems dealing with death and judgment occur in early 16th-century books printed by Gotfred of Ghemen in Copenhagen.

Ed.: **(a) Sweden:** Klemming, G. E., ed. *Svenska Medeltids dikter och rim*. Samlingar utgivna av Svenska fornskrift-sällskapet, 78–80. Stockholm: Norstedt, 1881–82; Klemming, G. E., ed. *Hymni, sequentiæ et piæ cantiones in regno Sueciæ olim usitatæ*. Stockholm: Norstedt, 1885–87; Undhagen, Carl-Gustaf, ed. *Birger Gregerssons Birgitta-officium*. Samlingar utgivna av Svenska fornskrift-sällskapet, ser. 2, Latinska skrifter, 6. Uppsala: Almqvist & Wiksell, 1960; Lundén, Tryggve, ed. *Sankt Nikolaus av Linköping Kanonisationsprocess*. Stockholm: Bonnier, 1963. **Lit.: (a) Sweden:** Moberg, Carl Allan. *Über die schwedischen Sequenzen. Eine musikgeschichtliche Studie*. Veröffentlichungen der Gregorian Akademie zu Freiburg in der Schweiz, 13. Uppsala: Almqvist & Wiksell, 1927; Lundén, Tryggve. "Sankt Brynolf, biskop av Skara." *Credo* (1945–46), 73–124; Lundén, Tryggve. "Medeltidens religiösa litteratur." In *Ny illustrerad svensk litteraturhistoria*. Ed. E. N. Tigerstedt. Stockholm: Natur och Kultur, 1955, vol. 1, pp. 122–222; Klockars, Birgit. "Medeltidens religiösa litteratur." In *Ny illustrerad svensk litteraturhistoria*. 2nd rev. ed. Stockholm: Natur och Kultur, 1967, vol. 1, pp. 125–225; Milveden, Ingmar. "Zu den liturgischen Hystorie in Schweden." Diss. University of Uppsala, 1972; Wright, Stephen K. "The Oldest Swedish Play: Sources, Structure, and Staging of the *De uno peccatore qui promeruit gratiam*." *Journal of English and Germanic Philology* 87 (1988), 49–72; **(b) Denmark:** Frandsen, Ernst. *Mariaviserne. Den lyriske Madonnadigtning fra Danmarks Middelalder, belyst gennem Bønnebøgernes Prosatexter*. Copenhagen: Levin & Munksgaard, 1926; Lehmann, Paul. *Skandinaviens Anteil an der lateinischen Literatur und Wissenschaft des Mittelalters*. 1. Stück. Sitzungsberichte der Bayerischen Akademie der Wissenschaften, Philosophisch-historische Abteilung, Jahrgang 1936, Heft 2. Munich: Bayerischen Akademie der Wissenschaften, 1936; 2. Stück. Jahrgang 1937, Heft 7. Munich: Bayerischen Akademie der Wissenschaften, 1937; Billeskov Jansen, F. J. *Danmarks Digtekunst*. Copenhagen: Munksgaard, 1944, vol. 1, pp. 44–51; Friis, Oluf. *Den danske litteraturs historie*. Copenhagen: Hirschprung, 1945–, vol. 1, pp. 162–77; Toldberg, Helge. "Lidt om Hr. Michaels and Per Ræff Lilles kilder." *Danske Studier* (1961), 17–39; Bruun, Henry. *Den middelalderlige dagvise*. Studier fra Sprog- og Oldtidsforskning, 257. Copenhagen: Gad, 1965.

Bridget Morris

[**See also:** Ansgar, St.; Ballads; Birgitta, St.; Erik, St.; Knud, St.; Nicodemus, Gospel of; Saints' Lives; Sunesen, Anders; Vadstena; Vadstena Language]

2. WEST NORSE. The earliest surviving examples of poetry on Christian themes are fragments of skaldic poetry from the conversion period (ca. A.D. 1000). Perhaps the oldest is Christian only by context: *Landnámabók* reports that Glúmr Þorkelsson, the grandson of the settler Svartkell, "prayed to the cross" with these lines (ed. Jakob Benediktsson 1968: 1:56):

Gott ey gǫmlum mǫnnum
gott ey œrum mǫnnum
[Good luck to the old; / Good luck to the young.]

There is no reason to doubt the authenticity of these lines, but their relationship to the cross remains to be demonstrated. An early *dróttkvætt* verse by Þorvaldr Koðránsson (ed. Finnur Jónsson 1912–15: 1A:110, 1B:105) on the difficulties of evangelization is preserved in *Kristni saga* (ed. Kahle 1905: 9) and *Óláfs saga Tryggvasonar en mesta* (ed. Ólafur Halldórsson 1958, 1961: A1:290–1). Þorvaldr complains about the mockery he received at the *Alþingi*, and concludes with a curse on the pagan priestess Friðgerðr. Three *helmingar* preserved in *Skáldskaparmál* also deal with 10th-century Christianity. Þorbjǫrn dísarskáld ("skald of the *dís*") describes the baptism of a Viking (ed. Finnur Jónsson 1912–15: 1A:144, 1B:135), and Eilífr Goðrúnarson's poem contains an obscure kenning for Christ (ed. Finnur Jónsson 1912–15: 1A:152, 1B:144). Þorleifr jarlsskáld ("earl's skald") tells how God helped Sven Haraldsson (Forkbeard) in battle (ed. Finnur Jónsson 1912–15: 1A:141, 1B:133; ed. Jónas Kristjánsson 1956: 219), but this poem may be later and wrongly attributed to Þorleifr.

Poetry from the 11th century reflects the growing acceptance and influence of Christianity in Iceland and Norway. The transition is typified by Hallfreðr Óttarsson, the favorite skald of Óláfr Tryggvason. Hallfreðr was inclined to paganism, but struggled to accept the new faith at his king's insistence. *Hallfreðar saga* records a series of four verses that show his gradual and reluctant response to Óláfr's command that he give up the old gods (ed. Finnur Jónsson 1912–15: 1A:168–9; 1B:158–9; ed. Einar Ól. Sveinsson 1939: 157–9). According to the saga, Hallfreðr composed a *vísa* suggesting that he preferred the old religion. Óláfr told him the poem was bad and ordered him to do better. Hallfreðr responded with two *vísur* reluctantly acknowledging that he was now a Christian, but Óláfr demanded a firmer assent and finally got it in two more *vísur* denouncing the old gods in favor of Christ. But this concession was not the end of the matter: a few years later, Hallfreðr was told to compose the now-lost *Uppreistardrápa as a penance for backsliding (ed. Einar Ól. Sveinsson 1939: 178). His last poem, composed on his deathbed, expresses his fear of hellfire and a somewhat shaky confidence that God will save him (ed. Finnur Jónsson 1912–15: 1A:173, 1B:163; ed. Einar Ól. Sveinsson 1939: 199).

The poets of the generation after Hallfreðr show a calmer attitude. *Skáldskaparmál* attributes a *helmingr* praising Christ as the creator of the world to the law-speaker Skapti Þóroddsson (ed. Finnur Jónsson 1912–15: 1A:314, 1B:291; ed. Finnur Jónsson 1931: 158). Sighvatr Þórðarson, the prolific skald favored by St. Óláfr Haraldsson, left two *lausavísur* on Christian themes: a prayer for his daughter on the occasion of her baptism (ed. Finnur Jónsson 1912–15: 1A:268–9, 1B:248; ed. Ólafur Halldórsson 1958: 2:699–700) and a poem on the afterlife (ed. Finnur Jónsson 1912–15: 1A:270, 1B:250; ed. Bjarni Aðalbjarnarson 1941–51: 2:295). More significant is his *Erfidrápa* or memorial lay on St. Óláfr (ed. Finnur Jónsson 1912–15: 1A:257–65, 1B:239–45; ed. Bjarni Aðalbjarnarson 1941–51: 2:267, 329–30, 366–7, 379–84, 386, 393–4, 406, 409–10; 3:20–1). According to *Den store saga* (ed. Ólafur Halldórsson 1958, 1961: 2:839–41), Sighvatr composed this poem on his deathbed. He had planned to use a *stef* from *Sigurðar saga*, but a woman who had seen Óláfr in a dream told him that the saint wanted a *stef* based on *uppreistarsaga* (the story of creation). Sighvatr presumably complied, although the *stef* does not survive in the fragmentary text. The *Erfidrápa* is a synthesis of the traditional encomiastic style and hagiography. It gives a lengthy and vivid account of Óláfr's victories in battle, but it also reports the miraculous solar eclipse associated with his death, and says that Óláfr, who now is with God, works many miracles and should be honored as a saint.

Þórarinn loftunga ("praise-tongue") developed this theme in his *Glælognskviða*, also composed shortly after Óláfr's death (ed. Finnur Jónsson 1912–15: 1A:324–7, 1B:300–1; ed. Bjarni Aðalbjarnarson 1941–51: 2:399, 406–8). If the poem was composed for Sven Álfífuson, as *Heimskringla* says, then it can be dated between 1031 and 1035. Its subject is Óláfr's sanctity: Þórarinn enumerates Óláfr's posthumous miracles and boldly urges Sveinn to pray to the saint for permission to rule Norway. *Glælognskviða* shows that within five years of Óláfr's death he was venerated not only as a saint, but also as *rex perpetuus*, the guardian of the land and the source of its prosperity. *Glælognskviða* is also remarkable for its meter, which is *kviðuháttr*, the syllable-counting development of *fornyrðislag* best known from *Ynglingatal* and the poetry of Egill Skalla-Grímsson. Perhaps Þórarinn used this meter ironically to insinuate that the bastard Sveinn's rule was an undesirable break in the Yngling line.

Arnórr Þórðarson did not compose poetry on specifically religious themes, but his poems are Christian in the sense that they presume a Christian point of view. Apart from a fragmentary *helmingr* on St. Michael's role in the Last Judgment (ed. Finnur Jónsson 1912–15: 1A:353, 1B:326), his poetry consists of conventional *drápur* in praise of the rulers who employed him. But three of these poems (*Rǫgnvaldsdrápa*, *Þórfinnsdrápa*, and the *Erfidrápa* on Haraldr harðráði ["hard-ruler"] Sigurðarson) conclude with a prayer for the salvation of the man celebrated. Arnórr may also be responsible for a metrical innovation that had tremendous influence on the development of Christian skaldic poetry. His poem *Hrynhenda*, on King Magnús inn góði ("the good") Óláfsson, is the earliest example of *hrynhent* meter, a modification of the *dróttkvætt* that expands the line to eight syllables and four stresses. The other features of the *dróttkvætt* are retained, but the longer line results in a falling meter, clearly in imitation of the trochaic dimeter used for Latin hymns and sequences. The *Hafgerðingadrápa* (ed. Finnur Jónsson 1912–15: 1A:177, 1B:167; ed. Jakob Benediktsson 1968: 132, 133, 134), a six-line fragment that *Landnámabók* ascribes to "a Christian man from the Hebrides," was long thought to be the earliest example of *hrynhent*, but recent scholarship suggests that this anonymous Christian's prayer for a safe voyage is much younger than the text surrounding it. It may have been composed as late as the 12th century. Another versified prayer, the famous *kredda* of Þrándr in Gata, is found in *Færeyinga saga* (ed. Finnur Jónsson 1912–15: 1A:211, 1B:202; ed. Ólafur Halldórsson 1987: 110). The form of the seven-line verse and its integrity have been disputed; it seems to be in a rough *ljóðaháttr* and may well be intact, the number of lines being symbolic. Far from being a *credo*, it is a simple, popular invocation of God, Christ, and the angels, to be prayed in the morning or at the beginning of a journey.

The 12th century was the great age of Christian skaldic poetry. This period included the consolidation of the Church in Iceland, and the establishment of the monasteries made possible both the learning on which the poetry is based and the preservation of texts. The 12th-century skalds had access to European education, but were not yet dominated by European literary tastes. Their poetry is utterly Christian yet authentically skaldic. These poems are significant for study of the *drápa* form because they are the earliest *drápur* preserved as intact units rather than as *vísur* scattered piecemeal through the prose texts. Most of them were recorded in MSS as soon as they were composed, so the texts are much less corrupt than the non-Christian poetry modified by the memories of generations of skalds. Even though their authors must have been known when they were copied down, the anonymity of the majority of these texts reflects the monastic ideal of humility and a sharp departure from a tradition in which the names of skalds were remembered longer than their verses. Two Christian *drápur* dating from the first half of the century are *Plácítus drápa* and *Geisli*. *Plácítus drápa*, the earliest written text of a skaldic poem, survives in AM 673b 4to, dated at about 1200 (ed. Finnur Jónsson 1912–15: 1A:607–18, 1B:606–22). The *drápa* lacks both its beginning and conclusion, but fifty-five *vísur* survive. It is closely related to *Plácítus saga*, which tells the legend of the Roman martyr Placidus (St. Eustace), who was converted when he realized that the hart he was hunting was Christ in disguise. The anonymous author of *Plácítus drápa* uses complex mythological kennings, although perhaps from an antiquarian point of view. But he augments the skaldic vocabulary by introducing words from everyday speech. Other innovations include the use of direct discourse and sentences that stretch across the boundaries of *helmingar* and even *vísur*.

Geisli, an encomium on St. Óláfr, is the earliest skaldic poem to which a definite date can be assigned, as well as the earliest *drápa* preserved intact (ed. Finnur Jónsson 1912–15: 1A:459–73, 1B:427–45). It was composed by Einarr Skúlason, who recited it at a gathering of dignitaries including kings Eysteinn, Sigurðr, and Ingi, and Archbishop Jón in the Trondheim cathedral in 1153. The complete text survives in two 14th-century codices, *Flateyjarbók* (GkS 1005 fol.) and *Bergsbók* (Stock. Perg. fol. no. 1). Einarr adheres strictly to the traditional *drápa* form, but he avoids mythological kennings and instead creates elaborate metaphors and symbols based on Scripture and the Latin poetry of his time. He was a priest, and the influence of theology and the liturgy is evident. The primary theme of *Geisli* is the typological relationship between Óláfr and Christ, and Einarr develops this theme with remarkable subtlety and complexity.

The MS AM 757a 4to, dating from the 14th century, is an anthology of Christian poetry of the 12th and 13th centuries, containing three long *drápur* and parts of three more. *Harmsól* (ed. Finnur Jónsson 1912–15: 1A:562–72, 1B:548–65), a late 12th-century *drápa*, is ascribed to the anonymous "Gamli kanóki" ("old canon"), presumably an Augustinian affiliated with the house at Þykkvabœr in Iceland. The theme of *Harmsól* is sin and redemption, but the skald also deals with salvation history from the birth of Christ to the Last Judgment, with particular emphasis on the latter. The tone is both personal and homiletic, and the style is traditionally skaldic. The author's diction shows the influence of *Plácítus drápa* and *Geisli*, but he also makes his own contribution to the development of a vocabulary for Christian poetry.

Leiðarvísan (ed. Finnur Jónsson 1912–15: 1A:618–26, 1B:622–33), an anonymous *drápa* roughly contemporary with *Harmsól*, is a skaldic version of the legend of the Sunday epistle. It tells of the letter that miraculously fell from heaven, urging the observance of Sunday as the sabbath. The skald proceeds to recount a series of events in salvation history that supposedly occurred on Sunday. *Leiðarvísan* lacks the beauty of *Harmsól*, but its structure is impressive. The *drápa* form is neatly symmetrical and is based on ingenious repetitions of the symbolic number three.

Líknarbraut (ed. Finnur Jónsson 1912–15: 2A:150–9,

2B:160–74) is a much later poem, probably composed in the late 13th century. Primarily a poem on the Cross, it reflects changing sensibilities in its portrayal of Christ as crucified and suffering rather than as creator or judge. The influence of earlier Christian *drápur* (especially *Harmsól* and *Leiðarvísan*) is apparent, but the poem also owes much to the Good Friday liturgy. The learned content of *Líknarbraut* leaves little doubt that the skald was a cleric, and its devotional tone suggests that it may have been composed for use in paraliturgical celebrations.

Heilags anda vísur (ed. Finnur Jónsson 1912–15: 2A:160–2, 2B:175–80) also dates from the 13th century. The poem is fragmentary, but the eighteen surviving *vísur* are a free translation of the Latin *Veni creator spiritus*, the earliest translation of a hymn into Icelandic and the only known translation of a foreign poem into the *dróttkvætt* meter. *Máríudrápa* (ed. Finnur Jónsson 1912–15: 2A:464–72, 2B:496–505) is a 14th-century *dróttkvætt* poem in praise of Mary. Its mood is joyful, and the themes conventional. It draws on Latin poetry, especially the *Gaude virgo gratiosa*, the *Ave Maria*, and the *Ave maris stella*, and emphasizes Mary's role as queen of heaven and mediatrix of grace. The last poem in AM 757a 4to is *Gyðingsvísur* (ed. Finnur Jónsson 1912–15: 2A:539–41, 2B:597–99), a fragmentary 14th-century poem of eight *vísur*. The verses tell the beginning of a well-known miracle of Our Lady: a Christian borrows from a Jew, giving a picture of the Virgin as security. When they later dispute the repayment of the loan, the picture testifies on the Christian's behalf, whereupon the Jew and his family are converted.

Sólarljóð (ed. Finnur Jónsson 1912–15: 1A:628–40, 1B:635–48), probably the best known of the Christian poems, is one of the most difficult. The earliest MSS date from the 17th century, but it may have been composed as early as the 13th. The meter of the poem is *ljóðaháttr*, an eddic meter rarely used by the skalds. *Sólarljóð* is an archaizing poem, an attempt to present a Christian theme in eddic style. It has affinities with *Hávamál* and *Vǫluspá* as well as with European vision literature. The speaker is a dead man who appears to his son in a dream to show him the way to salvation. The father gives precepts for good living and describes his own life and death, followed by a visionary account of the otherworld. The mythological imagery makes the poem vivid and powerful, but also adds an element of obscurity.

As the Church became more firmly established in Iceland and monastic education replaced the traditional skaldic training, the vernacular poets gradually abandoned the ideals of the old style and began to base their work more and more on continental models. The *dróttkvætt* gave way to *hrynhent* as the predominant meter, and kennings gradually disappeared. Eysteinn Ásgrímsson's *Lilja*, composed in the mid-14th century (ed. Finnur Jónsson 1912–15: 2A:363–95, 2B:390–416), epitomizes this development. *Lilja* is a *hrynhent drápa* of 100 *vísur* on the main events of salvation history, focusing especially on the conflict between good and evil. Its structure employs number symbolism, and the diction reflects principles of classical rhetoric. *Lilja* has been widely admired and imitated from the time of its composition down to the present; it gave the nickname *liljulag* to the *hrynhent* meter.

About the same time Eysteinn composed *Lilja*, there was a movement in the Icelandic Church to canonize Bishop Guðmundr inn góði ("the good") Arason. This development is significant for literary history because following the translation of his relics in 1344 a number of poets joined in the effort to promote his cause. In 1345, Arngrímr Brandsson, the abbot of Þingeyrar, composed a long *hrynhent* poem (ed. Finnur Jónsson 1912–15: 2A:348–62, 2B:371–89) in Guðmundr's honor as well as a few *dróttkvætt vísur* (ed. Finnur Jónsson 1912–15: 2A:362–3, 2B:389–90). Einarr Gilsson contributed a *dróttkvætt* poem on the bishop (ed. Finnur Jónsson 1912–15: 2A:397–404, 2B:418–29), a *hrynhent* poem (ed. Finnur Jónsson 1912–15: 2A:404–8, 2B:429–34), and his *dróttkvætt Selkolluvísur* (ed. Finnur Jónsson 1912–15: 2A:408–11, 2B:434–40) narrating one of the bishop's miracles. Árni Jónsson, the abbot of Munkaþverá, composed a very long (seventy-nine *vísur*) *Guðmundardrápa* in *hrynhent* (ed. Finnur Jónsson 1912–15: 2A:412–30, 2B:440–61), but all to no avail: Guðmundr's sanctity was never officially recognized. The poetry of Guðmundr's enemy Kolbeinn Tumason (ed. Finnur Jónsson 1912–15: 2A:38–40, 2B:47–9) also dates from this period. The subject of most of these *lausavísur* is Kolbeinn's troubled relationship with Guðmundr, but his three *vísur* in *runhent* (*fornyrðislag* with end-rhyming couplets), composed on his deathbed, rival the feeling and artistry of *Lilja*.

Lilja steered Icelandic poetry so powerfully out of the skaldic tradition and into the high Middle Ages that never again could *dróttkvætt* and the kenning regain their normative role. The poets of the 14th and 15th centuries, all anonymous, drifted nearer to the mainstream of European poetry. Their themes followed the trends of the times: they wrote about the saints (the apostles and Roman martyrs), the Cross, and above all, the Virgin Mary. There is metrical variation and experimentation, but all based on Latin hymn meters rather than on traditional skaldic measures. Two important anthologies of the poetry of the later Middle Ages are the MSS AM 713 4to and AM 721 4to; the poems have been edited by Finnur Jónsson (1912–15: 2) and Jón Helgason (1936–38). The 14th- and 15th-century poems have received almost no scholarly attention, and need much comparative study before their relationship to continental literature can be fully understood.

Ed.: Eiríkr Magnússon, ed. and trans. *Eysteinn Ásgrímsson. Lilja*. London: Williams & Norgate, 1870; Unger, C. R., ed. *Postola sögur. Legendariske fortællinger om apostlernes liv deres kamp for kristendommens udbredelse samt deres martyrdød*. Christiania [Oslo]: Bentzen, 1874; Gudbrand Vigfusson and F. York Powell, eds. *Corpus Poeticum Boreale: The Poetry of the Old Northern Tongue from the Earliest Times to the Thirteenth Century*. 2 vols. Oxford: Clarendon, 1883; Kahle, B., ed. *Isländische geistliche Dictungen des ausgehenden Mittelalters*. Heidelberg: Winter, 1898; Kahle, B., ed. *Kristnisaga, Þáttr Þorvalds ens Víðförla, Þáttr Ísleifs Biskups Gizurarsonar, Hungrvaka*. Altnordische Saga-Bibliothek, 11. Halle: Niemeyer, 1905; Rydberg, Hugo, ed. *Die geistlichen Drápur und Dróttkvætt Fragmente des Cod. AM 757, 4to*. Copenhagen: Møller, 1907; Finnur Jónsson, ed. *Den norsk-islandske skjaldedigtning*. Vols. 1A–2A (tekst efter håndskrifterne) and 1B–2B (rettet tekst). Copenhagen and Christiania [Oslo]: Gyldendal, 1912–15; rpt. Copenhagen: Rosenkilde & Bagger, 1967 (A) and 1973 (B); Björn M. Ólsen, ed. *Sólarljóð. Gefin út með skíringum og athugasemdum*. Safn til sögu Íslands og íslenzkra bókmenta, 5.1. Reykjavik: Hið íslenzka bókmentafjelag, 1915; Jón Þorkelsson and Sigurður Nordal, eds. *Kvæðasafn eptir nafngreinda íslenzka menn frá miðöld*. Reykjavik: Hið íslenzka bókmentafjelag, 1922–27; Finnur Jónsson, ed. *Edda Snorra Sturlusonar*. Copenhagen: Gyldendal, 1931; Jón Helgason, ed. *Íslenzk miðaldakvæði. Islandske digte fra senmiddelalderen*. Vols. 1.2–2. Copenhagen: Levin & Munksgaard; Munksgaard, 1936–38; Einar Ól. Sveinsson, ed. *Vatnsdœla Saga*. Íslenzk fornrit, 8. Reykjavik: Hið íslenzka fornritafélag, 1939; Johnsen, Oscar Albert, and Jón Helgason, eds. *Saga Óláfs konungs hins helga. Den store saga om Olav den hellige efter Pergamenthåndskrift i Kunghga Biblioteket i Stockholm nr. 2 4to, med varianter fra andre håndskrifter*. 2 vols. Oslo: Dybwad, 1930–33; Bjarni Aðalbjarnarson, ed. *Heimskringla*. 3 vols. Íslenzk fornrit, 26–8. Reykjavik: Hið íslenzka fornritafélag, 1941–51; Guðni Jónsson, ed. *Byskupa Sögur*. 3 vols. Reykjavik: Íslendingasagnaútgáfan; Haukadalsútgáfan, 1948; Mageröy, Hallvard, ed. *Glælognskvida av Toraren Lovtunge. Bidrag til nordisk filologi av studerende ved Universitetet i Oslo*, 12. Oslo: Aschehoug, 1948; Jónas Kristjánsson, ed. *Eyfirðinga sǫgur*. Íslenzk fornrit, 9. Reykjavik: Hið íslenzka fornritafélag, 1956; Ólafur Halldórsson, ed. *Óláfs saga Tryggvasonar en mesta*. 2 vols. Editiones Arnamagnæanæ, ser. A, vols. 1–2. Copenhagen: Munksgaard, 1958, 1961; Jakob Benediktsson, ed. *Íslendingabók. Landnámabók*. Íslenzk fornrit, 1. Reykjavik: Hið íslenzka fornritafélag, 1968; Black, Elizabeth Lynn. "*Harmsól*: An Edition." B. Litt. Thesis. Oxford University, 1971; Tate, George Sheldon. "*Líknarbraut*: A Skaldic *Drápa* on the Cross." Diss. Cornell University, 1974; Tucker, John. "A Study of the *Plácítus saga*, Including an Edition, and of Its Relation to the *Plácítus drápa*." B. Litt. thesis. Oxford University, 1974; Harry, Margaret Rose. "Kristni saga. AM 371, 4to (*Hauksbók*) and AM 105, fol.: An Edition of the Texts, with an Introduction, Notes, and an English Translation." Diss. University of Toronto, 1979; Chase, Martin. "Einar Skúlason's *Geisli*: A Critical Edition." Diss. University of Toronto, 1981; Stefán Karlsson, ed. *Guðmundar sögur biskups, 1: Ævi Guðmundar biskups: Guðmundar saga A*. Editiones Arnamagnæanæ, ser. B, vol. 6. Copenhagen: Reitzel, 1983; Ólafur Halldórsson, ed. *Færeyinga saga*. Reykjavik: Stofnun Árna Magnússonar, 1987. **Tr.**: Hollander, Lee M., trans. *Old Norse Poems: The Most Important Non-Skaldic Verse Not Included in the Poetic Edda*. New York: Columbia University Press, 1936; Turville-Petre, G., and E. S. Olszewska, trans. *The Life of Gudmund the Good, Bishop of Holar*. Coventry: Viking Society for Northern Research, 1942; Pilcher, Charles Venn, trans. *Icelandic Christian Classics*. Melbourne: Cumberledge; Oxford: Oxford University Press, 1950; Hollander, Lee M., trans. *Heimskringla: History of the Kings of Norway*. Austin: University of Texas Press; American-Scandinavian Foundation, 1964; Hermann Pálsson and Paul Edwards, trans. *The Book of Settlements (Landnámabók)*. University of Manitoba Icelandic Studies Series, 1. Winnipeg: University of Manitoba Press, 1972; Johnston, George, trans. *The Faroe Islanders' Saga*. [Ottawa]: Oberon, 1975. **Bib.**: Hollander, Lee M. *A Bibliography of Skaldic Studies*. Copenhagen: Munksgaard, 1958. **Lit.**: Jón Þorkelsson. *Om Digtningen på Island i det 15. og 16. Århundrede*. Copenhagen: Høst; Kahle, B. "Das Christentum in der altwestnordischen dichtung." *Arkiv för nordisk filologi* 17 (1900–01): 1–40, 97–160; Hjelmquist, Theodor. "Var Hallfreðr vandræðaskáld arian." *Arkiv för nordisk filologi* 24 (1908), 155–79; Paasche, Fredrik. *Kristendom og kvad: En studie i norrøn middelalder*. Oslo: Aschehoug, 1914; rpt. in his *Hedenskap og kristendom: Studier i norrøn middelalder*. Oslo: Aschehoug, 1948, pp. 29–212; Møller, Arne. *Islands Lovsang gennem tusind Aar*. Copenhagen: Gyldendal, 1923; Pilcher, Charles Venn. "*Sólarljóð*: An Icelandic Divine Comedy." *Canadian Journal of Religious Thought* 1 (1924), 499–508; Jón Helgason, "Bæn Glúms Þorkelssonar." In *Festskrift til Finnur Jónsson 29 Maj 1928*. Ed. Johs Brøndum-Nielsen et al. Copenhagen: Levin & Munksgaard, 1928, pp. 377–84; Sigurður Skúlason. "'At láta fyr(ir) róða.'" *Acta Philologica Scandinavica* 6 (1931–32), 199–202; Ohrt, F. "Sunnr at Urðarbrunni." *Acta Philologica Scandinavica* 12 (1937–38), 91–101; Einar Ól. Sveinsson. "Íslenzk sálmaþýðing frá 13. öld: Heilags anda vísur." *Skírnir* 116 (1942), 140–50; Hollander, Lee M. *The Skalds: A Selection of Their Poems with Introduction and Notes*. Princeton: Princeton University Press; American-Scandinavian Foundation, 1945; rpt. Ann Arbor: University of Michigan Press, 1968; Seip, Didrik Arup. "Plácítúsdrápa." *Studier i nordisk filologi* 39 (1949), 20–4 [vol. 39 ed. Carl-Eric Thors. Skrifter utgivna av Svenska

Litteratursällskapet i Finland, 323. Helsingfors: Mercator, 1949; Festschrift for Prof. Pipping]; Skard, Vemund. "Harmsól, Plácítusdrápa og Leiðarvísan." *Arkiv för nordisk filologi* 69 (1953), 97–108; Turville-Petre, G. *Origins of Icelandic Literature.* Oxford: Clarendon, 1953; rpt. 1967; Stefán Einarsson. *A History of Icelandic Literature.* New York: Johns Hopkins University Press; American-Scandinavian Foundation, 1957; Lange, Wolfgang. *Studien zur christlichen Dichtung der Nordgermanen 1000–1200.* Palaestra, 222. Göttingen: Vandenhoeck & Ruprecht, 1958; See, Klaus von. "Christliche Skaldendichtung." *Göttingische gelehrte Anzeigen* 213 (1959), 81–97; rpt. in his *Edda, Saga, Skaldendichtung: Aufsätze zur skandinavischen Literatur des Mittelalters.* Heidelberg: Winter, 1981; Foote, P. G. "Þrándr and the Apostles." In *Medieval Literature and Civilization: Studies in Memory of G. N. Garmonsway.* Ed. D. A. Pearsall and R. A. Waldron. London: Athlone, 1969, pp. 129–40; rpt. in *Aurvandilstá: Norse Studies.* Ed. Michael Barnes et al. Viking Collection, 2. Odense: Odense University Press, 1984, pp. 188–98; Foote, Peter G. "A Note on Þránd's kredda." In *Afmælisrit Jóns Helgasonar 30. júní 1969.* Ed. Jakob Benediktsson et al. Reykjavík: Heimskringla, 1969, pp. 355–63; rpt. in *Aurvandilstá,* pp. 199–208; Hill, Thomas D. "Eve's Light Answer: Lilja, Stanzas 16–17." *Mediaeval Scandinavia* 2 (1969), 129–31; Astås, Reidar. "Om Leiðarvísan: En studie i norrøn kristendomsforståelse." *Edda* (1970), 257–76; Hill, Thomas D. "Number and Pattern in Lilja." *Journal of English and Germanic Philology* 69 (1970), 561–7; Weber, Gerd Wolfgang. "Die Christus-Strophe des Eilífr Goðrúnarson." *Zeitschrift für deutsches Altertum und deutsche Literatur* 99 (1970), 87–90; Schottmann, Hans. *Die isländische Mariendichtung: Untersuchungen zur volkssprachigen Mariendichtung des Mittelalters.* Münchener germanistische Beiträge, 9. Munich: Fink, 1973; Foote, Peter G. "Observations on 'Syncretism' in Early Icelandic Christianity." *Árbók Vísindafélags Íslendinga* (1974), 69–86; rpt. in *Aurvandilstá,* pp. 84–100; Hallberg, Peter. *Old Icelandic Poetry: Eddic Lay and Skaldic Verse.* Trans. Paul Schach and Sonja Lindgrenson. Lincoln and London: University of Nebraska Press, 1975; Jón Helgason. "Heyr þú himna smiðr." *Opuscula* 5. Bibliotheca Arnamagnæana, 31. Copenhagen: Munksgaard, 1975, pp. 219–24; Marchand, James W. "Two Christian Skaldic Fragments." *Arkiv för nordisk filologi* 91 (1976), 138–52; Turville-Petre, E. O. G. *Scaldic Poetry.* Oxford: Clarendon, 1976; Frank, Roberta. *Old Norse Court Poetry: The Dróttkvætt Stanza.* Islandica, 42. Ithaca and London: Cornell University Press, 1978; Tate, George S. "Good Friday Liturgy and the Structure of Líknarbraut." *Scandinavian Studies* 50 (1978), 31–8; Jakob Benediktsson. "Hafgerðingadrápa." In *Specvlvm Norroenvm: Norse Studies in Memory of Gabriel Turville-Petre.* Ed. Ursula Dronke et al. Odense: Odense University Press, 1981, pp. 27–32; Louis-Jensen, Jonna. "Vǫndr er Máría mynduð." In *Specvlvm Norroenvm,* pp. 328–36; Foote, Peter G. "Latin Rhetoric and Icelandic Poetry: Some Contacts." *Saga och sed* (1982), 107–27; rpt. in *Aurvandilstá,* pp. 249–70; Tate, George S. "The Cross as Ladder: Geisli 15–16 and Líknarbraut 34." *Mediaeval Scandinavia* 11 (1978–79), 258–64; Frank, Roberta. "Skaldic Poetry." In *Old Norse–Icelandic Literature: A Critical Guide.* Ed. Carol J. Clover and John Lindow. Islandica, 45. Ithaca and London: Cornell University Press, 1985, pp. 157–96.

Martin Chase, S.J.

[See also: Arnórr Þórðarson jarlaskáld; Conversion; *Draumkvæde*; Einarr Skúlason; *Færeyinga saga*; Gamli kanóki; Hallfreðr Óttarsson; *Hallfreðar saga*; Kennings; *Landnámabók*; *Leiðarvísan*; *Lilja*; Miracles, Collections of; Óláfr, St.; *Óláfs saga helga*; *Óláfs saga Tryggvasonar*; *Plácítus saga* and *drápa*; Saints' Lives; Sighvatr Þórðarson; *Skáld*; Skaldic Meters; Skaldic Verse; *Snorra Edda*; *Sólarljóð*; Þórarinn loftunga]

Christian Prose

1. EAST NORSE: SWEDEN. Most of the extant religious prose was produced at the late 14th-century Brigettine foundation at Vadstena, and although other monastic and diocesan scriptoria did exist, few MSS from them survive. The great bulk of the vernacular prose literature consists of translations from Latin and in some cases from German, and was intended primarily for use by the Brigettine nuns. The surviving literature can be divided into several categories.

(a) Saints' lives, biographies, miracles, and canonization documents relating to the national saints are all in Latin, although some were later translated into the vernacular. The earliest saint's life is probably that of St. Botvid (d. ca. 1120), which was written in connection with the consecration of a church dedicated to him in 1176, although the earliest extant MS dates from the late 13th century. The most important collection of miracles concerns St. Erik, and contains some fifty miracles, many of which were written by a Dominican prior in Sigtuna, Israel Erlandsson, around 1300. The substantial material relating to the canonization of St. Birgitta, which took place in 1391, includes a life, testimonies of the many witnesses, and evidence of miracles after her death. In the vernacular, the oldest preserved religious work is a collection of saints' lives known as the *Fornsvenska legendariet* ("Old Swedish Legendary"), which was written by a Dominican cleric sometime between 1276 and 1307, and is based principally on Jacobus de Voragine's *Legenda aurea*.

(b) Revelation texts include some of the most original religious prose in Sweden. Petrus de Dacia (d. 1289), a Dominican from Visby who studied in Cologne and Paris, recorded his meetings and correspondence with the mystic Kristina of Stommeln in a work that reflects much of 13th-century spiritual and cultural attitudes. Two leaves containing St. Birgitta's revelations in her own hand survive in MS Cod. Holm A 65. The great bulk of her 700 or so revelations exists in copies in Latin, which are translations of her original utterances in Swedish, made by her confessors and gathered into eight books; there also exist translations of her revelations back into Swedish, which were undertaken during the 1380s for devotional use at Vadstena. A particular interest in mystical literature was shown by the Brigettine monk Jöns Budde of Nådendal monastery in Finland, who around 1480 translated into Swedish *Claustrum animae* (*Själens kloster*), some of the visions of St. Mechthild of Hackeborn, and the *Horologium sapientie* (*Gudeliga snilles väckare*) of Henry Suso. In the MS known as *Jöns Buddes bok* ("Jöns Budde's Book," MS Cod. Holm A 58, 1487–1491), there are, among other prose texts in Swedish, apocryphal legends, such as the vision of Tundale, the revelation concerning Guido's soul, excerpts from the work of St. Bernard, and part of Honorius of Autun's *Elucidarium*. Other mystical writings were translated into Swedish, most notably works by Bonaventure and Jean Gerson. Three works in particular, *Speculum virginum* (*Jungfruspegeln*, translated by Mathias Laurentii), Alanus de Rupe's meditation on the rosary (*Jungfru Marie psaltare*, translated by Johannes Matthei [d. 1521]), and the Vadstena Breviary *Cantus sororum* (*Jungfru Marie Örtagård*), are characterized by a marked asceticism and Marian devotion. Two tracts on the Passion date from the beginning of the 16th century: "Den korsfäste Jesu ljuvliga samtal med en syndare" ("The Wondrous Conversation of the Crucified Christ with a Sinner") and "Om Jesu lidandes bägare och hans blods utgjutelse" ("On the Cup of Jesus's Suffering and the Spilling of His Blood").

(c) Homiletic literature in Latin and Swedish comprises a significant part of the extant prose literature. Much of it is still unresearched. There are several collections of exempla that were available to preachers, such as the *Copia exemplorum* by Birgitta's confessor Mathias of Linköping (d. *ca.* 1350). The German collection *Seelentrost* (*Sjælinna thrøst*, "Solace of Souls") was translated around 1420 and is preserved in MS Cod. Holm A 108, which was written at Vadstena around 1440.

(d) Bible texts in Latin include parts of a commentary on the Apocalypse and a concordance to the Bible, both written by Mathias of Linköping. A Swedish paraphrase of the Pentateuch was written by an unidentified but certainly accomplished cleric at the beginning of the 14th century. It draws on patristic and scholastic writings, in particular Thomas Aquinas's *Summa theologicae*, but also shows considerable independence of its sources. There are translations of Judith, Esther, and 1 and 2 Maccabees by Jöns Budde in 1484, and of Joshua and Judges by Nikolaus Ragvaldi of Vadstena in about 1500. The New Testament translation was printed at the Royal Press in Stockholm in 1526, and the first translation of the entire Bible was the so-called *Gustaf Vasa's Bible*, printed in Uppsala in 1541, based mainly on Luther's 1534 translation.

(e) Theological manuals include *Summa de ministris et sacramentis ecclesiasticis* and *Suffragium curatorum*, guides to practical theology by the Dominican Laurentius Olavi (d. 1332), who was deacon in Uppsala; Bishop Brynolf of Skara's (d. 1317) work *Notulae Brynolfi*; and Mathias of Linköping's *Homo conditus*, a catechetical manual for preachers. In Swedish, there are a number of tracts for services and clerical instruction that deal with the sacraments, the mass, and Church ceremonies. There are also a number of prayer books in Latin and Swedish, many of them ornately decorated by Brigettine nuns.

DENMARK. Danish religious prose literature was produced in the diocesan and monastic schools, the most important scriptoria being at Lund and the Benedictine foundation of Skovkloster, near Næstved. The original collections are no longer intact, and very little of what is assumed to have been written now survives. Contemplation of the Passion and devotion to the Virgin are dominant features of later medieval prose literature.

(a) From the early Middle Ages, there are several saints' lives in Latin recording the pious deeds of devout clerics and kings, the most celebrated of whom is St. Knud (Cnut; d. 1086). Although not a candidate for canonization himself, Bishop Gunner of Viborg (d. 1251) had a biography written about him by a monk from the Cistercian monastery of Øm, near Silkeborg, and the same MS (DKB E don. var. 145 4to) contains a colorful account of the founding in 1165 of Øm monastery, entitled *Exordium carae insulae*. Several fragments of saints' lives and miracle collections survive in the vernacular; the most important are the collection known as *Hellige Kvinder* ("Holy Women"; MS SKB K 4), which contains several legends and miracles concerning female early Christian martyrs, and the *Mariager legendarium* (GkS [DKB] 1586 4to), which contains the lives of St. Jerome and St. Catherine of Siena, copied in 1488 by Niels Mogensen for a Brigettine nun, Lisbeth Hermansdatter, at Mariager monastery.

(b) Theological manuals and edificatory tracts include the Dominican Augustinus de Dacia's (d. 1285) guide to Christian doctrine entitled *Rotulus pugillaris* and an important collection of sermons by Matthias Ripensis, written at the end of the 13th century and preserved in two 15th-century copies, Cod. Ups. C 343 and C 356. Additional Dominican sermons and other religious

texts are contained in MS AM 76 8vo, dating from the end of the 15th century; this MS also includes the earliest extant copy of the *Elucidarium* in Danish, thought to have been translated around 1350. Another popular edificatory work, in similar style, is *Sydrak*. *Siæla trøst*, which was translated into Danish from Low German and is more popular in style than the Swedish version, is preserved in MSS Cod. Ups. C 529 and Cod. Holm A 109, both originally part of the same MS, written around 1425. Other edificatory works are included in the important MS AM 783 4to, written between 1430 and 1460 at the Augustinian monastery of Grinderslev. It contains contemplative works in Danish by St. Gregory, Thomas à Kempis, Bonaventure, and Suso. In fragmentary form, there are translations of the revelations of St. Birgitta.

(c) Of the Bible texts in the vernacular, only a fragment survives, dating from around 1475–1490 and containing a translation of the Vulgate from Genesis 2:9 to 2 Kings 23:18. It was probably translated in the late 15th century. In 1524, the New Testament was translated into Danish by Christiern Vinter and Hans Mikkelsen, and printed at Wittenberg; and the entire Bible, known as *Christian III's Bible*, was translated and printed in Copenhagen in 1550.

(d) Prayer books in the vernacular, which fostered private contemplation and prayer, were quite common among noblewomen in the later Middle Ages. The most ornately produced prayer book was that commissioned by Anna Brahe, abbess of the Brigettine monastery of Maribo, in 1497.

(e) Printing increased the distribution and number of religious books, especially liturgical books in Latin and Danish. In 1514, Christiern Pedersen (*ca.* 1480–1554) translated the prayers of the canonical hours, and in 1515, a book of homilies known as *Jærtegnspostil* ("Homilies with Exempla"), both of which were printed in Paris. Another influential pre-Reformation writer was Paul Helgesen (*ca.* 1480–1534).

Ed.: (a) Sweden: Most of the Swedish texts have been published in the series Samlingar utgivna av Svenska fornskrift-sällskapet, 1844–. **(b) Denmark**: Brandt, Carl Joakim, ed. *Dansk Klosterlæsning fra Middelalderen. 1. Henrik Susos Gudelig visdoms bog.* Copenhagen: Selskabet for Danmarks kirkehistorie, 1858–65; Knudsen, G., ed. *Sydrak.* Copenhagen: Universitets-jubilæets danske samfund, 1921–32; Nielsen, N., ed. *Sjælens trøst.* Copenhagen: Universitets-jubilæets danske samfund, 1937–52. **Lit.: (a) Sweden**: Gödel, Vilhelm. *Sveriges medeltidslitteratur. Proveniens. Tiden före Antikvitetskollegiet.* Stockholm: Nordiska Bokhandeln, 1916; Lundén, Tryggve. "Medeltidens religiösa litteratur." In *Ny illustrerad svensk litteraturhistoria.* Ed. E. N. Tigerstedt. Stockholm: Natur och Kultur, 1955, vol. 1, pp. 122–222; Klockars, Birgit. "Medeltidens religiösa litteratur." In *Ny illustrerad svensk litteraturhistoria.* Ed. E. N. Tigerstedt. 2nd rev. ed. Stockholm: Natur och Kultur, 1967, vol. 1, pp. 125–225. **(b) Denmark**: Gad, Tue. *Legenden i dansk middelalder.* Copenhagen: Dansk Videnskabs Forlag, 1961; Billeskov Jansen, F. J. *Dansk litteratur historie 1.* Copenhagen: Politiken, 1976; Kaspersen, Søren, et al. *Dansk litteraturhistorie. I. Fra runer til ridderdigtning, 800–1480.* Copenhagen: Gyldendal, 1984.

Bridget Morris

[**See also:** Amicus and Amileus; Bible; Birgitta, St.; *Elucidarius*; Erik, St.; Knud, St.; Miracles, Collections of; *Nicodemus, Gospel of*; *Old Swedish Legendary*; Petrus de Dacia; Prayer Books; Saints' Lives; Vadstena; Vadstena Language; *Visio Tnugdali*]

2. WEST NORSE. A considerable amount of religious prose has survived in Norse MSS in collections in Copenhagen, Reykjavik, Stockholm, Oslo, and elsewhere. Much of it was published in the 19th century, principally by C. R. Unger. Modern editions are available of some works; many of the MSS await publication. Any account of the religious prose must therefore be partial. New works are discovered from time to time, generally in fragmentary form: for example, the existence of a medieval version of the Book of Psalms, and of a Norse commentary on the Penitential Psalms, has been demonstrated in recent years. The earliest surviving MSS contain material of this kind: AM 732a VII 4to has an Easter Table, and dates from between 1121 and 1139; AM 237a fol., from the middle of the 12th century, contains fragments of homilies, while the somewhat younger AM 655 IX 4to has fragments of the sagas of the apostle Matthew and the saints Blasius and Placidus. It is not known for certain when religious prose began to be written in Norse; most probably, it followed on the establishment of schools and monasteries in Iceland and Norway, and thus dates from the middle of the 11th century onward. Much of it is anonymous: a few authors are known, particularly from Iceland in the latter part of the period, and some works have been attributed to known authors by critics past and present. Many Norse texts are little more than translations of Latin works, ancient and medieval; and some of those texts for which a precise source cannot be traced rely heavily on one, or several, Latin texts. Original works of religious prose are relatively uncommon.

Much of what has survived falls into the common medieval categories of homiletic and hagiographical literature. From the period around 1200, two books of homilies survive, commonly referred to as the "Icelandic homily book" (Stock. Perg. 4to no. 15) and the "Norwegian homily book" (AM 619 4to). The Norwegian book has a de tempore sequence that makes considerable use of the 8th-century homiliarium by Paulus Diaconus, which comprises homilies by Gregory, Augustine, Bede, and others. Gregory is particularly well represented in Norse literature. His thirty-fourth homily is found in a number of MSS, including the Norwegian and Icelandic books and the above-mentioned AM 237a fol., while there is a translation of his Dialogues in the defective MS AM 677 4to (early 13th century). The Icelandic book likewise contains homilies for particular days in the Church calendar, or concerning individual saints; many of these homilies can also be traced, in whole or in part, to known Latin homilies by the above authors and others. Homilies are also occasionally found incorporated into other works: for example, there are two Lenten homilies in the first part of Stjórn.

Hagiographical material, in different forms, appears in the 12th century and continues to be produced throughout the medieval period. In its earliest form, it probably represented close translation of Latin lives of the apostles and saints; the early 13th-century MS AM 645 4to contains relatively straightforward translations of Latin passio material on Peter, Paul, and other apostles, and on Pope Clement and Bishop Martin. Later, this kind of material was reworked and amplified, and a greater degree of freedom becomes apparent in the handling of source material. The Norse version of the legend of Barlaam and Josaphat is a case in point. Later still, a new approach became popular in which copious additions from the Church Fathers and more recent writers, such as Peter Comestor and Vincent of Beauvais, transformed the genre into a much more individualistic one. Grímr Hólmsteinsson's saga of John the Baptist and Bergr Sokkason's lives of Michael the

Archangel and Nicolas are just three instances of this kind. Akin to the lives of saints and apostles are those of some of the bishops of Iceland, with Jón, Þorlákr, Guðmundr Arason, and others receiving detailed treatment. Mention may also be made of such individuals as Earl Magnús of Orkney, Archbishop Dunstan, Edward the Confessor, and Thomas à Becket, whose lives relate closely to this genre.

Works of religious prose that fall outside these two categories include translation of parts of the Bible and a few individual works of various kinds. These works include a translation of Alcuin's Latin treatise De virtutibus et vitiis, which was made before, and perhaps well before, 1200; a translation of the Elucidarius of Honorius Augustodunensis; fragments of a translation of the Physiologus; Gregory's Dialogues; and a certain amount of liturgical and associated material, notably mass commentaries and a harmonized version of Christ's Passion. "Visio" literature is represented by a translation of Visio Pauli and by a vision of heaven and hell granted to a certain Dougal, a somewhat free translation of Visio Tnugdali. More peripheral to the genre are Veraldar saga, an Icelandic history book based partly on the Bible, and Konungs skuggsjá, in the second part of which the responsibilities of a king are illustrated with substantial reference to the Old Testament.

Ed.: [Jón Sigurðsson and Guðbrandur Vigfússon, eds.] Biskupa sögur. 2 vols. Copenhagen: Møller, 1858–78; Unger, C. R., ed. Stjórn: Gammelnorsk bibelhistorie fra verdens skabelse til det babyloniske fangenskab. Christiania [Oslo]: Feilberg & Landmark, 1862; Unger, C. R., ed. Thomas saga Erkibyskups. Christiania [Oslo]: Bentzen, 1869; Unger, C. R., ed. Maríu saga. Legender om Jomfru Maria og hendes jertegn. Christiania [Oslo]: Brögger & Christie, 1871; Wisén, Theodor, ed. Homiliu-bók. Isländska homilier efter en handskrift från tolfte århundradet. Lund: Gleerup, 1872; Unger, C. R., ed. Postola sögur. Legendariske fortællinger om apostlernes liv deres kamp for kristendommens udbredelse samt deres martyrdød. Christiania [Oslo]: Bentzen, 1874; Unger, C. R., ed. Heilagra manna søgur. Fortællinger og legender om hellige mænd og kvinder. 2 vols. Christiania [Oslo]: Bentzen, 1877; Þorvaldur Bjarnarson, ed. Leifar fornra kristinna fræða íslenzkra: Codex Arna-Magnæanus 677 4to auk annara enna elztu brota af íslenzkum guðfrœðisritum. Copenhagen: Hagerup, 1878; Gudbrand Vigfusson, ed., and George W. Dasent, trans. "Játvarðar saga." In Icelandic Sagas and Other Historical Documents Relating to the Settlement and Descents of the Northmen on the British Isles. 4 vols. Rolls Series, 88. London: Eyre and Spottiswoode, 1887–94, vol. 1, pp. 388–400; Gudbrand Vigfusson, ed. "Magnúss saga hin lengri." In Icelandic Sagas and Other Historical Documents, vol. 1, pp. 237–80; Dahlerup, Verner, ed. "Physiologus i to islandske bearbeidelser." Aarbøger for nordisk Oldkyndighed og Historie 4 (1889), 199–290; Indrebø, Gustav, ed. Gamal Norsk Homiliebok. cod. AM. 619 4°. Norsk historisk kjeldeskrift-institutt, Skrifter, 54. Oslo: Dybwad, 1931; rpt. Oslo: Universitetsforlaget, 1966; Jakob Benediktsson, ed. Veraldar saga. Samfund til udgivelse af gammel nordisk litteratur, 61. Copenhagen: Luno, 1944; Holm-Olsen, L., ed. Konungs skuggsjá. Utgitt for kjeldeskriftfondet. Gammelnorske tekster, nr. 1. Oslo: Norsk historisk kjeldeskrift-institutt, 1945; Kolsrud, Oluf, ed. Messuskýringar. Liturgisk symbolik frå den norsk-islandske kyrkja i millomalderen. Norsk historisk kjeldeskrift-institutt, Skrifter, 57.1. Oslo: Dybwad, 1952; Widding, Ole, ed. Alkuin i norsk-islandsk overlevering. Editiones Arnamagnæanæ, ser. A, vol. 4. Copenhagen: Munksgaard, 1960; Fell, C. E., ed. Dunstanus saga. Editiones Arnamagnæanæ, ser. B, vol. 5. Copenhagen: Munksgaard, 1963; Tveitane, Mattias, ed. En norrøn versjon av Visio Pauli. Årbok for Universitetet i Bergen, Humanistisk Serie, 1964, nr. 3. Bergen: Norwegian Universities Press, 1965; Uecker,

Heiko, ed. *Der Wiener Psalter: Cod. Vind. 2713.* Editiones
Arnamagnæanæ, ser. B, vol. 27. Copenhagen: Reitzel, 1980; Rindal,
Magnus, ed. *Barlaams og Josaphats saga.* Norrøne tekster, no. 4. Oslo:
Norsk historisk kjeldeskrift-institutt, 1981; Firchow, Evelyn Scherabon,
and Kaaren Grimstad, eds. *Elucidarius in Old Norse Translation.*
Reykjavik: Stofnun Árna Magnússonar, 1989: **Bib.**: Widding, Ole, *et al.*
"The Lives of the Saints in Old Norse Prose: A Handlist." *Mediaeval
Studies* 25 (1963), 294–337. **Lit.**: Mogk, Eugen. *Geschichte der
norwegisch-isländischen Literatur.* Grundriss der Germanischen
Philologie, 2.1. Strassburg: Trübner, 1904; Finnur Jónsson. *Den
oldnorske og oldislandske Litteraturs Historie.* 3 vols. 2nd ed.
Copenhagen: Gad, 1920–24; Turville-Petre, G. *Origins of Icelandic
Literature.* Oxford: Clarendon, 1953; rpt. 1967; Stefán Einarsson. *A
History of Icelandic Literature.* New York: Johns Hopkins University
Press; American-Scandinavian Foundation, 1957; Bekker-Nielsen, Hans,
*et al. Norrøn Fortællekunst. Kapitler af den norsk-islandske
middelalderlitteraturs historie.* Copenhagen: Akademisk Forlag, 1965;
Tveitane, Mattias. *Den lærde stil. Oversetterprosa i den norrøne
versjonen av Vitæ Patrum.* Årbok for Universitetet i Bergen, Humanistisk
Serie, 1967, no. 2. Bergen and Oslo: Norwegian Universities Press,
1968; Holm-Olsen, Ludvig, and K. Heggelund. *Norges litteraturhistorie.
I: Fra runene til norske selskab.* Oslo: Cappelen, 1974; Kirby, Ian J.
Biblical Quotation in Old Icelandic–Norwegian Religious Literature. 2
vols. Reykjavik: Stofnun Árna Magnússonar, 1976–80; Jón Helgason,
ed. *Byskupa sǫgur 2.* Editiones Arnamagnæanæ, ser. A, vol. 13.2.
Copenhagen: Reitzel, 1978; Kirby, Ian J. *Bible Translation in Old
Norse.* Université de Lausanne, Publications de la Faculté des Lettres,
27. Geneva: Droz, 1986.

I. J. Kirby

[**See also:** Alcuin: *De virtutibus et vitiis*; Bible; *Biskupa
sǫgur*, *Elucidarius*; Gregory, St.: *Dialogues*; *Guðmundar
sǫgur biskups*; *Gyðinga saga*; Homilies; *Hungrvaka*; *Jóns saga
ens helga*; *Konungs skuggsjá*; *Laurentius saga biskups*;
Miracles, Collections of; *Nicodemus, Gospel of*; *Páls saga
biskups*; *Physiologus*; *Postola sǫgur*; Prayer Books;
Reykjahólabók; Saints' Lives; *Stjórn*; *Þorláks saga helga*;
Veraldar saga; *Visio Tnugdali*; Visionary Literature]

Chronicles

1. DENMARK. Adam of Bremen's *Gesta Hammaburgensis
ecclesiae pontificum* provides the earliest description of a relatively long sequence of events in the history of Denmark. The
work aims at emphasizing the importance of the Hamburg-Bremen
archbishopric for missions in the Nordic countries, from the time
of its establishment in the 9th century until the change of archbishops in 1072. This emphasis leads to the inclusion of long
passages relating to Danish history. The last book of this work
contains useful information about the geography of the Nordic
countries. Both content and form of this work left their marks on
12th-century Danish historical writing.

Another work, *Gesta Cnutonis* or *Encomium Emmae*, written about 1040 by an anonymous monk at St. Omer in Flanders,
may also have been known in Denmark. The cornerstone of the
hagiology of St. Knud (Cnut; r. 1080–1086), Ælnoth's *Gesta
Swenomagni regis et filiorum eius et passio gloriosissimi Canuti
regis et martyris* (ca. 1120), is a kind of continuation of the *Gesta
Cnutonis* of the same literary character.

The first Danish chronicle, *Chronicon Roskildense* ("The
Chronicle of Roskilde"), however, is clearly modeled on Adam of
Bremen's book. Both begin with the arrival of Bishop Ansgar in
Denmark in 826; the *Chronicon Roskildense* then proceeds with

a description of the development of Christianity in Denmark until
about 1040, with a later addition ending in 1157. The first part is
to a great extent based on Adam's work, which stops in 1072, so
the Roskilde author had to build on local tradition. Although the
history of the Church is the main topic of the work, the importance of the kings to the Church, and here particularly to the
bishopric of Roskilde, is clearly stressed throughout the book, a
fact that makes it a kind of history of Denmark. The personal views
of the author are unmistakable: his sympathy lies with kings who
lend particular support to the bishopric of Roskilde, often at the
cost of other dioceses, especially the newly created archbishopric
of Lund. The Gregorian reforms pertaining to celibacy do not
enjoy the sympathy of the author. In other ways, the Roskilde
chronicle contrasts with those of Sven Aggesen and Saxo from the
late 12th century, both of which favor a powerful Crown.

The *Chronicon Lethrense* ("The Chronicle of Lejre"), a work
that treats legendary history, covers a period from the foundation
of the kingdom under King Dan "in the days of King David" to the
legendary battle of Bråvalla. None of the kings listed is historical,
but it is historiographically interesting to see that they all rule from
Lejre near Roskilde and were rulers of the entire country of Denmark. Here and there, the history of the kings is interspersed with
fairy-tale-like anecdotes.

The *Chronicon Lethrense* is usually dated to 1170 on the
basis of Saxo's having used the chronicle in his *Gesta Danorum*,
although the chronicle is found only in MSS of the *Annals of Lund*
from the 1250s. The entire idea of the "kingdom of Lejre" is central
to the pre-Christian part of the *Gesta Danorum*, which seems to be
an elaboration and adaptation of the *Chronicon Lethrense*. The
connections between Saxo and Sven Aggesen, however, are even
closer: they must have known each other, and Saxo borrowed
several new additions to the history of Denmark from Sven's
chronicle. Furthermore, both of them draw upon the Icelandic
tradition.

Sven Aggesen belonged to one of the powerful families of the
12th century, the Trugotsons, as did archbishops Asser (archbishop 1104–1137) and Eskil (archbishop 1137–1177). Despite
these ecclesiastical connections, the family was known primarily
as warlike aristocrats. Several of them belonged to the royal
housecarls, in whom Sven displays an interest. He wrote a *Lex
castrenis* ("law pertaining to a camp"), and in his writings many
details originate from housecarl circles, including his own family.
Whether he was in fact a royal housecarl himself is not known, nor
whether he was a member of the clergy, although his familiarity
with Latin indicates that he had enjoyed the best education of his
time. His book, *Brevis historia regum Dacie*, gives even less of a
clerical impression than Saxo's. Its title and likewise the entire text
are known only in postmedieval MSS.

The chronicle of Sven Aggesen begins with King Skjold,
probably based on an Icelandic pattern, and ends with a battle
against the Pomeranian princes in 1185. The chronicle was probably written shortly after that year. Long sequences are pure genealogy. The ordinary (*i.e.*, nonlegendary) history contains three
"short stories" with a literary stamp, and the legendary history also
includes one. Source study shows that Sven built on detailed
models: the legend about Uffe probably derives from an English
chronicle; the story of Queen Thyra and the German emperor
from Vergil's *Aeneid*; and the history of Sven Haraldsson
(Forkbeard) from Adam of Bremen and a saga about the
Jomsvikings.

As mentioned above, Saxo's *Gesta Danorum* is to a large extent
based upon earlier historical writings together with materials whose

sources are unknown. A great part of the latter group must be taken as the author's independent work. A number of poems are apparently independent treatments of sparsely attested sources.

Just as Saxo's work draws on previous historical writing, so succeeding chronicles tend to build upon *Gesta Danorum*. This is the case with the chronicle part of the *Annals of Ryd (Rydårbogen)*, the *Old Zealandic Chronicle (Den ældre Sjællandske krønike)*, which has several word-for-word quotations from Saxo, and especially the so-called *Jutish Chronicles (Jyske krønike)*, the beginning of which is simply an abbreviated version of Saxo's chronicle (*Compendium*, or *Abbreviatio Saxonis*).

The *Old Zealandic Chronicle* stops at the year 1307, and was presumably written shortly after this time. It was continued by the *New Zealandic Chronicle (Den yngre Sjællandske krønike)* until 1363, which for the last years expresses personal views upon the politics of its time and upon the character of King Valdemar Atterdag ("ever-day"). The *Jutish Chronicle* continues Saxo until 1340, with particular expansiveness about conditions in Jutland during the kingless period from 1332 until 1340.

In Denmark, as in other countries, the late Middle Ages are characterized by an ambition to write history in the vernacular. Like the *Jutish Chronicle*, the *Annals of Lund* ends in the beginning of the 14th century. This chronicle is known from two MSS from about 1400.

Finally, there is the Danish *Rimkrønike* ("Rhymed Chronicle") from 1460, again based on Saxo; each king (including [H]Amleth) steps forward to describe his deeds in *knittel* verse. The inspiration for this form may have come from Sweden, where rhymed chronicles flourished during the 14th and 15th centuries, directed against the Danish supremacy in the union of the Nordic countries. There are certain features of the Danish book that indicate it may have been meant as a reply to the Swedish chronicles.

In addition to the national chronicles, there is also a small group of local ones, all connected with religious institutions. One such chronicle, the *Exordium carae insulae*, describing the establishment of the Cistercian monastery at Øm, was begun in 1207 and continued until it ended abruptly in 1274. It gives a picture of life within the monastery and relations with the outside world, particularly with the bishop of Århus. This chronicle is occasionally lively and dramatic, in contrast to the contemporary chronicle of the diocese of Ribe, a survey of the long history of this diocese from about 860 until about 1230.

Ed.: Trillmich, Werner, ed. and trans. *Adam Bremensis Gesta Hammaburgensis ecclesiae pontificum*. In *Quellen des 9. und 11. Jahrhunderts zur Geschichte der hamburgischen Kirche und des Reiches*. Darmstadt: Wissenschaftliche Buchgesellschaft, 1978; *Saxonis Gesta Danorum* [see Saxo Grammaticus]; other chronicles are printed in Gertz, M. Cl., ed. *Vitae sanctorum Danorum*. 3 vols.. Copenhagen: Gad, 1908–12; Gertz, M. Cl., ed., *Scriptores minores historiae Danicae medii ævi*. 2 vols. Copenhagen: Gad, 1917–18; Kroman, Erik, *Corpus Codicum Danicorum Medii Ævi*. 4, *Chronica*. Copenhagen: Munksgaard, 1962. **Lit.**: Weibull, Lauritz. "Necrologierna från Lund, Roskildekrönikan och Saxo." *Scandia* 1 (1928), 84–112; Bolin, Sture. *Om Nordens äldsta historieforskning. Studier över dess methodik och källvärde*. Lund Universitets årsskrift, avd. 1, 27.3. Lund: Ohlsson, 1931; Jørgensen, Ellen. *Historieforskning og historieskrivning i Danmark indtil aar 1800*. Copenhagen: Luno, 1931; McGuire, Brian Patrick. *Conflict and Continuity at Øm Abbey: A Cistercian Experience in Medieval Denmark*. Opuscula Graecolatina, 8. Copenhagen: Museum Tusculanum, 1976; Christensen, Karsten. *Om overleveringen af Sven Aggesens værker*. Copenhagen: Dansk historisk forening, 1978;

Malmros, Rikke. "Blodgildet i Roskilde historiografisk belyst." *Scandia* 45 (1979) 43–66; Breengaard, Carsten. *Muren om Israels hus. Regnum og sacerdotium i Danmark, 1050–1170*. Copenhagen: Gad, 1984.

Inge Skovgaard-Petersen

[**See also:** Annals; Adam of Bremen; Aggesen, Sven; Chronicles, Rhymed; *Encomium Emmae reginae*; *Knittel(vers)*; Saxo Grammaticus]

2. SWEDEN. Sweden has no high-medieval historiography corresponding to the one that reaches its climax in Denmark with Saxo Grammaticus's *Gesta Danorum*, and in the Norse area with Snorri Sturluson's *konungasögur*. The oldest examples associate themselves through the literary vernacular with the Norse tradition. Around 1240, the three closely connected Västgöta chronicles about the Västgöta lawmen, the bishops in Skara, and Sweden's Christian kings came into existence. The chronicles go back to around 1000, but only for the last century are the brief notices now and then expanded into real portraits, such as of the lawmen Karl and Eskil, and of "the good" Bishop Bengt. *Guta saga*, an appendix to the *Guta Law (Gutalagen)*, describes the history of Gotland from a mythical origin until the 13th century, with the relations to the king of Sweden and the bishop of Linköping in view. The chronicle was written in 1285 at the latest, possibly as early as the first quarter of the 13th century.

The most distinguished chronicle in medieval Sweden, the *Erik's Chronicle (Erikskrönikan)*, which remained influential until the end of the epoch, belongs to quite a different tradition, the German rhymed chronicle. Its approximately 4,500 verses are composed in a subtly treated *knittel*. It presents the political course of events in Sweden from the middle of the 13th century until Magnus Eriksson's election as king in 1319. The main part deals with the period after the turn of the century, *i.e.*, the disputes between King Birger and his brothers; Duke Erik is the hero of the chronicle. Negotiations and feasts are presented according to the style of the courtly culture, but still with freshness and engagement. The chronicle is first known in a copy from the late 15th century. Much of the research on this chronicle has concentrated on its origin, milieu, sources, and authorship. The chronicle clearly came into existence in the aristocratic circles surrounding Duke Erik. It is primarily based on the oral tradition in these circles, and the author, a layman, worked during Magnus Eriksson's time of minority (–1331/2). The chronicle apparently had no immediate distribution and influence.

The other historical-political works of the 14th century do not take the form of the chronicle. This applies to *Konunga styrelsen*, an independent reworking of the widely known *De regime principum*, compiled as a "mirror" for the young Magnus Eriksson, or, rather, for his sons; the controversial pamphlet against Magnus Eriksson, *Qualiter regnavit rex Magnus*, which originated within an aristocratic circle that had Birgitta Birgersdotter (St. Birgitta) as *spiritus rector;* and several of Birgitta's revelations, which can be considered political treatises, directed against a tyrannical royal power. That there was a need at that time for historical-political literature of a more analytic nature is evident from the section of the Visby minorites annals called the *Visby Chronicle (Visbykrönikan)*, an elucidation of the political course of events in the Baltic area 1360–1395.

When the *knittel* rhymed chronicle from the 1430s appears as a historical-political mode of expression, it has changed character, even though the *Erik's Chronicle* is a model. It is now less courtly and stylized, addressing itself in less refined style; and its more openly propagandist content is directed toward a broader public. The revolt against the monarch of the Scandinavian union, Erik of Pomerania, created the immediate need. Work on the creation of an actual national chronicle can be followed closely from the original MS of the complete *Karl's Chronicle* (*Karlskrönikan*; SKB D 6), into which older MSS have been incorporated and revised.

The *Engelbrekt Chronicle* (*Engelbrektskrönikan*) is a presentation of the political developments from Queen Margrethe's accession in 1389 until the murder of the captain of the realm Engelbrekt in the spring of 1436. It is characterized partly by a juridical argumentation for the righteousness of the revolt, partly by a glorification of Engelbrekt. The author obviously had access to the documents of the Council of the Realm (*Riksråd*). Strong reasons suggest that he is the same person who wielded the pen in SKB D 6: Johan Fredebern, known as the scribe in the service of the Council. The *Engelbrekt Chronicle* came into existence soon after its final entry for the year 1436; the same applies to its continuation until the end of 1439. The latter was produced in the regent Karl Knutsson's (Bonde) chancellery, and gives a strongly biased picture of the Swedish power struggle. After Karl Knutsson became king, these two texts were incorporated into a larger chronicle of around 9,500 verses, the *Karl's Chronicle*, which continues to the fall of 1452; it is also a chancellery product, finished soon after the date of its final entry. Even though the chronicle is well informed, the added text is still a coarser production than the *Engelbrekt Chronicle*: Karl Knutsson is praised, and his enemies inside and outside the kingdom are attacked and slandered.

During his first period as a king (1448–1457), Karl Knutsson had great ambitions about building a Swedish national history. The next step was to combine the *Erik's Chronicle* with the new chronicle with the help of a newly written section for the period 1319–1389, *Förbindelsedikten* ("the Connection Composition"). This work possesses neither historical nor literary value. Of interest from a historiographical point of view are two brief chronicles from the same workshop: the *Prosaic Chronicle* (*Prosaiska krönikan*) and the *Small Rhymed Chronicle* (*Lilla rimkrönikan*). The history of Sweden is here traced back to mythical times, in the former even to the Flood, and a great number of ancient Gothic kings are included. The *Small Rhymed Chronicle* introduces the popular monologue form, in which the kings briefly characterize themselves and their time.

The national chronicle is continued by the *Sture Chronicle* (*Sturekrönikan*), in reality two chronicle works, one treating the years 1452–1487, the other the years 1487–1496. The former praises the regent Sten Sture and came into existence in his circle; the latter, thought to have been inspired by Archbishop Jakob Ulfsson, is critical of him. Its historical and literary value is not great. This judgment applies to an even higher degree to the chronicle texts that continue the national chronicle until 1520 (*Cronica Swecie*).

Historical-political works were written at the end of the Middle Ages outside the national leadership. Rhymed chronicles were written about Skara's and Linköping's bishops, and a prose chronicle was written about the Åbo bishops. A chronicle text in Latin, treating the unsettled years 1463–1467, is found included in *Diarium Vadstenense* ("The Memorial Book of Vadstena Abbey"). Widespread and authoritative for a long time, however, was

the main historical work of the epoch, *Chronicon regni Gothorum* ("Chronicle of the Gothic Kingdom"), written by Ericus Olai, prelate at the Uppsala cathedral, later professor in theology at the new (1477) university. Unlike its predecessors, this is a learned work, intended for a European public. It praises the ancient Swedish kingdom and its Christian Church, both centered in Uppsala. While the Gothic tradition is developed from literary sources, the historical material is compiled from annals and chronicles, most of which are still preserved. Most valuable is the description of contemporary times (–1467), which is characterized by a national religious sentiment.

The historiography of humanism finds expression in three works from the middle of the 16th century. Around 1540, Olaus Petri, the evangelic reformer, composed a *Swedish Chronicle* (*Svenska krönikan*) from ancient times until 1520. He joins the German humanists, and bases his work on comprehensive, varied, and well-selected material, which is used with critical acumen. The intention is religious, ethical, and didactic, combined with sharp criticism of the secular regime, but also with an understanding attitude toward the Church. The *Swedish Chronicle*, of great historical and literary value, was suppressed by the royal power.

The works that the two exiled prelates and brothers Johannes Magnus and Olaus Magnus completed in Rome paradoxically received greater importance in both Europe and Sweden. The *Historia de omnibus gothorum sveonumque regibus* (printed in Rome in 1554), a work of humanistic rhetoric, written by Johannes, introduced the Gothic historical tradition into the learned European debate with a large amount of scholarship and fantasy. Similar to Johannes Magnus's less well known *Historia metropolitanæ ecclesiæ Upsaliensis* (printed in Rome in 1557), about the archbishops at Uppsala until his own time, the Gothic history is a controversial pamphlet against the new political-religious regime in Sweden, that of Gustav Vasa. In the same spirit, Olaus Magnus gives in *Historia de gentibus septentrionalibus* (printed in Rome 1555) a varied, vivid description of "the Scandinavian peoples," primarily the Swedes, their way of life, institutions, material culture, and so on. The source material derives both from the classical authors and from personal knowledge and experience.

Lit.: Andersson, Ingvar. *Källstudier till Sveriges historia 1230–1436: Inhemska berättande källor jämte Libellus magnipolensis.* Lund: Skånska centraltryckeriet, 1928; Bolin, Sture. *Om Nordens äldsta historieskrivning. Studier över dess metodik och källvärde.* Lunds Universitets Årsskrift, 27.3. Lund: Ohlsson, 1931; Hagnell, Karin. *Sturekrönikan 1452–1496. Studier över en rimkrönikas tillkomst och sanningsvärde.* Lund: Lindstedt, 1941; Lönnroth, Erik. *Medeltidskrönikornas värld. En politisk miljöstudie.* Göteborgs Högskolas Årsskrift, 47. Gothenburg: Elander, 1941; Westin, Gunnar T. *Historieskrivaren Olaus Petri. Svenska krönikans källor och krönikeförfattarens metod.* Lund: Blom, 1946; Nygren, Ernst. "Ericus Olai." In *Svenskt biografiskt lexikon* 14. Ed. B. Hildebrand. Stockholm: Bonnier, 1953, pp. 216–42; Maliniemi, Aarno. "Biskopskrönika." *KLNM* 1 (1956), 627–8; Nygren, Ernst. "Cronica regni Gothorum." *KLNM* 2 (1957), 603–4; Rosén, Jerker. "Diarier." *KLNM* 3 (1958), 64–9; Rosén, Jerker. "Erikskrönikan." *KLNM* 4 (1959), 28–34; Andersson, Ingvar. *Erikskrönikans författare.* Stockholm: Norstedt, 1959; Wessén, Elias. "Gutasagan." *KLNM* 5 (1960), 602–4; Lindroth, Sten. "Göticismen." *KLNM* 6 (1961), 35–8; Carlsson, Gottfrid. "Historieskrivning: Sverige och Finland." *KLNM* 6 (1961), 587–91; Rosén, Jerker. "Karlskrönikan." *KLNM* 8 (1963), 290–4; Ronge, Hans H. "Krönikestil." *KLNM* 9 (1964), 496–7; Bolin, Sture. "Kungalängder."

KLNM 9 (1964), 509–10; Liedgren, Jan. "Lagmanslängder." KLNM 10 (1965), 165–6; Carlsson, Gottfrid. "Lilla rimkrönikan." KLNM 10 (1965), 568–70; Schück, Herman. "Linköpings biskopskrönika." KLNM 10 (1965), 600–1; Westin, Gunnar T. "Olaus Petris Svenska krönika." KLNM 12 (1967), 557–61; Ståhle, Carl-Ivar. "Medeltidens profana litteratur." In Ny illustrerad svensk litteraturhistoria. Ed. E. N. Tigerstedt. 2nd rev. ed. Stockholm: Natur och Kultur, 1967, vol. 1. pp. 37–124; Rosén, Jerker. "Politisk agitation." KLNM 13 (1968), 360–6; Westin, Gunnar T. "Prosaiska krönikan." KLNM 13 (1968), 504–5; Ronge, Hans H. "Rimkrönikor." KLNM 14 (1969), 303–5; Westin, Gunnar T. "Skara biskopskrönika." KLNM 15 (1970), 401–2; Jansson, Sven-Bertil. Medeltidens rimkrönikor. Studier i funktion, stoff, form. Studia litterarum Upsaliensia, 8. Stockholm: Läromedelsförlagen, 1971; Westin, Gunnar T. "Sturekrönikan." KLNM 17 (1972), 353–5; Paulsson, Göte. Annales Suecici medii aevi. Bibliotheca Historica Lundensis, 32. Lund: Gleerup, 1974; Lindroth, Sten. Svensk lärdomshistoria 1. Stockholm: Norstedt, 1975; Axelson, Sven. "Visbykrönikan." KLNM 20 (1976), 162–4; Schück, Herman. Rikets brev och register. Arkivbildande, kanslivâsen och tradition inom den medeltida svenska statsmakten. Skrifter utgivna av Svenska riksarkivet, 4. Stockholm: Liber, 1976; Kumlien, Kjell. Historieskrivning och kungadöme i svensk medeltid. Kungl. vitterhets-, historie- och antikvitetsakademien. Historiska serien, 20. Stockholm: Almqvist & Wiksell, 1979; Johannesson, Kurt. Gotisk renässans. Johannes och Olaus Magnus som politiker och historiker. Stockholm: Almqvist & Wiksell, 1982; Gejrot, Claes, ed. Diarium Vadstenense. The Memorial Book of Vadstena Abbey. Acta Universitatis Stockholmensis. Studia Latina Stockholmiensia, 33. Stockholm: Almqvist & Wiksell, 1988.

Herman Schück

[**See also:** Annals; Chancery; Chronicles, Rhymed; *Guta saga*; *Knittel(vers)*; *Konungastyrelsen*]

Chronicles, Rhymed.

In the European Middle Ages, different types of rhymed chronicles were composed, ranging from extensive "world chronicles" to chronicles about the history of a single abbey. The Scandinavian examples belong to the most frequent type, which relates the history of a country, county, town, or similar unit. Its representation of historical or pseudo-historical matters, however, is to a large extent limited to the deeds of the rulers and other powerful persons. The structure of a rhymed chonicle is generally additive. The lack of a definite ending made it possible to continue the narrative when desired. The genre emerged in 12th-century Europe, at the beginning flourishing especially in the Anglo-Norman monarchy, and reached Scandinavia in the 14th century. One Danish chronicle was composed in the 15th century; the rest of the Scandinavian works are Swedish. All rhymed chronicles mentioned below are composed in *knittel* verse, although the Danish works are more varied, using even stanzaic forms.

The bulk of the Scandinavian rhymed chronicles was composed in the 15th century, but the genre was introduced by about 1325 with *Erik's Chronicle* (*Erikskrönikan*). The subject of this chronicle is how "sires and princes" in Sweden have lived, and what they have done. The structural framework is the succession of Swedish kings from Erik Eriksson (d. 1250) to young Magnus Eriksson (elected 1319). The chronicle is an interpretation of Swedish history in the period from 1230 to 1320 as seen from an aristocratic point of view. The purpose may have been to give a positive background to the reign of Magnus Eriksson, whose election marks the end of the narrative. The sources of *Erikskrönikan* were written documents, oral traditions, and the author's own observations. Stylistically, the chronicle has its models in the Swedish romances (*Eufemiavisorna*), which were composed on the initiative of the Norwegian queen Eufemia, the mother-in-law of Duke Erik, the great hero of *Erikskrönikan*. German epic has also contributed to the stylistic arsenal of the author. *Erikskrönikan* is preserved in nineteen MSS, five from the 15th century (the oldest one from 1457), the rest from the 16th and the beginning of the 17th century.

The composition of rhymed chronicles was taken up on a large scale in the middle of the 15th century. Because of the contradictions in the union of Denmark, Sweden, and Norway (1397–1520), the propagandistic aim then became a dominant feature, pushing the chivalric ideals of *Erikskrönikan* in the background. Dating to the 1450s, the text preserved in the unique MS Stock. D 6 covers the period 1389–1452. It is usually called *Karl's Chronicle* (*Karlskrönikan*); the text, however, is a revised version, produced under the supervision of King Karl Knutsson. Most scholars now agree that the first section (vv. 1–2,765) originally was a separate chronicle, now called *Engelbrekt's Chronicle* (*Engelbrektskrönikan*), composed at the end of the 1430s. The main part of this text is a description of the Swedish insurrection against the king of the Union, led by Engelbrekt, whose death is described as that of a martyr. To a large extent, it is based on documents in the archives of the Swedish Crown.

In the 1450s, some 7,000 verses were added to *Engelbrektskrönikan*, and the text revised. Thus, *Karlskrönikan* undoubtedly came into existence in the government offices of King Karl, where many of the documents the author(s) used were found. Covering only sixteen years (1436–1452), *Karlskrönikan* is the most detailed of all Scandinavian rhymed chronicles. The protagonist is Karl Knutsson, Swedish marshal during the reign of Christoffer, then himself king. The chronicle is a result of the lively propaganda disseminated by Karl to confirm his position as king in the 1450s. As in all Swedish chronicle texts from the late Middle Ages, the versification of *Karlskrönikan* is rather poor. Stylistically, it is more heterogeneous than *Erikskrönikan*, mingling realistic features with those typical of metrical romance.

The period 1452–1496 is treated in *Sture's Chronicle* (*Sturekrönikan*), which was composed in three or more stages, shortly after the events. The political tendency of vv. 1–3,381, covering the period 1452–1487, goes in favor of Sten Sture, the leader of the group that wanted independence for Sweden; in the rest of the text, the tendency is against Sten. Among the sources were annals and propaganda pamphlets.

Most likely in the 1450s, the gap between *Erikskrönikan* and *Engelbrekskrönikan* was filled out with a text, now called *Förbindelsedikten* (The Connection Composition), covering the period 1319–1389. It thus became possible to create one large chronicle of Swedish history spanning the period 1230–1452 by combining the existing texts. This merging was undertaken on the initiative of Karl Knutsson. The combined chronicle is preserved in four MSS; in nine more, *Sturekrönikan* is added to it.

The *Small Rhymed Chronicle* (*Lilla rimkrönikan*; 451 lines composed in the 1450s) differs from the chronicles mentioned above because of its monologue form. Beginning with the kings of a mythological past, the Swedish regents up to King Christoffer briefly describe their own lives and how they died. At the very end of the Middle Ages, another large chronicle was put together. This chronicle combines versions of *Lilla rimkrönikan* with the great text suite (from *Erikskrönikan* to *Sturekrönikan*) and a new continuation up to 1520. The texts were recast in the monologue form of *Lilla rimkrönikan*, and a new prologue was composed. This text combination, often called the *Youngest Rhymed Chronicle* (*Yngsta rimkrönikan*), is preserved in three MSS.

The Danish chronicle, *Den danske Rimkrønike*, is also written in monologue form. In about 5,000 lines, it tells the life and death of the Danish kings, starting in the mythological past with the first king, Dan (and his father, Humle), and ending with Christian I (d. 1481). The main sources are the Latin *Compendium Saxonis* and its continuation the *Jutish Chronicle* (*Jyske krønike*; up to 1340) and annals. Scholars have argued that the main part was composed at the beginning of the 15th century, the concluding section added later. The most complete version, based on a now-lost MS ending with the year 1481, was printed in 1495 by Gotfred of Ghemen. Three MSS are preserved, offering more or less fragmentary versions, and there is a translation into Low German (up to 1477). As is the case with the Swedish chronicles, the author is unknown. According to Brøndum-Nielsen (1930), more than one author may have been at work during the reign of Christian I. The discussion about the time of composition has also been coupled with the question of form. There is no agreement about which chronicle, *Lilla rimkrönikan* or *Den danske rimkrønike*, introduced the monologue form to the Scandinavian chronicle. Another important problem, not yet solved, is raised by the resemblances between parts of the chronicle and ballad texts. Like the Swedish chronicles of the 15th century, the Danish one also bears witness to the contradictions of the Kalmar Union. Some sections of the text (such as the rhymes of Christian I) were revised so as to display hostility toward the Swedes.

Ed.: Klemming, G. E., ed. *Svenska medeltidens Rim-krönikor.* Samlingar utgivna av Svenska fornskrift-sällskapet, 17.1–3. 3 vols. Stockholm: Norstedt, 1865–67/8 [versions of all Swedish rhymed chronicles]; Nielsen, Holger, ed. *Den danske rimkrønike efter et håndskrift i Det Kgl. Bibliotek i Stockholm.* Universitets-jubilæets danske samfunds skriftserie. Copenhagen: Thiele, 1895–1911; Pipping, Rolf, ed. *Erikskrönikan enligt cod. Holm. 2.* Samlingar utgivna av Svenska fornskrift-sällskapet, 47. Stockholm: Almqvist & Wiksell, 1921; rpt. (with additions) Samlingar utgivna av Svenska fornskrift-sällskapet, 68. Stockholm, 1963 [standard edition of *Erikskrönikan*]; Toldberg, Helge, ed. *Den danske rimkrønike.* Universitets-jubilæets danske samfunds skriftserie, 382, 388, 402. Copenhagen: Schultz, 1958–61. 1. *Ghementrykket 1495 med variantapparat,* 1961; 2. *Danske fragmenter,* 1958; 3. *Nedertysk oversættelse (Københavns-hånd skriftet),* 1959; Jansson, Sven-Bertil, ed. *Erikskrönikan.* Stockholm: Tiden, 1985 [slightly revised text, with an introduction and historical commentaries]. **Lit.**: Landberg, Georg. "Om källorna till vår yngsta rimmade krönika 1452–1520." *Samlaren* (1926), 133–49; Pipping, Rolf. *Kommentar till Erikskrönikan.* Skrifter utgivna av Svenska Litteratursällskapet i Finland, 187. Helsinki: Svenska Litteratursällskapet i Finland, 1926; Bolin, Gunnar. "Till dateringen av Erikskrönikan." *Historisk tidskrift* (Sweden) 40 (1927), 288–309; Neuman, Erik. "Karlskrönikans proveniens och sanningsvärde." *Samlaren* (1927), 103–82; (1931), 97–190; (1934), 113–221; Andersson, Ingvar. *Källstudier till Sveriges historia 1230–1436.* Lund: Lindström, 1928; Brøndum-Nielsen, Johannes. *Om rimkrønikens sprogform og tilblivelse.* Copenhagen: Luno, 1930; Kraft, Salomon. "Erikskrönikans källor." *Historisk tidskrift* (Sweden) 52 (1932), 1–80; Lönnroth, Erik. "Sturekrönikan 1452–1487." *Scandia* 6 (1933), 173–92; Lönnroth, Erik. *Sverige och Kalmarunionen 1397–1457.* Gothenburg: Wettergren & Kerber, 1934; Brix, Hans. *Analyser og problemer* 3. Copenhagen: Gyldendal, 1936, pp. 132–61; Kraft,

Salomon. "Karlskrönikans datering." *Historisk tidskrift* (Sweden) 57 (1937), 1–24; Rosén, Jerker. *Striden mellan Birger Magnusson och hans bröder. Studier i nordisk politisk historia, 1302–1319.* Lund: Gleerup, 1939; Hagnell, Karin. *Sturekrönikan 1452–1496. Studier över en rimkrönikas tillkomst och sanningsvärde.* Lund: Lindstedt, 1941; Lönnroth, Erik. *Medeltidskrönikornas värld. En politisk miljöstudie.* Göteborgs Högskolas Årsskrift, 47.18. Gothenburg: Elander, 1941; Andersson, Ingvar. *Erikskrönikans författare.* Svenska akademiens minnesteckningar. Stockholm: Norstedt, 1958; Toldberg, Helge. "Den danske rimkrønike og folkeviserne." *Danske Studier* 53 (1958), 5–45; Ståhle, Carl Ivar "Medeltidens profana litteratur." In *Ny illustrerad svensk litteraturhistoria.* Ed. E. N. Tigerstedt. 2nd rev. ed. Stockholm: Natur och Kultur, 1967, vol. 1, pp. 37–124; Holzapfel, Otto. "Folkeviseformler i Den danske rimkrønike." *Danske Studier* 63 (1968), 94–7; Jansson, Sven-Bertil. *Medeltidens rimkrönikor. Studier i funktion, stoff, form.* Studia litterarum Upsaliensia, 8. Uppsala: Läromedelsförlag, 1971.

Sven-Bertil Jansson

[**See also:** Annals; Chronicles; *Eufemiavisorna*; *Knittel(vers)*; Sweden]

Church, Stave *see* Stave Church

Church Organization and Function

1. DENMARK. The expansion of the Frankish empire was followed by missionary efforts. Bishop Willibrord of Utrecht paid an unsuccessful visit to a Danish king in the early 8th century; a hundred years later, in 823, Archbishop Ebo of Reims had just as little luck even though the Danish pretender Harald embraced the Christian faith. However, the missionary Ansgar visited the Scandinavian kingdoms from 826 on, founding churches in the more important market towns, such as Schleswig, Ribe, and Birka (Sweden).

Of more lasting importance was the conversion of several Viking settlers on the British Isles, and the continual contacts between Danelaw Vikings and their relations at home had a significant impact.

The Ottonian emperors of Germany used the mission as a political instrument. In 948, Otto I founded missionary bishoprics with titular seats in Schleswig, Ribe, and Århus. Like the kings of Poland (968) and Bohemia, King Harald of Denmark was baptized at this time (as the runic stones at Jelling tell us). A bishop of Odense is recorded in 988, but little is known of this early period. The new Church was formally subordinated to the archbishops of Hamburg-Bremen, although the kings wanted a more independent Church.

When Sven Forkbeard and his son Knud (Cnut; r. 1013–1035) conquered England, the German influence was replaced by that of the Anglo-Saxon Church, whose importance can still be seen in the Danish language, where everyday Christian terms are generally of Anglo-Saxon origin. The German tradition was hostile to this encroachment upon the right of the archbishops of Hamburg. Bishops appear in Zealand (1022) and Scania (1048), and in the 1060s we find a regular ecclesiastical organization with the traditional eight dioceses of Lund, Roskilde, Odense, Schleswig, Ribe, Århus, Viborg, and "Vendsyssel" (originally in Vestervig, but in the 12th century translated to Børglum). The parish organization must have been completed before 1100, and from this time onward wooden churches were replaced by buildings in stone, later in brick.

The growing tension between Danish kings and German emperors made the subordination of the Danish bishops under the archbishop of Hamburg-Bremen intolerable. As several popes were sympathetic to any curtailment of imperial sovereignty, a Danish province was established in 1104 with Lund as the metropolitan center, originally for all Scandinavia. But since a Norwegian province (in Niðaróss, present Trondheim) was founded in 1152 and a Swedish province (in Uppsala) in 1164, the archbishops of Lund continued to claim the title of primate of Sweden.

It is reasonable to suppose that this early Danish Church had to accept increasing international ecclesiastical organization. According to tradition, King Knud tried to introduce some sort of ecclesiastical jurisdiction (and probably tithes too). With the establishment of a Danish province, the principle of paying tithes must have met with some success. When the sources become more specific, we find a Danish system in which the tithes were divided into three equal portions among bishop, mensa, and church (fabric). In the so-called Ecclesiastical Law of Zealand (1171) and of Scania (perhaps a few years later), we find an agreement by which the rights of the bishops were accepted in exchange for reduced fees for episcopal visitations, consecrations of churches, and so on. But in Jutland, the bishops had to be content with an "episcopal donation," which probably meant only that the farmers were in a better position to make a bargain, since commutation must have been common from the earliest-known evidence of tithe paying.

In the 11th century, the first monasteries were founded, especially by the Benedictine and Augustinian canons, and in the 12th century it is possible to see the outlines of ecclesiastical organization. Generally, a diocese was divided into several provostships with some archidiaconal functions, in Jutland often based on an older territorial system of a *syssel* (cf. English "shire" or German *Gau*), and cathedral chapters come into existence (in Ribe in 1145), initially wavering between a regular and a secular organization.

The changing foreign influences are especially evident in the history of the chapters; in the English tradition, the Benedictines in Odense became the cathedral chapter (1117); in Viborg, the canons took an Augustinian rule; and, after the translation of the Northern diocese from Vestervig (with an Augustinian house) to Børglum (after 1134), the diocese had a Premonstratensian house as its chapter.

The secular chapters of Århus and Ribe were led by an archdeacon, whereas Schleswig and Lund had a provost. Only Roskilde (probably after a reform in 1225) had a dean as its leader. In time, most secular chapters had several dignitaries (*e.g.*, Roskilde, with a dean, provost, archdeacon, and precentor) with different rules of precedent, even if precentors, generally the youngest dignitaries, invariably were of the lowest rank. A collegiate chapter (with dean and precentor) was founded in Copenhagen around 1200, and a smaller establishment, led by only a precentor, appears in Haderslev around 1250.

The early Church had to beg for royal support. But in the 12th century, the growing international influence resulted in an attempt to enforce celibacy, and, in the Gregorian tradition, many leading churchmen claimed total immunity from secular interference. In the turmoils of civil war, Archbishop Eskil (1137–1177) was in the front line of these reform movements, and he had to spend several years in exile at Clairvaux. At this time also, both the Cistercians (1144) and the Premonstratensians (1155) founded abbeys of great importance.

Crusades against the heathen Slavonic tribes on the Baltic coastlands added the island of Rugen to the diocese of Roskilde (1169), and several Cistercian houses in the north of Germany were founded from Denmark (*e.g.*, Colbatz in 1175 and Olivia in 1186). And at this time, the Hospitallers of St. John founded the priory of Dacia with its seat in Antvorskov.

During the time of archbishops Absalon (1177–1201) and his nephew Anders Sunesen (1202–1223), the Church worked hand in glove with the royal power, and the claims of an independent ecclesiastical legal system were fully accepted. When the Lateran Council of 1215 prohibited the use of ordeals, Danish law was changed at once in this respect. And as the folk laws (Zealand and Scanian Laws, *ca.* 1200; Jutland Law, 1241) make no mention of marriage and other matters of domestic relations, such problems must have been treated by ecclesiastical courts according to the principles of canon law (in its local application). The idea of *legitimatio per subsequens matrimonium* now became a permanent part of Danish law.

The crusade to Estonia in 1219 resulted in the foundation of the diocese of Reval, which at least formally continued to be part of the Danish ecclesiastical province, even if regular relations broke off when after 1340 the territory came under the military Order of the Brothers of the Sword (affiliated with the Teutonic Knights).

The friendly relations between secular and spiritual powers were suspended in the middle of the 13th century, in many respects a local parallel to the international antagonism between popes and emperors, the Investiture conflicts, and so on. The archbishops Jakob Erlendsen (1253–1274) and especially Jens Grand (1291–1302) strove to preserve and increase the ecclesiastical privileges and immunities against secular and especially royal pretentions.

Not intimidated by sacerdotal interdicts (*e.g.*, 1266–1275 and 1299–1303), the kings had the upper hand, since the bishops stood divided. The Jutland bishops, in particular, supported the kings, who could afford better lawyers and establish permanent ties to the Roman Curia. And not only did the popes have great political problems, they needed money. Accordingly, the kings succeeded in finding a working agreement with the papacy.

The kings were able to claim the rights of presentation to all rectories in chartered towns founded on royal lands, and, together with founder's right to several canonries and monasteries, the kings could later claim rights of presentation to about 10 percent of all parishes (especially in the diocese of Odense). But even if chapters and monasteries appropriated another 10–15 percent, most parishes were served by rectors appointed by the bishop (probably after local presentation) and administered by two churchwardens with annual visitation and auditing by the provost.

Most of the leading churchmen in this period studied abroad, especially in Paris. From 1200 onward, we find a whole group of Danish (at least Scandinavian) scholars in France, including philosophers (Boethius, Johannes, and Martinus de Dacia, the latter for a period as royal chancellor) and astronomers (Petrus Philomena, *ca.* 1300, and Johannes Simonis, 1417 in Vienne).

The chapters must have played an important role in training new clergy. By local statutes, scholars were obliged to maintain residence in the cathedral city for several years before taking up their vocations. In the high Middle Ages, the great abbeys were of considerable importance, assembling enormous landed wealth and appropriating churches and tithes. Even if many of the greater

Cistercian houses often were founded on an older Benedictine institution, we may later count about twenty-five Benedictine houses (about half of which were nunneries), eleven Cistercian houses (one nunnery), six Premonstratensian houses (one nunnery), and perhaps six Augustinian houses (especially among the poorer nunneries, it is extremely difficult to establish the order with any certainty).

There were enormous differences in wealth and importance between, for example, the Cistercian abbey of Sorø and the priory of the Hospitallers in Antvorskov and on the other hand the numerous nunneries, which often just managed to survive as "rest homes" for the wealthy gentry, and their daughter houses. In the early 13th century, the Mendicants arrived, and in time the Dominicans (arrived 1222) may have had as many as twenty houses (two nunneries) and the Franciscans (arrived 1232) perhaps twenty-eight, and in the later Middle Ages the Greyfriars had a provincial organization divided into five custodies.

In the early 13th century, the diocesan synod appears as a regular part of the ecclesiastical administration, generally as a bi-annual synod (e.g., with a Trinity and a Michaelmas term). Together with provincial councils, the synods played an important part in introducing and applying international canon law in Denmark.

At the end of this century (perhaps in 1298), officials were introduced. An official general took over most of the administrative affairs of the diocese, especially the legal business, but also economic matters and estate administration, while a local official was appointed for each hundred as a supervisor of the clergy (later "provost"); these officials were often chosen from among the local incumbents.

Already by the early 13th century, the archdiocese established its own administrative system. The older provosts (with some semiarchidiaconal powers) were supplanted by a system of rural deans in each hundred. Still remoter parts of the archdiocese (the province of Halland and the archiepiscopal palatine Lordship of Bornholm) had their own deans, who were members of the cathedral chapter, and they may have held some archdiaconal powers, perhaps by special delegation. In the later Middle Ages, the officials in Lund were by and large secular, often chosen from among the petty gentry, who made a career in the archiepiscopal household and the estate administration. Their office must have been a secular one, involving the collection of income (e.g., fines) and other duties. Little is known about the ecclesiastical courts here, which were headed by the anonymous *Curia Lundensis* (probably a group of delegated canons).

In the island diocese of Odense, we find special synods on the major islands of Lolland and Falster, held at the same time as the synod of Odense. When officials are introduced, we find not only hundred-officials here, but also special officials-general on all major islands.

Where the oldest provosts still survived, as in Ribe and Schleswig, we have evidence of concurrent jurisdiction, since the officials of both bishoprics and provosts claimed the fines. The bishops were probably victorious in the long run, since later only the provosts had undisputed rights of visitation of the parish churches.

In the wealthy diocese of Roskilde, the older provosts disappear in the 13th century (perhaps after the reform in 1225); but here the four prelates and the dean of the collegiate chapter of Copenhagen had divided the island of Zealand into five districts

where each dignitary claimed concurrent jurisdiction even in marriage cases, pretentions that the bishop tried to suppress. Even if the prelates in 1460 received papal confirmation of their time-honored right of jurisdiction (among others, in cases of incest, perjury, defloration), the diocesan statutes of 1517 granted them only the lesser (but probably more numerous) cases together with the visitation of the fabric.

As soon as we can establish a picture of the Danish Church, the scanty sources notwithstanding, we get an impression of the usual medieval piety. The popularity of special saints might change through the ages, but the worship of saints remained an integral part of the religion. From baptism to burial, the Church followed the people, and annual confession was mandatory. People who had been interdicted for a longer period without seeking absolution (in the 15th century, for a whole year) might simply be "signified" to the secular authorities, as this was considered a capital offense. Disputes over tithes and rectorial fees never involved the principles, but the exact amount might give rise to discussion during the negotiations on commutation and so on, and it must have been the general opinion that salvation could be obtained only through the power of the Church and its ordained clergy.

The 14th century was one of general decline, only partly through the plague, because a general agrarian crisis affected all landowners and especially the Church, which might have owned about one third of all landed property. Not all the 2,000 village churches could be maintained; in some parts of Jutland, several were closed down. In such areas, a parish priest might have to serve two or even three churches at the same time. And in the poorer chapters, as in Ribe, the number of canons might be cut by half.

The conflicts in the high Middle Ages between Church and state ended in a theoretical victory for the Church. But in its struggles for immunities and independence from the secular powers, the Danish Church had become increasingly dependent upon Rome. Instead of royal taxes, the bishops had to pay considerable amounts of annates for papal confirmation. The popes interfered in episcopal elections, claimed rights of provision, and through appeals to the Curia made their power felt in everyday life. Especially unpopular were the numerous papal crusade taxes; and since the 14th century was filled with crises, warfare, and civil war, culminating in an interregnum in 1332–1340, this might explain why the later-medieval clergy generally supported a strong monarchy as the only power that could protect the Church and thereby make its extensive privileges a reality.

The new king Valdemar IV (1340–1375) established friendly relations with the popes of Avignon, which gave him influence on the appointment of new bishops. His daughter Margrethe (*de facto* ruler 1375–1412) especially enjoyed strong support from the Church, and many bishops began their careers in the royal household or even as royal chancellors. Her founding of the Scandinavian Union (Kalmar, 1397), with her nephew Erik of Pomerania (1389–1439) as king of all three northern kingdoms, enhanced her influence, and the Scandinavian bishops were generally among her strongest supporters in the common councils (parliaments). Her wealth enabled her to make the last of the great donations to the Church. But her successor, King Erik, may not have possessed her diplomatic tact. The Swedish clergy, in particular, opposed his interference in episcopal elections, and in time this was one of the reasons why Sweden was plunged into a continuous civil war for or against the increasingly unpopular Union.

Since the bishops played such an important part in the affairs of state, they needed help in the administration of their dioceses, as consecration of new clergy, confirmations, and so on were episcopal prerogatives that could not be delegated to officials. Just before 1400, we find suffragans, at first with oriental titles. But since many bishops from the North Atlantic sees were frequent guests at court, they may have paid their episcopal hosts for hospitality received by performing suffragan work (such as consecrating churches), and as the Greenland routes were forgotten, the bishops of Gardar (Greenland) from then on were constantly found in Danish and Norwegian dioceses as ordinary suffragans.

Scandinavian bishops were also active in the great councils, in both Constance and in Basel; but when the councils had had their day, King Christian I (1448–1481) reestablished the former cordial relationship with the Curia, and during his visit to Rome in 1474 the Gold Rose was bestowed upon him together with substantial privileges, such as the presentation of all postpontifical dignitaries in chapters, and later his queen brought back the privilege of founding a university in Copenhagen (established 1479).

Since the Danish bishops were *ex officio* members of the Council (which held power during the interregnum, until a new king had been elected and signed a coronation charter, in which the privileges of the aristocracy were specified), the popes must have understood the importance of appointing only royal nominees. Generally, the chapters were cooperative, since most royal chancellors ended their careers as bishops. Especially during the Schism, when Denmark invariably supported Rome, later Pisa, and at last the Council, we find the annates, and so on, were considerably reduced.

The scanty evidence on diocesan synods in later-medieval Jutland makes it possible to conclude that they had disappeared here. But synods continued to play an important part in three eastern dioceses. The official-general in Roskilde has been studied in detail, and the results convey exactly the same picture of the importance of the spiritual courts in all aspects of daily life as elsewhere in northern Europe. These officials of Roskilde were generally picked from among younger university graduates, who returned from studies abroad (particularly in Rostock, Greifswald, and Erfurt). After holding office for three to five years, they went from the possession of an altar to a Copenhagen benefice, ending generally as members of the cathedral chapter. But behind these young and ambitious clerics, we find a group of assessors, often former officials, on whose experience the authority of the court might depend.

In the 1430s, the Augustinian chapter in Viborg was replaced by an ordinary secular one (with three dignitaries and twelve canons). But a similar experiment of replacing the Benedictines in Odense with a secular chapter in the 1480s was aborted, even though it had papal support, perhaps because the pious queen supported the monks.

As far as we may give credence to the mostly legal-economic sources, the later Middle Ages were characterized by a strong popular religious feeling. Old Romanesque village churches were rebuilt in Gothic style, often with tower, sacristy, and remodeled choir, and the old and aristocratic Romanesque mural frescoes were replaced by late Gothic scenes of a more popular genre, taken, for instance, from the *Biblia pauperum*. New altars were founded, and most guilds worshiped their own patron saint. Moreover, the guild might hold the right of presentation to its own altar. The Marian cult had made the formerly popular Virgin Mary

rather distant: accordingly, petitioners approached her through her mother, St. Anne, and the last provincial council of Copenhagen in 1425 introduced Anne's veneration (December 9).

Even if the older orders continued and even flourished in their traditional ways, public interest came to be attracted by new forms of worship. Of course, the Union monarchs supported the Brigettine Order, which founded two abbeys in Denmark. Through dynastic ties, this new order received houses in England (Syon), Germany, Poland, and Italy. King Erik took an interest in the Carmelite Order, which soon founded eight houses. The building of hospitals and other charitable institutions was especially popular. Not only did the hospital Order of the Holy Spirit establish six houses in the years 1451–1485, but its competitor, the Saint Anthony Order, established one house in Denmark and another in the duchy of Schleswig. Older charitable institutions were reformed, and new ones were established.

The general wave of reform was felt inside the older orders too, as the Benedictine house of Voer in East Jutland joined the Bursfeld congregation in 1486. The reform movement within the Franciscan order was extremely violent and ultimately led to its division. Supported by the royal family, the Spirituals gradually took over all Danish houses, while the opponents joined the Conventuals in Sweden.

Danish liturgy followed its North German neighbors in the traditions, which only gradually and to a lesser degree became influenced by Roman centralism (accordingly, much medieval church music is preserved in the post-Reformation Church). Together with the royal saints King Knud and Knud Lavard, traditional saints, such as Michael, Martin, and John, enjoyed uninterrupted worship, but for practical reasons village churches had to rely on the inexhaustible supply of relics from the 11,000 virgins or the 10,000 knights. Holy wells survived for centuries as places of veneration, and pilgrimages flourished. In the last century of the Middle Ages, the Church found its most popular saints in Severinus and Erasmus, whose worship is little known but who must have been extremely popular among the common people, as witnessed by name-giving practices among the peasantry.

Even if too little is known in detail, it is evident that the Church played an important part in the history of Danish law. Since the increasingly obsolete folk laws grew unable to cope with the problems of a modern society, the spiritual courts came to their assistance, especially in more sophisticated economic affairs. About 1376, the royal council referred matters of usury to the ecclesiastical courts, and the Church must have played an important part, since it was the only institution with courts that could, with the threat of excommunication, enforce the payments of debts.

In the later Middle Ages, the Danish Church depended on the royal power increasingly as its only protector in an often hostile and litigious world. Bishops often had difficult times dealing with local magnates or the independent Cistercian abbeys, which claimed immunity from the episcopal power. Most bishops were former royal officials, generally taken from the ranks of the lesser gentry, and the secular and spiritual affairs became so integrated that bishops took the secular fines from their own peasantry, and noble landowners seem to have kept the spiritual fines from the dependents.

When the evangelical preachers arrived in Denmark after 1517, they found a general interest in "reform." But with the exception of the Erasmian Bible humanist Paulus Helie (Poul Helgesen), who could follow Luther a long way but not into schism, they found few competent opponents. Most bishops were university graduates, but generally in canon or Roman law: able administrators and loyal royal councilors, but men not in a position to take part in a theological debate. Such matters were left in the hands of the suffragans and mendicant preachers.

Library lists give evidence that the Danish Church was well versed in its traditional and ordinary obligations, but without any pretentions of originality. When for purely political reasons King Frederik I (1523–1533) separated the Danish Church from Rome (1526/7), all his bishops and most of the clergy loyally followed the royal policies. A law reform began with a royal ordinance of 1527, which at last made it possible for secular courts to grant execution of debts. The secular and spiritual aristocracies happily competed in the supression of Franciscan houses (probably under suspicion of being loyal to Rome), and as the higher clergy felt more loyalty to the king and to their Danish aristocratic families than to Rome, the Danish Reformation arrived in 1536 by royal order and the peaceful resolution of a diet.

Lit.: Moltessen, L. J. *De avignonske Pavers Forhold til Danmark.* Copenhagen: Gad, 1896; *Acta pontificum Danica*, vols. 1–7. Copenhagen: Gad, 1904–43; Bachmann, Johannes. *Die päpstlichen Legaten in Deutschland und Skandinavien, 1125–1159.* Historische Studien, 115. Berlin: Ebering, 1913; rpt. Millwood: Kraus, 1965; Lindbæk, Johannes P. *De danske Franciskanerklostre.* Copenhagen: Gad, 1914; Koch, Hal. *Danmarks Kirke i den begyndende Højmiddelalder.* Copenhagen: Gyldendal, 1936; Gallén, Jarl. *La Province de Dacie de l'Ordre des frères prêcheurs.* Helsingfors: Söderström, 1946–; Dahlerup, Troels. *Studier i senmiddelalderlig dansk Kirkeorganisation.* Copenhagen: Gad, 1963; Seegrün, Wolfgang. *Das Papsttum und Scandinavien bis zur Vollendung der nordischen Kirchenorganisation (1164).* Neumünster: Wachholtz, 1967; Dahlerup, Troels. *Det dansk Sysselprovsti i Middelalderen.* Copenhagen: Gad, 1968; Losman, Beate. *Norden och Reformkoncilierna 1408–1449.* Studia historica Gothoburgensia, 11. Gothenburg: Akademieförlaget, 1970; Christensen, Aksel E., ed. *Danmarks Historie.* Copenhagen: Gyldendal, 1977–80 [contains complete and annotated bibliography]; Skyum-Nielsen, Niels. *Kirkekampen i Danmark, 1241–1290.* Copenhagen: Munksgaard, 1963; McGuire, Brian Patrick. *The Cistercians in Denmark.* Cistercian Studies Series, 35. Kalamazoo: Cistercian Publications, 1982.

Troels Dahlerup

2. NORWAY. The contact of the Vikings with Europe in the 9th and 10th centuries allowed Christian impulses to reach the coastal areas of Norway. In the middle of the 10th century, foreign missionaries were probably active in Viken and on Vestlandet. But it was the missionary kings Hákon Aðalsteinsfóstri ("Æthelstan's foster-son"), Óláfr Tryggvason, and Óláfr Haraldsson who adopted Christianity as the sole religion in Norway and who established the foundations for the oldest church organization, based, in the main, on English models. They had converted to Christianity abroad, and had both religious and political reasons for introducing Christianity. From other countries, they were acquainted with a pattern for collaboration between kingdom and Church under the king's leadership that they sought to adapt to Norwegian conditions. The introduction of a new religion could also break down a heathen social organization where it was in opposition to the king. The unification and christianization of Norway in the 11th century led to the confiscation of the farms of heathen landowners. Later, the royal power transferred a good portion of this property to the Church.

The missionary Church was under the leadership of the king. The christianization was part of the inclusion of the local communities under the royal power. The king had the first local churches built. The missionary bishops were members of the king's *hirð*, and were elected by him when the bishops from the reign of Óláfr kyrri ("peaceful," 1066–1093) began taking residence at established episcopal seats in Niðaróss (now Trondheim), Bergen, and perhaps somewhat later in Oslo. The first cathedrals were erected at or near central royal estates in the towns. In the earliest period, the bishops had several residences, and traveled either in the king's following or on their own missionary journeys. In the beginning, their activity was not territorially defined; but from the second half of the 11th century, we can glimpse an emerging episcopal organization based on the division into *logþing* regions. Like the king and his representatives, the bishops had close contact with the *logþings* in order to gain access to the farming society and have legal rules sanctioned as obligatory.

The king had Christianity adopted as the only permitted religion in Norway. However, the christianization of the people took centuries. Óláfr Haraldsson's *hirð*-bishop Grímkell was clearly active in the establishment of a Norwegian ecclesiastical organization and law. The missionary Church was a national Church ruled by the king, and the oldest ecclesiastical decisions for the individual *logþing* regions probably go back to Óláfr Haraldsson and Bishop Grímkell.

Not only did the king profit politically from introducing a new religion; he also found valuable advisers and helpers among the clergy. The priests could write, had contact with foreign countries, and could serve as the king's spokesmen to the people. Gradually, the country became covered with local churches, owned and administered either by the parishioners themselves jointly or by private church builders and their successors. The privately owned churches were called "convenience churches" (*hægendiskirkjur*), many of which later became parish churches. Gradually, the local churches came under the control of the bishops, thus laying a foundation for a nationwide church organization.

The king controlled the Church in the 11th century and the beginning of the 12th primarily through his appointing of bishops. At the same time, the farmers had influence on church and religious life. Christianity and church organization were made law at the secular *logþings*. The provincial laws included special church laws with provisions governing the relationship between the Church and the people, as well as religious life generally. They regulated the observance of festivals, mass-days, and fasts; set forth prohibitions against the exposure of deformed children, marriages of close relatives, and heathen cults; gave orders for burial in the churchyard; and the like. The Church still did not have any inner legislation based on the universally recognized canonical principles. With the help of the king's authority, it had to get its program and its organization sanctioned at the legal *logþing* by representatives of the free Norwegian farmer society. Therefore, the older church laws were formed differently for the individual *logþings*. Individual church laws came into existence for the Gulaþing Law in Vestlandet, the Frostuþing Law in Trøndelag, the Eiðsivaþing Law in Oppland, and the Borgarþing Law in Viken. The farmers also influenced the appointment of priests, who were gradually recruited from the local community and attached to it through marriage. The priests were supported by the farmers, who were responsible for the building and maintenance of the local churches, which were their common property.

In the first half of the 12th century, the Church became more independent of the Crown, and at the same time more firmly allied to the international papal Church. Originally, the Norwegian Church had been under the archbishop in Hamburg-Bremen, and since 1104 under the archbishop in Lund. In 1152 or 1153, the papal legate Nicolaus Brekespear came to Norway to establish a Norwegian archbishop's seat in Niðaróss. The Church received its own national organization with parishes and bishoprics under the leadership of the archbishop, and became a public authority parallel with the kingdom. The Norwegian church province comprised eleven bishoprics, five in Norway proper—Niðaróss, Bergen, Oslo, Stavanger (established in the 1120s), and Hamar (established at the time of the foundation of the archbishopric)—six in the Nordic island communities in the west—Skálholt and Hólar in Iceland, and in Greenland, the Faroe Islands, the Orkneys-Shetland, and Hebrides-Man. This new arrangement had its basis in the pope's policy of separating smaller provinces on the fringes of Europe and drawing them into a firmer subordinate relationship with Rome. In 1152/3 and under Magnús Erlingsson (1161–1184), the kingdom made concessions on three important points: the Church should have decisive influence on the choice of bishops and abbots; it should have administrative and financial jurisdiction over churches and church property; it should have jurisdiction over its own personnel and in ecclesiastical matters. From the earliest times, the Church had only had a certain judicial authority through the penitential discipline connected with confession.

The Church freed itself from its dependence on the farmer community. The proprietary church system gave way to an ecclesiastical proprietary right. During the 13th century, the farmers' influence on legislation disappeared. The more independent Church continued to be an important collaborator with the kingdom. Through support from King Magnús Erlingsson, the Church increased its freedom and rights. In collaboration with Archbishop Eysteinn Erlendsson (1161–1188), the king revised the Church laws. According to the law of succession of 1163, the bishops were to have a decisive influence on the accession of a new king.

King Sverrir Sigurðarson (1177–1202) refused on important points to accept the ecclesiastical reform of 1152/3 and the advantages the Church had achieved under Magnús Erlingsson. He demanded that the Church should submit to the king's leadership as it had earlier, and refused to accept the concessions that previously had been made to the Church to the extent the Church itself interpreted them. This applied primarily to the election of bishops, appointment of priests, ecclesiastical jurisdiction, and income derived from fines. This action led to the Church's political and military opposition to the king, and developed into the most bitter conflict between Crown and ecclesiastical authorities in medieval Norway. It was not until after Sverrir's death in 1202 that the conflict died down. King Hákon Sverrisson's reconciliation with the bishops in the same year was, however, more of a ceasefire than a solution. In the shelter of the ceasefire, it appears that the Church strengthened its position in the first half of the 13th century. In the collaboration with the Crown, the Church was probably the weaker partner, not least during Hákon Hákonarson's stable absolute monarchy after 1240 (r.1217–1263). But the king gradually accepted the notion of a more autonomous ecclesiastical organization with greater freedom and more extensive privileges than under King Sverrir.

Hákon's son and successor, Magnús lagabœtir ("law-mender"; 1263–1280) was more sympathetic than any previous king in his dealings with Archbishop Jón rauði ("the red"; 1268–1282). They resulted in a concordat in 1277, the Treaty of Tønsberg, where older ecclesiastical privileges were confirmed and new ones were made. The freedom of the Church in relation to the secular community was expressly recognized in a number of areas. Of the old privileges, the ecclesiastical election of bishops and the appointment of priests were reestablished as a matter of principle.

The new advantages were primarily financial. The clergy, which from the second half of the 12th century was exempted from military leiðangr service and leiðangr taxes, had later achieved tax relief also for laypeople in the service of the archbishop. It now obtained the provision that the episcopal setusveinar, or men fit for military service, such as the "king's men," should be exempted from leiðangr taxes. The archbishop received tax exemption for 100 men, the bishops for forty men each. The Church gained ground also in the area of independent jurisdiction, but it is debated to what extent this took place in relation to earlier theory and practice. Politically, King Magnús was unwilling to accept ecclesiastical influence to the detriment of the monarchy on the matter of succession to the throne and in legislation. His concessions were made from a strong royal position.

The barons and hirð officials, who, as members of the king's council, took over the reign for the underaged Eiríkr Magnússon in 1280, were unwilling to accept the Church's jurisdiction and economic gains even though they had participated in sanctioning them. Nor would they accept Archbishop Jón's demand for rule over the ecclesiastical legislation. This refusal led to a short but bitter struggle in the early 1280s. Archbishop Jón and two of his bishops were exiled. Shortly after, he died in Sweden. When the relations between the royal power and the Church had gradually become normal again, the Church could practice a high degree of autonomy, although not quite according to the agreement of 1277. During the rest of the high Middle Ages, there continued a struggle over the boundaries of this autonomy.

In the collaboration between Church and kingdom, significant advances had been made toward both an ecclesiastical and a royal national organization. The Church played an active role in the development of the royal ruling apparatus after the civil wars ended in 1240. With the exception of the struggle in the early 1280s, the bishops served as the king's advisers. Clerics served him on missions and in administrative matters. Nonetheless, only a small number of the Church's personnel were at the kingdom's disposal. The Church used the clerics first and foremost for its own purposes. This explains why the kings, from Hákon Hákonarson on, more systematically developed their own clergy associated with specific royal chapters.

Organization of the Church. The organization of the Church was hierarchical, with the local church parish as a basic unit. The church laws in the lǫgþing regions presuppose larger parish churches or main churches. In the beginning, it seems that there was such a church in each of the small Trøndelag counties. In the much larger counties on Vestlandet, it is likely that there was more than one main church. In Oppland, it seems that there was such a church for each third of a county, and in Viken two main churches in each county. The first county churches were most likely normally built on crown lands. In the 11th century, they probably had the status of a mother-church, and functioned as centers for baptism and burials for larger areas. In the 12th century, however, it appears that they had the same function and rights as parish churches. But they ranked higher, and the priest of the main church had both visitation and supervision rights over the other parish churches. The maintenance of the main or county churches was the farmers' responsibility.

A prerequisite for the arrangement with main churches is the existence of smaller parish churches with lower rank and for smaller areas. How far back status as a main church goes is uncertain, but certainly early in the 12th century local churches of a lower rank were common. "Convenience churches" are mentioned in all the church laws. They were built by magnates on their own farms and by the king on royal estates in the countryside and in the towns. In the 12th century, the convenience churches were increasingly converted into parish churches with churchyards. This process seems to have been particularly common in Oppland and in Trøndelag. Since there were relatively many main or county churches in these areas, we find here only main churches and converted convenience churches as parish churches. Nonetheless, there is reason to believe that most of the convenience churches also in Viken and on Vestlandet gradually received parish-church status. In addition, in Viken a number of churches have an intermediate position between the main churches and the convenience churches, the so-called heraðskirkjur ("district churches"), i.e., churches for a specific jurisdiction within a district (herað), which became parishes when a firmer parish division was introduced in the high Middle Ages. Heraðskirkjur appear also in the Gulaþing Law together with quarter and eight churches within a county, in an intermediate position between county and convenience churches. Because of the large and topographically divided Vestland counties, the quarter churches in the Bergen bishopric received certain administrative main-church functions in line with the main or county churches in Trøndelag and Oppland.

The local churches in Norway in the early 12th century were thus in the main of three kinds: main or county churches, smaller parish churches, and private convenience churches. Convenience churches were, along with the ground on which they stood, the property of the individual who built the church and his heirs; the others were the property of a farmer collective. The local churches were thus originally a kind of proprietary church, owned either individually or collectively. There is reason to believe that the county churches were originally royal proprietary churches. This system gave certain rights, for example in the appointment of priests. But it is unlikely that it was especially lucrative for the owners, and it hardly came into existence for that reason. Indeed, its abolition took place without struggle, in contrast to a number of other European countries. In Iceland, the Church managed only partially to abolish the proprietary-church system after conflicts in the 12th century and in the last decades of the 13th (Staðamál). Nevertheless, under King Sverrir, there were conflicts over the royal proprietary churches despite the fact that in 1152/3 the kingdom had renounced its proprietary-church authority.

In the high Middle Ages, the parish and diocese division assumed a definite form, and the administration came to be more in accordance with the norms of the Church. The proprietary-church system was replaced by the ecclesiastical proprietary right to the churches and their wealth. The bishops received the right to appoint priests, but the owners of the earlier convenience churches received patronage rights. The priests were to live in celibacy, although this was not really carried into effect. In the first half of the 14th century, churches in what is now Norwegian territory numbered approximately 1,200.

The central diocese organization had the bishop's office as its most important authority. During the high Middle Ages, the right to appoint bishops went first from the king to the clergy and people in the bishopric; finally, the chapters secured, after the

pattern of the universal Church, decisive authority in the election of bishops, but not without continued royal influence.

The church administration in each bishopric was brought under the bishop and, after 1152/3, the chapter clerical college of canons, or kórsbræðr, who were obligated to attend to the services in the cathedral and serve as the bishop's advisers. The bishops were consecrated by the archbishop. At the top of this nationwide hierarchical pyramid was (after 1152/3) the archbishop in Niðaróss (Trondheim). He was usually selected by the chapter in Niðaróss, but on several occasions the king appointed a new archbishop in the same way he retained the influence on the election of bishops. The archbishop was consecrated by the pope. The national assemblies of the high Middle Ages served also as national synods, but from 1280 they were replaced by a series of purely ecclesiastical provincial councils, which became an organ for ecclesiastical legislation.

Monasteries gained a foothold in Norway from the beginning of the 12th century. Monasteries and nunneries of the Benedictine order or its reformed branch, the Cluniacs, were established first. In the 1140s, the Cistercians gained a foothold from England. In the second half of the 12th century, the ordained Augustinians established monasteries, and from around 1240 the mendicant orders, Dominicans and Franciscans, established themselves in Norwegian towns. They were relatively independent of the episcopal Church.

In the first half of the 14th century, there were about thirty monasteries in Norway. They were few and small in comparison with southern countries, but played an important role as centers of learning and points of contact with European religious life. The expansion of monasteries took place in collaboration with the bishops, and monasteries contributed to the disengagement from the secular community and the strengthening of the episcopal Church. The independent mendicant orders soon came into a tense relationship with the secular clergy. Their aim was to propagate the faith among the people, and they poached on the secular clergy's preserves. They functioned in the towns, where the parish division was threatened by their activity. There were signs of struggle over rights and authority in the Norwegian Church from the end of the 13th century between individual bishops and chapters and between the bishops and the secular clergy, on one side, and, on the other, the royal free chapel clergy that the kingdom organized from the second half of the 13th century. A royal and an ecclesiastical national organization still could not have come into existence without the kingdom and the Church's having taken on important social functions and achieved a deep rooting in the broad layers of society.

Ecclesiastical functions. The initiative for the creation of a Norwegian ecclesiastical law lay with the Church and kingdom but with rights of resolution of the lǫgþing. After the establishment of the archbishop's seat, the influence of canon law increased. Through papal bulls and decisions at general councils, Norwegian church-meeting decisions or statutes, and the bishops' pastoral letters, canonical influence extended over a broad social range. Inner ecclesiastical legislation increased, and the right of decision of the lǫgþing disappeared during the high Middle Ages. From the 1260s, the Church demanded independent legislative power. Archbishop Jón rauði completed in the first half of the 1270s a specific ecclesiastical law for Trøndelag in the canonical spirit. King Magnús lagabœtir reacted strongly against this, and appears never to have accepted Archbishop Jón's ecclesiastical law. But since he could not agree with the archbishop on this matter, he abstained from completing the ecclesiastical legislation he had begun in 1267–1268, when he revised the lawbooks including the ecclesiastical laws for the western and eastern parts of the country. Magnús lagabœtir's *Landslǫg* (1274) thus does not contain a specific church law. In 1280, Archbishop Jón began the tradition of issuing the provincial statutes at purely ecclesiastical provincial councils. The push to an independent ecclesiastical church law legislation was repelled, and after 1290 the formal rule was that *forn* or old church law from before Magnús lagabœtir's and Archbishop Jón's time, should apply. In practical terms, the situation was unclear, however, with the existence of several concurrent versions of church law.

The Church could, as mentioned above, require atonement for sins through the penitential discipline. But punishment for breach of the church law had originally to be judged at the *þings*. From the time of the establishment of the archbishop's seat, the Church gradually developed independent judicial authority in clerical matters and also over laymen in the spiritual matters pertaining to church law. Ecclesiastical jurisdiction was headed by the bishop. Under his leadership, a judicial apparatus was developed with several similarities to the royal one. From earlier times, the bishop's bailiff (*ármaðr*) had to detect and examine breaches of church law, institute proceedings, and decide settlements. In the first half of the 13th century, the rural deans appear in the sources, clerics who were clearly considered superior to the bailiffs in the ecclesiastical administration of justice, with specific duties in the final phase: legal proceedings, judgment, and settlement. It is, however, only for the Oslo bishopric that a firm division into rural deaneries can be demonstrated. Otherwise, it seems that the priests at the main churches could look after functions pertaining to the office of the rural dean. From the end of the 13th century, an official also appears as the representative of the bishop. The establishment of the office of official probably aimed at centralizing the administration of justice within the bishopric in that the biggest cases and sinners were summoned to the bishop or official. Gradually, ecclesiastical assemblies got to institute proceedings, judge, and initiate punishment in addition to the imposition of atonement through the penitential discipline.

The Church became the country's greatest landowner in the late Middle Ages. Early in the 14th century, it owned approximately 40 percent of the nation's land estimated on the basis of the assessment of landholdings. It thus received extensive and varied economic rights and functions. It appears that from the beginning the king gave land for the episcopal churches. Moreover, the king and secular magnates established monasteries and local churches and donated lands to them. During the Middle Ages, the Church's property increased, especially through donations and by the Church's own purchase of land.

Under the proprietary-church system, the priest received his maintenance from the founders of the churches. The farmers paid a more or less firm annual amount of food, *prestreiða*, in addition to fees or once-only payments for specific ecclesiastical service. To replace this system, the tithe was introduced as the first fixed tax in Norway from the time of Sigurðr Jórsalafari ("Crusader"), and from the time of Magnús Erlingsson it became nationwide. The tithe was divided into four portions, with one quarter for the bishop, one for the priest, one for the parish church, and one for the poor. The tithe was to be one tenth of the yield of the field, and was paid mainly as corn tithe. A new regulation from 1277 decided pay-

ment for almost all economic activity, as well as trade and income from rents. But the Church had enormous difficulties in implementing this regulation in practical ways. Nonetheless, the tithe was the most significant tax in the medieval society and, after land rent, was the heaviest burden on the tenants.

The primary task of the Church was its religious function: to be instrumental in conversion to Christianity, to organize the worship of God, and to administer the Christian law. The Norwegian high-medieval Church managed to a great extent to affect the other forms of European, Catholic religious life. A sign that the ministry had deep roots is reflected in the contributions it received for prayers and masses for the deceased. As a religious institution, the Church was strong in the conscience of the people. Only in this way can one explain its power and influence, which it also used to pursue its earthly interests. The Church held a more important place in the individual's life than did the royal power, and contributed to developing a more integrated society.

Connected with the religious function of the Church were its social tasks. And here, as in many other things, it collaborated with the secular society. A quarter of the tithe was, as mentioned earlier, earmarked for the poor. The farmers themselves were to administer and distribute this tithe. Moreover, the Church received alms to distribute among the needy, and it administered hospitals for the poor and ill and provided medical help. Elderly people who could afford it could buy accommodation in ecclesiastical institutions.

The Church had an important cultural function. Christianity brought Norway into regular contact with European spiritual life. It was primarily clerics who received a higher education in Europe at the universities that became established from the time of the second half of the 12th century. The Church brought the art of reading and writing to the country, and thus established the basis for the written literature of the high Middle Ages. Together with the Crown, the Church created the milieu for this literature, and provided the impetus for some of the best examples of architecture and pictorial art. Preaching comprised the only contemporary vehicle for enlightenment of the people through the exposition of the Christian faith with rote learning of the Creed, the Lord's Prayer, and the Hail Mary. With their cathedral and monastic schools, the ecclesiastical institutions organized nearly all education in the Middle Ages. Education was aimed mainly at clerics, but the royal household, royal administration, and secular aristocracy profited from it as well.

In the 14th century, clerics numbered approximately 2,000. At the top of the hierarchy, there was a group of about 100 prelates: archbishop, bishops, abbots, abbesses, cathedral canons, chapel deans, and the college of priests at the most distinguished royal chapels. Most of the clerics had more modest economic and social positions.

The Church in the late Middle Ages. The Black Death, which in the years 1347–1351 decimated most of Europe, reached Norway in 1349 and spread over most of the country. The following decades saw new attacks, followed by scattered outbreaks until the middle of the 15th century, and possibly longer. The mortality rate is considered to be between half and two-thirds of the population. The economic, social, and political effects were enormous. Between half and two-thirds of the farms and about two-thirds of the holdings from the high Middle Ages were still deserted around 1520.

The decline in population and agricultural production was

followed by a drastic decline in land prices and land rental. The income on rent from inhabited farms fell to around one quarter of what it had been before 1350. If one includes the deserted farms, on which little or nothing was paid, the landowners received probably one fifth or less of the earlier land rent. All landowners, the Crown, the nobility and aristocracy, the Church, and clerics were affected. In addition, the Church and the Crown suffered in the decline in income from taxes: the tithe fell to around one third of what it had been before the plague, and the fixed state taxes to around half. But the farmers were in an economically better situation than earlier. They had more left for their own consumption because of better access to land as a result of reduced land rent and tax, which consequently allowed for increased production. The landowning aristocracy sank to the status of large farmers through the loss of land rent and income from royal service.

When the ecclesiastical basis for income became weakened, there were fewer clerics, and the organization became simpler, both centrally and locally. The loss in income and the decline in population resulted, at the local level, in more churches being served by a single priest. Centrally, there was a tendency to combine the income from several services in order to create an economic basis for a smaller number of clerical offices. The monasteries, which quite one-sidedly based their economy on income from land rents, were especially hard hit by the fall in land rent. In order to establish the religious service and tend to other duties, they needed convents of a certain size. When the economic prerequisite failed, the result was disintegration and reduced prestige. This is the main reason why several monasteries ceased to function before the Reformation.

The personnel of the Church was nonetheless so strong in numbers and the organization so closely woven that it could be regulated in relation to the decline in settlement and population without losing influence. It seems, in fact, that it became stronger in the late Middle Ages. The Church's part of the country's landed property grew to about half, not least through donations. The Church strengthened its position as an independent, official authority, and also increased its influence in the secular government. The Norwegian Council of the Realm, the country's ruling organ, gradually came to consist of a small number of high noble magnates together with the high clergy and with the archbishop as the council's leader.

On the whole, the Church was both in terms of organization and resources less hard hit by the late-medieval crisis than the kingdom and the secular aristocracy. When after the middle of the 14th century it tried to assert its rights according to the treaty of 1277, it met with less resistance. However, in Norway, as in the neighboring countries, the Church had to subject itself to the late-medieval papal right to appoint bishops and increase taxes.

The archbishop and some of the bishops received royal estates. The archbishops Aslak Bolt (1430–1450) and Olav Engelbrektsson (1523–1537) had funds to initiate large architectural projects, and they had at their disposal military resources. In 1458, King Christian I confirmed the treaty of 1277 as compensation for the Council of the Realm's agreeing to accept his son Hans as successor to the throne. The demands of the Church that had not previously been met with were thus partly granted. In the time that followed, the Norwegian Church governed its inner affairs with no interference from the royal power. Bishoprics and other important ecclesiastical positions had been filled largely by Norwegians. But during Christian II's Norwegian rule (1506–1513), the Church was pressured by a royal power that increasingly sym-

pathized with Lutheranism and wanted to decrease the Church's economic and political privileges. The economic basis of the Church was undermined and its organization weakened. From the end of the 1520s, the royal power prepared for the Reformation in Norway. Lutheran preachers were allowed to be active in the country, secular administrators were appointed in some of the monasteries, and the estates were taken away from the bishops. In the spring of 1537, Norway's last archbishop, Olav Engelbrektsson, fled with his battle fleet from Niðaróss to the Netherlands, where he died in exile the year after. In the course of just over one year, the Catholic bishop-church organization of the Middle Ages fell apart. The king appropriated the power earlier enjoyed by the pope and the bishop. Norway became a dependency within the Danish-Norwegian orthodox common state.

Lit.: Munch, P. A. *Det norske Folks Historie I–IV:2 og Anden Hovedafdeling. Unionsperioden*. 2 vols. Christiania [Oslo]: Tønsberg, 1852–63; Maurer, Konrad. *Die Bekehrung des norwegischen Stammes zum Christenthume*. 2 vols. Munich: Kaiser, 1855–56; rpt. Osnabrück: Zeller, 1965; Keyser, Rudolf. *Den norske Kirkes Historie under Katholicismen*. 2 vols. Christiania [Oslo]: Tønsberg, 1856–58; Lange, C. C. A. *De norske Klostres Historie i Middelalderen*. Christiania [Oslo]: Tønsberg, 1856; Taranger, Absalon. *Den angelsaksiske Kirkes Indflydelse paa den Norske*. Kristiania [Oslo]: Grøndahl, 1890; Bull, Edv. *Folk og kirke i middelalderen: Studier til Norges Historie*. Kristiania [Oslo]: Gyldendal; Copenhagen: Nordisk Forlag, 1912; Paasche, F. *Kristendom og kvad: En studie i norrön middelalder*. Kristiania [Oslo]: Aschehoug, 1914; Hübert, Margit. *Nogen undersøkelser om de norske domkapitler*. Kristiania [Oslo]: Grøndahl, 1922; Seip, Jens Arup. *Sættargjerden i Tunsberg og kirkens jurisdiksjon*. Oslo: Dybwad, 1942; Johnsen, Arne Odd. *Studier vedrørende Kardinal Nicolaus Brekespears Legasjon til Norden*. Oslo: Fabritius, 1945; Joys, Charles. *Biskop og Konge. Bispevalg i Norge 1000–1350*. Oslo: Aschehoug, 1948; *Nidaros erkebispestol og bispesete 1153–1953*. Oslo: Land og Kirke, 1955– [editors vary; English summaries]; Kolsrud, Oluf. *Noregs kyrkjesoga. I. Millomalderen*. Oslo: Aschehoug, 1958; Paasche, F. *Møtet mellom hedendom og kristendom i Norden*. Oslo: Aschehoug, 1958; Helle, Knut. *Norge blir en stat 1130–1319*. Handbok i Norges historie, 3. Bergen, Oslo, and Tromsø: Universitetsforlaget, 1964; 2nd ed., 1974 [with bibliographies of sources and more important literature]; Sandvik, Gudmund. *Prestegard og prestelønn*. Oslo: Universitetsforlaget, 1965; Wisløff, C. F. *Norsk kirkehistorie*. 3 vols. Oslo: Lutherstiftelsen, 1966–71, vol. 1; Hamre, Lars. *Norsk historie frå omlag 1400*. Oslo: Universitetsforlaget, 1968; Skånland, Vegard. *Det eldste norske provinsialstatutt*. Bergen: Universitetsforlaget, 1969; Hamre, Lars. *Norsk historie frå midten av 1400-åra til 1513*. Oslo: Universitetsforlaget, 1971; Gunnes, Erik. *Kongens ære. Kongemakt og kirke i "En tale mot biskopene."* Oslo: Gyldendal, 1971; Bagge, Sverre. *Den kongelige kapellgeistlighet 1150–1319*. Bergen: Universitetsforlaget, 1976; Mykland, Knut, ed. *Norges historie*. 15 vols. Oslo: Cappelen, 1976–80; Andersen, Per Sveaas. *Samlingen av Norge og kristningen av landet, 800–1130*. Handbok i Norges historie, 2. Bergen: Universitetsforlaget, 1977 [with bibliographies of sources and more important literature]; Sawyer, Birgit, et al., eds. *The Christianization of Scandinavia*. Alingsås: Viktoria, 1987; Bagge, Sverre, and Knut Mykland. *Norge i dansketiden*. Copenhagen: Politiken; Oslo: Cappelen, 1987; Tryti, Anna Elisa. *Kirkeorganisasjonen i Bergen bispedømme i første halvdel av 1300-tallet*. Bergen: [Historisk institutt, Universitetet i Bergen], 1987 [unpublished].

Magnús Stefánsson

[**See also:** Conversion; Denmark; Finland; Iceland; Monasticism; Norway; Sweden]

Churches, Stone. The first stone churches in Scandinavia were built in the second half of the 11th century. In Denmark, these churches comprise a group, especially around Roskilde, built of calcareous tufa. The most important was undoubtedly the bishop's church at Roskilde, built by Bishop Sven (1074–1088) as a basilica with transeptal chapels and a so-called "westwork" forming the western termination of the church. Another Roskilde church built by Bishop Sven was St. Mary's, a regular basilica without transepts.

Around 1090, a wooden church in Odense, dedicated to St. Alban, was replaced by a stone structure. Early Jutlandish stone churches include Asmild, Venge, and Tamdrup. Asmild was a basilica of Saxon design with a west choir, while Venge, which is still preserved, has a single nave with transeptal chapels, aspidal chancel, and a west tower. The details show English influence. In Århus, an aisled crypt, originally part of the 11th-century church of St. Nicolas, has been excavated.

In Scania, parts of an early bishop's church in Dalby (later an Augustinian foundation) are still preserved. The church was a basilica without transepts, terminated in the east by a square-ended chancel, all built of granite and sandstone.

In Sweden, St. Per in Sigtuna is the only surviving member of an early group of stone churches with aisled naves, transepts with aspidal chapels, small chancels with or without apses, and west towers furnished with galleries for the church patron. This group included the first bishop's church at Linköping and the royal churches of Gudhem and Vreta, later to become monastery churches. The earliest single-naved churches also had towers of this kind (*e.g.*, Rydaholm in Småland and Husaby in Västergötland, where the stone tower originally was added to a wooden church).

The first Norwegian stone churches were a series of 11th-century bishop's churches in Trondheim, Selje (on the west coast of Norway), and Bergen. The churches in Bergen and Trondheim have vanished, but Selje, which had an aisled nave, perhaps with a central tower resting on six slender piers, is still standing as a ruin. A little later, the present cathedral of Stavanger was built as a regular basilica with a west tower, but without transepts and with a small, square chancel. The first stone churches in East Norway, from around 1100 or a little later, seem to be a group in Oslo, including the cathedral of St. Halvard, a parish church dedicated to Clemens, and the royal chapel of St. Mary together with a small church at Hovedøy, later to form the core of a Cistercian abbey church just outside the town. Apart from St. Halvard's, which was a basilica with regular transepts, these churches were single-naved, although St. Clemens's and the church at Hovedøy had a series of pillars in the middle of the nave that carried roof beams, or, more probably, small vaults.

The most important buildings undertaken in Scandinavia in the 12th century were the new cathedrals erected especially in Denmark (including Scania). Among them, Lund in Scania, from 1104 the seat of an archbishop, was the first, and probably the most influential one. Here, masons of Rhenish-Lombardic origin built an aisled church with transepts. No central tower was built, but the nave was terminated by a western twin-tower front. The eastern part of the church was in many respects modeled on the cathedral of Speyer, Germany. The cathedral of Ribe, Jutland, reflects German influence from the Rhine-Maas area. It is even built of stone imported from Germany. Unlike Lund, the apse springs directly from the east wall of the transepts, the crossing of which is covered by a dome and crowned by a central tower. Besides

Lund and Ribe, new cathedrals were built in Viborg (heavily restored), in Århus (rebuilt) and, late in the century, in Roskilde. In Trondheim, Norway, the building of a new cathedral started around 1150 with the erection of a transept by English masons, probably from Lincoln. Monastic churches also played an important part in the development of Scandinavian stone architecture. St. Alban's, Odense, and Venge were early Benedictine foundations. Later foundations of great importance were Ringsted (Benedictine) and Sorø (Cistercian). Munkeliv near Bergen (Benedictine) is a key monument for understanding the 12th-century architecture of Bergen and West Norway. In Sweden, Cistercian abbeys like Alvastra and Varnhem become equally important.

The 12th century saw the building of many parish churches in stone. In Denmark alone, some 1,500 churches were built, the majority of them consisting of a single nave, a chancel with or without apse, and sometimes a west tower. Usually, their details reflect stylistic influence from the local cathedral. In Sweden, churches with east towers occur (*e.g.*, Hossmo, Småland). The churches of Gotland are characterized by masonry and sculptural details of especially high quality. At Bornholm, a special type of round church was built, obviously for defense purposes. In Norway, parish churches made of stone are found on both sides of the Oslo fjord, along the coast of West Norway and in Tröndelag, where a series of large parish churches reflect Anglo-Norman influence probably conveyed by masons from Trondheim.

Around 1160, brick was introduced as a new building material in Scandinavia, first in Denmark, a little later in Sweden, and from around 1250 in Norway. In Denmark, brick became the dominant building material; in Sweden, it was generally used except in northern Götaland and Gotland, where good building stone was abundant. In Norway, brick was to some extent used in the eastern part of the country and in Bergen and Trondheim, but the majority of the Norwegian stone churches were built in coursed rubble or dressed stone throughout the Middle Ages.

An early, unique Danish church made of brick is the church of Kalundborg, dating from the last quarter of the 12th century. It is built over a cruciform ground plan, probably Byzantine-inspired. The equally long cross-arms terminate in octagons that, together with the crossing, are crowned by towers.

Another early Danish brick building is the cathedral of Roskilde (1170–1220), the design of which seems to reflect Early Gothic stylistic ideals as manifested in some North French cathedrals (Noyon, Laon, Arras). Of a similar French design is the cathedral of Uppsala (*ca.* 1250–1350), which in part was built by the French architect Étienne de Bonneuil, who worked in Uppsala from 1287 to 1300. The cathedral of Trondheim (1180–1320) could, on the other hand, be labeled as typically English. It was built in dressed stone. Both general design and ornamental details show close resemblance with Lincoln and, as far as the western part of the building is concerned, Westminster Abbey. The octagonal termination of the choir is, however, a unique construction unparalleled among European cathedrals, while the choir extension of the cathedral in Stavanger (1273–1300) is less original. Its east front is probably inspired by Lincoln.

The cathedrals mentioned above were all basilicas. So was also one of the most important late 13th-century Danish churches, the cathedral of St. Knud (Cnut) in Odense, and two other large churches, the town churches of St. Peter's, Malmö and St. Mary's, Copenhagen, both built in the 14th century. In other Danish towns, a sort of "pseudo-basilica" with triforium galleries but without clerestory windows was built, *e.g.*, in Slagelse and Køge. Ordinary hall churches also occur, *e.g.*, St. Olav's, Elsinore.

In Sweden, hall churches were introduced by the mendicant orders, the Dominican church of St. Mary's in Sigtuna (1230–1240) being the first. The type became common, *e.g.*, St. Mary's in Visby, Gotland, the cathedrals of Linköping, Strängnäs, and Åbo in Finland. The Brigettine churches of Vadstena, Sweden, and Maribo, Jutland, both 15th-century, were also built as large hall churches. But the most spectacular Danish example is perhaps the 15th-century choir of Århus cathedral (1460–1470).

Apart from the cathedrals of Roskilde and Uppsala, which were inspired by French models, the majority of Danish and Swedish brick churches are offspring of North German brick architecture. St. Mary's, Visby, and other Gotlandish stone churches have their closest parallels in Rhineland-Westphalia. Masons from Gotland also introduced this style in Linköping and even in Uppsala.

The period 1300–1500 saw practically no church-building activity in Norway. In Sweden and Denmark, relatively few new churches were built, but many churches were enlarged and vaulted. New and larger choirs were built, and towers were added in the west. Some new churches of particular importance have already been mentioned. Others include the cathedral of Haderslev and the well-preserved Carmelite church of St. Mary's, Elsinore.

Lit.: Boethius, Gerda, and Axel Romdahl. *Uppsala domkyrka 1258–1435*. Stockholm: Almqvist & Wiksell, 1935; Fischer, Gerhard. *Domkirken i Stavanger*. Oslo: Dreyer, 1964; Fischer, Gerhard. *Domkirken i Trondheim*. 2 vols. Oslo: Land og Kirke, 1965; Krins, Hubert. "Die frühen Steinkirchen Dänemarks." Diss. University of Hamburg, 1968; Tuulse, Armin. *Romansk konst i Norden*. Stockholm: Bonnier, 1968; Anker, Peter. *L'Art scandinave*. 2 vols. La nuit des temps, 28–9. L'Abbaye Sainte–Marie de la Pierre-qui-vire [Yonne]: Zodiaque, 1968–69. [English translation: *The Art of Scandinavia*. London and New York: Hamlyn, 1970]; Cnattingius, Bengt. *Linköpings domkyrka*. 2 vols. Stockholm: Almqvist & Wiksell, 1987; for inventories see: *Sveriges kyrkor*. Stockholm: Almqvist & Wiksell, 1912–89; *Danmarks kirker*. Copenhagen: Christensen, 1933–89; *Norges kirker*. Oslo: Gyldendal, 1959–89.

Hans-Emil Lidén

[**See also:** Architecture; Stave Church]

Clári saga *see* **Klári (Clári) saga**

Climate. The exact nature of the climate of medieval Scandinavia has long been debated, and remains controversial. The pioneers in the field of historical climatology, such as Lamb and Flohn, believed that a warm period occurred in northern Europe around 1000–1200, similar to the warmth of the early 20th century, followed by a decline in temperatures culminating in the so-called Little Ice Age from about 1450 to 1750. That there was a cold period or periods around this latter time is certain; only the details and timing within different geographical regions remain a matter for debate and further research. Changes in climate prior to about 1450 are, unfortunately, much harder to verify, because, although advances have occurred in the availability and methods of interpretation of indirect or "proxy" climate data, such data are generally available only for isolated locations within continental Scandinavia, and often only for short, discrete periods. More information exists for Iceland and Greenland, but, even where proxy

data are available, they frequently pose problems of interpretation. The need for cautious and critical use of historical sources in particular has recently been emphasized. For these reasons, it is not possible to give a detailed description of medieval Scandinavian climate.

The available evidence can, however, give important clues as to how the climate may have varied. Because of lack of evidence for precipitation, the discussion will center on temperature variations. Over the entire period (*ca.* A.D. 500 to *ca.* 1700), decadal averages of annual-mean temperatures, while appearing quite variable, probably deviated by at most a few degrees Celsius from those prevailing during the 20th century.

Different types of proxy data include tree-line fluctuations, pollen records, documentary evidence, glacier oscillations, and tree rings. For example, the widths of annual growth rings of certain trees in continental Scandinavia correlate well with summer temperature. One interesting long tree-ring series, spanning 436 to 1981 and based on pine (*Pinus sylvestris*), has been produced by Bartholin for the area around Lake Torneträsk in northern Sweden. This series indicates a period of cold temperatures around 550. A warmer period then lasted to about 780. From that time, temperatures remained cooler until about 930. A warm period set in then and lasted for twenty to thirty years. From around 950 to 970, it was cooler again. From then to around 1140, a distinct mild period is suggested, followed by a short cold spell lasting perhaps ten years. From about 1150 to about 1560, the climate appears rather variable, but tending toward the mild side. The coldest summers of this time were probably around 1350, 1400, and 1470. The most marked cold period of the entire series is from about 1560 to about 1740. If these climate variations in northern Sweden are correct, similar conditions are likely to have prevailed in northern Finland. A study by Sirén, based on pines from a number of sites in northern Finland, concluded that the 1200s were colder than the 1300s, and the 1400s colder than the 1500s. An oak chronology from the Gotha River area in western Sweden suggests that temperatures between 1450 and 1700 were somewhat lower than those after 1700.

Indications of climate changes may also be drawn from studies of glacier moraine positions and mass balance estimates because glacial advance and growth generally signify a response to a colder climate. Conversely, a shrinking glacier suggests a time of warmer climate. There may, however, be a time lag of some years between a change in climate and a glacier's response. A number of methods are used to date glacier fluctuations, the most important of which are radiocarbon dating and lichenometry. Radiocarbon dating relies on measuring the proportion of the isotope C^{14} (radiocarbon) in the carbon contained in a particular material, for example, from buried soils or pieces of wood in glacier moraines. Lichenometry makes use of the fact that, in any given location, lichens, which can live for many centuries, grow at a rate that is roughly constant. Their size is therefore an indication of their age. Using these dating techniques, Karlén and other researchers have built up a guide to past glacier variations in Sweden and Norway. Several advances are indicated from about 550 to 950. Possible glacier advances between 800 to 900 would accord well with the dendrochronological evidence for a cooler climate in northern Sweden around 780 to 930. A radiocarbon date from Ritajekna in Sarek National Park points to another advance around 1290. It also seems likely that glaciers were relatively large during a period of cool summers from 1350 to 1400. Glaciers in Sweden probably reached their greatest extent in historical times in the 17th and early 18th centuries.

From 950 to 1590, glacial advances in Norway appear to have been better defined than in Sweden. Seven radiocarbon dates associated with moraines give ages around 1330 and 1490, and these data are believed to reflect periods of maximum glacier extent. The former of these dates is supported by a Norwegian document from 1340, which mentions a glacier advance of Jöstedalsbreen in southwestern Norway (see Eide 1955). Research by Karlén also shows evidence for an advance at this time from Vuolep Allakasjaure in northern Sweden. However, climatic changes in northern Sweden and southern Norway may not be synchronous. Following the advance of about 1490, it is possible that a warm spell occurred in southern Norway at the beginning of the 17th century, succeeded by a cold period. Another cold period is indicated from the late 17th century, with a warmer period separating the two.

Other documentary evidence from Norway includes sporadic references to weather in early sources, such as *Heimskringla*. This work refers to severe years around A.D. 961 to 965, 974, 1020, 1030–1035, 1047, 1207, and 1213. Good years are said to have occurred shortly after about 885 and from 1103 to 1130. These weather references cannot be regarded as reliable, however. A recent project led by Knud Frydendahl of the Danish Meteorological Office has attempted to gather all medieval historical references to climate in Denmark. Only isolated descriptions referring to individual years exist. Years that may have been severe in the Dano-Norwegian Baltic region include 1307, 1323, 1356, 1408, 1426, 1460, 1547, 1555, 1570, 1600, and 1608. However, the data sources used for this information have not all been historically verified.

Both Iceland and Greenland have high-resolution proxy-climate records that are among the longest in the world. The Iceland record is based on historical evidence, and Greenland has a number of records based on isotope data from deep ice cores. The evidence from Greenland will be considered first. The concentration of oxygen and deuterium isotopes in high-latitude precipitation is determined mainly by the temperature of its formation. This factor causes seasonal isotopic variations in snow and ice as well as long-term variations due to climatic changes. According to Dansgaard, ice-core data from Crête, central Greenland, suggests a considerable and rapid warming late in the 9th century. He argues that this rise may well have facilitated the Norse settlement of Iceland at this time. The name of Greenland, when this country was in turn settled by Eiríkr rauði ("the red") around 985, may have described reality. Dansgaard suggests that, when this happened, Greenland was at the end of a warm period longer than any that has occurred there since. A deterioration in the climate may have begun around 1030, with the climate remaining generally cold to about 1520. The coldest years of the period were around the late 1200s and the late 1300s. During this time, however, there were mild spells around the early 1100s and the early 1400s. From about 1520 to about 1740, temperatures remained on the cool side, but not markedly so. A cold period is seen from about 1740 to about 1900. Dansgaard suggests that the cold climate of the 14th century played an important part in the tragic end of the Greenland Norse colony. McGovern, however, while conceding that climate may have played a certain part, emphasizes the importance of economic and social factors.

As documents referring to climate in Iceland are both sparse and noncontemporary until the late 12th century, evidence for a mild climate for the first few centuries of settlement (from ca. 870 to 1170) is circumstantial only. The fact that the settlers not only traveled to Iceland but also chose to remain, and that they were able to grow barley, are examples of this evidence. From 1180 to 1210, sources suggest a period of cold climate, and from 1212 to 1232 a milder one. Over the next few decades, there are sporadic references to severe seasons. The 1280s and 1290s were undoubtedly severe, while the years 1300 to around 1320 were comparatively mild. The early 1320s, on the other hand, were harsh, with sea ice off the coasts and severe weather. The 1330s and 1340s are likely to have been mild. From around 1350, the climate seems to have become colder, and the 1370s were particularly harsh. The frequent presence of the sea ice off the Icelandic coast during the 14th century may also be inferred from two geographical descriptions; one is in a version of *Guðmundar saga*, the other is attributed to Ívarr Bárðarson. The period from about 1380 to 1430 was comparatively mild. There is some evidence for a mild climate between 1430 and 1560. For the latter part of the 16th century, sources suggest a comparatively harsh climate. The early and latter part of the 17th centuries were cold, but a mild spell occurred around 1640 to 1670.

From the research that has been done, it is evident that the climate of the Scandinavian regions varied considerably over the centuries from about 500 to 1700 and that these variations were spatial as well as temporal. It does seem likely, however, that there was a prolonged time of mild climate common to both the North Atlantic region (ca. 870 to 1050 or later) and to northern Scandinavia (ca. 950 to 1150). The available evidence is not yet sufficient for us to know whether southern Scandinavia was similarly affected. However, evidence for mild temperatures in places like England at this time suggests that this was possible. Subsequently, a number of alternating mild and colder intervals lasting for decades or longer occurred in the North Atlantic area. Over this period, the climate of northern Scandinavia also appears to have been variable, but may have remained milder than cooler. The "Little Ice Age" was undoubtedly a very real climatic event, but the time of its onset and duration appears to vary considerably in different geographical regions. According to Dansgaard's ice-core records from Crête, Greenland, the coldest years of the entire series (which runs from 600 to the present) occurred during 1150–1400. The period from about 1450 to 1700 was not particularly cold. The Iceland record suggests that the climate was always very variable on all time scales, and that cold periods from about 1610 to 1640, from about 1670 to 1700, and from about 1720 to about 1770 were interspersed with milder periods. In northern Sweden, however, a more protracted and very distinct cold period starts around 1570. In southern Norway, a cold period is indicated from around 1610, but it appears to have been relatively mild from the mid- to late 17th century, after which it became colder again.

Lit.: Bull, Edvard. "Islands klima i oldtiden." *Geografisk tidskrift* 23 (1915), 1–5; Thorodssen, Thorvaldur. *Árferði á Íslandi í þúsund ár.* 2 vols. Copenhagen: Hið íslenzka fræðafjelag, 1916–17; Finnur Jónsson, ed. *Det gamle Grønlands beskrivelse af Ívar Bárðarson (Ivar Bårdsson).* Udgiven efter håndskrifterne. Copenhagen: Levin & Munksgaard, 1930; Thórarinsson, Sigurður. "Tefrokronologiska studier på Island." *Geografiska Annaler* 26 (1944), 1–215 [English summary: "Tephrochronological Studies in Iceland"]; Eide, T. O. "Breden og Bygda." In *Norveg.* Ed. N. Lid. Oslo: Aschehoug, 1955, vol. 5, pp. 1–

42; Thórarinsson, Sigurður. "The Thousand Years Struggle Against Ice and Fire." *Museum of Natural History, Dept. of Geology and Geography, Miscellaneous Papers, No. 14.* Reykjavik: [s.n.], 1956; Sirén, Gustaf. "Skogsgränstallen som indikatör för klimatfluktuationera i norra Fennoskandien under historisk tid." *Communicationes Instituti Forestalis Fenniae* (Helsingfors) 54.2 (1961), 1–66 [English summary]; Friberg, Nils, *et al.* "Klimat." *KLNM* 8 (1963), 480–94; Andrae, Carl Göran. "Studier Kring Funbo Kyrkas räkenskaper 1395–1483." *Historisk tidskrift* (Sweden) 4 (1965), 385–440; Lamb, Hubert H. "The Early Medieval Warm Epoch and Its Sequel." *Palaeogeography, Palaeoclimatology, Palaeoecology* 1 (1965), 13–37; Flohn, Hermann. "Klimaschwankungen in historischer Zeit." In *Klimaschwankungen und Pendelungen des Klimas in Europa seit dem Beginn der regelmässigen Instrumenten-Beobachtungen (1670).* Ed. H. Von Rudloff. Braunschweig: Vieweg, 1967, pp. 81–90; Páll Bergþórsson. "An Estimate of Drift Ice and Temperature in 1000 Years." *Jökull* 19 (1969), 94–101; Dansgaard, Willy, *et al.* "Climatic Record Revealed by the Camp Century Ice Core." In *The Late Cenozoic Glacial Ages.* Ed. K. K. Turekian. Proceedings of Yale University Symposium. New Haven: Yale University Press, 1971, pp. 37–56; Le Roy Ladurie, Emmanuel. *Times of Feast, Times of Famine: A History of Climate Since the Year 1000.* Trans. Barbara Bray. London: Allen and Unwin, 1972; Dansgaard, Willy, *et al.* "Climatic Changes, Norsemen and Modern Man." *Nature* 255 (1975), 24–28; Fritts, Harold C. *Tree Rings and Climate.* London, New York, and San Francisco: Academic, 1976; Lamb, Hubert H. *Climate: Present, Past and Future. Vol. 2: Climatic History and the Future.* London: Methuen, 1977; Ingram, Martin J., *et al.* "Historical Climatology." *Nature* 276 (1978), 329–34; Bell, Wendy T., and Astrid E. J. Ogilvie. "Weather Compilations as a Source of Data for the Reconstruction of European Climate During the Medieval Period." *Climatic Change* 1 (1978), 331–48; La Marche, Valmore C., Jr. "Tree-Ring Evidence of Past Climatic Variability." *Nature* 276 (1978), 334–38; Þórhallur Vilmundarson. "Evaluation of Historical Sources on Sea Ice near Iceland." In *Sea Ice, Proceedings of an International Conference.* Ed. Þ. Karlsson. Reykjavik: National Research Council, 1972, pp. 159–69; Ogilvie, Astrid E. J. "Climate and Society in Iceland from the Medieval Period to the Late Eighteenth Century." Diss. University of East Anglia, 1981; Karlén, Wibjörn. "A Comment on John A. Matthews' Article Regarding C14–Dates of Glacier Variations." *Geografiska Annaler* 63, A:1–2 (1981), 19–21; McGovern, Thomas H. "The Economics of Extinction in Norse Greenland." In *Climate and History.* Ed. T. M. L. Wigley *et al.* Cambridge: Cambridge University Press, 1981, pp. 404–33; Karlén, Wibjörn. "Holocene Glacier Fluctuations in Scandinavia." In *Holocene Glaciers.* Ed. W. Karlén. *Striae* (Uppsala), 18 (1982), 26–34 [special issue]; Stuiver, Minzie. "High-Precision Calibration of the AD Radiocarbon Time Scale." *Radiocarbon* 24.1 (1982), 1–26; Bråthen, Alf. "Dendrokronologisk serie från västra Sverige 831–1975." In *Riksantikvarieämbetet och Statens Historiska Museer Rapport RAÄ 1.* Stockholm: Central Board of National Antiquities and the National Historical Museums, 1982; Bartholin, Thomas S., and Wibjörn Karlén. "Dendrokronologi i Lapland AD 436–1981." *Dendrochronologiska Sällskapet,* Meddelanden 5 (1983), 3–16; Wigley, Tom M. L., and Larry D. Williams. "A Comparison of Evidence for Late Holocene Summer Temperature Variations in the Northern Hemisphere." *Quaternary Research* 20 (1983), 286–307; Bartholin, Thomas S. "Dendrochronology in Sweden." In *Climatic Changes on a Yearly to Millennial Basis: Geological, Historical and Instrumental Records.* Ed. N.-A. Mörner and W. Karlén. Proceedings of the Second Symposium on Climatic Changes and Related Problems. Stockholm: Reidel, 1984, pp. 261–2; Ogilvie, Astrid E. J. "The Past Climate and Sea Ice Record from Iceland, Part 1: Data to A.D. 1780." *Climatic Change* 6 (1984), 131–52; Karlén, Wibjörn. "Dendrochronolgy, Mass Balance and Glacier Front Fluctuations in Northern Sweden." In *Climatic Changes on a Yearly to Millennial Basis,* pp. 263–71; Röthlisberger, Friedrich. *10.000 Jahre Gletschergeschichte der Erde.* Aarau, Frankfurt am Main, and Salzburg: Sauerländer, 1986; Alexandre, Pierre. *Le climat en Europe au moyen âge. Contribution à l'histoire des variations climatiques de 1000 à 1425, d'après les sources narratives de l'Europe occidentale.* Recherches d'histoire et de sciences sociales, 24. Paris: École des Hautes Études en Sciences Sociales, 1987; Lamb, Hubert H. "What Can Historical Records Tell Us About the Breakdown of the Medieval Warm Climate in Europe in the Fourteenth and Fifteenth Centuries—An Experiment." *Beiträge zur Physik der Atmosphäre* 60.2 (1987), 131–43; Grove, Jean M. *The Little Ice Age.* London and New York: Methuen, 1988; Schweingruber, Fritz Hans, *et al.* "Radiodensitometric—dendroclimatological conifer chronologies from Lapland (Scandinavia) and the Alps (Switzerland)." *Boreas* 17 (1988), 559–66; Ogilvie, Astrid E. J. "Climatic Changes in Iceland c. A.D. 865 to 1598." *Acta Archaeologica* [forthcoming].

Astrid E. J. Ogilvie

Clothmaking was in many respects similar among the Nordic countries. Tools are more common in Norwegian Viking Age graves than in graves in other countries, while implements used by professional crafts in central parts of Europe seem to be documented at an earlier date in Sweden. Finland seems to have been influenced by eastern neighbors as well as from the West.

The sources for knowledge of textile work are of three kinds: archaeological, including tools and cloth mainly from Viking Age graves and medieval settlements; written sources, such as laws, official documents, and literature; and living tradition, where tools known from the Middle Ages continued to be used alongside more modern equipment.

According to the sources known at present, it seems unlikely that any professional clothmaking existed in the Nordic countries in the Middle Ages. The production of cloth for everyday use seems to have been a home craft. Both archaeological finds and written sources suggest considerable importation of professionally produced textiles, including woolen cloth of different qualities, often named after the place of production, such as *amsterdamst* or *iperst.* It has not been possible, however, to identify any of these specific cloth types in archaeological finds, and it is often difficult to form an opinion about whether a fragment of cloth is imported or locally produced. The construction of the cloth is in most cases the same.

Sheep wool is the main domestic textile material. Some examples of very coarse goat-hair fabrics have been found in city excavations (Lund in Sweden: Blomqvist 1963: 228 *et passim;* Bergen in Norway: Schjølberg 1984: 79 *et passim*).

Finds of seed from vegetal fibers like flax (*Linum usitatissimum*) and hemp (*Cannabis sativa*) show that these plants were grown. Both were paid as tithes according to church law (Archbishop Jón's *Kristniréttr* [ecclesiastical law], Norway [rpt. in Keyser and Munch 1846–95: 2:355.19]. Sweden: *Upplandslagen* 6.5 [rpt. in Strömbäck 1960]—both 13th century). Vegetal fibers are seldom preserved in the soil in the northern countries, but importation of linen is known from the written sources. It seems likely that even nettle (*Urtica dioica*) was utilized for textiles.

Tools are the most important indication of local textile production. In most cases, only those made of imperishable material are preserved, but finds of wooden objects do occur, as in the famous Oseberg (Norway) barrow from the 9th century.

All stages of textile production were women's work, except fulling, which, at least in Iceland, seems to have been done by

14. Blanket in 2/2 twill. Detail of corner with starting border and selvage; 13th century. Skjoldehamn, Troms, Norway. University Museum, Tromsø. Courtesy of Norsk Folkemuseum, Oslo.

15. Traditional weaving on the warp-weighted loom, Stord, western Norway, 1956. The weaver beats up the weft with a sword beater while standing on a low bench to reach the first rows of the weft near the beam. Courtesy of Norsk Folkemuseum, Norway.

16. Swift from the Oseberg barrow; 9th century. Reconstruction. Courtesy of the University Museum of National Antiquities, Oslo.

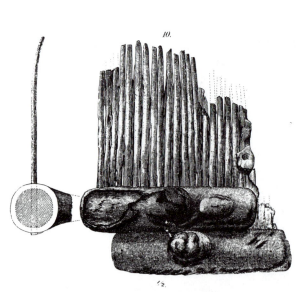

17. A pair of wool combs from Hyrt, western Norway (Hord). The handles are broken off. Viking Age. Historical Museum, University of Bergen, Norway. From Annual of Foreningen til norske fortidsminnesmerkers bevaring.

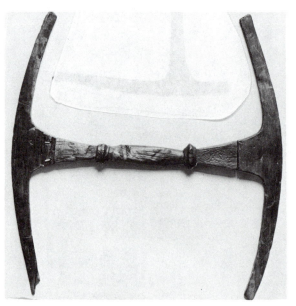

18. Skein-winding reel from the Oseberg barrow; 9th century. Courtesy of the University Museum of National Antiquities, Oslo.

men. For preparing wool for spinning, a pair of combs with long iron teeth were used to separate the long from the short wool and to lay the fibers even and parallel. Combs have been found in several Viking Age graves, even with wooden parts preserved, very similar to those known from professional clothmaking in more recent times. Wool combs are mentioned in the sagas (*e.g.*, *Grettis saga*). Cards are first mentioned at the beginning of the 16th century.

The wool was spun on a dropped spindle, one complete example of which was found in the Oseberg barrow. Finds of whorls made of stone, clay, or bone are common both in Viking Age graves and in medieval settlements. The Oseberg spindle had a carved notch in top for holding the thread, and the stone whorl was attached to the upper part of the spindle, much like those found in folk museums in Norway, Iceland, and other Nordic countries. Even the distaff for fastening the wool during spinning is of the same type as more recent ones, with notches carved along the upper part, as seen from the finds from excavations of Oslo.

The yarn was made into a ball or a skein, both of which are known from finds from prehistoric times. Bobbins of weft thread, a skein-winding reel of the "niddy-noddy" type, and a swift are documented in the Oseberg find.

In Iceland and Norway, in the Middle Ages and later, the warp-weighted loom was the common instrument for weaving ordinary everyday cloth, like wadmal (2/2 twill) and tabby. In Norway, loom weights have been found in abundance in Viking Age graves and also in medieval settlements, while they are rare in medieval sites in Sweden and Denmark. The great majority of the Norwegian loom weights are soapstone, easily worked and provided with a hole for fastening the warp threads. In Iceland, lava stones were used. Loom weights made of fired clay are the common type in all other countries.

The warp-weighted loom consists of two uprights, about 2.2 m. high, carrying a revolving beam, between 2 and 3 m. long. Along the beam is a row of holes. During warping, a band was woven that arranged the threads in a regular row. The band was sewn to the holes in the beam, forming a starting border, a third selvage. The loom stood in a slanting position, leaning against the wall or a beam. It was equipped with a shed rod and from one to three heddle rods. The weaving started at the top and proceeded downward, while the weaver walked back and forth along the loom, inserting the weft. The weft was beaten up with a sword-like beater made of iron, whalebone, or wood. Instead of a woven selvage, a corded band could hold the warp and be sewn to the beam; in both cases, a closed selvage was the result. Fragments of such starting borders can in many cases determine the use of the warp-weighted loom. In Iceland, this loom was the only one used until the 18th century, and the operating of it for weaving wadmal is known from written descriptions in the last century, when the tradition was still extant. The weaving of tabby is still practiced in certain areas of Norway, and the two types of binding, 2/2 twill and tabby, were representative of products of the warp-weighted loom.

This loom allowed a person to weave both cloth of great width as well as narrow pieces; very little was wasted by cutting. The pieces were short, perhaps up to 3 m. The long weaves for unspecified use belonged to the horizontal loom.

Iceland was the only Nordic country that had a large export of cloth to western and central Europe. Wadmal (vaðmál) was the main export article of the country, woven on the warp-weighted loom by women. Influenced by the long weaves in the European market, the Icelandic women succeeded in weaving up to twenty ells in one piece. Wadmal was woven in several qualities, one of which was a standard of value in Iceland, as it had been even in the other Nordic countries in the early Middle Ages. Length, width, thread count, and weight for different qualities were fixed by law (Hoffmann 1964: 194–226). As an example of export, the receipt for nine years of papal tithes from Iceland amounted in 1337 to 12,164 ells of wadmal in three different qualities.

In central parts of Europe, the warp-weighted loom had long since been replaced by the horizontal loom with treadles, operated by male weavers, as is documented from 11th-century France (Carus-Wilson 1971: 165 *et passim*). Around 1200, the new loom seems to have appeared in Sweden, as evidenced by a couple of finds of single pulleys, which have been interpreted as part of a horizontal loom. This evidence might perhaps mean that individual professional weavers, immigrant craftsmen with their new, effective loom, made their first appearance in the North at this time. Apparently, these weavers were isolated craftsmen. Weavers' guilds are unknown in Scandinavia in the Middle Ages. A new type of binding construction in twill seems to indicate a new technology connected with the horizontal loom. A great amount of asymmetrical twill, 2/1 or 1/2, has been brought to light in excavations in medieval cities (*e.g.*, Bergen and Oslo in Norway, Lund and Gamla Lödöse in Sweden). Very little of this material has as yet been published (see Lindström 1982: 180 *et passim*, Kjellberg 1979: 85, 102, *et passim*).

The quality of the twill varies a great deal, from coarse to very fine. The latter is a worsted, sometimes in a lozenge pattern, and both spinning and weaving are exquisite. The fabrics were doubtless imported from a well-established foreign center of professional weaving. The warp-weighted loom is not well suited for asymmetrical bindings, and it is inconceivable that the fine medieval three-shed twills could be woven on this implement. A few simple fragments of this construction, with the characteristic starting border of the warp-weighted loom, have been found in Sweden (Lund) and in Norway (Bergen and Oslo). They were most likely imitations of the imported cloth, woven by women who did not own the new horizontal loom. A recent theory, which must be regarded with skepticism, advocates that a group of very fine quality twills found in rich Viking Age graves, and similar to the ones mentioned above, were woven in western Norway (Bender Jørgensen 1987: 120).

Lit.: Keyser, R., *et al.*, eds., *Norges Gamle Love indtil 1387.* 5 vols. Christiania [Oslo]: Grøndahl, 1846–95; Grieg, Sigurd. "Kvindearbeide." In *Oseberg.* Oslo: Universitetets Oldsaksamling, 1928, vol. 2, pp. 173–205; Strömbäck, Dag, ed. *Lex Upplandiae (Upplandslagen).* Corpus Codicum Suecicorum Medii Aevi, 15. Copenhagen: Munksgaard, 1960; Hoffmann, Marta. "Garnvinde." *KLNM* 6 (1960), 206–7; Strömbäck, Dag, ed., *Lex Upplandiae.* Corpus Codicum Suecicorum Medii Aevi, 15. Copenhagen: Munksgaard, 1960; Granhall, Ingvar. "Hampa: Sverige." *KLNM* 6 (1961), 105–6 [*cf.* subsequent entries treating Finland, Denmark, and Norway, cols. 106–9]; Hoffmann, Marta. "Karding." *KLNM* 8 (1963), 278–9; Hoffmann, Marta. "Klede." *KLNM* 8 (1963), 457–8 [*cf.* subsequent entries on individual countries, cols. 458–74]; Blomqvist, Karin. "Vävnader." In *Thulegravningen 1961.* Ed. Ragnar Blomqvist and A. W. Mårtensson. Archaeologia Lundensia, 2. Lund: Kulturhistoriska Museet i Lund, 1963, pp. 227–32; Hoffmann, Marta. *The Warp-Weighted Loom: Studies in the History and Technology of an Ancient Implement.* Studia Norvegica, 14. Oslo: Universitetsforlaget, 1964; rpt. McMinnville: Robin and Russ

Handweavers, 1982; Lange, Johan. "Lin." *KLNM* 10 (1965), 578–9; Hoffmann, Marta. "Lin." *KLNM* 10 (1965), 579–80 [*cf.* subsequent entries, cols. 581–90]; Kaukonen, Toini-Inkeri. "Linberedning: Sverige och Finland." *KLNM* 10 (1965), 590–3; Hoffmann, Marta. "Linberedning: Norge." *KLNM* 10 (1965), 593–4; Geijer, Agnes. "Lärft." *KLNM* 11 (1966), 129–30; Kaukonen, Toini-Inkeri. "Lärft: Finland." *KLNM* 11 (1966), 130–1; Høeg, Ove Arbo. "Nesle." *KLNM* 12 (1967), 284–5 [*cf.* subsequent entries, cols. 285–6]; Hoffmann, Marta. "Oppstadvev." *KLNM* 12 (1967), 621–9; Hoffmann, Marta. "Renning." *KLNM* 14 (1969), 71–2; Carus-Wilson, Eleanora. "Haberget, a Medieval Conundrum." *Medieval Archaeology* 13 (1969), 148–66; Hoffmann, Marta. "Sengeutstyr." *KLNM* 15 (1970), 134–42 [*cf.* subsequent entries, cols. 142–9]; Hoffmann, Marta. "Spinning." *KLNM* 16 (1971), 499–500; Vilkuna, Kustaa. "Spinning: Finland." *KLNM* 16 (1971), 500–1; Hoffmann, Marta. "Toskaft." *KLNM* 18 (1974), 536; Hoffmann, Marta. "Ull og ullberedning." *KLNM* 19 (1975), 276–8 [*cf.* subsequent entries, cols. 278–9]; Hoffmann, Marta. "Vadmål." *KLNM* 19 (1975), 409–12 [*cf.* subsequent entries, cols. 412–16]; Hoffmann, Marta. "Valking." *KLNM* 19 (1975), 466–7; Berg, Gösta. "Valking: Sverige." *KLNM* 19 (1975), 467–8; Hoffmann, Marta. "Vever." *KLNM* 19 (1975), 679 [*cf.* subsequent entries, cols. 679–80]; Hoffmann, Marta. "Veving." *KLNM* 19 (1975), 680–1; Hoffmann, Marta. "Vevstol." *KLNM* 19 (1975), 681–2 [*cf.* subsequent entries, col. 683]; Lindström, Märta. "Textilier." In *Uppgrävt förflutet för PK banken i Lund.* Ed. Anders W. Mårtensson. Archaeologia Lundensia, 7. Lund: Kulturhistoriska Museet i Lund, 1976, pp. 279–92; Kjellberg, Anne. "Tekstilmaterialet fra Oslogate 7." In *De arkeologiske utgravninger i Gamlebyen, Oslo.* Ed. E. Schia *et al.* 2 vols. Oslo: Alvheim & Eide, 1977–79, vol. 2, pp. 83–104; Lindström, Märta. "Medieval Textile Finds in Lund." In *Textilsymposium Neumünster 1981.* Ed. L. B. Jørgensen and K. Tidow. Textilmuseum Neumünster, 1982, pp. 179–86; Schjølberg, Ellen. "The Hair Products." In *The Bryggen Papers.* Supplementary Series, 1. Ed. Asbjørn Herteig. Bergen: University Press, 1984, pp. 73–91; Bender Jørgensen, Lise. "A Survey of North European Textiles." In *Studien zur Sachsenforschung,* 6. Hildesheim: Lax, 1987, pp. 100–21; Kjellberg, Anne, and Marta Hoffmann. "Tekstilene." In *De arkeologiske utgravninger i Gamlebyenn, Oslo.* Mindets tomt, Søndre felt og deler av Nordre felt [forthcoming].

Marta Hoffmann

[**See also**: Crafts; Fashions; Guilds; Textiles, Furnishing]

Cnut, St. *see* **Knud (Cnut), St.**

Cnut the Great *see* **Knud (Cnut) the Great**

Codex Frisianus *see* **Fríssbók**

Codex Regius of the *Poetic Edda* is an Icelandic MS of ninety small quarto pages, but the fifth gathering, probably sixteen pages, is now lost. The MS is written by one hand not known elsewhere, and is dated palaeographically to about 1270–1280. *Codex Regius* is the most important MS of eddic poetry. It now contains twenty-nine poems in systematic order: the first ten lays are about the ancient Norse gods, but the remaining part is about ancient heroes. *Codex Regius* is a copy of an older MS now lost. The fragmentary AM 748 I 4to contains, in no particular order, seven eddic lays, and one of them, *Baldrs draumar*, is not preserved elsewhere. This MS is dated to about 1300 or a little later. The textual relationship between the two MSS points to a common written original. In the 1220s, Snorri Sturluson wrote a textbook on poetry, called *Snorra Edda* or the *Prose Edda.* It is almost certain that he used the text of the mythical poems *Vafþrúðnismál*

and *Grímnismál* from the common written source underlying the *Poetic Edda.* Finnur Jónsson believed (latest 1933) that Snorri had used a large collection of eddic poems when he compiled *Snorra Edda.* Bugge (1867) thought that the collection in *Codex Regius* was younger than *Snorra Edda* and from about 1240, but that older copies of some lays might have been used. Wessén believed that the writing of *Snorra Edda* gave the impetus for collecting the eddic poems. Researchers have concluded for literary (Heusler) or orthographical (Lindblad) reasons that *Codex Regius* is made from several collections of poems, the oldest from about 1200. Lindblad concludes that *Codex Regius* had two main sources, a heroic one from about 1200 and a mythological one from about 1240–1250. He considers influence from *Snorra Edda* to play a lesser role than do most other researchers.

It is not known whether *Codex Regius* had a name originally. In 1623, Jón Guðmundsson lærði ("the learned") mentioned for the first time an *Edda* by Sæmundr Sigfússon fróði ("the learned"; 1056–1133), older than *Snorra Edda.* In 1643, when Bishop Brynjólfur Sveinsson in Skálholt obtained *Codex Regius* (we do not now know from where), he believed that it was the *Edda* by Sæmundr, although it is now thought that Sæmundr played no part in collecting or writing *Codex Regius.* A name and a note in the MS indicate that it had been in Skagafjörður (in the north) or on the Reykjanes peninsula (southwest) during the previous years.

The last poem before the lacuna in *Codex Regius* is *Sigrdrífumál*, with the last part of it missing. This poem is preserved complete in paper copies from the 17th century. The explanation seems to be as follows. The lay is found in *Volsunga saga* as well, but in 1641 Brynjólfur Sveinsson received the only parchment MS of this saga, and at least two commentaries on *Sigrdrífumál* were written for him. It seems certain that there is a direct connection between the copying of the complete text of *Sigrdrífumál* and the activities in connection with *Volsunga saga* after 1641. The lacuna in *Codex Regius* accordingly occurred after 1641 but before 1643. Brynjólfur Sveinsson presented the MS to the king of Denmark in 1662, hence the name *Codex Regius* ("King's Book"). In the Royal Library, it was given the number GkS 2365 4to. It was brought back to Iceland on April 21, 1971, and is now in the Árni Magnússon Institute in Iceland.

Ed.: Bugge, Sophus, ed. *Norrœn fornkvæði.* Kristiania [Oslo]: Malling, 1867; rpt. Oslo: Universitetsforlaget, 1965; Wimmer, F. A., and Finnur Jónsson, eds. *Håndskriftet Nr. 2365 4to gl. kgl. samling på det store Kgl. bibliothek i København (Codex regius af den ældre Edda) i fototypisk og diplomatisk gengivelse.* Copenhagen: Samfund til udgivelse af gammel nordisk litteratur, 1891 [facsimile and transcription]; Heusler, Andreas, ed. *Codex Regius of the Elder Edda.* Corpus Codicum Islandicorum Medii Ævi, 10. Copenhagen: Munksgaard, 1937 [facsimile]. **Bib.**: Halldór Hermannsson. *Bibliography of the Eddas.* Islandica, 13. Ithaca: Cornell University Library, 1920; Jóhann S. Hannesson. *Bibliography of the Eddas: A Supplement to Bibliography of the Eddas (Islandica, XIII).* Islandica, 37. Ithaca: Cornell University Press, 1955. **Lit.**: Finnur Jónsson. *Seks afhandlinger om eddadigtene.* Copenhagen: Gad, 1933; Wessén, Elias. "Den isländska eddadigtningen: Dess uppteckning och redigering." *Saga och sed* (1946), 1–31; Lindblad, Gustaf. *Studier i Codex Regius av äldre Eddan.* Lundastudier i nordisk språkvetenskap, 10. Lund: Gleerup, 1954; Lindblad, Gustaf. "Snorre Sturlasson och eddadiktningen." *Saga och sed* (1978), 17–34; Lindblad, Gustaf. "Poetiska Eddans förhistoria och skrivskicket i Codex regius." *Arkiv för nordisk filologi* 95 (1980), 142–67; Harris, Joseph. "Eddic Poetry." In *Old Norse–Icelandic Literature: A Critical Guide.* Ed. Carol J. Clover and John Lindow. Islandica, 45. Ithaca and London: Cornell University Press, 1985, pp. 68–156 [essay with bibliography; supplement to Islandica 13 and 37 is in preparation by J. Harris]; Einar G. Pétursson. "Hvenær týndist kverið úr Konungsbók Eddukvæða?" *Gripla* 6 (1984), 265–91.

Einar G. Pétursson

[**See also:** *Baldrs draumar*; Eddic Poetry; *Grímnismál*; *Sigrdrífumál*; *Snorra Edda*; *Vafþrúðnismál*; *Vǫlsunga saga*]

Cogadh Gaedhel re Gallaibh

Cogadh Gaedhel re Gallaibh ("The War Between the Irish and the Foreigners") was written around 1114–1116, possibly in the monastery at Killaloe, Ireland. It survives in three imperfect MSS: L, a leaf of the *Book of Leinster* (1160); D, part of a 14th-century compilation MS (T.C.D. H.2 17); and B, a copy transcribed by Friar Michael O'Clery in 1635, now preserved in the Royal Library of Albert I, Brussels (MS 4639). Textual criticism reveals that while D and B were transmitted independently of each other, both ultimately derive from L.

Cogadh Gaedhel re Gallaibh is a propagandist work designed to enhance the prestige of Muirchertach O'Brien, king of Munster 1086–1118, by eulogizing Brian Boroimhe, his great-grandfather. The author made extensive use of written sources, primarily the exemplars of the *Annals of Ulster* and the *Annals of Inisfallen*, though he also exploited oral traditions. However, he manipulated these authentic records to dramatize the Vikings' depredations in order to highlight the prowess of Brian and his dynasty. *Cogadh Gaedhel re Gallaibh* greatly exaggerates the scale and intensity of the Viking onslaught on Ireland. It creates the illusion of a systematic invasion in which the whole country is subjugated, and the population is reduced to horrendous servitude, until Brian Boroimhe leads the Irish to freedom at the epic battle of Clontarf (1014).

In reality, the Danish conquest of Ireland is entirely ficticious, and *Cogadh Gaedhel re Gallaibh*'s climactic battle between the Irish and the Foreigners at Clontarf is a fraud. The actual battle of 1014 was merely another clash between Irish provincial kings (with Norse mercenaries) competing for national supremacy. Clontarf marked no turning point for the Irish and Hiberno-Norse communities.

Cogadh Gaedhel re Gallaibh and the poems it inspired, particularly *Cath Cluana Tairbh*, captured the imaginations of the Irish people during subsequent centuries of English oppression. More than any other work, it shaped the image of the Vikings in Ireland until very recent times.

Ed.: Todd, James H., ed. *Cogadh Gaedhel re Gallaibh: The War of the Gaedhil with the Gaill*. Rolls Series. London: Longmans, Green, Reader, and Dyer, 1867; Mac Neill, John, ed. *Cath Cluana Tairbh. Gaelic Journal* 7 (1896), 8–11, 41–4, 55–7. **Lit.**: Goedheer, Albertus Johannes. *Irish and Norse Traditions about the Battle of Clontarf*. Haarlem: Tjeenk Willink, 1938; Ryan, John. "The Battle of Clontarf." *Journal of the Royal Society of Antiquaries of Ireland* 68 (1938), 1–50; Ó Lochlainn, Colm. "Poets on the Battle of Clontarf—I." *Éigse* 3 (1942), 208–18; Leech, Roger H. "*Cogadh Gaedhel re Gallaibh* and *The Annals of Inisfallen*." *North Munster Antiquarian Journal* 11 (1968), 13–21; Hughes, Kathleen. *Early Christian Ireland: Introduction to the Sources*. Sources of History: Studies in the Uses of Historical Evidence. London: Hodder & Stoughton, 1972, pp. 288–300; Smyth, Alfred P. "The *Black* Foreigners of York and the *White* Foreigners of Dublin." *Saga-Book of the Viking Society* 19 (1975–76), 101–17.

Henry A. Jefferies

[**See also:** Ireland, Norse in]

Coins and Mints

Coins and Mints. Scandinavian coinage began in the Viking Age. The Vikings' worldwide expansion and enterprise brought foreign coins to their homelands. French *deniers*, Anglo-Frisian *sceattas*, and Anglo-Saxon pennies occur in some small finds of the early Viking Age from western Scandinavia. To Haithabu we can assign the earliest Scandinavian coinage, anonymous strikings imitating, from around 825, Carolingian *denier* types. This coinage developed, accompanied by declining weight standards, and spread to other, as yet unidentified Danish mints, perhaps at Jelling.

Around the year 1000, or shortly before, pennies were issued for the first time in the names of Scandinavian kings: Sven Haraldsson (Forkbeard; r. 985–1014) in Denmark, Óláfr Tryggvason (r. 995–1000) in Norway, and Olaf Skötkonung (r. ca. 995–1022) in Sweden. Sven and Óláfr had been commanders of the Viking army that attacked England and forced the English king, Æthelred II (978–1016), to pay tribute (Danegeld) to the aggressors. The two first Danegelds were paid in 991 and 994. The English penny type of that period, the CRVX-type, so named after the explanatory legend of the cross in the reverse field, became the prototype for the earliest pennies of the three Scandinavian kings. Some of their moneyers have Anglo-Saxon names. The late Anglo-Saxon circulation of pennies over a fixed period seems not to have been established in Scandinavia.

The many rich silver hoards from Viking Age Scandinavia reveal a significant increase in the import of Anglo-Saxon pennies to Scandinavia from the 990s onward. Within Scandinavia, the Anglo-Saxon coins mingled with German and other continental pennies.

With the Anglo-Saxon and German coins are also found, in declining percentage of the total number, Arab silver *dirhems* (also called "Kufic coins" from the epigraphy), originating almost without exception in the eastern parts of the Muslim world.

The period of essential import of Kufic coins was about 870–960. From the silver hoards, we learn that coins now played an important role as means of payment in Scandinavia. The Kufic coins, as later the Anglo-Saxon and German pennies, were convenient pieces of coveted silver, not difficult to adjust to accustomed weight units. Silver was the precious metal of value to the Scandinavians of the period, and these coins were usually of a high and stable fineness. Nonetheless, the foreign coins found in Scandinavian Viking Age hoards show that they have been tested for purity in many cases.

In this period, the native coinage continued in Denmark and Norway. In Sweden, however, coinage at the mint of Sigtuna came to a stop around 1030, and it was not taken up again until around 1180. On the island of Gotland, native coinage seems to have begun around 1140. In Norway, as we can see from the composition of the coin hoards and from the coins themselves, a national currency was definitely established during the reign of King Haraldr harðráði ("hard-ruler") Sigurðarson (r. 1047–1066). The Norwegian pennies were issued to a standard of about 0.89 grams, 1/240 of a Norwegian *mǫrk*. The silver content, at first remaining at the international level of about 90 percent silver, dropped successively down to a mean of about 33 percent silver. These coins of more than 50 percent copper are identified as the *Haraldsslátta* in *Morkinskinna*: "being mostly of copper, at its best, it was half silver." Coins of this low silver content were continuously issued in considerable quantities throughout the reign of Óláfr kyrri ("peaceful") Haraldsson (r. 1066–1093). Only a small number of these national pennies still have legible legends. We can see that *Nidarnes* (= Niðaróss, now Trondheim) was the mint of the earliest issues. The *Hamar* mint signature is found on three pennies of King Haraldr's later issue of lower silver content, and is written in the native Norse language: *Ólafr á Hamri* ("Ólafr at Hamar"). Nidarnes/Niðaróss is nevertheless supposed to have been the main Norwegian mint of the *Haraldsslátta* period. The same mint is also mentioned on specimens of the reformed pennies of Magnús berfœttr ("bare-leg") Ólafsson (r. 1093–1103), but is now called "Kaupangr." By this reform, the Norwegian penny had its weight reduced by half, 0.44 grams, but at the same time the approximately 90-percent silver content of the old standard was reintroduced.

The old coin reckoning (1 *mǫrk* = 8 *aurar* = 24 *ørtogar* = 240 pennies) was now changed, as far as the reckoned penny is concerned: 1 *mǫrk* = 8 *aurar* = 24 *ørtogar* = 480 pennies, the penny still being the only unit to be coined.

Within the Danish coinage, two parallel standards developed. In Jutland, a penny weight of 0.76 grams corresponded with a reckoning of 288 pennies to a Danish *mark* (*ca.* 0.218 grams). A different reckoning in the eastern provinces of the country (Funen, Zealand, and Scania), 192 pennies to the *mǫrk*, gave a heavier penny of 1.14 grams. The time of Sven Estridsen (r. 1047–1074) is famous for an impressive group of imitations of Byzantine coin types. The Byzantine prototypes rarely, if ever, occur in Scandinavian hoards, where Byzantine coins generally are not common. For a short period in the later part of Sven's reign, Danish pennies have legends in runic characters, which are also found on contemporary Norwegian pennies. During the reign of Harald Hen (r. 1074–1080), Denmark saw a development toward a national, exclusive coinage similar to, if not so distinct as, the Norwegian coinage under Haraldr harðráði. Down to King Niels (r. 1104–1134), coins had been issued at the following mints: Lund, Roskilde, Ringsted, Slagelse, Odense, Ribe, Viborg, Ørbæk, Gori? (presumably in Scania), Ålborg, Århus, Toftum, Borgeby, and Thumatorp.

The 12th century saw a development of bracteates within Scandinavian coinage. Bracteates are coins struck on one side only and on a flan so thin that the design is clearly visible in negative on the other side. Such one-faced coins were first struck in Norway for Ólafr Magnússon (r. 1103–1115). Some beautiful bracteates, obviously inspired by German models and their highly artistic execution, were issued in Denmark (Ålborg, Århus, Hjørring, and Horsens) about the middle of the 12th century. In the great period of the Valdemars, from Valdemar the Great (r. 1157–1182) to Valdemar the Victorious (r. 1202–1241), two-sided coins of normal penny weight and size occur again. As time went on, the coins were debased, and especially the following period, 1241–1340/77, saw a dramatic decline in the "Civil War coins," as they are usually called. The mints were in Lund, Roskilde, Schleswig, Ribe, and somewhere in North Jutland. Notable, too, is the counterfeit minting by outlaws on the island of Hjelm.

When the Swedish coinage was resumed around 1180, by King Knut Eriksson (r. 1167–1195), bracteates were the only coins to be issued both in Svealand (Uppsala) and Götaland (Lödöse, near present Gothenburg). Bracteates mention even Nyköping and Sigtuna as mints around 1230. In the testament of Magnus Birgersson (r. 1275–1290) from 1285, eight mints are mentioned in Svealand: Nyköping, Örebro, Uppsala, and Västerås; in Götaland: Jönköping, Skänninge, Skara, and Söderköping. Throughout Sweden, the reckoning of 1 *mǫrk* = 8 *aurar* = 24 *ørtogar* prevailed, but the number of pennies to the *mǫrk* varied: in Svealand 192, in Götaland 384, on Gotland and Öland with some neighboring part of continental Sweden 288. The Svealand reckoning was in-

troduced in Götaland around 1290, but Gotland stayed with its own reckoning until after 1361, when the Danes took over the island. In this period, Swedish coinage consists mainly of anonymous strikings, bracteates, and, during the reign of Birger Magnusson (r. 1290–1318), two-sided coins. These anonymous bracteates and coins bear no kings' names, only a single letter that may sometimes be interpreted as the initial of some coinage authority (*e.g.*, B = King Birger Magnusson; uncial E = Duke Erik, his brother; M = Magnus, Birger's son; R = *Rex*, W = Duke Valdemar, Birger's brother). Other letters are assumed to refer to mints (I = Jönköping; K = Kalmar; L = Lödöse; O = Örebro; S = Skara, Söderköping and/or Stockholm). Anonymous two-sided coins attributed to the reign of Magnus Eriksson (r. 1319–1364) have some parallel types of undisputably Norwegian provenance. Magnus was king of Norway as well (r. 1319–1355), and from the coins it has been demonstrated that there must have been a monetary union between the two countries down to the 1360s. The national provenance of some types of this period is still questionable.

In Norway, Sverrir Sigurðarson's (r. 1184–1202) two-sided pennies of the halfpenny standard supplemented the monotonous series of penny-fraction values (1/2 and 1/4 pennies); the same dies also produced bracteate strikings. Known mints were Niðaróss/Trondheim and Bergen; Oslo, Tönsberg, and Veøy have been suggested on the basis of questionable legends. The bracteates attributable to the reign include farthings of a mean weight of about 0.06 grams, among the smallest coins ever struck. Among the great variety of types is a large group of single letters (A, B, E, G, H, K, M, N, S, T, V), interpreted as initials of mints, earlier partly also as initials of princes with coining authority.

From the time of Hákon Hákonarson (r. 1217–1263), only anonymous bracteates are known, except for very few with the king's name and title (*Rex Hacu*, *Rex Haco*). The legend *Rex et Comes* ("King and Earl") may allude to the period of the king's minority (1217–1222/3), when Earl Skúli Bárðarson, the king's father-in-law and later opponent, acted as regent. The silver content of the bracteates now dropped to one third, which may have some connection with the value reckoning in *forngild mǫrk*, one third of a mark of fine silver.

Magnús lagabœtir ("law-mender") Hákonarson (r. 1263–1280) again introduced two-sided pennies, whose cross form and legend (*Benedictus Deus* and *Sit nomen Domini benedictum*) may reflect the *gros tournois*, introduced in France in 1266. The earliest penny type of Eiríkr Magnússon (r. 1280–1299), minted at Bergen and Tönsberg, is a very close imitation of the English sterling of the Long Cross type of 1279. The next type of Eiríkr, from around 1285, of unknown mint (Bergen?), is famous for showing for the first time the coat of arms of Norway, the lion rampant with an axe in its forepaws. This type was also issued in three denominations: penny, halfpenny, and farthing, as was also the corresponding type (profile bust) of Duke Hákon Magnússon, the king's brother and, as it seems from the evidence of the coins, the only Norwegian prince below the rank of king to enjoy the right of coining. Oslo was the ducal mint, and it was also one of the mints (with Bergen) of Hákon when he became king of Norway (Hákon V; r. 1299–1319). In 1319, his daughter's son, Magnus Eriksson, became king of both Sweden and Norway, which introduced a very long period (to 1905) when Norway stayed in union with one of the two other Scandinavian kingdoms, or both of them, political circumstances that necessarily had a decisive impact on the coinage.

In the late Middle Ages, from the 14th century, Scandinavian coinage was dominated by multiples of the *penny* value. The Gotland *ørtog*, or *gote*, was issued at Visby presumably from the second quarter of the 14th century. King Albrecht, of the Mecklenburg house (1364–1389), introduced shortly before 1370 the *ørtogar* on the Swedish mainland, minted at Stockholm and Kalmar. This *ørtog* coinage was to continue until 1534, the most important mints under the Swedish Crown in this period being Stockholm, Västerås, and Åbo (in Finland). In periods of native rebellion against the Scandinavian Union and the Danish Union king, the coin types aim at representing the patron of the realm, St. Erik the King; the Åbo coins, however, show St. Henrik the Bishop, the patron of Finland. Leaders of the anti-Danish movement, like Karl Knutsson (king of Sweden 1448–1457, 1464–1465, 1467–1470), Svante Nilsson Sture (r. 1504–1512), and Sten Sture the Younger (r. 1512–1520), added their family badges to the coin types. The latter, while not a king, put his own name in the obverse legend: *Steen Sture Ritter.*

The development in Denmark and Norway had a closer connection to the North German coinage of the Hanseatic League. The cities of Flensburg (Schleswig) and Ribe issued, before 1379, coins of the recently (*ca.* 1365) introduced North German *witten* denomination. The Danish King Erik, of the Pomeranian house, followed up with *witten* struck at Næstved around 1397–1405. He continued his coinage by striking, at Næstved and Lund, the sterling (= 3 pennies) of the same type as the previous *witten*; and later, he went on striking sterlings of pure copper. Because of this monetary policy, Erik came into a long-lasting conflict with the Hanseatic cities. His successor, Christoffer, of the Bavarian house, resumed the coinage of *witten*, or *hvid* as it was called in Danish. The Hanseatic *schilling* (= 12 pennies) was a model for the Danish *skilling* now introduced. In the interregnum following King Christoffer's death in 1448, the Privy Council issued coins with the obverse legend running *Moneta Regni Dacie.* Malmö (Scania) became the leading Danish mint, and continued to be so during the reign of Christian 1 (r. 1448–1481), renowned for a prolific coinage of *hvid* coins.

Hans 1 (r. 1481–1513) continued the *hvid* coinage at Malmö, but mints were established in Copenhagen and Ålborg as well. The *skilling* denomination was again issued, but this king is especially famous for having introduced a coinage in gold, comprising the values of noble and Rhenish *gulden.* The latter was also issued in Norway (a unique specimen in the Dresden collection), when Hans renewed the activity of the mints (Bergen, Niðaróss/Trondheim, and possibly Oslo), which had been idle for more than a century. With his noble dies, Christian II (r. 1513–1523) struck the first Scandinavian silver *gulden* (Malmö 1516, 1518). Silver coins of about the same size struck in Stockholm in 1512 for Sten Sture the Younger vary considerably in weight and have been regarded as multiples of the *mørk* value.

The introduction of larger silver coins, the forerunner of the Taler (*daler*), marks the end of medieval Scandinavian coinage. The borderline is usually drawn in Sweden by the year 1521, when Gustav 1 came into power, and in Denmark-Norway by 1540–1541, when Christian III began his monetary reform.

The three Scandinavian archbishops, and occasionally some bishops, apparently obtained coining rights or shares of the coinage. Some bracteates of ecclesiastical types (*e.g.*, a hand holding a crozier, a bishop's head facing a crozier) from around 1190–1215 were probably issued by the archbishop of Uppsala (Sweden). The archbishop of Niðaróss (Norway) was given the right of coining about 1220, according to a royal charter, although Norwegian coins of undoubtable ecclesiastical provenance are known only some fifty to sixty years later, when bracteates of a bishop's head facing were issued, most probably by Archbishop Jón rauði ("the red"; 1268–1282). King Eiríkr Magnússon withdrew the coining right of the Norwegian archbishop in 1281, and this right was not restored until 1458, at a time when the Norwegian mints were idle. Therefore, only the last three archbishops of Niðaróss, Gaute Ivarsson (1474–1510), Erik Valkendorf (1510–1522), and Olav Engelbrektsson (1523–1537), were able to make use of this right, issuing coins in the name of St. Óláfr, the patron of the country and the archbishopric. The last two also had their own names, titles, and family arms included in the coin design. The Danish archbishop of Lund (Scania) had a share in the coinage from the middle of the 12th century until about 1400, as had also the bishops of Roskilde and Ribe. The coin types clearly reflect the joint royal and episcopal coinage when the king, through his picture and/or symbol(s), occasionally with name and/or title, occupies one side of the coin and the (arch-)bishop the other. A coin with a crown on one side and a miter reads *Anno Domini MCCXXXIIII*, thus having a dating unique within European numismatics. The coin may have been struck for Bishop Niels Stigsen of Roskilde. While the bishop of Ribe had to give up his share in the coinage (1234–1280), the Roskilde bishop kept his, and perhaps he celebrated this event by issuing the *Anno Domini* coin.

Throughout the Middle Ages, foreign coins played an important part in Scandinavian numismatic history as prototypes to coin types and design, but also, especially in the Viking Age and the late Middle Ages, as means of payment. English sterlings (late 13th–14th centuries) and nobles (14th century), and German and Dutch *gulden* (14th–early 16th centuries) ought to be mentioned. North German coins of lower denominations also circulated within Scandinavia, one group, the "hole Pennies" of the Mecklenburgian (crowned) Bull Head type, so frequently that the the question has been raised if they were (partly) Scandinavian imitations.

The basic sources for the coin history of medieval Scandinavia are the coins themselves, as they are preserved and/or kept on file in their systematic context (even better if also in their find) in public and private collections. The three national Scandinavian coin collections are, ranked by seniority: The Royal Coin Cabinet (*Kungl. Myntkabinettet*), Stockholm; The Royal Collection of Coins and Medals (*Den Kongelige Mønt- og Medailliesamling*), The National Museum, Copenhagen; and The University Coin Collection (*Universitetets Myntkabinett*), Oslo. Supplementary evidence is available in preserved contemporary documents, such as law texts and diplomata (see *Diplomatarium Danicum, Diplomatarium Norwegicum,* and *Diplomatarium Suecanum*). For Denmark, a series of selected documentary sources to medieval coin history has been published: "Kilder til Danmarks Møntvæsen," *Nordisk Numismatisk Årsskrift* 1955, 1960, 1961, and 1982, with index.

Special surveys of research on Scandinavian medieval numismatics were published for the five latest International Numismatic Congresses: Rasmusson, N. L. *Relazioni* 1. Rome: International Numismatic Commission, 1961, pp. 291–335; Skaare, K. *A Survey of Numismatic Research 1960–1965.* Copenhagen: International Numismatic Commission, 1967, pp. 148–73; Skaare, K. *A Survey of Numismatic Research 1966–1971* 2. New York and Washington, D.C.: International Numismatic Commission, 1973, pp. 19–212; Jensen, J. S. *A Survey of Numismatic Research 1972–1977.* Bern: International Numismatic Commission, 1979, pp. 247–62; Jensen, J.

S. *A Survey of Numismatic Research 1978–1984*. London: International Numismatic Commission, 1986, pp. 346–64).

English abstracts of books, papers, and articles on Scandinavian numismatics (included in "Western and Central Europe"; see indices) are currently published in *Numismatic Literature*, edited semiannually by the American Numismatic Society, New York. The chief Scandinavian numismatic journals are *Nordisk Numismatisk Årsskrift/Nordic Numismatic Journal* (1936–) and *Nordisk Numismatisk Unions Medlemsblad* (Copenhagen 1936–).

KLNM (1956–78; 22 vols., including index) contains articles on numismatics in Scandinavian languages. An index to these articles is published in *Nordisk Numismatisk Unions Medlemsblad* (1979), 132–5.

Lit.: Schive, Claudius Iacob. *Norges Mynter i Middelalderen*. Christiania [Oslo]: Tönsberg, 1865 [see Skaare, Kolbjörn. "'Schive' er hundre år." *Nordisk Numismatisk Unions Medlemsblad* (1965), 69–74]; Hildebrand, Hans. "Sveriges mynt under medeltiden." In *Sveriges medeltid* 1:2. Stockholm: Norstedt, 1877; rpt. with index Stockholm: Gidlund, 1983; Hauberg, Peter. *Danmarks Myntvæsen og Mynter i Tidsrummet 1241–1377*. Copenhagen: Gyldendal, 1885; Hauberg, Peter. *Danmarks Myntvæsen i Tidsrummet 1377–1481*. Copenhagen: Gyldendal, 1886; Hauberg, Peter. *Gullands Myntvæsen*. Copenhagen: Gyldendal, 1891; Hauberg, Peter. *Myntforhold og Udmyntninger i Danmark indtil 1146*. Copenhagen: Luno, 1900; Hauberg, Peter. *Danmarks Myntvæsen i Tidsrummet 1146–1241*. Copenhagen: Luno, 1906; Bengt, Thordeman. "Sveriges medeltidsmynt." In *Mønt*. Ed. Svend Aakjær. Nordisk Kultur, 29. Stockholm: Bonnier; Oslo: Aschehoug; Copenhagen: Schultz, 1936, pp. 1–92; Holst, Hans. "Norges mynter til slutten av 16. århundrede." In *Mønt*, pp. 93–138; Galster, Georg. "Danmarks Mønter." In *Mønt*, pp. 139–200; Lindahl, Fritz. "Danmarks mønter 1377–1448." *Nordisk Numismatisk Årsskrift* (1955), 73–92; Malmer, Brita. "A Contribution to the Numismatic History of Norway During the Eleventh Century." In *Commentationes de nummis saeculorum IX–XI in Suicia repertis* 1. Ed. N. L. Rasmusson and L. O. Lagerqvist. Stockholm: Almqvist & Wiksell, 1961, pp. 223–376; Rasmusson, Nils Ludvig. "An Introduction to the Viking-Age Hoards." In *Commentationes de nummis saeculorum IX–XI in Suicia repertis* 1, pp. 1–16; Malmer, Brita. *Nordiska mynt före år 1000*. Acta Archaeologica Lundensia, ser. in 8°, no. 4. Lund: Gleerup; Bonn: Habelt, 1966; Skaare, Kolbjörn. "Die karolingischen Münzfunde in Skandinavien und der Schatzfund von Hon." *Hamburger Beiträge zur Numismatik* 20 (1966), 393–408; Lagerqvist, Lars O. "The Coinage at Sigtuna in the Names of Anund Jakob, Cnut the Great and Hathacnut." In *Commentationes de nummis saeculorum IX–XI in Suecia repertis* 2. Ed. Nils Ludvig Rasmusson and Brita Malmer. Stockholm: Almqvist & Wiksell, 1968, pp. 383–414; Skaare, Kolbjörn. "'Olav kyrre's myntreform." *Nordisk Numismatisk Årsskrift* (1969), 21–36; Skaare, Kolbjörn. "Norsk utmyntning på Håkon Håkonssons tid." *Nordisk Numismatisk Årsskrift* (1970), 5–36; Lagerqvist, Lars O. *Svenska mynt under vikingatid och medeltiden (ca. 995–1521) samt gotländska mynt (ca. 1140–1565)*. Numismatiska bokförlagets handbokserie, 4. Stockholm: Numismatiska bokförlaget, 1970; Jensen, Jörgen Steen. "Møntfundet fra Kirial på Djursland." *Nordisk Numismatisk Årsskrift* (1970), 37–168; Galster, Georg. *Unionstidens udmøntingere. Danmark og Norge 1397–1540, Sverige 1363–1521*. Copenhagen: Dansk numismatisk forening, 1972; Malmer, Brita. *King Canute's Coinage in the Northern Countries*. Dorothea Coke Memorial Lecture. London: Viking Society for Northern Research, 1974; Hatz Gertz. *Handel und Verkehr zwischen dem Deutschen Reich und Schweden in der späten Wikingerzeit. Die deutschen Münzen des 10. und 11. Jahrhunderts in Sweden*. Stockholm: Kungl. vitterhets-, historie-, och antikvitetsakademien; Almqvist & Wiksell, 1974; Jonsson, Kenneth. "Fastlandsmyntinger under Birger Magnusson (1290–1318)

med utgångspunkt från skatt- og lösfund." *Nordisk Numismatisk Årsskrift* (1975/76), 83–161; Malmer, Brita. "Mecklenburgian Bracteates with a Bull's Head and the Monetary History of Sweden." *Numismatica Stockholmiensia* 1 (1975/76), 9–11; Malmer, Brita, ed. *Corpus nummorum saeculorum IX–XI qui in Suecia reperti sunt*. Stockholm: Almqvist & Wiksell, 1. *Gotland*: 1.1. *Akebäck-Atlingbo*, 1975 (ed. with Nils Ludvig Rasmusson), 1.2. *Bal-Buttle*, 1977, 1.3. *Dalhem-Ethelhem*, 1982, 1.4. *Fardhem-Fröjel*, 1982; 3. *Skåne*: 3.1. *Århus-Grönby* 1985, 1.4. *Maglarp-Ystad*, 1987, 8. *Östergötland*: 8.1. *Älvsted-Viby*, 1983, 16. *Dalarna*: 16.1. *Falun-Rättvik*, 1979; Skaare, Kolbjörn. *Coins and Coinage in Viking-Age Norway: The Establishment of a National Coinage in Norway in the XI Century, with a Survey of the Preceding Currency History*. Oslo, Bergen, and Tromsø: Universitetsforlaget, 1976; Skaare, Kolbjörn. "Kong Sverres utmyntning." *Nordisk Numismatisk Årsskrift* (1979/80), 93–109; Jensen, Jörgen Steen. "Danish Finds of the So-Called Mecklenburg-Scandinavian Type." In *Proceedings of the International Numismatic Symposium: Warsaw-Budapest, 1976*. Ed. I. Gedai and K. Birö-Sey. Budapest: Akademiai Kaido, 1980, pp. 143–8; Malmer, Brita. *Den senmedeltida penningen i Sverige. Svenska brakteater med krönt huvud och krönta bokstäver*. Stockholm: Almqvist & Wiksell, 1980; Skaare, Kolbjörn. "Mints in Viking-Age Scandinavia." *Proceedings of the Eighth Viking Congress, Århus 1977*. Ed. Hans Bekker-Nielsen *et al*. Odense: Odense University Press, 1981, pp. 37–42; Malmer, Brita. "Monetary Circulation in South-Eastern Sweden c. 1350–1500 in the Light of Three Major Church-Finds." *Nordisk Numismatisk Årsskrift* (1981), 147–59; Skaare, Kolbjörn. "Coinage and Monetary Circulation in Norway from the Middle of the 14th Century till c. 1500." *Nordisk Numismatisk Årsskrift* (1981), 136–46; Jensen, Jörgen Steen. "Monetary Circulation in Denmark c. 1350–1500." *Nordisk Numismatisk Årsskrift* (1981), 160–70; Benedixen, Kirsten. "Sceattas and Other Coin Finds." In *Ribe Excavations 1970–1976* 1. Ed. Mogens Bencard. Trans. Barbara Bluestone. Esbjerg: Sydjysk Universitetsforlag, 1981, pp. 63–101; Malmer, Brita, and Inger Hammarberg. "The 1972 Västerås Hoard and Monetary History of Sweden 1470–1520." *Nordisk Numismatisk Årsskrift* (1982), 41–68; Jonsson, Kenneth. "Översikt över fastlandsmyntningen ca. 1180–1250." *Numismatiska Meddelanden* 39 (1983), 75–103; Skaare, Kolbjörn. "On Coins in Cumulative Finds from Medieval Churches." In *Proceedings of the Tenth International Numismatic Congress, London 1986* [forthcoming].

Kolbjörn Skaare

[**See also**: Hoards]

Commemorative Poetry. The survival of a quantity of skaldic poetry, much of which was committed to writing centuries after its supposed composition, attests to the genre's capacity to produce durable verbal memorials to significant events and figures, contemporary or otherwise. However, the combined, sometimes contradictory, testimony of fragmentary primary and comparatively late secondary sources to the original social, political, and artistic functions of individual skaldic compositions, and therefore to the contours of the memorial tradition as a whole, is all too often either unconvincing or inconclusive. Thus, while Bjarni Kolbeinsson's *Jómsvíkingadrápa* and Þorkell Gíslason's *Búadrápa* are confidently accepted as 12th–13th-century accounts of the unsuccessful 10th-century Norwegian enterprise of the Jómsvíkingar, the seven extant *helmingar* of Þórðr Særeksson's *drápa* on Þórálfr Skólmsson's heroic death at Fitjar (961) could belong either to a tribute rendered *in memoriam*, or to a later (11th-century) commemoration of Þórálfr's heroism.

Memorial compositions (*lausavísur* and strophic sequences) abound, ostensibly prompted by the deaths of those whose lives they commemorate. The drowning of his son Boðvarr, for example, apparently prompted Egill Skalla-Grímsson to reflect upon death's decimation of his family (*Sonatorrek*, 10th century). To Þormóðr Kolbrúnarskáld is attributed a 10th-century memorial (*Þorgeirsdrápa*) to the warrior life by which Þorgeirr Hávarsson lived and eventually died (Jón Helgason 1953 lists further examples).

Memorials to kings and leaders represent a particularly thematically consistent group. Individual treatments vary: contrast Markús Skeggjason's *Eiríksdrápa* with Gísl Illugason's tribute to King Magnús berfœttr ("bare-leg") Óláfsson, both from around 1103. The pressure of political and particularly religious circumstance may be marked; compare the thoroughly pagan tone of *Hákonarmál*, 10th century, with Ívarr Ingimundarson's *Sigurðarbolkr*, from around 1139. Characteristically, the extant texts supplement traditional skaldic panegyric with a sometimes terse, sometimes plaintive, occasionally plangent elegiac note, and thus seem to reflect the approaches of runic memorials (*Eiríksmál*, 10th century, and *Hákonarmál* are notable exceptions).

Distinguishing memorial sequences associated with the Norwegian kings from historical compositions, and particularly from nonposthumous panegyric, is frequently problematic. *Snjófríðardrápa*, for example, which is attributed in *Flateyjarbók* to King Haraldr hárfagri ("fair-hair") Hálfdanarson, seems, in fact, to reflect a later (12th–13th-century) antiquarian interest in Haraldr's legendary mourning of Snæfríðr. Treatments of the battle of Svolðr (Svold; 1000) include the tribute of Halldórr ókristni ("unchristian") to the (presumably still living) victor, Earl Eiríkr (d. 1016); Hallfreðr vandræðaskáld's memorial to the defeated Ólafr Tryggvason; and strophes mistakenly attributed in their source (*Bergsbók*) to Hallfreðr, but now dated to the 12th century.

While certain strophes, particularly those cited in *Íslendingasögur*, may be spurious, the extant primary evidence suggests that the tradition of composing memorial poems to recently deceased relatives, comrades, and prominent persons (*e.g.*, Þormóðr Trefilsson's *Hrafnsmál*; Sighvatr Þórðarson's *Erlingsflokkr*) survived the 12th-century emergence of a strongly antiquarian interest, and, for a time, the increasing post-Conversion dominance of religious themes, and thrived, both in Norway and in Iceland, until the late 13th century (see, for example, Ingjaldr Geirmundarson's *Brandsflokkr*, Skáld-Hallr's *Brandsdrápa*, and the anonymous *hrynhent* tribute to Magnús lagabœtir ["law-mender"] Hákonarson).

Ed.: Gullberg, Hjalmar, ed. *Ólafs drápa Tryggvasonar: Fragment ur "Bergsboken."* Lund: Berling, 1875; Finnur Jónsson, ed. *Den norsk-islandske skjaldedigtning.* Vols. 1A–2A (tekst efter håndskrifterne), 1B–2B (rettet tekst). Copenhagen and Christiania [Oslo]: Gyldendal, 1912–15; rpt. Copenhagen: Rosenkilde & Bagger, 1967 (A) and 1973 (B); Kock, Ernst Albin, ed. *Den norsk-isländska skaldediktningen.* 2 vols. Lund: Gleerup, 1946–49; Ohlmarks, Åke, ed. *Ivar skalds martyrkvad om trinkvären Sigurd slemmedjäknes död.* Uppsala: Geber, 1958; Edwards, Diana. "The Poetry of Arnórr jarlaskáld: An Edition and Study." Diss. Oxford University, 1979; Jón Skaptason, "Material for an Edition and Translation of the Poems of Sigvat Þórðarson, *skáld.*" Diss. State University of New York at Stony Brook, 1983. **Tr.:** Gudbrand Vigfússon and F. York Powell, eds. and trans. *Corpus Poeticum Boreale: The Poetry of the Old Northern Tongue from the Earliest Times to the Thirteenth Century.* 2 vols. Oxford: Clarendon, 1883; rpt. New York: Russell and Russell, 1965; Hollander, Lee M., trans. *Old Norse Poems:*

The Most Important Non-skaldic Verse Not Included in the Poetic Edda. New York: Columbia University Press, 1936; Hollander, Lee M., trans. *The Skalds: A Selection of Their Poems, with Introduction and Notes.* Princeton: Princeton University Press, 1945; rpt. Ann Arbor: University of Michigan Press, 1968; Turville-Petre, E. O. G., ed. and trans. *Scaldic Poetry.* Oxford: Clarendon, 1976 [includes texts and translations of *Sonatorrek*, strophes from Þormóðr Trefilsson's *Hrafnsmál*, and Sighvatr Þórðarson's *Erfidrápa Óláfs helga*, along with two elegiac *lausavísur* also attributed to Sighvatr, a strophe probably belonging to Arnórr Þórðarson's *Þorfinnsdrápa*, and a *fornyrðislag helmingr* attributed in *Landnámabók* to Hallsteinn Þengilsson]; Frank, Roberta. *Old Norse Court Poetry: The Dróttkvætt Stanza.* Islandica, 42. Ithaca and London: Cornell University Press, 1978. **Bib.:** Hollander, Lee M. *A Bibliography of Skaldic Studies.* Copenhagen: Munksgaard, 1958; Bekker-Nielsen, Hans, and Thorkil Damsgaard Olsen. *Bibliography of Old Norse–Icelandic Studies* 1– (1964); Frank, Roberta. "Skaldic Poetry." In *Old Norse–Icelandic Literature: A Critical Guide.* Ed. Carol J. Clover and John Lindow. Islandica, 45. Ithaca and London: Cornell University Press, 1985, pp. 157–96. **Lit.:** J. Þorkelsson. "Erfidrápa hrynhend om kong Magnús lagabœtir." *Småstykker 1–16.* Samfund til udgivelse af gammel nordisk litteratur [unnumbered volume]. Copenhagen: Møller, 1884–91, pp. 289–92; Olsen, Magnus. "Lovsigemanden Markus Skeggesons arvekvæde over kong Erik eiegod." *Edda* 15 (1921), 161–9; rpt. in his *Norrøne studier.* Oslo: Aschehoug, 1938, pp. 225–33; Holtsmark, Anne. "Bjarne Kolbeinsson og hans forfatterskap." *Edda* 37 (1937), 1–17; Heusler, Andreas. *Die altgermanische Dichtung.* Handbuch der Literaturwissenschaft 4. Berlin-Neubabelsberg: Akademische Verlagsgesellschaft Athanaion, 1923; 2nd ed., 1941, pp. 143–50 [on *erfidrápur* and elegy]; Vries, Jan de. *Altnordische Literaturgeschichte.* 2 vols. Grundriss der germanischen Philologie, 15–6. Berlin: de Gruyter, 1941–42; 2nd ed., 1964–67; Ohlmarks, Åke. "Til frågan om den fornnordiska skaldediktningens ursprung." *Arkiv för nordisk filologi* 57 (1944), 178–207; Petersen, Sven Aage. *Vikinger og vikingeånd: Sighvat Thordssøn og hans skjaldskab.* Copenhagen: Munksgaard, 1946; Jón Helgason. "Norges og Islands digtning." In *Litteraturhistorie. B: Norge og Island.* Ed. Sigurður Nordal. Nordisk kultur, 8B. Stockholm: Bonnier; Oslo: Aschehoug; Copenhagen: Schultz, 1953, pp. 3–179 [survey of historical and memorial poetry, pp. 134–42]; Lange, Wolfgang. *Studien zur christlichen Dichtung der Nordgermanen 1000–1200.* Palaestra, 222. Göttingen: Vandenhoeck & Ruprecht, 1958; Bessinger, J. B. "Maldon and the *Óláfsdrápa*: An Historical Caveat." In *Studies in Old English Literature in Honor of Arthur G. Brodeur.* Ed. Stanley B. Greenfield. Eugene: University of Oregon Books, 1963, pp. 23–35; Campbell, Alistair. *Skaldic Verse and Anglo-Saxon History.* Dorothea Coke Memorial Lecture. London: Viking Society for Northern Research, 1971 [contains reference to Þorkell Skallason's *Valþjóðsflokkr*, p. 16]; Jónas Kristjánsson. *Um Fóstbræðrasögu.* Reykjavik: Stofnun Árna Magnússonar, 1972, pp. 19–33; Ralph, Bo. "Om tillkomsten af *Sonatorrek*." *Arkiv för nordisk filologi* 91 (1976), 153–65; Sigrún Davíðsdóttir. "Old Norse Court Poetry." *Gripla* 3 (1979), 186–203; See, Klaus von. "Polemische Zitate in der Skaldendichtung: Hallfrøðr vandræðaskald und Halldórr ókristni." *Skandinavistik* 7 (1977), 115–9; rpt. in *Edda, Saga, Skaldendichtung: Aufsätze zur skandinavischen Literatur des Mittelalters.* Heidelberg: Winter, 1981, pp. 384–8; Fidjestøl, Bjarne. *Det Norrøne fyrstediktet.* Øvre Ervik: Alvheim und Eide, 1982 [esp. pp. 87–168, 193–8, 230–5, 244–6]; Poole, Russell. "Ormr Steinþórsson and the *Snjófríðardrápa.*" *Arkiv för nordisk filologi* 97 (1982), 122–37; Fidjestøl, Bjarne. "Arnórr Þórðarson: Skald of the Orkney jarls." In *The Northern and Western Isles in the Viking World: Survival, Continuity and Change.* Ed. Alexander Fenton and Hermann Pálsson. Edinburgh: Donald, 1984, pp. 239–57; Jansson, Sven B. F. *Runes in Sweden.* Trans. Peter Foote. [Stockholm]: Gidlund, 1987 [rev. ed. of *Runinskrifter i Sverige*. Stockholm: Almqvist & Wiksell, 1963].

Mary Malcolm

[**See also:** *Lausavísur*; *Skáld*; Skaldic Verse]

Conversion of the Scandinavian world occupied the whole of the Viking Age. Early 9th-century missionary attempts were hindered by Scandinavian aggression against the Saxon, Frankish, and English realms that supplied the missionaries. Subsequent Viking conquest in the British Isles, Ireland, and France resulted in mixed communities in which the Scandinavian element soon tended to conform to the Christian practice of the native population. Elsewhere, Norse pagans rubbed shoulders with Christians in markets, camps, and courts. Some added Christ to their pantheon, some were prime-signed (a preliminary to christening), and some baptized. The presence of Christian captives and traders in Scandinavia added diplomatic weight to missionary interest. Tenth-century conditions were more favorable, and by the beginning of the 11th century a decisive "moment" of conversion had been reached in Denmark, Norway, and the Atlantic islands. The pace was slower in Sweden.

Archaeological evidence can illustrate Christian encroachment and advance in the North, but it is haphazard, and its significance is often obscure. Native contemporary sources include runic inscriptions and poetry, as much as can be counted reliably transmitted. The two most substantial external sources are both recognizably tendentious: the *Vita Anskarii* (d. 865) by Rimbert (d. 888) and the *Gesta Hammaburgensis ecclesiae pontificum* by Adam of Bremen (*ca*. 1075). Some Norwegian and Icelandic laws of 11th-century origin shed light on the Christian norms imposed in the early "consolidation" period; some of the Norwegian articles show concessions made by churchmen to pre-Christian custom. Narrative sources from continental Scandinavia, almost all in Latin, date from around 1100 and later; the ample histories in Icelandic, from around 1220 and later. All should be approached with the greatest caution. By and large, trustworthy evidence of the conversion process is scanty, random, and enigmatic.

Christianity offered beliefs and practices that could answer in different ways to the religious forms and expectations of paganism, at the level of personal dedication and domestic cult, and, at a public level, in the ceremony needed to establish peace at assemblies and to make legal oaths effective. The Church could replace seasonal sacrifices and feasting with festivals, major and minor, of its own, and it introduced a perpetual cycle of intercession and a daily bloodless sacrifice for the well-being of all.

The "moment" of conversion came when men at the apex of society, whom missionaries most sought to influence, decided to abandon their sacrificial celebrations and to seek peace and prosperity by Christian rites only. We may take it that when the "moment" occurred, some larger or smaller sections of the community had already accepted Christianity, but it was only on its heels that any steady advance could be made, by persuasion or coercion or both, in changing the outward observance of the whole population.

In Denmark, the "moment" came in the 960s, when Harald Gormsson was baptized by Poppo, a German cleric who had undergone an ordeal to demonstrate the superiority of Christian belief. King Harald had buried his pagan parents in a great mound at Jelling; he now added a church to their memorial site and moved their bodies to it. He set up a grand rune stone, one face filled with a triumphant Christ crucified, and recorded on it, among other achievements, that he had "made the Danes Christian."

In Norway, the "moment" occurred in the reign of Óláfr Tryggvason, 995–999/1000; in Iceland, it happened in 999/1000, and at about the same time in the Faroes and Greenland. The conversion in these countries was fully confirmed in the reign of Óláfr Haraldsson, 1015–1030. He died in battle against his countrymen, but a year later his body was exhumed and his sainthood acknowledged; he was soon widely venerated. Both the Óláfrs became militant Christians while campaigning in the West, both had household bishops of Anglo-Saxon origin, and both appear to have found the doctrine of *compelle intrare* congenial to their own regnal ambitions.

A rune stone set up about 1030 on Frösön in Jämtland, a northerly buffer province between Norway and Sweden, proclaims that Austmaðr Guðfastarson "had Jämtland made Christian." Probably most of the chief men in Västergötland and on Gotland were Christian by 1050. Pagan and Christian coexistence lasted longest in central Sweden. Members of the ruling dynasty there were baptized from about 1000 onward, and rune stones show that many well-to-do families were Christian and that churches existed. But the heathen temple at Uppsala was still being used in the 1070s, and at about that same time the Christian king was ousted by a pagan kinsman, who reigned for a few years and was remembered as "Sacrifice" Sven.

Missionary work before and after the conversion "moment" was undertaken by Anglo-Saxon clerics, heirs to a long missionary tradition, and by others sent from the archiepiscopal church of Hamburg-Bremen. This center had been formed by amalgamation after the Danes sacked Hamburg in 845, and had the specific task (and, as the clergy there saw it, the specific prerogative) of bringing pagan Scandinavians and Slavs into the Christian fold. Christian terminology adopted in Scandinavia came from both English and Low German, but the two cannot always be distinguished, and dating the loanwords is often difficult.

The period of Christian "consolidation" lasted about 150 years in each of the northern countries. In that time, dioceses were organized, churches built, clergy trained, native bishops consecrated, tithes introduced, parishes formed, monasteries founded, and cults of native saints instituted. The development, though still rudimentary in many respects, culminated in the elevation to archiepiscopal rank of the see of Lund in Denmark in 1103/4 (it was the metropolitan see of all Scandinavia for half a century), of the see of Niðaróss (Trondheim) in Norway in 1152/3, and of the see of Uppsala in Sweden in 1164. Niðaróss had the bishops of Orkney, the Faroes, Iceland, and Greenland as suffragans along with those of Norway itself.

Simple instruction could lead to baptism, for which renunciation of the Devil (or old gods) and affirmation of the faith were requisite. Every Christian should know the *Pater noster* and Creed as a minimum, along with the formula for baptism in case of emergency, and should show punctilious respect for the fasting and other rules of the calendar; confession and communion were expected at least annually. Existing legal systems were used to punish breaches of church observance. The practices taught as essential for personal salvation also made part of the never-ending *opus Dei*, performed by consecrated men in consecrated houses, handling sacred paraphernalia and drawing liturgy and lore from sacred books in a special language incomprehensible to most people.

A church did not have to be big and was not difficult to build, but the owner would usually wait a long time to get it properly staffed. There must have been a vast outlay on relics, vestments, books, and other necessary equipment, and great efforts must have gone into education to provide enough men with sufficient knowledge of Latin, liturgy, and computus to maintain the services. One priest to every 150–200 inhabitants is a plausible estimate for the post-"consolidation" period, but the build-up to that figure was obviously gradual. Priests married and led ordinary laboring lives; their social status depended on their birth and means. Most were privately employed; many were menials. There were many other novelties in the new dispensation. Some kinds of food, including horsemeat, were forbidden; frequent periodic abstention from other kinds of food and from work were ordained. Private penance might have to be publicly performed; marriage within certain degrees of kinship and affinity became unlawful. Good works were preached as having assured benefit to the soul, with most emphasis on feeding the hungry, helping the traveler, redeeming captives, and freeing slaves. Rune stones and early laws reveal the strong impression made by the call to show charity. In the long run, of course, Christian teaching profoundly affected many other realms of thought, custom, and law.

Among the many Icelandic works that have some bearing on the conversion of Scandinavia, a few contain a limited amount of what must be judged authentic information about the progress of Christianity in Iceland from about 980 to 1120. They are *Íslendingabók* (ca. 1125–1130) by Ari Þorgilsson; *Hungrvaka* (ca. 1215); *Þorvalds þáttr Koðránssonar*; and a lost work from which matter is thought to be derived in *Kristni saga*, *Njáls saga* (ca. 1280), and *Óláfs saga Tryggvasonar en mesta* (the compilation made ca. 1300 that is also our only source for *Þorvalds þáttr*). The lost work and the *þáttr* were written before about 1250; both are thought to be related, in ways difficult to ascertain, to the lost Latin work on Óláfr Tryggvason that Gunnlaugr Leifsson (d. 1218/9) composed around 1200. *Kristni saga* survives only in *Hauksbók* (ca. 1300); it is usually ascribed to Sturla Þórðarson (d. 1284).

Two considerations make Ari's well-known account of the conversion "moment" at the *Alþingi* of 999/1000 remarkable. The first is that we can trace its source and transmission. Gizurr Teitsson, a baptized *goði*, was a Christian leader at that *Alþingi* meeting. He sent his son Ísleifr to school in Saxony; Ísleifr came back as a priest around 1025 and in 1056 became Iceland's first native bishop. His son Gizurr succeeded him as bishop (1082–1118). Another son, Teitr (d. 1110), was a priest who lived and taught in Haukadalr, where Ari was at school from the age of seven until he was twenty-one (1075–1089). Ari says that his account of the acceptance of Christianity was how Teitr told it. He also says that his *Íslendingabók* was approved by Sæmundr Sigfússon of Oddi (1054–1133), Bishop Þorlákr of Skálholt (1086–1133), and Bishop Ketill of Hólar (1075–1145). The learned Sæmundr was closely associated with Skálholt; Þorlákr had been educated in Haukadalr and was picked by Bishop Gizurr himself as his successor; and Ketill, a northerner, was married to Bishop Gizurr's daughter.

The conclusion that Ari's account, as far as it goes, has unassailable authority is reinforced by the second consideration. As a conversion narrative, his report is quite unconventional. He describes how pagans and Christians came to a sober compromise, thanks to the acumen of the lawspeaker, who was not baptized at the time, and to the desire for peace and respect for law of moderates on both sides. Baptism was to be universally accepted,

but private sacrifice, consumption of horsemeat, and exposure of infants remained lawful; some years passed before these practices were finally proscribed.

Hungrvaka is indebted to Ari but adds more material from the Skálholt-Haukadalr tradition, especially on missionary bishops in Iceland in the 11th century and on Bishop Ísleifr's problems. The other texts have material, more or less lurid, on the central conversion period, particularly on the mission of Friðrekr, a Saxon bishop, merely mentioned by Ari, who apparently met with some success in the four winters he is said to have spent in Iceland in the early 980s with his Icelandic companion, Þorvaldr; the mission of the Icelandic layman Stefnir Þorgilsson, emissary of Óláfr Tryggvason; and the mission of Þangbrandr, a Flemish or Saxon priest, also sent by King Óláfr. Ari says he spent one or two winters in Iceland just before the year of the decisive *Alþingi*. Some of what these accounts tell is evidently inferential embroidery on Ari's report, some of it is literary construction, and little can be tested against other sources. Some anecdotes have details hard to dismiss: Hjalti Skeggjason's mocking comment on Rúnólfr *goði* mumbling the salt he had to taste as part of the baptism ritual; northerners putting off baptism until they reached a hot-spring area after leaving the *Alþingi*. Accounts of stress on St. Michael in missionary preaching might rest on genuine reminiscence; runic inscriptions show the importance attached to his role as the protector and conveyer of souls in Sweden's conversion age. The most significant material in these texts is found in some skaldic stanzas in which the hostility that Christian preachers might meet from Icelanders appears to be authentically reflected: the kind of *níð* that, according to Ari, led the militant Þangbrandr to kill "two or three men" before returning to Norway to give Óláfr Tryggvason a gloomy report on the prospects of conversion in Iceland.

Ed.: Finnur Jónsson and Eiríkur Jónsson, eds. "Kristni saga." In *Hauksbók udgiven efter de Arnamagnæanske håndskrifter no. 371, 544 og 675, 4° samt forskellige papirshåndskrifter af det kongelige nordiske Oldskrift-selskab.* Copenhagen: Thiele, 1892–96; Kahle, B., ed. *Kristnisaga.* Altnordische Saga-Bibliothek, 11. Halle: Niemeyer, 1905; Ólafur Halldórsson, ed. "Þorvalds þáttr Koðránssonar." In *Óláfs saga Tryggvasonar en mesta.* 2 vols. Editiones Arnamagnæanæ, ser. A, vols. 1–2, Copenhagen: Munksgaard, 1958, vol. 1, pp. 280–300; Adam av Bremen. *Historien om Hamburgstiftet och dess biskopar.* Trans. E. Svenberg, with commentary by C. F. Hallencreutz *et al.* Stockholm: Proprius, 1984. **Lit.:** Thors, Carl Eric. *Den kristna terminologien i fornsvenskan.* Studier i nordisk filologi, 45. Helsingfors: Svenska Litteratursällskapet i Finland, 1957; Jansson, Sven B. F. *Runes in Sweden.* Trans. Peter Foote. [Stockholm]: Gidlund, 1987; Almqvist, Bo. *Norrön niddiktning.* 2:1. *Nid mot missionärer.* Stockholm: Almqvist & Wiksell, 1974; Strömback, Dag. *The Conversion of Iceland: A Survey.* Trans. and annotated by Peter Foote. Text series, 6. London: Viking Society for Northern Research, 1975; Jón Hnefill Aðalsteinsson. *Under the Cloak: The Acceptance of Christianity in Iceland.* Uppsala: Acta Universitatis Upsaliensis, 1978; Birkeli, Fridtjov. *Hva vet vi om kristningen av Norge?* Oslo: Universitetsforlaget, 1982; Roesdahl, Else. *Viking Age Denmark.* Trans. Susan Margeson and Kirsten Williams. London: British Museum, 1982; Foote, Peter. "On the Conversion of the Icelanders." In *Aurvandilstá: Norse Studies.* Ed. Michael Barnes *et al.* Viking Collection, 2. Odense: Odense University Press, 1984, pp. 56–64; Pizarro, Joaquín Martínez. "Conversion Narratives: Form and Utility." In *Sixth International Saga Conference 28/7–2/8 1985, Workshop Papers.* 2 vols. Copenhagen: Det arnamagnæanske institut, 1985, vol. 2, pp. 813–32; Moltke, Erik. *Runes and Their Origin: Denmark and*

Elsewhere. Trans. Peter G. Foote. Copenhagen: Nationalmuseet, 1985; Sawyer, Birgit, *et al.*, eds. *The Christianization of Scandinavia*. Alingsås: Viktoria, 1987.

Peter Foote

[See also: Adam of Bremen; Ansgar, St.; *Biskupa sögur*; Church Organization and Function; Harald Gormsson (Bluetooth); *Hauksbók*; *Hungrvaka*; *Íslendingabók*; *Njáls saga*: Óláfr, St.; Óláfr Tryggvason; *Óláfs saga Tryggvasonar*; Saints' Lives]

Coronation. Although the crown, the most important of the coronation symbols, is known in Scandinavia from coins, seals, and other artifacts from the 11th century, the coronation ceremony itself was introduced in the North only in the 12th century; it was, however, used extensively in Europe from the 8th century. Combining biblical and Roman themes, the Church had developed a complex coronation ritual to promote families to kingship who were favored by churchmen. Eagerly adopted by continental and Anglo-Saxon tribes, the ceremony was executed in close cooperation with church leaders. During the 12th century, German emperors in turn employed similar ceremonies as means of controlling Danish kings and subkings on whom they conferred crowns in return for oaths of obedience. Thus, Knud Lavard (d. 1131), Danish royal prince and count of Schleswig, was crowned by Lothair and awarded a German fief north of the Elbe. In 1134, Lothair used the excuse of Knud's murder by his rival Magnus Nielsen to exact an oath of obedience from Magnus, in return for which Magnus received a crown from the emperor. In a similar way, Sven Grate was crowned by Frederick Barbarossa in 1152. These secular coronations serve as the first Scandinavian contacts with the foreign ceremony.

In the following decades, full ecclesiastical coronations were introduced into Norway and Denmark as a consequence of the Church's increased power and the inability of native rulers to cope with the succession problem. The combination of these two elements is particularly clear in Norway in the 1160s, when in 1163 or 1164, Archbishop Eysteinn Erlendsson of Trondheim crowned the young boy Magnús Erlingsson in an attempt to stop the civil wars that had been devastating the country. In return, the Church received extensive privileges from Magnús and his father. Further demands were made by native churchmen in 1247 as a condition for the coronation of Hákon Hákonarson by a papal legate, but by then the monarchy was strong enough to decline the offer.

In Denmark, the first ecclesiastical coronation took place in 1170 in Ringsted, where the ruling king, Valdemar I, secured his lineage's claim to the throne in a double ceremony whereby his murdered father, Knud Lavard, who had not been a king himself, was elevated to sainthood, and Valdemar's young legitimate son Knud was crowned as future king. Similar conditions may have prevailed in Sweden when Karl Knutsson benefited from the first coronation in 1210.

International in origin, coronation rituals changed little over time. The lost medieval texts used in Scandinavia can be reconstructed from Reformation versions and seem to derive from Ottonian manuals of the 10th century. In the ceremony, the candidate swore an oath, was robed in special clothing and bore the royal insignia, including the crown, and was anointed with holy oil. Afterward, he or his father hosted a great banquet. The oath sworn by Magnús Erlingsson in Norway (preserved in a MS in the British Library from 1200) was given in Latin, as were similar

promises made by other European kings, but English kings used vernacular French. Of ecclesiastical origin, the special clothing was enumerated for Birger Magnusson's coronation in Sweden in 1310. The garments used in the crowning of the eight-year-old Magnús Erlingsson in the 1160s apparently traveled with him for the next twenty years, after which they were taken by his rival Sverrir as war booty in battle. Hákon Hákonarson's coronation in 1247 is fully described in *Hákonar saga (gamla) Hákonarsonar*.

As in Europe, Scandinavian queens were also crowned, although they were included in the ceremony at a later date. In Denmark, Margrethe of Pomerania, wife of Christoffer I, was crowned with him in 1252; in Norway, the Danish princess Ingeborg received a crown with her husband, Magnús Hákonarson, in 1261; and in Sweden, Helvig of Holsatia was crowned with King Magnus Ladelås in 1281. Anointing was the most important part of the coronation for queens because it was regarded as a fertility rite. This function is particularly clear for Magnús Hákonarson and Ingeborg. Magnús had already been accepted as king in 1257, but the mutual coronation took place three days after their wedding at the instigation of Magnús's father, Hákon, who was eager to secure the continuity of his lineage.

Ed.: Gudbrand Vigfusson and George W. Dasent, eds. and trans. *Icelandic Sagas and Other Historical Documents Relating to the Settlements and Descents of the Northmen on the British Isles*. 4 vols. Rolls Series, 88. London: Eyre and Spottiswoode, 1887–94; rpt. Millwood: Kraus, 1964, vol. 2; *cf.* chs. 247–55, 304–10 [trans. by Dasent in vol. 4]. **Lit.:** Holtzmann, Walther. "Krone und Kirche in Norwegen im 12. Jahrhundert." *Deutches Archiv für Geschichte des Mittelalters* 2 (1938), 341–400; Vandvick, Eirik. "Magnus Erlingssons Kroningseid." *Historisk tidsskrift* (Norway) 31 (1937–40), 453–88; 34 (1946–48), 625–37; Schramm, Percy Ernst, ed. *Herrschaftszeichen und Staatssymbolik*. 3 vols. Monumenta Germaniae historica, 13. Stuttgart: Hiersemann, 1954–55; Bouman, C. A. *Sacring and Crowning: The Development of the Latin Ritual for the Anointing of Kings and the Coronation of an Emperor in the Eleventh Century*. Groningen: Wolters, 1957; Hansen, J. Qvistgaard. "Regnum et sacerdotium. Forholdet mellem stat og kirke i Danmark 1157–1170." In *Middelalderstudier. Tilegnede Aksel E. Christensen på tresårsdagen 11. September 1966*. Ed. Tage E. Christiansen *et al.* Copenhagen: Munksgaard, 1966, pp. 57–76; Riis, Thomas. *Les institutions politiques centrales du Danemark 1100–1332*. Odense University Studies in History and Social Science, 46. Odense: Odense University Press, 1977; Nelson, Janet L. "Inauguration Rituals." In *Early Medieval Kingship*. Ed. P. H. Sawyer and I. N. Wood. Leeds: School of History, University of Leeds, 1977, pp. 50–71; Stafford, Pauline. *Queens, Concubines, and Dowagers: The King's Wife in the Early Middle Ages*. Athens: University of Georgia Press, 1983; Blom, Grethe Authén. "Kongekroninger og kroningsutstyr i norsk middelalder frem til 1300-årene." In *Kongens Makt og Ære: Skandinaviske herskersymboler gjennom 1000 år*. Ed. M. Blindheim *et al.* Oslo: Universitetets Oldsaksamling, 1985, pp. 71–7; Nelson, Janet L. *Politics and Ritual in Early Medieval Europe*. History Series, 42. London, Ronceverte: Hambledon, 1986.

Jenny Jochens

[See also: Hákon Hákonarson; *Hákonar saga gamla Hákonarsonar*; Margrethe I; Valdemar]

Cosmography. The oldest sources on the Nordic world as a distinct place in the cosmos are of foreign origin. To Romans like Tacitus and Arabs like Al-Mus'ūdī, the northern peoples were on the margins of civilization. They were "others" and "wild."

From the northern perspective, this view of the world was reversed. When the first local sources appear, they bear witness to a specific Nordic cosmography in which the Norsemen inhabited the center of the world, externalizing their own "others" to the periphery. The clue to the cosmology is found in Snorri's *Edda*. In *Gylfaginning*, he specifies a cosmological model of concentric circles. In the inner circle is *Miðgarðr*, "the middle yard," while the outer circle is *Útgarðr*, "the outer yard."

Miðgarðr is inhabited by humans and gods, while giants and other nonhumans reign in Útgarðr. According to the myths of creation, this initial division of cosmos into two separate spaces was made by the gods (*Æsir*), who subsequently built their own abode, Ásgarðr, somewhere inside Miðgarðr. There was no topological distinction between Miðgarðr and Ásgarðr, and consequently no absolute separation between humans and gods in this horizontal model of the cosmos. The model was supplemented by a vertical model, however, in which a distinction between an "upper" and a "lower" world placed gods and humans in separate regions. Above was Valhǫll, the abode of the gods and the place where heroic warriors who died on the battlefield spent their afterlife. Even here, men and gods could merge into one category of inhabitants of the "upper" world.

In regard to the social aspects of the cosmography, the horizontal model was by far the most significant, with a whole series of parallels in Nordic society. First and foremost, it was reflected in the distinction between law and non-law. Most medieval law books from the Scandinavian countries open with the proverb *með lǫg skal land byggja* ("with law shall the country be built"). This admonition was meant to be taken literally. The law was the defining feature of society, and bounded "the social" from "the wild" in a way that is clearly parallel to Snorri's cosmological model. At both levels, the central space was defined as controlled and familiar, while the peripheral space was uncontrolled and alien. Inside, law and peace reigned; outside, lawlessness and war flourished.

The outlaws were exiles from society. They had been expelled because of their nonsocial behavior, and had been absorbed into the wild. The general Norse word for outlaw is *útlagen*, which literally means "outside law." In Iceland, outlawry was known by the term *skóggangr* ("forest going"), and the outlaw was referred to as *skógarmaðr* ("forest man"). In this conceptual invention on the part of the Icelanders, there is an implicit recognition of the nonsocial as identical with the natural wilderness. This equation points to the significance of the opposition between society and nature at a general level.

Closely associated with the notion of *útlagi* is the Old Norse concept of *útilega* ("lying out"). Originally, the term was used about anyone who left ordinary human company and went his own ways. It relates to *liggja úti* ("lie out of doors"), and it gave rise to the notion of *útilegumaðr* ("out-lying man"). The original meaning of someone choosing to leave society on his own account later attained a more pejorative meaning, and the category came to embrace outlaws and supernatural beings in addition to robbers and pirates.

Clearly, the "outside" is associated with danger and lack of control. Once man left the social space defined by the law, he was reclassified as wild. Outside was also the space where the supernatural powers reigned, and where man had to capture them if he was to direct these forces to some purpose. Thus, there was a notion of *setja úti til fróðleiks* ("to sit out for wisdom"). Sitting out for wisdom implied that man temporarily left the social and vol-

untarily entered the wild to get into contact with the supernatural forces. "Wisdom" in this sense meant magical knowledge about, for instance, how to waken ghosts.

At yet another level of the social geography, the concentric model is operative also in distinguishing the farmstead and, by implication, the household from the nature in which it was embedded. The boundary was drawn at the *garðr*, meaning both "fence" and "enclosure". The separation between *innangarðs* ("inside the fence") and *útangarðs* ("outside the fence") had a whole series of legal implications. Inside was peace and social control; it was an inviolable space in which the members of the household worked and lived. It was nature domesticated. Outside the fence was the untamed nature, where man had to supplement the income of the household even at the risk of encountering the dark forces of the outside. Among the uncontrolled beings living outside the fence were the *huldufólk* ("the hidden people"). They were dangerous to women in particular; if women left the controlled social space at the farmstead and its immediate surroundings, they were liable to seduction by the *huldumenn*. Women attending the *saeter*, or summer shieling, at more or less distant mountain pastures were vulnerable to their assaults, and during the Middle Ages quite a number of pregnancies were the alleged result of such encounters.

The opposition between "inside" and "outside" in the Nordic cosmography thus mirrored an opposition between the familiar and the dangerous at a whole series of levels. The closer a person was to the center of the world, the less dangerous it was. Closest was the family, which was the social framework of daily life. The household consisted of those people who lived inside the same fence, which also meant "on the same farm." It was not only the most significant social unit for the people, but also the center of each individual's world view. In a more comprehensive circle around the individual was the kin group or the *ætt* as a whole. The kin group represented a "we-group" in relation to which all others were foreigners and potential enemies. One could also make allies with them, and marriage was an important means to this end. But in case of conflict, the individual often found himself in a defensive position, not unlike Þórr's when he had to defend Miðgarðr against the *Miðgarðsormr*, the giant serpent who lived in the sea separating Miðgarðr from Útgarðr.

There is a remarkable consistency in the horizontal model of the Nordic cosmography. The farmstead represents a microcosmos that confirms and continues the macrocosmic model depicted by Snorri. Both as an individual and as a species, the Norsemen lived in the center of their own world. This placement is directly attested to by the notion of *verǫld* ("world"). This word is composed from *verr* "man" and *ǫld* "age." The world was the age and the condition of mankind. Man himself was the ultimate center of the cosmos.

Lit.: Turville-Petre, E. O. G. *Myth and Religion of the North: The Religion of Ancient Scandinavia.* New York: Holt, Rinehart and Winston, 1964; rpt. Westport: Greenwood, 1975; Gurevich, A. J. *Categories of Medieval Culture.* Trans. G. L. Campbell. London: Routledge and Kegan Paul, 1985; Hastrup, Kirsten. *Culture and History in Medieval Iceland: An Anthropological Analysis of Structure and Change.* Oxford: Clarendon, 1985.

Kirsten Hastrup

[**See also:** Cosmology; Laws; Mythology; Outlawry; *Snorra Edda*]

Cosmology. Most of the surviving Norse scholarly texts on geography, cosmography, and astronomy date from the 14th century, but they reflect notions already prevalent in Iceland in the late 12th and 13th centuries. These notions are far removed from the heathen mythological cosmology of the early Middle Ages, although some old Germanic names both in astronomy and geography continued to be used for concepts and places now firmly embedded in Latin Christian learning. Like many of the sagas, nonfictional vernacular texts display a strong interest in geographical and cosmographical information. Abbot Nikulás from the North Icelandic Benedictine monastery in Þverá made an extensive journey to Rome and the Holy Land. Upon his return in 1154, he had the itinerary of his journey written down for the sake of later travelers; soon afterward, a cluster of geographical works began to accumulate around this text. These texts, although mostly very short, contained information on such matters as the various countries situated in each of the three continents of Asia, Africa, and Europe; the rivers and lakes in the world; which nations, derived from Noah's sons, live in which parts of the world; how many languages there are on every continent; what fabulous races live in foreign parts; which towns contain the most famous relics of holy men; which are the routes to Rome; where are the climatic zones; where the earthly paradise is and what it looks like; a map of Jerusalem and other matters of similar interest.

All these texts may have been included in a lost 13th-century MS, called *Gripla*, that comprised a collection of geographical works, including material on Greenland; from this MS, extracts were copied again and again, and are now partly preserved in various encyclopedic MSS of the early 14th century, such as *Hauksbók*. The popularity of these geographical texts can be seen from the short cosmographical text found among them, which is preserved in four different redactions in well over twenty MSS.

From a different tradition come the six preserved Old Icelandic *mappae mundi*, or highly stylized world maps, conforming to three basic patterns. Three are found in the fragments united in the MS GkS 1812 4to, which are obviously remnants of copies of an illustrated encyclopedic MS modeled closely on Latin illuminated encyclopedias. The largest is a rather detailed map of the inhabited world. A "T-O-type" with well over 100 entries, mostly in Latin, it is one of the very few double-page maps found in medieval European MSS. The same MS contains a colored astronomical drawing, which in its center shows the whole earth, divided into the climatic zones with an inhabited southern continent south of the equatorial ocean. A similar concept is found in the *mappae mundi* of three other MSS (AM 732b 4to and 736 I 4to, both from the 14th century, as well as in a young copy of the latter); at the center of an astronomical illustration showing the movement of the sun and moon, there is a *mappa mundi* roughly divided into the climatic zones, depicting the northern hemisphere with the three known continents, Asia, Africa, and Europe, while the southern hemisphere shows one big inhabited continent. These maps showing the climatic zones were modeled on maps found in the works of William of Conches and Lambert of St. Omer. A very small map of the inhabited northern hemisphere with the traditional tripartite division is found in a schematic drawing of the wind rose in GkS 1812 4to. Comparison with the corpus of over 1,200 continental *mappae mundi* shows that these few Icelandic maps cover more or less the whole range of iconographic possibilities.

The picture of the physical world that can be gleaned from medieval Icelandic scholarly texts is a fairly factual, but geocentric world view, as represented also by the mainstream Latin literature of the high Middle Ages, but revised to accommodate experiences collected by Scandinavians on their journeys.

This cosmography depicts a spherical world as the center of the universe, divided into the climatic zones much as we know them, containing the three known and inhabited continents. Asia, in the East, is by far the biggest, separated from Africa by the Nile. Europe, separated from Africa by the Mediterranean Sea and from Asia by the River Tanais (= Don), also includes the Atlantic isles as well as Greenland, which is connected with Bjarmaland east of the White Sea by a strip of land (making the Atlantic Ocean a sort of Scandinavian inland sea), and the islands of Helluland and Markland south of Greenland. Vinland is located south of these islands, and there is some speculation as to whether this area is an island or is connected with Africa. These three continents are thought to lie in the northern hemisphere; the smaller *mappae mundi* mentioned above, however, also show an unspecified inhabited area in the southern hemisphere.

Most of this geographical information was taken from well-known Latin handbooks, which were wholly or partly known in both Iceland and Norway in the Middle Ages, but rarely translated into Old Norse in their entirety, with the notable exception of *Elucidarius* (which contains little cosmographical information). The medieval Norwegians and Icelanders did, however, combine this knowledge with their own experiences acquired on their extensive voyages to the countries east, north, and west of Scandinavia. Thus, we find Old Norse texts derived and compiled from the writing of Honorius Augustodunensis, Bede, and Isidore, supplemented with details about the Baltic, the farthest North, and Vinland. The description of Europe, therefore, achieves far greater detail than in the Latin sources.

In cosmology and astronomy also, the scientific information handed down in the Middle Ages from antiquity through the Latin handbooks was enriched by popular knowledge. A portion translated from Honorius's *De imagine mundi* shows the cosmos built like an egg in which the earth is the yolk. From *Elucidarius*, one could learn that man was created as a microcosmos mirroring the macrocosmos; hence, his head is round, just as the earth is. But the roundness of the earth was obvious to northern seafarers, and is explained quite soundly in texts that describe the different range of visibility from a ship's deck as compared to the top of the mast.

Further popularization was achieved through native vernacular handbooks, such as the Norwegian *Konungs skuggsjá*, dating from about 1260. In this handbook for the education of a young prince, the earth is likened to an apple warmed and illuminated by a candle, giving the living image of the half-illuminated, spherical earth. Herein we also find an awareness of the climatic zones dividing the earth, and the cause of the seasons. The simile of the apple and the candle is also found in Old English texts, but many such notions, while distinctly tasting of native popular explanations, are in fact gleaned from Latin handbooks. A fetching explanation of the movement of the planets (contained in the same MS as the translation from Honorius) is found in Alexander Neckham's *De naturis rerum.*

Not all aspects of astronomy and cosmology lent themselves to popularization, and some aspects of the more sophisticated medieval science, which were part of the renaissance of the 12th century, were probably limited to a few clerics. The proper observance of Christian ritual demanded an accurate reckoning of the calendar synchronized with the solar and lunar cycles, and the knowledge of arithmetical reckoning of the time (computus) and astronomy needed for this reckoning was vital for the Church in Iceland as elsewhere. MSS surviving from the late 12th and 13th centuries show a distinct interest in these questions and a clear dependence on the encyclopedic and astronomical authorities of the Middle Ages: Isidore, Bede, Honorius, Helperic, Sacrobosco, and Gerlandus. In astronomy, the dependence on Latin texts was stronger than in general cosmology, and the astronomical terminology was either borrowed or translated from Latin, the role of the native authors being mostly limited to translating and compiling. Of these educated few practicing the arcane art of astronomy, only rarely have the names come down to us. In Iceland, one such person, Stjǫrnu-Oddi ("Star-Oddi") Helgason, was reported to have regularly taken lunar and solar observations in the late 12th century, recording azimuths in solar diameters and half-diameters, a measurement naturally suited to the task. At the same time, Abbot Nikulás used very simple methods to achieve quite an accurate reckoning of latitude while he was in the Holy Land. In the late 13th century, the Dane Petrus de Dacia became the first Scandinavian astronomer of continental fame, but he is an isolated phenomenon. By this time, however, there are records of observations made with the aid of an astrolabe in Denmark, and we can suppose that astronomy was becoming more sophisticated and a little more regularly practiced. Yet even as late as the 15th century, the Dominican Nicolaus de Dacia in Lund, who wrote about astronomy and astrology, was the only noteworthy Scandinavian astronomer of the period.

Ed.: Stephanus Björnsen, ed. *Rymbegla.* Havniæ: Suhm, 1780; Eiríkur Jónsson and Finnur Jónsson, eds. *Hauksbók udgiven efter de Arnamagnæanske håndskrifter no. 371, 544 og 675, 4° samt forskellige papirshåndskrifter af det kongelige nordiske Oldskriftselskab.* Copenhagen: Thiele, 1892–96; Kålund, Kr., and N. Beckman, eds. *Alfræði íslenzk: Íslandsk encyclopædisk litteratur.* Samfund til udgivelse of gammel nordisk litteratur, 37, 41, 45. Copenhagen: Møller, 1908–18. **Lit.:** Shackelford, J. R. "The Apple/Candle Illustration in *The King's Mirror* and the *South English Legendary.*" *Maal og minne* (1984), 72–84; Simek, R. "Die Übersetzung kosmographischer Begriffe in altnordischen enzyklopädischen und geographischen Texten." *Nordeuropa Studien* 21 (1987), 96–103; Simek, R. *Altnordische Kosmographie.* Berlin and New York: de Gruyter, 1990.

Rudolf Simek

[**See also:** America, Norse in; Cosmography; *Elucidarius; Hauksbók; Konungs skuggsjá; Leiðarvísir;* Petrus de Dacia; Vinland Map; Vinland Sagas]

Costume *see* Fashions

Council of the Realm (*Riksråd*). Among the best men of the Danish kingdom (*meliores regni*), a permanent group of councilors developed after the German pattern. This device may have been the king's answer to the National Assemblies (*Danehof*) and the annual meetings. Guardianship for a minor king may have contributed to strengthen this development that took place in Denmark at least from the time of Erik Menved, 1286–1319. The power struggle between the king and the aristocracy was, during the following centuries, the crucial subject of domestic policy in the history of Denmark. The evolution of councils in Scandinavia takes two main directions during the Middle Ages: the councilors' monarchical official duty, and increasingly their authority as an

aristocratic representative national assembly that replaced the *Danehof* or other National Assemblies.

King Valdemar Atterdag ("ever-day"; 1340–1375) created a strong Danish royal power. During the king's journeys abroad, the rule was entrusted to the Council of the Realm and to the Seneschal, the king's substitute. Symbolic of the shift in power, the term changed from the "king's councilors" to the "national councilors," and at the Peace of Stralsund in 1370 the authority of the Council culminated. The Council also played an important role in 1370, when Oluf was appointed successor of Valdemar. However, during the reign of Queen Margrethe, the Council, with new, aristocratic members, was pushed somewhat into the background. The queen chose, with a marked preference, the court officials in her administration. Even in Sweden and Norway, she felt free to appoint Danish and foreign officials. The Kalmar Union (established in 1397) of the three Nordic countries was gradually becoming a Danish supremacy.

In the reign of Erik of Pomerania, the Danish supremacy was extended within the Kalmar Union. The Crown tried to unite the kingdoms into one centralized state, by establishing, for example, council meetings for the entire Union. In these endeavors, Erik of Pomerania was actively supported by the Danish Council of the Realm especially from 1423–1425 and onward. The group of councilors had now become a more permanent organ. The councilors participated, to a still larger extent, in the administration, and a good relationship prevailed between the king and the councilors, until the Union crisis in the 1430s. Insight into the administration, the discontinuation of the National Assemblies, and the decreasing importance of the Landsting on behalf of the legal courts confirmed, together with the diffusion of the influence of the Council of Basel, the opinion of the Council as the representative of the kingdom and the people, and also the Council as court and judge vis à vis the Crown.

The members of the Council of the Realm were appointed by the king, and councilors took an oath to the king. Primarily, they were a well-educated aristocratic assembly of about thirty people who had ecclesiastical or secular status. The archbishop of Lund, together with his six ordinary bishops and the bishop of Roskilde, who held the office as the highest chancellor of Denmark, were members of the Council. In the reign of Erik of Pomerania, the abbots and the priors from the largest monasteries were appointed members of the Council; neither the king's chancellor nor the Chancellor of the Realm (*Rikskansler*) had status as councilor.

A concentration of families belonging to the high nobility took place in the reign of Erik of Pomerania, and the group of bishops belonged to the high aristocracy. For a number of the families, membership on the Council became somewhat hereditary. The councilors appeared as a homogeneous group by virtue of these family groups with interrelations in marriage. Their use of the lesser nobility, especially as servants and officials on the episcopal estates, together with their military position and their possession of the most important castles and the entailed estates, gave them a key position in society.

In the reign of King Christoffer of Bavaria (1440–1448), the Council of the Realm was dominated by the Gyldenstjerne, Rosenkrantz, Thott, Frille, and Rönnow families. They controlled most of the important castles and entailed estates. After the dethronement of Erik of Pomerania, the family of Gyldenstjerne and their supporters took up, to a considerable extent, a leading position, and, together with Archbishop Hans Laxmand (d. 1443) and other bishops, this family conducted the actual policies of the Council. The family Rosenkrantz strengthened their influence in the reign of King Christoffer, and so did the Thott, Frille, and Rönnow families. The number of secular councilors was sixteen in the second half of 1447, which was a fourth less than in the last years of the reign of Erik of Pomerania. During these years, the Council of the Realm resembled a landed, high-aristocratic government.

When Christian I was appointed Danish king in 1448, the position of power in the Council of the Realm was strengthened for the Rosenkrantz, Thott, Frille, and Rönnow families. Several new members of these families found their way into the council, and others were also admitted because of their support of the new king. In 1451, the number of ecclesiastical and secular councilors had increased to at least thirty-five, which marked a return to the size of the Council in the reign of Erik of Pomerania. The admittance of new members heralded a beginning of "democratization" of the Council. Several representatives from the middle layer of the nobility were admitted to the Council in these years, but also some who can be described as "the king's servants" because they owed their position mainly to the king. The means of strengthening the Danish Crown against the old families belonging to the high nobility was thus formed.

King Christian I's clash with the Thott family (1468–1469), his intervention against the entailed estates, and his shifted political course also had consequences for the Council of the Realm. The official element was intensified, and central power shifted back to the remaining elderly secular councilors and the bishops. The five leading families' share of the entailed estates decreased from a half to an eighth, and no new concentrations of castles around individuals or families were created.

Until Christian I became king, the Danish kings are, in connection with the election, known to have made a vow by word of mouth. However, the vow was so indefinite that, as early as the 14th century, a more explicit formulation of coronation charters was felt necessary (1320, 1376). King Christoffer of Bavaria promised in 1440 to issue a coronation charter, but this never happened. Between 1448 and 1536, the Council of the Realm demanded from every new king a coronation charter. The Council, which was responsible for the administration in periods of interregnum, in 1448 declared the country a "free country of election." This provision was carried into the coronation charters made by Frederik I and by Christian II, but the terms were made more rigorous: the king was not allowed to choose his son as his successor while he himself was alive. Moreover, the Council tried to strengthen its negotiating position from 1483 by making it a condition that the castles should revert to the Council of the Realm at the king's death. In the coronation charter of 1483, it was established that the members of the Council of the Realm should belong to the nobility. An appropriate distribution of members in the different parts of the country was sought.

The Council took over the legislative work of the old National Assembly and the *Danehof*, and the members acted as judges in the king's court. From 1448, the consent of the Council had to be obtained for appropriation of extra taxes; it was also applied when deciding on warfare.

In Sweden and Norway, the pattern of the Council of the Realm is very similar to the one found in Denmark. In Norway, foreigners, especially Danes, were admitted to the Council in the capacity of bishops and royal deans of monarchical chapels from the time of King Hákon VI and Queen Margrethe. While Margrethe's

and Erik of Pomerania's political goal had been to eliminate the Council in Norway as a factor of power, Christoffer of Bavaria tried, by enlarging the Council with new members, to gain influence on the Council's disposals; but after 1445, no new councilors were appointed. After the death of Christoffer of Bavaria, the Council in Norway was divided into two groups. However, the pro-Danish party asserted its political strength and had Christian I crowned king (1448–1450). During this period, the Norwegian Council became a numerous assembly. But after this time, the secular membership declined, and after the year 1500 there were probably not more than ten.

The Norwegian Council's political influence was in general declining after the middle of the 15th century, in spite of the short periods of independence and considerable royal concessions in relation to the accession of new kings to the throne. The *coup d'état* by Archbishop Olav Engelbrektsson in 1536 split the Council, and an incorporation of Norway into the Union with Denmark was desirable from the king's as well as from the Danish Council's point of view. Christian III's coronation charter (1536) made Norway a province under the Danish Crown. In reality, this provision implied that the Norwegian Council ceased to exist as an independent factor.

In Sweden, including Finland, Albrecht of Mecklenburg and Erik of Pomerania admitted a few Germans to the Council, and in the 15th century some Danish-born nobles appear as members of the Swedish Council. Several of Karl Knutsson's and Christian I's councilors belonged to the second or third generation of immigrant German or Danish families. In the reign of Sten Sture the Elder, the number of secular councilors is relatively constant, about thirty persons until 1494; but during the following three years, the number was halved. Primarily, the new recruiting of members to the Council took place especially in connection with the changes of the regent in 1504 and 1512. The old Council families were still dominant. At the beginning of the 1520s, the composition of the Council changed radically because Gustav Vasa appointed councilors mainly from families that had not previously belonged to the Council nobility. The struggle to control the entailed estates and the question of whether the king should be Danish or foreign characterized Swedish politics in the 15th century, especially the 1430s and 1460s. In the time of the Scandinavian Union, the Council in Sweden often exercised royal legal power and other functions when the king was absent.

Lit.: (a) Denmark: *Samling af Danske Kongers Haandfæstninger og andre lignende Acter.* Copenhagen, 1856–58; rpt. Copenhagen: Selskabet for udgivelse af kilder til dansk historie, 1974; Paludan-Müller, Caspar. *De første Konger af den Oldenborgske Slægt.* Copenhagen: Reitzel, 1874; rpt. Copenhagen: Selskabet for udgivelse af kilder til dansk historie, 1971; Matzen, Henning. *Danske Kongers Haandfæstninger.* Copenhagen, 1889; rpt. Copenhagen: Selskabet for udgivelse af kilder til dansk historie, 1977; Christensen, William. *Dansk Statsforvaltning i det 15. Århundrede.* Copenhagen: Gad, 1903; rpt. Copenhagen: Selskabet for udgivelse af kilder til dansk historie, 1974; Enemark, Poul. "Den økonomiske baggrund for de første Oldenborgske kongers udenrigspolitik: en arbejdshypotese." *Jyske Samlinger,* Ny Række 4.1 (1957), 1–20; Bruun, Henry, et al., *Studier over dansk politik i årene omkring 1500.* Copenhagen, 1959; rpt. Copenhagen: Selskabet for udgivelse af kilder til dansk historie, 1975; Christensen, Aksel E. *Kongemagt og Aristokrati. Epoker i middelalderlig dansk statsopfattelse indtil unionstiden.* Copenhagen, 1945; 2nd ed. Copenhagen: Munksgaard, 1968; Jørgensen, Poul Johs.

Dansk Retshistorie. Retskildernes og forfatningsrettens historie indtil sidste halvdel af det 17. århundrede. 5th ed. Copenhagen: Gad, 1971; *Rapporter til det nordiske historikermøde i København 1971, 9–12 august.* Vol. 2. *Den nordiske Adel i Senmiddelalderen. Struktur, funktioner og internordiske relationer.* Copenhagen: Nordisk Historikermøde, 1971; Linton, Michael. *Drottning Margareta. Fullmäktig fru och rätt husbonde.* Studia Historica Gothoburgensia, 12. Gothenburg: Akademiförlaget, 1971 [German summary]; Hoffmann, Erich. *Königserhebung und Thronfolgeordnung in Dänemark bis zum Ausgang des Mittelalters.* Berlin: de Gruyter, 1976; Riis, Thomas. *Les institutions politiques centrales du Danemark 1100–1332.* Odense University Studies in History and Social Sciences, 46. Odense: Odense University Press, 1977; Christensen, Aksel E., *et al.,* eds. *Gyldendals Danmarks historie.* 2 vols. Copenhagen: Gyldendal, 1977–80; Enemark, Poul. *Fra Kalmarbrev til Stockholms Blodbad: Den nordiske trestatsunions epoke 1397–1521.* Copenhagen: Nordisk ministerråd; Gyldendal, 1979; Olesen, Jens E. *Rigsråd—Kongemagt—Union 1434–1449.* Århus: Jysk selskab for historie, 1980 [German summary; comprehensive bibliography]; Christensen, Aksel E. *Kalmarunionen i nordisk politik 1319–1439.* Copenhagen: Gyldendal, 1980; Enemark, Poul. *Kriseår 1448–1451; en epoke i nordisk unionshistorie.* Copenhagen: Akademisk Forlag, 1981; Christensen, Harry. *Len og Magt i Danmark 1439–1481.* Århus: Jysk selskab for historie, 1983 [comprehensive bibliography]; Olsen, Jens E. *Unionskrige og Staendersamfund 1450–1481.* Århus: Jysk selskab for historie, 1983; Olesen, Jens E., ed. *Christoffer af Bayerns breve 1440–1448 vedrørende hans bayerske stamhertugdømme. Die Briefe Christoffers von Bayern 1440–1148 über sein bayrisches Stammherzogtum.* Copenhagen: Selskabet for udgivelse af kilder til dansk historie, 1986; Madsen, Uffe Geer. "Det danske rigsråds adelige medlemmer 1375–1412." *Historisk tidsskrift* (Denmark) 89 (1989), 1–37 [English summary]. **(b) Norway:** Aschehoug, T.H. *Statsforfatningen i Norge og Danmark indtil 1814.* Christiania [Oslo]: Feilberg & Landmark, 1866; Nielsen, Yngvar. *Det norske Rigsraad.* Kristiania [Oslo]: Den Norske Forlagsforening, 1880. Helle, Knut. *Norge blir en stat 1130–1319.* Handbok i Norges Historie, 3. Bergen, Oslo, and Tromsø: Universitetsforlaget, 1964; Blom, Grethe Authén. *Kongemakt og privilegier i Norge inntil 1387.* Oslo: Universitetsforlaget, 1967; Petersen, Erling Ladewig. "Henrik Krummedige og Norge. Studier over Danmarks forhold til Norge 1523–1533." *Historisk tidsskrift* (Denmark) 12.3 (1968), 1–82 [English summary]; Hamre, Lars. *Norsk Historie 1450–1513.* Oslo: Universitetsforlaget, 1971; Helle, Knut. *Konge og gode menn i norsk riksstyring ca. 1150–1319.* Bergen, Oslo, and Tromsø: Universitetsforlaget, 1972. **(c) Sweden:** Styffe, Carl Gustaf, ed. *Bidrag till Skandinaviens Historia ur utländska Arkiver.* 4 vols. Stockholm: Kongl. Boktryckeriet; Norstedt, 1859–75; Alin, Oscar. "Om Svenska Rådets Sammansättning under Medeltiden." *Uppsala Universitets Årsskrift* (1877), 1–19; Alin, Oscar. "Bidrag till Svenska Rådets Historia under Medeltiden." *Uppsala Universitets Årsskrift* (1882), 1–58; Skoglund, Alexandra. *De yngre Axelssönernas Förbindelser med Sverige 1441–1487.* Uppsala: Wretman, 1903; Westman, K. G. *Svenska rådets historia till år 1306.* Uppsala: Appelberg, 1904; Lönnroth, Erik. *Sverige och Kalmarunionen 1397–1457.* Studia Historica Gothoburgensia, 10. Gothenburg: Erlander, 1934; rpt. 1969; Löfqvist, K. E. *Om Riddarväsen och Frälse i Nordisk Medeltid.* Lund: Ohlsson, 1935; Löfqvist, K. E. "Rikets råd och män." *Historisk tidskrift* (Sweden) (1936), 406–9; Sjödin, Lars. *Kalmarunionens slutskede. Gustav Vasas befrielsekrig.* 2 vols. Uppsala: Almqvist & Wiksell, 1943–47; Jägerstad, Hans. *Hovdag och Råd under äldre medeltid. Den statsrättsliga utvecklingen i Sverige från Karl Sverkerssons regering till Magnus Erikssons regeringstillträde (1160–1331).* Lund: Blom, 1948; Wieselgren, Greta. *Sten Sture den Yngre och Gustav Trolle.* Lund: Gleerup, 1948; Palme, Sven Ulric. *Riskföreståndarvalet 1512. Studier i Nordisk Politik och Svensk Statsrätt*

1470–1523. Uppsala Universitets Årsskrift, 2. Uppsala: Lundequist, 1949; Palme, Sven Ulric. *Sten Sture den Äldre.* Stockholm: Wahlström & Widstrand, 1950; Gillingstam, Hans. *Ätterna Oxenstierna och Vasa under Medeltiden. Släkthistoriska Studier.* Stockholm: Almqvist & Wiksell, 1952; Carlsson, Gottfrid. *Kalmar Recess 1483.* Historisk Arkiv, 3. Stockholm: Kungliga vitterhets historia och antikvitetsakademien, 1955; Lundholm, Kjell-Gunnar. *Sten Sture den Äldre och stormännen.* Bibliotheca Historica Lundensis, 3. Lund: Gleerup, 1956; Westin, Gunnar T. *Riksföreståndaren och Makten. Politiska utvecklingslinjer i Sverige 1512–1517.* Publications of the New Society of Letters at Lund, 52. Lund: Gleerup, 1957 [German summary]; Anthoni, Eric. *Finlands Medeltida Frälse och 1500-Talsadel.* Skrifter Utgivna av Svenska Litteratursällskapet i Finland, 442. Helsinki: Svenska Litteratursällskapet i Finland, 1970; Andersen, Lizzie Wie, *et al., Uppsala-overenskomsten 1520. Magtstruktur och Magtkamp i Sverige januar-oktober 1520.* Odense: Universitetsforlaget, 1975 [English summary]; Schück, Herman. *Rikets brev och register.* Skrifter utgivna av Svenska Riksarkivet, 4. Stockholm: Liber, 1976 [German summary].

Jens E. Olesen

[**See also:** Coronation; Denmark; Margrethe I; Norway; Royal Administration and Finances; Sweden; Valdemar]

Crafts. The development of crafts in Scandinavia was to a great extent determined by the market and available resources: raw materials, tools, and materials for processing. The dominant materials in Scandinavia were hides and fur from domestic and wild animals, metal (iron and copper primarily from Sweden), clay (primarily in Denmark), wood, and coal. Written sources and archaeological evidence show a flourishing production of shoes, belts, purses, furs, kirtles made from hide, pottery, and iron and copper wares, but relatively few artisans working with precious metals and even fewer engaged in lacemaking, gold embroidery, and other fancy textile production. No trace of glass production has been found, although the materials (sand and fuel) were available.

Written sources for artisans exist, but only concerning those organized, a minority of artisans. Archaeological findings give a much broader picture of craft production but not of the producer. They show that specialized artisans existed in prehistoric times; a goldsmith named Lægæst carved his name in runes in the 5th century A.D. During the Middle Ages, there was a clear distinction between the artisan, who made a living by producing for a market, and the person engaged in handicraft for personal/household use, a distinction based on gender more than on work performed. The artisan producing for a market was male, the household producer female, such as the housewife making cloth and other items for her household. The woman's work in the household (weaving, sewing, baking, brewing) was performed by male artisans once it became a professional craft. An exception was the female brewer, who dominated the trade until the 16th century.

In Denmark, artisans tended to congregate in the cities. Artisans' quarters are found in the early towns of Ribe (8th century) and Hedeby (9th century). From the mid-14th century, urban authorities attempted to eliminate rural craft production, allowing only the village smith. This policy, continued by royal authorities in the 16th century, appears to have been fairly successful, partly because the city offered more opportunities for an artisan than rural areas. The rather dense urbanization, especially on Zealand and in Scania, meant that the rural population could comfortably reach a city regularly, providing a sizable consumer group.

This development was not true for the other Scandinavian countries. In Sweden, no attempts were made to keep craft production within city limits during the Middle Ages. Itinerant craftsmen were found as well as regional settlements of artisans, such as the workmasters of Dalarna, the stonecutters of Öland, and the coppersmiths of Hälsingland. In Norway, much of the craft production remained in the hands of the village artisans or the housewife, undermining the market for the urban artisan, whose customers were the relatively few urban inhabitants. The same held true for Finland. In Iceland, where raw materials were sparse, each farmstead produced what it needed or bought finished products from visiting merchants. References to Icelandic artisans are few and indicate that they were seasonal workers.

In the city, artisans had sales booths grouped together near or on the market square, but workshops scattered all over town, with certain processes (*e.g.*, tanning) taking place at the outskirts of the city to avoid pollution. Only the butchers of Copenhagen lived together in a compound. The artisans made up the middle layers of the urban population. In Denmark, a royal decree from 1422 prohibited any artisan from becoming a member of the city council and limited him to one craft. This prohibition seems to have created some dissatisfaction, and was possibly one of the causes for the generally peaceful uprisings of the urban population during the 15th century to protest the power of the city councilors, all members of the mercantile elite, but at no time did the situation change. Artisans also made up a majority of the stable taxpayers and formed a solid part of the city's economic base. Within the artisanate, a clear sense of social and economic ranking can be found in documents and tax records from the early 16th century. Goldsmiths were at the top of the ladder, with economic and marital ties to the mercantile elite. Bakers came second, followed by smiths, shoemakers, tailors, and cordwainers. On the bottom rungs were ropers, chandlers, coopers, and tinkers. Within each craft, even organized ones, there could be a great variation in the economic and social standing of the masters. Surnames of merchants and councilors indicate that it was not uncommon for sons of successful artisans to move upward socially. Downward social mobility is harder to discern in the sources.

The training of an artisan came through apprenticeship and a period as itinerant journeyman until the presentation and acceptance of a masterpiece made him a master. The training was primarily practical, though some skill at reading and writing or carving signs, numbers, and letters was also required. The Danish artisans used runic signs well into the 13th century, the best-known example being the smith Jakob Rød (early 13th century), who wrote Latin inscriptions and his name in runes on a group of censers. Guild statutes provide some details concerning the education of the organized masters, especially the length of apprenticeship (two to six years) and the relationship between masters and journeymen. Problems in this relationship seem to have arisen as a result of a generation rather than a class gap. There is no evidence that qualified journeymen were excluded from the ranks of the masters during the Middle Ages.

The much-studied and high-quality Viking artifacts may give the impression that craft production reached its peak artistically and technically during the Viking Age only to decline later. This picture may not be quite accurate, and as far as ceramic wares are concerned, positively false. The Viking raids and trade did bring more precious metals into the North than was brought in later,

and from these metals the jewelry was produced. It is not known if the producers were native or foreign workers. Artifacts from the high and late Middle Ages are of a much more varying quality and may seem less spectacular, especially against the broader European background.

Leather. Domestic and wild animals provided an abundance of fur and hide for shoes, belts, purses, gloves, saddles, reins, cords, and other items of leather. The most common artisan in the Scandinavian cities was the shoemaker, and shoemakers' guilds are most frequently mentioned in the sources. The northern climate demanded good footwear. When the Greyfriars arrived in Denmark in 1234, a chronicler noted with surprise that they came barefooted. Export of shoes seems not to have taken place, whereas Scandinavian hide and fur were in demand. The leatherworkers were specialized. By the late Middle Ages, the sources mention furriers, skinners, cordwainers, glovers, pursers, pouchmakers, saddlers, beltmakers, and slipper makers along with shoemakers. Tanning, in contrast, did not become a separate craft until the 17th century. Each leatherworker did his own tanning with some processes (chamoising, tawing) reserved for certain artisans (glovers, pursers).

Metal. Metalcraft was the most specialized craft in Scandinavia. The smith's guilds of Odense and Flensburg had as members by 1496 and 1514, respectively, blacksmiths, locksmiths, cutlers, lorimers, boilermakers, armorers, swordmakers, pewterers, and gunmakers. These artisans were found in practically all towns, even if not always organized in guilds. Production, ranging from sewing needles (made on small forges fired with acorn shells) to large brewing vats, was geared primarily toward the peasants (apparently the village blacksmith produced only horseshoes and ploughshares), the urban population, and the Church. Only the smiths of Odense and Copenhagen appear to have had noble and royal customers. While iron and copper could be found in Scandinavia, gold and silver had to be imported. Goldsmiths were closely supervised by royal magistrates to prevent cheating and forgery, but in return they received privileges and monopolies on their craft, and often belonged to the urban elite.

Wood. Turners, fletchers, wheelwrights, and cofferers are rarely mentioned in the written sources, but archaeological finds show extensive production of plates, cups, bowls, and chests for daily use, made from native as well as imported wood. The great fisheries at Skanør (the Scania Fair) and the Liim Fjord placed a heavy demand on barrels of a certain standard and weight for exporting the salted herrings. A few coopers' guilds were formed, but the merchants made certain that barrel production and prices did not present an obstacle to the profitable herring trade. Toward the end of the Middle Ages, cabinet makers and joiners appear in the sources and in the guilds, indicating a growing demand for furniture, fancily carved. But the joiners who in 1490 had formed a guild with the painters, master glaziers, and goldsmiths of Flensburg most likely had churches as their primary workplace. Combs for hair and weaving made from antlers and bones were also a commonly found craft, although the combmakers are rarely mentioned in the written sources. The same holds true—surprisingly, given the importance of ships and sailing to the Nordic people—for the shipwright. Archaeological excavations have unearthed a shipyard in the Danish countryside from the Viking Age and the early Middle Ages, indicating production of ships and boats for local trade and fishing.

Ceramics. Another rural craft that did not move into the cities was pottery. Near the clay deposits, on Zealand especially, pottery workshops arose, producing cups, bowls, plates, and jugs for the household. Most of this production was geared to the local market, but some inter-Scandinavian trade took place. In Norway, all ceramic and stone ware seems to have been imported during the Middle Ages, part of it from Denmark. Pottery was, in contrast to other craft production, at a fairly low stage during the Viking Age, but began flourishing during the high Middle Ages. The kilns also produced tiles and bricks for building once the arts of making them became known in Scandinavia (mid-12th century), and some Danish tiles were exported to Sweden.

Textiles. Textile production remained a home or cottage industry until the late 15th century. Archaeological finds of medieval textiles are few in contrast to the preceding periods (Bronze and Iron Ages). Prehistoric finds indicate that Nordic women knew how to use sophisticated spinning, weaving, and treatment techniques to produce a warm, durable, and presentable cloth. These techniques would in all likelihood have been preserved into the Middle Ages, whereas the price and scarcity of dyes would have limited the choice of colors. The horizontal loom was introduced into Scandinavia during the Middle Ages, except in Iceland, where the upright loom continued in use. Written sources refer only to imported Flemish and English cloth, a luxury item subject to taxation and coveted by the nobility and the urban elite. The locally produced cloth, known as *vaðmál*, must, however, have covered the needs of the majority of the population. According to Olaus Magnus (*Historia de gentibus septentrionalibus*, ch. 55), the Nordic women excelled in weaving wool and linen cloth (cotton remained a rarity in the North). Weaving became a professional craft during the final decades of the 15th century, when Scottish weavers settled in East Danish towns. Weavers' guilds were founded, the earliest in Copenhagen in 1550, in which women, rarely, could become masters and girls apprentices. Tailoring had earlier become a professional craft, and was closed to women who were not wives or daughters of masters. Seamstresses who made linen clothes (shirts and undergarments) were permitted to exercise their trade.

Food. Among the artisans of the medieval towns were also the bakers, butchers, and brewers. They are frequently mentioned in written sources, and their trades were closely supervised by the magistrates to ensure that bread and meat were available to the urban population at an affordable price. Bread riots appear to have been rare in Scandinavia, and the upswing in trade of oxen and increased cattle holdings in general during the late Middle Ages meant that meat, in Denmark at least, was relatively inexpensive, in fact, cheaper per pound than wheat bread. The variety of bread was not great, limited to wheat and rye breads of various shapes. But there are few references to cakes and pastries. The female baker appears to have been a common sight in Swedish towns, but rarely found in Danish sources. The brewer, who appears in the early towns, was not organized in guilds but licensed and supervised by the urban magistrates. During the 15th century, the merchants sought to gain a monopoly on brewing along with their control of the import of hops and German beer. By the 16th century, they had become successful, establishing brewers' guilds and reducing women who were not wives or widows of master brewers to working as tapsters and innkeepers, serving the beer imported by the merchants or brewed by the brewers.

Lit: Literature in English on Nordic crafts and artisans is sparse apart from the many books dealing with the Vikings, which usually include a discussion of the crafts. Else Roesdahl, *Viking Age Denmark*, trans. Susan Margeson and Kirsten Williams (London: British Museum,

1982), contains good chapters on crafts and craft production. Grethe Jacobsen, "Guilds in Medieval Denmark: The Social and Economic Role of Merchants and Artisans" (Diss. University of Wisconsin, Madison, 1980), and Grethe Jacobsen, "Women's Work and Women's Role: Ideology and Reality in Danish Urban Society, 1300–1550" (*The Second Scandinavian Economic History Review* 30.1 [1983], 3–20), deal primarily with guilds and women's roles and place in the craft, but contain some discussion of crafts. An excellent source for the latest gains in medieval Nordic archaeology including discussions of workshops and techniques of various artisans is the annual *Hikuin*, vol. 1– (1974–), which includes English abstracts of articles from vol. 3 (1977) onward. For works in the Scandinavian languages, see Grethe Jacobsen, *Håndværket kommer til Danmark. Tiden før 1555. 1. Håndværkets kulturhistorie* (Copenhagen: Håndværksrådets Forlag, 1982), and the following general articles in *KLNM*: Ljung, Sven, *et al.* "Hantverkare." *KLNM* 6 (1961), 216–25; Søgaard, Helge, *et al.* "Mester." *KLNM* 11 (1966), 563–6; *KLNM* also contains various articles on individual crafts.

Grethe Jacobsen

[See also: Carving; Clothmaking; Guilds; Wood Carving]

Crime and Punishment. Medieval Scandinavian laws were recorded in the Christian era, and with few exceptions the earlier extant MSS go back to the latter part of the 13th century. Because these laws were codified during a period of transition, which reflected the clash between an older system of customary law and the centralizing efforts of Church and monarchy, they present no uniform picture of the medieval Scandinavian penal system.

In pre-Christian Scandinavia, the power of the state was still relatively weak. The society was based on a system of kinship, and the guarantee for the legal protection of the individual was vested in the power of the autonomous extended family. If a family member inflicted an injury on another member of the household, he or she was subject to internal family discipline exercised by the head of the family. A grievance committed by an outside party against a member of the family was regarded as a crime against the family as a whole, and the ensuing vengeance could be directed at the offender's relatives as well as at the offender, *i.e.*, the responsibility was collective, and the reaction collective. The responsibility for crimes committed by a woman or a minor rested with the husband or guardian. Slaves were the liability of the owner, and, likewise, the owner bore the legal consequences of injuries inflicted by domestic or wild animals in his possession.

The observable consequences of a criminal action were punishable, but not intention and motives. Because the old law emphasized the effect of the crime, an action of self-defense was considered as punishable as other crimes committed. Accidents were punished according to the injury sustained, regardless of whether the perpetrator had acted with criminal intent.

The offended party obtained satisfaction through self-help (a legal term used to designate advocacy and execution of punishment), resulting in either blood vengeance (feud) or indemnification in the form of fines. Vengeance was not necessarily proportionate to the crime committed, and not just manslaughter, but also battery and assault could evoke a blood feud. Apart from those cases where the interest of the community had been violated, for example, in cases of treason, desertion, and sacrilege, there appears to have been no public intervention when crimes were committed.

The increased monarchical power and the growing influence of the Church in the 12th and 13th centuries brought about a change in the structure of the society. The old family community was dissolved, and the legal power that had been vested in the extended family was superseded by newer forms of royal legislation taken mainly from Roman canonical law. Collective responsibility was replaced by individual responsibility, and only the criminal was punished. In cases of manslaughter, however, the culprit's relatives were responsible for parts of the ensuing financial settlement (*wergild*). Efforts were made to restrict blood feud, and the old system of self-help was gradually replaced by public prosecution, although a form of self-help still remained in force in the sense that the execution of a sentence passed in court was usually left to the plaintiff. The criminal could be killed with impunity by the offended party only when he was caught in the act, for instance, in cases of theft, rape, or violation of domestic peace. As the people were compelled to refrain from using the ancient right of self-help, the king was obliged, in return, to punish the criminal by fines, outlawry, death, or corporal punishment.

Fines. In the Swedish and Danish provincial laws, as well as in the laws of the Icelandic free state (*Grágás*) and in Old Norwegian law, fines were the most common form of punishment. In earlier and more primitive stages of the law, fines had been one of the established means to settle an issue between two families. Because most injuries originally were regarded as an infringement of the individual's interests, fines were granted to the plaintiff as a form of moral satisfaction and financial compensation for the injury sustained. Later legislation often prescribes the division of the fine between the plaintiff and the king (the representative of the judicial system), or between the plaintiff and the Church (for church crimes). As the result of the influence from canonical law, a distinction was made between actions committed with criminal intent and accidents. The latter were judged more leniently than the former, and the fines incurred for such grievances went to the plaintiff in their entirety.

Outlawry. Medieval Scandinavian laws mention a series of crimes that could not be atoned for with fines; they incurred outlawry and loss of property. There is no legal evidence suggesting that outlawry could take effect without a prior legal verdict. In Denmark, outlawry as a form of punishment (*e.g.*, for manslaughter at the legal assembly, violation of peace of the household, arson, rape, and high treason) was probably introduced shortly before the codification of the provincial laws, reflecting the effort of Church and monarchy to confirm legal authority by intervening in criminal cases that violated society as a whole. The Swedish provincial laws mention two types of outlawry, an older, restricted form, according to which the criminal is outlawed from the province, and a more recent form that can be traced back to the royal peace legislation (*eþsøre*) from the middle of the 13th century. The latter prescribes full outlawry and loss of property. The Icelandic *Grágás* distinguishes among three types of outlawry: *skóggangr* (full outlawry and confiscation of property), *fjǫrbaugsgarðr* (lesser outlawry, *i.e.*, three years' exile and confiscation of property), and *heraðssekt* (exile from the district). In Norway, fines and outlawry were the oldest and most frequently used forms of punishment. Usually, fines could replace outlawry, and, conversely, outlawry could be incurred by fines outstanding. In Norway and Iceland, outlawry might be regarded as an alternative to the death penalty, because an outlawed individual could be killed with impunity.

Capital punishment. In pre-Christian times, the death penalty had a modest sphere of application. The punishment of a

crime usually bore the character of a private settlement, and the killing of the offender terminated (or perpetuated) the conflict. Gradually, the plaintiff's execution of the death penalty was legitimized by the jurisdiction of the popular courts. Later, when the execution became a public legal action, it was incumbent on the royal official to provide an executioner.

The Swedish and Danish provincial laws contain the following forms of the death penalty: beheading, hanging, breaking on the wheel, burning, stoning, and live burial. Often crimes that incurred capital punishment could be expiated with fines, especially if the plaintiff interceded on behalf of the defendant. In the Icelandic *Grágás*, there is no death penalty, but there are indications that executions took place as part of a private system of self-help, *e.g.*, in cases of rape and theft. Medieval Norwegian law contains little information about the execution of the death penalty by public authority, but certain sections in the penal codes prescribe, for example, drowning for sorcery, beheading for a slave caught stealing, and hanging for theft. On the whole, capital punishment appears to have been less important in Norway and Iceland than in Sweden and Denmark. Throughout the Middle Ages, there was increased recourse to the death penalty in Norse law. That development must be seen in light of the tendency to inflict more severe punishments as part of the general principle of deterrence.

Because certain crimes appear to have incurred certain forms of execution, scholars have attempted to establish a connection between penal actions and sacrificial rituals. Allegedly, specific types of criminal outrages, such as theft, murder, and rape, were liable to evoke the wrath of the gods, hence the perpetrators of such crimes were sacrificed to alleviate the guilt of the society and to placate the offended deities. This "Sacral Theory" was long favored by legal historians, but has since been rejected.

Corporal punishment. Corporal punishments were originally enacted on slaves and unfree members of society, and such forms of punishment carried very derogatory connotations. The Danish provincial laws give few examples of corporal punishment, but petty theft was punished with flogging or mutilation. The earliest Norwegian laws mention running the gauntlet as a form of punishment for petty theft, and bestiality was punished with castration. In the later laws, flogging was used as a means to punish petty theft (combined with branding and mutilation for repeated theft), failure to pay debts, and certain sex crimes. The Icelandic *Grágás* prescribes mutilation for a slave who murdered his owner or one of the owner's relatives, and the nature of the punishment, the loss of hands and feet, suggests that it was intended as a form of death penalty. In the Swedish provincial laws, corporal punishment was the most common form of punishment next to fines. Such crimes as petty theft, robbery, illicit intercourse, and the failure or inability to pay fines were often punished with mutilation, entailing the loss of such body parts as hands, ears, or nose. Petty theft, forgery, battery, and defamation could incur flogging.

Corporal punishments were executed in public and formed an important component in the systems of shameful punishments, *i.e.*, punishments that symbolically reflect the types of crimes they punish. Such punishments flourished during the later Middle Ages, probably as a result of the principles of deterrence and retaliation from Mosaic law.

Bib: Iuul, Stig, *et al. Scandinavian Legal Bibliography.* ACTA Instituti Upsaliensis Iurisprudentiae Comparativae, 4. Stockholm: Almqvist & Wiksell, 1961. **Lit.:** Björling, Carl G. E. *Om bötestraffet i den svenska* medeltidsrätten. Lund: Gleerup, 1893; Maurer, Konrad. *Altisländisches Strafrecht und Gerichtswesen*. Vol. 5 of his *Vorlesungen über altnordische Rechtsgeschichte*. 5 vols. Leipzig: Deichert, 1907–10; rpt. Osnabrück: Zeller, 1966; Heusler, Andreas. *Das Strafrecht der Isländersagas*. Leipzig: Duncker & Humblot, 1911; Amira, Karl von. *Die germanischen Todesstrafen: Untersuchungen zur Rechts- und Religionsgeschichte*. Abhandlungen der Bayerischen Akademie der Wissenschaften: Philosophisch-philologische und historische Klasse, 31, no. 3. Munich: Bayerische Akademie der Wissenschaften, 1922; Jørgensen, Poul J. *Manddrabsforbrydelsen i den skaanske ret fra Valdemarstiden*. Copenhagen: Universitetsbogtrykkeriet, 1922; Mayer, Ernst. "Die Entstehung der germanischen Todesstrafe." *Der Gerichtssaal* 89 (1924), 353–96; Hemmer, Ragnar. *Studier rörande straffutmätningen i medeltida svensk rätt*. Helsingfors: Mercator, 1928; Carlsson, Lizzie. "De medeltida skamstraffen: Ett stycke svensk kulturhistoria." *Rig* 17 (1934), 121–50; Gædeken, Poul. *Retsbrudet og reaktionen derimod i gammeldansk og germansk ret*. Copenhagen: Gad, 1934; Ólafur Larússon. "Die Popularklage der Grágás." In *Festskrift för professorn, jur. utr. dr. Otto Hjalmar Granfelt*. Helsingfors: Tilgmann, 1934, pp. 86–107; Wennström, Torstein. *Tjuvnad och förnæmi: Rättsfilologiska studier i svenska landskapslagar*. Lund: Gleerup; Leipzig: Reisland; Copenhagen: Gad, 1936; Almqvist, Jan Eric. *Tidelagsbrottet: En straffrätts-historisk studie*. 2nd rev. ed. Lund: Gleerup, 1938; Munktell, Henrik. "Om s.k. speglande straff." *Svensk juristtidning* 26 (1941), 254–70; Rehfeldt, Bernhard. *Todesstrafen und Bekehrungsgeschichte: Zur Rechts- und Religionsgeschichte der germanischen Hinrichtungsbräuche*. Berlin: Duncker & Humblot, 1942; Ström, Folke. *On the Sacral Origin of the Germanic Death Penalties*. Lund: Ohlsson, 1942; Skeie, Jon. *Den norske strafferett* 1. 2nd ed. Oslo: Norli, 1946; Iuul, Stig. "Den gamle danske strafferet og dens udvikling indtil slutningen af det 18. aarhundrede." In *Kampen mod forbrydelsen: Forbrydelsens historie, kriminalpolitiet, det politiske parti, strafferetten og dens udvikling gennem tiderne, kriminologi og kriminaltaktik samt fængselsvæsen* 1. Ed. Leif Beckman and Herluf Petersen. Copenhagen: Wiene, 1951; Lúðvíg Ingvarsson. *Refsingar á Íslandi á þjóðveldistímanum*. Reykjavik: Menningarsjóður, 1970; Fenger, Ole. *Fejde og mandebot: Studier over slægtsansvaret i germansk og gammeldansk ret*. Copenhagen: Juristforbundet, 1971; Gade, Kari Ellen. "Hanging in Northern Law and Literature." *Maal og minne* (1985), 159–83.

Kari Ellen Gade

[**See also:** *Grágás*; Laws; Outlawry]

Dámusta saga ("The Saga of Dámusti") is an anonymous *riddarasaga*, probably from the 14th century. With a total of only seventeen preserved MSS (only one fragmentary vellum MS, AM 557 4to, from the 15th century), *Dámusta saga* stands as one of the most sparsely transmitted *riddarasögur*. It is, however, extant in several redactions: an older redaction (14th century), an abridged redaction from the 17th century, and finally, a synopsis from the end of the 18th or beginning of the 19th century under the title *Sagan af Danusta Josephssyni* ("The Saga of Danusti Josephsson"). The *Dámusta rímur*, which probably date from the first half of the 15th century, belong to the oldest group of this Icelandic ballad genre.

Gratiana, the daughter of King Katalaktus of Greece, has until now rejected all suitors. Dámusti is the son of one of the king's wise men; he prays daily to the Virgin Mary. King Jón from Saxony courts Gratiana and obtains her consent. The marriage is scheduled to take place in the fall, but Dámusti, who also loves the princess, with the approval of the wise men kills the bridegroom in an ambush. The emperor forgives the murder, but Gratiana soon falls fatally ill. The Virgin Mary appears and instructs Dámusti to go to the graveyard where Gratiana is buried. There, Dámusti defeats the monster Alheimr, who caused Gratiana's death so that he could marry her. The giant gives Dámusti a potion that brings Gratiani back to life, and he soon marries her. After Katalaktus's death, Dámusti becomes emperor, but soon hands over the kingdom to his son, and he and Gratiana live out the rest of their lives as penitents.

The religious and moral elements of the saga make the work difficult to classify. It has been considered a pseudo-legend of Mary, and its author an unknown Icelandic clergyman. Nonetheless, *Dámusta saga* can be grouped with the Icelandic *riddarasögur*. Even though there are certain parallels, especially in the second part, between the saga and *Amadas et Ydoine* and other French works, the saga cannot be considered a translation. On the contrary, it represents an original Icelandic text, and shows how polyfunctional the structure of the medieval romances could be. The fairy tale bearing the title "Inntak úr söguþætti af Jóni Upplandakóngi" ("Contents of an Episode About Jón, King of the Uplands"), which is directly derived from *Dámusta saga*, demonstrates that many Icelandic popular tales had their origins in the late-medieval saga literature.

Ed.: Tan-Haverhorst, Louisa Fredrika, ed. *Þjalar Jóns saga. Dámusta saga.* Haarlem: Tjeenk Willink, 1939 [introduction in Dutch, pp. cxix–lxc; edition, pp. 48–108]; Finnur Jónsson, ed. "Dámusta rímur." In *Rímnasafn: Samling af de ældste islandske rimer.* 2 vols. Samfund til udgivelse af gammel nordisk litteratur, 35. Copenhagen: Møller & Jørgensen, 1905–22, vol. 2, pp. 771–800; "Inntak úr söguþætti af Jóni Upplandakóngi." In *Íslenzkar þjóðsögur og ævintýri.* 6 vols. Ed. Jón Árnason. Rev. ed. Árni Böðvarsson and Bjarni Vilhjálmsson. Reykjavik: Þjóðsaga, 1961, vol. 1, pp. 273–4. **Bib.**: Kalinke, Marianne E., and P. M. Mitchell. *Bibliography of Old Norse–Icelandic Romances.* Islandica, 44. Ithaca and London: Cornell University Press, 1985. **Lit.**: Kölbing, Eugen. "Über isländische Bearbeitungen fremder Stoffe." *Germania* 17, n.s. 5 (1872), 193–7; Jón Þorkelsson. *Om Digtningen på Island i det 15. og 16. Århundrede.* Copenhagen: Høst, 1888; Finnur Jónsson. *Den oldnorske og oldislandske Litteraturs Historie.* 3 vols. 2nd ed. Copenhagen: Gad, 1920–24, vol. 3, p. 57; Björn K. Þórólfsson. *Rímur fyrir 1600.* Safn Fræðafjelagsins um Ísland og Íslendinga, 9. Copenhagen: Möller, 1934, pp. 322–3; Schlauch, Margaret. *Romance in Iceland.* Princeton: Princeton University Press; New York: American-Scandinavian Foundation; London: Allen & Unwin, 1934; rpt. New York: Russell & Russell, 1973; Schlauch, Margaret. "The *Dámusta saga* and French Romance." *Modern Philology* 35 (1937), 1–13; Hermann Pálsson. *Sagnagerð. Hugvekjur um fornar bókmenntir.* Reykjavik: Almenna bókafélagið, 1982; Glauser, Jürg. *Isländische Märchensagas. Studien zur Prosaliteratur im spätmittelalterlichen Island.* Beiträge zur nordischen Philologie, 12. Basel and Frankfurt am Main: Helbing & Lichtenhahn, 1983; Kalinke, Marianne. "Norse Romance (*Riddarasögur*)." In *Old Norse–Icelandic Literature: A Critical Guide.* Ed. Carol J. Clover and John Lindow. Islandica, 45. Ithaca and London: Cornell University Press, 1985, pp. 316–63; Bibire, Paul. "From riddarasaga to lygisaga: The Norse Response to Romance." In *Les Sagas de Chevaliers (Riddarasögur). Actes de la Vᵉ Conférence Internationale sur les Sagas . . . (Toulon. Juillet 1982).* Ed. Régis Boyer. Civilisations, 10. Paris: Presses de l'Université de Paris-Sorbonne, 1985, p. 66; Jochens, Jenny M. "Consent in Marriage: Old Norse Law, Life, and Literature." *Scandinavian Studies* 58 (1986), 142–76; Kalinke, Marianne E. *Bridal-Quest Romance in Medieval Iceland.* Islandica, 46. Ithaca and London: Cornell University Press, 1990.

Jürg Glauser

[**See also:** Old Norse–Icelandic Literature, Foreign Influence on; *Riddarasögur*]

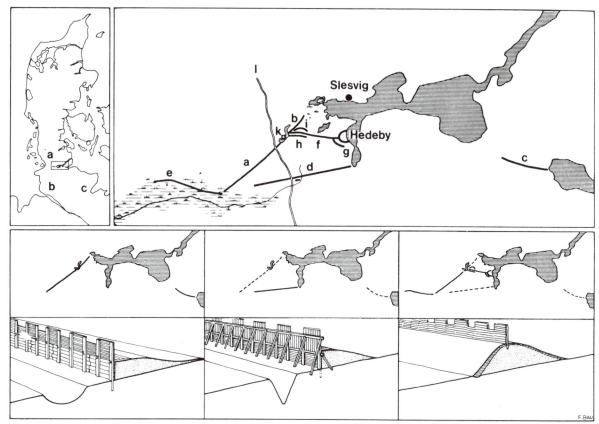

19. Danevirke

Danevirke is a set of ramparts protecting the southern border of medieval Denmark, one of the largest of northern Europe's ancient defensive works. The entire complex consists of several ramparts and ditches with a total length of about 30 km., built at various times. The ramparts functioned from about A.D. 737 into the 13th century. In 1864, the Danevirke was rebuilt and used against Prussia, and during World War II the German army constructed a tank trap there.

The oldest known versions of the name "Danevirke" date from the 12th century: *Danæwirchi* ("Defense of the Danes"), Latin form *opus danorum* (*Chronicon Lethrense*), and *daniuerki* (Sven Aggesen's *Brevis historia regum Dacie*).

The Danevirke runs from the head of Schlei (or Slien) fjord in the east to the rivers Rheide and Treene in the west. It effectively controlled the land approach to Denmark, because rivers and marsh areas already made a western approach difficult. The main north-south traffic route, the *Hærvej* ("army-road") or the Ox-road, passed through the Danevirke in the Hedeby area. Forests covered the 20-km.-wide areas down to the border river, the Eider. Beyond this lived the Saxons, to the west the Frisians, and to the east Slavic tribes.

Excavations over many years have yielded much information on the construction of the ramparts. By means of dendrochronology (tree-ring dating), the year of construction of some of the phases is now established. The political background of the Danevirke is illuminated by various written sources.

The Danevirke is best explained by dividing it into three successive complexes (Danevirke 1, 2, and 3), each functioning at different times.

Danevirke 1 consists of the North Wall (which has only one phase) and the earliest phase of the Main Wall. It was built in 737 and is, according to present knowledge, the oldest part of the Danevirke. It was constructed of earth faced with timber and was about 7 km. long, 10 m. wide, and 2 m. high. To the south was a ditch. No written sources say who had this great wall structure built or why, but probably the Danish king was responsible.

Danevirke 2 is also called "Kovirke," apparently raised during a single building phase and following an uncompromisingly straight line. It is about 6.5 km. long, constructed of earth faced with timber and with a ditch to the south. There is no definite dating evidence for Kovirke, but it is just possible that this is the rampart that, according to the Royal Frankish Annals, *s.a.* 808, the Danish King Godfred ordered built against threats from Charlemagne. There is, at present, no other good candidate for such a rampart.

Danevirke 3 comprises the Main Wall and to the west the Crooked Wall, to the east the Connecting Wall and the ramparts and ditches of Hedeby. It is about 14 km. long, forms a vast zig-zag line, and has many phases. The oldest phase seems to date from around 968; the construction of the Connecting Wall is dated by dendrochronology to that year. It was 12–13 m. wide and about 3 m. high, built of earth faced with turf and probably crowned with a wooden palisade. The political background for this vast construction must be the confrontations between Denmark and the German Empire described in the written sources (*e.g.*, Widukind and Thietmar).

Through the 11th and 12th centuries, the Danevirke was reinforced several times, and became more than 20 m. wide and 5 m. tall; the first time with turf fronts and later, at the Main Wall, with a stone front, and finally with a 7-m.-high brick front. This was the Valdemar's Wall, built by King Valdemar the Great (r. 1157–1182). At some stage, a fortress or castle, Thyraborg (undated), was built into the Danevirke. The political background to the 11th- and 12th-century phases of the Danevirke known from written sources, such as Sven Aggesen and Saxo, consists of threats from Slavic or German princes, or from the German Empire.

The Danevirke functioned as a military border rampart eleven times (in the years 815, 834, 974, 1043, 1066, 1113, 1131, 1147, 1156, 1171, and 1193) and was overrun four times (in the years 934, 974, 1043, and 1156). The last known occasion of a Danish army gathering at the Danevirke was in 1231.

With a Danish royal line ruling also as hereditary dukes of South Jutland, with close links to the South, and often hostile to Denmark, the political situation of the border area changed and the military significance of the Danevirke dwindled.

Lit.: Müller, Sophus, and Carl Neergaard. *Danevirke. Archæologisk undersøgt, beskrevet og tydet.* Copenhagen: Gyldendal, 1903; Jankuhn, Herbert. *Die Wehranlagen der Wikingerzeit zwischen Schlei und Treene.* Neumünster: Wachholtz, 1937; la Cour, Vilhelm. *Danevirkestudier. En arkæologisk-historisk undersøgelse.* Copenhagen: Haase, 1950; Hvidtfeldt, Johan. "Heinrich Himmler og mindesmærkerne ved Danevirke." *Sønderjyske Aarbøger* (1964), 467–76; Andersen, H. Hellmuth, *et al. Danevirke.* Jysk Arkæologisk Selskabs Skrifter, 13. Copenhagen: Gyldendal, 1976; Andersen, H. Hellmuth. *Jyllands Vold.* Højbjerg: Wormianum, 1977; Roesdahl, Else. *Viking Age Denmark.* Trans. Susan Margeson and Kirsten Williams. London: British Museum, 1982, pp. 139–46; Andersen, H. Hellmuth. "Danewerk." *Reallexikon der Germanischen Altertumskunde.* Ed. H. Beck *et al.* Berlin and New York: de Gruyter, 1982–84, vol. 5, pp. 236–43; Andersen, H. Hellmuth. "Das Danewerk als Ausdruck mittelalterlicher Befestigungskunst." *Chateau Gaillard* (Caen) 11 (1983), 9–17; Andersen, H. Hellmuth. "Zum neuen Schnitt am Hauptwall des Danewerks." *Archäologisches Korrespondenzblatt* 15, H. 4 (1985), 525–9.

Else Roesdahl

[**See also:** Fortification]

Darraðarljóð

Darraðarljóð ("Dǫrruðr's Lay"), a poem in praise of an unnamed "young king" who has won a victory over the Irish, survives only in *Njáls saga* (ch. 157). The young king is identified there as the Viking Sigtryggr silkiskegg ("silk-beard") and the battle as Clontarf, fought in 1014. These identifications are difficult to harmonize with the other sources on Clontarf; there is a better match with the victory won by Sigtryggr caech ("squinty") in the battle of Dublin of 919, although this identification also creates problems.

The central figures in *Darraðarljóð* are the valkyries who assist the young king in battle. The poem appears to be built on an extended metaphor in which the tenor is the valkyries' wielding of weapons and the vehicle their work on a piece of weaving. *Darraðarljóð* is consequently a uniquely rich source for medieval terminology related to the warp-weighted loom. In *Njáls saga*, the valkyries are depicted as literally engaged in weaving, apparently so as to determine the outcome of the battle by magic; this reading of the poem is probably overly literal.

The poem opens in the manner of a work song, with the valkyries as speakers. In verse 1, they describe the *skothríð*, or initial volleys of thrown weapons. In verses 2 and 3, they urge each other to join in the ensuing hand-to-hand fighting. In verses 4 to 6 occurs the famous refrain *Vindum, vindum / vef darraðar* "Let us wind, let us wind / the interweaving of the pennant[s]." Here, if the rare word *darrað*[*r*] is correctly interpreted as "pennant," the entire spectacle of battle is epitomized as an intertwining of the various banners carried by each force. In the terms of the metaphor, the valkyries as weavers wind up this "fabric" on the windlass-like beam at the top of the loom, so as to facilitate the weaving of a further length of fabric. The prose narrative introduces a person called Dǫrruðr, who hears the valkyries' song; the name Dǫrruðr probably represents a folk etymology on *darrað*[*r*]. Verses 7 and 8 announce the defeat of the Irish and the death of an earl, evidently on their side, and foreshadow the death of a "mighty king," presumably their high king; people hitherto confined to the coastal fringes (presumably the Vikings) will rule "the lands." In verses 9–11, the valkyries predict fresh victories for the "young king," concluding with an incitation to ride "out," interpreted in *Njáls saga* as meaning an exit from the hut where supposedly their loom is situated.

In meter and style, *Darraðarljóð* resembles the poems of the *Poetic Edda*. The narrative technique is the "running commentary" found in *Liðsmannaflokkr*, where the actions seem to unfold as the speakers speak. The original milieu for the poem was probably the British Isles, with special ties to the joint kingdom of York and Dublin. Walter Scott testifies, not very reliably, that a version of *Darraðarljóð* was still being recited on Orkney during the 18th century.

Ed.: Heusler, Andreas, and Wilhelm Ranisch, eds. *Eddica minora.* Dortmund: Ruhfus, 1903 [text, critical apparatus, and commentary]; Finnur Jónsson, ed. *Den norsk-islandske skjaldedigtning.* Vols. 1A–2A (tekst efter håndskrifterne) and 1B–2B (rettet tekst). Copenhagen and Christiania [Oslo]: Gyldendal, 1912–15; rpt. Copenhagen: Rosenkilde & Bagger, 1967 (A) and 1973 (B); Kershaw, Nora, ed. and trans. *Anglo-Saxon and Norse Poems.* Cambridge: Cambridge University Press, 1922 [text, translation, and analysis]; Einar Ól. Sveinsson, ed. *Brennu-Njáls saga.* Íslenzk fornrit, 12. Reykjavik: Hið íslenzka fornritafélag, 1954. Tr.: Magnus Magnusson and Hermann Pálsson, trans. *Njal's Saga.* Harmondsworth: Penguin, 1960. Lit.: Goedheer, Albertus Johannes. *Irish and Norse Traditions About the Battle of Clontarf.* Haarlem: Tjeenk Willink, 1938 [discussion of historical significance]; Holtsmark, Anne. "'Vefr Darraðar.'" *Maal og minne* (1939), 74–96 [discussion of weaving terminology and general interpretation]; Neumann, Eduard. *Der Schicksalsbegriff in der Edda.* Beiträge zur deutschen Philologie, 7. Giessen: Schmitz, 1955 [interpretation]; Genzmer, Felix. "Das Walkürenlied." *Arkiv för nordisk filologi* 71 (1956), 168–71 [discussion of historical significance]; See, Klaus von. "Das Walkürenlied." *Beiträge zur Geschichte der deutschen Sprache und Literatur* (Tübingen) 81 (1959), 1–15 [interpretation]; Hoffmann, Marta. *The Warp-Weighted Loom: Studies in the History and Technology of an Ancient Implement.* Studia Norvegica, 14. Oslo: Universitetsforlaget, 1964; rpt. McMinnville: Robin and Russ Handweavers, 1982 [discussion of weaving terminology]; Poole, Russell. "Darraðarljóð 2: ǫrum hrælaðr." *Maal og minne* (1985), 87–94 [discussion of weaving terminology]; Poole, R.G. *Viking Poems on War and Peace: A study in Skaldic Narrative.* Toronto, Buffalo, and London: University of Toronto Press, 1991, pp. 116–56.

Russell Poole

[**See also:** Eddic Meters; Eddic Poetry; *Liðsmannaflokkr*; *Njáls saga*]

De moribus et actis primorum normanniæ ducum
see **Dudo of St.-Quentin**

De virtutibus et vitiis *see* **Alcuin**

Demography. Historical demography studies populations in the past, with respect to size, composition, and distribution, but also with respect to the patterns and causes of change or stability. The latter fields of research involve the study of fertility, mortality, and migration, which are determined by biological and societal structures, and so must be examined within the framework of human physiology and society. This approach is called "social demography." Medieval demographic structures in Scandinavia were shaped by the basic socioeconomic fact that at least 90 percent of the population lived in the countryside and subsisted on the meager rewards of primary agricultural production. As all preindustrial and prescientific populations, they had only the most rudimentary rational knowledge of disease.

Medieval demography in Scandinavia has made tremendous progress during the last decades. This advance is due primarily to the development of a new scientific discipline, osteoarchaeology, which uses skeletal remains of people living in the past to determine sex, age at death, and health of their "producers."

The most important problem faced by osteoarchaeological research is that skeletons of infants and young children tend to disintegrate (see, *e.g.*, Holk 1970a, Sjøvold 1987b, Jensen 1979, Persson 1976, Persson and Persson 1981). Moreover, excavated skeletal populations tend to be unrepresentative reflections of the structure of mortality in living populations because death of infants and young children is so usual as to produce a significant frequency of irregular burials (Gräslund 1972–73, Holck 1987). Unwanted neonatals were exposed in pagan times and, probably still to some extent illegally after the introduction of Christianity in the 11th century (Benedictow 1985, Mundal 1987). Stillborn and unbaptized children, as well as suicides and some categories of criminals, were not buried in Christian cemeteries (Bøe 1963, Rosén 1969). The problems caused by underrepresentation of infants and young children in skeletal populations are usually overcome by comparison with populations with similar life expectancies for adolescents and adults, and good information on infants and children. Life tables have been produced providing such data on a regular and systematic basis (Coale and Demeny 1966, Henry 1970). This approach is acceptable when used with caution (Sjøvold 1987a).

On the basis of a general assessment of the osteoarchaeological data available in 1970, average life expectancy in medieval Scandinavia was determined to be between twenty and thirty years (Holck 1970a). Using the data produced in more recent studies and applying the life-table technique, we can now conclude that within this range of variation life expectancy most usually and on average was between twenty and twenty-five years (*cf.* Jensen 1979). This conclusion corresponds closely to the preplague results for England based on written sources (Ohlin 1966, Miller and Hatcher 1978, Razi 1980, Hatcher 1986).

A small medieval cemetery containing the skeletal remains of 364 individuals has been excavated at Fröson in Jämtland, a region of central Scandinavia that in the medieval centuries belonged territorially to the state of Norway, but ecclesiastically to the Swedish archbishopric of Uppsala. The cemetery had been used in the period around 1050/1100–1350 by a small but socially differentiated peasant population on a few nearby holdings containing twenty-five to forty-five persons: 184 of the individuals, 50.3 percent of the total cemetery population, had died before the age of seven; twenty-seven (7.4%) had died between the ages of seven and fourteen; fifteen (4.1%) between the ages of fourteen and twenty; sixty (19%) between the ages of twenty and forty; sixty-five (17.8%) between the ages of forty and sixty; and only five (1.4%) died at an age above sixty years (Gejvall 1960).

While the proportion of children dying below the age of seven may seem astonishing, one should note that an average life expectancy at birth of twenty years, the highest considered by the author, corresponds, according to life tables, to a death rate of children during the first seven years of life of about 625–650 per 1,000 (Coale and Demeny 1966, Henry 1970). This comparison suggests a significant deficit of children's skeletal remains in the graveyard at Fröson; a small deficit also of adults, mostly male, is probable. A country parish cemetery at Mære (central Norway) contained the analyzable skeletal remains of sixty-nine individuals buried between 1100 and 1550. Of these, 52 percent were children below the age of fifteen (Holck 1970b). The life expectancy of the adults, nonetheless, indicates a general level of mortality suggesting a probable deficit of infants.

A considerable increase in infant mortality must have been caused by a change in the pattern of breast feeding during the Middle Ages. Norwegian studies show that there was a shift away from immediate to delayed breast feeding and other means of feeding neonatals. The general view of physicians in classical antiquity was that the first milk of women, colostrum, was harmful to babies. This view, uncritically accepted by medieval physicians, was part of a massive importation of European culture into Scandinavia in the high Middle Ages (Weiser-Aall 1973). However, colostrum is highly important for the protection of neonatals against infections and also contains high amounts of important nutrients. The significance of such a change in breast-feeding customs can be surmised from the effects of the change back to immediate breast feeding (*ca.* 1680–1880). English data suggest that the change from immediate to delayed commencement of lactation caused an increase in medieval neonatal mortality during first month of life of between 50 and 100 percent, and in general infant mortality of between 10 and 25 percent (Fildes 1980, Benedictow 1985, Helgi Þorláksson 1986).

The high level of infant mortality must be seen in light of poor hygienic standards, causing frequent acute gastroenteritis and epidemics of dangerous intestinal diarrhoeal diseases like dysentery and typhoid fever. Epidemics of other children's diseases, such as measles, diphtheria, whooping cough, and scarlet fever, undoubtedly also took their toll, while smallpox probably did not arrive until about 1500 (Cartwright 1977).

The mortality level experienced by the peasant community at Fröson is on plausible grounds considered to have corresponded to an annual rate of forty to fifty per 1,000 (1.8–1.2 burials a year). This turnover had to be compensated for by the reproductive performance of women. Fertility may be measured as the number of births per 1,000 population per annum (producing crude birth rates that may be easily compared with mortality rates), as the number of births per 1,000 fertile women, or in a number of other ways (Hawthorn 1970). One should note that medieval populations do not seem to have known effective means of contraception, birth rates being the outcome of natural fertility.

A population will reproduce itself when fertile women on an average raise about 2.1 children who reach maturity. In a population with an average life expectancy at birth of twenty years, the maximum at Fröson, about 640 per 1,000 children will die before the age of twenty, implying an average number of six live births per fertile woman to compensate for this level of mortality. On average, about 35 percent of all persons reaching the age of twenty will die before attaining the age of forty (Coale and Demeny 1966). Moreover, a significant number of women will die from pregnancy-related causes. The implied substantial deficit of live births will have to be compensated for by the reproductive performance of other fertile women surviving to the age of forty to balance the pattern of death in the population. In all, the data suggest a mean number of about eight births per fertile woman surviving her reproductive period, in order to compensate for a general level of mortality producing a mean life expectancy at birth of twenty years. Medieval and early modern data from other parts of Europe and modern data from developing countries show that the average birth interval of poorly fed breast-feeding peasant women is about twenty-nine months, breast feeding causing a delay in resumption of ovulation of about eight months (*lactational amenorrhoea*) (Benedictow 1985). First confinement after wedding on average takes place after about seventeen months. According to this pattern of birth intervals, eight births, on average, require 220 months, or 18.3 years. Women beginning their reproductive performance well before the age of thirty will, on the average, have their last child before the age of forty. This means that a population experiencing an average life expectancy at birth of twenty years will not be able to reproduce itself if the average age at marriage for women is twenty years.

The solution to this problem of biological-genetic and social survival for populations experiencing such levels of mortality and life expectancy is early and (almost) universal marriage of women (Naraghi 1960, Hawthorn 1970). While in a society where average life expectancy at birth is twenty years, about 640 of 1,000 children born will die before the age of twenty, about 620 will die before the age of fifteen, about 7.8 live births being sufficient to produce a stationary population. However, we must take into account the considerable subfecundity of females during the first postmenarche years, making it likely that first confinement will occur at the age of seventeen. A reproductive career beginning at this age will quite likely satisfy the demands outlined above, *i.e.*, comprising, after the first at about age seventeen, seven births with mean intervals of about twenty-nine months, in all 203 months, or 16.9 years, still leaving room for one or two confinements. This alternative, therefore, also includes a potential for long-term population growth, *e.g.*, of the type experienced by the Scandinavian countries in the high Middle Ages of the magnitude of 0.2–0.3 percent a year. If life expectancy at birth was twenty-five years, 46 percent of children would survive to the age of fifteen, 44 percent to the age of twenty, easing noticeably the socially conditioned demands on the fecundity of women.

The lower the life expectancy at birth and the higher the mortality rates of infants and young children, the higher that birth rates will need to be to reproduce a family, lineage, kinship group, clan, or population, making *age at marriage* a crucial variable. The biological survival of social collectives will also be dependent on proportions of women married, female *nuptiality*. No registration of marriage existed in medieval Scandinavia. One may, however, note the strong view in both medieval and early modern Scandinavia that it was impossible for a single person to work a holding, and that in case of the death of one of the spouses rapid remarriage was a practical necessity (Benedictow 1985, Leijonhufvud 1921, Gaunt

1983). The *Íslendingasögur*, we are told, "contain not a single old maid" (Frank 1973), indicating universal marriage.

During classical antiquity, when average life expectancy at birth was about twenty years (Brunt 1971), the usual age at marriage for women was twelve to fifteen years (Hopkins 1965). In medieval Scandinavia, correspondingly, women might be expected to marry at an early age, in order to compensate for the high general level of mortality. In Scandinavia, no systematic data on age at marriage exist suitable for answering this question. It seems, according to Danish law, that girls might be expected to be married at the age of eighteen (Jacobsen 1982). The fact that the Icelandic sagas contain a considerable number of cases where girls married at the age of twelve or in the early teens (Sigurður Líndal 1976) is suggestive, and makes it clear that there was no normative resistance to such a practice. These indications of early marriage for women are strengthened by osteoarchaeologically obtained data showing supermortality for adolescent girls fourteen to nineteen years of age (Persson 1976). Age- and sex-specific structures of nuptiality, therefore, have probably been shaped by mortality and socioeconomic circumstances, the high mortality levels characteristic of these societies typically creating broad opportunities for early marriage by causing a low age of coming into inheritance and a good supply of vacant tenancies. As mentioned above, only 1.4 percent of the cemetery population at Fröson had reached the age of sixty. A medieval cemetery with 389 skeletons classified with respect to age as sixty-plus, two others classified as fifty to seventy, and one classified as fifty to sixty-five (Anderson 1986), indicating that proportion of population reaching the age of sixty years can hardly have been higher there than at Fröson. In England, in the 13th century, half of all boys of the feudal aristocracy were fatherless by the age of seventeen. As Berkener (1973) states: "Few parents lived to see their children marry, and even fewer lived to see more than one grandchild."

This conclusion may explain another important finding. In accordance with the usual conclusions of skeletal studies all over the world (*e.g.*, Acsádi and Nemeskéri 1970, Brothwell 1971, Hassan 1981), Scandinavian osteoarcheaological research pertaining to the medieval centuries regularly finds that men lived significantly longer than women (Holck 1970a, 1970b, 1986, 1987, Gejvall 1981, Persson 1976, Persson and Persson 1981, Jacobzon and Sjögren 1983, Tkocz 1985, Møller-Christensen 1982, Sellevold 1987 and 1989). An exception to this pattern has been registered in skeletal material from Danish grave mounds of the Viking period. The material is so small and socially skewed (Sellevold *et al.* 1987) that the modest difference in favor of female longevity seems to be covered by the fairly wide margins of uncertainty. However, it is likely that this finding reflects demographic reality and is caused by a high incidence of violent death in this belligerent upper-class population (*cf.* Hollingsworth 1957).

The typically longer life expectancy of men is usually explained by reference to confinement-related mortality (see, *e.g.*, Holck 1986, Anderson 1986, Högberg 1983; Sellevold 1989 disagrees). This argument is relevant but insufficient. Confinement-related mortality increases strongly with early marriage because young, often not fully grown females have a particularly marked pregnancy-related supermortality. Women at the end of their reproductive careers also experience a pronounced pregnancy-related supermortality as the health hazards due to a large number of pregnancy-related experiences increasingly manifest themselves, the number of such experiences obviously being connected with age at marriage. In developing countries of our own day that encourage early marriage of women, studies show a "natural maternal pregnancy-related" mortality rate of six to seven deaths per 1,000 births (see, *e.g.*, Kamel 1983, Chen *et al.* 1974), indicating that 4–7 percent of married fertile women will die from such causes. It has been suggested that female supermortality is due to food discrimination against women (*e.g.*, Wells 1971, Shorter 1984, Sellevold 1987 and 1989). A number of arguments dispute this view, only a few of which can be mentioned here. First, both Icelandic law of the Free State period (*Grágás*) and of the early modern period (*Búalög*) contain provisions specifically aimed at protecting the food intake of pregnant and lactating women, *i.e.*, most married fertile women. The southeastern Norwegian regional law code, the Borgarþing Law, exempts lactating women from two periods of Lent fasting for the same child (Jón Steffensen 1963, Benedictow 1985, 1988, 1989). Such provisions attest to a general concern for the nutrition and health of women and children. Second, medieval female skeletons do not generally exhibit more indications of malnutrition than those of men (Sellevold 1987). Third, no differences in stature have been registered exceeding the normal difference of 4–11 percent in favor of men (Gejvall 1960, Boldsen 1979, Persson and Persson 1981, Tkocz 1985, Sjögren 1983). In fact, the evidence rather supports the opposite case, as the stature of men falls significantly while the stature of women is steady. Fourth, women and girls also have as one of their particular tasks nursing of the sick, implying increased exposure to infectious diseases and resultant supermortality.

In international research, this point has been generally confirmed (Tabutin 1978, Henry 1987). The significance of the higher risk of exposure to infectious diseases is considerably strengthened by the phenomenon of pregnancy-related immunosuppression. This is a physiological reaction serving to prevent abortion due to the fact that fetuses differ genetically from the mother, but depressing at the same time the natural resistance to infectious diseases (immunodeficiency) (Weinberg 1984). One should note, however, that the tendency of female supermortality found regularly in osteoarchaeological studies and repeatedly in modern studies in developing countries seems to commence before the age of menarche (Henry 1970, Nagheri 1960, Stolnitz 1956). Socially conditioned causes may, therefore, be at work as well.

Although there exist no statistical data on family structure in medieval Scandinavia, it is clear that it predominantly was of the nuclear type. Persons living alone and all persons living in the same dwelling unit constitute a household. Nuclear family and household often were identical units, especially among the lower classes of peasants. However, lodgers, resident servants, and relatives quite frequently cohabited with nuclear families, making the household on average a somewhat larger social unit than the family. The degree of nuclearity is a historical and socioeconomic variable.

Families, at a given point in time, have only completed on average two-thirds of the process of raising children. An average of 1.5 children, consequently, indicates that completed families probably will comprise 2.25 children, and so implies population growth. If we add to this figure an average of two adults, which allows some to be widows or widowers and others to have extra adults in the family beyond a married couple, average household size will be 3.5 (Hollingsworth 1969). It is important that additions to this figure be specified and explained.

To approach more concretely the problem of household size in medieval Scandinavia, we have to rely partly on material from the 17th century and partly on osteoarchaeologically obtained demographic medieval data. Estimated on such premises, household size was much the same as in the rest of Europe, *i.e.*, containing on average between four and five persons in all (see, *e.g.*, Hollingsworth 1969), in the higher range in periods of population expansion, in the lower range in periods of stationary or diminishing population.

Norway. Useful data on the size of national population can be computed only in the case of Norway. This computation is possible because at least 90 percent of the population lived in the countryside and because the topography of the Norwegian landscape strongly restricts the choice of sites for farmsteads and cultivated areas. Holdings tend to be stable territorial units. Different types of sources, when brought together, allow quite a good enumeration of family holdings at the time of maximum expansion in the high Middle Ages, around 1330, and at the time of maximum contraction in the late Middle Ages, around 1450–1500. The figure is, within the present borders of Norway, 60,000 and 23–24,000 respectively, plus or minus 10 percent (Sandnes 1981).

Using a household multiplier of 4.5 (plus or minus about 10 percent), assuming a stationary population, and the median figure of holdings (60,000), we find 270,000 rural sedentary inhabitants in 1330. This figure covers about 90 percent of the population, and additions will have to be made to include town populations, fisher communities, hunters and gatherers, and mendicants, bringing the population total up to about 300,000. It is assumed that the territories lost to Sweden in the 17th century, mainly Bohuslän, Jämtland, and Härjedalen, constituted about one eighth of the total population (Lindstøl 1987), indicating a maximum for medieval Norway of about 343,000 persons, a figure that may be rounded upward to 350,000. This is the most plausible computation, but diverse factors of uncertainty indicate that the populations might have been as low as 275,000 and as high as 420,000. Although these margins of uncertainty are not exhaustive, this computation of the population of Norway can be usefully applied in many types of contexts and arguments.

The late-medieval minimum population, caused mainly by recurrent plague epidemics and reflected in mass desertion of holdings, caused comprehensive and far-reaching socioeconomic structural changes. Marginal holdings were massively abandoned, and the population concentrated on the good central holdings. The sharp reduction of population caused a high demand for labor, which produced strongly increased wages and a steep fall in land rents compared with the preplague levels, when demographic overexpansion caused intense competition for work and tenancies (Sandnes 1981). As labor became abundant and cheap during the high Middle Ages, resident servants probably became usual on the more substantial farms, tending to increase the average size of households. Some of the servants may have been married, increasing the proportion of holdings containing multiple households. At the time of the late-medieval minimum population, only the small and economically depressed secular and ecclesiastical aristocracies (Benedictow 1970, 1971, 1977, 1987) and very substantial peasants could finance resident servants. The average number of persons coming to join the basic biological family to form the household was probably quite small. The late-medieval population contraction coincides with the high point of the nuclear family holding. As the population concentrated on the best agricultural units and the resident households strongly tended to be constituted by nuclear families having to rely on their own working power, their ability to exploit the resources of the holdings diminished.

Assuming a stationary population at the time of population

minimum, everything considered, average household size probably tended to be somewhat smaller then than 150 years earlier. A reduction of the number of farmsteads within the present borders of Norway from 60,000 to 23,000–24,000, or by 60–62 percent, implies, using a multiplier of 4.25 and adding one-eighth for the areas ceded to Sweden in the 17th century, a population reduction within the medieval borders of Norway from 343,000 to about 125,000, or by around 63 percent. This magnitude of population decline corresponds remarkably closely to the conclusions of Hatcher with respect to England.

Denmark. In the last half-century, one serious attempt has been made to calculate the medieval population of Denmark (including Scania, Halland, and Blekinge, areas lost to Sweden at the middle of the 17th century) (Christensen 1938). The computation is founded mainly on four elements: (1) a tax register for Halland that is assumed to record accurately the number of adult men in 1232 (9,200–9,300 "rustici"); (2) the number of churches in Denmark; (3) the proportions of all Danish churches situated in Halland and the rest of Denmark, estimated to be 3.2 and 96.8 percent, respectively, preparing the ground for a calculation of 290,000 adult men; (4) this figure, when multiplied by the assumed quantitative relation between number of adult men and general population, 3.5, finally produces a computation of the size of the population of medieval Denmark at its maximum, around 1250–1300, of approximately one million inhabitants.

Iceland. Iceland was settled in historical times by culturally advanced people. *Landnámabók* contains, however, only the names of a small fraction of the early colonists, and osteoarchaeological studies and studies of blood types in the present Icelandic population make it clear that the number of immigrants of Irish and Scottish stock must have been substantial (Steffensen 1953, Jón Jóhannesson 1974).

The number of peasants liable to pay a duty to finance those participating at the meetings of the *Alþingi* (*þingfararkaup*) is said in *Íslendingabók* to have been 4,560 in 1097. This duty was paid by those not attending in person, and only those paying could participate at the *Alþingi* and at the local moots as moot-men. It was collected and the proceeds disbursed by the local chieftains. We do not know the amount paid or if the chieftains made a profit from it, or, as *Íslendingabók* points out, the proportion of those choosing to stay at home instead of going to the moot. And we do not know the quality of the process of registration and the social criteria used, *i.e.*, the rate of evasion and the rates of exemption because of poverty or social position, and how many were overlooked because of ignorance on the part of the recorders (Ólafur Lárusson 1936, Jón Steffensen 1963).

Such a piece of information may seem a rather foolhardy basis for the calculation of population size. What is further required is information as to household size. This type of information is provided by archaeologists, whose choice of sites for excavation usually is not governed by statistical notions of representativeness, but who tend to be attracted by the conspicuous and spectacular. On the basis of excavations of large farm sites, Icelandic archaeologists suggest fifteen to sixteen persons as household multiplier. This enormous figure requires particular comment. In the first centuries after settlement, the social scene in Iceland was dominated by intensive rivalries between kinship groups, making feuding, killings, and carnage an integral part of daily life. This situation acted as a strong incentive for people to seek collective solutions to their need for protection and defense, coming to

gether in expanded groupings consisting of multiple households, genetically related or not. Recently, arguments have been presented supporting a case for a significant incidence of joint families (Miller 1988). Calculation of household size on the basis of very uncertain notions as to the relation between space and household members inevitably comprises wide margins of uncertainty, margins compounded by extensive uncertainty connected with questions of representativeness. While household size may have been unusually large at those times, reflecting a considerable frequency of multiple households, the figure of fifteen to sixteen must be considered only as a "guestimate," and quite probably considerably exaggerated. The multiplicative effects of the wide margins of uncertainty involved in the constitutive assumptions may legitimately discourage researchers from seeing much use in such a computation.

This situation is not much improved by information as to the number of taxable peasants in 1311, which, revised to take account of the whole country, may be assessed at about 3,800. We do not know how many were exempted for reasons of poverty or immunity, and have no means of controlling the quality of registration, and other factors. This figure cannot, therefore, be taken to imply a population reduction since 1097. Some comfort may perhaps be derived from the fact that the figures do not differ by more than 17 percent.

According to Jón Steffensen (1967, 1968), a maximum population in medieval Iceland of close to 80,000 inhabitants was reached about 1200. The merits of this estimate are clearly subject to the qualifications of extensive margins of uncertainty, particularly downward. The highest estimates of the high-medieval Icelandic population suggest around 100,000 inhabitants. In our opinion, it never exceeded the population size recorded by the Census of 1703 of 50,400 persons (*Manntal* 1924, *Manntalið* 1960).

Iceland was hit by plague only twice, in 1402–1404 and 1494–1495. Although both epidemics were severe, the demographic consequences of two such episodes, as should be expected, were mostly temporary.

Sweden. No sources exist suitable for assessing the size of the medieval population of Sweden (Heckscher 1935–36, Schück 1938, J. Rosén 1969). The relative political and military strength of the Nordic countries indicates that the population of medieval Sweden was considerably smaller than Denmark's, while probably somewhat larger than Norway's. The population of Sweden must have been severely affected by the considerable number of plague epidemics that ravaged the country in the late-medieval period.

The size of the medieval population of Finland also remains unknown; it must have been quite small, exceeding only that of Iceland. The population of Finland consisted partly of Finns and partly of Swedes, who settled along the southern and southwestern coasts. Finland experienced population increase and settlement expansion in the late-medieval period, the only Nordic country and probably even the only European country to do so. The number of holdings at the middle of the 16th century is estimated at 33,000 (Orrman 1981). The probable explanation for this highly unusual pattern is that Finland, like Iceland, was relatively insulated from international trade, and so did not, or only rarely, import plague.

The relatively small size of Nordic populations has certain general epidemiological implications of considerable interest. Acute infectious diseases that cause permanent immunity, such as measles and smallpox, require populations of 500,000 to one million to become endemic. Smaller populations do not have a large enough annual input of susceptibles, and the disease will die out. When reintroduced, people born since the previous epidemic will all be susceptible (Black 1966, Anderson 1982). Diseases that seriously affect whole populations will often cause comprehensive disruptions of economic activities, preparing the ground for malnutrition, starvation, and related epidemic diseases. In epidemics of this type, parents will be affected as well as their children, giving rise to considerable supermortality, especially among infants and young children, as parents will not be able to take care of them. Adults will also suffer supermortality from lack of care. Endemicity ensures that adults are usually immune, transforming the social pattern of acute infectious diseases that cause permanent immunity into that of children's diseases. Thus, as population increases, these diseases tend to become endemic and common in childhood, and, as such, they are less lethal. Epidemic diseases, therefore, quite likely took a heavier toll on populations in the medieval period than later. This probability may help explain the low average life expectancy at birth and the high levels of child mortality in medieval Scandinavia, as exemplified by the finding in a medieval graveyard excavated in Trondheim of a proportion of young children that seemed surprising to the osteoarchaeologist (Anderson 1986). Árni Magnússon's dramatic description of the effects of an epidemic of smallpox in Iceland in 1707–1708 that caused a considerable desertion of holdings, reflecting substantial adult mortality, is well known. The special epidemiological background has been less well understood.

Lit.: Lindstøl, Tallak. *Mandtallet i Norge 1701 samt Oplysninger om Folkemængdens Bevægelse i Norge i det 16de og 17de Aarhundrede.* Kristiania [Oslo]: Cammermeyer, 1887; Árni Magnússon. *Embedsskrivelser og andre offentlige Aktstykker.* Ed. Kr. Kålund. Copenhagen and Kristiania [Oslo]: Gyldendal, 1916 [see p. 327]; Leijonhufvud, Karl K:son. "Pesten 1710–1711 och prästeskapet i Strängnäs stift." *Karolinska Förbundets Årsbok* (1921), 182–7; *Manntal á Íslandi 1703. Tekið að tilhlutun Árna Magnússonar og Páls Vídalín.* 17 vols. Reykjavik: Gutenberg, 1924–47; Heckscher, Eli F. *Sveriges ekonomiska historia från Gustav Vasa.* 2 vols. Stockholm: Bonnier, 1935–36; Ólafur Lárusson. "Island." In *Befolkning i oldtiden.* Ed. H. Shetelig. Nordisk kultur, 1. Stockholm: Bonnier; Oslo: Aschehoug; Copenhagen: Schultz, 1936, pp. 121–37; Christensen, Aksel E. "Danmarks befolkning og bebyggelse i middelalderen." In *Befolkning i middelalderen.* Ed. Adolf Schück. Nordisk kultur, 2. Stockholm: Bonnier; Oslo: Aschehoug; Copenhagen: Schultz, 1938, pp. 1–57; Schück, Adolf. "Ur Sveriges medeltida befolkningshistoria." In *Befolkning i middelalderen,* pp. 123–66; Sigurjón Jónsson. *Sóttarfar og Sjúkdómar á Íslandi 1400–1800.* Reykjavik: Hið íslenzka bókmentafélag, 1944; Rósen, Helge. "Begravningsbruk och dödstro." In *Livets högtider.* Ed. K. Rob. von Hikman. Nordisk kultur, 20. Stockholm: Bonnier; Oslo: Aschehoug; Copenhagen: Schultz, 1949, pp. 88–110; Jón Steffensen. "The Physical Anthropology of the Vikings." *Journal of the Royal Anthropological Institute* 83 (1953), 86–97; Stolnitz, G. J. "A Century of International Mortality Trends: II." *Population Studies* 10 (1956), 17–42; Hollingsworth, Ole Jørgen. "A Demographic Study of the British Ducal Families." *Population Studies* 11 (1957), 4–26; Gejvall, Nils-Gustav. *Westerhus: Medieval Population and Church in the Light of Skeletal Remains.* Lund: Ohlsson, 1960; Naraghi, Ehsan. *L'Étude des populations dans les pays à statistique incomplete.* Paris: Mouton, 1960; *Manntalið 1703.* Reykjavik: Hagskyrslur Íslands, 1960; Bøe, Arne. "Kirkegård." *KLNM* 8 (1963), 396–9; Black, F. L. "Measles Endemicity in Insular Populations; Critical Community Size and Its Evolutionary Implications." *Journal of Theoretical Biology* 11 (1966), 207–11; Ohlin, Goran. "No Safety in Numbers: Some Pitfalls of Historical Statistics." In *Industrialization in Two Systems: Essays in Honor of Alexander Gerschenkron by a Group of His Students.* Ed. H. Rosovsky. New York: Wiley, 1966, pp. 70–7; Coale, A. J., and P. Demeny. *Regional Model Life Tables and Stable Populations.* Princeton: Princeton University Press, 1966; rpt. New York: Academic, 1983; Lunden, Kåre. "Four Methods of Estimating the Population of a Norwegian District on the Eve of the Black Death (1349–1350)." *Scandinavian Economic History Review* 16 (1968), 1–18; Jón Steffensen. "Islands folkemængde gennem tiderne." *Medicinsk Forum* 16 (1963), 129–52; Jón Steffensen. "Population: Island." *KLNM* 13 (1968), 390–2; Rosén, Jerker. *Svensk historia* 1. 3rd ed. Stockholm: Svenska Bokforlaget, 1969; Hollingsworth, Thomas H. *Historical Demography.* Ithaca: Cornell University Press; London: Hodder and Stoughton, 1969; Benedictow, Ole Jørgen. *Hartvig Krummedikes jordegods. En studie i en senmiddelaldersk adelsøkonomi.* Oslo: Universitetsforlaget, 1970; Hawthorn, Geoffrey. *The Sociology of Fertility.* London: Collier-Macmillan, 1970; Henry, Louis. *Manuel de démographie historique.* Publications du Centre de recherches d'histoires et de philologie; Hautes études médiévales et modernes, 3. Geneva and Paris: Droz, 1970; Holck, Per. *Skjelettgraving. En innføring i antropologi for antropologer.* Oslo: Universitetsforlag, 1970 [1970a]; Holck, Per. "Ein Bericht über die Untersuchung der ausgegrabenen Skelette aus der Kirche auf Mære." In *Skrifter utgitt av Det Norske Videnskabs-Akademi,* Mat.-Nat. Kl., N.S. No. 28. Oslo: Universitetsforlaget, 1970, pp. 1–66 [1970b]; Acsádi, G. Y., and J. Nemeskréi. *History of Human Life Span and Mortality.* Budapest: Acadméiai Kiadó, 1970; Brothwell, Don R. "Palaeodemography." In *Biological Aspects of Demography.* Ed. W. Brass. London: Taylor and Francis, 1971, pp. 111–27; Wells, Calvin. "Ancient Obstetric Hazards and Female Mortality." *Bulletin of the New York Academy of Medicine* 51 (1971), 1235–49; Benedictow, Ole Jørgen. "Norge." In *Den nordiske Adel i Senmiddelalderen. Struktur, functioner og internordiske relationer.* Rapporter til det nordiske historikermøde i København 1971. Copenhagen: [n.p.], 1971; Sandnes, Jørn. *Ødetid og Gjenreisning.* Oslo: Universitetsforlaget; 1971; Brunt, P. A. *Italian Manpower 225 B.C.-A.D. 14.* Oxford: Clarendon, 1971; rpt. 1987; Gräslund, Anne-Sofie. "Barn i Birka." *Tor. Tidsskrift for nordisk fornkunskap* 15 (1972–73), 161–79; Weiser-Aall, Lily. "Det nyfødte barnets første føde." In her *Omkring de nyfødtes stell i nyere norsk overlevering.* Småskrifter fra norsk etnologisk granskning, 8. Oslo: Norske folkemuseum, 1973, pp. 5–51; Berkener, Lutz K. "Recent Research on the History of the Family in Western Europe." *Journal of Marriage and the Family* 35 (1973), 395–405; Frank, Roberta. "Marriage in Twelfth- and Thirteenth-Century Iceland." *Viator* 4 (1973), 473–84; Friberg, N., and I. Friberg. "Vikingatidens befolkning i Mälarlandskapen." In *Regionala utvecklingslinjer och strukturförändringar i Sveriges befolkningsgeografi* 4. Stockholm: Stockholms Universitet, Kulturgeografiska Institutionen, 1974; Jón Jóhannesson. *Íslendinga saga: A History of the Old Icelandic Commonwealth.* Trans. Haraldur Bessason. University of Manitoba Icelandic Studies, 2. Winnipeg: University of Manitoba, 1974; Petersen, William. "A Demographer's View of Prehistoric Demography." *Current Anthropology* 16 (1975), 227–45; Sigurður Líndal. "Ægteskab." *KLNM* 20 (1976), 495–501; Persson, Ove. "Undersökning av människoskelett." *Uppgrävt förflutet för PK banken i Lund.* Lund: Kulturhistoriska museet, 1976; Sandnes, Jørn. "Mannedauen og de overlevende." In *Norges historie* 4. Ed. Steinar Imsen and Jørn Sandnes. Oslo: Cappelen, 1977, pp. 148–247; Benedictow, Ole Jørgen. *Norges historie* 5. Oslo: Cappelen, 1977; 2nd rev. ed. Oslo: Bokkhaffen Nye Bøker, 1987; Hatcher, John. *Plague, Population and the English Economy 1348–1530.* London: Macmillan, 1977; rpt. 1987; Cartwright, Frederick F. *A Social History of Medicine.* London and New York:

Longman, 1977; Sjøvold, Torstein. "Inference Concerning the Age Distribution of Skeletal Populations and Some Consequence for Paleodemography." *Anthropologiai Közlemenyek* 22 (1978), 99–114; Tabutin, Dominique. "La surmortalité féminine en Europe avant 1940." *Population* 33 (1978), 121–48; Salvesen, Helge. *Jord i Jemtland.* Östersund: Wisénska bokhandelnsförlag, 1979; Boldsen, Jesper. "Liv og död i middelalderens Viborg." *MIV. Museerne i Viborg Amt* 8 (1979), 76–85; Razi, Zoi. *Life, Marriage and Death in a Medieval Parish.* Cambridge: Cambridge University Press, 1980; Gejvall, Gustav-Nils. "Skeletal Remains from Gårdlösa, Smedstorp Parish, Scania, Sweden." In *Gårdlösa: An Iron Age Community in Its Natural and Social Setting.* Ed. Berta Stjernquist. Acta Regiae Societatis Humaniorum Litterarum Lundensis, 75. Lund: Gleerup, 1981; Hassan, Febri A. *Demographic Archaeology.* New York: Academic, 1981; Orrman, Eljas. "The Progress of Settlement in Finland During the Late Middle Ages." *Scandinavian Economic History Review* 29 (1981), 129–43; Persson, Evy, and Ove Persson. "Medeltidsfolket från kvarteret Repslagaren." In *S:t Stefan i Lund. Ett monument ur tiden.* Ed. Anders W. Martensson. Gamla Lund forening for bevarande af stadens minnen, Årsskrift 62. Lund: Foreningen Gamla Lund, 1981, pp. 151–70; Sandnes, Jørn. "Settlement Developments in the Late Middle Ages (approx. 1300–1540)." In *Desertion and Land Colonization in the Nordic Countries c. 1300–1600. A Comparative Report from the Scandinavian Research Project on Deserted Farms and Villages.* Stockholm: Almqvist & Wiksell, 1981, pp. 78–114; Møller-Christensen, Vilhelm. *Æbelholt kloster.* Copenhagen: Nationalmuseet, 1982; Hørby, Kai. *Dansk socialhistorie* 2. Copenhagen: Gyldendal, 1982; Sjögren, Jane. "De döda åkeruppstås: kön, längd, ålder och sjukdomar hus ett urval av de på Helgeandsholmen gravladga." In *Helgeandsholmen. 1000 år i Stockholms ström.* Ed. Göran Dahlbäck. Stockholm: Liber Förlag, 1982, pp. 123–33; Welinder, Stig. *Paleodemography.* Reports, 26. Oslo: Norwegian Computing Centre for the Humanities, 1982; Jacobsen, Grethe. "Sexual Irregularities in Medieval Scandinavia." In *Sexual Practices & the Medieval Church.* Ed. Vern L. Bullough and James Brundage. Buffalo: Prometheus, 1982, pp. 72–85; Anderson, Roy M. *The Population Dynamics of Infectious Diseases: Theory and Applications.* London and New York: Chapman and Hall, 1982; Jacobzen, Lars, and Jane Sjögren. "Människor i stadens utkant. Helgeandshusets kyrkogård berätter om liv och död." In *Helgeandsholmen. 1000 år i Stockholm ström.* Ed. Göran Dahlbäck. Stockholm: Liber, 1982; Högberg, Ulf. "Mödradöd i förhistorisk tid." *Sydsvenska Medicinhistoriska sällskapets årsskrift* (1983), 103–14; Gaunt, David. *Familjeliv—Norden.* Stockholm: Gidlund, 1983; Sellevold, Berit Jansen, et al. *Iron Age Man in Denmark: Prehistoric Man in Denmark* 3. Nordiske Fortidsminder. Series B.8. Copenhagen: Kongelige nordiske Oldskriftselskab, 1984; Shorter, Edward. *A History of Women's Bodies.* Harmondsworth: Penguin, 1984; Benedictow, Ole Jørgen. "The Milky Way in History: Breast Feeding, Antagonism Between the Sexes and Infant Mortality in Medieval Norway." *Scandinavian Journal of History* 10 (1985), 19–53; Tkocz, Izabella. "Skeletal Material from a Layman's Churchyard." In *The Archaeology of Svendborg* 3. Ed. Michael Jansen. Odense: Odense University Press, 1985, pp. 26–63; Helgi Þorláksson. "Óvelkomin börn?" *Saga* 24 (1986), 79–120; Anderson, Trevor. "The Churchyard on the Folkebibliotekstomt (Library site), Trondheim: An Interim Osteological Report." In *Fortiden i Trondheim bygrunn. Meddelelser No. 2. Folkebibliotekstomten.* Trondheim: Riksantikvaren, Utgravningskontoret for Trondheim, 1986, pp. 1–16 [27 unnumbered pages containing tables, diagrams, and appendices]; Hatcher, John. "Mortality in the Fifteenth Century: Some New Evidence." *Economic History Review* 2nd ser. 29 (1986), 19–38; Holck, Per. *Cremated Bones: A Medical-Anthropological Study of Archaeological Material on Cremation Burials.* Antropologiske skrifter, 1. Oslo: Department of Anatomy, University of Oslo, 1986; Henry, Louis. "Mortalité des hommes et des femmes dans le passé." *Annales de démographie historique* (1987), 87–118; Mundal, Else. "Barneutbering." *Norskrift. Arbeidsskrift for nordisk språk og litteratur* 56 (1987), 1–78; Benedictow, Ole Jørgen. "Breast-feeding and Sexual Abstinence in Early Medieval Europe and the Importance of Protein-Calorie Malnutrition (Kurashiorkor and Marasmus)." *Scandinavian Journal of History* 13 (1987), 167–206; Sellevold, Berit Jansen. "Fokus på kvinner. Kvinners helse i middelalderen, belyst gjennom skjelettstudier." *KAN. Kvinner i arkeologi i Norge* 5 (1987), 50–83; Miller, W. I. "Some Aspects of Householding in the Medieval Icelandic Commonwealth." *Continuity and Change* 3 (1988), 321–55; Holck, Per. *Skjelettmaterialet fra Peterskirken, Tønsberg. En antropologisk rapport.* Antropologiske skrifter, 2. Oslo: Department of Anatomy, University of Oslo, 1989; Sellevold, Berit Jansen. "Fødsel og død. Kvinners dødelighet i forbindelse med svangerskap og fødsel i forhitorisk tid og middelalder, belyst ut fra studier av skjelettmaterialer." In *Kvinnors rosengård. Medeltidskvinnors liv och hälsa, lust och barnafödddande.* Ed. H. Griddeng et al. Stockholm: Stockholms Universitet, 1989, pp. 76–96; Benedictow, Ole Jørgen. "Breast Feeding and Sexual Intercourse in Medieval Norway." *Annales de démographie historique* (1989), 245–65.

Ole Jørgen Benedictow

[See also: Family Structure; Marriage and Divorce; Plague; Pregnancy and Childbirth]

Den utro Hustru *see* Drama

Denmark. Medieval Denmark was founded by its early Christian kings. Three major figures were Harald Blåtand ("Bluetooth"), who in the late 900s received baptism, Sven Estridsen, who in the mid-11th century divided his realm into bishoprics, and Knud, who in 1085 richly endowed the cathedral of Lund in Scania, which in 1104 became the first archiepiscopal see in the North. King Knud died in 1086 a Christian martyr. Christian Denmark, once founded, was shaped, primarily on the model of the kingdom of France, most effectively in the latter part of the 12th century by the Valdemar kings, after Valdemar den Store ("the great") ascended to the throne in 1157. In the course of a few centuries, Denmark gained all the features of European civilization in its social, political, and cultural life. In Danish historiography, the Middle Ages closed with the Protestant Reformation in 1536.

Politically, the Middle Ages in Danish history is a process of unification, up to 1157, and one of integration, then and later, into the affairs of the European continent. Not all Danish Viking Age kings had wielded authority over the whole realm, even if King Harald Blåtand in his famous Jelling inscription had declared himself to have "conquered all Denmark and Norway and christianized the Danes." Kings Sven Tveskæg ("Forkbeard") and Knud (Cnut) den Store ("the great") in the early decades of the 11th century were dominated in their politics by their English ambitions, and utilized their Danish territories only as bases of operation. Even if the British Isles remained within the Danish political sphere of interest, Danish involvement beyond the North Sea after 1066 became critical. Danish kings from about 1100 onward turned their attention to the Baltic, where they competed with growing German influence for supremacy in missionary efforts and mercantile ventures. The Baltic, a corridor between western Europe and the East in the Viking Age, became in the 12th century the object of a German invasion that subjected an older Slavic population of the region to Christianity. During the 12th century, a series of German mercantile cities were founded along the southern coast of the Baltic from Lübeck to Riga. Danish bishops and princes, along with German princes, took part in military and missionary efforts in the area. In the first decade of the 13th century, the Danish king Valdemar Sejr ("the victorious") was chosen overlord of the city of Lübeck, and from the mid-13th century the Hanseatic League became the most important factor in Danish foreign politics. Medieval political development in the North gradually resulted in a weakening of Denmark's ties with the British Isles, the North Atlantic, and the principalities of Inner Russia.

British culture, however, maintained a dominant influence upon church organizations in Denmark until the end of the 11th century. The account given by Adam of Bremen in his *Gesta Hammaburgensis ecclesiae pontificum* (ca. 1075) testifies to concurrent British and German missionary attempts with regard to Denmark, *e.g.*, in the years 1060–1066, when there were two bishops of Scania: Henrik, an Englishman, formerly bishop of the Orkneys, residing in Lund, and Egino, dependent on the Church of Hamburg and residing in Dalby. Adam's account, however, is hostile to British influence over Denmark, which was finally set aside by the establishment in 1104 of the archbishopric of Lund, and no impartial account of British ecclesiastical activity in Denmark during the earlier Middle Ages has survived. When in 1086 St. Knud was killed by his Danish subjects while preparing for a naval attack on England, his death was interpreted by official royal spokesmen as a death suffered in promulgating the Christian faith, *i.e.*, a martyrdom. And when, after 1095, his cult became established at Odense, English priests and monks were summoned to Denmark to establish an ecclesiastical center, a royal monastery (the monastery of St. Knud), which was to function also as cathedral chapter to the bishopric of Odense. The first substantial account of the martyrdom of St. Knud was written by Ailnoth, an English Benedictine, who wrote probably in the second decade of the 12th century, and who had no personal experience of the age of King Knud.

During the 12th century, Danish kings were confronted continuously with papal and imperial claims to supremacy over Denmark. King Valdemar den Store and his successors finally sided with the pope against the emperor in the Investiture Conflict, and thus managed to repel any imperial claims to taking their realm in fief of the Empire. Having obtained the throne in 1157, King Valdemar den Store succeeded in 1158 in having his friend and close ally Absalon elected bishop of Roskilde. The two set up the well-functioning kingdom of the Valdemars, conducted an imperialist policy in the Baltic, and succeeded in 1170 in having the king's father, Duke Knud Lavard, canonized. On the same day, the king's son, grandson of the new saint, appropriately named Knud, was proclaimed king, an event that represents the first culmination of the Valdemar Era. Before 1170, Absalon and King Valdemar faced an opponent to major features of their policy in Archbishop Eskil of Lund, a close friend of Bernard of Clairvaux, and to some extent spokesman for ecclesiastical independence. But 1170 also witnessed Archbishop Eskil's surrender to royal power, and in 1177, upon resigning from the archbishopric, obviously with papal consent, and with unanimous support of the king, the clergy, and the people, Eskil appointed Absalon his successor. As archbishop, Absalon continued to function as principal adviser to the king, and he commissioned Saxo, the historian, to write the *Gesta Danorum* to promulgate an authoritative view of modern Danish culture in terms compatible with 12th-century European state

philosophy and legal thinking, all to the glory of the Valdemar kings. Absalon belonged to a major Danish family, later known as the Hvide kin, and after having been elected archbishop, he was allowed for fifteen years to govern also his former diocese of Roskilde, where eventually he was succeeded by his nephew Peder Sunesen. After Absalon's death in 1201, Peder's elder brother, Anders Sunesen, succeeded him at Lund. Both of them, like Absalon himself, were educated at Paris and well versed in 12th-century political, theological, and legal thinking. Before his election to the archbishopric, Anders Sunesen had been chancellor to the king and was a prominent theologian and jurist. His major works were a poetical description of the seven days' work of Creation (the *Hexaemeron*), apparently a performance of his youth and intended for teaching young clergymen, and a Latin paraphrase of one of the most important legal works of medieval Denmark, the Law of Scania. Anders received his juridical education at the University of Bologna around 1190, under the guidance of Huguccio of Pisa, who was also the teacher of the later Pope Innocent III. Later, as archbishop of Lund, Anders, in collaboration with the king, created a modern crusading nation of Denmark, highly favored by the pope, who readily responded to all wishes put forward by King Valdemar and his archbishop to strengthen the inner structure of kingdom and Church in Denmark. However, the king's last desire, to depose bishop Valdemar of Schleswig, a descendant of one of his father's rivals for the throne, whom the king had held imprisoned for fourteen years, continuously met papal refusal.

Valdemar Sejr originally looked to the emperor for support and, on several occasions, obtained imperial concession of the overlordship over all territories north of the Elbe and Elde (confirmed 1214). But his aim was to gain the Baltic by military conquest and missionary campaigns, and for these objectives, papal benevolence was essential. During the first decades of the 13th century, he extended his power over the entire coastal region south of the Baltic, until finally in 1219 he conquered Estonia. This action gave rise to a German countermove. Count Henry of Schwerin captured the king in 1223 and imprisoned him for two years with his son and coregent, King Valdemar den Unge ("the young"). They were released on the condition that they refrained from any attempts at revenge, an obligation that, however, was set aside in 1227, when King Valdemar entered Holstein with an army, only to suffer his decisive defeat at Bornhøved (July 22, 1227). He was forced to relinquish all conquests in Germany, apart from the island of Rügen, which had come to Denmark in the day of Valdemar den Store (1169).

After the death of King Valdemar Sejr in 1241, the throne became an object of strife among three branches among his descendants. Kingship eventually fell to Christoffer 1, his son Erik Klipping, and his grandson Erik Menved, but twice in these years the archbishops of Lund sided with enemies of the realm. The controversies between Erik Klipping and Jakob Erlandsen, and between Erik Menved and Jens Grand, respectively, destroyed previous harmony between king and Church in Denmark and resulted in profound political crises. The conflicts were ended in favor of the royal position before papal tribunals of arbitration in 1274 and 1302. From substantial royal and aristocratic gifts in the foundation period, the Church of Denmark had become very rich. But at all stages of medieval political development in Denmark, the Church was under royal domination or, at least, under severe royal control. In the second decade of the 14th century, there was a minor outburst of the controversy once again, this time between

Erik Menved and Esjer Jul. King Valdemar Atterdag ("ever-day"), on succeeding to the realm in 1340, found all sources of royal income pawned to the counts of Holstein, but in twenty years the kingdom was completely restored. He managed, with the support of the Avignon popes, to bring all material church resources to his own political use. However, controversy between king and Church in Denmark remained latent throughout the Middle Ages. The Protestant Reformation of 1536 in its turn was accompanied by a total confiscation of episcopal estates in Denmark.

Socially, the Middle Ages signifies the transformation of Viking Age kinship society in Denmark into a commonwealth of four estates: clergy, aristocracy, burghers, and peasants. This process was launched and furthered by the kings, who, since the establishment of kingdom in Denmark, had tied all prominent individuals and families to their authority, substituting old kinship legal traditions with royal legislation and jurisdiction on the basis of written revisions of Danish common law. Originally, the bishops, like the secular aristocrats, had been members of the royal household, even if their recruitment followed rules other than those guiding succession among feudal lords. In fact, the development of ecclesiastical institutions and the inalienability of ecclesiastical property contributed highly to the transformation of Danish society during the Middle Ages. Members of noble families remained in a privileged position for obtaining ecclesiastical office, but the estates and income they were to administer as bishops or prelates were to be kept intact for their respective successors and could not be divided, or submitted to structural changes. Thus, ecclesiastical institutional estates would always have an heir whose rights and position were to be exactly the same as those of the actual holder. Nevertheless, several bishoprics in Denmark were in practice in the possession of the same kin for several generations, such as the diocese of Roskilde since the election of Absalon in 1158, and far into the 14th century.

Important stages in the social transformation processes are: (1) the revision in the late 12th century of the old military code for the king's men (Vederloven); (2) the codification by King Valdemar Sejr in 1241 of the old Law of Jutland, especially with its regulation of the ancient rules of the leding (leiðangr), the naval force that was to be at the disposal of the king for sixteen weeks every year; (3) the Royal Decree of 1276 concerning crimen laesae majestatis, which placed the king's men under more severe criminal jurisdiction than ordinary inhabitants of the realm; (4) the so-called Håndfæstning of 1282 (which has been termed the Danish Magna Carta), which restricted the king's prerogatives in respect to his men; (5) the conditions to which kings Christoffer II and Valdemar III submitted themselves upon their elections in 1320 and 1326, which further reinforced the rights to be enjoyed by the king's men and the king's obligations toward them; (6) the contract set up by King Valdemar Atterdag with his subjects in their various groupings in 1360 (Landefreden 1360); and (7) the acts of the Kalmar Union of 1397 (Unionsbrevet and Kronings-dokumentet), which in a Scandinavian context mark the establishment of aristocratic rights with regard to noblemen's disposal of their possessions, their participation in royal elections, and their eligibility to royal office. Unionsbrevet, although an act written on paper, in contrast to the Kroningsdokumentet (vellum), seems to have acquired constitutional status in the Union in the early 15th century, and was given a series of confirmations until the dissolution of the Union on the eve of the Reformation.

Economically, from the 13th century Denmark became integrated into the Baltic community, which came to furnish the areas of growth in western Europe (England, Flanders, and northern France) with necessary foodstuffs and raw material. From the Dark Ages, Denmark had, at the southwestern corner of Scania, an important international trading place that was remodeled from the beginning of the 13th century according to European standards into the Fairs of Scania on the peninsula of Skanør and Falsterbo. Like the Champagne Fairs in northern France, they furnished foreign trade with necessary conditions of security and favorable opportunities for international exchange of goods. The Scanian Fairs derive their existence from the abundant autumn fisheries of herring in the Sound, but they were not limited to the trade in herring. The fish was caught each year, from Midsummer's Day onward, by Danish peasants on leave from their landlords and on license from the king. It was prepared and salted down by Danish women and sold to German merchants at the fairs that opened each year on Assumption Day (August 15). Here, all trade was carried out in the king's coinage, for which the king imposed an exchange rate favorable to the Danes. During the entire Middle Ages, the Scanian Fairs constituted a major link between Danish and European economies. The Wendish cities, i.e., Lübeck, Wismar, Rostock, Stralsund, and Greifswald, came to constitute the most privileged group of Hanseatic cities at the Scanian Fairs. At an early stage, they were given autonomous jurisdiction on their allotted grounds (fed), and Lübeck was largely dealing in herring, which became a favored Lenten diet in most of northern Europe after Lübeck took pains to standardize measures and quality, and invested in the preservation process by procuring salt from Lüneberg. However, the other Hanseatic cities that won positions at the Fairs shortly after Lübeck were less interested in the trade in herring, and concentrated on grain and timber in exchange for western European cloth and other industrial or quasi-industrial products.

In the Middle Ages, Denmark underwent a process of urbanization. Archaeological evidence proves that the city of Ribe existed already in the late 8th century, Schleswig/Hedeby dates from about the same period, Århus, Viborg, and Ålborg existed in the 10th century, while Odense, Roskilde, and Lund can be documented with certainty only to the 12th century. When in the 12th century the Valdemar kings constructed a series of strong fortresses throughout the realm, new mercantile centers grew up under their protection. In the 13th century, a large number of minor mercantile cities were founded, characterized by their easy access to the sea and their orientation toward a central marketplace. Most Danish cities in the 13th century acquired some sort of autonomous governmental rights and specific trading privileges, under inspiration from urban conditions in nearby northern Germany. They adopted statutes providing for representative city councils resting mainly on the merchant class.

Medieval Denmark remained an agrarian economy, but, around 1300, emphasis shifted from corn production to the raising of cattle and the production of butter. German mercantile presence at the Scanian Fairs led to an intensive German representation in Danish cities, and permitted Danish peasants to obtain current world-market prices for their products. The 15th century experienced a heavy increase in the export of live cattle, primarily through Ribe and Kolding, to northwestern Europe, due not least to the involvement from the 14th century onward of the Holstein nobility with royal Danish administration, initiating also considerable immigration from Holstein into Denmark.

Danish medieval population figures can only be grossly estimated, but doubtless Denmark followed the general European pattern of development; in the 14th century, the country experienced its agrarian crisis like the major part of western Europe, with falling agrarian income and desertion of villages. This process seems to have been accompanied by a shift in population density from western toward eastern Denmark, and reduction in population seems to have begun before the Black Death.

In its lay and ecclesiastical culture, Denmark in the 10th and 11th centuries seemingly bore a strong British imprint, even if testimony is not abundant. This influence was substituted in the 12th and 13th centuries by French cultural and academic ideals, when sons of Danish noble families began to frequent the University of Paris in considerable numbers, qualifying not only in theology, but also in philosophy and natural sciences (e.g., the philosopher Boethius de Dacia, the astronomer Petrus Philomena, and the philospher-linguist Martinus de Dacia). The law school of Bologna was attended by Danes from the 12th and 13th centuries onward.

Furthermore, priests sought theological education at Rome, and Danish involvement in the Crusades resulted in a development especially of technical culture, medicine, and the art of warfare. Local Danish academic teaching is less well known, although schools of considerable importance must have existed at the cathedral chapters from about 1200. At Roskilde, Jens Grand, upon becoming archbishop of Lund, founded in 1290 a separate department of the chapter, consisting of six canons richly endowed and directed toward university studies, international pilgrimage, and diplomacy. Since 1253, Roskilde had offered a scholarship founded by Bishop Jakob Erlandsen to enable the Zealand diocese each year to send two of its best scholars for further training at Paris. Cathedral libraries, insofar as their contents are known to us, spanned all branches of medieval academic learning, and this is true also of several of the Danish Cistercian monastic libraries. The workings of the royal Chancery, the functions of royal diplomacy, and judicial practice under lay and ecclesiastical authority all implied continuous and systematic reference to current European conditions.

Danish political and commercial involvement in the affairs of the Baltic from the 13th century onward assimilated Denmark in various aspects of daily life and material culture to conditions in the German territories. This process of assimilation has special importance in the organization of trade, in military administration, and in the life of the cities. A list from about 1370 of burghers in Copenhagen indicates that an important German colony existed there; and at least about half of the Copenhagen burghers in 1370 bore German names. The Kalmar Union in the late 14th century may be interpreted also as a factor of political and cultural balance against German influence. Shortly after 1400, King Erik of Pomerania negotiated an English marriage for himself, which at the outset was intended to be a double marriage alliance, and eventually brought back a British orientation to Danish state life. With King Erik's deposition in 1439, the Danish kingdom went to a German prince, Christoffer of Bavaria. He died in 1448, however, without descendants and, on the initiative of the count of Holstein, was succeeded by King Christian 1, who became the founder of the Oldenburg Dynasty. In 1460, he even succeeded to the County of Holstein, and became deeply dependent in his financial policy upon the Holstein nobility and, likewise, upon German capital interest. The Oldenburg kings of Denmark up to the Reformation sought to contain Hanseatic influence in Danish

commerce and urban life, especially by compelling German merchants to join the Danish guilds if they wanted to remain in Denmark for more than one season. Hanseatic commercial initiative and German investment interests, however, remained of the utmost importance to Denmark until late into the Early Modern period, even if they were met with fierce Dutch competition from the middle of the 15th century. Low German must have been spoken in all major Danish medieval cities, and Dutch and English may also have been well known.

Ed.: Langebek, Jacob, ed. *Scriptores Rerum Danicarum Medii Aevi*. 9 vols. Hafniae [Copenhagen]: Godiche, 1772; Gertz, M. Cl., ed. *Vitae Sanctorum Danorum*. Copenhagen: Gad, 1908–12; Gertz, M. Cl.,ed. *Scriptores Minores Historiæ Danicæ Medii Ævi*. 2 vols. Copenhagen: Gad, 1917–22; Jørgensen, Ellen. *Annales Danici medii Ævi*. Copenhagen: Gad, 1920; Brøndum-Nielsen, Johs., and Poul Johs. Jørgensen. *Danmarks gamle landskabslove med kirkelovene*. 8 vols. Copenhagen: Gyldendal; Nordisk Forlag, 1933–61 [medieval Danish laws]; *Diplomatarium Danicum*. Copenhagen: Munksgaard, 1938– [published in Danish as *Danmarks riges breve*]; Blatt, Franz, and C. A. Christensen, eds. *Corpus diplomatum Regni danici auspiciis Societatis linguae et litterarum danicarum*. Hafniae [Copenhagen]: Munksgaard, 1938; Kroman, Erik, ed. *Danmarks gamle Købstadlovgivning*. 4 vols. Copenhagen: Rosenkilde & Bagger, 1951 [medieval city charters and statutes]; *Corpus Codicum Danicorum Medii Ævi*. Hafniae [Copenhagen]: Munksgaard, 1960–; Kroman, Erik. *Danmarks middelalderlige annaler*. Copenhagen: Selskabet for udgivelse af kilder til dansk historie, 1980. **Lit.**: Arup, Erik. *Danmarks historie*. Copenhagen: Hagerup, 1925–55 [inventory of Danish churches]; Nationalmuseet. *Danmarks kirker*. Copenhagen: Gad, 1933–; Bolin, Sture. "Mohammad, Charlemagne and Ruric." *Scandinavian Economic History Review* 1 (1953), 5–39; Christensen, Aksel E. "Scandinavia and the Advance of the Hanseatics." *Scandinavian Economic History Review* 5 (1957), 89–117; Damsholt, Nanna. "Kingship in the Arengas of Danish Royal Diplomas 1140–1223." *Mediaeval Scandinavia* 3 (1970), 66–108 [traces elements of common western ideology in royal Danish charters]; Riis, Thomas. *Les institutions politiques centrales du Danemark 1100–1319*. Odense: Odense University Press, 1977; Skyum-Nielsen, Niels, and Niels Lund, eds. *Danish Medieval History. New Currents*. Copenhagen: Museum Tusculanum, 1981 [contains useful surveys of recent research]; Roesdahl, Else. *Viking Age Denmark*. Trans. Susan Margeson and Kirsten Williams. London: British Museum, 1982.

Kai Hørby

[**See also:** Aggesen, Sven; Annals; Boethius de Dacia; Church Organization and Function; Chronicles; Conversion; Coronation; Council of the Realm; Danevirke; Demography; Gorm; Hanseatic League; Harald Gormsson (Bluetooth); Jelling; Johannes de Dacia; Kingship; Knud (Cnut) the Great; Knud (Cnut), St.; Laws; Leiðangr; Margrethe I; Martinus de Dacia; Royal Administration and Finances; Saxo Grammaticus; Social Structure; Succession; Sunesen, Anders; Sven Haraldsson (Forkbeard); Valdemar]

Dialects. From a strictly linguistic point of view, all the continental Scandinavian languages are dialects, since they are to a large degree mutually intelligible. This circumstance is partly due to their natural development from a common, North Germanic mother tongue, and partly to a set of common external influences from central and southern Europe in the Middle Ages.

Our earliest evidence for a Scandinavian language, Proto-

Scandinavian (PSc), is derived from some 150 inscriptions on stone, bone, and metal, written in a twenty-four-letter alphabet known as "the older runes" (called a *futhark* after the first six letters). The runic inscriptions date back at least as far as A.D. 200. A few loanwords in Finnish also reflect early Scandinavian forms, *e.g.,* *kuningas* 'king,' which has lost its final syllable in the later Scandinavian languages (*cf.* Old Icelandic *konungr*). The runic inscriptions are the earliest written evidence of any Germanic language, antedating even Gothic (4th century A.D.), but they do not permit any important conclusions about internal dialect divisions.

The Viking Age (800–1050) was marked by notorious raids of plunder, trade, and exploration from Scandinavia to the rest of Europe: Swedish raids across the Baltic, Norwegian across the Atlantic, and Danish in both directions. But this expansion also led to a gradual christianization, which brought with it writing in the Latin alphabet on parchment. Early documents in Icelandic refer to the language as "Danish" (*dǫnsk tunga*), perhaps because Denmark was the first Scandinavian country to receive Christian missionaries, from about 820.

The earliest preserved MSS (1150–1200) already show a dialectal split between East and West probably going back to at least 800: West Scandinavian (WSc) versus East Scandinavian (ESc). There were still overlappings, disputed areas, and no clear isoglosses, since internal wars were being fought, and borders were not fully stabilized until the 19th century. In general, ESc included Sweden and Denmark and parts of Finland; WSc included Norway and its Atlantic colonies, Iceland, Greenland, the Faroes, the Hebrides, the Orkneys, and parts of England known as "the Danelaw."

Some important isoglosses distinguishing WSc from ESc were: (1) Long *u* versus *o*: WSc *kū* 'cow' acc., *brū* 'bridge,' *trū* 'faith,' *būa* 'dwell' versus ESc *ko, bro, tro, bo.* (2) Varying rules for the application of umlaut (influence of unstressed vowels on preceding stressed vowels): WSc *tekr* 'takes,' *stendr* 'stands,' *gengr* 'goes' versus ESc *taker, stander, ganger,* Norwegian *odde* 'point of land,' *botn* 'bottom' versus Swedish *udde,* Danish *bund*; WSc *fǫrum* 'we go' versus ESc *farum.* (3) Breaking (following *a* or *u* causing *e* to break into two sounds): WSc *stela* 'steal,' *ek* 'I' versus ESc *stjæla, jak.* (4) Nasal assimilation before stops: WSc *bekkr* 'bench,' *klettr* 'cliff,' *soppr* 'mushroom' versus ESc *bänker, klinter, svamp.* (5) Pronominal lowering: WSc *vér* 'we,' *ér* 'you' pl. versus ESc *vir, ir.* (6) Monophthongization: WSc *graut* 'porridge,' *ey* 'island,' *bein* 'bone' versus ESc *grøt, ø, ben.* These relatively minor linguistic differences reflect the Baltic orientation of ESc and the Atlantic of WSc, with the Kjølen Mountains as a significant linguistic boundary.

While some of these isoglosses are later reflected in the standard languages that began appearing in the 1400s, the geographical and historical influences of the Middle Ages led to a quite different orientation of the spoken dialects. Icelandic maintained the grammatical structure of Old Norse (also known as Old Icelandic) and reflected its phonological structure. But it remained a virtually homogeneous dialect, with minor differences from south to north. The Faroe Islands, however, split into marked dialectal differences, while maintaining some of the old structure. The mainland areas developed a highly analytical grammar with the loss of inflections for nouns (cases) and verbs (person and number), except for local relicts. They also fell under the strong influence of their Low German neighbors, through invasion, immigration, and trade; and they participated in the general European

infiltration of classical (especially Latin) culture. The result through the medieval period was a popular speech that split into a great variety of local dialects used by the agricultural majority of the people, with islands of educated, *i.e.,* upper-class speech developed by the literate élite that ruled the countries. To clarify the picture, it will be necessary to discuss each country separately, as they developed into modern times. We may assume that by the end of the Middle Ages the dialects had become substantially what they are today.

The Middle Ages ended with a union of the Scandinavian peoples under the scepter of Queen Margrethe of Denmark from 1387. The union was a purely dynastic one, and it lasted only until 1520, when the young nobleman Gustav Vasa led the Swedes in a revolt against Danish rule. He succeeded in establishing himself as king of Sweden, and in 1527 led the country out of the Church of Rome into a national Swedish Church that accepted the leadership of Martin Luther. In 1537, the Danish king followed suit, thereby making all Scandinavia Lutheran; the last Catholic Icelandic bishop was beheaded in 1550. For the time being, Norway, Iceland, and the Faroes remained under Danish hegemony, and Finland was part of Sweden. Swedish rulers gradually overcame Danish preeminence, by taking an active part in the German religious wars and by defeating Danish forces. The art of printing was introduced, and a new, modern era dawned in the North with the Renaissance and the Reformation.

Danish. Today, the Danish dialects are divided into three areas: West, Central, and East. The West includes Jutland; the Central, the Danish islands Zealand, Funen, and the southern islands; and the East, the island of Bornholm. Actually, the East also includes the dialects of southern Sweden, which until 1638 was a part of the Danish realm. The speech of Scania, Halland, and Blekinge still shows strong traces of Danish influence. Swedish dialectologists refer to this area as "South Swedish." The East dialects are marked by having retained unstressed -*a*, while in the West and Central, all unstressed vowels are reduced to a schwa [ə]: *skriva* vs. *skrive.* The East has *ja* for "I," the Central *jæ,* the West *æ* or *a.* All Danish dialects have voiced postvocalic stops *p t k > b d g,* as in *krybe* 'creep,' *fod* 'foot,' *høg* 'hawk' (*cf.* Swedish *krjupa, fot, hök*); this includes also the south coast of Norway. In Danish proper, the voiced stops generally suffered a further weakening to become spirants, although the spelling remained the same: *b > w* (sometimes), *d > ð, g > w/j* (*cf. gribe* [griwə] 'seize,' *gade* [ga:ðə] 'street,' *bog* [bɔw] 'book,' *nøgle* [nøjlə] 'key'). Jutland is characterized by apocope of unstressed vowels: *bage* [bag] 'bake.' Jutland is divisible into West, East, and South Jutlandic. West Jutland is the only Scandinavian area with a separate definite article: *æ mand* 'the man,' *æ træ* 'the tree,' contrary to the usual postposition: *manden, træet.* It also lacks the usual gender distinction. Except for some southern dialects in Denmark that still distinguish two musical accents, most of the dialects in Denmark mark their Accent 1 with a glottal stop (*stød*), as in the word itself: [stø'ð]. In modern times, all Danish dialects have acquired a uvular *r* [R], as have the neighboring south-coast Norwegian and South Swedish dialects.

Norwegian. Norway remained united with Denmark after the Middle Ages until 1814. We shall not discuss here the considerable consequences of Danish hegemony. In spite of acquiring a Danish written form after 1450, most Norwegians continued to speak a variety of local dialects. In urban centers like Bergen and Oslo, a new modern standard arose, but the overwhelmingly ag-

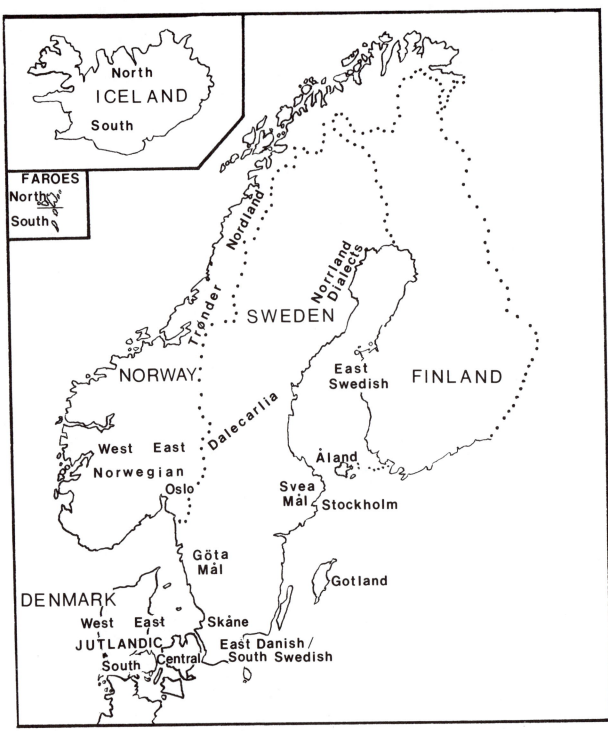

20. Location of dialects in the Scandinavian region.

ricultural and largely illiterate populations developed along lines of their own.

The Norwegian dialects remained closer to Swedish and did not share in the radical developments of Danish. Major lines of division coincided with the central mountain chain, which split the country into West and East Norwegian, with some mountain dialects in an intermediate "Midland" position. In the West, the dialects remained closer to Old Norse, although not maintaining the conservative grammatical structure of Icelandic. In the East, the innovations were closer to Swedish, including a tendency to retroflex *l* ("thick l" [ɫ]) and r before dentals [rd > ḍ or ɫ, rn > ṇ, rs > ṣ or š, rt > ṭ]. As in Swedish, the vowel system was shifted away from the European system to lower and fronted vowels. In the West, unstressed *a* and *u* remained, while in the East they split into leveling *a/u* (or *o*) after short syllables, but a schwa after long syllables: *fara > farra/fårrå* 'fare, go,' *vera > vara/varra/vårrå* 'be,' *vika, viku > vekka/vækka/vukku* 'week' vs. *bíta > bite* 'bite,' *kasta > kəste* 'throw.' As noted earlier, Norwegian generally retains the old diphthongs: *au, ei, ey* (> *øy*), which were lost in Swedish and Danish. Norwegian also retains the feminine gender of nouns; and the preterite and personal verb suffixes are reduced to a single vowel: *-a* (Old Norse *-aða*, etc.: *kastaða > kasta* 'threw, thrown'). Another dialect boundary is the Dovre Mountains in north-central Norway: north of this area are the Trønder dialects, characterized by many of the same features as East Norwegian, but also by apocope: *sitt* 'sit,' *kast* 'throw' inf., where East Norwegian has schwa. An isogloss runs across the northern parts of both East and West, and includes Trønder and Nordland dialects: extensive palatalization of double dentals: *dd > ḍḍ, ll > ʎʎ nn > ṇṇ, tt > ṭṭ* (*vidd* 'width,' *all* 'all' pl., *maṇṇ* 'man,' *siṭṭ* 'sit'). Case endings are lost, except in some northern dialects: *på daga* 'in the day,' *i husåm* 'in the houses.' Nearly all Norwegian dialects distinguish two tonal accents, known as Accent 1 and 2.

While the upper-class urban dialects have influenced the rural dialects in modern times, the latter are still extensively used, and are even promoted in the schools.

Swedish. The development of a standard Swedish around the court and administration in Stockholm has given the language of the east-central area great influence. But dialects persist in rural areas in daily speech. They are traditionally divided into South Swedish, coinciding with the once-Danish part of Sweden; Göta dialects around the great lakes Vänern and Vättern; Svea dialects around Mälar (including the Stockholm area), with sharply deviant dialects in western Dalecarlia; Norrland dialects north of this area, along the Baltic coast; Guta dialects, spoken on the island of Gotland; and East Swedish, spoken on the west coast of Finland (reflecting the usage of 17th- and 18th-century settlers). On the borders toward Norway there are Norwegian-type dialects (Jämtland, Härjedalen). Estonia once had a Swedish population, now almost gone. Dialect substrata are still clearly distinguishable in the intonation of speakers from these various areas.

In general, Swedish is more conservative than Danish, but has also changed from a synthetic to an analytic language. It has retained greater variety in its unstressed vowels (*a e o*), but like Norwegian, has shifted its stressed back vowels. All dialects except East distinguish clearly between Accent 1 and 2. The *r* and *l* are still those of Old Scandinavian, except in South Swedish, where *r* has become uvular. But after vowels both have been retroflexed (*l* and *rd > ɫ, rd rl rn rl rs* as in Norwegian). Masculine and feminine genders have been merged into a common gender having the form of the masculine: def. art. sg. *-(e)n*, as in *mannen* 'the man,' *solen*

'the sun' (*cf.* Norwegian *mannen, sola/soli,* etc.); 2nd person pl. pronouns have either become *ni* (from *i*) or are replaced by titles; weak verbs have been reduced from *-ade* to *-a* in speech: *kastade > kasta.* Like Norwegian, Central Swedish turns palatalized dentals and velars (before *j* or front vowels) into spirants or aspirates: *get* [je:t] 'goat,' *sked* [še:d] 'spoon,' *tjuge* [(t)çu:gə] 'twenty,' *stjärna* [šä:na] 'star.' North Swedish has much in common with northwestern Trønder dialects across the border, including a type of vowel "balance." The Guta dialects have retained the old diphthongs (*ai au øy*) and the stop quality of initial *g* and *k* (unpalatalized). They have diphthongized old long vowels. East Swedish has also preserved the diphthongs and the "hard" stops and has unaspirated voiceless stops (*p t k*) and only one tonal accent. These features are usually attributed to Finnish influence.

Faroese. Although the Faroes were settled by Norse Vikings in the 9th century, their language was not written until the 18th, first by J. C. Svabo (1746–1824). His admirably phonemic transcription was replaced in 1846 by a "properly" literary orthography that makes it look suspiciously like Icelandic. There is consequently no medieval written language, but the greatly fragmentized modern dialects must have developed in the Middle Ages. Until 1948, Danish was the official language and has become a second language of common use.

Unlike Icelandic, Faroese has not preserved the Old Norse spirants þ and ð: þ > t, or h; ð, though vanished, is still written. Other developments are reminiscent of West Norwegian: *ll > dl, nn > dn,* etc. Diphthongs have been preserved, although changed, and long vowels diphthongized. An intervocalic intrusion known as "sharpening" is characteristic: *eyjar* 'islands' > [åddjar], *bua* 'dwell' > [bygva]. The Faroes' seventeen inhabited islands show considerable dialectal deviation, with the chief division between South and North.

Icelandic. This is the most conservative of Scandinavian languages, having preserved the old grammar almost in its entirety. But its phonetic quality has changed considerably, especially its vowel system: *á* > [au], *æ* > [ai]; *au* > [øi], *ey* > [ei], *y* > [i]. Unifying forces, such as common fishing and grazing areas and the centuries-old meetings of the national *Alþingi,* have prevented the development of marked dialects, with only a few minor isoglosses separating South and North. In the vocabulary, purism has dominated Icelandic since the early 19th century: *e.g.,* "broadcasting" is *útvarp,* "airplane" is *flugvél.* Danish/Norwegian/Swedish is taught in the schools as a second language for Scandinavian contact, since Icelandic is not readily understood by other Nordic speakers.

The language of the other Norse colonies in the Shetlands and Orkneys in the Middle Ages is known as "Norn"; since it was never written, its form is relatively obscure.

Lit.: Bennike, Valdemar, and Marius Kristensen. *Kort over de danske folkemål.* Copenhagen: Gyldendal, 1898–1912; Hægstad, Marius. *Gamalt trøndermaal.* Videnskabs-selskabets Skrifter, 2. Hist.-filos. Klasse, 1899, no. 3. Kristiania [Oslo]: Dybwad, 1899; Ross, Hans. *Norske bygdemaal.* Videnskabs-selskabets Skrifter. Hist.-Filos. Klasse, 1905–09, no. 3. Christiania [Oslo]: Dybwad, 1905–09; Hægstad, Marius. *Vestnorske maalføre fyre 1350.* Videnskabs-Selskabets Skrifter, 2. Hist.-Filos. Klasse, 1907, no. 13.—1941, no. 1. Kristiania [Oslo]: Dybwad, 1907–42; Brøndum-Nielsen, Johannes. *Dialekter og dialektforskning.* Copenhagen: Schultz, 1927; Skautrup, Peter. *Det danske sprogs historie.* 5 vols. Copenhagen: Gyldendal, 1944–70; Wessén, Elias. *Våra folkmål.* Stockholm: Fritz, 1945; Lockwood, W. B. *An Introduction to Modern Faroese.* Copenhagen: Munksgaard, 1955;

Skautrup, Peter. "Dansk sprog." *KLNM* 2 (1957), 659–62; Skautrup, Peter. "Dansk tunge." *KLNM* 2 (1957), 662–4; Skautrup, Peter. "Dialekter." *KLNM* 3 (1958), 53–9; Matras, Chr. "Færøsk sprog." *KLNM* 5 (1960), 80–4; Hreinn Benediktsson. "Icelandic Dialectology: Methods and Results." *Islenzk tunga—Lingua Islandica* 3 (1961–62), 72–113; Hreinn Benediktsson. "Islandsk språk." *KLNM* 7 (1962), 486–93; Werner, Otmar. "Die Erforschung des Inselnordischen." *Zeitschrift für Mundartforschung.* Beihefte N. F., Nr. 6. Wiesbaden: Steiner, 1966; Hødnebø, Finn. "Norsk språk." *KLNM* 12 (1967), 357–63; Hagström, Björn. *Ändelsevokalerna i faröiskan.* Stockholm: Almqvist & Wiksell, 1967; Wessén, Elias. "Svenska språket." *KLNM* 17 (1972), 504–9; Bandle, Oskar. *Die Gliederung des Nordgermanischen.* Beiträge zur nordischen Philologie, 1. Basel and Stuttgart: Helbing & Lichtenhahn, 1973; Dahlstedt, Karl-Hampus. *Norrländska och nusvenska.* 2nd ed. Lund: Studentlitteratur, 1973; Haugen, Einar. *The Scandinavian Languages: An Introduction to Their History.* London: Faber and Faber, 1976; Holm, Gösta. "De nordiska dialekterna i Nordskandinavien och deras historiska bakgrund." In *Nord-Skandinaviens Historia i tvärvetenskaplig belysning.* Ed. Evert Baudou and Karl-Hampus Dahlstedt. Acta Universitatis Umensis, 24. Umeå: Umeå universitetsbibliotek,1980, pp. 151–74; Nordentoft, Annelise Munck. *Nordisk nabosprog.* Copenhagen: Gyldendal, 1981; Haugen, Einar. *Scandinavian Language Structures: A Comparative Historical Survey.* Minneapolis: University of Minnesota Press, 1982; Molde, Bertil, and Allan Karker, eds. *Språkene i Norden.* Nordisk Språksekretariat, 1. [Oslo]: Cappelen, 1983; Sandøy, Helge. *Norsk dialektkunnskap.* Oslo: Novus, 1985; Nes, Oddvar. *Norsk dialektbibliografi.* Oslo: Novus, 1986.

Einar Haugen

[See also: Alphabet; Language; Latin Language and Literature; Palaeography; Runes and Runic Inscriptions; Vadstena Language]

Dialogues *see* **Gregory, St.**

Diet and Nutrition. The lack of available source material from the 8th to the 16th century makes it difficult to describe in detail the everyday diet of the ordinary person in the Scandinavian areas. Written sources, such as accounts and pantry lists, show which foods were produced and which types of foodstuffs the larders of the upper class might contain; but they do not mention how they were eaten or the relations among the different foods. So we still know very little about the nutrition of the majority of the Scandinavian population during this period. The composition of the diet can be determined only through extensive analysis of the collected animal skeletal remains, plant remains, and pollen, resulting from well-documented archaeological excavations. Yet, analyses of this type have only been made at a few of the major town excavations, such as Svendborg in Denmark, Lund and Stockholm in Sweden, and Oslo in Norway (Jensen 1979, Jørgensen *et al.* 1986, Bergquist and Lepiksaar 1957, *etc.*). Roesdahl (1982) attempted a general description of the diet in Denmark during the Viking period. The description is based primarily on archaeological finds because the written sources from this period are scarce. Roesdahl contends that the diet consisted mainly of agricultural products: meat from oxen, pigs, sheep, and poultry; cereals; and dairy produce. Vegetables, such as peas and beans, together with fruit, nuts, and berries, were also eaten. The coastal populations could also add herring, cod, and flatfish to the diet, but bones from wild game, as later in the Middle Ages, are seldom found. Salt, honey, and various herbs were used as spices. Meat was pre-served by drying, smoking, or pickling in brine or whey, and somewhat less often by salting. Vegetables were preserved by being dried. Drink consisted primarily of fermented beverages; usually ale, but also mead and, more occasionally, the strong and sweet *bjórr*, although milk products and plain water were also consumed. The food was either prepared in clay or soapstone pots, or else roasted directly over the fire on a spit. Another popular way of preparing meat was to fill a pit halfway up with heated stones, place the meat wrapped in leaves or clay on top, and then fill the pit with soil or turf to conserve the heat. Fluids were heated by pouring them into suspended animal skins and dropping hot stones into them.

The medieval period is characterized by the striving toward self-sufficiency in the supply of foodstuffs, for which efficient storage was crucial. However, the task was impossible. For instance, the harsh climate in wide areas of Scandinavia altogether precluded the cultivation of grain. Furthermore, despite the great numbers of domestic animals being kept in the cities, and the various crops being grown in and around them, regular supplies from outside were essential. Effective preservation of foodstuffs and adequate storage were necessary to meet the need for provisions throughout the whole year. As in the Viking period, plants and fruit were dried. Fruit was also preserved in honey or sugar, and meat and fish were salted, dried, or smoked.

As imposed by the Church, fasting was a characteristic feature of the medieval diet. Fasting was observed during Lent, during a certain period prior to the other annual festivals and holidays, plus every Friday: 180 days altogether. The rules governing what might be eaten during a fast were not always interpreted the same way, but mostly they advocated total abstention from meat or poultry, and sometimes even from milk products or eggs. Eating fish was allowed. Seafish were the norm, although freshwater fish were probably preferred. Cod and herring, either fresh, dried, or salted, were the most commonly consumed saltwater fish in Scandinavia. Written sources, however, also mention a long list of other species found in surrounding waters, many of which have been confirmed through excavation. Some, such as the sturgeon or ling, are seldom seen today. Finds of shrimp, common mussels, and oyster shells indicate that shellfish were widely consumed. The Danish queen Christine enjoyed shrimp in 1504, while Peter Breughel's painting *The Poor Kitchen* of 1563 raises the question of whether mussels and oysters were really considered poor man's food. Marine mammals were also regarded as fish, which meant that such animals as porpoise and seal were eaten during a fast. While salmon is frequently referred to in written sources as becoming expensive toward the end of the period (Christensen 1904), perch and pike are the most commonly found freshwater fish at archaeological sites.

In areas where agriculture is dominant, meat comes most often from domestic animals, while game is only found in small amounts. However, in such areas as Norrland in northern Sweden, Troms in Finnmark, Nordland in northern Norway, and in the north of Finland, a prehistoric type of hunting still prevailed throughout the medieval period. In farming areas, skeletal remains indicate that pork was consumed just as much as beef. In monasteries, castles, and urban areas, though, pigs account for only about 20 percent of the skeletal remains, sheep and lambs for an additional 20 percent. While pigs, cattle, and sheep were often slaughtered in autumn to avoid feeding them during winter, fowl, such as hens and geese, presented the possibility of fresh meat throughout the year. Hens, of course, also provided eggs as a nourishing supplement to the diet. Remains of wild fowl, especially ducks, are not unusual in the excavated material either. As in the previous period, milk and dairy products played an important role in medieval society. Both cow's milk and sheep's or goat's milk were drunk or processed. It was often separated into curds and whey or buttermilk, and made into various other products besides cheese or butter, or else it was used in the preparation of other dishes.

The staple cereal was barley. In Iceland, it probably was the only grain cultivated until all grain growing was finally abandoned at the end of the 14th century. Much of the barley was used for brewing ale, by far the most common beverage, but together with rye it was also baked into bread. It was also excellent for making a sort of porridge. After barley in importance came rye, which was used for baking bread. According to the written sources, oats were used as animal feed, but at Hamar, in Norway, the remains of a kind of dry oatmeal bread have been found. Oats were probably used for porridge as well. Although wheat is known to have been grown in Denmark, Finland, Norway, and Sweden, none of these countries' domestic harvests had any significance. Wheat, as a nutrient, is mentioned in the written sources, but since it was rare and expensive, it seems to have had an impact only on the upper classes, who could afford the even rarer "white bread" (known as "wheat cake" or just plain "cake"). To a lesser extent, other cereals, like rice (imported from Italy), millet, and buckwheat, were also consumed.

Vegetables were probably far more common than the sources imply, and were presumably home-grown, since they are rarely mentioned. The terms *kål* ("kale" or "cabbage") and *kabudsekål* (common cabbage; "kabudse" from the Latin *caput* 'head') crop up, as do beets, which were used like cabbages, and onions. Peas and beans, which were well suited for storage when dried, are also mentioned, as are endives, which have been found at Svenborg on the island of Funen. Several different herbs were probably also grown, including lovage, dill, parsley, cress, horseradish, mint, marjoram, and thyme. Both mustard and vinegar were very popular as flavorings, as were hops and bog myrtle, which were used to flavor ale. Wild caraway is also mentioned in the written sources. Account books mention a number of imported spices, some from as far as the Moluccas. These include cumin, pepper, saffron, ginger, cardamom, grain of paradise, cloves, nutmeg, mace, cinnamon, aniseseed, and bay leaves, many of which were discovered by the Europeans during the Crusades. Since these spices were expensive, they probably had no great significance for the majority of the people. However, there are many indications that flavorings were widely used, not only sour (vinegar) and strong (mustard), but also sweet. The traditional sweetener was honey, used throughout the period. Sugar was known at least from the 14th century, but is seldom mentioned in accounts until the early 16th century. Like salt, sugar and honey were used liberally in many kinds of food, especially confectionary, which although expensive was quite popular.

As previously mentioned, ale was the staple drink of all the classes. Even children drank it daily (especially in urban areas). The wealthy, on the other hand, could also afford to drink wine, which was, of course, imported in limited quantities.

An important nutritional supplement was provided by fruit, berries, and nuts. Wild fruits, such as apples, pears, sour cherries, bullaces, cloudberries, blueberries, sloes, raspberries, brambles (blackberries), and woodland strawberries, could be picked by anyone wherever they grew. Cultivated fruits or imported fruits, like figs, grapes (raisins), or bitter oranges, would have been too expensive for the commoner, but the cultural layers of medieval towns have nevertheless turned up fig seeds and grape pips. Walnuts have also come to light in these layers, but the only known wild nut in Scandinavia at that time was the hazelnut. Account books also mention the use of almonds and chestnuts, which, like walnuts, had to be imported.

According to Kjersgaard (1978), the composition of the diet underwent a radical change in Denmark during the Middle Ages. He contends that the plague and the agricultural crises resulted in a remarkable decrease in cultivated land, which, among other things, prompted a shift in emphasis from growing grain to rearing livestock. Kjersgaard's hypothesis states that while in the 13th century the ratio between cereal and meat was 1:1, it developed into a ratio of 1:2 over the next two centuries. It is quite likely that this conclusion could apply generally to the rest of Scandinavia, even though the "Helgeandsholmen" survey in Stockholm shows a different result (Dahlbäck 1982: 276). Local variations might easily be the explanation for this difference.

No studies of the development of the Scandinavian diet from the 11th century to the 13th century are available. Archaeological evidence from northern Germany indicates that the proportion of cereals to meat in their diet grew during this period. For the rural population, this meant that their staple diet consisted of bread and other cereal products like groats at the time just before the agricultural crises set in (Janssen 1981). Surveys of southern Scandinavia would most likely yield similar results.

Three unique sources detail the cooking and serving of food. Two are cookery books recorded around 1300 and 1350, making them some of the oldest surviving records of medieval cookery in Europe (Kristensen 1908–20). The third is a list of meals served during the course of a year for the Swedish bishop Hans Brask around 1520 (Hildebrand 1885). The two cookery books share a common French origin, and contain recipes for sauces, milk and egg dishes, and chicken dishes. Characteristic of these dishes was the elaborate preparation involved. The ingredients were processed to the point of unrecognizability by either being cut, shredded, or ground to bits, or by being wrapped in pastry before being cooked. The list of meals records the composition of the menu at a wealthy table for most days of the year. The bishop ate two main meals every day. Each meal comprised several courses with meat, such as pork, beef, or mutton, either fried or boiled. During a fast, he ate fish, but generally avoided eggs and milk. Each meal was then rounded off with cheese and/or fruit.

Large numbers of different cooking utensils have been found at archaeological sites. At the same time, written sources provide us with descriptions of fully equipped kitchens, all of which indicates that cookery was already highly developed.

There is nothing to indicate that poor-quality food, or cookery, was accepted during the Middle Ages. Spices were not used to disguise the taste of food gone bad, but rather to enhance the taste. During the Middle Ages in Scandinavia, the possibility of a nourishing and varied diet existed, but we simply cannot say how much of the population was able to take advantage of it.

Lit.: Hildebrand, H., ed. "Matordningen i Biskop Hans Brask Hus." *Kongl. Vitterhets Historie och Antiqvitets Akademiens Månadsblad* (January, February–March 1885), 1–21, 141–2; Christensen, W., ed. *Dronning Christines Hofholdningsregnskaber.* Copenhagen: Gyldendal,

1904; Kristensen, M. *Harpestræng, Gamle danske Urtebøger, Stenbøger og Kogebøger*. Copenhagen: Thiele, 1908–20; Berquist, H., and J. Lepiksaar. *Animal Skeletal Remains from Medieval Lund*. Archaeology of Lund, 1. Lund: Museum of Cultural History, 1957; Kjersgaard, E. *Øl og mad i Danmarks middelalder*. Copenhagen: Nationalmuseet, 1978; Jensen, H. A. *Seeds and Other Diaspores in Medieval Layers from Svendborg*. Vol. 2 of *The Archaeology of Svenborg*. Odense: Odense University Press, 1979; Janssen, W. "Essen und Trinken im frühen und hohen Mittelalters aus archäologischen Sicht." In *Liber Castellorum, 40 variatias op het theme kastel*. Ed. T. J. Hoekstra *et al*. Zutphen: Walburg, 1981; Roesdahl, Else. *Viking Age Denmark*. Trans. Susan Margeson and Kirsten Williams. London: British Museum, 1982; Dahlbäck, G., ed. *Helgeandsholmen*. Stockholm: Liber, 1982; Jørgensen, G., *et al*. *Analyses of Medieval Plant Remains, Textiles and Wood from Medieval Svendborg*. Vol. 4 of *The Archaeology of Svendborg*. Odense: Odense University Press, 1986.

Bi Skaarup

[See also: Agriculture; Fishing, Whaling, and Seal Hunting]

Dínus saga dramblāta

Dínus saga dramblāta ("The Saga of Dínus the Haughty") is an Icelandic *riddarasaga* from the 14th century preserved in forty-five MSS. Like *Sigurðar saga þogla* or *Mágus saga*, for example, *Dínus saga dramblāta* is transmitted in three redactions that differ considerably from each other: (1) the oldest and lengthiest (the oldest vellum MS, AM 575a 4to, from the end of the 14th or the beginning of the 15th century); (2) a middle redaction, abridged, probably from the 17th century (MSS AM 184 fol. and AM 185 fol.) with independent interpolations especially from *Alexanders saga*; and (3) the youngest redaction, also abbreviated, which probably came into existence in the 18th century (MSS JS 270 8vo, Lbs. 2319 8vo, *etc*.). The distribution of the MSS suggests that *Dínus saga* had its origin in the western part of Iceland, perhaps in Reykhólar at Breiðafjörður, but that the youngest redaction came into existence in the southern part. *Dínus rímur* are transmitted from the 16th and 17th centuries.

The haughty Prince Dínus of Egypt is bound by a spell by the equally haughty Princess Philotemia of Bláland (Ethiopia), so that he is overcome by a burning desire for her. With his followers, Dínus goes to Bláland, but is duped by the princess. Dínus takes revenge with the help of a counterspell, which makes all the courtiers dance naked. Philotemia again binds the prince by a spell, and the men grow painful horns. Dínus counters by transforming Philotemia and her maids into crows. At the third encounter, Dínus holds her soldiers in check by a magic bag and succeeds in deflowering the princess. After a reconciliation, Dínus and Philotemia marry.

A Greek-oriental source for all of *Dínus saga* is out of the question. The sources that serve as a basis for this new, original story are translations of French and Latin works. *Klári saga* served as a model for the material and structure, but also *Kirialax saga*, *Alexanders saga*, *Rómverja saga*, and perhaps *Rémundar saga* and *Karlamagnús saga* were used.

Of central importance in this text is the bridal-quest plot connected with the *meykóngr* ("maiden-king") theme, whereby the extreme form of sexual aggression is considered sometimes as vulgar, sometimes as an expression of a mysogynic or general misanthropic violation in the universe of these sagas, and sometimes as parodic.

The special connection among *Dínus saga dramblāta* and *Klári*

saga, *Kirialax saga*, *Rémundar saga*, and also *Alexanders saga* was recognized long ago. On the basis of the close lexical parallels between *Dínus saga* and *Nikulás saga*, it has recently been suggested that Bergr Sokkason, abbot of the monastery of Munka-Þverá and author of *Nikulás saga*, or at least of its prologue, or some person within the abbot's circle, might have been the author of *Dínus saga*. This identification, however, would push back the date of the origin of the saga to the first half or the middle of the 14th century. Furthermore, the concentration of the MS tradition in the western part of Iceland makes it unlikely that *Dínus saga* originated in Eyjafjörður in northern Iceland.

The narrative style of *Dínus saga dramblāta* has been characterized as subjective, "ornate, opposed to [the] classical saga style," and rich in foreign words and loanwords.

Ed.: Finnur Jónsson, ed. "Dínús rímur." In *Rímnasafn: Samling af de ældste islandske rimer*. 2 vols. Samfund til udgivelse af gammel nordisk litteratur, 35. Copenhagen: Møller & Jørgensen, 1905–22, vol. 2, pp. 801–24; Jónas Kristjánsson, ed. *Dínus saga dramblāta*. Riddarasögur, 1. Reykjavik: Háskóli Íslands, 1960 [critical edition of the oldest and the middle versions]. **Tr**.: Leach, Henry Goddard, trans. "Dínus the Proud and Philotemia the Fair." In his *Angevin Britain and Scandinavia*. Harvard Studies in Comparative Literature, 6. Cambridge: Harvard University Press; London: Milford; Oxford: Oxford University Press, 1921; rpt. Millwood: Kraus, 1975, pp. 271–85 [English retelling of the "middle version" of the saga]. **Bib**.: Finnur Sigmundsson. *Rímnatal*. 2 vols. Reykjavik: Rímnafélagið, 1966, vol. 1, pp. 103–4; Kalinke, Marianne E., and P. M. Mitchell. *Bibliography of Old Norse–Icelandic Romances*. Islandica, 44. Ithaca and London: Cornell University Press, 1985. **Lit**.: Einar Ól. Sveinsson. *Verzeichnis isländischer Märchenvarianten. Mit einer einleitenden Untersuchung*. Folklore Fellows Communications, 83. Helsinki: Suomalainen Tiedeakatemia, Academia Scientiarum Fennica, 1929, pp. lii–liii; Björn K. Þórólfsson. *Rímur fyrir 1600*. Safn Fræðafjelagsins um Ísland og Íslendinga, 9. Copenhagen: Møller, 1934, pp. 398–9; Schlauch, Margaret. *Romance in Iceland*. Princeton: Princeton University Press; New York: American-Scandinavian Foundation; London: Allen & Unwin, 1934; rpt. New York: Russell & Russell, 1973; Wahlgren, Erik. "The Maiden King in Iceland." Diss. University of Chicago. University of Chicago Libraries, 1938; Jakob Benediktsson. "Dínus saga dramblāta. Jónas Kristjánsson bjó til prentunar." *Islenzk tunga* 3 (1961–62), 114–21 [review article]; Rossenbeck, Klaus. "Die Stellung der Riddarasögur in der altnordischen Prosaliteratur—eine Untersuchung an Hand des Erzählstils." Diss. Frankfurt am Main, 1970, pp. 117–20, 211; Tannert, Robert. "The Style of the *Dínus saga dramblāta*." *Scandinavian Studies* 52 (1980), 53–62; Nahl, Astrid van. *Originale Riddarasögur als Teil altnordischer Sagaliteratur*. Texte und Untersuchungen zur Germanistik und Skandinavistik, 3. Frankfurt am Main and Bern: Lang, 1981; Sverrir Tómasson. "Bergr Sokkason's Life of St Nicholas." In *Helgastaðabók. Nikulás saga. Perg. 4to nr. 16. Konungsbókhlöðu i Stokkhólmi*. Manuscripta Islandica Medii Aevi, 2. Reykjavik: Sverrir Kristinsson, 1982, pp. 161–76; Glauser, Jürg. *Isländische Märchensagas. Studien zur Prosaliteratur im spätmittelalterlichen Island*. Beiträge zur nordischen Philologie, 12. Basel and Frankfurt am Main: Helbing & Lichtenhahn, 1983; Amory, Frederic. "Things Greek and the *Riddarasögur*." *Speculum* 59 (1984), 509–23; Comolle, Heike. "Lehn- und Fremdwörter der Dínus saga dramblāta." *Nordeuropa, Studien* 19 (1985), Sonderreihe der Wissenschaftlichen Zeitschrift der Ernst-Moritz-Arndt-Universität Greifswald, pp. 112–7; Hallberg, Peter. "A Group of Icelandic 'Riddarasögur' from the Middle of the Fourteenth Century." In *Les Sagas de Chevaliers (Riddarasögur). Actes de la Vᵉ Conférence Internationale sur les Sagas . . . (Toulon. Juillet 1982)*. Ed.

Régis Boyer. Civilisations, 10. Paris: Presses de l'Université de Paris-Sorbonne, 1985, pp. 7–53; Kalinke, Marianne E. "Riddarasögur, Fornaldarsögur, and the Problem of Genre." In *Les Sagas de Chevaliers (Riddarasögur)*, pp. 77–91 [esp. p. 84]; Hermann Pálsson. "The Use of Latin Proverbs and Sententiae in the Riddarasögur." In *Les Sagas de Chevaliers (Riddarasögur)*, pp. 385–91; Kalinke, Marianne. "Norse Romance (*Riddarasögur*)." In *Old Norse–Icelandic Literature: A Critical Guide*. Ed. Carol J. Clover and John Lindow. Islandica, 45. Ithaca and London: Cornell University Press, 1985, pp. 316–63; Kalinke, Marianne E. "The Misogamous Maiden Kings of Icelandic Romance." *Scripta Islandica* 37 (1986), 47–71; Jochens, Jenny M. "Consent in Marriage: Old Norse Law, Life, and Literature." *Scandinavian Studies* 58 (1986), 142–76; Kalinke, Marianne E. *Bridal-Quest Romance in Medieval Iceland*. Islandica, 46. Ithaca and London: Cornell University Press, 1990.

Jürg Glauser

[**See also:** *Alexanders saga; Karlamagnús saga; Kirialax saga; Klári (Clári) saga; Rémundar saga keisarasonar; Riddarasögur; Rómverja saga*]

Diplomatics is the study of medieval diplomas (charters) and letters, especially as sources for historical research. In the Roman Empire, the Latin word *diploma* (Greek δίπλωμα) signified a pair of leaden or wax slabs with inscribed texts held together by a string and seals for the use of certain sorts of official documents. Since the publication of Jean Mabillon's *De re diplomatica* (1681), the word *diploma* came into common use as a technical term for medieval letters patent, especially documents of privileges. In medieval times, such a document was named *charta, instrumentum*, or *præceptum*, whereas other letters were named *litteræ*. Old Norse documents valid in law were in part named *skjal*. But in all Nordic languages, documents of this type as well as written information of other kinds most often were named *bréf*, or else *skript* or *skrift*. Modern Nordic languages generally use the words *diplom* or *brev* for all sorts of medieval documents and letters (also Swedish *urkund*, from German *Urkunde*).

The art of preparing written documents and letters in the Latin alphabet was inherited from Roman antiquity and spread to western and northern Europe together with Christianity and Latin writing. At the outset, Latin was the only language of diplomas in northern Europe. But around 1200, the Old Norse language began to be used in diplomas in the Norwegian kingdom and in Iceland. The medieval Norwegian written language lasted longest in practical use in diplomas. Royal *griðabréf* (charters of truce, delay of penalty) and *landsvistarbréf* (charters securing inviolability of a person within the kingdom) were written in the Norwegian language until the 1570s. Swedish and Danish languages came into use in diplomas in the 14th century.

In Carolingian times, a special handwriting was used in diplomas, in several respects different from the letters of books. In the 13th century, the older diploma writing was followed by Gothic cursive writing.

In northern Europe, parchment or skin, mostly from calves, was the common material for diplomas before 1200. After 1300, paper came into use alongside parchment in the Nordic countries.

The seals were usually made from wax. On parchment diplomas, they were attached to the lower edge of the diploma by means of parchment straps, on paper letters stamped to the paper beneath the text.

On the basis of the contents ("internal criteria") in diplomatics, a difference is drawn between two main types of documents, named *charta* and *notitia*.

The *charta* is a document of value by itself. In the *charta*, the expeditor notifies that he by means of the document accomplishes a disposition defined in the document, for example, transference of ownership, pronouncing of a testament, a sentence, an appointment, and so on (*dispositio*). In such documents, the expeditor normally names himself in the first person; in charters given by popes, bishops, and princes, in the first person plural. The *charta* is the most common type of document in western Europe, also in Denmark and Sweden. Such documents were destined to be preserved as constant evidence of the validity of the disposition that was introduced by means of the charter. The addressees of such documents are very often all persons living in a named area, and principally all these persons have to gain knowledge, or have the right to gain knowledge, of the contents of the document.

The *notitia*, as opposed to the *charta*, is principally a document that by itself has no value as an instrument of decision. A *notitia* only brings information of a valid disposition that has taken place beforehand. The partakers of the disposition are named in the third person, and the verbs have preterite form. Among Nordic diplomas, the examples of *notitia* in its strict sense are relatively few.

In the Old Norse area, however, especially in Norway and Iceland, a special type of document developed that has important qualities in common with the *notitia*, the *vitnebrev* ("letters of witnesses"). In these countries, Christianity and literature in Latin were introduced relatively late, and well-established legal communities existed long before the introduction of Latin writing. Legal institutions and traditions without the aid of script and knowledge of literature were especially well established. In these countries, the nonliterary judicial practice continued to work to the very end of the Middle Ages, several hundreds of years after the introduction of Latin writing. The use of script and written documents has to a great extent only a literary superconstruction upon a judicial practice that was principally still nonliterate, one that preserved old oral formulas and inherited juridical symbols. The *vitnebrev* was the common form of private document in the Old Norse area, especially in documents of lawful acquisition.

In the *vitnebrev*, one or, most often, more than one named witness report that they were present as certain named persons performed a judicial act or a disposition legally and solemnly, normally confirmed by *handa(r)band* ("shakehands"), and corroborate their witness by attaching their seals to the document. In the *vitnebrev*, the testimony with the verbs in preterite form replaces the *dispositio* of the *charta*. The *vitnebrev* was the normal way of preparing documents in the Old Norse area, but the document of disposition, the *charta*, was at times used by the clergy and the nobility. In the Swedish area, many documents from before 1350 had a structure that in its fundamental principles is consonant with the Old Norse *vitnisbréf*.

In late-medieval times, literature of letters became much more extensive and varied, not least by the constantly increasing number of letters that had no juridical function and that were less marked by formulas, *epistolary* letters.

In diplomatics, a difference is also drawn between two types of letters on the basis of the material form ("external criteria"). One type are the "open letters," *litteræ apertæ* or *patentes*, where the material is not folded together and not closed by seals, to the effect that all persons who are able to read, having got the document in their hands, can get knowledge of the contents.

Contrary to *litteræ apertæ* are the *litteræ clausæ*, closed letters, also named *missive*. Here, the parchment or paper is folded together and closed by the seal of the expeditor, the name of the addressee often written on the unused outside of the document. This arrangement was useful when the document had to be sent by letter carriers (*bréfamenn, bréfasveinar*) to an addressee far away (*sendibréf*), and also useful when the contents of the document were secret.

With regard to the contents, it can be generally stated that the nature of *litteræ apertæ* most often is dispositive, whereas *litteræ clausæ* normally were epistolary, i.e., contain a message especially addressed to the addressee.

The medieval art of preparing documents was influenced by medieval Latin rhetoric and stylistic construction, and became in time strongly marked by tradition and fixed formulas. The art of preparing a document was named *ars dictandi*. Often, older documents were used as patterns. But in medieval times, special instruction books on document formulation were written (*dictamen, summa dictaminis*). The system of formulas of the document, however, was marked in many ways by place and time of expedition and by schools of writing and seals; the formula system, therefore, is important for scholars who want to ascertain if a document is authentic or falsified.

As written documents were used as proofs of the validity of rights and advantages of many kinds, falsified documents always existed. Pope Innocent III (*ca.* 1200) is said to have tried to uncover false papal documents, and French Benedictines of the 17th century, the order to which Jean Mabillon, the founder of the modern study of diplomatics, belonged, defined diplomatics as *ars diplomata vera ac falsa discernendi* ("the art of discerning authentic diplomas from falsified").

In the year 1681, Mabillon brought out the fundamental study *De re diplomatica* in six volumes. This work had its origin in a dispute between Mabillon and the Dutch Bollandists on the authenticity of some old Benedictine documents. (Important contributions were also made early in German territory to the development of diplomatics.) Mabillon established that diplomas were built up by series of formulaic expressions, to which he assigned special designations. Since the 17th century, scholarship has developed the systematic and comparative analysis of medieval documents and the terminology that is specific to that study. Important subjects of research auxiliary to diplomatics are palaeography, or research on ancient writing; sfragistics, or research on seals; heraldics, or research on arms and devices; numismatics, or research on coins; and chronology.

The contents of a *diploma* are generally divided into three main parts: (1) *Protocol*, with the names of expeditor and addressee and greeting formula; (2) *Text*—here, the number of formulas can vary according to the nature of the document; and (3) the *Eschatocol*, which gives the names of the persons who have attached their seals to the document, if they are not named before, and also information on when and where the document was prepared.

In ancient times, the preparation of written documents was very expensive, and the documents were often of great value for a long time, especially documents warranting legal property and rights. Received documents and letters were therefore often preserved, not least in ecclesiastical and secular institutions. From the outset, the papal court was especially important in this connection. Thus, in many places, great collections of documents came into existence, developing in later times into regular archives. But it is generally supposed that regular royal archives did not exist in Nordic countries until the 13th century.

Older documents were not only preserved, but also copied. The copy was often framed by a new letter with new seals, confirming that the copy was a correct rendering of the substance of the original document (*vidisse, transcript*). But especially in permanent institutions, such as chanceries, in medieval times the production of copy books came into use, with copies or abstracts (*regesta*) of letters that had been sent from the institution.

In the Middle Ages and after, people's interest in old documents was mostly connected with their value as substantiation of private or political rights. The jurists were interested mainly in single documents. But the humanists' more critical attitude to historical tradition awoke an interest in old documents as sources of historical information. As a consequence of this development in the 18th century, the scholars of the Nordic countries began to gather and put in order extensive collections of old diplomas and letters, originals as well as copies. In Denmark, pioneers in this field were the famous Icelander Árni Magnússon and the Danes Hans Gram and Jakob Langebek; in Sweden, Sven Lagerbring. From this time on, the term *diplomatarium* was used to denote such unprinted or printed collections of old documents (chartularies).

The first printed *diplomatarium* was *Diplomatarium Arna-Magnæanum* (Copenhagen 1786), by the Icelander Grímur Thorkelin. After this printing, in the 19th century, the great Nordic edition series were started, *Diplomatarium Suecanum* (1829–), *Diplomatarium Norvegicum* (1847), and *Diplomatarium Islandicum* (1857). These series are still being continued or supplemented. Published in the 20th century are *Finlands medeltidsurkunder* (1910–35), *Diplomatarium Danicum* (1938), *Diplomatarium Færoense* (1907), *Diplomatarium Groenlandicum* (1936), and *Diplomatarium Orcadense et Hialtlandense* (1907–42). Comprehensive renderings of the contents of all sorts of written medieval historical sources are to be found in *Regesta Danica* (1938–), and in *Regesta Norvegica* (1898, and from 1978–).

Lit.: **(a) General**: Bresslau, Harry. *Handbuch der Urkundenlehre*. 2 vols. Berlin and Leipzig: de Gruyter, 1912–31; Bonenfant, Paul. *Cours de diplomatique*. 2 vols. Liège: Éditions Desoer, 1947–48. **(b) Nordic**: Agerholt, Johan. "Gamal brevskipnad." In *Meddelelser fra Det norske Riksarkiv*. Oslo: Gundersen, 1928–33; Blatt, Franz. *Under vor Haand og Segl*. Copenhagen: Munksgaard, 1943; Berulfsen, Bjarne. *Kulturtradisjon fra en storhetstid*. Oslo: Gyldendal, 1948; Ljungfors, Åke. *Bidrag till svensk diplomatik*. Lund: Gleerup, 1955; Kroman, Erik, *et al.* "Brev." KLNM 2 (1957), 226–9; Liedgren, Jan. "Diplom." *KLNM* 3 (1958), 80–2; Nygren, Ernst. "Diplomatarium." *KLNM* 3 (1958), 82–6; Johannesson, Gösta. "Diplomatik." *KLNM* 3 (1958), 87–90; Hamre, Lars. *Innføring i diplomatikk*. Oslo, Bergen, and Tromsø: Universitetsforlaget, 1972; Hamre, Lars, *et al.* "Vitnebrev." *KLNM* 20 (1976), 214–22; Fritz, Birgitta. "De svenska medeltidsbrevens tradering till 1800–talets børjan." In *Meddelanden från Svenska riksarkivet för åren 1976–1977*. Stockholm: Kungl. Boktryckeriet, 1976–77, pp. 68–135.

Hallvard Magerøy

[**See also**: Chancery; Palaeography; Seals]

Dísir *see* **Supernatural Beings**

Divine Heroes, Native

(1) *Harald Wartooth* (Hildiṭǫnn) is mentioned in Saxo's *Gesta Danorum* and in the defective *Sǫgubrot* derived from the lost **Skjǫldunga saga* (early 13th century). Whether Harald ever existed cannot be ascertained with certainty, and, if he did, he is difficult to place in history. Some scholars have assigned him to the 6th century, others to the 8th or 9th century.

According to the written sources, Harald was born through the intervention of Óðinn, who granted him victory in every battle. In return, Harald was to dedicate all who fell in his battles to Óðinn. Óðinn also taught Harald warfare, and, like Starkad, he was granted three times the span of a mortal life. While Harald was still a youth, two of his teeth were knocked out, and two enormous molars grew in their place, hence his nickname "wartooth."

Harald conquered Denmark, Sweden, and other areas, and placed Hring in charge of Sweden. According to Saxo (Book 7), Harald's servant Brun(i), who was in reality Óðinn, caused strife between Harald and Hring, and eventually the two met in battle at Bråvalla (Old Norse Brávellir). Seeing that Hring's army was deployed in wedge formation (*svínfylking*), Harald knew that only Óðinn could have taught them this tactic and that the god had now turned against him. Óðinn, who was acting as Bruni, Harald's charioteer, battered Harald to death with his own club. Hring gave Harald a magnificent funeral, which is described in great detail in both the Danish and Icelandic texts.

(2) *Hadding* (Hadingus) is not mentioned in Norse tradition. Apparently, he and his exploits are made up to introduce Scandinavian gods into Danish history. In Saxo's *Gesta Danorum*, he is the son of the Danish king Gram. After Gram's death at the hands of the Norwegian king Svipdag, Hadding was sent to Sweden, where he was raised by his giant foster-mother Harthgripa (Harðgreip). After her death, Óðinn appeared to Hadding and brought him into foster-brotherhood with the Viking Liser. The two were defeated by Loker, but Óðinn rescued his favorite, carrying him off on his supernatural horse. Óðinn taught Hadding how to deploy his forces and to break his fetters, and assured him that he would never fall into the hands of an enemy. Óðinn also told Hadding that he must kill a lion and eat its flesh and drink its blood, for this would give him strength. At first, Hadding lived as a Viking, but subsequently he killed Svipdag and won his hereditary kingdom.

Hadding's wife was Regnilda (Ragnhildr), daughter of a Norwegian king, who had been raped by giants. Hadding rescued her, and in gratitude she nursed his wounds and sealed up a ring in his leg. When her father later permitted her to choose a husband, Regnilda chose Hadding by the ring in his leg. The marriage was, however, an unhappy one. Hadding longed for the sea, but the shrieking seagulls were hateful to Regnilda, who longed for the mountains. One day, a woman appeared to Hadding bearing herbs. Hadding wanted to know where the herbs grew in winter, and went with the woman under the earth. The story as recorded by Saxo is difficult to understand, but Hadding's visit to the underworld echoes a number of tales known from Norse mythology, notably Hermóðr's journey to Hel to ransom Baldr (*cf. Gylfaginning*, ch. 34). The story is most similar to the sixth song of Vergil's *Aeneid*.

Hadding's death was fitting for a hero of Óðinn (*cf. Hávamál*, st. 138). King Hunding of the Swedes had heard false reports of Hadding's death. He then prepared a feast in Hadding's honor, and filled a gigantic jug with beer. During the feast, Hunding and Fjǫlnir, another king of the Swedes, fell into the jug and drowned. When Hadding heard this news, he hanged himself in public.

There are striking similarities between Hadding and Njǫrðr of the Vanir: Njǫrðr married the giantess Skaði, and Hadding took his wife from the giant world; Skaði chose Njǫrðr as her husband from his legs, and Regnilda recognized Hadding from the ring in his leg; Skaði and Regnilda complain of the shrieking gulls, and Njǫrðr and Hadding complain of the hills and the howling wolves. Njǫrðr took his own sister as his wife, and Saxo states that Harthgripa claimed Hadding's embraces. Saxo also records that Hadding established the annual sacrifice of Freyr in Sweden.

(3) *Starkad* (Old Norse Starkaðr) is a legendary hero mentioned in some *fornaldarsǫgur* and in Saxo Grammaticus's *Gesta Danorum*. The latter can be traced to an original written about 1200, whereas the Norse tradition is not known until 100 years later, though it seems to stem from narratives of the 12th century.

According to Saxo, rumor has it that Starkad was born a giant with six arms. The god Þórr cut off four of these arms and gave him human proportions. The god Óðinn taught him poetry and warfare, and rendered him three times the span of mortal life with the sinister provision that he was to commit a nefarious deed in each lifetime.

In his youth, Starkad lived as a Viking. At first, he was a follower of the Norwegian king Víkar, until Óðinn ordered him to kill Víkar treacherously. Later on, he raided in eastern Europe until one day, shipwrecked, he landed in Denmark. Here, he became a friend of the king, Frode IV (Old Norse Fróði); he was absent when Frode was killed by a Saxon rebel, Sverting. To Starkad's dismay, Frode's son Ingellus (Ingeld; Old Norse Ingjaldr) failed to avenge the murder. On the contrary, he made peace with Sverting's sons and married their sister. Starkad felt obliged to reestablish the honor of the Danish kingdom. He had to start by teaching Ingellus's sister to reject the courtship of a low-born goldsmith. Saxo describes this incident both in prose and in verse. In the same way, Saxo tells how Starkad exhorted Ingellus and helped him fight Sverting's sons. Into this "Lay of Ingellus" are woven verbal attacks upon various German customs, such as gluttony.

After fulfilling his mission, Starkad again deserted the Danish court to raid under the leadership of other kings. Once, he fled from a battle in Zealand without any obvious reason. Perhaps this was the second crime of the three Óðinn had prophesied. At last, he followed the Norwegian king Olo in the great battle of Bråvalla, about which Starkad is said to have composed a poem. Afterward, he was bribed to kill Olo. His repentance for this third crime and his longing for death are again told in prosimetrum. At last, he finds an ideal opponent, Hatherus. They fling invectives at each other; then Starkad gives Hatherus his sword, and sticks his neck out to be killed.

Some of the incidents from Saxo's tale are also found in Norse literature. Starkad's origin, the hanging of Víkar, and the Viking raids resemble what is told in the middle part of *Gautreks saga*. Saxo must have known at least this part of the saga, perhaps in a slightly different form. The Ingellus episode—the killing of Frode by Sverting, Starkad's exhortations, and the fight with Sverting's sons—are with some alterations rendered in the *Skjǫldunga saga*, as is the murder of Olo. There can be no doubt about the Norse origin of these parts of the Starkad story, even if the "Lay of Ingellus" is built on a long tradition mentioned in the Old English poems *Beowulf* and *Widsith*. Two separate stories may have been put together by

Saxo, who supplemented his version with some of his favorite topics.

Because of some curious similarities between the lives and characters of Starkad and Eskil, archbishop of Denmark from 1138 to 1177, it has been suggested that Saxo may have modeled his figure of Starkad on Eskil.

Lit.: (a) Harald Wartooth: Bjarni Guðnason, "Um Brávallaþulu." *Skírnir* 132 (1958), 82–128; Turville-Petre, E. O. G. *Myth and Religion of the North: The Religion of Ancient Scandinavia.* New York: Holt, Rinehart and Winston, 1964; rpt. Westport: Greenwood, 1975; Bjarni Guðnason, ed. *Danakonunga sǫgur.* Íslenzk fornrit, 35. Reykjavik: Hið íslenzka fornritafélag, 1982, pp. xxxvi–xlii, 46–71. **(b) Hadding**: Dumézil, Georges. *La Saga de Hadingus (Saxo Grammaticus I, v–viii): Du mythe au roman.* Paris: Presses Universitaires de France, 1953; Turville-Petre, E. O. G. *Myth and Religion of the North: The Religion of Ancient Scandinavia.* New York: Holt, Rinehart and Winston, 1964; rpt. Westport: Greenwood, 1975; Ward, Donald. *The Divine Twins: An Indoeuropean Myth in Germanic Tradition.* Berkeley and Los Angeles: University of California Press, 1968, pp. 75–6. **(c) Starkad**: Olrik, Axel. *The Heroic Legends of Denmark.* Trans. Lee M. Hollander. New York: American-Scandinavian Foundation, 1919; rpt. Millwood: Kraus, 1976; Herrmann, Paul. *Erläuterungen zu den ersten neun Büchern der dänischen Geschichte des Saxo Grammaticus.* Leipzig: Engelmann, 1901–22; Vries, Jan de. "Die Starkadsage." *Germanisch-romanische Monatschrift* 36, N.F. 5 (1955), 281–97; Dumézil, Georges. *Mythe et épopée. II: Types épiques indo-européens: Un héros, un sorcier, un roi.* [n.p.]: Gallimard, 1971; Skovgaard-Petersen, Inge. *Starkad in Saxo's Gesta Danorum: History and Heroic Tale.* Odense: Odense Unversitetsforlag, 1985; Skovgaard-Petersen, Inge. *Da Tidernes Herre var nær. Studier i Saxos historiesyn.* Copenhagen: Den danske historiske Forening, 1987; Friis-Jensen, Karsten. *Saxo Grammaticus as Latin Poet: Studies in the Verse Passages of the Gesta Danorum.* Analecta Romana Instituti Danici, Supplementum, 14. Rome: Bretschneider, 1987.

Inge Skovgaard-Petersen

[**See also:** *Fornaldarsǫgur*; *Gautreks saga*; *Hávamál*; Mythology; Saxo Grammaticus; *Skjǫldunga saga*; *Snorra Edda*]

Divorce *see* **Marriage and Divorce**

Doktor Hjælpeløs *see* **Drama**

Dorotheæ Komedie *see* **Drama**

Drama. Printed drama is not found in Scandinavia until about 1550; there is, however, evidence of early theatrical forms. Of special interest in this connection are some of the frescoes on walls and vaults in, for example, Danish churches from the 12th century and later (Kaspersen 1988).

In general, early European drama was closely connected with the Church and expressed a cosmological rather than an individual view: man as part of a universe, created by God. The sources of drama, especially in France and England, confirm this universal point of view. Although Scandinavian medieval history is not identical with European, the same universal idea and institutional praxis can be seen in the oldest Scandinavian sources. After the Reformation, a more individualistic and psychological view can be observed, as a consequence of new social, economic, and political

conditions, and perhaps influenced by Luther's psychological interpretation of the Christian creed (*sola fide, i.e.,* one can be saved only by personal faith). Most of the North European dramatic works from between 1550 and 1600 demonstrate a blending of the old and the new conception, thematically and formally.

The central idea of early-medieval drama is exemplified by two main forms: as an important part of the Catholic mass, and as folk customs with pre-Christian elements, ineffectually prohibited by the higher authorities. During the Easter mass, for instance, a regular drama was performed in the church, not for an audience but with the congregation actively taking part in the action. They are reported to have "run from Herod to Pilate," following the clergyman, monk, or layman who represented Christ in scenes depicting his torture and crucifixion, and ending up at the high altar, where the archangel cried out, "He is resurrected," and everyone sang "hosanna." The angel may well have become impatient when delayed by burlesque scenes in which, for example, the three Marys buy fragrant herbs at the apothecary on their way to the sepulcher on Easter morning. We know that such scenes were popular, and in one case were ordered not to continue for more than half an hour.

The whole Passion of Christ was reexperienced, past time lived through as present time, filled with hope for life and death in the future. Time was eternal, and place was universal. The set was visible during the whole play, with the church symbolizing the universe.

Later on, when the stage was placed outside the church, in the graveyard or the marketplace, the idea of simultaneity was shown according to a scenographic principle of houses: to the left the house of heaven, to the right the house, or mouth, of hell, and in the middle the house of earth. The staging provided a visible expression of the period's understanding of history: all times are now, and all the regions of the universe are here, within one and the same space.

Another main form of sacred drama, known from about 1100 especially in England and France, was the Feast of Fools (*festum stultorum, asinarium festa, festum subdiaconorum*). The presupposition of the comical, often obscene, and even blasphemous elements was a sincere belief of the participants in this drama as sacral, the idea of life as whole and holy, involving humor and sensual pleasure, although threatened by the Devil.

In Italy from about 1400 and in Scandinavia from the middle of the 16th century, a new understanding of history can be traced in architecture, writing, painting, and scenography, an empirical comprehension of nature and man (*ratio naturae*). The adoption of central perspective, for instance, gives evidence of an optic rather than a purely artistic point of view of art. In stage setting, simultaneity of time and space gave way to a principle of succession. The actors were not allowed to be visible on stage until the logically and chronologically constructed action demanded their presence. Instead of a stage with cosmological houses, the Terence stage was introduced: an elevated platform with a backstage curtain, split up and leading to various nonvisible localities, often private houses with signboards advertising family names, testifying to a more "realistic" (bourgeois) style. This drama form might be called "early modern," if by "modern" is meant before 1900.

As far as we know, the first printed drama in Sweden is *Tobiae Comedia* (1550). The preface mentions that drama has "always" been performed inside and outside the church "to inform layfolk about right and wrong." Theater, of course, is much older than printed drama. Jugglers, market artists, and mimics (*joculatores, scurrae, mimi*) had been active throughout Europe, often in connection with music and ballads, sung and danced. As for folk drama, in Scandinavia only a few traces are found of the Feasts of Fools. Perhaps the *Kjippardance*, still danced in Florø, Norway, has its origin in one of the New Year customs.

With regard to church drama, one of the oldest known Danish plays is based on an *ordinarium, i.e.*, rules for a Catholic mass, from Ringsted (1170). Another *ordinarium*, from Linköping, Sweden, gives evidence of a liturgical Easter drama (*Quem quaeritis in sepulchra, Christicolae*, "Whom are you seeking in the sepulcher, Christian women"). Two variants exist, both from about 1300. In Flensburg, Denmark (now Germany), a holy shrine "for the person of Jesus Christ" was used dramatically until 1527. In Århus in 1501 and at the University of Copenhagen in 1521, there were performances, probably acted in Latin by the students. In Norway, we read in a diary from Bergen: "I, Master Absolon, had a play acted on the churchyard with great pains and expense." And on March 25, 1506, Hans Jacobi, a priest in Söderköping, Sweden, records that he had procured a *ludus resurrectionis*, a resurrection play.

Each of the four oldest extant Danish dramatic texts represents one of the main genres of medieval drama: saint's play (about the legend of a saint), mystery play (about the Passion), morality play (an allegorical personification of virtues and vices), and farcical play or burlesque. The saint's play, *Ludus de Sancto Canuto Duce* ("A Play on the Holy Duke Knud," *i.e.*, Knud [Cnut] Lavard, 1096–1131) is known from a 16th-century transcript, but probably dates back to before 1500. It was performed outside the church, the scenography was simultaneous, and it contained a prologue and epilogue delivered by Preco, the messenger. *Dorotheæ Komedie* ("Dorotheae Comedy"), a mystery play, is a translation from a German prose drama in Latin (1507), about the chaste saint Dorothea and her terrible sufferings. It is called a "comedy" because of its happy ending, theologically speaking. The morality play is entitled *Paris' Dom* ("Paris's Judgment"), which draws upon the classical myth about Paris as judge in the contest among three Greek goddesses. The farcical play *Den utro Hustru* ("The Unfaithful Wife") is a witty and coarse burlesque on a theme from Boccaccio's *Decameron*; it was performed at Shrovetide. The three last-mentioned plays are written in *knittel, i.e.*, a four-beat rhythm with free use of varying numbers of weak syllables. They are preserved in a MS (DkB Thott 780 fol.) from Odense, about 1531; the burlesque, however, is definitely older than that.

A late printed text, dating from Århus (1637), is the Danish burlesque *Doktor Hjælpeløs* ("Doctor Helpless"), based on a farce from the 16th century and still found on "the farmer's bookshelf" in 1706. It is about a quack doctor healing a farmer's wife of her shrewishness; the last words are in Latin: *finis materiae, non malitiae* ("here the story ends, but not the problem").

The Danish *Dødedans* ("Dance of the Dead"), preserved in a printed edition from Copenhagen (1555), with wood engravings of the *dramatis personae*, doubtless was meant for performance, although none is known. The text is a dramatized Lutheran sermon with satirical undertones. The scenography probably was intended to be simultaneous; there are many examples of direct address to the public.

Scandinavian drama after the Reformation (in Denmark and Norway 1536, in Sweden 1527) is influenced by the Humanistic-Protestant secular drama in central and northern Europe (Austria, Switzerland, Germany, the Netherlands, and Scotland). Written in Latin and very soon in the national languages, this didactic drama was performed in close connection with grammar schools and universities; actors were students and their teachers. It was based on the model of the Roman comedy writers Plautus and Terence. The performances show, however, a dramatic and scenographical blending of new and old elements: devils, angels, and buffoons play an important role; burlesque and Protestant teaching are mixed; and simultaneous and successive scenography are both employed.

This "school theater" was very popular; it was played in the marketplace and the churchyard as well as in the town hall, and in Denmark at the court. From the middle of the 16th century, all the larger grammar schools in Denmark had performances, in Copenhagen, Odense, Ribe, Viborg, Randers, Ringsted, and Helsingør (Elsinore). It is, however, characteristic of the drama from the last decades of the 16th century, the secular comedy, that the audience is no longer a congregation taking part in the action, but a much more mixed group of citizens being entertained, more or less passively, by the play. The old anonymous drama is replaced by texts written by individual authors whose names are known, and who have left their personal stamp on the works.

The two most competent Danish dramatists of the period were Hieronymus Justesen Ranch (1539–1607) and Peder Jensen Hegelund (1542–1614). Both of them were clergymen, Ranch a vicar in Viborg, Hegelund bishop in Ribe, at the time a center of trade and culture, as well as witch burning. The known works by Ranch include *Kong Salomons Hylding* ("Homage to King Solomon"), performed in Copenhagen, 1585, and *Samsons Fængsel* ("Samson's Prison"), performed in 1599 and printed in Århus in 1633. Its original source was the Randers MS from 1599. It is a biblical drama with songs, a sort of early musical. A third work is *Karrig Niding* ("Avaricious Bastard"), a very well made original comedy in the manner of Plautus, probably printed in Århus in 1633. The edition is lost, but was used in preparing the 1664 edition. A Tobiae comedy may also be by Ranch.

Hegelund was very active as an organizer and leader of school theater. His own contribution as a dramatist is *Susanna*, performed in Ribe in 1576, and printed in Copenhagen in 1579. This "comicotragoedia" is a very complicated composition; the dialogue has the usual doggerel meter, supplied with many learned quotations and other marginal notes. The most original part is a long monologue by Calumnia, the *Fama Malum* from Vergil, the demon of slander. This personification of the wickedness in this world is depicted with shocking brutality.

Other Danish dramatists and theatrical practitioners from the last part of the 16th century include Søren Kjær, Peder Thøgersen, Hans Christensen Stehn, and Anders Tybo.

The Protestant-Humanistic drama and theater became, under the influence of Melanchthon, an educational instrument of the learned élite to advance civilization, answering to a new social and economic reality. But devils, angels, and buffoons, the heritage of the Middle Ages, continued to speak behind the didactic message. The burlesque-comical elements, jeering, devilish torture scenes, luxurious banquets, music, and the dance, made this theater extremely popular among all classes of people.

Rigid dogmatism triumphed, however, and from the beginning of the 17th century, the theatrical interest of the governing class shifted to opera, ballet, and foreign (English, German, and French) theater groups. Not until the middle of the 18th century, the time of the Norwegian-Danish Ludvig Holberg, did a revival of original Scandinavian drama take place.

Lit.: Rydqvist, J. E. "Oldest Nordic Play." *Skandia* 7 (1863), 167 [in Swedish]; Chambers, E. K. *The Mediaeval Stage*. 2 vols. London: Oxford University Press, 1903; rpt. 1963; Mantzius, Karl. *A History of Theatrical Art in Ancient and Modern Times*. 6 vols. Trans. Louis von Cossell. London: Duckworth, 1903–21 [in Danish 1897–1916]; Jacobsen, Jacob Peter. *Heros og helgen*. Copenhagen: Gyldendal, 1913; Nicoll, Allardyce. *The Development of the Theatre*. London: Harrap, 1927; 5th rev. ed. New York: Harcourt, Brace & World, 1968; Cohen, Gustave. *Le théâtre en France au moyen âge*. 2 vols. Paris: Rieder, 1928–31; Young, Karl. *The Drama of the Mediaeval Church*. 2 vols. Oxford: Clarendon, 1933; Krogh, Torben. *Ældre dansk teater*. Copenhagen: Munksgaard, 1940 [esp. for scenography]; Stender-Petersen, Ad. *Det Jyske Protestantisk-Humanistiske Skoledrama*. Århus: Humanister i Jylland, 1959; Kinderman, Heinz. *Theatregeschichte Europas 2*. Salzburg: Müller, 1959; Hale, J. R. *Renaissance Europe, Individual and Society, 1480–1520*. London: Fontana, 1971; rpt. Berkeley: University of California Press, 1977; Burke, Peter. *Popular Culture in Early Modern Europe*. London: Temple Smith, 1978; Murray, Alexander. *Reason and Society in the Middle Ages*. Oxford: Clarendon, 1978; Heller, Agnes. *Renaissance Man*. Trans. Richard E. Allen. London and Boston: Routledge & Kegan Paul, 1978; rpt. New York: Schocken, 1981; Hind, Tage. "Den humanistiske teaterbevægelse." In *Dansk Litteraturhistorie* 2. Copenhagen: Gyldendal, 1984, pp. 322–39; Risum, Janne. "Dødedansen." In *Dansk Litteraturhistorie 2*, pp. 126–31 [with original German woodcuts]; Kaspersen, Søren. "Bildende Kunst, Theater und Volkstümlichkeit im Mittelalterlichen Dänemark." In Andersen, Flemming G., *et al. Popular Drama in Northern Europe in the Later Middle Ages*. Odense: Odense University Press, 1988, pp. 201–50.

Tage Hind

[**See also:** *Knittel(vers)*]

Draugr *see* Supernatural Beings

Drauma-Jóns saga

Drauma-Jóns saga ("The Saga of Dream-Jón") is a very short Icelandic *riddarasaga* composed in Iceland, probably at the beginning of the 14th century. The hero, a young man named Jón, can interpret dreams and guess other people's dreams. Earl Heinrekr of Saxland is jealous of him, and thinks to obtain Jón's talent by eating his heart. But Heinrekr's wife, Ingibjǫrg, who has consented to murder Jón in his sleep, deceives her husband and helps Jón at the last moment by substituting a dog's heart and burying a wax image of Jón. The emperor of Saxland comes to Heinrekr with a dream, which Heinrekr admits he cannot interpret. He discovers from Ingibjǫrg that Jón is not dead. Jón is then brought before the emperor and tells him his story. He also interprets the dream, which signifies the queen's adultery with "the Flemish man." The two lovers are put on a ship, never to return, and Heinrekr is exiled from the country. The saga ends with the marriage of Ingibǫrg and Jón, who receives the earldom.

The tale must have been very popular in Iceland. In addition to five vellum MSS, the saga is presented in about forty-five paper MSS. Two *rímur* that were inspired by the saga date respectively from the 17th and 18th centuries.

The opinion of scholars has long been that Jón's story had an oriental origin, even though the role of dreams in the *Íslendingasǫgur* and many heroic eddic poems casts some doubt on this view. Davíð Erlingsson (1979) concludes that the composition of the saga is not the work of an Icelandic author, but that the story is foreign and a widely known folktale; the Icelandic author turned the saga into the style of an exemplum. It gives us,

accordingly, an interesting example of the way the sagamen could use popular as well as learned sources to create their works.

Ed.: Bjarni Vilhjálmsson, ed. *Riddarasögur*. 6 vols. Reykjavik: Íslendingasagnaútgáfan; Haukadalsútgáfan, 1949–54, vol. 6, pp. 147–70; Page, R. I., ed. "Drauma-Jóns saga." *Nottingham Medieval Studies* 1 (1957), 22–56. **Lit.**: Schlauch, Margaret. "'The Drauma-Jóns saga' and Its Sources." *Modern Language Review* 29 (1934), 421–33; Davíð Erlingsson. "Ætterni Drauma-Jóns sǫgu." *Opuscula* 7. Bibliotheca Arnamagnæana, 34. Copenhagn: Reitzel, 1979, pp. 172–218; Jorgensen, Peter A. "Drauma-Jóns saga." *Dictionary of the Middle Ages*. Ed. Joseph R. Strayer. New York: Scribner, 1982–89, vol. 4, pp. 289–90.

Régis Boyer

[**See also:** Exempla; *Riddarasögur*]

Draumkvæde

Draumkvæde ("Dream Poem") is the most common title of the best known of the Norwegian legendary ballads, being a description of an ecstatic otherworld journey recorded in many variants in Telemark from the 1840s onward, but most probably stemming from the high or late Middle Ages.

The more than 100 extant versions differ markedly in extent, sequence, and completeness of motifs. But one may follow Moe's reconstruction of what was probably the ballad's original structure: a certain Olav Åsteson went into a trance lasting from Christmas Eve to Epiphany, during which his soul came "up to the clouds above and down to the dark, blue sea" and saw "the flames of hell and of heaven likewise a part." He had to travel the difficult and painful route awaiting the souls of the deceased, "through briar and thorn," crossing "Gjallarbrú ['bridge'] . . . with sharp hooks in a row," wading "the miry marsh" until he reached "the shining paradise" without being allowed to enter into it. There follows a vision of the Preliminary Judgment: the devilish host from the north and the angelic host from the south under St. Michael meet in front of the Virgin's church to contend for the souls of the dead. Manifold are the retributions for evil deeds: the cope of lead, burning clay, the fiery pit, toads and serpents, which only the charitable need not fear.

Most features of *Draumkvæde* are found in the numerous Latin accounts of otherworld visions circulating during the Middle Ages, derived ultimately from the eschatology of the apocryphal apocalypses so popular in Judaism and Christianity especially between 200 B.C. and A.D. 200. But there are also some elements that reflect pre-Christian Germanic conceptions. The name Gjallarbrú and its golden decking are taken from Scandinavian mythology, but its function, *i.e.*, the punishment of sinners, comes from Christian visions, such as Tundale's vision (1149), or Thurkill's vision (1206), the one most comparable to *Draumkvæde*.

Draumkvæde's main content accords well with the more popular teachings of the medieval Catholic Church: there are allusions to the beatitudes of Christ, to St. Michael, to the Last Judgment, and so on, even if a special poetic touch often makes *Draumkvæde* stand out against the majority of that genre.

Comparison of the motifs and the structure of *Draumkvæde* with the corpus of medieval visionary literature suggests that the work was probably based on a lost account describing an ecstatic experience of an otherwise unknown nobleman, Olav Åsteson (or something similar), who may have lived in Norway sometime in the 13th to 15th centuries. Given that many of the medieval Latin prose visions were versified by clerics who used these texts for religious-didactic purposes, Olav's revelation may have received the same treatment. The vision would then have found its way into the repertory of the singers of folktales, as must have been the case with the other religious ballads. *Draumkvæde* presumably underwent the changes, amplifications, and shortenings usual in any oral tradition.

Ed.: Barnes, Michael, ed. *Draumkvæde: An Edition and Study.* Studia Norvegica, 16. Oslo, Bergen, and Tromsø: Universitetsforlaget, 1974 [with glossary]; Schmidt, Paul Gerhard, ed. *Visio Thurkilli.* Bibliotheca Scriptorum Graecorum et Romanorum Teubneriana. Leipzig: Teubner, 1978; Blom, Ådel G., *et al.*, eds. *Norske mellomalderballader* 1. Instituttet for sammenligende kulturforskning, Serie B, 66. Oslo: Universitetsforlaget, 1982 [full bibliography]; Cahill, Peter, ed. *Duggals leiðsla.* Reykjavik: Stofnun Árna Magnússonar, 1983. **Lit.**: Bugge, Sophus. "Mythologiske Oplysninger til Draumekvædi." *Norsk Tidsskrift for Videnskab og Litteratur* 7 (1854–55), 102–21, 192; Bø, Olav, and O. M. Sandvik. "Draumkvædet." *KLNM* 3 (1958), 303–5; Moe, Moltke. "Middelalderens visionsdigtning." In *Moltke Moes samlede skrifter.* 3 vols. Ed. Knut Liestøl. Institutet for sammenlignende kulturforskning, ser. B, 1, 6, 9. Oslo: Aschehoug, 1925–27, vol. 3, pp. 199–247 [English summary, pp. 385–8]; Liestøl, Knut. *Draumkvæde: A Norwegian Visionary Poem from the Middle Ages.* Studia Norvegica, 3. Oslo: Aschehoug, 1946 [with translation]; Liestøl, Knut. "Draumkvædet." *Syn og Segn* 54 (1948), 49–65; Midbøe, Hans. *Draumkvædet. En studie i norsk middelalder.* Oslo: Gyldendal, 1949; Barnes, Michael. "Draumkvæde—How Old Is It?" *Scandinavica* 11 (1972), 85–105; Bø, Olav. "Draumkvedet—Kentnisse und Vermutungen." *Norveg* 17 (1975), 155–72; Strömbäck, Dag. "Resan till den andra världen. Kring medeltidsvisionerna och Draumkvædet." *Saga och Sed* (1976), 15–29; Dinzelbacher, Peter. "Zur Entstehung von Draumkvæde." *Skandinavistik* 10 (1980), 89–96; Blom, Adel G. "Fra restitusjon til kildekritikk: En forskningshistorisk oversikt." *Tradisjon* 14 (1984), 91–102.

Peter Dinzelbacher

[**See also**: Ballads; *Visio Tnugdali*; Visionary Literature]

Droplaugarsona saga

Droplaugarsona saga ("The Saga of the Sons of Droplaug") is considered among the oldest *Íslendingasögur*, because of its primitive style and heroic materials, and its reference to a certain Þorvaldr, "er sagði sögu þessa" ("who told this story"). Unfortunately, the genealogy linking Þorvaldr with the characters appearing in the saga is corrupt, possibly omitting one or more generations; nor is it clear whether the narrative referred to is the saga in its entirety, or an oral or written source. Nevertheless, the saga's composition early in the 13th century is likely in view of the other sagas influenced by it: *Vápnfirðinga saga, Laxdæla saga, Ljósvetninga saga,* and, most notably, *Gísla saga,* which probably derives its account of Gísli's night killing of Þorgrímr Þorsteinsson from that of Helgi Ásbjarnarson by Grímr Droplaugarson.

After a preamble relating the marriage of Ketill Þrymr ("din") to an enslaved Hebridean noblewoman encountered abroad, the saga narrates the feud between Ketill's great-grandsons, the sons of Droplaug, and the chieftain Helgi Ásbjarnarson, a powerful litigant, but slow to take physical action. Exiled as a result of a lawsuit prosecuted by his namesake, Helgi Droplaugarson is ambushed and killed after a defense against heavy odds at Eyvindardalr. The battle is foreshadowed by prophetic dreams, and abounds in heroic devices and stoical rejoinders. It is balanced in the saga's structure by the revenge taken by Grímr Droplaugarson, who, apparently fatally wounded, is nursed back to health and awaits his opportunity. From an underground retreat near Helgi's home,

he attacks by night and, with his dead brother's sword, kills Helgi as he lies in bed with his wife. Grímr spends some time as an outlaw in Iceland before escaping to Norway, where he dies after killing a malevolent Viking in a duel.

Among the saga's sources were probably oral tales concerning historical persons and places in the east of Iceland at the end of the 10th century. Jón Jóhannesson (1950) considers Þorvaldr's narrative a short *ævi* ("life") of the sons of Droplaug, which formed the source of all or some of the main events of the saga. Three stanzas of Haukr Valdísarson's *Íslendingadrápa*, referring to the deaths of the two Helgis, must be based on traditions predating the saga. Folktale elements are discernible in the introductory story of Ketill and Arneiðr. The saga includes six *lausavísur* ("verses"), one spoken by Helgi Ásbjarnarson and five by Grímr. All but verse 3 are inappropriate to their contexts and thus unlikely to have been composed by the saga author; nor is it plausible that they originated with those to whom they are attributed. Verses 4 and 5 are believed to be interpolated (Jón Jóhannesson 1950: lxxi), and 4 and 6 show signs of 12th-century origin (de Vries 1967: 433).

The only complete text of the saga, in *Möðruvallabók*, is believed by Jón Jóhannesson to be an abridgment, with some omissions, of the original saga. The fragment AM 162c fol. preserves a longer, older, and stylistically simpler version of part of chs. 3 and 4, which, he argues, is closer to the original text.

Ed.: Kålund, K. "Droplaugarsona saga i den ved brudstykket AM 162, fol. repræsenterede bearbejdelse." *Arkiv för nordisk filologi* 3 (1886), 159–76; Jón Jóhannesson, ed. *Austfirðinga sǫgur.* Íslenzk fornrit, 3. Reykjavik: Hið íslenzka fornritafélag, 1950 [text, pp. 137–80; introduction, pp. 58–82]. **Tr.**: Gudbrand Vigfusson and F. York Powell, eds. and trans. *Origines Islandicae: A Collection of the More Important Sagas and Other Native Writings Relating to the Settlement and Early History of Iceland.* 2 vols. Oxford: Clarendon, 1905; rpt. Millwood: Kraus, 1976, vol. 2, pp. 533–61 [translation of chs. 9–14, under the name *Helganna saga*]; Schlauch, Margaret, and M. H. Scargill, trans. *Three Icelandic Sagas.* Princeton: Princeton University Press; Oxford: Oxford University Press, 1950, pp. 102–35; Haworth, Eleanor, and Jean Young, trans. *The Fljotsdale Saga and The Droplaugarsons.* Everyman's Library. London: Dent, 1990. **Bib.**: Halldór Hermannsson. *Bibliography of the Icelandic Sagas and Minor Tales.* Islandica, 1. Ithaca: Cornell University Library, 1909, pp. 8–9; Halldór Hermannsson. *The Sagas of Icelanders (Íslendinga sögur): A Supplement to Bibliography of the Icelandic Sagas and Minor Tales.* Islandica, 24. Ithaca: Cornell University Press, 1935, pp. 17–8. **Lit.**: Gordon, I. L. "The Murder of Þorgrímr in Gíslasaga Súrsonar." *Medium Ævum* 3 (1934), 79–94; Vries, Jan de. *Altnordische Literaturgeschichte.* 2 vols. Grundriss der Germanischen Philologie, 15–6. Berlin: de Gruyter, 1941–42; rpt. 1964–67, vol. 2, pp. 432–5; Heller, Rolf. "Droplaugarsona saga — Vápnfirðinga saga—Laxdæla saga." *Arkiv för nordisk filologi* 78 (1963), 140–69; Taylor, Arnold. "The Fight in Eyvindardalr." In *Specvlvm Norroenvm: Norse Studies in Memory of Gabriel Turville-Petre.* Ed. Ursula Dronke *et al.* Odense: Odense University Press, 1981, pp. 459–73; Perkins, Richard. "Droplaugarsona saga." In *Reallexikon der Germanischen Altertumskunde.* 2nd ed. Ed. Heinrich Beck *et al.* Berlin and New York: de Gruyter, 1985, vol. 6, parts 1–2, pp. 191–4.

Alison Finlay

[**See also**: *Brandkrossa þáttr; Fljótsdæla saga; Gísla saga Súrssonar; Íslendingadrápa; Íslendingasögur; Lausavísur; Laxdæla saga; Ljósvetninga saga; Möðruvallabók; Vápnfirðinga saga*]

Dudo of St.-Quentin: De moribus et actis primorum normanniæ ducum
("Concerning the Deaths and Deeds of the First Norman Dukes"). Dudo, born around 960, probably died before 1043. A monk from Vermandois, he was not a Norman, but a frequent visitor to the Norman court after 986 and a recipient of benefices from the dukes before 1015. Richard I (d. 996) commissioned him in 994 to write a history of the rulers of Normandy, and he was encouraged to continue by Richard II and his half-brother Rodulf, "hujus operis relator" ("the relator of this work"). He probably completed the first redaction by 1015 and an extended version before 1030.

Of fourteen surviving MSS, ten are 11th- and 12th-century, two are known to be lost, and not all are complete. Dudo's *De moribus et actis* was reproduced in abridged form by William of Jumièges, and much of its information recurs in other late histories. *De moribus et actis* was edited in 1619 by Duchesne, who gave it its title and divided it into a Prologue and three books, using two MSS. Lair's edition (1865) has a Prologue and four books, retaining Duchesne's title, collating seven MSS. The Prologue is dedicated to Archbishop Adalbero of Laon, and tells of the inception of *De moribus et actis*. Book 1 gives an account of the mythical, Trojan ancestry of the *Daci* (Danes), a description of their homeland and customs, and the exploits of a band of Danes marauding in Europe from about 850. Books 2–4 describe the expulsion of Rollo and his followers from *Dacia* (Denmark), their wandering in England and Flanders, arrival in what later became Normandy (876: Dudo's date), and subsequent events until the death of Richard I.

De moribus et actis is a panegyric and blatant political propaganda, which clearly attempts to establish Rollo's descendants as a legitimate dynasty and Normandy as a political and cultural entity. It is written in prolix Latin prose interspersed with fulsome verse apostrophes, contains many errors of fact and much information not supported by other evidence, and is difficult to use as a source. It has been much criticized and frequently dismissed as worthless. *De moribus et actis* is, however, the only surviving, consistent, inside source for early Norman history, and much of it appears based on eyewitness accounts and Norman family tradition. It may also contain information on 9th-century Viking activity in England and Europe; the nature and extent of the Scandinavian settlement in Normandy; the survival of Scandinavian language, customs, and institutions; the origin of the settlers and of Rollo (= Gǫngu-Hrólfr?); and Scandinavian laws, land tenure, warfare, marriage customs, and religion.

Ed.: Lair, Jules, ed. *Dudonis Sancti Quintini De moribus et actis primorum Normanniae ducum*. Mémoires de la Société des Antiquaires de Normandie, 23. Paris: Maisonneuve, 1865; Caen: Le Blanc-Hardel, 1865. **Tr.**: Albrectsen, Erling, ed. and trans. *Dudo. Normandiets historie under de første hertuger*. Odense: Odense Universitetsforlag, 1979 [Danish translation and commentary]. **Lit.**: Davis, R. H. C. *The Normans and Their Myth*. London: Thames and Hudson, 1976; Loud, G. A. "The *Gens Normannorum*—Myth or Reality?" In *Proceedings of the Battle Conference on Anglo-Norman Studies IV. 1981*. Ed. R. Allen Brown. Woodbridge: Boydell; Totowa: Biblio, 1982, pp. 104–16; Bates, David. *Normandy Before 1066*. London and New York: Longman, 1982; Williams, Kirsten. Review of Erling Albrectsen, trans. "*Dudo. Normandiets historie under de første hertuger*." *Saga-Book of the Viking Society* 21 (1982–83), 119–22; McKitterick, Rosamond. *The Frankish Kingdoms Under the Carolingians 751–987*. London and New York: Longman, 1983, pp. 228–57; Houts, Elizabeth M. C. van. "Scandinavian Influence in Norman Literature of the Eleventh Century." In *Anglo-Norman Studies VI: Proceedings of the Battle Conference 1983*. Ed. R. Allen Brown. Woodbridge: Boydell & Brewer; Wolfeboro: Longwood, 1984, pp. 122–35; Huisman, Gerda C. "Notes on the Manuscript Tradition of Dudo of St. Quentin's *Gesta Normannorum*." In *Anglo-Norman Studies VI*, pp. 107–21; Searle, Eleanor. "Fact and Pattern in Heroic History: Dudo of Saint Quentin" *Viator* 15 (1984), 119–37; Brown, R. Allen. *The Normans and the Norman Conquest*. 2nd ed. Woodbridge: Boydell & Brewer; Wolfeboro: Longwood, 1985; Searle, Eleanor. "Frankish Rivalries and Norse Warriors." In *Anglo-Norman Studies VIII: Proceedings of the Battle Conference 1985*. Ed. R. Allen Brown. Woodbridge: Boydell & Brewer; Wolfeboro: Longwood, 1986, pp. 198–213.

Kirsten Williams

[**See also**: William of Jumièges: *Gesta Normannorum ducum*]

Duggals leiðsla *see* Visio Tnugdali

Dunstanus saga
("The Saga of Dunstan") tells of St. Dunstan (*ca.* 909–988), Archbishop of Canterbury (feast day May 19). The saga was compiled by the monk Árni Laurentíusson (b. 1304), a son of Laurentíus Kálfsson (bishop of Hólar 1323–1330). Árni entered the monastery of Þingeyrar in about 1317, and was ordained a priest in 1323.

The saga is preserved in a single MS, AM 180b fol., from the 15th century. It was written on fols. 1r–5v; fols. 2 and 3 are damaged, and some of the text has been lost. A paper copy (NkS 267 fol.) was made from this MS in the 18th century by Guðmundur Ísfold. The saga begins with a prologue in the form of a letter in which Árni Laurentíusson identifies himself as the compiler, and gives reasons for composing a life of St. Dunstan. St. Dunstan's life is exemplified by a number of lections retelling some of his visions and miracles: his vision of his mother and father in heaven and his meeting with an angel who teaches him an antiphon; the miracle at Candelmas before Dunstan's birth when all the candles in the church are extinguished, but Dunstan's mother's candle is rekindled by a divine light; Dunstan's encounter with devils in the guise of dogs; his unorthodox entry into the monastery at Glastonbury via the scaffolding and roof; his vision of the apostles Peter, Paul, and Andrew, after he refuses a bishopric; the presence of the Holy Spirit in the likeness of a dove hovering over Dunstan; the death of Dunstan; and the miracle of the healing of a monk who was possessed by a devil.

Árni compiled and translated *Dunstanus saga* from a number of different Latin sources. The main source is a life of St. Dunstan written between 1006 and 1012 by Adelard, a monk of St. Peter's monastery in Ghent. Árni also used a life of Dunstan by Eadmer of Canterbury, written in the 12th century. Árni probably knew Eadmer's life, and also excerpts from Osbern of Canterbury's *Vita et miracula Sancti Dunstani* (written *ca.* 1080), via Vincent of Beauvais's *Speculum historiale*. For his reference to King Edgar, Árni uses the *Passio Sancti Eadwardi*. He probably also made use of Isidore of Seville's *Etymologiarum* for his account of the six ages of man. His digression on Thomas à Becket may have *Thomas saga erkibiskups* as its source. Árni may have known *Nikulás saga erkibiskups* and *Jóns saga helga* by the monk Gunnlaugr Leifsson of Þingeyrar.

Ed.: Gudbrand Vigfusson and George W. Dasent, eds. and trans. *Icelandic Sagas and Other Historical Documents Relating to the Settlements and Descents of the Northmen on the British Isles.* 4 vols. Rolls Series, 88. London: Eyre and Spottiswoode, 1887–94; rpt. Millwood: Kraus, 1964, vol. 2, pp. 385–408; Fell, Christine Elizabeth, ed. *Dunstanus saga.* Editiones Arnamagnæanæ, ser. B, vol. 5. Copenhagen: Munksgaard, 1963. **Bib.**: Widding, Ole, *et al.* "The Lives of the Saints in Old Norse Prose: A Handlist." *Mediaeval Studies* 25 (1963), 294–337. **Tr.**: Gudbrand Vigfusson, ed., and George W. Dasent, trans. *Icelandic Sagas and Other Historical Documents,* vol. 4, pp. 397–420. **Lit.**: Stubbs, William. *Memorials of St. Dunstan, Archbishop of Canterbury.* Rolls Series, 63. London: Longman, 1874; Bekker-Nielsen, Hans. "Duen uden galde. Et forslag til en tekstrettelse i Dunstanus saga." *Opuscula* 1. Bibliotheca Arnamagnæana, 20. Copenhagen: Reitzel, 1960, pp. 339–40; Harty, Lenore. "The Icelandic Life of St. Dunstan." *Saga-Book of the Viking Society* 15 (1961), 263–93; Hallberg, Peter. "Some Observations on the Language of *Dunstanus saga,* with an Appendix on the Bible Compilation *Stjórn.*" *Saga-Book of the Viking Society* 18 (1973), 324–53; O'Hare, Colman. "Dunstanus Saga: England and the Old Norse Church." *American Benedictine Review* 33 (1982), 394–422.

Helen Carron

[**See also:** *Jóns saga ens helga*; *Laurentius saga biskups*; Saints' Lives]

Dwarfs *see* Supernatural Beings

Dyrerim, De gamle danske ("The Old Danish Rhyming Bestiary") is a modern editor's name for an unnamed text in the Stockholm MS K 46 4to (pp. 45–114). The scribe was either the Næstved Franciscan Olauus Jacobi, who wrote the Stockholm MS K 31 4to (of *Mandevilles Rejse*) in 1459, or a contemporary from the same scriptorium. Because of a number of apparent misreadings, it must be a copy, but is probably not much younger than the original. The dialect has been identified as primarily that of South Zealand.

The *Dyrerim* are written in *knittelvers* without stanza division, but with a variable use of end-rhyme, which occasionally gives the impression of a stanza structure. The work begins with a prologue in the form of a dialogue about celibacy between a young girl, who disapproves of it, and a youth, the author of the book, who approves of it. Next follow 100 poems, which are all supplied with a bird or animal name as their title. Some poems have a concluding Latin prose commentary, which gives natural-historical information about the bird or animal of the title. According to the prologue, the aim of the poems is to describe the difficulties of bird life in order to contradict the girl's assertion that birds have an easier life than human beings, with their constant conflicts between soul and body. In accordance with this frame, the first poems are monologues, in which each bird describes the adversities of its species. Soon four-legged animals are also called upon to speak, and gradually the poems dissolve into independent, moralizing, or satirical short stanzas with social or sexual success or fiasco as their preferred themes. Some of the short stanzas are reminiscent of prophecies, which form part of actual books of prophecies (*e.g.,* the Danish *Lycke bogen,* printed in the 16th century).

No direct foreign model has been demonstrated for the text as a whole, but it is most nearly related to the German "Vogelparlamente" ("parliaments of fowls," *i.e.,* poems that describe a deliberation among birds). The Latin quotations are derived from two scientific compilations from the 13th century with roots in antiquity: Albertus Magnus's *Opus de animalibus* and Bartholomaeus Anglicus's *De proprietatibus rerum.* The uniformity of the poems, their use of native proverbs and popular beliefs, along with their popular, straightforward, and idiomatic language, suggest that the *Dyrerim* is an independent Danish work.

Ed.: Brøndum-Nielsen, Johs., ed. *De gamle danske Dyrerim.* Copenhagen: Thiele, 1908–09. **Lit.**: Bom, Kaj. "Dyrerim, De gamle danske." *KLNM* 3 (1958), 411–3.

Britta Olrik Frederiksen

[**See also:** *Knittel(vers)*; *Mandevilles Rejse*]

Dødedans *see* Drama

Ectors saga ok kappa hans ("The Saga of Ector and His Champions") is a native Icelandic *riddarasaga* dating from the late 14th or early 15th century. It is preserved in forty-five MSS, the most important of which are the fragmentary Cod. Stock. Perg. fol. no. 7 (15th century) and AM 152 fol. (*ca.* 1510), where the saga is preserved in its entirety.

After a brief summary of the events of the Trojan War, the saga relates how King Karnotius of Thecisia marries Gelfriðr, daughter of the king of India. Their son is named Ector, after the Trojan hero. He is educated in the liberal arts and dubbed a knight at age seventeen. At a tournament, Ector defeats six princes, who afterward offer him their service. They live together in a castle his father had built for him.

The seven knights decide to go off in search of adventure, agreeing to reunite after a year. Their seven adventures are then related in turn. Vernacius, for example, is defeated by the giant Nocerus and imprisoned. The princess Almaris, also a prisoner, gives him a sword with which he kills the giant. They are betrothed and Vernacius returns to Ector's castle. Of the other knights (Florencius, Fenacius, Alanus, Trancival, Ector, and Aprival), only Aprival is unable to return at the appointed time.

Aprival has been told of the great king Troilus and his beautiful daughter Trobil. Disguised as the merchant Valentínus, Aprival offends Troilus by praising Ector above all others. He agrees to meet Troilus's knights in a tournament, defeating all but the last. He is cast into prison, but is aided by Trobil and remains with her.

Reunited, the other heroes learn the whereabouts of the missing Aprival and decide to rescue him. Huge armies are assembled on both sides. Trobil and Aprival watch the spectacle. Ector's forces prevail. At Trobil's request, Ector agrees to release the prisoners, including her brother Eneas. In exchange, Trobil agrees to marry Ector. They all return to Ector's kingdom, and it is decided that Aprival will marry the princess Valdre, who had been rescued by Ector.

The saga concludes with the information that the author found his material in the *Trójumanna saga* and in the story of Ector as told by master Galterus de Castellione and gives the date of the great battle as July 1, 378 B.C.

This saga, with its seven tales of adventure, represents the sole Icelandic expression of the medieval frame narrative and, as such, invites comparison with such works as the *Seven Sages*, a medieval bestseller that may have been known in Iceland in the 14th century, but exists only in post-Reformation translations in German or Danish chapbooks. One is struck in *Ectors saga*, as in *roman à tirois* in general, by the structural similarity of the episodes. In *Ectors saga*, this basic structure is that of the most common type of folktale: the hero sets out, and either alone or with a helper defeats an opponent who is menacing a kingdom, and as a reward is granted the hand of a princess, returning finally to his point of departure (*cf.* Glauser 1983: 149ff.). Unity is achieved in the saga through the frame, but also through the device of interlacing, such as when the hero of the sixth adventure gets the bride of the seventh and vice versa.

The material used by the author of *Ectors saga* appears to originate from an unusually eclectic variety of sources, among them *Alexanders saga*, *Trójumanna saga*, and *Karlamagnús saga*. The lion and several other motifs derive apparently from Chrétien de Troyes's *Yvain*, which was widely known in Iceland, and possibly also *Le Chevalier de la charrette*, which appears not to have been (*cf.*, *e.g.*, Schlauch 1965).

Ed.: Loth, Agnete, ed. "Ectors saga." In *Late Medieval Icelandic Romances*. 5 vols. Editiones Arnamagnæanæ, ser. B, vols. 20–4. Copenhagen: Munksgaard, 1962–65, vol. 1, pp. 79–186. **Tr.**: Dodsworth, J. B., trans. In *Late Medieval Icelandic Romances*, vol. 1, pp. 81–186 [English paraphrase]. **Bib.**: Kalinke, Marianne E., and P. M. Mitchell. *Bibliography of Old Norse–Icelandic Romances*. Islandica, 44. Ithaca and London: Cornell University Press, 1985, pp. 51–2. **Lit.**: Björn K. Þórólfsson. *Rímur fyrir 1600*. Safn Fræðafjelagsins um Ísland og Íslendinga, 9. Copenhagen: Møller, 1934; Schlauch, Margaret. *Romance in Iceland*. Princeton: Princeton University Press; New York: American-Scandinavian Foundation; London: Allen & Unwin, 1934; rpt. New York: Russell & Russell, 1973; Schlauch, Margaret. "Arthurian Material in Some Late Icelandic Sagas." *Bulletin bibliographique de la Société internationale Arthurienne* 17 (1965), 87–91; Harris, Richard L. "The Lion-Knight Legend in Iceland and the Valþjófsstaðir Door." *Viator* 1 (1970), 125–45; Glauser, Jürg. *Isländische Märchensagas: Studien zur Prosaliteratur im spätmittelalterlichen Island*. Beiträge zur nordischen Philologie, 12. Basel and Frankfurt am Main: Helbing & Lichtenhahn, 1983; Kalinke, Marianne. "Norse Romance (*Riddarasögur*)." In *Old Norse–Icelandic Literature: A Critical Guide*.

Ed. Carol J. Clover and John Lindow. Islandica, 45. Ithaca and London: Cornell University Press, 1985, pp. 316–63.

M. J. Driscoll

[See also: *Alexanders saga*; *Karlamagnús saga*; *Riddarasögur*; *Trójumanna saga*]

Eddic Meters. The poetic forms of the *Codex Regius* are derived from common Germanic meter, which employs pairs of "verses" or "half-lines" joined into "long lines" by alliteration. The following four lines of *Þrymskviða* illustrate the essential features of this ancient metrical tradition, which was also inherited by Old English, Old Saxon, and Old High German poets:

> senn vóro Hafrar Heim um recnir,
> SCyndir at SCoclom, SCyldo vel renna;
> Biorg Brotnoðo, Brann iorð loga,
> Óc Óðins sonr í Iotunheima.
> [Neckel and Kuhn 1983: 114]
> [At once the goats were driven home, hurried into harness—they would have to run well—Mountains shattered, earth burned, Óðinn's son drove to the giants' land.]

The gap in the middle of each line indicates the boundary between half-lines. Alliterating stressed syllables are here indicated by capital letters. The first half-line of each line is called the "a-verse," the second half-line the "b-verse." An a-verse can have either one alliterating syllable (as in the first line above) or two (as in the others). A b-verse always has just one alliterating syllable. The rule for alliterative matching usually requires identity of the first consonant of the root syllable (lines 1, 3); but *sp-*, *st-*, *sc-* (= *sk-*) alliterate only with themselves (line 2). Any stressed syllable with an initial vowel is considered to alliterate with any other stressed syllable with an initial vowel. Note that the Norse *y*-glide spelled with an *i* or *j* in forms like *Iotunheima* (line 4) counts as a vowel for the purposes of alliteration.

Outside Scandinavia, alliterative poetry of the traditional Germanic type survived in a single meter. Three eddic meters are usually recognized, however: *fornyrðislag* or *fornyrðalag* ("old story meter"); *málaháttr* ("speech meter" or "sententious meter"); and *ljóðaháttr* ("song meter" or "stanzaic meter"). Snorri Sturluson used these terms in his *Háttatal*, which gives an example of each form.

The four lines quoted above are in *fornyrðislag*, the Norse meter most closely related to the meter of such West Germanic works as the Old English poem *Beowulf*. Half-lines of *fornyrðislag* usually fit into the familiar system of "five types" proposed by Sievers. Below are simple examples of each type, with a notation for the corresponding verse patterns.

> Type A: iarðar hvergi (/x|/x)
> ["neither on earth," *Þrymskviða* 2:6]
> Type B: oc Angantýr (x|/x\)
> ["and Angantýr," *Hyndluljóð* 9:4]
> Type C: oc qvennváðir (x|/ \x)
> ["woman's clothes," *Þrymskviða* 16:3]
> Type D: øxn alsvartir (/| \x)
> ["oxen all black," *Þrymskviða* 23:3]
> Type E: gullhyrnðar kýr (/ \x|/)
> ["golden-horned kine," *Þrymskviða* 23:2]

Three kinds of metrical position are distinguished in verse patterns: the *primary arsis* (/), usually occupied by a syllable with primary stress; the *secondary arsis* (\), usually occupied by a syllable with secondary stress; and the *weak position* (x), usually occupied by an unstressed syllable. The metrical positions of a given verse pattern are organized into two feet, with the boundary between feet indicated by a vertical bar (|). The treatment of types B and C above follows Pope (1966) and Taylor (1971) rather than Sievers (1893), who analyzes type B as x/|x/ and type C as x/|/x. For recent criticism of Sievers's analysis, see von See (1967: 5) and Russom (1987: 17–9, 141–4). Sievers's system allows for many "subtypes" differing significantly from the simple examples provided here.

Eddic *fornyrðislag* gives a general impression of brevity when compared with West Germanic verse. The Scandinavian material tends toward organization into succinct four-line stanzas, as opposed to the long verse paragraphs of works like *Beowulf*. Poetry in *fornyrðislag* is also relatively concise with respect to the number of syllables in the half-line. If we apply the procedures normally used for interpreting skaldic texts to Snorri's example of *fornyrðislag*, each half-line will fill just four metrical positions, with no "extrametrical" unstressed syllables or "expanded" verse types of the sort frequently encountered in Old English, Old Saxon, and Old High German poetry. Such concision is much less evident in the poems of the *Codex Regius*, however. The aggressive philology of emendation employed by Sievers and others to reconcile eddic texts with the paradigms in *Háttatal* has long since fallen into disrepute (Heusler 1925: 224–5).

Particularly puzzling to metrists are a number of *fornyrðislag* verses that do not fit into the five-types scheme. Verses like *Freyio at qvæn* ("Freya as bride," *Þrymskviða* 8:8) testify to a pattern /xx|/ that is rare in *Beowulf*. One also encounters a significant number of three-syllable verses like *breiddi faðm* (/x|/) ("braided the yarn," *Rígsþula* 16:3). It would be implausible to dismiss these as errors because they are subject to a special stylistic constraint favoring placement of a trochaic word before a monosyllable (Heusler 1925: 178).

In Snorri's *fornyrðislag* stanza, the a-verse always has single alliteration, and the b-verse always begins with an unstressed syllable. This arrangement is common in the *Codex Regius* poems, but it is not carried through with anything like the consistency found in skaldic poems.

Snorri's example of *málaháttr* consists entirely of lines that fill five metrical positions when interpreted according to the skaldic criteria. The only eddic poem employing lines of similar length consistently is *Atlamál*, and considerable emendation is necessary to "restore" a five-position meter in this work. Cautious modern opinion is represented by Turville-Petre (1976). The *Atlamál*-poet, he says, "seems to have been conscious that the number of syllables in his lines must not be less than five" (xiv).

Kuhn's studies of word placement in Germanic verse (1933, 1936, 1939) showed that several peculiarities of *málaháttr* can also be found in *fornyrðislag* based on legends from south of Scandinavia. Kuhn argued that the peculiarities resulted at least in part from translation of imported West Germanic poems into Scandinavian languages, and he consequently favored a distinction based on content rather than on Snorri's terminology. One distinction between *fornyrðislag* and eddic *málaháttr* is generally acknowledged, however. In *fornyrðislag*, the half-line tends to be a subject, predicate, or other subconstituent of a sentence, as in West Germanic verse. In *Atlamál*, on the other hand, the poet shows a strong preference for half-lines consisting of complete clauses, as in the following example (Neckel and Kuhn 1983: 249):

> Glǫð var oc Glaumvor,   er Gunnarr átti.
> ["glad was also Glaumvor, whom Gunnarr had married," *Atlamál* 6:5–6]

This line exemplifies two additional stylistic traits of *Atlamál*: (1) a strong preference for an a-verse with two alliterating syllables; and (2) employment in the b-verse of the pattern x‖/x|/x (type A with anacrusis).

In *ljóðaháttr*, the smallest repeated unit has a three-part rather than a two-part structure. Two alliterating half-lines resembling those of *fornyrðislag* are followed by a "full verse" with no prominent internal boundaries. The full verse normally has its own system of alliteration, which can involve two, three, or even four alliterating syllables. There is a strong tendency in *ljóðaháttr* toward pairing of two three-part structures to form a stanzaic unit expressing a complete thought, as in the following passage from *Hávamál* (Neckel and Kuhn 1983: 29):

> Deyr fé,   Deyia frœndr,
>   deyr Siálfr it Sama;
> Ec veit Einn,   at Aldri deyr:
>   Dómr um Dauðan hvern.
> [Cattle die, kinsmen die, one dies oneself as well; I know of only one thing that never dies: every man's fame.]

Sievers and others noticed a tendency toward regular metrical transformation within the three-part unit. The first half-line usually begins with an alliterating stressed syllable. The second half-line tends to begin with an unstressed syllable (*cf. at Aldri deyr*). The full verse shows a marked tendency toward rising rhythm, typically opening with a weak syllable and closing with a stressed monosyllable or "resolvable" disyllable. In *deyr Siálfr it Sama*, the short stressed syllable and following unstressed syllable of *Sama* are regarded as the "resolved" equivalent of a single long stressed syllable. Note that the weakly stressed verb *deyr*, by a general poetic convention, counts as unstressed when it appears without alliteration at the beginning of the verse. The first half-line of the three-part unit has in general the fewest syllables, while the full verse is generally longest. These features are all carried through consistently in Snorri's example stanza, but in poems like *Hávamál* such features are no more than tendencies.

Ed.: Neckel, Gustav, ed. *Edda: Die Lieder des Codex Regius nebst verwandten Denkmälern. I: Text.* 5th ed. rev. Hans Kuhn. Heidelberg: Winter, 1983. **Bib.**: Harris, Joseph. "Eddic Poetry." In *Old Norse-Icelandic Literature: A Critical Guide.* Ed. Carol Clover and John Lindow. Islandica, 45. Ithaca and London: Cornell University Press, 1985, pp. 68–156. **Lit.**: Sievers, Eduard. *Altgermanische Metrik.* Sammlung kurzer Grammatiken germanische Dialekte, Ergänzungsreihe, 2. Halle: Niemeyer, 1893; Heusler, Andreas. *Deutsche Versgeschichte mit Einschluss des altenglischen und altnordischen Stabreimverses.* 3 vols. Grundriss der germanischen Philologie, 8. Berlin and Leipzig: de Gruyter, 1925–29; rpt. 1956, vol. 1; Kuhn, Hans. "Zur Wortstellung und -betonung im Altgermanischen." *Beiträge zur Geschichte der deutschen Sprache und Literatur* 57 (1933), 1–109; rpt. in Kuhn 1969, pp. 18–103; Kuhn, Hans. "Die Negation des Verbs in der altnordischen Dichtung." *Beiträge zur Geschichte der deutschen Sprache und Literatur* 60 (1936), 431–44; rpt. in Kuhn 1969, pp. 124–34; Kuhn, Hans. "Westgermanisches in der altnordischen Verskunst." *Beiträge zur Geschichte der deutschen Sprache und Literatur* 63 (1939), 178–236; rpt. in Kuhn 1969, pp. 485–527; Lehmann, Winfred P. *The Development of Germanic Verse Form.* Austin: University of Texas Press and Linguistic Society of America, 1956; Pope, John. *The Rhythm of Beowulf: An Interpretation of the Normal and Hypermetric Verse-Forms in Old English Poetry.* 2nd ed. New Haven: Yale University Press, 1966; See, Klaus von. *Germanische Verskunst.* Sammlung Metzler, M 67. Stuttgart: Metzler, 1967; Kuhn, Hans. *Kleine Schriften: Aufsätze und Rezensionen aus den Gebieten der germanischen und nordischen Sprach-, Literatur- und Kulturgeschichte 1.* Ed. Dietrich Hofmann *et al.* Berlin: de Gruyter, 1969; Taylor, Paul B. "The Rhythm of Völuspá." *Neophilologus* 55 (1971), 45–57; Turville-Petre, E. O. G. *Scaldic Poetry.* Oxford: Clarendon, 1976; Russom, Geoffrey. *Old English Meter and Linguistic Theory.* Cambridge: Cambridge University Press, 1987.

Geoffrey Russom

[**See also**: Eddic Poetry; *Snorra Edda*]

Eddic Poetry.

Originally, the name *Edda* was applied only to Snorri Sturluson's treatise on mythology and poetic diction, written during the 1220s. The etymology and meaning of the term are disputed. In 1643, the Icelandic bishop Brynjólfur Sveinsson obtained an old codex with poems about Nordic gods and legendary heroes. He thought this anthology was compiled by his famous countryman Sæmundr fróði ("the learned") Sigfússon (1056–1133), and that the numerous quotations from the same poems in Snorri's *Edda* were extracts from Sæmundr's supposed work. Although this association with Sæmundr is completely unjustified, the name *Edda* (*Sæmundar Edda*) for contents of the newly discovered MS became conventional. To distinguish it from Snorri's prose *Edda*, it is nowadays usually referred to as the *Poetic Edda*.

This anthology, the *Codex Regius*, the main source of our knowledge of eddic poetry, is thought to date from the late 13th century. But characteristic scribal errors reveal that the MS is a copy of an older original no longer extant. A large number of eddic poems are also referred to and quoted in Snorri's *Edda*. The MS tradition goes back no farther. But most scholars assume that many eddic lays must have been preserved through oral tradition for a very long time, before they were finally recorded on parchment.

Much ingenuity has been devoted to trying to establish a chronology for the eddic poems, if not an absolute one, then at least a relative one. Among the criteria that have been applied are the relation of various poems to: the development of the Scandinavian languages; archaeological facts; the Scandinavian landscape with its flora and fauna; historical events; and Christian thoughts and beliefs. Scholars agree on the whole that the genesis of the eddic poems covers a considerable space of time, perhaps from the 9th to the 13th century.

Prosody and style. The two chief metrical verse forms of eddic poetry are *fornyrðislag* ("old story meter" or "epic meter") and *ljóðaháttr* ("song meter" or "chant meter"). The former is a stanza of eight lines, each of which has two stressed syllables and a varying number of unstressed syllables. The lines are joined together to form couplets by means of a regular application of alliteration, the only indigenous form of rhyme in Old Germanic and Norse poetry. In a few cases, we find a variant of *fornyrðislag* named *málaháttr*; it permits more syllables per line.

Ljóðaháttr differs from *fornyrðislag* by replacing the second and fourth couplets by a so-called "full line." Thus, this verse form has six rather than eight lines, and the full lines alliterate within themselves. In both *fornyrðislag* and *ljóðaháttr*, there is a marked tendency to make the half-stanza a syntactical and somewhat independent unit within the stanza.

The division into stanzas, which characterizes all eddic poetry, seems to be a distinguishing feature of Old Norse verse; it is otherwise extremely rare in the Germanic area.

The two main forms of stylistic adornment in Old Norse poetry are *heiti* and kennings. The former device simply means selected and unusual appellations for common concepts, for instance, archaisms that may perhaps have been preserved only in poetic diction. Far more specific are the kennings, the typical form of Old Norse imagery, also well known from Old English poetry. Primarily, the kenning consists of a main word plus a modifier in the genitive, which are sometimes welded together to form a compound noun. Blood may be called *hjǫrlǫgr* 'fluid of swords,' battle *naddél* 'storm of spears.' On the whole, eddic poetry makes sparse use of kennings, and always in simple and transparent forms, far from the complicated and enigmatic instances of skaldic *dróttkvætt*-stanzas.

As for style in a broad sense, both narrative and dialogue are extraordinarily terse and concentrated. Episodes usually follow one another abruptly, without connecting links, in sharp contrast to a more flowing epic form.

The poems in the *Codex Regius* are arranged according to a definite plan. First, there are poems about the ancient Norse world of the gods, followed by a section of poems with themes from heroic legend. Of these two major genres of eddic poetry, the mythological poems stand out as specifically Nordic. The heroic lays, on the other hand, have counterparts in other Germanic literatures.

Mythological poetry. Vǫluspá ("The Prophecy of the Sibyl") deserves its initial position. The creation of the world, the dissolution of the world order, the destruction of the world, and the emergence of a new world make up its theme. Its name derives from the *vǫlva* ("sibyl") who speaks in the poem, an aged seeress who remembers the ancient destinies of the world, and with her vision penetrates the veils of the future. In prophetic tones, she invokes the attention of all listeners. Many things she says are obscure to a modern audience, but the main line is clear. First, there is a description of the great void before the creation of the world. Then the thriving green earth, the Miðgarðr, the common home of gods and men, is raised out of the abyss. Three gods breathe life into the first pair of human beings, Askr and Embla, who correspond in Norse mythology to Adam and Eve. An essential element in the vision of the seeress is the picture of the World Tree, the ash Yggdrasill, which spreads its enormous crown over the earth, standing like a guardian of our whole existence. At its foot, three norns sit: "Laws they made there,/ and life allotted/ to the sons of men,/ and set their fates." Then follows the most difficult part of the poem, in which it is suggested that the gods have slain a sorceress and then broken agreements and oaths. The condition of innocence is past. Among the human beings, moral corruption will prevail; this dissolution portends doom and destruction. Giants and other terrifying creatures, enemies of gods and men, will be abroad. Finally, there will come the inevitable end: the destruction of the world, Ragnarǫk ("the extinction of the powers"). However, the seeress beholds a new creation still farther in the future. In this new world, the gods will meet again on the plain called Iðavǫllr, and take up their games of olden days, and

good people will enjoy eternal happiness. There are certain features of *Vǫluspá* that indicate a Christian influence. It has also been suggested that it was composed in the late 10th century, not long before Iceland officially adopted Christianity by a resolution of the General Assembly (*Alþingi*) in the year 1000. However that may be, this magnificent and serene poem has an unmistakably Norse stamp in both form and content.

Hávamál, which follows *Vǫluspá*, is in its preserved form the longest poem in the collection, with 164 stanzas. But it is far from homogeneous, probably compiled from various poems or parts of poems that can no longer be distinguished with certainty. Among them, we can discern fragments of several poems in which Óðinn himself relates his fortunes, for instance, the story of how he got possession of the poetic mead among the giants, or the description of how he hung for nine nights in a tree, wounded by a spear, sacrificed to himself by himself. Such mythical or ritual passages have given the entire poem its name: "The Words of the High One" (*i.e.*, Óðinn). But they have only slight or superficial connections with the major part of the poem, which consists of gnomic verse, rules of conduct of an everyday and sometimes rather trivial nature. *Hávamál* offers good common sense in abundance and coins it in sentences that often have the forceful brevity and graphic clarity of the proverb. If "much practical wisdom" is the wanderer's best travel ration, then, conversely, "too much beer" is the worst. Throughout, the ideal of the golden mean is proclaimed. Much interest is devoted to the problem of how to get along with one's fellows. The virtue of precaution, or rather distrust, is stressed. Treachery must be repaid, or, better yet, forestalled, with cunning and lies. Despite his misanthropy, however, the poet is well aware that "man is the joy of man," that human beings need each other. In an evil and hostile world, there is all the more reason to cultivate one's ties of friendship. *Hávamál* is strongly earth-bound. There is no hint of a life after death, and its philosophy of life completely lacks the heroic perspective. The demands of life are reduced to statements like: "The blind man is better / than one that is burned, / no good can come of a corpse." After being treated to such skeptical wisdom for more than seventy stanzas, one is quite surprised to be at last confronted with the following lines, some of the most magnificent in the whole *Edda*: "Cattle die, / and kinsmen die, / and so you die yourself; / one thing I know/ that never dies, / the fame of a dead man's deeds." In the end, even the poet of *Hávamál* directs his view from practical needs to that which transcends the life of the individual.

Vǫluspá and *Hávamál*, each in its own way, are the most universal poems in the *Codex Regius*. The remaining mythological lays present various episodes in the life of the gods. In two of them, Óðinn plays the principal part. Under the assumed name Grímnir ("the Disguised One"), in one of many such quick-change performances, he holds forth in a king's hall on the world of the gods and other elevated subjects (*Grímnismál*). On another occasion, he conquers, again incognito, the giant Vafþrúðnir in a dramatic duel of knowledge and wits (*Vafþrúðnismál*).

The poems with Þórr as protagonist usually have a humorous tone. In *Hymiskviða*, he goes out fishing with the giant Hymir, and terrifies his companion when he almost catches the huge Miðgarðsormr ("World Serpent") with a bull's head as bait on his hook. In *Þrymskviða*, Þórr has to visit the giant Þrymr, reluctantly disguised as the goddess Freyja, in order to deceive the lovesick giant and regain his stolen hammer. Thanks to the wits of his companion, the artful Loki in the shape of his bridesmaid, the pretended bride Þórr's astonishing carryings-on at the wedding feast can be explained away. With the famous hammer at last safely in his lap, he takes revenge for his ignominious role and reveals his true nature in the giant's hall.

In contrast to Þrymskviða, which is certainly among the youngest mythological poems, Skírnismál impresses one as being archaic. It deals with the god Freyr's consuming desire for the giant maiden Gerðr, whom he has only seen from a great distance. His servant Skírnir is sent to prevail upon her to grant Freyr his desire. The messenger is successful, but only after resorting to the most drastic of spells and threats. He can return home with the reply that Gerðr has promised to meet his master in the grove called Barri nine nights later. It has been suggested that Skírnismál should be interpreted as a cult poem, as the text for a fertility rite. Freyr, son of Njǫrðr and brother of Freyja, belongs to the family of the Vanir among the gods. He is the lord of sunlight, vegetation, and procreation. His cult seems to have had a strongly erotic character. If seen in the light of the Freyr cult, Skírnismál would represent the marriage of the earth-goddess (Gerðr) to the sun-god (Freyr).

Outside the Codex Regius, we find a few specimens of mythological eddic poetry, which for some reasons were not included in the collection. The two most important of these poems appear in MSS of Snorri's Edda. Rígsþula ("Rígr's list [of names]") treats the origin and structure of human society. Rígr is another name for the god Heimdallr. The poem relates that, while on a journey, Rígr visits three different farms, and that the housewife in each of them gives birth to a boy nine months later. At the first farm, the boy is named Þræll ("thrall"), at the second, Karl ("free-man"), and at the third, Jarl ("earl"). Rígsþula thus gives poetic form to a myth about three social classes and affords interesting glimpses into what was considered typical in appearance, food, and occupations for the different estates. Jarl and his wife raise twelve sons. The youngest is called Konr ungr ("young son"), with a name symbolism that can easily be interpreted as konungr 'king.' Thus, the poem sketches the social hierarchy from thrall to king.

Rígsþula reveals a certain sympathy for the aristocratic ideal. In Grottasǫngr, on the other hand, the point of view is that of the oppressed. According to Snorri's prose introduction, the Danish king Fróði had got possession of two enormously strong female slaves named Fenja and Menja. He made them turn a mill whose stones were so huge that no one else was strong enough to handle them. The mill, named Grotti, had an extraordinary quality: it could grind out whatever the owner wished for. The slaves first grind gold and happiness for King Fróði and peace in his kingdom. That is the famous period of the "Peace of Fróði." But the king yields to the temptation of exploiting his slaves too greedily and ruthlessly. At last, the oppressed rise from their debasement. Instead of gold and happiness, they will now grind out vengeance and destruction. The powerful intensity in this poem resembles the apocalyptic vision in Vǫluspá.

Heroic poetry. In the Codex Regius, Vǫlundarkviða has been placed in the penultimate position among the eleven poems in the mythological section, although it could as well have introduced the heroic section. In fact, it is difficult to place this lay in either of the two main categories of eddic poetry. It deals with the skillful smith Vǫlundr, known also from sources outside Scandinavia. He is captured by a king, who has Vǫlundr's knee sinews cut and isolates him on an islet. There he is compelled to forge treasures for the king. But Vǫlundr broods about revenge. He manages to cut the heads off the two young sons of the king and to violate his daughter. In due time, he escapes in flight on a pair of wings he has created. Vǫlundarkviða has a general resemblance to the Greek tale about Daedalus, who rose out of the labyrinth where he had been imprisoned, on wings that he had made himself. The similarity was observed quite early in the North; in Icelandic, a labyrinth is still called vǫlundarhús.

The heroic section proper of the Codex Regius is introduced by three poems about two exclusively Norse heroes, Helgi Hjǫrvarðsson and Helgi Hundingsbani ("killer of Hundingr"). The remaining sixteen poems and fragments revolve around Sigurðr Fáfnisbani ("slayer of Fáfnir"), the best-known hero of the entire cycle of Old Germanic legend. A genealogical link is established to Helgi Hundingsbani by making him Sigurðr's older half-brother. Both are said to be sons of a certain King Sigmundr, but by different mothers.

In a long sequence of poems, partly linked together and supplemented by short paragraphs in prose, one can follow Sigurðr's life from his youthful accomplishments, his slaying of the dragon Fáfnir and the acquisition of his enormous gold hoard, through his connection with the Gjúking dynasty and his marriage to the king's daughter, Guðrún, up to the time of his death at the hands of his brothers-in-law. The remaining poems deal mostly with Guðrún's later fortunes, her two subsequent marriages, first to King Atli and then to King Jónakr. The whole bloody chronicle comes to a close in Hamðismál, where Guðrún's sons with Jónakr are slain.

This main body of the heroic section originates in Old Germanic legends that reached Scandinavia early in some form. They reveal dim and very much transformed memories of historical persons and episodes from the 4th and 5th centuries among the Goths, Huns, and the South Germanic dynasty of the Gjúkings; the Gjúkings have been associated with the Burgundians, who had a kingdom on the Rhine at the beginning of the 5th century.

Various women are deeply involved in the tragic course of events. On his journey south, young Sigurðr meets the shield-maiden Brynhildr in a castle, and they fall passionately in love. Their meeting ends with an exchange of oaths, and Sigurðr gives her a ring as a token of fidelity. The next stage of his journey takes place at King Gjúki's court. Queen Grímhildr would like to have the hero and owner of the famous gold hoard as her son-in-law. One night, she gives him a drink from a horn, which makes him forget Brynhildr. He marries Gjúki's daughter, Guðrún, and enters into foster-brotherhood with his brothers-in-law, Gunnarr and Hǫgni. Queen Grímhildr urges her son Gunnarr to woo Brynhildr. But the wooer has to ride through the burning fire that surrounds her castle. Gunnarr tries, but fails. Then he and Sigurðr exchange appearances (Grímhildr has taught them to do this), and Sigurðr breaks through the barrier of fire. Afterward, the two men assume their normal appearances. Brynhildr is bewildered and somewhat suspicious. She had expected nobody but Sigurðr, "the one to whom I swore oaths on the mountain," "my first husband," to stand the test. She marries Gunnarr. Later on, in a dispute between the sisters-in-law Guðrún and Brynhildr, the former shield-maiden learns that she has been deceived. Consumed by jealousy and fury, she incites her husband to slay Sigurðr.

In a series of poems, the ladies bemoan the loss of the incomparable hero, with Brynhildr in a proud and hateful mood, Guðrún in a more elegiac vein. Brynhildr, while dying, gives directions that her body be placed on the funeral pyre beside Sigurðr. Guðrún lives on and marries Atli, king of the Huns. That marriage ends in catastrophe.

Atli invites his wife's brothers, Gunnarr and Hǫgni, to his court. The invitation is a trap. Atli is intent on acquiring the immense gold hoard, in the possession of the Gjúkings after Sigurðr's death. Guðrún warns her brothers by a message. But, according to the heroic standard, they defy the warning and set out on the journey. At Atli's court, they are both killed without having revealed the hiding place of the treasure. It will remain forever in the waters of the Rhine, never to be found again. Guðrún takes a horrible revenge on her husband. After having secretly slaughtered her two little sons with Atli and served them to him as a meat dish at his victory banquet, on the following night she burns her drunken husband and all his followers to death in the castle.

This episode is narrated in two parallel poems, the older *Atlakviða* and the younger *Atlamál*, which provides a unique opportunity for studying the same eddic motif in two different versions. Not only has *Atlamál* over twice as many stanzas as *Atlakviða* (105 versus forty-five), it is also the only eddic poem that makes use throughout of the fuller meter *málaháttr*. With its greater epic breadth, it appears as rather wordy and trivial in comparison with the concise heroism of *Atlakviða*.

Guðrúnarhvǫt (*hvǫt* 'incitement') and *Hamðismál*, closely related to each other, comprise the epilogue to the heroic poetry. Guðrún has married anew, to King Jónakr. Her daughter by Sigurðr, Svanhildr, married to Jǫrmunrekkr the Mighty, has been accused of adultery with her husband's son and shamefully executed, trampled to death under horses' hooves. Guðrún incites Hamðir and Sǫrli, her sons by Jónakr, to take revenge for her beloved daughter. They set out for Jǫrmunrekkr, succeed in mutilating him, but are themselves stoned to death. The *Poetic Edda* concludes with these laconic words: "There Sǫrli fell/ beside the gable,/ and Hamðir sank/ at the back of the house."

The traditions underlying eddic poetry were widespread in Scandinavia. Thus, for instance, Þórr's fishing adventure with the World Serpent in *Hymiskviða* is depicted on picture stones both in Denmark and Sweden. And a huge petroglyph on a rock face at Ramsundsberget in Sweden, in close accordance with the eddic poem, represents in great detail Sigurðr's killing of the dragon Fáfnir. But whatever share the other Nordic peoples may have had in the legendary traditions, it is a fact of literary history that it is in Iceland, and there only, that the poetry itself has been preserved.

Ed.: The MS *Codex Regius*, for centuries deposited in Copenhagen (GkS 2365 4to), is now in the care of the Stofnun Árna Magnússonar in Reykjavik, Iceland. Heusler, Andreas, ed. *Codex Regius of the Elder Edda*. Corpus Codicum Islandicorum Medii Aevi, 10. Copenhagen: Levin & Munksgaard, 1937 [facsimile]; Bugge, Sophus, ed. *Norrœn fornkvæði*. Christiania [Oslo]: Malling, 1867; rpt. Oslo: Universitetsforlaget, 1965; Finnur Jónsson, ed. *De gamle Eddadigte*. Copenhagen: Gad, 1932; Jón Helgason, ed. *Eddadigte*. 3 vols. Nordisk filologi, Tekster og lærebøger til universitetsbrug. A. Tekster. Oslo: Dreyer; Stockholm: Läromedelsförlagen; Copenhagen: Munksgaard, 1955; rpt. 1971; Dronke, Ursula, ed. and trans. *The Poetic Edda. 1: Heroic Poems*. Oxford: Clarendon, 1969 [*Atlakviða, Atlamál in grœnlenzko, Guðrúnarhvǫt, Hamðismál*]; Neckel, Gustav, ed. *Edda: Die Lieder des Codex Regius nebst verwandten Denkmälern. I: Text*. 5th ed. rev. Hans Kuhn. Heidelberg: Winter, 1983; *II: Kurzes Wörterbuch*. 3rd ed. rev. Hans Kuhn. Heidelberg: Winter, 1968. **Tr.**: Bellows, Henry Adams, trans. *The Poetic Edda*. New York: American-Scandinavian Foundation, 1923; rpt. 1969; Hollander, Lee M., trans. *The Poetic Edda, Translated with an Introduction and Explanatory Notes*. 2nd rev. ed. Austin: University of Texas Press, 1962; rpt. 1988; Terry, Patricia. *Poems of the Vikings: The Elder Edda*. Indianapolis and New York: Bobbs-Merrill, 1969; Auden, W. H., and Paul B. Taylor, trans. *Norse Poems* London: Athlone, 1981. **Bib.**: Halldór Hermannsson. *Bibliography of the Eddas*. Islandica, 13. Ithaca: Cornell University Library, 1920; Jóhann S. Hannesson. *Bibliography of the Eddas: A Supplement*. Islandica, 27. Ithaca: Cornell University Press, 1955. **Lit.**: Finnur Jónsson. *Den oldnorske og oldislandske Litteraturs Historie*. 3 vols. 2nd ed. Copenhagen: Gad, 1920–24; Craigie, William A. *The Art of Poetry in Iceland*. Oxford: Clarendon, 1937; Heusler, Andreas. *Die altgermanische Dichtung*. Berlin and Neubabelsberg: Athenaion, 1923; 2nd ed. Potsdam: Athenaion, 1941; 2nd rev. ed. Darmstadt: Gentner, 1957; Vries, Jan de. *Altnordische Literaturgeschichte*. 2 vols. Grundriss der germanischen Philologie, 15–6. Berlin: de Gruyter, 1941–42; rpt. 1964–67; Jón Helgason. "Norges og Islands digtning." In *Litteraturhistorie. B: Norge og Island*. Ed. Sigurður Nordal. Nordisk kultur, 8B. Stockholm: Bonnier; Oslo: Aschehoug; Copenhagen: Schultz, 1953, pp. 3–179; Einar Ól. Sveinsson. *Íslenzkar bókmenntir í fornöld* 1. Reykjavik: Almenna Bókafélagið, 1962; Hallberg, Peter. *Old Icelandic Poetry: Eddic Lay and Skaldic Verse*. Trans. Paul Schach and Sonja Lindgrenson. Lincoln and London: University of Nebraska Press, 1975 [extensive bibliography]; Glendinning, Robert J., and Haraldur Bessason, eds. *Edda: A Collection of Essays*. University of Manitoba Icelandic Studies, 4. Winnipeg: University of Manitoba Press, 1983; Harris, Joseph. "Eddic Poetry." In *Old Norse–Icelandic Literature: A Critical Guide*. Ed. Carol J. Clover and John Lindow. Islandica, 45. Ithaca and London: Cornell University Press, 1985, pp. 68–156 [extensive bibliography]; Jónas Kristjánsson. *Eddas and Sagas: Iceland's Medieval Literature*. Trans. Peter Foote. Reykjavik: Hið íslenska bókmenntafélag, 1988.

Peter Hallberg

[**See also:** *Alvíssmál; Atlakviða; Atlamál; Baldrs draumar; Codex Regius; Darraðarljóð;* Eddic Meters; *Grímnismál; Grípisspá; Grottasǫngr; Guðrúnarkviða I-III; Guðrúnarhvǫt; Hamðismál in fornu; Hárbarðsljóð; Hávamál;* Heiti; Helgi Poems; *Helreið Brynhildar; Hlǫðskviða; Hymiskviða; Hyndluljóð;* Kennings; *Lokasenna; Oddrúnargrátr; Reginsmál* and *Fáfnismál; Rígsþula; Sigrdrífumál; Sigurðarkviða in skamma; Sigurðarkviðu, Brot af; Skírnismál; Snorra Edda; Sólarljóð; Svipdagsmál; Þrymskviða; Vafþrúðnismál; Vǫlundarkviða;* Vǫlsung-Niflung Cycle; *Vǫluspá;* Women in Eddic Poetry]

Education. Scholarly education was introduced in the Nordic countries by the Church, which also remained the most important educational institution and the greatest "consumer" of educated personnel during the rest of the Middle Ages. In the first period after the introduction of Christianity, priests probably received elementary instruction in Latin, mass reading, and liturgical chant by the local priest they were going to succeed. Formal schools apparently began to be organized around 1100.

There were three kinds of such schools: cathedral schools, monastic schools, and town schools. The third Lateran Council (1179) decreed that every cathedral chapter should appoint a *magister* to give free education to the clergy and poor students of the diocese. Probably some education was given at most or all cathedral chapters in the Nordic countries, though lack of sources makes it difficult to tell when this practice started. The earliest evidence for Denmark and Iceland dates from the late 11th or early 12th centuries, for Norway from the late 12th century, and for Sweden and Finland respectively from the early 13th and early 14th centuries. Though the direct evidence is slight, we may assume that most priests were eventually educated at these schools.

By contrast, the monastic schools are little known and seem mainly to have been intended for members of the monasteries. Monastic schools for a broader public were apparently largely the products of competition or inspiration among the mendicant orders from the 13th century. The latter attached great importance to scholarly education, and there is evidence, even from the Nordic countries, that friars were sent for studies at the universities or were formally appointed teachers in the local houses.

As in the rest of Europe, there were numerous town schools in Denmark and Sweden during the later Middle Ages, while there seems to be no evidence of them from the other Nordic countries. These schools were founded by the city councils, but often received approval or financial support from ecclesiastical authorities. They served as a preparation for the cathedral school, but also had a more independent function in giving elementary instruction in reading, writing, and arithmetic to ordinary children of the town. According to Danish sources (from Malmö) from the early 16th century, such education seems to have been fairly normal at the time.

Less is known of the education of the laity in the earlier Middle Ages. It may be pointed out, however, that the higher aristocracy, at least in Iceland and from the mid-13th century also in Norway, was an administrative more than a military class, and that a considerable part of the Icelandic and Norwegian literature was written for and to some extent also by laymen. From this point of view, it is no coincidence that members of the Norwegian aristocracy are found as law students at Bologna around 1300. We do not know whether such men usually received their elementary education from private teachers or also attended ecclesiastical schools.

During most of the Middle Ages, studies abroad were necessary to create the kind of educated ecclesiastical elite that integrated the Nordic countries in the universal Church. Pope Gregory VII seems to have sketched a program to this effect in his letters from 1079 to the kings of Norway and Denmark, but the results of this initiative are unknown. A similar program, however, was carried out during the following century. Both the Norwegian and Danish higher clergy had close connections with the leading centers of learning in northern France in the 12th century, and several Icelandic bishops of the late 11th and early 12th centuries had studied in Germany or France. By contrast, the clergy of Sweden, including Finland, took part in this movement from a much later date, but established strong connections with the leading European universities from the second half of the 13th century. By the late 13th and early 14th centuries, it appears to have been fairly normal for members of the higher clergy to have some kind of university education, mostly some years at the lower, *artes* faculty in Paris. One may guess that about half of Norwegian canons had such an education, and the percentage was probably higher in Denmark and Sweden. The cathedral chapters gave some financial support for members who studied abroad.

In the later Middle Ages, a number of new universities grew up in Germany and eastern Europe, and most Nordic students went there. After a temporary drop because of the Black Death, the number of students seems to have risen during the 15th century and to have been considerably higher around 1500 than in the high Middle Ages, at least in Denmark and Sweden. We know the names of 2,146 Danish, 724 Swedish, 219 Norwegian, and ninety-seven Finnish students from the matricula of German, eastern European, and Dutch universities in the period 1350–1536. In addition, thirty-one Danes, thirty-one Swedes, one Norwegian,

and eighteen Finns are known to have studied in Paris during the same period. The foundation of the universities of Uppsala (1477) and Copenhagen (1479) indicate the importance the secular and ecclesiastical authorities attached to higher learning, but the institutions themselves were fairly insignificant as intellectual centers. Most students therefore continued to seek their education abroad.

The traditional disciplines in the schools, passed on from antiquity, were the seven liberal arts. They were divided into two groups, the *trivium* (grammar, rhetoric, and dialectics) and the *quadrivium* (arithmetic, geometry, music, and astronomy). But there was considerable variation, both locally and over time, in what was actually taught, and we know little of the particular Nordic varieties. Generally, scholarly education had a dual purpose, the transmission of the central values of European culture derived from both Christian and classical sources, and the practical purpose of giving future priests the necessary education to perform their duties. Since the educational standard of ordinary priests, as opposed to the higher clergy, was usually low in the Middle Ages, the success of the latter part of the program should not be overestimated. The content of the education and the success or failure of the program as a whole must be judged less from exact information on the teaching in schools than from examining the learning of the Nordic countries in general, as expressed, for example, in literature produced in these countries and the books that were available, and in the use of canon law and the Latin language.

Lit.: Olsson, Bror. "Katedralskole." *KLNM* 8 (1963), 347–54; Skovgaard-Petersen, Vagn, *et al.* "Skole." *KLNM* 15 (1970), 631–41; Sällström, Åke, *et al.* "Studieresor." *KLNM* 17 (1972), 329–42; Lindroth, Sten, and Jan Pinborg. "Universitet." *KLNM* 19 (1975), 312–9; Bagge, Sverre. "Nordic Students at Foreign Universities Until 1660." *Scandinavian Journal of History* 9 (1984), 1–29.

Sverre Bagge

Egill Skalla-Grímsson is the chief character of *Egils saga Skalla-Grímsonar*. According to this work, he died in old age a few years before Christianity was accepted by the Icelanders (A.D. 1000). Egill owes his fame as a poet (*skáld*) and hero entirely to the saga, which, however, must be considered a very unreliable biography. The historical authenticity of several of the *lausavísur* (occasional verses) spoken by Egill and a few others in the narrative, and even of the six poems ascribed to him there, has been questioned by several scholars.

As we have no means to discriminate between the historical Egill and the Egill of the saga, nor any safe criteria by which to identify authentic or non-authentic verse spoken by Egill and other persons, we are perhaps best advised to accept the poems as integrated parts of the saga and to set aside the question of their authenticity.

According to the saga, Egill composed six major poems. Three of them are found in various redactions of the saga, two others are quoted with one stanza from each, and a third is quoted with one stanza and and a refrain. In addition, the best redaction of the saga has Egill speak forty-eight stanzas (*lausavísur*), but the original may have had fifty in all, since in two cases a space for a stanza has been left blank.

The first of the three preserved poems is *Hǫfuðlausn* ("Head Ransom"), comprising twenty stanzas in *runhent* meter. The only other case of *runhent* in the saga is a stanza spoken much earlier by Egill's father, Skalla-Grímr, but scholars have tended to ignore that fact and grant Egill the honor of introducing end-rhyme in Norse poetry. Needless to say, the introduction of end-rhyme as early as the late 10th century is difficult to believe. According to *Egils saga*, Egill saved his life when he was in the power of King Eiríkr blóðøx ("blood-axe") Haraldsson in York by composing *Hǫfuðlausn* in one short night and reciting it before the king and his court. This poem is apparently preserved in its entirety, although its text in two redactions of the saga seems to have originated from two independent traditions, whether oral or written. As there is not one line of it quoted in the best redaction, and no space left for a first stanza as in the case of the two other preserved poems, it may mean that the text of it was not available when the original exemplar of this redaction was written.

Hǫfuðlausn is singularly empty of concrete material; the king is praised for his generosity and martial prowess, as was usual. He is called the enemy of the Scots, but no antagonist is named nor any specific battle. In this respect, the only comparable praise poem about a king is Snorri Sturluson's in honor of the young King Hákon Hákonarson (the first thirty stanzas of his poem *Háttatal*). This poem names no enemies or battlefield despite repeated descriptions of fighting and the king's prowess.

Sonatorrek is a memorial poem in honor of Egill's two sons, Bǫðvarr, a favorite who drowned at sea, and Gunnarr, who had died a little earlier. The poem comprises twenty-five stanzas in *kviðuháttr* meter. It is badly preserved in two almost identical 17th-century copies of a 15th-century MS. The first stanza is quoted in the *Egils saga* text of *Mǫðruvallabók*, and one stanza and a half are found in *Snorra Edda*. The poem concerns mainly Egill's own feelings, and it has been called the most lyrical product of Norse poetry. According to the saga, Egill had decided to starve himself to death after the drowning of Bǫðvarr, but was induced to compose a memorial poem and thus obtained control of his emotions. Toward the end, there is a remarkable reckoning with Óðinn. In stanza 22, Egill states that he had good relations with Óðinn before "the victory-lord broke friendship with me." But in stanza 23, Egill states that nevertheless the god has recompensed him for his injuries; and in stanza 24, he says that the god gave him *íþrótt vammi firrða* ("flawless art," i.e., the gift of poetry). In the last stanza, the poet says that although things are hard for him, the goddess of death is waiting, *skal ek þó glaðr / með góðan vilja / ok óhryggr / heljar bíða* ("yet I shall, glad with good will and in good heart, wait for death").

On the basis of this poem, there has been much speculation about Egill's religion. Some Christian ideas have been noted (*cf.* sts. 10, 21, and 25). For example, the sixth line of stanza 25, *með góðan vilja* ("with good will"), is reminiscent of the last words of Luke 2:14 in the Vulgate concerning men of good will (*bonae voluntatis*).

Arinbjarnarkviða is a poem in *kviðuháttr* meter, badly preserved in *Mǫðruvallabók*, on a page after the end of the saga. The two apparently last stanzas are only found in the *Third Grammatical Treatise*. Arinbjǫrn was Egill's lifelong friend, according to the saga. He was a Norwegian *hersir* ("chieftain"), a henchman of King Eiríkr blóðøx, and later of his son King Haraldr gráfeldr ("grey-cloak"), and his death in battle together with the king is mentioned in *Heimskringla*. In spite of its poor preservation, *Arinbjarnarkviða* is an impressive poem owing to its noble language and elevated style. In the final stanzas, the poet states that he has built a monument of praise that will long stand in the land of poetry, a statement that has often been compared with the famous lines of Horace: *Exegi monumentum aere perennius.*

Egill's *lausavísur* are spoken on various occasions in the saga. His first two stanzas, at the age of three, are spoken as a contribution to the entertainment at a feast at his grandfather's, and they are composed in intricate *dróttkvætt* meter, like most of his later *lausavísur*. His last *lausavísa*, about his helplessness as he is lying bedridden owing to old age, is in the simple *fornyrðislag* meter. Among the other stanzas is a deeply tragic stanza (17) about the death of his brother Þórólfr in the battle of Vínheiðr in England, two stanzas of very moderate passion, confessing to Arinbjǫrn his love of Ásgerðr, who becomes his wife (sts. 23–24), a stanza (28) in which he asks the gods to drive the king (Eiríkr) into exile, and a fine stanza (51) of dignified restraint about the loss of Arinbjǫrn.

A sign of Egill's self-centered interest is his inclination to describe his own looks with a metaphoric kenning, most often a metaphor from a mountain landscape: his drooping brows are called *hvarms hnúpgnípur* (literally "the stooping mountain peaks of the eyelid"), and *ennis þvergnípur* ("the cross-mountain peaks of the forehead"), and also with a longer kenning, *gerðihamrar grundar grímu* ("the enclosing rocks of the land of the mask," i.e., of the face). He calls the wrinkles on his forehead *ennis ósléttur* ("the unevenness of the forehead"), his nose *brúna miðstallr* ("the rise in the middle of the brows"), and his head *hjalma klettr* ("the rock of the helmets").

Many of Egill's kennings are very apt, as when he describes in stanza 6 of *Arinbjarnarkviða* his recitation of *Hǫfuðlausn* in the court of King Eiríkr blóðøx in York: "Yet I dared to offer the poetic mead to the king, so that the beer of Óðinn [the poem] came foaming to every man's mouth of hearing [the ears]." Another stanza with metaphors of extraordinary consequence is Egill's famous sailing stanza (32): "The furiously blowing enemy of the mast [the storm] cuts energetically with a storm chisel a file in front of the stem on the even road of the ship, and the enemy of the tree [the storm] files merciless with blasts the beak of the ship."

Bib.: Hollander, Lee M. *A Bibliography of Skaldic Studies*. Copenhagen: Munksgaard, 1958. **Lit.**: Jón Helgason. "Norges og Islands digtning." In *Litteraturhistorie: Norge og Island*. Ed. Sigurður Nordal. Nordisk kultur, 8B. Stockholm: Bonnier; Oslo: Aschehoug; Copenhagen: Schultz, 1953, pp. 3–179; Jón Helgason. "Hǫfuðlausnarhjal." In *Einarsbók. Afmæliskveðja til Einars Ól. Sveinssonar 12. desember 1969*. Ed. Bjarni Guðnason *et al*. Reykjavik: Nokkrir vinir, 1969, pp. 156–76; Halldór Laxness. "Nokkrir hnýsilegir staðir í fornkvæðum, VI Lúkas í Sonatorreki." *Tímarit Máls og menningar* 31.1 (1971), 1–24; Hofmann, Dietrich. "Das Reimwort *giǫr* in Egill Skallagrímssons Hǫfuðlausn." *Mediaeval Scandinavia* 6 (1973), 93–101; Turville-Petre, E. O. G. *Scaldic Poetry*. Oxford: Clarendon, 1976; Frank, Roberta. *Old Norse Court Poetry: The Dróttkvætt Stanza*. Islandica, 42. Ithaca and London: Cornell University Press, 1978; Frank, Roberta. "Skaldic Poetry." In *Old Norse–Icelandic Literature: A Critical Guide*. Ed. Carol J. Clover and John Lindow. Islandica, 45. Ithaca and London: Cornell University Press, 1985, pp. 157–96.

Bjarni Einarsson

[**See also:** Commemorative Poetry; *Egils saga Skalla-Grímssonar*; Kennings; *Lausavísur*; *Mǫðruvallabók*; *Skáld*; *Skáldasǫgur*; Skaldic Meters; Skaldic Verse; *Snorra Edda*]

Egils saga einhenda ok Ásmundar berserkjabana

("The Saga of the One-Armed Egill and the Berserk-Killer Ásmundr") is a late and fantastic *fornaldarsaga* dating from the 14th century. It comprises the three life stories of Egill, Ásmundr, and the giantess Arinnefja. The stories are set within a narrative frame consisting of the adventures they have in recapturing two princesses abducted by two giants in the shape of flying dragons (*flugdreki*). During the search in Jǫtunheimr, they tell each other their past adventures. Ásmundr tells of his exploits on Viking trips with his blood-brother Áran, and of the killing of two berserks, from which he derives his nickname. Egill's story reports how he is captured by a giant at the age of twelve and how he escaped by blinding the giant (a variant of the Polyphemus story); later, he loses his right arm in the fight with a giant, and is afterward called *einhendi*. Arinnefja's adventures are more colorful, as she has to procure three exotic treasures as a punishment for sorcery; in the course of the search, she has to fight three giantesses single-handedly and to sleep with the Lord of Darkness, whom she identifies as Óðinn. It turns out she is the giantess whom Egill tried to protect from the giant when he lost his arm, which she has miraculously preserved with magic herbs so that he can now be healed. All three set out to free the princesses, and they overcome the trolls with the help of Arinnefja's sorcery.

All parts of the saga are strongly reminiscent of fairy tales, and the author may have indeed connected the various fairy-tale plots and added a substantial number of fantastic elements as well as some rather gory details to create his saga. Quite a number of motifs show the interdependence of the text with other late *fornaldarsǫgur* (e.g., *Hálfdanar saga Eysteinssonar*), but it is difficult to establish any concrete links. Although this saga is far removed from the terse realism of the older sagas and has all the marks of escapist and trivial literature, the author has succeeded in creating an exciting story by skillfully combining elements of various origins and carefully avoiding loose ends in the plot.

Egils saga einhenda is well documented in over forty MSS, the oldest (AM 343a 4to, AM 557 4to, AM 589e 4to) dating from the 15th century.

Ed.: Lagerholm, Åke, ed. *Drei Lygisǫgur: Egils saga einhenda ok Ásmundar berserkjabana, Ála flekks saga, Flóres saga konungs ok sona hans.* Altnordische Saga-Bibliothek, 17. Halle: Niemeyer, 1927, pp. 1–83. **Tr.**: Hermann Pálsson and Paul Edwards, trans. *Gautrek's Saga and Other Medieval Tales.* New York: New York University Press; London: University of London Press, 1968, pp. 89–120; rpt. in *Seven Viking Romances.* Harmondsworth: Penguin, 1985, pp. 138–70; Simek, Rudolf, trans. *Zwei Abenteuersagas. Egils saga einhenda. Hálfdanar saga Eysteinssonar.* Altnordische Bibliothek, 7. Leverkusen: Literaturverlag Norden, 1989. **Lit.**: Fry, Donald. "Polyphemus in Iceland." In *The Fourteenth Century.* Ed. Paul E. Szarmach and Bernard S. Levy. Acta, 4. Binghamton: Center for Medieval and Early Renaissance Studies, State University of New York at Binghamton, 1977, pp. 65–86; Naumann, Hans-Peter. "Das Polyphem-Abenteuer in der altnordischen Sagaliteratur." *Schweizerisches Archiv für Volkskunde* 75 (1979), 173–89; Simek, Rudolf. "Zur Egils Saga Einhenda." *Österreichische Zeitschrift für Volkskunde,* N.S. 35, Gesamtserie 84 (1981), 154–62; Naumann, Hans-Peter. "Erzählstrategien in der Fornaldarsaga: Die Prüfungen des Helden." In *Akten der 5. Arbeitstagung der Skandinavisten des deutschen Sprachgebiets.* St. Augustin: Kretschmer, 1983, pp. 131–47.

Rudolf Simek

[**See also**: *Berserkr*; Folklore; *Fornaldarsǫgur*; *Hálfdanar saga Eysteinssonar*]

Egils saga Skalla-Grímssonar

Egils saga Skalla-Grímssonar ("The Saga of Egill Skalla-Grímsson") is one of the major *Íslendingasǫgur* from the golden age of saga writing, the 13th century. It is preserved in three main redactions from the 14th century and later. Their relationship is intricate, but the text of the 14th-century MS AM 132 fol. (*Mǫðruvallabók* = M) is the best redaction, since the other two are either fragmentary or defective texts that omit certain episodes and stanzas compared with the M-redaction. Nevertheless, the secondary redactions are valuable, since in many cases they have undoubtedly preserved more original phrases and single words than the text of M; and they are also useful in providing substitutes for missing words in M. Last but not least, they preserve two of the major poems ascribed to Egill in the saga, *Sonatorrek* and *Hǫfuðlausn*.

Although the text of the M-redaction is clearly superior to the other recensions, it appears to be the result of consistent stylistic abbreviation, sometimes even to the detriment of the content. It is fair to add that the writing of the stanzas in this text appears to be exceptionally conscientious, and in several cases a blank space has been left for a stanza to be filled in by an assistant scribe.

Egils saga is one of the so-called *skáldasǫgur* ("sagas of skalds"), because the chief character, Egill, acts as a skald. In the M-redaction, he speaks in all forty-eight stanzas (probably fifty originally, as a space for a stanza has in two cases been left blank); eight stanzas are spoken by other persons. Furthermore, according to the saga, Egill composed six major poems, and in the M-redaction a stanza is quoted in three of these cases and a stanza with one refrain in one. Also, a poem is written after the saga in the M-redaction: *Arinbjarnarkviða*, which has left no remnants in the other redactions. Of the two famous poems, the M-redaction has preserved only the first stanza of *Sonatorrek*, but nothing of *Hǫfuðlausn*.

Egill's birth is related in ch. 31 of the saga, and after that, the saga traces his career to his death and burial in ch. 86, and adds a concluding chapter about his descendants. The saga is unlike other *Íslendingasǫgur* in that most of it takes place abroad. Before the emigration from Norway to Iceland, Kveld-Úlfr, Egill's grandfather, a rich farmer and man of rank in Firðir, and his son Skalla-Grímr had become mortal enemies of King Haraldr hárfagri ("fairhair") Hálfdanarson of Norway, following the killing of Þórólfr Kveld-Úlfsson by the king and his men. Much later, Þórólfr, the son of Skalla-Grímr, travels abroad and becomes an intimate friend of the young King Eiríkr blóðøx ("blood-axe") Haraldsson of Norway. On his first travel abroad with his brother Þórólfr, Egill incurs the enmity of King Eiríkr, and many years later their enmity culminates with the king making Egill an outlaw in Norway. Egill subsequently kills one of the king's sons and some of his relatives and friends, and then utters the curse against the king and queen that they shall be driven out of the country. In a following chapter, the king and the queen are forced to leave the country after the arrival of the king's brother Hákon, who then becomes ruler of Norway.

After more travels abroad and various adventures, Egill settles at Borg, the family estate, as a peaceful farmer. The saga now describes him as an old man interested chiefly in poetry. But at a given occasion, he shows himself capable of defending his family's interests when they are threatened after he has handed over the estate to his son Þorsteinn.

Egill is said to have been dark-haired and very ugly like his father, while Þórólfr, his brother, is described as fair and handsome, and very much like his uncle Þórólfr Kveld-Úlfsson. The last chapter of the saga adds that among Skalla-Grímr's descendants were the handsomest people in Iceland, but more were very ugly. The older and the younger Þórólfr are both short of luck and are killed in the prime of life, while Skalla-Grímr and Egill remain the pillars of the family and die in old age. Both Skalla-Grímr and Egill and even his grandfather Kveld-Úlfr have the poetic vein in them, and Egill is versed in runic magic.

It has been suggested that the description of Egill and his father and grandfather is indebted to medieval descriptions of melancholy persons in the literature concerning humors, and that the author of *Egils saga* and the authors of the other *skáldasögur* were familiar with the Aristotelian connection between melancholia and poetic frenzy through the writings of the 12th-century authors.

Of all the poets in the *skáldasögur*, Egill fits this model by far the best. The strange thing is that the saga author has contrived to create a convincing character of extreme contrasts, in early years a ruthless fighting man who in mature years is occupied mainly with poetry.

Egill is described as avaricious and as a killer of men already in childhood. He is already a poet at the age of three. His verse is highly self-centered: he likes to describe his looks, and only there does he reveal his softer feelings.

The predominant view among scholars used to be that *Egils saga* must be considered a comparatively trustworthy biography of Egill, as his own verse together with family traditions were assumed to have been the main source of the saga author. On the other hand, it had been admitted that the prehistory of the family in its original home in Norway can hardly be reliable except in the outlines, especially the emigration to Iceland because of the enmity between them and Haraldr hárfagri.

As a matter of fact, the historical authenticity of much of the verse in *Egils saga* is highly questionable, and nothing can be known about the amount of family tradition available in the days of the saga author, nor about his dependence on it. On the other hand, a great deal can be inferred about his use of written sources of various kinds. For instance, the main model for the consequential slander episode beginning in ch. 12 is found in *Þinga saga*, which is preserved in *Morkinskinna* and related redactions of *konungasögur*, but has presumably been an independent work. The outlines and several details of the famous *dísablót* ("sacrifice to the *dísir*") episode (ch. 44) and others are appropriated from *Orkneyinga saga*. The sagas of the skalds Kormákr and Hallfreðr have also influenced episodes in *Egils saga*. The author had access to some redaction of *Landnámabók* and some works about King Haraldr hárfagri and King Hákon góði ("the good") Haraldsson, and most likely also *Ágrip*, *Morkinskinna*, and *Sverris saga*.

The author has in most cases refashioned the material he borrowed from his various sources to such a degree that it can be difficult to detect, but, once found, the source material as a rule appears obvious. The use of these sources for an entirely new artistic whole reveals the genius of the author. It is apparent that the verse in *Egils saga* is not among the sources of the author. The stanzas, whether spoken by Egill himself or somebody else, are an intrinsic part of the artistic fabric, and they are never quoted as evidence, which is almost the rule in *konungasögur*.

Egils saga's descriptions of events in the history of Norway have parallels, even verbatim, in *Heimskringla*, the sagas of the kings of Norway by Snorri Sturluson, which prove that there is some literary relation between *Egils saga* and *Heimskringla*, but it does not follow that *Egils saga* is a historical work on a par with *Heimskringla*. It is obvious that the author of *Egils saga* has arbitrarily connected Egill, and his forebears as well as his uncle Þórólfr, with well-known events of Norwegian history. It does not seem likely that Egill's connections with persons and events in English history are better founded.

Considering the political situation in Iceland in the first half of the 13th century and the growing interference of the king of Norway, *Egils saga* may be seen as a warning against intimate relations with the royal power, and on the other hand, a glorifying of the old aristocratic system in Iceland.

Above all, *Egils saga* may be considered a monument to the greater glory of Mýramenn ("men of Mýrar"), the descendants of Skalla-Grímr. It is noteworthy that the saga extends Skalla-Grímr's settlement (*landnám*) to the south bank of the river Hvítá and hints that he dominated most of the Borgarfjörður district on both sides of that great landmark, which contradicts the statement of the original text of *Landnámabók* (*cf.* chs. 28, 29, 39, and 83 of *Egils saga*). It is certainly no accident that the settlement in the south of Iceland of Ketill hœngr ("salmon"), a relative of Skalla-Grímr and, according to the saga, a great friend of Þórólfr Kveld-Úlfsson, is in *Egils saga* extended in a similar way. In the early 13th century, Ketill hœngr was counted among the ancestors of the Oddaverjar ("men of Oddi"), whose domain was coextensive with Hœngr's settlement as described in *Egils saga*.

At the end of ch. 84, it is stated that Tungu-Oddr, who had been the most dangerous of Þorsteinn Egilsson's adversaries, ruled over the Borgarfjörður district south of Hvítá, and that every man paid dues to the temple of which he was in charge.

The saga stresses repeatedly that all the descendants of Skalla-Grímr belong to his clan, the Mýramenn. In the early 13th century, a descendant of Skalla-Grímr resided in Reykjaholt, which had earlier replaced the former manor of Tungu-Oddr, south of Hvítá, and he dominated the Borgarfjörður district on both sides of the Hvítá for about thirty-five years. At the same time, he controlled the church of Reykjaholt, which had great revenues from the tithe and other sources. This man was Snorri Sturluson, the historian, who had as a young man and protégé of the Oddaverjar come to Borgarfjörður to marry a rich heiress and settle in Borg, her estate. Snorri gradually acquired the chieftainship over most of the Borgarfjörður district and moved to Reykjaholt.

Snorri may have considered it advantageous to consolidate his unique position in Borgarfjörður by writing a saga enhancing the renown of the Mýramenn, his clan according to the definition of the saga, and at the same time justifying his lucrative control of the church in Reykjaholt by alluding to a historical precedent.

It has been maintained that even if Snorri had written *Egils saga*, he could not have written (*i.e.*, composed) the best of the verse ascribed to Egill, as his own incontestable poetry did not indicate the necessary poetic ability. It has also been claimed that *Sonatorrek* is too imbued with personal grief to have been composed by any other man than Egill himself.

There is little doubt that Snorri has until recently been underestimated as a poet. Fidjestøl (1982) maintains that in *Háttatal* there are stanzas that are not inferior to the best in the genre. It should also be remembered that Snorri himself experienced the loss of a favorite son, when Jón murtr ("trout") died in Norway of a wound received in a drunken brawl. This tragic episode in the life of Snorri has its counterpart in ch. 38 of *Egils saga*, where Skalla-

Grímr tries to persuade his son Þórólfr to desist from his planned voyage to Norway. In both cases, the father offers to grant the son the means to establish himself in Iceland if he gives up the trip. The son nevertheless stands by his decision, travels to Norway, and is killed abroad.

A study of the vocabulary of *Heimskringla* and *Egils saga* has revealed considerable similarity in spite of the fact that both works are found only in comparatively late copies.

The poetic nature of *Egils saga* was demonstrated by Bley (1909). If, nevertheless, most scholars have in the past been unable to realize the true nature of the saga, it is not least owing to the saga author's accomplishment of a perfect artistic deception. Writers of fiction have always asserted that they tell nothing but the truth. The author of *Egils saga* makes no such statement, but sometimes when he feels that he is approaching the limits of plausibility, he states that "some people say." No one among his audience would have been able to impugn his story. Thus, Egill Skalla-Grímsson became the paragon of the old-world heathen hero and skald in the imagination of the Icelandic people.

Ed.: Finnur Jónsson, ed. *Egils saga Skallagrímssonar nebst den grösseren Gedichten Egils*. Altnordische Saga-Bibliothek, 3. Halle: Niemeyer, 1894 [with preface and commentary in German]; Sigurður Nordal, ed. *Egils saga Skalla-Grímssonar*. Íslenzk fornrit, 2. Reykjavik: Hið íslenzka fornritafélag, 1933; rpt. 1955; [a new edition with preface and notes in English is being prepared by Bjarni Einarsson for Stofnun Árna Magnússonar, Reykjavik; a diplomatic edition of the saga is in progress in Det arnamagnæanske Institut, Copenhagen]. **Tr.**: Eddison, E. R., trans. *Egils saga*. Cambridge: Cambridge University Press, 1930; rpt. New York: Greenwood, 1968; Jones, Gwyn, trans. *Egil's Saga*. Syracuse: Syracuse University Press, 1960; rpt. New York: Twayne, 1970; Fell, Christine, and John Lucas, trans. *Egil's Saga*. Toronto: University of Toronto Press; London: Dent, 1975; Hermann Pálsson and Paul Edwards, trans. *Egil's Saga*. Harmondsworth: Penguin, 1976. **Lit.**: Bley, A. *Eigla-Studien*. Gand: Van Goethem, 1909; Wieselgren, P. *Författarskapet till Eigla*. Lund: Blom, 1927; Vogt, W. H. *Von Bragi zu Egil. Ein Versuch zur Geschichte des skaldischen Preisliedes*. Breslau: Deutsche Islandsforschung, 1930; Jón Helgason. "Athuganir um nokkur handrit Egils sögu." In *Nordæla. Afmæliskveðja til Sigurðar Nordals sjötugs 14. september 1956*. Ed. Halldór Halldórsson *et al*. Reykjavik: Helgafell, 1956, pp. 110–48; Hallberg, Peter. *Snorri Sturluson och Egils saga Skallagrímssonar. Ett försök till språklig författarbestämning*. Studia Islandica, 20. Reykjavik: Menningarsjóður, 1962; Hallberg, Peter. "Snorri Sturluson och *Egils saga Skalla-Grímssonar*. Kommentar till en recension." *Maal og minne* (1964), 12–20; Vésteinn Ólason. "Er Snorri höfundur Egils sögu?" *Skírnir* 142 (1968), 48–67; Hallberg, Peter. *Stilsignalement och författarskap i norrön sagalitteratur. Synpunkter och exempel*. Nordistica Gothoburgensia, 3. Gothenburg: Elander, 1968; Bell, L. Michael. "A Computer Concordance to *Egils saga Skalla-Grímssonar*." In *Studies for Einar Haugen: Presented by Friends and Colleagues*. Ed. Evelyn Firchow *et al*. Janua Linguarum, Series Maior, 59. The Hague: Mouton, 1972, pp. 58–68; Bjarni Einarsson. *Litterære forudsætninger for Egils saga*. Reykjavik: Stofnun Árna Magnússonar, 1975; Bell, L. Michael. "Oral Allusion in Egils saga Skalla-Grímssonar. A Computer-Aided Approach." *Arkiv för nordisk filologi* 91 (1976), 51–65; Kristján Albertsson. "Egill Skallagrímsson í Jórvík." *Skírnir* 150 (1976), 88–98; Grimstad, Kaaren. "The Giant as a Heroic Model: The Case of Egill and Starkaðr." *Scandinavian Studies* 48 (1976), 284–98; Sørensen, Preben Meulengracht. "Starkaðr, Loki og Egill Skallagrímsson." In *Sjötíu ritgerðir helgaðar Jakobi Benediktssyni 20 júlí 1977*. 2 vols. Ed. Einar G. Pétursson and Jónas Kristjánsson. Reykjavik: Stofnun Árna Magnússonar, 1977, vol. 2, pp. 759–68; Clunies Ross, Margaret. "The Art of Poetry and the Figure of the Poet in Egils saga." *Parergon* 22 (1978),

3–12; Sørensen, Jan Sand. "Komposition og værdiunivers i Egils saga." *Gripla* 4 (1980), 260–72; West, Ralph. "Snorri Sturluson and *Egils saga*: Statistics of Style." *Scandinavian Studies* 52 (1980), 163–93; Fidjestøl, Bjarne. *Det norrøne fyrstediktet*. Øvre Ervik: Alvheim & Eide, 1982; Berman, Melissa A. "*Egils saga* and *Heimskringla*." *Scandinavian Studies* 54 (1982), 21–50.

Bjarni Einarsson

[**See also:** *Ágrip af Nóregs konunga sǫgum*; Egill Skalla-Grímsson; *Heimskringla*; *Íslendingasögur*; *Konungasögur*; *Landnámabók*; *Morkinskinna*; *Mǫðruvallabók*; *Orkneyinga saga*; *Skáldasögur*; Snorri Sturluson; *Sverris saga*; *Þinga saga*]

Eilífr Goðrúnarson. We owe almost everything we know of the skald Eilífr Goðrúnarson and his work to Snorri Sturluson's *Edda* (ca. 1225). The only other medieval text to mention him and his poetry is *Skáldatal*, where he is listed among the poets who composed in honor of Earl Hákon Sigurðarson (d. *ca.* 995), a ruler who strongly supported the cause of paganism against the increasing influence of Christianity in Norway. Eilífr's extant poetry shows his awareness of the religious diversity of his age, the late 10th century, though his major work, *Þórsdrápa* ("Þórr's lay") has been the subject of differing judgments of its religious perspective. Almost nothing is known of Eilífr's life, and it is not known for certain whether he was a Norwegian or an Icelander.

All of Eilífr's extant verse has been preserved in MSS of *Snorra Edda*. One half-stanza, quoted in *Skáldskaparmál* 11 among examples of kennings for poetry, is usually understood to contain a cryptic allusion to Earl Hákon, though Lie (1976) has argued that the allusion is to Þórr. Another half-stanza occurs in *Skáldskaparmál* 65 among skaldic terms for Christ, as an example of how early poets referred to Christ in both pagan and Christian terms. Eilífr's lines claim that the "powerful king of Rome" has established his rule over the lands and shrines of the heathen gods: "he is said to have his throne south at Urðr's well."

The political and religious upheaval of late 10th-century Norway is palpable in *Þórsdrápa*. This powerful, moving, but intensely difficult skaldic poem represents Þórr's journey to the home of the giant Geirrøðr, his crossing of a raging river, and his defeat of the giant and his two daughters. Snorri gives a prose account of this myth in *Skáldskaparmál* 27, and three *Edda* MSS (R, W, T) follow it with twenty *dróttkvætt* stanzas from *Þórsdrápa*. Two other half-stanzas, usually considered part of the poem, and conventionally numbered 21 and 16, are quoted elsewhere in *Skáldskaparmál*.

Our difficulty in gauging Eilífr's perspective on his subject stems partly from the poem's abstruse complexity and partly from our lack of an earlier treatment of the myth, apart from a couple of eddic stanzas that Snorri quotes in his text. Many of the *drápa*'s elaborate giant- and Þórr-kennings seem to carry contemporary political allusions. The overwhelming power the poem has for most modern readers derives from the fact that Eilífr was using myth to explore the common ground between Christ and Þórr in an age where the two were seen to be divine complements, the one harrowing hell and Satan with his cross, the other routing Geirrøðr and his giant crew with staff and hammer.

Ed.: Finnur Jónsson, ed. *Den norsk-islandske skjaldedigtning*. Vols. 1A–2A (tekst efter håndskrifterne) and 1B–2B (rettet tekst). Copenhagen and Christiania [Oslo]: Gyldendal, 1912–15; rpt. Copenhagen:

Rosenkilde & Bagger, 1967 (A) and 1973 (B), vol. 1A, pp. 148–52, vol. 1B, pp. 139–44; Finnur Jónsson, ed. *Edda Snorra Sturlusonar*. Copenhagen: Gyldendal, 1931; Frank, Roberta. *Old Norse Court Poetry: The Dróttkvætt Stanza*. Islandica, 42. Ithaca and London: Cornell University Press, 1978 [pp. 105–8, 112–5; 118–9]. **Tr.**: Faulkes, Anthony, trans. *Snorri Sturluson: Edda*. Everyman Classics. London and Melbourne: Dent, 1987. **Bib.**: Hollander, Lee M. *A Bibliography of Skaldic Studies*. Copenhagen: Munksgaard, 1958; Bekker-Nielsen, Hans. *Old Norse–Icelandic Studies: A Select Bibliography*. Toronto Medieval Bibliographies, 1. Toronto: University of Toronto Press, 1967. **Lit.**: Finnur Jónsson, ed. *Þórsdrápa Eilífs Goðrúnarsonar fortolket*. Oversigt over Forhandlinger, 5. Copenhagen: Det Kongelige danske Videnskabernes Selskab, 1900, pp. 369–410; Kock, Ernst. *Notationes Norrœnae: Anteckningar till Edda och skaldediktning*. Lunds Universitets Årsskrift, n.s., sec. 1. Lund: Gleerup, 1923–44, paras. 442–69 [entire work published in 27 parts]; Reichardt, Konstantin. "Die Thórsdrápa des Eilífr Goðrúnarson: Textinterpretation." *Publications of the Modern Language Association* 63 (1948), 329–91; Kiil, Vilhelm. "Eilífr Goðrúnarson's Þórsdrápa." *Arkiv för nordisk filologi* 71 (1952), 89–167 [to be used with care]; Weber, Gerd Wolfgang. "Die Christus-Strophe des Eilífr Goðrúnarson." *Zeitschrift für deutsches Altertum und deutsche Literatur* 99 (1970), 87–90; Lie, Hallvard. "Þórsdrápa." *KLNM* 20 (1976), 397–400; Clunies Ross, Margaret. "An Interpretation of the Myth of Þórr's Encounter with Geirrøðr and His Daughters." In *Specvlvm Norrœnvm: Norse Studies in Memory of Gabriel Turville-Petre*. Ed. Ursula Dronke et al. Odense: Odense University Press, 1981, pp. 370–91; Clunies Ross, Margaret. "Style and Authorial Presence in Skaldic Mythological Poetry." *Saga-Book of the Viking Society* 20 (1981), 276–304; Schier, Kurt. "Zur Mythologie der Snorra Edda: Einige Quellenprobleme." In *Specvlvm Norrœnvm*, pp. 405–20; Ström, Folke. "Poetry as an Instrument of Propaganda: Jarl Hákon and His Poets." In *Specvlvm Norrœnvm*, pp. 440–58; Kuhn, Hans. *Das Dróttkvætt*. Heidelberg: Winter, 1983 [esp. pp. 293–5]; Clunies Ross, Margaret, and B. K. Martin. "Narrative Structures and Intertextuality in *Snorra Edda*: the Example of Thor's Encounter with Geirrøðr." In *Structure and Meaning in Old Norse Literature: New Approaches to Textual Analysis and Literary Criticism*. Ed. John Lindow et al. Viking Collection, 3. Odense: Odense University Press, 1986, pp. 56–72; Frank, Roberta. "Hand Tools and Power Tools in Eilífr's Þórsdrápa." In *Structure and Meaning in Old Norse Literature*, pp. 94–109.

Margaret Clunies Ross

[**See also**: Kennings; *Skáld*; Skaldic Meters; Skaldic Verse; *Snorra Edda*]

Einarr Helgason skálaglamm was one of the most notable poets of the 10th century. He was of a distinguished family of western Iceland, the brother of Ósvífr, father of Guðrún, whose life is depicted in *Laxdœla saga*. Little is known about Einarr's life, except some episodes connecting him with Egill Skalla-Grímsson, whose influence is apparent in Einarr's poetry. Presumably, he spent a great part of his life at the court of Earl Hákon (d. 995). According to *Jómsvíkinga saga*, Einarr was first known as "skjaldmeyjar" ("shield-maiden") Einarr, but was later called "skálaglamm" ("scale-tinkle"), because Earl Hákon gave him a pair of scales that gave a tinkling sound and foretold the future. Apart from *Vellekla*, a panegyric on the Norwegian sovereign Earl Hákon, some other stanzas by Einarr have been preserved: two stanzas of a panegyric on the Danish king Harald Blåtand (Bluetooth), a stanza of another panegyric on Earl Hákon, and some *lausavísur*. *Vellekla* is one of the most important skaldic poems of the 10th century.

Unfortunately, the poem has not been preserved as a whole; yet, many of the stanzas are quoted in the biographies of the Norwegian kings Haraldr gráfeldr ("grey-cloak") Eiríksson and Óláfr Tryggvason in *Heimskringla* and in that of Earl Hákon in *Fagrskinna*. The introductory stanzas and those that deal with the battle of the Jómsvíkingar are preserved in *Snorra Edda*. Certainly, the poem in its present state is not complete; for example, the "stef"-stanza, which is essential for a *drápa*, is lacking.

Although the original structure of *Vellekla* is uncertain because of the poem's state of preservation, it is possible to offer a synopsis of its contents. After a comparatively long introduction (six stanzas) containing the customary elements, such as the request for silence, the praise of the sovereign, and the announcement of the theme, the *drápa* depicts the events that mark Earl Hákon's advance to power over the whole of Norway: the wars with Haraldr gráfeldr and his brothers, the sons of Eiríkr blóðøx ("blood-axe") Haraldsson, during which he took vengeance on his uncle Grjótgarðr and Haraldr for his father's, Earl Sigurðr's, death; the battles with Ragnfrøðr, another of Eiríkr's sons, who tried to reconquer Norway; the victorious battle at the Danevirke against the German emperor Otto II, which he fought in the service of the Danish king; the long expedition through the unknown Gautland back to Trondheim. It is doubtful whether the stanzas relating to the battle of the Jómsvíkingar under Earl Sigvaldi belong to this poem, since they are cited neither in *Heimskringla* nor in *Fagrskinna*; some of these stanzas describe the beneficial consequences of the earl's government. He restored the old pagan cults that had been abolished under Eiríkr's sons, which returned good harvests to the country. Usually, these stanzas are placed after the successful war against Haraldr in accordance with the historical accounts of *Heimskringla* and *Fagrskinna*. However, considering the present tense used in these stanzas, they could also be regarded as a praise of the earl's rule at the moment when the *drápa* was written, and therefore placed just before the concluding praise of the sovereign.

Thus far, no satisfactory explanations of the title of the poem, *Vellekla*, meaning "shortage of gold," have been found. Either it expresses the poet's hopes for a reward from the sovereign (but in the preserved stanzas this theme takes no more space than is usual in panegyrics), or it could be an ironic allusion to some unknown situation. There is a third possibilty: *Vellekla* could be part of a kenning for the sovereign (e.g., "remover of shortage of gold").

It is also somewhat difficult to date the poem. Supposing that the stanzas about the battle of the Jómsvíkingar were part of the original poem, it must be dated in the years after 985. In this case, chronological problems arise concerning the episodes related in *Egils saga*, but this objection may not prove serious, because these episodes are partly typical skaldic anecdotes whose content is historically doubtful. If the contested stanzas do not belong to the poem, it must be dated to the years after 975.

In *Vellekla*, Einarr skálaglamm proves to be a remarkable artist. He creates a brilliant poem by the sophistication of his language and metrics, especially by extensive and ingenious kennings, which he intended to equal the glory of his sovereign.

Vellekla is also important as evidence of the late Old Norse pagan religion. It shows the connection between political power and religion in the concept of the sovereign who is guided by the god, and who reintroduces the old cults that are the fundamental condition of the prosperity of the country. A literary allusion to *Vǫluspá* suggests that the poet wanted to praise Earl Hákon's rule as comparable to that of the god Baldr, who returns after Ragnarǫk.

Ed.: Finnur Jónsson, ed. *Den norsk-islandske skjaldedigtning*. Vols. 1A-2A (tekst efter håndskrifterne) and 1B-2B (rettet tekst). Copenhagen and Christiania [Oslo]: Gyldendal, 1912–15; rpt. Copenhagen: Rosenkilde & Bagger, 1967 (A) and 1973 (B), vol. 1A, pp. 122–31, 1B, pp. 117–24; Lindquist, Ivar, ed. *Norröna lovkväden från 800– och 900– talen. 1. Förslag till restituerad täxt jämte översättning*. Lund: Gleerup, 1929, pp. 44–55; Kock, Ernst A., ed. *Den norsk-isländska skaldediktningen*. 2 vols. Lund: Gleerup, 1946–50, vol. 1, pp. 66–9. **Tr.**: Hollander, Lee M., trans. *The Skalds: A Selection of Their Poems*. New York: American-Scandinavian Foundation; Princeton: Princeton University Press, 1945. **Lit.**: Björn M. Ólsen. "Skýring." *Árbók hins Íslenzka fornleifafélags* (1882), 154–6; Konráð Gíslason. *Forelæsninger over oldnorske Skjaldekvad*. Efterladte Skrifter, 1. Copenhagen: Gyldendal, 1895; Patzig, H. "Die Abfassung von Einars Vellekla." *Zeitschrift für deutsches Altertum und deutsche Literatur* 67 (1930), 55–65; Indrebø, Gustav. "Fylke og fylkesnamn." *Bergens Museums Árbok*, Hist.-ant. rekke nr. 1 (1931), 43–4; Finnur Jónsson. *Tekstkritiske Bemærkninger til Skjaldekvad*. Danske Videnskabernes Selskab. Historisk-filologiske Meddelelser, 20.2. Copenhagen: Levin & Munksgaard, 1934; Olsen, Magnus. "Eldste Forekomst av Navnet Hlaðir (Velleka 14)." *Maal og minne* (1941), 154–6; Turville-Petre, E. O. G. *Scaldic Poetry*. Oxford: Clarendon, 1976, pp. 59–63.

Edith Marold

[**See also**: Egill Skalla-Grímsson; *Egils saga Skalla-Grímssonar*; *Fagrskinna*; Harald Gormsson (Bluetooth); *Heimskringla*; *Jómsvíkinga saga*; Kennings; *Lausavísur*; *Laxdœla saga*; *Skáld*; Skaldic Meters; Skaldic Verse; *Snorra Edda*; *Vǫluspá*]

Einarr Skúlason was the most prolific skald of the 12th century. He was a favorite of Snorri Sturluson, who in his *Snorra Edda* and *Heimskringla* quotes twice as many verses from Einarr as from any other skald. In the surviving corpus of skaldic poetry, Einarr's verses are outnumbered only by those of Sighvatr Þórðarson.

Little is known of Einarr's life. He was a member of the Kveld-Úlfr family and, as a descendant of Skalla-Grímr, was a kinsman of Egill Skalla-Grímsson, Snorri, and Óláfr Þórðarson. The date and place of his birth are obscure, but he was probably born in the last decade of the 11th century in the area around the Borgarfjörður. By 1114, he was in Norway with King Sigurðr Jórsalafari ("crusader") Magnússon; *Þinga saga* reports that he was used as a messenger in a series of disputes between the king and Sigurðr Hranason that occurred between 1112 and 1114. *Morkinskinna* tells another anecdote concerning Einarr and Sigurðr Jórsalafari that took place when Sigurðr was awaiting the arrival of King Haraldr Gilli Magnússon in Norway, around 1124, although this passage may be an unreliable interpolation. We know that Einarr was with Haraldr Magnússon sometime during his reign (1130–1136), because he composed two poems in honor of Haraldr, and *Skáldatal* reports that he composed a poem (now lost) for Magnús blindi ("blind") Sigurðarson, who shared the rule with Haraldr from 1130 to 1135. By 1143, he was back in Iceland; his name appears in a list of priests in the west country compiled in that year. The position of his name in the list suggests that he lived in the Borgarfjörður district, probably at Borg. It is not clear where Einarr received his clerical education. The schools at Skálholt, Haukadalr, and Oddi were well established by this time, but he may have followed the example of the many learned Icelanders who studied in Germany and France.

Sometime during the joint reign of the Haraldssons, Einarr returned to Norway. He composed poems for all three, as well as a "Haraldssonakvæði." But his principal patron and great friend was Eysteinn, who, according to *Morkinskinna*, made Einarr his *stallari* ("marshall"). Einarr probably remained with King Eysteinn until Eysteinn's death in 1157, and then he may have left Norway to travel through Denmark and Sweden. *Skáldatal* reports that he composed poems for King Sørkvir of Sweden and his son Jón, and for King Sven of Denmark, although none of these poems survives. At some time, he returned to Norway and was with King Ingi and Grégoríus Dagsson: his poem *Elfarvísur* was composed for Grégoríus sometime between the battle of Elfr (1159) and the fall of Ingi and Grégoríus in 1161. It is not known whether Einarr then went home to Iceland or remained in Norway, but he would have been an old man and cannot have lived long after.

Einarr's masterpiece is *Geisli*, the long *drápa* on St. Óláfr Haraldsson, which he composed for a meeting in Trondheim in 1152 or 1153. The poem emphasizes Óláfr's sanctity by comparing him to Christ in an elaborately wrought typological parallel. *Geisli* may be the earliest of the Christian *drápur*; its influence can be seen in all the others. In addition to *Geisli*, a number of the poems Einarr made in praise of his patrons survive: fragments of the two *drápur* on Sigurðr and of two on Haraldr Gilli Magnússon (one in *tøglag* meter); the fragmentary *Haraldssonakvæði*; fragments of a poem in *runhent* meter on an unknown prince; the *Elfarvísur*, and the fragments of an *Eysteinsdrápa* and an *Ingadrápa*. His most difficult poem is the *Øxarflokkr*, containing extremely complex kennings, many in the metonymic style that Snorri calls *ofljóst* ("unclear"). Although the content of Einarr's poetry (apart from *Geisli*) is mundane, his verses show a remarkable facility with skaldic diction, rhyme, and meter.

Ed.: Finnur Jónsson, ed. *Den norsk-islandske skjaldedigtning*. Vols. 1A-2A (tekst eftir håndskrifterne) and 1B-2B (rettet tekst). Copenhagen and Christiania [Oslo]: Gyldendal, 1912–15; rpt. Copenhagen: Rosenkilde & Bagger, 1967 (A) and 1973 (B), vols. 1A, pp. 455–85, 1B, pp. 423–57; Finnur Jónsson, ed. *Morkinskinna*. Samfund til udgivelse af gammel nordisk litteratur, 53. Copenhagen: Jørgensen, 1932; Sigurður Nordal and Guðni Jónsson, eds. *Borgfirðinga sǫgur*. Íslenzk fornrit, 3. Reykjavik: Hið íslenzka fornritafélag, 1938; Bjarni Aðalbjarnarson, ed. *Heimskringla*. 3 vols. Íslenzk fornrit, 26–8. Reykjavik: Hið íslenzka fornritafélag, 1941–51; Chase, Martin. "Einar Skúlason's *Geisli*: A Critical Edition." Diss. University of Toronto, 1981. **Lit.**: Finnur Jónsson. *Den oldnorske og oldislandske Litteraturs Historie*. 2 vols. Copenhagen: Gad, 1894–1901, vol. 2, pp. 62–73; Paasche, Fredrik. *Kristendom og Kvad: En studie i norrøn middelalder*. Kristiania [Oslo]: Aschehoug, 1914, pp. 72–84; Paasche, Fredrik. *Norges og Islands Litteratur*. Kristiania [Oslo]: Aschehoug, 1924, pp. 288–90; Vries, Jan de. *Altnordische Literaturgeschichte*. 2 vols. Grundriss der germanischen Philologie, 15–6. Berlin: de Gruyter, 1941–42; rpt. 1964–67, vol. 2, pp. 15–23; Fidjestøl, Bjarne. *Det norrøne fyrstediktet*. Øvre Ervik: Alvheim & Eide, 1982, pp. 153–6; Tate, George S. "Einarr Skúlason." In *Dictionary of the Middle Ages*. Ed. Joseph R. Strayer. New York: Scribner, 1982–89, vol. 4, pp. 411–2.

Martin Chase, S.J.

[**See also**: Christian Poetry, West Norse; Egill Skalla-Grímsson; *Einars þáttr Skúlasonar*; *Heimskringla*; Miracles, Collections of; *Morkinskinna*; *Skáld*; Skaldic Meters; Skaldic Verse; *Snorra Edda*; *Þinga saga*]

Einars þáttr Skúlasonar ("The Tale of Einarr Skúlason") tells of Einarr, Icelander and court poet to a number of Norwegian kings in the first half of the 12th century. The tale was probably written about fifty years after the events it records. It is incorporated in the vellum collection of sagas of Norwegian kings known as *Morkinskinna*, dating from the second half of the 13th century. Written by two contemporary hands, *Morkinskinna* now contains thirty-seven leaves, though the original volume probably had fifty-three. In his introduction to the edition of 1932, Finnur Jónsson states that *Einars þáttr Skúlasonar*, found toward the end of the book among material concerned with the joint reign of the brothers Eysteinn (1103–1123) and Sigurðr Jórsalafari ("crusader") Magnússon (1103–1130), is clearly an interpolation, which is found nowhere else. It contains three anecdotes illustrating the verbal dexterity of Einarr as an improviser of occasional verses in the complex skaldic meter with its alliteration, full-rhyme, and half-rhyme, each incident being linked to a verse.

In the first anecdote, the poet comes late to a dinner at Trondheim, Norway, and is condemned to pay a sconce unless he can compose a verse before King Eysteinn has emptied his wine vessel. In the second, set in Bergen, a traveling player is to be flogged for eating meat on Friday. When Einarr vouches for him as a fellow entertainer, the king declares that the culprit shall be flogged for as long as it takes the poet to compose a verse. Einarr manages to complete the task by the time five strokes have been given. In the third anecdote, also set in Bergen, the king invites Einarr to compose a verse about a lady of unusually magnificent appearance who is sailing out of the harbor, and to complete it before her ship passes the island. As a fee, he agrees to give Einarr a pot of honey for every line of the eight-lined verse that neither he nor his guard can remember. Einarr then recites the poem, and the king can remember only the first and last lines, but the guard none.

Ed.: Finnur Jónsson, ed. *Morkinskinna*. Samfund til udgivelse af gammel nordisk litteratur, 53. Copenhagen: Jørgensen, 1932; Gimmler, Heinrich, ed. *Die Thættir der Morkinskinna: ein Beitrag zur Überlieferungsproblematik und zur Typologie der altnordischen Kurzerzählung*. Diss. Frankfurt am Main and Bamberg: Difo-Druck, 1976. **Tr.**: Boucher, Alan, trans. *A Tale of Icelanders*. Reykjavik: Iceland Review, 1980, pp. 91–3.

Alan Boucher

[**See also**: Einarr Skúlason; *Morkinskinna*; *Þáttr*]

Einars þáttr Sokkasonar ("The Tale of Einarr Sokkason") is preserved in *Flateyjarbók* in the latter part of the MS, written by Magnús Þórhallsson, under the heading *Grænlendinga þáttr*. The story takes place in Greenland. Two men of great authority are introduced at the beginning, Sokki Þórisson and his son, Einarr, who lived at Brattahlíð (Qagssiarssuk). Sokki obtains the Greenlanders' consent to try to get a bishop for Greenland, and for that purpose sends his son Einarr to Norway. In Norway, Einarr visits King Sigurðr Jórsalafari ("crusader"), who persuades a Norwegian priest, Arnaldr, to take on the bishopric. The same summer that Einarr and Arnaldr set off for Greenland, a Norwegian merchant, Arnbjǫrn, sails with a costly and splendid ship and heads for Greenland, but the ship and crew disappear. The ship and the men's bodies are later found in a firth near the glacier Hvítserkr by a Greenlandic huntsman, who brings the bones, the

ship, and the crew's valuables to Garðar and gives the ship to the bishop's see for the good of the dead men's souls. When news of this wreck comes to Norway, Arnaldr's kinsmen sail to Greenland and make a request to the bishop for Arnbjǫrn's inheritance, which the bishop refuses. This decision leads to a feud between the Greenlanders and Norwegian merchants, who at this time were present in great numbers in Greenland; the feud ends with a battle in which some of the men from both sides are killed, among them Einarr Sokkason. These events took place in the years 1124–1136.

There is every reason to believe that *Einars þáttr Sokkasonar* was composed by a man who had access to oral sources from both sides, the Greenlandic and the Norwegian. The þáttr contains quite a number of personal names and place-names, and the description of events and circumstances is frequently detailed to such an extent that one might conclude that some people who experienced these events were still alive when the þáttr was composed. There are some inconsistencies in the narration, but otherwise the þáttr is readable and well written. The author is unknown, but there are some striking similarities in style and vocabulary between the þáttr and *Morkinskinna*, in particular *Morkinskinna*'s insert from *Hryggjarstykki, indicating that the þáttr probably dates from the late 12th century.

Ed.: Guðbrandr Vigfússon and C. R. Unger, eds. *Flateyjarbók: En samling af norske Konge-Sagaer med indskudte mindre Fortællinger om Begivenheder i og undenfor Norge samt Annaler*. 3 vols. Christiania [Oslo]: Malling, 1860–68, vol. 3, pp. 445–54; Finnur Jónsson, ed. *Flateyjarbók (Codex Flateyensis). MS. No. 1005 fol. in the Old Royal Collection in the Royal Library of Copenhagen*. Corpus Codicum Islandicorum Medii Aevi, 1. Copenhagen: Levin & Munksgaard, 1930, cols. 847–50 [facsimile]; Rafn, C. C., and Finnur Magnússon, eds. *Grönlands historiske Mindesmærker*. 2 vols. Copenhagen: Brünnsch, 1838, vol. 2, pp. 669–724; Einar Ól. Sveinsson and Matthías Þórðarson, eds. *Eyrbyggja saga*. Íslenzk fornrit, 4. Reykjavik: Hið íslenzka fornritafélag, 1935, pp. 271–92; Sigurður Nordal et al., eds. *Flateyjarbók*. 4 vols. Akranes: Flateyjarútgáfan, 1944–45, vol. 4, pp. xi–xii, 231–41; Ólafur Halldórsson. *Grænland í miðaldaritum*. Reykjavik: Sögufélag, 1978, pp. 103–16, 401–5. **Bib.**: Halldór Hermannsson. *Bibliography of the Icelandic Sagas and Minor Tales*. Islandica, 1. Ithaca: Cornell University Library, 1908, p. 16; Halldór Hermannsson. *The Sagas of Icelanders (Íslendingasögur): A Supplement to Bibliography of the Icelandic Sagas and Minor Tales*. Islandica, 24. Ithaca: Cornell University Press, 1935; London: Oxford University Press, p. 24; Jóhann S. Hannesson. *The Sagas of Icelanders (Íslendingasögur). A Supplement to Islandica I and XXIV*. Islandica, 38. Ithaca: Cornell University Press, 1957, pp. 26–7. **Tr.**: Jones, Gwyn, trans. *The Norse Atlantic Saga: Being the Norse Voyages of Discovery and Settlement to Iceland, Greenland, and North America*. rev. ed. Oxford: Oxford University Press, 1986, pp. 236–41.

Ólafur Halldórsson

[**See also**: *Flateyjarbók*; *Morkinskinna*; *Þáttr*]

Eiríks saga rauða see **Vinland Sagas**

Eiríks saga víðfǫrla ("The Saga of Eiríkr the Far-traveler") is a short Icelandic saga, written probably around 1300 by an anonymous author. The story tells of Eiríkr, son of King Þrándr of Þrándheimr (Trondheim) in Norway, who makes a Christmas vow to find the heathen *Ódáins akr* ("pasture of immortality"). On his journey south and east, he stops in Constantinople, where he is taught about theology, geography, and cosmology by the king, and where he converts to Christianity. Eiríkr also learns that *Ódáins akr* is identical to the Christian earthly paradise and is told where to seek it. He continues his journey and comes to a river, beyond which he sees a beautiful country. In an attempt to pass the bridge leading there, Eiríkr is swallowed by a dragon guarding the bridge, and passes through darkness into a place he believes is paradise. However, in a dream conversation with his guardian angel, he is told that he is not in paradise, but in a place especially created to reward him for his toil. Given the choice of staying or returning, he chooses to go back to Norway in order to prepare the people there for the acceptance of the Christian faith. Ten years after his return, he is carried off by the spirit of God.

The saga exists in three medieval versions, A, B, and C, and is preserved in more than fifty MSS, the oldest of which is the B-manuscript AM 657c 4to (*ca.* 1350). All versions go back to one written original, and even though the C-version is extant only in two MSS from the 17th century, there can be little doubt that this version represents the original better than A and B, which are both reworked versions.

Eiríks saga víðfǫrla presents the (pseudo?) heathen concept *Ódáins akr*, also mentioned by the Danish historian Saxo Grammaticus (*ca.* 1200). Since this saga shares many of the characteristics of the *fornaldarsǫgur*, it has generally been classified with this group. It is doubtful, however, whether any Nordic traditional material is preserved in the saga. It seems obvious that the second part of the saga is thoroughly influenced by visionary literature, while the first part includes lavish paraphrases of such popular books of learning as the *Elucidarius* and *Imago mundi* (*ca.* 1125). In some places, the saga exhibits striking resemblances to *Barlaams ok Josaphats saga* and *Konráðs saga keisarasonar.* The saga could be considered a rather clever attempt to make an entertaining story out of a didactic and edifying topic, and it gained considerable popularity both in the Middle Ages and in later centuries.

Ed.: Rafn, C. C., ed. *Fornaldar sögur Norðrlanda.* 3 vols. Copenhagen: Popp, 1829–30, vol. 3, pp. 661–74; Guðbrandr Vigfússon and C. R. Unger, eds. *Flateyjarbok: En Samling af norske Konge-Sagaer med indskudte mindre Fortællinger om Begivenheder i og underfor Norge samt Annaler.* 3 vols. Christiania [Oslo]: Malling, 1860–68, vol. 1, pp. 29–36; Sigurður Nordal et al., eds. *Flateyjarbók.* 4 vols. Akranes: Flateyjarútgáfan, 1944–45, vol. 1, pp. 30–8; Jensen, Helle, ed. *Eiríks saga víðfǫrla.* Editiones Arnamagnæanæ, ser. B, vol. 29. Copenhagen: Reitzel, 1983. **Lit.**: Schlauch, Margaret. *Romance in Iceland.* New York: American-Scandinavian Foundation; London: Allen & Unwin, 1934; rpt. New York: Russell & Russell, 1973, pp. 49ff.; Patch, Howard Rollin. *The Other World According to Descriptions in Medieval Literature.* Smith College Studies in Modern Languages, n.s. 1. Cambridge: Harvard University Press, 1950, pp. 72f., 123; Simek, Rudolf. "Die Quellen der Eiríks saga víðfǫrla." *Skandinavistik* 14 (1984), 109–14; Jensen, Helle. "Eiríks saga víðfǫrla: Appendiks 3." In *The Sixth International Saga Conference 28/7–2/8 1985. Workshop Papers.* 2 vols. Copenhagen: Det arnamagnæanske Institut, 1985, vol. 1, pp. 499–512 [photocopies of papers distributed to participants]; Power, Rosemary. "Christian Influence in the *Fornaldarsǫgur Norðrlanda.*" In *The Sixth International Saga Conference*, vol. 2, pp. 843–57 [interpretation of the saga based on A].

†Helle Jensen

[**See also:** *Barlaams ok Josephats saga; Elucidarius; Fornaldarsǫgur, Konráðs saga keisarasonar,* Visionary Literature]

Eiríksdrápa *see* Þórðr Kolbeinsson

Eiríksmál ("The Lay of Eiríkr"), a panegyrical poem in honor of the late Norwegian Viking king Eiríkr blóðøx ("blood-axe") Haraldsson, has been handed down to us in *Fagrskinna* (Red. A) and one stanza in the MSS of Snorri's *Edda.* Unlike *Hákonarmál, Eiríksmál* is anonymous. Its brevity in comparison to *Hákonarmál* has led to the assumption that the stanzas preserved are no more than a fragment (*cf.* Hollander 1932–33).

The poem consists of one single scene taking place in Valhǫll, a conversation among Óðinn, Bragi, the god of poetry, and the hero Sigmundr. After a dream about preparations for a feast, Óðinn is now waiting for Eiríkr. When Eiríkr arrives with a loud noise, Bragi thinks that the god Baldr is coming back. Óðinn tells him that it is not Baldr but Eiríkr, whom he has chosen to be one of his warriors in Valhǫll. Sigmundr, who is assigned to welcome Eiríkr, asks the question that certainly also moved Eiríkr's followers: Why did Óðinn withhold victory from him? The answer hints at the imminent Ragnarǫk, embodied in the grey wolf who is threatening the gods' dwellings. The last stanzas contain the welcoming of Eiríkr, who gloriously marches in, followed by five kings, perhaps killed with or by him.

Fagrskinna relates that after the death of Eiríkr blóðøx during the battle of Stainmoor (Westmorland, England, 954), the king's widow ordered a poem to be made for his obsequies. Scholars have questioned whether this information is historically true. If one accepts the information given in *Fagrskinna*, the poem can be dated to the year 954. The language, strongly influenced by Anglo-Saxon (*cf.* Hofmann 1955) suggests that the poet lived in the Danelaw for a considerable time. But some scholars (Wadstein 1895, von See 1963) believe the poem is an imitation of *Hákonarmál.* In this case, it must have been written during the reign of Eiríkr's sons in Norway (after 961, the fall of Hákon góði ["the good"] Haraldsson). Their main arguments are the more archaic conception of Valhǫll in *Hákonarmál* and the higher poetic quality attributed to that poem (*cf.*, however, Wolf 1969, Marold 1972).

The poem is one of the "eddic poems," the others being *Hákonarmál* and *Haraldskvæði.* It differs in several respects from the skaldic panegyrics. The metrical form of the stanzas (*fornyrðislag* and *ljóðaháttr*) is typical of epic poetry, as is the scenic presentation of the events in dialogues. The vocabulary and the style also distinguish the poem from skaldic poetry.

The fact that Eiríkr was a baptized Christian did not prevent the poet from using the conception of the dead hero's glorious reception in Valhǫll as a means to praise the fallen Viking king. None of the dark sides of Óðinn as god of the dead is mentioned here, as is the case with *Hákonarmál.* The poem does not stress the terrible god, who himself inflicts death upon his own heroes, a characteristic trait of the "warriors of Óðinn." The emphasis lies on the hero's triumphant entry to Valhǫll as well as the eschatological theme of Ragnarǫk and the last battle against the monsters, for which Óðinn is gathering his heroes. By including these themes, the poem overcomes the terror of death, giving it a sense of purpose.

Ed.: Finnur Jónsson, ed. *Den norsk-islandske skjaldedigtning*. Vols. 1A-2A (tekst efter håndskrifterne) and 1B-2B (rettet tekst). Copenhagen and Christiania [Oslo]: Gyldendal, 1912–15; rpt. Copenhagen: Rosenkilde & Bagger, 1967 (A) and 1973 (B), vol. 1A, pp. 174–5; vol. 1B, pp. 164–6; Lindquist, Ivar, ed. *Norröna lovkväden från 800– och 900–talen*. Del 1. *Förslag till resitituerad täxt jämte översättning*. Lund: Gleerup, 1929, pp. 8–10; Kock, Ernst A., ed. *Den norskisländska skaldediktningen*. 2 vols. Lund: Gleerup, 1946–49, vol. 1, p. 89. **Tr.**: Hollander, Lee M. *Old Norse Poems: The Most Important Non-Skaldic Verse Not Included in the Poetic Edda*. New York: Columbia University Press, 1936; rpt. Millwood: Kraus, 1973; Leach, Howard G. *A Pageant of Old Scandinavia*. Princeton: Princeton University Press; New York: American-Scandinavian Foundation, 1946. **Lit.**: Wadstein, Elis. "Bidrag till tolkning och belysning av skalde- och Eddadikter." *Arkiv för nordisk filologi* 11 (1895), 64–92, esp. 87–8; Genzmer, Felix. "Das eddische Preislied." *Beiträge zur Geschichte der deutschen Sprache und Literatur* 44 (1919), 138–68; Noreen, Erik. "Eiríksmál och Hákonarmál." *Nordisk Tidskrift för vetenskap konst och industri, utg. av Letterstedska Föreningen* (1922), 535–42; Sahlgren, Jöran. *Eddica et Scaldica. Fornvästnordiska studier* 1. Nordisk Filologi, 1. Lund: Gleerup, 1927, pp. 1–37; Hollander, Lee M. "Is the Lay of Eric a Fragment?" *Acta Philologica Scandinavica* 7 (1932–33), 249–57; Hofmann, Dietrich. *Nordisch-englische Lehnbeziehungen der Wikingerzeit*. Bibliotheca Arnamagnæana, 14. Copenhagen: Munksgaard, 1955, pp. 42–52; See, Klaus von. "Zwei eddische Preislieder: Eiríksmál und Hákonarmál." In *Festgabe für Ulrich Pretzel zum 65. Geburtstag dargebracht von seinen Freunden und Schülern*. Ed. Werner Simon et al. Berlin: Schmidt, 1963, pp. 107–17; Wolf, Alois. "Zitat und Polemik in den *Hákonarmál* Eyvinds." In *Germanische Studien*. Ed. J. Erben and E. Thurnher. Innsbrucker Beiträge zur Kulturwissenschaft, 15. Innsbruck: Institut für vergleichende Sprachwissenschaft der Universität Innsbruck, 1969, pp. 9–32; Marold, Edith. "Das Walhallbild in den *Eiríksmál* und den *Hákonarmál*." *Mediaeval Scandinavia* 5 (1972), 19–33; Seeberg, Axel. "Five Kings." *Saga-Book of the Viking Society* 20 (1979–80), 106–13; See, Klaus von. *Edda, Saga, Skaldendichtung*. Heidelberg: Winter, 1981, pp. 522–5.

Edith Marold

[**See also:** Baldr; Commemorative Poetry; Eddic Meters; Eddic Poetry; Eyvindr Finnsson skáldaspillir; *Fagrskinna*; Óðinn; Skaldic Meters; Skaldic Verse; *Snorra Edda*; Þorbjǫrn hornklofi]

Eirspennill

Eirspennill ("copper-clasp") is a MS (AM 47 fol.) containing copies of four works: *Heimskringla* (the last third), *Sverris saga*, *Bǫglunga sǫgur*, and *Hákonar saga (gamla) Hákonarsonar*. The name *Eirspennill* refers to the copper clasp gracing the cover, and the generally high aesthetic quality of the volume clearly suggests that it was produced for a person of great wealth.

The MS is the product of two main hands. The first is responsible for the text of *Heimskringla*, the other for the remainder of the work. An early 14th-century origin may be confidently assumed. A marginal note shows that around the middle of the 14th century the volume belonged to Þrándr Garðarson, later archbishop of Niðaróss (Trondheim).

The spelling follows Icelandic conventions, but includes many Norwegianisms. Earlier scholarly opinion tended to favor the view that the MS was written in Norway by two Norwegians working from an Icelandic exemplar; but more recent research has shown that the copyists must have been two Icelanders imitating Norwegian conventions.

Eirspennill presents *Sverris saga*, *Bǫglunga sǫgur*, and *Hákonar saga* in condensed and abbreviated versions. *Eirspennill* takes care to leave out everything that may be filled in by an imaginative reader: the protagonists' thoughts and reflections, motives for deeds done, explanations of the purpose of actions performed, and various minor circumstances. A few of the omissions and changes in *Sverris saga* were evidently made with a view to eliminating any doubt as to Sverrir's royal ancestry.

It is difficult to determine whether the copyists worked from a MS containing all the four sagas mentioned above or from separate exemplars. A detailed linguistic investigation might settle the matter. Presumably, the second scribe was in charge of the abbreviations.

Ed.: Finnur Jónsson, ed. *Eirspennill*. Christiania [Oslo]: Den Norske historiske kildeskriftkommision, 1913. **Lit.**: Kålund, Kr. *Katalog over den Arnamagnæanske Håndskriftsamling*. 2 vols. Copenhagen: Gyldendal, 1889–94, vol. 1, pp. 33–5; Indrebø, Gustav, ed. *Sverris saga etter Cod. AM 327 4°*. Utgjevi av Den Norske Historiske Kildeskriftkommission. Kristiania [Oslo]: Dybwad, 1920; rpt. Oslo: Norsk Historisk Kjeldeskrift-Institutt, 1981, p. xxx; Seip, Didrik Arup. *Nye studier i norsk språkhistorie*. Oslo: Aschehoug, 1954, pp. 175–81; Louis-Jensen, Jonna. *Kongesagastudier. Kompilationen Hulda-Hrokkinskinna*. Bibliotheca Arnamagnæana, 32. Copenhagen: Reitzel, 1977, pp. 21–4; Stefán Karlsson. "Islandsk bogeksport til Norge i middelalderen." *Maal og minne* (1979), 1–17; Jakobsen, Alfred. "'Fusk' i en kongesagaavskrift?" *Opuscula* 8. Bibliotheca Arnamagnæana, 38. Copenhagen: Reitzel, 1985, pp. 134–40.

Alfred Jakobsen

[**See also:** *Bǫglunga sǫgur*; *Hákonar saga gamla Hákonarsonar*; *Heimskringla*; *Sverris saga*]

Elder Edda *see* Eddic Poetry

Elis saga ok Rósamundu

Elis saga ok Rósamundu ("The Saga of Elis and Rósamunda") is an Old Norse adaptation of an Old French *chanson de geste*, *Elie de Saint Gille*. The saga appears to derive from an earlier (probably 12th-century) version of the work than that preserved in the single extant French MS, BN 25516, dating from the 13th century. The first fifty-nine chapters of *Elis saga* are found, along with *Strengleikar*, in the Norwegian MS De la Gardie 4–7 fol. (ca. 1250). The *explicit* to this section names King Hákon Hákonarson (r. 1217–1263) as the commissioner of the work and the writer as "abbot Robert," probably to be identified with the "brother Robert" to whom the composition of *Tristrams saga* is attributed. The next eleven chapters, which deviate from the contents of the French *Elie*, are found only in Icelandic MSS, principally Stock. Perg. 4to no. 6 (ca. 1400), Stock. Perg. fol. no. 7, and AM 533 4to (both 15th century). These MSS provide *Elis saga* with a continuation and a second conclusion after the somewhat abrupt ending of the Norwegian text. They were probably inspired by the closing reference in ch. 59 to the further trials of Elis and Rósamunda, which are said to precede a happy outcome, but are not recorded ("þá er æigi á bók þessi skrifat").

Elis saga is written in the "court style" of a number of translated *riddarasögur* and marked by a high degree of alliteration. The retention of the narrating persona of the French source, with its initial direct address to the audience and later appeal for attention, is an unusual feature.

The saga combines the theme of Christian-pagan conflict, characteristic of French epic, with motifs more typical of original Icelandic *riddarasögur*, particularly in the last eleven chapters. As a whole, *Elis saga* conforms to the pattern of Exile-Testing-Return found in many medieval romances. The story concerns the testing of the newly dubbed Elis, who refuses a reconciliation and goes into exile after a quarrel with his elderly father, Duke Juliens of helga Egidie (French St. Gille). Juliens has publicly questioned his son's chivalric ability and been proved wrong. In the manner of a hero of chivalric romance, Elis travels alone, undergoing a series of tests of strength and courage that will provide ultimate refutation of his father's unwarranted criticism and eventually lead to marriage with the princess Rósamunda and a triumphant return to France. Elis begins by overcoming the heathen guards of four French knights, among them Vilhjálmr of Orengiborg (French Guillaume d'Orange), who have been taken prisoner after the defeat of the French by the advancing forces of Maskalbret. Captured by the enemy after a heroic stand, Elis escapes, and, in an episode more characteristic of romance than epic, acquires a helper figure in the form of Galopin, a reformed robber of noble birth. Wounded in a fight with a group of pagans beneath the walls of Sobrieborg, Elis is rescued and tended by the beautiful Rósamunda, who is already enamored of the description she has heard of him from her father, King Maskalbret. In single combat, Elis defeats her unwelcome suitor, Julien (a pagan king, not Duke Juliens of helga Egidie), refuses to marry the unconverted princess, but retires with her to a fortified tower to await reinforcements from France. Rósamunda agrees to be baptized after the inevitable defeat of the heathen. The Norwegian text ends here, at a point corresponding to line 2,417 in the French.

The Icelandic chapters describe Galopin's trip to France to seek the aid of Duke Juliens and Vilhjálmr, their arrival with an army, and resounding victory over the heathen, who surrender to Elis. At Rósamunda's request, he shows mercy to Maskalbret and restores his kingdom to him. In the tradition of medieval romance, but in contrast to the source, where the hero's role of godfather to the duly baptized Rosamonde prohibits marriage, they are wed. Juliens unhesitatingly grants Elis his patrimony and gives him the title of *hertogi* ("duke"). Also in keeping with the conventions of romance, Galopin is rewarded with a wife, lands, and the title of *jarl* ("count"). In the French version, Galopin marries Rosamonde, since Elie cannot. The final brief account of the reign of Elis and Rósamunda and the fine sons who succeed them resembles the ending of *Erex saga*.

The author's overtly partisan attitude toward the hero in his battles with the heathen, his fortitude, prowess, and mercy all serve to glorify Elis as a model knight and worthy Christian ruler.

Ed.: Kölbing, Eugen, ed. *Elis saga ok Rosamundu. Mit Einleitung, deutscher Übersetzung und Anmerkungen zum ersten Mal herausgegeben.* Heilbronn: Henninger, 1881; rpt. Wiesbaden: Sändig, 1971; Tveitane, Mattias. *Elis saga, Strengleikar and Other Texts: Uppsala University Library Delagardieska Samlingen Nos. 4–7 folio and AM 666b quarto.* Corpus Codicum Norvegicorum Medii Aevi. Quarto Serie, 4. Oslo: Selskapet til utgivelse af gamle norske håndskrifter, 1972 [facsimile]; Slay, Desmond. *Romances. Perg. 4:o nr 6 in The Royal Library, Stockholm.* Early Icelandic Manuscripts in Facsimile, 10. Copenhagen: Rosenkilde & Bagger, 1972. **Bib**: Kalinke, Marianne E., and P. M. Mitchell. *Bibliography of Old Norse–Icelandic Romances.* Islandica, 44. Ithaca and London: Cornell University Press, 1985, pp. 36–9. **Lit**: Kölbing, Eugen. "Die nordische Elissaga ok Rosamundu

und ihre Quelle." In *Beiträge zur vergleichenden Geschichte der romantischen Poesie und Prosa des Mittelalters unter besonderer Berücksichtigung der englischen und nordischen Litteratur.* Breslau: Koebner, 1876, pp. 92–136; Raynaud, Gaston, ed. *Elie de Sainte Gille. Chanson de geste publiée avec introduction, glossaire et index. Accompagnée de la rédaction norvégienne.* Paris: Didot, 1879 [contains a comparison of the contents of French and Norse versions and a French rendition of the German translation in Kölbing's edition]; Meissner, Rudolf. *Die Strengleikar. Ein Beitrag zur Geschichte der altnordischen Prosalitteratur.* Halle: Niemeyer, 1902; Hallberg, Peter. "Norröna riddarasagor. Några språkdrag." *Arkiv för nordisk filologi* 86 (1971), 114–38 [*Elis saga* and the "Tristram-Group"]; Barnes, Geraldine. "The *Riddarasögur*: A Medieval Exercise in Translation." *Saga-Book of the Viking Society* 19 (1977), 403–41 [pp. 416–8 are a review of Kölbing's and Meissner's assessments of the MSS]; Blaisdell, Foster W. "Elis saga ok Rósamundu: Holm 7—AM 119—Holm 17—Holm 46." *Opuscula* 8. Bibliotheca Arnamagnæana, 38. Copenhagen: Reitzel, 1985, pp. 153–7; Glauser, Jürg. "Vorbildliche Unterhaltung. Die Elis saga ok Rosamundu im Prozess der königlichen Legitimation." In *Applikationen. Analysen skandinavischer Erzähltexte.* Ed. Walter Baumgartner. Frankfurt am Main, Bern, and New York: Lang, 1987, pp. 95–129.

Geraldine Barnes

[**See also**: *Erex saga; Riddarasögur*]

Elucidarius (or *Lucidarius*) is a title given to two separate, popular medieval works. The first and older is a Latin *summa*, generally attributed to a monk calling himself Honorius Augustodunensis and dated to the very early 12th century. Written in the form of a dialogue between a master and a pupil, this *Elucidarius* was translated into a number of European languages, among them Old Icelandic and Swedish. The second work, entitled *Lucidarius*, was written in German in the late 12th century at the request of Henry the Lion. This work also uses the form of a dialogue between a master, who calls himself Lucidarius, and a student; it was translated into Danish, Dutch, Icelandic, and Bohemian. The German *Lucidarius* combines portions of Honorius's *Elucidarius* with other sources to produce a vernacular *summa*.

Both works are divided into three books and cover the general topic of theology in the thorough encyclopedic fashion typical of the medieval *summa*. Specific topics include the nature of the Trinity, the Creation, the Incarnation and Redemption, the role of the Church and the sacraments, the Last Judgment, and the end of the world. The German *Lucidarius* contains a lengthy survey of world geography in the first book, which is considerably shortened in the Danish translation. No doubt because they give simple and reassuring answers to a large number of common questions, both works achieved a popularity as reference sources among the unlearned laity that continued even after the Reformation. Among the earliest translations of Honorius's work into a European vernacular must have been the Old Icelandic *Elucidarius*. The oldest extant MS of this text, thought to be a copy of a copy of an original, is dated to around 1200. The MS evidence does not tell us clearly whether the original translator was an Icelander or a Norwegian. There is no complete version of the text in Old Icelandic, but portions of the translation, ranging in size from thirty-three leaves to a single paragraph, and in date from approximately 1200 to the 16th century, are preserved in eight parchment MSS. The two oldest defective MSS are extensive. AM 674a 4to, dated around 1200, consists of thirty-three leaves and was undoubtedly copied in Iceland, possibly from a Norwegian original. AM 675 4to, which now constitutes the third part of the *Hauksbók*, is dated to the early 14th century and consists of sixteen leaves. The following six Icelandic MSS contain portions of the text: AM 544 4to (early 14th century); AM 229 IV fol. (late 14th century); AM 685b 4to (second half of the 15th century); AM 685d 4to (second half of the 15th century); AM 238 XVIII fol. (16th century); AM 238 XIX fol. (15th century).

The Swedish translation of Honorius's work exists in two versions. The older, entitled *Lucidarius*, is extant in fragmentary form in the paper MS Cod. Holm D 4, housed in the Royal Library in Stockholm, and was written around 1430–1440. The younger version, entitled *Elucidarius*, covers the entire original text. It was translated in 1487 by the monk Jöns Raek (or Budde) in the cloister Nådendal, and is found in the paper MS A 58 4to in the Royal Library in Stockholm.

The German *Lucidarius* was probably translated into Danish around the turn of the 14th century. It exists in two versions: an older version found in the paper MS AM 76 8vo from the end of the 15th century, as well as in a printed edition by Gotfred of Ghemen; and a younger, shortened version suitable for a Protestant audience, published about 1534 in Roskilde and edited by the printer Hans Barth. The Icelandic translation is extant in two as yet unpublished MSS from the 17th century and later.

Ed.: Brandt, C. J., ed. *Lucidarius, en Folkebog fra Middelalderen.* Copenhagen: Berling, 1849; Hultman, O. F., ed. *Jöns Buddes bok. En handskrift från Nådendals Kloster.* Helsinki: Tidnings- & tryckeri-aktiebolaget, 1895; Jón Helgason, ed. *The Arna-Magnæan Manuscript 674A, 4to: Elucidarius.* Manuscripta Islandica, 4. Copenhagen: Munksgaard, 1957 [facsimile]; Konráð Gíslason, ed. "Brudstykker af den islandske Elucidarius." *Annaler for nordisk Oldkyndighed og Historie* (1858), 51–172; Kristensen, Marius, ed. *En klosterbog fra middelalderens slutning (AM 76, 8º).* Samfund til udgivelse af gammel nordisk litteratur, 54. Copenhagen: Jørgensen, 1933; Firchow, Evelyn S., and Kaaren Grimstad, eds. *Elucidarius in Old Norse Translation.* Reykjavik: Stofnun Árna Magnússonar, 1989. **Lit.**: The only survey of the Swedish and Danish translations is found in Schorbach, Karl. *Studien über das deutsche Volksbuch Lucidarius.* Quellen und Forschungen zur Sprach- und Kulturgeschichte der germanischen Völker, 74. Strassburg: Trübner, 1894; Salvesen, Astrid. *Studies in the Vocabulary of the Old Norse Elucidarium.* Oslo, Bergen, and Tromsø: Universitetsforlaget, 1968; Wolf, Kirsten. "A Note on the Date and Provenance of AM 229 fol. IV." *Maal og minne* (1991), 107–13.

Kaaren Grimstad

[**See also:** Bible; *Eiríks saga víðfǫrla*; Encyclopedic Literature; *Hauksbók*]

Elves *see* Supernatural Beings

Encomium Emmae reginae (or *Gesta Cnutonis regis*) deals

principally with Knud (Cnut) the Great and his progress to the English throne. It also tells something about Emma as Knud's queen, but nothing about her as the widow of King Æthelred II, Knud's adversary. Commissioned by Emma, the book was written in Latin prose around 1040–1041, probably in the monastery of St. Bertin in the city of St. Omer in Artois (Emma had been a refugee in Bruges). The text bore no title originally. The main MS (BL Add. 33241) and a number of copies are preserved. Its value as a historical source is debatable, because the narrative is heavily

biased in an effort to glorify Knud and conceal Emma's connection with Æthelred, as well as to denounce Harald, Knud's illegitimate son by Ælfgifu. The precise purpose of the text with respect to the relationship between Hardacnut, Emma's son by Knud, and Edward the Confessor, her son by Æthelred, remains open to debate. The text was written at a time when Emma had followed Hardacnut back to England, where he reigned only two years, until 1042. The last year, he reigned together with his half-brother, Edward the Confessor. This fact (but not Hardacnut's death) is recorded in an addition to the main MS. As the *Anglo-Saxon Chronicle* records (C1043, D1041 [1043]), tension rose between Emma and Edward because of her lack of support of his claims, by 1043 leading to King Edward's dispossession of his mother. As the bias in the text lies more in concealing some of the truth than in flagrant lying, some of the historical information it conveys may perhaps be trusted.

Ed.: Gertz, M. Cl., ed. "Gesta Cnutonis Regis (Encomium Emmæ)." *Scriptores minores historiæ Danicæ medii ævi.* Selskabet for Udgivelse af Kilder til dansk Historie. Copenhagen: Gad, 1917–20, vol. 2, pp. 375–426 [still the best edition with respect to variant readings]; Campbell, Alistair, ed. and trans. *Encomium Emmae Reginae.* Camden Society Third Series, 72. London: Royal Historical Society, 1949 [uses one unimportant secondary MS more than Gertz; does not give all variant readings]. **Tr.**: Campbell, Alistair [see above]. **Lit.**: Körner, Sten. *The Battle of Hastings, England, and Europe 1035–1066.* Lund: Gleerup, 1964; Lindqvist, Ole. "Encomium Emmae." *Scandia* 33 (1967), 175–81 [in opposition to Körner]; Stenton, F. M. *Anglo-Saxon England.* Oxford History of England, 2. 3rd ed. Oxford: Clarendon, 1971, pp. 426–7; Gransden, Antonia. *Historical Writing in England c. 550 to c. 1307.* London: Routledge & Kegan Paul, 1974; Campbell, Miles W. "The *Encomium Emmae Reginae*: Personal Panegyric or Political Propaganda." *Annuale Mediaevale* 19 (1979), 27–45.

Søren Balle

[**See also:** England, Norse in; Knud (Cnut) the Great]

Encyclopedic Literature. The medieval encyclopedia presented the arts and sciences that the Greeks considered essential to a liberal education in a form acceptable to the Christian Church. It was not arranged alphabetically, as modern encyclopedias are, to act as a repertory of information on all branches of knowledge, but concentrated on presenting a digest of all the *artes*.

In the period up to the 12th century, the two most influential Christian encyclopedists in western Europe were Isidore of Seville and Bede. Isidore's two major works in this field, the *Etymologiae* (ca. 600) and the *De natura rerum* (ca. 613), particularly the former, were widely known and used. There is some evidence that the *Etymologiae* was the ultimate source of certain Icelandic encyclopedic writings, including some of the texts in the encyclopedic section of *Hauksbók*.

The *Etymologiae sive origines* sets out in twenty books a succinct summary of the classical inheritance in the liberal arts, like grammar, music, and mathematics, as well as fundamental knowledge in fields that included the natural sciences, like geography, lists of the races and nations of men, kinds of animals, precious stones, and minerals, and the nature of agriculture and warfare. In *De natura rerum*, Isidore attempted a reconciliation of pagan science with Christian allegory. He was followed by the Anglo-Saxon scholar Bede, who, in a work of the same title from around 703, adapted classical natural science to the stringent requirements of the monastic vocations. He incorporated the study of natural science into that section of the curriculum dealing with computus, the reckoning of times, seasons, and astronomical occurrences, and in other of his works introduced elements of natural science into the genre of the exegetical biblical commentary, especially on the Book of Genesis. Hence, in Icelandic MSS as well as in those from other parts of western Europe, encyclopedic writing may appear in a variety of contexts and has connections with diverse bodies of knowledge, including biblical commentary, the lapidary, and the treatise on regions of the world and their inhabitants.

Elements of the classical encyclopedic tradition were also transmitted to the Middle Ages through a number of classroom sources, including glosses on hard words and unfamiliar terms, problems in the tradition of hexameral exegesis, and brief catalogues of encyclopedic subjects in works like Ovid's *Metamorphoses*, a text that was probably known in medieval Iceland. The ordering of the traditional encyclopedic subject matter in these and other medieval texts still bore a close relationship to that of the classical treatises, most of which were directly or indirectly modeled on Aristotle's *Meteorologica*.

In the 12th century, there arose a renewed interest in scientific enquiry, both for its own sake and for the light it might shed on the mysteries of the Book of Genesis and the nature of the cosmos. Thus, old myths and new science were often brought together by commentators on the sacred page, and the encyclopedia received a new lease on life in a more up-to-date form. We may detect its influence in writings as diverse as Bernardus Silvestris's *Cosmographia* (ca. 1147–1148), the *Speculum historiale* of Vincent of Beauvais (ca. 1190–1264), and the *Elucidarius* and *Imago mundi* (*De imagine mundi*) of Honorius Augustodunensis (ca. 1080–ca. 1137). The last two were extremely popular works known in Iceland, and several translations of the *Elucidarius*, more or less complete, exist in medieval Icelandic MSS. The *Elucidarius* was the only medieval Latin handbook translated into Old Norse in its entirety, but most other important encyclopedias and compendia seem to have been known in Iceland to some extent and were used by authors as sources both for scholarly knowledge and for the edifying or historical tales contained in them (others include Pliny's *Naturalis historia*, Solinus's *Collectanea rerum memorabilium*, Hrabanus Maurus's *De rerum naturis*, Lambert's *Liber floridus*, and Peter Comestor's *Historia scholastica*). It seems, for example, most likely that the author of *Stjórn*, the voluminous Old Norse Bible compilation, made use of all the above-named authors apart from Pliny, Lambert, and Hrabanus, but even these may have been known to some Icelandic scholars, possibly acquainted with them through various *florilegia*, if not directly.

Some encyclopedic writing appears in a group of Icelandic MSS that date from around 1200 or a little earlier. These texts are thus among the very earliest translations from Latin into Old Icelandic and include parts of *Veraldar saga*, the earliest MS of the Icelandic *Elucidarius*, AM 674a 4to, and the oldest parts of GkS 1812 IV 4to, which includes a treatise on computus with accompanying encyclopedic glosses. It seems likely that several other seminal encyclopedic works were translated into Icelandic during the late 12th century, even though we now know only fragments of them from much later MSS. In addition, a recent study of the *Edda* (ca. 1225) of Snorri Sturluson has indicated that encyclopedic writings probably had a formative influence on both the content and arrangement of material in that work, especially in *Gylfaginning* (Clunies Ross 1985).

Whereas the Old Norse *Elucidarius* is a rather close translation of the Latin dialogue of the same name, Icelandic compilers often found their own means of producing compendia combining both native Old Norse works and translations of Latin texts, rather than by direct translation of an existent Latin work. There are two major types of medieval encyclopedic literature: the collections and compendia aimed at producing micro-libraries; and the descriptions or "mirrors" of the whole world, represented by the voluminous continental encyclopedias of the 12th and especially 13th centuries. Medieval Norwegian and Icelandic authors seem to have been more interested in the former.

Traces of attempts at reproducing encyclopedic knowledge are to be found in the Norwegian *Konungs skuggsjá* (ca. 1260). This didactic dialogue combines chapters on secular topics (such as the shape of the world, the climatic zones, the geography and natural history of Iceland, Greenland, and Ireland, and the duties of traders and courtiers) with stories from the Old Testament and prayers, thereby creating a catechism of the basic secular and religious knowledge suitable for a Norwegian prince.

Hauksbók (1306–1308) contains a number of Old Norse translations of Latin historical works (like the *Trójumanna saga*, a translation of Dares Phrygius's *De excidio Troiae historia*, and the *Breta sǫgur*, an Old Norse version of Geoffrey of Monmouth's *Historia regum Britanniae*, including the poem *Merlínusspá* by Gunnlaugr Leifsson, a translation of Geoffrey's Book 7), as well as native Icelandic historical works (*Landnámabók*, *Kristni saga*, *Eiríks saga rauða*). Haukr also included (though possibly at a later date) the poem *Vǫluspá*, probably because of its summary of heathen cosmology and because he seems to have known the encyclopedias of Hrabanus or, more likely, Lambert, which also include prophetic poetry. To deal with Christian cosmology, he copied the Old Norse *Elucidarius* into his work. The rest of *Hauksbók* is given over to translations and compilations of Latin scholarly texts: a short cosmography and a plan of Jerusalem, a list of marvels of the East, an algorism, texts on computistics, and a lapidary. Jón Helgason (1960: xii–xiv) has summarized the contents of the encyclopedia section of *Hauksbók* and has noted that some of the texts of this 14th-century compilation are to be found in older MSS like GkS 1812 4to (item 1, on the course of the sun) and AM 673a 4to from around 1200 (item k, on the rainbow). The item on the course of the sun also serves to demonstrate that the Icelandic encyclopedic tradition was not entirely derivative but could generate original observations; the piece gives an account of Stjǫrnu-Oddi's astronomical observations in the north of Iceland. Christian religious learning plays a very minor part in this "gentleman's library" and is represented only by a few sermons and a dialogue between soul and body, a translation of another Latin text.

More religious lore is to be found in AM 764 4to (14th century, still unedited), which presents a mixture of historical and geographical writings (a short history of the world, extracts from Nennius's *Historia Brittonum*, annalistic notes, two versions of a cosmography) and saints' lives (*Remigius saga*, *Malcus saga*), as well as a substantial number of religious exempla.

A strong interest in natural history is the distinguishing feature of a small Old Norse handbook in AM 194 8vo, which, apart from annals, contains a great number of short texts comprising Old Norse writings on geography (a brief cosmography, a description of paradise, Abbot Nikulás's itinerary to the Holy Land, the origin of nations, marvels of the East), on history (the ages of the world, the Councils of the Church), and on computistics, but also on natural history itself (*e.g.*, stones, snakes, springs, rivers) and medicine. Although AM 194 8vo was written in 1387, most of its texts stem from the early 13th century at the latest. Abbot Nikulás's itinerary dates from the years between 1154 and 1159.

Fragments of an encyclopedic collection are preserved as part of the MS GkS 1812 4to. This collection appears to have been modeled on one of the few large illustrated encyclopedias, the earliest known MS of which is an 11th-century codex of Hrabanus Maurus's *De rerum naturis*; these were followed by the 12th-century encyclopedias like Lambert's *Liber floridus* and Herrad of Landberg's *Hortus deliciarum*. This Old Norse MS of thirty-six parchment leaves contains remnants of three older MSS, written by four hands between 1200 and 1350; the two younger parts still contain over twenty illuminations depicting the twelve signs of the zodiac and four constellations, as well as a number of astronomical drawings (*e.g.*, concerning the phases and the eclipse of the moon and the course of the planets) and also the three oldest existing examples of Old Norse world maps (*mappae mundi*), including a double-page map with well over 100 entries as well as a small map of climatic zones. These fragments of varying age, which also contain a schematic division of the seven liberal arts and a number of computistic and annalistic texts, were bound together in the later Middle Ages, but are in great part most likely the remains of copies of a more voluminous encyclopedic codex written in the late 12th century. Other fragments of copies of this Old Norse illustrated encyclopedia are found in AM 732b 4to and in AM 736 I & III 4to.

Additional encyclopedic texts are of varying MS age, mostly from the 14th and 15th centuries. Nevertheless, many of them probably had older exemplars, like the 15th-century AM 685d 4to, which is a free translation of the first part of Honorius's *Imago mundi* (1:1), where we find reference to the Platonic idea of the cosmic egg. An Icelandic translation of the *Imago mundi* is likely to have been made in the 12th century, and there seems to be a close correspondence between the *Imago mundi* and some parts of *Snorra Edda*.

Some of the cosmographical, astronomical, and other early scientific texts included in these Old Norse handbooks certainly date back to the 12th and early 13th century and were copied as independent texts in dozens of MSS down to the 18th century, but few other attempts were made to gather them in encyclopedic collections.

In all probability, medieval Icelandic knowledge of encyclopedic writings is likely to have been more extensive than the often fragmentary MS remains would indicate.

Ed.: Larsson, Ludvig, ed. *Áldsta delen af cod. 1812 4to gml. kgl. samling.* Samfund til udgivelse af gammel nordisk litteratur, 9. Copenhagen: Møller, 1883; Eiríkur Jónsson and Finnur Jónsson, eds. *Hauksbók udgiven efter de Arnamagnæanske håndskrifter no. 371, 544 og 675, 4° samt forskellige papirshåndskrifter af det kongelige nordiske Oldskrift-selskab.* Copenhagen: Thiele, 1892–96; Kålund, Kr., and N. Beckman, eds. *Alfræði Íslenzk. Islandsk encyclopædisk litteratur.* 3 vols. Samfund til udgivelse af gammel nordisk litteratur, 37, 41, 45. Copenhagen: Møller, 1908–18; Lindsay, W. M., ed. *Isidori Hispalensis Episcopi Etymologiarvm sive Originvm libri XX.* 2 vols. Oxford: Oxford University Press, 1911; Benediktsson, Jakob, ed. *Veraldar saga.* Samfund til udgivelse af gammel nordisk litteratur, 61. Copenhagen: Luno, 1944; Jón Helgason, ed. *Hauksbók: The Arna-Magnæan Manuscript 371, 4to, 544, 4to and 675, 4to.* Manuscripta Islandica, 5. Copenhagen: Munksgaard, 1960; Fontaine, Jacques, ed. *Isidore de Seville: Traité de la nature, De natura rerum.* Bibliothèque de l'École des Hautes Études Hispaniques, 28. Bordeaux: Féret, 1960;

Jones, C. W., ed. *Bedae Venerabilis Opera: Pars I, Opera Didascalica.* Corpus Christianorum Series Latina, 123A. Turnholt: Brepols, 1975. **Lit.**: Holtsmark, Anne. "Encyklopedisk litteratur." *KLNM* 3 (1958), 620–2; Salvesen, Astrid, and Allan Karker. "Ovid." *KLNM* 13 (1968), 63–6; Walter, Ernst. "Die lateinische Sprache und Literatur auf Island und in Norwegen bis zum Beginn des 13. Jahrhunderts. Ein Orientierungsversuch." *Nordeuropa Studien* 4 (1971), 195–230; Stock, Brian. *Myth and Science in the Twelfth Century: A Study of Bernard Silvester.* Princeton: Princeton University Press, 1972; Clunies Ross, Margaret. "The Influence of the Medieval Encyclopedia on Snorri's *Edda*." In *The Sixth International Saga Conference 28/7–2/8 1985. Workshop Papers.* 2 vols. Copenhagen: Det arnamagnæanske Institut, 1985, vol. 1, pp. 177–206 [photocopies of papers distributed to participants]; rpt. in her *Skáldskaparmál: Snorri Sturluson's Ars Poetica and Medieval Theories of Language.* Viking Collection, 4. Odense: Odense University Press, 1987, pp. 151–73; Scardigli, Piergiuseppe, and Fabrizio D. Rascellà. "A Latin-Icelandic Glossary and Some Remarks on Latin in Medieval Scandinavia." In *Idee, Gestalt, Geschichte. Festschrift Klaus von See.* Ed. Gerd Wolfgang Weber. Odense: Odense University Press, 1989, pp. 299–323 [GkS 1812 4to]; Simek, Rudolf. *Altnordische Kosmographie.* Berlin and New York: de Gruyter, 1990.

                              Margaret Clunies Ross and Rudolf Simek

[**See also:** *Breta sǫgur*; Conversion; *Eiríks saga rauða*; *Elucidarius*; *Hauksbók*; *Konungs skuggsjá*; *Landnámabók*; *Merlínusspá*; *Snorra Edda*; *Stjórn*; *Trójumanna saga*; *Veraldar saga*; Vinland Map; *Vǫluspá*]

England, Norse in. The history of Anglo-Saxon England is marked by over two centuries of Viking raids and Scandinavian settlement, culminating in the ascendancy of Sven Haraldsson (Forkbeard) to the throne in 1013 and of his younger son, Knud (Cnut) the Great, in 1016–1035 and ending with the successive reigns of Knud's sons, Harald and Hardacnut (d. 1042). The *Anglo-Saxon Chronicle* records the first attack by Norwegians in the entry from 787 (789), when three ships from "Hereða lande" (Hǫrðaland) put to shore near Portland and their companies killed the reeve who came to question them. The next raids followed in rapid succession: Lindisfarne in 793, Jarrow in 794, and Iona in 795. Alcuin, in a letter to King Æthelred, wrote of the attack upon the monastery at Lindisfarne: "Lo it is nearly 350 years that we and our fathers have inhabited this most lovely land, and never before has such terror appeared in Britain as we have now suffered from a pagan race, nor was it thought that such an inroad from the sea could be made. Behold, the church of St Cuthbert spattered with the blood of priests of God, despoiled of all its ornaments; a place more venerable than all in Britain is given as a prey to pagan peoples" (*English Historical Documents*, p. 842). In a section of the *Historia regum*, the account of the early raid drawn from Simeon of Durham's *History of the Church of Durham* reiterates more forcefully Alcuin's description: "In the same year the pagans from the northern regions came with a naval force to Britain like stinging hornets and spread on all sides like fearful wolves, robbed, tore and slaughtered not only beasts of burden, sheep and oxen, but even priests and deacons, and companies of monks and nuns. And they came to the church of Lindisfarne, laid everything waste with grievous plundering, trampled the holy places with polluted steps, dug up the altars and seized all the treasures of the holy church. They killed some of the brothers, took some away with them in fetters, many they drove out, naked and loaded with insults, some they drowned in the sea" (*EHD*, p. 273).

These early raids stand as isolated instances. But beginning in 835, England found itself under constant threat of attack by Danish armies, commencing with a raid on the Isle of Sheppey. Danish armies wintered on the Isle of Thanet in 850 and on Sheppey in 854. The period from 835 to 865 shows at least twelve raids in various parts of the country. But the autumn of the year 865 saw the arrival of the "Great Army," as the *Chronicle* states, in East Anglia, including among its leaders the sons of Ragnarr loðbrók ("hairy-breeches"), and initiating a campaign that would lead to Danish victory over the territory. Using East Anglia as a base, the invading force equipped itself, and within the next twelve months embarked on a campaign to conquer Northumbria. Where earlier attackers established winter quarters at river basins or offshore sites, the army of 865 was continually on the move each autumn and was now attacking vital centers within the Anglo-Saxon kingdom (Brooks 1978: 9): York in 866 (with its defeat in March 867), Nottingham in 867–868, York again in 868–869, Thetford in 869–870, Reading in 870–871, followed by a movement into the Berkshires, where the invaders encountered West Saxon troops led by the ealdorman and joined by larger forces under Alfred and King Æthelred. The Anglo-Saxon victory was short-lived, for soon afterward they were defeated by the Danes in a second encounter (Blair 1977: 71–2, Stenton 1971: 248–9). Subsequent attacks were launched by the Danes against London in 871–872, Torksey in 872–873, and Repton in 873–874. During the nine-year period of 865–874, the Danish army operated as a united force, moving between East Anglia and Northumbria and leading southwest from East Anglia to Wessex and thence to Mercia. In 874, the Danish host split into two forces. One force, under the leadership of Halfdan, turned toward establishing settlements, and the *Chronicle* for 876 relates that the Danish leader "shared out the lands of Northumbria, and they were engaged in ploughing and in making a living for themselves" (876A) in the area of southern Northumbria corresponding to modern Yorkshire. The remainder of the Great Army traveled south to Cambridge in 874–875 and began a series of renewed attacks upon Wessex at Wareham in 875–876, Exeter in 876–877, Chippenham in 877–878, and Cirencester in 879–880. The diminished Danish forces met with the West Saxon army at Wareham and were compelled upon their oath and with the exchange of hostages to leave Wessex, only to slip away in the night toward Exeter. Anticipated Danish reinforcements were destroyed when the fleet encountered storms off Swanage, and in 877 the army entered Gloucester in Mercia. Under the leadership of Guthrum, the Danish army again launched an invasion of Wessex in 878, forcing King Alfred (r. 871–899) to fall back to Selwood and establish a stronghold at Athelney. In joining with forces from Somerset, Wiltshire, and Hampshire, Alfred engaged the enemy in a decisive and victorious battle at Edington. After a brief interval during which the dispirited Danish forces retreated to Chippenham, Guthrum agreed to be baptized and to remove his forces from Wessex, finally establishing them in East Anglia.

The victory at Athelney did not bring an end to Viking attacks. In 884, Rochester was attacked, but the enemy was fended off with aid from Alfred's troops; and the threat remained that marauding Viking troops would be given support from Guthrum's army. Throughout this period, Alfred actively set about fortifying southern England, building fortresses and using earlier Roman walls, as at Bath and Winchester, as part of the defensive works.

The year 886, however, saw Alfred taking the initiative and securing London, followed by a treaty between Alfred and Guthrum. The treaty established the boundaries dividing Anglo-Saxon and East Anglian territories. Beginning at the Thames estuary, the boundary extended west along the Thames, then northerly along the River Lea, thence north to Bedford, where it turned westward to follow the River Ouse to Watling Street, and continuing northwest across the country. The territory north of the boundary became known as the "Danelaw." Alfred consolidated his position by entering into an alliance with Æthelred of Mercia, to whom he entrusted the defense of London. Threats from Danish armies nevertheless remained a constant reminder of the nebulousness of the boundary line. Compounding the uneasy situation was the presence of Danish forces off the southeastern coast who were meeting with increased resistance on the Continent.

Following Alfred's death in 899, his son, Edward the Elder, ascended the throne of Wessex. By the end of his reign (899–924), Edward succeeded in annexing to Wessex all Danish holdings south of the Humber. In 909, Edward took the offensive against the Northumbrian Danes and secured a peace on his own terms. The next year, however, the Danes, seeing that Edward was in Kent, harried extensively throughout Mercia, but were defeated near Tettenhall in Staffordshire. With the northern armies severely weakened, Edward could consolidate his movement against the southern Danes. An extended series of campaigns, coupled with the establishment of fortifications, extended Edward's control, and at his sister Æthelflæd's death in 918 he was chosen king of the Mercians. The remaining four Danish armies capitulated in the same year.

The climax of Edward's consolidation of power came in 920 with the submission of the Scots under Constantine, the Scandinavians under Rægnald (Rǫgnvaldr) of York, and the northern English under Ealdred of Bamborough, and also "of all the people of Northumbria, whether English, Danes, Norsemen, or others, and of the king of the Strathclyde Welsh and all his people" (Blair 1977: 81; cf. Stenton 1971: 333–5, Loyn 1977: 64).

Æthelstan (r. 924–939) extended Anglo-Saxon control farther west and north. In 927, his rule extended throughout Northumbria, including the Norse center at York. A decisive victory came in 937 in the battle of Brunanburh, where the combined forces of Olaf (Anlaf, Óláfr) Guthfrithson, ruler of Norse Dublin, Constantine, king of the Scots, and the king of the Strathclydes were routed. Although Olaf returned two years later and gained recognition from Edmund, Æthelstan's successor, of his overlordship of York and the Five Boroughs, his death in 941 allowed Edmund to recover his losses within the next three years. Edmund's death in 946, however, opened the gateway to Scandinavian rule of York once more: the Norwegian Eiríkr blóðøx ("blood-axe"), son of Haraldr hárfagri ("fair-hair"), gained control, followed by Olaf Sihtricson of Dublin, and by Eiríkr again, ending in 954. Eiríkr's death brought to a close Scandinavian power in the North and marked the beginning of a period of peace until renewed Scandinavian attacks in 980, two years after Æthelred Unræd ("unready, no-counsel") succeeded to the throne.

Following the death of King Eadred in 955, Edgar succeeded to the throne of Mercia and Northumbria, and at his brother Eadwig's death in 959 succeeded to the rest of the kingdom. Edgar's relationship with the Danelaw as expressed in his law code, IV Edgar, merits comment. Edgar was keenly aware of the autonomy of the Danelaw and that "for him to legislate for the Danelaw is a violation of legal privileges previously granted to that region" (Lund 1976: 184). IV Edgar does not legislate, but may in fact be confirmation of Danelaw privileges in recognition of support given him by the provinces (Lund 1976: 187), and thus ensure that he would not encroach upon these rights. After setting forth general principles of rights, Edgar repeats his assurance of a policy of nonencroachment: "Further, it is my will that there should be in force among the Danes such good laws as they best decide on, and I have ever allowed them this and will allow it as long as my life lasts, because of your loyalty, which you have always shown to me. And I desire that this one decree concerning such an investigation shall be common to us all, for the protection and security of all the nation" (*EHD*, p. 400).

The differences between the laws governing the Danelaw and those of Wessex and Mercia can be seen most clearly in the imposition of fines, which were much higher in the Danelaw, and in determining certain penalties (Stenton 1971: 507; *cf.* Fenger 1972, Kristensen 1975). It is perhaps, in part, as a result of Edgar's official recognition of Danelaw autonomy and his acknowledgment that the Danish territory was an integrated part of the realm (Stenton 1971: 371; *cf.* Stenton 1970: 163–4) that peace between Danelaw and Wessex and English Mercia was maintained for so long.

After the death of Edgar in 975 and of his son and successor Edward in 978, Æthelred, Edgar's son by Ælfthrythm, succeeded to the throne; and in 980, a new wave of attacks commenced. Southampton was, the *Chronicle* states, "plundered by a pirate-army, and most of the population slain or imprisoned." The Isle of Thanet and Cheshire suffered raids in the same year; in 981, Devon and Cornwall were attacked, and in 982 Dorset (*cf. Chronicle*). The records are silent for the next six years, until 988, when the southwest was attacked. Ipswich followed in 991, as did Maldon, an encounter memorialized in the Old English poem *The Battle of Maldon*. It is significant that the *Chronicle* for the same year records the first payment of tribute to the attackers: "In this same year it was resolved that tribute should be given, for the first time, to the Danes, for the great terror they occasioned by the seacoast. That was the first 10,000 pounds." The payment of "danegeld" became a common means of buying off the invaders throughout Æthelred's reign. Between 991 and 1018, a total of about 219,500 pounds was paid as tribute; the largest sum, 72,000 pounds plus an additional 10,500 pounds, was paid in 1018 after the succession of Knud the Great (see the *Chronicle* for the years 991, 994, 1002, 1007, 1009, 1012, 1018).

It is possible, too, as Lund (1976) suggests, that Æthelred exacerbated the situation by encroaching upon the privileges of the Danelaw in his attempts to introduce English law there (193) and thereby effect greater centralization of government (189).

Viking attacks following the battle of Maldon came with swiftness and precision, with larger numbers of forces than England had witnessed in the past. The *Chronicle* records a long series of raids culminating in Knud's succession to the throne. In 994, the Vikings harried Essex, Kent, Sussex, and Hampshire, taking winter quarters in Southampton and exacting 16,000 pounds in tribute. For the year 997, the *Chronicle* records the invaders in Cornwall, Devon, Liddyford, and Tavistock, and moving into Dorsetshire and to the Isle of Wight in 998. The *Chronicle* for the year 998 paints a picture of low English morale and poor leadership in the face of the powerful and sustained Viking onslaught: "Thus in the end these expeditions [of the English troops] both by sea and land served no other purpose but to vex the people, to waste their treasure, and to strengthen their enemies." The sentiment is forcefully reiterated in the entry for the year 1011: "All these disasters befell us through bad counsels." Æthelred's attempts to deal with the attackers betray not a decisive plan of defense and

attack, but a series of temporary measures, some perhaps unwisely undertaken, others coming too late to change the course of England's defeat. In 1002, Æthelred paid 24,000 pounds to the Viking fleet, and in the same year ordered that all Danes were to be slain: "This was accordingly done on the mass-day of St. Brice; because it was told the king, that they would beshrew him of his life, and afterwards all his council, and then have his kingdom without any resistance." The *Chronicle* report is confirmed by a royal decree that "all the Danes who had sprung up in this island . . . were to be destroyed by a most just extermination" (*EHD*, pp. 545–7). In 1004, Sven Haraldsson arrived with his fleet in Norwich and Thetford. But it was not until 1008 that, as the *Chronicle* records, Æthelred systematically set out to have ships built, only to find his navy divided and fighting one another: "Thus lightly did they suffer the labour of all the people to be in vain" (*Chronicle* 1009). The following year saw raids on London (a failed attempt), Oxford, Thetford, Cambridge, Bedford, and Northampton. The *Chronicle* for the year 1011 sums up the extent of their devastation: "They had now overrun East-Anglia, and Essex, and Middlesex, and Oxfordshire, and Cambridgeshire, and Hertfordshire, and Buckinghamshire, and much of Northamptonshire; and to the south of the Thames, all Kent, and Sussex, and Hastings, and Surrey, and Berkshire, and Hampshire, and much of Wiltshire."

Under the leadership of Sven Haraldsson, the events of the last fifteen years of renewed Viking attacks came to a speedy resolution. In 1013, Sven's fleet sailed to Sandwich, thence around East Anglia into the Humber to Trent and Gainsborough, securing the submission of the Northumbrians, the people of Lindsey and of the Five Boroughs, and then all the army to the north of Watling Street, the dividing line between the Danelaw and the southern kingdom. Soon after, Oxford also submitted and later London, giving hostages and tribute. Æthelred sent Queen Emma and his sons Alfred and Edward (later the Confessor) to Normandy; Æthelred himself soon followed. The political situation was again to change dramatically with the death of Sven on February 3, 1014, leaving an open gateway for Æthelred's return: "Then sent the king hither his son Edward, with his messengers; who had orders to greet all his people, saying that he would be their faithful lord—would better each of those things that they disliked—and that each of the things should be forgiven which had been either done or said against him; provided they all unanimously, without treachery, turned to him. Then was full friendship established, in word and in deed and in compact, on either side. And every Danish king they proclaimed an outlaw for ever from England" (*Chronicle* 1014). Æthelred returned to be acknowledged king once again; yet still he conceded to the attackers, paying 21,000 pounds to the army at Greenwich.

Sven's son Knud, meanwhile, having escaped to sea, soon returned to take the offensive, plundering in Sandwich in 1015, then in Dorset, Wiltshire, and Somerset. Æthelred lay ill at Corsham, leaving Edmund Ironside in command. But by then it was too late. Knud arrived in Mercia in 1016 with 160 ships and proceeded to Warwickshire. Edmund's efforts to gain the support of an army failed. Although Edmund was named king at his father's death in 1016, Knud's power was by now extensive and well matched against Edmund's. Peace was established between the two leaders, whereby Edmund was to rule Wessex and Knud Mercia and Northumbria. On November 30, 1016, however, Edmund died, and Knud succeeded to the throne of all England. For the next twenty-six years, England would remain under Danish rule.

Knud quickly applied himself to consolidating his power and

gaining the respect of the Church. After dispatching his enemies within the first year of his reign (see *Chronicle* for 1017), he married Æthelred's widow, Emma. In 1018, he engaged Wulfstan to draft a new set of laws modeled on the code of Edgar. In 1023, we find Knud attending the translation of St. Ælfheah's relics from London to Canterbury; in 1027, he visited Rome, issuing upon his return a letter reporting his journey, and reminding his subjects of his concern for their interests and of their obligations (*EHD*, pp. 414–6).

Along with his religious fervor, Knud remained a strong military leader. In 1019, he returned to Denmark to affirm his rule after the death of his brother, Harald, and again in 1023. In 1026 and 1028, he was forced to contend with possible attacks against Denmark from Sweden and Norway, ultimately gaining control of Norway and establishing his mistress Ælfgifu and his son Sven as his representatives. The arrangement failed in the face of Ælfgifu's imposition of heavy taxes and harsh penalties, and in 1035, shortly after Knud's death, Magnús Óláfsson succeeded to the throne of Norway. In England, Knud's consolidation of control was unimpeded, and in 1028 he invaded Scotland and secured the submission of Malcolm.

At Knud's death, Harald, Knud's son by Ælfgifu, was named king at a council meeting in Oxford in 1036, against the wishes of Emma and Earl Godwine, who supported the succession of Hardacnut, Knud's son by Emma. Alfred, Æthelred's son by Emma, arrived in England to visit his mother at Winchester, and was brutally tortured by Godwine. Harald was formally recognized as king in 1037. His death in 1040 cleared the way for Hardacnut's succession; his reign was to last only until 1042. On June 8, 1042, Edward the Confessor, Æthelred's son, came to the throne, thus bringing to an end Danish rule in England.

The effects of the Scandinavian presence in England were extensive, and can be most clearly observed through linguistic and place-name evidence. Linguistic influence is most clearly evidenced in loanwords, words showing semantic contamination, and words showing phonological influence. For example, English owes to Scandinavian influence such words as *egg* (Old Norse *egg*), *loan* (Old Norse *lána*), *skin* (Old Norse *skinn*), *call* (Old Norse *kalla*), *take* (Old Norse *taka*), *thrive* (Old Norse *þrífast*), *thrust* (Old Norse *þrýsta*), and *rotten* (Old Norse *rotinn*), to name but a few. Semantic contamination is shown in Modern English *dream*, which derives its meaning not from Old English *dream*, which means "joy," but from Old Norse *draumr*. Old English *steorfan* and *sweltan*, both meaning "to die," eventually lost their initial meanings, while Modern English "to die" derived from Old Norse *deyja*, its adoption receiving support from Old English *dead* (adjective) and *deaþ* (noun). Among personal pronouns, Old Norse *þeir* 'they' (nom. pl. masc.), *þeim* 'them' (dat. pl.), and *þeirra* (gen. pl.) replaced Old English *hie* 'they' (nom./acc. pl.), *him* 'them' (dat. pl.), and *hira*, *heora* 'their' (gen. pl.) (see Loyn 1977: 114–8, Baugh 1978: 96–106).

Personal names and place-names provide rich resources for the study of Scandinavian settlement. Place-names in -*by* and -*þorp*, for instance, not only reveal Scandinavian influence, but can also be used to document different stages of settlement. The forms are ubiquitous in the Danelaw area. In Yorkshire, of 402 Scandinavian habitative names, 196 are in -*by* and 176 in -*þorp*; in the East Midlands, of 467 names, 285 are in -*by* and 157 in -*þorp*; and in the Northwest, of 246 names, 100 are in -*by* and nine in -*þorp* (Fellows-Jensen 1985: 45). The evidence suggests that the first stage of Scandinavian colonization "is marked by the *býs*, while the

þorps and many other habitative names seem to derive on the whole from a later period, when there was an increase in the amount of land under exploitation" (Fellows-Jensen 1972: 251). The evidence of place-names indicates active Scandinavian colonization, with settlers at times establishing new settlements or taking over preexisting English settlements and compounding a Scandinavian name with an English one (*e.g.*, -*tun*), retaining the English names, or adopting new names. In her discussion of North Riding place-names, Fellows-Jensen concludes: "The majority of the hybrid and scandinavianized names are borne by older English vills whose names were partially adapted by the Vikings, while the majority of the *býs* mark the subsequent occupation by the Danes of the best available vacant land. A third stage in the Viking settlement, characterized by the exploitation of less favourable land, is marked by place-names in *thorp*" (1978: 38).

Although Scandinavian rule in England was short-lived, the more than 200 years of Scandinavian activity and influence contributed vitally to the development of English culture in the Middle Ages.

Ed.: Earl, John, ed. *Two of the Saxon Chronicles Parallel, with Supplementary Extracts from Others*. 2 vols. rev. ed. Charles Plummer. Oxford: Clarendon, 1892–99; rpt. 1952. **Tr.**: Garmonsway, G. N., trans. *The Anglo-Saxon Chronicle*. Everyman's Library, 624. London: Dent; New York: Dutton, 1953; rpt. 1967. **Bib.**: Rosenthal, Joel T. *Anglo-Saxon History: An Annotated Bibliography, 450–1066*. New York: AMS, 1985; Keynes, Simon. *Anglo-Saxon History: A Select Bibliography*. Old English Newsletter, Subsidia, 13. New York: Center for Medieval and Early Renaissance Studies, 1987. **Lit.**: Mawer, Allen. "The Redemption of the Five Boroughs." *English Historical Review* 38 (1923), 551–7; Whitelock, Dorothy. "The Conversion of the Eastern Danelaw." *Saga-Book of the Viking Society* 12 (1941), 159–76; Stenton, F. M. *Anglo-Saxon England*. The Oxford History of England, 2. Oxford: Clarendon, 1943; 3rd ed. 1971; Sawyer, P. H., *et al.* "The Two Viking Ages of Britain: A Discussion." *Mediaeval Scandinavia* 2 (1969), 163–207; Stenton, Doris Mary, ed. *Preparatory to Anglo-Saxon England*. Oxford: Clarendon, 1970; Fenger, Ole. "The Danelaw and the Danish Law: Anglo-Scandinavian Legal Relations During the Viking Period." *Scandinavian Studies in Law* 16 (1972), 85–96; Fellows-Jensen, Gillian. "The Vikings in England: A Review." *Anglo-Saxon England* 4 (1975), 181–206; Kristensen, Anne K. G. "Danelaw Institutions and Danish Society in the Viking Age." *Mediaeval Scandinavia* 8 (1975), 27–85; Wilson, David M. "Scandinavian Settlement in the North and West of the British Isles—An Archaeological Point-of-View." *Transactions of the Royal Historical Society*, 5th ser., 27 (1976), 95–113; Lund, Niels. "King Edgar and the Danelaw." *Mediaeval Scandinavia* 9 (1976), 181–95; Blair, Peter Hunter. *An Introduction to Anglo-Saxon England*. 2nd ed. Cambridge: Cambridge University Press, 1977; Loyn, H. R. *The Vikings in Britain*. New York: St. Martin, 1977; Sawyer, P. H. *From Roman Britain to Norman England*. New York: St. Martin, 1978; Baugh, Albert C., and Thomas Cable. *A History of the English Language*. 3rd ed. Englewood Cliffs: Prentice-Hall, 1978; Whitelock, Dorothy, ed. *English Historical Documents c. 500–1042*. 2nd ed. London and New York: Eyre Methuen; Oxford University Press, 1979 [*EHD*]; Brooks, N. P. "England in the Ninth Century: The Crucible of Defeat." *Transactions of the Royal Historical Society*, 5th ser., 29 (1979), 1–20; Sawyer, P. H. *Kings and Vikings: Scandinavia and Europe AD 700–1100*. London and New York: Methuen, 1982; Davis, R. H. C. "Alfred and Guthrum's Frontier." *English Historical Review* 97 (1982), 803–10; Lawson, M. K. "The Collection of Danegeld and Heregeld in the Reigns of Aethelred II and Cnut." *English Historical Review* 99 (1984), 721–38; Niles, John D., and Mark Amodio, eds. *Anglo-Scandinavian England: Norse-En-*

glish Relations in the Period Before the Conquest. Old English Colloquium Series, 4. Lanham, New York, and London: University Press of America, 1989. **Personal names and place-names**: Fellows-Jensen, Gillian. *Scandinavian Personal Names in Lincolnshire and Yorkshire.* Copenhagen: Akademisk Forlag, 1968; Fellows-Jensen, Gillian. *Scandinavian Settlement Names in Yorkshire.* Copenhagen: Akademisk Forlag, 1972; Cameron, Kenneth, ed. *Place-Name Evidence for the Anglo-Saxon Invasion and Scandinavian Settlements.* Nottingham: English Place-Name Society, 1975; Fellows-Jensen. *Scandinavian Settlement Names in the East Midlands.* Copenhagen: Akademisk Forlag, 1978; Fellows-Jensen, Gillian. "Place-Name Evidence for Scandinavian Settlement in the Danelaw: A Reassessment." In *The Vikings: Proceedings of the Symposium of the Faculty of Arts of Uppsala University June 6–9, 1977.* Ed. Thorstein Andersson and Karl Inge Sandred. Stockholm: Almqvist & Wiksell, 1978; Fellows-Jensen, Gillian. "Place-Names and Settlement in the North Riding of Yorkshire." *Northern History* 14 (1978), 19–46; Fellows-Jensen, Gillian. *Scandinavian Settlement Names in the North-West.* Copenhagen: Reitzel, 1985.

Phillip Pulsiano

[**See also**: *Encomium Emmae reginae*; Five Boroughs; Knud (Cnut) the Great; Old English Literature, Norse Influence on; Stamford Bridge, Battle of; York]

Erex saga ("Erex's saga") is an Old Norse prose version of the Old French chivalric romance *Erec et Enide*, by Chrétien de Troyes. Although the saga is complete only in 17th-century and later Icelandic transcripts, principally AM 181b fol. (*ca.* 1650) and Stock. Perg. fol. no. 46 (1690), it was probably originally written, along with the Norse adaptations of Chrétien's *Yvain* (*Ívens saga*) and *Perceval* (*Parcevals saga*), for the court of Hákon Hákonarson of Norway (r. 1217–1263).

In its present state, *Erex saga* is the most abbreviated of the translated *riddarasögur*, and structurally the most divergent from its source. There is some reordering of the hero's adventures, with two more added (in ch. 10). Another innovation in the saga is an epilogue that gives a brief account of Erex's later career and that of his descendants. *Erex saga* is also distinguished from its source by the addition of a number of overtly didactic passages about the moral responsibilities of kings and noblemen, spoken by or otherwise attributed to a number of characters, including King Arthur. The work has fewer rhetorical embellishments than some of the other translated *riddarasögur*, but it does contain a relatively high proportion of present participles, a feature more characteristic of Latin than of Old Norse prose style.

The story concerns the early success, followed by a knightly lapse, self-imposed exile, and eventual reintegration into chivalric society of the Round Table knight Erec (Old Norse Erex), who succumbs to uxoriousness after his marriage to Enide (Old Norse Evida). Stung by criticism from his bride for his self-indulgent withdrawal from public life, he embarks with her on a hazardous journey, which tests his prowess to the full. Finally, with reputation restored and enhanced, he resumes his rightful place in the Arthurian world and succeeds to the throne of his father, King Lac (Old Norse Ilax).

Erex saga limits itself to the question of the hero's damaged reputation and shows no interest in Chrétien's broader subject, the proper role of love and marriage in the chivalric life. This restriction of theme in the saga tends to resolve ambiguities in *Erec et Enide.* Chrétien, for example, deliberately obscures Erec's motives for ordering Enide to accompany him on his travels and to

remain silent in the face of approaching danger. The clear implication in the saga, however, is that she is joining him as an equal partner on the quest to regain his honor.

The saga's demystifying approach to the "courtly dilemma," *i.e.*, the problem of reconciling the often conflicting demands of love and chivalry, is clearly demonstrated in its treatment of the last of the hero's adventures, the enigmatic "Joy of the Court" (Old Norse *hirðar fagnaðr*). In this bizarre episode, Erex defeats a hitherto invincible knight whose sweetheart has compelled him to live with her in a walled garden and to remain there until he meets a challenger who can overcome him. In Chrétien's poem, this couple, whose selfish isolation parallels that of Erec and Enide in the early part of the work, seem to personify negative aspects of "courtly" love. The saga, however, rejects the love-inspired motive for their retreat and substitutes a simple social one: the aristocratic lady fears disgrace if anyone discovers that her lover is a mere knight.

In *Erec et Enide*, the hero's task is to find the proper balance between love and prowess, and to retrieve his honor. In *Erex saga*, he seeks only to restore his reputation. Whereas Chrétien is concerned with both the public life of his hero and heroine and the maturation of their relationship, the saga's interest is solely in the principles and demonstration of chivalric conduct.

Ed.: Cederschiöld, Gustaf, ed. *Erex saga.* Samfund til udgivelse af gammel nordisk litteratur, 3. Copenhagen: [s.n.], 1880; Blaisdell, Foster, W., ed. and trans. *Erex saga Artuskappa.* Editiones Arnamagnæanæ, ser. B, vol. 19. Copenhagen: Munksgaard, 1965. **Tr.**: Blaisdell, Foster W., Jr., and Marianne E. Kalinke, trans. *Erex saga and Ívens saga: The Old Norse Versions of Chrétien de Troyes's Erec and Yvain.* Lincoln: University of Nebraska Press, 1977. **Bib.**: Kalinke, Marianne E., and P. M. Mitchell. *Bibliography of Old Norse–Icelandic Romances.* Islandica, 44. Ithaca and London: Cornell University Press, 1985, pp. 39–41. **Lit.**: Kölbing, Eugen. "Die nordische Erexsaga und ihre Quelle." *Germania* 16, n.s. 4 (1871), 381–414; Blaisdell, Foster W. "The Composition of the Interpolated Chapter in the *Erex saga.*" *Scandinavian Studies* 36 (1964), 118–26; Blaisdell, Foster W., Jr. "Some Observations on Style in the *riddarasögur.*" In *Scandinavian Studies: Essays Presented to Dr. Henry Goddard Leach on the Occasion of His Eighty-fifth Birthday.* Ed. Carl F. Bayerschmidt and Erik J. Friis. Seattle: University of Washington Press, 1965, pp. 87–94; Blaisdell, Foster W. "A Stylistic Feature in the 'Erex Saga.'" In *Studies in Language and Literature in Honour of Margaret Schlauch.* Ed. Mieczyslaw Brahmer *et al.* Warsaw: Polish Scientific Publishers, 1966; New York: Russell & Russell, 1971, pp. 37–47; Kalinke, Sister Jane A., O.P. [Marianne E.]. "The Structure of the *Erex saga.*" *Scandinavian Studies* 42 (1970), 343–55; Kalinke, Marianne E. "A Structural Comparison of Chrétien de Troyes' *Erec et Enide* and the Norse *Erex saga.*" *Mediaeval Scandinavia* 4 (1971), 54–65; Kalinke, Marianne E. "Honor: The Motivating Principle of the *Erex saga.*" *Scandinavian Studies* 45 (1973), 135–43; Kalinke, Marianne E. "*Erex saga* and *Ívens saga*: Medieval Approaches to Translation." *Arkiv för nordisk filologi* 92 (1977), 125–44; Kalinke, Marianne E. *King Arthur North-by-Northwest: The matière de Bretagne in Old Norse–Icelandic Romances.* Bibliotheca Arnamagnæana, 37. Copenhagen: Reitzel, 1981; Kretschmer, Bernd. *Höfische und altwestnordische Erzähltradition in den Riddarasögur: Studien zur Rezeption der altfranzösischen Artusepik am Beispiel der Erex saga, Ivens saga, und Parcevals saga.* Hattingen: Kretschmer, 1982; Gouchet, Olivier. "Die altisländische Bearbeitung von Chrétiens Erec et Enide." In *Les Sagas de Chevaliers (Riddarasögur). Actes de la Vᵉ Conférence Internationale sur les Sagas . . . (Toulon. Juillet 1982).* Ed. Régis Boyer. Civilisations, 10. Paris: Presses de l'Université de Paris-

Sorbonne, 1985, pp. 145–55; Barnes, Geraldine. "Arthurian Chivalry in Old Norse." In *Arthurian Literature VII.* Ed. Richard Barber. Cambridge: Brewer, 1987, pp. 50–102.

Geraldine Barnes

[**See also:** Old Norse–Icelandic Literature, Foreign Influence on; *Riddarasǫgur*]

Erfidrápa Haralds harðráða *see* **Arnórr Þórðarson jarlaskáld**

Erfidrápa Óláfs helga *see* **Sighvatr Þórðarson**

Erik, St., was king of Sweden, and son of an unknown Jedvard (Edward). He was venerated as a saint in Uppsala from at least 1198 (the Vallentuna Calendar). In his legend, the oldest version of which is now dated to the 1180s (Sjögren 1983), he is said to have been killed by a Danish pretender to the Swedish throne, Magnus, son of Henrik Skadelår, an offspring of the Danish royal family, on Ascension Day, May 18, 1160, at the Mountain of the Holy Trinity in Uppsala after having heard mass. The legend characterizes his ten-year reign as model years of royal justice. But the chronology is erroneous. Ascension Day fell on the 5th of May in 1160, but on the 18th of May in 1167, one month after Erik's son Knut had slain his competitor for the Swedish throne, Karl Sverkerson. Thus, the legendary date is rather to be explained as the day of glorification of Knut's father as a saint in 1167. Numismatic evidence from the reign of Knut (1167–1196) proves that he promoted Erik's cult (Sjögren 1983). It must have received episcopal approbation by Stephen, archbishop 1164–1185. The saint's name was used as a symbol by aristocratic insurrections against later dynasties in the 13th century (Sjögren 1986). A rhymed liturgical office was created shortly before 1300 under Dominican influence, and from this period most of the miracles derive. The full version of his legend dates from 1344; new parts were composed for his office by Bishop Nils Hermansson (d. 1391).

St. Erik became a symbol of the Church in Sweden from the 14th century, and patron saint of Sweden and Stockholm in the 15th century. *Erik konungs lag* ("King Erik's Law") became a symbol for "old, good law." His relics are still kept in Uppsala cathedral. The feast of *translatio* of his relics was celebrated on January 24th, probably in memory of their transfer to the new cathedral in 1273 (Carlsson 1944). St. Erik was connected with a crusade for the propagation of faith to Finland. A Bishop Henrik, later venerated as a saint in Nousis and the patron saint of Finland, is supposed to have accompanied him and been killed at the campaign dated by historians to 1155/9. But there is no evidence outside the legend to support the crusade, and Henrik is not found among the bishops of Uppsala.

There is better evidence for Erik's origin in the province of Västergötland, where his son Knut probably supervised the building of Eriksberg church in memory of his father. Erik and his queen, Christina, tried to prevent the Cistercian foundation in Västergötland from moving from Lurö/Lugnås to Varnhem around 1158 (*Scriptores Minores Historiae Danicae Medii Aevi* 2:138, 141). Since Uppsala cathedral chapter followed *ordo monasticus* 1188/97, and since Erik's reign is the most probable period for the establishment of such a monastic chapter in Uppsala (Gallén 1976), we may see the reason for Erik's aversion to the Cistercians in his support for the Black Benedictines. Such a monastic chapter existed only in Odense, Denmark, so it cannot be ruled out that Erik had connections with Denmark, where we find *Ericus dux et eius filii Karolus et Kanutus* (jarl Erik and his sons Karl and Knut) in Lund 1145 (*Diplomatarium Danicum* 1:2, no. 88) and *Ericus* [lord of] *Falster* at Haraldsted 1131 (*Vita Sanctorum Danorum* 239; Gallén 1985). Erik's crusade may then tentatively be identified with the campaign mentioned under 1142 in the Novgorod chronicle.

Ed.: Fant, Eric Michael, ed. *Scriptores rerum svecicarum medii ævi* 2.1. Uppsala: Zeipel & Palmblad, 1828, pp. 270–320; Nelson, Axel, ed. *Vita et miracula Sancti Erici regis Sueciae. Latine et Suecice. Codex Vat. reg. lat. 525 Suecice et Britannice praefatus.* Corpus Codicum Suecicorum Medii Aevi, 3. Copenhagen: Munksgaard, 1944; Schmid, Toni, ed. "Erik den heliges legend på latin, fornsvenska och modern svenska." In *Erik den Helige. Historia, Kult, Reliker.* Ed. Bengt Thordeman. Stockholm: Nordiska rotogravyr, 1954, pp. xi–xx; Lundén, Tryggve, ed. "Eriksofficiet och Eriksmässen." In *Sankt Erik Konung.* Ed. Jarl Gallén and Tryggve Lundén. Svenska Katolska Akademiens Handlingar, 2. Stockholm: Niketryck, 1960, pp. 19–47. **Bib.:** Bohrn, Harald, and Percy Elfstrand. *Svensk historisk bibliografi 1936–1950.* Skrifter utgivna av Historiska Föreningen, 5. Stockholm: Norstedt, 1964, pp. 495–6; Rydbeck, Jan, ed. *Svensk historisk bibliografi 1951–1960.* Skrifter utgivna av Historiska Föreningen, 6. Stockholm: Norstedt, 1968, pp. 455–6; Bachman, Marie-Louise, and Yvonne Hirdman, eds. *Svensk historisk bibliografi 1961–1970.* Skrifter utgivna av Historiska Föreningen, 8. Stockholm: Almqvist & Wiksell, 1978, pp. 485–6. **Lit.:** Carlsson, Einar. *Translacio archiepiscoporum. Erikslegendens historicitet i belysning av ärkebiskopssätets förflyttning från Upsala till Östra Aros.* Uppsala Universitets Årsskrift, 1944:2. Uppsala: Lundequistska Bokhandeln, 1944; Bolin, Sture. "Erik den helige." *Svenskt biografiskt lexikon.* Ed. Bengt Hildebrand. Stockholm: Bonnier, 1953, vol. 14, pp. 248–57; Thordeman, Bengt, ed. *Erik den Helige: Historia, Kult, Reliker.* Stockholm: Nordiska rotogravyr, 1954; Schmid, Toni. "Erik den helige." *KLNM* 4 (1959), 13–16; Gallén, Jarl. "Erik den helige, Sveriges helgonkonung." In *Sankt Erik Konung*, pp. 1–15; Andersson, Ingvar. "Uppsala ärkestifts tillkomst." *Historisk tidskrift* (Sweden), 84 (1964), 389–410; Sibilia, Anna Lisa. "Erico (Erik) IX." *Bibliotheca Sanctorum* 4. Rome: Pontificia Università Lateranense, 1955, cols. 1322–6; Nyberg, Tore. "Eskil av Lund och Erik den helige." In *Historia och samhälle. Studier tillägnade Jerker Rosén.* Malmö: Studentlitteratur, 1975, pp. 5–21; Gallén, Jarl. "De engelska munkarna i Uppsala—ett katedralkloster på 1100-talet." *Historisk Tidskrift för Finland* 61 (1976), 1–21; Sjöberg, Rolf. "Via regia incedens. Ett bidrag till frågan om Erikslegendens ålder." *Fornvännen* 78 (1983), 252–60; Gallén, Jarl. "Knut den helige och Adela av Flandern. Europeiska kontakter och genealogiska konsekvenser." In *Studier i äldre historia tillägnade Herman Schück.* Stockholm: Gotab, 1985, pp. 49–66; Sjöberg, Rolf. "Rex Upsalie och vicarius—Erik den helige och hans ställföreträdare." *Fornvännen* 81 (1986), 1–13.

Tore Nyberg

[**See also:** Liturgy and Liturgical Texts; Miracles, Collections of; Monasticism; Saints' Lives]

Eufemiavisorna ("the Eufemia poems") are three epic poems of chivalry in the *knittel* meter translated into Old Swedish from prose or metrical foreign originals. According to statements in each of their conclusions, they were translated on the initiative of Queen Eufemia of Norway in the years 1303, 1308, and 1311–1312. Queen Eufemia had a daughter, Ingeborg, who was engaged in 1302 to the Swedish Duke Erik Magnusson. It is maintained, on good grounds, that it was in order to celebrate this event and to please her future son-in-law, that she employed some unknown Swede to translate into Old Swedish *knittel* the romance about Yvain, "the Knight of the Lion." The Old French poem *Yvain*, or *Le chevalier au lion*, by Chrétien de Troyes, had been translated into

Norwegian prose already in the first half of the 13th century, perhaps the main reason why the queen chose this very work for her intended gift. The dates 1308 and 1311–1312 may also be connected with certain important events in the history of the Swedish-Norwegian dynastic relations at that time. Eufemia was born a princess in Germany, and probably she had become acquainted with *knittel* poetry in her fatherland.

The European poetry of chivalry was known at an early time in Norway not only through *Yvain* but also through a number of other works, mainly French metrical romances, translated into Norwegian prose at the instance of King Håkon Håkonarson. But the *Eufemiavisorna* were the first representatives in Scandinavia of such literature in poetic form. They influenced to some extent the medieval literatures in the rest of Scandinavia, especially Denmark, where they were translated into Danish. In the later Swedish *knittel* epics of the Middle Ages, one can hear the echo of rhymes, formulas, and epithets introduced in the *Eufemiavisorna*.

The style, rhyme technique, and vocabulary of the *Eufemiavisorna* are to a great extent influenced by German patterns; the translator(s) must have been well acquainted with the culture of the South. Thus, French originals have had a surprisingly insignificant influence on the form of the *Eufemiavisorna*.

As suggested above, it is not quite certain whether all three poems were translated by the same person. According to V. Jansson (1945, summary, pp. 313–8), many facts speak in favor of the single-translator theory. Some details point to the possibility that the author-translator had a more than average interest in religion and was familiar with church services. Hence, it has been suggested that he was a priest.

Like the English adapters of the 13th and 14th centuries, the author of the *Eufemiavisorna* possessed a weak sensitivity to the subtle and refined aspects of courtly romance. The intricate analysis of the emotional life of characters, especially women, in the best French romances, was foreign to the author of the *Eufemiavisorna*. Instead, he was very fond of manly sports, *torney*, *dyost* ("tournaments, jousts"), and the like, fights, grand assemblies, and vivid scenes in the knights' castles. In short, the main themes of the *Eufemiavisorna* are adventures, fights, and love.

Herr Ivan, the oldest of the *Eufemiavisorna*, consists of no less than 6,645 lines. It describes the adventures of Ivan (Yvain), the bravest of the knights associated with King Arthur. In the presence of the queen, Ivan is scornfully accused by a fellow knight of having boasted while drunk of his intention to fight with a terrible knight, Wadein rødhe ("the red"), the owner and guardian of a miraculous fountain. In secret, he rides away, comes to the fountain, wounds its owner mortally, and pursues him into his castle, where Wadein falls dead in the courtyard. A maid, Luneta, hides Ivan from the vengeful inhabitants of the castle. After a time, he comes to know the châtelaine Laudine, Wadein's deeply mourning widow. He falls in love with the "fru(gha)" ("noble lady") and succeeds in winning her with the help of the cunning Luneta. But he loses her again, because he departs, together with his friend and kinsman Gawain, in search of adventures, and does not keep his promise to return within a year. In despair, he roves about in the wilderness, but is brought back to his senses thanks to the help of a merciful "frugha" and her healing unguent. He regains his knightly honor through a long series of noble and heroic deeds, much helped by his faithful lion, whose love he had won by saving him from being killed by a serpent. The combined achievements of the lion and Luneta enable Ivan to win back both Laudine and his honored place at King Arthur's court.

It is generally maintained that the Swedish translator used MSS both of the Old French *Yvain* and of the Old Norwegian *Íven(t)*. The end of the poem states that it was translated *aff valske tungo* ("from the French language"). The translator deals freely with his originals; he shortens, revises, and makes additions. The narration is more expansive in the latter part. The additions are often mechanical and especially frequent in rhyme position.

Hertig Fredrik (av Normandie), "Duke Frederic (of Normandy)," was written, according to its own declaration, in the year 1308, and comprises 3,310 lines. Like Ivan, the leading character, Duke Frederic, was one of the knights at the court of King Arthur. Once while hunting, he went astray and came to the realm of the dwarfs, who lived in a mountain. Like a medieval Gulliver, he helps their monarch, Malmrit, win back his kingdom from rebellious vassals and restore feudal order in the state, which gradually develops into an ideal society in miniature. The grateful King Malmrit gives Frederic a magic ring, capable of making people invisible. By means of that ring, Duke Frederic succeeds in entering a tower, where the king of Ireland had imprisoned his beautiful daughter, Floria. The invisible duke gets an opportunity to enjoy the favors of Floria. After a series of adventures and difficulties, he comes back to Normandy, bringing with him not only Floria but also a great fortune. Frederic and Floria, now married, become a good ruling couple, anxious about their subjects and the Church. Growing older, they become pious, and Floria enters a monastery.

It has been maintained that the poem was partly intended as a sort of King's Mirror, demonstrating how the good ruler should and should not behave. Certainly, however, the poem was appreciated not only by regents for its descriptions of feasts, erotic pleasures, and other popular entertainments. On the whole, it is more artistic than its Swedish forerunner, *Herr Ivan*.

The end of the poem states that it was first translated *aff walsko j tytzt mall* ("from French into German"), at the instance of Emperor Otto. This information is generally accepted by scholars, although no German text is known.

Flores och Blanzeflor, the youngest and shortest of the *Eufemiavisorna*, consists of 2,192 lines, and was written *ij then tima litith før aen [Eufemia] do* ("a short time before Eufemia died"), which was in 1312. Flores ("flower") is the son of the pagan king of "Apolis." During a ravaging expedition into Spain ("the land of St. James"), the king kills a French pilgrim, whose little daughter he brings with him back to his country. The girl is given the name Blanzeflor ("white flower"). She is brought up together with Flores. The two youngsters fall in love so passionately that they vow they will never be separated. Flores's father, King Fenix, strongly disapproves of his son's infatuation, because he has planned to marry him to a foreign princess. On a pretext, Flores is sent to a relative for some time, and Blanzeflor is handed over to a foreign merchant, who sells her to the king of Babylon. There, she is placed in his harem, and the king plans to make her his wife for the next year, at the end of which she will be killed in accordance with the king's peculiar habit. Flores, however, returns to his parents, who tell him that Blanzeflor is dead. Desperate, he threatens to kill himself, and the parents are forced to tell him the truth. He sets off to find his beloved, and his search is successful. Helped by a man in Babylon, Darias, and by the *portanär* (the guard at the castle gate), he manages to gain access to Blanzeflor's room in a tower, hidden in a basket of flowers. Unfortunately, the king happens to find the loving couple in bed. The situation is dangerous for Flores, but he saves both himself and Blanzeflor by killing in a tournament the most valiant of the knights at the court. Flores and Blanzeflor are allowed to leave Babylon. They come home to Apolis, where Flores's parents have recently died. Flores and Blanzeflor marry and take over the government of the kingdom, soon distinguishing themselves, like Frederic and Floria, as an ideal ruling couple, introducing Christianity and establishing charitable foundations. In the end, they entrust the government to their three sons, and join a monastery and a nunnery, respectively.

The poem is based, as *Herr Ivan* partly is, mainly on an Old Norwegian prose version of a French rhymed original, in this case a *roman d'aventure*, *Floire et Blancheflor*, from the 12th century, which, moreover, was the source of one of the stories in Boccaccio's *Decameron*.

The *Eufemiavisorna* are preserved, wholly or in part, in the following MSS: Cod. Holm. D4, (*ca.* 1410) [Ivan, Fredrik, Flores]; Cod. Holm. D 4a (1457) [Iv, Fr, Fl]; Cod. Holm. D 3 (1476) [Iv, Fr, Fl]; Cod. Skokloster 156 (*ca.* 1450) [Iv]; Cod. Skokloster 115, 116 (*ca.* 1500) [Fr]; Cod. Holm. K 45 (*ca.* 1500) [Fr]; Cod. Holm. D 2 (*ca.* 1523) [Fr]; AM 191 fol. (1492) [Fl]. An old but very small fragment of *Flores* from about 1350 is kept in the University Library, Helsinki.

The Danish translations exist in the following MSS: Cod. Holm. K 4 (*ca.* 1450) [Iv]; Cod. Holm. K 47 (*ca.* 1500) [Iv, Fr, Fl]. Furthermore, a now-lost Danish MS was used when *Flores* was printed in 1504 and 1509. Since the Danish texts are independent of any preserved Swedish MS, they are also valuable for the textual criticism of the original *Eufemiavisorna*.

Ed.: The Swedish *Eufemiavisorna* have been edited twice in the series Samlingar utgivna av Svenska fornskrift-sällskapet. The second set of these editions are: Olson, Emil, ed. *Flores och Blanzeflor. Kritisk upplaga*. Samlingar utgivna af Svenska fornskrift-sällskapet, 46. Lund: Berling, 1921; rpt. as Samlingar utgivna af Svenska fornskrift-sällskapet, 61; Noreen, Erik, ed. *Hertig Fredrik av Normandie. Kritisk upplaga på grundval av Codex Verelianus*. Samlingar utgivna af Svenska fornskrift-sällskapet, 49. Uppsala: Almqvist & Wiksell, 1927; Noreen, Erik, ed. *Herr Ivan. Kritisk upplaga*. Samlingar utgivna af Svenska fornskrift-sällskapet, 50. Uppsala: Almqvist & Wiksell, 1931; a short extract from *Herr Ivan* is to be found in Noreen, Erik, ed. *Fornsvensk läsebok. Andra bearbetade upplagan utgiven av Sven Benson*. Lund: Gleerup, 1962, pp. 62–70 [*Ur Herr Ivan: Kalegrewanz' berättelse*]; the Danish translations of the *Eufemiavisorna* are edited in Brandt, C. J. *Romantisk Digtning fra Middelalderen*. 3 vols. Copenhagen: Samfundet til den danske Literaturs Fremme, 1869–77 [*Ivan Løveridder*, vol. 1, pp. 1–204; *Hertig Frederik af Normandi*, vol. 1, pp. 204–84; *Flores og Blanseflor*, vol. 1, pp. 287–356; *Ivan Løveridder*, vol. 2, pp. 131–288; *Flores oc Blantzeflor*, vol. 2, pp. 289–348]. **Lit.**: Noreen, Erik. *Studier rörande Eufemiavisorna. 1. Textkritiska anmärkningar till Flores och Blanzeflor. 2. Bidrag till Hertig Fredriks textkritik. 3. Textkritiska studier över Herr Ivan*. Skrifter utgivna av Kungl. Humanistiska Vetenskapssamfundet i Uppsala 22.2, 22.7, 26.1. Uppsala: Almqvist & Wiksell, 1923, 1927, 1929; Sawicki, Stanislaw. *Die Eufemiavisor. Stilstudien zur nordischen Reimliteratur des Mittelalters*. Skrifter utgivna av Kungl. humanistiska vetenskapssamfundet i Lund, 28. Lund: Gleerup, 1939; Jansson, Valter. *Eufemiavisorna. En filologisk undersökning*. Uppsala Universitets Årsskrift 1945:8. Uppsala: Lundequist; Leipzig: Harrassowitz, 1945; Frappier, Jean. *Chrétien de Troyes*. Connaissance des lettres, 50. Paris: Hatier-Boivin, 1957; Hunt, Tony. "Herr Ivan Lejonriddaren." *Mediaeval Scandinavia* 8 (1975), 168–86.

Gösta Holm

[**See also:** *Flóres saga ok Blankiflúr*; *Ívens saga*; *Knittel(vers)*; *Riddarasögur*]

Exempla are short tales with explicit moralistic or didactic interpretations. The basic story could be drawn from history, legend, the Bible, saints' lives, classical or vernacular literature, folktales, and even from fables, bestiaries, lapidaries, and proverbs. Exempla were used by oriental and classical writers as well as by the early Fathers of the Christian Church. Pope Gregory the Great especially recommended the use of exempla and employed them in his homilies and in the *Dialogues*. Although collections of exempla are known from the beginning of the 12th century (*e.g.*, Petrus Alfonsi's *Disciplina clericalis* and William of Malmesbury's *Gesta regum Anglorum*), it was not until the advent of the preaching friars, who used exempla in their sermons (*e.g.*, Jacques de Vitry, *Sermones vulgares, Sermones communes*), that the popularity of the exemplum burgeoned all over Europe. From the 13th century, numerous collections of exempla were produced that circulated around the Continent, including Caesarius of Heisterback (*Dialogus miraculorum*), Jacobus de Voragine (*Legenda aurea*), Vincent of Beauvais (*Speculum historiale*), and Étienne de Bourbon (*Tractatus de diversis materiis praedicabilibus*).

Translations of Gregory's *Dialogues* served as an introduction to the genre in England by the late 9th century, and in Scandinavia, where the *Dialogues* were translated into Norwegian by 1150, although preserved only in Icelandic MSS after 1200. Other early West Norse examples of the genre in the vernacular occur in *Konungs skuggsjá*, where the exempla are drawn chiefly from the Bible, and in the miracles of the Virgin Mary. In East Norse, the exempla continued to be preserved in Latin with little divergence from the standard continental collections. A Low German source, *Seelentrost* (*ca.* 1350), was responsible for 15th-century translations into Old Swedish (*Siælinna thrøst*) and into Old Danish (*Siæla trøst*).

The influence of the preaching friars in Europe led to increased popularity of the exemplum in Scandinavia as well. Collections of exempla were preserved especially in Iceland, where over 150 such tales in the vernacular have been found and edited, although several different exempla can sometimes be found grouped under one rubric. The texts themselves often refer to the exempla by different names, including *ævintýr(i)*, *atburð*, *dæmi(saga)*, *exemplum*, *frásögn*, *(frá)saga*, and *ævisaga*, but they were evidently felt to be short tales quite distinct from the *þáttr*, which focused on local heroes, strong in the Germanic warrior tradition, as opposed in the exemplum to foreign characters with obvious weaknesses that allowed religious moralizing.

Close to two dozen complete and fragmentary vellum MSS containing exempla are preserved in Icelandic, although the number of medieval MSS as sources employed seems to have been considerably smaller. Twenty-eight exempla are directly indebted to the *Vitæ patrum*, and another fifty or so comprise a 15th-century translation from a Middle English prose MS indebted to *Handlyng Synne*, to the *Gesta Romanorum*, and to an expanded redaction of Odo of Cheriton. Many of the other exempla were probably 14th-century translations of a few Latin collections whose ultimate sources were Cæsarius of Heisterbach, Martin of Troppau, and Vincent of Beauvais. Over a dozen Icelandic exempla appear to be based on oral tradition, and some of these are attributed in the MSS themselves to Jón Halldórsson, a Norwegian Dominican monk who had studied in Paris and Bologna, and who left Bergen in 1323 to become bishop of Skálholt.

In Norway and Iceland, the exemplum also made its way from religious works into the secular literature. Exempla could be loosely attached to a saga (as in the beginning of just one MS of

Adonias saga), they could supply integrated episodes (*e.g.*, chs. 13–15 in *Víga-Glúms saga* from exempla nos. L and XC in Gering's edition; the Samarion and the flying-carpet interlude in *Viktors saga ok Blávus* from *Jónatas ævintýri*), and they could also be turned into *rímur* (*Jónatas rímur* from before 1600, and later poetic versions of exempla nos. LXXXII and LXIII in Gering's edition).

Ed.: Gering, Hugo. *Islendzk Æventyri*. 2 vols. Halle: Waisenhaus, 1882–83; Jakobsen, Alfred. "Noen tillegg til 'Islenzk æventyri.'" *Maal og minne* (1960), 27–47; Widding, Ole. "Om Rævestreger. Et kapitel i Adonius saga." *Opuscula* 1. Bibliotheca Arnamagnæana, 20. Copenhagen: Munksgaard, 1960, pp. 331–4; Jorgensen, Peter A. "Ten Icelandic Exempla and Their Middle English Source." *Opuscula* 4. Bibliotheca Arnamagnæana, 30. Copenhagen: Munksgaard, 1970, pp. 177–207; Jorgensen, Peter A. "Four Æventyri." *Opuscula* 5. Bibliotheca Arnamagnæana, 31. Copenhagen: Munksgaard, 1975, pp. 295–328; Einar G. Pétursson. *Miðaldaævintýri þýdd úr ensku*. Reykjavik: Stofnun Árna Magnússonar, 1976. **Lit.**: Mosher, Joseph A. *The Exemplum in the Early Religious and Didactic Literature of England*. New York: Columbia University Press, 1911; Tubach, Frederic C. *Index Exemplorum: A Handbook of Medieval Religious Tales*. Folklore Fellows Communications, 204. Helsinki: Suomalainen Tiedeakatemia, 1969; Schenda, Rudolf. "Stand und Aufgaben der Exemplaforschung." *Fabula* 10 (1969), 69–85; Jorgensen, Peter A. "The Icelandic Translations from Middle English." *Studies for Einar Haugen: Presented by Friends and Colleagues*. Ed. Evelyn Scherabon Firchow *et al.* Janua Linguarum, Series Maior, 59. The Hague and Paris: Mouton, 1972, pp. 305–20.

Peter A. Jorgensen

[**See also**: *Adonias saga*; Christian Prose; Gregory, St.: *Dialogues*; *Jóns þáttr biskups Halldórssonar*; *Konungs skuggsjá*; *Maríu saga*; *Rímur*; *Þáttr*; *Víga-Glúms saga*; *Viktors saga ok Blávus*]

Eyrbyggja saga ("The Saga of the Men of Eyrr") or, more accurately, "Saga Þórsnesinga, Eyrbyggja ok Álptfirðinga" ("The Saga of the Men of Þórnes, Eyrr, and Álptafjörðr") is one of the major *Íslendingasögur*. It tells the story of the people of Þórsnes, Eyrr, and Álptafjörður, all on the northern shores of the Snæfellsnes peninsula on the west coast of Iceland. The action begins in 884, the date of the arrival in Iceland of Þórólfr Mostrarskegg ("Mosterbeard"), and continues with an account of the feuds that take place in the neighborhood, most of which are concerned with or mediated by Snorri goði ("the priest"). At first, Arnkell goði, whose father, Þórólfr bægifótr ("lame-foot"), becomes a troublesome ghost after death, appears to be the more important figure; he is, however, killed in the course of his second quarrel with Snorri. A subplot concerns Snorri's sister, Þuríðr, her romance with Bjǫrn Breiðvíkingakappi ("champion of the Breiðvíkingar"), and the hauntings at the farm of Fróðá, where she lives. The action ends in 1031, the year in which Snorri died.

Three versions of the saga survive, the best in copies of the 14th-century codex *Vatnshyrna*; the original was lost in 1728 in a fire in the University of Copenhagen library. The middle part of another version of the saga is preserved in a 14th-century MS in the library in Wolfenbüttel, and there are fragments of yet a third version, the earliest of these being seven pages in the 15th-century *Melabók*.

Eyrbyggja saga was most likely composed in the middle of the 13th century. It must have been in existence before the fall of the Commonwealth (1262), since there are indications that certain republican institutions are in force, such as the allegiance of *þingmenn* ("liegemen") to their *goði* ("priest, chief") and the barring of women from the prosecution of a blood feud. A *terminus post quem* is provided by references to *Laxdœla saga*, composed probably between 1244 and 1248, and to the *Styrmisbók* version of *Landnámabók* (Styrmir died in 1245 and was probably writing 1235–1240). The style, more elegant than that of earlier sagas but still free of the influence of medieval chivalry and romanticism, and the diction, largely free of southern loanwords, also point to a mid-13th-century date. Accurate topographical references suggest that *Eyrbyggja saga* was composed in the area where the events described took place. The author may have been a monk at the Benedictine monastery at Helgafell. He appears to have had access to a library of sagas, for he summarizes and sometimes corrects material that had been treated in detail elsewhere; on two occasions, in the story of Víga-Styrr's slaying of the berserks and in chs. 13–15, he expands an incident. He shows a particular interest in the supernatural and in antiquarian lore. His description of a pagan temple and pagan worship are so convincing that they were long regarded as authentic; they are, however, adapted from Snorri Sturluson's *Hákonar saga góða*. The saga also contains a large number of skaldic stanzas (thirty-four).

The most remarkable feature of the *Eyrbyggja saga* is its lack of unity. Of all the *Íslendingasögur*, it is the only one that does not concentrate on the fate and fortunes of a single man or single family. Snorri goði is probably the most dominant figure, although events in which he played a major role are not mentioned, and his later life is treated cursorily. Equally unusual is the lack of traditional structure; the episodes in *Eyrbyggja saga* do not conform to the traditional pattern (in Andersson's [1967] terms) of Introduction, Conflict, Climax, Revenge, and Aftermath. Andersson has counted ten conflicts, and Hollander (1959) eight separate interwoven stories. Nineteenth-century scholars postulated interpolated chapters or a lost or unfinished ending, whereas modern critics have tried to find a unifying force in such varied elements as the location, the chronology, the history, the use of the supernatural, and the verses. The structure remains an enigma.

Ed.: Einar Ól. Sveinsson and Matthías Þórðarson, eds. *Eyrbyggja saga*. Íslenzk fornrit, 4. Reykjavik: Hið íslenzka fornritafélag, 1935; Scott, Forest S., ed. *Eyrbyggja saga*. Editiones Arnamagnæanæ [forthcoming]. **Tr.**: Schach, Paul, trans. *Eyrbyggja saga, Translated from the Old Icelandic*. Introduction and verse translations by Lee M. Hollander. Lincoln: University of Nebraska Press; American-Scandinavian Foundation, 1959; rpt. 1977; Hermann Pálsson and Paul Edwards, trans. *Eyrbyggja Saga*. Edinburgh: Southside, 1972; Toronto: University of Toronto Press, 1973; rev. ed. Harmondsworth: Penguin, 1989. **Lit.**: Hollander, Lee M. "The Structure of Eyrbyggja saga." *Journal of English and Germanic Philology* 58 (1959), 222–7; Hallberg, Peter. "Íslendinga saga och Egla, Laxdœla, Eyrbyggja, Njála, Grettla: Ett språktest." *Maal og minne* (1965), 89–105; Andersson, Theodore M. *The Icelandic Family Saga: An Analytic Reading*. Cambridge: Harvard University Press, 1967; Einar Ól. Sveinsson. "Eyrbyggja sagas kilder." *Scripta Islandica* 19 (1968), 3–18; Mabire, Jean-Pierre. *La composition de la Eyrbyggja Saga*. Publications du Centre de Recherches sur les Pays Nordiques de l'Université de Caen. Caen: Association des Publications de la Faculté des Lettres et Sciences Humaines de l'Université de Caen, 1971; Vésteinn Ólason. "Nokkrar athugasemdir um Eyrbyggja sögu." *Skírnir* 145 (1971), 5–25; Schach, Paul. "Some Observations on the Helgafell Episode in Eyrbyggja saga and Gísla saga." In *Saga og Språk: Studies in Language and Literature*. Ed. John M. Weinstock. Austin:

Jenkins, 1972, pp. 113–45; Scott, Forrest S. "The Icelandic Family Saga as a Precursor of the Novel, with Special Reference to Eyrbyggja Saga." *Parergon* 6 (1973), 3–13; Simpson, John. "Eyrbyggja Saga and Ninteenth Century Scholarship." In *Proceedings of the First International Saga Conference at the University of Edinburgh 1971*. Ed. Peter Foote *et al.* London: Viking Society for Northern Research, 1973, pp. 360–94; Heller, Rolf. "Das Alter der Eyrbyggja saga im Licht der Sprachstatistik." *Acta Philologica Scandinavica* 32 (1978), 53–66; McCreesh, Bernadine. "Structural Patterns in the *Eyrbyggja Saga* and Other Sagas of the Conversion." *Mediaeval Scandinavia* 11 (1978–79), 271–80; Hallberg, Peter. "Eyrbyggja sagas ålder—än en gång." *Acta Philologica Scandinavica* 32 (1979), 196–219; Kjartan G. Ottóson. *Fróðárlundur í Eyrbyggju.* Studia Islandica, 42. Reykjavik: Menningarsjóður, 1983; McCreesh, Bernadine. "Contrasting Christian and Pagan Motifs in Certain Family Sagas." In *The Sixth International Saga Conference 28/7–2/8, 1985. Workshop Papers*. 2 vols. Copenhagen: Det arnamagnæanske Institut, 1985, vol. 2, pp. 763–75 [photocopies of papers distributed to participants]; Rode, Eva. "Eyrbyggja saga: en sammenligning mellem A- og B-versionen." In *The Sixth International Saga Conference*, vol. 2, pp. 893–906; McTurk, Rory. "Approaches to the Structure of Eyrbyggja saga." In *Sagaskemmtun: Studies in Honour of Hermann Pálsson on His 65th Birthday, 26th May 1986*. Ed. Rudolf Simek *et al.* Vienna, Cologne, and Graz: Böhlau, 1986, pp. 223–38; D'Arcy, Julian Meldon, and Kirsten Wolf. "Sir Walter Scott and *Eyrbyggja Saga*." *Studies in Scottish Literature* 22 (1987), 30–43; Vésteinn Ólason. "'Máhlíðingamál': Authorship and Tradition in a Part of Eyrbyggja saga." In *Úr Dölum til Dala: Guðbrandur Vigfússon Centenary Essays*. Ed. Rory McTurk and Andrew Wawn. Leeds Texts and Monographs, n.s. 11. Leeds: University of Leeds, 1989, pp. 187–203.

Bernadine McCreesh

[See also: *Heimskringla*; *Íslendingasögur*; *Landnámabók*; *Laxdæla saga*; *Vatnshyrna*]

Eyvindr Finnsson skáldaspillir

Eyvindr Finnsson skáldaspillir ("the plagiarist"?) was a Norwegian poet of the 10th century, a man of noble descent from Hålogaland, whose mother was a descendant of Haraldr hárfagri ("fair-hair") Hálfdanarson. He was a skald at the court of Hákon góði ("the good") Haraldsson, and closely connected with the party of the earls of Hlaðir, who supported Hákon against the sons of Eiríkr, who were allied with the Danes. According to *Heimskringla*, Eyvindr seems to have been in a position of trust at the king's court. After Hákon's death, he was probably among the enemies of the new king, Haraldr gráfeldr ("grey-cloak") Eiríksson. Nevertheless, in the end, he became a skald at Haraldr's court, but the peaceful relations between them seem not to have lasted long, as his *lausavísur* make plain. The poem *Háleygjatal* shows him at the end of his life at the court of the victorious and powerful Earl Hákon Sigurðarson of the Hlaðir family.

Two poems by Eyvindr, *Hákonarmál* and *Háleygjatal*, and fourteen *lausavísur* (single stanzas) have been preserved. Nothing remains of a third poem, *Íslendingadrápa*, mentioned in *Heimskringla*.

The poem *Hákonarmál* is a panegyric on the dead Norwegian king Hákon góði (935–961), who was killed in the battle of Storð against the sons of Eiríkr blóðøx ("blood-axe") Haraldsson, his brother and adversary. The poem is contained in the MSS of *Heimskringla* (J, K, F) and some stanzas of it also appear in *Fagrskinna* (A, B) and in *Snorra Edda*.

The poem consists of three parts: the battle; the king's ensuing dialogue with the valkyries who have decided that he is to go to Óðinn, and the king's welcome in Valhǫll and among the gods;

and the concluding praise of the greatness and uniqueness of the late king, followed by words of grief over the situation of the country now enslaved. This three-part structure is also underlined by the meter. The traditional epic meter *fornyrðislag* is used for the battle section; the parts in which mythical persons are protagonists and the concluding praise use *ljóðaháttr* meter. For that reason, some scholars have assumed that two different poems have been combined in *Hákonarmál* (Sahlgren 1927). But this change of meter is characteristic of the genre of "eddic panegyrics," as well as the epic presentation and the use of mythical scenes and motifs for the purpose of praise. In the battle scenes, however, the poem is influenced to a greater extent by skaldic metaphors and kennings used to create impressive imagery.

As to the themes, the poem is cognate with *Eiríksmál*, although there are considerable differences. Whereas *Eiríksmál* is confined to a single scene, the entry of the king into Valhǫll, *Hákonarmál* also contains the battle and the praise of the king. There are also differences in religious attitudes. Valhǫll and Óðinn are presented very unfavorably. The valkyries, not Óðinn, choose the hero, and they also determine victory or defeat. Whether because of his Christian faith or his fear, the king does not want to go to Óðinn. Moreover, the king's welcome in Valhǫll is surpassed by his reception among the gods, for whom the poet uses the collective terms characteristic of the late-pagan religion of the environment of the earls of Hlaðir (*bǫnd, regin, rǫð, heiðin goð*). Unlike *Eiríksmál*, the poem reveals intense national feelings. The king is shown as a sovereign defending his kingdom, protecting the sanctuaries. His character is praised; there is no better king to come after him. And the gods who have invited him to join them are the gods worshiped in the environment of the earls of Hlaðir.

Taking into account the last stanza, where the poet speaks of the enslaved people, we have to assume that the poem was composed for the earls of Hlaðir after Hákon's death, when Haraldr gráfeldr's rule had become increasingly oppressive.

Most scholars accept the statement in *Fagrskinna* that *Eiríksmál* was the model for *Hákonarmál*. There are some very obvious parallels between the two poems. But there have also been voices in favor of the priority of *Hákonarmál* (Wadstein 1895, von See 1963); they argue that the poem's conception of Valhǫll is more archaic, and its poetic quality greater. Yet, both lines of argument are unconvincing, and it seems more correct to assume that the author of the *Hákonarmál* deliberately made his poem different from *Eiríksmál*, and had political motives for surpassing his model (Wolf 1969, Marold 1972).

Eyvindr's *Háleygjatal* was composed for Earl Hákon after his victory over the Jómsvíkingar in 985. This poem, as the opening stanza announces, traces the earl's ancestors to the gods. Only fragments are left: nine complete stanzas and seven half-stanzas are contained in *Heimskringla*, *Snorra Edda*, *Fagrskinna*, and *Flateyjarbók*. A 13th-century Icelandic MS (cf. Storm 1899: 111, Anm. 4), whose author probably used *Háleygjatal* to enumerate twenty-seven earls of Hlaðir, permits the conjecture that the poem also enumerated twenty-seven ancestors of Earl Hákon, just as *Ynglingatal*, which was presumably the model for *Háleygjatal*, does for the Ynglingar. The *kviðuháttr* meter also follows *Ynglingatal* (cf. Storm). The stanzas preserved show that *Háleygjatal* also relates how each of the princes met his death. The burial place of a prince is mentioned in only one case. The first of Hákon's ancestors is Sæmingr, the son of Óðinn and the giantess Skaði. The opening stanzas contain two traditional elements: the request for silence and the paraphrasing of "poem" by the myth of Óðinn's mead, the drink of poetical inspiration; this pattern shows clearly that the poem was composed as a panegyric.

The poem is connected with *Ynglingatal* by the meter, the genealogical content, and the concentration on the deaths of the princes. There are also certain similarities between the kennings and other metaphorical phrases in the two poems. Therefore, it has been generally supposed that *Háleygjatal* was composed for political reasons, following the model of *Ynglingatal*, in order to prove that the family of the earls of Hlaðir was just as old as the Ynglingar's, their rivals for the power in Norway, and that the earls were also descended from the gods. However, it has sometimes been argued that *Ynglingatal* is later than *Háleygjatal* (Wadstein 1895).

The fact that Eyvindr was called "skáldaspillir" plays a certain role in this discussion. The term was interpreted as "destroyer of skalds," and it was thought that this name implied that the poet had imitated older poems, especially their kennings. But since the style of skaldic poetry was highly traditional, we must beware of regarding these analogies from a modern point of view and dismissing them as lacking originality. It would be better to interpret the name of "skáldaspillir" as "who puts the other skalds in the shade" (Wadstein 1895, M. Olsen 1916).

Eyvindr's *lausavísur* are composed in *dróttkvætt* meter, the ceremonial, courtly style. The first six of them have to do with the battle of Fitjar: the first announces the arrival of the enemies' army to the king, the second calls the warriors to the battle. Stanzas 3–5 focus on one episode of the battle, the encounter of Hákon góði and Eyvindr skreyja ("bragger"). Stanza 6 is an answer to a well-known poem by Glúmr Geirason, skald of Haraldr gráfeldr, which praised his victory over Hákon. Eyvindr answered with a stanza recalling a previous victory of Hákon over the sons of Eiríkr.

Stanza 7 is a conventional praise of Haraldr gráfeldr. In stanza 10, the cool relation between king and skald is obvious. The remaining stanzas could be regarded as reflecting the author's critical attitude toward Haraldr's rule. In stanzas 8 and 9, he complains about the greed of the king, to whom he must even give his own gold (st. 10). Stanza 12 complains about the bad weather, for which in the contemporary view the king was responsible (*cf.* the fact that in *Vellekla* Earl Hákon was praised for bringing back good harvests). Stanzas 13 and 14 may also be read in this light: they deal with fishing and buying herring, partly in humorous paraphrases. In exchange for herring, the poet is forced to give a needle, which he had received as a present from the Icelanders. Seen in connection with the preceding stanzas, stanzas 13 and 14 could imply that the poet has lost his fortune as a consequence of his conflict with the king, and is forced in bad years to live by fishing for herring and selling his last possessions.

Ed.: Finnur Jónsson, ed. *Den norsk-islandske skjaldedigtning.* Vols. 1A-2A (tekst efter håndskrifterne) and 1B-2B (rettet tekst). Copenhagen and Christiania [Oslo]: Gyldendal, 1912–15; rpt. Copenhagen: Rosenkilde & Bagger, 1967 (A) and 1973 (B), vol. 1A, pp. 64–74, vol. 1B, pp. 57–65 [*Hákonarmál, Háleygjatal, lausavísur*]; Lindquist, Ivar, ed. *Norröna lovkväden från 800– och 900–talen.* 1. *Förslag till restituerad täxt jämte översättning.* Lund: Gleerup, 1929, pp. 10–7 [*Hákonarmál*], pp. 74–5 [*Háleygjatal 1–4*]; Kock, Ernst A., ed. *Den norsk-isländska skaldediktningen.* 2 vols. Lund: Gleerup, 1946–49, vol. 1, pp. 35–40 [*Hákonarmál, Háleygjatal, lausavísur*]. **Tr.**: Hollander, Lee M., trans. *Old Norse Poems: The Most Important Non-Skaldic Verse Not Included in the Poetic Edda.* New York: Columbia University Press, 1936; rpt. Millwood: Kraus, 1973; Leach, Howard G. *A Pageant of Old Scandinavia.* Princeton: Princeton University Press; New York: American-Scandinavian Foundation, 1946. **Lit.**: Wadstein, Elis. "Bidrag till tolkning och belysning av skalde- och Eddadikter." *Arkiv för nordisk filologi* 11 (1895), 64–92; Storm, Gustav. "Ynglingatal, dets Forfatter og Forfattelsestid." *Arkiv för nordisk filologi* 15 (1899), 107–41; Olsen, Magnus. "Fortjener Hákonarmáls digter tilnavnet 'skaldaspillir'?" In *Til Gerhard Gran, 9. des. 1916.* Kristiania [Oslo]: Aschehoug, 1916, pp. 1–9; Paasche, Frederik. "Hákonarmál." In *Til Gerhard Gran, 9. des. 1916*, pp. 10–6; Genzmer, Felix. "Das eddische Preislied." *Beiträge zur Geschichte der deutschen Sprache und Literatur* 44 (1919), 138–68; Noreen, Erik. "Anmärkninger till Eyvinds dikter." *Studier i fornvästnordisk diktning* (1921), 45–62; Noreen, Erik. "Eiríksmál och Hákonarmál." *Nordisk Tidskrift för vetenskap konst och industri, udg. av. Letterstedska Föreningen* (1922), 535–42; Sahlgren, Jöran. *Eddica et Scaldica. Fornvästnordiska studier* 1. Nordisk Filologi, 1. Lund: Gleerup, 1927, pp. 40–109; Flornes, H. M. "'Spåterne.' Merknader til ei lausavise av Eyvind Finnson." *Maal og minne* (1939), 15–16; Midtun, S. D. "En lausavísa av Øyvind Finnson." *Maal og minne* (1940), 143–4; Olsen, Magnus. "Skaldevers om nøds-år nordenfjells." *Festskrift til Konrad Nielsen på 70–årsdagen 28.8.1945.* Studia Septentrionalia, 2. Oslo: Brøgger, 1945, pp. 176–92; Lie, Hallvard. "Et upåaktet gammelnorsk ord: *hausi* og Hákonarmál 6." *Arkiv för nordisk filologi* 63 (1948), 200–3; Wolff, Ludvig. "Eddische-skaldische Blütenlese." In *Edda, Skalden, Saga: Festschrift zum 70. Geburtstag von Felix Genzmer.* Ed. Hermann Schneider. Heidelberg: Winter, 1952, pp. 92–107; Holm-Olsen, Ludvig. "Øyvind Skaldaspillir." *Edda* 53 (1953), 145–65; See, Klaus von. "Zwei eddische Preislieder: Eiríksmál und Hákonarmál." In *Festgabe für Ulrich Pretzel zum 65. Geburtstag dargebracht von seinen Freunden und Schülern.* Ed. Werner Simon et al. Berlin: Schmidt, 1963, pp. 107–17; Schier, Kurt. "Freys und Fróðis Bestattung." In *Festschrift für Otto Höfler zum 65. Geburtstag.* Ed. Helmut Birkhan et al. Vienna: Notring, 1968, pp. 389–409; Wolf, Alois. "Zitat und Polemik in den *Hákonarmál* Eyvinds." In *Germanische Studien.* Ed. J. Erben and E. Thurnher. Innsbrucker Beiträge zur Kulturwissenschaft, 15. Innsbruck: Institut für Vergleichende Sprachwissenschaft der Universität Innsbruck, 1969, pp. 9–32; Marold, Edith. "Das Walhallbild in den *Eiríksmál* und den *Hákonarmál.*" *Mediaeval Scandinavia* 5 (1972), 19–33; Schier, Kurt. "Háleygjatal." *Kindlers Literatur Lexikon* 5. Zurich: Kindler, 1970, pp. 1396–7; See, Klaus von. *Edda, Saga, Skaldendichtung.* Heidelberg: Winter, 1981, pp. 522–5.

Edith Marold

[**See also:** Commemorative Poetry; Eddic Meters; Eddic Poetry; *Eiríksmál; Fagrskinna; Flateyjarbók; Heimskringla; Íslendingadrápa;* Kennings; *Lausavísur;* Skaldic Meters; Skaldic Verse; *Snorra Edda*]

Fáfnismál *see* **Reginsmál and Fáfnismál**

Fagrskinna ("fair parchment") is a title employed since the 17th century for a history of the kings of Norway that appears to have been called *Nóregs konunga tal* ("Catalogue of the Kings of Norway") in the Middle Ages. It begins with Hálfdan svarti ("the black"), father of Haraldr hárfagri ("fair-hair"), and it ends with the battle of Ré in 1177, in which Magnús Erlingsson defeated Eysteinn Eysteinsson, the leader of the insurgent faction known as the *Birkibeinar* ("birch-legs"). Thus, both the author of *Fagrskinna* and of *Heimskringla* concluded their histories where they knew the continuation was to be found in *Sverris saga*.

Fagrskinna is preserved in various paper copies of two Norwegian vellums that perished in the Copenhagen fire of 1728. The older codex, of which a fragment exists (NRA 51 [Oslo]), was probably written about the middle of the 13th century, and the younger in the first half of the 14th century. The difference between the two versions is not great, but the younger one is transmitted almost complete, while the older one has several lacunae, amounting to about eighty printed pages. The younger redaction was, therefore, chosen as the basic text for the first edition in 1847. Nevertheless, the older redaction is preferable, and has since been published twice, with the lacunae filled in with text from the other redaction. Stanzas are quoted 272 times (including half-stanzas and two-line citations) when the sometimes supplemental skaldic material from both versions is counted; but the author knew many more stanzas and poems, and made use of their content without quoting. In general, he follows the practice of other *konungasögur*, quoting stanzas basically as evidence, although several stanzas are included as an integral part of the story.

Fagrskinna was probably written in the early 13th century, most likely in Niðaróss (Trondheim), or at least in Þrándheimr (Trøndelag), by either an Icelandic or a Norwegian scholar. There are many Norwegian word forms in the MSS, but they are no sure indication of Norwegian authorship, because we do not have the original text. The author had several written sources in more original versions than are now preserved, for instance: *Morkinskinna*, *Ágrip af Nóregs konunga sǫgum*, *Jómsvíkinga saga*, a saga about Óláfr Tryggvason, another about St. Óláfr, and most likely a saga about the earls of Hlaðir (**Hlaðajarla saga*). There are also indications that among *Fagrskinna*'s sources were the lost historical works by the Icelanders Ari Þorgilsson and Sæmundr Sigfússon. There are some striking parallels between *Fagrskinna* and *Heimskringla*, some verbatim, probably due to common sources. *Fagrskinna* is most likely the older of the two works, but there is no evidence that it was known in Iceland at the time of the composition of *Heimskringla*.

Fagrskinna is a well-written history; the narration is cogent and well arranged, without digression, free of superstition, and moderately pious. The author's chief interest is the high repute of the Norwegian regal line stemming from Haraldr hárfagri. It has been suggested that this work was commissioned by the young King Hákon Hákonarson (r. 1217–1263), who may have wished to have a complete history of the kings of Norway who preceded his grandfather Sverrir, whose saga he must have had.

Ed.: Finnur Jónsson, ed. *Fagrskinna: Nóregs konunga tal*. Samfund til udgivelse af gammel nordisk litteratur, 30. Copenhagen: Møller, 1902–03; Bjarni Einarsson, ed. *Ágrip af Nóregs konunga sǫgum; Fagrskinna—Nóregs konunga tal*. Íslenzk fornrit, 29. Reykjavik: Hið íslenzka fornritafélag, 1984. **Lit.**: Indrebø, Gustav. *Fagrskinna*. Avhandlinger fra Universitetets historiske seminar, 4. Kristiania [Oslo]: Grøndahl, 1917; Bjarni Aðalbjarnarson. *Om de norske kongers sagaer*. Skrifter utg. av Det Norske Videnskaps-Akademi i Oslo, II. Hist.-filos. klasse, 1936, 4. Oslo: Dybwad, 1937, pp. 173–236; Jakobsen, Alfred. "Om forholdet mellom Fagrskinna og Morkinskinna." *Maal og minne* (1968), 47–58; Jakobsen, Alfred. "Om Fagrskinna-forfatteren." *Arkiv för nordisk filologi* 85 (1970), 88–124; Jakobsen, Alfred, and Jan Ragnar Hagland. *Fagrskinna-studier*. Trondheim: Tapir, 1980 [also contains reprints of preceding two articles]; Fidjestøl, Bjarne. *Det norrøne fyrstediktet*. Øvre Ervik: Alvheim & Eide, 1982.

Bjarni Einarsson

[**See also**: *Heimskringla*; *Konungasögur*]

Family Sagas *see* **Íslendingasögur**

Family Structure. The concept of family denotes all relatives living together in the same dwelling and recognized as a single social unit. In its most basic sense, it comprises husband, wife, and their offspring, called "nuclear family" or "conjugal family." The term "extended family" denotes the addition of one or more relatives (however distant the relationship) other than offspsring; the extension may be either generationally vertical (grandparents, aunt, grandchildren, nephew, *etc.*) or lateral (brother, cousin, *etc.*) Vertical extensions often reflect the family developmental cycle, where successor offspring living at home marries while one or both of parents are still alive, often in connection with some form of retirement contract. This type is called "stem family."

Two or more nuclear families living together in the same dwelling, whether vertically or laterally organized, are usually called "joint families" or "multiple families." In Scandinavia, the term "grand family" (*storfamilie*) has generally been used in this sense. These terms denote a system of family organization that is principally different from the type based on the nuclear family. We will use the terms "joint family" and its Nordic equivalent, "grand family," to denote biologically related coresident families as defined by recent research, and the term "multiple family" to denote other types of coresident families (slave family–owner family, peasant family–lodger family, food-and-work community = *matlag*, *bolagsfamilj*).

Solitary persons and all persons living in the same household unit, biologically related or not, constitute a household. Household and nuclear family may be identical social units (simple family household). As servants, lodgers, and siblings with families may coreside with families, households will tend to be larger social units than nuclear families. The term "inmates" denotes coresident servants, lodgers, and other persons who are relatively casually connected with households. As the basic social and economic unit in large parts of the Nordic countries is the detached holding, and since a holding may be inhabited by two or more households dwelling in buildings at a distance from each other, the term "farmful" has been created by analogy to the established term "houseful" (Laslett 1972), when discussing the mean size and composition of the social unit inhabiting holdings. This term may cover all types of coresident social constellations defined above.

The concept of coresidential structure has demographic, sociopsychological, and sociological dimensions. We will here concentrate on the basic demographic connotations, mainly discussing the problem of size, composition, and development.

Grand family, joint family, multiple family. The concept of grand family has played a disproportionate role in Nordic historiography, often supposed to represent a primeval or early phase in the evolution of family organization prior to the emergence of the nuclear family, which is supposed to be closely related to modernization and industrialization. Recent Swedish and Finnish research has exposed the lax definitional classifications, unstringent analytical approaches, and undemanding empirical attitudes characteristic of this insouciant usage (Löfgren 1971: 4–10, Löfgren 1974a: 18–27, Löfgren 1974b: 59–61, Tornberg 1972: 4–17, Gaunt 1983).

Swedish ethnologists and historians commenting on problems relating to the grand family like to begin by quoting from a letter by King Gustav I (Vasa) (1523–1560), stating that in Norrland, Dalsland, and Värmland, "an evil and pernicious custom has arisen . . . that four, six, eight or more, occasionally a whole kin group, want to squeeze themselves into one holding and will not let their parts of the inheritance be bought off, but claim that they nowhere else can live as well as where they have grown up." The king then demands that siblings divide their inheritance and split it up to form new holdings. The purpose of the royal writ obviously is to increase the tax base. According to Löfgren (1972, 1974a, 1974b),

the purpose of those who formed these, as it seems, laterally organized grand families, was to avoid carving up the productive assets on which the social position of the kin group was dependent.

When the sources begin to flow more copiously, in the 17th and 18th centuries, the incidence of grand families is quite low, and is registered mostly in the forest districts of Norrland. These examples typically pertain to well-to-do peasants. However, many of the households labeled as grand families have probably reflected transitional stages in the family cycle (Löfgren 1972: 234). The seemingly higher incidence of grand families at the time of Gustav I may have been caused by the strong relative increase in animal husbandry and the price of hired labor in the late-medieval period, both reflecting the demographic and economic upheavals of large-scale population contraction.

The view that the grand-family system was the predominant domestic group from the Merovingian and Viking centuries down to the period of industrialization is, in Norwegian historiography, as in Swedish and Finnish, founded largely on conceptual ambiguities and anecdotal evidence recorded 1,000 years later (Frimannslund 1972: 231). In this tradition, it is erroneously assumed that the stem family represents a type of grand family, while modern demography, social history, and ethnology have pointed out that it reflects a cyclical phase of the nuclear family. Highly exaggerated relative frequencies of stem families in particular, but also of other types of multigenerational families, are arbitrarily assumed to be standard features of family organization in the past without any reference to substantiating demographic studies. We will, therefore, present some types of data and considerations that should be included in discussions of such problems in order to reach valid conclusions.

Outside Italy, medieval records containing systematic registration of agricultural populations, family by family, are exceedingly rare. However, three censuses made in 1268–1269 of the bondmen of the Benedictine priory at Spalding in the Lincolnshire fenland are extant. This is an area where a noticeable Nordic influence is still traceable at that time. Hallam (1957–58, 1961–62, 1963) has studied this unique census material for high-medieval northwestern Europe. We will use his findings to illustrate problems and perspectives relating to demographic structure of rural populations in the northern part of Europe about 1300.

Hallam (1957–58: 351–3) concludes that out of the 252 households surveyed, only four, or 1.6 percent, were three-generational. This figure is so low that under-registration of elderly people might be suspected, or a skewed social composition of the population due to influx of young adults. However, even if we assume gross under-registration, which is not suggested by any of the scholars who have examined these censuses, the resultant figure will still be quite small. Hallam's conclusion on this point agrees, in fact, roughly with the findings of the Scandinavian osteoarchaeologists, which indicate that only 1.5–3 percent of medieval populations in the Nordic countries reached the age of sixty years. According to the polyptych (survey of monastic estate) of the estates of St. Germain-des-Prés undertaken at the beginning of the 9th century, there are only twenty-six grandmothers among the 3,404 women recorded, making the researcher conclude that "the classical stem family was not present on the estates of St. Germain" (Herlihy 1978: 70–1).

In an agricultural population in modern Iran (1950) with demographic characteristics relatively similar to the one indicated by osteoarchaeology for medieval Scandinavia, the proportion of population above the age of forty-five was 15.5 percent (Naraghi 1960: 40–2). According to model life tables (South and East), the proportion of population above the age of forty-five in populations with life expectancy at birth of 22.5 years is 16 percent, 56 percent of all men reaching the age of twenty will die before the age of fifty. The corresponding rates for women will be still higher, due mostly to gender-specific reproduction-related supermortality, probably in the range of 4–7 percent, and a gender-specific increment in the level of exposure to infectious diseases due to the gender-specific role of nursing the ill. Mortality rates increased sharply after the age of forty. Hallam (1957–58: 349–50, 355–60) furnishes several telling indications of this high turnover rate of adult population.

Proportion of population above the age of forty-five or fifty years in medieval Scandinavia will, according to the skeletal studies, probably have been of the order of 15 percent to 10 percent, respectively. The proportion of those reaching this age and entering the role of grandparent in a household founded by offspring will depend on the chance of not being childless, and, if having mature offspring, on whether successor offspring was expected to postpone marriage until death or disablement of father (cf. Hallam 1957–58: 351). This material makes it clear that three-generational families, i.e., stem families, were a relatively marginal phenomenon in medieval Scandinavia.

Where the stem family is relatively common, a large mean household size is not implied. In the 18th century, mean household size in Alskog and Lye on Gotland was less than five, although more than a third of all households contained three generations or more at the time. Studies of socioeconomically "old-fashioned" agricultural communities in Central Sweden in the first half of the 17th century show 4.5 as mean household size, although more than 20 percent had a complex structure (extended, stem, joint, and multiple families), and almost 50 percent contained servants (Gaunt 1978: 74–8; cf. Friberg 1953: 229–38). A census was taken in 1645 of the population of five rural parishes on the Danish island of Møn (south of Zealand). This population likewise exhibits many archaic demographic features, i.e., corresponds in important respects relatively closely to the demographic structures uncovered by osteoarchaeologists on the basis of medieval skeletal materials. In this census, households contained on average of about four persons. The relative size of the earliest cohorts indicates a significant deficit of infants and young children in the registers. The proportion of people recorded as reaching the age of sixty in these communities was far higher than in any medieval-population studies by Scandinavian osteoarchaeologists, which is quite likely due in part to a tendency to exaggerate length of life at advanced ages because old age in these societies provides prestige.

In a population with a life expectancy at birth of 22.5 years, a man marrying at twenty-five years of age could (according to life tables), on average, expect to live for another thirty years at the most. As infant mortality correspondingly would be about 300 per 1,000, generational relations would typically not be strongly encumbered with clashes of interest over rights of disposal of productive resources and income and over opportunity for marriage. The high general mortality rates also caused a considerable number of vacant holdings, creating opportunities for marriage of younger siblings, who, therefore, would tend to move out of the parental household earlier than in the 17th and 18th centuries. This process is much enhanced by the custom of partible inheritance, which was generally practiced in all the Nordic countries.

No household consisting of three conjugal families of different generations, and so being a genuine vertically organized grand family, was registered by Hallam (1957–58: 352–3), and must have been a rarity also in the Nordic societies where mean life expectancy at birth was twenty to twenty-five years. Friberg (1956) registered on the basis of exceptionally good demographic material a proportion of only 3.4 percent above the age of sixty-five in the population of Grangärde in western Bergslagen in 1677, the proportion of the population older than fifty years being 11.5 percent. To the extent that grand families existed, they will mostly have had to consist of families and siblings practicing joint tenancy. This conclusion has been confirmed by much research on Nordic preindustrial peasantries.

The grand family in early modern Finland. Only in some districts of Finland, Österbotten, eastern Tavastland, and southeastern Karelia (Kexholm), has the grand family been shown to have been common, and so constituting an alternative system of family structure and organization to the otherwise overwhelmingly dominant nuclear-family type in the Nordic countries. Only in Karelia has this situation been shown to go back at least to 1500, the relative number of grand families and multiple families then being 23 percent. Of these complex families, more than 70 percent consisted of brother families and 14 percent of work-and-food communities (matlag, bolagsfamilj), which might or might not also contain biologically related parts. Some 80 percent of brother families consisted of the nuclear families of two brothers. This is the only part of the Nordic countries where the grand family has been shown to have been common and an alternative system of family organization at a time stretching back into the medieval period (Tornberg 1972: 4–17). Work-and-food communities are unstable social units tending to reflect temporal adaptations. Doubts have been voiced as to whether they should be considered a genuine subtype of family organization.

All notions of a linear evolutionary development of family organization throughout history from large domestic groups to simple nuclear families are dispelled by the Finnish material, showing that grand-family types of family organization developed in southeastern parts of Österbotten and Tavastland in the 17th century, constituting, in 1634, at most 20 percent and 5 percent, respectively, of all families. In central and northern Österbotten, the grand family originated in the 17th century and grew in relative importance throughout the 18th and into the next century, when the trend was reversed (Tornberg 1972: 7–9). Joint families/grand families ought to be viewed as special socioeconomic adaptations, not as representing a stage in a deterministic evolutionary process (Löfgren 1974a: 21–30).

Ethnological studies have shown that there is a close interaction between peasant ecotypes and the development of specific systems of family organization, in casu the grand family. As the institution of grand family is so intimately connected with particular periods and areas, those factors that have affected its occurrence may have varied greatly. It is, however, possible to discern common traits on a more generalized level of analysis: "The common distinguishing features of the Finnish areas of grand families were that those economic activities which demanded large input of labor power within the framework of the economic structure also were important as subsidiary sources of production and income." Slash-and-burn agriculture is characteristic of the old Karelian core areas of the grand family as well as of many areas where this institution developed in the 17th century. Later, when the grand family became more common, this development was closely connected with intensive animal husbandry (Tornberg 1972: 14–5).

This point has been developed by Löfgren, who emphasizes four categories of common features: (1) Grand families have mostly been registered in sparsely populated regions; (2) they are characterized by a high degree of economic differentiation within the household; (3) they are markedly associated with labor-intensive modes of production, particularly slash-and-burn agriculture, in which pooling of scarce family labor is highly advantageous; (4) they often represent the higher social classes of local peasant society, where families, by staying together, i.e., practicing joint tenancy or joint ownership, could avoid splitting up the means of production, keeping and running together, at least temporarily, land, cattle, and other productive assets in order to gain economies of scale (Löfgren 1972: 233–4, Löfgren 1974a: 21–2).

Recent research has uncovered interesting material in Icelandic law and sagas. Complex household types are indicated by the terms tvíbýli, félagsbú, búlag, and the phrase eiga bú saman. Tvíbýli seems to have involved unified management and separate ownership and use of cattle and tools by each bóndi. A félagsbú and a búlag seem to indicate partnership in work and property. We are also told in one of the sagas that "it is best for the property of brothers to be seen together." This introduced the concept of frèreche also in the Germanic part of the medieval Nordic area. The laws, moreover, assume occurrence of in-living married servants, partly corroborated by scattered saga evidence. In accordance with one of the main parameters of the Finnish pattern, joint and multiple households were closely related to intensive animal husbandry. There was some grain production in early high-medieval Iceland, but it was largely abandoned in the 13th century. Production of meat and dairy products was of paramount importance, shaping social and economic organization. Fishing and production of coarse woolen cloth played significant susidiary roles. As in Finland, there was a strong correlation between substantial holdings and wealthy households and occurrence of complex household arrangements. Not only economic conditions contributed to the forming of complex households. In Iceland, intensive feuding induced households to merge for reasons of defense. While there can be no doubt that single households were the dominant residential unit, a combination of law texts and incidental social information in sagas furnishes a good case for assuming a substantial frequency of complex households, and that intensive animal husbandry was the primary or basic cause of this phenomenon (Miller 1988: 321–35).

Modern Scandinavian medievalists without exception consider the mean household size in the medieval period to have been six persons or between six and seven persons, compared with the ten to thirteen persons suggested by many researchers for the Viking period, and more generally for the Merovingian period. However, even the much-reduced high-medieval mean-household size of six to seven persons claimed by Nordic historians seems to assume a record-breaking level.

Household size and composition: proportion of children.
According to the demographic pattern emerging in the data provided by osteoarchaeologists, children below fifteen years probably formed around 45 percent of the population. The number of children per family can be estimated only when the number of households is known, including the number of inmate families. What seems to be generally overlooked in studies of medieval demography is the effect of high general levels of mortality on the

distribution of children in households (see, however, Howell 1983: 212). As mentioned earlier, about 45–50 percent of those reaching twenty years of age would be dead before reaching their fiftieth birthday. The high turnover of adults implies a considerable frequency of marriages broken by the death of one of the spouses before completion of reproductive period, or even, to some extent, extinguished by the death of both spouses. Because there was a general opinion in old-time peasant society that neither a man nor a woman could run a holding single-handedly, remarriage usually followed quite soon after the death of a spouse (Hallam 1963: 349, Benedictow 1985: 49–50, Vejde 1938: 193–4, Leijonhufvud 1921: 183). The children of the former marriage(s), accordingly, were redistributed among new reproductive alliances, or in the case of the death of both parents, often among households headed by relatives. In short, households comprised a hidden demographic structure, the reproductive remains of broken and extinct families. The mean number of children per household reflects a larger number of reproductive alliances than those actually in function, and, correspondingly, the mean number of children per household is larger than the mean number of surviving children per reproductive alliance. Otherwise, the basic rule is that families at a given point will, on average, have completed only two-thirds of the process of rearing children (Hollingsworth 1969: 115), the figure of 1.4 indicating a stagnant or stationary population, 2.2 children per completed family. Such a figure indicates, of course, that completed families tended to have considerable reproductive success, but that the average number of surviving children per established reproductive alliance was being appreciably reduced by a large number of families who were reduced by mortality before their reproductive capacity had been exhausted, including also the proportion of young married girls who died at childbirth.

In the censuses of 1268–1269, Hallam (1957–58: 353–6) found 859 children distributed among 252 households, producing the enormous average of 3.4 living offspring per family, irrespective of age, marital status, and place of residence, in three manors at Spalding. Hallam does not seem to recognize the extraordinary (although not impossible) nature of this proportion of children living in the population, and that the mean number of 3.4 living children per household signifies explosive population growth, if taken at face value, i.e., as the children of the existing married couples.

The English demographic data, founded on written sources, and the Scandinavian data, founded on human skeletal sources, agree remarkably well. When roughly half of all married persons die while still having small or young children, roughly 40 percent of all marriages will be broken by the death of at least one spouse/parent, 10 percent extinguished by the death of both spouses/parents. In the case of the three manors at Spalding, the 859 living offspring recorded do not reflect the reproductive activities of the 252 married couples recorded, as Hallam thinks, but comprise the outcome of an additional number of marriages, perhaps not far from 100; in that case, the mean number of living children per household is about 2.5.

This is still a high figure, but can be explained by the intensive reclamation of wasteland and the attendant strong movement of colonization in the Lincolnshire fens, making it in these respects highly atypical in England at the time. The number of households increased six times at Spalding between 1086 and 1287; at nearby Pinchbeck, the corresponding growth rate was eleven times. These growth rates are typical for the Lincolnshire fenland (although much higher rates are known), and continued for some decades after the censuses of 1268–1269 (Hallam 1961–62, Miller and Hatcher 1978: 30–1, 35–6). This situation makes for considerable immigration of young adults at a time when population pressures elsewhere were becoming fierce (Titow 1961–62: 218–24), and permits universal marriage and low age at marriage. This scenario may also help to explain why Hallam found only four three-generational families among 252 households (1.6 percent).

Age distribution. The significance of the problem may be indicated by the age-related results of osteoarchaeological research. Although infants are greatly under-represented in the skeletal material exhumed in Tønsberg and Trondheim, adults above the age of forty constitute only 16 percent and 26.5 percent, respectively, of the total skeletal population. At Frösön in Jämtland, where children are satisfactorily represented in the skeletal remains, the corresponding figure is 19 percent (Gejvall 1960: 35–6, Anderson 1986: table 5, Holck 1987: 34–5; cf. Friberg 1956: 10).

The skeletal populations excavated in Lund, dating to around 1050–1100 and the last 100 years of the medieval period, respectively, exhibit a slightly different pattern, persons having died above the age of sixty constituting 5 percent and 4 percent, respectively, of the cemetery population. Children below the age of fifteen form close to 30 percent of both populations and so are markedly under-represented (Persson 1976: 173, Persson and Persson 1981: 151–70), although not as strongly as quite often is the case (Holck 1987: 34, Sjøvold 1978a: 167). This type of local variation is to be expected within the general pattern of demographic systems, the homogeneity of the other data giving more reason for surprise. In this case, the general commonality of demographic structure can, for example, be seen in life expectancies at birth of 26.9 and 24.9 years, respectively; and if the deficiency of children is compensated for by increasing proportion of children from 29 percent to about 45 percent, mean life expectancy at birth will be appreciably reduced. Such a correction of the deficiency of children will, correspondingly, cause the proportion of persons above the age of sixty to diminish substantially, bridging much of the age divergence in relation to the other data. The same type of distribution of the older parts of populations may be easily recognized also in "old-fashioned" populations in developing countries (Kpedekpo 1982: 40–1).

In light of this evidence, persons above forty-five years are assumed to constitute 15 percent of the population. After fifteen years, only 2.5 percent are left. We cannot assume that all marriages are complete at all times. In a society experiencing life expectancy at birth of 22.5–25 years, persons reaching twenty years of age will in the ensuing thirty years experience a mortality rate of about 50 percent and 45 percent respectively corresponding to, on average, about 1.66 percent and 1.5 percent per year. The parental generation (*i.e.*, comprising both parents and step-parents) is assumed to constitute roughly 42.5 percent of the total population.

The grandparental generation makes for only a small average addition to households or population according to the data presented above about the basic demographic structure of the medieval Scandinavian populations. Average life expectancy at birth of 22.5 years corresponds, according to the Life Tables South, for persons reaching twenty years of age, to a mortality rate of about 45 percent during the ensuing three decades. Persons above forty-five, fifty, and sixty years of age will constitute about 15 percent, 10 percent,

and 2.5 percent, respectively, of the population. We have assumed that the grandparental generation constitutes 5 percent of the population, perhaps only half of these living with their married children and grandchildren forming stem families, often because they do not have surviving offspring, or because offspring had left local society due to migration, vagabondage, and so on. These assumptions imply that about 10 percent of households were stem families, about 10 percent of these, or about 1 percent of all households, containing two grandparents. These assumptions are quite generous; compare, for example, the 1.6 percent of families registered by Hallam as containing a grandparent at Spalding in the Lincolnshire fenland, and none of them contained two grandparents.

Although this is a society characterized by high nuptiality, there will always be a social residue of persons who do not marry for various reasons.

The last category of persons to be considered is unmarried youth above the age of fifteen. The cohort of those fifteen to nineteen years is assumed to contain 10 percent of the population equally divided by gender. Universal marriage is assumed, and early marriage, particularly for girls. All girls are assumed to be married by the age of twenty, half of them at the age of 17.5 years, and this half will have to be considered as included in the estimate of the proportion constituted by the parental generation. Also a significant proportion of men will be married by the age of twenty, only a few by the age of 17.5. The remaining 7.5 percent of the population so far unaccounted for will have to be found in the category of unmarried youth and young adults.

We can thus conclude that the medieval population consisted mainly of children below the age of fifteen (45 percent) and (step)parents (42.5 percent), these two categories between them constituting roughly 87.5 percent of the population.

We may now calculate the mean household size and mean number of persons per *merkrból.* A Norwegian holding of average size, 1.5 *merkrból* (somewhat smaller in the west country), would, at a given point around 1300, on average be populated by 0.93 male (step)parent (*einvirki*) and 0.87 female (step)parent, having 1.91 live children below the age of fifteen, 0.32 unmarried youth, and 0.21 representatives of the grandparental generation, in all 4.24 persons.

On the basis of size and social distribution of holdings, it is possible to approach the question of incidence of multiple households in order to calculate the mean number of persons inhabiting holdings, *i.e.,* mean farmful size. Such a calculation has been performed for the district of Eidsvoll in southeastern inland Norway. The outcome indicates that we can assume twenty grand families and inmate-families of both categories in Eidsvoll around 1300, comprising eighty-five persons. This number represents an average addition of 0.38 persons per holding. While mean household size was 4.25 persons, mean farmful size was 4.6 persons. The addition is the outcome of an estimate considered to represent a realistic maximum, and so is quite probably on the high side, producing a somewhat exaggerated farmful size. However, these calculations have no pretense to an accuracy that permits fine-tuning of figures. One should note that the agricultural resources of the district of Eidsvoll, and the relative number of large holdings, were markedly above average in Norway.

A mean household size of 4.25 and a mean farmful size of 4.6 implies a slight population growth, which probably is correct with respect to inland southeastern Norway, where, at the time, there still was room for some colonization, but which may not reflect quite as accurately the apparently stagnant populations of western and central Norway. In the latter regions, the number of children per reproductive alliance represented by children in local society at a given point will have been around 1.4, the mean number permitting a population barely able to reproduce itself. This relative diminution of the proportion of children in the population probably reflects the workings of Malthusian pressure mechanisms, an increase in age at marriage reducing fertility, or an increase in mortality of infants and young children due to malnutrition, or both. Older elements of the population probably were little affected. Female mortality may actually have subsided slightly and female life expectancy have edged upward as marriage tended to be postponed, in the process reducing marginally maternal pregnancy-related mortality. For the country as a whole, therefore, slightly reduced mean household and farmful figures will probably better reflect the overall demographic situation, indicating, in rounded figures, mean household size and farmful size of four and 4.5 persons, respectively. This must be close to a minimum figure for the high Middle Ages, indicating a stationary population. Mean number of persons per *merkrból* correspondingly is 2.66.

Between 1050 and 1250, when the population of Norway generally was increasing briskly, mean number of children per actually reproducing family at any given point may at times have tended toward 1.8. The mean number of children per household including the children of broken or extinguished reproductive alliances will in that case tend toward 2.5. Mean household size, accordingly, will approach five persons, the proportion of children below the age of fifteen in the population consequently being about 50 percent, and mean farmful size being around 5.3.

In conclusion, our computations on the basis of the demographic structural indications provided by Scandinavian osteoarchaeologists and the economic structural indications provided by agricultural historians suggest that in the couple of centuries preceding the Great Pestilence, mean household size and mean farmful size in Norway may have varied between four and five persons and 4.5 and 5.5, respectively, the minimum figures probably being realistic around 1300.

Late-medieval developments. The dramatic reduction in the size of population caused by plague epidemics in the second half of the 14th century also affected the size and composition of households and farmfuls. Good holdings fell vacant in large numbers, and the rents were reduced to a small fraction of their level before 1348, to about 20–25 percent (Salvesen 1978: 137–40). Inmate households of both categories, therefore, might be expected to move out and establish themselves as independent substantial tenants.

The economic development in the same period is characterized by a marked change from arable farming to animal husbandry. According to the postmedieval Finnish experience, intensified animal husbandry might have stimulated a relative increase in frequency of grand families/joint families. In other European countries, there was a strong increase in the frequency of this type of coresident constellation after the Great Pestilence, particularly in southern France and in parts of Italy. It is remarkable that constellations of brother households increase particularly strongly. The close connection with the demographic and socioeconomic effects of the plague epidemics is not only suggested by coincidence in time, that the proliferation of this phenomenon commences around 1350, but is evident from the fact that the decline

is coincident with renewed population growth at the end of the 15th century, and that it almost disappears after the preplague population level had been reached around the middle of the ensuing century (Le Roy Ladurie 1966: 162–8, Klapisch and Demonet 1970: 415–28).

Whether a corresponding development took place in the Nordic countries in the late-medieval period, particularly in areas practicing intensive animal husbandry, is one of the questions that researchers should address in the future. A. E. Christensen's observation has been ignored: "A one-sided understanding of deserted holdings as a reflection of a deficit of peasants can be directly disproved, as it is not rare in the manorial rentals at the same time to find deserted holdings and holdings containing two tenants; indeed, coresidence of peasants, in fact, has been so usual that the archbishop of Lund, in the years 1499–1500, found himself compelled to issue provisions regulating the extent to which coresident tenants should pay dues" (1938: 36).

Possibly, the comprehensive fiscal registers and land registers compiled by government officials and some of the cadasters and rentals compiled by major ecclesiastical institutions and noblemen in the 16th century would yield interesting information if studied closely. The use of the word *ibidem* to denote additional household(s) may contain important clues. Undoubtedly, this usage mostly refers to divisions and subdivisions of a "named farm" (a term used to designate the originally colonized, individually named independent agricultual unit, that might or might not have become divided and subdivied into independent holdings [*gårdsbruk*]) and, consequently, to a separate household running an independent holding carved out from the original area of a "named farm." But some "named farms" not known to have been divided are recorded as containing more than one household.

Another indication of accumulation of persons within the framework of the nondeserted substantial holdings is the explosive growth of population registered in some Norwegian localities in the second half of the 16th century and the beginning of the 17th century, reflecting rates that can hardly be explained as the outcome of natural fertility alone (Holmsen 1939: 273–89, Fladby 1977: 112–22, Fladby 1978: 31–50, Fladby 1986: 71–81, Marthinsen 1979: 38–51, Aarsæther 1981: 400–8, 414–5). But that may be explained if part of the demographic dynamics is derived from the dissolution of grand families. This analysis indicates an interesting field of research that so far has been completely overlooked.

As in England, the late-medieval Norwegian society saw considerable upward mobility of the poorest sections of society, day laborers, *kotkarlar*, crofters, etc., as they moved into the best of the numerous vacant holdings produced by the recurrent plague epidemics. The extant Norwegian sources do not permit analysis of this social process, but only register its outcome. It is, nonetheless, as indicated above, probable that inmate-families now would move out and establish themselves as substantial independent tenants. Although the mean size of the late-medieval peasant household probably tended to diminish, this development may not have been so pronounced as might be assumed, because the effects of plague and out-migration of inmate-families might have been partly offset by an increased relative frequency of grand families.

In the 15th century, when population size was stationary or, more likely, in the long run slowly dwindling, mean household and farmful size may not have been much smaller than around

1300, perhaps only by a factor of about 0.25 percent. At least, caution seems advisable, and we will indicate 3.75–4.0 and 4.25, respectively, as sensible suggestions for the time being.

Lit.: Leijonhufvud, Karl K:son. "Pesten 1710–1711 och prästeskapet i Strängnäs stift." *Karolinska Förbundets Årsbok* (1921), 156–95; Skappel, S. *Om husmandsvæsenet i Norge. Dets oprindelse og utvikling.* Videnskapsselskapets Skrifter. II. Hist.-filos. Klasse 1922, no. 4. Kristiania [Oslo]: Dybwad, 1922; rpt. Blindern: Universitetsbokhandelen, 1979; Olsen, Magnus. *Ættegård og helligdom. Norske stedsnavn sosialt og religionshistorisk belyst.* Oslo: Aschehoug, 1926; rpt. Bergen: Universitetsforlaget, 1978; Steinnes, Asgaut. "Økonomisk historie." In *Romerike 1.* Bergen: Grieg, 1932, pp. 79–120; Johnsen, Oscar A. *Norges bønder. Utsyn over den norske bondestands historie.* Oslo: Aschehoug, 1936; Vejde, P. G. "Om pesten i Småland 1710–11." *Hyltén Cavalliusföreningens Årsbok* (1938), 159–95; Christensen, Aksel E. "Danmarks befolkning og bebyggelse i middelalderen." In *Befolkning i middelalderen.* Ed. Adolf Schück. Nordisk kultur, 2. Stockholm: Bonnier; Oslo: Aschehoug; Copenhagen: Schultz, 1938, pp. 1–57; Holmsen, Andreas. *Norges historie.* Oslo: Gyldendal, 1949; Friberg, Nils. "Dalarnas befolkning på 1600-tallet." *Geografiska Annaler* 3–4 (1953), 1–270; Hagen, Anders. *Studier i jernalderens gårdssamfunn.* Universitetets Oldsaksamlings Skrifter, 4. Oslo: Universitetets Oldsaksamling, 1953; Friberg, Nils. "Om mantalsskrivningen i Grangärde 1650–1750." *Ymer* 76 (1956), 1–24; Hallam, H. E. "Some Thirteenth-Century Censuses." *Economic History Review,* 2nd ser. 10 (1957–58), 340–61; Bjørkvik, Hallvard. "Envangsbruk." *KLNM* 3 (1958), 690–3; Gejvall, Nils-Gustaf. *Westerhus: Medieval Population and Church in the Light of Skeletal Remains.* Lund: Ohlsson, 1960; Skrubbeltrang, Fridlev. "Husmand." *KLNM* 7 (1962), 143–5; Hafström, Gerhard. "Husmand." *KLNM* 7 (1962), 145–6; Hallam, H. E. "Further Observations on the Spalding Serf Lists." *The Economic History Review,* 2nd ser. 10 (1963), 338–50; Lassen, A. *Fald og fremgang. Træk af befolkningsudviklingen i Danmark 1646–1960.* Århus: Universitetsforlaget, 1965; Ladurie, Emmanuel Le Roy. *Les paysans de Languedoc.* Paris: S.E.V.P.E.N.; Mouton, 1966; Hollingsworth, Thomas H. *Historical Demography.* London: Sources of History, 1969; Klapisch, Christiane, and Michel Dumonet. "A uno pane e uno vino. Structure et dévelopment de la famille rurale toscane (debut de 15ème siècle)." *Annales économies sociétés civilisations* 25 (1970), 873–901; Sandnes, Jørn. *Ødetid og Gjenreisning. Trønsk busetningshistorie ca. 1200–1600.* Oslo: Universitetsforlaget, 1971; Berkener, Lutz K. "The Stem Family and the Developmental Cycle of the Peasant Household: An Eighteenth-Century Austrian Example." *American Historical Review* 77 (1972), 398–418; Tornberg, Matleena. "Storfamiljinstitutionen i Finland. En sammanställning över finska forskningsresultat." *Nord-Nytt* (1972), 4–17; Löfgren, Orvar. "Familj och hushåll—Släkt och äktenskap." In *Land och stad. Svenska samhällstyper och livsformer från medtid till nutid.* Ed. Mats Hellspong and Orvar Löfgren. Lund: Gleerup, 1972, pp. 227–84; Dahlbäck, Göran, et al. *Det medeltida Sverige. 1.1. Uppland, Norra Roden.* Stockholm: Almquist & Wiksell, 1972; Laslett, Peter. "Introduction: The History of the Family." In *Household and Family in Past Time: Comparative Studies in the Size and Structure of the Domestic Group over the Last Three Centuries in England, France, Serbia, Japan, and Colonial America, with Further Materials from Western Europe.* Ed. Peter Laslett and Richard Wall. Cambridge: Cambridge University Press, 1972, pp. 1–89; Frimannslund, Rigmor. "Storfamilj." *KLNM* 17 (1972), 230–1; Berkener, Lutz K. "Recent Research on the History of the Family in Western Europe." *Journal of Marriage and the Family* 35 (1973), 395–405; Dahlbäck, Göran. "Landhöjning och bebyggelse i nordligaste Uppland." *Fornvännen* 69 (1974), 121–31; Löfgren, Orvar. "Family and Household Among Scandinavian Peasants: An Exploratory Essay." *Ethnologia Scandinavia* (1974), 17–52 [1974a]; Löfgren, Orvar. "Bondefamilie og

hushold i komparativt perspektiv." In *Familie, hushold og produktion. Punktundersøgelser i 5 danske lokalsamfund.* Ed. Orvar Löfgren. Copenhagen: Institutt for europæisk folkelivsforskning, 1974 [1974b]; Persson, Ove. "Undersökning av människoskelett." *Uppgrävt förflutet för PK banken i Lund. En investering i arkeologi.* Lund: Kulturhistoriska museet, 1976; Fladby, Rolf. *Norges historie* 6. Oslo: Cappelen, 1977; Fladby, Rolf. "Bosetnings- og befolkningsstudier i norske bygder på 1500- og 1600-tallet." In *Nordisk lokalhistoria: Mötesrapport* 2. Ed. W. Mårtensson. Helsingfors: Paikallishistoriallinen toimisto r.y, 1978, pp. 31–50; Salvesen, Helge. "Landskyld." In *Ødegårdstid i Norge. Det nordiske ødegårdsprosjekts norske undersøkelser.* Ed. J. Sandnes and H. Salvesen. Oslo: Universitetsforlaget, 1978, pp. 109–41; Gaunt, David. "Household Typology: Problems—Methods—Results." In *Chance and Change: Social and Economic Studies in Historical Demography in the Baltic Area.* Ed. S. Åkerman et al. Odense: Odense University Press, 1978, pp. 69–83; Herlihy, David, and Christiane Klapisch-Zuber. *Les Toscans et leurs familles. Une étude de catasto florentin de 1427.* Paris: Éditions de l'écoles des hautes études en sciences sociales, 1978; Miller, Edward, and John Hatcher. *Medieval England: Rural Society and Economic Change 1086–1348.* London: Longman, 1978; Sjøvold, Torstein. "Inference Concerning the Age Distribution of Skeletal Populations and Some Consequences for Paleodemography." *Anthropoloziai Közelmenyek* 22 (1978), 99–114; Salvesen, Helge. "Hoset-undersøkelsen. Kilder og metoder i analysen av bosetningsutviklingen i et marginalområde." In *På leiting etter den eldste garden.* Ed. R. Fladby and Jørn Sandnes. Oslo: Universitetsforlaget, 1979, pp. 131–50; Johansen, Olav Sverre. "Jernaldergårder i Nord-Norge." In *På leiting etter den eldste garden,* pp. 95–115; Marthinsen, Liv. "Kilder og bosetning på Østlandet 1500–1660." In *Distrikshistorie. Problemer, metode, organisering.* Ed. R. Fladby and L. Marthinsen. Oslo: Norsk Lokalhistorisk Institutt, 1979, pp. 38–50; Sandnes, Jørn. "Garden og Tunet." In *Norges kulturhistorie* 1. Ed. J. Semmingsen et al. Oslo: Aschehoug, 1980, pp. 39–68; Aarsæther, Ragnhild. "Bosettingsutviklinga i Salten fjerding fra høymiddelalderen til ca. 1660." In *Seinmiddelalder i norske bygder. Utvalgte emner fra Det nordiske ødegårdsprosjekts norske punktundersøkelser.* Ed. L. J. Hansen. Oslo: Universitetsforlaget, 1981, pp. 394–432; Persson, Evy, and Ove Persson. "Medeltidsfolket från kvarteret Repslagaren." In *S:t Stefan i Lund. Ett monument ur tiden.* Ed. Anders W. Mårtensson. Gamla Lund förening för bevarande av stadens minnen, Årsskrift 62. Lund: Föreningen Gamla Lund, 1981, pp. 151–70; Kpedekpo, G. M. K. *Essentials of Demographic Analysis for Africa.* London: Heinemann, 1982; Gaunt, David. *Familjeliv i Norden.* Stockholm: Gidlund, 1983; Howell, Cicely. *Land, Family and Inheritance in Transition: Kibworth Harcourt 1280–1700.* Cambridge: Cambridge University Press, 1983; Benedictow, Ole Jørgen. "The Milky Way in History: Breast Feeding, Antagonism Between the Sexes and Infant Mortality in Medieval Norway." *Scandinavian Journal of History* 10 (1985), 19–53; Anderson, Trevor. "The Churchyard on the Folkebibliotekstomt (Library Site), Trondheim. An Interim Osteological Report." In *Fortiden i Trondheim bygrunn. Meddelelser No. 2. Folkebibliotekstomten.* Trondheim: Riksantikvaren, Utgravningskontoret for Trondheim, 1986, pp. 1–16 + pls.; Fladby, Rolf. *Samfunn i vekst under fremmed styre, 1536–1660.* Handbok i Norges historie, 5. Bergen: Universitetsforlaget, 1986; Holck, Per. *Skjelettmaterialet fra Peterskirken, Tønsberg. En antropologisk rapport.* Antropologiske skrifter, 2. Oslo: Department of History, University of Oslo, 1987; Miller, W. J. "Some Aspects of Householding in the Medieval Icelandic Commonwealth." *Continuity and Change* 3 (1988), 321–55.

Ole Jørgen Benedictow

[See also: *Bóndi*; Demography; Marriage and Divorce; Plague; Pregnancy and Childbirth]

Faroe Islands. Until recent years, traditional work on the history of the Faroe Islands has connected the first Norse settlement with the Norwegian king Haraldr hárfagri ("fair-hair") Hálfdanarson's seizure of power in the battle of Hafrsfjǫrðr in the last years of the 9th century. The main source for this supposition was *Færeyinga saga*, written in Iceland about 1220, preserved and handed down as fragments in other sagas, especially *Flateyjarbók*, *Óláfs saga Tryggvasonar*, and *Heimskringla*.

The *Flateyjarbók* version mentions the name of the first settler of the Faroe Islands, Grímr kamban. The first name has a Norse origin, the second a Scottish-Gaelic origin, indicating that this man did not come directly from Norway, but from the Norse settlements in the Celtic areas in the South. The fact that *Landnámabók* counts Grímr's grandson among the first colonists in Iceland spoils the chronology of the saga, and the traditional Icelandic causal relations in general.

Recent studies in the saga material (Ólafur Halldórsson) have made a new interpretation possible. The most reliable source, *Óláfs saga Tryggvasonar*, makes no connection between Grímr's settlement in the Faroe Islands and mass emigration from Norway, caused by Haraldr's violent rule, thus eliminating all sure evidence of simultaneous Norse settlement in the Faroe Islands and Iceland.

Proofs of earlier settlement come from the Irishman Dicuil, living in the learned environment at the Carolingian court in Aix-la-Chapelle. In his *De mensura orbis terrae*, written about 825 and preserved in a MS from about 850, he describes a group of islands north of Scotland, having obtained his information from a devout Irish priest who had been there himself, and in a country farther north, which must be Iceland. The distance and the information that the group consists of many small islands separated by many narrow sounds and has an abundance of seabirds and sheep, make it certain that these are the Faroe Islands. Dicuil says that for 100 years hermits from Ireland (Scotia) had sought solitude there, but had by 825 fled from the islands because of the invasion by Norse bandits. He had never seen these islands mentioned by previous authors ("auctoritates").

This account is strengthened by the information given in *Íslendingabók* and *Landnámabók* that the first Icelandic settlers found Irish hermits, whom they called *papar*, in their new country. That fact is also made credible by philological evidence, especially in place-names beginning with *papa*.

This evidence should date the first habitation in the Faroe Islands back to about 700 and the first Norse settlement to about 800. However, archaeological research has not been able to find evidence of settlement earlier than about 900. Slabstones found in Skúvoy (one of the islands/villages mentioned in the *Færeyinga saga*) have carved wheel- or sun-crosses showing Celtic influence. But this influence should not be dated to the "papa-time" (Sverri Dahl), but rather is due to contact after the permanent Norse settlement.

The discussion about the time of the first settlement was renewed and intensified during the 1980s, when pollen analysis (Johannes Johansen) indicated permanent settlement as far back as 600–650. Botanic research has established the cultivation of oats and vegetational changes due to the grazing of sheep at that time, implying the presence of human beings. From about 950, there is a shift to the cultivation of barley. A historical evaluation of these provocative scientific results must await further archaeological research.

The first proof of Viking Age settlement was found in 1942 at the village of Kvívík: a farmstead comprising two parallel structures, one of them a hall (*skáli*), another the combined cowhouse and barn. The construction proved to be typical of the Viking Age: curved long walls, with the gable walls curved on the outside and straight inside. The walls are made of an outer and an inner layer of stones and turf, the space between filled with small stones and earth. In the Viking Age, or shortly thereafter, people settled in the outer fields of the original *landnám*-farmsteads, in inferior houses.

Until 1989, only one graveyard from the Viking Age had been found, near the village of Tjørnuvík. Here, the Celtic influence can be registered from a ringheaded pin of bronze with an ornamented head, a design well known in Scotland and the western Norse settlements. In 1989, an early medieval (Christian) graveyard was discovered at the village of Sandur, belonging to the first of six churches excavated on the same site; it can be dated to the first half of the 11th century. Recent excavations at the village of Leirvík have revealed bronze pins of the same kind. Typical finds in the houses are cooking vessels, train-oil lamps, spindle whorls, loom weights, sinkers for fishing lines, all made of soapstone or pumice. For some purposes, basalt and lead were also used. Finds of bones of sheep, cattle, pilot whales, seals, pigs, cod, and different kinds of birds give a clear picture of the diet of the Viking Age Faroese, which continued the same during the later Middle Ages and for centuries thereafter.

The lack of wood, iron, and grain made the Faroese especially dependent on foreign trade. They bartered for these commodities with cloth (as the many loom stones suggest), wool, and feathers. The find at Sandur of ninety-eight coins from many countries (dated to 950–1050) proves wide commercial contacts. Such trade implies ships and navigation, and while no ships or boats have been found, small toy ships reflect the reality of their existence.

Færeyinga saga, law texts, and comparison with analogous cultures give a fairly reliable picture of the social and political structures of the Viking Age and medieval Faroese society. This society was dominated by chieftains and large landowners whose extensive landed property was cultivated by people of inferior social status. Legislative, executive, and judicial powers were administered by the *Alting* (later *Løgting*), held in the capital, Tórshavn, and presided over by the Lawman (*løgmaður*), attended by thirty-six assessors (*løgrættumenn*). The court was in session every summer at St. Óláfr's Wake (July 29), which is still celebrated as the National Day in the Faroe Islands, marked by ceremonies connected with the new session of the *Løgting* (parliament).

Relations with Norway were always crucial. The incorporation of the islands into the Norwegian Church Province (1152) under the archbishopric of Niðaróss (Trondheim) also had political consequences. By 1180, the islands seem to have become a "taxland" under the Norwegian Crown (*Historia Norwegiae, Sverris saga*), as a result of continuous efforts by Norwegian kings to extend their power to include the islanders in the west. This *divide-et-impera* policy, instrumented by the imposition of taxes and the introduction of Christianity, is the theme of *Færeyinga saga*. However, the Faroese probably managed their own affairs, "paying off" direct Norwegian rule. The relations between the Faroese and the Norwegian Crown were not formalized until 1270 by a special treaty between King Magnús lagabœtir ("law-mender") Hákonarson and the Faroese, imposing mutual obligations. At the same time, Greenland (1261) and Iceland (1262–1264) were incorporated into the Norwegian Empire ("Noregsveldi"), not as provinces, but as "lands."

When in 1380 the Norwegian and Danish crowns were united

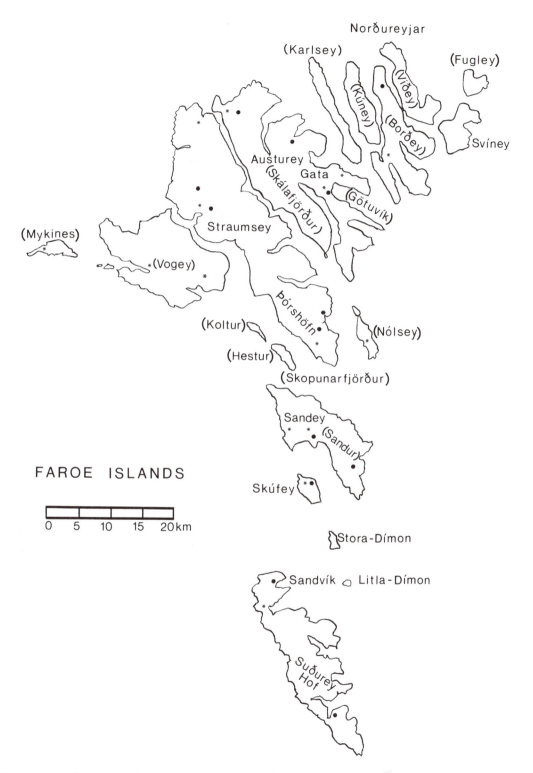

Norðureyjar

(Karlsey)

(Fugley)

(Kúney)

(Viðey)

(Borðey)

Svíney

Austurey

Gata

(Skálafjörður)

(Götuvík)

(Mykines)

Straumsey

*(Vogey)

Þórshöfn

(Koltur)

(Nólsey)

(Hestur)

(Skopunarfjörður)

FAROE   ISLANDS

Sandey

(Sandur)

Skúfey

| 0 | 5 | 10 | 15 | 20 km |

Stora-Dímon

Sandvík   Litla-Dímon

Suðurey
Hof

21. Place-names not in parentheses are mentioned in *Færeyinga saga.* An asterisk indicates places where archaeological research has proved or indicated settlement in the Viking Age and/or the early Middle Ages. A dot signifies "ærgi," a word of Gaelic origin meaning "shielings."

by dynastic accident, the Faroe Islands followed Norway, as did the other possessions in the west. But by that time, the Faroese had developed a culture of their own, expressed especially in their language, which has basically preserved its Old Norse origin. Later, the language became the most important element in the formation of the Faroese nation.

Ed.: "Historia Norwegiae." In Storm, Gustav, ed. *Monumenta historica Norvegiae*. Kristiania [Oslo]: Brøgger, 1880; Jakobsen, Jakob, ed. *Diplomatarium Færoense*. Tórshavn and Copenhagen: Jacobsen, 1907; rpt. 1985; Indrebø, Gustav, ed. *Sverris saga etter Cod. AM 327 4°*. Utgjevi av Den Norske Historisk Kildeskrift-kommission. Kristiania [Oslo]: Dybwad, 1920; rpt. Oslo: Norsk Historiske Kjeldeskrift-Institutt, 1981. Dicuil. *Liber de mensura orbis terrae*. Ed. J. J. Tierney. Scriptores latini Hiberniae, 6. Dublin: Dublin Institute for Advanced Studies, 1967; Ólafur Halldórsson, ed. *Færeyinga saga*. Reykjavik: Stofnun Árna Magnússonar, 1987. **Lit.**: Matras, Chr. *Stednavne paa de færøske Norðuroyar*. Copenhagen: Thiele, 1933; Matras, Chr. "Papbýli í Føroyum." *Varðin* 14 (1934), 185–7; Brøgger, A. W. *Løgtingssøga Føroya. 1sta bók. Hvussu Føroyar vóru bygdar*. Tórshavn: Føroya Løgting, 1937, pp. 20–49; Dahl, Sverri. "Fornar toftir í Kvívík. Heiðursrit til Rasmus Rasmussen." *Varðin* 29 (1951), 65–96; Dahl, Sverri, and Jóannes Rasmussen. "Víkingaaldargrøv í Tjørnuvík." *Fróðskaparrit* 5 (1956), 153–67; Matras, Chr. "Gammelfærøsk ærgi, n., og dermed beslægtede ord." *Namn och Bygd* 44 (1956), 51–67; Dahl, Sverri. "Toftarannsóknir í Fuglafirði." *Fróðskaparrit* 7 (1958), 118–46; Dahl, Sverri. *Fornminni. Føroyar, 1*. Copenhagen: Dansk-færøsk Samfund, 1958, pp. 119–53; Matras, Chr. "Føroyanavnið einaferð enn." *Fróðskaparrit* 8 (1959), 39–56; Matras, Christian. "Færøsk sprog." *KLNM* 5 (1960), 80–4; Hamre, Lars, et al. "Hirð." *KLNM* 6 (1961), 568–80; Foote, Peter. "Færeyinga saga, chapter forty." *Fróðskaparrit* 13 (1964), 84–98; Dahl, Sverri. "Víkingabústaður í Seyrvági." *Fróðskaparrit* 14 (1965), 9–23; Matras, Chr. "Írsk orð í føroyskum." *Úrval* 6 (1966), 121–39; Dahl, Sverri. *Fortidsminder*. Copenhagen: Gad, 1968, pp. 188–92; Foote, Peter, and David M. Wilson. *The Viking Achievement: The Society and Culture of Early Medieval Scandinavia*. London: Sidgwick & Jackson, 1970, pp. xv, xix, xxii, xxvi, 52–3; Dahl, Sverri. "The Norse Settlement of the Faroe Islands." *Mediaeval Scandinavia* 14 (1970), 60–73; West, John F. *The Emergence of a Nation*. London: Hurst; New York: Eriksson, 1972, pp. 5–15; Krogh, Knud. "Seks kirkjur heima á Sandi." *Mondul*. Tórshavn: Føroya Fornminnissavn, 1975, pp. 21–54; Thorsteinsson, Arne. "Forn búseting í Føroyum." *Fróðskaparrit* 26 (1978), 54–80; Young, G. V. C. *From the Vikings to the Reformation: A Chronicle of the Faroe Islands up to 1538*. Douglas, Isle of Man: Shearwater, 1979, pp. 1–9; Thorsteinsson, Arne. "On the Development of Faroese Settlements." *Proceedings of the 8th Viking Congress Århus 24–31 August 1977*. Ed. Hans-Bekker Nielsen et al. Odense: Odense University Press, 1981, pp. 189–202; Johansen, Johannes. "Kornvelting í Mykinesi 200 ár undan Grími Kamban." *Mondul* 1 (1982), 8–13; Johansen, Johannes. *Studies in the Vegetational History of the Faroe and Shetland Islands*. Tórshavn: Føroya Fróðskaparfelag, 1985, pp. 48–74; Arge, Símun V. "Det færøske landnám" Cand. mag. thesis, Århus, 1985, pp. 32–4 [unpublished]; Arge, Símun V. "Om landnamet på Færøerne." *Hikuin* 15 (1985), 103–28; Mahler, Ditlev. "Argisbrekka. Nye spor efter sæterdrift på Færøerne." *Hikuin* 15 (1985), 147–70; Hansen, Steffen Stummann. "Toftanes—en færøsk landnamsgård fra 9.– 10. årh." *Hikuin* 15 (1985), 129–46; Krogh, Knud. "Um Føroya elstu búseting." *Mondul* 1 (1986), 3–6; Johansen, Jóhannes. "Um Føroya fyrstu búseting—einaferð enn." *Mondul* 2 (1986), 3–6; Mahler, Ditlev. "Ærgi undir brekkuni." *Mondul* 3 (1986), 6–17; Mahler, Ditlev. "Argisbrekka. Nye spor efter sæterdrift på Færøerne." *Hikuin* 15 (1989), 147–70; Debes, Hans Jacob. *Føroya søga*. 2 vols. Tórshavn: Føroya Skúlabókagrunnur, 1990, pp. 55–113; Debes, Hans Jacob. "Problems Concerning the Earliest Settlement in the Faroe Islands" [forthcoming in *Fróðskaparrit*].

Hans J. Debes

[**See also:** Dialects; *Flateyjarbók*; *Færeyinga saga*; *Heimskringla*; *Íslendingabók*; *Landnámabók*; Language; *Ólafs saga Tryggvasonar*]

Fashions in the Nordic countries cannot have differed appreciably from those prevailing elsewhere in Europe, although they probably changed less rapidly than on the Continent, and the more extreme manifestations were probably less widespread here. During the Viking era and the early Middle Ages, men wore long trousers and tunics reaching down to about the knees. The full-length garments of Byzantine origin that became fashionable in central Europe during the 12th century also entered the Nordic countries eventually. The new fashion was adopted exclusively by kings and persons of princely rank, but by about 1200 it had been adopted by the Scandinavian magnates. Long trousers were unnecessary under these long garments, and so long stockings were worn instead. Long garments remained the fashion throughout the 13th century and into the 14th.

Women wore long gowns all through the Middle Ages. During the 13th century and the first half of the 14th, men and women dressed so similarly that the two sexes tend to be indistinguishable in pictures from the time, but women's garments were usually somewhat longer than men's, reaching all the way down to the floor, while the men's reached to the ankles or calves.

Continental fashions were radically transformed in the mid-14th century. Men's outer garments became so short that they ended at the small of the back, leaving the legs completely exposed. At the same time, the outer garment was made to fit more closely. It was open at the front and provided with buttons. The use of this new button-up garment in the Nordic countries from the mid-14th century onward is confirmed by written records of the period, which frequently mention costumes with silver buttons. For most of the medieval period, popular costume consisted of a short tunic and trousers.

Women's costume changed in the mid-14th century, when waists were drawn in, and skirts became wider.

Surviving garments. More medieval garments have survived in the Nordic area than in the rest of Europe combined.

The largest collection of garments comes from the Scandinavian colony in Greenland. Excavations in Herjólfsnes (Ikigait) churchyard in 1921 yielded fifteen more or less well-preserved body garments, seventeen hoods, an assortment of other headgear, and some stockings. No complete costume is extant. The garments were used as shrouds. The material is invariably woolen fabric, mostly in four-ended twill, less frequently tabby.

The cut and style of the body garments conform to European fashion. In terms of cut, they can be divided into two principal groups. The older and more numerous group consists of garments that were pulled over the head. These are usually cut in two parts, front and back, joined together by a seam at the shoulders. They have been widened at the bottom through the insertion of various numbers of gores, usually at the sides and in the middle, both front and back. The sleeves are generally cut in one piece, with a gore underneath. The other group, characterized by garments opening at the front, includes a man's costume consisting of long, narrow strips of cloth. This coat has a stand-up collar. The short men's costume that came into fashion in Europe in the mid-14th century is not represented at all in the Greenland material. Liripipe hoods are the main article of headgear, with two different kinds: a hood with a large shoulder-piece and gores inserted in the middle front and back, and hoods with a small shoulder-piece and shoulder gores. In addition to liripipe hoods, there are low, cylindrical caps with a flat upper part and a fairly high conical cap.

Hose are of various kinds: long stockings (reaching up to the thigh) with feet, long stockings with straps, short stockings with feet, and short stockings with straps. The Herjólfsnes garments are believed to date from the 14th and early 15th centuries.

Sweden has a virtually complete man's costume from the Bocksten bog. This outfit consists of a mantle, a liripipe hood, a tunic, and hose of what is now brown woolen fabric woven in three-ended twill, together with shoes and a belt of leather. The mantle is cut in a semicircle and held together at the right shoulder. The liripipe hood has a large shoulder-piece. The tunic has no shoulder seams. The hose are cut into a point at the front and extended far up the thigh. They were kept up by leather strips, secured to a belt. This costume probably dates from the first half of the 14th century.

A gown of Italian gold brocade, now in Uppsala cathedral, probably belonged to Margrethe, queen of Sweden, Denmark, and Norway (1353–1412).

Two garments that are probably of Swedish origin are now in other countries. Both are believed to have belonged to St. Birgitta (1302[1303?]–1373). The "cloak of St. Birgitta," as it is called, is in the convent of St. Lucia in Selci, Rome. This is an outer garment of dark blue cloth, made up of gores turned into a cloak. The other garment is a small linen tabby cap with delicate small braids at the ears, complete with strings. This cale or coif is now in the convent of Maria Refugie in Uden, Holland.

Norway has a medieval costume consisting of a hood, tunic, and shirt, plus breeches, all of woolen fabric woven in four-end twill. Both the dating and ethnic origin of this costume are uncertain.

Denmark has three garments recovered from peat bogs, two almost-complete outer garments from Kragelund and Moselund, respectively, and a fragmentary garment from Rønbjerg. The Kragelund garment has no shoulder seams. It has been dated to the 12th or 13th century, possibly later. The other two costumes have the same cut as some of the Herjólfsnes garments. They are both of uncertain date.

No complete garments have come down to us from Finland. The archaeological finds include quite a few fragments of costume, due not least to the practice, from the 9th century onward, of decorating garments with small rings and spirals of bronze wire, which have had the effect of conserving the textile material. The women wore long skirts, comparable to the ancient Greek *peplos*. This garment was a large, square piece of fabric that could be folded double at the shoulders and secured with buckles. Not until the 12th century did people begin sewing skirts together at the shoulders. In the east of Finland, the antiquated *peplos* skirt remained in use throughout the Middle Ages. Woolen coats, with small bronze buttons, began to be adopted by men at the end of the 11th century or the beginning of the 12th, an eastern innovation that did not become widespread in western Europe until later.

Lit.: Nørlund, Poul. "Buried Norsemen at Herjolfsnes." *Meddelelser om Grønland* 67 (1924), 1–270; Sandklef, A. "The Bocksten find." *Acta Ethnologica* 2 (1937), 1–64; Gjessing, G. "Skjoldehamndrakten." *Viking* 2 (1938), 27–81; Andersson, Aron, and Anne Marie Franzén. *Birgittareliker*. Stockholm: Almqvist & Wiksell, 1975 [English summary]; Hald, Margrethe. *Ancient Danish Textiles from Bogs and Burials*. Trans. Jean Olsen. Copenhagen: National Museum of Denmark, 1980; Lehtosalo-Hilander, Pirkko-Liisa. *Ancient Finnish Costumes*. Helsinki: Finnish Archaeological Society, 1984; Nockert, Margareta. *Bockstensmannen och hans dräkt*. Falkenberg: Hallands länsmuseer, 1985 [English summary]; Geijer, Agnes, *et al*. *Drottning Margaretas gyllene kjortel i Uppsala domkyrka*. Uppsala: Almqvist & Wiksell, 1985 [English summary].

Margareta Nockert

[See also: Clothmaking]

Feudal Influences and Tendencies

Feudal Influences and Tendencies. Feudalism is a difficult concept to define and has been used in divergent ways by scholars and students of medieval and early modern history. The term designates either a specific political system in which the personal relationship among lords, vassals, and subvassals is considered as the essential element, or a certain governmental structure based on the fiefs, with enfeoffment for services and centrifugal tendencies of the public power. Feudalism is also commonly used to describe a type of society resembling that of western Europe of the high Middle Ages. In the vocabulary of a Marxist theoretical tradition, the term stands for a specific mode of production, preceding capitalism and, generally considered, succeeding slavery, or, as in the Scandinavian case, a tribal society.

The problems concerning the existence of or the specific forms and characteristics of feudalism in medieval Scandinavia consequently depend on how feudalism is understood. Analyzed in whatever respect, Scandinavian feudalism is usually related to equivalent legal, political, economic, or social phenomena in western Europe. From this point of view, the societies of medieval Scandinavia produce features due to historical circumstances. As political realms, the three Scandinavian kingdoms developed rather late in comparison with the rest of western Europe. Political and social concepts and ideas were to a great extent brought in from abroad and adapted to social realities in Scandinavia. Considered as a jurisdictional and political system, the lord-vassal relationship as a legal institution never evolved in the Scandinavian kingdoms. During the 13th century, the privileged estates were established in all the Scandinavian kingdoms and became, at least in principle, exempted from taxes, performing services to the Crown and the realm instead. The predominantly military service was the determinant criterion for the aristocracy or nobility, which was composed of the successors of local chieftains and the new ministerial elements, as well as a wealthy stratum of the allodial peasantry with the ability to furnish a knight and mounted horse. A knightly culture was adopted by at least the upper stratum of the aristocracy, but the majority lived on rents from allodial possessions rather than by enfeoffment and feudal rights of fiefs.

The fief system, which is central in the western European feudal political system, played a significant role in the royal administrative systems especially in Denmark and Sweden from the 13th century. With some notable exceptions, especially the princely and ducal fiefs of Schleswig, the fief system never entailed political centrifugal implications, which is often considered as one of the main political results of feudalism. The fiefs seldom became inheritable, and the realms as political entities never disintegrated, although such tendencies became threateningly dominant in Denmark in 1241–1340, a period that has been regarded as having effective politically feudal tendencies that, however, never undermined the political structure. In general, fief holding in medieval Scandinavia was only temporary, and hereditary rights were not rooted. Many of the conflicts between kings or regents and various factions of the aristocracy in the later Middle Ages concerned control over the fiefs. The fief holders exercised fiscal and military authority in varying degrees over the fiefs, but they never acquired political, jurisdictional, and legal authority. From this point of view, Scandinavian feudalism can be regarded as either nonexistent or at least incomplete. The institutions and the political concepts derived from the European continent, but the fief-holding elites of the Scandinavian realms never acquired control over the public power and the executive-political governmental structure.

Regarding feudalism as a type of society with specific social and economic relations, medieval Scandinavia can definitely be regarded as feudal, although with its own peculiarities. The nobility and the clergy owned lands held by the peasantry. In medieval and feudal Scandinavia, a small-scale peasant production predominated. A manorial system is discernible from at least the 12th and the 13th centuries in Denmark and the central parts of Sweden. Demesne production was of some importance, but declined during the later Middle Ages. A determinant factor in many definitions of feudalism as a societal system is the presence of a dependent peasantry, performing labor services on the lord's demesne, a position of personal dependency toward the lord (villeinage or serfdom), subject to the jurisdictional power of the lord, and so on. In this respect, the Scandinavian feudal system exhibits some peculiarities. The manorial structure was very weak or even nonexistent in parts of Scandinavia. Labor services were in general insignificant. The nonallodial peasantry was personally and legally free. No manorial courts existed, with some minor exceptions. Contrary to the circumstances sometimes regarded as archetypal for feudal societies, the peasants in general never became subjects of the lord's jurisdictional power. The tenants held land on rather precarious conditions, at least in Norway and Sweden. The peasants were formally free to leave the land and could easily be evicted after rather short intervals. On Zealand and adjacent islands in Denmark, regulations were imposed during the 15th century aiming to tie the male population to the land (*vornedskab*). Since the peasantry was regarded as belonging to the land, it was a form of serfdom.

One of the most characteristic features of the medieval Scandinavian societies was that a large portion of the peasantry remained not only legally free, but also owned their land. The proportions of ownership varied in the three kingdoms and is difficult to estimate with accuracy for the medieval centuries. In the first decades of the 16th century, however, around 10 percent of the land was owned by the peasantry in Denmark, in Norway around 40 percent, and in Sweden (including Finland) around 50 percent, with great regional discrepancies, especially in Sweden. A free, allodial, and non-manorialized peasantry might be regarded as contrary to a feudal system. This allodial peasantry was, however, liable to fiscal and other duties to the Crown from the 12th to 13th century onward. They were, therefore, in a Marxist sense of the terminology, subject to feudal exploitation, not by a lord but by the Crown. Allodial and nonallodial peasants were equally free and legally competent.

Lit.: Koht, Halvdan. "Det nye i norderlendsk historie kringom år 1300." *Scandia* 4 (1931), 171–83; Bolin, Sture. "Medieval Agrarian Society in Its Prime: Scandinavia." In *The Cambridge Economic History of Europe. 1: The Agrarian Life of the Middle Ages.* Ed. M. M. Postan. 2nd ed. Cambridge: Cambridge University Press, 1966, pp. 633–59; Christensen, Aksel E. *Kongemagt og aristokrati. Epoker i middelalderlig dansk statsopfattelse indtil unionstiden.* 2nd ed. Copenhagen: Munksgaard, 1968; Gurevich, A. Ya. *Frihet og føydalisme. Fra sovjetisk forskning i norsk middelalderhistorie. Utdrag fra en avhandling av A. Ja. Gurevitsj "De frie bönder i det føydale Norge."* Ed. Steinar Supphellen. Oslo, Bergen, and Tromsø: Universitetsforlaget, 1977; Bernild, Ole, and Henrik Jensen. *Den feudale produktionsmådes historie i Danmark ca 1200 til ca 1800.* Studier i historie og tekstvidenskab fra Roskilde Universitetscenter, 1. Copenhagen: Dansk Universitets Presse, 1978; Lindkvist, Thomas. "Swedish Medieval Society: Previous Research and Recent Developments." *Scandinavian Journal of History* 4 (1979), 253–68; Helle, Knut. "Norway in the High Middle Ages: Recent Views of the Structure of Society." *Scandinavian Journal of History* 6 (1981), 161–89.

Thomas Lindkvist

[**See also:** Land Tenure and Inheritance; Landownership]

Finland. In Finland, settlement was established in the Stone Age during the so-called Suomusjärvi culture of approximately 6500–4200 B.C. From the linguistic point of view, the settlement of the subsequent cultural phase at the latest, that of the Comb-Ceramic culture (4200–2500 B.C.), is today regarded as Finno-Ugric. The European Battle-Axe culture reached Finland about 2500–2000 B.C. Finland received population from the Baltic area, which introduced more intensive agriculture and animal husbandry. After the subsequent Stone Age cultural phase of Kiukainen, Finland entered the Bronze Age (ca. 1500–500 B.C.). At that time, a vigorous culture was born on the west and south coasts of Finland, and this culture had close connections to Scandinavia. The Bronze Age in the inland areas had a strong eastern character. In the early Iron Age, the Germanic migration brought a great number of loanwords (of which 450 have been preserved) and other cultural influences to Finland. Grain cultivation increased considerably.

As the Iron Age began in Finland approximately 500 B.C., settlement decreased first, and the culture became poorer, but the connection to the culture of the Bronze Age and, in addition, to the Stone Age remained. Iron objects appeared alongside bronze objects, and the making of iron started also in Finland as early as about 500 B.C. The great rise of culture began in southwestern Finland during the Roman Iron Age (A.D. 1–400). People began to bury the deceased in rich graveyards. The graveyard culture spread inland to southern Ostrobothnia and Häme (Tavastland). The cultural connections to Estonia, the Weichsel and Elbe river mouths, and Sweden were close. A new influx of settlers came to Finland from these areas.

During the migration of peoples (ca. 400–600), the center of culture was still in southwestern Finland, but the settlement in Häme and southern Ostrobothnia increased and became wealthier because of the peak prosperity of fur trading. Small population centers were developed here and there even farther north, as far as southern Lapland, but here the culture did not yet become established. The Åland Islands inherited the culture of the Iron Age.

In the Merovingian era (600–800), Finnish culture became independent. Population grew and became more prosperous. The cultivated area was increased in Varsinais-Suomi (the southwest-

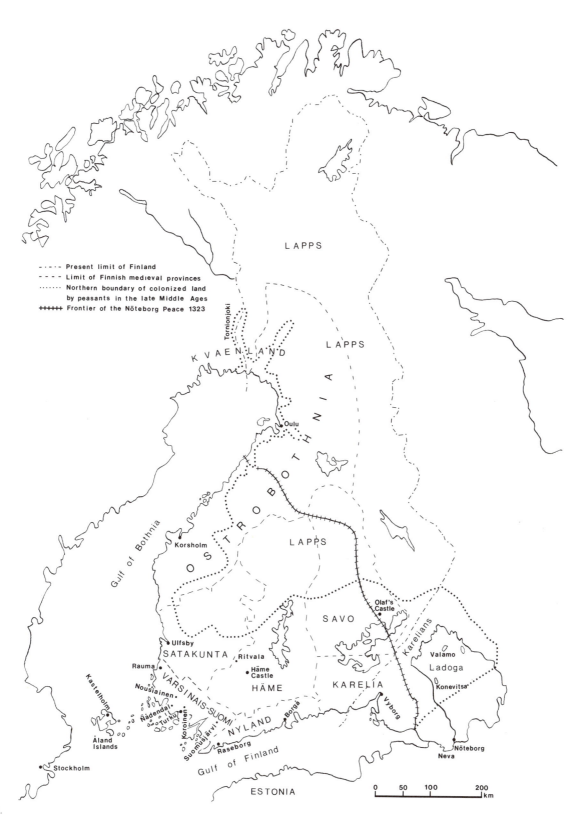

LAPPS

Present limit of Finland
Limit of Finnish medieval provinces
Northern boundary of colonized land
by peasants in the late Middle Ages
Frontier of the Nöteborg Peace 1323

Tornionjoki

KVAENLAND

LAPPS

Oulu

O
S
T
R
O
B
O
T
H
N
I
A

Gulf of Bothnia

Korsholm

LAPPS

SAVO

Olaf's
Castle

Karelians

Valamo

Ladoga

Ulfsby

SATAKUNTA

Ritvala

KARELIA

Konevitsa

Rauma

VARSINAIS-SUOMI

Häme
Castle

HÄME

Kastelholm

Nousiainen

Nådendal

Turku

Koroinen

NYLAND

Boga

Vyborg

Åland
Islands

Suomusjärvi

Raseborg

Gulf of Finland

Nöteborg
Neva

Stockholm

ESTONIA

0   50   100   200
km

22.

em corner of Finland) and Häme. Cultivation by burning was replaced by field cultivation to a considerable degree. Germanic migration was still going on; a few new cemeteries where graves are found in rows have their best equivalents in the Germanic graveyards of western Europe. At the end of the period, the rich culture of southern Ostrobothnia declined. In the east, however, West Finnish graveyard culture spread as far as the shores of Lake Ladoga. There, a powerful Karelian culture rose and developed from the local culture and from new West Finnish and, in the Viking Age, Scandinavian elements.

During the Viking Age (800–1050), the settlement in Finland became ever more powerful, consisting of three distinct areas: Varsinais-Suomi, Häme, and Karelia. The Åland Islands had already become fully Swedish. The areas inhabited by Finnish, Häme, and Karelian tribes constituted types of prehistoric provinces that were not yet politically strictly organized, but in which there was large cooperation under the lead of governors for purposes of cult, castle building, and organization of defense, as well as for military expeditions, hunting, and trade.

Areas north of the established agrarian settlement were inhabited by Lapps, who practiced hunting and to whom tradesmen and tax collectors traveled from the centers of the south. At this time, permanent settlement of Häme began to stretch into the great river valleys of southern Lapland, especially into the Tornionjoki river valley. During this and the subsequent periods, the people from Häme competed with the Norwegians for the taxation of the Lapps and for the fur trade in Lapland. The Norwegians used the name *kvenir* ("lowlanders") of the Finns and the name *Kvenland* ("Lowland") of the area populated by them on the east and north coast of the Gulf of Bothnia.

With the Viking raids to the east, Finnish tribes made fresh and active contact with the outside world on the southwestern and southern coasts. It was a question, above all, of commercial connections. In the heart of Häme, in the vicinity of the later medieval castle, there was a strong and long-lasting trade center, which has been excavated in recent years (Varikkoniemi). The position of Vikings as intermediaries in Finnish foreign trade in the early Middle Ages was inherited first and foremost by Gotland. But the Scandinavian governors also made expeditions to conquer Finland and to convert Finns to Christianity (*e.g.*, the expedition of St. Óláfr *ca.* 1007, and by Anundi, the son of the king of Sweden, *ca.* 1050).

Christian burials became common in the northern part of Varsinais-Suomi (Vakka-Suomi) by the middle of the 11th century and in the early 12th century throughout all Varsinais-Suomi and Häme. The period between 1050 and 1150 may be called "early Christian." Part of southwestern Finland was from time to time liable to pay taxes to Sweden (Svealand) as early as the 11th century and that the influence of Novgorod and the Eastern Church reached as far as eastern Häme.

Swedish domination. The victory of the Christian faith and the ecclesiastical order marked the end of prehistory in Finland and the beginning of the Middle Ages.

In the 1150s, Erik, king of Sweden, and Henrik, bishop of Uppsala, tried to introduce ecclesiastical and political order in Finland (the so-called "first crusade"). Sweden was not able to subjugate Finland, but missionary work and establishment of the first parishes were initiated in Lower Satakunta and the northern part of Varsinais-Suomi. The missions under the leadership of bishops, and perhaps also the crusades waged by the Swedish

aristocracy, continued in Finland all through the latter half of the 12th century. Ecclesiastical order was also established in spite of the harassment of Novgorod and paganism.

Because of the conquests by the Germans and the Danes in the Baltic countries, Sweden also launched her operations in the coastal countries of the Gulf of Finland at the beginning of the 13th century. They had been initiated mainly in the dioceses of Gotland and Linköping. From about 1220–1245, the bishop of Finland was the energetic Thomas; and as a result of his efforts, the diocese of Finland came to comprise the provinces of Varsinais-Suomi and Häme. Thomas sought support particularly from the German rulers in the Baltic countries, and probably also received armed assistance for his operations from the order of the Brethren of the Sword against paganism in Häme and against Novgorod during the 1230s. The diocese of Finland does not seem to have been under the authority of the bishop of Uppsala in his time, although the connection was established soon after Thomas at the end of the 1240s.

Around 1230, the bishopric of Finland was transferred from Nousiainen to Koroinen at the Aurajoki river mouth, from where it was transferred farther down the Aurajoki river mouth to Turku (*ca.* 1290). The significance of this river mouth grew with the arrival of German merchants. The Germans took over Finnish foreign trade during the 13th century, mainly via Visby, Riga, and Tallinn, and it remained under their control until the 16th century. A great number of German merchants settled down in Finland to act as merchant intermediaries, and they introduced the forms of the European town system to Finland. Turku, which received its town privileges in the 1290s, was at that time the only town in Finland. In addition, there were many important trading centers on the coast that still lacked the characteristics of a town.

Earl Birger, who was the virtual leader of Sweden 1248–1266, incorporated western Finland permanently into Sweden, to be governed by the Crown, Varsinais-Suomi in the late 1240s and Häme in the 1250s. Toward the end of the 1250s, he probably brought a fairly large group of Swedish crusaders to Häme to secure defense against Novgorod. He started to settle crusaders on the coast of the Gulf of Finland, named Nyland ("Newland"). The building of the strong Häme castle began. Swedish colonization continued later on the coasts of the gulfs of Finland and Bothnia in the 13th and 14th centuries.

The Häme and Turku castles were constructed as strong central crown castles around 1270–1300, and were the basis on which the castle-province administration under the leadership of governors was created. The control of the Swedish kings over Finland was thus strengthened. As a result of the conquest, Novgorod was forced to retreat from eastern Häme and even from western Karelia, which received a great number of settlers from western Finland. The Karelia of the Ladoga area was instead subjected to the permanent influence of Novgorod. The influence of Novgorod also stopped expanding in southern and northern Lapland because the Swedish authorities won the local Finnish settlement over to their cause by granting it large privileges to tax the Lapps and to trade with them. These were rights based on the old-established *birk* legal praxis; those who had been granted the privileges received the name *birkarlar* ("bircarlians").

In 1240, Bishop Thomas failed to conquer Karelia and to expand the sphere of interest of the west as far as the Neva River. King Magnus Ladelås had similar plans. In 1293, Torgils Knutsson, lord high constable of Sweden, organized a successful military expedition and had Viborg castle built to secure the conquest of western Karelia. After long conflicts, Novgorod acknowledged the conquest in the Treaty of Nöteborg made in 1323, the first written conclusion of peace between Sweden and Novgorod. The boundary between the countries was set northwest from the bottom of the Gulf of Finland through the wildernesses to the Gulf of Bothnia. Virtually, Finnish colonization and Swedish political expansion were permanently established across the border in Ostrobothnia and Savo as early as the latter half of the 14th century.

All of Finland, which was divided into several castle provinces, formed one diocese, the diocese of Turku. This situation created connections between different areas and made Turku the center of Finland. To assist the bishop, the cathedral chapter was founded in 1276. Finnish bishops were Swedes until 1291, when the first Finn, Magnus I, was elected bishop.

Finland as part of Sweden. Even in the Middle Ages, the name "Finland" meant primarily the southwestern part of the country (Varsinais-Suomi), the focus of settlement and economic life. But in the 15th century, the concept was extended to the whole area populated by Finnish tribes. The more accurate medieval term was "Österlandia" ("Eastland"), mentioned for the first time in 1344. Here, the name "Finland" is used for the whole Finnish territory.

Finland was not incorporated into Sweden as a country conquered, but became an equal part of the kingdom. When King Magnus Eriksson was under age, Finnish affairs were managed by the governors of the Turku and Viborg castles as "heads of Finland" (*capitaneus Finlandiae*) fairly independently. In the 1330s and 1340s, Magnus Eriksson pursued significant reforms in Finland in taxation, trade, and administration of justice; new national laws, common law, and city code were put into effect. Ulfsby and Borgå were granted a town charter in the 1340s.

Finland was an important stronghold for the king in the struggle against the aristocracy, and from Finland he attempted to extend Sweden's sphere of influence to the commercially important Neva line. In the 1350s, Finland was the duchy of Bengt Algotsson, favorite of Magnus Eriksson. Finland, or "Eastland," benefited from the internal power struggles of Sweden, so that the country and its inhabitants received full right to vote in the royal election on February 15, 1362.

Albrecht of Mecklenburg, who had been elected king in 1364, considered it important to assume strict control over Finland. For this purpose, he stayed almost the whole of the year 1365 in Finland. He made many decisions that particularly advanced trade. The king attempted to increase the efficiency of the feudalistic castle administration by having new castles constructed, but because of opposition from the peasants the project had to be abandoned. The Swedish heritage in Finnish administration and judicature remained strong. The germanization of the burghers in Finnish towns continued, however, and the castles of Finland often received German governors, but nowhere near as many as in Sweden.

In the 1370s, a significant feudalistic concentration of power took place when all Finnish castle provinces were placed in the charge of Bo Jonsson Grip, a Swedish aristocrat. Bo Jonsson made local administration more efficient by constructing Raseborg castle as the center of Uusimaa and by organizing Korsholm as the northernmost castle province. It comprised mainly the coast of the Gulf of Bothnia, which in the course of the Middle Ages became the object of intensive colonization, primarily from southwestern

Finland. A large part of the settlement and the castle province was on the Novgorod side of the boundary fixed in the Treaty of Nöteborg. In the contest in 1370, the ownership of the area was settled in Sweden's favor, but it was only in the Treaty of Täysinä in 1595 that Novgorod's successor in power, Moscow, finally recognized Swedish supremacy over northern Ostrobothnia.

When Bo Jonsson died in 1386, he tried with his will to keep his provinces in the hands of the Swedish aristocracy, but King Albrecht succeeded in thwarting the plan as far as Finland was concerned. He was supported by Bero II Balk, bishop of Finland, and Jeppe Djäkn, the Finnish governor of Turku castle. To forestall this development in other provinces, the aristocratic party of Sweden resorted to joint Nordic concentration of power against German and Mecklenburgian rule and also against the strong royal power.

When the Nordic troops of Queen Margrethe had defeated Albrecht, Jeppe Djäkn recognized Margrethe's domination in Finland in 1389, and all castle provinces except Viborg came under her control. Albrecht and his followers did not, however, give up easily, and in the conflicts that began, they aimed at isolating Finland from the country that was being concentrated in the hands of Margrethe with the support of the Vital Brethren. The western center of Finland came to Knut Bosson, a knight supporting the Mecklenburgian power, in 1395. The bishop of Finland and the lords of the Viborg and Raseborg castles were instead supporters of Margrethe and Erik of Pomerania; even Finns participated in the royal election in 1396. After the Union of Kalmar had been founded in 1397 and Margrethe had occupied Stockholm in 1398, the position of Knut Bosson and the Vitals in Finland lasted only to the year 1399.

Union of Kalmar. The country in a leading position in the Union of Kalmar was Denmark, where the ruler of the union also lived. The Union meetings held there were often attended by the leading figures of Finland. Formally, Finland was part of Sweden, but the Union rulers, Erik of Pomerania in particular, ruled Finland often as an entity unto itself. The ties of Finland to Sweden were loosened, and in practice Finland was almost "the fourth Union country."

Margrethe and Erik of Pomerania saw to it that Finnish castles came to be governed by men whom they trusted absolutely. Some of the governors were Danish and German, but a considerable number were Finnish. Erik of Pomerania practiced significant reform in Finland. He promoted settlement, restored tax-free landed property to the Crown, reformed taxation and local administration (division of castle provinces into administrative parishes), began to have coins minted for Finland (in Turku), and organized administration of justice in district courts, courts of appeal for civil cases in rural areas, and in the Common Court of Turku, which from now on represented the court of last resort, the justice of the king.

When the autocratic administration of Erik of Pomerania led to a revolt in Sweden in 1434, Finnish leaders under the strong bishop Magnus Tavast were loyal to the king to the very last, and made attempts at mediation. Finally, when Sweden had fully disclaimed the obstinate king, Finland did the same. In 1438–1439, peasants in Finland rose in local rebellion because they found their taxes heavy.

The new king, Christoffer of Bavaria, managed to have only the western part of Finland under immediate domination, for he was forced to enfeoff the eastern half of the country (the Viborg castle province) to Karl Knutsson, the head of the national party. Later, the feudalistic division of Finland lasted until the end of the Union. The foremost bishop in the Middle Ages in Finland, the prestigious Magnus II Tavast (1412–1450), was an important supporter of the king in Finland. The lord of the Viborg castle province was independently permitted to expend all tax revenue from his area, but in exchange he was responsible for defending his area and the whole of Finland and the country against Novgorod and Moscow. From Viborg, Karl Knutsson managed to become king of Sweden and the state leader several times after 1448.

For longer periods, only the western part of Finland was actual "Union Finland," whose tax receipts went to the king, but from time to time all Finnish castles were under the control of Karl Knutsson. After him, Erik Axelsson Tott (d. 1481), a Danish-born knight, became the virtual leader of Finland. For decades, he ruled the province of Viborg in particular, but every now and then also the province of Turku, and even the whole country as a protector. Erik Axelsson's eastern policy was fairly active; to secure the defense against the rising Moscow, he had Olaf's Castle built in 1475 in an area behind the boundary fixed in the Treaty of Nöteborg, where settlers from Savo had steadily arrived since the 14th century.

After the death of Erik Axelsson in 1491, Sten Sture, the protector of Sweden, finally took command of all the main castles in Finland. Under his leadership, the country for a short period changed over to a fairly centralized national state, a state that later on was realized by Gustav Vasa. The emphasis of foreign policy in the country shifted east when Moscow, which had annexed Novgorod to itself, took steps to claim that the old Treaty of Nöteborg be recognized and put into effect. The dispute was aggravated and developed into a war in 1495–1496. Finland suffered much from the war, but was spared conquest. A new boundary was not established, nor was a permanent and lasting peace.

In the final battle over the Union between Denmark and the protectors aiming at national Swedish kingship, Finland joined the latter particularly because Denmark had entered into alliance with the hated Moscow against Sweden. In the combat that ended in a military solution, Christian II, the king of Denmark, gained a victory. November 1520 marked the period of Danish occupation in Finland. However, the ferocious revenge that the king took on his opponents, the so-called Stockholm Massacre, aroused Sweden to violent rebellion against the Danish power. Finland was the last area to come into the hands of Denmark, for only in autumn 1523 did the forces of Gustav Vasa take command of the Finnish castles. The policy of Gustav Vasa to construct a national centralized state, and the fact that such supranational powers as the Union of Kalmar, the Hanseatic League, and the Catholic Church withdrew, marked the end of the Middle Ages and the beginning of modern times in Finland as well.

Economy and society. The foundation of Finnish medieval society consisted of free peasants who in the late Middle Ages owned well over 90 percent of the roughly 35,000 taxable farms of that time. Freehold estates owned by the peerage and other noblemen totaled some 3 percent (970 in number), of which 250 were farms cultivated and inhabited by the owners, and 720 were tenanted farms. In addition, the Church owned about 800 farms, or 2.5 percent of the total number. At the turn of the modern age, only about 50 percent of the farms were owned by peasants in Sweden.

In the Middle Ages, Finland also developed the structure of European class society; but toward the end of the period, the nobility, clergy, and burghers accounted for only a few percent of the population, which had increased perhaps to 300,000.

The leading noble families were of Swedish, German, and Danish descent. But in the late Middle Ages, many domestic families were also exempted from land dues to the Crown (*i.e.*, they rose to the freehold estate, the so-called *frälse*), and many of their members became holders of the highest posts. In the late 15th century, the flood of foreign noble families subsided, and the Finnish nobility began to be self-sufficient. The six towns in Finland in the Middle Ages (Turku, Ulfsby, Borgå, Viborg, Rauma, Nådendal) were triflingly small, and the regional differentiation they represented was insignificant. Many of the burghers, especially in Turku, Viborg, and Ulfsby, were of German and Swedish birth throughout the Middle Ages. During the Union, all Finnish bishops and nearly all members of the cathedral chapter were Finnish learned men.

Continuous colonization altered the dynamics of medieval Finnish society. The settlement became denser in the old hinterlands, whereas about half of the farms were in the southwestern center (Varsinais-Suomi, Satakunta, Häme) at the end of the Middle Ages. All the time, however, settlement and cultivation expanded to new areas in the northern and eastern directions in Ostrobothnia, Savo, and northern Karelia. In the 15th century, enthusiasm for settlement in central Finland was shown particularly by the tribe from Savo, a tribe that developed in an area between Häme and Karelia. Colonization from Savo was most intense in the 16th century, when it was also concentrated in the forests of central Scandinavia. There is no indication that the agrarian crisis of the late Middle Ages would have brought about an interruption in colonization in Finland, or such depopulation as in Scandinavia, although it is probable that development was retarded toward the end of the 14th century. But colonization was very vigorous again in the 15th and 16th centuries.

Finnish economic life was based on the trades of the peasants. The economy of the Crown and the Church, the existence of towns, and trade were all based on the yield from agriculture, fishing, and hunting. Peasant households were to a great extent self-sufficient, so there were many subsidiary trades, but usually there was one principal industry that yielded surplus for payment of taxes and trading.

Regional differences in the significance of different trades were great because of historical development and natural conditions. In southwestern Finland, field cultivation was the primary trade, and had great significance also in central Finland in the area inhabited by people from Häme, where hunting, fishing, and fowling were also important. In Savo and Karelia, the basis of economic life lay in cultivation by clearing and burning woodland, hunting, and fishing. In northern Finland, a fairly pure hunting economy was prevalent among both Finns and Lapps. Fishing was the chief industry on the coasts and the islands. Animal husbandry had great significance throughout medieval Finland. Tools, dishes, textiles and clothes, boats and small ships, iron, and so on were made by hand. Actual handicraft industry was reflected in the wooden-dish industry in Vakka-Suomi, where products were exported, for example, to Germany.

The importance of trade grew during the Middle Ages. Finland imported salt, cloth, hops, wines, spices, and various kinds of objects, as well as grain in bad years. The most important export articles were butter, fish (salted salmon, Baltic herring, dried pike), furs, pelts, seal oil, and horses (from Karelia). Foreign trade was mediated mainly by the Hanseatic towns (Danzig, Lübeck, Tallinn) and Stockholm, but peasants themselves took to the sea a good deal in trading affairs.

Culture. Medieval Finnish culture can be divided into "advanced culture," represented by the Church, nobility, and burghers, and the culture of the peasants. Influences passed mostly from the former to the latter, but, on the other hand, the upper social layer received many influences from abroad.

The most perceptible and impressive form of culture was represented by the building of castles and churches. Some 250 wooden and eighty stone churches were built in Finland in the Middle Ages. Of the wooden churches, the "St. Henrik's sermon room" in Kokemäki has been preserved. The first Finnish episcopal church in Koroinen was wooden. Around 1280, the construction of the Turku cathedral of brick began. Building and renovation of this impressive central church continued throughout the Middle Ages. Building and decoration (altars, sculptures, and wall paintings) of stone churches were influenced by European stylistic tendencies, which the master builders and artists brought particularly from Sweden, the Baltic countries, and Germany.

The first generation of Finnish castles is represented by six well-known early-medieval prehistoric castles in southwestern Finland from the 12th and 13th centuries. Around 1270–1300, three central castles were built (Turku, Häme, and Viborg). For the needs of administration and feudalistic exercise of power, six new castles were constructed mainly on the southwestern and western coasts in the 14th century. Of these, Raseborg in Uusimaa and Kastelholm on the Åland Islands became important central castles, but others fell into disuse. To defend the country against the rising state of Moscow, the strong Olaf's Castle was built on the eastern border in the 1470s, receiving stylistic features of the Renaissance. In the late Middle Ages, the high nobility had private stone dwellings built in southwestern Finland.

The Dominicans and Franciscans founded several monasteries in Finnish towns, and the Swedish order of the Brigettines founded a convent in Nådendal near Turku in the 1440. The Dominicans were a particularly significant factor in conveying the influences of religious culture from Europe to Finland. In the Karelia that lies behind the boundary fixed in the Treaty of Nöteborg, Orthodox monasteries were constructed, the most important of which were Valamo and Konevitsa on the islands of Lake Ladoga. A great number of Russian and Byzantine cultural influences spread there.

In Finland, the beginnings of education were provided by monastery schools, town schools, and the cathedral school of Turku. Reliable information exists that about 140 Finns continued their studies in foreign universities, at first particularly in Paris and Prague, but in the late Middle Ages mainly in Germany. The Finnish Olof Magnusson served as rector in the University of Paris twice in the 1430s. The coming of humanism to Finland is indicated by the fact that the schoolmaster of Viborg, Clement, taught his boys Vergil and Terence at the end of the 15th century.

The literary culture was based chiefly on literature from abroad. Finnish bishops and other men of power had considerable libraries ever since the early 13th century. Especially toward the end of the Middle Ages, a large number of texts were written in Finland in Latin, Swedish, and presumably even in Finnish, but only Swedish translations of Latin texts by the monk Jöns Budde 1461–1491 have been preserved. The Church of Finland had a missal printed in Lübeck in 1488 (*Missale Aboense*) and a manual in Halberstadt in 1522 (*Manuale Aboense*).

Finland enjoyed a rich indigenous peasant culture. Many of the teachings and views of the Church were adopted, but the old popular faith remained very strong. Although written medieval Finnish literature does not exist, the "unwritten literature," *i.e.*, folk poetry, was plentiful and rich in meaning. Epic and lyric poetry dating from the Viking Age and even earlier was sung, as well as magic verse. The poems were expressed in Finnish four-trochee meter, which is over 2,000 years old, the so-called "*Kalevala* meter." (The work known to modern readers as *The Kalevala* is a conflation of traditional oral songs, lyrics, and narrative first collected in the 19th century.)

Influenced particularly by Christianity, a new verse form was born, the *Kalevala*-type of legend poetry. Its themes were very international, but came into existence independently. The "Hymn to the Death of Bishop Henrik" is an important source from the early Christian time. In addition to legend, another medieval literary fashion, the ballad, was expressed in the *Kalevala* meter. Medieval ballads and legends reveal the rich world of the saints, knights, Hanseatics, priests, and monks. A massive spectacle of the presentation of ballads and legends was the Ritvala Whitsuntide Festival in Häme. A fine piece of Finnish poetry from the Middle Ages is the ballad "Death of Elina."

Ed.: Bunge, F. G. von, ed. *Liv-, Esth- und Curländisches Urkundenbuch* 1. Reval: [n.p.], 1852; Rydberg, O. S., ed. *Sveriges traktater med främmande magter jämte andra dit hörande handlingar* 1. Stockholm: Norstedt, 1877; *Detmar-Chronik von 1105–1276. Die Chroniken der deutschen Städte vom 14. bis ins 16. Jahrhundert* 19. Lubeck: [n.p.], 1884; Hausen, R., ed. *Registrum Ecclesiae Aboensis*. Helsingfors: Simalii, 1890; Hausen, R., ed. *Finlands medeltidsurkunder*. 8 vols. Helsingfors: Statsarkiv, 1910–28; Pipping, Rolf, ed. *Erikskrönikan enligt cod. Holm. 2. Samlingar utgivna av Svenska fornskrift–sällskapet*, 47. Stockholm: Almqvist & Wiksell, 1921; Nasovnova, A. N., ed. *Novgorodskaja pervaja letopis starsego i mladsego izvodov*. Moscow and Leningrad: Izdvo Akadamii, 1950. **Bib.**: *Suomen historiallinen bibliografia = Historical Bibliography of Finland 1544–1900* (1961), 1901–1925 (1940), 1926–1950 (1955), 1951–1960 (1968), 1961–1970 (1983), 1971–1980 (1988). **Lit.**: Donner, Gustaf Adolf. *Kardinal Wilhelm von Sabina, Bischof von Modena 1222–1234. Päpstlicher Legat in den Nordischen Ländern (+1251)*. Helsingfors: Finska vetenskaps-societeten, 1929; Gallén, Jarl. *La province de Dacia de l'Ordre des Frères Precheurs* 1. Helsingfors: Söderström, 1946; Dencker, Rolf. "Finnlands Städte und Hansisches Bürgertum (bis 1471)." *Hansische Geschichtsblätter* 77 (1959), 13–93; Jaakkola, Jalmari. *Suomen myöhäiskeskiaika*. 2 vols. *Suomen historia* 5–6. Helsinki: Söderström, 1950–59; Jutikkala, Eino, and Kauko Pirinen. *A History of Finland*. Trans. Paul Sjöblom. New York: Praeger, 1962; Pirinen, Kauko. *Kymmenysverotus Suomessa ennen kirkkoreduktiota*. Historiallisia tutkimuksia, 55. Helsinki: Suomen Historiallinen Seura, 1962; Kirkinen, Heikki. *Karjala idän kulttuuripiirissä. Bysantin ja Venäjän yhteyksistä keskiajan Karjalaan*. Historiallisia tutkimuksia, 67. Helsinki: Kirjayhtymä, 1963; Drake, Knut. *Die Burg Hämeenlinna im Mittelalter. Eine baugeschichtliche Untersuchung*. Trans. F. Nikolowski. Suomen Muinaismuistoyhdistyksen aikakauskirja, 68. Helsinki: Weilin & Göös, 1968; Gallén, Jarl. *Nöteborgsfreden och Finlands medeltida östgräns*. Svenska Litteratursällskapet i Finland, 427.1. Helsingfors: Svenska Litteratursällskapet i Finland, 1968; Anthoni, Eric. *Finlands medeltida frälse och 1500–talsadel.*

Svenska Litteratursällskapet i Finland, 442. Helsingfors: Svenska Litteratursällskapet i Finland; 1970; Sammallahti, Pekka. "Suomalaisten esihistoriankysymksiä." *Virittäjä* 1 (1977), 119–36; Saskolskij, I. P. *Borba Rusi protiv krestonosnoj agressii na beregach Baltiki v. XII–XVII vv.* Leningrad: Nauka, 1978; Huurre, Matti. *9000 vuotta Suomen esihistoriaa.* Helsinki: Otava, 1979; Suvanto, Seppo. "Medieval Studies in Finland: A Survey." *Scandinavian Journal of History* 4 (1979), 287–304; Vahtola, Jouko. "Tornionjoki—ja Kemijokilaakson asutuksen synty. Nimistötieteellinen ja historiallinen tutkimus." *Studia Historica Septentrionalia* 3. Ed. Kyösti Julku. Kuusamo: Pohjois-Suomen Historiallinen Yhdistys, 1980 [English summary, pp. 255–62]; Heininen, Simo, and Jussi Nuorteva. "Universitetsbesöken i utlandet före 1660: Finland." In *Studia Historica Jyväskyläensia* 22.1. XVIII Nordiska historikermötet. Juväskylä 1981. Mötesrapport 1. Jyväskylä: Jyväskylän yliopisto, 1981, pp. 67–118; Orrman, Eljas. "The Progress of Settlement in Finland During the Late Middle Ages." *Scandinavian Economic History Review* (1981), 129–43; Sundström, Hans, Pentti Koivunen, and Jouko Vahtola. "The Earliest Settlement in the Tornio (Torne) River Valley: An Example of Inter-Disciplinary Research." In *Desertion and Land Colonization in the Nordic Countries c. 1300–1600: Comparative Report from the Scandinavian Project on Deserted Farms and Villages.* Ed. Svend Gissel *et al.* Uppsala: Almqvist & Wiksell, 1981, pp. 244–71; Pirinen, Kauko. "Keskiajan kulttuurin välittyminen Suomeen." In *Suomen kulttuurihistoria* 1. Ed. Päiviö Tommila *et al.* 2nd ed. Porvoo: Söderström, 1983, pp. 11–39; Suomi, Vilho. "Katolisen keskiajan kirjalliset tuotteet." In *Suomen kulttuurihistoria* 1, pp. 40– 5; Lehtosalo-Hilander, Pirkko-Liisa. "Keski—ja myöhäisrautakausi." In *Suomen historia* 1. Espoo: Weilin & Göös, 1984, pp. 253–405; Vahtola, Jouko. "Finnlands kirchenpolitische Verbindungun im frühen und mittleren 13. Jahrhundert." *Jahrbücher für Geschichte Osteuropas* 32 (1984), 488–516; Suvanto, Seppo. "Keskiaika." In *Suomen historia* 2. Espoo: Weilin & Göös, 1985, pp. 9–225; Julku, Kyösti. *Suomen itärajan synty. Studia Historica Septentrionalia* 10. Jyväskylä: Pohjois-Suomen Historiallinen Yhdistys, 1987. [English summary, pp. 435–55]; Linna, Martti, ed. *Muinaisrunot ja todellisuus.* Historian Aitta, 20. Jyväskylä: Historian Ystäväin Liitto, 1987; Vahtola, Jouko. "Keskiaika." In *Suomen historian pikkujättiläinen.* Ed. Seppo Zetterberg. Porvoo: Söderström, 1987, pp. 39–125.

Jouko Vahtola

Finnboga saga ramma ("The Saga of Finnbogi the Strong") is classed as one of a group of younger, or "postclassical," *Íslendingasögur*, and is thought to have been composed in the first quarter of the 14th century. Primary MSS are AM 132 fol. (*Möðruvallabók*), written not later than 1350, and AM 510 4to (*Tómasarbók*), from the mid-16th century. A small part of the saga is preserved on one vellum leaf, AM 162c fol., dating from the 15th century. A number of paper MSS exist from the 17th century, all of which derive from the two primary MSS.

The eponymous hero, Finnbogi, is an Icelandic farmer's son, but his life is a particularly adventurous one, especially his exploits abroad. Finnbogi has all the traits of the true saga hero, in particular great physical strength, and his life is a series of feats of strength and responses to challenges. Many motifs in the saga are known from other sources, and similarities between *Finnboga saga* and other sagas (*e.g.*, *Gunnlaugs saga*, *Kjalnesinga saga*, and *Hallfreðar saga*) have been noted. Verbal parallels are few, however, and instances of direct borrowing are difficult to establish.

Finnbogi is a hero who is rejected as a child. He is exposed as an infant, but found by a poor, old couple. Later, through his valor, he gains his father's favor. His name and nickname ("the strong") are given to him by important men who value him highly. In Norway, he fights with bears and *blámenn* (literally "blue-men"),

and in Greece represents the king of Norway, at the same time converting to Christianity. Everywhere, his strength and noblemindedness win him admiration.

Events in Iceland are on the whole less grand. Finnbogi is involved in a series of disputes with the Ingimundarsons. This feud is also described in *Vatnsdœla saga*, where the account is very much biased in favor of the Ingimundarsons. Ólsen (1937–39) has suggested that *Finnboga saga* was written in response to *Vatnsdœla saga*, to exonerate Finnbogi, as it were; but it is equally plausible that the two versions represent oral variants of the same story (van Hamel 1934). In the end, Finnbogi is reconciled with his enemies and lives to an old age.

Finnbogi rammi is mentioned in *Landnámabók* and in the *Íslendingadrápa* of Haukr Valdísarson, and there can be little doubt that the character is based on a historical person, however fictionalized the account may be in its present form. Influence from the *fornaldarsögur* and *riddarasögur* is apparent both in the style of the saga and in a few incidental details, such as when Finnbogi is said to have lain under a silk blanket. One unusual aspect of the saga is its colloquial style, its use of words thought to have been common in the spoken language of the time, but rare in the literary language (Schach 1985).

Finnboga saga ramma is not one of the better-crafted *Íslendingasögur*. Characterization is flat, and the plot little more than a repetitive series of episodes designed to present the hero in a favorable light. The narrative is nevertheless lively and makes good reading.

The oldest *rímur* based on the saga were composed by Guðmundur Bergþórsson in 1686. A ballad found in the Faroe Islands is thought to have been based directly on the saga or another source common to both (Poulsen 1963).

Ed.: Gering, Hugo, ed. *Finnboga saga hins ramma.* Halle: Niemeyer, 1879; Jóhannes Halldórsson, ed. *Kjalnesinga saga.* Íslenzk fornrit, 14. Reykjavik: Hið íslenzka fornritafélag, 1959, pp. 251–340 [introduction, pp. lvii–lxix]. **Tr.**: Bachman, W. Bryant, Jr., and Guðmundur Erlingsson, trans. *The Saga of Finnbogi the Strong.* Lanham: University Press of America, 1990. **Lit.**: Hamel, A. G. van. "Vatnsdælasaga and Finnbogasaga." *Journal of English and Germanic Philology* 33 (1934), 1–22; Björn M. Ólsen. "Um Íslendingasögur. Kaflar úr háskólafyrirlestrum." In *Safn til sögu Íslands* 6.3. Ed. Sigfús Blöndal and Einar Ól. Sveinsson. Reykjavik: Hið íslenzka bókmenntafélag, 1937–39, pp. 336–48; Björn Sigfússon. "Finnboga saga ramma." *KLNM* 4 (1959), 280; Poulsen, Johan Hendrik. "Um Finnbogarímu færeysku." *Skírnir* 137 (1963), 46–58; Jón Helgason. "Syv sagablade (AM 162 C fol. bl. 1–7)." *Opuscula* 5. Bibliotheca Arnamagnæana, 31. Copenhagen: Munksgaard, 1975, pp. 1–97; Ólafur Halldórsson. "Rímur af Finnboga ramma." *Gripla* 1 (1975), 182–7; Schach, Paul. "Character Creation and Transformation in the Icelandic Sagas." In *Germanic Studies in Honor of Otto Springer.* Ed. Stephen Kaplowitt. Pittsburgh: K & S Enterprises, 1978, pp. 237–79; Schach, Paul. "Finnboga saga." In *Dictionary of the Middle Ages.* Ed. Joseph R. Strayer. New York: Scribner, 1982–89, vol. 5, pp. 64–5.

Margrét Eggertsdóttir

[**See also**: *Íslendingasögur*, *Möðruvallabók*, *Rímur*, *Vatnsdœla saga*]

Fishing, Whaling, and Seal Hunting. The fish resources along the Atlantic coasts of Scandinavia are special in a European, and perhaps also in a global, context because they are so rich and at the same time so close to the shore. In eastern Scandinavia, there are also fish resources close to the shore, although not as rich as in the west. Consequently, great quantities of fish could be taken with small boats and inexpensive fishing equipment by peasants along the coast. In Scandinavia, even commercial fishing was almost exclusively done by peasants who owned their own boats and sold the catch to merchants. This situation contrasts with England, Holland, Flanders, and Germany, where commercial fisheries were organized after 1370 by town merchants sending large fishing vessels out in the North Sea and to Icelandic waters on trips lasting for weeks.

The most important fish species for medieval Scandinavian fishermen were cod and coalfish in the west (Iceland, Faroe Islands, Norway, western Jutland), herring in the east (Bohuslän, Danish waters, the Baltic), and salmon in rivers and lakes. The richest catches were taken in seasonal fisheries on the spawning grounds. For cod, the principal ones were on the southwestern coast of Iceland, and in Norway from Troms to Möre, with the greatest concentration along the southern shores of the Lofoten Islands. The greatest shoals of spawning herring were found near the towns of Skanör and Falsterbo in Scania. The principal commercial fisheries took place on these spawning grounds. But for local consumption sufficient resources could be found along most of the Scandinavian coastline.

Boat and fishing tackle belonged mostly to the fishermen. In the cod fisheries, Scandinavian fishermen used lines with one or two hooks. In the herring fisheries, seines and nets were the tackle most commonly used. Lines and nets were so cheap that every farmer could afford them. The seine was divided into several parts, each of which could be owned by separate farmers. The fishing boats were usually manned by two to four men. Most coastal peasants owned boats of varying size. The members of the crew, which usually included the boat owner, divided the catch according to a prearranged share system. Servants were paid a fixed sum, and the share belonged to the master. The fish was partly consumed by the fishermen and their families, partly bartered or sold at local or international markets.

Coastal farmers in western Scandinavia ate astonishingly large quantities of fish. Along the northern and western coast of Norway in the 18th century, it was usual to have herring for breakfast and cod or coalfish at a meal later in the day. Fish must have provided about 25 percent of the caloric demand of these peasants' households in normal years. In years when the grain crops failed, fish could save the peasants from starvation. There are reports of peasants surviving difficult winters on fish and water. This large consumption of fish was most certainly the same in the Middle Ages and even earlier. In Denmark and Sweden, fish consumption was smaller, but still important.

Local barter, where coastal farmers gave fish in exchange for timber and other products from inland farmers, is found all along the Scandinavian coasts. The townsmen were important consumers of fish. In Norway and partly in Sweden and Denmark, peasants from the surrounding countryside caught the fish and sold it in the town. In Denmark and Sweden, fishermen often lived permanently in towns. In the fishing season, townsmen manned boats with their servants and sent them to fishing villages. For example, merchants of the Lake Mälar district traveled up to harbors along the Gulf of Bothnia, where they fished herring and traded with the local population.

The commercial revolution of 1100–1350 opened up European markets for Scandinavian fish. The development started at the Lofoten Islands, because here marketable fish was simplest to produce.

In northern Scandinavia, the climate is so cold and dry that it is possible to dry fish in the wind without the use of salt. The procedure required no investment and was so simple that the fishermen did it themselves. The dried cod was called stockfish because it hung over a rod, or stock, while drying. As early as 1100, cod was caught at the Lofoten Islands, dried there, brought to Bergen, and sold to exporters. This was the first fishery in northern Europe to acquire an international market. In the following period up to 1300, stockfish production spread southward to the coast of Möre.

The export of stockfish from Iceland via Bergen started around 1320–1340. The main fishing villages were on the Westman Islands and Snæfellsnes. In 1412, the first English merchants appeared in Icelandic waters. Icelandic fishermen got better prices from them than in Bergen, and in the following period stockfish production increased. The English built trading stations in the Westman Islands, Grindavík, Rif, Hafnarfjörður, and other places. In addition, in 1409, foreign fishermen started to fish in Icelandic waters with large fishing ships. They salted the fish on board and did not have bases ashore.

About 1450, stockfish production also spread to northern Troms and Finnmark. Earlier, there seem to have been no Norwegians living permanently there. Then Norwegian fishermen settled in fishing villages on the outer coast where the distance to the best fishing grounds was shortest. In 1520, there were fishing villages all along the coast to Vadsø. They had a population altogether of 2,000–3,000, which drew its main income from stockfish. Operating on a far smaller scale was the export of dried cod and flounder from western Jutland via Ribe to northern Germany at the end of the Middle Ages.

Herring for European markets was generally salted, some of it also smoked. Salting demanded salt and tuns, and this investment was risky because the herring shoals were irregular. The peasants could not afford it, and nearly all the salting was done by merchants. This situation gave the herring fisheries at Scania particular advantages. They were comparatively regular and were near the Hansa towns of northern Germany where the herring merchants lived. Commercial fisheries are first mentioned there around 1200. The value of the herring production at Scania soon surpassed the stockfish exports from Bergen. The fishermen sold the catch fresh to the merchants when they landed it at the end of the day. At Skanör and Falsterbo, the fishermen were peasants from Scania and above all from the Danish islands of Møn, Lolland, Falster, and southern Zealand. Although Skanör and Falsterbo were the two most important fishing villages, there were other smaller ones along the Sound. On Møn alone, there were eleven villages at the end of the Middle Ages. From 1370, at the latest, fishing boats from Hansa towns also participated, at the end of the 14th century, 400–500 from Lübeck alone. In the 1520s, the German bailiff at Scania claimed that one autumn a total of 7,515 boats participated with an average of five fishermen in each. Of all the fisheries of northern Europe in the Middle Ages, those of Scania probably had the largest participation. In value, however, the Dutch and English North Sea fisheries with larger fishing ships surpassed it in the 15th century.

Shoals of spawning herring came to the coast of Bohuslän in 1288–1341. The fisheries were organized in much the same way as at Scania, with foreign merchants and local fishermen. After 1400, the Hansa merchants also organized the salting of herring in the Liim Fjord. Fishing with nets in the fjord was open to all. Most of the fish was taken with seines and fish traps along the shore, but this area was reserved for the owners of the land.

Fish was important for the coastal population as a source of food and cash. With this money, they could buy, among other things, imported grain. It is therefore surprising to see how few professional fishermen there were in medieval Scandinavia. In Denmark, there were a few of them living in the towns. They provided the comparatively stable and protected town markets with daily provisions. In Germany, it was usual for town fishermen to form guilds; in Scandinavia, we find this trend only in Vejle. In the 15th century, we get the first reliable evidence of professional fishermen in the Icelandic and Norwegian fishing villages. Most of them lived in Finnmark, where we find about 500 fishermen's families at the end of the Middle Ages. But even on these barren settlements close to the ocean, people were reluctant to abandon all ties with agriculture. Almost all had some sheep and perhaps a cow that were fed on seaweed, fish, moss, and grass, which often was brought long distances by boat.

The great majority of medieval Scandinavian fishermen combined fishing with other occupations, above all with farming, because all the great fisheries were seasonal. The cod spawned in January to April and the Scania herring from the middle of August to October. In these periods, there was little to do on the farm. The peasants could thus skim the cream off the fishing resources without neglecting agriculture. It was also risky to rely exclusively on irregular fish shoals and on merchants who could be prevented from coming by war or accident. Coastal farmers consequently settled where they could find the best conditions for agriculture. But for some weeks or even months every year, they moved out to the best fishing districts. If there were farms there, they lodged in the farmhouses. But near the best fishing grounds, villages of fishermen's huts grew up that were used only in the fishing season. In Iceland and in Finnmark, they were built of stones and turf, farther south of timber.

Whaling. Several forms of whaling were practiced in Norway, Iceland, and the Faroe Islands. The oldest and most primitive method was to cut the blubber off dead or dying whales that had run themselves aground. Floating dead whales could be towed ashore. The laws give detailed rules for the division among the king, the landowner, and the finder. Many bays and inlets were so situated that whales often swam in, but did not find their way out again. Then it was easy for neighboring peasants to scare the whale aground or shoot it with poisoned arrows.

More active forms of whaling were also known. In the Old English *Orosius* (1:1), the chieftain Óttarr from northern Norway tells that he, with six of his men, hunted sixty large whales in two days. If the statement is true, they must have met a flock of smaller whales, such as pilot whales, scared them to the shore, and killed them there with knives and spears. This procedure is known in the Faroe Islands up to the present day.

The most risky form of whaling was harpooning on the open sea. Both Icelandic and Norwegian laws regulated it, but *Konungs skuggsjá* ascribes it to Icelandic waters only. In Norway, it is not mentioned in other medieval sources. It is safe to assume that harpooning on the open sea was very rare there.

In Iceland and the Faroes, whaling may have been economically important in parts of the islands. In Norway, the hunt was too passive and occasional to have any consequence.

Seal hunting. Before firearms made hunting more effective in the 16th century, there were more seals along the coasts than in recent centuries. Ice hunting of seals was important in the Baltic when the sea was frozen. In the Gulf of Bothnia, the peasants went out in teams equipped with sledges and small boats. When the seals lay on the ice far from open water, they could be killed easily with clubs or spears. Seals living under the ice had to breathe regularly in small holes in the ice, where they could be harpooned. In summer all over Scandinavia, they were clubbed or harpooned while lying on skerries or shores. Often, iron hooks were fastened to the rocks, and when the seals were scared and hurried to the sea, they were hooked. Special seal nets were commonly used.

On some skerries or shores, the seals lived for longer periods and bred their baby seals. Most such skerries were privately owned, with exclusive hunting rights. Seals were protected by law during two periods of the year, including the last weeks before they bred.

The most important seal product was blubber. It was eaten instead of butter, used for frying, in oil lamps, and to grease skin clothes. In coastal districts where wood was scarce (Greenland, Iceland, northern Norway), it was used instead of tar to smear boats. Seal meat was not valued highly, but was eaten by the peasants because other meat was scarce. Sealskins were used for shoes, gloves, caps, covers, bags, sacks, and watertight clothes. Seal products could in most cases be replaced by cattle and sheep products. Seals were of most use for the poorer part of the population.

Seal hunting and fishing have been subsidiary sources of income for coastal farmers up to modern times. But during the last two millennia, there has been a gradual shift from seal hunting toward fishing, first for local consumption and after 1100 also for an international market. Hunting had probably already reduced the number of seals in prehistoric times and throughout the Middle Ages, and certainly after 1500 and the introduction of firearms. Because seals consume vast quantities of fish, fewer seals meant more fish. Exploitation of sea resources has contributed to changing the ecological balance along the coast as far back as recorded history.

Lit.: Rafto, Thorolf, *et al.* "Englandshandel." *KLNM* 3 (1958), 658–76; Granlund, John, *et al.* "Fiske." *KLNM* 4 (1959), 302–7; Granlund, John, *et al.* "Fiskeläge." *KLNM* 4 (1959), 309–17; Volland, Odd, *et al.* "Fisker." *KLNM* 4 (1959), 318–20; Niitemaa, Vilho. "Fiskhandel." *KLNM* 4 (1959), 354–72; Stoklund, Bjarne, *et al.* "Garn og garnfiskeri." *KLNM* 5 (1960), 195–206; Granlund, John, *et al.* "Hamnordning." *KLNM* 6 (1961), 102–4; Johnsen, Arne Odd, *et al.* "Hvalfangst." *KLNM* 7 (1962), 160–72; Enemark, Poul. "Limfjordshandel." *KLNM* 10 (1965), 571–6; Volland, Odd, *et al.* "Sildefiske." *KLNM* 15 (1970), 245–57; Hørby, Kai. "Skånemarkedet." *KLNM* 16 (1971), 68–77; Vilkuna, Kustaa, *et al.* "Säljakt." *KLNM* 17 (1972), 686–703; Bernström, John. "Torskfiskar." *KLNM* 18 (1974), 513–8.

Arnved Nedkvitne

[**See also**: Trade]

Five Boroughs. Within the English East Midlands lies a group of five sites—Derby, Leicester, Lincoln, Nottingham, and Stamford—that became Scandinavian power centers following the Viking "Great Army's" settlement of this region in 877. Their individual importance is clear from the *Anglo-Saxon Chronicle* record of the English counterattack on the area in the second decade of the 10th century, which concentrated on capturing them either through direct attack or by intimidation and negotiation. They were first named as a group in the *Anglo-Saxon Chronicle* entry for 942, which celebrates in verse how King Edmund freed the Danes in the area from Norse tyranny, *i.e.*, from the rule of York's Viking kings. Subsequently, the people and territory of the Five Boroughs are mentioned in the *Chronicle* entry for 1013, while in 1015 the related phrase "the seven boroughs" occurs, although it is not made clear which two sites are grouped here with the original five.

To previous generations of historians, the Five Boroughs seemed primarily military and administrative centers of Danish origin, which provided the example for Alfred the Great's fortress-building policy, but more recent historical and archaeological research has thrown new light on their historical origins and function, although there is still much to be learned.

It is now clear that each of the Five Boroughs had a long pre-Viking pedigree as a local or regional center. Derby, Leicester, Lincoln, and Nottingham were all occupied to some extent in the Iron Age. Both Leicester and Lincoln became substantial Roman walled towns, and there were Roman fortifications within one km. of Derby at Little Chester. Pagan Saxon cemeteries are known at Little Chester, and a 4th–7th-century cemetery, perhaps continuously Christian, has been found at St. Paul-in-the-Bail, Lincoln. All five sites have produced evidence for occupation in the immediately pre-Viking, middle Saxon period. At Derby, there was an important church, and Leicester was the seat of the Middle Anglian bishopric from 737 and perhaps earlier. Defended enclosures have been located at both Nottingham and Stamford, ranging in area from approximately 1.1 hectares at Stamford to about 1.5–3 hectares at Nottingham. There is evidence of activity within the standing Roman walls at Lincoln. In spite of the limited and varied evidence, it may be suggested that each of these sites was a secular and ecclesiastical focus for its region in the 7th–9th centuries, a center of power and wealth requiring the provision of services, including the fabrication of objects, and attracting visitors, including interregional and perhaps even occasionally international merchants. Lincoln, for a mixture of geographical and historical reasons, perhaps saw more mercantile activity than the others, but on the present evidence none of the sites should be described as towns before the Vikings' arrival.

The development in the four decades of Viking rule until the recapture by the English is mostly unclear. A pottery kiln at Stamford suggests the initiation of the notable Stamford pottery industry at this time and thus signals burgeoning commercial activities, but only at Lincoln is there unequivocal evidence for settlement, with archaeological remains from Flaxengate showing the resettlement of a long-deserted site. Although no defenses have been discovered that can certainly be assigned to this phase, the assumption remains that at this time these places were principally defensive centers for surrounding immigrant landowners. Only at Nottingham do two Viking burials, recognizable through the presence of weapons, unequivocally attest to the presence of Scandinavians.

The "Viking" phase in the Five Boroughs effectively came to an end with their recapture by the English in the second decade of the 10th century. Yet the frequency with which moneyers' names of Norse derivation appear on the coinage minted there in the late 10th and early 11th century suggests that Scandinavians continued to form an important and numerically significant element in the population.

Lincoln's Flaxengate excavations provide the best index of urban and commercial development during this period, and indeed Lincoln was clearly the largest and most prosperous of the

Five Boroughs, rivaling York as the second city in England, after London, by the time of the Norman Conquest. Flaxengate has produced evidence for a range of manufacturing industries closely comparable in many respects to those discovered at Coppergate, York. Lincoln's inter-regional and overseas links also correspond to York's. Elsewhere in the Five Boroughs, there are again signs of manufacturing and trading activities, for example, pottery kilns at Leicester, Nottingham, and Stamford, which also has evidence of iron working.

By the Norman Conquest, the Five Boroughs embraced a series of places varied in their size and economy. Four had given their names to the surrounding shires that they served as administrative and legal centers, while the fifth, Stamford, may also have been once designated for that role. It is not clear whether their grouping together originated in their late 9th–early 10th-century Viking phase, or whether this designation was given by the English in an attempt to foster unity in a crucial buffer zone against the influence of York, but both their pre-Viking origins and their development into towns during the Anglo-Scandinavian phase of their existence are becoming more comprehensible.

Lit.: Biddle, Martin. "Towns." In *The Archaeology of Anglo-Saxon England*. Ed. David M. Wilson. London: Methuen, 1976, pp. 99–150; Hall, R. A. "The Five Boroughs of the Danelaw—A Review of Present Knowledge." *Anglo-Saxon England* 18 (1989), 149–206

R. A. Hall

[**See also:** England, Norse in; Stamford Bridge, Battle of; York]

Fjǫlsvinnsmál *see* Svipdagsmál

Flateyjarbók ("The Book of Flatey") is an Icelandic parchment (GkS 1005 fol.) consisting of 225 large folio sheets with two wide columns on each page, now bound in two volumes. *Flateyjarbók* was written by two priests, Jón Þórðarson and Magnús Þórhallsson, in 1387–1390, the annal entries for 1391–1394 at the back of the book being added piecemeal during those years. Magnús also illuminated the entire book and wrote a preface that describes the contents of the book and the division of labor between the two scribes. Here, the owner is named: Jón Hákonarson (1350–before 1416), a wealthy farmer in Víðidalstunga (northern Iceland), for whom it is presumed that the MS was written.

Nothing is known concerning the history of *Flateyjarbók* after the death of Jón Hákonarson until the latter half of the 15th century, when the book was in the possession of Þorleifur Björnsson, the governor at Reykhólar (western Iceland), who had twenty-three sheets with new material inserted into the original 202. The work was thereafter owned by Þorleifur Björnsson's descendants until 1647, when Jón Finnsson on Flatey, the island that gave its name to the book, in Breiðafjörður (western Iceland), gave the codex to Bishop Brynjólfur Sveinsson. In 1656, the bishop sent it as a gift to the king of Denmark, Frederik III. It remained in the Royal Library in Copenhagen until 1971, when it was deposited at the Árni Magnússon Institute in Reykjavik.

Flateyjarbók is the largest of all Icelandic parchments, and, with its Gothic illustrations, one of the most beautiful. The text is characterized by an attempt to present a continuous history of Norway by combining the biographies of individual Norwegian kings, into which are woven *þættir*, sections of other sagas, and even entire sagas that in some way concern the lives of the kings. The basic framework consists of four large sagas: *Óláfs saga Tryggvasonar en mesta* (the so-called *Longest Saga*), *Óláfs saga helga* (the so-called *Separate Saga*), *Sverris saga*, and *Hákonar saga Hákonarsonar*. The twenty-three more recent sheets contain, in addition to some *þættir*, the *Morkinskinna* version of the sagas of the kings Magnús góði ("the good") and Haraldr harðráði ("hard-ruler"). These sagas compensate somewhat for the fact that the MS originally contained no sagas of the kings who reigned between St. Óláfr and Sverrir, i.e. 1030–1177, possibly because Jón Hákonarson may already have owned a MS of kings' sagas covering this period, probably the MS now known as *Hulda* (AM 66 fol.). The sagas about the two Óláfrs are the most expanded of the four framework sagas. Related versions of these two sagas are preserved in other MSS, but nowhere with the same amount of expansion as in *Flateyjarbók*. Among the additions are *Jómsvíkinga saga*, *Færeyinga saga* (in a version that in the main seems to be original text, and that is not preserved elsewhere), *Orkneyinga saga* (including sections not found elsewhere), *Hallfreðar saga* (partially an independent version), *Grœnlendinga saga* (preserved nowhere else), and *Fóstbrœðra saga* (with sections not included in other MSS of the saga). Among the *þættir* are *Þorleifs þáttr jarlsskálds*, *Þorsteins þáttr uxafóts*, *Orms þáttr Stórólfssonar*, and *Vǫlsa þáttr*, none of which is preserved elsewhere. As a kind of conclusion for all the previous material and at the same time a bridge to the following *Sverris saga*, the poem *Nóregs konunga tal* is placed after *Óláfs saga helga*; this skaldic work is found nowhere else, and is especially noteworthy because it must be based on the oldest Icelandic historical writing, the lost work about the kings of Norway by Sæmundr fróði ("the learned") Sigfússon. Following the four framework sagas, there are, among other items, some passages from the otherwise lost saga about St. Óláfr by Styrmir Kárason, the only known version of *Grœnlendinga þáttr*, *Játvarðar saga hins helga*, and, finally, the Annals of Flatey. Preceding the sagas are, among other items, the only extant texts of the eddic poem *Hyndluljóð* and of *Óláfs ríma Haraldssonar*, the earliest recorded poem of the *rímur* genre.

The entire contents of *Flateyjarbók* could have been copied from some forty to fifty MSS; therefore, one must assume that the scribes of *Flateyjarbók* found their material in the library of a cloister or at an episcopal center, possibly the monastery at Þingeyrar, or at Reynistaðr, or the bishop's see at Hólar (northern Iceland).

Flateyjarbók preserves a great deal of material that exists nowhere else. Not least on this account, it has always been considered among the most exceptional MSS in Icelandic literature.

Ed.: Guðbrandr Vigfusson and C. R. Unger, eds. *Flateyjarbok: En Samling af norske Konge-Sagaer med indskudte mindre Fortællinger om Begivenheder i og udenfor Norge samt Annaler*. 3 vols. Christiania [Oslo]: Malling, 1860–68; Finnur Jónsson, ed. *Flateyjarbók (Codex Flateyensis): MS. No. 1005 fol. in the Old Royal Collection in the Royal Library of Copenhagen*. Corpus Codicum Islandicorum Medii Aevi, 1. Copenhagen: Levin & Munksgaard, 1930 [facsimile]; Sigurður Nordal et al., eds. *Flateyjarbók*. 4 vols. Akranes: Flateyjarútgáfan, 1944–45; Kolbrún Haraldsdóttir, ed. *Flateyjarbók: GkS 1005 fol.* Manuscripta Islandica Medii Aevi. Reykjavik: Lögberg [forthcoming facsimile]. **Bib.**: Halldór Hermannsson. *Bibliography of the Sagas of the Kings of Norway and Related Sagas and Tales*. Islandica, 3. Ithaca: Cornell University Library, 1910, pp. 10–1; Halldór Hermannsson. *The Sagas of the Kings (konunga sögur) and the Mythical-Heroic Sagas (fornaldar sögur): Two Bibliographical Supplements*. Islandica, 26. Ithaca: Cornell University Press, 1937, pp. 1–2. **Lit.**: Storm, Gustav, ed. *Islandske Annaler indtil 1578*. Christiania [Oslo]: Grøndahl, 1888; rpt. Oslo: Norsk Historisk Kjeldeskrift-Institutt, 1977, pp. xxxii–xxxviii; Finnur Jónsson. "Flateyjarbók." *Aarbøger for nordisk Oldkyndighed og Historie* ser. 3.17 (1927), 139–90; Munksgaard, Ejnar. *Om Flatøbogen og dens Historie*. Copenhagen: Levin & Munksgaard, 1930; Johnsen, Oscar Albert, and Jón Helgason, eds. *Saga Óláfs konungs hins helga: Den store saga om Olav den hellige efter pergamenthåndskrift i Kungliga biblioteket i Stockholm nr. 2 4to med varianter fra andre håndskrifter, utgitt for Kjeldeskriftfondet*. 2 vols. Oslo: Dybwad, 1930–41, vol. 2, pp. 1026–34; Louis-Jensen, Jonna. "Den yngre del af Flateyjarbók." In *Afmælisrit Jóns Helgasonar, 30. júní 1969*. Ed. Jakob Benediktsson et al. Reykjavik: Heimskringla, 1969, pp. 235–50; Louis-Jensen, Jonna. "Et forlæg til Flateyjarbók? Fragmenterne AM 325 IV β og XI,3 4to." *Opuscula* 4. Bibliotheca Arnamagnæana, 30. Copenhagen: Munksgaard, 1970, pp. 141–58; Westergård-Nielsen, Chr. "Nogle bemærkninger til Flatøbogens historie." In *Nordiska studier i filologi och lingvistik: Festskrift tillägnad Gösta Holm på 60-årsdagen den 8 juli 1976*. Ed. Lars Svensson et al. Lund: Studentlitteratur, 1976, pp. 432–44; Ólafur Halldórsson. "Á afmæli Flateyjarbókar." *Tímarit Háskóla Íslands* 2.1 (1987), 55–62; Ólafur Halldórsson. "Af uppruna Flateyjarbókar." *Ný saga* 1 (1987), 84–6; Würth, Stefanie. *Elemente des Erzählens: Die þættir der Flateyjarbók*. Beiträge zur nordischen Philologie, 20. Basel and Frankfurt am Main: Helbing & Lichtenhahn, 1991; Kolbrún Haraldsdóttir. *Um Hálfdanar þátt svarta og Haralds hárfagra: Konungasagnaathuganir*. Reykjavik: Stofnun Árna Magnússonar [forthcoming].

Kolbrún Haraldsdóttir

[**See also**: *Fóstbrœðra saga*; *Færeyinga saga*; *Hákonar saga gamla Hákonarsonar*; *Hallfreðar saga*; *Hyndluljóð*; *Játvarðar saga*; *Jómsvíkinga saga*; *Konungasögur*; *Morkinskinna*; *Óláfs saga helga*; *Óláfs saga Tryggvasonar*; *Orkneyinga saga*; *Rímur*; *Sverris saga*; *Þáttr*; *Þorleifs þáttr jarlsskálds*; Vinland Sagas]

Fljótsdœla saga ("The Saga of the People of Fljótsdalr"). What is now called *Fljótsdœla saga* probably never existed as a self-contained narrative, but was conceived as it now survives, as a sequel to *Hrafnkels saga Freysgoða*. It may be considered the youngest of the *Íslendingasögur*, dating from no earlier than the end of the 15th century, and assigned by its first editor (Kålund 1883) to the first half of the 16th. In the main surviving MS, a copy made in the 17th century, possibly from the author's own version, it forms the continuation of an altered and expanded text of *Hrafnkels saga*. The saga is incomplete, and may have been left unfinished by the author, although there are indications that he had intended to continue the narrative well beyond the point reached in the existing text.

Despite its late provenance, the saga is surprisingly lacking in the romance influence frequently found at the end of the classical period of saga composition. With the exception of the account of the rescue of a jarl's daughter from the bondage of the giant Geitir, perhaps derived from *Brandkrossa þáttr*, although there are few distinct parallels, the narrative is realistic, and almost entirely set in Iceland. Although he failed to achieve a comparable economy of style and clarity of structure, the author clearly modeled his work on the classical saga literature, in which he was demonstrably well versed. Internal evidence suggests acquaintance with

Laxdœla saga, Njáls saga, Hallfreðar saga, and Þorsteins saga hvíta, besides those works from which his narrative material is chiefly derived, Hrafnkels saga, Droplaugarsona saga, and Gunnars þáttr (saga) Þiðrandabana. He may have known the compilation Möðruvallabók, which incorporates many of these sagas.

The author's use of his sources is far from slavish, including variant versions of the characters' names and relationships, and adding much circumstantial detail. The main personages are those of Droplaugarsona saga, of which the author seems to have intended to produce an expanded version. The development of the feud between Helgi Ásbjarnarson and the sons of Droplaug is obscured, however, by the interpolation of the narrative of the killing of the blameless Þiðrandi, in this version the cousin of the sons of Droplaug, and the pursuit of his killer Gunnarr. Although the two Helgis espouse opposing sides in this affair, no original motivation is given for their enmity, and the involvement of such influential figures as Guðrún Ósvífrsdóttir renders their role peripheral. Derivation from Droplaugarsona saga is clearer in such incidents as the killing of Þorgrímr torðyfill ("dung-beetle"), and the clear anticipation of the killing by Helgi and Grímr of their stepfather Hallsteinn, at the point where the saga breaks off.

The saga in style and phrasing is frequently reminiscent of Hrafnkels saga, which Jón Jóhannesson (1950) judges to have been its model, but it lacks the moral weight of Hrafnkels saga. This fact, and the absence of concern for historical and topographical veracity, suggest that the saga was intended to be primarily an entertaining, fictional synthesis of material from older sagas, composed late as an attempt to revive rather than to continue the tradition that produced the Íslendingasögur.

Ed.: Kålund, Kristian, ed. Fljótsdæla hin meiri eller den længere Droplaugarsona-saga efter håndskrifterne. Samfund til udgivelse af gammel nordisk litteratur, 11. Copenhagen: Möller, 1883; Jón Jóhannesson, ed. Austfirðinga sögur. Íslenzk fornrit, 11. Reykjavik: Hið íslenzka fornritafélag, 1950 [Fljótsdœla saga is edited on pp. 215–96; introduction, pp. xcii–c]. Tr.: Haworth, Eleanor, and Jean Young, trans. The Fljotsdale Saga and The Droplaugarsons. Everyman's Library. London: Dent, 1990. Bib.: Halldór Hermannsson. Bibliography of the Icelandic Sagas and Minor Tales. Islandica, 1. Ithaca: Cornell University Library, 1908; rpt. New York: Kraus, 1966, p. 9; Halldór Hermannsson, The Sagas of Icelanders (Íslendinga sögur): A Supplement to Bibliography of the Icelandic Sagas and Minor Tales. Islandica, 24. Ithaca: Cornell University Press; London: Oxford University Press, 1935, p. 18; Jóhann S. Hannesson. The Sagas of Icelanders (Íslendinga sögur): A Supplement to Islandica I and XXIV. Islandica, 38. Ithaca: Cornell University Press, 1957, p. 21. Lit.: Schach, Paul. Icelandic Sagas. Twayne World Authors Series, 717. Boston: Twayne, 1984; Schach, Paul. "Fljótsdæla saga." In Dictionary of the Middle Ages. Ed. Joseph R. Strayer. New York: Scribner, 1982–89, vol. 5, p. 89.

Alison Finlay

[See also: Brandkrossa þáttr, Droplaugarsonar saga; Gunnars saga Þiðrandabana; Hallfreðar saga; Hrafnkels saga Freysgoða; Íslendingasögur; Laxdœla saga; Njáls saga; Þorsteins saga hvíta]

Flóamanna saga ("The Saga of the Men of Flói") focuses on the life and deeds of Þorgils Ørrabeinsfóstri ("-foster"). At the age of sixteen, his demand for his inheritance from his forefathers leads him to Norway. In the British Isles and Ireland, Þorgils wins

a precious sword and the sister of a Scottish earl. In Iceland, Þorgils marries again after giving his first wife to his best friend. His conversion to Christianity leads to conflict with the god Þórr, who appears in his dreams and threatens revenge. Þorgils staunchly defends his loyalty to the new faith. His attempt to settle in Greenland ends in disaster. Shipwrecked on a rough coast, Þorgils loses a large part of his crew to epidemic, and his wife is murdered by servants. Only after great difficulties do the survivors reach inhabited districts. Þorgils's relationship with Eiríkr rauði ("the red") becomes cold and unfriendly, so his stay in Greenland ends quickly. After adventures in Ireland and Hálogaland, he reaches Iceland. The last part of the saga reports on Þorgils's last marriage and on further conflicts with various opponents, until he finally dies at the age of eighty-five.

For the first nine chapters, the saga relies mainly on Sturla Þórðarson's version of Landnámabók. One episode in the story of Þorgils's youth indicates that the author was acquainted with Grettis saga. Þorgils's attempts to obtain his Norwegian inheritance recall those of Egill in Egils saga Skalla-Grímssonar. The related battles with revenants and Vikings are paralleled in Íslendingasögur, such as Reykdœla saga, Hávarðar saga Ísfirðings, or Víga-Glúms saga, and in fornaldarsögur, such as Ǫrvar-Odds saga and Friðþjófs saga. Models and analogues to the events in Greenland are found especially in those sagas that deal with this district, i.e., Grœnlendinga saga and Eiríks saga rauða. The saga uses hagiographical and religious literature, even the New Testament, for those passages that tell of Þorgils's conflicts with Þórr. The same is true for some of the thirteen dreams. In addition, the characterization of the hero shows the stylistic influence of riddarasögur. Even this brief survey shows the extent, otherwise unparalled among Icelandic sagas, to which "set pieces" drawn from widely divergent genres have been brought together here. Especially for a modern reader, this practice lends charm to the saga, even though it does not meet the aesthetic standards of the classical Íslendingasögur.

The saga survives in two versions. The shorter version is found in full in a number of late paper MSS. The most important are AM 517 4to, which Ásgeir Jónsson (ca. 1657–1707) prepared from the now-lost *Vatnshyrna (ca. 1375–1400) in the possession of P. H. Resen, and AM 516 4to, which is not, as was earlier assumed, a copy of *Vatnshyrna. The MS was written by Ketill Jörundarson (ca. 1603–1670); Árni Magnússon compared it with *Vatnshyrna and corrected it. The longer version has survived only in fragmentary form. Two pages of an extensive saga MS (the so-called Pseudo-Vatnshyrna) survive in AM 455b 4to (fols. 4–5rb; ca. 1390–1425) as well as in Einar Eyjólfsson's (ca. 1641–1695) copy (AM 515 4to) of two additional pages of the same MS, which he inserted into the text of the shorter version. Current scholarly opinion considers the longer version closest to the original, which probably dates from between 1290 and 1350.

Based on the hagiographical characteristics of the saga, scholars consider it likely that the author was an ecclesiastic from the south of Iceland. Perkins indicates a probable connection with Haukr Erlendsson (d. 1334) as well as with the farm Gaulverjabær.

Ed.: Guðbrandr Vigfússon and Theodor Möbius, eds. Fornsögur. Vatnsdælasaga. Hallfreðarsaga. Flóamannasaga. Leipzig: Hinrichs, 1860, pp. 117–61, 168–85; Finnur Jónsson, ed. Flóamannasaga. Samfund til udgivelse af gammel nordisk litteratur, 56. Copenhagen: Jørgensen, 1932; Perkins, Richard, ed. "An Edition of Flóamanna saga with a Study of Its Sources and Analogues." Diss. Oxford University, 1971; Þórhallur

Vilmundarson and Bjarni Vilhjálmsson, eds. *Harðar saga*. Íslenzk fornrit, 13. Reykjavik: Hið íslenzka fornritafélag, 1991, pp. 229–327. **Tr.**: Gudbrand Vigfusson and F. York Powell, eds. and trans. *Origines Islandicae: A Collection of the More Important Sagas and Other Native Writings Relating to the Settlement and Early History of Iceland*. 2 vols. Oxford: Clarendon, 1905; rpt. Millwood: Kraus, 1976, vol. 2, pp. 634–72. **Lit.**: Nijhoff, Piet Onno. *De Flóamanna saga. Een text-kritische beschouwing over de samenstelling en de bronnen*. Utrecht: Assen, 1937; Nijhoff, P. O. "Flóamanna saga and Landnáma." *Journal of English and Germanic Philology* 37 (1938), 3–6; Björn Sigfússon. "Tvær gerðir Flóamannasögu." *Saga* 2 (1954–58), 429–51; Perkins, Richard. "A Mediaeval Icelandic Rowing Chant." *Mediaeval Scandinavia* 2 (1969), 92–101; Perkins, Richard. "The Dreams of Flóamanna saga." *Saga-Book of the Viking Society* 19 (1974–77), 191–238; Perkins, Richard. "Kerganga." In *Sjötíu ritgerðir helgaðar Jakobi Benediktssyni 20. júlí 1977*. 2 vols. Ed. Einar G. Pétursson and Jónas Kristjánsson. Reykjavik: Stofnun Árna Magnússonar, 1977, vol. 2, pp. 640–53; Perkins, Richard. *Flóamanna saga, Gaulverjabær and Haukr Erlendsson*. Studia Islandica, 36. Reykjavik: Menningarsjóður, 1978.

Wilhelm Heizmann

[See also: *Egils saga Skalla-Grímssonar; Friðþjófs saga ins frœkna; Grettis saga; Hávarðar saga Ísfirðings; Íslendingasögur; Landnámabók; Reykjadœla saga (ok Víga-Skútu); Riddarasögur; Vatnshyrna; Víga-Glúms saga; Vinland Sagas; Qrvar-Odds saga*]

Flores och Blanzeflor *see* Eufemiavisorna

Flóres saga konungs ok sona hans ("The Saga of King Flóres and His Sons") is an Icelandic *riddarasaga* dating from the end of the 14th century. This text was very popular, since we know of at least forty paper and three vellum copies (AM 343a 4to, AM 577 4to [defective], and AM 586 4to, all from the 15th century). While certain motifs and characters point to a possible foreign influence, it does not seem that the saga is a translation or an adaptation, but an original composition.

King Flóres of Traktía kidnaps Elína of Kartagía, in Africa; she has three sons, Felix, Fenix, and Ajax. But her father, in Flóres's absence, takes her back with her children. The boat is shipwrecked. Flóres then marries the daughter of King Filipus of Sváva, Ermingerðr, who gives birth to a beautiful daughter named Elína. Duke Sintram falls in love with the princess, but his marriage proposal is met with refusal. With the help of his brothers, Reinald and Bertram, and three knights, Únus, Sekúndus, and Tertíus, he wages war on Flóres. After a fierce battle, Flóres is victorious. He kills Reinald and Bertram, and Sintram and the three knights are taken prisoner. The night before their execution, Flóres overhears Sintram and his three knights telling each other their life stories. He then recognizes that the knights are his three lost sons, and he pardons them all. Sintram marries Elína, and the three sons become, respectively, king of England (Felix-Únus), duke of Gaskónía (Fenix-Sekúndus), and king of Africa (Affríka; Ajax-Tertíus).

The author of *Flóres saga konungs* was familiar with many learned works, as well as other Icelandic sagas, such as *Blómstrvallasaga, Trójumanna saga,* and *Þiðreks saga*. But he clearly wanted to justify his composing a *riddarasaga*. He explains that he dislikes people who do not appreciate imaginary tales, and proposes a classification of such texts as this one into three categories: saints' lives, which he does not find very amusing; lives of kings,

which may be instructive because they teach rules of courtesy; and the sagas of kings known for their prowess and fame. He confesses that the events he tells "are considered by some as lies," but he dismisses such judgments.

It is difficult to trace the numerous sources of this rich and clearly composed text. Some motifs, such as the father who refuses to give his daughter in marriage and the fight against the drake, are ubiquitous in western literature. Some, such as the struggle between father and son(s), seem to be more Germanic. Still others, such as the exile of the hero during his youth, followed by his subsequent recognition, may be Byzantine in origin.

Ed.: Lagerholm, Åke, ed. "Flóres saga konungs ok sona hans." In *Drei Lygisǫgur. Egils saga einhenda ok Ásmundar Berserkjabana. Ála flekks saga. Flóres saga konungs ok sona hans*. Altnordische Saga-Bibliothek, 17. Halle: Niemeyer, 1927; Loth, Agnete, ed. *Fornaldarsagas and Late Medieval Romances: AM 586 and AM 589 a-f 4to*. Early Icelandic Manuscripts in Facsimile, 11. Copenhagen: Rosenkilde & Bagger, 1977. **Lit.**: Schlauch, Margaret. *Romance in Iceland*. Princeton: Princeton University Press; New York: American-Scandinavian Foundation; London: Allen & Unwin, 1934; rpt. New York: Russell & Russell, 1973; Einar Ól. Sveinsson. "Landvættasagan." In *Minjar og menntir. Afmælisrit helgað Kristjáni Eldjárn 6. desember 1976*. Ed. Guðni Kolbeinsson. Reykjavik: Menningarsjóður, 1976, pp. 117–29; Gísli Gestsson. "Riddarasaga úr Trékyllisvík." In *Sjötíu ritgerðir helgaðar Jakobi Benediktssyni 20. júlí 1977*. 2 vols. Ed. Einar G. Pétursson and Jónas Kristjánsson. Reykjavik: Stofnun Árna Magnússonar, 1977, vol. 1, pp. 208–20; Glauser, Jürg. *Isländische Märchensagas. Studien zur Prosaliteratur im spätmittelalterlichen Island*. Beiträge zur nordischen Philologie, 12. Basel and Frankfurt am Main: Helbing & Lichtenhahn, 1983.

Régis Boyer

[See also: *Blómstrvallasaga; Riddarasögur, Trójumanna saga; Þiðreks saga af Bern*]

Flóres saga ok Blankiflúr ("The Saga of Flóres and Blankiflúr") is a Christian romance about the young, loving couple Flóres and Blankiflúr, composed in Old Norwegian prose probably between 1220 and 1230. The saga has as its source *Floire et Blancheflor*, a French romance composed around 1150. The tale was a medieval bestseller; translations exist in the vernacular languages not only of Scandinavia and England, but also of Germany, Italy, Spain, Greece, the Netherlands, and other lands. Only the final part of the Old Norwegian saga, from the single combat onward, differs from the original French tale (ed. Leclanche 1980). This difference is due most likely to influence from European translations of the second French version of *Floire et Blancheflor* from around 1200 (Leclanche 1980).

Only one fragment of the Old Norwegian version survives: NRA 65, from the early 14th century; its text is close to, if not identical with, the original translation. Other Icelandic MSS are AM 575a 4to (fragmentary) and AM 489 4to, both from the 14th century. The name of the clerk who transformed the poem into a saga remains unknown.

The names of the couple are explained by the fact that the Christian Blankiflúr ("white flower") and the heathen (*i.e.*, Islamic) Flóres ("flower") were both born on Palm Sunday, the day on which Catholics carry blessed branches and flowers. Blankiflúr's mother is taken prisoner on her pilgrimage to Compostela in Spain, and Blankiflúr is brought up together with Flóres at the royal court of Flóres's father. Mutual love forms a natural part of their lives. Yet the king does not want his son to marry the daughter of a Christian prisoner, so behind the back of Flóres, he sells Blankiflúr and sees that she is transported to the King of Babylon. Flóres discovers the abduction and sets out to find her. After much traveling, he is successful. Only a short time before, however, Blankiflúr is compelled to marry the oriental king; the potentate keeps her prisoner in a tower, where forty young virgins are kept under lock and key. After a victorious single combat, Flóres returns home, is proclaimed king, and marries Blankiflúr. Thanks to the initiative of Blankiflúr, Flóres and his people adopt Christianity. The couple end their days in a nunnery and a monastery, and their son assumes rule of the kingdom.

Probably in the beginning of the 14th century, the Old Norse saga of Flóres and Blankiflúr served as source material for an Old Swedish metrical version, the *Flores och Blanzeflor*, which is the youngest of the three romances of the *Eufemiavisorna*.

Before 1500, the Swedish poem was translated into Danish. The Danish translation is found in two versions, one in Cod. Holm. K 47 from about 1500, the other in two printings from 1504 and 1509. These texts are based on a Swedish version older than the ones now extant.

Ed.: (a) Old Norse: Munch, P. A., ed. "Levninger af norsk Oldlitteratur, nylig opdagede i det norske Rigsarkiv." *Norsk Tidsskrift for Videnskab og Litteratur* 1 (1847), 25–42; Brynjolf Snorrason, ed. "Saga af Flóres ok Blankiflúr, i Grundtexten med Oversættelse." *Annaler for nordisk Oldkyndighed og Historie* (1850), 3–121; Storm, Gustav, ed. "Om Eufemiaviserne." *Nordisk Tidsskrift for Philologi og Pædagogik*, N.S. 1 (1874), 23–43; Kölbing, Eugen, ed. *Flóres saga og Blankiflúr*. Altnordische Saga-Bibliothek, 5. Halle: Niemeyer, 1896. **(b) Swedish**: Klemming, G. E. ed. *Flores och Blanzeflor. En kärleksdikt från medeltiden*. Samlingar utgivna av Svenska fornskrift-sällskapet, 1. Stockholm: Norstedt, 1844; Olson, Emil, ed. *Flores och Blanzeflor. Kritisk upplaga*. Samlingar utgivna af Svenska fornskrift-sällskapet, 46. Lund: Berling, 1921. **(c) Danish**: Brandt, C. J., ed. *Romantisk Digtning fra Middelalderen*. 3 vols. Copenhagen: Samfundet til den danske Literaturs Fremme, 1869–77; Olrik, J., ed. *Danske folkebøger* 6. Copenhagen: Gyldendal, 1925. **(d) French**: Krüger, Felicitas, ed. *Li romanz de Floire et Blancheflor, in beiden Fassungen nach allen Handschriften, mit Einleitung, Namenverzeichnis und Glossar*. Romanische Studien, 45. Berlin: Ebering, 1938; rpt. Nandeln: Kraus, 1967; Pelan, Margaret M., ed. *Floire et Blancheflor: Édition du Ms. 1447 du fonds français avec notes, variantes et glossaire*. Publications de la Faculté des lettres de l'Université de Strasbourg. Textes d'étude, 7. Paris: Les Belles Lettres, 1956; Pelan, Margaret M, ed. *Floire et Blancheflor: seconde version, edité du ms. 19152 du fonds français avec introduction, notes et glossaire*. Paris: Ophrys, 1975; Leclanche, Jean-Luc, ed. *Le conte de Floire et Blancheflor*. Les Classiques Françaises du Moyen Age, 105. Paris: Champion, 1980. **Bib.: (a) Old Norse**: Kalinke, Marianne E., and P. M. Mitchell. *Bibliography of Old Norse–Icelandic Romances*. Islandica, 44. Ithaca and London: Cornell University Press, 1985, pp. 41–5. **(b) Swedish**: Geete, Robert. *Fornsvensk Bibliografi*. Stockholm: Kungl. Boktryckeriet; Norstedt, 1903 [with supplements in 1919 and 1948]. **Lit.: (a) Old Norse**: Barnes, Geraldine Robyn. "The *Riddarasögur*: A Literary and Social Analysis." Diss. University of London, 1974, pp. 174–225; Barnes, Geraldine. "The *riddarasögur* and Mediæval European Literature." *Mediaeval Scandinavia* 8 (1975), 140–58. **(b) Swedish**: Herzog, Hans. "Die beiden Sagenkreise von Flore und Blanscheflur. Eine litteraturhistorische Studie." *Germania* 29, n.s. 17 (1884), 137–228; Olson, E. "Studier över rimmen i den fornsvenska Flores och Blanzeflor." In *Festskrift til K. F. Söderwall på hans sjuttioårsdag den 1 januari 1912*. Lund: Gleerup, 1911. Olson, E.

"Textkritiska studier över den fornsvenska Flores och Blanzeflor." *Arkiv för nordisk filologi* 32 (1916), 129–75, 225–66; Malin, Aarno. "Ett fragment från medeltiden av en hittills okänd textvariant av den fornsvenska Flores och Blanzeflor." *Studier i nordisk filologi* 12.2 (1921), 1–5; Noreen, Erik. *Studier rörande Eufemiavisorna. 1. Textkritiska anmärkningar til Flores och Blanzeflor*. Skrifter utgivna av Kungliga Humanistiska Vetenskapssamfundet i Uppsala, 22.2. Uppsala: Almqvist & Wiksell, 1923. **(c) Other vernacular languages:** Assende, Diederic van, ed. *Floris ende Blanchefloer. Mit Einleitung, Anmerkungen und Glossar hrsg. von Hoffmann von Fallersleben*. Leipzig: Brockhaus, 1836; Keyser, Paul de, ed. *Floris ende Blancefloer*. Klassieke Galerij, 25. Antwerp: Nederlandsche Boekhandel, 1961; Vries, F. C. de, ed. *Floris and Blauncheflur: A Middle English Romance Edited with Introduction, Notes and Glossary*. Groningen: Druk. V. R. B., 1966; Leclanche, Jean-Luc. "Contribution à l'étude de la transmission des plus anciennes oeuvres romanesque françaises. Un cas privilégié: Floire et Blancheflor." 2 vols. Diss. University of Lille, 1980 [bibliography, pp. 364–90].

Birte Carlé

[**See also:** *Eufemiavisorna*; *Riddarasögur*]

Flóvents saga Frakkakonungs ("The Saga of Flóvent, Ruler of the Franks"), a *riddarasaga* from the 13th century, survives in two main redactions, which often complement each other. These versions are represented best by the texts given by AM 580 4to (I) and Stock. Perg. 4to no. 6 (II), from 1300–1350 and around 1400, respectively. A sister MS to AM 580 4to, commonly referred to as "Ormr Snorrason's Book," also contained a text of the saga; however, this MS was lost in the Stockholm fire of 1697 and survives only in independent copies made prior to its destruction, AM 152 fol., AM 570a 4to, Stock. Papp. fol. no. 47, and in snatches of text excerpted therefrom by Swedish lexicographers in the 17th century. In all, twenty-one MSS are extant for the saga text (see Kalinke and Mitchell 1985), as well as a composite Latin translation, extant in two copies, made in the 18th century by Jón Ólafsson of Grunnavík on the basis of six MSS. Faroese ballads and Icelandic *rímur* based on *Flóvents saga* also survive.

At a yuletide feast in Rome, Flóvent, the fifteen-year-old nephew of Emperor Constantine, accidentally spills wine on a haughty duke. Enraged, the duke insults and strikes Flóvent, prompting the latter to strike back so forcibly that the duke's eyes spurt out. After Flóvent leaves the hall, the emperor swears an oath to have him killed and soon sets out after him. In single combat, Flóvent is victorious and takes the ruler's swift steed. Accompanied by his comrades, Otun and Jofrey, Flóvent rides north and finds lodgings at a hermit's house, where he learns that the heathen king Salatres has subjugated most of Frakkland (France), forcing King Flórent to flee to Paris. During the night, an angel appears to the hermit announcing that if Flóvent trusts in God's mercy, he will eventually defeat the heathen king and become ruler of Frakkland. After Flóvent defeats Korsablin, one of four petty rulers allied to Salatres, the heathen king dispatches his son Korduban to wreak vengeance, but he is duly routed at Kourbille. Salatres now enters the fray and is himself wounded in the battle. In a final battle, Salatres surrenders and promises the hand of his daughter Marsibilia to Flóvent. After Marsibilia is baptized, she is wed to Flóvent, now king of Frakkland, who has all the pagan temples either destroyed or turned into churches.

An epilogue recounts the victory of Flóvent over Ammiral, king of Spain; Flóvent's reconciliation with his uncle; his coronation in Rome by Pope Marcius; the marriage of Otun and Fauseta and that of Jofrey and Florenta, King Flórent's daughter; and concludes by mentioning that Marsibilia and Flóvent had splendid sons, and that he died of old age and was buried in Notre Dame.

Despite the insertion at one point in one vellum MS of a proverbial saying given in Old French and then freely rendered in the vernacular, *Flóvents saga* is probably not a translation but, as its rambling style indicates, an adaptation of a lost *chanson de geste*, made in all likelihood during the latter years of the reign of Hákon Hákonarson of Norway (1217–1263). There is no connection, other than that of the hero's name, with the *Chanson de Floovant*. The mischievous prank of cutting the sleeping tutor's beard that sets in motion the stock banishment of the hero found in the French work is quite unlike the evil deed that precipitates exile in the saga. There are some correspondences between *Flóvents saga* and later Middle Dutch and Italian versions, but not enough to indicate direct dependence. The saga operates with such stocks in trade of the *chanson de geste* as the rescue of the Christian warrior by a heathen princess, her conversion and marriage to the hero, the frequent suspension of combat for elevated prayer and lengthy declamation, the enumeration of military forces, the often lavish expressions of mutual admiration by brothers-in-arms, fondness for carnage and mutilation (a quarter of Korsablin's face and his left hand are slashed off), and loud tauntings and ravings, especially on the part of the infidels. But there are some features that are strikingly northern. Here belong such similes as "ýla sem hundar/vargar" ("howl like dogs/wolves"), "bleik sem nár" ("pale as a corpse"), "hǫggr Saxa sem næfrar" ("hews down Saxons like pieces of birch bark"), and certain touches of sly humor. The biblical references, Flovent's prayer in the Muslim temple, the description of the hermit's plain fare, and, above all, the general tone of the work, suggest a pious clerical author who turns to a make-believe world rich in adventure, in which Christianity is militantly triumphant.

Ed.: Cederschiöld, Gustaf, ed. "Flovents saga." In *Fornsögur Suðrlanda. Magus saga jarls, Konraðs saga, Bærings saga, Flovents saga, Bevers saga. Med inledning.* Lund: Berling, 1884, pp. 124–208 [texts of both redactions given in partly diplomatic transcription]. **Bib.**: Kalinke, Marianne E., and P.M. Mitchell. *Bibliography of Old-Norse Icelandic Romances.* Islandica, 44. Ithaca and London: Cornell University Press, 1985. **Lit.**: Bartsch, Karl. "Flovent, Bruchstücke eines mittelniederländischen epischen Gedichtes." *Germania* 9 (1864), 407–36; Darmesteter, Arsène. *De Floovante vetustiore gallico poemate et de merovingo cyclo. Scripsit et adjecit nunc primum edita Olavianam Flovents sagæ versionem et excerpta e Parisiensi codice "Il libro de Fioravante."* Paris: Vieweg, 1877 [provides Jón Ólafsson's Latin rendering (115–71), excerpts in Latin translation from Stock. Papp. fol. no. 47 and BN, Fonds scandinave 23 4to (172–3), and excerpts from *Il libro de Fioravante* as found in BN, Ital. 1,647 4to (174–90)]; Matras, Christian, ed. "Flóvinsríma." In *Svabos Færøske Visehaandskrifter.* Samfund til udgivelse af gammel nordisk litteratur, 59. Copenhagen: Luno, 1939, pp. 451–5; Andolf, Sven, ed. *Floovant. Chanson de geste du XIIᵉ siècle publié avec introduction, notes et glossaire.* Uppsala: Almqvist & Wiksell, 1941; Finnur Sigmundsson. "Flóventsrímur." In *Rímnatal.* 2 vols. Reykjavik: Rímnafélagið, 1966, vol. 1, pp. 143–4 [gives one of the eighteen fits from a 17th-century specimen]; Zitzelsberger, Otto J. "'Ormr Snorrason's Book' and *Flóvents saga Frakkakonungs.*" In *Les Sagas de Chevaliers (Riddarasögur). Actes de la Vᵉ Conférence Internationale sur les Sagas . . . (Toulon. Juillet 1982).* Ed. Régis Boyer. Civilisations, 10. Paris: Presses de l'Université de Paris-Sorbonne, 1985, pp. 265–86.

Otto J. Zitzelsberger

[**See also**: *Riddarasögur; Rímur*]

Folklore. The term "folklore" refers to the nonmaterial manifestations of belief, custom, and artistic creativity in the life of traditional communities. Each of these principal categories of folklore embraces a number of subcategories. Thus, the forms of traditional artistic expression include folk music, dance, and drama, as well as the various genres of what is usually termed folk literature. The genres of folk literature in their turn comprise not only narrative forms like folk epic, folktale, ballad, and legend, but also nonnarrative forms, such as the proverb, riddle, and other "minor genres," including traditional sayings, rhymes, and magic incantations.

Some information on the folklore of Scandinavia in the Middle Ages can be gleaned directly from the testimony of written sources surviving from the period, and more can be deduced from a comparison of this testimony with the folklore records of modern times. The text of this article deals chiefly with the testimony of Old Norse–Icelandic sources, and with the narrative forms of folk literature. The bibliography, on the other hand, lists source materials and studies of Scandinavian folklore in a much broader sense, including East Scandinavian (Danish and Swedish) tradition.

The repertoire of mythical and heroic poems of the *Poetic Edda*, preserved mainly in the *Codex Regius* of the late 13th century, must to a greater or lesser degree reflect traditions of medieval Scandinavian folk epic extending as far back as the Viking Age. These traditions were handed down orally until they were recorded in writing by Icelandic antiquarians of the time of Snorri Sturluson (1178/9–1241). The eddic lays deal with legends of Norse gods and ancient Germanic heroes, such as Sigurd and Ermanaric. They are compact and often allusive, and there is no evidence that the ancient Scandinavians developed long verse epics comparable to the poems of Homer. The sagas of medieval Iceland indicate a taste for extended prose narratives in epic style, but the relationship between existing saga texts and their postulated oral antecedents remains a matter of dispute.

Folktales. According to the international classification developed by Antti Aarne and Stith Thompson, the most important folktale types known to modern tradition can be categorized under the headings of animal tales (AT 1–299), tales of magic (AT 300–749), religious tales (AT 750–849), romantic tales (AT 850–999), and jokes and anecdotes (AT 1200–1999). The folktale as a genre flourished among the ordinary people of Iceland as early as the time of the antiquarian revival around 1200, when Oddr Snorrason in his *Óláfs saga Tryggvasonar* and the anonymous author or redactor of *Sverris saga* both referred condescendingly to popular tales about cruel stepmothers (*stjúpmœðrasǫgur*). This dating does not, of course, imply that all the folktale types known to modern Scandinavian tradition were already in existence in the high Middle Ages. The group of animal tales, for example, seems to have been little known prior to the translation of the international exemplum literature of the Church and of the collections of fables originating in Greek and Roman antiquity. Traces of the oriental tradition of animal tales have been seen in *Auðunar þáttr vestfirzka* and its analogues in *Gautreks saga* and Saxo's *Gesta Danorum*, which would point to an awareness of this tradition in the late 12th century. The main impact of the exemplum literature must, however, be dated to the 14th and 15th centuries, and the classical fable books did not penetrate Scandinavia until after the invention of printing. In general, there seems to be a marked discontinuity between the medieval and modern traditions of animal tales in Scandinavia. Thus, two international tale types probably deriving from the exemplum repertoire (AT 32 *The Wolf Descends into the Well* and AT 47E *Ass's Charter in His Hoof*) are extant in late-medieval Icelandic translation, but have left no trace in modern West Scandinavian tradition.

Reminiscences of popular tales of magic are more frequent in medieval sources. Saxo's story of Frotho can be linked with AT 300 *The Dragon-Slayer*; the frame tale in *Egils saga einhenda ok Ásmundar berserkjabana* resembles AT 301 *The Three Stolen Princesses*; the motif of the life-egg associates an episode in *Bósa saga ok Herrauðs* with AT 302 *The Ogre's (Devil's) Heart in the Egg*; and the *Bjarka þáttr* in *Hrólfs saga kraka* has several motifs in common with AT 303 *The Twins or Blood-Brothers*. The prose explanations accompanying *Vǫlundarkviða* and *Grottasǫngr* in the *Poetic Edda* seem to be early forms of the Swan Maidens (cf. AT 400 *The Man on a Quest for His Lost Wife*) and AT 565 *The Magic Mill*, respectively, while AT 510 *Cinderella* is recognizable in the plot of *Vilmundar saga viðutan*.

The literature of medieval Scandinavia is rich in religious tales. The attitude of the reformed Church was, however, doubtless partly to blame for the loss in more recent centuries of tales with a Roman Catholic flavor. It may be significant that the grateful guest in a genuine Icelandic folk variant of AT 750A-B *The Wishes; Hospitality Rewarded* is neither Christ nor St. Peter, but an anonymous stranger. This variant shares with Irish hagiography and with Snorri's *Gylfaginning* the distinctive motif of breaking the bones of a magic animal to extract the marrow, as related in the episode of Þórr's visit to the giant Útgarða-Loki. Reminiscences of folktales from the other major groups have also been discovered in Old Norse–Icelandic literature: the girl Kraka in *Ragnars saga loðbrókar* resembles the heroine of AT 875 *The Clever Peasant Girl*; the plot of *Klári saga* is a variant of AT 900 *King Thrushbeard*, and has entered modern Icelandic tradition from the saga text despite the fact that the latter bears the hallmarks of literary translation; and among the jokes and anecdotes, we find analogues to AT 1415 *Lucky Hans* in *Gautreks saga*, and to AT 1533 *The Wise Carving of the Fowl* in *Mágus saga*.

Examples like these allow us to form some notion, however hazy, of the content of the medieval folktale repertoire, but they tell us nothing whatsoever about form. As far as Iceland is concerned, it seems reasonable to assume that indigenous oral storytelling shaped the style of the sagas when they were not under the direct influence of foreign models; the evidence of recent folktale records hardly has independent weight in this context because of the uninterrupted reception of the sagas at all levels of Icelandic society right up to modern times.

Ballads. In the case of the ballads, we can have more confidence that the medieval form of the genre is reflected in existing records, though it is often difficult to prove that specific ballads in the documented tradition originated in the Middle Ages. Apart from the survival of some few MS fragments from the 15th century, the principal arguments for the existence of ballads in medieval Scandinavia are linguistic archaisms in some of the inherited texts, the apparent influence of the ballad style on the Swedish *Eufemia* romances from the early 14th century, and the striking fidelity to actual history in some of the ballads purporting to relate events from the 14th, 13th, or even 12th centuries. These arguments are supported by international parallels, especially in the thematically and stylistically related balladry of Scotland and England.

The consensus holds that the ballad genre was fully developed in continental Scandinavia and the Faroe Islands by the 14th century at the latest, whereas the evolution of the genre in Iceland may have been delayed until the end of the Middle Ages. The East Scandinavian ballad corpus is copiously recorded from the 16th century onward in the form of MS anthologies and broadside prints. Icelandic ballads begin to appear in significant quantities in MSS from the second half of the 17th century. In the Faroe Islands and Norway, records commence only with the romantic interest in peasant tradition that was awakened in the late 18th century and flourished in the 19th century. The ballad genre seems to have remained productive longest in the Faroe Islands, where it has maintained its functional relationship with the ring-dance on occasions of public festivity. Distinctively characteristic of the Faroese tradition is the evolution of an extended ballad form subdivided into cantos (*tættir*); a genetic relationship has been postulated between this form and the strophic narrative poetry of late-medieval Iceland (the *rímur*) and England (minstrel romances and ballads).

Following the principles established by the Danish folklorist Svend Grundtvig (1824–1883), modern Scandinavian ballad scholarship commonly classifies the traditional corpus thematically, with ballads of chivalry, legendary ballads, and ballads of the supernatural standing alongside historical, jocular, and heroic ballads. The last-mentioned class is apparently typical of the West Scandinavian area, and draws heavily on material supplied by the late-medieval *fornaldarsögur* and *riddarasögur*. Ballad singers of modern times have thus preserved the substance of narratives dating back four or five centuries, thanks to the remarkable stability of the song tradition in places remote from the main centers of cultural development. At the same time, the ballad repertoire has been enriched by many new compositions in explicit or implicit continuation of the medieval tradition.

Legends. Legends of the mythical and heroic variety are retold in Saxo's *Gesta Danorum*, in Snorri Sturluson's *Gylfaginning* and *Skáldskaparmál*, and in the *fornaldarsögur* and related ballads. The international corpus of medieval religious legends is extensively represented in Old Norse-Icelandic homiletic literature, and in the compilations conventionally referred to as *Maríu saga*, *Heilagra manna sögur*, and *Postola sögur*, while the regional traditions of the Church in Iceland are incorporated in such works as Ari Þorgilsson's *Íslendingabók* and the sagas of Icelandic bishops. The *Landnámabók* records innumerable legends connected with the settlement of Iceland; some are local etiological legends, such as the many explanations of place-names, while others are migratory legends, like the tale of a newly arrived settler's encounter with a prophetic merman, a creature of the fisherman's imagination still known until quite recently in Norway. Settlement legends also figure largely in the preambles to the *Íslendingasögur*, which can be viewed in a general way as the epic codification of legendary traditions attaching to the major landowning dynasties of the country. Such codifications of tradition based on local political and economic interests are also documented from Norway in the postmedieval period, although the level of epic elaboration is not comparable to that of the *Íslendingasögur*. Other points of contact between modern folk legend and the *Íslendingasögur* may be found in the anecdotes of the supernatural and of outlaw existence in works like *Eyrbyggja saga* and *Gísla saga Súrssonar*. A contributing factor in the preservation of ancient legends up to the time of the compilation of the *Íslendingasögur* in the 13th century seems to have been the circulation of skaldic strophes (*lausavísur*) in which the kernel of a given legend was encapsulated.

Nonnarrative genres. The nonnarrative genres of folk literature are more sporadically mirrored in medieval written sources. Proverbs are reproduced in some of the eddic lays, most strikingly in the first and third sections of *Hávamál*, a poem that expresses the cynicism of the Viking Age and undoubtedly transmits indigenous material. The proverbs scattered through legal texts, sagas, and other medieval Norse–Icelandic documents may also be partly indigenous, but at the same time we must reckon with the influence of the sententious literature in Latin that became known through the medieval school curriculum. An unusual literary composition is the *Málsháttakvæði*, an alliterative, rhymed poem of thirty strophes consisting largely of proverbial expressions. This humorous *jeu d'esprit* is often attributed to the 13th-century Orcadian skald Bjarni Kolbeinsson. Systematic collections of proverbs appear in the East Scandinavian area in the late Middle Ages in connection with the name of Peder Låle (original Danish redaction probably of the 14th, Swedish version of the 15th century). The first Icelandic proverb collection is written in the margin of a postmedieval MS of *rímur*. The reception of medieval proverbs in more recent folk tradition has unfortunately not been thoroughly investigated.

Old Norse–Icelandic literature does not preserve much in the way of popular riddles. Of the riddles quoted in a well-known episode of *Hervarar saga ok Heiðreks*, not more than one sixth are known to younger Nordic folk tradition. The situation resembles that in the examples of the riddling ballad known from mainland Scandinavia and the Faroe Islands. Another of the "minor genres" of folk literature about which little information can be extracted from medieval sources is the incantatory list of names associated with religious and magic practice; examples are, however, found in the so-called *þulur* embedded in the eddic lays of *Vǫluspá* and *Grímnismál*. Incantations recorded in modern times have a different frame of reference, often being constructed in imitation of the litanies and prayers of the Church.

Medieval men of letters were in a majority of cases didacticists and exegetes; they had no mission to preserve the lore of the people for its own sake and in unadapted form. Viewed from this perspective, our knowledge of medieval Scandinavian folklore is in fact greater than might have been expected. We owe it to two complementary factors: the eclecticism of medieval authors and compilers, and the relative stability and conservatism of the younger regional tradition.

Abbreviations: AT = type number in Aarne, Antti, and Stith Thompson. *The Types of the Folktale.* Rev. ed. Folklore Fellows Communications, 184. Helsinki: Academia scientiarum Fennica, 1961. **Ed.**: **(a) Iceland**: Jón Árnason and Ólafur Davíðsson, eds. *Íslenzkar gátur, skemtanir, vikivakar og þulur.* 4 vols. Copenhagen: Møller, 1887–1903; Finnur Jónsson, ed. *Íslenzkt málsháttasafn.* Copenhagen: Hið Íslenzka fræðafélag, 1920; Jón Árnason, ed. *Íslenzkar þjóðsögur og ævintýri.* 6 vols. Rev. ed. Árni Böðvarsson and Bjarni Vilhjálmsson. Reykjavik: Þjóðsaga, 1956–61; Jón Helgason, ed. *Íslenzk fornkvæði: islandske folkeviser.* 8 vols. Editiones Arnamagnæanæ, ser. B, vols. 10–17. Copenhagen: Munksgaard, 1962–70 (vols. 1–7); Copenhagen: Reitzel, 1981 (vol. 8). **(b) Faroe Islands**: Jakobsen, Jakob, ed. *Færøske Folkesagn og Æventyr.* Samfund til udgivelse af gammel nordisk litteratur, 27. Copenhagen: Møller, 1898–1901; Matras, Christian, and Napoleon Djurhuus, eds. *Føroya kvæði: Corpus carminum færoensium* 1–. Copenhagen: Universitets-Jubilæets danske Samfund, 1941–; Poulsen, Jóan Chr. *Føroysk orðafelli og orðtøk.* Tórshavn: Varðin,

1957. **(c) Norway**: Bø, Olav, and Svale Solheim, eds. *Norsk folkedikting.* 2nd ed. 7 vols. Oslo: Det norske Samlaget, 1960–71; Blom, Ådel Gjøstein, and Olav Bø, eds. *Norske balladar i oppskrifter frå 1800-tallet.* Oslo: Det norske Samlaget, 1973; Blom, Ådel Gjøstein, ed. *Norske mellomalderballadar. 1: Legendeviser.* Instituttet for sammenlignende kulturforskning, ser. B, vol. 66. Oslo, Bergen, and Tromsø: Universitetsforlaget, 1982. **(d) Denmark**: Grundtvig, Svend, et al., eds. *Danmarks gamle Folkeviser.* 12 vols. Ed. S. H. Grundtvig (vols. 1–5), Axel Olrik and Hakan Grüner-Nielsen (vols. 6–9), H. Grüner-Nielsen et al. (vol. 10), Hjalmar Thuren et al. (vol. 11), Sven H. Rossel et al. (vol. 12). Copenhagen: Samfundet til den danske Literaturs Fremme; Universitets-Jubilæets danske Samfund, 1853–1976; Kristensen, Evald Tang, ed. *Æventyr fra Jylland.* 4 vols. Copenhagen and Århus: Schønberg, 1881–97; Kristensen, Evald Tang, ed. *Danske Ordsprog og Mundheld, Skjæmtsprog, stedlige Talemåder, Slagord og Samtaleord.* Copenhagen: Gyldendal, 1890; Kristensen, Evald Tang, ed. *Danske Sagn som de har lydt i Folkemunde.* 1st ser., 8 vols. Copenhagen: Busck, 1980 [new edition of 1892–1901 publication]; 2nd ser., 7 vols. Copenhagen: Woel, 1928–39; Ohrt, F. *Danmarks Trylleformler.* 2 vols. Copenhagen and Christiania [Oslo]: Gyldendal; Nordisk Forlag, 1917–21; Kjær, Iver, and Bengt Holbek. *Ordsprog i Danmark.* Copenhagen: Paludan, 1969. **(e) Sweden/Swedish Finland**. *Finlands svenska folkdiktning.* Vols. 1–8. Helsingfors and Åbo: Svenska litteratursällskapet, 1917–67; Ström, Fredrik, ed. *Svenska folkgåtor.* Stockholm: Bonnier, 1939; Liungman, Waldemar, ed. *Sveriges samtliga folksagor i ord och bild.* 3 vols. Stockholm: Lindfors, 1949–52; Liungman, Waldemar, ed. *Sveriges sägner i ord och bild.* 7 vols. Stockholm and Djursholm: Vald litteratur, 1957–69; Klintberg, Bengt af, ed. *Svenska trollformler.* Stockholm: Wahlström och Widstrand, 1965; *Sveriges medeltida ballader.* Svenskt visarkiv, vols. 1–. Stockholm: Almqvist & Wiksell, 1983–. **Tr.**: Powell, George E. J., and Eiríkur Magnússon, trans. *Icelandic Legends.* 2 vols. London: Bentley, 1864–66; Craigie, William A., trans. *Scandinavian Folk-Lore.* Paisley and London: Gardner, 1896; Bay, Jens Christian, trans. *Danish Family & Folk Tales.* New York and London: Harper, 1899; Olrik, Axel, ed. *A Book of Danish Ballads.* Trans. E. M. Smith-Dampier. Princeton: Princeton University Press; New York: American-Scandinavian Foundation, 1939; Christiansen, Reidar Th., ed. *Folktales of Norway.* Trans. Pat Shaw Iversen. Chicago: University of Chicago Press; London: Routledge and Kegan Paul, 1964; Dal, Erik, ed. *Danish Ballads and Folk Songs.* Trans. Henry Meyer. Copenhagen: Rosenkilde & Bagger; New York: American-Scandinavian Foundation, 1967; Simpson, Jacqueline, trans. *Icelandic Folktales and Legends.* London: Batsford; Berkeley: University of California Press, 1972; Lindow, John, trans. *Swedish Legends and Folktales.* Berkeley: University of California Press, 1978; West, John F., trans. *Faroese Folk-Tales and Legends.* Lerwick: Shetland, 1980; Rossel, Sven H., trans. *Scandinavian Ballads.* Wisconsin Introductions to Scandinavia, 2.2. Madison: University of Wisconsin, Department of Scandinavian Studies, 1982; Simpson, Jacqueline, ed. and trans. *Scandinavian Folktales.* London: Penguin, 1988; Kvideland, Reimund, and Henning K. Sehmsdorf, eds. *Scandinavian Folk Belief and Legend.* Minneapolis: University of Minnesota, 1988. **Lit.**: Leyen, Friedrich von der. *Das Märchen in den Göttersagen der Edda.* Berlin: Reimer, 1899; Berge, Rikard. "Norsk Eventyrstil, I-VIII." *Norsk folkekultur* 1 (1915), 12–21; 3 (1917), 145–50; 4 (1918), 49–79; 5 (1919), 156–72; 7 (1921), 64–8; 12 (1926), 64–72; 16 (1930), 118–22; 19 (1933), 41–65; Olrik, Axel, and Hans Ellekilde. *Nordens Gudeverden.* 2 vols. Copenhagen: Gad, 1926–51; Einar Ól. Sveinsson. *Verzeichnis isländischer Märchenvarianten.* Folklore Fellows Communications, 83. Helsinki: Academia scientiarum Fennica, 1929; Leistøl, Knut, ed. *Folkevisor,* and Sydow, C. W. von, ed. *Folksägner och folksagor.* Nordisk kultur, 9A-9B. Stockholm: Bonnier; Oslo: Aschehoug; Copenhagen: Schultz, 1931; Götlind, Johan, ed. *Idrott och lek,* and

Nielsen, H. Grüner, ed. *Dans*. Nordisk kultur, 24A-24B. Stockholm: Bonnier; Oslo: Aschehoug; Copenhagen: Schultz, 1933; Jónas Jónasson. *Íslenzkir þjóðhættir*. Ed. Einar Ól. Sveinsson. Reykjavik: Ísafold, 1934; Andersson, Otto, ed. *Musik och musikinstrument*. Nordisk kultur, 25. Stockholm: Bonnier; Oslo: Aschehoug; Copenhagen: Schultz, 1934; Christiansen, Reidar Th. "Til de norske sjøvetters historie: vandring og stedegent." *Maal og minne* (1935), 1–25; Lid, Nils, ed. *Folketru*. Nordisk kultur, 19. Stockholm: Bonnier; Oslo: Aschehoug; Copenhagen: Schultz, 1935; Nilsson, Martin P:n, ed. *Årets högtider*. Nordisk kultur, 22. Stockholm: Bonnier; Oslo: Aschehoug; Copenhagen: Schultz, 1938; Wikman, K. Rob. von, ed. *Livets högtider*. Nordisk kultur, 20. Stockholm: Bonnier; Oslo: Aschehoug; Copenhagen: Schultz, 1949; Liungman, Waldemar. *Das wahrscheinliche Alter des Volksmärchens in Schweden*. Folklore Fellows Communications, 156. Helsinki: Academia scientiarum Fennica, 1955; Dal, Erik. *Nordisk folkeviseforskning siden 1800: Omrids af text- og melodistudiets historie og problemer især i Danmark*. Universitets-Jubilæets danske Samfund, 376. Copenhagen: Schultz, 1956; Christiansen, Reidar Th. *The Migratory Legends: A Proposed List of Types with a Systematic Catalogue of the Norwegian Variants*. Folklore Fellows Communications, 175. Helsinki: Academia scientiarum Fennica, 1958; rpt. New York: Arno, 1977; Bødker, Laurits. "Eventyr." *KLNM* 4 (1959), 71–6; Alver, Brynjulf, and Anne Holtsmark. "Gåter." *KLNM* 5 (1960), 648–53; Hermann Pálsson. *Sagnaskemmtun íslendinga*. Reykjavik: Mál og menning, 1962; Andersson, Theodore M. *The Problem of Icelandic Saga Origins: A Historical Survey*. Yale Germanic Studies, 1. New Haven and London: Yale University Press, 1964; Bødker, Laurits, *et al. The Nordic Riddle: Terminology and Bibliography*. Nordisk Institut for Folkedigtning, Skrifter, 3. Copenhagen: Rosenkilde & Bagger, 1964; Steindór Steindórsson. *Skrá um íslenzkar þjóðsögur og skyld rit*. Reykjavik: Þjóðsaga, 1964; Wikander, Stig. "Från indisk djurfabel till isländsk saga." *Vetenskaps-societeten i Lund. Årsbok* (1964), 87–114; Boberg, Inger M. *Motif-Index of Early Icelandic Literature*. Bibliotheca Arnamagnæana, 27. Copenhagen: Munksgaard, 1966; Kjær, Iver, *et al.* "Ordsprog." *KLNM* 12 (1967), 672–84; Hodne, Bjarne. *Personalhistoriske sagn: en studie i kildeverdi*. [Oslo]: Universitetsforlaget, 1973; Holzapfel, Otto. *Bibliographie zur mittelalterlichen skandinavischen Volksballade*. NIF Publications, 4. Turku: Nordic Institute of Folklore, 1975; Jonsson, Bengt R., *et al.*, eds. *The Types of the Scandinavian Medieval Ballad: A Descriptive Catalogue*. Institutet for sammenlignende kulturforskning, ser. B, vol. 59. Skrifter utgivna av Svenskt visarkiv, 5. Stockholm: Svenskt visarkiv; Oslo, Bergen, and Tromsø: Universitetsforlaget, 1978; Nolsøe, Mortan. "The Faroese Heroic Ballad and Its Relations to Other Genres." In *The European Medieval Ballad: A Symposium*. Ed. Otto Holzapfel *et al.* Odense: Odense University Press, 1978, pp. 61–6; Buchholz, Peter. *Vorzeitkunde: Mündliches Erzählen und Überliefern im mittelalterlichen Skandinavien nach dem Zeugnis von Fornaldarsaga und eddischer Dichtung*. Skandinavistische Studien, 13. Neumünster: Wachholtz, 1980; Vésteinn Ólason. *The Traditional Ballads of Iceland*. Reykjavik: Stofnun Árna Magnússonar, 1982; Hodne, Ørnulf. *The Types of the Norwegian Folktale*. Institutet for sammenlignende kulturforskning, ser. B, vol. 68. Oslo, Bergen, and Tromsø: Universitetsforlaget, 1984.

Michael Chesnutt

[**See also:** *Auðunar þáttr vestfirzka*; Ballads; *Bósa saga ok Herrauðs*; *Codex Regius*; Eddic Poetry; *Egils saga einhenda ok Ásmundar berserkjabana*; Eufemiavisorna; *Eyrbyggja saga*; Exempla; *Fornaldarsögur*; *Gautreks saga*; *Gísla saga Súrssonar*; *Grímnismál*; *Grottasǫngr*; *Hávamál*; *Hervarar saga ok Heiðreks konungs*; *Hrólfs saga kraka*; *Íslendingabók*; *Landnámabók*; *Lausavísur*; *Maríu saga*; Mythology; *Óláfs saga*

Tryggvasonar; *Postola sögur*; *Ragnars saga loðbrókar*; *Riddarasögur*; Riddles; *Rímur*; Saints' Lives; Saxo Grammaticus; *Snorra Edda*; *Vilmundar saga viðutan*; *Vǫlundarkviða*; *Vǫluspá*]

Forename *see* Fornafn

Fornafn (pl. *fornǫfn*) is an Old Norse noun occurring only in handbooks of grammar and poetics. There is good reason to believe (Tryggvi Gíslason 1967:110–1) that *fornafn* is an Old Icelandic calque on the Latin noun *pronomen* 'pronoun,' and is used in that sense by both Óláfr Þórðarson hvítaskáld ("white skald") in his *Third Grammatical Treatise* of about 1245–1252 (Björn M. Ólsen 1884:57) and, earlier, by his uncle Snorri Sturluson in the fourth section of his *Edda* (ca. 1225) named *Háttatal* or "List of Verse-forms" (ed. Finnur Jónsson 1931:214; trans. Faulkes 1987: 166). In the third section of the *Edda*, named *Skáldskaparmál* or "Poetic Diction," Snorri uses *fornafn* to refer to one of three major kinds of poetic diction in skaldic verse, the other two being *heiti* and *kenning* (Finnur Jónsson 1931:86; Faulkes 1987:64). Here, his usage is stylistic rather than grammatical.

Toward the end of *Skáldskaparmál*, Snorri differentiates two subclasses of *fornafn*, which he calls *viðrkenning* 'circumlocution, clear acknowledgment' and *sannkenning* 'true description,' saying that these terms "are put in place of men's names" (Finnur Jónsson 1931:188; Faulkes 1987:152). He gives some examples of *fornǫfn*. It would be *viðrkenning* to name a man by referring to his kin or his dwelling or his ship, if it has a name, or by one of his named possessions. So we might call the god Þórr the owner of his famous hammer Mjǫllnir. The *sannkenning* is a descriptive word or phrase, like "munificent one," for a man or woman.

Halldór Halldórsson (1975:25–7) argued that for the second, stylistic sense of *fornafn*, Snorri had in mind the trope known in Latin grammars and rhetorical handbooks as *pronominatio*. It could also be called *antonomasia*, the term Óláfr Þórðarson used (Björn M. Ólsen 1884:106). Snorri's cited examples of *fornǫfn* correspond fairly closely to the usage of treatises like the *Rhetorica ad Herennium*, which represents *pronominatio* as a descriptive epithet or a phrase referring to family connections instead of an individual's proper name, like "grandsons of Africanus" for the Gracchi. It is possible that Snorri used the term *fornafn* in both a grammatical and a stylistic sense because he was aware of the classical and medieval grammarians' understanding that the pronoun replaced only proper nouns in discourse, just as the figures he calls *viðrkenning* and *sannkenning* stood only for namable anthropomorphic referents of skaldic verse (Clunies Ross 1987:64–79).

Ed.: Björn Magnússon Ólsen, ed. *Den Tredje og Fjærde Grammatiske Afhandling i Snorres Edda. Tilligemed de Grammatiske Afhandlingers Prolog og To Andre Tillæg*. Samfund til udgivelse af gammel nordisk litteratur, 12. Islands grammatiske litteratur i middelaldren, 2. Copenhagen: Knudtzon, 1884; Finnur Jónsson. *Edda Snorra Sturlusonar*. Copenhagen: Gyldendal, 1931. **Tr.**: Faulkes, Anthony, trans. *Snorri Sturluson: Edda*. Everyman Classics. London and Melbourne: Dent, 1987. **Bib.**: Bekker-Nielsen, Hans. *Old Norse-Icelandic Studies: A Select Bibliography*. Toronto Medieval Bibliographies, 1. Toronto: University of Toronto Press, 1967. **Lit.**: Brodeur, Arthur G. "The Meaning of Snorri's Categories." *University of California Publications in Modern Philology* 36 (1952), 129–47; Collings, Lucy G. "The 'Málskrúðsfræði' and the Latin Tradition in Iceland." M.A. thesis,

Cornell University, 1967; Tryggvi Gíslason. "Íslenzk Málfræðiheiti miðalda-merking, þeirra fyrirmyndir og saga." Mag. art. diss., University of Iceland, 1967; Halldór Halldórsson. *Old Icelandic Heiti in Modern Icelandic.* University of Iceland Publications in Linguistics, 3. Reykjavik: Institute of Nordic Linguistics, 1975; Clunies Ross, Margaret. *Skáldskaparmál: Snorri Sturluson's ars poetica and Medieval Theories of Language.* Viking Collection, 4. Odense: Odense University Press, 1987.

Margaret Clunies Ross

[**See also:** Grammatical Treatises; *Heiti*; Kennings; *Snorra Edda*]

Fornaldarsögur ("sagas of antiquity"), also referred to as Mythical-Heroic Sagas and Legendary Sagas, comprise a group of approximately thirty late-medieval Icelandic texts. Neither the term *fornaldarsögur* nor the genre designation is traditional; both derive from modern treatments and collections of secular romances, especially those of Müller (1818) and Rafn (1829). Few critics would disagree, however, that these narratives, with their fondness for ancient settings, far-flung geographies, and one-dimensional heroes, do constitute a separate category of sagas. Although there is consensus as to the texts that should be regarded as *fornaldarsögur*, attempts to articulate a definition of the genre have been notably few. Based on the most important features the genre displays, the *fornaldarsögur* can, however, be characterized as Icelandic prose narratives based on traditional heroic themes, whose numerous fabulous episodes and motifs result in an atmosphere of unreality.

Any such designation must exclude tales that are similar in many formal respects, but that have borrowed their themes and heroes from abroad (*e.g.*, *Hjálmþés saga ok Ǫlvis, Eiríks saga víðfǫrla, Friðþjófs saga froekna,* all of which have at one time or another been included among the *fornaldarsögur*). Although tales with such foreign origins often center on quests and contain folkloric materials, recurrent characters, and stylized narration, they should not be confused with the indigenous *fornaldarsögur*, whose materials display a lengthy continuity within the Nordic cultural context and project a different ethos. While the fabulous nature of the *fornaldarsögur* can be evaluated only from the modern point of view, there is little doubt that similar judgments would have been made by contemporary Icelanders as well. The assessment of what a medieval Icelander would have believed possible or impossible is naturally a relative one, but one need only compare the soberness of the *Íslendingasögur* with the time compressions, talking animals, pagan theophanies, metamorphoses, and supernatural beings of the *fornaldarsögur* to see how uncomplicated this division is. Even where the *Íslendingasögur* treat the supernatural (*e.g.*, premonitions and visions), they tend to do so for specific dramatic effect, unlike the comic and mystifying impression often generated in the *fornaldarsögur*.

Temporally and spatially, the *fornaldarsögur* are unique among the native sagas as well. Time is frequently treated in the *fornaldarsögur* in the same way it is dealt with in folktales: it is simply ignored at the narrative level. When, for example, the hero of *Gǫngu-Hrólfs saga* has his feet cut off and later reattached, the text has no interest in letting us know whether this event takes place on the same day or several days, perhaps even weeks later. Likewise, the historical settings of the *fornaldarsögur* are either left unspecified or, where indicated, said to be some remote period before the colonization of Iceland. In either case, time references have a completely different nature from the nearly ubiquitous opening "þat var á dǫgum Haralds konungs ins hárfagra" ("It was in the days of King Haraldr Fair-hair") and the like of the *Íslendingasögur*. The treatment of geography in the *fornaldarsögur* is also reminiscent of folklore attitudes: although countries and cities are commonly named, they are merely ciphers for exotic settings, not carefully detailed locations. What they lack in precision, however, the *fornaldarsögur* make up in breadth, for the action of these sagas frequently occurs outside Scandinavia; France, Ireland, Russia, the Holy Land, and the otherworld all figure in them. But here, too, there is an air of unreality about these sagas that derives from what has been called the undefined landscape of Teutonic epic; it evokes a mood, but it does not detail a setting. Both features stand in stark contrast to the elaborate networks of temporal and spatial frames of reference in which the realistic saga genres, *Íslendingasögur, konungasögur, biskupasögur,* and *Sturlunga saga*, delight.

Several prominent, and occasionally overlapping, subcategories of *fornaldarsögur* exist: the "Adventure Tales" and the "Heroic Legends." To some degree, these designations correspond to comic and tragic modes within the genre. Occasionally, a third group ("Viking Sagas") is culled from among the previous two based on the hero's vocation. The "Adventure Tales" can be identified by such elements as the closeness of their structures and heroic biographies to the folktale and by the generally happy conclusion to the hero's quest: the acquistion of a wife and kingdom, the release of a companion, and so on. They include *Áns saga bogsveigis, Bósa saga, Egils saga einhenda ok Ásmundar berserkjabana, Gǫngu-Hrólfs saga, Gríms saga loðinkinna, Hálfdanar saga Brǫnufóstra, Hálfdanar saga Eysteinssonar, Hrólfs saga Gautrekssonar, Hrómundar saga Gripssonar, Illuga saga Gríðarfóstra, Ketils saga hoengs, Sturlaugs saga starfsama, Sǫrla saga sterka, Þorsteins þáttr boejarmagns, Þorsteins saga Víkingssonar,* and *Ǫrvar-Odds saga.* The "Heroic Legends," on the other hand, are usually tragic, with the hero's death often brought about through treachery, and their protagonists are frequently paralleled elsewhere in Germanic literature; they include *Ásmundar saga kappabana, Hálfs saga ok Hálfsrekka, Hervarar saga ok Heiðreks konungs, Hrólfs saga kraka, Ragnars saga loðbrókar, Sǫrla þáttr, Vǫlsunga saga, Yngvars saga víðfǫrla,* and *Þáttr af Ragnars sonum.* In addition, *Nornagests þáttr* and *Tóka þáttr Tókasonar* might well be added to this list. These two works deal with legendary figures (*e.g.*, Sigurðr Fáfnisbani, Hrólfr kraki, Hálfr Hjǫrleifsson), but such epic characters are used only as a means of establishing the venerable ages and remarkable careers of the protagonists. The placement of the tales among the "Heroic Legends" is troublesome, since while the *þættir* are clearly related to such works, they are themselves hardly "Heroic Legends."

Indeed, none of the assignments suggested above should be regarded as rigid; legitimate arguments can, for example, be advanced for designating a text like *Sǫrla þáttr* an "Adventure Tale" and for deleting *Yngvars saga víðfǫrla* from the "Heroic Legends," although it by no means fits easily into the "Adventure Tale" category. *Helga þáttr Þórissonar* has its closest structural and thematic analogues among saints' legends and local legends and cannot be easily placed within any of the normal subdivisions of the *fornaldarsögur*. A work like *Gautreks saga* defies simple classification: its first section, which treats the hero Starkaðr, belongs among the "Heroic Legends," while its latter portion, the so-called

Gjafa-Refs þáttr, neatly embodies the qualities of an "Adventure Tale." Moreover, three Old Norse texts, *Fundinn Nóregr, Hversu Nóregr byggðisk*, and *Sǫgubrot af fornkonungum*, are not properly *fornaldarsögur* since they are nonnarrative, but treat materials of great relevance to the *fornaldarsögur*. The number of *fornaldarsögur* would increase considerably if texts closely related by virtue of contents, but to a much lesser extent form and style, were to be included (*e.g., Ynglinga saga, Þiðreks saga af Bern*). However, other than similarity of subject matter, there appears to be little justification for reckoning these works among the actual *fornaldarsögur*. The difficulties involved in arranging the *fornaldarsögur* into neat subdivisions have led some modern critics to discuss the *fornaldarsögur* in terms of their relation to such external categories as myth, folktale, history, and heroic poetry.

In addition to the texts enumerated above, a number of "lost" *fornaldarsögur* are known to have existed. Most important among these vanished texts is **Skjǫldunga saga*, ample evidence of which exists to establish the outline of its contents. With varying degrees of certainty, the following texts can also be suggested as "lost *fornaldarsögur*": **Andra saga jarls, *Ásmundar saga flagðagæfu, *Gríms saga ok Hjálmars, *Haralds saga Hringsbana, *Hróks saga svarta, *Huldar saga, *Illuga saga eldhússgóða, *Ormars saga, Úlfhamssaga*, and **Þóris saga háleggs*. In some instances, these works are referred to in other sagas, while in others we have only the testimony of the lost saga's legacy in other, later genres.

The extant *fornaldarsögur* date largely from the Icelandic 14th and 15th centuries, but the *traditions* on which they are based are well attested throughout northern Europe and can, in some instances, be reliably dated to much earlier periods. Thus, while a well-known work like *Vǫlsunga saga* exists only in a single medieval MS, the narrative that forms its core is documented over vast expanses of time and space and in a wide array of media: in plastic representations (*e.g.*, the Ramsund petroglyph in Sweden, the Andreas carving on the Isle of Man, Norwegian stave-church carvings); in other genres of Norse literature (*e.g.*, the *Poetic Edda*, the *Prose Edda*); and in related Germanic traditions (*e.g., Beowulf, Das Nibelungenlied*).

Continuity or traditionality is, then, a key concept in the delineation of the *fornaldarsögur* as a group; but while the extant texts are traditional at base, they belong to an acquisitive and highly eclectic genre. Thus, while mythological, folkloric, and native literary traditions from earlier periods are used in composing these narratives, so too are literary texts from abroad and components of the learned clerical culture (*e.g.*, encyclopedic literature). It is difficult to read *Yngvars saga víðfǫrla*, for example, without believing that its authors were familiar with *Alfræði íslenzk* (AM 194 8vo) or some similar compendium of learned lore from which certain details have been culled. Typically, however, such foreign sources play only an ornamental, and not a substantive, role in the *fornaldarsögur*.

The *fornaldarsögur* enjoyed great and enduring popularity, a fact attested to by the substantial numbers of MSS in which they survive, including many from after the Reformation. Some of their titles even appear in inventories of the holdings of medieval Icelandic church libraries. The MS preservation of the *fornaldarsögur* as a group defies simple description, although it may be said that there are several medieval codices that tend to be made up solely of *fornaldarsögur* and other "romantic" sagas (*e.g.*, AM 152 fol., AM 343a 4to, GkS 2845 4to). In general, the MS histories of the individual *fornaldarsögur* are highly varied. *Hrólfs saga kraka* is

known only in post-Reformation MSS; *Hálfs saga ok Hálfsrekka* has but one extant medieval attestation; *Helga þáttr Þórissonar* is an embedded tale within the *Longest Saga of Óláfr Tryggvason* in *Flateyjarbók*; and *Ǫrvar-Odds saga* exists in five medieval MSS containing several highly distinct versions. As this last example indicates, the recensions of the *fornaldarsögur* can vary widely with regard to expansions, interpolations, and interpretations.

The considerable age of the settings of the sagas and the dates from which the historical figures occasionally encountered in them originate (*e.g.*, Ragnarr loðbrók ["hairy breeches"]) often result in the impression that the *fornaldarsögur* constitute the oldest group of sagas. In fact, the opposite situation obtains, for while the traditions on which the texts are based are typically archaic, the written *fornaldarsögur* themselves are among the most recent innovations of saga literature. There is evidence that *fornaldarsögur* were recited orally (*e.g., Þorgils saga ok Hafliða, Sturlu saga*), but of these oral versions we know little of substance, other than their existence. And despite the fact that the heroes and villains of the tales are commonly Norwegians, Danes, and Swedes, the *fornaldarsögur* are a decidedly Icelandic genre, although much can be learned about the traditions behind the *fornaldarsögur* from such non-Icelandic works as the *Gesta Danorum* of Saxo Grammaticus.

The fact that the *fornaldarsögur* flourished in the postclassical-saga period indicates a kind of revitalization in Icelandic literature. To a large extent, these sagas may justifiably be regarded as a literature intended to entertain, rather than to edify or inform. Unfortunately, the tendency of many modern critics has been to assume that the *fornaldarsögur* may thereby be dismissed as escapist literature (referred to as the "Verfall theory"). In fact, while there is little reason to doubt that these narratives were pleasantly diversionary, their function in late-medieval Icelandic literature was multifaceted. In a period of national distress and cultural retrogression due to geological, meteorological, political, and demographic factors, the *fornaldarsögur* represented a conduit to a glorious heroic past. As an antiquarian literature that developed in the postclassical-saga period, the *fornaldarsögur* fulfilled an important cultural and psychological function in addition to their robustly entertaining value. Certainly, leading Icelanders would have been well served by the recording of their legendary ancestors' exploits; such an argument may be made, for example, for the family of the Oddaverjar in the case of **Skjǫldunga saga*. No doubt, prominent Icelanders found the *fornaldarsögur* useful amplifications of information contained in family genealogies. One notes, for example, that Ari fróði ("the learned") does not hesitate to trace his own genealogy back to the legendary heroes and pagan gods in *Íslendingabók*; the impulse for the Icelanders to prove that they too, like their more established Nordic neighbors, had connections to the Scandinavian heroic age must have been powerful. One MS of *Landnámabók* suggests that just such a motivation accounts for the Icelanders' unparalleled interest in history and legend: "Enn uier þikiumst helldur suara kunna utlendum monnum. Þa er þeir bregda oz þui ad uier sieum komner af þrælum eda illmennum, ef vier vitum vijst vorar kynferdir sannar" ("But we can better answer the criticism of foreigners when they accuse us of coming from slaves or rogues, if we know for certain the truth about our ancestry"; *Melabók*, ch. 335).

The materials on which the *fornaldarsögur* are centered also find expression in the ballad traditions of the Faroes, Norway, Sweden, and Denmark and in the Icelandic metrical romances (*rímur*). In some instances, the relationships are fairly well understood, as when a now-lost *Hrómundar saga Gripssonar* gave rise to a *ríma*, a text on which the relatively modern *Hrómundar saga Gripssonar* was based. In other cases, such neat diachronic developments were surely not in force. Thus, any attempt to account for the evolutionary history of the materials relevant to *Hervarar saga ok Heiðreks konungs*, a group that includes eddic poetry, Saxo's *Gesta Danorum*, several *rímur*, the saga itself, as well as Faroese, Swedish, and Danish ballads, and even a refrain from the Icelandic ballad corpus, will demand a heavily reticulated stemma. Among the *fornaldarsögur* with *rímur* from before 1600 are *Áns saga bogsveigis*, *Bósa saga*, *Egils saga ok Ásmundar berserkjabana*, *Gǫngu-Hrólfs saga*, *Hálfdanar saga Brǫnufóstra*, *Hálfdanar saga Eysteinssonar*, *Hrólfs saga Gautrekssonar*, *Hrólfs saga kraka*, *Sǫrla þáttr*, *Sturlaugs saga starfsama*, *Vǫlsunga saga*, and *Þorsteins saga Víkingssonar*. The following *fornaldarsögur* are paralleled wholly or partially by non-Icelandic ballads: *Ásmundar saga kappabana*, *Hálfs saga ok Hálfsrekka*, *Hervarar saga ok Heiðreks konungs*, *Hrólfs saga Gautrekssonar*, *Illuga saga Gríðarfóstra*, *Ketils saga hœngs*, *Nornagests þáttr*, *Ragnars saga loðbrókar*, *Sǫrla saga sterka*, *Vǫlsunga saga*, and *Ǫrvar-Odds saga*. Curiously, only *Hrólfs saga Gautrekssonar* and *Vǫlsunga saga* are represented in both catagories, and it should be noted that only a very few texts do not have analogues or descendants in one or the other of these genres.

When modern, non-Icelandic interest in the sagas was ignited in Denmark and Sweden in the 17th century, the focus was largely on the *fornaldarsögur*, for they were believed to contain testimony about the earliest histories of the two kingdoms. Once the value of the *fornaldarsögur* as historical documents had been cast in doubt, however, the tales generally fared poorly in the hands of critics, except insofar as they were believed capable of shedding light on important heroic figures like Sigurðr-Siegfried. Modern critical reactions to the *fornaldarsögur* have been quite negative overall: judged by the Aristotelian views that are appropriate largely to the *Íslendingasögur*, the *fornaldarsögur* can hardly escape critical condemnation, given the affection they evince for recurrent tale types (*e.g.*, AT 1137, *The Ogre Blinded* [*Polyphemus*]), well-worn motifs (*e.g.*, R53.1 *Woman Hidden in Underground Chamber, Hill, or Mud Cabin*), and stock characters (*e.g.*, the "donor" figure). Part of this misevaluation of the *fornaldarsögur* can no doubt be traced to a generally inadequate appreciation for the relationship these texts bear to folklore forms. Moreover, there is a tendency to regard the *fornaldarsögur* as relics of the Viking Age, but they will only be understood when they are approached as the means by which late-medieval Icelanders themselves looked back at the Heroic Age. As these two aspects of the *fornaldarsögur* are incorporated into our views of them, the *fornaldarsögur* will take a more highly regarded place in our discussions of Icelandic literary and cultural history.

Ed. [see individual saga entries for critical editions]: Rafn, C. C., ed. *Fornaldar sögur Nordrlanda*. 3 vols. Copenhagen: Popp, 1829–30; Guðni Jónsson, ed. *Fornaldar sögur Norðurlanda*. 4 vols. Akureyri: Íslendingasagnaútgáfan, 1954. **Tr.**: Müller, R. E., trans. *Sagabibliothek* 2. Copenhagen: Schultz, 1818 [Danish; for English, see individual saga entries]. **Bib.**: Halldór Hermannsson. *Bibliography of the Mythical-Heroic Sagas*. Islandica, 5. Ithaca: Cornell University Library, 1912; rpt. New York: Kraus, 1966; Halldór Hermannsson. *The Sagas of the Kings (Konunga sögur) and the Mythical-Heroic Sagas (Fornaldar sögur): Two Bibliographical Supplements*. Islandica, 26. Ithaca: Cornell University Press, 1937; Einar Ól. Sveinsson. *Verzeichnis isländischer Märchenvarianten, mit einer einleitenden Untersuchung*. Folklore Fellows Communications, 83. Helsinki: Academia Scientiarum Fennica, 1929; *Bibliography of Old Norse–Icelandic Studies* 1– (1963–); Boberg, Inger M. *Motif-Index of Early Icelandic Literature*. Bibliotheca Arnamagnæana, 27. Copenhagen: Munksgaard, 1966. **Lit.**: Liestøl, Knut. *Norske trollvisor og norrøne sogor*. Kristiania [Oslo]: Norli, 1915 [see for ballads and legendary sagas]; Olrik, Axel. *The Heroic Legends of Denmark*. Trans. Lee M. Hollander. New York: American-Scandinavian Foundation, 1919; Schneider, Hermann. *Germanische Heldensage*. 3 vols. Grundriss der germanischen Philologie, 10. Berlin: de Gruyter, 1928–34; Reuschel, Helga. *Untersuchungen über Stoff und Stil der Fornaldarsaga*. Bausteine zur Volkskunde und Religionswissenschaft, 17. Bühl-Baden: Konkordia, 1933; Schlauch, Margaret. *Romance in Iceland*. Princeton: Princeton University Press; New York: American-Scandinavian Foundation; London: Allen & Unwin, 1934; rpt. New York: Russell & Russell, 1973; Genzmer, Felix. "Vorzeitsaga und Heldenlied." In *Festschrift Paul Kluckhohn und Hermann Schneider gewidmet zu ihrem 60. Geburtstag*. Tübingen: Mohr, 1948, pp. 1–31; Toorn, M. C. van den. "Über die Ethik in den Fornaldarsagas." *Acta Philologica Scandinavica* 26 (1964), 19–66; Holtsmark, Anne. "Heroic Poetry and Legendary Sagas." *Bibliography of Old Norse–Icelandic Studies* (1965), 9–21; Liestøl, Knut. *Den norrøne arven*. Oslo: Universitetsforlaget, 1970 [English summary, "The Norse Heritage"; see for ballads and legendary sagas]; Hermann Pálsson and Paul Edwards. *Legendary Fiction in Medieval Iceland*. Studia Islandica, 30. Reykjavik: Heimspekideild Háskóla Íslands, Menningarsjóður, 1971; Hermann Pálsson. "Early Icelandic Imaginative Literature." In *Medieval Narrative: A Symposium*. Ed. Hans Bekker-Nielsen et al. Odense: Odense University Press, 1979, pp. 20–30; Righter-Gould, Ruth. "The Fornaldar Sögur Norðurlanda: A Structural Analysis." *Scandinavian Studies* 52 (1980), 423–41; Buchholz, Peter. *Vorzeitkunde: Mündliches Erzählen und Überliefern im mittelalterlichen Skandinavien nach dem Zeugnis von Fornaldarsaga und eddischer Dichtung*. Skandinavistische Studien, 13. Neumünster: Wachholtz, 1980; Hallberg, Peter. "Some Aspects of the Fornaldarsögur as a Corpus." *Arkiv för nordisk filologi* 97 (1982), 1–35; Hermann Pálsson. "Fornaldarsögur." In *Dictionary of the Middle Ages*. Ed. Joseph R. Strayer. New York: Scribner, 1982–89, vol. 5, pp. 137–43; Kalinke, Marianne. "Norse Romance (*Riddarasögur*)." In *Old Norse–Icelandic Literature: A Critical Guide*. Ed. Carol J. Clover and John Lindow. Islandica, 45. Ithaca and London: Cornell University Press, 1985, pp. 316–63; Mitchell, Stephen A. *Heroic Sagas and Ballads*. Ithaca and London: Cornell University Press, 1991.

Stephen A. Mitchell

[**See also:** *Áns saga bogsveigis*; *Ásmundar saga kappabana*; *Bósa saga* (*Herrauðs saga ok Bósa*); *Egils saga einhenda ok Ásmundar berserkjabana*; *Eiríks saga víðfǫrla*; Folklore; *Friðþjófs saga ins frœkna*; *Gautreks saga*; *Gríms saga loðinkinna*; *Gǫngu-Hrólfs saga*; *Hálfdanar saga Brǫnufóstra*; *Hálfdanar saga Eysteinssonar*; *Hálfs saga ok Hálfsrekka*; *Helga þáttr Þórissonar*; *Hemings þáttr Áslákssonar*; *Hervarar saga ok Heiðreks konungs*; *Hjálmþés saga ok Herrauðs*; *Hrólfs saga Gautrekssonar*; *Hrólfs saga kraka*; *Illuga saga Gríðarfóstra*; *Ketils saga hœngs*; *Nornagests þáttr*; *Ragnars saga loðbrókar*; *Rímur*; *Skjǫldunga saga*; *Rímur*; *Sturlaugs saga starfsama*; *Sǫrla saga sterka*; *Sǫrla þáttr*; *Þáttr*; *Þiðreks saga af Bern*; *Þorsteins saga Víkingssonar*; *Þorsteins þáttr bœjarmagns*; *Vǫlsunga saga*; *Ynglinga saga*; *Yngvars saga víðfǫrla*; *Ǫrvar-Odds saga*]

Fornsvenskt Legendarium *see* **Old Swedish Legendary**

Fortification. During the Viking Age and the Middle Ages, a wide range of types of fortification were used in Scandinavia. The borders of the individual countries must be understood as their medieval borders; the area of modern Finland is, however, not considered in the present survey. Fortifications were built in response to particular political situations in the local areas, or in the kingdoms of Denmark, Norway, and Sweden. Their type, their shape and size, and the building materials reflect the local topography and the natural resources, the structure of society, the period's military and general technology, the social status and economic means of those who built them, and sometimes, particularly in the Middle Ages, fashions prevailing elsewhere in Europe. There were many fewer fortifications in Norway than in Denmark and Sweden, and fewer types; the main reason for this scarcity is the country's topography.

Some fortifications functioned for only a very short time. Others were reused and rebuilt after periods of desertion. Others again were in continuous use through several centuries, being modified or rebuilt time after time. But none is known to have functioned from the Viking Age until the end of the Middle Ages.

Remains of a very large number of fortifications are known, but it is often impossible to establish their period(s) and type(s), for only a small proportion have been investigated, and usually very little survives. It is often difficult to establish and date the various phases of the long-lived ones. Many excavations of important castles and other fortifications took place long ago and were often poorly documented, while the interpretations were often based on written sources barely mentioning the site or the area, or on foreign structural parallels, not on the excavated evidence itself. Modern comprehensive and critical studies are needed, especially for Sweden, as well as new excavations and a clear terminology.

Linear earthworks. Among the linear earthworks in Denmark, only the Danevirke is known to have functioned in the Viking Age and the (early) Middle Ages, but there may have been more. The Danevirke is by far the largest, and protected the country's southern border. In Norway and Sweden, such earthworks from Viking or medieval times are not known.

Sea barriers. Sea barriers, or ship blockages, prevented sudden attacks from sea-borne enemies by barring the passage of their ships and other floating means of attack. They are known from Europe and elsewhere over a wide span of time, and the Scandinavian evidence (archaeology, written sources, place-names, and pictures) comprise a number of barriers from both Viking and medieval times. One group seems to belong to the period of the Slav attacks in the 11th and 12th centuries.

A sea barrier might protect a particular harbor or town, for example in Hedeby, Birka, Kalundborg, Visby, Bergen, and Stockholm, and sometimes combined with a land fortification. Or it might protect an area, for example, around the inner Roskilde fjord or around Hellerumsviken in Blekinge. Sea barriers might be constructed in the forms of bridges, rows of piles, stone caissons, sunken ships, floating booms, solid chains, or combinations of these. Some were permanent, others temporary. People with local knowledge knew the openings in permanent barriers or used other, often very complicated sailing channels. Some types of barriers are vividly illustrated and described by Olaus Magnus (1555), as well as the means of overcoming them.

Fortified refuge camps. Temporary refuge camps for the inhabitants of a settlement or an area together with their animals and other important belongings, and used in times of unrest, existed in many regions of Scandinavia. A number of such fortifications have been identified: they were often to a large extent based on defensive elements provided by nature. Few are excavated, but while most are undoubtedly of Iron Age date, some have been demonstrated to be multiperiod structures, repaired and used in the Viking Age and/or the early Middle Ages. Others may have been constructed in these periods.

The fortified hill plateaus Borg and Hochburg, just outside Birka and Hedeby, respectively, were probably refuge places for the inhabitants of these trading centers until their ramparts were built in the 10th century; they also possibly housed semipermanent garrisons. The largest refuge camp known to have been refortified in the Viking Age is Torsburgen on Gotland, covering 112.5 hectares and situated on a cliff plateau with a 2-km.-long stone wall; perhaps it was meant for the whole population of Gotland. Gamleborg in Almindingen on Bornholm, also situated on a cliff, covered 2.5 hectares. It was probably used in the early Viking Age and certainly reinforced in the Middle Ages. Virket on Falster is another example; about 1,200 meters of its rampart is preserved. Saxo tells that it was used in the mid-12th century during Slav attacks. It appears from other written sources that some old fortified refuge camps were used in times of trouble in the late Middle Ages. But their main period was clearly earlier, before the time of castles, siege warfare, and large armies.

Fortified churches and churchyards. Defensive features of churches and churchyards have often been exaggerated, but there is no doubt that some fortified churches and churchyards did exist in parts of medieval Sweden and Denmark. None is known from Norway. In all three countries, however, a stone church was often the strongest building of a village or area, and also sacred, and the door could be barred from the inside by a heavy boom. An unfortified church might be used for refuge; examples are mentioned in written sources.

Fortified churches are mostly, but not exclusively, known from the Baltic area: Bornholm, Öland, and the coastal region of Småland around Kalmar. These are dated to around 1170–1250 and are commonly believed to have been built or fortified against pagan pirates from the East Baltic area. On Bornholm, they were round tower-like churches, while the defensive elements elsewhere were in the tower(s) of a rectangular church. Some of the freestanding stone towers in churchyards in Gotland and elsewhere probably also served defensive purposes. In the troubled 14th century, the churchyard of Malling (East Jutland) was fortified with a solid stone wall. Some other churchyard walls in this region and elsewhere may have had a similar, partly military function.

Urban defenses. The main forms of man-made urban defenses were earth ramparts, ditches, walls of stone or brick (12th or 13th century and later), sea barriers, and fortresses or castles (mainly 12th century and later). Complicated water defenses, sometimes in connection with a water mill, were also used (e.g., in Ribe). Trondheim was provisionally fortified with wooden structures about 1180, during the civil war between King Sverrir and Archbishop Eysteinn, but permanent urban earth ramparts or walls of Viking and medieval times are not known in Norway.

Ramparts and walls. The earliest known urban ramparts are of the mid 10th century and protected the great trading centers of Hedeby and Birka, while Århus, which was fortified at about the same time, was probably a fortress then. The ramparts were semicircular. They were built of earth, partly from the ditch, and

23. Sea barrier as illustrated in Olaus Magnus, *Historia de gentibus septentrionalibus* (Book 9, ch. 28) (Rome, 1555).

24. Part of Torsburgen, Gotland, and its south wall, seen from the east. The fortification (probably of late Iron Age date) was reused and the stone wall enlarged during the Viking Age. Photo: Peter Manneke, Riksantikvarieämbetets Gotlandsundersökningar (RAGU) (1975).

25. The medieval town wall of Visby, Gotland. Photo: Else Roesdahl (1970).

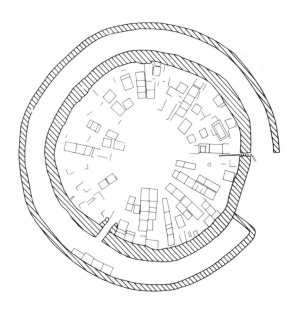

26. Eketorp on Öland. Plan of the late Viking and early-medieval fort.
After Borg, Näsman, and Wegræus (1976).

27. Hammershus, Bornholm. The central castle with the keep of *ca.* 1250. Photo: Birgit Als (1968). The Danish National Museum.

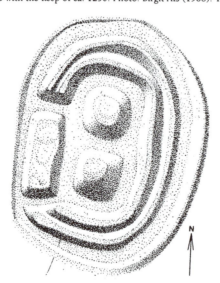

28. The earthworks of the castle Eriksvolde on Lolland, built in the 1340s. After Rikke Agnete Olsen (1986).

29. Reconstruction of Kalmar castle with its outer wards in the late 13th century. After Magnus Olsson (1944).

probably crowned by a timbered palisade; possibly there were also wooden towers. Timber-lined gateways were excavated at Hedeby, whose defenses were extended many times. Its 1,300–m.-long rampart is now about 8 m. high and 25 m. wide.

From about 1000 onward, the number of towns grew enormously. But not all were fortified. The purpose of many minor ramparts, ditches, or fences was rather to create a borderline between the jurisdiction of town and countryside, and a custom line, and to keep out thieves and unruly elements during the night.

A number of towns were, however, fortified and refortified, most of these in the medieval Danish area, and particularly during times of unrest. Some towns got an earth rampart during the Danish civil wars of the 12th century or just after (*e.g.*, Viborg, Roskilde, Copenhagen, Lund); and some towns were fortified or refortified during equally troubled times in the late 13th and the 14th centuries (*e.g.*, Ribe and Lund). Walls were expensive and only for very important towns: only Stockholm, Kalmar, and Visby in Sweden are known to have been entirely walled; in Denmark, only Copenhagen and Kalundborg. The 3.5-km.-long wall of Visby is well preserved. Its oldest parts are possibly of a late 12th-century date; it was strengthened and modernized several times during the Middle Ages.

Fortresses and castles. While a castle is today often defined as a fortification with a lord's private residence, or as a fortified lordly residence, this is not necessarily the case with a fortress or fort. Because of the often fragmentary evidence, the distinction is not always clear-cut; there is also a tendency to label too many fortifications as castles, if they date from after about 1100. The Scandinavian word for both is *borg*. Some forts or castles became the nucleus of a town.

Few fortresses have been identified, all of Viking or early-medieval date, and no castles are known in Scandinavia before the 12th century; these are characteristic medieval phenomena. There is no clear typology for Scandinavian castles, and they follow the western European lines only to some extent. For example, no motte (a tall earth mound for the support of a tower) is known to date from the 11th and 12th centuries; most of the many Danish mottes clearly belong to the late 13th or the 14th century. None is known in Norway; in Sweden, there are probably a few. And while the castles of Norway were built almost exclusively by kings, there are many in Denmark and Sweden built by the nobility, but very few before the 13th century. In 1396, Margrethe of Denmark, then the regent of all Scandinavian countries, forbade the building of private castles, and, in the case of Sweden, also ordered the demolition of existing ones. This ban lasted to 1483 and seems to have been effective in Denmark and Norway, while less is known about the effect in Sweden.

Strong houses and moated sites with a lordly residence and with a weak and sometimes partly symbolic fortification, perhaps just a moat, will be treated only in passing below. They are largely prestige architecture and not proper castles, although some are known to have withstood attacks of peasant revolts. They belong mainly to the late Middle Ages, during and after the ban on private castles. By this time, fortification and residence gradually separated.

Fortresses. One distinct group from the Viking Age is the four Danish geometrically planned Trelleborg fortresses built by the king around 980, with large equal-sized houses regularly placed in blocks within a circular rampart. Men, women, and children lived here, including craftsmen. These fortresses were probably

built to keep control of the country, and functioned for a short time. Around the mid-10th century, a semicircular rampart was built at Århus, which seems to have been mainly a fortress then, but developed into a town. At Borg (now Sarpsborg) in Østfold, Norway, St. Óláfr is said to have built a fortification in about 1016. Eketorp, one of the Iron Age fortifications of Öland, was rebuilt about 1000. It was constructed of local stone and had two ring-walls; the inner area had a diameter of 80 m. and long, close-set, radially placed buildings, leaving only the central area free. Eketorp functioned into the 13th century and probably held a garrison. The background must be this period's troubled situation in the Baltic and the exposed nature of the narrow, flat island. The larger Öland fortress of Gråborg was reused during the Viking Age and rebuilt in the Middle Ages, but little is known about it.

A German source of the 1120s, *Herbordi dialogus de Ottone episcopo Bambergensi*, says that in Denmark, *castra* were fortified with palisades (*ligno*) and moats (*fossatis*) and had no walls (*muros*) or towers (*turribus*). The exact meaning of *castra* is, however, uncertain. Saxo mentions, under a slightly later date, a tower near the harbor of Schleswig and a strange fortification near Roskilde, called Haraldsborg. Some fortifications built by the Danish king against pirates in the mid-12th century are also mentioned by Saxo, but their location and appearance are unknown, and they were perhaps forts rather than castles. The same may be true about the *castellum* built on the tiny island of Sprogø by King Valdemar I (1157–1182).

Castles, Denmark. The oldest castles seem to have been dominated by a tower; the largest is the stone tower at Bastrup, North Zealand, probably of the early 12th century. In the second half of this century, castles were built by King Valdemar I and his closest supporters for the protection of the realm and their own power after civil wars and pirate attacks. These castles were either tower castles or had a solid wall, *e.g.*, Tårnborg, Vordingborg, Kalundborg, and Copenhagen, all on Zealand. A town developed next to them. The Danevirke was modernized, and brick building was introduced in this period.

Many new castles were built during the century of political instability from around 1250. The archbishop built Hammershus on Bornholm about 1250; it had a strong keep and became one of the largest castles in Scandinavia. "The outlaws" built a castle on the island of Hjelm after the murder of King Erik Klippping in 1286. After a revolt in 1313, King Erik Menved built castles near the towns of Viborg and Horsens, and further, Ulstrup and Kalø, all in Jutland. During the dissolution of the realm under Christoffer II (1319–1332) and after, and during its reunion under King Valdemar IV (1340–1375), castles were built by the nobility, and built or reinforced by the Crown. There were many types, including wooden towers on mottes (*e.g.*, Kærsgård); artificial islands in lakes and swamps, with palisades and wood or turf buildings (Hedegård/Halkjær and Solvig); brick castles with walls and towers, including round wall towers for flanking fire (Kalø and Vordingborg). The earthworks were sometimes very large (*e.g.*, at Eriksvolde).

During the ban on private fortification (1396–1483), some bishops' castles remained castles, such as Hammershus. But the new Gjorslev on Zealand, for example, was not really fortified; it was an aristocratic residence. Among the few new castles built by the Crown were Krogen in Elsinore and Duborg in South Jutland. The abolition of the ban did not create a boom in private castle building. The well-preserved Glimmingehus in Scania, for example, was rather a strong house or a "mock castle." Because of the development of artillery, some castles were provided with earth ramparts and some with gun towers in the unstable times of the early 16th century, as at the Viborg bishop's Hald and Spøttrup in Jutland. After the establishment of a new regime under King Christian III (1534–1559), a systematic castle program for artillery warfare was launched, with new castles, for example, Landskrona, or modernizations of old ones, such as Malmøhus, both in Scania.

Castles, Norway. These castles were mainly royal and the number not large, the most important being in or near the towns of Trondheim, Bergen, Tønsberg, and Oslo, or along the borders, such as Vardøhus in Finnmark and Ragnhildsholmen and Bohus in the south. The walled town residences of kings and bishops, for example, in Trondheim and Oslo, can hardly be called castles. The same is true for the seats of the lay nobility.

Sagas mention a *kastala* at Kungahälla near Ragnhildsholmen built by King Sigurðr Jórsalafari ("crusader") Magnússon (1103–1130); it was destroyed in 1135. King Sverrir (1177–1202) realized the importance of castles and had one built near Trondheim (Sverresborg) and one at Bergen, both of stone. The first and best known was on a steep plateau, with walls following the natural features and a gate tower, a type that became common in Norway. These castles were soon destroyed but rebuilt by King Hákon Hákonarson (1217–1263) in Bergen with a prestigious residence, of which Håkonshallen is partly preserved. He also built a castle at Tønsberg; it developed into the largest in Norway. About the mid-13th century, Ragnhildsholmen was erected. This was of a regular, four-sided (*ca.* 37 x 40 m.) type unusual for Norway; a small outer ward and a tower were soon added. It played an important role for a short time in Scandinavian wars and politics.

Vardøhus and Bohus were built in the early 14th century. Bohus replaced Ragnhildsholmen and was a traditional castle. In Oslo, a new and more modern castle (Akershus) with many defense arrangements was erected on a long, narrow cliff plateau at the waterside. A modernization of Tønsberg castle of the 14th century included round wall towers for flanking fire. By 1319, royal power moved outside the country, and the great period of castle building ended. A last one, an artillery castle with gun towers, was built by the archbishop on the island Steinvikholm in Trondheim fjord in the unruly years around 1530.

Castles, Sweden. It is a current theory that King Knut Eriksson (1167–1196) started castle building by erecting a series of stone towers (Modern Swedish *kastaler*) to protect coastal areas against pirate attacks. The round early towers at Kalmar, Borgholm on Öland, and Tre Kronor in Stockholm are attributed to him and believed to have been forts, which soon developed into castles with walls and residences. Kruttornet, a four-sided stone tower at the harbor of Visby, probably of the 12th century, was also first freestanding but soon integrated into the town wall. A number of other freestanding stone towers are known, many of them on Gotland and all next to churches.

In the middle and the second half of the 13th century, a series of stone castles of regular four-sided plan were built, for example, in Stockholm (incorporating Tre Kronor), Nyköping in Södermanland, Örebro in Närke, and Aranäs in Västergötland, the last being a private castle of the powerful Torgils Knutsson. Kalmar castle was rebuilt by King Magnus Ladelås (1275–1290) and was given an irregular four-sided wall with two rectangular gate towers and round corner towers for flanking fire, probably the first in Scandinavia. It was the country's strongest and most modern castle.

Stäkeholm near Västervik, Småland, an almost square castle, was probably built by King Albrecht (1369–1389). At Visby, King Erik built Visborg in 1411, a large, four-sided castle, which included parts of the southwest corner of the town wall. Among the later medieval private castles (or strong houses) is Wiks hus in Uppland, a rectangular (40 x 20 m.) keep or tower house of nine stories with hanging corner turrets.

There were also castles built by bishops, and castles of irregular plan and, throughout the Middle Ages, timber castles. Even the important border castle Älvsborg at the mouth of Götaelven was of timber, as shown in a drawing from 1502. It was also provided with guns. Castles for modern artillery warfare were built, or old ones were modernized, by King Gustav Vasa (1523–1560), as at Kronoberg in Småland and Kalmar.

Lit.: (a) General: Tuulse, Armin. "Bastion." *KLNM* 1 (1956), 383–4; la Cour, Vilhelm, and Hans Stiesdal. *Danske voldsteder fra oldtid og middelalder. Hjørring amt. Thisted amt.* Copenhagen: Nationalmuseet, 1957, 1963; Tuulse, Armin, et al. "Blockhus." *KLNM* 2 (1957), 5–6; Tuulse, Armin, et al. "Borg." *KLNM* 2 (1957), 119–38; Ambrosiani, Björn, et al. "Fornborgar." *KLNM* 4 (1959), 508–14; Tuulse, Armin, et al. "Försvarskyrka." *KLNM* 5 (1960), 141–5; Lundberg, Erik B., et al. "Kastal." *KLNM* 8 (1963), 323–30; *Chateau Gaillard* 1– (1964–) [many articles in English]; Lundberg, Erik B., et al. "Port." *KLNM* 13 (1968), 397–407; Granlund, John, et al. "Pålning och pålkrans." *KLNM* 13 (1968), 616–21; Lundberg, Erik B., et al. "Ringmur." *KLNM* 14 (1969), 329–38; Lundberg, Erik B., and Anterio Sinisalo. "Rondell." *KLNM* 14 (1969), 399–400; Wikström, Lars, et al. "Stadens försvar." *KLNM* 16 (1971), 584–9; la Cour, Vilhelm. *Danske borganlæg til midten af det trettende århundrede.* 2 vols. Copenhagen: Nationalmuseet, 1972; Olsen, Rikke Agnete, et al. "Vold." *KLNM* 20 (1976), 224–6; Stiesdal, Hans, and Erik B. Lundberg, "Voldsted." *KLNM* (1976), 232–5; Roesdahl, Else. *Viking Age Denmark.* Trans. Susan Margeson and Kirsten Williams. London: British Museum, 1982, pp. 139–58; Olsen, Rikke Agnete. "Danish Medieval Castles at War." *Chateau Gaillard* 9–10 (1982), 223–35; Roesdahl, Else. "The End of Viking Age Fortification in Denmark and What Followed." *Chateau Gaillard* 12 (1985), 39–47; Liebgott, Niels-Knud. *Dansk middelalder arkæologi.* Copenhagen: Gad, 1989, pp. 52–116. **(b) Linear earthworks; Sea barriers; Fortified refuge camps**: Engström, Johan. *Torsburgen.* Archaeological Studies. Uppsala University Institute of North European Archaeology, 6. Uppsala: Institutionen för arkeologi, 1984; Crumlin-Pedersen, Ole. "Ship Finds and Ship Blockages AD 800–1200." In *Archaeological Formation Processes.* Ed. K. Kristiansen. Copenhagen: Nationalmuseet, 1985, pp. 215–28; [see also the bibliography for "Danevirke"]. **(c) Fortified churches and churchyards**: *Danmarks Kirker 7. Bornholm.* Copenhagen: Gad, 1954; Johannsen, Hugo, and Claus M. Schmidt. *Danmarks Arkitektur. Kirkens Huse.* Copenhagen: Gyldendal, 1981, pp. 49–61; Hinz, Hermann. "Die Schwedischen Kirchenkastale." *Chateau Gaillard* 9–10 (1982), 433–44; Andersson, Karin. "Kalmarkunstens kyrkor under tidig medeltid." *Hikuin* 9 (1983), 189–202; Boström, Ragnhild. "Ölands medeltida kyrktorn." *Hikuin* 9 (1983), 163–88; *Danmarks Kirker. Århus Amt* hft. 26. Copenhagen: Nationalmuseet, 1984, pp. 2305–11. **(d) Urban defenses**: Eckhoff, Emil, and Otto Janse. *Visby stadsmur.* 2 vols. Stockholm: Kungl. vitterhets historie- och antikvitets-akademien, 1922 [plates], 1936 [text]; Hansson, Hans. *Stockholms stadsmurar.* Stockholm: Stockholms Kommunalförvaltning, 1956; Andersen, H. Hellmuth, et al. *Århus Søndervold. En byarkæologisk undersøgelse.* Jysk arkæologisk selskabs Skrifter, 9. Copenhagen: Gyldendal, 1971; Jankuhn, Herbert. *Haithabu. Ein Handelsplatz der Wikingerzeit.* 8th ed. Neumünster: Wachholtz, 1986. **(e) Fortresses and castles**: Hahr, August. *Skånska* *borgar.* Stockholm: Norstedt, 1922; Olsson, Martin. *Kalmar slotts historia* 1–3. Stockholm: Kungl. vitterhets historie- och antikvitets-akademien, 1944–65; Fischer, Gerhard, and Dorothea Fischer. *Norske Kongeborger.* 2 vols. Oslo: Cappelen, 1951; Gyldendal, 1980; Erixon, Sigurd, ed. *Byggnadskultur.* Nordisk kultur, 17. Stockholm: Bonnier; Oslo: Aschehoug; Copenhagen: Schultz, 1953; Borg, Kaj, *et al.,* eds. *Eketorp: Fortification and Settlement on Öland Sweden. 1. The Monument.* Stockholm: Royal Academy of Letters History and Antiquities; Almqvist & Wiksell, 1976; Stiesdal, Hans. "Types of Public and Private Fortifications in Denmark." In *Danish Medieval History: New Currents.* Ed. N. Skyum-Nielsen and N. Lund. Copenhagen: Museum Tusculanum Press, 1981, pp. 207–20; "Burg." *Lexikon des Mittelalters* 2 (1981–82), 958–1003, esp. 991–4; Olsen, Rikke Agnete. "The Buildings on Danish Moated Sites in the 15th and Early 16th Century." *Chateau Gaillard* 9–10 (1982), 509–26; Olsen, Rikke Agnete. *Borge i Danmark.* Herning: Centrum, 1986; Roesdahl, Else. "The Danish Geometrical Viking Fortresses and Their Context." *Anglo-Norman Studies* 9. Proceedings of the Battle Conference. Ed. R. Allen Brown. Woodbridge: Boydell, 1987, pp. 208–26; Jaubert, Anne Nissen. "The Royal Castles During the Reign of Erik Menved (1286–1319)." *Journal of Danish Archaeology* 7 (1989) [forthcoming].

Else Roesdahl

[**See also**: Danevirke; Fortresses, Trelleborg]

Fortresses, Trelleborg.

The designation refers to four geometrically planned fortresses in Denmark: Trelleborg on Zealand, Nonnebakken (of which very little is known) on Funen, Fyrkat in northeastern Jutland, and Aggersborg in northern Jutland. They were all built around 980, of timber, turf, and earth, and they lasted for only a short time. They were never repaired.

The Trelleborg fortresses differed in size (the inner diameter of Aggersborg being 240 m., of Trelleborg 134 m., and of Fyrkat and Nonnebakken 120 m.) and in various details. But they had the same strict overall plan, for which no exact parallel is known: a circular rampart with gates at the four points of the compass; the inner area divided into four streets between the gates; large bow-sided houses arranged in regular quadrangles. A full-scale reconstruction of such a house was built at Trelleborg in 1948 and at Fyrkat in 1985. The cemeteries of these two fortresses have been found outside the ramparts. The Trelleborg fortresses are not mentioned in written sources, but the fact that they were constructed at the same time and at widespread locations in Denmark indicates that they must have been built by the king, most likely Harald (Bluetooth) Gormsson, known for many other achievements and large building enterprises (*e.g.,* Danevirke and Jelling).

The Trelleborg fortresses are the oldest known royal fortresses in Scandinavia, and their main purpose was probably to control Denmark. They were all situated on important inland roads and either had no access to or were a long way from the open sea. Consequently, the theory has been dismissed that they were winter barracks and training camps for the Vikings, who raided and finally conquered England under Harald's son Sven (Forkbeard) Haraldsson. Chronological reasons also argue against the theory. Perhaps the Trelleborg fortresses were abandoned after Sven's successful revolt against his father around 986.

Lit.: Nørlund, Poul. *Trelleborg.* Nordiske Fortidsminder, 4.1. Copenhagen: Det kgl. nordiske Oldskriftselskab, 1948; Olsen, Olaf, *et al. Fyrkat. En jysk vikingeborg.* 2 vols. Nordiske Fortidsminder. ser. B in quarto 3–4. Copenhagen: Det kgl. nordiske Oldskriftselskab, 1977;

Roesdahl, Else. "Aggersborg in the Viking Age." *Proceedings of the Eighth Viking Congress, Århus, 24–31 August 1977.* Ed. Hans Bekker-Nielsen *et al.* Odense: Odense University Press, 1981, pp. 107–22; Christiansen, Tage E. "Trelleborgs Alder. Arkæologisk datering." *Aarbøger for nordisk Oldkyndighed og Historie* (1982), 84–110 [full English translation]; Schmidt, Holger. "Om bygningen af et vikingetidshus på Fyrkat." *Nationalmuseets Arbejdsmark* (1985), 48–59; Roesdahl, Else. *Viking Age Denmark.* Trans. Susan Margeson and Kirsten Williams. London: British Museum, 1982, pp. 147–55; Roesdahl, Else. "The Danish Geometrical Viking Fortresses and Their Context." *Anglo-Norman Studies* 9. Proceedings of the Battle Conference. Ed. R. Allen Brown. Woodbridge: Boydell, 1987, pp. 208–26.

Else Roesdahl

[**See also**: Fortification]

Fóstbrœðra saga

Fóstbrœðra saga ("The Saga of the Sworn Brothers") relates the adventures of two arrogant ruffians, Þorgeirr and Þormóðr, who swear to avenge each other if need be. The first part recounts a series of killings beginning with Þorgeirr's vengeance for his father. Subsequently, when Þorgeirr asks which of them could overcome the other, Þormóðr dissolves their partnership. Þorgeirr goes to Norway and joins St. Óláfr's bodyguard. Þormóðr dedicates a poem to a woman named Þorbjǫrg Kolbrún ("coal brow"), which wins him the cognomen Kolbrúnarskáld ("Kolbrún's poet"). Later, he revises the poem to honor another woman named Þordís. When Þorbjǫrg discovers this revision, she causes Þormóðr's eyes to ache unbearably until he publicly confesses his disloyalty.

St. Óláfr asks Þorgeirr to avenge an injury inflicted on one of his retainers by an Icelander. Þorgeirr does so, and is killed in retaliation on a subsequent visit to Iceland. One of his killers, named Þorgrímr, flees to Greenland.

Þormóðr, who has become one of St. Óláfr's court poets, sails to Greenland, where he kills Þorgrímr and three of his sons. After recovering from his wounds, he rejoins St. Óláfr, with whom he remains during his exile. Before the battle of Stiklestad (1030), he recites *Bjarkamál in fornu* ("The Old Lay of Bǫðvar Bjarki"). The story may be an adaptation of William of Malmesbury's account of the singing of the *Song of Roland* before the battle of Hastings. Þormóðr fights without shield or armor in order not to be parted from his king even in death.

Fóstbrœðra saga has been preserved in two versions, MFR (*Möðruvallabók, Flateyjarbók, Codex Regius*), and H (*Hauksbók*). MFR is characterized by an ornate style, including personification and kennings, and by the use of anatomical, theological, and other digressions. H lacks almost all the digressions and has a simpler style. The question of the relationships between MFR and H is important for the history of the genre.

On stylistic grounds, H has been dated before 1200 and the digressions of MFR explained as later scribal interpolations. Likewise on stylistic grounds, Kroesen (1962) proposed the theory of dual authorship. Lachmann (1932) advocated the primacy of MFR, supported by Jansson (1944) and by Sigurður Nordal (1953), who dated MFR to about 1200. Jónas Kristjánsson (1972) urged the primacy of MFR and supported a late 13th-century date for the saga's composition. On the basis of his extensive study of the usage of the verbs *hittask* versus *finnask* ("to meet"), Hallberg (1972) assigned F and M to the early and H to the late 13th century. Conversely, von See (1976) favors Finnur Jónsson's view of H and explains the florid style and the digressions as expansions

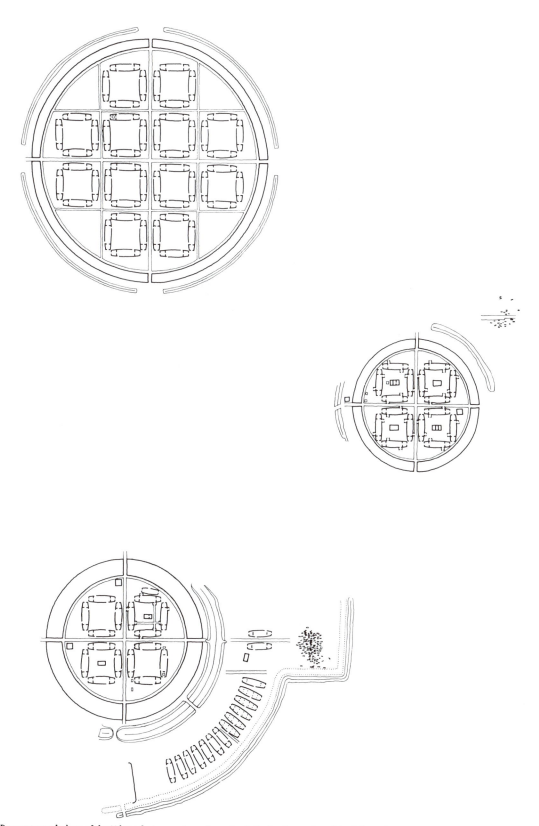

30. Reconstructed plans of the Viking fortresses Aggersborg (top), Fyrkat (center), and Trelleborg (bottom). Scale 1:4,000. Drawing: Holger Schmidt.

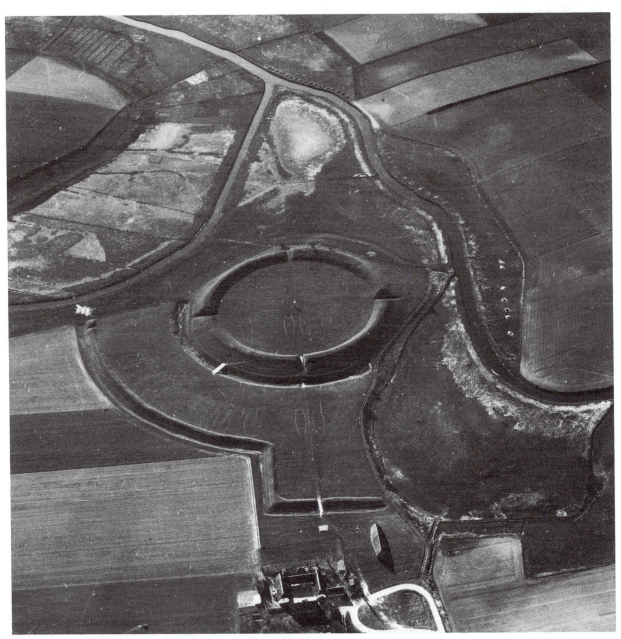

31. The Viking fortress of Trelleborg from the east, situated between two converging rivers. At the bottom of the photograph, outside the outer ward, is the reconstructed house from 1948. Photo: Hans Stiesdal, The National Museum of Denmark.

and accretions reflecting the gradual "spiritualization" of the saga by clerical copyists.

An early date for the original *Fóstbrœðra saga* is suggested by its primitive structure, ill-defined conflict, lack of motivation, and especially by its intimate relationship with the St. Óláfr legend. A dramatic *Þormóðar þáttr* comprises fragment II (5) of the oldest *Óláfs saga* and ch. 58 of the legendary saga of Óláfr; and the account of Þormóðr's death in this work is similar to that in his saga.

Major sources for the saga beside the Óláfr legend are Þormóðr's skaldic stanzas, especially those about Þorgeirr, but they were sometimes misinterpreted by the author. The sworn brothers play minor roles in *Grettis saga*, and Snorri Sturluson borrowed the death scene in *Fóstbrœðra saga* for his *Óláfs saga helga*. Although not a major saga, *Fóstbrœðra saga* does not lack dry humor, pithy dialogue, and memorable scenes, the most magnificent of which is Þormóðr's demonstration at Stiklestad of loyalty, which, as stressed by Schier (1964), is the unifying theme of the saga. The heroic nature of *Fóstbrœðra saga* inspired Halldór Laxness to write his satirical *Gerpla*, the English translation of which bears the apt title *The Happy Warriors* (1959).

Ed.: Björn K. Þórólfsson and Guðni Jónsson, eds. *Vestfirðinga sǫgur.* Íslenzk fornrit, 6. Reykjavik: Hið íslenska fornritafélag, 1943, pp. 119–276. **Tr.**: Hollander, Lee M., trans. *The Sagas of Kormák and The Sworn Brothers*. Princeton: Princeton University Press for the American-Scandinavian Foundation, 1949, pp. 73–176. **Lit.**: Lachmann, Vera. *Das Alter der Harðarsaga.* Leipzig: Mayer & Mayer, 1932, pp. 222–3 and *passim*; Jansson, Sven B. F. *Sagorna om Vinland.* Lund: Ohlsson, 1944, pp. 176–260; Sigurður Nordal, ed. *Literaturhistorie. B: Norge og Island.* Nordisk kultur, 8B. Stockholm: Bonnier; Oslo: Aschehoug; Copenhagen: Schultz, 1953, pp. 236–9; Kroesen, Jakoba M. C. *Over de Compositie der Fóstbrœðra Saga.* Leiden: Universitaire Pers, 1962; Hallberg, Peter. *The Icelandic Saga.* Trans. Paul Schach. Lincoln: University of Nebraska Press, 1962, pp. 68–9, 97–8, and *passim*; Schier, Kurt. "Fóstbrœðra saga." In *Kindlers Literatur Lexikon* 4. Zurich: Kindler, 1964, pp. 3634–5; Andersson, Theodore M. "Fostbrœðra saga." In *The Icelandic Family Saga: An Analytic Reading.* Harvard Studies in Comparative Literature, 28. Cambridge: Harvard University Press, 1967, pp. 186–92; Hallberg, Peter. "Nyare studier i isländsk sagalitteratur." *Samlaren* 93 (1972), 211–37 [esp. 212–5]; Jónas Kristjánsson. *Um Fóstbræðrasögu.* Reykjavik: Stofnun Árna Magnússonar, 1972 [English summary, pp. 311–26]; See, Klaus von. "Die Überlieferung der Fóstbrœðra saga." *Skandinavistik* 6 (1976), 1–18; See, Klaus von. "Hastings, Stiklastaðir und Langemark. Zur Überlieferung vom Vortrag heroischer Lieder auf dem Schlachtfeld." *Germanisch-romanische Monatsschrift* 26 (1976), 1–13; Schach, Paul. *Icelandic Sagas.* Twayne's World Authors Series, 717. Boston: Twayne, 1984, pp. 76–82.

Paul Schach

[See also: *Bjarkamál; Codex Regius; Flateyjarbók; Hauksbók; Íslendingasögur; Lausavísur; Möðruvallabók; Óláfs saga helga; Skáldasögur; Skaldic Verse*]

France, Norse in. From the beginning of the 8th century into the 10th century, France was one of the main targets of Norse raids in western Europe. In this period, the land that we call France today was part of the extensive Carolingian Empire, which ranged from the Atlantic to the Elbe, from the Danish border far into Italy. After long internal conflicts, this *Imperium Francorum* consisted of three parts: the western kingdom, which in time became France,

the eastern kingdom, which formed the basis of a later Germany, and the middle kingdom of Lotharingia (Lorraine), which extended on both sides of the Rhine from its estuary into Italy. Lotharingia soon disappeared as an independent kingdom. At the time, it comprised regions that today belong to Holland and Belgium, and that became the target of frequent Viking raids in the 8th–10th centuries. To simplify matters, the term "France" is used here to describe the whole territory from the Atlantic coast to the Rhine, even though it does not coincide with modern political borders.

Our main source for the activities of Norsemen in France are the reports of contemporary Frankish chroniclers, who wrote with bitterness about the heathen enemies from the North raiding their monasteries, churches, and towns to pillage and destroy. Naturally, their reports are not considered objective as defined by modern historical science; the chroniclers were personally affected and may well have exaggerated sometimes. But by examining hundreds of isolated descriptions, and with the aid of archaeological finds, it is possible to reconstruct the course of the Norse raids and the greed and toughness of the Vikings. Other sources, such as reports written by the Norsemen themselves at the time of their raids, are not available.

In 799, a small fleet of Norse ships appeared on the southwest coast of France to loot offshore islands. They may have been Norwegians, although in the following decades France was mostly ravaged by Danish Vikings. Other attacks at that time took place near the Rhine estuary. They were directed primarily against trading ports like Dorestad (near Utrecht), where people as well as all sorts of goods were seized. Even these first, limited raids showed quite clearly that loot was the main object of the Norsemen in France as well as elsewhere. Charlemagne organized coastal defenses. After his death in 814, however, there gradually began the long period of struggles against his heirs that frequently saw rights of supremacy contested on the battlefield and gradually came to break up the Carolingian Empire. For that reason, a united, vigorous defense against outside aggressors like the Vikings could not be maintained. The Norsemen could operate in France with less and less danger to themselves, while both their numbers and radius of action increased. They were not organized in a single fleet, but in several normally separate groups, although they united occasionally to achieve their objectives.

After the first attacks on coastal sites, a second phase began in the 830s. A considerable number of Norsemen established themselves on the island of Noirmoutier in the Loire estuary and turned it into fortified winter quarters that served as a base for raids in the spring and summer. Ultimately, the booty was hoarded in the camp, a Viking tactic observed all over western Europe. From 834 onward, the Norsemen raided up the Loire from Noirmoutier, attacking places like Nantes and Orleans. They occasionally left their ships for forays on land, returning to them afterward; this tactic also formed part of the usual Norse fighting style. The Vikings stayed in the Loire area for decades, until about 890. Despite local attempts at defense, no one could drive them off. They exercised regional control, but definitely did not settle as farmers.

Another important invasion target was the area between the mouths of the Seine and the Rhine. Here, too, the rivers served as gateways to the interior. From 834 onward, Frisia, a part of Lotharingia, was repeatedly attacked, while the domestic situation in France reached a critical state, as the Norsemen well knew. In this emergency, King Lothar I invested the Viking leader Rorik with part of Frisia, hoping (as it turned out, correctly) that this move would cause the attacks to abate. At the same time, increasing numbers of Norsemen arrived in France. Between 841 and 879/80, they plundered extensively in the whole area of the Seine and the Somme, with fortified camps like that on the Seine island Oscelle providing the necessary support according to Viking custom. Often the Franks had to pay large sums in tribute to buy peace at least for a while.

From 865 to 880, the Norsemen of northern France operated mostly in England. The return of a strong fleet in 879/80 introduced a third phase, namely that of the "Great Army," that was to last until 892. Several groups had joined forces to act together as a large unit under leaders like Sigfred and Godfred. This action affected particularly the area of Scheldt and the Meuse, where a camp was established in Elsloo on the River Meuse, and forays were undertaken in all directions. However, the period of violent fratricidal wars in France was coming to an end. In 881 and 891, the Norsemen for the first time suffered heavy defeats, which at least indicated an alteration, even though they did not yet bring about a complete change of the situation. To be sure, Emperor Charles III let slip the chance of annihilating the "Great Army" while it was surrounded in Elsloo; he turned to negotiations and permitted it to withdraw, an event that contributed to his own deposition.

A famine caused the Army, together with the Norsemen from the Loire, to leave France in 892. Some settled in England; the remainder returned. Thus, the last phase in France ended in serious defeats for the invaders. In 911, a treaty between the Norsemen and King Charles the Simple was agreed upon: the Norsemen became Christians, ceased their attacks, and in return were allowed to settle in an area that bears their name to this day, Normandy. In time, Normandy turned into a French duchy and the Vikings into French knights and peasants, thus bringing to an end their history in France.

Lit.: Haskins, Charles Homer. *The Normans in European History.* Boston: Houghton Mifflin, 1915; Arbman, Holger. *The Vikings.* Ed. and trans. Alan Binns. London: Thames & Hudson, 1961; Brøndsted, Johannes. *The Vikings.* Trans. Kalle Skov. Harmondsworth: Penguin, 1965; Jones, Gwyn. *A History of the Vikings.* 2nd. ed. Oxford and New York: Oxford University Press, 1984; Sawyer, Peter H. *The Age of the Vikings.* London: Arnold, 1971; Blair, Peter Hunter. *An Introduction to Anglo-Saxon England.* 2nd ed. Cambridge: Cambridge University Press, 1977; Wilson, David M. *The Vikings and Their Origins: Scandinavia in the First Millennium.* London: Thames & Hudson, 1980; Wilson, David M., and Ole Klindt-Jensen. *Viking Art.* 2nd ed. London: Allen & Unwin, 1980; Logan, Donald F. *The Vikings in History.* London: Hutchinson, 1983.

Horst Zettel

[**See also:** Norman Literature, Norse Influence on]

Freeprose Theory *see* **Bookprose/Freeprose Theory**

Freyja *see* **Freyr and Freyja**

Freyr and Freyja. In Norse mythology, the brother and sister Freyr and Freyja and their father, Njǫrðr, are the principal members of the Vanir. According to *Vǫluspá* and such other texts as Snorri Sturluson's *Edda* and *Ynglinga saga*, the Vanir and Æsir

fought a war near the beginning of mythic time. A female figure, perhaps Freyja, played an important but unclear role, and the cessation of hostilities involved an exchange of hostages that sent Freyr and Njǫrðr to the Æsir and ultimately led to the creation of the mead of poetry. The Vanir, therefore, were initially distinct from the Æsir and were incorporated with them by means of myth. Many observers regard the Æsir as gods of war and the Vanir as gods of fertility.

Ample evidence associates Freyr and Freyja with fertility. In his *Edda*, Snorri Sturluson remarks that both are fair of face and powerful. Freyr, the noblest of the gods, rules over rain, sunshine, and the growth of the earth, and may be invoked for good harvest and peace; he controls the wealth of men. Freyja, Snorri adds, is the noblest of goddesses. She dwells grandly, shares half the dead with Óðinn, travels behind a cart pulled by cats, and is invoked for love. She is equal in dignity to Frigg, Óðinn's wife, and is herself married to a mysterious figure called Óðr (perhaps a double of Óðinn). Their daughter was so fair that she was named "Hnoss," meaning "jewel." Freyr's mythic accoutrements include the ship Skíðblaðnir, which always has a fair wind and may be folded up and carried in a pocket, and the boar Gullinbursti or Slíðrugtanni, whose bristles illuminate even the darkest night. In poetry, Freyr sometimes bears the epithet "bright." Freyja's most important accoutrement is the *brísingamen*, a valuable object of unknown form, perhaps a necklace. She also possesses a shape-changing garment.

Freyr's greatest moment is his wooing of the giantess Gerðr, as told in the eddic poem *Skírnismál* and paraphrased in *Snorra Edda*. Even if one sets aside the interpretations associating the story directly with fertility ritual, there can be no doubt that sex and fertility lie at its core. In *Lokasenna*, Loki accuses Freyr of giving up his sword to obtain Gerðr, and Snorri makes much of Freyr's lack of a sword.

Freyja had marital problems, too. She wept tears of gold while Óðr was away and apparently gave herself to (or was taken by) Óðinn's brothers. Freyja, Loki says in *Lokasenna*, had slept with all the gods, including even her brother, Freyr; and Snorri notes that Njǫrðr had slept with his unnamed sister, for that was the custom among the Vanir. The giants' desire for Freyja is a mythic commonplace.

The sagas tell of horses sacred to Freyr (*e.g.*, Freyfaxi in *Hrafnkels saga*) and a cult based on a horse's phallus. Place-names like "Freyr's field" suggest, in turn, an association with fertility of the earth.

The names Freyr and Freyja mean simply "lord" and "lady," which suggests that they may recapitulate Njǫrðr and his unnamed sister/wife (perhaps Nerthus, mentioned by Tacitus, whose name is etymologically identical with Njǫrðr) or other earlier deities. Freyr is sometimes called Yngvi-Freyr and is therefore presumably connected with the Ynglingar, the first Swedish dynasty. Indeed, kennings in *Ynglingatal* and *Háleygjatal* with the meaning "Freyr's descendant" or "Freyr's relative" link the god with the Swedish kings and also with the Hlaðir earls. The name Ingunar-Freyr suggests association with the legendary Ing of Old English tradition. Freyja has apparently little to do with dynasties, but her shape-changing garment and association with the dead imply a connection with shamanism.

Bib.: Lindow, John. *Scandinavian Mythology: An Annotated Bibliography.* Garland Folklore Bibliographies, 13. New York: Garland, 1988. Lit.: Olsen, Magnus. "Fra gammelnorsk myte og kultus." *Maal og* minne (1909), 17–36; Schröder, Franz Rolf. *Germanentum und Hellenismus: Untersuchungen zur germanischen Religionsgeschichte*. Germanische Bibliothek, II. Abt., 17. Heidelberg: Winter, 1924; Schröder, Franz Rolf. *Untersuchungen zur germanischen und vergleichenden Religionsgeschichte, 1: Ingunar-Freyr*. Tübingen: Mohr, 1941; Vries, Jan de. *Altgermanische Religionsgeschichte*. 2 vols. Grundriss der germanischen Philologie, 12. 2nd ed. Berlin: de Gruyter, 1956, vol. 2, pp. 163–214, 307–13; Dronke, Ursula. "Art and Tradition in Skírnismál." In *English and Mediaeval Studies Presented to J. R. R. Tolkien on the Occasion of His Seventieth Birthday*. Ed. Norman Davis and C. L. Wrenn. London: Allen & Unwin, 1962, pp. 250–68; Ward, Donald. *The Divine Twins: An Indo-European Myth in Germanic Tradition*. Berkeley and Los Angeles: University of California Press, 1968; Dumézil, Georges. *Gods of the Ancient Northmen*. Ed. Einar Haugen. Trans. John Lindow *et al*. UCLA Studies in Folklore and Mythology, 1. Berkeley and Los Angeles: University of California Press, 1973, pp. 73–9 [translation of 1959 original]; Talbot, Annelise. "The Withdrawal of the Fertility God." *Folklore* 93 (1982), 31–46.

John Lindow

[**See also:** *Lokasenna*; Mythology; *Skírnismál*; *Snorra Edda*; *Vǫluspá*; *Ynglinga saga*]

Friðþjófs saga ins frœkna

Friðþjófs saga ins frœkna ("The Saga of Friðþjófr the Bold") concerns the love of Friðþjófr, the son of Þorsteinn, a prominent landowner in Sogn (Norway), for the beautiful Ingibjǫrg, daughter of Beli, the king of Sogn. While still a youth, Friðþjófr's prowess earns him the epithet *inn frœkni* ("the bold"). Friðþjófr and Ingibjǫrg fall in love while under the fosterage of a farmer in Beli's kingdom, and the rest of the saga relates the circuitous path by which they eventually join in marriage.

The first part of the saga treats the wooing of King Beli's daughter, Ingibjǫrg, by the low-born Friðþjófr. His action prompts the enmity of Ingibjǫrg's brothers, Helgi and Hálfdan, who have promised her in marriage to King Hringr. They assign Friðþjófr the task of collecting wedding tribute in the Orkneys, and while he is away, they destroy his hereditary estate. Upon his return, Friðþjófr starts a fight in the temple, setting the building on fire and destroying the images of Baldr and other gods. He is outlawed, and spends the next four years on Viking expeditions. In the second part of the saga, Friðþjófr returns in disguise and takes lodgings for the winter in Hringr's household. On his deathbed, Hringr leaves Ingibjǫrg to Friðþjófr, and entrusts his kingdom to him until Helgi and Hálfdan are old enough to rule. Insulted by the marriage, the brothers wage war against Friðþjófr. Helgi is slain, and Friðþjófr is victorious. Hálfdan is reduced to the position of chieftain under him.

Friðþjófs saga ins frœkna survives in two prose redactions: an older, shorter version composed in Iceland in the late 13th or early 14th century; a longer version composed probably in the early 15th century. The later version exhibits textual influence from *rímur* concerning Friðþjófr, which in turn draws elements from *Þorsteins saga Víkingssonar*. While the older version describes Hringr as a Swedish king, the later version situates the second half of the action in the Norwegian district of Hringaríki and supplies Norwegian place-names for locations otherwise unspecified in the earlier version; also, personal names are given for a number of characters otherwise nameless in the older version.

More than twenty MSS or MS fragments contain texts of this saga. The oldest surviving MS of the earlier redaction appears in

AM 510 4to (end of the 15th century), as well as in AM 568 4to (paper), along with two other younger paper MSS and three vellum fragments from the early 16th century (now in the Royal Library in Stockholm). The longer version exists only in paper MSS: AM 173 fol. and Stock. Papp. fol. no. 56.

The saga exhibits careful artistic craftmanship. Its plot uses the common romance device whereby a low-born character raises his status by marrying into nobility. The saga was widely translated during the 19th century, and achieved perhaps a greater than usual popularity among the *fornaldarsögur* largely as a result of Esaias Tegnér's dramatic poem "Fridthjof" (1825), which romanticized the saga material.

Ed.: Björner, E. J., ed. *Nordiska Kämpa Dater*. Stockholm: Horrn, 1737; Rafn, C. C., ed. *Fornaldar sögur Nordrlanda*. 3 vols. Copenhagen: Popp, 1829–30, vol. 2, pp. 63–100 [longer version]; Larsson, Ludvig, ed. *Sagan ock rimorna om Friðþiófr hinn frækni*. Samfund til udgivelse af gammel nordisk litteratur, 22. Copenhagen: Malmström, 1893; Larsson, Ludvig, ed. *Friðþjófs saga ins frœkna*. Altnordische Saga-Bibliothek, 9. Halle: Niemeyer, 1901; Guðni Jónsson, ed. *Fornaldar sögur Norðurlanda*. 4 vols. Akureyri: Íslendingasagnaútgáfan, 1954, vol. 3, pp. 75–104. **Tr.**: Eiríkr Magnússon and William Morris, trans. "Fridthjofs saga hins Froekna." In *Three Northern Love Stories and Other Tales*. London: Ellis & White, 1875; Anderson, Rasmus B., trans. "The Saga of Fridthjof the Bold." In *Viking Tales of the North*. Chicago: Griggs, 1882, pp. 75–111 [contains a translation of Tegnér's "Fridthjof"]; Sephton, John, trans. "A Translation of the Saga of Frithiof the Fearless." *Proceedings of the Literary and Philosophical Society of Liverpool* 48 (1893–94), 69–97; Schlauch, Margaret. *Medieval Narratives*. New York: Prentice-Hall, 1928; rpt. 1934; rpt. New York: Gordian, 1970, pp. 5–33. **Lit.**: Calaminus, Wilhelm. *Zur kritik und erklärung der altnordischen Frithjofssage*. Jena: Pohle, 1887; Kölbing, Eugen. "Über die verschiedenen Bearbeitungen der Friðþjófssaga und die Friðþjófsrímur." In *Beiträge zur vergleichenden Geschichte der romantischen Poesie und Prosa des Mittelälters*. Breslau: Koebner, 1878, pp. 207–17; Schier, Kurt. "Friðþjófs saga ins frœkna." In *Kindlers Literatur Lexikon* 3. Ed. Gert Woerner. Zurich: Kindler, 1967, pp. 300–2; Holm, Gösta. "Saltbränneren från Angr." In *Opuscula Septentrionalia. Festskrift til Ole Widding 10.10.1977*. Ed. Bent Chr. Jacobsen *et al*. Copenhagen: Reitzel, 1977, pp. 50–4.

Jonathan D. M. Evans

[**See also:** *Fornaldarsögur*; Old Norse–Icelandic Literature, Foreign Influence on; *Rímur*; *Þorsteins saga Víkingssonar*]

Frihetsvisan *see* Swedish Literature, Miscellaneous

Fríssbók

Fríssbók (*Codex Frisianus*), AM 45 fol. in the Arnamagnaean Collection in Copenhagen, was written about 1325 and contains sagas of the Norwegian kings, more specifically the first and third part of *Heimskringla* and *Hákonar saga Hákonarsonar* by Sturla Þórðarson. The codex consists of 124 leaves, about 31 x 24 cm., and is preserved intact. The text is written in two columns on each page. With the exception of three columns, the MS was written by a professional Icelandic scribe whose hand is also known from a psalter, now extant only in two fragments, AM 214a fol. and AM 249p fol., and also a MS of *Sverris saga* and *Bǫglunga sǫgur*, of which only two leaves are preserved in AM 325 VIII 4c 4to. The three columns written in another contemporary hand are on fols. 98ra and b and 98va. Although there is no doubt that the scribes were Icelandic, it is unclear whether the codex was written in

Iceland or Norway. If it was written in Iceland, it was most likely exported to Norway quite early, possibly even immediately after completion. In Norway, it was used both by Laurents Hansson and Mattis Størssøn in about the middle of the 16th century, probably in Bergen, but was exported to Denmark around 1600. The first known owner of the MS was the Dane Otto Friis from Salling, from whom it has taken its present name. The Danish nobleman Jens Rosenkrantz (1640–1695), his relative and a great book collector, obtained it from Friis. After Rosenkrantz's death, Árni Magnússon acquired all his MSS, with the purpose, it is said, of getting hold of *Fríssbók*.

In the first part of *Heimskringla*, completed with *Óláfs saga Tryggvasonar*, the text of *Fríssbók* belongs to the same class of MSS as "Kringla," and is more closely related to AM 39 fol. than any other extant MS. In this first part, there are two minor interpolations (23vb 37–24ra 3 and 33ra 1– 23, ed. 109.14–18 and 148.27–149.12). After this first part, there is a note: "her skal iⁿ koma saga Olafs *konungs* hins helga" ("St. Óláfs saga is to be inserted here"). But immediately thereafter follows *Magnúss saga góða*. The second part of *Heimskringla*, i.e., *Óláfs saga helga*, was never entered in the codex, probably because it was not to be found in its exemplar. In the text of most of the third part of *Heimskringla*, i.e., from *Magnúss saga góða* to *Haraldssona saga*, *Fríssbók* contains a series of interpolations drawn from a redaction of *Morkinskinna* older than the existing one. *Hákonar saga Hákonarsonar* in *Fríssbók* is related to the text preserved in *Eirspennill*, an abridged version compared with the more original redaction in other MSS, *e.g.*, *Flateyjarbók* and AM 81a fol.

Ed.: Unger, C. R., and A. C. Drolsum, eds. *Codex Frisianus. En Samling af norske Konge-Sagaer.* Norske historiske kildeskriftfonds skrifter, 9. Christiania [Oslo]: Malling, [1869]–71; *Codex Frisianus (Sagas of the Kings of Norway).* Corpus Codicum Islandicorum Medii Aevi, 4. Introduction by Halldór Hermannsson. Copenhagen: Levin & Munksgaard, 1932 [facsimile]. **Lit.**: Finnur Magnússon. *Fornmanna sögur* 9. Det kongelige nordiske Oldskriftselskab. Copenhagen: Möller, 1835, pp. xiii–xv; Finnur Jónsson, ed. *Heimskringla.* 4 vols. Samfund til udgivelse af gammel nordisk litteratur, 23. Copenhagen: Møller, 1893–1901, vol. 1, pp. xxi–xxiv; Bjarni Aðalbjarnarson, ed. *Heimskringla.* 3 vols. Íslenzk fornrit, 26–8. Reykjavik: Hið íslenzka fornritafélag, 1941–53, vol. 3, pp. lxxxvii–lxxxviii and xcii–xciv; Jakob Benediktsson. "Fríssbók." *KLNM* 4 (1959), 652–3; Louis-Jensen, Jonna. *Kongesagastudier. Kompilationen Hulda-Hrokkinskinna.* Bibliotheca Arnamagnæana, 32. Copenhagen: Reitzel, 1977, pp. 19–21, 34–43, and 83–97; Holm-Olsen, Ludvig. *Det arnamagnæanske håndskrift 81a fol. (Skálholtsbók yngsta).* Det Norske historiske kildeskriftsfonds skrifter, 38. Christiania [Oslo]: Malling, 1910–86, pp. xxviii and xxxii–xxxiv [parts 1–2 published in 1910–11; part 3 in 1926; part 4 in 1947; part 5 in 1986, issued with a new title page for the whole work].

Ólafur Halldórsson

[See also: *Eirspennill; Flateyjarbók; Hákonar saga gamla Hákonarsonar; Heimskringla; Morkinskinna*]

Fylgja *see* Supernatural Beings

Færeyinga saga ("The Saga of the Faroe Islanders") has to be assembled from passages incorporated in Snorri's *Óláfs saga helga* (separate and in *Heimskringla*) and in *Óláfs saga Tryggvasonar en*

mesta; the prime source is *Flateyjarbók*. The medieval editors of those compilations must have introduced changes, but not enough to obscure the distinctive attitude and technique of the original author. He wrote about 1200, certainly before Snorri composed his *Óláfs saga helga* in the 1220s. His themes are rivalry between Faroese chieftains from the mid-10th to the mid-11th century, conversion of the islanders to Christianity, and, interwoven with both these themes, the relations between Faroese leaders and Norwegian kings. The author cites no verse and apparently had no written sources; the anecdotes he built on must have come from the Faroes, but he evidently did not know the islands at first hand. The author succeeded in sustaining a narrative that did equal justice to imposing missionary kings, Óláfr Tryggvason and Óláfr Haraldsson, and to their wily Faroese antagonist, Þrándr í Gotu, presented as a man of superb cunning and supernatural power, who detests the Christianity forced on him. In the end, of course, Þrándr loses and dies, and paganism and Faroese independence, whatever that may have meant in the early Middle Ages, die with him. The author tells many entertaining tales, most of them too good to be true, often with Þrándr the trickster at the hub. We cannot tell whether the saga itself was especially influential, but it certainly belongs to a seminal "school" of narrative technique; *Orkneyinga saga* and *Jómsvíkinga saga* have some similar features and were written in the same generation. The author is particularly skillful in maintaining suspense by keeping his audience (and usually some of his cast) in ignorance or misled for as long as possible, a technique well known to saga writers, but seldom carried to such lengths as in *Færeyinga saga*. Another significant feature of the saga is the rounded romantic folktale that explains the origins of Þuríðr meginekkja ("the great widow"), and is told as a "story in the story" by her father, Þorkell. Both the manner and the matter of this episode (unconquerable love, abduction, death of father at hands of suitor, the forest life of an outlaw) offer further evidence of the variety and sophistication that existed in the literary milieu of the author of *Færeyinga saga*.

Ed.: Rafn, Carl Christian, ed. *Færeyinga saga.* Copenhagen: Schultz, 1832; rpt. Tórshavn: Emil Thomsen, 1972; Finnur Jónsson, ed. *Færeyinga saga.* Copenhagen: Thiele, 1927; Ólafur Halldórsson, ed. *Færeyinga saga.* Reykjavik: Stofnun Árna Magnússonar, 1987. **Tr.**: Powell, Frederick York, trans. *The Tale of Thrond of Gate, Commonly Called Færeyinga Saga.* London: Nutt, 1896; Johnston, George, trans. *The Faroe Islanders' Saga.* [Ottawa]: Oberon, 1975. **Lit.**: Ólafur Halldórsson. "Inngangur" [in his edition of *Færeyinga saga;* offers the best critical appraisal available]; Foote, Peter. "On the Saga of the Faroe Islanders." In *Aurvandilstá: Norse Studies.* Ed. Michael Barnes *et al.* Viking Collection, 2. Odense: Odense University Press, 1984, pp. 165–87; Foote, Peter. "Þrándr and the Apostles." In *Aurvandilstá,* pp. 188–98; Foote, Peter. "A Note on Þránd's *kredda*." In *Aurvandilstá,* pp. 199–208; Foote, Peter. "Færeyinga saga, Chapter Forty." In *Aurvandilstá,* pp. 209–21 [the last four works offer special studies with extensive bibliography].

Peter Foote

[See also: Christian Poetry, West Norse; Faroe Islands; *Flateyjarbók; Heimskringla; Óláfs saga helga; Óláfs saga Tryggvasonar*]

For Skírnis *see* Skírnismál.

Gamli kanóki, an Old Icelandic skaldic poet, is known as the author of a *drápa* in the *hrynhent* meter on St. John the Apostle, of which four stanzas are quoted in *Jóns saga postola IV* ("*Litla-Jóns saga*"), and of the *drápa Harmsól* ("Sun of Sorrow") in the *dróttkvætt* meter, which survives in its full length (sixty-five stanzas). Of Gamli himself, nothing is known, except that, according to the *Jóns saga postola*, he was a canon "austr í þyckabe" ("east in Þykkvabær"), an Augustinian cloister founded in 1168. The saga quotes from Gamli's *Jónsdrápa* between a quotation from Nikulás Bergsson (d. 1159) and another from Kolbeinn Tumason (d. 1208). Paasche took this ordering as an indication of chronology, implying a dating of this poem between 1168 and 1208. According to Skard, this date is corroborated by a comparison between Gamli's poetry, on the one hand, and *Leiðarvísan* and similar poems that seem to have influenced it, on the other.

Litla Jóns saga, with the fragments of *Jónsdrápa,* is preserved in the MS AM 649a 4to from the 14th century. As in the other poems quoted in the same context, the apostle is apostrophized in the poem. The final stanza, said in the saga to come "near the end" of the poem, is in *bænarform,* the form of prayer. The *stef* (refrain) seems to be lost, and nothing can be said of the original *drápa* form of the poem.

Besides alluding to Christ's particular love of the apostle John, who, in accordance with the legend, is considered the Lord's cousin, the poem mentions the unsuccessful persecution of the apostle by an evil king, identified in the saga as *Domicianus keisari,* as well as St. John's visions, recorded in the Book of Revelation. With the possible exception of *Hafgerðingadrápa,* this poem seems to be the oldest known religious poem in the *hrynhent* meter.

Harmsól is preserved in AM 757a 4to, a MS from around 1400 containing grammatical literature and religious poetry. The name of the skald, Gamli kanóki, is given in the MS.

The poem takes the form of a *drápa* with two *stefs,* each repeated three times (sts. 20, 25, 30 and 35, 40, 45), giving an *inngangr* (beginning) and a *slæmr* (end) of twenty stanzas each and a *stefjabálkr* (the "stave-section," consisting of several equal sets of verses) of twenty-five stanzas (provided that st. 20 is counted with the *inngangr; cf.* Schottmann 1973).

As in most cases, the ordering of the content corresponds only roughly to the *drápa* organization. After an introductory prayer to God for help in composing the poem, and a general statement on the importance of confession in stanzas 4–6, the poet confesses his sins in stanzas 7–16. General sinfulness in thought, word, and deed as well as particular sins, like swearing, taking part in the Holy Communion unworthily, and hypocrisy, are mentioned. Subsequently, Christ's work of salvation is described (sts. 17–29), his Incarnation and Birth, Passion and Crucifixion between the two thieves (who, by their constrasting deaths, announce the subsequent judgment theme), and finally Resurrection and Ascension.

Up to this point, the poem is a prayer, in which Christ is apostrophized in virtually every stanza (except *stef*-stanzas), whereas the following part is directed to the skald's fellow men, *systkin mín* (33). The following two *stefjamélar* describe Christ's return for the final judgment and the separation of God's children from the damned. The last *stefjamél* is an exhortation to the congregation for conversion.

The *slæmr* opens with a consoling series of examples of God's mercy on King David, Peter, and the penitent Mary. From stanza 53 on, the poem takes again the form of a prayer to Christ for mercy and a blessed departure from life, and to the Virgin Mary and all the saints for help and intercession. In stanza 64, the poet refers to the name of his poem, *Harmsól,* and begs his listeners to pray for him, a reason, incidentally, why the skald's name had to be transmitted together with the poem (Paasche). The last stanza gives a prayer for all Christians.

According to its content, *Harmsól* is a poem concerning confession and grace, corresponding to the two parts of the Christ-kenning in the poem's title. Mainly owing to its numerous kennings, it is, furthermore, a Christian praise poem, in which Christ is praised in more than eighty different kennings, most of them variations of the type "king of the heavenly hall," for example, *hreggtjalda stillir,* "king of the tent of the storms" (st. 1), and *éla ranns rítar gervir,* "maker of the shield of the house of storms" (st. 26). However, there are also kennings more closely connected with the main theme of the poem, like *ǫldu viggs runna angrstríðir,* "destroyer of the sorrow of men (the trees of the wave-horse)" (st. 21).

In the history of skaldic poetry, *Harmsól* occupies an important transitional position. The numerous kennings, which include a number of heathen base words, as well as the *dróttkvætt drápa* form, demonstrate the skald's commitment to the traditions of skaldic poetry. But his themes are new, and transform the poem into an important example of the religious inwardness characteristic of the late 12th century. Stylistically, quotations in direct speech (sts. 22–23) are also a comparatively new phenomenon.

Ed.: Unger, C. R., ed. *Postola sögur: Legendariske fortællinger om apostlernes liv deres kamp for kristendommens udbredelse samt deres martyrdød.* Christiania [Oslo]: Bentzen, 1874, pp. 466–513 [edition of *Jóns saga postola (Lítla Jóns saga), Jónsdrápa,* pp. 510–1]; Rydberg, Hugo, ed. *Die geistlichen Drápur und Dróttkvættfragmente des Cod. AM 757 4°.* Copenhagen: Møller, 1907, pp. 19–32 [strictly diplomatic edition of *Harmsól*]; Finnur Jónsson, ed. *Den norsk-islandske skjaldedigtning.* Vols. 1A-2A (tekst efter håndskrifterne) and 1B-2B (rettet tekst). Copenhagen and Christiania [Oslo]: Gyldendal, 1908–15; rpt. Copenhagen: Rosenkilde & Bagger, 1967 (A) and 1973 (B), vol. 1A, pp. 561–72; 1B, pp. 547–65 [basic edition]; Jón Helgason. "Til skjaldedigtningen." *Acta Philologica Scandinavica* 6 (1931–32), 195–8; 10 (1935–36), 250–64 [textual notes]. **Lit.**: Paasche, Fredrik. *Kristendom og kvad: En studie i norrøn middelalder.* Kristiania [Oslo]: Aschehoug, 1914, pp. 108–18, 173; rpt. in Paasche, Fredrik. *Hedenskap og kristendom. Studier i norrøn middelalder.* Oslo: Aschehoug, 1948, pp. 142–52, 210; Skard, Vemund. "Harmsól, Plácítusdrápa og Leiðarvísan." *Arkiv för nordisk filologi* 68 (1953), 97–108; Turville-Petre, G. *Origins of Icelandic Literature.* Oxford: Clarendon, 1953, pp. 161–3; Lange, Wolfgang. *Studien zur christlichen Dichtung der Nordgermanen 1000–1200.* Palaestra, 222. Göttingen: Vandenhoeck & Ruprecht, 1958, pp. 81–4, 143–50, 270–1; Weber, G. W. "Harmsól." In *Kindlers Literatur Lexikon* 3. Ed. Gert Woerner. Zurich: Kindler, 1967, pp. 1482–3; Schottmann, Hans. *Die isländische Mariendichtung.* Münchner Germanistische Beiträge, 9. Munich: Fink, 1973, pp. 204–9 [on the *drápa* form]; Frank, Roberta. *Old Norse Court Poetry: The Dróttkvætt Stanza.* Islandica, 42. Ithaca and London: Cornell University Press, 1978, pp. 98–100 [on *Harmsól*, st. 14]; Tate, George S. "Gamli kanóki." In *Dictionary of the Middle Ages.* Ed. Joseph R. Strayer. New York: Scribner, 1982–89, vol. 5, pp. 354–5.

Bjarne Fidjestøl

[**See also:** Christian Poetry, West Norse; Kennings; *Leiðarvísan; Postola sögur; Skáld;* Skaldic Meters; Skaldic Verse]

Gautreks saga is a *fornaldarsaga* that has come down to us in approximately thirty MSS, the oldest of which date from the beginning of the 15th century. The saga is often found in MSS as part of *Hrólfs saga Gautrekssonar* without a title of its own, but in some MSS the different parts are given subtitles like "Frá Gauta konungi enum milda" ("About King Gauti the Mild") or "Sǫguþáttr af Gjafa-Ref og Dala-Fíflum" ("A Story About Gift-Refr and the Dalir-Fools"). One such subtitle gave the saga its present name.

Gautreks saga exists in two main versions, a short one and a longer one, the chief difference being that "Víkars þáttr" is lacking in the short version. This version is generally considered the older, the longer version being the result of later additions; but the arguments are not very convincing. The stylistic material of several texts, both long and short ones, indicates clearly that the relationship between the two different versions is complicated.

Gautreks saga includes three stories: the first part deals with King Gauti of Gautland (Sweden), who is lost in the forest and is given shelter by a most peculiar family. They think it such an outrage to have to feed a guest that they decide to throw themselves over a cliff called Ætternisstapi ("Family Cliff"). The daughter Snotra, however, bears Gauti a son, Gautrekr, and comes to live

with him. The son, now King Gautrekr, appears in the second part of the saga, sometimes called "Gjafa-Refs þáttr," about the dealings between the simpleton Refr Rennisson and Earl Neri. Refr gives Neri a bullock, a very costly present, and expects a costly present in return. But Neri, although very wise, is very parsimonious and cannot bring himself to give away anything but good advice. This good advice nevertheless helps Refr to win both wealth and Gautrekr's daughter.

"Víkars þáttr," in the longer version of the saga, is about Víkarr, one of the minor Norwegian kings, and his foster-brother Starkaðr, who is compelled by the gods to betray Víkarr and sacrifice him to Óðinn. One of the very few links with the other parts of the saga is the presentation of Neri as a son of King Víkarr.

The saga is also connected to *Hrólfs saga Gautrekssonar.* The first chapters appear to continue and/or recapitulate the story of Refr and Gautrekr. Many scholars are convinced that *Hrólfs saga* is older than *Gautreks saga* and that the latter was written as a kind of introduction to the former.

The subject matter of the saga is related to certain folktales and fairy tales of the "Hans im Glück" type (Grimm) and also to certain Icelandic short stories, like *Auðunar þáttr vestfirzka* and even *Króka-Refs saga,* all having as a main theme the acquisition of wealth through the giving and receiving of presents. In both "Gauta þáttr" and "Gjafa-Refs þáttr," the theme is presented as sets of opposites: parsimonious versus generous, and wise versus unwise.

Gauti, Gautrekr, and Refr are also known to the Danish historian Saxo Grammaticus, as testified by a short story in Book 8 of his *Gesta Danorum.* King Gautrekr was famous for his generosity, as evidenced by this story and also by a stanza in the Icelandic poem *Háttalykill* (ca. 1150).

"Víkars þáttr" is based on a poem in *fornyrðislag* meter, called *Víkarsbálkr,* which is interwoven with the text of the þáttr. The poem is a monologue by the mythical hero Starkaðr about his life. It is thought to be older than the saga and usually supposed to date from the late 12th century. Starkaðr is also known from *Gesta Danorum* and from *Skjǫldunga saga.*

As a historical source, *Gautreks saga* has no importance. It was probably primarily meant to be "kátlig frásǫgn" ("an amusing story"), as its introduction says.

Ed.: Verelius, Olaus, ed. *Gothrici et Rolfi Westrgothiæ regum historia* [etc.]. Uppsala: Curio, 1664; Ranisch, W., ed. *Die Gautrekssaga in zwei Fassungen.* Berlin: Mayer & Müller, 1900; Guðni Jónsson, ed. *Fornaldar sögur Norðurlanda.* 4 vols. Akureyri: Íslendingasagnaútgáfan, 1954, vol. 4, pp. 1–50. **Tr.**: Hermann Pálsson and Paul Edwards, trans. *Seven Viking Romances.* Harmondsworth: Penguin, 1985, pp. 138–70 [revision of version in *Gautrek's Saga and Other Medieval Tales.* New York: New York University Press; London: University of London Press, 1968, pp. 23–55]. **Lit.**: Olrik, Axel. *Danmarks heltedigtning.* 2 vols. Copenhagen: Gad, 1903–10, vol. 2, pp. 181–219; Hollander, Lee M. "The Gautland Cycle of Sagas." *Journal of English and Germanic Philology* 11 (1912), 61–81, 209–17; Hollander, Lee M. "The Relative Age of the Gautrekssaga and the Hrólfssaga Gautrekssonar." *Arkiv för nordisk filologi* 29 (1913), 120–34; Götlind, Joh. "Valhall och ättestupa i västgötsk tradition." In *Folkeminne-studier tillägnade Hilding Celander den 17 juli 1926.* Gothenburg: Erlander, 1926, pp. 69–84; Wikander, Stig. "Från indisk djurfabel till isländsk saga." *Vetenskapssocieteten i Lund. Årsbok. 1964.* Lund: Gleerup, 1964, pp. 89–114; Milroy, James. "The Story of Ætternisstapi in Gautreks Saga." *Saga-Book of the Viking Society* 17 (1967–68), 206–23; Tveitane, Matthias. "Europeisk påvirkning på den norrøne sagalitteraturen.

Noen synspunkter." *Edda* 49.2 (1969), 73–95 [esp. pp. 84–7]; Amory, Frederick. "Pseudoarchaism and Fiction in Króka-Refs Saga." *Fourth International Saga Conference.* Munich: Institut für nordische Philologie der Universität München, 1979, 21 pp. [photocopies of papers distributed to participants]; Boyer, Régis. "How to Make a Good Fornaldarsaga." *Fourth International Saga Conference,* 14 pp.; Vermeyden, Paula. "Kanttekeningen bij de twee versies van de Gautreks Saga." *Amsterdamer Beiträge zur älteren Germanistik* 17 (1982), 163–77.

Paula Vermeyden

[See also: Divine Heroes, Native; Folklore; *Fornaldarsǫgur*; *Hrólfs saga Gautrekssonar*; *Þáttr*]

Geisli *see* Einarr Skúlason

Geographical Literature. Nordic medieval literature includes a considerable amount of geographical material, divisible into three main categories: descriptive accounts of regions, countries, and the world; travel writing; and miscellaneous geographic-ethnographic information.

Examples of the first category are found in Snorri's *Ynglinga saga* (ch. 1) and in the prologue to his *Edda* (ch. 2). AM 736 I 4to, from around 1300, also includes a brief description of the world. Saxo's *Gesta Danorum* is prefaced by a description of the geography and ethnography of the Nordic countries. Norway is described in the introduction to *Historia Norwegiae* and in *Óláfs saga Tryggvasonar* (ch. 22; AM 310 4to) by brother Oddr Snorrason. Snorri also accounts for the geography of Sweden and its dioceses in *Óláfs saga Haraldssonar* (ch. 77). *Knýtlinga saga* includes a chapter on Denmark and its administrative division, dioceses, and the number of its churches, obviously modeled on Snorri's chapter on Sweden. *Landnámabók* may be seen as a sort of coherent geographical survey of Iceland. The author of *Konungs skuggsjá* tells about "wonders" in Iceland, Ireland, Greenland, and the adjacent seas. Iceland is also the subject of ch. 2 of *Guðmundar saga biskups* by the abbot Arngrímr Brandsson (d. 1361). This passage was apparently written with a foreign audience in mind. An account of Greenland by the Norwegian Ívarr Bárðarson, dating from the middle of the 14th century, is extant in a Danish translation. Regional accounts include the Finnmark passage in *Egils saga* (ch. 14).

The second category, travel writing, is clearly the largest. One of the earliest contributions is the 9th-century story by Óttarr from Hálogaland about his journey past the northernmost tip of Norway to Kvitsjøen (Gandík). This story is extant in the Old English translation of Orosius's *Historiarum adversum paganos* by Alfred the Great. The sagas include numerous examples of travel writing. *Egils saga* tells of various kinds of sea voyages (Viking raids, military conquests, diplomatic missions, abductions, trading expeditions, colonization, foreign travel). *Grœnlendinga saga* and *Eiríks saga rauða* record voyages of discovery to America. Several accounts are extant of crusades to the Holy Land. *Orkneyinga saga* deals with Rǫgnvaldr Kali Kolsson's expedition there in 1151–1153, and the sagas of the Norwegian kings include the story of Sigurðr Jórsalafari ("crusader") Magnússon's crusade in 1108–1111. *Historia de profectione Danorum in Hierosolymam,* dating from around 1200, deserves special mention. This work records the crusades undertaken by Norwegian and Danish chieftains in 1191–1192.

The last category includes, for instance, *Fjarðatal*, a record of

the Icelandic fjords, and *Fylkjatal*, listing the districts of Norway (preserved in AM 415 4to and in *Hauksbók*). Greenlandic churches are recorded in *Flateyjarbók*. In *Norges gamle love indtil 1387* (2:487–91), the late 13th-century border between Norway and Sweden is drawn. Of special interest is *Leiðarvísir* (*itinerarium*), a guide to the Holy Land written by the Icelandic abbot Nikulás Bergsson around 1155 (in AM 194 8vo). *Hauksbók* includes a brief *Vegur til Róms*.

Norsemen drew this geographical material from erudite works in Latin by Solinus, Orosius, Isidore, Bede, and Honorius Augustodunensis. To these they added information acquired personally both at home and on journeys abroad as Vikings, traders, and pilgrims. On the whole, Scandinavia, the Atlantic islands, and the Baltic area are described fairly correctly, except for the assumption that an unbroken bridge of land extended all the way from Russia (Bjarmaland) to Greenland. In general, however, they adopted an uncritical attitude to the numerous fabulous and marvelous tales of remoter and unexplored parts, including tales of one-eyed creatures or humans with dogs' heads, and so on.

Of all Old Norse writers, Snorri best knew how to use geographical descriptions with maximum effectiveness. For example, *Heimskringla* makes several passing references to Kǫrmt (Karmøy) with its royal estate, Ǫgvaldsnes (Avaldsnes), merely recording their geographical names. Only in the context of Ásbjǫrn Sigurðarson's revenge mission against Þórir selr ("seal") do we find a more detailed description of the topography and settlement of the island.

Ed.: Keyser, R., *et al.,* eds. *Norges Gamle Love indtil 1387.* 5 vols. Christiania [Oslo]: Grøndahl, 1846–95; Eiríkur Jónsson and Finnur Jónsson, eds. *Hauksbók udgiven efter de Arnamagnæanske håndskrifter no. 371, 544 og 675, 4° samt forskellige papirshåndskrifter af Det kongelige nordiske Oldskrift-selskab.* Copenhagen: Thiele, 1892–96; Kålund, Kr., and N. Beckman, eds. *Alfræði íslenzk. Islandsk encyclopædisk litteratur.* 3 vols. Samfund til udgivelse af gammel nordisk litteratur, 37, 41, 45. Copenhagen: Møller, 1908–18; Finnur Jónsson, ed. *Det gamle Grønlands beskrivelse af Ívar Bárðarson.* Copenhagen: Levin & Munksgaard, 1930. **Lit.**: Finnur Jónsson. "Grønlands gamle Topografi efter Kilderne." *Meddelelser om Grønland* 20. Copenhagen: Luno, 1899, pp. 265–329; Finnur Jónsson. *Den oldnorske og oldislandske Litteraturs Historie.* 3 vols. 2nd ed. Copenhagen: Gad, 1920–24, vol. 2, pp. 932–6; Jón Jóhannesson. *Íslendinga saga I. Þjóðveldisöld.* Reykjavík: Almenna Bókafélagið, 1956, pp. 128–31; Simek, Rudolf. "Elusive Elysia or Which Way to Glæsisvellir." In *Sagnaskemmtun: Studies in Honour of Hermann Pálsson on His 65th Birthday.* Ed. Rudolf Simek *et al.* Vienna, Cologne, and Graz: Böhlau, 1986, pp. 247–75.

Alfred Jakobsen

[See also: *Egils saga Skalla-Grímssonar*; *Flateyjarbók*; *Guðmundar sǫgur biskups*; *Hauksbók*; *Heimskringla*; *Historia Norwegiae*; *Knýtlinga saga*; *Konungs skuggsjá*; *Landnámabók*; Laws; *Leiðarvísir*; *Óláfs saga helga*; *Óláfs saga Tryggvasonar*; *Orkneyinga saga*; *Profectio Danorum in Hierosolymam*; Saxo Grammaticus; *Snorra Edda*; Vinland Sagas; *Ynglinga saga*]

Germany, Norse in. The term "Germany" here implies territories of modern Germany. In the 9th century, part of this area, roughly speaking that between the Rhine and the Elbe, corresponded to the eastern parts of the Carolingian Empire.

The Norsemen's raids in Germany differ in various respects from their actions in France, England, and Ireland, where the major Viking groups established themselves, sometimes for decades, using fortified camps as their bases. The number of Norsemen operating in Germany also was smaller, all in all, than west of the Rhine. Nevertheless, the eastern part of the Frankish Empire did not remain free from Viking incursions.

In 845, a large fleet entered the Elbe estuary and proceeded to Hammaburg (Hamburg), then a small trading post and an episcopal see, the main base for mostly vain attempts to convert Scandinavia. However, the attack was certainly no pagan reaction to Christian efforts, but simply one of the usual Viking forays. Neither was there any question of a policy of military expansion by the Scandinavian kings. The East Frankish rulers had come to an agreement with the Danes by which the Eider was accepted as the border.

Intent on looting, the Norsemen raided Hamburg. Bishop Ansgar only just managed to have the most important relics taken to safety, while he, his clergy, monks, and part of the town's inhabitants had a narrow escape. But following the destruction of Hamburg, the Viking unit was defeated by a Saxon army centered on the northwest of present Germany, which in 854 belonged to the territories ruled by the East Frankish king, Louis the German.

Shortly afterward, negotiations took place between Louis and the Danish king Horik, who obviously feared being held responsible for the attack on Hamburg, since that blame implied the danger of a German attack on Denmark. The result of these negotiations is not known, but it must have been positive, since no military engagements took place on the Eider.

The year 858 saw another foray into Saxony. Reports concerning this raid are confused: Bremen may have been hit, the Weser offering as good a target to aggressors as the Elbe. Yet this attack was also finally repelled.

In 862/3, a Viking fleet sailed up the Rhine, ravaged Xanten, and established a short-lived camp on a Rhine island, presumably near Neuss. Cologne was looted, but attacks on territories east of the Rhine again achieved no result. The Norsemen realized that Saxon defense measures were after all quite effective, and that easier prey was available elsewhere. Only around 880 did Norsemen again appear in Saxony, and this time they were partially successful, managing to defeat a Saxon army. Even so, they were soon driven off.

The worst incursions into Germany involved the activities of the "Great Army," which had settled in the area of Meuse and Schelde between 880 and 892 and undertook devastating raids from its bases into the surrounding areas, sometimes including East Frankish territory. Many towns and monasteries in that region were affected, among them Aix-la-Chapelle, Bonn, Cologne, and Trier. Here, unlike Saxony, the marauders met with little resistance. But in 891, the German king Arnulf of Carinthia achieved a decisive victory over the Norsemen at Louvain. In 892, the "Great Army" retreated to England. By and large, this date marked the end of Norse raids in Germany, except for the occasional local incident. Basically, one has to differentiate between advancing groups of the "Great Army" and direct Danish invasions into Saxony. Elsewhere, no incursions took place. That is to say, the territories of the Rhine, Weser, and Elbe, particularly near the river mouths, were the Viking theater of operations in Germany.

The reason for this limitation probably lay in the numbers concerned. There simply were not enough Vikings to secure a good hold for any amount of time on the extensive German territories in addition to France, England, and Ireland. We are dealing not with hundreds of thousands, but rather some tens of thousands. Moreover, the Vikings were confronted with a very rigorous defense at least in Saxony, where the aristocracy enjoyed the king's full support. One may find evidence in many sources to corroborate the fact that the Norsemen were realists. They certainly did not court death. Where, as in Saxony, too many risks were involved, they retreated. There was less to be done against the large conglomerate of the "Great Army" than against the smaller groups appearing in northwestern Germany. Thus, the defenders triumphed in some places and suffered defeats in others.

Altogether, Germany was less affected by Norse raids than other countries. Yet where they did occur, the consequences were quite as terrible as elsewhere in Europe.

Lit.: Haskins, Charles H. *The Normans in European History.* Boston: Houghton Mifflin, 1915; Arbman, Holger. *The Vikings.* Ed. and trans. Alan Binns. London: Thames & Hudson, 1961; Brøndsted, Johannes. *The Vikings.* Trans. Kalle Skov. Harmondsworth: Penguin, 1965; Jones, Gwyn. *A History of the Vikings.* Rev. ed. Oxford and New York: Oxford University Press, 1984; Sawyer, Peter H. *The Age of the Vikings.* London: Arnold, 1971; Blair, Peter Hunter. *An Introduction to Anglo-Saxon England.* 2nd ed. Cambridge: Cambridge University Press, 1977; Wilson, David M. *The Vikings and Their Origins: Scandinavia in the First Millennium.* London: Thames & Hudson, 1980; Wilson, David M., and Ole Klindt-Jensen. *Viking Art.* 2nd ed. London: Allen & Unwin, 1980; Logan, Donald F. *The Vikings in History.* London: Hutchinson, 1983.

Horst Zettel

Gesta Danorum *see* **Saxo Grammaticus**

Gesta Hammaburgensis ecclesiae pontificum *see* **Adam of Bremen**

Gesta Normannorum ducum *see* **William of Jumièges**

Giants *see* **Supernatural Beings**

Gibbons saga ("The Saga of Gibbon") was composed in Iceland in the 14th century and is preserved in twenty-three MSS and fragments, the most important of which are AM 335 4to (vellum, *ca.* 1400), AM 529 4to (vellum, 16th century), and Cod. Stock. Perg. fol. no. 7 (late 15th century), a MS containing a total of eleven *riddarasögur.* There is also a very early fragment, AM 567 XVI 4to (one leaf, late 14th century). The remaining MSS are paper, dating for the most part from the 18th and 19th centuries.

Gibbon, son of King Vilhjálmr of France, pursues a beautiful deer while hunting one day and becomes separated from his companions. On the evening of the second day, unable to find the deer, he sees a cloth spread out on a cliff. Lying down upon the cloth, he is transported magically to Greece through the agency of Greka, the fairy-like daughter of King Filipus of Greece, who explains that she has chosen Gibbon of all the princes in the world as her husband. During the lengthy liaison that follows, Greka remains invisible to Gibbon, and he in turn invisible to the Greeks. She finally makes herself visible to him, but as a result he is made visible to the king, who forces him to return to France.

Back in France, Gibbon hears of the beautiful maiden-king Florentia of India, whom he vows to marry "or at least deflower."

Gibbon journeys to India and presents his suit. Realizing that his intentions are not honorable, Florentía challenges Gibbon to a harp-playing competition. Gibbon is victorious but must meet the giant Eskopart in single combat. He fatally wounds the giant, who asks that the son of Gibbon and Florentía be named after him. Furious at Gibbon's victory, Florentía assembles a huge army. After three days of fighting, only Gibbon and his companion Kollr remain. They are rescued by Greka and her flying carpet.

Returning to India, Gibbon, disguised as a monk, forces Florentía, the author at this point observing: "eigi var klaustra regula vel halldin a þessarri natt" ("the monastic rule was not well kept that night"). Gibbon remains with Florentía for a year, at the end of which she bears him a son, who is duly named Eskopart. Gibbon is again magically transported to Greece, and he and Greka are married.

Meanwhile, Eskopart grows to manhood, ignorant of his paternity. Having learned the truth from his mother, he vows to kill Gibbon, but following a hard battle in which each believes he has killed the other, the two are reconciled. Eskopart succeeds his father as king of France. According to one MS, Gibbon and Greka enter a cloister in their old age, and Eskopart becomes king of Greece.

As this synopsis makes clear, *Gibbons saga* is a not entirely successful amalgam of two basic motif patterns: maiden-king romances and tales of the union between human and fairy. For the latter, and indeed several other motifs, the saga is indebted to *Partalopa saga*. For the maiden-king elements, on the other hand, *Gibbons saga* is indebted to *Klári saga* (Wahlgren 1938). *Gibbons saga* also shares with *Rémundar saga keisarasonar* an overall plot structure and a number of incidental details, some of which probably represent cases of independent borrowing from the same source (*e.g.*, the name Eskopart occurs in *Bevis saga*). A number of elements also seem to have been borrowed from *Viktors saga ok Blávus* (*e.g.*, the flying-carpet motif) and from the shorter version of *Sigurðar saga þǫgla* (Einar Ól Sveinsson, 1964: cxxviiff.).

Ed.: Page, R. I., ed. *Gibbons saga*. Editiones Arnamagnæanæ, ser. B, vol. 2. Copenhagen: Munksgaard, 1960. **Bib.**: Kalinke, Marianne E., and P. M. Mitchell. *Bibliography of Old Norse–Icelandic Romances*. Islandica, 44. Ithaca and London: Cornell University Press, 1985, pp. 49–50. **Lit.**: Leach, Henry Goddard. "Is Gibbonssaga a Reflection of Partonopeus?" In *Medieval Studies in Memory of Gertrude Schoepperle Loomis*. Ed. R. S. Loomis. Paris: Champion; New York: Columbia University Press, 1927, pp. 305–20; Björn K. Þórólfsson. *Rímur fyrir 1600*. Safn Fræðafjelagsins um Ísland og Íslendinga, 9. Copenhagen: Møller, 1934; Schlauch, Margaret. *Romance in Iceland*. Princeton: Princeton University Press; New York: American-Scandinavian Foundation; London: Allen & Unwin, 1934; rpt. New York: Russell & Russell, 1973; Wahlgren, Erik. *The Maiden King in Iceland*. Chicago: University of Chicago Libraries, 1938 [private publication]; Einar Ól. Sveinsson. "*Viktors saga ok Blávus*: Sources and Characteristics." In *Viktors saga ok Blávus*. Ed. Jónas Kristjánsson. Riddarasögur, 2. Reykjavik: Handritastofnun Íslands, 1964, pp. cix–ccix; Glauser, Jürg. *Isländische Märchensagas: Studien zur Prosaliteratur im spätmittelalterlichen Island*. Beiträge zur nordischen Philologie, 12. Basel and Frankfurt am Main: Helbing & Lichtenhahn, 1983; Kalinke, Marianne. "Norse Romances (*Riddarasögur*)." In *Old Norse–Icelandic Literature: A Critical Guide*. Ed. Carol J. Clover and John Lindow. Islandica, 45. Ithaca and London: Cornell University Press, 1985, pp. 316–63; Kalinke, Marianne E. "The Misogamous Maiden Kings of Icelandic Romance." *Scripta Islandica* 37 (1986), 47–71.

M. J. Driscoll

[**See also:** *Klári (Clári) saga*; Old Norse-Icelandic Literature, Foreign Influence on; *Partalopa saga*; *Rémundar saga keisarasonar*; *Riddarasögur*; *Sigurðar saga þǫgla*; *Viktors saga ok Blávus*]

Gísla saga Súrssonar

Gísla saga Súrssonar ("The Saga of Gísli Súrsson") is the prototype of the Icelandic *skógarmanna sögur* ("outlaw sagas"). In the first part of the saga, we are told about the events that caused Gísli to be outlawed. Gísli was a staunch upholder of the honor and morality of his family. In this role, he clashed with his brother and sister, who showed a certain moral laxity. Consequently, the family is torn apart and Gísli is left alone, with only the support and devotion of his wife, Auðr.

After a short prologue about the hero's ancestors and their emigration to Iceland, Gísli's sister, Þórdís, marries Þorgrímr, a member of one of the most noble families in Iceland. Gísli and his brother, Þorkell, also marry. An illicit affair between Þorkell's wife and Vésteinn, Gísli's brother-in-law and close associate, is revealed during Vésteinn's absence from Iceland, which causes Þorkell to move to Þorgrímr's home. At Vésteinn's return, Gísli tries to warn him off, but in vain. During a great seasonal feast, Vésteinn is killed under mysterious circumstances. The murder is evidently a joint undertaking of Þorkell and Þorgrímr, who had shown unfriendliness to Vésteinn before, but it is not certain who the actual killer was. Gísli wants Vésteinn to be avenged, but since it is impossible for him to turn against his brother, Þorkell, he murders his sister's husband, Þorgrímr, while the latter is lying in bed at his wife's side. Gísli recites an incriminating stanza that is overheard by his sister, the victim's wife, and that revelation leads to his outlawry.

In the second part of the saga, Gísli defends himself against his enemies in a series of episodes reminiscent of folktales. The saga comes to a climax with Gísli's heroic death after a long fight with a band of enemies.

Scholars have seen affinities between *Gísla saga* and heroic poetry. Some important parallels in the Nibelungen story have been pointed out, such as the murder of Sigurðr in his bed. But the whole purport of the saga seems to be that the standards of heroic legends cannot be applied to an everyday Icelandic environment. In this respect, the author shows a marked individuality. Moreover, he is a master of focusing on certain matters, while in other cases leaving it to readers to decide what actually happened.

Gísli is said to have been a poet, and the saga contains many stanzas attributed to him. These stanzas must be later, although they cannot have been written by the author of the saga, since there are inconsistencies between the stanzas and the saga prose. Unique are the stanzas said to have been composed by Gísli during his outlawry, in which a dark woman, who resembles a valkyrie, embodies his fear and despair, whereas a white woman brings him hope of a better life in the hereafter. Here, the influence of Christianity is clear. The saga says that Gísli learned about this religion during a journey through Denmark, and accepted some of its values. This sympathy clashes with his conservative upholding of the old values and attitudes.

There are two versions of the saga. The shorter one is found in the vellum MS AM 556a 4to, dated to the 15th century. The longer one, now lost, must have been in a 14th-century vellum in the Royal Library in Copenhagen. It is known from two paper copies written by the librarian Ásgeir Jónsson (18th century) and one other paper copy. The prevailing opinion among scholars is that the shorter version is the more original one, and that the longer version is an elaboration of the shorter one. But not all agree with this view. Only in the prologue is there a marked difference: the story about the cursed weapon Grásíða that the family brought with them to Iceland is much longer in the longer version, and there are fantastic motifs in it, such as are usual in the *fornaldarsǫgur*. The vellum AM 761b 4to contains only some fragments. The fourteen other paper MSS are copies either from AM 556a 4to or from the copies of Ásgeir Jónsson.

Ed.: Finnur Jónsson, ed. *Gísla saga Súrssonar*. Altnordische Saga-Bibliothek, 10. Halle: Niemeyer, 1903; Finnur Jónsson, ed. *Gísla saga Súrssonar*. *Udgiven efter håndskrifterne af Det kongelige nordiske Oldskrift-Selskab*. Copenhagen: Thiele, 1929. Björn K. Þórólfsson and Guðni Jónsson, eds. *Vestfirðinga sǫgur*. Íslenzk fornrit, 6. Reykjavik: Hið íslenzka fornritafélag, 1943; Loth, Agnete, ed. *Gísla saga Súrssonar*. Nordisk filologi. Tekster og lærebøger til universitetsbrug. A. Tekster. 2. Oslo: Dreyer; Stockholm: Läromedelsförlagen; Copenhagen: Munksgaard, 1956. **Tr.**: Johnston, George, trans. *The Saga of Gisli*. London and Melbourne: Dent; Toronto: University of Toronto Press, 1963. **Lit.**: Prinz, Reinhard. *Die Schöpfung der Gísla Saga Súrssonar. Ein Beitrag zur Entstehungsgeschichte der isländischen Saga*. Veröffentlichungen der Schleswig-Holsteinischen Universitäts-Gesellschaft, 45. Breslau: Hirt, 1933; Holtsmark, Anne. *Studies in the Gísla Saga*. Studia Norvegica, 6. Oslo: Aschehoug: 1951; Seewald, Franz. *Die Gísla Saga Súrssonar: Untersuchungen*. Göttingen: Postberg, 1934; Foote, Peter. "An Essay on the Saga of Gisli and Its Icelandic Background." In *The Saga of Gisli*, pp. 93–134 [see above]; Andersson, Theodore M. "Some Ambiguities in *Gísla saga*: A Balance Sheet." *Bibliography of Old Norse–Icelandic Studies* (1968), 7–42; Hermann Pálsson. "Death in Autumn: Tragic Elements in Early Icelandic Fiction." *Bibliography of Old Norse–Icelandic Studies* (1973), 7–39; Thompson, Claiborne W. "*Gísla saga*: The Identity of Vestein's Slayer." *Arkiv för nordisk filologi* 88 (1973), 85–90; Clover, Carol J. "Gísli's Coin." *Bibliography of Old Norse–Icelandic Studies* (1977), 7–37; Guðni Kolbeinsson and Jónas Kristjánsson. "Gerðir Gíslasögu." *Gripla* 3 (1979), 128–62; Berger, Alan J. "Text and Sex in Gísla saga." *Gripla* 3 (1979), 163–8; Grønstol, Sigrid Bø. "Kjærleik og ættekjensle i konflikt: Om kvinnesyn og helteideal i Gisle-saga." *Edda* 79 (1979), 189–95; Hansen, Finn. "Punktum eller komma? Kommentar til ÍF-udgaven af Gísla saga Súrssonar." *Gripla* 3 (1979), 169–75; Hermann Pálsson. "Orð Vésteins." *Gripla* 3 (1979), 176–80; Kroesen, Riti. "The Enmity Between Þorgrímr and Vésteinn in the Gísla saga Súrssonar." *Neophilologus* 66 (1982), 386–90; Kroesen, Riti. "The Reforged Weapon in the Gísla saga Súrssonar." *Neophilologus* 66 (1982), 569–73.

Riti Kroesen

[See also: *Fornaldarsǫgur*; *Íslendingasǫgur*; Outlaw Sagas; Outlawry; Vǫlsung-Niflung Cycle]

Gísls þáttr Illugasonar

Gísls þáttr Illugasonar ("The Tale of Gísl Illugason") survives in two vellum MSS: AM 66 fol., known as *Hulda*, from the 14th century, and GkS 1010 fol., known as *Hrokkinskinna*, from the 15th century. Both MSS contain *konungasǫgur*, beginning with *Magnúss saga góða* and ending with *Magnúss saga Erlingssonar*. There are few textual differences between the two versions. In addition, three abbreviated and altered hagiographic accounts of the story form part of *Jóns saga helga*, the saga of bishop Jón Ǫgmundarson. The link between the *þáttr* and the hagiographic version is Jón Ǫgmundarson, who reputedly had a hand in saving Gísl's life at the court of Magnús berfœttr ("bareleg") Óláfsson (1093–1103).

The *þáttr* is usually considered a historic account, even if details are anachronistic and perhaps apocryphal. Two independent sources provide evidence that the protagonist was a historical personage. In *Skáldatal*, Gísl is listed as one of King Magnús's skalds. His genealogy is also found in the *Sturlubók* version of *Landnámabók*. Still, the story line of the *þáttr*, but not its treatment, is conventional. Gísl is one of many Icelanders who incur the king's wrath and ends up as one of his skalds. In Gísl's case, the king is furious when Gísl kills a retainer who had slain Gísl's father in Iceland.

The masterly treatment of the stereotyped plot provides the *þáttr*'s literary interest. Two premises inform the narrative. First, Gísl is a typical hero of the *Íslendingasǫgur*. He executes a moral duty in avenging the slaying of his father, an act that all, except the royal faction, admire and even condone. Second, a Christian sensibility informs the proceedings. Both Gísl and the king are judged as persons and as advocates of a judicial viewpoint opposed to the Christian concept of justice. Gísl is presented as heroic, magnanimous, and sincere; King Magnús is irate, headstrong, and vengeful, but ultimately acquires an understanding of the administration of justice in a Christian world. At first, it appears as if the story is an apologia for blood revenge. King Magnús has the legal right to punish the slaying of his retainer, but not in blind rage and in a spirit of vengefulness. Then he learns how to temper royal justice with Christian mercy. In effect, justice can be rendered only if the verdict takes into account the intent and the circumstances of the slaying. The *þáttr* thus illustrates a principle of canon law. Indeed, the structure of the story seems to be inspired by the canonistic aim to create harmony out of dissonance.

Ed.: Sigurður Nordal and Guðni Jónsson, eds. *Borgfirðinga sǫgur*. Íslenzk fornrit, 3. Reykjavik: Hið íslenzka fornritafélag, 1938, pp. 331–42. **Tr.**: Bachman, Bryant, Jr., trans. *Four Old Icelandic Sagas and Other Tales*. Lanham, New York, and London: University of America Press, 1985, pp. 139–49. **Lit.**: Ciklamini, Marlene. "The Literary Perspective of Gísl Illugason's Quest for Blood Revenge." *Scandinavian Studies* 38 (1966), 204–16; Gaiffier, Baudouin de. "Un thème hagiographique: Le pendu miraculeusement sauvé." In his *Études critiques d'hagiographie et d'iconologie*. Subsidia Hagiographica, 43. Brussels: Société des Bollandistes, 1967, pp. 194–226; Gaiffier, Baudouin de. "Liberatus a suspendio." In *Études critiques*, pp. 227–32; Louis-Jensen, Jonna. *Kongesagastudier. Kompilationen Hulda-Hrokkinskinna*. Bibliotheca Arnamagnæana, 32. Copenhagen: Reitzel, 1977, pp. 111–22; Magnús Fjalldal. "Um Gísls þáttr Illugasonar." *Skírnir* 160 (1986), 153–66.

Marlene Ciklamini

[See also: *Hulda-Hrokkinskinna*; *Íslendingasǫgur*; *Jóns saga ens helga*; *Landnámabók*; *Þáttr*]

Glass

Glass. Although never a part of the Roman Empire, Scandinavia maintained important trading links with the Roman world, and glass vessels were first introduced as a luxury commodity in the early centuries of the Christian era. Some of the earliest examples probably originated in Syria, and found their way into the rich inhumation burials of Denmark; but others, especially in the later 3rd and 4th centuries, were the product of glass centers based within the western empire itself. Their wider distribution in Scandinavia reflects both the development of the North Sea and Baltic trade routes and the increasingly commercial nature of glass output.

These new production centers appear to have been most dense in the Low Countries in the region bordered by the Rhine and the Seine, supplying both military and civilian needs. They seemed largely unaffected by the demise of the empire and continued to export to a new barbarian market, whose tastes in form and decoration differed vastly from the more sophisticated vessels of the old classical world. Scandinavia became an eager importer of prestige wares, typically tall beakers and small jars and flasks in light blue, green, or brown glass, often decorated with applied or marvered trailing. Unique designs, common throughout many regions in contact with established trading routes, included glass drinking horns, claw beakers (showing applied glass trails in the form of claws), and funnel beakers (so named because of their distinctive shape).

The ability to produce glass at this time appears to have languished somewhat, and there is only slight evidence to show manufacturing houses outside the former Roman centers. Similar typological sequences occur in all regions throughout the Continent, and common sources of manufacture must therefore be assumed. In this respect, Scandinavia is particularly important because the pagan burial, the single most useful archaeological context for the recovery of glass vessels, persisted in Scandinavia for several centuries after most of the rest of Europe had been converted to Christianity. After the beginning of the 7th century, therefore, Scandinavia is the only region where the output of the Rhineland glasshouses can be found in anything approaching complete form. The seriations show a marked deterioration in variety of types; generally, the drinking vessels become wider at the rim, lose the standing area, and ultimately emerge as the developed funnel beaker of the 10th century.

Throughout the first millennium, the materials of production seem to have remained largely unchanged. Like most glass found elsewhere in northwestern Europe, composition was of the high soda-lime-silica type produced by using a pure sand component and an alkali derived from natron, a saline evaporate, the closest source of which is located in Egypt. Although it seems improbable that natron continued to be shipped across Europe throughout the millennium, analysis of glasses has not identifed a substitute, and no other solution has been found. A more important change, however, took place in Europe between the 9th and 11th centuries; new materials were introduced as alkali sources, namely forest products, typically wood ash or the ashes of bracken, hence the term "forest" glass. The difference between the two types of glass is largely one of durability; the earlier glass tends to survive well in most buried contexts, whereas the later "forest" glass has a tendency to surface weathering, which causes opacity and eventual decomposition. The majority of glass of the medieval period proper is of this latter type, and its survival is often a matter of chance, giving rise to the poor record of glass-vessel remains known from Scandinavia during this period. Window glass, introduced at this time with the development of church building, suffers a similar fate and rarely survives in anything approaching its original condition. Both window and vessel fragments are frequently weathered to the extent that only a central core of opaque vitrification survives; in many cases, total disintegration must be assumed.

The use of these new alkali materials did, however, enable glass production to be decentralized and to occur in a much wider spectrum of locations where both sand and woodland supplies were plentiful. It effectively localized production, particularly in the forests of Germany and southern Sweden, and provided a semi-nomadic occupation for glass workers who might move from place to place according to the supplies of available woodland. Greater output of glass subsequently created new markets for window and vessel glass alike.

The manufacture of glass entails a chemical reaction between the two raw materials, sand and alkali, under specific redox conditions and according to strict timing. It was not an activity that could be carried out easily, and the processes were recorded in a number of manuals, notably by the monk Theophilus writing in the 12th century. In his *De diversis artibus*, he describes not only the materials to use, their amounts and coloring effects, but also the different methods necessary to produce vessel and window glass, respectively. The furnace, which contained separate compartments for fritting (the solid-state reaction between the two raw materials), melting, and cooling the finished products, seems to conform to a type found throughout northern Europe. The furnaces are poor archaeological survivors and, in the later period at least, were mostly temporary.

Furnace remains tend to be characterized by waste material from the production process, usually melted or twisted blobs of glass, and by the presence of cullet, fragments of vessels that were added to the glass melt to assist in the melting. These were sometimes imported specially for the purpose, and there are records of such trade. Many sites, particularly those occupied toward the end of the first millennium, undertook glassworking activity by melting down cullet and recycling it into beads, mounts, and other glass objects. This procedure could be carried out at a relatively low temperature, required considerably less skill than glassmaking proper, and was not dependent on specific locations for supplies of natural materials.

Tr.: Theophilus, P. *De Diversis Artibus: The Foremost Medieval Treatise on Painting, Glassmaking, and Metalwork.* Trans. John G. Hawthorne and Cyril S. Smith. [Chicago]: University of Chicago Press, [1963]; rpt. New York: Dover, 1979. **Lit.**: Arwidsson, Greta. "Some Glass Vessels from the Boat Grave Cemetery at Valsgärde." *Acta Archaeologia* 3 (1932), 251–66; Polak, Ada B. *Gammelt norsk glass.* Oslo: Gyldendal, 1953 [English summary]; Hunter, John. "Glasses from Scandinavian Burials in the First Millennium AD." *World Archaeology* 7.1 (1975), 79–86; Lundström, Agneta. *Bead-making in Scandinavia in the Early Middle Ages.* Early Medieval Studies, 9. Stockholm: Almqvist & Wiksell, 1976; Lundström, Agneta. "Survey of Glass from Helgö." In *Excavations at Helgö VI.* Ed. A. Lundström and H. Clarke. Stockholm: Kungl. vitterhets, historie och antikvitets akademien, 1981, pp. 1–38; Hunter, John. "The Medieval Glass Industry." In *Medieval Industry.* Ed. D. W. Crossley. Council for British Archaeology Research Report, 40. London: Council for British Archaeology, 1981, pp. 143–50; Näsman, Ulf. "Vendel-period Glass from Eketorp-II, Öland, Sweden." *Acta Archaeologia* 55 (1986), 55–116.

John Hunter

[See also: Painting]

Glossography denotes a scribal practice, widespread in antiquity and in the Middle Ages, consisting in providing particularly difficult or important texts with glosses, *i.e.*, words written between the lines of the text (interlinear glosses) or in the margins (marginal glosses) in order to explain words or passages. Sometimes, lists of glosses, not necessarily referred to any definite text, were written down on full pages or in the blank spaces of MSS;

collections of this kind are called glossaries. The explanations of words could be made either by means of synonyms and periphrases in the same language as the main text or by translation into another language. As far as the Christian West in the Middle Ages is concerned, most of the texts subject to glossing were written in Latin, the "language of culture" *par excellence*, while glosses were frequently written in the vernacular languages.

Compared with the rest of the Germanic-speaking areas, Scandinavia has not left us much evidence of glossographic activity from the medieval period.

The earliest relevant records come down to us from Iceland, where three MSS containing Latin-Icelandic glosses from about 1200 have been preserved. One MS is the renowned Icelandic *Hómilíubók* ("Book of Homilies"; cod. Stock Perg. 4to no. 15), showing on fol. 68rv interlinear and marginal glosses to the Latin *Credo*. The other two MSS, each containing a collection of glosses, are GkS 1812 4to (formerly in the Copenhagen Royal Library, now at the Árni Magnússon Institute of Iceland, Reykjavík) and the fragment AM 249l fol. (also in Reykjavík). Careful examination of the writing and composition of these two MSS has shown that the sections containing glosses were written by the same hand, and that they originally belonged to a single MS. This identification also applies to the glossaries themselves, which are only slightly later than the main text and may originally have been parts of a single glossary. A total of about 260 Latin words, for the most part nouns, with their respective Icelandic equivalents are included in the two MSS. In the former, they appear in two different places (fols. 24r and 34v) and are arranged in parallel columns, while in the latter they are inserted in the blank spaces of a calendar (fol. 4rv), also in columns. The content is miscellaneous, drawn mostly from domestic life and the world of artisans and peasants. Words are grouped, here as in other glossaries of this kind, according to diverse criteria (semantic affinity, metonymical relationship, rhyme, alliteration, *etc.*), which makes it impossible to trace them to a continuous Latin text. Rather, they are likely to be jottings made by some student or scholar for personal use. In other words, the glosses may reflect vocabulary exercises.

Bilingual glosses are also attested sporadically in later Icelandic MSS. For example, in the 14th-century AM 671 4to, interspersed among Latin marginal annotations in a section devoted to theological matters, appear several Icelandic glosses translating terms denoting "God's benefits" (fol. 5r). A series of Latin-Icelandic glosses are also found at p. 120 of AM 242 fol., currently known as the *Codex Wormianus* of Snorri's *Edda* (second half of the 14th century). The glosses, added to the MS by a mid-15th-century scribe, consist of three verbal forms and three adjectives.

As far as Norway is concerned, mention may be made of a small collection of Latin-Norwegian glosses written, presumably by a mid-14th-century hand, on wax tablets, known as *Hopperstadtavlerne*. Beside terms belonging to domestic and rural life, we find here names of animals, especially birds.

Comparatively richer and more varied is the evidence of gloss writing from East Scandinavia. In Denmark, two MSS deserve mention: AM 202 8vo and AM 11 8vo. The former, compiled in the course of the 14th century, comprises a miscellany of notes on Latin grammar and vocabulary. The glosses, mostly translating Latin words taken as examples to illustrate morphological and lexical features, are extremely varied in content. Some of them, however, especially those in the margins, do not bear any reference whatsoever to the main text, but exhibit a close link with foreign glossographic work, in particular with Old High German

glosses to Priscian's grammatical writings. AM 11 8vo, also dated to the 14th century, consists for the most part of a Latin translation of the Jutish Law (*Jyske lov*). A number of marginal annotations, including Latin and Danish glosses, were added in the 15th century.

The earliest evidence of glossing in Sweden is provided by the oldest extant Swedish MS, Stockholm codex B 59, a well-known MS of the so-called Older West-Götaland Law (*Äldre Västgötalagen*), written in the late 13th century. Latin-Swedish glosses, dating from the first half of the 14th century, are found in two different places in the MS (fols. 67v and 77v). Particularly interesting is the glossary on fol. 77v, divided into two sections, each of which has close correspondences with two analogous collections of glosses found in the Danish codex AM 202 8vo. The glosses in the first section (a list of verbs) also occur, with only slight variations, in a Swedish glossary from the second half of the 15th century (AM 792 4to, fol. 142v; the same glossary also includes many names of aromatic and medicinal plants). Finally, mention must be made of a Latin-Swedish glossary preserved in the early 15th-century codex C 22 of the Uppsala University Library (fols. 69r-77r). Its special importance lies in the fact that it represents the earliest extant collection of glosses of wider range from the Scandinavian Middle Ages, including some 800 words of miscellaneous content, almost a dictionary on a small scale.

Ed.: Schröder, J. H., ed. *Glossarii Latino-Svethici specimen vetustum.* Uppsala: Reg. Acad. Typographi, 1845 [glossary in the Uppsala codex C 22]; Wisén, Theodor, ed. *Homiliu-bók. Isländska homilier efter en handskrift från tolfte århundradet.* Lund: Gleerup, 1872 [Icelandic glosses on pp. 148–50]; Larsson, Ludvig, ed. *Äldsta delen af cod. 1812 4to Gml. kgl. samling på Kgl. biblioteket i København.* Samfund til udgivelse af gammel nordisk litteratur, 9. Copenhagen: Møller, 1883 [Latin-Icelandic glosses on pp. 41–51]; Lorenzen, M., ed. "Gammeldanske glosser i cod. Arn. Magn. 202, 8vo." In *Småstykker 1– 16.* Samfund til udgivelse af gammel nordisk litteratur [unnumbered volume]. Copenhagen: Møller, 1884–91, pp. 22–77 [includes an appendix on other minor East Scandinavian glosses]; Guðmundur Þorláksson, ed. "Islandsk-latinske gloser i et kalendarium i AM. 249, folio." In *Småstykker 1–16*, pp. 78–99; Hødnebø, Finn, ed. *Norske diplomer til og med år 1300.* Corpus Codicum Norvegicorum Medii Aevi, Folio serie, 2. Oslo: Selskapet til utgivelse af gamle norske håndskrifter, 1960, pp. 110–4 [Latin-Norwegian glosses in the so-called *Hopperstadtavlerne*]. **Lit.**: Scardigli, P., and F. D. Raschellà. "A Latin-Icelandic Glossary and Some Remarks on Latin in Medieval Scandinavia." In *Idee—Gestalt—Geschichte. Festschrift Klaus von See.* Ed. G.-W. Weber. Odense: Odense University Press, 1988, pp. 299–323 [on glosses in GkS 1812 4to].

Fabrizio D. Raschellà

[**See also:** Homilies (West Norse); Latin Language and Literature; Laws]

Glymdrápa *see* **Þorbjǫrn hornklofi**

Glælognskviða *see* **Þórarinn loftunga**

Goði (pl. *goðar*). In the Icelandic Free State, a *goði* was the holder of a *goðorð* (roughly translated "chieftaincy"), a position of political and social preeminence among the free landowners or *bœndr* (sing. *bóndi*). Originally, the *goðorð* appears to have been a sacral office, as its names implies (*goði* derives from *goð* 'god'), carrying the responsibility for maintaining a local temple and holding sacrificial feasts. In Free State Iceland, the official duties of the *goðar*, sometimes called *hǫfðingjar* 'leaders' (sing. *hǫfðingi*), primarily involved the functioning of the legal system.

During the early history of the Free State, a *goðorð* was a prize, in theory and sometimes in fact, within the reach of enterprising free farmers. The office could be bought, shared, traded, or inherited. At any given period, several people might share in the control of a chieftaincy, although only one individual at a time was permitted to fulfill the official responsibilities of each *goðorð* at the assemblies. If a woman inherited a *goðorð*, she had to let a man take charge of the office (*Grágás* Ia, p. 142).

The *goðar* were required to convene the local springtime district assembly (*várþing*); each local assembly district included three *goðorð*. The *goðar* were also required to hold the local fall assembly (*leið*), but they could do this individually for their own followers. At the *Alþingi*, the annual national assembly, the *goðar* were the voting members of the *lǫgrétta*. There, they reviewed the national laws and made new ones, determined forms of mulct (punishment or fines), commuted sentences of outlawry to banishments, and had the authority to represent the country in its rare foreign dealings. After the quarter courts (*fjórðungsdómar*) were established as part of the constitutional reforms of the mid-960s, the *goðar* nominated judges from among the *bœndr* for the *Alþingi* courts. The *goðar* also nominated judges to the court of appeals (*fimtardómr*) after it was established at the start of the 11th century.

Icelandic government lacked an executive branch, but a *goði* had a few formal executive duties, for instance, conducting the *féránsdómr* or "court of confiscation" to confiscate the property of someone who had been outlawed. The *goði* also had a large informal executive role: a *bóndi* who won a legal judgment against an opponent was then himself responsible for carrying out a sentence (for instance, killing an outlaw), and he often turned to his *goði*, who could command superior manpower, for aid.

The exact number of the first *goðorð* established at or after the founding of the *Alþingi* (ca. 930) is uncertain, although later Icelandic writings treat the number as having been fixed at thirty-six. About the year 965, as part of a series of constitutional reforms, the country was divided into quarters and the number of "full" chieftaincies was fixed at thirty-nine. The western, southern, and eastern quarters each had nine *goðorð*, but for geographical reasons, the northern quarter received an additional springtime assembly (*várþing*) and hence three additional *goðorð*. To balance these three extra *goðar*, three "new" *goðar* were added to each of the other quarters, but the powers of these additional chieftains were limited to participation in the *lǫgrétta*; they could not nominate judges to quarter courts or take part in local assemblies as *goðar*.

A *goði*'s relationship to his *þingmenn* or followers was a contract that could be canceled from either side. Every *bóndi* who owned a certain amount of property was required to be *í þing með* ("in the assembly with") a *goði*. But, according to the law and the sagas, he could choose which one (*Grágás* Ia, pp. 136–7; II, p. 273). A *þingmaðr* ("thing-man") must either accompany his *goði* to assemblies, including the *Alþingi*, or pay a thing-attendance tax called *þingfararkaup*, which the *goði* used to defray travel expenses for those who did attend. As frequently as once a year, a *bóndi* could break relations with one *goði* and transfer his allegiance to another. Likewise, a *goði* could sever relations with a particular *þingmaðr* (*Grágás* Ia, p. 140; II, pp. 277–8).

A chieftain's authority was derived from control of all or part of a *goðorð*, but his power was based on overlapping networks of political, friendship (*vinfengi*), and kinship ties. A *goðorð* was not a geographical unit; the *þingmenn* of different *goðar* often lived interspersed in a district. A *goði* looked to his *þingmenn* for armed manpower in pursuing feuds, exerting pressure in court cases, or carrying out legal sentences. A *bóndi* (and sometimes another *goði*) sought a chieftain's aid to bring his case before the courts, to help him enforce his rights, or to carry out his feuds. Successful *goðar* often played the role of power broker.

The *goðorð* is described in the laws as "power and not wealth" ("veldi er þat en æigi fe," *Grágás* III, p. 44; Ib, p. 206; II, p. 47), and, although otherwise treated as a private possession, it was exempted from being counted as taxable for the tithe. *Goðar* nevertheless often expected to be paid for their services to others, and the sagas show *goðar* frequently concerned with money matters. A crucial role of the *goðar* was to facilitate the redistribution of wealth. They held feasts, gave gifts, made loans, and extended hospitality. Through participation in feuds, they frequently had a decisive say in the transfer of land. The *goðar* were also largely responsible for pricing and helping to distribute imported goods.

By the 13th century, a new, smaller group of more powerful *goðar* emerged as five or six families gained control of all the country's *goðorð*. Called *stórgoðar* or *stórhǫfðingjar* in modern studies, these "large" *goðar* or "large leaders" often controlled several of the older *goðorð*. After 1220, the *stórgoðar* fought among themselves, seeking regional, or in some instances national, overlordship. Many of these later leaders sought to increase their power by becoming retainers of the Norwegian king, but their aspirations for independent rule ended when Iceland submitted to Norway's king in 1262–1264. The Crown abolished the chieftaincies.

Ed.: Vilhjálmur Finsen, ed. *Grágás*. 3 vols. Vol. 1a-b: *Grágás: Islændernes Lovbog i Fristatens Tid, udgivet efter det kongelige Bibliotheks Haandskrift*. Copenhagen: Berling, 1852; Vol. 2: *Grágás efter det Arnamagnæanske Haandskrift Nr. 334 fol., Staðarhólsbók*. Copenhagen: Gyldendal, 1879; Vol. 3: *Grágás: Stykker, som findes i det Arnamagnæanske Haandskrift Nr. 351 fol. og en Række andre Haandskrifter*. Copenhagen: Gyldendal, 1883. **Tr.**: Dennis, Andrew, et al., trans. *Laws of Early Iceland: Grágás I*. University of Manitoba Icelandic Studies, 3. Winnipeg: University of Manitoba Press, 1980. **Lit.**: Björn Sigfússon. "Full goðorð og forn og heimildir frá 12. öld." *Saga* 3 (1960), 48–75; Gunnar Karlsson. "Goðar og bændur." *Saga* 10 (1972), 5–57; Jón Jóhannesson. *A History of the Old Icelandic Commonwealth: Íslendinga saga*. Trans. Haraldur Bessason. University of Manitoba Icelandic Studies, 2. Winnipeg: University of Manitoba Press, 1974, pp. 53–63; Gunnar Karlsson. "Goðar and Höfðingjar in Medieval Iceland." *Saga-Book of the Viking Society* 19 (1977), 358–70; Helgi Þorláksson. "Stórbændur gegn goðum." In *Söguslóðir: Afmælisrit helgað Ólafi Hanssyni*. Ed. Bergsteinn Jónsson et al. Reykjavik: Sögufélag, 1979, pp. 227–50; Hastrup, Kirsten. *Culture and History in Medieval Iceland: An Anthropological Analysis of Structure and Change*. Oxford: Clarendon, 1985; Lúðvík Ingvarson. *Goðorð og goðorðsmenn*. Reykjavik: Oddi, 1986; Byock, Jesse L. "Governmental Order in Early Medieval Iceland." *Viator* 17 (1986), 96–104; Byock, Jesse L. *Medieval Iceland: Society, Sagas, and Power*. Berkeley, Los Angeles, and London: University of California Press, 1988.

Jesse L. Byock

[**See also:** *Alþingi*; *Bóndi*; *Grágás*; Iceland; Laws]

Gokstad is a Viking Age burial on a farm of the same name in Sandar, Vestfold, Norway, excavated in 1880 by N. Nicolaysen as the result of treasure seekers finding the stem of a ship. The burial is generally dated to around A.D. 900. For the burial, a ship 24 m. long (Fig. 32) was pulled ashore and let down into a shallow trench. A burial chamber was built aft of the mast, and grave goods placed in the chamber, in and around the ship. The grave was plundered at some time, and there was considerable damage to the burial chamber and its contents. It is believed that the dead person was placed in his bed in the chamber. Skeletal remains are of a sixty-to-seventy-year-old male, and show signs of rheumatism.

The grave goods included ship's equipment, oars for thirty-two rowers, sixty-four shields, a gangway, remains of the mast, and decayed textiles that are probably the remains of the sail. Three small boats (Fig. 33) and a sledge were intentionally broken during the burial. In the burial chamber were found remains of two finely carved beds, while fragments of at least five other beds lay in the ship. A large copper or bronze cauldron with a finely wrought iron chain may be part of the ship's regular equipment, while a large tub and several buckets made in white cooperage technique are probably additional equipment taken on board for the burial. The tent and beds may be part of the equipment carried on board. Gilt-bronze mounts for a horse harness (Fig. 34) show decoration in the Borre style, while some mounts recovered during restoration work on the site around 1930 are in Jelling style. The presence of both styles makes this an important find for the dating of early Viking Age art. Some iron tools and a number of unidentified wooden objects were also found.

For the burial, twelve horses, six dogs, and a peacock were sacrificed. Most of the organic material and the metals are excellently preserved because of the blue clay that was used for the mound. When the ship was restored in 1930, nearly all the wood could be reused; only the stem tops and parts of the ship damaged by the grave robbers had to be replaced by new wood where the old was missing. Two upper planks were also replaced, and the old brittle wood kept in storage. Two of the small boats have also been reconstructed. The ship, burial chamber, small boats, and most of the objects found are exhibited at the Viking Ship Museum, Bygdøy, Oslo, a department of Universitetets Oldsaksamling.

The ship was taken as typical for all Viking vessels, until the Skuldelev finds from Denmark, excavated in 1962. They showed that the late Viking Age had ships of different types for war and trade. The Gokstad ship may be of the type known as *karve*; according to the early-medieval sagas, these were the private traveling vessels of chieftains. The materials and workmanship of both the ship and all other grave goods are of very high quality, and the owner must have been in a position to demand the best. A replica of the Gokstad ship was sailed across the Atlantic to the Chicago World's Fair of 1893, and proved beyond a doubt that ships of this type were excellent seagoing vessels.

Lit.: Nicolaysen, N. *The Viking-Ship Discovered at Gokstad in Norway*. Trans. Thomas Krag. Christiania [Oslo]: Cammermeyer, 1882; rpt. Westmead: Gregg, 1971 [excavator's report; bilingual, English-Norwegian]; Hougen, Bjørn. *Studier i Gokstadfunnett* Universitetets Oldsaksamlings Årbok, 1931–32. Oslo: Universitetets Oldsaksamling, 1934; Brøgger, A. W., and Haakon Shetelig. *The Viking Ships: Their Ancestry and Evolution*. Oslo: Dreyer, 1951; rpt. 1971; Wexelsen, Einar, ed. *Centenary of a Norwegian Viking Find: The Gokstad Ex-cavations*. Trans. Karin C. Jenssen. Sandefjordmuseenes Årbok, 1979–80. Sandefjord: Sandefjordmuseene, 1981.

Arne Emil Christensen

[See also: Burial Mounds and Burial Practices; Graves; Ships and Shipbuilding; Viking Art]

Gorm was a 10th-century king of Denmark, and father of Harald Gormsson (Bluetooth).

According to Adam of Bremen, Gorm belonged to a dynasty that, coming from *Nortmannia*, displaced the so-called Swedish dynasty from Denmark in the second decade of the 10th century. From the text, it is difficult to ascertain whether the Hardegon mentioned is Gorm himself or, more likely, his father. If Gorm was no more than fifty years of age when he died in 958 (see below), he was born between 908 and 918.

Gorm is commemorated in two runic inscriptions at Jelling. One of them he himself made in memory of his wife, Thyre, "Denmark's ornament"; the other was erected by their son Harald in memory of his parents. Little more is known with certainty about Gorm than his marriage to Thyre and his fatherhood of his successor, Harald. His accession must have been sometime before 936, when he gave a hostile reception to Unni, archbishop of Bremen, who wanted to resume missionary work in Denmark. No source dates his death. According to Adam, Harald may have been Gorm's coruler for some time, but Adam was keen to highlight Christian Harald at the expense of pagan Gorm. Dendrochronology has now revealed that the timber used to build Gorm's burial chamber was felled in 958, which is, therefore, the likely year of death. Some years later, he was transferred to a new grave in the first wooden church in Jelling. Parts of his skeleton have been recovered, and show that he was forty to fifty years old when he died. He was about 172 cm. tall and, like most middle-aged Danes of the time, suffered from osteoarthritis in the lower part of the spine.

The extent of Gorm's power eludes us. There are no reasons to believe that the previous dynasty ruled only the Hedeby area, nor that the "Swedish" dynasty and the Jelling dynasty were contemporaneous. Gorm is thus likely to have had authority throughout Jutland. His son Harald claimed to have won for himself "all Denmark," but what that phrase actually means is much debated. Many solutions have been suggested, such as the reconquest of the Hedeby area from the German emperor, Zealand from the Norwegians, or the addition of the provinces east of the Great Belt to a Jelling-based kingdom of Jutland.

Ed.: Adam of Bremen. *Gesta Hammaburgensis Ecclesiae Pontificum*. In *Quellen des 9. und 11. Jahrhunderts zur Geschichte der hamburgischen Kirche und des Reiches*. Ed. Werner Trillmich and Rudolf Buchner. Ausgewählte Quellen zur deutschen Geschichte des Mittelalters, 11. Berling: Rütten & Loening, 1978. **Tr.**: Adam of Bremen. *History of the Archbishops of Hamburg-Bremen*. Trans. Francis J. Tschan. Records of Civilization: Sources and Studies. New York: Columbia University Press, 1959. **Lit.**: Krogh, Knud. "The Royal Viking-Age Monuments in Jelling in the Light of Recent Archaeological Excavations." *Acta Archaeologica* 53 (1982), 183–216; Jones, Gwyn. *A History of the Vikings*. 2nd ed. Oxford and New York: Oxford University Press, 1984; Moltke, Erik. *Runes and Their Origin, Denmark and Elsewhere*. Trans. Peter Foote. Copenhagen: National Museum of Denmark, 1985; Sawyer, Peter. *Da*

32. Reconstructed Gokstad ship in the Viking Ship Hall, Bygdøy, Oslo.
Photo: Jac. Brun. By permission of Universitetets Oldsaksamling.

33. Two of the three small boats (reconstructed) found with the Gokstad
ship. The smallest, 6.5 m. long, in the foreground. Photo: Jac. Brun. By
permission of Universitetets Oldsaksamling.

34. Bronze strap mounts from the Gokstad find. Photo by permission of Universitetets Oldsaksamling.

Danmark blev Danmark. Gyldendal og Politikens Danmarkshistorie, 3. Copenhagen: Gyldendal; Politiken, 1988.

Niels Lund

[**See also:** Adam of Bremen; Harald Gormsson (Bluetooth); Jelling; Runes and Runic Inscriptions]

Gotland. The name "Gotland" appears for the first time toward the end of the 9th century in Wulfstan's account in the Old English translation of Orosius's *Historiarum adversum paganos* (Book 1:i) of his travels from Hedeby across the Baltic to Truso. According to Wulfstan, Gotland was at that time loosely attached to Sweden. Not until the 11th century was a treaty made by which the island agreed to pay an annual tribute of sixty marks of silver to the Swedish king to have his protection and to be able to travel freely throughout all parts of his kingdom. During the 12th century, the island was also required to participate with six ships in sea expeditions, or to pay a fleet levy (*ledungslame*) of forty marks for each ship. After 1285, the *ledungslame* was established as an annual tax in addition to the yearly tribute. In this way, Gotland was formally included in the Swedish taxation system, even though the island retained its status as an independent republic.

Territorially, the island was divided earliest into three trisections, and a number of assizes (thing-moots), of which there were twenty in the 15th century. Each thing had a judge, elected by the people, who conducted the thing and represented it at the general thing (*landsting*). At the *landsting*, judgments in serious cases were delivered collectively under the direction of the High Court judge, new laws were established, and decisions regarding the island as a whole were made. The trisections were subdivided into parishes called "settings," with each parish paying ten marks silver of the tribute. The parishes had administrative duties, and were also required to equip the six ships or secure the *ledungslame*. A seventh ship was added later, and was equipped by the Visby guild.

During the Middle Ages, the farmers lived on individually situated farms, where a patriarchial great-family system prevailed. The farmers devoted themselves early to prolonged trade journeys. Silver minted in the Arab caliphate and the Byzantine Empire, especially from the time before the mid-10th century, were brought to Gotland through Russia. After the mid-10th century, German, Anglo-Saxon, and Bohemian coins were also brought to the island. The many magnificent medieval churches on Gotland bear witness to the wealth of the island.

The Gotland mercantile travelers were acquainted with Christianity early. According to tradition, the Norwegian St. Ólafr's visit played a decisive role in the christianization of the island, but this attribution is historically doubtful. The Danish king Valdemar Atterdag's ("ever-day") capture of Gotland in 1361 did not bring about radical changes in the conditions on the island. During the reign of King Valdemar (1340–1375) and Queen Margrethe 1 (1375–1412), there was continuous disagreement among Denmark, Mecklenburg, and Sweden about Gotland, with the result that the Tyska ("German") order intervened in 1398 and occupied the island, but handed it over to Erik of Pomerania (1397–1438) in 1408 as part of a ransom agreement. For Gotland, this situation led to great changes. King Erik had Visby castle built, and introduced a new annual tax to maintain it. In addition, royal bailiffs were installed on the island. After King Erik was dethroned, he resided at Viborg until 1449, when he handed over the island to

Denmark. Danish provincial governors were installed in his place. During the following years, the old system of self-government was further decreased. The central power received greater authority, thus diminishing the power of the thing-judges, and the royal edicts diminished the authority of the *landsting*. Gotland did not become Swedish again until 1645.

The mercantile journeys ceased in the first half of the 14th century. The main reason for the Visby trade had been the general rise of trade in the Baltic, which had its origin in the establishment of Lübeck. German merchants made use of Visby as a center for trade, and Visby soon became the most important transit port in the Baltic. In the 14th century, Visby's importance decreased. Reval, Riga, and Dorpat took over the control of the Novgorod trade, and the German merchant ships sailed less frequently to Novgorod. The wealth of Gotland thereby belonged to the past.

Lit.: Roosval, Johnny. *Den gotländske ciceronen. Vägvisare genom den gotländiska konsthistorien med huvudvikten lagd på medeltida kyrkokonst.* Stockholm: Centraltrykeriet, 1926; Hammargren, Henning. *Gotland, en försvarshistorisk och ekonomisk-geografisk studie.* Stockholm: Marinlitteraturföreningens Förlag, 1938; Yrwing, Hugo. *Gotland under äldre medeltid. Studier i baltisk-hanseatisk historia.* Lund: Gleerup, 1940; Lundberg, Erik. *Byggnadskonsten i Sverige 1: Under medeltiden 1000–1400.* Stockholm: Nordisk Rotogravyr, 1940; Yrwing, Hugo. "Gotlandskyrkan i äldre tid." In *Visby stift i ord och bild.* Stockholm: Idun, 1951, pp. 13–52; Björkegren, Rudolf. "Stiftets danska tid." In *Visby stift i ord och bild,* pp. 53–80; Havrén, Olof. "Från Brömsebrofreden till 1800-talet." In *Visby stift och bild,* pp. 81–118; Björkegren, Rudolf. *Gotländskt: Några bilder från Gotlands medeltid och danska tid.* Stockholm: Wahlström & Widstrand, 1951; Lagerlöf, Erland. *Kyrkor på Gotland. Garde ting södra delen. Konsthistoriskt inventarium.* Stockholm: Generalstabens litografiska anstalts förlag, 1965; Pernler, Sven-Erik. "Gotlands medeltida kyrkoliv." Diss. University of Uppsala, 1977; Yrwing, Hugo. *Gotlands medeltid.* Visby: Gotlandskonst, 1978; Yrwing, Hugo. *Visby, hansestad på Gotland.* Stockholm: Gidlund, 1986; Larsson, Lars. *Sören Norby och östersjöpolitiken 1523–1525.* Bibliotheca Historica Lundensis, 60. Malmö: Gleerup, 1986; Gardell, Carl Johan. *Handelskompani och bondearistokrati. En studie i den sociala strukturen på Gotland omkring 1620.* Studia Historica Upsaliensia, 44. Uppsala: Uppsala Universitet, 1986 [English summary].

Hugo Yrwing

[**See also:** *Guta saga*; *Leiðangr*; Margrethe I; Óláfr, St.; Sweden; Trade; Valdemar]

Gotlandsvisan *see* Swedish Literature, Miscellaneous

Grágás. The laws of the Icelandic Commonwealth are generally known by the name *Grágás* ("grey goose"), which dates back only to the 16th century. *Grágás* is not a unified corpus of law; the name applies to some 130 codices, fragments, and copies made during the centuries. The two principal MSS are GkS 1157 fol., usually named *Konungsbók* or *Codex Regius* because of its residence in the Danish Royal Library, and AM 334 fol., named *Staðarhólsbók,* after a farm in the West of Iceland. Both MSS are masterpieces of Icelandic bookmaking. They are generally dated mid-13th century, with *Staðarhólsbók* somewhat later than *Konungsbók*. The first scribal hand (pp. 1–26) of *Konungsbók* may, however, be as late as 1325.

We do not know who wrote these MSS or for whom. They

are quite different in the arrangement and their actual contents. *Konungsbók* contains sections on Christian law, assembly procedures, homicide, a *wergild* ring list, truce and peace speeches, sections on the lawspeaker, the law council, inheritance, incapable persons, betrothal, land claims, investments, searches, duties of communes, tithes, as well as a number of miscellaneous provisions. Certain sections and paragraphs can be found in both codices, others in only one; for example, *þingskapaþáttr*, the section on assembly procedures, *lǫgsǫgumannsþáttr*, the section on the lawspeaker, and *baugatal*, the *wergild* ring list, are not preserved in *Staðarhólsbók*, whereas its regulations are often more detailed than those in *Konungsbók*. According to Finsen, both versions are recensions of material relating to the same original MS. There was much dispute about the character of this original version, and our actual MSS, which are considered private collections, are thus more or less detailed at the whim or the memory of the scribe. Other sources have been suggested, such as lawspeakers' notes, customary practice, or judgments. Vilhjálmur Finsen (1852–83), on the other hand, conceived of *Grágás* as the laws accepted by the Law Council. Their development can be studied in some detail. Few laws can be dated. Many new laws are *nýmæli* ("novelty"); they were hardly considered definitive.

Grágás differs in certain respects from the Old Norwegian law that the settlers brought to Iceland. It is much more detailed, showing less alliteration and fewer picturesque and proverbial expressions than its early continental Scandinavian counterparts. It has been suggested that *Grágás* acquired a bookish appearance because of various revisions of the originally oral law, perhaps as early as 1117/8, when the laws were first committed to writing by Hafliði Másson as related in Ari's *Íslendingabók*, ch. 10. Our texts presumably represent the law of the 12th century basically in the form that was recited by the lawspeaker. Even if it is difficult to imagine that extensive passages had to be remembered in a style with few mnemonic devices, recent research points out that there is a correlation between the age of the texts and the amount of rhetoric applied to them.

After the Icelandic submission to the Norwegian king in 1262–1264, *Grágás* was soon superseded by *Járnsíða* (1271–1281), and eventually replaced by *Jónsbók*. Both law codes did not replace the Christian-law section of *Grágás*, which remained in force until 1354 in the diocese of Hólar, whereas in the diocese of Skálholt, Bishop Árni issued his own church law in 1275.

Ed.: Páll Eggert Ólason, ed. *The Codex Regius of Grágás.* Corpus Codicum Islandicorum Medii Aevi, 3. Copenhagen: Munksgaard, 1932 [facsimile]; Ólafur Lárusson, ed. *Staðarhólsbók: The Ancient Lawbooks Grágás and Járnsíða.* Corpus Codicum Islandicorum Medii Aevi, 9. Copenhagen: Munksgaard, 1936 [facsimile]; Vilhjálmur Finsen, ed. *Grágás.* 3 vols. Vol. 1a-b: *Grágás: Islændernes Lovbog i Fristatens Tid, udgivet efter Det Kongelige Bibliotheks Haandskrift.* Copenhagen: Berling, 1852; Vol. 2: *Grágás efter det Arnamagnæanske Haandskrift Nr. 334 fol., Staðarhólsbók.* Copenhagen: Gyldendal, 1879; Vol. 3: *Grágás: Stykker, som findes i det Arnamagnæanske Haandskrift Nr. 351 fol. Skálholtsbók og en Række andre Haandskrifter.* Copenhagen: Gyldendal, 1883. **Tr.**: Dennis, Andrew, *et al.*, trans. *Laws of Early Iceland: Grágás. I.* University of Manitoba Icelandic Studies, 3. Winnipeg: University of Manitoba Press, 1980. **Bib.**: Halldór Hermannsson. *The Ancient Laws of Norway and Iceland.* Islandica, 4. Ithaca: Cornell University Library, 1911; rpt. New York: Kraus, 1966; Townsend, J. A. B. "The Ancient Laws of Norway and Iceland: A Bibliographical Supplement to . . . Islandica 4." M.A. thesis, University of London,

1961. **Lit.**: Ólafur Lárusson. *Grágás og lögbækurnar.* Árbók Háskóla Íslands, 1922. Fylgirit. Reykjavik, 1923; Ólafur Lárusson. "On Grágás— The Oldest Icelandic Code of Law." *The Third Viking Congress.* Árbók hins íslenzka fornleifafélags. Fylgirit, 1957/8. Reykjavik, 1958, pp. 77–89; Widding, Ole. "Håndskriftanalyser, 5. GkS 1157 fol. Hånd A i Konungsbók af Grágás." *Opuscula* 2.1. Bibliotheca Arnamagnæana, 25.1. Copenhagen: Munksgaard, 1961, pp. 65–75. Ehrhardt, Harald. *Der Stabreim in altnordischen Rechtstexten.* Skandinavistische Arbeiten, 2. Heidelberg: Winter, 1977; Fix, H. *Grágás. Graphemische Untersuchungen zur Handschrift GkS 1157 fol.* Europäische Hochschulschriften, 1, 325. Frankfurt, *etc.*: Lang, 1979; Fix, H. "Poetisches im altisländischen Recht. Zur Zwillingsformel in Grágás und Jónsbók." In *Sprachen und Computer: Festschrift zum 75. Geburtstag von Hans Eggers, 9. Juli 1982.* Ed. Hans Fix *et al.* Sprachwissenschaft—Computerlinguistik, 9. Dudweiler: AQ-Verlag, 1982, pp. 187–206.

Hans Fix

[**See also**: *Jónsbók*; Laws]

Grámagaflím *see* Bjǫrn Arngeirsson Hítdœlakappi

Grammatical Treatises.

Old Icelandic literature has handed down some of the earliest and most remarkable instances of the application of medieval linguistic thought to the description of European vernaculars. This type of learning, which is the only direct evidence of native language studies in the whole of medieval Scandinavia, is essentially preserved in four writings, traditionally known as "grammatical treatises" (Icelandic *málfræðiritgerðir*).

This body of writings, datable approximately between the middle of the 12th and the middle of the 14th century, is transmitted in its entirety in only one MS, AM 242 fol. (from the second half of the 14th century), better known as the *Codex Wormianus* of Snorri's *Edda*. Here, the four treatises are introduced by a "Prologue," which is found only in this MS. Since none of these works bears a title of its own, they were named by early researchers according to their succession in the *Codex Wormianus*; the names "First," "Second," "Third," and "Fourth Grammatical Treatise" (here abbreviated FiGT, SGT, TGT, FoGT, respectively) have since become canonical, not least because for a long time it was taken for granted that this was their actual chronological order.

For two of the treatises, the FiGT and the FoGT, the *Codex Wormianus* also represents the only witness. The SGT is known in a somewhat different version, apparently nearer to the original and accompanied by two illustrative figures, also from the codex De la Gardie 11 in the Uppsala University Library (early 14th century), currently referred to as the *Codex Upsaliensis* of Snorri's *Edda*. More articulated and complex is the MS tradition of the TGT, which, in addition to being part of the collection in the *Codex Wormianus*, is also transmitted in two other Arnamagnæan MSS, AM 781 1 4to (early 14th century), in a version that is regarded as the nearest to the original, and AM 757a 4to (late 14th century). The tradition shows several lacunae and, even though a reciprocal integration of the three witnesses is possible in the majority of cases, a part of the text, albeit reasonably limited (about one MS page), is unrecoverable. All the witnesses of the Old Icelandic grammatical treatises invariably appear in MSS containing Snorri's *Edda* or parts of it, which clearly points to the fact that the ancient Icelanders used to associate them with this work and consequently with the theory of Old Norse versification.

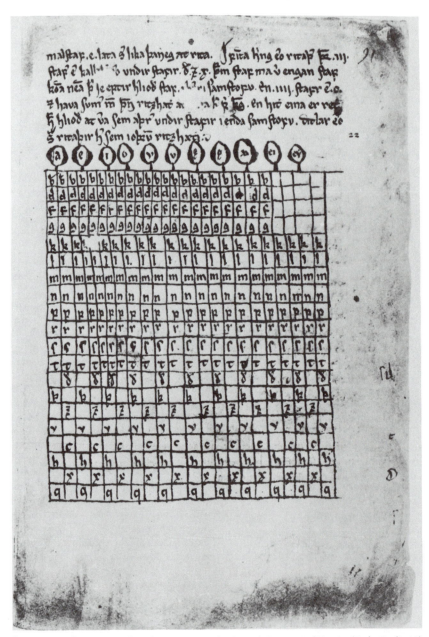

35. Figure showing the interaction between vowels and consonants in the *Second Grammatical Treatise* (De la Gardie 11).

The four treatises were written with the primary purpose of providing young Icelandic students with basic instruments for learning writing and the correct use of language, particularly in view of its application to literary composition, without resorting, at least in the initial stage of their curriculum, to Latin textbooks. Yet each treatise has a well-defined character that differentiates it from all the others, especially if we consider it beyond its merely didactic aspect.

The FiGT, written around the middle of the 12th century, may be viewed as an early attempt to establish a firm and unambiguous orthographic norm by adapting the Latin alphabet to the actual needs of the Icelandic language, on the example of what other western nations, notably the Anglo-Saxons, had already been doing for centuries. Yet the author went far beyond this practical aim, attaining results in the method of phonological analysis that were quite extraordinary for the time.

As to the aim of the SGT, scholars disagree. Some ascribe to it the predominant intention to reorganize and rationalize an orthographic practice that, since the introduction of writing into Iceland, had become increasingly inconsistent and confused; others have seen in it a sort of linguistic introduction to the *Háttatal*, *i.e.*, the section of Snorri's *Edda* dealing with types and structure of meters. More recently, others have inferred from its plain orthographic pattern a sophisticated treatment of distributional phoneme analysis and of minimal-syllable structure. Opinions also diverge concerning its date of composition: the datings proposed so far oscillate between the close of the 12th century and the last three decades of the 13th century.

The TGT is the only one with a known author. It was written around 1250 by Óláfr Þórðarson, the famous skald and Snorri Sturluson's nephew. Divided into two main sections, traditionally referred to as *Málfræðinnar grundvǫllr* ("the foundations of grammar") and *Málskrúðsfræði* ("the science of language ornament"), this is the most comprehensive of the four treatises and, in fact, the only one that fully deserves the name "grammatical." In its first section, in addition to a general treatment of the various types of sounds occurring in nature, of the letters, the syllable, and the eight parts of speech according to the Latin tradition, it includes a thorough comparison between the Latin alphabet and the Old Scandinavian (Danish) *fuþark*. The second section is entirely devoted to the exposition of the principal figures of speech, thoroughly in line with the tenets of classical rhetoric, but fully illustrated by examples drawn from Old Norse poetry.

The FoGT is practically a continuation and a completion of the second part of TGT. Since it was composed about one century later, it partly draws its illustrative material from later Icelandic poetry, often of a religious nature, and, when no suitable examples are available from tradition, the author introduces verses apparently composed *ad hoc* by himself.

The Prologue preceding the four grammatical treatises in the *Codex Wormianus*, whose function and significance are still a matter of discussion, seems to originate from the same author as the FoGT.

Concerning the sources, or, to use a more appropriate term, the theoretical foundations of the Old Icelandic grammatical treatises, it may be said, as a general rule, that they largely rely upon the classical grammatical tradition as transmitted by eminent medieval authors, such as Donatus Aelius, Priscian of Caesarea, Petrus Helias, Alexander of Villedieu, and Eberhard of Béthune. Nevertheless, all of them are characterized, to a more or less con-

siderable extent, by a marked tendency toward interpretative autonomy and originality of elaboration, as well as by the imprint, not always plainly observable on the surface, of a preexistent attitude toward an accurate linguistic analysis, fostered by an agelong acquaintance with runic epigraphy and skaldic poetry.

Ed.: Björn Magnússon Ólsen, ed. *Den Tredje og Fjærde Grammatiske Afhandling i Snorres Edda Tilligemed de Grammatiske Afhandlingers Prolog og To Andre Tillæg*. Samfund til udgivelse af gammel nordisk litteratur, 12; Islands grammatiske litteratur i middelalderen, 2. Copenhagen: Knudtzon, 1884 [TGT, FoGT, and the Prologue, with an ample introduction covering Old Icelandic grammatical literature as a whole]; Haugen, Einar, ed. *First Grammatical Treatise: The Earliest Germanic Phonology*. 2nd ed. London: Longman, 1972 [English translation]; Hreinn Benediktsson, ed. *The First Grammatical Treatise*. University of Iceland Publications in Linguistics, 1. Reykjavik: Institute of Nordic Linguistics, 1972 [the most comprehensive study of the FiGT to date, accompanied by English translation]; Albano Leoni, Federico, ed. *Il primo trattato grammaticale islandese*. Studi Linguistici e Semiologici, 5. Bologna: Il Mulino, 1975 [Italian translation]; Raschellà, Fabrizio D., ed. *The So-Called Second Grammatical Treatise: An Orthographic Pattern of Late Thirteenth-Century Icelandic*. Filologia Germanica: Testi e Studi, 2. Florence: Le Monnier, 1982 [English translation]. **Lit.**: Mogk, Eugen. "Untersuchungen zur Snorra-Edda. I. Der sogenante zweite grammatische traktat der Snorra-Edda." *Zeitschrift für deutsche Philologie* 22 (1889), 129–67; Holtsmark, Anne. *En islandsk scholasticus fra det 12. århundrede*. Skrifter utg. av Det Norske Videnskaps-Akademi i Oslo, II. Hist.-Filos. Klasse 1936, no. 3. Oslo: Dybwad, 1936 [on the intellectual background of the FiGT]; Raschellà, Fabrizio D. "Die altisländische grammatische Literatur. Forschungsstand und Perspektiven zukünftiger Untersuchungen." *Göttingische Gelehrte Anzeigen* 235 (1983), 271–315; Braunmüller, Kurt. "Fandtes der en fonotaktisk analyse i middelalderen?" In *The Nordic Languages and Modern Linguistics* 5. Ed. K. Ringgaard and V. Sørensen. Århus: Nordisk Institut, Aarhus Universitet, 1984, pp. 221–9 [on the alleged phonotactic analysis underlying the orthographic pattern of the SGT]; Albano Leoni, Federico. "Donato in Thule. *Kenningar* e *tropi* nel terzo trattato grammaticale islandese." *AION-Filologia Germanica* 28–9 (1985–86), 1–15 [on the reception of Latin rhetoric in the TGT].

Fabrizio D. Raschellà

[**See also**: *Snorra Edda*]

Graves. In northern Europe, numerous cemeteries with inhumation and cremation burials are known from the Viking Age, containing grave goods that can generally be dated to the 9th, 10th, and early 11th centuries. After christianization (from the end of the 10th century onward), cremation burials and grave goods disappear. In some regions, however, graves were equipped with goods up to the late 11th and 12th (Gotland, Dalarna, western Finland) and 13th centuries (Karelia), or even later (Saami regions in northern Fennoscandia). The diversity of cemeteries and grave forms may be illustrated by two local and regional examples in Hedeby and Viking Age Denmark (southern Scandinavia), as well as Birka and the Mälar region (middle Sweden).

Hedeby, Viking Age Denmark. In connection with the protourban settlement of Hedeby (late 8th–11th century), six cemeteries of varying size have been found (Fig. 36). The largest cemetery (Fig 36, F) was detected south of the semicircular wall surrounding the main settlement areas, where about 700 graves have been excavated: cremation deposits on the ground surface, in pits, and in urns, inhumation burials with or without coffins, rarely in wooden chambers (chamber graves), and in one case in a chamber, which was covered by a boat or ship. Most of the inhumation burials were oriented west-east (head of the deceased in the west); many of them were dug in a north-south direction. Both cremation and inhumation burials were set up as flat graves or covered by low earthen mounds that were limited by closed or interrupted ring ditches. Inside the main settlement area existed one cemetery (Fig. 36, C) with inhumation burials, mostly without coffins (about 350 excavated graves), another (Fig. 36, D) with chamber graves (ten excavated graves), and a third one (Fig. 36, E) with some inhumation burials not far from the harbor. North of the semicircular wall were found a cemetery (Fig. 36, A) with low mounds covering cremation deposits inside a walled area ("Hochburg") and some inhumation burials (Fig. 36, B) south of the Hochburg. Some single burials outside the settlement area proper may also be connected with Hedeby (Fig. 36, nos. 3–4).

Only a small part of the cemeteries has been investigated (about 1,500 excavated graves); the total number of graves is estimated at 7,000–13,000. In Hedeby, as in the adjacent South Scandinavian regions, cremation burials were usual in the late 8th and in the 9th centuries, whereas inhumation burials predominated in the 10th century, mostly in the form of oriented burials. Cremation burials in the form of deposits on the ground surface, in pits and urns, are known from more than fifty cemeteries in Schleswig-Holstein in Denmark, being flat graves covered by low mounds (diameter normally about 10 m., height about 0.3–1.0 m., often with limiting ring ditches), or set up as secondary burials in older mounds. In Denmark, one also finds stone settings of varying forms (circles, ovals, triangles, squares, rhombus or boat shapes; cf. the cemetery of Lindholm Høje), which can also be seen in Sweden, Norway, and, selectively, in the West Slavonic area. Cremation burials in wooden buckets came to light mainly on the North Frisian islands. In some cemeteries, cremation and inhumation burials are set up side by side (so-called biritual or mixed cemeteries).

Most of the cemeteries in southern Scandinavia (over 200) are characterized by inhumation burials, mainly in the form of graves with or without coffins. The orientation of the graves changes: north-south (south-north), west-east (southwest-northeast), the latter orientation current from the 10th century onward (Christian burials). The transition from heathen cemeteries with grave goods to Christian cemeteries and churchyards can be shown at several places in southern Scandinavia (Stengade, Thumby-Bienebek, Fyrkat, Trelleborg, Lund). In the 10th century, wooden chamber graves (length 1.8–3.0 m., breadth 1.0–2.2 m.) were reserved for members of leading families (male graves with weapons and horses, female graves in bodies-of-wagons, i.e., the upper or movable part of a wagon or cart). Royal monuments of this type are the chamber graves in the north mound and the early wooden church of Jelling. More than sixty burials in chambers and more than twenty burials in bodies-of-wagons are known from the Old Danish realm. Concerning the grave forms, analogies can be drawn to continental cemeteries of Merovingian times. On the other hand, boat and ship burials, as testified at Hedeby, Ladby on Funen, and other places, are characteristic of Scandinavia. Viking Age parallels to the grave monuments of Hedeby and Ladby (with warships, length 20 m. and more) include Borre, Gokstad, and Oseberg in southern Norway, all of them with burials of royal families. Stones with runic inscriptions are sometimes connected with burials, as at Svensberg near Hedeby, Jelling, Glavendrup, Funen, and other places.

Birka and the Mälar region. On the island of Björkö, several cemeteries are, as at Hedeby, connected with a Viking Age trading place, in this case Birka (9th–10th centuries). There are at least 2,300 graves, most of them visible; about 1,100 of these burials have been excavated (Fig. 37). The largest cemetery is situated east of the settlement (Svarta jorden, the Black Earth area) at Hemlanden (Fig. 37, 1), with at least 1,600 graves; the majority are circular mounds, some triangular, four-sided, or boat-shaped stone settings, containing cremation and inhumation burials. Flat graves with inhumation burials were found in the western part of the grave field. The cemetery north of the hill fort Borg contained almost exclusively flat graves with inhumation burials (Fig. 37, 2), whereas inside the hill fort were found one inhumation and some cremation burials (Fig. 37, 3). The cemetery south of Borg, with about 400 visible graves, consists mostly of circular mounds, several triangular, and some four-sided and boat-shaped stone settings. The excavated graves all revealed cremation burials (Fig. 37, 4). The Grindsbacka cemetery includes about sixty visible graves, consisting of circular and four-sided stone settings. Of the excavated graves, twenty-three were inhumation and twelve cremation burials. The cemetery was perhaps the youngest part of the Hemlanden cemetery after the decline of Birka (Fig. 37, 5). The Kärrbacka cemetery consists of stone settings with varying forms (mostly four-sided, some boat-shaped, circular, and triangular), most of them with inhumation burials, one with a cremation burial (Fig. 37, 6). The Ormknös cemetery probably does not belong to the Birka complex (Fig. 37, 7).

Inhumation burials (554 graves excavated) are recorded in the following forms: (1) graves in pits, without coffins, sometimes with fragments of a shroud or a cover, and underlay of textiles or birch bark; (2) graves in pits with coffins, which usually are rectangular, sometimes trapezoidal, with varying details (widest in the middle, slanting sides, rounded ends), one riveted coffin may have been a body-of-wagon; (3) graves in wooden chambers, measuring 1.5–3.95 m. in length and 0.9–2.8 m. in breadth. The inhumation burials are normally oriented west-east with the head of the body at the west end; some graves are oriented east-west and in other directions.

Cremation burials (566 excavated graves) are known in the following forms: (1) cremation deposits, with remains of the pyre with burned stones, fragments of grave goods, usually scattered on the ground surface, with or without urns, many of them with rivets, which may indicate the burning of a boat; (2) cremation burials without cremation deposits, the residue of the pyre being put into an urn or a pit; (3) cremations at the burial place (cremation *in situ*) or on a special site.

Concerning the external structure of the graves, low earth mounds are most common, while stone settings with circular, four-sided (rectangular, square shape), triangular, and boat-shaped forms represent only a small proportion. Most mounds contain cremation burials, but inhumation burials are also found since stone settings were raised over both inhumation and cremation burials. Flat graves with no external structure are generally represented by inhumation burials, but some cremation burials also occur.

By far the most common burial custom in the Mälar area in the late Iron Age (Migration Period to Viking Age) was the crema-

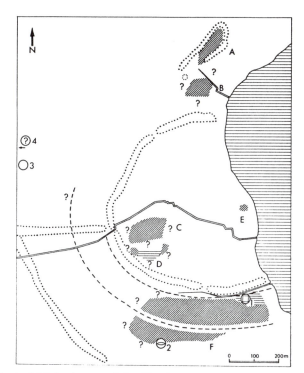

36. Hedeby. Cemeteries: (A) Cremation burials below low mounds (Hochburg). (B) Inhumation burials. (C) Inhumation burials. (D) Inhumation burials in wooden chambers. (E) Inhumation burials. (F) Cremation and inhumation burials, partly below low mounds. (1) Inhumation burials in wooden chambers. (2) Grave monument with wooden chamber and boat (ship) inhumations. (3-4) Single burials. Dotted lines: walls; hatched lines: ditches. After Heiko Steuer, "Zur ethnischen Gliederung der Bevölkerung von Haithabu anhand der Gräberfelder," *Offa* 41 (1984), 191, fig. 1.

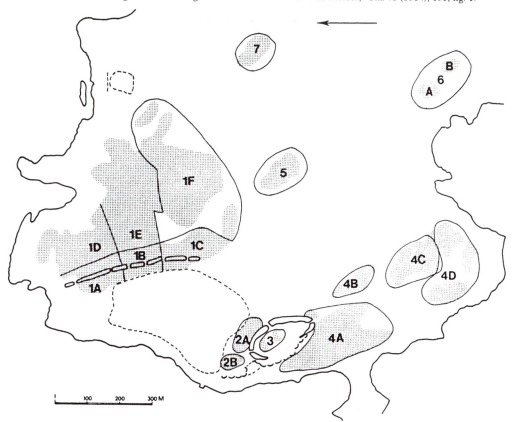

37. Cemeteries on Björkö. (1) Hemlanden. (2) Cemetery north of Borg. (3) Graves in Borg. (4) Cemetery south of Borg. (5) Grindsbacka. (6) Kårrbacka. (7) Ormknös. Hatched lines: settlement areas; closed lines: hill fort. After Anne-Sofie Gräslund, *Birka IV. The Burial Customs. A Study of the Graves on Björkö* (Stockholm: Almqvist & Wiksell, 1980), p. 4, fig. 4.

tion deposit within a mound or stone setting. The late Viking Age gives rise mainly to inhumation burials, often in rectangular stone settings. Viking Age inhumation burials in boats are known from several cemeteries; they continue a tradition from the Vendel Period.

Lit.: **(a) General**: Almgren, Oscar. "Vikingatidens grafskick i verkligheten och i den fornnordiska litteraturen." In *Nordiska studier tillegnade Adolf Noreen på hans 50–årsdag den 13 mars 1904, af studiekamrater och lärjungar.* Uppsala: Appelberg, 1904; Arbman, Holger, *et al.* "Begravning." *KLNM* 1 (1956), 409–17; Skov, Erik, *et al.* "Grav og gravskik." *KLNM* 5 (1960), 437–47; Bø, Olav, and Sune Lindqvist. "Hauglegging." *KLNM* 6 (1961), 246–50; Müller-Wille, Michael. "Bestattung im Boot. Studien zu einer nordeuropäischen Grabsitte." *Offa* 25/6 (1968/69), 1–203; Müller-Wille, Michael. "Boatgraves in Northern Europe." *International Journal of Nautical Archaeology and Underwater Exploration* 3 (1974), 187–204; Müller-Wille, Michael. "Königsgrab und Königsgrabkirche. Funde und Befunde im frühgeschichtlichen und mittelalterlichen Nordeuropa." *Bericht der Römisch-Germanischen Kommission* 63 (1982), 350–412; Capelle, Torsten. "Schiffsetzungen." *Prähistorische Zeitschrift* 61 (1986), 1–63. **(b) Hedeby, Viking Age Denmark**: Thorvildsen, Knud. *Ladby-skibet.* Nordiske Fortidsminder, 6.1. Copenhagen: Nationalmuseet, 1957; Müller-Wille, Michael. *Das Bootkammergrab von Haithabu.* Berichte über die Ausgrabungen in Haithabu, 8. Neumünster: Wachholtz, 1976; Müller-Wille, Michael. *Das wikingerzeitliche Gräberfeld von Thumby-Bienebek (Kr. Rendsburg-Eckernförde).* Offa-Bücher, Neue Folge, 36, 62. Neumünster: Wachholtz, 1976, 1982; Krogh, Knud J. "The Royal Viking-Age Monuments at Jelling in the Light of Recent Archaeological Excavations." *Acta Archaeologica* 53 (1982), 183–216; Roesdahl, Else. *Viking Age Denmark.* Trans. Susan Margeson and Kirsten Williams. London: British Museum, 1982, pp. 159–83; Müller-Wille, Michael. "Skandinavische Einwirkungen auf den Grabbrauch in Haithabu." In *Archäologische und naturwissenschaftliche Untersuchungen an ländlichen und frühstädtischen Siedlungen im deutschen Küstengebiet vom 5. Jahrhundert v. Chr. bis zum 11. Jahrhundert. Chr. 2. Handelsplätze des frühen und hohen Mittelalters.* Ed. Herbert Jankuhn *et al.* Acta Humaniora. Weinheim: Chemie, 1984, pp. 424–32; Steuer, Heiko. "Soziale Gliederung der Bevölkerung von Haithabu nach archäologischen Quellen." In *Archäologische und naturwissenschaftliche Untersuchungen,* pp. 339–66; Steuer, Heiko. "Zur ethnischen Gliederung der Bevölkerung von Haithabu anhand der Gräberfelder." *Offa* 41 (1984), 189–212; Jankuhn, Herbert. *Haithabu. Ein Handelsplatz der Wikingerzeit.* 8th ed. Neumünster: Wachholtz, 1986, pp. 100–17; Müller-Wille, Michael. "Wikingerzeitliche Kammergräber." In *Mammen. Undersøgelser 1868, 1871, 1986.* Ed. Mette Iversen *et al.* Jysk arkæologisk selskabs skrifter, 23. Århus, 1991 [forthcoming]. **(c) Birka and the Mälar region**: Ambrosiani, Björn. *Fornlämningar och bebyggelse. Studier i Attundalands och Södertörns förhistoria.* Uppsala: Kungl. vitterhets historie- och antikvitets akademien; Almqvist & Wiksell, 1964; Hyenstrand, Åke. *Ancient Monuments and Prehistoric Society.* Stockholm: Central Board of National Antiquities, 1979; Gräslund, Anne-Sofie. *Birka IV. The Burial Customs: A Study of the Graves on Björkö.* Stockholm: Almqvist & Wiksell, 1980.

Michael Müller-Wille

[**See also**: Birka; Burial Mounds and Burial Practices; Gokstad; Hedeby]

Greenland, Norse in.

From written sources and archaeological evidence, we know that people of Scandinavian extraction came to Greenland around the year 1000 and lived there for about five centuries. According to the written sources, these people came from Iceland and colonized two districts on the southwestern coast of the country, *Eystribyggð* (the Eastern Settlement, Julianehåb's district) and *Vestribyggð* (the Western Settlement, Godthåb's district). The earliest surviving record mentioning Greenland is a papal bull dated January 6, 1053 (Lappenberg 1842, no. 75), and some twenty years later, Adam of Bremen wrote a short notice about Greenland in his *Gesta Hammaburgensis ecclesiae pontificum.* Both sources count the inhabitants of Greenland among other Christian Scandinavian people.

The oldest Icelandic record of the discovery and settlement of Greenland is a small entry in *Íslendingabók* saying that Eiríkr enn rauði ("the red"), a man from Breiðafjörður (in western Iceland), went there, gave the land a name, and settled at Eiríksfjörðr (Eric's Fjord, Tunugdliarfik). The settlement is said to have taken place fourteen or fifteen years before Christianity came to Iceland, *i.e.,* 985 or 986, but the dating is not well founded. *Landnámabók* and *Eiríks saga rauða* contain fuller descriptions of Eiríkr rauði and the circumstances that led to his searching for Greenland. According to *Landnámabók,* fourteen ships with people from Iceland followed Eiríkr to Greenland; some of the settlers of the Eastern Settlement are named, but some are said to have gone to the Western Settlement.

Eiríks saga rauða and *Grœnlendinga saga* take place partly in Greenland, but because the main topic of these sagas is the description of the Vínland voyages, their information about the fate of the first settlers in Greenland is restricted to short remarks and anecdotes, such as the famous story about the sorceress Þorbjǫrg lítilvǫlva ("the little sybil") in *Eiríks saga rauða* and the description of the sickness in Lýsufjǫrðr in both, probably based on oral tales of Guðríðr Þorbjarnardóttir. But neither of these sagas gives any information about the growth of society or constitutional matters in Greenland. A national assembly (*þing*) at Garðar in Einarsfjǫrðr (Igaliko in Igaliko Fjord) is mentioned in *Fóstbrœðra saga* in the years 1025–1028. Although this source is not reliable, the Icelandic settlers may have founded their own national assembly shortly after the colonization. The earliest reliable source about these matters is *Einars þáttr Sokkasonar,* where special laws of Greenland are mentioned in connection with a dispute at the assembly at Garðar in the years around 1130. As in Iceland, this national assembly was called the *Alþingi;* it is last mentioned in a document written 1389 (*DI* 3, no. 367).

Written sources unanimously state that the first settlers of Greenland were pagans, and that the inhabitants of Greenland were converted to Christianity not many years after the colonization. This assertion has not been confirmed by archaeological evidence; neither heathen graves nor anything else to indicate that heathens of Scandinavian extraction ever lived there has been found in Greenland.

Churches in Greenland are listed in a small entry in *Flateyjarbók,* together with the names of firths and farms where they were situated, twelve in the Eastern Settlement and three in the Western. Another list of fjords and churches in Greenland has been adopted from an old parchment, now lost, in Arngrímur Jónsson's *Gronlandia* (written *ca.* 1600) and Jón Guðmundsson lærði's ("the learned") *Grænlands annál* (probably compiled in 1623). According to this source, which may have been written around 1200, there were 210 farms in the Eastern Settlement and ninety in the Western. This count tallies fairly well with the number of Norse ruins of farms and churches found in Greenland. A small entry in *Historia Norwegiae* says that Greenland was discovered, colonized, and strengthened with the Catholic faith by Icelanders. The Norwegian *Konungs skuggsjá* (*Speculum regale*) says the inhabitants are Christian and have their own churches and priests and even a bishop, although it is no more than one third of an ordinary bishopric. From other sources, deeds, and so on, we know that the first bishop of Greenland, Arnaldr, was consecrated to the bishopric of Garðar in the year 1124. An earlier bishop of Greenland, Eiríkr upsi Gnúpsson, is mentioned in *Landnámabók* and Icelandic annals, where he is said to have gone in search of Vínland in the year 1121, but otherwise nothing is known of him or where he had his bishop's seat. The last bishop known to have stayed in Greenland was Álfr (1368–1377, consecrated 1365).

From ruins of the cathedral and other buildings at Garðar, it can be deduced that this bishopric was relatively rich; according to a 14th-century description of Greenland attributed to Ívar Bárðarson, the cathedral of Garðar possessed the whole district of Einarsfjorðr and, besides other properties, various hunting grounds both in the inhabited and uninhabited parts of the country.

Information about the way of life of the Norse Greenlanders comes from archaeological investigation of the farmhouses and from written sources. *Konungs skuggsjá* says that the farmers in Greenland "raise cattle and sheep in large numbers, and make butter and cheese in great quantities. The people subsist chiefly on these foods and on beef; but they also eat the flesh of various kinds of game, such as reindeer, whales, seals, and bears." For grain, iron, and some of their timber, the Greenlanders had to depend on import. In exchange, they exported walrus and narwhal ivory, wool, ropes made of walrus hides, live polar bears, and falcons. The best hunting grounds were at the so-called *Norðrsetur* north of the Western Settlement in the environs of Disco, where they also obtained driftwood for their buildings, which otherwise were made of stones and turf.

In 1261, the Greenlanders accepted the sovereignty of the king of Norway, who afterward monopolized the Greenland trade. This political move, together with changes in the ice conditions of the shipping routes, caused less communication with other countries and diminishing import of supplies. The Western Settlement seems to have been abandoned about the middle of the 14th century; and at the beginning of the 15th century, many years passed without any merchant vessel coming to the Eastern Settlement. The last surviving record of a communication between the Norse Greenlanders and the outer world is an entry in an Icelandic annal telling of a party of Icelanders on a ship that was storm-driven to Greenland on its way from Norway to Iceland in 1406, who had to stay there for four years. It is, however, not unlikely that the Norse Greenlanders had contact with foreign ships after that time, such as English fishing vessels. But when the Englishman John Davis came to the Eastern Settlement in 1585, the Norse population had disappeared. How and exactly when it disappeared is still an unsolved riddle and will not be answered without extensive archaeological investigations of the Norse ruins.

Ed.: For editions and translations of the sources, see under the individual sagas. Lappenberg, Johann Martin, ed. *Hamburgisches urkundenbuch.* Hamburg: Voss, 1842; rpt. 1907. **Lit.**: Rafn, C. C., and Finnur Magnússon, eds. *Grønlands historiske Mindesmærker.* Copenhagen: Brünnich, 1838–45; rpt. Copenhagen: Rosenkilde & Bagger, 1976; Nansen, Fridtjof. *In Northern Mists.* Trans. Arthur G.

Chater. London: Heinemann, 1911; Roussell, Aage. *Farms and Churches in the Mediaeval Norse Settlements of Greenland.* Meddelelser om Grønland, 89.1. Copenhagen: Reitzel, 1941; Ólafur Halldórsson. *Grænland í miðaldaritum.* Reykjavik: Sögufélag, 1978; Garner, Fradley. "The Lost Colonies of Greenland." *Scandinavian Review* 67.2 (1979), 38–47; Jakob Benediktsson and Jón Samsonarson. "Um Grænlandsrit. Andmælaræður Jakobs Benediktssonar og Jóns Samsonarsonar við doktorsvörn Ólafs Halldórssonar 1. mars 1980." *Gripla* 4 (1980), 206–46; Krogh, Knud J. *Erik den Rødes Grønland.* 2nd ed. Copenhagen: Nationalmuseets forlag, 1982; Jones, Gwyn. *The Norse Atlantic Saga: Being the Norse Voyages of Discovery and Settlement to Iceland, Greenland, and North America.* Rev. ed. Oxford and New York: Oxford University Press, 1986 [all these works contain more or less detailed bibliographies].

Ólafur Halldórsson

[**See also:** Adam of Bremen; *Einars þáttr Sokkasonar; Flateyjarbók; Historia Norwegiae; Íslendingabók; Konungs skuggsjá; Landnámabók;* Vinland Sagas]

Gregory, St.: Dialogues,

Gregory, St.: Dialogues, or *Dialogi de vita et miraculis patrum Italicorum,* is the best-known work of St. Gregory the Great (ca. 540–604), who became pope after Pelagius in 590. The *Dialogues* relate moral tales and edifying anecdotes that became the model for the very popular genre of the exemplum. The *Dialogues* were translated into Icelandic as early as the end of the 12th century, although only a few fragments of the original survive (AM 677 4to, AM 921 IV 4to, NRA 71, 72, 72b, 76, 77). The *Dialogues* appear to have been common reading in medieval Iceland. Scholars have found traces of Gregory's work in many *Íslendingasögur,* including *Njáls saga.* The work also played an important part in the homiletic and hagiographical literature of Iceland.

Ed.: Migne, J.-P., ed. *Sancti Gregorii Papæ I, cognomento Magni, Opera omnia. Patrologiae Cursus Completus, Series Latina.* Paris: Garnier, 1862, vol. 77; Moricca, Umberto, ed. *Gregorii Magni Dialogi libri IV.* Rome: Tip. del Senato, 1924; Unger, C. R., ed. *Heilagra manna søgur. Fortællinger og legender om hellige mænd og kvinder.* 2 vols. Christiania [Oslo]: Bentzen, 1877; Hreinn Benediktsson, ed. *The Life of St. Gregory and His Dialogues: Fragments of an Icelandic Manuscript from the 13th Century.* Editiones Arnamagnæanæ, ser. B, vol. 4. Copenhagen: Munksgaard, 1963; Wolf, Kirsten. "A Fragment of a *Gregorius saga* in AM 238 fol. X." *Opuscula* 9. Bibliotheca Arnamagnæana, 39. Copenhagen: Reitzel, 1991, pp. 100–7. **Tr.**: Zimmerman, Odo John, trans. *Saint Gregory the Great: Dialogues.* New York: Fathers of the Church, 1959. **Bib.**: Widding, Ole, *et al.* "The Lives of the Saints in Old Norse Prose: A Handlist." *Mediaeval Studies* 25 (1963), 294–337. **Lit.**: Konráð Gíslason. *Um frumparta íslenzkrar túngu í fornöld.* Copenhagen: Trier, 1846; Einar Ól. Sveinsson. *Njáls saga: A Literary Masterpiece.* Trans. Paul Schach. Lincoln: University of Nebraska Press, 1971; Boyer, Régis. "The Influence of Pope Gregory's Dialogues on Old Icelandic Literature." In *Proceedings of the First International Saga Conference.* Ed. Peter Foote *et al.* London: Viking Society for Northern Research, 1973, pp. 1–27.

Régis Boyer

[**See also:** Exempla; Homilies (West Norse)]

Grettis saga

Grettis saga ("Grettir's Saga") is one of the four major *Íslendingasögur,* along with *Njáls saga, Egils saga,* and *Laxdœla saga. Grettis saga* differs from them and from other *Íslendingasögur* in its extensive use of supernatural creatures (ghosts, trolls, berserks) and folklore motifs. As in *Egils saga*, the focus is on a single hero, but Grettir seems more a figure from mythology than a realistic Icelander of the 11th century. There can be no doubt, however, that there was a real Grettir Ásmundarson who was born around the year 1000, for he is mentioned in other sources, some earlier than the saga. He seems to have been a well-known character, about whom many oral stories circulated. *Gísla saga*, which is earlier than *Grettis saga*, mentions casually (ch. 22) that only Grettir exceeded Gísli in the number of years spent in outlawry.

Grettis saga was composed sometime around 1310–1320; this date, late for the *Íslendingasögur*, can be deduced from internal evidence, especially a reference in ch. 49. The unknown author collected tales about Grettir from both written and oral sources and shaped them into the present saga, adding some preliminary matter about Grettir's forebears (especially his great-grandfather Ǫnundr tréfótr ["tree-foot"; chs. 1–13]) and some final chapters (83–93) telling how Grettir was avenged in Byzantium by his Norwegian half-brother Þorsteinn, and how Þorsteinn engaged in a love affair there with a married lady named Spes.

Extant today are four more or less complete vellum MSS of the saga and one vellum fragment of six leaves, all from the 15th and 16th centuries, as well as forty paper MSS. The vellums divide into two groups that go back to a single MS and do not differ from each other extensively, so there is in fact only a single version of the saga.

The main part of *Grettis saga* (chs. 14–82) is a biography of Grettir from his boyhood pranks to his death on the island of Drangey. It divides into two parts, the first leading up to his outlawry in ch. 46 and the second describing his nineteen years as an outlaw, many of them in the bleak central highlands of Iceland.

Grettir's youth begins with three sadistic pranks against his father (ch. 14), continues with a trial of strength (ch. 15), and culminates in the slaying of a servant, for which Grettir is sentenced to three years of exile (ch. 17). During his stay in Norway, he breaks into a burial mound and beheads the revenant ghost Kárr after a difficult fight (ch. 18). This is the first of Grettir's encounters with supernatural beings. He also slays twelve berserks and kills a troublesome bear (chs. 19–21). The latter episode brings him into conflict with a malicious Norwegian named Bjǫrn, whom Grettir is forced to kill (ch. 22). When he is also provoked to kill Bjǫrn's equally nasty brother (chs. 23–24), he is obliged to leave Norway.

Back in Iceland, he looks for opportunities to test his strength and soon takes on a revenant ghost named Glámr, whose murderous ways threaten all human life in Vatnsdal. This episode, which is prepared and described in careful detail (chs. 32–35), confirms Grettir as the strongest man in Iceland, but the dying Glámr places a curse on him that shapes the rest of Grettir's life: that Grettir will never increase in strength, that misfortune will dog him, that darkness will make him afraid to be alone.

On hearing that the new Norwegian king, Óláfr Haraldsson, rewards worthy men, Grettir goes again to Norway, but Glámr's curse has its effect when in a heroic attempt to bring fire to his freezing companions, he accidentally burns to death twelve men, including two sons of an Icelander named Þórir Skeggjason of Garðr (ch. 38). King Óláfr gives Grettir a chance to prove his innocence of evil intent, but changes his mind during a ceremony in Trondheim when Grettir, about to undergo the ordeal of bearing hot iron, strikes a mysterious boy who mocks him (ch. 39).

Back in Iceland, things go just as badly, and Þórir of Garðr manages to get Grettir declared an outlaw (ch. 46).

Grettir returns to Iceland (ch. 47) to find his father dead, his brother Atli slain, and himself outlawed, in effect a death sentence, for anyone could kill him with impunity. He first avenges his brother Atli (ch. 48) and then begins the long period of moving from one hiding place to another, fleeing from his enemies and coping with the dark. Some of his adventures belong in the realm of folklore: when Þórir of Garðr attacks him with a force of eighty men, Grettir wards them off with the unexpected aid of a powerful and shadowy man named Hallmundr, who lives in a cave with his daughter (ch. 57). Later (ch. 61), Hallmundr directs him to a warm and fertile valley within the glacier Geitland, presided over by a *blendingr* (half-troll, half-man) named Þórir, and Grettir spends a winter with him and his daughters. The slaying of the two trolls in Bárðardalur (chs. 64–66) is one of the high points of the saga (see below).

Eventually (ch. 69), Grettir, together with his brother Illugi and a servant named Glaumr, moves to the island of Drangey in Skagafjörður (north of Iceland), where he holds out against his enemies for three years. His enemies then enlist the services of a witch named Þuríðr, who curses him (ch. 78) and bewitches a tree stump by carving runes on it. In trying to chop it, Grettir inflicts a wound on his leg (ch. 79), which refuses to heal and so weakens him that his enemies are able to kill him.

The saga says that Grettir "was unlike other men when it comes to size and strength" (ch. 72), and that "he was more suited for slaying revenants and monsters than are other men" (ch. 93). Like the hero of the Old English *Beowulf*, he put his unusual strength to use as a protector of men, cleansing the land of bloodthirsty superhuman creatures. But he was dogged by bad luck, especially in being sentenced unjustly to outlawry, and the words of his uncle Jǫkull, "luck and prowess are two distinct things" (ch. 34), are a major theme in his saga. His enemies, gained through no malice on his part, are not able to get the better of him, however, and it is only by supernatural forces that he is overcome: Glámr's curse, the boy in the Trondheim church who is said to be an "unclean spirit," and the witchery of Þuríðr.

Several details of the saga relate to foreign literature, especially the resemblance of the troll slayings in Bárðardalr (chs. 64–66) to Beowulf's feats against Grendel and his mother. Both episodes consist of two separate fights, the first inside a building against a monster of one sex, and the second in a cave under or behind water against a monster of the other sex. In both works, the opponent of the first fight comes away alive, but having lost an arm. Both heroes are deserted by their companion(s) when blood comes to the surface of the water during the second fight. There are further resemblances that point to a connection, but the nature of that connection remains elusive.

The final section of the saga, the *Spesar þáttr* (chs. 83–93), is set in Byzantium and contains two motifs from the Tristan legend: the ambiguous oath by the unfaithful wife and the fragment broken from a sword, by which the killer is identified. Finally, Grettir's sexual adventure in Reykir (ch. 75) has been compared to Boccaccio's *Decameron* 3:1 (Glendinning 1970).

Ed.: Boer, R. C., ed. *Grettis saga Ásmundarsonar*. Altnordische Saga-Bibliothek, 8. Halle: Niemeyer, 1900; Guðni Jónsson, ed. *Grettis saga Ásmundarsonar*. Íslenzk fornrit, 7. Reykjavik: Hið íslenzka fornritafélag, 1936. **Tr.**: Hight, G. A., trans. *The Saga of Grettir the Strong*. Ed. with an introduction by Peter Foote. Everyman's Library. London: Dent, 1965; Fox, Denton, and Hermann Pálsson, trans. *Grettir's Saga*. Toronto: University of Toronto Press, 1974. **Lit.**: Gering, Hugo. "Der Béowulf und die isländische Grettis saga." *Anglia* 3 (1879), 74–87; Leach, Henry Goddard. *Angevin Britain and Scandinavia*. Harvard Studies in Comparative Literature, 6. Cambridge: Harvard University Press; London: Milford; Oxford: Oxford University Press, 1921, rpt. Millwood: Kraus, 1975, pp. 335–55; Hübener, Gustav. "Beowulf und nordische Dämonenaustreibung (Grettir, Herakles, Theseus u.s.w.)." *Englische Studien* 62 (1927–28), 293–327; Chambers, Raymond W. "Beowulf's Fight with Grendel and Its Scandinavian Parallels." *English Studies* 11 (1929), 81–100; Krappe, Alexander H. "A Viking Legend in England." *Anglia* 56 (1932), 432–5; Nordland, Odd. "Norrøne og europeiske litterære lån i Grettis saga." *Maal og minne* (1953) 32–48; Glendinning, Robert J. "*Grettis saga* and European Literature in the Late Middle Ages." *Mosaic* 4 (1970), 49–61; Hume, Kathryn. "The Thematic Design of *Grettis saga*." *Journal of English and Germanic Philology* 73 (1974), 469–86; Cook, Robert. "The Reader in *Grettis saga*." *Saga-Book of the Viking Society* 21.3–4 (1984–85), 133–54; Liberman, Anatoly. "Beowulf—Grettir." In *Germanic Dialects: Linguistic and Philological Investigations*. Ed. Bela Brogyanyi and Thomas Krömmelbein. Amsterdam and Philadelphia: Benjamins, 1986, pp. 353–401; Hastrup, Kirsten. "Tracing Tradition: An Anthropological Perspective on *Grettis saga Ásmundarsonar*." In *Structure and Meaning in Old Norse Literature: New Approaches to Textual Analysis and Literary Criticism*. Viking Collection, 3. Ed. John Lindow *et al.* Odense: Odense University Press, 1986, pp. 281–313.

Robert Cook

[See also: *Berserkr*; *Gísla saga Súrssonar*; *Íslendingasögur*; Old English Literature, Norse Influence on; Outlaw Sagas; Outlawry]

Grímnismál ("The Lay of Grímnir") is one of the anonymous mythological wisdom poems of the *Poetic Edda*. It is the fourth poem in the *Codex Regius* MS (GkS 2365 4to). MS AM 748 I 4to, designated A, also contains the full text of the poem. Snorri Sturluson quotes twenty-two stanzas in whole or in part in various places in his *Prose Edda* to illustrate particular myths, and draws on at least six other stanzas. Part of stanza 47 is quoted by Ólafr Þórðarson in the *Third Grammatical Treatise*. The meter is principally *ljóðaháttr*, but a few stanzas are in other meters, notably *fornyrðislag*. The number and selection of wisdom stanzas undoubtedly varied among oral performances of the poem, but there is no reason to discard stanzas as interpolations or to treat the extant written text as anything other than a coherent whole.

Grímnismál is preceded by a short prose narrative that is younger than the poem, but represents a reliable tradition. The prose tells how a young king's son, Geirrøðr, is fostered by Óðinn, and later claims his true father's kingdom. Frigg, Óðinn's consort, slanders Geirrøðr, telling Óðinn that he tortures his guests, and then tells the king he is to be visited by a magician. Óðinn (under the name Grímnir) visits Geirrøðr, who, thinking Grímnir is the magician of whom he has been warned, has him seized and set between two fires. As the poem begins, Grímnir has been pinned between the fires for eight nights. Geirrøðr's son brings Grímnir a drink, and the stranger rewards him with a recitation of mythological lore. This recitation, which makes up the bulk of the poem, concludes with lists of Óðinn's names, through which Grímnir's identity is gradually revealed, and with allusions to Geirrøðr's fate. A prose conclusion explains that Geirrøðr attempts to free Óðinn

when he learns who he is, but falls on his sword and dies.

Óðinn's torture and recitation has been interpreted as an example of shamanistic performance and as a reflection of the ritual education or consecration of a royal heir. It is more likely, however, that the myth is an abstract reflection of Scandinavian concepts of sovereignty rather than a report of an actual ritual. The frame story in *Grímnismál* is one variant of a widespread Scandinavian mythic pattern centered on the motif of Óðinn in disguise. The core of the myth is Óðinn's mastery of sacred knowledge; this knowledge warrants his sovereignty over gods and men. Other versions of this myth may be found in the eddic mythological poem *Vafþrúðnismál*, *Hervarar saga*, and in a number of other texts. An interesting parallel to the rivalry between Óðinn and his consort may be found in Paul the Deacon's *History of the Lombards* (Book 1, ch. 8), where the Lombards get their name as a result of a trick played by the goddess Frea on her husband Wodan to defeat his favorites, the Vandals.

Ed.: Neckel, Gustav, ed. *Edda. Die Lieder des Codex Regius nebst verwandten Denkmälern. I: Text.* 5th ed. rev. Hans Kuhn. Heidelberg: Winter, 1983. **Tr.**: Hollander, Lee M., trans. *The Poetic Edda, Translated with an Introduction and Explanatory Notes.* 2nd rev. ed. Austin: University of Texas Press, 1962; rpt. 1988; Auden, W. H., and Paul B. Taylor, trans. *Norse Poems.* London: Athlone, 1981, pp. 234–42. **Lit.**: Vries, Jan de. *Altnordische Literaturgeschichte.* 2 vols. Grundriss der germanischen Philologie, 15–6. Berlin: de Gruyter, 1941–42; rpt. 1964–67, vol. 1, pp. 45–7; Schröder, Franz Rolf. "Grímnismál." *Beiträge zur Geschichte der deutschen Sprache und Literatur* (Tübingen) 80 (1958), 341–78; Fleck, Jere. "Konr—Óttar—Geirrøðr. A Knowledge Criterion for Succession to the Germanic Sacred Kingship." *Scandinavian Studies* 42 (1970), 39–49; Fleck, Jere. "The 'Knowledge-Criterion' in the *Grímnismál*: The Case Against 'Shamanism.'" *Arkiv för nordisk filologi* 86 (1971), 49–65; Ralph, Bo. "The Composition of the Grímnismál." *Arkiv för nordisk filologi* 87 (1972), 97–118; Haugen, Einar. "The Edda as Ritual: Odin and His Masks." In *Edda: A Collection of Essays*. Ed. Robert J. Glendinning and Haraldur Bessason. University of Manitoba Icelandic Studies, 4. Winnipeg: University of Manitoba Press, 1983, pp. 3–24; Mazo, Jeffrey Alan. "Sacred Knowledge, Kingship, and Christianity: Myth and Cultural Change in Medieval Scandinavia." In *The Sixth International Saga Conference 28/7–2/8 1985. Workshop Papers.* 2 vols. Copenhagen: Det arnamagnæanske Institut, 1985, vol. 2, pp. 751–62.

Jeffrey A. Mazo

[See also: *Codex Regius*; Eddic Meters; Eddic Poetry; Folklore; Grammatical Treatises; *Hervarar saga ok Heiðreks konungs*; *Snorra Edda*; *Vafþrúðnismál*]

Gríms saga loðinkinna ("The Saga of Grímr with the Shaggy Chin") is a short *fornaldarsaga* composed in Iceland around the beginning of the 14th century. Along with *Áns saga bogsveigis*, *Ketils saga hœngs*, and *Ǫrvar-Odds saga*, *Gríms saga loðinkinna* tells about the Hrafnistumenn, a family living on the island of Hrafnista off the coast of Norway. Preserved in three vellum MSS from the 15th century, as well as in more than forty paper MSS, *Gríms saga loðinkinna* appears in almost every instance between *Ketils saga hœngs* and *Ǫrvar-Odds saga*. Apparently the youngest of the three, *Gríms saga* also has close parallels to *Hálfdanar saga Brǫnufóstra*, and these two sagas may go back to a common, now lost, written source, possibly the long saga of Grímr skógarmaðr ("the outlaw") mentioned in *Grettis saga*.

Grímr's story begins with the mysterious disappearance of his fiancée Lofthæna. Next follows an unrelated interlude in which Grímr kills some marauding trolls while staying at an isolated house, and then tracks an injured ogress to her cave, where he slays her father before wrestling with and decapitating the mother. On the next day, Grímr comes upon a beached whale, and, after slaying twelve men in defense of it, he is healed of his injuries by a particularly ugly ogress. After sharing her bed, he awakes to find Lofthæna at his side and learns that she had been cursed by her wicked stepmother. Grímr burns Lofthæna's troll-skin, returns home to have the evil stepmother stoned to death, and marries Lofthæna. Some twelve years later, Grímr defeats in single combat the unwanted suitor of his daughter Brynhildr.

Grímr's ancestry is not related in detail in the saga about him, but the first and third members of the *Hrafnistumanna* trilogy supply the story. *Ketils saga* relates that Grímr was the offspring of Ketill hœngr ("salmon") and a troll from Finnmark, and implies that his chin, hairy from birth and impervious to iron weapons, was due to his mother's heritage. *Qrvar-Odds saga* tells a similar story, but obscures the supernatural ancestry by attributing Grímr's hairy chin to the fact that while Ketill and Hrafnhildr were hiding in bed during a visit by some Finns to her father, she had peeked out and focused on the hairy chin of one of the guests.

Three different poetic treatments of the saga material are extant: a five-canto *rímur* by Þorvarður Hallsson (d. *ca.* 1758); a ten-canto *rímur* by Vigfús Jónsson (d. 1728) and his brother Magnús (d. 1684), which adds the material from *Ketils saga hœngs*; and a fragmentary *rímur* by an anonymous 19th-century poet, which includes the story of Qrvar-Oddr along with that of his two famous ancestors.

Ed.: Guðni Jónsson, ed. *Fornaldar sögur Norðurlanda*. 4 vols. Akureyri: Íslendingasagnaútgáfan, 1954, vol. 2, pp. 183–98; Guðni Jónsson and Bjarni Vilhjálmsson, eds. *Fornaldarsögur Norðurlanda*. 3 vols. Reykjavik: Bókaútgáfan forni, 1943–44, vol. 1, pp. 267–80. **Bib.**: Halldór Hermannsson. *Bibliography of the Mythical-Heroic Sagas*. Islandica, 5. Ithaca: Cornell University Library, 1912; rpt. New York: Kraus, 1966, p. 19. **Lit.**: Finnur Jónsson. *Den norsk-islandske skjaldedigtning*. Vols. 1A-2A (tekst efter håndskrifterne) and 1B-2B (rettet tekst). Copenhagen and Christiania [Oslo]: Gyldendal, 1912–15; rpt. Copenhagen: Rosenkilde & Bagger, 1967 (A) and 1973 (B), vol. 2A, pp. 287–9, 2B, pp. 308–10; Finnur Jónsson. *Den oldnorske og oldislandske Litteraturs Historie*. 3 vols. 2nd ed. Copenhagen: Gad, 1920–24, pp. 805–9; Jorgensen, Peter A. "The Two-Troll Variant of the Bear's Son Folktale in *Hálfdanar saga Brönufóstra* and *Gríms saga loðinkinna*." *Arv* 31 (1975), 35–43; Jorgensen, Peter. "The Gift of the Useless Weapon in *Beowulf* and the Icelandic Sagas." *Arkiv för nordisk filologi* 94 (1979), 82–90; Jorgensen, Peter A. "Literarisch verwandte Stellen in verschiedenen Fornaldarsagas." *Fourth International Saga Conference*. Munich: Institut für nordische Philologie der Universität München, 1979, 17 pp. [photocopies of papers distributed to participants]; Finnur Sigmundsson. *Rímnatal*. 2 vols. Reykjavik: Rímnafélagið, 1966, vol. 1, pp. 174–5, 306–7.

Peter A. Jorgensen

[**See also**: *Áns saga bogsveigis*; *Fornaldarsögur*; *Ketils saga hœngs*; *Rímur*; *Qrvar-Odds saga*]

Grípisspá ("The Lay of Grípir") dates from the end of the 12th century and was composed in Iceland. It is preserved in the *Codex Regius* and in a number of paper MSS, which supply the title. The poem was called *Sigurðarkviða Fáfnisbana in fyrsta* by earlier editors, and grouped with the legendary poems of the *Poetic Edda* that recount the life of Sigurðr Fáfnisbani. It is a later addition to the eddic corpus, and draws upon earlier poems. Apparently, it was included for summarizing purposes and as an example of the prophetic poem, or *spá*, a literary form popular in medieval Iceland. Both *Vǫluspá*, in the former, mythological section of the *Edda*, and *Grípisspá*, in the latter, legendary section, were used in Gunnlaugr Leifsson's (d. 1218/9) rendering of Geoffrey of Monmouth's *Prophetiae Merlini* (*ca.* 1200) into the Old Norse *Merlínusspá* in the late 12th century. A reference to the work in *Breta sǫgur* states that many knew the poem by heart, a fact more likely attributable to interest in the genre than in the somewhat confused content of that work itself.

The poem comprises about fifty verses in the eddic meter *fornyrðislag*. The young Sigurðr, on a visit to his maternal uncle Grípir, learns from his prescient kinsman of his heroic destiny. The ensuing episodic narrative, delivered as dialogue, is roughly divided into seven parts: Sigurðr's vengeance on the sons of Hundingr, Sigurðr's killing of Fáfnir and Reginn and seizure of the gold, the meeting with the king's daughter on the mountain, the visit to Heimir and meeting with Brynhildr, the visit to Gjúki and the marriage to Guðrún, the fetching of Brynhildr for Gunnarr, and the vengeance of Brynhildr with its aftermath. Much of the narrative of *Grípisspá* seems to be drawn from the now-lost portion of the *Codex Regius* containing *Sigurðarkviða in meiri*, for the content of which *Grípisspá* is seen as providing important evidence.

Ed.: Neckel, Gustav, ed. *Edda. Die Lieder des Codex Regius nebst verwandten Denkmälern. I: Text.* 5th ed. rev. Hans Kuhn. Heidelberg: Winter, 1983. **Tr.**: Hollander, Lee M., trans. *The Poetic Edda, Translated with an Introduction and Explanatory Notes.* 2nd rev. ed. Austin: University of Texas Press, 1962; rpt. 1988, pp. 205–15. **Lit.**: Vries, Jan de. *Altnordische Literaturgeschichte*. 2 vols. Grundriss der germanischen Philologie, 15–6. Berlin: de Gruyter, 1941–42; rpt. 1964–67, vol. 2, pp. 154–7; Einar Ól. Sveinsson. *Íslenzkar bókmenntir í fornöld* 1. Reykjavik: Almenna Bókafélagið, 1962, pp. 456–8; Harris, Richard. "A Study of *Grípisspá*." *Scandinavian Studies* 43 (1971), 344–55; Hallberg, Peter. *Old Icelandic Poetry. Eddic Lays and Skaldic Verse.* Trans. Paul Schach and Sonja Lindgrenson. Lincoln and London: University of Nebraska Press, 1975, pp. 71–2; Andersson, Theodore M. *The Legend of Brynhild*. Islandica, 43. Ithaca and London: Cornell University Press, 1980.

Richard L. Harris

[**See also**: *Breta sǫgur*; *Codex Regius*; Eddic Meters; Eddic Poetry; *Merlínusspá*; *Sigurðarkviðu, Brot af*; *Vǫluspá*]

Grógaldr *see* Svipdagsmál

Grottasǫngr ("The Mill Song"). This twenty-four-stanza poem in the meter *fornyrðislag* and its accompanying prose tale are variously preserved in MSS of the *Skáldskaparmál* section of Snorri Sturluson's *Prose Edda*. "Grotti," derived from "to grind," is the name for a mill (hence the usual English title). One version authenticates the prose tale by quotation of the opening stanza only in the midst of the prose narrative; this device probably represents Snorri's own style. The full poem is transmitted in two

MSS of the *Prose Edda* in a less integrated fashion appended to the end of the prose tale. Prose-only versions are found in three more MSS of the *Prose Edda*.

The prose tells how the mythical Danish king Fróði, son of Friðleifr, ruled during the world peace caused by the birth of Christ. In Sweden, Fróði acquired two huge slave women, Fenja and Menja, whom he set to work turning two gigantic millstones. The mill would grind out whatever it was commanded to. Fróði ordered the slaves to grind gold, peace, and happiness, but he granted them no rest. So, in the dead of night, they changed the course of their work song and produced a surprise attack by a Viking named Mýsingr, who killed Fróði, ending the era of Fróði's Peace. Mýsingr took the mill Grotti and the slave women aboard his ship and ordered them to grind salt. He too refused them rest, and Fenja and Menja ground on until the ship sank. This disaster caused the sea to be salty, and the currents passing through the enormous eye of the millstones still cause a maelstrom. The prose tale thus unites a story that explained Fróði's golden age and its demise with an etiological tale, "why the sea is salt" (Motif A1115.2), their common motif being the "wish mill" (D1601.21). One version locates the whirlpool in the Pentland Firth, and 19th-century Orkney folklore retained some memory of Grotti Finnie and Luki (or Grotti) Minnie and of a salt-quern there. Other obscure connections with Scandinavian folklore include the Sampo of the Finnish *Kalevala* (Motif F871). *Grottasǫngr* itself implies the destruction of the mill along with Fróði, antedating the composite versions with abduction by Mýsingr, salt milling, and *pourquoi* ending.

The poem is introduced and closed with mainly narrative stanzas (1–4, 23–24), but its core presents the action only through the song sung by the giant slaves; as such, it is a sophisticated derivative of primitive worksongs and contains at least one fragment of a simple mill song (3³⁻⁴). At first, the women grind blessing (5–6); when Fróði denies them sleep (7), they begin to reveal their giant nature (8–9); as girls, their playthings had been boulders (11–2); next, they lived as bloodstained valkyries (13–15); what a come-down to be Fróði's slaves (16). Their song modulates into prediction of the disaster they are now grinding out, an approaching enemy (18–20). At the same time, the mill begins to disintegrate (21, 23); the conclusion may be incomplete. In addition to worksongs, we recognize other underlying genres, including lullaby (5) and peace charm (6); 18⁴⁻⁸ seem to constitute a more than generic allusion to a famous Danish poem, *Bjarkamál*. The interpretive crux in stanza 22 is partly solved by associating stanzas 19–20 with dark prophecy, such as *Vǫluspá*; stanza 22, then, predicts shameful events in the life of Fróði's most famous descendant, Hrólfr kraki, as an ironic sort of "revenge" on Fróði. Datable skaldic kennings (*e.g.*, gold = "the meal of Fróði's sad slave women") prove that the legend was current in Norway before around 960. Whether the surviving poem is that old is debatable; de Vries (1941–42) argues that a Viking Age poem was thoroughly recast in late 11th-century Denmark before receiving a few Icelandic touches along with the language of its final form in the 12th century. Yet *Grottasǫngr* is artistically unified and, except for the analogous *Darraðarljóð*, conceptually unique among poems of the eddic type.

Ed.: Neckel, Gustav, ed. *Edda: Die Lieder des Codex Regius nebst verwandten Denkmälern. I: Text.* 5th ed. rev. Hans Kuhn. Heidelberg: Winter, 1983 [standard edition; for a fuller list see Harris 1985: 129–

30]. **Tr.**: Bellows, Henry Adams, trans. *The Poetic Edda, with Introduction and Notes.* New York: American-Scandinavian Foundation, 1923 [several reprintings, including 1969; for a fuller list, see Harris 1985: 130]; Hollander, Lee M., trans. *The Poetic Edda, Translated with an Introduction and Explanatory Notes.* 2nd rev. ed. Austin: University of Texas Press, 1962; rpt. 1988. **Bib.**: Harris, Joseph. "Eddic Poetry." In *Old Norse–Icelandic Literature: A Critical Guide.* Ed. Carol J. Clover and John Lindow. Islandica, 45. Ithaca and London: Cornell University Press, 1985, pp. 68–156 [bibliography, pp. 127–8, leads to earlier bibliography; for commentaries and recent literature not cited here, see pp. 130, 133–7, 145]. **Lit.**: Johnston, Alfred W. "Grotta Söngr and the Orkney and Shetland Quern." *Saga-Book of the Viking Society* 6 (1908–09), 296–304; Eiríkr Magnússon, ed. and trans. *Grottasǫngr.* Coventry: Viking Club; Curtis & Beamish, 1910 [rpt. from *Old Lore Miscellany of Orkney, Shetland, Caithness & Sutherland* 3 (1910)]; Olrik, Axel. *The Heroic Legends of Denmark.* Trans. Lee M. Hollander. New York: American-Scandinavian Foundation; London: Oxford University Press, 1919, pp. 261–82, 304–11, 476–81; Finnur Jónsson. *Den oldnorske og oldislandske Litteraturs Historie.* 3 vols. 2nd ed. Copenhagen: Gad, 1920–24, vol. 1, pp. 215–8; Malone, Kemp. "Note on *Grottasǫngr.*" *Acta Philologica Scandinavica* 5 (1929–30), 270; Schneider, Hermann. *Germanische Heldensage.* 2 vols. Grundriss der germanischen Philologie, 10.1–3. Berlin and Leipzig: de Gruyter, 1933, vol. 2, pt. 1: *Nordgermanische Heldensage*, pp. 31–6 [see also index]; Vries, Jan de. *Altnordische Literaturgeschichte.* 2 vols. Grundriss der germanischen Philologie, 15–6. Berlin: de Gruyter, 1941–42; rpt. 1964–67, vol. 1, pp. 95–8 [see also index]; Einar Ól. Sveinsson. *Íslenzkar bókmenntir í fornöld* 1. Reykjavík: Almenna bókafélagið, 1962, pp. 447–53; Harris, Joseph. "Reflections on Genre and Intertextuality in Eddic Poetry (with Special Reference to *Grottasǫngr*)." In *Poetry in the Scandinavian Middle Ages: Proceedings of the Seventh International Saga Conference.* Ed. Theresa Pàroli. Spoleto: Centro Italiano di Studi sull' Alto Medioevo, 1990, pp. 231–43.

Joseph Harris

[**See also**: *Bjarkamál; Darraðarljóð;* Eddic Meters; Eddic Poetry; Folklore; Kennings; *Snorra Edda*]

Grœnlendinga saga *see* **Vinland Sagas**

Guðmundar sögur biskups ("The Sagas of Bishop Guðmundr"). Guðmundr Arason, born in 1161, was a priest at various places in the north of Iceland, and bishop of Hólar from 1203 until his death in 1237. Guðmundr was renowned for his ascetic life, charity, and miracle working. Rigid in his striving for the rights of the Church, he fell out with most of the Icelandic chieftains after he became bishop. For periods of his episcopate, he was barred from his cathedral and had to stay in Norway or travel around Iceland, visiting friends together with a great number of followers. The Icelanders regarded Bishop Guðmundr as a saint, but he was never canonized or even beatified by the pope.

Probably a few years after Guðmundr's death, a chronicle of his life was initiated, possibly by the abbot Lambkárr Þorgilsson (d. 1249), who had served Guðmundr at a young age. This chronicle, however, offers an account only of Guðmundr's youth and priesthood, called *Prestssaga*, and ends abruptly in a description of Guðmundr's voyage to Norway in 1202 for his consecration. It is strictly chronological and contains annalistic notices up to 1199. It is preserved only as parts of *Guðmundar sögur* and abridged in *Sturlunga saga*.

The chief source for Guðmundr's career as bishop is *Íslendinga saga* by Sturla Þórðarson (d. 1284). Other sagas that inform us about shorter periods of Guðmundr's life are *Hrafns saga Sveinbjarnarsonar*, from about 1230, and *Arons saga Hjǫrleifssonar*, from the early 14th century. A miracle book, partly written as a supplement to Sturla Þórðarson's account of Guðmundr's life, was probably composed in the opening years of the 14th century and expanded about 1320 after the exhumation of the bishop's relics in 1315.

It is unlikely that any *Guðmundar saga* covering the bishop's whole life was written before the exhumation. There are four surviving *Guðmundar sögur*, A, B, C, and D, different mainly in style and structure. The designations do not necessarily mean that these four recensions were written in the order above, but they imply an assessment of how far they are removed from their principal sources.

Guðmundar saga A (the so-called "Oldest Saga") was written in the first half of the 14th century, perhaps most likely around 1320–1330. *A* is a compilation of the *Prestssaga*, *Hrafns saga*, *Íslendinga saga*, *Arons saga*, and annals, containing only a few original sentences from the compiler himself. The chief MS, AM 399 4to (*ca.* 1330–1350), is deficient, but the gaps, except at the end, can be filled from a later copy.

Guðmundar saga B (the so-called "Middle Saga") was probably written shortly after 1320. *B* is a compilation of the three first-mentioned sources of *A*, interpolated with some additional material and authorial comment; at the end, both parts of the miracle book were added. *B* represents an unsuccessful attempt to write a saint's life about Bishop Guðmundr. The chief MS, AM 657c 4to (*ca.* 1350), is deficient, and only the missing end of the miracle book can be supplied from other MSS.

Guðmundar saga C was written around 1320–1345, perhaps early in that period. It is based upon *B* and/or mainly the same sources together with some additional, partly written, material. Contrary to the compilers of *A* and *B*, who have copied their 13th-century sources, written in classical saga style without any conscious alterations, the author of *C* produced a consistent style by rewriting his sources according to a new taste, and rearranged the material, thus succeeding in writing a saint's life of a confessor, first a *vita* and then *miracula post mortem*. *C* has tentatively been ascribed to a known author of saints' lives, the Benedictine monk Bergr Sokkason. *C* is found only in deficient 17th-century copies, and the text has not been edited, except for the last preserved chapters (Foote 1961).

Guðmundar saga D was written after 1343 by the Benedictine monk Arngrímr (Brandsson?) (d. 1361 or 1362). *D*'s principal source was *C*, but Arngrímr reworked his material thoroughly, not only by adding new miracles and his own glosses, but also by omitting material that he did not find appropriate for the saint's image. The composition and especially the style have been altered and made still more florid than in *C*. *D* is preserved in several MSS that can be divided between two almost contemporary versions. The oldest MS, Stock. Perg. fol. no. 5 (*ca.* 1350–1360), represents a complete text of the less original version, containing many verses written by the author himself and another 14th-century poet. *D* was certainly written with a foreign audience in mind as an attempt to acquire a papal canonization of Bishop Guðmundr, but no Latin version has been found.

Ed.: [Jón Sigurðsson and Guðbrandur Vigfússon, eds.] *Biskupa sögur*. 2 vols. Copenhagen: Møller, 1858–78 [contains *A* with additional material from *B* (in vol. 1) and *D* (in vol. 2)]; Guðni Jónsson, ed. *Byskupa sögur*. 3 vols. Reykjavik: Íslendingasagnaútgáfan;

Haukadalsútgáfan, 1948, vols. 2–3 [contains the texts of *Biskupa sögur* 1858–78 with normalized orthography and without variants]; Jón Helgason, ed. *Byskupa sǫgur. MS Perg. fol. No. 5 in the Royal Library of Stockholm*. Corpus Codicum Islandicorum Medii Aevi, 19. Copenhagen: Munksgaard, 1950 [facsimile]; Stefán Karlsson, ed. *Sagas of Icelandic Bishops: Fragments of Eight Manuscripts*. Early Icelandic Manuscripts in Facsimile, 7. Copenhagen: Rosenkilde & Bagger, 1967 [facsimile]; Stefán Karlsson, ed. *Guðmundar sögur biskups I. Ævi Guðmundar biskups, Guðmundar saga A*. Editiones Arnamagnæanæ, ser. B, vol. 6. Copenhagen: Reitzel, 1983. **Bib.**: Halldór Hermannsson. *Bibliography of the Icelandic Sagas and Minor Tales*. Islandica, 1. Ithaca: Cornell University Library, 1908; rpt. New York: Kraus, 1966, pp. 34–5; Halldór Hermannsson. *The Sagas of Icelanders (Íslendinga sögur): A Supplement to Bibliography of the Icelandic Sagas and Minor Tales*. Islandica, 24. Ithaca: Cornell University Press; London: Oxford University Press, 1935, pp. 38–9; Jóhann S. Hannesson. *The Sagas of Icelanders (Íslendinga sögur): A Supplement to Islandica I and XXIV*. Islandica, 38. Ithaca: Cornell University Press, 1957, pp. 42–3; Widding, Ole, *et al.* "The Lives of the Saints in Old Norse Prose: A Handlist." *Mediaeval Studies* 25 (1963), 294–337 [esp. 312–3]. **Tr.**: Turville-Petre, G., and E. S. Olszewska, trans. *The Life of Gudmund the Good, Bishop of Hólar*. Coventry: Viking Society for Northern Research, 1942 [mainly a translation of *A*]. **Lit.**: Björn M. Ólsen. "Um Sturlungu." *Safn til sögu Íslands og íslenzkra bókmenta* 3 (1902), 193–510; Einar Ól. Sveinsson. "Jarteiknir." *Skírnir* 110 (1936), 23–48; Jón Jóhannesson. "Um Sturlunga sögu." In *Sturlunga saga*. 2 vols. Ed. Jón Jóhannesson et al. Reykjavik: Sturlunguútgáfan, 1946, vol. 2, pp. vii–lvi; Jakob Benediktsson. "Nokkur handritabrot." *Skírnir* 125 (1951), 182–90; Stefán Einarsson. *A History of Icelandic Literature*. New York: Johns Hopkins University Press, 1957, pp. 103–5; Magerøy, Hallvard. "Guðmundr góði og Guðmundr ríki: Eit motivsamband." *Maal og minne* (1959), 22–34; Widding, Ole. "Nogle problemer omkring sagaen om Gudmund den Gode." *Maal og minne* (1960), 13–26; Stefán Karlsson. "Um handrit að Guðmundar sögu bróður Arngríms." *Opuscula* 1. Bibliotheca Arnamagnæana, 20. Copenhagen: Munksgaard, 1960, pp. 179–89; Foote, Peter G. "Bishop Jörundr Þorsteinsson and the Relics of Guðmundr inn góði Arason." In *Studia Centenalia in honorem memoriae Benedikt S. Þórarinsson*. Ed. B. S. Benedikz. Reykjavik: Ísafold, 1961, pp. 98–114; Ólafía Einarsdóttir. *Studier i kronologisk metode i tidlig islandsk historieskrivning*. Bibliotheca Historica Lundensis, 13. Stockholm: Natur och Kultur, 1964; Hunt, Margaret Cushing. "A Study of Authorial Perspective in *Guðmundar saga A* and *Guðmundar saga D*: Hagiography and the Icelandic Bishop's Saga." Diss. Indiana University, 1985; Stefán Karlsson. "Guðmundar sögur biskups: Authorial Viewpoints and Methods." In *The Sixth International Saga Conference 28/7–2/8 1985. Workshop Papers*. 2 vols. Copenhagen: Det arnamagnæanske Institut, 1985, vol. 2, pp. 983–1005; Stefán Karlsson. "'Bóklausir menn': A Note on Two Versions of *Guðmundar saga*." In *Sagnaskemmtun: Studies in Honour of Hermann Pálsson on His 65th Birthday, 26th May 1986*. Ed. Rudolf Simek et al. Vienna, Cologne, and Graz: Böhlau, 1986, pp. 277–86.

Stefán Karlsson

[See also: *Arons saga Hjǫrleifssonar*; *Biskupa sögur*; Legenda; Miracles, Collections of; Saints' Lives; *Sturlunga saga*]

Guðrún *see* **Vǫlsung-Niflung Cycle**

Guðrúnarkviða I–III ("The Lay of Guðrún") is a group of three lays preserved in the *Codex Regius* together with other anonymous lays comprising the *Poetic Edda*. Numbered "First," "Second," and "Third," or "I," "II," and "III," for convenient reference by modern editors, the poems deal with the fate of Guðrún Gjúkadóttir after the murder of her husband, Sigurðr, by her brothers. The content of the three poems spans both halves of the Nibelung cycle: the murder of Sigurðr by Guðrún's brothers, and the murder of the same brothers by Atli, Guðrún's second husband. This fact bears witness to the Scandinavian striving to harmonize and unite the disparate, originally unconnected stories into a single continuous narrative. Yet a solution to the contradiction in the material such as that found in the German *Nibelungenlied* (the creation of a Guðrún who uses her second husband, Atli, to take vengeance on her brothers for the murder of Sigurðr) was never fully realized in Scandinavia, at least not in surviving texts. The dominant image of Guðrún in the *Poetic Edda* remains that based on the Atli poems. Despite her mourning for the murdered Sigurðr, Guðrún attempts to protect her brothers from Atli's scheming thirst for treasure, and murders Atli, her husband, to avenge his murder of her brothers.

The Guðrún lays are late elegiac poems of the 11th and 12th centuries. Like the majority of the eddic poems, they are composed in the *fornyrðislag* meter, which superseded the older *málaháttr* of the Atli poems. In their emotional tone, these compositions enshrine a quality seldom found in the earlier, more heroic poems. Moreover, in their choice and treatment of subject matter, their secondary motifs, their vocabulary, and their turn of phrase, they frequently show the influence of Danish and German ballads and *Spielmannslieder* ("minstrel's songs"). The enigmatic moral and psychological position of Guðrún in the three poems, especially in *Guðrúnarkviða II*, may thus be attributed at least in part to direct or indirect contact with the German "modernization" of the story.

Guðrúnarkviða I. The twenty-seven strophes of this 12th-century composition convey Guðrún's inconsolable grief as she sits at the bier of the murdered Sigurðr. Women of the court relate their own misfortunes, but the heroine is unable to weep, her feelings frozen in suffering. When the shroud is finally removed from the corpse and Guðrún is urged to kiss her beloved, she does so, and a torrent of tears bursts forth. Especially memorable in its dramatic and heroic tenor, contrasting but not conflicting with the earlier lyricism of the poem, is the final scene in which Guðrún is confronted by her rival, the tempestuous Brynhildr, with her eyes aflame with hatred and jealousy. Such rivalry and confrontation characterize the late German telling of the story, culminating in "Aventiure 14" of the *Nibelungenlied.* The stimulus for the composition of the poem appears to have been Guðrún's terse observation in *Guðrúnarkviða II* that she did not "weep and wail [for Sigurðr] like other women."

Guðrúnarkviða II or *Guðrúnarkviða forna* ("The Old Lay of Guðrún"). This poem appears to be the oldest, probably dating from the 11th century. Poorly preserved, its forty-four strophes are marred by many corrupt passages and lacunae. The theme of the poem is apparently the heroine's memory of and mourning for Sigurðr and her implacable hatred of her brothers. Her family, wishing to see her marry Atli, attempt to suppress these emotions by various means, including an *óminnisveig* ("draught of forgetfulness"). Notwithstanding their failure in this attempt, the marriage to Atli takes place; later, the brothers attend his court and are killed.

In view of the poem's dominant theme, Guðrún's murder of Atli at the end of the poem, as if to avenge his murder of her

brothers, appears illogical. There have been various scholarly attempts to find plausible psychological motivation for Guðrún's role. These interpretations invoke either the Scandinavian Guðrún, whose loyalty to her brothers is thought to take precedence over her grief for Sigurðr, or the late German Guðrún, who is irrevocably committed to taking vengeance on her brothers, with the aid of Atli, for the murder of Sigurðr. The latter reading leaves Guðrún's final killing of Atli an unexplained remnant of the Scandinavian tradition, unless, as in one interpretation, Atli is seen as implicated in the murder of Sigurðr.

Guðrúnarkviða III. Guðrún, now Atli's wife, is accused of adultery with Þjóðrekr, a German guest at the Hunnish court. She protests her innocence in lively fashion, and substantiates it by the ordeal of the boiling kettle, plucking a stone from the seething water with unscathed hand. Atli registers his pleasure, and the accuser, Atli's former concubine, after failing the same test, pays with her life in a "foul swamp." As in the case of *Guðrúnarkviða I*, the impulse for this lay appears to have come from *Guðrúnarkviða II*. Guðrún admits to having embraced Þjóðrekr "on one occasion," apparently the same on which she related her woes to Þjóðrekr (see *Guðrúnarkviða II* and its prose introduction). Whether Þjóðrekr is to be seen as having participated in the killing of the brothers at Guðrún's urging (as in the German version of *Þiðreks saga* and the *Nibelungenlied*), or in spite of her loyalty to them (as in the Scandinavian tradition) is difficult to ascertain. The poem contains evidence to support both conclusions. With its eleven stanzas, this 12th-century composition is the shortest of the Guðrún lays. Despite this brevity, a highly dramatic situation is evoked with an admirable economy of means. Presumably, the poem's present ambiguity did not exist for its original audience.

The three poems are not grouped together in the *Codex Regius*, but rather are placed among the other heroic lays in a manner reflecting the narrative context of these lays as a whole.

Ed.: Neckel, Gustav, ed. *Edda: Die Lieder des Codex Regius nebst verwandten Denkmälern. I: Text.* 5th ed. rev. Hans Kuhn. Heidelberg: Winter, 1983. **Tr.**: Terry, Patricia, trans. *Poems of the Vikings: The Elder Edda.* Indianapolis: Bobbs-Merrill, 1969. **Lit.**: Mohr, Wolfgang. "Entstehungsgeschichte und Heimat der jüngeren Eddalieder südgermanischen Stoffes." *Zeitschrift für deutsches Altertum und deutsche Literatur* 75 (1938–39), 217–80; Mohr, Wolfgang. "Wortschatz und Motive der jüngeren Eddalieder mit südgermanischem Stoff." *Zeitschrift für deutsches Altertum und deutsche Literatur* 76 (1939–40), 149–217; Zeller, Rose. *Die Gudrunlieder der Edda.* Tübinger germanische Arbeiten, 26. Stuttgart: Kohlhammer, 1939; Vries, Jan de. "Das zweite Guðrúnlied." *Zeitschrift für deutsche Philologie* 77 (1958), 176–99; Midderhoff, Hanns. "Zur Verbindung des ersten und zweiten Teils des Nibelungenstoffes in der Lieder-Edda." *Zeitschrift für deutsches Altertum und deutsche Literatur* 95 (1966), 243–58; Midderhoff, Hanns. "Übereinstimmungen und Ähnlichkeiten in den liedereddischen und epischen Nibelungen." *Zeitschrift für deutsches Altertum und deutsche Literatur* 97 (1968–69), 241–78; Harris, Joseph. "Elegy in Old English and Old Norse: A Problem in Literary History." In *The Vikings.* Ed. R. T. Farrell. London and Chichester: Phillimore, 1982, pp. 157–64; rpt. in *The Old English Elegies: New Essays in Criticism and Research.* Ed. Martin Green. Rutherford, Madison, and Teaneck: Fairleigh Dickinson University Press; London and Toronto: Associated University Presses, 1983, pp. 46–56; Glendinning, Robert J. "*Guðrúnarquiða Forna*: A Reconstruction and Interpretation." In *Edda: A Collection of Essays.* Ed. Robert J. Glendinning and Haraldur Bessason. University of Manitoba Icelandic Studies, 4. Winnipeg:

University of Manitoba Press, 1983, pp. 258–82; Cronan, Dennis. "A Reading of Guðrúnarqviða Ǫnnor." *Scandinavian Studies* 57 (1985), 174–87.

Robert J. Glendinning

[**See also:** *Codex Regius*; Eddic Meters; Eddic Poetry; Vǫlsung-Niflung Cycle]

Guðrúnarhvǫt ("Guðrún's Lament") is part of the Sigurðr-Guðrún cycle of poems contained in the *Codex Regius* of the *Poetic Edda* (13th century). The poem was written probably in the late 12th century by an anonymous poet, who appears to have borrowed from earlier lays on the subject, most notably *Hamðismál*.

Guðrún, Sigurðr's widow, incites her sons Hamðir and Sǫrli, to avenge their sister Svanhildr's death. Svanhildr, whose story is also recounted in *Sigurðarkviða in skamma* and *Hamðismál*, has been put to death by her husband, Jǫrmunrekkr, the king of the Goths, because he suspected her of adultery with his own son. Guðrún accuses her sons, born of her third marriage, to Jónakr, of cowardice, comparing them unfavorably to their uncles Gunnarr and Hǫgni. Hamðir accepts the challenge, and Guðrún, laughing, brings armor from the Hunnish treasure hoard. Hamðir predicts that he and his brothers will die in their attempt at vengeance. Guðrún's laughter turns to tears as she begins yet another bitter lament.

She lists the three hearths she has known, first as bride to Sigurðr, then as the unwilling wife of Atli, and finally as Jónakr's wife. She recounts her sorrows: the murder of Sigurðr, and of her brothers, Gunnarr and Hǫgni, the revenge she took on Atli by killing their sons, and her most recent sorrow, the brutal murder of her beautiful daughter. Now she realizes that her last two sons are to die as well, leaving her alone and unprotected. Guðrún concludes her lament by remembering the idyllic days with Sigurðr. She then commands that a funeral pyre be built for her. Only the flames can now melt the ice of her tormented heart.

The poem's theme is the epic magnitude of Guðrún's griefs and her inability to create happiness for herself. The most powerful moment in the poem is the contrast between her laughter as she brings armor out to her sons in order to avenge Svanhildr, and her weeping when she realizes that they, too, will die.

Ed.: Dronke, Ursula, ed. *The Poetic Edda. 1: Heroic Poems.* Oxford: Clarendon, 1969; Neckel, Gustav, ed. *Edda: Die Lieder des Codex Regius nebst verwandten Denkmälern. I: Text.* 5th ed. rev. Hans Kuhn. Heidelberg: Winter, 1983. **Tr.**: Hollander, Lee M., trans. *The Poetic Edda, Translated with an Introduction and Explanatory Notes.* Austin: University of Texas Press, 1962; rpt. 1988; Terry, Patricia, trans. *Poems of the Vikings: The Elder Edda.* Indianapolis: Bobbs-Merrill, 1969. **Bib.**: Harris, Joesph. "Eddic Poetry." In *Old Norse–Icelandic Literature: A Critical Guide.* Ed. Carol J. Clover and John Lindow. Islandica, 45. Ithaca and London: Cornell University Press, 1985, pp. 145–6. **Lit.**: See, Klaus von. "Guðrúnarhvǫt und Hamðismál." *Beiträge zur Geschichte der deutschen Sprache und Literatur* (Tübingen) 99 (1977), 241–9; rpt. in his *Edda, Saga, Skaldendichtung: Aufsätze zur skandinavischen Literatur des Mittelalters.* Heidelberg: Winter, 1981, pp. 250–8; Harris, Joseph. "Elegy in Old English and Old Norse: A Problem in Literary History." In *The Vikings.* Ed. R. T. Farrell. London and Chichester: Phillimore, 1982, pp. 157–64; rpt. in *The Old English Elegies: New Essays in Criticism and Research.* Ed. Martin Green. Rutherford, Madison, and Teaneck: Fairleigh Dickinson University Press; London and Toronto: Associated University Presses, 1983, pp. 46–56;

Glendinning, Robert J. "*Guðrúnarquiða Forna*: A Reconstruction and Interpretation." In *Edda: A Collection of Essays.* Ed. Robert J. Glendinning and Haraldur Bessason. University of Manitoba Icelandic Studies, 4. Winnipeg: University of Manitoba Press, 1983, pp. 258–82.

†Philip N. Anderson

[**See also:** *Codex Regius*; Eddic Poetry; *Hamðismál in fornu*; *Sigurðarkviða in skamma*; Vǫlsung-Niflung Cycle]

Guilds, corporations formed by merchants and artisans, are urban phenomena and in Scandinavia are thus found primarily in Denmark (including Scania), in a few Swedish towns, and in Bergen, Norway.

The medieval terms (spelling modernized) are *gilde* and *lav* (or *laug*), and are used interchangeably for the organization. Historians have used *gilde* to indicate confraternities and merchants' guilds, and *lav* for craft guilds. The term *embede* (*amt*) in contemporary sources refers to the craft itself (akin to the English "Mystery"). The term *skrå* refers to the statutes of a guild or fraternity.

Guild development in Denmark follows the continental pattern. The earliest guilds were established in the 12th century at the time of Danish trade hegemony in the Baltic. They were called "St. Knud (Cnut) guilds," and are first mentioned in a document from 1177, at which point there was a St. Knud's guild in many Danish towns. This document and the five oldest extant statutes, compiled during the 13th century, show that these were merchants' guilds. The patron saint was Duke Lavard (murdered 1130, canonized 1170). Prior to 1170, another murdered and canonized Knud (d. 1086, canonized 1100) may have been the patron saint. With the loss of trade hegemony to the Hanse merchants during the second half of the 13th century, the St. Knud guilds lost their commercial aspect and became exclusive confraternities for the urban elite during the later Middle Ages. Some guilds survived into the early modern period, and a few are still in existence. Any male merchant could become a member, whereas women could only participate in social and religious activities as wives and daughters.

Specific trade guilds with special rights and privileges for its members were formed during the late 14th and 15th centuries by the minor tradespeople, such as drapers, mercers, and fishmongers. Women could become full-fledged members as active traders during the 15th century, but this situation changed during the 16th century, when their access to guild membership was exclusively through marriage or birth.

Craft guilds were also founded in the 14th and 15th centuries, but may have begun as confraternities during the high Middle Ages. Early attempts by artisans to organize were suppressed. A 13th-century town law from Roskilde prohibits the bakers' guild. The first known craft guild is that of the Tailors and Shearers of Ribe, who in 1349 were granted permission to organize a guild with monopoly on cutting and sewing new clothing. The most frequently organized artisans were those working in leather (shoemakers, in particular), fur, and metal (smiths). Craft guilds were founded primarily in the larger towns of eastern Denmark (Zealand and Scania). By the early 16th century, some seventy Danish craft guilds are mentioned. In Sweden, twelve guilds existed in Stockholm by the 16th century (earliest guild founded 1356, most from the 15th century), one in Arboga (shoemakers, 1485) and one in Kalmar (cordwainers, 1428); in Norway, only the German shoemakers in Bergen organized.

Craft guilds were organizations of male masters. No women's guilds existed, but, as wives and daughters, women performed an important function as transmitters of workshops and privileges (through marriage) from one generation of masters to the next, and as partners in the workshop. Widows usually had the right to continue the workshop, but for a limited period only, between one and three years or until remarriage. As wives and unmarried daughters, women shared in the religious, social, and economic benefits enjoyed by the guild members.

Guilds played an important role in protecting urban craft production, and aided development and specialization within the individual craft. They appear to have had no political role. Disputes between the merchants and the craftsmen did occur during the 15th century, but no guild rule was ever imposed on Danish towns, where the merchants remained firmly in control.

Lit.: Jacobsen, Grethe. "Guilds in Medieval Denmark: The Social and Economic Role of Merchants and Artisans." Diss. University of Wisconsin–Madison, 1980; Friedland, Klaus, ed. *Gilde und Korporation in den nordeuropäischen Städten des späten Mittelalters*. Quellen und Darstellungen zur Hansischen Geschichte, N. F., Bd. 29. Cologne: Böhlau, 1984; Jacobsen, Grethe. "Economic Progress and the Sexual Division of Labor: The Role of Guilds in the Late-Medieval Danish City." *Alltag und Fortschritt im Mittelalter. Internationales Round-Table-Gespräch Krems a.d. Donau, 1. Oktober 1984*. Veröffentlichungen des Instituts für Mittelalterliche Realienkunde Österreichs, Nr. 8. Österreichische Akademie der Wissenschaften. Phil.-hist. Kl. Sitzungsb., Bd. 470. Vienna: Verlag der Österreichischen Akademie der Wissenschaften, 1986, pp. 223–36.

Grethe Jacobsen

[See also: Crafts; Hanseatic League]

Gull-Ásu-Þórðar þáttr ("The Tale of Gold-Ása-Þórðr").

The events behind this realistic story set in Norway during the reign of Eysteinn Magnússon (1103–1122) seem to have occurred about 1112. The story tells how a poor Icelander from the East Fjord area raised himself to a high social status in Norway through intelligence, good business sense, and friendship with a wealthy widow named Ása. Through a flattering praise-poem, Þórðr wins the support of Ása's powerful kinsman Víðkunnr Jónsson. But Þórðr's fortunes are threatened when he clashes with the most powerful noble in the kingdom, the violent Ingimarr af Aski. In the first stage of the stylized climax, Þórðr calls in his friend Víðkunnr. In the next stage, Víðkunnr calls in *his* friend, the powerful noble Sigurðr Hranason, reminding him of a past favor. In the third stage, Sigurðr calls in the most powerful friend in the kingdom, King Eysteinn. This process resolves the matter to the disadvantage of Ingimarr, who flees to Denmark. Þórðr marries Ása and lives out his life prosperously in Norway.

Ása is known only from the *þáttr*, but the other Norwegians are well attested. Þórðr is cited also in the *Skáldatal* ("List of Skalds"), but the bare information there could come from this story. One of Þórðr's verses in the story is an eight-line impromptu (*lausavísa*); the other is the refrain from his long eulogy (*drápa*) on Víðkunnr. Finnur Jónsson (1920–24) found the story "certainly historical"; de Vries (1941–42) was just as confident that it was a "freely invented tale." The *þáttr* is literature, not history, as the self-consciously escalating triad makes clear, but the evidence associated with Þórðr's poetry makes a historical kernel probable. Generi-

cally, the story belongs with a group that charts the fortunes of Icelanders in Norway. In these stories, the underdog Icelander overcomes hostility or prejudice, and several of the stories explore the value of friendship, an unsentimental reciprocity for favors given. The three proverbs in the story (two are actually Wellerisms) all have *double entendre* and serve to characterize Ingimarr. The *þáttr's* longer independent version in paper MSS of the 17th century and later is closer to the original, while the version in the *konungasögur* (*Morkinskinna, Hulda, Hrokkinskinna*) has been adapted somewhat to its larger context. If, as is usually assumed, the *þáttr* was present in the original of *Morkinskinna* (and not merely in the surviving copy of *ca*. 1280), it must have been written before about 1220.

Ed.: Jón Jóhannesson, ed. *Austfirðinga sǫgur*. Íslenzk fornrit, 11. Reykjavik: Hið íslenzka fornritafélag, 1950, pp. 337–49 [citations pp. cxiv–cxvii lead to all previous editions and to MS sources]; Ulset, Tor, ed. *Utvalgte þættir fra Morkinskinna*. Nordisk filologi. Oslo: Dreyer, 1978, pp. 81–6 ["Skipti Eysteins konungs ok *Ingimars um Ásu-Þórð"; *konungasaga* version]. **Tr.**: Bachman, W. Bryant, Jr., trans. *Four Old Icelandic Sagas and Other Tales*. Lanham, New York, and London: University Press of America, 1985, pp. 99–104 [longer, independent version from Jón Jóhannesson, above]. **Bib.**: Halldór Hermannsson. *Bibliography of the Icelandic Sagas and Minor Tales*. Islandica, 1. Ithaca: Cornell University Library, 1908; rpt. New York: Kraus, 1966, p. 35; Halldór Hermannsson. *The Sagas of Icelanders (Íslendinga sögur): A Supplement to Bibliography of the Icelandic Sagas and Minor Tales*. Islandica, 24. Ithaca: Cornell University Press; London: Oxford University Press, 1935, p. 39; Jóhann S. Hannesson. *The Sagas of Icelanders (Íslendinga sögur): A Supplement to Islandica I and XXIV*. Islandica, 38. Ithaca: Cornell University Press; London: Oxford University Press, 1957, p. 43. **Lit.**: Finnur Jónsson. *Den oldnorske og oldislandske Litteraturs Historie*. 3 vols. 2nd ed. Copenhagen: Gad, 1920–24, vol. 2, p. 544; Jón Jóhannesson, pp. cxiv–cxvii [see above]; Vries, Jan de. *Altnordische Literaturgeschichte*. 2 vols. Grundriss der germanischen Philologie, 15–6. Berlin: de Gruyter, 1941–42; rpt. 1964–67, vol. 2, p. 447; Harris, Joseph. "The King and the Icelander: A Study in the Short Narrative Forms of Old Icelandic Prose." Diss. Harvard University, 1969 [esp. pp. 133–7; on the proverbs in the *þáttr*]; Harris, Joseph. "Genre and Narrative Structure in Some *Íslendinga þættir*." *Scandinavian Studies* 44 (1972), 1–27 [esp. pp. 19–20]; Harris, Joseph. "Theme and Genre in Some *Íslendinga þættir*." *Scandinavian Studies* 48 (1976), 1–28 [esp. pp. 3, 7, and 15]; Louis-Jensen, Jonna. *Kongesagastudier: Kompilationen Hulda-Hrokkinskinna*. Bibliotheca Arnamagnæana, 32. Copenhagen: Reitzel, 1977, pp. 99–100; Harris, Joseph. "Þættir." In *Dictionary of the Middle Ages*. Ed. Joseph R. Strayer. New York: Scribner, 1982–89, vol. 12, pp. 1–6.

Joseph Harris

[See also: *Hulda-Hrokkinskinna; Konungasögur, Lausavísur, Morkinskinna; Þáttr*]

Gull-Þóris saga ("The Saga of Gold-Þórir")

is preserved in a single vellum MS, AM 561 4to, dating from around 1400, but was probably composed in the early part of the 14th century. It is thought to be a reworking of an older saga. There is a lacuna in the MS from the end of the 10th chapter to the beginning of the 12th. Since parts of the saga take place in northwestern Iceland, in the area around Þorskafjörður, it is also known as *Þorskfirðinga saga*.

Like *Finnboga saga ramma, Þórðar saga hreðu*, and other "postclassical" *Íslendingasögur, Gull-Þóris saga* contains a number of dissimilar elements and shows strong influence from the *fornaldarsögur* and *riddarasögur*, particularly in scenes set abroad, which contrast markedly with episodes taking place in Iceland.

The saga begins with a superficial description of the hero Þórir Oddsson: he is handsome and brave. Together with nine blood brothers, Þórir journeys to Norway during the reign of Haraldr hárfagri ("fair-hair") Hálfdanarson. At first, they occupy themselves with fishing, but feel it is little to their credit. They decide to break into a grave mound said to contain a berserk and large amounts of gold. The berserk turns out to be a kinsman of Þórir's named Agnarr, who tells him of another mound containing much gold, but warns him that the gold will not bring him luck. Þórir does not follow Agnarr's instructions exactly, however, and must fight a dragon, using marvelous articles given him by his father and a relative. He wins a great deal of gold, most of which he keeps for himself.

The story now turns to Iceland and tells of a feud in the area around Þorskafjörður. This part of the saga, although related to the rest because Þórir's avarice precipitates the conflict, has a much more realistic nature than the episodes in Norway. However, the events in Iceland include elements of the fantastic: men are changed into swine, and women put a cloak of invisibility over a ship and render weapons useless. Þórir seeks the advice of a sibyl, and in battle he and his opponents change shape.

Þórir's kinsman Gunnarr suddenly appears on the scene. Gunnarr is depicted as a troublemaker, and Þórir as a peacemaker interested primarily in his farm, unlike the young Þórir, who chose to look for gold rather than to fish. Toward the end of the story, Agnarr's prophecy regarding the curse on the gold hoard is fulfilled. Following a series of conflicts and difficulties and ultimate dishonor, Þórir becomes malicious and petulant, and finally vanishes with his gold, changing, some say, into a dragon lying on his hoard.

Gull-Þórir and the events in Þorskafjörður are mentioned in the *Sturlubók* version of *Landnámabók*, but in an account differing considerably from the story as presented in *Gull-Þóris saga*. In all likelihood, the account in *Sturlubók* is based on an older **Þorskfirðinga saga*, now lost, upon which the present saga was also based. There seem also to be connections between *Gull-Þóris saga* and *Hálfdanar saga Eysteinssonar* and *Skálda saga*, preserved in *Hauksbók* (ca. 1300). Many critics have compared the dragon and gold-hoard episodes to those in the Old English poem *Beowulf*.

Ed.: Maurer, Konrad, ed. *Die Gull-Þóris saga oder Þorskfirðinga saga.* Leipzig: Hinrichs'schen Buchhandlung, 1858; Kålund, Kr., ed. *Gull-Þóris saga eller Þorskfirðinga saga.* Samfund til udgivelse af gammel nordisk litteratur, 26. Copenhagen: Møller, 1898. **Tr.**: Garmonsway, G. N., *et al. Beowulf and Its Analogues.* London: Dent; New York: Dutton, 1968; rpt. 1971, pp. 324–7 [excerpt]; Evans, Mary Virginia. "*Beowulf* and *Gull-Þóris saga.*" M.A. thesis, Queen's University, 1972. **Lit.**: Kålund, Kr. "Om lakunerne i Gull-Þóris saga." *Arkiv för nordisk filologi* 1 (1882), 179–91; Þorleifur Jónsson. "Endnu lidt om lakunerne i Gullþóris saga." *Arkiv för nordisk filologi* 3 (1886), 286; Björn Magnússon Ólsen. "Landnáma og Gull-Þóris (Þorskfirðinga) Saga." *Aarbøger for nordisk Oldkyndighed og Historie* (1910), 35–61; Björn Sigfússon. "Gull-Þóris saga." *KLNM* 5 (1960), 594–5; Schach, Paul. "Gull-Þóris saga." In *Dictionary of the Middle Ages.* Ed. Joseph R. Strayer. New York: Scribner, 1982–89, vol. 6, p. 27.

Margrét Eggertsdóttir

[**See also:** *Berserkr; Finnboga saga ramma; Hálfdanar saga Eysteinssonar; Hauksbók; Íslendingasögur; Landnámabók; Riddarasögur; Þórðar saga hreðu*]

Gunnars saga Keldugnúpsfífls ("The Saga of Gunnarr, the Fool of Keldugnúpr").

The events related in the saga of Gunnarr Keldugnúpsfífl take place in the 11th century. The saga's date of composition is difficult to determine; the earliest preserved MSS date from the 17th century, and the saga contains a number of elements that indicate a rather late date of composition, probably not earlier than 1400. Four MSS preserve a text thought to be closest to the original, AM 496 4to, AM 156 fol., AM 443 4to, and AM 554i 4to. These MSS vary little in terms of plot, but there are significant differences in wording, particularly between the first and last named.

This short saga is characterized primarily by its use of episodes and motifs known from other sources. In the beginning of the saga, Gunnarr is the typical *kolbítr*, or "male Cinderella," despised by his father and ridiculed by others, until he proves himself by killing a man. He and his brother Helgi, who is unlike him in every respect, escape from those wishing to avenge the slaying by hiding in a cave. Gunnarr befriends a merchant, who has arrived in the district, and he and his brother take passage with him. Before leaving the country, however, Gunnarr betroths Helga, the sister of his enemies. In a curious, perhaps tongue-in-cheek scene, the saga relates how Gunnarr kills the two brothers one after another just outside the door, enters the farmhouse, and is greeted warmly by Helga. Gunnarr plights his troth and promptly departs, leaving Helga crying. They are shipwrecked, but manage to reach an unknown country of glaciers and polar bears. Gunnarr kills a bear and has dealings with giants, killing many of them, but befriending the giantess Fála, who later proves a valuable ally. This episode is reminiscent of the first chapter of *Jökuls þáttr Búasonar*. In Norway, the brothers meet Earl Hákon, who takes an immediate dislike to Gunnarr, for which no reason is given in the saga other than that he fears Gunnarr's strength. Gunnarr is made to fight a *blámaðr* (literally "blue-man"), whom he is able to defeat with the help of a magic cloak given to him by his friend, the merchant. Gunnarr and his brother now embark on a Viking expedition that ends in a great battle. This section corresponds closely to episodes in *Hjálmþés saga ok Ǫlvis* and *Þorsteins saga Víkingssonar*, both classed as *fornaldarsögur*. All three sagas are thought to derive from a single source, now lost. Gunnarr and his companions return first to Norway, where they are reconciled with Earl Hákon, then make their way back to Iceland, where Gunnarr is married. Gunnarr kills one of his old enemies, whose sister tries to avenge him through witchcraft, but without success. Gunnarr, however, offers a settlement, which is accepted in the end.

Parts of the saga are reminiscent of episodes in *Jökuls þáttr Búasonar*, a kind of continuation of *Kjalnesinga saga*, with which *Gunnars saga* also has many elements in common. Although much of the material in the saga is known from other sources, only one character, Earl Hákon, is mentioned elsewhere.

Gunnars saga Keldugnúpsfífls was written primarily as entertainment, and there is little original in it. Nevertheless, the story is well told with a fair share of quips.

The saga formed the basis for a number of *rímur*, the oldest of which, now lost with the exception of two verses, date from the 16th century. In addition, there are several groups of *rímur* from the 18th and 19th centuries (Björn K. Þórólfsson 1934:508–9).

Ed.: Guðni Jónsson, ed. "Gunnars saga Keldugnúpsfífls." In *Íslendinga sögur*. 13 vols. Reykjavik: Íslendingasagnaútgáfan, 1946–49, vol. 10, pp. 453–86; Jóhannes Halldórsson, ed. *Kjalnesinga saga*. Íslenzk fornrit, 14. Reykjavik: Hið íslenzka fornritafélag, 1959, pp. 343–79 [see also introduction, pp. lxx–lxxiv]; Björn K. Þórólfsson. *Rímur fyrir 1600*. Safn Fræðafjelagsins um Ísland og Íslendinga, 9. Copenhagen: Møller, 1934.

Margrét Eggertsdóttir

[**See also:** *Hjálmþés saga*; *Íslendingasögur*; *Jökuls þáttr Búasonar*; *Kjalnesinga saga*; *Rímur*; *Þorsteins saga Víkingssonar*]

Gunnars saga Þiðrandabana

("The Saga of Gunnarr, Slayer of Þiðrandi") is actually a *þáttr* rather than a saga. The central figure of the tale is more the object than the subject of the action, which is disjointed and largely unmotivated.

Björn Kóreksson gives Þiðrandi a horse as a token of friendship. A farm laborer named Ásbjörn becomes a small landholder, but is soon deeply indebted, especially to Björn and his brothers, usually referred to collectively as Kórekr's sons. A Norwegian named Gunnarr takes lodging at Njarðvík with Ketill, Þiðrandi's foster-father, and Þiðrandi goes to stay with Kórekr's sons. Ásbjörn finds refuge with Ketill, and Kórekr's sons and their companions, including Þiðrandi, go to Njarðvík to summon Ásbjörn for nonpayment of debt. On the way, they see Ásbjörn digging peat, and one of them hurls a spear through him. Ásbjörn manages to reach Njarðvík, and when the summoners arrive there, Ketill rushes out and kills one of them to avenge Ásbjörn. After Ketill and several other men have been slain, the summoners withdraw. A woman servant incites Gunnarr to kill Þiðrandi as fitting vengeance for Ketill's death, a common motif in saga literature. Þiðrandi finds shelter with a farmer named Sveinki, who successfully conceals him three times from his pursuers. Also a popular saga motif, this episode occupies over one fourth of the saga, followed by a second detailed concealment episode. Þiðrandi's final shelter is at Helgafell, where Guðrún protects him from her husband, Þorkell, and, with the help of Snorri goði ("chieftain, priest"), enables him to return to Norway, where Sveinki joins him.

Gunnarr's story is more fully told in *Fljótsdœla saga* than in his own *þáttr*. The Helgafell scene is well developed in *Laxdœla saga*, where the heroine Guðrún plays a much more prominent and independent role. As his source, the author of *Laxdœla saga* mentions *Njarðvíkinga saga*, which must be identical with *Gunnars saga*. This work was probably written around 1220 in western Iceland, since the author had scant knowledge of the scene of action, which takes place, for the most part, in eastern Iceland. The tale is preserved only in late paper transcripts of a lost MS about which nothing is known.

Ed.: Jón Jóhannesson, ed. *Austfirðinga sögur*. Íslensk fornrit, 11. Reykjavik: Hið íslenska fornritafélag, 1950. **Tr.**: Veblen, Thorstein, trans. *The Laxdæla Saga*. New York: Huebsch, 1925, pp. 289–302; Boucher, Alan, trans. *Tales from the Eastfirths*. Reykjavik: Iceland Review, 1981, pp. 68–79. **Lit.**: Schach, Paul. *Icelandic Sagas*. Twayne's World Authors Series, 717. Boston: Twayne, 1984, pp. 136–7.

Paul Schach

[**See also:** *Fljótsdœla saga*; *Laxdœla saga*; *Þáttr*]

Gunnlaugr ormstunga

("serpent-tongue"), an Icelandic skald, appears to have flourished around the year 1000. Any search for a "historical Gunnlaugr" is beset by problems. The main source for his life is the highly romantic *Gunnlaugs saga*, extant in a late 13th-century redaction, which centers upon his alleged rivalry with Hrafn Önundarson, a fellow skald, over Helga Þorsteinsdóttir. Some of the verses embedded in this saga appear to antedate the prose narrative and may have some historical value as sources. But convincing corroboration of their authenticity is lacking; only two of them are known elsewhere. Other minor sources are *Landnámabók*, *Skáldatal* (older redaction), *Egils saga*, and *Snorra Edda*. *Landnámabók* confirms the saga on Gunnlaugr's genealogy and on Hrafn's status as a poet, and supplements it by making Gunnlaugr a kinsman of the skalds Bragi Boddason and Tindr Hallkelsson. The older version of Snorri's *Skáldatal* includes Gunnlaugr in its list of the court poets of Earl Eiríkr of Hlaðir (d. ca. 1023) and King Olaf of Sweden (d. 1022), supporting the saga, which brings its hero into contact with these and other leaders and ascribes several fragments of political verse to him. One of these verses shows him as an itinerant poet planning visits to three kings (presumably Æthelred II of England, the "Unready"; Sigtryggr silkiskegg ["silk-beard"] of Dublin; and Olaf of Sweden) and two earls (Sigurðr Hlöðvisson of Orkney and Earl Eiríkr, although in the saga the latter has been replaced by an otherwise unknown Earl Sigurðr of Gautland). Only two fragments of poems for these patrons are cited, both datable to around 1002 according to the internal chronology of the saga. They afford a small insight into Gunnlaugr's political and poetic affiliations. The *stef* ("refrain") of his *Aðalráðsdrápa* has the ring of propaganda, extolling Æthelred's receipt of loyalty from his family and awe from his subjects. This expression of the "vicarius Dei" ideology of kingship belongs in a tradition of skaldic praises for English kings, stretching from Æthelstan to Knud (Cnut). The fragments of Gunnlaugr's *Sigtryggsdrápa*, a frankly petitionary poem, contain what seem to be reminiscences of Egill's *Höfuðlausn*, notably the rare *runhent* stanza form; a tradition special to the joint kingdom of York and Dublin is perhaps indicated.

Because of the uncertainties regarding the Gunnlaugr canon, little more can be said about his place in the history of skaldic poetry. Of the other political verses in the saga, one (doubtfully authentic) is a flyting (a ritualized insult) and the other a comparison of rival leaders, a genre exemplified in *Liðsmannaflokkr*. Where Gunnlaugr's later career is concerned, the story of tragic love told in the saga has the same stereotypic traits as the sagas of such skalds as Björn Hítdœlakappi, Hallfreðr Óttarsson, and Kormákr Ögmundarson. The prose narrative appears to be corroborated by frequent citations of verses purportedly by Hrafn Önundarson, Þórðr Kolbeinsson, Þorkell Hallkelsson, and Gunnlaugr himself. But one of these verses is a borrowing from *Kormáks saga*, and some others are probably 12th- or 13th-century compositions. External corroboration of the account of Gunnlaugr's rivalry with Hrafn appears in *Egils saga* and *Snorra Edda*. Snorri agrees with the saga in assigning a verse about this rivalry to Gunnlaugr: problematic, however, are the reliability of Snorri's attributions and the autobiographical status of the verse, even if correctly attributed. Whatever their authorship or date, some of the love verses contained in *Gunnlaugs saga*, with their bold dramatization of the speaker and striking combinations of kennings, rank among the finest skaldic compositions in that genre.

Ed.: Sigurður Nordal and Guðni Jónsson, eds. *Borgfirðinga sǫgur.* Íslenzk fornrit, 3. Reykjavik: Hið íslenzka fornritafélag, 1938. **Tr.**: Foote, P. G., ed., and R. Quirk, trans. *Gunnlaugs saga ormstungu: The Saga of Gunnlaug Serpent-Tongue.* Nelson's Icelandic Texts. London: Nelson, 1957 [parallel Icelandic and English text]. **Lit.**: Björn Magnússon Ólsen. *Om Gunnlaugs Saga Ormstungu: En kritisk Undersøgelse.* Det kongelige danske Videnskabernes selskabs skrifter, 7. Række, Historisk og filosofisk afdeling, 2.1. Copenhagen: Høst, 1911 [the Gunnlaugr canon]; Finnur Jónsson. "Sagaernes lausavísur." *Aarbøger for nordisk Oldkyndighed og Historie* (1912), 1–57 [the Gunnlaugr canon]; Finnur Jónsson. *Den oldnorske og oldislandske Litteraturs Historie.* 3 vols. 2nd ed. Copenhagen: Gad, 1920–24 [analysis of *Gunnlaugs saga* and of verses attributed to Gunnlaugr]; Bjarni Einarsson. *Skáldasögur: Um uppruna og eðli ástaskáldasagnanna fornu.* Reykjavik: Menningarsjóður, 1961 [fictional elements in the prose and verse of *Gunnlaugs saga*; connections with the literature of medieval Europe]; Vries, Jan de. *Altnordische Literaturgeschichte.* 2 vols. Grundriss der germanischen Philologie, 15–6. Berlin: de Gruyter, 1941–42; rpt. 1964–67 [analysis of *Gunnlaugs saga* and of the verses attributed to Gunnlaugr]; Turner, G. W. "The Verses in *Gunnlaugs saga ormstungu.*" *Journal of English and Germanic Philology* 76 (1977), 384–91 [literary analysis of verses attributed to Gunnlaugr]; Poole, Russell. "Compositional Technique in Some Verses from *Gunnlaugs saga.*" *Journal of English and Germanic Philology* 80 (1981), 469–85 [the Gunnlaugr canon; literary analysis of verses]; Fidjestøl, Bjarne. *Det norrøne fyrstediktet.* Øvre Ervik: Alvheim & Eide, 1982 [the praise poetry]; Poole, Russell. "Verses and Prose in *Gunnlaugs saga Ormstungu.*" In *The Sagas of the Icelanders: A Book of Essays.* Ed. John Tucker. New York and London: Garland, 1989, pp. 160–84 [treats the Gunnlaugr canon].

Russell Poole

[**See also:** *Egils saga Skalla-Grímssonar, Gunnlaugs saga ormstungu*; Kennings; *Kormáks saga*; *Landnámabók*; *Lausavísur, Skáld*; Skaldic Meters; Skaldic Verse; *Snorra Edda*]

Gunnlaugs saga ormstungu

Gunnlaugs saga ormstungu ("The Saga of Gunnlaugr Serpent-tongue") tells the story of an Icelandic skald in the early 11th century, his rivalry with another skald, Hrafn, over Helga in fagra ("the fair"), his visits as skald to foreign princes, and his death at the hand of his successful rival. *Gunnlaugs saga* belongs to the group of *Íslendingasögur* called *skáldasögur*, and has special relations with one of them, *Bjarnar saga Hítdœlakappa.* Both are written in the same pattern in the main plot, the love story. Two skalds meet at the court of a king. One of them has a betrothed maiden waiting for him in Iceland. The other skald goes back to Iceland and persuades the relatives of the girl to give her to him in marriage. The outlines of this pattern probably have their origin in a short story (*þáttr*) in *Morkinskinna.* In that story, an Icelandic skald and his brother are staying at the court of the king of Norway. The brother returns to Iceland, and before he leaves the skald asks him to take a message to an Icelandic maiden, asking her to stay unmarried until he returns. As soon as the brother arrives in Iceland, he proposes to the girl himself and is accepted. This sequence seems to be the plot in its most original form, a version of the well-known story of the wooer by proxy who becomes the lover of, in some variants marries, the desired maiden. The motif itself and the continuation of the story in *Morkinskinna* suggest that the original source is the romance of Tristan. The famous story of the thwarted love of Kjartan and Guðrún in *Laxdœla saga* follows the same pattern.

Gunnlaugs saga begins with a prophetic dream by Þorsteinn, son of Egill Skalla-Grímsson, and the father of Helga in fagra. The dream is interpreted to predict that a yet-unborn daughter of Þorsteinn's wife will be fought over by two valiant men, eventually killing each other, and that she would be married to a third man. The dream is modeled on a dream in *Trójumanna saga* and on another in *Nibelungenlied*, although the latter dream is only partially found in Old Icelandic literature (*Vǫlsunga saga*, ch. 26).

The author of *Gunnlaugs saga* knew many sagas and made use of some of them, not least *Egils saga Skalla-Grímssonar.* Nevertheless, the rivalry of Gunnlaugr and Hrafn over Helga is mentioned twice in *Egils saga* (chs. 79 and 87). This reference has been explained by oral tradition about this rivalry. The first half of the stanza spoken by Gunnlaugr in the saga (st. 19) is quoted in *Snorra Edda*, which has also been explained by oral traditions. Sagas of skalds entangled in a love triangle were apparently in vogue in Iceland in the early 13th century. Therefore, it is hard to believe that the mention of the rivalry of Gunnlaugr and Hrafn over Helga in *Egils saga* derives from oral tradition. The stanzas spoken by Gunnlaugr and others in the saga are as unlikely to be authentic (*i.e.*, early 11th-century poetry) as the content of the saga in general.

Gunnlaugs saga is preserved in two Icelandic parchment MSS, Stock Perg. 4to no. 18, probably written in the early 14th century, and defectively in AM 557 4to, probably from the early 15th century. The text of the older MS seems to be the better, more original, of the two, although both contain obvious errors. The MSS disagree most in ch. 1, where the older MS has some "learned" digressions and where the heading has the absurd information that *Gunnlaugs saga* has been told by Ari prestr inn fróði ("priest Ari the learned"). The text of the younger MS seems to be abbreviated.

The romantic and sentimental flavor of *Gunnlaugs saga*, together with its obvious use of early sagas as models (*Bjarnar saga Hítdœlakappa, Hallfreðar saga vandræðaskálds*) and direct and indirect references to others (*Laxdœla saga* and *Egils saga Skalla-Grímssonar*), have caused most scholars to assume that it must have been written late, *i.e.*, probably in the last decades of the 13th century. But Finnur Jónsson (1916) denied any romantic influence, and although he conceded that *Gunnlaugs saga* had affinities with other sagas, he maintained that they were mostly based on oral tradition. In his opinion, the saga was a "masterpiece," and belonged to the "best original saga-writing, around 1200."

The two conflicting views of the age of *Gunnlaugs saga*, early 13th and late 13th century, may both be partially right. *Gunnlaugs saga* may belong to the group of *Íslendingasögur* that Sigurður Nordal considered to be late adaptations of older sagas. The learned digressions and not least the curious naming of Ari fróði as the man who told the story, would fit well in this connection.

Ed.: Finnur Jónsson, ed. *Gunnlaugs saga ormstungu.* Samfund til udgivelse af gammel nordisk litteratur, 42. Copenhagen: Møller, 1916; Sigurður Nordal and Guðni Jónsson, eds. *Borgfirðinga sǫgur.* Íslenzk fornrit, 3. Reykjavik: Hið íslenzka fornritafélag, 1938, pp. 51–107; Strömbäck, Dag, ed. *The Arna-Magnæan Manuscript 557 4ᵗᵒ, Containing inter alia the History of the First Discovery of America.* Corpus Codicum Islandicorum Medii Aevi, 13. Copenhagen: Rosenkilde & Bagger, 1940 [facsimile]; Bjarni Einarsson, ed. *The Saga of Gunnlaug Serpent-Tongue and Three Other Sagas. Perg. 4:0 NR 18 Royal Library*

Stockholm. Early Icelandic Manuscripts in Facsimile, 16. Copenhagen: Rosenkilde & Bagger, 1986. **Tr.**: Jones, Gwyn, trans. *Erik the Red and Other Icelandic Sagas*. World's Classics, 582. London: Oxford University Press, 1961; rpt. 1980, pp. 171–217; Scargill, M. H., trans. "A Poet's Love: The Song of Gunnlaug and Hrafn: *Gunnlaugs saga Ormstunga*." In *Three Icelandic Sagas*. Trans. M. H. Scargill and Margaret Schlauch. Princeton: Princeton University Press; London: Oxford University Press, 1950, pp. 8–46; Foote, P. G., ed., and R. Quirk, trans. *Gunnlaugs saga ormstungu: The Saga of Gunnlaug Serpent-Tongue*. Nelson's Icelandic Texts. London: Nelson, 1957 [parallel Icelandic and English text]. **Lit.**: Björn Magnússon Ólsen. *Om Gunnlaugs saga ormstungu. En kritisk Undersøgelse*. Det Kongelige Danske videnskabers selskabs skrifter, 7. Række, Historiske og filosofiske afdeling 2.1. Copenhagen: Høst, 1911; Bjarni Einarsson. *Skáldasögur : Um uppruna og eðli ásta-skáldasagnanna fornu*. Reykjavik: Menningarsjóður, 1961; Bjarni Einarsson. "Bardaginn á Dinganesi." In *Mælt mál og forn fræði. Safn ritgerða eftir Bjarna Einarsson gefið út á sjötugsafmæli hans 11. apríl 1987*. Reykjavik: Stofnun Árna Magnússonar, 1987, pp. 91–9.

Bjarni Einarsson

[**See also**: *Bjarnar saga Hítdœlakappa; Egils saga Skalla-Grímssonar; Gunnlaugr ormstunga; Háttalykill; Morkinskinna; Skáld; Skáldasögur; Þáttr*]

Guta saga, an anonymous Old Gutnish legendary history of Gotland, survives as a text of about 2,000 words, primarily in prose, which follows immediately after the Laws of Gotland (*Gutalag*) in Codex B 64 of the Royal Library in Stockholm. The MS itself dates to the early 14th century, although *Guta saga* was almost certainly composed in something like its current form in the first quarter of the 13th century. In addition to *Guta saga*, five medieval translations, based on B 64, survive: three in Old Danish, one in Old Swedish, and one in German from the early 15th century.

The text takes the reader on a rapid journey through the history of the Baltic island-state, from its first settlement, when, according to legend, it sank by day and rose again by night, through some of the more important episodes in the island's history to events nearly contemporary with the compilation of the current text. *Guta saga* also relates how overpopulation forced the migration of a third of the residents and how these emigrants came to settle in the Byzantine Empire; it then tells something of the pagan rituals of the island, its christianization, and its ties to the Swedish kingdom. The last two sections detail the reciprocal obligations of the islanders to the Swedish king and the bishop of Linköping.

Guta saga has attracted considerable attention as one of the very few original, nonlegal prose works from the Old East Scandinavian area. In addition, the migration story, together with the claim that *enn hafa þair* [*i.e.*, the emigrants] *suint af waru mali* ("they still have something of our language"), have been much discussed. Some scholars hold that the story can be traced to Paul the Deacon, while others, basing themselves on the archaeological record and later reports concerning the Crimean "Goths," have maintained that the tale relates actual historical events.

Guta saga contains several verses in Nordic meters, although the exact proportion of verse is subject for debate. Based on an exploration of the text's stylistic levels (uncomplicated in the early sections, but highly complex and latinate in the last two) and verses, it has been suggested that the text was based on several indigenous traditions, to which have been added the concluding legal commentaries. The purpose of *Guta saga*, which everywhere promotes the idea of Gutnish independence and sovereignty, appears to have been to supplement the Laws of Gotland and to help the Gotlanders establish their relationship to the various powers that dominated the Baltic throughout the medieval period (*i.e.*, Sweden, Denmark, and the Hanseatic League).

Ed.: Pipping, Hugo, ed. *Gutalag och Gutasaga jämte ordbok*. Samfund til udgivelse af gammel nordisk litteratur, 33. Copenhagen: Møller, 1905–07. **Tr.**: Leach, Henry Goddard, ed. *A Pageant of Old Scandinavia*. Princeton: Princeton University Press; New York: American-Scandinavian Foundation, 1946, pp. 312–4 [partial translation]. **Lit.**: Mitchell, Stephen A. "On the Composition and Function of *Guta Saga*." *Arkiv för nordisk filologi* 99 (1984), 151–74; Maillefer, Jean Marie. "Guta Saga: Histoire des Gotlandais: Introduction, traduction, commentaires." *Études germaniques* 40 (1985), 131–40.

Stephen A. Mitchell

[**See also**: Gotland]

Gyðinga saga ("The Saga of the Jews") is found in its entirety or in fragments in five vellum MSS and sixteen paper MSS. The chief MS is codex AM 226 fol. from 1350–1360. A comparison of the two oldest MSS of *Gyðinga saga*, the fragments AM 655 XXV 4to from around 1300 and AM 238 XVII fol. from the beginning of the 14th century, with the corresponding sections in AM 226 fol. reveals, however, that *Gyðinga saga* in its original form was longer and that it is reduced by about one third in AM 226 fol.

In AM 226 fol., *Gyðinga saga* has no title. Árni Magnússon called the work "Historia Judaica" in his *Håndskriftfortegnelser* (AM 435a-b 4to) and "Historia Macchabeorum" in his note with AM 654 4to. The title "Gyðinga saga" seems to have first appeared in the 19th century (it is found in Jón Sigurðsson's catalogue, AM 394 fol.), and the saga was edited under this title by Guðmundur Þorláksson.

Gyðinga saga covers about 220 years of Jewish history. After an introduction sketching the conquests of Alexander the Great and the origin of the Seleucid Empire, it describes Antiochus IV's oppression of the Jews and their resistance under the Maccabees until Jewish independence in 142 B.C. The story then records the work of conquest and expansion as well as the rise and decline of the dynasty of Herod the Great and the reduction of Judaea to a Roman province. The actual historical narrative of *Gyðinga saga* ends with a note stating that Emperor Tiberius sent Pontius Pilate as procurator to Judaea, and the rest of the saga deals with events associated with the life and career of Pilate, including a short biography of Judas Iscariot.

In AM 226 fol., *Gyðinga saga* is divided into thirty-nine chapters. Although there are no other formal divisions, the saga falls naturally into three main parts. (1) The first twenty-one chapters form a unit and are based on 1 Maccabees with additions from 2 Maccabees and Peter Comestor's *Historia scholastica*. (2) Chs. 22–32 make up a middle section derived from *Historia scholastica*. (3) Chs. 33–38, giving an apocryphal story of the lives of Pontius Pilate and Judas Iscariot, are based on a certain "historia apocrypha," a precursor to the version of the legends in Jacobus de Voragine's *Legenda aurea*. There is no strong evidence that Flavius Josephus's *De bello Judaico* and *Antiquitates Judaicae* were sources for some of the additions in (1) and (2).

The last chapter contains a brief account of the Roman emperors from the death of Tiberius to Claudius, along with an epilogue that states that the work was translated from Latin into

Norse by the priest Brandr Jónsson (bishop of Hólar 1263–1264) at King Magnús Hákonarson's request. As Magnús assumed the title of king in 1257, and since Brandr is referred to as a priest rather than a bishop, the time of composition seems to be between 1257 and 1263. In 1262, Brandr went to Trondheim to be consecrated bishop; it is possible that *Gyðinga saga* was written in the time between his arrival in Norway in 1262 and his consecration as bishop on March 4, 1263.

The style of *Gyðinga saga* in AM 226 fol. is plain and unadorned; but the fragments AM 655 XXV 4to and AM 238 XVII fol., preserving a more original text, clearly show that it is wrong to deny *Gyðinga saga* all stylistic merits. In these fragments, the condensed style of the originals of *Gyðinga saga* is amplified to give a more diffuse narrative with a frequent use of alliteration.

Ed.: Guðmundur Þorláksson, ed. *Gyðinga saga: En Bearbejdelse fra Midten af det 13. árh. ved Brandr Jónsson.* Samfund til udgivelse af gammel nordisk litteratur, 6. Copenhagen: Møller, 1881; Wolf, Kirsten. "*Gyðinga saga.*" Diss. University of London, 1987; Wolf, Kirsten, ed. *Gyðinga saga* [forthcoming in the text series of Stofnun Árna Magnússonar]. **Tr.**: Fersch, Annabelle Flores. "*Gyðinga saga*: A Translation and Source Study." Diss. Tulane University, 1982; **Lit.**: Guðbrandur Vigfússon. "Um Stjórn." *Ný félagsrit* 23 (1863), 132–51; Storm, Gustav. "De norsk-islandske Bibeloversættelser fra 13de og 14de Aarhundrede og Biskop Brandr Jónsson." *Arkiv för nordisk filologi* 3 (1886), 244–56; Tryggvi Þórhallsson. "Brandur Jónsson biskup á Hólum." *Skírnir* 97 (1923), 46–64; Seip, Didrik Arup, ed. *Stjórn. AM 227 fol.* Corpus Codicum Islandicorum Medii Aevi, 20. Copenhagen: Munksgaard, 1956; Martin, Howard. "A Fragment of Gyðinga saga." *Opuscula* 5. Bibliotheca Arnamagnæana, 31. Copenhagen: Munksgaard, 1975, pp. 250–4; Jón Helgason. "Gyðinga saga i Trondheim." *Opuscula* 5. Bibliotheca Arnamagnæana, 31. Copenhagen: Munskgaard, 1975, pp. 343–76; Hallberg, Peter. "Några språkdrag i Alexanders saga och Gyðinga saga—med en utblick på Stjórn." In *Sjötíu ritgerðir helgaðar Jakobi Benediktssyni 20. júlí 1977.* 2 vols. Ed. Einar G. Pétursson and Jónas Kristjánsson. Reykjavik: Stofnun Árna Magnússonar, 1977, vol. 1, pp. 234–50; Wolf, Kirsten. "An Old Norse Record of Jewish History" *Jewish Quarterly Review* 77 (1986), 45–54; Wolf, Kirsten. "Lífssaga Pilati in Lbs. 4270 4to." *Proceedings of the PMR Conference* 12–13 (1987–88), 239–62; Wolf, Kirsten. "Gyðinga saga, Alexanders saga, and Bishop Brandr Jónsson." *Scandinavian Studies* 60 (1988), 371–400; Wolf, Kirsten. "The Judas Legend in Scandinavia." *Journal of English and Germanic Philology* 88 (1989), 463–76; Wolf, Kirsten. "Brandr Jónsson and Stjórn." *Scandinavian Studies* 62 (1990), 163–88; Wolf, Kirsten. "The Sources of Gyðinga saga." *Arkiv för nordisk filologi* 105 (1990), 140–55; Wolf, Kirsten. "Peter Comestor's *Historia Scholastica* in Old Norse Translation." *Amsterdamer Beiträge zur älteren Germanistik* 33 (1991), 149–66; Wolf, Kirsten. "An Extract of Gyðinga saga in Lbs. 714 8vo." *Opuscula* 9. Bibliotheca Arnamagnæana, 39. Copenhagen: Reitzel, 1991, pp. 189–202; Wolf, Kirsten. "A Note on the Date and Provenance of AM 229 fol. IV." *Maal og minne* (1991), 107–13; Wolf, Kirsten. "A Linguistic Peculiarity in Gyðinga saga." *Opuscula* 9. Bibliotheca Arnamagnæana, 39. Copenhagen: Reitzel, 1991, p. 146; Wolf, Kirsten. "A Note on *illska* in Gyðinga saga" [forthcoming in *Gripla*]; Wolf, Kirsten, "A Comment on the Dating of AM 226 fol." [forthcoming in *Gripla*].

Kirsten Wolf

[**See also**: *Alexanders saga*; Bible; Christian Prose; *Stjórn*]

Gǫngu-Hrólfs saga ("The Saga of Hrólfr the Stamper") is an anonymous *fornaldarsaga* from the beginning of the 14th century, preserved in AM 152 fol., AM 589f 4to, GkS 2845 4to, and BL Add. 4857.

The title of the saga refers to the size and weight of the supernatural hero, whom no horse can carry. He is identified as the Viking leader Rollo (Gǫngu-Hrólfr Rǫgnvaldsson), who in 911 was granted areas at the mouth of the Seine and who established the Norman duchy. Apart from the similarity between the names, there are, however, no historical points of connection. The saga represents to a much larger extent the type of the bridal-quest tale with numerous characters and scenes set in Scandinavia, Russia, and England.

The main theme is a fantastic journey of courtship to Garðaríki (Russia). Hrólfr, son of Sturlaugr and Ása (*Sturlaugs saga starfsama* includes them), undertakes the task for Earl Þorgnýr of Jutland after a swallow brings him a lock of Princess Ingigerðr's golden hair. During the journey, Hrólfr is outwitted by the Danish farmer's son Vilhjálmr, and undergoes a number of difficult tests as his servant. He manages to escape with Ingigerðr on the magical horse Dúlcifal. On his return, Hrólfr again falls into the hands of Vilhjálmr, who pricks him with a sleep-thorn and cuts off his feet. Ingigerðr heals him by a magical remedy, and, with the help of the dwarf Mǫndull, Hrólfr hangs the underhanded Dane. Before Hrólfr can get away with the princess, he must leave for Russia once more to avenge her father's death. He succeeds in this undertaking in a three-day battle described in detail. Finally, Hrólfr goes on a campaign to England to reestablish the deposed successor to the throne. In this concluding section, a detailed geographical digression on England and Denmark is incorporated from *Knýtlinga saga*.

The saga, which is rich in motifs, uses at least three fairy-tale sources to fulfill the bridal-quest pattern: the material of oriental origin about the demonic seducer in the figure of the dwarf, the tale about the unreliable servant (adopted as a German variant in the Grimm brothers' *Kinder- und Hausmärchen*), and finally the well-known tale from Egypt about the faraway maiden with the golden hair. The saga offers the oldest variant of the tale type of the unreliable servant, who forces his master to switch roles with him on a journey. The immediate source of the tale about the maiden with the golden hair has been debated; presumably the author knew a Norse version of the Tristan story.

The borrowings suggest a well-read author who also knew the learned and historical Icelandic works and related genres (*Sturlaugs saga starfsama, Yngvars saga víðfǫrla, Hrómundar saga Gripssonar*). Descriptions of parties with new musical instruments and exotic food (ch. 37), tournaments (ch. 21), courtly language, along with geographical digressions, indicate an attempt to expand the fictional potential of a *fornaldarsaga*, and to create an equally entertaining and instructive narrative.

Ed.: Rafn, C. C., ed. *Fornaldar sögur Nordrlanda.* 3 vols. Copenhagen: Popp, 1829–30; Guðni Jónsson, ed. *Fornaldar sögur Norðurlanda.* 4 vols. Akureyri: Íslendingasagnaútgáfan, 1954. **Tr.**: Hermann Pálsson and Paul Edwards, trans. *Göngu-Hrolfs Saga.* New Saga Library. Edinburgh: Canongate; Toronto and Buffalo: University of Toronto Press, 1980. **Lit.**: Hartmann, Jacob Wittmer. *The Göngu-Hrólfs saga: A Study in Old Norse Philology.* Columbia University Germanic Studies. New York: Columbia University Press, 1912; Schröder, Franz Rolf. "Gunthers Brautwerbung und die Gǫngu-Hrólfs saga." In *Festschrift*

Eugen Mogk zum 70. Geburtstag 19. Juli 1924. Halle: Niemeyer, 1924, pp. 582–95; Dünninger, Josef. "Untersuchungen zur Gǫngu-Hrólfs Saga." *Arkiv för nordisk filologi* 47 (1931) 309–46; 48 (1932), 31–60; Magoun, Francis P. "Whence 'Dúlcifal' in Gǫngu-Hrólfs Saga?" In *Studia germanica tillägnade Ernst Albin Kock den 6 December 1934.* Lund: Gleerup; Copenhagen: Levin & Munksgaard, 1934, pp. 176–91; Hermann Pálsson and Paul Edwards. *Legendary Fiction in Medieval Iceland.* Studia Islandica, 30. Reykjavik: Heimspekideild Háskola Íslands; Menningarsjóður, 1971.

Hans-Peter Naumann

[**See also:** *Fornaldarsǫgur; Hrómundar saga Gripssonar; Knýtlinga saga*; Old Norse-Icelandic Literature, Foreign Influence on; *Sturlaugs saga starfsama; Yngvars saga víðfǫrla*]

Hadding *see* **Divine Heroes, Native**

Haithabu *see* **Hedeby**

Hákon góði ("the good") Haraldsson (*ca.* 920–960)

was a younger son and successor of Haraldr hárfagri ("fair-hair") Hálfdanarson, who first brought Norway under a single kingship. Hákon was also called "Æthelstan's foster-son," because he was fostered in England at the Christian court of King Æthelstan of Wessex. Around 935, Hákon learned in England of his father's death, and returned to Norway to regain the throne from his half-brother, Eiríkr blóðøx ("blood-axe") Haraldsson. Hákon sought the support of Earl Sigurðr Hákonarson in Trondheim, and was named king in Trøndelag after promising the farmers that he would restore their patrimonial rights (*óðal*). When Hákon moved south and seized power in Oppland and Vík, Eiríkr, without further resistance, fled from Norway to York. Hákon became king over Norway, but in reality his power lay in the southwest; he allowed Earl Sigurðr to retain sovereignty in Trøndelag, and he gave his nephews, Tryggvi Óláfsson and Guðrøðr Bjarnarson, virtual autonomy over parts of southeastern Norway.

Hákon's popularity has been traditionally ascribed to his achievements as a lawgiver and organizer of military defense. The poet Sighvatr Þórðarson's *Bersǫglisvísur* ("Plain-speaking Verses," *ca.* 1038) extol Hákon for his justice and his laws. The histories *Ágrip*, *Fagrskinna*, and *Heimskringla* variously credit him with establishing the Gulaþing Law for the *fylkir* ("districts") of Rogaland, Hordaland, Sogn, and the Fjords, and the Frostuþing Law for the *fylkir* of Trøndelag together with Nordmøre, Namdal, and later Romsdal. But these histories are not wholly accurate, for the Gulaþing, at least, had probably been established in the 930s. It is more likely that Hákon reorganized existing law federations (the Gulaþing in western Norway, Frostaþing in northern Norway, and Eiðsivaþing around the southeastern Lake Mjøsa area) by extending their reach into neighboring districts and changing them into representative and consultive bodies. Each district was required to send a certain number of delegates (*nefndarmenn*) to the *þing*. The integration of *fylkir* into larger regions and the reorganization of the law federations on a more representative basis enabled the

monarchy to consult more easily with the several regions and thereby seek both legal and popular approval for national as well as local matters. Thus, Hákon can probably be credited with introducing the principle of representation into the Norwegian social order.

According to *Heimskringla* and *Fagrskinna*, Hákon also reorganized the military defense set up by his father, Haraldr Hálfdanarson, into a levy system (*leiðangr*), by which the king could summon on a proportional basis a levy of ships, warriors, weapons, and equipment. Hákon divided all the coastal lands into *skipreiður* ("ship-providing [districts]") and stipulated by law the number of warships and men to be supplied by each district. He also instituted a system of war signal fires along the mountaintops to warn of approaching enemies.

Although Hákon had been raised a Christian, his attempts to introduce Christianity into Norway did not succeed. According to *Heimskringla*, Hákon invited priests from England and built churches in western Norway. Further evidence of English mission activity in mid-10th-century Norway may be provided by the listing of a "Sigefridus norwegensis" among the names of Glastonbury monks who were bishops during the reign of King Edgar (d. 975). When Hákon proposed at the Frostaþing that the people accept Christianity, however, he reportedly met with great resistance and was forced to abandon his attempt. Hákon presumably left the faith himself, for the memorial poem *Hákonarmál* (*ca.* 961) commemorates him as a staunch upholder of pagan sanctuaries, although this poem may reflect the poet's sentiment more than the historical accuracy of Hákon's return to paganism.

Around 955, Hákon repelled the first of many attacks on Norway by his nephews, the Eiríkssons, who had taken refuge in Denmark with their uncle, King Harald Gormsson. Hákon retaliated with raids on Denmark, but when the Eiríkssons (*ca.* 960) renewed attacks at Fitje (Fitjar) on the island of Stord (Storð) off western Norway, Hákon was mortally wounded. *Heimskringla* reports that he was given a pagan burial, and lauds Hákon as a king who brought peace and good seasons. His famous eulogy *Hákonarmál* states: "Unbound against the dwellings of men / the Fenris-wolf shall go / before a king as good as he / walks on that empty path."

Lit.: Koht, Halvdan. "Haakon Adalsteinsfostre." *Norsk biografisk leksikon* 5. Oslo: Aschehoug, 1931, pp. 152–7; Birkeli, Fridtjov. "Hadde Håkon Adalsteinsfostre likevel en Biskop Sigfrid hos seg?" *Historisk tidsskrift* (Norway) 40 (1960–61), 113–36; Foote, Peter G., and David M. Wilson. *The Viking Achievement: The Society and Culture of Early Medieval Scandinavia.* London: Sidgwick & Jackson, 1970, pp. 36–42, 46–7, 280–2; Birkeli, Fridtjov. "The Earliest Missionary Activity from England to Norway." *Nottingham Mediaeval Studies* 15 (1971), 27–37; Holmsen, Andreas. *Norges historie fra de eldste tider til 1660.* 3rd ed. Oslo: Universitetsforlaget, 1971, pp. 141–51; Andersen, Per Sveaas. *Samlingen av Norge og kristningen av landet 800–1130.* Handbok i Norges historie, 2. Bergen: Universitetsforlaget, 1977, pp. 84–99, 247–73; Jones, Gwyn. *A History of the Vikings.* 2nd ed. Oxford and New York: Oxford University Press, 1984, pp. 92–6, 118–23.

Daphne L. Davidson

[**See also:** *Ágrip af Nóregs konunga sǫgum*; Eyvindr Finnsson skáldaspillir; *Fagrskinna*; *Heimskringla*; *Leiðangr*, Norway; Sighvatr Þórðarson]

Hákon Hákonarson, king of Norway 1217–1263, was born in 1204, the son of King Hákon Sverrisson, and grandson of Sverrir Sigurðarson.

After King Ingi Bárðarson's death in 1217, the Birkibeinar ("birch-legs") disagreed on his successor. The choice was among Hákon Hákonarson, Ingi's son Guttormr, and Ingi's brother Earl Skúli. Hákon was elected king but Skúli continued as earl and adviser to the young king, responsible for the rule of a third of Norway. In 1219, Hákon was engaged to Earl Skúli's daughter Margrét, and they were married in 1225.

During the 1220s, Hákon and Skúli had to fight a group of rebels, the Ribbungar from Viken. The fight lasted until 1227 and became a major reason why the king and Skúli supported each other. But gradually Hákon began to act increasingly independently, and during the 1230s open conflict broke out between Hákon and Skúli over the administration of the kingdom. In 1239, Skúli rebelled against Hákon, and assumed the title of king at Eyraþing in Niðaróss (Trondheim). Hákon crushed the resistance, and in 1240 Skúli was killed by the Birkibeinar. After that, Hákon was the uncontested king of Norway.

Practical cooperation between the archbishop and the kingdom characterized the greater part of Hákon Hákonarson's reign. In collaboration with the Church, hereditary succession to the throne was established. Hákon was recognized as the lawful successor to the kingdom of Norway at a meeting in Bergen in 1223. The archbishop confirmed the decision, and this act validated the principles concerning ecclesiastical influence on the succession; this influence had its roots in the Law of Succession to the Throne from 1163. In 1240, allegiance was sworn to Hákon's eldest legitimate son, Hákon, which proved a clear victory for the hereditary throne. At the same time, the principle of legitimacy was strengthened, since the son Hákon was preferred to an older, illegitimate half-brother. Papal assent that Hákon Hákonarson's successors were to rule Norway came in 1247, when Hákon was crowned by Cardinal William of Sabina.

In Hákon Hákonarson's time, European chivalric literature began its influence in Norway. Hákon Hákonarson, and later his son Magnús, wanted the Norwegian court to be comparable with those in Europe. Hákon had a number of European Latin works translated into Old Norse. The oldest of these translations is *Tristrams saga* from 1226. Five MSS containing *riddarasögur* expressly state that the works were translated at Hákon's request, and it is likely that Hákon also had *Konungs skuggsjá* written, modeled on the European *specula*. These translations were significant for the Norse cultural milieu, and among other things influenced a number of *Íslendingasögur*, among them *Laxdæla saga*. The *riddarasögur* became popular especially in Iceland, where as early as 1300 people began composing their own.

During Hákon's reign, the people of Lübeck began trading with Norway. The importance of this trade increased, and in 1250, Hákon signed a treaty with the city. The following year, an agreement was entered into with Novgorod concerning peace in the northern tributary countries. Hákon was also active in Scandinavian politics after 1248, when trouble arose in Denmark and Sweden. He married his son Hákon to Earl Birgir's daughter in Sweden, and his other son, Magnús, to King Erik's daughter in Denmark.

From 1220, Hákon Hákonarson had tried to subjugate the Norse islands in the west, but this conquest was impossible as long as there were conflicts in Norway. After Skúli's death, however, Hákon attempted to secure control over Iceland. Through the chieftains in Iceland, who were also his retainers, he succeeded in gaining control of the *goðorð* little by little. Thereafter, he could distribute the *goðorð* among the chieftains he found best suited to advancing his policies. In addition, he received support from the Norwegian bishops in Iceland; and in 1262–1264, he subjected Iceland and Greenland to the kingdom of Norway.

In the Hebrides and on the Isle of Man, there had been trouble throughout Hákon's reign, and·in 1262 the Scots attacked the islands. Hákon gathered a mercenary army and attacked Scotland in 1263. The result was meager, and he did not secure Norwegian control over the islands. Hákon then went to the Orkney Islands, where he died in the winter of 1263.

Lit.: Koht, Halvdan. "The Scandinavian Kingdoms Until the End of the Thirteenth Century." In *The Cambridge Medieval History* 6. Ed. J. R. Tanner *et al.* Cambridge: Cambridge University Press, 1929, pp. 362–92; Helle, Knut. "Tendenser i nyere norsk høymiddelalderforskning." *Historisk tidsskrift* (Norway) 40 (1960–61), 337–70; Helle, Knut. "Trade and Shipping Between Norway and England in the Reign of Hákon Hákonsson (1217–1263)." *Sjøfartshistorisk årbok* (Bergen) (1967), 7–33; Helle, Knut. "Anglo-Norwegian Relations in the Reign of Hákon Hákonsson (1217–63)." *Mediaeval Scandinavia* 1 (1968), 101–14; Bjørgo, Narve. "Om skriftlege kjelder for Hákonar saga." *Historisk tidsskrift* (Norway) 46 (1967), 185–229; Gunnes, Erik. "Kirkelig jurisdiksjon i Norge 1153–1277." *Historisk tidsskrift* (Norway) 49 (1970), 109–60; Crawford, Barbara E. "The Earls of Orkney-Caithness and Their Relations with the Kings of Norway and Scotland: 1150–1470." Diss. St. Andrews University, 1971; Helle, Knut. *Konge og gode menn i norsk riksstyring ca. 1150–1319.* Bergen: Universitetsforlaget, 1972; Crawford, Barbara E. "Weland of Stiklaw: A Scottish Royal Servant at the Norwegian Court." *Historisk tidsskrift* (Norway) 52 (1973), 329–39; Helle, Knut. *Norge blir en stat, 1130–1319.* Handbok i Norges historie, 3. 2nd ed. Bergen: Universitetsforlaget, 1974; Lunden, Kåre. *Norge under Sverreætten 1177–1319.* Norges Historie, 3. Oslo: Cappelen, 1976; Bagge, Sverre. "Kirkens jurisdiksjon i kristenrettssaker før 1277." *Historisk tidsskrift* (Norway) 60 (1981), 133–59; Helle, Knut. "Norway in the High Middle Ages: Recent Views on the Structure of Society." *Scandinavian Journal of History* 6 (1981), 161–89; Bagge, Sverre. "The Formation of the State and Concepts of Society in 13th Century Norway." In *Continuity and Change: Political*

Institutions and Literary Monuments in the Middle Ages. A Symposium. Ed. Elisabeth Vestergard. Odense: Odense University Press, 1986, pp. 43–61; Bagge, Sverre. "Borgerkrig og statsutvikling i Norge i middelalderen." Historisk tidsskrift (Norway) 65 (1986), 145–97; Bagge, Sverre. The Political Thought of the King's Mirror. Mediaeval Scandinavia Supplements, 3. Odense: Odense University Press, 1987.

Jón Viðar Sigurðsson

[See also: *Hákonar saga gamla Hákonarsonar, Konungs skuggsjá*; Norway; *Riddarasögur; Tristrams saga ok Ísǫndar*]

Hákon jarl ("earl") Sigurðarson (ca. 940–995), known

as Hákon inn ríki ("the great"), was the last pagan ruler of Norway (r. ca. 970–995). He was a member of the powerful Trondheim-based Hlaðajarlar ("earls of Lade"), who rose to prominence in Hålogaland in the 9th century, probably from wealth gained in the fur and ivory trade, and who enjoyed virtual sovereignty over northern Norway during the reigns of King Haraldr hárfagri ("fair-hair") Hálfdanarson and King Hákon góði ("the good") Haraldsson. Around 962, the Eiríkssons, successors to Hákon Haraldsson, treacherously burned Sigurðr Hlaðajarl in his hall, and his son Hákon vowed revenge. Earl Hákon fled to King Harald Gormsson in Denmark, and according to accounts in *Heimskringla* and *Fagrskinna* (probably based on the lost *Hlaðajarla saga*), he engineered through shrewd machinations the deaths of King Haraldr's two nephews, Haraldr Eiríksson and Haraldr Knútsson, both contenders for the Norwegian throne. King Haraldr rewarded Hákon with the restoration of his sovereignty over northern Norway, and gave him rule over southwestern Norway, in return for payment of tribute. When Hákon reestablished pagan sanctuaries that had been destroyed by the Christian Eiríkssons, his popular reign was accompanied by bountiful harvests and large catches of herring, according to *Fagrskinna* and *Heimskringla*.

Around 974, Hákon aided Denmark against the invasion of the German emperor Otto II, who reputedly forced the Christian baptism of King Harald and Earl Hákon as a condition of peace. On his return to Norway, however, Hákon cast off the Christian faith. Because Hákon had by now rejected Danish overlordship, King Harald Gormsson sent a fleet against him, but failed to recapture any territory. From this time on, Earl Hákon exercised full sovereignty over Norway (with the possible exception of the Danish-controlled Vík area in the southeast), but he never assumed the title of king, probably because of his strong family identity. The greatest threat to Hákon's rule came around 985, when a powerful naval force of Danes and Wendish Jómsvíkingar ("Vikings of Jóm") attacked Norway at Hjǫrungavágr (Liavåg). After a bitter fight, Hákon won the most important victory of his career and confirmed Norwegian independence. According to *Jómsvíkinga saga*, Hákon triumphed only after sacrificing his son to his tutelary goddess.

Heimskringla records that Hákon later forfeited his popularity with the people because of his greed, lawlessness, and lechery, but the real reasons for Hákon's eventual downfall may have been the rivalry of the northern Hlaðajarlar with the Yngling dynasty in the south, and the rise of Óláfr Tryggvason, great-grandson of Haraldr Hálfdanarson and son of the petty king Tryggvi Óláfsson of Vík. In 995, Óláfr Tryggvason attempted to seize the throne of Norway, and Hákon fled to Gaulardalr, where his mistress, Þóra, hid him in a pigsty. There the earl met an ignominious death by murder at the hand of his thrall.

Earl Hákon was famed as a brilliant political strategist and, above all, as a fervent champion of his ancestral pagan religion. According to his court poet Einarr skálaglamm ("scale-tinkle") in *Vellekla* (composed ca. 986), Hákon derived his mandate to rule directly from the pagan deities; the gods rewarded his correct religious performance with fertility in the land and success in war. A lasting legacy of Earl Hákon is the exceptional poetry that has survived from his unusually large retinue of skalds. The poems not only attest to the earl's sophisticated use of poetic propaganda to gain political ends, but are also in themselves a most valuable repository of pagan myths.

Lit.: Koht, Halvdan. "Haakon Sigurdsson." *Norsk biografisk leksikon* 5. Oslo: Aschehoug, 1931, pp. 187–91; Jones, Gwyn. "The Historian and the Jarl." *History Today* (1969), 232–9; Foote, Peter G., and David M. Wilson. *The Viking Achievement: The Society and Culture of Early Medieval Scandinavia*. London: Sidgwick & Jackson, 1970, pp. 36–43, 135–40; Holmsen, Andreas. *Norges historie fra de eldste tider til 1660*. 3rd ed. Oslo: Universitetsforlaget, 1971, pp. 151–3; Andersen, Per Sveaas. *Samlingen av Norge og kristningen av landet 800–1130*. Handbok i Norges historie, 2. Bergen: Universitetsforlaget, 1977, pp. 99–101; Ström, Folke. "Poetry as an Instrument of Propaganda: Jarl Hákon and His poets." In *Specvlvm Norroenvm: Norse Studies in Memory of Gabriel Turville-Petre*. Ed. Ursula Dronke et al. Odense: Odense University Press, 1981, pp. 440–58; Davidson, Daphne L. "Earl Hákon and His Poets." Diss. Oxford University, 1984; Jones, Gwyn. *A History of the Vikings*. 2nd ed. Oxford and New York: Oxford University Press, 1984, pp. 123–31.

Daphne L. Davidson

[See also: Einarr Helgason skálaglamm; *Fagrskinna*; Harald Gormsson (Bluetooth); *Heimskringla*; *Jómsvíkinga saga*; Norway]

Hákonar saga gamla Hákonarsonar ("The Saga of Hákon

Hákonarson the Old") is a biography of the Norwegian king, Hákon IV (r. 1217–1263), who was the son of Hákon Sverrisson (r. 1202–1204). Commissioned by Hákon's son Magnús lagabœtir ("law-mender"; r. 1263–1280), this detailed chronicle was compiled in 1264–1265 by Sturla Þórðarson (d. 1284). The trying circumstances under which the Icelandic poet and historian performed this task are recounted in *Sturlu þáttr* and in other parts of *Sturlunga saga*.

King Hákon had instigated the death of Sturla's uncle, Snorri Sturluson, in 1241. Sturla rightly regarded Hákon as his most dangerous enemy, for he had steadfastly resisted the king's subjugation of Iceland to Norway, which was accomplished in 1262–1264. Skúli Bárðarson (d. 1240), Hákon's most dangerous rival for royal power, was the maternal grandfather of Magnús, who supervised the composition of his father's biography, much as King Sverrir is said to have "sat over" Karl Jónsson as the Icelandic abbot wrote Sverrir's biography.

Although *Hákonar saga* lacks the vivid drama of *Sverris saga*, it has much in common with this work. Sverrir had succeeded in reestablishing the supremacy of the king over both the Church and the landed aristocracy, which often supported the Church, headed by the archbishop. Hákon IV maintained this royal supremacy and completed the unification of the country. The death of Skúli in 1240 is generally regarded as the end of the civil-war period in Norway (1130–1240).

During the reign of Hákon IV, Norway emerged as a European state. The Norwegian king was on good terms with Henry III of England, and trade between the two countries flourished during this time. Unlike Sverrir, Hákon was able to maintain a good relationship with the Church, while at the same time refusing its claims for independence. Several long passages emphasize the high regard in which Hákon was held by Emperor Frederick II (d. 1250). In 1250, Hákon concluded a treaty of commerce with Lübeck, and from then on trade with the Hanseatic cities increased. Hákon sent gifts of Icelandic falcons to the Bez of Tunis and to Henry III of England. Hákon's daughter Kristín married Prince Philip of Spain. Iceland and Greenland became tributary to Norway around the time of Hákon's death.

Quite aside from the fact that Sturla had to extol the virtues of his most feared enemy without severely condemning the king's most dangerous adversary, there is much irony in this work. The most obvious example is the ambivalent role played by Skúli: after successfully protecting Hákon for years against his enemies, Skúli's greed for power and prestige finally led him to open revolt and death. How skillfully Sturla dealt with this sensitive situation can be seen in Skúli's eulogy. Skúli would have been called one of the greatest men ever born in Norway, "if this unfortunate deed (ógiptuverk) had not overcome him in the last days of his life" (ch. 214, Guðni Jónsson, ed.).

There are several scenes and episodes in which Sturla waxes eloquent, such as the spirited exchange between Hákon and William of Sabina, the pope's envoy who crowned Hákon king of Norway. The chief importance of Hákonar saga, however, lies in the fact that it is an important historical document. This badly neglected chronicle has been preserved in three redactions found in Eirspennill, Codex Frisianus, and Flateyjarbók.

Ed.: Gudbrand Vigfusson, ed. "Hákonar saga Hákonarsonar." In Icelandic Sagas and Other Historical Documents Relating to the Settlements and Descents of the Northmen on the British Isles. 4 vols. Rolls Series, 88. London: Eyre and Spottiswoode, 1887–94; rpt. Millwood: Kraus, 1964, vol. 2, pp. 1–360, 374–82; Guðni Jónsson, ed. Konunga sögur. 3 vols. Reykjavik: Íslendingasagnaútgáfan, 1957, vol. 3, pp. 1–464; Mundt, Marina, ed. Hákonar saga Hákonarsonar etter Sth. 8 fol., AM 325 VIII,4°, og AM 304,4°. Norrøne skrifter, 2. Oslo: Norsk historisk kjeldeskrift-institutt, 1977 [supplement: James E. Knirk. Rettelser til Hákonar saga Hákonarsonar etter Sth. 8 fol., AM 325 VIII 4° og AM 304 4°. Norrøne tekster, 2. Oslo: Norsk historisk kjeldeskrift-institutt, 1982]. **Tr.**: Dasent, George W., trans. "The Saga of Hacon and a Fragment of the Saga of Magnus with Appendices." In Icelandic Sagas and Other Historical Documents Relating to the Settlements and Descents of the Northmen on the British Isles, vol. 4, pp. 1–373, 388–95. **Lit.**: Ker, William Paton. Sturla the Historian. Oxford: Clarendon, 1906; rpt. in Collected Essays. London: Macmillan, 1925, vol. 2, pp. 173–95.

Paul Schach

[**See also**: Eirspennill; Flateyjarbók; Fríssbók; Hákon Hákonarson; Konungasögur; Sturla Þórðarson; Sturlunga saga; Sverris saga]

Hákonar saga Ívarssonar ("The Saga of Hákon Ívarsson") and Morkinskinna recount two versions of Hákon Ívarsson's intermittent quarrel with King Haraldr harðráði ("hard-ruler") Sigurðarson (r. 1047–1066). The author of Hákonar saga Ívarssonar integrated material largely presented as unrelated episodes in Morkinskinna into a series of events motivated by ambition and vengeance. By representing Hákon, a belated Viking from eastern Norway, as a scion of the dynasty of the earls of Hlaðir (Lade, near Trondheim), the saga author identifies a petty personal dispute with a protracted feud of national significance. By relating Hákon to Einarr þambarskelfir ("paunch-shaker" or "bowstring-trembler"), he transforms Einarr's murder by the king, which remains inconsequential in Morkinskinna, into the impetus of the action. Thus, Hákon receives an earldom and the king's niece Ragnhildr in marriage, not as rewards for military support, but as compensation for the slaying of a kinsman. During the battle of Nissan River, King Sven Estridsen of Denmark narrowly eludes capture by King Haraldr, with the help of Earl Hákon, according to the saga. The king is enraged by people's praise of Hákon, and when he learns of the earl's complicity in Sven's escape, he launches a surprise attack upon the man he regards as a potential rival for the Norwegian throne. Hákon escapes, and the story ends with his return to Norway following Haraldr's death at Stamford Bridge (1066).

Composed around 1210, Hákonar saga Ívarssonar is preserved in four fragments (six leaves) of AM 570a 4to from around 1480. The lacunae can be filled from a Latin compendium in GkS 2434 4to (fols. 15r–18r), and from Snorri's account in Heimskringla. Snorri followed the saga in his presentation of these events in Haralds saga Sigurðarsonar, even though Morkinskinna is historically more reliable. Snorri abridged the saga account, condensed the circumstantial style, and purposely refined the character portrait of Hákon. Hákonar saga Ívarssonar is the only independent historical saga about a Norwegian who was not of royal status or a pretender to the throne.

Ed.: Jón Helgason and Jakob Benediktsson, eds. Hákonar saga Ívarssonar. Samfund til udgivelse af gammel nordisk litteratur, 62. Copenhagen: Jørgensen, 1952. **Lit.**: Bull, Edvard. "Håkon Ivarssons saga." Edda 27 (1927), 33–44.

Paul Schach

[**See also**: Heimskringla; Konungasögur; Morkinskinna]

Hákonardrápa see **Hallfreðr Óttarsson**

Hákonarmál see **Eyvindr Finnsson skáldaspillir**

Háleygjatal see **Eyvindr Finnsson skáldaspillir**

Hálfdanar saga Brǫnufóstra ("The Saga of Hálfdan, Foster-son of Brana") is a fornaldarsaga composed in Iceland around the year 1300 or shortly thereafter. It follows the life of young Prince Hálfdan in Denmark, whose father is killed by marauding berserks led by the evil Viking Sóti. Hálfdan and his sister, Ingibjǫrg, are hidden in a farmhouse protected from searchers by fortuitous snowstorms, before being sent by their foster-father to his brother in Bjarmaland. At the age of twelve, Hálfdan is given four ships of his own, but fog and storms combine to drive him and his lone surviving ship to Helluland. While hunting one day, he comes upon a cave containing two trolls, whom he slays with a gold-adorned sword found there. In a side cave, he finds a Scottish earl's abducted daughter and twin sons. While hunting with the latter, he encounters the half-troll Brana, daughter of an abducted princess from Valland. Since Brana has been badly treated by her troll family, Hálfdan and his two companions slay her sisters and numerous other trolls, but they are unable to kill her father, Járnnefr, vulnerable only to the sword given to Hálfdan by Brana, which she then wields herself to do him in. Hálfdan spends the winter with Brana, who, after informing him that she is carrying his child, gives him a ship she had made, as well as three magic gifts, and sends him off to marry the beautiful Marsibil, daughter of King Óláfr of England. He uses love-inducing herbs to overcome Marsibil's initial antipathy and enjoys favor at the court. The king's evil counselor Áki challenges Hálfdan, but loses badly in a swimming match and a joust. Áki then accosts Hálfdan's sister, but she invokes Brana, who uses a magic spell to transfix Áki to the door for the night while sending freezing weather to add to his discomfort. Somewhat later, Áki invites Hálfdan and his friends to a feast and sets fire to their quarters, but Brana miraculously appears to carry them all to safety.

On another occasion, Áki ambushes Hálfdan, but Hálfdan's clothing is impervious to all weapons except his own sword, and he easily slays all of Áki's men, while reserving for Áki one of the more thorough mutilations in Old Icelandic literature. Hálfdan sets off to avenge his father with twenty ships given him by Marsibil, but a curse by the dying Sóti prevents Hálfdan from returning to his love. Brana finally arrives to counter the curse, and the story ends in a flurry of marriages.

Many well-known folktale motifs can be found in *Hálfdanar saga Brǫnufóstra*, but these are not always skillfully juxtaposed. Also included are a ring able to detect an opponent's evil intentions (which is not used in the saga), a premonitory dream, and a spell making one unable to stand the sight of human blood. From a literary point of view, the most important passage is the hero's encounter with two trolls in a cave, a motif complex closer to the Old English epic *Beowulf* than corresponding passages in any other Norse saga, including the often-cited *Grettis saga*. Verbatim parallels to passages in this episode exist in *Gríms saga loðinkinna* and in *Ála flekks saga*, and indicate conscious literary borrowing in the writing of these sagas, possibly from an even older, lost original. It is also probable that *Hálfdanar saga Brǫnufóstra* was known to the author of *Sǫrla saga sterka*.

Hálfdanar saga Brǫnufóstra is preserved in three vellum MSS from the 15th century, but its later popularity is attested by some four dozen paper MSS. In addition, the material was given poetic form on three occasions, as *rímur* of sixteen, seventeen, and fourteen cantos from the first part of the 16th, the 18th, and the late 19th centuries, respectively. During the third quarter of the 18th century, the saga served as the model for the forgery *Hafgeirs saga Flateyings*.

Ed.: Guðni Jónsson, ed. *Fornaldar sögur Norðurlanda.* 4 vols. Akureyri: Íslendingasagnaútgáfan, 1954, vol. 4, pp. 287–318. **Tr.**: Hannah, Robert, trans. "The Saga of Halfdan, Foster-Son of Brana." *Seminar for Germanic Philology. Yearbook* 4 (1981), 9–27. **Bib.**: Halldór Hermannsson. *Bibliography of the Mythical-Heroic Sagas (Fornaldarsögur).* Islandica, 5. Ithaca: Cornell University Library, 1912; rpt. New York: Kraus, 1966, pp. 19–20. **Lit.**: Finnur Sigmundsson. *Rímnatal.* 2 vols. Reykjavik: Rímnafélagið, 1966, vol. 1, pp. 195–6; Jorgensen, Peter A. "The Two-Troll Variant of the Bear's Son Folktale in *Hálfdanar saga Brönufóstra* and *Gríms saga loðinkinna.*" *Arv* 31 (1975), 35–43; Jorgensen, Peter A. "*Hafgeirs saga Flateyings*: An Eighteenth-Century Forgery." *Journal of English and Germanic Philology* 76 (1977), 155–64; Jorgensen, Peter A. "Beowulf's Swimming Contest with Breca: Old Norse Parallels." *Folklore* 89 (1978), 52–9; Jorgensen, Peter A. "Literarisch verwandte Stellen in verschiedenen Fornaldarsagas." In *Fourth International Saga Conference.* Munich: Institut für Nordische Philologie der Universität München, 1979, 1–17 pp. [photocopies of papers distributed to participants].

Peter A. Jorgensen

[**See also**: *Ála flekks saga*; *Fornaldarsögur*; *Gríms saga loðinkinna*; *Jǫkuls þáttr Búasonar*; *Rímur*; *Sǫrla saga sterka*]

Hálfdanar saga Eysteinssonar

Hálfdanar saga Eysteinssonar ("The Saga of Hálfdan Eysteinsson"). This anonymous *fornaldarsaga* is transmitted in three principal recensions. The oldest and most original is represented by AM 343 4to and AM 586 4to. Its content was paraphrased several times in the form of the poetic *rímur* (*Hálfdanarrímur Eysteinssonar*).

The saga, consisting of four parts, treats the widespread maiden-king theme in an unusual fashion. After a genealogical introduction, Hálfdan, the son of the Norwegian king Eysteinn Þrándarson, is sent by his father to bring home Princess Ingigerðr from Garðaríki (Russia) as hostage and bride. The political marriage does not materialize, however, because Ingigerðr has switched roles with a maidservant by the same name and fled. Hálfdan is displeased with the false Ingigerðr and gives her to his servant Úlfkell, who becomes a usurper. During a party, the real Ingigerðr comes disguised to Hálfdan, and in the night she takes off her glove. Hálfdan looks with admiration at her beautiful hand with a sparkling gemstone on it, and falls asleep. He wakes up by the light of a torch and hears a voice saying: "For this hand, the ring, and the glove, you must search, and you must desire them, and you will never find peace until the one that now takes them away gives them freely into your hand" (ch. 8). Hálfdan follows this instruction, a motif reminiscent of the Cupid and Psyche story, but he becomes involved with Úlfkell's revolt and is defeated in a naval battle. Severely wounded, he receives three charms in a cottage of one of the foresters, with the help of whom he kills three giants one after the other, and finally arrives in the vicinity of the beloved. A glove is thrown to him from the battlement of the castle, although he does not get the hand that fits the glove until he has destroyed the enemy.

The main plot, which is rich in episodes and characters, and which takes place in northern Scandinavia, Russia, and the countries around the fictitious White Sea (Bjarmaland), combines in a complicated but clever way a stepmother tale with the leitmotif of a lost and retrieved beloved. The numerous borrowings from Icelandic as well as translated literature show the author was well read. Apart from historical works like *Landnámabók* and *Ynglinga saga*, the *fornaldarsögur*, such as *Gǫngu-Hrólfs saga* and *Vǫlsunga saga*, served especially as sources. As a kind of continuation, a later redactor incorporated the so-called *Vals þáttr*, a Viking story of Ragnarr, of Valr and his sons, and of Angarr and the giant Svaði, borrowed from *Bárðar saga*. The saga belongs to the later period of Icelandic narrative art, hardly before the middle of the 14th century.

Ed.: Rafn, C. C., ed. *Fornaldar sögur Nordrlanda.* 3 vols. Copenhagen: Popp, 1829–30; Schröder, Franz Rolf, ed. *Hálfdanar saga Eysteinssonar.* Altnordische Saga-Bibliothek, 15. Halle: Niemeyer, 1917. **Tr.**: Hermann Pálsson and Paul Edwards, trans. *Seven Viking Romances.*

Harmondsworth: Penguin, 1985; Simek, Rudolf, trans. *Zwei Abenteuersagas. Egils saga einhenda. Hálfdanar saga Eysteinssonar.* Altnordische Bibliothek, 7. Leverkusen: Literaturverlag Norden, 1989. **Lit.**: Schröder, Franz Rolf. "Untersuchungen zur Hálfdanar saga Eysteinssonar." Diss. University of Kiel 1917; Naumann, Hans-Peter. "Erzählstrategien in der Fornaldarsaga: Die Prüfungen des Helden." In *Akten der Fünften Arbeitstagung der Skandinavisten des deutschen Sprachgebiets.* Ed. H. Uecker. St. Augustin: Kretschmer, 1983, pp. 131–42.

Hans-Peter Naumann

[**See also:** *Bárðar saga Snæfellsáss; Fornaldarsögur; Gǫngu-Hrólfs saga; Landnámabók; Rímur; Vǫlsunga saga; Ynglinga saga*]

Hálfs saga ok Hálfsrekka

Hálfs saga ok Hálfsrekka ("The Saga of Hálfr and His Champions") is an Icelandic *fornaldarsaga*, preserved in one vellum MS (GkS 2845 4to, written around or after 1450) and in more than forty later paper MSS, all derived from the vellum.

The central part of the saga relates the story of the tragic fate of the Norwegian Viking King Hálfr and his warriors. After eighteen summers of successful plundering in distant countries, they fall victim to a treacherous invitation in their own country, Norway. Hálfr's stepfather, Ásmundr, sets fire to the hall when his guests have fallen asleep after much heavy drinking; they succeed in breaking out of the burning building, but in the ensuing battle Hálfr and most of his champions are killed.

This main part is preceded by a series of anecdotal accounts dealing mainly with Hálfr's ancestors, among them his father, Hjǫrleifr, and their adversaries, as well as a short chapter on a disastrous Viking expedition conducted by Hálfr's elder brother Hjǫrólfr. Following the main part, there is an account of how Hálfr's death was avenged and how his descendants settled in Iceland.

The story of Hálfr proper (Viking raids, final battle, revenge) consists of three longer poems in eddic style (*Innsteinskviða, Útsteinskviða, Hrókskviða*), connected by comparatively short prose paragraphs. The genealogical anecdotes at the beginning and the end of the saga consist of prose with interspersed *lausavísur* ("single stanzas").

The story of Hálfr's death is one of the earliest documented traditions in Old Norse: the skaldic poem *Ynglingatal* (9th century) uses the kenning *Hálfs bani* ("Hálfr's bane") for "fire." Hálfr is mentioned in various other Old Norse works, such as *Snorra Edda* and *Landnámabók*, but all these references are quite stereotypical, which indicates that the Hálfr tradition cannot have been very rich in literary times. The anecdotal parts rely on genealogies, and make use of motifs from folklore (*e.g.*, the laughing sage), mythology (Óðinn helping to brew ale), and heroic tradition (account of Víkarr's birth).

An older version of the saga, referred to as *Hróks saga svarta* ("The Saga of Hrókr the Black") in *Sturlunga saga*, seems to have been written between 1220 and 1280; the extant text very probably dates from the 14th century.

Ed.: Bugge, Sophus, ed. *Norröne Skrifter af sagnhistorisk Indhold.* Christiania [Oslo]: Det norske Oldskriftselskab, 1864–73, pp. 1–44; Andrews, A. Le Roy, ed. *Hálfs saga ok Hálfsrekka.* Altnordische Saga-Bibliothek, 14. Halle: Niemeyer, 1909; Jón Helgason, ed. *The Saga Manuscript 2845, 4to in the Old Royal Collection in the Royal Library of Copenhagen.* Manuscripta Islandica, 2. Copenhagen: Munksgaard, 1955 [facsimile]; Seelow, Hubert, ed. *Hálfs saga ok Hálfsrekka.* Reykjavik: Stofnun Árna Magnússonar, 1981. **Bib.**: Halldór Hermannsson. *Bibliography of the Mythical-Heroic Sagas.* Islandica, 5. Ithaca: Cornell University Library, 1912; rpt. New York: Kraus, 1966, pp. 20–1; Halldór Hermannsson. *The Sagas of the Kings (konunga sögur) and the Mythical-Heroic Sagas (fornaldar sögur): Two Bibliographical Supplements.* Islandica, 26. Ithaca: Cornell University Press, 1937, pp. 54–5. **Lit.**: Krappe, Alexander Haggerty. "Le rire du prophète." In *Studies in English Philology: A Miscellany in Honor of Frederick Klaeber.* Ed. Kemp Malone and Martin B. Ruud. Minneapolis: University of Minnesota Press, 1929, pp. 340–61; Krappe, Alexander Haggerty. "L'origine irlandaise d'un épisode de la 'Hálfs saga.'" *Revue celtique* 47 (1930), 401–5; Schneider, Hermann. "'Hálfssaga' und 'Hrólfssaga.'" In *Festschrift Theodor Siebs zum 70. Geburtstag 26. August 1932.* Ed. Walther Steller. Germanistische Abhandlungen, 67. Breslau: Marcus, 1933, pp. 179–98; Seelow, Hubert. "Páll Ketilssons Manuskript der Hálfs saga." *Opuscula* 7. Bibliotheca Arnamagnæana, 34. Copenhagen: Reitzel, 1979, pp. 254–9; Naumann, Hans-Peter. "Das Polyphem-Abenteuer in der altnordischen Sagaliteratur." *Schweizerisches Archiv für Volkskunde* 75 (1979), 173–89; Davíð Erlingsson. "Hjörleifur kvensami og Fergus Mac Léite." *Gripla* 4 (1980), 198–205.

Hubert Seelow

[**See also:** *Fornaldarsögur; Lausavísur; Sturlunga saga*]

Halldórs þáttr Snorrasonar

Halldórs þáttr Snorrasonar ("The Tale of Halldórr Snorrason") is the title of two *þættir* about Halldórr Snorrason, in modern times designated *I* and *II* according to the chronology of Halldórr's life. *I* is retained in MSS associated with *Óláfs saga Tryggvasonar*, primarily *Flateyjarbók*; *II* in *Morkinskinna* and *Hulda-Hrokkinskinna*. In *Halldórs þáttr I*, Halldórr is at odds with King Haraldr harðráði ("hard-ruler") Sigurðarson and seeks out the Norwegian noble Einarr þambarskelfir ("paunch-shaker" or "bowstring-trembler") for protection. Halldórr is insulted by one of Einarr's retainers, kills him, and appeals to Einarr's wife, Bergljót, for help. She advises Halldórr to throw himself on Einarr's mercy, and Einarr recounts this story: he was once released from slavery by a masked man who turned out to be Óláfr Tryggvason, who bade him apply the same mercy to someone later. That someone is Halldórr.

Halldórs þáttr II tells an entirely different story. Halldórr has served King Haraldr harðráði, but grows increasingly impatient in the king's service and increasingly less satisfied with his rewards. Finally, he bursts fully armed into the king's bedroom and takes a gold ring from him. Halldórr returns to Iceland and is never reconciled with Haraldr.

Several other medieval Icelandic sources mention Halldórr, including *Heiðarvíga saga, Laxdœla saga, Heimskringla, Hemings þáttr Áslakssonar,* and *Íslendings þáttr fróða. I* and *Íslendings þáttr* associate him with an oral saga about King Haraldr's stay in Constantinople, and *I* makes him a gifted raconteur. The historical Halldórr may therefore have been an important link in early Icelandic oral tradition.

Since Einarr met the disguised Óláfr Tryggvason after the battle of Svǫlðr (Svold), some scholars assigned *I* to circles around the monks at Þingeyrar in northwestern Iceland who wrote early sagas about Óláfr and perpetuated the notion that he survived the battle. Other scholars believe that *II* antedated *I*. Most would agree to date both texts to the 13th century.

Ed.: Einar Ól. Sveinsson, ed. *Laxdœla saga*. Íslenzk fornrit, 5. Reykjavik: Hið íslenzka fornritafélag, 1934, pp. lxxxii–xcii, 249–77. **Tr.**: Hermann Pálsson, trans. *Hrafnkel's Saga and Other Icelandic Stories*. Harmondsworth: Penguin, 1971, pp. 109–20 [*II* only]; Boucher, Alan, trans. *A Tale of Icelanders*. Reykjavik: Iceland Review, 1980, pp. 70–9 [*II* only]. **Lit.**: Harris, Joseph. "Christian Form and Christian Meaning in *Halldórs þáttr* I." In *The Learned and the Lewd: Studies in Chaucer and Medieval Literature*. Ed. Larry D. Benson. Harvard English Studies, 5. Cambridge: Harvard University Press 1974, pp. 249–64.

John Lindow

[**See also:** *Flateyjarbók; Hulda-Hrokkinskinna; Morkinskinna; Óláfs saga Tryggvasonar; Þáttr*]

Hallfreðar saga

Hallfreðar saga ("The Saga of Hallfreðr") belongs to that group of *Íslendingasögur* known as the *skáldasögur* ("skald sagas"). Like others of its kind (*e.g.*, *Kormáks saga*, *Fóstbrœðra saga*, and *Gunnlaugs saga*), it relates in a roughly biographical frame the life and deeds of a man renowned equally as a poet and an adventurer hero. Like his fellow skalds, Hallfreðr is physically flawed: large, strong, and chestnut-haired, but endowed with an unusually heavy brow and ugly nose. He was a fine poet, the saga tells us, but unpopular, thanks to his talent for poetic insult and his ornery nature. He was given his nickname *vandræðaskáld* ("troublesome skald") by King Óláfr Tryggvason, whose court he first visited around 996. On one occasion, the poet extemporized a *dróttkvætt* stanza in which every line contained the word "sword." So impressed was the king with Hallfreðr's poetic skill that he overlooked the poet's penchant for troublemaking and took him into his patronage. Pressed to convert to Christianity, Hallfreðr drove a hard bargain; he agreed on the condition that the king be his permanent and unequivocal mentor, indeed, that the king personally stand as godfather. At the bishop's urging, the king agreed, and Hallfreðr made ample use of his special status for years to come.

Hallfreðar saga is not one of the better-composed *Íslendingasögur*, but it has prompted attention on several grounds. One has to do with the insight it offers into the processes of the conversion and attitudes toward Christianity in the North. Both king and poet, and possibly bishop as well, seem to acknowledge the practical, not to say cynical, nature of Hallfreðr's conversion, and Hallfreðr's relationship to Christianity remains casual throughout his life. In an uncharacteristic aside, the saga notes that his chief manifestation of the faith was to blow crosswise over the cup before drinking; in any case, he "prayed little." Only at his death, when in a moving scene he rejects the fetch (his fate, in female form) that appears to him in his last moments, does Hallfreðr seem to break his pagan connections. One of the redactions pictures him uttering a stanza in which he expresses Christian repentance.

The other striking feature of *Hallfreðar saga* is its romantic interest. Hallfreðr pursues the woman Kolfinna both before and after her marriage to another man, and before and after his own marriage to another woman. In this respect also, *Hallfreðar saga* is typical of *skáldasögur*, most conspicuously *Kormáks saga*, in which an adulterous love triangle of just this kind is a standard element. In each case, the skaldic hero is the outsider who composes scorn poems against his rival and love poems to the woman. The theme of the lovelorn poet invites comparison with the contemporary troubadours of southern France. Indeed, the *skáldasögur*, as prose biographies studded with the highly technical poems of their heroes, invite comparison with the *vidas* of the troubadours, but no evidence for direct influence has yet been adduced.

Hallfreðar saga is preserved in two redactions: the relatively condensed one of *Möðruvallabók*, an important collection of sagas, chiefly Icelandic; and a fuller one, represented in discontinuous segments in *Óláfs saga Tryggvasonar en mesta*. The version in *Flateyjarbók*, also narrated in discontinuous segments, appears to be a conflation of the two. Its MS tradition thus reflects its intermediate generic status. Insofar as the saga concerns Hallfreðr's professional life as a skald in the court of Norway and hence the regency of Óláfr Tryggvason, it is related to the tradition of the *konungasögur*.

Together with *Kormáks saga*, to which it bears strong similarities, *Hallfreðar saga* is regarded as one of the oldest of the *Íslendingasögur*. Hallfreðr's verses, or those attributed to him (the authenticity has in some cases been questioned), are among the finest in the skaldic corpus, and they form the backbone of his saga.

Ed.: Einar Ól. Sveinsson, ed. *Vatnsdœla saga*. Íslenzk fornrit, 8. Reykjavik: Hið íslenzka fornritafélag, 1939 [based mainly on *Möðruvallabók; Hallfreðar saga*, pp. 133–200]; Bjarni Einarsson, ed. *Hallfreðar saga*. Reykjavik: Stofnun Árna Magnússonar, 1977 [based on all the MSS]. **Tr.**: Boucher, Alan. *The Saga of Hallfred the Troublesome Scald*. Reykjavik: Iceland Review, 1981. **Lit.**: Bjarni Einarsson. *Skáldasögur: Um uppruna og eðli ástaskáldasagnanna fornu*. Reykjavik: Menningarsjóður, 1961; Bjarni Einarsson. *To skjaldesagaer: En analyse af Kormáks saga og Hallfreðar saga*. Bergen, Oslo, and Tromsø: Universitetsforlaget, 1976.

Carol J. Clover

[**See also:** Christian Poetry; *Flateyjarbók;* Hallfreðr Óttarsson; *Íslendingasögur;* Love Poetry; *Möðruvallabók; Óláfs saga Tryggvasonar; Skáld; Skáldasögur*]

Hallfreðr Óttarsson

Hallfreðr Óttarsson, an Icelandic skald (966–1007), is the leading character of the *Hallfreðar saga*, and is mentioned in several other sagas and in historical documents such as *Flateyjarbók* and *Heimskringla*.

Hallfreðr lived during a stormy period of West Nordic history. Through his work as skald, first for the archpagan Earl Hákon Sigurðarson (d. 995) and then for his victorious adversary Óláfr Tryggvason (d. 1000), Hallfreðr was closely affected by the upheavals of this transitional period. He started his career as a court poet when he was scarcely twenty by celebrating Earl Hákon in a *drápa*. Nine strophes of this poem are preserved in Snorri's *Edda*. Four of them form a sequence where the king's conquest of the country is viewed in a cosmic perspective. Using erotic metaphors, the poet develops the idea, known from other parts of the world, of a holy wedding between the ruler and the land, the latter identical with the earth, seen also as a female being, the earth-goddess.

As court poet to King Óláfr, Hallfreðr began his service with his first *Óláfsdrápa*, of which a small number of strophes have been preserved. They make a conventional impression, perhaps because of the restraints the poet had to impose upon himself in his new spiritual environment. He admitted that he had deep roots in the religion of his fathers, and his poetic gifts were very dependent on the inspiration he could draw from pagan mythology. To serve a master who carried out his work of conversion with the zeal of a fanatic was bound to lead to complications, and in several *lausavísur* (occasional verses) Hallfreðr openly confesses his doubts and hesitations. The poet agreed to be baptized only on condition that the king himself would stand as his godfather. His final rejection of the old gods bears the stamp of a deep conflict of loyalties. A proof of the king's appreciation of his rebellious personality, however, is the fact that more than once he let clemency prevail when the poet went astray. On one such occasion, the king nicknamed him *vandræðaskáld* ("troublesome skald").

On another occasion, when the poet had been away for a long time in heathen Västergötland (western Gautland), the king demanded that he compose a poem as penance for his lack of faith; the poem, called *Uppreistardrápa*, was famous for its perfection but unfortunately has not survived. After Óláfr Tryggvason's death in the battle at Svǫlðr (Svold), Hallfreðr composed his memorial lay (*erfidrápa*), of which large fragments have been preserved.

Hallfreðr shows his literary personality most clearly in his *lausavísur*. Psychologically the most interesting are those that reflect the problems of his conversion. His last poems, from his deathbed, have a moving tone. Here, he confesses his fear of what hell might have in store for him.

Hallfreðr's erotic poetry is intimately linked with his satires. Like his older colleague Kormákr Ǫgmundarson, he was strongly attracted to a young woman, the beautiful Kolfinna. Even before his first journey abroad, he began to court her, but she was suddenly married off to a hated rival, Gríss Sæmingsson. In the same verses in which he sings the praises of Kolfinna's beauty, Hallfreðr excels in the coarsest satire directed against her husband.

Ed.: Einar Ól. Sveinsson, ed. *Vatnsdœla saga*. Íslenzk fornrit, 8. Reykjavik: Hið íslenzka fornritafélag, 1939; Bjarni Einarsson, ed. *Hallfreðar saga*. Reykjavik: Stofnun Árna Magnússonar, 1977. **Lit.**: Krijn, A. "Halfred Vandrædaskald." *Neophilologus* 16 (1931), 46–55, 121–31; Lie, Hallvard. *"Natur" og "Unatur" i skaldekunsten*. Avhandlinger utgitt av Det Norske Videnskaps-Akadademi i Oslo, 2. Hist.-filos. Klasse 1957, 1. Oslo: Aschehoug, 1957; Hallberg, Peter. *The Icelandic Saga*. Trans. Paul Schach. Lincoln: University of Nebraska Press, 1962; Bjarni Einarsson. "On the Rôle of Verse in Saga-Literature." *Mediaeval Scandinavia* 7 (1974), 118–25; Hallberg, Peter. *Old Icelandic Poetry: Eddic Lay and Scaldic Verse*. Trans. Paul Schach and Sonja Lindgrenson. Lincoln: University of Nebraska Press, 1975; Strömbäck, Dag. *The Conversion of Iceland: A Survey*. Trans. and annotated by Peter Foote. Text Series, 6. London: Viking Society for Northern Research, 1975; Bjarni Einarsson. *To skjaldesagaer. En analyse af Kormáks saga og Hallfreðar saga*. Bergen, Oslo, and Tromsø: Universitetsforlaget, 1976; Turville-Petre, E. O. G. *Scaldic Poetry*. Oxford: Clarendon, 1976; See, Klaus von. "Skaldenstrophe und Sagaprosa. Ein Beitrag zum Problem der mündlichen Überlieferung in der altnordischen Literatur." *Mediaeval Scandinavia* 10 (1977), 58–82; Frank, Roberta. *Old Norse Court Poetry: The Dróttkvætt Stanza*. Islandica, 22. Ithaca and London: Cornell University Press, 1978; Ström, Folke. "Hieros gamos-motivet i Hallfreðr Óttarssons Hákonardrápa och den nordnorska jarlavärdigheten." *Arkiv för nordisk filologi* 98 (1983), 67–79; Clover, Carol J., and John Lindow, eds. *Old Norse–Icelandic Literature: A Critical Guide*. Islandica, 45. Ithaca and London: Cornell University Press, 1985.

Folke Ström

[See also: Christian Poetry; Commemorative Poetry; *Hallfreðar saga*; *Lausavísur*; Love Poetry; *Skáld*; *Skáldasögur*; Skaldic Meters; Skaldic Verse; *Snorra Edda*]

Hamðismál in fornu ("The Old Lay of Hamðir") is a heroic poem preserved in the *Codex Regius* of the *Poetic Edda*. A "younger" *Hamðismál* is no longer extant, but attempts have been made to reconstruct it on the basis of *Snorra Edda* and *Vǫlsunga saga*. The first episode in *Hamðismál* tells, as in the eddic poem *Guðrúnarhvǫt*, how Guðrún incites Hamðir and Sǫrli, her two sons by her third husband, Jónakr, to avenge their sister Svanhildr's death on King Jǫrmunrekkr. On the journey, they meet their half-brother Erpr, who offers his help in words that they obviously misunderstand. After a short argument, they begin to fight, and Erpr is killed. Jǫrmunrekkr sits in his hall at a drinking bout, and when he hears of Hamðir's and Sǫrli's arrival, he laughs and boasts that he will hang them both. The avengers succeed in cutting off Jǫrmunrekkr's hands and feet. But then Jǫrmunrekkr roars like a bear that they must be stoned since weapons cannot harm them. Now they realize that they have caused their own death through the killing of Erpr. The poem reaches its climax with the words "Off would be his head now, if Erpr were living." The poem is then quickly, almost abruptly, brought to an end. After a heroic battle, Sǫrli falls at the gable end wall, Hamðir at the back of the hall.

The story treated in *Hamðismál* belongs to the oldest group of Germanic heroic legends. Jǫrmunrekkr has been identified as the historic king of the Goths, Ermanaric, who, according to Ammianus Marcellinus, committed suicide before the attack of the Huns in 375. Around 551, Jordanes gives a more detailed account of Ermanaric's end, which agrees with *Hamðismál* in terms of characters and motifs, so that we can hypothesize a Gothic poem in the 6th century.

The first evidence of the legend of Hamðir in Scandinavia is found in Bragi Boddason's *Ragnarsdrápa*; *Snorra Edda*, *Vǫlsunga saga*, and Saxo's *Gesta Danorum* give more detailed accounts.

No eddic text has been studied more critically than the thirty-one stanzas of *Hamðismál*. Several places are obscure; moreover, the text was considered defective and the order of the stanzas erratic. But recent studies suggest that on the whole its transmission is intact (Dronke 1969). The poem elucidates only the main incidents of the plot and presupposes knowledge of the legendary background of the saga. Metrically, *Hamðismál* presents a mixture of *fornyrðislag* and *málaháttr*. It has usually been regarded as belonging to the oldest group of heroic eddic poems (10th century). Von See argues that individual words suggest a relatively late date for the poem.

Throughout the poem, a reflective, antiheroic tone is combined with proverbial wisdom. The idea that sober-minded reason is more important than unrestrained heroism is stated several times. The climax is reached in stanza 29, a *ljóðaháttr* stanza, which is probably lifted from elsewhere without the meter being altered.

Ed.: Dronke, Ursula, ed. and trans. *The Poetic Edda. 1: Heroic Poems*. Oxford: Clarendon, 1969. **Bib.**: Clover, Carol J., and John Lindow. *Old Norse–Icelandic Literature: A Critical Guide*. Islandica, 45. Ithaca and London: Cornell University Press, 1985, pp. 146–7. **Tr.**: Hollander, Lee M., trans. *The Poetic Edda, Translated with an Introduction and Explanatory Notes*. 2nd rev. ed. Austin: University of Texas Press, 1962; rpt. 1988, pp. 316–21. **Lit.**: Brady, Caroline. *The Legends of Ermanaric*. Berkeley and Los Angeles: University of California Press, 1943; Henning, Ursula. "Gab es ein 'Jüngeres' Hamdirlied?" *Beiträge zur Geschichte der deutschen Sprache und Literatur* (Tübingen) 82 (1960), 44–69; See, Klaus von. "Die Sage von Hamðir und Sörli." In *Festschrift Gottfried Weber zu seinem 70. Geburtstag überreicht von Frankfurter Kollegen und Schülern*. Ed. Otto Burger and Klaus von See.

Frankfurter Beiträge zur Germanistik, 1. Bad Homburg, Berlin, and Zürich: Gehlen, 1967, pp. 47–75; rpt. in his *Edda, Saga, Skaldendichtung: Aufsätze zur skandinavischen Literatur des Mittelalters.* Heidelberg: Winter, 1981, pp. 224–49; See, Klaus von. "Guðrúnarhvǫt und Hamðismál." *Beiträge zur Geschichte der deutschen Sprache und Literatur* (Tübingen) 99 (1977), 241–9; rpt. in his *Edda, Saga, Skaldendichtung,* pp. 250–8; Andersson, Theodore M. "Hamðismál." In *Dictionary of the Middle Ages.* Ed. Joseph R. Strayer. New York: Scribner, 1982–89, vol. 6, pp. 87–8.

Otto Gschwantler

[**See also:** Bragi Boddason; *Codex Regius*; Eddic Meters; Eddic Poetry; *Guðrúnarhvǫt*; Saxo Grammaticus; *Snorra Edda*; *Vǫlsunga saga*]

Hanseatic League, or German Hansa, was a confederate association of cities and their merchants participating in the trade of regions extending inland from the Baltic and North seas. The Hanseatic League controlled much of the North European international commerce in the 13th, 14th, and early 15th centuries. It resembled a giant cartel, gradually evolving out of smaller associations formed in northern Germany during the 12th and 13th centuries.

The two principal *hansas*, or groupings of towns and merchants, were those in northwestern Germany and the Rhineland, led by Cologne, and those along the Baltic coast, led by Lübeck.

The Confederation of Cologne, named from the city in which it was convened, was formed in 1367 at a general meeting of delegates from the constituent organizations. The Articles of Agreement bestowed a formal institutional, and even a constitutional character, upon the league. Although occasionally distracted by internal disputes, the Confederation functioned as a major economic and political power in northern Europe for about a century and a half thereafter, waging war and signing treaties, conducting diplomatic missions, raising military and naval levies, and obtaining special trading rights for its merchants in four important port cities: London, Bruges, Novgorod, and Bergen. Commercial concessions granted to merchants from Hanseatic towns in each of the four ports included permanent quarters for their residence and business.

The towns belonging to the league lay, with few exceptions, in the regions known today as Germany, the Netherlands, Poland, Estonia, and Latvia, with a preponderance in Germany, as the term "German Hansa" suggests.

From the 11th century, movements of significant numbers of persons from the Low Countries and northern Germany eastward into Slavic and other territories and extending finally as far as the Gulf of Finland resulted in the formation of town settlements and landowning and mercantile classes of German origin. The demographic expansion was paralleled by increasing participation of German ships and merchants in the commerce of the North and Baltic seas, as well as the acquisition of exclusive rights to import and export of valuable commodities and products, such as the case of the four foreign ports where Hanseatic *Kontore*, or trading establishments, exercised strong influence on the economies of the host countries and hinterlands.

In the 11th and 12th centuries, Hanseatic maritime expansion gradually transcended in volume the international commerce carried on by Scandinavians. By the 14th century, the Hanseatic towns and merchants had arrived at a paramount position. Economic ascendancy was accompanied by the military victory of the league over Valdemar Atterdag ("ever-day") of Denmark, resulting in the Peace of Stralsund (1370), whereby the Hansa gained freedom of passage through the Sound, control of the Scanian region with its lucrative herring fisheries, and other valuable concessions. This agreement was probably the high-water mark of Hanseatic power. In the 15th and 16th centuries, the Dutch were expanding their industry, commerce, and shipping, becoming ever more competitive with the Germans. The rise of nationalistic aspirations in Denmark, the union of this kingdom with Sweden and Norway in 1397, and the aggressive pursuit of Baltic trade by English and Dutch merchants and ship captains contributed to the gradual dissolution of the quasi-monopoly held by the Hanseats. Tactics employed to protect their privileged position, such as embargoes, blockades, and favors to persons of high rank and influence, became less effective, and the position of the League more clearly defensive. Nature contributed to the League's difficulties with the silting up of the port of Bruges and the migration of the great herring catch from the Sound to the North Sea. In 1494, Ivan III of Moscow, having suppressed the independence of Novgorod, closed the *Kontor* there and expelled the German merchant monopoly. In 1556, the Germans lost their privileges in England, and by then the Dutch were the main carriers in the Baltic. Lübeck, which had been the leading city almost throughout the history of the Hansa, fought an unsuccessful war with Denmark. Decline continued until the final session of the Hanseatic diet, to which only six cities sent delegates in 1669, whereas at its height more than 100 towns had been enrolled as members of the League.

For more than four centuries, the Hanseatic city groupings were a potent force in the political and economic life of northern Europe. They initiated an increasingly viable, and in a sense, modern alternative to the dominance of that region by feudal and manorial interests. They promoted, even if sometimes by stimulating local or national opposition, the gradual emergence of artisan and mercantile classes, industrial and bourgeois society, a permanent result surviving the demise of the Hansa itself. This development is reflected in the domain of law, where its social contribution may have been inestimable. A few basic law codes bearing the names of principal towns became the underlying law of a great many Hanseatic cities, furnishing in part the practical equivalent of a constitutional apparatus, particularly in the judicial sphere and in the implementation of policies dictated by the convergent interests of the rising mercantile classes.

The original focus and purpose of the Hanseatic compacts had been the protection of intercity trade from attacks on land or sea, provision for safe navigation, and securing the most favorable terms and conditions possible for their business operations. For three or more centuries, the Hanseats were mostly responsible for the transport of commodities essential to the development of North European civilization: grain, furs, timber, wax, honey, pitch, tar, and potash from the East; copper and iron from Sweden; herring from Scania; salt from Lüneburg; Flemish and English cloth; and whale oil and cod from Norway.

Hanseatic history is intimately interwoven with virtually all the North European nations, perhaps, however, affecting Scandinavia the most. Bergen had one of the four great *Kontore*, and Stockholm had a large number of German merchants residing within its jurisdiction. With connections to Riga, Reval (Tallinn), and Novgorod, Visby on Gotland was, until its seizure by the Danes, the central *entrepôt* of the Baltic and the major emporium of Sweden. Tønsberg and Oslo in Norway and Ålborg in Denmark were local trading ports.

The great age of Hanseatic maritime and mercantile power lay between the decline of the world-roaming Scandinavian naval exploration, conquest, colonization, and trade, and the rise of the centralized monarchial state, which brought new political and economic vitality to the Nordic countries. In the interim, the Hansa played an important role in their trade and industries, handling much of the international traffic and transport, until it came to be regarded as an economically colonializing and exploiting organization, and its external commercial supremacy was progressively challenged and reduced by policies of the nationalistic Swedish and Danish monarchies.

Lit.: Meilink, Petrus A. *De Nederlandsche Hanzesteden tot het laaste Kwartaal der XIVe Eeuw*. The Hague: Nijhoff, 1912; Schäfer, Dietrich. *Die deutsche Hanse*. Monographien zur Weltgeschichten, 19. Bielefeld: Velhagen & Klassing, 1914; Hill, Charles E. *The Danish Sound Dues and the Command of the Baltic: A Study of International Relations*. Durham: Duke University Press, 1926; Bjork, David K. "The Peace of Stralsund." *Speculum* 7 (1932), 447–76; Laubinger, Heinrich. *Die rechtliche Gestaltung der deutschen Hanse*. Diss. University of Heidelberg, 1932; Westergaard, Waldemar. "Hansa Towns and Scandinavia on the Eve of Swedish Independence." *Journal of Modern History* 4 (1932), 349–60; Fink, Georg. *Die Hanse*. Leipzig: Bibliographisches Institut, 1939; Pagel, Karl. *Die Hanse*. Berlin: Deutsche Buch-Gemeinschaft, 1942; Schubart-Fikentscher, Gertrud. *Die Verbreitung der deutschen Stadtrechte in Osteuropa*. Forschungen zum deutschen Recht, 4, Nr. 3. Weimar: Böhlau, 1942; Bjork, David K. "Piracy in the Baltic: 1375–1398." *Speculum* 18 (1943), 39–68; Winter, William L. "Netherland Regionalism and the Decline of the Hansa." *American Historical Review* 52 (1948), 279–87; Gade, John Allyne. *The Hanseatic Control of Norwegian Commerce During the Late Middle Ages*. Leiden: Brill, 1951; Dollinger, Philippe. *La Hanse (XIIe–XVIIe siècles)*. Paris: Aubier, 1964; Winter, William L. "Problems of the North Germans and of the Hansa in the Later Medieval Baltic." *Bulletin of Baltic Studies* 8 (1971), 18–23; Winter, William L. "The Baltic as a Common Frontier of Eastern and Western Europe in the Middle Ages." *Lituanus: The Lithuanian Quarterly* 4 (1973), 5–39.

William L. Winter

[See also: Trade]

Harald Gormsson (Bluetooth),
a son of Gorm the Old and Thyre, was king of Denmark and Norway. Harald probably died on November 1, 985/8, having reigned fifty years, according to Adam of Bremen. Recent dendrochronological investigations of his father Gorm's grave mound at Jelling in Jutland suggest that Gorm died as late as around 958/9. This would indicate that Harald reigned less than thirty years, or perhaps he reigned simultaneously with his father.

Harald boasted that he won all Denmark and Norway and made the Danes Christians, and he is assumed to be the builder of the large fortresses Trelleborg and Fyrkat (ca. 980/1), Nonnebakken, and perhaps also the oversized Aggersborg, and the 1-km.-long Ravning Enge bridge (ca. 979). There is no need for connecting the "camps" in Denmark with the invasion of England by Harald's son Sven Haraldsson (Forkbeard). A sufficient explanation lies in the king's need for control of Denmark.

Harald apparently moved the royal seat to Roskilde in Zealand, where he built a wooden cathedral as his burial place. The famous legend of Poppo carrying glowing iron in order to convert the king to Christianity seems to date the conversion to the 960s, but the details vary, and none of the accounts are contemporary. Whereas recent findings raise doubts as to the beginning of Harald's reign, its ending is better known. Harald's son Sven led a revolt against him, forcing the king to flee to the Slavonic town of Jumne (probably a predecessor of Stettin/Szczecin), where he died from his wounds.

Bib.: Christensen, Aksel E. *Vikingetidens Danmark paa oldhistorisk baggrund*. Copenhagen: Gyldendal, 1969; Skovgaard-Petersen, Inge. *Danmarks historie. 1. Tiden indtil 1340*. Copenhagen: Gyldendal, 1977, pp. 15–209; Roesdahl, Else. *Viking Age Denmark*. Trans. Susan Margeson and Kirsten Williams. London: British Museum, 1982. Lit.: Bolin, Sture. *Om Nordens äldsta historieforskning. Studier över dess metodik och källvärde*. Lunds Universitets årsskrift n.f., avd. 1, bd. 27, nr. 3. Lund: Ohlsson, 1931, pp. 29–116; Weibull, Lauritz. *Kritiska undersökningar i Nordens historia omkring år 1000*. Copenhagen: Lybecker, 1911; rpt. in his *Nordisk historia 1*. Stockholm: Natur och Kultur, 1948, pp. 245–360; Weibull, Curt. *Källkritik och historia. Norden under äldre medeltiden*. Stockholm: Bonnier, 1964 [collection of articles]; Skovgaard-Petersen, Inge. "Sven Tveskæg i den ældste danske historiografi. En Saxostudie." In *Middelalderstudier. Tilegnede Aksel E. Christensen på tresårsdagen*. Ed. Tage E. Christiansen et al. Copenhagen: Munksgaard, 1966, pp. 1–37; Demidoff, Lene. "The Poppo Legend." *Mediaeval Scandinavia* 6 (1973), 39–67; Weibull, Curt. *Die Geaten des Beowulfepos und die dänischen Trelleburgen: Zwei Diskussionsbeiträge*. Acta Regiae Societatis Scientiarum et Litterarum Gothoburgensis, Humaniora, 10. Gothenburg: Kungl. Vetenskaps- och vitterhets-samhället, 1974; Sawyer, Peter. "The Christianisation of Scandinavia." In *Beretning fra femte tværfaglige vikingesymposium*. Ed. Torben Kisbye and Else Roesdahl. Århus: Forlaget Hikuin og Afdeling for middelalder-arkæologi ved Aarhus Universitet, 1986, pp. 23–37.

Søren Balle

[See also: Denmark; Fortification; Fortresses, Trelleborg; Gorm; Jelling]

Harald Wartooth *see* Divine Heroes, Native

Haraldr harðráði ("hard-ruler") Sigurðarson (1046–1066).
Haraldr harðráði ("hard-ruler") was the half-brother of St. Óláfr, the son of Óláfr's mother, Ásta, and her husband, Sigurðr sýr ("sow") Hálfdanarson. His hereditary claim to the Norwegian throne was thus dubious, but he lived in an age when hereditary rights were not paramount. According to *Heimskringla*, Haraldr "excelled other men in shrewdness and resourcefulness. . . . He was exceedingly skilled in arms, and victorious in his undertakings . . . a handsome man of stately appearance. He was light blond, with a blond beard and long mustaches, with one eyebrow higher than the other . . . ruthless with his enemies, and given to harsh punishment of all who opposed him . . . inordinately covetous of power and of valuable possessions of all kinds" (ch. 99). He succeeded to sole possession of the Norwegian throne in 1047.

Haraldr's career is recounted mainly in his saga in Snorri Sturluson's *Heimskringla*. At the age of fifteen, he fought alongside his half-brother in the battle of Stiklastaðir (Stiklestad), where Óláfr was killed. He then spent fifteen years away from Norway in the service of the Kievan prince Jaroslav, whose daughter he later married, and in the imperial service in Byzantium. The saga describes his years as leader of the Varangian Guard there in exaggerated terms: the empress Zóe falls in love with him; he captures cities using stratagems that are common folktale motifs. A Greek work written in the 1070s, *Logos nuthetikos*, also refers to his campaigns. Haraldr was also imprisoned in Byzantium for a time.

In 1045, Haraldr returned to Norway and made a treaty to share the rule with Óláfr's son Magnús inn góði ("the good") until the latter's death without male issue, when Haraldr became sole ruler. The years of Haraldr's rule in Norway are characterized by his repeated campaigns against Sven Estridsen in Denmark, including the burning of Hedeby in 1049. The two finally reached a treaty in 1064. Haraldr's mobilization against Denmark was made possible by his consolidation of control over Norway itself, in what Icelandic authors, at least, perceived as a harsh and overbearing manner. He was also known for his influence over the Norwegian Church, building churches and handpicking bishops and other officials. According to the sources, he founded Oslo and introduced coins as a common means of payment, although other rulers had struck coins previously. His reputation, which has come down to us mainly through Icelandic literature, is generally favorable, since he is credited with saving Iceland from famine. But some of the þættir included in the Morkinskinna version of his saga depict his personality rather unsympathetically. His nickname reflects the harshness many authors attributed to him.

Haraldr had a claim to the English throne by virtue of a treaty between his nephew Magnús and Hardacnut, son of Knud (Cnut) the Great. Upon the death of Edward the Confessor in January 1066, Haraldr saw an opportunity to make that claim. He landed in Yorkshire, and was eventually defeated by Harold Godwinsson at the battle of Stamford Bridge. But the English army's desperate ride north, losses sustained at Stamford Bridge, and rapid return south weakened it greatly just before Harold Godwinsson had to meet William the Conquerer at the battle of Hastings. Haraldr harðráði's invasion was thus the determining factor in Harald Godwinsson's loss to William, which changed the political face of Europe.

Haraldr's death at Stamford Bridge is often taken as symbolizing the end of the Viking Age in Scandinavia. His was not the last major overseas Viking campaign, but it was the last, perhaps, with some chance of success, and the sagas of subsequent kings do not paint the same sort of pictures of Viking heroes.

Ed.: Bjarni Aðalbjarnarson, ed. "Haralds saga Sigurðarsonar." In Heimskringla. 3 vols. Íslenzk fornrit, 26–8. Reykjavik: Hið íslenzka fornritafélag, 1941–51, vol. 3, pp. 68–202; Finnur Jónsson, ed. Fagrskinna: Nóregs konunga tal. Samfund til udgivelse af gammel nordisk litteratur, 30. Copenhagen: [s.n.], 1902–03; Finnur Jónsson, ed. Morkinskinna. Samfund til udgivelse af gammel nordisk litteratur, 80. Copenhagen: [s.n.], 1932. Tr.: Hollander, Lee M., trans. Heimskringla: History of the Kings of Norway. Austin: University of Texas Press, 1964, pp. 577–663; Magnus Magnusson and Hermann Pálsson, trans. King Harald's Saga: Harald Hardradi of Norway. Harmondsworth: Penguin, 1966. Lit.: Indrebø, Gustav. "Harald haardraade i Morkinskinna." In Festskrift til Finnur Jónsson 29. maj 1928. Ed. Johs. Brøndum-Nielsen et al. Copenhagen: Levin & Munksgaard, 1928, pp. 173–80; Blöndal, Sigfús. "The Last Exploits of Harald Sigurdsson in Greek Service: A Chapter from the History of the Varangians." Classica et Mediaevalia 1.2 (1939), 1–26; Bjarni Aðalbjarnarson. "Formáli." Heimskringla, vol. 3, pp. v–cxv; Turville-Petre, G. Haraldr the Hard-Ruler and His Poets. Dorothea Coke Memorial Lecture in Northern Studies. London: University College; Lewis, 1968; Ellis Davidson, H. R. The Viking Road to Byzantium. London: Allen & Unwin, 1976; Andersen, Per Sveaas. Samlingen av Norge og kristningen av landet 800–1130. Handbok i Norges historie, 2. Bergen: Universitetsforlaget, 1977; Jones, Gwyn. A History of the Vikings. 2nd ed. Oxford and New York: Oxford University Press, 1984;

Andersson, Theodore M. "Kings' Sagas (Konungasögur)." In Old Norse–Icelandic Literature: A Critical Guide. Ed. Carol J. Clover and John Lindow. Islandica, 45. Ithaca and London: Cornell University Press, 1985, pp. 197–238.

Ruth Mazo Karras

[See also: England, Norse in; Heimskringla; Morkinskinna; Norway; Stamford Bridge, Battle of; Varangian Guard]

Haraldr hárfagri ("fair-hair") Hálfdanarson is the king

credited with unifying Norway. According to his saga in Snorri Sturluson's Heimskringla, the fullest account of Haraldr's life although not to be taken as accurate in historical detail, he descended from the Yngling dynasty and came to the throne of his father's kingdom of Vestfold at the age of ten (scholars estimate the date of this accession at ca. 860–880). Haraldr desired to become king over all of Norway, and swore a vow not to cut or comb his hair until he had achieved this goal, hence his nickname. The story is legendary, and it is doubtful anyone had a concept of Norway as a unity before his conquest of the different regions.

The Heimskringla version is based on a lost *Haralds saga, as is a þáttr about him in Flateyjarbók. Haraldr's saga recounts a series of campaigns against various petty kings and his alliance with the powerful northern Earl Hákon Grjótgarðsson, as well as his conflicts with the Swedish king who was his rival for the eastern districts of Norway. At the battle of Hafrsfjörðr (Havsfjord), now dated between 885 and 890, Haraldr defeated a coalition of kings and earls and established his hegemony.

The political significance of Haraldr's unification of Norway was not as great as the Icelandic saga literature implies. Haraldr's hold upon northern and eastern Norway was never firm. Traditionally, the settlement of Iceland by Ingólfr Arnarson and others around 870 was attributed to their desire to escape from Haraldr's tyranny. However, the battle of Hafrsfjörðr cannot have been fought that early, and the settlers must have had motives other than fleeing the unified kingdom. Many leading Norwegians did flee after Hafrsfjörðr, to Shetland, Orkney, and the Hebrides, if not Iceland. According to Snorri, they continued to conduct raids upon Norway from there until Haraldr strengthened his navy and put a stop to this Viking activity. But scholars now doubt whether Haraldr actually made any expedition to Britain. Many of the original settlers of Iceland came not from Norway directly, but from the British Isles. To support the myth of Haraldr's tyranny as the cause of settlement, Icelanders probably invented an extension of Haraldr's power over the islands.

Snorri's account of Haraldr's establishment of a Norwegian state is most likely anachronistic. Haraldr was accused of having appropriated the óðal land of all the farmers, making them his tenants, and of imposing heavy taxation. The system of taxation and military organization Snorri describes, however, is probably a reflection of Snorri's own time. The accusations of tyranny may be due to an Icelandic tradition of hostility toward Haraldr, which allowed Icelanders to hearken back to a Golden Age of freedom. But society before Haraldr was dominated by chieftains, earls, or petty kings, and was not as egalitarian as Snorri indicates.

Haraldr's unified Norway did not survive his death (between 930 and 940), largely because he left so many sons, as many as twenty according to some sources. Snorri recounts his division of the realm among his sons and the sharing of his revenue with them before his death, assigning Eiríkr blóðøx ("blood-axe") to be high king. While this account is not likely to be accurate, the sons certainly all believed themselves entitled to the dignity of king. Upon Haraldr's death, his sons sought power in various of the petty kingdoms their father had controlled. Any governmental reforms he made collapsed with the end of his personal rule.

Ed.: Guðbrandr Vigfússon and C. R. Unger, eds. "Haralds þáttr hárfagra." In *Flateyjarbok. En Samling af norske Konge-Sagaer med indskudte mindre Fortællinger om Begivenheder i og undenfor Norge samt Annaler*. 3 vols. Christiania [Oslo]: Malling, 1860–68, vol. 1, pp. 567–76; Storm, Gustav, ed. *Monumenta historiae norvegiae: latinske kildeskrifter til Noregs historie i middelalderen*. Christiania [Oslo]: Brögger, 1880; Sigurður Nordal, ed. *Egils saga Skalla-Grímssonar*. Íslenzk fornrit, 2. Reykjavik: Hið íslenzka fornritafélag, 1933; Bjarni Aðalbjarnarson, ed. "Haralds saga ins hárfagra." In *Heimskringla*. 3 vols. Íslenzk fornrit, 26–8. Reykjavik: Hið íslenzka fornritafélag, 1941–51, vol. 1, pp. 94–149. **Tr**.: Hollander, Lee M., trans., *Heimskringla: History of the Kings of Norway*. Austin: University of Texas Press, 1964, pp. 59–95; Hermann Pálsson and Paul Edwards, trans. *Egil's Saga*. Harmondsworth: Penguin, 1976. **Lit**.: Bjarni Aðalbjarnarson. "Formáli." In *Heimskringla*, vol. 1.; Campbell, Alistair. "The Opponents of Haraldr Hárfagri at Hafrsfjorðr." *Saga-Book of the Viking Society* 12.4 (1942), 232–7; Ólafía Einarsdóttir. "Dateringen af Harald hårfagers død." *Historisk tidsskrift* (Norway) 47 (1968), 15–34; Gunnes, Erik. *Rikssamling og kristning 800–1177*. Oslo: Cappelen, 1976; Holmsen, Andreas. *Nye studier i gammel historie*. Oslo: Universitetsforlaget, 1976; Sawyer, P. H. "Harald Fairhair and the British Isles." In *Les Vikings et leur civilisation: problèmes actuels*. Ed. Régis Boyer. École des hautes études en sciences sociales, Bibliothèque Arctique et Antarctique, 5. Paris and La Haye: Mouton, 1976, pp. 105–9; Andersen, Per Sveaas. *Samlingen av Norge og kristningen av landet 800–1130*. Handbok i Norges historie, 2. Bergen: Universitetsforlaget, 1977; Berman, Melissa A. "*Egils saga* and *Heimskringla*." *Scandinavian Studies* 54 (1982), 21–50; Jones, Gwyn. *A History of the Vikings*. 2nd ed. Oxford and New York: Oxford University Press, 1984; Andersson, Theodore M. "Kings' Sagas (*Konungasögur*)." In *Old Norse–Icelandic Literature: A Critical Guide*. Ed. Carol J. Clover and John Lindow. Islandica, 45. Ithaca and London: Cornell University Press, 1985.

Ruth Mazo Karras

[**See also:** *Flateyjarbók; Heimskringla;* Norway]

Haraldskvæði *see* Þorbjǫrn hornklofi

Hárbarðsljóð

Hárbarðsljóð ("The Lay of Hárbarðr), one of the mythical lays contained in the *Poetic Edda*, has been preserved whole in the *Codex Regius* and, in part (from st. 17.7 to the end), in MS AM 748 4to. The lay combines prose and poetry, the latter characterized by a rather inconsistent metrical pattern. These peculiarities have suggested that the lay as received has been distorted in the transmission process, and derives from an original version that was more concise (Niedner 1887, Finnur Jónsson 1920–24). Other scholars, however, tend to regard the formal properties as the effects of fortunate choices by a poet who deliberately deviated from the prevailing system of poetic rules (Heusler 1923, Clover 1979).

Hárbarðsljóð contains a "flyting" (insult contest) between the gods Þórr and Óðinn, the latter disguised as the ferryman Hárbarðr (literally "grey-beard"). The outcome of the verbal match will determine whether Óðinn will ferry Þórr over the fjord. Several scholars see *Hárbarðsljóð* as a "character comedy" of sorts, humorously

contrasting the simpleminded Þórr with the clever and witty Óðinn; on a more general level of interpretation, this comedy could oppose spirit to strength, endorsing the preeminence of intellectual faculties (Finnur Jónsson 1920–24, Hallberg 1975). Other scholars impute the Þórr-Óðinn opposition to historical or sociological distinctions: Þórr then represents peasantry, whereas Óðinn represents the warrior caste (Liliencron 1856, Niedner 1887). In this interpretation, the lay clearly has a political impact, which Niedner relates to the exacerbated situation that the enslaved Norse peasants had to endure under the reign of Haraldr hárfagri ("fair-hair") Hálfdanarson (r. ca. 860–ca. 940). Given this historical argument, and also on the grounds of onomastic investigations (Lundberg 1944), it has been supposed that the lay originated in Norway, and consequently that it must be dated early; Olsen (1960), for instance, places the poem around the year 980.

In a more recent contribution, Clover (1979) regards the lay as a parody of the *senna-mannjafnaðr* (insult-contest) genre. According to Clover's analysis, two important rules of the genre are violated. Óðinn playfully violates the rule that sexual achievement is not a proper topic to boast about (see sts. 18, 20, 30). These departures so baffle dour Þórr that he can only react with lame rejoinders, thus violating the rule that each of the contenders should be eloquent.

Although pursuing the line of argumentation that Clover initiated, Bax and Padmos (1983) arrive at strikingly different conclusions. Approaching the dialogue from the perspective of pragmatics and discourse analysis, they contend that *Hárbarðsljóð* embodies elaborate and valuable versions of both the *senna* genre (sts. 1–14) and the *mannjafnaðr* genre (sts. 15–46). In the remaining stanzas (47–60), Þórr, having lost the verbal duel, withdraws from the encounter. The *senna* part makes clear that both Þórr and Óðinn are proficient flyters. The verbal interaction is tightly structured rather than a random collection of boasts and insults. At the end of the *senna*, the score is tied; the subsequent *mannjafnaðr* is then undertaken to settle the matter. This part of the duel consists of six marked rounds, each of which exposes the fixed basic pattern of interactional "moves" or speech actions. The match can be followed by the audience: the first two short rounds (sts. 15–18, 19–22) are won by Óðinn. But the third exchange (sts. 23–28) is harder for Óðinn to win, and in the fourth round (an even longer one, sts. 29–36), Þórr wins. Þórr quickly wins the fifth exchange, too (sts. 37–39), so that Óðinn has nearly lost his chance. Yet in the long and final encounter (sts. 40–46), Óðinn eventually manages to outwit his adversary (see Bax and Padmos 1983). In all, if one compares the exciting exchanges in *Hárbarðsljóð* to other *mannjafnaðar*, one is apt to conclude that the lay embodies the most developed version of this ancient verbal ritual.

Ed.: Neckel, Gustav, ed. *Edda: Die Lieder des Codex Regius nebst verwandten Denkmälern. I: Text*. 5th ed. rev. Hans Kuhn. Heidelberg: Winter, 1983. **Tr**.: Hollander, Lee M., trans. *The Poetic Edda, Translated with an Introduction and Explanatory Notes*. 2nd rev. ed. Austin: University of Texas Press, 1962; rpt. 1988; Taylor, Paul B., and W. H. Auden, trans. *The Elder Edda: A Selection*. London: Faber and Faber, 1969; rpt. 1970. **Lit**.: Liliencron, R. von. "Das Harbardslied." *Zeitschrift für deutsches Alterthum [und deutsche Literatur]* 10 (1856), 180–96; Niedner, Felix. "Das Hárbarðsljóð." *Zeitschrift für deutsches Alterthum und deutsche Literatur* 31 (1887), 217–82; Finnur Jónsson. *Den oldnorske og oldislandske Litteraturs Historie*. 3 vols. 2nd ed. Copenhagen: Gad, 1920–24; Heusler, Andreas. *Die altgermanische Dichtung*. 2nd ed. Potsdam: Athenaion, 1923; rpt. 1941; Lundberg,

Oskar. *Ön Allgrön. Ár Eddans Harbardsljod ett norskt kväde?* Arctos Svevica, 2. Stockholm: Geber, 1944; Olsen, Magnus. *Edda- og Skaldekvad Forarbeider til Kommentar. 1. Hárbarðsljóð.* Avhandlinger utgitt av Det Norske Videnskaps-Akademi i Oslo, 2. Hist.-filos. Klasse, 1. Oslo: Aschehoug, 1960; Hallberg, Peter. *Old Icelandic Poetry: Eddic Lay and Skaldic Verse.* Trans. Paul Schach and Sonja Lindgrenson. Lincoln and London: University of Nebraska Press, 1975; Clover, Carol J. "*Hárbarðsljóð* as Generic Farce." *Scandinavian Studies* 51 (1979), 124–45; Bax, Marcel, and Tineke Padmos. "Two Types of Verbal Dueling in Old Icelandic: The Interactional Stucture of the *senna* and the *mannjafnaðr* in *Hárbarðsljóð.*" *Scandinavian Studies* 55 (1983), 149–74.

Marcel Bax and Tineke Padmos

[**See also:** *Codex Regius*; Eddic Poetry; *Senna—Mannjafnaðr*]

Harðar saga ("The Saga of Hǫrðr") survives complete in only one medieval MS, AM 556a 4to, written late in the 15th century, where it is called *Hólmverja saga* ("The Saga of the Islet-Dwellers"), referring to the refuge in Hvalfjǫrðr in western Iceland used by the hero and his friends. There is also a single-leaf fragment of a shorter version of the beginning of the saga in AM 564a 4to, written about 1400, where the title is given as *Harðar saga Grímkelssonar.* There are about forty paper MSS written in the 17th century or later, all derived from AM 556a 4to. Four sets of *rímur*, composed in the 18th and 19th centuries, are based on the saga.

In the form in which it survives in AM 556a 4to, the saga contains many episodes involving the supernatural and sensational, with fantastic Viking adventures (covering fifteen years of the hero's life), encounters with heathen deities, and crude folklore motifs that link the story with *fornaldarsögur* and romance. This version seems typical of the kind of sagas written in the mid-14th century and later. The hero is a tragic figure, born into a hostile social environment, and doomed early in his life because of a cursed ring. He is led into misdeeds, outlawry, and eventual death by the folly and malice of friends and associates who are his moral inferiors; as well as being heroic and high-minded, Hǫrðr is unaffected by magically induced illusions. One of the more memorable episodes is the heroic escape of his wife, Helga, daughter of an earl in Gautland, from the islet after her husband's death, by swimming across the fjord with their two young sons.

Harðar saga is one of three Icelandic outlaw sagas, but unlike Grettir and Gísli, the heroes of the other two, Hǫrðr is not forced to endure loneliness and solitude in his outlawry. He lives with his wife, and together with his foster-brother Geirr, becomes leader of a band of outlaws (up to 180 people) who defy authority and set up an alternative society with its own rules and discipline, which lasts for three years.

Harðar saga is one of the few *Íslendingasögur* located (except for the Viking adventures abroad) in southwestern Iceland. The outline of the story is probably historical, though many of the adventures are obviously not. Hǫrðr's death must have taken place about 989, so that the story takes place entirely in heathen times. Reference is made to an otherwise-unknown **Álfgeirs þáttr* as a source.

The language confirms that the version of the saga in AM 556a 4to was not written before the 14th century, and the verses (some of which, in eddic meter, are attributed to supernatural characters) are clearly no older than the prose. But since the saga

is mentioned in Sturla's version of *Landnámabók* (*ca.* 1280), a version of it may have existed in the 13th century. The judgment on Hǫrðr by Styrmir Kárason (d. 1245) quoted at the end of the saga in AM 556a 4to has led some scholars to assume that the earlier version, the characteristics of which are impossible to reconstruct, was composed by Styrmir, though such references to statements by the learned men of the 12th and 13th centuries are not necessarily reliable attributions of authorship. The fragment in AM 564a 4to, which shows clear signs of having been shortened, does not include the verses in the corresponding part of AM 556a 4to; but it is uncertain whether the fragment, too, is based on the 14th-century version of the saga, or whether it is closer to the lost earlier version.

Ed.: *Agiætar Formmanna Søgur.* Hólar: Biørn Marcusson, 1756; Guðni Jónsson, ed. *Íslendinga sögur.* 13 vols. Reykjavik: Íslendingasagnaútgáfan, 1946–49, vol. 12; Hast, Sture, ed. *Harðar saga.* Editiones Arnamagnæanæ, ser. A, vol. 6. Copenhagen: Munksgaard, 1960; Þórhallur Vilmundarson and Bjarni Vilhjálmsson, eds. *Harðar saga.* Íslenzk fornrit, 13. Reykjavik: Hið íslenzka fornritafélag, 1991. **Tr.**: Boucher, Alan, trans. *The Saga of Hord and the Holm-Dwellers.* Reykjavik: Iceland Review, 1983 [with introduction by Anthony Faulkes]. **Lit.**: Lange, Joost de. *The Relation and Development of English and Icelandic Outlaw-traditions.* Haarlem: Tjeenk Willink, 1935 [contains a detailed summary of *Harðar saga*, pp. 91–5]; Einar Ól. Sveinsson. *Dating the Icelandic Sagas: An Essay in Method.* Viking Society, Text Series, 3. London: Viking Society for Northern Research, 1958, pp. 105–7.

Anthony Faulkes

[**See also:** *Fornaldarsögur, Íslendingabók, Íslendingasögur, Landnámabók, Lausavísur*, Outlaw Sagas; Outlawry; *Rímur*]

Harmsól *see* **Gamli kanóki**

Harpestreng, Henrik. A large body of medical work has been preserved from the Danish doctor Master Henrik Harpestreng, who died April 2, 1244, as a canon in Roskilde and physician-in-ordinary of King Erik Plovpenning ("plow-penny"). Two Latin works by a certain Henricus Dacus, presumably the same man, are known: a book about laxatives, *De simplicibus medicinis laxativis*, and a book about herbs, *Liber herbarum*, extant in several MSS from the 15th century.

His other works are written in older Middle Danish, according to the late MS Thott 710 4to (A, 1450), by the author's own efforts: "Here a medical book in Danish is begun, the one that Master Henrik Harpestreng composed from his great mastership." This is the prologue to Harpestreng's best-known work, *Urtebogen* ("The Book of Herbs"), which is known from late MSS and two MSS from around 1300. In one of these MSS (NkS 66 8vo by Brother Knud Juul, attorney of the monastery of Sorø), two books about herbs are followed by a *Stenbog* ("Book of Stones") about the curative properties of gemstones, and by a *Kogebog* ("Cookbook"), the oldest one with "French cuisine." The *Urtebog* is translated from a Latin poem in hexameters written under the French pseudonym Macer, *De viribus herbarum* (*ca.* 1090), and from Constantinus Africanus's *De gradibus liber*, a major work from the Salerno school (1050).

An astrological-prognostic work, which also contains the doctor's instructions for the bloodletting of King Erik Plovpenning, is still unedited (GkS 3656 8vo, from *ca*. 1500). Harpestreng also wrote about hygiene, bloodletting, and cupping, and may have collected his comprehensive knowledge in a leechbook. A Swedish leechbook (AM 45 4to, from *ca*. 1450) names Harpestreng as author, but his name had such a reputation in all of Scandinavia that it recommended any work. The provenance is thus uncertain, and more detailed examination of the authorship is lacking.

Harpestreng's works reveal him as a pupil of the international medical school in Salerno, Italy, which pursued Greek traditions (*e.g.*, Galen, 2nd century A.D.) and Arabic ones (*e.g.*, Avicenna's *Canon*, 1030). This antique system was based on a theory that the body was influenced by four cardinal liquids or humors, corresponding to the four elements and temperaments: air corresponding to blood (*sanguis*); fire to red or yellow gall (*cholera rubea*); soil to black gall (*melancholia*); and water to phlegm (*flegma*). Illnesses were caused by a lack of balance among these liquids, and medicine prescribed natural plants and minerals to restore the balance by a contrasting principle. Phlegm has, for example, the attributes of cold and moistness, and one gets pains if there is too much of it in the stomach. Harpestreng therefore suggests peas against stomach pains, because the attributes of peas are dryness and warmth like the yellow gall: "Pea is dry and warm; boiled and eaten it causes a good digestion and warms the stomach, but be careful not to eat it if you have an ulcer or abcess, because it increases the pain, and do not eat it during bloodletting nor when you suffer from pains in your eyes, because it brings about and increases warmth and infection and causes bad stitches and does not allow the unclean liquid to flow from one's eyes" (from *Liber herbarum*).

Ed.: Konráðr Gíslason, ed. *Fire og fyrretyve for en stor deel forhen utrykte prøver af oldnordisk sprog og literatur*. Copenhagen: Gyldendal, 1860; Klemming, G. E., ed. *Läke- och örteböker från Sveriges Medeltid*. Samlingar utgivna av Svenska fornskrift-sällskapet, 82, 84, 90. Stockholm: Norstedt, 1883–86; Hægstad, M. *Gamalnorsk fragment av Henrik Harpestreng*. Videnskabs-selskabets skrifter. II, Hist.-filos. Klasse 1906. Christiania [Oslo]: Dybwad, 1906; Harpestreng, H. *Gamle danske Urtebøger, Stenbøger og Kogebøger*. Ed. Marius Kristensen. Copenhagen: Thiele, 1908–20 [originally issued in 7 parts as Universitets-Jubilæets danske Samfund, Skrifter Nr. 182, 192, 200, 215, 226, 236, and 253; edits Stock. K 48 (S, *ca*. 1300), Knud Juul MS, NkS 66,8 (K, *ca*. 1300), a fragment of Linköping T67 (L, *ca*. 1350), NkS 7OR, 8vo (Q, after 1350), Stenbog from Stockholm K 4 (S, *ca*. 1450)]; Henricus Dacus. *De simplicibus medicinis laxativis*. Ed. J. W. S. Johnson. Copenhagen: Hofboghandel, 1914; Hauberg, P., ed. "*En middelalderlig dansk lægebog*." Copenhagen: Koppel, 1927; Harpestreng, Henrik. *Liber Herbarum*. Ed. Poul Hauberg. Copenhagen: Kretzschmer, 1936. Lit.: Hauberg, Poul. "Lidt om Henrik Harpestrængs Lægebog." *Danske Studier* 19 (1919), 111–28; Otto, Alfred. *Liber Daticus Roskildensis*. Tillæg 4. Copenhagen: Levin & Munksgaard, 1933; Møller-Christensen, Vilhelm. *Middelalderens Lægekunst i Danmark*. Copenhagen: Munksgaard, 1944 [English summary]; Skov, Sigv. "Henrik Harpestreng og middelalderens medicin." *Danske Studier* 45 (1945), 125–39; Gotfredsen, Edvard. *Medicinens historie*. 3rd ed. Copenhagen: Nyt Nordisk Forlag, 1973.

Sigurd Kværndrup

[See also: Medicine and Medical Treatment]

Háttalykill

Háttalykill ("Clavis metrica," or "Key to Meters") usually refers to the first Old Norse metrical treatise in verse. According to *Orkneyinga saga* (ch. 81), the poem was written around 1142 by Earl Rǫgnvaldr Kali Kolsson of the Orkneys in collaboration with his retainer, the Icelandic skald Hallr Þórarinsson breiðmagi ("broad-belly"). *Háttalykill* is found in two 17th-century paper MSS, Stock. Papp. 8vo no. 25 and Upp. R:683, both written by Jón Rugman. Whereas R:683 appears to be a later clean copy, Papp. 8vo no. 25 was apparently copied directly from an older, lost original.

Háttalykill consists of forty-one double stanzas. Each pair of stanzas exemplifies a certain meter or formal peculiarity, such as the number of syllables in the line, the placement and quality of internal rhymes and end-rhymes, clause arrangement within a stanza, and variation in poetic language. The original version of *Háttalykill* allegedly used five stanzas to illustrate each *háttr* ("meter"), but the poem was considered too long and was reduced to its present form (*Orkneyinga saga*, ch. 81). Both the metrical variations and the names for the different meters in *Háttalykill* correspond to a great extent to those given by Snorri Sturluson in his *Háttatal*, composed around 1220, and Snorri was undoubtedly familiar with Rǫgnvaldr's work. The exemplifying stanzas in *Háttalykill* are not as systematically arranged as those in *Háttatal*, and, unlike Snorri, Rǫgnvaldr does not provide an explanatory prose commentary.

In the opening stanzas of *Háttalykill*, the poet states his intention to tell "the tales of ancient heroes." The first thirty double stanzas describe the lives of champions from heroic lays and sagas. The rest of the poem is devoted to the military exploits of the kings of Denmark and Norway (from Haraldr hárfagri ["fair-hair"] Hálfdanarson to Magnús berfœttr ["bare-leg"] Óláfsson).

Háttalykill was written within the continental tradition of Latin *claves metricae*. During the 15th and 16th centuries, such verse keys became increasingly popular in Iceland, and from that period we find such poems as *Háttalykill* by Loptur ríki ("the rich"), *Maríulykill* by Jón Pálsson Maríuskáld ("Maria-skald"), *Háttalykill rímna* by Hallur Magnússon, and *Háttalykill* by Þórður Magnússon at Strjúgi.

Ed.: Sveinbjörn Egilsson, ed. *Edda Snorra Sturlusonar eða Gylfaginníng, Skaldskaparmál og Háttatal*. Reykjavik: Prentsmíðja Landsins, 1848–49 [see pp. 239–48 for *Háttalykill*]; Jón Þorkelsson, ed. *Om digtningen på Island i det 15. og 16. århundrede*. Copenhagen: Høst, 1888 [*Maríulykill*: pp. 255–69; Hallur Magnússon: pp. 361–7. See also the list of subsequent *háttalyklar*, p. 243, n. 1]; Jón Þorkelsson, ed. *Småstykker* 11–6. Samfund til udgivelse af gammel nordisk litteratur, 13. Copenhagen: Møller, 1884–91 [13: 203–82; Loptur Guttormsson: 15: 297–344; Þórður Magnússon: 16: 345–60]; Finnur Jónsson, ed. *Den norsk-islandske skjaldedigtning*. Vols. 1A–2A (tekst efter håndskrifterne) and 1B–2B (rettet tekst). Copenhagen and Christiania [Oslo]: Gyldendal, 1912–15; rpt. Copenhagen: Rosenkilde & Bagger, 1967 (A) and 1973 (B) [*Háttalykill*: 1A: 512–28, 1B: 487–505]; Jón Helgason, ed. *Íslenzk miðaldakvæði. Islandske digte fra senmiddelalderen*. Vols. 1.2–2. Copenhagen: Levin & Munksgaard, 1936–38 [*Maríulykill*: 2: 203–28]; Jón Helgason and Anne Holtsmark, eds. *Háttalykill enn forni*. Bibliotheca Arnamagnæana, 1. Copenhagen: Munksgaard, 1941; Kock, Ernst A., ed. *Den norsk-isländska skaldediktningen*. 2 vols. Lund: Gleerup, 1946–49 [*Háttalykill*: 1: 239–49]. Lit.: Finnur Jónsson. "Om Háttalykill, der tillægges Loptr Gutthormsson." *Arkiv för nordisk filologi* 48 (1932), 285–322.

Kari Ellen Gade

[See also: Bjarni Kolbeinsson; *Orkneyinga saga*; *Snorra Edda*]

Haukdœla þáttr *see* Sturlunga saga

Hauksbók ("Haukr's Book") designates a codex that Árni Magnússon possessed as a whole, which was later broken up into three parts: AM 371 4to (now in the Árni Magnússon Institute in Iceland), and AM 544 4to and AM 675 4to (both in the Arnamagnaean Institute in Copenhagen). The book is named after Haukr Erlendsson, who identified himself on a leaf in AM 371 4to, which was lost in the 17th century. All three parts of the book are defective, but especially AM 371 4to; of the original *Hauksbók*, which probably consisted of at least 210 leaves, 141 leaves are preserved.

Haukr Erlendsson was an Icelander by origin, and he is first mentioned in 1294 as lawman in Iceland. A few years later, he moved to Norway, where he served as lawman, and where he lived until his death in 1334. Two charters in which Haukr is mentioned, written in 1302 and 1310, are in the same hand as a considerable portion of *Hauksbók*. This hand is undoubtedly his own, the oldest known hand of an identified Icelander.

AM 371 4to is written entirely in Haukr's hand; in AM 544 4to, fols. 22–107, his hand alternates with the handwriting of Icelandic scribes, who must have been in his service. Judging from minor palaeographic variations between the above-mentioned charters, it appears likely that AM 371 4to, as well as AM 544 4to, fols. 22–59 and 69–107, were written in this period, possibly 1306–1308, when Haukr was on a mission to Iceland, and AM 544 4to, fols. 60–68, around or after 1310.

Those parts of the codex that Haukr either wrote himself or had written for him contain mainly three kinds of texts: first, historical or semihistorical works; second, mathematical treatises; third, philosophical or theological dialogues, translated from the Latin. Thus, AM 371 4to contains Haukr's copy of two texts on the history of Iceland, *Landnámabók* and *Kristni saga*. In AM 544 4to, Haukr copied, in the first place, translations of two semihistorical works, *Trójumanna saga* (fols. 22–33; a compilation of translations of Dares Phrygius's *De excidio Troiae*, *Ilias latina*, and other sources) and *Breta sǫgur* (fols. 36–53; a translation and adaptation of Geoffrey of Monmouth's *Historia regum Britanniae*) including also *Merlínusspá* ("Prophecy of Merlin") in verse translation attributed to the Benedictine brother Gunnlaugr Leifsson of Þingeyrar (d. 1219). In the second place, there are two sagas, both related to Greenland (and America), *Fóstbrœðra saga* (fols. 77–89) and *Eiríks saga rauða* (fols. 93–101). There are also two shorter stories, *Heiðreks saga* (fols. 72–76) and *Skálda saga* (fols. 101–104; a history of the poets of King Haraldr hárfagri ["fair-hair"]) and, finally, three *þættir*: *Hemings þáttr* (fols. 69–72), *Þáttr af Upplendinga konungum* (fols. 104–105), and *Ragnarssona þáttr* (fols. 105–107). AM 544 4to also includes in Haukr's hand two mathematical treatises, *Algorismus* (fols. 90–93; using Arabic numerals) and *Prognostica temporum* with other half-illegible pieces (fol. 107), and two dialogues grouped together as the so-called *Viðrœða líkams ok sálar* ("Dialogue Between Body and Soul") (fols. 60–68). The former dialogue, *Viðrœða æðru ok hugrekki* ["Dialogue Between Fear and Courage"] is a translation of the Pseudo-Senecan dialogue *De remediis*, which figures in a shortened form as the twenty-sixth chapter, "De fiducia et securitate," of the *Moralium dogma philosophorum*, attributed by some scholars to Galterus de Castellione; the latter dialogue is an interpolated translation of the *De arrha animæ* of Hugh of St. Victor.

The remaining part of *Hauksbók* can be divided into three sections, which are unconnected by scribal hand, contents, or gathering: (1) a collection of tracts and excerpts on geographical, chronological, and theological subjects, among them three sermons (AM 544 4to, fols. 1–14); (2) some pieces of the same kind, among them a plan of Jerusalem and *Vǫluspá* (AM 544 4to, fols. 15–21); (3) *Elucidarius* (AM 675 4to). The scribe of section (1) was most likely Norwegian, although some scholars have identified him as Faroese. The major portion of (2) is also Norwegian; section (3), which evidences an irregular, mixed orthography, is in all probability Icelandic. It is uncertain whether Haukr Erlendsson personally added some or all of these sections of his book or whether they were added later. With the exception of the last pages in (2), all of the above-mentioned sections were probably written about the same time as Haukr's own portions, *i.e.*, the beginning of the 14th century. But *Vǫluspá* (fols. 20–21) is written in an Icelandic hand from the middle of the 14th century, and the same is most likely true of the last lines on fol. 18v and perhaps also of fol. 19. These pieces were undoubtedly written after Haukr's death in 1334.

The history of the MS in the 14th–16th centuries is unknown, except for what has already been said concerning *Vǫluspá*. Sources indicate that around the year 1600 the MS was in the possession of a prosperous farmer in the Western Fjords, and in the first half of the 17th century it is known to have been used by historians working in the spirit of Renaissance humanism on the history of Greenland and Iceland, notably the two autodidacts Jón Guðmundsson lærði ("the learned") and Björn Jónsson of Skarðsá. In the 1650s, the MS collector and humanist Bishop Brynjólfur Sveinsson of Skálholt obtained AM 544 4to and had a copy of AM 371 4to made for himself, and Árni Magnússon obtained the second (and probably also the third) part of the MS in the 1690s from his heirs. The first part, or what remained of it, he obtained a little later, in the beginning of the 18th century.

In contrast to the practice most frequently encountered in medieval Icelandic MSS, in which works were collected in a book according to subject matter, *Hauksbók* from its inception was an entire private library, which Haukr, with assistance, wrote for himself. The *Hauksbók* version of *Landnámabók* is his own expanded version of this work, and research has shown that Haukr personally edited several of the other texts he wrote as well and that he usually condensed them. This procedure gives many of the texts in *Hauksbók* a special standing within the textual tradition.

Ed.: Eiríkur Jónsson and Finnur Jónsson, eds. *Hauksbók udgiven efter de Arnamagnæanske håndskrifter no. 371, 544 og 675, 4° samt forskellige papirshåndskrifter af Det kongelige nordiske Oldskriftselskab.* Copenhagen: Thiele, 1892–96; Jón Helgason, ed. *Hauksbók. The Arna-Magnæan Manuscripts 371,4°, 544,4°, and 675,4°.* Manuscripta Islandica, 5. Copenhagen: Munksgaard, 1960 [facsimile]. **Lit.**: Jón Þorkelsson. *Nokkur blöð úr Hauksbók og brot úr Guðmundarsögu.* Reykjavik: Hið íslenzka bókmentafélag, 1865; Kristensen, Marius. *"Nokkur blöð úr Hauksbók", et færøsk håndskrift fra o. 1300 undersøgt og bestemt med hensyn til dets sprogform.* Det Kgl. danske Videnskabernes Selskab. Historisk-filologiske Meddelelser, 9.5. Copenhagen: Høst, 1925; Jansson, Sven B. F. *Sagorna om Vinland I. Handskrifterna till Erik den rödes saga.* Lund: Ohlsson, 1944; Jón Helgason. "Til Hauksbóks historie i det 17. århundrede." *Opuscula 1.* Bibliotheca Arnamagnæana, 20. Copenhagen: Munksgaard, 1960, pp. 1–48; Stefán Karlsson. "Aldur Hauksbókar." *Fróðskaparrit* 13 (1964), 114–21; Taylor, Arnold, "*Hauksbók* and Ælfric's *De falsis Diis*." *Leeds Studies in English* n.s.3 (1969), 101–9; Sveinbjörn Rafnsson. *Studier i Landnámabók. Kritiska bidrag till den isländska fristatstidens* historia. Bibliotheca historica Lundensis, 31. Lund: Gleerup, 1974, pp. 13–7; Ólafur Halldórsson. *Grænland í miðaldaritum.* Reykjavík: Sögufélag, 1978, pp. 209–28, 280–92.

Gunnar Harðarson and Stefán Karlsson

[See also: *Algorismus*; Bible; *Breta sǫgur*; *Elucidarius*; Encyclopedic Literature; *Fóstbrœðra saga*; *Hemings þáttr Áslákssonar*; *Landnámabók*; *Merlínusspá*; *Trójumanna saga*; Vinland Sagas; *Vǫluspá*]

Haustlǫng *see* **Þjóðólfr of Hvin**

Hávamál ("The Speech of Hávi" [Óðinn]), is an anonymous "poem of information" consisting principally of didactic and gnomic matter, largely of a secular character, although material relating to pagan belief, especially the cult of Óðinn, appears in its latter part. It survives in the principal MS of the eddic poems, the *Codex Regius* (ca. 1270). The first strophe is also found near the beginning of Snorri's *Prose Edda* (ca. 1220), and the second half of stanza 84 is quoted as a *kviðlingr* ("ditty") in *Fóstbrœðra saga* (ch. 21). *Hávamál* comprises 164 strophes, mostly in ljóðaháttr meter, but *málaháttr* appears sporadically (e.g., 73, 85–87, 144). The end of stanza 145 is in *fornyrðislag*, and there are also strophes not in any recognizable meter (80, 142–143). This disjointedness extends to the poem's content; it is plainly not a unified composition, but the compilation of an "editor," perhaps no earlier than the 13th century, subsuming a number of distinct poems or strophe-sequences, some evidently disrupted in oral transmission. Six such sequences can be distinguished, although the boundaries are not always clear, and some strophes seem to fall outside the divisions altogether.

(a) The Gnomic Poem, as stanzas 1–77 (or 79) may be called, opens with advice to a traveler in a strange house, enjoining caution, alertness, and sobriety, and deprecating heedless loquacity, gluttony, sullen unsociability, and so on. After stanza 35, it passes to more varied advice, counseling friendship and the exchange of gifts, culminating in the famous lines: "cattle die, kin die, one dies oneself, renown alone is eternal." The tone is mundane and rationalistic, with no reference to cult or superstition. Fighting and weapons are barely mentioned, feuds and the duty of vengeance for kin not at all. Relations between the sexes are also ignored. Despite sporadic confusions, the Gnomic Poem has sufficient unity of substance and style to show that it descends essentially from a planned original composition and is not a mere anthology of preexisting strophes. Some references, notably to cremation (71) and *bautarsteinar* ("memorial stones," 72), indicate an origin in pre-Conversion Norway, and certain items of vocabulary are also Norwegian. Some scholars have minimalized the Gnomic Poem's links with the pre-Christian Norse world and see it rather as an expression of 12th- or 13th-century clerical moralizing, rooted in classical and biblical wisdom. But its marked dissimilarity from poems from that milieu (e.g., *Hugsvinnsmál*), notably in the absence of clear Christian allusions and in the quantity of lexical and other textual obscurities, tells heavily against that view.

The Gnomic Poem is followed by ten strophes (81–90), mostly in *málaháttr*, listing things to do and beware of. Among the latter are women, seen as deceitful, and this observation leads into a series of reflections (91–4) on the mutual faithlessness of the sexes.

(b) In stanzas 95–102, a first-person speaker, identified in 98

as Óðinn, tells how he was deceived in love by *Billings mær*, the wife (or daughter) of Billingr, a tale not otherwise known.

(c) Stanzas 104–10, to which 103 can be seen as an introduction, complement the preceding sequence and are probably by the same poet. Here, Óðinn tells how he seduced and then abandoned a woman, Gunnlǫð, to steal the sacred mead of poetry from her giant father, Suttungr (a tale already alluded to in stanzas 13–14, and told fully in Snorri's *Prose Edda*).

(d) *Loddfáfnismál.* In stanza 111, the poet proclaims that he has heard runes and counsels, in the hall of Hávi, which he will now pass on. There follow twenty-six strophes (112–137), mostly comprising a four-line formula in which Loddfáfnir (unknown outside *Hávamál*) is enjoined to heed advice, followed by three or more lines in which the advice is stated. This advice is often in the imperative, not used in the Gnomic Poem, but has much the same general character, differing in that it includes references to sexual relations, magic, and superstition. In places (128, 130, 135), the advice seems less self-interested than in the Gnomic Poem, perhaps through Christian influence, though there is nothing unambiguously Christian in the poem.

(e) *Rúnatal.* Stanzas 138–145 deal obscurely and incoherently with runes, ritual, and myth. Only the first four strophes form a clear sequence: here, Óðinn tells how, as he hung nine days on a "windy tree," pierced with a spear and sacrificed to himself, he "took up" runes, then grew and flourished. This account is not paralleled as such, but its various elements all have roots in Norse tradition. It is needless to invoke influence from the Crucifixion. The remaining four strophes are very miscellaneous, not least metrically, and are plainly a jumble of fragments.

(f) *Ljóðatal.* This numbered catalogue (146–163), the most clearly demarcated sequence in *Hávamál*, lists eighteen spells, of which the speaker claims sole knowledge (146) and describes what function each serves, but the spells themselves are not quoted. The speaker is not named, but Snorri was doubtless right, in using this sequence in *Ynglinga saga* (chs. 6 and 7), to identify him as Óðinn.

The final strophe (164) may well have been composed by the compiler of the existing text of *Hávamál*. When he worked is uncertain; the structure of the unified text seems to be reflected in *Sólarljóð*, itself, however, of uncertain date, and in Snorri's *Gylfaginning* (ca. 1220).

Ed.: Clarke, Daisy E. Martin, ed. *The Hávamál, with Selections from Other Poems of the Edda, Illustrating the Wisdom of the North in Heathen Times.* Cambridge: Cambridge University Press, 1923 [includes translation]; Finnur Jónsson, ed. *Hávamál.* Copenhagen: Gad, 1924 [with full commentary in Danish]; Neckel, Gustav, ed. *Edda: Die Lieder des Codex Regius nebst verwandten Denkmälern. I: Text.* 5th ed. rev. Hans Kuhn. Heidelberg: Winter, 1983; Evans, David A. H., ed. *Hávamál.* Text Series, 7. London: Viking Society for Northern Research, 1986 [includes introduction, commentary, and bibliography]. **Tr.**: Hollander, Lee M., trans. *The Poetic Edda, Translated with an Introduction and Explanatory Notes.* 2nd rev. ed. Austin: University of Texas Press, 1962; rpt. 1988. **Lit.**: Fleck, Jere. "Óðinn's Self-Sacrifice—a New Interpretation. I: The Ritual Inversion." *Scandinavian Studies* 43 (1971), 119–42; "II: The Ritual Landscape," pp. 385–413; See, Klaus von. *Die Gestalt der Hávamál. Eine Studie zur eddischen Spruchdichtung.* Frankfurt am Main: Athenäum, 1972.

D. A. H. Evans

[See also: *Codex Regius*; Eddic Meters; Eddic Poetry; Folklore; *Hugsvinnsmál*; *Snorra Edda*]

Hávarðar saga Ísfirðings

Hávarðar saga Ísfirðings ("The Saga of Hávarðr of Ísafjörður"), one of the shorter *Íslendingasögur*, tells the story of Hávarðr halti ("the lame") of Ísafjörður and his vengeance on Þorbjǫrn Þjóðreksson, who killed Hávarðr's son, Óláfr, for no good reason. At the time of Óláfr's death, Hávarðr is old and lame, and his two demands for compensation bring only insults from Þorbjǫrn. His wife, Bjargey, then goes to her brothers and solicits aid from her nephews. At that point, Hávarðr, suddenly imbued with the vigor of a young man, sets off with his nephews to kill Þorbjǫrn. Þorbjǫrn is about to kill Hávarðr with a rock, when the latter remembers hearing about the new religion preached by Óláfr Tryggvason and vows to be baptized. Þorbjǫrn then slips and falls, and Hávarðr kills him. To safeguard himself against reprisals, Hávarðr plans to kill Þorbjǫrn's brother, Ljótr, with the help of Steinþórr of Eyrr and his brother-in-law, Atli. Once Ljótr and his followers are dead, Hávarðr and Bjargey sail to Norway and are baptized by Óláfr Tryggvason.

The saga is preserved in paper MSS, the oldest and best of which (AM 160 fol. and AM 502 4to) date from the 17th century. These MSS are all believed to be copies of an earlier version, tentatively dated 1330. This version appears to be the reworking of an older lost saga, referred to in *Landnámabók* as the "saga þeira Þorbjarnar ok Hávarðar ins halta" ("saga of Þorbjǫrn and Hávarðr the lame," *Sturlubók*, ch. 117, *Hauksbók*, ch. 89) and as the "saga Ísfirðinga" ("saga of the people of Ísafjörður," *Sturlubók*, ch. 150, *Hauksbók*, ch. 121).

Stylistic features reminiscent of the *fornaldarsögur* add weight to the assumption that the extant *Hávarðar saga* is a late composition. Some of the characters are a little unconvincing. Hávarðr is suddenly transformed from a lame and helpless old man to a doughty warrior capable of great swimming feats. Atli changes from a miser to a brave and generous fighter. Óláfr is completely blameless when he is killed, whereas Þorbjǫrn appears to have no redeeming features. Óláfr's fight with the ghost is gratuitous adornment, and the author has sacrificed realism for humor when he sends the sorrowing Hávarðr to his bed for a year in three consecutive years. Christian influence can be seen in Hávarðr's vow to accept the faith and in his defeat of Þorbjǫrn, apparently by divine intervention.

The version of *Hávarðar saga* that has come down to us contains certain inaccuracies. The author has introduced an anachronistic lawman and confused Earl Hákon Sigurðarson (d. 995) and Óláfr Tryggvason (d. 1000) with Hákon Eiríksson (deposed 1014) and St. Óláfr (d. 1030). Geographical errors suggest that the author was not familiar with the Western Fjords. Discrepancies between *Hávarðar saga* and *Landnámabók* suggest that the author was working from memory and had neither the earlier lost saga nor *Landnámabók* in front of him. One of the most notable discrepancies appears with regard to the character Ljótr. *Landnámabók* has one person of this name, Ljótr inn spaki ("the wise") of Ingjaldssandr. *Hávarðar saga* divides this role between Gestr inn spaki ("the wise"), Hólmgǫngu-Ljótr ("holm-going") of Rauðasandr, and Ljótr Þjóðreksson.

There are also problems with the verses. Several do not fit in with the surrounding text. In one case, a superfluous tale of a thrall and an untied shoe is dragged in to give a *vísa* a *raison d'être*.

Another *vísa* was originally the work of a different poet, also nicknamed "the lame," and yet another is very similar to a stanza found in three other sagas.

The lateness and unreliability of *Hávarðar saga* may explain why critics have paid little attention to it.

Ed.: Guðni Jónsson, ed. *Vestfirðinga Sǫgur*. Íslenzk fornrit, 6. Reykjavik: Hið íslenzka fornritafélag, 1943, pp. 289–358. **Tr.**: Morris, William, and Eiríkr Magnússon, trans. *The Story of Howard the Halt*. Saga Library, 1. London: Quaritch, 1891, pp. 1–69; Gudbrand Vigfusson and F. York Powell, trans. *Origines Islandicae: A Collection of the More Important Sagas and Other Native Writings Relating to the Settlement and Early History of Iceland*. 2 vols. Oxford: Clarendon, 1905; rpt. Millwood: Kraus, 1976, vol. 2, pp. 245–74. **Lit.**: Wrenn, C. L. "The Text of *Hávarðar Saga Ísfirðings*." *Medium Ævum* 2 (1933), 71–2; Eeden, W. van. "Some Remarks About the *Hávarðar saga Ísfirðings*." *Neophilologus* 34 (1950), 44–8; Andersson, Theodore M. *The Icelandic Family Saga: An Analytic Reading*. Harvard Studies in Comparative Literature, 28. Cambridge: Harvard University Press, 1967.

Bernadine McCreesh

[See also: *Íslendingasögur*; *Landnámabók*; *Lausavísur*]

Hectors saga ok kappa hans *see* Ectors saga ok kappa hans

Hedeby

Hedeby. The Viking Age market, trading place, and proto-urban settlement of Hedeby, also called "Haithabu" after an Old Danish runic inscription, is situated at the inner part of the Schlei fjord, south and opposite the medieval town Schleswig in the northeastern part of Schleswig-Holstein, Germany, about 40 km. south of the present Danish-German border, and 40 km. southwest of the Baltic Sea (Fig. 38). Historical sources confirm the existence of the settlement between the year 808 (dislocation of Slavonic merchants from Reric to Hedeby under the rule of the Danish king Godfred) and 1066 (plundering of Hedeby by Slavonic people) as a trading and proto-urban center under the control of the Danish kingdom in the 9th, 10th, and 11th centuries, and of the German Empire in the 10th century. A successive series of dendrochronological dates covers the period between 811 and 1020; 783 is the oldest (isolated) dendrochronological date. The archaeological material can be fixed between the latter part of the 8th century and the 11th–12th centuries; the oldest coins belong to the late 8th–early 9th centuries (*sceattas*, coins of the older Carolingian type), the youngest to the years 1042–1066 (Edward the Confessor, minted at Lincoln).

A visible and outstanding monument of the former settlement (Fig. 39) is the semicircular wall (length 1,300 m., height 5.10 m.), which surrounded the main settlement areas (24 hectares) and was connected with the defense work of Danevirke. In 1897 and 1900, Sophus Müller identified the walled settlement with the historically known Hedeby. From 1900 to 1980, excavations took place in several parts of the main settlement and outside the semicircular wall. The excavations from 1930 to 1939 under the direction of Herbert Jankuhn and from 1962 to 1968 and 1979 to 1980 under the direction of Kurt Schietzel, were especially successful; they were supplemented by field surveys. About 6 percent of the walled settlement area has been investigated by large-scale and test excavations.

38. Southern Scandinavia. Viking Age early urban settlements and royal palaces. After Else Roesdahl, *Viking Age Denmark*. Trans. Susan Margeson and Kirsten Williams. (London: British Museum, 1982), p. 8, fig. 1.

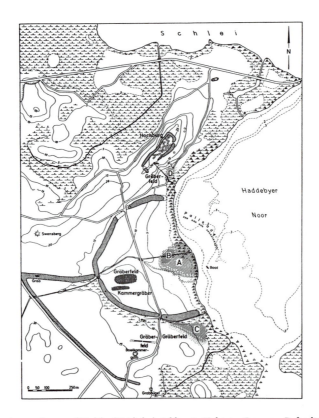

39. Viking Age trading and proto-urban settlement of Hedeby (Haithabu), Schleswig-Holstein, Germany. Defending walls, harbor, settlement areas (A–D), cemeteries, and single burials. After Herbert Jankuhn, *Haithabu. Ein Handelsplatz der Wikingerzeit*, 8th ed. (Neumünster: Wachholtz, 1986), p. 66, fig. 29.

The investigations yield a complex picture of the site. Settlement activity starts in the 8th century south of the semicircular wall (so-called "South-settlement" and "South-cemetery"). In the 9th century, probably three settlements with adjacent cemeteries existed in the south, the main area in the north. The main settlement area is well documented by timber structures and finds dating from the 9th century to the 11th–12th centuries. A harbor with several causeways and a semicircular palisade came to light, resembling the one known at Dorestad, the Netherlands. In the late 10th century, the main area was surrounded by a mighty wall. Unfortunately, we do not know the exact date of the walled area, to which belongs a cemetery on a hill ("Hochburg") north of the main settlement.

In moist layers of the main settlement, several parts of timber constructions were conserved, for example, buildings, wells, enclosures, gates, and facing of the riverside. The one-aisled houses of nonagrarian type (3 x 3 m. to 7 x 17.5 m.) built using several techniques (e.g., stave construction), are often divided into several rooms for dwelling, working, and sometimes for cattle. In the early "South-settlement," pithuts of South Scandinavian type were found. The structure of the main settlement is regular and obviously planned, probably by the royal administration. The six cemeteries (one in the south, three in the main settlement area, two in the north) reflect a stratified and polyethnic society of Danish, Scandinavian, Saxon, Frisian, Frankish, and Slavonic origin, partly Christian, partly heathen. Cremation and inhumation burials are found, sometimes under low mounds and surrounded by ditches. Only a few burials are equipped with grave goods; a richer inventory of grave goods is found in several chamber graves and the so-called "boat-chamber-grave," which may be the burial of a Danish king from about 900. Some single Viking Age graves are situated outside the settlement proper and gravefield complex, but presumably belong to Hedeby, as do the runestones in the neighborhood of Hedeby.

The innumerable archaeological finds, including osteological and botanical material, testify to multifaceted trade and handicraft production.

Hedeby served as a center of consumption for imported trading objects, as a production site for its own requirements and exports, and as a transfer place for transit trade, mainly from the Lower Rhine and the North Sea area to the Baltic Sea region. The supraregional connections are attested by imports from the Carolingian and Ottonian Empire, the British Isles, Scandinavia, the Baltic-Finnish region, the West and East Slavonic states, and the Byzantine Empire. Coins were struck from the early 9th century onward in Hedeby; there are also found, as in other places in northern Europe, coins of Arabian, insular, continental, and Byzantine origin.

Production of objects made of antler and bone, iron, metals, glass, leather, wood, and textiles is evidenced mainly by raw, unfinished, and waste material; workshops probably existed in the main settlement as well as in the outskirts near the inner side of the wall. The population, estimated at 800–1,000 persons, was mainly nonagrarian in occupation (merchants, craftsmen, sailors, etc.). Food had to be provided in the neighboring region by agriculture, cattle raising, and fishing.

In Carolingian and Ottonian times, Hedeby played an important role as a center of the Catholic Roman mission and christianization. Together with the contemporaneous trading places of Ribe, Kaupang, and Birka, Hedeby belongs to the earliest Scandinavian settlements with an urban character. It was succeeded by the town of Schleswig.

The documentation of the excavations and finds (e.g., the shipwreck from the harbor) is exhibited in the Wikinger Museum Haithabu, opened in 1985 near the historical site.

Lit.: (a) Surveys with bibliographies: Roesdahl, Else. Viking Age Denmark. Trans. Susan Margeson and Kirsten Williams. London: British Museum, 1982, pp. 70–7; Jankuhn, Herbert, et al. Archäologische und naturwissenschaftliche Untersuchungen an ländlichen und frühstädtischen Siedlungen im deutschen Küstengebiet vom 5. Jahrhundert v. Chr. bis zum 11. Jahrhundert n. Chr. Vol. 2: Handelsplätze des frühen und hohen Mittelalters. Acta Humaniora. Weinheim: Chemie, 1984; Jankuhn, Herbert. Haithabu. Ein Handelsplatz der Wikingerzeit. 8th ed. Neumünster: Wachholtz, 1986. (b) Monographs, special reports: Die Ausgrabungen in Haithabu. 9 vols. Neumünster: Wachholtz, 1937–87; Schietzel, Kurt, ed. Berichte über die Ausgrabungen in Haithabu. 26 vols. Neumünster: Wachholtz, 1969–89; Schriften aus der Archäologisch-Zoologischen Arbeitsgruppe, Schleswig-Kiel. 12 vols. Kiel: Archäologisch-Zoologische Arbeitsgruppe, 1976–88. (c) Cemeteries: Steuer, Heiko. "Zur ethnischen Gliederung der Bevölkerung von Haithabu anhand der Gräberfelder." Offa 41 (1984), 189–212. (d) Trade: Düwel, Klaus, et al. Untersuchungen zu Handel und Verkehr der vor- und frühgeschichtlichen Zeit in Mittel- und Nordeuropa. Vol. 4: Der Handel der Karolinger- und Wikingerzeit. Abhandlungen der Akademie der Wissenschaften. Phil.-Hist. Klasse 3, N. F., 156. Göttingen: Vandenhoeck & Ruprecht, 1987.

Michael Müller-Wille

[See also: Birka; Danevirke; Germany, Norse in; Kaupang; Trade]

Heiðarvíga saga ("The Story of the Moor Killings"), named for a skirmish in 1014 between men from the Húnavatn and Borgarfjörður districts, is probably the oldest extant Íslendingasaga. Evidence for its age are its awkward style and composition and its influence on later saga literature. The first fifteen chapters, which were destroyed in the fire of 1728 in Copenhagen, were reconstructed from notes and memory by Jón Ólafsson. The saga contains seventeen skaldic stanzas.

Víga-Styrr ("killer Styr") slays thirty-three men without reparation, including two berserks, whom he suffocates in a sauna (the episode occurs virtually unchanged in Eyrbyggja saga). Styrr is slain by Gestr, the young son of his last victim, whom he has offered a sick lamb in requital. Styrr's son tries three times to kill Gestr, but each time has his own life saved by the boy.

Following missions of revenge and counterrevenge, Hallr Guðmundarson is slain instead of an intended victim. Hallr's brother Barði three times seeks a peaceful settlement at the Alþingi. Rebuffed the third time with an insult, he prepares an excursion to Borgarfjörður according to detailed instructions from his foster-father, who correctly predicts that these instructions will not be properly executed. Barði's mother, who has cruelly goaded her sons to vengeance, intends to accompany them, but they cut her saddle girth so that she tumbles into a creek. (A less farcical version of this incitement-to-revenge episode is used by the author of Laxdœla saga.)

Since Barði is so deliberate in carrying out his plans, his enemies in Borgarfjörður more and more frequently ask each other the caustic question: "Don't you think Barði will come?" At the same time, however, they experience dreams and other foreboding omens. Even as Barði and his men approach, Gísli, one of the three brothers mowing the hay, asks this question. Barði kills him, and his brothers escape. As Gísli's father, Þorgautr, asks the scornful question, one of his sons casts Gísli's body before his feet with the answer: "Your son Gísli found out that he has come."

Barði now wants to withdraw to the defensive position recommended by his foster-father, but his companions insist on eating a large leisurely breakfast. Consequently, they have to defend themselves from an inferior site. After beating off three attacks, they retreat before an overwhelming force. They have lost four men and their opponents nine. During the litigation, Eiðr Skeggjason, who has lost both his sons, urges the litigants to avoid abusive language. Eiðr is more concerned about restoring peace than about recompense for his loss. This scene is the model for the one in Njáls saga in which Hallr of Síða offers to forgo compensation for his son in the interest of peace. Barði now seeks service in St. Óláfr's bodyguard, but is rejected because Christianity is still imperfect in Iceland. He is eventually killed after serving honorably in the emperor's bodyguard in Constantinople.

Ed.: Sigurður Nordal and Guðni Jónsson, eds. Borgfirðinga sögur. Íslenzk fornrit, 3. Reykjavik: Hið íslenzka fornritafélag, 1938; rpt. 1956. Tr.: Morris, William, and Eiríkur Magnússon, trans. The Story of the Ere-Dwellers with the Story of the Heath-Slayings as Appendix. London: Quaritch, 1892, pp. 191–259. Lit.: Hallberg, Peter. The Icelandic Saga. Trans. Paul Schach. Lincoln: University of Nebraska Press, 1962, pp. 119–32 and passim; Andersson, Theodore M. The Icelandic Family Saga: An Analytic Reading. Harvard Studies in Comparative Literature, 28. Cambridge: Harvard University Press, 1967, pp. 142–52; Schach, Paul. Icelandic Sagas. Twayne's World Authors Series, 717. Boston: Twayne, 1984, pp. 90–5.

Paul Schach

[See also: Eyrbyggja saga; Íslendingasögur; Lausavísur; Laxdœla saga; Njáls saga]

Heilagra manna sögur *see* Saints' Lives

Heimskringla

("The Circle of the World") comprises a Prologue and sixteen sagas of the kings of Norway. The first, Ynglinga saga, follows the rulers of Sweden and Norway from their divine origins to the half-light of 9th-century history, culminating in the reign of Hálfdan svarti ("the black") Guðrøðarson. The remainder trace the struggles of subsequent kings to establish a unified Norwegian realm and to maintain it against rivals at home and abroad. The work divides naturally into three parts: the story of the kings preceding Óláfr Haraldsson inn helgi ("the saint"), the saga of Óláfr helgi, and the history of the succeeding kings down to Magnús Erlingsson in 1177.

The work owes its fame as a masterpiece of medieval historiography to its grand scale, and to the artistry with which individual episodes are related and the larger whole integrated by recurrent themes and patterns of causation. The individual sagas vary greatly in length, in density of detail, and in more literary features, such as structure and use of direct speech. The longest part is Óláfs saga helga, which is clearly an adaptation of the so-called "Separate Saga." It is generally regarded as the greatest of all konungasögur for its dramatically realized episodes and its full and coherent treatment of character (especially Óláfr's), motivation, and theme.

Heimskringla, like the Separate Óláfs saga helga, is attributed with some certainty to Snorri Sturluson (d. 1241). Although no existing medieval MS names him as author, it is known, from Sturlunga saga, that Snorri compiled sögubœkr, "saga books," or possibly "story books" or "history books." The Oddaverja annáll, which is 16th-century, but based on earlier materials, also states, for the year 1241, that Snorri "compiled the Edda and many other learned books, Icelandic sagas" (samsetti Eddu ok margar aðrar fræðibækur, íslenzkar sögur). More specifically, several other works, including Orkneyinga saga and the sagas of Óláfr Tryggvason in Bergsbók and Flateyjarbók, cite Snorri as an authority for details of early Norwegian history. Since the writers of these works clearly knew at least some of the Heimskringla sagas, it is reasonable to count these citations among the evidence for Snorri's authorship. Further, two 16th-century translators of the work, Laurents Hanssøn and Peder Claussøn Friis, attribute the work to Snorri, and it has been argued that they based their claim on at least one medieval reference, now lost. As for more circumstantial evidence, Snorri twice spent two years in Norway, where he had important dealings with the Norwegian monarchy, and in Västergötland, Sweden. He was otherwise very well placed, materially and intellectually, to undertake such a vast task as the writing of Heimskringla. There are also similarities of content, style, and approach between Heimskringla and Snorra Edda.

Snorri's first stay in mainland Scandinavia was in 1218–1220; his second, 1237–1239, was too late to allow for the composing of Heimskringla on his return. The mention of saga books in Sturlunga saga refers to a period beginning in summer 1230, so that the time of composition is plausibly set in the 1220s or early 1230s. The Separate Óláfs saga helga was probably the first of Snorri's konungasögur to be written.

Although the archetype and several medieval copyings of Heimskringla are now lost, the work was evidently copied and circulated with more enthusiasm than any other konungasögur, with the exception of Snorri's own Separate Óláfs saga helga. Only a single leaf survives from Kringla, which is believed to be the oldest known MS (pre-1270) and the closest to Snorri's original. But its text is preserved complete in good transcripts, especially AM 35, 36, and 63 fol., by Ásgeir Jónsson, and these transcripts are used as the main MS for most printed editions. From the opening words of Kringla, "Kringla heimsins" ("the circle of the world"), the MS takes its name; Heimskringla itself was christened at least as early as the 17th century. Insofar as the medieval MSS suggest titles, they are less fixed and less flamboyant, in the style Konunga bók, Ævi, Sögur, or Bók Nóregskonunga.

All the other principal MSS of Heimskringla are more or less incomplete, and all date from the 14th century, usually early in the century. AM 39 fol. and AM 45 fol. (Codex Frisianus or Fríssbók) are vellums that, on the basis of their texts, are grouped with Kringla. The other main branch of the MS tradition, perhaps stemming from an exemplar that found its way to Norway, is the Jöfraskinna group. The main representatives of this branch are the vellum AM 47 fol. (Eirspennill) and AM 42 fol., a paper copy of the now-lost Gullinskinna, both of which contain only the third part of Heimskringla, and Jöfraskinna itself, which is now chiefly represented by the paper copies AM 37 fol. and 38 fol. There are further vellum and paper MSS, still more fragmentary.

The text of Heimskringla is not especially problematic. Disagreements among the MSS are mainly of a predictable and minor kind, and where there is a striking difference in content, there is usually little difficulty in establishing the original text. Codex Frisianus and some members of the Jöfraskinna group, for instance, contain some highly fabulous material that is not in character with the rest of *Heimskringla*, and that has apparently been interpolated from *Morkinskinna* by later scribes. There is reasonable, though not complete, agreement among MSS about where individual sagas and chapters begin and end. The titles for these parts vary considerably among the MSS, but those of *Kringla* (as preserved in the transcript Stock. Papp. fol. no. 18.) are often supported by other MSS and may be very old, even Snorri's own.

Snorri's first visit to mainland Scandinavia afforded him the chance to gather fresh oral materials for his work, and scholars have detected local traditions from Norway (especially the Trøndelag, Hålogaland, and Tønsberg) and from Sweden in his writing. He must also have learned much from some of his Icelandic contemporaries, notably his foster-father, Jón Loptsson, who had witnessed the coronation of Magnús Erlingsson in 1163/4. His most important sources were, however, skaldic verse and prose works, mainly Icelandic rather than Norwegian, on historical subjects.

Snorri's respect for the skalds as authorities and his realization of their limitations are voiced explicitly in the Prologue to *Heimskringla*, and he particularly values the work of such poets as Sighvatr Þórðarson and Þórarinn loftunga ("praise-tongue") who were present at some of the climactic events in Norwegian history. Accordingly, Snorri will often alter the details of events that he found in prose sources, bringing them into line with the skaldic evidence. He quotes around 600 verses from over seventy skalds, mainly in ones or twos, but sometimes in longer sequences, and elsewhere he uses more without directly quoting them. The verses are drawn mostly from formal panegyrics on rulers, both the *drápa* type containing refrains and the somewhat less pretigious *flokkr* type. Snorri's particular choices are often resourceful, not always suggested by his sources. In some parts of *Heimskringla*, skaldic verse is Snorri's principal, perhaps even his only, source; elsewhere, the main effect of the verse is to add graphic detail and perhaps more subjective comment, especially laudatory flourishes, to the normally detached prose narrative.

The prose sources used by Snorri rarely or never survive in exactly the form known to him, and Snorri, with a lack of helpfulness he shares with many medieval authors, gives extremely scant information about them. He refers in the Prologue to *konunga ævi* ("lives of kings") by Ari Þorgilsson, now lost. In *Haraldssona saga* (ch. 11), he refers to the *Hryggjarstykki by Eiríkr Oddsson, which covered the period 1130–1139 or later, and is also now lost but can be partially reconstructed. He praises both works highly for being based on reliable, often firsthand accounts, but they are in fact used relatively little in *Heimskringla*. Snorri's other references to sources consist only of passing mentions of *Skjǫldunga saga, *Jarla saga / sǫgur* (an early version of *Orkneyinga saga*), *Saga Knúts ins gamla* (a saga of the Danish Knud [Cnut] the Great), and a work written at King Sverrir's behest, presumably *Sverris saga* itself. Despite its difficulties, however, the study of what remains or can be reasonably reconstructed of Snorri's sources has been a major preoccupation of *Heimskringla* scholars, invaluable in revealing both Snorri's tremendous indebtedness to written tradition and the distinctive qualities of his kings' sagas.

Most of the prose sources used by Snorri are later than Ari Þorgilsson's and Eiríkr Oddson's writings, and were composed around the end of the 12th century and the beginning of the 13th. They divide broadly into two sorts: historical surveys spanning the reigns of several Norwegian kings or other Scandinavian rulers, and lives of individual kings. The most important surveys are *Morkinskinna* in an older version, *Fagrskinna*, the Norwegian *Ágrip af Nóregs konunga sǫgum*, *Orkneyinga saga*, *Skjǫldunga saga, and *Hlaðajarla saga, a now-lost saga of the earls of Hlaðir (Lade, near Trondheim). Among the lives of individual kings, those of Óláfr Tryggvason (r. 995–1000) by Oddr Snorrason and of St. Óláfr Haraldsson (r. 1015–1030) by Snorri's friend Styrmir Kárason, as well as something approximating to the *Legendary Saga of St. Óláfr*, have a special place. How many other early sagas of individual rulers existed before Snorri's time is unknown, but fragments survive from one saga about the 11th-century earl Hákon Ívarsson. Other works known to Snorri were genealogical lists, miracle tales about St. Óláfr, *þættir*, *Færeyinga saga*, and probably versions of *Jómsvíkinga saga* and *Hallfreðar saga*.

Although some sources, notably *Fagrskinna* and *Ágrip*, span most of the period covered by *Heimskringla*, the nature of the sources varies greatly from saga to saga. *Ynglinga saga* was probably composed from only exiguous preexisting materials, and much deduction and reconstruction was needed. In *Óláfs saga Tryggvasonar*, by contrast, Snorri's problem was to make sense of a wealth of traditions that were frequently fantastical or mutually discrepant. For the last few sagas of *Heimskringla*, he had the relatively full accounts of *Morkinskinna* and *Hryggjarstykki, and this fact may account for the impression of many readers that this part of the work is less clearly stamped as Snorri's own.

Snorri's method in adapting particular passages from his sources varies enormously. At times, he takes over a passage with little alteration, for example, the Snæfríðr episode in *Haralds saga hárfagra* (ch. 25), transcribed from *Ágrip*, or some of the miracle accounts in the third part of *Heimskringla*, whose content and persuasive "clerical" style closely echo the *Old Norwegian Homily Book* and the *Legendary Saga of St. Óláfr*. Many of the vivid details and trenchant speeches in such scenes as the battles at Hjǫrungavágr (Liavåg) or Svǫlðr (Svold; *Óláfs saga Tryggvasonar*, chs. 35–42 and 97–112), Stiklastaðir (Stiklestad; *Óláfs saga helga*, chs. 205–235), or Stamford Bridge (Stanforðabryggjur; *Haralds saga Sigurðarsonar*, chs. 87–94) derive from earlier accounts, although Snorri's version often surpasses theirs in economy and vigor. At other times, he radically departs from his sources in terms of content or presentation. He may, for instance, suppress details or whole episodes that he thinks far-fetched, add explanatory matter or conflate disparate accounts of the same events, while the inherited presentation of events may be changed by streamlining, dramatization, or rationalization. Further, several of the most celebrated episodes and characters in *Heimskringla* are unique to the work, among them the expulsion of Harald Gormsson's shape-shifting envoy by the guardian creatures of Iceland (*Óláfs saga helga*, ch. 33), Þórarinn Nefjólfsson and his ugly feet (*Óláfs saga helga*, ch. 85), or Einarr Eyjólfsson and his rousing speech against Norwegian encroachment on Iceland (*Óláfs saga helga*, ch. 125).

Because *Heimskringla* is concerned with major events of the past, it is fair to ask in what sense it may be regarded as history or historiography. Seen as a repository of historical tradition rather than historical fact, and as an unusually coherent 13th-century Icelandic view of the Norwegian past, it is probably the best of its kind. But judged by modern standards, it falls short. Its preoccupation with the deeds of great men, with political, rather than social and economic history, now appears old-fashioned, as do its use of dramatic reconstruction alongside sober narrative to present historical matters and its incorporation of anecdotes that may be revealing of character and motive, but otherwise (to modern taste) trivial. Snorri's grasp of causation is fine, and his writing, for its day, marked by plausibility and rationality; yet the occasional appearance of berserks, sorcerers, and soothsayers, not to mention heathen gods, ghosts, and monsters, is disconcerting to the modern eye.

Moreover, despite the methodological good intentions declared in the Prologue, the factual core of Snorri's work can be no better than its sources, and these sources are far from ideal. *Heimskringla* rests not on the kind of raw and rigorously controllable data, documentary, archaeological, and onomastic, favored by modern historians, but mainly on evidence that, like *Heimskringla* itself, has already been highly processed into narrative, interpretative historiography. Where Snorri does make learned references to archaeological remains, especially burial sites, or to etymologies of place-names or personal names, they do not always stand up to scrutiny. His discriminating use of skaldic verse is reassuring, but the skalds, as well as being vague and hyperbolical, can sometimes make errors, as when Sighvatr Þórðarson claims that there was an eclipse at the time of Óláfr Haraldsson's fall at Stiklastaðir.

Since the Icelandic traditions about Norwegian history preserved in *Heimskringla* and kindred works are often the fullest available, there is often no external means of checking their truth or of arbitrating between rival accounts when, for instance, *Heimskringla* disagrees with *Morkinskinna* and/or *Fagrskinna*. Where independent, foreign sources are available, they sometimes corroborate, sometimes undermine, the traditions preserved in *Heimskringla*. The late 11th-century Greek *Logos nuthetikos*, for example, substantiates the broad outlines of the adventures of Haraldr harðráði ("hard-ruler") Sigurðarson in the service of the Byzantine emperor as told in *Haralds saga Sigurðarsonar* (chs. 3–16). But the claim, buttressed by skaldic verse, that Haraldr blinded the emperor in revenge for being imprisoned by him seems from the Greek sources to be attached to the wrong emperor. Again, the *Heimskringla* account of Haraldr's fatal English campaign is partially confirmed by the *Anglo-Saxon Chronicle* and numerous chronicles written after the Norman Conquest (*e.g.*, by William of Malmesbury, Simeon of Durham, Henry of Huntingdon, Florence of Worcester, and Ordericus Vitalis), but its detail is often faulty, especially where the battle of Stamford Bridge has been given motifs belonging properly to the battle of Hastings, or other famous battles.

Heimskringla's impact on later centuries has been considerable, and not confined to the world of scholarship. In the development of the *konungasögur*, it is something of an end point, for the only new sagas that postdate are *Hákonar saga Hákonarsonar* and the now-exiguous *Magnúss saga lagabœtis*, about contemporary Norwegian kings, and *Knýtlinga saga*, about Danish royal history. As for lives of past Norwegian kings, instead of attempting new versions, makers of 14th- and 15th-century codices, such as *Hulda-Hrokkinskinna* and *Flateyjarbók*, copied parts of *Heimskringla*, expanding its text abundantly with material from other sources.

In the Nordic renaissance that began in the mid-16th century, *Heimskringla*, alongside other medieval Icelandic works, received its due share of attention. MSS were collected and copied, and the first printed texts published, in Peder Claussøn Friis's translation, the first complete one, published in Copenhagen (1633), and in Peringskiöld's edition, Stockholm (1697). In Norway, after mass printings at the turn of this century, it became known as a "second Bible," many Norwegians reputedly unaware that its author was actually an Icelander. Passages from *Heimskringla* provided a rallying call to those fighting for Icelandic and Norwegian national independence in the 19th and 20th centuries, and inspired creative artists both within Norway (Bjørnsen, Ibsen, Vigeland, Grieg) and outside (Carlyle, Longfellow, Elgar).

Ed.: Finnur Jónsson, ed. *Heimskringla*. 4 vols. Samfund til udgivelse af gammel nordisk litteratur, 23. Copenhagen: Møller, 1893–1901 [vols. 1–3: text and critical apparatus; vol. 4: interpretations of verses]; Finnur Jónsson, ed. *Heimskringla*. Copenhagen: Gad, 1911; rpt. 1925 [one-volume rev. rpt. of text in 1893–1901 ed.]; Bjarni Aðalbjarnarson, ed. *Heimskringla*. 3 vols. Íslenzk fornrit, 26–8. Reykjavik: Hið íslenzka fornritafélag, 1941–51. **Tr.**: [All have useful introductions.] Laing, Samuel, trans. *Snorri Sturluson. Heimskringla: Sagas of the Norse Kings*. rev. ed. Peter Foote. London: Dent, 1961; Simpson, Jacqueline, ed. *Snorri Sturluson. Heimskringla: The Olaf Sagas*. 2 vols. London: Dent; New York: Dutton, 1964 [also a revision of Laing's 1844 translation]; Hollander, Lee M., trans. *Heimskringla: History of the Kings of Norway*. Austin: American-Scandinavian Foundation; University of Texas Press, 1964; Magnus Magnusson and Hermann Pálsson, trans. *King Harald's Saga: Harald Hardradi of Norway*. Harmondsworth: Penguin, 1966 [*Haralds saga Sigurðarsonar*]. **Bib.**: Halldór Hermannsson. *Bibliography of the Sagas of the Kings of Norway*. Islandica, 3. Ithaca: Cornell University Library, 1910; Halldór Hermannsson. *The Sagas of the Kings (Konunga sögur) and the Mythical-Heroic Sagas (Fornaldar sögur): Two Bibliographical Supplements*. Islandica, 26. Ithaca: Cornell University Press, 1937. **Lit.**: Storm, Gustav. *Snorre Sturlassöns Historieskrivning*. Copenhagen: Luno, 1873; Sigurður Nordal. *Om Olaf den helliges saga*. Copenhagen: Gad, 1914; Sigurður Nordal. *Snorri Sturluson*. Reykjavik: Þór. B. Þorláksson, 1920; rpt. Reykjavik: Helgafell, 1973; Bjarni Aðalbjarnarson. *Om de norske kongers sagaer*. Skrifter utgitt av Det Norske Videnskaps-Akademi i Oslo. II. Hist.-filos. Klasse, 1936, no. 4. Oslo: Dybwad, 1937; Lie, Hallvard. *Studier i Heimskringlas stil: Dialogene og talene*. Skrifter utgitt av Det Norske Videnskaps-Akademi i Oslo. II. Hist.-filos. Klasse, 1936, no. 5. Oslo: Dybwad, 1937; Beyschlag, Siegfried. *Konungasögur: Untersuchungen zur Königssaga bis Snorri*. Bibliotheca Arnamagnæana, 8. Copenhagen: Munksgaard, 1950; Jakob Benediktsson. "Hvar var Snorri nefndur höfundur Heimskringlu?" *Skírnir* 129 (1955), 118–27; Sandvik, Gudmund. *Hovding og konge i Heimskringla*. Avhandlinger fra Universitetets Historiske Seminar, 9. Oslo: Akademisk Forlag, 1955; Gurevich, A. Ya. "Saga and History: The 'Historical Conception' of Snorri Sturluson." *Mediaeval Scandinavia* 4 (1971), 42–53; Almqvist, Bo. *The Uglier Foot: An Anecdote in Old Icelandic Literature and Its Counterparts in Irish Folk Tradition*. Folklore Studies Pamphlets, 1. Dublin: Comhairle Bhéaloideas Éireann, 1975; Ciklamini, Marlene. "*Ynglinga saga*: Its Function and Its Appeal." *Mediaeval Scandinavia* 8 (1975), 86–99; Kuhn, Hans. "Narrative Structures and Historicity in *Heimskringla*." *Parergon* 15 (1976), 30–42; Lönnroth, Lars. "Ideology and Structure in *Heimskringla*." *Parergon* 15 (1976), 16–29; Martin, John Stanley. "Some Aspects of Snorri Sturluson's View of Kingship." *Parergon* 15 (1976), 43–54; Sogge, Ingebjørg. *Vegar til eit Bilete. Snorre Sturlason og Tore Hund*. Nordisk Institutt, Universitetet i Trondheim, Skrifter, 1. Trondheim: Tapir, 1976; Stefán Karlsson. "Kringum Kringlu." *Landsbókasafn Íslands, Árbók 1976* (1977), 5–25; Andersson, Theodore M. "The Conversion of Norway According to Oddr Snorrason and Snorri Sturluson." *Mediaeval Scandinavia* 10 (1977), 83–95; Ciklamini, Marlene. *Snorri Sturluson*. Twayne's World Authors Series, 493. Boston: Twayne, 1978; Ciklamini, Marlene. "The Folktale in *Heimskringla* (*Hálfdanar saga svarta—Hákonar saga góða*)." *Folklore* 90 (1979), 204–16; Ciklamini, Marlene. "A Portrait of a Politician: Erlingr skakki in *Heimskringla* and in *Fagrskinna*." *Euphorion* 75 (1981), 275–87; Whaley, Diana. "The Miracles of S. Olaf in Snorri Sturluson's

Heimskringla." In *Proceedings of the Tenth Viking Congress*. Ed. James E. Knirk. Universitetets Oldsaksamlings Skrifter, Ny rekke, 9. Oslo: Universitetets Oldsaksamling, 1987, pp. 325–42; Bagge, Sverre. *Society and Politics in Snorri Sturluson's* Heimskringla. Berkeley, Los Angeles, and Oxford: University of California Press, 1991; Whaley, Diana. *Heimskringla: An Introduction*. London: Viking Society for Northern Research, 1991.

Diana Edwards Whaley

[See also: *Ágrip af Nóregs konunga sǫgum*; Annals; *Eirspennill*; *Fagrskinna*; *Flateyjarbók*; *Frríssbók*; *Færeyinga saga*; *Hákonar saga Ívarssonar*; *Hákonar saga gamla Hákonarsonar*; *Hallfreðar saga*; Homilies (West Norse); *Hulda-Hrokkinskinna*; *Jómsvíkinga saga*; *Knýtlinga saga*; *Konungasögur*; *Lausavísur*; *Magnúss saga lagabœtis*; *Morkinskinna*; *Óláfr Tryggvason*; *Óláfs saga helga*; *Óláfs saga Tryggvasonar*; *Orkneyinga saga*; Sighvatr Þórðarson; Skaldic Verse; *Skjǫldunga saga*; *Snorra Edda*; Snorri Sturluson; *Sturlunga saga*; *Sverris saga*; *Þáttr*; Þórarinn loftunga; *Ynglinga saga*]

Heiti (pl. *heiti*) is an uncommon Old Norse noun meaning "name, appellation," used as a technical term by Snorri Sturluson in his *Prose Edda* to refer to a large number of poetic synonyms employed by skaldic poets. Toward the end of the third section, named *Skáldskaparmál* ("Poetic Diction"), Snorri lists many *heiti* for the main referents of skaldic verse, such as deities, natural phenomena, a variety of animals, the sea, fire, men, and women. Many of the terms used occur only in poetry, and some allude to myth or legend, as when Fáfnir (the name of the man-turned-dragon killed by the hero Sigurðr) is given as a *heiti* for "serpent." Snorri cites a range of permissible terms for each of these key concepts; for example, he says a raven may be called "crow, Huginn, Muninn [these two after Óðinn's two ravens, *Grímnismál*, st. 20], secure-mood, early-flier, year-counter, flesh-marker" (trans. Faulkes 1987: 138).

Snorri differentiates three basic categories of skaldic diction, which he calls *heiti*, *fornafn*, and *kenning*, but immediately complicates this tripartite division by saying that certain kennings for Óðinn are called *kennt heiti*. Thus, the simplex *heiti* seems to be a cover term for at least two categories of poetic diction. Halldór Halldórsson (1975: 15–6) has suggested that Snorri probably had the medieval grammarians' definition of a synonym in mind when he used the term (*cf.* Old Norse *heita* 'to have a name, be called'). Snorri defines *heiti* as "to utter the name of each thing as it is called," *at nefna hvern lvt, sem heitir* (ed. Finnur Jónsson 1931: 86), and this definition is comparable to Priscian's formulation that synonyms signify one and the same thing (Clunies Ross 1987: 48–9). Snorri possibly preferred the term *heiti* over *nafn* 'name' because it was sometimes used in other Old Icelandic contexts for names whose forms betrayed the circumstances of their coinage (Clunies Ross 1987: 46–7).

The difference between a simple (*ókennt*) *heiti*, such as "sparkler" for "fire," and a *kennt heiti* or *kenning* like "Kraki's seed" for "gold" seems to be, first, that the kenning is a periphrasis (although the raven examples given above show that Snorri did not by any means consistently maintain this distinction), and, second, that the kenning signaled by its very formulation something of the circumstances that gave rise to the periphrasis.

Some of the MSS in which Snorri's *Edda* has been recorded also contain lists of versified poetic *heiti*, mostly in nonskaldic measures (*e.g.*, *fornyrðislag*, *ljóðaháttr*) called *þular*. Some of these lists are probably quite old, but others are likely to have been composed by people with antiquarian interests in the late 12th century or later (Halvorsen 1976, Amory 1984). Snorri quotes two sections from a *Þorgrímsþula* on horse- and ox-names respectively, and another on famous horses and their riders from a certain *Kálfsvísa* (trans. Faulkes 1987: 136–7). It is generally reckoned that these *þular* and some of the other list poems of the *Poetic Edda* (like *Alvíssmál*) may be reasonably old, and in some cases may display archaic principles of classification (Watkins 1970). Their purpose was probably to provide poets operating in an oral tradition with versified memory aids that functioned like rhyming dictionaries (Turville-Petre 1976: xli), so that they could keep the rich store of skaldic synonyms in mental play while composing.

Why did the poets need such an extensive repertoire of *heiti* and other kinds of poetic diction? It was argued in the last century, a thesis recently revived by Perkins (1984–85), that skaldic diction evolved from a kind of tabu-language associated with seafarers who dared not name the potentially destructive ocean or anything associated with it. Perkins further suggests that skaldic verse developed from rowing chants. Another argument is that the diversity of *heiti* and kennings evolved initially because there was a tabu on the outright naming of the gods; hence, a series of appellatives came into being that avoided naming them directly (Noreen 1921, Lie 1957: 42–59). Frank (1978: 40) has referred to *heiti* as "resonant archaisms" with a semimythological function.

Whatever the merit of these hypotheses, skaldic poetry first appears associated with the courts of late 9th-century Norwegian rulers. Its audience was a sophisticated and aristocratic one, and doubtless appreciated esoteric diction, metrics, and syntax partly for its own sake, partly because it confirmed their social and intellectual superiority to those who remained outside the court circle. The mental agility required to understand indirect references to myth and heroic legend, which *heiti* and kennings demand, was an appropriate quality to be displayed by an aristocratic elite, and this sociocultural phenomenon alone might be sufficient to explain the nature of skaldic diction (Lindow 1976).

Ed.: Finnur Jónsson, ed. *Edda Snorra Sturlusonar*. Copenhagen: Gyldendal, 1931. **Tr.**: Faulkes, Anthony, trans. *Snorri Sturluson. Edda*. Everyman Classics. London and Melbourne: Dent, 1987. **Lit.**: Noreen, Erik. *Studier i fornvästnordisk diktning*. Uppsala: A.-b. Akademiska bokhandeln, 1921; Brodeur, Arthur G. "The Meaning of Snorri's Categories." *University of California Publications in Modern Philology* 36 (1952), 129–47; Lie, Hallvard. *"Natur" og "unatur" i skaldekunsten*. Avhandlinger utg. av Det Norske Videnskaps-Akademi i Oslo. II. Hist.-filos. Klasse 1, 1957. Oslo: Aschehoug, 1957; rpt. in his *Om Sagakunst og Skaldskap. Utvalgte Avhandlinger*. Øvre Ervik: Alvheim & Eide, 1982, pp. 201–315; Lie, Hallvard. "Heiti." *KLNM* 6 (1961), 302–4; Watkins, Calvert. "Language of Gods and Language of Men: Remarks on Some Indo-European Metalinguistic Traditions." In *Myth and Law Among the Indo-Europeans*. Ed. Jaan Puhvel. Berkeley, *etc.*: University of California Press, 1970, pp. 1–17; Halldór Halldórsson. *Old Icelandic Heiti in Modern Icelandic*. University of Iceland Publications in Linguistics, 3. Reykjavik: Institute of Nordic Linguistics, 1975; Halvorsen, E. F. "Þulur." *KLNM* 20 (1976), 403–5; Lindow, John. *Comitatus, Individual and Honor: Studies in North Germanic Institutional Vocabulary*. University of California Publications in Linguistics, 83. Berkeley: University of California Press, 1976; Turville-Petre, E. O. G.

Scaldic Poetry. Oxford: Clarendon, 1976; Frank, Roberta. *Old Norse Court Poetry: The* Dróttkvætt *Stanza.* Islandica, 42. Ithaca and London: Cornell University Press, 1978; Amory, Frederic. "Things Greek and the *Riddarasögur.*" *Speculum* 59 (1984), 509–23; Perkins, Richard. "Rowing Chants and the Origins of *Dróttkvæðr Háttr.*" *Saga-Book of the Viking Society* 21.3–4 (1984–85), 155–221; Clunies Ross, Margaret. *Skáldskaparmál: Snorri Sturluson's ars poetica and Medieval Theories of Language.* Viking Collection, 4. Odense: Odense University Press, 1987.

Margaret Clunies Ross

[See also: Eddic Poetry; *Fornafn*; Kennings; Skaldic Verse; *Snorra Edda*; Snorri Sturluson]

Helga þáttr ok Úlfs

Helga þáttr ok Úlfs ("The Tale of Helgi and Úlfr"). This brief pseudo-historical tale is set in Orkney and the Celtic West at the time of Earl Sigurðr digri ("the fat") Hlǫðvisson, *i.e.*, in the early 11th century. It consists of two episodes: the confrontation between the Vikings Helgi and Úlfr illi ("the wicked") because of the slaying of Helgi's father by Úlfr, and the miraculous good fortune of Helgi's son, Bárðr, whom St. Peter rewarded for unquestioning generosity by giving him property and a bishopric in Ireland. The tale is preserved toward the end of *Flateyjarbók* (written 1387–1390) in the hand of the second scribe.

Sigurðr Nordal made the plausible suggestion that this *þáttr* found its way into *Flateyjarbók* by thematic association with *Orkneyinga saga*, which precedes it in the same section of the MS. Finnbogi Guðmundsson speculated that it might even be the work of the *Flateyjarbók* scribe, Magnús Þórhallsson. It is a primitively motivated combination of traditional revenge motifs in the first episode with a pious exemplum in the second episode, and there is certainly no reason to suppose that the text significantly antedates the vellum in which it was recorded. Apart from the remarks of its Icelandic editors, the *þáttr* has not attracted critical attention.

Ed.: Sigurður Nordal, *et al.*, eds. *Flateyjarbók.* 4 vols. Akranes: Flateyjarútgáfan, 1944–45, vol. 4, pp. xii, 242–5; Finnbogi Guðmundsson, ed. *Orkneyinga saga.* Íslenzk fornrit, 34. Reykjavik: Hið íslenzka fornritafélag, 1965, pp. cxxxviii–cxxxix, 385–91.

Michael Chesnutt

[See also: Exempla; *Flateyjarbók*; *Orkneyinga saga*; *Þáttr*]

Helga þáttr Þórissonar

Helga þáttr Þórissonar ("The Tale of Helgi Þórisson"), one of the legendary tales found in *Flateyjarbók* and in other Icelandic MSS, was probably written in the late 13th or early 14th century.

Helgi, the son of a Norwegian farmer, sails on a trading voyage to Finnmǫrk (Finnmark) one summer. On his way home, the ship comes to land one day, and Helgi goes alone into the forest. A darkness descends. Twelve women ride up and set up camp. The leader, Ingibjǫrg, the daughter of Guðmundr of Glæsisvellir, invites Helgi to eat with them and to sleep with her. After three days, she sends him away with gifts. He returns home, but the following Christmas, he is abducted and taken to Glæsisvellir. His father appeals to King Óláfr Tryggvason for help, and the following Christmas, Helgi appears at Óláfr's court with two men who bear gifts of two horns for Óláfr. Óláfr has them filled, the drink blessed and taken to the two men, but they extinguish the lights and disappear with Helgi. He returns alone the following Christmas, released by the power of Óláfr's prayers but blinded by Ingibjǫrg, who tells him that the women of Norway will not enjoy him for

long. He gives an ambiguous description of Guðmundr and his realm. He dies a year later.

The meeting of Helgi and Ingibjǫrg appears to be based on an episode in the *Lai de Lanval* of Marie de France, but Guðmundr and his realm are known from other Norse works, of which the closest is *Þorsteins þáttr bœjarmagns.* The origins seem to be largely in Celtic tales of a delightful otherworld inhabited by beautiful women, a concept with which the author was clearly uneasy. He endeavors to make the visit to Guðmundr's realm seem morally undesirable, and to show that Helgi is released because of the power of Óláfr's prayers. As in *Þorsteins þáttr*, two horns from the otherworld come into Óláfr's possession and vanish when he disappears from his ship in his final battle. The horns, like their bearers, are named Grímar: Grímr is the name used of another otherworld horn in *Þorsteins þáttr.* No literary relationship is discernible between the two *þættir.*

Ed.: Guðbrandr Vigfússon and C. R. Unger, eds. *Flateyjarbók: En Samling af norske Konge-Sagaer med indskudte mindre Fortællinger om Begivenheder i og undenfor Norge samt Annaler.* 3 vols. Christiania [Oslo]: Malling, 1860–68, vol. 1, pp. 359–62; Guðni Jónsson, ed. *Fornaldarsögur Norðurlanda.* 4 vols. Akureyri: Íslendingasagnaútgáfan, 1954, vol. 4, pp. 345–53. Tr.: Simpson, Jacqueline, trans. *The Northmen Talk: A Choice of Tales from Iceland.* London: Phoenix House; Madison: University of Wisconsin Press, 1965, pp. 175–80; Hermann Pálsson and Paul Edwards, trans. *Gautreks saga and Other Medieval Tales.* London: University of London Press; New York: New York University Press, 1968, pp. 141–7; rpt. in their *Seven Viking Romances.* Harmondsworth: Penguin, 1985, pp. 276–81. Lit.: Simpson, Jacqueline. "Grímr the Good—a Magical Drinking Horn." *Études celtiques* 10 (1962–63), 489–515; Simpson, Jacqueline. "Otherworld Adventures in an Icelandic Saga." *Folklore* 77 (1966) 1–20; Power, Rosemary. "*Le Lai de Lanval* and *Helga þáttr Þórissonar.*" *Opuscula* 8. Bibliotheca Arnamagnæana, 38. Copenhagen: Reitzel, 1985, pp. 158–61; Power, Rosemary, "Journeys to the Otherworld in the Icelandic *Fornaldarsögur.*" *Folklore* 96 (1985), 156–75.

Rosemary Power

[See also: *Flateyjarbók*; *Þáttr*; *Þorsteins þáttr bœjarmagns*]

Helgakviða Hjǫrvarðssonar *see* Helgi Poems

Helgakviða Hundingsbana I–II *see* Helgi Poems

Helgi Poems

Helgi Poems. The so-called "Helgi poems" comprise three lays in the *Poetic Edda: Helgakviða Hjǫrvarðssonar* ("The Lay of Helgi Hjǫrvarðsson") and *Helgakviða Hundingsbana I* and *II* ("The Lay of Helgi the Slayer of Hundingr"). The lays are independent units, but are linked by striking similarity of locality, theme, and treatment. Although they form a group by themselves within the category of heroic poems, they are linked with the Vǫlsungar and Niflungar by the poet's making Helgi Hundingsbani a half-brother of Sigurðr Fáfnisbani.

It is clear that *Helgakviða Hjǫrvarðssonar* is not of a piece. Lengthy prose passages unite the three sections of the lay into a loosely knit plot: (1) Hjǫrvarðr, who has three wives, woos Sigrlinn. Her son, dumb from birth, is given the name "Helgi" and a miraculous sword by his beloved-to-be, the valkyrie Sváva. Helgi, awakened to heroism, sets out to avenge his grandfather, and, under Sváva's protection, to do heroic deeds. (2) (*Hrímgerðarmál*) The slaying of the giant Hati introduces a popular flyting match with

Hati's daughter, Hrímgerðr, who, thirsty for revenge, demands intercourse with Helgi in recompense. The *senna* is self-sufficient, even divorced from the plot itself, and is used as a ruse to delay Hrímgerðr until she is petrified in the light of dawn. (3) A nocturnal threat, presented in Helgi's case by Hrímgerðr, appears to his brother, Heðinn, in the form of a witchwoman. She offers him her favors, but he refuses and thus provokes her revenge: Heðinn's fatal vow on the eve of Yuletide to obtain his brother's wife, Sváva. The curse of the witchwoman is thus fulfilled, but we are to understand that she was Helgi's *fylgja*, who has now left him because of his impending death. But the brothers do not come into conflict as threatened; Heðinn, struck with remorse, goes to Helgi and tells him what has happened. The doomed Helgi is soon mortally wounded in the battle. As he dies, he begs Sváva to marry the brother who will avenge him.

In the final form as preserved, *Helgakviða Hjǫrvarðssonar* is a complex of prose and verse in *fornyrðislag* and *ljóðaháttr* meter, without rigid structuring. In relying on prose inserts fleshed out with redundant *fornaldarsaga* motifs, the work resembles a scaled-down *fornaldarsaga* with verse inlays. The reconciliatory ending, with the remorseful hero, Heðinn, and the averted internecine conflict, shows a late conception of heroic poetry.

In *Helgakviða Hundingsbana II*, consisting of prose, stanza sequences, and verse fragments of various date, form, mood, and content, "revenge of kindred" is the leitmotif. (1) The opening part tells how Helgi killed Hundingr and so received his cognomen. (2) Sigrún is described as the valkyrie Sváva reborn. She comes to Helgi and confesses that she helped him in battle. (3) Sigrún is united with Helgi at Arasteinn ("Eagle Rock") after another ride "through air over sea." Meanwhile, he has killed four sons of Hundingr in extensive revenge of kin (prose). Sigrún, betrothed by her father to another, declares her love to Helgi. At Frekasteinn ("Wolf Rock"), he kills not only his rival, but also Sigrún's father, brother, and most of her kin. (4) Here, an abbreviated flyting match follows (cf. *Helgakviða Hundingsbana I*). (5) Helgi, transfixed by the spear that Óðinn lent to Dagr, falls (prose), and Sigrún's brother Dagr's revenge on his brother-in-law repeats the leitmotif. Sigrún, cursing, again turns against her kin, yielding her brother in revenge for Helgi. The speech culminates in Sigrún's threnody. (6) Helgi returns from Valhǫll, and the last passionate reunion of living and dead in the open mound introduces the grim climax of the poem. The preserved version is a problem-conscious, planned compilation. The leitmotif is revenge of kin. Kin-loyalty is opposed by individualistic love (wooing of wife and husband by Helgi and Sigrun, respectively), which itself is overtaken by Dagr's kin-revenge. The compiler is aware of similar problems in the "Hild Saga," to which he alludes.

Unlike *Helgakviða Hundingsbana II*, *Helgakviða Hundingsbana I* is an artistically composed, compactly structured, and thematically coherent work. The basic tale is altered to fit the new message. Tragic elements, such as the death of the bride's hostile father (the story of Hildr, cf. *Helgakviða Hundingsbana II*) and the dark side of heroism (Helgi's death and return) are withheld. This lay is a skaldic hymn to a primeval hero, whose life is glorified from his birth to the triumphant climax. (1) After a brief introduction, Helgi kills Hundingr and his four sons. (2) At Arasteinn, Helgi meets Sigrún, who begs him for help against the hated suitor Hǫðbroddr, promised Sigrún by her father. (3) Helgi assembles his army and sets sail. (4) Upon his arrival in enemy territory, there is a flyting match between Sinfjǫtli, Helgi's (and also Sigurðr's) half-brother, and Guðmundr, Hǫðbroddr's brother. (5) Hǫðbroddr

assembles his army, and they join in battle. (6) Helgi meets Sigrún a second time at Frekasteinn, and the poem ends abruptly, leaving him at the zenith of power, having won Sigrún and Hundingr's land.

The order of the works, *Helgakviða Hundingsbana I*, *Helgakviða Hjǫrvarðssonar*, *Helgakviða Hundingsbana II*, is problematic. The compiler of the *Edda* interposes *Helgakviða Hjǫrvaðssonar* between doublets. *Helgakviða Hjǫrvarðssonar* and *Helgakviða Hundingsbana II* are united by thought of the hero's "rebirth" and the beloved valkyrie (prose only). They thus fulfill the genealogical and chronological organizational criteria of the heroic poems: one heroic family with one reborn Helgi Hundingsbani, half-brother of Sigurðr, up to the characters of *Hamðismál*, Guðrún's last children. *Helgakviða Hundingsbana I* remains atypical, distinct from the other heroic poems of the compilation. Although the initial position of *Helgakviða Hundingsbana I* contradicts the compiler's principle of organization, *Codex Regius*, a copy of a lost exemplar, proves it to be intentional. It is possible that it forms a prologue to the heroic poems following the pattern of *Vǫluspá*, showing the symbolic beginning of the heroic era.

Ed.: Neckel, Gustav, ed. *Edda: Die Lieder des Codex Regius nebst verwandten Denkmälern. I: Text.* 5th ed. rev. Hans Kuhn. Heidelberg: Winter, 1983. **Tr.**: Hollander, Lee M., trans. *The Poetic Edda, Translated with an Introduction and Explanatory Notes.* 2nd rev. ed. Austin: University of Texas Press, 1962; rpt. 1988. **Lit.**: Klingenberg, Heinz. *Edda—Sammlung und Dichtung.* Beiträge zur nordischen Philologie, 3. Basel and Stuttgart: Helbing & Lichtenhahn, 1974; Harris, Joseph. "Eddic Poetry." In *Old Norse–Icelandic Literature: A Critical Guide.* Ed. Carol J. Clover and John Lindow. Islandica, 45. Ithaca and London: Cornell University Press, 1985, pp. 148–9.

Heinz Klingenberg

[See also: *Alvíssmál*; *Codex Regius*; Eddic Meters; Eddic Poetry; *Fornaldarsögur*; Maiden Warriors; *Senna–Mannjafnaðr*; Vǫlsung-Niflung Cycle; *Vǫluspá*; Women in Eddic Poetry]

Helreið Brynhildar

Helreið Brynhildar ("Brynhildr's Ride to Hel"). In the *Codex Regius*, the main MS preserving this anonymous eddic poem, the title reads *Brynhildr reið helveg* ("Brynhildr rode the way to Hel"); the title *Helreið Brynhildar* is a later one. The text of the poem is uncertain; it is probable that some sections are lost, and the order of the stanzas, as they appear in the *Codex Regius*, is questionable. Apart from the *Codex Regius*, the poem and its prose introduction are also cited, with some variations, in *Nornagests þáttr*. Both versions probably go back to the same original text. *Vǫlsunga saga*, which often makes use of eddic heroic poetry, does not use *Helreið Brynhildar*, but probably knew its introductory prose section.

The prose introduction to *Helreið Brynhildar* tells how Brynhildr and Sigurðr both were burned on funeral pyres, after which Brynhildr rode to the underworld on her way to Hel. A giantess prevents her from traveling through her region. The actual poem begins with the accusations of the giantess. She accuses Brynhildr of having brought Gjúki's sons bad luck. Brynhildr then begins her plea: she unintentionally offended Óðinn by helping a young hero, Agnarr, whom she loves, to win victory over an old suitor, Hjálm-Gunnarr. As punishment, Óðinn erected a wall of flame, behind which she was doomed to sleep until awakened by Sigurðr. Sigurðr spent eight nights sleeping next to Brynhildr with a sword separating them. Only when Guðrún, Sigurðr's wife, accuses Brynhildr of having slept in Sigurðr's arms does she realize they had tricked her into marrying Gunnarr; Sigurðr and Gunnarr had exchanged their outward forms. The poem ends with Brynhildr's hope that she now will be united with Sigurðr in death.

In *Helreið Brynhildar*, the stories concerning the awakening of the valkyrie and the wooing of Brynhildr are welded together, leading to contradictions within the narrative. In strophe 11.2, for example, the meeting between Brynhildr and Sigurðr is set at the hall of Brynhildr's foster-father, Heimir, which stands at odds with the statement in strophe 9 that Óðinn bound the valkyrie by a spell and raised up a wall of flames around her. Another peculiarity in the poem is that the wall of flame through which Sigurðr had to pass to awaken Brynhildr was originally presented as a test. In *Helreið Brynhildar*, however, the flames are turned into Óðinn's punishment for Brynhildr's disobedience.

In one sense, the poem's aim is to provide a justification for Brynhildr's actions in seeking vengeance for her supposed betrayal by Sigurðr. The narrative frame of the meeting between Brynhildr and the giantess thus serves to set the stage for Brynhildr's plea. The giantess appears as a representative of public opinion, and Brynhildr defends herself against the accusations. Brynhildr stands as the tragic heroine who turned against Óðinn and thereby unleashed his anger.

The story of Brynhildr's youth (sts. 6 and 7) was composed from older sources; the story of Óðinn's anger and of Brynhildr's sleep are taken from *Sigrdrífumál*. *Helreið Brynhildar* differs from *Sigrdrífumál*, in which the awakening of the valkyrie is treated, by the fact that Sigurðr does not awaken the sleeping valkyrie in order to have her himself, but to give her to his brother-in-law, Gunnarr, as his wife. Hlymdalir as the place of Hymir's home is found only in prose sources and was presumably invented by the author. Apart from *Fáfnismál* (sts. 42–46), *Helreið Brynhildar* is the only eddic poem that parallels Brynhildr with the valkyrie Sigrdrífa and connects the wall of shields with the flames. By equating Brynhildr with Sigrdrífa, it is possible to solve the mystery of Brynhildr's youth. Like Sigurðr, Brynhildr also grew up with a foster-father and does not know her parents.

Helreið Brynhildar is an elegiac, retrospective poem, characterized by sadness and pessimism. The account reaches its climax in Brynhildr's hopes to be reunited with Sigurðr after death.

Ed.: Neckel, Gustav, ed. *Edda: Die Lieder des Codex Regius nebst verwandten Denkmälern. I: Text.* 5th ed. rev. Hans Kuhn. Heidelberg: Winter, 1983. **Tr.**: Hollander, Lee M., trans. *The Poetic Edda, Translated with an Introduction and Explanatory Notes.* 2nd rev. ed. Austin: University of Texas Press, 1962; rpt. 1988, pp. 264–7. **Lit.**: Mohr, Wolfgang. "Entstehungsgeschichte und Heimat der jüngeren Eddalieder südgermanischen Stoffes." *Zeitschrift für deutsches Altertum und deutsche Literatur* 75 (1938), 217–80; Mohr, Wolfgang. "Wortschatz und Motive der jüngeren Eddalieder mit südgermanischem Stoff." *Zeitschrift für deutsches Altertum und deutsche Literatur* 76 (1939), 149–217; Hollander, Lee M. "Notes on Two Eddic Passages: *Helreið Brynhildar*, Stanza 14, and *Baldrs Draumar*, Stanza 12." *Scandinavian Studies* 22 (1950), 166–75; See, Klaus von. "Die Werbung um Brünhild." *Zeitschrift für deutsches Altertum und deutsche Literatur* 88 (1957), 1–20; rpt. in his *Edda, Saga, Skaldendichtung. Aufsätze zur skandinavischen Literatur des Mittelalters.* Heidelberg: Winter, 1981, pp. 194–213; Einar Ól. Sveinsson. *Íslenzkar bókmenntir í fornöld* 1. Reykjavik: Almenna, 1962, pp. 523–5; Hollander, Lee M. "Recent Work and Views on the Poetic Edda." *Scandinavian Studies* 35 (1963), 101–9; Finch, R. G. "Brunhild and Siegfried." *Saga-Book of the Viking Society* 17 (1966–69), 224–60; Andersson, Theodore M. *The Legend of Brynhild.* Islandica, 43. Ithaca and London: Cornell University Press, 1980; Jónas Kristjánsson. *Eddas and Sagas: Iceland's Medieval Literature.* Reykjavik: Hið íslenska bókmentafélag, 1988.

Stefanie Würth

[**See also**: *Codex Regius*; Eddic Poetry; Maiden Warriors; *Nornagests þáttr, Reginsmál* and *Fáfnismál; Sigrdrífumál*; Vǫlsung-Niflung Cycle; Women in Eddic Poetry]

Hemings þáttr Áslákssonar

Hemings þáttr Áslákssonar ("The Tale of Hemingr Ásláksson") tells the story of a legendary Norwegian athlete who incurs the enmity of King Haraldr harðráði ("hard-ruler") Sigurðarson by proving himself superior to the king in contests in archery, swimming, and skiing. He is saved from certain death by the intervention of St. Ólafr, takes refuge in England, and is instrumental in bringing about the death of Haraldr harðráði at the battle of Stamford Bridge in 1066. After the defeat and apparent death of King Harold Godwinsson at the battle of Hastings that same year, Hemingr retires with the secretly resuscitated king into a hermit's cell.

The *þáttr* is not recorded in complete form in any early manuscript. The first part, which describes the athletic contests, is obviously dependent on the same folklore motifs as accounts of the exploits of other legendary heroes, such as Vǫlundr's brother Egill, Saxo's Palnatóki, and the Swiss national hero, William Tell. This part is found in two related versions, one in a 15th-century hand in *Flateyjarbók* (GkS 1005 fol.) and the other in a 16th-century hand in *Hrokkinskinna* (GkS 1010 fol.). The second part of the *þáttr*, largely dependent on *Haralds saga Sigurðarsonar* but with much additional material, is found in *Hauksbók* (AM 544 4to) in Haukr Erlendsson's (d. 1334) hand.

Hemingr, the undoubted hero of the first part of the *þáttr*, plays a comparatively insignificant role in the second, while Haraldr harðráði, who is depicted as a cruel and ridiculously proud tyrant in the first part, appears as a doomed but noble hero in the second. It has therefore been suggested that the two parts did not originally belong together. There are, however, several textual links between them, and a transcript made in the winter of 1697–1698 of a now-lost leaf of *Hauksbók* contains text of the *þáttr* that overlaps with that surviving in *Hrokkinskinna*. The popularity of the *þáttr* in Iceland is shown by the survival of copies of more of less complete versions of it in over forty MSS, ranging in date from the 14th to the 18th century. It also formed the basis for two sets of *rímur*, one dating from the 16th century and the other composed by Benedikt Sigurðsson in 1729.

Ed.: Gudbrand Vigfusson, ed., and George W. Dasent, trans. *Icelandic Sagas and Other Historical Documents Relating to the Settlements and Descents of the Northmen on the British Isles.* 4 vols. Rolls Series, 88. London: Eyre and Spottiswoode, 1887–94; rpt. Millwood: Kraus, 1964, vol. 1, pp. 347–87; Fellows Jensen, Gillian, ed. *Hemings þáttr Áslákssonar.* Editiones Arnamagnæanæ, ser. B, vol. 3. Copenhagen: Munksgaard, 1962. **Tr.**: Gudbrand Vigfusson, ed., and George W. Dasent, trans. *Icelandic Sagas and Other Historical Documents*, vol. 3, pp. 374–415; Simpson, Jacqueline, trans. *The Northmen Talk: A Choice of Tales from Iceland.* London: Phoenix House; Madison: University of Wisconsin Press, 1965 [a translation under the title "The Battles of 1066" of the second part of the *þáttr* in Gudbrand Vigfusson's edition occupies pp. 101–18].

Gillian Fellows-Jensen

[See also: *Flateyjarbók*; *Hauksbók*; *Hulda-Hrokkinskinna*; *Rímur*; Stamford Bridge, Battle of; *Þáttr*]

Henrik Harpestreng *see* **Harpestreng, Henrik**

Hermanns saga ok Jarlmanns *see* **Jarlmanns saga ok Hermanns**

Hertig Fredrik av Normandie *see* **Eufemiavisorna**

Hervarar saga ok Heiðreks konungs ("The Saga of Hervǫr and King Heiðrekr") is a *fornaldarsaga* composed around 1250. The saga is extant in three basic versions: R, U, and H. Version R, which is probably closest to the original, is best represented by GkS 2845 4to, a late 14th- or early 15th-century vellum MS, with one page missing, containing the dialogue between Hervǫr [I] and Angantýr [II] and the greater part of *Hlǫðskviða*. Version U is known from several late paper MSS, especially a paper copy in Uppsala (R:715), AM 203 fol., and from an abstract made in the winter of 1596/7 by Arngrímur Jónsson (Jakob Benediktsson 1950: 350–4). Although H is generally close to U, it also makes use of a version close to the R text. Its basic text is *Hauksbók* (*ca.* 1330s; AM 544 4to).

The author of the saga attempted, not always successfully, to combine a number of stories and poems into a single coherent narrative. The various components are related to each other by a fictional genealogy and by the motif of the sword Tyrfingr, which must take a man's life whenever it is unsheathed. The main divisions of the saga are as follows:

(1) The origin of Tyrfingr (two prose versions), shorter in R (ed. Tolkien 1960: 2) and longer (U, H; ed. Tolkien 1960: 66–8).

(2) The battle of Sámsey (Samsø), in which Tyrfingr's owner, Angantýr, and his eleven brothers are defeated by Ǫrvar-Oddr and the Swedish Hjálmarr. Hjálmarr is also slain, but lives long enough to send a message to his love in "Hjálmarr's death song." A longer version of this poem is contained in *Ǫrvar-Odds saga*.

(3) Angantýr has a daughter, Hervǫr, who grows up with her grandfather, Earl Bjartmarr of Aldeigjuborg (Old Ladoga). Her father's identity has been kept from her; when she learns it, she dons armor and leads a Viking ship to Sámsey. The poem "The Waking of Angantýr" describes her visit to the grave mound and the recovery of Tyrfingr.

(4) Heiðrekr, son of Hervǫr and Guðmundr of Glæsisvellir, kills his brother with Tyrfingr. Exiled for this slaying, he receives from his father seven "wise counsels" (six in R and U), all of which he proceeds to break. Interwoven with the story of the broken counsels is that of the birth of his two sons, Angantýr (III), whose mother is a princess of Reiðgotaland, and the illegitimate Hlǫðr, whose mother is a princess of Húnaland. The episode ends with a riddle contest between Heiðrekr and the disguised Óðinn that results in Heiðrekr's death. While the frame story of this contest resembles those of other eddic wisdom poems, the riddles themselves (*Heiðreks gátur*) are among the few examples of the genre from medieval Scandinavia.

(5) In the final episode, Heiðrekr's two sons come to blows over the division of his kingdom. The narrative is adorned with the strophes of the poem called *Hlǫðskviða* or "The Battle of the Goths and Huns"; both describe the battle in which Angantýr slays his brother with Tyrfingr. While the story recounted has undoubtedly undergone many changes in the course of time, some of the place-names, eseially those mentioned in the poem, indicate their possible origin in the 5th or 6th century.

The main MS of the U version, AM 203 fol., follows the saga by a genealogy that relates Angyntýr to King Ingi II Hallsteinsson of Sweden (d. 1130). This material may well be derived from the works of Icelandic historians of the early 12th century (Ellehøj 1965, Pritsak 1981).

The first edition of the *Hervarar saga* (version U) was made by Olaus Verelius: *Hervarar saga på Gammal Götska* (Uppsala 1672). In 1873, Bugge edited the R-version (according to him, version II) with the combined H and U versions (his version I), but Heinzel (1887) proclaimed that Bugge's versions I and II should be rather regarded as two independent stories. This view was challenged by Ivan Šarovol's'kyj (1906–07), who argued that both H and R go back to the one and the same lost version of the saga, while U represents the contaminated version.

In a series of four articles (1913–27), Andrews resurrected version U, arguing that both U and R represent in their general makeup the original saga, while H was the product of the later scribe.

Jón Helgason (1924) distinguished two versions of the saga. His *Heiðreks saga* contains a diplomatic edition of R, with H printed under it (pp. 1–88) and U following (pp. 89–161). According to Tolkien (1960), R is the closest witness of the original called A (composed *ca.* 1250), while U and H descend from the next version of the saga (X, *ca.* 1300); H, however, is nothing but a careless abridgment of X.

Ed.: Bugge, Sophus, ed. *Norrøne Skrifter af sagnhistorisk Indhold 3*. Christiania [Oslo]: Det norske Oldskriftselskab, 1873; Jón Helgason, ed. *Heiðreks saga. Hervarar saga ok Heiðreks konungs*. Samfund til udgivelse af gammel nordisk litteratur, 48. Copenhagen: Jørgensen, 1924; rpt. 1976; Turville-Petre, Gabriel, ed. *Hervarar saga ok Heiðreks*. Introduction by Christopher Tolkien. Text Series, 2. London: Viking Society for Northern Research, 1956; Tolkien, Christopher, ed. and trans. *Saga Heiðreks konungs ins vitra; The Saga of King Heidrek the Wise*. London: Nelson, 1960. **Lit.**: Heinzel, Richard. *Über die Hervararsaga*. Vienna: Gerold, 1887; Heusler, Andreas. "Die altnordischen Rätsel." *Zeitschrift des Vereins für Völkerkunde* 11 (1901), 117–49; Šarovol's'kyj, Ivan. *Skazanie o meče Tjurfinge*. 2 vols. Kiev: [n.p.], 1906; Boer, R. C. "Om Hervararsaga." *Aarbøger for nordisk Oldkyndighed og Historie* (1911), 1–80; Andrews, A. LeRoy. "Studies in the Fornaldarsögur Norðrlanda, II: The Hervarar Saga." *Modern Philology* 11 (1913–14), 313–78; 18 (1920), 93–100; 21 (1923), 187–99; 25 (1927), 149–61; Löwenthal, F. *Studien zum germanischen Rätsel*. Heidelberg: Winter, 1914, pp. 6–14; Schück, H. *Studier i "Hervararsagan."* Uppsala: Almqvist & Wiksell, 1918; Liestøl, K. "Die guten Ratschläge in der Hervararsaga." In *Festschrift für Eugen Mogk zum 70. Geburtstag 19. Juli 1924*. Halle: Niemeyer, 1924, pp. 841–98; Malone, Kemp. "Widsith and the Hervararsaga." *Publications of the Modern Language Association* 40 (1925), 769–813; Genzmer, F. "Vorzeitssaga und Heldenlied." In *Festschrift für P. Kluckhohn und Heinrich Schneider gewidmet zu ihrem 60. Geburtstag*. Tübingen: Mohr, 1948, pp. 1–31; Dickins, Bruce. "Two Little-Known Renderings of the Old Norse 'Waking of Angantýr.'" *Saga-Book of the Viking Society* 16 (1962–65), 80–8; Ellehøj, Svend. *Studier over den ældste norrøne historieskrivning*. Bibliotheca Arnamagnæana, 26. Copenhagen: Munksgaard, 1965 [esp. pp. 85–108]; Pritsak, O. *The Origin of Rus': 1. Old Scandinavian Sources Other than the Sagas*. Cambridge: Harvard University Press, 1981, pp. 188–225, 753–60.

Omeljan Pritsak

[See also: *Folklore*; *Fornaldarsögur*; *Hauksbók*; *Hlǫðskviða*; *Riddles*; *Ǫrvar-Odds saga*]

Hirð is a common term for the retinue of warriors accompanying kings or great men in the Nordic countries. The word is derived from Anglo-Saxon *hīred* 'family, household.' Most of what is known of the institution concerns the king's *hirð*. As it appears in Danish sources of the 11th and 12th centuries and Norwegian ones of the 12th and 13th, this group was a corporation with a special ceremony of reception for new members and regular meetings, which functioned as a court of law for its members and eventually came to serve as a council for the king. The Danish law of the *hirð* (the *Vederlov*) claims to have been issued by Knud (Cnut) the Great, but this ascription is uncertain. The most detailed information comes from Norway (*Hirðskrá*). The Norwegian *hirð* of the 12th and 13th centuries was divided into three groups: the *hirðmenn* ("hirð-men"); the *gestir* ("guests"), who did police work for the king; and *kertisveinar*, young men who served as pages. The first group was further divided into several different ranks, with the *hirð* officials on top; then the *lendir menn* ("landed men"), after 1277 named barons; the *skutilsveinar* (men who carry dishes at the table), after 1277 named knights; and finally the ordinary *hirðmenn*. In Sweden, "men" in the service of the king, duke, or bishop are referred to in the laws, but we have no definite information on the *hirð* as an organization. Even the Icelandic chieftains had their retainers, but the term *hirð* seems not to have been used of them until the mid-13th century, near the end of the Free State period. In addition, prominent Icelanders were often attached to the *hirð* of the Norwegian king.

We can distinguish three stages in the evolution of the *hirð*. During the first, in Denmark until the 12th century, in Norway until the first half of the 13th, the *hirð* was primarily a warrior organization, attached to the king's person. Most of its members probably lived near the king. The relationship between the king and his men was based on some sort of contract, which could be terminated by both parties. During the Norwegian civil wars, a king's *hirð* was usually dissolved at his death. The king's *hirð* was not the only one that existed, though it had clearly surpassed those of other great men in importance from the end of the Viking Age.

In the second stage, with the growing centralization of the Nordic kingdoms, this body of retainers changed into an organization of the aristocracy of the realm. Both Danish and Norwegian sources distinguish quite early between resident and nonresident members of the *hirð*. In the early Middle Ages, the former were the normal category, but most members became nonresident in Denmark from the 12th century and in Norway at least from the mid-13th, after the civil wars. On the other hand, the attachment to the king became permanent, and an ideology was developed that strongly emphasized the *hirðmaðr*'s ("hirð-man's") submission to the king and the loyal service owed to him. In both countries, the *hirð* served as an instrument in attaching the majority of the leading men to the king's direct service. The change in Denmark coincides with the change in military organization from the popular levy to an elite army of heavily armed men, who were rich enough to become professional warriors and in addition received tax compensation. These men became *hirðmenn* without ever residing at court.

Although there was also some military professionalization in Norway during the civil wars, no corresponding change took place there. The development of the royal administration, however, had partly the same effect as in Denmark. A large number of the *hirðmenn* became local administrators. In addition, the king sought to attach prominent men in the districts to his service by making

them *hirðmenn*. Thus, the *hirð* grew numerically, but only a relatively small percentage remained at court: on the one hand, the most prominent members of the royal household and the central administration; and on the other, younger members of the aristocracy who served at court for a shorter period.

This development then logically led into the third stage, the dissolution of the *hirð*. The *hirð* had served to create an aristocracy of the realm. The members of this aristocracy, however, were now distinguished from the rest of the population through arms and privileges rather than membership in an organization. There was also a growing tendency, above all in Denmark, for membership of the aristocracy in practice to become dependent on birth. Although its formal organization still existed in Denmark in the late 13th century, the *hirð* had lost its importance long before that. The development went more slowly in Norway, but the unions with the other Nordic countries from 1319, and the fact that the king usually lived abroad, precipitated the decline of the *hirð*, although the term *hirðmaðr* occurs in the sources as late as the 15th century.

Lit.: Löfqvist, Karl-Erik. *Om riddarväsen och frälse i nordisk medeltid*. Lund: Ohlsson, 1935; Hamre, Lars, *et al*. "Hird." *KLNM* 6 (1961), 568–80; Benedictow, Ole J. "Norge." In *Den nordiske adel i senmiddelalderen. Struktur, funtioner og internordiske relationer. Rapporter til det nordiske historikermøde i København 1971.* Copenhagen: [s.n.], 1971; Helle, Knut. *Norge blir en stat 1130–1319.* 2nd ed. Bergen, Oslo, and Tromsø: Universitetsforlaget, 1974; Skovgaard-Petersen, Inge, *et al*. *Danmarks historie* 2. Copenhagen: Gyldendal, 1977; Lund, Niels, and Kai Hørby. *Dansk socialhistorie.* Copenhagen: Gyldendal, 1979.

Sverre Bagge

Historia de antiquitate regum Norwagiensium *see* **Theodoricus**

Historia Norwegiae. Together with the *Historia de antiquitate regum Norwagiensium* of Theodoricus monachus, the *Historia Norwegiae* can be considered among the most ancient documents concerning the history of Norway. The *Historia Norwegiae* is a minor work found at fols. 1–12r of a paper MS containing other historical texts and documents concerning the Orkney Islands, Scotland, and Norway. The MS was discovered in the library of the baron of Panmure in Scotland and was published for the first time in Oslo in 1850. Storm considered the Dalhousie MS (the name of the owner) to have been composed between 1443 and 1460; however, recent examination by Chesnutt (1985) demonstrates that it cannot have been compiled before about 1500.

The text of the *Historia Norwegiae* is much older than the age of the MS. A reference to a volcanic earthquake and eruption as contemporaneous suggests 1211 as a *terminus a quo*.

We do not know the name or the nationality of the author; all facts that can be deduced depend upon internal evidence. Munch (1850) and Bugge (1873) contend that the detailed description of the Orkney Islands provides evidence for the author's birthplace. Storm (1873) argues to the contrary, that such a description is no more accurate than for other areas, and that the strong nationalistic stamp of the author denotes Norwegian origin.

The work consists of a prologue addressed to a certain Agnellus, who has not been identified with certainty, followed by a geographical description of Norway, the Faroe Islands, the Orkney

Islands, and Iceland, with a digression on the custom and dress of the Lapps. This geographical section is followed by a summary of a history of Norway beginning with the royal house of the Ynglingar and ending with the return from England in 1015 of St. Óláfr. Because of the fragmentary state of the MS, it cannot be said how far the story continued in its original form. However, it seems from the prologue that a third section followed that was dedicated to the struggle between paganism and Christianity. The chronicle was probably composed in Norway.

The problem of the sources is very complex. Among the Latin sources can be mentioned Adam of Bremen's *Gesta Hammaburgensis ecclesiae pontificum* and works by Honorius Augustodunensis and Solinus. When the author traces the pedigree of the kings of England, he clearly follows an English chronicle known from the great compilation of Roger of Hoveden. In the chapter on the Lapps, there is a description of the beaver, hunted by the Lapps, closely resembling that given by Giraldus Cambrensis in the *Itinerary Through Wales*, and which suggests that the two descriptions probably descend from a common source. It is generally believed that the *Historia Norwegiae* is based largely on an older Latin work, which was also one of the sources of the *Ágrip af Nóregs konunga sǫgum*. Ulset (1983: 150), however, recently proposed a stemma showing that the *Historia Norwegiae* and Theodoricus's work were among the sources used by the author of *Ágrip*, thus confirming an earlier proposal by Storm.

The style is characterized by florid rhetoric, which attests to the wide range of the author's reading.

Ed.: Munch, P. H., ed. *Symbolae ad historiam antiquiorem rerum Norvegicarum*. Kristiania [Oslo]: Warner, 1850; Storm, Gustav, ed. *Monumenta historica Norwegiæ*. Kristiania [Oslo]: Brøgger, 1880; rpt. 1973, pp. 69–124, 203–24. **Lit.**: Storm, Gustav. "Norske historieskrivere paa kong Sverres tid." *Aarbøger for nordisk Oldkyndighed og Historie* 6 (1871), 410–31; Bugge, Sophus. "Bemærkninger om den i Skotland fundne latinske Norges krønike." *Aarbøger for nordisk Oldkyndighed og Historie* 8 (1873), 1–49; Storm, Gustav. "Yderligere Bemærkninger om den skotske Historia Norvegiae." *Aarbøger for nordisk Oldkyndighed og Historie* 8 (1873), 361–85; Finnur Jónsson. "Ágrip." *Aarbøger for nordisk Oldkyndighed og Historie* 63 (1928), 261–317; Skard, E. "Målet i Historia Norwegiae." In *Skrifter utgitt av Det Norske Videnskaps-Akademi i Oslo*. Hist.-filos. Klasse, 1930, 5; Lehmann, P. *Skandinaviens Anteil an der lateinischen Literatur und Wissenschaft des Mittelalters*. 2. Stück. Sitzungsberichte der Bayerischen Akademie der Wissenschaften, Philosophisch-historische Abteilung, Jahrgang 1937, Heft 7. Munich: Bayerischen Akademie der Wissenschaften, 1937; Turville-Petre, G. *Origins of Icelandic Literature*. Oxford: Clarendon, 1953, pp. 169–75; Ellehøj, Svend. *Studier over den ældste norrøne historieskrivning*. Bibliotheca Arnamagnæana, 26. Copenhagen: Munksgaard, 1965, pp. 142–74; Ulset, Tor. *Det genetiske forholdet mellom Ágrip, Historia Norwegiæ og Historia de antiquitate regum Norwagiensium: En analyse med utgangspunkt i oversettelsesteknikk samt en diskusjon omkring begrepet "latinisme" i samband med norrøne tekster*. Oslo: Novus, 1983; Chesnutt, Michael. "The Dalhousie Manuscript of the Historia Norvegiae." *Opuscula* 8. Bibliotheca Arnamagnæana, 37. Copenhagen: Reitzel, 1985, pp. 54–95.

Carlo Santini

[**See also:** Adam of Bremen; *Ágrip af Nóregs konunga sǫgum*; *Konungasögur*, Theodoricus: *Historia de antiquitate regum Norwagiensium*]

Hjálmþés saga ("The Saga of Hjálmþér") probably dates from the 15th century. Its primary MS, AM 109a III 8vo, a paper book, was produced in the 17th century by Ólafur Jónsson, probably in Eyjafjörður in the north of Iceland. Some of its verses predate the surrounding prose. Comparisons by Kölbing and Björn K. Þórólfsson of the late 14th-century *Hjálmþés rímur* with the extant text of *Hjálmþés saga* suggest the existence of an earlier, more original version of the story, probably composed around 1300.

Best classified as a *lygisaga*, *Hjálmþés saga* was, ironically, first published for its supposed historical value by Peringskiöld at Uppsala in 1720 because of what he regarded as its evidence of Sweden's noble past. This publication fell among a spate of editions of later, fantastic sagas produced at the Antikvitetsarkiv during the late 17th and early 18th centuries in that fervor of Rudbeckian scholarship supporting Sweden's Stormaktstid ("time of great power"). Editions from the early 19th century on, however, have regarded the saga's historicity in a less enthusiastic light. Aside from the hero's homeland, Mannheimar, equated by Rudbeck with Atlantis and thus with Sweden, the place-names of *Hjálmþés saga*, including such items as Syría, Arabia, Serkland, and Bláland, are entirely foreign to Scandinavia. Personal names are also largely of foreign origin: Marsibil, Lúða, and Núdus.

The saga's importance lies in its folk motifs, which have analogues in continental Scandinavian tradition but more interestingly in Celtic folklore. The narrative presents the adventures of Hjálmþér, son of King Ingi of Mannheimar, and his friend Ǫlvir. The hero is in conflict with Lúða, a wicked and amorous stepmother who places upon him a spell called an *álǫg* (related to the Celtic *geis*) that forces him to seek out a princess, Hervǫr Hundingr's daughter. Once Hjálmþér locates her, Hundingr assigns him a dangerous task called a *forsending* ("dangerous mission"), in this instance, initially to obtain the horns of a dangerous ox, although the requirements eventually become threefold. The narrative abounds in folk motifs, the wicked stepmother, the *álǫg*, and the *forsending* having been examined most closely for Celtic analogues. In particular, "Kulhwch and Olwen," in the *Mabinogion*, and "The Adventures of Art son of Conn, and the Courtship of Delbchaen" have been viewed as close to some parts of *Hjálmþés saga*. Two passages have been shown to be later interpolations, in particular a crudely inserted Viking episode, in chs. 4 and 5, from ch. 20 of *Þorsteins saga Víkingssonar*. Both style and content suggest a diversity of sources, with part of the work sounding like later Icelandic sagas generally, but the amorous stepmother Lúða sounding in her more intense moments as if she came from a Greek romance.

Ed.: Peringskiöld, Johan Fredrich, ed. *Hjalmters och Olvers saga*. Stockholm: Horrn, 1720; Guðni Jónsson, ed. *Fornaldar sögur Norðurlanda*. 4 vols. Akureyri: Íslendingasagnaútgáfan, 1954, vol. 4, pp. 179–243; Harris, Richard. "Hjálmþérs saga: A Scientific Edition." Diss. University of Iowa, 1970. **Lit.**: Kölbing, Eugen. *Beiträge zur vergleichenden Geschichte der romantischen Poesie und Prosa des Mittelalters*. Breslau: Koebner, 1874, pp. 200–7; Gould, Chester. "The Source of an Interpolation in the Hjalmtérs saga ok Olvis." *Modern Philology* 7 (1909), 207–16; Björn K. Þórólfsson. *Rímur fyrir 1600*. Fræðafjelagsins um Ísland og Íslendinga, 9. Copenhagen: Møller, 1934; Einar Ól. Sveinsson. *Um Íslenzkar Þjóðsögur*. Reykjavik: Ísafold, 1940, pp. 217–25, 241–50; Nilsson, Gun. "Den isländska litteraturen i Stormaktstidens Sverige." *Scripta Islandica* 5 (1954), 19–41; Einar Ól. Sveinsson. "Celtic Elements in Icelandic Tradition." *Béaloideas* 16 (1959), 3–24; Hermann Pálsson. "Hjálmþérs saga ok Ölvis." In *Dictio-*

nary of the Middle Ages. Ed. Joseph R. Strayer. New York: Scribner, 1982–89, vol. 6, pp. 266–7.

Richard Harris

[See also: *Fornaldarsögur*; *Lygisaga*; *Þorsteins saga Víkingssonar*]

Hlǫðskviða ("The Lay of Hlǫðr"), or "The Battle of the Goths and the Huns," although not included in the *Codex Regius*, is regarded as one of the anonymous heroic lays of the *Poetic Edda*. It is preserved in MSS of *Hervarar saga ok Heiðreks konungs* in the epic meter *fornyrðislag*, and traces of the poetic language are still perceptible in the accompanying prose.

Only the first ten strophes are preserved in the oldest and best version of the poem, R, from the 14th century; the remainder has been transmitted in a 17th-century MS of the U version, which is corrupt in many places.

There is no general agreement where the poem begins. Some scholars argue for the strophe where Angantýr avenges his father's slayers (ed. Tolkien 1960, no. 74), some for the *þula* enumerating the names of those "who ruled over the lands in these days" (no. 75), and others for the strophe where the Hunnish kingdom, the birthplace of Hlǫðr, is mentioned (no. 76). Hence, the number of strophes (or fragments of strophes) varies from thirty-one to thirty-four, depending on the perception of the given scholar.

As in much heroic poetry, the poem presents a war between two peoples as a family conflict, in this case a war between half-brothers, also a common heroic motif. In *Hlǫðskviða*, Angantýr (representing the Goths) and Hlǫðr (representing the Huns) fight over the division of their inheritance, which includes "Tyrfingr," considered by the author of *Hervarar saga* to be an accursed sword, with which Angantýr kills Hlǫðr. "Tyrfingr" is derived from, and must originally have referred to, the Visigothic tribe of the Tervingi.

Hlǫðskviða presents its main characters as if they were historical figures, but there are various schools of thought about their identity. The first is the "plain historical" school, best represented by Nerman (1928), who believed that he had successfully established the heroes of the saga as the ruling dynasty of Reiðgotaland. That Germanic state encompassed, he believed, northeastern Germany, northern Poland, and eastern Prussia. Taking as the basis for chronology the hypothetical date of Ívarr víðfaðmi ("wide-fathoming") Hálfdanarson's death (*ca.* 675) and thirty years for a generation, Nerman arrived at a "historical" genealogy, according to which Angantýr, Hlǫðr, and Hervǫr lived in the first half of the 6th century.

The second, the "epic-historical" school, tried to identify the heroes of the saga and of *Hlǫðskviða* with important personalities of the age of migrations, *i.e.*, the Germanic epic age, thereby blending several personalities into one, or splitting one personality into several, depending on their roles. Heinzel (1887) initiated this approach, following an idea first expressed by Müller (1858) that the "Battle of the Goths and the Huns" was the great historical battle of the year 451 on the Mauriac/Catalaunian Plains, in which Attila the Hun (Humli of the saga and *kviða*), together with the Gepids under Ardaric, the Ostrogoths, and other Hunnic subjects, were decisively defeated by the Roman patrician Aetius, assisted by the Visigoths. From this starting point, Heinzel created an extremely complex and ingenious system of fusions, for example, the name Angantýr derived from Aetius (Agetius), and Hlǫðr from the Frankish Chlodio. Hlǫðr as a character, however, he identified with the Roman general Litorius, a rival of Aetius. Gizurr, Angantýr's adviser, is a composite figure in that he represents three historical personages: the Vandal king Geiseric (d. 477), who instigated Attila's attack on the Visigoths (Gizurr owes his name to him); the bishop of Orleans, St. Anianus, the organizer of the city's defense against the Huns; and a certain anchorite who predicted to Attila his defeat on the eve of the battle of 451.

According to Much (1889), Angantýr and his valkyric sister, Hervǫr, are to be identified with the Langobardic dynasty, specifically, with King Agelmundus (*ca.* 360–400), mentioned in the Old English poem *Widsith*, and his daughter, who, as Paul the Deacon relates, fought against the Vulgars (representing the Huns) in a battle in which the king was killed and the daughter carried off as a prisoner. The battle that inspired the saga was, however, the victory of Lamissio, Agelmundus's successor, over the said Vulgars.

Schück (1918) found a historical prototype for the battle in the struggle between Vinitharius, the king of the Goths and successor of Ermanaric (last quarter of the 4th century), and Balamber, the king of the Huns, who helped the Goth Gesimund. Schütte (1905), who in principle defended the Catalaunian theory, nevertheless proposed his own correction to Heinzel's system. His Heiðrekr was the king of the Gepids (H)Ardaric (Schütte 1933), and the name Hervǫr (Her-vǫr) was originally that of the Hreiðgotic hero Wyrm-here, with the two elements transposed, named in *Widsith* (119a), in other words, the female Hervǫr is in fact the male hero Ormarr (Wyrm-here; Schütte 1935).

Malone (1932; *cf.* 1923) identified the Angantýr of the saga and the *kviða* with the Beowulfian character Ongenþeow of Sweden, and Hlǫðr (*Widsith* Hliþe) with the Beowulfian character Hreðel. Hlǫðr, not Heiðrekr (*Widsith* Heaþoric < *Hǫðrekr), of the saga corresponds to the Geatish leader Hæðcyn of *Beowulf*. Malone then assumes a fusion of Hreðel and Hæðcyn under the name Hlǫðr, since the Beowulfian character Angantýr (Ongenþeow) killed Hæðcyn in battle (Malone 1925, 1939).

No less complex is the hypothesis of Lukman (1946), who decided to pass over Jordanes (who wrote in 551) in favor of the original sources of the 4th century, including Ammianus Marcellinus (*ca.* 330–391). Heiðrekr is Athanaric (Haithanarich; r. *ca.* 369–381), the ruler of the Visigoths; the battle refers to the events of the year 386, when the Ostrogoths under Odotheus appeared on the Danube, and were defeated by a stratagem. The Hlǫðr of the saga is Odotheus.

Rosenfeld (1955) expressed the idea that the only period when the inheritance claims based on a Gothic-Hunnic mixed marriage would be contested was the time of the Gothic-Hunnic struggles after Attila's death. Without dealing with the names of the *Hlǫðskviða*, he suggests that its historic background was the war of 456 conducted by Valamer (Theodoric's uncle) with the Huns coming from the east, over the newly colonized Pannonia.

Tolkien has argued correctly that "to pick about in old histories, looking for names that begin with the same letter or contain one or two of the same consonants as those in one's text, will attain nothing" (1953–57: 155). From this principle, it is clear that the long scholarly battle over the historicity of the *Hlǫðskviða*, the exact date, and the location of the battle of the Goths and the Huns has so far managed only to create a galaxy of diverse, uncompromising opinions and no objective criteria that could be used to settle the dispute. The reason behind this confusion is the dogmatic refusal to part with the idea that the "battle" *must* reflect an important historical event.

It would seem, however, that *Hlǫðskviða* is simply an epic lay governed by its own laws and rules, which are different from the ones that govern historical writing. Like every true epic, *Hlǫðskviða* has telescoped several centuries of history, and transformed its main characters into archetypes. The poet did not use the proper names of historical peoples, but topical appellations symbolizing the role of the characters in the epic's plot, for example, Heiðrekr = Old Norse *heið-rekr* 'the king of the [*Dún* 'Don'] heath'; Angantýr = Old Norse *angan Týr* 'joy, happiness Týr'; Hervǫr = Old Norse *her-vǫr* 'protector of the host' (= the Goths); and Hlǫðr = Old Norse *hlǫðr* 'destroyer, vanquisher.'

The only "historical" aspect of *Hlǫðskviða* is its set of topographic names. These, in fact, do reflect the geography of the Gotish Ukraine during the period of the great migrations, for example, *Danparstaðir* '(Gotish) homestead on the River Dnieper' (its ruins, from the 4th–5th century B.C., comprise the Kamjans'ke Horodyšče on the left bank of the lower Dnieper); *Dúnheiðr* 'the Don[ec'] heath'; *Jassarfjǫll* 'the Jas/Alanian mountains' to the south of the Donec and north of the Suxyj Torec River (Pritsak 1981: 206–14, Beck 1986). But the "Reið-Gothic" layer of the ethnic and geographic names (*Reið*-Gotaland, identified with Jutland, and Garðaríki) must be from about 750–850, and was probably collected later in West Götland.

Ed.: Turville-Petre, Gabriel, ed. *Hervarar saga ok Heiðreks*. Introduction by Christopher Tolkien. Text Series, 2. London: Viking Society for Northern Research, 1956; Jón Helgason, ed. *Kviður af Gotum og Húnum*. Reykjavik: Heimskringla, 1967, pp. 217–46; Tolkien, Christopher, ed. and trans. *Saga Heiðreks konungs in vitra; The Saga of King Heidrek the Wise*. London: Nelson, 1960. **Lit.**: Müller, Peter Erasmus. *Saxonis Grammatici Historia Danica*. Havniae [Copenhagen]: Gyldendal, 1839–58; Heinzel, Richard. "Über die Hervararsaga." *Sitzungsberichte der Wiener Akademie der Wissenschaften* 114 (1887), 417–519; Much, R. "Askibourgion oros." *Zeitschrift für deutsches Alterthum und deutsche Literatur* 33 (1889), 1–13; Much, Rudolf. "Askibourgion oros." *Zeitschrift für deutsches Alterthum und deutsche Literatur* 53 (1889), 1–13; Schütte, Gudmund. "Anganty-Kvadets Geografi." *Arkiv för nordisk filologi* 21 (1905), 30–44; Schück, Henrik. *Studier i Hervararsagan*. Uppsala: Almqvist & Wiksell, 1918; Nerman, Birger. "Forsök till datering av Reidgoternas konungaätt." In *Festkrift til Finnur Jónsson 29. maj 1928*. Ed. Johs. Brøndum-Nielsen et al. Copenhagen: Levin & Munksgaard, 1928, pp. 206–12; Malone, Kemp. "The Hervararsaga." *The Literary History of Hamlet* 1. Heidelberg: Winter, 1923, pp. 150–78; Malone, Kemp. "Widsith and the Hervararsaga." *Publications of Modern Language Association* 40 (1925), 769–813; Malone, Kemp. "Hliþe and Hlǫðr." *Acta Philologica Scandinavica* 6 (1932), 328–31; Schütte, Gudmund. "The Problem of the Hraid-Goths." *Acta Philologica Scandinavica* 8 (1933), 247–61; Schütte, Gudmund. *Gotthiod und Utgard. Altgermanische Sagengeographie in neuer Auffassung*. 2 vols. Copenhagen: Aschehoug, 1935–36; Malone, Kemp. "Humblus and Lotherus." *Acta Philologica Scandinavica* 13 (1939), 201–14; Lukman, N. "Goterne i Heidreks saga. En tradition om Athanaric (†381)?" *Aarbøger for nordisk Oldkyndighed og Historie* (1946), 103–20; Rosenfeld, H. "Wielandlied—Lied von Frau Helchen Söhnen und Hunnenschlachtlied." *Beiträge zur Geschichte der deutschen Sprache und Literatur* 77 (1955), 204–48; Tolkien, Christopher. "The Battle of the Goths and Huns." *Saga-Book of the Viking Society* 14 (1953–57), 141–63; Pritsak, Omeljan. *The Origin of Rus': 1. Old Scandinavian Sources Other than the Sagas*. Cambridge: Harvard University Press, 1981, pp. 188–225, 753–60.

Omeljan Pritsak

[**See also**: Eddic Meters; Eddic Poetry; *Hervarar saga ok Heiðreks konungs*]

Hoards. Deliberate deposits of precious metal in the form of treasure hoards are an important source of evidence for the study of the overseas contacts and the domestic economy of medieval Scandinavia, most notably during the Viking Age; gold and silver, however, were not the only metals hoarded. The medieval hoards may be divided into (1) those that were concealed by the owners with intent to recover them later; and (2) those that were deposited permanently for ritual purposes, as religious offerings. The great majority of hoards dating to the medieval period fall into category (1); in that period it is probable that much treasure was normally kept hidden, unlike the situation in the Bronze and Iron Ages, when there are many impressive metal deposits of a ritual nature known from Scandinavia, particularly in watery places.

Some examples of category (2), ritual hoards, will be considered first. The votive-deposit type of hoard may result from a single act or be the product of accumulation from continuous offerings. Ritual hoards of iron weapons, as found in southern Scandinavia during the Migration Period, are virtually unknown during the Viking Age outside of Gotland; but in 1964, a large find of nearly 300 objects, mostly arrowheads, dating from the 7th to the 10th centuries, was made in Estuna churchyard in Uppland, Sweden. Deposits of *gullgubber*, small gold foils impressed with a design of a man and a woman embracing, are thought to be pagan fertility offerings, such as those found beneath the church at Mære in Trøndelag, Norway. This practice also represents a native religious continuity from the pre-Viking period into the 9th and 10th centuries.

In Lapland, Saami sacrificial sites have accumulated deposits of metal objects (ornaments and arrowheads) from the 11th to the 14th century.

The phenomenon of votive hoards did not end with the conversion of Scandinavia to Christianity, for there are various indications of continuity of belief. An early example is the offering of 110 coins placed beneath the foundations of the first stone church at Sankt Jørgensbjærg in Roskilde, Denmark (*ca.* 1040), while accumulations of coins are regularly revealed by archaeologists excavating beneath wooden floors in medieval Scandinavian churches.

All silver in the Viking Age was imported into Scandinavia either as Viking plunder and tribute or as a result of trade. Viking treasure hoards may be broadly grouped into those that represent an individual's personal ornaments as opposed to commercial wealth, the accumulated capital of a merchant, chieftain, or family. In certain instances, other explanations may have to be sought, such as a metalworker's or tradesman's stock. For instance, hoards of iron blanks, with axe- or spade-shaped blades, were used from the Merovingian period onward as raw material for trade in a form that also came to serve for taxation purposes.

The Viking Age silver-hoard material can be divided into four categories of objects: (1) coins, (2) ingots, (3) ornaments (chiefly rings and brooches), and (4) hack-silver (deliberately cut-up fragments of ingots and ornaments used as "small change"). The characteristic Viking-type hoard, which continued to be deposited in some areas in Scandinavia into the 12th century, is a mixture of most of these elements, although it changed over time, due to the developing sophistication of the Scandinavian economy. Early hoards tend to have a higher proportion of complete ornaments and fewer coins than later hoards, with their numerous coins and highly fragmented hack-silver, often heavily pecked and nicked as the silver quality was checked during transactions.

This development reflects the fact that much of the silver reaching Scandinavia as a result of early Viking activity was converted into ornaments that denoted the status of the wearers, even if the ornaments were later cut up for use in economic transactions. Increasing economic activity required more silver in circulation, and increasing familiarity with the use of coin led to the establishment of Scandinavian coinages.

However, it was only during the 11th century that Scandinavian rulers began to mint their own coins in any quantity, and it was not until the second half of the century that the Danish and Norwegian kings seem to have been able to exclude foreign coin and hack-silver in the transition to a coined-money economy. In Sweden, the process took even longer, and the Viking-type hoard deposited at Burge, Lummelunda, on Gotland (ca. 1140), weighing 10.36 kg. is one of the latest. This hoard is only about a quarter the weight of the greatest Viking treasure known, which was deposited around 905 at Cuerdale in northwestern England, derived from the wealth of the Viking kingdoms of York and Dublin.

Silver hoards continued to be deposited in Scandinavia in the high Middle Ages, but their contents, aside from coins, are rather different, comprising new forms of European ornaments and tableware (*e.g.*, spoons) and Scandinavian folk-costume jewelry. There are, however, four 14th-century hoards known fom Gotland, probably hidden during the raids of the Danish invaders in 1361 (battle of Visby), which contain objects dating back to the 12th century, representing family wealth accumulated over several generations.

In the 9th and 10th centuries, very large numbers of Islamic *dirhams* reached Scandinavia from the East, by way of the Russian river routes to the Baltic, spilling over into the Scandinavian settlements in Britain and Ireland, where twenty hoards have been found containing these Kufic coins. It has been estimated that of the approximately 250,000 foreign Viking Age coins found in Sweden, as many as 100,000 are Islamic, with those of the Sāmānid dynasty in the majority; the mints of Tashkent, Samarkand, and Bukhārā are particularly well represented. Toward the end of the 10th century, this flow of eastern silver was replaced by one of similar size from England and Germany, so that over 60,000 Anglo-Saxon coins are known from some 1,000 northern European finds.

Coins are the commonest artifacts surviving from the Viking Age, and rank as one of its most important sources of historical and economic data, apart from their significance to medieval numismatic studies. For the medieval archaeologist and art historian, the wealth of mixed hoards of coin and bullion allows a chronological framework to be established for the deposition of different types of object and for the changing fashions in decorative art. There are inevitably numerous difficulties in determining the exact date of a hoard's deposition from its coin contents, but even the presence of a single identifiable coin in a hoard gives a date at or after which it must have been buried or lost.

It is important to remember that most accumulated or savings hoards have failed to come down to us because they were recovered by the rightful owners or their heirs. It is another matter with emergency hoards, those buried during a disturbance or in wartime by owners who were then prevented by death from regaining their property. The extent to which variations in hoard deposition and nonrecovery fluctuate according to times of unrest

has been much debated. Certain documented periods of stress, such as the movement of the "Great Army" of Danes through England during the decade of around 865–875, the events leading up to the Irish defeat of the Vikings at the battle of Tara in 980, and the 1361 battle of Visby, are clearly marked in the archaeological record by the discovery of greater numbers of hoards than during other periods of the Middle Ages. On the other hand, the Kirial hoard, Denmark's largest, consisting of 81,422 coins weighing 33.5 kg., in two domestic iron cauldrons, was concealed within a year or two of 1365, when Denmark was not at war. There is, therefore, no simple equation to be made between widescale disturbance and hoard loss, when so many accidental and unknowable factors need also to be taken into account.

However, the very existence of hoards, whether deliberately hidden, ritually deposited, or accidentally lost, will always reveal something of the changing wealth and fortunes of an area, for where there is no wealth, there can be no hoards, even if increased wealth is not necessarily reflected in an increase in known hoards. All things considered, the medieval hoards of Scandinavia, including those from the Scandinavian Viking Age settlements in the East and West, reveal most strikingly the Vikings' great appetite for silver and their success in satisfying it.

Lit.: **(a)** For general introductions in English to medieval Scandinavian hoards, notably the Viking Age silver hoards and their contents, see: Rasmussen, Nils. "An Introduction to the Viking-Age Hoards." *Commentationes de nummis saeculorum IX-XI in Suecia repertis* 1 (1961), 1–16; Sawyer, Peter. *The Age of the Vikings.* 2nd ed. London: Arnold, 1971, ch. 5; Hårdh, Birgitta. "Trade and Money in Scandinavia in the Viking Age." *Meddelanden från Lunds Universitets Historiska Museum* (1977–78), 157–71; Graham-Campbell, James. *Viking Artefacts: A Select Catalogue.* London: British Museum, 1980; Blackburn, Mark, and David Metcalf, eds. *Viking-Age Coinage in the Northern Lands: The Sixth Oxford Symposium on Coinage and Monetary History.* British Archaeological Reports, International Series, 122. Oxford: B.A.R., 1981; Graham-Campbell, James. "Viking Silver Hoards: An Introduction." In *The Vikings.* Ed. R. T. Farrell. London and Chichester: Phillimore, 1982, pp. 32–41; Sawyer, Peter. *Kings and Vikings: Scandinavia AD 700–1100.* London and New York: Methuen, 1982; Malmer, Brita. "Circulation of Monetary Silver in the Baltic Area During the Viking Age." In *Society and Trade in the Baltic During the Viking Age: Papers of the VIIth Visby Symposium Held at Gotlands Fornsal, Gotland's Historical Museum, Visby, August 15th–19th, 1983.* Ed. Sven-Olof Lindquist. Acta Visbyensia, 7. Visby: Gotlands Fornsal, 1985, pp. 185–94; Kruse, Susan. "Ingots and Weight Units in Viking Age Silver Hoards." *World Archaeology* 20.2 (1988), 285–301; Clarke, H., and E. Schia, eds. *Coins and Archaeology: Medieval Archaeology Research Group, Proceedings of the First Meeting at Isegran, Norway 1988.* British Archaeological Reports, International Series, 556. Oxford: B.A.R., 1989. **(b)** Major surveys and inventories of medieval silver hoards and their contents in Scandinavia include: Grieg, Sigurd. "Vikingetidens skattefund." *Universitetets Oldsaksamlings Skrifter* 2 (1929), 177–311; Ugglas, Carl af. *Gotländska silverskatter från Valdemarstågets tid.* Ur Statens Historiska Museums Samlingar, 3. Stockholm: Wahlström & Widstrand, 1936; Skovmand, Roar. "De danske Skattefund fra Vikingetiden og den ældste Middelalder indtil omkring 1150." *Aarbøger for nordisk Oldkyndighed og Historie* (1942), 1–275; Stenberger, Mårten. *Die Schatzfunde Gotlands der Wikingerzeit.* 2 vols. Stockholm: Kungl. vitterhets historie och antikvitets akademien, 1947–58; Hatz, Gustav. *Handel und Verkehr zwischen dem deutschen Reich und Schweden in der späten Wikingerzeit. Die deutschen Münzen des 10. und 11. Jahrhunderts in Schweden.*

Stockholm: Kungl. vitterhets historie och antikvitets akademien, 1974; Malmer, Brita, ed. *Corpus nummorum saeculorum IX-XI qui in Suecia reperti sunt.* Stockholm: Almquist & Wiksell, 1975– [in progress]; Hårdh, Birgitta. *Wikingerzeitliche Depotfunde aus Südschweden. Probleme und Analysen.* 2 vols. Acta Archaeologica Lundensia, series in 4°, 9, and series in 8° minore, 6. Bonn: Habelt; Lund: Gleerup, 1976; Skaare, Kolbjørn. *Coins and Coinage in Viking-Age Norway: The Establishment of a National Coinage in the XI Century, with a Survey of the Preceding Currency History.* Oslo: Universitetsforlaget, 1976; Glob, P. V., ed. *Danefæ. Til Hendes Majestæt dronning Margrethe II, 16 April 1980.* Copenhagen: Nationalmuseet, 1980; Zachrisson, Inger. *De samiska metalldepåerna år 1000–1350 i ljuset av fyndet från Mörtträsket, Lappland.* Archaeology and Environment, 3. Umeå: University of Umeå, 1984; Thunmark-Nylén, Lena. "Hedningar, kristna och silverskatter." *Götlandskt Arkiv* 58 (1986), 23–44; Jonsson, Kenneth. *Viking-Age Hoards and Late Anglo-Saxon Coins.* Stockholm: GOTAB, 1987; Thurborg, Märit. "Regional Economic Structures: An Analysis of the Viking Age Silver Hoards from Öland, Sweden." *World Archaeology* 20.2 (1988), 302–24. **(c)** Selected references to the Viking Age silver hoards of Britain and Ireland, for comparative purposes: Dolley, R. H. Michael. *The Hiberno-Norse Coins in the British Museum.* Sylloge of Coins of the British Isles. London: British Museum, 1966; Graham-Campbell, James. "The Viking-Age Silver and Gold Hoards of Scandinavian Character from Scotland." *Proceedings of the Society of Antiquaries of Scotland* 107 (1975–76), 114–35; Graham-Campbell, J. A. "The Viking-Age Silver Hoards of Ireland." In *Proceedings of the Seventh Viking Congress, Dublin 15–21 August 1973.* Ed. Bo Almqvist and David Greene. Dublin: Royal Irish Academy, 1976, pp. 39–74; Graham-Campbell, James. "The Viking-Age Silver Hoards of the Isle of Man." In *The Viking Age in the Isle of Man.* Ed. Christine Fell *et al.* London: Viking Society for Northern Research, 1983, pp. 53–80; Boon, George. *Welsh Hoards, 1979–1981.* Cardiff: National Museum of Wales, 1986; Brooks, Nicholas, and James Graham-Campbell. "Reflections on the Viking-Age Silver Hoard from Croydon, Surrey." In *Anglo-Saxon Monetary History: Essays in Memory of Michael Dolley.* Ed. Mark Blackburn. Leicester: Leicester University Press, 1986, pp. 91–110; Grierson, Philip, and Mark Blackburn. *Medieval European Coinage. 1. The Early Middle Ages.* Cambridge: Cambridge University Press, 1986; Graham-Campbell, James. "Some Archaeological Reflections on the Cuerdale Hoard." In *Coinage in Ninth-Century Northumbria: The Tenth Symposium on Coinage and Monetary History.* Ed. David Metcalf. British Archaeological Reports, British Series 180. Oxford: B.A.R., 1987, pp. 329–44; Kenny, Michael. "The Geographical Distribution of Irish Viking-Age Coin Hoards." *Proceedings of the Royal Irish Academy* 87C (1987), 507–25.

James Graham-Campbell

[**See also:** Coins and Mints]

Hoaxes *see* Viking Hoaxes

Hólmganga ("island-going") was a duel or single combat governed by rules, in contrast to *einvígi*, single combat not governed by rules. Despite this distinction, the two words are often used interchangeably. The rules governing *hólmganga* varied and were probably set by the combatants in many cases. Most of our information about *hólmganga* comes from *Íslendingasögur*, although we do not know how much of this source material is based on actual custom and how much is purely fiction.

Occasions for *hólmganga* include the breakdown of court proceedings or a court judgment unacceptable to one party (*Njáls saga*, ch. 8; *Egils saga Skalla-Grímssonar*, ch. 56; *Ljósvetninga saga*, ch. 30); quarrels over women (*Kormáks saga*, chs. 9–10; *Gunnlaugs saga*, ch. 11) or, according to the Swedish 13th-century *Hednalagen* ("Pagan Law"), insults to one's honor or manhood. In practice, *hólmganga* could constitute a form of legalized brigandage. Some men, including "berserks," traveled about challenging men to duels for their property and women (*Egils saga Skalla-Grímssonar*, ch. 64; *Grettis saga*, ch. 19; *Gísla saga*, ch. 1). *Landnámabók* reports that several early settlers of Iceland won land in this way (S70; S86, H74; S389, H343). Duels are reported during the Conversion period at the end of the 10th century to test the relative merits of the pagan and Christian religions. A pagan poetess told the redoubtable Christian missionary Þangbrandr that the god Þórr challenged Christ to a duel, and Christ refused to fight (*Njáls saga*, ch. 102). Þangbrandr himself dueled with pagans (*Njáls saga*, ch. 101).

As the name implies, *hólmganga* was normally held on an island. In Iceland, it frequently took place at local *þing*-meetings and during the yearly *Alþingi*, where a certain island in the middle of the Öxará ("Axe River") was used for duels. The participants' cloaks or another piece of cloth might demarcate the fighting zone (*Svarfdœla saga*, ch. 9). *Kormáks saga* (ch. 10) gives an elaborate description of the preparation of the site in the *hólmgǫngulǫg* ("law of the *hólmganga*," although it is unclear how widely it applied). A cloth five ells square was spread out and staked at the corners with pegs called *tjǫsnur*. Three-foot-wide furrows were dug around the cloak and bounded on the far side by cords. If a combatant set one foot outside the cords, he was said to be yielding; if he put both feet outside, he was fleeing (*Kormáks saga*). In *Egils saga Skalla-Grímssonar* (ch. 64), the *hólmganga* takes place on an island inside a circle of stones. *Hednalagen* specifies that the combat should be held where three roads meet.

Weapons varied. According to *Kormáks saga* (ch. 14), the sword allowed in *hólmganga* could not exceed a certain length. Egill went to a *hólmganga* with an extra sword at hand, in case the first one broke (*Egils saga Skalla-Grímssonar*, ch. 64). A contestant was allowed three shields (*Kormáks saga*, ch. 10). Combatants might have other men to hold their shields for them (*Kormáks saga*, chs. 10 and 14; *Gunnlaugs saga*, ch. 11).

If a man failed to appear for the duel, he was publicly disgraced; he was called *níðingr*, a term implying the worst possible scorn and insult (*Kormáks saga*, ch. 21; *Vatnsdœla saga*, chs. 33–34; *Hednalagen*). According to *Hednalagen*, he lost the right to swear oaths or to bear witness. In *Gísla saga* (ch. 2), when the challengee was slow to appear, the challenger planned to make a wooden statue of him in a posture implying sodomy.

According to *Egils saga Skalla-Grímssonar* (ch. 64), if the challenger won the victory, he received as his prize that for which he had issued the challenge. If he lost the fight, he might ransom himself at an agreed-upon price. If he was killed, all his possessions were inherited by his slayer. In *Hednalagen*, if the man who had first insulted his opponent felled him in the duel, he only had to pay half the normal compensation for manslaughter. If the other man succeeded in killing his insulter, he owed no compensation. Sometimes a duel concluded when the first wound was received, according to *Kormáks saga* (ch. 10), when the first blood fell on the cloak spread as an arena. The loser might buy himself off from the *hólmganga* by paying three marks of silver (*Kormáks saga*, ch. 10; *Gunnlaugs saga*, ch. 11; *Svarfdœla saga*, ch. 9) or a ring (*Kormáks saga*, ch. 23).

In Scandinavia, the duel was apparently not regarded as a

trial by ordeal or judgment of God, as it was in many parts of Europe. There are, however, possible traces of pagan rites in connection with *hólmganga*. According to *Kormáks saga* (ch. 10), the man who drove the *tjǫsnur* or pegs to hold down the cloth for an arena must look between his legs and hold his earlobes while speaking the spell that was later called the *tjǫsnublót* ("*tjǫsnur-sacrifice*"). There are reports of sacrificing an ox after a duel (*Kormáks saga*, ch. 22; *Egils saga*, ch. 65). *Einvígi* also appears to have had pagan connections. According to Snorri Sturluson's *Gylfaginning*, the god Ullr was the patron god of *einvígi*.

Hólmganga was abolished in Iceland in the first or second decade of the 11th century, and in Norway in 1014.

Lit.: Jones, Gwyn. "The Religious Elements of the Icelandic 'Hólmganga.'" *Modern Language Review* 27 (1932), 307–13; Jones, Gwyn. "Some Characteristics of the Icelandic 'Hólmganga.'" *Journal of English and Germanic Philology* 32 (1933), 203–24; Lundberg, Oskar. "Holmgång och holmgångsblot." *Arv* 2 (1946), 125–38; Ciklamini, Marlene. "The Old Icelandic Duel." *Scandinavian Studies* 35 (1963), 175–94; Bø, Olav. "*Hólmganga* and *Einvígi*: Scandinavian Forms of the Duel." *Mediaeval Scandinavia* 2 (1969), 132–48; Foote, Peter G., and David M. Wilson. *The Viking Achievement: The Society and Culture of Early Medieval Scandinavia*. London: Sidgwick & Jackson, 1970, pp. 379–81; Radford, R. S. "Going to the Island: A Legal and Economic Analysis of the Medieval Icelandic Duel." *Southern California Law Review* 62.2 (1989), 615–44.

Jesse L. Byock

Homilies (West Norse).

The two principal collections of Old West Norse sermons, Stock. Perg. 4to no. 15 (the "Stockholm" or "Old Icelandic Homily Book") and AM 619 4to (the "Old Norwegian Homily Book"), both dated to around 1200, are among the oldest monuments of Old West Norse prose. They have eleven items in common, all based on earlier exemplars. Two of the sermons included in these collections, one for the feast of the dedication of a church (the so-called "Stave-church Homily"), and another for St. Michael's Day based on Gregory the Great's thirty-fourth gospel homily on the nine orders of angels, are also preserved in what is perhaps the oldest Icelandic MS fragment, AM 237a fol., written around 1150, and itself probably a remnant of a homiliary of considerable size. These sermons, at least, can be dated to the early part of the 12th century.

The ultimate provenance of both collections is obscure. Linguistic evidence suggests that AM 619 4to was composed in the vicinity of Bergen, Norway, perhaps at either of the Benedictine monasteries of Munkalíf or Sancti Albani on Selja, or at the Augustinian house of Jónskirkja. Stock. Perg. 4to no. 15 appears to have been owned by a descendant of the scholarly cleric Gottskálk Jónsson of Glaumbær (*ca.* 1524–1590) before it was purchased by the MS collector Jón Eggertsson for the Swedish College of Antiquities in 1682.

While the core of AM 619 4to is a cycle of homilies organized *per circulum anni*, the less orderly arrangement of Stock. Perg. 4to no. 15 reflects copying from several different collections. Both anthologies are homiletic handbooks rather than homiliaries in the strict sense of the word: In addition to expositions of the pericopes for particular feast days, they include admonitory and catechetical sermons to be read *quando volueris*, as well as commentaries on the Lord's Prayer and the service of the mass. Stock. Perg. 4to no. 15 also contains an allegorical interpretation of the

eight church modes, a translation of part of pseudo-Ambrose's *Acta Sancti Sebastiani*, two versions of the Apostles' Creed, an Easter gospel harmony, excerpts from a *Stephanus saga*, and prayers to Christ and Mary. AM 619 4to preserves a complete translaton of Alcuin's *De virtutibus et vitiis*, a "Debate Between the Body and the Soul" probably based on the Old French poem *Un samedi par nuit*, a homily on St. Óláfr derived from a *vita* older than Eysteinn Erlendsson's *Passio Olavi*, and a vernacular version of the extended series of twenty *Miracula Beati Olavi*, which dates from the 1160s.

Whole and partial sources for many of the texts in AM 619 4to and Stock. Perg. 4to no. 15 have been identified among the works of Augustine, Maximus of Turin, Fulgentius of Ruspe, Caesarius of Arles, Gregory the Great, Bede, Ambrosius Autpertus, Paschasius Radbert, Haymo of Auxerre, and Honorius Augustodunensis, but the Latin background of many sermons still awaits investigation. Much of the source material exploited by the Scandinavian homilists was available in standard homiliaries, such as those compiled by Alan of Farfa (before 770) and Paul the Deacon (*ca.* 790), but the homilists doubtless made use of other sorts of collections as well. Stock. Perg. 4to no. 15, for instance, contains a close translation of a penitential sermon that circulated in the "Pembroke-type" homiliary, a Carolingian preacher's anthology most fully represented by the 11th-century Anglo-Saxon MS Cambridge, Pembroke College 25. The Scandinavian translator may have had access to a version of this collection or to a *florilegium* containing material from it. Many of the sermons for which proximate sources have not yet been identified are very likely original though eclectic compositions based on reading and reminiscence. The dedication homily mentioned above, for instance, is built around a set of conventional allegorical interpretations of the parts of a church building, parallels for all of which can be found in various Latin sources, but which the Norse homilist adapts to a local setting, and applies to the wooden interior of a Scandinavian turf- or stave-church.

In order to make Christian teaching as accessible to their congregations as possible, the homilists adopted a simple, idiomatic prose style, occasionally adorned with native proverbs and similitudes from everyday life. Particularly in paraphrases of gospel passages, sudden changes of tense and shifts from indirect to direct speech are reminiscent of the terse, homespun narrative of the *Íslendingasǫgur*. The latinate diction and syntax characteristic of much later Old West Norse religious prose are, on the whole, not found in the early homilies, though in some passages (particularly in perorations) rhetorical devices, such as isocolon, antithesis, chiasmus, anaphora, alliteration, and word pairs, are exploited to achieve a high style. A few alliterative rhythmical sequences, such as the following catalogue of vices from Stock. Perg. 4to no. 15, can be scanned as verse: *lygi oc lausung / oc lester marger / scopon oc scialsemi / oc skeitun optlega / giálp oc gáleysi / glepi ófallin / gildingr oc geþleysi / grand er þat andar* ("lying and falsehood / and many vices, / railing and gossiping / and frequently scorn (?), / boasting and heedlessness, / unbecoming merriment, / bragging and capriciousness, / that is the soul's harm").

Vernacular sermons and sermon fragments are also preserved in many other early Icelandic MSS. AM 677 4to (*ca.* 1200) contains ten homilies from what was probably a complete translation of Gregory the Great's forty *Homiliae in evangelia*. The miscellany of learned and theological writings in the AM 544 4to section of *Hauksbók* includes a sermon based on the Old English homily *De falsis diis* by Ælfric of Eynsham, a tract on the evils of sorcery partially related to the same author's *De auguriis*, and a homily on the Ember Days also found in Stock. Perg. 4to no. 15 and AM 114 4to (mid-14th century). A spiritual interpretation of the rainbow in the same section of *Hauksbók* was doubtless also intended for the use of preachers. A parallel version of this text is found in the "Physiologus" MS, AM 673a 4to (*ca.* 1200), which also contains a version of the commonplace allegory of a ship and its parts in sermon form. A partial catalogue of other Arnamagnaean MSS containing texts that have been tentatively identified as "homilies" is found in Knudsen 1961, col. 659.

Ed.: Unger, Carl R., ed. *Gammel norsk homiliebog (codex Arn. Magn. 619 qv.)*. Norsk oldskriftselskabs samlinger, 1.5. Christiania [Oslo]: Brøgger & Christie, 1862–64; Wisén, Theodor, ed. *Homiliu-bók. Isländska homilier efter en handskrift från tolfte århundradet*. Lund: Gleerup, 1872; Þorvaldur Bjarnarson, ed. *Leifar fornra kristinna fræða íslenzkra: Codex Arna-Magnæanus 677 4to auk annara enna elztu brota af íslenzkum guðfrœðisritum*. Copenhagen: Hagerup, 1878; Eiríkur Jónsson and Finnur Jónsson, eds. *Hauksbók udgiven efter de Arnamagnæanske håndskrifter no. 371, 544 og 675, 4° samt forskellige papirshåndskrifter af det kongelige nordiske Oldskrift-selskab*. Copenhagen: Thiele, 1892–96, pp. cxviii–cxxii, 156–64, 167–9, 172–5; Flom, George T., ed. *Codex AM 619 quarto. Old Norwegian Book of Homilies. . . .* University of Illinois Studies in Language and Literature, 14, no. 4. Urbana: University of Illinois, 1929; Indrebø, Gustav, ed. *Gamal norsk homiliebok. cod. AM. 619 4°*. Norsk historisk kjeldeskrift-institutt, Skrifter, 54. Oslo: Dybwad, 1931; rpt. Oslo: Universitetsforlaget, 1966; Paasche, Fredrick, ed. *Homiliu-bók (Icelandic Sermons), Perg. 4to No. 15 in the Royal Library, Stockholm*. Corpus Codicum Islandicorum Medii Aevi, 8. Copenhagen: Levin & Munksgaard, 1935 [facsimile]; Seip, Didrik Arup, ed. *The Arna-Magnæan Manuscript 677, 4°. Pseudo-Cyprian Fragments. Prosper's Epigrams. Gregory's Homilies and Dialogues*. Corpus Codicum Islandicorum Medii Aevi, 18. Copenhagen: Levin & Munksgaard, 1949 [facsimile]; Knudsen, Trygve, ed. *Gammelnorsk homiliebok etter AM 619 qv*. Corpus Codicum Norvegicorum Medii Aevi, Series in Quarto, 1. Oslo: Selskapet til utgivelse av gamle norske håndskrifter, 1952 [facsimile]; Kolsrud, Oluf, ed. *Messuskýringar. Liturgisk symbolik frå den norsk-islandske kyrkja i millomalderen*. Norsk historisk kjeldeskrift-institutt, Skrifter, 57.1. Oslo: Dybwad, 1952; Jón Helgason, ed. *Hauksbók; the Arna-Magnæan manuscripts 371,4to, 544,4to, and 675,4to*. Manuscripta Islandica, 5. Copenhagen: Munksgaard, 1960, pp. xii–xiii, xix [544 4to, fols. 4r-8r, 9v-10v, 12r-13v]; McClung, Pope J., ed. "An Edition of the Stockholm Homily Book, Sthm. 15,4°." Diss. University of North Carolina, Chapel Hill, 1974; Arkel-de Leeuw van Weenen, Andrea van, ed. "The Manuscript Sthm. Perg. 15 4°: A Diplomatic Edition and Introduction." Diss. Rijksuniversiteit te Utrecht, 1977; [a new facsimile edition of Stock. Perg. 4to no. 15, to be published by Stofnun Árna Magnússonar, is in preparation]. **Lex.**: Larsson, Ludvig, ed. *Ordförrådet i de älsta isländska handskrifterna*. Lund: Lindsted; Collin & Zickerman, 1891; Holtsmark, Anne, ed. *Ordforrådet i de eldste norske håndskrifter til ca. 1250*. Oslo: Dybwad, 1955. **Tr.**: Salvesen, Astrid, trans. *Gammelnorsk Homiliebok*. Introduction and commentary by Erik Gunnes. Oslo: Universitetsforlaget, 1971. **Lit.**: Larsson, Ludvig. *Studier över den Stockholmska homilieboken I–II*. Lund: Malmström, 1887; Wisén, Theodor. *Några ord om den Stockholmska homilieboken. Ett genmäle*. Lund: Berling, 1888; Wisén, Theodor. "Textkritiska Anmärkningar till den Stockholmska homilieboken." *Arkiv för nordisk filologi* 4 (1888), 193–239; Larsson, Ludvig. *Svar på professor Wiséns "Textkritiska Anmärkningar till den Stockholmska Homilieboken."* Lund: Malmström, 1888; Neckel, Gustav. "Zum Stockholmer Homilienbuch." *Beiträge zur Geschichte der deutschen Sprache und Literatur* 38 (1913), 459–500;

Vrátný, Karel. "Literarische Kleinigkeiten." *Arkiv för nordisk filologi* 29 (1913), 163–80; Vrátný, Karel. "Enthält das Stockholmer Homilienbuch durchweg übersetzungen?" *Arkiv för nordisk filologi* 32 (1916), 31–49; Vrátný, Karel. "Textkritische Nachlese zum Stockholmer Homilienbuch." *Arkiv för nordisk filologi* 33 (1917), 141–57; Holtsmark, Anne. "En gammel norsk homilie i AM 114a qv." *Arkiv för nordisk filologi* 46 (1930), 259–72; Reichborn-Kjennerud, I. "Et kapitel av Hauksbók." *Maal og minne* (1934), 144–8; Holtsmark, Anne. "Sankt Olavs liv og mirakler." In *Festskrift til Francis Bull*. Oslo: Gyldendal, 1937, pp. 121–33; rpt. in her *Studier i norrøn diktning*. Oslo: Gyldendal, 1956, pp. 15–24; Turville-Petre, G. "The Old Norse Homily on the Assumption and *Maríu Saga*." *Mediaeval Studies* 9 (1947), 131–40; rpt. in his *Nine Norse Studies*. London: Viking Society for Northern Research, 1972, pp. 102–17; Turville-Petre, G. "The Old Norse Homily on the Dedication." *Mediaeval Studies* 11 (1949), 206–18; rpt. with a postscript in his *Nine Norse Studies*, pp. 79–101; Turville-Petre, G. *Origins of Icelandic Literature*. Oxford: Clarendon, 1953, pp. 115–21; Magnús Már Lárusson. "Nokkrar úrfellur í homilíu." In *Afmæliskveðja til Alexanders Jóhannessonar . . . frá samstarfsmönnum og nemendum*. Reykjavik: Helgafell, 1953, pp. 159–63; rpt. in his *Fróðleiksþættir og Sögubrot*. Hafnarfjörður: Skuggsjá, 1967, pp. 73–8; Bekker-Nielsen, Hans. "En norrøn adventsprædiken." *Maal og minne* (1959), 48–52; Widding, Ole. "De norrøne homiliebøgers prædiken på Stephansdag." *Maal og minne* (1959), 42–7; Widding, Ole, and Hans Bekker-Nielsen. "A Debate of the Body and Soul in Old Norse Literature." *Mediaeval Studies* 21 (1959), 272–89; Bekker-Nielsen, Hans. "Den gammelnorske paaskeprædiken og Gregor den store." *Maal og minne* (1960), 99–104; Bekker-Nielsen, Hans. "Fra Ordbogens Værksted: 3. 'Homiletisk haandbog?'" *Opuscula* 1. Bibliotheca Arnamagnæana, 20. Copenhagen: Munksgaard, 1960, pp. 343–4; Jón Helgason. "Vers i homiliebøgerne." *Opuscula* 1. Bibliotheca Arnamagnæana, 20. Copenhagen: Munksgaard, 1960, pp. 357–9; Turville-Petre, Joan. "Sources of the Vernacular Homily in England, Norway and Iceland." *Arkiv för nordisk filologi* 75 (1960), 168–82; Bekker-Nielsen, Hans. "Cæsarius af Arles som kilde til norrøne homilier." *Opuscula* 2.1. Bibliotheca Arnamagnæana, 25.1. Copenhagen: Munksgaard, 1961, pp. 10–6; Bekker-Nielsen, Hans. "Et overset brudstykke af en af Gregor den Stores homilier." *Opuscula* 2.1. Bibliotheca Arnamagnæana, 25.1. Copenhagen: Munksgaard, 1961, pp. 37–47; Knudsen, Trygve. "Homiliebøker." *KLNM* 6 (1961), 657–66; Gjerløw, Lilli. "Imbredagene." *KLNM* 7 (1962), 361–3; Turville-Petre, Joan. "Translations of a Lost Penitential Homily." *Traditio* 19 (1963), 51–78; Bekker-Nielsen, Hans. "Kyrkofäderna och kyrkolärarna i vestnordisk litteratur." *KLNM* 9 (1964), 690–3; Tveitane, Mattias. "Vár dróttenn kann allar tungur." *Maal og minne* (1964), 106–12; Bekker-Nielsen, Hans. "Den ældste tid." In *Norrøn Fortællekunst. Kapitler af den norsk-islandske middelalderlitteraturs historie*. Ed. Hans Bekker-Nielsen et al. Copenhagen: Akademisk Forlag, 1965, pp. 16–23, 148–51; Tveitane, Mattias. "Irish Apocrypha in Norse Tradition? On the Sources of Some Medieval Homilies." *Arv* 22 (1966), 111–35; Benediktsson, Jakob. "Traces of Latin Prose-Rhythm in Old Norse Literature." In *The Fifth Viking Congress, Tórshavn, July 1965*. Ed. Bjarni Niclasen. Tórshavn: Føroya Landsstýri, Tórshavnar Býráð, Føroya Fróðskaparfelag, and Føroya Fornminnissavn, 1968, pp. 17–24; Bekker-Nielsen, Hans. "The Old Norse Dedication Homily." In *Festschrift für Konstantin Reichardt*. Ed. Christian Gellinek. Bern: Francke, 1969, pp. 127–34; Taylor, Arnold. "*Hauksbók* and Ælfric's *De Falsis Diis*." *Leeds Studies in English*, n.s. 3 (1969), 101–9; Ottósson, Róbert A. "Das musiktheoretische Textfragment im Stockholmer Homilienbuch." *Opuscula* 4. Bibliotheca Arnamagnæana, 30. Copenhagen: Munksgaard, 1970, pp. 169–76; Jakob Benediktsson. "*Cursus* in Old Norse Literature." *Mediaeval Scandinavia* 7 (1974), 15–21; Westlund, Börje. *Skrivarproblemet i Isländska Homiliboken*. Stockholm Studies in

Scandinavian Philology. New Series 10. Stockholm: Almqvist & Wiksell, 1974; Lindblad, Gustaf. "Den rätta läsningen av Isländska homilieboken." *Scripta Islandica* 26 (1975), 25–45; Marchand, James W. "The Old Icelandic Allegory of the Church Modes." *Musical Quarterly* 61 (1975), 553–9; Marchand, James W. "The Old Norwegian Christmas Homily and the Question of Irish Influence." *Arv* 31 (1975), 23–34; Tveitane, Mattias. "'Første Julepreken' i *Gamal Norsk Homiliebok*. En språklig oversikt." *Maal og minne* (1975), 20–9; Kirby, I. J. "On the Fragmentary 'History of the Passion' in the Icelandic Homily Book." *Arkiv för nordisk filologi* 91 (1976), 130–7; Marchand, James W. "Two Notes on the Old Icelandic Physiologus Manuscript." *Modern Language Notes* 91 (1976), 501–5; Marchand, James W. "The Ship Allegory in the *Ezzolied* and in Old Icelandic." *Neophilologus* 60 (1976), 238–50; Walter, Ernst. *Lexikalisches Lehngut im Altwestnordischen: Untersuchungen zum Lehngut im ethisch-moralischen Wortschatz der frühen lateinisch-altwestnordischen Übersetzungsliteratur.* Abhandlungen der sächsischen Akademie der Wissenschaften zu Leipzig. Phil.-hist. Klasse, Band 66, Heft 2. Berlin: Akademie-Verlag, 1976; Arkel-de Leeuw van Weenen, Andrea, and Gilles Quispel. "The Diatessaron in Iceland and Norway." *Vigiliae Christianae* 32 (1978), 214–5; Arkel, Andrea van. "Scribes and Statistics: An evaluation of the statistical methods used to determine the number of scribes of the Stockholm Homily Book." *Scripta Islandica* 30 (1979), 25–45; Rode, Eva. "Svar på artiklen 'Scribes and Statistics.'" *Scripta Islandica* 30 (1979), 46–50; Westlund, Börje. "Skrivare och statistik. Ett genmäle" *Scripta Islandica* 30 (1979), 51–62; Rode, Eva. "Et fragment af en prædiken til askeonsdag. AM 655 XI, 4to." *Opuscula* 7. Bibliotheca Arnamagnæana, 34. Copenhagen: Reitzel, 1979, pp. 44–61; Frederiksen, Britta Olrik. "Til engleafsnittet i Gregors 34. evangeliehomilie i norrøn oversættelse." *Opuscula* 7. Bibliotheca Arnamagnæana, 34. Copenhagen: Reitzel, 1979, pp. 62–93; Gjerløw, Lilli. *Liturgica Islandica. I. Text.* Bibliotheca Arnamagnæana, 35. Copenhagen: Reitzel, 1980, pp. 21–6, 83–6; Kirby, Ian J. *Biblical Quotation in Old Icelandic–Norwegian Religious Literature.* 2 vols. Reykjavik: Stofnun Árna Magnússonar, 1976–80, vol. 2, pp. 51–74, 91–6, 101, 106; Spencer, Helen L. "Vernacular and Latin Versions of a Sermon for Lent: 'A Lost Penitential Homily' Found." *Mediaeval Studies* 44 (1982), 271–305; McDougall, David. "Studies in the Prose Style of the Old Icelandic and Old Norwegian Homily Books." Diss. University of London, 1983; Magerøy, Hallvard. "In dedicatione ecclesiæ sermo. Om overleveringa av 'Stavkyrkjepreika.'" *Opuscula* 8. Bibliotheca Arnamagnæana, 38. Copenhagen: Reitzel, 1985, 96–121.

David McDougall

[**See also:** Alcuin: *De virtutibus et vitiis*; Bede; Christian Prose; *Hauksbók*; *Óláfs saga helga*; *Physiologus*; Saints' Lives]

Houses.

1. RURAL. Our knowledge of rural medieval houses in Scandinavia is based mainly on archaeological data, but buildings from the high Middle Ages are still standing in some districts and can be studied *in situ*. Traditionally, the houses of farms and villages have been most intensively studied, and large-scale excavations carried out during the last decades have presented new information. But the research activity has been concentrated in certain regions, leaving other regions more or less blank. The rural architecture of the high and late Middle Ages, especially, is little studied from an archaeological point of view.

Recent research has shown that the development of the rural house was not a unilinear evolution from a simple to a more complex type of building. Scandinavia is divided into different ecological and economic zones with different resources, and societies with different economic and social structures can be found. The study of houses has undergone a change from an evolutionistic and diffusionistic view to a more fundamental one, taking into account local ecological and economic contexts. In recent years, much attention has also been paid to the social and symbolic value of a house and its effect on the construction, shape, and form of buildings (Stoklund 1980).

In parts of Sweden and Norway, permanent farms, often divided into several holdings, existed in the Roman and Migration periods, while in Denmark, large villages with more than twenty holdings have been found. A similar village-like settlement has recently been excavated in southwest Norway (Løken 1987). The individual farm or holding was, however, surprisingly similar in most of Scandinavia about A.D. 500. Normally, each farm had one main rectangular longhouse divided by partition walls into several rooms that had different functions. In most regions, the byre with cowsheds was placed at one end of the house, with the living rooms, and sometimes rooms for cooking and storage at the other end. The buildings were usually 5–7 m. broad, while the length may vary between 15 m. and 75 m., according to the farmer's social position. Many farms also had smaller houses with special functions, such as cooking rooms, smithy, byre, barn or storehouses, grouped around the main building (Carlsson 1979, Beskow-Sjöberg 1977, Hvass 1978, 1983, Løken 1987, Myhre 1982, Ramquist 1983).

The houses were always three-aisled, with two inner rows of wooden posts carrying beams that ran both transversally and longitudinally and that were fastened into a construction called *grind* in Norway and *højrem* in Denmark. This construction was strong enough to support the roof, leaving the outer walls without a supporting function. The walls were built in different techniques. Hewn planks or logs standing side by side in wall ditches, called "stave-work," were common, as well as wattle-work or bulwark constructions. In some regions, outer walls of stone or turf were added for isolation purposes and to protect the woodwork. For outhouses or smaller farmhouses, walls made only of stone or turf have been found.

The *grind*- or *højrem*-construction was in use in some parts of Scandinavia throughout the Middle Ages, and may even be found today (Gjærder 1982, Vensild 1982). Longhouses with a byre and different living rooms under the same roof were common in some districts until modern times. But new building techniques and a new layout of houses and rooms were introduced on other farms during the Viking and high Middle Ages. The late-medieval rural houses became more differentiated in Scandinavia, depending on geographical and social factors.

During the Migration Period, some longhouses had curved side walls, and this shape became a model during the Viking Age. On the larger farms or estates in Denmark, huge buildings or halls, more than 40 m. long and 10 m. broad, have recently been excavated. This type of house is well known from the Danish royal forts like Trelleborg and Fyrkat. Smaller buildings with curved walls were common also on ordinary farms in Norway, South Sweden, and Denmark, and the house type was introduced by Norse settlers on the North Atlantic islands: Shetland, the Faroes, Iceland, and Greenland. But these houses were used alongside the traditional rectangular longhouse, and the curve-sided house went out of use in the high Middle Ages (Hvass 1979, Johansen 1982, Albrethsen 1982, Myhre 1982, Näsmann 1984, Olsen and Schmidt 1977, Nielsen 1979).

Two other new trends in house construction should be pointed out: (1) On many farms, the byre was separated from the main building and was built as one of several freestanding houses. (2) Gradually, the *grind*-construction was replaced in the living rooms by reducing the number of posts, letting stronger wall constructions support the weight of the roof. One solution to this problem was to set up oblique supporting posts on the outside of the walls, as can be found on many Danish house sites from the Viking Age (Olsen and Schmidt 1977, Schietzel 1981), but which seldom occur on houses of the high Middle Ages. In Denmark, South Sweden, and West Norway, houses usually had walls built in bulwark or stave-work, while timber houses with cross-jointing were introduced in Sweden and East Norway in the late Viking Age and became common during the high Middle Ages (Hauglid 1980, Rosander 1986).

In Jutland, the longhouse with *højrem*-construction still existed in the late Middle Ages, and this tradition from prehistoric times can be found up to the 20th century (Vensild 1982). Also, in South and West Norway, the longhouse with several living rooms and sometimes also a byre was common during the 18th and 19th centuries; this type of building has a continuous tradition extending back to the high Middle Ages and even to the Iron Age (Myhre 1982, Brekke 1982).

The old truism that the introduction of proper timber buildings at the end of the Viking Age brought an end to the longhouse tradition still seems to be correct, however, for most parts of Sweden and Norway. Many of the medieval timber buildings are still standing, making it possible to admire their high-quality workmanship. They were specialized buildings, built, for instance, for living purposes only (*stove/stuga*), for storage (*loft* or *bur*), for cooking (*eldhus*), or for other purposes (Hauglid 1980, Rosander 1986). But in the western parts of Scandinavia and in the mountain valleys where timber was scarce, timber buildings were rarer, and cross-jointing was used for special rooms in longhouses only, on upper-class farms, and in the towns. Where longhouses were used, the different rooms had the same specialized functions as each separate timber building, and were called by the same names, for example, *stove*, *eldhus*, and *bu* (Brekke 1982).

At the end of the medieval period, two main building traditions may be found in Scandinavia: the western parts followed a general trend of the North Sea countries, where longhouses built in stave-work or bulwark were usual. The eastern parts, however, received their main influence from the eastern parts of Europe, and proper timber buildings were most common.

Lit.: Beskow-Sjöberg, Margaretha. *The Archaeology of Skedemosse IV: The Iron Age Settlement of the Skedmosse Area on Øland, Sweden.* Stockholm: Almqvist & Wiksell, 1977; Olsen, Olaf, and Holger Schmidt. *Fyrkat. En jysk vikingeborg.* Nordiske Fortidsminder B, 3. Copenhagen: Lynge, 1977 [English summaries]; Hvass, Sten. "Die Völkerwanderungszeitliche Siedlung Vorbasse, Mitteljütland." *Acta Archaeologica* 49 (1978), 61–111; Hvass, Sten. "The Viking Age Settlement at Vorbasse, Central Jutland." *Acta Archaeologica* 50 (1979), 137–72; Carlsson, Dan. *Kulturlandskapets utveckling på Gotland.* Visby: Press, 1979 [English summary]; Nielsen, Leif Christian. "Omgård: A Settlement from the Late Iron Age and Viking Period in West Jutland." *Acta Archaeologica* 50 (1979), 173–208; Hauglid, Roar. *Laftekunst. Laftehusets opprinnelse og eldste historie.* Norske Minnesmerker. Oslo: Dreyer, 1980; Stoklund, Bjarne. "House and Culture in the North Atlantic Isles: Three Models of Interpretation." *Ethnologica Europea* (1980), 113–32; Schietzel, Kurt. *Stand der siedlungsarchäologischen Forschung in Haithabu. Ausgrabungen im*

Haithabu, 16. Neumünster: Wachholtz, 1981; Brekke, Nils Georg. "Samanbygde hus i Hordaland." *Fortidsforeningens Årbok* 137 (1982), 51–114; Myhre, Bjørn, et al., eds. *Vestnordisk byggeskikk gjennom to tusen år: tradisjon og forandring fra romertid til det 19. århundre.* Arkeologisk Museum i Stavanger, Skrifter, 7. Stavanger: Arkeologisk Museum i Stavanger, 1982; Vensild, Henrik. "Højremhuse i Nord- og Nordvest-Jylland i historisk tid." In *Vestnordisk byggeskikk gjennom to tusen år*, pp. 119–29; Albrethsen, Svend Erik. "Træk af den norrøne gårds udvikling på Grønland." In *Vestnordisk byggeskikk gjennom to tusen år*, pp. 269–87; Gjærder, Per. "Om stavverk og lafteverk." In *Vestnordisk byggeskikk gjennom to tusen år*, pp. 31–67; Myhre, Bjørn. "Bolighusets utvikling fra jernalder til middelalder i Sørvest-Norge." In *Vestnordisk byggeskikk gjennom to tusen år*, pp. 195–217; Johansen, Olav Sverre. "Viking Age Farms: Estimating the Number and Population Size." *Norwegian Archaeological Review* 15 (1982), 45–69; Hvass, Sten. "Vorbasse: The Development of a Settlement Through the First Millennium AD." *Journal of Danish Archaeology* 2 (1983), 127–36; Ramquist, Per. Gene. *On the Function, Origin and Development of Sedentary Iron Age Settlement in North Sweden.* Archaeology and Environment, 1. Umeå: Department of Archaeology, University of Umeå, 1983; Näsmann, Ulf. "Husforskning i Norden. En skisse av situasjonen för yngre järnåldern och medeltiden." *Kulturgeografist Seminarium* 2/84 (1984), 79–95; Rosander, Göran, ed. *Kuttimring i Norden. Bidrag till dess äldre historia.* Falun: Dalarnas Museum, 1986; Løken, Trond. "The Settlement at Forsandmoen—an Iron Age Village in Rogaland, SW Norway." *Studien zur Sachsenforschung* 6 (1987), 155–68.

Bjørn Myhre

2. URBAN. Houses in Scandinavian cities were of varied size and construction depending on their functions. Wood was mostly used, with an increasing use of stone and brick, especially in the later-medieval period, and in South Scandinavia. Monumental buildings, such as churches, monasteries, and kings' and bishops' palaces, were built mostly in stone, but such buildings will be excluded here, as the main subject of this study is the ordinary house for the city dweller.

From written sources in Norway, we have information about such houses as the living house (*stue*), kitchen house (*eldhus*), storehouse (*bod*), byre (*fjøs*), stable (*stall*), and hayloft/barn (*forhus/løe*), together with rooms or buildings for commercial purposes, various crafts, general storage, and social meetings. These buildings were organized in a special layout forming a unit, with boundaries of fences or eaves drip-gaps between the buildings (Schia 1987a: 86). This unit, in Norway called *bygård*, perhaps best translated into English as "townyard," consisted of a parcel of land, or plot, with several buildings of various functions and a courtyard; it was a densely built-up area of relatively limited dimensions when compared with the typical farm. These townyards could belong to a single owner, or be divided among two or more owners or into subordinate divisions as tenements, properties, or holdings.

There are no wooden houses of medieval age standing in Norwegian cities today. In Bergen, however, there are buildings from the 18th century that show the medieval layout of the townyards in the area of the Hanseatic wharf: (1) two rows of houses on either side of a courtyard or passage (Fig. 41) (Herteig 1985: 11), the "double-yard" (*dobbeltgård*), or (2) one row of houses and a passage/courtyard (Fig. 40, left), the "single-yard" (*enkeltgård*). Archaeological excavations in the wharf area since 1955 have shown that this layout has a medieval origin (Herteig

40. 18th-century houses from the wharf area in Bergen. The two white buildings to the right form a "double-yard" with a gate in the middle. To the left is the fronthouse of a "single-yard." Photo: E. Schia.

41. The interior of a "double-yard" seen from the gate. Photo: E. Schia.

42a

42b

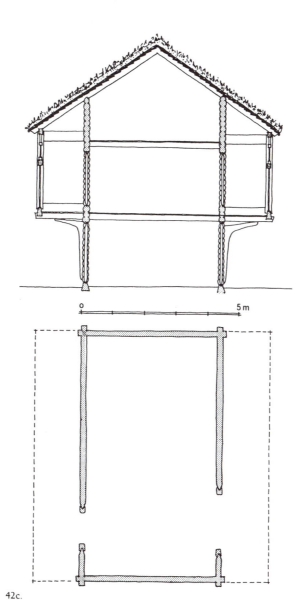

0   5 m

42c.

Archaeological remains and reconstruction of the so-called "door-house" in Bergen; second half of the 13th century. Reconstruction: H. Christie, A. Herteig, O. A. Svendsen.

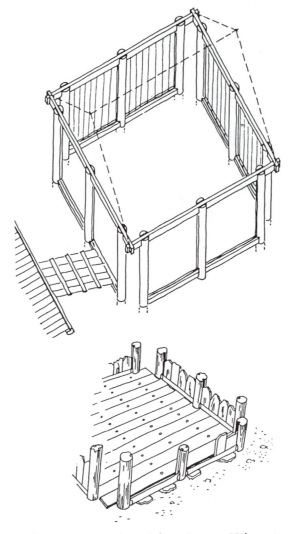

43. The "open corner house" from Bergen; 12th century.
Reconstruction: E. Reimers.

44. Reconstruction of excavated townyards in Oslo from the end of the 13th century. Reconstruction: Ø. Hansen, E. Schia.

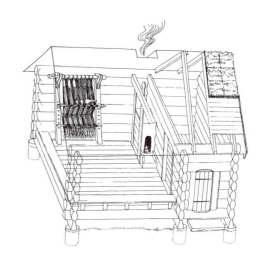

45a

45b

45a–b. Typical single-storied living or kitchen house. Excavated remains and reconstruction from Oslo. Photo: D. Skre; reconstruction: Ø. Hansen, E. Schia.

47. Single-storied one-room house from Oslo; early 12th century. To the right, remains of house with central hearth. Photo: E. Schia.

46. Building with three rooms, probably two-storied; end of the 13th century. Oslo. Photo: E. Schia.

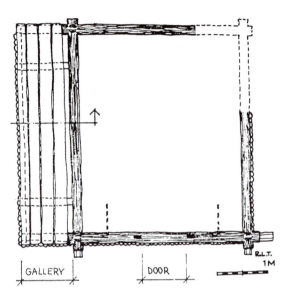

GALLERY   DOOR   R.L.T. 1M

48. One-room single-storied house from Tønsberg, with external gallery. Drawing: R. L. Tollnes.

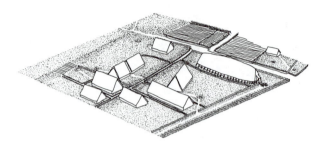

50. Reconstruction of excavated settlement (*ca.* 1200) in Lund. Drawing: Anders Andren.

49. Small building (latrine?) with internal pit. In the back, a sill beam with remains of wattlework. Photo: C.D. Long.

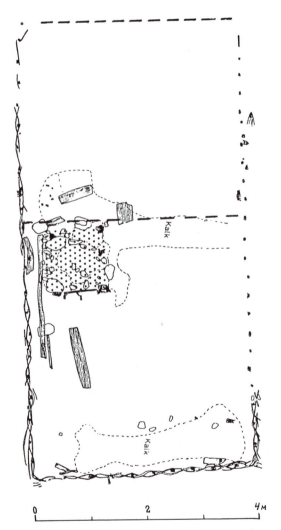

0   2   4 M

51. Plan of wattle house from Lund divided into two rooms with oven in the corner; from *ca.* 1020.

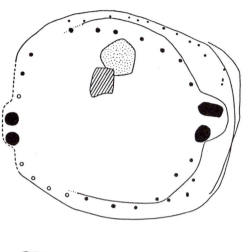

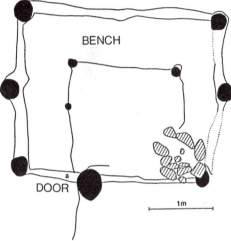

53. Plan of two small sunken huts from Århus (11th century), one with a fireplace in the corner, roof-carrying posts, and vertical planks in the wall (bottom). The wall of the other was made of wattle, with a fireplace in the middle of the wall. After H. Helmuth Andersen.

52. Medieval stone building from Visby. Photo: Hans Hemlin.

1959, Harris 1973). From the second half of the 13th century are the unique remains of a house with two doors at the ground level and two external galleries or pentices (*sval*) on the upper floor (Figs. 42a–c). The reconstruction is based on a bracket and a corner post from the gallery, as well as on the remains of two doors and walls at ground level (Herteig 1959: 180, 1969: 40). Parallels to this construction are found both in Bergen in the 18th century and in medieval rural houses still standing (*loft*). The "door-house" shows a strong continuity in the Norwegian tradition of house building. From the mid-12th century is a house consisting of a wooden sill beam, vertical wall planks, and roof-bearing posts dug into the ground (Fig. 43). Strangely enough, the corners, which consisted of a pair of posts set apart, were left open. The construction is not primitive, and must be related to some special function (Reimers 1976: 104).

In medieval Oslo, excavations have been carried out 150–200 m. from the waterfront (Fig. 44), in an area dominated by activities different from the wharf (Lidén 1977, Schia 1987). Typical here are single-story houses with two rooms (Figs. 45a–b), a good example of which was found in 1987, from the early 13th century. This building has a narrow room, an antechamber, with a wooden floor and entrance on the right side (Fig. 45a). From the narrow room, there was a door to the main room, with a threshold and mortises for the door posts (*beitski*) at either side of the door opening, as seen in the middle of the internal wall. In the right corner of the main room, there was a fireplace (oven?) of stone and clay with a corner post (*ovnskall*), which supported a short plank wall holding the stones of the fireplace/oven in position. The main room had a wooden floor, and against the wall (left side in Fig. 45) were the remains of an earth-filled bench (*moldbenk*), with a vertical plank in the front. It was originally covered with planks. Such benches were made for sitting, and were sometimes used for sleeping, depending on the width of the bench. They also prevented drafts from the wall. Houses like this probably functioned as either a living house or a kitchen house. A few examples (11th century) of houses with a central hearth and an earth floor have also been found (Fig. 47, right). The general rule is, however, a fireplace in the corner, combined with a wooden floor. Excavations in Oslo have also revealed buildings with three rooms and probably two stories (Fig. 46), in addition to smaller single-story houses of one room only (Fig. 47). The latter were probably storehouses. A similar building has also been found in Tønsberg with an external gallery (Fig. 48).

Another type of building (ca. 2–3 x 3–4 m.) consisted of four roof-bearing corner posts dug into the ground, post-and-wattle walls, and a pit of varying depth inside (Fig. 49). They are found alone, and sometimes built up against buildings as shown in Figs. 45a–b (Schia 1987b: 110, 142). Such buildings (11th–13th centuries) have been found in Tønsberg, Trondheim (Long 1975: 206), and Oslo. Very often, the pits were filled with moss and human excrement, and have been interpreted as latrines. Normally, wooden houses were made of horizontal logs, notched at the corners (*laft*). In early-medieval times, however, houses were also post-built, with a stave-constructed wall. Wattle houses are rare in Norwegian cities, and occur only in early-medieval layers. From Trondheim, there is an example of a sill beam with small holes for the posts in the wattle construction, preserved together with the remains of wattle-work (Fig. 49, in the background).

In Sweden, various excavations have shown that wattle houses from the early-medieval period were quite common. In Lund, houses of different function and size have been found, including

a longhouse (21 x 5.5 m.) of the same type as the Danish Viking Age fortresses (Fig. 50). Smaller houses, however, were more common, and the house shown in Fig. 51, probably used by a metalworker, was divided into two rooms, with an oven in the corner and benches filled with limestone along two of the walls in the living room. The other room probably functioned as an antechamber or storage room (Nilsson 1976: 55–7). The excavations in Lund also show a building technique developing throughout the Middle Ages: wattle houses were replaced by more solid post-built constructions, walls of standing timber, which in the early 13th century were replaced by timber-framed buildings and wall fillings of clay or brick. As in Norway, there are also examples of medieval log buildings with notched corners, as shown from excavations, for instance, in Uppsala (Ehn and Gustafsson 1984), Söderköping (Tesch 1987), and Lödöse (Ekre 1968). In the high Middle Ages, buildings begin to appear in stone, several examples of which are still standing in Stockholm and Visby. The Hanseatic wharf area in Visby was developed in the 13th century with stone buildings up to eight stories (Fig. 52), thus making Visby a kind of medieval "Nordic Manhattan."

From Denmark, our knowledge of urban houses is based mostly on surviving late-medieval brick houses, of various size and function, since there has been less archaeological excavation. In Århus, however, at a site close to the southern city wall, several small sunken huts from the 10th century have been recovered, each with different specialized functions: kitchen house and living house with fireplaces, and huts for various handicrafts, among which weaving is documented by concentrations of loom weights. These sunken-feature buildings, about 70 cm. below the contemporary surface, undoubtedly provided good protection against the cold winter temperature. In the 13th century, houses in Århus were still made of post and wattle, and from the 14th century, post-built constructions with vertical planks in the walls have been documented (Andersen 1971). From other Danish excavations, there are examples of sill stones on which timber-framed buildings have been constructed.

Lit.: Herteig, Asbjørn. "The Excavation of 'Bryggen,' the Old Hanseatic Wharf in Bergen." *Medieval Archaeology* 3 (1959), 177–86; Ekre, Rune. *Ny bild av medeltidens Lödöse.* Göteborgs Hembygdsförbunds skriftserie, Göteborg förr och nu, 5. Gothenburg: Förenade tryckerier, 1968; Bugge, Gunnar, and Christian Norberg-Schulz. *Stav og Laft i Norge. Early Wooden Architecture in Norway.* Oslo: Byggekunst. Norske Arkitekters Landsforbund, 1969; Herteig, Asbjørn. *Kongers havn og handels sete.* Oslo: Aschehoug, 1969; Andersen, H. Helmuth. "Århus Søndervold. En byarkeologisk undersøkelse." *Jysk arkæologisk selskaps skrifter* 9 (1971), 30–63; Harris, Edward C. "Bergen. Bryggen 1972: The Evolution of a Harbour Front." *World Archaeology* 5 (1973), 61–71; Lidén, Hans-Emil. "Development of Urban Structure in the 12th and 13th Centuries." In *Archaeological Contributions to the Early History of Urban Communities in Norway.* Ed. Asbjørn E. Herteig *et al.* Institute for Comparative Research in Human Culture, 27. Oslo: Universitetsforlaget, 1975, pp. 90–106; Long, Clifford D. "Excavations in Trondheim." *Zeitschrift für Archäologie des Mittelalters* Jahrgang 3 (1975), 183–207; Nilsson, Thorvald. *Hus och huskonstruktioner. Uppgrävt förflutet för PK banken i Lund.* Archaeologica Lundensia, 7. Malmö: Kulturhistoriska museet i Lund, 1976; Reimers, Egill. "Einige Mittelalterliche Hauskonstruktionen in Bergen. Häuser und Höfe." *Acta Visbyensia* 5 (1976), 89–106; Lidén, Hans-Emil. "Stratigrafisk-topgrafisk beskrivelse av feltet 'Mindets tomt.'" In *De arkeologiske utgravninger i Gamlebyen, Oslo* 1. Oslo, Bergen, and Tromsö:

Universitetsforlaget, 1977, pp. 11–71; Ehn, Ola, and Jan Helmer Gustafsson. "Kransen. Ett medeltida kvarter i Uppsala." *Uppland Fornminnesförenings Tidskrift* 50 (1984), 14–57; Herteig, Asbjørn. "The Archaeological Excavations at Bryggen: 'The German Wharf.'" In *The Bryggen Papers. Main Series.* Bergen, Oslo, Stavanger, and Tromsø: Universitetsforlaget, 1985, vol. 1, pp. 9–46; Schia, Erik. "Reconstructing Townyards on the Periphery of the European Urban Culture." *Norwegian Archaeological Review* 20 (1987), 81–96 [1987a]; Schia, Erik. "Stratigrafi bebyggelserester og daterende funngrupper. 'Søndre felt.'" In *De arkeologiske utgravninger i Gamlebyen. Oslo* 3. Øvre Ervik: Alvheim & Eide, 1987, pp. 41–228 [1987b]; Tesch, Sten. "Söderköping." In *7000 år på 20 år. Arkeologiska undersökningar i Mellansverige.* Ed. Tiiu Andræ *et al.* Stockholm: Riksantikvarieämbetet, 1987, pp. 271–98.

Erik Schia

[**See also:** Architecture]

Hrafnkels saga Freysgoða

("The Saga of Hrafnkell, Freyr's *Goði*") was probably written in the late 13th century, toward the end of the most fruitful period in the history of the sagas. It is, however, extant only in late paper MSS, except for one leaf of a parchment MS that dates from the early 15th century.

The saga is novella-length (about 9,200 words), and its locale is the northeastern corner of Iceland. Hrafnkell is a powerful and ruthless chieftain (*goði*) and large landowner who is a worshiper of the god Freyr. He kills a young shepherd, Einarr, for riding a horse, Freyfaxi, that Hrafnkell has forbidden anyone to ride because he has dedicated it to Freyr.

The boy's father, Þorbjǫrn, demands satisfaction. Hrafnkell, who in the past has never paid compensation for his killings, makes him a very generous offer, but Þorbjǫrn refuses, demanding *sjálfdœmi*, or the right to set his own terms. Everyone thinks he should accept Hrafnkell's terms, but he finally talks his nephew, Sámr, into taking his case to the *Alþingi*, the annual assembly in southwestern Iceland where lawsuits were settled, generally in favor of the side with the greater number of powerful adherents. Sámr and Þorbjǫrn soon find that no one wishes to tangle with Hrafnkell, and their case seems hopeless until they gain the support of Þorkell and Þorgeirr, two brothers who are powerful chieftains from the northwest. With their aid, they are able to have Hrafnkell outlawed. After the *Alþingi* is over, they hold a "court of execution" at Hrafnkell's dwelling, and give him a choice of death, or life stripped of his land and most of his possessions. Hrafnkell chooses life because, he says, he does not want to desert his family.

Sámr takes over Hrafnkell's property, and Hrafnkell moves away to settle in a district to the east. By hard labor and good luck, he builds himself up again and becomes a chieftain even more powerful than he had been before. He gives up his worship of Freyr and becomes more amiable in his dealings. All is quiet for six years, when a relative of Sámr's, Eyvindr, returns from a successful merchant trip abroad and docks in the nearby fjord. Egged on by a servant woman to gain revenge, Hrafnkell waylays Eyvindr and kills him after a hard battle. Sámr tries to prevent the killing, but gets there too late. The next morning, Hrafnkell captures Sámr and forces him to give up the farm and other property he took from him. Sámr, however, is allowed to return to his first residence. He hurries off to the west and asks Þorkell and Þorgeirr for their assistance in getting his property back, but they refuse, as they had warned him that not to kill Hrafnkell would have dire consequences. Sámr leaves in high dudgeon, returns to his farm, and never contests Hrafnkell's power.

Because of its length and a certain amount of verifiable historical fact and accurate geographical detail, *Hrafnkels saga* had long been used as an example of a saga that could well have been orally transmitted. When it was discovered that some of the history and geography was incorrect, it became the center of the long-lasting controversy over the manner of composition and transmission of the sagas of Icelanders in general. Sigurður Nordal maintained that it was historical fiction of the 13th century. Hermann Pálsson argued that it was a kind of *roman à clef*, and that it was meant to exemplify Christian virtues. Neither of these positions can be maintained, as Óskar Halldórsson and Kratz have argued. It now seems evident that there must have been an oral component in the transmission. Kratz maintains that the large amount of alliteration in many sections of the work indicates that it was based on a lost narrative poem of the eddic type.

With its tight narrative structure and its deft characterization, the work stands among the best of the genre. If it has a message, it seems to be that only some are called to be leaders, but those who are must always exercise restraint.

Ed.: Cawley, Frank Stanton, ed. *Hrafnkels saga Freysgoða.* Cambridge: Harvard University Press, 1932; Jón Jóhannesson, ed. *Austfirðinga sǫgur.* Íslenzk fornrit, 11. Reykjavik: Hið íslenzka fornritafélag, 1950, pp. 95–133; Jón Helgason, ed. *Hrafnkels saga Freysgoða.* Nordisk filologi, Tekster og lærebøger til universitetsbrug, A: Tekster, vol. 2. Copenhagen: Munksgaard; Oslo: Dreyer; Stockholm: Bonnier, 1950; Taylor, A. R., ed. "Hrafnkels saga Freysgoða." In E. V. Gordon. *An Introduction to Old Norse.* 2nd ed. rev. A. R. Taylor. Oxford: Oxford University Press, 1957, pp. 58–86. **Bib.**: Kratz, Henry. *Frühes Mittelalter: Vor- und Frühgeschichte des deutschen Schrifttums.* Handbuch der deutschen Literaturgeschichte. Zweite Abteilung: Bibliographien, 1. Ed. Paul Stapf. Berne and Munich: Francke, 1970, p. 117; Fidjestøl, Bjarne. "Hrafnkels saga etter 40 års gransking." *Maal og minne* (1983), 1–17; Clover, Carol J. "Icelandic Family Sagas (*Íslendingasögur*)." In *Old Norse–Icelandic Literature: A Critical Guide.* Ed. Carol J. Clover and John Lindow. Islandica, 45. Ithaca and London: Cornell University Press, 1985, pp. 239–315. **Tr.**: Hermann Pálsson, trans. *Hrafnkel's Saga and Other Icelandic Stories.* Harmondsworth: Penguin, 1971. **Lit.**: Gordon, E. V. "On *Hrafnkels saga Freysgoða.*" *Medium Ævum* 8 (1939), 1–32; Sigurður Nordal. *Hrafnkatla.* Studia Islandica, 7. Reykjavik: Ísafold; Copenhagen: Munksgaard, 1940 [trans. R. George Thomas as *Hrafnkels saga Freysgoða.* Cardiff: University of Wales Press, 1958]; Scovazzi, Marco. *La saga di Hrafnkell e il problema delle saghe islandesi.* Arona: Paideia, 1960; Hermann Pálsson. "Höfundur Hrafnkels sögu." In *Til Kristins E. Andréssonar 12. júní 1961.* Reykjavik: Hól, 1961, pp. 109–12; Hermann Pálsson. *Hrafnkels saga og Freysgyðlingar.* Reykjavik: Þjóðsaga, 1962; Hermann Pálsson. *Art and Ethics in Hrafnkel's Saga.* Copenhagen: Munksgaard, 1971; Óskar Halldórsson. *Uppruni og þema Hrafnkels sögu.* Rannsóknastofnun í bókmenntafræði við Háskóla Íslands. Fræðirit, 3. Reykjavik: Hið íslenzka bókmentafélag, 1976; Kratz, Henry. "Poetry and Truth: The Poetic Source of *Hrafnkels saga.*" In *Wege der Worte: Festschrift für Wolfgang Fleischhauer.* Ed. Donald C. Riechel. Cologne and Vienna: Böhlau, 1978, pp. 189–209; Hughes, Shaun. Rev. of Óskar Halldórsson. *Uppruni og þema Hrafnkels sögu. Scandinavian Studies* 52 (1980), 300–8; Kratz, Henry. "*Hrafnkels saga*: Thirteenth-Century Fiction?" *Scandinavian Studies* 53 (1981), 420–46; Fulk, R. D. "The Moral System of *Hrafnkels saga Freysgoða.*" *Saga-Book of the Viking Society* 22.1 (1986), 1–32; Wolf, Kirsten. "On the Authorship of *Hrafnkels saga.*" *Arkiv för nordisk filologi* 106 (1991), 104–24.

Henry Kratz

[**See also:** *Goði; Íslendingasögur*]

Hrafns saga Sveinbjarnarsonar *see* **Sturlunga saga**

Hrafns þáttr Guðrúnarsonar ("The Tale of Hrafn Guðrúnarson"), a short Old Icelandic tale, is a part of *Magnúss saga góða*. However, the tale appears in only one version, in the compilation *Hulda-Hrokkinskinna* from the 15th century, where it stands among five stories appended to *Magnúss saga*.

The first part takes place in Iceland. While Hrafn is still a child, his father is murdered by a neighbor. Guðrún, Hrafn's mother, conceals the killing from her son. The truth is revealed to Hrafn when he grows up, and he kills the murderer's son. Hrafn is outlawed and barely gets away on a trading ship. When he arrives in Norway, he is permitted residence by the king's steward, Ketill, but is soon disgraced when he gets on too friendly terms with Ketill's wife and daughter. In the end, Hrafn is forced to kill Ketill, and King Magnús Óláfsson becomes the prosecutor of the case. Hrafn thereafter seeks reconciliation with all his might, and is brought back into favor by his achievement in a sea battle against the Danes. Advice given to Magnús in a dream by St. Óláfr also influences the course of events. Hrafn becomes a *hirðmaðr* ("king's man"), marries Ketill's daughter, and settles his outlawry in Iceland.

Hrafns þáttr probably came into being late and under influence from previous sagas, even though it has been assigned by some scholars to as early as about 1200. Completely unknown main actors perform side by side with famous characters like King Magnús, the skald Sighvatr Þórðarson, Einarr þambarskelfir ("the string-shaker") and his son Eindriði. Guðrún is said to be a sister of Sighvatr, but nowhere else is such a sister mentioned. According to the *þáttr*, she resides at Melar in Hrútafjǫrðr, but other sources describe other people living there at the time. Further, a couple of Norwegian place-names are otherwise unknown.

Hrafns þáttr was probably written to accompany *Magnúss saga góða*, drawing on popular motifs. The text refers to another tale in *Magnúss saga*, and there are some striking resemblances to the Danish folksong "Svend af Vollersløv." However, one need not assume a direct connection between the two. Óláfr's intervention at the end has a touch of miracle saga to it.

Ed.: Einar Ól. Sveinsson, ed. *Vatnsdœla saga*. Íslenzk fornrit, 8. Reykjavik: Hið íslenzka fornritafélag, 1939, pp. cxvii–cxx, 317–33. **Tr.**: Niedner, Felix, trans. "Hrafn aus dem Widderford." In *Norwegische Königsgeschichten* 1. Thule, 17. Jena: Diederich, 1928; rpt. 1965, pp. 175–87. **Lit.**: Finnur Jónsson. *Den oldnorske og oldislandske Litteraturs Historie*. 3 vols. 2nd ed. Copenhagen: Gad, 1920–24, vol. 1, p. 613; vol. 2, p. 542; Harris, Joseph. "Theme and Genre in Some *Íslendinga þættir*." *Scandinavian Studies* 48 (1976), 1–28 [esp. pp. 11–2]; Louis-Jensen, Jonna. *Kongesagastudier. Kompilationen Hulda-Hrokkinskinna*. Bibliotheca Arnamagnæana, 32. Copenhagen: Reitzel, 1977, pp. 110–1; Danielsson, Tommy. *Om den isländska släktsagans uppbyggnad*. Skrifter utgivna av Litteraturvetenskapliga institutionen vid Uppsala universitet, 22. Stockholm: Almqvist & Wiksell, 1986, pp. 67–9.

Tommy Danielsson

[**See also**: *Heimskringla*; *Hirð*, *Hulda-Hrokkinskinna*; Outlawry; Sighvatr Þórðarson; *Páttr*]

Hrafnsmál *see* **Sturla Þórðarson**

Hreiðars þáttr heimska ("The Tale of Hreiðarr the Foolish") is found in *Morkinskinna* and *Hulda-Hrokkinskinna*, with stylistic variations but essentially the same plot. It tells of the deceptively simple Icelander Hreiðarr, who badgers his merchant brother into taking him to the court of Magnús inn góði ("the good") Óláfsson in Norway. There he behaves strangely but manages to join the court. He is innocent of anger until a visit to Haraldr harðráði ("hard-ruler") Sigurðarson, whose retainers bully Hreiðarr until he kills one. When Haraldr later confronts him, Hreiðarr seems about to win over the king by making a metal pig for him, but he turns the gift into an insult by referring to Haraldr's father as Sigurðr sýr ("sow"). Hreiðarr escapes back to Magnús, composes and recites a poem for the king, receives awards, returns to Iceland, and becomes a great man.

Typologically, *Hreiðars þáttr* is a so-called *útanferðar þáttr*, because it describes an Icelander's journey to Norway, encounter with a king (doubled in this instance), subsequent reward, and return to Iceland. The protagonist's improvement in social status typifies such *þættir*. *Hreiðars þáttr* takes a special place, however, because of the implausibility of much of the narrative (Hreiðarr is, for example, supernaturally swift of foot) and because of Hreiðarr's verbal cleverness. About half of the text is dialogue, and Hreiðarr wins every verbal encounter.

Many of the *þættir* exhibit characteristics of folktale, and *Hreiðars þáttr* is no exception. Besides his speed of foot, Hreiðarr possesses unusual strength, and his journey from buffoonery to social respectability after being tested by kings parallels that of many unpromising folktale heroes. The tale of "The Youth Who Wanted to Learn What Fear Is" (tale type 326 in Aarne and Thompson; no. 4 in Grimm) seems particularly close. In any case, it appears unlikely that the story could have any historical basis.

Occasional archaisms in the language of *Hreiðars þáttr* have tempted some scholars to assign the story to the oldest layer of Old Icelandic literature, around the beginning of the 13th century. All agree, however, that it is told with great zest and skill.

Ed.: Björn Sigfússon, ed. *Ljósvetninga saga*. Íslenzk fornrit, 10. Reykjavik: Hið íslenzka fornritafélag, 1940, pp. xci–xciv, 245–60; Faulkes, Anthony, ed. *Two Icelandic Stories: Hreiðars þáttr, Orms þáttr*. Text Series, 4. London: Viking Society for Northern Research, 1968. **Tr.**: Simpson, Jacqueline, trans. *The Northmen Talk: A Choice of Tales from Iceland*. London: Phoenix House; Madison: University of Wisconsin Press, 1965, pp. 119–32; Hermann Pálsson, trans. *Hrafnkel's Saga and Other Icelandic Stories*. Harmondsworth: Penguin, 1971, pp. 94–108; Boucher, Alan, trans. *A Tale of Icelanders*. Reykjavik: Iceland Review, 1980, pp. 56–67. **Lit.**: Grimm, Jakob, and Wilhelm Grimm. *Kinder- und Haus-Märchen*. Berlin: Realschulbuchhandlung, 1812–15; Aarne, Antti, and Stith Thompson. *The Types of the Folk-tale: A Classification and Bibliography*. Folklore Fellows Communications, 184. Helsinki: Suomalainen Tiedeakatemia, 1961; Lindow, John. "*Hreiðars þáttr heimska* and AT 326: An Old Icelandic Novella and an International Folktale." *Arv* 34 (1978), 152–79.

John Lindow

[**See also**: *Hulda-Hrokkinskinna*; *Morkinskinna*; *Páttr*]

Hrings saga ok Tryggva ("The Saga of Hringr and Tryggvi") is an Icelandic saga generally considered a *riddarasaga*. Only two 15th-century vellum fragments survive, AM 489 4to and AM 586 4to. The original probably dates from the 14th century. *Hrings rímur ok Tryggva* were composed after the saga in the 16th century and probably tell the same story, although they put the stress on the *skapraun*, or trial of the hero's temper. These *rímur* could have existed by 1400. They, too, are fragmentary, at least in their earliest version. The *rímur* were in turn the basis of a prose saga found in MSS dating from the 18th and 19th centuries.

Brynhildr, daughter of King Hertryggr in Garðaríki, has been brought up together with Hringr. After a few years spent in Viking expeditions during his youth, Hringr becomes king of Greece. In the meantime, a Viking wants to marry Brynhildr: he will be ousted thanks to the help of the king of Saxony, Tryggvi, who, as a consequence, gets Brynhildr. Then a war arises between Hringr and Tryggvi, but it soon ends, and Hringr marries Tryggvi's sister, Brynveig. But Tryggvi is treacherously murdered because of a false friend, and Brynveig dies of sorrow. Thus, since there is no longer any obstacle to the love between Hringr and Brynhildr, they marry.

Supposing the *rímur* faithfully reproduce the plot of the saga, the text could be a useful tool to help solve the difficult and complex problem of defining the nature of the categories of sagas known as *riddarasögur*, *fornaldarsögur*, and *lygisögur*. *Hrings saga ok Tryggva* is not a real *riddarasaga*, despite the fact that the heroes are princely persons and that they express feelings that supposedly belong to the courtly sphere. There is no "knight," properly speaking, nor conventionally chivalric themes in this text. On the other hand, the plot is too simple and the adventures not sufficiently fantastic to allow us to speak of a *fornaldarsaga* in the best meaning of the term. Consequently, we have here a good instance of what King Sverrir is supposed to have called *lygisögur*, an intermediary between *riddarasögur* and *fornaldarsögur*.

Ed.: Finnur Jónsson, ed. *Rímnasafn: Samling af de ældste islandske rimer.* 2 vols. Samfund til udgivelse af gammel nordisk litteratur, 35. Copenhagen: Møller, 1905–22; Loth, Agnete, ed. "Hrings saga ok Tryggva." In *Late Medieval Icelandic Romances.* 5 vols. Editiones Arnamagnæanæ, ser. B, vols. 20–4. Copenhagen: Munksgaard, 1965, vol. 5, pp. 235–8 [English paraphrase by Gillian Fellows-Jensen]; Loth, Agnete, ed. *Fornaldarsagas and Late Medieval Romances. AM 586 4to and AM 589 a–f 4to.* Early Icelandic Manuscripts in Facsimile, 11; Copenhagen: Rosenkilde & Bagger, 1977 [facsimile]; Blaisdell, Foster W. *The Sagas of Ywain and Tristan and Other Tales: AM 489 4to.* Early Icelandic Manuscripts in Facsimile, 12. Copenhagen: Rosenkilde & Bagger, 1980 [facsimile]. **Bib.**: Kalinke, Marianne E., and P. M. Mitchell. *Bibliography of Old Norse–Icelandic Romances.* Islandica, 44. Ithaca and London: Cornell University Press, 1985, pp. 54–5. **Lit.**: Björn K. Þórólfsson. *Rímur fyrir 1600.* Safn Fræðafjelagsins um Ísland og Íslendinga, 9. Copenhagen: Møller, 1934; Schlauch, Margaret. *Romance in Iceland.* Princeton: Princeton University Press; New York: American-Scandinavian Foundation; London: Allen & Unwin, 1934; rpt. New York: Russell & Russell, 1973.

Régis Boyer

[**See also:** *Fornaldarsögur, Lygisaga; Riddarasögur, Rímur*]

Hrólfs saga Gautrekssonar ("The Saga of Hrólfr Gautreksson") is a *fornaldarsaga* dating from the end of the 13th century. It is preserved in numerous MSS, which form two main groups: a longer recension represented by AM 152 fol. and AM 590 b-c 4to, and a shorter and more original recension represented by SKB 7 4to. Although the first leaf containing the opening of the saga is missing, this early 14th-century MS offers the most reliable text. The *Hrólfs rímur Gautrekssonar* are composed on the basis of the last part of the saga.

The saga is structured around a fourfold bridal quest involving Hrólfr's father, Gautrekr, Hrólfr himself, his brother, Ketill,

and his blood-brother, Ásmundr. The saga begins with the courtship by King Gautrekr of Gautaland of a Norwegian princess and the subsequent birth of their sons, Hrólfr and Ketill. The opening section, which presents a genealogical connection between the father of Hrólfr and *Gautreks saga*, is followed by three additional wooing expeditions that are decisive for the pattern of the text. The first courtship journey leads Hrólfr to Sweden, where he woos Princess Þornbjorg. However, she reveals herself as a valkyrie-like heroine, whom he wins sexually after a hard battle. When Hrólfr accompanies Ketill to Russia on the second courtship journey, they meet a cannibal-giant who eats their followers and also threatens the brothers with death. They manage to blind the sleeping cyclops with an iron fork, and they escape with the magic sword Risanautr ("giant's companion"), which Hrólfr later uses considerably. He undertakes the third and most dangerous bridal quest to Ireland together with his blood-brother, Ásmundr. Before Ásmundr can win the daughter of the king of Ireland, they must undergo further adventurous trials, such as a fight with a lion, which, as in the previous bridal quests, reveals Hrólfr as a helpful, clever, and cautious hero. In general, the anonymous author emphasizes the characterization of the protagonist but without reaching the level of the art of the *Íslendingasögur*. At the end of the saga, the author comments on the possibilities of the oral transmission of the saga material, and he addresses his audience directly with the following noteworthy reflection: "Whether this is true or not, let those who can, enjoy the story; but those who cannot, had better find some other amusement."

Although the saga attempts to capture the Viking atmosphere of the Scandinavian *forn ǫld* through names and scenes, it is difficult to classify the saga. Both the plot and the motifs give it the imprint of a fairy tale. In the threefold wooing expedition, one also finds the typical bridal-quest saga, which is interspersed with clear chivalric or romantic elements, such as courtly speech, the maiden-king, duels, and tournaments. The reworking of the Polyphemus material probably comes from a nonliterary version of the medieval European folk tradition that differs somewhat from Homer. The many similarities in motifs found within Norse literature, especially in *Qrvar-Odds saga* and *Hyndluljóð*, have not yet been fully investigated by scholars.

Ed.: Rafn, C. C., ed. *Fornaldar sögur Nordrlanda.* 3 vols. Copenhagen: Popp, 1829–30; Detter, Ferdinand, ed. *Zwei Fornaldersögur (Hrólfssaga Gautrekssonar und Ásmundarsaga kappabana) nach Cod. Holm. 7, 4to.* Halle: Niemeyer, 1891. **Tr.**: Hermann Pálsson and Paul Edwards, trans. *Hrolf Gautreksson: A Viking Romance.* New Saga Library. Edinburgh: Southside; Toronto: University of Toronto Press, 1972. **Lit.**: Hollander, Lee M. "The Gautland Cycle of Sagas." *Journal of English and Germanic Philology* 11 (1912), 61–81, 209–17; Hollander, Lee M. "The Relative Age of the Gautrekssaga and Hrólfssaga Gautrekssonar." *Arkiv för nordisk filologi* 29 (1913), 120–34; Hermann Pálsson and Paul Edwards. *Legendary Fiction in Medieval Iceland.* Studia Islandica, 30. Reykjavik: Heimspekideild Háskóla Íslands; Menningarsjóður, 1971; Fry, Donald K. "Polyphemus in Iceland." *The Fourteenth Century.* Ed. Paul E. Szarmach and Bernard S. Levy. Acta 4. Binghamton: Center for Medieval and Early Renaissance Studies, State University of New York at Binghamton, 1977, pp. 65–86; Naumann, Hans-Peter. "Das Polyphem-Abenteuer in der altnordischen Sagaliteratur." *Schweizerisches Archiv für Volkskunde* 75 (1979), 173–89; Kalinke, Marianne. "Norse Romance (*Riddarasögur*)." In *Old Norse–Icelandic Literature: A Critical Guide.* Ed. Carol J. Clover and John Lindow. Islandica, 45. Ithaca and London: Cornell University

Press, 1985, pp. 324–6, 328–31; Kalinke, Marianne E. *Bridal-Quest Romance in Medieval Iceland*. Islandica, 46. Ithaca and London: Cornell University Press, 1990, pp. 25–65.

Hans-Peter Naumann

[See also: *Fornaldarsögur; Gautreks saga; Hyndluljóð;* Old Norse-Icelandic Literature, Foreign Influence on; *Qrvar-Odds saga*]

Hrólfs saga kraka ("The Saga of Hrólfr the Pole-ladder"), next to *Vǫlsunga saga* probably the best known of the *fornaldarsögur*, concerns King Hrólfr and his twelve champions at the early Danish stronghold Hleiðargarðr (associated with modern Lejre), on Zealand in Denmark. Hrólfr's importance in the legendary history of Denmark is corroborated by accounts in Saxo's *Gesta Danorum, *Skjǫldunga saga,* Snorri's *Skáldskaparmál* and *Ynglinga saga,* and the *Chronicon Lethrense.* The Old English poem *Widsith* mentions him in its list of early Germanic heroes by the name "Hróþwulf," who is named in *Beowulf* as a nephew of King Hrothgar ("Hróar" in the saga). *Langfeðgatal* (AM 415 4to; 14th century) traces Hrólfr's ancestry from Óðinn through Skjǫldr, Danr, Hálfdan, and Helgi, his father, although genealogical details in other sources differ. *Hrólfs saga kraka* is preserved in thirty-eight MSS, none dating to before the early 17th century; the saga is known to be older, however, because a copy was listed among a collection of "Norse books" in the Icelandic cloister at Möðruvellir in 1461, and Snorri's *Skáldskaparmál* (ca. 1225) refers to *frásagnir* ("narratives") about Hrólfr.

Hrólfs saga kraka has been edited six times; of these editions, four are based upon AM 9 fol. The *editio princeps* (1737) used only the MSS then available in Sweden, which included Stock. Papp. 4to no. 17. The most recent diplomatic edition (1960) reproduces AM 285 4to, which has been described by its editor as "a careful, sensible copy of the saga" and which "serves as well as any as a basis for reconstructing the common original."

Although the saga centers upon the Danish court, much of the action takes place elsewhere in the legendary landscape of northern Europe. *Hrólfs saga kraka* opens upon a dynastic struggle between Fróði and his brother Hálfdan, king of Denmark. Hálfdan is killed and his throne usurped. Although his sons Helgi and Hróar manage to escape, later to reclaim the throne, Helgi is the victim of an evil fate. His first sexual partner is Ólof, a bellicose and unsubmissive queen who returns home to Germany immediately after her forced stay with Helgi. Their daughter, Yrsa, becomes Helgi's wife, and their offspring is Hrólfr, the saga's hero Helgi's third partner is an elf-woman, with whom he conceives Skuld, a sorceress later instrumental in the downfall of her half-brother, Hrólfr, and his splendid court.

When her incestuous marriage with Helgi is revealed, Yrsa leaves Denmark to join her mother in Germany, where she is taken against her will to Uppsala as the wife of the Swedish king Aðils. Helgi goes after her but is ambushed by Aðils, who emerges as Hrólfr's chief enemy in the Scandinavian dynastic conflict that serves as the saga's central theme. The major heroes in this conflict, Hrólfr's twelve champions, are gathered from throughout Scandinavia. Among them are Svipdagr, a Swede who has been betrayed by Aðils in his wars against the berserks, and Bǫðvarr bjarki ("little bear"), whose father has been turned into a bear by his stepmother and slain by the king of Norway. After reaching Hrólfr's court, Bǫðvarr kills a winged troll that has wrought much carnage in Denmark and allows the coward Hǫttr to take the credit.

He forces Hǫttr to eat the troll's heart and drink its blood; as a result, Hǫttr is marvelously emboldened, and Hrólfr renames him "Hjalti" ("hilt").

Once his court is assembled, Hrólfr and his men take revenge upon Aðils and reclaim the Danish patrimony lost at Helgi's death. Hrólfr's court attains the height of splendor, but it is destroyed and Hrólfr is killed when his sorceress half-sister, Skuld, wages war against him with the aid of supernatural creatures. Bǫðvarr's brothers soon exact revenge upon Skuld and return the throne to Hrólfr's descendants. Hrólfr receives his nickname *kraki* ("pole, pole-ladder") from his servant Vǫggr, who is struck by the king's slender appearance.

Hrólfs saga kraka has attracted the attention of scholars interested in the legendary history of the North and in the "Bear's Son" folk motif. The section about Bǫðvarr is taken as a significant example of the motif and an analogue of *Beowulf.* Bǫðvarr's parents' names, Bjǫrn and Bera, mean "bear" and "she-bear," respectively, and his nickname "bjarki" means "little bear." His fight with the troll parallels Beowulf's victory against Grendel, and the addition of wings to the description of the monster appears to represent late contamination with the dragonslayer episode, of which there are numerous medieval Scandinavian examples.

Hrólfs saga kraka abounds in folktale and romance elements, including named swords and heirlooms; supernatural creatures, including elves, norns, berserks, sorcerers, and trolls; magical weapons; and enchantments. Its climax includes tragic-heroic speeches nearly as striking as those found in the Old English poem *The Battle of Maldon.* The list of Hrólfr's twelve champions suggests awareness of Arthurian material, and the narrator's ascription of Hrólfr's final defeat to his failure to worship the true Creator resembles similar passages elsewhere in medieval literature. *Hrólfs saga kraka's* alleged authority for this inference is "master Galterus," or Galterus de Castellione, whose history of Alexander the Great was translated into Icelandic as *Alexanders saga* in the mid-13th century.

Ed.: Björner, E. J., ed. *Nordiska Kämpa Dater.* Stockholm: Horn, 1737; Rafn, C. C., ed. *Fornaldar sögur Nordrlanda.* 3 vols. Copenhagen: Popp, 1829–30, vol. 1, pp. 3–109; Finnur Jónsson, ed. *Hrólfs saga kraka og Bjarkarímur.* Samfund til udgivelse af gammel nordisk litteratur, 32. Copenhagen: Møller, 1904; Guðni Jónsson, ed. *Fornaldar sögur Norðurlanda.* 4 vols. Akureyri: Íslendingasagnaútgáfan, 1954, vol. 1, pp. 1–105; Slay, Desmond, ed. *Hrólfs saga kraka.* Editiones Arnamagnæanæ, ser. B, vol. 1. Copenhagen: Munksgaard, 1960. **Tr.**: Mills, Stella M., trans. *The Saga of Hrolf Kraki* Oxford: Blackwell, 1933; Jones, Gwyn, trans. *Eirik the Red and Other Icelandic Sagas.* Oxford: Oxford University Press, 1961; rpt. 1980, pp. 221–318. **Lit.**: Olrik, Axel. *Danmarks heltedigtning. En oldtidsstudie 1.* Copenhagen: Thiele, 1903 [trans. Hollander, Lee M. *The Heroic Legends of Denmark.* New York: American-Scandinavian Foundation, 1919]; Panzer, Friedrich Wilhelm. *Studien zur germanischen Sagengeschichte 1.* Munich: Beck, 1910; Olson, Oscar L. "The Relation of the *Hrólfs saga Kraka* and the *Bjarkarímur* to *Beowulf." Scandinavian Studies and Notes* 3 (1916), 5–99; Chambers, R. W. *Beowulf: An Introduction to the Study of the Poem with a Discussion of the Stories of Offa and Finn.* 3rd ed. with supplement by Charles L. Wrenn. Cambridge: Cambridge University Press, 1959 [see esp. pp. 16–30, 54–61; English translation of *Hrólfs saga,* ch. 23, pp. 142–6]; Klaeber, Fr. *Beowulf and the Fight at Finnsburg.* 3rd ed. with supplement. Boston: Heath, 1950, pp. xvii–xx; Caldwell, James Ralston. "The Origin of the Story of Bǫthvar-Bjarki." *Arkiv för nordisk filologi* 55 (1940), 223–75; Slay, D. *The Manuscripts* of *Hrólfs saga kraka*. Bibliotheca Arnamagnæana, 24. Copenhagen: Munksgaard, 1960; Jones, Gwyn. *A History of the Vikings*. 2nd ed. Oxford and New York: Oxford University Press, 1984, pp. 34–54; Hughes, S. F. D. "The Literary Antecedents of *Áns saga bogsveigis*." *Mediaeval Scandinavia* 9 (1976), 198–235; Jorgensen, Peter A. "The Gift of the Useless Weapon in *Beowulf* and the Icelandic Sagas." *Arkiv för nordisk filologi* 94 (1979), 82–90.

Jonathan D. M. Evans

[**See also:** Folklore; *Fornaldarsögur*; Old English Literature, Norse Influence on; Old Norse-Icelandic Literature, Foreign Influence on; Saxo Grammaticus; *Skjǫldunga saga*; *Snorra Edda*; *Ynglinga saga*]

Hrómundar saga Gripssonar

("The Saga of Hrómundr Gripsson") dates from the 17th century and is almost certainly based on *Griplur*, late-medieval *rímur* on the same subject. The *Griplur* were probably based on a now-lost saga of Hrómundr Gripsson. This lost saga has been the focus of much scholarly debate. Interest centers on the description in *Þorgils saga ok Hafliða* (ch. 10) of the entertainment at the wedding feast at Reykjahólar in 1119, where "Hrólfr of Skálmarnes told a saga about Hrǫngviðr the Viking, and about Óláfr king of warriors, and the breaking of the mound of Þráinn the berserk, and Hrómundr Gripsson, with many verses in it." The text further notes that "Hrólfr composed this saga himself." *Þorgils saga* cannot be dated more precisely than to the first half of the 13th century, but it was clearly composed long after the events described. If it does contain a genuine tradition about the Reykjahólar wedding, its account provides evidence for an oral stage in the development of *fornaldarsögur* well before such sagas were generally written down, and suggests that early *fornaldarsögur* were composed in a mixture of prose and verse. Even if the account in *Þorgils saga* is based on a written saga circulating at the time rather than on older traditions, the lost *Hrómundar saga* remains one of the oldest written *fornaldarsögur*.

The summary of *Hrómundar saga* given in *Þorgils saga* corresponds closely to the first half of *Griplur*. We can thus be reasonably sure that the lost saga contained the following: (1) introduction of King Óláfr and his men, including Hrómundr; (2) a battle at Elfarsker between the king and Hrǫngviðr, in which the latter is killed by Hrómundr; (3) while on a Viking raid with Óláfr, Hrómundr breaks into the grave mound of a certain Þráinn, kills him, and acquires treasure and a sword. Other episodes recounted in the *Griplur* that we cannot be sure were in the lost saga include: (4) Hrómundr is accused of seducing the king's sister, Svanhvít; (5) the king and his followers fight a battle against Hrǫngviðr's brother, Helgi, and two kings; Hrómundr is wounded, but the battle is won; (6) Hrómundr marries the princess. The narrative is thus in the mainstream of the *fornaldarsaga* tradition.

Ed.: Finnur Jónsson, ed. *Rímnasafn: Samling af de ældste islandske rimer*. 2 vols. Samfund til udgivelse af gammel nordisk litteratur, 35. Copenhagen: Møller, 1905–22, vol. 1, pp. 351–410 [*Griplur*]; Rafn, C. C., ed. *Fornaldarsögur Nordrlanda*. 3 vols. Copenhagen: Popp, 1829–30, vol. 2, pp. 363–80 [*Hrómundar saga Gripssonar*]. **Tr.:** Kershaw, Nora, trans. *Stories and Ballads of the Far Past*. Cambridge: Cambridge University Press, 1921, pp. 58–78. **Lit.:** Brown, Ursula. "The Saga of Hrómund Gripsson and Þorgilssaga." *Saga-Book of the Viking Society* 13 (1946–53), 51–77; Foote, Peter G. "Sagnaskemtan: Reykjahólar 1119." *Saga-Book of the Viking Society* 14 (1953–57), 226–39; See, Klaus von. "Das Problem der mündlichen Erzählprosa im Altnordischen."

Skandinavistik 11 (1981), 89–95; rpt. in his *Edda, Saga, Skaldendichtung: Aufsätze zur skandinavischen Literatur des Mittelalters*. Heidelberg: Winter, 1981; Foote, Peter. "Sagnaskemtan: Reykjahólar 1119. Postscript." In *Aurvandilstá: Norse Studies*. Ed. Michael Barnes *et al*. Viking Collection, 2. Odense: Odense University Press, 1984, pp. 76–83; Jesch, Judith. "Hrómundr Gripsson Revisited." *Skandinavistik* 14 (1984), 89–105.

Judith Jesch

[**See also:** *Fornaldarsögur*, *Rímur*, *Sturlunga saga*]

Hrómundar þáttr halta

("The Tale of Hrómundr with the Limp") is a short, anonymous *þáttr* incorporated into *Óláfs saga Tryggvasonar* in *Flateyjarbók*; it appears also in a condensed form in the *Sturlubók* version of *Landnámabók* composed by Sturla Þórðarson (d. 1284). An extract from the original text is transmitted also in *Hauksbók*. The date for the composition of the *þáttr* can thus be established on the basis of the date of *Sturlubók*. According to Einar Ól. Sveinsson (1939), the language and style of the tale suggest an early date. Although the texts in *Flateyjarbók* and *Sturlubók* go back to a common original, there are divergences that can be attributed either to Sturla's editing or to his source. Only in *Flateyjarbók* is the narrative called a *þáttr*.

The *þáttr* tells the story of twelve Norwegian Vikings who steal horses from Icelandic farmers, including the farmer Hrómundr. Hrómundr decides to pursue the crime, but wants to come to a solution in a friendly way. The horse thieves pay little attention to Hrómundr's accusations and attack the Icelander at his farm. Hrómundr reveals himself as an undaunted hero in his fight against the Norwegians, in which he is finally killed. Hallsteinn, Hrómundr's son, then goes to Norway to King Óláfr's court, becomes one of his men, and falls by his side in the battle of Svǫlðr (Svold).

Within the context in which it appears in *Óláfs saga Tryggvasonar* in *Flateyjarbók*, *Hrómundar þáttr halta* displays a moral meaning set against a political background. The political dimension of the *þáttr* is reflected in Hallsteinn's relationship with King Óláfr, his baptism, and his death in the battle of Svǫlðr.

Elements of the *þáttr* are mentioned also in *Vatnsdœla saga* (ch. 29) and *Grettis saga* (ch. 30). In all of the MSS of *Landnámabók*, Hrómundr's son is called Hásteinn. In the lists of the participants in the battle of Svǫldr in *Óláfs saga* by Oddr and in *Heimskringla*, there is no Hásteinn, but two men by the name of Hallsteinn. A later scribe most likely identified Hrómundr's son with one of these men.

Ed.: Rafn, C. C., *et al*., eds. *Fornmanna sögur*. 12 vols. Copenhagen: Popp, 1828–46, vol. 3, pp. 142–51; Guðbrandr Vigfússon and C. R. Unger, eds. *Flateyjarbók: En Samling af norske Konge-Sagaer med indskudte mindre Fortællinger om Begivenheder i og undenfor Norge samt Annaler*. 3 vols. Christiania [Oslo]: Malling, 1860–68, vol. 1, pp. 409–14; Þorleifr Jónsson, ed. *Fjörutíu Íslendinga þættir*. Reykjavik: Sigurður Kristjánsson, 1904, pp. 163–72; Guðni Jónsson, ed. *Íslendinga þættir*. Reykjavik: Sigurður Kristjánsson, 1935, pp. 133–43; Einar Ól. Sveinsson, ed. *Vatnsdœla saga*. Íslensk fornrit, 8. Reykjavik: Hið íslenzka fornritafélag, 1939, pp. 303–15; Sigurður Nordal *et al.*, eds. *Flateyjarbók*. 4 vols. Akranes: Flateyjarútgáfan, 1944–45, vol. 1, pp. 455–60; Guðni Jónsson, ed. *Íslendinga sögur*. 13 vols. 2nd ed. Akureyri: Íslendingasagnaútgáfn, 1953, vol. 5, pp. 411–23. **Lit.:** Jónas Kristjánsson. *Eddas and Sagas: Iceland's Medieval Literature*. Trans. Peter Foote. Reykjavik: Hið íslenska bókmenntafélag, 1988, p. 303; Würth, Stefanie. *Elemente des Erzählens: Die þættir der Flateyjarbók*. Beiträge zur nordischen Philologie, 20. Basel and Frankfurt am Main: Helbing & Lichtenhahn, 1991.

Stefanie Würth

[**See also:** *Flateyjarbók; Grettis saga; Hauksbók; Landnámabók, Óláfs saga Tryggvasonar, Þáttr, Vatnsdœla saga*]

Hryggjarstykki *see* Konungasögur

Hrynhenda *see* Arnórr Þórðarson jarlaskáld

Hugsvinnsmál ("The Speech of the Wise-Minded One") is an

anonymous loose rendering in some 148 strophes of the *Disticha* (or *Dicta*) *Catonis*, a collection of didactic Latin couplets in which a father gives advice to his son, dating from the second or third century A.D. The *Disticha* were widely celebrated throughout Europe in the Middle Ages and later, and translated into many vernacular tongues. In Iceland, they were known at least by the 12th century; one of the couplets is quoted with a prose translation in the *First Grammatical Treatise*. The use of *Hugsvinnr* in the Icelandic title is probably a rendering of the Latin adjective *catus* 'shrewd,' which the translator apparently associated with the name *Cato*. The popularity of *Hugsvinnsmál* in Iceland is evidenced by the large number of surviving MSS, of which forty-two are known, although most are paper MSS from the 17th century onward, and many contain only a small portion of the text. The oldest MS, AM 624 4to, a vellum from the 15th century, forms the basis of modern editions, although it omits a number of strophes found in some other MSS; the order of the strophes also varies somewhat in the MSS and hence in modern editions. The poem's style is plain to the point of flatness, and its vocabulary has been described by Gering as meager. The text presents no serious problems of interpretation. The meter, as usual in Old Norse didactic verse, is *ljóðaháttr*. The translation is very free, and, although the Latin original is pagan, as the translator observes in his introductory strophe, sentiments of a manifestly Christian character appear. The poem shows a number of verbal resemblances to *Hávamál* and to *Sólarljóð; Hávamál* is certainly older than *Hugsvinnsmál* and is probably consciously echoed. But the precedence between *Hugsvinnsmál* and *Sólarljóð* is less clear; Ólsen suggested common authorship. Extensive claims for the influence of *Hugvinnsmál* have been made by Hermann Pálsson (1985), who sees echoes widely in Icelandic saga literature and even in the Norwegian *Konungs skuggsjá* (ca. 1250); but it is more likely that all these works, *Hugsvinnsmál* included, draw on a general Norse stock of sententious phraseology. The poem can be tentatively assigned to the 13th century; its use of the negative verbal suffix *-a, -at* surely precludes any later date.

Ed.: Gering, Hugo. ed. *Hugsvinnsmál. Eine altisländische Übersetzung der Disticha Catonis*. Kiel: Lipsius & Tischer, 1907; Finnur Jónsson, ed. *Den norsk-islandske skjaldedigtning*. Vols. 1A-2A (tekst efter håndskrifterne) and 1B-2B (rettet tekst). Copenhagen and Christiania [Oslo]: Gyldendal, 1912–15; rpt. Copenhagen: Rosenkilde & Bagger, 1967 (A) and 1973 (B) [vol. 2A, pp. 167–97, presents a diplomatic text, with variants; vol. 2B, pp. 185–210, has a normalized text with Danish translation]; Halldór Hermannsson, ed. *The Hólar Cato: An Icelandic Schoolbook of the Seventeenth Century*. Islandica, 39. Ithaca: Cornell University Press; Tuvestrand, Birgitta, ed. *Hugsvinnsmál. Handskrifter*

och kritisk text. Lundastudier i nordisk språkvetenskap, A.29. Lund: Studentlitteratur, 1977 [English summary]. **Lit.:** B. M. Ólsen, ed. *Sólarljóð. Safn til sögu Islands og íslenskra bókmenta*, 5.1. Reykjavik: Hið íslenzka bókmentafélag, 1915, pp. 66–70; Alexander, Gerhard. "Studien über die Hugsvinnsmál." *Zeitschrift für deutsches Altertum und deutsche Literatur* 68 (1931), 97–127; Hermann Pálsson. *Áhrif Hugsvinnsmála á aðrar fornbókmenntir*. Studia Islandica, 43. Reykjavik: Menningarsjóður, 1985 [brief English summary; includes text of poem and Latin original].

D. A. H. Evans

[**See also:** Eddic Meters; *Hávamál; Konungs skuggsjá; Sólarljóð*]

Hulda-Hrokkinskinna is the name usually applied to the

version of the sagas of the kings of Norway between approximately 1035 and 1177 contained in the medieval Icelandic MSS *Hulda* ("the secret [vellum]"; AM 66 fol., 14th century) and *Hrokkinskinna* ("the wrinkled vellum"; GkS 1010 fol., 15th century). This version is a compilation based on *Morkinskinna* and the relevant part of *Heimskringla*, with a number of additions from other works. The compilation was made after 1268, perhaps after 1280, but hardly much later than 1300, from MSS no longer extant. *Hulda* and *Hrokkinskinna* are sister MSS, derived directly or indirectly from the lost original compilation.

The MSS of *Heimskringla* fall into two main classes, the "Kringla" class and the "Jöfraskinna" class. The MS that was available to the compiler of *Hulda-Hrokkinskinna* belonged to the latter class, together with such MSS as *Eirspennill, Jöfraskinna*, and *Gullinskinna;* the latter two are known to us in 16th- and 17th-century transcripts, while only stray fragments are left of the originals. In 1599, the sagas of the kings of Norway were translated into Danish by the Norwegian cleric Peder Claussøn Friis; the last third of *Heimskringla* was certainly translated either from the very MS that was used by the compiler of *Hulda-Hrokkinskinna* or from a descendant of it.

The name *Morkinskinna* designates the MS GkS 1009 fol., and, by extension, the version of the sagas of the kings of Norway preserved almost completely in this MS, and partly or fragmentarily in two other MSS, notably the more recent part of *Flateyjarbók* (15th century). Genetically, the *Morkinskinna* text used by the compiler of *Hulda-Hrokkinskinna* was more closely related to the more recent part of *Flateyjarbók* than to GkS 1009 fol. Stylistically, the *Morkinskinna* text in *Hulda-Hrokkinskinna* differs considerably from that of both the other MSS of *Morkinskinna* text, as a result of a revision that seems to have been undertaken around 1300 and that affected the vocabulary as well as the narrative technique. This revision aimed at achieving a slightly "florid" style and a stricter chronological order of presentation.

While the main constituents of the compilation are *Morkinskinna* and *Heimskringla, Hulda-Hrokkinskinna* draws on other sources for three complete *þættir* and a number of shorter passages. Two of the *þættir, Þorgríms þáttr Hallasonar* and *Hrafns þáttr Guðrúnarsonar*, are not found elsewhere, while *Gísls þáttr Illugasonar* has parallel texts in the three versions of *Jóns saga helga*.

Ed.: Rafn, C. C., *et al.*, eds. *Fornmanna sögur*. 12 vols. Copenhagen: Popp, 1828–46, vols. 6–7; Louis-Jensen, Jonna, ed. *Hulda: Sagas of the Kings of Norway 1035–1177*. Early Icelandic Manuscripts in Facsimile,

8. Copenhagen: Rosenkilde & Bagger, 1968 [facsimile]; a critical edition by Jonna Louis-Jensen will appear in Editiones Arnamagnæanæ, ser. A, vols. 11–2. **Lit.**: Louis-Jensen, Jonna. "Introduction." In *Hulda*, pp. 9–24; Louis-Jensen, Jonna. *Kongesagastudier: Kompilationen Hulda-Hrokkinskinna*. Bibliotheca Arnamagnæana, 32. Copenhagen: Reitzel, 1977 [with references].

Jonna Louis-Jensen

[**See also:** *Eirspennill; Flateyjarbók; Gísls þáttr Illugasonar; Heimskringla; Hrafns þáttr Guðrúnarsonar, Jóns saga ens helga; Konungasögur, Morkinskinna; Þorgríms þáttr Hallasonar*]

Hungrvaka ("Hunger-waker"), named by its anonymous author in its preface, survives in six 17th-century transcripts and later copies of these. The primary MSS represent three versions: (1) AM 380 4to, AM 379 4to (B); (2) AM 205 fol., AM 375 4to, AM 378 4to (C); (3) AM 110 8vo (D). Probably none of these versions preserves the medieval original. The text is short, about 7,800 words, and gives an account of the first five bishops of Iceland in the southern diocese of Skálholt: Ísleifr Gizurarson (bishop 1055–1080), Gizurr Ísleifsson (bishop 1082–1118), Þorlákr Rúnólfsson (bishop 1118–1133), Magnús Einarsson (bishop 1134–1148), and Klœngr Þorsteinsson (bishop 1152–1176). Its final paragraph seems intended to link it to a following life of St. Þorlákr Þórhallsson. Because of references to the sanctity of St. Þorlákr (acknowledged 1198) and of St. Jón Ǫgmundarson (acknowledged 1200), and references to Gizurr Hallsson (d. 1206) as immediate informant, the text was probably written in the first or second decade of the 13th century, but perhaps after 1206. It was probably written at or near Skálholt, since it may use documents likely to have been preserved in the cathedral archive, particularly a copy of a papal letter. It used *Íslendingabók* as a primary source concerning Bishops Ísleifr and Gizurr, although the author probably also had access to other material, since it gives supplementary material that sometimes conflicts with *Íslendingabók*. It also used material derived, probably indirectly, from Adam of Bremen's *Gesta Hammaburgensis ecclesiae pontificum*. It is the most important primary historical source for the other three bishops with whom it deals, although there is no certain evidence that other medieval texts used it as such. However, *Auðunar þáttr vestfirzka*, preserved in *Morkinskinna* and *Flateyjarbók*, may employ motifs and wording taken from it.

The text has a fairly consistent method of presentation. It gives the origin and person of each bishop, a detailed and dated account of his consecration, a general account of his personal qualities and any specific ways he enriched or enlarged the establishment at Skálholt, a detailed account of his death, and a list of historical memoranda of events, mostly deaths, abroad and in Iceland during the bishop's episcopacy. These memoranda are normally undated but given in chronological order.

The style of the text is distinctive. Sometimes rather ornate, it makes use of sententious moral comments and proverbs. Its descriptions tend to be formulaic, and are often composed of alliterating pairs of adjectives. Because of close similarities of structure and style, and shared peculiarities of chronology, it is normally considered that the author of *Hungrvaka* also composed *Páls saga biskups*. He may also have composed a number of passages preserved in *Þorláks saga helga*.

Ed.: Jón Ólafsson, ed. *Hungurvaka . . . Páls biskups saga*. Copenhagen: Godiche, 1778; [Jón Sigurðsson and Guðbrandur Vigfússon, eds.] *Biskupa sögur*. 2 vols. Copenhagen: Möller, 1858–78; Stefán Sveinsson, ed. *Saga Páls Skálholts biscups oc Hungrvaka*. Winnipeg: [n.p.], 1889 [rpt. of 1778 edition, with notes]; Kahle, B., ed. *Kristni saga, Þáttr Þorvalds ens víðfǫrla, Þáttr Ísleifs biskups Gizurarsonar, Hungrvaka*. Altnordische Saga-Bibliothek, 11. Halle: Niemeyer, 1905; Gudbrand Vigfusson and F. York Powell, eds. and trans. *Origines Islandicae: A Collection of the More Important Sagas and Other Native Writings Relating to the Settlement and Early History of Iceland*. 2 vols. Oxford: Clarendon, 1905; rpt. Millwood: Kraus, 1976, vol. 1, pp. 420–58; Jón Helgason, ed. *Byskupa sǫgur* 1. Det kongelige nordiske oldskriftselskab. Copenhagen: Munksgaard, 1938, pp. 25–115; Guðni Jónsson, ed. *Byskupa sögur*. 3 vols. Akureyri: Íslendingasagnaútgáfan; Haukadalsútgáfan, 1948, vol. 1. **Tr.**: Gudbrand Vigfusson and F. York Powell, eds. and trans., *Origines Islandicae*, vol. 1, pp. 425–58. **Lit.**: Kahle, B. "Die Handschriften der Hungrvaka." *Arkiv för nordisk filologi* 20 (1904), 228–54; Stefán Einarsson. *A History of Icelandic Literature*. New York: Johns Hopkins University Press; American-Scandinavian Foundation, 1957; Jón Helgason. "Småstykker 3. Et sted i Hungrvaka." *Opuscula* 1. Bibliotheca Arnamagnæana, 20. Copenhagen: Munksgaard, 1960, pp. 352–3; Bekker-Nielsen, Hans. "*Hungrvaka* and the Medieval Icelandic Audience." *Studi Germanici* N.S. 10 (1972), 95–8; Schach, Paul. *Icelandic Sagas*. Twayne's World Authors Series, 717. Boston: Twayne, 1984; Köhne, R. "Wirklichkeit und Fiktion in dem mittelalterlichen Nachrichten über Isleif Gizurarson." *Skandinavistik* 17 (1987), 24–30.

Paul Bibire

[**See also:** Adam of Bremen; *Biskupa sögur; Ísleifs þáttr biskups; Íslendingabók; Páls saga biskups; Þorláks saga helga*]

Hunting in Scandinavia provided a subsidiary income for peasants in many inland districts. The game can be divided into animals hunted for their furs, those hunted for their meat, and beasts of prey hunted because they killed domestic animals. Among the fur-bearing animals, squirrel was by far the most important, followed by ermine, both hunted mainly north of Trondheim in Norway and of Stockholm in Sweden. Deer, elk, reindeer, and hare were the most important animals hunted for meat. In the northernmost parts of Norway and Sweden and on the mountain plateaus of southern Norway, there were herds of tens of thousands of reindeer. In the woodlands of southern Scandinavia, elk and deer were common. Among beasts of prey, foxes and wolves were found all over Scandinavia, bears in Norway and Sweden. In Iceland, arctic fox was the main game, supplemented by an occasional polar bear coming across from Greenland on drift ice.

The weapons used were bow and spear, and, from the 13th century, the crossbow. From the 16th century, guns were used. The simplest and perhaps most common procedure was for the hunter to stalk as near the game as possible before shooting or throwing the spear, but it was also common to chase game. In snow-rich districts, the best hunting season was late winter, when the snow crust was hard enough to support a hunter on skis, but not the quarry. In Denmark, southern Sweden, and some northern districts, dogs were used in the chase. Reindeer, elk, and deer were chased over cliffs or into trenches that were often dug in long rows across the traditional tracks of these animals. A wide variety of traps were used. Traps for elk, deer, wolves, and foxes clamped around their legs. Such traps were usually made of wood, in the later Middle Ages occasionally of iron. Traps for squirrel and other fur animals fell over the animal. Traps with automatically launched arrows or spears were also used. Likewise, trees bowed to the ground with a rope around the top functioned as snares.

The right to hunt generally belonged to the owner of the land. In Norway and Sweden, the best hunting grounds were in the commons (*almenningar*). They included the mountain plateaus of southern Norway and most inland areas of northern Norway and northern Sweden, where great flocks of reindeer lived. The commons also included large forests for fur and elk hunting. Here, hunting was free for all, but huts, walls, or trenches for hunting purposes belonged to the persons who had built them. If they were unused for ten years, anyone could repair them and start using them without compensation.

In many European countries, princes and nobles reserved hunting for themselves. In Scandinavia, this restriction was a late development. In the 13th century, the Danish king reserved certain geographic areas for his own hunting. Both the Danish and Swedish kings issued several regulations to reserve deer hunting for kings and nobles. It is not clear how far this policy really succeeded in limiting the hunting rights of peasants before 1500. In Norway, there were no such limitations to the peasants' hunting rights; there were fewer nobles and more game.

In Sweden, the peasants were legally bound to participate in the hunt for wolves, bears, and foxes at certain times of the year. The peasants of a certain district spread over a large area and chased the wolves into a net or a trap. These publicly organized chases are not known in Norway and Denmark before 1500.

The majority of the hunters were farmers who received most of their income from agriculture. Hunting gave them an extra supply of cash or meat. In Denmark and southern Sweden, professional hunters are found only at the courts of the great landowners. In northern Norway and Sweden, however, the Lapps drew their main incomes from hunting reindeer and fur animals, giving them both food and cash. The Viking Age chief Óttarr, who lived in northern Norway, received in tribute fifteen furs of marten, five of reindeer, one of bear, and a coat of bear- or otter-skins from the richest Lapps in this area. Reindeer meat was their staple food. In the Middle Ages, the reindeer were caught mainly through an extensive system of trenches. In the 16th century, the Lapps learned to use firearms, resulting in decimation of the wild reindeer. The Lapps then started to keep large herds of domesticated reindeer.

In the Viking Age, furs were perhaps the main commodity of Scandinavian merchants. Only a small portion of these furs were produced in Scandinavia. Gotland merchants bought their furs in the eastern Baltic, particularly Novgorod. Norwegian merchants got them from the White Sea area.

Lit.: Granlund, John, *et al.* "Jakt." *KLNM* 7 (1962), 533–52; Granlund, John, *et al.* "Skalljakt." *KLNM* 15 (1970), 391–3.

Arnved Nedkvitne

Húsdrápa *see* Úlfr Uggason

Hymiskviða ("The Lay of Hymir") is one of the mythological eddic poems, which is also extant in AM 748 I 4to (*ca.* 1300), and which in a frame plot pieces together a number of myths concerning Þórr. In order that Ægir can brew beer for the gods, Þórr and Týr go to the giant Hymir, who alone has command over the great beer cauldron. In the evening, Þórr eats two of the giant's oxen, so

that food must be brought in for the next day. With an ox-head as bait, which Þórr has torn off one of the giant's animals, Þórr and Hymir go fishing. Hymir catches two whales at the same time, but Þórr lures the Miðgarðsormr ("World Serpent"), which snatches at the ox-head; Þórr raises it with force to the surface and hits it on its head with his hammer, but then the "fish" sinks back into the ocean. Contrary to the *Snorra Edda*, the poem says nothing about the fact that Hymir, out of fear, cuts Þórr's fishing line before he could give the serpent its final blow. After further displays of strength, Þórr carries away the cauldron. On the way, he kills giants, who pursue him. Now Ægir's drinking bout can begin.

Bragi and other skalds gave accounts of Þórr's fishing expedition; *Snorra Edda* gives a detailed description. In addition, there are pictorial representations of the story on stones: Ardre VIII (Gotland), Altuna (Sweden), Hørdum (Denmark), and the stone of Gosforth (Cumberland). The *First Grammatical Treatise* alludes to the stealing of the cauldron. The attempt to prove an old connection between Þórr's fishing expedition and the stealing of the cauldron with the help of the Indra myth (stealing and drinking of the Soma and the following fight against the Chaos monster) remains problematic. The cup test (Þórr smashes a cup on Hymir's head) has a striking parallel in the Swedish tale about Knös. In this fusion of myths about Þórr, *Hymiskviða* would appear to be relatively young. The fact that Snorri does not mention *Hymiskviða* is no argument for the theory that the poem was composed later than Snorri's *Edda* (Reichardt 1933: between 1225 and 1250). It may have come into existence in the first half of the 12th century (Del Zotto 1979).

The account of Þórr's encounter with the Miðgarðsormr reveals borrowings from skaldic poems, and takes on cosmic dimensions reminiscent of the cosmic processes in the gods' final battle in *Vǫluspá* (esp. st. 52, perhaps also st. 57). Þórr's greed (st. 15) has a parallel in *Þrymskviða* (st. 15). Apart from the traditional eddic stylistic features, *Hymiskviða* distinguishes itself by a wealth of kennings, variations, and *hapax legomena*, some of which are very archaic; and also by a strikingly small proportion of direct speech. Many words never or rarely appear in poetry, but in prose or modern Icelandic. Metrical and syntactical peculiarities suggest skaldic influences (Del Zotto 1979). The poet was concerned with welding together individual episodes, although he did not succeed very well; the vague mention of the lameness of one of Þórr's goats (st. 37f.) seems quite unmotivated. Perhaps both stanzas are an interpolation, and were added by the redactor of the collection of poems in order to create a transition to the following poem, *Lokasenna* (Klingenberg 1983). Then, it would be necessary to assume that AM 748 I 4to, which contains both stanzas, goes back to a text with the same order of the poems as in the *Codex Regius* of the *Poetic Edda*, which is improbable. Þórr's fishing expedition forms the middle of the poem, even though it is just a myth among others, around which the other episodes and the frame plot are concentrically arranged (Glendinning 1980).

Ed.: Neckel, Gustav, ed. *Edda: Die Lieder des Codex Regius nebst verwandten Denkmälern. I: Text.* 5th ed. rev. Hans Kuhn. Heidelberg: Winter, 1983. **Tr.**: Hollander, Lee M., trans. *The Poetic Edda, Translated with an Introduction and Explanatory Notes.* 2nd rev. ed. Austin: University of Texas Press, 1962; rpt. 1988. **Bib.**: Harris, Joseph. "Eddic Poetry." In *Old Norse–Icelandic Literature: A Critical Guide.* Ed. Carol J. Clover and John Lindow. Islandica, 45. Ithaca and London: Cornell University Press, 1985, p. 150; Lindow, John. *Scandinavian Mythol-*

ogy: An Annotated Bibliography. Garland Folklore Bibliographies, 12. New York and London: Garland, 1988. **Lit.**: Vogt, Walther Heinrich. "Þórs Fischzug. Eine Betrachtung über ein Bild auf Bragis Schild." In Studier tillägnade Axel Kock, tidskriftens huvudredaktör, 1888–1928. Lund: Gleerup, 1929, pp. 200–16; Reichardt, Konstantin. "Hymiskviða. Interpretation. Wortschatz. Alter." Beiträge zur Geschichte der deutschen Sprache und Literatur 57 (1933), 130–56; Schröder, Franz Rolf. "Das Hymirlied. Zur Frage verblasster Mythen in den Götterliedern der Edda." Arkiv för nordisk filologi 70 (1955), 1–40; Brøndsted, Johannes. "Thors Fiskeri." Nationalmuseets arbejdsmark (1955), 92–104; Gschwantler, Otto. "Christus, Thor und die Midgardsschlange." In Festschrift für Otto Höfler zum 65. Geburtstag. Ed. Helmut Birkhan and Otto Gschwantler. Vienna: Notring, 1968, pp. 145–68; Weber, Gerd Wolfgang. "Das Odinsbild des Altunasteins." Beiträge zur Geschichte der deutschen Sprache und Literatur 94 (1972), 323–34; Schier, Kurt. "Die Húsdrápa von Úlfr Uggason und die bildliche Überlieferung altnordischer Mythen." Minjar og menntir, Afmælisrit helgað Kristjáni Eldjárn 6. desember 1976. Ed. Guðni Kolbeinsson. Reykjavik: Menningarsjóður, 1976, pp. 425–43; Kabell, Aage. "Der Fischfang Þórs." Arkiv för nordisk filologi 91 (1976), 123–9; Wolf, Alois. "Sehweisen und Darstellungsfragen in der Gylfaginning. Thors Fischfang." Skandinavistik 7 (1977), 1–27; Zotto, Carla Del. La Hymiskviða e la pesca di Þórr nella tradizione nordica. Testi e studi di filologia, 1. Rome: Istituto di Glottologia della Università di Roma, 1979; Glendinning, Robert J. "The Archetypal Structure of Hymisqviða." Folklore 91 (1980), 92–110; Klingenberg, Heinz. "Types of Eddic Mythological Poetry." In Edda: A Collection of Essays. Ed. Robert J. Glendinning and Haraldur Bessason. University of Manitoba Icelandic Studies, 4. Winnipeg: University of Manitoba Press, 1983, pp. 134–64; Sørensen, Preben Meulengracht. "Thor's Fishing Expedition." In Words and Objects: Towards a Dialogue Between Archaeology and History of Religion. Ed. Gro Steinsland. Institute for Comparative Research in Human Culture, Oslo. Ser. B: Skrifter. 71. Oslo: Universitetsforlaget, 1986, pp. 257–78.

Otto Gschwantler

[**See also:** Codex Regius; Eddic Meters; Eddic Poetry; Grammatical Treatises; Snorra Edda; Þórr; Þrymskviða; Vǫluspá]

Hyndluljóð

Hyndluljóð ("The Lay of Hyndla") is one of the "additional lays" of the Poetic Edda that were not incorporated into the Codex Regius and are known only from the MS Flateyjarbók of the end of the 14th century.

The goddess Freyja wakes up the giantess Hyndla, rides with her to Valhǫll, and asks her about the forefathers of Óttarr, whom Freyja protects. Óttarr needs to know his pedigree to win the lawsuit with a certain Angantýr. The main part of Hyndluljóð is a list of nearly seventy names, all of them belonging to Óttarr's pedigree. Some of the names are known from heroic lays and tales, some seem to be fictitious, and some are borrowed from real West Norwegian genealogies. It is therefore possible to deduce that Óttarr was a Norwegian or Icelandic chieftain for whom Hyndluljóð was composed. However, the pedigree is rather complicated and contradictory. At the end of the lay, Freyja demands that Hyndla give Óttarr the ale of memory, but the giantess mixes it with poison. Freyja is not, however, frightened by this deed, because she asks the gods to help Óttarr.

Stanzas 29–44 of Hyndluljóð are known as Vǫluspá in skamma ("The Short Prophecy of the Sybil"), an imitation of the Vǫluspá; and stanza 33 is cited in Snorra Edda.

The majority of scholars date Hyndluljóð to the 12th century. Some of them see in it the influence of Christianity. The living man who visits the otherworld is a character from medieval Christian visions; Hyndla seems more like a witch than a giantess.

It is possible to conjecture that certain juridical representations of the Northmen could be discerned under the sacral mythopoetical visions in Hyndluljóð. We need to distinguish between the two layers in the genealogical enumeration recited by the ecstatic Hyndla, Óttarr's pedigree, which includes five generations of his forefathers, and subsequent extensive genealogies of the noble kin, which include the tales and legends of heroes and heathen gods. Thus, the authentic pedigree passes into myth and prophecy about the coming Ragnarǫk, the destruction of the gods. Óttarr had to know his genealogy to defend his inheritance rights to his paternal estate just as Northmen did when they litigated in the law court on the matter of the óðal right. It seems permissible to interpret the inclusion of Óttarr's pedigree in the legend that unites illustrious clans of Skjǫldungar, Skilfingar, Ǫðlingar, Ynglingar, hersar, and hǫldar into one consanguineous circle of "the best men in Miðgarðr" (Middle Earth, the world of humans) as a tendency inherent in ancient mentality to mythologize and poeticize property relations. Óttarr asserts his rights to his paternal estate with the help of Freyja, whose protection he enjoys, whereas the giantess does not regard him with favor, but is compelled to disclose his descent to him. It is possible to surmise that the giantess does not want Óttarr's victory in the lawsuit, because by seeking his inheritance right he defends eo ipso the cause of the whole Miðgarðr, for the best people in Miðgarðr are his kinsmen. Thus, Miðgarðr, the world of humans, friends of æsir, versus Útgarðr, the world of giants and monsters, represents the disposition of enemy forces forming the basis of Hyndluljóð. Óttarr's defense of his property rights is treated as if raised to the level of the world conflict depicted in Vǫluspá. Asserting his óðal right, Óttarr (if such a man really existed and fought a lawsuit about landed estate) had to be conscious of the fact that he defended the legacy of all his forefathers, beginning with the old heroes and his patron æsir. Poetization and mythologization of the property relations shed new light on their essence.

Ed.: Neckel, Gustav, ed. Edda: Die Lieder des Codex Regius nebst verwandten Denkmälern. I: Text. 5th ed. rev. Hans Kuhn. Heidelberg: Winter, 1983; pp. 288–96. **Tr.**: Hollander, Lee M., trans The Poetic Edda, Translated with an Introduction and Explanatory Notes. 2nd rev. ed. Austin: University of Texas Press, 1962; rpt. 1988. **Lit.**: Bergmann, F. W. Rig's Sprüche (Rigs mål) und das Hyndla-Lied (Hyndlu lióð). Zwei sozial-ethische Gedichte der Saemunds-Edda. Strassburg: Trübner, 1876; Holtsmark, Anne. "Hyndluljóð." KLNM 7 (1962), 200–1; Vries, Jan de. Altnordische Literaturgeschiche. 2 vols. Grundriss der germanischen Philologie, 15–6. Berlin: de Gruyter, 1941–42; rpt. 1964–67, vol. 2, pp. 107–10; Fleck, Jere. "Konr—Óttarr—Geirroðr. A Knowledge Criterion for Succession to the Germanic Sacred Kingship." Scandinavian Studies 42 (1970), 39–49; Gurevich, Aron Ja. "Edda and Law: Commentary upon Hyndlolióð." Arkiv för nordisk filologi 88 (1973), 72–84.

A. Ya. Gurevich

[**See also:** Eddic Poetry; Flateyjarbók; Snorra Edda; Vǫluspá]

Hœnsa-Þóris saga

Hœnsa-Þóris saga ("The Saga of Hen-Þórir"), like Hrafnkels saga Freysgoða, has attracted much attention from literary historians, in part because Ari Þorgilsson, in his *Íslendingabók*, chose to give a synopsis of the same dispute that provides the plot of the saga. Ari's account differs in some details of genealogy and other matters, but the broad account is the same. For Ari, the significance of the story is that the difficulties of prosecuting a killing case provided the catalytic incident for a constitutional reform that led to the division of the country into quarters; for the saga author, the constitutional reform is, according to one MS tradition, of no concern at all. Another stemma of MSS incorporates Ari's account of the reform verbatim, but even in this version national political issues are subordinated to local politics and disputes, and to the moral and practical problems of transferring fodder in time of need. The saga account exhibits the effects of an authorial reworking of historical events. Commentators believe the saga account to be intimately connected to the furor caused by a provision in the *Jónsbók* law code that mandated forced sales of hay in hard times from those who had surpluses to those in need. The earlier laws of the Icelandic commonwealth had no such provision. If the commentators are correct, the saga must have been written sometime after the introduction of *Jónsbók* in 1281. Such an ascription assumes that the norms governing the distribution of food and fodder during famine times were unproblematic prior to 1281 and thus incapable of giving rise to sagaworthy disputes. There is, however, no reason to believe that the relations between haves and have-nots in times of hardship were any less tense when the haves possessed the formal legal entitlement to the surpluses. The saga's *terminus post quem* simply cannot be dated very confidently.

The plot of the saga follows the vagaries and transformations of a dispute originated in a failed attempt to purchase hay during a hard winter. Blund ("sleep")-Ketill Geirsson, a wealthy and popular farmer, attempts to purchase hay on behalf of his impoverished tenants from the miserly farmer Hœnsa-Þórir, who is blessed with substantial supplies. Þórir counters generous offers for his surpluses with surly refusals, leading Blund-Ketill to force a sale simply by expropriating the surplus and leaving behind a fair price. After being rebuffed by two chieftains, Arngrímr and Tungu-Oddr ("Oddr from Tunga"), Þórir succeeds in buying the support of Oddr's son, Þorvaldr, to help prosecute his claim against Blund-Ketill. The summoning leads to disaster. Arngrímr's son, Helgi, is killed by a Norwegian merchant lodging with Blund-Ketill, and Þórir manipulates this misfortune by using it to provoke the summoning party into burning Blund-Ketill in his home. The rest of the saga details the mustering of support for vengeance and legal action on behalf of Blund-Ketill. Blund-Ketill's son, Hersteinn, recruits Þorkell trefill ("fringe"), who in turn recruits Gunnarr

Hlífarson by imposing a hasty betrothal of Hersteinn to Gunnarr's daughter. Gunnarr then tricks the girl's maternal uncle Þórðr gellir ("yeller") into allying himself with the cause. Once Þórðr enters the scene, the saga concerns itself with his power struggle with the rival chieftain Tungu-Oddr, who had highhandedly claimed the right to Blund-Ketill's property after his death. By way of anticlimax, the saga narrates Hersteinn's killing of Þórir and the outlawry of the burners. The saga concludes with an account of how Tungu-Oddr's son woos and marries Gunnarr's second daughter contrary to the wishes of both his and her father.

The saga has long been noted for its exemplum-like qualities. Blund-Ketill's virtue and Þórir's meanness approach the allegorical. The saga author also derives humorous effects and plot impetus from the commonplace of asking visitors for the latest news. But allegory never deflects the saga from the social and cultural constraints imposed by the disputing process. Like so many of the *Íslendingasögur*, *Hœnsa-Þóris saga* deals with the competition for power among chieftains and *bœndr* ("householders") and how this competition is mediated by feud and legal action.

Ed.: Baetke, Walter, ed. *Hœnsa-Þóris saga*. Altnordische Textbibliothek, N. F., 2. Halle: Niemeyer, 1953; Sigurður Nordal and Guðni Jónsson, eds. *Borgfirðinga sǫgur*. 2nd ed. Reykjavik: Hið íslenzka fornritafélag, 1956. **Tr.**: Jones, Gwyn, trans. *Erik the Red and Other Icelandic Sagas*. London: Oxford University Press, 1961; rpt. 1980, pp. 3–38; Hermann Pálsson, trans. *The Confederates & Hen-Thorir*. Edinburgh: Southside, 1975. **Lit.**: Maurer, Konrad. "Ueber die Hœnsa-Þóris saga." *Abhandlungen der philos.-philol. Classe der königlichen bayerischen Akademie der Wissenschaften* 12.2 (1871), 157–216; Berger, Alan J. "Old Law, New Law, and *Hœnsa-Þóris saga*." *Scripta Islandica* 27 (1976), 3–12; Jónas Kristjánsson. "Landnáma and Hænsa-Þóris saga." In *Opuscula Septentrionalia: Festskrift til Ole Widding, 10.10.1977*. Ed. Bent Chr. Jacobsen *et al*. Copenhagen: Reitzel, 1977, pp. 134–48; Ebel, Uwe. "Zum Erzählverfahren der mittalalterlichen isländischen Prosaerzählung: Das Beispiel der 'Hønsa-Þóris saga.'" *Beiträge zur nordischen Philologie*. Frankfurt: Haag & Herchen, 1982, pp. 26–55; Miller, William Ian. "Gift, Sale, Payment, Raid: Case Studies in the Negotiation and Classification of Exchange in Medieval Iceland." *Speculum* 61 (1986), 18–50.

W. I. Miller

[See also: *Íslendingabók; Íslendingasögur*]

Hǫfuðlausn *see* Egill Skalla-Grímsson

Hǫfuðlausn *see* Óttarr svarti

Iceland was the last country in Europe to be settled. Major sources like Ari fróði's ("the learned") *Íslendingabók*, from about 1130, and *Landnámabók*, from about the same time but preserved in much later versions, provide only one possible interpretation of the oldest history. Settlement is said to have begun about 870, and these oldest sources were not written down until 250 years later. No traces of human habitation have been found that can with certainty be dated before the middle of the 9th century.

The Norse colonization of Iceland, invariably referred to in early sources as *landnám*, "landtaking" or "land claim," can be regarded as an extension of the Viking settlements in the Scottish islands and elsewhere in the British and northern isles.

Before the Norse settlement, some Irish hermits, *papar*, had lived there for a while. Dicuil, a 9th-century Irish scholar, states in his geographical treatise *De mensura orbis terrae* (*ca.* 825) that such hermits had sailed north to the island shortly before the end of the 8th century. Depending on ancient Greek and Roman works of geography, Dicuil identified the island as *Thule*, a term used by classical geographers to designate a country in the extreme north. The *papar* are mentioned also in *Íslendingabók* and *Landnámabók*. According to Ari, they left Iceland when the Norse settlers arrived. They did not want to live among heathens.

Most of the settlers (*landnámsmenn*) came directly from western Norway, although some evidently sailed from the Norse settlements in the British and northern isles, where they had mingled with the indigenous Celtic and Pictish population. Some of the settlers brought Celtic slaves with them. The question of the Celtic element in the Icelandic population has been a matter of controversy. However, anthropological research has shown that Icelandic blood types suggest a much closer affinity with the Celts than with the Norwegians. Consequently, it seems safe to assume that people of Celtic stock must have represented a considerable part of the original population.

The Norse expansion west over sea in the Viking period has been linked with an increase in the population of Norway from the 8th century onward. Love of adventure and lust for plunder must have been contributory factors, as well as trade, which became increasingly important. Iceland was, however, situated far away from the goals of the Viking raids, and the colonization was, as the word *landnám* indicates, a search for land. The medieval Icelandic literary tradition gave as one of the reasons for the settlement of

Iceland the oppression, *ofríki*, of Haraldr hárfagri ("fair-hair") Hálfdanarson in his attempts to unify Norway politically. Immigration probably increased after Haraldr's victory in the battle on Hafrsfjǫrðr toward the end of the 9th century and his alleged raid on the Viking settlements in the west shortly afterward. But King Haraldr cannot be responsible for the entire immigration to Iceland. Correspondence in time may have created an impression of a causal relationship. The migration from the western and northern isles has been explained as the consequence of the dense population, if not overpopulation, in the islands, at the end of the 9th century. Certain defeats suffered by the Vikings (*e.g.*, at Dublin in 902) may serve to explain why some of the Norsemen there chose to immigrate to Iceland.

Population and settlement figures. According to *Íslendingabók*, Iceland was fully settled, *albyggt*, within sixty winters, "so that there was no further settlement made afterward." These sixty years (870–930) are called *landnámsöld*, the time of settlement. It was probably Ari's opinion that all the land had by then been claimed, and that the settlement had the same extent as at the time he wrote *Íslendingabók*. The leading settlers acquired vast areas and established big farms where they engaged in extensive farming, particularly animal husbandry. The density of settlement increased after 930, and it should be noted that some of the largest estates in the country were not founded until the 10th, or even the 11th, century. By the beginning of the 12th century, the settlement pattern that has survived to our times had become firmly established. As in Norway, the salient feature is the wide scattering of individual farms, each being located some distance away from its neighbors. There were never any villages in medieval Iceland. The farms were concentrated near the coast, in the interior lowlands, and in the river valleys. The interior plateau has always been uninhabitable. Few farms are situated higher than 200 m. above sea level; most of them are below the 100-m. contour. In the earliest period, farms were established up to about 450 m. above sea level, especially in the northeast, where the climate is relatively dry. Climatic conditions at that time were generally more favorable than in later centuries. Between two-fifths and three-quarters of the land may have been covered with grass, as compared with a little more than one fifth now. According to Ari, Iceland was covered with wood from the mountains to the coast at the time of the settlement. Scientific investigations seem to confirm that large parts of the country were covered with trees and scrub birch, which the settlers used for the grazing of animals and for firewood, or burned off to clear pastures. Continuous grazing on loose, sandy ground in a climatically marginal area soon resulted in the reduction of grassland. After 1100, erosion increased noticeably. Conditions were made worse by the gradually deteriorating climate from the last decades of the 12th century onward.

Landnámabók mentions about 400 settlers and about 600 farms. A number of these, to be sure, were abandoned almost immediately. On the other hand, Landnámabók provides information about only a fraction of all the settlers and farms, and there is no solid basis for estimating the size of the Icelandic population at any time in the Middle Ages.

The census of 1703 gives the first reliable information about the total population. At that time, the country had about 50,000 inhabitants, divided into about 8,100 households. There were about 4,000 registered farms, lögbýli, which made up the core of the medieval settlement. The lögbýli of 1703 were divided into about 5,900 farmer holdings, bœndabýli, units of production run by individual families. In addition, there were about 1,500 households of smallholders and fishermen, and about 750 households were lodgers. The average family size on a farmer holding was six in 1703; the households of smallholders and fishermen were much smaller.

The figures of 1703 may be compared with two pieces of information on taxpayers in the Middle Ages. Íslendingabók states that around 1100 the bishop of Skálholt had a count made of the farmers who were to pay þingfararkaup to the goðar, a tax intended to finance the trip to the Alþingi. The total number came to about 4,560. In 1311, there were 3,812 taxable farmers. These are minimum figures to which may be added at least 15 percent nontaxable farmers. The number of farmers on ordinary holdings cannot, in any case, have exceeded 6,000. The few contemporary hints do not indicate that the size of medieval households differed from those of 1703. Even if we increase the average number of persons in single holdings to seven to eight and in double or multiple holdings to six to seven, the medieval population would not exceed 40,000. It is unlikely that it ever exceeded 50,000, and it was possibly much lower. There are several indications that the maximum was reached in the late 14th century or around 1400. Viewed against this background, a recent estimate of about 80,000 inhabitants around 1200 appears rather unrealistic, and even higher earlier estimates can safely be dismissed.

In the high Middle Ages, there is no indication of overpopulation or pressure on the natural resources, as has been assumed in contemporary Norway and other parts of Scandinavia. The individual farm, usually a one-family holding, was predominant. Double holdings, tvíbýli, existed during the time of the Free State and later, but we do not know how common they were. On such holdings, the outlying meadows as well as the home field and the buildings were shared by the two families. Multiple holdings may also have existed, although there is no contemporary mention of them.

Iceland was spared when the Black Death reached the other Scandinavian countries in the years 1349–1350. But "The Great Plague," plágan mikla, ravaged the country from 1402 to 1404. It is not known how large a part of the population died. Estimates range from one-third to two-thirds. About the middle of the 15th century, the population had probably reached its former level, since the country avoided further outbreaks of the plague until the years 1494–1495, when "The Last Plague," plágan síðari, ravaged the land. The mortality rate during this plague is also unknown. Since the plague did not become endemic, there was neither permanent desertion of farms nor an agricultural crisis, as in large parts of Norway, Sweden, and Denmark. Abandonment appears to have been temporary and confined to farms in the interior and marginal settlements. Farms could also be deserted because people were attracted to the fishing areas.

Economy. The settlers brought with them domestic animals, particularly sheep, cattle, goats, and horses, and from the beginning animal husbandry was the principal occupation. What the farms yielded, however, failed to provide all the food that was needed, so the limited natural resources available had to be exploited to the full, including fishing and fowling. To compensate for the lack of suitable wood for building purposes, driftwood was gathered assiduously. The major part of the production was consumed domestically, and the goal was as much self-sufficiency as possible. Up to about 1300, the main emphasis was on animal husbandry and some agriculture, with fishing as an additional food supply in the coastal areas, all of which influenced the pattern of settlement. Most of the major farms, including the episcopal sees of Skálholt and Hólar, were situated a good distance from the coast. It is usually claimed that cattle breeding was more extensive during the high Middle Ages than in later centuries. Increased sheep raising is said to have followed the deterioration of the climate from the last decades of the 12th century, which made it more difficult to maintain large herds of cattle. The depopulation after the plagues probably had the same effect. Sheep raising required less labor, although it was not until about 1500 that it became the principal occupation of Icelandic farmers. The production of homespun, vaðmál, remained important in the high Middle Ages, not only for domestic use, but also for export abroad, as was the case with furs and hides. At least from the 12th century onward, homespun, together with kúgildi, the value of a cow, became a legal unit of value, six ells of vaðmál being the equivalent of an ounce of silver.

Climatically, Iceland is marginal for the purpose of raising crops. But the original settlers were used to that kind of agriculture, and the favorable climate during the first part of the high Middle Ages (before ca. 1150–1200) made it possible to grow barley, and to a lesser extent oats. The deterioration of the climate made growing crops impossible in the north, but it was more reliable in the south and west, and increased temporarily at the end of the 14th century. However, cereals were always scarce and had to be imported.

The decline of agriculture was presumably caused by factors other than the deterioration of the climate. In the early 14th century, Icelandic dried fish entered the European market, and the country received grain and grain products in exchange. Fish became a lucrative export. With the growth of urban life and trade in Europe, together with stricter observation of religious fasting, the demand for dried fish increased steadily. As a result, coastal farms in Iceland, particularly those with natural harbors, were much sought after by religious houses and wealthy landowners alike. As early as the first half of the 12th century, the bishop of Skálholt had bought up the Westman Islands, probably the largest fishing settlement in Iceland. At the end of the 13th century, the monastery of Helgafell gained control of the best coastal fishing farms at the extreme end of Snæfellsnes. The success of fishing influenced the pattern of settlement around Faxaflói and Breiðafjörður, and especially in the

Vestfirðir, which until then had been a poor, sparsely populated, isolated area. In the course of a few decades, the settlements there grew in importance economically and, before long, politically. This growth is clearly indicated by the fact that the number of tax-paying householders in Vestfirðingafjórðungur (-"quarter") in 1311 shows a considerable increase in the figure from about 1100, although their number in the other quarters had either declined or remained unchanged. Strategically located major farms in Vestfirðir and around Breiðafjörður attracted much greater wealth than ever before. Still, there is no reason to believe that fishing was more important than agriculture. But the fishing stations and other coastal settlements attracted labor, and the degree of self-sufficiency decreased. The Danish-Norwegian monarchy also gradually acquired numerous coastal farms and harbor rights. From about 1400, it controlled the Westman Islands, and after the Lutheran Reformation in 1540–1550, all monastic property was confiscated by the Crown, including the important fishing settlements on Snæfellsnes and Reykjanes. At the same time, the see of Skálholt lost several coastal farms to the Crown in exchange for inland farms.

In the 10th and 11th centuries, wealthy farmers and chieftains engaged in foreign trade, using harbors as close to home as possible. Traders from Norway, Orkney, and possibly from the western isles also sailed to Iceland. In the course of the 12th century, foreign trade by Icelanders more or less came to an end. However, the trade itself continued to expand, becoming more regular and better organized, and increasingly connected to Norway. Seagoing ships had become larger, and consequently could call only at certain ports. The Norwegian merchants who took over trade with Iceland to an increasing extent naturally gravitated toward the more central ports. Trade in Iceland thus became limited to fewer market centers, and in Norway to the growing towns, first Niðaróss (Trondheim), then Bergen, which, during the 13th century, actually, and later also legally, became the center of trade with Iceland. The growing income of the chieftains, because of lending and leasing and their lucrative administration of local churches, increased their need for trade. The surplus produce had to be exchanged for other goods, not least foreign luxuries, enabling the chieftains to maintain their status and lifestyle. Even though they had given up commercial shipping, they still controlled the ports in Iceland. In the 13th century, about ten ports were in use, some of them only intermittently. Because trade was generally seasonal, its volume small and limited, conditions were lacking for the ports to develop into permanent villages or towns.

The volume of trade in the decades following the annexation to the Norwegian Crown in the years 1262–1264 is unknown in detail, but we have numerous examples of sailings between Iceland and Norway, mostly Bergen. Political contact was regular and intimate, and so probably were trade relations, even though the Icelanders around 1300 complained of insufficient shipping. The exportation of dried fish from Iceland did not start seriously until well into the 14th century, leading to a sudden increase in the number of ships bound for Iceland during the 1330s and especially 1340s. The Bergen traders mostly exchanged Baltic grain for the fish. The economic boom was short-lived. The Black Death in Norway in the years 1349–1350 brought trade to a standstill, and commerce with Iceland never reached its extent prior to the plague. The period from about 1260 to the end of the 14th century is called the Norwegian Age, *norska öldin*.

Around 1400, the English started fishing off Iceland, and soon also trading. Because of irregular importation from Norway after the middle of the 14th century, the English were well received by the Icelanders. The volume of their trade quickly increased, and evidently grew larger than the Norwegian trade had ever been. Indeed, the English trade practically put an end to shipping between Iceland and Bergen. The English merchants could offer the Icelanders much better trading terms. The price of dried fish increased by more than 70 percent. This trade was probably an important source of the growing prosperity of the coastal regions of the west and northwest in that period. The Danish-Norwegian king tried in vain to keep the Icelanders from trading with the English, and occasionally there was open conflict. From about 1440, the king capitulated and allowed the English to engage in trade in return for a tax, which was not always paid. The English were in charge of most of the Icelandic trade until about 1540, when the Hanseatics, who, since the end of the 15th century, had competed with the English for the Iceland trade, gradually took over. The 15th century is called the English Age, *enska öldin*.

The Icelandic Free State. The settlement was brought about by chieftains and rich farmers from western Norway and to a lesser extent from the Norse Viking settlements in the west. Some of them, as leaders of one or two ships' crews, claimed possession of vast areas, which they distributed among relatives and dependents or gave to people who came later. Our knowledge of the earliest social and political relationships is fragmentary, but it appears that society was, from the beginning, run by chieftains who saw themselves as first among equals.

We do not know how the independent groups of settlers got on with each other or how they created a society, but as more and more of the habitable land was settled, some form of social and political organization was needed. According to tradition, assemblies or *þing*-meetings were held after about 900. Around 930, a nationwide assembly, the *Alþingi*, was established, in which the main characteristics of the social and political structure were given legal expression. Apparently, this founding was the result of peaceful negotiations and was an expression of the will to balance the power of the rulers and of the various parts of the country, reflecting the division of power among many chieftains in the Age of Settlement. As no individual person or family had sufficient resources to control the whole country, a balance of power between a few oligarchs was the natural way to secure peace and order. The *Alþingi* was favorably situated at Þingvellir in the interior of the southwest, with good connections to other parts of the land. The period from about 930 to 1262/4 is commonly called the "Age of the Free State" in foreign historical research. Icelandic historians usually call the Free State *þjóðveldi*, which has given rise to the term "Old Icelandic Commonwealth." None of these terms is adequate.

From about 930, social and political power was divided among thirty-six chieftaincies, called *goðorð*, each of which was headed by one or more chieftains, *goðar*. The number of *goðar* must have roughly corresponded to the number of influential families. The *goðar* were equals. The man in charge of the *goðorð* belonging to the family of Ingólfr Arnarson, Iceland's first settler, was called *allsherjargoði*, "the *goði* of all the people," and had the sacred task of hallowing the *Alþingi* at its opening session every summer. About 965, the country was divided into quarters, or *fjórðungar*. Quarter courts, *fjórðungsdómar*, were established, and the number of *goðar* was increased to thirty-nine. Norðlendingafjórðungur then was allowed twelve *goðar*; Austfirðingafjórðungur, Sunnlendinga-fjórðungur, and Vestfirðingafjórðungur each had nine. The purpose was probably to strengthen the balance of power among the parts of the country. In order to create a balance at the functions of the *Alþingi*, each group of *goðar* of the three quarters other than Norðlendingafjórðungur elected three additional men, soon called "new *goðar*." But in the local districts, there were thirty-nine *goðorð*. The sphere of interest of the individual *goði* was restricted through a decision that he could not have thingmen, *þingmenn*, outside his quarter.

The original figure of thirty-six *goðar*, three groups of twelve, may express their judicial and administrative functions at the thing-meetings; groups of twelve were common in Scandinavia when courts of law were established. Sentencing occurred at the *Alþingi* and at the regional springtime assemblies, the *várþing*. The judicial system consisted of the regional *várþing*-courts, the quarter courts, and, shortly after 1000, the Fifth Court, *fimmtardómr*, the latter two, at the *Alþingi*. The *goðorð* were the basic units and the *goðar* the leading authorities. Each *várþing* was the joint responsibility of three *goðar*, each of whom nominated twelve assessors to the *várþing*-court, which thus consisted of thirty-six men. The quarter courts functioned as courts of appeal from the *várþing*. Thirty-six men sat here and in the Fifth Court. The *goðar* also named people to the courts at the *Alþingi*, but they had no formal judicial authority or responsibility for the legal proceedings or the execution of sentences. If one of the men of a *goði* was found guilty, the latter had no legal obligation to see that the man was punished or paid a fine. But the mutual personal relationship implied that in practice the *goði* would help his thingman, *þingmaðr*, to obtain his rights. If the *goði* neglected to do so, the thingman could turn to another *goði* and become his thingman.

All forty-eight *goðar*, each of them with two thingmen, took part in the activities of the legislative *lǫgrétta*, or Law Council, at the *Alþingi*. They made up 144 of the members, which also included the lawspeaker, *lǫgsǫgumaðr*, and later the two bishops. The lawspeaker was the chairman of the *Alþingi*, and this institution was established together with the *Alþingi* and existed until 1271. The lawspeaker was the only secular official for the whole people. Every year, he had to declare the rules of procedure for the thing-meeting. He also had to recite the rest of the laws in the course of three summers, his term of office. His was an office of great responsibility, especially before the laws were written down in 1117–1118. The person elected had to be a highly qualified man who had great prestige and a solid family background. The laws of the Free State are extant in two law books, both written in the years 1250–1270, *Konungsbók* and *Staðarhólsbók*. They vary in content, organization, and expression. The combined laws of the Free State are called *Grágás*.

In the *lǫgrétta*, only the forty-eight *goðar* had the right to vote. Its most important tasks were to pass new laws, *nýmæli*, to interpret the laws, and to make amendments to and exemptions from the law. The *goðar* were helped by their thingmen in the execution of their functions at the thing. Every ninth thingman followed his *goði* to the *Alþingi*. The others paid him *þingfararkaup*. The respect for a *goði* increased with the size of his following when riding to the thing or traveling around the country. Outside the thing-sessions, his authority was restricted to his thingmen, *mannaforráð*. Only during the thing-sessions did he possess territorial power and influence, regionally at the *várþing*, nationally at the *Alþingi*. At the autumn assembly, the *leið*, he had to provide information about new legislation and pass on other important announcements and news from the recent *Alþingi*.

The authority exercised by the *goðar* could, as time went on, provide the basis for a certain local power outside the thing-sessions. The *goðorð* were originally nongeographical units. The thingmen of one *goði* might live scattered among the thingmen of other *goðar* within the quarter. In practice, however, the *goðorð* gradually became restricted more or less to clearly defined core areas. The population was organized in *goðorð*, based on voluntary mutual trust, not on obedience between lord and subject. Every farmer had the duty as the head of his household to be a thingman for a *goði*. The *goði* had to be able to wield his power in such a way that it was in the interest of the thingmen to belong to his *goðorð*. These conditions put the *goði* under certain obligations. They also created the basis for manipulation that eventually led to the destruction of the original balance of power.

Church and religion. The fact that the chieftains were called *goðar* has led to the assumption that their office originated from their function as religious leaders, "sacrificial priests," in the pre-Christian era. Sources giving the *goði* a leading position in religious practices are problematic. Even if several place-names indicate cult functions, they are too numerous to imply a connection between them and the *goðar* and *goðorð*. Nor were the things held close to the supposed heathen temples. It is unclear why it was only in Iceland that the terms *goði/goðorð* were linked to the institution of the chieftain. Even scholars inclined to believe in the theory that *goðar* were religious leaders admit that it is difficult to see any connection between their supposed religious functions and their purely secular judicial, administrative, and legislative tasks, which we know from the laws and other contemporary sources concerning events and relations in the 12th and 13th centuries. It seems unreasonable that the chieftains who established the constitution would base their rule and political authority on heathen concepts and functions. They came from the areas of Norway most infiltrated by Christianity and from the Norse Viking settlements in the west, where Christianity had gained a firm foothold. Many had been Vikings, who, after contact with Christianity, had become "mixed in their faith." Some had also been marked with the sign of the cross before baptism, *prima signatio*, which made it possible for them to have free contact with Christians. During heathen times, the *goðar* may have hallowed the things, as the *allsherjargoði* did at the *Alþingi* during Christian times. They may also have held sacrificial feasts for their households and thingmen. But these are only assumptions. The theory of the pre-Christian religious leadership of the *goðar* is based on sources as uncertain as those that form the basis of the theory of a Germanic *Eigentempelwesen*, a system of proprietary temples considered the forerunner of the later *Eigenkirchenwesen*, a proprietary church system. This theory has generally been rejected by recent research.

Christianity was introduced in the years 999–1000 through an agreement at the *Alþingi* following tough negotiations and pressure from the Norwegian king. In contrast to what happened in parts of the king's own country, this acceptance occurred without armed conflict or bloodshed. Such a political adoption of the new faith followed by mass baptism was, however, not as unique and spectacular as many scholars have assumed. In connection with the adoption of Christianity, we have a glimpse, for the first time, of the power constellation that characterized the later history of the Free State. The leader of the *Haukdœlir*, Gizurr inn hvíti ("the white"), together with his son-in-law Hjalti Skeggjason and Hallr Þorsteinsson of Síða in the eastern part of the country, the leader of the so-called *Síðumenn*, spearheaded the adoption of the new faith. Using the theories of the origin and religious character of the *goði*-chieftaincy as a point of departure, scholars have often claimed that the Christian faith removed the foundation for the power of the *goðar*. But the *goðar* were the very persons who first adopted the new faith at the *Alþingi*, and the institutions of *goði* and *goðorð* survived the christianization without being weakened. The *goðar*, in fact, increased their power and influence with the help of the Church. The leading *goðar* were probably well informed about how domination over the Church had strengthened the power of secular chieftains and princes in western Europe.

Initially, the introduction of Christianity did not imply a close relationship with Rome. The Church of Iceland evolved as a national church in which secular magnates had extensive power and influence. At first, it was placed under the archbishop of Hamburg/Bremen. In 1104, Iceland and Scandinavia came under the archbishop of Lund, and after 1152/3, Iceland, along with other Norse settlements in the west, became part of the Norwegian ecclesiastical province. Not until then did the pope and archbishop start to interfere with ecclesiastical affairs in Iceland.

Ísleifr, the son of Gizurr inn hvíti, became the first native bishop, in 1056, with a seat in the family farm of Skálholt in the heart of Árnesþing, the sphere of authority of the Haukdœlir. At the end of the 11th century, his son and successor, Gizurr, donated Skálholt as the permanent bishopric. Gizurr not only performed a pious act, he also secured the Haukdœlir's control over the bishopric as long as they preserved their power in Árnesþing. They largely monopolized the office of bishop in Skálholt throughout the period of the Free State in the second half of the 12th century, together with their neighbors and allies the Oddaverjar. For a long time, bishops were elected on their terms. At the peak of their power, they had Þorlákr Þórhallsson (1178–1193) elected bishop of Skálholt. After him came the Oddaverji Páll Jónsson (1195–1211). Both elections apparently occurred with the consent of the Haukdœlir. When a bishopric for the north of Iceland was established at Hólar at the beginning of the 12th century, they had major influence there too; Jón Qgmundarson was succeeded by Ketill Þorsteinsson (1122–1145), who was married to the daughter of Bishop Gizurr. From 1163 to 1201, the Oddaverji Brandr Sæmundarson was bishop. After his death, the most powerful family in northern Iceland, the Ásbirningar, had Guðmundr Arason elected bishop (1203–1237). His election broke the hegemony of the Haukdœlir and the Oddaverjar, and allowed the Ásbirningar to attain a dominant position in northern Iceland.

Until 1104, Iceland and the rest of Scandinavia belonged to the archdiocese of Hamburg/Bremen, and from 1104 to 1152/3, to that of Lund. After 1152/3 and up to the Reformation, Iceland belonged to the archdiocese of Niðaróss. In 1237, the archbishop rejected the candidates chosen by the Icelanders, and the chapter at Niðaróss instead chose two Norwegians. This action was part of the archbishop's and the chapter's efforts to secure for themselves the right to fill the episcopal seats on the Norse islands in the west. After Iceland came under the king of Norway in the years 1262–1264, both bishoprics were again occupied by Icelanders. The bishop of Skálholt, Árni Þorláksson, worked to abolish secular influences within the Church and to reestablish the authority of the bishop granted by canon law. He instituted a new ecclesiastical law, which was adopted by the Skálholt bishopric in 1275 and in 1354 made valid for the Hólar bishopric.

In 1380, after Iceland followed Norway into the Dano-Norwegian monarchy and in 1397 into the Kalmar Union, Danish clergy became eligible for Icelandic bishoprics. It was important to Queen Margrethe and her government to appoint bishops to Iceland without involving the Norwegian authorities, since the bishops occupied seats on the Norwegian State Council and since she needed their support. The first Danish clergyman was appointed to Skálholt in 1382 by a papal commission, a practice that was continued in the consecration of bishops at Skálholt until 1466 and at Hólar until 1442. Later, the bishoprics were given to Englishmen, Dutchmen, and Germans, many of whom never occupied their posts. From 1420 to 1460, bishops resided at Skálholt for a total of only fourteen years. At Hólar, where church authority was stricter, the bishops served for somewhat longer periods. The power of the bishopric at Hólar increased when in 1442 the Norwegian Gottskálk Kæneksson was consecrated by Archbishop Aslak Bolt. He was succeeded by his nephew Óláfr Rögnvaldsson (1460–1495). In 1524, Jón Arason became the last Catholic bishop at Hólar. He was beheaded in 1550. In 1541, Ögmundr Pálsson was forced to relinquish his office and was replaced by a Lutheran. The Reformation in Iceland became a fact.

In its early development, the Church expanded locally as chieftains or wealthy farmers built churches on their farms. They then controlled them. This proprietary-church system was at the outset universal in Iceland at a time when it was about to break down in the rest of Europe. The church-farmer had to maintain the church building and procure a priest. At first, when priests were not expected to be well educated, he himself or someone in his household commonly functioned as a priest. Tithe was introduced in 1096/7, earlier than in the other Scandinavian countries. This income provided the economic foundation for the activities of the Church. As a result of the proprietary-church system, the church-farmers administered the property and income of the local church. They received half the tithes themselves, that is, the church- and priest-tithes. The other half went to the bishop and the poor. The tithe for the poor was administered by the leaders of local groups known as *hreppar*. The church-farmer also administered the part of his farm that he had given to the church as its endowment, *heimanfylgja*, *dos*, and any other farms that had been acquired by the church, most often as alms. All this property was exempt from tithe. It often happened that eventually the church-farmer gave his church the whole farm where it was built. This joint ecclesiastical institution then became a private foundation and an independent economic unit. It was called a *staðr*, *locus religiosus*, or *sacer*, and was in many cases very lucrative. Usually, a condition for establishing a *staðr* was that the donor and his successors had the right to continue to administer it and benefit from its economic resources. If they did not, the heirs could reclaim the gift. Sometimes, however, the church-farmer gave control of the *staðr* to the bishop, who then assigned its administration to one of the local chieftains. On a large farm, it could happen that the *staðr* might include only the half of the farm where the church was built, if this half was large enough to be considered a meaningful economic unit.

Secular political developments. The spokesmen for Christianity, led by the Haukdœlir, dominated Icelandic politics in the 11th century, the period in which power began to be concentrated in fewer hands, as well as the first stage in the formation of territorial lordships, *ríki*. *Ríki* meant, first, domination over a district, then the district itself with fairly fixed boundaries. It included at least three *goðorð* and one *várþing*-parish. There is much to indicate that the territorialization of the *goðorð* began with a *goði* controlling two *goðorð* in his *várþing* district, thereby gaining authority over two core areas. It then became difficult for the thingmen of the third *goði* to gain the necessary support. In modern studies, a *goði* who ruled a *ríki* is often called *stórgoði*, big chieftain. At this time in some parts of the country, the *mannaforráð* had become territorially demarcated, turning into more stable units of power.

We can now speak of local government, *héraðsstjórn*. In the 11th century, the Haukdœlir in Árnesþing, the Ásbirningar in Hegranesþing (Skagafjörður), the Svínfellingar, and the Austfirðingar of Austfirðir managed to establish *ríki*. We know only the result of this first phase of the concentration of power, but the scarce information we do have indicates that it was a slow and peaceful process, achieved partly by gifts and marriages. In the 11th and early 12th centuries, the Haukdœlir were the most powerful family. They dominated Árnesþing, a compact area of settlement strategically located for the concentration of power. Þingvellir, where the *Alþingi* was held, was close to their district. It was easy for them to mobilize their thingmen to ride to the *Alþingi* with them. Eyrar, one of the two most important commercial centers in Iceland during the time of the Free State, was within their sphere of power.

Tithe transferred wealth from the lesser farmers to the bigger ones, and probably contributed, more than anything else, to deepening the social gap between the aristocracy of the *goðar* and the lesser landowners and the increasing number of those who leased land. It is reasonable to connect the second phase of the concentration of power and the formation of *ríki*, which began around 1100 or at the beginning of the 12th century, with the tithe income. Two of the leaders responsible for the introduction of tithes were Bishop Gizurr and the priest Sæmundr fróði Sigfússon in Oddi. The origin of the Oddaverjar's *ríki* in Rangárþing, the neighboring district of Árnesþing, at the beginning of the 12th century, is obviously connected with the transfer of income consequent upon tithing. The power of the Oddaverjar in the middle of the 12th century was clearly manifested when the Oddaverji Brandr Sæmundarson became bishop of Hólar, 1163–1201, and shortly afterward when their protégé, Þorlákr Þórhallsson, became bishop of Skálholt, 1178–1193. He was succeeded by the Oddaverji Páll Jónsson, 1195–1211. These elections coincided with the culmination of their power in Rangárþing in the second half of the 12th century. These episcopal elections also reflect the intimate cooperation of the Haukdœlir and Oddaverjar that began in the time of Sæmundr fróði and Bishop Gizurr at the end of the 11th century and persisted until about 1220. This alliance dominated secular and ecclesiastical politics in Iceland, as well as the economy and trade, during this period. The Haukdœlir retained their influence over the bishopric at Skálholt: while an Oddaverji held the office of bishop, a Haukdœli was steward, *ráðsmaðr*, of the bishopric, *i.e.*, the administrator of its property and income. At the same time as the *ríki* of the Oddaverjar arose, the Ásbirningar in Skagafjörður gained control over their fourth *goðorð*, in Húnavatnsþing. The rich and powerful Hafliði Másson owned the other two *goðorð* there. He may have tried to establish a *ríki* in the district, but did not succeed. The confrontations between the *goðar* in Húnavatnsþing and elsewhere where *ríki* had not been established, Vestfirðingafjórðungur, Eyjafjörður, and Þingeyjarþing, in the 12th century and the beginning of the 13th, were a consequence of their attempts to acquire more *goðorð* in order to form their own *ríki*.

The third phase in the concentration of power and the formation of *ríki* came in the last quarter of the 12th century and the first quarter of the 13th. A new family, the Sturlungar, now came to the fore. They were the sons of the *goði* Hvamm-Sturla in Dalir, who was active and acquisitive in the second half of the 12th century. The development of *ríki* in Eyjafjörður and Þingeyjarþing, which began at the end of the 1180s, was completed in 1215 when Sighvatr Sturluson had gained control of the six *goðorð* in the district. At the beginning of the 13th century, his brother, Snorri Sturluson, established a *ríki* in Borgarfjörður on both sides of the boundary between the quarters Sunnlendingafjórðungur and Vestfirðingafjórðungur. The rule that a *goði* could have thingmen only within his quarter had not been respected for a long time. During this period, the Svínfellingar also gained control of all the *goðorð* in Austfirðingafjórðungur.

Around 1220, most of the *ríki* had taken shape. Only in the divided, and in many ways backward, Vestfirðir had the development come no farther than to show a tendency toward the formation of a *ríki*. It was not until late in the 1240s that Hrafn Oddsson, who had a family background in the district, managed to establish firm control over Vestfirðir. In Árnesþing, Rangárþing, Hegranesþing (Skagafjörður), and Austfirðingafjórðungur, the concentration of power had, as far as we know, been a long, steady process. In other districts, such as Eyjafjörður, along with Þingeyjarþing and Borgarfjörður, the development started later and was faster, partly because of pressure and coercion.

The development of *ríki* led to the use of new methods of government by the *stórgoðar*. They usually sought the model in Norway. Trusted men functioned as their advisers and probably also represented them in the local government, while their followers were bodyguards and police who formed a coercive force if necessary. Both functioned as the extended arm of the *stórgoðar*. The power base of the *stórgoðar* also changed when the *ríki* evolved. Earlier, the farmers had been able to choose a *goði* relatively freely. Now, all the farmers within a *ríki* were, in reality, subjected to one *stórgoði* as his thingmen. What had formerly been essentially a leadership based upon family and friendship now became a territorial, political authority. At the same time, the *stórgoðar* gained control over the judicial activites in the district and decided all cases between their thingmen at the farm where they resided. The local and regional things declined. The *stórgoðar* aimed at ever-increasing power and influence. Their success in utilizing the economic resources and manpower in the *ríki* was, in the end, the factor that determined whether they would survive in the power struggle that became increasingly bitter and destructive in the final phase of the Free State.

The chieftains had a strong economic power base in their authority over local ecclesiastical institutions, the *staðir*, and the rich farmers' churches, that were, at least later, called *bœndakirkjur*. Snorri Sturluson is a good example of a chieftain who managed to acquire several *goðorð* and vast economic resources, mainly through the *staðir* and the rich farmers' churches; and by these means, he established his *ríki* in Borgarfjörður. Riches begat riches. The *goðar* could buy more farms, expand their economic activities, and thereby strengthen their position as *stórgoðar*. The concentration of power was parallel to the concentration of economic resources. The sons of Hvamm-Sturla, Þórðr, Sighvatr, and Snorri owned at least ten times as much property as their fathers, and their power corresponded to their wealth. Bishop Þorlákr Þórhallsson had, in his time, tried to establish a rule that the bishop should have authority, *forræði*, over the local churches, while the laymen could continue to have the administration, *varðveizla*, of them and their economy as benefices, *lén*, under his supervision. The attempt failed because of opposition from the laymen after the bishop had to give in to the Oddaverji Jón Loptsson, the most powerful man in Iceland at the time. Prior to this confrontation with Jón, Þorlákr had for the most part implemented his policy in Austfirðir, and the great number of *staðir* there, about two-thirds of the local churches compared with about one third elsewhere in the country, probably dates back to Þorlákr's efforts.

The fourth and final phase in the concentration of power came after the year 1220, in the Age of the Sturlungar. Five families, the Ásbirningar, Sturlungar, Oddaverjar, Haukdœlir, and Svínfellingar, controlled almost all the thirty-nine *goðorð*. Most of the *ríki* had taken shape. The conflict concerned *ríki*, not *goðorð* as before. The battle of Qrlygsstaðir in 1238 was fought between the firmly established *ríki* of the Haukdœlir in Árnesþing and the Ásbirningar in Hegranesþing/Húnavatnsþing, on the one side, and the new, as yet incomplete *ríki* of the Sturlungar in Eyjafjörður, along with Þingeyjarþing, Dalir, Borgarfjörður, Húnavatnsþing, and Vestfirðir, on the other side. In spite of the much greater population of their area, the Sturlungar managed to mobilize no more than approximately half as many troops as the Haukdœlir and Ásbirningar. The Sturlungar were defeated. The Ásbirningar gained control over the last two *goðorð* in Húnavatnsþing, the whole *ríki* of Sighvatr Sturluson, Eyjafjörður, and Þingeyjarþing; their *ríki* now included the entire Norðlendingafjórðungur. At the same time, the Haukdœli Gizurr Þorvaldsson gained a dominating position in southern and western Iceland. But the victory of the Haukdœlir and Ásbirningar was not final. A few years after the battle of Qrlygsstaðir, the Sturlungi Þórðr Kakali, son of Sighvatr Sturluson, was in the process of reconstituting the power of the Sturlungar, with support from the Norwegian king.

In the 13th century, the Norwegian monarchy played an increasing role in political developments in Iceland. After 1220, when Snorri Sturluson became King Hákon's and Duke Skúli's *lendr maðr* ("landed man," later called "baron"), the king attached one Icelandic chieftain after another to his court. After Snorri had been assassinated in 1241 for committing treason against the king of Norway, the king claimed his property and his *goðorð* as forfeit to the Crown. This act served as his springboard for interfering in the politics of the Free State. From 1238 until after the end of the Free State, the two bishops of Iceland were Norwegians, and served as active supporters of the king's policies. The words of Cardinal William of Sabina in 1247, when he was in Norway to crown King Hákon, probably reflect the attitude toward Iceland in the king's circle. The cardinal said that "it was unreasonable that that country did not serve under a king like all other countries in the world" (Sturla Þórðarson's *Hákonar saga [gamla] Hákonarsonar*). The Icelandic constitution, with *goðar* and *goðorð*, was, despite the evolution of the *ríki* as a stage on the way toward organized statehood, considered an anomaly. The destructive civil wars justified the king's plan to subject the country to his secular power, a parallel to the subjection to the ecclesiastical power of the archbishop of Niðaróss after 1152/3. The Icelandic chieftains, on their side, considered it advantageous to be the king's men in their political efforts. They were stronger with his support. At the same time, the Norwegians had monopolized trade and shipping to and from Iceland, so that the Icelanders were becoming more and more dependent upon Norway, economically and politically. The chieftains probably had to pay for the king's support by gradually handing over their *goðorð* to him. About 1250, he had obtained nearly all the *goðorð* and could decide who was to control them. In reality, he could be considered as the farmers' superior in the *goðorð*.

It was only a question of time before Iceland became part of the Norwegian kingdom. In 1258, the Haukdœli Gizurr Þorvaldsson was appointed earl, with the duty of completing the subjection of Iceland to Norway. As he was not active enough, in 1261, the king sent a Norwegian courtier, Hallvarðr Gullskór, to Iceland to speed the mission. Hallvarðr played the chieftain of Vestfirðir, Hrafn Oddsson, who now gained control of Snorri Sturluson's Borgarfjörður-*ríki*, against Earl Gizurr, forcing him to act on the king's behalf.

Iceland as a Norwegian tributary country. In the years 1262–1264, the Icelanders swore to give the Norwegian king their land, their taxes, and their obedience. Iceland became a part of the Norwegian kingdom. The monarchy had conquered Iceland by making most of the chieftains the king's liege men, while at the same time exploiting internal divisions and power struggles, the desire for peace, and the economic dependence on Norway. This development influenced the conditions the Icelanders wrote into the agreement (*Gamli sáttmáli*) when they accepted Hákon Hákonarson as their king: the king had to let them enjoy peace and Icelandic law, and to maintain sufficient shipping between the two countries.

Iceland was of primary importance to King Magnús lagabœtir ("law-mender") Hákonarson and his two sons. The law book of the Free State, *Grágás*, was replaced by new law books: *Járnsíða*, 1271–1273, and *Jónsbók*, 1281, corresponding to the two stages of Magnús lagabœtir's contemporary revision of Norwegian law. The first book, in particular, was strongly influenced by Norwegian law, but no common legal system was established between the two countries. *Jónsbók* and successive law amendments became Icelandic law for the rest of the Middle Ages.

The constitution had to be adapted to the monarchy, and the authority of the king had to be more precisely defined. The institution of the *goðorð* was abolished. Iceland got an administration run by officials appointed by the king. They took over the former functions of the *goðar*, represented the state, and administered the king's monopoly of coercion. The earldom ceased to exist after Gizurr's death in 1268, and one or two superior commissioners, *valdsmenn*, governed the country. At least from 1320, they were called *hirðstjórar*. They were supported by sheriffs, *sýslumenn*; according to *Jónsbók*, there had to be one for every quarter. This system used the old institution of the things as its basis. The tax roll of 1311 distinguishes nine tax-collection districts, which possibly made up the sheriff's districts, *sýslur*, at the time, and which seem to conform to the borders of the *ríki* toward the end of the period of the Free State. The lawspeaker was replaced by a lawman, *lögmaðr*, appointed by the king; from 1283, there were two of them. The *Alþingi* was reorganized. The *lögrétta* became a court of law with thirty-six members, following the Norwegian model, and the old quarter courts and the Fifth Court disappeared. When the courts pronounced sentences, they consisted of six, twelve, or twenty-four assessors, depending on the importance of the cases. The old assembly of the *Alþingi* was replaced by a Norwegian system of designated men, *nefndarmenn*.

The chieftains became the king's men, executed his orders, and received their power and authority from him. New men and new families came to the fore, while those who had dominated during the Age of the Sturlungar receded into the background.

There were no more armed conflicts. The Icelanders were loyal to the monarchy. At the same time, they carefully guarded their rights. In the beginning of the 14th century, they reacted against the king's practice of sending only Norwegians to act as *sýslumenn* and *hirðstjórar*. As a result, the *hirðstjórar* thereafter were either Norwegians or Icelanders, while the sheriffs and the lawmen were usually Icelanders. In 1375, the Icelanders acted to protect their traditional political and economic rights, and made them the condition for swearing the king allegiance in 1377.

The royal revenue from Iceland, which included judicial penalties as well as taxes, was managed by the royal treasury in Bergen. Iceland was governed from Bergen, the capital of the Norwegian kingdom and the staple port of the trade with the Norwegian "tributary lands." There was a clear link between trade and economics on one side, and politics on the other.

Conflict over local churches. The decades following the submission of the Icelanders to the Norwegian king were dominated by a sharp controversy, the *staðamál*, concerning the control of the local churches and church property, in particular the richest *staðir*. Prompted by the Norwegian archbishop, the bishop of Skálholt, Árni Þorláksson (1269–1298), reintroduced the demands of his predecessor, Þorlákr Þórhallsson, in a more aggressive form. In a judgment declared in Bergen in 1273, the archbishop gave Árni full support. The controversy was renewed after the death of Magnús lagabœtir in 1280, when a council of barons functioned as the regency for the young King Eiríkr, and the archbishop had been forced to leave the country. It was finally settled by a compromise in 1297, the concordat of Ǫgvaldsnes, which stated that *staðir* on farms that were church properties in their entirety were to be subjected to the bishop's authority. They became beneficial churches, *lénskirkjur*, administered by the bishop and assigned to priests or, less often, lay favorites for a certain number of years. But churches on farms, half or more of which were owned by laymen, *i.e.*, all the farmers' churches and a few *staðir*, were to remain in the hands of the laymen, provided they abided by the obligations laid down by the donors; the bishop could make no further claims in such cases. Although Bishop Árni did not achieve all his aims, it was still a significant victory for the Church. The provisions of the concordat were gradually put into effect, and the power, influence, and wealth of the Church grew throughout the late Middle Ages. The bishops gradually gained the authority they were entitled to according to canon law.

Late Middle Ages. One result of the joint monarchy of Norway and Sweden after 1319 was that Iceland became increasingly peripheral to the royal government. During the regency in the 1320s, Bergen maintained its position as the political center of the kingdom; but after Magnús Eiríksson had come of age, its status as a royal residence was greatly reduced, and in 1340 the king ordered that the royal sources of income "from the north and from the west," *i.e.*, from Iceland and other tributary lands and regions, were to go directly to him, not to the royal treasury in Bergen. When in 1350 Magnús shared his kingdoms between Eiríkr, who received Sweden, and Hákon, who received Norway, he reserved Iceland, the Faroes, Shetland, and Hálogaland for himself, certainly for purely financial reasons.

Magnús continued to administer Iceland, not only after Hákon came of age in 1355, but also after Hákon had himself taken charge of the government in 1358. Magnús's motives continued to be purely financial. Even though shipping to Iceland had collapsed after the ravages of the plague in the years 1349–1350, it was probably hoped throughout the 1350s that it would improve again. The rich fisheries led the king to try to increase the number of taxpayers in Iceland, and he levied a tax on the cargos of ships coming to Bergen from Iceland. The arrangement with the *leiguhirðstjórar* from 1354 was also economically motivated. In return for a fixed annual sum, they administered the king's entire income from Iceland for a certain number of years. The result was a stricter political and economic regime; but when the Norwegian *hirðstjóri* was killed in 1361, this arrangement was abolished. Instead, the *hirðstjórar* received a fixed share of the royal income, which was, after 1350, again administered by the royal treasury in Bergen, but as separate royal income. The Icelanders continued to communicate with the king's government and with foreign countries through Bergen because of its stable functions and monopoly. Long after the Norwegian Age had ended, and the Bergen monopoly had irrevocably ceased to exist, Icelandic secular and ecclesiastical magnates continued to communicate with counselors of the realm in Bergen and Niðaróss.

When Norway and Denmark became joint kingdoms in 1380, Iceland and the other Norwegian tributary lands followed suit. This development was not accompanied by any changes in the constitution or status of the countries involved.

The 15th and early 16th centuries were characterized by conflicts between the Danish-Norwegian king and the English concerning the right to sail to Iceland in order to fish and trade. The Icelanders began by demanding free trade and an end to the Bergen monopoly. During the period from about 1425 to about 1470, the English acted, more or less, as they wished around and in Iceland. The monarchy had to acknowledge that Iceland could no longer be governed from Bergen. The English also established bases in the land, and around 1460 the English king referred to the country as *terra nostra Islandia*, "our country of Iceland." The main English bases were the Westman Islands, Grindavík, and Hafnarfjörður on Reykjanes, and Rif on Snæfellsnes. They had, however, no bases in Vestfirðir, where contending chieftains were in control. On Snæfellsnes, the point of intersection between the spheres of interest, confrontations with the English occurred.

Shortly before 1480, the *Alþingi* adopted the regulation that only foreigners born in the kingdoms of the Norwegian king had the right to winter in Iceland. In 1490, the *Alþingi* by the so-called "*pínings*-verdict" once more prohibited foreigners from spending the winter in Iceland. Foreign merchants were not allowed to fish or to hire Icelanders. The background for these measures was that foreign activity had increased more than was in the interests of the chieftains. In the early 15th century, they were happy to trade with the English, and had become rich in the process. Now they feared an increase in wages as a result of the competition for labor; they feared undue winter sales and a rise in the price of imports. The Danish-Norwegian king supported the chieftains. During the first decades of the 15th century, when Iceland was only loosely affiliated with the joint kingdom, royal government was disordered and to some extent illusory. Toward the end of the 15th century, the government regained strength, and for the first time the king was able to send ships to Iceland to control what went on there, particularly seeing that foreigners did not gain a foothold. The *hirðstjórar* had contact on a regular basis with both the king in Denmark and the Council of the Realm in Norway. Most of the *hirðstjórar* were Icelanders, and they used the royal service to strengthen their own economic and political status.

The Church was also faithful to the king. John Craxton, an English cleric, who in 1425 was appointed bishop of Hólar by the pope and was allowed to take over the bishopric of Skálholt a few years later, was expelled from the country in 1435 after he had tried to make the Church of Iceland more independent of the archiepiscopal see of Niðaróss. When the Norwegian cleric Gottskálk Kæneksson became bishop of Hólar in 1442, the contact with Niðaróss, the Council of the Realm in Norway, and the Danish-Norwegian court was reestablished. Gottskálkr was succeeded by his nephew, Óláfr Rögnvaldsson (1460–1495). After 1465, the bishops of Skálholt were Icelanders. The last two Catholic bishops, Ögmundur Pálsson of Skálholt from 1521, and Jón Arason of Hólar from 1523, were both Icelanders. After the Reformation had been accomplished in Denmark and Norway in the years 1536–1537, their struggle for the Catholic Church in Iceland was doomed to failure. In 1541, the bishop of Skálholt was arrested and taken to Denmark, where he died shortly afterward. In 1550, Jón Arason was beheaded along with two of his sons. If one single year marks the end of the Middle Ages in Iceland, it must be 1550, the year that paved the way for the Lutheran monarchy with its state church and its strong economic and political basis.

Lit.: Maurer, Konrad. *Island. Von seiner ersten Entdeckung bis zum Untergange des Freistaats (ca. 800–1264)*. Munich: Kaiser, 1874; rpt. Aalen: Scientia, 1969; Jón Helgason. *Islands kirke fra dens Grundlæggelse til Reformationen*. Copenhagen: Gad, 1925; Ólafur Lárusson. *Yfirlit yfir íslenzka rjettarsögu*. Reykjavik: [n.p.], 1932 [photocopy]; Einar Ólafur Sveinsson. *Sturlungaöld*. Reykjavik: Kostnaðarmenn nokkrir Reykvíkingar, 1940 [English translation: *The Age of the Sturlungs: Icelandic Civilization in the Thirteenth Century*. Trans. Jóhann S. Hannesson. Islandica, 36. Ithaca: Cornell University Press, 1953]; Sigurður Nordal. *Íslenzk menning* 1. Reykjavik: Mál og menning, 1942 [English translation: *Icelandic Culture*. Trans. Vilhjálmur T. Bjarnar. Ithaca: Cornell University Library, 1990]; Ólafur Lárusson. *Byggð og saga*. Reykjavik: Ísafold, 1944; Björn Þorsteinsson. *Íslenzka þjóðveldið*. Reykjavik: Heimskringla, 1953; Björn Þorsteinsson. *Íslenzka skattlandið. Fyrri hluti*. Reykjavik: Heimskringla, 1956; Jón Jóhannesson. *Íslendinga saga 1: Þjóðveldisöld*. Reykjavik: Almenna, 1956 [English translation: *A History of the Old Icelandic Commonwealth: Íslendinga saga*. Trans. Haraldur Bessason. University of Manitoba Icelandic Studies, 2. Winnipeg: University of Manitoba Press, 1974]; Ólafur Lárusson. *Lög og saga*. Reykjavik: Hlaðbúð, 1958 [Norwegian translation: *Lov og ting. Islands forfatning og lover i fristatstiden*. Trans. Knut Helle. Universitetsforlagets Islandsserie. Bergen and Oslo: Universitetsforlaget, 1960]; Jón Jóhannesson. *Íslendinga saga 2: Fyrirlestrar og ritgerðir um tímabilið 1262–1550*. Reykjavik: Almenna, 1958; Skovgaard-Petersen, Inge. "Islandsk egenkirkevæsen." *Scandia* 26 (1960), 230–96; Ólafía Einarsdóttir. *Studier i kronologisk metode i tidlig islandsk historieskrivning*. Bibliotheca Historica Lundensis, 13. Stockholm: Natur och Kultur, 1964; Magerøy, Hallvard. *Norsk-islandske problem. Omstridde spørsmål i Nordens historie*, 3. Oslo: Universitetsforlaget, 1965; Hermann Pálsson. *Eftir þjóðveldið. Heimildir annála um íslenzka sögu 1263–98*. Reykjavik: Heimskringla, 1965; Olsen, Olaf. *Hørg, hov og kirke. Historiske og arkæologiske vikingetidsstudier*. Copenhagen: Gad, 1966; Björn Þorsteinsson. *Ný Íslandssaga. Þjóðveldisöld*. Reykjavik: Heimskringla, 1966; Foote, Peter, and David M. Wilson. *The Viking Achievement: The Society and Culture of Early Medieval Scandinavia*. London: Sidgwick & Jackson, 1970; Björn Þorsteinsson. *Enska öldin í sögu Íslendinga*. Reykjavik: Mál og menning, 1970; Sawyer, Peter H. *The Age of the Vikings*. 2nd ed. London: Arnold, 1971; Kuhn, Hans. *Das alte Island*. Düsseldorf and Cologne: Diederichs, 1971; Magnús Stefánsson and Björn Teitsson. "Um rannsóknir á íslenzkri byggðarsögu tímabilsins fyrir 1700." *Saga* 10 (1972), 134–78 [Norwegian version: "Islandsk ødegårdsforskning." *Nasjonale forskningsoversikter. Det nordiske ødegårdsprosjekt. Publikasjon nr. 1*. Copenhagen: Landbohistorisk Selskab, 1972]; Gunnar Karlsson. "Goðar og bændur." *Saga* 10 (1972), 5–57; Sveinbjörn Rafnsson. *Studier i Landnámabók. Kritiska bidrag till den isländska fristatstidens historia*. Bibliotheca historica Lundensis, 31. Lund: Gleerup, 1974; Jón Steffensen. "Uppruni Íslendinga." In *Menning og meinsemdir. Ritgerðasafn um mótunarsögu íslenzkrar þjóðar og baráttu hennar við hungur og sóttir*. Reykjavik: Sögufélag, 1975, pp. 15–33; Jón Steffensen. "Tölfræðilegt mat á lífffræðilegu gildi frásagna Landnámu af ætt og þjóðerni landnemanna." In *Menning og meinsemdir*, pp. 92–106; Jón Steffensen. "Fólksfjöldi á Íslandi í aldanna rás." In *Menning og meinsemdir*, pp. 434–49; Strömbäck, Dag. *The Conversion of Iceland: A Survey*. Trans. and annotated by Peter Foote. Text Series, 6. London: Viking Society for Northern Research, 1975; Gunnar Karlsson. "Goðar and Höfðingjar in Medieval Iceland." *Saga-Book of the Viking Society* 19 (1977), 358–70; Saugstad, Letten Fegersten, *et al.* "The Settlement of Iceland." *Norwegian Archaeological Review* 10 (1977), 60–81; Sørensen, Preben Meulengracht. *Saga og Samfund. En indføring i oldislandsk Litteratur*. Copenhagen: Berling, 1977; Björn Þorsteinsson. *Íslensk miðaldasaga*. Reykjavik: Sögufélag, 1978; Tomasson, Richard F. *Iceland: The First New Society*. Minneapolis: University of Minnesota Press, 1980; Gelsinger, Bruce E. *Icelandic Enterprise: Commerce and Economy in the Middle Ages*. Columbia: University of South Carolina Press, 1981; Gissel, Svend, *et al. Desertion and Land Colonization in the Nordic Countries c. 1300–1600: Comparative Report from the Scandinavian Research Project on Deserted Farms and Villages*. Stockholm: Almqvist & Wiksell, 1981; Helgi Þorláksson. "Stéttir, auður og völd á 12. og 13. öld." *Saga* 20 (1982), 63–113; Sawyer, P. H. *Kings and Vikings: Scandinavia and Europe, A.D. 700–1100*. London and New York: Methuen, 1982; Byock, Jesse L. *Feud in the Icelandic Saga*. Berkeley, Los Angeles, and London: University of California Press, 1982; Blom, Grethe Authén. *Magnus Eriksson og Island. Til belysning av periferi og sentrum i nordisk 1300–talls historie. Det Kongelige Norske Videnskabers Selskab. Skrifter no. 2, 1983*. Trondheim: Universitetsforlaget, [1983]; Björn Þorsteinsson. *Island. Politikens Danmarks Historie*. Århus: Politikens, 1985; Hastrup, Kirsten. *Culture and History in Medieval Iceland: An Anthropological Analysis of Structure and Change*. Oxford: Clarendon, 1985; Byock, Jesse L. "Cultural Continuity, the Church, and the Concept of Independent Ages in Medieval Iceland." *Skandinavistik* 15.1 (1985), 1–14; Byock, Jesse L. "Governmental Order in Early Medieval Iceland." *Viator* 17 (1986), 19–34; Magnús Stefánsson. "Bergen—Islands første hovedstad." *Kjøpstad og rikssentrum. Onsdagskvelder i Bryggens Museum*, 2. Ed. Ingvild Øye. Bergen: Bryggens Museum, 1986; Lúðvík Ingvarsson. *Goðorð og goðorðsmenn* 1–3. Egilsstaðir: [n.p.], 1986–87; Byock, Jesse L. *Medieval Iceland: Society, Sagas, and Power*. Berkeley, Los Angeles, and London: University of California Press, 1988 [contains a comprehensive and up-to-date bibliography of medieval Icelandic history]; Jón Thor Haraldsson. *Ósigur Oddaverja*. Ritsafn Sagnfræðistofnunar, 22. Reykjavik: Sagnfræðistofnun Háskóla Íslands, 1988; Jón Viðar Sigurðsson. *Frá goðorðum til ríkja. Þróun goðavalds á 12. og 13. öld*. Reykjavik: Menningarsjóður, 1989; Helgi Þorláksson. *Gamlar götur og goðavald. Um fornar leiðir og völd Oddaverja í Rangárþingi*. Ritsafn Sagnfræðistofnunar, 25. Reykjavik: Sagnfræðistofnun Háskóla Íslands, 1989.

Magnús Stefánsson

[**See also:** Agriculture; *Alþingi*; *Bóndi*; Church Organization and Function; Climate; Conversion; Cosmography; Crime and Punishment; Demography; Family Structure; Fishing, Whaling, and Seal Hunting; *Goði*; *Grágás*; Hákon Hákonarson; Hanseatic League; Haraldr hárfagri ("fair-hair") Hálfdanarson; *Ísleifs þáttr biskups*; *Íslendingabók*; *Landnámabók*; Laws; *Leiðangr*; Óláfr, St.; Óláfr Tryggvason; Plague; Settlement, Age of; Snorri Sturluson; Social Structure; Sturlung Age; Temples, Heathen; Trade]

Iconography. The surviving pagan monuments are few and scattered, with concentrations of memorial stones with pictorial programs on the island of Gotland from the late 8th and early 9th centuries, Cumbria from the first half of the 10th, the Isle of Man in the 10th and early 11th, and Gotland again in the second half of the 11th. In addition, there are some fragments of pictorial representations in textile and wood carving from Norway (9th and early 10th centuries), and a couple of memorial stones from mainland Sweden of the 9th century. Three skaldic poems of the 9th and 10th centuries, moreover, describe pictures, and some further poetic fragments may also come from ekphrases.

The 8th–9th-century memorial stones on Gotland constitute the only homogeneous group of monuments. A manned ship under sail and a horse and rider are the dominating pictures both numerically and in size; together, the representations may depict the journey of the deceased to Valhǫll. Most stones have surrounding, much smaller scenes with motifs based on myths and sagas. Using the contemporary poem by Bragi Boddason, *Ragnarsdrápa*, scholars have identified one of these scenes as the battle of the Haddings, while others have with less certainty been taken to represent Þórr's fishing expedition and the slaying of Jǫrmunrekkr. Further pictures of this period are the memorial stone at Sparlösa, Västergötland, Sweden (rider with sword and animals, ship, birds, building: a mythical hunt? journey to Valhǫll?); the textile fragments from Tune (ship and figures) and Oseberg, Norway (laden horses, riders, carriages, walking men and women: procession? migration myth?); the Oseberg carriage (end: man attacked by snakes and lizard-like beast, identical iconography on Hunninge stone I, Gotland; side: rider and man on foot confronting each other in battle, woman intervening or egging on: connected with the battle of the Haddings?).

There is a hiatus of pictures from Scandinavia between the mid-9th and the mid-10th centuries. This can to some extent be bridged by using the skaldic poems describing pictures painted on shields and walls: Bragi Boddason's *Ragnarsdrápa* (first half of the 9th century), Þjóðólfr of Hvin's *Haustlǫng* (10th century), and Úlfr Uggason's *Húsdrápa* (980s). Þórr's fishing expedition is described by both Bragi and Úlfr, and the Fishing Stone at Gosforth, Cumbria, probably reflects a Scandinavian iconography, but it is only with the stones at Hørdum, Denmark, and Altuna in Uppland, Sweden, that an iconography corresponding to the poem's descriptions of the scene survive from Scandinavia proper. The Altuna memorial stone of the second half of the 11th century is one of the few outspokenly pagan pictures among the Upplandic memorials (which are predominantly Christian: around 65 percent have a cross and 25 percent a Christian invocation). The saga of Sigurðr on two memorials of the mid-11th century may reflect an honorific subject matter taken up in the period of conversion. No certain Ragnarǫk scene survives from Scandinavia, and the combination of this theme with a Crucifixion on the cross at Gosforth, Cumbria, may reflect the iconography of a mixed Scandinavian-insular culture.

The earliest Christian representation in Scandinavia is the filigree cross of the first half of the 10th century from grave 660 at Birka, Uppland, Sweden. The figure of Christ on this and later pectoral crosses is stylized, but easily recognizable and uncontaminated by pagan pictures. The vine-entwined Crucifixion is used on the royal memorial stone at Jelling, Denmark (third quarter of the 10th century), illustrating the part of the inscription where Harald Gormsson commemorates the conversion of the Danes. The vine-entwined Crucifixion is West European iconography that underwent modifications of style only when it was transplanted to Scandinavia. The fragmentary panels from Flatatunga, Iceland, of the mid-11th century, show a row of standing saints below a frieze of plant ornament, and are probably the oldest surviving church decorations in Scandinavia. Christian narrative representations are few in the surviving material, the most important being the Adoration of the Magi on the stone from Dynna, Norway (first half of the 11th century), which probably depends ultimately on continental prototypes but with stylistic transformations that have influenced the iconography.

Ecclesiastical art. Architecture carries pictures mainly in Denmark and Sweden. The most frequently occurring representations are the Crucifixion, the Deposition, and the Majestas Domini, normally in tympana, but occasionally as separate reliefs in the walls of the 12th-century churches. Other frequent representations are Samson and the lion, the Expulsion, Herod, and various saints. Narrative representations with themes drawn from the Old and New Testaments occur especially in the school of Horder in northern Jutland, in the diocese of Skara, Västergötland, in Scania emanating from the works in Lund, and on Gotland, which probably also had the cathedral workshop in Lund as a starting point. Both the quality of the carvings and the relative purity of their iconography vary, but no more than normal in European Romanesque stone carving.

Elaborate programs of a very high artistic quality survive above all on the metal altar fronts from Denmark and Sweden, and the cross of walrus ivory carved by Liutger for Gunhild in Denmark (ca. 1100) demonstrates one of the ways in which fairly complicated allegorical concepts were introduced into Scandinavia through artists working for, among others, royal patrons and using costly materials. The iconography of the Gunhild cross consists of the Crucifixion flanked by allegories of Life and Death, the Church, and the Synagogue, on one face; and on the other face, Christ in Judgment surrounded by angels, Abraham with the souls of the blessed, the elect, and the damned, and the torments of hell. Similarly, high-quality and very close European iconographic ties are demonstrated by the Danish wall-painting of the 12th century. Mostly, the iconographic programs follow continental models, but some types, notably the Majestas in Sønder Jernløse and the Hodegetria in Maaløv, both in Zealand, are of indisputably Byzantine origin, whether transmitted directly or by way of Germany cannot be ascertained. Contemporaneous Gotlandic murals, notably in Garde, are both stylistically and iconographically closely related to Russo-Byzantine painting. There is no doubt that the Danish schools of painting employed indigenous artists, but both their style and their iconographic programs show that they kept closely in touch with Germany and England throughout the 12th century. The most frequently recurring pictorial theme is Christ in Majesty (in apse or on chancel arch). Where the program has been fairly well preserved, the early decorations have scenes mainly from the New Testament (*e.g.*, Raasted), while stories from the lives of saints and unidentified battles seem to be introduced from the late 12th century onward (*e.g.*, Højen). Again, this pattern forms part of the normal European development.

Scandinavian altar fronts survive from the mid-12th century, beginning with the Danish metal fronts in the Carolingian and Ottonian tradition. The thirty-one painted fronts from Norway date from the mid-13th century to the early 15th, by which time they seem to have been made redundant by the reredos. The development of their iconographical programs reflects the general European tendency to let stories from legends and saints' *vitae* play an increasingly important role. The earliest Norwegian front, from Ulvik, has Christ in Majesty surrounded by apostles in a normal, Romanesque tradition. Similarly, Crucifixion representations of the later 13th century are of straightforward types, the most interesting of them being the front from Kinsarvik, where the Crucifixion is flanked by St. Paul and the vanquished Synagogue on the left, St. Peter and Ecclesia on the right, the whole framed by a Latin inscription quoting Baudri of Bourgueil on iconolatry. With the 14th century, far more emphasis is given to narrative scenes, such as the Passion of Christ on the front from Eid, apocryphal and legendary Marian cycles on the fronts from Odda and Nes, Emperor Heraclius recovering the True Cross on the front from Nedstryn, and St. Óláfr flanked by scenes from his passion on a front now in Trondheim cathedral. These fronts were evidently produced by urban workshops with good access to current, European iconographical prototypes and instructed by a clergy educated in the use of pictures.

Wooden crucifixes survive mainly from Sweden and Norway, and the iconography follows the main continental types. The suffering Christ of the Gero tradition is rare; the magnificent crucifix from Danderyd, Uppland, is probably an import, but there are local copies preserved from Låby and Husby-Långhundra, Uppland. Another late Ottonian tradition survives in the splendid crucifixes from Forsby (probably *ca.* 1135), and Svenneby, both Västergötland, where Christ wears a colobium and, in Forsby, apparently also originally a crown, being identified as *rex et sacerdos*. A much later version of Christ wearing a colobium, from Grong, Norway, seems, on the other hand, to reflect the *Volto Santo* type, as does the crucifix from Våversunda, Sweden (*ca.* 1200). The *Rex Triumphans* type was current in the second half of the 12th century, with Christ standing upright and wearing a royal crown. The extremely fine crucifix from Tryde, Scania (*ca.* 1160), is the most famous example, while that from Horg, Norway ("Horg crucifix II"), represents the most primitive versions. The closely connected *Christus Patiens* type, with S-shaped body, royal crown, loincloth, and eyes either open or closed, survives in greater numbers and was used certainly until the mid-13th century, possibly even later; the crucifixes in Hemse, Gotland, and Urnes, Norway, exemplify the type. Peculiar to a small group of this type of Scandinavian crucifixes is the association of painted shoes with loincloth. The Gothic type of Christ crucified, with closed eyes, body hanging, crown of thorns, and feet overlying, appears to have been introduced in the first third of the 13th century. Among the earliest examples is the crucifix from Hablingbo, Gotland, based on Saxon models. Distinctive of the Gotlandic crucifixes of the late 13th century is the *flabellum* type with narrative and allegorical representations within the ring, of which the Öja version is the most splendid. The development of the suffering Christ in the Scandinavian crucifixes follows that of western Europe, with the

14th-century cross from Fana, Norway, as a particularly expressive example. Calvary groups survive sporadically; the stylistically earliest version of the mourning Virgin and St. John are from Kjerstad, Västergötland; while the group from Bro, Gotland, and the Norwegian groups from Giske and Balke represent different stylistic and emotional interpretations without having iconographical distinctions.

Representations of the Virgin, like the Crucifixion, followed European types. The earliest surviving type is the *Sedes Sapientiae*, which predominates in 12th- and early 13th-century sculpture and is used also on the oldest altar front, from Lisbjerg, Denmark, of the mid-12th century. The great number of stylistic varieties testifies to the popularity of the type, iconographic differences being confined to hair, headdress, and the shape of the throne. The Virgin from Urnes, Norway, sits on a folding chair, while the Viklau and related representations have a chair comparable to that used in Saxon and Westphalian *Sedes Sapientiae* representations. The Child sitting sideways on the Virgin's lap was also introduced early. The Virgin from Varnum, Sweden, was probably imported from England shortly after 1150, and the same date is given to the indigenous version from Vreta, Östergötland. But the Gothic versions result from new West European models, stylistically attributable as German, English, and French. The maternal and playful postures of Virgin and Child increase from the late 13th century onward, but are rarely accentuated in either sculpture or painting. The *Maria Lactans* is very rare, though the type occurs on the 14th-century altar front from Vanylven, Norway. In sculpture, the sitting Virgin with standing Child and the standing Virgin are confined mainly to Swedish art; both types seem to have been introduced to Gotland through German prototypes in the 14th century, although there are stylistic indications also of English models for the standing type of the Virgin.

Seated saints appear to have been introduced in the late 12th century. The oldest examples are a group of unidentified bishops in Sweden: Sts. Nicholas, Thomas à Becket, and Sigfrid of Växjö have all been suggested. There are minor variations of age and type of pallium, otherwise they form a homogenous group and are seated on a chair identical to that used for the most common type of *Sedes Sapientiae*. Statues of St. Óláfr survive from the first half of the 13th century onward. The earliest type shows him seated, bearded, crowned, wearing tunic and mantle, and carrying the orb in his left hand and a scepter or an axe in his right, for example, the St. Óláfr from Tydal, Norway (now National Museum, Copenhagen; the axe is a modern reconstruction). An early Swedish example from Dädesjö depicts a young warrior under the saint's feet, and this figure became a normal attribute for the Óláfr iconography. Several explanations have been attempted, more or less fanciful or based on late-medieval legends: the saint's pagan youth, his half-brother Haraldr harðráði ("hard-ruler") Sigurðarson, a troll. Probably, the young warrior is an allegory of vanquished paganism in the same tradition as the Romanesque iconography of Constantine the Great. Approximately twenty statues of St. Óláfr of later types have the warrior exchanged for a dragon with crowned head, possibly a conflation with the attribute of St. George, although the same type of dragon occurs with the Virgin and a number of different saints, and can probably be taken as a general symbol of hell vanquished. High Gothic versions of St. Óláfr frequently show his left hand holding the strap of his mantle instead of an orb, a courtly gesture unlikely to have conveyed specific meaning, and the orb continued as an attribute to the end of the

Middle Ages. Unless they have definite attributes, like the axe or the proskynetic man, standing royal saints are not necessarily identifiable as St. Óláfr. Sts. Erik or Knud, or a European kingly saint, are possible alternatives. But the certain examples demonstrate that the standing representations of St. Óláfr had been introduced by the mid-13th century, and they came to predominate in the late Middle Ages. The dress of both the sitting and the standing types was changed into armor and mantle in most of the 15th-century versions. Contemporaneously, the king's age is frequently marked as advanced. Both iconographic changes seem to reflect the contemporary ideal of royalty in German art rather than reinterpretations of the saint's role. Approximately 250 statues of St. Óláfr survive from all Nordic countries, more than half of them from Sweden, testifying to the general popularity of the saint. The late Romanesque and Gothic types were presumably Scandinavian inventions based on contemporary European representations of kings in church sculpture, royal seals, and so on. It is noteworthy that dress, posture, and features were subject to the changing fashions of courtly ideal. The late-medieval versions are certainly made in North German workshops, but the high number of these sculptures surviving in Scandinavia testifies to the popularity of these modernized iconographical types.

The other Scandinavian saint of international importance was St. Birgitta of Sweden (1302 [1303?]–1373). Italian sources document that portraits of her existed there in the 1370s and that they had a certain likeness. The earliest Swedish statues of the saint, in Skederid and Vadstena, are normally assumed to have been based on such Italian portraits. The Vadstena statue depicts her as an authoress inspired, with her book of revelations held open by one hand and presumably a pen in her raised right hand (damaged); her dress is contemporary, and the remains of polychromy correspond with the colors she is recorded to have worn. Most of the later statues preserve the pose of writing, but the emotional impact is changed by giving the features a more youthful, blissfully meditating, and idealized rendering. As is the case with most saints, late-medieval versions show her standing, but retaining her book.

Import of sculpture from North Germany and the Netherlands may have started in the second half of the 14th century, but from the early 15th century onward it dominates completely over indigenous production. The patrons' role in influencing the iconographical programs may to some extent be inferred from the presence of indigenous saints like Óláfr, Birgitta, Knud, Erik, and Sunniva, and one of Bernt Notke's masterpieces, St. George in Stockholm, was commissioned to commemorate Sten Sture's victory at Brunkeberg in 1471. Nevertheless, iconographic types and details seem to owe little to Scandinavian traditions. Although the absence of peculiarly Scandinavian iconographic types is characteristic of most medieval art from the region, it becomes even more striking when coupled with the absence of indigenous styles and local iconographic preferences.

Lit.: Nygren, Olga Alice. *Helgonen i Finlands medeltidskonst. En ikonografisk studie.* Suomen miunaismuistoyhdistyksen Aikakauskrirja. Finska fornminnesföreningens Tidskrift, 46.1 Helsingfors: [s.n.], 1945; Eldjárn, Kristján. "Carved Panels from Flatatunga, Iceland." *Acta archaeologica* 24 (1953), 81–101; Tuulse, Armin. *Den ikonografiska forskningen i Sverige.* Stockholm: Kungl. vitterhets-, historie- och antikvitetsakademien, 1972; Lassen, Erik. *Dansk Kunsthistorie: Billedkunst og skulptur. 1. Fra runesten til altertavle, ca. 900–1500.* Ed.

Vagn Poulsen *et al.* Copenhagen: Politiken, 1975, Banning, Knud, ed. *A Catalogue of Wall-Paintings in the Churches of Medieval Denmark: Scania, Halland, Blekinge.* 4 vols. Copenhagen: Akademisk Forlag, 1976; Haastrup, Ulla. "Die seeländischen, romanischen Wandmalereien in Slagelille, Sonderup und Fjenneslev. Studien über Technik, Ikonographie und Werkstattzusammenhang der Finja-Gruppe." *Hafnia-Copenhagen Papers in the History of Art* 6 (1979), 106–43; Anderson, Flemming G., *et al.*, eds. *Medieval Iconography and Narrative: Proceedings of the Fourth International Symposium at Odense University 1979.* Odense: Odense University Press, 1980; Fuglesang, Signe Horn. "Crucifixion Iconography in Viking Scandinavia." In *Proceedings of the Eighth Viking Congress, Århus, 24–31 August 1977.* Ed. Hans Bekker-Nielsen *et al.* Odense: Odense University Press, 1981, pp. 73–94; Zeitler, Rudolf, and Jan O. M. Karlsson, eds. *Imagines medievales. Studier i medeltida ikonografi, arkitektur, skulptur, måleri och konsthantverk. Mit ausfürlichen deutschen Zusammenfassungen.* Acta Universitatis Upsaliensis, Ars Suetica, 7. Uppsala: Institutionen för konstvetenskap vid Uppsala Universitet, 1983; Lindahl, Fritze. *Middelalderlige fingerringe med ikonografiske motiver.* Taidehistoriallisia tutkimuksia konsthistoriska Studier, 8. Helsinki: [n.p.], 1985. Düwel, K. "Zur Ikonographie und Ikonologie der Sigurddarstellungen." In *Zum Problem der Deutung frühmittelalterlicher Bildinhalte: Akten des 1. Internationalen Kolloquiums in Marburg a. d. Lahn, 15. bis 19. Februar 1983.* Ed. Helmut Roth. Sigmaringen: Thorbrak, 1986, pp. 221–71; Fuglesang, Signe Horn. "Ikonographie der skandinavischen Runensteine der jüngeren Wikingerzeit." In *Zum Problem der Deutung frühmittelalterlicher Bildinhalte,* pp. 183–210.

Signe Horn Fuglesang

[**See also**: Birka; Bragi Boddason; Carving: Bone, Horn, and Walrus Tusk; Ironwork; Jelling; Oseberg; Painting; Saints' Lives; Þjóðólfr of Hvin; Úlfr Uggason; Viking Art; Wood Carving]

Illuga saga Gríðarfóstra ("The Saga of Illugi, Foster-son of Gríðr").

The oldest MS of this saga (AM 123 8vo) dates from about 1600, and there is some doubt as to whether it is a genuine medieval *fornaldarsaga.* It relates the adventures of Illugi, a Norwegian farmer's son and friend of the king's son Sigurðr. The central episode concerns Illugi's encounter in the far north of Norway with the troll-wife Gríðr and her daughter, who turn out to be human women under a spell. Illugi frees them from enchantment, killing a number of real trolls in the process, and he and Sigurðr marry them.

The saga is shorter than most *fornaldarsögur,* and simpler in both structure and style, consisting largely of the one episode, with attendant preliminaries and the happy ending. The hero's rescue of a princess from a troll is a common folktale motif, but the saga version is most closely paralleled in Danish, Faroese, and Norwegian ballads about Illugi. The motif of the shipwreck and ensuing search for fire (the cause of Illugi's journey to the troll-woman's cave), with the telling of three truths as a condition for being given the fire, is paralleled in Saxo's account of Thorkillus's expedition to visit Utgarthilocus (*Gesta Danorum,* Book 8). The Icelandic saga may be based on a variant of the ballad combined with this motif, making it not a true *fornaldarsaga* but a pastiche (Davíð Erlingsson 1975). Although the origins of *Illuga saga* are obscure, it is clear that the saga, the ballads, and Saxo's account all derive from the same pool of material reworked in a number of different genres at different times throughout Scandinavia.

Ed.: Rafn, C. C., ed. *Fornaldar sögur Nordrlanda.* 3 vols. Copenhagen: Popp, 1829–30, vol. 3, pp. 648–60. **Lit.**: Davíð Erlingsson. "Illuga saga og Illuga dans." *Gripla* 1 (1975), 9–42 [English summary]; Jesch, Judith. "Ásmundar saga Flagðagæfu." *Arv* 38 (1984 for 1982), 103–31.

Judith Jesch

[See also: *Fornaldarsögur*; Saxo Grammaticus]

Ireland, Norse in. Viking attacks on Ireland were first noted in 795, and became annual occurrences from 822. In the 830s and 840s, Ireland was widely raided by several fleets that came inland via the many navigable rivers. These fleets were under the command of Norwegian earls. From 841, they operated from winter camps. The annals mention a *longphort*, or ship camp, in Dublin by the River Liffey, in Waterford by the Barrow, in Limerick by the Shannon, and in Anagassan by the Boyne. Later camps included Wexford and Cork.

The Viking hold on the waterways was, however, endangered by heavy defeats by the Irish and the advent of a rival Danish fleet. In 853, Óláfr, son of the king of "Lochlann" (possibly Rogaland in southwestern Norway), asserted Norwegian power over the remnants of the camps. He abandoned the practice of Viking hit-and-run operations, and placed his fleets in the service of the highest bidder.

From 853, Norse activity must be analyzed within the wider framework of the complex diplomatic schemes of the internal Irish power struggle. Until the Norman Conquest in 1170, Ireland was divided among three or four rival over-kingdoms, and mercenary troops were in high demand. The Norsemen were out of a job only during momentary truces, and only then resorted to more or less random Viking attacks. A momentary Irish truce seems indeed to be the explanation of the expulsion of the Norsemen from Ireland in 902. They dispersed to England and France to take part in the conquest of new territories.

By 914, a new generation of warriors sought land for themselves in Ireland, and took up the old campsites by the rivers. They were under the leadership of the grandsons of Ívarr the Boneless. Ívarr was a coregent of Dublin with Óláfr from 857 to 873, and his descendants had established themselves as kings of York. In the 920s, the grandsons of Ívarr controlled the entire Irish Sea area from their strongholds in York and Dublin. For a brief moment, the Viking kingship was a major political force in the history of both England and Ireland. In 927, Godfred was ousted from York by Æthelstan, king of the Anglo-Saxons, but the Dublin king recaptured York in 939 and held it almost continually to 952. The Dublin-York kingship was, however, repeatedly attacked, because it never managed to obtain a truce with any of its neighbors. For all practical intents, it was a kingship of the sea and the rivers, based on camps, and it did not secure a firm territorial grip. In the Irish context, Dublin and its allied camps ceased to have an independent political status after heavy defeats in the 940s. Norse warriors were once again reduced to mercenaries in the Irish power struggle.

The last outbursts of Norse political aspirations came under the rule of Sigtryggr silkiskegg ("silk-beard"; r. 989–993, 995–1042). From 980, Dublin had to recognize the over-kingship of the Irish king of Meath, and Sigtryggr repeatedly allied with the king of Leinster to establish his sovereignty. However, he was forced to pay tribute to Meath in 995, 998, and 1000. Even though he probably was the engineer of the great alliance in 1014 of Leinster and the Orkney earl, he wisely kept out of the battle of Clontarf, thus saving Dublin from total defeat. By his death in 1042, Dublin was a minor political power, but a growing merchant town.

The luxuries of the Dublin market and the profits to be gained by controlling it attracted the interest of Irish kings for direct control. In 1052, Dublin was forced to acknowledge a son of the king of Leinster as regent. Except from 1078 to 1094, when Dublin was controlled by the Norse king of Man and the Isles (the Hebrides), the city was held by Irish kings.

The other Norse camps also came under Irish control, Limerick by 968 and Waterford in 1035. The history of the camps at Wexford and Cork is not known, whereas camps at Strangford and Carlingford Loughs, including Anagassan, were evacuated during the contraction of Dublin power in the 940s.

Even though Dublin ceased to be a political unit, the city continued to have a mercenary fleet. It was used by Irish and sometimes Scottish, Welsh, and even Norman warlords, and was only dissolved by the Norman Conquest.

Prey and tribute. The objective of a Viking hit-and-run attack was the taking of valuable goods. The Irish used the monasteries as sanctuaries for persons, wealth, and livestock during their own internal wars, and even in peacetime monasteries would be storerooms of ecclesiastical as well as secular wealth. The Vikings therefore concentrated attacks on religious sites as a practical matter of course. The first settlements to feel the threat were isolated coastal settlements, such as Iona, which had to be temporarily abandoned in the 830s and 840s, and small settlements, such as Skellig Michael. Larger establishments were better able to defend themselves and would indeed be protected by their secular overking. Nevertheless, a large seat like Kildare, which was even at times regarded as the capital of Leinster, was plundered no less than fifteen times by the Norse between 836 and 1000. A series of eleven attacks on Armagh, the prime ecclesiastical center of the North, must also be noted. Settlements near the Viking camps probably paid tribute as protection money. Long lists in the 11th-century *Book of Rights* seem to reflect a complicated pattern of tributes paid in allegiance between Irish and Norse lords. In fact, Viking warfare was but one additional feature in the complex matrix of Irish power struggles. Overlords and rival contenders were locked in conflicts that failed to produce one victor who would have shaped an Irish state. Thus, breaches of sanctuary and payment of tribute were not new phenomena to the Irish. The Viking contribution was, however, an escalation of the means of warfare. They introduced the longship, which the Irish kings used from the 10th century to control the large navigable rivers. The Vikings also introduced superior weaponry, such as hand-axes and long swords.

Slaving and trading. The activities of the Viking Age proper, the 9th century, may be said to concentrate on the extraction of portable wealth, accumulated in the monasteries, and the payment of tributes and mercenary money. The Viking camps were semipermanent structures, easily abandoned. The 10th-century creation of the York-Dublin axis coincided with an upward trend in international trade. The Dublin Vikings engaged in this trade in luxuries and handicrafts, as is well attested by the excavations of Dublin, which will, when eventually published, add considerably to our knowledge. Irish kings and churches were ready buyers of wine and wheat, metalwork and craftsmanship, made available to them via the Norse ports and trading ships. Ireland had no mineral wealth, and was forced to pay in hides and slaves. Very little is known about the actual trade mechanisms and balances, but one indicator is the growing number of instances recorded in the annals of the taking of slaves by the Irish. Rival lords seem to have waged war in part with the object of taking slaves to be sold at the Dublin slave market in return for foreign commodities. In the 11th century, Dublin was probably the prime slave market of western Europe, furnishing customers in the British Isles, Anglo-Saxon as well as Norse, and the Scandinavian countries and Iceland. The trade (and Irish slave raids) seems to have petered out in the early 12th century, when the Normans banned slave trade. Indeed, the Irish synod of 1170 welcomed the Norman Conquest as just punishment for the abuses of the slave trade. By then, however, trade had shifted to the export of hides to be used as parchment, and Dublin control of the Irish Sea area had already succumbed to the growing power of Bristol.

Norse traditions. Conversion to Christianity was already in evidence by the late 9th century, and the York-Dublin king was forced to become baptized in 926. Heathen cults were still in evidence around 1000. The reign of Sigtryggr silkiskegg, however, signaled a steady growth of Anglo-Saxon cultural influence in Dublin. The Dublin mint was opened in 997 to English standards, and when Cnut (Knud) the Great took the English throne, Sigtryggr seems to have followed his example. He undertook a pilgrimage to Rome in 1028 and founded Christchurch cathedral within the bounds of the city, probably quite near the royal hall. Archaeological evidence underlines the growing Anglo-Saxon influence on the material culture of the Norse and through them on the Irish. Nevertheless, the court of Sigtryggr was in close contact with the earl of Orkney and the Norwegian king, and many settlers in Iceland probably had family relations in Ireland.

Dublin must have had, then, a thriving skaldic tradition that was conveyed to Iceland and thus preserved. Pride of place must go to the "saga of Brian Bóramha," which tells the story of the battle of Clontarf in 1014. In fact, Dublin wisely kept out of this struggle between the Leinster and Munster kings, but the earl of Orkney and many other Norse noblemen fell as mercenaries. They were remembered in stories that are now incorporated into *Njáls saga*. Dublin's role in skaldic and saga traditions is, however, still largely unresearched.

In the 12th century, Dublin was losing contact with the Norse world, and was increasingly seen as the capital of the king of Leinster. Nevertheless, the city retained a large Norse population that was even able to preserve the identity of settlers who chose to move to the growing economic area around the Bristol channel and brought their Norse language to such places as Swansea and Bardsey. The Norse merchants and handicraftsmen in Dublin were increasingly absorbed into Irish society, and even obtained landholds. The Norman Conquest, however, brought disaster to this easily recognizable segment of the population. The Norse of Dublin were ousted to Ostmantown and were deprived of their privileges. By the middle of the 13th century, the Norse were wholly assimilated in Irish society, but the Viking experience was never forgotten, as evidenced in a number of Irish tales.

Lit.: **(a) Source criticism**: Goedheer, A. J. *Irish and Norse Traditions About the Battle of Clontarf.* Haarlem: Willink, 1938; Ó Cuiv, Brian. "Literary Creation and Irish Historical Tradition." *Proceedings of the British Academy* 49 (1963), 233–62; Hughes, Kathleen. *Early Christian Ireland: Introduction to the Sources.* London: Hodder & Stoughton, 1972; Ó Corráin, Donnchadh. "Caithréim Chellacháin Chaisil: History or Propaganda?" *Ériu* 25 (1974), 1–69; MacNiocaill, Gearoid. *The Medieval Irish Annals.* Medieval Irish History Series, 3. Dublin: Dublin Historical Association, 1975. **(b) General history**: Bugge, Alexander. "Bidrag til det sidste Afsnit af Nordboernes Historie i Irland." *Aarbøger for nordisk Oldkyndighed og Historie* (1904), 248–315; Curtis, Edmund. "The English and the Ostmen in Ireland." *English Historical Review* 23 (1908), 209–19; Ó Corráin, Donnchadh. *Ireland Before the Normans.* Dublin: Gill and Macmillan, 1972; Byrne, Francis John. *Irish Kings and High-kings.* London: Batsford, 1973; Smyth, Alfred P. *Scandinavian York and Dublin. I: The History and Archaeology of Two Related Viking Kingdoms.* Dublin: Templekieran, 1975; Smyth, Alfred P. *Scandinavian Kings in the British Isles, 850–880.* Oxford: Oxford University Press, 1977; Smyth, Alfred P. *Scandinavian York and Dublin. II: The History and Archaeology of Two Related Viking Kingdoms.* New Jersey: Humanities Press; Dublin: Templekieran, 1979; Ó Corráin, Donnchadh. "High-Kings, Vikings and Other Kings." *Irish Historical Studies* 21 (1979), 283–323. **(c) Archaeology**: Dolley, Michael. *The Hiberno-Norse Coins in the British Museum.* Sylloge of Coins of the British Isles, 1. London: British Museum, 1966; Graham-Campbell, J. A. "The Viking-Age Silver Hoards of Ireland." In *Proceedings of the 7th Viking Congress, Dublin 15–21 August 1973.* Ed. Bo Almqvist and David Greene. Dublin and London: Dundalgan, 1976, pp. 39–74; Wallace, Patrick. "The Archaeology of Viking Dublin." In *The Comparative History of Urban Origins in Non-Roman Europe: Ireland, Wales, Denmark, Germany, Poland, and Russia from the Ninth to the Thirteenth Century.* Ed. Helen B. Clarke *et al.* Oxford: British Archaeological Reports, 1985, pp. 103–42. **(d) Art**: Henry, Françoise. *Irish Art During the Viking Invasions (800–1020 A.D.).* Ithaca: Cornell University Press, 1967; Henry, Françoise. *Irish Art During the Romanesque Period (1020–1170 A.D.).* London: Methuen, 1970; Ryan, Michael, ed. *Ireland and Insular Art A.D. 500–1200: Proceedings of a Conference at University College Cork, 31 October–3 November 1985.* Dublin: Royal Irish Academy, 1987. **(e) Raids and trade**: Gwynn, Aubrey. "Medieval Bristol and Dublin." *Irish Historical Studies* 5.20 (1947), 275–86; Lucas, A. T. "Irish-Norse Relations: Time for a Reappraisal?" *Journal of the Cork Historical and Archaeological Society* 61 (1966), 62–75; Lucas, A. T. "The Plundering and Burning of Churches in Ireland, 7th to 10th Century." In *North Munster Studies: Essays in Commemoration of Monsignor Michael Moloney.* Ed. Etienne Rynne. Limerick: Thomond Archaeological Society, 1967; Doherty, Charles. "Exchange and Trade in Early Medieval Ireland." *Journal of the Royal Society of Antiquaries of Ireland* 110 (1980), 67–89; Holm, Poul. "The Slave Trade of Dublin, Ninth to Twelfth Centuries." *Peritia* 5 (1986), 317–45. **(f) Religion**: Marstrander, Carl J. S. "Thor en Irelande." *Revue celtique* 36 (1916), 241–53; Gwynn, Aubrey. "The Origins of the See of Dublin." *Irish Ecclesiastical Record* 5.57 (1941), 40–55, 97–112; Gwynn, Aubrey. "The First Bishops of Dublin." *Reportorium Novum. Dublin Diocesan Historical Record* 1.1 (1955), 1–26; Hughes, Kathleen. *The Church in Early Irish Society.* London: Methuen, 1966. **(g) Philology**: Marstrander, Carl J. S. *Bidrag til det Norske Sprogs Historie i Irland.* Videnskapsselskapets Skrifter. II. Hist.-Filos. Klasse. Christiania [Oslo]: Dybwad, 1915; Greene, David. "The Evidence of Language and Place-Names in Ireland." In *The Vikings: Proceedings of the Symposium of the Faculty of Arts of Uppsala University, June 6–9, 1977.* Uppsala: Almqvist & Wiksell, 1978, pp. 119–24; Ó Corráin, Donnchadh. "The Semantic Development of Old Norse *Jarl* in Old and Middle Irish." In *Proceedings of the Tenth Viking Congress, Larkollen, Norway, 1985.* Ed. James E. Knirk. Universitetets Oldsaksamlings Skrifter, ny rekke, 9. Oslo: Universitetets Oldsaksamling, 1987, pp. 287–93. **(h) Literature and folklore**: Christiansen, Reidar Th. *The Vikings and the*

Viking Wars in Irish and Gaelic Tradition. Skrifter utg. av det Norske Videnskaps-Akademi i Oslo. Oslo: Dybwad, 1931; Sommerfelt, A. "The Norsemen in Present Day Donegal Tradition." *Journal of Celtic Studies* 1.2 (1959), 232–8; Christiansen, Reider Th. *Studies in Irish and Scandinavian Folktales.* Copenhagen: Rosenkilde & Bagger, 1959; MacCana, Proinsias. "The Influence of the Vikings on Celtic Literature." In *The Impact of the Scandinavian Invasions on the Celtic-speaking Peoples c. 800–1100 A.D.* Dublin: Institúid Ard-Léinn Bhaile Átha Cliath, 1962, pp. 78–118; rpt. 1975 [Proceedings of the International Congress of Celtic Studies, Dublin, 6–10 July 1959]; Chesnutt, Michael. "An Unsolved Problem in Old Norse–Icelandic Literary History." *Mediaeval Scandinavia* 1 (1968), 122–37; Almqvist, Bo. "Scandinavian and Celtic Folklore Contacts in the Earldom of Orkney." *Saga-Book of the Viking Society* 20 (1978–79), 80–105; Mackenzie, Bridget Gorden. "On the Relation of Norse Skaldic Verse to Irish Syllabic Poetry." In *Specvlvm Norroenvm: Norse Studies in Memory of Gabriel Turville-Petre.* Ed. Ursula Dronke *et al.* Odense: Odense University Press, 1981, pp. 337–56; Gísli Sigurðsson. *Gaelic Influence in Iceland: Historical and Literary Contacts. A Survey of Research.* Studia Islandica, 46. Reykjavik: Menningarsjóður, 1988.

Poul Holm

[**See also**: Slavery]

Ironwork. Modern Swedish researchers (Ambrosiani 1983, Hyenstrand 1979) have stressed the vital importance of the economic development of, for example, Uppland in the Vendel and Viking ages (*ca.* A.D. 600–1050). Rich finds have been made of furnaces and iron blanks, whereas there remain very few finished forged products from those early days, apart from weapons. In the well-known Oseberg grave in South Norway, from the 9th century, there are two iron-mounted chests, which are very simple. Their plain iron bands have never been the object of aesthetic consideration.

The earliest preserved Scandinavian ironwork images or ornaments date no farther back than the Missionary period, *i.e.*, the decades around the year 1100, and are found on church doors. The corresponding secular smithing is considerably younger, and belongs mainly to the centuries after the Reformation.

On the doors of some Norwegian stave churches, early Romanesque lock- and ringhandle-plates remain, often dominated by long-necked animal heads extending from the corners of the plates (Fig. 54). Those heads have apotropaic purposes. The fear of evil powers was immense, after as well as before the arrival of Christianity, and many of the signs and images on medieval doors sprang from that fear. Their task was to scare off the Devil and his demons.

According to medieval conceptions, the keyhole particularly attracted the demons. This belief explains why the lock-plate from Lomen is surrounded by four monsters whose guard-keeping, with roots in ancient heathen times, has been reinforced by a Christian cross (Fig. 54). At Sala, a dragon has posted itself below the keyhole (Fig. 55). Apart from dragons and crosses, there were applied apotropaic signs of pagan origin, as well as biblical quotations, prayers, Christograms, and names of saints, all for the same evil-averting purpose. Such representations have been repeated on innumerable doors down to the present time.

In some medieval legends, the archangel Michael guards the gate of paradise; he "cast out that old serpent, called the Devil and Satan" (Revelation 12:9). The step between the gate of paradise and the church door was never very long, and Michael often appears on or near the door (Figs. 56, 57). Michael's mission as guardian could also be taken over by other famous warriors and dragonslayers, such as St. George and Sigurðr Fáfnisbani (Fig. 58).

Michael as gatekeeper and other representations for that purpose formed an important part of the repertory of Scandinavian smiths, but they fancied other motifs as well. No pre-Christian forgings of that kind remain, so it is difficult to know how much builds on native tradition and how much has been borrowed from abroad. But some trends in the development can be distinguished.

The ironwork of the oldest doors was sparse and simple, but executed with aesthetic awareness and a developed sense of the possibilities of the craft. A hinge strap at Garde has a broad central groove, whose ridges continue into the gently bent terminal split curls (Fig. 59). That type of forging probably issued from the native form tradition.

The influx of foreign forms and motifs increased when Lund, at the beginning of the 12th century, became the archiepiscopal see of all Scandinavia. No ironwork has been preserved in Lund cathedral, but in South Swedish parish churches, there are doors that imply a well-known finished prototype. The only possible place for such a prototype is Lund itself. In those days, Scania was part of Denmark, and several Scanian places have such "Lundensic imitations." The impulses spread farther to Småland via Växjö cathedral, which started building after the middle of the 12th century. A characteristic specimen of the latter group comes from Vetlanda (Fig. 60). Its lower portions are covered with a regular lattice, over which rises a strictly conventionalized arcade. The latter, as well as the openings of the lattice, contains vegetative forms intended to represent Trees of Life. The church door was meant to mirror the gate of paradise, and these ornamental forms present a picture of the eschatological paradise, the prospect of an eternal life held out by the Church.

Paradisaical allusions of a different kind appear on the door at Väversunda. In its top panel, side by side, stand the two poles in the Christian doctrine of salvation, the Fall and the Crucifixion (Fig. 61). The first event drove the two sinners out of paradise and caused its gate to be shut. Christ's sacrificial death on the Cross opened it anew. The churchgoer is again reminded that the church door is the gate of paradise, the road to salvation. As at Väversunda, Christ is often pictured on the church door or very near it. Sometimes, there is a direct reference to John 10:9, where Jesus says, "I am the door: by me if any man enter in, he shall be saved."

The Väversunda door (Fig. 61) consists of additive representations in horizontal panels, one on top of the other. The protagonists of the picture scenes are shaped as thin sheet-iron silhouettes. Michael and the dragon on the door at Rogslösa (Fig. 56) have been made in the same technique, which is characteristic of Swedish ironwork and which remained vigorous until the 15th century. A grill at Strängnäs consists of similar thin silhouettes, whose surfaces, like the above-mentioned ones, have been enlivened by dots and lines, made with punch and chisel (Fig. 62). Many Swedish doors and chests are covered with hunting scenes in this technique, which was also known in Finland (Fig. 63).

Only in exceptional cases have Scandinavian smiths given a marked in-the-round character to their figure representations. We have already seen a Michael with his head *en ronde bosse* (Fig. 57), and on some doors there are crucifixes with a certain plasticity (Fig. 64).

The medieval ringhandles are also plastic. Some Norwegian

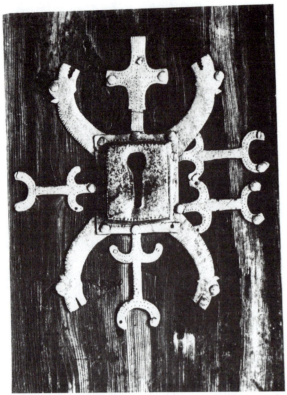

54. Lomen, Norway. Lock-plate of stave-church door; 12th century.

55. Sala, Sweden. Dragon guarding the keyhole of a church door; 15th century.

56. Rogslösa, Sweden. St. Michael and the dragon on a church door. The door contains several similar picture scenes; *ca.* 1200.

57. Reinli, Norway. St. Michael between two protruding dragon heads. Ringhandle-plate of a stave-church door; 12th century.

59. Garde, Sweden. Hinge strap of old Scandinavian type; *ca.* 1100.

58. Kungslena, Sweden. St. George and the dragon placed near the keyhole of a church door; *ca.* 1200.

60. Vetlanda, Sweden. Door with paradise motif; early 13th century.

61. Våversunda, Sweden. Door with pictures of the Fall and the Crucifixion; *ca.* 1200.

62. Strängnäs, Sweden. (Top) Grille with silhouettes of fable animals and coats of arms inside circular frames; first half of the 15th century. (Bottom) Detail. Pelican symbolizing Christ.

63. Hollola, Finland. Man with hunting horn and prey placed high up on a church door; 15th century.

64. Romfartuna, Sweden. Crucifix on entirely ironclad door; *ca.* 1500.

65. Noderhof, Norway. Ringhandle consisting of two winged dragons with intertwined tails; *ca.* 1200.

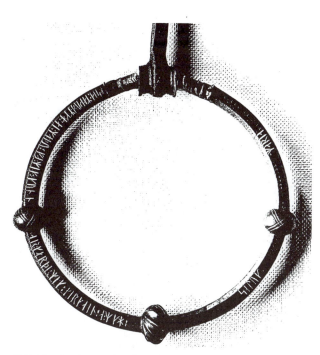

66. Delsbo, Sweden. Ringhandle with three upsets, two animal heads, and a runic inscription; *ca.* 1200.

67. Björksta, Sweden. Animal's head on a ringhandle. The handle is of a Romanesque type, but sits on a 15th-century door.

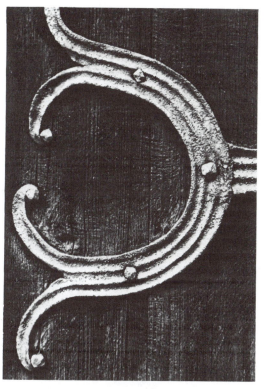

68. Källunge, Sweden. Church door dominated by a typically Gotlandic motif; end of the 13th century.

69. Martebo, Sweden. C-shape terminating a typically Gotlandic motif; shortly before middle of the 14th century.

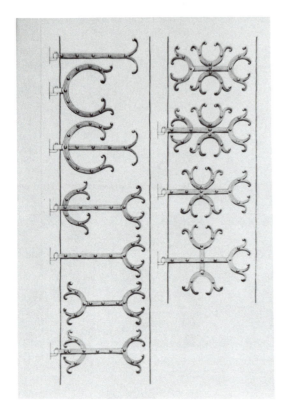

70. Iron straps and C-shapes in combinations that occur on Gotlandic doors.

72. Søndersø, Denmark. Door with Latin inscription; 1483.

(a)

(b)

71 a–b. Prototype and successor. (a) Pontigny, France; 12th century. (b) Fole, Sweden; late 12th century.

variants are shaped like two winged dragons that twine around each other (Fig. 65), whereas the Swedish handles have only dragons' heads (Fig. 66), some of them well elaborated (Fig. 67). Both in Norway and Sweden, ringhandles are often furnished with runic inscriptions. One from Delsbo reads: "You may look at me. You shall not get me. Gunnar made me. The church owns me. Holy Mary" (Fig. 66).

Very early, Gotland developed a motif that did not exist in other parts of Scandinavia. In Gotlandic forging, however, it was predominant for over a hundred years from the middle of the 13th century. In the course of that period, doors were made larger and larger, often some 5 m. high and divided into two leaves. Each door leaf was furnished, all the way up, with horizontal iron straps, at both ends terminating in C-shapes with split curls. The middle section of each strap has two additional C-shapes (Fig. 68). Straps and C-shapes are enlivened by three deep, chiseled grooves (Fig. 69).

In theory, preliminary stages of this motif can be said to exist on Gotland as early as the 12th century. By combining straight horizontal hinge straps (Fig. 70a) and C-shaped ones (Fig. 70b), one arrives at a number of variations (Figs. 70c–g) which could be regarded as precursors of the fully developed Gotlandic motif (Fig. 70h). But everything points to the latter having another origin.

In 1164, a Cistercian abbey was founded in the middle of Gotland by monks from Nydala in Småland, whose mother abbey, in its turn, was Clairvaux in France. Clairvaux was one of the principal establishments of the Cistercian order, and its economy was based on iron production (Fossier 1961, Graves 1957, Sprandel 1968). Clairvaux's English daughter abbeys are to a large extent located near known ore deposits, and Nydala's unlimited supply of lake ore, charcoal, and water power decided Clairvaux's choice of that place for its first Swedish daughter monastery.

In other words, the Clairvaux monks were mining experts and skilled smiths, and everything indicates that they brought this typically French-Cistercian motif to Scandinavia. No Romanesque ironwork remains at Clairvaux, but at Pontigny, a sister establishment in the neighborhood, the prototype of the Gotlandic motif (Fig. 71a) can still be studied.

The Black Death and Valdemar Atterdag's ("ever-day") forays caused a stagnation on Gotland after the middle of the 14th century. On the Swedish mainland, artistic activity had culminated around the year 1200 with a large group of picture doors (Figs. 56, 61). Then followed a period of decline for 200 years. Not until the first half of the 15th century was there a certain recovery with such products as the Strängnäs grill (Fig. 62). During the decades before the Reformation, there was again an increase, at least in quantity. The quality, however, remained uneven; apart from a small number of aesthetically and technically remarkable products, the smithing was primitive. Because of the protracted stagnation, smiths often lacked current and prevalent models, and instead had to repeat ancient Romanesque patterns and motifs. This conservatism has led to many doors being regarded as being much older than they are.

The development in Denmark was different. Apart from Scania, now a Swedish province, hardly any Romanesque ironwork remains, and the Gothic specimens, except for some areas, bear a rustic and primitive stamp. The most interesting exception is Funen, where a large group of doors covered by inscriptions in beautiful, well-wrought letters was created in the decades around the year 1500 (Fig. 72). The door reproduced here bears a Latin inscrip-

tion that can be translated: "Our lady Cecilia in the year of the Lord 1483. As soon as you enter the temple, consider why you were born human. So read and sing and to Christ pronounce prayers. This is the door of the Lord. The just shall enter into this church of the holy apostles Peter and Paul."

Lit.: Romdahl, A. L. "Rogslösadörren och en grupp romanska smiden i de gamla Götalandskapen." Fornvännen 9 (1914) 231–45; Holmér, F. "Stildrag i järnsmideskonsten under romansk tid." Tidskrift för konstvetenskap 16 (1932), 86–99; Mackeprang, M. "Fyenske jærnbundne kirkedøre fra middelalderen. Aarbøger for nordisk Oldkyndighed og Historie (1943), 1–30; Graces, C. "The Economic Activities of the Cistercians in Medieval England (1128–1307)." Analecta Sacri Ordinis Cisterciensis 13 (1957), 3–60; Sprandel, Rolf. Das Eisengewerbe im Mittelalter. Stuttgart: Hiersemann, 1968; Hauglid, Roar. Norske stavkirker, dekor og utstyr. Oslo: Dreyer, 1973; Thømt-Bjærke, T. "Problemer omkring en gruppe smijernbeslås i Sogn, Valdres og Gudbrandsdalen." Diss. University of Oslo, 1978; Hyenstrand, Å. "Iron and Iron Economy in Sweden." In Iron and Man in Prehistoric Sweden. Ed. and trans. Helen Clarke. Stockholm: Jernkontoret, 1979, pp. 134–56; Nordman, C. A. Finlands medeltida konsthantverk. Helsingfors: Museiverket, 1980; Ambrosiani, B. "Background to Boat-Graves in the Mälaren Valley." In Vendel Period Studies: Transactions of the Boat-Grave Symposium in Stockholm, February 2–3, 1981. Ed. J. P. Lamm and H.-A. Nordström. Stockholm: Museum of National Antiquities, 1983, pp. 17–22; Karlsson, Lennart. Medieval Ironwork in Sweden. Stockholm: Almqvist & Wiksell, 1988 [with exhaustive references to medieval ironwork throughout Scandinavia].

Lennart Karlsson

[See also: Iconography; Oseberg]

Isle of Man *see* **Man, Isle of**

Ísleifs þáttr biskups ("The Tale of Bishop Ísleifr") concerns Ísleifr Gizurarson, first bishop of the Icelanders (1056–1080). Ísleifr was a son of Gizurr inn hvíti ("the white") Teitsson and his third wife, Þórdís Þóroddsdóttir. His son, Gizurr, succeeded him as bishop (1082–1118).

The þáttr is preserved in two vellum MSS: Flateyjarbók (GkS 1005 fol., ca. 1400) and AM 75e fol. no.5. In Flateyjarbók, the þáttr is interpolated in Óláfs saga helga. AM 75e fol. no.5 is a 15th-century vellum, of which fifteen leaves or parts of leaves have survived. Ísleifs þáttr appears on fols. 9v–10. It is also found in the 17th-century paper MS AM 554h α 4to, thought to have been copied from AM 75e fol. no.5 while it was still complete.

The þáttr relates two episodes from Ísleifr's life. The first tells of his meeting with St. Óláfr in Norway. At that time, Ísleifr was a priest and short of money. His meeting with the king is brought about by the charitable act of another Icelander, Brandr Vermundarson, who makes the priest a gift of a cloak the king had previously given to him. Óláfr's curiosity is aroused upon hearing of this act, and he determines to see Ísleifr himself. When priest and king meet, Óláfr himself gives the cloak to Ísleifr.

The second episode is set in Iceland, and concerns Ísleifr's marriage to Dalla Þorvaldsdóttir. Ísleifr requested Dalla's hand in marriage from her father, Þorvaldr, but was unwilling to agree to the condition stipulated by Þorvaldr that he should leave Skálholt and move to the north of Iceland. Dalla, foreseeing that Ísleifr will make her the best husband in Iceland, persuades Þorvaldr to drop the condition, and she and Ísleifr are married. Their three sons

(Gizurr, Teitr, and Þorvaldr) are named.

The *þáttr* concludes with a reference to St. Jón Ǫgmundarson (bishop of Hólar 1106–1121), who thought of his foster-father Ísleifr whenever he heard good men mentioned. Similar accounts appear in both versions of his saga: the older *Jóns saga helga* and *Jóns saga helga* by Gunnlaugr Leifsson.

Ed.: Hannes Finsson, ed. *Kristni-saga, sive Historia Religionis Christianae in Islandiam introductionae; nec non Páttr af Isleifibiskupi, sive Narratio de Isleifo Episcopo.* Hafniae [Copenhagen], 1773; [Jón Sigurðsson and Guðbrandur Vigfússon, eds.] *Biskupa sögur.* 2 vols. Copenhagen: Møller, 1858–78, vol. 1, pp. 51–6; Guðbrandur Vigfússon and C. R. Unger, eds. *Flateyjarbók: En Samling af norske Konge-Sagaer med indskudte mindre Fortællinger om Begivenheder i og undenfor Norge samt Annaler.* 3 vols. Christiania [Oslo]: Malling, 1860–68, vol. 2, pp. 140–2; Gudbrand Vigfusson and F. York Powell, eds. *An Icelandic Prose Reader.* Oxford: Clarendon, 1879, pp. 148–9 [includes the account of Ísleifr's marriage only]; Kahle, B., ed. *Kristnisaga, Þáttr Þorvalds ens víðfǫrla, Þáttr Ísleifs biskups Gizurarsonar, Hungrvaka.* Altnordische Saga-Bibliothek, 11. Halle: Niemeyer, 1905, pp. xxii, 83–6; Jón Helgason, ed. *Byskupa sǫgur* 1. Det kongelige nordiske oldskriftselskab. Copenhagen: Munksgaard, 1938. **Tr.**: Leith, Mary Charlotte Julia, trans. *The Stories of Thorwald the Far-farer and of Bishop Isleif.* London: Masters, 1894, pp. 27–30; rpt. in her *Stories of the Bishops of Iceland.* London: Masters, 1895, pp. 27–30; Gudbrand Vigfusson and F. York Powell, eds. and trans. *Origines Islandicae: A Collection of the More Important Sagas and Other Native Writings Relating to the Settlement and Early History of Iceland.* 2 vols. Oxford: Clarendon, 1905; rpt. Millwood: Kraus, 1976, vol. 1, pp. 595–6; Loth, Agnete, trans. *To islandske bispekrøniker.* Odense: Odense Universitetsforlag, 1989 [in Danish]. **Lit.**: [Jón Sigurðsson and Guðbrandur Vigfússon, eds.] *Biskupa sögur*, vol. 1, pp. 154, 219; Jóhann Kristjánsson. "Ætt Döllu biskupsfrúar." *Skírnir* 85 (1911), 378–84; Hannes Þorsteinsson. "Nokkrar athuganir um íslenzkar bókmentir a 12. og 13. öld." *Skírnir* 86 (1912), 140; Ragnar Ólafsson. "Hvaðan var Dalla kona Ísleifs biskups?" *Saga* 7 (1969), 137–9; Köhne, Roland. "Wirklichkeit und Fiktion in den mittelalterlichen Nachrichten über Isleif Gizurarson." *Skandinavistik* 17.1 (1987), 124–30.

Helen Carron

[**See also**: *Biskupa sögur, Flateyjarbók, Þáttr*]

Íslendingabók ("The Book of Icelanders") is a concise history of Iceland from the Age of Settlement until 1118, written by the priest Ari Þorgilsson (1068–1148) during the years 1122–1132. It is preserved in two 17th-century copies of a now-lost codex from about 1200 (AM 113a and b fol.). According to the preface, Ari had written an earlier version that he revised at the suggestion of bishops Þorlákr and Ketill and Sæmundr Sigfússon "the learned" (d. 1133), omitting the *Ættartala ok konunga ævi* ("Genealogies and Life of Kings"). From later *konungasögur*, it can be concluded that the omitted *Ættartala ok konunga ævi* most probably recorded years of reigns for Norwegian kings. Ari's earlier version is lost, but it was used by Snorri Sturluson and probably in other historical works. The extent and character of the omitted sections and their later use have been discussed in detail by many scholars, most recently by Ellehøj (1965), but their opinions have differed considerably (*cf.* Andersson 1985).

Íslendingabók tells of the Settlement, the establishment of the *Alþingi* and the first laws, the division of the country into quarters, the establishment of the calendar, and the discovery of Greenland. The most detailed account concerns the introduction of Christianity and the history of the Icelandic Church. Here, the foreign missionary bishops and the first Icelandic bishops are listed, with the main emphasis on the description of Gizurr Ísleifsson (bishop of Skálholt 1082–1118) and his efforts in the organization of the Icelandic Church, for instance, by introducing tithes (1097) and establishing the other episcopal see in Hólar (1106), along with the writing down of the first law book (1117–1118).

The chronological backbone of the work is the list of Icelandic lawspeakers, whose names and terms of office are recorded from the establishment of the *Alþingi* (930) until the 1120s. This chronology is connected with the general time reckoning from the birth of Christ by the mention of three specific years: the death of St. Edmund in 870, the fall of Óláfr Tryggvason in 1000, and the beginning of a new moon cycle in 1120. The Icelandic dates were fixed in relation to these years. In so doing, Ari had established the chronology for Iceland's oldest history, upon which later historians built.

Ari refers to a number of native informants for his narrative, and emphasizes their knowledge and trustworthiness. The oldest was born in 995, and several others remembered events from most of the 11th century and had known persons born in the latter half of the 10th century. Ari undoubtedly knew some Latin historical literature; he did not use it as a source for the history of Iceland, but to a certain extent as a model. He quotes directly only one "saga" about St. Edmund in connection with the year of the saint's death. Scholars have disagreed on Ari's use of foreign literature; several have assumed, for instance, a direct or indirect acquaintance with the Anglo-Saxon Bede, while others have asserted that the arguments for this influence are untenable.

For the Icelandic recording of history, however, it was of decisive importance that Ari did not follow his supposed models by writing in Latin, but chose instead to write his book in Icelandic.

Ed.: *Schedæ Ara Prestz Froda Vm Island.* Skálholt: Kruse, 1688; Gudbrand Vigfusson and F. York Powell, eds. and trans. *Origines Islandicae: A Collection of the More Important Sagas and Other Native Writings Relating to the Settlement and Early History of Iceland.* 2 vols. Oxford: Clarendon, 1905; rpt. Millwood: Kraus, 1976, vol. 1, pp. 278–306; Halldór Hermannsson, ed. and trans. *The Book of the Icelanders (Íslendingabók) by Ari Thorgilsson.* Islandica, 20. Ithaca: Cornell University Press; London: Milford; Oxford University Press, 1930; rpt. ed. *Íslendingabók.* Tilegnet Islands Alting 930–1930 af Dansk-Islandsk Forbundsfond. Copenhagen: Jørgensen, 1930; Finnur Jónsson, ed. *Íslendingabók.* Tilegnet Islands Alting 930–1930 af Dansk-Islandsk Forbundsfond. Copenhagen: Jørgensen, 1930; Holtsmark, Anne, ed. *Íslendingabók.* Nordisk Filologi. Tekster og Lærebøger til Universitetsbrug. A Tekster. 5. bind. Oslo: Dreyer, 1952; Jón Jóhannesson, ed. *Íslendingabók Ara fróða AM. 113a and 113b, fol.* Reykjavik: University of Iceland, 1956 [facsimile]; Jakob Benediktsson, ed. *Íslendingabók. Landnámabók.* Íslenzk fornrit, 1.1. Reykjavik: Hið íslenzka fornritafélag, 1968. **Lit.**: Turville-Petre, G. *Origins of Icelandic Literature.* Oxford: Clarendon, 1953, pp. 88–108; Ólafía Einarsdóttir. *Studier i kronologisk metode i tidlig islandsk historieskrivning.* Bibliotheca Historica Lundensis, 13. Stockholm: Natur och Kultur, 1964; Ellehøj, Svend. *Studier over den ældste norrøne historieskrivning.* Bibliotheca Arnamagnæana, 26. Copenhagen: Munksgaard, 1965; Bekker-Nielsen, Hans. "The Use of *Rex* in *Íslendingabók.*" In *Studies for Einar Haugen: Presented by Friends and Colleagues.* Ed. Evelyn Scherabon Firchow *et al.* Janua Linguarum, Series Maior, 59. The Hague and Paris: Mouton, 1972, pp. 53–7; Christensen, Aksel E. "Om kronologien i Aris Íslendingabók og dens laan fra Adam af Bremen." In *Nordiske Studier. Festskrift til Chr. Westergård-Nielsen.* Ed. Johs.

Brøndum-Nielsen *et al.* Copenhagen: Rosenkilde & Bagger, 1975, pp. 25–34; Sverrir Tómasson. "Tækileg vitni." *Afmælisrit Björns Sigfússonar.* Ed. Björn Teitsson *et al.* Reykjavik: Sögufélag, 1975, pp. 251–87; Louis-Jensen, Jonna. "Ari og Gregor." In *Nordiska Studier i filologi och lingvistik. Festskrift tillägnad Gösta Holm.* Ed. Lars Svensson *et al.* Lund: Studentlitteratur, 1976, pp. 273–9; Andersson, Theodore M. "Ari's *konunga ævi* and the Earliest Accounts of Hákon Jarl's Death." *Opuscula* 6. Bibliotheca Arnamagnæana, 33. Copenhagen: Reitzel, 1979, pp. 1–17; Skårup, Povl. "Ari frodes dødsliste for året 1118." *Opuscula* 6. Bibliotheca Arnamagnæana, 33. Copenhagen: Reitzel, 1979, pp. 18–23; Mundal, Else. "Íslendingabók, ættartala og konunga ævi." In *Festskrift til Ludvig Holm-Olsen på hans 70-årsdag den 9. juni 1984.* Ed. Bjarne Fidjestøl *et al.* Øvre Ervik: Alvheim & Eide, 1984, pp. 255–71; Andersson, Theodore M. "Kings' Sagas (*Konungasögur*)." In *Old Norse–Icelandic Literature: A Critical Guide.* Ed. Carol J. Clover and John Lindow. Islandica, 45. Ithaca and London: Cornell University Press, 1985, pp. 197–238 [esp. pp. 200–1]1.

Jakob Benediktsson

[**See also**: Iceland; *Konungasögur*]

Íslendingadrápa

("The *drápa* of Icelanders") by Haukr Valdísarson is an Icelandic poem belonging to a group of skaldic verse celebrating kings and heroes who are, as a rule, well known from preserved Icelandic sagas (*e.g.*, *Jómsvíkingadrápa* and *Krákumál*). The poet is otherwise unknown, and the poem is preserved only in the MS AM 748 I 4to from the early 14th century. This MS has mixed contents; the first gathering contains six eddic lays, and is thus the most important collection of eddic verse after the *Codex Regius.* Next comes various learned material, and then *Íslendingadrápa* is written on the last leaf, but it ends abruptly with the first couplet of the twenty-seventh stanza.

In its present state, the poem names twenty-seven illustrious Icelanders, all but two known from *Íslendingasögur* and *konungasögur*. Ten men, Icelandic and foreign, appear in connection with the feats of the heroes. In general, each hero is given a stanza, and, with one remarkable exception, they are praised for their courage and fighting valor. The exception is Síðu-Hallr, who in stanza 22 is described as a lawmaker who upheld his right against any man. But his chief merit was as the father of "worthy sons to whom the glorious Lord of Heaven granted true honor." Síðu-Hallr is known from *Íslendingabók* as the leader of the Christian party at the *Alþingi* in the year 1000 when Christianity was adopted, and from *Njáls saga* as the great peacemaker. His son Þorsteinn, known from a separate saga and a *þáttr*, is spoken of in the next stanza. But the extraordinary content of stanza 22, together with the solemn and pious words about the true honor granted by the Lord to Hallr's sons, the *höfuðsmenn* (persons of high rank), may suggest that the poet is alluding to Hallr as the great-grand-father of St. Jón Ögmundarson, bishop of Hólar, who was made an Icelandic saint in 1200. Hallr was also the ancestor of two other bishops in the 12th century.

The dating of the *Íslendingadrápa* has not been resolved. Jónas Kristjánsson (1975) claims that the poem dates from the 12th century, *i.e.*, probably earlier than the *Íslendingasögur*, and that Haukr accordingly had recourse only to oral sources. As a matter of fact, very little can be known about oral sources in this case. Much of what Haukr says about the feats and the fate of his heroes is in general terms, but the facts are with rare exceptions in agreement with preserved sagas. There is no reason to believe that

if he had recourse to saga MSS, he would have worked like a historian. His poem is more like a poetic adaptation of saga material, and the few deviations might be both intended and unintended. On the other hand, linguistic arguments are not conclusive, owing to the difficulty in establishing the linguistic norms of the 12th and 13th centuries. It is clear that Haukr imitates the poetry preserved in the sagas, including archaic word forms and old-fashioned kennings, but a poetic spark is lacking.

Ed.: Möbius, Th., ed. *Íslendingadrápa Hauks Valdísarsonar. Ein isländisches Gedicht des XIII. Jahrhunderts.* Kiel: Mohr, 1874. **Lit.**: Finnur Jónsson, ed. *Den oldnorske og oldislandske Litteraturs Historie.* 3 vols. 2nd ed. Copenhagen: Gad, 1920–24, vol. 2, pp. 107–8; Björn M. Ólsen. *Um Íslendingasögur. Kaflar úr háskólafyrirlestrum.* In *Safn til sögu Íslands og íslenzka bókmennta* 6.3. Ed. Sigfús Blöndal and Einar Ól. Sveinsson. Reykjavik: Hið íslenzka bókmenntafélag, 1937–39, pp. 219–20; Vries, Jan de. *Altnordische Literaturgeschichte.* 2 vols. Grundriss der germanischen Philologie, 15–6. Berlin: de Gruyter, 1941–42; rpt. 1964–67, vol. 2, pp. 49–53; Jón Helgason. "Norges og Islands digtning." In *Litteraturhistorie. B. Norge og Island.* Ed. Sigurður Nordal. Nordisk kultur, 8B. Stockholm: Bonnier; Oslo: Aschehoug; Copenhagen: Schultz, 1953, pp. 3–141 [esp. p. 141]; Jónas Kristjánsson. "Íslendingadrápa and Oral Tradition." *Gripla* 1 (1975), 76–91; Kuhn, Hans. *Das Dróttkvætt.* Heidelberg: Winter, 1983, pp. 319–21; Bjarni Einarsson. "Íslendingadrápa." *Tímarit Háskóla Íslands* 4 (1989), 127–31.

Bjarni Einarsson

[**See also**: *Droplaugarsona saga*; Skaldic Verse]

Íslendinga saga *see* Sturlunga saga

Íslendingasögur

("sagas of Icelanders," or "family sagas") is the modern term for a group of sagas about Icelandic farmer-chieftains from the period of Settlement (870–930) to the mid-11th century. The main setting for the action is, with one exception (*Egils saga*), Iceland, but many of these sagas begin in Norway before the Settlement, and many of them also describe journeys abroad and contacts with kings and noblemen in Scandinavia and the British Isles.

In medieval literature, the *Íslendingasögur* are distinctive for telling tales in a heroic spirit about nonaristocrats. Contemporary sagas from the 13th century tell tales about the same class of people. But while the pursuit of honor lies at the heart of the *Íslendingasögur*, the actors in the contemporary sagas seem more concerned with power.

The *Íslendingasögur*, between thirty-five and forty in number, are anonymous, and no saga is preserved in an author's original MS. A few fragments date from the 13th century, but the oldest MSS containing complete or nearly complete sagas date from about 1300 onward, and a number of sagas are preserved in 14th- and 15th-century MSS. Some sagas exist only in paper MSS from the 16th or 17th centuries. Consequently, the quality of the texts and their proximity to their originals vary greatly.

Dating of the *Íslendingasögur* is controversial. Most scholars agree that the majority date from the 13th century. In some cases, this assumption can be deduced from the age of the oldest MSS. In other cases, it is deduced from connections with other texts as well as knowledge of the laws and customs of the old pre-State society that was dissolving in the mid-13th century, and was gradually replaced by a new state from the 1260s onward. If the theory is accepted that *Egils saga* was written by Snorri Sturluson (1179–1241), facts of his biography place the saga in the period 1220–1240. There are good grounds to believe that *Njáls saga* was written 1275–1290. Other datings are much more uncertain. It has been common practice to classify a group of sagas thought to be older than *Egils saga* as preclassical, but scholars disagree about which sagas should be placed in this group. A considerable number of the classical sagas have influenced the version of *Landnámabók* written by Sturla Þórðarson no later than 1280. Another group of sagas is considered postclassical and dated in the 14th century or even later. As a rule, these sagas are more fantastic than the classical sagas and draw a more diffuse image of the old society. Some of these late sagas are thought to be revisions of classical versions now lost. The best known of the postclassical sagas is *Grettis saga*; among the others are *Kjalnesinga saga*, *Harðar saga*, *Hávarðar saga*, *Þórðar saga hreðu*, *Finnboga saga ramma*, *Svarfdæla saga*, *Fljótsdæla saga*, *Flóamanna saga*, *Bárðar saga*, *Króka-Refs saga*, and *Víglundar saga*.

Background in history and oral tradition. The sagas present themselves as history, and many of the characters are no doubt historical. In most sagas, there are frequent references to characters known from other texts, and often characters are connected with later generations through genealogies. Moreover, in most sagas, the chronology has several ties to historical events, and as a rule the inner chronology is consistent. There is also a high degree of consistency in the information about persons and events in the sagas as a whole. All these characteristics suggest that the sagas were created as historical rather than fictional works. It does not necessarily follow, however, that they are historical documents of the same kind as modern history. The question of historicity has been much debated. From the time the *Íslendingasögur* became objects of study and continuing into this century, scholars (with some notable exceptions) had great faith in their value as sources for history. But the strict demands of source criticism in this century led to sagas being rejected altogether by historians, first because they were considered unreliable and even pure fiction, and second because they dealt with private matters in which the historians were not particularly interested. Many historians now think that the sagas can be used with caution as sources about social mechanisms and mental attitudes operative between the time of writing and the time in which events are supposed to have occurred.

The question of historicity is closely related to the question of orality. The sagas exist only as written literature, but are they primarily oral tales recorded more or less exactly as they were told, or are they works of authors who created them out of diverse materials, such as older written texts, oral tales, and their own fantasy? The question is still controversial, although no scholar would deny that the writer had some influence on the final form of the work. The majority of scholars would probably agree with this statement: the consistency of the saga canon as a whole, with regard to the world described and its inhabitants, is best explained by the existence of a continuous oral tradition about persons and events in the first centuries after the Settlement. Moreover, the uniformity of themes and their treatment, as well as the style, indicate that the narrative form of this tradition was already highly developed when it was adapted by the writers of sagas. However, the macrostructure of *Íslendingasaga* must have been inspired by older literary genres, such as saints' lives and *konungasögur*. There is no evidence or likelihood that an oral saga ever existed coming anywhere near the scope of the average *Íslendingasaga*, let alone

the longest ones. We must assume that the medium of the written word enabled the authors to refine their style and narrative technique, compose sagas of greater complexity and length than the oral tales, and give individual events and the saga as a whole a meaning or a thematic structure not present in the oral tales.

If such a description is accepted, it is still important not to confuse saga writers with modern writers of fiction. The author of a saga could not treat his material with the freedom of a writer of contemporary fiction. The saga writer was bound by tradition and most likely had no wish to be free from it.

At first reading, the sagas resemble each other closely, and they do indeed have a great many characteristics in common, testifying to the strength of the tradition. However, the sagas also differ from one another in many respects. A part of the explanation may lie in the tradition itself. The events narrated in the sagas are supposed to have taken place about 200–400 years before the time of writing. A difference in the degree of stylization and heroic idealization in the sagas could partly reflect their place in a process whereby oral tradition gradually has transformed into heroic tales the chaotic narratives of recent events, such as those on which *Sturlunga saga* is based. On the other hand, if the *Íslendingasögur* are compared with the heroic lays of the *Poetic Edda*, which are undoubtedly among the influences forming the *Íslendingasögur*, they appear realistic and full of extraneous material. However, individual sagas most likely differ not only because the authors had different traditions to work with, but also because they had different backgrounds and education, different values and interests, and different ability and desire to develop something out of their material. Sagas like *Reykdæla saga* or *Víga-Glúms saga* are crude and often clumsily told, and seem likely to be formed more by the traditions at hand than by the craft of the writer, while works like *Njáls saga* or *Laxdæla saga* transcend the limits set by tradition through conscious artistry and thematic interpretation of the subject matter.

Social and ethical norms. Whatever degree of sophistication we can detect in an *Íslendingasaga*, the action dominates, developed and formed through conflicts. The nature of these conflicts is conditioned by the social and ethical norms in the society depicted, as idealized by tradition. The Icelanders of the 13th century must have looked to the past, seeing there a society where living and dying with honor was a possibility, although never cheaply or easily realized. Most of them probably felt that chances of living with honor in their own tumultuous times were small.

For a saga hero, seeking and preserving his own and the family's honor is a categoric imperative more important than the preservation of property or life itself. As with most other social matters, honor is the responsibility of the adult males of a family, although women frequently spell out the demands of the code of honor at crucial moments. The sagas depict a society with considerable differences in social status, wealth, and power, but in this society every free man has a choice to live, or at least to die, honorably. It goes without saying that not every man in the sagas lives up to this ideal.

In the preservation of honor, a man may be forced to use violence, even to kill. But it is not considered honorable to initiate a conflict by abusing other people or treating them unjustly. Persons who so behave are called *ójafnaðarmenn* and thought worthy of contempt. An honorable man is not easily upset and usually delays his revenge until the community begins to wonder at his equanimity; then he strikes relentlessly, but is always open to the possibility of a settlement, if that can be acquired without dishonor. The conflicts in the sagas are usually started by men who are either overbearing and greedy, or rash and inconsiderate. The initial causes are various: disagreement about property, disgrace to a female member of a family, unprovoked attack, verbal insult. However, it is important to realize that such behavior is almost immediately interpreted in terms of honor. In real life, a farmer who suffered losses from aggressive neighbors may have had quite material reasons to be angered, but in a saga he is so much more likely to be interested in getting revenge than "his money back" that he promises to give the property at stake to a chieftain willing to help him retrieve it from the aggressor.

It must be emphasized that while the code of honor lies at the core of saga ethics, individual sagas reveal a varying degree of influence from Christian values, and some of them show a conflict between the Christian idea of forgiveness and the old duty of revenge.

Types of conflict. In most sagas, we find instances of what can be called a "typical feud": a conflict between two individuals or kin groups with alternating clashes and attempts at resolution, usually climaxing with manslaughter followed by revenge, and, in the end, settled through the help of mediators or courts. A settlement during the course of a feud is often considered unsatisfactory by one of the parties involved, and this dissatisfaction then leads to a new phase. At the end of a saga, however, all feuds have been reconciled. As a rule, brokers and mediators play an important role in the typical feud.

In some sagas, conflict arises among close relatives or in-laws, creating what could be called a "tragic feud." Such sagas are closely related to eddic heroic poetry and are probably influenced by it. Here, people face a tragic situation: both or all alternatives open to them are disastrous. In *Laxdœla saga*, Kjartan provokes his cousin and foster-brother, Bolli, until Bolli's wife and brothers-in-law force him to kill Kjartan. In revenge, he is attacked by his cousins and killed. In *Gísla saga*, Gísli kills his brother-in-law in revenge for another brother-in-law and a foster-brother; in revenge, Gísli is killed, having been persecuted by men hired by his third brother-in-law. In *Njáls saga*, a similar sense of tragedy is created when conflict arises between thirst for revenge and ties created through friendship and fosterage.

Sagas about skalds often describe conflicts more individually oriented than a "typical" feud. A skald is often rash and inconsiderate of other people's honor, for example, the honor of the family of the woman he falls in love with. This behavior initiates conflict, where the skald is only reluctantly supported by his kin and usually goes his own way. The sagas of Kormákr and Hallfreðr show heroes governed by their impulses rather than a developed sense of honor. The same applies to *Gunnlaugs saga* and *Fóstbrœðra saga*, and partly to *Bjarnar saga Hítdœlakappa.*

Feud is conflict within the framework of society. When a person has been outlawed as a result of feud, he is no longer a part of society, and cannot be legally assisted or avenged. Therefore, the sagas of outlaws, *Gísla saga* and *Grettis saga*, describe heroes praiseworthy for their ability to escape revenge, sometimes through rather unheroic behavior. Typically, the outlaw tends to get assistance from women and men of low status. The outlaw is treated sympathetically in his own saga, but people standing or placing themselves outside society because of contemptible behavior are treated as outcasts. In many sagas, there are incidents where individuals or families, usually of low birth, do harm by stealing and

witchcraft. Such persons are without honor, "outsiders" who are killed or driven away by good people, but often only when they have caused considerable harm. "Land-cleansing" episodes are found in many sagas, among them *Laxdœla saga*, *Eyrbyggja saga*, and *Grettis saga*; and in one saga, *Vatnsdœla saga*, this type of conflict is the dominant one.

In order to conduct a feud, an alliance with a *goði* or an influential chieftain is necessary, and usually feuds end up involving such persons, although the conflict may have begun at a lower stage in society. A conflict between people who are not equal always ends either in reconciliation before an important person is killed, or by the defeat of the lower person. In the *þættir* about the dealings of Icelanders with a king, the end is almost always a reconciliation in which the Icelander pledges his loyalty to the king, and the king rewards him. Such conflicts, or pseudo-conflicts, also appear in the travel episodes of sagas and in *þættir* set in Iceland, like *Þorsteins þáttr stangarhöggs*. In *Egils saga*, such a conflict is described between the family of Kveld-Úlfr and his descendants and the kings of Norway, but it is atypical because the kings suffer heavy losses through the actions of this chieftain family without really receiving compensation. However, a reconciliation of sorts is brought about in York when Egill ransoms his head from Eiríkr blóðøx ("blood-axe") with a poem. Kveld-Úlfr and his descendants do not recognize the new kind of king who is more than a *primus inter pares*, as the old kings were, and they get away with it because they have sanctuary in Iceland and because they have influential helpers at the court.

Structure and composition. Each *Íslendingasaga* describes several conflicts more or less closely tied to each other. In a number of sagas, the conflicts are subordinated to an overall scheme of composition moving from introduction of the characters and the situation, often including some anticipatory conflicts, through the development of the main conflict to a climax, followed by revenge and eventually final reconciliation, and ending with an aftermath accounting for the fate of some characters and their descendants. This model applies best to the structure of a saga when the climax and revenge can be defined easily. Within each of these segments of the narrative, excluding the aftermath, conflicts can arise, and one can even see this same structure repeated many times as a microstructure. The small units of conflict can also be made the points of departure for analysis of saga plot. It then appears that feud can be analyzed into recurrent constituents: conflict, advocacy, and resolution. With its stress on advocacy (the implications of a third party in a conflict, either on one of the sides or as mediator), this model reveals the social nature of feud, but it cannot account for the structure of the saga as a whole. These structural models can be supplemented with an analysis of the interweaving strands of narrative. The matter of one saga is often complex, and the general method of composition then is to interweave the stories by jumping from one to the other and back, rather than finishing one story and then starting a new one.

Style and narrative technique. In their style and narrative technique, the *Íslendingasögur* have much in common with *konungasögur* and other sagas based on native tradition. The writer or sagaman never speaks in the first person, nor is a reader or listener ever addressed. This technique has given the sagas a reputation for "objectivity" or *impassibilité*. Their objectivity should not be understood too literally, however. More often than not, sympathies and antipathies are quite clear, although they are conveyed to the reader by discreet means. Presentation of character appears as an objective fact, although it often includes judgment and evaluation, and biases the reader. Individual acts are often commented upon indirectly by reference to common opinion. However, many sagas present important characters and their actions with such detachment that it is hard to see any sort of bias. *Egils saga* is a good example: no attempt is made to hide faults in the protagonist's appearance or character. As in many other sagas, the characterization is humorous rather than moral or psychological.

The saga style is dominated by parataxis, and the reporting of fact is usually brisk and lucid. As a rule, narrative pace slows down considerably when peaks of the action are being prepared and can become quite slow with changes of scene and detailed description of movement when violent confrontation is being prepared. There is not much pure description. Nature or other material surroundings are described only to the extent necessary for the understanding of the action, but in some cases individuals are described in considerable detail.

Dialogue is extremely important in the *Íslendingasögur*, and it is more varied in form than the narration. Dialogues are usually brief and interspersed with action, but many sagas also have speeches of some length. The function of the dialogue is varied. At the peaks of action, it enlivens the characters' confrontation with each other and expresses reasons for antagonism or alliance. Comments made by characters are, as a rule, no less cool and detached than the voice of the sagaman, but at the same time they are personal. One of the most important functions of the dialogue is to give an act a historical dimension by connecting it with past events or pointing to the future through warning and prediction. Important characters in the saga are individualized to some extent through their speech, although more in the direction of general characteristics than any kind of idiosyncrasy.

Historical context. The classical *Íslendingasögur* were written in an age when Icelandic society had been through a profound crisis and was changing radically. The social mechanisms established soon after the initial settlement, which seem to have functioned quite well for about three centuries, were disturbed, and Iceland was taking steps toward a mainstream European form of government by subjecting itself to the king of Norway. The *Íslendingasögur* as a whole embody a myth of Iceland as a bastion of the free and often heroic farmer in no need of king or state. The roots of this myth are difficult to trace, but it is only natural that it was strengthened when people felt that an era was coming to an end. However, the interests and anxieties that can be seen as the driving forces behind the writing of the sagas are much more complex. One of the driving forces that had affected the Icelandic society most deeply was the Church, and the Icelandic writers were not only learned in the teaching of the Church, but also deeply affected by it in their whole way of thinking and feeling. The tension between these two worldviews explains why the *Íslendingasögur* are so different from traditional literature that reflects a fixed and static society. Conflict and contradiction is the vital nerve that connects them with the present age.

Ed.: Íslenzk fornrit, 2–14. Reykjavik: Hið íslenzka fornritafélag, 1933–59; Guðni Jónsson, ed. *Íslendingasögur.* 13 vols. Reykjavik: Íslendingasagnaútgáfan, 1946–49. **Bib.:** Halldór Hermannsson. *Bibliography of the Icelandic Sagas and Minor Tales.* Islandica, 1. Ithaca: Cornell University Library, 1908; rpt. New York: Kraus, 1966; Halldór Hermannsson. *The Sagas of Icelanders (Íslendinga sögur): A Supplement to Bibliography of the Icelandic Sagas and Minor Tales.* Islandica, 24. Ithaca: Cornell University Press; London: Oxford University Press, 1935; Jóhann S. Hannesson. *The Sagas of Icelanders (Íslendinga sögur): A Supplement to Islandica I and XXIV.* Islandica, 38. Ithaca: Cornell University Press; London: Oxford University Press, 1957. **Lit.:** Ker, W. P. *Epic and Romance: Essays on Medieval Literature.* 2nd ed. London: Macmillan, 1908; rpt. New York: Dover, 1957; Craigie, W. A. *The Icelandic Sagas.* Cambridge: Cambridge University Press, 1913; Liestøl, Knut. *Upphavet til den islendske ættesaga.* Instituttet for sammenlignende kulturforskning. Serie A: Forelesninger. Oslo: Aschehoug, 1929; Heusler, Andreas. *Die altgermanische Dichtung.* 2nd ed. Potsdam: Athenaion, 1941; 2nd rev. ed. Darmstadt: Gentner, 1957; Sigurður Nordal. "Sagalitteraturen." In *Litteraturhistorie: B. Norge og Island.* Ed. Sigurður Nordal. Nordisk kultur, 8:B. Stockholm: Bonnier; Oslo: Aschehoug; Copenhagen: Schultz, 1953, pp. 180–273; Einar Ól. Sveinsson. *Dating the Icelandic Sagas: An Essay in Method.* Viking Society, Text Series, 3. London: Viking Society for Northern Research, 1958; Hallberg, Peter. *The Icelandic Saga.* Trans. Paul Schach. Lincoln: University of Nebraska Press, 1962; Andersson, Theodore M. *The Problem of Icelandic Saga Origins: A Historical Survey.* Yale Germanic Studies, 1. New Haven and London: Yale University Press, 1964; Andersson, Theodore M. *The Icelandic Family Saga: An Analytic Reading.* Harvard Studies in Comparative Literature, 28. Cambridge: Harvard University Press, 1967; Schier, Kurt. *Sagaliteratur.* Sammlung Metzler, M78. Stuttgart: Metzler, 1970; Lönnroth, Lars. *Njáls Saga: A Critical Introduction.* Berkeley: University of California Press, 1976; Röhn, Hartmut. *Untersuchungen zur Zeitgestaltung und Komposition in der Íslendingasögur: Analysen ausgewählter Texte.* Beiträge zur nordischen Philologie, 5. Basel: Helbing & Lichtenhahn, 1976; Byock, Jesse L. *Feud in the Icelandic Saga.* Berkeley, Los Angeles, and London: University of California Press, 1982; Clover, Carol J. *The Medieval Saga.* Ithaca and London: Cornell University Press, 1982; Bürling, Coletta. *Die direkte Rede als Mittel der Personengestaltung in den Íslendingasögur.* Texte und Untersuchungen zur Germanistik und Skandinavistik, 7. Frankfurt am Main: Lang, 1983; Schach, Paul. *Icelandic Sagas.* Twayne World Authors Series, 717. Boston: Twayne, 1984; Clover, Carol J. "Icelandic Family Sagas (*Íslendingasögur*)." In *Old Norse–Icelandic Literature: A Critical Guide.* Ed. Carol J. Clover and John Lindow. Islandica, 45. Ithaca and London: Cornell University Press, 1985, pp. 239–315 [extensive bibliography, pp. 294–315]; Byock, Jesse L. *Medieval Iceland: Society, Sagas, and Power.* Berkeley, Los Angeles, and London: University of California Press, 1988.

Vésteinn Ólason

[**See also:** *Bandamanna saga; Bárðar saga Snæfellsáss; Bjarnar saga Hítdœlakappa;* Bookprose/Freeprose Theory; *Droplaugarsona saga; Egils saga Skalla-Grímssonar; Eyrbyggja saga; Finnboga saga ramma; Fljótsdœla saga; Flóamanna saga; Fóstbrœðra saga; Gísla saga Súrssonar; Goði; Grettis saga; Gull-Þóris saga; Gunnars saga Keldugnúpsfífls; Gunnars saga Þiðrandabana; Gunnlaugs saga ormstungu; Hallfreðar saga; Harðar saga; Hávarðar saga Ísfirðings; Heiðarvíga saga; Hrafnkels saga Freysgoða; Hœnsa-Þóris saga;* Iceland; *Kjalnesinga saga; Kormáks saga; Króka-Refs saga; Laxdœla saga; Ljósvetninga saga; Njáls saga;* Outlaw Sagas; *Reykdœla saga (ok Víga-Skútu);* Saga; *Skáldasögur; Svarfdœla saga; Þáttr; Þórðar saga hreðu; Þorsteins saga hvíta; Þorsteins saga Síðu-Hallssonar; Valla-Ljóts saga; Vápnfirðinga saga; Vatnsdœla saga; Víga-Glúms saga; Víglundar saga;* Vinland Sagas; Women in Sagas]

Íþróttir. Old Norse *íþrótt* (pl. *íþróttir*) is probably derived from *ið* 'deed, feat' and *þrótt(r)* 'strength' (for detailed discussion, see Crozier 1986). Unlike modern Icelandic *íþrótt*, which means "sport, athletics," the Old Norse term had the more general significance of its proposed etymology: "feat-strength, ability in a respected skill." Athletic achievements certainly qualified as *íþróttir* in medieval Scandinavia, but the term could also denote mastery of crafts, fine arts, games of skill, traditional lore, law, and book learning. *Íþróttir* are so diverse that it may seem difficult to formulate a principle of exclusion. Skills particularly associated with mercantile or agrarian activity seem to have been excluded quite systematically, however (Russom 1978: 13). Games particularly associated with children were probably excluded as well. Skill in the use of the top (*skapt-kringla*, *hreyti-speldi*) or in the throwing of the snowball (*snæ-kǫkkr*) would probably not be regarded as an *íþrótt* (Tillhagen 1956, Alver 1962). On the other hand, almost any talent qualified as an *íþrótt* if it was somehow associated with the aristocratic milieu of the chieftain's household and the *þing*, or public assembly.

Texts discussing *íþróttir* make the connection with aristocratic life quite clear. In Snorri Sturluson's well-known story of Þórr and Útgarða-Loki (*Gylfaginning*, ch. 48), the giant chieftain says that no one can join his household unless he knows some kind of *íþrótt*. The visiting Æsir then attempt to show their prowess in a wrestling match, a foot race, an eating contest, and a drinking contest. The latter two activities may seem ignoble today, but they had important associations with heroic society, in which the chieftain was supposed to be generous with food and drink, while the retainers showed their appreciation by consuming what was offered.

Rǫgnvaldr Kali, earl of the Orkneys, and Haraldr Sigurðarson, king of Norway, composed skaldic verses listing their *íþróttir* (*Orkneyinga saga*, ch. 58; Finnur Jónsson 1912–15, vol. 1A, p. 357; vol. 1B, p. 329). Subjects mentioned include horsemanship, swimming, versecraft, *tafl*, runes, book learning, crafts (*smíðir*), skiing, rowing, and harping. The term *smíðir* encompasses a wide variety of crafts, including carpentry and jewelsmithing, as well as weapons manufacture. There were at least two varieties of *tafl*: *skák-tafl*, probably a type of "war game" analogous to modern chess (Du Chaillu 1890: 353), and *hnefa-tafl*, probably a type of "hunting game" in which one or more pieces attempted to escape from a larger number of "hunters" (Tolkien 1960: 88). Runic knowledge involved not only skill in carving and interpreting runic characters, but also use of these characters in magic charms of the sort described in the eddic poems *Rígsþula* (st. 43) and *Sigrdrífumál* (sts. 5–19).

The Old Norse *mannjafnaðr* "man-comparison" involved frequent references to *íþróttir*. In a verbal duel between Eysteinn and Sigurðr, joint kings of Norway, each antagonist argues that his gifts make him most fit to rule (*Heimskringla: Magnússona saga*, ch. 21). Sigurðr boasts of his physical strength, as displayed in hand-to-hand encounters and in use of weapons, especially the bow. Eysteinn claims to be the more accurate archer, and prides himself on his ability in public speaking, law, skiing, and use of bone skates. Three types of swimming skill are distinguished. Eysteinn is best at diving and long-distance swimming, while Sigurðr excels at the type of contest in which two swimmers try to duck (*kefja*) each other.

Saga writers often include brief portraits of chieftains listing *íþróttir* along with other noble gifts. In *Heimskringla*, for example, we learn that King Óláfr Tryggvason excelled in mountain climbing and in juggling with knives (*handsaxaleikr*). Óláfr was also famous for his ability to dance along the oars outside the railing of his longship while his mèn were rowing (*Óláfs saga Tryggvasonar*, ch. 85). A similar passage in *Njáls saga* (ch. 19) informs us that the Icelandic champion Gunnarr was unbeatable in sports of all kinds. Gunnarr was ambidextrous in his use of weapons, swam like a seal, and could jump amazing distances forward, backward, and vertically.

Although games restricted to childhood did not qualify as *íþróttir*, children often participated in adult sports or imitated other types of significant adult activities. In *Njáls saga* (ch. 8), for example, two boys and a girl carry out a mock legal procedure of divorce. Both children and adults participated in the Icelandic *knattleikr*, which was played with a bat (*knatt-drepa*, *knatt-tré*) and ball (*knǫttr*) on a smooth field of ice. The connection of this game with social status is particularly emphasized in *Gísla saga Súrssonar* (ch. 18), where the evaluative role of male and female spectators is represented. The players' concern for reputation often produced brawls and even killings, as in *Egils saga Skalla-Grímssonar* (ch. 40), where the seven-year-old Egill kills his opponent Grímr with an axe. A similar intensity of competition is evident in descriptions of the horse fight (*hesta-víg*), as for example in ch. 29 of *Grettis saga Ásmundarsonar*, although in this type of contest the *íþrótt* might more properly be credited to the animals than to the men who goaded them. Ch. 72 presupposes that competitive sports were frequently practiced at public assemblies, and gives a detailed account of wrestling matches.

There was apparently no hard-and-fast rule forbidding women to participate in *íþróttir*. Both sexes played *tafl* (*Gunnlaugs saga ormstungu*, ch. 4). The skaldic poets known to history include women like Steinunn and Steingerðr (Frank 1978: 24, 97, 168). Use of weapons by dedicated warrior women like Brynhildr is a well-known feature of ancient Germanic legend (see, *e.g.*, the eddic poem *Helreið Brynhildar*). The description of Guðrún's deadly swordplay in the eddic *Atlamál* (sts. 49–51) suggests that aristocratic women with no special dedication to warfare might also have some training in martial arts.

Lit.: Weinhold, Karl. *Altnordisches Leben*. Berlin: Weidmann, 1856; Du Chaillu, Paul. *The Viking Age*. 2 vols. New York: Scribner, 1890; Finnur Jónsson, ed. *Den norsk-islandske skjaldedigtning*. Vols. 1A-2A (tekst efter håndskrifterne) and 1B-2B (rettet tekst). Copenhagen and Christiania [Oslo]: Gyldendal, 1912–15; rpt. Copenhagen: Rosenkilde & Bagger, 1967 (A) and 1973 (B); Tillhagen, C.-H. "Barnlek." *KLNM* 1 (1956), 349–52; Alver, Brynjulf. "Idrottsleikar." *KLNM* 7 (1962), 322–29; Tolkien, Christopher, ed. and trans. *Saga Heiðreks konungs ins vitra; The Saga of King Heidrek the Wise*. London: Nelson, 1960; Frank, Roberta. *Old Norse Court Poetry: The Dróttkvætt Stanza*. Islandica, 42. Ithaca and London: Cornell University Press, 1978; Russom, Geoffrey. "A Germanic Concept of Nobility in *The Gifts of Men* and *Beowulf*." *Speculum* 53 (1978), 1–15; Crozier, Alan. "Old West Norse *íþrótt* and Old English *indryhtu*." *Studia Neophilologica* 58 (1986), 3–10.

Geoffrey Russom

[**See also:** *Senna—Mannjafnaðr*]

Ivan Lejonriddaren *see* Eufemiavisorna

Ívens saga ("Íven's Saga") is an Old Norse prose version of Chrétien de Troyes's chivalric romance *Yvain*, or *Le chevalier au lion*. The oldest MS of *Ívens saga*, Stock. Perg. 4to no.6 (early 15th century), attributes the commissioning of the translation from the

French to *Hákon konungr gamli* ("King Hákon the Old"), presumably Hákon Hákonarson (r. 1217–1263). The work is probably contemporary with the other Old Norse versions of Chrétien's narratives, *Erex saga* and *Parcevals saga*. *Ívens saga* is also found, incomplete, in AM 489 4to (*ca.* 1450) and, in somewhat abbreviated form, in Stock. Papp. fol. no. 46 (1690).

While remaining faithful to the substance of its source, *Ívens saga* conforms to the pattern found in other translated *riddarasögur* of omitting authorial intrusion and internal monologue, and reducing description. The sole intrusion by the saga writer involves some antifeminist remarks in ch. 7 about female fickleness. Stylistically, its most distinctive feature is alliteration, a characteristic of *riddarasögur* "court style," which, in this case, serves to highlight crucial scenes as well as to link synonymous or collocating doublets. Present participles also occur in emotionally charged passages or at significant turns of the narrative, although not with the frequency of the similarly structured *Erex saga*.

Like *Erex saga*, *Ívens saga* concerns the efforts of a knight to expiate a chivalric lapse. Whereas Erex fails to find the proper balance between love and prowess by neglecting the latter, Íven errs in the opposite direction and causes the breakdown of his marriage by forgetting to return at the stipulated time after a triumphant year of combat in the company of Valven (French Gauvain). After a series of adventures in which the hero, accompanied by a lion that he rescues from a dragon, proves himself a knight of exceptional valor and worth, the couple are reconciled. In Íven's case, but not in the French Yvain's, the loss of honor in failing to meet the deadline is as devastating as the estrangement from his wife. The saga's elimination of Chrétien's internal monologues, in which the allegorical personification *Amors* ("Love") plays a major role, restricts its thematic focus to Íven's retrieval of honor through knightly prowess.

Yvain is a witty and complex work in which the Arthurian world is simultaneously idealized and treated ironically. Chrétien treats his heroine with good-humored irreverence, and the behavior of Arthur and his knights reveals discrepancies between the theory and practice of chivalry. The laudatory introduction of the Round Table, for example, is undercut in the opening scene when the king abruptly absents himself from the assembled court to retire to bed with Guinevere, and some of his knights conduct themselves less than courteously. Small but significant changes make Arthur a more impressive and dignified figure in the saga: he is introduced as a future emperor of Rome, and his exit from the company is explicity attributed to fatigue. The hero is also a more admirable figure than his French model, never falling prey to the *folie* ("rashness, excess") or arrogance that overtakes Yvain in the first part of the work. *Ívens saga* loses the dimension of comedy and irony in *Yvain* and becomes a straightforward story of honor temporarily lost and regained by a knight who, apart from his conduct toward a woman portrayed as demanding and irrational, is an exemplary, if colorless, representative of chivalric ideals.

Ívens saga and *Erex saga* are sources of the Swedish verse romance *Ivan Lejonriddaren* (alternatively *Herr Ivan*), composed for Eufemia, queen of Hákon V of Norway, in 1303. The appearance of the lion-knight motif in some independent Icelandic *riddarasögur*, like *Sigurðar saga þogla* and *Vilhjálms saga sjóðs*, may also have been directly inspired by *Ívens saga*.

Ed.: Kölbing, Eugen, ed. *Riddarasögur. Parcevals saga. Valvers þáttr. Ívents saga. Mírmans saga.* Strassburg: Trübner, 1872, pp. 73–136; Kölbing, Eugen, ed. *Ívents saga.* Altnordische Saga-Bibliothek, 7. Halle: Niemeyer, 1898; Slay, Desmond, ed. *Romances. Perg. 4:o nr 6. Royal Library Stockholm.* Early Icelandic Manuscripts in Facsimile, 10. Copenhagen: Rosenkilde & Bagger, 1972; Blaisdell, Foster W., ed. *Ívens saga.* Editiones Arnamagnæanæ, ser. B, vol. 18. Copenhagen, Reitzel, 1979; Blaisdell, Foster W., ed. *The Sagas of Ywain and Tristan and Other Tales. AM 489 4to.* Early Icelandic Manuscripts in Facsimile, 12. Copenhagen: Rosenkilde & Bagger, 1980. **Tr.**: Blaisdell, Foster W., and Marianne E. Kalinke, trans. *Erex saga and Ívens saga: The Old Norse Versions of Chrétien de Troyes's Erec and Yvain.* Lincoln: University of Nebraska Press, 1977. **Bib.**: Kalinke, Marianne E., and P. M. Mitchell. *Bibliography of Old Norse–Icelandic Romances.* Islandica, 44. Ithaca and London: Cornell University Press, 1985, pp. 56–60. **Lit.**: Harris, Richard L. "The Lion-Knight Legend in Iceland and the Valþjófsstaðir Door." *Viator* 1 (1970), 125–45; Kalinke, Marianne E. "*Erex saga* and *Ívens saga*: Medieval Approaches to Translation." *Arkiv för nordisk filologi* 92 (1977), 125–44; Kalinke, Marianne E. "Alliteration in 'Ívens saga.'" *Modern Language Review* 74 (1979), 871–83; Kalinke, Marianne E. *King Arthur North-by-Northwest: The matière de Bretagne in Old Norse–Icelandic Romances.* Bibliotheca Arnamagnæana, 37. Copenhagen: Reitzel, 1981; Hunt, Tony. "The Medieval Adaptations of Chrétien's *Yvain*: A Bibliographical Essay." In *An Arthurian Tapestry: Essays in Memory of Lewis Thorpe.* Ed. Kenneth Varty. Glasgow: University of Glasgow French Department, 1981, pp. 203–13; Patron-Godefroit, Annette. "La transmission scandinave d'*Yvain*." In *An Arthurian Tapestry*, pp. 239–47; Marold, Edith. "Von Chrestiens *Yvain* zur *Ívenssaga*. Die *Ívenssaga* als rezeptionsgeschichtliches Zeugnis." In *Les Sagas de Chevaliers (Riddarasögur). Actes de la Ve Conférence Internationale sur les Sagas . . . (Toulon. Juillet 1982).* Ed. Régis Boyer. Civilisations, 10. Paris: Presses de l'Université de Paris-Sorbonne, 1985, pp. 157–92; Schosmann, Rémy. "Yvain-Ívens saga: Translation or Travesty?" In *Les Sagas de Chevaliers*, pp. 193–203; Barnes, Geraldine. "Arthurian Chivalry in Old Norse." In *Arthurian Literature VII.* Ed. Richard Barber. Cambridge: Brewer, 1987, pp. 50–102.

Geraldine Barnes

[See also: *Erex saga*; *Eufemiavisorna*; Old Norse–Icelandic Literature, Foreign Influence on; *Riddarasögur*]

Jarlmanns saga ok Hermanns ("The Saga of Jarlmann and Hermann") is an indigenous Icelandic *riddarasaga* presumably composed in the 14th century. *Jarlmanns saga* is transmitted in approximately sixty MSS, the oldest from the 15th century, the youngest from the beginning of the 20th century. The large number of extant MSS suggests the extraordinary popularity of the saga.

Jarlmanns saga follows the bridal-quest pattern in which there is a proxy wooer, and is structured around multiple wooings, rival wooers, and abduction of the bride.

Hermann inherits the throne of France. Jarlmann, the son of the wealthy Earl Roðgeirr, who had fostered Hermann, assists his foster-brother in the affairs of the kingdom. The plot unfolds when Jarlmann observes that Hermann is the perfect ruler in every respect but one: he has no wife. Jarlmann suggests that Ríkilát, daughter of King Katalatus of Mikligarðr (Constantinople), who is more beautiful and intelligent than other women, and noted for leechcraft, is Hermann's equal in every way.

The saga is bipartite, and focuses on Jarlmann's two journeys to obtain Ríkilát for Hermann. His first quest is as proxy wooer, and he returns to France with the bride. Jarlmann's second quest is also for Ríkilát, but this time because she had been mysteriously abducted during preparation for the wedding festivities. Although the bridal quest is the focus of *Jarlmanns saga*, its peculiar character derives from the relationship of the foster-brothers. Whereas the proximate cause of the second quest is the abduction of the bride, the ultimate cause is Jarlmann's estrangement from his foster-brother, leading to his subsequent departure from court, because Hermann had suspected his wife of loving Jarlmann, and Jarlmann of wanting to seduce her.

Jarlmanns saga is dominated by the double quest for Ríkilát, but this quest is punctuated by the quests of rival wooers. Jarlmann's proxy wooing is impeded by the appearance of an antagonistic wooer, a heathen, who resorts to war, but is defeated by Jarlmann. The unwelcome suitor for Ríkilát is paralleled by an unwelcome heathen suitor for Herborg, Hermann's sister. He is rejected and also resorts to war, but is defeated by Hermann. The quest for Ríkilát in the second part of the saga has a false conclusion, a double wedding, that of the heathen king Rúdent of Serkland with Ríkilát, and of Austvestan, alias Jarlmann, with Rúdent's mother's

sister Þorbjǫrg, a giantess. The two antagonists, Rúdent and Þorbjǫrg, are killed in their bridal beds, the former by Norðsunnan, alias Hermann, who as Austvestan's brother attended the royal couple, the latter by the "husband" Austvestan. The saga culminates in the marriage of Hermann to Ríkilát, and Jarlmann to Herborg. In a conclusion, we learn that Jarlmann and his wife withdrew from the world and entered monasteries. Hermann and Ríkilát had two sons, one of whom, Ríkarðr, was said to have been the father of the eponymous hero of *Konráðs saga keisarasonar*.

The author of *Jarlmanns saga ok Hermanns* was acquainted not only with indigenous Icelandic romances, such as *Konráðs saga*, but also with the Old Norse translation *Tristrams saga ok Ísǫndar*, from which the proxy wooing, the bride as leech, and the problem of the proxy wooer as lover presumably derive. The hall-of-statues episode in *Tristrams saga* seems to have been the inspiration for the scene in which Jarlmann draws a picture of Hermann for Ríkilát to obtain her consent to the marriage.

Ed.: Bjarni Vilhjálmsson, ed. "Jarlmanns saga ok Hermanns." In *Riddarasǫgur*. 6 vols. [Reykjavík]: Íslendingasagnaútgáfan; Haukadalsútgáfan, 1949–54, vol. 6, pp. 171–235; Loth, Agnete, ed. "Jarlmanns saga ok Hermanns." In *Late Medieval Icelandic Romances*. 5 vols. Editiones Arnamagnæanæ, ser. B, vols. 20–4. Copenhagen: Munksgaard, 1962–5, vol. 3, pp. 1–66. **Bib.**: Kalinke, Marianne E., and P. M. Mitchell. *Bibliography of Old Norse–Icelandic Romances*. Islandica, 44. Ithaca and London: Cornell University Press, 1985, pp. 52–4. **Lit.**: Glauser, Jürg. *Isländische Märchensagas: Studien zur Prosaliteratur im spätmittelalterlichen Island*. Beiträge zur nordischen Philologie, 12. Basel and Frankfurt am Main: Helbing & Lichtenhahn, 1983; Kalinke, Marianne. "Norse Romance (*Riddarasǫgur*)." In *Old Norse–Icelandic Literature: A Critical Guide*. Ed. Carol J. Clover and John Lindow. Islandica, 45. Ithaca and London: Cornell University Press, 1985, pp. 316–63; Kalinke, Marianne E. *Bridal Quest Romance in Medieval Iceland*. Islandica, 46. Ithaca and London: Cornell University Press, 1990.

Marianne E. Kalinke

[**See also:** *Konráðs saga keisarasonar*; Old Norse–Icelandic Literature, Foreign Influence on; *Riddarasǫgur*; *Tristrams saga ok Ísǫndar*]

Játvarðar saga ("Játvarðr's Saga"), the saga of St. Edward the Confessor (1003–1066), is chiefly preserved in the vellum MSS Stock. Perg. fol. no. 5 (1350–1360) and *Flateyjarbók* (GkS 1005 fol., *ca.* 1400). A single vellum fragment from the 15th century is found in AM 238 XVI fol. This fragment includes the beginning of an account of Magnús góði's ("the good") claim to the throne of England, and Edward's reply. Of importance also is the 17th-century paper MS, AM 663b 4to.

The saga can be divided into four sections. The first contains a genealogy of Edward and comments on the purity of his life. William of Normandy is then introduced, with an account of his wooing and marriage to Mathilda.

Section 2 contains Edward's vision of the death by drowning of a Danish king who was planning to attack England; the story of Edward, his coronation ring, and St. John the Evangelist; Edward's vision of the Seven Sleepers of Ephesus; and brief mention of some of Edward's miracles.

Section 3 concerns the question of succession after Edward's death. It includes an account of Earl Godwine's death, and mentions the battles of Stamford Bridge and Hastings. It also refers to the tradition that King Harold Godwinsson survived the battle of Hastings.

Section 4 deals with the emigration to Byzantium of some English noblemen and their men, said to have been led by Sigurðr, earl of Gloucester. After the death of King Harold, they were unwilling to remain in England under William's rule.

Játvarðar saga was probably compiled in the 14th century from a number of different sources. The compiler alludes to English works and a history of the kings of Norway, and makes reference to Gizurr Hallsson in his text. Among his sources were the Latin lives of St. Edward; Osbert of Clare's *Vita beati Eadwardi regis Anglorum*, written 1138; Ailred of Rievaulx's *Vita sancti Edwardi regis et confessoris*, written between 1161 and 1163; and William of Malmesbury's *Gesta regum Anglorum*, written in about 1125. The compiler of *Játvarðar saga* probably knew these sources only in some abbreviated form. The excerpts from Ailred and Osbert stem from a service book containing lessons for St. Edward's feast day; St. Edward's vision of the Seven Sleepers of Ephesus derives from William of Malmesbury via Vincent of Beauvais's *Speculum historiale*. The compiler used *Haralds saga Sigurðarsonar* and the *Chronicon Laudunensis*, a world chronicle up to the year 1219, written by an English monk at Laon. Among the material with its source in the latter is the story of Edward and St. John the Evangelist, the account of Earl Godwin's death, and the account of the emigration to Byzantium.

Ed.: Rafn, C. C., and Jon Sigurdsson, eds. "Saga Játvarðar konúngs hins helga." *Annaler for nordisk Oldkyndighed og Historie* (1852), 3–43; Guðbrandr Vigfússon and C. R. Unger, eds. *Flateyjarbók: En Samling af norske Konge-Sagaer med indskudte mindre Fortællinger om Begivenheder i og undenfor Norge samt Annaler.* 3 vols. Christiania [Oslo]: Malling, 1860–68, vol. 3, pp. 461–72; Gudbrand Vigfusson and George W. Dasent, eds. and trans. *Icelandic Sagas and Other Historical Documents Relating to the Settlements and Descents of the Northmen on the British Isles.* 4 vols. Rolls Series, 88. London: Eyre and Spottiswoode, 1887–94; rpt. Millwood: Kraus, 1964, vol. 1, pp. 388–400. **Tr.**: Gudbrand Vigfusson and George W. Dasent, eds. and trans. *Icelandic Sagas and Other Historical Documents*, vol. 3, pp. 416–28. **Lit.**: Powell, F. Y. "A Northern Legend of the English Conquest." *English Historical Review* 4 (1889), 87–9; Smith, A. H. "The Early Literary Relations of England and Scandinavia." *Saga-Book of the Viking Society* 11.3 (1936), 215–32; Jón Helgason, ed. *Byskupa sǫgur. Ms. Perg. fol. no. 5 in the Royal Library of Sweden.* Corpus Codicum Islandicorum Medii Aevi, 19. Copenhagen: Munksgaard, 1950; Rogers, H. L. "An Icelandic Life of St. Edward the Confessor." *Saga-Book of the Viking Society* 14.4 (1956–57), 249–72; Ashdown, Margeret. "An Icelandic Account of the Survival of Harold Godwinson." In *The Anglo-Saxons: Studies in Some Aspects of Their History and Culture Presented to Bruce Dickins.* Ed. Peter Clemoes. London: Bowes & Bowes, 1959, pp. 122–36; Widding, Ole, *et al.* "The Lives of the Saints in Old Norse Prose: A Handlist." *Mediaeval Studies* 25 (1963), 294–337; Fell, Christine. "The Icelandic Saga of Edward the Confessor: The Hagiographic Sources." *Anglo-Saxon England* 1 (1972), 247–58; Fell, Christine E. "A Note on Pálsbók." *Mediaeval Scandinavia* 6 (1973), 102–8; Ciggaar, Krijnie N. "L'émigration anglaise à Byzance après 1066. Un nouveau texte en Latin sur les Varangues à Constantinople." *Revue des études Byzantines* 32 (1974), 301–42; Fell, Christine. "The Icelandic Saga of Edward the Confessor: Its Version of the Anglo-Saxon Emigration to Byzantium." *Anglo-Saxon England* 3 (1974), 179–96; Fell, Christine. "English History and Norman Legend in the Icelandic Saga of Edward the Confessor." *Anglo-Saxon England* 6 (1977), 223–36.

Helen Carron

[**See also:** England, Norse in; *Flateyjarbók*; Legenda; Saints' Lives; Stamford Bridge, Battle of]

Jelling is the location of royal pagan and Christian dynastic monuments of the mid- and late 10th century in Jutland, Denmark. The monuments known today comprise two rune stones, a stone-setting, two mounds, burials, and a church (Fig. 73). There have been many excavations, most recently in the 1970s and in 1981.

The smaller rune stone must belong among the oldest elements, but its original place and context are unknown. The runes on the stone translate: "King Gorm made this monument in memory of Thorvi [Thyre], his wife, Denmark's adornment." Only parts of the large stone-setting are preserved, under the southern mound (Fig. 73). It is composed of two converging rows of standing stones, was probably a ship-setting, and seems to relate to the northern mound. This largest burial mound in Denmark held the remains of a rich pagan burial in a wooden chamber. The date of the burial was probably 958/9 (by dendrochronology), and the grave had clearly been broken into at a later stage. The evidence suggests that this was the grave of the pagan King Gorm, father of King Harald Gormsson (Bluetooth).

Written sources imply that King Harald and the Danes were converted between 958 and 965. The southern mound, which is larger than the northern mound, was probably started and certainly finished after the conversion, although mounds were basically pagan. No grave was found here, in spite of extensive excavations. The large rune stone is clearly Christian. It was placed exactly between the centers of the two mounds: a large three-sided boulder with most of the script on one side, a lion entwined with a snake on the other, and Christ on the third (Fig. 74). The inscription reads: "King Harald commanded this monument to be made in memory of Gorm, his father, and in memory of Thorvi [Thyre] his mother—that Harald who won the whole of Denmark for himself, and Norway, and made the Danes Christian." Between this rune stone and the northern mound, a large wooden church was built, planned with a wooden burial chamber. This building was found during excavations of the floor of the present stone church of around 1100. The grave contained the skeletal remains of a middle-aged man, who had first been buried

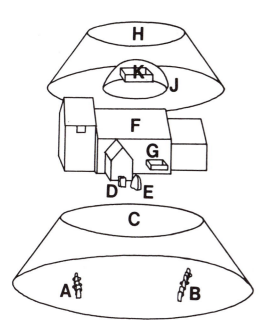

73. Schematic drawing of the Jelling monuments. (A–B) Remains of stone setting. (C) Southern mound. (D) King Gorm's rune stone. (E) King Harald's rune stone. (F) Present stone church, which had three wooden predecessors. (G) Grave in the first church. (H) Northern mound. (J) Older mound. (K) Viking burial chamber dug into the older mound. Drawing: Knud J. Krogh.

74. The royal rune stones in Jelling, raised by King Gorm (left) and King Harald (right). Photo: The National Museum of Denmark.

elsewhere, as well as remains of rich textiles and two fine strapends. The evidence available suggests that after the conversion King Harald had his father translated from the pagan burial mound to the prominent grave in the new church, to make him "Christian."

With the large rune stone, the church, and this burial, the originally pagan dynastic monument was converted into a grand Christian dynastic monument with the focus on King Harald himself.

Lit.: Kornerup, J. *Kongehøiene i Jellinge og deres undersøgelse efter Kong Frederik VII's befaling i 1861*. Copenhagen: Det Kongelige nordiske Oldskrift Selskab, 1875; Nielsen, Karl Martin, *et al.* "Jelling Problems: A Discussion." *Mediaeval Scandinavia* 7 (1974), 156–234; Christensen, Askel E. "The Jelling Monuments." *Mediaeval Scandinavia* 8 (1975), 7–20 + pl.; Roesdahl, Else. *Viking Age Denmark*. Trans. Susan Margeson and Kirsten Williams. London: British Museum, 1982, pp. 164–79; Krogh, Knud J. "The Royal Viking-Age Monuments at Jelling in the Light of Recent Archaeological Excavations: A Preliminary Report." *Acta Archaeologica* 53 (1982), 183–216; Moltke, Erik. *Runes and Their Origin: Denmark and Elsewhere*. Trans. Peter G. Foote. Copenhagen: National Museum of Denmark, 1985, pp. 202–23; Christensen, Kjeld, and Knud J. Krogh. "Jelling-højene dateret." *Nationalmuseets Arbejdsmark* (1987), 223–31; Roesdahl, Else. *The Vikings*. Trans. Susan Margeson and Kirsten Williams. London: Lane, 1991.

Else Roesdahl

[See also: Burial Mounds and Burial Practices; Conversion; Gorm; Harald Gormsson (Bluetooth); Iconography; Runes and Runic Inscriptions]

Jewelry. Our knowledge about jewelry in the early Middle Ages derives from treasure trove and items found scattered in the earth. In recent years, metal detectors have brought to light a considerable amount of jewelry, especially amulets with animal figures.

Only a small amount of jewelry has been found in graves, because the conversion to Christianity in the period around the year 1000 eliminated burial deposits, apart from pectoral crosses and, if the person was a bishop, a finger ring. Heavy jewelry, such as neck rings and bracelets, went out of use during the 12th century. Medieval jewelry is is characterized by economy of precious metal.

The use of finger rings became common in the early Middle Ages. They were worn on all fingers, by both men and women. Some finger rings adopted the shape of the plain or twisted Viking bracelets; others had precious stones inserted, especially stones or gems accorded symbolic significance or magical power, such as the sapphire, ruby, or amethyst. Many bishops' rings had sapphires, for example, the one found in the grave of the Danish archbishop Absalon (d. 1201), perhaps the one by which he had been consecrated. The oldest dated signet ring belonged to the Swedish king Knut Eriksson (r. 1167–1196). From the late 13th century onward, many rings with engraved or openwork pictures of Christ and saints and with religious inscriptions have survived, and, from the 15th century, signet rings with coats of arms or housemarks.

Among the finds from the early Middle Ages are openwork amulets of silver and bronze with animal figures in the late Viking Urnes style, and with *Agnus Dei*. Round amulets with pictures of Christ and the saints were either engraved or made of coins. Amulets could also hold relics, such as a round capsule with the Virgin depicted, in a hoard, dated before 1066, from Valbo, Gästrikland (SHM = Statens Historiska Museum, Stockholm); in the same treasure were other specimens of jewelry with granulation and filigree. Some crosses are encolpiums with cavities for relics. Most of them were bronze, and were brought from Byzantium and the near Orient. Three excellent 11th- to 12th-century encolpiums belong to the National Museum of Denmark, Copenhagen (= DNM): the Queen Dagmar Cross of gold with enamel in bright colors, found in Ringsted church and imported from Byzantium; the Roskilde Cross of gold with precious stones and granulation, from Byzantium or northern Italy; and the Orø Cross, a Byzantine or Near Eastern reliquary cross with Nordic engravings (perhaps all through a Nordic replica). A silver reliquary cross of the Orø-type was found at Gullunge, Uppland, and another with rounded cross ends was found at Gåtebo, Öland. The latter was modeled on a Byzantine cross, but the nielloed figure of Christ is reminiscent of the art of the runic stones (SHM). Small pendant crosses of gold, silver, or bronze were either made of plain sheet metal, with engravings, like some crosses from Hågerup, about 1050 (DNM), or were cast with a crucifix in relief like a group represented by crosses from Valbo in Gästrikland, Sandgårda in Gotland, Ryd in Öland, Johannishus in Blekinge, Haukøy near Troms, and several others, among them Store Tårnby, Zealand, all dated to about 1050–1150. Pendant crosses may also have ornaments consisting of three flat buckles at the cross ends; this type is especially found in Sweden and other countries in the Baltic. In Trondheim, two silver crucifixes with filigree were found with coins from about 1040. Of nearly the same date is a cross in openwork Ringerike style, found at Bonderup, Zealand (DNM).

The early-medieval amulets and pendant crosses hung on chains consisting of 8–shaped, bent rings of gold or silver, or made of thin "knitted" (Ösenstich) silver thread, techniques already used in the Viking Age and known from the Birka graves. Some of the chains are connected to the pendants by cast animal heads.

Round brooches (fibulae) with filigree of a workmanship close to Viking Age specimens and influenced by Carolingian and Ottonian goldsmiths' art were found at Kolund near Flensburg Fjord, at Frederiksborg, Zealand, (DNM), and Johannishus, Blekinge (SHM), all dated to about 1050–1075. Round brooches of different sizes were used throughout the Middle Ages, the early ones to fasten the mantle on the shoulders. The later ones in openwork were placed on the breast, as shown in Queen Eufemia's bronze effigy (ca. 1350) in Sorø church. The pectorale, a rich representation of the round brooch, was used for clasping the bishop's cope. A splendid specimen of gold with jewels and ornaments with grotesque figures, lions, and eagles, of Parisian goldsmith's art about 1300, was found in the Motala River in Sweden (SHM). A gilded copper pectorale with the Annunciation derives from a Danish church, about 1400 (DNM).

In the 14th century, ring brooches became very common, often with the inscription: "AVE MARIA GRA(CIA)." Some of them are divided into two halves and joined together by cast, clasped hands; they were called Hanttruwebrazen and were used as engagement and wedding gifts. Two specimens of gold have been found in Denmark, one of them in a treasure from the town of Slagelse in 1883, and dated by coins contained in the find to before 1375 (DNM). A spectacular silver ring brooch, formed like a gear wheel, with the name of a mintmaster and his tools engraved in eight flaps around the brooch, was found in Bornholm, and dates from about 1300 (DNM)

In the 14th century, the upper classes demanded luxury, and silver jewels, often gilded, were sewn on the clothing. The predilection for heraldry influenced jewels, and stamped sheet silver or cast silver was formed as coats of arms, surrounded by stylized lions, eagles, and fleurs-de-lis, and provided with eyes and hooks for sewing onto the garment. This sort of jewelry was strongly represented in the Slagelse treasure. Other specimens of dress jewelry were spherical buttons and buckles, which could be divided into two parts to be hooked together, often in cast openwork with flowers, leaves, and, as central figures, the Virgin, St. George with the dragon, or other saints. Such dress accessories were represented in the rich hoards, deposited about 1361, at Dune and Amunde on Gotland. A beautiful buckle from Dune, with reliefs in gilded silver representing a young knight and his lady (13th century), belongs to the best goldsmiths' work of the period (SHM).

The Nordic kings and queens may have worn crowns even before the first coronation took place, in Norway 1163, in Denmark 1170, and in Sweden 1210. Over the centuries, royal crowns were presented to churches as ornaments for Madonna statues, Queen Margrethe's to Børglum in 1407 and Queen Philippa's to Vadstena in the 1430s. None of these crowns is extant. Noblemen and noblewomen could wear head jewelry, either of gold and silver with fleurs-de-lis and other ornaments, or ribbons with silver roses. A silver chaplet of a noblewoman, worked in repousée, was included in a hoard from Badeboda in Småland (14th century; SMH). A crown with fleurs-de-lis in openwork gilded silver sheet was found together with a magnificent pectoral cross in the town of Middelfart on Funen, from about 1500 (DNM). The items may have belonged to a Madonna statue, but were possibly used as a bridal crown and a bridegroom's cross.

Beads of filigree work for rosaries have been found in several places, as in the Slagelse hoard and in Nyborg church; a complete rosary of gold and silver belonged to an abbess, Anna Reinholdsdatter Leuhusen in Stockholm, who died in 1550 (SHM).

The same abbess was the owner of a beautiful belt consisting of a chain in filigree gold (SHM). In the later Middle Ages, belts were often made of cloth or leather, with buckles and furnishings of silver. In the Dune hoard were found 14th-century belt fittings of gilded silver (SHM). The so-called "Belt of Erik of Pomerania" of woven silk has a silver buckle from about 1450 and furnishings 150 years older (DNM).

Matrixes and patrixes of bronze for round brooches and other jewelry from the transitional period between the Viking Age and the Middle Ages have been found at Hedeby, Schleswig, and in the towns of Viborg and Lund. Matrixes for later medieval jewelry have been excavated at Tønsberg, Norway, and at various places in Sweden.

Lit.: Kielland, Thor. *Nordisk guldsmedkunst i middelalderen*. Oslo: Steenske forlag, 1926; Ugglas, Carl R. *Gotländska silverskatter från Valdemarstågets tid*. Ur Statens historiska museums samlingar, 3. Stockholm: Wahlström & Widstrand, 1936; Skovmand, Roar. *De danske skattefund fra vikingetiden og den ældste middelalder indtil omkring 1150*. Aarbøger for nordisk Oldkyndighed og Historie (1942) [entire issue; French summary]; Serning, Inga. *Lapska offerplatsfynd från järnålder och medeltid i de svenska lappmarkerna*. Acta Lapponica, 11. Stockholm: Geber, 1956; Holmqvist, Wilhelm. *Övergångstidens metallkonst*. Kungl. vitterhets historie och antikvitets akademiens handlingar. Antikvariska serien, 11. Stockholm: Almqvist & Wiksell, 1963; Oldeberg, Andreas. *Metallteknik under vikingetid och medeltid*. Stockholm: Seelig, 1966; Karling, Sten, *et al*. *Nordisk medeltid: Konsthistoriska studier tillägnade Armin Tuulse*. Stockholm: Almqvist & Wiksell, 1967, pp. 34–43 [English summary]; Nylén, Erik, *et al*. *Gotlands största silverskatt funnen vid Burge i Lummelunda*. Götländskt arkiv. Visby: Gotlandstryck, pp. 1–60; Andersson, Aron, *et al.* "Smykker." *KLNM* 16 (1971), 278–86, 291–6, 298–301; Hovstadius, Barbro. *Brudkronor i Linköpings stift.* Nordiska museets Handlingar, 87. Stockholm: Nordiska museet, 1976; Mårtensson, Anders W. *Medeltida metallhantverk i Lund. En årsbok till medlemmarna av Kulturhistoriska föreningen för södra Sverige.* Lund: Berling, 1972, pp. 125–50; Lindahl, Fritze. *Dagmarkorset, Orøkorset og Roskildekorset.* Copenhagen: Nationalmuseet, 1980; Lindahl, Fritze, and Jørgen Steen Jensen. "Skattefundet fra Slagelse 1883." *Aarbøger for nordisk Oldkyndighed og Historie* (1983), 123–82 [English summary]; Lindahl, Fritze. *Middelalderlige fingerringe med ikonografiske motiver.* Taidehistoriallisia tutkimuksia Konsthistoriska Studier, 8. Helsinki: [n.p.], 1985, pp. 187–96; Duczko, Wladyslaw. *The Filigree and Granulation Work of the Viking Period: An Analysis of the Material from Björkö.* [*Birka* 5]. Stockholm: Kungl. vitterhets historie och antikvitets akademien, 1985; Jensen, Jørgen Steen, *et al. Danmarks Middelalderlige Skattefund ca. 1050–ca. 1550.* 2 vols. Nordiske Fortidsminder, Serie B, Bind 12 [forthcoming Copenhagen: Det Kongelige nordiske Oldskriftselskab; English introduction].

Fritze Lindahl

[**See also**: Graves; Hoards; Viking Art]

Johannes de Dacia (John of Denmark) taught in Paris around 1280, although nothing is known about his life. In Latin, he wrote *Summa grammatica* and *Sophisma de gradibus formarum.* The latter work deals with a metaphysical problem much discussed in the 13th century, whether one substance (*e.g.*, a man) has one or several substantial forms. Johannes argues for several substantial forms, for example, one by which a man is a living being, another by which he is an animal, and a third by which he is a man. His *Summa*, which was composed in 1280, is a voluminous collection of *quaestiones* dealing with linguistic problems seen in the light of the then-fashionable theory of *modi significandi.* Johannes was no independent thinker, but a competent compiler who drew material from his predecessors, including his compatriots Boethius de Dacia and Martinus de Dacia, as well as the Englishman Robert Kilwardby. The work is prefaced with an extensive treatise on science and its division into separate disciplines. This "Divisio scientie" was soon detatched from the body of the work and had a considerable independent diffusion.

Ed.: Johannes Dacus. *Opera.* Ed. A. Otto. Corpus Philosophorum Danicorum Medii Aevi, I.1–2. Danish Society of Language and Literature. Copenhagen: Gad, 1955 [French preface]. Lit.: Pinborg, Jan. *Die Entwicklung der Sprachtheorie im Mittelalter.* Beiträge zur Geschichte der Philosophie und Theologie des Mittelalters, Texte und Untersuchungen, 42.2. Münster and Copenhagen: Aschendorff & Frost-Hansen, 1967.

Sten Ebbesen

[**See also**: Boethius de Dacia; Martinus de Dacia]

Jómsvíkinga saga ("The Saga of the Jómsvíkingar") was written in Iceland around or possibly before 1200. For the most part, the scene of the action is late 9th- and 10th-century Denmark. Structurally, the saga falls into two parts, the first of which deals with the Danish kings, in particular King Harald Gormsson and his parents, Gorm the Old and Thyre. This part is to some extent based on two now-lost written sources, **Óláfs saga Tryggvasonar* by Gunnlaugr Leifsson and **Skjǫldunga saga.* Dreams and omens

play a major role in this section, predicting, among other things, the conversion of Denmark, described at the end of the section, and the conflict between Harald and his son Sven Haraldsson, which is the subject of the latter part of the saga. The principal characters in the latter part of the saga are the leaders of a band of Vikings called "the Jomsvikings," and its main theme is their strained relations with the Danish royal house. Pálnatóki from Funen is said to have founded the stronghold at Jómsborg on the Baltic coast of Wendland and to have been the first leader of the Viking community there. He was succeeded by Sigvaldi Strút-Haraldsson from Scania. The Jomsvikings are praised for their boldness and fortitude, but their activities are not described in any detail until they invade Norway and fight the famous sea battle in Hjǫrungavágr (Liavåg?) against Earl Hákon Sigurðarson and his sons. They are defeated at last, after Earl Hákon has invoked his protector, the goddess Þorgerðr Hǫrðabrúðr ("bride of the Hordaland"). Those who did not fall or flee are captured, and many of them beheaded; but a few are pardoned by Earl Eiríkr Hákonarson, among others, Vagn Ákason, Pálnatóki's grandson, the bravest of them all.

The problems surrounding the preservation of *Jómsvíkinga saga* are among the most complex in the history of Icelandic literature. If we assume there was originally one written saga, based on oral traditions and to a lesser extent on older written sources, this saga would seem to have split into two redactions quite soon after its composition. The alternative is to allow for two sagas composed separately, but both based on oral traditions. In any case, two substantially different redactions are discernible in some MSS and in the parts of the saga incorporated into other works. These two redactions may be designated A and B. The A-version is preserved uncontaminated in one Icelandic MS only, AM 291 4to, the oldest and undoubtedly best MS preserving the saga, written in the latter half of the 13th century. The saga is not complete, however, because the last and third-to-last leaves of this MS are lost, and the first page is illegible and the last page nearly so. The same version, with a number of omissions, was incorporated into the saga of Óláfr Tryggvason in *Flateyjarbók*, but with some alteration of style and minor interpolations from other sources. The third MS is Stock. Perg. 4to no. 7, written in the early 14th century. In this MS, the text of the A-version has been in part shortened and includes interpolations from other sources. A different redaction of the saga is found in AM 510 4to, written about the middle of the 16th century. Here, the first section of the saga is omitted, and the text is a combination of the A- and B-versions. Still another redaction is the Latin translation of Arngrímur Jónsson, made in 1592–1593 after a now-lost MS, the text of which seems to have been a combination of the A- and B-versions. In the MS AM 310 4to, there are two sections of *Jómsvíkinga saga* incorporated into *Óláfs saga Tryggvasonar*, taken from a MS closely related to AM 291 4to. *Fagrskinna* and *Heimskringla* both use the B-version of *Jómsvíkinga saga*, and the same version was probably also used by Bjarni Kolbeinsson, the author of the poem *Jómsvíkingadrápa.* The most characteristic feature of the redaction of AM 291 4to is its contempt for the Danish kings, especially Harald Gormsson. In the other redactions, this maliciousness is either somewhat softened or completely effaced, but there are also several other textual discrepancies among the MSS.

The saga itself is in no way outstanding for its characterization, but the story is vivid and well told. Throughout, the saga is interspersed with grotesque humor, even in the most grisly scenes, as, for example, the description of the beheading of the Jomsvikings after the battle in Hjǫrungavágr. Some of the events described in the saga are historical facts, although they did not happen in the same way as recorded, and most of the characters are attested in historical sources. But as a whole, the saga is far from being a historical work. It must be classified as an entertaining fiction, and as such, it is one of the highlights of medieval Icelandic saga literature.

Ed.: Hammarsköld, L. *Jomswikinga-Sagan, eller Historia om kämparne från Jomsborg. På Isländska och Swenska.* . . . Stockholm: Elmén & Granberg, 1815 [text from Stock. Perg. 4to no. 7 and copies of AM 510 4to]; *Jomsvikinga saga, útgefin eptir gamalli kálfskinnsbók í hinu konúngliga bókasafni í Stockhólmi.* Copenhagen: Popp, 1824 [latter section, copied from Stock. Perg. 4to no. 7]; Rafn, C. C., *et al.*, eds. *Fornmanna sögur.* 12 vols. Copenhagen: Popp, 1828–46, vol. 11, pp. 1–158 [mainly based on AM 291 4to]; Guðbrandr Vigfússon and C. R. Unger, eds. *Flateyjarbók: En Samling af norske Konge-Sagaer med indskudte mindre Fortællinger om Begivenheder i og udenfor Norge samt Annaler.* 3 vols. Christiania [Oslo]: Malling, 1860–68, vol. 1 [text of *Jómsvíkinga saga* interwoven with the text of *Óláfs saga Tryggvasonar* and other sources, pp. 96–210; see ed. 1969, p. 9]; Cederschiöld, Gustaf, ed. *Jómsvíkinga saga, efter skinnboken no. 7, 4:to å Kungl. Biblioteket i Stockholm.* Lund: Berling, 1875; Gjessing, A., ed. *Jómsvíkinga-saga i latinsk oversættelse af Arngrim Jonsson.* Kristianssand: Steed, 1877; Petersens, Carl af, ed. *Jómsvíkinga saga (efter cod. AM 510, 4:to) samt Jómsvíkinga drápa.* Lund: Gleerup, 1879; Petersens, Carl af, ed. *Jómsvíkinga saga efter arnamagnæanska handskriften N:o 291. 4:to i diplomatarisk aftryck.* Copenhagen: Berling, 1882; Jakob Benediktsson. *Arngrimi Jonae opera Latine conscripta.* 4 vols. Bibliotheca Arnamagnæana, 9–12. Copenhagen: Munksgaard, 1950–57, vol. 1, pp. 87–140; Blake, N. F., ed. and trans. *Jómsvíkinga saga—The Saga of the Jomsvikings.* Nelson's Icelandic Texts, 3. London: Nelson, 1962; Ólafur Halldórsson, ed. *Jómsvíkinga saga.* Íslenzkar fornbókmenntir. Reykjavik: Jón Helgason, 1969 [normalized text from AM 291 4to with the lacunae filled from *Flateyjarbók* and Stock. Perg. 4to no. 7]. **Tr.**: Sveinbjörn Egilsson, trans. *Historia de piratis Jómensibus.* . . . Scripta historica Islandorum, 11. Copenhagen: Möller, 1842, pp. 1–146; Hollander, Lee M., trans. *The Saga of the Jómsvíkings.* Austin: University of Texas Press, 1955; rpt. Freeport: Books for Libraries, 1971; Blake, N. F., ed. and trans. [see above]; Degnbol, Helle, and Helle Jensen, trans. *Jomsvikingernes saga.* Copenhagen: Gad, 1978 [Danish]. **Lit.**: Storm, Gustav. "Om Redaktionerne af Jomsvikingasaga." *Arkiv för nordisk filologi* 1 (1883), 235–48; Krijn, Sophia Adriana. *De Jómsvíkingasaga.* Leiden: Ijdo, 1914; Indrebø, Gustav. *Fagrskinna.* Avhandlinger fra Universitetets historiske seminar, 4. Oslo: Grøndahl, 1917; Hollander, Lee M. "Studies in the Jómsvíkingasaga." *Arkiv för nordisk filologi* 33 (1917), 193–222; Krijn, Sophia Adriana. "Nogle bemærkninger om Jómsvíkinasaga." *Arkiv för nordisk filologi* 34 (1918), 166–71; Hollander, Lee M. "Gjenmæle." *Arkiv för nordisk filologi* 35 (1919), 207–8; Hempel, Heinrich. "Die Formen der Iómsvíkinga saga." *Arkiv för nordisk filologi* 39 (1922–23), 1–58; rpt. in his *Kleine Schriften.* Ed. Heinrich Matthias Heinrichs. Heidelberg: Winter, 1966; Bjarni Aðalbjarnarson. *Om de norske kongers sagaer.* Skrifter utgitt av Det Norske Videnskaps-Akademi i Oslo, II. Hist.-filos. Klasse 1936. No. 4. Oslo: Dybwad, 1937, pp. 201–17; Larsson, Ludvig. *Glossar till codex AM 291, 4:to.* Utgivet av Sture Hast, Lundastudier i nordisk språkvetenskap, 13. Lund: Gleerup, 1956; Jakob Benediktsson, ed. *Arngrimi Jonae Opera Latine conscripta,* vol. 4, pp. 117–40 and 171–80; Jakob Benediktsson. "Jómsvíkinga saga." *KLNM* 7 (1962), 607–8; Foote, Peter G. "Notes on Some Linguistic Features in AM 291 4to." *Íslenzk tunga* 1 (1956), 26–46; Halldór Laxness. "En islandsk roman om Danmark." In *Yfirskygðir staðir.* Reykjavik: Helgafell, 1971, pp. 172–86; Bjarni Einarsson. *Litterære forudsætninger for Egils saga.* Reykjavik:

Stofnun Árna Magnússonar, 1975, pp. 105–47; Degnbol, Helle. "Jómsvíkinga saga." In *Dictionary of the Middle Ages.* Ed. Joseph R. Strayer. New York: Scribner, 1982–89, vol. 7, pp. 144–5.

Ólafur Halldórsson

[**See also:** Bjarni Kolbeinsson; *Fagrskinna; Heimskringla; Konungasögur; Óláfs saga Tryggvasonar; Skjǫldunga saga*]

Jómsvíkingadrápa *see* Bjarni Kolbeinsson

Jon Præst

Jon Præst ("Priest John") is the Danish rendering of Latin "Presbyter Johannes," the name of a legendary Christian priest-king of the Indies, called "Prester John" in English; his Swedish name is Joan präst av Indialand ("Priest John of India"). Wishful rumors of his victory over the Saracens, a misinterpretation of Yeh-lü Ta-shih's victory over the Seljuk Sultan in 1141, were supported by a personal letter that the Byzantine emperor Emanuel Komnenos received from him, probably in 1165. The letter, a literary fiction written in Latin by a westerner, describes the marvels of the priest-king's lands, and boasts of his fabulous wealth and power.

The Latin text of this letter survives in nearly 100 MSS, a dozen of which date from the 12th century. In his standard edition, Zarncke distinguished an original from five later interpolated versions (A–E) created within a century. The letter was translated into several vernaculars, among them possibly Old Norse (Holm-Olsen 1945: 13–4, 132–3). One Old Swedish and two Old Danish translations are extant.

The Swedish translation is preserved in two MSS, Ups. C 213 from about 1450 and the almost identical Stock. D 27 from 1550–1600. It belongs to the same tradition as the Danish translation printed by Gotfried of Ghemen in 1510, namely the Latin C-version. The second Danish translation, in a Royal Library MS, Thott 585 8vo from about 1500, represents the Latin B-version, the main difference being the placing of an interpolated description of Jon Præst's second palace, either finally (B) or somewhat earlier in the text (C). Although they are both heavily abbreviated (in some places even obscure), the Uppsala/Ghemen and the Thott versions differ greatly in their omissions. The Uppsala and Ghemen texts also have a number of transpositions and additions in common, whereas the Thott text stays close to its Latin original. One corruption in the Ghemen text (*stegheton*; cf. in the Uppsala text *stengøthom* dat. pl., literally "stone goats," *i.e.*, "ibexes") suggests that its intermediate source was Swedish, though not the Uppsala text, which is corrupt in some places where the Ghemen text is correct (*e.g., aff thet nesthe land* corresponding to Latin *de proximis regionibus*, "from the nearby regions," but in the Uppsala text *vesthan off landene*, "west of the country"). The Thott version has several rare or unique words. Probably, the Scandinavian translations (in both versions) were first made at the beginning of the 15th century.

Ed.: Zarncke, Friedrich. "Der Priester Johannes," ch. 2. *Abhandlungen der philologisch-historischen Classe der Königlich Sächsischen Gesellschaft der Wissenschaften* 7 (Leipzig, 1879), 909–34 [Latin text]; *Facsimile-Udgave af En lysthelighe Historie aff Jon Presth.* Copenhagen: Hermann-Petersen, 1910; Karker, Allan. *Jon Præst. Presbyter Johannes' Brev til Emanuel Komnenos.* Copenhagen: Reitzel, 1978 [Latin, Swedish, and two Danish texts, bibliography; cf. review by M. C. Seymour in *Medium Ævum* 48 (1979), 150–1]. **Lit.**: Holm-Olsen, Ludvig. *Konungs skuggsiá.* Utgitt for Kjeldeskriftfondet. Gammelnorske tekster, nr. 1.Oslo: Norsk Historisk Kjeldeskrift–Institutt, 1945; 2nd rev. ed. 1983; Toldberg, Helge. "Traditionen om Presbyter Johannes i Norden." *Arkiv för nordisk filologi* 76 (1961), 231–57; Edsman, Carl-Martin, *et al.* "Joan präst av Indialand." *KLNM* 7 (1962), 583–7 [with extensive bibliography]; Florovsky, Georges V. "Prester John." In *The New Encyclopædia Britannica.* 15th ed. Chicago, *etc.*: Encyclopædia Britannica, 1986, vol. 9, pp. 686–7.

Allan Karker

Jóns saga ens helga contains the *vita et acta* of the priest St. Jón Ǫgmundarson (1052–1121), consecrated in 1106 as first bishop of the diocese of Hólar, coterminous with Iceland's Northern Quarter. In 1198, his bones were disinterred and washed; in 1200, they were enshrined at Hólar, and the *Alþingi* officially endorsed his cult (*dies natalis* April 23). The translation ceremony seems to have been closely modeled on the procedure followed at Skálholt when St. Þorlákr Þórhallsson was enshrined in 1198; and the oldest *Jóns saga*, now lost, was also influenced by the first *Þorláks saga.*

The oldest *Jóns saga* was a vernacular work produced at the same time as a Latin life and probably in some association with it. The Latin life was written by Gunnlaugr Leifsson (d. 1218/9), a Benedictine of Þingeyrar. Koppenberg has argued that the Latin life never existed, but not persuasively; he overlooks the entry in the Munkaþvéra inventory of 1429, "jons sagha holabiscups j latino. onnor i norrœno" ("The Saga of Jón, bishop of Hólar, in Latin. Another in Norse"; *DI* 4, 374). A dossier of miracles kept at Hólar provided material for the *acta* of the oldest *Jóns saga.*

Jóns saga now exists in three recensions: A (chief MSS AM 221 fol., *ca.* 1300, AM 234 fol., *ca.* 1340); B (Stock. Perg. fol. no. 5, *ca.* 1360, AM 219 fol., *ca.* 1380); and C (Stock. Papp. 4to no. 4, *ca.* 1630). A, with a fluent, decorously ceremonial style, best represents the oldest *Jóns saga*, but has been abridged. Early in the 14th century, an editor, plausibly linked with Bergr Sokkason, refurbished the oldest *Jóns saga* to produce B, incorporating fresh matter from Gunnlaugr's Latin life and from a lost **Gísls saga Illugasonar*, rearranging the sequence of some episodes, and re-writing in a florid style. Another 14th-century editor produced C, a more or less straightforward conflation of the A and B versions. His text of A was very like that of AM 234 fol., and his text of B was fuller than that in Stock. 5, more like that in the AM 219 fol. fragments.

The author of the oldest *Jóns saga* had little information about Bishop Jón's career, and he attractively supplemented it with matter drawn from hagiographic commonplaces as well as learned and popular storytelling to illustrate Jón's personal piety, pastoral care, and educational zeal. The picture he draws of school life at Hólar in Jón's time, with two foreign clerics as the chief masters, may be idealized but must contain a core of truth. The description gives some idea of how Christian and classical learning flowed into early Iceland. The whole work is enlivened by anecdotes, and these and the *post mortem* miracle reports often bring us in close touch with everyday life in 12th-century Iceland.

Ed.: [Jón Sigurðsson and Guðbrandr Vigfússon, eds.] *Biskupa sögur.* 2 vols. Copenhagen: Møller, 1858–78 [texts rpt. in Guðni Jónsson, ed. *Byskupa sögur.* 3 vols. Reykjavik: Íslendingasagnaútgáfan; Haukadalsútgáfan, 1948]; Jón Helgason, ed. *Byskupa sögur. MS Perg. fol. No. 5 in the Royal Library of Stockholm.* Corpus Codicum Islandicorum Medii Aevi, 19. Copenhagen: Munksgaard, 1950; Stefán

Karlsson, ed. *Sagas of Icelandic Bishops: Fragments of Eight Manuscripts.* Early Icelandic Manuscripts in Facsimile, 7. Copenhagen: Rosenkilde & Bagger, 1967. **Tr.**: Gudbrand Vigfusson and F. York Powell, eds. and trans. "The Life of S. John the Bishop." In *Origines Islandicae: A Collection of the More Important Sagas and Other Native Writings Relating to the Settlement and Early History of Iceland.* 2 vols. Oxford: Clarendon, 1905; rpt. Millwood: Kraus, 1976, vol. 1, pp. 534–67 [*Jóns saga* A]; Simpson, Jacqueline, trans. *The Northmen Talk: A Choice of Tales from Iceland.* London: Phoenix House; Madison: University of Wisconsin Press, 1965, pp. 65–76 [extracts from *Jóns saga* B]. **Lit.**: Hallberg, Peter. "Jóns saga helga." In *Afmælisrit Jóns Helgasonar 30 júní 1969.* Ed. Jakob Benediktsson *et al.* Reykjavik: Heimskringla, 1969, pp. 59–79. Koppenberg, Peter. *Hagiographische Studien zu den Biskupa sögur: Unter besonderer Berücksichtigung der Jóns Saga Helga.* Scandia Wissenschaftliche Reihe, 1. Bochum: Scandia, 1980.

Peter Foote

[See also: *Biskupa sögur*, Miracles, Collections of; Saints' Lives]

Jóns saga leikara *see* **Jóns saga leiksveins**

Jóns saga leiksveins ("The Saga of Jón the Playmate"), alternatively known under Árni Magnússon's title, *Jóns saga leikara* ("The Saga of Jón the Player"), is an Icelandic knightly romance closely related to the French *lais* and composed probably in the 14th century. The saga is extant only in 12 paper MSS, of which the oldest is AM 174 fol. from 1644. The version of the saga in ÍB 260 8vo (1826) and Lbs. 678 4to (1852–1854) differs from that in the other MSS in that it belongs to a separate redaction representing a prose paraphrase of certain *rímur*, although not the ones in Lbs. 861 4to (see below). No complete edition of the saga has yet appeared in print. An excerpt from the saga based on AM 174 fol. was, however, published by Jiriczek (1893–94); other sections likewise based on AM 174 fol. were published by Loth (1982); and in his unpublished dissertation, Soderbach (1949) edited the full saga based on Stock Papp. 8vo no. 17 II (*ca.* 1650). The *Jóns rímur leiksveins* (ed. Finnur Jónsson 1905–22) from the first half of the 16th century, which are extant only in Lbs. 861 4to (1695) and Lbs. 862 4to (a copy), represent an abridged rendering of the saga.

The saga tells of Jón, a noble French youth, who sets out in search of adventure. On his journey, he kills a dragon and brings its tongue to the king. At a royal banquet, during which Jón courts the king's daughter, peculiar events take place, and the next morning a savage wolf that has long ravaged the king's court is caught. When asked by the king to name his reward for killing the dragon, Jón requests the wolf. He departs with the beast and releases it. It turns out that the wolf is Sigurðr, son of the king of Flæmingjaland (Flanders), upon whom a wicked stepmother had placed a spell. Jón and Sigurðr enter sworn brotherhood, and Jón marries the king's daughter.

Some of the motifs of *Jóns saga leiksveins*, such as the dragon, the evil stepmother, and the werewolf, rest on old and well-known traditions. But material is also found in the saga that points to foreign contacts little in evidence in Icelandic literature. The motif of the adulteress (here the queen) forced to have her lover's head before her at meals, for example, shows a striking resemblance with the Welsh-Latin *Arthur and Gorlagon*, and this connection is strengthened by other parallels. Influence from Dante's *Divine Comedy* has also been suggested in the inscription above the gate behind which the dragon lives. Finally, a number of parallels exist between *Jóns saga leiksveins* and certain *fornaldarsǫgur*, above all, *Hrólfs saga kraka*.

The style of the saga is simple and the story well structured. It moves swiftly from event to event, with little description, and mystery and suspense heighten the interest.

Ed.: Jiriczek, Otto Luitpold. "Zur mittelisländischen Volkskunde: Mitteilungen aus ungedruckten Arnamagnäanischen Handschriften." *Zeitschrift für deutsche Philologie* 26 (1893–94), 16–7; Finnur Jónsson, ed. *Rímnasafn: Samling af de ældste islandske rimer.* 2 vols. Samfund til udgivelse af gammel nordisk litteratur, 35. Copenhagen: Møller & Jørgensen, 1905–22, vol. 2, pp. 825–41; Soderbach, Martin. "*Jóns saga leikara.*" Diss. University of Chicago, 1949; Loth, Agnete. "Utroskabs hævn: Motivet Stith Thompson Q478.1.4 i nogle islandske kilder." *Gripla* 5 (1982), 216–56. **Bib.**: Finnur Sigmundsson. *Rímnatal.* 2 vols. Reykjavik: Rímnafélagið, 1966, vol. 1, p. 293; Kalinke, Marianne E., and P. M. Mitchell. *Bibliography of Old Norse–Icelandic Romances.* Islandica, 44. Ithaca and London: Cornell University Press, 1985, pp. 60–1. **Lit.**: Kittredge, G. L. "Arthur and Gorlagon: Versions of the Werewolf's Tale." *Harvard Studies and Notes in Philology and Literature* 8 (1903), 149–275; rpt. New York: Haskell House, 1966; Leach, Henry Goddard. *Angevin Britain and Scandinavia.* Harvard Studies in Comparative Literature, 6. Cambridge: Harvard University Press; London: Milford; Oxford: Oxford University Press, 1921; rpt. Millwood: Kraus, 1975, pp. 213–5, 382; Finnur Jónsson. *Den oldnorske og oldislandske Litteraturs Historie.* 3 vols. 2nd ed. Copenhagen: Gad, 1920–24, vol. 3, p. 119; Lagerhold, Åke, ed. *Drei Lygisǫgur. Egils saga einhenda ok Ásmundar kappabana. Ála flekks saga. Flóres saga konungs ok sona hans.* Altnordische Saga-Bibliothek, 17. Halle: Niemeyer, 1927, p. lxiii; Einar Ól. Sveinsson. *Verzeichnis isländischer Märchenvarianten. Mit einer einleitenden Untersuchung.* Folklore Fellows Communications, 83. Helsinki: Suomalaien Tiedeakademia. Academia Scientiarum Fennica, 1929, pp. liii–liv, xxx; Schlauch, Margaret. *Romance in Iceland.* Princeton: Princeton University Press; New York: American-Scandinavian Foundation; London: Allen & Unwin, 1934; rpt. New York: Russell & Russell, 1973, pp. 82–5; Glauser, Jürg. *Isländische Märchensagas: Studien zur Prosaliteratur im spätmittelalterlichen Island.* Beiträge zur nordischen Philologie, 12. Basel and Frankfurt am Main: Helbing & Lichtenhahn, 1983, pp. 14, 16, 304.

Kirsten Wolf

[**See also**: *Ridddarasǫgur*; *Rímur*]

Jóns saga Svipdagssonar ok Eireks forvitna see Þjalar-Jóns saga

Jóns þáttr biskups Halldórssonar ("The Tale of Bishop Jón Halldórsson"),

extant in AM 657 4to, from the 14th century, and AM 624 4to, from the 15th century, is a short biography of the Norwegian Jón Halldórsson, bishop of Skálholt from 1322 to 1339. He was raised in the Dominican monastery in Bergen, and went to Paris and Bologna to study at an early age. He is further said to have come "from school so mature, that he was the wisest clerk to have come to Norway," which explains his subsequent election as bishop. Also included in the *þáttr* are an account of his strange vision on the eve of his departure from Iceland to Bergen and a detailed report of his illness and last days in Bergen, where he died.

The *þáttr* tells that Jón would orally recount *ævintýri* (shorter, moralizing narratives with motifs drawn from legend, fiction, or fairy tales) that he had "learned abroad both from letters and from his own experience." In retelling them, he would adapt them to suit the taste of his audience so as to please as many listeners as possible. Furthermore, we are told that some men in Iceland collected "his narratives for their own and other people's delight"; three of the tales from his collection are provided as specimens of his repertoire. Such tales were frequently used as exempla in sermons, and in fact the third tale was inserted into a sermon delivered at Staðarhóll. The three tales take up well over one half of the *þáttr*, evidently, this aspect of the bishop's activities was of great concern to the biographer. In *Islendzk ævintýri*, Gering published around 100 *ævintýri*. Besides the three tales mentioned above, at least four others may confidently be traced to Jón.

Jón also translated *Klári saga* from Latin into Old Norse. Oddly, the biographer makes no specific reference to it. A likely explanation is that apart from its length, *Klári saga* does not deviate from *ævintýri* in theme and subject matter. Moreover, Jón may well have condensed it for use as an exemplum in his sermons.

The author of *Jóns þáttr* was probably a cleric and a personal acquaintance of the bishop. Hallberg (1968) suggests on the basis of linguistic and stylistic evidence that the author may be the abbot Bergr Sokkason, an interesting but unprovable hypothesis.

Ed.: [Jón Sigurðsson and Guðbrandr Vigfússon, eds.] *Biskupa sögur.* 2 vols. Copenhagen: Møller, 1858–78; Gering, Hugo, ed. *Islendzk ævintyri.* 2 vols. Halle: Waisenhaus, 1882–84; Guðni Jónsson, ed. *Byskupa sögur.* 3 vols. Akureyri: Íslendingasagnaútgáfan; Haukadalsútgáfan, 1948. **Lit.**: Jakobsen, Alfred. *Studier i Clarus saga: Til spørsmålet om sagaens norske proveniens.* Årbok for Universitetet i Bergen, Humanistisk Serie, 1963, No. 2. Bergen and Oslo: Universitetsforlaget, 1964; Hallberg, Peter. *Stilsignalement och författarskap i norrön sagalitteratur. Synpunkter och exempel.* Nordistica Gothoburgensia, 3. Gothenburg: Almqvist & Wiksell, 1968.

Alfred Jakobsen

[**See also**: Exempla; *Klári (Clári) saga*; *Þáttr*]

Jónsbók ("Jón's Book")

is named after the lawspeaker Jón Einarsson (d. 1306), one of its main authors, who brought the law code from Norway to Iceland in 1280, to have it accepted by the General Assembly (*Alþingi*). Although the original MS is lost, some 260 copies are preserved. These copies fall into two classes, one being closer to the original than the other, which has numerous interpolations from later times. Equally old MSS from both classes have come down to us, the earliest from the first half of the 13th century.

After the Icelanders submitted to the Norwegian King Hákon Hákonarson and his son Magnús in 1262–1264, the law of the Icelandic Commonwealth, *Grágás*, was abolished. *Jónsbók*, however, was prepared to supersede the interim (1271–1281) *Járnsíða*, a law code disliked by the Icelanders, as it incorporated mainly Norwegian law and did not pay enough attention to Icelandic conditions. About 1275, King Magnús lagabœtir ("lawmender") had completed his second revision of the national law code for Norway (*landslǫg*), in which Icelanders must have taken part, since the *landslǫg* shows influence from *Grágás* and *Járnsíða*. Magnús's national code of law became a more acceptable model for a new code of law, *Jónsbók*. Yet the national law was not followed in every detail; the paragraphs on escheatage are quite different in both codes, and the section on nautical law in *Jónsbók* is modeled on Magnús's town law (*bœjarlǫg*). *Jónsbók*'s ability to combine various sources and expand important sections is noteworthy. Although it is only half the size of *Grágás*, the section on inheritance rights is much more detailed.

The controversial debate about accepting *Jónsbók* is related in some detail in *Árna saga biskups* (chs. 28–31). The main points of disagreement concerned confiscation of property in cases that cannot be atoned for by money; unsuitability of the law to Icelandic conditions; and incompatibility to church law. The new law was accepted eventually, yet not unanimously. Points of dissent were reconciled by three amendments to the law (*réttarbœtr*) during the following thirty years. Finally, in 1314, *Jónsbók* took the form that remained valid for 400 years. The ten sections of *Jónsbók* deal with assembly attendance, Church and king, allegiance to the king, sanctuary and peace, marriage and inheritance, land claims, land rents, contracts, nautical law, and theft.

Jónsbók was among the first books printed in Iceland (Hólar 1578). Even today, some parts of this medieval law code remain in full force, primarily agriculture rights and the rights over the foreshore. There are also some thirty translations into Danish from the 17th–18th centuries in MS, and one in print (Copenhagen, 1763).

Jónsbók is thought to have had much influence on the preservation of the Icelandic language; it was among the essential reading materials for the young. However, the influence of medieval (Latin) rhetoric on the style of *Jónsbók* is obvious. It extends far beyond the opening invocational letter by King Magnús and is considerably stronger than in *Grágás*.

Ed.: Jakob Benediktsson, ed. *Skarðsbók. Jónsbók and Other Laws and Precepts. MS. No. 350 fol. in the Arna-Magnæan Collection.* Corpus Codicum Islandicorum Medii Aevi, 16. Copenhagen: Munksgaard, 1943 [facsimile]; Westergård-Nielsen, Chr., ed. *Skálholtsbók eldri. Jónsbók etc. AM 451 Fol.* Early Icelandic Manuscripts in Facsimile, 9. Copenhagen: Rosenkilde & Bagger, 1971; Ólafur Halldórsson, ed. *Jónsbók.* Copenhagen: Møller, 1904; rpt. with a postscript by Gunnar Thoroddsen. Odense: Odense Universitetsforlag, 1970; Jónas Kristjánsson *et al.*, eds. *Skarðsbók. Codex Scardensis. AM 350 fol.* Manuscripta Islandica Medii Aevi, 1. Reykjavik: Lögberg, 1981 [facsimile]. **Bib.**: Halldór Hermannsson. *The Ancient Laws of Norway and Iceland.* Islandica, 4. Ithaca: Cornell University Library, 1911; Townsend, J. A. B. "The Ancient Laws of Norway and Iceland: A Bibliographical Supplement to . . . Islandica 4." M.A. thesis, University of London, 1961. **Lit.**: Hertzberg, E. "Glossarium." In *Norges Gamle Love indtil 1387.* Ed. R. Keyser *et al.* 5 vols. Christiania [Oslo]: Grøndahl, 1846–95, vol. 5, pp. 57–834; Ólafur Lárusson. *Grágás og lögbækurnar.* Árbók Háskóla Íslands, 1922. Fylgirit. Reykjavik: Gutenberg, 1923; Halldór Hermannsson. *Illuminated Manuscripts of the Jónsbók.* Islandica, 28. Ithaca: Cornell University Press, 1940; Ole Widding. "Jónsbóks to ikke-interpolerede håndskrifter. Et bidrag til den islandske lovbogs historie." *Scripta Islandica* 18 (1967), 3–20; Fix, H. "Poetisches im altisländischen Recht. Zur Zwillingsformel in Grágás und Jónsbók." In *Sprachen und Computer. Festschrift zum 75. Geburtstag von Hans Eggers, 9. Juli 1982.* Ed. Hans Fix *et al.* Sprachwissenschaft—Computerlinguistik, 9. Dudweiler: AQ-Verlag, 1982, pp. 187–206; Fix, H. *Wortschatz der Jónsbók.* Texte und Untersuchungen zur Germanistik und Skandinavistik, 8. Frankfurt, *etc.*: Lang, 1984.

Hans Fix

[**See also:** *Alþingi*; *Árna saga biskups*; *Grágás*; Laws]

75. The Järsta stone. Valbo parish, Gästrikland, Sweden.

Järsta Stone, by the Upplandic rune master Asmund Karasun, is a commemorative monument containing one of the most puzzling 11th-century memorial inscriptions. The monument, classified as GS11 in Jansson's *Gästriklands runinskrifter*, was raised on a grave site in Valbo parish, Gästrikland, Sweden, and is still standing.

Analysis of the Järsta stone within the context of the runic tradition in Denmark and Sweden reveals that the inscription on this stone accords grammatically and orthographically with Asmund's other inscriptions and follows the patterns of formulation in structure and content traditional to runic carving. The Järsta stone, along with the other stones signed by Asmund, is characterized by an inscription carefully placed in a text band integrated with the ornamentation and the contours of the stone.

A reading that smoothly follows the text band around the two zoomorphic figures on this carving provides the key to the meaning:

Þiuðgæiʀʀ ok Guðlæifr ok Karl, þæiʀ brøðr alliʀ, letu

retta stæin þenna. Þa satti Æimundr runaʀ rettaʀ æftiʀ Þiuðmund, faður sinn. Guð hialpi hans salu ok Guðs móðiʀ. En Asmundr Karasun markaði.
[Þiuðgæiʀ and Guðlæif and Karl, all those brothers, had this stone raised. Then Æimund wrote right runes after Þiuðmund, his father. May God and God's mother help his soul. And Asmund, son of Kara, carved.]

In *Aimuntrunoʀ*, for *Æimundʀrunaʀ* or *Aimundr runaʀ*, Asmund uses a single rune to represent two similar consecutive sounds, here the palatal [ʀ] and the dental [r]. He may simply have chosen the digraph *ai* from the many ways of representing the sound, resulting from the elision of the unstressed [i] of *satti* and the stressed [æi] of *Æimund*. His use of a common rune for two similar consecutive sounds could thus explain both orthographic ambiguities: the missing nominative -*r* of *aimunt* and the unstressed -*a* of *sata*.

Lit.: Wessén, Elias, and Sven B. F. Jansson, eds. *Upplands runinskrifter*. Sveriges runinskrifter, 6–9. Kungl. vitterhets historie och antikvitets akademien. Uppsala: Almqvist & Wiksell, 1940–58; Thompson, Clairborne W. *Studies in Upplandic Runography*. Austin and London: University of Texas Press, 1975; Jansson, Sven B. F., ed. *Gästriklands runinskrifter*. Sveriges runinskrifter, 15.1. Kungl. vitterhets historie och antikvitets akademien. Uppsala: Almqvist & Wiksell, 1981, pp. 89–107; Trygstad, Anne. "The Järsta Stone." *Publications of the Modern Language Association* 100 (1985), 9–19.

Anne Trygstad

[**See also:** Runes and Runic Inscriptions]

Jǫkuls þáttr Búasonar ("The Tale of Jǫkull Búason"). According to *Kjalnesinga saga*, Jǫkull Búason was fostered in Norway by his mother, the giantess Fríðr. Jǫkull then traveled to Iceland, where he killed his father in a combat caused by Búi's refusal to acknowledge Jǫkull as his son. In the groups of the *Kjalnesinga saga* MSS called A and B, it is plainly stated that nothing certain is known about Jǫkull's later destiny. MS group C, on the other hand, appends a story, *Jǫkuls þáttr Búasonar*, a tale of Jǫkull's subsequent adventures.

For a long time, Jǫkull and his men are adrift at sea. The ship is wrecked in a storm off the coast of Greenland, and the men survive only because Jǫkull carries them ashore. One night, he discovers the witches Geit and Gnípa on the beach. He decapitates Geit and defeats Gnípa at wrestling, winning her as a friend and helper. Later on, Jǫkull and his comrade Úlfr kill Gnípa's parents and brothers in a fierce fight at the trolls' cave. As penance, Jǫkull helps Gnípa get the troll-king's son as a husband. By means of a ring, Jǫkull becomes invisible and starts a riot in the king's mountain; the bewildered trolls soon kill each other. After being wrestled down, the son is forced to agree to marry Gnípa. Jǫkull also liberates a prince and a princess of Serkland, imprisoned by the trolls in a mountain cave. He then accompanies them home, marries the princess, and soon becomes king of Serkland.

Jǫkuls þáttr was probably written by someone who had read *Kjalnesinga saga*, and who thought that Jǫkull should have a saga of his own. Possibly, the story came into being in the 15th century. It is strongly influenced by the *fornaldarsögur* for the adventures in Greenland, and by the *riddarasögur* for the stay in Serkland. The parallels to *Hálfdanar saga Brǫnufóstra* are especially obvious; the lines of action are as a whole the same. Moreover, the princess is named Marsibilla in *Jǫkuls þáttr* and Marsibil in *Hálfdanar saga*. The king of Serkland also appears in some *riddarasögur*, among them *Bevers saga*.

Jǫkuls saga is an adventure tale, totally devoid of the realistic background of many *Íslendingasögur*. Still, the story is quite entertaining, not least because of its burlesque style and dialogue.

Ed.: Jóhannes Halldórsson, ed. *Kjalnesinga saga*. Íslenzk fornrit, 14. Reykjavík: Hið íslenzka fornritafélag, 1959, pp. xx–xxiii, 45–59. **Lit.**: Finnur Jónsson. *Den oldnorske og oldislandske Litteraturs Historie*. 3 vols. 2nd ed. Copenhagen: Gad, 1920–24, vol. 3, p. 79.

Tommy Danielsson

[**See also:** *Fornaldarsögur*; *Hálfdanar saga Brǫnufóstra*; *Kjalnesinga saga*; *Riddarasögur*; *Þáttr*]

K

Karlamagnús saga ("The Saga of Charlemagne") is a collection of Old Norse prose translations of texts about Charlemagne, most of them Old French *chansons de geste*.

The beginning (branch I in Unger's edition) and the original ending seem to be parts of a translation of the same text, a lost *Life of Charlemagne* in Old French, which consisted mainly of summaries of different *chansons de geste*, including a *Chanson de Basin*. This *Life* can scarcely have been written before the second third of the 13th century, and is thus later than the other texts translated in *Karlamagnús saga*, which all date from the 12th century. It is important to distinguish between the *chansons de geste* used by the French author of the *Life* and those used directly by the Norwegian or Icelandic translators.

Between the two parts of this translated *Life of Charlemagne*, a compiler placed translations of the following texts (branch numbers follow Unger's edition): III: *Enfances d'Ogier le Danois*; IV: *Pseudo-Turpin Chronicle* (the only translation made from Latin in the older version of *Karlamagnús saga*) and *Aspremont* (the beginning of the latter is lost and has been replaced by the former); V: *Saxons*, a version lost in French, but perhaps identical to the source of Jean Bodel's *Chanson des Saisnes*; VI: *Otinel*; VII: *Pèlerinage/Voyage de Charlemagne*; VIII: *Roland*.

The end of the branch of Roland seems to stem from the *Life of Charlemagne*, and so does what follows: the retelling of the *Moniage de Guillaume* (branch IX) and an account of Charlemagne's death. This account is now extant only in the Danish translation (see below).

The texts no doubt came from Britain, and they were translated in the 13th century; the *Pseudo-Turpin Chronicle* may have been translated before 1200. We do not know under what circumstances they arrived or were translated, nor under what circumstances the translations were assembled. We do not even know whether the translators and the compiler were Norwegians or Icelanders.

All of the extant copies were written by Icelanders, including a fragment of branch VIII written in the second half of the 13th century; we do not know whether this fragment was already a part of the collection. The first version of this text, α, is extant in a fragment from the 14th century and in two copies from about 1400 or a little later; the end is missing in both.

The α-text was revised in Iceland. The revised version, β, was used for Icelandic *rímur* and Faroese *kvæði*, and was the basis of further revisions extant in Icelandic copies from the 14th century and later. The most important innovations are the addition of the translation of an English version of *Doon de la Roche* (branch II, *Olif ok Landres*), a rewriting of branch IV, and a new text of Charlemagne's death (stemming indirectly from the *Speculum historiale* of Vincent of Beauvais).

A Swedish translation of the α-version of VII and VIII, *Karl Magnus*, was made about 1400. There is no evidence that other branches were translated as well.

An abridged Danish translation of the entire α-version, *Karl Magnus' Krønike*, was made in the 15th century. It is extant in a MS from 1480, a printed edition from 1509, and a revised edition from 1534, which was often reprinted during the following centuries.

Ed.: Unger, C. R., ed. *Karlamagnus saga ok kappa hans. Fortællinger om Keiser Karl Magnus og hans Jævninger i norsk Bearbeidelse fra det trettende Aarhundrede.* Christiania [Oslo]: Jensen, 1860; Kornhall, David, ed. *Karl Magnus enligt Codex Verelianus och Fru Elins bok.* Samlingar utgivna av Svenska fornskrift-sällskapet, Häft 219, Bd. 63. Lund: Blom, 1957; Hjorth, Poul Lindegård, ed. *Karl Magnus' Krønike.* Copenhagen: Schultz, 1960; Loth, Agnete, ed. *Karlamagnús saga, Branches I, III, VII og IX. Edition bilingue projetée par Knud Togeby et Pierre Halleux. Texte norrois édité par Agnete Loth. Traduction française par Annette Patron-Godefroit. Avec une étude par Povl Skårup.* Copenhagen: DSL, La Société pour l'étude de la langue et de la littérature danoises; Reitzel, 1980; Halvorsen, Eyvind Fjeld, ed. *Karlamagnus saga and Some Religious Texts, AM 180 a and b fol.* Early Icelandic Manuscripts in Facsimile, 18. Copenhagen: Rosenkilde & Bagger, 1989 [facsimile of MS "a," ed. Unger]. **Tr.**: Hieatt, Constance B., trans. *Karlamagnús saga: The Saga of Charlemagne and His Heroes.* 3 vols. Mediaeval Sources in Translation, 13, 17, 25. Toronto: Pontifical Institute of Mediaeval Studies, 1975–80. **Bib.**: Kalinke, Marianne E., and P. M. Mitchell. *Bibliography of Old Norse–Icelandic Romances.* Islandica, 44. Ithaca and London: Cornell University Press, 1985, pp. 61–71. **Lit.**: Halvorsen, E. F. *The Norse Version of the Chanson de Roland.* Bibliotheca Arnamagnæana, 19. Copenhagen: Munksgaard, 1959; Kornhall, David. *Den fornsvenska sagan om Karl Magnus.*

Handskrifter och Texthistoria. Lundastudier i nordisk språkvetenskap, 15. Lund: Gleerup, 1959; Hjorth, Poul Lindegård. *Filologiske Studier over Karl Magnus' Krønike.* Copenhagen: Schultz, 1965.

Povl Skårup

[**See also:** Old Norse–Icelandic Literature, Foreign Influence on; *Riddarasögur*]

Karrig Niding *see* Drama

Kaupang (Skíringssalr) was a marketplace, dated to the period around 750–920, by the Viksfjord, Tjølling, Vestfold, Norway.

In his report to King Alfred the Great (*Orosius* 1:i), the North Norwegian merchant Ohthere (Óttarr) mentions a port in southern Norway by the name of "Sciringesheal" (Old Norse Skíringssalr). The information given about this port is sparse, apart from some reliable geographical facts. These facts point to Skíringssalr being located somewhere on the coast of Vestfold, the most important of the ancient kingdoms of Norway. Philological and historical considerations point to the county of Tjølling in South Vestfold as earlier Skíringssalr. Here we find a group of farms called "Kaupang." In 1850, it was pointed out that on these farms there were "grave mounds beyond number." In 1867, a great many mounds were opened. All contained cremation graves. The grave goods were partly burned beyond recognition, but artifacts of western and Baltic origin could be identified. The dating could be established entirely in the Viking Age. But the material was not sufficient to demonstrate that the graves had to belong to the population of a *kaupang*, or marketplace.

In 1947, a series of new inhumation graves was found on the Kaupang land. An excavation campaign begun in 1950 first concentrated on this cemetery, which comprised mainly boat graves for men, women, and children. The grave goods contained a higher percentage of imported artifacts: weapons, jewelry, shards of glass and pottery, and amber and jet beads. Altogether, some sixty persons have been unearthed in this cemetery. Two or three persons had often been interred in the same boat. Some graves were indeed richly furnished, but none of the Kaupang graves was of the highest standard found in Birka. It could be deduced that these graves must belong to merchant families rather than to ordinary farmers, and to the same period as the 1867 graves. This information again testifies to an unusually large population in the Kaupang area in the Viking Age. The dating of the graves corresponds well enough with Ohthere's visit to Skíringssalr in the 890s. But rich and numerous grave finds do not constitute a *kaupang*. Lacking material from a habitation proper, material representing something more than a mere farming community, one would still be without decisive archaeological evidence for the identification of Ohthere's port.

The only possible locality in the Kaupang area was a long, narrow strip of land between the cemeteries. The soil was markedly black here (*cf.* the Black Earth in Birka). The first trenches, cut in 1956, proved promising. In 1957–1967, a complex of six houses was uncovered in the area. Only one of them had a hearth, and this was also better constructed than the other five, which may have been workshops. Between the houses, there were three wells. Cobbled paths led from the houses down to stone piers alongside the Kaupang bay. An 80-kg. anchor indicates that fairly large boats might run into this bay. The Viking Age shoreline was 3 m. higher than today, and there was an excellent harbor. The Black Earth was extremely thin compared, for instance, with that of Hedeby. But it was so closely packed with artifacts that a highly concentrated intensity of habitation could be deduced. It seems as if this habitation was confined to one period only. But some of the houses had obviously been altered during the habitation period, which can be dated from the end of the 8th to the beginning of the 10th century. This dating is firmly established by a series of twenty-nine (?) coins, mainly Kufic; but Anglo-Saxon, Franconian, and one Scandinavian coin are also included, covering the years 720–890 (Skaare 1975). Some 2,000 pottery fragments show mainly pots thrown on the wheel and mainly of Rhenish origin. But there is also a group of Baltic origin and groups from the North Sea region. The coins and the pottery groups provide better evidence than any other material from Kaupang's Black Earth that this settlement was of a nonagrarian type. The groups of material from the habitation site have not been given the intensive analysis they deserve. There can be no doubt that they reflect various forms of workshop industry for something more than household consumption. Two groups are conspicuous: processing of soapstone and metal production. A more detailed study of the first showed a much more complex picture with regard to production, transportation, and fairs than the fairly simple picture (import of raw material, export of products fabricated on Kaupang) so far taken for granted (Resi 1979). The same complex picture also has emerged from the study of the whetstones, abundant in the Kaupang material, but perhaps not produced there. It would seem that Kaupang's role in the Viking Age trade was in some cases more that of a distribution than that of a production center (Resi 1987).

Archaeological criteria more than anything else point to the community at Viksfjord being the "Sciringesheal" Ohthere visited on his way to King Alfred. It was much smaller in area than, for instance, Birka (4 hectares to Birka's 12 hectares), but it served as a port for the immediate hinterland as well as for oversea markets in Jutland (Hedeby), the Baltic, and particularly western Europe.

Lit.: Blindheim, Charlotte. "Kaupang in Skiringssal: A Norwegian Port of Trade from the Viking Age." In *Vor- und Frühformen der europäischen Stadt im Mittelalter. Bericht über ein Symposium in Reinhausen bei Göttingen 1972.* 2 vols. Ed. Herbert Jahnkuhn *et al.* Abhandlungen der Akademie der Wissenschaften in Göttingen. Phil.-hist. Kl. 3. Folge. Nr. 84. Göttingen: Vandenhoeck & Ruprecht, 1974, vol. 2, pp. 40–57; Blindheim, Charlotte. "Kaupang by the Viks Fjord in Vestfold." In *Archaeological Contributions to the Early History of Urban Communities in Norway.* Instituttet for sammenlignende kulturforskning. Serie A: Forelesninger 27. Ed. E. Asbjørn *et al.* Olso, Bergen, and Tromsø: Universitetsforlaget, 1975, pp. 125–73; Skaare, Kolbjørn. *Coins and Coinage in Viking-Age Norway: The Establishment of a National Coinage in Norway in the XI Century, with a Survey of the Preceding Currency History.* Oslo, Bergen, and Tromsø: Universitetsforlaget, 1976; Resi, Heid Gjøstein. *Die Specksteinsfunde aus Haithabu.* Berichte über Ausgrabungen in Haithabu, 14. Neumünster: Wachholtz, 1979; Blindheim, Charlotte, *et al. Kaupang-funnene* 1. Norske Oldfunn, 11. Oslo: Universitets Oldsaksamling, 1981; Düwel, Klaus, *et al.*, eds. *Untersuchungen zu Handel und Verkehr der vor- und frühgeschichtlichen Zeit in Mittel- und Nordeuropa. Teil IV. Der Handel der Karolinger- und Wikingerzeit.* Abhandlungen der Akademie der Wissenschaften in Göttingen. Phil.-hist. Kl. 3. Folge. Nr. 156. Göttingen: Vandenhoeck & Ruprecht, 1987; Resi, Heid Gjøstein. "Reflections on Viking Age Local Trade in Stone Products. In *Proceedings of the Tenth Viking Congress, Larkollen, Norway, 1985.* Ed. James E. Knirk.

Universitetets Oldsaksamlings Skrifter, Ny rekke, 9. Oslo: Universitetets Oldsaksamling, 1987, pp. 95–102.

Charlotte Blindheim

[**See also:** Birka; Coins and Mints; Graves; Trade]

Kennings were already a matter for discussion in Old Norse culture, either by puzzled auditors of skaldic poetry, or by literary experts, such as Snorri Sturluson and Óláfr Þórðarson. Even the experts could be mistaken, as today, but nevertheless the Norsemen's general understanding and appreciation of kennings far outweighed their occasional errors of interpretation. It is the other way around for the modern readers of skaldic poetry. The fact that the complications of kennings, then as now, have to be unriddled has suggested that the kenning had the same intellectual function in Old Norse culture as the riddle, of which the Norsemen were equally fond. Kenning and riddle indulged a love of wordplay and of contests of wit in the culture.

Kenning (pl. *-ar*) is a feminine noun derived regularly from the weak verb *kenna*, which in the verb phrase *kenna X við Y* means "to call X by Y's name," or designate X by Y. In its simplest form, a kenning consists of two noun members compounded together in a base word, or head noun, and a determinant, with or without genitive linkage between them, for example, *benregn* or *benja regn* ("wound-rain" or "rain of wounds" = "blood"). In this form, the kenning is distinguished from the uncompounded *heiti* (pl. *heiti*), a poetic appellative (like English "blade" for "sword") that was said to be *ókennt*, i.e., "undesignated." There are, however, borderline kennings, the *viðrkenningar* and *sannkenningar* ("by-kennings" and "true kennings"), which merely denote persons by their qualities of character, relations to others, and possessions, just as they are, and so refer to them more or less directly in the manner of the *ókennt heiti*. Where formal distinctions fail, the real difference between kennings and *úkennd heiti* lies in their modes of reference.

Since the generic term for any epithet in skaldic poetry was *heiti* ("appellation," from *heita* 'to call by name'), kennings were set off from all other epithets as *kennt heiti*, because of their peculiar designations of their referents.

In Snorri's *Skáldskaparmál* (7), three grades of skaldic diction are given: (1) "To name everything the way it is called." The ordinary *heiti* does so with poetic words for man, fire, sea, sword, and so on.

(2) "The second branch is what is termed substitution for names [= *fornọfn*]." Here, Snorri seems to translate by *fornafn* the Latin rhetorical term *pronominatio* for a classical figure that will match either the "by-" or the "true kenning." By *pronominatio*, the Roman Gracchi were known rhetorically as "the grandsons of Scipio Africanus"; cf. the *viðrkenning* for Þórr, *Jarðar burr* ("son of Earth"). Hence, this division includes the borderline *viðrkenningar* and *sannkenningar*.

(3) "The third branch of diction is what is termed kenning, and the branch is so set up that if we denominate Óðinn or Þórr or Týr or some one of the gods or the elves, and to each of them that I give a name, I then transfer with an appellative the property of another god or mention some of his deeds, therewith the first becomes the possessor of the name and not the one who was named for him; thus, when we allude to Victory-Týr or Týr of the Hanged or Týr of Ships' Cargoes, those are Óðinn's names." The crucial point in this definition of kenning is the transfer of names

that the kenning effects, so that Týr, the sharer in Óðinn's sovereign power, can stand for Óðinn, while Óðinn "possesses" his name. This kind of transference, or *translatio*, may have prompted Óláfr Þórðarson to claim in the *Third Grammatical Treatise* (3:16) that every kenning was constructed with a metaphor.

To summarize, we may say that the heightened language of the ordinary *heiti* (grade 1) requires no special mode of reference, whereas the "pronominal" periphrases and metaphors of the kennings (grades 2 and 3) must designate their referents within one remove or at one remove and more from them. As between the low and high grades of kenning, the metonymic principle of syntagmatic proximity predominates in the formation of "by-kennings" and "true kennings," and the metaphorical principle of paradigmatic similarity in that of bona fide kennings. But the latter kennings will also often combine a metaphorical head noun with a metonymic determinant, as in the Týr-kennings for Óðinn above: "victory," "hanged men," and "ships' cargoes" are metonyms detailing circumjacent areas of Óðinn's presence in battle, beside the gallows, and aboard ship; "Týr," of course, is Óðinn's metaphorical name.

Great but not unlimited variability is to be expected in the more complex morphology of kennings. Some kennings, notably for women, dispense with their determinants to form half-kennings, for example, *óskmær* ("chosen maid" = valkyrie), which lacks the determinant, Óðinn, chief of the valkyries. But the main stylistic tendency of kennings is to elaborate on themselves and concatenate kenning with kenning in multiple noun compounds, not unlike the "gripping beasts" motifs of Viking art. Doubled kennings were said to be twice-designated (*tvíkennt*), and further expansions were covered by a jeweler's term, "enchased" (*rekit*).

Snorri and his critical successors agreed that the kennings within a kenning should not exceed the number of five, and yet six-unit kennings were not out of reach of the skalds. Þórðr Særeksson's man-kenning, *nausta blakks hlémána gífrs drífu gimslọngvir* ("the sword-swinger in driven snow [= battle], with the troll [= axe] of the shield, like a protective moon on the side of the steed of the boathouse [= ship]") may be the longest kenning on record (as in *Þórálfs drápa Skolmssonar* 1).

One last refinement, on top of these, was mysteriously termed *ofljóst* ("over-light"); it added a pun on the name of whoever might be the referent of a personal kenning. Thus, since Grettir happens to be the name of a snake as well as of a human being, the name can be rendered with various snake-kennings. And if Icelanders were to be named, they could be represented in an anagrammatic kenning as *álhimins lendingar*, of which *álhiminn* means "sky of the eel" or river ice, so that *íss* ("ice") plus *lendingar* equals "Icelanders" (*Íslendingar*).

In the larger context of the *dróttkvætt* stanza of court poetry, the skalds freely mixed metaphors in their kennings, though Snorri, who considered that practice a "monstrosity" (*nykrat*), would have preferred to see in the stanzaic framework more unified kenning images, "new creations" (*nýgervingar*), as he called them in his *Háttatal* commentary (at ch. 6). But, again, skaldic practice did not conform to critical precept.

Kennings were not all form and verbal tricks; content also had significance, especially in connection with Old Norse mythology. The so-called "mythological kennings" were in point of content narrative precipitates from the stories told immemorially of the gods and their doings. Even the faded metaphor of "tree" for a man or a woman, which enters into countless nonmythological kennings, has a creation myth behind it (as in Snorri's *Gylfaginning*, ch. 9), relating how men and women were fashioned from trees. Consequently, when Snorri Sturluson in an antiquarian and critical spirit undertook to expound the kenning system to the Norse Christian skalds of the 13th century, he not only delved into the traditional forms of skaldic diction, but also retold some of the ancient myths that were encapsulated in the content of the pagan kennings. Thereby, he could show that the mythological kennings were not altogether arbitrary but were well motivated in the system. If we must find a remote source of origin for the majority of kennings, it probably lies in the mythologizing of the Norsemen; but that still would not account for purely poetic kennings, such as Þórðr Særeksson's kenning above.

Ed.: Björn Magnússon Ólsen, ed. *Den Tredje og Fjærde Grammatiske Afhandling i Snorres Edda. Tilligemed de Grammatiske Afhandlingers Prolog og To Andre Tillæg*. Samfund til udgivelse af gammel nordisk litteratur, 12. Islands grammatiske litteratur i middelaldren, 2. Copenhagen: Knudtzon, 1884 [the *Third* and *Fourth Grammatical Treatises* by Óláfr Þórðarson and an anonymous author, respectively]; Finnur Jónsson, ed. *Edda Snorra Sturlusonar*. Copenhagen: Gyldendal, 1931 [Snorri Sturluson's *Gylfaginning*, *Skáldskaparmál*, and *Háttatal*]; Turville-Petre, E. O. G. *Scaldic Poetry*. Oxford: Clarendon, 1976 [a selection of skaldic verse, with introduction and notes to verse; on kennings, pp. xlv–lix]; Frank, Roberta. *Old Norse Court Poetry: The Dróttkvætt Stanza*. Islandica, 42. Ithaca and London: Cornell University Press, 1978 [a selection of skaldic verse, with introduction and notes to the verse; on kennings, pp. 39–49]. **Lex.**: Finnur Jónsson, ed. *Lexicon poeticum antiquæ linguæ septentrionalis: Ordbog over det norsk-islandske skjaldesprog. Oprindelig forfattet af Sveinbjörn Egilsson*. 2nd ed. Copenhagen: Møller, 1931; rpt. Lynge, 1966 [Danish translation of 1860 Latin original]. **Tr.**: Brodeur, Arthur Gilchrist, trans. *Snorri Sturluson. The Prose Edda*. New York: American Scandinavian Foundation, 1916; rpt. 1967 [*Gylfaginning* and *Skáldskaparmál*]; Faulkes, Anthony, trans. *Snorri Sturluson. Edda*. Everyman Classics. London and Melbourne: Dent, 1987 [*Prologue, Gylfaginning, Skáldskaparmál*, and *Háttatal*]. **Lit.**: Meissner, Rudolf. *Die Kenningar der Skalden: Ein Beitrag zur skaldischen Poetik*. Rheinische Beiträge und Hülfsbücher zur germanischen Philologie und Volkskunde, 1. Bonn: Schroeder, 1921; Heusler, Andreas. Review of *Die Kenningar der Skalden*, by R. Meissner. *Anzeiger für deutsches Altertum und deutsche Literatur* 41 (1922), 127–34; Lindow, John. "Riddles, Kennings, and the Complexity of Skaldic Poetry." *Scandinavian Studies* 47 (1975), 311–27; Spamer, James Blakeman. "The Kenning and the Kend Heiti: A Contrastive Study of Periphrasis in Two Germanic Poetic Traditions." Diss. Brown University, 1977; Marold, Edith. *Kenningkunst: Ein Beitrag zu einer Poetik der Skaldendichtung*. Quellen und Forschungen zur Sprach- und Kulturgeschichte der germanischen Völker, 80. Berlin: de Gruyter, 1983; Clunies Ross, Margaret. *Skáldskaparmál: Snorri Sturluson's ars poetica and Medieval Theories of Language*. Viking Collection, 4. Odense: Odense University Press, 1987; Amory, Frederic, "Kennings, Referentiality, and Metaphors." *Arkiv för nordisk filologi* 103 (1988), 87–101.

Frederic Amory

[**See also**: Eddic Poetry; *Fornafn*; Grammatical Treatises; *Heiti*; Skaldic Meters; Skaldic Verse; *Snorra Edda*]

Kensington Stone

Kensington Stone is the name given to an inscribed, 92-kg. slab of graywacke, measuring approximately 76 x 40 x 15 cm., that first came to attention near the village of Kensington, Douglas County, Minnesota, in August 1898. Supposedly found under the roots of a poplar tree by the Swedish-born farmer Olof Ohman and his Norwegian-born neighbor Nils Flaten, the stone attracted local attention because of the curious lettering. The inscription was said to be in Scandinavian runes and to chronicle a disastrous expedition made by eight "Goths" (Swedes) and twenty-two Norwegians to Minnesota in 1362. If genuine, the Kensington stone would contain the earliest known written record of American history.

Shallowly carved and relatively unweathered, the runes are of mixed types used from the 9th to the 11th century, in addition to several homemade symbols. The date 1362 in runes is anachronistically based on the Arabic system with place value. The language used is a mixture of modern Swedish and Norwegian, together with misapplied "medieval" trimmings. Diligent promotion has made the Kensington inscription the kingpin of "Viking Romanticism" in North America, with a host of by-products, including an elaborate cryptogram theory. From 1899 to the present, however, specialists in Scandinavian linguistics and runology have characterized it as a late 19th-century hoax, perpetrated by Minnesotans in the interest of ethnic prestige.

Lit.: Andersen, Harry, and Erik Moltke. "Kensington-stenen, Amerikas runesten." *Danske Studier* (1949–50), 37–60; Jansson, Sven B. F. "'Runstenen' från Kensington i Minnesota." *Nordisk tidskrift för vetenskap, konst och industri utgiven av Letterstedtska föreningen*. Årg. 25, Häft 7–8, 1949 (Stockholm, 1950), 377–405; Holand, Hjalmar R. *Explorations in America Before Columbus*. New York: Twayne, 1956; Wahlgren, Erik. *The Kensington Stone: A Mystery Solved*. Madison: University of Wisconsin Press, 1958; Steefel, Lawrence M. Review of Erik Wahlgren, *The Kensington Stone: A Mystery Solved. Minnesota Archaeologist* 23 (1965), 97–115; Blegen, Theodore C. *The Kensington Rune Stone: New Light on an Old Riddle*. St. Paul: Minnesota Historical Society, 1968; Liestøl, Aslak. "Cryptograms in Runic Carvings: A Critical Analysis." *Minnesota History* 41 (1968), 34–42; Landsverk, O. G. *Runic Records of the Norsemen in America*. New York: Friis; Twayne, 1974; Hall, Robert A. *The Kensington Rune-Stone Is Genuine*. Columbia: Hornbeam, 1981; Wahlgren, Erik. "American Runes: From Kensington to Spirit Pond." *Journal of English and Germanic Philology* 81 (1982), 157–85.

†Erik Wahlgren

[**See also**: America, Norse in; Viking Hoaxes]

Ketils saga hœngs

Ketils saga hœngs ("The Saga of Ketill Salmon") is a minor *fornaldarsaga*. Ketill, a typical hero, was endowed with superhuman strength, fearlessness, and an enterprising spirit. He acquired his byname *hœngr* 'salmon,' after he had slain a dragon. When asked by his father what he had been up to, he replied in self-deprecation that he had killed a salmon. The nickname alludes to his giant ancestry and to his role as a giant/*berserkr* killer and as an ally of giants.

Ketill's father, Hallbjǫrn, was a demitroll, and many of Ketill's adventures took place in Hallbjǫrn's territory. Ketill thus lived in a pagan environment and ambience. Still, in the description of Ketill's love affair with the giantess Hrafnhildr, the mother of his son, Grímr loðinkinni ("shaggy-chin"), the saga exhibits a curiously antipagan bias.

Typically, these giantesses were protectresses of their lovers, or so-called foster-mothers. The motif is rooted in the pagan belief that giants and giantesses were minor deities and eponymous ancestors. But there is no reminiscence of this belief in *Ketils saga hœngs*. On the contrary, Ketill, though pagan, is singularly divorced from pagan beliefs or worship. Ketill's love affair with Hrafnhildr is described largely in human terms. Although his father disliked the liaison, and, upon Hrafnhildr's appearance at their manor, ruptured it, Ketill had no interest in other women. His arranged marriage left him cool but proved lasting because of the patience of his wife. Still, he named his daughter Hrafnhildr, an act that expressed his love for the giantess and that may have reflected his and his kin's ties to a giant cult. Later, in a series of verses, Ketill stated unequivocally that he did not fear Óðinn. The implication is that Ketill was not a worshiper of the gods. Of course, he did not have to trust in the fickleness of Óðinn. In all of his trials and combats, he could safely rely on his strength, his wits, and his magic sword and arrows.

Structurally, the saga consists of a string of adventures interlaced with eddic verses. The interest of the saga resides less in its literary merit than in its use of the same folk motifs that lie at the heart of such masterpieces as *Grettis saga Ásmundarsonar*. Whereas Ketill's boorishness, indolence, and sloth as a child are the paradoxical telltale signs of his future greatness, these qualities in Grettir also cause tragedy, loneliness, and persecution. In *Ketils saga hœngs*, folk motifs are exclusively structural elements in an adventure story. In *Grettis saga Ásmundarsonar*, the folk motifs that link Grettir's life to the typical career of a giant killer have a psychological function and humanize the hero.

Ketils saga hœngs forms a cycle with three other sagas, generally referred to as the *Hrafnistumanna sǫgur* ("sagas of the men of Hrafnista"), in which the heroes, Grímr loðinkinni, Ǫrvar-Oddr, and Án bogsveigir ("bow-swayer") are Ketill's descendants. The saga dates probably from the 13th century. The main MSS are AM 343a 4to and AM 471 4to, both from the 15th century.

Ed.: Guðni Jónsson, ed. "Ketils saga hængs." In *Fornaldar sögur Norðurlanda*. 4 vols. Akureyri: Íslendingasagnaútgáfan, 1954, vol. 2, pp. 149–81. **Lit.**: Ellis, Hilda R. "Fostering by Giants in Old Norse Saga Literature." *Medium Ævum* 10 (1941), 70–85; Chadwick, Nora K. "The Monsters and Beowulf." In *The Anglo-Saxons: Studies in Some Aspects of Their History and Culture Presented to Bruce Dickins*. Ed. Peter Clemoes. London: Bowes and Bowes, 1959, pp. 171–203; Ciklamini, Marlene. "Grettir and Ketill Hængr, the Giant-Killers." *Arv* 22 (1966), 136–55.

Marlene Ciklamini

[**See also**: *Áns saga bogsveigis*; *Fornaldarsögur*; *Grettis saga*; *Gríms saga loðinkinna*; *Ǫrvar-Odds saga*]

Kings' Sagas *see* Konungasögur

Kingship in medieval Scandinavia poses the question of whether its Christian manifestations maintain continuity from pre-Christian times in respect of sacral kingship, a concept broadly defined in terms of "an aura of specialness" that is believed to surround a king (McTurk 1975–76: 156). Whereas Christian sacral kingship, which becomes well attested in Scandinavia from the earliest reports of the cult of St. Óláfr onward (Hoffmann 1975: 58–89), implies kings ruling by divine grace and representing God on earth, pre-Christian sacral kingship in Scandinavia, if it existed at all, may have involved one or more of the following: (1) the belief that kings were descended from gods (attested, according to Turville-Petre 1978–79 and others, by Þjóðólfr of Hvin's *Ynglingatal*; cf., however, Baetke 1964: 69–170 and Faulkes 1978–79); (2) the

dedication of princes for purposes of vengeance to gods or semideified kings (attested, according to Höfler 1952, by the runic inscription on the Rök stone; see, however, Kuhn 1954–55 and Kratz 1978–79); (3) the ritual education of kings in numinous knowledge (attested, according to Fleck 1970 and Mazo 1985, in *Rígsþula*, *Hyndluljóð*, *Grímnismál*, and *Vafþrúðnismál*); (4) the ritual marriage of a king to a bride who personifies the well-being of his realm (attested, according to Svava Jakobsdóttir 1988, in the Gunnlǫð-episode of *Hávamál*, sts. 104–10); (5) the priestly function of kings, attested in Eyvindr skáldaspillir's ("the plagiarist") *Hákonarmál* and Einarr skálaglamm's ("scale-tinkle") *Vellekla* (though was this the exclusive prerogative of kings, or enough to grant them the necessary "aura of specialness"? Baetke 1964: 54–68, McTurk 1975–76); (6) the attribution to kings of a *mana*-like quality of luck, supposedly reflected in the words *gipta*, *gæfa*, *hamingja* (Ström 1967, Hallberg 1973), and also of supernatural powers, as suggested by legends of St. Óláfr and Saxo's account of Valdemar I (Gunnes 1974; however, cf. B. Sawyer 1985); (7) and the sacrificial slayings of kings in order to bring fertility, supposedly attested in *Ynglingatal*'s account of the slaying of King Dómaldi (Ström 1967, Lönnroth 1986).

While the uncertainty of the evidence would lead some scholars to dispense with the term "sacral" in connection with pre-Christian Scandinavian kingship (Martin 1990; cf. Lönnroth 1986), others continue to use it in that context in making comparisons with Irish kingship (Wormald 1982; cf. Ström 1981, Sayers 1985, Svava Jakobsdóttir 1988); or in using *Rígsþula* to argue for a pre-Christian Scandinavian counterpart to the idea of the king's "two bodies" (Dronke 1989); or in claiming that the earls of Hlaðir were the true inheritors of pagan sacral kingship in Norway, while Haraldr hárfagri ("fair-hair") Hálfdanarson, with his decidedly nonreligious kingship, eased the transition from paganism to Christianity as the basis for royal power (Fidjestøl 1987).

Many of these alleged aspects of pre-Christian Scandinavian kingship served Dumézil as evidence for his division of Indo-European ideology into the three functions of sovereignty, force, and fecundity, represented respectively by Óðinn, Þórr, and Freyr, as well as by priests, warriors, and farmers (*e.g.*, Dumézil 1958: 54–8), a scheme that, however, Haugen (1967) and Page (1978–79) have criticized, particularly with regard to Dumézil's subdivision (1948; cf. Polomé 1984) of the first function into the roles of magician and jurist, represented respectively by Óðinn and Týr (though see Strutynski 1974). Maillefer (1981), on the other hand, following Dumézil's view (1971; cf. 1958: 33) that the Indo-European king combines all three functions, finds that pre-Christian Swedish kingship, at least, exemplifies the third function more than the other two.

Pre-Viking Scandinavian kingship has been compared with pre-Migration Germanic kingship with regard not only to sacrality, but also to the king's dependence on an assembly, a feature reflected in the sociopolitical status of the Icelandic *goði* (which Sawyer 1982 compares with Irish kingship). Just as kingship among the Germans became increasingly competitive and military with the diplomatic, commercial, and predatory activity brought about by economic growth and contact with Rome, so did Scandinavia's 8th-century economic expansion and subsequent contact with the Franks in particular lead to a development among its peoples from tribal kingship (*Volkskönigtum*) to military kingship (*Heerkönigtum*), a development described as "both cause and effect of Viking activity" (Wormald 1982: 147).

The adoption by royal families of saint-kings as their chief ancestors provides a framework for studying the subsequent development of medieval Scandinavian kingship, and need not derive from any pre-Christian belief in the descent of kings from, or their dedication to, gods (despite recent claims, see Hoffmann 1975; cf. von See 1978). The "warrior-martyr" and "innocent murder victim" types of royal saint, knowledge of which appears to have reached Scandinavia from Merovingian Francia by way of Anglo-Saxon England, combined in the posthumously developed cult figure of St. Óláfr, whose adoption by the descendants of his half-brother, Haraldr harðráði ("hard-ruler") Sigurðarson, as their chief ancestor (in place of Haraldr hárfagri Hálfdanarsson), helped to secure their tenure of the Norwegian throne until, with Magnús Erlingsson's election in about 1165, legitimacy came to the fore as a criterion for the succession (Hoffmann 1975: 58–9, Jochens 1987).

The pattern established in Norway recurs in Denmark with Sven Estridsen's (d. 1074) attempt to give prominence among his ancestors to the convert Harald Gormsson (Bluetooth) in place of the latter's pagan father, Gorm the Old; with the fostering by two of Sven's sons, Erik Ejegod ("ever-good"; 1095–1103) and Niels (1104–1134), of the cult of their brother, St. Knud (Cnut; d. 1086), to secure their own and their descendants' royal claims; with the combined adoption by Valdemar I (d. 1182) of his son Knud (VI) as coruler and his father, Knud Lavard (son of Erik Ejegod), as chief ancestor (the latter development reflecting a new preference for the "victim" to the "warrior" type of royal saint); and with the comparable attempts of Christoffer I (1252–1259; son and grandson respectively of Valdemars II and I) to secure his line's succession by appointing his son, Erik Klipping, as coruler and promoting the cult of his brother, Erik Plovpenning ("plow-penny"; d. 1250), with the result that Erik Klipping (1259–1286) and the latter's son, Erik Menved (1286–1319), ruled after him (Hoffmann 1975: 89–196).

In Sweden, the same pattern is seen in the use of St. Erik Jedvardsson's (d. ca. 1160) cult by his descendants, down to and including Magnus Ladulås Birgersson (1275–1290), his great-granddaughter's second son by Earl Birger, to ward off rival claimants to the throne (Hoffmann 1975: 197–204).

Lit.: Dumézil, Georges. *Mitra-Varuna. Essai sur deux représentations indo-européennes de la souveraineté*. 3rd ed. Collection La Montagne Sainte-Geneviève, 7. Paris: Gallimard, 1948, pp. 142–74; Höfler, Otto. *Germanisches Sakralkönigtum. 1: Der Runenstein von Rök und die germanische Individualweihe* Tübingen: Niemeyer; Münster and Cologne: Böhlau, 1952; Kuhn, Hans. Review of Höfler, *Germanisches Sakralkönigtum. Anzeiger für deutsches Altertum* 67 (1954–55), 51–61; Dumézil, Georges. *L'idéologie tripartie des Indo-Européens*. Collection Latomus, 31. Brussels: Latomus, 1958; Baetke, Walter. *Yngvi und die Ynglinger. Eine quellenkritische Untersuchung über das nordische "Sakralkönigtum."* Sitzungsberichte der sächsischen Akademie der Wissenschaften zu Leipzig. Philologisch-historische Klasse, 109, part 3. Berlin: Akademie, 1964; Haugen, Einar. "The Mythical Structure of the Ancient Scandinavians: Some Thoughts on Reading Dumézil." In *To Honor Roman Jakobson: Essays on the Occasion of His Seventieth Birthday, 11 October 1966*. 3 vols. Janua Linguarum, Studia Memoriae Nicolai van Wijk dedicata, Series maior, 31–3. The Hague and Paris: Mouton, 1967, vol. 2, pp. 855–68; Ström, Folke. "Kung Domalde i Svitjod och 'kungalyckan.'" *Saga och sed* (1967), 52–66; Fleck, Jere. "Konr—Óttarr—Geirroðr. A Knowledge Criterion for Succession to the Germanic Sacred Kingship." *Scandinavian Studies* 42 (1970), 39–49; Dumézil, Georges. *Mythe et épopée*. 3 vols. Paris: Gallimard, 1968–73. Vol. 2, *Types épiques indo-européens: un héros, un sorcier, un roi*, 1971 [see p. 358]; Hallberg, Peter. "The Concept of *gipta-gæfa-hamingja* in Old Norse Literature." In *Proceedings of the First International Saga Conference, University of Edinburgh, 1971*. Ed. Peter Foote et al. London: University College; Viking Society for Northern Research, 1973, pp. 143–83; Gunnes, Erik. "Divine Kingship: A Note." *Temenos: Studies in Comparative Religion* 10 (1974), 149–58; Strutynski, Udo. "History and Structure in Germanic Mythology: Some Thoughts on Einar Haugen's Critique of Dumézil." In *Myth in Indo-European Antiquity*. Ed. Gerald James Larson et al. Publications of the UCSB Institute of Religious Studies. Berkeley, Los Angeles, and London: University of California Press, 1974, pp. 29–50; Hoffmann, Erich. *Die heiligen Könige bei den Angelsachsen und den skandinavischen Völkern. Königsheiliger und Königshaus*. Quellen und Forschungen zur Geschichte Schleswig-Holsteins, 69. Neumünster: Wachholtz, 1975; McTurk, R. W. "Sacral Kingship in Ancient Scandinavia: A Review of Some Recent Writings." *Saga-Book of the Viking Society* 19 (1975–76), 139–69 [esp. p. 156]; Chaney, William A. Review of Hoffmann, *Die heiligen Könige. Speculum* 52 (1977), 991–3; Christiansen, Eric. Review of Hoffmann, *Die heiligen Könige. English Historical Review* 92 (1977), 182–4; See, Klaus von. Review of Hoffmann, *Die heiligen Könige. Skandinavistik* 8 (1978), 72–5; Kratz, Henry. "Was Vamoþ Still Alive? The Rök-stone as an Initiation Memorial." *Mediaeval Scandinavia* 11 (1978–79), 9–29; Faulkes, Anthony. "Descent from the Gods." *Mediaeval Scandinavia* 11 (1978–79), 92–125; Page, R. I. "Dumézil Revisited." *Saga-Book of the Viking Society* 20 (1978–79), 49–69; Turville-Petre, Joan. "On Ynglingatal." *Mediaeval Scandinavia* 11 (1978–79), 48–67; Maillefer, J.-M. "Recherche sur l'ancienne royauté suédoise et l'idéologie des trois fonctions." *Études germaniques* 36 (1981), 371–92; Moisl, Hermann. "Anglo-Saxon Royal Genealogies and Germanic Oral Tradition." *Journal of Medieval History* 7 (1981), 215–48; Ström, Folke. "Poetry as an Instrument of Propaganda: Jarl Hákon and His Poets." In *Specvlvm Norroenvm: Norse Studies in Memory of Gabriel Turville-Petre*. Ed. Ursula Dronke et al. Odense: Odense University Press, 1981, pp. 440–58 [esp. p. 454, n. 46]; Sawyer, Peter. "The Vikings and Ireland." In *Ireland in Early Mediaeval Europe: Studies in Memory of Kathleen Hughes*. Ed. Dorothy Whitelock et al. Cambridge: Cambridge University Press, 1982, pp. 345–61; Wormald, C. Patrick. "Viking Studies: Whence and Whither?" In *The Vikings*. Ed. R. T. Farrell. London and Chichester: Phillimore, 1982, pp. 128–53 [esp. pp. 144–8]; Polomé, Edgar. "The Indo-European Heritage in Germanic Religion: The Sovereign Gods." In *Athlon. Satura grammatica in honorem Francisci R. Adrados*. Ed. A. Bernabé et al. Madrid: Editorial Gredos, 1984, vol. 1, pp. 401–11; Boyer, Régis. "Pagan Sacral Kingship in the Konungasögur." In *The Sixth International Saga Conference 28/7.–2/8. 1985. Workshop Papers*. 2 vols. Copenhagen: Det arnamagnæanske Institut, 1985, vol. 1, pp. 71–87; Mazo, Jeffrey Alan. "Sacral Knowledge, Kingship, and Christianity: Myth and Cultural Change in Medieval Scandinavia." In *The Sixth International Saga Conference*, vol. 2, pp. 751–62; Sawyer, Birgit. "Valdemar, Absalon and Saxo: Historiography and Politics in Medieval Denmark." *Revue belge de philologie et d'histoire* 63 (1985), 685–705 [esp. pp. 696–9]; Sayers, William. "Konungs skuggsjá: Irish Marvels and the King's Justice." *Scandinavian Studies* 57 (1985), 147–61; Lönnroth, Lars. "Dómaldi's Death and the Myth of Sacral Kingship." In *Structure and Meaning in Old Norse Literature: New Approaches to Textual Analysis and Literary Criticism*. Ed. John Lindow et al. Viking Collection, 3. Odense: Odense University Press, 1986, pp. 73–93; Fidjestøl, Bjarne. "Skaldediktinga og trusskiftet. Med tankar om litterær form som historisk kilde." In *Proceedings of the Seventh Biennial Conference of Teachers of Scandinavian Studies in Great Britain and Northern Ireland Held at University College London,

March 23–25, 1987. Ed. R. D. S. Allan and M. P. Barnes. London: University College London, 1987, pp. 58–77; Jochens, Jenny M. "The Politics of Reproduction: Medieval Norwegian Kingship." *American Historical Review* 92 (1987), 327–49; Svava Jakobsdóttir. "Gunnlǫð og hinn dýri mjǫður." *Skírnir* 162 (1988), 215–45; Dronke, Ursula. "Marx, Engels, and Norse Mythology." In *Studies in Honour of H. L. Rogers.* Ed. Geraldine Barnes *et al. Leeds Studies in English*, n.s., 20 (1989), 29–45; Martin, John Stanley. "Some Thoughts on Kingship in the Helgi Poems." In *Poetry in the Scandinavian Middle Ages: Proceedings of the Seventh International Saga Conference.* Ed. Theresa Pàroli. Spoleto: Centro Italiano di Studi sull' Alto Medioevo, 1990, pp. 369–82.

Rory McTurk

[**See also:** Einarr Helgason skálaglamm; Eyvindr Finsson skáldaspillir; *Grímnismál; Hávamál; Hyndluljóð,* Óláfr, St.; *Rígsþula;* Rök Stone; Þjóðólfr of Hvin; *Vafþrúðnismál*]

Kirialax saga ("The Saga of Kirialax"). Like some of the classical *Íslendingasǫgur,* this romantic saga deals with three generations of a family, although the bulk of the story is devoted to the eponymous hero. *Kirialax saga* first tells how Kirialax's father, Laicus, king of Thessaly, wins the daughter of King Dagnus of Syria by assembling a large force of men, conquering some Syrian towns, and defeating the princess's brother, Egias, who then becomes his friend and helps to secure the marriage. The offspring of this union is Kirialax, who is trained in both the liberal and martial arts, and then begins a life of adventure and travel. His first deed, which constitutes the longest episode in the saga, is to aid King Soba of Phrygia against the powerful invading force of King Solldan of Babylon. Kirialax displays great prowess here and also cleverness in devising the scheme by which Solldan's army is routed: knowing that elephants fear mice, Kirialax arranges for fragile boxes containing mice to be thrown at the enemy's elephants, who then flee in terror. Kirialax next aids King Lodovicus of Sicily and the emperor Zeno by driving off a marauder from the North named Eugenius. The hero then wins as a bride the princess of Constantinople, Florencia, in a way that echoes his father's bride winning. Refused at first, he brings an army and overcomes Florencia's brother, who then persuades the emperor to grant his daughter's hand. Interspersed among these adventures are Kirialax's visits to historical sites in Troy and Jerusalem, and his travels to India, Africa, Asia, and even the columns of Hercules at the end of the world (*i.e.,* Gibraltar). The third generation is presented through a single adventure involving Kirialax's sons, Valterus and Villifer, and their fight with a stranger, who turns out to be their cousin. The saga ends with a notice by the narrator that he will now turn to heroes of the North, but apart from a few lines preserved in one MS, nothing seems to have come of this intention.

Kirialax saga exists in three fragmentary MSS from the 15th century and some fourteen later copies. The date of composition was probably in the 14th century. The plot of the saga is repetitious and without interest or suspense. It is further marred by irrelevant digressions, such as Kirialax's travels and Egias's fight with the monster Honocentaurus in a labyrinth, by means of which he gains a bride. In fact, the main thread seems to be a series of three bride winnings (by Dagnus, Egias, Kirialax), all by force. The "court style" in which the saga is written has a tedious abundance of alliterating word chains. The redeeming feature of the saga is the amount of learned lore, ultimately of foreign origin but borrowed by the saga from Norse texts, such as the story of the elephants and the mice, of ancient origin but here derived from *Stjórn.* Other examples include the story of the labyrinth or "Domus Dedali" (house of Dedalus), which the author reminds us is called *Vǫlundar hús* ("house of Vǫlundr") in the North; the story of the slaying of Hector by Achilles; an account of marvelous birds in India; and the description of the fabulous palace of the emperor in Constantinople. A massive use of such details makes *Kirialax saga* unique among Icelandic *riddarasǫgur,* a saga in which the plot merely serves as an excuse for a display of learning.

Ed.: Kålund, Kristian, ed. *Kirialax saga.* Samfund til udgivelse af gammel nordisk litteratur, 43. Copenhagen: Møller, 1917; Loth, Agnete, ed. *Fornaldarsagas and Late Medieval Romances. AM 486 and AM 589 a–f 4to.* Early Icelandic Manuscripts in Facsimile, 11. Copenhagen: Rosenkilde & Bagger, 1977; Blaisdell, Foster W., ed. *The Sagas of Ywain and Tristan and Other Tales. AM 489 4to.* Early Icelandic Manuscripts in Facsimile, 12. Copenhagen: Rosenkilde & Bagger, 1980. **Lit.:** Kålund, Kristian. "Kirjalax sagas kilder." *Aarbøger for nordisk Oldkyndighed og Historie,* 3rd ser., 7 (1917), 1–15; Cook, Robert. "*Kirialax saga:* A Bookish Romance." In *Les Sagas de Chevaliers (Riddarasǫgur). Actes de la Vᵉ Conférence Internationale sur les Sagas . . . (Toulon. Juillet 1982).* Ed. Régis Boyer. Civilisations, 10. Paris: Presses de l'Université de Paris-Sorbonne, 1985, pp. 303–26; Hallberg, Peter. "A Group of Icelandic 'Riddarasǫgur' from the Middle of the Fourteenth Century." In *Les Sagas de Chevaliers,* pp. 7–53.

Robert Cook

[**See also:** *Leiðarvísir; Riddarasǫgur; Stjórn;* Style]

Kjalnesinga saga ("The Saga of the Men of Kjalarnes") is preserved in four groups of MSS (A–D). Only AM 471 4to, representing A, is on parchment; it dates from the latter half of the 15th century. The rest are late paper MSS. The B-group is supposedly closely related to the lost version in *Vatnshyrna.* The C-group contains a number of additions to the original text.

The introduction to *Kjalnesinga saga* is proportionally long, telling of *landnám* ("land taking") and family relationships on Kjalarnes, below Mount Esja north of Reykjavík. The main actor of the saga is Búi Andríðsson. Búi is persecuted by the chief Þorgrímr because of his reluctance to sacrifice. Eventually, he is provoked into killing Þorgrímr's son and burning down his temple. This act leads Þorgrímr to attack and kill Búi's innocent father. A conflict begins among Búi, the Norwegian Ǫrn, and Kolfiðr over the beautiful Ólǫf. Ǫrn waylays Kolfiðr, but is himself killed in the ensuing fight. Búi defeats Kolfiðr in a duel. He prepares to leave for Norway, but is attacked on his way to the ship by some relatives of Þorgrímr. Outsiders intervene, and Búi departs for the islands of Orkney and later visits King Haraldr hárfagri ("fair-hair") Hálfdanarson. Here, in order to make amends for the temple fire, he is assigned the task of collecting a backgammon board from Haraldr's foster-father, the mountain-giant Dofri. Búi gets help from Dofri's daughter, Fríðr, with whom he soon has an affair. At the end of the winter, when he wants to return, it appears that Fríðr is pregnant. At the parting, she promises to send the child, if a boy, to Búi. Dofri gives him the board as a gift. However, upon Búi's return, Haraldr demands one more achievement; he is to fight a *blámaðr* (literally "blue man"). Búi emerges victorious from the fierce combat and is reconciled to Haraldr. Back in Iceland, after some further entanglements, he is also reconciled to Þorgrímr.

Some years later, Jǫkull, Fríðr's son, arrives, but Búi refuses to acknowledge him and proposes a wrestling match as a test. In spite of Jǫkull's attempts at a peaceful agreement, the fight goes on until Búi is fatally wounded. Jǫkull leaves Iceland, ill at ease.

Kjalnesinga saga takes place early, around 900, when Haraldr was king of Norway. But the saga was written down late. A few references in the text point to an origin at the beginning of the 14th century. As the author knew Kjalarnes very well, he may have resided there or at the monastery of Viðey. The cultural situation resembles that in *Hauksbók*, initiated by the lawman Haukr Erlendsson. Moreover, there are some connections between *Kjalnesinga saga* and *Finnboga saga ramma*, which may have been written down by Haukr's relative Gizurr Bjarnarson.

Kjalnesinga saga seems an eclectic work of art. There are a number of borrowings from other written sources, a large quantity of revised motifs from other *Íslendingasögur*, and quite a lot of romantic material of a kind often to be found in *fornaldarsögur* and *riddarasögur*.

The description of the pagan temple at Hof resembles accounts in, among other works, *Eyrbyggja saga*, the *Hákonar saga góða* of *Heimskringla*, and *Alexanders saga*. The section may have come from learned or oral sources. The account of Ørlygr leaving Ireland and taking land in Iceland is found in *Landnámabók* and *Óláfs saga Tryggvasonar en mesta* as well. The existing divergences can be explained in different ways; either *Kjalnesinga saga* treated its written sources freely, or it presents an independent story, based on oral tales. The life-and-death struggle between father and son has many non-Icelandic parallels, for instance in *Hildebrandslied*. The most important similarities are found in Irish sagas about Cuchulainn. Possibly, Irish traditions have had a more general influence on *Kjalnesinga saga*. However, it is hard to determine whether these influences reach as far back as to the age of *landnám*; they may have arrived later with, for example, merchants, or they may be just an expression of an individual author's special interest in Ireland.

Ed.: Jóhannes Halldórsson, ed. *Kjalnesinga saga*. Íslenzk fornrit, 14. Reykjavik: Hið íslenzka fornritafélag, 1959, pp. v–xx, 1–44. **Tr.**: Jones, Gwyn, trans. "The Saga of the Men of Keelness." In *Four Icelandic Sagas*. Princeton: Princeton University Press; New York: American-Scandinavian Foundation, 1935, pp. 103–32. **Lit.**: Finnur Jónsson. "Hofalýsingar í fornsögum og goðalíkneski." *Árbók hins íslenzka fornleifafélags* (1898), 28–38; Posthumus, Johanna Arina Huberta, ed. *Kjalnesinga saga*. Akademisch proefschrift (Universiteit van Amsterdam). Groningen: de Waal, 1911, pp. i–xxxv; Schlauch, Margaret. *Romance in Iceland*. Princeton: Princeton University Press; New York: American-Scandinavian Foundation, 1934; rpt. New York: Russell & Russell, 1973, pp. 114–8; Helgi Guðmundsson. *Um Kjalnesinga sögu*. Studia Islandica, 26. Reykjavik: Menningarsjóður, 1967; Hallberg, Peter. "Ett par språknotiser till Kjalnesinga saga." *Maal og minne* (1968), 26–31; Danielsson, Tommy. *Om den isländska släktsagans uppbyggnad*. Skrifter utgivna av Litteraturvetenskapliga institutionen vid Uppsala universitet, 22. Stockholm: Almqvist & Wiksell, 1986, pp. 45–50.

Tommy Danielsson

[**See also:** *Alexanders saga*; *Eyrbyggja saga*; *Finnboga saga ramma*; *Hauksbók*; *Heimskringla*; *Íslendingasögur*; *Jǫkuls þáttr Búasonar*; *Landnámabók*; *Óláfs saga Tryggvasonar*; *Vatnshyrna*]

Klári (Clári) saga ("The Saga of Klárus"). According to an introductory passage in one group of MSS, this story was "found" in France, written in Latin meter, by Jón Halldórsson; Jón then "told" the story that is now written down. This passage tells us at once too much and not enough. It gives us an approximate date (*ca.* 1300, when Jón, a Norwegian who later served as bishop in Skálholt from 1322 to 1339, was a student in Paris) and informs us that the Norse text was based on a Latin poem (now lost). But it does not tell us when or even whether Jón made the written translation that is called *Klári saga*. Jón is known to have brought back exempla from France, which he told orally and which were later written down (Gering 1882–83). The most likely interpretation of the introductory passage is that Jón made a written translation from a Latin MS while he was a student in Paris.

The editions of Cederschiöld (1879, 1907) and the study by Jakobsen (1964) mention ten MSS divided into two groups, one group descending from AM 657b 4to (late 14th century) and the other descending from Stock. Perg. 4to no. 6 (*ca.* 1400). These two main MSS derive independently from a common original (see Jakobsen 1964: 13–14). The bibliography by Kalinke and Mitchell, however, lists twenty-four MSS, mostly late; we need to study these MSS to see whether or not they fit into the present two-group stemma.

The saga belongs to the category of "maiden-king romances" (Walhgren 1938) and indeed seems to have given rise to that genre in Old Icelandic, which also includes *Dínus saga drambláta*, *Nitida saga*, *Sigrgarðs saga frœkna*, *Sigurðar saga þogla*, and *Viktors saga ok Blávus*.

The story concerns Klárus (or Clárus), prince of Saxland, and his efforts at winning the haughty Serena, princess of France. On Klárus's first visit to her, he is entertained courteously in her tower, until she suddenly causes him to spill an egg on his tunic and then expels him from her presence with colorful language (*e.g.*, *vándr þorpari*, roughly "dumb hick"). With the help of his wise teacher from Arabia, Master Perus, Klárus visits Serena in disguise, eventually gets the better of her, and marries her (although on his first two attempts she tricks him into drinking a sleeping potion and then has him whipped). On the morning after the marriage, Serena awakes to find herself destitute and in the company of an ugly vagabond. For the next year, she accompanies this vagabond, in reality Perus, on his wanderings, steadfastly enduring much humiliation and hardship, and is eventually rewarded by being reunited with Klárus.

It has long been recognized that this "taming of the shrew" tale belongs to the type exemplified by the Brothers Grimm story of "King Thrushbeard" and the Norwegian tale "Håkon Borkenskjegg" collected by Asbjørnsen and Moe. *Klári saga* shares with the latter the use of precious treasures (three tents drawn by animal figures in the saga, a golden spinning wheel and its accessories in the tale) to appeal to the princess's avarice on three successive visits.

The saga is written in the learned style, with a number of absolute constructions and latinisms, some of which may derive from the Latin original.

Ed.: Cederschiöld, Gustaf, ed. *Clarus saga. Clari fabella. Islandice et latine*. Lund: Gleerup, 1879; Cederschiöld, Gustaf, ed. *Clári saga*. Altnordische Saga-Bibliothek, 12. Halle: Niemeyer, 1907; Bjarni Vilhjálmsson, ed. "Clari saga." In *Riddarasögur*. 6 vols. Reykjavik: Íslendingasagnaútgáfan, 1949–54, vol. 5, pp. 1–61; Slay, Desmond, ed. *Romances: Perg. 4:o nr 6, Royal Library, Stockholm.* Early Icelandic Manuscripts in Facsimile, 10. Copenhagen: Rosenkilde & Bagger, 1972 [English introduction]. **Bib.**: Kalinke, Marianne E., and P. M. Mitchell. *Bibliography of Old Norse–Icelandic Romances.* Islandica, 44. Ithaca and London: Cornell University Press, 1985. **Lit.**: Gering, Hugo. *Islendzk æventyri.* 2 vols. Halle: Waisenhaus, 1882–83 [contains some exempla supposedly brought to Iceland by Jón Halldórsson; introduction to volume 2 has an account of his life as well as extensive comments on the style of *Klári saga* in relation to that of the *æfintýri*]; Philippson, Ernst. *Der Märchentypus von König Drosselbart.* Folklore Fellows Communications, 50. Greifswald: Academia Scientiarum Fennica, 1923 [the most comprehensive study to date of the Thrushbeard story and its European analogues]; Schlauch, Margaret. *Romance in Iceland.* Princeton: Princeton University Press; London: Allen & Unwin, 1934; rpt. New York: Russell & Russell, 1973; Wahlgren, Erik. *The Maiden King in Iceland.* Chicago: University of Chicago Libraries, 1938 [private publication]; Jakobsen, Alfred. *Studier i Clarus saga: Til spørsmålet om sagaens norske proveniens.* Årbok for Universitetet i Bergen, Humanistisk Serie, 1963, No. 2. Bergen and Oslo: Universitetsforlaget, 1964.

Robert Cook

[**See also**: Exempla; *Jóns þáttr biskups Halldórssonar*; Old Norse–Icelandic Literature, Foreign Influence on; *Riddarasögur*; Style]

Knittel(vers)

Knittel(vers) (from German *Knittel, Knüttel[vers]*, from *Knüttel* 'bludgeon,' after Latin *versus rhopalicus*, from Greek *rhópalon* 'bludgeon') The Latin name belongs to a sort of verse in which each word in a line had a syllable more than the preceding one, so that the words became "thicker and thicker" like a bludgeon. Thus, the name *knittel* is an inappropriate one, since these characteristics do not apply to the Scandinavian meter. The *knittel* was the normal metrical form of Scandinavian (except Icelandic) epic poetry during the Middle Ages. The average line had four stresses and a varying number of unstressed syllables; but lines with three stresses did occur. The lines were rhymed in pairs, as illustrated by the following example from the Old Swedish *Herr Ivan*:

> Thet wár forsníman ok ække lángo
> iak fóor ok wílde nýmære fánga,
> væpnadher wæl til fóot ok hánda,
> ok léta æn mík thordhe nákar bestánda.

Literally:

> It was recently and not long ago,/ that I went away and
> wanted to meet with new experiences/ well armed on
> both legs and hands,/ and sought to find somebody who
> dared to fight with me.

Most *knittel*-lines began with an unstressed syllable (more seldom two), although in some lines the first syllable was stressed (such as *væp*- in l. 3 above).

The requirements of the rhymes varied from poem to poem, but as a rule they were fairly exact. In all of the *knittel*-poems, however, there occur off-rhymes, such as *mila* 'miles' and *skridha* 'glide'; *sant* 'true' and *langt* 'long, far away'; *meen* 'detriment,' *etc.* and *heem* 'home.' Different final vowels in a rhyme pair were especially common, for example, *blidha* (pl.) 'in good humor'; *qwidho* (acc.); 'grief'; *wara* 'be'; *skare* 'crowd' (see also *lángo* and

fánga in ll. 1 and 2 in the passage quoted above).

Poems written in *knittel* characteristically employed stereotyped phrases, often owing to the need for a rhyming word, for example, *badhe minna ok swa mere* ("both smaller and bigger [tokens]"), *hwa thet wil forstanda* ("whoever will understand it") *vtan alt meen* ("without every deficiency, excellently"). For the same reason, the poems employ variation by means of synonyms or negated antonyms: *badhe medh snille ok swa medh skæl* ("both with prudence and also with judgment"), *han war feet ok ække magher* ("he was fat and not lean"; see also l. 1 quoted above).

As the name indicates, *knittel* was brought to Scandinavia from Germany, where it was already in use by the 12th century. In accordance with its origin, the Scandinavian *knittel* shows a rather strong German influence on its style and vocabulary (e.g., such words as *stolt* 'splendid,' *ædel* 'noble,' *æuintyr* 'story'). Another stylistic influence came from the ballads.

Knittel was composed in all of the Scandinavian countries except Iceland, least often in Norway, most often in Sweden. Two kinds of *knittel* poems were especially popular in Sweden, romantic epic poetry based on foreign patterns (e.g., *Eufemiavisorna* and *Karl Magnus*) and rhymed chronicles (e.g., *Erikskrönikan*). A third genre involved turning prose novels into poetry (e.g., *Konung Alexander*). The *Eufemiavisorna* were translated into Danish, *Herr Ivan* into Norwegian.

In addition to the *Eufemiavisorna*, there exist three Old Danish *knittel* poems, *Dvergekongen Lavrin* ("Lavrin, the King of the Dwarfs"), *Den kyske dronning* ("The Chaste Queen"; written by Jep[pe] Jensen, presumably a monk, in 1483), and *Persenober og Konstantianobis* (written in 1483, perhaps by Jep[pe] Jensen). No immediate foreign originals of these poems are known; but they employ widespread motifs. Perhaps they were transmitted orally to their authors. *Persenober and Konstantionobis* goes back to a well-known French romance. In addition, a fragment of a poetic rendering of *Evangelium Nicodemi* in *knittel* survives from about 1325 (SKB A 115).

The genre *Rimkrönikor* ("rhymed chronicles") is represented in Denmark by a single work, *Den danske Rimkrønike*, the greatest part of which, however, is not in *knittel*.

Ed.: The Danish texts are printed in Brandt, C. J., ed. *Romantisk Digtning fra Middelalderen.* Copenhagen: Samfundet til den danske Literaturs Fremme, 1869–77 [*Dvergekongen Lavrin*, pp. 1–31; *Persenober and Konstantinobis*, pp. 33–86; *Den kyske Dronning*, pp. 87–128]. **Lit.**: Lie, Hallvard. "Knittel." *KLNM* 8 (1963), 583–6.

Gösta Holm

Knud (Cnut) the Great

Knud (Cnut) the Great was king of England (1016/7–1035), Denmark, Norway, and perhaps parts of Sweden, a son of Sven Haraldsson (Forkbeard) and grandson of Harald Gormsson (Bluetooth). His mother was a sister of King Boleslav Chrobry of Poland (only sagas name her as Sigríðr). Knud was born in the 990s and followed his father on his last conquering expedition to England in 1013, when Sven became king. Sven died on February 3, 1014, and when the English counselors (*witan*) recalled King Æthelred, Knud's forces were expelled, with no help given to either side by the mercenary fleet of Danes under Earl Þorkell. Knud's brother, Harald, had been left with the Danish throne and fortresses, and refused to share his power with Knud. Earl Þorkell was reconciled with Knud, whose fleet, strengthened by the Norwegian Earl Eiríkr of Hlaðir (Lade), numbered about 160 ships. It arrived in the summer or autumn of 1015 on the southern coast of England, where it had several encounters with the English levies. The ealdorman Eadric of Mercia rebelled and joined Knud with forty ships. In the spring, a rapid move on horseback secured Northumbria for Knud, and by the beginning of April the ships approached London. King Æthelred died in London on April 23 before the arrival of the fleet, while his son, Edmund Ironside, collected armies against Knud, partly in rebellion against his father. Æthelred's queen, Emma of Normandy, negotiated some sort of armistice with Knud for London. In the final battle of Assandun, Knud had the victory, and the peace treaty of Alney in October or November 1016 provided Knud with Mercia and huge tax revenues from all of England. Edmund was to reign over Wessex, but he died on November 30, 1016, and the English *witan* were left with no alternative but to elect Knud as king of England.

The subsequent division of England into four great earldoms suggested itself: Eiríkr already possessed Northumbia, and Eadric held Mercia; then Þorkell got East Anglia, and Knud retained Wessex. But soon there were many smaller earldoms, and King Knud and Earl Þorkell appear as two almost equally strong competitors for power, while Eadric was killed. In 1017, Knud married Emma, thus removing the Norman support for the refugee princes, Alfred and Eadward. In 1018, Danes and English made an agreement in Oxford, including a renewal of legislation in close cooperation with Archbishop Wulfstan, the famous homilist, a legislation to be elaborated upon before the mid-1020s (Liebermann, *I–II Cn*). Large gifts to churches and monasteries and the solemn transfer to Canterbury in 1023 of the remains of St. Ælfheah, slain by the Danes in London 1012, again reveal Knud's early alliance with the Church.

In 1019, Knud returned to Denmark for the winter and probably was elected king; nothing more is heard of his brother, Harald. In Norway, King Óláfr (later St. Óláfr) had assumed power, but was expelled by Knud in an expedition in 1025. Óláfr was killed on his return in 1030 (or 1028?) in the battle of Stiklestad (Stiklarstaðir) near Niðaróss (Trondheim). King Óláfr also appeared as the ally of the Göta-Swedish king Onundr (Anund) Jakob, and even if the Anglo-Danish forces had no success against the Swedes in the battle of the Helgeå (Holy River) in Skåne (Scania), some agreement seems to have secured the reign over parts of Sweden for Knud (also suggested by the coin of Sigtuna in Uppland-Sweden); he may also have had some influence in Götaland. Now Knud could appear as the equal of the German emperor Conrad and the pope, both of whom he met in Rome in Easter of 1027, securing toll reductions for English and Danish clerics traveling to Rome. Perhaps also the marriage between Knud's daughter, Gunnhild/Kunigunde, and the emperor's son, Henry, was agreed upon, possibly combined with the recognition of Danish possession of the later duchy of Sønderjylland (Schleswig).

Not much is recorded about the later years of Knud's reign. Some skirmishes with Scots and Welsh are recorded. With the tax paid in 1017, Knud was a wealthy man from the outset, able to bestow rich gifts and obtain loyal retainers. Taxation was perhaps continued, but on a much lower level. The large payments to Scandinavians and the new coinage struck by English minters in Denmark and Norway established the beginnings of monetary economy, but the political structure was fragile. Earl Þorkell was exiled from England in 1021, but he and Knud were reconciled again in 1023, now with the exchange of their sons as a pledge. Knud's son Hardacnut reigned in Denmark with his mother Queen Emma, even striking coins in his own name before Knud's death.

Knud died in Shaftesbury on November 12, 1035, and was buried in Winchester; his body was later moved to the present cathedral. Knud's empire then disintegrated. Knud's two sons by his mistress Ælfgifu of Northamptonshire, Sven and Harald, reigned in Norway and England, respectively, for a short while, and Hardacnut reigned over England for two years.

After the Norman Conquest in 1066, monastic historians of the 12th century came to assess Knud's reign along several lines. He was viewed as the last good Anglo-Saxon king, his codes were studied carefully, and his long, peaceful reign and pious acts were praised. Alternatively, the old narratives were given a further bias, with the Danes cast as an image of the oppressive Normans. In more recent times, historians have reproached Knud for the loss of an empire, but credit him with founding the Royal Navy. The use of Knud as a symbol has thus given the legends about him a more lasting life than the few known facts.

Ed.: Liebermann, F[elix], ed. *Die Gesetze der Angelsachsen.* 3 vols. Halle am Saale: Niemeyer, 1903–16. **Tr.**: Robertson, Agnes J., ed. *The Laws of the Kings of England from Edmund to Henry I.* Cambridge: The University Press, 1925; Whitelock, Dorothy, ed. *English Historical Documents c. 500–1042.* 2nd ed. London: Methuen; Oxford: Oxford University Press, 1979. **Bib.**: Stenton, F. M. *Anglo-Saxon England.* Oxford History of England, 2. 3rd ed. Oxford: Clarendon, 1971; Gransden, Antonia. *Historical Writing in England c. 550 to c. 1307.* London: Routledge & Kegan Paul, 1974; Skovgaard-Petersen, Inge. *Danmarks historie. Tiden indtil 1340.* Copenhagen: Gyldendal, 1977, vol. 1, pp. 15–209; Roesdahl, Else. *Viking Age Denmark.* Trans. Susan Margeson and Kirsten Williams. London: British Museum, 1982; Sawyer, Peter H. *Gyldendal og Politikens Danmarkshistorie. 3: Da Danmark blev Danmark. Fra ca. år 700 til ca. 1050.* Copenhagen: Gyldendal; Politiken, 1988. **Lit.**: Liebermann, F. "Wulfstan and Cnut." *Archiv für das Studium der neueren Sprachen und Literaturen* 102 (1899), 47–54; Larson, Laurence Marcellus. "The King's Household in England Before the Norman Conquest." *Bulletin of the University of Wisconsin,* no. 100, History Series, vol. 1, no. 2. Madison, 1904, pp. 55–204; Larson, L. M. "The Political Policies of Cnut as King of England." *American Historical Review* 15 (1909–10), 720–43; Larson, Laurence Marcellus. *Canute the Great 995 (circ)–1035 and the Rise of Danish Imperialism During the Viking Age.* Heroes of the Nations. New York and London: Putnam, 1912; rpt. New York: AMS, 1970 [obsolete in many respects]; Moberg, Ove. *Olav Haraldsson, Knut den store och Sverige. Studier i Olav den heliges förhållande till de nordiska grannländerne.* Lund: Gleerup; Copenhagen: Munksgaard, 1941; Rosén, Jerker. "Knut den store och ärkebiskopen av Hamburg-Bremen. Ett forsök." In *Vetenskaps-societeten i Lund, Årsbok (Yearbook of the New Society of Letters at Lund)* 1941. Lund: Gleerup, 1941, pp. 113–29; Moberg, Ove. "Två historiografiska undersökningar. 1. Knut den stores Romresa. 2. Danernes kristnande i den isländska litteraturen." *Aarbøger for nordisk Oldkyndighed og Historie* (1945), 5–45; Weibull, Lauritz. "Dråpen i Roskilde i Knut den stores och Sven Estridsens tid." In *Nordisk historia.* Stockholm: Natur och Kultur, 1948, vol. 1, pp. 375–90 [originally printed in *Historisk tidskrift för Skåneland* 4 (1910)]; Weibull, Lauritz. "Knut den stores skånska krig." In *Nordisk historia,* pp. 391–404 [originally printed in *Historisk tidskrift för Skåneland* 4 (1910)]; Whitelock, Dorothy. "Wulfstan and the Laws of Cnut." *English Historical Review* 63 (1948), 433–52; Weibull, Curt. *Källkritik och historia: Norden under äldre medeltiden.* Stockholm: Aldus, 1964 [collection of articles]; Becker, C. J. "The Coinages of Harthacnut and Magnus the Good at Lund c. 1040–c. 1046." In *Studies in Northern Coinages of the Eleventh Century.* Ed. C. J. Becker. Det Kongelige

Danske Videnskabernes Selskab, Historisk-filosofiske Skrifter, 9.4. Copenhagen: Munksgaard, 1981, pp. 119–74; Stafford, Pauline. "The Laws of Cnut and the History of Anglo-Saxon Royal Promises." *Anglo-Saxon England* 10 (1982), 173–90; Balle, Søren. "Ulf Jarl og drabet i Roskilde." In *Historisk årbog fra Roskilde amt 1983.* Roskilde: Historisk Samfund for Roskilde amt, 1983, pp. 23–59; Lawson, M. K. "The Collection of Danegeld and Heregeld in the Reigns of Aethelred II and Cnut." *English Historical Review* 99 (1984), 721–38; Poole, Russell. "Skaldic Verse and Anglo-Saxon History: Some Aspects of the Period 1009–1016." *Speculum* 62 (1987), 265–98.

Søren Balle

[See also: *Encomium Emmae*; Harald Gormsson (Bluetooth); *Knýtlinga saga*; England, Norse in; Óláfr, St.; Sven Haraldsson (Forkbeard)]

Knud (Cnut), St.,

was a Danish king, son of King Sven Estridsen (1047–1075) and an unknown mother, killed in Odense at an insurrection on July 10, 1086. His remains were first elevated from the tomb in April 1095. His cult was approved by Pope Paschal II in 1099 and solemnly inaugurated on April 19, 1100, in Odense. The examination of his relics in Odense cathedral crypt has not led to any conclusion about his age, and, since genealogical evidence is insufficient, estimates vary between about 1036 and 1054 as possible years of birth.

Knud participated in sea-raids in the Baltic (according to Saxo) and against England in 1069 (*Anglo-Saxon Chronicle*), although not as commander-in-chief. At the death of King Sven on April 28, 1074/5, Knud became a candidate for the succession, although he was not the eldest son. But his brother Harald took power, and not until Harald's death in 1080 was Knud taken for king. Leading a Viking fleet against England in 1075, he decided not to attack but turned to Flanders, where he entered into a political alliance with Count Robert I (d. 1093) and ultimately (*ca.* 1080?) married his daughter Adela. The common enemy in the alliance was William the Conquerer, who after 1066 made it increasingly difficult for Scandinavian rulers to reestablish their North Sea empire. King Knud must have realized that the Danish aim of reconquering England was an illusion, and his policy of establishing an economy based on inland resources by means of new taxes rather than war booty is to be understood from this perspective.

Another main concern was Knud's effort to secure Denmark's southern border against King Henry IV, who during Knud's reign had broken with Pope Gregory VII and established his own papacy, thereby enabling his own coronation as an emperor in Rome in 1084. By remaining on the southern border, Knud was unable to join the fleet allegedly preparing for an attack against England in northern Jutland in 1085, which in turn led to the insurrection against him and to his violent death in Odense. The rebels were aristocrats and farmers furnishing the Viking fleet (*leiðangr*).

In church matters, Knud had to balance between the schismatic pope of Henry IV and the defeated Gregory VII (d. May 1085). He openly followed the directives formulated by Gregory VII in letters to his brother King Harald in 1077–1080 (DD 1,2 Nr. 17–20) in securing better economic conditions for the clergy by means of taxation and donations, such as the one to the cathedral in Lund, May 21, 1085 (DD 1,2 Nr. 21). He also introduced social improvements for the poor, liberated slaves, women, and foreigners (Breengaard 1982). The inevitable trend toward royal autocratic government and at the same time the insufficiency of its administrative personnel gave birth to the decisive dissatisfaction among the landowning groups of society.

St. Knud had furnished the church in Odense with relics of St. Alban and St. Oswald (brought home in 1075?) and inaugurated the construction of the Romanesque cathedral that was later dedicated to him and served from around 1095 by Benedictines from Evesham. As a saint, Knud was the uniting force behind the diocese of Odense, comprising all islands between Jutland, Scania, and the German coast except Zealand, Møn, and Rügen.

Knud's biography was written around 1122 by Ælnoth, one of the English monks in Odense; his liturgical office must have been created by the English monks, taking its inspiration from the cult of English royal saints (Hoffmann 1975). In the 13th century, the cult was limited to Odense diocese and Lund, while St. Knud Lavard (d. 1131), the father of King Valdemar I (1157–1182), became the patron saint of Zealand. From around 1400, by analogy to Norway's and Sweden's royal saints, St. Knud of Odense took preeminence under the inspiration of the Scandinavian Union of Kalmar (1397–1520). His relics were walled in during the centuries of Lutheran orthodoxy and restored together with the crypt in the 19th century.

Ed.: (a) *Passio S. Canuti* and *Gesta* by *Ælnoth*: Sollerius, Joannes B., ed. *Acta Sanctorum, Iulii.* Antwerp: Moulin, 1723, vol. 3, pp. 121–43; Langebek, Jakob, ed. *Scriptores Rerum Danicarum Medii Aevi* 3. Copenhagen: Godiche, 1774, pp. 325–90; Gertz M. Cl., ed. *Vitae Sanctorum Danorum.* Copenhagen: Gad, 1908–12, pp. 27–166. (b) *Knýtlinga saga*: Bjarni Guðnason, ed. *Danakonunga sǫgur.* Íslenzk fornrit, 35. Reykjavík: Hið íslenzka fornritafélag, 1982, pp. 91–321. Tr.: Hermann Pálsson and Paul Edwards, trans. *Knýtlinga saga: The History of the Kings of Denmark.* Odense: Odense University Press, 1986. Bib.: Oxenvad, Niels, *et al.*, eds. *Knuds-bogen 1986: Studier over Knud den Hellige.* Fynske Studier, 15. Odense: Odense Bys Museer, 1986, pp. 181–90. Lit.: Hoffmann, Erich. "Knut der Heilige und die Wende der dänischen Geschichte im 11. Jahrhundert." *Historische Zeitschrift* 218 (1974), 529–70; Hoffmann, Erich. *Die heiligen Könige bei den Angelsachsen und den skandinavischen Völkern. Königsheiliger und Königshaus.* Quellen und Forschungen zur Geschichte Schleswig-Holsteins, 69. Neumünster: Wachholtz, 1975, pp. 89–139; Breengaard, Carsten. *Muren om Israels hus. Regnum og sacerdotium i Danmark 1050–1170.* Copenhagen: Gad, 1982, pp. 108–80, 328–33; Nyberg, Tore. "König Knut der Heilige, Teuzo und der Peterspfennig aus Dänemark." *Archivum historiae pontificiae* 23 (1985), 359–65.

Tore Nyberg

[See also: England, Norse in; *Knýtlinga saga*; Miracles, Collections of; Liturgy and Liturgical Texts; Saints' Lives]

Knútsdrápa see Óttarr svarti; Sighvatr Þórðarson

Knýtlinga saga

("The Saga of the Knýtlingar") is an Icelandic compilation about the Danish kings from the 10th century to 1187. The name *Knýtlinga saga* is found in Árni Magnússon's copy from around 1700 of a parchment codex from around 1300, but is probably not a medieval title. The text is transmitted in two recensions; A is complete, B truncated, beginning with the reign of Sveinn Úlfsson (Sven Estridsen). To the A-group belong the lost parchment from around 1300 (and numerous paper copies, all deriving from Árni Magnússon's copy) plus fragments of another parchment MS. The B-group encompasses a parchment codex from the 15th century, sixteen paper copies, and three fragments of another parchment MS.

Knýtlinga saga provides important historical information about the expansion of the Danish empire to include parts of England and Wendland (eastern Germany), while Danish-Norwegian hostilities receive less attention. Of the fifty-nine skaldic stanzas in this saga, fifty are transmitted nowhere else; the saga thus stands as an important repository for Old Norse poetry. *Knýtlinga saga* is to a large extent based on lost works, many of which were employed as sources elsewhere. Like *Heimskringla*, *Knýtlinga saga* used the *Konunga ævi* ("life history of kings") by Ari Þorgilsson, *Jómsvíkinga saga*, and an *Óláfs saga helga*, which is thought to be by Styrmir Kárason. Through this last work, or directly, *Knýtlinga saga* quotes a detailed saga with many skaldic stanzas about Knud (Cnut) the Great's conquest of England. Moreover, *Knýtlinga saga* mentions sagas about the Norwegian kings Magnús góði ("the good") Óláfsson (d. 1047) and Haraldr harðráði ("hard-ruler") Sigurðarson (d. 1066), and for the 12th century an *Ævi Nóregskonunga* ("life history of the kings of Norway"), possibly Eiríkr Oddsson's *Hryggjarstykki* and some *Sǫgur Nóregskonunga* ("sagas of the kings of Norway"). Since *Knýtlinga saga* makes independent use of *Heimkringla*'s older sources, the question of whether it also used *Heimskringla* itself remains open. The account of Erik Ejegod ("ever-good"; r. 1095–1103) is based on Markús Skeggjason's poem *Eiríksdrápa*. For the period 1134–1187, a translation of a 12th-century chronicle is quoted; known also by Saxo Grammaticus and by younger annalists, this chronicle distinguishes itself in *Knýtlinga saga* by its exact relative chronology, by its thorough knowledge of the persons and place-names of the period, and by its independent political attitude, which is different from that of Saxo in his *Gesta Danorum*, but characteristic of Denmark during the last half of the 12th century.

While half of *Knýtlinga saga* is compiled on the basis of older works, a younger, well-composed saga of the king St. Knud (Cnut; r. 1080–1086) constitutes the central part of the work. With the hagiographer's knowledge of Snorri's *Óláfs saga helga* and a number of Danish works (Ælnoth's *Gesta Swenomagni regis et filiorum ejus*, the Danish source of Radulfus Niger's *Chronicon universale*, popular legends from eastern Denmark, and a Danish catalogue of ships [*Knýtlinga saga*, ch. 32]), a charming and highly integrated account of St. Knud's life and canonization is given. The saga distinguishes itself by its excellent narrative technique and its fine treatment of discourse, which both characterize the persons and carry the action forward. This long, well-composed work is followed by a short saga with a looser structure about another Danish saint, the duke Knud Lavard, and his parents. These two sagas are written in a more "courtly" style and bear a close linguistic and ideological resemblance to *Laxdœla saga*.

The individual kings' biographies are tied together by a chronological framework common to *Knýtlinga saga* and the so-called *Ágrip af sǫgu Danakonunga* ("Summary of the History of the Kings of Denmark") and based on Ari Þorgilsson's work supplemented with Danish records. Among *Knýtlinga saga*'s many genealogical notes, the youngest mentions the wedding of a Swedish descendant from the Danish royal house and the Norwegian king Hákon ungi ("the young") in 1251. The politically important wedding of the Norwegian king Magnús lagabœtir ("law-mender") Hákonarson (Hákon ungi's brother) and the Danish princess Ingiborg in 1261 is not mentioned and was probably not known

to the compiler. The cautious treatment of Danish-Norwegian controversies places *Knýtlinga saga* in the period after 1257, when a treaty created a precarious peace between the two countries after generations of conflict. Scholars traditionally maintain that *Knýtlinga saga* was composed in imitation of *Heimskringla*, with St. Knud seen as the equivalent of St. Óláfr. Hallberg (1963) suggests that the author of the entire saga was Óláfr Þórðarson hvítaskáld ("white-skald"; d. 1259), Snorri Sturluson's nephew and brother of Sturla Þórðarson, although this view has been contested.

Ed.: Petersen, Carl, and Emil Olson, eds. *Sǫgur Danakonunga. 1: Sǫgubrot af fornkonungum. 2: Knytlinga saga.* Samfund til udgivelse af gammel nordisk litteratur, 46. Copenhagen: Ohlsson, 1919–25, pp. 29–294 [standard critical edition]; Bjarni Guðnason, ed. *Danakonunga sǫgur.* Íslenzk fornrit, 35. Reykjavik: Hið íslenzka fornritafélag, 1982, pp. 91–321 [edition with extensive commentaries in modern Icelandic and with bibliographical notes]. **Tr.**: Hermann Pálsson and Paul Edwards, trans. *Knytlinga saga: The History of the Kings of Denmark.* Odense: Odense University Press, 1986. **Lit.**: Finnur Jónsson. "Knytlingasaga, dens Kilder og historiske Værd." *Det Kongelige Danske Videnskabernes Selskabs Skrifter* 6 Rk. Hist. Phil. Afd. 6, nr. 1 (1900), 1–41; Weibull, Curt. "Saxo." *Historisk tidskrift för Skåneland* 6 (1915), 179–236; Moberg, Ove. "Två historiografiska undersökningar. 1. Knut den stores Romresa." *Aarbøger for nordisk Oldkyndighed og Historie* (1945), 5–25; Albeck, Gustav. *Knytlinga, Sagaerne om Danmarks Konger.* Copenhagen: Nyt Nordisk forlag, 1946; Campbell, Alistair. "Knúts Saga." *Saga-Book of the Viking Society* 13 (1946–53), 238–48; Hallberg, Peter. *Óláfr Þórðarson hvítaskáld, Knýtlinga saga och Laxdæla saga. Ett försök till språklig författarbestämning.* Studia Islandica, 22. Reykjavik: Heimspekideild Háskóla Íslands; Menningarsjóður, 1963; Ellehøj, Svend. "Omkring Knýtlingas kilder." In *Middelalderstudier tilegnede Aksel E. Christensen.* Ed. Tage E. Christiansen et al. Copenhagen: Munksgaard, 1966, pp. 39–56; Heller, Rolf. "Knytlinga saga: Bemerkungen zur Entstehungsgeschichte des Werkes." *Arkiv för nordisk filologi* 82 (1967), 155–74; Bjarni Guðnason. "Aldur og uppruni Knúts sögu helga." In *Minjar og menntir: Afmælisrit helgað Kristjáni Eldjárn.* Ed. Guðni Kolbeinsson et al. Reykjavik: Menningarsjóður, 1976, pp. 55–77; Weibull, Curt. "Knytlingasagan och Saxo: En källkritisk undersökning." *Scandia* 42 (1976), 5–31; Malmros, Rikke. "Blodgildet i Roskilde historiografisk belyst: Knytlingesagas forhold til det tolvte århundredes danske historieskrivning." *Scandia* 45 (1979), 43–66; Heller, Rolf. "*Knýtlinga saga* und *Laxdœla saga*: Schöpfungen *eines* Mannes?" *Mediaeval Scandinavia* 11 (1978–79), 163–78; Hallberg, Peter. "Ja, *Knýtlinga saga* und *Laxdœla saga* sind Schöpfungen *eines* Mannes." *Mediaeval Scandinavia* 11 (1978–79), 179–92; Bjarni Einarsson. "On the 'Blóð-Egill' Episode in *Knýtlinga saga*." In *Sagnaskemmtun: Studies in Honour of Hermann Pálsson on His 65th Birthday, 26th May 1986.* Ed. Rudolf Simek et al. Vienna, Cologne, and Graz: Böhlau, 1986, pp. 41–7.

Rikke Malmros

[See also: *Ágrip af sǫgu Danakonunga*; England, Norse in; *Heimskringla*; *Jómsvíkinga saga*; Knud (Cnut) the Great; Knud (Cnut), St.; *Konungasögur*; *Laxdœla saga*; *Óláfs saga helga*; Óttarr svarti; Saxo Grammaticus]

Kong Solomons Hylding *see* Drama

Konráðs saga keisarasonar ("The Saga of Konráðr, Son of an Emperor") is a fine specimen of an early indigenous *riddarasaga*

that combines elements from native tradition with newer and more fashionable ones from the Continent. Presumably composed by an Icelandic cleric in the early 14th century, sometime after *Ívens saga* had been adapted from the French, the saga exists in two main redactions, an older one represented by Stock. Perg. 4to no. 7 (*ca.* 1350) and Stock. Perg. fol. no. 7 (*ca.* 1460), and a somewhat reduced later version, from which description and dialogue have been pared away, respresented by Stock. Perg. 4to no. 6 (*ca.* 1400), the only vellum MS providing a full text of the saga. In all, forty-eight MSS of the saga are extant as well as eight sets of *rímur*, or rhyming ballads (ranging from the 16th to the 19th centuries), and a 15th-century Faroese poem, *Koralds kvæði*, that are based on its story line.

Konráðr is sent by his father, the emperor of Saxland, to the learned Earl Róðgeirr for instruction. Konráðr excels in deeds requiring agility and strength, surpassing in these even the earl's own son, his foster-brother Róðbert, who, seeing himself outdone, devotes himself instead to the study of foreign languages, at which he becomes quite adept. When Konráðr returns home, his father advises him not to depend on the knowledge of others but to rely on himself. The advice, as matters turn out, goes unheeded. After Konráðr's sister is made pregnant by Róðbert, Konráðr, having won clemency from his enraged father for Róðbert, sails with the latter to Constantinople. On their arrival, Konráðr, ignorant as he is of Greek, blindly enters into a name and role exchange with Róðbert ostensibly to open communication with the Greek emperor. Róðbert, however, utilizes his command of Greek and the false identity to further his own sinister ends and bring about Konráðr's downfall. He tells the jealous monarch that Konráðr is a potential seducer of his daughter Mathilda, and as such should be disposed of. A series of perilous trials, each more severe than the one preceding, is imposed upon Konráðr. However, Mathilda recognizes Róðbert for what he really is, and provides Konráðr with warning counsel. When Konráðr visits her, the two are able to converse in a third language found in a compendium, and Konráðr is able to reestablish his princely identity, proclaim it subsequently at a public assembly, and prove it beyond all doubt by successfully accomplishing an impossible task, the bringing back from a serpent-infested land of a particular green gem. His prize is none other than Mathilda, whom he foolishly had allowed his proxy Róðbert to woo.

The entertaining quality of the saga derives largely from the succession of ever more frightening situations that Konráðr faces. The dominant thematic note struck in the saga is not that ignorance of foreign languages is the basic fault, but that naiveté and blindness toward life, as exemplified in Konráðr's actions, inevitably lead, unless corrected, to great peril. While the hero can speak to his father at length of the purposefulness of life as part of a grand celestial design, his own activity as demonstrated by his various "circus acts" is purposeless and for a considerable length of time given over to sporting and self-gratification. The relinquishing of personal identity to Róðbert marks the culmination of Konráðr's self-contained unawareness of life. It is not until he visits Mathilda on his own initiative and listens to her sage counsel that he embarks on meaningful activity from which, at the end, he can emerge triumphantly.

Ed.: **(a)** Gunnlaugur Þórðarson, ed. *Konráðs saga keisarasonar, er fór til Ormalands.* Copenhagen: Páll Sveinsson, 1859 [normalized text based on AM 179 fol., a 17th-century paper copy of Stock. Perg. 4to no. 6]; Cederschiöld, Gustaf, ed. "Konráðs saga." In *Fornsögur Suðrlanda.*

Magus saga jarls, Konraðs saga, Bærings saga, Flovents saga, Bevers saga. Med inledning. Lund: Berling, 1884, pp. 43–84 [eclectic text, largely based on Stock. Perg. 4to no. 7]; Zitzelsberger, Otto J., ed. *Konráðs saga keisarasonar.* New York and Bern: Lang, 1988 [diplomatic texts of Stock. Perg. 4to no. 7 and Stock. Perg. fol. no. 7 given on split page; diplomatic text of Stock. 6 4to given separately]. **(b)** Wisén, Theodor, ed. "Konráðs Rímur." In *Riddara-rímur.* Copenhagen: Berling, 1881, pp. 91–171; Matras, Christian, ed. "Konráðs kveai." In *Svabos Færøske Visehaandskrifter.* Copenhagen: Luno, 1938, pp. 334–43. **Tr.**: Zitzelsberger, Otto J., trans. "Konráðs saga keisarasonar." *Seminar for Germanic Philology: Yearbook* 3 (1980), 38–67 [based on Cederschiöld's text]. **Bib.**: Kalinke, Marianne E., and P. M. Mitchell. *Bibliography of Old Norse–Icelandic Romances.* Islandica, 44. Ithaca and London: Cornell University Press, 1985, pp. 75–7 [entries to 1981]. **Lit.**: Zitzelsberger, Otto J. "Six MSS of *Konráðs saga* Unlisted in Printed Catalogues." *Amsterdamer Beiträge zur älteren Germanistik* 18 (1982), 161–77 [description of MSS not mentioned in an earlier article]; Kalinke, Marianne E. "The Foreign Language Requirement in Medieval Icelandic Romance." *Modern Language Review* 78 (1983), 850–61.

Otto J. Zitzelsberger

[See also: Old Norse–Icelandic Literature, Foreign Influence on; *Riddarasögur; Rímur*]

Konung Alexander

Konung Alexander ("King Alexander") is an Old Swedish epic poem about the life and deeds of King Alexander the Great of Macedonia (d. 323 B.C.). The text is preserved in a single MS, Cod. Stock. D 4, a product of the famous monastery at Vadstena, written by five different hands over a long period of time. The part containing *Konung Alexander* was probably written down about 1415. Three leaves of the text are missing.

The poem was composed about 1380. The epilogue states that it was translated from Latin on behalf of the *riksdrots* (*i.e.*, the highest royal official) Bo Jonsson Grip, Sweden's richest and most powerful nobleman at the time. The Latin original was one of the recensions of *Historia de preliis*, a group of various interpolated and modified versions of archipresbyter Leo's *Nativitas et victoria Alexandri Magni*. Closely related to the lost MS used for *Konung Alexander* is no. 14169 in the Bibliothèque Nationale in Paris. The translator-author of *Konung Alexander* is unknown; he was certainly a learned man and a skillful latinist. Probably, he belonged to the retinue of Bo Jonsson Grip.

The Alexander novel was popular throughout Europe, perhaps because it overflows with tales of heroic deeds, battles, buried treasures, and exotic creatures.

The meter of *Konung Alexander* is the common medieval epic *knittel*. The *knittel* of *Konung Alexander* is influenced by *Eufemiavisorna* (and *Erikskrönikan*) both as far as rhyming, metrical padding, reiterations, and hyperboles are concerned. The rhymes of *Konung Alexander*, however, are more often incongruent than those of the forerunners (*e.g.*, *thørst* 'thirst' rhyming with *fisk* 'fish'; *wægh* 'way' with *gladh* 'merry'; *hugh* 'mind' with *op* 'up'). Some of the incongruent rhymes in the MS may be due to copying errors or simply to conscious alternations of copyists speaking a different dialect or using younger forms.

The author of *Konung Alexander* has been called "one of the few real author personalities of medieval Sweden." His style is praised as strong and visual, personal and often acrid, spiced with proverbs and concrete metaphors. The vocabulary contains many unique words, such as *enbændin* 'stubborn,' *halfgrat* 'somewhat unfriendly,' *swepil* 'swaddling clothes.' Many of the uncommon words are borrowed from Low German. By comparing the language of *Konung Alexander*, especially the vocabulary, with modern dialect conditions, one can maintain with some certainty that the translator-author had grown up in some part of eastern Götaland.

Ed.: Ahlstrand, J. E. [on the title page wrongly: G. E. Klemming], ed. *Konung Alexander. En medeltidsdikt från latinet vänd i svenska rim omkring år 1380 på föranstaltande af rikdrotset Bo Jonsson Grip.* Samlingar utgifna af Svenska fornskrift-sällskapet, 12. Stockholm: Norstedt, 1855–62 [corrections of errors and additions are given by Ronge 1957: 74–85]; Noreen, Erik, ed. *Ur Konung Alexander.* In *Fornsvensk läsebok.* 2nd rev. ed. Sven Benson. Malmö: Gleerup, 1954, pp. 84–9 [107 lines]. Lit.: Bure, Nils. *Rytmiska studier öfver knittelversen i medeltidens svenska rimverk.* Lunds Universitets Årsskrift, 34, afd. 1, nr. 6. Lund: Malmström, 1898; James, M. R. *The Romance of Alexander: A Collotype Facsimile of Ms. Bodley 264.* Oxford: Clarendon, 1933. Cary, George. *The Medieval Alexander.* Ed. D. J. A. Ross. Cambridge: Cambridge University Press, 1956; Ronge, Hans H. *Konung Alexander. Filologiska studier i en fornsvensk text.* Skrifter utgivna af Institutionen för nordiska språk vid Uppsala universitet, 3. Stockholm: Almqvist & Wiksell, 1957; Holm, Gösta. "Några problem i Alexanderforskningen." *Arkiv för nordisk filologi* 73 (1958), 210–44; Ronge, Hans H. *Rimlista till Konung Alexander.* Acta Universitatis Upsaliensis, Studia Philologiae Scandinavicae Upsaliensia, 4. Stockholm: Almqvist & Wiksell, 1964; Bergmeister, Hermann-Josef, ed. *Die Historia de preliis Alexandri Magni.* (Der lateinische Alexanderroman des Mittelalters): synoptische Edition der Rezensionen des Leo Archipresbyter und der interpolierten Fassungen J¹, J², J³ (Buch I und II). Beiträge zur klassischen Philologie, 65. Meisenheim am Glam: Hain, 1975.

Gösta Holm

[See also: Chronicles; *Eufemiavisorna*; *Knittel(vers)*; Vadstena]

Konungastyrelsen.

Um styrilsi kununga ok höfdhinga, or *Konungastyrelsen* ("The Royal Rule"), as the work is commonly known, is Sweden's contribution to the *Speculum regale* literature, which was so widespread and popular in the Middle Ages. It contains no explicit information as to when, by whom, or for whom it was written. The unknown author's main source and model was Aegidius Romanus's politico-pedagogical treatise *De regimine principum* (ca. 1280); a number of other writers, named and unnamed, also left their mark in his work. *Konungastyrelsen* is a compilation and can in a sense be considered part of the literature of translation. The Swedish compiler, however, shows what for medieval times is a remarkable independence in relation to his sources, and his prose style is of the very highest order.

Konungastyrelsen comprises four chapters. The first discusses rule by one versus rule by many, and hereditary versus elective monarchy. Arguments on both sides are set forth in the familiar manner of scholasticism. The author plainly endorses royal rule by one; to him, rule by many is the same thing as rule by the nobility. He also argues for hereditary monarchy, which is remarkable in view of the fact that the kings of medieval Sweden were elected. The remaining chapters give instructions on how a king should live and act in accordance with wisdom and moral principles; how he should organize his immediate surroundings, his court, and his servants; and how he should govern his country and his people. The overriding principle is that royal government should be to the credit of the king and to the benefit of the people.

The style of *Konungastyrelsen*, in its basic structure, is one of fullness and breadth, with a predominance of parallel expressions (pairs of synonyms or near-synonyms) and other redundant features. Ultimately, this style goes back to classical rhetoric. At the same time, it is simple and clear. The author has almost entirely managed to avoid the distracting latinisms, intricate periods, and constructions alien to Swedish generally, which are so common in Old Swedish translated prose. The text is larded with numerous proverbs and other sententious sayings.

Konungastyrelsen, in its entirety, is known only through a printed edition from 1634, based on a MS that shortly afterward disappeared without a trace. The MS was probably transcribed in the mid-15th century. All that is left of *Konungastyrelsen* in medieval MSS is a short fragment that can be dated to approximately 1440; it had not been part of the lost MS used for the printed edition of 1634. The original was at least a century older. With the help of its language and certain statements in the work, it can be deduced that *Konungastyrelsen* was composed at roughly the same time as the national law code, *i.e.*, in the 1340s. The work may have been intended for Magnus Eriksson's sons, Erik and Hákon. In 1344, the former, then five years old, was appointed successor to the Swedish throne. A possible candidate for authorship is perhaps St. Birgitta's confessor, Magister Mathias, the foremost Swedish theologian of the Middle Ages. However, we are here on very precarious ground.

Ed.: Klemming, G. E., and Robert Geete, eds. *Småstycken på forn svenska.* 2 vols. Stockholm: Norstedt, 1868–81; Geete, Robert, ed. *Um Styrilsi Kununga ok Höfþinga. Normaliserad upplaga.* Stockholm: Norstedt, 1878; Bure, Johan [Bureus, Johannes]. *En nyttigh Bok om Konunga Styrilse och Höfdinga.* Ed. Lennart Moberg. Samlingar utgivna af Svenska fornskrift-sällskapet, 235. Uppsala: Almqvist & Wiksell, 1964 [facsimile of 1634 edition]. Lit.: Söderwall, K. F. *Studier öfver Konunga-Styrelsen.* Lunds universitets årsskrift. Lund: Berling, 1880; Schück, Henrik. "Konungastyrelsens författare." *Samlaren* 29 (1909), 45–55; Lönnroth, Erik. *Sverige och Kalmar-unionen, 1397–1457.* Gothenburg: Elander, 1934; Svanberg, Nils. "Konungastyrelsen. En stilkarakteristik." *Nysvenska studier* 18 (1938), 190–209; Ståhle, Carl Ivar. "Medeltidens profana litteratur." In *Ny illustrerad svensk litteraturhistoria.* Ed. E. N. Tigerstedt. 2nd ed. Stockholm: Natur och Kultur, 1967, pp. 37–124; Moberg, Lennart. "Några anteckningar till ordspråken i Konungastyrelsen." In *Nordiska studier i filologi och lingvistik. Festskrift tillägnad Gösta Holm.* Ed. Lars Svensson et al. Lund: Studentlitteratur, 1976, pp. 302–9; Drar, Kristin. *Konungens herravälde såsom rättvisans, fridens och frihetens beskydd.* Bibliotheca historico-ecclesiastica Lundensis, 10. Stockholm: Almqvist & Wiksell, 1980; Moberg, Lennart. *Konungastyrelsen: En filologisk undersökning.* Samlingar utgivna av Svenska fornskrift-sällskapet, 69:2. Uppsala: Almqvist & Wiksell, 1984 [English summary].

Lennart Moberg

[See also: *Konungs skuggsjá*]

Konungasögur

("kings' sagas") is the term used for a category of Old Norse sagas distinguished specifically by subject matter, namely the life stories of Scandinavian royalty. *Konungasögur* concern especially the Viking Age and medieval kings of Norway from the 9th to the 13th centuries, and also the kings of Denmark from roughly the same period, and, by extension, the earls of Orkney. The kings of Sweden appear incidentally in these works, but no tales were written about them in particular, save *Ynglinga saga*, which derives the Norwegian ruling line from prehistoric

Swedish kings. The literary form is almost exclusively Icelandic, and royal biography was seminal in the development of the entire saga genre. The texts represent basically the codification in 12th- and 13th-century Iceland of historical traditions concerning non-Icelandic happenings, with Icelandic events appearing chiefly as digressions. A few works were composed in Latin and then translated into Old Norse, but most were vernacular compositions. The texts range from accounts of individual regents to collections of life stories covering several generations of rulers, from speculations concerning the mythical beginnings of prehistoric Scandinavian royal lines to presentations of contemporary sovereigns based in part on documentary material, and from works preserved in many MSS to fragments, lost texts, and hypothetical constructions. In contrast to many other types of sagas, especially the anonymous Íslendingasögur, the authors are often named.

Although konungasögur can be defined literally and delimited narrowly, the definition is often broadened to include some other closely related writings. The term encompasses, in addition, saga accounts of the Norse colonies in the North Atlantic, specifically the Orkneys and the Faroes, tales of the half-legendary Baltic warrior community of the Jómsvíkingar, and chronicles in the medieval Latin historical tradition. One could also include the non-saga presentations of early Icelandic history and genealogies, and perhaps even the stories about the discovery and settlement of Greenland and Vinland, although the latter are probably better classified as Íslendingasögur.

Research into this material centers mainly on philological questions concerning genesis and development, and on the complex textual relationships among various works. This is true especially when the same story is told several times, such as in the various recountings of the reign of a particular sovereign. In spite of reservations as to their reliability, these sagas still provide the basis of any historical speculation about the period.

Beginnings of historical writing (1120–1190). Historical writing in Iceland, which was among the first types of literature practiced there, began in the early 1100s. Around 1130, Ari Þorgilsson (1067/8–1148) composed a short epitome of Icelandic history called Íslendingabók, which deals with events from the beginning of the Scandinavian settlement around 870 down to Ari's own day, with an emphasis on ecclesiastical concerns. According to the prologue, the preserved work is a second edition and apparently omits the genealogy (*ættartala) and kings' lives (*konunga ævi) of the previous version. The lost genealogies may be the earliest form of Landnámabók, a topographical account of the colonization that includes the ancestral lines of the first settlers. The lost kings' lives probably dealt with the rulers of Norway from the time of Haraldr hárfagri ("fair-hair"), contemporary with the settlement of Iceland, down to Sigurðr Jórsalafari ("crusader"; d. 1130). According to the poem Nóregs konunga tal, Ari's somewhat older contemporary Sæmundr Sigfússon (1056–1133) also wrote a now-lost history of the Norwegian kings from Haraldr hárfagri to Magnús góði ("the good"; d. 1047). Since Snorri Sturluson in his prologues to the Separate Óláfs saga helga and to Heimskringla states that Ari was the first to write history in the vernacular, it is assumed that Sæmundr wrote in Latin. Later references indicate the authority these two pioneers represented for subsequent medieval historical authors, but it has proven difficult to evaluate the extent and nature of their lost works. A main achievement was the establishment of a chronological framework for early history. In addition, they collected historical lore and

placed it within this framework, at the same time setting examples for the critical evaluation of material. Both Sæmundr and Ari earned the byname fróði ("learned," especially in historical lore), and this stage of writing has been termed the period of the "learned men."

The recording of political history in Norway began about half a century later and represented more directly the tradition of medieval European Latin chronicles. The Norwegian historical works from around 1170–1190, which are sometimes referred to as the "Norwegian synoptics," include the anonymous Historia Norwegiae, the Historia de antiquitate regum Norwagiensium by the unidentified monk Theodoricus, and the so-called Ágrip af Nóregs konunga sǫgum. Ágrip ("summary"), a 19th-century misnomer based on the idea that the work was a compendium of individual sagas about each of the kings, is defective initially and toward the end, and exists only in an Icelandic copy of a Norwegian original. Like Theodoricus's work, it probably began with Haraldr hárfagri, but whereas Theodoricus stopped in 1130, as did Ari, Ágrip apparently continued until the arrival of Sverrir Sigurðarson in Norway in 1177. The Historia Norwegiae, which also reviews the legendary kings of Scandinavian prehistory, breaks off defective with Óláfr Haraldsson's arrival in Norway in 1015. Ágrip is partially a translation or paraphrase of Theodoricus's text and of the Historia Norwegiae (or of a Latin source common to the two of them), but is more saga-like in tone. Among its vernacular innovations is the inclusion of skaldic verse. The interrelationships of the "Norwegian synoptics," and their possible dependence on the lost works by Ari and Sæmundr, are debated. The significance of the later question is whether the Norwegian historical tradition is independent of the Icelandic or simply derivative. Theodoricus acknowledges Icelandic historical traditions, but also refers to a lost, probably Norwegian *Catalogus regum Norwagiensium.

While authors in Norway were mainly adapting the genre of European chronicle to native material, the saga genre itself developed in Iceland. The first saga may well have been Eiríkr Oddsson's *Hryggjarstykki (literally "back-piece," maybe "[single] piece of calfskin"), composed sometime around the mid-12th century. The work is lost, but was used as a source in 13th-century compendia of Norwegian history (Heimskringla, Morkinskinna, and Fagrskinna). References indicate that the work covered at any rate the initial period of the Norwegian civil wars encompassing the strife in 1130–1139 among the sons and grandsons of Sigurðr Jórsalafari, and it may have continued until 1161. Recent scholarship (Bjarni Guðnason 1978), however, views the work as a life history of Sigurðr slembir ("sham deacon"), especially from 1136 when he killed King Haraldr gilli ("Gilchrist") until he was killed himself by Haraldr's sons in 1139. The work apparently combined secular and hagiographic elements, and presented Sigurðr slembir's death as a martyrdom.

Latin hagiographic writing had been practiced since the 11th century in both Norway and Iceland, and foremost among the native saints whose history had been put on parchment was St. Óláfr. An early vita is lost, but one from the mid-12th century is preserved in vernacular translation, followed by a collection of miracles, in the Old Norwegian Book of Homilies, and also as a source for a shorter and a longer Latin account by Archbishop Eysteinn Erlendsson (d. 1188) of the saint's life, death, and miracles. A Latin life story of St. Magnús of the Orkneys (d. 1115), *Vita sancti Magni, which was written in conjunction with his canonization around 1135 by a Master Robert, may have served both as a source and a model for Eiríkr Oddsson's *Hryggjarstykki, especially in the presentation of the martyrdom. Pieces of the *vita* are preserved in vernacular translation in particular in the longer version from about 1300 of *Magnúss saga eyjajarls*.

In the mid-1180s, a priest turned king in Norway, Sverrir Sigurðarson (r. 1177/84–1202), took a sometime Icelandic abbot of the monastery at Þingeyrar who was visiting Norway, Karl Jónsson, into his service as the author of the tale of his early years as a pretender to the throne. The king directed the composition himself. The resultant text, *Grýla* ("bug-bear"), no longer exists as a separate work, but comprises the first part of the entire saga of the king, *Sverris saga*. Among other things, it includes dreams, premonitions, and dramatic scenes with direct discourse. From the early 1190s comes the *Historia de profectione Danorum in Hierosolymam*, a Latin recounting of contemporary preparations for a crusade undertaken mainly by Danes who traveled via Norway and had an audience with King Sverrir. This work was probably written by a Norwegian monk living in Denmark at the time.

Formative period (1190–1220). The three main roots of *konungasaga* composition were compact Latin chronicles covering long periods of time, brief Latin legends of individual saints, and vernacular and Latin accounts of relatively contemporary history covering short periods of time. The confluence of secular royal biography, religious saints' lives, and recountings of contemporary events are obvious in, for example, **Hryggjarstykki*. The sources from which Old Norse historians had to draw their material were many and varied. Ari had trustworthy informants, some of whose firsthand knowledge went back to the period of the Conversion around 1000, and in the prologue to *Sverris saga* and also in Snorri's prologues to the Separate *Óláfs saga helga* and to *Heimskringla*, the value of eyewitness accounts is stressed. Snorri emphasizes the traditions from Ari, and also the value of skaldic poetry. These poems, whose stylistic and metrical intricacies facilitated their preservation during the period of oral transmission, were often cited as confirmation of events. Skaldic strophes were perhaps transmitted with accompanying prose describing in more detail the happenings referred to, and this prose could lie behind the relation of events recorded in the poems. Oral tradition is otherwise not often mentioned, but must have been important. In addition, motifs and descriptions were borrowed from other literature, both native and foreign.

Part of the formative period of *konungasaga* composition is connected with the Benedictine monastery at Þingeyrar in northern Iceland. Abbot Karl Jónsson (d. 1212/3), who wrote about the first years of Sverrir's reign, may have collected additional material about the king and may have been the author of the entire *Sverris saga*. During the last decade or so of the 12th century, two monks at the monastery composed Latin biographies of Óláfr Tryggvason (r. 995–1000), the king of Norway whom the Icelanders viewed as being responsible for the conversion of Iceland and therefore held in esteem in much the same way the Norwegians revered St. Óláfr. The texts were translated into Old Norse, and three different MSS exist of Oddr Snorrason's *Óláfs saga Tryggvasonar*. Gunnlaugr Leifsson's work, probably a revision and expansion of Oddr's text, is preserved only as incorporated in a 14th-century compilation about the king.

Various saga accounts of St. Óláfr (r. 1015–1028) survive from this formative period. The earliest known one, preserved in only six MS fragments, was dubbed the Oldest *Óláfs saga helga* and may well date to around 1200. A later revised and augmented version of this text is found in the so-called Legendary *Óláfs saga helga*, preserved in a MS from central Norway (Trøndelag) dated

to about 1250. Among other things, a legendary section with miracles has been added, hence the modern name. Styrmir Kárason (d. 1245), prior of the Augustinian house of Viðey, composed a *lífssaga* ("biography") of St. Óláfr certainly before 1230 and based on the Oldest *Óláfs saga helga*. Pieces of his work survive only as excerpts quoted in an appendix to *Óláfs saga helga* in *Flateyjarbók*, but it is also believed to have been Snorri Sturluson's chief source for his saga of the saint. Styrmir's work was apparently somewhat hagiographic in tone, presenting Óláfr as a holy man who already worked miracles in his youth.

Icelanders composed not only royal biographies, but also provincial or regional histories during the first two decades of the 13th century. These include: (1) the compilation *Orkneyinga saga*, a record of the earls of Orkney from the time of Haraldr hárfagri down to around 1170 (accounts of individual events were likely written down as early as the late 12th century); (2) *Færeyinga saga*, about happenings in the Faroe Islands, especially a powerful and wily local chieftain's political dealings there in the years shortly before and after 1000 (the work is in many ways more like an *Íslendingasaga* than a *konungasaga*); (3) *Jómsvíkinga saga*, the tale of the semi-legendary adventures of heroes from a warrior community in the Baltic with connections to the Danish rulers, whose exploits culminate in their dashing defeat at the battle of Hjǫrungavágr (ca. 980) against Earl Hákon ríki ("the mighty") of Norway and thus impinge on Norwegian history (this work has much in common with *fornaldarsögur*); (4) the lost **Skjǫldunga saga*, known mainly from a 17th-century Latin retelling, which presented a history of the prehistoric kings of Denmark through some twenty generations down to the mid-10th century (in content more akin to *fornaldarsögur* than to *konungasögur*); (5) the history of the earls of Hlaðir (Lade, near Trondheim), the chief rivals of the kings of Norway in the 10th and 11th centuries, which has been dubbed **Hlaðajarla saga* by scholars who claim its existence, although it is known only as it was absorbed in 13th-century compendia (*Fagrskinna* and *Heimskringla*); and (6) *Hákonar saga Ívarssonar*, the only saga about a Norwegian who was neither of royal status nor a pretender to the throne, although in this version he is presented as a scion of the earls of Hlaðir.

Sverris saga was probably completed soon after the monarch's death in 1202, most likely by around 1210. This masterpiece marks a literary high point in *konungasaga* composition, and had a substantial influence on later works, among other things in the employment of public oratory. Another saga about more or less contemporary events belonging to this period is *Bǫglunga sǫgur*, the story of the period of strife following Sverrir's death, existing in two related but politically varying redactions. A shorter and probably more original version covers the period 1202–1209, and a longer, probably revised and extended version continues until 1217.

Classical period (1220–1280). During the formative period of *konungasaga* composition, a great diversity of texts and types was represented. The classical period encompasses especially the years 1220–1240, and is characterized particularly by the composition of large, more compendious histories of long periods of time. The existence of *Sverris saga* was a prerequisite for the composition of these compendia, since they all end or probably ended in 1177, the year when Sverrir arrived in Norway and advanced his claims to the throne. The so-called **Oldest Morkinskinna*, a comprehensive version of Norwegian history from Magnús góði (r. 1035–1047) until probably 1177, set the stage for the works of this period. Written by an Icelander in the early

1220s, its account is best reflected, although somewhat shortened, in the latter part of *Fagrskinna*. *Fagrskinna* is a rather sober and sometimes skeletal presentation of Norwegian royal history from Hálfdan svarti ("the black," Haraldr hárfagri's father) to 1177. The realistic account is based mainly on written materials, perhaps also a now-lost independent *Haralds saga hárfagra*, and contains much skaldic poetry. It is thought that the work was composed in Norway by an Icelander, perhaps for King Hákon Hákonarson.

The Icelander Snorri Sturluson (1178–1241) is identified by two 16th-century Danish translations as the author of *Heimskringla*, and his writing of "saga-books" in 1230–1231 is mentioned in *Sturlunga saga*. Snorri apparently first wrote a saga about St. Óláfr, now termed the Separate *Óláfs saga helga*, in the 1220s. This work was prefaced by a prologue and a summary presentation of the preceding kings in the royal line, and followed by a recounting of miracles that the saint worked after his death. Then, around 1230, Snorri composed a continuous presentation of the individual histories of the kings of Norway to the year 1177, using a slightly revised version of the Separate *Óláfs saga helga* as the central text and middle third of the work. The modern title for this compendium, *Heimskringla* (literally "Circle of the World"), is derived from the first two words in an initial geographical presentation in the earliest extant MS of the work, which lacks Snorri's prologue. The account begins with *Ynglinga saga*, which, based on the genealogical poem *Ynglingatal* by Þjóðólfr of Hvin, recounts the fates of some twenty-six generations of ancestors of the Norwegian royal line, starting with the gods in prehistoric times and continuing down to Hálfdan svarti in the 9th century. *Heimskringla* is the crowning work of *konungasaga* composition. Snorri's critical historical judgment of cause and effect and his literary skills at structuring a story and modeling dramatic dialogue are everywhere evident.

The composition of an Icelandic compendium about the kings of Denmark from the 10th century until 1187, *Knýtlinga saga*, belongs to the time after 1257. Danish histories in Latin and skaldic poetry were among the sources used, in addition to sagas of the kings of Norway. Embedded in this anonymous compilation is a well-composed and extensive saga of St. Knud (Cnut; r. 1080–1086), *Knúts saga helga*, for which *Heimskringla*'s *Óláfs saga helga* functioned as both source and model, the protagonists in both instances being at once kings and martyred saints.

The time frame for the classical period of *konungasaga* composition may be extended until the latter part of the 13th century and encompasses then the composition of sagas about contemporary regents. *Hákonar saga Hákonarsonar*, the story of Hákon Hákonarson (r. 1217–1263), was commissioned by Hákon's son and successor, Magnús, and was completed by Snorri's nephew, Sturla Þórðarson, within two years of Hákon's death. The somber account, which lacks the narrative power of earlier *konungasögur*, is based on a wealth of written historical sources and documentary material, and includes as embellishment many skaldic verses, most of which were composed by the saga author himself. Soon after the death of Magnús lagabœtir ("law-mender") in 1280, Sturla (d. 1284) wrote his biography, *Magnúss saga lagabœtis*, which is only fragmentarily preserved and was apparently quite dry.

Postclassical period (1280–1390). After about 1280, *konungasaga* composition as such ceased, but texts of existing works continued to be copied by scribes, often in large MSS containing several *konungasögur*. During the postclassical period, more original editorial activities concentrated on the encyclopedic

collection and expansion of material and its stylistic embellishment. The text of the preserved *Morkinskinna* heralds the advent of these procedures. In this MS, the presentation of the *Oldest *Morkinskinna* was somewhat redone stylistically, and more skaldic strophes were added, but the main distinction is the inclusion of *þættir* (sing. *þáttr*), short stories about Icelanders and their relationships with the Norwegian kings. These tales are usually only loosely connected with the main story, and are often woven piecemeal into the narrative. Snorri's Separate *Óláfs saga helga* is also interpolated with *þættir* in various MSS from the 1300s.

Beyond the inclusion of short stories, redactors attempted to combine extensive histories of individual epochs or sovereigns, and one such product is the text of *Hulda-Hrokkinskinna*, a conglomeration mainly of the last third of *Heimskringla* with *Morkinskinna* text. The most striking such compilation, however, is the so-called Longest *Óláfs saga Tryggvasonar*. To make this work, every known version of the story of Óláfr Tryggvason was employed, including the vernacular translation of the otherwise lost Latin version from around 1200 by Gunnlaugr Leifsson. The stylistic embellishments of the "florid style" (*i.e.*, alliteration, synonymous variation, rhythmic word placement, and syntactic parallelism), which became popular in the 1300s, characterize especially the sections from Gunnlaugr's text. The encyclopedic conflation and compilation of *konungasögur* in the 1300s culminates in *Flateyjarbók* (ca. 1390). This MS, the largest of all Icelandic parchments, includes, among other works, the Longest *Óláfs saga Tryggvasonar*, the Separate *Óláfs saga helga*, *Sverris saga*, and *Hákonar saga Hákonarsonar*, in addition to a 15th-century addition consisting of *Morkinskinna* text. Other individual sagas and *þættir* in independent versions have been interlarded, especially in the Longest *Óláfs saga Tryggvasonar*.

Ed. and **Tr**: For editions and translations of *konungasögur*, see the bibliographies following separate articles about individual works and MSS. **Bib**.: Halldór Hermannsson. *Bibliography of the Sagas of the Kings of Norway and Related Sagas and Tales*. Islandica, 3. Ithaca: Cornell University Library, 1910; Halldór Hermannsson. *The Sagas of the Kings (konunga sögur) and the Mythical-Heroic Sagas (fornaldar sögur): Two Bibliographical Supplements*. Islandica, 26. Ithaca: Cornell University Press, 1937; Andersson, Theodore M. "Kings' Sagas (*Konungasögur*)." In *Old Norse–Icelandic Literature: A Critical Guide*. Ed. Carol J. Clover and John Lindow. Islandica, 45. Ithaca and London: Cornell University Press, 1985, pp. 197–238 [esp. 227–38]. **Lit**.: For additional literature, especially concerning works, see the bibliographies following separate articles on each of the *konungasögur*. Storm, Gustav. *Snorri Sturlassöns Historieskrivning: En kritisk Undersøgelse*. Copenhagen: Luno, 1873; Sigurður Nordal. *Om Olaf den helliges saga: En kritisk undersøgelse*. Copenhagen: Gad, 1914; Koht, Halvdan. "Sagaernes opfatning av vor gamle historie." *Historisk tidsskrift* (Norway) ser. 5.2 (1914), 379–420; rpt. in *Rikssamling og kristendom*. Norske historikere i utvalg, 1. Ed. Andreas Holmsen and Jarle Simensen. Oslo: Universitetsforlaget, 1967, pp. 41–55; Johnsen, Oscar Albert. "Snorre Sturlasons opfatning av vor ældre historie." *Historisk tidsskrift* (Norway), ser. 5.3 (1916), 213–32; Paasche, Fredrik. "Heimskringlas Olavssaga: Komposition-Stil-Karaktertegning." *Edda* 6 (1916), 365–83; Indrebø, Gustav. *Fagrskinna*. Avhandlinger fra Universitetets historiske seminar, 4. Oslo: Grøndahl, 1917; Sigurður Nordal. *Snorri Sturluson*. Reykjavík: Þór B. Þorláksson, 1920; Paasche, Fredrik. "Tendens og syn i kongesagaen." *Edda* 17 (1922), 1–17; Berntsen, Toralf. *Fra sagn til saga: Studier i kongesagaer*. Oslo: Gyldendal, 1923; Schreiner, Johan. *Tradisjon og saga om Olav den hellige*. Avhandlinger utg. av Det Norske

Videnskaps-Akademi i Oslo, II. Hist.-fílos. Kl., 1926, 1. Oslo: Dybwad, 1926; Schreiner, Johan. *Saga og oldfunn: Studier til Norges eldste historie*. Avhandlinger utg. av Det Norske Videnskaps-Akademi i Oslo, II. Hist.-fílos. Kl., 1927, 4. Oslo: Dybwad, 1927; Lie, Hallvard. *Studier i Heimskringlas stil: Dialogene og talene*. Skrifter utgitt av Det Norske Videnskaps-Akademi i Oslo. II. Hist.-fílos. Kl., 1936, 5. Oslo: Dybwad, 1937; Bjarni Aðalbjarnarson. *Om de norske kongers sagaer*. Skrifter utg. av Det Norske Videnskaps-Akademi i Oslo, II. Hist.-fílos. kl., 1936, 4. Oslo: Dybwad, 1937; Einar Ólafur Sveinsson. *Sagnaritun Oddaverja: Nokkrar athuganir*. Studia Islandica, 1. Reykjavik: Ísafóld, 1937; Holtsmark, Anne. "Om de norske kongers sagaer: Opposisjonsinnlegg ved Bjarni Aðalbjarnarsons doktordisputats 23. september 1936." *Edda* 25 (1938); 145–64; Beyschlag, Siegfried. *Konungasögur: Untersuchungen zur Königssaga bis Snorri: Die älteren Übersichtswerke samt Ynglingasaga*. Bibliotheca Arnamagnæana, 8. Copenhagen: Munksgaard, 1950; Beyschlag, Siegfried. "Möglichkeiten mündlicher Überlieferung in der Königssaga." *Arkiv för nordisk filologi* 68 (1953), 109–39; Turville-Petre, G. *Origins of Icelandic Literature*. Oxford: Clarendon, 1953, [esp. pp. 88–108, 166–227]; Sandvik, Gudmund. *Hovding og konge i Heimskringla*. Avhandlinger fra Universitetets historiske seminar, 7. Oslo: Akademisk Forlag, 1955; Ólafía Einarsdóttir. *Studier i kronologisk metode i tidlig islandsk historieskrivning*. Bibliotheca Historica Lundensis, 13. Stockholm: Natur och kultur, 1964; Ellehøj, Svend. *Studier over den ældste norrøne historieskrivning*. Bibliotheca Arnamagnæana, 26. Copenhagen: Munksgaard, 1965. Olsen, Thorkil Damsgaard. "Kongekrøniker og kongesagaer." In *Norrøn Fortællekunst: Kapitler af den norsk-islandske middelalderlitteraturs historie*. Ed. Hans Bekker-Nielsen *et al*. Copenhagen: Akademisk Forlag, 1965, pp. 42–71; Schier, Kurt. *Sagaliteratur*. Sammlung Metzler, M78. Stuttgart: Metzler, 1970, pp. 9–33; Louis-Jensen, Jonna. *Kongesagastudier: Kompilationen Hulda-Hrokkinskinna*. Bibliotheca Arnamagnæana, 32. Copenhagen: Reitzel, 1977; Bjarni Guðnason. *Fyrsta sagan*. Studia Islandica, 37. Reykjavik: Menningarsjóður, 1978; Hallberg, Peter. "Hryggjarstykki: Några anteckningar." *Maal og minne* (1979), 113–21; Sverrir Tómasson. "Hryggjarstykki." *Gripla* 3 (1979), 214–20; Knirk, James E. *Oratory in the Kings' Sagas*. Oslo, Bergen, and Tromsø: Universitetsforlaget, 1981; Fidjestøl, Bjarne. *Det norrøne fyrstediktet*. Øvre Ervik: Alvheim & Eide, 1982; Clover, Carol J. *The Medieval Saga*. Ithaca and London: Cornell University Press, 1982, pp. 148–88; Ulset, Tor. *Det genetiske forholdet mellom Ágrip, Historia Norwegiæ og Historia de Antiquitate Regum Norwagiensium: En analyse med utgangspunkt i oversettelsesteknikk samt en diskusjon omkring begrepet "latinisme" i samband med norrøne tekster*. Oslo: Novus, 1983; Andersson, Theodore M. "Kings' Sagas (*Konungasögur*)." In *Old Norse-Icelandic Literature: A Critical Guide*, pp. 197–238 [above]; Andersson, Theodore M. "Norse Kings' Sagas." In *Dictionary of the Middle Ages*. Ed. Joseph R. Strayer. New York: Scribner, 1982–89, vol. 9, pp. 175–8; Jónas Kristjánsson. *Eddas and Sagas: Iceland's Medieval Literature*. Trans. Peter Foote. Reykjavik: Hið íslenska bókmenntafélag, 1988, pp. 147–75; Sverrir Tómasson. *Formálar íslenskra sagnaritara á miðlödum*. Reykjavik: Stofnun Árna Magnússonar, 1988 [esp. pp. 261–90, 347–50, 374–83, 386–7, 388–94].

James E. Knirk

[**See also**: *Ágrip af Nóregs konunga sǫgum*; *Bǫglunga sǫgur*; *Eirspennill*; *Fagrskinna*; *Flateyjarbók*; *Fríssbók*; *Færeyinga saga*; *Hákonar saga gamla Hákonarsonar*; *Hákonar saga Ívarssonar*; *Heimskringla*; *Historia Norwegiae*; *Hulda-Hrokkinskinna*; *Íslendingabók*; *Jómsvíkinga saga*; *Knýtlinga saga*; *Landnámabók*; *Magnúss saga helga eyjajarls*, *Magnúss saga lagabœtis*; *Morkinskinna*; *Óláfs saga helga*; *Óláfs saga Tryggvasonar*; *Orkneyinga saga*; Political Literature; *Profectio Danorum in Hierosolymam*; Saints' Lives; *Skjǫldunga saga*; Snorri Sturluson; *Sverris saga*; Sæmundr Sigfússon inn fróði; Theodoricus: *Historia de antiquitate regum Norwagiensium*; *Páttr*; *Pinga saga*; *Ynglinga saga*]

Konungs skuggsjá

Konungs skuggsjá ("King's Mirror"), or *Speculum regale* (both titles are found in the prologue) is a didactic work composed in Norway during the reign of King Hákon Hákonarson (1217–1263), probably in the 1250s. As with many medieval textbooks, *Konungs skuggsjá* is a dialogue, not between teacher and pupil as usual in such works, but between father and son. The work was probably written for the sons of King Hákon. One of them, Magnús, followed his father as king (1263–1280); he received the nickname *lagabœtir* ("law-mender") owing to the important revision of the laws that he organized, and which were influenced by *Konungs skuggsjá*.

Konungs skuggsjá is preserved in many MSS, most of them Icelandic. One of the oldest and best is AM 243β fol., written in Norway, probably in Bergen around 1275.

The author is anonymous, and many unsuccessful attempts have been made to attribute the work to persons more or less well known from historical sources. The work itself, however, gives a picture of an author working in close connection with the royal court. He was probably a man in holy orders, and by Norwegian standards he had a substantial theological background. Whether he had achieved this learning in Norway or had studied abroad is uncertain.

The first part of *Konungs skuggsjá* deals with subjects of importance to traders who sail with their merchandise to foreign countries. Different scientific matters are treated, and there are chapters on Ireland, Iceland, and Greenland, where there was a thriving Norse population in the Middle Ages. In the second part, the author gives firsthand and detailed information about the king's retainers, their daily life, and their duties. He then concentrates on the king, his dignity, and his duties, especially as the highest judge. To instruct him in this capacity, the author gives a series of examples from the Old Testament of judgments pronounced by God, and the problem of capital punishment is thoroughly discussed.

According to the prologue, *Konungs skuggsjá* should also deal with the clergy and finally with the peasants and the common people. But in the work as we now have it, there are no separate chapters dealing with these matters. It is a much discussed problem whether the work was left unfinished or whether the final part is lost. As a third solution, it has been suggested that the prologue in its present form has been rewritten by a scribe who knew that both clergy and peasants are mentioned in the work, and who formulated his words in a somewhat misleading way. There is reason to believe that *Konungs skuggsjá* is complete in its present state.

Konungs skuggsjá has its place in a series of works from different countries written to be of use to kings or sons of kings. Some are called *specula*, but, as far as is known, none is the direct model for *Konungs skuggsjá*. Among the author's sources was doubtless the Vulgate, and he must have known some of the many commentaries on the books of the Bible. He mentions Isidore and the *Dialogues* of Pope Gregory, and he certainly knew other learned works, but to point out exactly what he may have read has proved difficult.

Konungs skuggsjá is the most important work composed in

medieval Norway. It gives unique insight into the cultural life of the country in the middle of the 13th century, and offers discussion of a king's position and duties, seen from a Norwegian point of view, against the background of European *rex justus* ideology. In *Konungs skuggsjá*, the Old Norse language is treated with great stylistic skill as a flexible instrument for the author's thoughts. A theory that two separate works by two different authors are brought together in *Konungs skuggsjá* is based on very weak arguments.

Ed.: Flom, George, ed. *The Arnamagnæan Manuscript 243 β, folio: The Main Manuscript of Konungs skuggsjá in Phototypic Reproduction with Diplomatic Text*. Urbana: University of Illinois Press, 1915; Finnur Jónsson, ed. *Konungs skuggsjá. Speculum regale*. Udgivet efter håndskrifterne af Det kongelige nordiske oldskriftselskab. Copenhagen: Gyldendal, 1920–21; Holm-Olsen, Ludvig, ed. *Konungs skuggsiá*. Utgitt for Kjeldeskriftfondet. Gammelnorske tekster, nr. 1. Oslo: Norsk Historisk Kjeldskrift-Institutt, 1945; 2nd rev. ed., 1983. **Tr.**: Larson, Laurence Marcellus, trans. *The King's Mirror (Speculum Regale— Konungs skuggsjá): With Introduction and Notes*. New York: Twayne; American-Scandinavian Foundation, 1917. **Lit.**: Tveitane, Mattias, ed. *Studier over Konungs skuggsiá. I utvalg*. Bergen, Oslo, and Tromsø: Universitetsforlaget, 1971 [with bibliography]; Vandvik, Eirik. "A New Approach to the Konungs Skuggsiá." *Symbolae Osloenses* 29 (1952), 99–109; rpt. in Tveitane, *Studier over Konungs skuggsiá*, pp. 71–9; Holm-Olsen, Ludvig. "The Prologue to The King's Mirror: Did the Author of the Work Write It?" In *Specvlvm Norroenvm: Norse Studies in Memory of Gabriel Turville-Petre*. Ed. Ursula Dronke *et al*. Odense: Odense University Press, 1981, pp. 223–41; Holm-Olsen, Ludvig. "Kongespeilet." In *Norges litteraturhistorie*. Ed. Edvard Beyer. Oslo: Cappelen, 1974; 3rd ed., 1982, vol. 1, pp. 151–73; Bagge, Sverre. *The Political Thought of the King's Mirror*. Mediaeval Scandinavia Supplements, 3. Odense: Odense University Press, 1987.

†*Ludvig Holm-Olsen*

[See also: Bible; Cosmology; *Hugsvinnsmál*; *Konungastyrelsen*; Political Literature]

Kormákr Qgmundarson

Kormákr Qgmundarson was an Icelandic poet (*ca*. 930–970), the chief character of *Kormáks saga*. The name (Irish *Cormac*) suggests Celtic family connections. According to Haukr Valdísarson's *Íslendingadrápa*, Kormákr was of high birth (*kynstórr*). The saga belongs to the category of *skáldasögur*, and is particularly remarkable for the large number of verses (*lausavísur*) it contains scattered throughout. Sixty-four of the eighty-five verses are spoken by the hero. Of the remaining ones, fifteen are attributed to his chief rival, Bersi. A few verses are faked, corrupt, or of doubtful origin (in particular 6, 24, 61, 73, and 79). The prose story of the saga, the biography of the poet, is unusually short and constitutes little more than a connecting framework around the many verses. There are linguistic indications that it was composed at the beginning of the 13th century, the earliest period of saga writing.

Its all-dominating theme is the hero's unhappy love story, a love that is never consummated. Right from the start, it contains bizarre elements. A glimpse of a young girl's beautiful ankles is enough to make the poet fall in love and causes a flow of poetic inspiration. He realizes that love for the young Steingerðr is to be his fate for the rest of his life. But although his feelings are reciprocated, and, after incidents in which blood is shed, her father's resistance is overcome, the planned marriage falls through. Paradoxically enough, the direct cause of the failure is Kormákr himself: when the time comes, he does not turn up at the wedding that has already been prepared. According to the saga, the real reason is the harmful spell put upon him by a woman whose sons the poet had killed. Against her will, Steingerðr is married to the scarred warrior Bersi. With the arrogance that always characterizes him, Kormákr insists on his first right to the girl and challenges Bersi to single combat, but after a slight wound has to admit defeat. Scornful verses, challenges, and single combats follow. Steingerðr leaves Bersi and later marries again, this time a peaceful man whom Kormákr deeply despises and mocks.

Off on his Viking journeys, the poet dreams of his beloved and sings the praises of her beauty. What seems to be a promising meeting between the two occurs when Kormákr visits his country, but a night spent with Steingerðr ends in a frustrating anticlimax: the physical role of a lover seems to have been something denied to Kormákr.

One thing is certain: no Icelandic skald can compete with Kormákr as the master of love poetry, which is not, however, his only genre. *Skáldatal* informs us that Kormákr had sung the praises of both Earl Sigurðr in Hlaðir and Haraldr gráfeldr ("grey-cloak") Eiríksson. Only a part of the former's poem has survived; there are seven half-strophes from *Sigurðardrápa*, cited in *Skáldskaparmál* in Snorri's *Edda*, and one complete strophe in *Heimskringla*. An original artistic device of the poet is his way of replacing the *drápa*'s refrain (*stef*) by varying mythological allusions that do not seem to have any connection with the content of the rest of the poem. In Snorri's *Háttatal*, this variety of *dróttkvætt* is called *hjástælt*.

A much-discussed theory would have us believe that *Kormáks saga* is an entirely literary product, with prose and poetry as equally authentic literary components. The author, it is suggested, was a 13th-century writer who had been influenced by continental European troubadour poetry and the medieval love poetry of which Tristan is the hero (Bjarni Einarsson 1976). This theory has been contested on both linguistic and literary-historical grounds (Einar Ól. Sveinsson 1966–69, Andersson 1969, Hallberg 1975).

Ed.: Einar Ól. Sveinsson, ed. *Vatnsdæla saga*. Íslenzk fornrit, 8. Reykjavik: Hið íslenzka fornritafélag, 1939. **Lit.**: Wood, Cecil. "Kormak's Stanzas Called the *Sigurðardrápa*." *Neophilologus* 43 (1959), 305–19; Hallberg, Peter. *The Icelandic Saga*. Trans. Paul Schach. Lincoln: University of Nebraska Press, 1962; Einar Ól. Sveinsson. "Kormákr the Poet and His Verses." *Saga-Book of the Viking Society* 17 (1966–69), 18–60; Andersson, Theodore M. "Skalds and Troubadours." *Mediaeval Scandinavia* 2 (1969), 7–41; Frank, Roberta. "Onomastic Play in Kormákr's Verse: The Name Steingerðr." *Mediaeval Scandinavia* 3 (1970), 7–34; Bjarni Einarsson. "The Lovesick Skald: A Reply to Theodore M. Andersson (*Mediaeval Scandinavia* 1969)." *Mediaeval Scandinavia* 4 (1971) 21–41; Hallberg, Peter. *Old Icelandic Poetry: Eddic Lay and Skaldic Verse*. Trans. Paul Schach and Sonja Lindgrenson. Lincoln: University of Nebraska Press, 1975; Turville-Petre, E. O. G. *Scaldic Poetry*. Oxford: Clarendon, 1976; Bjarni Einarsson. *To skjaldesagaer. En analyse af Kormáks saga og Hallfreðar saga*. Bergen, Oslo, and Tromsø: Universitetsforlaget, 1976; See, Klaus von. "Skaldenstrophe und Sagaprosa. Ein Beitrag zum Problem der mündlichen Überlieferung in der altnordischen Literatur." *Mediaeval Scandinavia* 10 (1977), 58–82; Frank, Roberta. *Old Norse Court Poetry: The Dróttkvætt Stanza*. Islandica, 42. Ithaca and London: Cornell University Press, 1978; See, Klaus von. "Mündliche Prosa und Skaldendichtung. Mit einem Exkurs über Skaldensagas und

Trobadorbiographien." *Mediaeval Scandinavia* 11 (1978–79), 82–91; Schottmann, Hans. "Der Bau der Kormáks saga." *Skandinavistik* 12 (1982) 22–36; Lie, Hallvard. *Om sagakunst og skaldskap. Utvalgte avhandlinger.* Øvre Ervik: Alvheim & Eide, 1982; Clover, Carol J., and John Lindow, eds. *Old Norse–Icelandic Literature: A Critical Guide.* Islandica, 45. Ithaca and London: Cornell University Press, 1985.

Folke Ström

[See also: *Heimskringla*; *Íslendingadrápa*; *Kormáks saga*; *Lausavísur*; Love Poetry; *Skáld*; *Skáldasögur*; Skaldic Meters; Skaldic Verse; *Snorra Edda*]

Kormáks saga ("The Saga of Kormákr"). The life and work of the 10th-century Icelandic poet Kormákr Qgmundarson are noted briefly both in the *Skáldatal* and in Snorri Sturluson's *Prose Edda*. *Kormáks saga*, probably written in the early 13th century, is a dramatic prose account of his life. The work is preserved *in toto* in the mid-14th-century MS *Möðruvallabók* and in fragments in AM 162 fol. (*ca.* 1400). Like *Bjarnar saga Hítdœlakappa*, *Gunnlaugs saga*, *Hallfreðar saga*, and *Fóstbrœðra saga* (all *Íslendingasögur* constructed as skaldic biographies), *Kormáks saga* intersperses poetic samples in its prose account, including no fewer than sixty-four stanzas of *dróttkvætt* attributed to Kormákr himself. Most of these verses are presented as *lausavísur* improvised on specific, informal occasions; the saga neither cites nor quotes Kormákr's "official" production for his patrons, Sigurðr Hlaðajarl ("Earl of Hlaðir") Hákonarson or King Haraldr gráfeldr ("grey-cloak") Eiríksson (*ca.* 960–970). Indeed, the saga is in general little concerned with Kormákr's professional or political career or indeed his travels and adventures. Rather, its interest lies in his secular life, above all, his unhappy love for Steingerðr.

The saga proper begins when Kormákr falls in love with Steingerðr at his first glimpse of her feet, which show under a partition separating the two at their first meeting. She returns the feeling, but their marriage is thwarted when Kormákr, thanks to a curse laid on him by a woman whose sons he had slain, fails to appear at the wedding. Steingerðr then marries and eventually divorces Bersi, and soon after marries Þorvaldr. Kormákr persists in his attentions, exchanging hostilities with her husbands, and visiting on Steingerðr both love poems and welcome and unwelcome displays of affection. The saga ends with fantastic adventures in which Kormákr saves Steingerðr from Vikings by jumping overboard with her and swimming to land. He dies at the hands of a Scottish giant, with Steingerðr's name on his lips.

Although the *skáldasögur* as a group show some interest in romantic matters, *Kormáks saga* alone is structured from first to last around its hero's obsessive quest for a woman. No matter where he is or where he goes, fighting the king's battles in Ireland, escaping a shipwreck, or grappling with a giant, Kormákr has only Steingerðr on his mind. "There is no danger so great for you," says his brother Þorgils, "that you aren't always thinking of Steingerðr." The image of the "lovesick skald" is so extraordinary in the context of saga literature that some scholars have doubted the authenticity of the poems, the saga, or both, suspecting instead medieval workmanship under the direct influence of southern models, specifically the Tristan legend (translated into Norse around 1226) and troubadour poetry. The suggestion requires us to imagine a forger accomplished in the composition of archaic poetic language, however, and the factual inconsistencies between the verse and prose further require us to suppose that the saga forger and the stanza forger were different people. Such difficulties as these, together with the existence of legal injunctions against the composition of love poetry (albeit less passionate in tone) in the North, lead other scholars to reject the "southern" hypothesis in favor of a more or less authentic native product.

Ed.: Einar Ól. Sveinsson, ed. *Vatnsdœla saga.* Íslenzk fornrit, 8. Reykjavik: Hið íslenzka fornritafélag, 1939 [*Kormáks saga*, pp. 201–302]. **Tr.**: Hollander, Lee M., trans. *The Sagas of Kormák and the Sworn Brothers.* Princeton: Princeton University Press; American-Scandinavian Foundation, 1949. **Lit.**: Bjarni Einarsson. *Skáldasögur: Um uppruna og eðli ástaskáldasagnanna fornu.* Reykjavik: Menningarsjóður, 1961; Einar Ól. Sveinsson. "Kormakr the Poet and His Verses." *Saga-Book of the Viking Society* 17 (1966), 18–60; Andersson, Theodore M. "Skalds and Troubadours." *Mediaeval Scandinavia* 2 (1969), 7–41; Frank, Roberta. "Onomastic Play in Kormákr's Verse: The Name Steingerðr." *Mediaeval Scandinavia* 3 (1970), 7–34; Bjarni Einarsson. "The Lovesick Skald: A Reply to Theodore M. Andersson (*Mediaeval Scandinavia* 1969)." *Mediaeval Scandinavia* 4 (1971), 21–41; Bjarni Einarsson. *To skjaldesagaer. En analyse af Kormáks saga og Hallfreðar saga.* Bergen, Oslo, and Tromsø: Universitetsforlaget, 1976.

Carol J. Clover

[See also: Kormákr Qgmundarson; *Lausavísur*; *Möðruvallabók*; Old Norse–Icelandic Literature, Foreign Influence on; *Skáldasögur*; *Snorra Edda*]

Krákumál means "lay of Kráka ('crow')," a nickname of Ragnarr loðbrók's ("hairy-breeches") second wife, Áslaug. This anonymous heroic skaldic poem was composed in the 12th century as part of an antiquarian revival. It was frequently called "Deathsong of Ragnarr lodbrók" and belongs to the genre of *ævikviða* ("poem of life"), represented by about five poems, all of them transmitted in connection with *fornaldarsögur*, in this case with *Ragnars saga loðbrókar*. The dying hero, Ragnarr, overwhelmed by his enemy, the English king Ælla, and thrown into a snake pit, reports that he fought fifty-one battles and now is waiting for the valkyries to take him to Óðinn's hall. He hopes that his sons will avenge him.

The poem consists of twenty-nine stanzas in the meter of *dróttkvætt* ("court poetry"), mostly in its less strict form of *háttlausa*, which means that the internal rhymes are neglected. Each stanza, excepting 23 and 29, has ten lines as against eight in the usual *dróttkvætt* stanza. The first line of each stanza is a *stef*, or refrain: *Hjoggum vér með hjǫrvi!* ("We struck with a sword!"). After the description of battles in the first twenty-one stanzas, the latter part contains educational and mythological reflections. There are reasons to believe that the poem was composed in the Orkney Islands (de Vries 1967, Frank 1978).

Scholars disagree on the value of the poem. But even if it is not among the foremost examples of skaldic poetry, it definitely needs a new evaluation (Heinrichs 1978). The fact that it was highly admired during the 18th century and that it took some time before the worst errors of interpretation were rectified probably led to its neglect in later times.

In the course of the Scandinavian Renaissance, Ole Worm published the poem for the first time in 1636 (second edition, 1651), in an appendix to his *Literatura Runica*, transcribed in runes of the younger *fuþark* (runic alphabet) and accompanied by a Latin translation. In the 18th century, it was translated into several European languages: Dutch (Lambert ten Kate, 1723), Swedish

(Erik Julius Björner, 1737), French (Paul Henri Mallet, 1756; ten stanzas), English (Thomas Percy, 1763), Danish (B. C. Sandvig, 1779), and German (Friedrich David Gräter, 1789), not to mention numerous quotations, especially of the last two stanzas containing the impressive last line: *læjandi skalk deyja* ("laughing I shall die"). The *ridens moriar* and the longstanding misinterpretation of a kenning in stanza 25.6, meaning drinking out of a horn, but misunderstood as saying that the heroes in Óðinn's hall drank from the skulls of their enemies, influenced the Romantic view of Germanic heroism for nearly 200 years.

The main MS is NkS 1824b 4to from around 1400. Another important MS, kept in Uppsala University Library, R 702, is a copy of a lost MS by Magnús Ólafsson (17th century), an Icelander, who actually was the author behind Ole Worm's edition, translation, and commentary. The third MS that must be considered is AM 6 fol., a copy by Jón Erlendsson.

Ed.: Wormius, Olaus [Worm, Ole], ed. *Runer, seu Danica literatura antiquissima*. Amsterdam: Jansonius, 1636, pp. 197–227; 2nd ed. Copenhagen: Martzan, 1651, pp. 182–207; Rafn, C. C., ed. *Krakas Maal eller Kvad om Kong Ragnar Lodbroks Krigsbedrifter og Heltedød*. Copenhagen: Schultz, 1826, pp. 89–152; Finnur Jónsson, ed. *Den norsk-islandske skjaldedigtning*. Vols. 1A–2A (tekst efter håndskrifterne) and 1B–2B (rettet tekst). Copenhagen and Christiania [Oslo]: Gyldendal, 1912–15; rpt. Copenhagen: Rosenkilde & Bagger, 1967 (A) and 1973 (B), vol. 1A, pp. 641–51; 1B, pp. 649–56; Kock, Ernst A., ed. *Den norsk-isländska skaldediktningen*. 2 vols. Lund: Gleerup, 1946–50, vol. 1, pp. 316–21. **Bib.**: Halldór Hermannsson. *Bibliography of the Mythical-Heroic Sagas*. Islandica, 5. Ithaca: Cornell University Library, 1912, pp. 36–9; rpt. New York: Kraus, 1966; Halldór Hermannsson. *The Sagas of the Kings (Konunga sögur) and the Mythical Heroic Sagas (Fornaldar sögur): Two Bibliographical Supplements*. Islandica, 26. Ithaca: Cornell University Press, 1937, pp. 61–2. **Tr.**: Schlauch, Margaret, trans. *The Saga of the Volsungs, the Saga of Ragnar Lodbrok Together with the Lay of Kraka*. New York and London: American-Scandinavian Foundation; Norton, 1930; 3rd ed. 1964. **Lit.**: Beck, Thor J. "Ragnar Lodbrok's Swan Song in the French Romantic Movement." *Romanic Review* 22 (1931), 218–22; Vries, Jan de. *Altnordische Literaturgeschichte*. 2 vols. Grundriss der germanischen Philologie, 15–6. Berlin: de Gruyter, 1941–42; rpt. 1964–67, vol. 2, pp. 37–41; Terpstra, J. U. "Ten Kates Übersetzung von Ragnar Lodbroks Sterbelied (*Krákumál*) und ihre literarhistorische Bedeutung." *Neophilologus* 44 (1960), 135–46; Heinrichs, Anne. "Von Ole Worm zu Lambert ten Kate. Frühe Rezeption der 'Krákumál.'" In *Sprache in Gegenwart und Geschichte: Festschrift für Heinrich Matthias Heinrichs zum 65. Geburtstag*. Ed. Dietrich Hartmann et al. Cologne and Vienna: Böhlau, 1978, pp. 294–306; Frank, Roberta. *Old Norse Court Poetry: The* Dróttkvætt *Stanza*. Islandica, 42. Ithaca and London: Cornell University Press, 1978.

Anne Heinrichs

[**See also:** *Ragnars saga loðbrókar*; Skaldic Meters; Skaldic Verse]

Kristni saga *see* **Conversion**

Króka-Refs saga ("The Saga of Refr the Wily") is a postclassical *Íslendingasaga* written in the 14th century by an anonymous author who probably lived in western Iceland. The saga is found in its entirety in one 15th-century vellum MS (AM 471 4to) and many paper MSS. Fragments of the saga are also found in two 15th-century vellum MSS, Stock. Perg. 4to no. 8, and AM 586 4to. Differences among the MSS are small, and the vellum MSS best preserve the original text. The oldest known MS of the saga, a section of the late 14th-century vellum MS *Vatnshyrna*, is no longer extant.

Refr Steinsson, a *kolbítr* ("coal biter," *i.e.*, layabout) in his youth, is an Icelander with the unfortunate habit of being slow to anger, but excessive in his vengeance. Although a remarkable craftsman, he spends most of his life fleeing one country after another in order to avoid counter-retribution for his justifiable acts of revenge. First, Refr flees Breiðafjörður because he slew his widowed mother's importunate neighbor. Later, he has to leave the uncle who sheltered him because he kills an overbearing neighbor. Refr settles in Greenland, takes a wife, and raises a family. Eventually, he and his household flee to the wilderness to escape the counter-revenge for slaying a neighboring family that had slandered him. A Norwegian trader visiting Greenland is drawn into the case, and despite useful advice from King Haraldr Sigurðarson, Refr is only flushed from his fortress (possibly the first in medieval literature to be equipped with a sprinkler system), while the Norwegian is killed. Making their escape from the fortress to the sea by means of a boat with wheels, Refr and his household flee to Norway, visiting Trondheim in disguise, perhaps to plead their case before the king. However, he kills one of Haraldr's retainers who tries to seduce his wife. Refr goes to the king, announces in puns and riddling speech what has happened, and takes his family to Denmark. Haraldr unravels the puns and concludes that this must be the same Icelander who had caused so much trouble in Greenland. He outlaws Refr and sets the dead retainer's brother after him. Refr gains the favor of the Danish king, Sveinn (Sven), by means of a gift of polar bears and gyrfalcons, and is able to trick his Norwegian pursuer into swearing to leave him in peace. Sveinn encourages him to keep the name that he adopted as his latest disguise, "Sigtryggr." He eventually goes on a pilgrimage to Rome, falls sick, and is buried at a French monastery. One of his sons, who stays in Denmark, is the ancestor of Bishop Absalon.

As is common with postclassical *Íslendingasögur*, *Króka-Refs saga* has very little connection with historical traditions. Some characters are mentioned in other sources, such as *Landnámabók*, *Gísla saga*, and *Hávarðar saga*, but most are not. The saga's chronology also seems to be taken from earlier *Íslendingasögur* rather than from history. For example, although Hákon Aðalsteinsfóstri ("Æthelstan's foster-son") and Haraldr Sigurðarson ruled ninety years apart, the occurrence of both names in *Gísla saga* may have given the author of *Króka-Refs saga* the impression that they ruled sequentially. However, archaeological excavations in Greenland have provided the saga with some historical corroboration: waterworks similar to those described in the saga have been unearthed in Narssaq.

Króka-Refs saga has its place in the group of stories that describe a clever or lucky man, usually an Icelander, who benefits from the king of Denmark at the expense of the king of Norway by means of a well-placed gift of a valuable animal. This group of narratives includes *Auðunar þáttr vestfirzka* and the so-called *Gjafa-Refs þáttr* of *Gautreks saga*. The presence of another Refr may indicate a more direct literary relationship between the two sagas, or it might simply be that *Refr* (*i.e.*, "fox") was considered an appropriate name for a cunning man. Despite his pilgrimage to Rome, Refr's cleverness has neither the spiritual overtones of Auðunn's "luck" and generosity, nor the folktale effect of Gjafa-

Refr's. Yet Refr also stands in contrast to saga heroes like Grettir and Gísli, who are similarly known for their skill in word- and smithcraft. Although the injustice of Refr's situation could easily be turned into tragedy, he in fact overcomes his bad luck by means of his wits. In contrast to 13th-century depictions of fate as always ineluctable and usually tragic, the 14th-century *Króka-Refs saga* seems to imply that a man's fate is in his own hands, and that when those hands are as skilled as Refr Steinsson's, his story is sure to have a happy ending.

Ed.: Jóhannes Halldórsson, ed. *Kjalnesinga saga.* Íslenzk fornrit, 14. Reykjavik: Hið íslenzka fornritafélag, 1959. **Tr.**: Jones, Gwyn, trans. *Four Icelandic Sagas.* Princeton: Princeton University Press; New York: American-Scandinavian Foundation, 1935; Bachman, W. Bryant, Jr., trans. *Four Old Icelandic Sagas and Other Tales.* Lanham: University Press of America, 1985. **Lit.**: Schach, Paul. *Icelandic Sagas.* Twayne's World Authors Series, 717. Boston: Twayne, 1984.

Elizabeth Ashman Rowe

[**See also:** *Auðunar þáttr vestfirzka; Gautreks saga; Gísla saga Súrssonar; Hávarðar saga Ísfirðings; Íslendingasögur; Landnámabók; Vatnshyrna*]

Land Registers. Medieval land registers (Danish *jordebøger*), *i.e.*, accounts of the incomes enjoyed by individuals or institutions from landed property, are found from Norway, Denmark, and Sweden, but not from Iceland or Finland. In some cases, the original documents survive to the present day, while other registers survive only in postmedieval transcripts. The existence of additional land registers can be deduced from references to them in medieval or later sources, but nothing is known about the contents of these lost records.

In the medieval period, a great deal of landed property was held by ecclesiastical institutions, so that some of the most significant of the land registers contain information about the dues and services owed to churches and religious houses.

Among the most famous of the church registers from Norway are *Bergens kalvskinn* from about 1350, which describes the revenues of the diocese of Bergen, *Aslak Bolts jordebok* from the 1430s for the archdiocese of Niðaróss (Trondheim), and *Biskop Eysteins jordebok* or *The Red Book* from about 1400, which records the revenues of the diocese of Oslo.

Similar land registers from Denmark are *Roskildebispens jordebog* from the 1370s, *Århusbogen* from 1313, *Ribe Oldemor* from the 13th and 14th centuries, and *Slesvigbispens jordebøger* from the 14th and 15th centuries. These registers contain descriptions of the revenues of the dioceses of Roskilde in Zealand and Århus, Ribe, and Schleswig in Jutland. Most of the landed property of the archdiocese of Lund in Scania is registered in *Palteboken* dating from the beginning of the 16th century.

Even more sparse than the Danish registers are the surviving medieval registers of the Swedish Church. Examples are *Registrum ecclesie Lincopensis* from the 14th and 15th centuries, and *Registrum prediorum* from 1376, covering the building fund of the diocese of Uppsala.

The second great ecclesiastical property-owning institution in the medieval period was religious houses, from whose archives several important medieval registers derive. A number of registers from the 15th century survive from Munkeliv cloister near Bergen in Norway. From North Zealand in Denmark, we have *Esrum klosters jordebog* (1497), while from Swedish houses are found registers from Vårfruberga from the middle of the 13th century, Sko cloister from the 14th and 15th, and Vadstena from the 15th.

The most important register of secular property in medieval Scandinavia is the 13th-century Danish *Kong Valdemars jordebog*, which survives in a transcript from about 1300. This work contains a number of lists, the most significant one dating from 1231, which record the revenues from crown lands (*kongelev*) and from the king's private property (*patrimonium*). Registers of the property of noblemen, mostly dating from the late-medieval period, include from Norway *Hartvig Krummediges jordebok* (1456), and from Sweden Arvid Trolle's and Karl Knutsson's registers from the end of the 15th century and *Sten Stures jordebok* from 1515.

Since the practical reason for the keeping of land registers was to obtain a record of land property on which dues and services were owed, they naturally form an important source of information for the social historian. They provide a picture of the economic structure of an area and consequently of the allocation of power and influence there. The information they yield as to what was paid, by whom, and how much, as well as to how the dues were paid and how the various properties were otherwise organized, turns them indirectly into very significant sources of information about cultural history. They contribute to architectural history by their descriptions of the buildings on estates (farms, houses, mills, churches); to agricultural and industrial history by their accounts of the exploitation of fields and meadows, the construction of bridges, landing places, saltworks, and fish weirs; to administrative history by their information about how the cultivation of the land was organized, how the dues were paid (to stewards or bailiffs), and how the services were distributed among the able-bodied members of the population; and to metrology (the science of weights and measures) and to numismatics (the study of coinage) by the registration of assessments. Land registers are important sources of information for name research because of the huge number of place-names and personal names they record.

Ed.: (a) Norway: Munch, P. A., ed. *Björgynjar Kalfskinn*. Kristiania [Oslo]: [n.p.], 1843; Munch, P. A., ed. *Codex Diplomaticus Monasterii Sancti Michaelis . . . vulgo Munkalif*. Kristiania [Oslo]: [n.p.], 1845; Munch, P. A., ed. *Aslak Bolts jordebok*. Kristiania [Oslo]: Grøndahl, 1852; Huitfeldt, H. J., ed. *Biskop Eysteins jordebok*. Kristiania [Oslo]: Gundersen, 1878; Kjær, A. ed. "Fortegnelser over Hartvig Krummediges norske gods." In *Sproglige og historiske Afhandlinger viede Sophus Bugges Minde*. Kristiania [Oslo]: Aschehoug, 1908. **(b) Denmark:** Langebek, J., et al., eds. *Slesvigbispens jordebøger*. Scriptores Rerum

Danicarum Medii Aevi, 7. Hafniæ [Copenhagen]: Møller, 1792; rpt. Quellensammlung der Gesellschaft für Schleswig-Holsteinische Geschichte, 6. Kiel: Kommissions-Verlag des Universitäts-Buchhandlung, 1904; Nielsen, O., ed. Samling af Adkomster, Indtægtsangivelser og kirkelige Vedtægter for Ribe Domkapittel og Bispestol, nedskrevet 1290–1518, kaldet "Oldemoder." Copenhagen: Thiele, 1869; Nielsen, O., ed. Codex Esromensis. Esrom Klosters Brevbog. Copenhagen: Jørgensen, 1880–81; Aakjær, S., ed. Kong Valdemars jordebog. 3 vols. Samfund til udgivelse af gammel nordisk litteratur, 50. Copenhagen: [s.n.], 1926–45; Christensen, C. A., ed. Roskildebispens jordebog. Danmarks middelalderlige Regnskaber, 3 Rk. 1. Copenhagen: Gad, 1956; Rasmussen, Poul, ed. De middelalderlige jordebøger. Århus Domkapitels jordebøger, 3. Copenhagen: Landbohistorisk Selskab, 1975. (c) Sweden: Almquist, J. A., ed. Arvid Trolles jordebok 1498. Stockholm: Kungl. samfundet för utgifvande af handskrifter rörande Skandinaviens historia, 1938; Nygren, E., ed. Registra ecclesie Lincopensis. Linköping: Linköping biblioteks handlingar, 1941–44; Dovring, F. ed. Fogdö (Vårfruberga) klosters jordebok. Vetenskapssocietetens i Lund årsbok. Lund: Gleerup, 1945; Peetre, Arthur, ed. Sko klosters medeltida jordeböcker. Skrifter utg. av Vetenskapssocieteten i Lund, 42. Lund: Gleerup, 1953.

John Kousgård Sørensen

Land Tenure and Inheritance.

In the main part of Scandinavia (excluding some regions of southern Sweden and Denmark), natural conditions worked against the development of agriculture. Even now, the percentage of area under tillage is very small (3 percent in Norway, 9 percent in Sweden). Cattle breeding, hunting, and fishing prevailed. Tillage, where it was possible, was conducted by relatively primitive methods, often by hand. The productivity of soil was secured not so much by the regular rotation of crops, as by intensive manuring. The scanty possibilities for agriculture offer one explanation why the large-scale landownership that triumphed in medieval Europe was much more modest in Scandinavia.

Nowhere else in early-medieval Europe can we observe the archaic social structures of man's relation to the land in such high relief as in the Scandinavian countries. It is impossible to understand this relation if one applies to it the notion of "private property" (in a Roman or bourgeois sense). The land tiller felt himself an integral part of nature, as well as of a human collective. The land was an appurtenance of the family or kinship group that lived on it and tilled it from generation to generation. The land was perceived as homeland; patrimonium was indistinguishable from patria. The world was, in the eyes of the ancient Scandinavians, an aggregate of farmsteads, and, at the same time, a well-organized and defensible farm. Scandinavian mythology had a pair of notions, Miðgarðr ("middle-yard") and Útgarðr ("the space beyond the fence"), that were applied to the universe and expressed the opposition of culture and socially organized life, on the one hand, and chaos and evil monsters and giants, on the other hand. This pair of mythopoetic notions found a correspondence in law in the pair of terms, innangarðs-útangarðs being "the land inside the fence" and "the land beyond the fence that is singled out of the common fund." Similarly, the term heimr had both meanings, "world, fatherland, home" and "farmstead, dwelling." Thus, the tilled and humanized world was modeled on house and estate.

The key word that reveals the inner content of landownership, as seen by Scandinavians, is óðal. From the study of the old Norwegian law sources, we can see that óðal represents both the belonging of the land to man and his group, and their belonging

to the land. Óðal was thought of as an inalienable property of the man. Even when óðal changed hands, its former owners did not forfeit all their rights. Land alienation was restricted to a series of solemn procedures and presupposed the preference right of the owner's relatives (the right of preemption) and the redemption right.

The óðal right was one of the main qualities of a freeman. The social category of hǫldar, the peasants who enjoyed full rights, was that of óðalsmenn, those who hereditarily possessed óðal land. The story told by some Icelandic sagas about "the confiscation of all Norwegian óðal" that King Haraldr hárfagri ("fair-hair") Hálfdanarson was supposed to have undertaken when he united Norway (Óláfs saga helga, ch. 1; Heimskringla: Haralds saga hárfagra, ch. 6; Hákonar saga góða, ch. 1; Egils saga Skalla–Grímssonar, ch. 4) provoked a prolonged discussion among historians. It seems possible to interpret it as reminiscences about the king's encroachment upon old liberties and personal freedom of the population. This encroachment was thought of, in the period of composition of the sagas at the beginning of the 13th century, as the king's attempt to take away the óðal, though there was not, and could not be, any general confiscation of land possessions, and Haraldr took away estates only from some of his noble enemies. Óðal and personal freedom were understood by saga tellers as equivalent.

The óðal's belonging to the family was thought of as age-old, and in the Norwegian law of the 13th century we find the expression haugóðal, the land that was possessed by the family from the times when there were burial mounds, i.e., from the heathen times. The proof of the óðal right consisted in the testimony that the land was possessed by family continuously during several generations (four or even six, according to Norwegian law). A noble was called óðalsborinn maðr ("a man who was born with the óðal right").

The óðal was a very archaic institution common not only to Scandinavian peoples but also to the Germanic peoples in general (compare Gothic haim-ōþil, Old English ēðel, Old Frisian ēthel, Old Saxon ōthil, and Old High German uodal).

To acquire a new plot of land, it was necessary to sanctify it by means of special magic rituals. A torch was carried around its boundaries, or bonfires were built at certain points on them. The Icelandic term helga sér (landit) ("to acquire the land, to consecrate") retains the memory of this magic procedure. The ancient Scandinavians' ability to poeticize and mythologically interpret property relations found its expression in the eddic lay Hyndluljóð.

Old Scandinavian law codes, especially detailed in Norway and Sweden (the so-called provincial laws), characterize óðal as an object of family possession. This group was not wholly isolated from the more extensive kindred circle. A hypothesis about the existence, in ancient Scandinavia, of a large family that included three generations of relatives who led joint husbandry seems to find some confirmation in the historical sources. The óðal right belonged mainly to the male kinsmen, although in certain cases (especially in the absence of the masculine offspring), the land could be inherited by females. The earlier forms of landownership are not fixed in the written records, but some traces of them are found by archaeologists. The remains of "ancient fields" (fornåkrar, oldtidsagre) from the last centuries B.C. and the first centuries A.D. have been discovered in Jutland, Gotland, and in some regions of Sweden and Norway. There were allotments of family lands, separated by turf and stone boundaries. These landholdings belonged to the population of separate farmsteads and small villages that developed from them. Ancient Germans and Scandinavians seem to have lacked the communal property of arable land. Community, a collective regulating the village agriculture, developed during the Middle Ages (a rural form of settlement was spread mainly in Denmark). Meanwhile, pastures and forests were subjected to community rules, and separate farmers did not have exclusive rights on their plots of wood or meadow. The neighbors' collectives ruled the common meadows and forests (almeninngr), as well as mountain pastures (setr).

The specific forms of landed property corresponded to certain peculiarities of the development of large landownership. One of its characteristics was the origin of the kings' and nobles' estates as a result of the transformation of the system of gifts and feasts. It was an ancient custom that the peasant population had to afford a provision for the chieftain and his bodyguard when they visited the countryside, and to arrange a feast for them. The king could grant his right to receive veizla, entertainment, to his retainer, and the lendir menn mentioned by Icelandic sagas and Norwegian law codes were, as a matter of fact, not large landowners, although they possessed their own estates, but the king's officials who were endowed by him with the revenues from the peasants of certain regions. Because of these grants, the term veizla was applied not only to the feast, but to territory, or more exactly, to the complex of the peasants' farms from which provision was gathered by the veizlumaðr or lendr maðr, and which because of the king's bestowal came under the control of this veizlumaðr. The veizla was one of the sources of the development of noble landownership. Certain parallels to this phenomenon can be found elsewhere in Europe of the early Middle Ages, from Anglo-Saxon "bookland" to Old Russian kormlenie. Veizla was not equivalent to the western European fief, being rather its embryo.

Another feature of the large land-property development in Scandinavian countries was inner colonization, the clearing of new lands, on which petty holders were settled. They did not own their plots on the óðal right and were only lease holders, leiglendingar in Norway, landbor in Sweden and Denmark. Landbor differed radically from the land tenants in other countries of feudal Europe. They did not enjoy a competency, but, nevertheless, retained certain elements of personal freedom and were not attached to their lord or to his estate. Their landholding was leased only on a very limited term, from one to six or eight years, according to the country and the period under consideration. The landlord had a right to expel the tenant and to give his plot of land to another man. In fact, the landbo tilled his land over a long period of time, even hereditarily, on condition that he paid all his rents, mostly in kind. But the short term of lease made the leiglendingr's condition very precarious and unstable from a legal point of view, and the landlord had the option of raising the rent. The status of landholder had drawn nearer to the status of the personally dependent peasant only in Denmark, and the system of vornedskab during the 15th, 16th, and 17th centuries deprived Danish peasants of any civil rights. Attempts by the nobility to introduce the continental forms of landownership and exploitation in Norway and Sweden met with the peasants' stubborn resistance and were unsuccessful. The separate small husbandry remained dominant, and it was not accidental that in Norway it was not destroyed, but, on the contrary, strengthened. During the 16th, 17th, and 18th centuries, the main part of Norwegian church lands, as well as lands of nobility, passed into the hands of wealthy peasants.

Lit.: Hertzberg, Ebbe. "Lén og veizla i Norges sagatid." In Germanistische Abhandlungen zum LXX. Geburtstag Konrad von Maurers. Ed. Oscar Brenner et al. Göttingen: Dieterich, 1893; rpt. Aalen: Scientia, 1974, pp. 283–331; Beauchet, Ludovic. Histoire de la propriété foncière en Suède. Paris: Larose, 1904; Maurer, Konrad. Vorlesungen über altnordische Rechtsgeschichte. 3 vols. Leipzig: Deichert, 1907–08; Haff, Karl. Die dänischen Gemeinderechte. Leipzig: Deichert, 1909; Taranger, A. "The Meaning of the Words Óðal and Skeyting in the Old Laws of Norway." In Essays in Legal History Read Before the International Congress of Historical Studies Held in London in 1913. Ed. P. Vinogradoff. Oxford: Oxford University Press, 1913, pp. 159–73; Johnsen, Oscar Albert. Norges bønder. Utsyn over den norske bondestands historie. Oslo: Aschehoug, 1936; Haff, Karl. "Zu den Problemen der Agrargeschichte des germanischen Nordens." Historische Zeitschrift 155 (1937), 98–106; Frost, J. Das norwegische Bauernerbrecht. Odels- und Aasätesrecht. Jena: Fischer, 1938; Hatt, Gudmund. The Ownership of Cultivated Land. Det Kgl. Danske Videnskabernes Selskab, Hist.-filol. Meddelelser, 26.6. Copenhagen: Munksgaard, 1939; Wührer, Karl. Beiträge zur ältesten Agrargeschichte des germanischen Nordens. Jena: Fischer, 1935; Steensberg, A. Den danske landsby. Fra storfamilie til adelssamfund. Copenhagen: Schultz, 1942; Holmsen, Andreas. "Problemer i norsk jordeiendomshistorie." Historisk tidsskrift (Norway) 34.3 (1947), 220–55; Dorving, Folke. "Agrarhistorisk forskning och svensk medeltidshistoria." Historisk tidskrift (Sweden) 36.4 (1953), 384–409; Steinnes, Asgaut. "Utskyld." Historisk tidsskrift (Norway) 36.4 (1953) 301–411; Hatt, Gudmund. "Das Eigentumsrecht an bebautem Grund und Boden." Zeitschrift für Agrargeschichte und Agrarsoziologie 3.2 (1955), 118–28; Holmsen, Andreas, et al. "The Old Norwegian Peasant Community." Scandinavian Economic History Review 4 (1956), 17–81; Robberstad, Knut, et al. "Odelsrett." KLNM 12 (1957), 493–503; Borgedal, Paul. "Jordeiendommens historie i Norge." Jordskifteverket gjennom 100 år, 1859–1958. Oslo: Det Kgl. Landbruksdepartment, 1959, pp. 9–166; Rasmussen, Poul, et al. "Jordejendom." KLNM 7 (1962), 654–77; Christensen, Aksel E. Vikingetidens Danmark. Copenhagen: Gyldendal, 1969; Wührer, Karl. "Agrarverfassung." Reallexikon der germanischen Altertumskunde 1. Berlin and New York: de Gruyter, 1973, pp. 100–10; Gurevich, A. "Representations of Property During the High Middle Ages." Economy and Society 6, (1977), 1–30; Gurevich, A. Ja. "Zu Begriffsbildungen in vorkapitalistischen Gemeinwesen und ihre gesellschaftlichen Motivation: 'Hof,' 'Grund und Boden,' 'Welt.'" Anhang mittelalterlicher skandinavischer und angelsächsischer Quellen. Jahrbuch für Wirtschaftsgeschichte 1 (1979), 113–24; Lindkvist, Thomas. Landborna i Norden under äldre medeltid. Uppsala: Almqvist & Wiksell, 1979.

Aaron Ja. Gurevich

[See also: Agriculture; Cosmography; Family Structure; Hyndluljóð; Land Registers; Landownership; Laws]

Landnámabók ("The Book of Settlements") is an account of the discovery and settlement of Iceland. It deals in continuous topographical order with roughly 430 settlers, their families, and their successors around the country. Landnámabók is preserved in five redactions, three medieval and two from the 17th century. (1) Sturlubók was composed by Sturla Þórðarson (d. 1284), preserved in AM 107 fol., a copy from the 17th century of a later lost vellum MS. (2) Hauksbók is preserved, although only fourteen leaves, in a codex by the same name (AM 371 4to), written by Haukr Erlendsson (d. 1334) during the years 1306–1308. A copy from the 17th century (AM 105 fol.) was made while the MS lacked only two leaves. (3) Melabók was written in the beginning of the 14th century. Only two leaves are preserved in a MS from around 1400 (AM 445b 4to); this MS was in a more complete condition used in Þórðarbók. (4) Skarðsárbók is a compilation of Sturlubók and Hauksbók, made from the vellums in the 1630s by Björn Jónsson in Skarðsá (d. 1655). The chief MS is AM 104 fol. (5) Þórðarbók is a compilation of a MS of Skarðsárbók and Melabók, made by the priest Þórður Jónsson (d. 1670), preserved in AM 106 and 112 fol.

The relationship among the redactions was debated for a long time, and most thoroughly examined by Jón Jóhannesson (1941). According to an epilogue to Hauksbók, this redaction is compiled from Sturlubók and an older redaction written by Styrmir Kárason (d. 1245). According to Jón Jóhannesson (1941), this redaction, Styrmisbók, which is now lost, was also the basis for Sturlubók and Melabók. This theory was disputed by Sveinbjörn Rafnsson (1974), but hardly refuted. It is certain that Melabók represents the oldest preserved redaction, unfortunately only in fragments. In Melabók, the list of settlement begins with the eastern boundary of the Southern Quarter and continues clockwise around the country, while Sturlubók and Hauksbók begin with the discovery of Iceland and the first settlement in the southwestern part and continue around the country so that the Southern Quarter becomes divided into two parts. This obviously first took place in Sturlubók. The oldest redaction of Landnámabók must go back to the beginning of the 12th century. The epilogue to Hauksbók says that Ari Þorgilsson and Kolskeggr inn vitri ("the wise one") were the first to write about the settlement; and the text of Landnámabók states that Kolskeggr has sagt fyrir ("dictated" or "written about") the settlement in the southern section of the Eastern part. According to genealogies, Kolskeggr was an older contemporary of Ari. The original redaction was probably based on the information from several people acquainted with local conditions.

The preserved Landnámabók redactions are expanded in relation to the original; Melabók, however, least so. Sturlubók and Hauksbók adopted material from sagas, genealogies, and so on. It has been asserted that Landnámabók was originally written to ensure the proprietary right of certain chieftains to landownership (Sveinbjörn Rafnsson 1974), which would reduce the trustworthiness of Landnámabók's accounts. This view may be partly correct, but it does not exclude the possibility that certain traditions concerning the settlement existed, and that, by force of analogy, the accounts of the settlements should cover the whole country, especially in instances where the economic interests of certain families cannot be demonstrated.

In Landnámabók, over 3,500 personal names and almost 1,500 farm names are mentioned, which form an important source for onomastics. Moreover, Landnámabók contains many brief accounts, often extremely well told, most of which probably go back to the 13th century. Many sagas relied on Landnámabók as a source for genealogical and other biographical information.

Sturla Þórðarson presumably imagined Sturlubók as an introduction to an account of the history of Iceland, continued with Kristni saga, Þorgils saga ok Hafliða, Sturlu saga, and his own Íslendinga saga.

Ed.: Einar Eyjólfsson, ed. Sagan Landnama vm fyrstu bygging Islands af nordmønnum. Skálholt: Kruse, 1688 [based on Skarðsárbók]; Finnur Jónsson, ed. Landnámabók I–III. Hauksbók. Sturlubók. Melabók. Udgiven af det Kongelige nordiske Oldskrift-selskab. Copenhagen: Gyldendal, 1900; Gudbrand Vigfusson and F. York Powell, eds. and trans. Origines Islandicae: A Collection of the More Important Sagas and Other Native Writings Relating to the Settlement and Early History of Iceland. 2 vols. Oxford: Clarendon, 1905; rpt. Millwood: Kraus, 1976, vol. 1, pp. 2–236; Finnur Jónsson, ed. Landnámabók. Melabók A.M. 106. Udgiven af Kommissionen for det Arnamagnæanske Legat. Copenhagen: Gyldendal, 1921; Jakob Benediktsson, ed. Skarðsárbók. Landnámabók Björns Jónssonar á Skarðsá. Reykjavik: Háskóli Íslands, 1958 [with variants from Þ]; Jakob Benediktsson, ed. Íslendingabók. Landnámabók. Íslenzk fornrit, 1. Reykjavik: Hið íslenzka fornritafélag, 1968; Landnámabók. With an introduction by Jakob Bendiktsson. Icelandic Manuscripts, Series in Folio, 3. Reykjavik: Stofnun Árna Magnússonar, 1974 [facsimile]. **Tr.**: Hermann Pálsson and Paul Edwards, trans. The Book of Settlements: Landnámabók. University of Manitoba Icelandic Studies, 1. Winnipeg: University of Manitoba Press, 1972. **Lit.**: Jón Jóhannesson. Gerðir Landnámabókar. Reykjavik: Hið íslenzka bókmenntafélag, 1941; Einar Ólafur Sveinsson. Dating the Icelandic Sagas: An Essay in Method. London: Viking Society for Northern Research, 1958; Jón Helgason. Fortællinger fra Landnámabók. 1. udg., 2. opl. med ændringer og tillæg. Nordisk filologi; Tekster og lærebøger til universitetsbrug, 3. Copenhagen: Munksgaard, 1963; Jakob Benediktsson. "Landnámabók: Some Remarks on Its Value as a Historical Source." Saga-Book of the Viking Society 17 (1966–69), 275–92; Sveinbjörn Rafnsson. Studier i Landnámabók: Kritiska bidrag till den isländska fristatstidens historia. Bibliotheca historica Lundensis, 31. Lund: Gleerup, 1974 [see also the review by Jakob Benediktsson in Saga-Book of the Viking Society 19 (1974–77), 311–8]; Sveinbjörn Rafnsson. "Aðferðir og viðhorf í Landnámurannsóknum." Skírnir 150 (1976), 213–38; Bandle, Oskar. "Die Ortsnamen der Landnámabók." In Sjötíu ritgerðir helgaðar Jakobi Benediktssyni 20. júlí 1977. 2 vols. Ed. Einar G. Pétursson and Jónas Kristjánsson. Reykjavik: Stofnun Árna Magnússonar, 1977, vol. 1, pp. 47–68; Sigurður Þórarinsson. "Jarðvísindi og Landnáma." Sjötíu ritgerðir helgaðar Jakobi Benediktssyni, vol. 2, pp. 665–76; Jónas Kristjánsson. "Landnámabók and Hænsa-Þóris saga." In Opuscula Septentrionalia. Festskrift til Ole Widding, 10. 10. 1977. Ed. Bent Chr. Jacobsen et al. Copenhagen: Reitzel, 1977, pp. 134–48.

Jakob Benediktsson

[**See also:** Conversion; Hauksbók; Iceland; Íslendingabók; Landownership; Sturlunga saga]

Landownership. Little is known about landownership, or about Scandinavian society as a whole, during the Viking Age. It is likely that the family group was the most important institution. Most families probably cultivated their own land, but certainly some families possessed much land, which must have been cultivated by thralls. Kings, "chieftains," and other men of wealth probably had many persons dependent upon them. If so, it would account for the great number of peasants later to be found as tenants, and would help to explain the enormous regional differences in the distribution of landed wealth in later centuries.

In the early Middle Ages, 11th–13th centuries, Scandinavia developed along European lines into a feudal society insofar as authority, royal and clerical, and differentiation between privileged and unprivileged estates were concerned. Landownership, however, did not become feudal in the strictest sense of the word, but was basically allodial. Much land in Denmark was made church property before 1200, no doubt nearly all of it as endowments from kings and lords. Their generosity reflects their great wealth. We have concrete evidence, however, only of a few royal estates and of the renowned Hvide family, especially Sune Ebbesen, whose wealth, as far as we know, was unsurpassed until the end of the Middle Ages.

The Church's demand for land was a major factor in determining the rules of inheritance in the provincial laws (*ca.* 1200). Every son inherited from his father and from his mother one portion, every daughter half a portion, while the Church under a will could inherit up to half a portion. Marriage, death, and childbirth could change the size of a family's property radically. At the same time, selling and pawning of land became common.

The time of the Valdemars (1157–1241) saw the formation of a class of men serving the king or the bishops. The military service of the peasants became obsolete and was converted into taxes. The new nobility was recruited from the old aristocracy as well as from ordinary freemen and thus became a very heterogeneous class. It was, however, united through its service and privileges, which by about 1300 exempted all its servants, whether demesne farmers and cottars, or freeholders, from royal taxation.

The growing demands of the Crown tempted the free peasants to seek protection under the privileged classes, although this protection meant that they lost their property and became tenants. We do not know how much land passed in this way into the hands of the privileged, especially the nobility, because we have no way of determining the importance of the landowning peasantry in the early Middle Ages. But we do know that after 1350 only around 15 percent of the peasant holdings were owned by peasants, *i.e.*, the same percentage as in 1536.

Norway and Sweden developed similarly to Denmark, acquiring the same medieval institutions. As in Denmark, daughters inherited half in proportion to sons. It is, however, characteristic that this rule was introduced later than in Denmark. Sweden especially lagged behind, and slavery still existed around 1300. But thereafter development was rapid. In approximately 1350, the king made serious attempts to prevent the nobility from acquiring control of peasant property. The Norwegian Church became a rich institution, helped to a considerable degree by gifts or purchases from peasants, often in the form of partial holdings. The Crown succeeded in retaining the taxes from the nobility's tenants; in a country with such small resources, it would otherwise have been impossible to maintain a medieval royal power.

The decline in population after 1349 hit landowners hard. It caused a drop in feudal rents due to desertion (especially in Norway) and peasants forcing down the rents. In Norway, many noblemen lost their status, and the royal power was consequently weakened, with the result that the Danish kings assumed power. In Denmark, the estates of the nobility were concentrated in fewer hands. At the same time, the practice of acquiring land from the free peasants was stopped by Valdemar IV and Margrethe, who took the free peasants under royal protection. Furthermore, they confiscated or bought noble estates, thus doubling crown land, which, since the 12th century, had been small. The king was now able to live off his own properties (which included the "Crown's free peasants"), and was usually able to refrain from extraordinary taxation. As sovereign of Sweden, Margrethe pursued the same policy as in Denmark, securing the crown estates and forcing the nobility to return acquisitions of free peasant land.

Three features of Danish landownership in the late Middle Ages warrant attention. First, many noblemen did not derive their income solely from their own land. Petty noblemen served as bailiffs for the Church, the Crown, or better-off peers, and the stewards of the castles were often men of the highest aristocracy. If they were at the same time pledgees (*i.e.*, if the king had pawned the castle to them), they received the royal income in full. Second, the peasants' dues to their lord consisted of two types, the land rent

and a variety of small dues received by the lord in his capacity as lord protector. This difference is apparent with regard to village churches, where the church would often only get the land rent and a nobleman or bishop the lordly income. Third, the allodial peasantry, now "the Crown's free peasants," was a very restricted class. They could not alter the size of their holdings, and compulsory inheritance could force the heir to cultivate the land or find someone who would do so.

Scandinavian land distribution is well documented at the end of the Middle Ages. For Sweden, the figures are derived from the complete tax assessments of 1544. The Danish figures are estimated from information from institutional, personal, and regional sources:

Landowners ca. 1530 (percentage of peasant holdings in Sweden and Denmark, and of rent in Norway):

	Sweden	Denmark	Norway
Crown	5.5	*ca.* 10	4
Allodial peasants	51.7	*ca.* 15	40
Church	21.0	35–40	44
Nobility	21.8	35–40	12

The proportion between the owner categories, at least in Denmark, was nearly stable from 1412 until the Reformation, the slight instability being due to the Church's continued acquisition of land. Note the small figures for free peasants in Denmark and nobility in Norway. The number of peasants' holdings is a good yardstick in determining individual wealth, as the holdings after the population crisis tended to uniformity in size.

Within the owner categories, the differences were enormous. The bishop of Roskilde possessed 2,500–3,000 holdings, his cathedral more than 1,000, but the Odense bishop and cathedral held only 700. Sorø monastery in Zealand had 600, Grinderslev in northern Jutland, 35. Many rural vicars possessed only the "glebe" land (*i.e.*, the vicarage farm). Some noblemen possessed hardly any land, while others had 500–800 holdings. Mogens Gøye and his first wife had in 1532 as many as 1,600, 2 percent of the country. Geographically, Zealand was dominated by the Church, most of Jutland by the nobility, Djursland by the major nobility, and Salling by the minor nobility. In remote parts of the country, such as Bornholm and Blekinge, there were many free peasants. Undoubtedly, regional land distribution often had ancient roots.

Lit.: Holmsen, Andreas. *Norges historie* 1. Oslo: Gyldendal, 1939; 4th ed. 1977; Lönnroth, Erik. *Statsmagt och statsfinans i det medeltida Sverige.* Gothenburg: Elander, 1940; Christensen, Aksel E. *Kongemagt og aristokrati.* Copenhagen: Munksgaard, 1945; rpt. 1968; Iuul, Stig. "Arveret." *KLNM* 1 (1956), 258–67; Rasmussen, Poul, *et al.* "Jordejendom." *KLNM* 7 (1962), 654–77; Ulsig, Erik. *Danske adelsgodser i middelalderen.* Copenhagen: Gyldendal, 1968; Dahlerup, Troels. "Lavadelens krise." *Historisk tidsskrift* (Denmark) 12 (1969), 1–43; Gissel, Svend, *et al. Desertion and Land Colonization in the Nordic Countries c. 1300–1600.* Stockholm: Almqvist & Wiksell, 1981; Sawyer, P. H. *Kings and Vikings.* London and New York: Methuen, 1982; Ulsig, Erik. "Kronens kamp for bevarelsen af skattegodset 1241–1396." In *Profiler i nordisk senmiddelalder og renaissance. Festskrift til Poul Enemark.* Ed. Svend E. Green-Pedersen *et al.* Arusia-historiske Skrifter, 2. Århus: Arusia, 1983, pp. 203–17.

Erik Ulsig

[**See also:** Land Tenure and Inheritance]

Language. At the beginning of the Viking Age, Scandinavian was spoken over an area roughly comprising present-day Denmark and southern and central Norway and Sweden (including Bornholm, Gotland, and Åland). During the Viking Age and the early Middle Ages, Scandinavian-speaking communities established themselves in Normandy, the British Isles, the Faroes, Iceland, Greenland, the Finnish and Estonian coastal regions, and parts of Russia. In some of these places, Scandinavian became the dominant language: Orkney and Shetland, the Faroes, Iceland, and, in the areas of Scandinavian settlement, Greenland. Except where it gained total dominance, it was only in Finland and Estonia that Scandinavian survived beyond the Middle Ages, and even in Orkney and Shetland and Greenland it succumbed, in competition with Lowland Scots in the first two (ca. 1650–1750), and as a result of the extinction of the Norse colony in the third (early 16th century).

Sources. No Viking Age or medieval Scandinavian texts have been preserved from Normandy, Finland, or Estonia, and the British Isles (Man, Orkney, and Shetland excepted) and Russia have little to show other than a few brief runic inscriptions. Evidence for Scandinavian-speaking communities in these areas therefore comes mainly from place-names, remnants of Scandinavian influence on the vernacular, archaeological discoveries, and historical documents. From Man, we have over thirty runic inscriptions, most of them dated to the Viking Age, a few to the 12th century. Orkney and Shetland provide us with about thirty-five runic inscriptions from the period 1000–1200, and thirteen documents from the period 1299–1509. Verse composed in Orkney, mostly in the 12th and early 13th centuries, has been preserved in later Icelandic MSS. Three runic inscriptions have been found in the Faroes, the earliest said to be from the 10th, the latest from the 13th century; from the 14th and 15th centuries, a small number of documents survive, some of which may and some of which do exhibit Faroese linguistic features. From Greenland, over seventy-five runic inscriptions are known, the bulk from around 1300 or a little later, but a few possibly from as early as 1000; the eddic poem *Atlamál* is called "the Greenlandic" in the Icelandic MS in which it is preserved.

From Iceland and mainland Scandinavia, there is a wealth of sources. For the period before the earliest preserved vernacular MSS (Iceland and Norway ca. 1150, Denmark and Sweden ca. 1250–1275), we have to rely principally on runic inscriptions (altogether some 5,000 are known from the period 700–1500, about half of which predate 1150). Eddic and skaldic verse, personal and place-names in foreign sources or in Latin documents written in Scandinavia, and Scandinavian loanwords in foreign languages offer additional evidence.

All these sources have drawbacks. Only runic inscriptions and eddic and skaldic verse provide us with complete sentences and are free from the interference of other languages. The verse, although some of it is undoubtedly much older than 1150, is preserved in MSS of the 13th century or (much) later, the skaldic poetry in particular often in garbled form. There are also problems about the dating of many eddic poems (most of them, though, were composed not later than the 12th century), and doubts about the authenticity of some skaldic verse. The runic inscriptions of the Viking Age suffer from having been written in the sixteen-character younger *fuþark*; this system provides only the crudest guide to phonemic contrasts, and interpretation is often difficult. Iceland has no inscriptions demonstrably older than the oldest MSS.

It is not certain when the Latin alphabet was first used for writing Scandinavian, but there is some evidence that in Iceland and Norway this development must have taken place at least in the second half of the 11th century. A few extant MSS (containing texts of religious, historical, legal, or scientific character) are generally reckoned to be from the period 1150–1200; two of the longest and most important are the Icelandic and Norwegian homily books. Much information about 12th-century Icelandic phonology and orthography is to be found in the so-called *First Grammatical Treatise*, probably written about 1130–1140, but preserved in a MS of Snorri's *Edda* from around 1360. The oldest Swedish MSS are from the period 1250–1300 and consist entirely of provincial law texts; most Swedish MSS from the next half-century are also legal in character. The earliest Danish MSS follow a similar pattern: those from the period 1250–1300 contain texts of the provincial law of Scania; those from around 1300 and the following decades are predominantly law MSS, although leech books and religious and historical works also appear. Original diplomas are important linguistic sources since they normally give their date and place of issue, but only Norway shows any significant number before well into the 14th century. After 1200 (Iceland and Norway) and 1350 (Denmark and Sweden), we find great numbers of MSS containing texts on a wide variety of subjects, although from Norway there is little besides diplomas and copies of older MSS after around 1350. By the time of the Reformation, Norwegian had been almost completely ousted as a written language by Danish.

Status ca. 700. As far as we can tell, the basic structure of Scandinavian around the year 700 did not differ greatly from that of other contemporary Germanic languages. Stressed syllables could be short (VC), long ($\overline{V}C$ or $V\overline{C}$), or overlong ($\overline{V}\overline{C}$), while unstressed syllables were almost universally short; Scandinavian had also developed the front rounded vowels [y] and [ø] and the low front vowel [æ] through a process of mutation. In morphology, it retained a four-case system in nouns (with the usual differences between stem classes), adjectives (both strong and weak declensions), and pronouns, and a full range of indicative and subjunctive personal endings in the verb. Syntactically, Scandinavian had almost certainly become an SVO (Subject-Verb-Object) language, but null-subjects occurred widely; the order "head + modifier" had begun to give way to the reverse, but this was just the beginning of a slow process, which in the Faroes, Iceland, and Norway is not even complete today (cf. Norwegian *huset deres* 'their house,' Icelandic *fegurð náttúrunnar* 'the beauty of nature'). Many characteristically Scandinavian features had developed by 700, although generally they can be observed only in much later sources. *U*-mutation, especially of [a] > [ɔ], seems to have taken place over virtually the whole Scandinavian-speaking area, and, like the other mutations, to have been phonemicized by 700. But the runic and other sources bear few traces of this innovation, and by the time of the first MSS, it appears to have been largely reversed in Denmark and Sweden (Old Icelandic *ǫll*, Old Swedish *all* 'all' n. pl.). The *-sk* (*-s*) form of the verb and the suffixed definite article are thought to have developed during the syncope period (ca. A.D. 500–700), but the first examples do not appear before the 11th century.

Development. It is generally assumed that Scandinavian around 700–1050 was a relatively uniform and static language. The linguistic period is often referred to as "Common Scandinavian." However, the appearance of uniformity may be illusory and depend on scarcity of data; the preserved material can hardly represent more than a tiny proportion of the total features, and as soon as material becomes abundant in the 12th century and later, numerous linguistic differences appear among the various parts of Scandinavia. Nor was this a period without linguistic change: monophthongization of the falling diphthongs /ei/ /au/ /øy/ spread through Denmark and into many parts of Sweden, the clusters /hl/ /hn/ /hr/ were simplified to /l/ /n/ /r/ in the whole of mainland Scandinavia, the -sk form of the verb was simplified to -s in Denmark and Sweden, to mention just two phonological and one morphological change that we can follow in the sources. These changes themselves created dialectal variation since they did not spread over the whole Scandinavian area, but there must also have been numerous other isoglosses.

Scandinavian in the period around 1050–1300 is commonly divided into East Norse (EN) and West Norse (WN). EN is broadly the language of Denmark, Sweden, the colonies across the Baltic, and the Danelaw; WN is the language of Norway, Iceland, and the other Atlantic colonies. The division is based almost entirely on certain phonological and morphological criteria as they appear in MSS and to a lesser extent in runic and other sources. Monophthongization of /ei/ /au/ /øy/, lack of u-mutation, and the simplification of the verbal ending -sk > -s have been mentioned above. Other criteria are: EN /u/ vs. WN /o/ (buþ : boð 'message, command'); EN lack of front mutation in specific cases (present tense of strong verbs, EN kom(b)er : WN kømr 'comes,' past subjunctive of strong verbs, EN väre : WN væri 'would be,' before the combinations /gi/ /ki/, EN takin : WN tekinn 'taken,' where conditioned by original /z/, EN glar : WN gler 'glass'); additional occurrences of breaking in EN (EN jak : WN ek 'I'); additional types of breaking in EN (EN siunga : WN syngva '[to] sing'); EN nasal + /p/ /t/ /k/ : WN /p:/ /t:/ /k:/ (EN krumpin : WN kroppinn 'crooked, bent,' EN branter : WN brattr 'steep,' EN ænkia : WN ekkja 'widow').

How far the EN versus WN division represents the real state of affairs at any period has increasingly been questioned. While Icelandic and most forms of Norwegian apparently remain very similar until the 13th century, many differences must have developed between Swedish and Danish by the same period. The earliest Danish MSS show that Jutlandic apocope and Zealandic reduction of unstressed vowels to /ə/ had taken place, and that, doubtless in part as a consequence of this phonetic reduction, the inflectional system in these areas had been drastically simplified (resulting in a system not unlike that in modern Danish). It is also widely argued that stød, the glottal catch characteristic of most forms of modern Danish, had developed by the 12th century. The reduction of unstressed vowels and inflectional simplification are not features of the earliest Swedish MSS, and most scholars agree that the pitch-accent contrast (tones 1 and 2) characteristic of modern Norwegian and Swedish existed in those types of Scandinavian long before the Middle Ages.

Each isogloss naturally has its own extension, which may constantly change. Therefore, we find that broad dialectal divisions like EN and WN, irrespective of their overall aptness, tend to be misleading (see, for example, the "Checklist of Dialectal Criteria in O[ld] Sc[andinavian] Manuscripts (1150–1350)" in Haugen 1976: 210–3, which shows some EN features in the WN area and vice versa), and that in time they shade into other distinctions. By the 13th century, it is probably more accurate to see Scandinavian in terms of central (most Swedish and many Norwegian) and peripheral (other) dialects; by the time of the Reformation, however, a division into mainland and insular Scandinavian seems more appropriate. During the Middle Ages, many forms of Swedish and

Norwegian came to share such features as the vowel shift (which gives modern standard Norwegian and Swedish "å," "o," "u," "y" their characteristic pronunciations), vowel balance (/'fa'ra/ : /'bi:tə/), the development of retroflex consonants, affrication and spirantization of velar stops, and the loss of /-n/ in inflectional endings. Eventually, however, the spread of inflectional simplification northward from Denmark into most areas of Norway and Sweden, and the profound lexical, morphological, and even syntactic influence on the mainland Scandinavian dialects by Middle Low German meant that at the end of the Middle Ages the biggest gulf was between (most forms of) Danish, Norwegian, and Swedish on the one hand, and Faroese and Icelandic on the other (insofar as we know what late 15th-century Faroese was like). This difference arose not merely because Faroese and Icelandic retained the four-case system, personal inflection in verbs, null-subjects (disappearing or shortly to disappear from Danish, Norwegian, and Swedish), and so on, and were less affected by the flood of Middle Low German loanwords, but also because the Faroese and Icelandic phonological systems had developed in separate ways, the vowels in particular undergoing numerous changes of quality and much diphthongization.

A number of changes affected all or virtually all forms of Scandinavian. One of the most important was the lengthening of short stressed syllables, which seems to have begun in Denmark in the 12th century or earlier and to have reached Iceland by the time of the Reformation. As a result, all stressed syllables in modern Faroese and Icelandic, modern standard Norwegian and Swedish, and in the great majority of dialects are long (V̄C or VC̄; overlong syllables were shortened); in modern standard Danish, stressed monosyllables may still be short, cf. Danish /gør/, Norwegian, Swedish /jø:r/, Faroese /dʒe:r/ 'does.'

Attempts to reconstruct the history and form of the spoken dialects of Scandinavia in the period 700–1500 are based on written texts, and these sources give a very imperfect picture of the linguistic situation at any given time or place. Most MSS are copies (often copies of copies of copies), and the language in them is usually a mixture of the language of the original(s), the practices of the scriptorium in which the scribe had learned to write or in which he worked, or both, and the scribe's own dialect. In addition, as time went on, standards or norms developed in connection with secular or ecclesiastical centers. As the court and chancellery in Norway moved from Trondheim to Bergen and finally around 1300 to Oslo, we find a form of written language developing that ultimately contained elements from all three areas. In 15th-century Sweden, the Brigettine monastery of Vadstena developed distinctive habits of writing, often referred to as "Vadstena language." The syntax of much medieval literature is also patently dependent on Latin models. The distinction made between "learned" and "popular" style seems often far from clear, but it is unlikely that the most marked characteristics associated with the learned were ever a significant part of the spoken language anywhere in Scandinavia.

Outside Denmark, the Faroes, Iceland, Norway, and Sweden, we know little of linguistic developments in the Middle Ages. Gotlandic has runic texts going back to the 10th century and MS records as old as around 1350; from these sources we can see that Gotlandic was as different as Danish and Norwegian from other forms of Swedish, and was characterized both by archaic features (e.g., the retention of the falling diphthongs /ai/ /au/ /oy/) and innovations (e.g., diphthongization /iu/ > /iau/, a general tendency to raise vowels, the verb forms al, ulu for scal, sculu 'shall'). Orkney and Shetland Norn seem to have shared a number of phonological developments with Faroese and Icelandic, especially the former (e.g., /rn/ and /n:/ > /dn/, the intercalation of /g/ (Faroese /gv/) after the reflexes of Old Norse /o:/ and /u:/, /θ/ > /h/ sporadically in initial position). Greenlandic runic inscriptions exhibit a mixture of Icelandic and Norwegian features, which may have characterized an emergent Greenlandic form of Scandinavian (/θ/ > /t/ initially in some pronouns seems the only recorded Greenlandic innovation). The modern Swedish of Finland and Estonia shows some influence from Finnish and Estonian, especially on the phonological level, but it is uncertain how old this influence is. These dialects also possess a number of archaic features (e.g., retention of the old falling diphthongs, of the consonant clusters /nd/ /mb/ /ld/, and, in some areas, of short stressed syllables). Scandinavian spoken on Man and in the Hebrides was possibly influenced by Gaelic before its demise sometime in the Middle Ages.

Lit.: The principal work is Einar Haugen, *The Scandinavian Languages: An Introduction to Their History* (London: Faber and Faber, 1976); it deals with the history of all the Scandinavian languages from their origins to the present day and includes a 28-page bibliography that goes up to about 1970. Included below are **(a)** bibliographical works, **(b)** the principal histories of individial Scandinavian languages (in some respects now out-of-date), and **(c)** a few important contributions in English that have appeared since 1970.

(a) Haugen, Einar, and Thomas L. Markey. *The Scandinavian Languages: Fifty Years of Linguistic Research.* The Hague and Paris: Mouton, 1972; Haugen, Einar, ed. *A Bibliography of Scandinavian Languages and Linguistics 1900–1970.* Oslo, Bergen, and Tromsø: Universitetsforlaget, [1974]. **(b)** Skautrup, Peter. *Det danske sprogs historie.* 5 vols. Copenhagen: Gyldendal, 1944–70; Indrebø, Gustav. *Norsk målsoga.* Ed. Per Hovda and Per Thorson. Bergen: Grieg, 1951; Seip, Didrik Arup. *Norsk språkhistorie til omkring 1370.* 2nd ed. Oslo: Aschehoug, 1955; Skautrup, Peter. "Dansk sprog." *KLNM* 2 (1957), 659–62; Matras, Chr. "Færøsk sprog." *KLNM* 5 (1960), 80–4; Hreinn Benediktsson. "Islandsk språk." *KLNM* 7 (1962), 486–93; Wessén, Elias. *Svensk språkhistoria.* 3 vols. Stockholm: Almqvist & Wiksell, 1965 [7th, 4th and 2nd impressions, respectively]; Andersen, Per Sveaas. "Normanner." *KLNM* 12 (1967), 338–42; Oftedal, Magne. "Norn." *KLNM* 12 (1967), 345–7; Hødnebø, Finn. "Norsk språk." *KLNM* 12 (1967), 357–63; Skard, Vemund. *Norsk språkhistorie.* 3 vols. Oslo, Bergen, and Tromsø: Universitetsforlaget, 1967 [in progress, 3rd ed. vol. 1, 1976]; Bergman, Gösta. *Kortfattad svensk språkhistoria.* Stockholm: Prisma, 1968 [*A Short History of the Swedish Language.* Trans. Francis P. Magoun, Jr., and Helge Kökeritz. 2nd ed. Stockholm: Swedish Institute for Cultural Relations, 1973]; Wessén, Elias. "Svenska språket." *KLNM* 17 (1972), 504–9. **(c)** Stoklund, Marie. "Greenland Runic Inscriptions." *Michigan Germanic Studies* 7 (1981), 138–47; Liberman, Anatoly. *Germanic Accentology. 1: The Scandinavian Languages.* Minneapolis: University of Minnesota Press, 1982; Haugen, Einar. *Scandinavian Language Structures: A Comparative Historical Survey.* Sprachstrukturen, A5. Tübingen: Niemeyer, 1982; Page, Raymond I. "The Manx Rune-Stones." In *The Viking Age in the Isle of Man.* Ed. Christine Fell *et al.* London: Viking Society for Northern Research, 1983, pp. 133–46; Barnes, Michael P. "Norn." *Scripta Islandica* 35 (1984), 23–42; Hansen, Bente H. "The Historical Implications of the Scandinavian Linguistic Element in English: A Theoretical Evaluation." *Nowele* 4 (1984), 53–95; Söderlind, Stefan. "The Realm of the Rus': A Contribution to the Problem of the Rise of the East-Slavic Kingdom." In *Scandinavian Language Contacts.* Ed. P. Sture Ureland and Iain Clarkson. Cambridge: Cambridge University Press, 1984, pp.

133–70; Platzack, Christer. *The Scandinavian Languages and the Null Subject Parameter.* Working Papers in Scandinavian Syntax, 20. Trondheim: Linguistics Department, University of Trondheim, 1985.

Michael P. Barnes

[**See also:** Alphabet; *Atlamál*; Dialects; Eddic Poetry; Grammatical Treatises; Latin Language and Literature; Palaeography; Runes and Runic Inscriptions; Skaldic Verse; Vadstena Language]

L'Anse aux Meadows, now a small fishing village on the northern tip of the Great Northern Peninsula in Newfoundland, was the site of the first Norse settlement in North America. The settlement was located on a shallow bay, now known as Epaves Bay. It faces west across the Strait of Belle Isle to the Labrador coast, which is clearly visible in fair weather.

The Norse settlement was discovered in 1960 by the Norwegian explorer and writer Helge Ingstad, and excavated by his archaeologist wife, Anne Stine Ingstad, 1960–1968. Additional excavations were conducted 1973–1976 by the Canadian Parks Service. The site is now a national historic park. It was declared a World Heritage Site by UNESCO in 1978, the first site to obtain this distinction.

The Norse settlement, which took place around the year 1000, comprised three building complexes located close together by a brook on a narrow terrace encircling a sedge peat bog 100 m. inland from the shore. Each complex consisted of a large hall flanked by a small hut. The southernmost complex also contained a small house. Each complex had been the site of a specialized activity: one hall contained a smithy for the forging of boat nails; another hall had a carpentry shop, where replacements were made for damaged wooden boat parts; and in the third complex, boats were repaired with the new parts produced in the other two compounds. Away from the dwellings and closer to the shore was an open-ended hut with a bloomery furnace of stone and clay for the smelting of iron. A kiln for the making of charcoal to fuel the furnace lay nearby. This is the first evidence of iron manufacture in North America. The iron was made from local bog iron ore. The production was small, sufficient only for making about 100 boat nails.

The large halls were built in a specifically Icelandic architectural style characteristic of the Commonwealth Period, the same style as introduced into Greenland by the first Icelandic settlers there. The chief construction material was sod over a massive frame of wood. Each hall contained living quarters for about thirty people, as well as large storage rooms. The small huts were "pit buildings" partially set into the ground. They were used as workshops and possibly living quarters for slaves.

The settlement was not a normal colonizing venture but a base for exploration and exploitation of Vinland's resources farther south. As all exploration was coastal, the coast of the Gulf of St. Lawrence would probably have been the chief goal. From northern Newfoundland, one can circumnavigate this large inland sea, beginning and ending at L'Anse aux Meadows. The importance of the passage through the Strait of Belle Isle to the Norse settlement is made evident by the very location of the settlement on the outer coast facing the strait, rather than on one of the sheltered harbors nearby. That the Norse occupants of L'Anse aux Meadows did in fact venture farther south is demonstrated by the presence in the

Norse deposits of butternuts, *Juglans cinerea*, a North American walnut found in the St. Lawrence valley and along the Miramichi River in New Brunswick. The distribution of this nut coincides with that of wild grapes. The two fruits ripen at the same time, so that the Norse who picked the butternuts are likely to have observed and perhaps harvested wild grapes as well.

Although not Vinland *per se*, L'Anse aux Meadows would have a place in Vinland, guarding the northern entrance to this vast and rich region where hardwoods may have been the major attraction. The rigid organization of the site implies that it was a carefully planned and strictly controlled venture, authorized and executed by the leader of the Greenland colony, Leifr Eiríksson and his family. Whoever controlled and owned L'Anse aux Meadows controlled the resources of Vinland.

The L'Anse aux Meadows settlement lasted only a few years. Its great distance from Greenland was probably the chief factor in its abandonment. This distance was almost as great as that to Europe, and Europe had so much more to offer in the way of metals, luxury goods, family, and friends, as well as the necessary ties with the Church.

Lit.: Lindsay, Charles S. "Was L'Anse aux Meadows a Norse Outpost?" *Canadian Geographic Journal* (February–March 1977), 36–43; Wallace, Birgitta Linderoth. "The L'Anse aux Meadows Site." Appendix 6 in Jones, Gwyn. *The Norse Atlantic Saga: Being the Norse Voyages of Discovery and Settlement to Iceland, Greenland, and North America.* Oxford: Oxford University Press, 1964; rev. ed. 1986, pp. 285–304, figs. 26–30; Ingstad, Anne Stine, and Helge Ingstad. *The Norse Discovery of America.* 2 vols. *1: Excavations at L'Anse aux Meadows, Newfoundland 1961–1968; 2: The Historical Background and the Evidence of the Norse Settlement Discovered in Newfoundland.* Oslo: Norwegian University Press, 1986; Harris, R. Cole, and Geoffrey J. Matthews. *Historical Atlas of Canada.* Toronto, Buffalo, and London: University of Toronto Press, 1987, vol. 1, pl. 16 [contains up-to-date site maps and all of the radiocarbon dates]; Wallace, Birgitta Linderoth. "L'Anse aux Meadows: Gateway to Vinland" [forthcoming in *Acta Archaeologica*].

Birgitta Linderoth Wallace

[**See also:** America, Norse in; Greenland, Norse in; Vinland Map; Vinland Sagas]

Lapland. The geographical term "Lapland" has been used in two senses, a broader one, denoting the area of northern Scandinavia with adjacent territories of Finland plus the Kola Peninsula (sometimes called Russian Lapland), and a more restricted one, meaning the Swedish-Finnish Province of Lapland. In its broader sense, Lapland corresponds fairly well to the Old Norse term "Finnmǫrk," the name that appears in western Scandinavian sources.

The name "Lapland," prevailing in eastern Scandinavian sources, has a relatively recent origin. It occurs for the first time in Saxo Grammaticus's *Gesta Danorum* (ca. 1200) in the form of *utraque Lappia*, i.e., western and eastern Lapland (*Lappia* is the Latin equivalent of Lapland). The origin of the word *Lapp* is uncertain. According to one etymology it is of Finnish, according to another of Swedish origin. The word was probably taken into use to avoid confusion between the two earlier meanings of Finn: (1) a *Saami* (Lapp) and (2) a *Suomalainen* (an inhabitant of Finland). In Swedish, *finne* was used in the latter sense. In Old Norse, and still in Norwegian, there is confusion as to the meaning of the word *finn(r)*.

In the Middle Ages, the district of Lapland was sparsely populated. The inhabitants were Saamis who lived by hunting, fishing, and reindeer breeding. Before the Peace of Nöteborg between Sweden-Finland and Novgorod (1323), there was a rivalry among three powers over the sovereignty of these vast districts of the North, i.e., between Norway, Sweden-Finland, and Karelia (northwestern Russia and adjoining border country of Finland). The interests of the Karelians were taken over by Novgorod, which in the war preceding the Peace of Nöteborg more or less fully subdued their Karelian allies. It is very difficult to state the precise border established in the Peace of Nöteborg. The extant copies of the documents of the treaty are rather late, and have, in all probability, been falsified in details. There has not been full agreement among historians whether the border went from the Gulf of Finland to the Arctic Ocean or to the Gulf of Bothnia. It is, however, a fairly common opinion nowadays that the border went from the Gulf of Finland via the Karelian Isthmus to the Gulf of Bothnia, and terminated somewhere to the south of Oulu (Uleåborg). As the circumstances were not clear, the Swedish Crown tried to push its domains northward into the Karelian zone of interest. In the long run, the Novgorod-Karelians could not maintain their claims in the neighborhood of the Gulf of Bothnia. In the eastern parts of Finnish Lapland, representatives of both the Swedish Crown and the Karelians levied taxes. In other parts, both the Danish-Norwegian and Swedish-Finnish Crown forced the Saamis to pay taxes. In some districts in eastern Finland, the Saamis paid taxes to three nations: Denmark-Norway, Sweden-Finland, and Novgorod (Moscow).

The taxation of the Saamis of Sweden-Finland was given to a certain group of people called *birkarlar*, who collected the taxes for the Swedish king, not without some profit to themselves. According to an old but unsure tradition, this privilege was given to the *birkarlar* by the Swedish king Magnus Birgersson (r. 1275–1290).

For the purpose of taxation, Swedish-Finnish Lapland was divided into minor districts called *Lapmarks*. These districts were named after the great rivers of Lapland: Ume, Lule, Torne, and Kemi Lapmark. The taxation of Ume Lapmark, the southernmost of them all, did not belong to the *birkarlar*, but stood directly under the Crown. Therefore, the Saamis of this Lapmark were called "the King's Lapps."

The coastal areas around the Gulf of Bothnia are not looked upon as belonging to the historical province of Lapland. Here, we find in olden times another historical province called Bothnia, divided into two parts, West Bothnia (Västerbotten), and East Bothnia (Österbotten). These historical provinces (*landskap*) had a rather unofficial character. They are not now and were not then administrative provinces or counties (*län*). (*Västerbottens län* is something different from the historical province mentioned here, i.e., *landskapet* Västerbotten.)

From prehistoric times, there was a border, archaeologically substantiated, between the historical province of Jämtland to the south and Lapland to the north through the valley of Ströms Vattudal (roughly in latitude 64° north). The present-day border is a little farther to the north.

The more precise borders of the historical province of Swedish-Finnish Lapland are of late origin. The border with Norway was defined only in 1751, and the demarcation between the historical provinces of Lapland and Västerbotten was established in the same year. The latter border is called *lappmarksgränsen* (the Lapmark boundary), and runs parallel to the coastline, roughly 100 km. inland. It was intended as a demarcation line between the coastland farmers and the Saamis, and followed an old traditional boundary.

The ultimate division into Swedish and Finnish Lapland dates from 1809, and the present border between Finnish and Russian Lapland dates from after World War II.

Lit.: Ziegler, Jacob. *Terrae Sanctae, quam Palaestinam nominant, Syriae. Arabiae, Aegypti & Schondiae doctissima descripto*. Argentorati: apud Vuendelinum Rihelium, 1536, pp. xciii–xcvi; Goes, Damianus à. *Deploratio Lappianae gentis & Lappiae descriptio*. Lovanii: ex officina Rutgeri Rescii, 1540; Ahnlund, Nils. "Västerbotten." *Svenska Turistföreningens Årsskrift* (1937), 25–40 [map on p. 33]; Itkonen, T. I. *Suomen lappalaiset vuoteen 1945*. Porvoo and Helsinki: Söderström, 1948, vol. 1, pp. 27–57; Collinder, Björn. *The Lapps*. Princeton: Princeton University Press, 1949; Ahnlund, Nils. "Västerbotten före Gustav Vasa." *Västerbotten* (1955), 1–15; Jutikkala, Eino, and Kauko Pirinen. *A History of Finland*. Trans. Paul Sjöblom. New York: Praeger, 1962; Bylund, Erik. "Koloniseringen av Lappland." In *Natur i Lappland*. Ed. Kai Curry-Lindahl. Stockholm: Svensk natur, 1963, vol. 1, pp. 102–19; Baudou, Evert. "Orsaker till bebyggelseförändringar i Norrland under medeltiden." In *Arkivet, historien, rörelsen. Sven Lundkvist 60 år*. Skara: Sober, 1987, pp. 67–79 [map on p. 75]; Julku, Kyösti. "The Early History of Finland's Eastern Boundary" (= Summary). In his *Suomen itärajan synty*. Studia Historica Septentrionalia, 10. Jyväskylä: Rovaniemi, 1987, pp. 435–55.

Tryggve Sköld

[See also: Finland]

Latin Language and Literature.

The Latin language came to Scandinavia with the Christian missionaries (9th and following centuries), and the Church and its institutions remained the center of Latin culture until the Reformation. Latin also played an important role in secular administration and as the language of learning, but here regional differences were important. In Iceland and Norway, the position of the vernacular was much stronger than in other countries.

The Latin written and spoken in Scandinavia shares all the characteristics of medieval Latin in general with regard to pronunciation, spelling, morphology, syntax, vocabulary, and stylistic differentiation. Legal Latin, however, developed some neologisms particular to Scandinavia and its various regional laws.

The style of medieval Latin texts varies with their purpose or genre and with the contemporary or classical models chosen by the author. The language of most charters, annals, and scholastic texts is straightforward and its vocabulary formulaic, while some 12th-century historical works are stylistically ambitious, such as Sven Aggesen's *Brevis historia*, Saxo Grammaticus's *Gesta Danorum*, and the anonymous *Historia Norwegiae* and *De profectione Danorum*. The use of prose rhythm (cursus) and of rhymed prose was introduced in the second half of the 12th century, but we do not yet know precisely how widespread they were.

Latin verse was written regularly from the beginning of the 12th century. A wealth of rhythmical and rhymed meters were used along with quantitative meters, with or without rhyme. Ecclesiastical poetry is mainly rhythmical and rhymed. The poems of Saxo's *Gesta Danorum* are a virtuoso display of twenty-four different unrhymed classical quantitative meters, while the 14th-

century poet Jacobus Nicholai de Dacia varied the rhymed dactylic hexameters and distichs in almost as many ways in his *Liber de distinccione metrorum*; 14th-century Icelandic poets experimented with Latin verse written according to Old Norse metrics (Finnur Jónsson 1884–91, Kålund 1917–18). There are a number of texts in prosimetrum (a mixture of prose and verse), for example, Ælnoth, Saxo, and Pauper Olavus (Shetland, 15th century).

The ecclesiastical texts were of mixed origin. Besides imported liturgical texts, a whole literature soon grew up around local saints, to be used in the liturgy and for edification. Lives and passions of the saints Knud (Cnut) the king (Denmark, the first written *ca.* 1100), Óláfr (Norway, 12th century), Þorlákr (Iceland, early 13th), Botvid and Erik (Sweden, 12th and 13th), and Henrik (Finland, late 13th) were among the first texts written in Latin in each country. A number of complete saints' offices with prose readings and hymns have been transmitted, such as those for St. Knud (Cnut) Lavard (Denmark, 1170) and St. Birgitta (Önnerfors 1966). The most original Scandinavian contribution to ecclesiastical literature is St. Birgitta's *Reuelaciones*. Jacobus Nicholai de Dacia's rhythmic Mary poem (*ca.* 1350; ed. Lehmann, pp. 394–412) is unusually long.

In Denmark and Sweden, charters and official documents were originally written in Latin, in the other countries normally in the vernacular, except for international correspondence. The first transmitted Swedish charters written in the vernacular date from the 1280s, the first Danish one from 1371. A number of private Latin letter collections are extant, such as those by Abbot Wilhelm of Æbelholt (d. 1203, Denmark) and the Swede Petrus de Dacia (d. 1289).

Historical texts in Denmark were often written in Latin, in the other countries less frequently so. The lives of the king-saints form a transition to secular Latin historiography, which flourished in the 12th century in Denmark and Norway. A shortened and "medievalized" version of Saxo was composed in the early 14th century, and this *Compendium Saxonis* soon became more popular than the rather difficult original. The first Icelandic historian, Sæmundr fróði ("the learned"; d. 1133), wrote a now-lost Latin history of the Norwegian kings. The main work in Latin by a Swedish historian is Ericus Olai's *Chronicon regni Gothorum* (*ca.* 1470).

Law texts were sometimes translated into Latin, and although having no legal status, the translations served to clarify the vernacular text: Anders Sunesen wrote a paraphrase of the Scanian Law, a 14th-century Latin translation of the Jutish Law was commented upon in Latin by Bishop Knud Mikkelsen of Viborg around 1465, and King Magnus Eriksson's Swedish Law was translated around 1500 by Archdeacon Ragvald Ingemundsson of Uppsala.

Scandinavians made a significant contribution to 13th- and 14th-century scholastic literature, which had Paris as its most important center. Anders Sunesen's didactic poem *Hexaemeron* (*ca.* 1200) is an early example of theological scholasticism, and Magister Mathias (14th century, St. Birgitta's confessor) wrote a rhetorical handbook and a *Poetria* using Aristotle's works in Latin translations. But the larger part of this literature is about speculative grammar, mathematics, and astronomy.

Secular Latin poetry has not been transmitted in large quantities. Saxo's paraphrases of vernacular poetry in the *Gesta Danorum* (*ca.* 1200), inspired by Vergil, Horace, and other classical authors, are an early, sophisticated example, and Jacobus Nicholai de Dacia's poems in the *Liber de distinccione metrorum*, written around 1360 and thematically inspired by the initial on-slaught of the Black Death (1349–1350), is the only known collection of poems. Many verse epitaphs and other inscriptions are preserved, written on stone or transmitted in MSS, as well as a small number of secular songs occasioned by various political disasters (Denmark and Sweden, 13th–16th centuries). The proverbs of Peder Låle exist in a double version, of which the Latin version has a metrical form.

Bib.: Önnerfors, Alf, ed. *Mittellateinische Philologie*. Wege der Forschung, 292. Darmstadt: Wissenschaftliche Buchgesellschaft, 1975 [Scandinavia, pp. 447 ff.]; Pfaff, Richard W. *Medieval Latin Liturgy: A Select Bibliography*. Toronto Medieval Bibliographies, 9. Toronto: University of Toronto Press, 1982 [Scandinavia, pp. 118 ff.]; Olsen, Thorkil Damsgaard. "Dansk middelalderlitteratur ca. 1977–1987." *Danske Studier* 82 (1987), 108–40. **Lit.: (a) Language**: Strecker, Karl. *Introduction to Medieval Latin*. Rev. Robert B. Palmer. Berlin: Weidmann, 1957; 3rd ed. 1965; Löfstedt, Einar. *Late Latin*. Oslo: Aschehoug; Cambridge: Harvard University Press, 1959; Norberg, Dag. *Manuel pratique de latin médiéval*. Paris: Picard, 1968; Langosch, Karl. *Lateinisches Mittelalter. Einleitung in Sprache und Literatur*. 3rd ed. Darmstadt: Wissenschaftliche Buchgesellschaft, 1975. **(b) Metrics**: Norberg, Dag. *Introduction à l'étude de la versification latine médiévale*. Studia Latina Stockholmiensia, 5. Stockholm: Almqvist & Wiksell, 1958; Janson, Tore. *Prose Rhythm in Medieval Latin from the 9th to the 13th Century*. Studia Latina Stockholmiensia, 20. Stockholm: Almqvist & Wiksell, 1975; Klopsch, Paul. *Einführung in die mittellateinische Verslehre*. Darmstadt: Wissenschaftliche Buchgesellschaft, 1972. **(c) Dictionaries and glossaries**: Hammarström, Magnus. *Glossarium till Finlands och Sveriges latinska medeltidsurkunder jämte språklig inledning*. Helsinki: Finska litteratur-sällskapets tryckeri, 1925; Blatt, Franz. *Saxonis Gesta Danorum. 2: Index verborum*. Copenhagen: Levin & Munksgaard, 1957; Hakamies, Reino. *Glossarium latinitatis medii aevi Finlandicae*. Suomalaisen Tiedaakatemian julkaisemia Pohhjoismaiden historiaa valaisevia asiakirjoja, 10. Helsinki: [n.p.], 1958; Westerbergh, Ulla. *Glossarium till medeltidslatinet i Sverige. Glossarium mediae latinitatis Sueciae*. Stockholm: Almqvist & Wiksell, 1968–; Blatt, Franz, *et al. Lexicon mediae latinitatis Danicae*. Århus: Aarhus University Press, 1987–. **(d) Studies**: Finnur Jónsson. "Lønskrift og lejlighedsoptegnelser fra et par islandske håndskrifter." In *Småstykker*. Samfund til udgivelse af gammel nordisk litteratur, 13. Copenhagen: Møller, 1884–91, p. 193; Kålund, Kristian, and N. Bechman, eds. *Alfræði íslenzk: Íslandsk encyclopædisk litteratur*. 3 vols. Samfund til udgivelse af gammel nordisk litteratur, 37, 41, 45. Copenhagen: Møller, 1908–18, vol. 3, p. 64; Vandvik, Eirik. "National Admixture in Medieval Latin." *Symbolae Osloenses* 23 (1944), 81–101; Lehmann, Paul. *Skandinaviens Anteil an der lateinischen Literatur und Wissenschaft des Mittelalters*. 1. Stück. Sitzungsberichte der Bayerischen Akademie der Wissenschaften, Philosophisch-historische Abteilung, Jahrgang 1936, Heft 2. Munich: Bayerischen Akademie der Wissenschaften, 1936; 2. Stück. Jahrgang 1937, Heft 7. Munich: Bayerischen Akademie der Wissenschaften, 1937; Önnerfors, Alf. "Zur Officiendichtung im schwedischen Mittelalter." *Mittellateinisches Jahrbuch* 3 (1966), 55–93; Kabell, Aage, ed. *Iacobus Nicholai de Dacia, Liber de distinccione metrorum. Mit Einleitung und Glossar*. Monografier utgivna av Kungl. humanistiska vetenskapssamfundet i Uppsala, 2. Uppsala: Almqvist & Wiksell, 1967; Tengström, Emin. *Latinet i Sverige*. Lund: Bonnier, 1973; Skard, Sigmund. *Classical Tradition in Norway: An Introduction with Bibliography*. Oslo: Universitetsforlaget; New York: Columbia University Press, 1980; Bäärnhielm, Göran, ed. "Magnus Erikssons landslag. Latinsk översättning (ca år 1500) av Ragvald Ingemundsson, lib. V–XV." Diss. University of

Stockholm, 1980; Öberg, Jan. "Brief, Brieflitteratur, Briefsammlungen. ˌkandinavien." *Lexikon des Mittelalters*. Munich: Artemis, 1983, vol. 2, pp. 677 ff.; Friis-Jensen, Karsten. *Saxo Grammaticus as Latin Poet: Studies in the Verse Passages of the Gesta Danorum*. Analecta Romana Instituti Danici, Supplementum, 14. Rome: Bretschneider, 1987.

Karsten Friis-Jensen

[**See also:** Aggesen, Sven; Birgitta, St.; *Biskupa sögur*; Boethius de Dacia; Erik, St.; *Historia Norwegiae*; Johannes de Dacia; Knud (Cnut), St.; Martinus de Dacia; Óláfr, St.; Petrus de Dacia; *Profectio Danorum in Hierosolymam*; Saints' Lives; Saxo Grammaticus; Sunesen, Anders; Theodoricus; *Þorláks saga helga*]

Laurentius saga biskups

Laurentius saga biskups ("The Saga of Bishop Laurentius") is the youngest of the original Icelandic *Biskupa sögur* written in the Middle Ages. It records the life of Laurentius Kálfsson, born in 1267 and bishop of Hólar from 1324 until his death in 1331. The saga tells of his youth and education in both Hólar and Niðaróss (Trondheim), and of the quarrels he had with his superiors after he became a priest in Iceland and in Norway. He seems to have been more honest than the bishop of Hólar and the canons of Niðaróss considered desirable. As bishop, he proved to be very strict, making no distinctions because of an individual's status. He did seem to have a sense of humor, however, because his lively stories about comical characters, along with practical jokes and plays on words, are found woven into the saga.

The author of the saga is almost certainly Einarr Hafliðason (1307–1393), who was Laurentius's student and later assistant after Laurentius became a bishop. Einarr became a priest in 1332 and was often administrator of the Hólar episcopal seat. He went to the pope's court in Avignon in 1345–1346, traveled in France, and stayed for a while in Paris. He is thought to have translated the legend *Atburðr á Finnmǫrk* ("An Event in Finnmark") from Latin in 1381. Einarr wrote the so-called *Lǫgmannsannáll* up until 1362, the MS of which is preserved in his own hand. A number of phrases in *Laurentius saga* and the annal are almost identical. The saga seems to have been written after 1346, to judge by its reports of Árni, archbishop of Niðaróss from 1346 to 1349. Generally, the saga seems historically authentic, but is, of course, somewhat biased in favor of the main character.

The saga is preserved almost complete in two vellum MSS, AM 406a I 4to (A) from the first half of the 16th century and AM 180b fol. (B) from around 1500. They are both connected with Skagafjörður in the northern part of Iceland, but are independent of each other. In the first quarter of the saga, their texts are very similar, but after that, B is considerably more sparing of words. In both of these MSS, there are some small lacunae, one of which is common to both. This missing chapter can be supplied from the paper MS AM 404 4to (Þ), which was copied for Bishop Þorlákr Skúlason of Hólar around 1640 from MS B, while the now-missing leaves were still in the MS. The copyist of Þ drew upon A to fill in lacunae in B. The end of the saga is missing in all the MSS, but cannot have amounted to more than a few lines, since the main character at this point is on his deathbed.

In addition to the three main MSS, two vellum leaves survive from the 16th century, which seem to be copied from B, and nineteen paper MSS from the 17th and 18th centuries, derived from A, B, or Þ, and thus of no independent value.

Ed.: [Jón Sigurðsson and Guðbrandur Vigfússon, eds.] *Biskupa sögur.* 2 vols. Copenhagen: Møller, 1858–78, vol. 1, pp. 787–914; Árni Björnsson, ed. *Laurentius saga biskups.* Reykjavik: Ísafold, 1969. **Tr.**: Elton, Oliver, trans. *The Life of Laurence, Bishop of Hólar in Iceland (Laurentius saga), by Einar Haflidason.* London: Rivingtons, 1890; Jørgensen, Jørgen Højgaard, trans. *Historien om Biskop Laurentus på Holar.* Odense: Odense Universitetsforlag, 1982. **Lit.**: Storm, Gustav, ed. *Islandske Annaler indtil 1578.* Christiania [Oslo]: Grøndahl, 1888; rpt. Norsk historisk kjeldeskrift-institutt, 1977, pp. 262–70; Magnús Már Lárusson. "Laurentius saga" *KLNM* 10 (1965), 354–5; Bekker-Nielsen, Hans. "Laurentius saga." In *Dictionary of the Middle Ages.* Ed. Joseph R. Strayer. New York: Scribner, 1982–89, vol. 7, pp. 386–7.

Árni Björnsson

[**See also:** *Biskupa sögur*]

Lausavísur ("loose verses"), *i.e.*, single-stanza poems, occur intermittently in many medieval Norwegian and Icelandic prose works. The single-stanza norm is not absolute; still shorter units, termed *kviðlingar*, occur. In addition, one character may speak a series of *lausavísur*, different characters may exchange them, in a type of repartee, or the saga may present them as "work in progress" (to be subsequently gathered into an extended poem). *Lausavísur* are presented as if spoken in an immediate reaction to the speaker's situation, even one so extreme as impending death. Some of the situations described are highly specific, for instance, a pilgrimage to the Holy Land and a voyage to Vinland. But the situations can also be stereotypical: speakers on the battlefield brooding over their wrongs, inciting their comrades, gloating over the enemy dead, or at sea lamenting their discomfort as compared with the sexual or other pleasure of some rival on land. To mark this alleged spontaneity, *lausavísur* are prefaced in the sagas by the formula *þá segir [skáldit]* ("then the skald says") (or something similar), whereas an excerpt from a longer poem is announced by *svá segir [skáldit]* ("so says the skald") (or similar), without implying a temporal marker.

Sometimes, the verse form or arrangement of clauses has a simplicity that suggests extempore composition, but simple verses have not been plentifully preserved, perhaps because they were not highly valued. By far the commonest verse form in *lausavísur* is the very complex *dróttkvætt*. Indeed, many of the extant *lausavísur* are in every way highly finished miniature poems, vivid in their kennings and metaphors and encompassing the same range of topics as the extended poem: love, revenge, battle, elegy, praise, ritual insult, travel, dreams, religious beliefs, and prophecy; *Egils saga* exemplifies most genres.

Virtually all *lausavísur*, of which hundreds survive, are preserved in connection with saga texts, in a type of prosimetrum whose origin is uncertain. Some are incidental to the saga plot, but others have a material effect on it. In a few cases, such as *Kormáks saga*, they form the backbone of the saga. Some verses corroborate historical statements in the prose. They often complement the largely external viewpoint of the prose narrative by suggesting emotion and psychological depth; notable here are the elegies and laments about old age or sickness attributed to Egill, the love verses attributed to Kormákr, the dream verses attributed to Gísli, and the invective traded between rival factions during the Conversion period. Verses also complement the prose at a stylistic level, with their deviant lexis and syntax. Their presence often retards the pace of narration, creating suspense and marking climaxes. Their lexical richness adds a certain grandiloquence, evocative of the heroic age. Partial paraphrase in the prose probably helped to ensure intelligibility.

Although most *lausavísur* are attributed to professional skalds, ascriptions extend right through society, to include marginalized groups and even the dead. Extempore verse making is well attested in postmedieval Iceland, but how far it was a genuine part of Viking and medieval Icelandic culture is a largely insoluble problem. References to *lausavísur* outside the sagas (*Grágás* and *Snorra Edda*) are scanty, although supplemented by fuller and more convincing testimony in the *samtíðarsögur* ("contemporary sagas").

The treatment of *lausavísur* in the *Íslendingasögur* and *konungasögur* seems unhistorical in some respects. Some purported *lausavísur* are actually excerpts from extended poems. Sometimes, *lausavísur* are paraphrased inaccurately in the prose or linked with more than one context or author. Such features as metaphors, kennings, the present tense, apostrophes, and repetitions may be interpreted in an overliteral fashion. But in criticizing the saga testimony, we have to reckon with the relative unconcern for organic unity in the medieval aesthetic and with the uncertainties of oral and scribal tradition, which may have distorted the prose author's intention. Linguistic and metrical criteria may point to a different dating from that implied in the saga, but are of limited value because deliberate archaizing or partial modernization may have occurred. A work like *Egils saga* seems to contain different strata of *lausavísur*, ranging in age from the hero's own time to the writing down of the saga in the 13th century. Possible strata include composition (1) by the person and in the situation identified in the saga, (2) retrospectively on the part of the saga character, remembering the situation, (3) on the part of a near-contemporary of the saga character, composing either *lausavísur* or an extended poem that was subsequently broken up to provide *lausavísur*, (4) on the part of a 12th-century skald, composing in order to embellish an early (perhaps oral) version of the saga, (5) on the part of the author of a version of the saga prose (either oral or written), or (6) on the part of a later redactor or interpolator, reworking a written version of the saga (as in *Njáls saga*).

Lit.: **(a) General introductions**: Jón Helgason. "Norges og Islands digtning." In *Litteraturhistorie: Norge og Island.* Ed. Sigurður Nordal. Nordisk kultur, 8B. Stockholm: Bonnier; Oslo: Aschehoug; Copenhagen: Schultz, 1953, pp. 3–179 [detailed introduction to the topic]; Lie, Hallvard. "Lausavísur." *KLNM* 10 (1965), 355–6 [brief introduction]; Frank, Roberta. "Skaldic Poetry." In *Old Norse–Icelandic Literature: A Critical Guide.* Ed. Carol J. Clover and John Lindow. Islandica, 45. Ithaca and London: Cornell University Press, 1985; Poole, Russell. "Verses and Prose in *Gunnlaugs saga ormstungu*." In *The Sagas of Icelanders: A Book of Essays.* Ed. John Tucker. New York and London: Garland, 1989, pp. 160–84 [general essay on the origin and role of *lausavísur* in *Gunnlaugs saga*]. **(b) Discussions of authenticity and related problems**: Finnur Jónsson. "Sagaernes lausavísur." *Aarbøger for nordisk Oldkyndighed og Historie* (1912), 1–57 [supports the authenticity of most *lausavísur*, partly on linguistic grounds]; Sigurður Nordal, ed. *Egils saga Skalla-Grímssonar.* Íslenzk fornrit, 2. Reykjavik: Hið íslenzka fornritafélag, 1933 [argues that Egill may have retrospectively composed some of the verses attributed to him]; Foote, Peter. "An Essay on the *Saga of Gísli*." In *The Saga of Gísli.* Trans. George Johnston. Toronto: University of Toronto Press, 1963, pp. 112–9 [expresses skepticism concerning the authenticity of the verses attributed to Gísli]; Jónas Kristjánsson. *Um Fóstbræðrasögu.* Reykjavik: Stofnun Árna Magnússonar, 1972 [full discussion of means of assessing authenticity of *lausavísur*, with application to the Þormóðr attributions]; See, Klaus von. "Skaldenstrophe und Sagaprosa: Ein Beitrag zum Problem der mündlichen Überlieferung in der altnordischen Literatur." *Mediaeval Scandinavia* 10 (1977), 58–82; rpt. in his *Edda, Saga, Skaldendichtung: Aufsätze zur skandinavischen Literatur des Mittelalters*. Heidelberg: Winter, 1981, pp. 461–85 [argues that the explanations of *lausavísur* in the saga prose do not necessarily rest on oral tradition and may be misleading]; Poole, Russell. "The Origins of the *Máhlíðingavísur*." *Scandinavian Studies* 57 (1985), 244–85 [argues that the author of an early version of *Eyrbyggja saga* dismembered a poem to provide *lausavísur* for separate episodes in the saga]; Poole, Russell. "Some Royal Love Verses." *Maal og minne* (1985), 115–31 [deals with migratory verses attributed to various Norwegian kings]; Poole, R. G. "The Cooperative Principle in Some Medieval Interpretations of Skaldic Verse: Snorri Sturluson, Þjóðólfr Arnórsson, and Eyvindr skáldaspillir." *Journal of English and Germanic Philology* 87 (1988), 159–78 [argues that interpretation of verses in the sagas sometimes rests on the application of norms used in the interpretation of ordinary conversation]. **(c) Discussions of the prosimetrum form**: Hruby, Arthur. *Wann sprechen die Personen der isländischen Saga eine Strophe? Eine Studie zur Technik der Saga*. Vienna: Manzsch, 1932 [the part played by verses in the saga literature]; Wolf, Alois. "Zur Rolle der *Vísur* in der altnordischen Prosa." In *Festschrift Leonhard C. Franz zum 70. Geburtstag*. Ed. Osmund Menghin and Hermann M. Ölberg. Innsbrucker Beiträge zur Kulturwissenschaft, 11. Innsbruck: Institut für Vergleichende Sprachwissenschaft der Universität Innsbruck, 1965, pp. 459–84; Clover, Carol J. "Scene in Saga Composition." *Arkiv för nordisk filologi* 89 (1974), 57–83 [the placing of *lausavísur* in saga scenes and episodes]; Bjarni Einarsson. "On the Role of Verse in Saga-Literature." *Mediaeval Scandinavia* 7 (1974), 118–25 [argues that verses in the sagas of Icelanders should be treated as embellishment rather than as evidential support for the prose narrative]; Magerøy, Hallvard. "Skaldestrofer som retardasjonsmiddel i islendingesogene." In *Sjötíu ritgerðir helgaðar Jakobi Benediktssyni 20. júlí 1977*. 2 vols. Ed. Einar G. Pétursson and Jónas Kristjánsson. Reykjavik: Stofnun Árna Magnússonar, 1977, vol. 2, pp. 586–99 [verses as a means of creating arrest in the prose narrative]. **(d)** The following four entries form a debate concerning the origin and role of the *lausavísur* in *Kormáks saga*: Bjarni Einarsson. *Skáldasögur: Um uppruna og eðli ástaskáldasagnanna fornu*. Reykjavik: Menningarsjóður, 1961 [argues that the verses and prose in *Kormáks saga* and other sagas concerning skalds were influenced by the Tristan story]; Einar Ól. Sveinsson. "Kormakr the Poet and His Verses." *Saga-Book of the Viking Society* 17 (1966), 18–60 [argues that the verses in *Kormáks saga* are older than the prose and to some extent authentic]; Andersson, Theodore M. "Skalds and Troubadours." *Mediaeval Scandinavia* 2 (1969), 7–41 [supports Einar Ól. Sveinsson on dating and native origin of verses in *Kormáks saga*]; Bjarni Einarsson. "The Lovesick Skald: A Reply to Theodore M. Andersson (*Mediaeval Scandinavia* 1969)." *Mediaeval Scandinavia* 4 (1971), 21–41 [contests the use of linguistic evidence as a means of dating]. **(e)** Another debate, on verses attributed to Torf-Einarr: See, Klaus von. "Der Skalde Torf-Einar Jarl." *Beiträge zur Geschichte der deutschen Sprache und Literatur* (Tübingen) 82 (1960), 31–43; rpt. in his *Edda, Saga, Skaldendichtung*, pp. 367–79 [argues that the verses attributed to Torf-Einarr are constituent stanzas in a poem, composed retrospectively]; Hofmann, Dietrich. "Sagaprosa als Partner von Skaldenstrophen." *Mediaeval Scandinavia* 11 (1982 for 1978–79), 68–81 [dissents from von See's conclusions concerning Torf-Einarr]; See, Klaus von. "Mündliche Prosa und Skaldendichtung. Mit einem Exkurs über Skaldensagas und Trobadorbiographien." *Mediaeval Scandinavia* 11 (1982 for 1978–79), 82–91; rpt. in his *Edda, Saga, Skaldendichtung*, pp. 496–505 [reply to Hofmann].

Russell Poole

[**See also**: *Heiti*; Kennings; *Skáld*; Skaldic Meters; Skaldic Verse]

Laws

1. DENMARK. In his *Gesta Danorum* (ca. 1200), the Danish historian Saxo tells us about the achievements of early Danish kings as lawmakers. Some of these kings are purely legendary figures, and as for the rest of them, their laws are hardly the result of what posterity has called legislation, but rather an expression of the maintenance of peace that the Church required of the kings, and that started in the kingdom of the Franks in the 9th century and then spread from there under the name of "God's Peace" and later "Peace of the Land." Such laws of peace, which can be better characterized as agreements than as legislation, originated under St. Knud (Cnut; r. 1080–1086). In the biography of this king as a saint, there is talk of an *edictum regale*, which contains punitive provisions (*vindicta*); but the purpose was to ensure "observance of holy days and the legal periods of fasting as they are otherwise observed throughout the world." A rebellion broke out, and the king was killed. His attempts to make laws may be the explanation. At any rate, we hear of no more attempts of a similar nature for the next 100 years.

Saxo and other sources talk about a law called the *Vederlov* ("Veder Law"), which consisted of rules for the warriors in the king's guard, his personal army (*lex castrensis*). It is supposed to have been written down around the year 1180 at the request of King Knud VI and Archbishop Absalon, but it is said to go back to a law that King Knud (Cnut) den Store ("the great"; r. 1018–1035) had issued for his guard when he became king of Denmark, Norway, and England. It is not unlikely that some of the rules in the *Vederlov* originate from the time of Knud; but others are more recent, and several have been inspired by the ecclesiastical law of the 12th century. The law further establishes the mutual rights and duties in the contractual agreement between the guard and the guard's sovereign, the king. The duty to obey the commands of the king and to observe mutual tolerance within the brotherhood of the guard are the most important rules.

It was not the first time that Absalon became occupied with laws and rights. In Paris, he had studied not only theology and philosophy, but also ecclesiastical law and the political theory. Late in the year 1157, he returned and took up residence with Knud Lavard's son, Valdemar, who at the time was king of Jutland together with King Niels's grandson, Knud Magnussen. There is evidence that Absalon then began recording the Jutish law, for when the kingdom was unified under Valdemar den Store ("the great"), the Jutish rules of inheritance seem to have been transferred to and incorporated into the "Law of Zealand." The written privileges for the city of Schleswig, which, according to the Latin municipal law of this town dating from about 1200, goes back to Sven Grathe, also originate from about the middle of the 12th century.

The recording of the laws of the Danish lands seems to have continued under Valdemar den Store (r. 1157–1182): under the year 1170, the *Ryd Yearbook* (*Annales Ryenses*) says: *Leges Danorum edite sunt*, "the laws of the Danes are published." But except for the *Vederlov* and some lesser ecclesiastical laws for Scania and Zealand, we do not know the results of these efforts to create written laws. The provincial laws that have been transmitted appear to have been recorded between about 1200 and 1241; but no preserved MSS are older than about 1250, and most of them date from the 1300s and later.

Judging from its content, the Law of Scania was recorded between 1202 and 1216; it mentions Valdemar II, who became king in 1202. In the law, there are rules about the testimony of ordeal by fire, which was prohibited by the Church in 1215, so that it must have been abolished soon after that by royal edict, which we know of in undated form. Archbishop Anders Sunesen's Latin paraphrase, an explication and interpretation of the Law of Scania, closely resembles the 241 chapters of the Law of Scania. It was possibly meant for the internal use of the Church: in several papal letters, information is requested concerning local customary laws; but the Latin version could also have been written for the use of foreign clergy operating in Scania. For the legal historian, it is important to study the Latin translation of the Old Danish legal concepts of the Archbishop Sunesen, who was well versed in Roman law and canon law. But it is just as important for Danish philologists, of course, that all the provincial laws from the 13th century were recorded in the mother tongue.

The oldest preserved laws of Zealand appear to have been recorded after the Law of Scania. They exist in three different editions, collectively called Valdemar's Zealandic Law. As already mentioned, Jutish dialect indicates that some rules pertaining to inheritance were transferred from Jutland in the middle of the 12th century; the royal name of Valdemar may therefore have been attached to this complex of laws, whose age is confirmed by several rules concerning ordeal by fire. By contrast, there is only one rule about ordeal by fire in Erik's Zealandic Law, whose content and language are not more recent than the laws of Valdemar from this island. Jurors have replaced the ordeal by fire, and many rules supplement and expand the older rules in Valdemar's Zealandic Law. It is not known which King Erik is being referred to; from 1234 to 1246 there were two ruling kings by this name, and from 1259 to 1319 there were again two Eriks. A late posterity must have related the recorded customary rights in the provincial laws to the royal names, thereby endowing them with a legislative power unknown in the 13th century, not only in Denmark, but also in all of western Europe.

The above seems to be contradicted by the fact that King Knud VI, in the year 1200, issued a law in Latin concerning homicide in Scania, which stated that "the monarchy is entitled to make and change laws." But it was added that the law in question is not new, but only and simply forgotten; furthermore, the rules in the law pertain to the maintenance of peace, which was the duty assigned to the king by the Church. Archbishop Absalon also witnessed the execution of the law.

This limited competence of the monarchy is in accordance with the Jutish Law, the only one among the provincial laws that has been dated (to 1241) as well as provided with a prologue. The originator of the recording of the law seems to be Bishop Gunnar of Viborg, who witnessed the making of the law together with the other bishops of the kingdom, and who was the king's closest adviser in this matter according to a contemporary source. The prologue emphasizes the necessity of the law and the duties of the authorities. Concerning the king's relationship to the law, it states that he cannot change or abolish the law of the land unless it is in direct violation of God's commandments. Concerning the organization of society, it states that the government of the Church is the model for the government of the country. The king must be obeyed because he has to maintain peace for everyone and especially protect the Church. Most of the sentences in the prologue are a free rendition of rules from the canon law, which Bishop Gunnar had studied in Paris in his youth.

Although the content of the Jutish Law resembles the other provincial laws in many areas, resembling the Scanian law most, in other areas it is a product of the political situation toward the

middle of the 13th century. Also, linguistically it appeared as the most recent of the old Danish laws and was to become the foundation for the states of the law, not just in the late Middle Ages but all the way up to the law book for the entire country, during the absolute monarchy, King Christian V's Danish Laws from 1683.

Two legal texts, from the middle of the 13th century, became valid for all of Denmark. They establish strict penalties for certain breaches of the peace, prescribing the death penalty and confiscation for high treason. The great magnates seemed to have reacted against these rules, not least as the king demanded the right to appoint jurors in cases concerning high treason. The result was a defeat for the king; in 1282, King Erik Klipping had to sign a charter, a royal promise, that severely limited the power of the king, and especially his opportunity to make laws, to the advantage of the nobility, who insisted upon the inherited state of the law. Up until the inauguration of the absolute monarchy in 1660, each succeeding king had to sign a royal pledge establishing the constitution written by the State Council. Thus, the king was obliged to maintain peace in accordance with ordinances issued for each individual country.

Thord's Articles, written in Latin, closely resemble the Jutish Law. They were supposedly written by Thord Litle, who, around 1300, was a provincial judge in Viborg in Jutland. Several of the articles appear to have been worked out in legal practice.

Except for coronation charters, peace regulations, and privileges for the towns, Denmark in the late Middle Ages is deficient in laws. The court practices filled in the deficiencies in the provincial laws; and especially the royal court, which consisted of the king and the State Council, performed a judicial function in sentencing.

The Middle Ages in Denmark ended with King Christian II's (r. 1513–1523) comprehensive attempt at legislation. A complex of laws consisting of a unified law for the country and one for the towns was elaborated in 1521–1522. But the aristocracy reacted against the policy of the king; he was driven from the throne in 1523, and his laws were abolished. Under his successor, Frederik I (r. 1523–1533), the laws reflected those changes in the Church and society that resulted in the Reformation in 1536.

Ed.: Brøndum-Nielsen, Johs., and Poul Johs. Jørgensen, eds. *Danmarks gamle Landskabslove med Kirkelovene*. 8 vols. Copenhagen: Gyldendal; Nordisk Forlag, 1933–61; Kroman, Erik, and Stig Iuul, eds. *Danmarks gamle Love paa nutidsdansk*. 3 vols. Copenhagen: Gad, 1945–48; Kroman, Erik, ed. *Danmarks gamle Købstadslovgivning*. 5 vols. Copenhagen: Rosenkilde & Bagger, 1951–61; Kroman, Erik, ed. *Den danske Rigslovgivning indtil 1513*. 2 vols. Copenhagen: Munksgaard, 1971–91. **Lit**.: Jørgensen, Poul Johs. *Dansk Retshistorie*. Copenhagen: Gad, 1947; Fenger, Ole. *Gammeldansk ret. Dansk rets historie i oldtid og middelalder*. Viborg: Centrum, 1983.

Ole Fenger

2. ICELAND. Iceland was settled in the decades shortly before and after the year 900. Toward the end of the settlement period, according to Ari Þorgilsson's *Íslendingabók* (ch. 2), a Norwegian named Úlfljótr brought the law from Norway to Iceland. Presumably, Úlfljótr acted as the first lawspeaker until about 930, modeling his laws after the West Norwegian *Gulaþingslǫg* and enjoying the counsel of Þorleifr Hǫrða-Kárason. This initial law of Iceland, *Úlfljótslǫg*, is lost. It must have incorporated the ideas of the General Assembly, the Law Council, and the lawspeaker. Among the early activities of the Law Council (ca. 965) was the division of the country into quarters with Quarter Assemblies and

Quarter Courts, as related in *Íslendingabók* (ch. 5). A well-known piece of legislation is the acceptance of Christianity in the year 1000, when the law required that all men should become Christians and be baptized (*cf. Íslendingabók*, ch. 7). Ch. 8 relates that during Skapti Þóroddsson's time as lawspeaker (1004–1030), dueling was abolished and the Fifth Court established. Legislation was a difficult process that required the agreement of chieftains, prominent members of the Law Council, and their followers who shared the Quarters' seats.

Tithe law was introduced in 1096 by Bishop Gizurr Ísleifsson, who also had laws made to establish the sees at Skálholt in 1082 and at Hólar in 1106. A new law requiring that the laws be written down in a book was passed at the General Assembly of 1117. This task was to be carried out by Hafliði Másson, the lawspeaker Bergþórr Hrafnsson, and other wise men. According to *Íslendingabók* (ch. 10), they were to introduce such new laws as seemed better to them than the old ones. They were to announce them during the next session and retain all those that were not opposed. The homicide section and much else were written and read to the Law Council, and everyone was pleased with it, and nobody spoke against it. *Hafliðaskrá*, however, as this code was called, is also lost, but we have reason to assume that much of it is preserved in *Grágás*, whose oldest fragment, AM 315d fol., is only about thirty years younger.

The preserved laws of the Icelandic Commonwealth are generally known as *Grágás* ("grey goose"). *Grágás* is not a unified corpus of law, but refers to some 130 codices, fragments, and copies incorporating the tithe law of 1096 and the old Christian law (*Kristinn réttr forni*), originally drawn up by Bishop Þorlákr Rúnólfsson (1118–1133) under the guidance of Archbishop Asser of Lund, according to *Hungrvaka* (ch. 11).

After the Icelanders' submission to the Norwegian king in 1262–1264, *Grágás* was soon superseded by the unpopular *Járnsíða* (1271–1281), which is preserved in a single 13th-century MS, AM 334 fol., and a few copies, and eventually replaced by the long-enduring *Jónsbók*, which received several amendments and has come down to us in more than 260 MSS. Both these law codes did not immediately replace the old Christian law section *Kristinna laga þáttr* of *Grágás*. Bishop Árni Þorláksson issued his new church law (*Kristinn réttr nýi*) in 1275 and had it accepted by the General Assembly for the diocese of Skálholt, whereas in the diocese of Hólar the old Christian law remained in force until 1354.

Ed.: Keyser, R., et al., eds. *Norges Gamle Love indtil 1387*. 5 vols. Christiania [Oslo]: Grøndahl, 1846–95, vol. 1, pp. 259–300 [*Járnsíða*], vol. 5, pp. 16–56 [*Kristinn réttr nýi*]; Páll Eggert Ólason, ed. *Staðarhólsbók: The Ancient Lawbooks Grágás and Járnsíða*. Corpus Codicum Islandicorum Medii Aevi, 9. Copenhagen: Munksgaard, 1936 [facsimile; contains *Kristinn réttr nýi*]; Jakob Benediktsson, ed. *Skarðsbók. Jónsbók and Other Laws and Precepts. MS. No. 350 fol. in the Arna-Magnæan Collection*. Corpus Codicum Islandicorum Medii Aevi, 16. Copenhagen: Munksgaard, 1943 [facsimile]; Westergård-Nielsen, Chr., ed. *Skálholtsbók eldri. Jónsbók etc. AM 451 Fol*. Early Icelandic Manuscripts in Facsimile, 9. Copenhagen: Rosenkilde & Bagger, 1971; Jónas Kristjánsson et al., eds. *Skarðsbók. Codex Scardensis. AM 350 fol*. Manuscripta Islandica Medii Aevi, 1. Reykjavik: Lögberg, 1981. **Bib.**: Halldór Hermannsson. *The Ancient Laws of Norway and Iceland*. Islandica, 4. Ithaca: Cornell University Library, 1911; Townsend, J. A. B. "The Ancient Laws of Norway and Iceland: A Bibliographical Supplement to . . . Islandica 4." M.A. thesis, University of London, 1961.

Hans Fix

3. NORWAY. The oldest legislation known in Norway can be traced to the assemblies (*lǫgþing*) of each law province. In the 11th century, Norway had four law provinces, known by their assembly names: "Gulaþing," established around 950, covering western Norway; "Frostuþing," established around 950, covering Trøndelag; "Eiðsifaþing," established around 1020, covering the inland area of eastern Norway; and "Borgarþing," established somewhat later, covering the Oslofjord regions.

At the assemblies, the laws were probably recited by "lawspeakers" or "lawmen" (*lǫgmenn*). The laws were at first transmitted orally but began to be recorded in the latter part of the 11th century. We now have only the Gulaþing and the Frostuþing laws in complete form. Only one complete medieval MS is preserved containing the Gulaþing laws, *Codex Rantzovianus* (E donatione variorum no. 137 4to), written 1250–1300 in a West Norwegian dialect. Additionally, twelve fragments dating from the 13th century are preserved. One contains a part of the laws for eastern Norway.

The provincial laws contain regulations based partly on custom, partly on decision, made at the provincial assemblies. The contents of these laws are mostly the same as in the *Landslǫg* (see below).

Tradition says that the old laws were revised by St. Óláfr (r. 1015–1028). In the preserved Gulaþing laws, scholars distinguish an "Óláfr-text" from a "Magnús-text" (Magnús Erlingsson, r. 1161–1184). In the Frostuþing laws, there is an older version called *Grágás* ("grey goose"). (The name "Grágás" appears in a medieval source and is used of a collection of Norwegian laws; it later came to be applied to Icelandic texts.)

The first section of each of the old provincial laws concerns matters of Christian observance. Such regulations were included among the laws in the course of the 11th century; there are some references in the Gulaþing laws to provisions agreed between St. Óláfr and his attendant bishop Grímkell. The earliest Christian laws bear some resemblance to Anglo-Saxon church legislation.

In the early trading centers, separate laws were developed. They go by the name of "Bjarkøy laws" (*Bjarkeyjarréttr*). These laws became a municipal code, which was first recorded toward the end of the 12th century. Only two medieval fragments of the Niðaróss (Trondheim) version of these laws have survived, the oldest dating from around 1250.

A Norwegian metropolitan see was established at Niðaróss in 1152/3. At that time, ecclesiastical statutes with national validity were promulgated. The second archbishop of Niðaróss, Eysteinn Erlendsson (1161–1188), took the initiative in securing a revision of the Christian laws of the old law provinces; the outcome was a volume called *Gullfjǫðr* ("gold-feather").

In King Magnús Erlingsson's reign, an extensive revision of legislation was undertaken, and the influence of the provincial assemblies reduced. King Hákon Hákonarson (r. 1217–1263) began to revise the Frostuþing laws, but it fell to one of his sons, Magnús (r. 1263–1284), to complete his work.

The development of legislation on a national scale went hand in hand with the general political evolution in Norway. King Haraldr hárfagri ("fair-hair") conquered western Norway at the end of the 9th century. In the following century or so, coastal Norway remained a more or less united kingdom under Haraldr's descendants, but definitive control over the rich inland regions of eastern Norway and Trøndelag was not achieved until after the death of St. Óláfr at Stiklestad in 1030, when the monarchy was strengthened by the power of the Church. A period of comparatively peaceful development was then interrupted by intermittent wars of succession, especially in the century from about 1130 onward. And when these wars finally came to an end in 1240, the national monarchy, personified in Hákon Hákonarson, emerged as the sovereign power. The unification of the realm was completed and the ground prepared for the creation of a national legal code.

Initially, King Magnús got his counselors to revise the Gulaþing laws (1267) and those of the East Norwegian provinces (1268). Only the Christian law sections of these revisions survive. In June 1269, King Magnús and Archbishop Jón (1268–1282) met at the Frostuþing. The Icelandic annals report: "Then King Magnús got the agreement of all the men of Frostuþing that he should compose the Frostuþing book in everything pertaining to secular affairs and the monarchy as he thought best" (Storm 1888: 138). The king was thus not authorized to revise the Christian law section.

Soon afterward, work was begun on a code for the whole of the country (Landslǫg). Decisions promulgated by national assemblies held in 1271 and 1273 were included in the new code, which was completed in time to be adopted by the Gulaþing in 1274 and by the Frostuþing probably in the following year. It was accepted by the Eiðsifaþing and the Borgarþing in 1276. Although a common secular code had now been created, it actually existed in four separate versions, one for each of the old law provinces. But the differences between them were only minor and have to do mainly with the name and organization of the assembly. In later copies of the code, this ground was covered in general terms.

King Magnús's Landslǫg starts with a prologue and is then divided into the following sections: þingfararbǫlkr (on the organization of assemblies), kristinsdómsbǫlkr (the Christian law section), landvarnarbǫlkr (on the defense of the realm), mannhelgarbǫlkr (on personal rights), erfðatal (on inheritance), landabrigði (on tenancies), kaupabǫlkr (on contracts), þjófabǫlkr (on theft), and a last section containing statutes.

The contents of the Landslǫg go back mainly to the older laws of the Gulaþing and Frostuþing. The East Norwegian laws are lost, but they probably supplied a certain amount of material to the Landslǫg, especially in the section on land tenancies. A couple of instances in the sections on personal rights and inheritance show traces of borrowing or influence from Icelandic laws. Influence from canon law is discernible in the sections on personal rights and theft. A principle of subjective guilt is sometimes applied, and in general the attitude is more humane than in the older provincial codes. In this attitude, the influence of Roman law is also detectable. By reforming the law on rights of preemption and redemption of family land, and by restricting freedom of donation, King Magnús sought to limit a growing concentration of landownership in the Church's hands. Several matters not previously regarded as the province of the Crown are brought under state control.

King Magnús's zeal in his work on the Landslǫg earned him the nickname Law-mender (lagabœtir). But he must have been assisted by men learned in law. We learn from the prologue and conclusion that the king compiled the Landslǫg "with the advice of the best men." These "best men" must have belonged among the king's counselors. We have a few clues to their identity. It has been suggested that Auðunn Hugleiksson (baron from 1277, d. 1302) and the chancellor Þórir Hákonarson were the chief men behind the revision of the laws.

Thirty-nine fairly complete medieval MSS of the Landslǫg exist. Two date from the end of the 13th century and three from after 1350; the others date from the first half of the 14th century. Thirty-one fragments of Landslǫg MSS are also preserved. Six of them probably date from the end of the 13th century, one is from

the latter part of the 14th century, and the rest from around 1300–1350. The majority of the more or less complete MSS appear to have been written in Bergen, Oslo, and Tønsberg. We know very little about the scribes except the names of two of them: Þorgeirr Hákonarson and Eiríkr Þróndarson, both working around 1300. No original of the Landslǫg survives, and we must assume that many copies have disappeared. According to Storm (1879: 11), at least eighty copies must have existed in the 16th century.

King Magnús's legislative work was not confined to the Landslǫg. His name is also connected with the Hirðskrá ("retinue-book") preserved in ten medieval MSS and four fragments, all dating from the 14th century, and to a new municipal code, preserved in twenty-five MSS and three fragments, the oldest from the end of the 13th century.

King Magnús was authorized to revise only the secular part of the laws. Archbishop Jón initiated work on an ecclesiastical code (completed 1273), based on principles of canon law. Archbishop Jón's ecclesiastical code is preserved in seven MSS, five of them dating from the 14th century. The result of the ensuing discussions between king and Church was a concordat in Tønsberg in 1277. The final stage in ecclesiastical legislation in medieval Norway is represented by a code issued in the reign of King Hákon VI (ca. 1355–80).

Ed.: Keyser, R., et al., eds. Norges gamle love indtil 1387. 5 vols. Christiania [Oslo]: Grøndahl, 1846–95; Flom, George T., ed. The Borgarthing Law of the Codex Tunsbergensis. University of Illinois Studies in Language and Literature, 10.4. Urbana: University of Illinois Press, 1925; Flom, George T., ed. The Old Norwegian General Law of the Gulathing According to Codex Gl.k.S. 1154 Folio. Illinois Studies in Language and Literature, 20.3–4. Urbana: University of Illinois Press, 1937; King Magnus Håkonsson's Laws of Norway and Other Legal Texts. Gl. kgl. Saml. 1154 fol. Introductions by Magnus Rindal and Knut Berg. Corpus Codicum Norvegicorum Medii Aevi, 7. Oslo: Society for Publication of Old Norwegian Manuscripts, 1983 [facsimile]. **Tr.**: Larson, Lawrence M., trans. The Earliest Norwegian Laws, Being the Gulathing Law and the Frostathing Law. Records of Civilization, 20. New York: Columbia University Press, 1935. **Lit.**: Storm, Gustav. Om Haandskrifter og Oversættelser af Magnus Lagabøters Love. Christiania Videnskabsselskabs Forhandlinger 1879, 14. Christiania [Oslo]: Dybwad, 1879; Storm, Gustav, ed. Islandske Annaler indtil 1578. Christiania [Oslo]: Grøndahl, 1888; rpt. Norsk historisk kjeldeskrift-institutt, 1977; Helle, Knut. Norge blir en stat 1130–1319. Handbok i Norges historie, 3. Bergen, Oslo, and Tromsø: Universitetsforlaget, 1974; Robberstad, Knut. Rettssoga. 3rd rev. ed. Oslo, Bergen, and Tromsø: Universitetsforlaget, 1976; Andersen, Per Sveaas. Samlingen av Norge og kristningen av landet 800–1130. Handbok i Norges historie, 2. Bergen, Oslo, and Tromsø: Universitetsforlaget, 1977.

Magnus Rindal

4. SWEDEN. Sweden's medieval laws constitute laws for the various provinces, a state law, and a municipal law. The state law is found in an older and a younger version.

Two provincial laws have royal assent, the Law of Uppland (Upplandslagen) of 1296 and the Law of Södermanland (Södermannalagen) of 1327; both applied to the areas north and south of Stockholm. The Law of Västmanland (Västmannalagen) governed the area west of Stockholm, and the Law of Hälsingland (Hälsingelagen), northern Sweden. The Law of Dalecarlia (Dalalagen) received its name in more recent times, and it is uncertain if it governed the present province of Dalarna, although this is the generally accepted opinion. A new theory says that it governed the provinces of Värmland and Dalsland (Sjöholm 1988). In certain sources, a Law of Närke (*Närkeslagen*) is mentioned, but no MSS of it are extant. The above-mentioned laws go under the common designation of the "Svea Laws."

The Göta Laws governed South Sweden, and contain the Law of Östergötland (*Östgötalagen*) and two versions of the Law of Västergötland (*Västgötalagen*), normally called the "older" and "younger" Västgöta Law. Moreover, there is a canon law for the Växjö diocese as an addition to a MS of the state law. This canon law generally is referred to as the ecclesiastical section of the "Law of Småland" (*Smålandslagen*). However, no MSS of this law have been preserved. The Laws of Västergötland distinguish themselves from the other laws by the fact that the MSS in which they are found also contain other texts primarily concerned with Västergötland. The Law of Gotland (*Gutalagen*), which governed the island of Gotland outside the town of Visby, is also regarded as a Swedish law.

The older state law is normally called "Magnus Eriksson's state law" (*Landslag*) after the king at that time, but it lacks royal assent. It came into existence around 1350. A revised, codified version appeared in 1442 as Christoffer's state law. During Magnus Eriksson's reign, a municipal law also appeared. It has a predecessor in the "Bjärkö Law" (*Bjärköarätten*), which originally governed Stockholm, but in the form preserved in MSS it is adapted to the town Lödöse near present-day Gothenburg. Because of controversies with the Church, the state law lacks a canon law. The provincial laws were also used side by side with the state law throughout the Middle Ages.

There are no preserved original MSS of Swedish medieval laws, except the younger state law. The copies are not older than from around 1300, except for some fragments. Inner criteria confirming an older age are also lacking. The *Östgötalagen* was thoroughly revised when the older state law came into existence. Everything indicates that there were written collections of laws at an earlier date, but that they were modified in different ways. Even a codified law like the *Upplandslagen* received many later additions.

The Swedish medieval laws, like those of the other Scandinavian countries, show a general agreement with western European medieval law. The similarities are so detailed that there must have been a direct influence. Noteworthy agreements have been found, above all, with the Langobard Law, which was particularly popular with the Church. It was systematically revised during the late Middle Ages with the same apparatus as the Roman and canon law. All these legal systems have had a decisive importance for the Scandinavian medieval laws.

Current research presumes that the laws were transmitted orally for centuries before they were committed to writing. This view of the sources goes back to the German historical law school from the beginning of the 19th century. The influence of foreign law, according to this view, first came at a late stage in the development of law. There should, therefore, be traces of an old Scandinavian or "Germanic" law in the Scandinavian laws. The basis for all western medieval law is, however, the Bible, in particular the Mosaic Law (Sjöholm 1988). Here, there are general agreements both in the main principles and in details. As in the Mosaic Law, the suspect is guilty until he has proven his innocence. The law of evidence is the same as in medieval law, as are the categories of crime and the kinds of punishment. Vendetta is proscribed in the Mosaic Law, while it is, to a varying degree,

permitted in the medieval law. Given the fact that oaths and sworn evidence were taken on the Bible or relics in the presence of a priest, the Church had control over the process. From the beginning, the Church played an integral role in the "secular" law establishment, *i.e.*, laws that governed the layman. In the western European theocratic state, ecclesiastical and secular law establishment are two sides of the same coin.

Sweden's medieval laws form a part of this European legal tradition. Virtually all of their content is also found in the above-mentioned legal systems or in later continental law. Of the neighboring countries, the similarity is greatest to Danish law, especially the Scanian and Zealand law. The southern and western Swedish areas belonged to Denmark in the Middle Ages, and the Danish archbishop was for a long time the primate of Sweden. It is likely that the influence upon Swedish law took place in part via the episcopal see in Lund. The production and dissemination of MSS were greatly advanced by the growth of monasticism in the 12th century in Denmark and Sweden.

Ed.: Schlyter, C. J., and H. S. Collin, eds. *Corpus iuris Sueo-Gotorum antiqui. Samling af Sweriges gamla lagar.* 13 vols. Stockholm: [various publishers], 1827–77 [imprint varies; vols. 1–2 ed. Schlyter and Collin, 3–13 ed. Schlyter]; Friesen, Otto von, ed. *Upplandslagen efter Ångsöhandskriften.* Samlingar utgivna af Svenska fornskrift-sällskapet, 122. Uppsala: Akademisk Forlag, 1902; Karlsson, Karl Henrik, ed. *Södermannalagen efter Cod. Havh. Ny Kgl. Saml 4:0 N:o 2237.* Samlingar utgivna af Svenska fornskrift-sällskapet, 126. Stockholm: Norstedt, 1904; Henning, Sam., ed. *Upplandslagen enligt Codex Esplunda.* 2 vols. Samlingar utgivna av Svenska fornskrift-sällskapet, 169–70. Uppsala: Almqvist & Wiksell, 1934; Holmbäck, Åke, and Elias Wessén, eds. *Magnus Erikssons landslag i nusvensk tolkning.* Rättshistoriskt bibliotek, 6. Stockholm: Nordiska bokhandeln, 1962; Holmbäck, Åke, and Elias Wessén, eds. *Magnus Erikssons stadslag i nusvensk tolkning.* Rättshistoriskt bibliotek, 7. Stockholm: Nordiska bokhandeln, 1966. **Lit.**: Sjöholm, Elsa. *Sveriges medeltidslagar. Europeisk rättstradition i politisk omvandling.* Lund: Institutet för rättshistorisk forskning, 1988; Sjöholm, Elsa. "Sweden's Medieval Laws. European Legal Tradition—Political Change." *Scandinavian Journal of History* 15 (1990), 65–87.

Elsa Sjöholm

[**See also:** Aggesen, Sven; Denmark; *Grágás*; Hákon Hákonarson; Haraldr hárfagri ("fair-hair") Hálfdanarson; Iceland; *Íslendingabók*; *Jónsbók*; Magnús Hákonarson; Norway; Sweden]

Laxdœla saga

Laxdœla saga ("The Saga of the Laxdœlir") is one of the greatest *Íslendingasögur*, probably composed about the middle of the 13th century. It has come down to us in six medieval MSS and MS fragments. The oldest is the fragment AM 162 D2 fol., most likely written in the last quarter of the 13th century. *Laxdœla saga* is also preserved in a couple of paper MSS, some of which are thought to be copies of vellum MSS, now lost. The MSS of *Laxdœla saga* are divided into two groups, *y* and *z*; the main difference between the two groups is that the latter lacks the so-called *Bolla þáttr*. Editions of *Laxdœla saga* are based on the *y*-group of MSS, especially *Möðruvallabók* (mid-14th century), which preserves the saga in its fullest form.

The author of *Laxdœla saga* appears to have used written sources concerning the settlement of Iceland, and he also refers to two Icelandic sagas as well as Ari Þorgilsson. Some influences from the romance literature of the time are also apparent, especially in descriptions of customs, costumes, and weapons.

The action takes place over about 200 years, in the general area of Breiðafjörður, especially in the district known as Dalir (the Dales). At the beginning, the saga tells us of Ketill flatnefr ("flat-nose"), a Norwegian chieftain who was forced to flee from Norway when King Haraldr hárfagri ("fair-hair") Halfdanarson came to power (ca. 872). Ketill dies in Scotland, but his sons, Bjǫrn and Helgi, and daughter, Unnr, become settlers in Iceland. The feuds of Bjǫrn's and Unnr's descendants form the main subject matter of the saga.

At the beginning of the saga, peace prevails in the Dales under the leadership of Unnr. With the fourth generation, however, the disagreement between friends and relatives starts and gradually grows into feudal war, ending with the slaying of Kjartan by Bolli, his foster-brother.

The treatment is very often similar to that of romances, especially in its moral undertones. Unlike other Icelandic sagas, the main theme is the life and loves of a woman, Guðrún Ósvífrsdóttir, and deals with her affairs with Kjartan and Bolli in a way similar to that in which the triangular love affair among Brynhildr, Sigurðr, and Gunnarr is handled in eddic heroic poetry. At the end of the saga, Guðrún looks back and comments on her life: "Þeim var ek verst, er ek unna mest" ("To him I was worst whom I loved most"), a sentiment that has been interpreted in a variety of ways.

It has been suggested that Óláfr Þórðarson hvítaskáld ("white-skald"; d. 1259) was the author of Laxdœla saga. Some scholars, however, have thought that it was probably composed by a woman.

Ed.: Kålund, Kr., ed. Laxdœla Saga. Samfund til udgivelse af gammel nordisk litteratur, 19. Copenhagen: Møller, 1889–91; Kålund, Kr., ed. Laxdœla saga. Altnordische Saga-Bibliothek, 4. Halle: Niemeyer, 1896; Einar Ól. Sveinsson, ed. Laxdœla saga. Íslenzk fornrit, 5. Reykjavik: Hið íslenzka fornritafélag, 1934. **Tr.**: Press, Muriel A. C., trans. Laxdœla Saga. London: Dent, 1899; rpt. London: Dent; New York: Dutton, 1964; Arent, Margaret A., trans. The Laxdoela Saga. Seattle: University of Washington Press; New York: American-Scandinavian Foundation, 1964; Magnus Magnusson and Hermann Pálsson, trans. Laxdæla Saga. Harmondsworth: Penguin, 1969. **Bib.**: Halldór Hermannsson. Bibliography of the Icelandic Sagas and Minor Tales. Islandica, 1. Ithaca: Cornell University Library, 1908; rpt. New York: Kraus, 1966 [and supplements in Islandica 24 and 38]; Bekker-Nielsen, Hans, ed. Bibliography of Old Norse–Icelandic Studies 1– (1963–); Fry, Donald K. Norse Sagas Translated into English: A Bibliography. AMS Studies in the Middle Ages, 3. New York: AMS, 1980. **Lit.**: Heller, Rolf. "Studien zu Aufbau und Stil der Laxdœla Saga." Arkiv för nordisk filologi 75 (1960), 113–67; Heller, Rolf. Laxdœla Saga und Königssagas. Saga. Untersuchungen zur nordischen Literatur- und Sprachgeschichte. Halle: Niemeyer, 1961 [monograph]; Hallberg, Peter. Óláfr Þórðarson hvítaskáld, Knýtlinga saga och Laxdœla. Ett försök till språklig författarbestämning. Studia Islandica, 22. Reykjavik: Heimspekideild Háskóla Íslands; Menningarsjóður, 1963; Bredsdorf, Thomas. Kaos og kærlighed. En studie i islændingesagaens livsbillede. Copenhagen: Gyldendal, 1971; Njörður P. Njarðvík. "Laxdœla saga—en tidskritik?" Arkiv för nordisk filologi 86 (1972), 72–81; Madelung, Margaret Arent. The Laxdœla Saga: Its Structural Patterns. University of North Carolina Studies in the Germanic Languages and Literatures, 74. Chapel Hill: University of North Carolina Press, 1972; Ólafur Halldórsson. "Morgunverk Guðrúnar Ósvífursdóttur." Skírnir 147 (1973), 125–8; Heller, Rolf. Die Laxdœla Saga. Die literarische Schöpfung eines Isländers des 13. Jahrhunderts. Abhandlungen der sächsischen Akademie der Wissenschaften zu Leipzig. Philologisch-historische Klasse 65.1. Berlin: Akademie, 1976; Beck, Heinrich. "Laxdœla saga—

a Structural Approach." Saga-Book of the Viking Society 19 (1977), 383–402; Dronke, Ursula. "Narrative Insight in Laxdœla saga." In J. R. R. Tolkien, Scholar and Storyteller: Essays in Memoriam. Ed. Mary Salu and Robert T. Farrell. Ithaca and London: Cornell University Press, 1979, pp. 120–37; Conroy, Patricia. "Laxdœla saga and Eiríks saga rauða: Narrative Structure." Arkiv för nordisk filologi 95 (1980), 116–25; Kress, Helga. "'Mjǫk mun þér samstaft þykkja.' Um sagnahefð og kvenlega reynslu í Laxdæla sögu." In Konur skrifa: Til heiðurs Önnu Sigurðardóttur. Ed. Valborg Bentsdóttir et al. Reykjavik: Sögufélag, 1980, pp. 97–109; Clover, Carol J., and John Lindow, eds. Old Norse-Icelandic Literature: A Critical Guide. Islandica, 45. Ithaca and London: Cornell University Press, 1985; Hermann Pálsson. Leyndarmál Laxdælu. Reykjavik: Menningarsjóður, 1986; Conroy, Patricia, and T. C. S. Langen. "Laxdœla saga: Theme and Structure." Arkiv för nordisk filologi 100 (1988), 118–41.

Sverrir Tómasson

[**See also:** Íslendingasögur; Möðruvallabók; Women in Sagas]

Legenda, the gerund form (treated as fem. sing.) of the Latin verb legere, means "what shall or must be read." In scientific technical usage, legenda designates inscriptions on a coin or medal, words on a map, and captions below a picture in a book. In the domain of religion, legenda has come to mean an entertaining or edifying narrative about a saint. The use of legends in the Christian Church led to this transmission in meaning: on his feast day, the passion (passio) of a martyr or eulogy of a confessor was read as part of the lectiones in the daily office. Originally, only the lectiones of the lives (vitae) of confessors, i.e., saints who were not martyrs, were called legenda, as opposed to the passiones of martyrs (cf. the statement by the 12th-century liturgist John Beleth: "Legendarius vocatur liber ille ubi agitur de vita et obitu confessorum, qui legitur in eorum festis, martyrum autem in passionariis" [De divinis officiis 60, Patrologia Latina 202, p. 66]: "A book that relates the life and death of confessors, to be read on their feasts, is called a legendary; in the case of martyrs, it is a passionary"). This distinction between liber legendarius and liber passionarius gradually became blurred, however; the Legenda aurea confirms the wider meaning, which includes in legenda the acts of martyrs as well as the biographies of other saints. At the same time, the ecclesiastical use of legenda in public reading receded in favor of private edification. In the 15th century, legenda also came to be used about an improbable account, and in the 16th century with the connotation of a fictitious tale. The Reformation led to the defamation and pseudo-etymological alteration of legenda as Lügend ("lie-gend"); the close semantic relationship between legenda and fictitious tale is also evident in French, in which only one word, légende, exists for both concepts: légende hagiographique and légende populaire (or folklorique). In modern times, the word legenda is generally used to designate a fictitious tale about a historical personage or event. It is, therefore, subjected to the same truth-criteria as fanciful tales and fictions in general. In literary scholarship, legenda means a religious narrative about the life and/or death of a Christian saint, with special emphasis on the elements that bear witness to holiness (Rosenfeld 1982).

An essential element of legenda is that it presupposes a basis in historical fact, linking imaginary events and stories to real persons and places. This historical basis is often embellished or distorted by popular imagination and by the various motives of the writers. The proportions of these two elements may be very unequal, and as fact or fiction preponderates, the narrative may be classified as history or *legenda*. Such subjective (and even unconscious) reworking of material obscures the historical evidence, often almost suppressing it completely.

Legenda is formed by two distinct influences. On the one side stands the individual anonymous creator or, more generally, the people or cultural milieu that generates the disordered, fragmented compositional elements. On the other side stands the hagiographer, as editor and compiler, who gives shape and definition to the narrative, basing it on written, oral, or pictorial tradition combined with historical and empirical evidence, such as documents, relics, or shrines. The hagiographer writes with clear purpose: to interest and, above all, to edify his audience. Thus, the narrative brings together biography and panegyric, and combines them with a moral lesson (Delehaye 1927)

Because of its origin within popular culture, a *legenda* generally lacks invention, variety, and originality. Complexity yields to simplicity, and the supernatural is made concrete. Yet the supernatural element appeals only when it is combined with the marvelous; consequently, popular legends abound with wonders (*miraculae*). The number of heroes and events is usually limited, and the scope of the hero's activities is exaggerated, often incorporating a wealth of items dislodged from their historical context, or he is credited with the achievements of his predecessors. An idealized figure thus takes the place of a sharply defined historical portrait; often, he becomes no more than the personification of an abstraction. It is therefore not surprising that there are striking similarities among many *legendae* (Delehaye 1927).

In Norse, no distinction was generally made among *legendarium*, *passionarium* (or *passionale*), and *vitae sanctorum*, or between *legenda* and saint's life. The terms were used for the life (or lives) of a saint (or saints), often with appended *miraculae*.

Lit.: Zoepf, Ludwig. *Das Heiligen-Leben im 10. Jahrhundert*. Beiträge zur Kulturgeschichte des Mittelalters und der Renaissance, 1. Leipzig and Berlin: Teubner, 1908; rpt. Hildesheim: Gerstenberg, 1973; Delehaye, Hippolyte. *Les légendes hagiographiques*. 3rd rev. ed. Subsidia Hagiographica, 18. Brussels: Société des Bollandistes, 1927 [*The Legends of the Saints*. Trans. Donald Attwater. New York: Fordham Books, 1962]; Gad, Tue. *Legenden i dansk middelalder*. Copenhagen: Dansk videnskabs forlag, 1961; Gad, Tue. "Legende." *KLNM* 10 (1965), 413–23; Gad, Tue, and Toni Schmid. "Legendarium." *KLNM* 10 (1965), 412–13; Gad, Tue. *Helgener: Legender fortalt i Norden*. Copenhagen: Rhodos, 1971; Carlsson, Thorsten. "Norrön legendforskning—en kort presentation." *Scripta Islandica* 23 (1972), 31–56; Rosenfeld, Hellmut. *Legende*. Sammlung Metzler, 9. 4th rev. ed. Stuttgart: Metzler, 1982.

Kirsten Wolf

[**See also:** *Postola sögur*, Saints' Lives]

Leiðangr

Leiðangr (Old Norse), *lething* (Old Danish), *lethung* (Old Swedish), *expeditio* (Latin) designates any military expedition, but is used more specifically for the official fleet levied by the three Scandinavian countries from the late Viking Age to the early high Middle Ages. *Leiðangr* appears in the skaldic court poetry of the 10th and 11th centuries, in the provincial laws of the 12th and 13th centuries, and in Latin chronicles from *Encomium Emmae* (*ca.* 1040–1041) to Saxo Grammaticus (*ca.* 1200), while the Norse sagas of the 13th century appear to describe later military conditions. *Leiðangr* was a public fleet levy of the free farmers of the countries under the leadership of the king or the earl of Hlaðir. *Leiðangr* was

the main organizing bond between the king and the farmers, who in *leiðangr* fought as his personal "men."

Each country was divided into districts (Old Norse *skipreiða*, Old Danish *skipæn*, Old Swedish *skiplagh*, Latin *navis*, *navigium*); the district farmers were obliged to own the necessary arms and to build and equip a rowed sailing ship of forty or forty-two (later occasionally fifty) oars. In Norway, there were 279 such districts in 1277, in Denmark probably 600–800. Originally, these larger districts were divided into smaller areas (Old Norse *manngerð*, *liði*, Old Danish *hafnæ*, Old Swedish *hamna*, *ar*) with the obligation to provide one man per oar. Legislation emphasized that the ships were to be built and equipped in the same way, so that they could function in unison as large, fast fleet formations. Only royal ships were built somewhat more magnificently and faster than the others, and with more oars; the longships Skuldelev 2 and Hedeby 1 belong to this category.

In the 11th century, *leiðangr* was a successful military institution. Sections of the Danish and Norwegian *leiðangr* conquered England under the leadership of Knud (Cnut) the Great. Their strength lay in their discipline and in the versatility of their ships. The ships were fast, propelled both by sail and oars. They were so light that they could be pulled overland from one river to another, and they could, in addition to the crew, carry provisions for more than a month. In Scandinavian waters, the fleets fought great naval battles, where the ships were tied together, and where the crew then engaged in hand-to-hand combat. More frequently, however, they served as an organization for amphibious warfare: the ships sailed in a fast, broad formation and moored simultaneously at a shore, or sailed up a river to a suitable camping site. The surrounding area was then plundered, and the opposing force attacked by an established phalanx of infantry equipped with bows and arrows, spears, swords, or battle-axes, and large, round shields. Before offensive campaigns were begun, the king summoned the crew to give its opinion and to select a part of the *leiðangr* that was to stay behind and defend the home country. The *leiðangr* was called to arms to fend off all threats from invading forces; and detachments of *leiðangr* from smaller areas fought against each other in civil wars. In the 11th century, earls are mentioned as lesser chieftains of *leiðangr*; in the 12th century, the bishops are the fleet levy's local leaders. Breach of duty to participate in *leiðangr* was punished by fines due to the king, forty marks for the shipmaster, three for farmers.

After 1066, and especially during the 12th century, *leiðangr* and its armed farmers met with increasing resistance from the new professional military systems. From 1134, German cavalry appeared in Denmark, and before 1169 it had become compulsory for each Danish shipmaster to bring a horse and a crossbow on the *leiðangr* ship. In 1169, the Danish farmers' *leiðangr* dissolved and was replaced by a smaller, professional army of the so-called *herræmæn*. This new military organization and its levy were also called *lething* or *expeditio*, but it probably did not contain any farmers after 1169. In Sweden, a similar professional system was introduced before 1281. In Norway toward the end of the 12th century, a new strategy for warfare was introduced that centered on a few heavy "grand ships," and, in contrast to Denmark, the farmers could still be called upon for active service, although in smaller numbers than earlier (for example, six men out of a forty-man ship in 1273). In all three Scandinavian countries, *leiðangr* then became the name of a certain tax, in Norway paid by all farmers until the 19th century, in Denmark and Sweden paid by independent farmers until early modern times.

Lit.: Hafström, Gerhard, et al. "Hamna." KLNM 6 (1961), 96–101; Rasmussen, Poul, et al. "Herred." KLNM 6 (1961), 488–95; Hafström, Gerhard. "Hundare." KLNM 7 (1962), 74–8; Yrwing, Hugo, et al. "Landvärn." KLNM 10 (1965), 302–11; Bjørkvik, Halvard, et al. "Leidang." KLNM 10 (1965), 432–59; Bjørkvik, Halvard. "Lide." KLNM 10 (1965), 534–7; Bjørkvik, Halvard. "Manngjerd." KLNM 11 (1966), 323–4; Hafström, Gerhard. "Skeppslag." KLNM 15 (1970), 471–2; Hafström, Gerhard. "Skeppsvist." KLNM 15 (1970), 472–5; Rasmussen, Poul. "Skiben." KLNM 15 (1970), 477–9; Bjørkvik, Halvard. "Skipreide." KLNM 15 (1970), 546–51; Robberstad, Knut, et al. "Styresmann." KLNM 17 (1972), 368–77; Malmros, Rikke. "Leding og Skjaldekvad. Det elvte århundredes nordiske krigsflåder, deres teknologi og organisation og deres placering i samfundet, belyst gennem den samtidige fyrstedigtning." Aarbøger for nordisk Oldkyndighed og Historie (1985), 89–139 [English summary]; Lund, Niels. "The Armies of Swein Forkbeard and Cnut: leding or lið?" Anglo-Saxon England 15 (1986), 105–18; Larson, Mats G. Hamnor, husbyar och ledung. University of Lund, Institute of Archaeology, Report Series, 29. Lund: University of Lund, 1987 [English summary].

Rikke Malmros

[See also: Royal Administration and Finances; Ships and Shipbuilding; Warfare]

Leiðarvísan ("Way-Pointing" or "Guidance") is an anonymous Icelandic praise poem of forty-five stanzas in dróttkvætt meter, a drápa. It is transmitted in extenso in AM 757 4to (14th century); the first thirty-five stanzas also survive in AM 624 4to (15th century).

An introduction and final section each comprise twelve stanzas. The middle section of twenty-one stanzas contains two four-lined staves, making up the latter half of stanzas 13, 17, 21, and 25, 29, 33, respectively. The poem is composed around the number three, in honor of the Holy Trinity. It is crammed with kennings, only a few of which are pre-Christian, and it contains as many as forty-one hapax legomena.

Leiðarvísan has its origin in the latter half of the 12th century, the occasion possibly being a local church feast. The poet himself names his poem (st. 44). He most likely had his background in the same monastic circles as the abbot Nikulás Bergsson. Some minor metrical lapses and the mention of a clerical adviser named Rúnolfr (st. 43), obviously the priest Rúnolfr Dálksson, have led to the supposition that the author was a young person, perhaps a clerical student. He is very familiar with contemporary and earlier vernacular poetry and homilies, and reveals a thorough knowledge of the Bible.

Leiðarvísan provides its audience with ethical guidance. The poem exhorts its audience to show penitence, to avoid vices, and especially to observe the Lord's day, the sanctity of which has been verified by the many salvatory events occurring on just that day of the week. In the final section, the poet paints a vivid picture of the Last Judgment (Matthew 25). He refers to a version of the "Heavenly Letter," or the "Sunday Letter" (purported to be a letter by Christ Himself, and written in His own blood), which falls to Jerusalem (sts. 6–8). In Leiðarvísan, the "Heavenly Letter" was most likely put into verse for the first time.

The poem begins and ends with a prayer addressed to Christ, the almighty Ruler of heaven and earth, and the birth of Christ stands as the poem's axis (st. 23). He triumphed over the Devil through deliberate submission to pain and death. He is the maker and warrant of peace between God and man, and is eager to give comfort and joy to those who submit to Him.

Ed.: Finnur Jónsson, ed. Den norsk-islandske skjaldedigtning. Vols. 1A–2A (tekst efter håndskrifterne) and 1B–2B (rettet tekst). Copenhagen and Christiania [Oslo]: Gyldendal, 1912–15; rpt. Copenhagen: Rosenkilde & Bagger, 1967 (A) and 1973 (B). Lit.: Priebsch, Robert. Letter from Heaven on the Observance of the Lord's Day. Oxford: Blackwell, 1936; Lange, Wolfgang. Studien zur christlichen Dichtung der Nordgermanen, 1000–1200. Palaestra, 222. Göttingen: Vandenhoeck & Ruprecht, 1958, pp. 150–7; Astås, Reidar. "Om Leiðarvísan: En studie i norrøn kristendomsforståelse." Edda (1970), 257–76; Jones, W. R. "The Heavenly Letter in Medieval England." Medievalia et Humanistica, n.s. 6 (1975), 163–78; Astås, Reidar. "Forkynnelse og diktning på 1100-tallet." Edda (1980), 129–37; Lees, Clare A. "The 'Sunday Letter' and the 'Sunday Lists.'" Anglo-Saxon England 14 (1985), 129–51.

Reidar Astås

[See also: Christian Poetry; Kennings; Skaldic Meters; Skaldic Verse]

Leiðarvísir ("Guide"). Only one complete vernacular itinerary survives from medieval Iceland: an account of a pilgrimage to the Holy Land, which was dictated, as the last sentence tells us, by a certain "Abbot Nikulás." Nineteenth-century scholars identified him as Nikulás Sæmundarson, who died in 1158 as abbot of the Benedictine monastery of Þingeyrar, but modern scholars are generally agreed on Nikulás Bergsson, who became abbot of the Benedictine monastery of Þverá soon after its foundation in 1155. This Abbot Nikulás died in 1159 or 1160. Although the account was dictated during his abbacy, Nikulás must have made the journey some years earlier: his comment that the Saracens still held Ascalon shows that he left the Holy Land before August 1153, when the town was captured by the Crusaders. The itinerary is embedded in an encyclopedic miscellany, AM 194 8vo, where it begins and ends abruptly, with no indication that it is in any way different from the material surrounding it. The date of the MS is 1387. A single folio from another copy of the itinerary survives, made around 1400, AM 736 II 4to.

Nikulás traveled from Iceland to Norway, on to Denmark, and overland to Rome, then to Bari to begin his crossing to the Holy Land via the islands of the eastern Mediterranean, evidently taking passage in local coasting vessels. This extraordinarily enterprising pilgrimage is described in doggedly factual terms and often gives us little more than a list of cities, sites, and the distances between them; but it is enlivened from time to time by brief comments on such diverse topics as heroic legend, Scandinavian history, the beauty of the women, and the classical monuments of Rome. Most famous of all is the explanation of how, by the banks of the Jordan, he lay on his back and used his knee, fist, and thumb to measure the angle of elevation of the Pole Star. In the same MS is a modern detailed account of the holy places in and around Jerusalem, which Kedar and Westergård-Nielsen believe may also originate with Nikulás Bergsson. The dating evidence for this "Variant Description of Jerusalem" is not conclusive, but it is clear that the unnamed pilgrim-author saw the Church of the Holy Sepulchre after 1149, when the Crusaders' radical rebuilding was completed. The "Variant Description" was later used, often verbatim, for the unhistorical description of Kirialax's visit to the Holy Land in Kirialax saga.

Ed.: Kålund, Kr., and N. Beckman, eds. *Alfræði Íslenzk: Islandsk encyklopædisk litteratur*. 3 vols. Samfund til udgivelse af gammel nordisk litteratur, 37, 41, 45. Copenhagen: Møller, 1908–18, vol. 1; Kålund, Kr. "En islandsk Vejviser for Pilgrimme fra 12. Århundrede." *Aarbøger for nordisk Oldkyndighed og Historie* 3.3 (1913), 51–105. **Lit.**: [includes **Tr.**]: Magoun, Francis Peabody, Jr. "The Rome of Two Northern Pilgrims: Archbishop Sigeric of Canterbury and Abbot Nikolás of Munkathverá." *Harvard Theological Review* 33 (1940), 267–89; Magoun, Francis P., Jr. "The Pilgrim-Diary of Nikulás of Munkathverá: The Road to Rome." *Mediaeval Studies* 6 (1944), 314–54; Kedar, Benjamin Z., and Chr. Westergård-Nielsen. "Icelanders in the Crusader Kingdom of Jerusalem: A Twelfth-Century Account." *Mediaeval Scandinavia* 11 (1978–79), 193–211; Hill, Joyce. "From Rome to Jerusalem: An Icelandic Itinerary of the Mid-Twelfth Century." *Harvard Theological Review* 76 (1983), 175–203; Wilkinson, John, with Joyce Hill and Will Ryan. *Jerusalem Pilgrimage 1099–1185*. The Hakluyt Society Second Series, 167. London: Hakluyt Society, 1988.

Joyce Hill

[**See also:** Cosmology; Encyclopedic Literature; Geographical Literature; *Kirialax saga*]

Liðsmannaflokkr

Liðsmannaflokkr ("Household Troop's Poem") is a skaldic praise-poem of ten *dróttkvætt* stanzas. It recounts some of the battles fought by Knud (Cnut) and Þorkell inn hávi ("the tall one"; an independent Danish warlord) in England from 1009 to 1016. It is preserved fragmentarily in *Knýtlinga saga* and entire in two compilations concerning St. Óláfr, the *Legendary Saga* and Styrmir's fragmentarily extant *Óláfs saga. Knýtlinga saga*, apparently relying on the lost *Knúts saga, attributes the poem to the *liðsmenn* ("household troops") of Knud, hence the editorial name *Liðsmannaflokkr*. The Óláfr compilations contain an evidently secondary attribution of authorship to Óláfr himself. An early 11th-century English milieu is indicated by two linguistic forms influenced by Anglo-Saxon; the presence of one East Norse lexical item accords with the East Scandinavian origins of many of the *liðsmenn*. Verses 1–3 describe a landing on the English coast and preparations for a battle recounted in verse 4: the battle is *á heiði* ("on a heath") and led by Þorkell, and so probably to be identified with the 1010 action at Hringmaraheiðr ("Ringmere heath"). In verse 5, attention shifts from Þorkell to Knud, with a politically astute assessment of their respective contributions to the conquest of England. Verses 5 and 6 describe an unidentified battle fought under Knud's command by the Thames near London against Ulfcetel, an outstanding commander who is normally associated with the defense of East Anglia. Verses 7–9 show Knud conducting a siege of London, with the implication that this attack led directly to the occupation of the city (described in verse 10). The crucial battle of Assandun and the negotiated settlement between Knud and Edmund Ironside at Olanige are not mentioned. Verse 8 corroborates some minor sources in suggesting that the defense of London had assistance from a "British" (probably Welsh) quarter, and that Queen Emma, widow of Æthelred and subsequently Knud's wife, was in the city during the siege. *Liðsmannaflokkr* has great literary interest for its very free "running commentary" narrative technique, its *mansǫngr* ("love-song") refrain, and its adoption of a purportedly rank-and-file point of view.

Ed.: Guðbrandr Vigfússon and C. R. Unger, eds. *Flateyjarbók: En Samling af norske Konge-Sagaer med indskudte mindre Fortællinger om Begivenheder i og udenfor Norge samt Annaler*. 3 vols. Christiania [Oslo]: Malling, 1860–68 [contains text of Styrmir's *Óláfs saga helga*]; Bjarni Guðnason, ed. *Danakonunga sǫgur*. Íslenzk fornrit, 35. Reykjavik: Hið íslenzka fornritafélag, 1982 [contains text of *Knýtlinga saga*]; Heinrichs, Anne, *et al.*, eds. and trans. *Óláfs saga hins helga. Die "Legendarische Saga" über Olaf den Heiligen (Hs. Delagard. saml. nr. 8¹¹)*. Heidelberg: Winter, 1982. **Lit.**: Finnur Jónsson. *Den oldnorske og oldislandske Litteraturs Historie*. 3 vols. 2nd ed. Copenhagen: Gad, 1920–24, vol. 1 [this and the following items contain, *inter alia*, discussions of the editorial problems]; Ashdown, Margaret, ed. *English and Norse Documents Relating to the Reign of Ethelred the Unready*. Cambridge: Cambridge University Press, 1930; Holtsmark, Anne. "Olav den Hellige og 'seierskjorten.'" *Maal og minne* (1954), 104–8; Hofmann, Dietrich. *Nordisch-englische Lehnbeziehungen der Wikingerzeit*. Bibliotheca Arnamagnæana, 14. Copenhagen: Munksgaard, 1955; Vries, Jan de. *Altnordische Literaturgeschichte*. 2 vols. 2nd ed. Grundriss der germanischen Philologie, 15–6. Berlin: de Gruyter, 1941–42; rpt. 1964–67, vol. 1; Fidjestøl, Bjarne. *Det norrøne fyrstediktet*. Øvre Ervik: Alvheim & Eide, 1982; Poole, Russell. "Skaldic Verse and Anglo-Saxon History: Some Aspects of the Period 1009–1016." *Speculum* 62 (1987), 265–98 [contains text, translation, and historical commentary]; Poole, R.G. *Viking Poems on War and Peace: A Study in Skaldic Narrative*. Toronto, Buffalo, and London: University of Toronto Press, 1991, pp. 86–115.

Russell Poole

[**See also:** England, Norse in; Knud (Cnut) the Great; *Knýtlinga saga*; *Óláfs saga helga*; *Skáld*; Skaldic Meters; Skaldic Verse]

Líknarbraut see Christian Poetry

Lilja

Lilja ("Lily") is an Old Norse–Icelandic poem composed in the middle of the 14th century and traditionally ascribed to an otherwise unknown poet, Eysteinn Ásgrímsson. The title *Lilja* is one of the traditional appellations of the Virgin Mary, and the poem is written specifically in her honor. Although the poet focuses on the Virgin Mary and addresses her specifically and at length, the poem is a summary of all Christian history from Creation until the end of history. The poet begins and ends with an invocation of the triune God, stanzas 2–4 appeal for inspiration, and then the poet narrates the events of creation history up to the Annunciation in stanza 25. Stanzas 25–50 are concerned with the events of Christ's life and preaching up to the Passion; stanzas 50–75 concern the defeat of Satan in the Passion, the Harrowing of Hell, the Ascension and the Last Judgment. The final twenty-five stanzas are prayers for forgiveness on the part of the poet, and praise of Mary and God as Father, Son, and Holy Ghost. The ordering of the narrative is reflected in a formal metrical pattern in that the poem consists of 100 *hrynhent* stanzas in symmetrical *drápa* form. The first twenty-five stanzas form a prologue (the *upphaf* or *inngangr*), the next fifty stanzas a refrain section (the *stefjabálkr*) divided between two refrains recurring five times each, and the last twenty-five stanzas form the conclusion (the *slœmr*).

Lilja is a metrical and rhetorical *tour de force*, in which Eysteinn Ásgrímsson shows extraordinary technical facility (*e.g.*, st. 55 in which the consonant cluster -dd- is repeated sixteen times), but the language of the poem as a whole is clear and transparent. The tone varies from the serenity of the invocation of the triune God in stanzas 1 and 100 to the poet's abject and emotional confession in stanzas 75–80, or the dramatic representation of the Crucifixion as a combat in which the World Serpent was caught on the hook of the Cross (sts. 60–66).

The poem is, however, more than an extraordinary monument of skaldic craftsmanship. It also reflects a very subtle and sophisticated understanding of Christian theology and poetry. For example, stanza 33 narrates the birth of Christ, stanza 66 the completion of the atonement, and stanza 99, which addresses Mary, completes the poem, since stanza 100 repeats the first stanza. Thus, the poem reflects a triadic, triangular pattern based on the correspondences between 33/66/99 as well as the larger pattern based on the number 100 reflected in the formal pattern of the refrains. There are thus two numerical patterns, one triadic and one circular, and these numerical patterns suggest the iconographic figure of the "triangular circle," a famous emblem of the Incarnation, the joining of God and man made possible by the mediation of the Virgin Mary, the *Lilja* to whom the poem is addressed.

The popularity of the poem in Icelandic tradition inspired the proverb *öll skáld vildu Lilja kveðið hafa* ("every poet wishes he had composed *Lilja*"), and the more carefully one reads and studies the poem the more fully one can appreciate the force of this maxim.

Ed.: Finnur Jónsson, ed. *Den norsk-islandske skjaldedigtning*. Vols. 1A–2A (tekst efter håndskrifterne) and 1B–2B (rettet tekst). Copenhagen and Christiania [Oslo]: Gyldendal, 1912–15; rpt. Copenhagen: Rosenkilde & Bagger, 1967 (A) and 1973 (B), vols. 2A: 263–95, 2B: 390–416; Gunnar Finnbogason, ed. *Lilja*. Reykjavik: Stafafell, 1974. **Lit.**: Hill, Thomas D. "Number and Pattern in *Lilja*." *Journal of English and Germanic Philology* 69 (1970), 561–7; Schottmann, Hans. *Die isländische Mariendichtung: Untersuchungen zur volkssprachigen Mariendichtung des Mittelalters*. Münchener germanistische Beiträge, 9. Munich: Fink, 1973, pp. 188–251; Foote, Peter. "Latin Rhetoric and Icelandic Poetry: Some Contacts." In *Aurvandilstá: Norse Studies*. Ed. Michael Barnes *et al*. Viking Collection, 2. Odense: Odense University Press, 1984, pp. 249–70.

Thomas D. Hill

[**See also:** Christian Poetry; *Nicodemus, Gospel of*; Skaldic Meters; Skaldic Verse]

Liturgy and Liturgical Texts. Up to the year 1104, the Scandinavian countries came under the archbishop of Bremen. In 1104, a Nordic ecclesiastical province with its archbishopric in Lund was founded. A Norwegian ecclesiastical province was begun in 1153 with its archbishopric in Niðaróss (Trondheim), and in 1164 a Swedish province was founded with its archbishopric in Uppsala.

Every diocese had its own rites and its own liturgy. The difference could be considerable, especially with regard to the veneration of saints. Liturgical uniformity in one and the same diocese was not reached until the end of the Middle Ages, when the liturgical books were printed.

Within the Swedish ecclesiastical province, four missals, or massbooks, were printed: for the dioceses of Uppsala in 1484 and in 1513, Strängnäs in 1487, and Åbo diocese in 1488. The rest of the dioceses in the ecclesiastical province (Linköping, Skara, Västerås, Växjö) never received their own printed missal book.

A number of missal MSS survive in Swedish archives and libraries, among them the oldest missal fragments of the country from the early 12th century (in the Skara diocese and the national library). Within the Danish ecclesiastical province, three massbooks were printed: for Copenhagen in around 1484, for Schleswig in 1486, and for Lund in 1514. The rest of the dioceses (Roskilde, Odense, Ribe, Viborg, Århus, and Børglum) never received printed

missals. From the Norwegian ecclesiastical province, only one printed missal exists, for the Niðaróss archdiocese, printed in 1519. Several fragments are kept in the national archive in Oslo.

The Nordic missals are all rather similar. All contain a calendar, ordinary masses, propers of the time, of the saints, and of the common of saints. Older missal MSS sometimes contain further rituals that later were excluded or were moved to other liturgical books.

In addition to missals, several breviaries or handbooks for the Hours were printed in the Nordic countries. In Sweden, such books were printed for Uppsala in 1496, for Skara in 1498, for Strängnäs in 1495, for Linköping in 1493, and for Västerås in 1513. The Skara breviary is especially interesting since, apart from the ritual for the Hours, it also contains rituals for baptism, weddings, funerals, and several masses. The Skara breviary was, in other words, used at the same time as a missal and a manual, unique within the Nordic history of liturgy.

In Denmark, there are kept five printed breviaries: for Lund in 1517, for Roskilde in 1517, for Odense in around 1482, 1497, 1510, for Århus in 1519, and for Schleswig in 1512. In Norway, a breviary for Niðaróss was printed in 1519, and was used throughout the ecclesiastical province. A breviary for Hólar in Iceland was printed in 1534. Except for the Skara breviary, the Nordic breviaries share the general arrangement prevalent during the Middle Ages, but with different propers of saints.

The manual (today the ritual) contained formulas for baptism, weddings, visits to the sick with communion, extreme unction, funerals, and some benedictions. The term *liber agendarum* was also used. In Sweden, three manuals were printed: for Uppsala in 1487, for Åbo in 1522, and for Linköping in 1525. The Skara breviary, printed in 1498, was also used as a manual. Some manuals in MSS are preserved in Swedish libraries, among them the oldest (about 1400) from the church of Hemsjö in the diocese of Skara. In Denmark, two printed manuals were edited: for Schleswig in 1512, and for Roskilde in 1513. From the diocese of Odense, there is a manual in MS from about 1400. In Norway, three manual MSS from the 13th to the 14th century are preserved.

Two of the sacraments of the Church, confirmation and ordination, were reserved for the bishop. The ritual was contained in the pontifical. From the Nordic medieval period, only two such handbooks are preserved, both in MSS. One of them, housed in the University of Uppsala library, from the latter part of the 15th century, belonged to the archdiocese of Lund; the other, in the library of the University of Lund, dates from the beginning of the 16th century, and was used in the diocese of Roskilde. A copy of a pontifical printed in Rome in 1497 has numerous notes in the margin showing that it had been used in Lund. For the rest, only fragments are preserved from the Nordic pontifical tradition.

A gradual containing the songs of the mass was printed in 1493 for the diocese of Västerås. Several fragmentary gradual MSS are preserved from various Nordic dioceses. The book of antiphons contained the music for the Hours. From the Nordic medieval period, a number of antiphonal books have been preserved, several of them in fragments.

The *ordinarium* offered a means of assistance in the use of the liturgical books, above all in the regulation of the complicated medieval ecclesiastical year. A Niðaróss *ordinarium* in MS from the 13th century is preserved, along with two *ordinaria* from Linköping (15th century).

The missionary activity in the Nordic countries emanated from England in the west and from Germany and France in the south. In all of Nordic liturgy, there are easily observed influences from these two directions, somewhat varying in some dioceses, depending on situation and development. At the end of the medieval period, these foreign influences had been united within the Swedish liturgy. All this can be observed in the veneration of the saints.

One more characteristic element was the regular liturgy for religious orders. Cistercians, Dominicans, and Franciscans were numerous in all Nordic contries. As an example of such influence, the Åbo missal from the year 1488 may be mentioned, in which Dominican elements dominate.

The liturgical handbooks were completed by synodal statutes. The bishop, however, had the right to promulgate statutes within the frame of the canon law and within his diocese. These statutes regulated new circumstances or strengthened the observance of earlier prescriptions. Such statutes have been preserved in all Nordic countries. Many statutes are still unedited, or their editions are antiquated. These statutes are important sources for the pious life in medieval Scandinavia.

The veneration of saints constituted an important part of the medieval liturgy, having been established when Christianity reached the Nordic countries in the 11th century. Later on, new continental and English saints gained a foothold in the North. Such saints followed new currents of culture, such as the establishment of monastic orders. Nordic saints played an important part in the liturgy. Several of them belong to the missionary period or the 11th century. Their status varied somewhat in different dioceses in different times.

In the 11th century, the English missionaries Sigfrid (February 15) and Eskil (October 8) were active in Sweden, Sigfrid in the south of Sweden and Eskil in Södermanland. About the same time, David (June 25) and Botvid (July 28) worked in the middle part of Sweden. In the 12th century, we meet St. Erik (May 18) and Henrik (January 19); Helena of Skövde (July 30 in Skara, in other dioceses July 31) also belongs to this epoch.

Best known of Swedish saints is Birgitta of Vadstena, who died in 1373 and was canonized in 1391. She founded the Brigettine Order, and her worship spread throughout the North and beyond. Her festival days were October 7 (canonization), July 23 (death), and May 28 (translation in Linköping).

The most important saint of Norway was St. Ólafr, martyred in 1030. His day, July 29, was the most distinguished day in the North. In Sweden, Ólafr was sometimes venerated more than St. Erik.

Other more local saints of Denmark were Knud (Cnut), king and martyr (July 10; d. 1086; canonized 1101) and also Knud Lavard, duke and martyr (January 7; d. 1131; translated 1170). The veneration of Knud spread not only in Denmark, but also to the south of Sweden.

The complex medieval ecclesiastical year with its movable and fixed parts was necessarily regulated in the liturgical handbooks. At synods and convocations of clergy, special statutes for different dioceses were promulgated, many of them of French origin.

Ed.: Freisen, J. *Manuale curatorum secundum usum ecclesie Roskildensis.* Paderborn: [n.p.], 1898; Freisen, Joseph, ed. *Liber agendorum, ecclesie et diocesis Sleszvicensis.* Paderborn: Junfermann, 1898; Freisen, J., ed. *Manuale Lincopense, Breviarium Scarense, Manuale Aboense.* Paderborn: Junfermann, 1904; Collijn, I, ed. *Manuale Upsalense.* Kungliga bibliotekets handlingar. Bilagor. Ny följd, 1. Uppsala: Almqvist & Wiksell, 1918; *Missale Lundense av år 1514.* Laurentius Petri sällskapets urkundsserie, 4. Facsimile edition with afterword and index by Bengt Strömberg. Malmö: Kroon, 1946; Peters, Knut, ed. *Breviarium Lincopense.* Laurentius Petri sällskapets urkundsserie, 5.1–4. Lund: Ohlsson, 1950–58; Schmid, Toni, ed. *Graduale Arosiense impressum.* Laurentius Petri sällskapets urkundsserie, 7.1–7. Lund: Berling, 1959–65; Gjerløw, Lilli, ed. *Ordo Nidrosiensis ecclesiae.* Libri Liturgici Provenciae Nidrosiensis Medii Aevi, 2. Oslo: Universitetsforlaget, 1968. **Lit**: Lindberg, Gustaf. *Die schwedischen Missalien des Mittelalters: Ein Beitrag zur vergleichenden Liturgik. 1. Kalendarium, proprium de tempore, proprium de sanctis, commune sanctorum.* Uppsala: Almqvist & Wiksell, 1923; Johansson, Hilding. *Hemsjömanualet. En liturgihistorisk studie.* Samlingar och studier till Svenska kyrkans historia, 24. Stockholm: Svenska Kyrkans Diakonistyrelses Bokförlag, 1950; Strömberg, Bengt. *Den pontifikala liturgien i Lund och Roskilde under medeltiden.* Studia Theologica Lundensia, 9. Lund: Gleerup, 1955; Johansson, Hilding. *Den medeltida liturgien i Skara stift. Studier i mässa och helgonkult.* Studia Theologica Lundensia, 14. Lund: Gleerup, 1956; Björkman, Ulf. *Stilla veckan i gudstjänst och fromhetsliv.* Bibliotheca Theologiae Practicae, 2. Lund: Gleerup, 1957; Helander, Sven. *Ordinarius Lincopensis ca. 1400 och dess liturgiska förebilder.* Bibliotheca Theologiae Practicae, 4. Lund: Gleerup, 1957; Frihtz, Carl-Gösta. *Till frågan om det s. k. Helgeandshusmissalets liturgihistoriska ställning.* Bibliotheca Theologiae Practiae, 34. Uppsala: Gleerup, 1976.

Hilding Johansson

[**See also**: Birgitta, St.; Church Organization and Function; Erik, St.; Knud (Cnut), St.; Monasticism; Ólafr, St.; Prayer Books; Saints' Lives]

Ljósvetninga saga ("The Saga of the Ljósavatn Family") is a medium-length *Íslendingasaga.* The main theme of the saga is the rivalry and battles between two chieftain families in northern Iceland, the Möðruvellir family in Eyjafjörður and the Ljósavatn family in the district just to the east. The saga is divided into two main parts. The first part starts with the great friendship between the two famous chiefs, Guðmundr ríki ("the mighty") of Möðruvellir and Þorgeirr of Ljósavatn (the latter especially well known from his important role as lawspeaker when Christianity was introduced into Iceland). There is constant conflict between Guðmundr and the sons of Þorgeirr, the most prominent of them being attacked in his home and slain by Guðmundr. In the second part of the saga, the conflict continues between the descendants of Guðmundr and Þorgeirr. The climax of this part is the battle of Kakalahóll, where the noblest and most beloved of Guðmundr's sons is killed. Most of the events of the saga took place from about 990 to 1066, that is, over two to three generations. *Ljósvetninga saga* is thus a true "Family Saga." At least some of the main characters must represent genuine historical personages, but many of the events are fictional and sometimes reflect literary borrowings and traditional motifs. The author's sympathies obviously lie with the Ljósvetninga family. The most dominating personality in the saga, Guðmundr inn ríki (d. ca. 1025), is known as a great chieftain in a number of other sagas, but is described here in *Ljósvetninga saga* with malicious irony.

It is generally assumed that *Ljósvetninga saga* was written around 1260. But the saga has suffered greatly during transmission. It now exists in two versions. The A-version is represented by only one MS, AM 561 4to (vellum, ca. 1400), covering most of the first part of the saga. A fuller, but not complete, version is C, which existed in a vellum codex written in the 15th century. Of the *Ljósvetninga saga* text of this codex, only three folios (six pages) remain (in AM 162c fol.), but the complete *Ljósvetninga saga* text of this codex is transmitted in more than thirty paper MSS. In the C-version, the saga is extended to include a number of separate small tales (*þættir*), which are regarded as later additions.

For a time, *Ljósvetninga saga* played an important role in the great controversy between the supporters of "Freeprose" as against "Bookprose," since it was maintained that the two versions of this saga represent exceptionally reliable examples of separate records of oral tradition. But this viewpoint has now been largely discredited.

Ed.: Björn Sigfússon, ed. *Ljósvetninga saga.* Íslenzk fornrit, 10. Reykjavík: Hið íslenzka fornritafélag, 1940. **Tr.**: Gudbrand Vigfusson and F. York Powell, trans. "The Story of the Men of Lightwater." In *Origines Islandicae: A Collection of the More Important Sagas and Other Native Writings Relating to the Settlement and Early History of Iceland.* 2 vols. Oxford: Clarendon, 1905; rpt. Millwood: Kraus, 1976, vol. 2, pp. 355–427; Andersson, Theodore, and William Ian Miller. *Law and Literature in Medieval Iceland:* Ljósvetninga saga *and* Valla-Ljóts saga. Stanford: Stanford University Press, 1989, pp. 121–255. **Lit.**: Björn Sigfússon. *Um Ljósvetninga sögu.* Studia Islandica, 3. Reykjavík: Ísafold, 1937; Magerøy, Hallvard. *Sertekstproblemet i Ljósvetninga saga.* Oslo: Aschehoug, 1957; Magerøy, Hallvard. "Guðmundr góði og Guðmundr ríki." *Maal og minne* (1959), 23–34; Magerøy, Hallvard. "Den samanhengen i Ljósvetninga saga." In *Afmælisrit Jóns Helgasonar: 30 júní 1969.* Ed. Jakob Benediktsson *et al.* Reykjavík: Heimskringla, 1969, pp. 118–46; Magerøy, Hallvard. "Eventyrvariantar og sagaversjonar. Ei jamføring" In *Einarsbók: Afmæliskveðja til Einars Ól. Sveinssonar: 12 desember 1969.* Ed. Bjarni Guðnason *et al.* Reykjavík: Nokkrir vinir, 1970, pp. 233–54; Danielsson, Tommy. *Om den isländska släktsagans uppbygnad.* Skrifter utgivna av Litteraturvetenskapliga institutionen vid Uppsala universitet, 22. Stockholm: Almqvist & Wiksell, 1986; Andersson, Theodore M. "Guðbrandur Vigfússon's Saga Chronology: The Case of *Ljósvetninga saga.*" In *Úr Dölum til Dala: Guðbrandur Vigfússon Centenary Essays.* Ed. Rory McTurk and Andrew Wawn. Leeds Texts and Studies, n.s. 11. Leeds: School of English, University of Leeds, 1989, pp. 1–10.

Hallvard Magerøy

[**See also:** Bookprose / Freeprose Theory; *Íslendingasögur*]

Lokasenna ("Loki's Quarrel") is one of the masterpieces of the eddic tradition. Also called *Ægisdrekka* ("Ægir's Banquet"), and found in the *Poetic Edda*, it was composed by an unknown author who drew on a much older oral tradition.

The poem is set at the time just before Ragnarǫk, after Loki's misdeeds have tainted all the gods and caused the death of Baldr. The prose prologue, which, like the epilogue, was probably added when the originally oral poem was written down, reports that Loki has just been thrown out of the gods' banquet in Ægir's hall for killing a servant. With scorn for the hypocrisy that he says characterizes the gods, Loki marches arrogantly back into the hall. Bragi rebukes him, but Loki invokes his blood-brotherhood with Óðinn. When Bragi attempts to apologize, Loki accuses him of cowardice. Bragi's wife, Iðunn, steps in to calm her husband, only to have Loki maliciously point out that she has committed adultery with Loki himself. This abuse continues around the banquet table as Loki accuses Gefjon, Frigg, Freyja, Skaði, and Beyla of adultery and other misdeeds, and Óðinn, Njǫrðr, Týr, Freyr, Byggvir, and Heimdallr of cowardice, referring in each case to a well-known story about that particular god or goddess. In most cases, it was Loki himself who instigated the incidents.

Þórr's wife, Sif, then offers Loki a cup of mead as a bribe to leave her out of the diatribe, but to no avail. Loki points out that even she is as guilty of infidelity as the rest. Suddenly, Þórr appears. Faced with the angry thunder-god, Loki flees the hall with a final curse, anticipating his ultimate defeat at the end of the world.

The poem consists of sixty-five stanzas, written mostly in *ljóðaháttr* ("chant meter"), a six-line verse form common to eddic poems. There is a variation of this stanza called, significantly, *galdralag* ("incantation meter"). Here, a seventh line takes the listener by surprise. This stanza assumes a power that the standard *ljóðaháttr* stanzas lack. Four *galdralag* verses are spoken by Loki, and reflect his attempts to use magic to increase his power. Óðinn tries to outdo him with an eight-line verse, but Loki is able to turn it against him. Only when Loki uses Þórr's name in a *galdralag* verse does his magic prove to be too strong even for him, for he conjures Þórr into his presence, and this act leads to his banishment.

The poet's probable purpose was to recite a catalogue of the important stories of the gods, and, in particular, the legends of Loki. The catalogue form, perhaps intended for other poets to help them remember the old myths and kennings, also appears in *Vǫluspá*, *Vafþrúðnismál*, *Grímnismál*, and *Hárbarðsljóð*. But *Lokasenna* stands apart for its dramatic quality, for its more skillful weaving of the catalogue concept with the story, and for its succinct and effective portraits of the individual gods.

Ed.: Neckel, Gustav, ed. *Edda: Die Lieder des Codex Regius nebst verwandten Denkmälern. I: Text.* 5th ed. rev. Hans Kuhn. Heidelberg: Winter, 1983. **Tr.**: Hollander, Lee M., trans. *The Poetic Edda, Translated with an Introduction and Explanatory Notes.* 2nd rev. ed. Austin: University of Texas Press, 1962; rpt. 1988; Taylor, Paul B., and W. H. Auden, trans. *The Elder Edda: A Selection.* London: Faber & Faber; New York: Random House, 1967; Terry, Patricia, trans. *Poems of the Vikings: The Elder Edda.* Indianapolis: Bobbs-Merrill, 1969. **Lit.**: Dumézil, Georges. "Two Minor Scandinavian Gods: Byggvir and Beyla." Trans. John Lindow. In his *Gods of the Ancient Northmen.* Ed. Einar Haugen. Center for the Study of Comparative Folklore and Mythology, 3. Berkeley, Los Angeles, and London: University of California Press, 1973, pp. 89–117; Heinrichs, Heinrich Matthias. "Lokis Streitreden." *Island. Deutsch-Isländisches Jahrbuch* 6 (1970), 41–65; Harris, Joseph. "The *senna*: From Description to Literary Theory." *Michigan Germanic Studies* 5 (1979), 65–74; Anderson, Philip N. "Form and Content in the *Lokasenna*: A Re-evaluation." *Edda* (1981) 215–25; Klingenberg, Heinz. "Types of Eddic Mythological Poetry." In *Edda: A Collection of Essays.* Ed. Robert J. Glendinning and Haraldur Bessason. University of Manitoba Icelandic Studies, 4. Winnipeg: University of Manitoba Press, 1983, pp. 134–64; Harris, Joseph. "Eddic Poetry." In *Old Norse–Icelandic Literature: A Critical Guide.* Ed. Carol J. Clover and John Lindow. Islandica, 45. Ithaca and London: Cornell University Press, 1985, pp. 68–156 [see p. 150 for bibliography on *Lokasenna*]; McKinnell, John. "Motivation in *Lokasenna.*" *Saga-Book of the Viking Society* 22 (1987–88), 234–62.

†Philip N. Anderson

[**See also:** *Codex Regius*; Eddic Meters; Eddic Poetry; Loki]

Loki is one of the most vivid and frequently discussed gods in the old Scandinavian mythology. The various sources present incidents that seem to relate to more than one personality. On the one hand, Loki is said to be the murderer by advice (*ráðbani*) of Baldr, whose killing is said to be the worst incident among gods and men (*Gylfaginning*, ch. 33). Both Loki and his children play a central part in Ragnarǫk on the side of the enemies of the gods, and many other calamities that strike the gods are caused by Loki, too. On the other hand, he is the blood relation of Óðinn and a figure who, by his own will or not, brings the gods some of their most precious objects, without which they could not fulfill their function as defenders of the cosmos.

The sources tell us that Loki is intelligent and cunning, and that he is deceitful (*Gylfaginning*, ch. 19; *Skáldskaparmál*, ch. 24; *Lokasenna*, st. 54; *Hymiskviða*, st. 37; *Vǫluspá*, st. 35; *Haustlǫng*, sts. 5–9; *Þórsdrápa*, st. 1; *Húsdrápa*, st. 2). As to his appearance, he is said to be beautiful (*Gylfaginning*, ch. 19). He is able to transform himself into all kinds of animals, both male and female, and into a woman as well (*Gylfaginning*, chs. 25, 33, 35, 36; *Skáldskaparmál*, chs. 3, 16, 44; *Lokasenna*, sts. 23, 33, and end prose; *Þrymskviða*, sts. 3, 20; *Hyndluljóð*, st. 40; *Haustlǫng*, st. 12).

His father and mother are said to be the giant Fárbauti and Laufey or Nál, and his brothers are Býleistr and Helblindi. His wife is Sigyn, and their sons are Nari (or Narfi) and Váli. With a giantess, he has the children Fenrir, the World Serpent, and Hel. In the shape of a mare, he gave birth to the stallion Sleipnir, which became Óðinn's horse and on which it is possible to ride to the world of the dead (*Gylfaginning*, chs. 19, 25, 36; *Lokasenna* end prose; *Sǫrla þáttr*).

Loki plays an important role in many myths, often as the companion of Þórr and Óðinn. Often, his role is first to create a dangerous situation, but in the end to resolve it. Significant myths include his mingling blood with Óðinn in the beginning of time (*árdaga*; *Lokasenna*), the killing of Baldr (*Gylfaginning*, ch. 33), and his punishment. In the mythical present, he is chained to a rock, on which a snake drops poison in his eyes. Sigyn catches the poison in a bowl, but when it is full she has to empty it, and Loki trembles with pain, thereby causing earthquakes (*Gylfaginning*, ch. 36; *Lokasenna* end prose). Finally, his part in Ragnarǫk is significant, since he and his children are the main opponents of the gods (*Gylfaginning*, chs. 37–38; *Vǫluspá*, sts. 53–56).

Some scholars believe that Loki is identical with the god Lóður, whom we know from the anthropogonic myth of *Vǫluspá*, stanza 18, and in a kenning for Óðinn (*Lóðurs vinr* ["Lóður's friend"] in *Háleygatal* and *Íslendingadrápa*). But although etymological arguments have been put forward, neither these nor the role played by Lóður in the anthropogony are sufficient proof for an identity.

"Loki" is very problematic etymologically, and this difficulty is also true for his surname "Loptr" (*Gylfaginning*, ch. 19; *cf.* Jan de Vries, *Altnordisches etymologisches Wörterbuch* [Leiden: Brill, 1962]). There is nothing to suggest that Loki was ever worshiped, since there is no trace of a Loki cult and his name cannot be found in place-names. So the only way to understand his meaning and function in Nordic mythology is through his role in the myths and mythical references.

What were the meaning and function of this god in the pantheon of the old Scandinavians? During the 19th and early 20th centuries, many scholars linked Loki and most other gods with some natural phenomenon. He was seen as a fire-demon by some or a water-demon by others. Others looked upon him as a newcomer in the pantheon and inspired by the Christian Devil. None of these proposals is supported by modern scholars, although certain traits of the Loki figure may be explained in these ways; but

almost everybody agrees that they do not explain the essential significance of this god.

In 1933, de Vries put forward a theory of Loki as a trickster. By denying any authenticity to those traits that also can be found outside the North, the Swedish scholar Rooth (1961) finds that the most constitutive trait is the making of the net as he was caught after the killing of Baldr (*Gylfaginning*, ch. 36). Combining this with later folkloristic material, she maintains that Loki was in fact a deified spider. In 1956, Folke Ström suggested that Loki originally was a hypostasis of Óðinn and thus was a representative of Óðinn's "evil" aspect. In 1975, another Swede, Å. V. Ström, saw Loki as the dark side of Óðinn; he compares this god with the Iranic god Vayu, who also has both a good and evil aspect. Most of the scholars here mentioned have not been able to make the whole material fit into their theories, and they have therefore dismissed much of it as "nonauthentic." Dumézil's book on Loki (1948), however, uses all the material at hand. By comparing it with Ossetic and other Indo-European material, he succeeds in proving, for instance, that the role of Loki in the myth of Baldr is very old and dates back to Indo-European times. Dumézil's analysis leads him to see Loki as "the impulsive intelligence," a psychological interpretation not very typical of Dumézil. Elsewhere, Dumézil proposed in an analysis of the myths of Baldr and Ragnarǫk that Loki is an archdemon, parallel to other Indo-European figures. With this theory as a point of departure, Schjødt (1981) has attempted to see Loki as the demon of our cosmic age. He shows how Loki becomes more and more evil concurrently with the deterioration of the world, culminating with the murder of Baldr and his role in Ragnarǫk. This position is due to his mediating role where male and female, culture and nature, good and evil, and many other oppositional pairs are intermingled.

Whether or not this theory can be accepted, it seems necessary to agree that Loki is a god who has changed his role radically. The problem is whether it is the conception of him that has changed or whether this change is constitutive for his mythic function.

Lit.: Vries, Jan de. *The Problem of Loki.* Folklore Fellows Communications, 110. Helsinki: Societas Scientiarum Fennica, 1933; Krogmann, Willy. "Loki." *Acta Philologica Scandinavica* 12 (1938), 59–70; Dumézil, Georges. *Loki. Les dieux et les hommes*, 1. Paris: Maisonneuve, 1948; rev. ed. [Paris]: Flammarion, 1986; Ström, Folke. *Loki. Ein mythologisches Problem.* Gothenburg: Almqvist & Wiksell, 1956; Rooth, Anna Birgitta. *Loki in Scandinavian Mythology.* Skrifter utgivna av Kungl. Humanistiska Vetenskapssamfundet i Lund, 61. Lund: Gleerup, 1961; Holtsmark, Anne. "Loki—En omstridt skikkelse i nordisk mytologi." *Maal og minne* (1962), 81–9; Turville-Petre, E. O. G. *Myth and Religion of the North: The Religion of Ancient Scandinavia.* New York: Holt, Rinehart and Winston, 1964; rpt. Westport: Greenwood, 1975, pp. 126–46; Ellis Davidson, H. R. *Gods and Myths of Northern Europe.* Harmondsworth: Penguin, 1964; Ström, Åke V., and H. Biezais. *Germanische und baltische Religion.* Die Religionen der Menschheit, 19.1. Berlin, *etc.*: Kohlhammer, 1975; Schjødt, Jens Peter. "Om Loke endnu engang." *Arkiv för nordisk filologi* 96 (1981), 49–86; Dumézil, Georges. *Loki.* 3rd ed. Paris: Flammarion, 1986.

Jens Peter Schjødt

[**See also:** Eddic Poetry; Eyvindr Finnsson skáldaspillir; *Hymiskviða*; *Hyndluljóð*; *Íslendingadrápa*; *Lokasenna*; Mythology; *Snorra Edda*; *Sǫrla þáttr*; Þjóðólfr of Hvin; *Þrymskviða*; Úlfr Uggason; *Vǫluspá*]

Love Poetry

1. EAST NORSE. A portion of East Norse love poetry is found in Old Swedish runic inscriptions. These poems are not creations of erotic passion, but evidence of tender feelings and genuine love between husband and wife. The poems of this kind are very short, one stanza and a half, or a pair of lines, as on a rune stone erected by the yeoman farmer Holmgautr, owner of the estate of Hasvimyra, Fläckebo parish, Västmanland, to the memory of his deceased wife. The inscription ends in a stanza, the first half of which runs:

Kumbʀ hifrøya
til Hasvimyra
æigi bætri
þan byi raðr.

[Never will come / to Hasvimyra / a better mistress / to manage the house.]

On the old þing-place at Bällsta in Vallentuna, Uppland, stand two stones erected to the memory of Ulf, with fourteen lines of poetry. The last four lines run:

Auk Gyriði
gats at veri.
þy man i grati
getit lata.

[Likewise Gyrid / loved her husband. / So in an elegy / she aims to have it mentioned.]

Love poetry is found primarily in the ballads, the majority of which have a love story as the principal theme. The story or mood of these ballads is often condensed or mirrored in the burdens (refrains), some of which have the character of subjective love lyrics (e.g., DgF 431 A, SMB 22 D). In the main, the lyric love poetry proper shares the same fate as the ballad: poems of medieval origin are, with a few exceptions, found only in sources from the 16th century onward, the Danish printed in *Danske Viser* (1912–31), the Swedish in *1500– och 1600–talens visböcker* (1884–1919). Like the ballads, the lyrical poems draw heavily upon a stock of set expressions and formulas, although the building elements in the lyrics are smaller and even more interchangeable than in the epic songs. It is, accordingly, often somewhat inadequate to talk about definite or fixed "types" in the lyrics as in narrative poetry. However, the general style as well as specific stylistic features and stanzaic forms (not to mention many single lines, rhymes, and groups of lines, appearing in a considerable number of postmedieval texts) may with a high degree of probability be regarded as medieval, more exactly belonging to the 13th and especially to the 14th and 15th centuries. We can conjecture about this dating with more confidence because we actually possess some lyrical love poems preserved in MSS from the Middle Ages. The oldest example, from about 1250 (Dombibliothek, Cologne) is Danish rather than Swedish:

iac wet en frugha i wæreldet wære
hænna lif tha wil iac æra.

[I know of a lady in this world / I wish to honor her life.]

It has indeed been suggested that this is not a secular love poem, but a religious one, the *frugha* meaning "Our Lady." This view can hardly be upheld in this specific case, even if the two genres admittedly have very much in common, an erotic vocabulary with roots in the Song of Songs. This ambiguity is evident in some of the poems found in a MS from about 1480 and attributed to the Danish friar Peder Ræff:

iek wil tegh prisæ fraa top til thoo
och ther i mellom, om iek kan foo,
thu speyell och ædhelæ quinnæ.

[I will praise you from top to toe / and in between, if I can get / you, mirror and honorable woman.]

These and similar lines are directed to the Holy Virgin. It is significant that the sensuality in Peder's poems to the Virgin Mary is lacking in the only undoubtedly secular love poem attributed to him, the most famous one, "Reth elscuens dydh mz sangh oc frydh" (Frandsen, *Mariaviserne*, no. 21). This is the only Danish love poem preserved in a source from before the Reformation, while we have at least four such Swedish items. In a MS from about 1450, there is one, "Glädhe oc frögd oc hiertans hug" (ed. Klemming 1881–82). In another MS of the same age, there are two: "Jak wil qwedha ena wiso" and "Kristh for syn dödh" (ed. Jonsson 1976); in the latter, we see the intonation from Peder Ræff. From about 1500, there is one text, "J mith hiarta der yppas änh sorgh" (ed. Klemming 1881–82), which seems to consist of two, probably three, different poems.

External evidence as well as internal, for example, the use of the term *visa* for the poem, makes it clear that, at least as a rule, the love lyrics were sung and might thus rightly be called "love songs." Several stanzaic forms are represented in the material, among them the sequence (as in "Jak wil qwedha ena wiso," the first example of acrostic in Swedish verse) and structures from the German *Minnesang* and *Meistersang* (as in "Glädhe oc frögd oc hiertans hug," with two *Stollen* and an *Abgesang*). German patterns lie more or less behind the entire genre.

The East Nordic love poetry had probably left traces in the Swedish *Eufemiavisor* from the early 14th century, although one cannot exclude the possibility that the lyrical phrases in question are taken directly from German poetry.

Ed.: Klemming, G. E., ed. *Svenska medeltids dikter och rim*. Samlingar utgivna av Svenska fornskrift-sällskapet, 25. Stockholm: Norstedt, 1881–82; Noreen, Adolf, *et al.*, eds. *1500– och 1600–talens visböcker*. Stockholm and Uppsala: Svenska litteratursällskapet, 1884–1919; Grüner-Nielsen, H., ed. *Danske Viser fra Adelvisebøger og Flyveblade, 1530–1630*. Copenhagen: Gyldendal, 1912–31; rpt. Copenhagen: Reitzel, 1978–79 [with postscript by I. Piø]; Frandsen, Ernst. *Mariaviserne. Den lyriske Madonnadigtning fra Danmarks Middelalder, belyst gennem Bønnebøgernes Prosatexter*. Copenhagen: Levin & Munksgaard, 1926; Wessén, Elias, and Sven B. F. Jansson. *Upplands runinskrifter*. Kungl. vitterhets historie och antikvitets akademien, 6. Uppsala: Almqvist & Wiksell, 1953, pp. 346–75; Jansson, Sven B. F., and Elias Wessén. *Gotlands runinskrifter*. Kungl. vitterhets historie och antikvitets akademien, 11. Uppsala: Almqvist & Wiksell, 1962, pp. 202–3; Janson, Sven B. F. *Västmanlands runinskrifter*. Kungl. vitterhets historie och antikvitets akademien, 13. Uppsala: Almqvist & Wiksell, 1964, pp. 69–76; Jonsson, B. R., ed. "Några gamla kärleksvisor." *Sumlen* (1976), 20–34. **Bib.**: Jón Helgason. "Bällsta-inskriftens 'i grati.'" In *Festskrift till Jöran Sahlgren 8.4.1944*. Ed. K. G. Ljunggren *et al.* Lund: Gleerup, 1944, pp. 479–82. **Lit.**: Brøndum-Nielsen, Johs. "Skriververset i Kölner Dombibliotheks Codex CXXX." *Acta Philologica Scandinavica*, 4 (1929–30), 65–71; rpt. in his *Studier og tydninger*. Copenhagen: Schultz, 1951; Frandsen, Ernst. *Folkevisen*. Århus: Universitetsforlaget; Copenhagen: Levin & Munksgaard, 1935; Savicki, St. *Die Eufemiavisor*. Lund and Leipzig: Gleerup, 1939; Frandsen, Ernst. "Middelalderlig lyrik." *Danske Studier* (1954), 75–108; Hildeman, Karl-Ivar. *Medeltid på vers*. Skrifter utgivna av Svenskt visarkiv, 1. Stockholm: Almqvist & Wiksell, 1958.

Gösta Holm and Bengt R. Jonsson

2. WEST NORSE. In general, Old Norse love poetry may be divided into two groups, that which may be considered autochthonous, and that which was composed under the influence or in

imitation of foreign models, *i.e.*, classical authors like Ovid or the troubadours and their imitators. The distinction is by no means clear.

The native-foreign question is particularly vexed in the case of skaldic verse. There are altogether about fifty stanzas dealing with the subject of love (Finnur Jónsson 1912–15, "Erotiske digte og vers"). A clear case of troubadour influence are the verses composed by Rǫgnvaldr Kali, earl of Orkney, and two of his companions (both Icelanders) while visiting Narbonne in the Languedoc on their way to the Holy Land in 1151 and cited in *Orkneyinga saga*. These verses are something of an anomaly in the skaldic canon, but show at least how contact could have taken place. Of the remainder, over half are by the poet Kormákr Ǫgmundarson, and a further six by Hallfreðr vandræðaskáld ("troublesome skald"), both heroes of sagas bearing their names, two of the so-called *skáldasǫgur*, or skaldic biographies. Dronke (1968) uses a number of their verses to argue the universality of what is commonly called *amour courtois*, the skalds in question ostensibly antedating the troubadours of Provence by some hundred years. Bjarni Einarsson (1961), on the other hand, argues that the same verses cannot be much older than the sagas in which they are preserved, *i.e.*, from the 13th century, going so far as to suggest that they were probably composed by the saga authors themselves. He cites linguistic evidence (refuted by Einar Ól. Sveinsson 1966), and also musters what may be called literary-critical evidence, *i.e.*, aspects of the skaldic verses that may be traced more readily to troubadour than to native practice, but also looks at the complex question of the relationship between prose and verse in the sagas. Andersson (1969), however, argues that the similarities are not close enough to indicate dependence and that most of the verses in question represent native Norse tradition in that they are inspired by a particular situation, as is normally the case with skaldic poetry, as opposed to being of a general nature, "not bound by any particular moment," a characteristic of troubadour poetry. Bjarni Einarsson (1971) has countered Andersson's arguments, and the question remains open.

The subject of origins has unfortunately obscured the real achievement of poets like Kormákr, whose verses, genuine or spurious, based solely on native tradition or inspired by continental models, represent a high point in skaldic poetry.

The theme of love is treated in a number of poems in the *Edda*, but differently handled in the heroic poems and in the mythological poems. In the heroic poems, the woman expresses her love, more specifically her sorrow at lost love (*e.g.*, *Helgakviða Hundingsbana II*). In the mythological poems, there are a number of examples of male characters suffering from the pangs of love. Freyr in *Skírnismál*, for example, on seeing Gerðr for the first time, experiences *móðtregi mikill* ("great longing"). Óðinn himself becomes consumed with passion for "Billings mær," the daughter (or possibly wife) of Billingr (*cf. Hávamál* 96–102).

The term *mansǫngskvæði* (from *man*, originally a servant of either sex but subsequently used only of young maidens) appears in a number of early sources in reference to amorous or erotic verses. *Grágás* states that the penalty for composing such verses (*mansǫngr*) to a woman was outlawry, the heaviest penalty, but that the woman herself was guilty if twenty or older. This law may be quite old, but need not be much older than *Grágás* itself (13th century). Numerous references to *mansǫngskvæði* in the sagas and other sources indicate the existence of love lyrics in Iceland at least as early as the 12th century. None of these poems survives, but then conditions for the survival of poetry of this type are seldom

good: it was "popular," and thus rarely committed to parchment, and was viewed by ecclesiastical authorities as immoral. As elsewhere in Europe, much of the evidence we have concerning medieval love poetry is the direct result of the Church's attempts to stamp it out. Among other improvements attributed to Bishop Jón Ǫgmundarson, elected 1106, was a ban on the then-popular game (*leikr*) in which a man and a woman recited or sang to each other "disgraceful and ludicrous verses, unworthy of hearing." The bishop is also said to have banned the composition of love songs (*mansǫngsvísur*), but was not entirely successful in his attempt. The source of this information, *Jóns saga helga*, testifies at least to the existence of these practices at the time of its composition (early 13th century). But to what extent these verses represent an indigenous tradition is difficult to determine.

Young clerics in the Commonwealth period would have been familiar with Latin poets, as a reference in *Jóns saga helga* shows. There, the young Klœngr Þorsteinsson, subsequently bishop at Skálholt, is rebuked for reading Ovid's *Ars amatoria*. Some indication of what these early lyrics were like is provided by a single line preserved in *Sturlunga saga: Mínar eru sorgir þungar sem blý* ("Mine are sorrows heavy as lead"), referred to as a "dance" (*dans*) in the saga, but in view of its subjective, personal nature, certainly from some kind of love lyric, perhaps a carol (*vikivakakvæði*; the term is postmedieval), or, less likely, a ballad, but in any case, one decidedly "southern."

The term *mansǫngr* came eventually to be used exclusively of the subjective, nonnarrative introductions to the *rímur*, in which the poet addresses the audience directly. The *mansǫngvar* deal most often with the subject of love, women's inconstancy being an especially favorite theme. Other common topoi were reflections on old age and its effect vis à vis love, or references to classical lovers or Ovid. Although the presence of *mansǫngvar* did not become fixed until after the Reformation, they appear sporadically in even the earliest *rímur* (14th century). The use of kennings and *heiti* in the *mansǫngvar*, as in the *rímur* in general, descends directly from skaldic practice; but in style and theme, they derive from the medieval European love lyric, and show a particular affinity with the German *Minnesang*. However, the *rímur* poets use only the themes of love in the *mansǫngvar*, but eschew the other great themes of troubadour poetry, for instance, nature and the coming of spring, perhaps for simple climatic reasons.

From this same period, *i.e.*, the late Middle Ages down to the early 17th century, we have indications of the existence of what must have been a large body of love lyrics. These were the *afmorskvæði* (from *amour*), the usual name for lyrics dealing with love after the term *mansǫngr* became associated with the *rímur*. They were also known as *brunakvæði* (literally "burning poems"), a term favored by ecclesiastics, whose vehemence in condemning them attests their popularity. Only a handful of poems and fragments have survived, often as marginalia in saga and other MSS, but what does remain gives us some idea of what these poems were like: the poet, separated from his loved one, describes his longing for her. A few lyrics present the woman's side, and may with some certainty be ascribed to women. In form, the *afmorskvæði* show unusual variety, for the most part derived from continental models.

Most of the ballads (*fornkvæði* or *sagnadansar*) and many carols (*vikivakakvæði*) also deal in one way or another with the theme of love. Although probably of medieval provenance, they are preserved only in full versions dating from after the Reformation. The ballads fall squarely within the larger context of northern

European balladry, while the relationship between the *vikivakakvæði* and other European dance lyrics has yet to be fully investigated, although their kinship with the English carol seems clear. Like their European counterparts, the Icelandic ballads are essentially narrative in nature, impersonal and objective, composed of short stanzas. The *vikivakakvæði*, on the other hand, are lyrical, personal, and subjective, and characterized by the presence of a burden (refrain).

Although perhaps not great literature, many of the carols, ballads, *mansöngvar*, and *afmorskvæði* have a simple beauty, and are deserving of more sympathetic treatment than that given them in most literary histories.

Ed. Finnur Jónsson, ed. *Den norsk-islandske skjaldedigtning*. Vols. 1A-2A (tekst efter håndskrifterne) and 1B-2B (retter tekst). Copenhagen and Christiania [Oslo]: Gyldendal, 1912–15; rpt. Copenhagen: Rosenkilde & Bagger, 1967 (A) and 1973 (B). **Lit**.: Björn K. Þórólfsson. *Rímur fyrir 1600*. Safn Fræðafjelagsins um Ísland og Íslendinga, 9. Copenhagen: Møller, 1934; Bjarni Einarsson. *Skáldasögur: Um uppruna og eðli ástaskáldasagnanna fornu*. Reykjavik: Menningarsjóður, 1961 [English summary]; Holtsmark, Anne. "Kjærlighetsdiktning." In *KLNM* 8 (1963), 438–43; Jón Samsonarson, ed. *Kvæði og dansleikir*. 3 vols. Reykjavik: Almenna, 1964; Einar Ólafur Sveinsson. "Kormakr the Poet and His Verses." *Saga-Book of the Viking Society* 17 (1966), 18–60 [English translation of "Kormakur skáld og vísur hans." *Skírnir* 140 (1966), 163–201]; Dronke, Peter. *Medieval Latin and the Rise of European Love-Lyric*. Oxford: Clarendon, 1968; Andersson, Theodore M. "Skalds and Troubadours." *Mediaeval Scandinavia* 2 (1969), 7–41; Bjarni Einarsson. "The Lovesick Skald: A Reply to Theodore M. Andersson (*Medieval Scandinavia* 1969)." *Mediaeval Scandinavia* 4 (1971), 21–41; Bjarni Einarsson. *To skjaldesagaer: En analyse af Kormáks saga og Hallfreðar saga*. Bergen, Oslo, and Tromsø: Universitetsforlaget, 1976; Turville-Petre, E. O. G. *Scaldic Poetry*. Oxford: Clarendon, 1976; Vésteinn Ólason. *The Traditional Ballads of Iceland*. Reykjavik: Stofnun Árna Magnússonar, 1982; Hughes, Shaun F. D. "Rímur." *Dictionary of the Middle Ages*. Ed. Joseph R. Strayer. New York: Scribner, 1982–89, vol. 10, pp. 401–7.

M. J. Driscoll

[**See also:** Ballads; Bjǫrn Breiðvíkingakappi; Eddic Poetry; *Eufemiavisorna*; Hallfreðr Óttarsson; *Hávamál*; *Heiti*; Helgi Poems; Kennings; Old Norse–Icelandic Literature, Foreign Influence on; Kormákr Ǫgmundarson; *Orkneyinga saga*; *Rímur*; Runes and Runic Inscriptions; *Skáldasögur*; Skaldic Verse; *Skírnismál*]

Lucidarius *see* **Elucidarius**

Ludus de Sancto Canuto Duce *see* **Drama**

Lygisaga ("lying saga, fictional saga"). In Old Norse, the term *lygisaga* generally signifies an invented, fictitious story (as, for example, *Jómsvíkinga saga*, ch. 28 [*Flateyjarbók* 1, 184]), or refers to a more or less distinctly literary narrative of fantastic, unhistorical content. King Sverrir (r. 1184–1202) used the term in the latter sense when he spoke about sagas like the now-lost **Hrómundar saga Gripssonar*; he found "slíkar lygisǫgur skemtiligstar" ("such *lygisǫgur* the most amusing [of all sagas]" [*Þorgils saga ok Hafliða*, ch. 10]).

Lygisaga was first used as a technical term in modern times chiefly by German and American scholars in the 19th and first half of the 20th centuries to designate a more or less narrowly defined group of texts. *Lygisaga* referred to sagas of the late Middle Ages that were composed in Iceland after the model of the translated *riddarasögur*. The basis for classification resides primarily in the contrast between translated *riddarasögur* and original *lygisögur*. Some scholars extended the designation to late groups of *fornaldarsögur*.

Owing chiefly to the pejorative connotations of the word, recent scholars have increasingly avoided the term *lygisaga*. In English, the designation "romances" is preferred; in German scholarship, "Icelandic" or "original" (in the sense of "not translated") *riddarasögur* or "Märchensagas" is preferred. In both cases, scholars agree about a core group of sagas, although the classification of individual texts on the border between *lygisaga* and *riddarasaga*, or else between *lygisaga* and *fornaldarsaga*, is in dispute.

Lit.: Andrews, A. LeRoy. "The Lygisǫgur." *Publications of the Society for the Advancement of Scandinavian Studies* 2 (1914–15), 255–63; Andrews, A. LeRoy. "Studies in the Fornaldarsögur Norðrlanda." *Modern Philology* 9 (1911–12), 371–97 [esp. 386–8]; Leach, Henry Goddard. *Angevin Britain and Scandinavia*. Harvard Studies in Comparative Literature, 6. Cambridge: Harvard University Press; London: Milford; Oxford: Oxford University Press, 1921; rpt. Millwood: Kraus, 1975, pp. 163–4; Schlauch, Margaret. *Romance in Iceland*. Princeton: Princeton University Press; New York: American-Scandinavian Foundation; London: Allen & Unwin, 1934; rpt. New York: Russell & Russell, 1973; Jakob Benediktsson. "Lygisǫgur." *KLNM* 11 (1966), 18; Schier, Kurt. *Sagaliteratur*. Sammlung Metzler, M 78. Stuttgart: Metzler, 1970, pp. 105–6; Jónas Kristjánsson. "Text Editions of the Romantic Sagas." In *Les relations littéraires franco-scandinaves au moyen âge. Actes du Colloque de Liège (avril 1972)*. Bibliothèque de la Faculté de Philosophe et Lettres de l'Université de Liège, 208. Paris: Les Belles Lettres, 1975, pp. 275–88; Nahl, Astrid van. *Originale Riddarasǫgur als Teil altnordischer Sagaliteratur*. Texte und Untersuchungen zur Germanistik und Skandinavistik, 3. Frankfurt am Main and Bern: Lang, 1981, pp. 3–10; See, Klaus von. "Das Problem der mündlichen Erzählprosa im Altnordischen: Der Prolog der Þiðriks saga und der Bericht von der Hochzeit in Reykjahólar." *Skandinavistik* 11 (1981), 91–5; rpt. in his *Edda, Saga, Skaldendichtung. Aufsätze zur skandinavischen Literatur des Mittelalters*. Heidelberg: Winter, 1981, pp. 506–10; Glauser, Jürg. *Isländische Märchensagas. Studien zur Prosaliteratur im spätmittelalterlichen Island*. Beiträge zur nordischen Philologie, 12. Basel and Frankfurt am Main: Helbing & Lichtenhahn, 1983, pp. 17–8; Kalinke, Marianne. "Norse Romance (Riddarasögur)." In *Old Norse–Icelandic Literature: A Critical Guide*. Ed. Carol J. Clover and John Lindow. Islandica, 45. Ithaca and London: Cornell University Press, 1985, pp. 316–63 [esp. p. 324].

Jürg Glauser

[**See also:** *Fornaldarsögur*; *Riddarasögur*]

Magic seems to be volitive symbolic behavior to effect or to prevent changes in the environment by means of extraordinary communicative acts with paranormal factors. Magic is a way for certain human beings to make things happen that ordinarily could not be made to happen. Generally, it is distinguished from religion by the fact that the will of the magician is paramount. The magician makes the environment do his bidding, whereas in religion the human community generally attempts to harmonize its behavior with a universal paradigm.

In Viking Age accounts, there is a self-conscious division between two types of magic: Old Norse *galdr* and *seið(r)*. *Galdr* is derived from the verb *gala* 'to make the sound of a crow or raven,' while the etymology of *seið(r)* remains somewhat obscure (de Vries 1962). It may have something to do with vocal performance, such as singing or chanting. By the Viking Age, however, *seið(r)* had developed a reputation for being somehow "shameful." *Ynglinga saga* (ch. 7) relates how the Vanir goddess Freyja taught the god Óðinn the art of *seiðr*. It may be that *seiðr* was thought to be "shameful" or unmanly because it sometimes involved sexual activity, or perhaps more plausibly because it involved the loss of consciousness and induction of trance states. *Galdr*, on the other hand, appears to be a more straightforward use of symbolic vocal utterances, perhaps accompanied by visible signs, to impress the will of the magician directly onto the environment. The saga literature is rich with accounts of magic; extensive studies have been made by Dillmann (1986), Eggers (1932), Ellis Davidson (1973), Jaide (1937), and Strömbäck (1935).

The most discussed aspect of medieval Scandinavian magic is certainly "rune magic," *i.e.*, the notion that the runes, the early Germanic writing system, were essentially a magicoreligious tool. Early literature on this subject suffered from a theoretically imprecise basis (Olsen 1916, Linderholm 1918, Lindquist 1923, Agrell 1927). In 1952, Bæksted raised the first serious objections to the simple equation that runes are magic. More recently, Schneider (1956) and Klingenberg (1973) have continued speculation in the field of rune magic, while other runologists, such as Page (1964) and Antonsen (1980), have remained more skeptical. The problems are summarized by Flowers (1986: 48–61).

Whether or not runes are in and of themselves magical, they were used almost exclusively for magical ends in the older runic period (1st–8th centuries A.D.). A review of the inscriptions of this period shows that there is not a single one of them that could be interpreted in a purely secular, nonmagical sense (Krause 1966). In the later period (9th–12th centuries), such profane communications become more common, while in the following medieval period they become more common still.

As far as the theory and practice of magic with runes are concerned, it is clear that this writing system was used as an aid in objectifying the will of the magician in graphic form. Formulas that until the introduction of the runes were perhaps performed only vocally were now made symbolically more objective, and hence more effective magically, by means of writing. The fact that the word used to class these signs, Proto-Germanic *rūnō*, Old Norse *rún*, seems to have basically meant "secret" or "mystery," adds to the credibility of those who see in the runes something intrinsically magical. In the history of magic in Scandinavia, there seems to have been no set of symbolic behaviors more important than a vocal performance followed by an execution of a graphic sign or set of signs to reinforce the will of the magician. In this process, the runes became a primary tool of the magician in pre-Christian times.

After the introduction of Christianity into Scandinavia, indigenous cultural features, such as the runes, began to erode slowly. In the field of magic, there arose a new tradition, certainly inspired by continental models, of recording magic "recipes" in *grimoires*, or *galdrabœkur*, books of magic, as they were commonly called in Icelandic. The kind of magic practiced from these books is recorded in two significant ways. First, there is the tradition of the Icelandic folktales having their origins in this period (12th–17th centuries), in which the exploits of famous magicians who are said to have used such manuals are recounted. Second, there are the few remains of these books themselves. The most complete of these is the so-called *Galdrabók* (ed. Lindquist 1921).

The theoretical basis for the practice of magic in these sources is essentially unchanged from the heathen period. The magician is usually supposed to speak a vocal formula and then draw or carve a special abstract sign, called *galdrastafir* or *galdramyndir* in Old Icelandic. This procedure varies greatly from the standard forms of magic being commonly practiced at the same time on the Continent, in which supernatural entities are invoked and coerced into doing the bidding of the magician.

The practice of magic in the Scandinavian Middle Ages was

greatly shaped by the traditions of magical practice inherited from the heathen age, and especially conditioned by the forms of symbolic action bound up with the use of runes for magical purposes. The basis of this practice is the belief that certain persons have the power to effect their will directly on the environment with the aid of the traditional lore, such as mythic references, poetic formulas, runes, or abstract graphic signs.

Ed.: Lindqvist, N. *En isländsk Svartkontsbok från 1500 talet (Galdrabók)*. Uppsala: Appelberg, 1921. **Tr.**: Flowers, Stephen E. *The Galdrabók: An Icelandic Grimoire*. York Beach: Weiser, 1989. **Lit.**: Olsen, Magnus. "Om troldruner." *Edda* 5 (1916), 225–45; Linderholm, Emanuel. *Nordisk magi*. Stockholm: Norstedt, 1918; Lindquist, Ivar. *Galdrar: De gamla germanska trollsångernas stil undersökt i samband med en svensk runinskrift från folkvandringstiden*. Göteborgs högskolas årsskrift, 1. Gothenburg: Wettergren & Kerber, 1923; Agrell, Sigurd. *Runornas Talmystik och dess antika förbild*. Lund: Gleerup, 1927; Eggers, Hans Jürgen. *Die magischen Gegenstände der altisländischen Prosaliteratur. Form und Geist*. Arbeiten zur germanischen Philologie, 27. Leipzig: Eichblatt, 1932; Strömbäck, Dag. *Sejd. Textstudier i nordisk religionshistoria*. Nordiska texter och undersökningar, 5. Stockholm: Gerber; Copenhagen: Levin & Munksgaard, 1935; Jaide, Walter. *Das Wesen des Zaubers in den primitiven Kulturen und in den Islandssagas*. Leipzig: Noske, 1937; Bæksted, Anders. *Målruner og Troldruner: Runmagiske Studier*. Copenhagen: Gyldendal, 1952; Schneider, Karl. *Die germanischen Runennamen: Versuch einer Gesamtdarstellung: Ein Beitrag zur idg./germ. Kultur- und Religionsgeschichte*. Meisenheim: Hain, 1956; Vries, Jan de. *Altnordisches etymologisches Wörterbuch*. 2nd rev. ed. Leiden: Brill, 1962; Page, R. I. "Anglo-Saxons, Runes, and Magic." *Journal of the Archaeological Association* 27 (1964), 14–31; Krause, Wolfgang. *Die Runeninschriften im älteren Futhark*. Abhandlungen der Akademie der Wissenschaften in Göttingen, Phil.-hist. Kl., Dritte Folge, 65. Göttingen: Vandenhoeck & Ruprecht, 1966; Ellis Davidson, H. R. "Hostile Magic in the Icelandic Sagas." In *The Witch Figure: Folklore Essays by a Group of Scholars in England Honouring the 75th Birthday of Katharine M. Briggs*. Ed. Venetia Newell. Boston and London: Routledge and Kegan Paul, 1973, pp. 20–41; Klingenberg, Heinz. *Runenschrift, Schriftdenken, Runeninschriften*. Germanische Bibliothek, 3. Reihe. Untersuchungen und Einzeldarstellungen. Heidelberg: Winter 1973; Antonsen, Elmer H. "Den ældre fuþark: en gudernes gave eller et hverdagsalfabet?" *Maal og minne* (1980), 129–43; Dillmann, François-Xavier. "Les magiciens dans l'Islande ancienne: Études sur la représentation de la magie islandaise et de ses agents dans les sources littéraires norroises." Diss. University of Caen, 1986; Flowers, Stephen E. *Runes and Magic: Magical Formulaic Elements in the Older Runic Tradition*. American University Studies, Series 1: Germanic Languages and Literature, 53. New York, Bern, and Frankfurt am Main: Lang, 1986.

Stephen E. Flowers

[See also: Runes and Runic Inscriptions]

Magnús Hákonarson,

son of Hákon Hákonarson, ruled Norway 1263–1280; he became king in 1257, and ruled together with his father until Hákon died in 1263.

Magnús Hákonarson and his closest advisers, the "good men," concentrated on the domestic conditions of Norway. Legislative and organizational work characterized Magnús Hákonarson's reign, and secured him the name *lagabœtir* ("law-mender"). During his reign, the State Council was more firmly structured than before. Furthermore, he saw to it that a staff of civil servants was educated at the royal chapel, the Apostolic Church in Bergen. We are able to distinguish a group of diplomats employed in his service during his reign.

The object of his legislation was a comprehensive revision of the old law books. The legal revision was a continuation of the State Laws dating from the time of Magnús Erlingsson (1161–1184) and Hákon Hákonarson (1217–1263). The latter had initiated the revision of the Frostuþing Law. The revision of the law went through two stages. The first one included a revision of the law books for Gulaþing in 1267, and Eiðsifa- and Borgarþing in 1268. The latter consisted of the working out of the National Law in 1274 (which also came to apply to the Faroe Islands), a Town Law in 1276, and two law codes for Iceland, *Járnsíða* in 1271 and *Jónsbók* in 1281. An older court law was expanded and revised, and became the *Hirðskrá* (1273–1277).

The object of this legislative work was to create uniform laws for the entire country. The legislation increased the authority of the king with regard to the administration and execution of the laws, as well as the public regulation of society. At the same time, it entailed important reforms, regulation of the tax system and of the institutions for the poor. There is no actual Christian Law in the National Law. The reason for this exclusion was a major conflict between the monarchy and the Church concerning Christian legislation, dating from the end of the 1260s. Magnús Hákonarson claimed that the king and the Church should administer the Christian legislation in unison. On the basis of this claim, Christian legislative decisions were publicized in a statute dating from the middle of the 1260s. The revision of the Gulaþing Law and the Eiðsifa- and Borgarþing Law in 1267 and 1268 included the Christian Law. During the revision of the Frostuþing Law, the king was strongly opposed by the new archbishop, Jón rauði ("the red"), who independently started to make a Trondic Christian Law in accordance with purely ecclesiastical principles. The conflict between the king and the archbishop was difficult, but an agreement was reached in Tønsberg in 1277.

Magnús Hákonarson's first task as absolute monarch was to conclude a peace treaty with Scotland. Thus, he abandoned his father's expansive foreign policy. The negotiations with the Scottish king began in 1264, and an agreement was reached two years later, the Treaty of Perth. Magnús Hákonarson gave up his claim to the contested islands, the Hebrides and the Isle of Man, in return for a one-time compensation of 4,000 pounds sterling and 100 pounds sterling annually in perpetuity; at the same time, Norwegian control over the Orkney Islands and the Shetland Islands was secured. Magnús Hákonarson preserved the contact his father had established with neighboring countries and with Europe. His relations with Sweden and Denmark were peaceful, even though he became involved in the dispute over the throne in Sweden in the 1270s and in inheritance claims in Denmark. He also extended legal rights of all German-speaking merchants in Norway, surpassing the rights of native and other foreign merchants. This was the first step in the development of special privileges for the Germans in Norway, based upon their special role in the economy of the country.

Lit.: Koht, Halvdan. "The Scandinavian Kingdoms Until the End of the Thirteenth Century." In *The Cambridge Medieval History* 6. Ed. J. R. Tanner *et al*. Cambridge: Cambridge University Press, 1929, pp. 362–92; Seip, Jens Arup. *Sættargjerden i Tunsberg og kirkens jurisdiksjon*. Oslo: Det Norske Videnskaps-akademi i Oslo, 1942; Helle, Knut. "Tendenser i nyere norsk høymiddelalderforskning."

Historisk tidsskrift (Norway) 40 (1960–61), 337–70; Helle, Knut. "Trade and Shipping Between Norway and England in the Reign of Håkon Håkonsson (1217–1263)." Sjøfartshistorisk årbok (Bergen) (1967), 7–33; Helle, Knut. "Anglo-Norwegian Relations in the Reign of Håkon Håkonsson 1217–63." Mediaeval Scandinavia 1 (1968), 101–14; Gunnes, Erik. "Kirkelig jurisdiksjon i Norge 1153–1277." Historisk tidsskrift (Norway) 49 (1970), 121–60; Crawford, Barbara E. "The Earls of Orkney-Caithness and Their Relations with the Kings of Norway and Scotland: 1150–1470." Diss. St. Andrews University, 1971; Helle, Knut. Konge og gode menn i norsk riksstyring ca. 1150–1319. Bergen: Universitetsforlaget, 1972; Crawford, Barbara E. "Weland of Stiklaw: A Scottish Royal Servant at the Norwegian Court." Historisk tidsskrift (Norway) 52 (1973), 329–39; Helle, Knut. Norge blir en stat 1130–1319. 2nd ed. Handbok i Norges historie, 3. Bergen: Universitetsforlaget, 1974; Lunden, Kåre. Norge under Sverreætten 1177–1319. Norges historie, 3. Oslo: Cappelen, 1976; Bagge, Sverre. "Kirkens jurisdiksjon i kristenrettssaker før 1277." Historisk tidsskrift (Norway) 60 (1981), 133–59; Helle, Knut. "Norway in the High Middle Ages: Recent Views on the Structure of Society." Scandinavian Journal of History 6 (1981), 161–89; Bagge, Sverre. "The Formation of the State and Concepts of Society in 13th Century Norway." In Continuity and Change: Political Institutions and Literary Monuments in the Middle Ages. A Symposium. Ed. Elisabeth Vestergaard. Odense: Odense University Press, 1986, pp. 43–61; Bagge, Sverre. "Borgerkrig og statsutvikling i Norge i middelalderen." Historisk tidsskrift (Norway) 65 (1986), 145–97; Sandvik, Gudmund. "Sættargjerda i Tunsberg og kongens jurisdiksjon." In Samfunn. Rett. Rettferdighet. Festskrift til Torstein Eckhoffs 70–årsdag. Ed. A. Bratholm et al. Oslo: Tano, 1986, pp. 563–85; Bagge, Sverre. The Political Thought of the King's Mirror. Mediaeval Scandinavia Supplements, 3. Odense: Odense University Press, 1987.

Jón Viðar Sigurðsson

[See also: Gyðinga saga; Hákon Hákonarson; Jónsbók; Laws; Magnúss saga lagabœtis; Norway]

Magnússdrápa see Arnórr Þórðarson jarlaskáld

Magnúss saga helga eyjajarls ("The Saga of St. Magnús, Orkney-earl"). The Norse Life of St. Magnús, earl of Orkney (d. probably 1117) survives in three textually related Norse versions. These are, first, the one incorporated into Orkneyinga saga, probably composed at the end of the 12th century, revised in the 13th century to accommodate it to the sagas of the kings of Norway in Heimskringla, and surviving as interpolations into the sagas of the Norwegian kings in Flateyjarbók (written ca. 1387), and also in a few other MS fragments. The account of Magnús occupies chs. 33, 39–40, and 44–52 of Orkneyinga saga as normally edited, and the miracle book, presented as a discrete section, forms ch. 57. Second and third, the Longer and Shorter versions of a separate Magnúss saga helga survive, the longer, a text of thirty-five chapters, primarily in AM 350 4to, a paper copy, made about 1700, of a vellum MS written around 1400, now almost completely destroyed, and the shorter, twenty chapters, in AM 235 fol., written at the end of the 14th century. All these Norse versions were preserved in Iceland, and were almost certainly composed there. A short Latin Legenda de s. Magno also survives in AM 670f 4to, an early 18th-century paper copy of a lost vellum fragment. The Breviarium Aberdonensis also preserves a very brief Latin account.

The Shorter Saga of St. Magnús is very closely related to Orkneyinga saga, and may be directly derived from it, probably after its 13th-century revision relating it to Heimskringla. The

Shorter Saga may preserve fuller wording than that of the surviving version of Orkneyinga saga. The Longer Saga was probably composed in its present form about or soon after the beginning of the 14th century, in the cultural context of the Benedictine monasteries of northern Iceland, and possibly by Abbot Bergr Sokkason of Þverárklaustr. It seems to be based upon a text of Orkneyinga saga close to Flateyjarbók, but it further cites as its source a Latin Life of St. Magnús, composed by a "Master Robert" twenty-eight years after Magnús's martyrdom. The Longer Saga is also textually related to the Breviarium Aberdonensis, which could also be derived from Master Robert's text.

All the Norse texts give an account of Magnús's ancestry, and describe an incident in his youth, when he was conscripted by King Magnús berfœttr ("bare-leg") Óláfsson of Norway on an expedition into the Irish Sea (1098). He refused to fight, reading his psalter instead, and then absconded. Nothing else of his life is narrated other than his martyrdom at the hands of his cousin Earl Hákon Pálsson, which is described in detail. There follows a miracle book of the healings performed at his shrine. The Legenda makes only indirect reference to the story of the Irish Sea expedition, and omits the miracle book. The Longer Saga (ch. 27) and the Legenda preserve the detail of Magnús's double wounding at martyrdom, although only the Longer Saga describes the double blow as struck from in front into the same wound on the head. Orkneyinga saga (ch. 50) and specifically the Shorter Saga (ch. 13) mention only a single blow. The double blow from in front into a single wound has been strikingly confirmed from the skull of St. Magnús, discovered at the cathedral in Kirkwall in 1919. Underlying all the texts, therefore, is a Passio, to which a miracle book is normally appended. This text may well be that of Master Robert. The account in Orkneyinga saga is probably based directly or indirectly upon this text, as may be the much-abridged texts of the Legenda and the Breviarium. The Shorter Saga represents a separate redaction of the account in Orkneyinga saga, but the Longer Saga of St. Magnús seems to be a reworking of that account by reference back to Master Robert's text.

Ed.: Gudbrand Vigfusson, ed., and George W. Dasent, trans. Icelandic Sagas and Other Historical Documents Relating to the Settlements and Descents of the Northmen on the British Isles. 4 vols. Rolls Series, 88. London: Eyre and Spottiswoode, 1887–94; rpt. Millwood: Kraus, 1964 [contains both versions of Magnúss saga helga and the Legenda de s. Magno]; Finnbogi Guðmundsson, ed. Orkneyinga saga. Íslenzk fornrit, 34. Reykjavik: Hið íslenzka fornritafélag, 1965. Tr.: Hermann Pálsson and Paul Edwards, trans. Magnus' Saga: The Life of St Magnus Earl of Orkney 1075–1116. Oxford: Perpetua Press, 1987. Lit.: Mooney, John. "Discovery of Relics in St. Magnus' Cathedral." Proceedings of the Orkney Antiquarian Society 3 (1924–25), 73–8; Mooney, John. St. Magnus, Earl of Orkney. Kirkwall: Mackintosh, 1935; Magnús Már Lárusson. "Sct. Magnus Orcadensis Comes." Saga (1962), 470–503.

Paul Bibire

[See also: Flateyjarbók; Heimskringla; Legenda; Miracles, Collections of; Orkney, Norse in; Orkneyinga saga; Saints' Lives]

Magnúss saga lagabœtis ("The Saga of Magnús the Law-mender"; r. 1263–1280) was written by the Icelandic historian Sturla Þórðarson (d. 1284). Sturlu þáttr, a short account of the latter part of Sturla's life, relates that Sturla, who held a high rank at the Norwegian court, began writing the saga of Magnús

Hákonarson during his second stay in Norway around 1266–1271. During his third visit there in the summer of 1278, he acquired additional material for the work, which he finished in Iceland shortly after the king's death.

The saga is a contemporary account of Magnús lagabœtir's reign over a realm that spread widely across the North Atlantic. It is structured in the same way as Sturla's saga on King Hákon (*Hákonar saga Hákonarsonar*), Magnús's father, using the regnal years to establish a chronological framework. The chronology of these two sagas runs much along the lines of West European chronicles, especially the English kings' chronicles of the 12th and 13th centuries. But the Icelandic tradition prevails in Magnús's saga with its strong realism; apart from statements of fact, the narrative is parsimonious. The saga was written under the guidance of King Magnús, who decided what it should contain.

Magnúss saga lagabœtis is preserved in two fragments in a vellum from around 1400 (AM 325 X 4to), which were accidentally found by Árni Magnússon around 1700. Only a century earlier, the saga as such was still available in Iceland, judging by the works of Arngrímur Jónsson. In the Middle Ages, Magnús's saga must have been well known, as the various annalists of the 14th century have made abundant entries from it, some of which apparently represent long passages from lost parts of the saga. The two original fragments deal with the years 1263–1264 and 1271 and verify that the image as a prince of peace, which King Magnús attempts to give his father, is very much the same as the one he favors for himself. Foreign policy is the dominating theme in the saga, as it is in the latter part of the saga of his father, likewise written under Magnús's guidance.

His great achievements in law and administration seem to play only a minor role in the presentation of Magnús as an arbitrator in Scandinavian politics. The main sources for this work were the king's and Sturla's memoranda (the reader senses the author's closeness to the events), as well as interviews, letters, itineraries, and the royal archives in general; poems are absent from the saga.

Ed.: Rafn, C. C., *et al.*, eds. *Fornmanna sögur*. 12 vols. Copenhagen: Popp, 1828–46, vol. 10; Gudbrand Vigfusson, ed., and George W. Dasent, trans. *Icelandic Sagas and Other Historical Documents Relating to the Settlements and Descents of the Northmen on the British Isles*. 4 vols. Rolls Series, 88. London: Eyre and Spottiswoode, 1887–94; rpt. Millwood: Kraus, 1964, vol. 2, pp. 361–8; Storm, Gustav, ed. *Islandske annaler indtil 1578*. Christiania [Oslo]: Grøndahl, 1888; rpt. Oslo: Norsk Historisk Kjeldeskrift-institutt, 1977, pp. 332–6 [annalistic excerpts from the saga]; Jakob Benediktsson, ed. *Arngrimi Jonae: Opera latine conscripta*. 4 vols. Bibliotheca Arnamagnæana, 9–12. Copenhagen: Munksgaard, 1950–57, vol. 9, pp. 305–11, vol. 10, pp. 170–6, vol. 12, pp. 217–21 [material from the saga in Arngrímur Jónsson's works]. **Tr.**: Gudbrand Vigfusson, ed., and George W. Dasent, trans. *Icelandic Sagas and Other Historical Documents*, vol. 4. **Lit.**: Ólafía Einarsdóttir. *Studier i kronologisk metode i tidlig islandsk historieskrivning*. Bibliotheca Historica Lundensis, 13. Stockholm: Natur och Kultur, 1964, pp. 156–7; Ólafía Einarsdóttir. "Hvornår forfattedes sagaen om Magnus lagabøter." *Historisk tidsskrift* (Norway) 46 (1967), 59–67; Ólafía Einarsdóttir. "Om de to håndskrifter af Sturlunga saga." *Arkiv för nordisk filologi* 83 (1968) 44–80; Ólafía Einarsdóttir. Review of K. Lunden, *Norge under Sverreætten. Historisk tidsskrift* (Denmark) 80 (1980), 122–3.

Ólafía Einarsdóttir

[**See also:** Annals; Hákon Hákonarson; *Hákonar saga gamla Hákonarsonar*; *Konungasögur*; Magnús Hákonarson; Sturla Þórðarson; *Sturlunga saga*]

Mágus saga jarls ("The Saga of Earl Mágus") is preserved in approximately seventy-five vellum and paper MSS. This comprehensive transmission, without parallel among the *riddarasögur*, comprises a shorter and a longer version from around 1300 and 1350, respectively. The former can be assigned together with *Konráðs saga keisarasonar*, *Mírmanns saga*, and *Bærings saga* to the oldest period of the nontranslated Icelandic *riddarasögur*. But the more detailed later version enjoyed the greater popularity in Iceland down to the early 20th century. The anonymous *Mágus saga jarls* may be one of the *riddarasögur* that had its origin in Reykhólar in western Iceland.

Parts of the material of the saga are also found in *Mágus rímur* and *Geirarðs rímur*, in the Faroese ballad *Karlamagnus kvæði* (*Karlamagnus og Jógvan kongur*, CCF 106), and in Norwegian ballads (*Dei tri vilkári, The Types of the Scandinavian Medieval Ballad*, TSB D 404).

The arrogant Emperor Játmundr of Saxland is killed in the course of a dispute by the vehement Vígvarðr, son of Earl Ámundi. For three years, he hides in a forest together with his brothers, Rǫgnvaldr, Markvarðr, and Aðalvarðr. By a trick, his brother-in-law Mágus manages to release the brothers from captivity and from the persecution of Játmundr's son, Emperor Karl. In the end, Mágus reconciles the two parties. Because of his skills, Mágus is also called Bragða-Mágus ("the trickster") and the saga *Bragða-Mágus saga*.

Even though *Mágus saga jarls*, like *Karlamagnús saga*, *Flóvents saga*, *Elis saga ok Rósamundu*, and *Bærings saga*, belongs among the group of Old Norse *riddarasögur* that can be classified as the *matière de France* group, it hardly presents, at least in its present form, a close translation of a lost *chanson de geste*. Nonetheless, a part of it shows a very close thematic relation to *Pèlerinage de Charlemagne* (ch. 1: "Travel to Constantinople"), to the fairy-tale type AaTh 1552 (ch. 2: "The Wise Carving of the Owl"), to *Decameron* 3:9 (the test of the unloved woman, chs. 2–4; cf. Shakespeare's *All's Well That Ends Well*), and in the main part (chs. 5–22) to *Renaud de Montauban* (also known as *Maugis d'Aigremont* or *Fils d'Haymon*). In the *Geirarðs þáttr* of the younger version, a story from *Gesta Romanorum* is also used. Among the Old Norse texts used by the author of *Mágus saga jarls* are *Þiðreks saga*, *Karlamagnús saga*, *Hálfs saga ok Hálfsrekka*, and *Snorra Edda*. The younger version shows in the added *þættir* many similarities in content to the *fornaldarsögur*. The origin of the older *Mágus saga* may be oral tradition, or it may be, as in the case of *Tristrams saga*, that a translation made in Norway was revised in Iceland and gave rise to a new version. In any case, the two different versions present an interesting example of how a source that was considered stylistically unsatisfactory (*i.e.*, the older version) was adapted to changed poetic and stylistic models (the younger version). Similar characteristics can be found with regard to *Qrvar-Odds saga*, to which *Mágus saga* appears to have a connection. The narrative style of the older and shorter *Mágus saga* has been compared with the classical *Íslendingasögur*. The younger version is characterized by an active, obtrusive narrator, seen also in a large number of the *riddarsögur* and *fornaldarsögur* of the 14th and 15th centuries.

Ed.: Gunnlaugur Þórðarson, ed. *Bragða-Mágus saga með tilheyrandi þáttum*. Copenhagen: Páll Sveinsson, 1858 [longer version]; Cederschiöld, Gustaf, ed. *Fornsögur Suðrlanda. Magus saga jarls, Konraðs saga, Bærings saga, Flovents saga, Bevers saga. Med inledning*. Lund: Berling, 1884, pp. lxxx–cxxxviii, 1–42 [shorter version]; Páll Eggert Ólason, ed. *Mágus saga jarls ásamt þáttum af Hrólfi skuggafifli, Vilhjálmi Laissyni og Geirarði Vilhjálmssyni*. Riddarasögur, 1. Reykjavík: Fjallkonuútgáfan, 1916 [longer version]; Bjarni Vilhjálmsson, ed. "Mágus saga jarls (hin meiri)." In his *Riddarasögur*. 6 vols. Reykjavík: Íslendingasagnaútgáfan; Haukadalsútgáfan, 1949–54, vol. 2, pp. 135–429 [longer version]. **Bib**.: Kalinke, Marianne E., and P. M. Mitchell. *Bibliography of Old Norse–Icelandic Romances*. Islandica, 44. Ithaca and London: Cornell University Press, 1985; Finnur Sigmundsson. *Rímnatal*. 2 vols. Reykjavík: Rímnafélagið, 1966, vol. 1, pp. 88–90, 158–9. **Lit**.: Leach, Henry Goddard. *Angevin Britain and Scandinavia*. Harvard Studies in Comparative Literature, 6. Cambridge: Harvard University Press; London: Milford; Oxford: Oxford University Press, 1921; rpt. Millwood: Kraus, 1975; Schlauch, Margaret. *Romance in Iceland*. Princeton: Princeton University Press; New York: American-Scandinavian Foundation; London: Allen & Unwin, 1934; rpt. New York: Russell & Russell, 1973; Lane, George S. "A Note on the Icelandic MSS of the Mágus Saga." *Journal of English and Germanic Philology* 33 (1934), 498–501; Halvorsen, E. F. "Mágus saga jarls." *KLNM* 11 (1966), 239–41; Rossenbeck, Klaus. "Die Stellung der Riddarasǫgur in der altnordischen Prosaliteratur—eine Untersuchung an Hand des Erzählstils." Diss. Frankfurt am Main, 1970; Togeby, Knud. "L'influence de la littérature française sur les littératures scandinaves au moyen âge." In *Généralités*. Ed. Hans Ulrich Gumbrecht. Grundriss der romanischen Literaturen des Mittelalters, 1. Heidelberg: Winter, 1972, pp. 377–8; Hamer, Andrew. "Mágus saga—Riddarasaga or Fornaldarsaga?" In *Fourth International Saga Conference*. Munich: Institut für Nordische Philologie der Universität München, 1979, 13 pp. [photocopies of papers distributed to participants]; Kalinke, Marianne E. *King Arthur North-by-Northwest: The matière de Bretagne in Old Norse–Icelandic Romances*. Bibliotheca Arnamagnæana, 37. Copenhagen: Reitzel, 1981; Nahl, Astrid van. *Originale Riddarasögur als Teil altnordischer Sagaliteratur*. Texte und Untersuchungen zur Germanistik und Skandinavistik, 3. Frankfurt am Main and Bern: Lang, 1981; Glauser, Jürg. *Isländische Märchensagas. Studien zur Prosaliteratur im spätmittelalterlichen Island*. Beiträge zur nordischen Philologie, 12. Basel and Frankfurt am Main: Helbing & Lichtenhahn, 1983; Amory, Frederic. "Things Greek and the Riddarasögur." *Speculum* 59 (1984), 509–23; Kalinke, Marianne E. "Riddarasögur, Fornaldarsögur, and the Problem of Genre." In *Les Sagas de Chevaliers (Riddarasögur). Actes de la V⁰ Conférence Internationale sur les Sagas . . . (Toulon. Juillet 1982)*. Ed. Régis Boyer. Civilisations, 10. Paris: Presses de l'Université de Paris-Sorbonne, 1985, pp. 77–91; Kalinke, Marianne. "Norse Romance (Riddarasögur)." In *Old Norse–Icelandic Literature: A Critical Guide*. Ed. Carol J. Clover and John Lindow. Islandica, 45. Ithaca and London: Cornell University Press, 1985, pp. 316–63; Kalinke, Marianne E. "The Misogamous Maiden Kings of Icelandic Romance." *Scripta Islandica* 37 (1986), 47–71; Kalinke, Marianne E. "Mágus saga jarls." In *Dictionary of the Middle Ages*. Ed. Joseph R. Strayer. New York: Scribner, 1982–89, vol. 8, pp. 45–6.

Jürg Glauser

[**See also**: *Fornaldarsögur*; *Hálfs saga ok Hálfsrekka*; *Karlamagnús saga*; Old Norse–Icelandic Literature, Foreign Influence on; *Riddarasögur*; *Snorra Edda*; *Þiðreks saga af Bern*; *Ǫrvar-Odds saga*]

Máhlíðingavísur *see* **Þórarinn svarti**

Maiden Warriors. Old Norse literature has a common conception of women who, fully armed, participate in battle like men. These women thus encroach upon a preserve that, both earlier and later, has been considered a male one in European conceptual history. They show themselves in a sphere where strength and initiative are demanded and where it is possible to gain honor and immortality, at least in the world of words; great deeds in battle are commemorated in skaldic verse or in the later *Íslendingasögur*.

In the younger sources (*fornaldarsögur* and *riddarasögur*), these women are met with reprisals. Often they are forced out of the male sphere because their suitors defeat and sometimes rape them (*cf*. the fairy-tale motif *König Drosselbart*). In the younger sources, the women are described as being provocatively sexually hostile. They prefer to fight rather than to love, and are exceedingly proud, independent, and unsympathetic. In the older sources, the *Poetic Edda* and the *Íslendingasögur*, the strong, proud woman is capable of both fighting or loving, of showing both strength and tenderness (*cf*. Sigrún in *Helgakviða Hundingsbana* I). The primary positive or negative attitude toward the fighting women is thus decided by the date of the sources. The appearance of such women is determined by whether the material is treated realistically or not, or whether the plot takes place in distant lands or in local surroundings. The type therefore appears in the *Poetic Edda* and in the *fornaldarsögur* with the common-Germanic or common-Nordic mythic material and in the exotic *riddarasögur*. The type does not exist in the local *Íslendingasögur*, where armed women would have been a breach of style. Guðrún in *Laxdœla saga*, however, may be a successor to the type.

Whether the Norse maiden warriors are related to the Greek Amazons is not known. Nor is it known if maiden warriors in Scandinavia had a historical basis. No woman's grave containing weapons has yet been discovered.

In Old Norse literature, an armed maiden warrior is called *valkyrja*, *skjaldmær*, or *meykóngr*.

The term *valkyrja* has the etymology *kjósa val*, and refers to the fact that she chooses the warriors who are to fall in battle. The *valkyrja* is a supernatural being in the shape of an armor-clad earthly woman, or she may be an earthly woman in the service of Óðinn, god of war and death. The *valkyrja* has two functions: she is present on the battlefield where the "choice" is to be made, and she is in Valhǫll, where the fallen warriors gather. The *valkyrja* was able to fly through the air. The word *valkyrja* is used both in *Snorra Edda* and in the *Poetic Edda*, which also uses it about female figures independent of Óðinn, like Sigrún in *Helgakviða Hundingsbana* and Brynhildr in the poetic cycle about Sigurðr Fáfnisbani. It is possible that Vǫlundr's vanished wife, Svanhvítr, is related to the type. In her capacity as swan maiden, she can at least fly. And an obscure line, *ørlǫg drýgia* ("in wars to try them"), can perhaps be translated as if she and her vanished sisters have been associated with warfare.

Skjaldmær is used especially in *fornaldarsögur*, and the maiden warriors are here totally Nordic, but can, like all of the characters of this saga type, be involved in supernatural events. The same Brynhildr, who in the *Poetic Edda* is called a *valkyrja*, is called *skjaldmær* in the *Vǫlsunga saga*, a *fornaldarsaga* that treats the same material. This identification shows that the designations *valkyrja* and *skjaldmær* at least sometimes could apply exactly to the same female character.

Meykóngr is used only in *riddarasögur*. This variant of the type "maiden warrior" is always a ruling queen and unwilling to share her power with a man. Most commonly, she appears totally sexually hostile and wants to fight against her suitors. She is then with force and/or cunning made to change her mind.

Lit.: Wahlgren, Erik. *The Maiden King in Iceland*. Chicago: University of Chicago Libraries, 1938 [private publication]; Heller, Rolf. *Die literarische Darstellung der Frau in den Isländersagas*. Halle: Niemeyer, 1958; Diner, Helen. *Mothers and Amazons: The First Feminist History of Culture*. Ed. and trans. John P. Lundin. New York: Julian, 1965; Andersson, Theodore M. *The Legend of Brynhild*. Islandica, 43. Ithaca: Cornell University Press, 1980; Strand, Birgit. *Kvinnor och män i Gesta Danorum*. Kvinnohistoriskt arkiv, 18. Gothenburg: Historiska institutionen, Göteborgs Universitet, 1980; Sørensen, Preben Meulengracht. *Norrønt nid*. Odense: Odense Universitetsforlag, 1980; Præstgaard Andersen, Lise. "Oehlenschläger, de norrøne kilder og de norrøne kvinder." *Danske Studier* (1981), 5–31; Præstgaard Andersson, Lise. *Skjoldmøer—en kvindemyte*. Copenhagen: Gyldendal, 1982; Damico, Helen. *Beowulf's Wealhtheow and the Valkyrie Tradition*. Madison: University of Wisconsin Press, 1984.

Lise Præstgaard Andersen

[See also: *Fornaldarsǫgur*; Helgi Poems; *Íslendingasǫgur*; *Laxdœla saga*; *Riddarasǫgur*; *Snorra Edda*; Vǫlsung-Niflung Cycle; *Vǫlsunga saga*; *Vǫlundarkviða*; Women in Eddic Poetry; Women in Sagas]

Maine Coin is a weathered, barely decipherable coin, originally considered English, but now firmly identified as having been issued by King Óláfr kyrri ("the peaceful") Haraldsson of Norway (r. 1067–1093). The coin was found by amateur archaeologist Guy Mellgren in 1957, in association with Indian artifacts, at Naskeag Point, just east of the mouth of the Penobscot River, Maine. The spot is now referred to as the "Goddard site." Measuring 16.4 mm. in diameter and apparently at one time pierced so that it could be worn as a pendant, it has been analyzed by the numismatic scholar Kolbjørn Skaare at Oslo University. Tested at the Atomic Institute at Kjeller, the coin has a composition of 22 percent silver. Initially, the find was regarded as evidence of Norse exploration in Maine, possibly by the Icelandic bishop Eiríkr Gnúpsson, who, according to Icelandic chronicles, set sail "in search of Vinland" about 1121. But the coin is now believed to have come south by stages through trade among Indian tribes.

Lit.: Skaare, Kolbjørn. "An Eleventh Century Norwegian Penny Found on the Coast of Maine." *NNF-NYTT. Meddelelser fra Norsk Numismatisk Forening* (May 1979), 12–7; Wahlgren, Erik. "The Norse Coin from Maine: Philology and Navigation." *NNF-NYTT. Meddelelser fra Norsk Numismatisk Forening* (March 1980), 24–30; McKusick, Marshall, and Erik Wahlgren. "The Norse Penny Mystery." *Archaeology of Eastern North America* 8 (1980), 1–10; Bourque, Bruce J., and Steven L. Cox. "Maine State Museum Investigation of the Goddard Site, 1979." *Man in the Northeast* 22 (Fall 1981), 3–27; Ingstad, A. S. *The Norse Discovery of America*. Trans. Elizabeth S. Seeberg. Oxford: Oxford University Press, 1985, pp. 429–34.

†Erik Wahlgren

[See also: America, Norse in; Vinland Sagas]

Málsháttakvæði *see* **Bjarni Kolbeinsson**

Mandevilles Rejse ("Mandeville's Travels"). The fictitious Sir John Mandeville's travels from St. Albans in England to the Holy Land and beyond appealed to the North as to most of Europe for its dynamic synthesis, within a historical narrative, of a traveler's report from the Holy Land, an itinerary for a pilgrimage in the spirit, an affirmation of Scripture's historicity, a world perspective on Christendom, crusade polemic, and an account of marvels of the East, authorized by such writers as Orosius, Solinus, and Pliny. The North also claimed its proprietary stake in the Dane Otgerus (Holger Danske), conqueror for Christendom of lands between Jerusalem and the Earthly Paradise. The Latin work was known to Claudius Clavus, a Danish cartographer, in 1427. A translation into Danish, probably done about 1440, perhaps by Peder Hare, cleric in Roskilde diocese, was copied by Olauus Jacobi for the Franciscan community at Næstved, Zealand, in 1459 (SKB 307). Two further copies and an uncompleted summary of this translation are extant: Odense, Landsarkivet for Fyn, Karen Brahes Bibliotek E III 6 (mid-16th century); SKB M 306 (1584); and GkS 3559 (late 16th century). The text is thus a monument of Danish literary prose. No vernacular versions are known for other Scandinavian countries, though the influence of Mandeville is seen in the Icelandic *lygisögur*. Its diverse appeal is suggested by its varied contexts: in the monastic milieu of Latin and vernacular religious literature; alongside the lists of relics, many implicitly authenticated by Mandeville, held in religious houses; in the scriptorium that also produced *Dyrerim* ("Rhyming Bestiary") and the *Krønike* ("Legendary Chronicle"); later, paired with the *Udvandrere* (a catalogue of ancient Scandinavian emigrants who achieved worldly rule); in the tradition of such itineraries as Abbot Nikulás Bergsson's (d. 1159 or 1160) of Munkaþverá and the anonymous *De profectione Danorum in terram sanctam* (from Børglum monastery, Jutland, 1190); and against the background of actual pilgrimage from Scandinavia to the Holy Land.

Ed.: Lorenzen, M. *Mandevilles Rejse i gammeldansk Oversættelse*. Samfund til udgivelse af gammel nordisk litteratur, 5. Copenhagen: Møller, 1882. Lit.: Toldberg, H. "*Mandevilles rejse*." *KLNM* 11 (1966), 309–11; Bradley, S. A. J. "The Translator of *Mandevilles Rejse*: A New Name in Fifteenth-Century Danish Prose?" In *Medieval Literature and Civilisation: Studies in Memory of G. N. Garmonsway*. Ed. D. A. Pearsall and R. A. Waldron. London: Athlone, 1969; Bradley, S. A. J. "Mandevilles Rejse: Some Aspects of Its Changing Role in the Later Danish Middle Ages." *Medieval Scandinavia* 9 (1976), 146–63.

S. A. J. Bradley

[See also: Chronicles; *Dyrerim, De gamle danske*; Lygisaga; *Profectio Danorum in Hierosolymam*]

Man, Isle of. Set in the middle of the Irish Sea, easily visible on a clear day from all the surrounding countries, Man offered great potential to the politically ambitious of the region. Few historical sources survive from the Viking Age itself, but the period after the late 11th century until Man passed out of control of the Scandinavian kings in 1265 is rather better documented in *Chronica regum Manniae et insularum* (first compiled in the 13th century). By using standing monuments and archaeological investigation alongside historical sources, we can produce a reasonable narrative of the Scandinavian epoch.

The polity of Man before the Scandinavians came cannot be reconstructed coherently. By the 9th century, Norse settlement is evidenced by the presence of a number of furnished graves of pagan character. The graves are of two types: major accompanied burials in isolated mounds, and ordinary accompanied flat graves in preexisting Christian cemeteries (*e.g.*, at Peel Castle). The graves contain material with a Scottish or Norwegian taint. At some stage in the 10th century, the Scandinavians became Christian, and some seventy carved memorial stones, some of which are inscribed with runes, witness both to the Scandinavian character of the culture and to the fact that the original Manx population still played a role in the structure of society, particularly in that the inscriptions bear both Scandinavian and Manx names.

Excavated settlement sites of the Viking Age in Man tell us little. The major excavations on St. Patrick's Isle, Peel, have revealed a major 12th-century building. Earlier houses can be seen at the Braaid, which shows continuity from the pre-Norse period. This continuity is also evidenced at some of the promontory forts set along the coastline, some of which continued in use during the Middle Ages.

The prosperity of the island in the Viking Age is demonstrated by the presence of nineteen silver hoards, which date mostly from between 960 and 1070. These hoards may reflect the proximity of Dublin, the major economic center of the Scandinavians in the West. But when Dublin's trade shifted toward the southeast, and after Godred Crovan had established the Kingdom of Man and the Isles around 1079 with its northern bias, Man's prosperity declined.

The Church's presence in the Viking Age is attested by the sculptured crosses, by the Christian burials, and by the supposition that an ecclesiastical organization existed, a thesis based on the survival of ecclesiastical buildings where the crosses are found. There was a bishop in Man before 1079, but the parochial organization clearly belongs to a later period, and the bishopric of Sodor and Man was established in the mid-12th century.

From 1079 until 1265, a Norse dynasty reigned in Man, becoming more closely bound to Norway as time went on, particularly as the Western Isles (part of the kingdom of Man and the Isles) were gradually conquered by the Scots. The Norwegian interest in the Western Isles and in Man was purchased by the Scottish Crown after the battle of Largs, and, although Alexander III allowed Magnus to continue as king, a rebellion led by Godred Magnusson brought about the defeat and death of Godred, the last Norse king, at the battle of Ronaldsway in 1275.

The secular administration of the kingdom was carried out from Castle Rushen from the late 12th century onward, and this strong and impressive castle remained the administrative center of the island until the 19th century. The Norse administration is traced also in Tynwald, the present governing body of Man. This assembly, which still meets in a form that reflects its Scandinavian origins in the open air on St. John's Day, has its roots in the all-island (and originally all-kingdom) *þing* of the Norse period, of which there are good secondary records.

The chief language of the island in the Norse period was apparently Scandinavian, but a substream of Brythonic Manx seems to have survived throughout the period as the language of the peasantry. Place-names do not seem to be pre-Norse, although claims are made for one or two early Celtic examples. Norse elements are strong in the surviving place-names, particularly in settlement names.

Lit.: Bersu, Gerhard, and David M. Wilson. *Three Viking Graves in the Isle of Man*. Society for Medieval Archaeology, Monograph Series, 1. London: Society for Medieval Archaeology, 1966; Davey, Peter. *Man and Environment in the Isle of Man*. 2 vols. British Archaeological Reports, British Series, 54.1–2. Oxford: British Archaeological Reports, 1978 [provides all the relevant sources; David Freke will shortly produce a monograph on the Peel Castle excavations (to be published

by Liverpool University)]; Fell, Christine, *et al.*, eds. *The Viking Age in the Isle of Man: Select Papers from the Ninth Viking Congress, Isle of Man, 4–14 July 1981*. London: Viking Society for Northern Research, 1983.

David M. Wilson

[**See also:** Manx Crosses]

Mannjafnaðr *see* Senna—Mannjafnaðr

Manx Crosses. The Viking Age crosses decorated with pictures of human figures and animals reflect the mixture of Norse and Celtic traditions so characteristic of this period of the Isle of Man's history. The crosses also show strong links with northwestern England. Some scenes represent pagan and heroic themes popular in the Vikings' homelands, while others show Christian subjects.

The crosses are made of local slate, which fractures easily. Many survive only as fragments, making identifications difficult. In addition, the craftsmen used a cryptic style where several scenes might be shown on the same part of the cross, rather than divided into separate episodes. For these reasons, the pictures, particularly those on the fragmentary crosses, must be looked at very carefully to determine which scenes belong together and which attributes are distinctive of a particular figure or episode.

76. Kirk Andreas Cross (121) with carvings of the Sigurðr legend. By permission of Manx Museum.

The crosses with pictures date to the second half of the 10th century, most from soon after about 950. Literary sources must be used with caution when making identifications, since most are considerably later than the carvings. As only a tiny proportion of 10th-century literature survives, it is not possible to link every picture with a known story.

Some figures have been identified as pagan gods of Norse mythology: among others, Heimdallr, the watchman of the gods, Gerðr, who was wooed by Freyr, the god of fertility, and Þórr. However, only Óðinn can be identified with any certainty: he is shown on a cross fragment from Kirk Andreas (128, following the reference numbers in use at the Manx Museum) with a raven on one shoulder and a spear alongside (both attributes of Óðinn), and his foot in the jaws of the wolf Fenrir, his foe at Ragnarǫk. On the reverse is a figure with a cross, a book, and a fish, trampling on a serpent, a figure of undoubted Christian meaning.

The great cross at Bride (124) is one of the few complete pictorial crosses, yet it remains an iconographic puzzle. There is no reason to identify the god Þórr among the host of motifs, as has been done in the past. One of the supposed Þórr figures has in fact an incised satchel on his chest. There is probably a Christian source for this figure, as similar ones appear on Irish and North English crosses. Both Norse and Celtic traditions play their part in the complicated decoration on the Bride cross, but the identification of many motifs remains elusive.

The most important group iconographically are four crosses decorated with scenes from the Sigurðr legend: Jurby (119), Malew (120), Kirk Andreas (121), and Maughold (122, from Ramsey). The cross at Kirk Andreas is the best preserved and the clearest to "read": it shows Sigurðr at the base of the cross on the left killing the dragon Fáfnir, depicted as a serpent. Sigurðr is shown crouching in the curve of the serpent's body, thus effectively beneath it, as told in literature. This composition illustrates well the skill of the craftsmen in using the limited space on each side of the cross shaft to good effect. Above, Sigurðr roasts Fáfnir's heart cut into three slices on a spit above flames. Here, Sigurðr has his thumb in his mouth, referring to a detail known from literature. In testing the heart to see if it was ready, Sigurðr burned his fingers, put them into his mouth, and thus understood the speech of the birds who warned him that the smith Reginn would betray and kill him. A bird's head is shown above Sigurðr's shoulder, and the head of his horse, Grani, is visible at the top of the panel.

The cross at Jurby shows the dragon-killing scene, and on the Malew cross the dragon killing and the heart roasting are depicted. Among other related motifs on the Ramsey cross, there is a unique occurrence of an episode that occurs early in the Vǫlsung legend, in which the otter eats a fish.

The Manx Sigurðr carvings reveal the form of the Sigurðr legend in the 10th century, containing most of the key elements of each episode as shown in the later pictures, such as the Norwegian stave-church doorways, and as told in literature. Together with the Halton cross in Lancashire, they are the earliest pictures of the Vǫlsung legend that can be identified with any certainty.

Other Manx crosses are decorated with swordsmen, men on horseback, women in characteristic trailing dresses, rows of animals depicted quite naturalistically, and hunting scenes. There are also a few Christian scenes, such as the Christ figures on two crosses at Kirk Michael (126 and 129).

All the crosses are Christian, and the cross itself dominates, with the pictures usually confined to the narrow fields on each side of the cross shaft. The pictures of heroic legend were obviously thought appropriate for Christian memorial stones. What, then, do they mean?

The pictures have been interpreted in various ways, as a survival of paganism in a Christian framework, as an elaborate allegory of the triumph of Christianity over paganism, or as equivalents in two different traditions. This latter interpretation would explain the Kirk Andreas cross, where Óðinn seems to counterbalance a Christian figure.

This interpretation can be taken farther. The rows of animals and hunting scenes, as on Sandulf's cross at Kirk Andreas and Joalf's cross at Kirk Michael, may have been meant to recall the wealth and status of the man or woman in whose memory the cross was erected. Perhaps, the heroic deeds of Sigurðr and stories of the gods were intended likewise to enhance the memory of the dead.

Lit.: Kermode, P. M. C. Manx Crosses: The Inscribed and Sculpted Monuments of the Isle of Man from About the End of the Fifth to the Beginning of the Thirteenth Century. London: Bemrose, 1907; Bailey, Richard. Viking Age Sculpture in Northern England. London: Collins, 1980; Margeson, Sue. "On the Iconography of the Manx Crosses." In The Viking Age in the Isle of Man: Select Papers from the Ninth Viking Congress, Isle of Man, 4–14 July 1981. Ed. Christine Fell et al. London: Viking Society for Northern Research, 1983, pp. 95–106; Wilson, David M. "The Art of the Manx Crosses of the Viking Age." In The Viking Age in the Isle of Man, pp. 175–87.

Sue Margeson

[See also: Man, Isle of]

Margrethe I (1353–October 27, 1412), queen of Norway, Sweden, and Denmark, was the daughter of King Valdemar IV Atterdag ("ever-day") of Denmark and Queen Helvig. At the age of six, she was betrothed, and at the age of ten married, to King Hákon of Norway, son of King Magnus of Sweden of the Folkungs dynasty. Rebellion in Sweden brought Albrecht of Mecklenburg to the throne, but Hákon kept a firm grip on the western parts of the country. Thus, by marriage, Margrethe acquired the additional titles of queen of Norway and Sweden. The upbringing of the young queen was overseen by the Swedish noblewoman Merethe Ulfsdotter, together with that of Merethe's own daughter, and "both often tasted the same birch." Merethe herself was of notable birth; her father was a Swedish nobleman, and her mother St. Birgitta of Vadstena. The young Queen Margrethe was from the very beginning made familiar with current political themes, and was raised in an environment that doubtless shaped her opinion of the possibilities for women in society.

In 1370, around Christmas, she gave birth to her only child, Óláf (Óláfr), the legitimate heir to the crown of Norway and, more or less, Sweden. In Denmark, the problem of succession was deliberately kept undecided. Margrethe's rebellious brother, Christoffer, had died, and King Valdemar had made vague promises to the son of Margrethe's sister Ingeborg, Albrecht of Mecklenburg (not to be confused with King Albrecht of Sweden, his father's brother). When King Valdemar died on October 24, 1375, the Danish Council was faced with a difficult choice, since the Mecklenburg candidate was heavily supported by the German emperor, Charles IV. Margrethe acted swiftly, as if she were the recognized ruler of the realm. After many negotiations, the Danes elected Olaf king in May 1376. But under the military threat by Albrecht, an agreement was reached in September that opened the way for recognition of Albrecht's rights, without detracting from Olaf's, by submitting the issue to arbitration by a number of German princes. Margrethe thwarted this accord by claiming that all arbitration had to follow Danish rules of succession, of which there were none, since Danish kings were elected freely. The death of Emperor Charles in November 1378 and of Duke Albrecht in February 1379 left Margrethe to skirmish only with Albrecht of Sweden. King Hákon died in the late summer of 1380, only forty years old. The next summer, Olaf was acclaimed with all rights as hereditary king of Norway.

In 1386, diplomacy separated the Holsteinians from the Mecklenburg party, albeit at the cost of concessions regarding the status of the duchy of Schleswig under the Crown, but, as usual, with an enfeoffment of doubtful character, supplemented with clauses that cried out for interpretation. In Sweden, Albrecht gradually lost control over the main fiefs to the councilors. Details of their contacts with Margrethe are not known. But Olaf's sudden death on August 3, 1387, for the moment upset all possible plans. Then, on August 10, Margrethe established herself as "authorized lady and husband and guardian of all of the realm of Denmark," until a new king could be elected according to her proposal. The following year, she performed a similar "coup d'état" in Norway, and managed to secure similar recognition from a number of Swedish magnates. The resulting war with King Albrecht was decided on February 24, 1389, by her victory at Axevall and Åsle, where Albrecht was captured while the German faction still kept Stockholm. The same year, Margrethe adopted her sister's maternal grandson, Bugislav of Pomerania, now renamed Erik, who would become king of all three kingdoms. Everything seemed settled, when a war of revenge with Mecklenburg broke out. The peace in 1395 secured the release of Albrecht, who put up Stockholm as a pledge for the release sum. As this sum was not paid, Stockholm finally fell into the hands of Margrethe by 1398. Margrethe had already instituted her famous Union of Kalmar the year before. The resulting document, when compared with the coronation document for Erik, suggests that the outcome was not fully in accord with her ideas of monarchial reign. This may explain why the document was written only as a semivalid paper draft, kept secret in Denmark. The stipulated parchment copies to be sent to all three countries were never made, but the document was later used to curb the government of Erik of Pomerania. The lack of a son and the varying rules of succession in the three kingdoms would eventually prove to be the ultimate obstacle for Erik and thus for the life work of Margrethe. Nevertheless, the union between Denmark and Norway lasted until 1814, and with Sweden until the 1520s, indirectly giving fuel to the wars of the 17th and 18th centuries, and playing a major role in the politics of Scandinavia from the 19th century to the present day.

Lit.: Erslev, Kristian. Danmarks Historie under Dronning Margrethe og hendes nærmeste Efterfølgere 1375–1448. 1. Dronning Margrethe og Kalmarunionens Grundlæggelse. Copenhagen: Erslev, 1882; Lönnroth, Erik. Sverige och Kalmarunionen 1397–1457. Gothenburg: Elander, 1934; rpt.: Akademiförlaget, 1969; Linton, Michael. Drottning Margareta. Fullmäktig fru och rätt husbonde. Studier i kalmarunionens förhistoria. Studia Historica Gothoburgensia, 12. Gothenburg: Akademiförlaget, 1971; Christensen, Aksel E. Kalmarunionen og nordisk politik 1319–1439. Copenhagen: Gyldendal, 1980 [with extensive references to scholarly literature]; Hørby, Kai. Danmarks historie. 2.1: Tiden 1340–1648. Copenhagen: Gyldendal, 1980 [with extensive bibliography in vols. 2.1 and 2.2]; Albrectsen, Esben. Herredømmet over Sønderjylland 1375–1404. Studier over Hertugdømmets lensforhold og indre opbygning på dronning Margrethes tid. Copenhagen: Den danske historiske forening, 1981; Etting, Vivian. Margrethe den Første. Copenhagen: Fogtdal, 1986 [lavishly illustrated].

Søren Balle

[See also: Denmark]

Maríu saga ("The Saga of Mary") tells the life story of Mary, the mother of Jesus. The biography focuses on the time up to the return of the holy family from Egypt: the story of Mary's parents, Joachim and Anne; Mary's conception and release from original sin in the womb; her birth; the first years of life and the stay at the temple in Jerusalem; her betrothal to Joseph; the Annunciation and Immaculate Conception; the visit to Elizabeth; the birth of Jesus; the Adoration of the Magi; and the flight into Egypt. The saga merely touches on later events in her life, and then goes into detail about the circumstances of her death and the Assumption. The biographical data about Mary are accompanied by a detailed description of Herod's reign. This *vita* contains numerous theological opinions and commentaries, which give the saga its distinctive stamp. Among other points, the saga treats the following: Mary's original sin, the name "Mary," the significance of the fifteen steps of the temple in Jerusalem and the psalms associated with them, the mystery of Jesus's human and divine nature, Mary's freedom from sin, the painless virgin birth, the gifts of the three Magi, the Slaughter of the Innocents in Bethlehem, the resurrection of the body at the Last Judgment, and man as the likeness of God.

Unger's edition (1871) reproduces the text of two related versions (pp. 1–62: Stock. Perg. 4to no.11, with variant readings from AM 232 fol., AM 633 4to, AM 634 4to, and Stock. Perg. 4to no. 1; pp. 339–401: AM 234 fol., with variant readings from AM 240 I, II, X, XI, XIV fol.). Apart from the saga, the edition prints a number of miracles attributed to Mary (*jarteiknir*) that were often transmitted together with the saga in varying forms and numbers. Since the edition has the same title as the saga, one must distinguish among edition, saga, and miracles. In contrast to the saga, Mary's miracles belong to a number of chronologically and stylistically distinct groups. New collections of miracles were added in the course of transmission until, as in Stock. Perg. 4to no.1 and AM 635 4to, they achieved a form that has no parallel. Unger's edition brings together miracles from these different collections, often juxtaposing three stylistically divergent versions of the same story.

If one considers the MS tradition of the saga and the miracles, the following picture emerges: the miracles can be found in thirty-nine MSS, while there are nineteen MSS of the saga; fourteen MSS of the saga also contain miracles; the remaining five MSS are fragments. The same holds true for the twenty-five MSS that contain only miracles. Thus, it cannot be determined from the MS tradition whether the saga and miracles were transmitted separately. The oldest evidence for the saga dates from the second half of the 13th century, and can be found in the MSS NRA 78 (1r; *ca.* 1250–1300) and AM 240 XI fol. (1r-v; *ca.* 1275–1300). The complete saga is contained in AM 232 fol. (55ra-66va; *ca.* 1350), AM 234 fol. (28vb-39vb; *ca.* 1340), AM 633 4to (1r-59v; *ca.* 1700–1725), AM 634 4to (1r-19r, 49r-57v; *ca.* 1700–1725), Stock. Perg. 4to no. 1 (1ra-16vb; *ca.* 1450–1500), and Stock. Perg. 4to no.11 (1va-26vb; *ca.* 1325–1375). The MS tradition of the miracles of Mary goes back as far as the beginning of the 13th century with AM 655

II 4to (1r–4v; *ca.* 1200–1225). The following MSS also date from the 13th century: AM 655 XIX 4to (1r–2v; *ca.* 1225–1250), AM 656 II 4to (1r–v; *ca.* 1250), NRA 78 (1r–v; *ca.* 1250–1300), and AM 240 II fol. (2ra–3vb; *ca.* 1300).

Icelandic tradition considers the distinguished cleric Kygri-Bjǫrn Hjaltason the author of *Maríu saga* (*Biskupa sǫgur*, vol. 1, p. 186). Having been chosen bishop of Hólar in 1236, he died in 1237 or 1238 on his return from a journey abroad (*Sturlunga saga*, vol. 1, pp. 486 ff.; *Islandske Annaler*, p. 130), during which he had possibly visited Rome to receive the confirmation of his investiture. The statement in *Guðmundar saga* does not necessarily mean that Kygri-Bjǫrn was the author of the surviving *Maríu saga*. It is possible that different versions of the Life of Mary were in circulation in Iceland and Norway. There is, however, no indication of this in the MS tradition. Only in *Reykjahólabók* in the 16th century do we find an extensive Life of Mary (*Emmerencia Anna og Maria*), which is based on Low German models (*Reykjahólabók*, vol. 2, pp. 305–468). Consequently, if no more convincing arguments should be found, there is no reason to doubt Kygri-Bjǫrn's authorship. Furthermore, according to *Guðmundar saga*, he was in Rome at the time of the Lateran Council (1215) (*Biskupa sǫgur*, vol. 2, p. 92). The date of the council provides a *terminus post quem*, since *Maríu saga* (ch. 23) offers a detailed report on this council. The probable time of composition thus lies between 1216 and 1236, perhaps even between 1224 and 1236 (Turville-Petre 1972: 107).

It is not the literary quality of *Maríu saga* that accords it a special place within the genre of Marian *vitae*, but the unusual, or even eccentric, way of interweaving *vita* and theological commentary. The arrangement of the biography is based on a whole series of sources of which the chief ones are the apocryphal gospels *Liber de ortu beatae Mariae et infantia salvatoris* (Pseudo-Matthew) and *De nativitate Mariae*, which depends on the former (both works were attributed to Jerome, who is probably for this reason named in the prologue to the saga, pp. 1 and 339). Minor sources for the description of Jesus's childhood are the canonical gospels of Matthew and Luke. The *Trinubium Annae* (the legend, known from at least the 9th century, about Anne's three marriages, with Joachim, Salome, and Cleophas), often referred to in secondary literature, is found only in Stock. Perg. 4to no.11 (p. 17); all other MSS mention only Cleophas as Anne's second husband. The historical background in the *vita* is based for the most part on Flavius Josephus's *Antiquitates Judaicae*, Books 16 and 17. The sources are often mentioned by name. Biblical authorities from the Old Testament are Moses, Isaiah, Solomon, and David; from the New Testament, Matthew, Luke, John, and Paul. Additional sources are the Church Fathers Jerome, Gregory the Great, Augustine, and John Chrysostom. The numerous theological commentaries, the sources of which are still mostly unknown, remain an unsolved problem. It is here that the author reveals himself to be astonishingly well read and knowledgeable, capable of independent reflection. Only a comprehensive investigation of all the commentaries would lead to detailed conclusions about a man who, with *Maríu saga*, created a work that is unique within the continental medieval tradition on Mary's life.

Ed.: [Jón Sigurðsson and Guðbrandur Vigfússon, eds.] *Biskupa sǫgur*. 2 vols. Copenhagen: Møller, 1858–78; Unger, C. R., ed. *Mariu saga: Legender om Jomfru Maria og hendes jertegn*. Christiania [Oslo]: Brøgger & Christie, 1871; Storm, Gustav. *Islandske Annaler indtil 1578*. Christiania [Oslo]: Grøndahl, 1888; rpt. Norsk Historisk Kjeldeskrift-institutt, 1977; Kålund, Kristian. *Sturlunga saga*. 2 vols. Copenhagen: Gyldendal, 1906–11; Loth, Agnete, ed. *Reykjahólabók. Islandske helgenlegender*. 2 vols. Editiones Arnamagnæanæ, ser. A, vols. 15–6. Copenhagen: Munksgaard, 1969–70. **Lit.**: Turville-Petre, G. "The Old-Norse Homily on the Assumption and *Maríu saga*." *Mediaeval Studies* 9 (1947), 131–40; rpt. in his *Nine Norse Studies*. London: Viking Society for Northern Research, 1972, pp. 102–17; Widding, Ole. "Om de norrøne Marialegender." *Opuscula* 2.1. Bibliotheca Arnamagnæana, 25.1. Copenhagen: Munksgaard, 1961, pp. 1–9; Widding, Ole, and Hans Bekker-Nielsen. "The Fifteen Steps of the Temple. A Problem in the *Maríu saga*." *Opuscula* 2.1. Bibiotheca Arnamagnæana, 25.1. Copenhagen: Munksgaard, 1961, pp. 80–91; Widding, Ole, *et al.* "The Lives of the Saints in Old Norse Prose: A Handlist." *Mediaeval Studies* 25 (1963), 294–337; Bekker-Nielsen, Hans, *et al. Norrøn fortællekunst: Kapitler af den norsk-islandske middelalderlitteraturs historie*. Copenhagen: Akademisk Forlag, 1965, pp. 127–36; Widding, Ole. "Marialegender: Norge og Island." *KLNM* 11 (1966), 401–4; Heizmann, Wilhelm. "Zur typologischen Interpretation des Magnificat in Maríu saga." In *The Sixth International Saga Conference 28/7–2/8. 1985. Workshop Papers*. 2 vols. Copenhagen: Det arnamagnæanske Institut, 1985, vol. 1, pp. 469–81 [photocopies of papers distributed to participants].

Wilhelm Heizmann

[**See also:** Christian Poetry; Christian Prose; Miracles, Collections of; *Reykjahólabók*; Saints' Lives; Visionary Literature]

Marriage and Divorce

Marriage and Divorce. Sharing a common pagan heritage, the Scandinavians, like other Germanic peoples, were confronted with a new set of values concerning marriage and divorce with the appearance of the Church. As Christianity gained recognition and churchmen increased their authority, these new ideas were reluctantly accepted by the native populations.

Modern German scholars have argued at length that marriage by capture (Old Norse *herfang*) was the original pagan form of marital union in the North. Some Scandinavian men did acquire women through warfare, since the practice was prohibited by the Church as late as 1176. It rarely seems to have taken place on native soil, however, but mainly in foreign wars. Most often taken as concubines, such women were frequently of aristocratic background and joined native females in providing Viking men with casual sexual unions, extending over periods of varying lengths. These features of polygyny were more pronounced at the higher levels of society, particularly among kings, where they seem to have lasted longer because of greater resistance to Christian morality. Another Germanic concept, the *Friedelehe*, which was a union less binding than formal marriage between a man and a free concubine, finds little support in the Nordic sources, although it is still touted by some historians.

Marriage, however, provided the most lasting sexual union for pagan Scandinavians. With a native word only for the ceremony (Old Norse *brúðlaup* or *brúðkaup*), but lacking a term for the institution, pagan marriage is best known from the Scandinavian law codes and from the *Íslendingasögur*. The arrangement consisted of two distinct steps: the betrothal and the wedding. The initiative was taken by the man directly or by his father, while the woman's father was unable to start proceedings for his daughter, but had to wait for a suitor to appear. The betrothal was essentially a contract between the two men, in which the groom promised to pay a minimum sum, known as "the bride price," in order to obtain the woman. In return, her father or guardian declared his right to give her away, and promised to hand over at the wedding a dowry, the sum of the woman's inheritance. The two men shook hands on the bargain, and the date of the marriage was fixed most often within the next year. Celebrated at either the bride's or the groom's house, the wedding consisted of an elaborate festivity lasting several days. It was considered binding in law when at least six witnesses saw the couple openly go to bed.

The most important of these rules was the stipulation of the bride price (Old Norse *mundr*) paid by the groom, which became the shorthand for legal marriage. The commercial character of the transaction is underlined by the use of the same formula (the agreeing on a price, the witnesses, the handshake) that was used in negotiations for other important acquisitions, such as land or ships.

Little if any room existed for the woman's own opinion in the pagan settlement. Providing the most detailed rules, the legal sources imply that male decision (or even coercion) was normal. Men often used marriage alliances to cement agreements between formerly feuding parties. Exchanged like pawns, wives started new lives among people whom they hitherto had considered their enemies. The marriages of orphans were arranged by other male relatives, but only widows enjoyed somewhat more freedom, since they required only their father's approval.

Once married, the couple stayed together, working on their farm and creating their new family. If the marriage did not work out, a divorce could be obtained, a right that extended to both men and women. In the earliest times, it may have been sufficient for the party desiring a divorce to summon witnesses and to declare himself or herself divorced from the spouse, but divorce does not seem to have been common. Both divorced and bereaved people usually remarried quickly, because farm life demanded the work of a couple.

In the pagan context, therefore, unions between men and women were characterized by male control or coercion and accompanied by casualness throughout the duration of the union. Marriage, the most fundamental arrangement, remained basically a commercial transaction between two families.

On this issue, the most telling difference between paganism and Christianity was that, for the latter, marriage was not a commercial contract but a sacrament, the feature that gave Christian marriage its unique character. It was a monogamous union that could not be dissolved, because the couple promised faithfulness to each other for life. The notion of equality of spouses already implicit in the obligation of mutual fidelity became even clearer in the concept of consent.

Consent was developed by continental canon lawyers in the middle of the 12th century. Derived from Roman law and writings of the Church Fathers, consent had originally involved the father, but eventually Roman and Christian writers began to show concern that the bride should also agree with her father's plans. This change was adopted by canon lawyers, and consent in the Christian context eventually came to mean that of the young couple, not of the father. In the Germanic world, boys were liberated from parental control at puberty, but girls escaped their father's protection only to be placed under their husband's control. Therefore, forced agreements weighed more heavily on women than on men. In accord with the freedom given to Germanic young men, churchmen extended it to women as well. Icelandic and Norwegian documents repeatedly stressed that true marriage exists as soon as a man has asked a woman to become his wife, and witnesses have heard her say yes. In some of the *Íslendingasögur*, female consent is accorded to pagan women, undoubtedly an attempt by the clerical authors to educate their audience to this novel idea. In other ways, however, the Church shaped its marriage regulations to accommodate former native patterns. The pagan twofold division between the betrothal and the wedding was retained in the Christian program by the exchange of promises (the engagement) and the wedding ceremony, which now was moved from the private house, first to the door of the church and later inside. Performed by churchmen, the wedding ceremony was preceded by the reading of banns, which were established to prevent people from unwittingly overstepping the new incest rules, now extended by churchmen beyond the former native limits. Churchmen also participated in the ritual of leading the couple to bed, emphasizing the procreative function in marriage. In Sweden, this custom came to rival the marriage ceremony itself. In place of the pagan model characterized by male coercion and fluidity, the Christian marriage model promised female consent and stability.

It is impossible to determine how far these rules were implemented. Among the lower classes, men and women undoubtedly cohabited informally, disregarding both pagan and Christian ceremonies. Although churchmen labored hard to induce the upper classes to accept the new rules, as late as the 13th century a Danish man was still reminded in law that if he lived with a woman openly for three years she was considered his wife. As illustrated in *Sturlunga saga*, Icelandic men were notorious for the frequency of their extramarital unions, and many high-born women in Norway continued to be married by their male relatives without their own approval. By the time of the Reformation, however, the rules of monogamy, consent, and indissolubility finally gained general acceptance.

Lit.: Finsen, Vilhjálmur. "Fremstilling af den islandske familieret efter Grágás." *Aarbøger for nordisk Oldkyndighed og Historie* (1849), 150–321; (1850), 121–272; Esmein, A. *Le mariage en droit canonique.* 2nd ed. rev. R. Génestal and J. Dauvillier. Paris: Recueil Sirey, 1929–35; Schwerin, Claudius Freiherrn von. "Die Ehescheidung im älteren isländischen Recht." *Deutsche Islandforschung* 1 (1930), 283–99; Köstler, Rudolf. "Raub-, Kauf-, und Friedelehe bei den Germanen." *Zeitschrift der Savigny-Stiftung für Rechtsgeschichte, Germanistische Abteilung* 63 (1943), 92–136; Bras, Gabriel le. "Le mariage dans le théologie et le droit de l'Église du XIᵉ au XIIIᵉ siècles." *Cahiers de civilisation médiévale* 11 (1968), 191–202; Eames, Elizabeth. "Mariage et concubinage légal en Norvège à l'époque des Vikings." *Annales de Normandie* 2 (1952), 195–208; Carlsson, Lizzie. *"Jag giver dig min dotter." Trolovning och äktenskap i den svenska kvinnans äldre historia.* 2 vols. Skrifter utg. af Institutet för rättshistorisk forskning, 8.1. Stockholm: Nordiska Bokhandlen, 1965–72; Kalifa, Simon. "Singularités matrimoniales chez les anciens germains: le rapt et le droit de la femme à disposer d'elle-même." *Revue historique de droit français et étranger* 48 (1970), 199–225; Frank, Roberta. "Marriage in Twelfth- and Thirteenth-Century Iceland." *Viator* 4 (1973), 473–84; Wikman, K. Rob. V. "Patterns of Marriage Among the Old Scandinavians." *Ethnologia Europaea* 8 (1975), 68–84; Jochens, Jenny M. "The Church and Sexuality in Medieval Iceland." *Journal of Medieval History* 6 (1980), 377–92; Wemple, Suzanne Fonay. *Women in Frankish Society: Marriage and the Cloister 500–900.* Philadelphia: University of Pennsylvania Press, 1981; Jacobsen, Grethe. "Sexual Irregularities in Medieval Scandinavia." In *Sexual Practices and the Medieval Church.* Ed. Vern Bullough and James Brundage. Buffalo: Prometheus, 1982, pp. 72–85; Jochens, Jenny M. "The Medieval Icelandic Heroine: Fact or Fiction?" *Viator* 17 (1986), 35–50; Jochens, Jenny M. "Consent in Marriage: Old Norse Law, Life, and Literature." *Scandinavian Studies* 58 (1986), 142–76; Howell, Martha. "A Documented Presence: Medieval Women in Germanic Historiography." In *Women in Medieval History & Historiography.* Ed. Susan Mosher Stuard. Philadelphia: University of Pennsylvania Press, 1987, pp. 101–31; Jochens, Jenny M. "The Politics of Reproduction: Medieval Norwegian Kingship." *American Historical Review* 92 (1987), 327–49; Karras, Ruth Mazo. "Concubinage and Slavery in the Viking Age." *Scandinavian Studies* 62 (1990), 141–62.

Jenny Jochens

Martinus de Dacia, born Morten Mogensen, was a Dane who studied and taught in Paris in the 1270s–1280s, obtaining the degree of master of theology. In 1288, he appears as chancellor to King Erik VI Menved, probably appointed on the king's succession in 1287. In the king's struggle with Archbishop Jens Grand, he was the king's (unsuccessful) candidate for the see of Roskilde in 1290; and in 1296/7, he was one of the king's two plenipotentiary *procuratores* in the process between king and archbishop at the pope's court. It is uncertain whether he returned from Rome to Denmark. He may have gone to Paris instead; he died there in 1304 and was buried in Notre Dame, of which he was a canon. In Denmark, he held canonries in Lund (now in Sweden), Roskilde, and Schleswig.

Martinus's writings, all in Latin, date from the time he taught at Paris (1270s). They comprise some *quaestiones* on the Old Logic, *i.e.*, Porphyry's *Isagoge,* Aristotle's *Categories* and *Perihermeneias,* the anonymous *Liber sex principiorum,* and Boethius's *De differentiis topicis;* and *Modi significandi,* a work that provides an admirably clear exposition of the linguistic theory of *modi significandi* ("ways of signifying") and enjoyed popularity for more than a century. Several later grammarians wrote commentaries on it, among them Albertus Schwebelinus, Gentilis de Cingulo, and one Simon (*ca.* 1285–1300).

Ed.: *Martini de Dacia Opera.* Ed. Henricus Roos. Corpus Philosophorum Danicorum Medii Aevi, 2. Copenhagen: Danish Society of Language and Literature; Gad, 1961. Tr.: Rosier, Irène. "Traduction d'un extrait de la syntaxe du traité De modis significandi de Martin de Dacie." *Archives et Documents de la Société d'Histoire et d'Epistémologie des Sciences du Language* 3 (1983). Lit.: Roos, Heinrich. *Die Modi significandi des Martinus de Dacia. Forschungen zur Geschichte der Sprachlogik im Mittelalter.* Beiträge zur Geschichte der Philosophie und Theologie des Mittelalters, Texte und Untersuchungen, 37.2. Münster: Aschendorff; Copenhagen: Frost-Hansen, 1952; Pinborg, Jan. *Die Entwicklung der Sprachphilosophie im Mittelalter.* Beiträge zur Geschichte der Philosophie und Theologie des Mittelalters, Texte und Untersuchungen, 42.2. Münster: Aschendorff; Copenhagen: Frost-Hansen, 1967.

Sten Ebbesen

Martyrologies are lists of saints, arranged according to the calendar, with extracts from the legends of the various saints named (the martyr's *passio* and the confessor's *vita*), and with space reserved for the entry of obituaries. The Scandinavian martyrologies are based on the texts of Ado, bishop of Vienne, France (850–860), and of the monk Usuardus, from St. Germain-des-Prés in Paris (*ca.* 875).

Several fragments of martyrologies, but only five complete ones, are preserved from the Scandinavian region. Three of the complete ones were used in Sweden: two in the cathedrals of Lund and Strängnäs, and a third in the Brigettine monastery of Vadstena. Two were used in Denmark: one in the cathedral of Ribe, and one in the Franciscan convent of Nysted, on the isle of Lolland.

The Lund cathedral martyrology, *Liber daticus vetustior,* was established in 1146, and is the oldest in Scandinavia. It follows Ado's list of saints in abbreviated form, but from the beginning also included certain Nordic saints' names, such as St. Óláfr of Norway; St. Ansgar, Denmark's apostle; and St. Lucius, pope and patron of the Roskilde diocese of Zealand, Denmark. At some time before 1200, the consecration dates of the Lund cathedral's altars were added to the calendar, *i.e.*, the altars of St. John the Baptist, Our Lady, St. Lawrence, and St. Mary Magdelene. During the first decades of the 13th century, the names of a few Danish saints were incorporated, among them St. Knud (Cnut) Lavard and St. Wilhelm, as well as St. Dominic, St. Francis, St. Thomas of Canterbury, and later St. Catherine.

The Ribe martyrology was established at the end of the 13th century; like the rest of Scandivanian martyrologies, it is based on the texts of Usuardus. Its lists of saints, however, reveals that it is directly dependent on an English version from the New Minster of Winchester. From the beginning, the martyrology included a significant number of Danish saints: St. Knud the Holy, St. Knud Lavard, St. Thøger, St. Kjeld, St. Wilhelm, and St. Ansgar. During the 14th and 15th centuries, a number of universal saints were added, among them St. Francis, St. Clara, St. Anthony of Padua, St. Bernard of Clairvaux, and St. Anna. However, only one Nordic saint, St. Birgitta, was added.

The Scandinavian martyrologies clearly reflect the differences among Nordic church provinces. The Strängnäs and Vadstena martyrologies thus include a list of local Swedish saints who do not occur in the Danish versions, for example, St. Sigfrid, St. Eskil, St. Botvid, St. Erik, and St. Helena. And while the Strängnäs martyrology was originally built around a Dominican version from the middle of the 14th century, the Nysted MS, from the beginning of the 14th century, is distinguished by its inclusion of the Franciscan saints' days: St. Bernard, St. Bonaventure, and the date of the consecration of the church in Portiuncula.

By means of palaeographic analysis and through the study of MS additions, it can be shown how individual saints, national as well as international, gained popularity within the Scandinavian Church during the Middle Ages, not least under the influence of the new religious orders (the Friars) from the 13th century onward. In those cases where the feast category of a saint's day is indicated, a change of category may reflect the growing or declining importance of the saint. In the Strängnäs martyrology, for instance, the feast categories of St. Dominic and of St. Peter the Martyr were lowered, perhaps because the originally Dominican martyrology was later used in a secular clerical context.

The martyrologies are an important source for the study of the medieval calendar, and the name lists of the obituaries can provide valuable information concerning the general history of the period.

MSS.: Lund Cathedral: (*Liber daticus vetustior*). The University Library, Lund, MS no. 7; Ribe Cathedral: The Danish Royal Library, MS GkS 849; Nysted Convent: Museum Meermanno-Westreenianum, Den Haag, MS 10 D 7; Strängnäs Cathedral: The Swedish Royal Library, MS A 28; Vadstena Monastery: The University Library, Uppsala, MS C 34. Ed.: Langebek, Jacobus, *et al. Necrologium Ripense.* In *Scriptores rerum Danicarum medii ævi,* 5. Copenhagen: Godiche, 1783, pp. 534–

70; Weeke, C., ed. *Libri memoriales Capituli Lundensis: Lunds Domkapitels Gavebøger ("Libri datici Lundenses")*. Copenhagen: Selskabet for Udgivelse af Kilder til Dansk Historie, 1884–89; rpt. 1973. **Lit.**: Jørgensen, Ellen. *Fremmed Indflydelse under den danske Kirkes tidligste Udvikling*. Det Kongelige Danske Videnskabernes Selskabs Skrifter, 7. Copenhagen: Luno, 1908, pp. 80–1; Schmid, Toni. *Strängnäs stifts kalendarium under medeltiden*. Nordisk Tidsskrift för Bok- och Biblioteksväsen, 19. Stockholm: Almqvist & Wiksell, 1932, pp. 83, 89; Gad, Tue. *Martyrologier i Det kgl. Bibliotek og martyrologiet fra Nysted*. Fund og Forskning, 13. Copenhagen: Det kongelige Bibliotek, 1966.

Niels-Knud Liebgott

[**See also:** Ansgar, St.; Birgitta, St.; Christian Poetry; Christian Prose; Erik, St.; Knud (Cnut), St.; Legenda; Monasticism; Óláfr, St.; *Postola sögur*; Saints' Lives]

Medicine and Medical Treatment. The fact that most of the inhabitants of the Nordic countries lived in quite small settlements or on separate farms scattered over a large area obviously had its impact on health and medicine. Cities were small and few. Distances were substantial; forests, moors, and mountains severely hampered internal communication, especially in the northern regions. Sailing on rivers, lakes, and coastal waters could be hazardous or impossible during several months of the year. Infections undoubtedly dominated the prevailing diseases in the Nordic Middle Ages, as they did in later periods, although sources documenting morbidity are scarce. The relative isolation in separate settlements provided a certain protection against larger epidemics and established a sort of immunity balance between the individuals and the infective germs of the endemic diseases. However, the same isolation left the population rather unprotected when a new disease was imported to the local society. Thus, infections that passed on mildly elsewhere could ravage and severely take their toll, giving local mortality peaks. The population in many areas lived on a subsistence minimum, making it especially vulnerable to infections and other ailments. Short-term and long-term climatic fluctuations or variations in the supply of fish and game could cause under- or malnutrition and even endanger the lives of the inhabitants through famine and decreased resistance. There are clues that deficiency diseases, such as scurvy, were frequent, especially in winter times. Many patients probably suffered from more than one disease, which makes a historical assessment of the health conditions difficult.

Ships sailing to foreign countries maintained connections with the rest of the world, bringing back disease as well as medical knowledge. The Viking campaigns, raiding distant shores, were also part of this contact.

Sources are few as to how disease was perceived by the Scandinavian population of the Middle Ages. Animistic attitudes seem to have prevailed in religion and in medicine, to be replaced only gradually by ideas from Christianity and natural science. The poems of the *Edda* contain sayings and proverbs of medical interest, supplying indications of contact with foreign, scientific medicine as well as ideas from local folklore.

Educated medical practitioners were rare. The sagas mention men, probably old warriors, who had special skills in the treatment of battle wounds. A much-cited story from *Magnúss saga góða* tells about the battle at Lyrskov (1043), in which King Magnús, lacking a sufficient number of surgeons, selected men with especially soft hands to dress the wounds of their fellow soldiers.

Many of these men subsequently acquired reputations as medical men. The Icelander Hrafn Sveinbjarnarson (d. 1213) was regarded as a famous surgeon, and it seems probable that he had a certain command of the principles of contemporary Salernitan medicine. Women practicing war surgery are mentioned several times, for example, at the battle of Stiklestad (1030).

Osteoarchaeological findings from medieval burial sites also confirm that fairly advanced surgery was performed from time to time. Several surgical instruments from the Middle Ages are preserved, such as blood-letting equipment, needles, forceps, and catheters. In addition to wound and fracture treatment, operations for gallstones and cleft palates, for example, are mentioned, together with trepanations. The resistance of the Christian Church toward the practice of surgery hampered its development in Scandinavia as elsewhere.

In ordinary situations, however, most of the population had to rely on themselves or on local persons with special abilities in curing casualties or diseases. After the introduction of Christianity, a certain degree of medical service was provided by men of the Church, since many of them had medical knowledge and were able to practice according to the principles of the monastery medicine of southern Europe. In Scandinavia, medical doctors were not educated until the establishment of the first universities offering such training (Uppsala 1477, Copenhagen 1479).

Among the medical remedies used in the Middle Ages, several herbs or drugs from classical Greek and Roman medicine were known in the North in the Viking Age. This knowledge was intermingled with the local tradition and the use of local herbs. The same plants and vegetables could be used for nutrition, for their pleasant taste, and for the prevention and cure of diseases, an example being the highly valued *hvǫnn* (*Angelica officinalis*).

Herbals and medical books from ancient Scandinavia as a rule are collections of material somewhat revised and supplemented from MSS from central Europe. A much-cited author in Scandinavia is Henrik Harpestreng (d. 1244) from Roskilde in Denmark. After the introduction of the printed book, compilations of foreign herbals were published, such as the books of Christiern Pedersen (1533 and 1534) and Henrik Smid (from 1537).

Due to the geography and social structure of the Nordic countries, hospitals of significant size were not established until the 18th century. However, hospitals were erected in connection with churches and monasteries. In Denmark, they are reported from the 11th century. In Norway, the first hospital seems to have been founded in Trondheim around 1170–1180. The history of the early hospitals is often unclear, as sources and definitions are vague in many cases. The medieval monasteries in Scandinavia had a special function in taking care of leprous patients. Leprosy was common, and hospitals that treated the disease were founded all over Scandinavia in the Middle Ages. Excavations performed by Vilhelm Møller-Christensen (1903–1988) of the cemeteries of such hospitals have enriched our knowledge of Nordic medieval medicine in general.

Lit.: Grøn, Fredrik. *Altnordische Heilkunde*. Harlem: Bohn, 1908; Møller-Christensen, Vilhelm. *The History of the Forceps*. Copenhagen: Levin & Munksgaard, 1938; Møller-Christensen, Vilhelm. *Bone Changes in Leprosy*. Trans. Anita Engelbreth-Holm. Copenhagen: Munksgaard, 1961. Additional references can be found in *KLNM*.

Øivind Larsen

[**See also:** Harpestreng, Henrik; Plague]

Melkólfs saga ok Salomons konungs

Melkólfs saga ok Salomons konungs ("The Saga of Melkólfr and King Solomon") is preserved fragmentarily in only one MS, AM 696 III 4to from around 1390, consisting of two leaves. The first leaf contains the beginning of *Melkólfs saga*, the second a fragment of *Plácítus saga*.

The saga tells how God revealed to King Solomon that He would grant him any boon. Solomon asked for wisdom, and was made the wisest man in the world. However, in Jerusalem, there was a youth, Melkólfr (or Malcolfus), who was very clever. Fearing that Solomon would take him away, his parents kept him locked in a loft with no windows. One day while out hunting with his hawks, the king rode to the house to test Melkólfr's cleverness. He put out one of his horse's eyes and one of his hawk's, and asked how many eyes there were. Melkólfr correctly replied that there were six eyes: "You have two eyes, your horse one eye, and your hawk has one eye, and I have two eyes." Accordingly, Melkólfr became one of Solomon's prized men, and was left to rule in his stead when the king was away.

The narrative now shifts back to the king's castle and relates an episode, in which Melkólfr does not figure, about two of the king's men who bore grudges against each other. The one was rich and wise, but cunning and false; the other was poorer, but kinder and had the greater honor from the king. Accordingly, his colleague was jealous of him and wished to destroy him. He suggested that they should try to improve their relationship. The poorer man agreed, and said that as a token of their reconciliation, he would buy some meat from him and pay him later: "I will take a side from you, and you shall have a side from me later." Because of the lacuna, the saga ends *in medias res* at the point when the creditor asks for repayment, but the words of the rich man clearly suggest that he will demand the flesh of the debtor as payment. The scene would seem to record an early version of the "pound of flesh" motif in Shakespeare's *The Merchant of Venice*. In the now-lost continuation of the saga, Melkólfr perhaps fulfilled a role analogous to that played by Portia.

The immediate source of the saga has not been established, and no parallels for the saga have been found among the numerous Marcolfus stories on the European continent. Certain details suggest well-known folk motifs; thus, the riddle to test cleverness approximates Stith Thompson H583.1 and H583.1.1, and the incomplete story about the meat bears a vague resemblance to Stith Thompson E341 and E341.1.

The saga is closely related to the humorous and well-known *Dialogus Salomonis et Marcolfi*, which is found in Danish and Swedish chapbooks and in Icelandic in some twenty MSS from the mid-15th century to the 19th century, including two *rímur* cycles (all unedited). This *Dialogus* consists of two different parts. The first, the dialogue proper, parodies the *disputatio*, with the wise and learned Solomon being aped by, and finally yielding to, the clever and insolent Marcolfus. The second comprises a series of anecdotes in most of which Marcolfus provides proofs for his riddling pronouncements. There is a striking similarity between the saga and the first tale in the appended anecdotes, for which no source has been demonstrated. It is tempting to see *Melkólfs saga ok Salomons konungs* as our only extant evidence in any language of the anecdote in its early stage before it became associated with, adapted, and appended to the dialogue proper.

Ed.: Jackson, Jess H., ed. "Melkólfs saga ok Salomons Konungs." In *Studies in Honor of Albert Morey Sturtevant*. University of Kansas Publications, Humanistic Studies, 29. Lawrence: University of Kansas

Press, 1952, pp. 107–18 [with English translation]. **Lit.**: Bäckström, P. O. *Svenska Folkböcker, sagor, legender och äfventyr*. 2 vols. Stockholm: Bohlin, 1845–48, vol. 2, p. 64; Kemble, John M., ed. *The Dialogue of Salomon and Saturnus*. London: Ælfric Society, 1848; rpt. New York: AMS, 1974, pp. 1–133; Finnur Jónsson. *Den oldnorske og oldislandske Litteraturs Historie*. 3 vols. 2nd ed. Copenhagen: Gad, 1920–24, vol. 3, p. 112; Leach, Henry Goddard. *Angevin Britain and Scandinavia*. Harvard Studies in Comparative Literature, 6. Cambridge: Harvard University Press; London: Milford; Oxford: Oxford University Press, 1921; rpt. Millwood: Kraus, 1975, pp. 166, 384; Paulli, R., ed. *Marcolfus*. Danske folkebøger, 13. Copenhagen: Gyldendal, 1936, pp. iii–lxxxvi; Menner, Robert J., ed. *The Poetical Dialogues of Solomon and Saturn*. New York: Modern Language Association of America; London: Oxford University Press, 1941, pp. 21–35; Thompson, Stith. *Motif-Index of Folk Literature*. 6 vols. Rev. ed. Bloomington and Indianapolis: Indiana University Press, 1955–58; Boberg, Inger M. *Motif-Index of Early Icelandic Literature*. Bibliotheca Arnamagnæana, 27. Copenhagen: Munksgaard, 1966, pp. 153–4; Schultz, James A. "Solomon and Marcolf." In *Dictionary of the Middle Ages*. New York: Scribner, 1982–89, vol. 11, pp. 366–70; Wolf, Kirsten. "Some Comments on *Melkólfs saga ok Salomons konungs.*" *Maal og minne* (1990), 1–9.

Kirsten Wolf

[**See also:** Riddles]

Merlínusspá

Merlínusspá ("Prophecy of Merlin") is a versified translation of the *Prophetiae Merlini*, consisting of two poems written about 1200 by the monk Gunnlaugr Leifsson, who lived in Þingeyrar monastery and died in 1218/9.

The prophecies of Merlin are contained in Book 7 of Geoffrey of Monmouth's *Historia regum Britanniae* (chs. 3–4). According to Geoffrey, he had translated these prophecies from the British original into Latin in 1135 before writing the *Libellus Merlini*. This "Libellus," however, has been preserved only as part of the *Historia*, which has led to doubts whether an independent version of Merlin's prophecies ever existed (Tatlock 1950; cf., however, Leach 1921). The prophecies refer to the wars between the Anglo-Saxons and the Britons under their king Vortigern. They are pronounced by a young man named Merlin, who is said to be the son of a British princess and a demon (Merlinus is the Latin form of the Welsh name Myrddhin). The story of Merlin combines the youth of a certain Ambrosius (taken from Nennius) with the figure of a famous 6th-century Welsh poet and prophet.

Gunnlaugr's translation follows Geoffrey's text closely, except for some added stanzas and half-stanzas, which contain descriptions of battles in the stereotyped skaldic style, showing the translator's liking for scenes and kennings for warfare and battle. Gunnlaugr also adds an introduction to the first part, mentioning his reasons for translating the text, a prayer concluding the first part, and an introduction to the second part, giving the context of Merlin's prophecies, namely the explanation of the mysterious disappearance of the foundations of a tower the king wants to build. This story is told by Geoffrey earlier in Book 6, leading to the conclusion that Gunnlaugr knew not only the independent version of the "Libellus," but the complete text of the *Historia*. This theory seems to be supported also by the interpretative additions and translations (J.S. Eysteinsson 1953–57; cf., however, Leach 1921, who supposed that Gunnlaugr used only the "Libellus").

Gunnlaugr's two poems were later inserted into the Icelandic prose translation of the *Historia regum Britanniae*, the *Breta sǫgur*, in the same place where the prophecies appear in Geoffrey's text.

But the sequence of the poem is inverted, for which a reason has not yet been found. It is contested whether there is a connection between the *Merlínusspá* and the translation of the *Historia*, and if so, what. The *Breta sǫgur* have been handed down to us in *Hauksbók*. In the second version (AM 573 4to), the scribe omits the poems, saying that many people know them by heart anyway.

The Latin versions of the prophecies are written in prose, but Gunnlaugr used verse for his translation. He chose the *fornyrðislag*-stanza of ten to twelve lines, presumably because the meter was used in Icelandic poems of prophecy. His model was *Vǫluspá*, shown by several borrowings from this poem.

The author was a skillful versifier who had a good command of the eddic and skaldic techniques and traditions. But his poetry lacks inspiration; it is the poetry of "a book-man who had not a spark of poetic talent in him" (Finnur Jónsson).

Ed.: Eiríkur Jónsson and Finnur Jónsson, eds. *Hauksbók udgiven efter de Arnamagnæanske håndskrifter no. 371, 544 og 674, 4° samt forskellige papirshåndskrifter ad Det kongelige nordiske Oldskrift-selskab.* Copenhagen: Thiele, 1892–96, pp. 272–83; Finnur Jónsson, ed. *Den norsk-islandske skjaldedigtning.* Vols. 1A-2A (tekst efter håndskrifterne) and 1B-2B (rettet tekst). Copenhagen and Christiania [Oslo]: Gyldendal, 1912–15; rpt. Copenhagen: Rosenkilde & Bagger, 1967 (A) and 1973 (B), vol. 2A, pp. 10–36; 2B, pp. 10–45; Kock, Ernst A., ed. *Den norsk-isländska skaldediktningen.* 2 vols. Lund: Gleerup, 1946–50, vol. 2, pp. 6–28. **Lit.**: Finnur Jónsson, ed. *Hauksbók*, pp. cxi–cxiii; Leach, Henry Goddard. *Angevin Britain and Scandinavia.* Harvard Studies in Comparative Literature, 6. Cambridge: Harvard University Press, 1921; London: Milford; Oxford: Oxford University Press; rpt. Millwood: Kraus, 1975, pp. 137–9; Kock, Ernst A. *Forngermansk forskning.* Lunds Universitets Årsskrift N. F. avd. I, Bd. 18. Lund: Gleerup, 1922, vol. 1, pp. 3, 25; vol. 2, p. 87; Finnur Jónsson. *Den oldnorske og oldislandske Litteraturs Historie.* 3 vols. 2nd ed. Copenhagen: Gad, 1920–24, vol. 2, pp. 173–4; Tatlock, J. S. P. *The Legendary History of Britain.* Berkeley and Los Angeles: University of California Press, 1950, pp. 418–21; Jón Helgason. "Norges og Islands digtning." In *Litteraturhistorie: Norge og Island.* Ed. Sigurður Nordal. Nordisk kultur, 8:B. Stockholm: Bonnier; Oslo: Aschehoug; Copenhagen: Schultz, 1953, p. 99; Turville-Petre, G. *Origins of Icelandic Literature.* Oxford: Clarendon, 1953; rpt. 1967, pp. 200–2; J. S. Eysteinsson. "The Relationship of *Merlínússpá* and Geoffrey of Monmouth's *Historia*." *Saga-Book of the Viking Society* 14 (1953–57), 95–112; Halvorsen, E. F. *The Norse Version of the Chanson de Roland.* Bibliotheca Arnamagnæana, 19. Copenhagen: Munksgaard, 1959, p. 23; Jakob Benediktsson. "Merlínússpá." *KLNM* 11 (1966), 556–7; Frank, Roberta. "*Merlínússpá*." In *Dictionary of the Middle Ages.* Ed. Joseph R. Strayer. New York: Scribner, 1982–89, vol. 8, pp. 275–6.

Edith Marold

[**See also:** *Breta sǫgur*; Eddic Meters; *Hauksbók*; Skaldic Poetry; *Vǫluspá*]

Meykóngr *see* **Maiden Warriors**

Miracles, Collections of. The Old Norse *jarteikn* (pl. *-ir*) originally denoted an object that a messenger kept as proof of his identity. Later, it was used to name a miraculous event attributed to the intercession of a saint. Thus, it acquired the meaning "miracle" or "wonder" (Latin *signum*, *miraculum*). *Jarteiknir* are usually short stories about a person who is ill or in danger, and subsequently healed or rescued. *Jarteiknabœkr* are collections of such stories,

usually about the same saint. Local *jarteiknabœkr* were frequently used as the basis for a request for canonization. Medieval Latin literature includes large collections of miracles attributed to the Virgin Mary and the various saints. These have been wholly or partly translated into vernacular languages. Often, *jarteiknir* were used in homiletic literature as *exempla*.

In Scandinavia, collections of miracles were translated from the Latin, and original miracle stories were written in both Latin and the vernacular. In content, the miracle stories composed in Scandinavia do not differ essentially from those composed in other countries, so we can hardly speak of national characteristics.

The richest miracle literature has been handed down in West Norse, including collections of miracles attributed to the intercession of "international" saints (*Postola sögur*) and the Virgin Mary (*Maríu saga*). Other collections of miracles are about local saints. Miracles about St. Óláfr were first told in skaldic poetry (*Glælognskviða*, *Erfidrápa*), and in *Geisli* fourteen miracles are mentioned. It is generally assumed that a collection of Óláfr's miracles was already in existence, and that in the 1160s, Archbishop Eysteinn Erlendsson of Niðaróss (Trondheim) collected and translated into Latin a great number of Óláfr's miracles; this collection is now extant in a shorter and longer version. Shortly after the death of Þorlákr Þórhallsson, bishop of Skálholt, his miracles were written at the initiative of his successor, Bishop Páll Jónsson, and read at the *Alþingi* in 1199. They were translated into Latin by Gunnlaugr Leifsson, monk of Þingeyrar, but most of them are preserved only in Icelandic. Miracles of Earl Magnús Erlendsson are found in *Orkneyinga saga*, translated largely from the *Vita sancti Magni*. In addition, there are accounts of miracles attributed to the bishops Jón Ǫgmundarson and Guðmundr góði ("the good") Arason; these accounts are appended to the sagas of the two bishops.

The oldest Danish collections of miracles date from the 13th century and are written in Latin (ed. Gertz), including collections of miracles attributed to the intercession of St. Vilhelm, St. Knud (Cnut), Knud (Cnut) Lavard, King Erik Plovpenning, St. Thøger, St. Kjeld, and St. Niels. Only three miracles from a collection of miracles about the Virgin Mary are preserved; these miracles date from about 1300. Remnants from the same collection are found in the legendary *Hellige Kvinder*.

The oldest Swedish miracle collection is about St. Erik, written in Latin toward the end of the 13th century. From the 1370s onward, miracles about the native saints Birgitta, Brynolf, Nikolaus, and Katarina were collected. In a codex from 1385, a miracle collection is found containing nearly 200 miracles attributed to the various international saints. In Cod. Upps. C 9 (*ca.* 1450) and SkB A 3 (1502), a legend of St. Anna including a number of miracles is found. From the mid-15th century, we have the *Svensk Järteckens Postilla.* A number of miracles attributed to the Virgin Mary are found in younger MSS.

Ed.: (a) Iceland and Norway: [Jón Sigurðsson and Guðbrandur Vigfússon, eds.] *Biskupa sögur.* 2 vols. Copenhagen: Møller, 1858–78; Unger, C. R., ed. *Mariu saga: Legender om Jomfru Maria og hendes jertegn.* Christiania [Oslo]: Brögger & Christie, 1871; Unger, C. R., ed. *Postola sögur: Legendariske fortællinger om apostlernes liv deres kamp for kristendommens udbredelse samt deres martyrdød.* Christiania [Oslo]: Bentzen, 1874; Unger, C. R., ed. *Heilagra manna søgur: Fortællinger og legender om hellige mænd og kvinder.* 2 vols. Christiania [Oslo]: Bentzen, 1877; Storm, Gustav, ed. *Monumenta Historica Norvegiae.* Christiania [Oslo]: Brøgger; Norsk Historisk

Kjeldeskrift-Institutt, 1880; Metcalfe, Frederick, ed. *Passio et miracula beati Olavi*. Oxford: Clarendon, 1881; Johnson, Oscar Albert, and Jón Helgason, eds. *Saga Olafs konungs hins helga: Den store saga om Olav den hellige efter Pergamenthåndskrift i Kungliga Biblioteket i Stockholm nr. 2 4to, med varianter fra andre håndskrifter.* 2 vols. Oslo: Dybwad, 1930–33; Indrebø, Gustav, ed. *Gamal norsk homiliebok. cod. AM 619 4°.* Norsk historisk kjeldeskrift-institut, Skrifter, 54. Oslo: Dybwad, 1931; rpt. Oslo: Universitetsforlaget, 1966; Holtsmark, Anne, ed. *A Book of Miracles: MS No. 645 4to of the Arna-Magnæan Collection in the University Library of Copenhagen.* Corpus Codicum Islandicorum Medii Aevi, 12. Copenhagen: Munksgaard, 1938; Jakob Benediktsson. "Nokkur handritabrot." *Skírnir* 125 (1951), 182–98 [esp. pp. 190–6]; Finnbogi Guðmundsson, ed. *Orkneyinga saga.* Íslenzk fornrit, 34. Reykjavik: Hið íslenzka fornritafélag, 1965; Jon Helgason, ed. *Byskupa sǫgur* 2. Editiones Arnamagnæanæ, ser. A, vol. 13.2. Copenhagen: Reitzel, 1978. **(b) Denmark:** Gertz, M. Cl., ed. *Vitae sanctorum Danorum.* Copenhagen: Gad, 1908–12; Diderichsen, Paul, ed. *Fragmenter af gammeldanske Haandskrifter.* Copenhagen: Schultz, 1931–37. **(c) Sweden:** Berlin, E. E., ed. *Legenda svecana vetusta S. Magni comitis Orcadensium.* Uppsala: [excudebant regiae academiae typographi], 1839; Stephens, G., ed. *Ett forn-svenskt legendarium.* 2 vols. Samlingar utgifna af Svenska fornskrift-sällskapet, 7.1–2. Stockholm: Norstedt, 1847–58; Rietz, Ernst, ed. *Svensk Järteckens Postilla. Efter en gammal handskrift från Norrige första gången utgifven.* 4 vols. Lund: Berling, 1850; Klemming, G. E., ed. *Klosterläsning.* Samlingar utgifna af Svenska fornskrift-sällskapet, 22. Stockholm: Norstedt, 1877–78. **Bib.:** Widding, Ole, *et al.* "The Lives of the Saints in Old Norse Prose: A Handlist." *Mediaeval Studies* 25 (1963), 294–337. **Tr.: (a) Iceland and Norway:** Hermann Pálsson and Paul Edwards, trans. *Orkneyinga Saga: The History of the Earls of Orkney.* London: Hogarth, 1978; rpt. Harmondsworth: Penguin, 1981; Wolf, Kirsten. "A Translation of the Latin Fragments Containing the Life and Miracles of St. Þorlákr along with Collections of *Lectiones* for Recitation on His Feast-Days." *Proceedings of the PMR Conference* 14 (1989), 261–76. **Lit.: (a) Iceland and Norway:** Sverdrup, Jakob. "De gammelnorske adjektiver paa -*ligr* og adverbier paa -*liga*, -*la.* En studie i gn. orddannelse." *Arkiv för nordisk filologi* 27 (1911), 1–50 [esp. p. 2]; Maliheimi, A. *Zur Überlieferung der lateinischen Olafslegende.* Ann. Societatis Scientiarum Fennicæ, B.11. Helsingfors: Acta Societatis Scientiarum Fennicæ, 1920; Holtsmark, Anne. "Sankt Olavs liv og mirakler." In her *Studier i Norrøn Diktning.* Oslo: Gyldendal, 1956, pp. 15–24; Widding, Ole. "Om de norrøne Marialegender." *Opuscula* 2.1. Bibliotheca Arnamagnæana, 25.1. Copenhagen: Munksgaard, 1961, pp. 1–9 ; Schottman, Hans. *Die isländische Mariendichtung. Untersuchungen zur volkssprachigen Mariendichtung des Mittelalters.* Münchener Germanistische Beiträge, 9. Munich: Fink, 1973; Whaley, Diana. "Heimskringla and Its Sources: The Miracles of Óláfr helgi." In *The Sixth International Saga Conference 28/7–2/8 1985. Workshop Papers.* 2 vols. Copenhagen: Det arnamagnæanske Institut, 1985, vol. 2, pp. 1083–1103 [photocopies of papers distributed to participants]. **(b) Denmark:** Gad, Tue. *Legenden i dansk middelalder.* Copenhagen: Dansk Videnskabs Forlag, 1961. **(c) Sweden:** Lundén, T. "Om de medeltida svenska mirakelsamlingarna." *Kyrkohistorisk Årsskrift* 50 (1950), 33–60.

Gryt Anne Piebenga

[See also: Birgitta, St.; *Biskupa sǫgur*; Christian Poetry; Christian Prose; Erik, St.; *Guðmundar sǫgur biskups*; Homilies (West Norse); *Jóns saga ens helga*; Knud (Cnut), St.; Legenda; *Magnúss saga helga eyjajarls*; *Maríu saga*; Óláfr, St.; *Óláfs saga helga*; *Orkneyinga saga*; *Postola sǫgur*; Saints' Lives; *Þorláks saga helga*]

Mírmanns saga ("The Saga of Mírmann"; also *Mírmants saga*) was composed in Iceland, probably in the 14th century, and is unique among the *riddarasǫgur* in that the hero's conversion to Christianity plays an important role in the development of the plot. *Mírmanns saga* is preserved in some thirty-two MSS and fragments. Both the early vellums are defective, Cod. Stock. Perg. 4to no. 6 (*ca.* 1400), preserving the first half, and AM 59a 4to (15th century), the last two-thirds of the saga. Two small vellum fragments from around 1500 (now Lbs. 1230 8vo), containing parts of the end of the saga, were recently discovered in the binding of a 17th-century book now in the National Library in Iceland. The remainder are paper MSS, the majority of which date from the 18th and 19th centuries.

The saga takes place in the time of Nero, when Clemens was pope in Rome. Mírmann, son of the heathen Earl Hermann of Germany, is brought up at the court of King Hlǫðver (Clovis) of France. Following the death of his first wife, Hlǫðver marries the young princess Katrín of England, who becomes enamored of the young hero. Along with the rest of France, Mírmann is converted to Christianity (Hlǫðver is said to be Jewish!). He returns, but his attempt to convert his father ends in Mírmann killing Hermann. Mírmann's mother avenges her husband by infecting Mírmann with leprosy. He returns briefly to France, but leaves in search of a cure, disguised as Jústínus. He is advised to seek out the Sicilian princess Cecilía, whose powers as a healer are said to be unsurpassed. Mírmann makes the journey to Sicily, and in a bizarre scene Cecilía coaxes the evil from his body and cures him. Mírmann remains with Cecilía. He distinguishes himself as a knight and is offered her hand in marriage. He returns to France, and following the death of Hlǫðver, is seduced by the widow Katrín, who through false letters and slander has convinced Mírmann that Cecilía has been unfaithful to him in his absence. They marry. Learning of this, Cecilía disguises herself as the earl Híringr and journeys to France with an army. In single combat, she defeats Mírmann and leads him away captive. The wicked queen's tongue is cut out. They return to Sicily, and following a long and happy reign, both retire from the world and end their lives in a cloister.

Early scholars assumed the saga to be a translation rather than a native Icelandic composition. Kölbing (1872) found in the saga *echt deutsche Sagenstoff* ("genuine German saga-material"), but postulated a (lost) Latin original, also citing parallels in the Italian chapbook *Reali de Francia.* Mogk (1909) suggested a French original, and Leach (1921) classed the saga as a 14th-century importation, part of his so-called "Merovingian cycle." In fact, there is no evidence that the saga is not an Icelandic composition. Like other native *riddarasǫgur*, it borrows and adapts themes and motifs from continental sources, but, unlike many, this first-rate story successfully shapes the borrowed material into a finely wrought whole with a strong narrative thread.

Perhaps the most unusual aspect of *Mírmanns saga* is the active role played by the three female characters and the correspondingly passive role of Mírmann himself. *Mírmanns saga* is written in a fine, terse prose style for the most part devoid of rhetorical elaboration.

Ed.: Kölbing, Eugen, ed. *Riddarasǫgur. Parcevals saga. Valvers þáttr. Ívents saga. Mírmans saga.* Strassburg: Trübner, 1872, pp. 137–213; Bjarni Vilhjálmsson, ed. *Riddarasǫgur.* 6 vols. Reykjavik: Íslendingasagnaútgáfan, 1949–54, vol. 3, pp. 1–94; Slay, Desmond, ed. *Romances. Perg 4:o nr 6 in The Royal Library, Stockholm.* Early

Icelandic Manuscripts in Facsimile. Copenhagen: Rosenkilde & Bagger, 1972 [facsimile]. **Bib**.: Kalinke, Marianne E., and P. M. Mitchell. *Bibliography of Old Norse–Icelandic Romances*. Islandica, 44. Ithaca and London: Cornell University Press, 1985, pp. 80–2. **Lit**.: Kölbing, Eugen, ed. *Riddarasögur*, pp. xxxix–xlvii; Zinzow, Adolf. *Die erst sächsisch-fränkische, dann normannische Mirmannsage nach Inhalt, Deutung und Ursprung*. Pyritz: Bache'shen, 1891; Mogk, Eugen. *Geschichte der norwegisch-isländischen Literatur*. 2nd ed. Strassburg: Trübner, 1904; Leach, Henry Goddard. *Angevin Britain and Scandinavia*. Harvard Studies in Comparative Literature, 6. Cambridge: Harvard University Press; London: Milford; Oxford: Oxford University Press, 1921; rpt. Millwood: Kraus, 1975; Björn K. Þórólfsson. *Rímur fyrir 1600*. Safn Fræðafjelagsins um Ísland og Íslendinga, 9. Copenhagen: Møller, 1934; Schlauch, Margaret. *Romance in Iceland*. Priceton: Princeton University Press; New York: American-Scandinavian Foundation; London: Allen & Unwin, 1934; rpt. New York: Russell & Russell, 1973; Halvorsen, E. F. "Mírmanns saga." *KLNM* 11 (1966), 639–40; Glauser, Jürg. *Isländische Märchensagas: Studien zur Prosaliteratur im spätmittelalterlichen Island*. Beiträge zur nordischen Philologie, 12. Basel and Frankfurt am Main: Helbing & Lichtenhahn, 1983; Kalinke, Marianne. "Norse Romance (*Riddarasögur*)." In *Old Norse–Icelandic Literature: A Critical Guide*. Ed. Carol J. Clover and John Lindow. Islandica, 45. Ithaca and London: Cornell University Press, 1985, pp. 316–63; Kalinke, Marianne E. "Mírmanns saga." In *Dictionary of the Middle Ages*. Ed. Joseph R. Strayer. New York: Scribner, 1982–89, vol. 8, pp. 432–3.

M. J. Driscoll

[See also: *Riddarasögur*]

Monasticism. Christianity came to Scandinavia from monastic circles when Ansgar (d. 865), a Benedictine monk of Corvey (Westphalia), preached among Danes and Swedes around 830–850. But no monasteries grew up on the basis of this early mission, the results of which were annihilated by the period of the Viking raids around 850–950. After Christianity had been adopted in Denmark by Harald Gormsson (Bluetooth) and had started to infiltrate Norway and West Sweden from the west and the Lake Mälaren area from the east, the old monastic traditions of insular (Celtic and Anglo-Saxon) Christendom had a direct impact upon the next stage of mission in the 11th century. Knud (Cnut) the Great (r. 1016–1035), king of England and Denmark, directed missionary bishops with monastic education to Denmark, and we find the same process among Norwegians under Ólafr Haraldsson (d. 1030) and among Swedes. Unlike the situation in Germany some centuries earlier, however, it has not been possible to trace any later existing monastic community back to a foundation in this first missionary period. The efforts of earlier historians to ascribe to Knud the Great the introduction of English Benedictines in Denmark cannot be verified. David (d. 1082?), supposedly a Cluniac abbot from England, preached on the northern shore of Lake Mälaren in Sweden and was venerated as a saint in Munktorp, where the legend places his monastery, but no conclusive evidence has been produced.

Benedictines and the first Austin Canons. It seems, then, that the cradle of monasticism in western Scandinavia was the monastic center of Selja outside Bergen, Norway, established around 1100 and dedicated to St. Alban, still existing until the third quarter of the 15th century; the Benedictine cathedral chapter of Odense, Denmark, founded by monks from Evesham, England, upon the call of King Erik Ejegod ("ever-good") around 1095, the church in Odense where King Knud the Holy was martyred in 1086 and

which was dedicated to St. Alban, protomartyr of Britain; and Niðarholmr (Nidarholm), on an island outside Trondheim (Niðaróss) in Norway, founded around 1100.

It is impossible to establish the date of foundation of a number of Benedictine monasteries. Those near the three cathedral cities of Schleswig, Ribe, and Lund may be older. But around 1150, the following Benedictine foundations were in existence: (1) the cathedral chapter, St. Knud's, in Odense, Denmark; (2) Selja and Niðarholmr close to the episcopal sees of Bergen and Trondheim in Norway, and the third Norwegian foundation, Munklífi (Munkaliv), Bergen, founded around 1110; (3) All Saints' Abbey (Allehelgenskloster, Allhelgona) outside the city boundary of Lund, the archiepiscopal see of all Scandinavia since 1104, later of Denmark alone; (4) Veng in the east of mid-Jutland (the existing church has English models and has been dated to *ca.* 1125), probably the start of the Benedictine monastic branch in eastern Jutland comprised later of Voerkloster ("de Oratorio"), Glenstrup, Essenbæk, and Alling. Veng was extinct by about 1150; (5) Seem outside the fence of the episcopal city of Ribe, which, like Schleswig with its St. Michael's Abbey, were missionary centers already in the time of Ansgar; (6) Ringsted on Zealand, a foundation of King Erik II 1135, entrusted with the cult of St. Knud the Duke (d. 1131), and Næstved also on Zealand, a foundation of the powerful Hvide family, also in 1135 (even Esrom seems to have belonged to this group of Benedictine foundations before it became Cistercian); (7) a Benedictine monastic chapter at the cathedral of Uppsala, Sweden, probably founded by King Erik Jedvardson (d. 1160) upon the Odense model, where Erik was venerated as a saint like St. Knud in Odense; it was extinct and transformed into a secular cathedral chapter in the beginning of the 13th century; possibly also Vreta, the later nunnery in Östergötland, Sweden, was at first a Benedictine monastery (Ahnlund 1945); and (8) two abbeys in Iceland: Þingeyrar and Munkaþverá. Nun's convents were established in the areas of groups (1) (Odense, Nonnebakken; from *ca.* 1200 Dalum), (2) (Gimsøy, Nonneseter/Bergen, Nonneseter/Oslo, Bakke), (3) (Bosjö), (4) (several; see Smith 1973), (5) (Seem as a "double monastery" with monks and nuns), and (8) (Kirkjubœr), and in Greenland.

The Rule of St. Augustine had spread to canonical communities in Denmark in the 11th and 12th centuries, and we find the Austin Canons in two ecclesiastical centers: Vestervig in North Jutland, diocese of Børglum, with its cult of St. Thøger (Theodegarius, 11th century), and Dalby in Scania, diocese of Lund, following a short period of Dalby as episcopal see in the 1060s.

Evidence of historical writing (Iceland: *Sverris saga*, the two *Óláfs saga Tryggvasonar*, *Jóns saga helga*, etc.; Norway: *Historia de antiquitate regum Norwagiensium*) and liturgical texts for royal saints in Odense, Ringsted, and maybe Uppsala are among the sources for the important position of the Black Benedictines in the early development of Christian culture in Scandinavia.

Reformed Benedictine and Regular Canons. The monastic "reform movement" of the 12th century partly expanded upon what had been achieved. Cistercians (Cîteaux and Clairvaux lines) settled from the mid-century on Zealand (Esrom, Sorø, nuns in Roskilde and Slangerup), in Scania (Herrevad/Herrisvad), on Funen (Holme/Brahetrolleborg), in Jutland (Vitae schola/Vitskøl; Cara insula/Øm; Tuta vallis/Tvis; Locus Dei/Løgum, replacing Seem; Rus regis/Ryd, replacing St. Michael's); Ås in Halland (today Sweden); and in Norway (Hovedøya on an island in the Oslo fjord; Lyse close to Bergen and before 1500 also Nonneseter/Bergen for nuns; Tautra close to Trondheim). Thanks to foundation narratives and charters, this chapter of monastic expansion in Denmark and Norway is better known than the Benedictine one. In the 13th century, it gave rise to conflicts with the episcopal power in Jutland (Øm, bishops of Århus). Norbertines were called in to establish a cathedral chapter in North Jutland (Børglum, or possibly Vrejlev at an early stage after *ca.* 1139/43, as recent excavations indicate; from *ca.* 1200, we find canonesses of St. Norbert in Vrejlev), in Scania (Lund, with the excavated St. Drotten's church from the 12th century with its wooden predecessors; Tommarp; Vä, moved to Bäckaskog; Öved, probably as a successor of Lund) and in Norway (Tønsberg; Dragsmark/Bohuslän, today in Sweden). The two reform orders soon engaged in colonizing activities on the southern shore of the Baltic: Cistercians in Kolbacz, Dargun, Eldena (West Pomerania), Oliva (East Pomerania), and Norbertines in Belbuk (and even in Kolbacz?).

In Norway, the position of the black Benedictines was challenged by the Austin Canons' strong position there: Jonskloster in Bergen (*ca.* 1150); Kastelle kloster near Konghelle/Kungahälla in Bohuslän, founded shortly before 1181; Elgeseter in Trondheim, founded not later than 1183. They existed also in Iceland (Þykkviboer) and Greenland. Students from Paris brought the Austin Canons of St. Victor to Norway: Olavskloster in Stavanger (*ca.* 1150), which moved to Utstein not later than around 1280, and was closely connected with the episcopal see of Stavanger, and Halsnøy (*ca.* 1164), closely connected with the bishops of Bergen.

In the spirit of the reform movement, two cathedral chapters in Jutland adopted the rule of St. Augustine: Ribe under the Flemish-born bishop Elias (d. 1162) and Viborg. But only Viborg remained a regular cathedral chapter throughout the Middle Ages (secularized 1437). The important reformer of the Austin Canons in Denmark was William, canon of St. Geneviève in Paris, active in Denmark for several decades, a reformer of Eskilsø priory in the Roskilde bay, which he moved to Æbelholt on Zealand, where he became abbot, renowned for his collection of exemplary letters. He died in 1202, and was canonized in 1224. This center of pilgrimage became especially renowned for the medical skill of its canons. Other Austin priories were Grinderslev and Tvilum in Jutland. Some of the nuns' convents in Jutland may have followed the same rule, although this is certain only for Asmild opposite Viborg.

There are some indications that the cathedral chapter of Skara, Sweden, also tried to introduce the rule of St. Augustine (Schück 1983–84). The spirit of the reform movement also induced Archbishop Andreas Sunesøn (Anders Sunesen) of Lund to call for the establishment of Benedictine General Chapters for Denmark (1206). Several documents concerning Benedictine students of Odense going abroad in the middle of the 14th century may have received their impulse from the reform bull of Pope Benedict XII 1334 for the promotion of studies in the Benedictine abbeys.

Monasticism in Sweden. In Sweden, the Cistercians of the Clairvaux line were alone to set the complete monastic landscape by their foundations Alvastra (Östergötland, 1143); Varnhem (Västergötland); Viby (Uppland), moved to Julita (Södermanland); Nydala (Småland, 1144); Roma (Gotland); with a number of nuns' convents partly attached to the monks, partly under episcopal jurisdiction: Vreta, Gudhem, Sko, Vårfruberga, Askeby, Riseberga, and Solberga. The Bernhardine Cistercians profited from the spirit of expansion of the Baltic crusading period and were active in the Danish and Swedish missionary efforts in the Baltic area: Padis in Estonia and St. Michael's nunnery in Tallinn may have been initiated by Danish sovereigns and Cistercian monks, perhaps from the Roma kloster, Gotland.

In this connection, the arrival of the Hospitallers of St. John is significant. The Danish Antvorskov, Zealand, was their main house, founded before 1170; Eskilstuna in Sweden followed before 1185, and Varna/Værne in Norway, probably before 1177, not later than 1194 (Nyberg 1985). The Danish flag, said to have descended from heaven on the battle for Estonia in 1219, is basically identical with the war flag of the Hospitallers of St. John.

It is difficult to characterize the social basis of this first wave of monastic culture in Scandinavia. Kings and the high nobility took the initiative for foundations and donated property; but we may assume that at least the recruitment of lay personnel (*conuersi* and *conuersae*) also touched the lower layers of society. There are no traces of popular movements of religious enthusiasm ultimately finding its form in monasticism, as, for example, that attached to Robert of Arbrissel, with the possible exception of the preaching of the Hospitallers of St. John before the arrival of the mendicants.

Mendicants. Due to the still-undeveloped state of city life in Scandinavia, the mendicants had to settle at the episcopal sees (Dominicans) and in coastal and inland trading centers (Franciscans). We might assume that they in turn contributed to the development of an urban lifestyle based on the continental European models. St. Dominic showed an explicit interest in Denmark, and sent the Danish-born brother Salomon to Copenhagen in 1221 so that convents could be established in Lund (1221), Ribe (1228), and Visby, Gotland (1228). Now the Dominicans created a province for all Scandinavia named "Dacia," possibly after the model of the Hospitallers of St. John, whose tendency toward popular preaching they adopted, enriching it by theological learning in assistance to bishops and cathedral clergy. Foundations in the highly developed towns of Roskilde, Trondheim, Sigtuna, and Skänninge soon followed. The complete list of Dominican (Blackfriars, *sortebrødre/svartbröder*) convents founded until 1253 numbers no less than twenty-two, of which fourteen were situated in episcopal towns, including Reval in Danish Estonia. Denmark, including Estonia, had eleven; Sweden, including Gotland and Finland, eight; and Norway, three convents. This pattern must have meant a change in old cathedral cities with monastic life, like Lund, Odense, Bergen, and Trondheim; in cathedral towns hitherto without monasticism, like Ribe and Århus in Denmark, Skara and Västerås in Sweden, and Oslo in Norway; and in merchant settlements, like the Danish Åhus (Scania) and Haderslev (South Jutland). Certainly, they stimulated the urban spirit and the introduction of an independent town administration, which had been kept back due to the dominating power of the king's sheriff in city life.

Correspondingly, the Franciscan friars (Greyfriars, *gråbrødre/gråbröder*) evoked and channeled strong tendencies toward an intensified popular piety in new settlements, gradually generating an urban lifestyle. Only eight of their convents out of a total of twenty-four for the first thirty-five years (1232–1267) were situated in episcopal towns, although the two important Swedish episcopal towns of Linköping and Uppsala were among them, both lacking a Dominican convent. In 1267, Denmark had seventeen Franciscan convents (Odense followed in 1279), Sweden had five already by 1250, with Stockholm in 1270 as the next one, and Norway had two or three at the close of the reign of King Hákon Hákonarson (d. 1263).

The distribution of the two mendicant orders that found their way to Scandinavia in the 13th century shows that in some important cities there was room for both of them: Schleswig, Ribe, Lund, Oslo, Bergen, Trondheim, Skara, and Stockholm, and in a second wave also Visby, Halmstad, Odense, Viborg in Denmark, and Viborg in Finland. These were exceptions, however, since a number of developing settlements had only one (Franciscan) convent and stayed that way until the end of the Middle Ages; for example, in Denmark: Ålborg, Randers, Horsens, Kolding, Tønder, Flensburg, Svendborg, Kalundborg, Ystad, Trelleborg; in Sweden: Söderköping, Enköping. Later foundations were Helsingør (Elsinore), Malmø, and Nyköping on Falster, Denmark; Nyköping, Jönköping, and Arboga in Sweden, and Kökar on the Åland islands, also belonging to Sweden; Kongshelle/Kungahälla and Marstrand in Bohuslän, which was at that time in Norway. Sites around an abbey of one of the old orders with a Franciscan convent were Næstved and Tønsberg. Franciscans formed their Scandinavian province Dacia like the Dominicans, but not until 1432/8 did they try to make Lund their common study house, while the Dominicans very early had made Sigtuna one of their main centers for theological studies.

Since, from the monastic point of view, North Sweden and Finland were "empty" missionary areas, the Dominicans to a large extent became a substitute for original monasticism, especially in Finland with its important convent in Åbo/Turku. From here as well as from other centers, the Dominicans strongly influenced the liturgical practice of the secular clergy through the cathedral liturgy (Parvio 1980). In all Scandinavia, eighteen Dominicans were promoted to bishop until 1378.

Important centers of female monasticism were the convent of the Dominican nuns in Skänninge, where St. Ingrid was a remarkable personality toward the end of the 13th century. A daughter foundation came later in Kalmar. The St. Clare convent just north of old Stockholm played an important role for this developing capital of Sweden. Most remarkable was the concentration of three nunneries in Roskilde: Cistercian nuns in Vor Frue (Our Lady's), Dominican nuns in St. Agnete, and the St. Clare nuns. Cistercian nuns were also found in Slangerup and in Bergen on the island of Rügen, then part of the diocese of Roskilde.

While Cistercian Sorø was a center of literary activity (e.g., it owned an early MS of Adam of Bremen's *Gesta Hammaburgensis* and produced the 15th-century *Rhymed Chronicle*), the Dominicans took interest in annal writing, where Lund gave impulses to other houses, such as Sigtuna and Skänninge. They cultivated philosophical, theological, and scientific as well as devotional and spiritual literature. The Franciscans in Visby kept a valuable chronicle covering the period 815–1412, and the *Younger Zealand Chronicle* (mid-14th century) may have a Franciscan as its author (Oksbjerg 1987).

Brigettines of Vadstena. In the third phase of Scandinavian monasticism, an original contribution was made: the Order of the Holy Savior (*Ordo Sancti Salvatoris*), conceived by St. Birgitta of Sweden shortly before 1350, approved 1370 and 1378, and centered in Vadstena, a royal manor that King Magnus Eriksson and his wife, Blanche of Namur, assigned to Birgitta's planned monastery in their will of May 1, 1346. A new type of female contemplative monastic life arose with a group of priests and brothers attached to the monastery. The task of the males was to guide the sisters and to preach and administer the sacraments to multitudes of faithful gathering as pilgrims. Only five out of a total of twenty-five such abbeys, each governed by an abbess and a confessor general, were situated in Scandinavia: Vadstena 1370/84; Maribo in Lolland, Denmark, 1416; Bergen, Norway, the former Benedictine abbey of Munkaliv, 1421; Mariager in Jutland and Nådendal/Naantaali in Finland, both in the 1440s. The Brigettines changed the map of monasticism by introducing a new spirituality

that adopted characteristics of Cistercian, Dominican, and Franciscan traditions in combination with pastoral work by the priests. The grandiose outline of their Gothic abbey churches intended to shelter large crowds at the regular annual pilgrimage gatherings made a strong impact, and their symbolic localization with the entrance in the east and a freshwater lake on the west side was copied as far as topographical features allowed. The evidence of preserved accounts from Vadstena from the period 1529–1570 proves that pilgrim groups arrived in Vadstena from very distant areas of Sweden, and that this practice, despite the Reformation, continued well into the 1540s, when the priests' convent was suppressed. After a late flourishing under Jesuit assistance, the last nuns were exiled from Vadstena, their last refuge in Scandinavia, in 1595.

In most of their abbeys, the Brigettine fathers collected large libraries, and the bulk of the Vadstena MSS is today preserved in the Uppsala University Library. The Brigettines observed a strictly cloistered, severe lifestyle and promoted the new devotional spirit of the 15th century. Thus, they represent a reform movement for monasticism under royal protection, leading to a reassessment of monastic life among the Cistercians and some of the Black Benedictines, for example, Voer Abbey in Jutland, which joined the Bursfeld reform congregation, whereas other Benedictine abbeys (Munkaliv, Glenstrup/Nørrekloster) were dissolved, and their property transferred to the new order.

15th and 16th centuries. The reform movement of the 15th century came to the Dominican province Dacia from the Netherlands, and several convents were reformed. Among the Franciscans, the Observants in fifty years took over all Danish convents, the last one in 1519, whereas the Swedish and Norwegian convents remained conventual. The Antonites and the Carmelites arrived in the same period, partly under the protection of the Union kings Erik of Pomerania (1412–1436) and the Olderburger Christian I (1448–1483), his wife, Dorothea (d. 1495), and their son, King Hans (1483–1513). The Carmelites' college in Copenhagen became closely attached to the university, founded 1479. Also, the Order of the Holy Spirit now spread in Denmark and established six houses. The Hospitallers of St. John increased the number of their houses in Denmark (one of them was Dueholm in North Jutland), and in Sweden they gained a strong position in Stockholm, where they built a new church, the first to be destroyed in the Reformation. The Carthusians settled in Scandinavia in 1493 (Pax Marie/Mariefred on the southern shore of the Lake Mälaren in Sweden), after three efforts in Denmark (12th and 15th centuries) had failed. A new Cistercian abbey was founded in Sweden farther to the north, Gudsberga in Dalarna.

The dissolution of mendicant convents began in Denmark under Frederik I (1523–1533) and was confirmed by law in 1537. In Sweden, it was quickly accomplished after the Diet of Västerås 1527 by King Gustav Vasa, in Norway after 1536. In Denmark and Norway, life in the proper monastic settlements, especially in the countryside (abbeys, *herreklostre*) was allowed to continue until the last inhabitant died, although the use of Latin and old ceremonies was restricted, and new members were not accepted. In Sweden, monks were treated harshly, and all monasteries except Vadstena and some nuns' convents were dissolved by 1550 (Ivarsson 1970).

In Denmark, in a few cases, female monasticism continued for another century in Lutheran forms for unmarried daughters of the nobility, as in the old Brigettine convent of Maribo (*det adelige jomfrukloster*, cf. Johansen 1985). Remarkable representatives for the mendicant recusants were Paulus Heliæ (Paul Helgesen), a Carmelite and lecturer at the University of Copenhagen, author of apologetic literature and the *Skiby Chronicle*, dealing with the events leading up to the Reformation; the historian Petrus Olai (Peder Olsen), the Franciscan who collected all possible information on the origin and the houses of his order in Denmark (Rasmussen 1976); and Jacobus de Dacia (Jakob of Denmark), active as a missionary in Mexico until his death 1566/7.

Ed. (including sources): Langebeck, Jacobus, ed. "Annales Fratrum Minorum Wisbyenses ab Anno 67. ad An. 1525." In *Scriptores Rerum Danicarum Medii Ævi* 1. Hafniæ [Copenhagen]: Godiche, 1772; rpt. Nendeln and Lichtenstein: Kraus, 1969, pp. 251–66; Langebeck, Jacobus, and P. F. Suhm, eds. "Historia Sanctorum in Selia insula Norvegiæ," "Historia Fundationis Monasterii Lysensis in Norvegia," "Anonymi Commentariolus de Coenobiis Norvegie," "Liber Donationum Monasterii Sorensis," "Monumenta Sorana varia," "Necrologium Monasterii Loci Dei." In *Scriptores Rerum Danicarum Medii Ævi* 4. Hafniæ [Copenhagen]: Godiche, 1776; rpt. Nendeln and Lichtenstein: Kraus, 1969, pp. 1–22, 406–21, 463–587; Langebeck, Jacobus, and P. F. Suhm, eds. "Regula B. Augustini, cum Statutis Ordinis S. Augustini in Dania 1275–1357." In *Scriptores Rerum Danicarum Medii Ævi* 5. Hafniæ [Copenhagen]: Godiche, 1783; rpt. Nendeln and Lichtenstein: Kraus, 1969, pp. 638–44; Fant, Ericus Michael, ed. "Diarium Fratrum Minorum Stockholmensium ab anno 1008 ad annum 1502." In *Scriptores Rerum Suecicarum Medii Aevi* 1.1. Uppsala: Zeipel & Palmblad, 1818, pp. 67–83; Langebeck, Jacobus, *et al.*, eds. "Diplomata ad monasterium Loci Dei pertinentia," "Catalogus reliqvarum conventuum Fratrum minorum . . ." [Copenhagen, Roskilde], "Varia de monasterio Dalbyensi," "Summa processus in causa Ecclesiæ Ottoniensis B. Canuti ordinis B. Benedicti, 1489." In *Scriptores Rerum Danicarum Medii Ævi* 8. Hafniæ [Copenhagen]: Godiche, 1834; rpt. Nendeln and Lichtenstein, 1969, pp. 1–258, 269–312, 464–5, 475–8; Nielsen, O., ed. *Dueholms diplomatarium. Samling af Breve 1371–1539 der i sin tid ere opbevarede i St. Johannesklostret Dueholm paa Morsø.* Copenhagen: Gyldendal, 1872; Gertz, M. Cl., ed. "De Monasteriis Cisterciensium," "Exordium Monasterii Caræ Insulæ," "Petrus Olai: De Ordine Fratrum Minorum," "De Expulsione Fratrum Minorum," "De Ordine Predicatorum in Dacia," "De Profectione Danorum in Hierosolymam." In *Scriptores minores historiæ Danicæ medii ævi* 2. Copenhagen: Gad, 1922; rpt. Copenhagen: Selskabet for udgivelse af kilder til dansk historie, 1970; Nygren, Ernst, ed. *Liber privilegiorum monasterii Vadstenensis. E codice Archivi Reg. Holm. A 19 (olim A 23).* Corpus Codicum Suecicorum Medii Aevi, 11. Copenhagen: Munksgaard, 1950; Nygren, Ernst, ed. *Diarium Vadstenense ("Vadstena klosters minnesbok"). E codice membr. Bibl. Univ. Upsal. C 89.* Corpus Codicum Suecicorum Medii Aevi, 16. Copenhagen: Munksgaard, 1963; Garner, H. N. *Atlas over danske klostre.* Copenhagen: Nyt Nordisk Forlag, 1968; Larsson, Anna, ed. *Vadstena klosters två äldsta jordeböcker.* Samlingar utgivna av Svenska fornskrift-sällskapet, 245. Uppsala: Almqvist & Wiksell, 1971; Roth, Stig. *Gudhems klosterruin. Grävningsberättelse avseende planform och murverk, altaren, stendekor och gravar.* Acta Regiae Societatis Scientiarum et Litterarum Gothoburgensis: Humaniora 8. Gothenburg: Kungl. vetenskaps- och vitterhets samhället, 1973; Paulsson, Göte, ed. *Annales Suecici Medii Aevi.* Bibliotheca Historica Lundensis, 32. Lund: Gleerup, 1974; Eklund, Sten, ed. *Sancta Birgitta. Opera Minora. 1: Regvla Salvatoris.* Samlingar utgivna av Svenska fornskrift-sällskapet, ser. 2. Latinska skrifter, 8.1. Stockholm: Almqvist & Wiksell, 1975; Christensen, C. A., and Herluf Nielsen, eds. "Epistolæ abbatis Willelmi de Paraclito." In *Diplomatarium Danicum* 1. række, 3. Bind. Copenhagen: Reitzel, 1976–77, pp. 411–576; Kroman, Erik,

ed. *Danmarks middelalderlige annaler.* Copenhagen: Selskabet for udgivelse af kilder til dansk historie, 1980; Parvio, Martii, ed. *Manuale seu exequiale Aboense 1522.* Suomen kirkkohistoriallisen seuran toimituksia, 115. Helsinki: Societas historiae ecclesiasticae Fennica, 1980; Knutsson, Knut, and Göte Paulsson, eds. *Dalby klosters intäktsbok 1530–1531.* Skånsk Senmedeltid och Renässans, 10. Lund: Gleerup, 1983; Andersson-Schmitt, Margarete, and Monica Hedlund, eds. *Mittelalterliche Handschriften der Universitätsbibliothek Uppsala. Katalog über die C-Sammlung.* Acta Bibliothecae R. Universitatis Upsaliensis, 26.1. Uppsala: Almqvist & Wiksell, 1988–; Gejrot, Claes, ed. *Diarium Vadstenense. The Memorial Book of Vadstena Abbey.* Acta Universitatis Stockholmiensis. Studia Latina Stockholmiensia, 33. Stockholm: Almqvist & Wiksell, 1988; Henriksén, Christer, ed. *De Culpis.* Studia seminarii Latini Upsaliensis, 1. Uppsala: Department of Classical Philology, 1990. **Lit.**: Daugaard, Jacob Brøgger. *Om de danske Klostre i Middelalderen.* Copenhagen: Seidelin, 1830; Lange, Christian C. A. *De norske Klostres Historie i Middelalderen.* Christiania [Oslo]: Feilberg & Landmark, 1847; Severinsen, P. *Viborg Domkirke med Stad og Stift i 800 Aar.* Copenhagen: Lohse, 1932; Helms, Hans Jørgen. *Næstved St. Peders Kloster (Skovkloster).* Næstved: Haase, 1940; Ahnlund, Nils. "Vreta klosters äldsta donatorer." *Historisk tidskrift* (Sweden) 65 (1945), 301–51; Gallén, Jarl. *La province de Dacie de l'ordre des frères prêcheurs. 1: Histoire générale jusqu'au grand schisme.* Helsingfors: Söderström, 1946; Cnattingius, Hans. *Studies in the Order of St. Bridget of Sweden. 1: The Crisis in the 1420's.* Acta Universitatis Stockholmiensis, Stockholm Studies in History, 7. Uppsala: Almqvist & Wiksell, 1963; Johansson, Hilding. *Ritus cisterciensis. Studier i de svenska cisterciensklostrens liturgi.* Bibliotheca theologiae practicae, 18. Lund: Gleerup, 1964; Johnsen, A. O. *Om pave Eugenius III's vernebrev for Munkeliv kloster av 7. januar 1146.* Avhandlinger udg. av Det Norske Videnskaps-Akademi i Oslo, II. Hist.-filos. Kl. Ny ser., 7. Oslo: Universitetsforlaget, 1965; Ivarsson, Gustaf. *Johan III och klosterväsendet.* Bibliotheca theologiae practicae, 22. Lund: Gleerup, 1970; Backmund, Norbert. *Die mittelalterlichen Geschichtsschreiber des Prämonstratenserordens.* Bibliotheca Analectorum Praemonstratensium, 10. Averbode: Praemonstratensia, 1972, pp. 244–52; Nyberg, Tore. "Lists of Monasteries in Some Thirteenth-Century Wills. Monastic History and Historical Method: A Contribution." *Mediaeval Scandinavia* 5 (1972), 49–74; Smith, Gina G. "De danske nonneklostre indtil ca. 1250." *Kirkehistoriske Samlinger* (1973), 1–45; Gallén, Jarl. "De engelska munkarna i Uppsala—ett katedralkloster på 1100–talet." *Historisk Tidskrift för Finland* 61 (1976), 1–21; McGuire, Brian Patrick. *Conflict and Continuity at Øm Abbey: A Cistercian Experience in Medieval Denmark.* Opuscula Graecolatina, 8. Copenhagen: Museum Tusculanum, 1976; Jexlev, Thelma. *Fra dansk senmiddelalder. Nogle kildestudier.* Odense University Studies in History and Social Sciences, 29. Odense: Odense Universitetsforlag, 1976; Rasmussen, Jørgen Nybo. *Broder Peder Olsen som de danske franciskaneres historieskriver.* Skrifter udgivet af Det Historiske Institut ved Københavns Universitet, 6. Copenhagen: Den Danske Historiske Forening, 1976; Johnsen, Arne Odd. *De norske cistercienserklostre 1146–1264.* Avhandlinger udg. av Det Norske Videnskaps-Akademi i Oslo, II. Hist.-filos. Kl. Ny ser., 15. Oslo: Universitetsforlaget, 1977; Nyberg, Tore. "Die skandinavische Zirkarie der Prämonstratenserchorherren." In *Secundum regulam vivere. Festschrift für P. Norbert Backmund O. Praem.* Ed. Gert Melville. Windberg: Poppe, 1978, pp. 265–79; Sterum, Niels, ed. *Festskrift til Olga Bartholdy på 80–årsdagen 20. juli 1978.* Løgumkloster-Studier, 1. Løgumkloster: Refugiets kulturforening, 1978; Johnsen, Arne Odd, and Peter King. *The Tax Book of the Cistercian Order.* Avhandlinger udg. av Det Norske Videnskaps-Akademi i Oslo, II. Hist.-filos. Kl. Ny ser., 16. Oslo: Universitetsforlaget, 1979; Sigsjö, Ragnar. "Klosterstaden Varnhem." *Västergötlands Fornminnesförenings Tidskrift* (1979–80),

103–56; Nyberg, Tore. "Birgitta/Birgittenorden." *Theologische Realenzyklopädie* 6. Ed. Gerhard Krause and Gerhard Müller. Berlin and New York: de Gruyter, 1980, pp. 648–52; Nyberg, Tore. "St. Knud and St. Knud's Church." In *Hagiography and Medieval Literature: A Symposium.* Ed. Hans Bekker-Nielsen *et al.* Odense: Odense University Press, 1981, pp. 100–10; McGuire, Brian Patrick. *The Cistercians in Denmark: Their Attitudes, Roles, and Functions in Medieval Society.* Cistercian Studies Series, 35. Kalamazoo: Cistercian Publications, 1982; Schück, Herman. "Det augustinska kanikesamfundet vid Skara domkyrka. En studie om den västgötska kyrkan och dess förbindelser under 1200–talet." *Västergötlands Fornminnesförenings Tidskrift* (1983–84), 136–93; Nyberg, Tore. "Zur Rolle der Johanniter in Skandinavien. Erstes Auftreten und Aufbau der Institutionen." In *Die Rolle der Ritterorden in der mittelalterlichen Kultur.* Ed. Zenon Nowak. Ordines militares. Colloquia Torunensia Historica, 3. Torun: Uniwersytet Mikotłaja Kopernika, 1985, pp. 129–44 [also in *Dacia* 54 (1988), 3–9]; McGuire, Brian Patrick. "Anders Sunesen og klostervæsenet: Kontinuitet eller brud?" In *Anders Sunesen; Stormand—teolog—administrator—digter.* Ed. Sten Ebbesen. Copenhagen: Gad, 1985, pp. 27–41; Green-Pedersen, Svend E. "De danske cistercienserklostre og Generalkapitlet i Cîteaux til ca. 1340." In *Festskrift til Troels Dahlerup.* Ed. Aage Andersen *et al.* Århus: Arusia, 1985, pp. 37–53; King, Peter. "Attendance at the Cistercian Chapter General During the Fourteenth Century." In *Festskrift til Troels Dahlerup,* pp. 55–63; Fritz, Birgitta. "Den heliga Birgitta och hennes klosterplaner." In *Festskrift til Thelma Jexlev. Fromhed og verdslighed i middelalder og renaissance.* Ed. Ebba Waaben *et al.* Odense: Odense Universitetsforlag, 1985, pp. 9–17; Johansen, Marianne. "Beginer i Danmark." In *Festskrift til Thelma Jexlev,* pp. 18–25; Lafrenz, Deert. "Michaeliskirche." In *Die Kunstdenkmäler der Stadt Schleswig. 3: Kirchen, Klöster und Hospitäler.* Ed. Deert Lafrenz. Die Kunstdenkmäler des Landes Schleswig-Holstein, 11. Munich and Berlin: Deutscher Kunstverlag, 1985, pp. 71–92; Radtke, Christian. "St. Michael." In *Die Kunstdenkmäler der Stadt Schleswig,* vol. 3, pp. 6–10; Nyberg, Tore. *Die Kirche in Skandinavien. Mitteleuropäischer und englischer Einfluss im 11. und 12. Jahrhundert. Anfänge der Domkapitel Børglum und Odense in Dänemark.* Beiträge zur Geschichte und Quellenkunde des Mittelalters, 10. Sigmaringen: Thorbecke, 1986; Oksbjerg, Erik. "Sjællandske Krønike 1355–59." *Scandia* 53 (1987), 35–75, 199; Tollin, Clas. "Nydala kloster och den tidigmedeltida nyodlingen." *Bebyggelsehistorisk tidskrift* 13 (1987), 129–40; Winroth, Anders. "Den värdsliga grundvalen för Gudsberga kloster." *Bebyggelsehistorisk tidskrift* 13 (1987), 141–56; *Aarbok for Foreningen til Norske Fortids Mindesmærkers Bevaring* 141 (1987) [issue devoted to Norwegian monasticism]; *Skånes Hembygdsförbunds Årsbok* (1987/88) [issue devoted to monasticism in the province of Skåne]; Hørby, Kai. "Søro Klosters Gavebog." In *Kongemagt og samfund i middelalderen. Festskrift til Erik Ulsig.* Ed. Poul Enemark *et al.* Århus: Arusia, 1988, pp. 55–62; Nielsen, Ingrid. "Brude- eller nonneslør. Om grundlæggerne af Sankt Clara og Sankt Agnes klostre i Roskilde." In *Kongemagt og samfund i middelalderen,* pp. 101–15; Nyberg, Tore. "Der Birgittenorden als Beispiel einer Neugründung im Zeitalter der Ordensreformen." In *Reformbemühungen und Observanzbestrebungen im spätmittelalterlichen Ordenswesen.* Ed. Kaspar Elm. Berliner Historische Studien, 14. Berlin: Duncker & Humblot, 1989, pp. 373–96; Hedlund, Monica, & Alf Härdelin, eds. *Vadstena klosters bibliotek—The Monastic Library of Medieval Vadstena.* Acta Bibliothecae R. Universitatis Upsaliensis, 29. Stockholm: Almqvist & Wiksell, 1990; Götlind, Anna. *The Messengers of Medieval Technology? Cistercians and Technology in Medieval Scandinavia.* Occasional Papers on Medieval Topics, 4. Alingsås: Viktoria Bokförlag, 1990; Nyberg, Tore. "Monastische Regionen und Zentren Skandinaviens im Mittelalter." In *Naissance et fonctionnement des réseaux monastiques et canoniaux.* Saint–Etienne: Centre Européen de Recherches sur les Congrégations et Orders Religieux; Publications Université Jean Monnet, 1991, pp. 235–57; Rajamaa, Ruth. *Systramas verksamhet, undervisning och uppfostran i Vadstena kloster 1384–1595.* Stockholm: Pedagogiska institutionen, Stockholms Universitet, 1992; Nyberg, Tore, ed. *Birgitta, hendes værk og hendes klostre i Norden. Brigitta, Her Works, and Her Five Abbeys in the Nordic Countries.* Odense University Studies in History and Social Sciencies, 10. Odense Universitetsforlag, 1992; Drar, Kristin. *Medeltida kvinnokloster på Östgötaslätten* [forthcoming]; Johansson, Jan Kenneth. *Medeltida manskloster på Östgötaslätten* [forthcoming].

Tore Nyberg

[See also: Ansgar, St.; Birgitta, St.; *Biskupa sögur*; Church Organization and Function; Conversion; Erik, St.; Knud (Cnut), St.; Ólafr, St.; Saints' Lives; Vadstena]

Morkinskinna ("the rotten vellum") is the not particularly appropriate name given by Thormodus Torfæus to the MS later to be designated GkS 1009 fol. in the Royal Library in Copenhagen. The MS was brought to Copenhagen by Torfæus in 1662 as a gift to the Danish king from Bishop Brynjólfur Sveinsson at Skálholt. The name *Morkinskinna* is also applied to the sagas of the kings of Norway contained in this MS that cover the period between about 1035 and the second half of the 12th century.

The MS was written around 1275 by two Icelandic scribes, probably in the scriptorium of some clerical institution. It has several lacunae and lacks a conclusion. In its present condition, it consists of thirty-seven leaves, but probably about one third of the book is missing.

Parts of the *Morkinskinna* text are also preserved in the more recent part of *Flateyjarbók* (15th century) and in AM 325 IV β and XI 3 4to (two 14th-century fragments, in all likelihood remnants of the very MS from which the more recent part of *Flateyjarbók* was transcribed). The more recent part of *Flateyjarbók* is intact, but contains only the sagas of kings Magnús góði ("the good") and Haraldr harðráði ("hard-ruler"), *i.e.,* approximately the first half of *Morkinskinna.* The extensive lacuna following the first leaf of the *Morkinskinna* MS can thus be filled in from the more recent part of *Flateyjarbók* and AM 325 4to, but there is no parallel text to fill in the lacuna at the end. It is assumed, however, that *Morkinskinna,* like *Fagrskinna* and *Heimskringla,* ended with the battle of Ré in 1177, just before the advent of King Sverrir.

The preserved *Morkinskinna* is a reworking of a lost older work, known in the literature as the "Oldest Morkinskinna," which differed from the surviving version in not containing a number of shorter interpolations from *Ágrip af Nóregs konunga sǫgum* and most or all of the *þættir* about Icelanders, which are a distinctive feature of *Morkinskinna* as we have it. The "Oldest Morkinskinna" was used by the author of *Fagrskinna* as the main source of the latter part of his work and was also an important source of the last third of *Heimskringla.*

The "Oldest Morkinskinna" has been dated to the early 13th century; Storm (1873), on external criteria, dates it as narrowly as 1217–1222. It is probable that it was written to fill a gap between two earlier works, the saga of St. Ólafr (d. 1030) and the saga of King Sverrir. Certain archaic features of its style and language testify to its early origin, and an uneven presentation marked by repetition, contradiction, and infelicities in chronology add to the impression of a preclassical work. The hypothesis that *Morkinskinna* was based on a group of otherwise unattested separate sagas of Norwegian kings can hardly be defended; apart from the section based on Eiríkr Oddsson's lost *Hryggjarstykki*, dealing with the years 1136–1139 (perhaps 1136–1161?), the sources were probably oral rather than written. The references to "Knúts saga" (*Knúts saga helga*) and "Jarla sǫgur" (*Orkneyinga saga*) are likely to be unoriginal.

Text from *Morkinskinna* (with interpolations) forms part of various compilations from the 13th and 14th centuries. A number of *þættir* and shorter anecdotes have been interpolated from a *Morkinskinna* redaction into the archetype of one of the two main classes of MSS of *Heimskringla* (the "Jöfraskinna" class), and a similar but independent augmentation is evident in *Codex Frisianus*, which belongs to the "Kringla" class. The late 13th-century compilation *Hulda-Hrokkinskinna* is based on texts of *Morkinskinna* and *Heimskringla* (among others) in a ratio of approximately two to one. The style of this text of *Morkinskinna* has been revised, either prior to or contemporary with its incorporation in *Hulda-Hrokkinskinna*. Two MSS of the *Óláfs saga Tryggvasonar en mesta*, AM 62 fol. (14th century) and AM 54 fol. (an addition made in the 16th century), contain a short interpolation from an apparently expanded *Morkinskinna* redaction.

Ed.: Unger, C. R., ed. *Morkinskinna: Pergamentsbog fra første Halvdel af det trettende Aarhundrede. Indeholdende en af de ældste Optegnelser af norske Konge-sagaer.* Christiania [Oslo]: Bentzen, 1867; Finnur Jónsson, ed. *Morkinskinna.* Samfund til udgivelse af gammel nordisk litteratur, 53. Copenhagen: Jørgensen, [1928–]1932; Jón Helgason, ed. *Morkinskinna: MS. No. 1009 fol. in the Old Royal Collection of The Royal Library, Copenhagen.* Corpus Codicum Islandicorum Medii Aevi, 6. Copenhagen: Levin & Munksgaard, 1934 [facsimile]. **Lit.**: Storm, Gustav. *Snorre Sturlassöns Historieskrivning. En kritisk Undersögelse.* Copenhagen: Luno, 1873 [esp. pp. 28–31]; Indrebø, Gustav. *Fagrskinna.* Avhandlinger fra Universitetets historiske seminar, 4. Kristiania [Oslo]: Grøndahl, 1917 [esp. pp. 11–34]; Indrebø, Gustav. "Aagrip." *Edda* 17 (1922), 18–65 [esp. pp. 23–59, 63–5]; Bjarni Aðalbjarnarson. *Om de norske kongers sagaer.* Skrifter utg. av Det Norske Videnskaps-Akademi i Oslo, II. Hist.-filos. Kl., 1936, 4. Oslo: Dybwad, 1937, pp. 135–73; Hreinn Benediktsson. *Early Icelandic Script as Illustrated in Vernacular Texts from the Twelfth and Thirteenth Centuries.* Icelandic Manuscripts, series in folio, 2. Reykjavik: Manuscript Institute of Iceland, 1965, nos. 57–8; Louis-Jensen, Jonna. "Den yngre del af Flateyjarbók." In *Afmælisrit Jóns Helgasonar. 30. júní 1969.* Ed. Jakob Benediktsson et al. Reykjavik: Heimskringla, 1969, pp. 235–50; Louis-Jensen, Jonna. "Et forlæg til Flateyjarbók? Fragmenterne AM 325 IV β og XI,3 4to." *Opuscula* 4. Bibliotheca Arnamagnæana, 30. Copenhagen: Munksgaard, 1970, pp. 141–58; Louis-Jensen, Jonna. *Kongesagastudier: Kompilationen Hulda-Hrokkinskinna.* Bibliotheca Arnamagnæana, 32. Copenhagen: Reitzel, 1977 [esp. pp. 62–108].

Jonna Louis-Jensen

[**See also:** *Ágrip af Nóregs konunga sǫgum*; *Fagrskinna*; *Flateyjarbók*; *Fríssbók*; *Heimskringla*; *Hulda-Hrokkinskinna*; *Konungasögur*; *Óláfs saga Tryggvasonar*; *Þáttr*]

Music and Musical Instruments.

Information about musical life in medieval Scandinavia is not plentiful, but the literary sources (the *Eddas*, the sagas, and the chronicles) make clear at least that even in Viking times music was recognized as an art, a civilized and civilizing accomplishment that belonged to the ideal education of a cultured man. Thus, in *Orkneyinga saga* we read that Earl Rǫgnvaldr Kali Kolsson (d. 1158) counted harp playing among his "nine accomplishments" (*cf.* the eight accomplishments that purport to be claimed, some in identical terms, by King Haraldr harðráði ["hard-ruler"] Sigurðarson in *Morkinskinna*). Furthermore, it was understood that music affected the inner man, his mind and soul, to such a degree that, in especially skilled hands, it was believed to be capable of exerting a magical power, even over small animals and inanimate objects. Such a view, of course, received encouragement and respectability from the biblical account of David playing his harp to calm Saul. In *Vǫluspá*, the god Óðinn was willing to give one of his eyes as security for knowledge of the "nine holy songs" with which he could work wonders, such as making the earth open before him. In *Vǫlsunga saga* (drawing upon *Atlakviða* and *Atlamál*), we are told of Gunnarr, son of Gjúki, who, when inspired, could play the harp so that women would weep; and of how Gunnarr, cast into a snake pit with hands bound, played his harp with his toes so wonderfully that the snakes were lulled to sleep. So popular were Gunnarr's musical exploits that they gave their names to several tunes an itinerant musician played before King Óláfr Tryggvason in Trondheim, as recounted in *Nornagests þáttr*. In *Bósa saga*, the adventurer Bósi (in the guise of King Goðmundr's harp player Sigurðr) played tunes at the wedding party held at King Goðmundr's court, which caused not only the guests who were present but also "the knives and dishes and everything that wasn't held down" to begin to move about and dance. These tunes also have particular names, the last being "Rammaslag." This name is printed in the margin beside Arild Huitfeldt's retelling, in *Danmarckis Rigis Krønike* IV (1603), of Saxo's account of King Erik Ejegod ("evergood") being driven berserk by the playing of a visiting harper and then killing four men (*Gesta Danorum*, Book 12). Referring to *Bósa saga*, Sven Lagerbring reported (*Svea Rikes Historia* I) that in 1769 the belief was still current in some peasant areas that a particular dance or piece of music had such powers. Others (see Levy 1974), calling attention to the fact that for "Rammeslag" Bósi resorted to the use of a special string "that lay across the other strings," would relate it to the group of dance melodies called "Ramme slåtter" or "Gorrlause [*i.e.*, loose-string] slåtter," so-called because to play them the musician must tune down (loosen) the lowest string of the fiddle from G to F. These melodies have survived in Setesdal in Norway to the present day.

At the beginning of his Book 3, Saxo describes Hotherus, the foster-son of King Gevarus, who "through the ear captured people's hearts and filled them with joy or horror," as a master of all sorts of stringed instruments, naming as examples "harp and lyre, lute and fiddle." The names of a variety of other string, wind, and percussion instruments are mentioned elsewhere in the literary sources as well (*e.g.*, "pipar, bumbur, gígjur eðr salterium eðr hǫrpur" in *Kirialax saga*), but it is usually difficult to determine with certainty how such designations are to be interpreted and to what extent they are to be taken as representing actual use or seen as literary conventions, often anachronistic. Similarly, the numerous pictorial representations of musical instruments, especially in church wall-paintings, cannot be taken as evidence that all the instruments so depicted were familiar from local usage. One of the latest and most comprehensive examples is the unusually large instrumentarium in the mid-16th-century wall-paintings of an angelic orchestra playing no fewer than thirty-one different instruments, uncovered during the restoration of Rynkeby church on the island of Funen in Denmark in 1965. Allowance must be made for the possibility that the artist of such works came from abroad, and that he may have drawn on the example of other similar works of decoration elsewhere, or worked from a collection of standard patterns. On the other hand, nonangelic representations, such as the stone figure of a musician playing a stringed instrument on the choir vaulting in Niðaróss (Trondheim) cathedral, often give a living impression of musical performance.

Unfamiliar musical instruments (such as the *gígja*, perhaps) and songs from other parts of Europe may have been introduced by the itinerant musicians (*leikarar*) who visited the courts of the great men, as we read in the literary accounts (*e.g., Ynglinga saga, Sverris saga, Eufemiavisor, Erikskrönikan, Karlskrönikan*), where they are often spoken of with contempt, as, for example, by Saxo (*e.g.*, in Book 1, at King Huglek's court in Ireland). As a class, they were much lower than the singers and poets (the skalds, and, for example, the German Minnesingers Reimer von Zweter, Tannhäuser, Rumelant, and Frauenlob, who visited the Danish courts and celebrated several of the Danish kings). *Leikarar* are treated in many accounts as little better than beggars, and in the older *Västgötalag* (*ca.* 1225) and the later *Östgötalag*, as beyond the pale without actually being outlaws. Nevertheless, they were indispensable to weddings, public festivals, and market gatherings. With the passage of time, the more qualified musicians among them achieved a certain status above that of the jugglers and clowns, apparently by the 15th century being accorded the recognition of a kind of guild organization with a scale of fees.

No instrumental music has survived from the Middle Ages in Scandinavia and, in the nature of things, probably none was ever written down. Some singers were no doubt better educated, but only a couple of pieces of secular vocal music are known from medieval sources. One (in Uppsala, Univ. Bibl. MS C 233) is a song, beginning *Ex te lux oritur dulcis Scotia*, in honor of the marriage between King Eiríkr Magnússon of Norway and Princess Margaret, daughter of Alexander III of Scotland, which took place in Bergen between August 30 and September 8, 1281. This song is perhaps the only surviving example of what can be called "court music" from medieval Scandinavia. The other surviving example of secular vocal music is for a fragment of a Danish ballad written at the bottom of a page of a late 13th-century MS containing, among other things, the Laws of Scania (*Codex runicus*, Copenhagen, AM MS 28, 8vo). The text, beginning *Drømdæ mik æn drøm inat* ("I dreamed a dream last night"), is written in runic characters, whereas the music, like the previous example, is written in rhythmically undifferentiated notation on a four-line staff. Many other Scandinavian folksongs and ballads are undoubtedly also of medieval origin, but were first written down later, starting in the mid-16th century, and then with melodies only exceptionally before the 19th century. One of these, a melody to which *Voluspá* was purportedly still being sung by Icelanders in the late 18th century, was among the examples of Icelandic music noted down by Johann Ernst Hartmann in Copenhagen and communicated to J. B. de la Borde for publication in his *Essai sur la musique ancienne et moderne* (Paris, 1780). Latin school songs and Maria-songs (some macaronic or entirely in the vernacular) occur with melodies in collections made earlier, however. Examples include the mid-15th-century Danish, probably Franciscan, collection AM 76 8vo; the early 16th-century collection made by Gísli Jónsson, later bishop of Skálholt (AM 622 4to); the Swedish-Finnish collection *Piae cantiones ecclesiasticae et scholasticae*, made by Theodoricus Petri of Åbo (Greifswald, 1582); and a 17th-century Icelandic collection (Rask 98).

English missionaries played an important role in the christianization of Scandinavia, and their influence is to be observed in the earliest liturgical traditions, for example, at Niðaróss (Trondheim) in Norway and Odense in Denmark, and in the earliest additions to the liturgy, required for the celebration of new local and national saints, such as the royal martyrs St. Ólafr (d. 1030), St. Knud *rex* (d. 1086), and St. Knud *dux* (d. 1131). Because of the Reformation, only comparatively few, and late, medieval liturgical books have survived entire in Scandinavia; however, many thousands of fragments from them have survived in the national archives of all the Scandinavian countries, the parchment folios having been used, among other things, as binding material and as wrappers for public records. Despite Haapanen's pioneering work in Helsingfors and the brave efforts of palaeographers in the other capitals, these fragments are still far from being thoroughly catalogued. Yet, we must look to them for knowledge of medieval Scandinavian church music. From such sources, Reiss (1912) was able largely to reconstruct the Offices and Mass of St. Ólafr; the services for Knud *rex* are known from late printed sources, but without music; quite exceptionally, the Offices and Masses of St. Knud (Lavard) *dux*, perhaps prepared for his translation and canonization in 1170, survive intact in a late 13th-century copy (now Kiel, Univ. Bibl. MS S.H. 8 A 8vo). A certain influence from Germany was inevitable, in view of the fact that Scandinavia first belonged to the church province of Hamburg-Bremen, but this influence became less direct with the establishment by Pope Paschal II of a separate archbishopric with its seat in Lund in 1103, and of a second province of Niðaróss by Pope Anastasius IV in 1154. In the 12th century, important connections were established with Paris, first with the collegiate churches of St. Geneviève and St. Victor, later with the newly established university. The special cultivation of sequence composition at St. Victor is perhaps reflected in the three sequences added around 1170 to the *Liber daticus Lundensis* (Lund, Univ. Bibl.), the earliest complete pieces of music surviving in a Danish source, and certainly in the great sequence for St. Ólafr, *Lux illuxit letabunda* (*ca.* 1200), which quotes several melodic phrases from sequences associated with Adam of St. Victor. Additional influence from Paris came with the activities of Dominicans and Franciscans in Scandinavia in the 13th century, clearly to be seen in the use of Dominican models for the texts and music of various liturgical pieces, for St. Erik of Sweden and St. Henrik of Finland, for example, and in particular for virtually the entire liturgy for the feast of St. Þorlákr of Skálholt in Iceland.

In his endowment (*ca.* 1080) of St. Lawrence church in Lund (the later cathedral), King Knud made provision for a cantor. After the dedication of the cathedral in 1145, Archbishop Eskil Sunesen issued choral statutes, the first in Scandinavia, for the archdiocese of Lund. If the assistance of foreign musicians was needed to establish a proper musical practice, their names are not now known, with the exception of one Ríkini, a French clerk engaged by Bishop Jón of Hólar in Iceland to teach church music in the school founded by him in 1107. In view of the close contacts of churchmen from Scandinavia with Paris in the 12th and 13th centuries, it would be reasonable to expect church music in Scandinavia to include the new polyphony cultivated there; evidence of this development is almost totally lacking, however. The choral statutes of Uppsala cathedral from 1298 are of particular interest in this regard, inasmuch as they stipulate that on the occasions when "that kind of polyphonic song which is called *organum*" is performed, the singers are to receive an extra fee. The term *organum* is ambiguous: it can refer to the use of an organ, and it is known that various churches had organs, for example, Ribe cathedral in Denmark by around 1290, Lund and Niðaróss before 1330. Arngrímr Brandsson brought an organ to Iceland in 1329 that he had himself built in Trondheim (*Biskupa sögur*). *Organum* can also refer to the style of singing in which a second part is added to an existing tune in accordance with certain rules that can be learned so that it can be done extempore. The term can also mean the compositions in what came to be called the *ars antiqua* style, although it was modern in the early 13th century. Moberg (1947) argued persuasively that the reference to *organum* in the Uppsala statutes must be to the latter kind of music in order to justify special remuneration for the skill involved, and he supported his argument with three early 14th-century music theoretical treatises (in Uppsala Univ. Bibl. C 55 and C 543) which could have been used to teach such skills. However, no example of such music, or of music written in mensural notation, has been found in a Scandinavian MS written before the 16th century, and we have no knowledge of the music in the lost book *continentem discantus et tripleta* given to the school in Lund in 1358.

Biskupa sögur record that Laurentius Kálfsson, bishop of Hólar (1322–1331), forbade singing in two and three parts in church; since he referred to such singing as *leikaraskapr*, it may be to the practice of the earlier, improvised kind of polyphony that he took exception. In any case, the few examples of polyphonic music that have survived in Scandinavian sources are all of a kind that could have been improvised. These include: (1) the proper hymn, *Gaudet mater ecclesia*, in the Office of St. Knud Lavard (Kiel, Univ. Bibl. MS. S. H. 8 A 8vo), which has two melodies, both of which, although written as single melodies, can be sung in two parts as *rondellus*; (2) the well-known "hymn" to St. Magnús of the Orkneys, *Nobilis humilis*, remarkable for its use of parallel thirds (nos. [1] and [2] are probably 12th-century pieces, although found in late 13th-century MSS); (3) and (4) the beginnings of two antiphons to which parts in parallel *organum* have been added, apparently in the 15th century, in fragments of two liturgical MSS, Swedish and Finnish respectively (Uppsala, Univ. Bibl. C 23 and Stockholm, Kammararkivet, Baltiska fogderäkenskap F. 365); (5) part of a troped *Agnus Dei* and a *Credo* on a fragment of a noted missal copied for a Benedictine monastery in Iceland in 1473 (AM 80 8vo); (6) three Latin songs in two parts, one in three parts, a *Sanctus* and a *Credo* in two parts in a MS from Iceland dated to around 1500 (AM 687b 4to); (7) five Latin songs and one mixed Latin and Danish in two parts in a MS from about 1425–1475 (AM 76 8vo). To this list may be added the several polyphonic pieces, of a character similar to the above, contained in *Piae cantiones* (Greifswald, 1582).

Ed.: [Jón Sigurðsson and Guðbrandur Vigfússon, eds.] *Biskupa sögur.* 2 vols. Copenhagen: Møller, 1858–78; Þorsteinsson, Bjarni, ed. *Íslenzk þjóðlög.* Copenhagen: Møller, 1906–09; Kålund, Kristian, ed. *Kirialax saga.* Samfund til udgivelse af gammel nordisk litteratur, 43. Copenhagen: Møller, 1917; Kristensen, Marius, ed. *En Klosterbog fra Middelalderens Slutning.* Copenhagen: Jörgensen, 1933 [AM 76 8vo; music edited by E. Abrahamsen; a new edition of this MS is in preparation]; Ottósson, Robert Abraham, ed. *Sancti Thorlaci episcopi officia rhythmica et proprium missae in AM 241 A folio.* Bibliotheca Arnamagnæana Supplementum, 3. Copenhagen: Munksgaard, 1959;

Eggen, Erik, ed. *The Sequences of the Archbishopric of Nidarós.* 2 vols. Bibliotheca Arnamagnæana, 21–2. Copenhagen: Munksgaard, 1968; Knudsen, Thorkild, *et al.*, eds. *Danmarks gamle Folkeviser XI: Melodier.* Copenhagen: Universitets-jubilæets danske samfund; Akademisk Forlag, 1976; Gjerløw, L., ed. *Antiphonarium Nidrosiensis Ecclesiae.* Libri liturgici Provinciae Nidrosiensis Medii Aevi, 3. Oslo: Norsk Historisk Kjeldeskrift Institutt, 1979 [no transcriptions, but many photographs]; Gjerløw, Lilli, ed. *Liturgica Islandica.* 2 vols. Bibliotheca Arnamagnæana, 35–6. Copenhagen: Reitzel, 1980. **Lit.**: Hammerich, Angul. "Studien über isländische Musik." *Sammelbände der Internationalen Musikgesellschaft* 1 (1899/1900), 341–71; Finnur Jónsson. "Das Harfenspiel des Nordens in der alten Zeit." *Sammelbände der Internationalen Musikgesellschaft* 9 (1907/08), 530–7; Reiss, Georg. *Det norske Rigsarkivs middelalderlige Musikhaandskrifter. En Oversigt.* Videnskabs-selskabets Skrifter, 2. Hist.-filos. Kl., 1908, 3. Christiania [Oslo]: Dybwad, 1908; Hammerich, Angul. *Musik-Mindesmærker fra Middelalderen i Danmark.* [English ed. *Medieval Musical Relics of Denmark.* Trans. Margaret W. Hamerik. Leipzig: Breitkopf & Härtel, 1912]; Reiss, Georg. *Musiken ved den middelalderlige Olavsdyrkelse i Norden.* Videnskaps-selskapets Skrifter, 2. Hist.-filos. Kl., 1911, No. 5. Kristiania [Oslo]: Dybwad, 1912; Kolsrud, Oluf, and Georg Reiss. *Tvo norrøne latinske kvæde med melodiar.* Videnskaps-selskapets Skrifter, 2. Hist.-filos. Kl. 5. Kristiania [Oslo]: Dybwad, 1913; Hammerich, Angul. *Dansk Musikhistorie indtil ca. 1700.* Copenhagen: Gad, 1921; Abrahamsen, Erik. *Éléments romans et allemands dans le chant grégorien et la chanson populaire en Danemark.* Copenhagen: Haas, 1923; Haapanen, Toivo. *Verzeichnis der mittelalterlichen Handschriftenfragmente in der Universitätsbibliothek zu Helsingfors.* 3 vols. Helsingfors Universitetsbiblioteks Skrifter, 4, 7, 16. Helsingfors: [n.p.], 1922, 1925, 1932; Haapanen, Toivo. *Die Neumenfragmente der Universitätsbibliothek Helsingfors. Eine Studie zur ältesten nordischen Musikgeschichte.* Helsingfors Universitetsbiblioteks Skrifter, 5. Helsingfors: [n.p.], 1924; Haapanen, Toivo. "Dominikanische Vorbilder im mittelalterlichen nordischen Kirchengesang." In *Gedenkboek D. F. Scheuerleer.* The Hague: Nijhoff, 1925, pp. 129–34; Moberg, Carl-Allan. *Über die schwedischen Sequenzen.* 2 vols. Veröffentlichungen der Gregorianischen Akademie zu Freiburg in der Schweiz, 13. Uppsala: Almqvist & Wiksell, 1927; Moberg, Carl-Allan. "Kleine Bermerkungen zum Codex Upsal. C 23." *Svensk tidskrift för musikforskning* 12 (1930), 37–52; Andersson, Otto, ed. *Musik og musikinstrumenter.* Nordisk kultur, 25. Stockholm: Bonnier; Oslo: Aschehoug; Copenhagen: Schultz, 1934; Handschin, Jacques. "Die älteste Dokument für die Pflege der Mehrstimmigkeit in Dänemark." *Acta Musicologica* 7 (1935), 67–9; Beveridge, John. "Two Scottish Thirteenth-Century Songs." *Music & Letters* 20 (1939), 352–64 [see also "Correspondence" from M. Bukofzer, *Music & Letters* 21 (1940), 202–3]; Kolsrud, Oluf. "Korsongen i Nidarosdomen." In *Festskrift til O. M. Sandvik.* Oslo: Aschehoug, 1945, pp. 83–121; Norlind, Tobias. "Sång och harpspel under vikingatiden." In *Festskrift til O. M. Sandvik,* pp. 173–83; Moberg, Carl-Allan. *Die liturgischen Hymnen in Schweden.* Vol. 1. Copenhagen: Munksgaard, 1947; Vol. 2.1–2 [with Ann-Marie Nilsson] Uppsala: Almqvist & Wiksell, 1991; Norlind, Tobias. *Bilder ur Svenska Musikens Historia från äldsta tid till medeltidens slut.* Stockholm: Musikhistoriska museet, 1947; Schiørring, Nils. *Det 16. og 17. Århundredes verdslige danske Visesang.* 2 vols. Copenhagen: Thaning & Appel, 1950; Sandvik, Agnar. "Messe- og tidesang i den norske middelalderkirken." In *Nidaros Erkebispestol og Bispesete 1153–1953.* Oslo: Land og Kirke, 1955, pp. 633–57; Raasted, Jørgen. "Middelalderlige håndskriftsfragmenter i Danmark I." *Scandia* 26 (1960), 145–50; Wallin, Nils. "Hymnus in honorem Sancti Magni comitis Orchadiae: Codex Upsaliensis C 233." *Svensk tidskrift för musikforskning* 43 (1961), 339–54; Milveden, Ingmar. "Die schriftliche Fixierung eines Quintorganums in einem Antiphonar-fragment der

Diözese Åbo." *Svensk tidskrift för musikforskning* 44 (1962), 63–5;
Horton, John. *Scandinavian Music: A Short History.* London: Faber,
1963; Milveden, Ingmar. "Manuskript, Mönch und Mond. Ein Hauptteil
des Cod. Upsal. C 23 in quellenkritischer Beleuchtung." *Svensk
tidskrift för musikforskning* 46 (1964), 9–25; Ottósson, R. A., *et al.*
"Koral, Gregoriansk." *KLNM* 9 (1964), 116–32; Milveden, Ingmar.
"Organum." *KLNM* 12 (1967), 684–92; Ling, Jan. "Musik." *KLNM* 12
(1967), 27–30; Milveden, Ingmar. "Rimofficium." *KLNM* 14 (1969),
305–19; Milveden, Ingmar. "Sekvens." *KLNM* 15 (1970), 86–102;
Andersson, Otto. "The Bowed Harp of Trondheim Cathedral and
Related Instruments in East and West." *Galpin Society Journal* 23
(1970), 5–34; Grinde, Nils. *Norsk musikkhistorie.* Oslo:
Universitetsforlaget, 1971 [English translation: *A History of Norwegian
Music.* Lincoln and London: University of Nebraska Press, 1991];
Møller, Dorte Falcon. "Den himmelske lovprisning." *Den iconographiske
post* 4–5 (1971), 26–35; Salmen, Walter. *Musikgeschichte Schleswig-
Holsteins von der Frühzeit bis zur Reformation.* Neumünster:
Wachholtz, 1972; Schiørring, Nils. "Flerstemmighed i dansk
middelalder." In *Festskrift til Jens Peter Larsen.* Ed. Nils Schiørring *et
al.* Copenhagen: Hansen, 1972, pp. 11–27; Milveden, Ingmar. *Zu den
liturgischen "Hystorie" in Schweden.* Uppsala: Skriv Service, 1972;
Bergsagel, John. "Anglo-Scandinavian Musical Relations before 1700."
In *Report of the Eleventh Congress of the International Musicological
Society, Copenhagen 1972.* 2 vols. Ed. Henrik Glahn *et al.* Copenhagen:
Hansen, 1974, vol. 1, pp. 263–71; Levy, Morten. *Den stærke slått.*
Højbjerg: Wormianum, 1974; Marchand, James W. "The Old Icelandic
Allegory of the Church Modes." *Musical Quarterly* 61 (1975), 553–9;
Bergsagel, John. "Liturgical Relations Between England and Scandinavia:
As Seen in Selected Musical Fragments from the 12th and 13th
Centuries." In *Föredrag och diskussionsinnlägg från Nordiskt
Kollokvium III i Latinsk Liturgiforskning.* Kåytånnöllisen Teologian
Julkaisuja A 3/1975. Helsingfors: Institutionen för Praktisk Teologi,
Helsingfors Universitet, 1976, pp. 11–26; Møller, Dorte Falcon. "Folk
Music Instruments in Danish Iconographic Sources." In *Studia
instrumentorum musicae popularis: Bericht über die 4. Internationale
Arbeitstagung der Study Group on Folk Musical Instruments des
International Folk Music Council in Balatonalmáli 1973.* Ed. Erich
Stockmann. Stockholm: Musikhistoriska museet, 1976, pp. 73–6;
Müller, Mette. "Der himmlische Lobgesang in Rynkeby. Eine dänische
ikonographische Quelle des 16. Jahrhunderts." In *Studia
instrumentorum musicae popularis,* vol. 4, pp. 70–3; Schiørring, Nils.
Musikkens Historie i Danmark. Copenhagen: Politiken, 1977–78;
Johansson, K. "Gunnars harpa." *Den iconographiske post* (1979), 33–
6; Andersen, Merete Geert. "Colligere fragmenta, ne pereant." *Opuscula*
7. Bibliotheca Arnamagnæana, 34. Copenhagen: Reitzel, 1979, pp. 1–
35; Bergsagel, John, and Niels Martin Jensen. "A Reconsideration of the
Manuscript Copenhagen A.M. 76, 8°." In *Festskrift Henrik Glahn.* Ed.
Mette Müller. Copenhagen: Fog, 1979, pp. 19–33; Bergsagel, John.
"Songs for St. Knud the King." *Musik & Forskning* 6 (1980), 152–66;
Bergsagel, John. "Remarks Concerning Some Tropes in Scandinavian
Manuscripts." In *Nordisk Kollokvium V for Latinsk Liturgiforskning
1981.* Århus: Institut för Kirkehistorie, Aarhus Universitet, 1982, pp.
187–205; De Geer, Ingrid. *Earl, Saint, Bishop, Skald—and Music: The
Orkney Earldom of the Twelfth Century: A Musicological Study.*
Uppsala: Institutionen för Musikvetenskap, 1985; Bergsagel, John.
"The Practice of *Cantus planus binatim* in Scandinavia in the 12th to
16th Centuries." In *Le polifonie primitive in Friuli e in Europa. Atti del
congresso internazionale, Cividale del Friuli, 22–24 agosto 1980.* Ed.
Cesare Corsi and Pierluigi Petrobelli. Rome: Orfeo, 1989, pp. 62–83.

John Bergsagel

[See Also: Ballads; Love Poetry]

Mythical-Heroic Sagas *see* **Fornaldarsögur**

Mythology. Scandinavia was unusual among medieval cultures in that it recorded a body of texts about the pagan gods who had been displaced by the conversion to Christianity, which brought writing and made possible the recording of such texts. Most of these texts were first recorded in vernacular MSS from the 13th century in Iceland, more than two centuries after Iceland's conversion to Christianity; but in many cases, an oral tradition running back to pagan times may be surmised. The *Gesta Danorum* of the Danish cleric Saxo Grammaticus comprises another important textual source. Besides these textual sources, scholars use the evidence of such disciplines as onomastics and archaeology to reconstruct Scandinavian mythology and early religion.

The system was apparently polytheistic, with an emphasis on male gods with probable Indo-European and definite Germanic cognates. It comprises a myth of origin, numerous myths detailing the acts of the gods, primarily against the related race of the *jǫtnar* (usually rendered "giants," but see below), a myth of the destruction of the current race of gods, and the beginning of a new cycle of gods. This recorded mythology bears many similarities with Christianity.

Sources. The body of texts is small. Some of the earliest skaldic poetry is mythological in nature and may therefore reflect genuine paganism, since it is believed that skaldic verses underwent very little alteration in oral transmission. Bragi Boddason, according to scholarly tradition the oldest known of the skalds (9th century?), described scenes inscribed on a shield in his *Ragnarsdrápa*, one of them the encounter between Þórr and the Miðgarðsormr ("Midgard serpent"). Another very early shield poem, the *Haustlǫng* of Þjóðólfr of Hvin, has two mythological scenes: the rape of Iðunn, and Þórr's encounter with Hrungnir. Úlfr Uggason's *Húsdrápa*, which probably dates from the decades before the conversion to Christianity, describes the decorative scenes carved inside an Icelandic farmhouse, among which were Þórr's encounter with the Miðgarðsormr, Loki's with Heimdallr, and Baldr's funeral. Several other skaldic poems and fragments exist with mythological subjects, of which the most important may be Eilífr Goðrúnarson's *Þórsdrápa*, a poem about Þórr's visit with Geirrøðr. Of particular interest are single stanzas by the Icelandic poets Vetrliði Sumarliðason and Þorbjǫrn dísarskáld, which address Þórr in the second person and thus give the only indication in textual format of the possible nature of ritual or prayer.

Þórr is the most represented god in this brief survey of the skaldic evidence. Óðinn and the other gods play a major role, however, in verse composed in nonskaldic forms. The anonymous *Eiríksmál* describes the arrival of Eiríkr blóðøx ("blood-axe") in Valhǫll, and was presumably therefore composed shortly after his death in 954. Eyvindr Finnsson's *Hákonarmál* describes a similar arrival for Hákon the Good, who died around 960; the depiction of the warrior culture in Valhǫll points toward Óðinn.

However, the strictly eddic poems have the most to report with respect to Scandinavian mythology. Each of these poems has its own textual history, and the dating of them is uncertain. Some observers have felt confident in dating all of them to paganism, while others are equally convinced that at least some are products of the high Middle Ages. The problem is complex, for the material is clearly old, and, just as clearly, it had to have existed for two centuries in Christian oral tradition in Iceland before being recorded, and, most importantly, had to make sense to contemporary audiences in order to remain in oral tradition. Most of the important mythological eddic poems were collected into the main MS of the *Poetic Edda* by an unknown redactor, who followed a conscious plan. The book opens with the synoptic *Vǫluspá*, which gives the entire sweep of mythic history, from the creation, through the war between the two groups of gods, Æsir and Vanir, and the death of Baldr (omitted from a version of the poem recorded in a different MS), through the fall of the gods (Ragnarǫk) and rebirth of the universe. A group of poems about Óðinn then follows: *Hávamál* (gnomic wisdom; amorous adventures; acquisition of the mead of poetry; self-sacrifice and acquisition of wisdom), *Vafþrúðnismál* (contest of wisdom with a giant), and *Grímnismál* (ecstatic wisdom performance in the hall of a human king). The next poem, *Fǫr Skírnis*, or *Skírnismál*, tells of the wooing of the giantess Gerðr for Freyr by his servant Skírnir. Thereafter, the redactor placed a series of poems about Þórr: *Hárbarðsljóð* (duel of wits with Óðinn), *Hymiskviða* (encounter with the Miðgarðsormr and acquisition of kettle for brewing mead), *Lokasenna* (Loki's insults to the gods; a Þórr poem because Þórr is the only one who can quiet Loki), and *Þrymskviða* (retrieval of his hammer from a giant). Þórr is also the divine actor in *Alvíssmál* (dwarf sues for hand of Þórr's daughter), which the redactor apparently classified as a poem about beings of the lower mythology, because *Vǫlundarkviða*, with elfin characteristics, intervenes between *Þrymskviða* and it. Since the remaining poems in the MS are heroic, one may infer an intended historical progression from the sacred prehistory of the gods to the human prehistory of the heroic poetry. A historical or at least linear progression is suggested even among the mythological poems, since the order of gods celebrated in them follows the order in which, according to the mythology, they perished at Ragnarǫk: Óðinn, Freyr, and Þórr. However, the *Poetic Edda* makes a clear break between mythological and heroic poems.

Many of these poems are also gathered in a second MS, which lacks the careful plan of the *Poetic Edda*, and a few other mythological eddic poems were retained in other MSS. These include *Baldrs draumar* (Óðinn seeks information from a seeress regarding Baldr's fate) and *Rígsþula* (origin of the social classes).

Of the various sources, the *Edda* of Snorri Sturluson (1179–1241) is by far the most important. It is, in fact, the only text called "Edda" during the Middle Ages; application of the term to the poems just described was a learned conjecture of the 17th century. The work consists of a prologue followed by three major sections: *Gylfaginning* ("Deluding of Gylfi"), *Skáldskaparmál* ("Poetic Diction"), and *Háttatal* ("Enumeration of Meters").

The prologue offers a version of learned prehistory, in which the human king Óðinn emigrates from Troy to the North, establishes his sons as monarchs over various kingdoms there, and himself settles in Sigtuna in Sweden. The prologue is radically different from what follows, and earlier observers doubted whether Snorri could have written it. But it is not difficult to imagine it having been written after the rest of the work was composed, as a defense against those who would criticize the retelling of pagan myths in *Gylfaginning* and the opening pages of *Skáldskaparmál*.

Gylfaginning contains a frame in which the Swedish king Gylfi journeys to visit the Æsir. Precisely what the term means in this context has been a hotly debated issue, but Gylfi's interlocutors are called "High," "Just-as-High," and "Third," names that point clearly to Óðinn. Gylfi asks them questions, and the answers are most of the major myths. Gylfi begins with creation and then moves to cosmology before beginning to ask about individual gods. Óðinn receives the greatest amount of attention, but a dozen or so gods and an equal number of goddesses are surveyed, some of them very briefly. Ragnarǫk and its aftermath are the last topics treated. *Gylfaginning* may be read in a variety of ways, depending on one's view of Snorri's aims, and the range has been enormous, from authentic Germanic paganism to 13th-century fiction. All contemporary readings, however, begin from Snorri's use of euhemerism, the view that the pagan gods were once human.

The prologue and particularly *Gylfaginning* are the most famous parts of Snorri's *Edda*, but they represent no more than a third of the entire work. *Skáldskaparmál*, by far the longest section, adds a few more myths, of which the most important is that of the origin of the mead of poetry, and it also recounts some heroic legend. But nearly all of *Skáldskaparmál* is a discussion of the poetic figures used in the older poetry; *Háttatal* is a *clavis rhythmica*, with commentary, enumerating 100 primarily metrical possibilities.

Snorri's *Edda* is thus in its entirety properly viewed as a handbook of poetics, since the myths in *Gylfaginning* and *Skáldskaparmál* are keys to understanding the kennings of the older skalds. Indeed, these kennings themselves represent a secondary source of our knowledge of Scandinavian mythology, since they often build on myth: for example, the earth may be called "flesh of Ymir" after the creation myth, or gold may be called "headpiece of Sif" after her golden hair. *Skáldskaparmál*, in fact, includes lists of kennings for many of the gods.

Snorri Sturluson also apparently composed the other major mythological source in Iceland: *Ynglinga saga*, the first in his cycle of sagas, *Heimskringla*, about Norwegian kings. *Ynglinga saga* chronicles briefly the reigns of the early Swedish kings known as Ynglingar, and in doing so generally follows the poem *Ynglingatal* by Þjóðólfr of Hvin. However, Snorri traces the line all the way back to mythic prehistory and has it begin with the emigration of Óðinn from Asia. The presentation of the learned prehistory here bears similarities with the prologue to Snorri's *Edda*, but there is a good deal of additional valuable mythological information, especially concerning Óðinn and the war between the Æsir and the Vanir.

Other Old Norse–Icelandic prose sources are more recondite. Indeed, if one adopts a strict definition of myth as stories about gods, virtually no text will qualify. The closest is perhaps the *Sǫrla þáttr* of the late 14th-century compilation *Flateyarbók*; the opening pages of *Sǫrla þáttr* report that Freyja slept with some dwarfs to obtain the *Brísinga men* necklace. Many texts refer to alleged pagan ritual, and these references have precipitated a vigorous debate on their trustworthiness and meaning.

An important Latin source is the *Gesta Danorum* of Saxo Grammaticus, who was associated with the Danish bishopric at Lund. *Gesta Danorum* is a verse history of Denmark up to 1202. The first nine of its sixteen books treat prehistory and contain a certain amount of euhemerized mythology. Although *Gesta Danorum* was composed within Danish circles, Saxo relied heavily on Icelandic sources, and it is seldom easy to distinguish Icelandic from Danish.

To these textual sources may be added the evidence of onomastics, archaeology, and the history of religions. Theophastic place-names abound in Scandinavia, and they reveal much about the chronology and distribution of the cults of the various gods. Archaeological evidence includes objects and images that have been identified as portrayals of or sacred to various of the gods.

The history of religions provides a comparative perspective for interpretation of all these kinds of evidence.

The mythology. Although each text must be approached and evaluated individually, the systematizing efforts of Snorri and the redactor of the *Poetic Edda* invite discussion of the mythology as a system. Broadly speaking, Scandinavian mythology is about the ongoing struggle between two groups of beings, the Æsir and the *jǫtnar*, traditionally taken for gods and giants, and symbolically to be understood as forces of order and of chaos. Both terms seem to refer to something like what we would call tribes; other terms existed to indicate divine beings or beings with unusually large stature. In any case, the two groups are inextricably linked from the start, because the Æsir create the cosmos out of the body of Ymir, the hermaphroditic progenitor of the *jǫtnar*.

The Æsir were not permanently opposed to all other groups, since early in mythic time they struck a peace with the group known as the Vanir, from whom came to them a number of the more important gods, especially those associated with fertility: Njǫrðr, Freyr, and Freyja. Some scholars have regarded the war between the Æsir and the Vanir and the incorporation of Vanir among Æsir in connection with the truce as a reflection of an actual religious war or of the replacement of one cult with another; such a surmise cannot be proven. Others hold that the war and ensuing peace symbolically explain the existence of different aspects of divinity.

In the "mythic present," then, Æsir contend with *jǫtnar*. This combat is generally envisioned as struggles between single gods and giants, although sometimes others are peripherally involved. A brief survey of the individual struggles serves to indicate the nature of the various gods. Óðinn generally uses his wisdom as his weapon. Thus, he wins a contest of wisdom with the giant Vafþrúðnir, at the end of which, recognizing his adversary, the giant forfeits his head. In the hall of the human king Geirrøðr, Óðinn gives an ecstatic wisdom performance when he is tortured between two fires; at the end, he reveals his godhead, and Geirrøðr falls on his sword. Since the subject of both of these myths is mythic history and cosmology, we may infer that wisdom and power are associated. Óðinn's control of wisdom had in part to do with this mastery of poetry, an accomplishment associated with his theft of the mead of poetry from the giants. The mead is a powerful symbol concerning the interaction of various groups of beings, since it was fermented from the spittle of Æsir and Vanir at their truce, with the intervention of the chthonic dwarfs, but ended up among the giants. Óðinn's retrieval of it exists in variant forms, but the salient point seems to be invasion of the giant world, seduction of a giant maiden, and a return to the world of the gods in bird form.

Where Óðinn uses wisdom and sometimes guile against the forces of chaos, Þórr generally uses his hammer; in other words, Óðinn uses strategy, and Þórr, force. The two little poetic fragments addressed to Þórr catalogue some of the giants and giantesses he killed, and nearly all of the myths in which he figures end with his killing one or many of them.

Two of Þórr's struggles stand out as particularly significant. The first is against the Miðgarðsormr, a snake lying coiled about the earth deep in the ocean. Þórr fished up this serpent and threw his hammer at it, killing it, according to some sources, but failing to do so, according to Snorri. The outcome seems perhaps to have been less important than the struggle, which was popular in poetry and also apparently in rock carving. The poetic sources connect Þórr's struggle against the Miðgarðsormr with a journey to acquire

a large kettle to brew beer. Here again, one may note a contact with Óðinn; Óðinn acquires the mead of poetry, whose value is symbolic, and Þórr acquires a kettle for brewing, whose role is more concrete.

Þórr's second important opponent was Hrungnir, strongest of the giants. According to Snorri, Hrungnir and Þórr fought a formal duel, and both sides realized the importance of it, for Hrungnir was the strongest of the giants and was equipped with a heart of stone. Þórr triumphed when his shieldbearer Þjálfi tricked the giant into standing on his shield, enabling Þórr to cast his hammer at the giant without impediment. However, the closeness of the duel is indicated by the fact that Þórr got a fragment of the giant's stone heart in his head and was unable without help to remove the dead giant's leg, which had fallen over him.

That Þórr relies on his shieldbearer is not unusual, for he generally operates with some kind of assistant. Especially in the Hrungnir story, it is tempting to regard this assistant as the mythic representation of a youth being initiated into warrior society.

Þórr also kills many giantesses. The most important of the myths involves his visit to the home of the giant Geirrøðr, not identical to the human king visited by Óðinn. Along the way, he is nearly swept away in a river of urine or menstrual fluids being created by one of the giant's daughters, and later she and a sister attempt to rise up under Þórr and crush him against the ceiling. He resists and breaks their backs. Þórr's enmity with giantesses remains obscure; he killed many more, but most of the myths are now lost. Þórr himself dressed as the goddess Freyja when he went off to the world of the giants to regain his hammer, which had, according to the late and parodic eddic poem *Þrymskviða*, been stolen by the giant Þrymr.

Freyr has only one major moment in the mythology, his longing for and apparently winning the giantess Gerðr. However the myth is to be interpreted, it connects him with fertility and, because he gives up his sword, removes him from the sphere of war and battle.

The female Æsir play small roles. The two most significant, Frigg and Freyja, seem to represent the Æsir and Vanir, respectively. From statements by Snorri and by inference, it is possible to discern connections with magic, wisdom, and the dead, which other sources confirm for human seeresses. With the mythology, however, the goddesses often function as no more than objects desired by the *jǫtnar*.

The most enigmatic figure in the mythology is Loki, who is of giant extraction but functions uneasily among the gods. Comparative analysis makes clear that he plays the common mythological role of the trickster figure, that is, one whose violation of boundaries and lack of forethought are dangerous, but also may confer benefits on society. In the systematized mythology of the recorded texts, however, it is plain that he sides ultimately with the enemies of the gods, perhaps through association with Satan. Loki arranged the slaying of Baldr by his half-brother Hǫðr, a slaying that apparently first brought death among the Æsir and that could not be avenged, given the close family relationship of slayer and slain. Loki leads the forces of chaos against the Æsir at Ragnarǫk. Although Ragnarǫk is conceived as a massive battle, in fact it involves individual combats in which the various gods are defeated by their major adversaries, followed by the destruction of the cosmos. Thereafter, however, the next generation of Æsir will rule. Baldr and Hǫðr will be reconciled, and there is no mention of the presence of *jǫtnar*.

Interpretation. Many of the greatest scholars of myth, religion, and folklore have written on Scandinavian mythology, including Jakob Grimm, Sir James Frazer, Axel Olrik, Kaarle Krohn, and a great many others. The earliest serious scholarship, that of the 19th century, understood the myths as representations of seasonal change and the gods as such natural phenomena as storms, thunder, fire, and the like, sometimes in connection with hypothetical ritual activity. Ritual activity was the focus of some later interpretations, such as those of Otto Höfler, who argued the existence of a cult group of warriors linked with Óðinn, while other scholarship involved not so much interpretation as a search after borrowings from other traditions. In general, however, the major trends of the middle decades of this century might be described as "historicist" and "comparative," the former referring to work that focuses on philological and archaeological detail in the context of Germanic religion (Karl Helm is a major name here), and the latter referring to work undertaken by Georges Dumézil and his followers attempting to show a tripartite structure allegedly characteristic of Indo-European mythologies. A more recent trend has involved the search for the learned, medieval context of the mythology, often in Christian theology. Such a focus both clarifies the material and renders less significant the gulf between pagan Scandinavia and the recording of the mythology centuries later during Christianity.

Bib.: Lindow, John. *Scandinavian Mythology: An Annotated Bibliography.* Garland Folklore Bibliographies, 13. New York and London: Garland, 1988. **Lit.**: Höfler, Otto. *Kultische Geheimbünde der Germanen.* Frankfurt: Diesterweg, 1934; Baetke, Walter. *Die Götterlehre der Snorra-Edda.* Berichte über die Verhandlungen der sächsischen Akademie der Wissenschaften zu Leipzig, philo.-hist. Kl., 97.3. Berlin: Akademie-Verlag, 1950; Helm, Karl. "Mythologie auf alten and neuen Wegen." *Beiträge zur Geschichte der deutschen Sprache und Literatur* (Tübingen) 77 (1955), 333–65; Vries, Jan de. *Altgermanische Religionsgeschichte.* 2 vols. 2nd ed. Grundriss der germanischen Philologie, 12.1–2. Berlin: de Gruyter, 1956–57; Ellis Davidson, H. R. *Gods and Myths of Northern Europe.* Harmondsworth: Penguin, 1964; Holtsmark, Anne. *Studier i Snorres mytologi.* Skrifter utg. av Det Norske Videnskaps-Akademie i Oslo, II. Hist.-philos. Kl., ny serie, 4. Oslo: Det Norske Videnskaps-Akademie i Oslo, 1964; Turville-Petre, E.O.G. *Myth and Religion of the North: The Religion of Ancient Scandinavia.* New York: Holt, Rinehart and Winston, 1964; rpt. Westport: Greenwood, 1975; Dumézil, Georges. *Gods of the Ancient Northmen.* Ed. Einar Haugen. Trans. John Lindow *et al.* Publications of the UCLA Center for the Study of Comparative Folklore and Mythology, 3. Berkeley, Los Angeles, and London: University of California Press, 1973 [trans. of 1959 original]; Klingenberg, Heinz. *Edda—Sammlung und Dichtung.* Beiträge zur nordischen Philologie, 3. Basel and Stuttgart: Kohlhammer, 1974; Ström, Åke V. "Germanische Religion." In Ström, Åke V., and Haralds Biezais. *Germanische und baltische Religion.* Die Religionen der Menschheit, 19.1 Stuttgart: Kohlhammer, 1975; Gottfried, Lorenz. *Snorri Sturluson: Gylfaginning: Texte, Übersetzung, Kommentar.* Texte zur Forschung. Darmstadt: Wissenschaftliche Buchgesellschaft, 1984; Simek, Rudolf. *Lexikon der germanischen Mythologie.* Kröners Taschenausgabe, 368. Stuttgart: Kröner, 1984; Lindow, John. "Mythology and Mythography." In *Old Norse–Icelandic Literature: A Critical Guide.* Ed. Carol J. Clover and John Lindow. Islandica, 45. Ithaca and London: Cornell University Press, 1985, pp. 21–67; Clunies Ross, Margaret. *Skáldskaparmál: Snorri Sturluson's ars poetica and Medieval Theories of Language.* Viking Collection, 4. Odense: Odense University Press, 1985.

John Lindow

[**See also:** *Alvíssmál*; Baldr; *Baldrs draumar*; Bragi Boddason; Eddic Poetry; Eilífr Goðrúnarson; *Eiríksmál*; Eyvindr Finnsson skáldaspillir; Freyr and Freyja; *Grímnismál*; *Hárbarðsljóð*; *Hávamál*; *Hymiskviða*; Kennings; *Lokasenna*; Loki; Maiden Warriors; Óðinn; Religion, Pagan Scandinavian; *Rígsþula*; Saxo Grammaticus; Skaldic Verse; *Skírnismál*; *Snorra Edda*; Supernatural Beings; *Sǫrla þáttr*; Þjóðólfr of Hvin; Þórr; *Þrymskviða*; Úlfr Uggason; *Vafþrúðnismál*; *Vǫlundarkviða*; *Vǫluspá*; *Ynglinga saga*]

Märchensagas *see* **Lygisǫgur**

Mǫðruvallabók ("The Book of Mǫðruvellir"), AM 132 fol., is an Icelandic MS that consists of 200 parchment leaves, bound in wooden plates; 189 leaves were written in the middle of the 14th century.

Mǫðruvallabók contains exclusively *Íslendingasǫgur*: (1) *Njáls saga*, with lacunae filled on eleven leaves from the 17th century; (2) *Egils saga Skalla-Grímssonar*, defective; (3) *Finnboga saga*; (4) *Bandamanna saga*; (5) *Kormáks saga*; (6) *Víga-Glúms saga*; (7) *Droplaugarsona saga*; (8) *Ǫlkofra saga*; (9) *Hallfreðar saga*; (10) *Laxdœla saga*; and (11) *Fóstbrœðra saga*, very defective.

The first seven of these sagas are in the same geographical order as the original *Landnámabók*, starting in the South and ending in the East, and after (1) a place was meant for another southern saga, the now-lost *Gauks saga Trandilssonar*, which was never copied in *Mǫðruvallabók*.

Almost the whole original part of *Mǫðruvallabók* is written by a single scribe, whose meticulous handwriting is known from several other, mainly fragmentary, MSS. For some reason, this scribe has left an open space for sixteen stanzas (and two lines in a 17th) in (2), but fourteen of these stanzas (and the two lines) have been written by another contemporary scribe, whose hand is also known from other MSS.

The scribes have not been identified, but several things point to the north of Iceland as *Mǫðruvallabók*'s place of origin. The MS's name is derived from the farm name Mǫðruvellir in Eyjafjörður, where its owner at that time, the lawman Magnús Björnsson, wrote his name in it in 1628. In the late 17th century, the MS was brought to Copenhagen and came into the possession of Professor Árni Magnússon. It belongs to the Arnamagnæan Collection, which Árni bequeathed to the University of Copenhagen and which is currently being transferred in part to the University of Iceland; since 1974, *Mǫðruvallabók* has been back in Iceland.

Mǫðruvallabók is by far the most comprehensive collection of *Íslendingasǫgur*, and in many cases it contains sagas or parts of sagas that are not found elsewhere, except in copies that are derived from *Mǫðruvallabók*. Our knowledge of this important branch of Old Icelandic literature is thus based to a large degree on this MS.

Ed.: Einar Ól. Sveinsson, ed. *Mǫðruvallabók (Codex Mǫðruvallensis), MS. No. 132 fol. in the Arnamagnæan Collection in the University Library of Copenhagen.* Corpus Codicum Islandicorum Medii Aevi, 5. Copenhagen: Munksgaard, 1933 [facsimile]; Arkel-de Leeuw van Wenen, Andrea van. *Mǫðruvallabók, AM 132 Fol. Volume Two. Text.* Leiden, etc.: Brill, 1987. [See also editions of individual texts.] **Lit**.: Jón Helgason. "Gauks saga Trandilssonar." In *Heidersskrift til Gustav Indrebø.* Ed. Hjørdis Johannessen *et al.* Bergen: Lunde, 1939, pp. 92–

100; rpt. in Jón Helgason. *Ritgerðakorn og ræðustúfar.* Reykjavik: Félag íslenzkra stúdenta í Kaupmannahöfn, 1959, pp. 100–8; Jón Helgason. *Handritaspjall.* Reykjavik: Mál og Menning, 1958, pp. 59–62; Mageröy, Hallvard. "Dei to gjerdene (versjonane) av Bandamanna saga.—Tillegg om Möðruvallabók-skrivaren." *Arkiv för nordisk filologi* 81 (1966), 100–8; Stefán Karlsson, ed. *Sagas of Icelandic Bishops: Fragments of Eight Manuscripts.* Early Icelandic Manuscripts in Facsimile, 7. Copenhagen: Rosenkilde & Bagger, 1967, pp. 26–9; Arkel-de Leeuw van Wenen, Andrea van. *Möðruvallabók, AM 132 fol. Volume One. Index and Concordance.* Leiden, *etc.*: Brill, 1987 [introduction and printed text together with microfiches containing an index with complete references and a concordance].

Stefán Karlsson

[**See also:** *Bandamanna saga; Droplaugarsona saga; Egils saga Skalla-Grímssonar, Finnboga saga ramma; Fóstbrœðra saga; Hallfreðar saga; Íslendingasögur; Kormáks saga; Landnámabók; Laxdœla saga; Njáls saga; Víga-Glúms saga; Qlkofra þáttr*]

Mottuls saga, or *Skikkju saga* (both mean "Saga About the Cloak"), is an Old Norse prose translation of the Old French *fabliau Le Lai du cort mantel.* This rather frivolous piece by Old Norse standards tells the story of a magic cloak brought to King Arthur's court, by means of which the chastity of the women at his court can be tested. Of course, all of them fail in one way or another, until Karradin's shy lady is brought forward and passes the test.

This saga belongs to the group of Arthurian romances translated into Old Norse at the Norwegian court of Hákon Hákonarson around the middle of the 13th century, but surely does not aspire to the educative purpose ascribed to the other works of this genre. It is also the only known translation into Old Norse prose of an Old French *fabliau.* The subject matter of the chastity-testing cloak was extremely popular both on the Continent, where translations were made into all major vernacular languages, and in Iceland, where the 14th- or 15th-century *Samsons saga fagra* was composed to reveal, among other things, the history of the cloak before it reached King Arthur's court, and which actually refers to the MS using the title *Skikkju saga.* The popularity of the saga in Iceland is also shown by the fourteen MSS still extant, dating from the time around 1300 to the 19th century, and by a *rímur* version of the saga called *Skikkju rímur* composed in the 15th century.

Ed.: Cederschiöld, Gustav, and F.-A. Wulff, eds. *Versions nordiques du fabliau francais Le mantel mautaillié. Textes et notes.* Lund: Gleerup, 1877 [contains also *Skikkjurímur*]; Kalinke, Marianne E., ed. *Mottuls saga: With an Edition of* Le Lai du cort mantel *by Philip E. Bennett.* Editiones Arnamagnæanæ, ser. B, vol. 30. Copenhagen: Reitzel, 1987. **Tr.**: Simek, Rudolf, trans. *Zwei Rittersagas. Die Saga vom Mantel und die Saga vom schönen Samson. Mottuls saga und Samsons saga fagra.* Fabulae medievales, 2. Vienna: Braumüller, 1982. **Lit.**: Kalinke, Marianne. "Amplification in *Mottuls saga:* Its Function and Form." *Acta Philologica Scandinavica* 32 (1979), 239–55; Friesen, Marilyn Joan Ardis. "*Le Cort Mantel* and *Mottuls saga:* A Literary Comparison." Diss. University of Illinois, 1983.

Rudolf Simek

[**See also:** Old Norse–Icelandic Literature, Foreign Influence on; *Riddarasögur*]

Namnlös och Valentin see Swedish Literature, Miscellaneous

Navigation. There is no evidence whatsoever that any sort of instrument was used in Viking navigation. The "sun-board" to determine latitude from sun altitude, the sun-compass set by the shadow cast by a central pin, and the sun-stone to find the sun's position from polarization even when it was hidden by cloud are all imaginary modern creations. The wood fragment with unequally spaced roughly radial lines from a Benedictine monastery in Greenland (Vebæk 1956) is far too small to be used as a sun-compass. The *sólarsteinn* or sun-stone, if it were a piece of Iceland feldspar with polarizing properties as some assume, would work only when the observer's zenith was unclouded and would not help the orientation of the equally hypothetical sun-compass in any case. To establish direction from the sun, one would need an independent source of time.

The sun was evidently used in navigation, but not in this quasi-modern way. Stjornu-Oddi ("Star-Oddi") Helgason's *Oddatala* shows that in Iceland in the early 12th century the sun's noon altitude and bearing at sunrise and sunset had been established for every day of the year. The information in the Vinland sagas that even on the shortest day the sun was above the horizon at *dagmál* ("mid-morning") and *eykt* ("mid-afternoon") certainly looks like an attempt to define the latitude of a place on the American coast well south of Iceland, where this would not be the case, but cannot be used to calculate an exact latitude, as some enthusiasts have attempted (Næss 1954). But the Króksfjarðarheiðr observation in Greenland suggests that sun altitudes in one place were on occasion compared with those in another to establish the difference in latitude between them, though the crudeness of this method (the shadow of the boat's gunwale on a man lying across the bottom boards) sufficiently demonstrates the absence of any instruments for determining it (Næss 1954).

The Canterbury portable sundial (*ca.* A.D. 1000) gives 9:00 A.M., noon, and 3:00 P.M. from the sun's altitude, and has been interpreted as showing that the necessary correction for sun declination North or South in different months had been reduced to a simple, easily remembered formula in successive months. This works only in the latitude between 50 and 60° North, but

men who knew it could form a good idea of time or latitude from differences in the length of a shadow, and of direction at sunrise and sunset. In between, they probably relied on keeping a steady course by reference to wind and sea, and making allowance for the sun's progress across the sky. As recent orientation experiments have shown that the directional sense of humans and birds is interfered with by magnets, it is likely that they also relied on some sense of the earth's magnetic field long before the introduction of the magnetic compass, and backed it up with the interpretation of wave patterns and bird flight, such as is recorded from later whalers and contemporary primitive navigators in the Pacific (Binns 1971).

Most Viking navigation was not over long ocean voyages but along a coast at a safe distance offshore ("so that the sea came halfway up the mountains," as *Hauksbók* says, ch. 2) from one known point to another, and keeping a careful dead reckoning of distance run in terms of *dœgr siglingar*, or day's sailings. A normal value for this measure of 24 *vikur* ("shifts") of 6 nautical miles gives good agreement between the Old Norse texts and a modern chart, although under favorable conditions a Gokstad ship could cover half as much again. Sailing all night along coasts was avoided when possible. When it had to be done, the navigator attempted to sense from the bow the reflection of the seas off the land.

There is no evidence of any charts for sea use before the 15th century, but texts show the navigators had a clear mental picture of the layout of their world. Iceland is "opposite" one point on the Norwegian coast, Shetland opposite another, Scotland opposite a third; and if one sailed from these traditional departure points, one could assume that "at the expected time on the second day" (*Beowulf*, v. 219) the destination, identifiable by its characteristics (wooded, rocky, sandy, *etc.*) would be in sight. Wulfstan on his voyage to the east along the south coast of the Baltic evidently thought of himself as sailing across a grid whose North-South lines were identified by the islands on them, for he records progress by saying that he had on his port side Øland or Bornholm, although they were far out of sight, 50 or 100 miles north of his track. As he sailed at night, it seems possible, as Crumlin-Pedersen suggests (1984), that he followed the 10–fathom line, which in turn suggests that his navigational method was more English (where sounding is well recorded at this period) than Scandinavian (where on steep coasts it seems naturally to have been little used). This distinc-

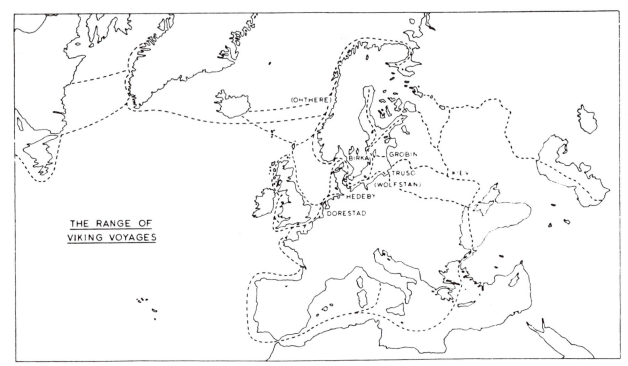

77. The range of Viking voyages.

tion is obviously not without interest for the old question whether Wulfstan was a Scandinavian like Ohthere or (Craigie's suggestion) an Angle. It is striking that *Grœnlendinga saga* (ch. 3) has Leifr Eiríksson repeat Bjarni Herjólfsson's landfalls consistently in the reverse order, as if he were feeling his way back down a route along a common frame of reference. This frame does not agree with modern charts as well as do the distances of days' sailings. If one follows the *Landnámabók* sailing directions for Greenland from Hernar in Norway, and sails due west, north of the Shetlands so they are barely visible and south of the Faroes so that the sea is halfway up the mountains, one will not in fact reach Greenland without a drastic alteration of course to due north. Either they thought of Greenland as farther south than it is, or of the Faroes as farther north. The weakness of the frame of reference over long stretches of open ocean is clear, and tells against much modern position finding that has been imported into the period. Along coasts that could be connected with one another without large gaps, it seems to have worked well enough, on the west side of the Atlantic or the east. In particular, the great ports of the period like Birka, Skíringssalr, and Haithabu were evidently able to rely on the substantial local knowledge necessary to bring a merchant ship to harbor. All lie well out of the way at the end of a fairly awkward approach, and the main qualification of any navigator to find them can only have been that he had been there before. In an illiterate age, the knowledge of the navigator must always have been acquired by experience and survival.

Ed.: Kålund, Kr., and N. Beckman, eds. *Alfræði Íslenzk. Islandsk encyclopædisk litteratur.* 3 vols. Samfund til udgivelse af gammel nordisk litteratur, 37, 41, 45. Copenhagen: Møller, 1908–18. **Lit.**: Næss, Almar. *Hvor lå Vinland. En studie over solobservasjoner i de norrøne sagaer.* Oslo: Dreyer, 1954; Vebæk, Christen. "Topographical and Archaeological Investigations in Norse Settlements in Greenland." Third Viking Congress, Reykjavík, 1956. *Árbók hins Íslenzka Fornleifafélags,* Fylgirit (1958), 107–22; Ramskou, Thorkild. *Solstenen, primitiv navigation i Norden før Kompasset.* Copenhagen: Rhodos, 1969 [English summary, pp. 83–96]; Binns, A. L. "Sun Navigation in the Viking Age, and the Canterbury Portable Sundial." *Acta Archaeologica* 62 (1971), 23–34; Lewis, David. *We the Navigators: The Ancient Art of Landfinding in the Pacific.* Honolulu: University Press of Hawaii, 1972; Schnall, Uwe. *Navigation der Wikinger.* Schriften des Deutschen Schiffahrtsmuseums, 6. Hamburg: Stalling, 1975 [best general account; no English summary]; Binns, Alan. *Viking Voyagers: Then and Now.* London: Heinemann, 1980 [a survey of the same material]; Crumlin-Pedersen, Ole. "Ships, Navigation and Routes in the Reports of Ohtere and Wulfstan." In *Two Voyagers at the Court of King Alfred: The Ventures of Ohtere and Wulfstan Together with the Description of Northern Europe from the Old English Orosius.* Ed. Niels Lund. York: Sessions, 1984.

Alan Binns

[**See also:** Ships and Shipbuilding]

Nesjavísur *see* Sighvatr Þórðarson

Nicodemus, Gospel of. Translations of the apocryphal gospel *Evangelium Nicodemi* are found in Old Norse, Old Swedish, and Old Danish. This gospel originates in two independent Greek traditions. One, named in Latin *Gesta Pilati*, relates to Pilate's trial of Christ and the subsequent Crucifixion. The other, commonly known as *Descensus Christi ad inferos*, relates Christ's harrowing of hell. Probably in the 5th century, both traditions were joined in an apocryphal gospel that relates the betrayal of Christ by the Jews and the glorious victory of Christ. Here, Satan is outwitted and driven from hell, while Christ raises Adam and all the righteous souls to eternal bliss in paradise. The gospel, originally entitled *Gesta salvatoris* or *Passio domini*, was later renamed *Evangelium Nicodemi* after its alleged author, the Pharisee Nicodemus, who assisted during Christ's burial (John 19:39).

In Old Norse, the second half of the Latin gospel, *Descensus*

Christi ad inferos, was translated from Latin under the title *Niðrstigningar saga*. Although the saga translates only this part, the opening and concluding lines show that the translator probably had access to the whole text of the gospel. The translation is based on Tischendorf's A-group of texts. The Old Norse text has survived in four medieval MSS, of which three probably have a common ancestor: AM 645 4to (complete text), AM 623 4to (beginning missing), and AM 233a fol. (fragmentary). The fourth and youngest MS, AM 238 V fol. (also fragmentary), is a revision of the older recension based on the Latin text. As Magnús Már Lárusson (1955) has shown, an additional source text is the copy of a medieval MS made by Ólafur Jónsson í Arney in 1780 (JS 405 8vo). Seip believed that the original translation was Norwegian, but the linguistic evidence for this view does not seem conclusive. Although the question of national origin may not be definitely solved, the four medieval MSS are all Icelandic. There is also an independent Icelandic translation of the Gospel, probably postmedieval, extant in seventeen MSS from the 18th and 19th centuries (in chronological order: Lbs 1258 8vo, JS 280 4to, JS 219 8vo, JS 36 4to, Lbs 786 8vo, Lbs 526 8vo, JS 456 8vo, ÍB 98 8vo, Nks 68 4to, Lbs 2636 8vo, Lbs 2144 8vo, ÍB 393 8vo, Lbs 509 4to, ÍB 212 8vo, Lbs 1036 8vo, Lbs 1160 8vo, Lbs 1333 8vo).

The story of Christ's harrowing of hell, spectacular as it is in the Latin text, is further dramatized by the Old Norse translator. The Vulgate-like style of the Latin text is rendered in a free translation, which on the linguistic level is paratactical, sometimes clumsy, and almost naive. On the narrative level, however, the translator amplifies the text and adapts it to a northern setting. In the three oldest MSS, the triad of Christ, Satan, and Inferus (reflecting the shadow-like character of Hades) is transformed into an opposition between Christ and Satan, while Inferus appears as a host of ungodly officials, giants, devils, and trolls. A unique feature of the Old Norse text is two interpolations relating how Christ outwits Satan and turns the inhabitants of hell against him. Triumphantly entering on a white horse and dressed like a king (*cf.* Revelations 19:11–14), Christ tricks Satan into believing that he is no more than a human being, fearful of death, and thus an easy prey. Satan, who changes into the shape of the Miðgarðsormr ("World Serpent"), rises to the bait and tries to swallow Christ, but is immediately defeated by his divine opponent *sem fiskr á øngli eða mús undir tréketti* ("like a fish on a hook or a mouse in a trap"). Christ's stratagem reflects the medieval motif of pious fraud (*pia fraus*), according to which Christ was allowed to use human cunning to defeat his enemy. This motif is also known from the 14th-century Old Icelandic poem *Lilja* (st. 42).

There are references to Christ's descent in several Old Norse sources, primarily in the religious poetry. *Geisli* (composed by the Icelandic skald Einarr Skúlason ca. 1153) states that a multitude of dead rose with Christ (st. 4); in *Leiðarvísan* (second half of the 12th century), it is told that Christ himself bound the ingenious Devil (st. 31); *Líknarbraut* (late 13th or perhaps 14th century) recounts that Christ descended into hell to visit the devils with Satan (st. 22); and, finally, *Lilja* paints a dramatic picture of Christ in combat with Satan (sts. 60–64). The late Icelandic poem *Niðurstigningsvísur* by Jón Arason (1484–1550) gives a free rendering of Christ's harrowing of hell (sts. 24–36), and makes explicit reference to *Gesta salvatoris* (st. 11). A reference to the descent is also found in the apostolic creed contained in the Christian law section of King Magnús's *landslǫg*, where the relevant passage reads *fór niðr til helvítis at leysa þaðan alla sína menn*

("descended into hell, thence to release all his men"). Iconographically, the descent into hell is reflected in the religious art of Norwegian stave churches, for example, the ceiling decorations in Vang and Ål, and altar frontals from Volbu, Eid, and Årdal.

A fragment of an Old Danish poetic rendering of the *Evangelium Nicodemi* survives in SKB A 115 from around 1325, consisting of two leaves. The linguistic form of the poem is Scanian. The home of the anonymous author and the provenance of the MS are thought to be in Lund or its close vicinity. From a number of scribal errors, it is clear that SKB A 115 is a copy of an older MS. Whether this MS was the original or also a copy cannot be ascertained, but it is reasonable to assume that it was written in the same Scanian linguistic form as SKB A 115. The metrical form of the poem is *knittel*. It contains altogether 103 lines of verse, and covers the conclusion of the *Gesta Pilati* and the very beginning of *Descensus Christi ad inferos*. The poem appears to be based on Tischendorf's D-group of texts. Brøndum-Nielsen (1955: 11) suggests that the poem may also to some extent rely on a now-lost German poetic adaptation of the *Evangelium Nicodemi*.

An Old Swedish prose translation of the entire *Evangelium Nicodemi* survives in three MSS: Codex Skokloster 3 4to (now in SRA), SKB A 110 (Codex Oxenstiernianus), and SKB A 3. Codex Skokloster 3 4to (also called "Passionarius") contains the *Old Swedish Legendary*. The MS dates from 1450–1470 and is presumably from Vadstena. The translation of the *Evangelium Nicodemi* most probably did not originally belong to the *Old Swedish Legendary*, since it is not found in the two older MSS of the legendary, SKB A 34 and Upps. C 528. SKB A 110 is from Vadstena; it is not a single book as such, but a collection of six MSS or parts of MSS. The translation of the *Evangelium Nicodemi* is found in the last part in a hand no younger than the beginning of the 15th century. SKB A 3 is a Vadstena MS written in 1502. It originally consisted of three volumes containing a legendary arranged according to the church year; only the first volume has survived.

Ed.: **(a) Latin**: Tischendorf, Constantinus, ed. *Evangelia apocrypha.* 2nd ed. Leipzig: Mendelssohn, 1876, pp. 389–416; Kim, H. C., ed. *The Gospel of Nicodemus. Gesta Salvatoris. Edited from the Codex Einsidlensis, Einsiedeln Stiftsbibliothek, MS 326.* Toronto: Pontifical Institute of Mediaeval Studies, 1973. **(b) Old Norse**: Unger, C. R., ed. *Heilagra manna søgur: Fortællinger og legender om hellige mænd og kvinder.* 2 vols. Christiania [Oslo]: Bentzen, 1877, vol. 2, pp. 1–20 [all medieval MSS]; Finnur Jónsson, ed. *AM 623, 4°: Helgensagaer.* Samfund til udgivelse af gammel nordisk litteratur, 52. Copenhagen: Jørgensen, 1927; Holtsmark, Anne, ed. *A Book of Miracles: MS No. 645 4to of the Arna-Magnæan Collection in the University Library of Copenhagen.* Corpus Codicum Islandicorum Medii Aevi, 12. Copenhagen: Munksgaard, 1938 [facsimile of AM 645 4to]; Haugen, Odd Einar, ed. *Niðrstigningar saga* [forthcoming]. **(c) Old Danish**: Brøndum-Nielsen, Johs., ed. *Et gammeldansk Digt om Christi Opstandelse efter Fragment Stockh. A 115 (c. 1325).* Det Kongelige Danske Videnskabernes Selskab, Historisk-filologiske Meddelelser, vol. 35, no. 1. Copenhagen: Munksgaard, 1955. **(d) Old Swedish**: Klemming, G. E., ed. *Klosterläsning.* Samlingar utgifna af Svenska fornskrift-sällskapet, 22. Stockholm: Norstedt, 1877–78, pp. 375–419 [SKB A 110]; Klemming, G. E., ed. *Svenska medeltidens bibelarbeten.* 2 vols. Samlingar utgifna af Svenska fornskrift-sällskapet, 9. Stockholm: Norstedt, 1848–55, vol. 2, pp. 371–411 [Cod. Skokloster 3 4to]. **Lit.**: **(a) General**: Kroll, Josef. *Gott und Hölle. Der Mythos vom Descensuskampfe.* Leipzig: Teubner, 1932, pp. 83–95; Turner, Ralph V. "*Descendit ad inferos*: Mediaeval

Views on Christ's Descent into Hell and the Salvation of the Ancient Just." *Journal of the History of Ideas* 27 (1966), 173–94; Izydorczyk, Zbigniew. "The Unfamiliar *Evangelium Nicodemi*." *Manuscripta* 33 (1989), 169–91; Wolf, Kirsten. "The Influence of the *Evangelium Nicodemi* on Norse Literature: A Survey" [forthcoming in *Mediaeval Studies*]. **(b) Old Norse**: Turville-Petre, G. *Origins of Icelandic Literature*. Oxford: Clarendon, 1953; rpt. 1967, pp. 126–8; Magnús Már Lárusson. "Um Niðurstigningarsögu." *Skírnir* 129 (1955), 159–68; Aho, Gary Lawrence. "A Comparison of Old English and Old Norse Treatments of Christ's Harrowing of Hell." Diss. University of Oregon, 1966; Aho, Gary. "*Niðrstigningarsaga*: An Old Norse Version of Christ's Harrowing of Hell." *Scandinavian Studies* 41 (1969), 150–9; Marchand, James W. "Leviathan and the Mousetrap in the *Niðrstigningarsaga*." *Scandinavian Studies* 47 (1975), 328–38; Haugen, Odd Einar. "The Evaluation of Stemmatic Evidence: Recension and Revision of *Niðrstigningar saga*." In *The Sixth International Saga Conference 28/7–2/8 1985. Workshop Papers*. 2 vols. Copenhagen: Det arnamagnæanske Institut, 1985, vol. 1, pp. 423–50 [photocopies of papers distributed to participants]; Wolf, Kirsten. "Om en 'tabt' islandsk oversættelse af Nikodemusevangeliet." *Arkiv för nordisk filologi* 107 (1992), 167–79; Haugen, Odd Einar. "Stamtre og tekstlandskap: Studiar i resensjonsmetodikk med grunnlag i *Niðrstigningar saga*." 2 vols. Diss. University of Bergen, 1992. **(c) Old Danish**: Gad, Tue. *Legenden i dansk middelalder*. Copenhagen: Dansk Videnskabs Forlag, 1961. **(d) Old Swedish**: Gödel, Vilhelm. *Sveriges medeltidslitteratur: Proveniens*. Stockholm: Nordiska Bokhandlen, 1916; Jansson, Valter. *Fornsvenska legendariet: handskrifter och språk*. Nordiska texter och undersökningar, 4. Uppsala: Almqvist & Wiksell, 1934.

Odd Einar Haugen

[**See also**: Bible; Christian Poetry; Christian Prose; Einarr Skúlason; *Knittel(vers)*; *Leiðarvísan*; *Lilja*; Old Swedish Legendary]

Niðrstigningar saga *see* Nicodemus, Gospel of

Nitida saga

Nitida saga ("The Saga of Nitida") is a native Icelandic *riddarasaga* composed probably in the 14th century. It is preserved in some sixty-five MSS and fragments, making it one of the most popular sagas. Apart from one leaf (Cod. Stock. Perg. 8vo no. 10 VII) from the late 15th century, the earliest vellum, AM 529 4to, dates from the 16th century. The vast majority of the MSS, however, are paper, dating from the 18th and 19th centuries.

The saga opens with a description of Nitida of France, the most famous maiden-king in the northern hemisphere, whose beauty and intelligence are without peer. Together with Hléskjǫldr, son of her foster-mother, Egidia, queen of Apulia, Nitida journeys to Visio, an island near the edge of the world ruled over by a wise earl named Virgilius. They succeed in stealing a stone vessel, a number of magic stones, apples, and curative herbs before returning to France.

Nitida's hand in marriage is sought, in turn, by Ingi, son of King Hugon of Mikligarðr, Heiðarlogi and Vélogi, both sons of King Soldán of Serkland, and Liforinus, whose sister, Sýjalín, becomes a close friend of Nitida. While Hugon and Liforinus each succeed in abducting Nitida, she is able to escape with the aid of a magic stone. Heiðarlogi and Vélogi mount an attack after being rejected by Nitida, and are subsequently outwitted and killed. Seeking to avenge his sons, Soldán attacks Nitida's army, but Liforinus comes to their aid, killing Soldán and taking the wounded Hléskjǫldr with him to India, where he nurses him back to health. Liforinus returns to France, and Nitida agrees to marry him. Ingi then makes another attempt to win Nitida, but is wounded by

Liforinus and nursed back to health by Sýjalín, whom Ingi now wishes to marry. Liforinus agrees on the condition that Ingi's sister Listalín marry Hléskjǫldr. The saga ends with a description of the triple marriage celebrations, the magnificence of which the narrator says, "it is not easy for a simple tongue on the fringe of the world to describe."

The saga falls squarely within the tradition of maiden-king romances described by Wahlgren (1938), sharing their overall motif structure. One important difference, however, is the character of Nitida herself. *Nitida saga* is the only one of the pre-Reformation maiden-king sagas to bear the name of a female protagonist. Nitida is portrayed throughout as a good and popular ruler; we are told time and time again how the people rejoice when she returns from captivity. She is, more importantly, no virago. Although adverse to the idea of marriage, she in no way humiliates her suitors. When her suitors resort to violence, she is obliged to outwit them. Nor is she herself humiliated. In the end, she agrees to marry Liforinus, because he has succeeded in winning her respect, not because her has broken her.

The narrative is in good prose style with only the occasional flourish; the plot is straightforward and uncluttered by superfluous characters and motifs.

Ed.: Loth, Agnete, ed. "Nitida saga." In *Late Medieval Icelandic Romances*. 5 vols. Editiones Arnamagnæanæ, ser. B, vols. 20–4. Copenhagen: Munksgaard, 1962–65, vol. 5, pp. 3–37. **Tr.**: Fellows Jensen, Gillian. In Loth, Agnete. *Late Medieval Icelandic Romances*, vol. 5, pp. 3–37 [English paraphrase]. **Bib.**: Kalinke, Marianne E., and P. M. Mitchell. *Bibliography of Old Norse–Icelandic Romances*. Islandica, 44. Ithaca and London: Cornell University Press, 1985, pp. 85–6. **Lit.**: Schlauch, Margaret. *Romance in Iceland*. Princeton: Princeton University Press; New York: American-Scandinavian Foundation; London: Allen & Unwin, 1934; rpt. New York: Russell & Russell, 1973; Wahlgren, Erik. *The Maiden King in Iceland*. Chicago: University of Chicago Libraries, 1938 [private publication]; Einar Ólafur Sveinsson. "*Viktors saga ok Blávus*. Sources and Characteristics." In *Viktors saga ok Blávus*. Ed. Jónas Kristjánsson. Riddarasögur, 2. Reykjavik: Handritastofnun Íslands, 1964, pp. cix–ccix; Glauser, Jürg. *Isländische Märchensagas: Studien zur Prosaliteratur im spätmittelalterlichen Island*. Beiträge zur nordischen Philologie, 12. Basel and Frankfurt am Main: Helbing & Lichtenhahn, 1983; Kalinke, Marianne. "Norse Romance (*Riddarasögur*)." In *Old Norse–Icelandic Literature: A Critical Guide*. Ed. Carol J. Clover and John Lindow. Islandica, 45. Ithaca and London: Cornell University Press, 1985, pp. 316–63; Bibire, Paul. "From *riddarasaga* to *lygisaga*: The Norse Response to Romance." In *Les Sagas de Chevaliers (Riddarasögur). Actes de la V* *Conférence Internationale sur les Sagas . . . (Toulon. Juillet 1982)*. Ed. Régis Boyer. Civilisations, 10. Paris: Presses de l'Université de Paris-Sorbonne, 1985, pp. 55–74; Kalinke, Marianne. "The Misogamous Maiden Kings of Icelandic Romance." *Scripta Islandica* 37 (1986), 47–71.

M. J. Driscoll

[**See also**: Old Norse–Icelandic Literature, Foreign Influence on; *Riddarasögur*]

Njáls saga

Njáls saga ("The Saga of Njáll") is the longest and most widely acclaimed of the *Íslendingasögur*. It is a tale of the two friends, Gunnarr and Njáll, and their families in the south of Iceland, but a great number of other people are involved, directly or indirectly, and the action is set in various parts of Iceland, Scandinavia, and the British Isles.

After a gloomy introductory section (chs. 1–18) describing

three failed marriages (one ending in divorce, two with the killing of the husband by the wife's foster-father), the protagonists are introduced: Gunnarr is tall, handsome, and brave, a great fighter and athlete; Njáll has great knowledge of the law, is wise, prescient, and peace loving; both are rich and generous. Their friendship is put to a test when Gunnarr has married the twice-widowed Hallgerðr, and she gets into conflict with Njáll's wife, Bergþóra. This conflict escalates from insults to mutual killings of slaves and free men, until Njáll's sons, led by the grim-faced and quick-tempered Skarpheðinn and egged on by their mother, kill one of Gunnarr's close relatives. After each clash, Gunnarr and Njáll settle the case between themselves. Hallgerðr resents this peacemaking, but can do nothing while Gunnarr lives. Chs. 46–80 describe how Gunnarr's prosperity causes envy among neighboring chieftains, and how he is, against his will, drawn into feuds where he kills a great many adversaries in self-defense. Each time, Njáll succeeds in negotiating compensations until Gunnarr is finally outlawed for three years. He defies the sentence and stays at home, against Njáll's advice, and is killed after a glorious defense. Skarpheðinn and Gunnarr's eldest son, Hǫgni, kill several of his enemies in revenge.

The second part of the saga centers on Njáll's family. In an intermediary sequence, set abroad, the sons of Njáll and Gunnarr's relatives, led by Þráinn, Hallgerðr's son-in-law and ally, reopen their feud, and back in Iceland it escalates until Skarpheðinn kills Þráinn. Njáll succeeds in settling the case, and to ensure peace he fosters Þráinn's son, Hǫskuldr, raising him in his own spirit and making him a chieftain superior to others in the two families.

In these years, Iceland has been christianized, but envy and hatred have not been uprooted, and Mǫrðr, a sly and smooth-tongued chieftain, who previously turned people against Gunnarr, now succeeds in making Njáll's sons mistrust their foster-brother Hǫskuldr, and they slay him cruelly. This is a heavy blow to Njáll. He attempts to reconcile his sons with Hǫskuldr's relatives but fails. Realizing at last that his struggle against evil is in vain, he goes with open eyes to his death, when he and his wife, his sons, and a grandson are burned and killed in their home. This event, seen as tragic even by the leader of the attackers, is a magnificent climax of the whole saga. The repercussions are great and seem to have national significance when a great battle breaks out at the Alþingi. However, good men succeed in making the relatives accept compensation, all but the son-in-law Kári, who had managed to escape from the burning farmhouse. Alone, he traces the burners and kills them one after the other inside and outside Iceland. In the end, he is reconciled with the leader of the burners, Flosi.

The numerous threads of this complex narrative are skillfully woven into a picture that gives the impression of an integrated whole, although many details stand out and demand attention in their own right. The scope of the saga is exceptional, with the long introduction, two great feud stories, each ending in an impressive climax with the killing of the protagonist, and then a long final movement of revenge incorporating a great battle in Ireland (Clontarf, A.D. 1014). To link the strands together, the author uses several kinds of foreshadowing along with other narrative devices to create the impression of a coherent and fatal chain of events.

Njáls saga surpasses other sagas in the number and variety of clearly, and often humorously, delineated characters. Even Gunnarr, who comes close to being a "cliché," the blond hero, is individualized by his emotionally charged and vivid utterances about his aversion to killing and about his reasons for staying at home when he has been outlawed. The unheroic but wise and sometimes cunning Njáll forms a contrast to him, as does Skarpheðinn, who, through his giant stature, ugly grin, and witty and sarcastic comments, is one of the most memorable figures in the saga, keeping his secrets to his death in the fire. The mistresses of these houses, Hallgerðr and Bergþóra, are no less memorable. Neither of them is faultless, and Hallgerðr is indeed one of the villains, but they are proud and active women, not afraid to play their own game. Sexuality, seen as a dangerous and even destructive force, is here more openly dealt with than in most or all sagas.

The style of Njáls saga is simple at first sight, but has in fact great variation. As a rule, summary of events is paratactic with a relatively high frequency of formulaic expressions, especially at the beginning and ending of the chapters and at other important junctures. Authorial bias is manifest in the presentation of characters, and it is often expressed through ironic comments, for example, "Gunnarr's sons, Hǫgni and Grani, were fully grown by this time. They were men of very different natures; Grani took after his mother, but Hǫgni was a fine man" (ch. 75). The stylistic versatility of the saga appears most vividly in the dialogue, which ranges from brief comments of epigrammatic wit and compression to personal statements illuminating the whole drama, like Njáll's seemingly contradictory statements in the fire. He consoles his people by saying: "Be of good heart and speak no words of fear, for this is just a passing storm, and it will be long before another like it comes. Put your faith in the mercy of God, for He will not let us burn both in this world and in the next." But his final statement belongs to the world he cannot renounce, although he has understood its limitations. Invited by Flosi to leave his sons and save himself, he answers: "I have no wish to go outside . . . for I am an old man and ill equipped to avenge my sons; and I do not want to live in shame" (ch. 129).

The presence of an author is more strongly felt in Njáls saga than in most other sagas, and his engagement in the fate of the characters and, above all, in Njáll's struggle for peace is unmistakable. It can be deduced from Njáll's final statements, quoted above, that the values inspiring the author form no harmonious hierarchy. The author is strongly tied to the basic values of the old and vanishing society, as he sees it, with its ideas of family honor and solidarity. He desperately wants peace and harmony, but accepts that in extreme cases honor can be preserved only by blood revenge. In the new faith, Njáll and the author see hope for the individual, and this hope is symbolized by the contrasting images we get of the two friends after their death: the heathen Gunnarr sits in his mound reciting poetry, stubbornly confirming the pride that led to his fall, a sad and gloomy picture. Njáll's death is even more tragic, but one of the chieftains most active in getting Iceland christianized says about his corpse: "Njáll's countenance and body appear to have a radiance that I have never seen on a dead man before" (ch. 132).

Whoever wrote Njáls saga must have been thoroughly versed in the narrative traditions of his age, both oral and literary. It seems overwhelmingly likely that tales were told about Gunnarr and Njáll, about whose existence there is no doubt, before the saga was written, and the author may well have been one of the storytellers. But it is also obvious that the saga is the work of an author who, with much deliberation and artistic skill, created a great literary work from material now for the most part unavailable.

References to law and legal practice in the saga show influence from laws introduced in Iceland in 1271. The oldest MS and fragments of MSS are dated to around 1300. These and other arguments have been used to date the saga to the years 1275–1290. There are almost twenty MSS from the Middle Ages, and a great many paper MSS from the post-Reformation era. This confirms the fact that *Njáls saga* has always been one of the most popular of the *Íslendingasögur*. It was first published in Copenhagen in 1772, and in the 19th century it was translated into Latin and several European languages.

Ed:. Konráð Gíslason *et al.*, eds. *Njála, udgivet efter gamle Håndskrifter.* 2 vols. Copenhagen: Gyldendal, 1879–96; Einar Ól. Sveinsson, ed. *Brennu-Njáls saga.* Íslenzk fornrit, 12. Reykjavik: Hið íslenzka fornritafélag, 1954; Jón Helgason, ed. *Njáls saga: The Arnamagnæan Manuscript 468, 4°* (*Reykjabók).* Manuscripta Islandica, 6. Copenhagen: Munksgaard, 1962 [facsimile]. **Tr.**: Magnus Magnusson and Hermann Pálsson, trans. *Njal's saga.* Harmondsworth: Penguin, 1960. **Lit.**: Finnur Jónsson. "Om Njála." *Aarbøger for nordisk Oldkyndighed og Historie* 19.2 (1904), 89–166; Einar Ól. Sveinsson. *Um Njálu* 1. Reykjavik: Menningarsjóður, 1933; Einar Ól. Sveinsson. *Á Njálsbúð. Bók um mikið listaverk.* Reykjavik: Hið íslenzka bókmenntafélag, 1943; Einar Ól. Sveinsson. *Studies in the Manuscript Tradition of Njáls saga.* Studia Islandica, 13. Reykjavik: Leiftur, 1953; Maxwell, I. R. "Pattern in *Njáls saga.*" *Saga-Book of the Viking Society* 15 (1957–61), 17–47; Fox, Denton. "*Njáls saga* and the Western Literary Tradition." *Comparative Literature* 15 (1963), 289–310; Saxon, Anne Martha. "Unity and Narrative Technique in the *Brennu-Njáls saga.*" Diss. University of California, Berkeley, 1964; Heimir Pálsson. "Rittengsl Laxdælu og Njálu." *Mímir* 6 (1967), 5–16; Greenway, John L. "The Wisdom of Njál: The Representation of Reality in the Family Sagas." *Mosaic* 4.2 (1970), 15–26; Lönnroth, Lars. "Hetjurnar líta bleika akra. Athuganir á Njáls sögu og Alexanders sögu." *Skírnir* 144 (1970), 12–30; Allen, Richard F. *Fire and Iron: Critical Approaches to Njáls saga.* Pittsburgh: Pittsburgh University Press, 1971; Einar Ól. Sveinsson. *Njáls saga: A Literary Masterpiece.* Ed. and trans. Paul Schach, with an introduction by E. O. G. Turville-Petre. Lincoln: University of Nebraska Press, 1971; Bolton, W. F. "The *Njála* Narrator and the Picture Plans." *Scandinavian Studies* 44 (1972), 186–209; Clover, Carol. "*Óláfs saga helga, Runzivals þáttr,* and *Njáls saga*: A Structural Comparison." Diss. University of California, Berkeley, 1972; Heimir Pálsson. "Hjónin á Hlíðarenda." *Skírnir* 146 (1972), 147–58; Rulfs, Jane Lee. "Narrative Techniques in *Njáls saga.*" Diss. Rice University, 1974; Lönnroth, Lars. "Structural Divisions in the *Njála* Manuscripts." *Arkiv för nordisk filologi* 90 (1975), 49–79; Lönnroth, Lars. *Njáls saga: A Critical Introduction.* Berkeley, Los Angeles, and London: University of California Press, 1976; Nanna Ólafsdóttir. "Nokkur menningarsöguleg dæmi úr Njálu." *Skírnir* 151 (1977), 59–72; Kress, Helga. "Manndom og misogyni: Noen refleksjoner omkring kvinnesynet i Njáls saga." *Gardar* 10 (1979), 35–51; Dronke, Ursula. *The Role of Sexual Themes in Njáls saga.* The Dorothea Coke Memorial Lecture. London: Viking Society for Northern Research, 1981; Berger, Alan John. "The Meaning of Njáls saga." *Scandinavistik* 11 (1981), 1–8; Hermann Pálsson. "Eftir Njálsbrennu." *Andvari* n.s. 25 (1983), 47–50; Hermann Pálsson. *Uppruni Njálu og hugmyndir.* Reykjavik: Menningarsjóður, 1984.

Vésteinn Ólason

[See also: *Darraðarljóð*; *Íslendingasögur*; Women in Sagas]

Nóregs konunga tal *see* Fagrskinna

Norman Literature, Scandinavian Influence on.
Scandinavian influence can be found in several works written by authors in Normandy in the 11th century. It can be traced in stories about the Viking past of Normandy, in accounts of contemporary events concerning Scandinavia or persons coming from northern Europe, and in legends originating from Scandinavian or Anglo-Scandinavian sources. In about the year 1000, the poet Garnier of Rouen wrote a Latin satire against the Irish poet Moriuth. The Irishman and his wife had been captured by the Vikings and taken away separately. After many adventures, the poet finally was reunited with his wife in Normandy after the intercession of the Duchess Gunnor, herself of Danish origin. According to Garnier, the Irish poet consulted the pagan gods three times during his long search for his wife: he consulted the intestines of a woodpecker, sacrificed a young girl, and invoked the help of the gods for a third time. These pagan rituals are strongly reminiscent of Viking ceremonial practices. The poem itself may well be related to the *flyting*, a form of dialogue in Norse and Irish vernacular literature.

Dudo of St.-Quentin (d. after 1015) wrote the first history of the Viking settlement and early dukes of Normandy, in Latin, *De moribus et actis primorum normaniæ ducum.* Dudo included passages on pagan sacrificial rituals similar to the ones Garnier described. He wrote about Vikings sacrificing human blood to their war-god Þórr, and about their priest consulting the intestines of an ox to know beforehand the outcome of the next Viking raid. He also depicts other Scandinavian customs. Rollo, the first Viking leader of Normandy, divided land among his followers by way of the *funiculus* (a rope). He mentions Rollo's trick of scaring off an attack of Franks near Chartres by using animal carcasses. He also describes how Rollo's son, William Longsword, and thirty of his followers acted like berserks while taking an oath with a great deal of noise and performing the Scandinavian *vápnatak* ("weapon taking"). He may have used an eyewitness account for his story of the attack on Lisbon in 966 by pagan Vikings expelled from Normandy.

During the third quarter of the 11th century, the Norman historians writing about the Norman Conquest of England in 1066 included Scandinavian material. Bishop Guy of Amiens, the author of the *Carmen de Hastingae proelio,* describes the burial of King Harold Godwinsson of England by Duke William of Normandy as a purely Viking funeral. The duke ordered that Harald's body be buried under a heap of stones on top of a cliff as *custos littoris et pelagi* ("guardian of the shore and the sea"). It has been suggested that the burial mound (the heap of stones) symbolizes the king's mound, because according to the *Carmen* the Norman duke becomes king at the same spot and at the same moment when his predecessor was buried. William of Poitiers, the biographer of William the Conquerer, who wrote around the years 1073–1077, refers to the same story: "It is said by way of mockery that the duke would rather install him [Harald] as guardian of the shore and sea" than hand him over for burial by his mother.

The author most influenced by Scandinavian tradition is William of Jumièges, who wrote a continuation of Dudo of St.-Quentin's history of the dukes of Normandy around 1060–1070. In the first book of *Gesta Normannorum ducum,* concerning the Viking invasions of Normandy, William gives prominence to the Anglo-Scandinavian Bjǫrn Ironside, son of King Lothbroc. The king forced his son Bjǫrn into exile together with his tutor, Hastingus, and a multitude of young men. Bjǫrn acquired his nickname "Ironside" because of his invulnerability, which the historian William explains as follows: "And therefore he was called Ironside, because when his shield did not protect him and when he stood unarmed in the battlefield, he was invulnerable, despised whatever force of arms, for his mother had him infected with very strong magic poison." According to William, Bjǫrn and Hastingus ravaged France for thirty years and then conquered the Italian city of Luni near Pisa, thinking it was Rome. Bjǫrn returned to the North, suffered shipwreck near England, then went to Frisia, where he died. Hastingus returned independently to Chartres.

Bjǫrn Ironside's name is first mentioned by William of Jumièges, and thereafter (ca. 1145) in the skaldic poem *Háttalykill.* Bjǫrn's Mediterranean trip shows striking resemblances to the *Fragmentary Annals* (Ireland, mid-11th century). Bjǫrn's magic invulnerability is a Scandinavian saga motif, and Frisia in connection with Lothbroc's sons was known in Jumièges as well as in Northumbria from the 10th century onward.

William of Jumièges is the first authority to mention Lothbroc, who may be the legendary Ragnarr loðbrók, and therefore his story is an important stage in the development of the famous Scandinavian saga. Other written sources mentioning the name Lothbroc are Adam of Bremen's *Gesta Hammaburgensis ecclesiae pontificum* (Hamburg, ca. 1075), the *Annals of St. Neots* (East Anglia, early 12th century), and Ari Þorgilsson's *Íslendingabók* (ca. 1122–1133), the first to combine the names Ragnarr and Lothbroc. This evidence, combined with other elements, suggests that William of Jumièges had access to an (Anglo-)Scandinavian source.

More passages in the *Gesta Normannorum ducum* show Scandinavian influence. The mysterious *Haigroldus rex Daciae,* mentioned by Dudo, is said to have come from Denmark to Normandy to assist Richard I in his struggle against the French king. He is identified by William of Jumièges as King Harald (Bluetooth) of Denmark (941–988) in Book 4. Both Dudo and William of Jumièges mistook the temporary Viking leader of Bayeux in about 845 for his royal contemporary namesake Harald Bluetooth. William adds that King Harald had been expelled from Denmark by his son Sven. Two other sources mention this story: the *Encomium Emmae* (ca. 1040–1041) and Adam of Bremen's *Gesta Hammaburgensis.* Considering the fact that only a mainly English source like the *Encomium* and a German source like Adam, who got his information directly from King Sven's grandson, knew about the dissension between Harald and Sven, William of Jumièges must have taken his information from an (Anglo-)Scandinavian source.

William is the only non-Scandinavian source to pay attention to the early career of Óláfr the Viking, the later king and martyr of Norway (d. 1030). The account in *Gesta Normannorum ducum* shows a striking resemblance to the poetry of Óláfr's skald Sighvatr, not only as far as the attack on Dol in Brittany is concerned, but also in that William and Sighvatr agree that Óláfr had assisted Knud (Cnut) the Great in his struggle to obtain the throne of England after his father died in 1014. Sighvatr visited Normandy in 1025–1026, and it is very likely that he imported the Norse version of Óláfr's early Viking career that William subsequently wrote down (Books 4–5). With regard to the marriage in 1017 of King Knud and Emma, widow of King Æthelred of England and daughter of Duke Richard I of Normandy, William of Jumièges describes the union as a Scandinavian marriage by seizure. The Christian ceremony followed a few days later (Book 5). William's date is incorrect, but the tradition he represents is an interesting example of Scandinavian influence in Normandy. Another example may be the blood-brotherhood relationship depicted in *Gesta Normannorum ducum* among Duke Robert the Magnificent, Ed-

ward (later the Confessor), and Alfred during their exile in Normandy (1013–1036/40; Book 6).

Finally, the B-redaction of *Gesta Normannorum ducum,* written around 1100, contains the legendary story that Duke Robert the Magnificent had visited the Byzantine emperor in 1035 (Book 6). The story contains three motifs that have long been regarded as belonging to a common Norman-Scandinavian literary stock. They are the mule with the golden horseshoes, the ban on buying or selling firewood, and the use of walnuts as fuel. Together or separately, these motifs occur in stories about Normans or Scandinavians who traveled to southern Italy or Byzantium, the most famous of whom are Duke Robert of Normandy, Haraldr harðráði ("hard-ruler") Sigurðarson of Norway, and the Norse Sigurðr Jórsalafari ("crusader") Magnússon.

Ed.: Lair, Jules, ed. *Dudonis Sancti Quentini. De moribus sue actis primorum Normanniae ducum.* Mémoires de la Société des Antiquaires de Normandie, 23. Caen: Le Blanc-Hardel, 1865; Omont, H., ed. "Satire de Garnier de Rouen contre le poète Moriuth (Xe–XIe siècle)." *Annuaire-Bulletin de la Société de l'histoire de France* 21 (1891), 193–210; Foreville, Raymonde, ed. *Guillaume de Poitiers. Histoire de Guillaume le Conquérant.* Paris: Les Belles Lettres, 1952; Morton, C., and H. Muntz, eds. *The "Carmen de Hastingæ Proelio" of Guy, Bishop of Amiens.* Oxford: Oxford University Press, 1972. **Tr.**: See Foreville; Morton and Muntz [above]. **Lit.**: Musset, L. "Le satirists Garnier de Rouen et son milieu (début du XIe siècle)." *Revue du Moyen Age Latin* 10 (1954), 237–67; Musset, L. "L'image de la Scandinavie dans les oeuvres Normandes de la période ducale (911–1204)." In *Les relations littéraires Franco-Scandinavies au Moyen Age.* Paris: Bibliothèque de la Faculté de Philosophie et Lettres de l'Université de Liège, 1975, vol. 208, pp. 193–215; Van Houts, E. M. C. "Scandinavian Influence in Norman Literature." In *Anglo-Norman Studies: Proceedings of the Battle Conference* 6 (1983). Ed. R. Allen Brown. Woodbridge: Boydell and Brewer; Wolfeboro: Longwood, 1984, pp. 107–21.

Elisabeth M. C. van Houts

[**See also**: Dudo of St.-Quentin: *De moribus et actis primorum normanniæ ducum*; France, Norse in; William of Jumièges: *Gesta Normannorum ducum*]

Nornagests þáttr ("The Tale of Nornagestr") is an anonymous *fornaldarsaga* written probably in the early 14th century, and incorporated into one of the earliest versions of the *Óláfs saga Tryggvasonar.* The two chief MSS containing the þáttr are *Flateyjarbók,* AM 62 fol., and GkS 2845 4to. The þáttr contains two prose sections from the *Prose Edda,* and the poems *Reginsmál* and *Helreið Brynhildar,* along with their prose introductions. The þáttr also includes reference to a now-lost *Sigurðar saga.* Verbal agreements between the þáttr and the *Poetic Edda* confirm that that author relied on a MS closely related to the *Codex Regius.*

The tale is structured as a frame story. A very old man, Gestr, appears at the royal Norwegian court of Óláfr Tryggvason and asks for shelter for the night. This Gestr ("guest") entertains the court with stories from the Scandinavian past. When the king asks him about his faith, he answers that he was marked with the sign of the cross in Denmark, but that he has not yet been baptized. Óláfr encourages him to relate his 300-year life story. Nornagestr tells about all the known rulers in the Scandinavian past whom he visited. Gestr's old age is attributed to the three norns, who prophesied his future at his birth (cf. his name, Norn). The youngest norn felt herself slighted, and predicted that he should live no longer than the candle burned that was lit beside the cradle. But, in fact, this fate resulted in a long life, for another older sibyl immediately put out the candle and preserved it unburned. Gestr now tells Óláfr that he came to the Norwegian court because he had heard many favorable things about Óláfr. At the king's instigation, Gestr is baptized and lights his candle. As the candle goes out, the old man dies.

The focus of the *þáttr* is the praise of Christianity, which is personified through Óláfr Tryggvason. *Nornagests þáttr* can thus be placed alongside the other *þættir* within *Óláfs saga Tryggvasonar* that present the king as advocate and teacher of the new faith, and that place his political function in the background.

Ed.: Rafn, C. C., ed. *Fornaldar sögur Nordrlanda*. 3 vols. Copenhagen: Popp, 1829–30, vol. 1, pp. 311–42; Guðbrandr Vigfússon and C. R. Unger, eds. *Flateyjarbók: En Samling af norske Konge-Sagaer med indskudte mindre Fortællinger om Begivenheder i og udenfor Norge samt Annaler*. 3 vols. Christiania [Oslo]: Malling, 1860–68, vol. 1, pp. 346–59; Bugge, Sophus, ed. "Söguþáttr af Norna-Gesti." In his *Norröne skrifter af sagnhistorisk indhold*. Christiania [Oslo]: Det norske Oldskriftselskab, 1864, pp. 45–79; Wilken, Ernst, ed. *Die prosaische Edda im Auszuge nebst Völsungasaga und Norna-Gests-þáttr*. Paderborn: Schöningh, 1912, pp. 235–61; Guðni Jónsson, ed. *Fornaldar sögur Norðurlanda*. 4 vols. Akureyri: Íslendingasagnaútgáfan, 1954, vol. 1, pp. 305–35; Sigurður Nordal et al., eds. *Flateyjarbók*. 4 vols. Akranes: Flateyjarútgáfan, 1944–45, vol. 1, pp. 384–98. **Tr.**: Kershaw, Nora, trans. *Stories and Ballads of the Far Past*. Cambridge: Cambridge University Press, 1921, pp. 14–37. **Lit.**: Hollander, Lee M. "Notes on the *Nornagests þáttr*." *Scandinavian Studies* 3 (1916), 105–11; Panzer, Friedrich. "Zur Erzählung von Nornagest." In *Vom Werden des deutschen Geistes. Festgabe Gustav Ehrismann*. Ed. Paul Merker and W. Stammler. Berlin and Leipzig: de Gruyter, 1925, pp. 27–34; Jónas Kristjánsson. *Eddas and Sagas: Iceland's Medieval Literature*. Trans. Peter Foote. Reykjavik: Hið íslenska bókmenntafélag, 1988, pp. 353 ff. *et passim*; Würth, Stefanie. *Elemente des Erzählens: Die þættir der Flateyjarbók*. Beiträge zur nordischen Philologie, 20. Basel and Frankfurt am Main: Helbing & Lichtenhahn, 1991.

Stefanie Würth

[See also: *Codex Regius; Flateyjarbók; Fornaldarsögur; Helreið Brynhildar; Óláfs saga Tryggvasonar; Reginsmál* and *Fáfnismál; Snorra Edda; Þáttr*]

Norns *see* **Supernatural Beings**

Norway. The first clear mention of Norway and its inhabitants occurs around 890 in the geographical survey prefacing King Alfred's Old English translation of Paulus Orosius's *Historiarum adversum paganos*, which includes a carefully recorded account of the voyages of the Norwegian Ohthere (Óttarr). He told the king "that he lived northernmost of all Northmen." From his home, he sailed southward along "the land of the Northmen," which he also called *Norðweg*, the "north way." The name is commonly thought to allude to the long and mostly protected sailing route that united Norwegian territory at a time when land, with its mountains and forests, tended to divide.

Óttarr describes Norway as a long and narrow stretch of territory extending from the land of the "Finns" or Lapps in the north (present-day Finnmark) to Denmark (*Denamearc*) in the

south. East of Norway, Óttarr knew of the land of the Swedes, *Sweóland*, and farther north *Cwéna land*, the land of the West Finnish *Cwénas* (Old Norse *kvænir*). Norway thus enters history in a clear Scandinavian context. It appears that the country comprised most of its present territory, and that Óttarr regarded its inhabitants as a separate ethnic group, the Norsemen or Norwegians. At that time, the political unification of the country under a single monarch had as yet barely started, so that the idea of a Norway settled by Norwegians must have been rooted in more general geographic and sociocultural features.

Extensive forests separated southeastern Norway from Swedish settlements to the east. Farther north, the long mountain range called "the Keel" (Old Norse *Kjolrinn*, Norwegian *Kjølen*) took over as a natural border. There was closer contact with Danish-settled areas to the south, across the water and along the coast of present West Sweden, which to Óttarr formed part of Denmark. In the Viking Age and the early Christian period, the Danes often claimed, and sometimes had political supremacy over the Víkin or Oslofjord area. Still, in Óttarr's account most of this area was apparently thought to be Norwegian territory, including the port of Skíringssalr or Kaupang west of the mouth of the Oslofjord.

Inside Norway, communications at sea brought people from various parts of the country together. From the fjords cutting inland, traffic and settlement would follow river valleys and lakes toward higher ground, and people would traverse high plateaus and mountain passes between the main regions. This network of communications favored barter between areas of different natural and economic conditions, and helped to forge social links between regions. The Norsemen of Óttarr's days were also bound together by the cult of the same Nordic deities and by the common Old Norse language, which was characterized by traits of its own as compared with Danish and Swedish dialects.

More distinct Norwegian boundaries were a consequence of the long medieval process of political unification coming to an end in the 13th century. The Old Norse kingdom then included present Norway and the later Swedish provinces of Jämtland and Härjedalen to the east and Bohuslän to the south. South of Bohuslän, the three kingdoms of Scandinavia converged at the mouth of the Göta River. In the early 1260s, the Norse-speaking inhabitants of Iceland and Greenland placed themselves under the Norwegian Crown. Farther south, the Western Isles from the Faroes to the Hebrides and Isle of Man had, like Iceland, been settled from Norway in the Viking Age and had later been made tributary territories of the Norwegian kingdom. The Hebrides and Isle of Man were ceded to Scotland in 1266, while farther north Norwegian dominion continued. This was the total extension of the Norwegian realm until the Orkneys and Shetland were pledged to the Scottish king in 1468–1469. Formally, the rest of the "tributary lands" west over sea belonged to Norway past the end of the Middle Ages.

Settlement and population. Medieval Norway was a predominantly agrarian society in which towns were few and scattered, and in which the agricultural population was settled on individual farms. Over the years, these farms were divided into varying numbers of holdings, that is to say, units of production run by individual households, usually families. In the coastal districts from South to North Norway, the houses of the various holdings of a divided farm would often stay clustered together in a hamlet-like complex. But regular villages in the common European sense did not exist in medieval Norway. No more fundamental socioeconomic dividing line can be drawn through medieval Scandinavia than the one between the areas of individual farms, mainly to the north and west, in Norway, Iceland, and peripheral parts of Sweden, and the best agricultural regions with their village settlement to the south and east, in Central and South Sweden and most of Denmark. In the areas first mentioned, large, compact estates were never feasible, and society in general was less aristocratic than in the village regions.

The fact that the rural population of Norway was attached to single farms, whose names and property boundaries have to a large degree been preserved up to the present day, makes it possible to measure the volume of settlement in the form of a number of farms with their own names at given times, as they are indicated by datable place-names and other information in both contemporary and later sources.

From the Viking Age to the first half of the 14th century, there was a considerable extension of agrarian settlement. In the oldest and best agricultural areas, settlement became denser through the increasing division of farms and the exploitation of less accessible resources. At the same time, new farms and whole farm districts were cleared in less favorable or central areas; there was a general expansion of settlement toward the interior, onto higher ground, and farther north. This process can only be explained as connected with a steady increase in population. The evidence suggests that the increase was greater in East Norway, where the reserves of agricultural land were most extensive. In the southern and western coastal districts, the growing population found an outlet through the Viking colonization of the Atlantic isles to the west and even part of the British Isles. When this outlet had been closed, a particularly extensive division of farms took place in those districts.

The total number of named farms in Norway has been estimated at about 36,500 in the first half of the 14th century. It cannot be ascertained how far the division of those farms into holdings had progressed by this time. Nor do contemporary sources provide a solid basis for estimating the average number of persons per holding. These and other uncertainties make it difficult to produce a reliable estimate of Norway's total population at the end of the high Middle Ages more precise than somewhere between 275,000 and 550,000, including the provinces later ceded to Sweden. The population was probably less than half of the population of the contemporary Danish kingdom and considerably less than that of the kingdom of Sweden.

As a consequence of the population crisis of the latter half of the 14th century, the number of farms in Norway may have been reduced by one half to two-thirds. The number of holdings may have gone down to one third. This would suggest a loss of at least half of the high-medieval population. The consequent contraction of agrarian settlement was, to a large extent, the reverse process of the earlier expansion. Gradually, the population was concentrated in the best and most central agricultural districts and, within each district, on the best farms. The coastal districts of West and North Norway did, however, keep more of their population than the inland districts of the same regions, and there was even a clear expansion of Norwegian settlement northward and eastward along the coast of Troms and Finnmark, the northernmost areas of present Norway. The increased economic importance of fishing is the obvious explanation for the last development. In general, agrarian settlement and population do not show any signs of renewed growth until the second half of the 15th century or, over large parts of the country, until the first half of the 16th century.

Land tenure and social structure. Agriculture in the form of mixed farming was the dominant means of subsistence in medieval Norway, although it must be stressed that subsidiary economic activities like fishing, hunting, forestry, and the extraction of bog iron were important for most farmers. Fishing, above all, made an indispensable contribution to diet and economy in the coastal districts to the north and west. Since agricultural land was by far the most important means of production, the ownership of such land and the right to use it were decisive in shaping the structure of medieval Norwegian society.

By the early 14th century, the majority of Norwegian peasants were tenants or part-tenants of clerical or lay landowners. Only a minority belonged to the class of peasants who held their land by óðal right, as inherited family land. Such freemen were called hauldar (sing. hauldr) in the old provincial codes of West Norway and Trøndelag, and in the National Code of 1274. Most of the peasants had the lower legal status of bóndi, that is to say, a person who rented or had, at the most, bought his land.

At this time, the distribution of land in terms of value has been roughly estimated as follows: 7 percent for the Crown, 20 percent for the lay aristocracy, 40 percent for the Church, and 33 percent for freeholding peasants and burghers. These percentages do not, however, allow the simple conclusion that one third of Norwegian peasants were freeholders. Some well-to-do peasants had acquired small collections of farms and holdings that would be cultivated by other peasants as their tenants. And there had developed an extensive part-ownership of farms and holdings, not least through the rules of inheritance and marriage settlement, so that many small parcels of land would be rented by peasants to peasants. Consequently, many peasants would work their holdings partly as freeholders and partly as tenants. Quite a few would, in addition, be the owners of inherited or otherwise acquired parts of land rented by other peasants.

There is no solid evidence for when and how this pattern of landownership came about. Over the last fifty years, an influential school of materialist historians have postulated a society of free, equal farmers as the point of departure for Norwegian social history. In the course of the high Middle Ages, from the 11th or 12th to the 13th century, the majority of peasants were reduced from being freeholders to tenants of clerical and lay landowners. This development created a lay and clerical aristocracy that separated itself from the broad mass of the population and ruled the people through the state and the Church. Fundamentally, Crown and Church were the instruments of this aristocracy, and the monarchical and ecclesiastical ideologies served its needs. The politico-ideological superstructure of society in its turn influenced the relations of production. By increasing the public burdens on the people, the Crown and the Church weakened the peasantry and accelerated the transition from a freeholding to a tenancy system.

The materialist view took issue with an older approach that had argued that the tenancy system had developed quite far as early as the prehistoric period, or at the latest in the early Christian period, before the middle of the 12th century. A core of the tenancy system appears to have existed in the Viking Age or the early Christian period. Nor is there any empirical basis for the belief that the great mass of Norwegian peasants were freeholders and that society was generally less aristocratic in an earlier period. In the Viking Age and early Christian period, local aristocratic families commanded the support of peasants not only by means of traditional and personal loyalties and ability to protect and reward followers, but probably also in part by means of the control landowners could exercise over tenants.

There is no doubt that the tenancy system became increasingly important in the following period, not least through the growth of part-ownership of farms and holdings. Consequently, the proportion of freeholders was reduced. But it must be stressed that the striking growth of church land from nil at the start of the missionary period to about 40 percent in the first half of the 14th century was due largely to royal and aristocratic donations of land that was probably worked in advance by tenants. In other words, a great deal of what has been regarded as growth of the tenancy system as such may actually have been the transfer and reorganization of tenant holdings.

In the high Middle Ages, the centralization of Church and monarchy produced a development away from an old clan aristocracy, whose power base was overwhelmingly local, toward a service aristocracy that based its social position mainly in the government of state and Church. Still, high-medieval Norway was not a particularly aristocratic society compared with the neighboring Scandinavian kingdoms and most of the rest of Europe. Since the agricultural resources of the country were scarce and scattered, there were few really great landholders. The clergy and royal service aristocracy were certainly placed well above ordinary people in wealth and status, but the boundary between these two groups and peasant society was a fluid one, and both groups were recruited from the peasantry. In general, the clerical and lay aristocracy lacked the private economic power base that would have made it strong enough in number and influence to strive for independent control of society.

On the other hand, the situation of the Norwegian tenant of the Middle Ages was, in European terms, quite favorable. Not only would tenants of Crown, Church, and aristocracy farm the best land of the country, so that they would not rarely be better off than many freeholders, the tenant was also, in legal terms, a free man who worked the soil he leased on a contract basis. The landowner exercised no private jurisdiction over him, he was not obliged to perform labor services, and he was not tied to the soil. In other words, there was no serfdom or villeinage in Norway. Regular slavery had largely ebbed away by the late 12th century, probably not least for economic reasons. The growth of population led to increased demand for agricultural land, and such land could be leased at a better profit than would derive from cultivation by means of slave labor. This circumstance may have led to emancipation of slaves as well as growth of the tenancy system.

The evidence suggests that the land rent was a relatively heavy burden at the end of the high Middle Ages, constituting perhaps one fifth to one sixth of the yield. Moreover, in some districts the demand for land made it possible to extract payments over and above the rent. The law codes of the 12th and 13th centuries refer to short leases (one to three years), but they also open the way for longer contracts. Most of the written contracts that have survived before 1350 are leases for life, and some of them even provide for the right of the son to inherit the lease from his father. Leases of this type appear to represent the normal practice of central church institutions, and they were used by other landholders as well. To the degree that shorter leases were applied, they would normally be prolonged as long as the tenant and his heirs fulfilled their basic economic obligations.

As a consequence of the catastrophic decline of population in the late Middle Ages, land became plentiful. Land rents may on average have dropped to one fourth or one fifth of what they had been before the Black Death. At this low rent, there was more and better land for each tenant. Thus, the standard of living of the average peasant must have been considerably higher than it had been before the middle of the 14th century. In economic terms, the crisis of the late Middle Ages was a crisis for the recipients of land rents, taxes, and other dues from the agrarian population, that is, the Crown, the Church, and private landlords. The high aristocracy was strongly reduced in number and became more clearly separated from the rest of the population as a birth aristocracy. This decline had partly to do with the fact that royal service could no longer sustain an important low aristocracy. Thus, society below a few great families became more egalitarian than before.

Political unification. In Óttarr's days, there was as yet no political organization for more than parts of Norway. Territorial unification under one monarchy started seriously with King Haraldr hárfagri ("fair-hair") Hálfdanarson in the decades around 900. It was achieved by two main stages of military struggle with a more peaceful period in between.

The first stage came to an end shortly after the middle of the 11th century. Throughout most of this phase, a monarchy with its chief power base in the coastal region of West Norway tried to gain a more permanent foothold in other parts of the country as well. A king like Óláfr Haraldsson (r. 1015/6–1028), the later St. Óláfr, managed to make his power felt over most of Norwegian territory. Still, his reign was only an episode in a period when Danish power was paramount in southeastern Norway. Not until the disintegration of the Danish North Sea empire after the death of Knud (Cnut) the Great in 1035 did it become possible for Norwegian monarchs to control the whole of Norway more permanently. Under Magnús I Óláfsson (r. 1035–1047) and Haraldr III harðráði ("hard-ruler") Sigurðarson (r. 1046–1066), Norwegian territory was secured southward through Bohuslän to the mouth of the Göta River. And the inland agricultural regions of East Norway, called Upplǫnd (Uplands), and Trøndelag were brought under more effective royal rule.

A period of comparative stability and peace followed. But frequent reigns of two or three joint rulers, commanding support from different regions and interest groups, indicate that political unity was far from achieved.

In the 1130s began a century of wars of succession, termed "the civil wars" by posterity. This was the second stage of the unification struggle, ending in victory for the kings of the line of Sverrir Sigurðarson (r. 1177–1202). The civil wars ebbed in the 1220s under Sverrir's grandson, Hákon IV Hákonarson (r. 1217–1263). The territorial divisions and social and political tensions that had for so long provided support for rival pretenders and their parties were now finally overcome by a national system of government.

One cornerstone of this system was the incorporation of the magnates and leading freemen of the country in the royal *hirð* or retinue as members of a royal service aristocracy. As a consequence of this process, *hirð* membership became the criterion of lay aristocratic status. During the civil wars, the *hirð* aristocracy was divided between rival kings and pretenders. The wars ended when the aristocracy had been united under one king.

Another cornerstone of the national system of government was the collaboration of the Church and the clergy with the monarchy. The oldest Norwegian Church was a national church, led by the king and incorporated into peasant society by his help. By the establishment of a separate Norwegian church province in 1152 or 1153, governed from the metropolitan see of Niðaróss (Trondheim), and covering also the six dioceses of the Western Isles from Greenland to the Hebrides and Isle of Man, the Norwegian Church broke away from its heavy dependence on monarchy and peasant society and became more firmly incorporated in the universal Church under papal leadership. By means of its national hierarchical organization, the Church developed into an almost state-like public authority at the side of the monarchy, contributing greatly to the unification of Norwegian society, not least in the wider, cultural sense.

The more independent Church continued to collaborate with the monarchy, although there were also passing clashes between the two parties, developing into bitter conflicts in the days of King Sverrir and again in the early 1280s. The consolidated monarchy of the 13th century would not accept a politically autonomous Church. But the monarchy was, by and large, prepared to grant the Church internal autonomy, judicial powers in spiritual matters, and financial privileges.

The clergy continuously furnished the king with able, literate helpers in the government. After the civil wars, the bishops generally acted as counselors and political guarantors for the monarchy. Clerics of lower rank served the king in embassies and administrative tasks, particularly members of the mendicant orders and cathedral chapters. Still, the Church used most of its personnel and considerable revenue for its own purposes. This pattern helps to explain why Hákon Hákonarson and his successors worked more systematically to create a clergy of their own within the framework of the royal chapel, which was again part of the hirð.

The clerical helpers of the king must have contributed essentially to the formulation of royal political ideology as expressed in Oratio contra clerum Norvegiae and Konungs skuggsjá. The latter work emphasizes the king's likeness to God and his function as God's chosen representative on earth. The position of the king is presented as so elevated and superior in relation to other temporal authorities that the work must be said to defend a near-absolutist ideology. A related ideology pervades the extensive royal legislation of the following period, culminating in the great law codes of King Magnús VI lagabœtir ("law-mender") Hákonarson (r. 1263–1280). Both in this legislation and in the official saga biographies of King Sverrir and his successors, the position of the king as the heir of St. Ólárf, the national patron, is stressed.

Even if the hirð aristocracy and the clergy played key roles in the state-building process of the high Middle Ages, they were in themselves too slender a basis on which to build national royal power. Norwegian society was predominantly a peasant society, and no public authority of importance could be established and maintained without the acceptance of the agrarian population. Fundamental for the political unification of the country and the development of a nationwide political system was the peasant society's need for at least a minimum of peace and order. From this need stemmed the two main functions of medieval monarchy in society: enforcer of justice and military leader.

Centrally placed in the relations between king and peasants were the popular assemblies, or þings. They functioned locally in judicial and partly also political matters throughout the Middle Ages. Politically, some of them acquired special importance by the "taking" or acclamation of a new king. From the days of Haraldr hárfagri, the monarchy was active in promoting the so-called logþings as representative assemblies of larger regions and su-

preme forum of legislation and judicial decisions. The provincial law codes sanctioned by the logþings regulated the king's role in the enforcement of justice, with the right to legal fines and confiscation, and his role as military leader, commanding the important naval levy of the leiðangr, which was supplied by the peasantry.

The national monarchy of the high Middle Ages reduced the judicial and political influence of peasant society through the þings. In the law codes of Magnús lagabœtir, the king assumes the role as the highest judge and legislator in the land. The participation of the logþings in legislation had by now been reduced to more formal assent to royal enactments that would have been sanctioned in advance by central royal assemblies or parliaments. Although freemen representing local districts were sometimes summoned to such assemblies at the side of prelates and magnates, their participation was hardly decisive for the outcome of discussions and negotiations; it was intended more to bind peasant society.

Still, the monarchy attached importance to the preservation of the legal basis and support it had acquired from the agrarian population at an early stage of the unification process. The relationship between monarchy and peasantry was never free from tension, because of the economic and military burdens placed on the people and infringements by local royal representatives. But royal taxation in the form of a partial conversion of the leiðangr was lighter in Norway than in the neighboring kingdoms, at the same time as the peasantry kept its military function. Royal legislation also reveals that the monarchy tried to protect its subjects from abuses on the part of royal officials and private landowners. It is debatable how far this policy was carried out in practice. But it is hard to see how the monarchy, on a comparatively weak financial basis, could have been built up to its strength and influence at the end of the high Middle Ages without some form of positive functional relationship with the great majority of the population. This relationship would include the participation, under the control of royal officials, of the best men of rural districts and towns in local public affairs.

The establishment of a national system of government required more solid points of support than the royal estates visited by an itinerant king and his hirð at the first stage of the unification process. The role of the kings as promoters of towns must be viewed in this light. In the rise and development of Norwegian towns from the 11th century onward, attention should be drawn not least to the towns' function as administrative and fiscal centers of monarchy and Church in which were gathered, increasingly, revenues in kind from the agrarian countryside. In the 13th century, the international commercial center of Bergen, by far the largest and most important of medieval Norwegian towns, became the first town to deserve the name of a national capital. From the beginning of the 14th century, it was rivaled by Oslo as a coordinate political and administrative center for the increasingly important eastern part of Norway.

Toward the end of the high Middle Ages, the Crown exerted a greater political influence than its power apparatus and revenues by themselves would suggest. The cause of this increased power may well have been that there was a certain balance between the main sociopolitical groups of the country in the sense that none of them was strong enough to dominate the others and to act against the interests of the kingdom as a whole; they were all to a certain extent dependent on the Crown. But this equilibrium proved fragile. When the consolidated monarchy of the 13th century directed its new-found strength into an active and at times aggressive foreign policy, it was shown after some time to have insufficent re-sources in open confrontations with the far more populous and economically stronger neighboring kingdoms and with the North German seaports that were later united in the Hanseatic League. In the end, Norway was reduced to a mere pawn in the ambitious game into which it had entered as an active player, and became for 600 years the weaker partner in a series of Scandinavian unions starting in 1319.

Late Middle Ages. When Hákon V Magnússon died in 1319, Magnus VII Eriksson (r. 1319–1355), the son of his daughter in her marriage with a brother of the Swedish king, inherited the Norwegian crown. In the same year, his election to the throne of Sweden as Magnus II led Norway into a little more than personal union with that kingdom. The union lasted until the second son of Magnus, Hákon VI (r. 1355–1380), became Norwegian king. In this period, Norway suffered most acutely from the population and production crises of the late Middle Ages. The already weak financial basis of the Crown was now so reduced that the question has been raised whether the preconditions of a fairly effective and independent Norwegian state authority any longer existed.

Hákon VI married Margrethe, the daughter of the Danish king, Valdemar IV, and was drawn into Valdemar's ill-fated struggle with the Hanseatic League. His son with Margrethe, Óláfr IV (r. 1380–1387), was accepted as Danish king before he inherited his father's throne. This was the origin of the Danish-Norwegian union that was to last for more than four centuries; for some periods of the late Middle Ages, it also included Sweden.

Norway entered the union with Denmark as a kingdom of her own, represented by her "council of the realm," an aristocratic representative and sanctioning body that derived from the con-sultative and executive royal council of the high Middle Ages. However, the weak Norwegian aristocracy was not capable in the long run of defending its own and other Norwegian interests in relation to the Danish-Norwegian monarchs, governing from Denmark, and the strong conciliar aristocracy of that kingdom. On the other hand, the disintegration of a central Norwegian political power and the more private exercise of local administration by the holders of royal *lén*, or fiefs, led to greater autonomy for local rural districts and towns.

In 1536, on the eve of the Lutheran Reformation and after an unsuccessful revolt by the last Catholic archbishop of Norway, Olaf Engelbrektsson, the much-reduced council that he led ceased to function. Norway was formally, albeit never fully in practice, incorporated into the Danish realm, ruled by the king and his Danish council.

Bib.: The annual volumes of *Bibliography of Old Norse–Icelandic Studies* (1963–) list recent studies of medieval Norwegian history. Bibliographies of sources and more important literature are found in Andersen, Per Sveaas. *Samlingen av Norge og kristningen av landet, 800–1130.* Handbok i Norges historie, 2. Bergen: Universitetsforlaget, 1977; and in Helle, Knut. *Norge blir en stat 1130–1319.* Handbok i Norges historie, 3. 2nd ed. Bergen: Universitetsforlaget, 1974. For a complete annual bibliography of works on Norwegian history, see *Bibliografi til Norges historie.* Oslo: Den norske historiske forening, 1916–. **Lit.**: Recent comprehensive treatments of Norwegian medieval history are the two above-mentioned works by Sveaas Andersen and Helle. For the late Middle Ages, they are supplemented by two works by Lars Hamre: *Norsk historie frå omlag 1400* (Oslo: Universitetsforlaget, 1968); *Norsk historie frå midten av 1400-åra til 1513* (Oslo, Bergen, and Tromsø: Universitetesforlaget, 1971). Comprehensive treatments of Norwegian history in non-Scandiavian languages are extremely scarce and brief, as is the case with Larsen, Karen. *A History of Norway.* Princeton: Princeton University Press; American-Scandinavian Foundation, 1950; a more up-to-date survey of early-medieval Scandinavian history and culture is to be found in Foote, Peter G., and David M. Wilson. *The Viking Achievement: The Society and Culture of Early Medieval Scandinavia.* London: Sidgwick & Jackson, 1970; Holmsen, Andreas. *Nye studier i gammel historie.* Oslo: Universitetsforlaget, 1976; Mykland, Knut, ed. *Norges historie.* 5 vols. Oslo: Cappelen, 1976–77; Holmsen, Andreas. *Norges historie fra de eldste tider til 1660.* 4th ed. Oslo: Universitetsforlaget, 1977; Gissel, Svend, *et al. Desertion and Land Colonization in the Nordic Countries c. 1300–1600: Comparative Report from the Scandinavian Research Project on Deserted Farms and Villages.* Stockholm: Almqvist & Wiksell, 1981; Helle, Knut. "Norway in the High Middle Ages: Recent Views on the Structure of Society." *Scandinavian Journal of History* 6 (1981), 161–89; Salvesen, Helge. "The Strength of Tradition: A Historiographical Analysis of Research into Norwegian Agrarian History During the Late Middle Ages and the Early Modern Period." *Scandinavian Journal of History* 7 (1982), 75–133.

Knut Helle

[**See also:** Agriculture; *Bóndi*; Church Organization and Function; Council of the Realm; Demography; Family Structure; Fishing, Whaling, and Seal Hunting; Hákon góði ("the good") Haraldsson; Hákon Hákonarson; Haraldr harðráði ("hard-ruler") Sigurðarson; Hákon jarl ("earl") Sigurðarson; Haraldr hárfagri ("fair-hair") Hálfdanarson; *Hirð*; Hunting; Kingship; *Konungs skuggsjá*; Land Tenure and Inheritance; Landownership; Laws; *Leiðangr*; Magnús Hákonarson; Margrethe I; Monasticism; Óláfr, St.; Óláfr Tryggvason; *Oratio contra clerum Norvegiae*; Plague; Royal Administration and Finances; Royal Assemblies; Settlement, Rural; Slavery; Social Structure; Trade; *Þing*]

Numerals. Roman numerals were introduced into Scandinavia together with Latin script. They were often distinguished from letters by a point before and after the numeral in question, for example, .xv. = 15. Arabic numerals were known from at least the second half of the 13th century, but Roman numerals prevailed throughout the Middle Ages, even in accounts.

The words denoting the numerals from 1 to 100 in the Indo-European languages have a common origin, the constitutive unit being 10. While 1 to 10 are denoted by simplex words, all other numerals are expressed by compounds containing derivatives of the word for 10. This pattern includes the word for 100 (Latin *centum*, Gothic *hund*, Old Norse *hund-rað*, etc.), the etymological interpretation of which is "ten decades," and the Scandinavian word for 1,000 (Old Norse *þúsund*), etymologically "a great hundred" (Proto-Germanic *þūs-hund*).

The decimal system is perceptible in the medieval Scandinavian languages, for example, Old Norse *þrettán* '13' (etymologically "three-ten"), *þrír tigir* or *þrjátigi* '30' (etymologically "three decades"), *etc.* Less evident is Old Swedish and Old Danish *tiughu* '20' where the original first component is lost; *cf. tuair tikiʀ* 'two decades' in the runic inscription on the Rök stone in Östergötland, Sweden, from about 800.

However, the decimal system is intermingled with a duodecimal counting system based on the number 12, and a vigesimal system based on the number 20. Thus, in Old Norse, the word *hundrað* normally represents the numerical value "120" and *þúsund* "1,200." The numerical value 100 may be expressed by *tíu tigir* 'ten decades' or *hundrað tírætt* 'a hundred according to the decimal counting,' sometimes expressly opposed to *hundrað tólfrætt* (120, or a hundred according to the duodecimal system). For instance, in *Konungs skuggsjá*, a leap year is said to consist of *iijͨ daga tolfræd og vj dagur. . . . Enn at bokmáli þá verda oll hundrud tijræd kollud. og verdur þat þá at riettu tali iijͨ tijræd og lx dagar og vi dægar* ("300 days according to the duodecimal counting and 6 days. . . . But in the literary language, all hundreds belong to the decimal system, and then the correct expression will be 300 days according to the decimal counting and 50 days and 6 days"; *Konungs skuggsjá*, p. 10); the "literary language" is Latin. Quoting a Norwegian speaker in his *Gesta Danorum* (ca. 1200), Saxo Grammaticus noted this peculiarity: *Volebat autem millenarium mille ac ducentorum capacem intellegi* ("he wanted a thousand to be understood as twelve hundred"; Book 5, ch. 7:4).

In Old Danish, the component *-tiugh(æ)* in numerals is ambiguous, meaning a set of either ten (a decade) or twenty (a score). For instance, a Zealand MS from about 1300 has *siutyugh* 'seven decades', *i.e.*, 70, while a contemporary Jutland MS has *fiyrsin tiughæ* 'four times twenty', *i.e.*, 80. The latter usage became dominant in the 14th century, resulting in, for example, *halffiærdhasinstiwo* 'three and a half times twenty' for 70, sometimes even *femsynnætyffwæ* 'five times twenty' for 100, *fiorthen*

oc tywæ 'fourteen and twenty' for 34, and the like. In Modern Danish, the words for 20, 30, and 40 preserve etymological decades: *tyve, tredive, fyrre(tyve)*, whereas the words for 50–90 are etymologically multiples of 20, for instance, *firsindstyve* (normally abbreviated *firs*) "80." Whether the Danish vigesimal counting is a premedieval relic or a medieval innovation can hardly be established. Vigesimal counting of unknown age occurs in several European languages, such as Irish, Basque, and Albanian. In French, the vigesimal element (*e.g.*, *soixante-dix* '70,' *quatre-vingts* '80') is an 11th-century innovation spreading from Normandy, but there is no evidence that it originated with the Viking settlers. Nor is the role of the number 12 confined to Scandinavian; the common denominator of Roman fractions was 12.

Lit.: Noreen, Adolf. *Altschwedische Grammatik*. Halle: Niemeyer, 1904, sects. 479–88; Holm-Olsen, Ludvig, ed. *Konungs skuggsiá*. Utgitt for Kjeldeskriftfondet. Gammelnorske tekster, nr.1. Oslo: Norsk Historisk Kjeldeskrift-Institutt, 1945; 2nd rev. ed. 1983; Szemerényi, O. *Studies in the Indo-European System of Numerals*. Heidelberg: Winter, 1960; Brøndum-Nielsen, Johs. *Gammeldansk Grammatik 4*. Copenhagen: Schultz, 1962, sects. 540–51; Noreen, Adolf. *Altisländische und altnorwegische Grammatik*. Tübingen: Niemeyer, 1970, sects. 444–53.

Allan Karker

Oddrúnargrátr ("Oddrún's Lament") is another in the Sigurðr-Guðrún cycle of poems contained in the *Codex Regius* of the *Poetic Edda* (13th century). Oddrún, here the (half?)-sister of Atli and Brynhildr, appears nowhere else in the texts, and is probably an invention of the late 12th-century poet. Oddrún, skilled in magic and witchcraft, hears of the difficult labor of Borgný, King Heiðrekr's daughter. She rushes to her aid because she has pledged to help all in distress. When Borgný thanks her for safely delivering twins, Oddrún replies bitterly that it was not love for Borgný that brought her there. In fact, she has never forgiven Borgný for having accused her publicly at a banquet of having an illicit love affair. And now Borgný herself has just borne twins to her own illicit lover.

Oddrún then proceeds to tell her tale. After Sigurðr's and Brynhildr's deaths, Gunnarr asks Atli for Oddrún's hand in marriage. But Atli is furious about Brynhildr's fate, and forbids the marriage. Love proves to be too strong, however, and Oddrún and Gunnarr become secret lovers. They are betrayed to Atli, who has Gunnarr and Hǫgni imprisoned. Oddrún escapes into exile.

From the snake pit where he has been thrown, Gunnarr plays his magic harp. The sound carries to Oddrún, who races to her lover's aid. But she arrives too late. As she rushes into the room, she watches in horror as Atli's mother transforms herself into a serpent and kills Gunnarr with a bite to the heart. The poem concludes with a reminder that love dictates destiny.

The juxtaposition of the two women, Borgný and Oddrún, forms the focus of the poem: Borgný at Oddrún's mercy, guilty of the same sin of which she had accused Oddrún, and Oddrún bitter and, like Borgný, rejected by her family because of love.

Ed.: Neckel, Gustav, ed. *Edda: Die Lieder des Codex Regius nebst verwandten Denkmälern.I: Text.* 5th ed. rev. Hans Kuhn. Heidelberg: Winter, 1983. **Tr.**: Hollander, Lee M., trans. *The Poetic Edda, Translated with an Introduction and Explanatory Notes.* 2nd rev. ed. Austin: University of Texas Press, 1962; rpt. 1988; Terry, Patricia, trans. *Poems of the Vikings: The Elder Edda.* Indianapolis: Bobbs-Merrill, 1969. **Lit.**: Andersson, Theodore M. *The Legend of Brynhild.* Islandica, 43. Ithaca: Cornell University Press, 1980; Glendinning, Robert J. "*Guðrúnarqviða Forna*: A Reconstruction and Interpretation." In *Edda: A Collection of Essays.* Ed. Robert J. Glendinning and Haraldur Bessason. University of Manitoba Icelandic Studies, 4. Winnipeg: University of Manitoba, 1983, pp. 258–82; Harris, Joseph. "Eddic Poetry." In *Old Norse-Icelandic Literature: A Critical Guide.* Ed. Carol J. Clover and John Lindow. Islandica, 45. Ithaca and London: Cornell University Press, 1985, pp. 91, 101, 151.

†*Philip N. Anderson*

[**See also:** *Codex Regius*; Eddic Poetry; Vǫlsung-Niflung Cycle; Women in Eddic Poetry]

Odds þáttr Ófeigssonar ("The Tale of Oddr Ófeigsson"), a short Old Icelandic tale, is included in the versions of the king's saga *Haralds saga harðráða* in *Morkinskinna*, the later part of *Flateyjarbók*, and *Hulda-Hrokkinskinna*. It is found at the end of a section concerning domestic conflicts between Haraldr and, among others, Hákon jarl ("earl") Ívarsson.

In spite of an embargo, Oddr's men have been trading with Finns in the north of Norway. The king's man Einarr Háreksson arrives and searches through Oddr's ship, but finds nothing. Einarr informs King Haraldr, who continues the search. By using advice from his friend the *hirðmaðr* ("king's man") Þorsteinn, Oddr stays continuously a step ahead of Haraldr. Each time, the king finds out the hiding place of the treasure a little bit too late. At last, Oddr succeeds in escaping to Iceland. He sends horses as gifts to Þorsteinn, which makes Haraldr understand how things happened. He commands the death of Þorsteinn, but nobody is willing to execute the order. Therefore, Þorsteinn is allowed to leave the king's bodyguard.

The three versions of the *þáttr* are very much alike. However, a strange speech, made by Oddr to his men in connection with the escape, is missing in the version in *Hulda-Hrokkinskinna*.

Odds þáttr probably dates from the beginning of the 13th century and is based on oral tales. Perhaps, the motif of cunning has been traditionally associated with the historical personage Oddr. A statement concerning a famine in Iceland makes it possible to place the events in 1056.

Oddr also appears in *Bandamanna saga* and in *Hemings þáttr Ásláksssonar*. There are few connections between *Odds þáttr* and the saga, but the character of Oddr can still be easily recognized. *Bandamanna saga* takes place some years earlier, but is younger than *Odds þáttr*. Einarr Háreksson performs a similar role in the supposedly older *Sneglu-Halla þáttr*. The course of events in *Odds þáttr* is paralleled in *Njáls saga*, in the section where Hákon jarl is looking for Hrappr, whom Þráinn hides on three separate occasions. Like Oddr, Þráinn always stays one step ahead of his adversary. *Njáls saga* may have borrowed the motif from *Odds þáttr*.

According to many scholars, *Odds þáttr*, which is told in a prominent saga style, was probably written down independently before being incorporated into the *konungasögur*

Ed.: Guðni Jónsson, ed. *Grettis saga Ásmundarsonar*. Íslenzk fornrit, 7. Reykjavik: Hið íslenzka fornritafélag, 1936, pp. xcix–civ, 365–74. **Tr.**: Morris, William, and Eiríkr Magnússon, trans. "An Adventure of Odd Ufeigson with Harald Hardradi." In *The Story of Howard the Halt*. Saga Library, 1. London: Quaritch, 1891, pp. 167–75; Lowe, Pardee, Jr., trans. *King Harold and the Icelanders*. Lincoln: Penmaen, 1979, pp. 35–43; Boucher, Alan, trans. *A Tale of Icelanders*. Reykjavik: Iceland Review, 1980, pp. 80–4. **Lit.**: Finnur Jónsson. *Den oldnorske og oldislandske Litteraturs Historie*. 3 vols. 2nd ed. Copenhagen: Gad, 1920–24, vol. 2, pp. 542–3; Vries, Jan de. *Altnordische Literaturgeschichte*. 2 vols. 2nd ed. Grundriss der germanischen Philologie, 15–6. Berlin: de Gruyter, 1941–42; rpt. 1964–67, vol. 2, pp. 411–2; Gimmler, Heinrich. *Die Thættir der Morkinskinna. Ein Beitrag zur Überlieferungsproblematik und zur Typologie der altnordischen Kurzzählung*. Diss. Frankfurt am Main; Bamberg: Difo-Druck, 1976, pp. 76–7, 127; Danielsson, Tommy. *Om den isländska släktsagans uppbyggnad*. Skrifter utgivna av Litteraturvetenskapliga institutionen vid Uppsala universitet, 22. Stockholm: Almqvist & Wiksell, 1986, pp. 75–6.

Tommy Danielsson

[See also: *Bandamanna saga*; *Flateyjarbók*; *Hemings þáttr Áslákssonar*; *Hulda-Hrokkinskinna*; *Morkinskinna*; *Njáls saga*; *Sneglu-Halla þáttr*]

Óðinn (Proto-Germanic **Wōþanaz*) appears in medieval Scandinavian sources as the chief figure of pagan Nordic mythology. He is also mentioned in Anglo-Saxon and German sources, where variations of his name include "Woden" and "Wotan." Óðinn's name is almost certainly to be traced to the same form (**wātós*) from which the Old Norse adjective *óðr* ('mad, frantic, vehement'; cf. German *wut*) is derived. In the 11th century, for example, Adam of Bremen remarks "Wodan, id est furor" ("Wodan, that is fury"; *Gesta Hammaburgensis ecclesiae pontificum* 4:26). Although the narrative sources of information about Óðinn are generally late and of questionable reliability, the image that emerges of this deity matches this association with "fury."

Óðinn's career is treated most fully in the *Prose Edda* and the *Poetic Edda*. Among the god's prominent deeds are his acquisition of the poetic mead for the gods and mankind (*Skáldskaparmál*, chs. 4–6; *Hávamál*, sts. 104–110); his self-sacrifice on the World Tree (Yggdrasill), which results in his appropriation of runic wisdom (*Hávamál*, sts. 138–144); his pivotal role in the shaping of the world and in creating mankind (*Gylfaginning*, chs. 5–6; *Vǫluspá*, sts. 4, 17–18; *Grímnismál*, sts. 40–41); the death of his son Baldr with its implications for the gods (*Gylfaginning*, chs. 33–35; *Vǫluspá*, sts. 31–33; cf. the very different version in Book 3 of Saxo's *Gesta Danorum*); and his own demise at Ragnarǫk (*Gylfaginning*, chs. 36–39; *Vǫluspá*, st. 53; *Vafþrúðnismál*, sts. 52–53). An array of kennings also allude to these adventures. Odinic theophanies occur in the *konungasögur* and are common in the *fornaldarsögur*. In the *konungasögur*, especially those of missionary kings (e.g., *Óláfs saga Tryggvasonar en mesta*), he is portrayed as an old man bent on revivifying paganism through his misdeeds. The image in the *fornaldarsögur* is usually that of a much more robust character who frequently acts as a donor figure (e.g., *Vǫlsunga saga*).

Nearly all of Óðinn's activities revolve around his search for wisdom. In addition to self-mutilation by hanging and impalement on Yggdrasill, he allows himself to be tortured between two fires in *Grímnismál*. The result of both experiences is an ecstatic state in which Óðinn spouts forth numinous knowledge. Furthermore, the god gained wisdom by giving up an eye for a drink at Mímir's well (*Gylfaginning*, ch. 8; *Vǫluspá*, st. 28), while elsewhere he confers with the embalmed head of the wise Mímir (*Vǫluspá*, st. 46; *Ynglinga saga*, chs. 4, 7). He is often found on journeys, the sole purpose of which is to grow in wisdom from knowledge gained through confrontations with otherworldly beings (*Vafþrúðnismál*, *Vǫluspá*). Moreover, he is a master of two kinds of magic (*galdr*, *seiðr*). Óðinn asks tidings of the dead (*Hávamál*, st. 157), and is referred to as "god of the hanged" (*hangaguð*, *hangatýr*). Such references, together with evidence from the archaeological record (the Gutnish Lárbro stone) and early (Tacitus, *Germania*, ch. 39), as well as late (*Gautreks saga*, ch. 7) literary testimony, imply that Óðinn's cult may have involved human sacrifice.

The interplay between knowledge and poetry ran deep in early Scandinavian culture, because history was recorded and transmitted largely in the form of skaldic verse (cf. the prologue to *Heimskringla*). In addition to Óðinn's obtaining the poetic mead, which he apportions to gods and men, Óðinn speaks in verse (*Ynglinga saga*, ch. 6). He and his priests are called "song-smiths" (*ljóðasmiðir*; *Ynglinga saga*, ch. 6). This association between Óðinn and poetry, and particularly the special relationship poets had with Óðinn, has important ramifications for our understanding of the deity, since much of the textual record concerning him survives in works of poetry or in writings dealing with poetic art (i.e., eddic and skaldic poetry, *Snorra Edda*). This fact may explain why the image of Óðinn that emerges from the written testimony does not always seem in accord with other sources of information.

Óðinn's ecstatic experiences, his quest for wisdom, and his self-sacrifice on the World Tree, along which he could then travel to the other worlds, have suggested to some that Scandinavian paganism was influenced by the shamanistic practices of the neighboring Lapps or of Siberian tribes. It is doubtful that anything like the shamanism of northern Asia was practiced by the Scandinavians; there is, for example, no evidence of such typical shamanistic activities as dancing, the use of drums, or healing. But it is difficult to deny traces of what appear to be shamanistic elements in the figure of Óðinn. In addition to his association with ecstasy-producing elements, such as intoxicants, self-sacrifice, and torture, Óðinn has two ravens that he sends out to collect information (*Gylfaginning*, ch. 25), and he frequently appears as a shape changer (*Ynglinga saga*, ch. 7; *Skáldskaparmál*, ch. 6).

Óðinn was also a god of battle, and in that context was affiliated with the valkyries and the berserks. The valkyries of Old Norse poetry and sagas are armed attendants who ride into battle, where they give victory according to Óðinn's will. They place invisible fetters on the warrior, often a hero whom Óðinn had earlier championed, thus giving rise to Óðinn's reputation as a fickle patron. The berserks appear to have a long history in Scandinavia. By the time of the sagas, however, whatever cultural reality they may once have had as members of elite military bands had given way to literary use as stock figures, usually comic or villainous, sometimes both.

Among Óðinn's notable possessions are his spear (Gungnir), his eight-legged horse (Sleipnir), his ravens (Huginn, Muninn), his wonderfully reproductive ring (Draupnir), and the high-seat from which he sees into all the worlds (Hliðskjálf). He is the father of several of the most important deities, such as Þórr and Baldr, and is married to Frigg, with whom he periodically carries on a rivalry (*e.g.*, the prose introduction to *Grímnismál*). Óðinn is also the blood-brother of the complex and troublesome Loki (*Lokasenna*, st. 9).

Óðinn's status in the Nordic pantheon has been the matter of much debate. Certain aspects of our information about him, such as the paucity of Odinic place-names in the West Norse area, have led some scholars to conclude that he is a relative newcomer (presumably from the south), whose worship to some extent replaced the indigenous Týr (<*Tîwaz*). Pioneered by Dumézil, however, recent comparative research has indicated how Óðinn would fit into an inherited Indo-European mythological scheme.

Ed.: Finnur Jónsson, ed. *Edda Snorra Sturlusonar*. Copenhagen: Gyldendal, 1931; Neckel, Gustav, ed. *Edda: Die Lieder des Codex Regius nebst verwandten Denkmälern. I: Text*. 5th ed. rev. Hans Kuhn. Heidelberg: Winter, 1983. **Tr.**: Hollander, Lee M., trans. *The Poetic Edda, Translated with an Introduction and Explanatory Notes*. 2nd rev. ed. Austin: University of Texas Press, 1962; rpt. 1988; Faulkes, Anthony, trans. *Snorri Sturluson: Edda*. Everyman's Library. London and Melbourne: Dent, 1987. **Bib.**: Lindow, John. *Scandinavian Mythology: An Annotated Bibliography*. Garland Folklore Bibliographies, 13. New York and London: Garland, 1988. **Lit.**: Davidson, Hilda R. E. *The Road to Hel: A Study of the Conception of the Dead in Old Norse Literature*. Cambridge: Cambridge University Press, 1943; Helm, Karl. *Wodan: Ausbreitung und Wanderung seines Kultes*. Giessener Beiträge zur deutschen Philolgie, 85. Giessen: Schmidt, 1946; Vries, Jan de. *Altgermanische Religionsgeschichte*. 2 vols. 2nd ed. Grundriss der germanischen Philologie, 12. Berlin: de Gruyter, 1956–57; Turville-Petre, E. O. G. *Myth and Religion of the North: The Religion of Ancient Scandinavia*. New York: Holt, Rinehart and Winston, 1964; rpt. Westport: Greenwood, 1975; Ellis Davidson, H. R. *Gods and Myths of Northern Europe*. Harmondsworth: Penguin, 1964; Buchholz, Peter. "Shamanism—the Testimony of Old Icelandic Literary Tradition." *Mediaeval Scandinavia* 4 (1971), 7–20; Fleck, Jere. "The 'Knowledge-Criterion' in the *Grímnismál*: The Case Against Shamanism." *Arkiv för nordisk filologi* 86 (1971), 49–65; Fleck, Jere. "Óðinn's Self-Sacrifice—a New Interpretation." *Scandinavian Studies* 43 (1971), 119–42, 385–413; Weber, Gerd Wolfgang. "Das Odinsbild des Altunasteins." *Beiträge zur Geschichte der deutschen Sprache und Literatur* (Tübingen) 94 (1972), 323–34; Dumézil, Georges. *Gods of the Ancient Northmen*. Ed. Einar Haugen. Trans. John Lindow *et al*. Publications of the UCLA Center for the Study of Comparative Folklore and Mythology, 3. Berkeley, Los Angeles, and London: University of California Press, 1973 [trans. of 1959 original]; Ellis Davidson, H. R. *The Viking Road to Byzantium*. London: Allen & Unwin, 1976, pp. 281–312; Dillmann, François-Xavier. "Georges Dumézil et la religion germanique: l'interprétation de dieu Odhinn." In *Georges Dumézil à la découverte des indo-européens*. Ed. Jean-Claude Rivière. Paris: Copernic, 1979, pp. 259–71; Haugen, Einar. "The *Edda* as Ritual: Odin and His Masks." In *Edda: A Collection of Essays*. Ed. Robert J. Glendinning and Haraldur Bessason. University of Manitoba Icelandic Studies, 4. Manitoba: University of Manitoba Press, 1983, pp. 3–24; Lindow, John. "Mythology and Mythography." In *Old Norse–Icelandic Literature: A Critical Guide*. Ed. Carol J. Clover and John Lindow. Islandica, 45. Ithaca and London: Cornell University Press, 1985, pp. 21–67; Mitchell, Stephen A. "'Nú gef ek þik Óðni': Attitudes Toward Odin in the Mythical-Heroic Sagas." In *The Sixth International Saga Conference 28/7–2/8, 1985. Workshop Papers*. 2 vols. Copenhagen: Det arnamagnæanske Institut, 1985, vol. 2, pp. 777–91 [photocopies of papers distributed to participants]; Boyer, Régis. "Óðinn d'après Saxo Grammaticus et les sources noroises: Étude comparative." In *Festschrift Oskar Bandle zum 60. Geburtstag am 11. Januar 1986*. Ed. Hans-Peter Naumann *et al*. Beiträge zur nordischen Philologie, 15. Basel and Frankfurt am Main: Helbing & Lichtenhahn, 1986, pp. 143–57; Edwards, Paul. "Alcohol into Art: Drink and Poetry in Old Icelandic and Anglo-Saxon." In *Sagnaskemmtun: Studies in Honour of Hermann Pálsson on His 65th Birthday, 26th May 1986*. Ed. Rudolf Simek *et al*. Vienna, Cologne, and Graz: Böhlau, 1986, pp. 85–97; Puhvel, Jaan. *Comparative Mythology*. Baltimore: Johns Hopkins University Press, 1987; Glosecki, Stephen O. *Shamanism and Old English Poetry*. New York and London: Garland, 1989; Mitchell, Stephen A. *Sagas and Ballads*. Ithaca and London: Cornell University Press, 1991, pp. 60–4.

Stephen A. Mitchell

[**See also:** Adam of Bremen; *Berserkr*; Eddic Poetry; *Gautreks saga*; *Grímnismál*; *Hávamál*; *Lokasenna*; Maiden Warriors; Mythology; *Óláfs saga Tryggvasonar*; Runes and Runic Inscriptions; Saxo Grammaticus; *Snorra Edda*; *Vafþrúðnismál*; *Vǫlsunga saga*; *Vǫluspá*; *Ynglinga saga*]

Óláfr, St. The sources of our knowledge of the saint are contemporary or younger skaldic poetry, secular sagas of the king (especially those from the hand of Snorri Sturluson), liturgical texts, church legends, and miracles.

Óláfr Haraldsson, Norwegian king and martyr, was born about 995. He seems to have been eager and vindictive, severe and proud, in many respects far from the medieval Christian ideal of humility. But in most sources, he is more or less portrayed after a model common to saints and martyrs, with some features patterned after Christ.

Óláfr descended from Haraldr hárfagri ("fair-hair") Hálfdanarson and was the son of Haraldr inn grenski ("the Greenlandish"), a local king in southeast Norway. At the age of twelve, he sailed out for his first Viking expedition. During a winter stay at Rouen in France some years later, he was baptized. Shortly after that, he went home claiming Norway as his patrimony (1015), and within a year, he had defeated the Danish and Swedish rulers.

King Óláfr wanted to found his rule on Christian legislation, with the Church as his ally and Charlemagne as his ideal. To this end, he brought English clerics with him. He built churches and divided Norway into church regions, but because of his violent behavior he grew unpopular among the powerful local chieftains. They joined forces with the Christian King Knud (Cnut) the Great of Denmark and his Norwegian vassal, the earl Hákon Eiríksson, and expelled Óláfr from his domain (1028).

The king fled to Grand Duke Jaroslav of Garðaríki (Novgorod). Encouraged by the message that Hákon Eiríksson had been drowned, Óláfr left his asylum two years later, raised a small army in Sweden, and crossed over to Norway. There, he encountered a large peasant army, and fell in battle at Stiklastaðir (Stiklestad) on July 29, 1030. His body was secretly carried to Niðaróss (Trondheim) by loyal peasants and buried in a sandbank by the River Nið.

Immediately after the king's fall, healing miracles were said to be performed where his body rested: light shined over its location, and the coffin moved upward in the sand. Grímkell, missionary bishop and counselor of Óláfr, was sent for. He came and opened the coffin, and the king's body was buried close by St. Clement's church in Niðaróss.

One year later, Grímkell opened the coffin anew. Witnesses reported that the king's face still had a fresh color, and that hair and nails had grown after his death. The bishop now proclaimed Óláfr a saint, and his mortal remains were enshrined and placed near the high altar of the church. The king was, however, never officially canonized. In the high Middle Ages, a cathedral was built in Niðaróss to shelter the shrine of the saint.

The violent death of King Óláfr led to a sudden change in popular opinion of him. Many people grew discontented with the exploiting Danish rulers, and years of crop failure were regarded as a divine response to the evil deed of killing their king. Submission to the dead king became an act of repentance and penitence.

The cult of the new saint made rapid progress and spread widely also outside Norway. Many churches were dedicated to St. Óláfr. Crowds of supplicants came to see his shrine and to profit from his healing powers.

Like his pre-Christian ancestors, Óláfr was thought to possess supernatural influence on harvest and fortune. He was ascribed features from Freyr, the god of vegetation, and from the thunder-god Þórr. Springs with healing water were said to have welled forth where the king or his body had been. Folk traditions about the king's successful fight against trolls and giants proliferated. For centuries, the saint played a dominant role as protector against evil forces.

In the 1160s, King Magnús Eiríksson declared himself to be the saint's vassal and substitute. Óláfr had become an embodiment of the biblical idea of a just king, and was referred to as "Norway's king of all eternity." Church and kingdom shared a common interest in the saint as founder and unifier of a Christian national state.

Lit.: Bukdahl, Jørgen. "St. Olav and Norway." *American Scandinavian Review* 18 (1930), 405–13; Dickins, Bruce. "The Cult of S. Olave in the British Isles." *Saga-Book of the Viking Society* 12 (1940), 53–80; Turville-Petre, Gabriel. *The Heroic Age of Scandinavia*. London: Hutchinson, 1951, pp. 140–64; Turville-Petre, G. *Origins of Icelandic Literature*. Oxford: Clarendon, 1953; rpt. 1967; Simpson, Jacqueline. "Introduction." In her ed. *Snorri Sturluson. Heimskringla: The Olaf Sagas*. 2 vols. Trans. Samuel Laing. London: Dent; New York: Dutton, 1964, vol. 1 [esp. pp. xxii–xxxi]; Gunnes, Erik. "Divine Kingship: A Note." *Temenos* 10 (1974), 149–58; Svahnström, Gunnar, ed. *St. Olav—seine Zeit und sein Kult*. Acta Visbyensia, 6. Visby: Museum Gotlands Fornsal, 1981; Henriksen, Vera. *St. Olav of Norway: King, Saint—and Enigma*. Oslo: Tano, 1985.

Reidar Astås

[**See also:** Iconography; Liturgy and Liturgical Texts; Miracles, Collections of; Norway; *Óláfs saga helga*; Saints' Lives]

Óláfr Tryggvason

Óláfr Tryggvason was king of Norway 995–999/1000. He was the son of Tryggvi Óláfsson, grandson of Haraldr hárfagri ("fair-hair") Hálfdanarson, a petty king of Viken or the Upplands.

Before Óláfr Tryggvason became king, he led great Viking raids to England, Scotland, and Ireland. The *Anglo-Saxon Chronicle* for the years 991 and 994 states that Óláfr led a large Viking fleet to attack the eastern and southern coast of England. In both cases, the English king paid large amounts of silver, "Danegeld," to buy off the Vikings.

Just before Óláfr Tryggvason went to Norway, controversy arose in Trøndelag between Earl Hákon, who was the actual ruler of the country, and the Tronds. According to *Heimskringla*, the earl constantly abused their wives and daughters, "and the farmers began to grumble just as the Tronds are wont to do over anything which goes against them" (*Heimskringla* 1:343). One of the rich peasants who had refused to give up his wife to the earl gathered the farmers and set out against Hákon. The earl fled and was killed by his own slave, Karkr, while escaping. Óláfr Tryggvason, who was on his way to Niðaróss (Trondheim), inadvertently encountered one of the earl's sons and killed him in battle; the two other sons fled. Óláfr was chosen king by the people of Trøndelag at the Eyraþing. After that, he traveled throughout the country and was made king of all Norway. In 996, Óláfr was in Víkin (Viken), and from there he carried out his plans to introduce Christianity in Norway and to secure complete control over the country.

With the help of his paternal relatives, he succeeded in making the farmers of Viken accept the new faith in 996/7. Those who refused or disagreed with him, "he dealt with hard; some he slew, some he maimed, and some he drove away from the land" (*Heimskringla* 1:362). Gradually, his actions led to a conflict between the king and the farmers. In the summer of 997, he went to the southwestern part of the country, made the Rogalenders embrace the new faith, and secured their support by marrying his sister to one of the chieftains there, Erlingr Skjálgsson, at Sóli (Sole). In the west, he introduced Christianity through the support of his maternal relatives while securing control over this province. The introduction of Christianity in these provinces, the west, and Viken, was facilitated by long-lasting contact with Christian western Europe, especially the British Isles.

In the fall of 997, Óláfr Tryggvason went to Trøndelag. There and in the north, paganism was stronger than in the other provinces. Óláfr Tryggvason met with strong opposition from the farmers and was forced to acquiesce. He returned one year later, killed the leader of the farmers, Járn-Skeggi, and made the Tronds embrace the new faith. Some of the rich farmers refused to accept the new order. They fled and went to Sweden, joining Eiríkr, son of Earl Hákon. Óláfr Tryggvason tried to secure control over Trøndelag and the good-will of the Tronds by marrying Guðrún, Járn-Skeggi's daughter. He did not succeed; Guðrún attempted to murder him on their wedding night. In 999, he made the people of Háleygjaland (Hålogaland) accept Christianity. Thus, he had christianized the entire coastal area of Norway. Óláfr Haraldsson later christianized the interior.

But it was not only in Norway that Óláfr Tryggvason tried to spread Christianity. His pressure on the Icelandic chieftains was undoubtedly one of the main reasons why the Icelanders accepted the new faith at the Alþingi in 999/1000. He also made the Greenlanders accept Christianity.

Óláfr Tryggvason's strengthening of the power of the king involved not only an expansion of the king's territorial control over the country, but also an attempt to develop the internal organization of the kingdom. It was most likely Óláf Tryggvason who introduced the office of district governor, a service rendered by a chieftain who received royal land in return. He was also the first Norwegian king to mint coins.

Óláfr Tryggvason died in the battle of Svǫlðr (Svold) in 999/1000, where he fought the Danish king Sven Haraldsson (Forkbeard), who had been forced to give up Viken, the Swedish king who wanted control of Gautaland, and Eiríkr, son of Earl Hákon.

Lit.: Finnur Jónsson, ed. *Heimskringla*. 4 vols. Samfund til udgivelse af gammel nordisk litteratur, 23. Copenhagen: Møller, 1893–1901; Koht, Halvdan. "The Scandinavian Kingdoms Until the End of the Thirteenth Century." In *The Cambridge Medieval History* 6. Ed. J. R. Turner *et al.* Cambridge: Cambridge University Press, 1929, pp. 362–92; Baetke, Walter. *Christliches Lehngut in der Saga-religion. Das Svolder-Problem. Zwei Beiträge zur Saga-kritikk.* Berichte über die Verhandlungen der sächsischen Akademie der Wissenschaften zu Leipzig. Philol.-hist. Klasse, 98.6. Berlin: Akademie-Verlag, 1951; Ellehøj, Svend. "The Location of the Fall of Olaf Tryggvason." *Árbók hins íslenzka fornleifafélags*, Fylgirit (1958), 63–73; Gunnes, Erik. *Rikssamling og kristning 800–1177.* Norges historie, 2. Oslo: Cappelen, 1976; Andersen, Per Sveaas. *Samlingen av Norge og kristningen av landet, 800–1130.* Handbok i Norges historie, 2. Bergen: Universitetsforlaget, 1977; Helle, Knut. "Norway in the High Middle Ages: Recent Views on the Structure of Society." *Scandinavian Journal of History* 6 (1981), 161–89; Birkeli, Fridtjov. *Hva vet vi om kristningen av Norge?* Oslo: Universitetsforlaget, 1982; Bagge, Sverre. *Society and Politics in Snorri Sturluson's* Heimskringla. Berkeley and Los Angeles: University of California Press, 1991.

Jón Viðar Sigurðsson

[See also: Conversion; *Heimskringla*; Norway; *Óláfs saga Tryggvasonar*]

Óláfs saga helga

("The Saga of St. Óláfr"). Óláfr Haraldsson, king of Norway 1015–1028, died fighting at Stiklastaðir (Stiklestad) on July 29, 1030. His death was quickly interpreted as a martyrdom for the true faith in Norway, and one year after the battle his uncorrupted remains were translated from a grave just outside Niðaróss (Trondheim) to St. Clemens church in town, and his sanctity proclaimed. The cult of St. Óláfr spread rapidly, and miracles were worked, not only in Niðaróss, but throughout Norway, and even in remote countries. The story of this king and saint, *Óláfs saga helga*, developed from the confluence of two lines of historical writing in medieval Norway and Iceland, the religious-historical tradition of saints' lives and the secular-historical tradition of royal biography; the saga found many different realizations during the period 1180–1230.

The religious tradition includes a Latin *officium* (*The Leofric Collectar*) for the feast of St. Óláfr (July 29) from about 1050, but this work contains only biblical quotations and provides no historical information. Two skaldic poems from the decade after St. Óláfr's death, *Glælognskviða* ("Calm-sea Lay") by Þórarinn loftunga ("praise-tongue") and *Erfidrápa* (the "Memorial Lay") by Sighvatr Þórðarson, describe the king's death and some miracles. But not until Einarr Skúlason's poem *Geisli* ("Sunbeam"), composed around 1152, does the historical element really play a role in a preserved literary monument. For his poem, Einarr Skúlason is thought to have used a now-lost *Translatio sancti Olavi* and an official *vita* from the mid-12th century. An Old Norse rendering of the *vita* is found in the *Old Norwegian Homily Book*; the *vita* formed the basis of Archbishop Eysteinn's *Passio et miracula beati Olavi*, which exists in two versions, an older and shorter version, and a younger and expanded version made during his exile in England 1179–1182. The shorter version became very popular and is found in a number of foreign sources. The oldest is a legendary from the Benedictine monastery of Anchin, MS Douai 295, from about 1200; the miracles are followed by William of Jumièges's *Gesta Normannorum ducum* (5:11–12), which describes Óláfr's baptism in Rouen. Oxford,

Bodleian Library, Rawlinson C 440, a legendary written in the beginning of the 14th century, adds a mass for Óláfr after the miracles. All Scandinavian breviaries are based on the shorter version. The longer version is found in only one MS from around 1200, Oxford, Corpus Christi College 209, from Fountains Abbey. Apart from the material drawn from the *Old Norwegian Homily Book*, it contains a collection of miracles from the time after 1152/3 and from Archbishop Eysteinn's own time.

The secular-historical tradition of royal biography includes sections of the monk Theodoricus's *Historia de antiquitate regum Norwagiensium*, a synoptic history of the kings of Norway from Haraldr hárfagri ("fair-hair") Hálfdanarson to Haraldr Gilli Magnússon (d. 1163), written around 1180. Theodoricus mentions a written account of the translation and miracles of St. Óláfr (*i.e.*, the *Translatio sancti Olavi*), saying that he has omitted details about these subjects because they had already been committed to posterity by others. The secular-historical tradition also includes sections of the (now-defective) *Historia Norwegiae* (*ca.* 1200), a history of Norway beginning with the Ynglingar and ending with a fragmentary account of Óláfr's return from England (1015), and of *Ágrip af Nóregs konunga sǫgum* ("Compendium of the History of the Kings of Norway"), a survey of the period from Haraldr hárfagri through much of the 12th century, composed at the end of the 12th century. It is based primarily on Theodoricus and, most likely, on a Latin precursor of the *Historia Norwegiae*. *Ágrip* provides only a sketch of Óláfr's life as part of a series of vernacular kings' biographies.

The first really full-scale saga rendition of the history of Óláfr is the so-called *Oldest Saga of St. Óláfr* from the end of the 12th century. The text is preserved in only six fragments, NRA 52 (Oslo), dating from about 1225; the seventh and eighth fragments, AM 325 IVa 4to, are from a different MS, and Louis-Jensen (1970) has demonstrated that they do not belong to the *Oldest Saga*. The language of the *Oldest Saga* is Icelandic. The six fragments comprise only events from the king's reign until his departure from the country for his exile in Russia; but the saga must also have included his early years, the battle of Stiklastaðir, and an acknowledgment of his sanctity. Flaws in composition include curious repetitions, contradictions in details, and a clumsy order of events; the work is composed of anecdotes, *þættir*, skaldic strophes (six stanzas and two additional lines), and reports of historical facts.

Closely related to the *Oldest Saga* is a Norwegian revision known as the *Legendary Saga of St. Óláfr*, which contains a great deal of clerical or legendary matter, hence its name. The *Legendary Saga* presents a history of the saint's life from birth to death: his childhood and youth, his Viking years in England, his return to Norway and overthrow of the earls from Lade, his reign and the christianization of Norway, his exile in Russia, his return and death at Stiklastaðir, and the miracles attributed to him. This saga is preserved in only one MS, De la Gardie 8 (Uppsala), from central Norway (Trøndelag) in the mid-13th century. The *Legendary Saga* has shortened the text considerably and improved upon the composition, although many incongruities are still left, probably due to the great variety of oral and written sources that were incorporated. The author often combined two variants of the same episode or reported them in different places. Two major sections were added: (1) the so-called *Kristni þáttr*, inserted in two parts at different places, and containing stories of the king's missionary activities, especially his christianization of the inhabitants of Gudbrandsdal, and (2) the *Legendarium*, *i.e.*, the miracles of the saint after his death, which on the whole follow the *Old Norwe-gian Homily Book*. Short passages are also interpolated from *Ágrip*, though these may have been in the *Oldest Saga*. The *Legendary Saga* attempts to combine the king's secular history with his spiritual importance as a saint. Although the facts of his history are presented, the larger part of the saga consists of episodes and *þættir* constructed around historical characters, among them a number of Icelanders (*e.g.*, skalds and persons known from the christianization of Ice-land) and containing much fictional or legendary matter. The saga quotes some sixty skaldic stanzas, about sixteen by Sighvatr Þórðarson and fifteen by Þormóðr Kolbrúnarskáld.

The *Legendary Saga* was not the immediate source for later histories of St. Óláfr. Other sagas about St. Óláfr's life must have existed. The presentation of St. Óláfr's life in *Fagrskinna* is de-pendent on one of these lost sagas; no special prominence is given to his story in this collection of kings' lives. Fragments of the priest Styrmir Kárason's *lífssaga* ("biography") of St. Óláfr, dated to about 1220, are preserved in *Flateyjarbók* as a list of twenty-eight "ar-ticles" in an appendix to the version of *Óláfs saga helga* presented there (the *Separate Saga*). The fragments reveal that it had a more amplified and rhetorical style than the *Legendary Saga* or the *Oldest Saga*. The versions of *Óláfs saga helga* culminate in Snorri Sturluson's *Separate Saga of St. Óláfr*, which was later incorpo-rated in a slightly revised version as the central part of his collection of histories of the Norwegian kings, *Heimskringla*. His version was probably based on Styrmir Kárason's text, but Snorri also drew material from a number of other sources, among them *Orkneyinga saga* and *Færeyinga saga*. Interestingly, the *Kristni þáttr* that was interpolated into the *Legendary Saga* is also quoted by Snorri, and there is a greater degree of word-for-word correspondence. Snorri did not use *þættir* that he deemed too fanciful, for instance, *Óláfs þáttr Geirstaðaálfs*. The interpolated 14th-century MSS of the *Separate Saga* constitute the final stage in the development of the sagas about St. Óláfr. In these later redactions, Snorri's version was used as the basic text, but it was expanded through the introduction of much of the material that Snorri discarded from his sources.

Ed.: Keyser, R., and C. R. Unger, eds. *Olafs saga hins helga*. Christiania [Oslo]: Feilberg & Landmark, 1849 [first edition of the *Legendary Saga*, with appendix containing the six fragments of the *Oldest Saga*]; Storm, Gustav, ed. *Otte brudstykker af den ældste saga om Olav den hellige*. Det norske historiske kildeskriftfonds skrifter, 29. Kristiania [Oslo]: Grøndahl, 1893 [notes, facsimile, and introduction]; Johnsen, Oscar Albert, ed. *Olafs saga hins helga. Efter pergamenthaandskrift i Uppsala Universitetsbibliotek, Delagardieske samling nr. 8 II*. Det norske historiske kildeskriftfonds skrifter, 47. Kristiania [Oslo]: Dybwad, 1922 [note introduction and the investigation of dialect by Marius Hægstad]; Holtsmark, Anne, ed. *Legendarisk Olavssaga*. Corpus Codicum Norvegicorum Medii Aevi, Quarto serie, 2. Oslo: Dreyer, 1956 [facsimile]; Guðni Jónsson, ed. "Helgisaga Óláfs Haraldssonar." In *Konunga sögur*. 3 vols. [Reykjavik]: Íslendingasagnaútgáfan, 1957, vol. 1, pp. 201–400 [see pp. 403–26 for "Brot úr elztu sögu"; normalized Icelandic texts, the second containing Storm's eight frag-ments]; Heinrichs, Anne, *et al.*, eds. and trans. *Olafs saga hins helga: Die "Legendarische Saga" über Olaf den Heiligen*. Heidelberg: Winter, 1982 [slightly normalized Norwegian; helpful index and introduction]. **Tr.**: Heinrichs, Anne, *et al.*, eds. and trans. *Olafs saga hins helga* [see above; German translation of the *Legendary Saga*]. **Bib.**: Halldór Hermannsson. *Bibliography of the Sagas of the Kings of Norway and Related Sagas and Tales*. Islandica, 3. Ithaca: Cornell University Library, 1910; rpt. New York: Kraus, 1966, pp. 45–6; *Supplement*: Islandica 26 (1937), p. 26.

Lit.: Sigurður Nordal. *Om Olaf den helliges saga: En kritisk undersøgelse*. Copenhagen: Gad, 1914; Turville-Petre, G. *Origins of Icelandic Litera-ture*. Oxford: Clarendon, 1953; rpt. 1967, pp. 175 ff.; Andersson, Theodore M. "Lore and Literature in a Scandinavian Conversation Episode." In *Idee—Gestalt—Geschichte: Festschrift Klaus von See*. Ed. Gerd Wolfgang Weber. Studien zur europäischen Kulturtradition. Studies in European Cultural Tradition. Odense: Odense University Press, 1968, pp. 261–84 [refers to *Kristni þáttr*]; Louis-Jensen, Jonna. "'Syvende og ottende brudstykke.' Fragmentet AM 325 IVα 4to." *Opuscula* 4. Bibliotheca Arnamagnæana, 30. Copenhagen: Munksgaard, 1970, pp. 31–60; Jónas Kristjánsson. *Um Fóstbræðrasögu*. Reykjavik: Stofnun Árna Magnússonar, 1972, pp. 151–216 [English summary]; Jónas Kristjánsson. "The Legendary Saga." In *Minjar og menntir: Afmælisrit helgað Kristjáni Eldjarn 6. desember 1976*. Ed. Guðni Kolbeinsson *et al.* Reykjavik: Menningarsjóður, 1976, pp. 281–93; Heinrichs, Anne. "'Intertexture' and Its Function in Early Written Sagas: A Stylistic Observation of *Heiðarvíga saga*, *Reykdæla saga* and the *Legendary Olafssaga*." *Scandinavian Studies* 48 (1976), 127–45; *Papers of the Third International Saga Conference. Oslo, July 26th–31st, 1976* [photocopies of papers distributed to participants; contains the following relevant articles: Anderssen, Per Sveaas. "On the Histo-ricity of Certain Passages in the Saga of Olaf Haraldsson"; Frankis, John. "An Old English Source for the Guðbrandsdal Episode in Óláfs saga helga"; Heinrichs, Anne. "Episoden als Strukturelemente in der Legendarischen Saga und ihre Varianten in anderen Olafssagas"]; Hallberg, Peter. "Direct Speech and Dialogue in Three Versions of Óláfs saga helga." *Arkiv för nordisk filologi* 93 (1978), 116–37; Schach, Paul. *Icelandic Sagas*. Twayne's World Authors Series, 717. Boston: Twayne, 1984, pp. 48–55; Heinrichs, Anne. "Christliche Überformung traditioneller Erzählstoffe in der 'Legendarischen Olafssaga.'" In *The Sixth International Saga Conference 28/7–2/8 1985. Workshop Papers*. 2 vols. Copenhagen: Det arnamagnæanske Institut, 1985, vol. 1, pp. 451–67 [photocopies of papers distributed to participants]; Whaley, Diana. "Heimskringla and Its Sources: The Miracles of Óláfr helgi." In *The Sixth International Saga Conference*, vol. 2, pp. 1083–103; Andersson, Theodore M. "Kings' Sagas (*Konungasögur*)." In *Old Norse–Icelandic Literature: A Critical Guide*. Ed. Carol J. Clover and John Lindow. Islandica, 45. Ithaca and London: Cornell University Press, 1985, pp. 212 ff.; Jónas Kristjánsson. *Eddas and Sagas: Iceland's Medieval Litera-ture*. Trans. Peter Foote. Reykjavik: Hið íslenska bókmenntafélag, 1988, pp. 154–63; Heinrichs, Anne. *Der Óláfs þáttr Geirstaðaálfs—Eine Variantenstudie*. Heidelberg: Winter, 1989; Poole, Russell. "Skaldic Praise Poetry as a Marginal Form." In *Poetry in the Scandinavian Middle Ages: The Seventh International Saga Conference*. Ed. Teresa Pàroli. Atti del 12 Congresso Internazionale di Studi sull'Alto Medioevo. Spoleto: La sede del Centro Studi, 1990, pp. 169–85 [refers to *Liðsmannaflokkr*].

Anne Heinrichs

[**See also:** *Ágrip af Nóregs konunga sǫgum*; Christian Poetry; Christian Prose; Conversion; Einarr Skúlason; *Flateyjarbók*; *Heimskringla*; *Historia Norwegiae*; Homilies (West Norse); *Konungasögur*; Miracles, Collections of; Óláfr, St.; Political Literature; Saints' Lives; Sighvatr Þórðarson; Theodoricus: *Historia de antiquitate regum Norwagiensium*; Þórarinn loftunga; William of Jumièges: *Gesta Normannorum ducum*]

Óláfs saga Tryggvasonar, the saga(s) of King Óláfr Tryggvason of Norway (r. 995–999/1000), developed from short passages in the oldest Icelandic and Norwegian *konungasögur*, such as *Historia Norwegiae*, *Ágrip*, and *Historia de antiquitate regum*

Norwagiensium by Theodoricus Monachus. The saga, which describes his life and deeds in detail, has many different realizations. The oldest *Óláfs saga Tryggvasonar* was composed in Latin about 1190 by the monk Oddr Snorrason at the monastery of Þingeyrar (northern Iceland), but is preserved only as three different redactions of an Icelandic translation, each represented by a single MS: AM 310 4to, written in 1250–1275 (incomplete); Stock. Perg. 4to no. 18, written about 1300 (incomplete); and a fragment consisting of two folios, De la Gardie 4–7, written about 1270. The version in AM 310 4to is expanded with interpolations from Ari Þorgilsson's *Íslendingabók* and from *Jómsvíkinga saga*; as a rule, the text is wordier in this redaction than in the others. Which of these three redactions represents the original translation best has, however, not been determined with full certainty.

Oddr collected his material from both oral and written sources, among others the now-lost works of Sæmundr Sigfússon and Ari Þorgilsson. Correspondances between Oddr's and Theodoricus's texts indicate that Oddr must have used Theodoricus's work or a common source. In the written sources, Oddr found the main historical and pseudo-historical knowledge about Óláfr Tryggvason's life, as follows. After his father was treacherously killed by his kinsmen, Óláfr's mother bore him in exile and sent him on a perilous journey to Novgorod, where he was fostered. At twelve years old, he was made the leader of warriors, and later became the chief of Vikings who harassed the coasts of the Baltic Sea, the Netherlands, and the British Isles. He was baptized in England and shortly thereafter went to Norway, where he ruled as a king for five years, during which time he christianized five countries. He was killed in a battle at sea in the year 1000.

Oddr's chief concern was to glorify Óláfr Tryggvason as the first missionary king of Norway and the person who christianized Iceland; as John the Baptist was the forerunner of Christ, Óláfr Tryggvason was the forerunner of St. Óláfr, not a saint himself, but chosen by God for salvation of Norsemen from the delusion of heathendom. Although Oddr based his saga on written and oral sources, he found himself free to expand the story with anecdotes modeled on the Bible and hagiographic literature.

Oddr's *Óláfs saga Tryggvasonar* is, together with skaldic poetry, the main source of *Fagrskinna*'s passage about Óláfr Tryggvason, in which the description of his last battle constitutes the bulk of the account. This version excludes all the legendary and hagiographic material. Likewise, Snorri Sturluson's *Óláfs saga Tryggvasonar* in *Heimskringla* has as its main sources Oddr's *Óláfs saga Tryggvassonar* and skaldic poetry; but, in addition, Snorri used *Jómsvíkinga saga* and probably a now-lost saga about the earls of Hlaðir (**Hlaðajarla saga*). Snorri also pruned the diction of all hagiographic characteristics.

Gunnlaugr Leifsson, a monk at Þingeyrar (d. 1218 or 1219), also used Oddr in his *Óláfs saga Tryggvasonar* and most likely expanded it with separate *þættir* and other material concerning the king's missionary activity. His *Óláfs saga Tryggvasonar*, written in Latin, is lost, except for some passages in *Óláfs saga Tryggvasonar en mesta* (the *Longest Saga*), which was probably composed in the early 14th century and was modeled on Snorri Sturluson's *Separate Saga* of St. Óláfr. The main source of the *Longest Saga* was *Heimskringla* in a MS closely related to *Jöfraskinna*, but material from various sagas and *þættir* with reference to the introduction of Christianity was inserted, including *Færeyinga saga*, *Hallfreðar saga*, *Landnámabók*, a lost saga of the Danish kings, Gunnlaugr's *Óláfs saga Tryggvasonar*, and so on. The original version of the saga is preserved in AM 61 fol., AM 53 fol., and AM 54 fol., all written in the late 14th century. In *Bergsbók* (Stock. Perg. fol. no. 1, early 15th century, descending from AM 54 fol.), the saga is attributed to Bergr Sokkason, abbot of the monastery at Munkaþverá (northern Iceland) during the second quarter of the 14th century. The *Longest Saga* was later altered considerably, with changes in the sequence of episodes; two independent *þættir* (*Nornagests þáttr* and *Helga þáttr Þórissonar*) were interpolated. This later version is preserved (incomplete) in AM 62 fol. and partly in *Flateyjarbók*, where a new revision has been undertaken, in particular by the addition of fresh material, such as *Grœnlendinga saga*. Instead of the abridged saga texts of the original *Longest Saga*, large parts of the sagas in question have been copied from independent MSS, among others *Færeyinga saga* and *Jómsvíkinga saga*.

Ed.: Finnur Jónsson, ed. *Saga Óláfs Tryggvasonar af Oddr Snorrason munk*. Copenhagen: Gad, 1932; Ólafur Halldórsson, ed. *Óláfs saga Tryggvasonar en mesta*. 2 vols. Editiones Arnamagnæanæ, ser. A, vols. 1–2. Copenhagen: Munksgaard, 1958–61 [vol. 3 forthcoming]; Holtsmark, Anne, ed. *Olav Tryggvasons saga etter AM 310 qv*. Corpus Codicum Norvegicorum Medii Aevi, Quarto serie, 5. Oslo: Selskapet til utgivelse av gamle norske håndskrifter, 1974. **Tr.**: Sephton, John, trans. *The Saga of King Olaf Tryggwason Who Reigned over Norway A.D. 955 to A.D. 1000*. Northern Library, 1. London: Nutt, 1895 [the *Longest Saga*]. **Lit.**: Finnur Jónsson. "Óláfs saga Tryggvasonar (hin meiri)." *Aarbøger for nordisk Oldkyndighed og Historie* (1930), 119–38; Bjarni Aðalbjarnarson. *Om de norske kongers sagaer*. Skrifter utg. av Det Norske Videnskaps-Akademi i Oslo, II. Hist.-filos. Kl., 1936, 4. Oslo: Dybwad, 1937 [esp. pp. 55–135]; Holtsmark, Anne. "Om de norske kongers sagaer: Opposisjonsinnlegg ved Bjarni Aðalbjarnarsons doktordisputats 23. september 1936." *Edda* 25 (1938), 145–64; Gordon, Erma. *Die Olafssaga Tryggvasonar des Odd Snorrason*. Berlin: Pfau, 1938; Beyschlag, Siegfried. *Konungasögur: Untersuchungen zur Königssaga bis Snorri: Die älteren Übersichtswerke samt Ynglingasaga*. Bibliotheca Arnamagnæana, 8. Copenhagen: Munksgaard, 1950, pp. 180–202, 256–62; Jones, Gwyn. *The Legendary History of Olaf Tryggvason*. The W. P. Ker Memorial Lectures, 22. Glasgow: Jackson & Son, 1968; Lönnroth, Lars. "Studier i Olaf Tryggvasons saga." *Samlaren* 84 (1963), 54–94; Ellehøj, Svend. *Studier over den ældste norrøne historieskrivning*. Bibliotheca Arnamagnæana, 26. Copenhagen: Munksgaard, 1965; Andersson, Theodore M. "The Conversion of Norway According to Oddr Snorrason and Snorri Sturluson." *Mediaeval Scandinavia* 10 (1977), 83–95; Hoffmann, Dietrich. "Die Vision des Oddr Snorrason." In *Festskrift til Ludvig Holm-Olsen på hans 70-årsdag den 9. juni 1984*. Ed. Bjarne Fidjestøl *et al*. Øvre Ervik: Alvheim & Eide, 1984, pp. 142–51; Holm-Olsen, Ludvig. "Forfatterinnslag i Odd munks saga om Olav Tryggvason." In *Festskrift til Alfred Jakobsen*. Ed. Jan Ragnar Hagland *et al*. Trondheim: Tapir, 1987, pp. 79–90.

Ólafur Halldórsson

[**See also**: *Ágrip af Nóregs konunga sǫgum*; Christian Poetry; *Fagrskinna*; *Flateyjarbók*; *Hallfreðar saga*; *Heimskringla*; *Helga þáttr Þórissonar*; *Historia Norwegiae*; *Íslendingabók*; *Konungasögur*; *Landnámabók*; *Nornagests þáttr*; Óláfr Tryggvason; Theodoricus: *Historia de antiquitate regum Norwagiensium*; *Þáttr*; Vinland Sagas]

Óláfsdrápa see **Hallfreðr Óttarsson**

Óláfsdrápa sœnska see **Óttarr svarti**

Old English Literature, Norse Influence on. It is not surprising that the vernacular literature of Anglo-Saxon England would to some extent come under Scandinavian influence, considering the tremendous impact of the Scandinavians upon English history, from the first raids of the Vikings upon Lindisfarne in 793, to the treaty between Alfred and Guthrum in 886 establishing the "Danelaw," to the succession of Knud (Cnut) to the throne of England in 1016, which he held until his death in 1035, and of the successive reigns of his two sons, ending in 1042.

Such historical events provided the impetus and subject matter for a number of Old English poems, such as *The Battle of Maldon* and two poems contained in the *Anglo-Saxon Chronicle: The Battle of Brunanburh* and *The Capture of the Five Boroughs*.

The Battle of Maldon describes a battle fought in 991 between an English levy led by Byrhtnoth and a Viking fleet that made its way down from Ipswich to the estuary of the Blackwater and the small island of Northey on the east coast of England. The *Parker Chronicle* describes the event thus: "In this year Anlaf [Óláfr Tryggvason?] came with ninety-three ships to Folkestone, and harried outside, and sailed to Sandwich, and thence to Ipswich, overrunning all the countryside and so to Maldon. Ealdorman Byrhtnoth came to meet them with his levies and fought them, but they slew the earldorman and there had possession of the place of slaughter." Despite suggestive evidence in *Óláfs saga Tryggvasonar* (Gordon 1987: 13–5) and a treaty among King Æthelred and Anlaf, Justin (Jósteinn), and Guðmundr in 991 or 994, it is uncertain that Óláfr was actually at Maldon, even though he was engaged in military campaigns in England around that time. Scholars now generally hold that the poem was composed some years after the event (*ca.* 1020–1042) (McKinnell 1975, Blake 1978, Anderson 1986), with some possibility of influence from *Bjarkamál* (Phillpotts 1929), the *Vita Oswaldi* (composed *ca.* 995–1005; McKinnell 1975), and possibly the *Encomium Emmae* (Anderson 1986). The work must be counted as an imaginative poetic creation based on accounts of the battle, and not as a firsthand report. Notable is the poem's portrait of Byrhtnoth and his troop as they defend their position in the best of heroic traditions, as well as its swift pace, individual speeches, and battle clashes.

The two *Chronicle* poems commemorate victories over invading forces. *The Capture of the Five Boroughs* is recorded in the *Anglo-Saxon Chronicle* for the year 942, and tells in its ten lines of Edmund's freeing of the Five Boroughs of Leicester, Lincoln, Nottingham, Derby, and Stamford from the Norsemen at York. More noteworthy is *The Battle of Brunanburh* (in the *Chronicle* for 937), which relates the victory of the English forces under the command of Æthelstan and Edmund over the combined forces of Scots, commanded by Constantine, and Norsemen, commanded by Anlaf, son of the Viking king of Dublin Guthfrith. After the initial clash, the invading forces flee; five kings and seven earls of the Norse forces are killed, although Anlaf and Constantine escape. Scholars have identified the battle on Vínheiðr described in *Egils saga Skalla-Grímssonar* (chs. 50–55) as another account of the battle at Brunanburh, although some of the details are incorrect (*e.g.*, Anlaf [Óláfr] and Constantine are made into one person: "Óláfr rauði ['the red'] was the name of the king of Scotland").

Other works within the corpus of Old English may have come under direct Scandinavian influence, or drawn upon a larger Scandinavian or Germanic tradition of catalogues or encyclopedic writing. The *Rune Poem* contains a number of parallels with the Icelandic and Norwegian rune poems. For example, where the

Old English poem reads (*hægl*) *byþ hwitust corna* ("hail is the whitest of grains"), the Icelandic poem has (*hagall*) *er kaldastr korna* ("hail is the coldest of grains"), and the Norwegian (*hagall*) *er kaldakorn* ("hail is cold grain"); where the Old English reads (*man*) *byþ on myrgþe his magan leof* ("man rejoicing in life is cherished by his kinsmen"), the Icelandic has (*maðr*) *er manns gaman* ("man is the joy of man"). Yet, as the poem's most recent editor remarks, the poems reveal "disparities in content, style, and purpose" (Halsall 1981: 38); more likely, the poems simply draw from a larger tradition of rune lore and shared vocabulary. The Scandinavian relations of another poem, *The Rhyming Poem*, have also been the subject of recent discussion, with Earl (1987) suggesting that the poet was familiar with verse techniques of skaldic poetry. The claim was rejected in a response by Amory (1987), who asserted "that the Anglo-Saxon rhymer knew neither the Old Norse language nor its literature." Still another work, the poetic *Solomon and Saturn*, a dialogue on miscellaneous topics, has been said to exhibit stylistic affinities with *Vafþrúðnismál* (Dobbie 1942: 6: 161). The poem *Widsith*, a catalogue poem in which a ficticious *scop* recounts his experiences among various tribes, suggests parallels with Saxo's *Gesta Danorum* and with versified name lists contained in *Hervarar saga* and *Ǫrvar-Odds saga* (Malone 1962). Finally, early scholarship on *Wulf and Eadwacer* suggests a Norse model for the poem, citing the use of *ljóðaháttr* meter (v. 3) and similarities in Old English and Old Norse diction (*e.g.*, Old English *on þreat cymeð*, Old Norse *at þrotum koma*) (Lawrence 1902, Schofield 1902). The use of the word *hwelp* 'hwelp' in a sense corresponding to Old Norse *vargdropi* 'wolf's cub' may also point to Norse influence (Pulsiano and Wolf 1991).

Among the prose works, the question of the relationship of *The Prose Phoenix* to the Old Norse version contained in AM 764 4to (14th century) and AM 194 8vo (15th century) has recently been reopened. Larsen (1942) maintained that the Old Norse version derived from the Old English version or from a common source, which Förster (1920) took to be a Latin sermon or homily (*cf.* Blake 1964: 96). Yerkes (1984), however, suggests that on the evidence of shared errors and the appearance of *hapax legomena* in the Old English version (*e.g.*, Old English *carlfugol* 'male bird' where Old Norse reads *karlfugl*), the Old Norse version possibly came first. With regard to the prose *Solomon and Saturn* and its companion, *Adrian and Ritheus*, Cross and Hill (1982) have argued that although one of the questions is found elsewhere only in *Alfræði Íslenzk*, it is more likely that both the Old English works and the Old Norse work had contact with a Latin list or text of the *Joca monachorum* type.

Two additional works merit mention here, *Deor* and *Waldere*, both of which draw upon legends widely circulated in the Middle Ages. The matter concerning Weland and Beadohild in *Deor* is also related in *Vǫlundarkviða*, although it is clear from the Weland story carved on the Franks Casket (8th century) that the legend was inherited in Old English from a native tradition (Malone 1933). The Walter legend that forms the core of *Waldere* is known, among other works (*e.g.*, *Waltherius*, *Nibelungenlied*), from *Þiðreks saga* (chs. 241–44).

The most important work exhibiting Scandinavian parallels is the epic poem *Beowulf*. Scandinavian history is central to the narrative, and the work displays a wide range of parallels to and influences from Scandinavian history, literature, myth, and folklore.

The nearest parallel to Beowulf's fight with Grendel in the

hall Heorot and his fight with Grendel's mother in the mere (ll. 662–709, 1492–1590) is found in chs. 64–66 of *Grettis saga*. A parallel to the descent into the mere and the subsequent battle is found in *Samsons saga fagra*; for analogues to fights with creatures in a hall or cave, we can look to *Orms þáttr Stórólfssonar* (chs. 6–9), *Þorsteins þáttr uxafóts* (chs. 10–11), *Gull-Þóris saga*, and *Þorsteins saga Víkingssonar* (ch. 13). For the dragon fight that concludes *Beowulf*, scholars have suggested a possible Danish origin, particularly as reflected in Frotho's fight with a dragon in Saxo's *Gesta Danorum*.

For the character of Beowulf himself, scholars have noted affinities with Bǫðvarr in *Hrólfs saga kraka*; so close are the parallels that scholars have seen in the combination of these characters "a confirmation of the original identity of the two heroes" (Klaeber 1950: xix ff.). Hroðgar's character in the Old English poem is similar to that of Hrólfr in *Hrólfs saga kraka*. Other parallels with episodes and references to characters appearing in *Beowulf* have been seen in such works as *Skjǫldunga saga, Heimskringla*, Sven Aggesen's *Brevis historia*, and *Vǫlsunga saga*, to name but a few (see also Jorgensen 1978, 1986)

Ed.: Readers should consult the introductions to Krapp, George Philip, and Elliott Van Kirk Dobbie, eds. *The Anglo-Saxon Poetic Records*, 6 vols. New York: Columbia University Press, 1931–53; Malone, Kemp, ed. *Deor*. London: Methuen, 1933; rpt. Exeter: University of Exeter, 1983; Gordon, E. V., ed. *The Battle of Maldon*. London: Methuen, 1937; rpt. 1957; Klaeber, Fr., ed. *Beowulf and The Fight at Finnsburg, Edited, with Introduction, Bibliography, Notes, Glossary, and Appendices*. Lexington: Heath, 1922; 3rd ed. 1950 [see introduction, pp. xii–xlviii and bibliography, pp. cxxxv–clv]; Malone, Kemp, ed. *Widsith*. Anglistica, 13. Copenhagen: Rosenkilde & Bagger, 1962; Blake, N. F., ed. *The Phoenix*. Old and Middle English Texts. Manchester: Manchester University Press, 1964 [for Old Norse version, see Appendix II, pp. 96–9]; Halsall, Maureen, ed. *The Old English Rune Poem: A Critical Edition*. McMaster Old English Studies and Texts, 2. Toronto: University of Toronto Press, 1981; Cross, James E., and Thomas D. Hill, eds. *The Prose Solomon and Saturn and Adrian and Ritheus*. McMaster Old English Studies and Texts, 1. Toronto: University of Toronto Press, 1982. **Tr.**: Garmonsway, G. N., *et al.*, eds. *Beowulf and Its Analogues*. New York: Dutton, 1971; Bradley, S. A. J., trans. *Anglo-Saxon Poetry*. London: Dent, 1982. **Bib.**: Donald K. Fry. *Beowulf and The Fight at Finnsburh: A Bibliography*. Charlottesville: University Press of Virginia, 1969; Greenfield, Stanley, and Fred C. Robinson. *A Bibliography of Publications on Old English Literature to the End of 1972*. Toronto: University of Toronto Press, 1980; Douglas D. Short. *Beowulf Scholarship: An Annotated Bibliography*. Garland Reference Library of the Humanities, 193. New York and London: Garland, 1980; Pulsiano, Phillip. *An Annotated Bibliography of North American Doctoral Dissertations on Old English Language and Literature*. Medieval Texts and Studies, 3. East Lansing: Colleagues, 1988; readers should also consult the *Old English Newsletter*, vol. 1– (1967–) and *Bibliography of Old Norse–Icelandic Studies* (1963–). **Lit.**: The literature on the subject is extensive; readers should consult the bibliographies listed above. Only studies referred to in this article are listed below: Lawrence, William Witherle. "The First Riddle of Cynewulf." *Publications of the Modern Language Association* 17 (1902), 247–61; Schofield, William Henry. "Signy's Lament." *Publications of the Modern Language Association* 17 (1902), 262–95; Phillpotts, Bertha. "The Battle of Maldon: Some Danish Affinities." *Modern Language Review* 24 (1929), 172–90; McKinnell, John. "On the Date of *The Battle of Maldon*." *Medium Ævum* 44 (1975), 121–36; Jorgensen, Peter A. "Beowulf's Swimming Contest with Breca: Old Norse Parallels." *Folklore* 89 (1978), 52–9;

Yerkes, David. "The Old Norse and Old English Accounts of the Phoenix." *Journal of English Linguistics* 17 (1984), 24–8; Anderson, Earl R. "*The Battle of Maldon*: A Reappraisal of Possible Sources, Date, and Theme." In *Modes of Interpretation in Old English Literature: Essays in Honour of Stanley B. Greenfield*. Ed. Phyllis Rugg Brown *et al.* Toronto: University of Toronto Press, 1986, pp. 247–72; Jorgensen, Peter A. "Additional Icelandic Analogues to *Beowulf*." In *Sagaskemmtun: Studies in Honour of Hermann Pálsson on His 65th Birthday, 26th May 1986*. Ed. Rudolf Simek *et al.* Vienna, Cologne, and Graz: Böhlau, 1986, pp. 201–8; Earl, James W. "Hisperic Style in the Old English 'Rhyming Poem.'" *Publications of the Modern Language Association* 102.2 (1987), 187–96; Amory, Frederic. "Hisperic Style." *Publications of the Modern Language Association* 102.5 (1987), 843–4 [letter to the editor; see Earl's response, p. 844]; Pulsiano, Phillip, and Kirsten Wolf. "The 'hwelp' in *Wulf and Eadwacer*." *English Language Notes* 28.3 (1991), 1–9; Pulsiano, Phillip, and Kirsten Wolf. "*Exeter Book* Riddle 57: Those Damned Souls, Again." *Germanic Notes* 22.1–2 (1991), 2–5.

Phillip Pulsiano

Old Norse–Icelandic Literature, Foreign Influence on,

includes translations, adaptations, and recreations of English, French, German, and Latin literature; the incorporation of motifs, episodes, and themes; and the adaptation of narrative structures from non-Scandinavian works. The impact of foreign literature can be perceived in genres that were cultivated primarily in France, England, and Germany, such as the *lai*, romance, and *chanson de geste*, Old Norse–Icelandic translations of which are known as *riddarasǫgur*, and also in the indigenous eddic poetry, primarily the heroic lays, in the *Íslendingasǫgur, konungasǫgur*, and *fornaldarsǫgur*.

The dissemination of foreign matter in Old Norse–Icelandic literature was both literary and oral, embracing (1) the fairly accurate translation of known masterpieces of continental literature, such as the *lais* of Marie de France or Thomas of Britain's *Tristan*; (2) translations and adaptations of foreign literature for which the translator's/adaptor's source is not known, for example, *Mágus saga jarls*, which is related to the French poem *Quatre fils Aimon*; or *Þiðreks saga*, the source of which was a collection of German epics belonging to the Dietrich von Bern cycle; or the "Landrés þáttr" of *Karlamagnús saga*, which derives from an English romance that is no longer extant; (3) the inclusion in Old Icelandic literature of foreign motifs and episodes, known either through oral or written transmission, such as the faithful-lion motif introduced into Scandinavia through the Old Norse translation of Chrétien de Troyes's *Yvain*; (4) the retelling or generic recasting of translated literature, such as *Tiódels saga*, the Icelandic redaction of the Old Norse *Bisclaretz ljóð*, itself a translation of the *lai Bisclaret*; or *Tristrams kvæði*, a ballad belonging to the Tristan matter; or the many *rímur* that derive ultimately from continental literature via Old Norse or Old Icelandic prose translations, such as the *Skikkju rímur*, the metrical version of *Mǫttuls saga*; (5) the adaptation of foreign structures, forms, and themes, such as the structure and theme of maiden-king sagas or the multi-tier structure of bridal-quest narratives.

The least problematic evidence for foreign influence in Old Norse–Icelandic literature is provided by the translations: in the sacred realm, prayers, homilies, saints' lives, and biblical literature, such as *Stjórn*; in the secular realm, certain learned and historiographical works, such as the *Elucidarius* or *Gyðinga saga*, collections of exempla, such as those ascribed to Jón Halldórsson (bishop of Skálholt, 1322–1339), and the *riddarasǫgur*. The subsequent influence of the translated *riddarasǫgur* is limited for the most part to the transmission of non-Scandinavian names, motifs, themes, and episodes primarily in indigenous Icelandic romances, but also in the narratives traditionally known as *fornaldarsǫgur*, and sporadically in the *Íslendingasǫgur*. The Tristan matter was well known in the North, not only through the Old Norse translation *Tristrams saga ok Ísǫndar* by Brother Robert, but also through a 14th-century Icelandic adaptation entitled *Saga af Tristram ok Ísodd*. Nonetheless, neither the Tristan legend nor the translated Arthurian matter engendered romances of the tragic Tristan type that focus on an adulterous relationship, or of the marital-romance type favored in the Arthurian tradition.

Many motifs essential to the Tristan legend, however, were incorporated into Icelandic literature. Although most of the Tristan motifs presumably became known through Brother Robert's translation of Thomas's *Tristan*, some Icelandic authors, as Bjarni Einarsson (1961, 1976) has pointed out, also seemed to have been acquainted with the Béroul/Eilhart-branch of the legend. Schach (1962, 1964, 1968) has amply documented the impact of *Tristrams saga* on the romances as well as the *Íslendingasǫgur*. An analogue to the ambiguous-oath episode occurs in the "Spesar þáttr" of *Grettis saga*. Isolde's abduction by a harp-playing Irishman, her rescue by Tristan, and return to her husband inspired a similar episode in *Kormáks saga*. Princesses skilled in leechcraft, like Isolde, appear in *Jarlmanns saga ok Hermanns*, *Rémundar saga keisarasonar*, and *Sturlaugs saga starfsama*. *Rémundar saga* also borrowed from the hall-of-statues episode in *Tristrams saga* the motif of fashioning a likeness of the beloved. The author of *Gǫngu-Hrólfs saga* knew the Tristan legend, and incorporated into his bridal-quest romance both the sword-between-the-lovers motif, a variant of which also appears in *Kormáks saga* and *Sturlaugs saga starfsama*, and the golden hair dropped by a swallow, the latter motif known from the Béroul-branch, but not the Thomas-branch, of the legend. The unusual figure of a giant wearing a mantle fashioned of the beards and moustaches of his slain opponents, who confronts King Arthur in *Tristrams saga*, surfaces in the person of Ǫgmundr Eyþjófsbani in one redaction of *Ǫrvar-Odds saga*, which is also indebted to the Tristan legend for the love-death of Ingibjǫrg. These Tristan loans suffice to show the considerable popularity of the romance and its impact on Icelandic authors.

The Tristan legend also appears to have influenced a certain type of Icelandic composition. Although no group of narratives emerged in Iceland that focuses on the adulterous love triangle, as happened in France and Germany, a group of sagas, such as *Kormáks saga*, which present the dilemma of a woman desired by two men, may have been inspired by acquaintance with *Tristrams saga* or other versions of the legend. Such romances as *Jarlmanns saga ok Hermanns* and *Haralds saga Hringsbana* may reflect criticism of the adulterous relationship glorified in the Tristan legend; indeed, Schlauch considered the latter "a deliberate reply to the French romance." In any case, in both sagas, the surrogate wooer refuses to take the bride for himself in order not to betray his lord. The rather enigmatic hero of *Friðþjófs saga frœkna*, which has defied satisfactory interpretation to date, is a protagonist who loves a married woman but refuses to commit adultery. His virtuous behavior may have been intended by the author as a corrective to Tristan, and may be interpreted as an indirect criticism of the amorality espoused by *Tristrams saga*.

In addition to the appearance of essential motifs associated

with the Tristan legend and the adaptation of the narrative situation of the love triangle, but realized in a manner quite different from that in the Tristan tale, two anonymous Tristan texts were produced in the 14th century: the *Saga af Tristram ok Ísodd* and the ballad *Tristrams kvæði*. The two works are worlds apart, not only in form, the one a prose account, the other a metrical narrative, but especially in character. The saga has been criticized as a bungled narrative effort, the result of an imperfect recollection of the Tristan legend, but recent scholarship prefers to see it as a deliberate parody of the romance. *Tristrams kvæði*, however, which focuses on the death of the lovers, faithfully transmits the original's tragic tone.

Of the fiction translated in Norway and Iceland, no other work had the impact of *Tristrams saga*. The translations of Chrétien de Troyes's Arthurian romances neither generated a spate of imitations, as they did in Germany, nor did they prove as productive a source of motifs as *Tristrams saga*. Nonetheless, *Ívens saga* and *Mǫttuls saga* enriched the repertoire of motifs in Old Icelandic literature. The faithful-lion episode from *Ívens saga* is incorporated into *Ectors saga*, *Grega saga*, *Kára saga Kárasonar*, *Konráðs saga keisarasonar*, *Vilhjálms saga sjóðs*, *Sigurðar saga þǫgla*, and even a post-Reformation folktale, *Vígkæns saga kúahirðis*. The dragon in *Ívens saga* was also borrowed in other works, and took on features from a similar dragon appearing in *Þiðreks saga*. Quite a different faithful lion appears in *Hrólfs saga Gautrekssonar*, a lion that one can bully into submission by making pig-like noises. An analogous fearful elephant appears in *Konráðs saga keisarasonar*. The lore that elephants fear the grunting of pigs was transmitted by ancient and medieval writers (Pliny, Thomas of Cantimpré). It is also found in the Icelandic version of *Epistola Alexandri ad Aristotelem* (*Sendibréf Alexanders*), which may have been the source for the romances.

Other motifs underwent modification at the hands of Icelandic authors. The mantle of *Mǫttuls saga*, which can expose unfaithful women, reappears in *Samsons saga fagra*, with the additional virtue of being able to detect thieves. Like *Tristrams saga*, *Mǫttuls saga* generated a metrical version, the *Skikkju rímur*. *Mǫttuls saga* contributed the body of the narrative, but the author also borrowed matter from *Erex saga* and apparently was also familiar with oral Arthurian traditions, for he depicts the Round Table, which is not mentioned in any of the translated Arthurian romances. Other translated works, such as *Karlamagnús saga* and *Amícus saga ok Amilíus*, also generated *rímur*, but the primary sources of inspiration for the *rímur* were the indigenous romances, such as *Dámusta saga* and *Viktors saga ok Blávus*, which themselves had been inspired by continental romance.

Both translation and oral transmission played a role in incorporating foreign matter into Icelandic literature. On the one hand, the Old Norse translation *Januals ljóð* of the French *lai Lanval* presumably was the source of the opening episode in *Helga þáttr Þórissonar*. On the other hand, the *lai Eliduc*, which was not translated, surfaces in an episode in *Vǫlsunga saga*, itself indebted, like *Þiðreks saga* and portions of the *Poetic Edda* (e.g., the dream sequence in *Atlamál*, which derives from the *Somniale Danielis*), not only to South Germanic heroic matter but also to non-Germanic sources.

The authors of indigenous Icelandic romances borrowed material from various genres and literary traditions. The "Herrgottsschnitzer" ("carver of crucifixes") motif in *Sigurðar saga turnara*, for example, is not original; it appears in earlier French and German *fabliaux*, notably in *Le prestre crucefié*. The authors of *Gibbons saga* and *Viktors saga ok Blávus* presumably were acquainted with a tale belonging to the "Tristan-in-disguise" group of narratives, notably the German *Tristan als Mönch*. In *Dámusta saga*, an analogue appears to an episode found in the French romance *Amadas et Ydoine*, while the authors of *Gongu-Hrólfs saga* and *Konráðs saga* seem to have known a narrative about an exchange of identities, which is otherwise transmitted only in Elisabeth von Nassau-Saarbrücken's 15th-century German translation of a French *chanson de geste*, *Loher und Maller*.

The influence of foreign literature in Iceland, in written or oral form, can be seen not only in an originally foreign genre, the *riddarasögur*, but also in the indigenous Icelandic genres. The *Rauðúlfs þáttr* of *Óláfs saga helga*, for example, transmits a version of Charlemagne's oriental travels that is independent of that preserved in *Karlamagnús saga*. Judging from an analogue to the Harpins de la Montaingne episode in *Egils saga*, the author presumably was acquainted with Chrétien de Troyes's *Yvain* before the romance could have reached Iceland in translated form. The influence of *Beowulf* on *Grettis saga* has sometimes been argued, and Gregory's *Dialogues* may have contributed matter to *Njáls saga*, *Egils saga*, and the sagas of St. Óláfr and Óláfr Tryggvason, among others.

There is overwhelming evidence that Icelanders were acquainted with the anecdotal repertoire of Europe. An incident recounted in both *Haralds saga harðráða* and *Sigurðar saga Jórsalafara* (in the compilation *Morkinskinna*), where for lack of firewood the respective king uses walnuts as kindling matter, has literary antecedents, including Wace's *Roman de Rou*.

Icelanders also adopted foreign structures, forms, and themes. They resisted using the Arthurian paradigm as a model for their romances, and instead imitated the structure of *Klári saga*, a narrative attributed to Jón Halldórsson, who is said to have become acquainted with the tale in a Latin metrical version, no longer extant. Unlike the Arthurian marital romances, *Klári saga* is a bridal-quest romance that focuses on a misogamous woman. The wiles and machinations employed by the prospective bride to obstruct her marriage are used by the wooer to promote it. The structure and essential narrative elements of *Klári saga* recur in a group of Icelandic romances called *meykóngr*-sagas, since their female protagonist is a maiden-king: *Sigurðar saga þogla*, *Nitida saga*, *Viktors saga ok Blávus*, *Sigrgarðs saga frœkna*, and *Dínus saga drambláta*. The author of the Helgi/Ólof portion of *Hrólfs saga kraka* employs the maiden-king pattern in a tragic mode in keeping with his heroic sources. *Ála flekks saga*, *Gibbons saga*, *Mágus saga jarls*, and *Hrólfs saga Gautrekssonar* contain important maiden-king episodes. Although the structure and the narrative details of the maiden-king romances are chiefly indebted to *Klári saga*, the maiden-king type appears in *Hrólfs saga Gautrekssonar*, a work that presumably antedates *Klári saga*. There is evidence to suggest that the Latin source of *Klári saga* was in turn indebted to oriental literature. Indeed, the combination shield-maiden/maiden-king encountered in *Hrólfs saga Gautrekssonar*, which strikes us as "Nordic," appears in the much older tale of ed-Datma in *The Thousand and One Nights*. This oriental tale includes the important motif of the avenging wooer in disguise and as trickster that is essential to *Klári saga*. Polygenesis is one explanation for the appearance of identical female types, plots, and narrative structures in both Icelandic and oriental literature. Nonetheless, given the considerable impact of Muslim culture on medieval Europe, nota-

bly through seven centuries of Spanish occupation and its prominent role at the Sicilian court of Emperor Frederick II (1194–1250), where translations were made from Arabic and Greek, a more plausible explanation is that Icelanders became acquainted with certain oriental narratives, in oral or written form, and presumably in translation, during their sojourns and travels on the Continent.

Not only the narratively conservative and hence predictable maiden-king romances appear to be indebted to foreign sources, both written and oral, for their structure, but also other bridal-quest narratives. Andersson (1985) has convincingly argued that the multigenerational bridal-quest tales found in eddic poetry (*Helgakviða Hjǫrvarðssonar*) and in some *fornaldarsögur* (*Vǫlsunga saga*, *Hrólfs saga Gautrekssonar*, *Þorsteins saga Víkingssonar*) were inspired by a combination of written sources (*Tristrams saga ok Ísǫndar* and *Þiðreks saga*) and oral infiltration of bridal-quest patterns and motifs from German *Spielmannsdichtung* (minstrel epic). Bridal-quest narrative was the most popular form of romance in Iceland, but in the adoption of this genre, just as in the adoption of narrative matter, Icelandic authors imbued their compositions with a peculiarly Icelandic sensibility. Unlike continental romance, for example of the Arthurian type, which is fairly predictable, many Icelandic romances, like the sagas of Icelanders, strike us as quite modern because the hero's behavior is not based on exigencies of plot, but rather derives from his character, his positive as well as negative qualities.

In addition to matter and structure, some formal aspects of Icelandic literature may well be indebted to the Continent. The similarity between plot interlace in the French prose compilations of romance and the *Íslendingasögur* is striking, although the influence of the former on the latter cannot be demonstrated. Certain stylistic traits in Icelandic prose, such as cursus, owe their origin to foreign sources. The *rímur*, many of which are based on foreign matter or Icelandic narratives imitative of foreign literature, are full of figures of speech that approximate kennings and that seem to be an indigenous development. Nonetheless, it is more likely that the genitive periphrasis, which is a distinctive trait of the *rímur*, is an expression of a common European tendency toward a florid poetic diction in the later Middle Ages. Furthermore, an indispensable component of the *rímur*, the *mansöngr*, a love lyric, which functions as prologue to each *ríma*, presumably arose under the influence of German love poetry. Thus, these Icelandic love poems probably attest Icelandic familiarity with the continental love lyrics of the high Middle Ages.

Bib.: Kalinke, Marianne E., and P. M. Mitchell. *Bibliography of Old Norse–Icelandic Romances*. Islandica, 44. Ithaca and London: Cornell University Press, 1985. **Lit.**: Leach, Henry Goddard. *Angevin Britain and Scandinavia*. Harvard Studies in Comparative Literature, 6. Cambridge: Harvard University Press; London: Milford; Oxford: Oxford University Press, 1921; Schlauch, Margaret. *Romance in Iceland*. Princeton: Princeton University Press; New York: American-Scandinavian Foundation; London: Allen & Unwin, 1934; rpt. New York: Russell & Russell, 1973; Turville-Petre, G. *Origins of Icelandic Literature*. Oxford: Clarendon, 1953; rpt. 1967; Bjarni Einarsson. *Skáldasögur: Um uppruna og eðli ástaskáldasagnanna fornu*. Reykjavik: Menningarsjóður, 1961; Schach, Paul. "Tristan in Iceland." *Prairie Schooner* 36 (1962), 151–64; Schach, Paul. "Tristan and Isolde in Scandinavian Ballad and Folklore." *Scandinavian Studies* 36 (1964), 281–97; Lönnroth, Lars. *European Sources of Icelandic Saga-Writing: An Essay Based on Previous Studies*. Stockholm: Thule, 1965; Turville-

Petre, Gabriel. "Dream Symbols in Old Icelandic Literature." In *Festschrift Walter Baetke: Dargebracht zu seinem 80. Geburtstag am 28. März 1964.* Ed. Kurt Rudolph *et al.* Weimar: Böhlau, 1966, pp. 343–54; Boberg, Inger M. *Motif-Index of Early Icelandic Literature.* Bibliotheca Arnamagnæana, 27. Copenhagen: Munksgaard, 1966; Schach, Paul. "Some Observations on the Influence of *Tristrams saga ok Ísǫndar* on Old Icelandic Literature." In *Old Norse Literature and Mythology: A Symposium.* Ed. Edgar C. Polomé. Austin and London: University of Texas Press, 1968, pp. 81–129; Tveitane, Mattias. "Europeisk påvirkning på den norrøne sagalitteraturen. Noen synspunkter." *Edda* 69 (1969), 73–95; Glendinning, Robert J. "*Grettis saga* and European Literature in the Late Middle Ages." *Mosaic* 4 (1970), 49–61; Harris, Richard L. "The Lion-Knight Legend in Iceland and the Valþjófsstaðir Door." *Viator* 1 (1970), 125–45; Jorgensen, Peter. "The Icelandic Translations from Middle English." In *Studies for Einar Haugen: Presented by Friends and Colleagues.* Ed. Evelyn Scherabon Firchow *et al.* Janua Linguarum, Series Major, 59. The Hague and Paris: Mouton, 1972, pp. 305–20; See, Klaus von. "Disticha Catonis und Hávamál." *Beiträge zur Geschichte der deutschen Sprache und Literatur* (Tübingen), 94 (1972), 1–18; rpt. in his *Edda, Saga, Skaldendichtung: Aufsätze zur skandinavischen Literatur des Mittelalters.* Heidelberg: Winter, 1981, pp. 27–44; Davíð Erlingsson. *Blómað mál í rímum.* Studia Islandica, 33. Reykjavik: Menningarsjóður, 1974; Jakob Benediktsson. "Cursus in Old Norse Literature." *Mediae-val Scandinavia* 7 (1974), 15–21; Bjarni Einarsson. *Litterære forudsætninger for Egils saga.* Reykjavik: Stofnun Árna Magnússonar, 1975; *Les relations littéraires franco-scandinaves au moyen âge: Actes du colloque de Liège (avril 1972).* Bibliothèque de la Faculté de Philosophie et de Lettres de l'Université de Liège, 208. Paris: Société d'Edition "Les Belles Lettres," 1975; Bjarni Einarsson. *To skjaldesagaer: En analyse af Kormáks saga og Hallfreðar saga.* Bergen: Universitetsforlaget, 1976; Lönnroth, Lars. *Njáls saga: A Critical Introduction.* Berkeley, Los Angeles, and London: University of California Press, 1976; Fry, Donald K. "Polyphemus in Iceland." In *The Fourteenth Century.* Acta, 4. Ed. Paul Szarmach and Bernard S. Levy. Binghamton: Center for Medieval and Early Renaissance Studies, State University of New York at Binghamton, 1977, pp. 65–86; Kalinke, Marianne E. *King Arthur North-by-Northwest: The matière de Bretagne in Old Norse–Icelandic Romances.* Bibliotheca Arnamagnæana, 37. Copenhagen: Reitzel, 1981; Clover, Carol. *The Medieval Saga.* Ithaca: Cornell University Press, 1982; Vésteinn Ólason. *The Traditional Ballads of Iceland.* Reykjavik: Stofnun Árna Magnússonar, 1982; Andersson, Theodore M. "'Helgakviða Hjǫrvarðssonar' and European Bridal-Quest Narrative." *Journal of English and Germanic Philology* 84 (1985), 51–75; Kalinke, Marianne E. "Norse Romance (*Riddarasögur*)." In *Old Norse–Icelandic Studies: A Critical Guide.* Ed. Carol J. Clover and John Lindow. Islandica, 45. Ithaca and London: Cornell University Press, 1985, pp. 316–63; Clover, Carol J. "*Vǫlsunga saga* and the Missing Lai of Marie de France." In *Sagnaskemmtun: Studies in Honour of Hermann Pálsson on His 65th Birthday, 26th May 1986.* Ed. Rudolf Simek *et al.* Vienna, Cologne, and Graz: Böhlau, 1986, pp. 79–84; Gísli Sigurðsson. *Gaelic Influence in Iceland: Historical and Literary Contacts. A Survey of Research.* Reykjavik: Menningarsjóður, 1988; Hughes, Shaun F. D. "Rímur." In *Dictionary of the Middle Ages.* Ed. Joseph R. Strayer. New York: Scribner, 1982–89, vol. 10, pp. 401–7; Kalinke, Marianne E. *Bridal-Quest Romance in Medieval Iceland.* Islandica, 46. Ithaca and London: Cornell University Press, 1990.

Marianne E. Kalinke

[**See also:** *Ála flekks saga*; *Alexanders saga*; Amicus and Amileus; *Dámusta saga*; *Dínus saga drambláta*; *Ectors saga ok kappa hans*; Eddic Poetry; *Egils saga Skalla-Grímssonar*; *Elucidarius*; *Erex saga*; *Fornaldarsögur*; *Friðþjófs saga frœkna*; *Gibbons saga*; *Grettis saga*; *Gyðinga saga*; *Gǫngu-Hrólfs saga*; *Hrólfs saga Gautrekssonar*; *Íslendingasögur*; *Ívens saga*; *Jarlmanns saga ok Hermanns*; *Karlamagnús saga*; *Klári (Clári) saga*; *Konráðs saga keisarasonar*; *Konungasögur*; *Kormáks saga*; Love Poetry; *Mágus saga jarls*; *Mǫttuls saga*; *Nitida saga*; *Njáls saga*; *Óláfs saga helga*; *Rémundar saga keisarasonar*; *Riddarasögur*; *Rímur*; *Samsons saga fagra*; *Sigrgarðs saga frœkna*; *Sigurðar saga turnara*; *Sigurðar saga þǫgla*; *Stjórn*; *Sturlaugs saga starfsama*; *Tiódels saga*; *Tristrams saga ok Ísoddar*; *Tristrams saga ok Ísǫndar*; *Þiðreks saga af Bern*; *Þorsteins saga Víkingssonar*; *Viktors saga ok Blávus*; *Vilhjálms saga sjóðs*; *Vǫlsunga saga*; *Qrvar-Odds saga*]

Old Swedish Legendary (*Fornsvenska legendariet*) is a chronologically arranged collection of legends from the earliest Christian time to the middle of the 13th century. It begins with the Virgin Mary, John the Baptist, and Jesus, and ends with Peter Martyr (d. 1252). We also learn something, though mostly in summary form, about emperors and popes from the same period. The Nordic countries play a very small part in the legendary. There are a number of legends about Nordic saints (Sigfrid, Óláfr, Earl Magnús of the Orkneys, Erik), but these are certainly later additions.

The material of the legends was for the most part taken from the *Legenda aurea* of Jacobus de Voragine. For the material about emperors and popes, the author used Martinus Oppaviensis's *Chronicon pontificum et imperatorum* in a version from 1276. Another important source was the *Sächsische Weltchronik*. No close study has been made of the author's treatment of his sources, but it seems to have been rather free.

The legendary cannot be dated earlier than 1276, the date of Martinus's *Chronicon*. Nor can it be dated later than 1312, because it mentions Frederick II among the Roman emperors, but does not mention his successor Henry VII, who was crowned in 1312. Thus, the legendary would seem to date from around 1300, which makes it one of the oldest Swedish-language texts written in the Latin alphabet.

The author's or compiler's name is not known, but he was most likely a Dominican friar, since the collection is introduced with a dedication to St. Dominic. Linguistic evidence suggests that the collection came into being in the county of Östergötland, where there was early a Dominican friary in the town of Skänninge.

The Old Swedish Legendary is essentially preserved in three MSS, all of them of considerably later date than the presumed original. The oldest of the three is SKB A 34, usually referred to as the *Codex Bureanus*, from the middle of the 14th century or somewhat later, but much of the legendary is missing from it. Next comes the Upps. C 528, or *Codex Bildstenianus*, probably from the first half of the 15th century. Finally comes Skokloster 3 4to (now in SRA), or *Codex Passionarius*, probably from the middle or second half of the 15th century. In addition to these three MSS, there is, among others, a short fragment, SKB A 124, which may be somewhat older than the *Codex Bureanus*.

The legendary is an important source not only for ancient ecclesiastical history but for ancient history in general. Furthermore, its age makes it an important source for the history of the language (Jansson 1934).

There are other collections of legends in Swedish, for instance, the one known as the "Linköping legendary" (ca. 1500), most of which was edited by Dahlgren and appeared in *Ett forn-svenskt legendarium*, vol. 3 (1865–74). Despite the title, however, these legends are not in the strict sense a part of the *Old Swedish Legendary*.

Ed.: Stephens, G., ed. *Ett forn-svenskt legendarium*. 2 vols. Samlingar utgifna af svenska fornskrift-sällskapet, 7.1–2. Stockholm: Norstedt, 1847–58; Dahlgren, F. A., ed. *Ett forn-svenskt legendarium 3*. Samlingar utgifna af svenska fornskrift-sällskapet, 7.3. Stockholm: Norstedt, 1865–74; Jansson, Valter, ed. *Fornsvenska legendariet*. Samlingar utgifna af svenska fornskrift-sällskapet, 181. Uppsala: Almqvist & Wiksell, 1938– [partial edition]; Jansson, Valter, ed. *Legendarium Suecanum ("Fornsvenska legendariet"). E Codice Membr. Bibl. Univ. Upsal. C 528 ("Codice Bildsteniano")*. Corpus Codicum Suecicorum Medii Aevi, 19. Copenhagen: Munksgaard, 1966 [English introduction]. Lit.: Ottelin, Odal. *Studier öfver Codex Bureanus*. 2 vols. Uppsala universitets årsskrift, 1900, 1904. Uppsala: Berling, 1900–05; Jansson, Valter. *Fornsvenska legendariet: handskrifter och språk*. Nordiska texter och undersökningar, 4. Uppsala: Almqvist & Wiksell, 1934 [thorough discussion of phonology, but little of accidence, syntax, stylistics, and vocabulary]; Jansson, Valter. "*Fornsvenska legendariet*." *KLNM* 4 (1959), 518–22; Klockars, Birgit. "*Skänningelegendariet*." In *Ny illustrerad svensk litteraturhistoria*. Ed. E. N. Tigerstedt. 2nd ed. Stockholm: Natur och Kultur, 1967, vol. 1, p. 156.

Börje Tjäder

[See also: Christian Prose; Legenda; *Nicodemus, Gospel of*; Saints' Lives]

Om ett gyllene år see Swedish Literature, Miscellaneous

Oratio contra clerum Norvegiae ("A Speech Against the Norwegian Clergy"), also known as *En tale mot biskopene* ("A Speech Against the Bishops"), is an anonymous anticlerical pamphlet, written during the conflict between King Sverrir and the Church around 1200. *Oratio* is preserved in only one MS, AM 114a 4to, from the early 14th century. As a piece of propaganda, *Oratio* compares favorably with most European works of the period. It is written in a vivid style and has a clear and logical composition, which is well suited to bringing home its central message. It opens with the allegory of the body politic, quite popular in contemporary Europe, according to which the various ranks and functions in society correspond to the limbs and organs of the human body. The author identifies the king with the heart and the whole body with the Church, thus placing himself within the Carolingian tradition of an extensive secular-religious community governed by the king. Next, he describes the illness that has affected the body, because its members, in practice those representing the clergy, have failed to perform their function; he sets out to correct this evil by presenting the right doctrine on the government of the Church. As the king is God's representative on earth, all men, including the clergy, owe him obedience. In support of this doctrine, the author refers to the duty of all men to pay taxes to the emperor and to the law of advowson (the right of presentation of a priest to a church), which allows even ordinary laymen to govern churches. In addition, he defends the contemporary Norwegian king against some of the charges brought against him by the clergy. The excommunication passed against King Sverrir

in 1194 is invalid, because the king is in the right. The king did not resign his government of the Church when the archdiocese was established (in 1152/3), and even if he had done so, such a resignation would have been against the "sacred laws" and thus null and void. Finally, the author points out that heresy has normally originated in the clergy, while the kings have supported the right doctrine, and he cites examples to this effect.

Oratio contains a doctrine of royal superiority over the Church that was decidedly old-fashioned by the late 12th century, when most royalist propagandists based their claims on the doctrine of the two swords and tried to defend the independent authority of the king in purely secular matters. The author of *Oratio* supports his arguments by extensive quotations, both in the original and translation, from "the sacred writings," *i.e.*, sources contained in the *Decretum Gratiani*. He exploits this source very skillfully, despite the fact that its general attitude to the king's position within the Church is the very opposite of his own.

Although it is preserved in only one MS, *Oratio* seems to have exerted some influence. The author of *Konungs skuggsjá* clearly drew upon *Oratio*, although he is less extreme in his doctrine of royal superiority over the Church. Together, the two works suggest a quite original tradition of political thought in the Norwegian court milieu, which was used actively by the monarchy, not only to defend its rights against the Church but also to make the people at large accept a stronger royal government.

Ed.: Holtsmark, Anne, ed. *En tale mot biskopene: En sproglig-historisk undersøkelse*. Skrifter utgitt av Det norske vitenskaps-akademi i Oslo, II. Hist.-filos. Kl., 1930, 9. Oslo: Dybwad, 1931 [text, introduction, etc.]. Lit.: Gunnes, Erik. *Kongens ære. Kongemakt og kirke i "En tale mot biskopene."* Oslo: Gyldendal, 1971; Bagge, Sverre. *The Political Thought of The King's Mirror*. Odense: Odense University Press, 1987.

Sverre Bagge

[See also: *Konungs skuggsjá*; Norway; Political Literature; *Sverris saga*]

Orkney, Norse in. The history of Viking Orkney is as distorted as it is dominated by *Orkneyinga saga*; unfortunately, few other documentary sources for the Viking period survive. Until Haraldr Maddaðarson rebelled against King Sverrir Sigurðarson of Norway at the end of the 12th century, the Orkney earldom included Shetland, which also experienced Viking occupation but in even more obscure circumstances.

The splendid neolithic monuments of the Northern Isles demonstrate that Orkney had a distinguished past, but modern opinion is almost as baffled as the 12th-century author of *Historia Norwegiae*: "From where the people of Orkney came, we are entirely ignorant." At the time of the first raids in the late 8th century, the population is thought to have consisted largely of Bronze Age natives ruled by a Pictish nobility that may not have been very numerous. The *Historia* relates that in the time of King Haraldr hárfagri ("fair-hair") Hálfdanarson, a group of Norwegian pirates destroyed the Picts, seized their lands, and subdued the islands. Such an account would appear to be confirmed by place-name evidence, which reflects the total obliteration of Pictish influence.

Archaeological evidence, for example, from the site of Buckquoy, has tended to suggest more peaceful contact and assimilation. The finding flies in the face of ample documentation to the contrary throughout those areas that were subjected to the misery of the Viking attacks. It is difficult to believe that the ferocity of the Viking assaults on the Scottish mainland and on the Hebrides was not paralleled by an earlier experience in Orkney.

Historical sources and onomastic evidence agree that Celtic monks (*papae*) had established a presence in Orkney, and that, as elsewhere, the monastic communities and hermitages seem largely to have survived the initial onslaught, doubtless through the payment of tribute. The saga tradition relates that Orkney was converted to Christianity by King Óláfr Tryggvason, but clearly the process was both earlier and more gradual. Viking pragmatism probably dictated some accommodation with the *papae*; nominal acceptance of Christianity may have been acquired along with other cultural baggage adopted, and adapted, by the invaders.

There is no evidence to suggest that Orkney was occupied much before the late 8th century. But it became an important base for attacks on the British mainland, and it remained a highly important link on the golden road between Norway, Ireland, and the Mediterranean.

It is doubtful whether Haraldr hárfagri's much-cited expedition "west-over-sea" ever took place. He allegedly sought to displace Orkney-based Vikings who were using the islands as a refuge from which to attack Norway, and, consequently, he granted an earldom to the family of Rǫgnvaldr, earl of Møre. The earldom, which probably replaced a Pictish kingship, testifies to Orkney's central importance in the Scandinavian world as a link between Norway, the Celtic West, and the Scandinavian kingdom of York. The earls' *de facto* possession of Caithness brought the Norsemen into conflict with the Celtic tribes of northern Scotland, but also resulted in the creation of some Celto-Norse kindreds.

The earldom achieved its zenith under Þorfinnr Sigurðarson (d. *ca.* 1065), who feuded with the Scottish king MacBeth. After a pilgrimage to Rome, Þorfinnr established an important cathedral or minster on the tidal island of Birsay alongside his Bu, or palace. Archaeology is beginning to reveal much about the parish of Birsay, the place-names of which have been extensively surveyed. Remarkable complexes have been excavated on the east coast between Skaill and the Brough of Deerness as well as at Westness in Rousay. All three sites suggest that the Vikings occupied areas and apparently sometimes holdings that had already been settled. Some of the structures that postdate the Viking Age proper, including such fortified sites as Cubbie Roo's castle on Wyre, are being reassessed. Archaeology is also contributing to the history of the development of the Church from the 11th century, since the physical evidence, such as the numerous chapel sites, can be matched with that of place-names and medieval estate rentals.

If the Viking Age in Orkney is usually taken to have ended with Earl Þorfinnr, the late Norse, or Scandinavian, era lasted much longer. The men who built the exquisite Kirkwall cathedral (founded 1137) were accustomed to reliving the exploits of their Viking ancestors through the medium of poetry and saga. Posterity should perhaps not presume the temporal division of a world that represented a unity to the people who lived in it.

Modern archaeologists rightly consider the Viking period to be the final phase of Orkney's prehistory, since it is otherwise comparatively poorly documented. The gradual recovery of information may further illuminate the position of splendor and centrality that Orkney enjoyed in the Viking Age.

Lit.: Anderson, Alan Orr, ed. and trans. *Early Sources of Scottish History A.D. 500 to 1286*. Edinburgh: Oliver and Boyd, 1922 [esp. pp. 330–1] [translates most of the standard historical sources—sagas, annals, *etc.*]; Wainwright, F. T., ed. *The Northern Isles*. Edinburgh: Nelson, 1962 [esp. chs. 8–10]; Marwick, Hugh. *The Place-names of Birsay*. Ed. W. F. H. Nicolaisen. Aberdeen: Aberdeen University Press, 1970; Sawyer, Peter H. "King Harald Fairhair and the British Isles." In *Les Vikings et leurs civilisation*. Ed. Régis Boyer. Paris: Mouton, 1976; *Birsay: A Centre of Political and Ecclesiastical Power. Orkney Heritage* 2 (1983) [entire issue devoted to Birsay]; Morris, Christopher. "Viking Orkney: A Survey." In *The Prehistory of Orkney*. Ed. Colin Renfrew. Edinburgh: Edinburgh University Press, 1985, pp. 210–42; Crawford, Barbara E. *Scandinavian Scotland*. Scotland in the Early Middle Ages, 2. Leicester: Leicester University Press, 1987; Thomson, William P. L. *History of Orkney*. Edinburgh: Mercat, 1987; Crawford, Barbara, ed. *St Magnus Cathedral and Orkney's Twelfth-Century Renaissance*. Aberdeen: Aberdeen University Press, 1988.

Edward J. Cowan

[**See also:** Birsay; Caithness; *Historia Norwegiae*; *Magnúss saga helga eyjajarls*; *Orkneyinga saga*]

Orkneyinga saga ("The Saga of the Orkney Islanders") is otherwise known as *Jarla sǫgur* ("The Sagas of the [Orkney] Earls"), which is a more precise and probably the historically more correct title. It was compiled by an Icelandic author at the end of the 12th or the beginning of the 13th century. This original redaction, no longer extant, was one of the sources exploited by Snorri Sturluson in his first, independently composed biography of St. Óláfr. About 1230, a new redaction of *Orkneyinga saga* was produced, apparently under the influence of Snorri's *Heimskringla*; here, the original text was supplemented by a mythical-genealogical introduction, a sequence of miracles of St. Magnús the Orcadian martyr, and two continuations dealing with the history of the Norse community in Caithness on the Scottish mainland. The most recent editor of *Orkneyinga saga* argues, not wholly convincingly, that the introduction to the new redaction was written by Snorri Sturluson. The other additions would seem to stem through literary and oral channels from the local tradition of Orkney and Caithness, respectively.

The text of the saga is badly preserved. There are three fragmentary witnesses from around 1300, and a fairly full text interpolated into the sagas of Óláfr Tryggvason and St. Óláfr as these appear in the great codex *Flateyjarbók* from the end of the 14th century. Fragments of a vellum MS of early date, the remnants of which were destroyed in the Copenhagen fire of 1728, were transcribed around 1700 by the amanuensis of the famous historian Torfæus. A century earlier, this vellum MS, when still complete, was translated into Danish, and this textually important translation survives in a good copy.

Orkneyinga saga is an early example of the type of historical writing generally classified under the heading *konungasǫgur*, and several attempts have been made to put a name to its anonymous author. It seems likely that the saga was written in the intellectual environment of Oddi in the south of Iceland, the seat of a great family that had extensive relations with Orkney. Of the various conjectures regarding the identity of the author, Hermann Pálsson's (1965) advocacy of Snorri Grímsson (d. 1208) is circumstantially the most persuasive. Other candidates who have been proposed by earlier scholars are Bjarni Kolbeinsson, bishop of Orkney;

Sighvatr, the brother of Snorri Sturluson; and the priest Ingimundr Þorgeirsson from Eyjafjörður in the north of Iceland.

Whoever the author may have been, he did not succeed in creating a harmonious whole out of the sources at his disposal. These sources evidently ranged from sketchy recollections of the early period of the islands' history to detailed secondhand or even firsthand accounts of events in the 12th century. This passive reliance upon a multiplicity of sources explains why the life story of the Viking chieftain Sveinn Ásleifarson, whose death in 1170/1 brought the original saga to an end, is told at much greater length than the histories of the early earls. The sections dealing with the life of St. Magnús and with the pilgrimage to the Holy Land of Earl Rǫgnvaldr Kali Kolsson are reworked in whole or in part from preexisting written materials, thus further contributing to the lack of stylistic homogeneity in the saga.

Though not a monument of literary genius, *Orkneyinga saga* constitutes a most valuable repository of historical tradition. Its author worked in the spirit of enlightened antiquarianism promoted by Ari Þorgilsson, and plainly followed the example of Ari in drawing upon the testimony of reputable informants. His knowledge of skaldic poetry extended to verses by and about some of the Orkney earls; the most notable skalds quoted in the saga are Arnórr Þórðarson jarlaskáld ("earls' skald"; 11th century) and Rǫgnvaldr Kali (d. 1158).

Ed.: *Orkneyinga Saga sive Historia Orcadensium . . . edidit Jonas Jonæus Isl.* Hafniæ [Copenhagen]: Sumtibus Illustriss. P. Frid. Suhm, 1780; Gudbrand Vigfusson, ed., and George W. Dasent, trans. *Icelandic Sagas and Other Historical Documents Relating to the Settlements and Descents of the Northmen on the British Isles.* 4 vols. Rolls Series, 88. London: Eyre and Spottiswoode, 1887, vol. 1, pp. 1–231; rpt. Millwood: Kraus, 1964; Sigurður Nordal, ed. *Orkneyinga saga.* Samfund til udgivelse af gammel nordisk litteratur, 40. Copenhagen: Møller, 1913–16; Finnbogi Guðmundsson, ed. *Orkneyinga saga.* Íslenzk fornrit, 34. Reykjavik: Hið íslenzka fornritafélag, 1965. **Tr.**: Jón Hjaltalín and Gilbert Goudie, trans., Joseph Anderson, ed. *The Orkneyinga Saga.* Edinburgh: Edmonston and Douglas, 1873; Gudbrand Vigfusson, ed., and George W. Dasent, trans. *Icelandic Sagas and Other Historical Documents*, vol. 3, pp. 1–236; Taylor, Alexander Burt, trans. *The Orkneyinga Saga: A New Translation with Introduction and Notes.* Edinburgh and London: Oliver and Boyd, 1938; Hermann Pálsson and Paul Edwards, trans. *Orkneyinga Saga: The History of the Earls of Orkney.* London: Hogarth, 1978; rpt. Harmondsworth: Penguin, 1981. **Lit.**: Einar Ól. Sveinsson. *Sagnaritun Oddaverja: nokkrar athuganir.* Studia Islandica, 1. Reykjavik: Ísafold, 1937; Hermann Pálsson. "Höfundur *Orkneyinga sögu.*" *Tímarit Máls og menningar* 26 (1965), 98–100; Seip, Didrik Arup. "Some Remarks on the Language of the Magnus Legend in the *Orkneyinga Saga.*" In *Nordica et Anglica: Studies in Honor of Stefán Einarsson.* Ed. Allan H. Orrick. Janua Linguarum Series Major, 22. The Hague and Paris: Mouton, 1968, pp. 93–6; Taylor, A. B. "Orkneyinga Saga—Patronage and Authorship." In *Proceedings of the First International Saga Conference, University of Edinburgh 1971.* Ed. Peter Foote *et al.* London: Viking Society for Northern Research, 1973, pp. 396–410; Chesnutt, Michael. "*Haralds saga Maddaðarsonar.*" In *Specvlvm Norroenvm: Norse Studies in Memory of Gabriel Turville-Petre.* Ed. Ursula Dronke *et al.* Odense: Odense University Press, 1981, pp. 33–55; Smith, Brian. "Shetland in Saga-Time: Rereading the *Orkneyinga Saga.*" *Northern Studies* 25 (1988), 21–41.

Michael Chesnutt

[**See also:** Arnórr Þórðarson jarlaskáld; Caithness;

Flateyjarbók; *Konungasögur*; *Magnúss saga helga eyjajarls*; *Óláfs saga helga*; *Óláfs saga Tryggvasonar*; Orkney, Norse in]

Oseberg is a Viking Age ship burial on a farm of the same name in Slagen, Vestfold, Norway. G. Gustafson excavated the site in 1904, after a farmer had found carved wood when digging for treasure in the mound. The burial is usually dated to around A.D. 850. The date of the ship, wagon, and some of the other grave goods is generally placed at 800. Because of the blue clay subsoil and the tightly stacked turves of the mound, the burial has had nearly hermetic conditions, and the preservation of both metals and organic materials is remarkable. Oseberg is by far the richest burial from the Scandinavian Viking Age, and offers much information on material culture and art. The burial was placed in a 23-m. ship, pulled ashore, and lowered down into a shallow trench in the clay. During the burial ceremony, a central cairn of large stones was thrown into the ship. The combined weight of the stones and the mound pressing down into the soft subsoil caused much mechanical damage to the grave goods. Most objects are broken, and some are incomplete. The grave was robbed at some time, and the robbers' trench damaged the ship's prow and the burial chamber. Originally, the bodies of two women were placed in the burial chamber. The remains indicate that they were fully dressed, placed in beds, and the chamber hung with textiles. The skeletons are incomplete; most of the bones were found in the robbers' trench. One is of a woman fifty to sixty years old, the other between twenty and thirty years. The grave goods contain ship's equipment, objects from the "royal manor" that symbolize most of the activities of a large Viking Age farm, and a number of finely carved wooden objects, some of which may have had cultic use.

The largest and most impressive single object is the ship. Together with Gokstad, it is our main source for knowledge about early Viking Age shipbuilding. It is also of great importance in the study of Viking art. Shetelig (1971), who studied the Oseberg carvings, attributed the ship and wagon to the same master, and identified several other craftsmen on the basis of stylistic and technical details.

Before the Oseberg excavation, Viking art was known mainly from small metalwork. Oseberg gave the first information on art of monumental character. Precise dating, stylistic affinities, and development of Viking art are still under debate; nevertheless, all scholars include Oseberg in any discussion of these issues.

The find supplies information on nearly all aspects of Viking Age material culture. Most Viking graves lack organic material, either because the body was cremated with the grave goods included on the funeral fire, or because of decay. Oseberg has an abundance of wooden artifacts. Besides the ship and wagon, four sledges were found, three of them carved and with sledgepoles that are among the finest pieces of art in the find. Five animal-head posts are also richly decorated, although their exact use is unknown. Buckets, troughs, and ladles come from kitchen and table; chests and boxes were used for storage. A plain work sledge, hoe, dung fork, and wooden shovels represent the farmwork. Many of the wooden artifacts are paralleled by objects in use until only a couple of generations ago, and Norwegian ethnology draws heavily on Oseberg for the oldest dated example when various groups of artifacts are analyzed. In addition to the woodwork, Oseberg contains textiles, both imported and local. Of special value are fragments of tapestries, extremely fine woolen twills, and Byzan-

78. The ship during excavation. All equipment has been lifted, and the ship is ready to be recorded and lifted. Photo: Væring. By permission of Universitetets Oldsaksamling.

79. The wagon is the only wheeled vehicle of Viking Age date from Norway. It was probably for ceremonial rather than practical use. Photo: L. Smestad. By permission of Universitetets Oldsaksamling.

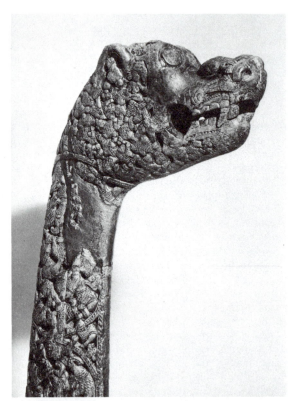

80. The "Carolingian" head-post is a good example of the intricate carving on many of the wooden objects found with the Oseberg ship. Photo: Holst. By permission of Universitetets Oldsaksamling.

81. A "collage" of kitchen and table equipment from Oseberg. The two brass-bound buckets are surely imports, while the rest is locally made. Photo: A. Liestøl. By permission of Universitetets Oldsaksamling.

tine silks. The textiles were placed mostly in the burial chamber, and were badly damaged when the grave was robbed. Tools for textile work include a frame for *sprang* (a braiding or plaiting technique used in textile work), spindles, sheep shears, wooden tablets for tablet weaving, and small wooden beaters that may have been used for processing flax. Of the personal equipment, two pairs of leather shoes are remarkably intact, while basketry made from birch roots and a box of thin bent wood survived only as small fragments.

Metalwork of high quality was also found, of both iron and copper alloys. The three yew buckets are believed to be of Irish or English manufacture; their mountings are iron and brass for the largest, brass or bronze for the two others. Two of the oak chests had iron mounts. There were two axes, and a knife, all with wooden handles intact, strap mounts, horse trappings, and dog chains, in addition to the 2,000–3,000 iron rivets of the ship and its anchor.

The remarkable conditions in the mound have led to the conservation of plant remains. Some are part of the grave goods, others are preserved in and on the turves used to build the mound. The latter indicate that the mound was built and the burial took place in late summer or early autumn. This notion is also supported by the find of wild apples (*Pirus malus*) in a bucket in the burial chamber. They are ripe, and must be part of the food included in the grave goods. Wheat (*Triticum sativum*), oats (*Avena sativa*), flax (*Linum usitatissimum*), and hemp (*Cannabis sativa*) were represented by a few seeds each, found in various parts of the burial. All were cultivated during the Viking Age. Hazelnuts (*Corylus avellana*) were probably picked from wild bushes, while the half of a walnut shell (*Juglands regia*) must be an import, probably from France or Britain.

In a small box in one of the chests lay fruits of woad (*Isatis tinctorina*), widely grown for its blue dye prior to the introduction of indigo. Another small box was full of cress seeds (*Lepidum sativum*), probably cultivated as a kitchen herb.

The name "Oseberg" has been tentatively and hypothetically linked with Queen Ása, mentioned in Snorri Sturluson's *Heimskringla*. We can be fairly certain that a burial as rich as this must have been for a member of the ruling dynasty, which in Vestfold at that time was the Yngling family, who later united Norway into one kingdom. Ingstad (1982) has suggested that the grave is that of Álfhildr Álfarinsdóttir, first wife of Guðrøðr veiðikonungur ("the hunter") Hálfdanarson.

The Oseberg ship has often been interpreted as a luxury yacht, intended for inshore use only, as opposed to the seaworthy Gokstad ship. An exact replica of Oseberg was launched in 1987, and sailing trials in the summer of 1987 showed that the replica, with a reconstructed rig, is fast, but very difficult to handle and not safe under certain conditions. Continued trials will add to our knowledge of Viking Age ships and seamanship.

The ship and equipment can be seen at Vikingskipshuset, Bygdøy, Oslo, a department of Universitetets Oldsaksamling.

Lit.: Brøgger, A. W., et al. *Osebergfundet*. 3 vols. Kristiania [Oslo]: Universitetets Oldsaksamling, 1917–27 [the standard publication on the find; vol. 4, on textiles, is forthcoming]; Brøgger, A. W., and Haakon Shetelig. *The Viking Ships: Their Ancestry and Evolution*. Trans. Katherine John. Oslo: Dreyer, 1951; rpt. 1971; Blindheim, Charlotte. "Da Osebergfunnet ble gravet. Et 75-års jubileum." *Viking* 43 (1980), 5–19; Ingstad, A. S. "Osebergdronningen—hvem var hun?" *Viking* 45 (1982), 49–65; Christensen, A. E. *Husfruen på Oseberg*. Tønsberg: Vestfoldminne, 1987, pp. 4–10.

Arne Emil Christensen

[See also: Burial Mounds and Burial Practices; Iconography; Ships and Shipbuilding; Viking Art]

Óttarr svarti ("the black"). Our information on Óttarr's career comes from *Skáldatal*, supplemented by stray and not always reliable references in *Heimskringla*, the *Legendary Saga of St. Óláfr*, and other *konungasögur*. An Icelander, Óttarr was the nephew of Sighvatr and so, like some other skalds, had a famous skald in his lineage. His other family affiliations are unknown. A typical itinerant poet, he composed praises of various rulers. *Skáldatal* shows his career beginning with Sven Haraldsson (Forkbeard; d. 1014), but according to the *Legendary Saga*, his first patron was Óláfr sœnski ("Swedish"). Óttarr's *Óláfsdrápa sœnska* (from ca. 1018) is now represented only by six half-stanzas in *Snorra Edda*. They are unique in the corpus of extant skaldic praise poetry in being composed in the rare *hálfhneppt* form. An Irish origin for *hálfhneppt*, with its final monosyllable in each line and free arrangement of the other accented syllables, has been claimed: Óttarr's words seem to draw attention to the form as an innovation. An otherwise unknown poem about Óláfr's son, Qnundr Jakob, is mentioned by the Uppsala version of *Skáldatal*.

The story of Óttarr's move to Norway after the Swedish king's death in 1022 is a highly romantic one. A too-amorous poem about Ástríðr, the daughter of Óláfr sœnski and (from 1019) wife of Óláfr helgi ("the holy") Haraldsson, is said to have offended the Norwegian king; Sighvatr rescued his nephew by encouraging him to present Óláfr with an encomium and a toned-down version of the Ástríðr poem. This anecdote seems to build upon a stereotypical characterization (skald as lover) and upon such stories as Egill's risky encounter with Eiríkr blóðøx ("blood-axe") Haraldsson at York, but cannot altogether be discounted, since it appears in the *Oldest Saga of St. Óláfr*. The opening two stanzas of the resulting *Óláfsdrápa*, or *Hofuðlausn* ("head-ransom"), are probably a semi-independent prelude to the main *drápa*; they echo lines composed by Sighvatr some seven years earlier, asking for acceptance as a court poet. For the documentary content, Óttarr is evidently indebted to Sighvatr's *Víkingarvísur* and to the anonymous *Liðsmannaflokkr*. The surviving stanzas contain valuable historical data on Óláfr's campaigns in England and rise to power in Norway. No traces of the Ástríðr poem or of a poem about Dala-Guðbrandr (mentioned in *Skáldatal*) remain.

We soon afterward hear of Óttarr at the court of Óláfr's archenemy, Knud (Cnut) the Great, who legendarily rewarded him for *Knútsdrápa* with a helmet full of silver pennies. The extant stanzas (known chiefly from *Knýtlinga saga*, which here supplements *Heimskringla*) deal with Knud's campaigns in England in 1015–1016 and with the battle of Helgeå (datable between 1025 and 1027). Although apparently later than and indebted to Þórðr Kolbeinsson's *Eiríksdrápa*, *Knútsdrápa*, with its liberal mentions of place-names, helps to fill out the other historical sources concerning the period 1015–1016 in England. The relative simplicity of the style may indicate a special effort toward intelligibility in a mixed English-Scandinavian milieu.

Ed.: Finnur Jónsson, ed. *Den norsk-islandske skjaldedigtning*. Vols. 1A-2A (tekst efter håndskrifterne) and 1B-2B (rettet tekst). Copenhagen and Christiania [Oslo]: Gyldendal, 1912–15; rpt. Copenhagen: Rosenkilde & Bagger, 1967 (A) and 1973 (B); Kock, Ernst A., ed. *Den norsk-isländska skaldediktningen*. 2 vols. Lund: Gleerup, 1946–50 [text contains some improvements on Finnur Jónsson's edition]; Bjarni Guðnason, ed. *Danakonunga sogur*. Íslenzk fornrit, 35. Reykjavik: Hið

Íslenzka fornritafélag, 1982 [text and analysis of stanzas from *Knútsdrápa*]. **Tr.**: Campbell, Alistair. *Skaldic Verse and Anglo-Saxon History*. London: Lewis, 1971 [translation of Óttarr's verses on English topics with discussion of their historical value]; Whitelock, Dorothy, ed. *English Historical Documents c. 500–1042*. 2nd ed. London and New York: Eyre Methuen; Oxford University Press, 1979 [English translation of Óttarr's verses on English topics]. **Lit.**: Finnur Jónsson. *Den oldnorske og oldislandske Litteraturs Historie*. 3 vols. 2nd ed. Copenhagen: Gad, 1920–24 [brief discussion of Óttarr's career and poems]; Moberg, Ove. *Olav Haraldsson, Knut den Store och Sverige*. Lund: Gleerup, 1941 [historical content of Óttarr's verses]; Campbell, Alistair. *Encomium Emmae reginae*. Camden Society, Third Series, 72. London: Royal Historical Society, 1949 [historical value of Óttarr's verses on English topics]; Nordland, Odd. *Hǫfuðlausn i Egils saga, ein tradisjonskritisk studie*. Oslo: Det norske samlaget, 1956 [comparative study of "hǫfuðlausn" stories in skaldic tradition]; Vries, Jan de. *Altnordische Literaturgeschichte*. 2 vols. 2nd ed. Grundriss der germanischen Philologie, 15–6. Berlin: de Gruyter, 1941–42; rpt. 1964–67 [brief discussion of Óttarr's career and poems]; Einar Ól. Sveinsson. "An Old Irish Verse Form Wandering in the North." In *Proceedings of the Seventh Viking Congress, Dublin 15–21 August 1973*. Ed. Bo Almqvist and David Greene. Dublin: Royal Irish Academy, 1976, pp. 141–52 [discussion of the origins of *hálfhneppt*]; Fidjestøl, Bjarne. *Det norrøne fyrstediktet*. Øvre Ervik: Alvheim & Eide, 1982 [Óttarr's place within the corpus of praise-poetry]; Poole, Russell. "Skaldic Verse and Anglo-Saxon History: Some Aspects of the Period 1009–1016." *Speculum* 62 (1987), 265–98 [text and historical content of some stanzas from *Hǫfuðlausn* and *Knútsdrápa*].

Russell Poole

[**See also:** *Heimskringla*; *Knýtlinga saga*; *Liðsmannaflokkr*; *Óláfs saga helga*; Sighvatr Þórðarson; *Skáld*; Skaldic Meters; Skaldic Verse; *Snorra Edda*; Þórðr Kolbeinsson]

Outlaw Sagas. Many sagas contain accounts of men living in outlawry, since full outlawry (permanent) or lesser outlawry (three years) were the only legal sanctions for antisocial behavior in medieval Iceland apart from the system of fines. In *Gísla saga*, *Grettis saga*, and *Harðar saga*, the principal character lives as an outlaw for a considerable part of the narrative. Full outlawry involved the loss of legal status, and the outlaw would generally live abroad. Some outlaws, however, like the heroes of the three outlaw sagas, remained in Iceland and managed to survive, in some cases for many years, either hiding with friends or in uninhabited parts of the country. Generally, this option meant a solitary existence, though Grettir had dealings both with other outlaws and with nonhuman beings. But in *Harðar saga*, Hǫrðr took up with a group and lived as leader of an organized outlaw band.

Lit.: Lange, Joost de. *The Relation and Development of English and Icelandic Outlaw-traditions*. Haarlem: Tjeenk Willink, 1935; Turville-Petre, G. "Outlawry." In *Sjötíu ritgerðir helgaðar Jakobi Benediktssyni 20. júlí 1977*. 2 vols. Ed. Einar G. Pétursson and Jónas Kristjánsson. Reykjavik: Stofnun Árna Magnússonar, 1977, vol. 2, pp. 769–78.

Anthony Faulkes

[**See also:** *Gísla saga Súrssonar*; *Grettis saga*; *Harðar saga*; *Íslendingasögur*; Outlawry]

Outlawry (in Free State Iceland). The Norsemen conceived of society as synonymous with law; the Icelanders referred to their society as *vár lǫg* ("our law"), and the same concept is evident in the name given to the Danish settlements in England, "the Danelaw." An outlaw was outside the bounds of society, a nonperson. Some terms for outlaw denote nonhuman status by equating the individual with a wild animal. The word *vargr* means both wolf and outlaw. *Skógarmaðr* ("forest man") and *urðarmaðr* ("man of the wilds") are words for outlaws that refer to their hideouts in the wilderness, far from human habitations, but also point up their likeness to wild beasts. Outlaws, for example, Grettir (*Grettis saga*, ch. 38), might also be equated with supernatural creatures of the wild, such as trolls.

In Iceland, outlawry was the harshest punishment during the Free State (*ca.* 930–1264). The Free State laws made no provisions for the imposition of corporal punishment, execution, or incarceration, a situation linked to the nature of Icelandic government, which functioned without executive powers and maintained no policing body. Individuals who won a legal judgment against others in the courts were responsible for enforcing the penalty, whether fine or outlawry. The latter could amount to a death sentence, since a full outlaw might be slain with impunity.

There were two basic types of outlawry in Iceland, usually referred to as "lesser outlawry" and "full outlawry." In addition, the sagas frequently refer to a third type, which exiled an individual from specific regions of the island. Called *héraðssekt* ("district outlawry") or *fjórðungsútlegð* ("quarter outlawry"), this third type of outlawry is not mentioned in the laws.

The property of an outlaw, whether a lesser or a full outlaw, was subject to confiscation at a *féránsdómr*, a court of confiscation, that took place at the farmstead of the convicted person fourteen days after the end of the assembly where he was outlawed. There, claims were made on his property to cover his debts, and compensation was awarded to the victims of his offenses. The chieftain who conducted the court received a cow or an ox, and the rest of the property was divided between the man who brought charges against the outlaw and the men of the quarter, or of the assembly district; this last was to be used by them to support the outlaw's dependents or to provide relief to the poor (*Grágás* Ia, pp. 83–8, 108, 112 ff., 118, 120).

Lesser outlawry was a sentence of a three-year exile from Iceland. This punishment of temporary banishment was known as *fjǫrbaugsgarðr*, a word composed of *fjǫrbaugr* 'life-ring' and *garðr* 'fence, enclosure.' The lesser outlaw was called a *fjǫrbaugsmaðr*. He had to pay a ransom for his life to the chieftain who presided over the confiscation of his property at the *féránsdómr*; originally, this payment was a silver ring, but later it was set at one *mǫrk* (*Grágás* Ia, p. 88). The law entitled the lesser outlaw to stay at three different farmsteads, no more than a day's journey apart, not venturing beyond bowshot from them. As often as once a month, he was allowed to travel the public road connecting the three dwellings; if men approached him, he could venture off the road beyond the range of a spear (*Grágás* Ia, pp. 88–9).

Each summer for three successive years, the outlaw was required to make three attempts to secure passage on outgoing ships. The law protected him as he traveled to the harbor. A ship's captain who refused him was liable to a fine. If after three summers the *fjǫrbaugsmaðr* had not succeeded in leaving the country, he became a full outlaw. The *fjǫrbaugsmaðr* had to remain abroad for three years, after which he could return to Iceland and resume his position as a full member of society (*Grágás* Ia, pp. 89–92). While abroad, a lesser outlaw had legal immunity from attack (*Grágás* Ia, p. 96).

Full outlawry was known as *skóggangr* ("going into the forest"), and the outlaw was called a *skógarmaðr*. Since there were no forests to speak of in Iceland, the term probably originated in continental Scandinavia. A full outlaw was also called *óheilagr*, meaning "unholy" or "unprotected." The phrase *vargr í véum* ("wolf in consecrated places"), which applied to outlaws, conveys a similar idea.

The *skógarmaðr* lost all of his rights. No one was allowed to sustain or help him in any way or to give him passage (*Grágás* la, pp. 12, 94–5, 121; II, pp. 13, 198, 359; III, p. 11). If the outlaw succeeded in leaving Iceland, he could never return. Anyone could slay him with impunity, either in Iceland or abroad (*Grágás* la, p. 96; II, p. 397). A full outlaw was denied burial in a churchyard (*Grágás* la, p. 12; II, p. 13; III, p. 11), and children born to an outlaw, whether man or woman, had no inheritance rights (*Grágás* la, p. 224).

The *lǫgrétta* or legislative council at the *Alþingi* could mitigate a sentence of full outlawry to permanent exile. In such an instance, the outlaw was given the same protection and advantages in seeking passage abroad as a lesser outlaw (*Grágás* la, pp. 95–6). Also, full outlaws could win reduction of their sentences or reprieve by killing other outlaws, and other individuals could win mitigation on their behalf by killing outlaws in their name (*Grágás* la, pp. 187–8). Such rules probably fostered distrust among outlaws, dissuading them from banding together and becoming dangerous to settled society.

Ed.: Vilhjálmur Finsen. *Grágás*. 3 vols. *la-b: Grágás: Islændernes Lovbog i Fristatens Tid, udgivet efter Det Kongelige Bibliotheks Haandskrift*. Copenhagen: Berling, 1852; *2: Grágás efter det Arnamagnæanske Haandskrift Nr. 334 fol., Staðarhólsbók*. Copenhagen: Gyldendal, 1879; *3: Grágás: Stykker, som findes i det Arnamagnæanske Haandskrift Nr. 351 fol. Skálholtsbók og en Række andre Haandskrifter*. Copenhagen: Gyldendal, 1883. **Tr.**: Dennis, Andrew, et al., trans. *Laws of Early Iceland: Grágás I*. University of Manitoba Icelandic Studies, 3. Winnipeg: University of Manitoba Press, 1980. **Lit.**: Lúðvík Ingvarsson. *Refsingar á Íslandi á þjóðveldistímanum*. Reykjavik: Menningarsjóður, 1970, pp. 94–173; Foote, Peter G., and David M. Wilson. *The Viking Achievement: The Society and Culture of Early Medieval Scandinavia*. London: Sidgwick & Jackson, 1970, pp. 381–3; Hastrup, Kirsten. *Culture and History in Medieval Iceland: An Anthropological Analysis of Structure and Change*. Oxford: Clarendon, 1985, pp. 136–45.

Jesse L. Byock

[**See also:** Cosmography; Crime and Punishment; *Grágás*; *Grettis saga*; Iceland; Laws; Outlaw Sagas]

P

Pagan Scandinavian Religion *see* **Religion, Pagan Scandinavian**

Painting. To a greater degree than elsewhere in Europe, Nordic medieval art has escaped the destruction of later times. The sculptured images of the saints were frequently banished to church attics, or even less appropriate surroundings, after the Reformation. Some sculptures remained in the body of the church. In certain instances, wall-paintings were covered with new images that better reflected the Lutheran faith, but more often they seem to have remained on display until, shabby or discolored, they were whitewashed over. They thereby avoided the fate of paintings in more strictly reformed countries, such as Holland, where they were destroyed altogether. In many Nordic churches, medieval paintings have been uncovered, and though often pale and fragmented, they can be studied and sometimes even aesthetically enjoyed. Presumably for reasons of economy, the vault-paintings frequently escaped overpainting, and are therefore better preserved than the wall-paintings, which are often spoiled through incautious uncovering or restoration. Those paintings exposed in the later decades of the 19th century and the first years of the 20th are sometimes completely repainted. In many cases, however, the overpainting was removed in later years.

The painting preserved in the North is mainly sacred. The profane painting of the Middle Ages has largely been lost, probably because the dwelling houses of the time, to a considerable extent, were wooden, and seldom survived down to our time. Furthermore, secular buildings were generally more exposed to deterioration and rebuilding than churches. Thus, the extent of the profane painting during the Middle Ages cannot be appreciated. Among the few surviving remains are some figures in Bollerup's stronghouse in Scania (Fig. 82). As on the Continent, even in dwellings, people liked to depict saints and other sacred themes on their walls, and profane images have documentary witness, for example, the now-vanished 15th-century paintings in Ålholm castle in Denmark. However, one can also find pictures with profane content inside the church, such as depictions of various occupations—masons or carpenters at work, the painter in his studio, the nobleman riding to the hunt with a falcon on his wrist,

the farmer shooting a bird with an arrow, horse trading, plowing, and the like (Figs. 83-84). The painter could also depict jests and fancies.

The painting discussed below belongs to the churches where one finds both wall-paintings and painted altars. Medieval stained glass is preserved only to a limited extent, and no book illumination of significance was created in the Nordic lands. Painting with oil as a fixing agent can be seen as early as the 12th century, for example, on the crucifixes in Hemse and Alskog on the island of Gotland. The Norwegian antemensals (altar frontals) of the High Gothic period were once believed to be the oldest examples of oil painting in Europe. Mural painting was carried out largely on a dry ground with lime as a fixative.

Danish and Swedish medieval painting derived most of its artistic impulses from the German-speaking lands south of the Baltic, while the Norwegians, especially during the High Gothic period, received inspiration from Britain. However, with the increasing importance of the Hanseatics in Norway's trade, a German influence began to appear here also, especially obvious in altar art. Swedish influence was strong in Finland, which belonged to Sweden for the whole of the Middle Ages. Influences came from other directions as well, though these sources have not been completely explored. Finland had direct contacts with other Baltic countries than Sweden.

The different style periods are unequally represented. Denmark and the southern Swedish province of Scania, which was Danish during the Middle Ages, reveal the richest stock of Romanesque painting, admittedly often in fragmentary condition, but frequently of high quality. In Sweden, few examples of Romanesque painting survive, mainly in the southern and central areas along with the islands of Gotland and Åland, which together form the eastern outposts of Romanesque painting in the Nordic region. There are no Romanesque paintings on the Finnish mainland, and, strangely enough, none in Norway, if one does not count the paintings of Hackås church in Jämtland, which belonged to Norway during the Middle Ages. However, they probably existed, at least in Norway, in now-vanished or time-ravaged Romanesque churches. Even in Denmark and Sweden, we do not find the full scope of Romanesque painting. Much may be concealed under layers of whitewash.

Among the oldest and most outstanding paintings in Scandinavia from the Romanesque period are those in Vä, Scania, where parts of a series have been preserved in the choir and the westernmost part of the church (Figs. 85, 86). Above all, the apse's *Majestas Domini*, with surrounding evangelist symbols, draws the viewer's attention. Now dated to the 1120s, the paintings in Vä have been connected with the Italo-Byzantine style, which spread over Europe via North Italy. As the paintings stand rather isolated in Danish art, they were possibly executed by a foreign master summoned for the occasion. A Byzantine influence is noticeable in other 12th-century painting in Denmark (*e.g.*, the older series of paintings in Kirke-Hyllinge, Sæby, and Sønder Jærnløse in Zealand, together with Finja in Scania), but it is not clear by which routes it reached the country. The majority of older 12th-century paintings in Denmark survive in Zealand, the now-Swedish Scania, and eastern Jutland. After 1175, the distribution became more even over the whole country. Even when Byzantine influence is apparent, other influences may appear, as, for example, in Førslev, Zealand, and the heavily restored Bjäresjö series in Scania (Figs. 87, 88). These paintings are dated to before 1225, and have been compared with contemporaneous painting in France and Germany. However, even in Bjäresjö, the Byzantine influence is obvious (Fig. 89).

Associated with the Byzantine-influenced paintings in Sweden are those in Garda and Källunge on Gotland (Fig. 90) and in Torpa, Södermanland. The Gotland examples originated under influences from Novgorod, and were perhaps painted by Russian artists who sojourned on the island. This idea has been contested by Swedish byzantinists, who maintain a direct influence from Constantinople as more plausible. The Torpa paintings may have received their Byzantine influence by way of southern Italy or Sicily, possibly intermediated by the Knights of St. John in the adjacent Eskilstuna. The restoration-disfigured paintings in Mästerby, Gotland, the few but high-quality fragments in Kaga, Östergötland (Fig. 91), the remains of paintings in Asby in the same province, and several other examples belong to a more western-oriented tradition, and originated around 1200 and later. The paintings in Hejdeby, Gotland, from 1270–1280 blend Romanesque and Gothic characteristics (Fig. 92), as do a number of contemporary fragments in Norwegian churches, for example, Nes in Telemark.

High Gothic painting, like the Romanesque, is sparsely represented, but may be richest in Norway. Besides a preserved wall-painting from the Ål stave church, now in the Oldsaksamlingen in Oslo, together with a famous altar canopy in Torpo (Fig. 93), several antemensals of wood from the 13th and 14th centuries are preserved (Fig. 94). Among the oldest is the antemensal from Kinsarvik in Hordaland (1260–1290), which depicts the Crucifixion. The scene is reminiscent of English book illumination during the 13th century. The same applies to much art produced in Norway from 1250 to 1350. Tall, slender figures, often with smiling faces, are outlined in graceful S-curves on the later antemensals. The earlier material is characterized by a stricter language of form, with a higher degree of stylization in the depiction of garments and persons, less movement in the composition, and sometimes lingering traces of the Romanesque. The antemensals often have the Crucifixion as the main motif (Figs. 94, 95). However, this motif gradually met competition from, for example, the Virgin and Child, although a number of similar Mary antemensals may have belonged to the Mary altar. Other motifs may occur on the main altar's antemensal, such as the *Majestas Domini* in Ulvik (*ca.* 1250–

1280). Among the Danish examples, an antemensal from Løgumkloster, now in the National Museum of Copenhagen, dated to around 1325, shows Christ as judge as its central scene and, in addition, the Nativity and childhood of Jesus. The picture is assumed to have been painted in the abbey's own workshop. The style is reminiscent of French miniature painting. No equivalent survives in Sweden, which, however, has paintings on wood. Among the finest examples is the painted ceiling in the abandoned church of Dädesjö, Småland, from around 1275 (Fig. 96). The childhood of Jesus is depicted in a series of medallions. Apocryphal material has been added to the Gospel accounts here. Stylistically, the paintings stand on the border between Romanesque and Gothic art. The choir-painting from 1323 in Södra Råda, Värmland (Fig. 97), should also be mentioned, together with the roughly contemporary work in the now-demolished church at Björsäter in Östergötland, parts of which have been preserved in the Museum of National Antiquities in Stockholm. The series has been compared stylistically with French book illumination, while the Björsäter paintings have been considered closer to the English ideal. Both cases show painting of a high standard, especially in Södra Råda.

High Gothic mural painting does not exist in Norway, and only to a modest extent in Denmark and the Swedish mainland (Fig. 98). On Gotland, however, it is abundant. Here, the vaults were already built by the time the paintings of the High Gothic period were made, while the construction of vaults on the mainland occurred largely during the 15th century, and the need for repainting arose. The figure painting often consists of single, large-scale saints or the apostles, sparsely distributed about the body of the church. Sometimes, large-scale figure scenes occur, for example, the Archangel Michael weighing souls or fighting the dragon (Fig. 99), or friezes with scenes from the Bible, framed by arcades (Fig. 100). An architecturally toned ornamental painting already existed during the Romanesque period, often imitating masonry, as in Ribe cathedral, Denmark, from about 1200 (Fig. 101). Ornamental painting also appears during the High Gothic period, and is abundantly represented on Gotland at Vallstena, Lummelunda, Stenkyrka, and other locations. In the crown of the vaults, one often finds an ornamental foliate decor, sometimes combined with figures (Fig. 102).

The High Gothic period was also the high point for stained glass. Little of this material has been preserved, and most of it is in museums. On Gotland, however, one can still find stained glass in its original place (Fig. 103). Both figures and patterns appear in intense colors, as well as in *grisaille.*

There is little painting preserved in Scandinavia from the later half of the 14th century and the period around 1400. Some was without doubt overpainted, but the difficult times during the 14th century may also have had an inhibiting effect on the production of art. The reduction could also result from the fact that most churches were now provided with adornment, which did not yet need to be renewed. Among the paintings that survive from around 1400 are the Bohemian-influenced examples in Bunge, Gotland (Fig. 104), undoubtedly executed by a foreign artist. The Passion series in Bunge has close parallels in the churches of Silesia, now in Poland. The apostles in Othem, Gotland (Fig. 105), and the elegant ones in Fogdö, Södermanland (Fig. 106), both influenced by the so-called "beautiful style," can also be mentioned. There is more from this period preserved in Denmark than in Sweden; examples are the paintings in Vester Broby (1380–1400) and Undløse (1400–1425; Fig. 107), which belong to the better-known Danish series. A connection between Undløse and the Swedish Fogdö paintings has been noted. It has also been claimed that the Bergen Maria church in Norway received its paintings during the early 15th century.

The period from 1425 to the end of the Middle Ages is rich in preserved murals in Denmark, Sweden, and Finland. To a certain degree, this survival is due to the fact that few churches received later painting, but were simply whitewashed when medieval paintings deteriorated. There are almost 100 churches with late-medieval paintings in the Swedish province of Uppland alone, some only fragmentarily preserved, but also many in more complete form. Native altar art survives from this time, especially in Sweden, although imported work dominates (Fig. 108). The importation from northern Germany and the Netherlands was especially great, but South German altarpieces also appear. Flemish and North German altarpieces can thus be studied to advantage in the Nordic countries (Fig. 109), especially Sweden, where a large proportion of this art is preserved.

The most outstanding paintings in early 15th-century art were uncovered in 1980–1981 in the church of Brönnestad in Scania. The series has been dated to about 1425–1440/50. In large-scale scenes, the childhood and Passion of Jesus are depicted in the vaults of the church. Their rare beauty of line is combined with an unusual interest in a realistic depiction of the milieu. An example is the archaic scene in Romanesque manner with Mary in her bed (Fig. 110), which shows how she, like real women in confinement, is given a substantial meal after the rigors of giving birth. Another picture shows how Jesus learns to walk with the aid of a chair on wheels, while the aged Joseph gently prevents the chair from running away. Usually, the quality of Nordic mural painting, although not low, is not as fine as at Brönnestad. There are examples of painting without artistic merit, in some cases quite primitive, and these have direct reference to the everyday peasant life (Fig. 111), the calendar, and the seasons of the year. Much of this painting has been preserved in Finland. A unique representation of a virgin in a labyrinth in the church of Sibbo, Nyland, may be mentioned here, a work undoubtedly associated with folk customs or rites.

Until around 1450, Nordic art bears traces of the "beautiful style," which to varying degrees manifests itself in the various schools of painting (Figs. 112, 113). In Sweden, it is still visible in Ärentuna (ca. 1435) or Tensta (1437), both in Uppland. After the middle of the 15th century, its soft drapery is replaced by a more angular type of folding, analogous to those applied by Martin Schongauer or Meister E.S. in the continental material that found its way to the North through copperplate and woodcut prints. In Denmark, the broken-fold style was practiced by the painter in the Chapel of the Three Kings in Roskilde cathedral, from about 1464 (Fig. 114), in Sweden by Johannes Ivan, 1451 (Fig. 115), and by Albert the Painter (Albertus pictor) from the 1460s and later (Fig. 116). The figure drawing becomes more realistic with the passage of the century. The slender, graceful S-curved figures of the "beautiful style" have already disappeared in the earlier part of the century.

A new tendency toward the greater use of accessible areas for figure painting appears early in the 15th century, and becomes, especially in Sweden, more obvious in the course of the century. In the case of such artists as Albert the Painter, even the smallest corner is generally used for figure painting, if one excludes the ribs

of the vaults and comparable places, where vine ornamentation or other decor is more suitable. The impression is often that of a many-colored, picture-rich fabric stretched over the interior of the church (Fig. 117). There are, however, series of paintings less rich in pictures even toward the end of the Middle Ages. In Roskilde (1464), one experiences, for example, a pleasing balance between figures and foliate ornamentation (Fig. 118), even if all the surfaces bear painting of some kind, such as stenciled medallions reminiscent of wallpaper patterns. The same balance may be found in the Tierp Master's series in Uppland, Sweden, from the period around 1470, and in Lars the Carpenter's paintings in Rimito (Rymättylä) near Åbo (Turku) in Finland, from around 1514 (Fig. 119).

Renaissance characteristics appear during the last quarter of the 15th century, for example, attempts at perspectivist structuring of space or heightened realism in the depiction of the milieu (Fig. 120). However, no Renaissance analogue to the Italian occurs: Gothic survives well into the 16th century. Ribe cathedral in Denmark, with paintings from around 1530, is probably one of the first monuments in the Nordic countries that received a picture series of Renaissance character (Fig. 121). The changes of style in native altarpiece painting in the Nordic countries proceed mainly parallel with those in mural painting. Both arts lag behind the tone-setting artistic centers.

Iconography. Nordic iconography generally conforms to international models until sometime in the 15th century. The choice of saints naturally varies, and we have early pictures of Óláfr (Figs. 122, 123), Erik, and Knud, the national saints (Figs. 124, 125), but the oldest images of them are sculpted. One of the early painted pictures of St. Knud is found in Dädesjö (ca. 1275; Fig. 124). However, paintings most often concern the international saints and their legends. Among the most popular are Nicholas of Myra, whose legend is developed in a painted series in Lemland on Åland (ca. 1275–1300), and Margaret of Antioch, represented in the 13th-century paintings in the church of Hackås, Jämtland (Fig. 126), a Norwegian province in the Middle Ages, and in the above-mentioned canopy in the Torpo stave church, Norway, painted around 1250 (Fig. 93). The stained glass in Dalhems church on Gotland has a picture of Margaret from about 1230.

The band of saints grows as the Middle Ages draw to a close. Many more local saints appear, not least in Sweden, where virtually every province in the 15th century has some saint or martyr of its own (Fig. 127). Among the most popular is Birgitta (Fig. 128), the Swedish patron saint along with Erik and a cult figure in western Christianity. In the Mälar provinces alone, pictures of her are preserved in at least thirty churches. The cult of St. Anne leaves conspicuous traces in art toward the end of the Middle Ages (Fig. 129).

In the late Middle Ages, Old Testament motifs (aside from the Prophets) occur infrequently in Denmark and Finland. From Romanesque times onward, the stories of Moses, David, and Samson are found alongside those of Noah. These figures should be interpreted as prototypes of Christ. Old Testament motifs had an upsurge in popularity in the Mälar provinces from the 1470s, when Albert the Painter emerged as an independent master (Figs. 130, 131). Albert gained inspiration for these compositions from the so-called *Biblia pauperum* and edifying works of a similar typological construction. Perhaps inspired by Albert's work, other masters applied similar principles of composition. (Albert's contemporaries in the so-called Tierp School avoided Old Testa-

82. Bollerup stronghouse, Scania, St. Andrew; *ca.* 1475–1500. Photo: Jan Johansson.

83. Gothem, Gotland. Knight on horseback; *ca.* 1300. Photo: N. Lagergren, by permission of Antikvarisk-topografiska arkivet.

84. Vendel, Uppland. The master builder fortifies himself from a tankard while working on the small roof steeple. Painted by Johannes Ivan, 1451–1452. Photo: Anna Nilsén.

85. Vä, Scania. Enthroned on a rainbow in the sky, the mighty Christ-figure raises his hand in a gesture of benediction. A flap of clothing flares out from his waist, reinforcing the impression of power. The figure is displayed frontally in the usual way and is surrounded by a mandorla. His white tunic and golden-brown mantle are outlined against an ultramarine background. The downward-tapering face with the long, strongly accentuated nose and the large, dark eyes, the stylized folds of the tunic, and the drape of the mantle all point toward a Byzantine influence; *ca.* 1121–1130. Photo: Lennart Karlsson.

86. Vä, Scania. Symbol of the evangelist Matthew. Detail of apse's *Majestas* picture. Photo: Lennart Karlsson.

87. Førslev, Zealand. The figure in the circle has its roots in Roman portraiture; *ca.* 1150–1200. Photo: Danmarks kirker.

88. Nylars, Bornholm. Adam and Eve in the story of the Fall.
Photo: Anna Nilsén.

89. Bjäresjö. One of the Virtues. The figure shows clear Byzantine
influence. Photo: National Museum, Copenhagen.

90. Garde, Gotland. Saint. Photo: Anna Nilsén.

91. Kaga, Östergötland. Angel. Photo: Antikvarisk-topografiska arkivet.

92. Hejdeby, Gotland. St. Martin. Photo: Antikvarisk-topografiska arkivet.

93. Torpo, Buskerud. Altar canopy with, among other things, the Apostles and the legend of St. Margaret; *ca.* 1260–1290. Photo: Anna Nilsén.

94. Kinsarvik, Hordaland. Antemensal with Crucifixion, framed by the Apostles Peter and Paul, flanked by *Ecclesia* and *Synagoga*. The Crucifixion picture shows simultaneously how Jesus is nailed to the Cross, how Stephaton extends the vinegar-filled sponge to him, and how Longinus pierces his side. On each side of the Cross stand Mary and John, mourning the already dead Savior. The scene is surrounded by angels who swing censers in allusion to the Eucharist; *ca.* 1260–1290. Photo: Historical Museum, University of Bergen.

95. Årdal, Sogn og Fjordarne. Antemensal with Crucifixion from *ca.* 1320–1350. While the Kinsarvik antemensal, with its elegant, almost floating Christ-figure, characteristic of the 13th-century Gothic style, hardly expresses great suffering, here we find him hanging heavily from the Cross, bleeding profusely from his wounds. The didactic, demonstrative features of the Kinsarvik picture are gone. Mary, with a sword in her breast, and John, with a gesture of pain, stand sorrowing alone at the Cross, a picture that appeals to the compassion of the viewer. Photo: Historical Museum, University of Bergen.

96. Dädesjö, Småland. St. Stephen, watering his foals, sees the Star of Bethlehem. A scene from the Swedish variant of the legend of the proto-martyr Stephen; *ca.* 1275. Photo: J. Andersson, by permission of Antikvarisk-topografiska arkivet.

98. Schleswig Cathedral. The cloister. The Burial of Christ. Photo: Anna Nilsén.

97. Södra Råda, Värmland. The Dormition of the Virgin; 1323. Photo: Anna Nilsén.

99. Lojsta, Gotland. The Archangel Michael fighting the dragon; *ca.* 1300–1350. Photo: Antikvarisk-topografiska arkivet.

100. Othem, Gotland. Virgin and Child; beginning of 14th century. Photo: Anna Nilsén.

101. Ribe Cathedral, Jutland. Painting imitating masonry. Photo: National Museum, Copenhagen.

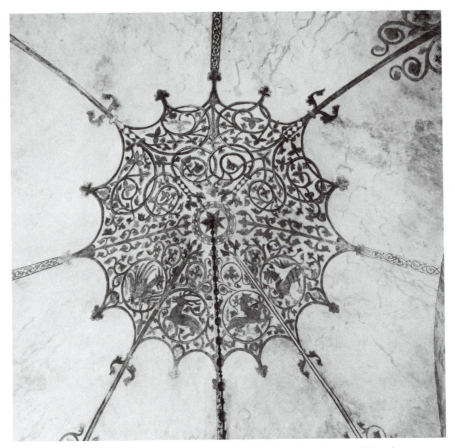

102. Fröjel, Gotland. Ornamental vault painting; *ca.* 1300. Photo: Antikvarisk-topografiska arkivet.

103. Endre, Gotland. Stained glass. Baptism of Christ; *ca.* 1250. Photo: A. Edle, by permission of Antikvarisk-topografiska arkivet.

104. Bunge, Gotland. Descent from the Cross; second half of the 14th century. Photo: Anna Nilsén.

105. Othem, Gotland. St. Paul. Photo: Anna Nilsén.

106. Fogdö, Södermanland. The Apostle Bartholomew; ca. 1400–1425. Photo: Anna Nilsén.

107. Undløse, Zealand. The Drunkard; ca. 1425. Photo: Danmarks kirker.

108. Lena, Uppland. Triptych with Joachim and Anne's meeting in the Golden Gate. Lars Germundsson, an Uppland master; 1491. Photo: Anna Nilsén.

109. Vårmdö, Uppland. Triptych, probably from Lübeck; 1475–1500. Detail from the Dormition of the Virgin. The triptych was long thought to be made in Sweden by an artist from Lübeck. Since immigrant artists were responsible for some of the altar art in Sweden and other pieces were imported from their places of origin, it is difficult to ascertain the extent of the domestic production. Photo: Anna Nilsén.

110. Brönnestad, Scania. Epiphany; *ca.* 1425–1440/50. Photo: Lennart Karlsson.

111. St. Marie, Åbo (Turku). Ship painting from 15th century.
Photo: Anna Nilsén.

113. Norra Fågelås, Västergötland. Wings of the Mary triptych; *ca.*
1400. Now in the Museum of National Antiquities, Stockholm. Photo:
Anna Nilsén.

112. Årentuna, Uppland. Creation of Eve; *ca.* 1435.
Photo: Anna Nilsén.

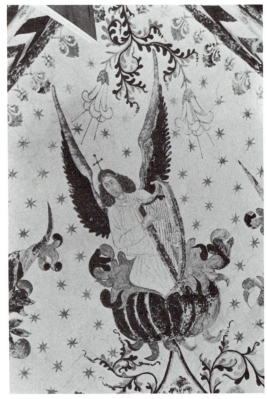

114. Roskilde Cathedral, Zealand. Three Kings Chapel. Angel playing harp; *ca.* 1464. Photo: Danmarks kirker.

115. Vendel, Uppland. Virgin and Child. Johannes Ivan; 1451–1452. Detail. Photo: Anna Nilsén.

116. Härkeberga, Uppland. Virgin on a crescent moon. Albert the Painter; *ca.* 1485. Photo: Anna Nilsén.

117. Dannemora, Uppland. Legend of St. John the Baptist; *ca.* 1520. Photo: Anna Nilsén.

119. Rimito, near Åbo (Turku). Church interior, painted by Lars the Carpenter, who also made an Olof triptych in Värmdö, Uppland; *ca.* 1514. See pl. 122. Photo: Anna Nilsén.

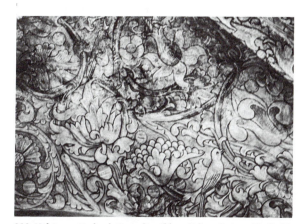

118. Helsingør, Zealand. Carmelite Abbey. Foliate design with Gothic fantasy flowers and birds; first quarter of 16th century. Photo: Anna Nilsén.

120. Helsingør, Zealand. Carmelite Abbey. The Rich Man's Dinner; *ca.* 1500. Photo: Danmarks kirker.

121. Ribe Cathedral, Jutland. Apostles. Photo: Danmarks kirker.

122. Värmdö, Uppland. St. Óláfr's Sailing Trip. Detail. Painted by Lars the Carpenter; 1514. Photo: Anna Nilsén.

123. Trondheim Cathedral. Antemensal with St. Óláfr from Haltdalen church; 1320–1340. Photo: Oldsaksamlingen, University of Oslo.

124. Dädesjö, Småland. St. Knud (Cnut); *ca.* 1275. Photo: Antikvarisk-topografiska arkivet.

125. Tortuna, Västmanland. St. Apollonia with tongs and St. Sunniva of Norway, here with three stones instead of the usual piece of rock. The series of paintings in Tortuna is one of the richest in saints in Scandinavia, showing many of the native Scandinavian saints, and also international saints, a number of them relatively unusual, as, for example, Brendan and Ottilia (Odil); *ca.* 1500. Photo: Anna Nilsén.

126. Hackås, Jämtland. Legend of Margaret. Detail; end of 13th century. Photo: Antikvarisk-topografiska arkivet.

129. Risinge, Östergötland. Legend of St. Anne; 1410–1420. Photo: Anna Nilsén.

127. Vendel, Uppland. St. Sigfrid of Växjö, a Swedish local saint. Johannes Ivan, 1451–1452. Photo: Anna Nilsén.

128. Hov, Östergötland. St. Birgitta intercedes successfully for a soul at the Archangel Michael's weighing of souls; *ca.* 1515. Photo: Anna Nilsén.

130. Härkeberga, Uppland. Noah sleeps off his drunkenness. The sons see their father exposed, and Ham makes a fool of him. Prototype for the Mocking of Christ; *ca.* 1485. Photo: Anna Nilsén.

132. Sagu (Sauvo), near Åbo (Turku). The priest Petrus Petri turns to the Mother of God with a prayer for mercy. Painting by Petrus Henriksson; 1472. Photo: Anna Nilsén.

131. Almunge, Uppland. Left, the Ascension of Christ, and right, its prototype in the Old Testament: Enoch being taken up to heaven together with Elijah on the way to heaven in the chariot of fire. Below him, Elisha receiving his mantle. On the far right, a picture of Moses receiving the tablets of the law, which is not connected with the Ascension but is probably painted as a formal appendage to Enoch for purposes of symmetry. The heavenly sphere is symbolized by the four angels. Workshop of Albert; *ca.* 1490. Photo: Anna Nilsén.

133. Södra Råda, Värmland. The Holy Trinity, or Seat of Grace; 1323. Photo: Anna Nilsén.

134. Vendel, Uppland. *Imitatio.* Christ's followers at the foot of the cross. Detail from Crucifixion. Johannes Ivan, 1451–1452. Photo: Anna Nilsén.

136. Härnevi, Uppland. The worship of the pious and the worldly. The lines show how the pious and poor man directs his thoughts to the five wounds of Christ and the crown of thorns, while the worldly and rich man, with his banderole bearing signs devoid of meaning, lets his thoughts go to the glories of the world, symbolized by the treasures in the house behind him. Albert the Painter; 1485–1490. Photo: Anna Nilsén.

135. Hattula, Tavastland (Häme). The pelican alludes in this context to Christ's sacrifice, as does Abel's offering, which is depicted above; 1510s. Photo: Anna Nilsén.

137. Mørkøv, Zealand. The horrors of hell are depicted here, not without relish, by the Danish Isefjords workshop; *ca.* 1460–1480. Photo: Danmarks kirker.

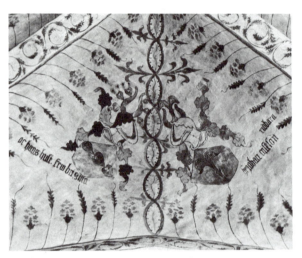

139. Östra Ryd, Uppland. Patron's arms with accompanying inscriptions. Johannes Ivan; 1459. Photo: Anna Nilsén.

138. Almunge, Uppland. The parable of the mote and the beam. Detail. Workshop of Albert; *ca.* 1490. Photo: Anna Nilsén.

140. Gerlev, Zealand. Martin the Painter has placed his signature over the picture of the Last Supper, in the crown of the easternmost vault of the nave; *ca.* 1425. Photo: Danmarks kirker.

141. Tortuna, Västmanland. The Last Judgment. Detail. One of the seven mouths of hell. Photo: Anna Nilsén.

142. Sketch of the Judas kiss from the high Gothic period. This formula continues throughout the Middle Ages. From the Icelandic MS AM 673a 4to. After Harry Fett.

143. Hattula, Tavastland (Häme). The Miracle of the Painter. Mary saves the painter from the Devil's wrath by stretching out her hand; 1510s. Photo: P.O. Welin, Museiverket, Helsingfors (Helsinki).

144. Lojo (Lohja), near Helsingfors (Helsinki). The Miracle of the Painter. The painter saves himself from the wrath of the Devil by seizing a corner of Mary's robe; 1510s. Photo: Anna Nilsén.

145. Björklinge, Uppland. Drollery; *ca.* 1450. Photo: Anna Nilsén.

146. MS AM 673a 4to in the University Library of Copenhagen. This leaf shows two different sketches of St. Christopher. After Harry Fett.

ment scenes.) No absolute equivalent to the Middle Swedish typological painting series exists in the other Nordic lands or on the Continent. Nevertheless, traces may be discerned in Denmark, Finland, and south of the Baltic, where, for example, the cathedral in Kolberg had a typological painting series (destroyed by bombing during the Second World War). However, there is no comparison with the world of Old Testament motifs of the rich and diversified kind left by Albert and his successors. A total of 130 different motifs from the Old Testament have been registered among the late-medieval paintings in the three Mälar provinces.

The wall- and vault-paintings of the churches were meant to beautify the house of God, while the donor sought to secure God's grace in the life to come. Several series of paintings arose in relation to the donors' weddings, presumably in hope of blessing. The program, whether wall-paintings or altarpieces, was usually composed by people with theological training. Sometimes, the priest of the church documented his collaboration with an inscription or his portrait (Fig. 132). A gift to God should be beautiful, and an expression of the highest knowledge. A perfectly beautiful sermon may have been the model closest to the mind of the designer of the program.

Right up to the middle of the 15th century, or directly after, the painting series generally have an epic character. The story of salvation is told from the Creation and Fall through to the Last Judgment. Variations in fullness of detail, choice of subject, and number of pictures naturally occur. The Romanesque program represents Christ as king and victor (Fig. 85), and emphasizes His power. In the Gothic period, the *majestas* representation disappears, to be replaced by the Trinity, with God the Father holding out the sacrificed Son, and the dove of the Holy Ghost in between (Fig. 133). The focus is on the Passion. There is a shift from didactic clarity to mysticism. Devotional images depicting the suffering Christ appear, intended for contemplation. *Imitatio* and *compassio* become living concepts (Fig. 134), encouraged by the preachers, especially the mendicant friars. The later programs also resemble sermons of the mendicants in construction. The method of composition described above, in which Old Testament scenes illuminate a New Testament picture, have their equivalents in sermons, which use examples drawn not just from the Bible (Fig. 135), but also from fables, legends, folktales, heroic sagas, and the like. By depicting Abraham preparing to sacrifice his son alongside the picture of Christ, the painter emphasizes the idea of sacrifice, while a corresponding depiction of Samson or David emphasizes that of triumph. The heroes of the folk saga may have the same function.

Moralizing pictures are abundant, especially in the late-medieval material (Fig. 136). The pedagogic clarity and the visible placement of these pictures make it probable that their function was to remind the viewer of the guiding light of the Church's teaching. The devotional pictures, which are also most frequently placed so that they may be seen, may have been intended as recipients of prayer to the depicted saint. Other pictures are aimed at inspiring reflection, for example, the Last Judgment, which generally receives a central position in the program of pictures (Fig. 137). Sometimes it is placed directly in front of the entrance, sometimes on the triumphal arch toward the aisle, sometimes on the western or eastern wall. The format is usually large.

The interior of the church must have had an uplifting and inspiring effect on those entering. In the Nordic churches, with their few and small windows, sometimes with stained glass, it would hardly have been possible to see all the paintings even by straining one's eyes. The totality of the program is often indicated,

however, by the choice of pictures for the best-illuminated places (Fig. 138). The well-conceived unity of all its components was, as revealed by many inscriptions, directed to God, a fact that explains why many pictures were painted in places where it was difficult for the congregation to see them.

Donors and painters. It was an expensive undertaking to provide the churches with altar art and wall-paintings. A poor parish was dependent on donors. That such donors existed among the nobility and the richer burghers is often indicated by painted coats of arms, and sometimes by inscriptions or donors' portraits (Fig. 139). One may thus imagine the undertaking of a commission as a cooperation among donors, program designers, and artists.

Several painters have left their names to posterity in the form of signatures. Probably all, or the majority, signed their work, but possibly in places like portal or window niches, or other areas that were later reworked, so that the signatures were lost. The claim that medieval painters wished to remain anonymous is contradicted by the large number of signatures that have been preserved, sometimes prominently placed, and sometimes followed by comments that bear witness to self-esteem. In Denmark, the painter Martin, who has left his signature in several churches (Fig. 140), more than once expressed his pride, for example, in Gerlev, where one can read in a most prominent place: *Martinus malera bene fecit* ("Martin the painter did this well"). Örjan the Painter's self-portrait in Valö, Sweden, also witnesses to self-esteem; here, one sees the master with an air of satisfaction lay the last touches to his painting of his patron saint, Luke.

The painters sometimes used models for their pictures, such as sketches made during the travels of their apprenticeship, woodcuts, and other printed sources. These models have seldom been followed slavishly. Sometimes, however, as in Tortuna church near Västerås in Sweden, one can see that the painter had at hand a print depicting the legend of St. Erasmus, which he followed fairly closely. The scene of the Last Judgment in the same church (Fig. 141), with a hell composed of seven mouths and a heavenly citadel with the nine choirs of angels, each on its own story, may be the painter's own invention, possibly deriving from a text. In this context, it should also be stressed that certain picture formulas were established at an early point, and vary little over time (Fig. 142). One should not, however, deny the artists the ability to innovate. Witness several of the miracles of Mary, depicted in the Finnish churches of Hattula and Lojo (Lohja), where the same workshop of painters has represented the same miracle in different ways in both churches (Figs. 143, 144). In such cases, the starting point had been written or orally transmitted material. Sometimes, in work pictures, for example, or the depiction of clothing, the painter gained inspiration from contemporary reality. A good number of the drolleries that occur on the remaining surfaces are thought to be free compositions (Fig. 145). No painters' workshop with its sketchbooks and graphic prints has been preserved. One is almost totally reliant on comparative studies to find the sources of inspiration. In Iceland, however, a sketchbook, the so-called *Teiknibók* in AM 673a 4to, unique in the Nordic context, was preserved. Obviously used over a long period, it contains pictures with both High Gothic and Late Gothic style characteristics (Fig. 146).

The origins of the painters can seldom be determined. As the older material often has an international character in respect to both style and content, it is thought to have often involved masters and workshops summoned for the purpose. The nearer the end of the Middle Ages, the greater the number of local variations that can be discerned, and the more often the painters have indigenous names. The borrowing of skillful artists from foreign parts and the importation of altar art, however, by no means ceased at the end of the Middle Ages.

Bib.: Gram, M. "Henrik Cornells skrifter—en bibliografi." *Iconographisk post* 4 (1981) [separate publication]; Engström, Margit. "Aron Anderssons tryckta skrifter." In *Den ljusa medeltiden. Studier tillägnade Aron Andersson*. Ed. Lennart Karlsson *et al.* Museum of National Antiquities. Studies, 4. Stockholm: Statens Historiska Museum, 1984, pp. 353–9. **Lit.**: Fett, Harry. *En islandsk tegnebog fra middelalderen*. Videnskabs-Selskabets Skrifter. II. Hist.-filos. Kl., 1910, no. 2. Christiania [Oslo]: [n.p.], 1910; *Sveriges kyrkor. Konsthistoriskt inventarium*. Stockholm: Kungl. vitterhets, historie och antikvitetsakadamien, 1912-; Lindblom, Andreas. *La peinture gothique en Suède et en Norvège: Étude sur les relations entre l'Europe et les pays scandinaves*. Stockholm: Wahlström & Widstrand, 1916; *Danmarks kirker*. Ed. Nationalmuseet. Copenhagen: Gad, 1933–; Wennervirta, Ludvig. *Suomen keskiaikainen kirkkomaalaus*. Porvoo: Söderström, 1937; Stange, A. *Deutsche Malerei der Gotik*. 10 vols. Berlin: Deutscher Kunstverlag, 1934–60, vol. 6; rpt. Nerdeln: Kraus, 1969; Söderberg, Bengt G. *De gotländska passionsmålningarna och deras stilfränder. Studier i birgittinskt muralmåleri*. Stockholm: Wahlström & Widstrand, 1942; Nygren, Olga Alice. *Helgonen i Finlands medeltidskonst. En ikonografisk studie*. Suomen muinaismuistoyhdistyksen Aikakauskirja. Finska fornminnesföreningens Tidskrift, 46.1. Helsingfors: [n.p.], 1945; Nygren, Olga Alice. *Gudsmodersbilden i Finlands medeltidskonst*. Helsingfors: Söderström, 1951; Söderberg, Bengt G. *Svenska kyrkomålningar från medeltiden*. Stockholm: Natur och Kultur, 1951; Cornell, Henrik, and Sigurd Wallin. *Schwedische Kirchenmalereien des 16. Jahrhunderts*. 2 vols. Stockholm: Humanistiska sällskapet, 1954–60; Borelius, Aron. *Romanesque Mural Paintings in Östergötland*. Stockholm: Norstedt, 1956; Cornell, Henrik, and Sigurd Wallin. *Kirchenmalereien von Johannes Iwan*. Stockholm: Humanistiska sällskapet, 1957; Nygren, Olga Alice. *En medeltida frälsningsspegel*. Tammerfors: Söderström, 1957; *Finlands kyrkor*. Helsingfors: Finska Fornminnesföreningen, 1959–; *Norges kirker*. Oslo: Land og kirke, 1959–; Cornell, Henrik. *Stockholmer Malerschulen des 15. Jahrhunderts*. Stockholm: Humanistiska sällskapet, 1961; Cornell, Henrik. *Johannes Rosenrod, ein schwedischer Maler von 1437*. Stockholm: Bonnier, 1962; Cornell, Henrik, and Sigurd Wallin. *Roslagmästaren*. Stockholm: Bonnier, 1964; Andersson, Aron, *et al. Die Glasmalereien des Mittelalters in Scandinavien*. Corpus Vitrearum Medii Aevi. Skandinavien. Stockholm: Kungl. vitterhets-, historie- och antikvitetsakademien, 1964; Cornell, Henrik, and Sigurd Wallin. *Die Malerschule von Tierp*. Stockholm: Bonnier, 1965; Broby-Johansen, R. *En dansk billedbibel*. 3rd ed. Copenhagen: Gyldendal, 1967; Blindheim, Martin. "De malte antemensaler i Norge." *Årsbok för svenska staten konstsamlingar* 15 (1968), 28–50; Tuulse, Armin. *Romansk konst i Norden*. Stockholm: Bonnier, 1968; Anker, Peter, and Aron Andersson. *L'Art scandinave*. 2 vols. La nuit des temps, 28–9. L'Abbaye Sainte-Marie de la Pierre-qui-vire [Yonne]: Zodiaque, 1968–69 [English translation: *The Art of Scandinavia*. 2 vols. London and New York: Hamlyn, 1970]; Moltke, Erik. *Bernt Notkes altertavle i Århus Domkirke og Tallinntavlen*. 2 vols. Copenhagen: Gad, 1970; Söderberg, Bengt G. *Gotländska kalkmålningar 1200–1400*. Uppsala: Föreningen Gotlands Fornvänner Visby; 1971; Tuulse, Armin. *Den ikonografiska forskingen i Sverige*. Stockholm: Kungl. vitterhets, historie och antikvitetsakademien, 1972; Odenius, Oloph. "Der Mann im Brunnen und der Mann im Baum. Ein ikonographischer Beitrag." In *Festschrift für Robert Wildhaber zum 70. Geburtstag am 3.*

August 1972. Ed. Walter Escher *et al.* Basel: Krebs; Bonn: Habelt, 1972; Stigell, Anna-Lisa. *Kyrkans tecken och årets gång*. Finska fornminnesföreningens tidskrift, 77. Helsingfors: Finska fornminnesföreningen 1974; Norberg, Rune. "Nordisk medeltid." In *Bildkonsten i Norden*. 5 vols. 2nd ed. Stockholm: Prisma, 1974, vol. 1; Plahter, Leif E., *et al. Gothic Painted Altar Frontals from the Church of Tingelstad*. Oslo, Bergen, and Tromsø: Universitetsforlaget, 1974; Lassen, Erik. *Dansk Kunsthistorie: Billedkunst og skulptur. 1. Fra runesten til altertavle, ca. 900–1500*. Ed. Vagn Poulsen *et al.* Copenhagen: Politiken, 1975; Ahlstedt-Yrlid, Inger. *Och i hopp om det eviga livet. Studier i Skånes romanska muralmåleri*. Lund: Corpus inris, 1976 [English summary]; Banning, Knud, ed. *A Catalogue of Wall-Paintings in the Churches of Medieval Denmark: Scania, Halland, Blekinge*. 4 vols. Copenhagen: Akademisk Forlag, 1976–1982; Nyborg, Ebbe. *Fanden på væggen*. Højbjerg: Wormianum, 1978; Haastrup, Ulla. "Die seeländischen, romanischen Wandmalereien in Slagelille, Sonderup und Fjenneslev. Studien über Technik, Ikonographie und Werkstattzusammenhang der Finja-Gruppe." *Hafnia-Copenhagen Papers in the History of Art* 6 (1979), 106–43; *Medieval Iconography and Narrative: Proceedings of the Fourth International Symposium at Odense University 1979*. Ed. Flemming G. Andersen *et al.* Odense: Odense University Press, 1980; Nordhagen, Per Jonas. "Senmiddelalderens billedkunst 1350–1537." In *Norges kunsthistorie*. 7 vols. Ed. Knut Berg. Oslo: Gyldendal, 1981, vol. 2, pp. 375–433; Wickström, Anne. "Maleriet i højmiddelalderen." In *Norges kunsthistorie*, vol. 2, pp. 252–374; Cornell, Henrik. *Albertus Pictor. Sten Stures und Jacob Ulvssons Maler. Seine Stellung innerhalb der europäischen Kunst. Seine Bedeutung in Schwedens künstlerischem und religiösem Leben*. Stockholm: Kungl. vitterhets, historie och antikvitetsakademien, 1981; Zeitler, Rudolf, and Jan O. M. Karlsson, eds. *Imagines medievales. Studier i medeltida ikonografi, arkitektur, skulptur, måleri och konsthantverk. Mit ausführlichen deutschen Zusammenfassungen*. Acta Universitatis Upsaliensis, Ars Suetica, 7. Uppsala: Institutionen för konstvetenskap vid Uppsala universitet, 1983; Lagerlöf, Erland. "Bysantinskt måleri från en gotländsk stavkyrka." In *Den ljusa medeltiden. Studier tillägnade Aron Andersson*. Ed. Lennart Karlsson *et al.* Museum of National Antiquities. Studies, 4. Stockholm: Statens Historiska Museum, 1984, pp. 123–32; Haastrup, Ulla, and Robert Egevang. *Danske kalkmalerier*. Copenhagen: Nationalmuseet, 1985- [*Romansk tid 1080–1175*, 1987; *Senromansk tid 1175–1275*, 1987; *Tidlig gotik 1275–1375*, 1989; *Gotik 1375–1475*, 1985; *Sengotik 1475–1500*, 1991; *Sengotik 1500–1536*, 1992; *Efter reformationen 1536–1700* (forthcoming)]; Reuterswärd, Patrik. *The Forgotten Symbols of God*. Stockholm Studies in History of Art, 35. Stockholm: Almqvist & Wiksell, 1986; Tångeberg, Peter. *Mittelalterliche Holzskulpturen und Altarschreine in Schweden. Studien zu Form, Material und Technik*. Stockholm: Kungl. vitterhets historie och antikvitets akademien, 1986; Nilsén, Anna. *Program och funktion i senmedeltida kalkmåleri. Kyrkmålningar i Mälarlandskapen och Finland*. Stockholm: Kungl. vitterhets historie och antikvitets akademien, 1986; Nilsén, Anna. "Johannes Rosenrod—ein deutscher Maler in Schweden." In *Beiträge zur Geschichte und Kunst im Ostseeraum*. Homburger Gespräch, 8. Ed. L. O. Larsson. Kiel: Christian-Albrechts-Universität, 1988, pp. 43–60; Hammer, Karen Elisabeth. *Sakrale Wandemalerei in Dänemark und Norddeutschland im ausgehenden Mittelalter. Eine Studie zu den Malereien der Elmelundegruppe in Sakralräumen Süddänemarks unter besonderer Berücksichtigung der Kirche zu Fanefjord sowie der norddeutschen Wandmalerei*. Hamburg: Verlag an der Lottbek, Peter Jensen, 1990.

Anna Nilsén

[**See also**: Iconography; Viking Art]

Palaeography is the scientific study of old writing, of the history and evolution of its techniques and forms. It is especially concerned with the forms of script used in medieval MSS and their reading and interpretation. The word "palaeography" was coined from the Greek *palaiós* 'old' and *-graphia* 'writing, script' by the Benedictine monk Bernard de Montfaucon, who in 1708 published a book on Greek scripts entitled *Palaeographia Graeca sive De Ortu et Progressu Literarum*. In practice, however, palaeographic studies had already been begun by his confrère Jean Mabillon, whose pioneering work *De re diplomatica libri VI* appeared in 1681. Whereas epigraphy deals mainly with texts written on lasting material like stone, palaeography is concerned with texts on paper, parchment, papyrus, linen, and wax. These can be written with a reed or straw pen (Latin *harundo* or *calamus*), a brush, quill (Latin *penna* 'feather'), or stylus (Latin *stilus* or *graphium*) of metal or bone. They can be written either in formal book script for literature or in cursive everyday script for official or private purposes.

Palaeography is an important auxiliary science for philology and history. The palaeographer's main tasks are interpreting texts, determining the date of MSS, and identifying and differentiating scripts. Palaeographic analysis of a script examines the appearance of the letters, abbreviations, the slant of writing, the movement of the pen, the size of the letters, the penstrokes, the nature of the writing material, and the nature of the text. Medieval palaeography overlaps or has points of contact with other disciplines; besides epigraphy, these include diplomatics (from which it developed), sphragistics (seals), papyrology, and numismatics.

In the Middle Ages, the most important writing material was parchment, the dressed skin of calves (vellum), goats, or sheep. Writing was done with quill pens, normally made from goose or swan feathers. There were also many different kinds of ink; the normal color was black.

The most usual form of parchment book is the codex, a book comprising one or more folded sheets. In the 14th century, it became customary to label or foliate the pages of books with letters and roman numerals, for example Ai, Aii, up to Axvi, followed by Bi, Bii, and so on. Continuous pagination did not become standard practice until early modern times. In the right bottom corner, each page normally had a *custos*, or catchword, the first letter or syllable of the word beginning the next page; this sign made it easier to check that the pages were bound in the correct order. Book formats were classified as folio, quarto (4to), octavo (8vo), duodecimo (12mo), sextodecimo (16mo), according to whether the sheet was folded to make two, four, eight, twelve, or sixteen leaves. The codex was usually bound in wooden boards covered with leather and often fitted with a clasp. Titles and headings were written, often by special rubricators, in red ink after the MS was finished.

MSS, especially liturgical ones, could also be embellished with miniatures in gold, silver, and other colors. Illuminations included the adornment of initials, which were sometimes used to frame little pictures, and the creation of larger illustrations. An early example of Nordic book-painting is the illuminated gospel harmony known as *Dalbyboken* (DKB, GkS 1325 4to) from around 1050. Icelandic book-painting, which flourished in the 13th and 14th centuries, is conservative in character but also shows originality. There are also exquisite illustrations from the 15th and 16th centuries. Primarily law codices and religious books were illustrated. From Norway and Sweden, there are examples of illu-

minated law codices from the 14th century; the mid-15th-century *Magnus Erikssons landslag* (SKB B 172) has great artistic and cultural interest.

Paper, a Chinese invention that came to the West via the Arabs and Spain, gradually replaced parchment as a writing material. Paper came into use in Spain and Italy in the 12th and 13th centuries, reaching Scandinavia in the 14th. A feature of European paper is the watermark, a design or pattern visible when held up to the light. Watermarks are important dating aids.

In order to save work and parchment, Roman script used abbreviations and ligatures. The following abbreviation methods came into general use throughout western Europe: (1) suspension, *i.e.*, omission of one or more letters at the end of a word, the abbreviation being marked by a point or colon or by a stroke over or under the word; (2) contraction, *i.e.*, omission of one or more letters in the middle of a word, the abbreviation being marked by a stroke over the word as in *ds* for *deus*; (3) superscript or interlinear letters (a kind of contraction), the omitted letter(s) being written above the word or between the lines; (4) special abbreviaton signs, known as Tironian notes, a system devised by Cicero's freedman Tiro, in which, for example, "depressed" 7 stood for *et* 'and,' 5 for *con* 'with'; a curved or zigzag line represented *er* or *re*, and a bar over a letter indicated the omission of a following nasal.

Vernacular medieval texts from Denmark and Sweden show a limited use of abbreviations. Those most commonly found are the nasal bar for *m* and *n*, the curved sign for *er* and *re*, "depressed" 7 for *ok* 'and,' and 3 for *-et(h)* (*th3* = *thet[h]*). An interlinear open *a* is used for *ar*, *ra*, *er*, and *re*. Suspension is indicated by a point or colon, or by a stroke that was variously curving or wavy. The use of abbreviations decreases around the middle of the 16th century, the longest to survive being the nasal bar and the use of interlinear letters.

Medieval West Norse writing employs considerably more abbreviations in vernacular texts than does contemporary East Norse script. Latin abbreviations are used even for native words with the same meaning, for instance "depressed" 7 for *ok* 'and,' *n* (= *non*) for *eigi* 'not.' As in East Norse script, the nasal bar and interlinear letters occur. The abbreviation for *er* has many other meanings. Suspension was common. Scribes often wrote just the initial letter followed by a point or some other sign; the letter could also be written between two points, as in *.b.* for *biskup* 'bishop,' *.e.* for *eða* 'or.' Abbreviations became less common in Iceland and Norway in the 16th century.

Ligatures of two (or three) letters sharing a common feature, such as the central upright in NB (= *N[ota] B[ene]*), are much more frequent in West Norse than in East Norse texts. A ligature can stand for a single sound, such as *æ*, but the letters can also retain their individual values, as in *k* (*s* + *k*). Carolingian script, in contrast to Merovingian, restricted the use of ligatures, retaining virtually none except those for *st*, *ct*, and *&* (= *et*). These ligatures were adopted into Nordic writing at an early date.

All western European script goes back to Roman writing. The development of Roman script can be sketched as follows. An original archaic script of a majuscular type gradually evolved into a book script known as *scriptura capitalis*, usually divided into classical *capitalis rustica* (a form with tall, narrow letters; Fig. 147) and *capitalis quadrata* or *elegans* (with almost square letters, which survived until the 6th century A.D.; Fig 147). At an early stage, almost certainly before the 3rd century B.C., a cursive script evolved, and in the first half of the 3rd century A.D., this cursive formed the basis for the first book script of minuscule type, known as the original or primitive minuscule. The typical book script of the early Middle Ages was uncial, with its rounded stems and lines. The letters *A, E, D, H, M, Q,* and *V* are particularly characteristic of uncial script (Fig. 147). Magnificent uncial MSS survive from the 4th to the 9th century. Around the year 400, scribes developed the contemporary everyday writing into yet another book script, half-uncial. A variety of national scripts (Beneventian in Italy, Merovingian in France, Visigothic in Spain, Insular in the British Isles; Fig. 147) gradually developed out of half-uncial and cursive script. From the time of Charlemagne until the end of the 12th century, the West (with the exception of the British Isles) was dominated by Caroline minuscule (Fig. 147), a development of the book script of late antiquity. This script, the prototype of our lower-case alphabet, is clear and legible, with each letter written separately. The short letters, as well as the ascenders and descenders, were all the same height, and abbreviations and ligatures were used sparingly. At the end of the 12th century, Caroline minuscule was reformed to a laterally compressed script with tall, narrow, angular, "broken" shapes; bowed letters like *d* and *p* were joined to the following round letter like *o*. From this Gothic book script was gradually developed *Fraktur*, the German blackletter type. German handwriting is a direct continuation of cursive Gothic script. Toward the end of the Middle Ages, there was a return to the clear Carolingian script. Humanistic book script (*antiqua*) became the model for our Roman type, while humanistic cursive evolved into our italic type.

Latin script came to Scandinavia along with Christianity. Denmark, like Sweden, mostly learned the art of writing from Germany. The following periods can be distinguished:

Caroline minuscule (ca. 1050–1250). The sources, in Latin, comprise MSS, books, and diplomas. Significant books include Denmark's oldest liturgical MS, the *Dalbyboken* mentioned above, and the 12th-century *Necrologium Lundense* (LUB, medeltidshs. no. 6 4to), with about eighty different hands, showing the development of writing over nearly a century; the numerous names have great interest to philologists and historians. Documentary script is more conservative than book script, having preserved older features going back to Merovingian script. It is not a true cursive. It is characterized by its long ascenders and descenders and the looping decoration of the minims and abbreviation signs. The oldest surviving diploma is from 1135.

Early Gothic (ca. 1250–1350). Latin sources include diplomas, chronicles, annals, necrologies, and town charters. The compilation *Kong Valdemars jordebog* has some brief passages in Danish; of particular value is the abundant place-name material. Abbreviations are frequent in these MSS. Danish sources include law texts, medical books, and religious literature. The oldest extant MS in Danish is *Skånske lov* (SKB B 74) from around 1250. These texts, like contemporary Swedish MSS, have few abbreviations. Documentary script differs from book script by becoming cursive: more letters are written continuously without lifting the pen.

Later Gothic (ca. 1350–1525). There are many Danish sources of various kinds: legal texts, diplomas, chronicles, medical works, and religious literature. True book script (Fig. 148) is found particularly in liturgical MSS. Up until 1450, the predominant script in books and diplomas is a semicursive form known as Gothic hybrid (*lettre bâtarde*) in which the different letters are written with broad penstrokes and only partly joined, and have

elegant, rounded, sweeping lines (Fig. 148). True cursive script occurs both in books and in documents after 1450 (Fig. 148). During this period, Danish takes over from Latin and Low German as the language of diplomas. The oldest surviving vernacular diplomas from Denmark are from the 1370s. After the Reformation, Denmark was dominated by the neo-Gothic script developed in Germany, found in textual and cursive forms. This functioned as a national script, alongside Latin or humanistic script, mainly in names and for texts in Latin and Romance languages. Neo-Gothic script was used in Denmark and Norway until 1875.

The development of writing in Sweden was similar to that in Denmark. The oldest extant original Swedish diploma dates from 1165. A fragment of the older *Västgötalagen* (SKB B 193) from 1225–1250 shows the influence of Insular and West Norse writing. The oldest surviving book in Sweden, a complete text of the older *Västgötalagen* (SKB B 59), from around 1285, is written in Gothic minuscule. The later Middle Ages (ca. 1370–1526) are dominated by a Gothic hybrid script (Fig. 148). As in Denmark, neo-Gothic script achieved currency at the time of the Reformation and remained the national script until the early 19th century. The German letters *ä* and *ö* were introduced with the Reformation, and *å* was adopted in 1526; these innovations distinguished Swedish from Danish, which retained its medieval letter forms.

Iceland's writing has a twin origin: Caroline minuscule from the Continent and Insular from England (partly introduced via Norway). The oldest surviving texts in Icelandic, from the latter half of the 12th century, are written in Caroline minuscule adapted for Icelandic (Fig. 148); the script lacks Insular letters, with the exception of þ (thorn). However, judging by the *First Grammatical Treatise* (written in the 1130s) and Ari fróði's ("the learned") *Íslendingabók* (1120s), both of which are preserved only in later transcripts, Insular script appears to have been known in Iceland before 1150. From the Carolingian period (around 1150–1225), there are about twenty-five MSS in Icelandic. Only one MS is certainly older than this period: an Easter table (AM 732a VII 4to), written between 1121 and 1139. The table contains an almost complete alphabet (minuscules and capitals). From the Carolingian-Insular period (ca. 1225–1300), there are several MSS of various kinds in Icelandic, including one of the oldest known MSS, a fragment of *Egils saga* (AM 162 A ð fol.; Fig 148). The *Second Grammatical Treatise* (written ca. 1200, preserved in later MSS) enumerates almost the entire Latin alphabet as well as ǫ, ę, ø, y, and þ. During this period, there is a strong East Norse influence on Icelandic script. During the Gothic period (ca. 1300–1550), the Icelandic sources consist of a large number of MS books (including the *Codex Regius* of Snorri's *Prose Edda*) and numerous diplomas, the oldest of which dates from 1315. Diplomas in Iceland were written mostly in the native language, but in the 15th century there is sometimes a mixture of Icelandic, Danish, and Norwegian. Cursive script does not become common in diplomas until 1400; before this, the script used in diplomas and books was essentially the same. The Gothic hybrid never achieved any currency in Iceland. As in the rest of Scandinavia, neo-Gothic script was adopted at the Reformation for native Icelandic texts. Latin and French words, however, are written in Latin cursive script. In the mid-19th century, German script is wholly given up in favor of Latin. Distinctive features of medieval Icelandic scripts are the frequent use of abbreviations and ligatures, and the many functions of capital letters and accents. Capital letters are used for the following purposes: to emphasize words and names, such as sa-

DESPECTVS·TIBI·SVM·NEC·
DEVCALIONVACVVM
REMISIT EUM/ AD HERODEM
a a b c d e e d f f g h
a b c d e e f g h i l l m n o p q r s t
Hadriano summo papae patrique beato·
Rex carolus salue mando ualeque pater.

147. Line 1: rustic capital, 5th–6th century; line 2: square capital, 4th century; lines 3–4: uncial, 7th century; line 5: insular round, 8th century; line 6: insular pointed, 8th century; line 7: Caroline minuscule, 8th century. Reproduced from Lars Svensson, *Nordisk paleografi* (1974)

148. Lines 1–2: Caroline minuscule, Iceland. From *Reykjaholtsmáldagi*. Hand 1, the end of 12th century. Reykjavík. Line 3: Caroline-Insular minuscule, Norway. From *Jordebok från Munkelivs kloster*. Ca. 1200. KKB, codex 1347 4to (old collection). (Note insular *f, r, v*). Lines 4–5: Caroline-Insular minuscule, Iceland. From the fragment of *Egils saga*. Mid-13th century. AM 162 A. ð fol. (Note the numerous abbreviations.) Lines 6–10: Gothic minuscule, Sweden. From *MEL*. The latter part of the 14th century. LUB, medeltidsh. no 17, p. 83 verso. Lines 11–12: Gothic hybrid, Sweden (Vadstenakursiv). From *Vitae patrum*. The end of the 14th century. SKB A 110 (Codex Oxenstiernianus), 4to, p. 381. Line 13: Gothic Cursive, Norway. *Dipl. norv.* XXV, 19. 1484. Line 14: Gothic cursive, Denmark. From Korsør Kirkes Arkiv. DRA, 26/7 1490. Reproduced from Lars Svensson, *Nordisk paleografi* (1974)

cred names sometimes written with more than just the initial letter in capitals (e.g., MaRia); to indicate the start of a new sentence or section; for calligraphic reasons, especially R, N, S (e.g, utaN); to indicate geminate consonants (þaN); for clarity; and as initials. Accents, usually acute, are used as a diacritic mark over i (not systematically); as a diaeresis over one or both vowels in hiatus; over little words (e.g., ér); over vowels in stressed syllables; as rhythmic markers; to mark vowel quality; as a correction sign; over y instead of a dot; to mark long vowels; as a transposition mark; and as a hyphen at the end of a line. A specifically Icelandic feature is the writing of a dot over a consonant to mark length, a usage that survives, side by side with gemination, throughout the Middle Ages. Furthermore, it should be noted that medieval Latin in Iceland never achieved the dominant position that it enjoyed in so much of the rest of Europe. Most of the country's medieval literature is written in Icelandic.

In Norway, too, literature written in Latin has a subordinate position in the Middle Ages. From around 1200, Latin is used mainly, and to a decreasing extent, in diplomas and ecclesiastical documents. Other literature was written in the vernacular. The oldest surviving books, written in Carolingian-Insular script, date from the mid-12th century (Fig. 148). The oldest extant original diploma in Norwegian (with formulas adopted from English documentary language) dates from around 1210. Norwegian was long the documentary language, developed in Bergen and Niðaróss (Trondheim), after 1314 in Oslo. Swedish or Swedish-influenced language is encountered in Norwegian diplomas during the period when the two kingdoms were united (1319–1355). In the first half of the 15th century, a mixture of Swedish and Norwegian was written in the Brigettine monasteries. Pure Danish became customary in royal rescripts after 1450, and in episcopal letters from Niðaróss and Oslo after 1500. After the Reformation, Danish also became the language of literature and of the Church in Norway. Medieval Norwegian script is, like Icelandic, rich in abbreviations and ligatures. Capital letters and accents are also used in a similar way. In Norway, as in the rest of Scandinavia, neo-Gothic script came into use at the time of the Reformation. The change to Latin script occurred at the same time in Norway as in Denmark, in 1875.

Bib.: Brown, J. T. "Palaeography." In *The New Cambridge Bibliography of English Literature.* 5 vols. Ed. George Watson et al. Cambridge: Cambridge University Press, 1974–77, vol. 1, cols. 209–21; John, James J. "Latin Paleography." In *Medieval Studies: An Introduction.* Ed. James M. Powell. Syracuse: Syracuse University Press, 1976, pp. 1–68 [see bibliography, pp. 53–68]; Tjäder, Jan-Olof. "Latin Palaeography [1975–83]." *Eranos. Acta philologica Suecana* 75 (1977), 131–61; 78 (1980), 65–97; 80 (1982), 63–92; 82 (1984), 66–95 [critical bibliograpical surveys in English]; Bischoff, Bernhard. "Literaturverzeichnis." In *Paläographie des römischen Altertums und des abendländischen Mittelalters.* Grundlagen der Germanistik, 24. Berlin: Schmidt, 1979, pp. 299–323; Boyle, Leonard E. *Medieval Latin Palaeography: A Bibliographical Introduction.* Toronto Medieval Bibliographies, 8. Toronto, Buffalo, and London: University of Toronto Press, 1984; rpt. 1986 [with copious annotations and a comprehensive index]; John, James J. "Paleography, Western Europe." In *Dictionary of the Middle Ages.* Ed. Joseph R. Strayer. New York: Scribner, 1982–89, vol. 9, pp. 334–51 [accompanied by annotated bibliography]. **Lit.: (a) Latin palaeography:** Battelli, Giulio. *Lezioni di paleografia.* 3rd ed. Rome: Città del Vaticano, 1949; rpt. 1978; Cencetti, Giorgio. *Compendio di paleografia latina per le scuole universitarie e archivistiche.* Naples: Istituto editoriale mezzogiorno, 1966; Bischoff, Bernhard. *Paläographie* [see above]; John, James J. "Latin Paleography" [see above]. **(b) Scandinavian palaeography.** Hægstad, Marius. "Nordische (altnordische) Schrift." In *Reallexikon der germanischen Altertumskunde.* Ed. Johannes Hoops. Strassburg: Trübner, 1915–16, vol. 3, pp. 331–41; Brøndum-Nielsen, Johannes. "Den nordiska—västnordiska och danska—skriften." In *Svend Dahls bibliotekshandbok.* Ed. Samuel E. Bring. Uppsala and Stockholm: Almqvist & Wiksell, 1924, vol. 1, pp. 75–106; Jansson, Sam. "Svenskt skrivskick under medeltiden och fram till våra dagar." In *Svend Dahls bibliotekshandbok,* vol. 1, pp. 107–26; Spehr, Harald. *Der Ursprung der isländischen Schrift und ihre Weiterbildung bis zur Mitte des XIII. Jahrhunderts.* Halle: Niemeyer, 1929; Nielsen, Lauritz. *Danmarks middelalderlige Haandskrifter.* Copenhagen: Gyldendal, 1937; Kroman, Erik. "Dansk palæografi." In *Palæografi. A. Danmark og Sverige.* Ed. Johannes Brøndum-Nielsen. Nordisk kultur, 28:A. Stockholm: Bonnier; Oslo: Aschehoug; Copenhagen: Schultz, 1944, pp. 36–81; Jansson, Sam. "Svensk paleografi." In *Palæografi. A. Danmark og Sverige,* pp. 82–130; Björn Þórólfsson. "Nokkur orð um íslenzkt skrifletur." In *Landsbókasafn Íslands. Árbók 1948–1949* (1950), pp. 116–52; Seip, Didrik Arup. *Palæografi. B. Norge og Island,* 28:B. Ed. Johannes Brøndum-Nielsen. Nordisk kultur, 28:B. Stockholm: Bonnier; Oslo: Aschehoug; Copenhagen: Schultz, 1954; Jansson, Sam. "Latinska alfabetets utveckling i medeltida svensk brevskrift. De enskilda bokstävernas historia." *Acta Philologica Scandinavica,* 22 (1954), 81–148; Hreinn Benediktsson. *Early Icelandic Script as Illustrated in Vernacular Texts from the Twelfth and Thirteenth Centuries.* Icelandic Manuscripts, series in folio, 2. Reykjavik: The Manuscript Institute of Iceland, 1965; Svensson, Lars. *Nordisk paleografi. Handbok med transkriberade och kommenterade skriftprov.* Lundastudier i nordisk språkvetenskap, ser. A, no. 28. Lund: Studentlitteratur, 1974. **(c) Dated Scandinavian vernacular MSS with sample facsimiles:** Hildebrand, Emil, et al., eds. *Svenska skriftprof från Erik den heliges tid till Gustaf III:s. Medeltiden 1.* Stockholm: Norstedt, 1894; Kålund, Kristian, ed. *Palæografisk Atlas. Dansk Afdeling.* Copenhagen: Gyldendal, 1903; Kålund, Kristian, ed. *Palæografisk Atlas. Oldnorsk-islandsk Afdeling.* Copenhagen and Kristiania [Oslo]: Gyldendal, 1905; Kålund, Kristian, ed. *Palæografisk Atlas. Ny serie. Oldnorsk-islandske Skriftprøver c. 1300–1700.* Copenhagen and Kristiania [Oslo]: Gyldendal, 1907; Swedlund, R., and O. Svenonius, eds. *Svenska skriftprov 1464–1828. Texter och tolkningar.* 2nd ed. Stockholm: Geber, 1948; Hreinn Benediktsson. *Early Icelandic Script* [see above]; Svensson, Lars. *Nordisk paleografi* [see above]. **(d) Abbreviations:** Cappelli, Adriano. *Lexicon abbreviaturarum: Dizionario di abbreviature latine ed italiane.* 6th ed. Milan: Hoepli, 1973; Cappelli, Adriano. *The Elements of Abbreviation in Medieval Latin Paleography* [Cappelli's introduction]. Trans. David Heimann and Richard Kay. University of Kansas Publications. Library Series, 47. Lawrence: University of Kansas Libraries, 1982; see also Bischoff, Bernhard. *Paläographie,* p. 316 [above], and Boyle, Leonard E. *Medieval Latin Palaeography,* nos. 1762–812 [above]. **(e) Encyclopedias and glossaries treating writing and palaeographic terms:** Birkelund, Palle, et al. *Nordisk lexikon for bogvæsen 1–2.* Copenhagen: Busck; Oslo: Dreyer; Stockholm: Forum, [1946]-1962; *KLNM.* 22 vols. Copenhagen: Rosenkilde & Bagger; Helsingfors: Örnförlaget; Reykjavik: Ísafold; Oslo: Gyldendal; Malmö: Allhem, 1956–78; Glaister, Geoffrey Ashall. *Glaister's Glossary of the Book: Terms Used in Papermaking, Printing, Bookbinding and Publishing with Notes on Illuminated Manuscripts and Private Presses.* 2nd rev. ed. London: Allen & Unwin, 1979; Strayer, Joseph R., ed. *Dictionary of the Middle Ages.* 12 vols. New York: Scribner, 1982–89.

Lars Svensson

[See also: Alphabet; Dialects; Diplomatics; Grammatical Treatises; Language; Latin Language and Literature; Vadstena Language]

Páls saga biskups

Páls saga biskups ("The Saga of Bishop Páll") survives in three MSS of the 17th century, Stock. Papp. 4to no. 4, AM 204 fol., and AM 205 fol., and in later transcripts of these. All surviving MSS represent a single version of the text, which most likely was medieval. In all these MSS, the saga comes after *Hungrvaka* and *Þorláks saga helga*, and, to judge from its abrupt introduction, may have been intended to form a sequel to them in a cycle of sagas about the bishops of Skálholt. The saga presents a fairly short biography of Páll Jónsson, bishop of Skálholt in Iceland (born 1155, consecrated 1195, died November 29, 1211). Because of similarities in style and structure, peculiarities of chronology, and favorable references to Gizurr Hallsson (d. 1206), *Páls saga* has been attributed to the author of *Hungrvaka*, which was probably composed during the first decade of the 13th century. Consequently, *Páls saga* was probably composed in the second decade of the 13th century, shortly after the bishop's death. It has no known written sources, although it names Ari Þorgilsson as an authority for the account of the death of Bishop Gizurr Ísleifsson. Its author probably had personal knowledge of Bishop Páll and other individuals whom he mentions; he includes himself among the surviving intimates of the bishop (ch. 19). Although *Páls saga* mentions Guðmundr Arason, bishop of Hólar, references to his turbulent episcopacy are very different from those in the various Guðmundr sagas. The saga's accuracy was strikingly confirmed in 1954 when the stone coffin described in the saga (ch. 6) was found containing Bishop Páll's remains.

Ed.: Jón Ólafsson, ed. *Hungurvaka . . . Páls biskups saga.* Copenhagen: Godiche, 1778; [Jón Sigurðsson and Guðbrandur Vigfússon, eds.] *Biskupa sögur.* 2 vols. Copenhagen: Möller, 1858–78; Stefán Sveinsson, ed. *Saga Páls Skálholts biscups oc Hungurvaka.* Winnipeg: [n.p.], 1889 [rpt. of 1778 edition, with notes]; Gudbrand Vigfusson and F. York Powell, eds. and trans. *Origines Islandicae: A Collection of the More Important Sagas and Other Native Writings Relating to the Settlement and Early History of Iceland.* 2 vols. Oxford: Clarendon, 1905; rpt. Millwood: Kraus, 1976; Guðni Jónsson, ed. *Byskupa sögur.* Akureyri: Íslendingasagnaútgáfan; Haukadalsútgáfan, 1948; Jón Helgason, ed. *Byskupa sǫgur.* Editiones Arnamagnæanæ, ser. A, vol. 13.2. Copenhagen: Reitzel, 1978. **Lit.:** Ólafur Lárusson. "Kirknatal Páls biskups Jónssonar." *Skírnir* 99 (1925), 16–37; Stefán Einarsson. *A History of Icelandic Literature.* New York: Johns Hopkins University Press; American-Scandinavian Foundation, 1957; Schach, Paul. *Icelandic Sagas.* Twayne's World Authors Series, 717. Boston: Twayne, 1984.

Paul Bibire

[See also: *Biskupa sögur*; *Guðmundar sögur biskups*; *Hungrvaka*; *Þorláks saga helga*]

Pamphilus ok Galathea

Pamphilus ok Galathea is a 13th-century translation of an anonymous poem, the *Pamphilus de amore*, written toward the end of the 12th century presumably in northern France. The poem is in elegiac verse and presented in a dialogue form approaching drama, *fabliau*, didactic poetry, and handbooks of love rather than romance (Schlauch 1933). The work, which focuses on the idea of courtly love, and which draws heavily on Ovid's *Ars amatoria* and *Remedia amoris*, tells of Pamphilus, who falls in love with Galathea. He appeals to Venus for help, who gives the young man advice regarding the rules of the games of love. Pamphilus finally wins Galathea's heart with the help of an old woman. The poem was very popular in the 13th century; it was translated into a number of European languages and was included in Eberhard's *Laborintus*.

The chief MS of *Pamphilus ok Galathea* is De la Gardie nos. 4–7, from around 1250–1300, which represents a copy of a now-lost prose translation. The MS contains only the first two-thirds of the original rendering due to a lacuna in the MS. In addition, copies are found in a number of paper MSS from the 17th–19th centuries (AM 391 fol.; AM 948c 4to; Stock. Papp. 4to no. 34; Rask 692 4to).

The anonymous translator adhered closely to his original. No attempt is made, however, to imitate the metrical form of the Latin. Alliteration appears now and then, but otherwise examples of stylistic embellishments to match the Latin are few. The frequent errors in the Norse texts are presumably due to the copying, not to the translator himself. De Morawski (1917: 50, n. 1) suggests that the close translation was made by a student as an exercise.

Ed.: Kölbing, Eugen, ed. "Bruchstück einer altnordischen Bearbeitung von Pamphilus und Galathea." *Germania* 23, n.s. 11 (1878), 129–41; Holm-Olsen, Ludvig, ed. *Den gammelnorske oversettelse av Pamphilus med en undersøkelse av paleografi og lydverk.* II Hist.-filos. Kl. 1940, No. 2. Avhandlinger utgitt av Det Norske Videnskaps-Akademi i Oslo. Oslo: Dybwad, 1940; Mattias Tveitane, ed. *Elis saga, Strengleikar and Other Texts: Uppsala University Library Delagardieska samlingen Nos. 4–7 folio and AM 666b quarto.* Corpus Codicum Norvegicorum Medii Aevi, quarto serie 4. Oslo: Selskapet til utgivelse af gamle norske håndskrifter, 1972 [facsimile]; Hermann Pálsson. "Pamphilus de amore í norrænni þýðingu (ný útgáfa með skýringum)." *Gripla* 6 (1984), 12–48. **Bib.:** Kalinke, Marianne E., and P. M. Mitchell. *Bibliography of Old Norse–Icelandic Romances.* Islandica, 44. Ithaca and London: Cornell University Press, 1985, pp. 86–7. **Lit.:** Morawski, Joseph de. *Pamphile et Galatée par Jehan Bras-de-Fer de Dammartin-en-Goële poème français inédit du xive siècle.* Paris: Librairie ancienne Honoré Champion, 1917; Schlauch, Margaret. *Romance in Iceland.* Princeton: Princeton University Press; New York: American-Scandinavian Foundation; London: Allen & Unwin, 1933; rpt. New York: Russell & Russell, 1973, pp. 46–7, 184; Bekker-Nielsen, Hans, *et al. Norrøn fortællekunst: Kapitler af den norsk-islandske middelalderlitteraturs historie.* Copenhagen: Akademisk Forlag, 1965, pp. 108–9; Olsen, Thorkil Damsgaard. "Pamphilus." *KLNM* 13 (1968), 91; Sverrir Tómasson. "Hugleiðingar um horfna bókmenntagrein." *Tímarit Máls og menningar* 50.2 (1989), 211–26.

Kirsten Wolf

[See also: *Riddarasögur*]

Parcevals saga

Parcevals saga ("Parceval's Saga") is an Old Norse prose version of Chrétien de Troyes's chivalric romance *Perceval*, or *Le Conte du Graal.* The saga was probably composed, along with the other Arthurian *riddarasögur*, at the court of Hákon Hákonarson of Norway (r. 1217–1263). *Parcevals saga* is preserved in one vellum MS, Stock. Perg. 4to no. 6 (*ca.* 1400), which also contains *Ívens saga*, a fragment (*ca.* 1350), and a number of postmedieval paper transcripts. A lacuna in the vellum and also in the paper transcripts covers some 180 lines of Chrétien's poem.

The story concerns the chivalric education and adventures of a rustic but promising youth. Unschooled but enthusiastic, the knight aspirant leaves home, enjoys the hospitality of the ailing Fisher King, proves himself worthy as a Round Table knight, delivers the lady Blanchefleur (Norse Blankiflúr) from her enemies, and undertakes the quest for the Grail and the Bleeding Lance, mysterious objects that he has glimpsed but reprehensibly failed to ask about at the Fisher King's castle. The significance of the Grail is eventually explained to him one Easter by a hermit, who identifies himself as Perceval's uncle.

Parcevals saga retains a pattern of fidelity to its source similar to that of the other translated riddarasögur; only at the beginning and end does it diverge from Chrétien's Perceval. In its introductory family history of the hero, which makes his mother an abducted princess and his deceased father's rural exile voluntary, the saga deviates from Chrétien's grim account of killing, maiming, and dispossession as the background to their forest existence. The saga also appends a brief conclusion to that section of Perceval where Chrétien interrupts, and never resumes, his tale of the knight's adventures. Parceval, as promised, returns to and marries Blankiflúr, becoming lord of her land and an invincible knight. Gauvain's adventures, which take up the rest of Chrétien's unfinished narrative, become the separate Valvers þáttr.

Unlike its source, the saga is indifferent to the complicated network of relationships that influence Perceval's predicted "destiny." The Norse version eliminates the blood tie between his family and the Grail King's, and, although providing a conclusion to the story, offers no answer to Chrétien's unresolved question of the restoration of the Fisher King's health and lands. The saga's perplexing definition of the Grail as a gangandi greiði (possibly "walking purveyor of hospitality") has elicited a number of suggestions as to how the saga writer conceived it.

Parcevals saga focuses on the educative aspect of the story, with detailed and sometimes amplified attention paid to those episodes where the hero receives instruction in chivalric theory and practice. Injected into Chrétien's roman courtois is a vein of practical, worldly instruction in manners and morals, which has its affinity with the ethic of the Norwegian Konungs skuggsjá ("King's Mirror") and the didactic Icelandic poem Hugsvinnsmál, a Norse version of the Latin Disticha Catonis. The saga also contains a number of proverbial statements (sententiae), some of them rhymed, an unusual stylistic feature in a work that is otherwise typical of the translated riddarasögur in its use of alliterative collocating or synonymous word pairs (e.g., skomm ok skaða 'shame and harm'; synd né svívirðing 'sin nor dishonor') and, sometimes at sententious or significant turns of the narrative, present participles.

Parcevals saga lacks the comic irony that underlies the presentation of the hero and Gauvain in Perceval. The latter's amorous exploits and polished manners often carry courtoisie to excess, but pointedly contrast with Perceval's gaucherie; the division of Chrétien's narrative into saga and þáttr removes this comparison from the Norse. And despite a series of tutors in the art of chivalry, the French hero remains naive throughout; his Norse counterpart, although uneducated and heima alinn ("home-bred") is never entirely foolish or boorish, and ends his days gloriously.

Attitudes toward and conceptions of chivalry differ in the two works. Perceval is somewhat ambivalent from the outset about the merits of the chivalric life, which has caused the death or disablement of Perceval's father and brothers, whereas in the saga, riddaraskapr ("chivalry") is wholeheartedly endorsed. Chivalry in Parcevals saga is a straightforward code of valor, loyalty, piety, and humility, uncomplicated by the religious mysticism in Chrétien's

Perceval and developed further by other writers of Grail romances.

Ed.: Kölbing, Eugen, ed. *Riddarasögur. Parcevals saga. Valvers þáttr. Ívents saga. Mírmans saga.* Strassburg: Trübner, 1872, pp. 1–71; Maclean, Helen Susan, ed. "A Critical Edition, Complete with Introduction, Notes, and Select Glossary of *Parcevals saga* from the Stockholm Manuscript Codex Holmiensis no. 6, Pergament quarto." M.Phil. thesis. University of Leeds, 1968; Slay, Desmond, ed. *Romances: Perg. 4:o nr 6. Royal Library, Stockholm.* Early Icelandic Manuscripts in Facsimile, 10. Copenhagen: Rosenkilde & Bagger, 1972. **Bib.**: Kalinke, Marianne E., and P. M. Mitchell. *Bibliography of Old Norse–Icelandic Romances.* Islandica, 44. Ithaca and London: Cornell University Press, 1985, pp. 87–90. **Lit.**: Kölbing, Eugen. "Die nordische Parzivalsaga und ihre Quelle." *Germania* 14 (1869), 129–81; Mitchell, P. M. "The Grail in the Parcevals Saga." *Modern Language Notes* 73 (1958), 591–4; Loomis, R. S. "The Grail in the *Parcevals Saga*." *Germanic Review* 39 (1964), 97–100; Foote, P. G. "Gangandi greiði" In *Einarsbók. Afmæliskveðja til Einars Ól. Sveinssonar. 12. desember 1969.* Ed. Bjarni Guðnason et al. Reykjavik: Nokkrir vinir, 1969, pp. 48–58; Kratz, Henry. "The *Parcevals saga* and *Li contes del Graal.*" *Scandinavian Studies* 49 (1977), 13–47; Kratz, Henry. "*Textus, Braull,* and *Gangandi Greiði.*" *Saga-Book of the Viking Society* 19 (1977), 371–82; Kalinke, Marianne E. *King Arthur North-by-Northwest: The* matière de Bretagne *in Old Norse–Icelandic Romances.* Bibliotheca Arnamagnæana, 37. Copenhagen: Reitzel, 1981; Barnes, Geraldine. "Parcevals Saga: Riddara Skuggsjá?" *Arkiv för nordisk filologi* 99 (1984), 49–62; Álfrún Gunnlaugsdóttir. "Quelques aspects de Parcevals Saga." In *Les Sagas de Chevaliers (Riddarasögur). Actes de la Ve Conférence Internationale sur les Sagas . . . (Toulon. Juillet 1982).* Civilisations, 10. Ed. Régis Boyer. Paris: Presses de l'Université de Paris-Sorbonne, 1985, pp. 217–33; Weber, Wolfgang. "The Decadence of Feudal Myth: Towards a Theory of *riddarasaga* and Romance." In *Structure and Meaning in Old Norse Literature. New Approaches to Textual Analysis and Literary Criticism.* Ed. John Lindow et al. Viking Collection, 3. Odense: Odense University Press, 1986, pp. 415–54; Barnes, Geraldine. "Arthurian Chivalry in Old Norse." In *Arthurian Literature VII.* Ed. Richard Barber. Cambridge: Brewer, 1987, pp. 50–102.

Geraldine Barnes

[**See also:** *Hugsvinnsmál; Konungs skuggsjá; Riddarasögur*]

Paris' Dom *see* Drama

Partalopa saga ("The Saga of Partalopi") is the Old Norse version of the story about Partenopeus de Blois from 1182–1185, which was translated into a number of European languages. The oldest known but now-lost MS is *Ormr Snorrasons bók* (extant in copies in Stock. Perg. fol. nos. 46, 47, 48, and 58). The saga is extant in thirty-two MSS, of which ten have textual significance. These MSS can be divided into two redactions, A and B. The most important MSS belonging to the A-redaction are AM 533 4to, Stock. Perg. fol. no. 7, JS 27 fol., Lbs. 272 fol., and AM 109a 8vo. The MS Stock. Perg. fol. no. 46 represents the B-redaction.

The only certain fact about the date and provenance of the saga is that it is an Old Norse translation of a French source made before the 14th century in Norway or Iceland. It is possible that the saga came into existence along with other translations of courtly literature in Norway around 1250.

The source is either the preserved French or a now-lost French version. The preserved texts can be divided into two main groups: *y* and *z* (Bødtker 1904). The preserved French and several more or less direct translations of this work into English, Italian, High

German, Low German, and Dutch belong to the *y*-group, in which the story begins in France, the hero's native country. The Old Norse version, the Danish poem (see below), a Spanish prose version, a Catalonian translation of it, and an English version belong to the *z*-group, in which the story begins in Greece, the heroine's native country (Bødtker 1912). The main difference between the two groups, *i.e.*, the country where the story begins, may be due to a deliberate change from *ordo artificialis* to *ordo naturalis*, which theoretically may have been made independently of each other within the *z*-group. Verbal agreements within the *z*-group also support the theory about a close relationship between these versions, however. *Partenopeus de Blois* is a *roman courtois* sharing characteristics with stories of the type *romans d'antiquité* as well as *romans bretons*. The name of the protagonist is drawn from *Roman de Thebes*, and the main motif has its origin in Apuleius's story about Amor and Psyche.

The story evolves from the motif "the breach of the order," which relates how a mortal falls in love with a supernatural being (in the *Partalopa saga* the heroine, Marmoria, is not supernatural, but she is skilled in astronomy and magic, and, as the ruling empress of Constantinople, she is very mighty). The lovers are together only in the shelter of the dark of the night. In the daytime, the supernatural being disappears, and his full identity remains hidden to his partner. The mortal is persuaded by jealous or worried relatives to breach the promise to the lover not to try to meet again. The supernatural being disappears in anger, and the mortal must endure many trials before they can be united.

What is special about *Partenopeus de Blois* and *Partalopa saga*, however, is that the man and the woman have exchanged roles. The woman is not the one who takes the erotic initiative, while the man is the one who humbly worships her, who is cast off, and who is finally restored to her favor. This shift is probably due to influence from Breton stories and Marie de France's *lais*. The Old Norse version has also added a motif not found in any other: the proud princess who humiliates and rejects all lovers until she is finally overcome by one of them (*cf.* the fairy-tale motif, *König Drosselbart*).

In the French text, the heroine promises the hero marriage after two and a half years. In the saga, she does not want to marry Partalopi or any other man; she only wants to have a secret lover, because she does not want to lose her position as maiden-king, *meykóngr*. She finally realizes, however, that she misses Partalopi and that she must engage in a general, public marriage.

The saga is written in normal Norse prose, or what Halvorsen (1962) calls "translator's prose" without the embellishing effects found in other prose treating courtly topics, such as *Elis saga*, *Tristrams saga*, and *Strengleikar*.

The Danish poem *Persenober og Konstantianobis* is found in the MS SKB 47 (younger than 1484), also containing the Danish versions of Chrétien de Troyes's *Yvain* and the *Floire et Blancheflor*. The plot is more or less the same as in the Old Norse version, but is somewhat simplified, and the names differ considerably. The French prince is called Persenober and the Greek princess Konstantianobis, and in this version her empire is Konstantia. There is no direct connection between the Danish and Old Norse versions, but it has been suggested that they ultimately go back to the same Norse version. A printed edition from 1572 appears to be based on a now-lost edition from 1560.

Ed.: Robert, A. C. M., and G.-A. Crapelet, eds. *Partonopeus de Blois*. 2 vols. Paris: Crapelet, 1834 [French version]; Brandt, C. J., ed. "Persenober og Konstantionobis." In *Romantisk digtning fra middelalderen*. 3 vols. 1869–77, vol. 2. Copenhagen: Samfund til den danske literaturs fremme, 1870 [Danish version]; Dalamere, Lord, ed. *Fragment of Partonope of Blois from a Manuscript at Vale Royal in the Possession of Lord Delamere*. London: Roxburghe Club; Nichols, 1873; rpt. in *The Middle English Versions of Partonope of Blois*. Ed. Trampe Bödtker. Early English Text Society, e.s, 109. London: Trübner, 1912 [Middle English version]; Klockhoff, Oskar, ed. *Partalopa saga för första gången utgifven*. Upsala [*sic*] Universitets Årsskrift. Uppsala: Edquist, 1877 [Old Norse version]; Olrik, Jørgen, ed. "Persenober og Konstantianobis." In *Danske Folkebøger* 12. Copenhagen: Gyldendal, 1925 [Danish version]; Gildea, Joseph, ed. *Partonopeu de Blois*. 2 vols. Villanova: Villanova University Press, 1967–70 [French version]; Præstgaard Andersen, Lise, ed. *Partalopa saga*. Editiones Arnamagnæanæ, ser. B, vol. 28. Copenhagen: Reitzel, 1983 [Old Norse version; English translation by Foster W. Blaisdell, pp. 127–98]. **Lit.**: Kölbing, Eugen. "Über die verschiedenen Gestaltungen der Partonopeus-Saga." *Germanistische Studien* 2 (1875), 55–114; Kölbing, Eugen. "Ueber die englischen versionen der Partonopeussage." In *Beiträge zur vergleichenden Geschichte der romantischen Poesie und Prosa des Mittelalters unter besonderer Berücksichtigung der englischen und nordischen Litteratur*. Breslau: Koebner, 1876, pp. 80–91; Bødtker, A. Trampe. *Parténopeus de Blois. Étude comparative des versions islandaise et danoise*. Videnskabs-Selskabets Skrifter. II. Hist.-filos. Kl. 1904. No. 3. Christiania [Oslo]: Dybwad, 1904; Newstead, Helaine. "The Traditional Background of *Partonopeus de Blois*." *Publications of the Modern Language Association* 61 (1946), 916–46; Fourrier, Anthime. *Le courant réaliste dans le roman courtois en France au moyen-âge*. Paris: Nizet, 1960; Halvorsen, Eyvind Fjeld. "Høvisk stil." *KLNM* 7 (1962), 315–18; Halvorsen, E. F. "Lærd og folkelig stil: Island og Norge." *KLNM* 11 (1966), 119–23; Halvorsen, E. F. "Partalopa saga." *KLNM* 13 (1968), 121–2; Halvorsen, E. F. "Riddarsagaer." *KLNM* 14 (1969), 175–83; Præstgaard Andersen, Lise. *Skjoldmøer—en kvindemyte*. Copenhagen: Gyldendal, 1982.

Lise Præstgaard Andersen

[**See also:** Maiden Warriors; *Riddarasögur*]

Persenober og Konstantianobis *see* Partalopa saga

Personal Names in medieval Scandinavia, *i.e.*, forenames and by-names, were used not only in Scandinavia itself but also in the regions of the British Isles and France that had been colonized by settlers from Scandinavia in the Viking period. The personal names occur not only as the names of characters in medieval works of literature and history, but also as elements in place-names.

The development of the Scandinavian personal nomenclature in the late-medieval period is, as far as forenames are concerned, characterized on the one hand by an increase in the number of names borrowed from Latin and German, and on the other hand by a degree of stability, which is in part at least a result of the practice of calling a child after the grandparent or some other relation. As far as by-names are concerned, the most significant development in the medieval period is that the by-names of the nobility could become hereditary and thus turn into family names.

Forenames. The medieval nomenclature is made up in part of Scandinavian names handed down from earlier times and in part of names borrowed from, in particular, southern and central Europe as a result of religious and commercial activity. The statistical relationship between the native Scandinavian names and the names of foreign origin varies from time to time and place to place. Foreign influence made itself felt earliest and strongest in Denmark and Sweden, while the Scandinavian names survived better in the rural districts of Norway, in the Faroes, and in Iceland.

It is usual to distinguish between compound (dithematic) forenames and simplex (monothematic) ones. The compound names are made up of two words from such categories of meaning as heathen mythology (Gudmund / Guðmundr, Thorstein / Þorsteinn, Asløgh / Áslaug), warfare (Gunnar / Gunnarr, Bothild / Ragnhildr, Sigrid / Sigríðr), or the animal world (Ødbjørn / Arinbjǫrn, Arngrim / Arngrímr). Unlike other compound words, compound names are not supposed to have a meaning. The combination of the two elements in a forename is generally the result of a naming practice according to which the name of the child had to contain at least one of the elements in the names of its parents, the principle of variation.

The simplex names consist of one linguistic element. This element can be an original by-name, which assumed the function of a forename at an early date (Sten / Steinn, Gun(n), Gerd / Gerðr). This type of forename is assumed to be typologically the most archaic. Such simplex names can, however, be hypocoristic short forms of compound names (Thorsten / Þorsteinn, Stenkil / Steinkell, Gunnar / Gunnarr, Thorgun / Þorgunnr, Asgerd / Ásgerðr). To these simplex names is sometimes added a derivative ending. The most common of these are -i (masc.) and -a (fem.) (Thori, Gunna; Tumi, Þóra). Such formations are also assumed to have originated as hypocorisms, or pet names. The same stylistic effect could be achieved by the use of various consonant developments, particularly geminations (Tokke < Þorkell, Ebbe < Esbjørn, Tubbi < Þorbjørn, Tobba < Þorbjǫrg, Sigga < Sigrid, Sigríðr). The hypocoristic nature of these names became obscured at an early date, however, and they end by being stylistically neutral.

The first names of foreign origin to be adopted into the nomenclature in the medieval period reflect the conversion of the Scandinavians to Christianity in the 11th century. At this time, the population of Scandinavia was introduced not only to the Bible but also to the great band of saints to whom the churches of the new faith were mainly dedicated and whose feast days were recorded in the calendar. Many of the names of personages in the New Testament and the legends of the saints were taken into use as Christian names, and in the course of a century or a century and a half, they became extremely popular. Such names as Johannes, Petrus, Nicolaus, Andreas, Birgitta, Katarina, Margareta, and Maria in their scandinavianized forms eventually became the most commonly occurring forenames throughout most of the North.

Toward the end of the 13th century, the Low German influence on the culture and language of eastern Scandinavia in particular began to make itself felt. This influence resulted in the borrowing of a number of German forenames (Vilhelm / Vilhjálmr, Henrik / Heinrekr, Matilde / Matthilda). Low German influence in Scandinavia was a result of commercial and economic relationships, and the German forenames occur most frequently among the nobility and the merchant classes. They did not penetrate to the medieval peasant society.

By-names. In contrast to forenames, by-names must have a lexical meaning. They must characterize their bearers. From this point of view, the very large body of heterogeneous by-name material from medieval Scandinavia can be placed into three main groups. The names can point to the bearers' characteristics, to their relationship to places or other people, or to their function in society.

Characteristic by-names can describe physical characteristics (physionyms), for example, Lille ("little") Peter, Anders Blind ("blind"), or Jens Fyrtårn ("resembles a lighthouse"). They can also describe mental characteristics (psychonyms), for example, Dumme ("stupid") Peter, Óláfr kyrri ("peaceful"). Without supplementary information about the bearer, it can sometimes be difficult to decide whether a by-name is a physionym or a psychonym, for example, Lars Ræv ("who is as red-haired as a fox" or "who is as cunning as a fox").

By-names of relationship are very numerous. Of those that refer to relationship to another person, patronymics are the most significant group. These are by-names that consist of the father's name (normally his forename) plus the word for son or daughter, Jørgen Pederssøn, Ane Andersdatter, Egill Skalla-Grímsson, Helga Þorsteinsdóttir. The masculine patronymics lie behind the extremely common modern Scandinavian family name in -sen, -son. Another important subgroup consists of names expressing relationship to a place, normally the bearer's birthplace. Such by-names can take the form of an inhabitant's name or folk name, for example, Lars Falstring ("from Falster"), Per Jude ("from Jutland"), or of a place-name, for example, Lars Falster, Jens Rønninge.

Occupational by-names indicate the occupation or social status of their bearers. The most important of these is the group of by-names that reveal their bearer's occupations. This type of name occurs particularly frequently in the towns, where the trades and crafts were separated out into specialized occupations, for example, Hans Væver ("weaver"), Ole Smed ("smith"), Jens Møller ("miller").

By-names form the basis for family names, which are by-names that have been inherited and therefore no longer necessarily characterize their bearers. The establishment of a proper system of family names in Scandinavia did not take place until well after the end of the medieval period; and in Iceland, where patronymics predominate, such a system has never taken root. Medieval family names in Scandinavia were to be found almost only among the nobility, and even among the members of this class they were not universal. By-names that have already developed into family names among the nobility in the medieval period include physionyms: Hvide ("white"), Krumpen ("crouched"), Brok ("badger"); psychonyms: Glob ("fool"), Hvas ("sharp"); relationship to person: Stensen; relationship to place: Urne, Friis; occupational: Munk ("monk").

Lex.: Lundgren, M. F., and Erik Brate. *Personnamn från medeltiden*. Uppsala: Almqvist and Wiksell, 1892–1934 [Sweden]; Lind, E. H. *Norsk-isländska dopnamn och fingerade namn från medeltiden*. Uppsala: Lundequist, 1905–14; Supplement. Oslo: Dybwad, 1931; Lind, E. H. *Norsk-isländska personbinamn från medeltiden*. Uppsala: Lundequist, 1920–21; Hornby, R., *et al. Danmarks gamle Personnavne*. 2 vols. Copenhagen: Gad, 1936–64; *Sveriges medeltida personnamn*. Ordbok utgiven av Kungl. vitterhets historie och antikvitets akademiens personnamnskommitté. Vol. 1–. Uppsala: Almqvist & Wiksell, 1967–; Stemshaug, Ola, ed. *Norsk personnamnleksikon*. Oslo: Det norske Samlaget, 1982. **Lit.: (a) General**: Janzén, Assar, ed. *Personnavne*. Nordisk kultur, 7. Stockholm: Bonnier; Oslo: Aschehoug; Copenhagen: Schultz, 1947 [contains treatments of Primitive Norse personal names, West Scandinavian, Danish and Swedish forenames, and Scandinavian by-names]. **(b) Denmark**: Hald, K. *Personnavne i Danmark. II Middelalderen*. Copenhagen: Dansk historisk Fællesforening, 1974; Hornby, R. *Danske personnavne*. Copenhagen: Gad, 1978; Søndergaard, G. *Bogen om personnavne*. Copenhagen: Politiken, 1979; Kousgård Sørensen, John. *Patronymer i Danmark. I: Runetid og middelalder*. Copenhagen: Akademisk Forlag, 1984 [English summary]. **(c) Sweden**: Modéer, Ivar. *Svenska personnamn.* Kungl. Vetenskapssamhällets i Uppsala handlingar, 10. Uppsala: Almqvist & Wiksell, 1964; Otterbjörk, Roland. *Svenska förnamn.* Stockholm: Norstedt, 1964. **(d) Danelaw**: Feilitzen, Olof von. *The Pre-Conquest Personal Names of Domesday Book.* Uppsala: Almqvist & Wiksell, 1937; Fellows-Jensen, Gillian. *Scandinavian Personal Names in Lincolnshire and Yorkshire.* Copenhagen: Akademisk Forlag, 1968. **(e) Normandy**: Adigard des Gautries, Jean. *Les noms de personnes scandinaves en Normandie de 911 à 1066.* Lund: Blom, 1954.

John Kousgård Sørensen

[**See also**: Place-names]

Petrus de Dacia

Petrus de Dacia (*ca.* 1230–1289) is called Sweden's first author. While studying at the *studium generale* of the Dominicans in Cologne (1267–1269), Petrus visited the nearby village of Stommeln, where he met the German beguine Christina of Stommeln in 1267. As Christina's confessor, he often witnessed her remarkable and even terrifying experiences: ecstasies, stigmatizations, and visions that convinced him that Christina was a saint capable of showing him the right way to God. In 1269–1270, when studying in Paris, Petrus began the correspondence with Christina that continued until his death. In 1270, he returned to Sweden, revisiting Stommeln on his way home, and in 1271 he was appointed lector of the Dominican convent of Skänninge. Not earlier than 1277, he was transferred to Västerås, where he became lector and then prior, until 1280, when he was made lector of the convent of Visby in his native island of Gotland. In 1279, while staying a month in Cologne, he again paid several visits to Christina. Having become prior in Visby, he was also appointed *socius* of the provincial for the General Chapter at Bordeaux in summer 1287. On his way home from Bordeaux, Petrus met Christina at Stommeln for the last time. In a letter of September 9, 1289, Christina was informed that Petrus had died during the Lent of that year.

Two literary works in Latin by Petrus are known, both in the *Codex Juliacensis* from about 1300, now in the Bischöfliches Diözesanarchiv in Aachen. In the *Vita Christinae Stumbelensis* ("Life of Christina of Stommeln"), Petrus describes his visits to Stommeln and his strong emotional reactions to Christina's mystical experiences. The book also contains their correspondence and a biography of Christina written by the parish priest of Stommeln, who used to read and translate Petrus's letters to Christina and write down her letters. Although Petrus was deeply attached to Christina, he repeatedly emphasizes that their love is a spiritual one, having Christ for its true object.

Petrus's other known work is *De gratia naturam ditante sive De virtutibus Christinae Stumbelensis* ("On Grace Enriching Nature, or On the Virtues of Christina of Stommeln"). It consists of a poem of forty-three hexameters praising Christina's virtues and a long theological treatise commenting on each word of the poem. The greater part of this work is lost. Petrus exploits his philosophical and theological learning to find theoretical explanations of Christina's behavior. The work presents few original thoughts, being mainly a compilation of the ideas of Petrus's masters in Cologne and Paris, Albertus Magnus and Thomas Aquinas.

Ed.: Petrus de Dacia. *Vita Christinae Stumbelensis.* Ed. Johannes Paulson. Scriptores Latini Medii Aeui Suecani, 1, fasc. 2. Gothenburg: Wettergren & Kerber, 1896; Petrus de Dacia. *De gratia naturam ditante sive De virtutibus Christinae Stumbelensis. Edition critique avec une* introduction par Monika Asztalos. Acta Universitatis Stockholmiensis. Studia Latina Stockholmiensia, 28. Stockholm: Almqvist & Wiksell, 1982 [review by Eva Odelman in *Archivum Latinitatis Medii Aevi,* 43 (1984), 166–76]; [a new edition of Petrus's letters with a Swedish translation is being prepared by Monika Asztalos]. **Lit.**: Schück, Henrik. *Vår förste författare. En själshistoria från medeltiden.* Stockholm: Geber, 1916; Lehmann, Paul. *Skandinaviens Anteil an der lateinischen Literatur und Wissenschaft des Mittelalters.* 1. Stück. Sitzungsberichte der Bayerischen Akademie der Wissenschaften. Philosophisch-historische Abteilung, Jahrgang 1936, Heft 2. Munich: Bayerische Akademie der Wissenschaften, 1936, pp. 44–47; Gallén, Jarl. *La province de Dacie de l'ordre des Frères Prêcheurs. 1: Histoire générale jusqu'au grand schisme.* Helsinki: Söderström, 1946; Olsen, T. D. "Petrus de Dacia." *New Catholic Encyclopedia.* New York: McGraw-Hill, 1967, vol. 11, p. 247; Lindroth, Sten. *Svensk lärdomshistoria.* 4 vols. Stockholm: Norstedt, 1975–81, vol. 1, pp. 64–71; Nieveler, Peter. *Codex Iuliacensis. Christina von Stommeln und Petrus von Dacien, ihr Leben und Nachleben in Geschichte, Kunst und Literatur.* Veröffentlichungen des Bischöflichen Diözesanarchivs Aachen, 34. Mönchengladbach: Kühlen, 1975; Asztalos, Monika. "Les lettres de direction et les sermons épistolaires de Pierre de Dacie." In *The Editing of Theological and Philosophical Texts from the Middle Ages: Acts of the Conference Arranged by the Department of Classical Languages, University of Stockholm, 29–31 August 1984.* Acta Universitatis Stockholmiensis. Studia Latina Stockholmiensia, 30. Stockholm: Almqvist & Wiksell, 1986, pp. 161–84; *Den Svenska Litteraturen. 1: Från forntid till frihetstid 800–1718.* Stockholm: Bonnier, 1987, pp. 66–71.

Eva Odelman

Physiologus

Physiologus (or *Bestiarius*) is a natural history written originally in Greek probably in the 4th century. The work became very popular, with early Latin renderings serving as the originals for a number of later translations into several European languages. The *Physiologus* contains descriptions of natural and supernatural beings and objects, with religious and moral lessons drawn from their appearance and behavior.

In Scandinavia, the work is known only in an Old Icelandic rendering, but the influence of the *Physiologus* manifests itself in several works, such as the Danish *Lucidarius,* the Swedish *Siælinna thrøst, Konungs skuggsjá,* and Anders Sunesen's poem *Hexaemeron.* The Old Icelandic translation is not preserved in its entirety; only two small fragments are extant: AM 673a I and II 4to. Both fragments date from about 1200, and both appear to be copies; judging from the orthography of these fragments, the originals probably dated from the 12th century. The fragments represent the first illustrated books made in Iceland still extant. The illustrators based their pictures upon foreign models, possibly of English origin.

Fragment I (two leaves) contains allegorical interpretations of five animals: phoenix, hoopoe, siren, horsefly, and onocentaur. The author does not describe the physical attributes of the animals, but dwells only upon the moral symbolism to be drawn from them. The second leaf has only pictures that appear to have no connection to the *Physiologus* text.

Fragment II consists of eight adjoining leaves plus one separate leaf. Only leaves 1–6 contain the *Physiologus* text (descriptions of fifteen animals and their allegorical significance, *i.e.,* the *Physiologus* proper): *hydris* (watersnake, but here a kind of bird), goat, wild ass, monkey, falcon, coot, panther, *aspedo* (turtle, but here a kind of whale), partridge, onocentaur, weasel, adder, turtledove, deer, and lizard. Fragment II also treats four animals in the

Bible: *milvus* (kite), *porcus silvae* (wild boar), *nycticorax* (nightraven), and *elephans* (elephant). These four creatures derive from commentaries on the Bible rather than from *Physiologus*. Leaves 8–9 contain allegorical explanations, first of the ship and its individual parts, and next of the rainbow and its colors.

Ed.: Dahlerup, Verner, ed. "Physiologus i to islandske bearbejdelser." *Aarbøger for nordisk Oldkyndighed og Historie* 4 (1889), 199–290; Halldór Hermannsson, ed. *The Icelandic Physiologus*. Islandica, 27. Ithaca: Cornell University Press, 1938; Hreinn Benediktsson. *Early Icelandic Script as Illustrated in Vernacular Texts from the Twelfth and Thirteenth Centuries*. Icelandic Manuscripts, series in folio, 2. Reykjavik: Manuscript Institute of Iceland, 1965 [pls. 9 and 10]; [n.a.]. "Faksimile af de islandske Physiologus-fragmenter [with Danish translation by Jonna Louis-Jensen]." *Romanske stenarbejder* (Højberg) 2 (1984), 23–57. **Lit.**: Marchand, James W. "Two Notes on the Old Icelandic Physiologus Manuscript." *Modern Language Notes* 91 (1976), 501–5; Vellev, Jens. "De islandske Physiologus-billeder og den romanske stenskulptur." *Romanske stenarbejder* (Højberg) 2 (1984), 7–22; Louis-Jensen, Jonna. "Forklaringer til den islandske Physiologus-tekst." *Romanske stenarbejder* (Højberg) 2 (1984), 59–62; Kolstrup, Inger-Lise. "Physiologus- og bestiariefremstillinger i dansk romansk stenskulptur." *Romanske stenarbejder* (Højberg) 2 (1984), 63–118; Faraci, Dora. "The *gleða* Chapter in the Old Icelandic Physiologus." *Opuscula* 9, Bibliotheca Arnamagnæana, 39. Copenhagen: Reitzel, 1991, pp. 108–26.

Kirsten Wolf

[**See also:** Christian Poetry; *Elucidarius*; Homilies (West Norse); *Konungs skuggsjá*; Sunesen, Anders]

Place-names. In the Middle Ages, Scandinavian place-names were found in the two countries of the Scandinavian peninsula, Norway and Sweden, together with Denmark and Schleswig, and also in the colonies established by Norwegians and Danes in Iceland, the Faroes, the British Isles, and Normandy, and by Swedes in the Åland islands and the western and southern parts of the Finnish mainland, around Uleåborg, Vasa, Åbo, and Helsinki.

Settlement history. There is no stratum of place-names in central and southern Scandinavia that can be proved to have been coined by people speaking a non-Germanic language. So a place-name chronology for the region is dependent partly on such internal evidence as their lexical content and linguistic expression, partly on a study of the names found in the colonies, and partly on comparison with the nomenclature of the rest of northwestern Europe, where names containing elements cognate with those found in Scandinavian place-names can be stratified between names of, for example, Celtic, Romance, or Slavic origin. We can assume that place-name elements found in all the countries in which Germanic tribes settled were current in the Migration Period, while elements found only in Scandinavia may be archaic elements that dropped out of use very early, or elements that did not come into use until the migrations were completed, or elements that were applicable only to the topography or settlement situation in Scandinavia. Elements shared by Scandinavia and one or more of the other Germanic countries may reflect a colonizing movement or the influence of trading contacts.

The problems associated with establishing a chronology of settlement in Scandinavia on the basis of the place-name evidence are thus very complicated, but it is nevertheless possible to draw some tentative conclusions. The oldest surviving place-names, dating from before the Migration Period, would seem to be those

borne by a number of islands, lakes, and rivers. These names are either old appellatives (words for water, land-elevations, *etc.*) functioning as names, or names formed by the addition of a derivative suffix to a root form, which can seldom be identified with certainty, for example, the Danish island names *Als* and *Mors*, formed with an *s*-suffix, and the Swedish lake name *Åsnen* and the Norwegian river name *Mesna*, formed with an *n*-suffix.

The Germanic tribes who settled in northwestern Europe in the Migration Period brought with them not only methods of name forming but also an appropriate place-name vocabulary. At first, they evidently gave names not to individual farms or nucleated settlements but to areas of dispersed settlement. These names were often formed by adding an *ing*-suffix to a theme, and many of them apparently originated as tribal names before being transferred to the tribal territory. In Denmark and in southern and eastern Sweden, place-names derived from tribal names in *-ingaR* with appellatival themes, for example, Swedish *Märinge* (< **mar* 'lake'), occur frequently, but place-names derived from tribal names based on personal names, which are fairly common in England and Germany, such as *Hastings* (< *Hæsta*), *Sigmaringen* (< *Sigimar*), do not occur. Singular *ing*-names formed on appellatival or verbal themes, for example, *Stevning* (< *stafn* 'promontory') and *Pebringe* (< **pipr-* 'trickle'), have a more general distribution over Scandinavia, being also found in Norway. Many of these names were originally appellatives in *-ing*, and such place-names are not necessarily old.

Heimr is a generic element used to coin district names in the Migration Period. This element occurs particularly frequently in the names in Norway, for example, *Trondheim* (< tribal name *Þrændr*), but there are also many instances in southern and central Sweden and Jutland, where *heimr* usually has the meaning "village," while in the Danish islands, names in *-heimr* occur comparatively rarely.

Although names in *-ingaR*, *-ing*, and *-heimr* occur frequently in the Scandinavian homelands, there is little evidence for their use to coin names in the Viking colonies. There are some few names in *-heimr* in Iceland and Shetland, but these instances are mostly stereotype names, such as **Sól-heimr* and **Vind-heimr*. The few apparent instances of Scandinavian names in *-ing* or *-heimr* recorded in sources from the Danelaw can be more satisfactorily explained as the result of adaptation by Scandinavian-speaking settlers of earlier English names in *-ing* and *-hām*.

Lev/löv is a generic that evidently had its period of currency early in the Migration Period. This element originally seems to have denoted "something left behind." It is used of nucleated settlements and seems to point to private ownership of land. Names containing this element are found only in Denmark and southern Sweden, while names containing the related German element *leben* also have a restricted distribution, being found mainly within the old territory of Thüringen. The names in Scandinavia may reflect a movement from Thüringen. If so, the route followed must have been over Brandenburg, Mecklenburg, Lolland, and Falster, for there is a broad belt without *lev*-names in Schleswig-Holstein.

Two other old generics with restricted distributions within Scandinavia, *løse* and *vin*, would both seem originally to have denoted "pasture-land," although they survive in names of settlements, many of high status. Their distribution patterns are more or less complementary, with the *løse*-names being very common in the Danish islands and spreading from there to southern Sweden, while the *vin*-names are most numerous in Norway and fairly common in western Sweden.

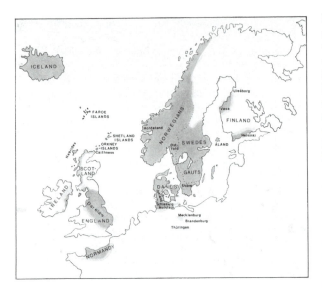

149. Distribution of Scandinavian place-names in the medieval period.

Of the three old generics with restricted distributions in the homelands, the two elements characteristic of Denmark and southern Sweden, *lev* and *løse*, have left no trace on the nomenclature of the colonies in the west, while the typically Norwegian and West Swedish *vin* was evidently taken in fossilized form to Orkney and Shetland in the compound appellative *leik-vin* 'playing-field,' which appears as a place-name in these islands, but not in the Faroes or Iceland.

Names in *-staðir* (Danish *sted*, Norwegian *stad*, Swedish *sta*) are found over most of Scandinavia, although they are particularly common in the parts of Norway in which names in *-heimr* and *-vin* are rare. The cognate elements *stede* and *stedt* are fairly common in England and Germany. There are no Scandinavian names in *-sted* in the Danelaw, but there are a fair number of names in *-staðir* in the Northern and Western Isles and Man. Such names are extremely common in Iceland, although the generic does not occur in settlement names in the Faroes. In the colonies, *-staðir* was evidently used to coin names for small secondary settlements detached from an older estate center. The absence of *-staðir* from the areas of Scandinavian settlement in England probably results from its role there being played by another Scandinavian generic, *bý*, while in the Faroes the lack of space for expansion of settlement onto outfields meant that the element was inappropriate for the Faroese nomenclature.

The generic *bólstaðr* 'site of farm or vill' frequently occurs in names along the west coast of Norway, and Norwegian settlers took the element with them to the Northern and Western Isles and Caithness, where it is the most frequently occurring Scandinavian generic. It is not found in names in Denmark, but there are a number of instances in Sweden, where *bólstaðr* would seem to

have developed a secondary significance: "site of deserted settlement." It has been suggested that the names in *-bólstaðr* in Åland were given by Swedes in the 9th century to settlements established on sites that had been deserted by the earlier inhabitants of the islands. This secondary significance of the generic might lie behind its frequent occurrence in the Northern and Western Isles and Caithness, where the Viking settlers displaced the earlier Celtic inhabitants. The generic *toft*, *tomt*, however, which was certainly used with the denotation "site of a deserted settlement," not only has a much wider distribution than *bólstaðr* in the Scandinavian homelands but also occurs in all the colonized areas, although it is much less common than *bólstaðr* in the areas where the latter element occurs.

Names in *-þorp*, a generic that denoted a "dependent secondary settlement," are extremely common in both Denmark and Sweden, but rarely occur in Norway outside of Østfold. The numerous Scandinavian compounds in *-þorp* in eastern England were most probably coined by the Danish settlers there. In the other areas of Viking colonization, names in *-þorp* occur comparatively rarely. Some of the place-names in *-þorp* in the Scandinavian homelands seem to date from after the Viking Age, since they often have personal names of biblical origin as their specifics.

The Scandinavian generic occurring most frequently in place-names in the Danelaw is *bý*. This is also one of the most common habitative generics in Åland. Both in the Danelaw and in Åland, the generic *bý* is often compounded with a personal name, presumably because an influx of settlers to these areas had led to a sudden need to coin a large number of new names for small independent agricultural units. In Caithness, the Northern and Western Isles, Man, and Iceland, areas where small detached settlement units otherwise tended to be given names in *-staðir* or *-bólstaðr*, scattered instances of names consisting of a personal name plus *-bý* may reflect contact between the Norwegian colonies and the Danelaw in the Viking period. In the Scandinavian homelands, place-names in *-bý* with personal names as specifics have a fairly restricted distribution; and many of them would seem to have been coined after the Viking period. It has been suggested that they reflect trading contacts with the Danelaw.

A recurrent compound in *-bý*, *Hus(e)by* (< **húsa-bý*), which would seem to have denoted some kind of administrative center, has a characteristic distribution in Scandinavia. There are nine instances in Denmark, forty-six in Norway, and about seventy in Sweden. With the exception of four instances in Orkney, the name *Hus(e)by* does not occur in the Scandinavian colonies. It seems likely that this name, both in the Scandinavian homelands and in Orkney, replaced older names. Its absence from the Danelaw and Åland can be explained by the fact that the **húsa-bý* institution did not develop until about the year 1000.

Tún is another generic that would sometimes seem to have been used to coin names in replacement of older names for administrative centers. Names in *-tún* are quite common in Sweden but rare in Norway and very rare in Denmark. The related Old English generic *tūn* is by far the commonest habitative generic in place-names in England, and there is early evidence in this country for its use to denote a "royal vill." It is possible that the *tún*-names in Scandinavia were associated with an administrative reorganization in the 10th or 11th centuries.

Such generics as *setr* and *sætr*, which would both seem originally to have been associated with a pastoral economy, occur much more frequently in the mountainous areas of Norway and Sweden than in the low-lying and fertile Denmark. They were also taken to the Northern Isles and northwestern England by the Norwegians, but they are not found in the Inner Hebrides, Man, or Iceland. Their absence from the Inner Hebrides and Man probably reflects the survival there of the Gaelic generic *áirge*, adopted by the Vikings as *ærgi* and taken by them to some of their other colonies, where it occurs in such place-names as *á Argjum* in the Faroes and *Grimsargh* in England. In Iceland, on the other hand, the terms *setr* and *sætr* may simply not have been applicable to the forms of agricultural exploitation employed.

Settlements established in Scandinavia in the Viking period and later on newly cleared land were evidently given names in either *-þveit* or *-rud*. The distribution patterns of these two elements are complementary. *Þveit* is particularly common in a broad belt running from Hordaland in Norway to southern Zealand, for example, Danish *Tingtved*. In northeastern Zealand, however, there is not a single name in *-þveit*, and the clearing of land for settlement is commemorated here by a concentration of names in *-rød* (< *rud*), such as *Birkerød*. Names of this type spill across the Sound to Scania (*e.g., Ekeröd*) and southern and central Sweden and eastern Norway (*e.g., Nakkerud*). Of the two generics denoting clearings, only *þveit* is at all common in the colonies, occurring reasonably frequently in the Danelaw, northwestern England, southwestern Scotland, and Normandy (*e.g.,* English *Thwaite*, Norman *Le Thuit*).

Administrative history. A study of the names borne by the administrative districts known as *herreds* in Denmark and *härads* in Sweden distinguishes between primary and secondary *herred* names. Primary *herred* names are based on place-names or names of inhabitants, such as *Bobergs härad, Albo härad*, and given to *herreds* that were the result of an artificial division of land in, for example, areas where the topography is not marked. Secondary *herred* names are old names for natural districts that were converted into *herreds* when the division of a country into such units took place, as *Tjusts härad*, older *Thiust*. In Denmark and southern Sweden, the term *herred* was added to original district names earlier than was the case farther north, and this pattern suggests that the Scandinavian institution of the *herred* originated in Denmark.

In Jutland, there was also an administrative district known as a *syssel*. Each *syssel* included a number of *herreds*. The division into *syssels* is probably older than that into *herreds* and must go back at least to the 10th century. The *syssel* names in northern Jutland are based on the names of districts (*e.g., Ommersyssel*), or of inhabitants (*e.g., Vendsyssel*), while those in southern Jutland are based on settlement names (*e.g., Istedsyssel*), suggesting that the divisions in this latter area were artificial creations.

Communications. Place-names are one of the best sources of information about means of communication in early times. Such names as Danish *Bavnehøj*, containing *bavn* 'beacon-fire,' Norwegian *Vorda*, containing *varða* 'beacon, cairn,' and Swedish *Snäckviken*, containing *snäck* 'warship,' have been used as evidence of defensive measures taken against attack from the sea. Place-names also reveal that conspicuous features were used as landmarks not only along the coast but also inland on mountain tracks. Field names have been used to trace the course of lost roads and tracks, to date the construction of roads or the period when these were abandoned, and to locate old crossing places over rivers and streams.

Agricultural history. Many names point to the exploitation of mountain pastures in the summer months. Place-names provide information as to which crops were cultivated and which animals bred in the various regions. Names reveal, for example, that in the Faroes, pigs were kept not only on the infields close to the houses but also on the outfields, often at a great distance from the settlement. Place-names also show that in the mountainous areas of Norway kilns were used to dry the corn. Names can also provide information about changes in the flora not instigated by humans. A study of names in central and eastern Norway containing the specific *gran* 'spruce,' for example, indicates that this tree spread into Norway from Sweden earlier than the date in the 13th or 14th century suggested by pollen studies.

Paganism. Names are one of the best sources of information about the worship of the heathen gods in Scandinavia. The existence of cults of Óðinn, Þórr, Njǫrðr, Freyr, and Freyja over the whole of Scandinavia is shown by such names as *Odense* and *Torslunde* in Denmark, *Njærheim* and *Frøyset* in Norway, and *Onsjö* and *Fröböke* in Sweden. The gods Ullr and Frigg, on the other hand, while appearing in several names in Norway and Sweden, such as *Ulleväl* and *Friggeråker*, have left no trace in the place-names of Denmark. The god Týr, who is commemorated in many names in Denmark, such as *Tislund* and perhaps *Thisted*, occurs only in a single one in Norway, *Tysnes*, and does not appear at all in names in Sweden.

Linguistic history. Place-names supply some of our best evidence for linguistic developments in Scandinavia in early times because they can be located exactly. The changes revealed can be dramatic, as when an examination of field names from two Danish-named parishes south of the present Danish-German frontier, *Svavsted* and *Mildsted*, shows that the inhabitants must still have been Danish-speaking in the Middle Ages, but that Danish was replaced by German as the local language in the 13th century in Svavsted and in the 14th century in Mildsted. Even when there has not been a change of language, place-names are an important source of information about the relative conservatism of the various Scandinavian languages and dialects. The contribution made by place-names to the history of the vocabulary can have broader cultural implications, as when a study of Saamish-Finnish place-names in northern Sweden reveals how a Slav cultural influence must have been transmitted by the Finns, probably in connection with the trade in furs in the Viking period.

Bib.: Fellows-Jensen, Gillian. "Place-name Research in Scandinavia 1960–1982, with a Select Bibliography." *Names* 32 (1984), 267–324. **Lit.:** Steinnes, Asgaut. "The 'Huseby' System in Orkney." *The Scottish Historical Review* 38 (1959), 36–46; Hald, Kr. "The Cult of Odin in Danish Place-names." In *Early English and Norse Studies Presented to Hugh Smith in Honour of His Sixtieth Birthday.* Ed. Arthur Brown and Peter Foote. London: Methuen, 1963, pp. 99–109; Andersson, Thorsten. *Svenska häradsnamn.* Nomina Germanica, 14. Lund, 1965; Thors, Carl-Eric. "The Baltic as a Separating and a Unifying Element in the Formation of Place-names." In *Proceedings of the Eighth International Congress of Onomastic Sciences.* Ed. D. P. Blok. The Hague and Paris: Mouton, 1966, pp. 529–41; Pamp, Bengt. *Ortnamnen i Sverige.* Lundastudier i nordisk språkvetenskap, B2. Lund: Studentlitteratur, 1970; Kousgård Sørensen, John. "Toponymic Evidence for Administrative Divisions in Denmark in the Viking Age." In *The Vikings.* Ed. Thorsten Andersson and Karl Inge Sandred. Symposia Universitatis Upsaliensis Annum Quingentesimum Celebrantis, 8. Stockholm: Almqvist & Wiksell, 1978, pp. 133–41; Kousgård Sørensen, John.

150. Vin •; Løse °

"Place-Names and Settlement History." In *Names, Words, and Graves: Early Medieval Settlement*. Ed. P. H. Sawyer. Leeds: The School of History, University of Leeds, 1979, pp. 1–33; Sandnes, Jørn, and Ola Stemshaug, eds. *Norsk Stadnamnleksikon*. 2nd ed. Oslo: Det Norske Samlaget, 1980; Jørgensen, Bent. *Dansk Stednavneleksikon*. 3 vols. Copenhagen: Gyldendal, 1981–83; Helleland, Botolv. "Evidence of Cultural History in the Place-names of a Fjord Community in the West of Norway (Eidfjord)." In *Topothesia: Essays Presented to T. S. Ó Máille*. Ed. B. S. Mac Aodha. Galway: RTCOG, 1982, pp. 131–43; Matras, Christian. "Faroese Place-Names." In *Topothesia*, pp. 102–10; Fellows-Jensen, Gillian. "To Divide the Danes from the Norwegians: On Scandinavian Settlement in the British Isles." *Nomina* 11 (1988 for 1987), 35–60.

Gillian Fellows-Jensen

[**See also:** England, Norse in; Personal Names; Religion, Pagan Scandinavian]

Plácítus drápa see Plácítus saga

Plácítus saga ("The Saga of Plácítus") and *Plácítus drápa* ("The Poem of Plácítus") both tell the story of St. Eustace, a Roman warrior named Placidus before his conversion by a crucifix-bearing stag. Agreeing to be tested, he is stripped of everything, including his wife, who is taken from him by a sailor, and his sons, who are seized by animals as he is transporting them across a flooding river. Years of exile follow. Then Eustace returns to power, and the family is reunited, only to be martyred together in an ox-shaped oven of brass. Ancient sources and analogues have been proposed for all parts of the story, which is also strongly influenced by the Bible. It exists in several Greek and two Latin prose versions, the longer of which (*Bibliotheca Hagiographica Latina*, 2760) seems to be the immediate or ultimate source of all the Old Norse–Icelandic versions.

Plácítus saga exists in four versions: (1) a translation preserved fragmentarily in AM 655 IX 4to, written about 1150 in Trondheim (the only non-Icelandic MS among those mentioned here); (2) a different translation preserved fragmentarily in AM 655 X 4to, from about 1260, and completely or partly in six paper

MSS written between 1651 and 1878, the most important of which is the earliest, Stock. Papp. 8vo no. 8; (3) a version that freely reworks the Latin and is independent of version 2 (though they may descend from the same translation) found in two paper MSS from the 19th century; and (4) an abbreviated version preserved incompletely in AM 696 III 4to, from about 1390, whose source has not been determined. The early translation of the legend points to the narrative appetite of the period, and the richness of the material on which it fed. The numerous paper MSS, in which it is treated as an exemplum, attest to a popularity that endured the Reformation.

Plácítus drápa is found in AM 673b 4to, from about 1200. Owing to the loss apparently of a first and last leaf, only fifty-nine stanzas survive of what must have been a seventy-eight-stanza drápa. The thirty-six-stanza stefjabálkr (central section) opens with a refrain, then is divided into two groups of seven stanzas by means of two refrains which combine to form stanza 32. If we assume construction in multiples of seven, ten stanzas remain of an original twenty-one-stanza upphaf (introduction) and thirteen of an equally long slœmr (conclusion). The poetic merit of the poem has been considered slight, but the difficulties of telling a story in dróttkvætt may account for its mechanical kennings.

Interest in the poem has centered on its relation to other Christian skaldic poems and to the saga. Vocabulary shared with Harmsól, Geisli, and Leiðarvísan has been used to argue either for or against the priority of Plácítus drápa. It is equally difficult to determine how it relates to the prose versions. Although it scarcely overlaps with version 1, its wording and narrative agree by turns with both versions 2 and 3. Since the drápa may have influenced later copies of the saga version that was its source, and the poet might have used more than one prose version or the hypothetical common source of 2 and 3, locating the drápa within the prose stemma will remain problematical.

Ed.: Unger, C. R., ed. *Heilagra manna søgur: Fortællinger og legender om hellige mænd og kvinder.* 2 vols. Christiania [Oslo]: Bentzen, 1877, vol. 2, pp. 193–210; Finnur Jónsson, ed. *Den norsk-islandske skaldedigtning.* Vols. 1A-2A (tekst efter håndskrifterne) and 1B-2B (rettet tekst). Copenhagen and Christiania [Oslo]: Gyldendal, 1912–15; rpt. Copenhagen: Rosenkilde & Bagger, 1967 (A) and 1973 (B), vol. 1A, pp. 607–18, vol. 1B, pp. 606–22; Murray, Jessie, ed. *La vie de Saint Eustace.* Les classiques français du moyen âge, 60. Paris: Champion, 1929; Tucker, John. "A Study of the *Plácítus saga*, Including an Edition, and of Its Relation to the *Plácítus drápa*." B.Litt. thesis. Oxford University, 1974. [An edition is in preparation for Editiones Arnamagnæanæ]. **Lit.**: Jón Helgason. "Til Skaldedigtningen." *Acta Philologica Scandinavica* 7 (1932–33), 150–68; Tucker, John. "St. Eustace in Iceland: On the Origins, Structure, and Possible Influence of the *Plácítus saga*." In *Les Sagas de Chevaliers (Riddarasögur). Actes de la Vᵉ Conférence Internationale sur les Sagas . . . (Toulon, Juillet 1982).* Civilisations, 10. Ed. Régis Boyer. Paris: Presses de l'Université Paris-Sorbonne, 1985, pp. 327–39; Tucker, John. "The Relation of the Plácítus drápa to the Plácítus saga." In *The Sixth International Saga Conference 28/7–2/8 1985. Workshop Papers.* 2 vols. Copenhagen: Det arnamagnæanske Institut, 1985, vol. 2, pp. 1057–66 [photocopies of papers distributed to participants].

John Tucker

[**See also:** Christian Poetry; Einarr Skúlason; Gamli kanóki; Leiðarvísan; Saints' Lives; Skaldic Meters]

Plague is a disease caused by a bacterium called *Yersinia pestis*. The intensive study of this disease by historians and demographers reflects its extraordinary powers to shape the development of populations by causing mass mortality, and by doing so, often causing radical economic and social change in the short and long term. In European medieval history, plague ravaged populations and affected historical developments in two protracted series of epidemics, one beginning in 541 and ending in 767 (Biraben and Le Goff 1969), the other beginning in 1347, lasting throughout the remainder of the medieval period, and persisting throughout most of the early-modern period as well. Such series of waves of epidemics are called "pandemics."

Plague is originally and basically a rodent disease transmitted by fleas. In many areas of the world where wild rodents live in great density, plague circulates continuously in the population (sylvatic plague). Such a rodent population is called a plague focus (Pollitzer and Meyer 1961). Pandemics may occur, when the causal pathogenic agent is disseminated from a natural focus to populations of rats living in close contact with humans, commensal rats.

Plague in human beings and in animals has two main forms: bubonic plague and pneumonic plague, both having highly varied clinical manifestations. The basic form is bubonic plague. According to the place of the bite wound, the infective material is usually drained through a lymphatic tract to one or more lymph glands, most often in the groin, but also quite often in one of the axillas and relatively frequently in the submaxillary areas and behind the ears (e.g., Pollitzer 1954; cf. Block 1711). The infection produces buboes, inflamed swellings of the lymphatic glands.

Occasionally, the infectious material is regurgitated directly into the bloodstream, or the infection is so overwhelming that it passes directly through the lymphatic system and into the bloodstream, causing bacteraemia (sepsis) and a condition called "primary septicaemic plague." In these cases, the bacteria propagate very rapidly, and the patients usually die the same day, quite often even in a few hours (Philip and Hirst 1917). This form explains the many terror-stricken descriptions of sudden death observed in late-medieval and early-modern plague epidemics. As emphasized by Block (1711), the Swedish physician who wrote a book about his observations during the plague epidemic in Norrköping in 1710–1711, plague without external clinical manifestations is the most dangerous form. In reality, this is a special case of bubonic plague where death occurs before buboes have had time to develop. The term "primary" refers to the fact that usually, in about half of all bubonic cases, bacteria eventually pass from the buboes into the bloodstream, causing secondary septicaemic plague, i.e., secondary in relation to the basic or primary bubonic condition. In most of these cases, bacteria reach the peripheral blood circulation and capillary vessels (Chun 1936), where their tendency to clot and the weakening of the walls of the vessel by bacterial toxins tend to cause subcutaneous hemorrhages. These are the petechiae, the dark spots often described in historical sources; people soon learned that this phenomenon signified certain and imminent death. Also, the eyes may be affected (conjunctivitis), as is probably the case with the Norwegian nobleman Sigurðr Hafþórsson, who, during the epidemic in Oslo in 1371, was in bed "because of inflammation in his eyes" (Benedictow 1992, DN 6, no. 278; cf. Block 1711).

In cases of secondary septicaemic plague, bacteria are transported with the bloodstream also to the lungs, where they may cause pneumonia, a condition called "secondary pneumonic plague," *i.e.*, secondary to the primary bubonic plague infection. This development seems to take place in about 10–25 percent of bubonic cases (Hirst 1953: 222, Leads 1984: 1400, Welty *et al.* 1985: 646). Such patients often develop a cough and bloody expectoration containing plague bacteria, which occasionally may infect others by droplet infection (*cf.* influenza).

Persons contracting plague directly by droplet infection are said to suffer from primary pneumonic plague. Secondary and primary pneumonic plague, then, spread by cross-infection, the primary being markedly more contagious than the secondary. Primary pneumonic plague is one of the most virulent diseases known. It is doubtful if any person has survived this condition without administration of antibiotics. The average duration of the illness is about 1.8 days, the infective cough emerging after about twenty-four hours, little time, therefore being left for spread. Moreover, not a few cases die before developing the dangerous cough, especially toward the end of outbreaks. Pneumonic plague, therefore, is characterized by weak powers of spread and small and episodic outbreaks, usually at the familial or neighborhood levels, rarely comprising more than a few tens of victims (Wu 1913, 1926, and 1927–28, Klimenko 1910, Chun 1936). However, as cases of pneumonic plague arise from cases of bubonic plague, they normally constitute a few percent of the victims of epidemics of bubonic plague.

Studies of the wave of plague epidemics in Sweden in 1710–1713 suggest the possible occurrence of small local epidemics with a substantial proportion of such cases, or possibly even epidemics of primary pneumonic plague, within the usual pattern of predominant bubonic plague (Moseng 1990). This pattern may have been the case in parts of Scandinavia in the late-medieval centuries as well. The case for this model is strengthened by descriptions in Nordic sources of some important aspects of social life. We are told, for example, that it was the custom "among the populace in the countryside that the whole household slept together in the same chamber during nights"; they used to have "farm animals like calves and pigs" in the houses where they lived (Vejde 1938). The first custom should be expected to increase the incidence of transmission by droplet infection from cases of secondary pneumonic plague, and also to increase the powers of spread of primary pneumonic plague significantly. The second custom would tend to increase the number of rats and rat fleas living in the immediate proximity of a household, which should increase (1) infection doses and so lethality rates; (2) the occurrence of overwhelming infections and so the incidence of primary septicaemic plague (repeatedly observed by Block 1711); and (3) the proportion of household members affected as evidenced by a conspicuous frequency of extinction of households (Leijonhufvud 1921, Vejde 1938).

As rats are social animals defending territories, the dispersed pattern of farm settlement implies a pattern of at least one rat colony per household-farmhouse and a higher ratio of rats and their fleas relative to the numbers of human beings than in urban settlements, where more households would tend to live within the area of the same rat colony. This feature explains why morbidity and mortality rates in rural areas are far higher than in towns in preindustrial Europe (Benedictow 1987, 1992).

Clinical symptomatic references to sharp pangs of pain and bloody expectoration, as in the account in the Icelandic *Lögmannsannáll* of the Great Pestilence in Norway in 1349–1350 (*Islandske Annaler*, p. 275), are not, as hitherto commonly supposed, unambiguous references to primary pneumonic plague (see,

e.g., Jón Steffensen 1974). Bloody expectoration is definitionally a clinical symptom of secondary pneumonic plague, which is developed from bubonic plague. Sharp pangs of pain are the usual description of the extreme tenderness of buboes (see, *e.g.*, Block 1711: 21, Benedictow 1990: 28–30, 1992). Also, bubonic plague is a fast killer, causing a considerable frequency of hasty and sudden deaths. As a matter of fact, the Swedish word for sudden death, *brådöda*, became a name for plague (Block 1711, Ottosson 1986 and 1989).

While plague is disseminated directly between rodents by the agency of fleas, this case is rare with human beings. Bacteraemia in human beings occurs only in about half of the cases and is very much weaker than in rats, making people a poor source for infected blood conducive to growth of blocks in the ventricular system of fleas (Benedictow 1992). In plague epidemics, human beings become the fortuitous victims of an epizootic among commensal rats, the "black rat," which prefers living close to human beings because of its strong predeliction for grain.

It has recently been maintained that this type of rat cannot survive in substantial numbers in countries of temperate or cool climates, and so cannot have provided the rodent basis for epidemics of plague in the parts of Europe with these climatic types (Walløe 1982, Davis 1986, Oeding 1988). However, until the 1790s, the black rat was the only rat in Sweden and Finland, the countries of Scandinavia with the coldest winters. At the beginning of this century, it was found in a number of urban and rural areas (Nybelin 1928, Bernström 1969, Vilkuna 1969). Large numbers of skeletal remains of the black rat dating back to the 13th century and the late-medieval period have recently been found during excavations in Stockholm, illustrating the need for rat catchers mentioned by Olaus Magnus (Vretemark 1982). Other medieval findings have been reported going back to *ca.* A.D. 1000 (see, *e.g.*, Bergquist 1957). "During the late-medieval period, rats and mice are mentioned as generally known vermin in and around human buildings" (Bernström and Vilkuna 1969). Moreover, the brown or grey rat was not observed in Scandinavia before the 1750s, first in Norway. Many findings of skeletal remains of the black rat in North Germany and in England antedating the high Middle Ages, in England even going back to the Roman period (Armitage *et al.* 1984, Teichert 1985, Reichstein 1987), strengthen the case for assuming a long presence of this type of rat in Scandinavia. This fact supports the plague explanation put forward by Norwegian, Swedish, and Finnish archaeologists of indications of depopulation and mass occurrence of deserted farms in some areas in the 6th and 7th centuries (Benedictow 1992:22).

The steady flea parasite of the black rat, *Xenopsylla cheopis*, has, because of the predeliction of this rat for grain, developed through evolutionary selection the ability to subsist on grain, dependent only on blood for laying eggs. Transport of grain is a usual mechanism of interregional and interlocal spread of plague in the preindustrial society. As rats rapidly die from plague, the pathogen is usually transported in the bodies of rat fleas that primarily seek rat hosts at the place of arrival. A plague epidemic, then, usually begins with a few sporadic cases (endemic phase), as some rat fleas, having left dead rats and not succeeding in finding a new rat host, are offered the opportunity of a human substitute. As rats die off in large numbers, making it increasingly difficult to find new rat hosts, fleas gather on the remaining rats, which soon become ill and unable to defend themselves by the usual self-cleansing activities, causing the usual flea count to grow from about seven to often between fifty and 100 on sick rats (Indian

Plague Research Commission, 1 [1906], 24 [1907], 29 [1908], Busvine 1976). The death of rats in this phase, therefore, turns loose hundreds of fleas in the close proximity of human beings. This ecological pattern explains the typical explosive development pattern of plague epidemics with suddenly skyrocketing mortality rates.

This ecological pattern also explains what might at first seem an epidemiological puzzle, the ability of plague to penetrate and permeate sparsely populated local societies, reaching the many small and peripheral agricultural farmsteads and villages where large parts of the population of medieval Europe lived, as certainly was the case in Scandinavia. Medieval Norway, for example, which at the time of maximum population density around 1300, contained roughly 350,000 inhabitants in an area about three times the size of England, living typically in small nuclear-family-based households on detached or semidetached holdings. Norway suffered disastrously from the onslaughts of plague. The decisive point is that people lived in closely knit local societies where experience and necessity had developed a strong spirit of interdependence and mutual assistance. Occurrence of disease and death was met with neighborly work assistance, nursing care, and visits of consolation (Hagberg 1937, Vejde 1938). People visited the ill and dying to assist them, and in the case of plague, often brought with them to their own farmsteads dangerous rat fleas in their clothing. A Norwegian priest testifies that he was present when Anund Helgason died in the Great Pestilence, and that his death occurred also "in the presence of Ragndid Simonadottir and Alvald Sveinkason and *many other good persons*" (*DN* 1, no. 355; translation supplied). This pattern of social behavior is also highlighted in Sweden in 1710–1713, when there was much social unrest and rioting in the countryside as a reaction to the efforts of the government to prohibit and prevent social interaction between healthy and diseased people (Leijonhufvud 1921, Vejde 1938, Ottosson 1986a).

The powers of spread of diseases disseminated by cross-infection are weakened by the death of those who contract them. Death actually strengthens the dynamics of spread of bubonic plague, because bubonic plague is not spread by cross-infection but by ecological mechanisms. First, when people die, relatives and neighbors congregate to mourn and commemorate the deceased. Second, the Norse word for funeral feast can be directly translated as "inheritance feast." When people die, others inherit, and the funeral feast was ordinarily the occasion when the inheriting relatives agreed upon their portions and often began to share out the valuables and possessions (Bø 1960: 450–2). The situation in the wake of a great plague epidemic is well illustrated by a passage in the account of the *Fitjaannáll* of the second plague epidemic in Iceland: "Much property then came in the hands of many; almost everybody received inheritance from relatives, third cousins, or closer relations" (*Annales Islandici Posteriorum Sæculorum* 1927–32: 27–8). Preindustrial societies were characterized by widespread and pronounced poverty; clothing, bedding, and so forth were valuable and eagerly inherited (see, *e.g.*, Leijonhufvud 1921, Vejde 1938). The inheritance mechanism in this way intensified the spread of dangerous infected and infective rat fleas between farmsteads and local societies. Within this epidemiological framework, the rapid course of the disease itself was a factor increasing the dynamics of spread.

These are probably the most important mechanisms of local spread of plague in the parts of the Nordic countries with dispersed farm settlement. In village settlements and urban localities, intralocal spread through contact between rat colonies probably has played an important role as well (Benedictow 1992).

The class system yields another important mechanism of local epidemic spread. During the period of rapid population growth in the high Middle Ages, a great number of inferior settlements of a clearly proletarian character, in English associated with the concepts of croft and cottage, was established on marginal lands, often in the periphery of the old settlements. The occupants had to earn most of their income working as hired labor on the old, substantial farms, and undoubtedly often received much of their income in the form of grain (Benedictow 1986, 1992).

Three epidemiological mechanisms were probably the most important for interlocal dissemination of plague in the Scandinavian countries and Iceland. First, people fleeing from areas ravaged by plague and unwittingly bringing infected and infective rat fleas with them in clothing or luggage. Second, transport of grain containing such fleas. Third, in quite a number of patients, bubonic plague is clinically characterized by a marked *Wandertrieb* ("urge to wander"). Persons who are away from home because of trade or work migration will often feel a compulsive urge to set out for home (Chun 1936). Resident servants and workers in aristocratic households and on substantial farms will in this way disseminate the epidemic, increasing particularly the capacity of plague to reach the peripheral and small settlements and the cottages and crofts of the poor on the outskirts of local society, which otherwise tend to be passed over by epidemic diseases. Where significant distance is involved, another danger emerges: muscular efforts promote the development of serious types of secondary pneumonic plague. Traveling or wandering plague-infected persons are often the origin of outbreaks of primary pneumonic plague (Wu 1926, Wakil 1932).

Particularly during the latter part of the high Middle Ages, population pressure inspired the establishment of thousands of settlements founded on the specialized exploitation of extensive resources in marginal and peripheral areas, mostly animal farming in highland areas. This development presupposes the concomitant development of a network of trade in grain, allowing procurement of vital grain from fertile lowland districts in exchange for animal products, implying a considerable profit in terms of calories, the most vital category of nutrition (Martens 1989). It may have been closely connected with a similarly fine-meshed network of trade in salt, an indispensable product for conservation of animal produce. This pattern of exchange may explain the extraordinary powers of plague to reach the most peripheral and widely dispersed settlements and localities: the more peripheral and dispersed the localities, the more specialized their husbandry tended to be, and the more they would be integrated in commercial activities, and then first of all in the grain trade, a type of goods particularly suited to dissemination of plague (Benedictow 1992). In the late-medieval period, fishing communities in northern Norway established a firm connection with Hanseatic merchants in Bergen, trading fish and grain, making themselves vulnerable to import of plague from North German towns (Benedictow 1992).

Contemporary chroniclers and annalists agree that the late-medieval pandemic of plague arrived in Scandinavia by boat from England, where the disease began to spread in the summer of 1348. The disease was first introduced at the end of 1348 (*Annales Danici Medii Aevi* 1920: 174–5), it is said in an old folktale, by a Norwegian ship coming from England and running aground in Vendsyssel in Jutland, because the crew had died of plague

(Christensen 1938: 39). Next autumn, according to the Icelandic annalists, the disease arrived in Bergen. One should, however, note that the Icelandic annalists writing about the arrival of plague in Norway received their information from Bergen and the western part of Norway, and generally seem to have been poorly informed about what occurred in other parts of Norway, particularly the southeast. An altar for the most prestigious of all plague saints, St. Sebastian, was mentioned as having been founded in the cathedral of Oslo at the end of February 1349, and the townsmen, perhaps somewhat later, are said to have donated money to it (*DN* 2, no. 298; *DN* 4, no. 348). Possibly, therefore, southeastern Norway may have been infected from Denmark at the end of 1348. The commercial exchange of Norwegian timber for Danish grain (Nielsen 1933) may have served as a mechanism of spread of infection. As the story about the ship suggests, it may also have been imported directly from England. Norwegian ships brought the disease to Shetland, the Orkneys, and the Faroe Islands.

Recent research (Benedictow 1990, 1992) has established that there must have been (at least) two independent introductions of the Great Pestilence in Norway. There was one in the Oslofjord area, in all likelihood in Oslo. The spatiotemporal pattern of territorial spread conforms to the role of Oslo as the point of introduction and epicenter of the outbreak. The epidemic commenced its spread out from this feeder outbreak at the latest in the first half of July 1349, but probably in May–June. This is confirmed by a later source referring to the "Summer of the Great Mortality" (*DN* 3, no. 298). It may also have been introduced from England or, possibly, from Denmark, with ship transport toward the end of 1348, and have been smouldering in the rat populations until warmer weather triggered the flea-based dynamics of dissemination of this disease. There was also one independent introduction of plague in Bergen, possibly around mid-August, but probably not much earlier.

The spread of the Great Pestilence in southern Norway followed the main roads, and branched off along secondary and eventually tertiary communication lines, eventually reaching the peripheral communities and settlements. In the Hamar area and, as it seems, also in Borgarsysla (Østfold), the plague raged in August. At the end of September, it broke out at Toten on the western side of Lake Mjøsa. Metastatic spread with ship transport seems to have occurred in a southwesterly direction along the coast, and reaching, evidently, the south country (Sørlandet) at a time when Stavanger, 150 km. to the south of Bergen, remained uncontaminated. Stavanger probably was contaminated from this southerly source. This underscores the fact that the outbreak of plague in the Oslofjord area was considerably earlier than the outbreak in Bergen. On the other hand, in all likelihood, the contagion was brought to Niðaróss (Trondheim) from Bergen, making itself felt toward the end of September or the beginning of October.

In southern Norway, the Great Pestilence petered out in the border area between Telemark and Buskerud in December. No evidence exists indicating that the plague epidemic continued into 1350 and raged during the winter months. The last known fatality of plague was the bishop of Stavanger, who died on January 7, 1350. This fact probably mirrors the relatively late introduction of the Great Pestilence in the west country (Vestlandet), and suggests that this most notorious of all epidemics died out around the turn of the year also in this region.

This seasonal pattern agrees closely with the general European pattern, where plague characteristically rages in summer and autumn, reflecting the crucial role of fleas in dissemination and transmission. This interpretation of type of plague on the basis of the seasonal pattern agrees closely with the clinical description of the plague symptoms provided by the Icelandic annalists, unambiguously indicating bubonic plague.

The determination of the epidemic as bubonic plague, which has a lethality rate of around 80 percent, furnishes the opportunity to suggest morbidity rates relative to given mortality rates. If one third of the population died, the morbidity rate was 40 percent.

The Great Pestilence reached Sweden from southwestern Denmark (Scania) in 1349, from Norway in the west, and by shipping contacts with North German commercial towns in 1350. Finland is the only country in Europe that seems to have escaped plague epidemics altogether, or to have been hit only rarely during the Middle Ages (Ilmoni 1846–49, Orrmann 1981).

The demographic effects of the arrival of plague in Scandinavia can be assessed only in Norway, and then only approximately. On the most plausible assumptions, we have estimated the maximum population of medieval Norway around 1300 at roughly 350,000 inhabitants. The minimum population, probably in 1450–1500, is estimated at about 125,000 inhabitants, a contraction of 64 percent. This result is conspicuously similar to Hatcher's (1977) conclusions with respect to England. Evidence indicating population contraction and widespread desertion of holdings and villages is also found in Denmark and Sweden (Christensen 1963–66, Norborg 1979, Sandnes 1981), without, however, allowing quantification at a national level.

A plague explanation of the process of depopulation presupposes recurrent epidemics satisfying the following model: the effects of a demographic crisis increasing normal mortality four times without significant differentiation with respect to age and sex cannot be compensated for by the age groups below the age of fifteen even if they exhausted their powers of reproduction, the reproductive potential of those older being so small as to allow their being disregarded (Del Panta and Livi Bacci 1977). This model means that, even according to theoretical considerations, a population will need at least fifteen years to recuperate from the losses of an epidemic crisis of this magnitude and pattern of impact. In reality, no population exhausts its reproductive potential, and many studies have shown that it will usually take twenty-five to thirty years for a population to recuperate from such a crisis on the basis of its own reproductive resources. If crises of this magnitude and structure recur within shorter intervals of time, the size of a population will diminish. Plague is a bacterial disease and characteristically provokes only transitory and weak immunity in survivors. This property ensures that the whole population is at risk at each recurrence, and prevents the development of pronounced age-specific patterns of the type caused by viral diseases inducing permanent or long-lasting immunity, as in the case of so-called "children's diseases" like measles or mumps. Many examples of reinfections by plague have been registered, even within the same epidemic (Sticker 1910, Benedictow 1992). A case of reinfection was also registered by Block (1711) in the epidemic in Norrköping 1710–1711. As with other acute epidemic diseases hitting populations without much difference with respect to age and sex, plague causes a significant supermortality from lack of nursing care, as parents cannot attend to their sick children or each other because of concomitant illness.

It seems clear that plague generally satisfies the conditions set by the model outlined above both with respect to powers of dissemination, severity, sociology of impact, and recurrence (Hatcher

1977, Benedictow 1987a and b, 1992). Recurrent epidemics in Norway were recorded by the Icelandic annals in 1360, 1370–1371, 1379, 1390, and 1392. Several are mentioned also in the 15th century, in spite of dependence on other types of source material poorly suited to registering such events (Benedictow, 2nd ed. 1987). In the 15th century, plague epidemics appear in Sweden at least in 1413, 1422, 1439, 1440, 1455, 1465, 1484, and 1495 (Norborg 1968).

Iceland was hit by plague epidemics only twice, in 1402 and 1495. Although both onslaughts were severe and undoubtedly caused considerable population reduction in the short term, there is no reason to assume more lasting demographic effects. The same is probably the case with Finland, which seems to have experienced a noticeable settlement expansion and corresponding population increase during the late-medieval period as a whole. The main reason for the relatively mild fate of these two countries must be seen in their relatively isolated territorial position and relatively sparse contacts with other countries (Hornborg 1938: 117, Jón Steffensen 1974).

The arrival of plague in Scandinavia, 1348–1350, was arguably the most important event in the late-medieval period, causing strong and protracted population reduction in most of the region. The reduction of population produced a high demand for labor and tenants, which in turn caused substantial reduction in land rent and increase in wages. Material living standards of ordinary people accordingly improved considerably, while the incomes of the social elites and governments were much reduced. In Norwegian historiography, the plague is usually considered the principal cause of the decline and fall of the sovereign Norwegian state (Benedictow 1977, 1987a).

Ed.: *Diplomatarium Norvegicum. Oldbreve til kundskab om Norges indre og ydre forhold, sprog, slægter, sæder, lovgivning og rettergang i middelalderen*, vols. 2, 3, 4, 6. Christiania [Oslo]: Malling, 1852, 1857–58, 1858, 1864; Mansa, Frederik Vilhelm. *Bidrag til Folkesygdommenes og Sundhedspleiens Historie i Danmark.* Copenhagen: Gyldendal, 1873; Storm, Gustav, ed. *Islandske Annaler indtil 1578.* Christiania [Oslo]: Grøndahl, 1888; rpt. Norsk historisk kjeldeskrift-institutt, 1977; Jørgensen, Ellen, ed. *Annales Danici Medii Aevi.* Copenhagen: Selskabet for udgivelse af kilder til dansk historie, 1920. **Lit.**: Block, Magnus G. *Åtskillige Anmärkingar öfwer närvarande Pestilentias Beskaffenhet, Motande, Botande och Utrotande uti Östergötland.* Linköping: [n.p.], 1711; Ilmoni, Immanuel. *Bidrag till Nordens sjukdoms-historia.* 2 vols. Helsingfors: Simelii, 1846–49; Dörbeck, Franz. *Geschichte der Pestepidemien in Russland von der Gründung des Reiches bis auf die Gegenwart.* Breslau: Kern, 1906; Indian Plague Research Commision, Reports on Plague Investigations in India, 1. "Experiments upon the Transmission of Plague by Rats." *Journal of Hygiene* 6 (1906), 425–82; Indian Plague Research Commission . . . 24. "General Considerations Regarding the Spread of Infection, Infectivity of Houses etc. in Bombay City and Island." *Journal of Hygiene* 7 (1907), 858–74; Indian Plague Research Commission . . . 29. "Observations of the Bionomics of Fleas with Special Reference to *P. cheopis.*" *Journal of Hygiene* 8 (1908), 221–35; Klimenko, V. S. "O chumnykh epidemiyakh v Rossii [On plague epidemics in Russia]." *Voenno-medicinskiy Zhurnal* 229 (1910), 659–63; Sticker, Georg. *Abhandlungen aus der Seuchengeschichte und Seuchenlehre. 1.2. Die Pest.* Giessen: Töpelmann, 1910; Hult, O. T. "Pesten i Sverige 1710." *Hygienisk tidskrift* 8 (1915), 79–197; Philip, W. M., and L. F. Hirst. "A Report on the Outbreak of the Plague in Colombo, 1914–1916." *Journal of Hygiene* 15 (1917), 527–64; Leijonhufvud, Karl K:son. "Pesten 1710–1711 och prästeskapet i Strängnäs stift." *Karolinska Förbundets Årsbok* (1921), 156–95; MacArthur, William P. "Old-time Plague in Britain." *Transactions of the Royal Society of Tropical Medicine and Hygiene* 19 (1925–26), 355–71; Wu, Lien-Teh. *A Treatise on Pneumonic Plague.* Geneva: League of Nations, 1926; *Annales Islandici Posteriorum Sæculorum.* Reykjavik: Hið íslenzka bókmentafélag, 1927–32, vol. 2 [*Fitjaannáll*, pp. 1–385]; Christensen, C. A. "Nedgangen i landgilden i det 14. aarh." *Historisk tidskrift* (Denmark), 10th ser., 1 (1930), 446–65; Wakil, A. W. *The Third Pandemic of Plague in Egypt: Historical, Statistical, and Epidemiological Remarks on the First Thirty Years of Its Prevalence.* The Egyptian University. The Faculty of Medicine. Publication No. 3. Cairo: Egyptian University, 1932; Nielsen, Axel, ed. *Dänische Wirtschaftsgeschichte.* Jena: Fischer, 1933; Chun, J. W. H. "Clinical Features." In *Plague: A Manual for Medical and Public Health Workers.* Ed. Lien-Teh Wu et al. Shanghai: Weishenghu National Quarantine Service, Shanghai Station, 1936, pp. 309–33; Hagberg, Louise. *När döden gästar. Svenska folkseder och svensk folktro i samband med död och begravning.* Stockholm: Wahlström & Widstrand, 1937; Vejde, P. G. "Om pesten i Småland 1710–11." *Hyltén Cavallius Föreningens Årsbok* (1938), 159–95; Christensen Aksel E. "Danmarks befolkning og bebyggelse i middelalderen." In *Befolkning i middelalderen.* Ed. Adolf Schück. Nordisk kultur, 2. Stockholm: Bonnier; Oslo: Aschehoug; Copenhagen: Schultz, 1938, pp. 1–57; Hornborg, Eirik. "Svenskarna i Finland och Estland." In *Befolkning i middelalderen*, pp. 106–22; Reichborn-Kjennerud, Ingjald. *Vår gamle trolldomsmedsin.* Skrifter utgitt av Det norske Videnskabs-Akademi i Oslo II. Hist.-filos. Kl., 1940, No. 1. Oslo: Dybwad, 1940; Reichborn-Kjennerud, Ingjald. "Black Death." *Journal of the History of Medicine and Allied Sciences* 3 (1948), 359–60; MacArthur, William P. "The Identification of Some Pestilences Recorded in the Irish Annals." *Irish Historical Studies* 6 (1949), 169–88; Reincke, Heinrich. "Bevölkerungsprobleme der Hansestäde." *Hansische Geschichtsblätter* 70 (1951), 1–33; Hirst, L. F. *The Conquest of Plague: A Study of the Evolution of Epidemiology.* Oxford: Clarendon, 1953; Pollitzer, Robert. *Plague.* World Health Organization, Monograph Series, 22. Geneva: World Health Organization, 1954; Bergquist, Harry. "Skeletal Finds of Black Rat from the Early Middle Ages." *Archaeology of Lund* 1 (1957), 98–103; Norborg, Lars-Arne. *Storföretaget Vadstena kloster. Studier i senmedeltida godspolitik och ekonomiförvaltning.* Bibliotheca Historica Lundensis, 7. Lund: Gleerup, 1958; Fenyuk, B. K. "Experience in the Eradication of Enzootic Plague in the North-West Part of the Caspian Region of the USSR." *Bulletin of the WHO* 23 (1960), 263–73; Christensen, C. A. "Krisen på Slesvig domkapitels jordegods 1352–1437." *Historisk tidskrift* (Denmark), 11th ser., 6 (1960), 161–244; Bø, Arne. "Gravøl." *KLNM* 5 (1960), 450–2; Pollitzer, Robert, and Karl F. Meyer. "The Ecology of Plague." In *Studies in Disease Ecology.* Ed. Jacques M. May. Studies in Medical Geography, 2. New York: Hafner, 1961, pp. 433–590; Christensen, C. A. "Ændringerne i landsbyens økonomiske og sociale strucktur i det 14. og 15. århundrede." *Historisk tidskrift* (Denmark), 12th ser., 1 (1963), 257–349; Keyser, Erich. "Die Pest in Deutschland und ihre Erforschung." In *Actes du colloque international de démographie historique. Liège (Université de Liège), 18–20 avril, 1963.* Ed. P. Harsin and É. Hélin. Liège: Génin, 1965, pp. 369–77; Lassen, A. "The Population in Denmark in 1660." *Scandinavian Economic History Review* 13 (1965), 1–30; Norborg, Lars-Arne. "Pest. Sverige." *KLNM* 13 (1968), 246–48; Bernström, John, and Kustaa Vilkuna. "Råttor och möss." *KLNM* 14 (1969), 577–84; Biraben, Jean-Noël, and Jacques Le Goff. "La peste dans le haut moyen âge." *Annales Economies, Sociétés, Civilisations* 24 (1969), 1484–510; Gräslund, Bo. "Åring, näring, pest och salt." *Tor. Tidskrift för nordisk fornkunskap* 15 (1972–73), 274–93; Jón Steffensen. "Plague in Iceland." *Nordisk medicinhistorisk Årsbok* (1974), 40–50; Biraben, Jean-Noël. *Les hommes et la peste en France et dans les pays européens et méditerranéens.* Paris: Mouton, 1975, vol. 1; Busvine, James R. *Insects,*

Hygiene and History. London: Athlone, 1976; Magnus, Bente, and Bjørn Myhre. *Forhistorien*. Norges Historie, 1. Oslo: Cappelen, 1976; 2nd ed. 1986 [esp. pp. 404–8]; Norris, John. "East or West? The Geographic Origin of the Black Death." *Bulletin of the History of Medicine* 51 (1977), 1–24; Del Panta, Lorenzo, and Massimo Livi Bacci. "Chronologie, intensité et diffusion des crises de mortalité en Italie: 1600–1850." *Population* 32 (September 1977), 401–42; Hatcher, John. *Plague, Population and the English Economy, 1348–1530*. London: Macmillan, 1977; rpt. 1987; Lund, Niels, and Kai Hørby. *Samfundet i tidlig vikingtid og tidlig middelalder*. Dansk socialhistorie, 2. Copenhagen: Gyldendal, 1980; Petersen, Erling Ladewig. *Fra standssamfund til rangssamfund 1500–1700*. Dansk socialhistorie, 3. Copenhagen: Gyldendal, 1980; Orrmann, Eljas. "The Progress of Settlement in Finland During the Late Middle Ages." *Scandinavian Economic History Review* 29 (1981), 129–43; Sandnes, Jørn. "Settlement Developments in the Late Middle Ages. (Approx. c. 1300–1600)." In *Desertion and Land Colonization in the Nordic Countries c. 1300–1600: Comparative Report from the Scandinavian Research Project on Deserted Farms and Villages*. Ed. Svend Gissel *et al.* Stockholm: Almqvist & Wiksell, 1981, pp. 78–114; Walløe, Lars. "Pest og folketall 1350–1750." *Historisk tidsskrift* (Norway) 61 (1982), 1–45; Vretemark, Maria. "Svartråttan—snyltgäst och pestspridare." In *Helgeandsholmen. 1000 år i Stockholms ström*. Ed. Göran Dahlbäck. Stockholm: Liber, 1982, pp. 294, 467; Seger, Tapi. "The Plague of Justinian and Other Scourges: An Analysis of the Anomalies in the Development of the Iron Age Population in Finland." *Fornvännen* 77 (1982), 184–97; Nielsen, Alf Ragnar. "Pest og geografi. Synspunkt på Lars Walløes artikkel 'Pest og folketall 1350–1750.'" *Historisk tidsskrift* (Norway) 62 (1983), 216–26; Nielsen, Alf R. "Svartedauen i Nord-Norge. Om utforskinga av seinmiddelalderens ødegårdsdannelse i landsdelen." *Håløygminne* 16 (1984), 504–14; Armitage, Philip, *et al.* "New Evidence of Black Rat in Roman London." *London Archaeologist* 4 (1984), 375–83; Holmsen, Andreas. *Den store manndauen*. Oslo: Universitetsforlaget, 1984; Benedictow, Ole Jørgen. "Walløe, Juhasz og pestens sosiologi." *Historisk tidsskrift* (Norway) 64 (1985), 84–93; Teichert, Manfred. "Beitrag zur Faunengeschichte der Hausratte, *Rattus rattus* L." *Zeitschrift für Archäologie* 19 (1985), 263–9; Davis, David E. "The Scarcity of Rats and the Black Death: An Ecological History." *Journal of Interdisciplinary History* 16 (1986), 455–70; Benedictow, Ole Jørgen. "Den store manndauen og dødsregisteret fra Sigdal." *Historisk tidsskrift* (Norway) 65 (1986), 3–15; Ottosson, Per-Gunnar. *Pestskrifter i Sverige 1572–1711*. University of Linköping Studies on Health and Society, 7. Linköping: Universitetet, 1986; Benedictow, Ole J. *Fra rike til provins 1448–1536*. Norges Historie, 5. Oslo: Cappelen, 1977; 2nd ed. 1987 [1987a]; Benedictow, Ole J. "Morbidity Rates in Historical Plague Epidemics." *Population Studies* 41 (1987), 401–31 [1987b]; Reichstein, Hans. "Archözoologie und die prähistorische Verbreitung von Kleinsäugern." *Sitzungsberichte der Gesellschaft Naturforschender Freunde zu Berlin*, n.s. 27 (1987), 9–21; Oeding, Per. "Pest på Island i det 15. århundre." *Tidsskrift for den Norske Lægeforening* 108 (1988), 3196–201; Martens, Irmelin. "Middelaldergårder i Fyresdal—arkeologiske registreringer og historiske kilder." *Collegium Medievale* 2 (1989), 73–91; Benedictow, Ole Jørgen. "The Great Pestilence in Norway: An Epidemiological Study." *Collegium Medievale* 3 (1990), 19–55; Moseng, Ole G. "Nordens siste pestepidemi: En punktstudie av Allerum 1710–1711." Thesis, Department of History, University of Oslo, 1990; Benedictow, Ole Jørgen. *Plague in the Late Medieval Nordic Countries: Epidemiological Studies*. Oslo: Universitetsforlaget, 1992.

Ole Jørgen Benedictow

Poetic Edda *see* **Eddic Poetry**

Political Literature (West Norse). It is not always easy to make a clear distinction between political literature from Norse times and other Norse literature. All religious literature was written in the service of the Church and inevitably had the effect of consolidating its political power. A main category of skaldic poetry, poems in honor of princes, and a main category of saga literature, the *konungasögur*, expressed a positive attitude toward princes, the Norwegian kings in particular. Iceland's status as an independent nation and its principal political and religious institutions, the *Alþingi* and the bishoprics of Skálholt and Hólar, were supported by a well-developed sense of national self-respect, which both gave birth to and absorbed new impulses from the rich literature about the Icelanders' own past, such works as *Íslendingabók*, *Landnámabók*, and the saga literature. In this connection, the term "political literature" refers to the literature characterized by a definite intention on the part of the author to influence the political powers' measures of government in specific historical situations, or the opinion of important groups of the community in relation to political conditions and controversial political issues.

Norse literature also contains examples of political poetry from preliterary times that was written down much later. Thus, the sagas tell us that princes were sometimes given important political advice from skalds in the form of poems. *Óláfs saga helga* tells how the belief that King Óláfr was a saint gained ground after his death (1030). At that time, the Icelandic poet Þórarinn loftunga ("praise-tongue") composed *Glælognskviða* ("calm-sea lay"), where he advises King Óláfr's successor, the Danish-English King Sven, to support the worship of the king as a saint. In the poem *Bergsoglisvísur* in the saga about King Óláfr's son Magnús inn góði ("the good"), the Icelandic skald Sighvatr Þórðarson persuades King Magnús to stop persecuting those who had opposed his father.

In the saga literature dealing with historical events in the Nordic countries, a distinction is made between "sagas about the past" and "contemporary sagas." In principle, the sagas about the past could not be defined as political literature in our meaning of the term. But certain accounts in the sagas about the past have been interpreted as disguised contributions by the authors to the political debates of their own time. In *Óláfs saga helga*, Einarr from Þverá at the *Alþingi* dissuaded the Icelanders from yielding to King Óláfr's demand for taxes, and from letting him establish a military base on the small island of Grímsey off the north coast of Iceland. This speech has been interpreted as an attempt by the author, Snorri Sturluson, to warn the Icelanders against subjecting themselves to the rule of King Hákon Hákonarson of Norway (r. 1217–1263).

However, political literature in the true meaning of the term comprises that part of the *konungasögur* that can be classified as contemporary sagas. The oldest of these is **Hryggjarstykki* by Eiríkr Oddsson (12th century). Only small fragments of this saga remain, incorporated into the accounts of Magnús blindi ("the blind"), Haraldr Gilli, and the sons of Haraldr Gilli in *Morkinskinna*, *Fagrskinna*, and *Heimskringla*. It is thought that this part was written in defense of the pretender to the throne Sigurðr slembidjákn ("sham deacon"; killed 1139). The other sagas belonging to this category are *Sverris saga* (at least the first part written by the abbot Karl Jónsson, d. 1212/3), *Bǫglunga sǫgur*, *Hákonar saga Hákonarsonar*, and *Magnúss saga lagabœtis* (only some fragments remain). The last two sagas were written by Sturla Þórðarson (d. 1284). The central figures in all these sagas are the *birkibein*-kings; *birkibeinar* ("birch-legs") was originally a nickname denoting the warriors of the anticlerical party during the civil wars from the 1170s on until King Hákon Hákonarson's definite safeguarding of his royal supremacy in the 1240s, whereas the warriors of the clerical party were named *baglar* ("croziers"). The sagas about King Sverrir and King Hákon Hákonarson put forward strong arguments supporting their legitimacy. In the *Bǫglunga sǫgur*, the legitimacy of the *birkibein* kings is indisputable. This saga has been handed down in two versions, a longer version covering the period 1202–1217 and a shorter version covering 1202–1210. The longer version takes a positive view of the *birkibein* kings, but portrays the *baglar* king Erlingr steinveggr ("stone wall") as an impostor. The shorter version is more positive toward the *baglar*, and regards Erlingr steinveggr as the true son of King Magnús Erlingsson, as he claimed to be.

King Sverrir was probably the initiator of a controversial document, *Oratio contra clerum Norvegiae* (ca. 1200), which supports King Sverrir's case in his fight with the authorities of the Church by means of arguments from canon law. The comprehensive anonymous educational work *Konungs skuggsjá* (probably from the 1250s) is also to some extent political literature because, like the *Oratio*, it presents the view that the monarchy is superior to the ecclesiastical authorities, and that only one heir to the throne at a time shall be chosen king. The stylistic requirement for objectivity in the saga literature tended to limit the political propaganda in the sagas telling about events in Iceland in the 12th and 13th centuries. But such sagas as *Hrafns saga Sveinbjarnarsonar* and *Þorgils saga skarða* are so biased in support of their respective heroes as to merit being called political propaganda. The *Sturlunga saga* also contains verses that distinctly express dislike at the thought of the Icelanders becoming subject to the Norwegian kings.

Ed.: Indrebø, Gustav, ed. *Sverris saga etter Cod. AM 327 4°.* Utgjevi av Den Norske Historiske Kildeskriftkommission. Kristiania [Oslo]: Dybwad, 1920; rpt. Oslo: Norsk Historisk Kjeldeskrift-Institutt, 1981; Holtsmark, Anne, ed. *En tale mot biskopene: En sproglig-historisk undersøkelse.* Skrifter utgitt av Det norske videnskaps-akademi i Oslo, II. Hist.-filos. Kl. 1930, 9. Oslo: Dybwad, 1931; Magerøy, Hallvard, ed. *Soga om birkebeinar og baglar: Bǫglunga sǫgur.* Norsk Historisk Kjeldeskrift-Institutt, Norrøne tekster, 5. Oslo: Kjeldeskriftfondet; Solum, 1988. **Lit.**: Holm-Olsen, Ludvig. *Studier i Sverres saga.* Avhandlinger utgitt av det Norske videnskaps-akademi i Oslo. II. Hist.-filos. Kl. 1952, 3. Oslo: Dybwad, 1953; Helle, Knut. *Omkring Bǫglungasǫgur.* Universitetet i Bergen, Årbok 1958, Historisk-Antikvarisk rekke Nr. 7. Bergen: Grieg, 1959; Holm-Olsen, Ludvig, and Kjell Heggelund. *Norsk litteraturhistorie* 1. Oslo: Cappelen, 1974; Jón Jóhannesson. *A History of the Old Icelandic Commonwealth: Íslendinga saga.* Trans. Haraldur Bessason. University of Manitoba Icelandic Studies, 2. Winnipeg: University of Manitoba Press, 1974; Bjarni Guðnason. *Fyrsta sagan.* Studia Islandica, 37. Reykjavík: Menningarsjóður, 1978; Lárus H. Blöndal. *Um uppruna Sverrissögu.* Reykjavik: Stofnun Árna Magnússonar, 1982; Bagge, Sverre. *The Political Thought of The King's Mirror.* Odense: Odense University Press, 1987; Sverrir Tómasson. *Formálar íslenskra sagnaritara á miðöldum.* Reykjavík: Stofnun Árna Magnússonar, 1988; Jónas Kristjánsson. *Eddas and Sagas: Iceland's Medieval Literature.* Trans. Peter Foote. Reykjavík: Hið íslenska bókmenntafélag, 1988.

Hallvard Magerøy

[**See also:** *Bǫglunga sǫgur; Fagrskinna; Hákonar saga gamla Hákonarsonar; Heimskringla; Íslendingabók; Íslendingasögur; Konungasögur; Konungs skuggsjá; Landnámabók; Magnúss saga lagabœtis; Morkinskinna; Óláfs saga helga; Oratio contra clerum Norvegiae;* Sighvatr Þórðarson; *Skáld;* Skaldic Verse; *Sturlunga saga; Sverris saga;* Swedish Literature, Miscellaneous; Þórarinn loftunga]

Postola sǫgur ("Apostles' Sagas"). In the 2nd century, legends about the apostles began to appear, many originating from the desire of the devout to satisfy their curiosity. The biblical Acts provides little information about the lives of the apostles, and this lack of biographical detail allowed ample opportunity for fantasy to augment the sparse actual knowledge about their backgrounds, careers, miracles, and martyrdom. The oldest of these legends are the *Acts of John* from the middle of the 2nd century and the *Acts of Paul* from about A.D. 160, followed by the *Acts of Peter* from about A.D. 200, and then the *Acts of Andrew* and of *Thomas*, both from the 3rd century. These five lives were put together by Leucius Charinus in a collection that existed in Greek and also in Latin under the title *Actus apostolorum*. To these lives, legends about the other apostles were added later. "Complete" collections in Latin of the lives of all the apostles existed around A.D. 600 and are usually known as Abdias's *Historia apostolica*. Abdias was said to have been bishop of Babylon and ordained by Simon and Jude. The supposed Abdias collection was edited by W. Lazius in 1551 under the title *Abdiæ episcopi Babyloniæ historia certaminis aspostolorum* on the basis of two MSS. This edition was reprinted in J. A. Fabricius's *Codex Apocryphus Novi Testamenti* 2 (1719) under the title *Abdiæ historia apostolica*. In the MSS, however, Abdias is mentioned as the author of the last legend only, the "Passio Simonis et Judae" (Unger 1874: 787[11-18]); moreover, Lazius's text is haphazardly pieced together from MSS, and expanded and revised by Lazius himself. Accordingly, the Abdias collection found here is not by Abdias and is not a medieval Vulgate edition of apostle legends, but an unreliable 16th-century edition of only partly representative versions (Gad 1961).

In Norse, lives of all the apostles, including Paul and Matthias, are extant. The Latin lives probably came to Iceland and Norway soon after Christianity had become firmly rooted and belong among the very first texts that were translated into Norse. This dating is evident from a leaf of *Matheus saga postola* in AM 655 IX 4to from the second half of the 12th century; a comparison of the text of this fragment with other (younger) MSS containing an identical text reveals a number of errors in the old fragment and indicates that the original translation must date from before 1150.

The most complete collection of apostles' sagas is found in the *Codex Scardensis* from around 1360, containing the lives of Peter (fols. 1v–27v), Paul (fols. 27v–36r), Andrew (fols. 36v–39v), a composite life of the two sons of Zebedee, John and James (fols. 40r–81v), the lives of Thomas (fols. 82r–85v), Philip (fols. 85v–86r), James the Lesser (fol. 86), Bartholomew (fols. 86r–88v), Matthias (fols. 88v–89r), a composite life of Simon and Jude (fols. 89r–92), and a life of Matthew (fols. 92r–94). All the lives in this codex (or rather Eyjólfur Björnsson's copy in AM 628 4to, AM 631 4to, AM 636 4to made before the codex fell into obscurity for some thirty years) were either printed *in extenso* or used to supply variants in the *apparatus criticus* of Unger's edition. The largest part of the codex (fols. 1–81) appears to be based on MSS little older than the codex itself. The exemplar of the composite life of

John and James, for instance, is AM 239 fol., which is hardly more than a few years older than the codex. From the language of the lives found in this part of the codex, it seems probable that these versions cannot be much older than about 1300. The lives found on fols. 82–94 are based on older texts; the life of Matthias, for instance, could be from the beginning of the 13th century. From the orthography in this part, it seems clear that the originals were not younger than roughly 1300, probably somewhat older. The older texts are characterized by their close adherence to the Latin source and their artistic simplicity; the younger texts contain a considerable amount of extraneous doctrinal and hagiographic material, and are characterized by a certain elegance of expression. Other collections or fragments of collections of apostles' sagas include AM 645 4to from the beginning of the 13th century, AM 655 XII–XIII 4to from 1200–1250, and AM 652 4to from 1250–1300 (see also Widding et al. 1963).

Pseudo-Abdias has generally been considered the primary source for most of the Old Norse postola sögur, but information drawn from such works as Peter Comestor's Historia scholastica, Honorius Augustodunensis's Speculum ecclesiae, Vincent of Beauvais's Speculum historiale, and the Pseudo-Turpin Chronicle is also found in a number of the lives. The exact sources for a number of sections or passages in the apostles' sagas remain obscure, despite efforts to trace them by Widding et al. (1963) and later by Collings (1969) in her analysis of the Codex Scardensis. Many of the Norse lives are extant in several versions; Pétrs saga postola, for example, is found in six versions, Andreas saga postola in five, and Páls saga postola in three. In some instances, the versions are mutually independent renderings of a common Latin source; in others, they are translations of different Latin sources. Matheus saga postola, for example, is found in two versions, which are separate translations of the same source, presumably the vita of Lambertus a Legio. Philippus saga postola is extant in three versions, the first of which is based on Pseudo-Abdias, the second on the Legenda aurea, and the third probably on a Low German source.

At the end of his edition, Unger printed the text of two versions of a life of John the Baptist, because this saga often accompanies the lives of the apostles in the old collections. The first life (pp. 842–9) is edited from the defective MS AM 625 4to from the early 14th century. The text is largely dependent on the Gospels, but no immediate source has been found. The second version (pp. 849–931) is based on the 14th-century MS AM 232 fol., which is complete apart from a prologue (letter), supplied from AM 23a fol. from the mid-14th century. According to this letter, the saga was written by the priest Grímr Hólmsteinsson (d. 1298) at the request of Runólfr Sigmundsson (d. 1306), abbot of the Benedictine monastery of Þykkvabær. The work is a compilation of information about John, in which his life story according to the Gospels is filled out with material from, for example, Bede, Comestor, Vincent of Beauvais, and the Church Fathers Gregory, Augustine, Ambrose, and Jerome.

Finnur Jónsson (1920–24) has pointed out that Unger's division of the sagas into the genres heilagra manna sögur ("saints' lives") and postola sögur ("apostles' sagas") may be practical, but not original, and lacks a basis in medieval times. Finnur Jónsson refers to a statement in Tveggja postola saga Philippus ok Jacobs: ". . . en Phillippus var sva fiarlægr þeim monnum, er heilagra manna sogur hafa samsettar, ok er þvi fra honum fatt sagt" (". . . but Philippus was so far away from the men who composed the lives of holy men, and therefore little is said about him").

Ed.: Unger, C. R., ed. Postola sögur: Legendariske fortællinger om apostlernes liv deres kamp for kristendommens udbredelse samt deres martyrdød. Christiania [Oslo]: Bentzen, 1874; Larsson, Ludvig, ed. Isländska Handskriften No. 645 4° i Den Arnamagnæanske Samlingen på Universitetsbiblioteket i København: I. Handskriftens äldre del. Lund: Malmström, 1885; Finnur Jónsson, ed. AM 623, 4°: Helgensagaer. Samfund til udgivelse af gammel nordisk litteratur, 52. Copenhagen: Jørgensen, 1927, pp. 9–25; Holtsmark, Anne, ed. A Book of Miracles: MS No. 645 4° of the Arna-Magnæan Collection in the University Library of Copenhagen. Corpus Codicum Islandicorum Medii Aevi, 12. Copenhagen: Munksgaard, 1938 [facsimile]; Agerschou, Agnes, ed. "Et fragment af Jóns saga baptista." Opuscula 1. Bibliotheca Arnamagnæana, 20. Copenhagen: Munksgaard, 1960, pp. 97–104; Slay, Desmond, ed. Codex Scardensis. Early Icelandic Manuscripts in Facsimile, 2. Copenhagen: Rosenkilde & Bagger, 1960; Hreinn Benediktsson. Early Icelandic Script as Illustrated in Vernacular Texts from the Twelfth and Thirteenth Centuries. Icelandic Manuscripts, series in folio, 2. Reykjavik: Manuscript Institute of Iceland, 1965, pls. 27, 28, 36, 43, 44, 56, 64, 67 [facsimiles]; Ólafur Halldórsson, ed. Sögur úr Skarðsbók. Reykjavik: Almenna bókafélagið, 1967. Bib.: Widding, Ole, et al. "The Lives of the Saints in Old Norse Prose: A Handlist." Mediaeval Studies 25 (1963), 294–337. Lit.: Lipsius, Richard Adelbert. Die apokryphen Apostelgeschichten und Apostellegenden. 2 vols. and suppl. Braunschweig: Schwetsch, 1883–90; Eiríkr Magnússon. "Kodex Skardensis af postulasögur." Arkiv för nordisk filologi 8 (1892), 238–45; Mogk, Eugen. Geschichte der norwegisch-isländischen Literatur. Strassburg: Trübner, 1904, pp. 887–9; Finnur Jónsson. Den oldnorske og oldislandske Litteraturs Historie. 3 vols. 2nd ed. Copenhagen: Gad, 1920–24, vol. 2, pp. 863–73; James, Montague Rhodes. The Apocryphal New Testament. Oxford: Clarendon, 1924; corr. ed. 1953; Lehmann, Paul. Skandinaviens Anteil an der lateinischen Literatur und Wissenschaft des Mittelalters. 2. Stück. Sitzungsberichte der bayerischen Akademie der Wissenschaften, Philosophisch-historische Abteilung, Jahrgang 1937, Heft 7. Munich: Bayerischen Akademie der Wissenschaften, 1937; Vries, Jan de. Altnordische Literaturgeschichte. 2 vols. 2nd ed. Grundriss der germanischen Philologie, 15–6. Berlin: de Gruyter, 1941–42; rpt. 1964–67, vol. 2, p. 468; Paasche, Fredrik. Norges og Islands Litteratur 1. Rev. ed. Anne Holtsmark. Oslo: Aschehoug, 1957, pp. 292–5, 445–6; Turville-Petre, G. Origins of Icelandic Literature. Oxford: Clarendon, 1953; rpt. 1967, pp. 128–31; Foote, Peter G. The Pseudo-Turpin Chronicle in Iceland. London Medieval Studies, Monograph No. 4. London: University College, 1959; Foote, Peter G. "A Note on the Source of the Icelandic Translation of the Pseudo-Turpin Chronicle." Neophilologus 43 (1959), 137–42; Gad, Tue. Legenden i dansk middelalder. Copenhagen: Dansk Videnskabs Forlag, 1961, pp. 70–84; Johannessen, Ole-Jörgen. "Litt om kildene til Jóns saga baptista II." Opuscula 2. Bibliotheca Arnamagnæana, 25. Copenhagen: Reitzel, 1961–77, pp. 100–16; Bekker-Nielsen, Hans. "On a Handlist of Saints' Lives in Old Norse." Mediaeval Studies 24 (1962), 323–34; Bekker-Nielsen, Hans, et al. Norrøn Fortællekunst: Kapitler af den norsk-islandske middelalderlitteraturs historie. Copenhagen: Akademisk Forlag, 1965, pp. 121–4, 136; Collings, Lucy Grace. "The Codex Scardensis: Studies in Icelandic Hagiography." Diss. Cornell University, 1969; Carlsson, Thorsten. "Norrön legendforskning—en kort presentation." Scripta Islandica 23 (1972), 31–56; Kirby, Ian J. Biblical Quotations in Old Icelandic–Norwegian Religious Literature. 2 vols. Reykjavik: Stofnun Árna Magnússonar, 1976–80, vol. 2, pp. 22–38; Kirby, Ian J. Bible Translation in Old Norse. Université de Lausanne Publications de la Faculté des Lettres, 27. Geneva: Droz, 1986.

Kirsten Wolf

[See also: Christian Poetry; Christian Prose; Legenda; Saints' Lives; Skarðsbók]

Pottery. Despite a long tradition of study of prehistoric pottery in Scandinavia, systematic research into medieval pottery has not been carried out until comparatively recently, and there are still considerable gaps in knowledge.

Special problems are connected with the establishment of narrow dating criteria. The medieval archaeologist makes greater demands of "fine-chronology" than the prehistorian, but the find material and sequences of relatively dated pottery are often of the same nature. Sequences of relatively dated pottery can be established with advantage out of the finds from the thick culture layers in towns. But both in these cases and where samples from more limited settlement deposits are concerned, there are difficulties in generalizing about a perhaps local pattern of shapes and decoration. Coin datings and, to a growing extent, dendrochronological datings, play a decisive role. In relation to pottery, coin dating can consist of, for example, dating finds on the basis of the oldest and youngest coins found. The castle mound of Næsholm in the Holbæk area is the best-known example; its period of activity can be specified from a large number of coins found as the years around 1240–1340. To this evidence can be added the group of "coin-dated" pottery, *i.e.*, pottery vessels used as containers for treasure including coins hoarded in the Middle Ages. So far, only the Danish material has been published. From Denmark, a little over fifty pieces of medieval coin-dated pottery are known; the time at which they were deposited is established as after the date of the youngest coin contained in the particular find. On the basis of this material, it is possible to outline the main characteristics of the development of medieval pottery.

In the first centuries of the Middle Ages up to the beginning of the 13th century, domestic pottery still had prehistoric features in production technique and firing. The pottery during this period was still built up by hand without the use of the potter's wheel, and the black or grey earthenware was fired at relatively low temperatures, perhaps 600°–700° C, in stacks, or pit ovens, dug into the soil. However, this type of oven from this period has not yet been found in Scandinavia.

The pottery from the early Middle Ages differs in important respects from the pottery of the Viking Age and the Late Iron Age. Both in quality and in design, the pottery of late-prehistoric times deteriorates, and Scandinavia must then have become open to influences from the outside world. The new influences first arrived in the Jutland peninsula from the south and west, in the form of the *Kugeltopf*, with its globe-shaped corpus, rounded base, and narrowing, sometimes grooved, neck with outward-curving rim. The vessels differ in size, and functioned as both cooking and storage pots. The *Kugeltopf*, which also occurs in versions with three small legs, and with or without lugs, was produced throughout the Middle Ages. From the 13th century onward, the *Kugeltopf* was made on the potter's wheel, and the fabric was fired harder in actual pottery kilns, as has been illustrated in later years through the finds of kilns in Barmer and Hellum in northern Jutland. At the same time, the *Kugeltopf* became common all over southern Scandinavia.

In eastern Denmark, on the Islands, in Scania, and in southern Sweden, innovations in pottery came from the Slavonic areas along the south coast of the Baltic. The type of pottery that originally developed in central Europe is characterized by its flat base, urn-shaped vessels, with high shoulder angle and narrowing rim. The pots occur in all sizes and were used for various purposes in the household. This Slavonic pottery type, which was earlier named

"Wendic pottery," is now, with reference to its archaeological distribution, most commonly called "Baltic pottery." Besides its more or less biconical shape, the Baltic pottery is characterized by its low-fired ware and the addition of micaceous sand. Most conspicuous is the stamped or drawn decoration, hatching, wave lines, imprints with a fingernail, and so on, usually concentrated on the shoulder or rim area of the vessel, sometimes supplemented by a drawn line running in a spiral down the corpus.

One may assume that in the beginning the new pottery types were imported to Scandinavia, but since, for instance, the Baltic pottery, from the 11th century and for a couple of centuries onward, seems to have been almost completely dominant in the area, at least at that stage, it must have been made extensively in Scandinavia. In the countries of origin of this type of pottery, Germany and Poland, attempts have been made to establish a fine chronology, but this dating is not transferable to the Scandinavian context as a whole. Although it seems clear that the Baltic pottery was in use during the period from about 950 to the beginning of the 13th century, it is still difficult to date the individual finds within this relatively long span of time. There seems, however, to be one indication, based on the decoration: the above-mentioned spiral line on the corpus has not been found on material older than the 11th century. The lack of spiral line, on the other hand, cannot be used as a criterion of age. A tendency to simpler rim profiles in the latter types of vessels may be discernible in larger finds, and the decoration, particularly the wave line, may seem more imprecise or careless. Nevertheless, it must be stressed that, for Baltic as for prehistoric pottery, local factors, no doubt due to the domestic nature of pot making, make it difficult to draw parallels between different finds.

In step with the professionalization of pot making from the beginning of the 13th century, *i.e.*, the introduction of the potter's wheel and actual pottery kilns, which allowed firing temperatures up to 900°–1000° C, the Baltic pottery with its prehistoric features was ousted by the *Kugeltopf*. In eastern Denmark, the tradition of Baltic design could still be traced; hard-fired grey pots with flat bases turned on the potter's wheel were still produced well into the 13th century, using the wave and spiral lines as popular elements of decoration.

The major innovation of the 13th century, however, is the red-fired glazed pottery. The potter's kiln and new technical knowledge made firing with the help of oxygen possible. This technique gave a reddish color and made it possible to achieve the high temperatures necessary for glaze firing. So far, pottery kilns have been found and excavated only in Denmark, and Zealand probably took the lead in the production of the new types of pottery. Pottery kilns from the 13th and 14th centuries have been investigated in Farum Lillevang and Faurholm, both in North Zealand. In both places, particularly in Farum Lillevang, the finds give a clear impression of the potter's repertoire during the high Middle Ages. Red-fired glazed globular pots, with or without legs or lugs, formed the largest mass product, but the outstanding object in the finds is the big decorated jug. Although the glazed jug occurs commonly in western Danish finds, at least from the 14th century, unglazed grey-fired variations of the jug are commonly found on Funen and in Jutland.

The chronological distribution of the red-fired glazed jug is thought to be confined to the period 1250–1350, mainly on the basis of the series of coin-dated vessels, the pottery from Næsholm, and a group of other finds. Recent observations in Ribe (Denmark)

and Lund (Sweden) indicate, however, that the starting point should perhaps be moved closer to 1200. But apart from that, the red-fired glazed jug must still be regarded as a relatively sure archaeological "dating standard."

The domestic pottery of the 15th century is still little researched. From this century, there are a few examples of glazed jugs, but apart from these pieces there is one distinct type of vessel, the "tail pot," a red-fired globular pot on three legs with a vertical pipe-shaped handle. The tail pot was produced without interruption for the next 300–400 years, but the early examples are characterized by the red-fired fabric covered by a clear or faintly greenish glaze on the inside and by the rim curved inward, so that the pots have a more distinctly globular shape than the later pots, which as a rule have a vertical rim, most often decorated with a roll stamp.

Imported pottery can probably be found among the early *Kugeltopfs* and the Baltic ware, but they are with few exceptions difficult to identify without mineralogical analyses. The pottery from the Netherlands and the Rhine region, such as the hard-fired graphite-like *Blau-graue Ware* and the whitish *Pingsdorf Ware* with red painting, constitutes an extremely small part of the total Scandinavian pottery material from the Middle Ages. Imported pottery plays a decisive role in Norway, however, where no local pottery production seems to have existed. English and Danish products in particular are dominant.

From the middle or the end of the 13th century onward, the hard-fired pottery from the Rhine region occurs more often in Scandinavia. Mugs of greyish-brown fabric, and jugs and jars of yellowish or brownish fabric, covered by a shiny reddish-brown or purple slip, go under the name of *Fast Steinzeug*. It is not until the years around 1340 that the mass-produced greyish-white stoneware from Siegburg in the Rhineland occurs commonly in Scandinavian finds.

Lit.: Selling, Dagmar. *Wikingerzeitliche und frühmittelalterliche Keramik in Schweden*. Stockholm: Petterson, 1955; LaCour, Vilhelm. *Næsholm*. Copenhagen: Nationalmuseet, 1961; Bencard, Mogens, and Else Roesdahl. *Dansk middelalderlertøj, 1050–1550*. Jysk Arkæologisk Selskabs håndbøger, 1. Copenhagen: Gyldendal, 1972; Bencard, Mogens. *Medieval Pottery Imported into Denmark*. Chateau Gaillard, 5. Caen: Centre de recherches archéologiques médiévales, Université de Caen, 1972; Liebgott, Niels-Knud. *Medieval Pottery Kilns at Faurholm in North Zealand, Denmark*. Acta Archæologica, 46. Copenhagen: Munksgaard, 1975; Wahlöö, Claes. *Keramik 1000–1600 i svenska fynd*. Archæologica Lundensia, 6. Lund: Kulturhistoriska museet, 1976; Liebgott, Niels-Knud. *Danske fund af møntdateret keramik ca. 950–1450*. Nationalmuseets Skrifter, Arkæologisk-historisk række, 18. Copenhagen: Gyldendal, 1978 [German summary]; Liebgott, Niels-Knud. *Keramik fra vikingetid og middelalder*. Copenhagen: Gyldendal, 1978; Liebgott, Niels-Knud. *Keramik fra voldstedet Pedersborg ved Sorø*. Aarbøger for nordisk Oldkyndighed og Historie, 1977. Copenhagen: Det Kongelige Nordiske Oldskriftselskab, 1979; Magnus, Bente, and Siri Myrvoll, eds. *Mångahanda slags kärl finnas hos Nordborna. Bruk av keramik i middelalderen*. Riksantikvarens Rapporter, 8. Øvre Ervik: Alvheim & Eide, 1983; Augustsson, Jan-Erik. *Keramik i Halmstad ca. 1322–1619. Produktion-distribution-funktion*. Hallands Länsmuseers skriftserie, 2. Varberg: Stiftelsen Hallands Länsmuseer, 1985; Madsen, Per Kristian. "A Survey of the Research of Danish Medieval Pottery." *Medieval Ceramics* 10 (1986), 57–84.

Niels-Knud Liebgott

Prayer Books

1. EAST NORSE. Prayer books are collections of prayers and similar texts for private devotion. It is a universal Christian genre, and the Swedish and Danish prayer books, all from the period around 1450–1550, can be regarded as local representatives of the genre in its last stage of development. The genre had its origin in the Psalter (the 150 Old Testament psalms), passages of which were recited at fixed hours of prayer in the monasteries, and whose use spread out from there to the private devotions of laypeople. In the first stage of the development (9th century), prayers from the breviary (the book containing the official prayers for the canonical hours) were incorporated into the Psalter. Later, other prayers were added, and, finally, the prayers were detached from the Psalter. Thus, in the 14th–16th centuries, independent prayer books came into existence, first in Latin, later also in the vernacular. They include (1) books of hours, in which the connection with the breviary and prayers at the canonical hours still survives, since a calendar (a record of the days of the year with notes about the festivals of the Church, the feast days of saints, *etc.*) and psalms and prayers for fixed hours of the day always form part of it, along with the litany and prayers for saints; (2) books of common prayer or prayer books proper, in which the selection of material is dependent on the writer's or the owner's personal interests, and whose arrangement of material is sometimes random, sometimes in accordance with the place of the addressee in the hierarchy of the litany (*i.e.*, first prayers to the Trinity, then to the Virgin Mary, and then to groups of other saints, with local variations); and (3) hybrid forms of these two types.

From Sweden, around fifteen MSS with prayers as their main content are preserved. The majority (*e.g.*, Berlin Theol. Lat. 71 8vo, Giessen 881, Stock. A 38 and A 43, Upps. C 12 and C 68) derive from Vadstena, being written by or for Vadstena nuns, and they belong to the hybrid type with hour-book material in Latin and individually composed prayers in Swedish, occasionally arranged according to the litany. A few, mostly in Latin, belong to the book-of-hour type (*e.g.*, Upps. C 475), while a few are entirely in Swedish and composed freely (*e.g.*, Stock. A 37). Among printed books, there are a few minor works for laypeople containing, among other things, prayers for indulgence, in addition to books of hours for official use.

From Denmark are preserved about twenty MSS with prayer material as their main content. These MSS also seem to have originated in a homogeneous circle, primarily nuns and other religious women from among the nobility or the wealthier townspeople, several with Brigettine affiliations. Only one MS, mostly in Latin, belongs more or less to the book-of-hours type (Kalmar 33). A small group includes the hybrid type (*e.g.*, Stock. A 40 and A 42, Lund 35, GkS 1615 4to), but in contrast to the corresponding Swedish MSS the Danish ones normally have the book-of-hours material in the vernacular. The rest are the common prayer-book type, some without any clear arrangement (*e.g.*, GkS 1614 4to), others partially arranged according to the litany (*e.g.*, Thott 553 4to, the only MS in which the female saints come before the male ones). Two MSS containing the same text, *Visdoms Spejl* ("Mirror of Wisdom"; AM 782 4to and AM 784 4to), follow the ecclesiastical year. Among printed books, there is first and foremost *Vor Frue Tider* ("Our Lady's Hours"; Paris, 1514), a combined book of hours and prayers in Christiern Pedersen's thoroughly revised redaction.

Although the sources have not all been identified, it is certain that much of the content of the prayer books is dependent on foreign sources, especially Latin and Low German sources, which have been translated, revised, or excerpted more or less freely. A great deal of material in the Danish prayer books came via Sweden, while a reverse movement has not been demonstrated. Where the authors are known, they are mostly the major names of the Church: Church Fathers, scholastics, mystics, and the founders of the Catholic orders (Birgitta of Vadstena is the only Scandinavian founder). The addressees for the prayers are the same as elsewhere (first and foremost the celestial hierarchy, with Jesus and the Virgin Mary as the most frequently invoked); the character of the addresses is the same also (praise, thanks, requests for intercession for the salvation of the soul, or for protection against earthly misfortunes); and the content can be, for example, of a mainly dogmatic or ethical character, as in the penitentials, with their instructions on how to search one's conscience before confession. The prayer can be of an epic-contemplative character or lyrical-mystical-ecstatic; the form can be prose or verse. Following foreign models, the prayers may also be accompanied by rubrics containing statements about authors, promises of indulgence, instructions on the use of pictures at devotion, and other magic elements.

In contrast to the foreign models, the Danish and Swedish prayer books are modest in appearance. The ornament consists of illuminated initials, a few marginal drawings, and miniatures of a poor quality; the Danish MS AM 421 12mo distinguishes itself from its fellows by its forty-eight full-page miniatures in gold and colors depicting, for example, scenes from the life of Jesus.

East Norse prayer material is also found sporadically outside the prayer books, for instance, in MSS containing religious material of various kinds, as in the Swedish MS Upps. C 23 (ca. 1500) and the Danish MS AM 76 8vo (ca. 1450–1500).

Ed.: Geete, Robert, ed. *Skrifter till uppbyggelse från medeltiden: En samling af moralteologiska traktater på svenska.* Samlingar utgifna af Svenska fornskrift-sällskapet, 36. Stockholm: Norstedt, 1904–05; Geete, Robert, ed. *Svenska böner från medeltiden.* Samlingar utgifna af Svenska fornskrift-sällskapet, 38. Stockholm: Norstedt, 1907–09; Nielsen, Karl Martin, ed. *Middelalderens danske bønnebøger.* 5 vols. Copenhagen: Gyldendal, 1945–82. **Bib.**: Gallén, Jarl. "Bönböcker." *KLNM* 2 (1957), 507–8. **Lit.**: Frandsen, Ernst. *Mariaviserne. Den lyriske Madonnadigtning fra Danmarks Middelalder, belyst gennem Bønnebøgernes Prosatexter.* Copenhagen: Levin & Munksgaard, 1926; Schmid, Toni, and Ernst Nygren. *En bönbok från Vadstena Kloster. Tvenne uppsatser om en år 1950 nyupptäckt handskrift.* Stockholm: Thulin, 1952; Szövérffy, J. *Volkskundliches in mittelalterlichen Gebetbüchern. Randbemerkungen zu K. M. Nielsens Textausgabe.* Historisk-filologiske Meddelelser, udg. af Det Kongelige Danske Videnskabernes Selskab, 37, no. 3. Copenhagen: Munksgaard, 1958; Frederiksen, Britta Olrik. *En dansk Mechtild-tradition? En undersøgelse af nogle gammeldanske bønner.* Universitets-jubilæets danske samfunds skriftserie, 493. Copenhagen: Akademisk Forlag, 1984 [English summary].

Britta Olrik Frederiksen

2. WEST NORSE. Few Icelandic prayer books survive from the Middle Ages. The oldest is Upps. R 719 from around 1525–1550. It contains no hours, but instead the following seven prayers in Icelandic: *O bone Jesu; Conditor celi*; a prayer about the Cross (of unknown origin); a continuation of no. 3; a prayer for the church officials, relatives, and benefactors (of unknown origin); an extract from the king's prayer in *Konungs skuggsjá* called "A Good Prayer"; and a *brynjubœn* (literally "byrnie-prayer," *i.e.*, prayer for protection) belonging to the prayers entitled *Lorica*. This MS includes an illumination of the martyr Erasmus. Add. 4895 12mo from the 15th century contains the Erasmus prayer and also another prayer in Icelandic, *De cruce*. It is uncertain if *De cruce* dates from before the 14th century, but the Erasmus prayer may have been translated from Scandinavian in the 14th century.

The prayer book Thott 181 8vo from the 16th century is one of the closest to Catholic prayer books of all the prayer books of the Reformation. It contains, among other items, a calendar, a prayer in Latin, the *Domine labia* in Icelandic, as well as a book of hours, *Anima Christi*, and the seven penitential psalms.

Similar in content are two prayer books from the latter half of the 16th century, Bodl. MS Icel. g. 1 and Register House 22 in Edinburgh. From the 16th century, there are fragmentary books with prayer material of various kinds, such as ÍB 363 8vo from about 1550 (four leaves of the same MS are in the National Archives, Þjms 619). Parallels to the prayers are found in *Svenska böner* and Danish medieval prayers, among others, Johanne Nielsdatter's book of hours from around 1480.

Most of the prayer books appear to have been written for women. This applies to ÍBR 1 8vo, ÍB 363 8vo / Þjms 619, the first half of Thott 181 8vo, Register House no. 22 (although with exceptions). Bodl. MS Icel. g. 1 is, however, written in large part for a man. It is probable that the prayer books were originally written for nuns (*Svenska böner* 30).

Marian hours did, of course, exist in the Middle Ages. Now they are extant only in poetry (*cf. Íslenzk miðaldakvæði*).

The medieval Icelandic prayer material has been little investigated, and no comprehensive edition exists. The origin of the prayers is unknown, but it is probable that they stem from Latin, Low German, or Scandinavian, especially Swedish, sources.

The external appearance of the prayer books is not conspicuous; only Upps. R 719 is illuminated. Some MSS contain ornate initials.

As far as we know, there are no medieval Norwegian prayer books. However, it is likely that Swedish and Danish prayer books found their way to Norway and were copied. This hypothesis is supported by the fact that in 1520 there was a book with a Danish Marian prayer in Vinje Church in Telemark.

Lit.: Geete, Robert, ed. *Svenska böner från medeltiden.* Samlingar utgifna af Svenska fornskrift-sällskapet, 38. Stockholm: Norstedt, 1907–09; Jón Helgason, ed. *Íslenzk miðaldakvæði. Islandske digte fra senmiddelalderen.* Vols. 1.2–2. Copenhagen: Levin & Munksgaard, 1936–38; Kolsrud, Oluf. *Noregs kyrkjesoga. 1: Millomalderen.* Oslo: Aschehoug, 1958, p. 366; Widding, Ole. "Til Konungs Skuggsjá. Kongens bøn efter R:719." *Opuscula* 1. Bibliotheca Arnamagnæana, 20. Copenhagen: Munksgaard, 1960, pp. 327–30; Bekker-Nielsen, Hans. "En god bøn." *Opuscula* 2.1. Bibliotheca Arnamagnæana, 25.1. Copenhagen: Munksgaard, 1961, pp. 52–8; Svavar Sigmundsson. "Handritið Uppsala R:719." In *Opuscula septentrionalia. Festskrift til Ole Widding 10.10. 1977.* Ed. Bent Chr. Jacobsen *et al.* Copenhagen: Reitzel, 1977, pp. 207–20; Stefán Karlsson. "Sex skriffingur." *Opuscula* 7. Bibliotheca Arnamagnæana, 34. Copenhagen: Reitzel, 1979, pp. 36–43.

Svavar Sigmundsson

[See also: Bible; Birgitta, St.; Christian Poetry; Christian Prose; *Konungs skuggsjá*; Liturgy and Liturgical Texts; Saints' Lives; Vadstena]

Pregnancy and Childbirth

Pregnancy and Childbirth are the most gender-determined historical experiences. Most women have experienced them, willingly or unwillingly. In the Middle Ages, women could avoid pregnancy by choosing a religious life, if the family permitted, or if they were strong or wealthy enough to do as they wished. Men have a vested interest in controlling the sexual activities of women, not least their reproductive abilities. This interest has shaped the historical experience of women and men differently and determined the sources available to the historian. Literature, folklore, and religious rites provide evidence about women's experience; laws and scientific writings depict primarily the men's role and perceptions.

Old Norse terms for pregnancy include *vera eigi ein saman* ("not to be alone") and *eigi heil* ("not well"). Most words concern the physical aspect: *digrast í gerðunum* ("to become big around the waist") or *fara/vera með barni* ("to walk/be with child"), the latter common to the other Scandinavian languages. The sources reveal ambivalence by the women toward the condition, as one filled with danger but also offering some privileges. In sermons (mostly late-medieval), husbands were urged to show consideration, and pregnant women were exempt from fasting regulations. The laws show that the pregnant woman could be considered especially valuable. Early Icelandic and Swedish laws set a fine for the killing of a pregnant woman double that for other kinds of woman- or manslaughter.

Scholars have commonly believed that pregnancy and childbirth took a heavy toll on adult women. An examination of the sources does not bear out this notion. Successful pregnancies depended on nutrition, age, number of previous pregnancies, skill of helpers, and sanitary conditions, all determined by the socioeconomic conditions of the woman. The wealthier had a better chance for survival and recovery. Royal women, however, may have been at greater risk due to marriage at an early age. Scandinavian skeletal remains do not show a higher mortality for pregnant and parturient women than for nonpregnant cohorts. A higher mortality for adult women (fifteen to twenty years) apparent in some skeletal material seems due to inferior living conditions (relative to men), *i.e.*, less food, harder work.

Prevention is not mentioned in Scandinavian sources. A Swedish law and a Danish synodal statute refer to induced abortion, the former by some form of massage. Herbals mention plants that can cause ceased menstruation to resume. The degree of popular use and effectiveness of these herbs is a matter of speculation.

The birth took place in the bath chamber or other separate place, which would limit the risk of infection. In contrast to other European countries, birth chairs were not in use in Scandinavia. Instead, the parturient woman knelt or sat on the stronger of the women present, supported by the others. The birth was exclusively a female affair in the village and towns. The husband took part on more isolated farmsteads. Women also gave evidence in legal disputes involving pregnant women and infants, usually concerning inheritance, suspicious stillbirths, or deaths of infants.

Exposure of children was apparently practiced in heathen times. The sagas refer to it, and the oldest Norwegian laws make it permissible in case of severe deformity. The Church frowned on exposure, but infanticide did take place, with economic reasons apparently weighing more heavily than the sex of the child. In the Christian period, the mother was responsible for the well-being of the infant, once she had recovered from the birth, and was a prime suspect if the only child died. Giving birth in secret was prohibited in one early Norwegian law, but not elsewhere, and did not become a capital offense until the 17th century.

Divine and human helpers are mentioned in pre-Christian and Christian sources. In the heathen period, the divine helpers were always female (*dísir, nornir*). In the Christian period, the primary divine helpers were the Virgin Mary and the saints Margaret and Dorothea, but a few male saints were also called on for help. Small MSS containing the *vita* of St. Margaret were used in Iceland as birth amulets as late as the 17th century. Other Christian magic was used, such as rune sticks with a prayer to Mary and Elizabeth, a kirtle said to have belonged to Mary, and chants, formulas, and songs invoking Mary and the saints (used secretly after the Reformation). Some of these rituals probably go back to heathen chants and birth runes, mentioned in the *Oddrúnargrátr* and the *Sigrdrífumál*.

Human helpers were usually neighbors or relatives, although some of the Old Norse terms imply that they could be specially skilled women. The caesarian section performed on the dead queen Dagmar (d. 1215) in the famous ballad seems to have been carried out by one of the women present. Caesarians were performed, although the Church prohibited them. Midwives, as clearly defined professional birth helpers, appear in the sources during the 15th century. After the Reformation, they were enlisted by the reformers in the crusade against "popish" superstition and rites connnected with childbirth, and used by the authorities to control and maintain social mores and order. Trained midwives may, however, have been available only for urban women.

The *kvindegilde*, the women's feast mentioned from the 13th century to the 19th century, was a celebration of a successful birth by the female helpers. The feast entailed drinking, dancing, and mocking of a male figure made of straw, and could develop into a raucous affair ending with aggressive behavior toward any man who encountered the women on their way home. Baptism feasts, on the other hand, included both men and women, and took place shortly after the birth. The recovery period ideally lasted six to eight weeks, although it is doubtful that many women could afford to rest so long; it ended with the *kirkegang* (church-going), a religious celebration of the recovery of the woman, at times developing into a demonstration of social status.

Lit.: Jacobsen, Grethe. "Pregnancy and Childbirth in the Medieval North: A Typology of Sources and a Preliminary Study." *Scandinavian Journal of History* 9.2 (1984), 91–111 [contains references to sources and studies used above].

Grethe Jacobsen

Profectio Danorum in Hierosolymam

Profectio Danorum in Hierosolymam is an exciting *Historia* about a group of Danish crusaders who reach Jerusalem in 1192 after dire hardships and loss of life. It has been transmitted in three MSS, all transcripts of a lost parchment MS in Lübeck. The work was written before 1202 by a "frater X canonicus" (Brother Christianus, canon), as the author calls himself in a pompous dedication to a "dominus K." Christianus displays an intimate knowledge of Norway; he quotes two Norwegian proverbs, and his nominal forms manifest Norwegian diphthongization. As a Norwegian canon, he could be from the Premonstratensian monastery in Tønsberg, come to pay a longer visit to a Danish sister monastery, such as the one at Børglum in Vendsyssel. The significance of the work consists not least in its ideal picture of the spiritual development of the new class of knights, in accordance with the crusade ideology of Pope Urban II.

Profectio Danorum begins with the author ascertaining that the world is now approaching destruction. The judgment of God is drawing near. Since all peace has disappeared, the desire to sin has increased tremendously, while all modesty is gone. The punishment is, then, that the "center of the world," Jerusalem, has been conquered by the heathens in the year 1187. The pope invokes the Third Crusade, and in the same year his edict reaches lords and sons of chieftains who are gathered at the court of King Knud VI in Odense. Esbem Snare, the brother of Archbishop Absalon, challenges the court to follow the edict of the pope and participate in "the holy war" as the true defenders of "Christianity" against the infidels. His challenge takes the form of an appeal to national and historical consciousness by conjuring up the heroic past of the Danes: as defenders attached to the bodyguard of the Greek emperor, as Langobards, the conquerers of the Roman Empire, and as the conquerers of Normandy, England, Norway, and Vendland.

Fifteen housecarls follow his suggestion. Through Norway, where there is trouble in the large, drunken city of Bergen, and where several Norwegian crusaders join, the Danes venture out onto the ocean in their open boats and sail toward Jerusalem. The voyage follows a dramatic course, and many perish during a raging storm, here brilliantly, if bombastically, described by the author. The rest continue overland to Venice and from there by boat to the Holy Land. Here, however, an armistice has been agreed upon, so the crusaders must content themselves with being redirected to the holy places as mourning tourists. The climax of the journey becomes instead the reception at the court of the emperor in Constantinople, and especially the moving encounter with the gigantic portrait of "the Holy Mother of God," which is carried through the city.

Profectio Danorum sometimes employs a twofold biblical interpretation and has an allegorical character. It can be interpreted allegorically as the history of the Danish warrior: from Viking, with material and honor-bound objectives, to his debacle as ruler of the oceans. After that, the men revive "that old seed from the times of the ancient Church, that all things should be common to them, all according to the need to each one." They continue as Christian knights who have been saved from the raging elements by God, and as members of the European community in the struggle of Christianity against the infidels. Finally, in the presence of the Virgin Mary's portrait, they attain spiritual insight as warriors.

Ed.: Gertz, M. Cl., ed. *Scriptores minores historiæ Danicæ medii ævi* 2. Copenhagen: Gad, 1922; rpt. Copenhagen: Selskabet for udgivelse af kilder til dansk historie, 1970. **Tr.**: Olrik, Jørgen. *Krøniker fra Valdemarstiden.* Copenhagen: Schønberg, 1900–01; Svara, B. *Jorsal-ferda åt Danene.* Norrøne bokverk, 31. Oslo: Det norske samlaget, 1934; Kværndrup, Sigurd, ed. *Antologi af nordisk litteratur. 1: 800–1300.* 2nd ed. Copenhagen: Samleren, 1985. **Lit.**: Riant, Paul. *Skandinavernes Korstog og Andagtsreiser til Palæstina (1000–1350).* Copenhagen: Schubothe, 1868; Skånland, Vegard. *Einige Bemerkungen zu der Historia de Profectione Danorum in Hierosolyman. 1: Mandant und Verfasser; 2: Textkritisches.* Symbolae Osloenses, 33 and 36. Oslo: Fabritius, 1957, pp. 137–55 (vol. 33); Oslo: Universitetsforlaget, 1960, pp. 99–115 (vol. 36); Kaspersen, Søren, et al., eds. *Dansk litteraturhistorie 1: Fra runer til ridderdigtning o. 800–1480.* Copenhagen: Gyldendal, 1984.

Sigurd Kværndrup

[**See also**: Geographical Literature; *Konungasögur*]

Prose Edda *see* **Snorra Edda**

Punishment *see* **Crime and Punishment**

Ragnars saga loðbrókar ("The Saga of Ragnarr Hairy-breeches"), an Old Icelandic *fornaldarsaga*, survives in two major redactions: X, dating from around 1250, and preserved fragmentarily in AM 147 4to (*ca.* 1490) with *Krákumál* incorporated in its text; and Y, dating from later in the 13th century, deriving largely from X, and preserved complete in NkS 1824b 4to (*ca.* 1400) with *Krákumál* as an appendix. The existence of a third redaction, here called the "oldest" and composed independently of *Krákumál*, may be deduced from the combined evidence of X and *Ragnarssona þáttr*, a mainly prose compilation preserved in *Hauksbók*. This oldest redaction was perhaps complete by 1230. Like Y, X appears to have been written as a sequel to *Vǫlsunga saga*, but only Y is preserved as such.

The oldest redaction clearly depended heavily on the same verse and prose oral traditions as were drawn on independently by *Krákumál*, which dwells on Ragnarr's battles, and by Saxo in his *Gesta Danorum* (Book 9), which concentrates on Ragnarr's wives (other than Áslaug) and sons. The oldest redaction described his winning of Þóra by slaying a serpent; his marriage after Þóra's death to Áslaug, daughter of Sigurðr and Brynhildr; the deaths in Sweden of his two sons by Þóra (Eiríkr and Agnarr), and the resulting revenge mission led by Áslaug and her own sons by Ragnarr (Ívarr, Bjǫrn, Hvítserkr, and Sigurðr); Ragnarr's death in King Ælla's snake pit after his abortive invasion of England; and his sons' revenge, involving the cutting of a blood-eagle on Ælla's back. Items added in X include the herdswoman Kráka at Spangereid in Norway, in whose guise Áslaug first meets Ragnarr; another son by this marriage, Rǫgnvaldr, and his heroic death; and the hostile cows slain by Ívarr. Y adds an introductory account of Áslaug-Kráka's childhood and three chapters at the end describing, respectively, the deaths and descendants of Ragnarr's sons; an exchange of verses in which two warriors recognize each other as followers of Ragnarr and Bjǫrn; and a *trémaðr* ("wooden man") on the island of Samsø, who claims in verse to have been placed and worshiped there by sons of Loðbróka.

The Faroese ballad sequence *Ragnars kvæði* (first recorded in the 18th century), dealing with Ragnar(r)'s marriages to Tóra (*sic*) and Ásla(ug), derives partly from Y, but also from oral traditions descended from those underlying the oldest redaction. From these oral traditions also derive the Norwegian and Danish ballads edited as Landstad XI and DgF 24 about a serpent-slaying exploit,

and DgF 22–23 about a princess brought up as a herdswoman before marrying a king.

Ívarr, Bjǫrn, and Sigurðr are arguably 9th-century historical figures and among the sons of a woman named Loðbróka. Since *bróka* is a *heiti* for *kona* 'woman,' *Loðbróka* may be seen as a variant of **Loþkona*, a goddess name deducible from the Swedish place-name *Locknevi* (<*Loþkonuvé*). Through confusion of her name with the common noun *loðbrók* 'hairy-breeches,' applicable as a nickname to a man (*cf. hábrók* 'high-and-mighty') as well as a woman (*cf. langbrók* 'long-legs'), and in particular to a typical warrior (witness the 7th-century bronze plates from Torslunda, Öland), Loðbróka came to be regarded as the father rather than the mother of her sons, and identified with her contemporary Reginheri, the leader of the Viking attack on Paris in 845, who, however, cannot certainly be regarded as their historical father. Legends developed about Ragnarr loðbrók, his serpent slaying, and his sons. The historical Loðbróka was soon largely forgotten, but is perhaps dimly remembered in the figure of Áslaug.

Though more anchored in history than many *fornaldarsögur*, *Ragnars saga* combines heroic and Viking legend with folktale in a manner characteristic of the genre.

Ed.: Landstad, M. B., ed. *Norske Folkeviser*. Christiania [Oslo]: Tønsberg, 1853, pp. 139–45 [edition of Landstad XI, "Lindarormen"]; *Danmarks gamle Folkeviser*. Ed. S. H. Grundtvig (vols. 1–5), Axel Olrik and Hakon Grüner-Nielsen (vols. 6–9), H. Grüner-Nielsen *et al.* (vol. 10), Thorkild Knudsen *et al.* (vol. 11), Sven H. Rossel *et al.* (vol. 12). Copenhagen: Samfundet til den danske Literaturs Fremme, 1853–1976, vol. 1, pp. 327–48 [editions of DgF 22, "Regnfred og Kragelil"; DgF 23, "Karl og Kragelil"; and DgF 24, "Ormekampen"]; Eiríkur Jónsson and Finnur Jónsson, eds. *Hauksbók, udgiven efter de Arnamagnæanske håndskrifter no. 371, 544 og 675, 4°, samt forskellige papirshåndskrifter af Det kongelige nordiske Oldskrift-selskab*. Copenhagen: Thiele, 1892–96, pp. 458–67, *cf.* pp. xci–xciii [edition of *Ragnarssona þáttr*]; Olsen, Magnus, ed. *Vǫlsunga saga ok Ragnars saga loðbrókar*. Samfund til udgivelse af gammel nordisk litteratur, 36. Copenhagen: Møller, 1906–08; Finnur Jónsson, ed. *Den norsk-islandske skjaldedigtning*. Vols. 1A-2A (tekst efter håndskrifterne) and 1B-2B (rettet tekst). Copenhagen and Christiania [Oslo]: Gyldendal, 1912–15; rpt. Copenhagen: Rosenkilde & Bagger, 1967 (A) and 1976 (B), vol. 2A, pp. 232–42; vol. 2B, pp. 251–61 [editions of the verses of the saga]; Matras, Christian, and Napoleon Djurhuus, eds. *Føroya kvæði: Corpus* *carminum Færoensium* 1–. Copenhagen: Universitets-Jubilæets danske Samfund, 1941–, vol. 1, pp. 215–43 [edition of *Ragnars kvæði*]; Bjarni Guðnason, ed. *Danakonunga sǫgur.* Íslenzk fornrit, 35. Reykjavik: Hið Íslenzka fornritafélag, 1982, pp. 78–90, cf. pp. xliv–li [partial edition of *Ragnarssona þáttr*]. **Tr.**: Prior, R. C. Alexander, M. D., trans. *Ancient Danish Ballads Translated from the Originals.* London and Edinburgh: Williams and Norgate; Leipzig: Hartmann, 1860, vol. 1, pp. 246–68 [translations of DgF 22, "Regnfred og Kragelil"; DgF 23, "Karl og Kragelil"; and DgF 24, "Ormekampen"]; Smith-Dampier, E. M., trans. *Sigurd the Dragon-Slayer: A Faroese Ballad-Cycle.* Oxford: Blackwell, 1934; rpt. New York: Kraus, 1969, pp. 135–52 [translation of *Ragnars kvæði*]; Schlauch, Margaret, trans. *The Saga of the Volsungs. The Saga of Ragnar Lodbrok Together with The Lay of Kraka.* Scandinavian Classics, 35. New York: American-Scandinavian Foundation; Norton; London: Allen and Unwin, 1930, pp. 185–256, cf. pp. xxxi–xxxix. **Bib.**: Halldór Hermannsson. *Bibliography of the Mythical-Heroic Sagas (Fornaldarsögur).* Islandica, 5. Ithaca: Cornell University Library, 1912, pp. 34–6, 39; Halldór Hermannsson. *The Sagas of the Kings (Konunga Sögur) and the Mythical-Heroic Sagas (Fornaldar Sögur): Two Bibliographical Supplements.* Islandica, 26. Ithaca: Cornell University Press, 1937, pp. 60–1. **Lit.**: Smith, A. H. "The Sons of Ragnar Lothbrok." *Saga-Book of the Viking Society* 11 (1935), 173–91; McTurk, Rory. "The Relationship of *Ragnars saga loðbrókar* to *Þiðriks saga af Bern.*" In *Sjötíu ritgerðir helgaðar Jakobi Benediktssyni 20 júlí 1977.* 2 vols. Ed. Einar G. Pétursson and Jónas Kristjánsson. Reykjavik: Stofnun Árna Magnússonar, 1977, vol. 2, pp. 568–85; McTurk, Rory. "An Irish Analogue to the Kráka-episode of *Ragnars saga loðbrókar.*" *Éigse: A Journal of Irish Studies* 17 (1978), 277–96; Wormald, C. Patrick. "Viking Studies: Whence and Whither?" In *The Vikings.* Ed. R. T. Farrell. London and Chichester: Phillimore, 1982, pp. 128–53 [esp. pp. 141–4]; Frank, Roberta. "Viking Atrocity and Skaldic Verse: The Rite of the Blood-eagle." *English Historical Review* 99 (1984), 332–43; Bjarni Einarsson. "De Normannorum atrocitate, or on the Execution of Royalty by the Aquiline Method." *Saga-Book of the Viking Society* 22 (1986), 79–82; Frank, Roberta. "The Blood-eagle Again." *Saga-Book of the Viking Society* 22 (1988), 287–9; McTurk, R. W. *Studies in Ragnars saga loðbrókar and Its Major Scandinavian Analogues.* Medium Ævum Monographs (New Series), 15. Oxford: Society for the Study of Mediæval Languages and Literature, 1991.

Rory McTurk

[**See also:** Ballads; *Fornaldarsögur*; *Hauksbók*; *Heiti*; *Krákumál*; Saxo Grammaticus; Vǫlsung-Niflung Cycle; *Vǫlsunga saga*]

Ragnarsdrápa *see* **Bragi Boddason**

Reginsmál and **Fáfnismál** ("The Speech of Reginn" and "The Speech of Fáfnir") are the titles given by editors to a section of text in the *Codex Regius* of the *Poetic Edda* that follows *Grípisspá.* The division of this material into two separate texts is entirely the work of editors and based solely on evidence from late paper MSS; the *Codex Regius* contains only a faded title, which the Neckel/Kuhn edition reads as *Frá Sigurði*, introducing the entire section, and the designation *Capitulum* preceding the prose description of Sigurðr's victory over the sons of Hundingr in *Reginsmál.* Both texts are a mixture of prose and verse used to summarize the action, and verse used for the dialogues; most of the verse is in *ljóðaháttr* meter, although there are a few stanzas in *fornyrðislag.*

The story told by these texts covers Sigurðr's youth. *Reginsmál* tells of the encounter of the gods Óðinn, Hœnir, and Loki with Hreiðmarr and his sons. Seeing an otter eating on a riverbank, the gods kill and skin it, and show its pelt to their host Hreiðmarr, who reveals himself as the father of the otter and demands monetary compensation or else threatens death to the three gods. Loki travels back to the river and catches a dwarf, Andvari, living there in the shape of a fish. Andvari, in turn, is forced to redeem his life by surrendering his considerable gold treasure, including a potent ring, but not without pronouncing a curse of death to subsequent owners of the treasure. This curse is repeated by Loki, as the gods hand over the gold and ring to Hreiðmarr. Hreiðmarr's son Fáfnir kills him for the gold, and, refusing a share to his brother Reginn, transforms himself into a dragon and hoards the treasure. Reginn rears Sigurðr and incites him to kill Fáfnir. After successfully avenging the death of his father, Sigmundr, Sigurðr slays the dragon with a sword forged from the remnants of his father's weapon. *Fáfnismál* contains a brief prose description of the dragonslaying and a long dialogue in verse between the dying Fáfnir and his slayer, in which Fáfnir repeats the curse on the treasure. Birds then advise Sigurðr to kill Reginn as well, take the treasure, and set off to seek both the shield-maiden on the mountain and the beautiful daughter of King Gjúki.

Although the legend of Sigurd is known throughout the medieval Germanic literary world, this particular sequence of events is unique to the Norse tradition. The tale is summarized in Snorri's *Edda* (*Skáldskaparmál*), which includes stanzas 32 and 33 of *Fáfnismál*, expanded in the *Vǫlsunga saga*, which includes stanzas 1, 2, 6, and 18 of *Reginsmál*, and occurs in a cycle of Faroese ballads, the *Sjúrðarkvæði.* The German tradition, represented by the *Nibelungenlied* and *Þiðreks saga*, contains a dragon- or serpent-slaying episode, but no story of the gods' ransom of their lives. In the Old English poem *Beowulf*, the dragonslaying is attributed to Sigemund/Sigurðr. If the legend of Sigurðr originated in Germany, as is generally agreed, then the Norse version of the origin of the treasure and the specific details of the dragon fight can be considered innovations. The motif of a great hero slaying a dragon or other monster is common in Indo-European mythological tradition; the addition of the gods' adventures to the story may be attributed to a technique much employed in the *Edda* of linking divine and heroic legend. Snorri told the tale to explain why gold is called "the otter's ransom."

Scholars can do no more than speculate on the date and form of the original texts. In their present form, the texts date from the second half of the 13th century, when the *Codex Regius* was written. However, Heusler (1819) suggested that *Reginsmál* and *Fáfnismál* developed out of two earlier hypothetical poems, one dealing with the hoard (*Hortlied*), the other telling how Sigurðr took revenge for his father's death (*Vaterrachelied*). To explain variation in the meter, Andersson (1980) proposed that yet a third poem in *fornyrðislag* surveying the events of the story may have existed, and that an early redactor combined the two sources where he saw fit. Arguing the case for artistic unity, Kragerud (1981) considers the variation in meter as a stylistic technique and examines the catechism, gnomes, and prophecy contained in the dialogues against the background of other thematically similar eddic poems, such as *Hávamál*, *Vafþrúðnismál*, *Grímnismál*, and *Baldrs draumar.*

Ed.: Neckel, Gustav, ed. *Edda: Die Lieder des Codex Regius nebst verwandten Denkmälern. I: Text.* 5th ed. rev. Hans Kuhn. Heidelberg: Winter, 1983. **Tr.**: Hollander, Lee M., trans. *The Poetic Edda, Trans-*

lated with an Introduction and Explanatory Notes. 2nd rev. ed. Austin: University of Texas Press, 1962; rpt. 1988, pp. 216–32. **Bib.**: Harris, Joseph. "Eddic Poetry." In *Old Norse–Icelandic Literature: A Critical Guide.* Ed. Carol J. Clover and John Lindow. Islandica, 45. Ithaca and London: Cornell University Press, 1985, pp. 145, 151. **Lit.**: Heusler, Andreas. "Altnordische Dichtung und Prosa von Jung Sigurd." In *Sitzungsberichte der Preussischen Akademie der Wissenschaften,* phil.-hist. classe 1919, pp. 162–95; rpt. in his *Kleine Schriften.* 2 vols. Ed. Helga Reuschel. Berlin: de Gruyter, 1969, vol. 1, pp. 26–64; Andersson, Theodore M. *The Legend of Brynhild.* Islandica, 43. Ithaca and London: Cornell University Press, 1980, pp. 84–99; Kragerud, Alf. "De mytologiske spørsmål i Fåvnesmål." *Arkiv för nordisk filologi* 96 (1981), 9–48.

Kaaren Grimstad

[**See also:** *Baldrs draumar; Codex Regius;* Eddic Meters; Eddic Poetry; *Grímnismál; Hávamál; Snorra Edda; Þiðreks saga af Bern; Vafþrúðnismál;* Vǫlsung-Niflung Cycle; *Vǫlsunga saga*]

Religion, Pagan Scandinavian.

The pre-Christian religion or religions of Scandinavia and North Germany, especially Schleswig-Holstein, span the period from the Iron Age (*ca.* 500 B.C.) to medieval times. The Old Norse–Icelandic texts were written or recorded from the 12th to the 15th century.

There was probably no single, uniform, pagan Scandinavian religion in the sense the word "religion" has acquired in Christianity or Islam. Evidence survives for religious similarities in the areas where Germanic dialects were probably spoken, however, such as the names of some gods (*e.g.,* those contained in the designations for the days of the week). There may have been some religious continuity from the Late Bronze to Early Iron Age. (For Indo-European traces in Germanic religion, see de Vries 1956–57, Ström 1975, Polomé 1985, and Dumézil 1924, 1939, 1940, 1956a, 1956b, 1959, 1971; cf. Turville-Petre 1964, Buchholz 1968b, Clover and Lindow 1985.) Scholars should use caution in applying to Scandinavian sources theories developed in other areas. The history of research shows that such all-encompassing theories often develop a momentum of their own, not always suited to the circumstances of a particular time and place (de Vries 1956–57: 1.54 ff., Buchholz 1968b, 1972a, 1972b, 1975).

The sources. The sources on which most handbooks are based are medieval Icelandic MSS, containing prose narratives and verse of different kinds. This material, decisively influenced by its medieval writers or redactors, can nevertheless be used with caution and strict methodology to unravel some aspects of pagan Scandinavian religion and mythology. Some runic inscriptions from the 2nd century A.D. through the Middle Ages are also valuable as contemporary testimony of magic and religious practices, although their often fragmentary state makes interpretation difficult.

Place-name study is valuable for mapping out a "religious geography" of pagan Scandinavia. Significant for our purposes are place-names whose second component denotes a holy place or sanctuary of some kind, or a piece of land whose religious "use" or dedication is indicated by the first component being the name or designation of a god (theophorous place-names, cf. list in de Vries 1956–57: 2.475–9). Examples of second components designating pieces of land (or administrative units in the case of -*tún*) are Old Norse -*vin,* -*heimr,* -*land,* -*akr,* -*vangr,* -*ey,* -*lundr,* -*berg,* and -*sjór.* The first three, together with -*tún,* are the oldest in relative

chronology, and may have originated in the Roman Iron Age. Second components denoting a sanctuary are, for example, Old Norse -*vé,* Gothic *alhs* ("temple"; Old Norse cognates possible, but uncertain), Old Norse -*hof* ("temple, building"; late?), -*stallr* ("sacrificial altar"), -*hǫrgr* (stone heap as altar and/or supporting an idol), -*hjallr* (a platform or scaffold), and -*stafr* ("staff"; idol?). The distribution of such names in the Scandinavian countries and regions varies widely. Furthermore, the exact locations to which such names refer may be unknown or may have shifted in the course of prehistory. Cooperation with other disciplines is thus essential.

Archaeology is indispensable to any account of pagan Scandinavian religion. Apart from the general sociological significance of settlement excavations, cemeteries and other burials can sometimes provide examples of beliefs and customs; witness, for example, grave goods, the "Charon's coin" (placed in the dead person's mouth to pay for the journey to the beyond), burial sacrifices (horses, even humans "accompanying" the dead), and the position of the corpse in the grave (*e.g.,* in relation to the location of the underworld). The beliefs connected with cremation or inhumation are not at all clear, nor are the reasons for the frequent shifts and transitions from one to the other.

Apart from pictorial monuments, the most important group of archaeological finds is connected with excavations of sanctuaries and places of public sacrifice of local and regional significance (Olsen 1966, Ström 1967, Glob 1969, Lidén 1969, Jankuhn 1977, Hauck 1987). Places that have yielded most in this respect are the bogs and fens in Denmark, southern Sweden, and northern Germany. This pattern may, however, be due only to the excellent conditions for preservation offered by bogs, so that our picture may well be deceptive. There are two clearly distinguished categories of finds: (1) men and women killed in various ways and then thrown or submerged in the lake or bog, sometimes with precautions to prevent them from "rising" (*e.g.,* fixing the corpse to the ground by a kind of scaffold), and (2) the great bog sacrifices (Celtic and Roman Iron Ages) of partly agricultural, partly aristocratic-warlike character (Thorsberg in northern Schleswig-Holstein; Nydam, Vimose, Ejsbøl, Kragehul, Illerup, and Rappendam in Denmark; Skedemosse, Röekillorna, and Gårdlösa in Sweden; and Oberdorla in Thuringia, Germany). The excavations of sacrificial places like these have considerably advanced our knowledge of public cult and sacrifice in early Germanic times.

Spectacular advances have been made since about 1970 in the field of pictorial monuments, such as the Migration Age gold bracteates, together with about 2,500 rectangular "guldgubber," and, to a lesser degree, the Gotland picture stones with their scenes from cult and heroic legend. There are also pictorial weavings (Oseberg, Överhogdal) and statues of gods, from large wooden idols to small metal "pocket gods." The wooden idols were occasionally found near or in a heap of stones reminiscent of the *hǫrgr.* Furthermore, there are the scenes on the sacrificial kettle from Gundestrup, thought to be of Celtic provenance, and on the now-lost golden horns from Gallehus, with a Germanic inscription, possibly influenced by Celtic conceptions. The Late Bronze Age rock carvings have recently been compared with Celtic material, such as horned gods and the cult of the head (see Görman 1987 and also Buchholz 1984 on other Celtic influences).

Apart from the Gotland stones, only some of which have been convincingly "read," the most significant subgroup comprises the roughly 900 gold bracteates, made from almost 500 different dies. The complicated systems of religious beliefs and cults that must have been prevalent in Migration Age South Scandinavia are embodied in these amulets, which probably were made in some of the main sanctuaries (*e.g.*, in Odense, Old Norse *Óðinsvé*). These small works of art were deciphered only recently with the aid of advanced photographic and enlargement techniques (Hauck 1970). They show a remarkable continuity between medieval Old Norse word traditions and Migration Age beliefs, as well as significant traits not exhibited in the medieval texts, though this fact does not necessarily mean they were then unknown. One central religious complex is connected with the god Óðinn and his characteristics, and centers on shamanism as a widespread cluster of techniques establishing contact with the supernatural world, a contact indispensable to any archaic religion (Buchholz 1968, 1984, Hauck 1970, 1980). For cultic phenomena, the data at our disposal are incomplete and fragmentary.

Sacred localities. There are two etymologically distinct Germanic and Old Norse groups of terms denoting the concept of "holy." One is Old Norse *heilagr* (adj.). This word clearly indicates a sacrality referring to the gods. Some early attestations of the word prove this denotation: *heilagt tafn* ("the holy sacrifice," *i.e.*, the god Baldr; Úlfr Uggason, *Húsdrápa*, st. 9); *heilagt full Hrafnásar* ("the holy cup of the Raven-God," *i.e.*, the mead of poetry; Hofgarða-Refr, st. 2); and *heilagt land* ("the holy land," *i.e.*, the realm of the gods; *Grímnismál*, st. 4). *Helgi* denotes (1) holiness, inviolability (*hofshelgi* 'holiness of the temple,' *þinghelgi* 'holiness of the assembly'), and is (2) a personal name of kings and heroes, which must indicate some kind of "holiness," for example, that due to holding an office ("sacral kingship"?) or having been dedicated to a god.

The second group of terms appears as the Old Norse noun *vé* and the verb *vígja*. *Vé* clearly has the meaning "sanctuary," which is attested not only from early skaldic poetry onward, but also in place-names (mostly theophorous ones), where it denotes the sanctuary of a god (*e.g.*, *Óðinsvé*, "Óðinn's sanctuary," Odense on Funen, Denmark). The runic stone of Glavendrup, Funen (10th century), probably mentions a *kuþa uia* (Old Norse *goða véa*), a "priest of the sanctuaries." The verb *vígja* is used in the Christian sense of "to bless, consecrate." The exact connotations of this word are not clear (was there Christian influence in the inscriptions?), nor is the "sanctifying" of dead men as a protection against them (*Hervarar saga*), but the transfer of some power may well be the intention. Such an interpretation suggests magical associations.

Sacred localities, which include sanctuaries and temples, are as a rule situated near some special feature of the landscape, as a mountain, grave mound (some prehistoric burials are of considerable size), stone, tree, spring, or lake. It is quite conceivable that contact with the unseen power was thought to be facilitated by elevation (mountains) or subterranean connections (wells, lakes, also trees and stones). The dead in their burial mounds also provided a separate "point of contact" with the beyond. Óðinn was apparently also worshiped on mountains. Wells and lakes are probably the most important group of sacred localities, evident mainly from excavations of South Scandinavian bog and lake sanctuaries (Jankuhn 1970), but also, for example, from Adam of Bremen's *Gesta Hammaburgensis ecclesiae pontificum* (4:26, 27, and schol. 138, 139, 141), which mentions human sacrifices in a well for oracular purposes (schol. 138). Near that well there stood a huge perennially green tree said to be of unknown origin (schol. 138). Forests could also be regarded as sacred (*e.g.*, place-names

in -*lundr*). Cultivated fields very probably were used for seasonal vegetation or fertility cults (*cf.*, *e.g.*, place-names in -*akr* and -*vin*) linked by the place-names to specific gods connected with fertility (Njǫrðr, Freyr, Freyja).

It makes sense to assume that a sanctuary was somehow demarcated in the landscape. This demarcation could be achieved by a fence or poles (Old Gutnish *stafgarþr*?). The one category of "nature sanctuaries" best investigated by archaeologists comprises lake or bog sanctuaries (Jankuhn 1970). Such sanctuaries are known in South Scandinavia and North Germany from the Bronze Age until just after the Late Roman Iron Age. Apart from different kinds of sacrifices, many contain idols, some of which were still standing in or on stone heaps. Such a stone heap was probably called a *hǫrgr* in Old Norse (occurring also in place-names). In a most important eddic text (*Hyndluljóð*, st. 10), the goddess Freyja says of a hero:

> He a high altar made me
> of heaped stones—
> all glary have grown
> the gathered rocks
> and reddened anew them
> with neats' fresh blood;
> for ay believed Óttar
> in the ásynjur.
> (Lee M. Hollander, trans., *The Poetic Edda* [Austin: University of Texas Press, 1962; rpt. 1988], p. 131)

The *hǫrgr* was thus intimately connected with bloody sacrifices and apparently also with fire (*cf.* "glary" rocks). We do know that sacrifices connected with fire were also performed in the sanctuaries of Gårdlösa and Röekillorna (Jankuhn 1970).

Structures of some kind, such as enclosures or a roof, could be erected so that the *hǫrgr* was the center (*cf. Grímnismál*, st. 16, where the god Njǫrðr rules over a "high-timbered *hǫrgr*"). Such structures could be small, or larger in the case of more important sanctuaries that could sometimes be forerunners of a Christian church (Lidén 1969, Olsen 1966); examples may be the temple of Uppsala as described by Adam of Bremen (Turville-Petre 1964: 244 ff.), or the temple of Mære in Trøndelag (Lidén 1969), where the post holes were apparently "consecrated" by burying amulets in them. An early Christian church was not always erected on exactly the same site as a pagan temple, and one must bear in mind that a temple building was just one of the many forms of sanctuary.

Quite a number of pagan Scandinavian idols have been excavated (de Vries 1956–57, Jankuhn 1970, and particularly Hauck 1976), dating from the Bronze Age to early-medieval times. Most are archaic wooden sculptures, distinguished from a mere pole by faces and distinct sexual attributes. One (Rude Eskildstrup, 6th century A.D.) displays a triple neck ring, perhaps a ruler's attribute. Medieval historical and literary sources also mention idols of gods with specific attributes. It is possible that some idols had clothes put on them for specific occasions. One saga describes the anointing of idols, and later folklore also preserves traces of sacrifices to wooden figures. Idols may have been carried around in processions.

Old Norse *stallr* or *stalli* was apparently a general term for the location where the sacrifice took place, a kind of pagan "altar" about which we do not know anything exact (*cf.*, however, the *hǫrgr* above, and the "altar" of Stora Hammars, pl. 5 in Buchholz 1972: 26). In *Ynglingatal* (st. 12), a king is called *vǫrðr véstalls* ("the guardian of the holy altar"). An important requisite was the ring, apparently both part of the priest's attire and also kept on or near the altar. Oaths were sworn "on the ring" (perhaps touching it). Such rings could be dedicated to specific gods (Þórr, Ullr). Another important cult object was the kettle, evidently necessary for cooking sacrificial meat and for collecting the blood. Such kettles could also be called *hlautbolli* ("oracular bowl"), because the blood could be used for oracles.

Sacrifice, animal and human. The information provided by our sources is insufficient to establish a sacrality or worship of animals. Some animals, such as the bear, were probably regarded with awe. Gods, especially Óðinn, could appear in animal shape (bear, horse, snake, boar, bird, *etc.*), as could warriors or magicians through special procedures. It was also thought possible to have sexual relations with such real or imaginary animals.

The sacrificial animal *par excellence* of the warrior and aristocratic class was the horse. Eating horse meat was part of the sacrificial meal, and was expressly allowed to continue after the conversion of Iceland. Aristocratic burials and the mass sacrifices in Danish bogs contain numerous horses. Horse racing connected with burial ceremonies and/or periodic cults could explain place-names like *Skedevi* and *Skedemosse* (Old Norse *skeið* 'race, race course') and even some Bronze Age pictorial monuments (as in the Kivik grave).

In the "ordinary," agricultural milieu, the main sacrificial animal was the sheep (Old Norse *sauðr*). It was cooked (Old Norse *sjóða* 'to cook': *sauðr*) and eaten as part of the sacrificial meal. A text from medieval Gotland informs us that smaller cult communities were called *suþnautar* 'cooking companions.'

Images of such animals as snakes and ravens served as insignia in battle. It is quite likely that weapons were thought to have, or to be given (by naming or inscribing them), attributes of beasts or birds of prey as "attackers." Weapons could also be given to kings and heroes by gods, especially Óðinn.

The purposes of a sacrifice were mainly to placate the gods (who were thought to be dependent on the sacrifices), to avert catastrophes, to secure success in war, and to procure "a good harvest and peace" (Old Norse *ár ok friðr*). This practice was often connected with the universal desire to know the future. Predictions could be based on the behavior of the victim or on properties of its blood or specific organs. The etymological connection between German *Los*, English *lot*, and Old Norse *hlaut* 'sacrificial blood' makes it reasonable to assume the casting of lots and performing of other rites to learn one's future "lot" in connection with sacrifices to which the gods were thought to be attracted.

Apart from the sacrifice itself as the main ceremony, there were most probably hymns to the gods and also dances. We only have traces: some hymns to Þórr (de Vries 1956–57) and possibly invocations of other gods (*e.g.*, *Sigrdrífumál*, sts. 3–4, possibly from a hymn to all gods?). One can speculate that there were songs to induct new priests into their office (*Hávamál*, st. 144), or to test their runic knowledge (*Hávamál*, sts. 146–63, *Sigrdrífumál*, sts. 6–13, 15–17, *etc.*). There was certainly dancing, but the written sources are almost silent (*cf.*, however, *Gesta Danorum*, Book 5:154, about the lascivious body movements connected with the cult at Uppsala). Gold bracteates show that, as in shamanic practice, dance was one of the techniques necessary to attain ecstasy (Hauck 1970, 1980, Buchholz 1968a). We can assume that the priests made use of such techniques.

Sacrifices could be inanimate (agricultural produce like butter or seed, parts of utensils like plows, horses' trappings, weap-

ons) or animate (sheep, horses, even, at important occasions, human beings). Animal sacrifices were connected with a sacrificial meal establishing a communion among the participants. The sacrifice itself could apparently be conducted with the blood flowing, or without, by choking, to judge from the sacrificial terminology (Jankuhn 1970). Some parts of the animal, such as heads and hooves, were reserved for the gods. The bones were sometimes split to get at the marrow, sometimes left intact (perhaps to "resuscitate" the animal in order to secure abundance of meat). Drinking was evidently connected with the sacrificial meal; the drinks could be dedicated to specific gods.

There is abundant archaeological evidence of human sacrifices in pagan Scandinavia in the bog and lake sanctuaries (Jankuhn 1970). Adam of Bremen, *Guta saga*, and the *Gutalag* are also considered reliable witnesses. People were killed by hanging, stabbing, drowning, or breaking of the backbone. The sacrifice was evidently not an everyday occurrence, but was linked to important occasions like ceremonies in major sanctuaries relating to "matters of state," such as successes or failures of the king, a crisis (drought, famine, invasion), or perhaps in respect of the reenactment of some primordial event, such as Baldr's death, or the creation of the world from the dismembered giant Ymir. We even have indications of ritual cannibalism (splitting of human bones in some early sanctuaries). Human sacrifice to Óðinn is depicted on the Gotland picture stone of Stora Hammars (Buchholz 1972b: 26), and several times described or alluded to in the literature (*e.g.*, *Gautreks saga*, ch. 7).

Celebrations could be conducted every nine years, as at Uppsala and Lejre. In the course of one year, there were probably three main sacrifices with local and regional differences regarding the exact time: in autumn, in midwinter (Yule), and at the beginning of spring. In some cases, there was a fourth sacrifice in midsummer. In the 1st century A.D., the Roman historian Tacitus (*Germania*, ch. 40) described the Danish cult of a goddess Nerthus, equated with *Terra mater*, "Mother Earth." The idol is carried around the country in a wagon; finally everything is ritually washed, and the assisting slaves are drowned. The name "Nerthus" is connected with Old Norse *Njǫrðr*, a male god also connected with fertility (Beck 281).

The question of priesthood. There has been some controversy over whether there were Germanic and pagan Scandinavian priests. Much of that controversy, however, revolves around questions of priesthood as a sacral "office" in the sense of the more fixed social and religious structures of India and pagan Gaul, with their rigidly separated castes and highly organized priestly class. There certainly were pagan Scandinavian priests in the sense of persons, male and female, with priestly functions. Such priests are mentioned by, among others, Tacitus (*Germania*, chs. 7, 10, 11, and 40), and quite frequently in Icelandic sagas. The term is Old Norse *goði*, unambiguously connected with *goð* 'god.' The dignity of *goði* could be inherited, and was perhaps originally connected with ownership of the place of sacrifice. Besides the *goðar*, the sagas mention *gyðjur* 'priestesses.' The texts support the assumption that these people were particularly active in fertility cults. On the function of the 10th-century *goði*, see Jón H. Aðalsteinsson (1985).

Also significant are place-names, not only theophorous place-names connected with important administrative centers (Hellberg 1986; note the connection here between "secular" and sacral), but also names containing apparently priestly designations.

Furthermore, we have to consider some runic inscriptions, such as that at Glavendrup (10th century): *kuþa uia* (Old Norse *goða véa*), "the priest of the sanctuaries"; Rök (early 9th century): *uiauari*, "the guardian of the sanctuaries"; Snoldelev (early 9th century): *þulaʀ a Salhaugum*, "of the 'speaker' at S." (see below); and Nordhuglen (*ca.* A.D. 400): *ek gudija ungandir*, "I, the priest, immune against sorcery."

The priest in this inscription cannot be harmed by evil sorcery because he is the stronger magician. The Old Norse word *þulr* 'speaker' points in the same direction: the speaker of magical and sacral formulas, often at assemblies. *Hávamál* (st. 111) expresses it thus (Buchholz 1984): "It is time to speak from the speaker's chair, at the spring of knowledge from the past. I saw and was silent, I saw and took thought; I listened to the speeches of men. I heard them consider the mysteries of the past, nor were they silent about the future, at the High One's hall, in the High One's hall."

The designation *þulr*, the inscription of Nordhuglen, numerous aspects of the cult of Óðinn (Buchholz 1984), the "magic" described in Old Norse sources (Buchholz 1968a), and the scenes on gold bracteates (Hauck 1970, 1980) all point in the same direction: the fundamental significance of shamanism in Old Norse religion and cult. It was essential for the person initiated into the contact with the unseen to have a command of these techniques that helped him to reach the state of ecstasy that was desirable or even necessary to perform sacrificial or other tasks most efficiently. Ecstasy as a means of establishing contact with the beyond is much older than pagan Scandinavian religion. That it remained so much alive in pagan Scandinavian pictorial monuments and even in texts committed to parchment in the 13th century is proof of its fundamental significance in religious anthropology.

Bib.: Buchholz, Peter. *Bibliographie zur alteuropäischen Religionsgeschichte 1954–1964: Literatur zu den antiken Rand- und Nachfolgekulturen im aussermediterranen Europa unter besonderer Berücksichtigung der nichtchristlichen Religionen.* Arbeiten zur Frühmittelalterforschung, 2. Berlin: de Gruyter, 1967; vol. 2. Ed. Jürgen Ahrendts. Berlin and New York: de Gruyter, 1974 [bibliography for 1965–1969]; vol. 3. Ed. Wilfried Flüchter. Berlin and New York: de Gruyter, 1985 [bibliography for 1970–1975]; Lindow, John. *Scandinavian Mythology: An Annotated Bibliography.* Garland Folklore Bibliographies, 13. New York and London: Garland, 1988. **Lit.**: Dumézil, Georges. *Le festin d'immortalité: Étude de mythologie comparée indo-européenne.* Annales du Musée Guimet, bibliothèque d'études, 34. Paris: Geuthner, 1924; Olsen, Magnus. *Farms and Fanes of Ancient Norway: The Place-Names of a Country Discussed in Their Bearings on Social and Religious History.* Institutet for sammenlignende kulturforskning, ser. A: Forelesinger, 9. Oslo: Aschehoug; Leipzig: Harrassowitz; Paris: Champion, 1928; Dumézil, Georges. *Mythes et dieux des germains: Essai d'interprétation comparative.* Mythes et religions, 1. Paris: Presses Universitaires de France, 1939; Dumézil, Georges. *Mitra-Varuna: Essai sur deux représentations indo-européennes de la souveraineté.* Bibliothèque de l'Ecole des Hautes Etudes, Sciences Religieuses, 46. Paris: Presses Universitaires de France, 1940; Dumézil, Georges. *Aspects de la fonction guerrière chez les indo-européens.* Bibliothèque de l'Ecole des Hautes Etudes, Sciences Religieuses, 68. Paris: Presses Universitaires de France, 1956 [1956a]; Dumézil, Georges. "L'étude comparée des religions des peuples indo-européens." *Beiträge zur Geschichte der deutschen Sprache und Literatur* (Tübingen) 78 (1956), 173–80 [1956b]; Vries, Jan de. *Altgermanische Religionsgeschichte.* 2 vols. 2nd ed. Grundriss der germanischen Philologie, 12.1–2. Berlin: de Gruyter, 1956–57; Dumézil, Georges. *Les dieux des germains: Essai sur la formation de la religion scandinave.* Mythes et religions, 38. Paris: Presses Universitaires de France, 1959; Turville-Petre, E. O. G. *Myth & Religion of the North: The Religion of Ancient Scandinavia.* New York: Holt, Rinehart and Winston, 1964; rpt. Westport: Greenwood, 1975; Olsen, Olaf. "Hørg, hov og kirke. Historiske og arkæologiske vikingetidsstudier." *Aarbøger for nordisk Oldkyndighed og Historie* (1966), 1–307 [see review by C. J. Becker and A. E. Christensen in *Historisk tidsskrift* (Denmark) (1967), 439–52]; Ström, Folke. *Nordisk hedendom. Tro och sed i förkristen tid.* 2nd ed. Gothenburg: Gumpert, 1967; Buchholz, Peter. "Schamanistische Züge in der altisländischen Überlieferung." Diss. Münster, 1968 [see his "Shamanism—the Testimony of Old Icelandic Literary Tradition," *Mediaeval Scandinavia* 4 (1971), 7–20]; Buchholz, Peter. "Perspectives for Historical Research in Germanic Religion." *History of Religions* 8 (1968–69), 111–38; Glob, P. V. *The Bog People: Iron Age Man Preserved.* Trans. Rupert Bruce-Mitford. Ithaca and London: Cornell University Press, 1969; Jankuhn, Herbert, ed. *Vorgeschichtliche Heiligtümer und Opferplätze in Mittel- und Nordeuropa: Bericht über ein Symposium in Reinhausen bei Göttingen in der Zeit vom 14. bis 16. Oktober 1968.* Abhandlungen der Akademie der Wissenschaften in Göttingen, Phil.-hist. Klasse, 3, Nr. 74. Göttingen: Vandenhoeck & Ruprecht, 1970; Hauck, Karl. *Goldbrakteaten aus Sievern: Spätantike Amulett-Bilder der "Dania Saxonica" und der Sachsen-"Origo" bei Widukind von Corvey.* Münstersche Mittelalter-Schriften, 1. Munich: Fink, 1970; Dumézil, Georges. *Mythe et épopée. Types épiques indo-européens: Un héros, un sorcier, un roi.* [n.p]: Gallimard, 1971; Buchholz, Peter. "Im Himmel wie auf Erden: Gedanken zu Heiligtum und Kultprovinz in der frühgeschichtlichen Religion Skandinaviens." *Acta Germanica* 7 (1972), 1–17 [1972a]; Buchholz, Peter. "The Religious Geography of Pagan Scandinavia." *Mediaeval Scandinavia* 5 (1972), 89–91 [1972b]; Stemshaug, Ola. *Namn i Noreg.* Oslo: Det Norske Samlaget, 1973; Buchholz, Peter. "Forschungsprobleme germanischer Religionsgeschichte." *Christiana Albertina—Forschungsberichte und Halbjahrsschrift der Universität Kiel,* N.F., 2 (1975), 19–29; Ström, Åke V., and Haralds Biezais. *Germanische und baltische Religion.* Stuttgart: Kohlhammer, 1975 [to be used with caution]; Hauck, Karl. "Bilddenkmäler zur Religion." In *Reallexikon der germanischen Altertumskunde* 2. Ed. Heinrich Beck et al. Berlin and New York: de Gruyter, 1976, pp. 577–90; Jankuhn, Herbert. "Archäologische Beobachtungen zur Religion der festländischen Angeln." In *Studien zur Sachsenforschung.* Hildesheim: Lax, 1977, pp. 215–34; Hauck, Karl. "Brakteatenikonologie." In *Reallexikon der germanischen Altertumskunde* 3 (1978), 361–401; Sandnes, Jørn, and Ola Stemshaug. *Norsk Stadnamnleksikon.* Oslo: Det Norske Samlaget, 1980; Hauck, Karl. *Überregionale Sakralorte und die vorchristliche Ikonographie der Seegermanen.* Nachrichten der Akademie der Wissenschaften in Göttingen 1. Phil.-hist. Kl. 1981, Nr. 8. Göttingen: Vandenhoeck & Ruprecht, 1981 [esp. pp. 205–53 (pls. 1–17)]; Boyer, Régis. *Yggdrasill: La religion des anciens Scandinaves.* Bibliothèque historique. Paris: Payot, 1981; Jørgensen, Bent. *Dansk Stednavneleksikon.* 3 vols. Copenhagen: Gyldendal, 1981–83; Buchholz, Peter, "Odin: Celtic and Siberian Affinities of a Germanic Deity." *Mankind Quarterly* 25 (1984), 427–37; *Frühmittelalterliche Studien* 18 (1984) [entire volume treats sacrifice in prehistoric central and northern Europe]; Hauck, Karl. "Varianten des göttlichen Erscheinungsbildes im kultischen Vollzug erhellt mit einer ikonographischen Formenkunde des heidnischen Altares." *Frühmittelalterliche Studien* 18 (1984), 266–313 [pls. 11–20]; Dalberg, Vibeke, et al., eds. *Bebyggelsers og bebyggelsenavnes alder. NORNAs niende symposium i København 25–27 oktober 1982.* Uppsala: NORNA, 1984; Jón Hnefill Aðalsteinsson. "Blót and Þing: The Function of the Tenth Century goði." *Temenos* 21 (1985), 23–38; Moltke, Erik. *Runes and Their Origin: Denmark and Elsewhere.* Trans. Peter G. Foote. Copenhagen: National Museum of Denmark, 1985; Polomé, Edgar C.

"Germanic Religion and the Indo-European Heritage." *Mankind Quarterly* 26 (1985), 19–55; Clover, Carol J., and John Lindow, eds. *Old Norse–Icelandic Literature: A Critical Guide*. Islandica, 45. Ithaca and London: Cornell University Press, 1985; *Die Goldbrakteaten der Völkerwanderungszeit. 1.1: Einleitung; 1.2: Ikonographischer Katalog* (Text); *1.3: Ikonographischer Katalog* (Plates). Münstersche Mittelalter-Schriften, 24. Munich: Fink: 1985; *Nordisk samarbeidsnemd for humanistisk forskning (NOS-H). Innstilling om førkristen nordisk religion*. Oslo: Norges Allmennvitenskapelige Forskningsråd, 1986 [unpublished MS]; Beck, Heinrich, ed. *Germanenprobleme in heutiger Sicht*. Berlin and New York: de Gruyter, 1986; Hellberg, Lars. "Hedendomens spår i uppländska ortnamn." *Ortnamnssällskapets i Uppsala Årsskrift* (1986), pp. 40–71; Polomé, Edgar C. "Germanic Religion." In *The Encyclopedia of Religion* 5. Ed. Mircea Eliade. New York: Macmillan, 1987, pp. 521–36; Sawyer, Birgit, *et al.*, eds. *The Christianization of Scandinavia: Report of a Symposium Held at Kungälv, Sweden 4–9 August 1985*. Alingsås: Viktoria, 1987; Hauck, Karl. "Gudme in der Sicht der Brakteatenforschung." *Frühmittelalterliche Studien* 21 (1987), 147–81 [pls. 22–5]; Görman, Marianne. "Nordiskt och keltiskt. Sydskandinavisk religion under yngre bronsålder och keltisk järnålder." Diss. University of Lund, 1987; Edsman, Carl Martin. "Opening Address." In *Old Norse and Finnish Religions and Cultic Place-Names: Based on Papers Read at the Symposium on Encounters Between Religions in Old Nordic Times and on Cultic Place-Names Held at Åbo, Finland, on the 19th–21st of August 1987*. Ed. Tore Ahlbäck. Scripta Instituti Donneriani Aboensis, 13. Stockholm: Almqvist & Wiksell, 1990.

Peter Buchholz

[See also: Adam of Bremen; Baldr; Burial Mounds and Burial Practices; Freyr and Freyja; *Gautreks saga*; *Goði*; Graves; *Grímnismál*; *Guta saga*; *Hávamál*; *Hervarar saga ok Heiðreks konungs*; *Hyndluljóð*; Loki; Magic; Mythology; Óðinn; Oseberg; Place-names; Runes and Runic Inscriptions; Rök Stone; Saxo Grammaticus; *Sigrdrífumál*; *Snorra Edda*; Supernatural Beings; Temples, Heathen; Þórr; Úlfr Uggason]

Reliquaries are containers for relics of saints. The Scandinavian reliquaries can be classified in four main types: shrines of saints, *sepulchra*, portable reliquaries, and jewel reliquaries.

Shrines of saints usually consist of body-sized caskets that contain the whole body or parts of a saint. From written sources, it is known that a large number of such shrines existed in Scandinavia during the Middle Ages. From Denmark can be mentioned, for instance, the shrines of St. Kjeld in Viborg, St. Thøger in Vestervig, and St. Knud Lavard in Ringsted. In Norway, St. Óláfr's shrine in the cathedral of Trondheim was the most famous. In Sweden, the national saint, St. Erik (d. *ca.* 1160), was kept in a shrine in Uppsala cathedral; and in Vadstena, a shrine contained the body of St. Birgitta (*translatio* 1381). Only three of the body-sized shrines have survived the Lutheran Reformation. Those are St. Knud the Holy's shrine in Odense cathedral, and a similar shrine in the same church, which contained the relics of St. Alban or St. Oswald, or possibly of St. Knud's brother, Benedikt. Both shrines are made of oak and have been mounted with gilt-copper plates in repoussé technique. St. Birgitta's shrine is a 1.8-m.-long, house-shaped coffin, but all its ornaments are postmedieval.

The most frequently occurring type of reliquary is the *sepulchrum, i.e.*, the small capsule containing relics, preferably of three martyrs, which since the Council of Nicea in 787 had to be incorporated in an altar at its consecration. About fifty small leaden capsules of this type are now in the Danish National Museum. In many cases, the bone relics are preserved wrapped in silk or other precious textiles with indications of the saint's name written on a strip of parchment. Occasionally, the leaden capsule has an incised ornament or a runic inscription, for example, the one from Stokkemarke church on Lolland, *episcopus gisiko*, which refers to Bishop Gisike of Odense (1286–1304). There are also examples of capsules with magic formulas.

The portable reliquaries served in churches to house the relics and to present them on special feast days, and were often lavishly ornamented and frequently made of costly materials. House-shaped wooden caskets from the 13th century, mounted with gilt-copper plates, seem to have been particularly well preserved in the West Nordic area, with the best examples in the Danish National Museum, the University Historical Museum in Bergen, and the University Collection of Antiquities in Oslo.

From the end of the 12th century onward, and particularly during the 13th century, a considerable number of *champlevé* enamel reliquaries manufactured in Limoges, France, found their way to Scandinavia. Several completely preserved examples and many fragments, some of high quality, are now in the Danish National Museum and in the State Historical Museum in Stockholm. A few of these reliquaries have been used as portable altars, such as the 12th-century *champlevé* enamel casket found in Frøslev bog, South Jutland.

Among the portable reliquaries, a certain group can be described as "narrative." These are also often made of precious metal, with gems, jewels, and rock crystals. What makes them distinctive is that their shape reflects the part of the saint's body they contain. The head reliquaries widespread in western Europe also seem to have been common in Scandinavia, but it is most often the arm reliquary, shaped like a sleeve with an upward-pointing hand, that is mentioned. Two silver arm reliquaries, from Linköping cathedral, with relics of St. Eskil and St. Birgitta, are now in the State Historical Museum in Stockholm. An enameled arm reliquary containing relics of St. Óláfr, now in the Danish National Museum, was manufactured in Cologne around 1200, and is closely related to a St. Gereon arm reliquary preserved there. The main Scandinavian museums possess a large number of portable reliquaries of different shapes and made of different materials. The cross reliquary is the most common, but there are also examples of carved-out rock crystals.

Jewel reliquaries have likewise been preserved in large numbers, in the shape of pendants made of silver and gold, often decorated with enamel. The pictorial crosses containing a splinter of the True Cross are the most frequently encountered. The most famous among them are the Dagmar Cross, a Byzantine *cloisonné* enamel from the 12th century, found in 1685 in Queen Dagmar's grave (d. 1212) in the Benedictine abbey of Ringsted, Denmark, and the Roskilde Cross, a 12th-century South Italian encolpion with gold filigree and gems, still containing a fragment of the Cross. This reliquary was found in 1807 in a cavity in the head of the Christ figure on the late Romanesque crucifix of Roskilde cathedral, Denmark.

Lit.: Kielland, Thor. *Norsk guldsmedkunst i middelalderen*. Oslo: Steen, 1927; Ugglas, Carl R. *Bidrag till den medeltida guldsmedekonstens historia*. 2 vols. Stockholm: Wahlström & Widstrand, 1948; *Reliker* *och relikvarier från svenska kyrkor.* Stockholm: State Historical Museum, 1951 [exhibition catalogue]; Thordeman, Bengt, ed. *Erik den helige.* Stockholm: Nordisk rotogravyr, 1954; Lindblom, Andreas. *Birgittes gyllene skrin.* Stockholm: Almqvist & Wiksell, 1963; Andersson, Britt-Marie. *Émaux limousins en Suède. Les châsses, les croix.* Antikvarisk Arkiv, 69. Stockholm: Almqvist & Wiksell, 1980; Lindahl, Fritze. *Dagmarkorset, Orø- og Roskildekorset.* Copenhagen: Nationalmuseet, 1980; Liebgott, Niels-Knud. *Hellige Mænd og Kvinder.* Højbjerg: Wormianum, 1982; Lindahl, Fritze. "Hellige Olafs arm eller en anden helgens. . . ." In *Festskrift til Thelma Jexlev. Fromhed og verdslighed i middelalder og renaissance.* Ed. Ebba Waaben *et al.* Odense: Odense Universitetsforlag, 1985, pp. 45–60; Oxenvad, Niels, *et al. Knuds-bogen 1986: Studier over Knud den Hellige.* Fynske Studier, 15. Odense: Odense Bys Museer, 1986; Liebgott, Niels-Knud. *Middelalderens emaljekunst.* Copenhagen: Nationalmuseet, 1986 [English summary].

Niels-Knud Liebgott

[**See also:** Birgitta, St.; Erik, St.; Knud (Cnut), St.; Óláfr, St.; Saints' Lives; Vadstena]

Rémundar saga keisarasonar ("The Saga of Rémundr, Son of an Emperor").

Rémundr, the son of the Christian king of Saxland (Germany), is a young man well trained in both bookish and martial arts. After a feast, he dreams of a strange country with three fabulous buildings, the third of which is a castle with a revolving chamber on its top. In the dream, he sees himself exchanging rings in a wedding ceremony with a beautiful maiden, and then he is put into a golden bed with her, inside the revolving chamber. Just as they are about to embrace, he wakes up. On his finger is the ring.

In grief because of his dream, Rémundr first consoles himself with a lifelike statue of the maiden. In a fight with a giant named Eskupart, who claimed that the statue represented *his* sweetheart, Rémundr is wounded by the point of the giant's sword, which (according to Eskupart's dying curse) will remain lodged in his head until the maiden of the dream removes it.

Carried in a gold and silver chariot and called "the afflicted man of the cart" (*hinn kranki kerrumaðr*), Rémundr sets out for Africa with two companions, one of whom, Víðfǫrull, was sent by the maiden of his dream to fetch him. In Africa, he spurns the advances of the king's daughter, and as a consequence is attacked by the king's men, whom he defeats with the aid of her brother. His sickness worsens until, in India, an archbishop sends the maiden of his dream, whose name is Elína, to remove the iron piece from his head. With the aid of a stone that renders him invisible, he is able to pay nightly visits to Elína. When the prince of Sicily comes to demand her hand, Rémundr defeats him.

At the urging of the archbishop, Rémundr returns home to prepare for a proper wedding with Elína. Back in Saxland, his father has been killed and the kingdom has been overrun by pagans from Tartary and Russia, whom he defeats after lengthy fighting. With 20,000 knights, he returns to India by way of Jerusalem, marries Elína, and then returns to Saxland to be crowned.

This romantic saga dates from the middle of the 14th century, and two MS fragments from that century are preserved, as well as about forty later copies. It is the longest (372 pages in Broberg's edition) of the indigenous Icelandic *riddarasögur*, with much of its space devoted to stereotyped battle descriptions. Its plot is a bridal-quest romance, of which there are some twenty in Old Icelandic, and it shares features with *Gibbons saga, Viktors saga ok Blávus,* and *Klári saga.* Among Icelandic bridal-quests, it

has the peculiar feature of being initiated by a dream that comes to both the hero and the heroine. In this respect, it resembles the Old French prose romance *Le petit Artus de Bretagne,* with which it probably shares a source. Rémundr's quest is not generated by his passion, however, as is Arthur's. A more passive person than Elína (who sends Víðfǫrull to bring him), he is content to stay at home caressing the statue, and sets out only when wounded and in need of a cure. The motifs connected with the deviation from the French analogue (statue of the beloved, embedded sword fragment, voyage to a distant land to seek a cure for a poisoned wound) all come from the story of Tristan. But where Tristan sets out in a boat, Rémundr goes off in a cart, which suggests influence from a tale about Lancelot, the "knight of the cart."

The style is closer to that of the *Íslendingasögur* than to the "court" style of the *riddarasögur,* and the plot is well constructed, although with one weak point: until he is cured by Elína in India, Rémundr is hardly fit for the adventures he undergoes in Africa.

Ed.: Broberg, Sven Grén, ed. *Rémundar saga keisarasonar.* Samfund til udgivelse af gammel nordisk litteratur, 38. Copenhagen: Møller, 1909–12; Bjarni Vilhjálmsson, ed. *Riddarasögur.* 6 vols. Reykjavik: Íslendingasagnaútgáfan; Haukadalsútgáfan, 1949–54, vol. 5, pp. 163–339. **Lit.**: Schlauch, Margaret. "The 'Rémundar saga keisarasonar' as an Analogue of Arthur of Little Britain." *Scandinavian Studies* 10 (1929), 189–202; Einar Ól. Sveinsson. "Viktors saga ok Blávus: Sources and Characteristics." In *Viktors saga ok Blávus.* Riddarasögur, 2. Ed. Jónas Kristjánsson. Reykjavik: Handritastofnun Íslands, 1964, pp. cxxvii-cxxviii, cciv–ccvi; Schach, Paul. "Some Observations on the Influence of *Tristrams saga ok Ísöndar* on Old Icelandic Literature." In *Old Norse Literature and Mythology: A Symposium.* Ed. Edgar C. Polomé. Austin: University of Texas Press, 1968, pp. 81–129; Skårup, Povl. "Forudsætter Rémundar saga en norrøn Lancelots saga kerrumanns?" *Gripla* 4 (1980), 76–80; Hallberg, Peter. "A Group of Icelandic 'Riddarasögur' from the Middle of the Fourteenth Century." In *Les Sagas de Chevaliers (Riddarasögur). Actes de la Vᵉ Conférence Internationale sur les Sagas . . . (Toulon, Juillet 1982).* Ed. Régis Boyer. Civilisations, 10. Paris: Presses de l'Université de Paris-Sorbonne, 1985, pp. 7–53; Heinrichs, Anne. "*Amor hereos* als Gestaltungsprinzip der *Rémundar saga keisarasonar.*" *Skandinavistik* 18.2 (1988), 125–39.

Robert Cook

[**See also:** *Gibbons saga; Klári (Clari) saga; Riddarasögur; Viktors saga ok Blávus*]

Reykdœla saga (ok Víga-Skútu) ("The Saga of the People of Reykjadalr [and of Killer-Skúta]")

is preserved only in one vellum MS (AM 561 4to) from about 1400, which is now defective in the beginning and has two lacunae. But about thirty paper MSS were copied from AM 561 4to during the 17th century, and these MSS can be used to fill in the missing parts. Like all *Íslendingasögur,* *Reykdœla saga* is anonymous and poses difficulties in dating. Two proposals for its date have been made: the middle of the 13th century (Jónas Kristjánsson 1988), and between 1210 and 1220 (Hofmann 1972). The difference turns on varying opinions concerning the author's indebtedness to oral tradition.

Reykdœla saga consists of two parts connected by characters from two succeeding generations. The first part, called *Reykdœla saga* in ch. 19, is centered on Vémundr kǫgurr ("coverlet"), a young man of good family who always looks for trouble and regularly receives assistance from his wise uncle Áskell goði ("chieftain" or "priest"). Áskell is finally killed in a skirmish. In the second part, Áskell's death is avenged by his son, Skúta.

The composition of the saga is uneven, containing a string of episodes, sometimes only loosely connected, with many repetitions of motifs, mostly of a rural character. Stylistically, there are two distinctive features that do not occur in other sagas to the same degree. The first is an unusually large number of formulas, more than 100, of the type: "it is said that," "it is not told whether," and the like, which apparently point to oral tradition, but can also be considered as a written literary device (Andersson 1966). A special type of these formulas contains references to variants of tradition, for example: "Some people say what is told here: that it was an axe and was called Fluga, and some people say that it was a sword and was called Fluga. But whatever it was, Skúta carried that weapon always, and so it was now this time." The narrator knew two traditions, originally oral, reports both, and is uncertain about which to follow.

The second distinctive characteristic is the use of indirect speech; only 8.5 percent of the saga consists of direct speech, which is by far the lowest rate ever found in an *Íslendingasaga*. Liestøl (1928) sees the author as a sort of district historian from the northeast of Iceland, whose geographical statements are very accurate, and who was really not an artist, but a conscientious reporter of past events, as he believed them to be true.

The most impressive character in the saga is Áskell goði, who represents the type of the noble heathen seen from a Christian perspective. In a time of famine, people discuss whether conditions might be improved by exposing babies and killing old people. But Áskell knows a better solution: "He said that it was more advisable to honor the Creator by helping the old people through a gift of money and raising up the children" (ch. 7). His life is devoted to peacemaking, and his death is a self-sacrifice.

The problem of oral or literary origin hinges largely on the fact that ch. 26 in *Reykdœla saga* is nearly identical with ch. 16 in *Víga-Glúms saga*. Most critics agree that the relationship must be literary, but disagree whether *Reykdœla saga* or *Víga-Glúms saga* was the source, or whether they shared a common source in the form of an independent *þáttr*. Doubtless, the version in *Reykdœla saga* is better fitted into the context than in the version in *Víga-Glúms saga*. After a careful examination of all arguments, Hofmann (1972) pleads for *Reykdœla saga* as the source and gives further evidence to strengthen the case for its oral origin. If he is right, *Reykdœla saga* belongs to the earliest written sagas. Despite clumsiness of composition and style, the saga shows a skillful treatment of certain narrative techniques (Heinrichs 1974 and 1976).

Ed.: Þorgeir Guðmundsson and Þorsteinn Helgason, eds. *Íslendinga sögur*. 2 vols. Copenhagen: Møller, 1829–30, vol. 2, pp. 7–8, 229–320; Finnur Jónsson, ed. *Íslenzkar fornsögur*. 2 vols. Copenhagen: Møller, 1880–81, vol. 2, pp. 1–152; Björn Sigfússon, ed. *Ljósvetninga saga*. Íslenzk fornrit, 10. Reykjavik: Hið íslenzka fornritafélag, 1940, pp. 149–243. **Tr.**: Vogt, Walter Helmut. "Die Geschichte von den Leuten aus dem Rauchtal." In *Thule: Altnordische Dichtung und Prosa*. 15 vols. Ed. Felix Niedner and Gustav Neckel. Düsseldorf-Köln: Diederichs, 1921; rpt. 1964, vol. 11, pp. 297–372. **Bib.**: Halldór Hermannsson. *Bibliography of the Icelandic Sagas and Minor Tales*. Islandica, 1. Ithaca: Cornell University Library, 1908, p. 91; Halldór Hermannsson. *The Sagas of Icelanders (Íslendinga sögur): A Supplement*. Islandica, 24. Ithaca: Cornell University Press; London: Oxford University Press, 1935, p. 65; Jóhann S. Hannesson. *The Sagas of Icelanders (Íslendinga sögur): A Supplement*. Islandica 38. Ithaca: Cornell University Press, 1957, p. 73. **Lit.**: Lotspeich, C. M. "The Composition of the Icelandic Family Sagas." *Journal of English and Germanic Philology* 8 (1909), 217–24; Liestøl, Knut. "Reykdœla saga: Tradisjon og forfattar." In *Festskrift til Finnur Jónsson 29. Maj 1928*. Ed. Johs. Brøndum-Nielsen et al. Copenhagen: Levin & Munksgaard, 1928, pp. 29–44; rpt. in his *Saga og folkeminne*. Oslo: Norli, 1941, pp. 18–32; Turville-Petre, G., ed. *Víga-Glúms saga*. 2nd ed. Oxford: Clarendon, 1960; rpt. 1967 [discussion of *Reykdœla saga* in introduction]; Vries, Jan de. *Altnordische Literaturgeschichte*. 2 vols. Grundriss der germanischen Philologie, 15–6. Berlin: de Gruyter, 1941–42; rpt. 1964–67, vol. 2, pp. 424–7; Bouman, Ari C. "Observations on Syntax and Style of Some Icelandic Sagas: With Special Reference to the Relation Between Víga-Glúms saga and Reykdœla saga." In *Studia Islandica* 15. Reykjavik: Menningarsjóður, 1956, pp. 5–72; Baetke, Walter. "Die Víga-Glúms-Episode in der Reykdœla-Saga." In *Beiträge zur deutschen und nordischen Literatur: Festgabe für Leopold Magon zum 70. Geburtstag, 3. April 1957*. Ed. Hans Werner Seiffert. Deutsche Akademie der Wissenschaften zu Berlin: Veröffentlichungen des Instituts für deutsche Sprache und Literatur, 11. Berlin: Akademie-Verlag, 1958, pp. 5–21; rpt. in his *Kleine Schriften*. Weimar: Böhlau, 1973; Andersson, Theodore M. *The Problem of Icelandic Saga Origins: A Historical Survey*. Yale Germanic Studies, 1. New Haven: Yale University Press, 1964; Andersson, Theodore M. "The Textual Evidence for an Oral Family Saga." *Arkiv för nordisk filologi* 81 (1966), 1–23; Andersson, Theodore M. *The Icelandic Family Saga: An Analytic Reading*. Harvard Studies in Comparative Literature, 28. Cambridge: Harvard University Press, 1967; Hofmann, Dietrich. "Reykdœla saga und mündliche Überlieferung." *Skandinavistik* 2.1 (1972), 1–26; Heinrichs, Anne. "Perspektivität in der altisländischen Sagakunst. Eine stilistische Untersuchung." *Colloquia Germanica* 3 (1974), 193–208; Heinrichs, Anne. "'Intertexture' and Its Functions in Early Written Sagas: A Stylistic Observation of *Heiðarvíga saga*, *Reykdœla saga*, and the Legendary Olafssaga." *Scandinavian Studies* 48 (1976), 127–45; Clover, Carol J. "Icelandic Family Sagas (*Íslendingasögur*)." In *Old Norse–Icelandic Literature: A Critical Guide*. Ed. Carol J. Clover and John Lindow. Islandica, 45. Ithaca and London: Cornell University Press, 1985, pp. 239–315; Simek, Rudolf, and Hermann Pálsson. *Lexikon der altnordischen Literatur*. Kröners Taschenausgabe, 490. Stuttgart: Kröner, 1987, pp. 290–1; Jónas Kristjánsson. *Eddas and Sagas: Iceland's Medieval Literature*. Trans. Peter Foote. Reykjavik: Hið íslenska bókmenntafélag, 1988, pp. 243–4.

Anne Heinrichs

[**See also:** Bookprose/Freeprose Theory; *Íslendingasögur*; *Þáttr*; *Víga-Glúms saga*]

Reykjahólabók ("The Book of Reykjahólar"; Stock. Perg. fol. no. 3) is an Icelandic legendary containing twenty-five saints' lives. The codex now consists of 168 leaves; a number of leaves are missing at the beginning and end, and there are several lacunae. The MS is written all in one hand, a hand also found in AM 667 4to fragments V, X, XI, and in twenty-six charters. The scribe has been identified as Björn Þorleifsson at Reykjahólar (after 1467– before 1554). The codex has been dated to around 1525.

Contained in the volume are legends of the Three Holy Kings, Henry and Cunegund, Oswald, Barlaam and Josaphat, Roch, Sebastian, Lazarus, the Seven Sleepers, Stephen the Deacon, Laurence of Rome, Christopher, George the Great, Silvester, Gregory on the Stone, Gregory the Great, Ambrose, Augustine, Erasmus, Nicholas of Tolentino, John Chrysostom, Servatius, Jerome, Anthony, Dominic, and Anne. The legendary includes lives of saints who had not hitherto enjoyed much veneration among Icelanders (*e.g.*, the Magi and SS. Henry, Cunegund, Dominic, Roch, George, and Christopher). It looks not to Latin models, but primarily to Low German sources. Widding and Bekker-Nielsen (1960, 1962) argue that the compiler of the collection drew most of his material from one of the revised and expanded versions of Jacobus de Voragine's *Legenda aurea* into Low German, known as the *Passional* or *Der heiligen Leben*, which has survived in a number of printed editions. Widding and Bekker-Nielsen note that of editions older than *Reykjahólabók*, Stephen Arndes's edition of the *Passionael* (Lübeck 1488, 1492, 1499, 1507) comes nearest to the text of *Reykjahólabók*.

> **Ed.**: Jón Sigurðsson. "Saga Ósvalds konúngs hins helga." *Annaler for nordisk Oldkyndighed og Historie* (1854), 3–91 [includes Danish translation by Thorleif Gudm. Repp.]; Loth, Agnete, ed. *Reykjahólabók: Islandske helgenlegender.* 2 vols. Editiones Arnamagnæanæ, ser. A, vols. 15–6. Copenhagen: Munksgaard, 1969–70. **Bib**: Widding, Ole, et al. "The Lives of the Saints in Old Norse Prose: A Handlist." *Mediaeval Studies* 25 (1963), 294–337. **Lit.**: Widding, Ole, and Hans Bekker-Nielsen. "En senmiddelalderlig legendesamling." *Maal og minne* (1960), 105–28; Widding, Ole, and Hans Bekker-Nielsen. "Low German Influence on Late Icelandic Hagiography." *Germanic Review* 37 (1962), 237–62; Bekker-Nielsen, Hans. "St. Anna i islandsk senmiddelalder." *Fróðskaparrit* 13 (1964), 203–11; Kalinke, Marianne E. "Osvalds saga konungs." In *The Audience of the Sagas: The Eighth International Saga Conference, August 11–17, 1991, Gothenburg University.* 2 vols. Gothenburg: Göteborgs Universitet, 1991, vol. 1, pp. 268–77 [photocopies of papers distributed to participants]; Kalinke, Marianne E. "'Gregorius saga biskups' and 'Gregorius auf dem Stein.'" *Beiträge zur Geschichte der deutschen Sprache und Literatur* 113 (1991), 67–88.

> ***Kirsten Wolf***

[**See also**: Legenda; *Maríu saga*; Saints' Lives]

Rhymed Chronicles *see* Chronicles, Rhymed

Riddar Paris och Jungfru Vienna *see* Swedish Literature, Miscellaneous

Riddarasögur

1. INDIGENOUS. In the prologue to *Flóres saga konungs ok sona hans*, a 14th-century *riddarasaga*, or chivalric romance, the author establishes three categories of sagas: saints' lives, which most people do not find very entertaining; sagas that tell of mighty kings from which one can learn courtly manners and how one is to comport oneself in the service of chieftains; and sagas that tell of kings who won great renown through their deeds. The last category presumably subsumes two established types of Icelandic sagas, the *fornaldarsögur* and the *riddarasögur*.

The designation *riddarasögur* ("knights' sagas") is attested in the Middle Ages; the redactor of the younger *Mágus saga jarls* refers to such *riddarasögur* as *Þiðreks saga* and *Flóvents saga*. The name *riddarasögur* is not a generic term, however; it is descriptive and refers to the courtly milieu that the narratives describe. The *riddarasögur* embrace a heterogeneous literature. The designation applies, on the one hand, to translations of courtly romances, *lais*, and *chansons de geste*, and, on the other hand, to indigenous Icelandic narratives composed in the wake of and under the influence of the translations. The former group came into being in Norway and Iceland primarily in the 13th and early 14th centuries, the latter in Iceland in the late 13th but predominantly 14th centuries. The indigenous Icelandic *riddarasögur* have on occasion also been called *lygisögur* ("fictitious sagas") and *fornsögur Suðrlanda* ("ancient sagas of southern lands"). German scholars refer to them as *Märchensagas* ("fairy-tale sagas"). Since the Icelan-

dic *riddarasögur* are the equivalent of the continental and English courtly romances, we use the terms *riddarasögur* and "Icelandic romances" interchangeably. As is the case with the translated *riddarasögur*, the indigenous romances are in prose; at times, this prose is quite florid, characterized by extensive alliteration.

Despite recent interest in the Icelandic *riddarasögur* and *fornaldarsögur*, valid and convincing criteria for assigning some sagas to one group rather than to the other have not yet been advanced. Consensus as to what constitutes the canon of Icelandic *riddarasögur* is wanting, although most scholars let themselves be guided by the contents of Loth's five-volume edition, *Late Medieval Icelandic Romances*, and Bjarni Vilhjálmsson's six-volume *Riddarasögur*, the latter containing both translated and indigenous sagas. In their respective articles on the *fornaldarsögur* and the *riddarasögur*, Einar Ól. Sveinsson (1959) and Halvorsen (1969) concur that certain sagas appear to be borderline cases that partake of characteristics of both groups. The sagas in question are *Ála flekks saga*, *Hrings saga ok Tryggva*, *Sigrgarðs saga frœkna*, *Sigurðar saga fóts*, and *Vilmundar saga viðutan*. It is uncertain what criteria were applied in this selection. To be sure, the presence of such elements as trolls and shapeshifters in *Ála flekks saga* and *Vilmundar saga viðutan* does impart a strong folkloristic element that is generally foreign to the *riddarasögur*. But the bridal-quest structure and theme of *Hrings saga ok Tryggva* and of *Sigurðar saga fóts* are in the best tradition of the *riddarasögur*. In studying the Icelandic *riddarasögur*, which are acknowledged to be romances, it might serve us well to keep in mind what Hermann Pálsson (1982–89) wrote about the *fornaldarsögur*: "In terms of general literary theory, the *fornaldarsögur*, particularly the 'adventure tales,' probably could best be regarded as secular romances."

Our discussion of the *riddarasögur* includes those sagas that represent the Icelandic equivalent of medieval romance, *i.e.*, those sagas that were inspired mainly by the translated romances for their plot, structure, and style, at the same time that they incorporated certain traditionally Nordic motifs into their compositions. The translated *riddarasögur* derive from works belonging to different genres: *chanson de geste*, such as *Karlamagnús saga* and *Elis saga ok Rósamundu*; *lai*, such as *Mǫttuls saga* and the *Strengleikar*; Arthurian and other romance, such as *Tristrams saga ok Ísǫndar*, *Ívens saga*, and *Flóres saga ok Blankiflúr*. Whereas the translated *riddarasögur* cannot be said to constitute one genre, the indigenous Icelandic *riddarasögur* are a fairly homogeneous group; their plot and structure are determined by the quest. Unlike the late-medieval romances on the Continent, the Icelandic *riddarasögur* did not continue the tradition of Arthurian romance, although it was well known, to judge by the number of Arthurian romances translated and Arthurian motifs incorporated in the indigenous Icelandic romances. Instead, Icelandic authors favored bridal-quest romance. Basic to the indigenous *riddarasögur*, even those that are not bridal-quest sagas, is a quadripartite structure consisting of (1) the hero's youth; (2) motivation for the quest and the hero's departure; (3) adventure cycle with conflict; and (4) return of the hero and wedding. The structural pattern may be multiplied in one work, as, for example, in *Jarlmanns saga ok Hermanns* or *Hrólfs saga Gautrekssonar*, which respectively double and quadruple the bridal quest, which is basic to the plot. If one includes the aforementioned hybrid sagas, then the corpus of medieval Icelandic romance consists of some thirty-five works.

The quest and the adventures encountered by the hero during the quest are the substance of Icelandic romance, which can be divided into two main groups: bridal-quest romances and sagas in which the plot is generated by some injustice suffered by the hero or one of his relatives, and which consists of the hero's quest to right the wrong. Ten sagas belong to this latter category. In several sagas, the plot revolves around the search for and the reunion of lost relatives: in *Valdimars saga* and in *Blómstrvallasaga* a sister and a brother, respectively, are abducted by a flying dragon, and the hero sets out in search. Trolls abduct the hero's father in *Vilhjálms saga sjóðs*. *Flóres saga konungs ok sona hans* deals with the abduction of a bride, her retrieval, and the eventual reunion of the protagonist and his three sons believed to be dead. The other two sagas deal with the usurpation of a throne and its repossession. In *Adonias saga*, the eponymous hero avenges the slaying of his father, the king of Spain, and in *Bærings saga* the protagonist flees from the murderer of his uncle and the rejected suitor of his widowed mother. Two other sagas, *Jóns saga leiksveins* and *Mírmanns saga*, tell about evil mothers: the iniquitous stepmother of Jón, who changes the hero into a werewolf, and Mírmann's evil mother, who causes her son to be stricken with leprosy, and his equally evil foster-mother, who causes Mírmann to forget that he already has a wife and to marry the foster-mother.

Ectors saga and *Kirialax saga* differ from the other sagas in that they lack a unifying quest. In *Ectors saga*, the eponymous protagonist and his knights set out separately to seek adventures and agree to meet again after a year. The saga best approximates the structure of Arthurian romance with its sequence of adventures. The plot of *Kirialax saga* is rather amorphous; it consists of a sequence of incidents, including two bridal quests, but without a unifying goal. The learned author uses the romance as a vehicle for describing the wonders of the Near East.

Most of the Icelandic *riddarasögur* are bridal-quest romances, however, works in which the quest for a bride is not merely one theme among many, but rather the motivating force of the entire plot. In his 1955 monograph, Geissler distinguished three types of bridal quest: the quest by a woman for a man with matrimony as the goal; the quest by a man for a woman with matrimony as a goal; and a man and woman woo each other but whose goal is not matrimony but sexual union. Only the first of these categories applies to the *riddarasögur*. Occasionally, a woman does woo a man, as in *Bærings saga*, but this courtship occurs merely as an isolated motif rather than as the driving force of the narrative.

In the bridal-quest sagas, the conflict derives either from the hero himself or from others. If the hero himself is the source of the conflict, it arises because of his low social standing, his phlegmatic personality, or his unethical or otherwise unworthy behavior. If other persons are the source of the conflict, then the impediments are the bride herself, the relatives, most frequently the father, or one or more rivals for the bride.

The quintessential Icelandic bridal-quest romance is *Hrólfs saga Gautrekssonar*, a so-called *fornaldarsaga*. The work is outstanding for its well-drawn characters, male as well as female, and its tight quadripartite structure, and is exemplary for the types of bridal quest, the possibilities of conflict, and the variety of protagonists and antagonists.

If the hero is his own worst enemy in the quest for a bride, the cause may be his psychic weakness. What characterizes the protagonists of a group of bridal-quest romances, among them *Friðþjófs saga ins frœkna* and *Gǫngu-Hrólfs saga* (two so-called *fornaldarsögur*), *Dámusta saga*, and *Gibbons saga*, is their extraordinary passivity. They reach their goal only because in the last analysis their life is determined and their happiness ensured by

forces beyond them. Although Friðþjófr, Dámusti, Gibbon, and Gǫngu-Hrólfr are distinct in their behavior and personalities, they resemble each other in that the successful conclusion of their respective bridal quests is the result primarily not of their own aggressive wooing, but rather the interference of another: the generosity of a rival in *Friðþjófs saga ins frœkna*; the protection and guidance of the Virgin Mary in *Dámusta saga*; the control exercised by a strong-willed woman in *Gibbons saga*; and the interaction of the realm of the dead with that of the living in *Gǫngu-Hrólfs saga*.

The conflict in several sagas stems from rivals, presumed or real, for the hand of the same princess. In most bridal-quest sagas, at least one rival appears on the scene, but he may not always be the determining factor in the development of the plot. Such is the case, for example, in the first section of *Hrólfs saga Gautrekssonar*, where old King Gautrekr has a rival in young King Óláfr, or in *Konráðs saga keisarasonar*, where the traitor Roðbert takes advantage of the protagonist's ignorance of Greek to present the bridal suit for himself rather than his lord. *Sigurðar saga fóts* has an unusual plot in that Ásmundr, the rival for the hand of Signý, daughter of the king of Sjólǫnd ("the Sealands"), abducts the bride on her wedding day. When the wronged bridegroom refuses to accept compensation, the rivals decide to settle the matter by single combat. The battle is inconclusive, and to the reader's surprise the abductor offers to relinquish the bride after all. The erstwhile rivals become sworn brothers, and the second part of the romance tells how Sigurðr aids his blood-brother in obtaining the daughter of the king of Ireland for his wife. Somewhat similar to *Sigurðar saga fóts* is the plot of the fragmentary *Hrings saga ok Tryggva*. The heroine is betrothed to Hringr, whom she loves, but then given in marriage to Tryggvi, who has rescued her and her father's kingdom from the unwanted attentions of a Viking. As in *Sigurðar saga fóts*, the rivals engage in combat, are grievously wounded, and then reconciled. Unlike Sigurðr, however, Hringr is not given his beloved but rather the sister of his former rival in marriage. Tryggvi is killed in battle; his sister, Hringr's wife, dies of grief; and Hringr gets his beloved after all.

Also centered on the problem of rival suitors is *Jarlmanns saga ok Hermanns*. Whereas the rivalry in the above-named sagas is real, it exists only in the mind of Hermann, who accuses his foster-brother Jarlmann of having an amatory interest in the bride he has wooed and brought back for him. Jarlmann is hurt and insulted, and leaves the court. The unjustified accusation is the indirect cause of the abduction of the bride by a rival suitor, for had Jarlmann not been absent, the abduction would have been foiled. *Jarlmanns saga ok Hermanns* may be interpreted as a counterpart to *Konráðs saga keisarasonar*. While the conflict in the latter is generated by the protagonist's unwarranted trust in his treacherous foster-brother, in *Jarlmanns saga ok Hermanns* the opposite happens: an unwarranted mistrust of the foster-brother leads to the crisis.

The most unusual obstacle that confronts the suitors of the Icelandic bridal-quest romances is the desired woman herself. Only in the Icelandic *riddarasögur* and in some of the so-called *fornaldarsögur*, which we include here if they are bridal-quest romances, do we find a motif, otherwise unknown in medieval literature, of the maiden-ruler who does not wish to marry, that is, the *meykongr* ("maiden-king") motif. No other medieval literature appears to have cultivated a subgenre of bridal-quest romance that focuses on the misogamous woman and the hero's attempt to trick her into marriage. To be sure, there exist such isolated figures as Brünhilt in the *Nibelungenlied* or the anonymous ruler of

Edinburgh in the *lai* of *Doon*, who wish to marry only the man who can pass certain tests, but the woman who categorically refuses to marry because marriage undermines her position as sovereign is an Icelandic phenomenon. In all, there are six sagas that are maiden-king romances from beginning to end: *Klári saga keisarasonar, Sigurðar saga þögla, Nitida saga, Viktors saga ok Blávus, Dínus saga drambláta,* and *Sigrgarðs saga frœkna.* In another group of sagas, a maiden-king episode forms a substantial part of the plot: *Ála flekks saga, Gibbons saga, Hrólfs saga Gautrekssonar,* and *Hrólfs saga kraka.*

Klári saga keisarasonar belongs among the translated *riddarasögur.* The work is supposed to be based on a Latin metrical narrative brought to Iceland by Jón Halldórsson, bishop of Skálholt (1322–1339), when he returned from his studies in Paris and Bologna. No such Latin tale is extant. In any case, it was presumably an isolated maiden-king romance on the Continent, which may, however, ultimately derive from Arabian tales. A major figure in *Klári saga keisarasonar* is a Master Perus of Arabia, and the narrative type involving the haughty princess who does not want to get married and who mistreats her suitors has analogues in *The Thousand and One Nights.*

The bridal-quest narratives that center on the misogamous woman have three distinguishing motifs: the arrogant female ruler who opposes marriage (solely in *Klári saga keisarasonar* does the female protagonist not rule a kingdom or part of a kingdom by herself); the rejection and cruel treatment of all suitors; and the humiliation and taming of the recalcitrant woman by the hero. The *meykongr*-sagas are distinct from other bridal-quest tales in that there is always a direct confrontation between the wooer and the wooed. Whereas the relatives of the desired bride or rivals are the impediments to the hero's successful quest in other bridal-quest tales, in the *meykongr*-sagas the woman herself is the source of conflict. Her misogamy does not derive from hatred of men, however, but rather from the fear that her realm may fall into the hands of a man who is not equal to the task.

Some of the authors of the *riddarasögur* were probably acquainted with each other's work. They made references in one saga to characters in another; they borrowed matter from other sagas; and they composed their sagas as continuations of or responses to each other's work. The variation on the theme of trust in one's foster-brother that is common to both *Konráðs saga keisarasonar* and *Jarlmanns saga ok Hermanns* has been noted. The affinity of these two sagas is documented at the conclusion of *Jarlmanns saga ok Hermanns:* Hermann turns out to be the paternal grandfather of Konráðr. A third saga in which the plot is generated in part by the relationship of the protagonist to another man, in this case, a sworn brother, is *Þjalar-Jóns saga,* also known as *Jóns saga Svipdagssonar ok Eireks forvitna.* Jón chooses, as it were, Eirekr as husband for his sister to prevent her from being married to an evil earl. The prospective bridegroom's interest in the maiden is roused when Jón shows him an image of her. (The motif, which is known from the hall-of-statues episode in *Tristrams saga ok Ísǫndar,* notably generates the bridal quest in *Rémundar saga keisarasonar,* in which the maiden appears in a dream.) *Þjalar-Jóns saga* turns out to be a continuation, so to speak, of *Konráðs saga keisarasonar,* because the evil earl is none other than the traitor Roðbert. In *Konráðs saga keisarasonar,* we learn only that Roðbert eventually acquired a realm of his own. In *Þjalar-Jóns saga,* he finally gets his just deserts while Eirekr obtains a bride.

The romances also borrowed from each other. The second bridal quest of *Sigurðar saga fóts* for the daughter of King Hrólfr of Ireland is greatly indebted to *Hrólfs saga Gautrekssonar.* In both sagas, the name of the wooer is identical, Ásmundr, as is the name Hrólfr and the character of the nasty ruler of Ireland. As happens in the fourth bridal quest of *Hrólfs saga Gautrekssonar,* the wooer in *Sigurðar saga fóts* is attacked, vanquished, and imprisoned by the evil father of the desired bride. As happens to his namesake, the Ásmundr of *Sigurðar saga fóts* is rescued by the king's daughter and avenged by his foster-brother.

In the past, scholars have dismissed the indigenous *riddarasögur* as products of a period of decadence in Icelandic literature. The chronology does not bear out this assessment, since the earliest *riddarasögur* presumably are contemporary with or at the most slightly younger than some classical Icelandic sagas. The contents of the MS Stock. Perg. 4to no. 7 (Royal Library, Stockholm), dated 1300–1325 by the Arnamagnæan Dictionary Project in Copenhagen, reveal the sweeping taste of Icelanders at the height of their literary productivity: together with *Egils saga* and *Jómsvíkinga saga,* the codex contains, *inter alia, Bærings saga, Hrólfs saga Gautrekssonar,* and *Konráðs saga keisarasonar.* None of these sagas in the codex is an original text, and we assume that the three romances were already popular enough to have led the person responsible for the contents of the codex to include them. If the MS was produced around the earlier possible date, *i.e.,* around 1300, then it is not out of the question that some of the Icelandic romances were composed at the same time as *Njáls saga* and *Hrafnkels saga Freysgoða.*

Ed.: Cederschiöld, Gustaf, ed. *Fornsögur Suðrlanda. Magus saga jarls, Konráðs saga, Bærings saga, Floventz saga, Bevers saga. Med inledning.* Lund: Berling, 1884; Tan-Haverhorst, Louisa Frederika, ed. *Þjalar Jóns saga. Dámusta saga.* Haarlem: Tjeenk Willink, 1939; Bjarni Vilhjálmsson, ed. *Riddarasögur.* 6 vols. Reykjavik: Íslendingasagnaútgáfan; Haukadalsútgáfan, 1949–54; Guðni Jónsson, ed. *Fornaldar sögur Norðurlanda.* 4 vols. Akureyri: Íslendingasagnaútgáfan, 1954; Jónas Kristjánsson, ed. *Dínus saga drambláta.* Riddarasögur, 1. Reykjavik: Háskóli Íslands, 1960; Loth, Agnete, ed. *Late Medieval Icelandic Romances.* 5 vols. Editiones Arnamagnæanæ, ser. B, vols. 20–4. Copenhagen: Munksgaard, 1962–65; Jónas Kristjánsson, ed. *Viktors saga ok Blávus.* Riddarasögur, 2. Reykjavik: Handritastofnun Íslands, 1964. **Bib.**: Kalinke, Marianne E., and P. M. Mitchell. *Bibliography of Old Norse–Icelandic Romances.* Islandica, 44. Ithaca and London: Cornell University Press, 1985. **Lit.**: Schlauch, Margaret. *Romance in Iceland.* Princeton: Princeton University Press; New York: American-Scandinavian Foundation; London: Allen & Unwin, 1934; rpt. New York: Russell & Russell, 1973; Wahlgren, Erik. *The Maiden King in Iceland.* Chicago: University of Chicago Libraries, 1938 [private publication]; Einar Ól. Sveinsson. "Fornaldarsögur Norðrlanda." *KLNM* 4 (1959), 49–507; Geissler, Friedmar. *Brautwerbung in der Weltliteratur.* Halle: Niemeyer, 1955; Halvorsen, E. F. "Riddersagaer." *KLNM* 14 (1969), 175–83; Naumann, Hans-Peter. "Die Abenteuersaga als eine Spätform altisländischer Erzählkunst." *Skandinavistik* 8 (1978), 41–55; Nahl, Astrid van. *Originale Riddarasögur als Teil altnordischer Sagaliteratur.* Frankfurt am Main and Bern: Lang, 1981; Hermann Pálsson. "Fornaldarsögur." In *Dictionary of the Middle Ages.* Ed. Joseph R. Strayer. New York: Scribner, 1982–89, vol. 5, pp. 137–43; Glauser, Jürg. *Isländische Märchensagas: Studien zur Prosaliteratur im spätmittelalterlichen Island.* Beiträge zur nordischen Philologie, 12. Basel and Frankfurt am Main: Helbing & Lichtenhahn, 1983; Kalinke, Marianne. "Norse Romance (*Riddarasögur*)." In *Old Norse–Icelandic Literature: A Critical Guide.* Ed. Carol J. Clover and John Lindow. Islandica, 45. Ithaca and London: Cornell University Press, 1985, pp. 316–63; Kalinke, Marianne E. "The Misogamous Maiden Kings of

Icelandic Romance." *Scripta Islandica* 37 (1986), 47–71; Weber, Gerd Wolfgang. "The Decadence of Feudal Myth: Towards a Theory of riddarasaga and Romance." In *Structure and Meaning in Old Norse Literature: New Approaches to Textual Analysis and Literary Criticism.* Ed. John Lindow *et al.* Viking Collection, 3. Odense: Odense University Press, 1986, pp. 415–54; Kalinke, Marianne E. *Bridal–Quest Romance in Medieval Iceland.* Islandica, 46. Ithaca and London: Cornell University Press, 1990.

Marianne E. Kalinke

2. TRANSLATED. Translated *riddarasögur* are prose translations and adaptations, the majority made in 13th-century Norway, of a diverse collection of Old French verse epic (*Elis saga ok Rósamundu*, from the *chanson de geste Elie de Saint Gille*; *Karlamagnús saga*, in ten "branches," deriving in the main from Carolingian *chansons de geste*) and chivalric narrative, the latter including Old Norse versions of *lais* (*Strengleikar*), *romans courtois* (*Erex saga, Ívens saga, Parcevals saga / Valvers þáttr*, from Chrétien de Troyes's *Erec et Enide, Yvain, Perceval; Mottuls saga*, from *Le mantel mautaillé*), *romans d'aventure* (*Flóres saga ok Blankiflúr*, from the earlier of two versions of *Floire et Blancheflor*; *Bevers saga* [or *Bevis saga*], from the Anglo-Norman *Boeve de Haumtone*), and the now-fragmentary romance of *Tristan* by Thomas of Britain (*Tristrams saga*). *Riddarasögur* whose immediate sources cannot be positively established are *Partalopa saga* (a version of the *roman d'aventure Partenopeus de Blois*) and *Flóvents saga*, which does not correspond to the extant *Chanson de Floovant*. Sometimes included in discussions of *riddarasögur* is *Þiðreks saga*, a compilation of tales of German origin about Dietrich of Bern. *Mágus saga jarls*, a 14th-century Icelandic work, has some connection with, but is not an adaptation of, the *chanson de geste Les quatre fils Aimon* (or *Renaud de Montauban*).

The reliability of the extant MSS of their presumed Norwegian originals is a matter of some debate. With the exception of *Strengleikar*, the first fifty-nine chapters of *Elis saga* (both preserved in the Norwegian MS De la Gardie 4–7 II fol., dating from ca. 1250), and fragments of *Flóres saga ok Blankiflúr* and *Karlamagnús saga*, the *riddarasögur* exist only in Icelandic copies dating from the early 15th to the 19th century. Where the comparison with Norwegian MSS is possible, however, the majority of extant texts evidently preserve the substance of their exemplars. Shared patterns of style and syntax among a number of *riddarasögur* (the "Tristram-Group") suggest that radical editing was not always common practice among later scribes.

Scholars generally agree that Hákon Hákonarson of Norway (r. 1217–1263) initiated the production of the *riddarasögur*. The king's ambition to propel himself and Norway into the mainstream of international affairs is well documented in his biography, *Hákonar saga gamla Hákonarsonar*, and the *riddarasögur* are the literary evidence of his desire to keep in step with European culture. Hákon is named as the commissioner of *Elis saga, Ívens saga, Mottuls saga, Strengleikar*, and *Tristrams saga*. Even if some of the statements to this effect at the beginnings or endings of these works are those of later scribes, they are probably historically true. The immediate sources of the *riddarasögur* are likely to have been Anglo-Norman MSS, since Norway's links with continental Europe were largely through the intermediary of Angevin Britain, with which there were long-established ecclesiastical and economic ties. The name of the cleric, Robert, to whom the composition of *Elis saga* and *Tristrams saga* is attributed, is Anglo-Norman. But the works give no indication that the mother tongue of Robert or any other *riddarasaga* writer was French, and the texts contain occasional apparent mistranslations or misunderstandings of the original language.

As translations and adaptations, the *riddarasögur* belong to a venerable tradition in Norwegian and Icelandic literature. Norse versions of Latin religious works date from the early 12th century, and the Anglo-Norman Body and Soul debate poem *Un samedi par nuit* was translated into Norwegian (and is contained in the Norwegian Homily Book) around 1200. A variety of historical and pseudo-historical material provides the sources for *Breta sögur, Trójumanna saga, Rómverja saga*, and *Veraldar saga*, all dating from the first half of the 13th century. In addition to *Elis saga* and *Strengleikar*, MS De la Gardie 4–7 contains an incomplete translation of the Latin poem *Pamphilus de amore*.

The translation of French "courtly" narrative (*lais, romans courtois*) seems to have been a phenomenon restricted to the reign of Hákon Hákonarson, but Norse versions of Latin romances and pseudo-histories, like *Alexanders saga* (from Galterus de Castellione's *Alexandreis*) and *Amícus saga ok Amilíus* (from the account of the legend in the *Speculum historiale* by Vincent of Beauvais), continued through the reigns of Hákon's son, Magnús (r. 1263–1280), and grandson, Hákon Magnússon (r. 1299–1319). Extant texts lend no substance to the assertion in the late 14th-century Icelandic romance *Viktors saga ok Blávus* that Hákon Magnússon had a number of *riddarasögur* translated from Greek and French. The Icelandic *Klári saga* (mid-14th century) purports to be a translation of an unnamed Latin source. Apart from Bjarni Erlingsson of Bjarkey, who is said to have found the now-lost Middle English story of Olive and Landres (Branch II of *Karlamagnús saga*) on a trip to Scotland in 1286–1287, the only names associated with the translated *riddarasögur* and secular narratives that have or claim Latin sources are of kings and clerics: Hákon Hákonarson, two of his successors, the unidentified "Robert" (called "brother" in *Strengleikar* and "abbot" in *Elis saga*), and two Icelandic bishops, Brandr Jónsson of Hólar, author of *Alexanders saga*, and Jón Halldórsson of Skálholt, author of *Klári saga*.

From a stylistic viewpoint, the *riddarasögur* present a curious blend of Norse form and French content. Prose was the preferred medium for long narratives in Old Norse, although it has been suggested that its employment for the *riddarasögur* is due to a contemporary lack of native meters equivalent to the verse forms of Old French epic and romance. It was not until the development of the *rímur* that Iceland acquired a form of poetic narrative corresponding to the metrical romances of other European literatures, but a distinctive Old Norse prose style was well developed by the time *chansons de geste* and *romans courtois* reached Norway. On the Old Norse literary time scale, the *riddarasögur* are contemporary with the writing of the *Íslendingasögur*. The style of the translations, which often resembles but is, in varying degrees, more rhetorical than that of the *Íslendingasögur*, is often called the "court style," and is characterized by the use of antithesis, parallelism, and alliteration, especially in rhyming or assonanced word pairs, often occurring in chains (e.g., *brenna ok bæla, vitrleikr ok fróðleikr, skomm ok skaða*). Participial constructions, a feature of the "learned style" of religious translations from Latin, also appear in the *riddarasögur* with a much higher frequency than in the *Íslendingasögur*, especially at points of dramatic intensity. The rhetorical training of the translator-adaptors is evident in their independent prefaces to *Strengleikar* and *Mottuls saga*, which are modeled on the traditional medieval *exordium*, or prologue, a convention otherwise foreign to Old Norse secular narrative.

Comparison of *riddarasögur* with available MSS of their sources shows a relationship that ranges from word-for-word translation to free adaptation. By and large, the *riddarasögur* are faithful to the content of their originals, although there are occasional major deviations, like the ending of *Flóres saga ok Blankiflúr*, the Icelandic chapters that continue the Norwegian *Elis saga*, and the incorporation of an additional chapter into *Erex saga*. Extended descriptions of physiognomy, dress, and social ritual, characteristic of French romance but alien to Norse narrative tradition, are usually eliminated or abbreviated. Occasionally, there is amplification of source material, as in *Eskia*, the version of Marie de France's *Lai la fresne* in *Strengleikar*, and *Mǫttuls saga*. Authors sometimes make additions to the existing framework, like the prologues to *Strengleikar* and *Mǫttuls saga* and the epilogue to *Equitan* (from Marie's *lai* of the same name) and *Erex saga*.

While the *Erex saga* epilogue, with its reference to Erex's later career and that of his sons, is similar to many epilogues in *þættir* and *Íslendingasögur*, the ending of the Norwegian *Equitan* is one of a number of overtly didactic passages in the *riddarasögur*, which are either not found or are less prominent in their originals. The *Equitan* conclusion is a lengthy, exhortatory piece on the vices of greed and injustice, which gives the story of the ignoble King Equitan the appearance of an exemplum. *Erex saga* expands passages in Chrétien's *Erec et Enide* that are concerned with the obligations of kings and noblemen; *Parcevals saga* emphasizes the educational aspect of Chrétien's romance; *Tristrams saga* has a moralizing quality not present in the extant fragments of Thomas's work; *Flóres saga ok Blankiflúr* has an evangelical fervor that exceeds the Christian-pagan conflict in *Floire et Blancheflor* and is more reminiscent of the crusading spirit of *Karlamagnús saga*.

Elis saga and *Karlamagnús saga* treat French epic with due gusto, but the Norse versions of romances, particularly of *romans courtois*, differ radically in tone from their sources. A shift from works that combine, in Chrétien's case, comedy, eroticism, and implicit didacticism, not always in easily discernible parts, to Norse renditions that are essentially exemplary in mode is effected by various modifications to structure, theme, and character. In addition to the element of explicit moralizing in the *riddarasögur*, their elimination of two narrative conventions that are fundamental to the *roman courtois* but alien to Old Norse saga, the nonomniscient narrator and internal monologue, plays a significant part in this process. The transition from the liveliness of the octosyllabic couplet of the *lai* and *roman courtois* to a rhetorically embellished prose also gives the *riddarasögur* a stylistic ponderousness at odds with the lightness of touch of their sources.

Riddarasögur authors make occasional independent interventions in the course of the narrative to explain unfamiliar terms, for example, dates in the church calendar like Pentecost (Old French *pantecoste*: "þikkisdagr, which we call *hvítasunna*" in *Ívens saga*) and Palm Sunday (Old French *jour de la Pasque flori*: "*palmasunnudagr . . . is called *blómapáskir* abroad" in *Flóres saga ok Blankiflúr*). But the constant, intrusive presence of a narrator is absent (*Elis saga* is something of an exception), and a typically 13th-century outburst against women in *Ívens saga*, which adds a condemnatory note to some wry comments on *Yvain*, is unusual. The departure of the loquacious narrator, with his running commentary on the action, takes with it the means by which Chrétien establishes a sense of audience complicity and underlines discrepancies between the theory and practice of Arthurian chivalry,

thereby giving his romances an ironic dimension lacking in the *riddarasögur*. Problems of conflicting loyalties, usually between love (often personified as *Amors*) on the one hand and the demands of chivalry on the other, are explored through the medium of internal monologue by Chrétien and other writers of French romance. *Flóres saga ok Blankiflúr* is unique in its retention of such a passage of "psychological allegory" in which Love and Reason vie for the hero's allegiance; other *riddarasögur* largely ignore the inner life of their characters and the problematic side of literary chivalry. Love has only minor interest in *Erex saga* and *Ívens saga*, for example, whereas their sources concern the proper role of love and marriage in the chivalric life; large portions of the French text examining the private thoughts of hero and heroine are left out, but descriptions of combat are rendered in detail. Similarly, in *Flóres saga ok Blankiflúr*, Flóres wins Blankiflúr not, like French Floire, through the appealing strength of their mutual love, but by force of arms.

Unbecoming or undignified conduct on the part of Arthur and his knights tends to be omitted, glossed over, or otherwise excused in the *riddarasögur*. Any satire in *Mǫttuls saga*, the tale of a chastity test, is aimed at the ladies rather than the knights of Arthur's court. Heroic preconceptions of Arthur and his knights deriving from *Breta sǫgur*, Norse conceptions of the hero as found in eddic poetry and *Íslendingasögur*, a likely imperviousness to or a possible distaste for "courtly" irony, and idealized expectations of the heroes of French romance on the part of translators and audience may all have influenced the presentation of character in the *riddarasögur*. Clerical authorship may be responsible for their overtly didactic element. Chivalry in the *riddarasögur* is "feudal" rather than "courtly," with the emphasis on the virtues of courage, loyalty, piety, and modesty, along with a lack of interest in the ritual and emotion of love.

These modifications to their sources flatten *riddarasögur* characters, turn heroes into types, and make the tales straightforward accounts of knightly virtue rewarded or, occasionally, as in the case of *Equitan*, sin punished. The tendency to improve and exemplify character and to simplify "courtly" and, in the case of *Parcevals saga*, mystical enigma is one feature that the *riddarasögur* share with some other adaptations of French romance: for example, the Middle English *Ywain and Gawain* (from *Yvain*), an ideological companion piece to *Ívens saga*, and *Sir Perceval of Galles* (indirectly from *Perceval*), and the 15th-century Burgundian prose *Erec*.

The extant MSS testify to the popularity of the translated *riddarasögur* in Iceland, but the extent of any direct influence they may have exerted on the *Íslendingasögur* is difficult to establish. The contribution of the *Íslendingasögur* to the style, form, and ethic of the *riddarasögur* may have been greater than any influence in the opposite direction. Some scholars see the effects of the *riddarasögur* on the development of Icelandic saga narrative as superficial only, limited to the occasional uncharacteristically "chivalric" description (for example, the initial portrait of Kari Sǫlmundarson in *Njáls saga*) or motifs like the "ambiguous oath" in the Þorsteinn and Spes story in *Grettis saga*, which parallels an episode in *Tristrams saga*. Other scholars have argued that French romance, and the Tristan story in particular, had a more profound impact on the *Íslendingasögur*, particularly on "skald sagas" like *Kormáks saga*.

The independent Icelandic *riddarasögur*, most of which date from the 14th century, take their inspiration in part from the translated *riddarasögur*, but differ from them markedly in tenor. Whereas the latter are restrained in their treatment of love, the exotic, and the supernatural, hyperbole is the keynote of the Icelandic romances, which owe more to the Norse versions of *chansons de geste* and *romans d'aventure* than to those of *lais* and *romans courtois*. Certain characters and motifs from the translated *riddarasögur* reappear in the Icelandic romances, although some of these may have been familiar in Iceland from other sources. The Tristan legend, for example, is the subject of *Tristrams saga ok Ísoddar*, and the lion-knight story, which appears in *Ívens saga*, is found in a number of the independent *riddarasögur*. *Sigurðar saga þögla* is typically eclectic in its use of motifs from the translated romances: set in the days of King Arthur, it contains an account of the tale of Flóres and Blankiflúr, and has a hero who rescues a lion from a dragon.

Although many of the heroes of these independent romances are the subject of Icelandic *rímur*, only *Karlamagnús saga*, *Mǫttuls saga*, and *Tristrams saga* appear to have inspired medieval *rímur* and ballads. *Flóres saga ok Blankiflúr* and *Ívens saga* are sources of the Swedish verse romances (known as *Eufemiavisorna*), *Flores och Blanzeflor* and *Ivan Lejonriddaren*, composed for Eufemia, wife of Hákon Magnússon of Norway, in the early years of the 14th century.

Ed.: Bjarni Vilhjálmsson, ed. *Riddarasögur*. 6 vols. Reykjavik: Íslendingasagnaútgáfan; Haukadalsútgáfan, 1949–54. **Bib.**: Kalinke, Marianne E., and P. M. Mitchell. *Bibliography of Old Norse–Icelandic Romances*. Islandica, 44. Ithaca and London: Cornell University Press, 1985. **Lit.**: Meissner, Rudolf. *Die Strengleikar. Ein Beitrag zur Geschichte der altnordischen Prosalitteratur*. Halle: Niemeyer, 1902; Leach, Henry Goddard. *Angevin Britain and Scandinavia*. Harvard Studies in Comparative Literature, 6. Cambridge: Harvard University Press; London: Milford; Oxford: Oxford University Press, 1921; rpt. Milwood: Kraus, 1975; Halvorsen, E. F. *The Norse Version of the Chanson de Roland*. Bibliotheca Arnamagnæana, 19. Copenhagen: Munksgaard, 1959; Mitchell, Phillip M. "Scandinavian Literature." In *Arthurian Literature in the Middle Ages: A Collaborative History*. Ed. Roger Sherman Loomis. Oxford: Clarendon, 1959, pp. 462–71; Knudson, Charles A. "Les versions norroises des romans de Chrétien de Troyes: le cadre." In *Mélanges de langue et de littérature du Moyen Age et de la Renaissance offerts à Jean Frappier par ses collègues, ses élèves et ses amis*. 2 vols. Geneva: Droz, 1970, vol. 1, pp. 533–41; Hallberg, Peter. "Norröna riddarsagor. Några språkdrag." *Arkiv för nordisk filologi* 86 (1971), 114–38 [on the "Tristram-Group"]; Halvorsen, Eyvind Fjeld. "Norwegian Court Literature in the Middle Ages." *Orkney Miscellany* (King Hákon Commemorative Number) 5 (1973), 17–26; Blaisdell, Foster W., Jr. "The So-Called 'Tristram-Group' of the *Riddarasögur*." *Scandinavian Studies* 46 (1974), 134–9; Hallberg, Peter. "Is There a 'Tristram-Group' of the *Riddarasögur*?" *Scandinavian Studies* 47 (1975), 1–17; *Les relations littéraires franco-scandinaves au moyen âge. Actes du colloque de Liège (avril 1972)*. Bibliothèque de la Faculté de Philosophie et Lettres de l'Université de Liège, 208. Paris: Société d'Edition "Les Belles Lettres," 1975 [articles in English and French]; Zink, Georges. "Les poèmes arthuriens dans les pays scandinaves." In *Les relations littéraires franco-scandinaves*, pp. 77–95; Barnes, Geraldine. "The *riddarasögur* and Mediæval European Literature." *Mediæval Scandinavia* 8 (1975), 140–58; Barnes, Geraldine. "The *Riddarasögur*. A Medieval Exercise in Translation." *Saga-Book of the Viking Society* 19 (1977), 403–41; Sverrir Tómasson. "Hvenær var Tristrams sögu snúið?" *Gripla* 2 (1977), 47–78 [English summary]; Kalinke, Marianne E. *King Arthur North-by-Northwest: The* matière de Bretagne *in Old Norse–Icelandic Romances*. Bibliotheca Arnamagnæana, 37. Copenhagen: Reitzel, 1981; Kalinke, Marianne E. "Scribes, Editors, and the *riddarasögur*." *Arkiv för*

nordisk filologi 97 (1982), 36–51; Kretschmer, Bernd. *Höfische und altwestnordische Erzähltradition in den Riddarasögur. Studien zur Rezeption der altfranzösischen Artusepik am Beispiel der* Erex saga, Ívens saga *und* Parcevals saga. Hattingen: Kretschmer, 1982; Boyer, Régis, ed. *Les Sagas de Chevaliers (Riddarasögur). Actes de la Ve Conférence Internationale sur les Sagas . . . (Toulon, Juillet 1982)*. Civilisations, 10. Paris: Presses de l'Université de Paris-Sorbonne, 1985 [articles in English, French, German]; Bibire, Paul. "From *riddarasaga* to *lygisaga*: The Norse Response to Romance." In *Les Sagas de Chevaliers*, pp. 55–74; Jónas Kristjánsson. "The Court Style." In *Les Sagas de Chevaliers*, pp. 431–40. Reichert, Hermann. "King Arthur's Round Table: Sociological Implications of Its Literary Reception in Scandinavia." In *Structure and Meaning in Old Norse Literature: New Approaches to Textual Analysis and Literary Criticism*. Ed. John Lindow *et al.* Viking Collection, 3. Odense: Odense University Press, 1986, pp. 394–414; Barnes, Geraldine. "Arthurian Chivalry in Old Norse." In *Arthurian Literature VII*. Ed. Richard Barber. Cambridge: Brewer, 1987, pp. 50–102; Almazan, Vincent. "Translators at the Castilian and Norwegian Courts in the Thirteenth Century: Parallels and Patterns." *Mediaeval Scandinavia* 12 (1988), 213–32; Barnes, Geraldine. "Some Current Issues in Riddarasögur Research." *Arkiv för nordisk filologi* 104 (1989), 73–88.

Geraldine Barnes

[**See also:** *Adonias saga*; *Ála flekks saga*; *Alexanders saga*; Amicus and Amileus; *Bevis saga*; *Blómstrvallasaga*; *Bærings saga*; *Dámusta saga*; *Dínus saga drambláta*; *Drauma-Jóns saga*; *Ectors saga ok kappa hans*; *Elis saga ok Rósamundu*; *Erex saga*; *Eufemiavisorna*; *Flóres saga konungs ok sona hans*; *Flóres saga ok Bankiflúr*; *Flóvents saga Frakkakonungs*; *Fornaldarsögur*; *Friðþjófs saga ins frœkna*; *Gibbons saga*; *Grettis saga*; *Gǫngu-Hrólfs saga*; *Hrings saga ok Tryggva*; *Hrólfs saga Gautrekssonar*; *Íslendingasögur*; *Ívens saga*; *Jarlmanns saga ok Hermanns*; *Jóns saga leiksveins*; *Karlamagnús saga*; *Kirialax saga*; *Klári (Clári) saga*; *Konráðs saga keisarasonar*; *Kormáks saga*; *Lygisaga*; *Mágus saga jarls*; Maiden Warriors; *Mírmanns saga*; *Mǫttuls saga*; *Nitida saga*; *Njáls saga*; Old Norse–Icelandic Literature, Foreign Influence on; *Pamphilus ok Galathea*; *Parcevals saga*; *Partalopa saga*; *Rémundar saga keisarasonar*; *Rímur*; *Rómverja saga*; *Saulus saga ok Nikanors*; *Samsons saga fagra*; *Sigrgarðs saga frœkna*; *Sigrgarðs saga ok Valbrands*; *Sigurðar saga fóts ok Ásmundar Húnakongs*; *Sigurðar saga turnara*; *Sigurðar saga þögla*; *Skáldasögur*; *Strengleikar*; Style; *Tiódels saga*; *Tristrams saga ok Ísoddar*; *Tristrams saga ok Ísǫndar*; *Þáttr*; *Þjalar-Jóns saga*; *Valdimars saga*; *Veraldar saga*; *Viktors saga ok Blávus*; *Vilhjálms saga sjóðs*; *Vilmundar saga viðutan*; Women in Sagas]

Riddles. A riddle is a question that involves a rewriting of a concrete, objective description in an exact but novel way. Each word is intended to be equally clear and adjusted as in a logical definition, but the rewriting is made to complicate and puzzle. It is, therefore, difficult to see immediately what is spoken of, and the solution is usually rather difficult. The more unclear a riddle is, the better it is; but it must still give a completely correct description of what it concerns.

Riddles are known in most countries and have a long history. Generally, a distinction is made between the riddles that survive among the people and concern everyday matters, and those that have their origin in mythological and literary allegories and kennings, and have been transmitted from generation to generation in literature.

One of the oldest riddles in Scandinavia is found in the runic inscription on the Eggja stone in Sogn in Norway from the middle of the 8th century. The runes have not been interpreted definitively, but a name may be hidden in a riddle in them.

In Old Norse works, riddles appear widely, especially in the eddic poems (*Vafþrúðnismál, Alvíssmál, Grímnismál, Fjǫlsvinnsmál*), in Saxo's *Gesta Danorum*, and in the *fornaldarsǫgur*. There are some differences among the riddles in these works. In the eddic poems, they tend to be questions about mythological matters rather than actual riddles, but nonetheless questions and answers are asked as in the riddle contests. In Saxo, the riddles are mainly in prose, but in the *fornaldarsǫgur* real riddles are found as they are known from elsewhere, both riddles of a literary origin and riddles that have their origin among the people.

The eddic poems that include riddles or tell of quizzes similar to the riddle contests are *Vafþrúðnismál* and *Alvíssmál*. In *Vafþrúðnismál*, Óðinn goes to match his own lore with that of the giant Vafþrúðnir. After an initial test, they continue the wager with the loser's head as the stake. Óðinn finally propounds the unanswerable question: "What did Óðinn whisper in the ear of his son, before Baldr was placed on the funeral pyre?"

Alvíssmál tells of a wisdom contest between Þórr and the dwarf Alvíss. The former promises his consent to the marriage between his daughter and Alvíss provided the dwarf can answer all his questions. Þórr says that he has never met a man so learned in ancient lore; but this wisdom does not help the dwarf, for when he answers the last question, daylight surprises him and transforms him into stone.

Saxo gives an account of the riddles that Eiríkr asked King Fróði. Eiríkr describes his journey in riddles and uses proper names with the intention of misleading the king. The solution to these riddles involves solving name-riddles and puns.

The most famous riddles in medieval Scandinavian works are those of Gestumblindi and Heiðrekr, preserved in *Hervarar saga ok Heiðreks*. Six of the thirty-five riddles appear widely in later times, but the others are known only from this story of the contest between King Heiðrekr and Gestumblindi. The riddles are incorporated into a "head-ransom" framework. Gestumblindi was King Heiðrekr's enemy, but Óðinn exchanged clothes with him, went to the king, and competed with him in a riddle contest. The events are described in a vein similar to Óðinn's contest with Vafþrúðnir. One of Gestumblindi's riddles that is known from elsewhere is the way-riddle:

> From home I went
> and left my home
> and saw the roads on the road;
> a road was above,
> a road was below;
> solve my riddle
> correctly, King Heiðrekr.

Here, Gestumblindi stood on a bridge, a river was under him, and birds flew in all directions over him.

The leek-riddle is widely known. The riddle asks what it is that

> turns its feet
> toward the sun
> but its head toward Hel.

In the course of the contest, Gestumblindi comes up with a riddle that shows that he is perhaps not who he pretends to be:

> What marvel was that
> which I saw outside
> Delling's doors?
> It has ten tongues
> and twenty eyes;
> with forty legs
> the creature moves forward.

Heiðrekr solves the riddle as a sow in the yard, and he has it killed to know if the number of piglets is correct. Now he suspects whom he is competing with, and is certain when Gestumblindi asks:

> What did Óðinn speak
> in Baldr's ear,
> before he was placed on the pyre?

Many of the riddles in *Hervarar saga* are known from other languages and have parallels outside Scandinavia.

Riddles to test cleverness are also found in *Melkólfs saga ok Salomons konungs*. A remnant of a riddle appears in the *Prose Edda*. The story of Bil and Hjúki in ch. 11 of Snorri's *Gylfaginning* may be based on a riddle asking who they are (Holtsmark 1945).

Riddles have been studied from many points of view. Scholars, for example, have divided riddles into a number of categories according to their content. In the first category are puns; in the second, riddles that contain a direct question about a certain topic; in the third, riddles that involve a metaphor or a simile; in the fourth, riddles that tell of what the questioner has witnessed; and in the fifth, riddles about numbers. Scholars have also analyzed riddles according to their form, as well as to the roles that they played in the cultures where they once flourished.

Educational and instructive riddles deliberately effect a certain knowledge. Many of Gestumblindi's riddles belong to this category, and such riddles are generally thought to have come to Europe from Asia. A riddle about the year has been traced all the way back to the ancient religious text in *Rigveda*. The lore in *Alvíssmál* and *Vafþrúðnismál* is of the same kind, and several other mythological poems of the *Poetic Edda* contain profound wisdom from far away. Learned or educational riddles are also found in an Icelandic MS from the 13th century (*Alfræði Íslenzk*, vol. 3, pp. 36 f.); a list of questions contains the riddle, "Which four grains make the soil wet?" The answer is "Rain, hail, snow, and dew."

Riddles were well suited as entertainment in the homes of farmer societies, when the families gathered in the evenings or on holidays. The description in many popular riddles is taken directly from everyday life, and the meaning and interpretation of the riddle were thus easy for everyone. But this meant, on the other hand, that the riddles could not travel unchanged to another cultural setting where conditions were different. "Ambiguous" riddles fall within this category. These can be interpreted in two different ways; sometimes, they have a normal vocabulary but a meaning that can be vulgar and allude to sex.

"Head ransom" is one of the most common purposes of riddles in narratives and literature. The doomed man is given the choice between escaping his fate by solving the riddles presented, or by posing riddles that cannot be solved. In the sagas, it is often said that the doomed have enjoyed the help of good spirits in solving these contests.

The solution of a riddle is a mental contest that tests a person's intelligence to the utmost. The solution of a riddle appears to be a philosophical problem. The riddle-contest is also an exercise in the use of language and is thus in many ways associated with the philosophy of language.

Ed.: Hammershaimb, V. U. "Færöiske gaader." *Antiquarisk tidsskrift* (1849–51), 315–22 [72]; Jón Árnason and Ólafur Davíðsson, eds. *Íslenzkar gátur, skemtanir, vikivakar og þulur.* 4 vols. Copenhagen: Møller, 1887–1903; Kålund, Kr., and N. Beckman, eds. *Alfræði Íslenzk. Islandsk encyclopædisk litteratur.* 3 vols. Samfund til udgivelse af gammel nordisk litteratur, 37, 41, 45. Copenhagen: Møller, 1908–18. **Bib.**: Bødker, Laurits, *et al. The Nordic Riddle: Terminology and Bibliography.* Nordisk institut for folkediktning. Skrifter, 3. Copenhagen: Rosenkilde & Bagger, 1964; Taylor, Archer. *A Bibliography of Riddles.* Folklore Fellows Communications, 126. Helsinki: Academia scientiarum Fennica, 1939. **Lit.**: Aarne, A. *Vergleichende Rätselforschungen.* 3 vols. Folklore Fellows Communications, 26–8. Helsinki: Suomalaisen Tiedeakatemian Kustantama, 1918–19; Holtsmark, Anne. "Bil og Hjuke." *Maal og minne* (1945), 139–54; Alver, B. "Norrøne gåter frå mellomalderen." *Syn og segn* (1954), 29–36; Alver, B. "Ikring spørsmålet om eit felles-nordisk system for klassifisering av gåter." In *Nordisk seminar i folkediktning i Ålborg 10.-11. September 1961.* Ed. Laurits Bødker. Copenhagen: Rosenkilde & Bagger, 1962; Rooth, A. B. *Gåtan som diktart.* Lund: Studentlitteratur, 1976; Grambo, Ronald. *Models of Metaphorical Riddles: Preliminary Considerations on Cognitive Folkloristics.* Acta Ethnographica Academiae Scientiarum Hungaricae, 28. Budapest: Akadémiai Kiadó, 1979; Ellis Davidson, H. R. "Insults and Riddles in the *Edda* Poems." In *Edda: A Collection of Essays.* Ed. Robert J. Glendinning and Haraldur Bessason. University of Manitoba Icelandic Studies, 4. Winnipeg: University of Manitoba Press, 1983, pp. 25–46; Wolf, Kirsten. "Some Comments on *Melkólfs saga ok Salomons konungs.*" *Maal og minne* (1990), 1–9.

Jón Hnefill Aðalsteinsson

[See also: *Alvíssmál; Folklore; Fornaldarsögur, Grímnismál; Hervarar saga ok Heiðreks konungs; Kennings; Melkólfs saga ok Salomons konungs; Saxo Grammaticus; Snorra Edda; Svipdagsmál; Vafþrúðnismál*]

Rígsþula ("The Lay of Rígr") is an incomplete poem of approximately forty-eight stanzas traditionally considered to be "eddic," although it is preserved in a MS of the *Prose Edda* (*Codex Wormianus*, AM 242 fol.). In style, meter, narrative content, and language, *Rígsþula* is quite similar to the mythological poems preserved in the *Poetic Edda*, but questions about the origin and circulation of this poem before it was copied into the *Codex Wormianus* are even more problematic than, and quite distinct from, similar questions concerning the other mythological eddic poems.

The text is introduced by a prose preface that identifies the main protagonist, Rígr, with the god Heimdallr, an identification sometimes supported by comparison with *Vǫluspá* (st. 1), in which the *helgar kindir* ("the holy races") are identified as the "kin" of Heimdallr. The parallel, however, is not exact, and we cannot accept the identification as anything other than an early learned gloss on the text as we have it.

The myth that the poem narrates concerns Rígr, a figure who is identified in the poem as an *áss kunnigr* ("a wise god"). During his travels, Rígr came upon the house of Ái and Edda, "great-grandfather" and "great-grandmother." The house was simple and poor, but Rígr spent three nights there sharing the bed of the married couple. The woman then gives birth to *þræll* ("slave"), who marries a woman of low status and begets the race of *þrælar*, or "slaves." The narrative sequence is repeated at the houses of Afi and Amma, "Grandfather" and "Grandmother," and Faðir and Móðir, from whom the races of the *karlar* ("free men") and *jarlar* ("aristocrats") originate. In the concluding stanzas of the poem, Rígr is apparently preparing Konr, the youngest son of Jarl, to become king. *Konr, ungr* ("young") will become the *konungr*. The poem breaks off without any conclusion.

In discussing *Rígsþula*, it is appropriate to distinguish between the poem itself as the artistic realization of the narrative and the myth or myths that are narrated in the poem. And it is also useful to distinguish between these myths and ideas concerning the "right" ordering of society that they implicitly express. A medieval Icelandic or Norwegian Christian, for example, might have thought incredible and absurd the myth of the divine being Rígr who fathers the three orders of society, but he might nonetheless have readily agreed that society is or should be ordered according to this pattern. Given these distinctions, the poem itself is stylistically and linguistically comparable to the other eddic poems, and a simple although not, strictly speaking, necessary assumption is that the general framework of possibilities that scholars have discussed in dating the other eddic poems is relevant here as well. The poem might be much older than the MS in which it was preserved, and a product of a pre-Christian period, or it might be the work of 11th- or 12th-century Icelandic or Norwegian poets of a somewhat antiquarian disposition. The latest dating proposed is von See's (1957), who argues that the poem is a mid-13th-century work composed in Norway. Such a date seems quite late for a poem this archaic in content and in its social ideology. These myths reflect apparent archaic insular influences in certain significant respects.

The first and most striking is the name *Rígr*, which corresponds well to Old Irish *rí* (*ríg*, gen. dat. acc. sing.), the standard Old Irish term for "king." A second feature of *Rígsþula* that seems to reflect Celtic influence is the implicit sanction the poem concedes to allowing distinguished visitors to have sexual relations with the wife of the host, a social custom that can be paralleled readily in early-medieval secular Irish literature, and that would seem to conflict with both Christian and pre-Christian normative values in Iceland and Norway. On the Celtic, specifically Irish, aspect of *Rígsþula*, see Young (1983).

The "tripartite" or implicitly "quattuor-partite" structure of society that *Rígsþula* sanctions ("slaves," "freemen," "nobles," and then a "king") can be paralleled in Celtic social structures, but there are also Germanic parallels. Any structure or ordering of society of this sort is a fiction imposed on a complex and refractory reality, but if we could localize and date *Rígsþula* with more confidence, we could read the poem as a rich source of social ideology, of implicit attitudes toward such topics as class and work in the social circle in which it was produced and appreciated. As it is, we may see the poem as reflecting a specifically aristocratic and secular ideology, although we cannot be confident how widely the ideals implicit in the poem were ever shared in Scandinavian antiquity. On the later influence and the dissemination of the myth of the "three" classes, see Hill (1986).

Ed.: Neckel, Gustav, ed. *Edda: Die Lieder des Codex Regius nebst verwandten Denkmälern. I: Text.* 5th ed. rev. Hans Kuhn. Heidelberg: Winter, 1983. **Tr.**: Hollander, Lee M. *The Poetic Edda, Translated with an Introduction and Explanatory Notes.* 2nd rev. ed. Austin: University of Texas Press, 1962; rpt. 1988. **Lit.**: Young, Jean. "Does Rígsþula Betray Irish Influence?" *Arkiv för nordisk filologi* 49 (1933), 97–107; See, Klaus von. "Des Alter der Rígsþula." *Acta Philologica Scandinavica* 24 (1957–61), 1–12; Haugen, Einar. "The Mythical Structure of the Ancient Scandinavians: Some Thoughts on Reading Dumézil." In *To Honor Roman Jakobsen: Essays on the Occasion of His Seventieth Birthday 11 October 1966.* Janua Linguarum, series major, 31–3. The Hague: Mouton, 1967, pp. 855–68; Harris, Joseph. "Eddic Poetry." In *Old Norse–Icelandic Literature: A Critical Guide.* Ed. Carol J. Clover and John Lindow. Islandica, 45. Ithaca and London: Cornell University Press, 1985, pp. 68–156 [esp. 94–7 (bibliography, p. 151)]; Hill, Thomas D. "*Rígsþula*: Some Medieval Christian Analogues." *Speculum* 61 (1986), 76–87.

Thomas D. Hill

[**See also:** Eddic Poetry; Vǫluspá]

Rímur are Icelandic narrative poems, usually long enough to be divided into cantos or fits, with each such division (*ríma*, fem. sing.) displaying different and usually complicated patterns of rhyme, alliteration, and strict counting of stressed and unstressed syllables. Probably arising in the first half of the 14th century, the *rímur* proved to be the most popular literary form in Iceland from the 15th century until well into the 1800s.

Plots for the *rímur* are derived from prose sources, usually sagas of various kinds. Although members of the genre are commonly called "metrical romances" in English, the thematic material can be quite varied. Of the roughly seventy-eight *rímur* composed before 1600, a commonly employed cutoff date for the premodern members of the genre, almost half are based on the *riddarasögur* of both foreign and domestic provenance, and a score of others deal with material from the *fornaldarsögur*. *Íslendingasögur* and *konungasögur* provide material for only nine *rímur*, and the remainder are based on folktales, exempla, and tales from the *Eddas*. Original thematic material is found only in two parodies of the heroic ideal, *Skíða ríma* and *Fjósa ríma*.

While the oldest of the *rímur*, *Óláfs ríma Haraldssonar* (composed ca. 1350), comprises just a single canto of sixty-five stanzas, the number of cantos among *rímur* prior to 1600 averages around eight, with the largest number (thirty) in *Pontus rímur*. There is likewise considerable variation in the number of stanzas per canto. *Skíða ríma* contains by far the largest number with 202 stanzas, but being a parody of heroic adventure, its stanzaic abundance may also be satirizing what might have seemed to contemporaries an endless string of monotonous verses in the *rímur*. In a corpus of thirty other, old cycles comprising 181 *rímur*, the average number of stanzas was fifty-two, with a differing number from canto to canto being the rule rather than the exception. *Landrés rímur* has a rather large spread, with several cantos containing stanzas in the low thirties and other cantos with just over 100, while a narrow range of stanzas per canto is represented by *Þrymlur* (twenty-three to twenty-nine) and *Óláfs rímur Tryggvasonar* [B] (thirty-three to thirty-five).

Early in the development of the *rímur*, a series of nonnarrative stanzas called a *mansǫngr* (masc. sing.), "love-song," previously extant as occasional poetry, could be affixed to the beginning of each canto. In content, these verses echo continental European courtly poetry, singing the praises of women in general or of one woman in particular, or lamenting the adversity occasioned by love. In later *rímur*, nonamorous subjects could be broached. While some of the earliest *rímur* have no *mansǫngvar* and others affix the *mansǫngr* only to the first canto, a vacillation between roughly two and twelve stanzas in each canto of a poem is not uncommon for the bulk of medieval *rímur*. By far the greatest fluctuation is demonstrated by *Pontus rímur*, in which the *mansǫngvar* can vary between zero and eighty-seven stanzas per canto.

All the stanzas in a single canto have the same meter, although in very late *rímur* the final stanzas could sometimes be made more difficult. Theoretically, the total number of prosodic combinations was very large, since the placement of alliterating staves and rhyme, and the number of syllables in a line or in a rhyme could all be varied. By the end of the 19th century, Helgi Sigurðsson counted more than 2,000 possibilities divided among twenty-three major types. The most common prosodic patterns, however, especially in the older *rímur*, are *ferskeytt*, *stafhent*, *braghent*, *skáhent*, and *samhent*.

Ferskeytt is by far the most common meter. In its most basic form, its four-line stanza is characterized by uneven-numbered lines containing four stressed syllables, two alliterating staves on any combination of stressed syllables except the first and second, and monosyllabic end-rhyme. Even-numbered lines contain three stressed syllables, the first of which must begin with the same alliterating stave employed in the preceding line. Ideally, each line contains three unstressed syllables. Trochaic rhyme combines the final two syllables of the even lines, as in the following example:

> Synina bæði og sína frú
> sikling til sín kallar
> biðr sér hlýða bræðr nú
> býtir frænings vallar.
> (*Jónatas rímur* 1:14)

Stafhent differs from *ferskeytt* in having four stressed syllables in each line, monosyllabic rhyme also in the even lines, and a rhyme scheme of *aabb*:

> Jonatas segir auðar ná
> ekki er gott að segja frá
> burt er hafin besta þín
> en brotin í sundr kistan mín
> (*Jónatas rímur* 2:15)

Samhent resembles *stafhent* meter except that the rhyme is the same in all four lines (*aaaa*). *Skáhent* differs from *ferskeytt* in having the second and fourth stressed syllables rhyme in the first and third lines, while eliminating rhyme in the odd lines.

The only three-line stanza in the early *rímur*, first attested in the 15th century, is *braghent*, which contains three lines connected by trochaic rhyme. The final two lines each contain four stressed (and ideally four unstressed) syllables, with alliteration as in the preceding meters. The initial line contains six stressed syllables (with three of these alliterating with each other) and six unstressed syllables:

> Létti aldri leiðum fyrri lestir branda
> heldr en karskur kljúfur randa
> kastala sér á velli standa.
> (*Jónatas rímur* 3:24)

Characteristic of the language of the *rímur* is the heavy use of *heiti* and kennings (one- and multiple-part metaphors, respectively) as well as special poetic vocabulary. For example, a woman is often referred to as a "goddess of riches" (*auðar Ná*), gold can be called the "home-field of the snake" (*frænings vǫllr*), and a warrior or a man in general can be a "cleaver of shields" (*kljúfr randa*) or "destroyer of swords" (*lestir branda*). While the earliest use of these figures of speech corresponds closely to their codification in Snorri Sturluson's *Prose Edda*, later usage showed some innovation.

Both skaldic and eddic poetry influenced the earliest *rímur*. The prosodic complexity and metaphoric diction show the influence of skaldic poetry, while the narrative, stanzaic eddic poetry, with its treatment of heroic and mythological themes, very likely encouraged the development of the *rímur* in Iceland. Poets often refer to their poetry as *eddu list* or *eddu regla* (eddic art or rules). In the verses cited above, for example, the resolution of two short syllables to represent a long, stressed syllable (*syni-, ekki, brotin*) and the alliterating of any vowel with any other vowel, including *j* (*jonatas, auðar, ekki*) are also eddic characteristics. Although it is possible to derive all the necessary elements of the *rímur* from native Icelandic literary material, the sudden appearance of the genre and lack of any evidence for a period of development leading to the basic features of diction and meter indicate that outside influence provided the models for the earliest *rímur*.

The name of the genre itself is a borrowing, cognate with French *rime*, a term that spread to all the Germanic languages, including Middle English, Middle Low German, and Middle Dutch, where the meaning was expanded to refer to an entire poem. The term was finally chosen over other loanwords, such as *vísa, dans*, or *spil*, which were sometimes also employed in the *rímur* themselves probably due to Middle English influence, where the sense of "story" is also present (*cf.* Old English *ríman* 'to recount'). Because some of the meters found in medieval Latin, Irish, English, and German are similar to the simpler, earlier *rímur* meters, probably one or more of these languages supplied the impetus for the adoption of the genre in Iceland, but there is little doubt that skaldic and eddic poetry soon influenced the imported poetry.

In addition, the influence of the older, French-inspired dance (Icelandic *dans, dansleikr, hringleikr*) cannot be lightly discounted. Dances are mentioned in Iceland from the 12th century, and the fact that church leaders disapproved of them so vigorously indicates that dancing must have been enjoying great popularity at that time. Dances might have encouraged the use of straightforward word order and set the stage for the rapid acceptance of the introductory amorous verses in the *rímur*. Even the term *mansǫngr* is known from the dances.

Melodies, which also accompanied the dances, may have influenced the recitation of the *rímur*. Although the oldest musical notation for *rímur* is preserved in 17th-century MSS, melodies for the individual *rímur* are apparently much older. They extended over the entire stanza, being repeated for each successive stanza until the end of the canto. The reciter (*kvæðamaður*) chanted *a capella*, although he might be joined in harmony by a second reciter.

Before the Reformation, it was unusual for poets to identify themselves in their work, indicating that the newer poetry might at first have been considered inferior to skaldic verse. After 1600, the practice of having a poet name himself in his work becomes quite common, although identification is often made difficult because the names might be obscured by the use of synonyms for a

name that had been broken down either into its compounding elements or into the runic equivalents of its letters.

After 1600, *rímur* continued to increase in popularity in Iceland, with over 1,000 such poems having been preserved. About half that number were composed in the 19th century, and although the popularity of *rímur* subsequently declined sharply, these poems continued to be composed and performed into the 20th century. After the Reformation, the saga-derived *rímur* became the source for *rímur*-derived sagas, but the exact number of these works is currently unknown.

Ed.: Finnur Jónsson, ed. *Rímnasafn. Samling af de ældste islandske rimer*. 2 vols. Samfund til udgivelse af gammel nordisk litteratur, 35. Copenhagen: Møller, 1905–22; Craigie, W. A. *Skotlands Rímur: Icelandic Ballads on the Gowrie Conspiracy*. Oxford: Clarendon, 1908; Craigie, W. A., ed. *Sýnisbók íslenzkra rímna: Specimens of the Icelandic Metrical Romances*. 3 vols. London and New York: Nelson, 1952; Ólafur Halldórsson, ed. *Íslenzkar miðaldarímur*. 4 vols. Reykjavik: Stofnun Árna Magnússonar, 1973–75; Homan, Theo, ed. *Skíðaríma*. Amsterdam: Rodopi, 1975. **Lit.**: Jón Þorkelsson. *Om digtningen på Island i det 15. og 16. århundrede*. Copenhagen: Høst, 1888; Helgi Sigurðsson. *Safn til bragfræði íslenzkra rímna að fornu og nýju*. Reykjavik: Ísafold, 1891; Finnur Jónsson. *Den oldnorske og oldislandske Litteraturs Historie*. 3 vols. 2nd ed. Copenhagen: Gad, 1920–24; Björn K. Þórólfsson. *Rímur fyrir 1600*. Safn Fræðafjelagsins um Ísland og Íslendinga, 9. Copenhagen: Møller, 1934; Craigie, W. A. *The Art of Poetry in Iceland*. Oxford: Clarendon, 1937; Craigie, W. A. *The Romantic Poetry of Iceland*. Glasgow: Jackson, 1950; Sveinbjörn Benteinsson. *Bragfræði og háttatal*. Reykjavik: Leiftur, 1953; Stefán Einarsson. "Report on Rímur." *Journal of English and Germanic Philology* 40 (1955), 255–61; Stefán Einarsson. *A History of Icelandic Literature*. New York: Johns Hopkins University Press; American-Scandinavian Foundation, 1957; Rokkjær, Carl C. "Rímur og Folkeviser." *Acta Philologica Scandinavica* 26 (1964), 100–8; Finnur Sigmundsson. *Rímnatal*. 2 vols. Reykjavik: Rímnafélagið, 1966; Hallfreður Örn Eiríksson. "On Icelandic Rímur: An Orientation." *Arv* 31 (1975), 139–50; Hughes, S. F. D. "'Vǫlsunga rímur' and 'Sjúrðar kvæði': Romance and Ballad, Ballad and Dance." In *Ballads and Ballad Research: Selected Papers of the International Conference on Nordic and Anglo-American Ballad Research. University of Washington, Seattle, May 2–6, 1977*. Ed. Patricia Conroy. Seattle: University of Washington Press, 1978, pp. 37–45; Vésteinn Ólason. "Ballads and Romance in Medieval Iceland." In *Ballads and Ballad Research*, pp. 26–36; Hughes, S. F. D. "Rímur." In *Dictionary of the Middle Ages*. Ed. Joseph R. Strayer. New York: Scribner, 1982–89, vol. 10, pp. 401–7; Jorgensen, Peter. "The Neglected Genre of *Rímur*-Derived Prose and Post-Reformation Jónatas Saga." *Gripla* 7 (1990), 187–201.

Peter A. Jorgensen

[**See also:** Eddic Meters; Eddic Poetry; *Heiti*; Kennings; Love Poetry; Skaldic Meters; Skaldic Verse; *Snorra Edda*]

Romances *see* **Riddarasögur**

Rómverja saga ("The Saga of the Romans") is an Icelandic translation of Sallust's *Bellum Iugurthinum* and *Coniuratio Catilinae*, and Lucan's *Pharsalia*. The saga is preserved in two redactions: the older (A) in AM 595a-b 4to (second quarter of the 14th century), the younger (B) in AM 226 fol. (second half of the 14th century), of which AM 225 fol. is a copy, and in some younger fragments. The A-redaction is fragmentary; the beginning and ending, among other parts, are lost. B is complete, but revised and abridged. Nonetheless, B preserves a few more original readings than A, which shows that it does not reproduce the common original without alterations.

The translation of Sallust in the A-redaction is quite accurate, so that it has been possible to determine to which group of Sallust MSS the Latin original belonged. The transition between Sallust's two works is based on Lucan's second book and the Lucan scholia. The translation of Lucan is much freer than that of Sallust and greatly abbreviated. It opens with a section on the oldest history of Rome and history prior to *Pharsalia*. Only the beginning of this introduction is preserved in A, but a longer section is rendered in AM 764 4to (printed in the 1980 facsimile edition), which continues with a short extract from the Lucan text. In the B-version, this introduction is much abridged. Here, the narrative extends beyond Lucan's account and ends with Augustus's victory and the birth of Christ. The extracts in AM 764 4to show that this was also the case in the A-version. In AM 594 4to, on two originally blank pages preceding the Lucan material, there is inserted in a slightly younger hand another section on the oldest history of Rome ending with the account of Romulus ("Upphaf Rómverja," printed by Konráð Gíslason, 1860: 381–5). This section is based on the original introduction to Lucan and on Martin of Troppau's chronicle, and was obviously added to the saga later. Meissner (1903) incorrectly asserted that both introductions were later additions, and accordingly omitted the introduction to Lucan in his edition (1910).

Hofmann (1986) has convincingly argued that *Veraldar saga* borrowed a number of direct quotations from *Rómverja saga* in the section on the history of Rome. Accordingly, the composition of *Rómverja saga* must be dated to the 1180s at the latest, and probably originated in the same milieu as *Veraldar saga*, i.e., in the circle of the episcopal see in Skálholt.

The style of *Rómverja saga* (in A) is classical. Rhetorical adornments and poetic embellishments are left out (especially in the Lucan text); Latin technical terms are often aptly translated, although misunderstandings do occur. The translator shows a certain independence in toning down Lucan's strong criticism of Caesar and in a more objective treatment of the civil war.

Ed.: Konráð Gíslason, ed. *Fire og fyrretyve for en stor Deel forhen utrykte Prøver af oldnordisk Sprog og Litteratur*. Copenhagen: Gyldendal, 1860, pp. 108–386 [prints both redactions]; Meissner, Rudolf, ed. *Rómveriasaga (AM 595, 4°)*. Palaestra, 88. Berlin: Mayer & Müller, 1910 [with introduction and commentary]; Jakob Benediktsson, ed. *Catilina and Jugurtha by Sallust and Pharsalia by Lucan in Old Norse: Rómverjasaga AM 595 a-b 4to*. Early Icelandic Manuscripts in Facsimile, 13. Copenhagen: Rosenkilde & Bagger, 1980 [a diplomatic edition is in preparation by Þorbjörg Helgadóttir]. **Lit.**: Meissner, Rudolf. "Untersuchungen zur Rómverjasaga. I. Upphaf Rómverja." *Nachrichten von der königl. Gesellschaft der Wissenschaften zu Göttingen*. Phil.-hist. Klasse, 1903, pp. 657–72; Paasche, Fr. "Über Rom und das Nachleben der Antike im norwegischen und isländischen Schrifttum des Hochmittelalters." *Symbolae Osloenses Auspiciis Societatis Graeco-Latinae* 13 (1934), 114–45; Þorbjörg Helgadóttir. "Sallust oversættelsen i *Rómverja saga*, AM 595a-b 4to." Cand. mag. Diss. University of Odense, 1984; Hofmann, Dietrich. "Accessus ad Lucanum: Zur Neubestimmung des Verhältnisses zwischen Rómveria saga und Veraldar saga." In *Sagnaskemmtun: Studies in Honour of Hermann Pálsson on His 65th birthday, 26th May 1986*. Ed. Rudolf Simek *et al.* Vienna, Cologne, and Graz: Böhlau, 1986, pp. 121–51; Þorbjörg Helgadóttir. "On the Sallust Translation in *Rómverja saga*." *Saga-Book of the Viking Society* 22 (1987–88), 263–77; Jakob Benediktsson. "To stiltræk i Rómverja saja" [forthcoming in *Eyvindarbók: Festskrift til Eyvind Fjeld Halvorsen*].

Jakob Benediktsson

[**See also**: *Veraldar saga*]

Royal Administration and Finances

1. DENMARK. During the Middle Ages, Denmark developed from a domain household into a tax-levying state. This process was not completed until the latter half of the 16th century, and although this development cannot be followed in all details, its importance can hardly be doubted. Major stages in this development are the breakdown after 1227 of the realm of King Valdemar Sejr ("the victorious"), complete upon his death in 1241. His death left his successors, his three sons with Berengaria, to compete among themselves for supremacy, aided by various German princes who, in return for military assistance, obtained royal estates in Denmark in fief. From 1332 until 1340, Denmark was totally given in pawn to the counts of Holstein, and it was not until the years after 1360 that King Valdemar Atterdag ("ever-day") succeeded in restoring an autonomous Danish state on a new basis.

After kingship had been established in the late Viking period, royal administration seems to have been based upon the large estates belonging to the king himself and those of his major chieftains. Military defense was the most important objective of all royal administrations, and the *leding*, or levy, developed into a strong and well-adjusted organization of maritime warfare. Its origins in ancient Scandinavian kinship society have long been debated, but no conclusions have been arrived at, except perhaps for a recent theory that the *skipæn* as a unit in the *leding* framework can be identified with the ancient estates of major Viking chieftains. The *leding* fleet, given each year to the king at his disposal, is one ship built and furnished for sixteen weeks by each *skipæn*, and manned by peasants divided into *havner*, one *havne* consisting of from three to eight men who were to alternate in rendering actual military service on board the ship. To govern this whole process, there were strict rules for the division of burdens among the peasants, and a strong role of leadership on the part of a royal *styresmand*, who supervised the delivery of foodstuffs and furnishings to the campaign, and who was also responsible for manning the ship. If there were insufficient men, he had the power to order people out, even if the peasant in question had the right to refuse if there was anyone in his *havne* who had not served on the ship since he himself had served last.

From 1157, when King Valdemar den Store ("the great") obtained the Crown, the dynasty of the Valdemar kings built strong castles throughout the realm and conscripted peasants to maintain them. In Old Danish, the word *inne* may have covered all forms of taxation, but it may also have meant specifically peasants' work on the king's fortifications in the realm. *Ægt* points linguistically to burdens of transportation of the king and his household in their endless traveling throughout the realm. *Redskud* is presumably delivery of foodstuffs on requisition of royal officials, while *stud*, to be yielded in the spring and during the winter, normally is paid in oats for the king's horses.

A survey of royal income in the year 1231 has come down to us in a MS from about 1300 called *Hovedstykket*, i.e., the main part of "King Valdemar's Land Register," which has sometimes inappropriately been considered a Danish counterpart to the English *Domesday Book*. The MS is a copy of, among other things, texts from the royal chancery; but why the copy was made at such a relatively late date and why in the monastery of Sorø are questions that have never been answered. The *Hovedstykket* proves that estates at the disposal of the king were of three kinds; they were property of the Crown, or they were *kongelev* and belonged to whoever occupied the Danish throne at a given time, or they were the king's hereditary estates, his *patrimonium*. The *Hovedstykket* illustrates how royal estates were administered from castles and other strongholds in the realm, and it is an important source of information about their relative size and value.

Several estates would furnish specific yearly deliveries to the king's household, and all of them were obliged to provide housing and maintenance for the king on his travels; *gæsteri* ("maintenance") is normally measured in nights. Our insight into the functionings of royal administration in the time of the Valdemars, however, is dimmed by the fact that the *leding, gæsteri, ægt, stud, inne,* and *redskud* in the course of time all came to mean simply taxes.

From the outset, the *leding* was probably intended to be replaced by mere taxation, as in years when the king had no enemy to move against, and when he profitably might use the peasants' prestations for other purposes. He would then dispose of deliveries and services from all *leding* districts corresponding to an actual sixteen-week campaign. Even in years when the *leding* was actually ordered out, there were payments made by those who lived too far from the sea to give service in person; they were charged with a tax called *kværsæde* (for sitting-behind). From the middle of the 1200s, when warfare changed to favor professional cavalry, the *leding* may be supposed to have been absolved continuously.

Cities founded on ground belonging to the king or the Crown were often granted favorable conditions for a certain period of time, but were later taxed with a yearly contribution, *midsommergæld* or *arnegæld*, a tax on hearths to be paid on Midsummer's Day, resting on the theory or reality that the cities were royal property.

In the 1200s, when royal power in Denmark was the object of continuous strife among branches of the royal family after the death of King Valdemar Sejr, royal estates, with all their normal income, were often pawned to princes in the service of the king who then were obliged to serve the king in warfare on conditions corresponding to the value of their pawns. A series of misfortunes in royal Danish foreign policy in the years leading up to 1332 resulted in all royal estates and incomes being given in pawn to the counts of Holstein for a sum of 200,000 silver marks; Danish royal castles fell into the possession of Holstein noblemen, who themselves were the counts' creditors.

From 1340 onward, King Valdemar Atterdag, who had spent his youth abroad and now accepted the realm on conditions set up by the counts of Holstein and their allies, managed to restore the kingdom of Denmark financially in the course of little more than twenty years. He established a strong military organization on the basis of the royal estates, intended both for inner coercion and for international warfare, and he entered into close cooperation with the Church, which allowed him to dispose of ecclesiastical property nearly as if it had been royal in return for concessions in other ecclesiastical rights and duties. In this way, King Valdemar was able to draw revenue from taxation, in money or in kind from his other subjects. His success in creating a financial structure was favored by a shift in population from the countryside to the cities,

which allowed him and other feudal lords to redistribute their holdings in a way favorable to their intentions, to collect large estates, and at the same time to normalize the minor dependent holdings in size and yield. Another important factor was growing dependence upon the Hanseatic cities, which became the gateway to world economy for Danish commercial and speculative enterprises. From the 1330s until the end of the century, no Danish coinage was issued, and foreign coin circulated freely in Denmark.

Under Valdemar and his daughter, Margrethe, who succeeded to the realm in 1375 on behalf of her minor son Olaf, the royal holdings grew in size and value because of vast acquisitions that, at least officially, were termed reductions of lost crown property to its former state. They laid the basis for a more consolidated royal economy in the 1400s, even if administration of royal estates and income henceforth, for internal political reasons, had to be given to magnates of the realm on more liberal terms and for longer periods of time than had hitherto been normally the case. Gradually, in the later Middle Ages, the corporation of the Council of the Realm (the *Rigsråd*) came to consider itself, in its capacity as representative of all servants of the Crown, as major guarantor of the Crown's integrity, to be observed especially when royal power was handed over from one monarch to another.

One constant and important source of royal income comprised dues and customs from the Scanian Fairs. They had existed apparently from time immemorial, based upon the abundant autumn herring fisheries in the Sound, but they were reorganized along western European models in the middle of the 1200s. The king issued his coinage each year during the market period, and he enforced an exchange rate with foreign currency most favorable to Denmark. At the same time, he levied dues on all grants yielded to foreign visitors to the market, to be paid in Danish coinage, and an export customs payment, to be paid in Flemish coinage for the traffic to western Europe or in Hanseatic coinage, *i.e.*, Lübeck coinage for the traffic across the Baltic. The Scanian customs system no doubt is a precursor of the Sound Toll dues, its importance being mainly that it was paid in foreign currency.

During the entire Middle Ages, the king levied a trading and consumption tax in all cities and marketplaces, and the chancery would levy dues on all judicial decisions, the issuing of charters, and the like. These taxes, however, could never have reached the levels of income derived from royal estates and foreign trade.

Lit.: Christensen, William. *Dansk Statsforvaltning i det 15. Aarhundrede.* Copenhagen: Gad, 1900; rpt. Copenhagen: Selskabet for udgivelse af kilder til dansk historie, 1974; Jørgensen, Paul Johs. *Dansk Retshistorie.* Copenhagen: Gad, 1947; Christensen, Aksel E. *Kongemagt og aristokrati. Epoker i middelalderlig dansk statsopfattelse indtil unionstiden.* 2nd ed. Copenhagen: Akademisk Forlag, 1968; rpt. 1976; Christensen, Aksel E., et al., eds. *Danmarks Historie.* 2 vols. Copenhagen: Politiken, 1977–80; Riis, Thomas. *Les institutions politiques centrales du Danemark 1100–1332.* Odense University Studies in History and Social Sciences, 46. Odense: Odense University Press, 1977; Lund, Niels, and Kai Hørby. *Samfundet i tidlig vikingetid og tidlig middelalder.* Dansk Socialhistorie, 2. Copenhagen: Gyldendal, 1980.

Kai Hørby

2. NORWAY. The early Norwegian monarchy developed no machinery of government by which various parts of the kingdom could be held together beyond the lifespan of each king. The monarchs were hardly capable of ruling directly more than a core

territory, through which they would progress with their *hirð*, or retinue, to consume the proceeds in kind of royal estates and other sources of income. But there were limits to the size of territory that could be controlled by a single king in this way.

A king who wanted to unite the land under his rule could not do so without the help of local chieftains, who possessed an inherited power base that the king as yet lacked in many districts. At best, he could make the chieftains exercise public authority on his behalf and render military support in return for a share of royal income and power. Such a system of government would, however, cut both ways. The chieftains tended to cooperate with the king only as far as it served their own interests.

From the reign of King Óláfr II Haraldsson (1015/6–1028) can be traced the title of *lendr maðr* ("landed man"), a person who in return for fealty and service was provided with the income of royal land in addition to his own. Both local chieftains and prominent freemen of the peasant society were made *lendir menn* and thus tied closer to the monarchy. In this fashion started the incorporation of the magnates of the country into the *hirð* as royal liegemen and the leading rank of a service aristocracy. Over the years, the *hirð* came to function as a corps of administrative personnel. Within its framework was built up a machinery of both local and central government, in the end covering the whole of Norway, together with the "tributary" islands west over the sea.

From Óláfr Haraldsson's reign is also attested the local office of royal *ármaðr* ("servant, messenger"). In the sagas, the *ármaðr* appears as a manager of royal estates whose authority would also extend over public matters. In the 12th-century provincial codes, he represents the king locally in fiscal, judicial, and military matters. There were hardly enough *ármenn* to take care of local administrative tasks all over the country, since the law code of the *Gulaþingslǫg* implies that there would not be such an official in every large county (*fylki*) of West Norway. This lack may help to explain why the provincial law codes cast the *lendr maðr* in much the same role as the *ármaðr*. He was probably to represent the king in districts without *ármenn*, and otherwise to support the *ármaðr* in carrying out his duties as a more regular royal servant.

In the more important towns of the kingdom, a royal official called a *gjaldkeri* can be traced back to at least the first decade of the 12th century (in Trondheim). Like the *ármaðr*, he represented the king in a general civil and military capacity. He was head of urban administration and organized the urban assembly, the *þing* or *mót*.

A regular system of local administration that covered the whole country was only gradually established from the latter half of the 12th and throughout the 13th centuries. The mainstay of the system was the office of *sýslumaðr*, comparable to that of the English sheriff. The *sýslumaðr* was charged with more extensive fiscal, legal-administrative, and military duties than the *ármaðr*. He combined the regular administrative service of the *ármaðr* with the social standing of the *lendr maðr*, which is revealed by the fact that most *lendir menn*, or "barons," as they were also called from the 1270s, served as *sýslumenn*. In the course of the 13th century, the kingdom was fairly systematically subdivided into administrative districts called *sýslur* (sing. *sýsla*), each controlled by one or two *sýslumenn*. Altogether there were more than fifty such officials, being paid mainly by a share of the legal fines they collected on behalf of the king. If the *sýsla* contained a town, the *sýslumaðr* would take up residence there and head the town administration. In the more important towns, he would support and partly control the *gjaldkeri* in his function as a more direct urban official.

From the late 12th century, the local administration of justice was increasingly handled by the royal *lǫgmaðr* ("lawman"). His original task was to instruct the *þing* courts on points of law. But his instruction increasingly acquired the character of judgment, and was legally defined as such from 1260. The law codes of King Magnús lagabœtir ("law-mender") from the 1270s define in greater detail the role of the lawman as well as that of the *sýslumaðr*, with whom he was to act in concert in the enforcement of law. In the following period, ten lawmen, each within his own law province, delivered judgments and passed sentences, partly in sessions of their own courts, partly within the framework of local and regional *þings*. Like the *sýslumenn*, the lawmen tended to take up residence in towns. The larger towns of Bergen and Trondheim were given special urban lawmen.

In 1308, a regional royal treasurer or *féhirði(r)* resided in the royal castle or palace of each of the four most important towns of the kingdom: Bergen, Trondheim, Oslo, and Tønsberg. Into his treasury, the *sýslumenn* and other officials of the pertaining region paid the royal incomes for which they were accountable, and from here payments were made on behalf of the king.

In the early kingdom, there was no other organ of central government than an itinerant king and his private *hirð*. The development of a more elaborate system of central administration took place on well-known European lines. Within the *hirð*, offices of the royal household, above all that of the *stallari* ("marshal"), were entrusted with public functions and gradually acquired the character of offices of state. In the latter half of the 13th century, the chancellor emerged as head of a royal writing office, which developed into what may be termed the first "department of state" in Norway. Writing had been put to use in royal administration at least from the mid-12th century. But it took more than a century before writing became a regular means of accounting, record keeping, and communication between the central government and local districts.

In the Middle Ages, the king never completely ceased to be itinerant. But from the late 12th century, he would rarely stay outside the leading towns of the kingdom for long periods. Bergen in the 13th century became what may be termed the first real political capital of Norway, in its capacity as the most important royal residential town, the chief meeting place of royal assemblies, and the rallying point of incipient agencies of central government.

In the reign of King Hákon V Magnússon (1299–1319), Oslo became the center of the royal chancery. In the late Middle Ages, when the monarchy moved abroad, the two towns functioned as more or less coordinate centers of administration, Bergen for North and West Norway with the tributary Atlantic islands, Oslo for East Norway. Sections of the permanent royal council, later the "Council of the Realm" (Old Norse *ríkisins ráð*, Latin *consilium regni*), were resident in Bergen from the beginning of the 14th century, later also in Oslo.

The early monarchy probably to some extent based itself on riches acquired by the Viking methods of plunder and trade. Still, the permanent and stable element of its economy must have been the yield of royal estates, supplemented by contributions of food, lodging, and transport from the peasants during the progress of king and *hirð*. The maintenance of peace and order by an itinerant king was probably an early additional source of income, in the form of legal fines and confiscations (*sak[ar]eyrir*). The population also contributed economically to the defense system of the *leiðangr*.

During the prolonged military struggle for territorial unification, the monarchy confiscated considerable quantities of land from defeated opponents as it gained footholds in various parts of the country. In the 11th and 12th centuries, agricultural land was no doubt the main source of royal income. Over the years, however, it was given away at greater speed than it accrued, above all in the form of donations to ecclesiastical institutions. In the first half of the 14th century, the Crown, according to the latest estimate, hardly had at its disposal more than about 7 percent of the land of the country in terms of value. It may by this time have received more of its revenue from the *sakeyrir*. Its third main source of income was the part of the *leiðangr* that, from the 12th century onward, had gradually been converted into an annual tax, the first state tax of Norway.

The economy of the Crown also rested on regal rights of uncertain fiscal importance. The king claimed ownership of what nobody else possessed: commons (in the sense that people who started new farms there became his tenants), property without heirs, treasure trove, flotsam, and jetsam. His monopoly of minting could be turned to account. He claimed the right of preemption of all goods arriving at Norwegian ports. From 1294, he imposed a fixed duty on foreign ships calling there. Foreign traders had some time earlier been subjected to an export duty on herring from East Norway, and for a period in the first half of the 14th century had to pay both import and export duties on further goods.

The royal revenues from territories outside Norway proper are little known. After the annexation of Iceland in 1262–1264, the peasants there paid a tax of homespun (*vaðmál*) to the Norwegian Crown, but information is lacking about the taxes paid from the other tributary islands of the Atlantic. The king had the right to *sakeyrir* from Iceland, Greenland, the Faroe Islands, Shetland, and Orkney, and had estates in some of the islands. The right to trade with and to exact tribute from the "Finns" or Lapps (Saami) in the north became a royal monopoly of some importance.

The royal revenues were paid mainly in a narrow selection of goods. Consequently, it was necessary for the king and his servants to trade in order to procure other commodities and cash.

The financial basis of the high-medieval Norwegian Crown was rather weak. The decline of population and production in the latter part of the 14th century must have altered the fiscal situation drastically for the worse. As a consequence of the financial crisis, the administrative machinery of Norwegian state government was strongly reduced. As the monarchy moved abroad, the central government of Norway came more and more to be directed from Denmark. The prelates and magnates of the Council of the Realm, who were to function as a consultative and sanctioning body at the king's side in the government of Norway, had no central administrative apparatus at their disposal. The Norwegian chancellor was largely reduced to an issuer of certain formalized judicial documents, and the surplus of royal revenues was sent to Denmark from the regional treasures. During throne vacancies, royal minorities, and longer royal absences, there functioned up to 1387 a chairman of the council and leader of Norwegian state government in the person of the chancellor or the *dróttseti* ("steward"), corresponding to the Danish *drost* and the Swedish *drots*. A *dróttseti* was also appointed for further periods up to 1483. The archbishop of Trondheim occupied a strong position in the council, and acted as its *de facto* leader toward the end of the Middle Ages.

In local administration, the *sýslumenn* in the late Middle Ages were generally replaced by the private bailiffs (Norwegian *fogder*, sing. *fogd*) of holders of larger royal *lén*, or fiefs. These "vassals" were generally more autonomous royal representatives and held

their *lén* on more favorable fiscal terms than the high-medieval *sýslumenn*. The captains of the royal castles of Bergen, Trondheim, Oslo, and Tønsberg came to combine the earlier functions of local *sýslumaðr* and regional treasurer. They exercised direct authority over a castle *lén* that tended to expand toward the end of the Middle Ages, and indirectly controlled other *lén* by virtue of their superior fiscal authority and greater military resources. Thus, they functioned as especially trusted and often rather independent middlemen between a king who resided in Denmark and his Norwegian subjects. The captain of the strategically important Bohus castle at the Göta River also acquired a dominant position, while the castle of Tønsberg lost its importance toward the end of the Middle Ages.

The disintegration of a central Norwegian administration and the more private exercise of local administration by the *lén* holders led to a greater autonomy for local districts and towns. The leading members of local society came to play a more important part in public affairs, in the capacity of town councilors and men sworn to take part in the decisions of local and regional *þing*s (Norwegian *lagrettemenn*). In local rural districts, so-called *lensmenn*, recruited from peasant society, increasingly functioned as helpers of the *fogder*. And the royal *gjaldkeri* changed into the *fogd* of the town (Norwegian *byfogd*), functioning under the town council.

Lit.: Johnsen, Arne Odd, and Jerker Rosén. "Drottsete." *KLNM* 3 (1958), 338–48; Blom, Grethe Authén. "Fehirde." *KLNM* 4 (1959), 210–2; Blom, Grethe Authén. "Gældker." *KLNM* 5 (1960), 673–8; Hamre, Lars, et al. "Hird." *KLNM* 6 (1961), 568–80; Rasmussen, Poul, et al. "Jordejendom." *KLNM* 7 (1962), 654–77; Carlsson, Gottfrid, et al. "Kansler." *KLNM* 8 (1963), 232–9; Carlsson, Gottfrid, et al. "Kansli." *KLNM* 8 (1963), 239–43; Hamre, Lars, et al. "Kapelgeistlighet." *KLNM* 8 (1963), 256–64; Peetre, Arthur, et al. "Kronans finanser." *KLNM* 9 (1964), 412–28; Hammarström, Ingrid, et al. "Kronans handel." *KLNM* 9 (1964), 428–34; Hafström, Gerhard, et al. "Lagman." *KLNM* 10 (1965), 150–63; Bjørkvik, Halvard, et al. "Leidang." *KLNM* 10 (1965), 432–59; Bøe, Arne. "Lendmann." *KLNM* 10 (1965), 498–505; Hamre, Lars. *Norske historie frå omlag 1400.* Oslo: Universitetsforlaget, 1968; Nielsen, Herluf, et al. "Rigsråd." *KLNM* 14 (1969), 220–34; Helle, Knut. "Riksmøter." *KLNM* 14 (1969), 252–7; Jørgensen, Jens Ulf. "Sagefald." *KLNM* 14 (1969), 651–7; Rasmussen, Poul, et al. "Skatter." *KLNM* 15 (1970), 413–41; Blom, Grethe Authén. "Skattland." *KLNM* 15 (1970), 446–50; Hamre, Lars. *Norsk historie frå midten av 1400-åra til 1513.* Oslo: Universitetsforlaget, 1971; Hamre, Lars, et al. "Stallar." *KLNM* 17 (1972), 34–8; Andersen, Per Sveaas, et al. "Syssel." *KLNM* 17 (1972), 645–51; Andersen, Per Sveaas, and Björn Þorsteinsson. "Sysselmann." *KLNM* 17 (1972), 651–8; Helle, Knut, ed. *Norge blir en stat, 1130–1319.* Handbok i Norges historie, 3. 2nd ed. Bergen: Universitetsforlaget, 1974; Modéer, Kjell Å., et al. "Ting." *KLNM* 18 (1974), 334–68; Enemark, Poul, et al. "Told." *KLNM* 18 (1974), 431–49; Holmsen, Andreas. *Nye studier i gammel historie.* Oslo: Universitetsforlaget, 1976; Mykland, Knut. *Norges historie.* 5 vols. Oslo: Cappelen, 1976–80; Andersen, Per Sveaas. *Samlingen av Norge og kristningen av landet, 800–1130.* Handbok i Norges historie, 2. Bergen: Universitetsforlaget, 1977; Helle, Knut. "Norway in the High Middle Ages: Recent Views on the Structure of Society." *Scandinavian Journal of History* 6 (1981), 161–89.

Knut Helle

3. SWEDEN. An account of the finances of the Crown and the royal administration as well the administrative divisions in Sweden during the medieval period must begin with the new art of castle building introduced in the 13th century. Originally built by the king for purely military purposes, the castles also came to

play an important role in the local government throughout the Middle Ages.

With the introduction of a heavily armed and armored cavalry patterned after the international model, and with the construction of completely new castles, the Crown came to have different financial needs, since building and furnishing permanent houses and maintaining permanent garrisons were costly enterprises. The castles also served as residences for the ambulatory court. As a consequence, standing taxes and different fees replaced personal service, leading to new collection systems and administrative districts. Such military and administrative changes had great importance for the consolidation of royal power, which at the same time was strengthened through cooperation with the Church.

Administrative procedures and enlargement of the administration from the middle of the 13th century came as a direct consequence of the new military need. The construction of defensive works had to be maintained, and soldiers required weapons, clothing, food, and money, as well as feed for the horses. To fill these and other needs, the incomes in money and payment in kind, which until then had been collected in storage houses in the demesne of the Crown in the district, were sent to the castle of the province. The castle thus became the center of the territory, defended and administered by a commander responsible for that territory. If the castle lay directly under the king's control, it was administered by his bailiff. If it was granted by the king to a nobleman, the captain stood in the latter's service. The main duty of the captain was to act as commander and be responsible for the defense of the castle and the surrounding territory; he thus had certain financial and administrative duties.

The king directly disposed of income from a Crown-administered bailiwick. The bailiff was required to maintain accounts of incomes and expenses. How the bailiff was paid is not clear, but some part of the tax collection must have fallen to his share. Or he may have had a separate fief of estate and income inside or outside the bailiwick in addition to the income (immunity from taxation) he received for his ordinary service.

Male members of the royal family, especially the younger brothers of the reigning king, received duchies. Even female members of the royal family received maintenance provinces (*donatio propter nupitas*), comprising a demesne of the Crown with income from the district. In the beginning of the 14th century, a castle was given along with a province, but this eventually came to pose a threat to the reigning king, and was later forbidden by law. Provinces with or without a castle to defend and maintain consisting of fiefs of estates and income were also given to individuals outside the royal family in recognition of service to the Crown or in pledge.

In the Middle Ages, the kings were always short of money, and to pay their debts bailiwicks as well as certain sources of income were pawned. Such territory was given with all the king's ordinary sources of income. The right to impose extra taxes and high fines, however, was reserved for the king. The possessor of the pledge was guaranteed a certain yearly minimum yield from the province in question. The pledge conditions could be set up either in such a way that the annual collection was deducted from the main debts, or else it was paid in one lump, at which time the pledge reverted to the king. In the first case, it was a question of amortizing the debt. Otherwise, the collection functioned as the holder's interest. Even if the heirs of the province holder were included in the pledge agreement, as was often the case, few ex-

amples from the period show that the fee passed to the heirs of the province holder. That a province was pledged again by the holder was common.

The pledged fief gave the province holder a free hand. The defense and administration of the territory passed completely to him. He manned and equipped the castle and had his own bailiffs and civil servants. The promise to keep the castle to assist the king or his heirs was the only connection between the Crown and the province holder.

The earliest castles were built presumably as protection against external enemies in the east and west, and then at watercourses leading into key districts in the interior. Nature itself offered a good defense. The country was, on the whole, sparsely populated; mountains and forests made the terrain difficult to penetrate. Lakes and bogs formed a natural defense in the summertime; during the winter, sledges made passage on the frozen waterways relatively easy.

The first citadel-type fortresses were located at such key positions. In Stockholm, the castle was placed at the outflow of Lake Mälaren into the Baltic. Nyköpingshus was located farther south, and Stäkeborg even farther down the coast, protecting the rich central districts of Östergötland. Kalmar appears in contemporary sources as the most important castle on the east coast. It was situated just north of the contemporary border with Denmark, and at the same time guarded the passageway through Kalmarsund. Borgholm on the isle of Öland was similarly situated. The fortification found in Jönköping at the southern shore of Lake Vättern guarded the south of the realm, and farther south forests formed natural barriers. As a consequence of political conditions during this period, there was not a particularly large territory for the Swedish Crown to defend on the west coast. The old town Lödöse at the Göta River had a castle, and somewhat later Axvall was built not far from the episcopal see of Skara.

All these fortresses had large bailiwicks, because the income of the king and the Crown was quite limited. In other words, a large territory was required to support the castle. This does not mean, however, that all territories at this time were bailiwicks of the castle.

The struggles for the throne within the reigning dynasty during the first decades of the 14th century involved these castles; Nyköpingshus and Stäkeborg were destroyed. After Magnus Eriksson was elected king in 1319, a relatively peaceful period followed, with few castles being built. Finances in any case did not allow the construction of large buildings, especially not after the redemption of the former Danish provinces Scania and Blekinge in 1332. On the contrary, Kalmar castle was pawned, something that was possible because it was no longer a boundary castle. Lödösehus lost its importance and came to be replaced by fortresses at Lindholm and Älvsborg at the mouth of the Göta River.

The period is distinguished by extensive, consolidated territories, resulting in part from the disappearance of several castles. Thus, not only the old Nyköping bailiwick, but almost all of middle Sweden was under the castle in Stockholm. During the civil wars of 1350 and 1360, castles were again constructed. During the German regime from 1363, a number of small private castles were built that would later be transferred to the king's possession and become an integral part of the administration division. Nyköpingshus was rebuilt, and the castle became the center of a large pawn-province complex. To Nyköpinghus now belonged not only the bordering parts of Södermanland, but also the more distant territories of Dalarna and Norrland in the north. For protection of the important iron and copper export from the mines in middle Sweden, castles were built in Örebro, Köping, and, later, Västerås.

Under King Albrecht of Mecklenburg, nephew of King Magnus Eriksson, the administration came under strong German influence. Nevertheless, the struggle with the deposed kings Magnus Eriksson and Håkon Magnússon, who held territory in the west, and their followers continued a long time. Toward the end of this period, after the Mecklenburgs had been driven out in 1388/9, and Queen Margrethe, and later Erik of Pomerania, had ascended the throne, the division of the country into several smaller administration units had progressed far. In Södermanland, for example, a new castle was built by Bo Jonsson (Grip), a wealthy magnate who had been the leader of the opposition to German dominion in the years 1370–1380. During this period, Norrland became more prominent. Some fortresses were built there, but the coastal territories farthest north were under the administration of Korsholm, a castle on the eastern shore of the Gulf of Bothnia, in the Finnish territory, which then belonged to Sweden.

The process of administrative division suddenly came to a halt during the 1434 revolt of the people under the leadership of Engelbrekt Engelbrektsson. The first assault was directed against Borganäs, the center of a hated bailiwick in Dalarna, not far from Kopparberg and the copper mine. Almost half of the castles of the realm were completely destroyed or seriously damaged. The result was a return to the maintenance of larger territories under the remaining citadels, which on the whole were the strongest and most important ones.

The Swedish Crown typically administered house and land through its own bailiffs, which at least in principle meant that the income went directly to the national treasury (fiscus). But in practice, the collection was often already mortgaged long before it was received by the bailiwick and the officials in the districts. The Crown suffered from a constant lack of liquid assets and income from the relatively primitive agrarian society. The agrarian crisis of the 14th century worsened the situation. At the same time, the Scandinavians started to lose international merchant shipping to the Hanseatic ports. During the second half of the 14th century, the pledge fee became the predominant form of administration.

Queen Margrethe understood the need to assert royal power, however, and looked after the interests of the Crown by confiscating provinces and estates, and by levying harsh taxes. During her reign, when Sweden practically was ruled from Copenhagen, crown administration with strong centralization was firmly asserted. But at the death of the queen, when Erik of Pomerania, a young relative whom she had selected as her successor, came to the throne, the strength of the Crown diminished.

At the end of the Middle Ages, about half of the farms were owned by fee holders. The rest of the soil was farmed for landowners. Aristocratic and ecclesiastical land holders were exempt from crown tax, while at the same time they could collect taxes from their own lands. And although the Crown placed certain restrictions on tax exemption, the income from taxation was nonetheless comparatively insignificant. Given the often precarious financial situation of the Crown, however, the revenue duty was a standard theme in domestic politics. In view of its financial needs, the Crown imposed additional taxes, which tended to become permanent. Typically, the taxes overlapped, and were constantly changed in different ways. Thus, the new tax paid in kind, which

was added to the old legal taxes in 1403, is considered to have been a severe additional tax, which nevertheless became part of the standing structure.

There were, as well, significant variations in the taxes imposed within local districts. Much rested on local agreement between the representatives of the Crown and the taxpayers. The organization in the administrative territories, and local regulations and statutes, settled what was to be considered the ordinary tax in a given region. Bailiffs and others were responsible for overseeing the details of the taxation system. Yet the Crown had only a general idea about its sources of income or revenues, and accounts were maintained showing only approximate sums expected from the bailiwicks.

While the preserved source material illuminating the tax system is fragmentary, we do know that, at times, the taxes were burdensome. Grievances over hard taxes and tax collection are common in contemporary sources, not least in connection with the Engelbrekt insurrection in 1434. But how these taxes affected the private individual is impossible to determine. The Crown also received income in money (as opposed to goods or service in kind) from customs, minting coins, and the taxation of certain towns.

During the 15th and early 16th century, Sweden joined the other Nordic countries in a union. The period was characterized by incessant fighting for control between the king of the Union and the Swedish aristocratic council members. Events came to a head with the election of a regent to lead the council and govern the country as a republic, thus bringing to a halt for a long time the king's demand for control of Sweden. The Swedish council in turn attempted to curtail the power of the king through constitutional means.

The period after Erik of Pomerania's fall is characterized by a decentralized province administration. Most of the castles and provinces were in the possession of members of the State Council as fiefs in exchange for service. This arrangement implied that the feudal lords received Crown income from their respective provinces for their part in the defense and administration of these provinces. As during the Mecklenburg regime in the 14th century, the territory of the province of the Crown was often limited. There was again a danger of the kingdom being dissolved. Attempts at the middle of the century to subjugate the provinces under the Crown and royal bailiwick administration were in vain.

The period after 1504, like that before 1434, has been the object of special studies of the administrative system. To coordinate and increase the financial resources of the central power, territories that lacked a castle to maintain were consolidated. Income from the territories in the central, northern, and eastern (Finnish) areas went to maintain the castles in Västerås, Åbo (now Turku in Finland), and especially Stockholm, which functioned as administrative center. This Crown-administered territory was composed in such a way that most of the collected income was received in cash, iron, and grain, although other goods, such as bulls from farms and provinces in Götaland, also formed an integral part of the tax collection.

The bailiffs of these castles stood in the service of the national manager (riksföreståndaren), from whom they took orders with regard to tax conveyance, sale of goods, and other aspects of tax collection. Thus, the bailiff at Västerås castle had to relinquish most of the iron revenue as well as a part of his other collected taxes to the central administration. From there, the goods were easily transported to Stockholm, either on the ice of the Mälaren in winter or by boat in summer. Because of this arrangement, the Västerås bailiff was dependent upon Stockholm to replenish deficiencies in his stores.

The whole taxation structure, with its strong centralization, was intended to keep Stockholm as strong as possible. Furthermore, in order to ensure continued surplus, those provinces that were best connected with Stockholm, providing easy access to available revenue, were centrally administered. Other provinces were granted exemption from taxes in lieu of service, implying that the national manager could not make financial claims upon the feudal lords in the form of a province collection for the national treasury, but could only collect extra taxes.

The process of stabilizing the finances of the Crown that continued from the end of the 15th century came to be completed under King Gustav Vasa. Confiscation of church property and accumulated revenue after the Reformation in 1527 added considerably to the national treasury. With the sweeping reforms of about 1540, the medieval administrative pattern finally dissolved, and a more uniform tax system along with a central bookkeeping system was established, thus allowing the Crown, for the first time, to form a complete picture of its sources of income.

Lit.: Styffe, Carl Gustaf, ed. *Bidrag till Skandinaviens historia ur utländska arkiver*. 5 vols. Stockholm: Norstedt, 1875–84; Styffe, Carl Gustaf. *Skandinavien under unionstiden. Med särskildt afseende på Sverige och dess förvaltning åren 1319 till 1521. Ett bidrag till den historiska geografien.* Tredje upplagan. Stockholm: Norstedt, 1911; Lönnroth, Erik. *Statsmakt och statsfinans i det medeltida Sverige. Studier över skatteväsen och länförvaltning.* Gothenburg: Acta Universitatis Gothoburgensis, 1940; Rosén, Jerker. *Kronoavsöndringar under äldre medeltid.* Kungl. humanistiska vetenskapssamfundet i Lund, Skrifter 46. Lund: Gleerup, 1949; Dovring, Folke. *De stående skatterna på jord 1400–1600.* Kungl. humanistiska vetenskapssamfundet i Lund, Skrifter 49. Lund: Gleerup, 1951; Rosén, Jerker. "Drottning Margaretas svenska räfst." *Scandia* 20.2 (1951), 169–246; Hammarström, Ingrid. *Finansförvaltning och varuhandel 1504–1540. Studier i de yngre Sturarnas och Gustav Vasas statshushållning.* Diss. Uppsala: Akademisk avhandling, 1956; Bjurling, Oscar. *Das Steuerbuch König Eriks XIII. Versuch einer Rekonstruktion.* Skrifter utgivna av Ekonomisk-historiska föreningen i Lund, 4. Lund: Berling, 1962; Fritz, Birgitta. *Hus, land och län. Förvaltningen i Sverige 1250–1434.* 2 vols. Stockholm Studies in History, 16, 18. Stockholm: Almqvist & Wiksell, 1972–73; Dahlbäck, Göran, *et al.*, eds. *Det medeltida Sverige. Uppland.* Stockholm: Almqvist & Wiksell, 1972–88, vol. 1, parts 1–6; Folin, Nina, and Göran Tegnér, eds. *Medeltidens ABC.* Stockholm: Gidlund; Statens historiska museer, 1985; Dahlbäck, Göran, ed. *Svensk medeltidsforskning idag. En forskningsöversikt utarbetad på uppdrag av Humanistisk-samhällsvetenskapliga forskningsrådet.* Stockholm and Uppsala: Humanistiska samhällsvetenskapliga forsknings rådet, 1987.

Birgitta Fritz

[See also Chancery; Coins and Mints; Council of the Realm; Denmark; Feudal Influences and Tendencies; *Hirð*; Iceland; *Leiðangr*; Norway; Royal Assemblies (Parliaments, Estates); Sweden; *Þing*]

Royal Assemblies (Parliaments, Estates).

The royal assemblies in the three Scandinavian kingdoms cannot be grouped under one designation. They flourish in different epochs in different forms. On the whole, they correspond to the development that, in the rest of Europe, can be observed from the feudal curia in an expanded form to the organized assembly of the estates of the realm.

In Norway, the royal meeting (a contemporary term does not exist) received a firm form in connection with the establishment of the archiepiscopal see in Niðaróss (Trondheim) in 1152/3 and the coronation of Magnús Erlingsson in 1163/4. The new law of succession demanded an assembly of bishops, abbots, and men who constituted the *hirð*, plus twelve farmers from each of the five dioceses. This assembly was clearly meant to take over the role of the *þing* in the taking of a king, the acceptance of new laws, and agreements with the Church. The domestic disturbances during the following half-century allowed no opportunity for this royal assembly. It reached its climax during the reigns of Hákon Hákonarson and Magnús lagabœtir ("law-mender"): fifteen known assemblies from 1218 to 1281 with up to eighty participants ("good men"). The number of farmers remains unknown. However, the law of succession was probably not followed strictly. The assemblies were dominated by the king and the archbishop; decisions were made in a smaller circle, but were sanctioned through the acceptance of the participants in the form of acclamation. Any real influence by the farmers, who were not always summoned, cannot be demonstrated. The royal assembly diminishes in importance because of the schism between the state and Church, and does not take place after 1302. It is replaced partly by the Council of the Realm (*riksråd*), partly by the synods of the Norwegian church province. However, certain swearings of allegience to kings, *e.g.*, in 1344 and 1442, took place through assemblies of a similar character.

In Denmark, the king's *hirð*-assembly became a meeting (*consilium*) with the magnates of the nation around the middle of the 13th century. Erik Klippping committed himself in his charter of assurance of 1282 to hold an annual *parlamentum quod dicitur hof* at Mid-Lent; the domestic designation later became *danehof*. The most distinguished men of the Church and the secular society (*meliores regni*) were summoned. But representatives of towns and rural communities could also participate, although without any real influence on the decisions, which were mostly legislation and legal matters. *Danehof* was the supreme authority of the nation: it could judge between the king and his subjects. It normally met in Nyborg (Funen) in the early summer. Although the meeting appeared again in later coronation charters, it took place more and more irregularly and infrequently, the last time in 1413. The need of the monarch for advice was normally satisfied through the Council of the Realm, in special cases through *herredager*. In special cases, an appeal was made to the *landsting*.

So far, with a certain displacement in time, the development is parallel to that seen in Norway. But at the end of the Middle Ages, there was a new royal assembly. In 1468, Christian I summoned the Council of the Realm to Kalundborg (Zealand) along with the nobles, town men, and farmers to judge between him and a group of magnates. The meeting gave sanction to the king's expansion of rights in relation to the vassals. The sporadic royal assemblies, which were later held in Kalundborg from 1482, were formally assemblies of the estates of the realm gathered in order to support the royal power in extraordinary situations. The Council of the Realm and the nobility, bishops, abbots, and representatives of the chapters, plus leading men from the towns and rural communities were summoned. The procedures appear simple; the meeting never obtained a strong position in the political life of the nation. The last assembly of the estates of the realm was held in Copenhagen in 1536, where the term *rigsdag* (parliament) was used, implying that the power of the Church was broken.

The development in Sweden varied considerably from those in Norway and Denmark. The existence of meetings among the king, the bishops, and the magnates is certainly known from the middle of the 12th century, now and then in the form of the ecclesiastical concilium, but there were no established forms. After a Council of the Realm came into existence in the 1280s, it is difficult to distinguish in the source material between the meetings (*parlamentum, consilium*) with this group and the meetings with a bigger circle. In the 16th century, the domestic term for the latter was still *herredag, i.e.,* meeting of the lords. The meeting in 1319, where Magnus Eriksson was chosen as king, can be seen as the first real national assembly. In the national landlaw adopted around 1350, the king-nominating assembly was the only prescribed national assembly; decisions about legislation and taxation took place in the various "countries." The representation was federal, with delegations from seven jurisdictions ("countries"), and from 1362 also from Finland. An assembly similar to the *danehof* is seen in Magnus Eriksson's summons to a meeting in 1359; apart from the general participants in the *herredag*, representatives of the chapters, the towns, and the jurisdictions were also summoned. The task was to reestablish order in the nation, and the groups affected were to certify and strengthen the decisions. Further, two types of national assemblies, with a tendency to merge, can be seen: the king-nominating assembly, which until 1523 was summoned according to the law (in 1544, the hereditary realm was introduced); and assemblies summoned by the Council of the Realm during the periods in which this was governing (1435–1441, 1464–1467, 1470–1497, 1501–1512). In documents and chronicles, these later assemblies are often described as assemblies of the estates of the realm: "bishops, prelates, barons, and knights, town men and all commoners." But here it is without doubt the old *herredag*, to which the Council of the Realm, or incidental rulers, summoned the nobility and, more or less explicitly stated, representatives of the towns, the *Bergslag* (the mining areas in Västmanland and Dalarna), and the rural communities. The actual participation of the various provinces and categories was extremely uneven. The Council needed the support from these groups but made the decisions that concerned politics and policy itself; the assembly as such had no sphere of authority.

A change took place in the 1510s, when the regent used the assembly to strengthen his position against the Council of the Realm. The meeting in Västerås in 1527, where the power of the Church was broken, became epoch making: it is the first meeting that was in reality a meeting of the estates of the realm, but totally directed by the king, Gustav Vasa. During the rest of the 16th century, the royal meetings play an increasingly important role in the nation's political life. In 1544, the term *ständer* ("estates") and in 1561 the term *riksdag* ("parliament") were first used. The development is thus to a certain degree contrary to the development in Denmark and Norway.

Lit.: Jörgensen, Poul Johs. *Dansk Retshistorie. Retskildernes og Forfatningsrettens Historie indtil sidste Halvdel af det 17. Århundrede.* Copenhagen: Gad, 1947; Jägerstad, Hans. *Hovdag och råd under äldre medeltid. Den statsrättsliga utvecklingen i Sverige från Karl Sverkerssons regering till Magnus Erikssons regeringstillträde (1160–1319).* Lund: Blom, 1948 [with review by Jerker Rosén in *Scandia* 19 (1950), 299–320]; Christensen, Askel E. *Kongemagt og aristokrati. Epoker i middelalderlig dansk statsopfattelse indtil unionstiden.* 2nd ed. Copenhagen: Akademisk Forlag, 1968; rpt. 1976; Helle, Knut. *Konge og gode menn i norsk riksstyrning ca. 1150–1319.* Bergen: Universitetsforlaget, 1972; Lönnroth, Erik. "Representative Assemblies in Medieval Sweden." In *Scandinavians: Selected Historical Papers.* Ed. Å. Holmberg et al. Gothenburg: Gothenburg University; Eckerstein, 1977, pp. 85–91; Christensen, Aksel E., et al., eds. *Danmarks Historie.* 2 vols. Copenhagen: Politiken, 1977–80; Blom, Grethe Authén. "Hyllingen av Håkon (VI) Magnusson, Båhus 17. juli 1344." *Historisk tidsskrift* (Norway) 59 (1980), 333–54; Jexlev, Thelma. "Kalundborgmødet 1468—stændermøde eller særdomstol?" In *Festskrift til Troels Dahlerup på 60-årsdagen den 3 december 1985.* Ed. Aage Andersen et al. Arusia-historiske skrifter, 5. Århus: [n.p.], 1985, pp. 277–86; Schück, Herman. "Sweden's Early Parliamentary Institutions from the Thirteenth Century to 1611." In *The Riksdag: A History of the Swedish Parliament.* Ed. Michael F. Metcalf. New York: St. Martin, 1987, pp. 5–60.

Herman Schück

[**See also:** *Hirð*; Royal Administration and Finances]

Runes and Runic Inscriptions

1. INTRODUCTION. Runes are the individual letters of the runic alphabet, the oldest and only native system of writing used by the Germanic peoples. This alphabet, called the *futhark* after its first six letters (*th = þ*), is attested in an older version from about A.D. 150–750 and in later variants. Latin letters, which came in the wake of Christianity, competed with and gradually replaced runes, and only in Scandinavia, because of the late christianization (10th and 11th centuries), did runic writing continue into the Middle Ages. Inscriptions with runes, though often obscure or scanty, are valuable primary sources for the study of primitive Germanic and especially old Scandinavian culture and language. Of about 6,000 known inscriptions, over half are found in Sweden, 1,600 in Norway, and 800 in Denmark.

The older runes (ca. A.D. 150–750). The runic forms were possibly originally meant to be carved with a knife on wooden surfaces, since horizontal lines, which would not be clearly distinguishable from the grain of the wood, were apparently avoided as a rule. Runes have appropriate characteristics for incised letters, consisting basically of straight lines: vertical staves, slanting branches, pointed loops, and angular crooks. The older *futhark* encompassed twenty-four letters, with some variations in form. (See the standardized representation, with transliteration, in Fig. 151.)

The runic alphabet as such must predate the earliest inscriptions, and its invention has traditionally been fixed around the birth of Christ. Obviously related to the letters in Mediterranean alphabets, runes must owe their creation to the contact of Germanic tribes with literate cultures to the south, and various theories have been produced as to which alphabet was the model: Latin (especially Latin capitals, which is most likely), Greek, or Etruscan/North Italic alphabets (see Düwel 1967: 90–5, Moltke 1985: 38–73). Apparently, some older runic writers believed that the runes were "of divine origin," as they are termed on the Noleby stone and the Sparlösa stone from Västergötland, Sweden; and in the eddic poem *Hávamál*, they are connected with Óðinn and seem to be considered his invention. Although the etymology of the word "rune" is disputed, its early uses in Germanic languages indicate a relationship with mystery and secrecy.

Each rune had a fixed place in the order of the alphabet and a name that was also a meaningful word. The early names must be reconstructed from later MS sources: *fehu 'cattle, wealth,' *ūruz 'aurochs,' *þurisaz 'giant,' *ansuz 'god,' and so on. In spite of attempts to derive them from a Germanic cosmology, neither the special order nor the particular choice of name is understood. The initial sound of each rune name was in principle the sound the rune represented, and the names could thus help carvers to remember which sounds the runic symbols denoted. The runic alphabet has its own graphic and orthographic conventions, which were often typical of early stages of literacy. They include freedom of direction in writing runes (left to right, which predominates as time goes on, right to left, or alternating), the reversing or inverting of individual letters, and the possibility of combining two or more signs, usually with a common stave, into ligatures called "bind runes." Words and sentences are frequently run together, and the same character is as a rule not written twice in succession, even where one word ends and the next begins with identical sounds. The runic alphabet could be divided into three groups, in Old Norse called ættir (sing. ætt/átt) 'families' (or 'groups of eight'?), divisions that Viking Age and medieval ciphers used.

The older futhark was well suited for rendering the distinctive sounds of the older Germanic languages. There are nearly 200 known inscriptions in this alphabet, not including bracteate legends (see below). Most are short, consisting of only one or a few words, and many defy interpretation. They reveal few dialectal features in spite of wide geographic spread; the majority are, however, found in Scandinavia, and are usually considered to be in Proto-Scandinavian. They occur mainly on weapons, jewelry, tools, and stones, poor conditions for preservation probably responsible for the dearth of wooden objects. On precious, military, or everyday objects, one often finds names: of the owner, of the workman who crafted the object, or of the object itself. From the time about 450–550 and with Denmark as their center of distribution come numerous bracteates, thin medallions of gold stamped with a design and frequently an inscription, many of which are garbled or more rune-like than runic (ca. 150 different rune-bearing stamps are represented). Also from Denmark come the golden horns from Gallehus (Jutland), elaborate, presumably cult objects, with the simple legend on one: "I, Hlewagastiʀ from Holt (?; holt dweller?; son of Holta-?), made the horn." Several stone inscriptions commemorate deceased persons, while some simply declare who wrote the runes. A few have pictorial additions. The text on the Tune stone from eastern Norway begins, as it is usually read, "I, Wiwaʀ, in memory of Woduridaʀ, the bread-warden (=lord), wrought [the runes]" and continues with statements referring to the stone, three daughters among the heirs, and apparently the funeral feast. The enigmatic inscription on the Eggja stone, from a cenotaph in western Norway dated to around 700, appears to be a necrology, and constitutes, with its nearly 200 runes, the longest text in the older futhark. The tracing of the head of a horse also adorns the slab.

Repeatedly, runic writers using the older futhark call themselves erilaʀ or irilaʀ (probably related to "earl," and perhaps also to "Heruli," the name of a Germanic tribe). These writers often give their name, or nickname, or describe themselves, and sometimes claim they are another person's erilaʀ, or state that they wrote the runes or performed some other action. The term was apparently a designation of rank or position, and is often considered to represent a priest or rune-master. The formula alu recurs on bracteates and on one stone. This word probably literally means "ale," and may owe its supposed protective nature to the significance of this drink in cult celebration. Like any other script, the runic alphabet could be used for purposes of magic, but that use does not necessarily imply that the runes themselves were essentially magic.

The roughly seventy native Anglo-Saxon and around twenty Frisian runic inscriptions belong largely to the 5th to 9th centuries. The Anglo-Saxon runic objects include mainly small artifacts, coins, and stones. Foremost among them is the Ruthwell Cross, a large 8th-century stone cross containing in its more than 320 runes portions of an Anglo-Saxon poem also preserved in the *Vercelli Book* and known as *The Dream of the Rood*. Also outstanding is the Auzon or Franks Casket, a box of whalebone on which various religious, historical, and legendary situations are presented in carved pictures and long, mainly runic inscriptions, but including some Latin with Roman letters. The Frisian inscriptions all come from artificial mounds in the marshy coastal landscape. The Anglo-Saxon and Frisian *futhorks* (the fourth letter had undergone a sound change: *a > o*) are closely related, the alphabet being extended in both places to encompass signs for new sounds that had arisen due to phonological changes. Around 800, the Anglo-Saxon *futhork* reached a total of thirty-one distinct characters used in inscriptions.

The Viking Age (ca. 750–1050). Toward the end of the period of use of the older *futhark*, major linguistic changes occurred in Scandinavia. Certain vowels, and hence syllables, were lost in a process known as syncope; as a result, independent status was achieved by the new vowel sounds resulting in particular from mutation (umlaut); in addition, the distribution of various consonants was altered. These phonological changes left the older *futhark* less suited to render the current speech sounds, and the transitional period (*ca.* 600–750) is characterized by orthographic experimentation. Around 600, initial *j* disappeared, and the *j*-rune, in accordance with the phonological change in its name, became an *a*-rune. The original *a*-rune, also following the linguistic development of its name, later mainly signified a nasalized *a*-sound (*ą*).

Although the linguistic changes led to an increase in the inventory of distinctive sounds in the language, the Scandinavian response was an apparently deliberate reform of the runic alphabet with a reduction in the number of letters and a simplification of many of the forms. Sometime before the year 800, the younger *futhark* with only sixteen runes emerged. One symbol, therefore, had to represent many sounds: the *k*-rune, for example, was used for both *k* and *g*, and the *u*-rune stood for *u, o, y, ø,* or *w*. The paucity of signs and their ambiguity made the reader's task more difficult. The carver's task was made easier, however, as the apparent principle behind the graphical forms of the new letters, and perhaps the entire reform, was economy. In general, the characters took less room and were easier to write.

There were two closely related initial variants of the sixteen-rune alphabet: the "short-twig runes," which are of simpler form, and the "long-branch" or normal younger runes, which resemble more closely the older runes. See the standardized representation in Fig. 152, where the primary sound value of each sign is listed. Based on their general distribution, the short-twig runes are often called the "Norwegian-Swedish runes," whereas the long-branch runes are known as the "Danish runes." It has usually been assumed that the short-twig runes represented a simplification of

ᚠᚢᚦᚨᚱᚲᚷᚹᚺᚾᛁᛃᛈᛇᛉᛊᛏᛒᛖᛗᛚᛜᛞᛟ

f	u	þ	a	r	k	g	w	h	n	i	j	p	ë	R	s	t	b	e	m	l	ŋ	d	o
	th																				ng		

151. The older, 24-rune *futhark*.

a) ᚠᚢᚦᚬᚱᚴᚼᚾᛁᛅᛋᛏᛒᛘᛚᛦ

f u þ ą r k   h n i a   s t b m l R

b) ᚠᚢᚦᚬᚱᚴᚼᚾᛁᛅᛋᛏᛒᛘᛚᛦ

f u þ ą r k   h n i a s t b m l R

152. The younger, 16-rune (Viking Age) *futharks*: (a) the normal runes;
(b) the short-twig runes.

153. The Gripsholm stone.

ᚠᚢᚦᚮᚱᚴᚼᚾᛁᛂᛋᛏᛒᛘᛚᠣ   ᛂᛆᚯᚵᛑᛔᛜᚴᛋ

f	u	þ	o	r	k	h	n	i	a	s	t	b	m	l	y		e	æ	ø	g	d	p	z
																							c

154. The medieval runes, the 16-rune alphabet, plus extensions.

155a.

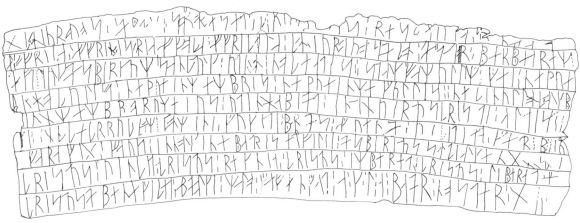

155b.

156.

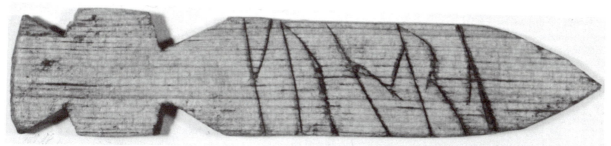

157. Ownership tag reading "Gunnar owns."

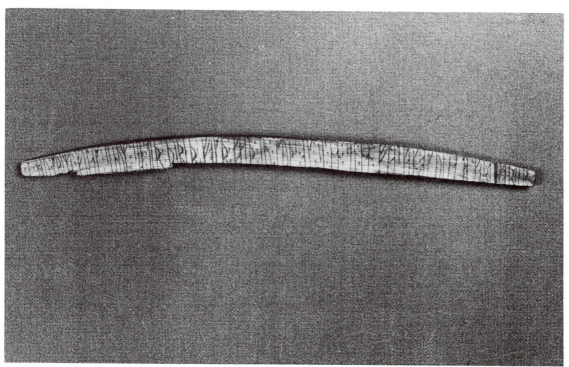

158. A runic "letter," addressed by one Tore the Fair to his business partner, Havgrim, in Bergen, about 1330.

the long-branch runes, but recently strong arguments have been advanced for the primacy of the short-twig runes (see Liestøl 1981, Barnes 1987). The long-branch runes are then viewed as a contamination of the short-twig runes and what remained of the older *futhark*.

The two initial younger *futharks* appear to be functional variants: the short-twig forms were probably designed as a cursive script for the practical business of everyday communication, whereas the fuller forms of the long-branch runes were more decorative and thus better suited for epigraphic use on stone monuments. Further graphic simplification, far beyond that of the short-twig forms, led to the "staveless" runes, often called "Hälsinge" runes, a Swedish shorthand where the staves have basically been removed and only characteristic strokes of the branches and pockets appear. Regional variations of the sixteen-rune *futhark* soon developed from the mixing of the two initial variants. In Norway and Sweden, for instance, the long-branch forms of the *h-*, *b-*, *m-*, and *ʀ-*runes became standard with time.

From Viking and medieval times, there are inscriptions that employ ciphers. Various systems are used, *e.g.*, the replacement of a rune by the following sign, or the indication of a rune by its "family" and number within the family, *e.g.*, *3/2 = u* (that is, the family of six runes beginning with *f*, which is usually called the third family, and the second symbol in that family, which is *u*). Both these systems are found on the 9th-century Rök stone from Östergötland in Sweden (Ög136), an impressive monument commemorating a dead kinsman, with all five faces completely covered with runes; the text, which is partially in verse, contains allusions to Germanic heroic legends. (Concerning the citation of runic inscriptions, *e.g.*, Ög136, see "Ed." following the subarticles about medieval inscriptions below.)

Rune stones are a hallmark of the Viking Age. As a rule, they are memorial, erected not necessarily on a grave, although many are near grave sites, but in public places or by roads or bridges, and thus visible for those who passed by. Rune stones are usually raised stones, but inscriptions on glacial boulders or faces of bedrock also occur. The legends were probably often colored, as statements in various inscriptions imply and remains of pigment on some stones confirm. Runes on stones, especially in the early Viking Age, were cut in successive lines arranged as a rule in vertical rows and often between incised frames; they could be placed along narrow edges or off-center on broad faces. In the later Viking Age, especially in Sweden, they were placed in a band or bands, commonly in the form of a snake with head and tail, on a flat portion of the stone, often toward the edge, and sometimes with added ornamentation in the form of a cross or drawings. The most famous pictures are the illustrations from the legend of Sigurðr the Dragonslayer found on the Ramsund rock in Södermanland, Sweden. Memorial inscriptions state who commissioned or sponsored the monument and who was honored by it, usually indicate the relationship between the two, and often contain a description of the dead person or other additions. In spite of their stereotyped nature, they are invaluable sources of knowledge about the Viking Age: development of the language and poetry; genealogy, inheritance, and habits of name giving; settlement, government, and communication; Viking raids and peaceful trading expeditions; and the spread of Christianity and pilgrimages.

The custom of raising rune stones in memory of dead kinsmen or comrades is found early in Denmark, where a total of around 200 are known. The most famous of all Danish rune stones

is the 10th-century larger Jelling stone in Jutland (D42), raised by King Harald Gormsson (called "Bluetooth") to honor his parents, although equally an exaltation of the king himself and often called "Denmark's certificate of baptism." It has horizontal lines of runes on all three faces, with, however, pictures of Christ and a beast wrestling with a serpent dominating two of them. The text reads: "King Harald commanded this monument to be made in memory of Gorm, his father, and in memory of his mother, Þorvi (Thyre)— that Harald who won the whole of Denmark for himself, and Norway, and made the Danes Christian."

Rune stones predominate in the rich Swedish material. Those from the southern provinces of Västergötland, Östergötland, and Småland are more or less contemporary with the Danish ones, whereas those from farther north are generally somewhat younger. In the province of Uppland alone, where the fashion of raising rune stones reached its apex during the 11th century, some 1,300 such monuments are recorded. There were a number of professional rune carvers in Uppland who signed their inscriptions, the most prolific among them, Øpir, with over eighty stones to his credit. Nearly thirty stones are found in the Lake Mälar area raised in memory of men who followed Yngvarr víðfǫrli ("the far-traveler") on an ill-fated exploit to the East during the 11th century. The noblest monument to this expedition, at Gripsholm in Södermanland, reads (Sö179; see Fig. 153): "Tola had this stone set up in memory of her son Haraldr, Ingvarr's brother. [In verse:] They fared like men / far after gold / and in the East / gave the eagle food. / They died southward / in Serkland (the Arab caliphates)." Jarlabanki, an 11th-century landed aristocrat from Täby in Uppland, constructed a causeway and recorded his enterprise, as well as an advertisement for himself, on four rune stones. Originally, two stood at each end of the road, and all had more or less the same text (*e.g.*, U164): "Jarlabanki had these stones put up in memory of himself in his own lifetime. And he made this causeway for his soul's sake. And he owned the whole of Täby by himself. May God help his soul." The fashion of erecting rune stones ended in Sweden around 1100, due not to Christianity *per se* (many of the later stones are definitely Christian), but perhaps due to the new custom of burying the dead in a Christian graveyard at a church and erecting memorials to them at the grave with a text suiting the occasion.

The Viking Age rune stones in Norway date mainly to the 10th and 11th centuries, and number only some sixty. The 3.5-m.-high stone at Oddernes on the southern tip of the country has two inscriptions (N209–10), the older one, from the 10th century, in memory of a deceased person. The younger one, on a narrow side, commemorates the construction of a church on ancestral property during the early 11th century by a man named Eyvindr, who appears to be called the godson of St. Óláfr. The stone from Dynna, just north of Oslo, is a magnificent red sandstone monument decorated with pictures of the Magi under the Christmas star riding to find the Christ child. According to the inscription along one narrow side (N68), it was erected by a woman in memory of her daughter, "the most skillful maiden in Hadeland (the particular region of eastern Norway in which the stone stood)." Norwegian Viking Age objects with runic inscriptions include a wooden pole and bucket from the Oseberg ship burial, a copper kettle from the Gokstad ship burial, and, from the 1060s, coins stamped with moneyers' names in runes.

The Scandinavians took their script with them as they plundered, traded with, and settled or visited other areas, from Russia in the East and Turkey and Greece in the South, to Greenland and Ireland in the North and West. Inscriptions are scattered throughout the British Isles and the Faroes, with the only concentration on the Isle of Man. The some thirty Manx inscriptions are mainly on stone crosses from the 10th and 11th centuries with the common memorial formula (which can be extended): "X put up the cross in memory of Y." The personal names on the crosses reveal a mixed society of Celts and Scandinavians who intermarried.

Medieval runes and runic inscriptions (ca. 1050–1500). Changes in both form and sound value for many runes mark the runological transition about 1020–1100 to the Middle Ages. The original *a*-rune, which in an altered form in the Viking Age usually denoted a nasalized *a*-sound, came to denote *o*, in accordance with a further sound change in its name. As an alphabet, the *futhark*, or more properly *futhork* after this sound change, still consisted of sixteen symbols, but more signs came into existence and could be used when writing texts. The medieval runes were based on the modified mixtures of short-twig and long-branch runes of the late Viking period, with differentiations and additions making possible the denotation of a greater number of distinctive speech sounds. New symbols were created partly through the practice of adding dots to existing rune forms, a system already in limited use in late Viking times: a dotted *i*-rune signified *e*, a dotted *k*-rune *g*, and so on. Other new forms came about by specialization of variants; *e.g.*, when the short-twig *a*-rune was used for *a*, the long-branch variant could denote *æ*. The basic inventory of standard medieval runes is presented in Fig. 154. The representation does not reflect all regional variations in form and sound value.

The introduction of Latin letters during the late 10th or 11th century constituted a cultural gain, but for some time this alphabet was used solely in connection with the Christian faith, and initially only for the writing of Latin. Throughout the Middle Ages, writing with the Latin alphabet was mastered only by a small elite, mainly clerics and nobility. In contrast, the ability to read and write runes must have been widespread. The variety of runic objects found during recent excavations in medieval towns demonstrates that runes were used for a great spectrum of activities. The relationship between Roman letters and runes must have been complementary, the choice of alphabet being partially dependent on the type of message: notes of temporary significance were inscribed with runes on pieces of wood, whereas texts of more permanent character (deeds, royal edicts, voluminous legal, historical, or literary texts) were written in Roman letters on parchment. Some 10 percent of all medieval runic inscriptions are in Latin, mainly those with religious content, such as invocations of saints and prayers.

Runic inscriptions from the Middle Ages are found mainly in the medieval towns and churches of Norway, Sweden, and Denmark (see the individual subarticles below). Runic writing in Scandinavia apparently thrived during the 12th and 13th centuries, continued into the 14th, and declined during the 15th. In the Swedish province of Dalarna, an offshoot of the medieval runic tradition persisted until the early 20th century. Elsewhere in Scandinavia, postreformational runic practices are basically learned reconstructions rather than genuine traditions.

Runic inscriptions are found in the entire medieval Scandinavian realm. Iceland has over seventy, but strangely enough none are preserved much before 1200, the time of the one on the church door from Valþjófsstaðir. Icelandic inscriptions are usually found on grave slabs or small artifacts, or as marginalia in MSS. Norwe-

gian finds from Bergen and Trondheim sometimes apparently attest to the use of runes by Icelanders who traded in Norway. From Greenland come some seventy-five runic inscriptions that seem to show special phonological and (ortho)graphic characteristics. Notable among the Greenlandic inscriptions are eight wooden runic crosses with Latin or Old Norse texts and the small stone from Kingittorsuaq, Baffin Bay, with a message complete with cryptic runes. From Orkney, there are over thirty inscriptions consisting mainly of 12th-century Norwegian(?) graffiti in the neolithic stone-built grave chamber at Maeshowe, some of which have erotic or humorous content. One carver at Maeshowe terms himself "the most rune-wise man west of the sea [North Sea]." None of the North American "runic" inscriptions, including the Kensington stone from Minnesota, has proven genuine.

Ed.: [Runic inscriptions in the respective Scandinavian countries are registered at Runologisk-epigrafisk laboratorium (Nationalmuseet, Copenhagen), Runearkivet (Oldsaksamlingen, Oslo), and Runverket (Riksantikvarieämbetet, Stockholm). For editions of Danish, Norwegian, and Swedish inscriptions, see the literature lists after the subarticles below.] Bæksted, Anders. *Islands Runeindskrifter.* Bibliotheca Arnamagnæana, 2. Copenhagen: Munksgaard, 1942; Olsen, Magnus. "Runic Inscriptions in Great Britain, Ireland and the Isle of Man." In *Viking Antiquities in Great Britain and Ireland* 6. Ed. Haakon Shetelig. Oslo: Aschehoug, 1954, pp. 151–233; Krause, Wolfgang, with contributions by Herbert Jankuhn. *Die Runeninschriften im älteren Futhark.* Abhandlungen der Akademie der Wissenschaften in Göttingen, Phil.-hist. Kl., Dritte Folge, 65. Göttingen: Vandenhoeck & Ruprecht, 1966 [inscriptions in the older *futhark*]; Stoklund, Marie. "Greenland Runic Inscriptions." In *Proceedings of the First International Symposium on Runes and Runic Inscriptions.* Ed. Claiborne W. Thompson. *Michigan Germanic Studies* 7.1 (1981), 138–47 [a survey, with references to editions with English text in *Meddelelser om Grønland* 67 (1924), 273–90; 76 (1930), 173–9; 88.2 (1936), 223–32, pl. 1–6]; Page, R. I. "The Manx Rune-Stones." In *The Viking Age in the Isle of Man: Select Papers from The Ninth Viking Congress, Isle of Man, 4–14 July 1981.* Ed. Christine Fell *et al.* London: Viking Society for Northern Research, 1983, pp. 133–46. **Bib.**: Arntz, Helmut. *Bibliographie der Runenkunde.* Leipzig: Harrassowitz, 1937; Krause, Wolfgang, ed. *Bibliographie der Runeninschriften nach Fundorten.* Abhandlungen der Akademie der Wissenschaften in Göttingen, Phil.-hist. Kl., Dritte Folge, 48 and 80. Part 1: Marquardt, Hertha. *Die Runeninschriften der britischen Inseln.* Göttingen: Vandenhoeck & Ruprecht, 1961. Part 2: Schnall, Uwe. *Die Runeninschriften des europäischen Kontinents.* Göttingen: Vandenhoeck & Ruprecht, 1973; Knirk, James E. "Runebibliografi 1985–." *Nytt om runer* 1– (1986–) [see "Lit." below]; Knirk, James E. "Supplement til Runebibliografi 1985–." *Nytt om runer* 2– (1987–). **Lit.**: [For literature concerning specifically Danish, Norwegian, and Swedish inscriptions, see the subarticles below.] Friesen, Otto von, ed. *Runorna.* Nordisk kultur, 6. Stockholm: Bonnier; Oslo: Aschehoug; Copenhagen: Schultz, 1933; Elliott, Ralph W. V. *Runes: An Introduction.* Manchester: Manchester University Press, 1959; 2nd ed. 1963; rev. ed. 1989; Musset, Lucien. *Introduction à la Runologie.* Bibliothèque de Philologie Germanique, 20. Paris: Aubier-Montaigne, 1965; Düwel, Klaus. *Runenkunde.* Sammlung Metzler, 72. Stuttgart: Metzler, 1967; rev. ed. 1983; Krause, Wolfgang. *Die Sprache der urnordischen Runeninschriften.* Heidelberg: Winter, 1971; Page, R. I. *An Introduction to English Runes.* London: Methuen, 1973; Antonsen, Elmer H. *A Concise Grammar of the Older Runic Inscriptions.* Sprachstrukturen, A, 3. Tübingen: Niemeyer, 1975; Thompson, Claiborne W. *Studies in Upplandic Runography.* Austin and London: University of Texas Press, 1975; Haugen, Einar. *The Scandinavian*

Languages: An Introduction to Their History. London: Faber and Faber, 1976, pp. 118–31, 142–79, 191–4, 223–9, 244; Liestøl, Aslak. "The Viking Runes: The Transition from the Older to the Younger *fuþark.*" *Saga-Book of the Viking Society* 20.4 (1981), 247–66; Thompson, Claiborne W., ed. *Proceedings of the First International Symposium on Runes and Runic Inscriptions. Michigan Germanic Studies* 7.1 (1981), 1–213; Flowers, Stephen E. *Runes and Magic: Magical Formulaic Elements in the Older Runic Tradition.* American University Studies, Ser. 1: Germanic Languages and Literature, 53. New York, Bern, and Frankfurt am Main: Lang, 1986; Knirk, James E., ed. *Nytt om runer: Meldingsblad om runeforskning.* Oslo: Oldsaksamlingen, 1986– [newsletter with yearly reports of new finds, bibliography, etc.]; Barnes, Michael. "The Origins of the Younger *fuþark*—A Reappraisal." In *Runor och runinskrifter,* pp. 29–45 [see below]; *Runor och runinskrifter: Föredrag vid Riksantikvarieämbetets och Vitterhetsakademiens symposium 8–11 september 1985.* Kungl. vitterhets historie och antikvitets akademien, Konferenser, 15. Stockholm: Almqvist & Wiksell, 1987 [proceedings of the Second International Symposium on Runes and Runic Inscriptions]; Page, R. I. *Runes.* Reading the Past, 4. London: British Museum, 1987; Thompson, Claiborne W. "Runes." In *Dictionary of the Middle Ages.* Ed. Joseph R. Strayer. New York: Scribner, 1982–89, vol. 10, pp. 557–68.

James E. Knirk

2. DENMARK. The custom of erecting rune stones in memory of dead kinsmen or comrades seems to have died out in Denmark around 1025, with a few exceptions, mainly due to Swedish influence, on the island of Bornholm. Around 1065–1075, runes were used on coins, in competition, however, with Latin letters. One finds, for example, *Magnus rex* (Magnus was King Sven Estridsen's Christian name) in Roman capitals on the obverse, and on the reverse, in runes, the mint master's name (*ca.* sixty different moneyers' names occur, many of them English) and the place where the coin was struck (chiefly Lund). On the early, flat Christian grave slabs, which superseded standing rune stones, we find similar linguistic competition, runes being used for inscriptions in the vernacular (Bjolderup church in Jutland, D14: *ketilurnæligirhir,* "Ketil Urne lies here") or in Latin (Føvling church in Jutland, D25, a hexameter: *p:æsbirnik:langsum:kubaþ:in:kristo:rekuiæscæns,* "P. [= Pastor/dean?] Esbern Langsum ["the slow"] here lies at rest in Christ"). In this last inscription, some extremely complicated ligatured runes, inspired by Latin epigraphy, have been used. Other examples of the epigraphic use of runes occur in Romanesque churches, where one finds patron's inscriptions or maker's formulae hewn into the hard granite or cut into the softer limestone blocks. On the Søndbjerg plinth stone, Jutland (D148), patron's and builder's signatures are combined with a Latin quotation: *:iakob:uulæ:skialm:gurþæ:ubiara / ibiokulus,* "(Old Danish:) Jakob caused [*i.e.,* commissioned]. Skjalm made. (Latin:) Where the altar, there the eye."

The fixed order of the runes allowed them to be used for ordering by carpenters or construction workers, as can be seen in their use for numbering roof beams in churches like those at Hviding and Brøns. One also finds nonepigraphic inscriptions of a more informal character, often prayers or just graffiti, scratched into the wet clay of bricks before they were fired, or into the damp or dry plaster of the walls. One reads, for example, at Tjæreby church on Zealand: "Priest Thomas, pray for me," and at Tornby church in Jutland (D169): "Þorsteinn Bre . . . cut these runes at Whitsun . . . He had much delight from the tones (= choir songs) in the morning there." Linguistic features indicate that Þorsteinn was a Norwegian. Ecclesiastical fixtures could also be furnished with runic

inscriptions, for instance, baptismal fonts, bells, and censers. There are twelve censers made by Master Jakob Red in Svendborg on Funen with different but similar inscriptions in Latin or in Old Danish, each consisting of a master formula along with a sacred name or devotional phrase, like the following in the vernacular on the censer from Hesselager church (D175): "Master Jakob Red of Svendborg made me. Jesus Christ."

Nonepigraphic inscriptions are found especially on objects excavated from medieval Danish towns, particularly Lund, Ribe, and Schleswig, as well as on a few items found elsewhere. These inscriptions are usually on wood, bone, antler, or lead, and consist of *futharks* (twelve alone from Lund), owner's inscriptions (like "Bovi owns the graver" on the bronze stylus from Dalby in Scania), identifications of the items (*e.g.,* tinbl:bein 'twining bone' [for twisting yarn] or *skefnikr,* Old Danish *skæfningr,* a kind of polished needle, on bone tools from Lund and Ålborg respectively), and finally magic charms, some of them just pretending to be inscriptions, others, mainly on lead, in Latin with roots in the rich liturgical stock of the Catholic Church. The Blæsinge inscription, Denmark's longest with well over 400 runes (discovered in 1983), in Latin on a lead plate, begins with a conjuration of the seven sisters (of fever?) and goes on: "I conjure you and invoke you by the Father, the Son, and the Holy Ghost, that you harm not this servant of God, neither in eyes nor in limbs nor in marrow nor in any joint of limbs, [but rather] that the strength of the most high Christ may inhabit you. Behold the cross of the Lord! Flee, you hostile adversaries! The Lion of the tribe of Judea, the Root of David, has conquered. In the name of the Father and the Son and the Holy Ghost. Amen. Christ conquers, Christ reigns, Christ rules, Christ liberates, Christ blesses you, defends you from all evil. AGLA. Our Father." ("AGLA" is a religious charm word.) Frequently, the spells are in corrupt Latin; the lead plate from Odense (D204), for instance, contains a few of the same elements as the Blæsinge inscription, but is generally rather confused. The most important charm in the vernacular is Denmark's third-longest runic inscription, on the Ribe rune stick, Jutland, dated to around 1300. It begins with an invocation in the eddic meter *fornyrðislag:* "Earth I pray guard / and the heaven above, / sun and St. Mary / and himself the Lord God, / that he grants me hands to make whole / and healing tongue / to cure the Trembler / when treatment is needed." There follows an exorcism to cast out the demon malaria (the Trembler), a brief narrative section, a threat, and the closing: "Amen, so be it!"

Around 1300, antiquarian interest led to some isolated instances of the writing of runes on parchment, notably in the so-called *Codex Runicus* of the *Scanian Law,* and in another MS for a translation of a religious text (*Planctus Mariae*).

Ed.: *Det Arnamagnæanske Haandskrift No 28, 8vo, Codex Runicus.* Ed. Kommissionen for det Arnamagnæanske Legat. Copenhagen: Gyldendal, 1877 [photolithographic edition]; Brøndum-Nielsen, Johs., and Aage Rohmann, eds. *Mariaklagen efter et runeskrevet Haandskrift-Fragment i Stockholms Kgl. Bibliotek.* Copenhagen: Schultz, 1929; Jacobsen, Lis, and Erik Moltke, in collaboration with Anders Bæksted and Karl Martin Nielsen. *Danmarks runeindskrifter: Text, Atlas.* 2 vols. Copenhagen: Munksgaard, 1941–42 [corpus edition, including inscriptions from Schleswig, Scania, Halland, Blekinge; dictionary, grammar, lexicon, bibliography; inscriptions are cited with D plus their publication number]. **Lit.**: Moltke, Erik. *Runes and Their Origin: Denmark and Elsewhere.* Trans. Peter G. Foote. Copenhagen: National Museum of Denmark, 1985, pp. 391–500 [revised and updated translation of Erik Moltke's *Runerne i*

Danmark, deres historie og brug (Copenhagen: Forum, 1976), which presents all runic inscriptions from the Old Danish realm]; Stoklund, Marie. "Runefund." *Aarbøger for nordisk Oldkyndighed og Historie* (1986; published 1988), 189–211.

Marie Stoklund

3. NORWAY. Some 500 medieval runic inscriptions were known in Norway in the mid-1950s, for the most part having ecclesiastical associations, and encompassing largely markers in church graveyards, carvings on church walls, statements on church furnishings, and religious formulas on amulets.

Over forty medieval gravestones with runic inscriptions are known. Some of the earlier ones have epitaphs reminiscent of those on Viking Age memorials, while others bear simple pious wishes (*e.g.*, "May God help the soul of") or the vernacular equivalent of the standard Latin expression *hic iacet* ("here lies"). Although a number of the Christian runic tombstones were erected monuments, especially the earlier ones, the majority were horizontal slabs. An example is the large tablet from St. Mary's church in Oslo (N19, 1100s), which is inscribed "Ǫgmundr skjálgi ('squint-eyed') had this stone laid over Gunna Guðúlfr's daughter, and the anniversary of her death [is] the mass of St. Luke [October 18]."

The majority of inscriptions occurring in an ecclesiastical context are carved into the church buildings themselves. Of the roughly 300 such inscriptions, over two-thirds are in stave churches, the rest in stone churches. A small number commemorate the structure itself. On parts of the interior of the stave churches in Torpo (N110) and Ål (N121), for instance, a 12th-century Þórólfr had written impressive runic legends naming himself as the master builder and listing others who worked on his crew. A prayer that God might bless the builder and the benefactors of "God's house" was among the runic inscriptions saved when the stave church in Atrå was torn down (N149), but the foremost epigraph concerns the consecration of the church around 1180 by Bishop Ragnarr of Hamar (N148). The runic lettering cut into a stave in the church at Høre (N564) apparently dates the lumbering for the church building to the summer when Earl Erlingr fell in Niðaróss, *i.e.*, 1179.

Most inscriptions carved into the woodwork or stonework of churches are not monumental, however, but plain graffiti. Although some of these inscriptions originate with the building crews (like the name "Ásgrímr" painted on a ceiling beam at Høre), the scribblings, which usually consist simply of signatures or short prayers, are not generally contemporary with the construction. Names are often found in the standard carver's formula "X wrote these runes," apparently the runic equivalent of "Kilroy was here." The stave church at Borgund in Sogn boasts over thirty-five inscriptions (N350–383, A307–309, and A297 in the bell tower), including statements naming the church, two expanded carver's formulas, perhaps a riddle, some ciphered runes, magical formulas, possibly abbreviations for liturgical words, numerous short prayers and requests, several individual names, the first seven runes of the *futhark* (which were used to indicate days in the runic calendar), and a number of indecipherable scrawls. The walls of the Nidaros cathedral in Trondheim bear somewhat more graffiti than those in Borgund, and similar categories are represented (N469–506).

Various church furnishings carry runic inscriptions, the largest single category being nine bells and one clapper. The bell from Bønsnes speaks (N92): "Þorgeirr the priest had me made, Jón made me, with God's grace," as does the statue on the crucifix from Lunder (N108, *ca.* 1250): "My name is Jesus of Nazareth; I suffered a hard death." Other ecclesiastical items with inscriptions encompass baptismal fonts, wooden chests, an altar cloth, a psalterium, and several keys, rings, and mounting irons for doors. Loose finds from churches include amulets of wood or lead, usually with Latin or apparently Latin texts, such as the two small wooden pieces from Borgund stave church (N348–349), one of which is inscribed with, among other things, a list of names for God. Over twenty lead amulets, a few in the shape of a cross, have turned up, often in some sort of ecclesiastical context (see Fig. 156). Although a number have correct Latin, such as the folded sheet from Ulstad with the entire Lord's Prayer and the names of the Evangelists (N53), many are corrupt, and several are inscribed with meaningless runes or rune-like signs.

In the 1950s, inscriptions from a secular setting comprised a relatively small number of the total. Among them were various stones, usually with mundane or jocular messages, six medieval farmhouses, and such items as combs and drinking horns. Then in 1955, a conflagration destroyed part of Bryggen (the old German wharf) in Bergen, and subsequent archaeological excavations brought to light over 550 rune-inscribed objects, more than doubling the inventory of inscriptions from the Middle Ages. Excavations in the 1970s and 1980s in other medieval towns have also contributed to the corpus and further shifted the overall weight from ecclesiastical associations to an urban environment. The number of medieval runic inscriptions in Norway, over 1,400, now exceeds the total for all the other Scandinavian countries combined.

More than 600 runic inscriptions, mostly dating to 1150–1350, are registered from Bryggen. The great majority are on wood, especially small sticks whittled flat on several sides, as a rule four, in order to serve as runic writing material. Runic inscriptions are also found on utensils and other objects not primarily intended to bear texts. Of the entire corpus, over 25 percent can either no longer be read, due to the poor state of preservation, or make little or no sense.

The largest group of inscriptions from Bryggen deals with mercantile transactions. Some 110 ownership tags have been identified by text or shape; they are pieces of wood, usually with an inscription like "Einarr owns," "Lucía Grímsdóttir owns," or "Þorsteinn owns me," or simply a personal name like "Eiríkr," and whittled in such a way that they can be attached directly or tied to merchant's wares (see Fig. 157). Several other inscriptions from Bryggen indicate ownership but not commercial activities, since they are inscribed directly on the item itself, such as "Jóhann owns" (B4) on an ornamentally carved walrus skull.

More than fifteen business letters and notes were uncovered, including accounting records and packing slips. The letter dispatched by Þórir fagr ("the fair") around 1330 from the southwestern coast of Norway to his business partner in Bergen employs many of the formulaic phrases of medieval correspondence and concerns, among other things, the difficulties Þórir has acquiring beer and fish to send to town and a request for gloves, probably to be sold in the district (N648; see Fig. 158). Another letter, which dates to the end of the 12th century and was written or dictated by Sigurðr lávarðr ("lord"), the son of King Sverrir, is addressed to a smith and states specifications for the fabrication of spearheads (B448).

Several inscriptions consist of stereotyped carver's formulas or requests and prayers similar to ones cut into church walls, whereas others provide rare glimpses into private lives and human relationships. On one surface of a rune stick is carved "Gyða says that you should go home" (B149), perhaps a message from a wife to a carousing husband, and on yet another, "Ingibjǫrg made love with me when I was in Stavanger" (B390). Folk poetry is also included among the inscriptions, such as the ditty (B493) *bylli min unn mer an ek þer af astom auk af allum huga* ("My swain! Love me; I love you, with all my heart and [ciphered runes:] all my mind").

Over thirty pieces of poetry written in runes, many very fragmentary, were unearthed at Bryggen. They range from the simple ditty just quoted to examples of eddic meters and skaldic strophes. The greater part of these verses is erotic, and only one of the metrical texts is otherwise known, a quotation from a stanza by King Haraldr harðráði ("hard-ruler") Sigurðarson, B88. Although some skaldic poems could reflect the activity of Icelanders in Norway, it appears that this art form had not generally died out among Norwegians, as previously assumed. The eddic verses include the following, which is probably a quotation from an older poem, rather than a reflection of genuine pagan feelings (B380): *hæil:seþu:ok:ihuhum:goþom / þor:þik:þig:gi:oþen: þik:æihi:* ("Hail to you, and be of good cheer! May Þórr receive you; may Óðinn own you").

The over sixty runic inscriptions in Latin include a taste of goliardic poetry, with one inscription (N603) consisting of fragments from two poems preserved in the *Carmina Burana*. A popular line from Vergil appears a few times, but only once complete (in conjunction with a skaldic love song, B145): *Omnia vincit Amor, et nos cedamus Amori* ("Love conquers all; let us too yield to Love"). Many of the Latin texts reflect the Christian liturgy, including the Lord's Prayer and the "Hail Mary," although these two usually appear very truncated. The Latin inscriptions also encompass incantations to stop bleeding, protect against blindness, or help during difficult childbirth. Latin-like gibberish appears on magical sticks or amulets, including one sequence of runes having close parallels among charms known from medieval English sources. Two recurring international formulas are the protective word "AGLA" and the palindrome *sator arepo tenet opera rotas*.

Some sixty inscriptions from Bryggen contain the runic alphabet itself, or parts thereof, including those consisting of only the rune *f*. These *futhark* inscriptions are almost always in standard runic order, and usually consist, when complete, of only the sixteen alphabetic letters. The row of runes sometimes occurs in conjunction with other inscriptions, notably personal names. Although alphabet magic cannot be ruled out, many of these inscriptions may be didactic demonstrations or instances of writing practice, of which other examples based on syllabaries are known.

The over 100 runic finds from recent excavations in Trondheim are roughly comparable to the ones from Bryggen, although a number of them predate the Bryggen finds, Bergen being a somewhat younger town. Lacking are business correspondence and poetry. In Oslo, over fifty runic inscriptions have been found during the past two decades, and in Tønsberg, thirty. The inventories from these towns, which also partly predate those from Bryggen, lack basically the mercantile inscriptions, and include a much higher percentage of inscriptions on bones and bone utensils, and also a higher percentage of nonsense inscriptions and nonrunic or rune-like signs. The nonurban finds during the past decades include the runic letter of proposal to a betrothed woman discovered under the floor of the stave church in Lom (A74).

Prior to the Norwegian finds of the past thirty-five years, scholars had been largely unaware of the extent to which runes were used for everyday communications in the Middle Ages.

Ed.: *Norges Innskrifter med de yngre Runer* 1–. Oslo: Kjeldeskriftfondet, 1941– [ongoing publication, with vols. 1–5 by Magnus Olsen (and Aslak Liestøl) containing the inventory known in the mid-1950s and vol. 6 (1980–90) by Aslak Liestøl, Ingrid Sanness Johnsen, and James E. Knirk containing most of the Latin and mercantile texts from Bryggen; inscriptions are cited by N plus their publication number; those from Bryggen not yet published in the corpus edition are referred to by B plus a registration number, those from elsewhere in Norway by A plus a number]. **Lit.**: Liestøl, Aslak. "The Runes of Bergen." *Minnesota History* 40.2 (1966), 49–58; Liestøl, Aslak. "Correspondence in Runes." *Mediaeval Scandinavia* 1 (1968), 17–27; Liestøl, Aslak. "Runic Voices from Towns of Ancient Norway." *Scandinavica* 13 (1974), 19–33; Dyvik, Helge J. J. "Addenda runica latina: Recently Found Runic Inscriptions in Latin from Bryggen." In *The Bryggen Papers*. Supplementary Series, 2. [Bergen]: Norwegian University Press, 1986, pp. 1–9; Seim, Karin Fjellhammer. "A Review of the Runic Material" and "Runic Inscriptions in Latin: A Summary of Aslak Liestøl's Fascicle (Vol. VI, 1) of Norges Innskrifter med de yngre Runer." In *The Bryggen Papers*, pp. 10–23, 24–65; Gosling, Kevin. "The Runic Material from Tønsberg." *Universitetets Oldsaksamling, Årbok* (1986–88), 175–87.

James E. Knirk

4. SWEDEN. There are around 800 medieval runic inscriptions known in Sweden, of which some eighty have Latin texts. The majority come from the provinces of Västergötland, Småland, and Gotland, while the area around Lake Mälar (the Stockholm/Uppsala area), which has the highest concentration of Viking Age rune stones, has relatively few. On Gotland, legends on grave slabs and carvings or paintings on the plaster of medieval churches dominate, while inscriptions elsewhere show greater variation. The number of medieval inscriptions has increased substantially because of the recent systematic excavations of medieval town centers (especially Old Lödöse, Skara, Nyköping, Söderköping, and Uppsala), the restoration of churches, and scientific fieldwork in connection with the ongoing publication of the corpus. The runic finds encompass objects of wood, bone, and metal, plus brick, and plaster. Old Lödöse, which is located some 40 km. northeast of Gothenberg, has provided the greatest number of inscriptions from one locality, almost fifty, but the combined interpretable texts would fill fewer than ten lines.

The texts on the early-medieval grave slabs are closely related to those on late Viking Age raised rune stones. A grave slab from the old churchyard at Rådene provides an example of a burial legend in its shortest form (Vg93, 1100s): *+:rani:læt. gæra:sten:þænna: / :a:pætar:faþur:sin:* ("Rani had this stone made in memory of Peter, his father"). During the later Middle Ages, the basic text is often a Swedish translation of the Latin formula *hic iacet* ("here lies"), for instance, at Västerhejde church (G210, 1300s): *+hier:likr:kairualtr:iberhi:ok:hans:hus:froya* ("Here lies Gairvaldr from Berg [present-day Bjärs] and his wife").

Carvings in the plaster walls of churches are mostly short prayers or signatures. A few important signatures of church builders occur on Gotland and in Västergötland, and the almost illegible inscription from Torpa church (Sö337), "Ødulfr made the church," provides the name of a stonemason associated with five remarkable 12th-century churches. A tragic event in the history of Hejde church was mentioned on a floor stone that has disappeared (G171): "The church burnt during a procession(?) on (Easter) Saturday; at that time *h* was the Sunday (rune) and *s* the prime (rune) in the 13th row [of the Easter table, (*i.e.*, 1492)]."

Church doors, baptismal fonts, and church bells are ecclesiastical fixtures that sometimes bear runic inscriptions, either signatures or more extensive and less stereotyped texts. On an iron door mounting from Hörsne church, one reads (G155, 1100s): "Gairvaldr attached the iron to the door." On the Burseryd baptismal font is written (Sm50, 1200s): "Arinbjorn made me, Viðkunnr the priest wrote me, and here I shall stand for a while." The runic bell from Saleby church, one of twelve from Västergötland, is Sweden's oldest self-dated bell and the oldest with Swedish text (in addition to Latin; Vg210): ∴þa:iak:uar:gør:þa:uar:þushu ndraþ:tu:hundraþ:tiuhu:uintr:ok:atta:fra:byrþ:gus:+a+g+l+a+∴/ :aue:maria:gracia:plena:/:dionisius:siþ:benediktus : "[Old Swedish]: When I was made, it was one thousand two hundred twenty and eight winters (= years; 1228) from God's birth. AGLA. (Latin:) Hail Mary, full of grace. Dionysius be blessed." "AGLA" is a protective formula; Dionysius, the name that follows the beginning of the "Hail Mary" (Ave Maria), probably refers to St. Denis, the patron saint of France. Four bells from Västergötland have the futhark, and four others the prayer "Ave Maria, Jesus," while one has a poetic runic inscription in Latin (Vg248).

The use of runes for purposes of magic is attested by many small metal sheets, which are often found in connection with graves and Christian graveyards. Remarkable is the Högstena magic formula (Vg216, 1100s), a charm with a heathen air that, freely translated, reads: "I conjure against the spirit of the dead, the revenant, whether he comes riding or running, reveals himself sitting or sinking down (reclining?), comes traveling or flying; in every form the ghost shall deteriorate and die." The antithesis to this incantation is a little, fragmentary lead cross from Lödöse, a burial amulet whose runic inscription in Latin is a close quotation from the Catholic burial ritual (Vg264, 1200s; normalized and reconstructed as far as possible): Domine Iesu [Christe, l]ibera de igni[bus sicut] liberasti t(r)es [pueros] de camino ignis ("Lord Jesus Christ, save [the soul] from the flames, as you saved the three young men from the burning oven" [cf. Daniel 3]).

The persons responsible for the inscriptions quoted above were obviously literate. In the profane texts preserved on a number of everyday items made of wood, bone, or metal, such as tools and utensils, the common people express themselves, often succinctly, with signatures, prayers, and futhark magic. (The following examples all come from Old Lödöse.) Statements of ownership like "Helga owns me" (Vg239, 1200s) on a small wooden spade (butter knife?) are quite common; the expression "owns me" is gradually dropped in preference for just the name, as on the other side of the spade: "Helga." Sometimes, an object is labeled by a runic carver. Examples are a fairly unidentifiable wooden fragment bearing the inscription (Vg272, 1200s; the first letter a Latin capital) Prhl 'swingle, thrashing stick,' and a small lead sheet with the runes (Vg234, 1200s) unmarka 'one mark [a unit of weight].' Occasionally, a longer profane text appears, for example on a weaver's knife (Vg279, 1100s): "Think of me, I am thinking of you; love me, I love you," a little love verse also found in the Norwegian material. A wooden calendar (Vg233, 1100s) uses runes as numbers. The runic calendar, an eternal calendar for popular reckoning of time employed from the Middle Ages until the 1800s, is largely a Swedish phenomenon; the first seven runes indicate weekdays and are repeated for the 365 days of the year, and the entire row of sixteen runes plus three new rune-like signs signify the nineteen years of the lunar cycle. Runes could also be used as numbers in late-medieval counting games.

Ed.: Sveriges runinskrifter 1–. Ed. Kungl. vitterhets historie och antikvitets akademien. Stockholm: [various publishers, now:] Almqvist & Wiksell, 1900– [the ongoing corpus publication, by county, e.g., vol. 5 is Västergötlands runinskrifter, inscriptions are cited by an abbreviation for the province plus their registration or publication number, e.g., Vg93 (= Västergötland no. 93); similarly, G (= Gotland), Sm (= Småland), Sö (= Södermanland)]; "Runfynd 19XX." Fornvännen [yearly reports of new finds beginning with: Svärdström, Elisabeth. "Runfynd 1966." Fornvännen 62 (1967), 261–5]; Svärdström, Elisabeth. Runfynden i Gamla Lödöse. Lödöse—västsvensk medeltidsstad, 4.5. Stockholm: Almqvist & Wiksell, 1982. **Lit.**: Svärdström, Elisabeth. "Svensk medeltidsrunologi." Rig 55 (1972), 77–97; Jansson, Sven B. F. Runes in Sweden. 2nd rev. ed. Trans. Peter Foote. [Stockholm]: Gidlund; Royal Academy of Letters, History and Antiquities; Central Board of National Antiquities, 1987, pp. 162–73.

Elisabeth Svärdström

[**See also:** Alphabet; Eddic Meters; Harald Gormsson (Bluetooth); Hávamál; Järsta Stone; Jelling; Kensington Stone; Language; Magic; Manx Crosses; Óðinn; Palaeography; Rök Stone Inscription; Viking Hoaxes; Yngvars saga víðfǫrla]

Rural Houses see **Houses, Rural**

Rural Settlement see **Settlement, Rural**

Rus'. The term Rus- first appears around 830–840 in both western and eastern sources as a designation for traders dealing in slaves, precious furs, and swords, who developed trade routes from the Baltic along the Volga to Baghdad. Their first trading centers were in Old Ladoga (Aldeigjuborg); a locality referred to in Arabic as Arthāni (near modern Jaroslavl'); Kiev (Kœnugarðr); and Novgorod, the "New Town" (Old Norse Holmgarðr), founded by 900, followed by Polotsk (Palteskjuborg) and Smolensk (Smalenskja). Political upheavals in the mid-10th century led to the replacement of the Volga route by one along the Dnieper, known in the sources as "the route from the Varangians to the Greeks."

The origin of the word Rus', which does not occur in Old Norse sources, and the ethnic group(s) to which it referred have been the subject of much debate (Pritsak 1981, vol. 1). That there was a significant "Scandinavian" component in Rus' is indicated not only by written sources, but also by the bilingual names of the waterfalls on the river Dnieper (Benediktz 1978: 9–12), one group of which is most easily explained as deriving from Old Norse.

In medieval Slavic sources, Rus' refers first and foremost to a dynastic, political-geographical entity that first appeared on the upper Volga in the mid-10th century as a seminomadic (Khazarian type) khaganate (empire). In about 930, the Rus' polity moved to newly conquered Kiev. After a few decades of struggle with the Slavs on the right bank of the Dnieper, the Rus' converted to Christianity of the Byzantine rite in 988, followed by a shift to the (Bulgarian) Slavonic rite in 1036, and remained the crucial political, economic, and cultural force in Eurasia until it fell to the Tatars in 1240. The Scandinavian term for the region, known from rune stones and in skaldic verse, was Garðr/Garðar ("town[s]/enclosure[s]"); medieval Icelandic writings refer to it as "Garðaríki," the "kingdom of the towns."

According to Pritsak, both names were movable geographic names that shifted with the interests of the Norsemen. Originally, they referred to the Franco-Frisian towns of Quentovic and Dorestad (ca. 750–850), and later became associated with the territory that encompassed first Ladoga and Novgorod, and later Kiev. The earlier designation for this territory and the lands east of the Baltic in general was *austrvegr*, the "eastern way." This term included the territories Kúrland, Eistland, Aðalsýsla, Eysýsla, and later Bjarmaland and the northern Dvina (Vína). Expeditions to this area are prominent in *Egils saga Skalla-Grímssonar* and *Landnámabók*.

The earliest rulers of the territory bore Scandinavian names, starting with Rurik (Hrœrekr, ca. 860) through Olga (Helga, regent 945–964). The next prince, Svjatolav (964–972), was the first to have a Slavic name. In the oldest chronicle of the Rus', the *Povĕst'vremennykh let*, this situation is accounted for by a legendary account of how the war-torn Slavs and Finns invited Scandinavians from across the seas to come and rule them. This account, known as the "Calling of the Varangians," has led to the spilling of much scholarly ink; its supporters are referred to as "Normanists," its opponents, who claim that Rus' is of purely Slavic origin, as "anti-Normanists." In its present form, the story of the "Calling of the Varangians" is reminiscent of other origin legends, for example, Vortigern's request for aid from Hengist and Horsa in Geoffrey of Monmouth's *Historia regum Britanniae*. The precise events leading to the establishment of the *khaganate* and later of the kingdom are still subjects of scholarly discussion; it is, however, clear that Scandinavians, both merchants and warriors, must have played an important part in its foundation along with the Khazars and the Slavs.

Even after the capital moved south to Kiev, the ruling families of Scandinavia maintained ties with the rulers of Novgorod, who usually were the sons of the kings of Kiev. Óláfr Tryggvason was brought up at the court of Valdemar (Volodimir, 970–1015) in the 970s, and Óláfr Haraldsson (later known as St. Óláfr) sought refuge at the court of his successor, Jaroslav (1018–1054), during the winter of 1029–1030, leaving his son, Magnús, in his care. Óláfr's half-brother, Haraldr harðráði ("hard-ruler"), spent some time in Jaroslav's service on his way to and from Greece, and married one of his daughters, Elizabeth (Old Norse Ellisif). Jaroslav himself was married to a Swedish princess, Ingigerðr; his grandson, Vlademir (Monomach, 1113–1125), married Gyða, daughter of the last Anglo-Saxon king, Harold Godwinsson, slain at Hastings in 1066. Gyða was raised at the court of the Danish king Sven Estridsen (1047–1076). The daughters of their son, Mstislav (Haraldr, according to the sagas), also married Scandinavians: Málmfríðr was the wife first of King Sigurðr Jórsalafari ("crusader") of Norway (d. 1130) and then of King Erik II of Denmark (d. 1137); Ingeborg married Knud Lavard, king of the Obotriti (d. 1131).

In the sagas, Garðaríki served as the setting for numerous harrying expeditions, historical and otherwise. The locations most commonly named are Holmgarðr and Aldeigjuborg, closest to Scandinavia and familiar from the *konungasögur*. *Eymundar þáttr*, which appears to reflect the fratricidal wars that followed Valdemar's death (1015), leaves its hero in possession of the kingdom of Palteskja. Another Icelander said to have visited Garðaríki is Bjǫrn Hítdœlakappi. Merchants to and from this part of the world are described as "Holmgarðsfari" ("traveler to Holmgarðr") or "gerzkr," although the latter term was easily confused with the "girzkr" ("Greek"). "Rus'ian [conic] hats" (sing. *gerzkr hǫttr*) appear in a number of sagas.

As a country peopled by monsters and giants, perhaps because of its location within the classical "Scythia," perhaps because of confusion over the fact that the Latin "Ruzzia"/"Rucia," which often appears in Icelandic as "Rucialand," could easily be confused with "Risaland" (giantland), or a combination of the two, Garðaríki is a place of sorcery and adventure in *fornaldarsögur* and *riddarasögur*.

Ed. and **Tr**.: Likhachev, D. S., ed. *Povĕst' vremennykh let (Tale of Bygone Years)*. 2 vols. Moscow and Leningrad: Akademiin Nauk, 1950 [also referred to as the "Russian Primary Chronicle" or "Nestor Chronicle," the most important source for the history of Rus' to the 12th century]; Cross, Samuel Hazzard, and Olgerd P. Sherbowitz-Wetzor, eds. and trans. *The Russian Primary Chronicle: Laurentian Text*. Cambridge: Medieval Academy of America, 1973. **Lit.**: Braun, F. "Das historische Russland im nordischen Schrifttum des X.–XIV. Jahrhunderts." In *Festschrift Eugen Mogk zum 70. Geburtstag 19. Juli 1924*. Halle: Niemeyer, 1924, pp. 150–96; Schmidt, Knud Rahbek, ed. *Varangian Problems: Report on the First International Symposium on the Theme The Eastern Connections of the Nordic Peoples in the Viking Period and Early Middle Ages, Moesgaard, University of Aarhus, 7th–11th October 1968. Scando-Slavica*. Supplementum, 1. Copenhagen: Munksgaard, 1970; Sigfús Blöndal. *The Varangians of Byzantium: An Aspect of Byzantine Military History*. Trans. and rev. Benedikt S. Benediktz. Cambridge and New York: Cambridge University Press, 1978; Pritsak, Omeljan. *The Origin of Rus'. 1: Old Scandinavian Sources Other than the Sagas*. Cambridge: Harvard University Press, 1981 [vol. 2 forthcoming]; Noonan, Thomas. "Kievan Rus'." In *Dictionary of the Middle Ages*. Ed. Joseph R. Strayer. New York: Scribner, 1982–89, vol. 7, pp. 244–52; Pritsak, Omeljan. "The Origin of the Name Rus/Rus'." In *Passé Turco-Tatar, Présent Soviétique: Études offerts à Alexandre Bennigsen*. Ed. Ch. Lemercier-Quelquejay et al. Louvain: Éditions Peeters; Paris: Éditions de l'École des Hautes Études en Sciences Sociales, 1988, pp. 45–65.

Omeljan Pritsak

[See also: Russia, Norse in; Trade; Varangians]

Russia, Norse in. Did Scandinavians found, or dominate, or merely visit and serve, the early Russian state? After a quarter-millennium debate, there is still no consensus, partly due to the politically charged nature of the debate itself. The Slavs had been "living like savage beasts and birds" before the advent of the civilizing Norsemen, according to the German-born Moscow academician Schlözer in 1802, a view adopted by several subsequent scholars and nonscholars alike, including Adolf Hitler, who saw in Russia "a wonderful instance of the state-organizing capability of the Germans among an inferior race." Thoroughly provoked, many Russian and Soviet historians have countered by downplaying, questioning, or even denying any Scandinavian influence on the rise of early Russia. In short, noises emanating from more modern racist assumptions have often "jammed" signals from a distant past.

Written sources inspired the "Normanist" side. The *Bertinian Annals* of the Frankish court state that envoys from the prince of Rhos visting Byzantium in 839 were Swedes. The treatise *De administrando imperio* by the Byzantine emperor Constantine Porphyrogenitos (ca. 950) distinguishes "Rhos" from "Slavs" and gives not only Slavonic names for the cataracts down the Dnieper, but also "Rhos" ones, which have proven to be Old Swedish. Likewise, Bishop Liutprand of Cremona in 968 identifies the Rhos with (Germanic) Northmen. Finally, the *Russian Primary Chronicle*, edited by the monk Nestor around 1112, asserts that two Slavonic tribes and two Finnish ones from the Ladoga–Novgorod–Upper Volga area, locked in internecine strife, around 860 invited in the very foreigners who had been dominating them earlier, "Varangians called Rus' . . . from across the sea," to restore order and rule them all.

Other philological arguments have also been marshaled to substantiate that Norsemen founded or were a dominant force in ancient Russia. Thus, the name "Russia" (Slavonic *Rus'*, Latin *Rhos*, Greek *'Rōs*, Arabic *Rūs*) has been derived from Finnish *ruotsi* 'Swede,' or originally Swedish "rower," as reflected in *Roths*-lagen, "the Rowers' Law-reach," the area around what is now Stockholm. The names of Russia's early rulers, as well as their envoys, as enumerated in the *Primary Chronicle*, are overwhelmingly Norse. Place-names around Novgorod in particular reflect a one-time presence of the *Varjagi* 'Varangians,' and so on.

The "Anti-Normanist" side has taken varying exception to all these arguments. Following the Russian revolution, there has been an increasing emphasis on archaeology. Basing themselves on the "solid (arti)facts" unearthed, Soviet scholars demonstrated that the Slavs in the south, around the Don and Dnieper, were more advanced economically and culturally than the tribes in the forested north. In keeping with Marxist historical materialism, Soviet scholars generally concluded that the Russian state must have arisen from the inner societal needs of this more developed and sophisticated south, around Kiev.

This "Moscow school" view has lately been challenged by a "Leningrad school" of archaeologists (Dubov *et al.* 1978). The oldest excavated part of Old Ladoga comprises a Scandinavian smithy from 754. The Old Ladoga Plakun cemetery, likewise Nordic, dates from around 830–840. The entire town was razed in a fire around 860 (*cf.* the *Primary Chronicle*'s words on tribal and intercommunal warfare). A Nordic king held court there and moved south, to Gorodišče close by Novgorod, where there are cultural layers from about 860–890, whereas Novgorod itself appears to date from about 900 (Nosov 1984). Scandinavians are well represented in the Upper Volga settlements from the same time (which tallies well with the Arab Ibn Faḍlān's description of a Scandinavian "Rūs" boat pyre by the Volga in 921), as well as in, *e.g.*, the great Gnĕzdovo warriors' cemetery right outside Smolensk, north of Kiev.

This argument is part of what we may see as a long-term tendency toward reappraising the whole Normanist controversy. In this reappraisal, there are three main constituents: the "Nordic-Fennic equation"; the question of what Nordic warriors *did* around 839–1030 in relation to the Slavs; and the question of lasting Nordic influence on the Slavs, and vice versa.

First, still unresolved is the question of what relationship(s) Norse immigrants had to the aboriginal Baltic Fennic (Finnish, Estonian, Vepse, *etc.*) and Volga Fennic (Merja) tribes, along the Baltic–Ladoga–Onega–Upper Volga waterway. Here, Scandinavians and Slavs alike were intruders, lured by the world market of Islam. In the caliphate, far-northern luxury articles, furs for clothing, walrus teeth for scabbards, and so on, were in high demand. Such articles prompted, on the one hand, Fennic, especially Vepse, expansion northward (the *Wisu* of Arab sources, the *Bjarmar* of Norse sagas), and on the other hand, both Scandinavian and Slav expansion in Fennic (Vepse) areas, beginning with Old Ladoga, and ending in the White Sea area ("Bjarmaland," from Vepse *Perämaa* 'hinterland,' *Perm'*). The *Wisu* describe North Norwegian

walrus hunters fighting each other around 926. Indeed, Norwegian expansion northward ("Nor-*way*") to Kola may be explained by these market forces. As late as 1222, a Norwegian sailed through "Bjarmaland" and eastern Europe to Jerusalem and home.

Second, there are indications that the Rhos of the *Bertinian Annals* both came from and returned to Old Ladoga. And great numbers of Islamic coins, first in the Ladoga-Novgorod woodlands around 750–860, then in Sweden (Rothslagen and Gotland) 860–950, point to something drastic occurring around 860. Did Slav colonization and domination induce a joint Scandinavian-Vepse reaction? Vepse cemeteries near Ladoga show a Vepse-Scandinavian symbiosis around 860–950. Did the victors in an Old Ladoga "civil war" in 860 both call in mercenaries from Sweden (*cf.* the Islamic coinage from Russia going there) and proceed south, to Novgorod, Kiev, and Constantinople, which in 866 barely withstood the *'Rōs*? The name *Rūs'* may with some difficulties be derived from *ruotsi*, but points perhaps instead to Greek *'Rōs* (from the 839 contact) as influenced by a Vepse milieu, *cf.* other Fennic tribal names in Russian, *Em'*, *Lib'*, *Sum'*, *Ves'*, *etc.* Greek *'Rōs* is in turn biblical, but its application to the 839 Swedes may also have been inspired by archival materials on the 3rd- to 6th-century blond (*'rūsioi*) Scandinavian proto-Vikings known as the Erules ("Earls") or Rosomones.

Whatever the ethnic origins of these original *Rus'* (and there were certainly many Slavs among them), it is important to distinguish the early Nordic arrivals and Old Ladoga, Upper Volga settlers from the later "Varangians." Mentioned in Arabic in about 1020 (*Warānk*), in the Old Russian Law Code 1015 (*Varjagi*, alongside *Kolbjagi*), and in Byzantine Greek from 1030 (*Varanggoi*, alongside *Koulpinggoi*), they may have comprised both traders and warriors. Their name may bespeak their farthest northern trading haunts at *Varanger*, as indicated by al-Bīrūnī and al-Qazwīnī. The enigmatic *Kolbjagi* (in al-Qazwīnī al-*Kilābiyya*, Old Norse *kylfingar*) may be their Fennic partners (*cf.*, *e.g.*, Vepse Ladogan artifacts in Arctic Scandinavia, including Varanger, and Norwegian state intervention against marauding *kylfingar*). The early rulers of Russia in Kiev used Scandinavian elite troops. Six thousand were removed from Kiev in 988 to Constantinople, where they formed the beginnings of the emperor's Varangian guard. After the Norman invasion of England in 1066, fugitive Anglo-Saxons also served as Varangians.

Third, and most important, the old "Normanist" assumptions that Scandinavians introduced civilization among the subject Slavs, must be totally revised. The Norsemen were few in relation to Slav and non-Slav natives alike. Only in areas colonized by Novgorod, up toward the White Sea, is their racial type still dominant today, alongside the Vepse (Onega-Saima) type. Otherwise, Norsemen were drops in a Slavonic sea. They took up "Russian" (meaning Eastern Slavonic), had weapons made by Slav smiths, married locally. Tales and folklore motifs in Russia thought to have been Scandinavian have been shown instead to have originated in Byzantium and traveled northward. Less than ten Norse loanwords have been established in Russian (*e.g.*, *jabednik* 'official'; *Sud* 'the Golden Horn' found at Constantinople; *cf.* Thomsen 1877); nearly the same number are found, less known, in Vepse (*e.g.*, *murgneita* 'to breakfast'; *sur* 'big'; *kurta* 'shirt'). Some fifteen Russian words, however, penetrated Scandinavian (*tolk* 'interpreter,' *cf.* English *talk*; *torg* 'marketplace'; *græns* 'border'; *etc.* [*cf.* Mel'nikova 1984]; plus possibly *moln* 'cloud' and *Mjǫlnir* 'Þórr's hammer' from *molnija* 'lightning'; *brynje* 'coat-of-mail' from *bronjá*;

tapar-yx 'an axe' from *topor*; the deity *Kvasir* from *kvas*; *etc.*)

Generally, the Norsemen absorbed culture in, and via, Russia, Novgorod, Kiev, and Constantinople and, seldom realized, down the Volga, traversing the Muslim Bulgar state and Jewish Khazaria to Zoroastrian-and-Shia-Muslim Iran and Shia-and-Sunni Iraq in the 9th–11th centuries. A few details of late Norse paganism may even have been inspired in the East (*e.g.*, the deity Heimdallr, the Bifrǫst bridge, Þórr's abode, Freyja's name), although this connection remains to be proven. The Norse sources on *væringjar* (Varangians) and travelers to and through Russia are few, the most notable being some 100 rune stones, thirty-two of which commemorate the ill-fated expedition of Yngvarr víðfǫrli ("the widely traveled"; *cf. Yngvars saga víðfǫrla*) in 1041, which may have made it all the way to *Karusm*, Muslim Khwārizm, in present-day Uzbekistan.

Lit.: Thomsen, Vilhelm. *The Relations Between Ancient Russia and Scandinavia and the Origin of the Russian State.* London and Oxford: Parker, 1877; rpt. New York: Franklin, 1965; Stender-Petersen, Adolf. *Varangica.* Århus: Universitetets slaviske institut, 1953; Avdusin, Daniil. "Smolensk and the Varangians According to the Archaeological Data." *Norwegian Archaeological Review* 2 (1969), 52–62; *Varangian Problems: Report on the First International Symposium on the Theme The Eastern Connections of the Nordic Peoples in the Viking Period and Early Middle Ages, Moesgaard, University of Aarhus, 7th–11th October 1968.* Scando-Slavica, Supplementum 1. Copenhagen: Munksgaard, 1970 [special issue containing proceedings of a symposium held at the Moesgaard Museum, University of Aarhus, 1968]; Bulkin, V. A. "On the Classification and Interpretation of Archaeological Material from the Gnezdovo Cemetery." *Norwegian Archaeological Review* 6 (1973), 10–13; Klejn, L. S. "Soviet Archaeology and the Role of the Vikings in the Early History of the Slavs." *Norwegian Archaeological Review* 6 (1973), 1–4; Lebedeu, G. S., and V. A. Nazarenko. "The Connections Between Russians and Scandinavians in the 9th–11th Centuries." *Norwegian Archaeological Review* 6 (1973), 5–9; Dubov, I. V., *et al.* "Russo-Scandinavian Connections in the Founding Phase of the Russian State." *Scando-Slavica* 24 (1978), 63–89 [in Russian with English summary]; Pritsak, Omeljan. *The Origin of Rus'. 1: Old Scandinavian Sources Other than the Sagas.* Cambridge: Harvard University Press, 1981 [vol. 2 forthcoming]; Nielsen, Jens Peter. "Boris Grekov and the Norman Question." *Scando-Slavica* 27 (1981), 69–92; Mel'nikova, E. A. "Drevnerusskie leksičeskie zaimstvovanija v švedskom jazyke." In *Drevnejsie gosudarstva na territorii SSSR—1982.* Moscow: Nauka, 1984, pp. 62–75 [English summary]; Nosov, E. N. "Novgorod i novgorodska okruga." *Novgorodskij istoričeskij sbornik* 1984, pp. 3–28; Shepard, Jonathan. "Yngvarr's Expedition to the East and a Russian Inscribed Stone Cross." *Saga-Book of the Viking Society* 21 (1984–85), 222–92; Sedov, V. V., *et al. Srednevekova Ladoga.* Leningrad: Nauka, 1985; Cook, Robert. "Russian History, Icelandic Story, and Byzantine Strategy in *Eymundar þáttr Hringssonar*." *Viator* 17 (1986), 65–89; Larsson, Mats G. "Yngvarr's Expedition and the *Georgian Chronicle*." *Saga-Book of the Viking Society* 22 (1987), 98–108; Stang, Haakon A. "The Naming of Russia." Diss. University of Oslo [in progress].

Haakon Stang

[**See also:** *Rus'*; Varangians; *Yngvars saga víðfǫrla*]

Rök Stone Inscription. The runic inscription on the huge stone in the cemetery of Rök parish in southeastern Sweden, containing some 750 characters, is the longest and most complicated of all ancient Scandinavian inscriptions. The stone is almost 4 m. high, 1 1/2 m. wide, and 1/2 m. thick, and is covered with runes on all four sides as well as the top. The inscription appears to date

from the early 9th century, and is composed mainly in "short-twig runes" of the later *futhark*, which contained sixteen letters. However, it also contains a number of cipher runes of various types, including some that use runes of the older twenty-four-letter *futhark*. The inscription features the oldest *fornyrðislag* strophe in existence. The work of generations of scholars has deciphered most of the writing, although there is much uncertainty about detail, including the order in which the five surfaces should be read. There is wide disagreement about the meaning and intent of the inscription as a whole.

Ostensibly, it is a memorial stone raised in honor of Væmoð by his father, Varin. The inscription then makes a series of cryptic references to memorable matters of the past, including "two articles of booty that were taken twelve times in battle"; Theoderic on horseback on the shores of the "Hreið Sea"; twenty kings dead on a battlefield; (another?) twenty kings having only four names among them, each five of the same name being sons of one of four brothers; the sacrifice of a mother for one of the "Ingeldings"; a son born to Vilin, who could fell a giant; Þórr; Sibbi, ninety years old, who fostered Væmoð or engendered him.

One interpretation (von Friesen 1920) sees the stone as an announcement by Varin that in his old age he has engendered a son to avenge Væmoð, even as Sibbi, at the age of ninety, had done. The great deeds mentioned are to serve as inspirations for the avenger against the twenty sea-kings who caused Væmoð's death. Höfler (1975) modified this theory, claiming that *sibbi* means "father," and that Varin himself was ninety, and was dedicating the

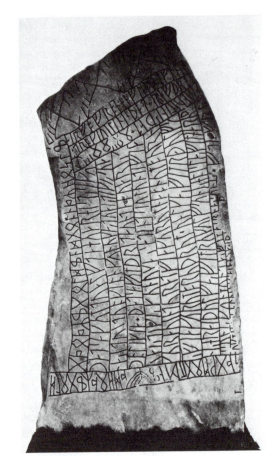

159. Rök Stone

avenging son to a quasi-divine Theodoric the Great. The kings were members of a "warrior guild," such as the one evidenced by the Trelleborg remains. Other scholars (Wessén 1964, Jacobsen 1961) consider all the material except the first two sentences to be unrelated episodes present merely for ornament and to demonstrate the rune master's knowledge and versatility. Nielsen (1969) contends that the inscription contains two religious segments, one an invocation to Óðinn, one to Þórr. Lönnroth (1977) claims to see a tripartite form, each section containing a riddle pertaining to a heroic legend and its answer. Kratz (1978–79) views it an an initiation memorial, Væmoð being only ritually dead, and inaugurated into a brotherhood of warriors divided into groups where each one has the same ritual name and is subservient to a "father," in Væmoð's case, Vilin. The memorable matters pertain to the brotherhood, some of them so secret they cannot be mentioned (the inscription skips over from memorable matter three to memorable matter twelve). The brotherhood is dedicated to Þórr, and wise old Sibbi is Væmoð's mother.

Ed.: Brate, Erik, ed. *Östergötlands runinskrifter, granskade och tolkade.* Stockholm: Wahlström & Widstrand, 1911–18, pp. 231–55; Friesen, Otto von, ed. *Rökstenen.* Svenska Fornminneplatser, 23. Stockholm: Wahlström & Widstrand, 1934. [Most studies listed below furnish the text of the inscription.] **Bib.**: Pipping, Hugo. "Rökstensinskriften en rättsurkund." *Studier i nordisk filologi* 22 (1932), 131–7; Nielsen, Niels Åge. *Runerne på Rökstenen.* Odense University Studies in Scandinavian Languages, 2. Odense: Odense University Press, 1969, pp. 65–8; Kratz, Henry. *Frühes Mittelalter: Vor- und Frühgeschichte des deutschen Schrifttums.* Handbuch der deutschen Literaturgeschichte. Zweite Abteilung: Bibliographen, 1. Ed. Paul Stapf. Bern and Munich: Francke, 1970, p. 83; Wessén, Elias. "Rök, ett fornminne och ett ortnamn." *Fornvännen* 70 (1975), 14–5. **Lit.**: Bugge, Sophus. *Der Runenstein von Rök in Östergötland, Schweden.* Ed. Magnus Olsen *et al.* Stockholm: Hæggström, 1910; Friesen, Otto von. *Rökstenen: Runstenen vid Röks kyrka Lysings härad läst och tydd.* Stockholm: Kungl. vitterhets historie och antikvitets akademiens handlingar, 1920; Höfler, Otto. *Der Runenstein von Rök und die germanische Individualweihe. 1: Germanisches Sakralkönigtum.* Tübingen: Niemeyer; Cologne: Böhlau, 1952; Wessén, Elias. *Runstenen vid Röks kyrka.* Kungl. vitterhets historie och antikvitets akademiens handlingar, Filologisk-filosofiska serien, 5. Stockholm: Almqvist & Wiksell, 1958; Jacobsen, Lis. "Rökstudier." *Arkiv för nordisk filologi* 76 (1961), 2–50; Höfler, Otto. "Der Rökstein und die Sage." *Arkiv för nordisk filologi* 78 (1963), 1–121; Wessén, Elias. "Teoderik—myt eller hjältesaga?" *Arkiv för nordisk filologi* 79 (1964), 1–20; Höfler, Otto. "Der Rökstein und Theoderich." *Arkiv för nordisk filologi* 90 (1975), 92–110; Nielsen, Niels Åge. *Runerne på Rökstenen* [see above]; Lönnroth, Lars. "The Riddles of the Rök-Stone: A Structural Approach." *Arkiv för nordisk filologi* 92 (1977), 1–57; Kratz, Henry. "Was Vamoþ Still Alive?: The Rök-Stone as Initiation Memorial." *Mediaeval Scandinavia* 11 (1978–79), 9–29.

Henry Kratz

[**See also:** Eddic Meters; Runes and Runic Inscriptions]

Saga is an Icelandic word borrowed into English to designate an Old Norse prose narrative. The oldest sagas are *postola sögur* ("apostles' sagas") and *heilagra manna sögur* ("saints' lives"), anonymous translations of Latin biographies of apostles and saints, the earliest from about 1150. Turville-Petre (1953) stressed the importance of these works, over 100 of which are extant, as models for later subgenres.

Although the forerunners of *konungasögur* ("kings' sagas") are also quite old, the major biographies and compendia were compiled around 1190–1230. Skaldic stanzas were important sources for these works, some of which include tales about Icelandic poets. The most important *konungasaga* is *Heimskringla* ("Orb of the World"), a history of Norway to 1177, by the Icelandic scholar Snorri Sturluson (1178/9–1241).

Best known are the *Íslendingasögur* ("sagas about Icelanders"), of which forty have been preserved. The best of these anonymous works, such as *Njáls saga*, are among the finest literary creations of the Middle Ages. Most were composed during the 13th century. The oldest, biographies of poets, such as *Egils saga*, seem to be offshoots of the *konungasögur*. There has been much speculation about the nature of their oral sources. Structurally, the *Íslendingasögur* resemble romances, characterized by plot interlace and sophisticated foreshadowing.

Riddarasögur ("sagas about knights") are prose adaptations of romances. *Tristrams saga ok Ísǫndar*, perhaps the oldest, is a translation of Thomas's *Tristan* made in 1226 at the behest of Hákon Hákonarson (r. 1217–1263). *Tristrams saga* exerted a strong influence on saga writing, and the subgenre inspired a spate of mediocre Icelandic imitations.

Fornaldarsögur ("sagas of ancient times") comprise two groups, heroic legends and adventure tales. The most important member of the first group is *Vǫlsunga saga*. Characteristic of the second group is *Gǫngu-Hrólfs saga*, whose hero bears the same name as the conqueror of Normandy. Most of the *fornaldarsögur* are products of the 14th century. Many *fornaldarsögur* are retold by Saxo Grammaticus in his 13th-century *Gesta Danorum*.

Bib.: Halldór Hermannsson. *Bibliography of the Icelandic Sagas and Minor Tales.* Islandica, 1. Ithaca: Cornell University Library, 1908; rpt. New York: Kraus, 1966; Halldór Hermannsson. *Bibliography of the Mythical-Heroic Sagas.* Islandica, 5. Ithaca: Cornell University Library, 1912; rpt. New York: Kraus, 1966; Halldór Hermannsson. *The Sagas of Icelanders (Íslendinga sögur): A Supplement to Bibliography of the Icelandic Sagas and Minor Tales.* Islandica, 24. Ithaca: Cornell University Press, 1935; Halldór Hermannsson. *The Sagas of the Kings (Konunga sögur) and the Mythical-Heroic Sagas (Fornaldar sögur): Two Bibliographical Supplements.* Islandica, 26. Ithaca: Cornell University Press, 1937; Jóhann S. Hannesson. *The Sagas of Icelanders (Íslendinga sögur): A Supplement to Islandica I and XXIV.* Islandica, 38. Ithaca: Cornell University Press, 1957; Fry, Donald K. *Norse Sagas Translated into English: A Bibliography.* New York: AMS, 1980; Kalinke, Marianne E., and P. M. Mitchell. *Bibliography of Old Norse–Icelandic Romances.* Islandica, 44. Ithaca and London: Cornell University Press, 1985. **Lit.**: Schlauch, Margaret. *Romance in Iceland.* Princeton: Princeton University Press; New York: American-Scandinavian Foundation; London: Allen & Unwin, 1934; rpt. New York: Russell & Russell, 1973; Turville-Petre, G. *Origins of Icelandic Literature.* Oxford: Clarendon, 1953; rpt. 1967; Andersson, Theodore M. *The Icelandic Family Saga: An Analytic Reading.* Harvard Studies in Comparative Literature, 28. Cambridge: Harvard University Press, 1967; Hallberg, Peter. *The Icelandic Saga.* Translated with an Introduction by Paul Schach. Lincoln: University of Nebraska Press, 1962; Schier, Kurt. *Sagaliteratur.* Sammlung Metzler, M78. Stuttgart: Metzler, 1970; Hermann Pálsson and Paul Edwards. *Legendary Fiction in Medieval Iceland.* Studia Islandica, 30. Reykjavik: Heimspekideild Háskóla Íslands; Menningarsjóður, 1971; Kalinke, Marianne E. *King Arthur North-by-Northwest: The matière de Bretagne in Old Norse–Icelandic Romances.* Bibliotheca Arnamagnæana, 37. Copenhagen: Reitzel, 1981; Clover, Carol J. *The Medieval Saga.* Ithaca and London: Cornell University Press, 1982; Schach, Paul. *Icelandic Sagas.* Twayne's World Authors Series, 717. Boston: Twayne, 1984; Clover, Carol J., and John Lindow. *Old Norse–Icelandic Literature: A Critical Guide.* Islandica, 45. Ithaca and London: Cornell University Press, 1985.

Paul Schach

[**See also:** Bookprose/Freeprose Theory; *Egils saga Skalla-Grímssonar*; *Fornaldarsögur*; *Gǫngu-Hrólfs saga*; *Heimskringla*; *Íslendingasögur*; *Konungasögur*; *Njáls saga*; *Postola sögur*; *Riddarasögur*; Saints' Lives; Saxo Grammaticus; *Tristrams saga ok Ísǫndar*; *Vǫlsunga saga*]

Saints' Lives

1. DENMARK. Along with chronicles, saints' lives constitute one of the most important literary genres in the early Middle Ages. Indeed, most of the early Danish works in Latin were legends, based on the lives of holy men and women and patterned on international models.

Saints' cults were used in missionary work and in the establishment of political institutions, *e.g.*, to advance the feudal society, which became a political prerequisite of the Catholic Church after Pope Gregory VII. An important link in this process was that the monarchy was sanctified through the Church. In the centuries between the introduction of Christianity and the Reformation in 1536, the following people were canonized in Denmark: the king Knud, who was killed in Odense Cathedral (1086), the martyr Knud (Cnut) Lavard, the son of King Erik Ejegod ("evergood") and the father of King Valdemar den Store ("the great"; r. 1157–1182); the missionary Theodgar (Thøger) from Thüringen, who was venerated especially in North Jutland; Margrethe, a martyr from Zealand, killed by her husband after an argument (she was related to Bishop Absalon, King Valdemar's brother-in-arms); and Abbot Vilhelm, a French Augustinian abbot, summoned to the country by Bishop Absalon. The following were venerated as saints but without canonization: Niels of Århus, housecarl of King Valdemar the Great, son of King Knud Magnussen, his comrade-in-arms during the civil wars (he thus represents a collateral branch to the victorious royal family); King Erik Plovpenning ("plowpenny"), Valdemar den Store's grandson, killed by his brother Abel in the Schlei; and the popular saint Anders from Zealand (d. 1205), priest in St. Peter's church in Slagelse, who until recent times was still venerated as a saint in western Zealand, as was Niels in Århus.

The victorious feudal central power was able to raise many saints from the grave among its own people. As holy figures and concrete, worldy people, the saints, not least the national and local ones, could give visible and purposeful content to religious belief. In so doing, the saint's cult could ally itself with the nature-religious cult forms that continued to exist even after the Reformation. The distance created between the monotheistic confessional dogma of Christianity and the natural-religious, magic forms of understanding was considerably reduced by the hidden "polytheism" of the Catholic Church in hagiography and by the rites and conceptions that developed in connection with the holy men and women: relics, pilgrimages, saints' days, saints' feasts with dances (French *ballado*), and so on.

From the Middle Ages, eleven Danish legends and fragments are known, comprising four passions, the anonymous *Passio Sancti Kanuti regis et martiris* (ca. 1090), a fragment of the Englishman Robert of Ely's legend about Knud Lavard (ca. 1135), from which material is used in the anonymous *Passio de Sct. Canuto duce* (ca. 1170). There survive, moreover, two short accounts of St. Margrethe's death and enshrinement (ca. 1205). There are six *vitae*, including: "The Life of St. Kjeld" (ca. 1350), "The Life of St. Knud" (ca. 1220), "St. Anders' Miraculous Ride" (ca. 1350), and "The Life of St. Thøger" (ca. 1260). There is also a large collection of miracles linked to King Erik Plovpenning and the Anglo-Saxon Ailnoth's king's-mirror legend and historical chronicle about King Sven Estridsen and his five sons, with special emphasis on St. Knud (ca. 1120).

Apart from the legends about King Knud, the most interesting of the original Danish legends in Latin is the long *vita* about a Victorine abbot, the Frenchman Vilhelm (*Vita et miracula S. Guillermi*). The *vita* demonstrates the great cultural differences between the center (France) and the periphery (Denmark) noticed by the Parisian monk, who comes upon an almost abandoned monastery that lacks almost everything (Eskildø), but who, with Bishop Absalon's help, creates a flourishing cultural center (Æbelholt). An interesting collection of letters is preserved from the abbot.

The legend about Knud Lavard is both beautiful and well composed. Duke Knud is depicted as the seed that must die and be buried so that a new (religious) life can bloom. His life is a long preparation for his voluntary martyrdom, where he, in spite of many warnings, is treacherously murdered by his cousin, Prince Magnus Nielsen, whose motive is *invidia*. At the place of the murder, a well gushes out, and miracles are said to take place at the grave. Knud's son, Valdemar den Store, has the body translated. After a victory in the civil war of 1134–1157 and his accession to the throne, Valdemar also manages to obtain the Pope's canonization of Knud Lavard (1170).

On the borderline of the original Danish saints' lives is Rimbert's *Vita Anskarii*, an account of Ansgar, "the Apostle of the North," who, with the support of the Frankish emperor Louis the Pious, undertook a comprehensive mission in Scandinavia from 832 onward.

Ed.: Gertz, M. Cl., ed. *Vitae Sanctorum Danorum.* Copenhagen: Gad, 1908–12. **Tr.**: Olrik, Hans, trans. *Danske helgeners levned.* 2 vols. Copenhagen: Schønberg, 1893–94; Fenger, P. A., trans. *Ansgars Levned.* Copenhagen: Kristeligt Folkebibliothekt, 1926. **Lit.**: Olrik, Hans. *Knud Lavards Liv og Gærning.* Copenhagen: Wroblewski, 1888; Jørgensen, Ellen. *Helgendyrkelse i Danmark. Studier over kirkekultur og kirkeligt liv fra det 11te aarhundredes midte til Reformationen.* Copenhagen: Hagerup, 1909; Gad, Tue. *Legenden i dansk middelalder.* Copenhagen: Dansk videnskabs forlag, 1961; Gad, Tue. *Helgener. Legender fortalt i Norden.* Copenhagen: Rhodos, 1971; Skyum-Nielsen, Niels. *Kvinde og slave.* Copenhagen: Munksgaard, 1971; Hoffmann, Erich. *Die heiligen Könige bei den Angelsachsen und den skandinavischen Völkern. Königsheiliger und Königshaus.* Neumünster: Wachholtz, 1975; *Catholica* 27 (1978) [issue on St. Knud Lavard]; Damsholt, Nanna. "Abbed Vilhelm af Æbelholts brevsamling." *Historisk tidsskrift* (Denmark) 78 (1978), 1–22; Bekker-Nielsen, Hans, *et al.*, eds. *Hagiography and Medieval Literature: A Symposium.* Odense: Odense University Press, 1981 [proceedings of Fifth International Symposium organized by the Center for the Study of Vernacular Literature in the Middle Ages, November 17–18, 1980]; McGuire, Brian Patrick. *The Cistercians in Denmark: Their Attitudes, Roles, and Functions in Medieval Society.* Cistercian Studies Series, 35. Kalamazoo: Cistercian Publications, 1982; Breengaard, Carsten. *Muren om Israels hus. Regnum og sacerdotium i Danmark 1050–1170.* Copenhagen: Gad, 1982; Kaspersen, Søren, *et al. Dansk litteraturhistorie. 1: Fra runer til ridderdigtning, o. 800–1480.* Copenhagen: Gyldendal, 1984; Damsholt, Nanna. *Kvindebilledet i dansk højmiddelalder.* Copenhagen: Borgen, 1985.

Sigurd Kværndrup

2. ICELAND AND NORWAY. Translated saints' lives are among the oldest records of vernacular literature that have come down to us from Norway and Iceland, some fragments dating from the middle of the 12th century. Many other MSS are extant from the late 12th and early 13th centuries, some from Norway, but the great majority from Iceland, although the originals were

often composed in Norway and show Norwegian traces in the language.

Over 100 different saints' lives are included in this corpus, drawn primarily, but not exclusively, from Latin sources. These sources include the apocryphal books of the New Testament, *legendaria* like Jacobus de Voragine's *Legenda aurea*, Gregory's *Dialogues*, and the lives of many saints, from the early "desert saints" down through the centuries. Much of the material concerns the lives of the apostles, both from the canonical *Acta apostolorum* and from the New Testament apocrypha. The "Harrowing of Hell" from the *Evangelium Nicodemi* was popular, as were legends of the Virgin Mary. Lives of the martyred saints, such as Catherine, Sebastian, and Thomas à Becket, are found along with the lives of the confessors, such as Nicolas and Anthony, known for their exemplary lives and miracles rather than their martyrdoms.

Until recently, little has been done to organize this material or to explore the connections among the various texts, due in no small part to the large corpus of secular material in Old Norse, which has been so fascinating to scholars that they have unduly neglected religious writings. There is also little of value in the contents of most of these lives, as they are well known from other sources, except for ones where the Latin original is lost.

Whatever their intrinsic value might be, these works are extremely important for the history of the language and the development of Old Norse literature, although scholars have begun to see this potential only recently. In his seminal work, *Origins of Icelandic Literature*, Turville-Petre maintained that religious writings had taught Icelanders how to write secular sagas, but he had little to say directly about the language of the saints' lives. Unlike early translations from Latin and Greek into other vernaculars, the earliest Old Norse saints' lives show little influence of Latin syntax and few loanwords from Latin. Unnatural constructions, such as appositional participial phrases, the ablative absolute, and the accusative with the infinitive, are replaced by native constructions. Even the Greek and Roman gods are replaced by pagan Norse gods, such as Óðinn for Mercury, Þórr for Jupiter, and Frigg for Venus. The style is lively and colloquial, and little different from that of the secular sagas in Iceland. In a second stage, from the mid-13th to the 15th century, many of the saints' lives were written in a more ornate style (the so-called "florid style"), deliberately imitating Latin, and often translating Latin constructions literally. While the florid style was adopted by Icelandic writers in the 13th century, as in the priest Grímr Hólmsteinsson's (d. 1298) *Jóns saga baptista*, the style flourished in the 14th century, with Bergr Sokkason as its best-known exponent. The simple style, however, was not made obsolete, as demonstrated by, *e.g.*, MS Stock. Perg. fol. no. 2 (late 14th century), which contains twenty-six legends, none written in the florid style.

The lives of the native Norwegian and Icelandic saints contain many elements of the earlier Latin lives. Generally, however, they tend to be more realistic. Some of the accounts stress worldly events more than religion, and go beyond the scope of hagiography. The exception is one of the recensions of the life of St. Óláfr, the most popular of Norwegian saints.

Latin lives of the other Norwegian saints (Hallvarðr, Sunniva, and Magnús) are extant, but we have little in the vernacular about the last two. There is only one fragment (*ca.* 1300) of a life of Hallvarðr (d. 1043) in the vernacular, and a short account of the life of Sunniva is embedded within *Óláfs saga Tryggvasonar* of Oddr Snorrason (*Seljumanna þáttr*). There are three different vernacular

redactions of the life of St. Magnús of the Orkneys (d. 1115), one contained in *Orkneyinga saga*, all apparently descended ultimately from a lost Latin account ascribed to Rodbert of Cricklade, who lived in the 12th century.

Lives of the three Icelandic saints, all bishops, Jón Ǫgmundarson (d. 1121), Þorlákr Þórhallsson (d. 1193), and Guðmundr Arason (d. 1237), are extant in the vernacular. The saga of St. Þorlákr was composed in Icelandic, although fragments of a Latin life of the saint are also in evidence; the other two are translated from lost Latin originals. Jón's life was originally composed by Gunnlaugr Leifsson (d. 1218) and translated into Icelandic not much later. This translation and a later revised one have both survived. Guðmundr's saga was composed in Latin by Arngrímr Brandsson (d. 1361), and probably translated soon after. The ending, however, is missing in the MS we have, and must be supplied from a collection of small pieces about Guðmundr found in a different MS.

The lives of these Icelandic saints mostly emphasize their exemplary lives and piety. They are supplemented by collections of miracles (*jarteiknir*) that take place through their benign influence after they are dead.

Ed.: Keyser, R., and C. R. Unger, eds. *Barlaams ok Josaphats saga.* Christiania [Oslo]: Feilberg & Landmark, 1851; [Jón Sigurðsson and Guðbrandr Vigfússon, eds.] *Biskupasögur.* 2 vols. Copenhagen: Møller, 1858–78; Unger, C. R., ed. *Thomas saga erkibyskups: Fortællinger om Thomas Becket Erkebiskop af Canterbury.* Christiania [Oslo]: Bentzen, 1869; Unger, C. R., ed. *Mariu saga: Legender om Jomfru Maria og hendes jertegn.* Christiania [Oslo]: Brögger & Christie, 1871; Unger, C. R., ed. *Postola Sögur: Legendariske fortællinger om apostlernes liv, deres kamp for kristendommens udbredelse samt deres martyrdød.* Christiania [Oslo]: Bentzen, 1874; Unger, C. R., ed. *Heilagra manna søgur: Fortællinger og legender om hellige mænd og kvinder.* 2 vols. Christiania [Oslo]: Bentzen, 1877; Þorvaldur Bjarnarson. *Leifar fornra kristinna frœða íslenzkra: Codex Arna-Magnæanus 677 4to auk annara enna elztu brota af íslenzkum guðfrœðisritum.* Copenhagen: Hagerup, 1878; Larsson, Ludvig, ed. *Isländska Handskriften No. 645 4° i Den Arnamagnæanske Samlingen på Universitetsbiblioteket i København: I. Handskriftens äldre del.* Lund: Malmström, 1885; Morgenstern, G., ed. *Arnamagnæanische Fragmente. Ein Supplement zu den Heilagra Manna Sögur.* Leipzig and Copenhagen: Graf, 1893; Finnur Jónsson, ed. *AM 623, 4°: Helgensagæer.* Samfund til udgivelse af gammel nordisk litteratur, 52. Copenhagen: Jørgensen, 1927; Finnur Jónsson, ed. *Oddr Snorrason. Saga Óláfs Tryggvasonar.* Copenhagen: Gad, 1932, pp. 100–3; Holtsmark, Anne, ed. *A Book of Miracles: MS No. 645 4° of the Arna-Magnæan Collection in the University Library of Copenhagen.* Corpus Codicum Islandicorum Medii Aevi, 12. Copenhagen: Munksgaard, 1938 [facsimile]; Guðni Jónsson, ed. *Byskupa sögur.* Reykjavik: Íslendingasagnaútgáfan; Haukadalsútgáfan, 1948; Seip, Didrik Arup, ed. *The Arna-Magnæan Manuscript 677, 4to.* Corpus Codicum Islandicorum Medii Aevi, 18. Copenhagen: Munksgaard, 1949 [facsimile]; Jón Helgason, ed. *Byskupa søgur. MS Perg. fol. No. 5 in the Royal Library of Stockholm.* Corpus Codicum Islandicorum Medii Aevi, 19. Copenhagen: Munksgaard, 1950 [facsimile]; Overgaard, Mariane, ed. *The History of the Cross-tree down to Christ's Passion: Icelandic Legend Versions.* Editiones Arnamagnæanæ, ser. B, vol. 26. Copenhagen: Munksgaard, 1968; Foote, Peter, ed. *Lives of Saints: Perg. fol. Nr. 2 in the Royal Library, Stockholm.* Early Icelandic Manuscripts in Facsimile, 4. Copenhagen: Rosenkilde & Bagger, 1962; Hreinn Benediktsson, ed. *The Life of St. Gregory and His Dialogues: Fragments of an Icelandic Manuscript from the 13th Century.* Editiones Arnamagnæanæ, ser. B, vol. 4. Copenhagen: Munksgaard,

1963; Fell, Christine Elizabeth, ed. *Dunstanus saga*. Editiones Arnamagnæanæ, ser. B, vol. 5. Copenhagen: Munksgaard, 1963; Loth, Agnete, ed. *Thomasskinna. Gl. kgl. Saml. 1008 fol. in the Royal Library, Copenhagen*. Early Icelandic Manuscripts in Facsimile, 6. Copenhagen: Rosenkilde & Bagger, 1964; Finnbogi Guðmundsson, ed. *Orkneyinga saga*. Íslenzk fornrit, 34. Reykjavík: Hið íslenzka fornritafélag, 1965; Stefán Karlsson, ed. *Sagas of Icelandic Bishops: Fragments of Eight Manuscripts*. Early Icelandic Manuscripts in Facsimile, 7. Copenhagen: Rosenkilde & Bagger, 1967; *Helgastaðabók. Nikulás saga. Perg. 4to NR 16*. Manuscripta Islandica Medii Aevi, 2. Reykjavik: Lögberg, 1982 [with introduction by Selma Jónsdóttir, Stefán Karlsson, and Sverrir Tómasson]; Stefán Karlsson, ed. *Guðmunar sögur biskups. I: Ævi Guðmundar biskups, Guðmundar saga A*. Editiones Arnamagnæanæ, ser. B, vol. 6. Copenhagen: Reitzel, 1983. **Bib.**: Widding, Ole, *et al.* "The Lives of the Saints in Old Norse Prose: A Handlist." *Mediaeval Studies* 25 (1963), 294–337; Schier, Kurt. *Sagaliteratur*. Sammlung Metzler, M78. Stuttgart: Metzler, 1970, pp. 68–71, 124–9. **Lit.**: Nygaard, Marius. "Den lærde stil i den norrøne prosa." In *Sproglig-historiske studier tilegnede professor C. R. Unger*. Kristiania [Oslo]: Aschehoug, 1896, pp. 153–70; Turville-Petre, G. "The Old-Norse Homily on the Assumption and *Maríu Saga*." *Mediaeval Studies* 9 (1947), 131–40; Turville-Petre, G. *Origins of Icelandic Literature*. Oxford: Clarendon, 1953; rpt. 1967; Widding, Ole, and Hans Bekker-Nielsen. "The Virgin Bares Her Breast." *Opuscula* 2.1. Bibliotheca Arnamagnæana, 25.1 Copenhagen: Munksgaard, 1961, pp. 76–9; Widding, Ole, and Hans Bekker-Nielsen. "The Fifteen Steps of the Temple: A Problem in the Maríu saga." *Opuscula* 2.1. Bibliotheca Arnamagnæana, 25.1 Copenhagen: Munksgaard, 1961, pp. 80–91; Foote, Peter G. "On the Fragmentary Text Concerning St Thomas Becket in Stock. Perg. Fol. Nr. 2." *Saga-Book of the Viking Society* 15 (1961), 403–50; Magerøy, Hallvard. "Helgensoger." *KLNM* 6 (1961), 350–3; Harty, Lenore. "The Icelandic Life of St. Dunstan." *Saga-Book of the Viking Society* 15 (1961), 263–93; Widding, Ole, and Hans Bekker-Nielsen. "An Old Norse Translation of the 'Transitus Mariae.'" *Mediaeval Studies* 23 (1961), 324–33; Bekker-Nielsen, Hans. "On a Handlist of Saints' Lives in Old Norse." *Mediaeval Studies* 24 (1962), 323–34; Widding, Ole. "Et norsk fragment af Barlaams saga. Et bidrag til Barlaamsagaens tekstkritik." *Maal og minne* (1963), 37–46; Widding, Ole, and Hans Bekker-Nielsen. "Legende. Norge og Island." *KLNM* 10 (1965), 421–3; Bekker-Nielsen, Hans, *et al. Norrøn Fortællekunst. Kapitler af den norsk-islandske middelalderlitteraturs historie*. Copenhagen: Akademisk Forlag, 1965; Loth, Agnete. "Egidius saga hins helga. Fragmentet AM 238 XVI, fol." *Opuscula* 3. Bibliotheca Arnamagnæana, 29. Copenhagen: Munksgaard, 1967, pp. 62–73; Hallberg, Peter. "Jóns saga helga." In *Afmælisrit Jóns Helgasonar 30. júní 1969*. Ed. Jakob Benediktsson *et al.* Reykjavik: Heimskringla, 1969, pp. 59–79; Fell, Christine. "English History and Norman Legend in the Icelandic Saga of Edward the Confessor." *Anglo-Saxon England* 6 (1977), 223–36; Jorgensen, Peter A. "St. Julian and Basilissa in Medieval Iceland." In *Sjötíu ritgerðir helgaðar Jakobi Benediktssyni 20. júlí 1977*. 2 vols. Ed. Einar G. Pétursson and Jónas Kristjánsson. Reykjavik: Stofnun Árna Magnússonar, 1977, vol. 2, pp. 473–80; Jónas Kristjánsson. "Learned Style or Saga Style?" In *Specvlvm Norroenvm: Norse Studies in Memory of Gabriel Turville-Petre*. Ed. Ursula Dronke *et al.* Odense: Odense University Press, 1981, pp. 260–92; Kratz, Henry. "The Vocabulary of Paganism in the *Heilagra manna sǫgur*." In *The Sixth International Saga Conference 28/7–2/8 1985: Workshop Papers*. 2 vols. Copenhagen: Det arnamagnæanske Institut, 1985, vol. 2, pp. 629–43 [photocopies of papers distributed to participants]; Sverrir Tómasson. *Íslenskar Nikulás sögur og kaflar úr Nikulás sögu Bergs Sokkasonar*. Reykjavik: [n.p.], 1985; Wolf, Kirsten. "'Lífssaga Pilati' in Lbs. 4270 4to." *Proceedings of the PMR Conference* 12–13 (1987–88), 239–62; Wolf, Kirsten. "The Judas Legend in Scandinavia."

Journal of English and Germanic Philology 88 (1989), 463–76; Wolf, Kirsten. "A Translation of the Latin Fragments Containing the Life and Miracles of St. Þorlákr along with a Collection of *Lectiones* for Recitation on His Feast-days." *Proceedings of the PMR Conference* 14 (1989), 261–76; Wolf, Kirsten. "A Fragment of a *Gregorius saga* in AM 238 fol. X." *Opuscula* 9. Bibliotheca Arnamagnæana, 39. Copenhagen: Reitzel, 1991, pp. 100–7.

Henry Kratz

3. SWEDEN. The earliest saints' lives, all written in Latin, are for the most part standardized legends of limited historical value, often written long after the death of the saint, in connection with the rise of the cult. The 11th-century missionaries include the English-born Sigfrid, who traveled to Västergötland to the court of Sweden's first Christian king, Olaf (Skötkonung) Eriksson, leaving three nephews behind in the district of Värend, where they were martyred. Sigfrid is regarded as the founder of the see of Växjö, which was the center of his cult. Another of the 11th-century English missionaries was Eskil, who preached in Södermanland during the reign of the Christian king Inge the Elder, but was stoned to death in Strängnäs during a heathen uprising under Blot-Sven ("Sacrificer-Sven"), and was buried in the trading center that later took the name Eskilstuna. Also in the 11th century, the English Cluniac monk David, who was inspired by the example of Sigfrid's nephews, but was probably himself never martyred, traveled to Sweden, where he worked as a missionary in Västmanland. His legend is late and based wholly on foreign models.

The Swedish saint Botvid, born in Södermanland, accepted Christianity while on a journey to England and, although never ordained, worked to convert his native province upon his return to Sweden. His legend contains two main stories, one concerning his catching large quantities of fish, and the other depicting his martyrdom around 1120 at the hand of a Wendish slave, whom he had freed from captivity and intended to send back to his own land to preach the gospel. The life of the saint-king Erik bears similarities to that of Knud of Denmark, and its historical reliability has been the subject of debate. He is portrayed as a supporter of the Church, a good ruler and judge, and an undertaker of the *justum bellum* against the heathen in Finland. A life was also written of Henrik, the English-born bishop of Uppsala, who accompanied Erik to Finland, remained behind as a missionary, and was eventually martyred there.

In the late 13th and 14th centuries, as individual saints' cults grew, early legends were reworked and additional ones written. Brynolf Algotsson, bishop of Skara 1278–1317, wrote legends that were incorporated into his offices in honor of St. Eskil and the wrongfully murdered widow, Helena of Skövde. Ingrid of Skänninge's biography (d. 1282) was written at the beginning of the 15th century. Nikolaus Hermansson, bishop of Linköping 1375–1391, wrote the offices in honor of St. Erik and of St. Ansgar (d. 865), who led the first mission to Sweden around 830 and built the first Christian church at Birka.

Swedish saints' lives of the later Middle Ages are more fully authenticated *vitae*, usually incorporated into a formal application for canonization. They emanate chiefly from the circles of Birgitta Birgersdotter, who died in 1373 and was canonized in 1391. The earliest life of St. Birgitta was written by her two confessors, Petrus Olofsson of Alvastra and Petrus Olofsson of Skänninge. Exactly what form their *Vita* originally took is uncertain. The extant text tells episodically of her pious childhood and married life, her vision calling her to become the "bride and mouthpiece" of Christ, her life of devotion during her widowhood in Sweden, and her death in Rome. Two further lives of Birgitta, written before her canonization, were incorporated into offices, one by Birger Gregersson, archbishop of Uppsala 1367–1383, which is known by its opening antiphon *Birgitte matris inclite*, and the other by Nikolaus Hermansson, known as *Rosa rorans*. Birger's legend contains mainly biographical details relating to her life in Sweden and Rome, and miracles after her death, whereas that of Nikolaus contains several excerpts from her revelations. In the 15th century, Margareta Clausdotter, abbess of the Brigettine foundation at Vadstena 1472–1480, wrote a colorful but historically dubious account in Swedish of Birgitta's family.

Many of the Brigettine circle were revered as local saints in Sweden. The *vita* of Nikolaus Hermansson containing seventy-seven miracles was presented as part of an application for canonization in 1414; he was beatified in 1515. St. Birgitta's daughter, Katarina Ulfsdotter, was beatified in 1489. Her life, written in the 15th century by the general confessor at Vadstena, Ulf Birgersson, emphasizes her chaste marriage and strict obedience to her mother's wishes. Ulf Birgersson also wrote a life of Petrus Olofsson of Skänninge. Brynolf of Skara's life does not survive, but only the testimonies concerning miracles that occurred after his death.

Some of the biographies of Swedish saints were translated into Swedish, most notably a life of St. Birgitta, based chiefly on existing biographies, although it contains additional details, in particular relating to Brigettine iconography, and a life of her daughter, Katarina, translated by Jöns Budde of Nådendal monastery in Finland. Of the non-Scandinavian saints' lives, there are several substantial collections in the vernacular. The *Fornsvenska legendariet* ("Old Swedish Legendary"), which uses the *Legenda aurea* as its main source but arranges the saints in chronological order, exists in several MSS. Additional early Christian saints' and martyrs' lives occur in other collections, the most important of which are: *Codex Oxenstierna* (Cod. Holm. A 110, written at Vadstena *ca.* 1385), which, in addition to the above-mentioned life of St. Birgitta, contains a translation of the *Vitae patrum*; *Nådendals klosterbok* (Cod. Holm. A 49, *ca.* 1442); Cod. Holm. A 10 (written at Vadstena *ca.* 1500); and the *Linköping Legendarium* (Cod. Linc. B 70a, written at Vadstena *ca.* 1500), parts of which were translated by the general confessor Nikolaus Ragvaldi.

Ed.: Fant, Erik Mikael, et al., eds. *Scriptores rerum svecicarum medii aevi.* 3 vols. Uppsala: Zeipel & Palmblad, 1818–76; Collijn, Isak, ed. *Acta et processus canonizacionis beate Birgitte.* Samlingar utgivna av Svenska fornskrift-sällskapet, 2.1. Uppsala: Almqvist & Wiksell, 1924; Collijn, Isak, ed. *Processus seu Negocium canonizationis B. Katerine de Vadstenis.* Samlingar utgivna av Svenska fornskrift-sällskapet, 2.3. Uppsala: Almqvist & Wiksell, 1942–46; Collijn, Isak, ed. *Birgerus Gregorii. Legenda sancte Birgitte.* Samlingar utgivna av Svenska fornskrift-sällskapet, 2, Latinska skrifter, 4. Uppsala: Almqvist & Wiksell, 1946; Undhagen, Carl-Gustav, ed. *Birger Gregerssons Birgitta-officium.* Samlingar utgivna av Svenska fornskrift-sällskapet, 2, Latinska skrifter, 6. Uppsala: Almqvist & Wiksell, 1960. **Lit.**: Schmid, Toni. "Eskil, Botvid och David. Tre svenska helgon." *Scandia* (1931), 102–15; Oppermann, Charles James August. *The English Missionaries in Sweden and Finland.* London: Society for Promoting Christian Knowledge; New York: Macmillan, 1937; Brilioth, Yngve. *Svenska kyrkans historia. II: Den senare medeltiden 1274–1521.* Stockholm: Almqvist & Wiksell, 1941; Ekwall, Sara. *Vår äldsta birgittabiografi och dennas viktigaste varianter.* Kungl. vitterhets–, historie– och antikvitetsakademiens handlingar, hist. ser., 12. Stockholm: Almqvist & Wiksell, 1965; Lundén, Tryggve. "Medeltidens religiösa litteratur." In *Ny illustrerad svensk litteraturhistoria.* Ed. E. N. Tigerstedt. Stockholm: Natur och Kultur, 1955, vol. 1, pp. 122–222; Cross, J. E. "St. Erik of Sweden." *Saga-Book of the Viking Society* 15.4 (1961), 294–326; Klockars, Birgit. "Medeltidens religiösa litteratur." In *Ny illustrerad svensk litteraturhistoria.* Ed. E. N. Tigerstedt. 2nd rev. ed. Stockholm: Natur och Kultur, 1967, vol. 1, pp. 125–225; Lundén, Tryggve. *Nikolaus Hermansson. Biskop av Linköping. En litteratur- och kyrkohistorisk studie.* Lund: Gleerup, 1971; Lundén, Tryggve. *Svenska helgon.* Stockholm: Verbum, 1972; 2nd ed., 1973; Milveden, Ingmar. "Zu den liturgischen 'Hystorie' in Schweden." Diss. Uppsala University, 1972; Sawyer, Birgit, et al., eds. *The Christianization of Scandinavia.* Alingsås: Viktoria, 1987.

Bridget Morris

[**See also**: Ansgar, St.; *Barlaams ok Josaphats saga*; Birgitta, St.; *Biskupa sögur*; Christian Poetry; Christian Prose; *Dunstanus saga*; Erik, St.; Gregory, St.: *Dialogues*; *Guðmundar sögur biskups*; *Jóns saga ens helga*; Knud (Cnut), St.; Legenda; *Magnúss saga helga eyjarls*; *Maríu saga*; Martyrologies; Miracles, Collections of; Monasticism; *Nicodemus, Gospel of*; *Óláfs saga helga*; *Óláfs saga Tryggvasonar*; Old Swedish Legendary; *Orkneyinga saga*; *Páls saga biskups*; *Postola sögur*; *Reykjahólabók*; *Thómas saga erkibiskups*; *Þorláks saga helga*; Vadstena; Visionary Literature]

Samsons Fængsel *see* Drama

Samsons saga fagra

Samsons saga fagra ("The Saga of Fair Samson") is a *riddarasaga* probably composed late in the 14th or early 15th century. It has two clearly distinctive parts. The first is a romance in the Arthurian style, mingled with motifs from fairy tales, modeled mainly on some version of the romance of Lancelot, although no actual translation into Old Norse is known of any version of the romance of Lancelot. The second part (the so-called "Sigurðar þáttr") resembles other late and fantastic *fornaldarsögur*, but shows knowledge not only of Snorri's *Edda* and older *fornaldarsögur*, but also of scholarly literature (with information taken from encyclopedic texts, such as those represented in the ethnographic texts of the *Hauksbók*) in its treatment of the far North and its inhabitants. The extraordinary popularity of this interesting saga in postmedieval Iceland is shown by the existence of about forty MSS.

The first part tells how Samson, supposedly the son of King Arthur, falls in love with the Irish princess Valentina, who, however, is soon abducted by the evil harper Kvintelin, but rescued shortly afterward by Samson's foster-mother, the sorceress Olimpia. While searching for his fiancée, Samson has to fight Kvintelin's mother under a waterfall, reminiscent of similar troll fights in *Beowulf* and *Grettis saga*. While Samson and Valentina think each other dead, she is abducted again by a dwarf, driving a cart, in the pay of Kvintelin, but is rescued after a chase. To make up for his evil actions, Kvintelin is sent out to search for the magic cloak.

The second part tells of Sigurðr, the son of King Guðmundr of Glæsisvellir and of a woman of the fabulous race of the *Smámeyjar* ("little girls"), who by killing Skrýmir, King of the Giants, becomes the king of Giantland and gains a treasure trove. Among his treasures is the chastity-testing cloak. When Sigurðr, aged 100, tries to marry a Russian princess, Kvintelin kills old Sigurðr, steals the cloak, and brings it to Samson. The saga ends in stereotypical fashion with a number of marriages.

Ed.: Wilson, John, ed. *Samsons saga fagra*. Samfund til udgivelse af gammel nordisk litteratur, 65. Copenhagen: [s.n.], 1953. **Tr.**: Simek, Rudolf, trans. *Zwei Rittersagas. Die Saga vom Mantel und die Saga vom schönen Samson: Möttuls saga und Samsons saga fagra*. Fabulae medievales, 2. Vienna: Braumüller, 1982. **Lit.**: Cederschiöld, G., and F.-A. Wulff, eds. *Versions nordiques du fabliau français Le mantel mautaillié. Textes et notes.* Lund: Gleerup, 1877, pp. 90–1; Simek, Rudolf. "Lancelot in Iceland." In *Les Sagas de Chevaliers (Riddarasögur).* Actes de la Vᵉ Conférence Internationale sur les Sagas . . . (*Toulon. Juillet 1982*). Ed. Régis Boyer. Civilisations, 10. Paris: Presses de l'Université de Paris-Sorbonne, 1985, pp. 205–16; Simek, Rudolf. "Elusive Elysia, or Which Way to Glæsisvellir? On the Geography of the North in Icelandic Legendary Fiction." In *Sagnaskemmtun: Studies in Honour of Hermann Pálsson on His 65th Birthday, 26th May 1986.* Ed. Rudolf Simek *et al.* Vienna, Cologne, and Graz: Böhlau, 1986, pp. 247–75.

Rudolf Simek

[**See also:** *Fornaldarsögur; Grettis saga; Hauksbók; Riddarasögur; Snorra Edda*]

Satiren om Abbotarna *see* Swedish Literature, Miscellaneous

Saulus saga ok Nikanors

Saulus saga ok Nikanors ("The Saga of Saulus and Nikanor") was composed in Iceland in the 14th century, and is preserved in twenty-six MSS and fragments, the most important of which are three vellum MSS, AM 343a 4to (15th century), where the saga is preserved in full, and the two fragments AM 162c fol. (15th century, four leaves) and AM 570a 4to (second half of the 14th century, two separate leaves). The remainder are paper MSS, the majority of which date from the 18th and 19th centuries.

King Helesius in Liberum Domum (Santiago de Compostela) in Galicia has a son, Saulus. Excellent in knightly skills and all other accomplishments, his only shortcoming is vanity. Nikanor is a powerful duke ruling over the city of Bár (Bari). His sister Potentiana surpasses in beauty all other women north of the Greek archipelago. The two meet at a splendid feast held by Timoteus, emperor of Rome, where Saulus, jealous of the attention afforded Nikanor, challenges him to a chess match. He is defeated, and in anger strikes Nikanor, who in turn challenges him to meet him the following day in a tournament. Neither can defeat the other, and the two become sworn brothers. It is also arranged that Saulus marry Potentiana. Before the wedding can take place, however, two heathen dukes, Abel of Cappadocia and Mattheus of Phrygia, arrive in Bár, demanding that Potentiana marry the latter. A battle ensues, in which Nikanor's army is defeated and forced to retreat into the city, which the dukes then besiege. Nikanor sends word to Saulus, who assembles an army but arrives too late. The city has fallen. Potentiana is abducted, and Nikanor cast into the dungeon. Saulus succeeds in retaking the city and freeing Nikanor. The two then journey to North Africa, arriving on the very day of the wedding. By posing as entertainers, they succeed in gaining access to the bridal chamber, drug Mattheus, and free Potentiana, leaving in her place a clay figure. Saulus and Potentiana are now wed.

Meanwhile, realizing who the perpetrators of the deception were, Mattheus and Abel gather an invincible army. Saulus and Nikanor hear of these preparations and amass a mighty army, numbering nearly a million men from many kingdoms. They assemble in Rome. The two dukes make their way toward Rome, burning and destroying everything in their path. A tremendous battle follows in which the two heathen dukes are killed and their army dispersed. Nikanor now decides to seek the hand of Luneta, daughter of King Benjamin of Akaia in Greece. Saulus presents the suit on Nikanor's behalf and is accepted. The wedding festivities, which take place in Rome, last more than a fortnight. Saulus and Nikanor return to their respective kingdoms, where they rule until their deaths in old age.

The saga is characterized by a fondness for blow-by-blow battle descriptions (over a third of the narrative is taken up with such scenes) and by an unusually large number of biblical and classical allusions. Thus, we are informed that Saulus is from Galicia, "where James the Apostle is buried," and Nikanor from Bár, "burial place of St. Nicholas." Abel, who is first said to be from Cappadocia, is later said to be from Mesopotamia, "which is where Jacob fled in order to escape his brother Esau." Abel's shield, which depicts scenes from the lives of several classical and biblical worthies, is described in detail (nearly 600 words).

Rossenbeck (1970: 120ff., 210–1) and, following him, Glauser (1983: 130ff.) have analyzed the way in which simultaneous action is handled in the saga by managing point of view. The older version of the saga, as edited by Loth, shows clearly how the narrative style of the original *riddarasögur* is midway between that of the *Íslendingasögur* and the translated *riddarasögur.*

Ed.: H. Erlendsson and Einar Þórðarson, eds. "Sagan af Sálusi og Nikanor." In *Fjórar riddarasögur.* Reykjavik: E. Þórðarson, 1852, pp. 34–93 [edition based on a young paper MS]; Loth, Agnete, ed. "Saulus saga ok Nikanors." In *Late Medieval Icelandic Romances.* 5 vols. Editiones Arnamagnæanæ, ser. B, vols. 20–4. Copenhagen: Munksgaard, 1962–65, vol. 2, pp. 3–91. **Tr.**: Dodsworth, J. B. *Late Medieval Icelandic Romances*, vol. 2, pp. 3–91 [English paraphrase]. **Bib.**: Kalinke, Marianne E., and P. M. Mitchell. *Bibliography of Old Norse–Icelandic Romances.* Islandica, 44. Ithaca and London: Cornell University Press, 1985, pp. 93–4. **Lit.**: Björn K. Þórólfsson. *Rímur fyrir 1600.* Safn Fræðafjelagsins um Ísland og Íslendinga, 9. Copenhagen: Møller, 1934; Schlauch, Margaret. *Romance in Iceland.* Princeton: Princeton University Press; New York: American-Scandinavian Foundation; London: Allen & Unwin, 1934; rpt. New York: Russell & Russell, 1973; Rossenbeck, Klaus. "Die Stellung der Riddarasögur in der altnordischen Prosaliteratur—eine Untersuchung an Hand des Erzählstils." Diss. Frankfurt am Main, 1970; Glauser, Jürg. *Isländische Märchensagas: Studien zur Prosaliteratur im spätmittelalterlichen Island.* Beiträge zur nordischen Philologie, 12. Basel and Frankfurt am Main: Helbing & Lichtenhahn, 1983; Kalinke, Marianne. "Norse Romance (*Riddarasögur*)." In *Old Norse–Icelandic Literature: A Critical Guide.* Ed. Carol J. Clover and John Lindow. Islandica, 45. Ithaca and London: Cornell University Press, 1985, pp. 316–63.

M. J. Driscoll

[**See also:** *Riddarasögur*]

Saxo Grammaticus

Saxo Grammaticus. Toward the end of the 12th century, the Danish historian Sven Aggesen wrote that his old associate Saxo was composing a full-length history of the Danish kings of the previous century. Four MS fragments of this work (one, from Angers, probably autograph), a compendium of around 1345, and an edition printed at Paris in 1514 from a lost MS provide the surviving evidence for Saxo's achievement. It was printed under the title of *Danorum Regum Heroumque Historiæ* ("The History of the Kings and Heroes of the Danes"), but is usually known by the earlier description *Gesta Danorum* (alias *De Gestis Danorum*).

Saksi was not an uncommon name in medieval Denmark, and the historian cannot be identified for sure with any who bore it. *Grammaticus* "the learned" and *Longus* "the tall" are posthumous by-names. From his own words, we learn that he came from a warrior family, and that he joined the household of King Valdemar I's foremost adviser, Absalon, bishop of Roskilde (1158–1192) and archbishop of Lund (1178–1201), who encouraged him to write history. His partiality for Zealand suggests that he came from that island. He may have been educated abroad, and his familiarity with church business argues that he became a clerk of some sort, but probably not a monk. He was also familiar with war and seamanship. In Absalon's will, "my cleric Saxo" was forgiven a small debt, and required to send two borrowed books to the Cistercians of Sorø. Saxo completed his work under the patronage of Archbishop Anders (1201–1223), probably after 1216, and dedicated it to Anders and King Valdemar II.

During Saxo's lifetime, Denmark achieved dominance over the Baltic lands; Danes also came into closer contact with the intellectual life of the southern countries their ancestors had raided. Saxo aimed to provide them with a national history in Latin comparable to those of other European peoples. The only foreign historians he mentions are Bede, Dudo of St.-Quentin, and Paulus Diaconus; he was less influenced by them in his concept of the nation than by Vergil's *Aeneid*, and by the historical abridgments of the Roman authors Valerius Maximus and Justin. His view of morals and mythology owed much to Horace, Ovid, and Cicero; and the tone of his work coincides with the humanistic scholarship of the 12th century as expounded in the schools of northern France (*e.g.*, by William of Conches and John of Salisbury), as well as with the contemporary epics of Galterus de Castellione (*Alexandreis*) and Geoffrey of Monmouth (*Historia regum Britanniae*).

Other Danish authors (*e.g.*, the Roskilde Chronicler, the Lejre Chronicler, Sven Aggesen) had made pioneer attempts to record the Danish past in Latin, but Saxo found them inadequate. He had no use for the annalists of Lund, nor for conventional chronology, and the northern genealogists failed to provide him with enough kings. He claimed to be restoring lost native traditions and interpreting runic memorials, but these claims seem unfounded. He took most of his legendary and heroic material from wandering Icelanders and their MSS, relocating stories from their international repertoire within Denmark. He claimed that Archbishop Absalon's own words were his main source for modern history, but he must have used other written sources now lost. His debt to biblical ideas and language was small.

The work published in 1514 begins with a preface including a geographical description of the northern world, and is divided into sixteen books of unequal length. Books 1–4 deal with the Danes before the birth of Christ, 5–8 with the period down to the establishment of the Church in Denmark. Books 9–12 cover events from the Conversion to the promotion of Lund as a metropolitan see, and 13–16 run from 1104 to 1187.

The first eight books differ from the rest in the greater fluency of the prose and the inclusion of verse in a variety of meters. The basic subdivisions are the reigns of over seventy kings. Saxo begins with the election of the eponymous Dan as the first ruler, and the dethronement of the first two kings, Humblus and Lotherus, by unjust and justified violence. Then Skioldus and Hadingus appear as types of the heroism, luck, and virtue essential for effective kingship even in a pagan world. These kings, and Frotho I in Book 2, are names derived from Old Norse poetry and invested with attributes and episodes. With Kings Ro (Book 2) and Høtherus (Book 3), he made versions of the legends now found in the *Snorra Edda* and *Skjǫldunga saga*'s epitome. Amlethus, the prototype of Hamlet, whose career appears in Books 3 and 4, was imported from an undiscovered source, and served as a type of cunning hero dogged by the unkindness of fate and human corruption, a pattern for both kings and tyrannicides. The rest of Book IV tells of the patriotic duelist Uffo, already celebrated by Sven Aggesen as vindicator of the Danish frontier, and known in Anglo-Saxon sources (*e.g.*, *Widsith*, *Beowulf*, and the Mercian genealogy). The heathen gods, introduced in Book 1 as malign but fallible illusionists, enslave men's minds and lust for their daughters (Baldr and Nanna, Óðinn and Rinda, Book 3).

King Frotho III, an imaginary Danish Caesar contemporary with Christ, takes up Book 5. Helped by his witty companion Erik the Eloquent, he builds an empire over the northern world and civilizes it by enforcing two law codes. His story is enlivened by romance, adventure, and horror, but illustrates the power of words over weapons. In Book 6, this power is taken to excess, when the Danes elect the rustic poet Hiarno to rule them. This same power becomes beneficial and invigorating in the case of the degenerate Ingellus (see Ingjaldr of *Skjǫldunga saga*) and his dauntless and poetic champion Starcatherus, whose satire shamed the king into doing his duty and destroying his enemies. Stories of love, magic, and murder occupy the reign of Halfdanus in Book 7, which ends with the revival of the Danish empire under Haraldus Hyldetan, who is taught the secret of military success by Óðinn. The great fight of Brávalla, in which Óðinn betrays Haraldus to his enemies, begins Book 8; and later on, Starkatherus contrives his own death after a poetic outburst on the duty of vengeance. Jarmericus (Ermanaric the Goth) then appears, as the victim of another treacherous counselor, and in the reign of Snio, famine drives the Lombards to emigrate from Denmark. In two voyages to the underworld, Danish adventurers witness the malign and morbid condition of the old gods and giants. The mighty King Gøtricus is prevented from overthrowing Charlemagne by assassination, and Saxo's "Old Testament" ends with Viking heroism betrayed by the heathen gods, powerless against fate.

In Book 9, the supreme Viking Regnerus (Ragnarr loðbrók ["hairy-breeches"]) achieves empire over the whole North, including the British Isles, only to die in Ella's snake pit as a punishment for persecuting the new faith accepted by his less successful rival Haraldus. His avenging sons fail to preserve his empire, and efforts to hold England by a succession of alternately Christian and pagan kings culminate with Gormo's marrying the English heiress Thyra. The English throne falls to their sons by inheritance, but Gormo dies of grief at the death of the elder. More tribulations afflict his successors Haraldus and Sveno in Book 10 (echoes here of Adam of Bremen and the *Roskilde Chronicle*), until both king and people accept the true faith, and Sveno's son Kanutus wins a Christian empire over the whole northern world, including England. He leaves a vigorous Church and a military law code to posterity, and after his son's death the Danes show their probity by accepting the Norwegian Magnús as king in observance of a sworn pact.

In these two books, written sources are distorted and augmented by Nordic legend: tales of Ragnarr, Ívarr, Gorm, the Jómsvíkingar, and Palnatoki. From 11 onward, more Latin sources were available, and in 11 to 13 the reigns of Sven 11 and his five sons (1047–1134) are presented with an eye to earlier accounts, modified or rejected at will. Each ruler serves as an example of good or bad kingship according to his effectiveness against the Slavs and the unruly nobility and people of Denmark. Kings purge their own guilt by spectacular penances, and the people incur death and destruction for the slaying of King Knud (Cnut) the Saint (1086) and Knud (Cnut) Lavard (1131). Book 14 (four times as long as any other) covers the period of civil wars, conspiracy, and dissension among king, bishops, and nobles from 1134 to 1178, when Valdemar I and Absalon succeeded in conquering the Rugian Slavs and restoring unity to the kingdom. Book 15 covers Absalon's first years as archbishop of Lund (1178–1182) and the rebellion of the Scanians against his authority. Book 16 relates how his political mission was fulfilled in the early years against Knud (Cnut) VI (1182–1187) by the declaration of Danish independence against the Emperor Frederick Barbarossa, and by the subjugation of the Pomeranian Slavs.

In the last three books, a copious narrative is enlivened by reported speech and digressions on Norwegian, German, and Slavic affairs. The main source may have been Absalon's own words, but Saxo and the compiler of Knýtlinga saga (ca. 1260) perhaps used an earlier written source now lost. Books 9–16 are usually supposed to have been written first, before 1201; and the earlier books in the time of Valdemar II. Much of the text must relate to contemporary issues and personalities, but it is difficult to find Saxo advocating any official policy. His patrons were the most powerful men in the kingdom, but he was an idiosyncratic critic of the times, hoping to inspire his fellow countrymen to political unity and civic virtue by the example of former days, as well as to impress learned foreigners. Simplified and excerpted versions of his work were current in Denmark in the later Middle Ages, but it was only after 1514 and the appearance of Anders Sørensen Vedel's Danish translation in 1575 that his view of the Nordic past was widely received both at home and abroad.

Ed.: Pedersen, Christian, ed. *Danorum Regum Heroumque Historiæ.* Paris; Badius, 1514 [based on complete MS; Books 10–16 reproduced in E. Christiansen's trans.; the whole edition was reprinted with minor alterations at Basel in 1534 and Frankfurt in 1576]; Stephanius, Stephanus J., ed. *Saxonis Grammatici Historiæ Danicæ Libri XVI.* Søro: Crusius, 1645 [usually bound with the following work]; Stephanius, Stephanus J. *Notæ Uberiores in historian Danicam Saxonis.* Soro: Crusius, 1645. Reproduced (ed. H. D. Schepelern) by Museum Tusculanum, Copenhagen, 1978. [There were further editions by C. A. Klotz (Leipzig, 1771), P. E. Müller (Copenhagen, 1839, with Prolegomena and Notæ Uberiores by J. M. Velschow, 1858), and A. Holder (Strassburg, 1886).]; Olrik, Jørgen, and H. Ræder, eds. *Saxonis Gesta Danorum.* Vol. 1. Copenhagen: Levin & Munksgaard, 1931. Vol 2. *Indicem Verborum Continens*, by Franz Blatt. Copenhagen: Levin & Munksgaard, 1957. For the 14th-century abridgment, of which four MSS survive, see: Langebek, J., ed. *Thomæ Gheysmeri Compendium Historiæ Danicæ.* In SRD, vol. 2, pp. 286–400. Copenhagen: Godiche, 1773; Gertz, M. Cl., ed. *Scriptores Minores Historiæ Danicæ.* 2 vols. Copenhagen: Gad, 1917–18. Vol. 1 rpt. by Selskabet for Udgivelse af

Kilder til Dansk Historie, Copenhagen, 1970. The four Saxo MS fragments appear in facsimile in vol. 5 of Corpus Codicum Danicorum Medii Aevi. Ed. Johannes Brøndum-Nielsen. Copenhagen: Munksgaard, 1962. **Tr.**: Elton, Oliver, trans. *The First Nine Books of the Danish History of Saxo Grammaticus.* Folklore Society Publications, 33. London: Nutt, 1893; rpt. 2 vols. New York: Norrœna Society, 1905; Ellis Davidson, Hilda, ed., and Peter Fisher, trans. *Saxo Grammaticus. The History of the Danes. Books I–IX.* 2 vols. Cambridge: Brewer; Totowa: Rowman and Littlefield, 1979–80; Fisher, Peter. "On Translating Saxo into English." In Friis-Jensen, Karsten, ed. *Saxo Grammaticus: A Medieval Author Between Norse and Latin Culture.* Copenhagen: Museum Tusculanum, 1981, pp. 53–64; Christiansen, Eric, trans. *Saxo Grammaticus: Danorum Regum Heroumque Historia. Books X–XVI: The Text of the First Edition with Translation and Commentary.* 3 vols. British Archaeological Reports, International Series, vols. 84 and 118 (in two parts). Oxford: B.A.R., 1980–81. **Bib.**: A survey of the most important work done to 1930 was given by Jørgen Olrik in the Latin and Danish Prolegomena to his edition. See further: Skovgaard-Petersen, Inge. "Saxo." *KLNM* 15 (1970), 49–50, and "Saxo" in *Dansk Biografisk Lexicon* 12 (1982), 641–3; Laugesen, Anker Teilgaard. *Introduktion til Saxo.* Copenhagen: Gyldendal, 1972, pp. 86–7 [meager]. **Lit.**: Two collections of articles contain much recent work: Boserup, Ivan, ed. *Saxostudier. Saxo-kollokvierne ved Københavns universitet.* Copenhagen: Museum Tusculanum, 1975; Friis-Jensen, Karsten, ed. *Saxo Grammaticus: A Medieval Author Between Norse and Latin Culture* [see above]. These are referred to below as *Saxostudier* and *Saxo-Culture*. **(a) Myth and Legend**: Turville-Petre, E. O. G. *Myth and Religion of the North: The Religion of Ancient Scandinavia.* New York: Holt, Rinehart and Winston; rpt. Westport: Greenwood, 1975, pp. 27–34; Ellis Davidson, H. R. *Gods and Myths of Northern Europe.* Harmondsworth: Penguin, 1964; Dumézil, Georges. *La Saga de Hadingus.* Paris: Presses Universitaires, 1953 [trans. by D. Coltman as *From Myth to Fiction: The Saga of Hadingus* (Chicago: University of Chicago Press, 1973) and reviewed by E. O. G. Turville-Petre in *Saga-Book of the Viking Society* 14 (1953–55), 131–4]; Andersson, Theodore M. "*Niflunga saga* in Light of German and Danish Materials." *Mediaeval Scandinavia* 7 (1974), 22–30; Dollerup, Cay. *Denmark, Hamlet and Shakespeare.* 2 vols. Salzburg Studies in English Literature, Elizabethan and Renaissance Studies, 47. Salzburg: Institut für englische Sprache und Literatur, Universität Salzburg, 1975; Lukman, Niels. "Ragnar loðbrók, Sigfrid, and the Saints of Flanders." *Mediaeval Scandinavia* 9 (1976), 7–50; Smyth, Alfred P. *Scandinavian Kings in the British Isles 850–880.* Oxford: Oxford University Press, 1977 [on Ragnarr and his sons]; Strand, Birgit. *Kvinnor och Män i Gesta Danorum.* Kvinnohistoriskt arkiv, 18. Gothenburg: [n.p.], 1980 [English summary]; Bjarni Guðnason. "The Icelandic Sources of Saxo Grammmaticus." In *Saxo-Culture*, pp. 79–93; Martinez-Pizarro, Joaquin. "An *Eiríks þáttr málspaka*? Some Conjectures on the Source of Saxo's Ericus Disertus." In *Saxo-Culture*, pp. 105–19; Skovgaard-Pedersen, Inge. "The Way to Byzantium: A Study in the First Three Books of Saxo's History of Denmark" In *Saxo-Culture*, pp. 121–33; Strand, Birgit. "Women in Gesta Danorum." In *Saxo-Culture*, pp. 135–67. **(b) History and Ideology**: Skovgaard-Petersen, Inge. "Saxo, Historian of the Patria." *Mediaeval Scandinavia* 2 (1969), 54–77; Damsholt, Nanna. "Kongeopfattelse og kongeideologi hos Saxo." In *Saxostudier*, pp. 148–55; Riis, Thomas. "Bruddet mellem Valdemar den Store og Eskil 1161. Søborg, diplomerne og Saxo." In *Saxostudier*, pp. 156–66; Skyum-Nielsen, Niels. "Saxo som kilde til et par centrale institutioner i samtiden." In *Saxostudier*, pp. 175–92; Weibull, Curt. "Vem var Saxo?" *Historisk tidsskrift* (Denmark) 78 (1978) 87–96; Riis, Thomas. *Les institutions politiques centrales du Danemark 1100–1332.* Odense University Studies in History and Social Sciences, 46. Odense: Odense University Press, 1977, pp. 14–31, 86–150; Johannesson, Kurt. *Saxo*

Grammaticus. *Komposition och världsbild i Gesta Danorum.* Stockholm: Almqvist & Wiksell, 1978 [in Swedish, but for an English summary see his "Order in Gesta Danorum and Order in the Creation," in *Saxo-Culture,* pp. 95–104]; Malmros, Rikke. "Blodgildet i Roskilde historiografisk belyst." *Scandia* 45 (1979), 46–66 [English summary]; Weibull, Curt. "Saxos berättelser om de danske vendertågen 1158–1185." *Historisk tidsskrift* (Denmark) 83 (1983), 35–70; Sawyer, Birgit. "Saxo-Valdemar-Absalon." *Scandia* 51 (1985), 33–60 [English summary]; Sawyer, Birgit. "Valdemar, Absalon and Saxo: Historiography and Politics in Medieval Denmark." *Revue Belge de philologie et d'histoire* 63 (1985), 685–705; Skovgaard-Pedersen, Inge. *Da Tidernes Herre var nær. Studier i Saxos historiesyn.* Copenhagen: Den danske historiske Forening, 1987. **(c) Latinity, Verse, and Manuscripts:** Blatt, Franz [Indledning and Præfatio to the Index (vol. 2) of Olrik and Ræder's 1931 edition]; *Saxostudier,* pp. 1–114, contains thirteen articles in Danish on the language, construction, and analogues of Saxo's work; Friis-Jensen, Karsten. *Saxo og Vergil.* Copenhagen: Museum Tusculanum, 1975 [French summary]; Boserup, Ivan. "The Angers Fragment and the Archetype of Gesta Danorum." *Saxo-Culture,* pp. 9–26; Friis-Jensen, Karsten. "The Lay of Ingellus and Its Classical Models." *Saxo-Culture,* pp. 65–78; Friis-Jensen, Karsten. *Saxo Grammaticus as Latin Poet: Studies in the Verse Passages of the Gesta Danorum.* Analecta Romana; Instituti Danici, Supplementum 14. Rome: Bretschneider, 1987; Friis-Jensen, Karsten. "Was Saxo a Canon of Lund?" *Cahiers de l'institut du moyen-âge grec et latin* 59 (1989), 331–57.

Eric Christiansen

[See also: Aggesen, Sven; *Brávallaþula;* Chronicles; Denmark; Divine Heroes, Native; Dudo of St.-Quentin: *De moribus et actis primorum normanniæ ducum;* Gorm; Harald Gormsson (Bluetooth); Knud (Cnut) the Great; Knud (Cnut), St.; *Knýtlinga saga;* Latin Language and Literature; *Ragnars saga loðbrókar; Skjǫldunga saga; Snorra Edda;* Sunesen, Anders; Sven Haraldsson (Forkbeard); Valdemar]

Schacktavelslek ("The Game of Chess") was composed by an unknown author, using as his main sources a version of Jacobus de Cessolis's *De ludo scaccorum* in Latin and a North German verse adaptation of it by Meister Stephan. It belongs to the genre of political commentary, and discusses the organization of the state and the ways of ruling it. The text contains no description of chess as a game; the pieces are nothing but representatives of the various estates and professions. Thus, under the heading "De disposicione regis" (all headings are in Latin), the author presents his view of the virtues of the righteous king. The queen, according to the author, should be wise, chaste, tolerant, and modest. The bishops represent the judges, who help the king make laws. The knights are taught to be loyal and wise, brave and generous, to defend the right, and protect the common people. The rooks represent the high officials of the state (Swedish *marsk* and *drots*), who exercise their power with wisdom, righteousness, mercy, and humility. The first pawn in front of the right rook represents the peasants; the second the craftsmen; the third the butchers and tanners, but above all the scribes (all deal with animal skin); the fourth the merchants and the money changers. The longest Swedish MS ends at this point, so the treatment of the remaining pawns is lacking. The presentation of the estates and professions is made through a direct statement of virtues necessary to each, and through illustrative exempla from Roman and Greek history.

The Swedish author often deviates from his sources; some portions seem to be his own additions. References to well-known political circumstances, such as the existence of a political union, the rivalry among several persons for the throne, and even the dethronement of the king and his flight abroad, point to the anarchic period about 1465 as the time of composition. The opinions expressed by the author are close to those of the opposition against King Karl Knutsson VIII.

The author can be described as a learned man, most likely a high functionary of the Church, although not of noble birth. Politically, he takes a constitutionist standpoint. He adapts Jacobus de Cessolis's advocacy of the hereditary kingdom to the Swedish practice, according to which the king was elected, but from within the ruling dynasty. He is also anxious to remind the king of his oath to the people to consult his council. The council in its turn has to guarantee the right to the people. Remarkably, the author pleads for education of young knights even in reading and writing. He also shows more understanding of the conditions of the peasants than his precursors do, even quoting the widespread "democratic" proverb *ho war tha en ädela man, tha adam groff ok eua span* (in Middle English, "Whan Adam delf, and Eve span, who was thanne a gentilman?," vv. 1751ff.).

Compared with its model, *Schacktavelslek* shows considerable literary merits. The author displays a satirical talent lacking in his forerunners. He criticizes the poor education that spoils the young knights, he expresses his contempt for women, and he warns the reader of the tricks of love. Most remarkable is the fact that he adds a lyrical song, now called *Äktenskapsvisan* (possibly based on a Danish or German model), which in a very naturalistic way shows what dangerous adventures love and marriage are.

Schacktavelslek is preserved in two MSS (MS A, AM 191 fol., from 1492, MS B, Cod. Stock. D 3, from 1476), both copies of the lost Swedish original. Despite its modest length (1,504 lines), B has some better readings than A with its 3,322 lines.

Ed.: Klemming, G. E., ed. *Svenska medeltids dikter och rim.* Samlingar utgivna av Svenska fornskrift-sällskapet, 25. Stockholm: Norstedt, 1881–82, pp. 201–309. **Lit.:** Blomquist, Gunnar. *Schacktavelslek och Sju vise mästare. De ludo scaccorum, De septem sapientibus. Studier i medeltidens litteraturhistoria.* Stockholm: Geber, 1941; Ståhle, Carl Ivar. "Medeltidens profana litteratur." In *Ny illustrerad svensk litteraturhistoria.* Ed. E. N. Tigerstedt. 2nd rev. ed. Stockholm: Natur och Kultur, 1967, vol. 1, pp. 37–124.

Sven-Bertil Jansson

Scotland, Norse in. The history of Viking Scotland has yet to be written, but there is no doubt that the Norwegian and Danish attacks had a crucial impact upon the country's political and social development. For several centuries, the Scandinavian earldom of Orkney controlled the north, while a Celto-Norse kingdom was established in the Western Isles. Viking activity in Ireland and England also had an impact upon Scotland, which experienced a Scandinavian presence until 1266, when King Magnús lagabœtir ("law-mender") Hákonarson ceded Hebrides to the Scots in the treaty of Perth. Orkney and Shetland remained Norwegian possessions until the 15th century. Place-names, linguistic influence upon both the Scots and Gaelic languages, folktales, and archaeological evidence all reflect the heritage of Scotland's Viking Age.

The first recorded raids date to the 790s, when Lindisfarne, and, therefore, Scotland's eastern seaboard, was attacked in 793, and Iona and Skye in the following year. Monastic sites, often conveniently situated on or near the coast, yielded much plunder. Despite the severe setback in 806, when sixty-eight members of the Iona community were slaughtered, and notwithstanding several other assaults, the monastery founded by St. Columba survived. The *Life of Blathmac* implies that the remaining monks, as elsewhere, bought off their attackers. Orkney and Islay served as bases for the early raids, and both places continued to serve as important centers of power.

Early-medieval Britain was composed of diverse peoples. In 839, the Danes won a battle in which "the flower of the Pictish nobility was destroyed." Kenneth mac Alpin, king of Scottish Dalriada, whose own western kingdom was hard pressed by Vikings, made himself first ruler of the united peoples of the Picts and the Scots. He transferred some of St. Columba's relics to Dunkeld, but the new ecclesiastical caput was also threatened by Danes raiding up the River Tay from the east and thus halfway across Scotland.

In subsequent years, Viking activity greatly intensified. Hálfdan broke away from the Great Danish Army to push into eastern Scotland. With the consolidation of the Orkney earldom, Viking settlers approached the shores of the Moray Firth; in 900, they captured the mighty fortress of Dunottar, south of Aberdeen. In the west, a hybrid Celto-Norse population known as "Gall-Gael" was mounting assaults that were especially dreaded because the mixed-bloods were regarded by contemporary chroniclers as more base and bloodthirsty than the Vikings themselves. There is no evidence for their traditional association with Galloway. Southwestern Scotland was devastated by Olaf and Augisl from Ireland. In 870, they successfully besieged Dumbarton, carrying off prisoners and much booty. This important episode, noted in the Irish and Welsh sources, may be interpreted as an attempt to establish an alternative commercial center to Dublin.

The infant kingdom of Scotland almost perished in the midst of such overwhelming hostile attention, but a savior appeared in King Constantine mac Aed (900–943), who battled both Vikings and Anglo-Scandinavians throughout his long reign. Several defeats at Scandinavian hands persuaded him to attempt pacification through marriage alliances; such a measure, at least, is suggested by the occurrence of Scandinavian personal names among some of his successors. He also worked hard to create a common identity for his ethnically diverse people. He and his successors took advantage of English weakness resulting from Scandinavian attacks to push his Scottish frontier farther to the south.

Viking activity was by no means over, but it was no longer the potent threat it had once represented. In the mid-10th century, a fleet of summer raiders was destroyed in the district of Buchan. Very soon, Somerled, or Sorley, came to be used as a personal name in the Hebrides. On Christmas Eve 986, the Vikings massacred fifteen monks on Iona. A year later, the men of Dalriada exacted powerful vengeance on 300 of the raiders under their chief Godfrey mac Harald, *ri Innse Gall* ("king of the Islands of the Foreigners"). In the north, the men of Moray continued to battle with the Orcadians, whose leader, earl Sigurðr digri ("the stout") Hlǫðvisson, perished on the field of Clontarf in 1014. In Icelandic and Irish tradition, the battle marked the end of the Viking Age. The portents described in *Njáls saga* as having been seen throughout the Atlantic community tell the same tale: doom for the men of the North. As *Darraðarljóð* expresses it (and the poem was probably composed in Caithness), the Norns were indeed weaving the fates of the last of the Vikings.

Place-name evidence indicates that Viking settlement of the Scottish mainland was most dense in Caithness. Although for a time a presence was established in Dingwall, Strathoykel was regarded as the southern frontier. Archaeological excavations at Freswick in Caithness testify to Norse hegemony to the 12th century. Much evidence is being recovered from the impressive site at the Udal in North Uist. Archaeology and place-names alike suggest a considerable presence in the Hebrides. Place-names and personal names also indicate Scandinavian penetration into the south of Scotland in population movements best regarded as secondary.

The Vikings introduced Scotland to a world of unprecedented wide horizons. Scots took part in the Vinland voyages, and Orcadians adventured in the Holy Land. For some 400 years of its history, Scotland could no longer be considered to be on the road to nowhere. Indeed, had there been no Viking Age, it is conceivable that there might have been no Scotland.

Lit.: Anderson, Alan Orr, ed. and trans. *Early Sources of Scottish History A.D. 500 to 1286*. 2 vols. Edinburgh: Oliver and Boyd, 1922 [indispensable guide to the primary sources that are often available in more modern editions and translations]; Smyth, Alfred P. *Warlords and Holy Men: Scotland A.D. 80–1000*. The New History of Scotland, 1. London: Arnold, 1984 [a lively study, full of stimulating, if mischievous and idiosyncratic, interpretations]; Morris, Christopher. "Viking Orkney: A Survey." In *The Pre-history of Orkney*. Ed. Colin Renfrew. Edinburgh: Edinburgh University Press, 1985, pp. 210–42; Crawford, Barbara E. *Scandinavian Scotland*. Scotland in the Early Middle Ages, 2. Leicester: Leicester University Press, 1987 [useful bibliography].

Edward J. Cowan

[See also: Caithness; *Darraðarljóð*; Orkney, Norse in]

Seal Hunting *see* Fishing, Whaling, and Seal Hunting

Seals. The science dealing with seals is called sigillography (*sigillum* 'seal,' diminutive of *signum*) or sphragistics (Greek *sfragis* 'seal'). Since antiquity, imprints of a stamp in clay, wax, or sealing wax have been used as a personal or official mark. One can seal up, *i.e.*, close a folded letter, a parcel, or a door, or seal, *i.e.*, confirm the authenticity of, a document with a seal, placed on or hanging under the document. In the Middle Ages, a signature was replaced by seals, the use of which became common, especially in the 12th and 13th centuries.

In Scandinavia, a seal is first mentioned in 1072–1073, and Danish kings have used seals from the end of the 11th century, the Norwegian and Swedish kings probably somewhat later. For judgments issued in the king's name, court seals (*sigillum ad causas*) were used. Soon after, the Church (bishops, chapters, monasteries, *etc.*), towns, districts, guilds, and livery companies, individuals (first the nobility, later the clergy, commoners, and peasants) began to use seals as well. From around 1400, seals were combined with signatures, which, especially from around 1800, completely replaced the seal (except for very special purposes), just as the gummed envelope rendered it as superfluous as a letter closer.

In the Middle Ages, the stamp itself was a flat plate, the back of which was equipped with a raised crest with the lug or a handle. The plate could be circular, shield-shaped, multiangular, or pointed oval, the last-mentioned frequently used by women and the clergy. The stamps, which were usually made by goldsmiths, were often broken up or made useless in other ways after the owner's death. Many stamps are, however, preserved in museums. For imprints of smaller seals, a signet was used, but the transition between the two designations is vague. The signet could be set into a ring, and instead of an actual signet, gems could be used, *i.e.*, carved stones. The word "signet" is also used for the seal imprinting itself. With a clip, double seals could be made with both an obverse and a reverse side, so-called "coin seals." The word "clip" may also refer to the seal itself, usually a king's large seal, called the "clip of the kingdom"; the term gradually came to be used about certain large, one-sided seals as well.

Institutional stamps and signets in particular could be in use for a very long time, which makes it difficult to date them if their existence is known only from seal imprints. One can distinguish between big seals (*sigillum*) used for important documents, and the usually smaller and more private types: privy seals and signets. Already in the Middle Ages, the distinctions became unclear, and often the small seals replaced the big ones. The royalty and the upper clergy could use a counterseal printed on the reverse side of the actual seal with a smaller stamp. Medieval seals were most often made of wax, occasionally colored, and frequently placed in a larger lump of wax or in a wooden cap. In the 15th century, the paper seal came into existence. A thin layer of wax or sealing wax was placed on the document; then it was covered with a piece of paper, and the stamp was pressed into it. Wax seals became common from the 16th century, and also metal seals are found. Best known are the papal bulls, most often made out of lead, which has given the name to the document itself.

The oldest seals hang under the letters in parchment straps or strings, which are stuck through holes in the letter. Often the bottom part of the letter is folded, a *plica*, in order to strengthen the suspension. Plicas can also be used to protect the seals, as it gradually became common to imprint them directly on the letters. The sealers of a letter were often listed in the text, but not necessarily in the same order as the seals, and the sealing with borrowing signets is found. The abbreviation *l.s.* for *locus sigilli* ("the place of the seal") can be used on copies to show the place of the seal on the original document. The seals show a legend and a picture. The legend states the name of the owner of the stamp (and possibly his position), and often it begins with S (= *signum, sigillum, secretum,* or *signetum*). The letters were originally majuscules, from the middle of the 14th century also minuscules, and from about 1500, majuscules or capitals. The language was originally Latin, later possibly German or Low German, and thereafter the native language of the individual countries. The picture shows the owner of the seal or a symbol of his person. The kings could be on a horse (cavalry seal) or on a throne, or the seal could simply be heraldic, showing the royal coat of arms. Bishops could stand or sit enthroned, and other members of the clergy could kneel in a niche under an image of a saint. Biblical motifs and symbols are found in ecclesiastical seals, not infrequently accompanied by the owner's own coat of arms. Noble seals usually contained the owner's coat of arms, in some instances also with a helmet and a crest, which can also appear alone. Commoners' seals and peasants' seals could also be heraldic, but often they contain marks, letters, or symbols. Town and district seals are much varied; often pictures occur that allude to the name of the locality, its appearance, or topography. In guild seals, many kinds of tools are found. Seal pictures can thus elucidate changing styles, depict the development in clothes, tools, or ships, and contain topographic information. Personal seals are an important source of information for genealogies and social history until around 1700. In both personal and institutional seals, the picture could be replaced by letters (initials). More recent seals of office often contain simply the name of the institution.

Ed.: **(a) Denmark**: Petersen, Henry. *Danske gejstlige Sigiller fra Middelalderen.* Copenhagen: Reitzel, 1896; Petersen, Henry. *Danske adelige Sigiller fra det XIII og XIV Aarhundrede.* Copenhagen: Reitzel, 1897; Thiset, A. *Danske adelige Sigiller fra det XV, XVI og XVII Aarhundrede.* Copenhagen: Reitzel, 1889–1905; Petersen, Henry. *Danske kongelige Sigiller samt sønderjydske Hertugers og andre til Danmark knyttede Fyrsters Sigiller, 1085–1559.* Copenhagen: Reitzel, 1917; Grandjean, Poul Bredo. *Danske Købstæders Segl indtil 1660.* Copenhagen: Schultz, 1937; Grandjean, Poul Bredo. *Danske Herreders Segl indtil 1660, herunder Lands- og Birkesegl, med Supplement til Danske Købstæders Segl.* Copenhagen: Schultz, 1946; Grandjean, Poul Bredo. *Danske Gilders Segl fra Middelalderen.* Copenhagen: Schultz, 1948; Grandjean, Poul Bredo. *Danske Håndværkerlavs Segl.* Copenhagen: Schultz, 1950; Grandjean, Poul Bredo. *Slesvigske Købstæders og Herreders Segl indtil 1660, herunder Landskabers Segl.* Copenhagen: Schultz, 1953. **(b) Iceland**: Magnús M. Lárusson and Jónas Kristjánsson. *Sigilla Islandica.* 2 vols. Reykjavik: Handritastofnun Íslands, 1965–67. **(c) Norway**: Huitfeldt-Kaas, H. J. *Norske Sigiller fra Middelalderen. 1: Verdslige Segl indtil Aar 1400.* Kristiania [Oslo]: Aktie-Bogtrykkeriet, 1899–1902; Brinchmann, Christopher. *Norske Konge-Sigiller og andre Fyrste-Sigiller fra Middelalderen.* Kristiania [Oslo]: Malling, 1924. **(d) Sweden**: Hildebrand, Bror Emil. *Svenska Sigiller från Medeltiden.* 3 vols. Stockholm: Kongl. witterhets historie och antiqvitets akademiens förlag, 1862–67; Fleetwood, Harald. *Svenska medeltida Kungasigill.* 3 vols. Stockholm: Lindberg, 1936–47; Fleetwood, Harald. *Svenske medeltida biskopssigill. 1: Ärkebiskopars av Lund sigill.* Stockholm: Lindberg, 1951. **Bib.**: Achen, Sven Tito, and Ole Rostock. *Bibliografi over heraldisk litteratur i Danmark og om Danmark 1589–1969.* Copenhagen: Dansk Historisk Fællesforening, 1971. **Lit.**: Grandjean, Poul Bredo. *Dansk Sigillografi.* Copenhagen: Schultz, 1944; Prange, Knud. *Heraldik og Historie.* 2nd ed. Copenhagen: Dansk Historisk Fællesforening, 1977.

Knud Prange

[See also: Chancery]

Senna—Mannjafnaðr.

Both the words *senna* and *mannjafnaðr* refer to hostile verbal matches in which two or more contenders by boasts and insults, imputations and rebukes, or other degrading devices try to injure each other's honor, or encroach upon each other's social prestige. Although it is generally accepted that verbal dueling originates in real-life practices, scholars have reached no consensus about its generic status. It has been suggested that a *mannjafnaðr* ("comparison of men") constitutes "a somewhat more formalized version" of the *senna* genre, practiced on special social occasions (such as at the "drinking table"; see Lönnroth 1979: 97). Clover, on the other hand, asserts that "we have not two classes but one, itself a distinct category which English scholarship long ago labelled a flyting" (1980: 445).

Yet *senna* and *mannjafnaðr* clearly represent native categories, and recent contributions to the study of these flyting traditions have shed light on the generic features of each category (Harris 1979, Bax and Padmos 1983). Flytings can be compared with temporarily, geographically, and culturally distinct forms of verbal dueling in order to clarify their fundamental aspects (witness the sounding tradition in the Black English vernacular [Labov 1972], verbal dueling rhymes in the Near East [Dundes *et al.* 1972], or ritual challenges among chivalric knights in the West European Middle Ages [Bax 1981, 1983, 1984]). The alleged forms of Norse flyting can be defined as specific "speech events," and analyzed in terms of purpose of the interaction (or "outcome"), participants, setting, message form, and message content. Once these features are scrutinized, one arrives at the conclusion that the *senna* and the *mannjafnaðr* as received in written documents do in fact constitute different types of verbal dueling. Old Norse literary texts seem to present us with information about the performance of these "rituals" in their contemporary context.

Examples of the *senna* tradition are numerous in the medieval literature of Scandinavia, and can be found in Saxo's *Gesta Danorum*, *Ketils saga hœngs*, *Hárbarðsljóð*, *Gríms saga loðinkinna*, *Hjálmþés saga ok Ǫlvis*, *Lokasenna*, and the Helgi poems of the *Poetic Edda*.

A *senna* can be practiced for several reasons, among them diversion, as in *Lokasenna*, where Gefjon advises the gods not to take Loki's insults seriously (st. 19). Second, a *senna* may help to define social status, as in the contest between Ericus and Grep (in Saxo), which serves to reveal who has the greater verbal ability, hence social prestige. Third, a *senna* functions as a means to impress an opponent. In several texts, a *senna* precedes a physical fight, probably to intimidate the opponent and thus cause him to withdraw from the encounter. In this respect, the *senna* can be compared with the insulting sequences in a judicial context (*e.g.*, *Njáls saga*, ch. 119).

A *senna* begins with a preliminary exchange: a "summons" by the first speaker, who uses a deprecatory term of address (thus challenging the other to a verbal contest), and an "answer," comparable in form or content, that counts as an acceptance of the challenge. The verbal interaction develops according to a small set of comparatively simple principles: each contender confronts the other with personal insults, and defends himself against the offenses that are addressed to him in reply. Such a defensive move can consist of a denial of the content of an insult, or may take the form of a counterattack in which the speaker "mirrors" or surpasses the foregoing outrage, thus sending it back to its originator (for particulars, see Bax and Padmos 1983: 154–6). Contrary to the *mannjafnaðr* genre, the propositions put forth in a *senna* must always relate to the other speaker. Further, the insults that are uttered in this context are *ritual* in character, that is, they are not "heard" as truly meant offenses. Their impact draws upon their tactical merits within the ongoing duel rather than on their truth value (Bax and Padmos 1983: 154–5, 165–6).

Examples of *mannjafnaðr* are found in *Hárbarðsljóð*, *Ǫrvar-Odds saga*, *Heimskringla*, *Hálfs saga*, and *Ólafs saga helga*. They share with the *senna* the same purpose and ritual nature. There are, however, several features that suggest that the *mannjafnaðr* stands apart as a speech genre. A *mannjafnaðr* cannot be practiced, as a *senna* often is, among strangers. The contenders must know each other by name, as in the oldest version of *Ǫrvar-Odds saga* (p. 78); when Oddr's opponents propose to give him a name for the occasion, he reveals his own name. In *Hárbarðsljóð*, Þórr and Hárbarðr have identified themselves before engaging in the *mannjafnaðr*. Another precondition is that the contenders must be equal in relevant aspects; this demand of equality is expressed by

Eysteinn in *Heimskringla* (3, ch. 21: 259). *Hárbarðsljóð* is a special case in that the *mannjafnaðr* starts after a *senna* that has ended "undecided"; this outcome means that the opponents have proved to be equal in verbal skill (see Bax and Padmos 1983: 157).

Yet what makes a *mannjafnaðr* truly distinct are its formal properties. Propositions necessarily refer to the actual speaker; moreover, they constitute a claim by the speaker about his own competence in a certain field, for instance, boasts pertaining to his warlike spirit, virility, physical or verbal abilities, or magic cunning. In the context of the duel, such a claim is heard as abuse, an implicit attempt to reduce the prestige of the hearer. The obligatory response to this action is either a mere rejection of the claim or a rejection accompanied by a counterclaim that "tops" the original claim. In *Hárbarðsljóð*, we find this typical sequence: in stanza 15, Þórr boasts about his fight against the giant Hrungnir, and lays claim to the fact that he is a competent warrior. In its context, this claim entails the speaker's conviction that the hearer, Hárbarðr, is not as competent in this respect (compare the conceited "Meanwhile, what were you doing?"). Hárbarðr reacts by boasting about his own heroic exploits: "I was with Fjǫlvarr for five winters. . . . We fought battles, felled heroes, / And wooed maidens: we had much to do" (st. 16). This boast mirrors Þórr's claim, which is thus rejected: Hárbarðr argues against Þórr's supposition that Hárbarðr is not an able warrior; but the latter also adds a new topic, women. This new element is challenging in character in that Hárbarðr indicates that he, unlike Þórr, is not only competent in the field of armor, but also in the field of *amour*. In stanza 17, Þórr comes up with a defying question: "How were the women you won there?," showing that he, so far, is not impressed, thus rejecting the counterclaim. Hárbarðr then gives a more detailed account of his affairs: "With seven sisters I dallied / And had my way with them all. / Meanwhile, what were you doing?" And this formula indicates the next round in the verbal contest (see Bax and Padmos 1983).

The *senna* and *mannjafnaðr* also differ in their complexity. The *senna* employs a series of "two-turn" exchanges, but one "round" in a *mannjafnaðr* can consist of as many as eight turns linked by observable sequencing rules (see *Hárbarðsljóð*, sts. 29–36).

Ed.: Boer, R. C., ed. *Ǫrvar-Odds saga*. Altnordische Saga-Bibliothek, 2. Halle: Niemeyer, 1892; Le Roy Andrews, A., ed. *Hálfs saga ok Hálfsrekka*. Altnordische Saga-Bibliothek, 14. Halle: Niemeyer, 1909; Olrik, Jørgen, and H. Ræder, eds. *Saxonis Gesta Danorum*. Vol. 1. Copenhagen: Levin & Munksgaard, 1931. Vol. 2. *Indicem Verborum Continens*, by Franz Blatt. Copenhagen: Levin & Munksgaard, 1957; Bjarni Aðalbjarnarson, ed. *Heimskringla*. 3 vols. Íslenzk fornrit, 26–8. Reykjavik: Hið íslenzka fornritafélag, 1941–51; Guðni Jónsson, ed. "Ketils saga hœngs." In *Fornaldarsögur Norðurlanda*. 4 vols. Akureyri: Íslendingasagnaútgáfan, 1954, vol. 2, pp. 149–81; Neckel, Gustav, ed. *Edda: Die Lieder des Codex Regius nebst verwandten Denkmälern. I: Text*. 5th ed. rev. Hans Kuhn. Heidelberg: Winter, 1983 [*Hárbarðsljóð* and *Lokasenna*]. **Lit.**: Labov, William. "Rules for Ritual Insults." In his *Language in the Inner City: Studies in the Black English Vernacular*. Philadelphia: University of Pennsylvania, 1972, pp. 297–353; Dundes, A., *et al.* "The Strategy of Turkish Boys' Verbal Dueling Rhymes." In *Directions in Sociolinguistics*. Ed. John J. Gumperz and Dell Hymes. New York: Holt, Rinehart and Winston, 1972, pp. 130–60; Lönnroth, Lars. *Den dubbla scenen: muntlig diktning från Eddan till ABBA*. Stockholm: Prisma, 1978; Clover, Carol J. "*Hárbarðsljóð* as Generic Farce." *Scandinavian Studies* 51 (1979), 124–45; Harris, Joseph. "The *senna*: From Description to Literary Theory." *Michigan Germanic Studies* 5 (1979), 65–74;

Lönnroth, Lars. "The Double Scene of Arrow-Odd's Drinking Contest." In *Medieval Narrative: A Symposium*. Ed. Hans Bekker-Nielsen *et al.* Odense: Odense University Press, 1979, pp. 94–119; Clover, Carol J. "The Germanic Context of the Unferþ Episode." *Speculum* 55 (1980), 444–68; Bax, Marcel. "Rules for Ritual Challenges: A Speech Convention Among Medieval Knights." *Journal of Pragmatics* 5 (1981), 423–44; Bax, Marcel. "Die lebendige Dimension toter Sprachen. Zur pragmatischen Analyse von Sprachgebrauch in historischen Kontexten." *Zeitschrift für germanistische Linguistik* 11.1 (1983), 1–21; Bax, Marcel, and Tineke Padmos. "Two Types of Verbal Dueling in Old Icelandic: The Interactional Structure of the *senna* and the *mannjafnaðr* in *Hárbarðsljóð*." *Scandinavian Studies* 55 (1983), 149–74; Bax, M. M. H. "Conversatieanalyse als filologisch instrument. De tweegesprekken in het Oudhoogduitse *Hildebrandslied* en het Middelnederlandse *Vanden ouden Hillebrant*." In *In ga daer ic hebbe te doene*. Ed. J. J. Th. M. Tersteeg and P. E. L. Verkuyl. Groningen: Wolters-Noordhoff, 1984, pp. 15–44.

Marcel M. H. Bax and Tineke Padmos

[**See also:** *Hárbarðsljóð*; *Íþróttir*]

Settlement, Age of.

The Icelandic Age of Settlement spans the decades 870–930, with 874 traditionally accepted as the symbolic year of the founding of Iceland, when Ingólfr Arnarson, the first settler, "took land" in the southwestern part of the island. Before the middle of the 10th century, all the pastureland in Iceland had been taken. According to Ari fróði ("the learned"; 1067–1148), who wrote the *Íslendingabók*: "Wise men have said . . . that in the space of sixty years Iceland was fully occupied, so that after that there was no further taking of land." At this time, the population of the country was probably between 20,000 and 30,000.

It is clear from *Landnámabók*, first completed early in the 12th century, that most of the settlers were Norwegian, with a minority of Irish and Scots. Most of the Norwegian settlers did not migrate directly from Norway but came to Iceland indirectly after spending some years in Britain, Ireland, the Hebrides, and Orkney. Many brought Celtic wives and slaves. Of those who came directly from Norway, most came from the southwest, particularly from Sogn and Hordaland. Some also came from northern Norway, but few people came from the eastern part of the country. There were also a handful of Swedes and Danes, and a few from other places.

The settlement of Iceland was a part of the dispersion of the Nordic peoples, a movement that occupied the Scandinavians from the late 8th century into the 11th. Scholars propose different reasons for this outpouring from the North. Some stress the shortage of land and the pressure of a growing population; others emphasize the desire for adventure, plunder, and honor, values strong among the ancient Scandinavians. According to tradition, the migration out of Norway was prompted by the desire to escape the rule of Haraldr hárfagri ("fair-hair") Hálfdanarson, who had succeeded in unifying Norway during the second half of the 9th century and who was trying to force all of the petty chieftains to submit to his rule, which many refused to do.

The culture that took root in Iceland was Scandinavian. Irish influences are apparent in a few proper names, some place-names, and a few words in the language. However, some students of Icelandic literature claim that Irish culture had a larger impact on the culture and literature (Stefán Einarsson 1957: 5–6).

Our main source of information on pre-Christian Iceland, its legal system, material conditions of life, relations between the sexes, kinship names and naming patterns, and social structure in general

are the *Íslendingasögur*. While most of these historical fictions were not written down until the late 12th and 13th centuries, social and material conditions had not changed much since the Age of Settlement; and the authors, when they dealt with this period, were "conscious of the distance in time, and they had a considerable historical sense" (Sigurður Nordal 1957: 29).

Lit.: Ker, W. P. *The Dark Ages*. Edinburgh and London: Blackwood, 1904; Sigurður Nordal. *The Historical Element in the Icelandic Family Sagas*. Fifteenth W. P. Ker Memorial Lecture Delivered in the University of Glasgow, 19th May 1954. Glasgow: Jackson, 1957; Stéfán Einarsson. *A History of Icelandic Literature*. Baltimore: Johns Hopkins University Press; New York: American-Scandinavian Foundation, 1957; Brøndsted, Johannes. *The Vikings*. Trans. Kalle Skov. Harmondsworth: Penguin, 1960 [published originally in Danish]; Jones, Gwyn. *The Norse Atlantic Saga: Being the Norse Voyages of Discovery and Settlement to Iceland, Greenland, and North America*. London: Oxford University Press, 1964; 2nd ed. 1986; Foote, Peter G., and David M. Wilson. *The Viking Achievement: The Society and Culture of Early Medieval Scandinavia*. London: Sidgwick & Jackson, 1970; Hermann Pálsson and Paul Edwards, trans. *The Book of Settlements, Landnámabók*. University of Manitoba Icelandic Studies, 1. Winnipeg: University of Manitoba Press, 1972; Jón Jóhannesson. *A History of the Old Icelandic Commonwealth: Íslendinga saga*. Trans. Haraldur Bessason. University of Manitoba Icelandic Studies, 2. Winnipeg: University of Manitoba Press, 1974 [originally pubished in Icelandic in 1956]; Tomasson, Richard F. *Iceland: The First New Society*. Minneapolis: University of Minnesota Press, 1980; Byock, Jesse L. *Feud in the Icelandic Saga*. Berkeley, Los Angeles, and London: University of California Press, 1982; Hastrup, Kirsten. *Culture and History in Medieval Iceland: An Anthropological Analysis of Structure and Change*. Oxford: Clarendon, 1985; Byock, Jesse L. *Medieval Iceland: Society, Sagas, and Power*. Berkeley, Los Angeles, and London: University of California Press, 1988.

Richard F. Tomasson

[**See also:** Iceland; *Íslendingabók*; *Íslendingasögur*; *Landnámabók*]

Settlement, Rural.

During prehistoric times and the medieval period, the major feature of the Nordic region was a preponderance of forest, broken up by a large number of minor lakes and swamps. The establishment of settlements was dependent upon the natural resources available for arable farming and/or cattle raising.

Cattle raising was the predominant feature in the economy of settlements during the late Iron Age and the Viking Age. The large number of swamp areas made access to water relatively easy; there was land suitable for grazing and for the collection of winter fodder.

The number and size of settlements increased during the later Viking Age and the early-medieval period as a result of the rising population. It is possible to estimate the age of a settlement from its name. Place-names ending in -*thorp*, -*arp*, -*rup*, and -*ryd* were most probably established during this period. Settlements in Denmark, and most probably the rest of the Nordic region, were not stable during the early Iron Age. As the land became exhausted, villagers moved on to fresh pastures. Beginning in the 1970s, principally in Denmark, archaeological excavations have examined a number of village sites dated from A.D. 1 to the late Iron Age. This work has established that during certain periods, villages ceased to exist, only to become reestablished within the same area at a later stage.

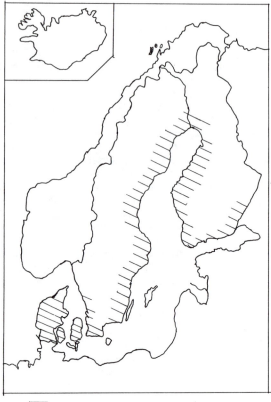

= areas which are dominated by villages settlements.

160. Distribution of types of villages and farms in Scandinavia.

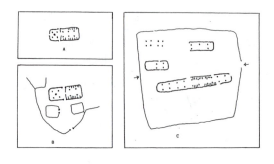

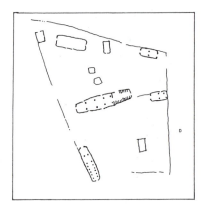

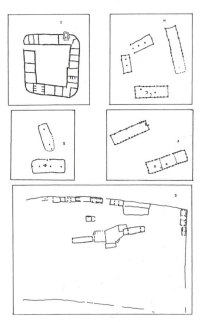

161. Development of farms in Denmark. (A) Grøntoft; Pre-Roman Iron Age. (B) Hodde. Year A.D. 1. (C) Vorbasse; A.D. 400. (D) Vorbasse; A.D. 900. (E) Vorbasse; A.D. 1000. (F) Store Valby; Middle Ages. (G) Astrup; 15th century. (H) Store Valby; 17th century. (I) Hatterød; ca. 1800. After Gröngaard-Jeppesen (1981).

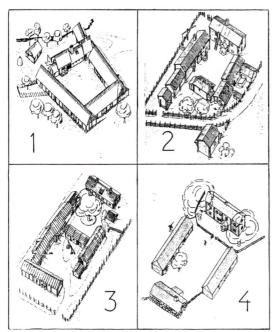

162. Swedish farm types. (1) South Swedish farm. (2) North Swedish farm.
(3) Central Swedish farm. (4) The "Götisk" farm. After *Geografiska notiser*
(1949).

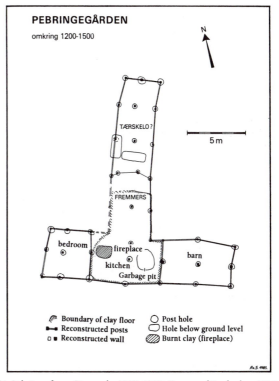

PEBRINGEGÅRDEN

omkring 1200-1500

N

5 m

TÆRSKELO?

FREMMERS

bedroom

fireplace

barn

kitchen

Garbage pit

🜂 Boundary of clay floor   ○ Post hole
▬ Reconstructed posts   ◯ Hole below ground level
▫▪ Reconstructed wall   ▨ Burnt clay (fireplace)

A.S. 1985.

164. Pebringe farm, Denmark, 1200–1500. Excavated in the late 1930s.
After Steensberg (1986).

163. Approximate spread of Swedish farm types.
Nos. 5 and 6 are mixed villages of types 3 and 4.
After *Geografiska notiser* (1949).

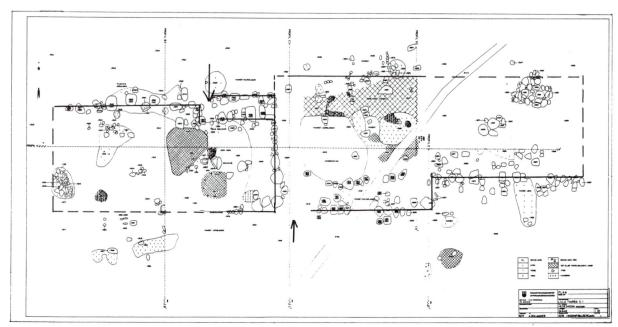

165. Farm in Lilla Tvären, Scania, Sweden; middle of 14th century. Excavated 1976, by the author. Scale 1:100. (Tärsklo = threshing barn; Fremmers = hall.)

About A.D. 1000, this mobility ceased and villages became fixed. Two factors influenced this development: the changing face of agriculture and the organizational structure imposed by the monarchy, the Church, and a growing aristocracy.

Medieval sources describe three main types of farming undertaken during this period: one-field, two-field, and three-field systems. The types are differentiated in terms of their cropping systems and were dependent upon the nature of the land. Areas of fertile and easily cultivated soil, for example in Denmark and the Swedish plains, had most probably established as early as the Viking Age a system of rotation farming where the ratio of crops to fallow land was 2:1 (*i.e.*, in the three-field system). The principal crops were barley and rye; wheat and oats became important during the later-medieval period. Evidence for this trend has been found in the analysis of fruits and seeds. A prerequisite for this type of farming is the ability of the farm workers to work cooperatively. Sandy soils were cultivated using an ard, which made shallow furrows. The development of the wheel-plow during the period 1000–1100 enabled larger areas of land to be plowed, and facilitated the cultivation of the previously forest-clad heavier clay soils.

It is difficult to give a definitive picture of rural settlements during the medieval period. The type of settlements already established during the Iron Age form part of the picture, of course, as do individual farms. These latter were often situated in areas of poorer soil, unsuitable for more extensive farming. Exceptions to this pattern can be seen on, for example, Bornholm, where factors concerning inheritance, landownership, and the organization of society produced a settlement picture consisting only of individual farms.

Medieval villagers were usually concentrated on plains with fertile soil where it was easy to use the wheel-plow. A village is defined as a settlement of at least three farms.

Probably the best picture of settlement patterns can be gained from certain 17th- and 18th-century maps, which show conditions prior to the agricultural reforms. It is possible to study the different methods of farming used and get an overview of the countryside. Certain of these conditions can be presumed valid for the Middle Ages. The Danish book *Cadestre of King Waldemar* (*ca.* 1230) records the king's estates and taxes in such detail that reconstructions of the settlement patterns can be made.

The laws current at that time have been preserved to a greater or lesser extent. These laws regulated the daily life, settling disputes among the villagers. Place-names also play a part in an overview of the development of village settlements over a large area, and the density of these settlements.

From the evidence above, together with other written material, it is possible to build an overview of the settlement of villages and individual farms. In Denmark, the villages were situated on the large plains with good soil, where solitary farms were found in marginal areas: northern and western Jutland, and the northern parts of Funen, Zealand, and Scania. As mentioned above, on the island of Bornholm the settlement consisted only of individual farms. In Sweden and Finland, the situation was similar, with villages on easily cultivated land, especially along the coasts and rivers. In southeastern Finland, influence from the east can be seen in the occurrence of large groups of houses functioning as individual farms. In Norway, the settlements often comprised a large number of buildings. They were, however, not villages, but farms with one or several buildings for each function. These buildings could be placed regularly or irregularly on the site. In Iceland, the settlements consisted only of individual farms.

An individual farm in the early Iron Age would consist of several buildings, each with a different function. Archaeological examinations have confirmed that there would be a long house with a central hearth, a dwelling house. There are also examples of long houses divided into a living area and a byre. The farms also featured one or more pit houses, together with several huts.

Archaeological investigations of medieval farms have been made in Denmark by one of the pioneers of rural archaeology, Axel Steensberg. His excavations during the middle of the 20th century were for a long time the only ones concerned with medieval farms. However, the 1980s saw the initiation of several projects in both Sweden and Denmark, studying rural settlements, with an emphasis on environmental analysis.

Archaeological investigations of medieval villages in both Scania and Denmark have shown that the same type of long houses and pit houses constructed in the late Viking Age also appear in the early-medieval period. Not until the second half of the 13th century were long houses replaced by houses constructed using foundations made of stones. Pit houses also ceased to be constructed during this period. At this time, too, there were changes in the proportion of livestock types.

One of the few farms from the period 1200–1400 examined by archaeologists is the village Lilla Tvären (Fig. 165). The building that formed the dwelling place was constructed on a foundation of stones at the end of the 13th century. During the 14th century, the length of the building was extended.

The appearance and exact function of the different buildings of the medieval farms are not known in detail. The distribution map of farm types in Sweden (Fig. 163) is based primarily on material from the 17th and 18th centuries. It probably also indicates what the situation was like in the medieval period, because preserved older farmhouses fit well into the picture.

Lit.: Erixon, Sigurd. *Svensk Bygnadskultur.* Stockholm: Aktiebolaget Bokverk, 1947; Nikander, B. "Kultursheden och en etnografisk översikt." *Folkliv* (1950–51), 103–29; Steensberg, Axel. *Bondehus og vandmöller i Danmark genom 2000 år.* Copenhagen: Hassing, 1952 [English summary]; Steensberg, Axel. "Bebyggelsen paa landet i Danmark i historisk tid." In *Landbrug og bebyggelse.* Ed. Sigurd Erixon. Nordisk kultur, 13. Stockholm: Bonnier; Oslo: Aschehoug; Copenhagen: Schultz, 1956, pp. 254–64; Vreim, Halvor. "Den lantlige bebyggelse i Norge under historisk tid." In *Landbrug og bebyggelse,* pp. 265–74; Erixon, Sigurd. "Bebyggelsestruktur och bysamfällighet i Sverige." In *Landbrug og bebyggelse,* pp. 275–94; Göransson, S. "Field and Village on the Island of Öland." *Geografiska annaler* 40 (1958), 101–58; Christensen, Aksel E. *Danmarks historie.* Vol. 1. Copenhagen: Gyldendal, 1977; Gröngaard-Jeppesen, Torben. *Landsbyens opståen. Indledende studier over middelalderlandsbyernes pladskontinuitet.* Skrifter fra historisk institut, Odense Universitet. Odense: Historisk Institut, Odense Universitet, 1979; Randsborg, Klaus. *The Viking Age in Denmark: The Formation of a State.* New York: St. Martin, 1980; Gröngaard-Jeppesen,Torben. *Middelalderlandsbyens opståen, kontinuitet og brud i den fynske agrarbebyggelse mellem yngre jernalder og tidlig middelalder.* Odense: Odense bymuseer, 1981; Steensberg, Axel. *Pebringegården.* Højbjerg: Wormianum, 1986 [English summary]; Porsmose, Erland. *De fynske landsbyers historie.* Odense: Odense Universitetsforlag, 1987 [English summary].

Ingmar Billberg

[See also: Agriculture; Houses, Rural; Houses, Urban]

Shetland, Norse in.

Shetland is called "Hjaltland" in the sagas and medieval documents. This group of around thirty inhabitable islands and numerous grazing islets and rocks lies 360 km. west of Bergen and 338 km. north of Aberdeen in Scotland. From the period of the Viking migrations until the Reformation, Shetland's relationship with Scandinavia was close and complex, but eventually waned in intensity.

Until the 13th century, there is next to no documentary or literary evidence concerning Shetland's polity and economy. Crawford (1987) has argued that until the 11th century, the kings of Norway may have granted Shetland to favored individuals, and that Earl Þorfinnr II of Orkney may well have acquired Shetland for his earldom after defeating one individual so favored, Rǫgnvaldr Brúsason, in 1046. However, there is some evidence that Shetland was an important, albeit relatively poor, "third" (*þriðjungr*) of the Orkney earldom, used by claimants like Rǫgnvaldr Brúsason and Rǫgnvaldr Kali Kolsson as a stepping-stone to power (Smith 1988).

In the absence of documentary evidence, we have to look to archaeology and settlement toponymy for information about the first 400 years of Norse society in Shetland. Hamilton's excavations at "Jarlshof" (the name was invented in the early 19th century by Sir Walter Scott), a medium-sized and probably typical township at the southmost tip of the Shetland mainland, uncovered seven phases of settlement from about 800 to the 13th century, revealing a peasant community *par excellence*, with much evidence of fishing activity (Hamilton 1956). Jakobsen's work (1936) on Shetland farm names, and Nicolaisen's (1969) on their chronology, give us a picture of a society overwhelmingly Norse; there is no evidence of any pre-Norse place-name anywhere in Shetland. Thanks to the amount of low-lying land in the islands, Shetland's settlement toponymy is far more complex than that of the Faroes.

In 1195, King Sverrir Sigurðarson of Norway removed Shetland from the control of the Orkney earls, and he and his successors henceforth administered the islands directly from Norway (Crawford 1983). In the late 13th and early 14th centuries, Shetland adopted political and economic institutions characteristic of Norway at that period. We have records of the Shetland lawthing from 1299 and 1307, the latter showing that the law administered in the islands was Magnús lagabœtir ("law-mender") Hákonarson's landlaw (Robberstad 1983). Recent research has shown that a new system of land valuation, rent, and taxation was probably introduced in Shetland at the same time, based on the East Norwegian *markebol* unit (Smith forthcoming). There is evidence from the late 13th and early 15th centuries of close political and family links between Shetland and the Faroes, the latter group of islands administered from Norway in precisely the same way as Shetland.

Before the 15th century, Shetland fish, always the main export commodity, was channeled through the Hanseatic *kontor* in Bergen. During that century, individual merchants from North Germany ignored Hansa rules and began to trade directly with the Shetlanders, thus breaking an important economic link between Shetland and Norway (Friedland 1983). In 1469, Christian 1 of Denmark and Norway mortgaged his royal rights in Shetland to the king of Scotland; and during the next 150 years, Norse and Scots administrators and forms of administration and law jostled and intermixed in the islands. Norwegian aristocrats, known as the "Lords of Norway" in Shetland, continued to own large estates in the islands, but were gradually ousted by Scots in the late 16th and early 17th centuries (Smith 1990). Shetlanders finally ceased to speak a Scandinavian language in the 18th century (Jakobsen 1928).

In the late 19th century, Shetland intellectuals formulated a romantic theory of Shetland's Norse past, contrasting that era favorably with what they called the period of "semi-serfdom" endured by Shetlanders in the 18th and 19th centuries (Cohen 1983).

Lit.: Jakobsen, Jakob. *An Etymological Dictionary of the Norn Language in Shetland.* 2 vols. London: Nutt, 1928, vol. 1; Jakobsen, Jakob. *The Place-Names of Shetland.* London: Nutt, 1936; Hamilton, J. R. C. *Excavations at Jarlshof, Shetland.* Ministry of Public Building and Works, Archaeological Reports, no. 1. Edinburgh: Her Majesty's Stationery Office, 1956; Nicolaisen, W. F. H. "Norse Settlement in the Northern and Western Isles." *Scottish Historical Review* 48 (1969), 6–17; Cohen, Bronwen. "Norse Imagery in Shetland: An Historical Study of Intellectuals and Their Use of the Past in the Construction of Shetland's Identity, with Particular Reference to the Period 1800–1914." Diss. Manchester University, 1983; Friedland, Klaus. "Hanseatic Merchants and Their Trade with Shetland." In *Shetland and the Outside World 1469–1969.* Ed. Donald J. Withrington. Aberdeen University Studies Series, 157. Oxford: Oxford University Press, 1983, pp. 86–95; Crawford, Barbara. "The Pledging of the Islands in 1469: The Historical Background." In *Shetland and the Outside World,* pp. 32–48; Robberstad, Knut. "Udal Law." In *Shetland and the Outside World,* pp. 49–68; Crawford, Barbara. *Scandinavian Scotland.* Scotland in the Early Middle Ages, 2. Leicester: Leicester University Press, 1987; Smith, Brian. "Shetland in Saga-Time: Rereading the *Orkneyinga Saga.*" *Northern Studies* 25 (1988), 21–41; Smith, Brian. "Shetland, Scotland, Scandinavia, 1300–1700: The Changing Nature of Contact." In *Scotland and Scandinavia.* Ed. Grant Simpson. Edinburgh: Donald, 1990; Smith, Brian. *Toons and Tenants: Rural Communities in Shetland, 1200–1800* [forthcoming].

Brian Smith

Ships and Shipbuilding.

Ships and Shipbuilding. Until the epoch-making excavation of the Skuldelev ships (Denmark) in 1962, the royal burial ship from Gokstad on the Oslofjord (Brøgger 1951) had dominated thinking about the ships of the period, and its presumed character was attributed to all ships mentioned in the sources. This association was partly because of the superbly uncompromising craftsmanship with which the Gokstad ship achieves its evident aim of a fast, necessarily ultra-lightweight, and therefore necessarily flexible, seaworthy hull. Since it is not an extreme longship war vessel like Ladby or Skuldelev 2 or 5 (Olsen and Pedersen 1967), and since Magnus Andersen's Atlantic crossing in his facsimile *Viking* ran 360 km. on his best day, the Gokstad ship seemed to be a fast ocean clipper and an ideal shallow-draught landing-craft combined. Although merchant ships were known from the texts, they had little influence on the common picture of the "Viking" ship. In fact, Andersen's *Viking,* with its continuous, watertight deck, extra stability ensured by built-on buoyancy fender, deeper keel, and quite unhistoric rig including staysails, cannot seriously be used as evidence for the original. Andersen's account is quite frank, but highly selective quotation by enthusiasts without understanding of his original text led to unrealistic adulation of the Gokstad ship. Some modern, superficially scientific enthusiasts even assert that the Gokstad ship, whose open hull puts its rail under water if it heels more than 15°, could carry full sail of 90 sq. m. in Beaufort Storm Force 10, ignoring the potentially 12-m.-high waves with their virtual gravity effect that accompany such unusual storms. Even accurate modern replica Viking ships must be treated with caution as historical evidence, for they are usually sailed by dedicated and gifted seamen with modern backup, and are not really representative of the Viking Age. But because the ship's capabilities are so central to many questions of the period, over- or underestimates can seriously affect the value of hypotheses about it.

The Skuldelev find gave a convincing demonstration on one site of the variety of Viking ship types. Skuldelev 1 (length 15.8 m., breadth 4.4 m., draught 1.3 m., sail area 91.5 sq. m.) was capable of crossing the North Atlantic to Iceland or Greenland with 13.6 metric tons of cargo, but was not very fast under sail nor easily rowed. The smaller Skuldelev 3 (length 13.4 m., breadth 3.5 m., draught 0.9 m., sail area 41.2 sq. m.) was equally seaworthy, with a crew of six to seven but room for twice as many, and is probably representative of the maid-of-all-work of many estates of the period. The Skuldelev war vessels 2 (length 28 m., breadth 4.4 m., draught 0.9 m.) and 5 (length 18.3 m., breadth 2.6 m., draught 0.6 m.) had much larger crews, of a minimum fifty and twenty-five respectively, with 100 or fifty needed for continuous operation, requiring larger supplies of food and water scarcely to be carried in these light-displacement hulls, making them less independent, with a smaller operational radius. They are developments of pre-Viking types of the 5th and 7th centuries, such as Nydam (Akerlund 1963) or Sutton Hoo (Bruce-Mitford 1975), which carried no sail but evidently made successful North Sea crossings under oars alone. The division in the Skuldelev craft between capable sailing vessels with auxiliary oars, and primarily oared war vessels with auxiliary sails disposes of the difficulty that the Gokstad ship is underpowered under sail and oars in most believable reconstructions, leading to a variation between them of 150 percent in sail area and displacement. The warships could easily raise or lower their mast and rig when rowing to windward; in the merchant ships, the mast was a fixture, which may suggest that it was higher, with a higher aspect ratio, more efficient rig, suiting a ship with a smaller crew and less oar power to call on. But since no rigs survive, there can be no proof.

The variety of craft at Skuldelev is important in other ways. Once the Gokstad ship ceases to be the sole model, the skepticism of some historians about the size of certain ships (*e.g.,* King Óláfr's Long-Serpent) or certain fleets (*e.g.,* the A.D. 851 fleet of 350 ships) seems less justified. If we enlarge it to a length of 51.8 m. with eighty rowers, or envisage 20,000 men in a fleet of such expensive masterpieces, we may well have doubts. But a longship like Skuldelev 2 would at such a length have only twice the tonnage of the Gokstad ship (Banbury 1975), with the same power per ton available from its oars, and a fleet made up of Skuldelev 3 need not have numbered more than 7,000 men, a good deal more credible than the 20,000 involved if they were all in Gokstad ships. The contemporary accounts are less open to the charge of possible exaggeration.

Existing ships make a bigger impression than deductions, however legitimate, from fragments. But the evidence from Staraja Ladoga and Hedeby of merchant ships of Scandinavian type of 24.4 m. long and one from Bergen 27.4 m. long shows that some were larger than later cogs, such as that from Bremen, which is 23.2 m. long (Crumlin-Pedersen 1983). There is thus no reason to use the nature of the vessels as evidence that Viking ships carried only small luxury cargoes, and the bulk shipment of grain and other low-value loads later produced a different ship type, the Hansa cog. The development of ships of this size in Scandinavia is evidence that bulk cargoes were carried on a scale that made such ships worthwhile before the Hanseatic period.

Whether the later, larger oared warships were a similar improvement on their predecessors is doubtful. Since the maximum speed for a given power depends on waterline length, and an

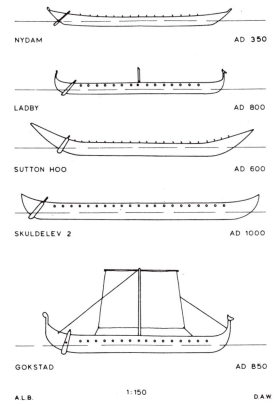

166. The evolution of the seagoing oared warship in Scandinavia to A.D. 1000.

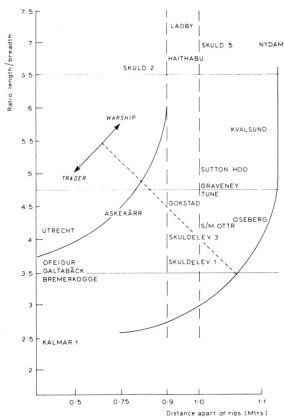

168. Sailing ships (bottom left) are wide in proportion to length, and are good load carriers, but not fast. Oared warships are narrow for their length and fast. Gokstad, incorporating both traditions, stands on the dotted "borderline" between war galleys and merchant sailing ships.

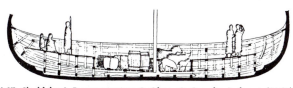

167. Skuldelev 1. Reconstruction: O. Olsen, O. Crumlin-Pedersen (1969).

oarsman produces approximately 0.5 hp. and requires a yard of rail to row over (less in the later, more crowded ships), the motive for increasing length beyond the limit of structural strength of a shallow hull is clear. The hull had to be shallow for its length to enable the oars to be applied effectively without entering the water at too steep an angle. In the Gokstad ship, this ratio was combined with a seaworthy freeboard by adding two strakes of planking above the oarports, with covers to close the oarports when the ship was under sail; without this feature, the permissible heel would have been too small for sailing in a seaway.

Estimates of the ability under sail of the Gokstad ship have been naturally as various as estimates of its sail area and displacement where the variation between upper and lower estimates, appropriate to different roles, is 150 percent. Some scholars thought Gokstad always needed a following wind, while others thought it

could sail 4° off the wind at 7 knots, far surpassing a modern ice-yacht! The latter is certainly a misunderstanding of Andersen's 4 points (45°), itself hard to believe even as a heading, to which must be added the optimal 10° leeway required to produce the turbulence of water flowing under the shallow keel toward the windward side, which adds a virtual keel of water, shown in tank tests and sailing with replicas. The side rudder, not very effective for large course alterations, but easily handled because it is balanced about its axis, functions as a trim tab to control this angle of attack. Two alternative tiller holes in some rudders suggest it was used in the "half-up" position to control the ship even at the last minute before beaching, which was the normal way of loading, unloading, or spending the night.

The speeds to be expected from the waterline length can be substantially exceeded. *Odin's Raven*, a two-thirds replica version of the Gokstad ship, very similar to Skuldelev 3, was timed at a speed of 12.5 knots, $2\sqrt{L}$, and under a conservative seagoing rig tacked through the wind reliably and repeatedly without using oars or making sternway. At such speeds, England was barely a night and a day from Denmark, but of course such speeds imply that the wave making as the ship races through the water is not that of a displacement hull. Whether we explain this by planing, semiplaning, the flexibility of the hull, or fine sections and ultra-light weight (all have been suggested; Binns 1980), the puzzling fact is well established. Light is thrown on the necessary sail trimming by the practice in contemporary North Norwegian *femboring* (five oars a side) of using a priare, or three-armed sheet in the middle of the foot, used to control the curve and therefore the power of the sail. The interlace at the foot of the sail being held by crewmen in depictions of Viking ships on Gotland stones, such as that from Hejnum, seems to show this as a Viking Age feature, which implies skilled fine tuning to get the best speed possible as close to the wind as possible.

Shipbuilding. Seasoned timber has proved difficult to work as required in modern replica construction, and it seems likely that the timber was cut in the fall and moved through the forest on the winter snow to some convenient place close to the beach, where in spring it was built into a ship that sailed that summer. No hull has shown any sign of the use of a saw, and planks were split from a trunk radially, giving perhaps six narrow oak planks, or across a diameter, giving two wide pine planks. This process is important for the interpretation of hull shape, as shrinkage along the radius of a trunk is only half that across it (McGrail 1974). When allowance for this distortion is made, early ships like Nydam can be restored to much more seaworthy forms than those presently exhibited. The relative stability of split planks was required by the constructional method of all Viking Age hulls, the lapstrake or clinker form in which the hull shell is first completed from overlapping planks, and afterward strengthened by inserting frames and crossbeams. The extra flexibility needed in the devotedly and expensively lightened warships, where the thickness of the frames is carefully varied to suit the load, was achieved by tying the planking to the frames; but in merchant ships, it was fastened rigidly with metal or wooden spikes.

Ease of beaching required a shallow keel and relatively wide midship section, and seaworthiness required a curving high prow with reserve buoyancy. The ability to keep up speed with little power input required fairly fine ends so that the ship was not stopped by seas hitting a bluff bow. In the smaller craft in which the method is most at home, the crossbeams provided seats for the oarsmen. In ships the size of the Gokstad ship and larger, crossbeams were supports for a deck of loose boards on which the oarsmen probably sat on their sea chests. In the largest ships, a double row of such beams was needed. The cog was built on thicker planking secured to a skeleton or keel and straight stems, which was built first, with a fairly flat bottom giving a much greater volume on a given length, altogether more suitable for carrying large cargoes in tidal waters where oared propulsion was less important.

Lit.: Brøgger, A. W., and Haakon Shetelig. *The Viking Ships.* Trans. Katherine John. Oslo: Dreyer, 1951; Akerlund, Harald. *Nydamskeppen. En studie i tidig skandinavisk skepps byggnadskonst.* Gothenburg: Gothenburg Sjöfartsmuseum, 1963 [English summary, pp. 154–60]; Olsen, Olaf, and Ole Crumlin-Pedersen. "The Skuldelev Ships." *Acta Archaeologica Scandinavica* 38 (1967), 73–174; Ellmers, Detlev. *Frühmittelalterliche Handelsschiffahrt in Mittel- und Nordeuropa.* Neumunster: Wachholtz, 1972; McGrail, Sean. *The Gokstad Færing.* Maritime Monographs, 11. London: National Maritime Museum, 1974; Bruce-Mitford, Rupert. *The Sutton Hoo Ship-Burial. 1: Excavations, Background, the Ship Dating and Inventory.* London: British Museum, 1975; Banbury, Philip. *Man and the Sea: From the Ice Age to the Norman Conquest.* London: Coles, 1975; Binns, Alan. *Viking Voyagers: Then and Now.* London: Heinemann, 1980; Crumlin-Pedersen, Ole. *From Viking Ships to Hanseatic Cogs.* Occasional Lecture, 4. London: National Maritime Museum, 1983.

Alan Binns

[**See also:** Gokstad; Navigation; Oseberg; Transport]

Sighvatr Þórðarson. With more than 160 stanzas and half-stanzas, Sighvatr's *oeuvre* is the most fully attested of all the skalds. Even so, the original context of many stanzas is uncertain and only one poem, *Bersoglisvísur* ("Plain-speaking Verses"), approaches complete preservation. Although no saga centering on Sighvatr exists, his distinguished career is documented by numerous episodes, some anecdotal and perhaps dubiously reliable, in the various versions of *Óláfs saga helga.* An Icelander born near the turn of the 11th century, Sighvatr belonged to a skaldic kindred, being the son of Þórðr Sigvaldaskáld and the uncle of Óttarr svarti ("the black"). His childhood was spent independently of his father, who seems to have been attached to the Jómsvíkingar, and in a non-Snorri anecdote his legendary fluency in poetic improvisation is attributed to his having caught and eaten a miraculous fish. Following a successful petition to St. Óláfr to accept him as a court poet, his adult career began with his *Víkingarvísur* ("Verses on the Viking Expedition"; the title is editorial). Here, Sighvatr used information from eyewitnesses (including his father?) to enumerate Óláfr's battles in the Baltic, England, France, and Spain. *Nesjavísur* ("Nesjar Verses"), by contrast, is based on Sighvatr's own participation in Óláfr's victorious sea-battle against Earl Sveinn Hákonarson (1016). Sighvatr also became personally involved in peace missions. His embassy (ca. 1017) to Earl Rǫgnvaldr of Västergötland is described in *Austrfararvísur* ("Verses on a Journey to the East"). This collection of verses gives vivid, humorous, almost chatty impressions of a difficult route, inhospitable heathen people, and a favorable diplomatic outcome, although its exact documentary significance remains controversial. Subsequently, with the high rank of *stallari* ("marshall"), Sighvatr went to England to gather intelligence about Knud (Cnut) the Great's designs in Norway. He described this mission in a sparsely preserved sequence entitled *Vestrfararvísur* ("Verses on a Journey to the West"; 1025–1026). Sighvatr's close relationship with Óláfr, richly documented in the *lausavísur* and other compositions, brought him landed property and also benefited other Icelanders, including his nephew Óttarr. Tradition has it that he was instrumental in the naming of Óláfr's son Magnús, and in return the king sponsored Sighvatr's daughter at baptism. A pilgrimage to Rome (1029–1030) precluded his participation in the king's final battle at Stiklastaðir. His sorrow is expressed in some very eloquent and touching memorial *lausavísur.* His *erfidrápa* ("memorial lay"), perhaps composed some years later, appears to have focused on Óláfr's battles, sainthood, and miracles. Spurning an invitation from Sveinn, the temporary regent of Norway, Sighvatr attached himself to Óláfr's widow, Ástríðr, in exile in Sweden, and composed verses eulogizing her political efforts on behalf of Magnús, her stepson. Returning to Norway with Magnús (1035), he forestalled civil war with the poem entitled *Bersoglisvísur,* which, by mingling candid admonition with sweet persuasion, brought the new king to recognize the grievances of Sveinn's erstwhile supporters. He also mediated between Ástríðr and Álfhildr, the mother of Magnús. Despite his declaration to Knud that he could serve only one lord at a time, Sighvatr was capable of political independence. Most notably, he composed a *drápa* and an affectionate memorial *flokkr* in honor of Erlingr Skjálgsson, Óláfr's brother-in-law and long-time foe (d. 1028). Some MSS connect his name with a poorly attested *Tryggvaflokkr* for Tryggvi Óláfsson (son of Óláfr Tryggvason, and an unsuccessful contender against Earl Sveinn);

poems praising Earl Ívarr and the Swedish king Ǫnundr Jakob are also reported. His *Knútsdrápa* ("Lay in Honor of Knud") was composed after Knud's death (1035), perhaps on the occasion of Magnús's reconciliation with Hardacnut (1038). Its coverage included Knud's English campaign, the battle of Helgeå, and the king's pilgrimage to Rome. It is distinctive formally for its *klofastef* ("broken refrain") and very restrictive *tøglag* versification. Sighvatr's death probably occurred around 1043. His verse distinguishes itself by sincerity, loyalty, humor, and general strength of personality. Such is the air of spontaneity that his poems appear to be retrospective assemblages of occasional or anecdotal verses. Colloquial and proverbial touches sit side by side with foreign words, which, combined with the breadth of geographical references, give his verse a somewhat cosmopolitan feel. Mythological kennings occur seldom, except in *Erlingsflokkr*, perhaps because they were out of keeping with the newly Christian ethos. Also scarce are obscure, neologistic compound nouns and kennings, of the sort so often found in other skalds' work. The general effect is simplicity, commonly offset by a difficult word order or an intricate plaiting of several short sentences within the one *helmingr*. With Sighvatr, then, skaldic discourse seems to be both in touch with its traditions and also opening itself to international contacts, in conformity with the expansion of Norwegian and Danish hegemony during his lifetime.

Ed.: Finnur Jónsson, ed. *Den norsk-islandske skjaldedigtning*. Vols. 1A-2A (tekst efter håndskrifterne) and 1B-2B (rettet tekst). Copenhagen and Christiania [Oslo]: Gyldendal, 1912–15; rpt. Copenhagen: Rosenkilde & Bagger, 1967 (A) and 1973 (B); Kock, Ernst A., ed. *Den norsk-isländska skjaldediktningen*. 2 vols. Lund: Gleerup, 1946–50 [contains some improvements on Finnur Jónsson's edition]; Jón Skaptason. "Material for an Edition and Translation of the Poems of Sigvat Þórðarson, *skáld*." Diss. State University of New York at Stony Brook, 1983. **Tr.**: Hollander, Lee M. *The Skalds: A Selection of Their Poems with Introduction and Notes*. Princeton: Princeton University Press, 1945; 2nd ed. Ann Arbor: Michigan University Press, 1968 [brief biography, together with translations of selected stanzas, with emphasis on *Austrfararvísur*, *Vestrfararvísur*, and *Bersǫglisvísur*]; Campbell, Alistair. *Skaldic Verse and Anglo-Saxon History*. London: Lewis, 1971 [translation of Sighvatr's verses on English topics and discussion of their historical value]; Turville-Petre, E. O. G. *Scaldic Poetry*. Oxford: Clarendon, 1976 [brief biography, with small selection of stanzas and translations]; Whitelock, Dorothy, ed. *English Historical Documents c. 500–1042*. 2nd ed. London and New York: Eyre Methuen; Oxford University Press, 1979 [English translation of Sighvatr's verses on English topics]; Fell, Christine. "*Víkingarvísur*." In *Specvlvm Norroenvm: Norse Studies in Memory of Gabriel Turville-Petre*. Ed. Ursula Dronke et al. Odense: Odense University Press, 1981, pp. 106–22 [text, translation, and discussion of *Víkingarvísur*]. **Lit.**: Finnur Jónsson. *Den oldnorske og oldislandske Litteraturs Historie*. 3 vols. 2nd ed. Copenhagen: Gad, 1920–24 [account of Sighvatr's career and poems]; Vestlund, Alfred. "Om strofernas ursprungliga ordning i Sigvat Tordarsons Bersǫglisvísur." *Arkiv för nordisk filologi* 46 (1929), 281–93 [analysis and rearrangement of stanza order in *Bersǫglisvísur*]; Moberg, Ove. *Olav Haraldsson, Knut den Store och Sverige*. Lund: Gleerup, 1941 [historical account of Sighvatr's verses]; Campbell, Alistair. *Encomium Emmae reginae*. Camden Society Third Series, 72. London: Royal Historical Society, 1949 [historical value of Sighvatr's verses on English topics]; Holtsmark, Anne. "Uppreistarsaga." *Maal og minne* (1958), 93–7 [the theme of betrayal in *Erfidrápa*]; Hallberg, Peter. *Den fornisländska poesien*. Verdandis skriftserie, 20. Stockholm: Bonnier, 1962 [selections, chiefly from *Austrfararvísur*]; Vries, Jan de. *Altnordische Literaturgeschichte*. 2 vols. Grundriss der germanischen Philologie, 15–6. Berlin: de Gruyter, 1941–42; rpt. 1964–67, vol. 1 [general account of Sighvatr's career and compositions]; Bǫðvar Guðmundsson. "Rǫðin á Bersǫglisvísum." *Mímir* 9.1 (1970), 5–8 [reply to Vestlund, urging conservative approach to the prose sources]; Hǫskuldur Þráinsson. "Hendingar í dróttkvæðum hætti hjá Sighvati Þórðarsyni." *Mímir* 9.1 (1970), 9–29 [Sighvatr's practice with *hendingar*]; Frank, Roberta. *Old Norse Court Poetry: The Dróttkvætt Stanza*. Islandica, 42. Ithaca and London: Cornell University Press, 1978 [detailed analyses of selected stanzas from *Austrfararvísur*, the memorial *lausavísur*, and the *Erfidrápa*]; Fidjestøl, Bjarne. *Det norrøne fyrstediket*. Øvre Ervik: Alvheim & Eide, 1982 [discussion of stanza allocation and sequence in the known praise poems].

Russell Poole

[**See also**: Christian Poetry; Commemorative Poetry; Kennings; *Lausavísur*; Óláfr, St.; *Óláfs saga helga*; Óttarr svarti; *Skáld*; Skaldic Meters; Skaldic Verse]

Sigrdrífumál ("The Lay of Sigrdrífa") is preserved in the *Codex Regius* of the *Poetic Edda* (GkS 2365 4to; written in Iceland *ca.* 1270; now in Reykjavik) and in much later paper MSS. It does not constitute a single poem, but is part of a mass of heterogeneous prose and verse concerning "young Sigurðr" that begins with *Reginsmál*, continues through *Fáfnismál*, and ends when *Sigrdrífumal* breaks off in the great lacuna after stanza 29.2. The title is found only in some of the paper MSS. The lacuna resulted from the removal of the fifth of the *Codex Regius*'s originally seven gatherings. Although no copy antedates the loss, the contents of the eight lost leaves can be determined from a 13th-century paraphrase (*Vǫlsunga saga*) in prose, with many verse quotations. This paraphrase confirms the paper MSS that continue the poem through stanza 37.

Introductory prose tells how Sigurðr, fresh from killing the dragon and removing its treasure, rode up to the mountain Hindarfjall, where he saw a great light like a fire. In it was an enclosure of shields, and within that lay a sleeping person in armor. Sigurðr removed the helmet, saw that it was a woman, and cut the chain mail from her body. In narrative verse (*fornyrðislag*, st. 1), she asks who freed her from the dark fetters of sleep, and Sigurðr identifies himself with a reference to the slaying of Fáfnir. In chant meter (*ljóðaháttr*, st. 2), she says that her long sleep was due to Óðinn. Prose: she gave him a drink of mead, the memory cup. *Ljóðaháttr* (sts. 3–4): Her invocation of day and the gods, a blessing on the two of them. Prose with *fornyrðislag* inlay: She was a valkyrie called Sigrdrífa. (The word seems to be an appellative in *Fáfnismál*, st. 44: "the victory-showering one" may be a periphrasis for a valkyrie.) She defied the will of Óðinn, who stabbed her with a sleep-thorn and cursed her so that she would lose her valkyrie powers in marriage, but she swore to marry only a man without fear. *Fornyrðislag* (st. 5): She says she is presenting her interlocutor with beer filled with magical powers for good. *Ljóðaháttr* (sts. 6–13): Sigrdrífa teaches Sigurðr a series of runes, such as "victory runes" and "ale runes," their use, and where they are to be cut. A mixture of charm meter (*galdralag*, a by-form of *ljóðaháttr*) and *fornyrðislag* (sts. 14–19): Cryptic references to the mythological history and use of runes. *Ljóðaháttr* (sts. 20–21): Sigrdrífa asks Sigurðr in a challenging way whether she should speak further; he answers that he has no fear of his fate and will value her "loving advice" as long as he lives. Stanzas 22–37 in *ljóðaháttr* give eleven numbered items of advice and five similar unnumbered expansions or additions; the rules for the conduct of life touch on loyalty, oaths, wisdom, honor, witches, women, drinking, and the dead, among other subjects.

Many conflicting analyses of this material have been argued, but a typical one might distinguish the following components: (1) The remains of a *fornyrðislag* narrative poem specific to Sigurðr that told of the awakening of the valkyrie (st. 1, prose and verse after st. 4, and st. 5). (2) The *ljóðaháttr* poem on runes (sts. 6–13.6) may have been introduced by stanza 8, in which Sigrdrífa offers beer; nothing ties it specifically with Sigurðr. (3) The *ljóðaháttr* poem of ethical advice might have included the beautiful and ancient invocations in stanzas 3–4, the valkyrie's explanation of her sleep (st. 2), the exchange regarding knowledge and fate (sts. 20–21), and the advice stanzas (22–37, perhaps minus interpolations); it is difficult to imagine this poem as separate from the Sigurðr story. (4) Finally, an assortment of bits of wisdom tradition accounts for stanza 13.7–18.

The various elements reflect diverse cultural periods: the invocation stanzas (3–4) are at least modeled on very ancient ritual poetry; some advice may reflect Christian influence (33–34). Although firm datings are impossible, a consensus of contemporary scholarship might assign the rune poem and the advice poem substantially to the 11th century and the *fornyrðislag* narrative to the 12th. *Sigrdrífumál* is an important witness to stages in the story of Sigurðr and Brynhildr. But such questions as the origin of the identification of Brynhildr with Sigrdrífa or of Sigurðr's "prior betrothal" to Brynhildr can only be answered after intricate and hypothetical reconstruction of lost written versions just preceding the preserved monuments. In general, it seems that both a pamphlet of Sigurðr poems and a separate prose saga of Sigurðr must be postulated for about 1200 (see Andersson 1980 for summaries and references).

Ed.: Neckel, Gustav, ed. *Edda: Die Lieder des Codex Regius nebst verwandten Denkmälern. I: Text.* 5th ed. rev. Hans Kuhn. Heidelberg: Winter, 1983. **Tr.**: Hollander, Lee M., trans. *The Poetic Edda, Translated with an Introduction and Explanatory Notes.* 2nd rev. ed. Austin: University of Texas Press, 1962; rpt. 1988, pp. 233–42. **Lit.**: Clarke, D. E. Martin, ed. and trans. *The Hávamál, with Selections from Other Poems of the Edda, Illustrating the Wisdom of the North in Heathen Times.* Cambridge: Cambridge University Press, 1923 [esp. pp. 15–30]; Vries, Jan de. *Altnordische Literaturgeschichte.* 2 vols. Grundriss der germanischen Philologie, 15–6. Berlin: de Gruyter, 1941–42; rpt. 1964–67, vol. 1, pp. 296–9; vol. 2, pp. 525–6 [see also index]; Hallberg, Peter. *Old Icelandic Poetry: Eddic Lay and Skaldic Verse.* Trans. Paul Schach and Sonja Lindgrenson. Lincoln and London: University of Nebraska Press, 1975, pp. 75–7; Andersson, Theodore M. *The Legend of Brynhild.* Islandica, 43. Ithaca and London: Cornell University Press, 1980 [esp. pp. 81–4, 98–102]; Andersson, Theodore M. "The Lays in the Lacuna of Codex Regius." In *Specvlvm Norroenvm: Norse Studies in Memory of Gabriel Turville-Petre.* Ed. Ursula Dronke et al. Odense: Odense University Press, 1981, pp. 6–26; Einar G. Pétursson. "Hvenær týndist kverið úr Konungsbók Eddukvæða?" *Gripla* 6 (1984), 265–91; Harris, Joseph. "Eddic Poetry." In *Old Norse–Icelandic Literature: A Critical Guide.* Ed. Carol J. Clover and John Lindow. Islandica, 45. Ithaca and London: Cornell University Press, 1985, pp. 68–156 [esp. pp. 99, 152].

Joseph Harris

[See also: *Codex Regius*; Eddic Meters; Eddic Poetry; Maiden Warriors; *Reginsmál* and *Fáfnismál*; Volsung-Niflung Cycle; *Volsunga saga*; Women in Eddic Poetry]

Sigrgarðs saga frœkna ("The Saga of Sigrgarðr the Brave") is an anonymous Icelandic *riddarasaga* composed probably in the third quarter of the 15th century, perhaps in Oddi in South Iceland. *Sigrgarðs saga frœkna* thus belongs to the youngest period of the genre, and with a total of more than fifty preserved MSS from the 15th to the beginning of the 20th century, is one of the most heavily transmitted *riddarasögur*. Two cycles of *Rímur af Sigrgarði frœkna* date from the 17th century.

Prince Sigrgarðr from Garðar courts the arrogant maiden-queen Ingigerðr of Taricia, who, along with her two sisters, has been bound in a spell cast by their wicked stepmother, Hlégerðr. Three times he is rejected by Ingigerðr, and returns home in low spirits. On his way home after a second visit, he kills the Viking Knútr, takes on the dead man's shape, and lets the report spread of his own death. He spends the winter with Ingigerðr together with his two men. In the spring, he and his men are sent on a difficult errand. They prevail in fierce fights with animals, giants, and dragons, accomplish the task, and thus break the spell in which the three sisters are bound. Sigrgarðr reassumes his own shape, subdues Ingigerðr, and takes her as his wife.

The thematic relationship between *Sigrgarðs saga frœkna* and the *fornaldarsögur* is so striking that the saga has often been placed in a group of sagas bordering the original *riddarasögur* and the *fornaldarsögur*. Especially characteristic is the stepmother motif with its detailed spell plot. The devices of the spell (*álog*) and the maiden-king (*meykóngr*) determine the narrative structure of the text. Direct loans from *Bósa saga* (two-brother motif) and especially *Viktors saga ok Blávus* are probable. From the latter, *Sigrgarðs saga frœkna* most likely appropriated the bridal-quest story, which makes it possible to date an Icelandic *riddarasaga* with some certainty. *Sigrgarðs saga frœkna* can probably be dated to the time between around 1440 (*Viktors saga*) and the last quarter of the 15th century (the oldest MS of *Sigrgarðs saga*, AM 566a 4to). The saga also includes familiar motifs, such as magic weapons, flying carpets, a guest in the disguise of a merchant, a winter guest, and shape shifting. In one of the central incidents in the saga, the hero and the Viking taunt one another with *níð*, or sexual insults.

Ed.: Einar Þórðarson, ed. *Sagan af Sigrgarði frœkna.* Reykjavik: E. Þórðarson, 1884; Loth, Agnete, ed. "Sigrgarðs saga frœkna." In *Late Medieval Icelandic Romances.* 5 vols. Editiones Arnamagnæanæ, ser. B, vols. 20–4. Copenhagen: Munksgaard, 1962–65, vol. 5, pp. 39–107 [English summary]. **Bib.**: Finnur Sigmundsson. *Rímnatal.* 2 vols. Reykjavik: Rímnafélagið, 1966, vol. 1, pp. 430–2; Kalinke, Marianne E., and P. M. Mitchell. *Bibliography of Old Norse–Icelandic Romances.* Islandica, 44. Ithaca and London: Cornell University Press, 1985, pp. 97–99. **Lit.**: Jiriczek, Otto Luitpolt. "Zur mittelisländischen Volkskunde. Mitteilungen aus ungedruckten Arnamagnäanischen Handschriften." *Zeitschrift für deutsche Philologie* 26 (1893–94), 2–25; Finnur Jónsson. *Den oldnorske og oldislandske Litteraturs Historie.* 3 vols. 2nd ed. Copenhagen: Gad, 1920–24; Leach, Henry Goddard. *Angevin Britain and Scandinavia.* Harvard Studies in Comparative Literature, 6. Cambridge: Harvard University Press; London: Milford; Oxford: Oxford University Press, 1921; rpt. Millwood: Kraus, 1975; Schlauch, Margaret. *Romance in Iceland.* Princeton: Princeton University Press; New York: American-Scandinavian Foundation; London: Allen & Unwin, 1934; rpt. New York: Russell & Russell, 1973; Wahlgren, Erik. *The Maiden King in Iceland.* Chicago: University of Chicago Libraries, 1938 [private publication]; Einar Ól. Sveinsson. "*Viktors saga ok Blávus*: Sources and Characteristics." In *Viktors saga* ok *Blávus*. Ed. Jónas Kristjánsson. Riddarasögur, 2. Reykjavik: Handritastofnun Íslands, 1964, pp. cxxxviii–cxliv; Stefán Einarsson. "Heimili (skólar) fornaldarsagna og riddarasagna." *Skírnir* 140 (1966), 272; Jorgensen, Peter A. "The Icelandic Translations from Middle English." In *Studies for Einar Haugen: Presented by Friends and Colleagues*. Ed. Evelyn Scherabon Firchow *et al*. Janua Linguarum, Series Maior, 59. The Hague and Paris: Mouton, 1972, pp. 305–20; Hermann Pálsson. "Towards a Definition of *Fornaldarsögur*." In *Fourth International Saga Conference München, July 30th–August 4th, 1979*. Munich: Institut für Nordische Philologie der Universität München, 1979, 17 pp. [photocopies of papers distributed to participants]; Buchholz, Peter. *Vorzeitkunde. Mündliches Erzählen und Überliefern im mittelalterlichen Skandinavien nach dem Zeugnis von Fornaldarsaga und eddischer Dichtung*. Skandinavistische Studien, 13. Neumünster: Wachholtz, 1980; Nahl, Astrid van. *Originale Riddarasögur als Teil altnordischer Sagaliteratur*. Texte und Untersuchungen zur Germanistik und Skandinavistik, 3. Frankfurt am Main and Bern: Lang, 1981; Glauser, Jürg. *Isländische Märchensagas: Studien zur Prosaliteratur im spätmittelalterlichen Island*. Beiträge zur nordischen Philologie, 12. Basel and Frankfurt am Main: Helbing & Lichtenhahn, 1983; Bibire, Paul. "From riddarasaga to lygisaga: The Norse Response to Romance." In *Les Sagas de Chevaliers (Riddarasögur). Actes de la Vᵉ Conférence Internationale sur les Sagas . . . (Toulon. Juillet 1982)*. Ed. Régis Boyer. Civilisations, 10. Paris: Presses de l'Université de Paris-Sorbonne, 1985, pp. 55–74 [esp. p. 67]; Kalinke, Marianne E. "Riddarasögur, Fornaldarsögur, and the Problem of Genre. In *Les Sagas de Chevaliers (Riddarasögur)*, pp. 77–91; Kalinke, Marianne. "Norse Romance (*Riddarasögur*)." In *Old Norse–Icelandic Literature: A Critical Guide*. Ed. Carol J. Clover and John Lindow. Islandica, 45. Ithaca and London: Cornell University Press, 1985, pp. 316–63; Kalinke, Marianne E. "The Misogamous Maiden Kings of Icelandic Romance." *Scripta Islandica* 37 (1986), 47–71; Kalinke, Marianne E. *Bridal-Quest Romance in Medieval Iceland*. Islandica, 46. Ithaca and London: Cornell University Press, 1990.

Jürg Glauser

[See also: *Bósa saga ok Herrauðs; Fornaldarsögur; Maiden Warriors; Riddarasögur; Rímur; Viktors saga ok Blávus*]

Sigrgarðs saga ok Valbrands

Sigrgarðs saga ok Valbrands ("The Saga of Sigrgarðr and Valbrandr") is an anonymous Icelandic *riddarasaga*, composed probably in the 15th century, perhaps in Oddi in South Iceland. The transmission of the saga is extremely poor. Of the extant vellum MSS (Stock. Perg. 8vo no. 10, II, III from the 16th century), only two small fragments are preserved; the remaining seventeen MSS are all late paper MSS. In the 17th century, a *rímur* cycle based on the material of the saga came into existence.

The eminent Prince Sigrgarðr of England chases a hind, and is led by it to the dwarf Gestr. Sigrgarðr receives a wonderful harp and gloves from him, and promises in return his firstborn son. Sigrgarðr later marries Princess Florida of Villisvínaland ("wild boar country"), having defeated the wicked Duke Valbrandr in a duel and beaten Florida in harp playing. However, during the wedding night, Sigrgarðr is stabbed and killed by Valbrandr. Later, Valbrandr abducts Sigrgarðr's two sons, killing one of them. Gestr removes the elder son and Florida to safety in England, and trains the boy, named Sigrgarðr like his father, to become a brave knight. At the age of fifteen, he takes revenge on Valbrandr, defeating him with Gestr's help in a furious battle. Valbrandr is tortured to death, and young Sigrgarðr becomes king. At Gestr's advice, he courts

the beautiful Princess Porfila of Ungaria (Hungary?), and takes her as his wife.

Although *Sigrgarðs saga ok Valbrands* contains ancient elements, it is not based on a foreign source, but undoubtedly belongs to the youngest group of the pre-Reformation sagas. In structure and content, there are clear parallels with *Bærings saga* and *Adonias saga*, and influence from *Gibbons saga* is also evident.

The saga represents an adaptation of a rich corpus of international narrative patterns. For the extensive first part and the short third part of the saga, the bridal-quest theme constitutes the plot. Several common motifs of the narrative literature of medieval Europe, such as the chase of the hind (*Placidas*), the meeting with the dwarf, the magic instrument, the test of the suitor, and the magic flute, determine the fairy-tale-like character of *Sigrgarðs saga ok Valbrands*. The emphasis placed upon the courtly aspect is striking. In addition, an unusually distinctive narrator comments upon the events, divides his sympathy among the characters, sides with the hero, and curses the wicked Valbrandr.

Ed.: Loth, Agnete, ed. "Sigrgarðs saga ok Valbrands." In *Late Medieval Icelandic Romances*. 5 vols. Editiones Arnamagnæanæ, ser. B, vols. 20–4. Copenhagen: Munksgaard, 1962–65, vol. 5, pp. 109–94 [English summary]. **Bib.**: Finnur Sigmundsson. *Rímnatal*. 2 vols. Reykjavik: Rímnafélagið, 1966, vol. 1, p. 432; Kalinke, Marianne E., and P. M. Mitchell. *Bibliography of Old Norse–Icelandic Romances*. Islandica, 44. Ithaca and London: Cornell University Press, 1985, pp. 99–100. **Lit.**: Schlauch, Margaret. *Romance in Iceland*. Princeton: Princeton University Press; New York: American-Scandinavian Foundation; London: Allen & Unwin, 1934; rpt. New York: Russell & Russell, 1973; Wahlgren, Erik. "Quinatus, Porfila, and Sigurðr." *Scandinavian Studies* 18 (1944–45), 195–201; Stefán Einarsson. "Heimili (skólar) fornaldarsagna og riddarasagna." *Skírnir* 140 (1966), 272; Togeby, Knud. "L'influence de la littérature française sur les littératures scandinaves au moyen âge." In *Généralités*. Ed. Hans Ulrich Gumbrecht. Grundriss der romanischen Literaturen des Mittelalters, 1. Heidelberg: Winter, 1972, vol. 1, pp. 333–95 [esp. p. 383]; Nahl, Astrid van. *Originale Riddarasögur als Teil altnordischer Sagaliteratur*. Texte und Untersuchungen zur Germanistik und Skandinavistik, 3. Frankfurt am Main and Bern: Lang, 1981; Glauser, Jürg. *Isländische Märchensagas: Studien zur Prosaliteratur im spätmittelalterlichen Island*. Beiträge zur nordischen Philologie, 12. Basel and Frankfurt am Main: Helbing & Lichtenhahn, 1983; Bibire, Paul. "From riddarasaga to lygisaga: The Norse Response to Romance." In *Les Sagas de Chevaliers (Riddarasögur). Actes de la Vᵉ Conférence Internationale sur les Sagas . . . (Toulon. Juillet 1982)*. Ed. Régis Boyer. Civilisations, 10. Paris: Presses de l'Université de Paris-Sorbonne, 1985, pp. 55–74 [esp. p. 66]; Kalinke, Marianne E. *Bridal-Quest Romance in Medieval Iceland*. Islandica, 46. Ithaca and London: Cornell University Press, 1990.

Jürg Glauser

[See also: *Adonias saga; Bærings saga; Gibbons saga; Riddarasögur; Rímur*]

Sigurðar saga fóts ok Ásmundar húnakongs

Sigurðar saga fóts ok Ásmundar húnakongs ("The Saga of Sigurðr Foot and Ásmundr King of the Huns") was composed in Iceland, presumably in the 14th century. This short saga is preserved in over forty MSS and fragments, but only one vellum, Stock. Perg. fol. no. 7, dating from the late 15th century.

King Knútr of Sjólond has a beautiful daughter named Signý. The young King Ásmundr of Húnaland is unmarried. His retainers jestingly suggest that the lack of a suitable wife impairs his honor, and Signý is mentioned as a wife who would be to his credit. Ásmundr presents his suit to Signý, who, although favorably disposed toward Ásmundr, is loath to accept in her father's absence. Not content with such an answer, Ásmundr declares himself betrothed to Signý. Meanwhile, King Knútr has met the fleet-of-foot Sigurðr fótr, king of Valland, who has asked for and been granted his daughter's hand. At the wedding, Ásmundr and one of his men abduct the bride, not entirely against her will. All attempts at a settlement fail, Sigurðr refusing to accept anything short of Signý. The kings meet in single combat. Although defeated, Sigurðr once more refuses a settlement, and Ásmundr agrees to give up Signý. Signý and Sigurðr are married, and he and Ásmundr become sworn brothers.

Ásmundr now turns his attention to Elena, daughter of King Hrólfr of Ireland. Hrólfr considers Ásmundr unworthy of his daughter, and will not hear of the union. Ásmundr challenges the Irish to battle, but is badly defeated. In a dream, Signý sees what has befallen Ásmundr and urges Sigurðr to go to his aid. He and his men sail to Ireland and defeat Hrólfr. Unknown to them, Ásmundr has been released by Elena. King Hrólfr is spared at Elena's request, in return for which he agrees to the marriage.

Sigurðar saga fóts is generally classed as a *riddarasaga*, presumably on the grounds that the action takes place outside Scandinavia. It has, however, more in common with the *fornaldarsögur*: the names are all Nordic, and although the setting is not Scandinavia proper, it is limited to the Viking North Sea area. There is also a complete absence of the magic stones and other marvelous objects much favored by *riddarasögur* authors; and although the two heroes meet in single combat, there is no tournament, otherwise *de rigueur* in the *riddarasögur*. There is, in any case, no clearcut distinction between the two, the present saga being one of the four or five often cited as borderline cases.

A few scholars have seen a correspondence between the saga and the Middle High German *Kudrun*, a view rejected by Liestøl (1933), who argues that the saga is not a firsthand treatment of the Hilde-Gudrun theme, but rather draws heavily on a number of *fornaldarsögur*, in particular *Hrólfs saga Gautrekssonar* and *Ásmundar saga kappabana*.

For this type of saga, critical opinion has been unusually favorable, Liestøl (1933) calling it one of the best and Jackson (1931) the most readable of its kind. This favor is no doubt due to its brevity and its similarity to the more "respectable" (because more "native") *fornaldarsögur*. The narrative is uncluttered by superfluous characters and motifs and written in a straightforward, if somewhat uninspired, style.

Ed.: Jackson, J. H., ed. "Sigurthar saga fóts ok Ásmundar Húnakongs." *Publications of the Modern Language Association* 46 (1931), 988–1006; Loth, Agnete, ed. "Sigurðar saga fóts." In *Late Medieval Icelandic Romances*. 5 vols. Editiones Arnamagnæanæ, ser. B, vols. 20–4. Copenhagen: Munksgaard, 1962–65, vol. 3, pp. 231–50. **Tr.**: Fellows-Jensen, Gillian. In *Late Medieval Icelandic Romances*, vol. 3, pp. 233–50 [English summary]. **Bib.**: Kalinke, Marianne E., and P. M. Mitchell. *Bibliography of Old Norse–Icelandic Romances*. Islandica, 44. Ithaca and London: Cornell University Press, 1985, pp. 100–1. **Lit.**: Liestøl, Knut. "Det litterære grunnlaget for Sigurðar saga fóts ok Ásmundar húnakóngs." In *Festskrift til Halvdan Koht på sekstiårsdagen 7de juli 1933*. Oslo: Aschehoug, 1933, pp. 154–8; Glauser, Jürg. *Isländische Märchensagas: Studien zur Prosaliteratur im spätmittelalterlichen Island*. Beiträge zur nordischen Philologie, 12. Basel and Frankfurt am Main: Helbing & Lichtenhahn, 1983.

M. J. Driscoll

[See also: *Ásmundar saga kappabana*; *Fornaldarsögur*; *Hrólfs saga Gautrekssonar*; *Riddarasögur*]

Sigurðar saga turnara ("The Saga of Sigurðr the Jouster"), was composed in Iceland, probably in the 14th century, and survives in thirty MSS and fragments. The oldest of these is Stock. Perg. fol. no. 7, dating from the second half of the 15th century, in which the saga is defective. Two early paper MSS, AM 585d 4to (1691) and AM 122 8vo (*ca.* 1700), preserve the saga in full.

Sigurðr, son of Vilhjálmr, king of France, having by the age of twelve surpassed all others at book learning and knightly pursuits, travels abroad in search of adventure. In Greece, he disguises his identity and offers his services to King Valdimarr in return for winter lodging. Count Hermóðr of Spain arrives and challenges the king and his men to a tournament. After initially professing his ignorance of the sport, Sigurðr goes on to distinguish himself, defeating Hermóðr and routing his army. During the tournament, Sigurðr notices a beautiful veiled woman watching from a tower, whom he suspects is the king's daughter. Through his skill at climbing and picking locks, Sigurðr gains access to the tower, and there follows an extended liaison between the two, during which Sigurðr reveals his true identity to the princess.

Having overextended himself financially through his generosity, Sigurðr is obliged to seek a loan from Þrándr, the king's adviser and a cunning and wicked man. He reveals the secret of his liaison with the princess to Þrándr, who betrays him to the king. Sigurðr escapes capture in the princess's bedchamber on three consecutive nights, first by hiding in a hollow seat, next by hiding in a secret place under the bed, and finally by standing with arms outstretched in front of a life-sized crucifix over the bed. Sigurðr is then asked to relate his exploits to Þrándr's "parents," realizing too late that the "father" is really the king himself. Sigurðr kills Þrándr and forces the king to allow the marriage, which he does gladly once Sigurðr has revealed his true identity. The wedding takes place, and Sigurðr becomes king of both countries.

The plot of *Sigurðar saga turnara*, like those of most *riddarasögur*, is composed of conventional motifs and episodes borrowed from a wide variety of sources, native and foreign. Thus, although initially described in terms befitting a perfect knight, Sigurðr becomes in battle the archetypal Viking hero, while in his dealings with the king's daughter taking on characteristics commonly associated with the figure of the trickster in medieval legend. Schlauch (1934) recognized in the saga a general indebtedness to the *fabliaux*. Spaulding (1982) suggests that a 12th-century *fabliau*, *Du prestre crucifie*, could have provided a source for the crucifix incident in *Sigurðar saga*. Similarly, Sigurðr's escapes from detection in the princess's bedchamber are reminiscent of, and may be based on, the *sjávarlopt* episodes told by King Haraldr harðráði ("hard-ruler") Sigurðarson and Þorsteinn Ásmundarson in *Grettis saga*.

Despite this eclecticism, *Sigurðar saga turnara* functions well as a literary work: it is a good story, well told. Both style and plot are straightforward and free of rhetorical elaboration.

Ed.: Loth, Agnete, ed. "Sigurðar saga turnara." In *Late Medieval Icelandic Romances*. 5 vols. Editiones Arnamagnæanæ, ser. B, vols. 20–4. Copenhagen: Munksgaard, 1962–65, vol. 5, pp. 195–232; Spaulding, Janet Ardis. "Sigurdur [sic] saga turnara: A Literary Edition." Diss. University of Michigan, 1982. **Tr.**: Fellows-Jensen, Gillian. In *Late Medieval Icelandic Romances*, vol. 5, pp. 197–232 [English summary]. **Bib.**: Kalinke, Marianne E., and P. M. Mitchell. *Bibliography of Old Norse–Icelandic Romances*. Islandica, 44. Ithaca and London: Cornell

University Press, 1985, pp. 101–2. **Lit.**: Schlauch, Margaret. *Romance in Iceland*. Princeton: Princeton University Press; New York: American-Scandinavian Foundation; London: Allen & Unwin, 1934; rpt. New York: Russell & Russell, 1973; Einar Ól. Sveinsson. "*Viktors saga ok Blávus*: Sources and Characteristics." In *Viktors saga ok Blávus*. Ed. Jónas Kristjánsson. Riddarasögur, 2. Reykjavik: Handritastofnun Íslands, 1964; Glauser, Jürg. *Isländische Märchensagas: Studien zur Prosaliteratur im spätmittelalterlichen Island*. Beiträge zur nordischen Philologie, 12. Basel and Frankfurt am Main: Helbing & Lichtenhahn, 1983; Kalinke, Marianne. "Norse Romance (*Riddarasögur*)." In *Old Norse–Icelandic Literature: A Critical Guide*. Ed. Carol J. Clover and John Lindow. Islandica, 45. Ithaca and London: Cornell University Press, 1985, pp. 316–63.

M. J. Driscoll

[**See also:** *Grettis saga*; *Riddarasögur*]

Sigurðar saga þogla ("The Saga of Sigurðr the Silent"), a *riddarasaga* composed in Iceland in the 14th century, relates the tale of Seditíána, daughter of King Flóres and Queen Blankiflúr of France, who refuses all suitors and, having succeeded her father to the throne, insists on being called king. Her hand is sought by Hálfdan, Sigurðr's brother, whom she humiliates. Sigurðr has an unpromising youth; he is still unable to speak at age seven, hence his sobriquet "the silent." But under the tutelage of his foster-father, Count Lafranz of Lixion, he becomes a paragon of medieval masculinity. Following a series of adventures, he succeeds, with help from the supernatural, in chastising Seditíána and winning her for himself.

The saga is one of a number of native romances dealing with the theme of the "maiden-king," a popular subgenre of the bridal-quest narrative. Added to the basic plot are names, objects, topoi, and entire episodes freely borrowed from other sources. The acquisition of a grateful lion, for example, is a motif present in other *riddarasögur* (and elsewhere), but which derives ultimately from Chrétien de Troyes. In addition, *Sigurðar saga* can be shown to have borrowed directly from, or been influenced by, the following sagas: *Flóres saga ok Blankiflúr*, *Klári saga*, *Bevis saga*, *Viktors saga ok Blávus*, and *Gibbons saga*. The list could be extended. The prologue, a kind of apologia for the romances, is also found in two MSS of *Gongu-Hrólfs saga*, but cannot be shown to be more original there. This extraneous material is for the most part carefully woven into the plot and is seldom perfunctory. Moreover, much of it is characterized by a humor not found in other sources.

The saga's popularity is attested by sixty MSS and fragments, the majority paper from the 18th and 19th centuries. There are two early vellums, AM 152 fol., dating from the early 16th century, which preserves the saga in its entirety, and the fragmentary AM 596 4to, comprising two separate fragments, the first from the middle of the second half of the 14th century, the second somewhat later. AM 596 4to preserves a version of the saga substantially different from the other MSS, shorter by several episodes and differing in a number of incidental details, but differing also from AM 152 fol. and related MSS in terms of style. All extant paper MSS stem from AM 152 fol., while AM 596 fol. (or a MS closely related to it) clearly formed the basis for the *Sigurðar rímur þogla*, composed probably in the 14th century and preserved in four MSS. While Björn K. Þórólfsson (1934) argued that the longer version must be the more original, the opposite conclusion was reached by Einar Ól. Sveinsson (1964). A comparison of the two texts indicates that neither, as preserved, can be the source of the other, for while AM 152 fol. and related MSS contain material not

found in AM 596 fol., the wording of AM 596 fol. is consistently more elaborate. Rather, both appear to derive from a common source, AM 152 fol. showing evidence of material amplification, AM 596 fol. of rhetorical amplification.

The style of *Sigurðar saga* is not as far removed from that of the *Íslendingasögur* as some critics have suggested. On the whole, the saga shows few characteristics of the "courtly style" commonly associated with the romances.

Ed.: Einar Þórðarson, ed. *Sagan af Sigurði þogula*. Reykjavik: E. Þórðarson, 1883; Bjarni Vilhjálmsson, ed. "Sigurðar saga þogla." In *Riddarasögur*. 6 vols. Reykjavik: Íslendingasagnaútgáfan; Haukadalsútgáfan, 1949–54, vol. 3, pp. 95–267; Loth, Agnete, ed. "Sigurðar saga þogla." In *Late Medieval Icelandic Romances*. 5 vols. Editiones Arnamagnæanæ, ser. B, vols. 20–4. Copenhagen: Munksgaard, 1962–65, vol. 2, pp. 93–259; Driscoll, M. J, ed. *Sigurðar saga þogla: The Shorter Redaction*. [forthcoming]. **Tr.**: Dodsworth, J. B. In *Late Medieval Icelandic Romances*, vol. 2, pp. 95–259 [English summary]. **Bib.**: Kalinke, Marianne E., and P. M. Mitchell. *Bibliography of Old Norse–Icelandic Romances*. Islandica, 44. Ithaca and London: Cornell University Press, 1985, pp. 102–5. **Lit.**: Björn K. Þórólfsson. *Rímur fyrir 1600*. Safn Fræðafjelagsins um Ísland og Íslendinga, 9. Copenhagen: Møller, 1934; Schlauch, Margaret. *Romance in Iceland*. Princeton: Princeton University Press; New York: American-Scandinavian Foundation; London: Allen & Unwin; 1934; rpt. New York: Russell & Russell, 1973; Wahlgren, Erik. *The Maiden King in Iceland*. Chicago: Chicago University Libraries, 1938 [private publication]; Einar Ól. Sveinsson. "*Viktors saga ok Blávus*: Sources and Characteristics." In *Viktors saga ok Blávus*. Ed. Jónas Kristjánsson. Riddarasögur, 2. Reykjavik: Handritastofnun Íslands, 1964, pp. cix–ccviii; Harris, Richard L. "The Lion-Knight Legend in Iceland and the Valþjófsstaðir Door." *Viator* 1 (1970), 125–45; Glauser, Jürg. *Isländische Märchensagas: Studien zur Prosaliteratur im spätmittelalterlichen Island*. Beiträge zur nordischen Philologie, 12. Basel and Frankfurt am Main: Helbing & Lichtenhahn, 1983; Kalinke, Marianne E. "Norse Romance (*Riddarasögur*)." In *Old Norse–Icelandic Literature: A Critical Guide*. Ed. Carol J. Clover and John Lindow. Islandica, 45. Ithaca and London: Cornell University Press, 1985; Kalinke, Marianne E. "The Misogamous Maiden Kings of Icelandic Romance." *Scripta Islandica* 37 (1986), 47–71.

M. J. Driscoll

[**See also:** *Bevis saga*; *Flóres saga ok Blankiflúr*; *Gibbons saga*; *Gongu-Hrólfs saga*; *Klári (Clári) saga*; *Riddarasögur*; *Viktors saga ok Blávus*]

Sigurðar þáttr Hranasonar *see* **Þinga saga**

Sigurðardrápa *see* **Einarr Skúlason**

Sigurðarkviða in skamma ("The Short Lay of Sigurðr") is an anonymous poem in the *Poetic Edda* comprising seventy-one stanzas in *fornyrðislag* meter. Despite its name, *Sigurðarkviða in skamma* is one of the longest eddic poems: the term "short" distinguishes it from a lost *Sigurðarkviða in meiri* ("The Long Lay of Sigurðr"), which occupied much of the lost fifth gathering of *Codex Regius*, the chief MS of the *Edda*. Since the third Sigurðr poem in the *Edda* (*Brot af Sigurðarkviðu*) also fell partly into the lost gathering, the short lay is the only complete extant Norse poem on Sigurðr's death. Unfortunately for our knowledge of Germanic legend, it is also probably the latest, and abbreviates its narrative by skipping over the older central parts of the story.

The poem begins with a sketchy account of Sigurðr's arrival at the court of Gjúki, his sworn brotherhood with Gjúki's sons Gunnarr and Hǫgni, and his assisting Gunnarr in wooing Brynhildr. It continues with Brynhildr's determination to see Sigurðr dead. In other sources, Brynhildr is jealous of Sigurðr's wife, Guðrún, because Sigurðr is a preeminent hero, or angered at the deceit by which Sigurðr helped Gunnarr win her hand, or intent on vengeance because Sigurðr promised to marry her but then jilted her. In the short lay, Brynhildr's motive is unstated, but appears to be jealousy and/or unrequited love. Brynhildr threatens to leave Gunnarr if he does not kill Sigurðr; Hǫgni resists the idea, then agrees and suggests they incite their youngest brother, Guttormr, to kill Sigurðr, since he has sworn no oaths of brotherhood with him. Guttormr kills Sigurðr in his bed, the Scandinavian version of Sigurðr's death; in German versions, he is killed in the forest. But Sigurðr is able to kill Guttormr and comfort Guðrún before he dies. When Brynhildr hears Guðrún weeping, she laughs feverishly and begins to remind Gunnarr how he, Hǫgni, and Sigurðr all deceived her when she married Gunnarr. She prepares to commit suicide, invites her servants to share her funeral pyre, and prophesies the future troubles of Gunnarr, Guðrún, and Sigurðr's daughter, Svanhildr. Gunnarr will fall in love with Brynhildr's sister, Oddrún, but her brother, Atli (Attila), will kill Gunnarr in a snake pit, whereupon Guðrún will kill Atli. She will then be carried across the sea, where she will bear a son to the king Jǫrmunrekkr (Ermanaric), and Svanhildr will be murdered by her stepfather. Finally, Brynhildr requests that Gunnarr build one pyre for Brynhildr and Sigurðr to share, as they had shared a bed long ago.

The concentration on Brynhildr's psychology, the allusive account of the basic story, the broad and detailed narrative of Brynhildr's death, and the fascination with prophecy all suggest that the short lay is one of the later eddic poems, as do many lines that the poet appears to have borrowed from other eddic poems. From these borrowings, we can probably date *Sigurðarkviða in skamma* between 1200 and 1250. In style, the poem often seems inferior, with strained images and empty phrases needed to fill out the verses; some images, however, notably those of Guðrún awakening drenched in blood, and of Brynhildr and Sigurðr together on the pyre, are among the most vivid in the Sigurðr-Brynhildr legend.

Ed.: Neckel, Gustav, ed. *Edda: Die Lieder des Codex Regius nebst verwandten Denkmälern. I: Text.* 5th ed. rev. Hans Kuhn. Heidelberg: Winter, 1983. **Tr.**: Hollander, Lee M., trans. *The Poetic Edda, Translated with an Introduction and Explanatory Notes.* 2nd rev. ed. Austin: University of Texas Press, 1962; rpt. 1988. **Lit.**: Finnur Jónsson. *Den oldnorske og oldislandske Litteraturs Historie.* 3 vols. 2nd ed. Copenhagen: Gad, 1920–24, vol. 1, pp. 291–2; Vries, Jan de. "Het korte Sigurdlied." *Mededeelingen der Koninklijke Nederlandsche Akademie van Wetenschappen.* Afd. Letterkunde, N.R., 2 (1939), no. 11, pp. 1–75 (367–441); Vries, Jan de. *Altnordische Literaturgeschichte.* 2 vols. Grundriss der germanischen Philologie, 15–6. Berlin: de Gruyter, 1941–42, vol. 2, p. 155; rpt. 1964–67, vol. 2, pp. 147–50; See, Klaus von. "Die Werbung um Brünhild." *Zeitschrift für deutsches Altertum und deutsche Literatur* 88 (1957), 1–20; rpt. in his *Edda, Saga, Skaldendichtung: Aufsätze zur skandinavischen Literatur des Mittelalters.* Heidelberg: Winter, 1981, pp. 194–213; Andersson, Theodore M. *The Legend of Brynhild.* Islandica, 43. Ithaca and London: Cornell University Press, 1980, ch. 1 [esp. pp. 29–36]; Sperberg-McQueen, C. Michael. "The Legendary Form of *Sigurðarkviða in Skamma.*" *Arkiv för nordisk filologi* 100 (1986), 16–40.

C. M. Sperberg-McQueen

[**See also:** *Codex Regius*; Eddic Meters; Eddic Poetry; *Sigurðarkviðu, Brot af*; Vǫlsung-Niflung Cycle]

Sigurðarkviðu, Brot af ("Fragment of a Sigurðr Lay"), also called "Sigurðarkviða in forna" ("The Old Lay of Sigurðr"), is an anonymous heroic poem in the *Poetic Edda*, of which nineteen stanzas in *fornyrðislag* meter are preserved. Part of the poem (thirty stanzas?) was lost in the missing fifth gathering of the MS *Codex Regius*; hence the conventional name.

Brot af Sigurðarkviðu provides our earliest northern version of the Sigurðr-Brynhildr legend; by comparing it with the 13th-century *Vǫlsunga saga*, which paraphrases the *Edda*, we can reconstruct the rough contents of the missing parts as well as those of other poems lost in the lacuna of *Codex Regius*, notably the long, detailed **Sigurðarkviða in meiri* ("The Long Lay of Sigurðr").

The untruncated *Brot af Sigurðarkviðu* evidently told how Sigurðr arrives at the court of Gjúki, swears blood-brotherhood with Gjúki's son Gunnarr, and marries Gjúki's daughter, Guðrún. He helps Gunnarr woo the "shield-maiden" Brynhildr, who has vowed to marry the hero who can ride to her through the undying flames surrounding her hall. Gunnarr's horse balks, and Sigurðr and Gunnarr exchange external appearances so that Sigurðr can ride the flames and marry Brynhildr as Gunnarr's proxy. He does so, but places a sword between Brynhildr and himself on the bridal bed.

Years later, in anger, Guðrún reveals the deception to Brynhildr. Brynhildr is desolate. She tells Gunnarr that Sigurðr betrayed him and consummated their marriage. Brynhildr refuses "to have two husbands in one hall"; she, Sigurðr, or Gunnarr must die. Gunnarr confers with his brother Hǫgni.

Here the fragment begins. Told that Sigurðr must die, Hǫgni surmises that Brynhildr has incited the murder out of jealousy of Guðrún. With wolf and snake meat, Gunnarr and Hǫgni embolden their brother, Guttormr, who kills Sigurðr. When they return, Guðrún asks after Sigurðr; Hǫgni tells her they have cut him down and that his horse now mourns over his head. Brynhildr congratulates them and laughs loudly; Guðrún predicts vengeance for Sigurðr's death. In a flashback, the poet announces that Sigurðr was killed "south of the Rhine" and that a raven cried out that Atli (Attila) would avenge the brothers' broken oaths to Sigurðr. The forest murder follows the German form of the legend and suggests a German or Danish source.

That night, Gunnarr lies awake, tormented by the memory of the raven's cry. Brynhildr awakens weeping just before day, telling a dream of Gunnarr riding fettered among his enemies. She then reveals the truth: Sigurðr did not consummate the marriage with her at all, so Gunnarr, not Sigurðr, has betrayed his oaths.

The poem breaks off abruptly here; it once probably continued with an account of Brynhildr's death, omitted from *Codex Regius* because the following poems (notably *Sigurðarkviða in skamma*) told the story more fully.

Brot af Sigurðarkviðu combines the terse, dramatic narrative style of the oldest Germanic heroic lays with motifs reminiscent of ballads and late eddic poetry, such as the raven's prophecy, the warning dreams, and the image of Grani mourning over Sigurðr's body. Like *Sigurðarkviða in skamma*, it shows more interest in Brynhildr than in Sigurðr; this emphasis may reflect continental influence. Some lines show the metrical light line filling of late eddic poetry. Datings range from the 10th to the 12th century; 1100 to 1150 seems plausible for the poem as we have it.

Ed.: Boer, R. C., ed. *Die Edda mit historisch-kritischem Commentar.* 2 vols. Haarlem: Tjeenk Willink, 1922; Sijmons, B., and H. Gering, eds. *Die Lieder der Edda.* 3 vols. Germanistiche Handbibliothek, 7.1–5. Halle: Waisenhaus, 1903–31; Neckel, Gustav, ed. *Edda: Die Lieder des Codex Regius nebst verwandten Denkmälern. I: Text.* 5th ed. rev. Hans Kuhn. Heidelberg: Winter, 1983. **Tr.**: Hollander, Lee M., trans. *The Poetic Edda, Translated with an Introduction and Explanatory Notes.* 2nd rev. ed. Austin: University of Texas Press, 1962; rpt. 1988. **Lit.**: Heusler, Andreas. "Die Lieder der Lücke im Codex Regius der Edda." In *Germanistische Abhandlungen Hermann Paul zum 17. märz 1902 dargebracht.* Ed. Friedrich von der Leyen *et al.* Strassbourg: Trübner, 1902, pp. 1–98; rpt. in his *Kleine Schriften.* 2 vols. Ed. Stefan Sonderegger. Berlin: de Gruyter, 1969, vol. 2, pp. 223–91; Vries, Jan de. *Altnordische Literaturgeschichte.* 2 vols. Grundriss der germanischen Philologie, 15–6. Berlin: de Gruyter, 1941–42; rpt. 1964–67, vol. 2, pp. 299–303; See, Klaus von. "Die Werbung um Brünhild." *Zeitschrift für deutsches Altertum und deutsche Literatur* 88 (1957–58), 1–20; rpt. in his *Edda, Saga, Skaldendichtung: Aufsätze zur skandinavischen Literatur des Mittelalters.* Heidelberg: Winter, 1981, pp. 194–213; See, Klaus von. "Freierprobe und Königinnenzank in der Sigfridsage." *Zeitschrift für deutsches Altertum und deutsche Literatur* 89 (1959), 163–72; rpt. in his *Edda, Saga, Skaldendichtung,* pp. 214–23; Andersson, Theodore M. *The Legend of Brynhild.* Islandica, 43. Ithaca and London: Cornell University Press, 1980 [esp. ch. 1]; Andersson, Theodore M. "The Lays in the Lacuna of *Codex Regius.*" In *Specvlvm Norroenvm: Norse Studies in Memory of Gabriel Turville-Petre.* Ed. Ursula Dronke *et al.* Odense: Odense University Press, 1981, pp. 6–26.

C. M. Sperberg-McQueen

[**See also**: *Codex Regius*; Eddic Meters; Eddic Poetry; *Sigurðarkviða in skamma*; Vǫlsung-Niflung Cycle; *Vǫlsunga saga*]

Sigurðr *see* Vǫlsung-Niflung Cycle

Sju vise mästare

Sju vise mästare ("Seven Wise Masters") exists in three different versions in Old Swedish, one (A) approximately from 1350–1400, the other two (B and C) probably somewhat younger. The translators are unknown. The texts, all complete, are preserved in Cod. Holm. D 4 (from *ca.* 1420), Cod. Holm. A 49 (from *ca.* 1450), and Cod. AM. 191 fol. (before 1492), respectively. A and B belong to the same group, but C differs, the original presumably being Low German. A Latin text, Cod. Ups. C 7, to which A and B are closely related, was edited by Blomquist (1941: 265–92).

Sju vise mästare is a collection of diminutive tales with some similarity both to *The Thousand and One Nights* and Boccaccio's *Decameron.* Originating in India, the collection spread to Europe. It was divided into three main versions and an abundance of subgroups, one of them existing *inter alia* in *Historia septem sapientium Romæ* and in *Sju vise mästare.*

The tales are unified within a frame story. The son of the emperor of Rome has rejected his stepmother's allurements (*cf.* Joseph and Potiphar's wife). She accuses him of attempted rape and repeatedly calls upon the emperor to have him executed. Each time, the young man is saved by one of the seven wise men who have brought him up and educated him. Both the empress and the wise men try to persuade the emperor by telling him appropriate stories. In the end, the young man is exonerated, and the empress condemned to death.

The fact that the text was translated into Old Swedish at least three times shows that it must have been as popular in Sweden as it was in the rest of Europe, even something of a bestseller. The reason might be that some of the stories are a bit dramatic, while others have comic details, and one or two touch upon sexual matters.

The description of individuals is primitive, schematic, and unrealistic. The author's capability for variation is limited, and the reactions of his characters stereotyped.

Language and style, especially those of text A, have been praised for simplicity and freshness. However, there are also examples of latinisms common to most Old Swedish translations from Latin, *e.g.*, present participles with a direct object (such as *Tha negh sonen honom einkte swarande,* literally "Then bowed the son him nothing answering") and *hwiliker* 'who' as a relative pronoun.

Ed.: Klemming, G. E., ed. *Sju vise mästare.* In *Prosadikter från Sveriges medeltid.* Samlingar utgifna av Svenska fornskrift-sällskapet, 28. Stockholm: Norstedt, 1887–89, pp. 111–246; Noreen, Erik, ed. "Ur *Sju vise mästare.*" In *Fornsvensk läsebok.* 2nd ed. rev. Sven Benson. Lund: Gleerup, 1954, pp. 95–9 [presents one short story]. **Lit.**: Campbell, Killis. *A Study of the Romance of the Seven Sages.* Baltimore: Modern Language Association of America, 1898; Noreen, Erik. "Om 'Sju vise mästare' på fornsvenska." *Samlaren* 35 (1914), 67–70; Blomqvist, Gunnar. *Schacktavelslek och Sju vise mästare. De ludo scaccorum, De septem sapientibus. Studier i medeltidens litteraturhistoria.* Stockholm: Geber, 1941; Ståhle, Carl Ivar. "Sju vise mästare." In *Ny illustrerad svensk litteraturhistoria.* Ed. E. N. Tigerstedt. Stockholm: Natur och Kultur, 1955, vol. 1, pp. 112–3.

Gösta Holm

Skáld is the main Old Norse word for a poet. *Greppr* 'man' also occurs, but only infrequently in verse in this specific sense. *Skáld* presumably referred, as it does in modern Icelandic, to any kind of poet. But since nothing is directly known about the authorship of eddic poems or the contexts in which they were composed, it is only possible to speak about the makers of skaldic verse, and this is the normal usage of the loanword "skald/scald" in modern English, and of German *Skald(e)* and Scandinavian *sk(j)ald.*

Insight into the role of the skald can be gained from various sources: the verses themselves, the prose narratives involving skalds, and the laws, which, however, are concerned only with poetry as a medium for libel or illicit protestations of love. The *lausavísur,* or occasional verses, are obviously promising sources, since they are supposedly extemporized comments on battles, sea voyages, love affairs, or other situations in which the skald was personally involved, although the authenticity of some, especially those quoted in *Íslendingasögur,* may be questioned. But the more extended and "official" *drápur* and *flokkar,* which eulogize the deeds of others, also contain hints about the skalds' art and status. It is indeed a proud and highly self-conscious art. The skalds attributed its genesis to the god Óðinn, producing fascinating elaborations of the myth of the "mead of poetry." They counted one of their predecessors, Bragi Boddason, among the gods; and they frequently punctuated their poems with exuberant references to the composition and performance of verse (for which Kreutzer 1977 is an invaluable source). The importance of verse making is also publicly affirmed by the considerable number of nicknames that refer to it, among them Þórarinn loftunga ("praise-tongue") and Auðun illskælda ("bad-poet, ?plagiarist").

In addition to producing verbal art, the skalds became the subject of it in brief anecdotes and fuller, detachable *þættir,* which are preserved in versions of the *konungasögur*. These anecdotes and *þættir* are especially numerous in the sagas of Magnús góði ("the good") and Haraldr Sigurðarson in such MSS as *Morkinskinna* and *Hulda-Hrokkinskinna*. Moreover, there are six complete sagas of skalds (*skáldasögur*): *Egils saga Skalla-Grímssonar*, *Gunnlaugs saga ormstungu*, *Kormáks saga*, *Hallfreðar saga*, *Fóstbrœðra saga* (the skald is one of the two foster-brothers, Þormóðr Kolbrúnarskáld), and *Bjarnar saga Hítdœlakappa* (Bjǫrn's rival Þórðr Kolbeinsson). Some of these sagas are counted among the earliest of the *Íslendingasögur*. A now-lost saga of Ormr Barreyjarskáld appears to have existed in some form by 1119, for a reading of it is among the entertainments at the wedding of Reykjahólar recorded for that year in *Þorgils saga ok Hafliða* (ch. 10). There is also the *Skálda saga*, from the mid-13th century at the earliest, whose heroes are highly fictionalized versions of three skalds of Haraldr hárfagri ("fair-hair").

The dynamic of these prose narratives depends partly on the power of poetry itself. Egill Skalla-Grímsson in his saga assuages the wrath of King Eiríkr blóðøx ("blood-axe") by means of the panegyric *Hǫfuðlausn* ("Head-ransom"); he pours out and purges his angry grief at the deaths of his sons in *Sonatorrek* ("Cruel Loss of Sons"). The *níð*, or verse slander, of Þorleifr jarlsskáld ("earl's skald") is, according to the *þáttr* about him, so potent that Hákon jarl Sigurðarson equips an assassin with magical powers and sends him to Iceland to do away with the poet. However, there is also an evident fascination with the figure of the poet himself, whose frequently awkward, even turbulent, temperament can produce interesting confrontations with royal patrons or neighbors at home in Iceland. Hallfreðr is given his nickname *vandræðaskáld* ("troublesome-poet") by King Ólafr Tryggvason in memory of his anguished conversion from paganism to Christianity. The principal theme of the *skáldasögur*, however, is rivalry and unhappiness in love, a central theme in *Kormáks saga*, and dominant in all the rest except *Egils saga*.

Skaldic verse is resolutely and, for the medieval period, unusually, not anonymous, although some verses lack known authors, while some named skalds lack extant verses, including several of the 146 poets named in *Skáldatal* (ca. 1260), the "List of Poets," and categorized according to their royal patrons. Estimates vary as to the total number of names of skalds that are recorded, but Kuhn (1983: 240) reckons on over 300 for the period to 1200. There is interesting diversity among the practitioners of the skaldic art. Haraldr Sigurðarson was the most prolific of a handful of verse-making Norwegian kings, and Rǫgnvaldr Kali, earl of Orkney, shared his gift, as did the Orcadian bishop Bjarni Kolbeinsson. Icelandic skalds included such lawspeakers as Markús Skeggjason and Snorri Sturluson, the outlaws Grettir and Gísli, and several women. Some attributions and verses, however, are suspect, the supernatural ones being the most obvious case. *Haralds saga Sigurðarsonar* in *Heimskringla*, for example, contains verses spoken in dreams by the ghost of Ólafr Haraldsson and by troll-women.

Little is known about the training of skalds, and it is not until Snorri Sturluson's *Edda* (ca. 1220) that we see possible teaching materials on meter, diction, and mythological background. Some skalds are the sons of skalds, among them Sighvatr, son of Þórðr Sigvaldaskáld ("Sigvaldi's skald"), and Arnórr jarlaskáld ("earls' skald"), son of Þórðr Kolbeinsson, but there are not enough to suggest a definite pattern of heredity. There are also skaldic friendships on record, but only very imprecise references to tutoring. Einar Helgason skálaglamm ("scale-tinkle") visited Egill

Skalla-Grímsson and discussed poetry with him (*Egils saga*, ch. 78); Gunnlaugr ormstunga ("serpent-tongue") was a friend of Hallfreðr and rival of Hrafn Ǫnundarson, both in poetry and in love. Hofgarða-Refr's memorial poem for his foster-father, Gizurr gullbrárskáld ("poet of goldbrow"), includes thanks for passing on to him the gift of poetry. Would-be skalds doubtless began memorizing and studying existing verses, and established skalds retained these verses in their repertoire. Þormóðr Kolbrúnarskáld ("Kolbrún's skald"), called upon to recite something to King Ólafr before the battle of Stiklastaðir in 1030, readily declaims *Bjarkamál* (whose authenticity, however, has been questioned). *Stúfs þáttr* shows the skald entertaining Haraldr Sigurðarson with the verses of others before proceeding to his own.

Similarly, although references to making and uttering verses are numerous within the skaldic corpus, they yield only imprecise insights into the skald's craft. There is a distinction between composition (for which the verb *yrkja* is especially favored) and performance (*kveða*, *flytja*, *fœra fram*), and skalds frequently arrive at court with their eulogies ready-made. For *lausavísur*, on the other hand, the claims of rapid extemporization may in many cases be true, for the verses often depend for their effect on their immediacy within a particular situation, whether it be a witty exchange of insults, or a sighting of Constantinople from an approaching ship. Some such claims, however, are dubious, as when Egill makes his first *dróttkvætt* utterances at the age of three (*Egils saga*, ch. 31). Skaldic verses were certainly delivered with panache (often *skǫruliga* 'splendidly'), and although the manner of recitation probably differed from everyday speech, poems were not sung. There is no evidence of musical accompaniment.

Whether rightly or wrongly, the notion of skaldship is above all associated with the poets composing for Scandinavian, especially Norwegian, rulers from the 9th century (Bragi Boddason) to the 13th century (Sturla Þórðarson and his brother Ólafr hvítaskáld ["white-skald"]). The court poets are, to begin with, Norwegians, but in the mid-10th century Egill becomes the first known Icelander to compose at a foreign court, and Glúmr Geirason the first to enjoy an established position, with King Haraldr gráfeldr ("grey-cloak"). By the end of the 10th century, the Norwegians had been displaced, for reasons not now understood.

The relationship of poet and royal patron is nowhere systematically defined. The skald's position at court was probably never full-time or lifelong, but the existence of the term *hirðskáld* ("court poet") might suggest at least a semiofficial role. *Egils saga* (ch. 8) claims that Haraldr hárfagri's poets were given seats of honor opposite the king; Arnórr jarlaskáld enjoyed similar favor at the feasts of Þorfinnr, earl of Orkney, and married a relative of his. Here, as often, the specific role of court poet fused with the general one of royal retainer. Sighvatr Þórðarson's position of trust with Ólafr Haraldsson helgi ("the saint") was such that he went on diplomatic missions for him, commemorated in the *Austrfararvísur* and *Vestrfararvísur* ("Verses on a Journey to the East/West"), and later gave outspoken advice to Ólafr's son (and Sighvatr's godson) Magnús in the *Bergsǫglisvísur* ("Plain-speaking Verses"). Sighvatr's position was exceptional, but many skalds fought and died alongside their patrons. At Stiklastaðir, Ólafr Haraldsson, according to his saga in *Heimskringla* (ch. 206), places his skalds Þormóðr Kolbrúnarskáld, Gizurr gullbrá ("gold-brow"), and Þorfinnr munnr ("mouth") in the shield wall in front of him, so that they might compose about the battle afterward from firsthand knowledge. They pledge support for the king in *dróttkvætt* stanzas, which are immediately memorized by the men around them. All three skalds fall with their lord in the battle.

As well as providing commemoration, praise, and propaganda in their panegyrics and blame in their satires, skalds could supply less lofty forms of entertainment, and Máni skáld, at the end of the 12th century, feared displacement by jugglers and minstrels. Þjóðólfr Arnórsson, a leading skald at the poetically lively court of Haraldr Sigurðarson, was called upon by the king to extemporize a verse about a tanner and a smith, and took part in a three-way verse-making contest. Sneglu-Halli, a specialist in insulting verses, responded to a challenge to make a snapshot in verse when Haraldr Sigurðarson put his armor on a Frisian dwarf.

The rewards for poetry were hospitality (although Sneglu-Halli complains of Haraldr Sigurðarson's meanness with food) and gifts of treasure or armor, to which the skalds frequently refer (e.g., Haraldskvæði, sts. 18–19), as well as occasionally hinting at their impecunious state or uttering complaints about rulers who fail in generosity.

Ed.: Finnur Jónsson, ed. Den norsk-islandske skjaldedigtning. Vols. 1A–2A (tekst efter håndskrifterne) and 1B–2B (rettet tekst). Copenhagen and Christiania [Oslo]: Gyldendal, 1912–15; rpt. Copenhagen: Rosenkilde & Bagger, 1967 (A) and 1973 (B). Lit.: Hollander, Lee M. The Skalds: A Selection of Their Poems with Introduction and Notes. Princeton: Princeton University Press, 1945; 2nd ed. Ann Arbor: University of Michigan Press, 1968; Almqvist, Bo. Norrön Niddiktning: Traditionshistoriska studier i versmagi. 1: Nid mot furstar. Nordiska texter och undersökningar, 21. Stockholm: Geber, 1965; Turville-Petre, Gabriel. Haraldr the Hard-Ruler and His Poets. Dorothea Coke Memorial Lecture. London: Viking Society for Northern Research, 1968; Wright, Dorena Allen. "The Skald as Saga-Hero." Parergon 6 (1973), 13–20; Almqvist, Bo. Norrön niddiktning: Traditionshistoriska studier i versmagi. 2.1–2: Nid mot missionärer: Senmedeltida nidtraditioner. Nordiska texter och undersökningar, 23. Stockholm: Geber, 1974; Kreutzer, Gert. Die Dichtungslehre der Skalden: Poetologische Terminologie und Autorenkommentare als Grundlage einer Galtungspoetik. Kronberg Taunus: Scriptor, 1974; 2nd ed. Meisenheim am Glan: Hain, 1977; Clover, Carol J. "Skaldic Sensibility." Arkiv för nordisk filologi 93 (1978), 63–81; Dronke, Ursula. "The Poet's Persona in the Skalds' Sagas." Parergon 22 (1978), 23–8; Clunies Ross, Margaret. "The Art of Poetry and the Figure of the Poet in Egils saga." Parergon 22 (1978), 3–12; rpt. in Sagas of the Icelanders. Ed. John Tucker. New York and London: Garland, 1989, pp. 126–45; Ström, Folke. "Poetry as an Instrument of Propaganda: Jarl Hákon and His Poets." In Specvlvm Norroenvm: Norse Studies in Memory of Gabriel Turville-Petre. Ed. Ursula Dronke et al. Odense: Odense University Press, 1981, pp. 440–58; Kuhn, Hans. Das Dróttkvætt. Heidelberg: Winter, 1983.

Diana Edwards Whaley

[See also: Arnórr Þórðarson jarlaskáld; Bjarkamál; Bjarni Kolbeinsson; Bjǫrn Arngeirsson Hítdœlakappi; Bjǫrn Breiðvíkingakappi; Bragi Boddason; Christian Poetry; Commemorative Poetry; Egill Skalla-Grímsson; Eilífr Goðrúnarson; Einarr Helgason skálaglamm; Einarr Skúlason; Eyvindr Finnsson skáldaspillir; Gamli kanóki; Gunnlaugr ormstunga; Hallfreðr Óttarsson; Kormákr Ǫgmundarson; Lausavísur, Love Poetry; Óttarr svarti; Sighvatr Þórðarson; Skáldasögur; Skaldic Meters; Skaldic Verse; Skáldkonur; Snorri Sturluson; Stúfs þáttr; Sturla Þórðarson; Þáttr; Þjóðólfr of Hvin;

Þórarinn loftunga; Þórarinn svarti; Þorbjǫrn hornklofi; Þórðr Kolbeinsson; Þorleifs þáttr jarlsskálds; Úlfr Uggason; Víga-Glúmr Eyjólfsson]

Skald Sagas see Skáldasögur

Skáldasögur ("Sagas of Skalds") is a modern name given to a group of Íslendingasögur that have famous skalds as principal characters: Kormáks saga, Hallfreðar saga, Bjarnar saga Hítdœlakappa, Gunnlaugs saga ormstungu, Egils saga Skalla-Grímssonar, and Fóstbrœðra saga. The first four are also sagas of tragic love. Kormáks saga is probably the oldest, and the outlines of its love story and several minor traits apparently influenced Hallfreðar saga. In the saga, Kormákr improvises more than sixty stanzas, some indisputably the finest stanzas on love in skaldic poetry. Altogether, there are eighty-five stanzas, including half-stanzas and couplets, in Kormáks saga. Here and in the following four sagas, the stanzas form a part of the artistic fabric of the saga and are never quoted as evidence.

On the other hand, fifteen stanzas from Þormóðr Kolbrúnarskáld's erfidrápa ("elegy") about his foster-brother Þorgeirr are quoted as evidence or confirmation of the story in Fóstbrœðra saga, while about twenty, depending on the redaction, are quoted as entertainment only. In this saga, there is a special episode of love, where Þormóðr improvises two stanzas.

In Bjarnar saga and Gunnlaugs saga, the outlines of the love story are the same, and in both sagas the principal character dies at the hands of the man, also a skald, who had married his betrothed. It should be noted that the plot of the love story in Laxdœla saga follows the same pattern.

Egils saga is a very different skald saga, although it contains an episode of passionate love, which later has great consequences for Egill. And Egill himself plays the lovesick skald in a short episode.

It has been suggested that the dominant theme of Kormáks saga, the skald's lifelong love of a woman both before and after she has married another man, may have its roots in some version of the originally French romance of Tristan, and that the plot of Bjarnar saga and Gunnlaugs saga may originate in an episode in the same romance through the medium of a þáttr in Morkinskinna. The short but intricate love episode in Fóstbrœðra saga appears to have affinities with an episode in the Tristan romance. It can hardly be expected that stanzas that constitute an inherent part of these love stories are authentic 10th-century poetry.

Ed.: Sigurður Nordal, ed. Egils saga Skalla-Grímssonar. Íslenzk fornrit, 2. Reykjavik: Hið íslenzka fornritafélag, 1933; rpt. 1955; Sigurður Nordal and Guðni Jónsson, eds. Borgfirðinga sǫgur. Íslenzk fornrit, 3. Reykjavik: Hið íslenzka fornritafélag, 1938; Einar Ól. Sveinsson, ed. Vatnsdœla saga. Íslenzk fornrit, 8. Reykjavik: Hið íslenzka fornritafélag, 1939; Björn K. Þórólfsson and Guðni Jónsson, eds. Vestfirðinga sǫgur. Íslenzk fornrit, 6. Reykjavik: Hið íslenzka fornritafélag, 1943; Bjarni Einarsson, ed. Hallfreðar saga. Reykjavik: Stofnun Árna Magnússonar, 1977. Lit.: Kinck, H. E. Mange slags kunst. Kristiania [Oslo]: Aschehoug, 1921; Schoepperle, Gertrude. Tristan and Isolt: A Study of the Sources of the Romance. 2 vols. 2nd ed. New York: Franklin, 1959–60, vol. 2, pp. 544–5; Bjarni Einarsson. Skáldasögur: Um uppruna og eðli ástaskáldsagnanna fornu. Reykjavik: Menningarsjóður, 1961; Andersson, Theodore M. "Skalds and Troubadours." Mediaeval Scandinavia 2 (1969), 7–41; Bjarni Einarsson. "The Lovesick Skald: A

Reply to Theodore M. Andersson (*Mediaeval Scandinavia* 1969)." *Mediaeval Scandinavia* 4 (1971), 21–41; Bjarni Einarsson. "On the Rôle of Verse in Saga-Literature." *Mediaeval Scandiavia* 7 (1974), 118–25; Bjarni Einarsson. *To skjaldesagaer. En analyse af Kormáks saga og Hallfreðar saga*. Bergen, Oslo, and Tromsø: Universitetsforlaget, 1976; Bjarni Einarsson. "Um Þormóð skáld og unnusturnar tvær." *Gripla* 5 (1982), 66–76.

Bjarni Einarsson

[**See also:** *Bjarnar saga Hítdælakappa; Egils saga Skalla-Grímssonar; Fóstbrœðra saga; Gunnlaugs saga ormstungu; Hallfreðar saga; Íslendingasögur; Kormáks saga; Laxdœla saga; Morkinskinna; Skáld;* Skaldic Verse; *Þáttr*]

Skaldic Meters. The skaldic verse of the 9th to the 14th century is mostly composed in meters that are strophic, stress counting, and syllable counting, with tightly regulated alliteration and internal rhyme.

Dróttkvætt. The highly elaborate *dróttkvæðr háttr* or *dróttkvætt* "court meter" is the meter of some five-sixths of the skaldic corpus and the basis of most other skaldic meters. Its kinship with the eddic *fornyrðislag* and Old English, Old High German, and Old Saxon alliterative verse is obvious and undisputed; whether its special characteristics show influence from Latin, Irish, or Welsh verse is less certain. The following half-strophe from the memorial poem for Haraldr Sigurðarson (d. 1066) by Arnórr jarlaskáld ("earls' skáld") illustrates the meter:

> Vítt fór **v**olsungs hei*ti*;
> **v**arð marglofaðr har*ð*a,
> sás skau*t* ór Nið **n**ý*t*la
> **n**or*ð*an herskips bor*ð*i.

[Wide went the prince's name; praised most highly was he who skillfully launched from the Nið southward the warship's plank.]

The following notation is customary in scanning lines:

> / full stress
> / half/secondary stress
> x unstressed element
> - long syllable
> ⌣ short syllable

In the quotation above, boldface indicates alliteration, and italics indicate internal rhyme.

The rules of the *dróttkvætt* are, in summary, as follows (the fullest, most recent account being Kuhn 1983):

(1) The strophe (*vísa*) consists of eight lines (*vísuorð*). However, the half-strophe (*vísuhelmingr*) forms a complete metrical unit, and is usually independent in syntax and often in meaning. Many skaldic half-strophes are preserved alone in MSS, as is the specimen verse above.

(2) Each of the two couplets (*vísufjórðungar*) in the half-strophe is united by alliteration, just as the strakes of a boat are joined by their nails, as Óláfr hvítaskáld ("white-skald") said. (a) Alliteration is normally carried by strongly stressed syllables, *e.g.,* the first syllables of nouns and adjectives. (b) In each odd line there are two alliterating sounds or *stuðlar* ("props," "supporters"). (c) In every even line, the first syllable carries the *höfuðstafr* ("main post"), a sound alliterating with the *stuðlar* of the previous line. (d) Each consonant alliterates with itself, and the clusters *sk, sp,*

and *st* count as units, alliterating only with themselves. *Hl, hn, hr,* and *hv* normally alliterate with themselves or with *h*. Any vowel alliterates with any other vowel, though preferably an unlike one, and *j* counts as a vowel.

(3) Individual lines carry internal rhyme or *hendingar* ("?catches, links"). (a) *Hendingar* fall on stressed, or sometimes half-stressed, syllables, which may or may not be the same as those bearing alliteration. (b) The second member of the rhyming pair in each line, called *viðrhending* ("after-rhyme"), must fall on the penultimate syllable. The first of the pair is called *frumhending* ("fore-rhyme"). If this falls on the first syllable, as it most commonly does, it is further called *oddhending* 'edge-/point-rhyme'; mid-line it is called *hluthending* '?chance-rhyme.' (c) There is commonly, but not invariably, a caesura at some point between the two rhyming syllables. (d) Two types of *hending* alternate, so that pairs of odd and even lines are demarcated, although not by means of common sounds as in the case of alliteration. Odd lines contain an *aðalhending*, a "chief/full rhyme" of vowel or diphthong and following consonant(s). Even lines contain a *skothending* ("?shot-rhyme"), a half-rhyme of postvocalic consonant(s) only. (e) In both types of *hending*, a consonant group or geminate consonant may rhyme in full or only on its first element; consonants belonging to inflectional or derivational syllables are very frequently left out of the rhyme. Certain clusters, however, can rhyme only with themselves, notably *ng*. (f) Older skalds couple *a, á, e, i* and *í* with their *u*-mutated counterparts *ǫ, ǫ́, ø, y,* and *ý* respectively in both *skothendingar* and *aðalhendingar, e.g., allr* rhyming with *fjǫllum*. It was apparently only around 1200 that the mutated and nonmutated sounds became so distinct that they could not be coupled in *aðalhendingar*.

(4) The number of syllables in an individual line is regulated. The norm is six, and exceptions usually fall into one of a few definite categories: (a) "Resolution," in which a pair of syllables, of which at least the first is short, "resolves," or counts as metrically equivalent to a long syllable, stressed or unstressed. A long syllable is defined as a long vowel or diphthong followed by one or more consonants, or a short vowel followed by two or more consonants. Thus, *þríma vas þvígit skemmri* is equivalent to *vé bað vísi knýja*. Resolution most commonly occurs in the first foot of a line, never in the third. (b) *Bragarmál* ("fusion"; literally "poetic language"), in which an enclitic becomes nonsyllabic by dropping its vowel. Thus, *þar es/ em ek, etc.* become *þars/ emk, etc.* In the specimen verse above, *sás* is an editorial restoration from MS *sa er* (*er* being the younger form of *es*). (c) Elision is common when the second, word-initial vowel occurs in an unstressed syllable, *e.g., hefr afreka ens øfra*. (d) Some apparently overlong lines probably contain modernized forms in the MS texts, so that restoration of the appropriate older forms, *e.g.,* prepositions *fyr, ept, of,* for MS *fyrir, eptir, yfir,* or verb *hefr* for *hefir*, yields the normal six syllables. (e) Snorri Sturluson allows the possibility of a five-syllable line where there are *seinar samstǫfur* ("slow syllables"); (Commentary to *Háttatal,* st. 7). However, most such lines contain a monosyllable that at an earlier stage was disyllabic, *e.g., blóm/blám* from *blóum* in the line *jafnþarfr blóum hrafni*.

(5) The stress patterns of the *dróttkvætt* line are more controversial than the other metrical features outlined above, although insofar as all metrical features are interdependent, virtually all can be disputed. The following description is based on the analysis of Sievers (1893), which, although by no means unchallenged, remains the best known and most widely used: (a) Each line has

three main stresses, *i.e.*, there are three metrical feet. In certain cases, secondary stress supplements the first two main stresses. (b) Stress most frequently falls on a long syllable. Stress on a short syllable is especially common in lines containing an additional secondary stress. (c) The first syllable of an even line always carries stress and alliteration. (d) All lines end with a trochee (/x), usually provided by an independent disyllabic word. (e) Because the third foot is predetermined, only the stress patterns of the first two feet need further classification. Sievers's system of classification into Five Types, minimally summarized below, therefore applies both to *dróttkvætt* and to Norse *fornyrðislag* and other early Germanic poetry. Type A, scanning / x / x, e.g., *harri fekk í hverri*, is the commonest, although whether the *dróttkvætt* line is predominantly trochaic is disputed. Types B and C are relatively rare, and, having unstressed openings, can occur only in odd lines. B scans x / x /, e.g., *at framm í gný grimmum*; C is x / / x, e.g., *at áleggjar Yggjar*. D and E both contain two full stresses and one secondary stress. D scans / / \ x, e.g., *hraustr þjóðkonungr austan*; E scans / \ x /, e.g., *hjǫrþey á Skáneyju*.

The lines of the specimen verse are A, D, B, and A with additional secondary stress. The relative frequency with which the various line types are used tends to be quite similar among different skalds (for figures, see Hollander 1953, Kuhn 1983, sects. 58–65). In the corpus as a whole, there is a marked difference between metrical usage in odd and even lines. Certain verbal fillings are characteristic of particular metrical types (see J. Turville-Petre 1969, Kuhn 1983: ch. 3). For instance, E lines are commonly filled by a trisyllabic nominal or adjectival compound ending with an inflectional syllable, plus a monosyllabic finite verb, e.g., *snarfengjan bar þengill*. Some critics believe that the types can yield particular aesthetic effects, the trochaic beat of the A lines, for instance, being suitable for depicting quick, resolute action.

Difficulties of skaldic scansion. These difficulties are many, both practical and theoretical. The written texts, mostly 13th century or later, are often far removed in time from the skald's lifetime. The tight verse form reduces but does not remove the possibility of scribal corruption, and older linguistic forms may need restoring, although metrical and linguistic arguments can become circular. There is no help from the medieval theoreticians (the authors of *Háttalykill*, *Háttatal*, and the *Third Grammatical Treatise*), who recognize variations in length of line and of syllables, but are silent about the stress patterns of skaldic meter. We also lack exact knowledge of the stress patterns of spoken Old Norse.

There are therefore areas of doubt about the relative stress of words in the metrical line. There are, *e.g.*, lines in which the (presumed) normal clause stress would yield only two full stresses rather than three, and in which there are two candidates, say a second element of a compound and a finite verb, for raising to full stress in order to conform to the metrical "rules." Assigning such problem lines to one of Sievers's Five Types can become somewhat arbitrary, especially when the choice is among certain subtypes of A, D, and E lines. More generally, must we assume that the "natural" stress ranking of words was modified to fit the rules, as the highlighting of syntactically unimportant words by alliteration and rhyme would suggest, or that meter as practiced by the skalds was more flexible than such systems as Sievers's would imply? Still more fundamental is the problem of the verse's rhythmic properties, *i.e.*, the temporal relations of syllables. The Five Type classification provides a rationale of the distribution of stress and syllable length in the line, but it assigns no time values. The at-

tempts of Heusler and others (including Sievers himself) to discover rhythmic principles for speaking the *dróttkvætt* line have not met with widespread acceptance. It remains likely that there were no set time values and no regular beats.

Variants of dróttkvætt. The rules of *dróttkvætt* are reasonably stable throughout its five or so centuries of use. However, some points, such as the presence and placing of *hendingar* and alliteration, are not totally fixed until the 11th century, and some flexibility remains even within the strict *dróttkvætt*, e.g., in the incidence of casual additional assonances. Moreover, there are "official" variants with separate names in which variation is formalized. The following (*bragar-*)*hættir* ("[poetic] meters") and many more, some of them stylistic rather than strictly metrical, are named and exemplified in *Háttalykill* and *Háttatal*, although some of the theoreticians' meters may have been rarely or never used.

(1) Variation in line length. *Hrynhenda/hrynhent/hrynjandi* (*cf.* vb. *hrynja* 'rush, flow, resound') is the most important meter after *dróttkvætt*, and is the meter of the major 14th-century poems. It has an extra trochee, and the line tends to settle into trochaic tetrameter; influence from octosyllabic Latin hymns or metrical prayers has been suggested. Another meter, *draughent*, has a seven-syllable line, while the three *stúfar* meters have one or more five-syllable lines per half-strophe.

(2) Variation in quantity, quality, and placing of *hendingar*. *Alhent* has two pairs of *aðalhendingar* per line, while at the opposite extreme, *háttlausa* ("meter-less") has all its lines rhymeless, and the *hǫfuðstafr* is not necessarily on the first syllable of even lines. *Munnvǫrp* has rhymeless odd lines and *skothendingar* in even lines. In *dunhent*, the last word of each odd line is echoed in the first of each even line, so that the couplet is united by rhyme as well as by alliteration. In *fleinsháttr* (named in *Háttatal* only), the rhyming syllables always fall on the first and second stresses.

(3) End-rhyme. The meter of the rare examples of end-rhyming strophic verse is called *runhent* irrespective of its other metrical properties.

(4) *The eddic-skaldic boundary.* The use of eddic meters in noneddic poetry, such as *ljóðaháttr* in *Hákonarmál* by Eyvindr skáldaspillir ("plagiarist"; *ca.* 961), *fornyrðislag* in Gísl Illugason's memorial poem for Magnús berfœttr ("bare-leg"; *ca.* 1104), is one factor that makes the definition of "skaldic" verse very difficult. There are, moreover, meters with resemblances to both *dróttkvætt* and eddic meters. For instance, *tøglag* and the ancient *kviðuháttr* have, in common with *fornyrðislag*, a two-foot alliterative line, but are syllable counting (*kviðuháttr* having alternation of three- and four-syllable lines). *Tøglag* has some tightening of alliteration and addition of *hendingar*.

Bib.: Hollander, Lee M. *A Bibliography of Skaldic Studies.* Copenhagen: Munksgaard, 1958; Frank, Roberta. "Skaldic Poetry." In *Old Norse-Icelandic Literature: A Critical Guide.* Ed. Carol J. Clover and John Lindow. Islandica, 45. Ithaca and London: Cornell University Press, 1985, pp. 157–96. **Lit.**: Sievers, Eduard. *Altgermanische Metrik.* Sammlung kurzer Grammatiken germanischer Dialekte, Ergänzungsreihe, 2. Halle: Niemeyer, 1893; Heusler, Andreas. *Deutsche Versgeschichte mit Einschluss des altenglischen und altnordischen Stabreimverses.* 3 vols. Grundriss der germanischen Philologie, 8. Berlin and Leipzig: de Gruyter, 1925–29; rpt. 1956, vol. 1; Hollander, Lee M. *The Skalds: A Selection of Their Poems with Introduction and Notes.* Princeton: Princeton University Press, 1945; 2nd ed. Ann Arbor: University of Michigan Press, 1968; Lie, Hallvard. "Skaldestil-studier." *Maal og minne* (1952), 1–92; rpt. in his *Om sagakunst og skaldskap:*

Utvalgte avhandlinger. Øvre Ervik: Alvheim & Eide, 1982, pp. 109–200; Hollander, Lee M. "Some Observations on the *dróttkvætt* Meter of Skaldic Poetry." *Journal of English and Germanic Philology* 52 (1953), 189–97; Lie, Hallvard. "Hrynhenda." *KLNM* 7 (1962), 26–8; Lie, Hallvard. "Hrynhent." *KLNM* 7 (1962), 28–30; Lie, Hallvard. "Kviðuháttr." *KLNM* 9 (1964), 559–61; See, Klaus von. *Germanische Verskunst.* Sammlung Metzler, M67. Stuttgart: Metzler, 1967, pp. 37–60; Turville-Petre, Joan. "The Metre of Icelandic Court Poetry." *Saga-Book of the Viking Society* 17 (1969), 326–51; Lie, Hallvard. "Runhent." *KLNM* 14 (1969), 479–80; Lie, Hallvard. "Tøglag." *KLNM* 19 (1975), 218–19; Turville-Petre, E. O. G. *Scaldic Poetry.* Oxford: Clarendon, 1976; Jakob Benediktsson. "*Hafgerðingadrápa.*" In *Specvlvm Norroenvm: Norse Studies in Memory of Gabriel Turville-Petre.* Ed. Ursula Dronke *et al.* Odense: Odense University Press, 1981, pp. 27–32; Kuhn, Hans. *Das Dróttkvætt.* Heidelberg: Winter, 1983.

Diana Edwards Whaley

[See also: Eddic Meters; Grammatical Treatises; *Háttalykill; Lausavísur; Skáld;* Skaldic Verse; *Snorra Edda*]

Skaldic Verse.

In Old Norse, the word *skáld* (or *skald*) means "poet," and the word *skáldskapr*, "poetry" or, in a narrower sense, "a libel in verse." This narrower meaning is possibly the original one, as the most widely accepted etymology associates the word with Old High German *skeldan* 'to scold.'

In modern use, skaldic poetry is defined primarily as Old Norse poetry distinct from eddic poetry. This distinction is not known in Old Norse, however, where the word *skáld* may be used indiscriminately of authors of both genres. Since eddic poetry is anonymous, there was little need for the word *skáld* in this context, and therefore it naturally would be used more commonly of authors of skaldic verse.

In view of the difficulty of constructing a neat definition of skaldic poetry that rules out overlap (*cf.* Frank 1985: 160), it is tempting to define as skaldic verse everything contained in Finnur Jónsson's authoritative edition (1912–15; *cf.* von See 1980: 19). A more serious definition covering this corpus will have to use partly conceptual and partly chronological criteria, applying the term skaldic verse to all Old West Norse alliterative poetry that is neither eddic nor belonging to the Icelandic *rímur* genre, and that is composed before about 1400. In contrast to eddic poetry, which is "timeless" (Turville-Petre 1976: xvi), skaldic poetry is in principle historical and situated within a definite historical context. In most cases, the name of the skald is known and very often the poem's original addressee or audience.

Secondary to this historical criterion are metrical and stylistic criteria. Typical skaldic verse has a highly elaborate form, strictly regulated in rhyme, meter, and the number of syllables and lines. Nevertheless, some skaldic poems are also composed in an eddic-like manner.

Nearly all skaldic verse is unambiguously strophic. Eddic poetry, which is more loosely strophic, is supposed to have been influenced by skaldic verse in this respect. Typically, a skaldic stanza consists of eight lines, which mainly by syntactic means are divided into two halves (*helmingar*). By means of different rhyming devices, the halves are divided into two "long lines," each consisting of two "short lines," and probably the "short lines" are divided into two still smaller rhythmical units ("cola") by means of a caesura (Kuhn 1983). In the short lines, stresses and syllables, or rather metrical positions, are counted. A stanza in *dróttkvætt* meter thus will consist of (2x2x2x2=) 16 cola and of (8x6=) 48 syllables or metrical positions, 24 of which are stressed. Above the strophe level, there are no strict compositional rules, except for the *drápa* form, which is characterized by a systematic use of recurring refrains, or *stef.*

In addition to strictly regulated alliteration, skaldic poetry makes lavish use of internal rhymes, called *hendingar*, and occasionally of end-rhyme in the meter *runhent.*

The principal skaldic meters are not numerous, but by regularization of stylistic phenomena, new varieties are easily created, as Snorri Sturluson demonstrated in his metric model poem, *Háttatal.* The number of possible meters is thus another difference between eddic and skaldic poetry.

Stylistically, skaldic verse is characterized by its tendency to vary its vocabulary, particularly its nouns, by using *heiti* instead of plain words, and especially by prolific use of the kenning, a device that often gives the genre a riddle-like character. There is also extraordinary liberty in word order and clause arrangement. The constituent parts of kennings may be split and separated, and several clauses are frequently interlaced and intercalated within the limits of the half-strophe.

The chronological limit of skaldic verse is arbitrarily set by Finnur Jónsson (1912–19) at 1400, while Jón Helgason suggests the date of the composition of *Lilja* about 1350 by Eysteinn Ásgrímsson as a more suitable limit, because of the polemics found in this poem against the traditional skaldic aesthetics. The author propounds his own Christian aesthetic of "clear words" in preference to the "darkness" of the *forn* ("old, heathen") poetry (Jón Helgason 1953: 102). On the other hand, Christian skaldic poetry of the 14th century continued until the Reformation (ed. Jón Helgason 1936–38; *cf.* Jón Þorkelsson 1888). As these poems in many cases cannot be dated with certainty, it is probable that some of them may antedate 1400. Another solution to the delimitation problem would therefore be to consider Jón Arason (1484–1550), the last Catholic bishop of Iceland, as the last skald as well.

Normally, *rímur* are not regarded as part of the corpus of skaldic verse. Finnur Jónsson thus includes the skaldic poetry of Einarr Gilsson in his edition, but he excludes his *Óláfs ríma Haraldssonar* preserved in *Flateyjarbók.* Icelandic ballads (*fornkvæði*) are excluded as not alliterative.

Preservation. The greater part of skaldic poetry is preserved as quotations in prose works from the 12th to the 14th century. Poetry previous to these dates must have been transmitted orally, as stated by Snorri Sturluson in the introduction to *Heimskringla.* In written form, skaldic poetry is found mainly in five types of literature, namely *konungasögur, Íslendingasögur* (including the Sturlunga collection), poetical treatises (including Snorri's *Edda*), *fornaldarsögur*, and religious sagas (including *biskupa sögur* and *postola sögur*). Religious poetry may also be found in separate MSS, like AM 713 4to. A few stanzas are preserved in runic form, the most important being a *dróttkvætt* stanza on the Karlevi stone (10th or 11th century) and a group of verses carved on wood from Bryggen in Bergen (13th and 14th centuries).

Subgenres. Skaldic poetry may be divided into a number of subgenres according to its content and historical value. A survey of the subgenres will also involve some comments on the definition given above as well as on the history of skaldic verse.

As we have chosen the poems' historical character as our main defining criterion, the panegyrical poems (*mærð, lof*), composed by court poets in honor of kings and earls will have to be considered the main genre of skaldic verse. From the 9th to the 13th century, poems and fragments of poems are known on about forty princes (kings and earls) from the Scandinavian countries, England, and the Orkneys, in addition to a handful of Icelandic chiefs. A catalogue of court poetry from about 1260, Skáldatal, mentions the works of 146 skalds, bearing witness to a great quantity of praise poems now lost; but several of its entries are probably apocryphal. The typical content of a praise poem is an enumeration of battles and other feats of prowess, and the person in question is praised for his generosity and boldness, above all as a sea warrior. The praise may be expressed in plain words, or it may be alluded to in the kennings.

An important subgroup of praise poems are the erfikvæði (funeral poems). It has been argued that skaldic verse in general had its origin in this group (Ohlmarks 1944), but this is uncertain (cf. Fidjestøl 1982: 198). There is no clearcut difference in style or content between erfikvæði and other praise poems, except for occasional expressions of mourning or the like.

Another subgenre of praise poems is a small group of genealogical poems, recalling the ancestors of a king or prince, beginning in a mythical past and above all giving information on the death and burial place of each pedigree (cf. the Prologue of Heimskringla on Ynglingatal [and Háleygatal]: "in this poem, his ancestors are mentioned, and it is told about their death and burial place"). The genealogical poems are composed in the meter kviðuháttr.

Three praise poems from the 9th–10th centuries (Haraldskvæði, Eiríksmál, Hákonarmál) are called eddic praise poems, on metric and stylistic grounds. They are skaldic, however, insofar as they are composed in praise of historical kings, and the authors of the poems (except Eiríksmál) are known. In the 12th century, praise poems are also composed in skaldic variants of eddic meters.

Poems describing pictures, mostly decorated shields, may be considered eulogies insofar as they implicitly praise the giver of the owner of the object. The shield poem Ragnarsdrápa by Bragi, which probably is the oldest preserved skaldic poem, contains some metrical irregularities not found in classical skaldic verse, suggesting that the stricter rules were laid down only somewhat later, possibly by Þorbjǫrn hornklofi.

Mansǫngvar are love poems, or praise poems on women. According to Icelandic law (in a passage supposed to belong to its younger layers), mansǫngvar were forbidden under heavy penalty. Níðvísur, the opposite of praise poems, were likewise strictly forbidden, because níð was supposed to have a real injurious influence on the person against whom it was directed (cf. Almqvist 1965).

Another group of skaldic verse attested in the oldest period are poems narrating a story from the mythical or heroic past. To a certain extent, this group overlaps with the poems that describe mythological pictures. Outside this group, narration is seldom found in skaldic poetry, and in their legendary or mythological content, these poems are akin to eddic poetry and thus have no relevance for actual history. But normally the name of the skald is known, and they are distinct from eddic poems in meter and style. This group includes four major poems (Ragnarsdrápa, Haustlǫng, Þórsdrápa, Húsdrápa) and a number of fragments. Stray strophes may have a heathen hymnic content, e.g., a lausavísa by Vetrliði Sumarliðason praising the god Þórr by means of an enumeration of his forceful deeds in slaying monsters (cf. Lindow 1988).

The third main group of skaldic verse known from the 9th century onward comprises the so-called lausavísur, occasional verses on any subject from everyday life, often preserved together with an anecdote in prose recounting the circumstances leading up to the composition of the stanza in question. Since a large number of occasional verses preserved in the Íslendingasögur are under suspicion of being forgeries, Finnur Jónsson, in his edition of skaldic verse, makes a distinction between stanzas believed to be original poetry from the saga age (before ca. 1050) and spurious stanzas from the Íslendingasögur, supposed to stem from the 12th to the 14th century (Finnur Jónsson 1A: 603–7, 2A: 198–208, 430–61). This distinction must remain hypothetical, however.

Although skaldic verse typically is concerned with contemporary history, except the mythological-heroic group mentioned above, in the 12th century a new genre appeared, the historical poem, or sǫgukvæði, dealing with persons and events from the past, like Ragnarr loðbrók, the Jómsvíkingar, or heroes from the Íslendingasögur (Krákumál, Jómsvíkingadrápa, Íslendingadrápa), or from the more recent past, like Óláfr Tryggvason (Rekstefja by Pseudo-Hallfreðr). Jómsvíkingadrápa was composed by Bjarni Kolbeinsson, bishop in the Orkneys 1188–1223, and there are reasons to believe that the genre may have originated in the Orkneys. Stanzas and poems quoted in fornaldarsögur (Finnur Jónsson 2A: 219–344) are frequently attributed to heroes from these sagas, and thus they can also be qualified as sǫgukvæði. However, to a great extent, the fornaldarsaga poetry is in eddic meter and style, and parts of it might more properly be counted among the eddic poetry ("eddica minora").

The historical poems bear witness to a revival of the interest in the national past of the Nordic countries in the 12th century, corresponding to the 12th-century renaissance in Europe. Another genre that likewise may qualify as a poetry of learning comprises the two claves metricae from the middle of the 12th and the first quarter of the 13th century, Háttalykill and Háttatal. These works reveal an attempt to keep alive the classical art of skaldic poetry. Snorri Sturluson's Háttatal is incorporated in his Edda, the cornerstone of the medieval art of commentary on skaldic verse, and remains the most influential introduction to skaldic studies.

After the introduction of Christianity in the beginning of the 11th century, Christian themes gradually replace the heathen themes of the earlier religious poetry. In particular, after the establishment of a Scandinavian church province (the archbishopric of Lund 1103, Niðaróss [Trondheim] 1152/3), skaldic verse tends to be dominated by Christian poetry. The meter hrynhent, which resembled contemporary European meters, gained ground at the expense of dróttkvætt. Eiríksmál, a hrynhent eulogy on the founder of the archbishopric of Lund, the Danish king Erik Ejegod ("ever-good"), is an interesting blend of traditional panegyrics and a new, Christian feeling for the virtues of the soul. The dróttkvætt poem Geisli, dealing with the national saint of Norway, Óláfr Haraldsson, was composed by the court poet Einarr Skúlason on the occasion of the establishment of the archbishopric of Niðaróss, and is the first major representative of the legendary poem. From the second half of the 12th century onward, legendary poetry becomes the dominant genre, including poems to Christ and the Virgin Mary, the apostles and other universal as well as local saints, and poems on the holiness of Sunday, on the importance of repentance, and on other themes.

Ed.: Finnur Jónsson, ed. *Den norsk-islandske skjaldedigtning* Vols. 1A-2A (tekst efter håndskrifterne) and 1B-2B (rettet tekst). Copenhagen and Christiania [Oslo]: Gyldendal, 1912–15; rpt. Copenhagen: Rosenkilde & Bagger, 1967 (A) and 1973 (B); Jón Helgason, ed. *Íslenzk miðaldakvæði: Islandske digte fra senmiddelalderen*. Vols. 1.2–2. Copenhagen: Levin & Munksgaard; Munksgaard, 1936–38; Kock, Ernst A., ed. *Den norsk-isländska skaldediktningen*. 2 vols. Lund: Gleerup, 1946–50; Liestøl, Aslak. "Runer frå Bryggen." *Viking* 27 (1963), 5–53; Turville-Petre, E. O. G. *Scaldic Poetry*. Oxford: Clarendon, 1976 [text, translation, and commentary of selected poems]; Frank, Roberta. *Old Norse Court Poetry: The* Dróttkvætt *Stanza*. Islandica, 42. Ithaca and London: Cornell University Press, 1978 [text, translation, and commentary of selected poems]. **Tr.**: Hollander, Lee M., trans. *The Skalds: A Selection of Their Poems, with Introduction and Notes*. Princeton: Princeton University Press, 1945; 2nd ed. Ann Arbor: University of Michigan Press, 1968. **Bib.**: Hollander, Lee M. *A Bibliography of Skaldic Studies*. Copenhagen: Munksgaard, 1958; Frank, Roberta. "Skaldic Poetry." In *Old Norse–Icelandic Literature: A Critical Guide*. Ed. Carol J. Clover and John Lindow. Islandica, 45. Ithaca and London: Cornell University Press, 1985, pp. 157–96 [bibliograhy and bibliographical essay]; Fidjestøl, Bjarne. "Skaldestudier. Eit forskingsoversyn." *Maal og minne* (1985), 53–81 [bibliographical essay]. **Lex.**: Finnur Jónsson. *Lexicon poeticum antiquæ linguæ septentrionalis. Ordbog over det norsk-islandske skjaldesprog oprindelig forfattet af Sveinbjörn Egilsson*. Copenhagen: Møller, 1913–16; 2nd ed. 1931; rpt. 1966. **Lit.**: Jón Þorkelsson. *Om digtningen på Island i det 15. og 16. århundrede*. Copenhagen: Høst, 1888; Wadstein, E. "Bidrag till tolkning ock belysning av skalde- ock Edda-dikter. II." *Arkiv för nordisk filologi* 11 (1895), 64–92 [on the etymology of *skáld*, pp. 88–90]; Paasche, Fredrik. *Kristendom og kvad. En studie i norrøn middelalder*. Oslo: Aschehoug, 1914, pp. 108–11, 173; rpt. in his *Hedenskap og kristendom. Studier i norrøn middelalder*. Oslo: Aschehoug, 1948, pp. 142–52, 210; Noreen, Erik. *Studier i fornvästnordisk diktning*. Uppsala Universitets Årsskrift, 1921. Filosofi, Språkvetenskap och Historiska Vetenskaper, 4. Uppsala: Academiska Bokhandlen, 1921–23; Meissner, Rudolf. *Die Kenningar der Skalden. Ein Beitrag zur skaldischen Poetik*. Bonn and Leipzig: Schroeder, 1921; rpt. Hildesheim, Zurich, and New York: Olms, 1984; Reichardt, Konstantin. *Studien zu den Skalden des 9. und 10. Jahrhunderts*. Palaestra, 159. Leipzig: Mayer & Müller, 1928; Kock, Ernst A. *Notationes norrœnae: Antekningar till Edda och skaldediktning*. Lunds Universitets Årsskrift, n.s., sec. 1. Lund: Gleerup, 1923–44 [entire work published in 27 parts]; Ohlmarks, Åke. "Till frågan om den fornnordiska skaldediktningens ursprung." *Arkiv för nordisk filologi* 57 (1944), 178–207; Jón Helgason. "Norges og Islands digtning." In *Litteraturhistorie: Norge og Island*. Ed. Sigurður Nordal. Nordisk kultur, 8B. Stockholm: Bonnier; Oslo: Aschehoug; Copenhagen: Schultz, 1953, pp. 3–179; Lie, Hallvard. "Billedbeskrivende dikt." *KLNM* 1 (1956), 542–5; Lie, Hallvard. "Dråpa." *KLNM* 3 (1958), 351–2; Lange, Wolfgang. *Studien zur christlichen Dichtung der Nordgermanen 1000–1200*. Palaestra, 222. Göttingen: Vandenhoeck & Ruprecht, 1958; Holtsmark, Anne. "Háttalykill." *KLNM* 6 (1961), 242–3; Liestøl, Aslak, *et al.* "Drottkvætt-vers fra Bryggen i Bergen." *Maal og minne* (1962), 98–108; Holtsmark, Anne. "Kjærlighetsdiktning." *KLNM* 8 (1963), 438–43; Jakob Benediktsson *et al.* "En ny drottkvættstrofe fra Bryggen i Bergen." *Maal og minne* (1964), 93–100; See, Klaus von. "Skop und Skald. Zur Auffassung des Dichters bei den Germanen." *Germanisch-romanische Monatsschrift* 45, N.F. 14 (1964), 1–14; rpt. in his *Edda, Saga, Skaldendichtung. Aufsätze zur skandinavischen Literatur des Mittelalters*. Heidelberg: Winter, 1981, pp. 347–60; Lie, Hallvard. "Lausavísur." *KLNM* 10 (1965), 355–6; Holtsmark, Anne. "Lovkvad." *KLNM* 10 (1965), 700–4; Almqvist, Bo. *Norrön niddiktning. Traditionshistoriska studier i versmagi. 1: Nid mot furstar*. Nordiska texter och undersökningar, 21. Stockholm: Geber, 1965; Steblin-Kamenskij, M. I. "On the Etymology of the Word Skáld." *Afmælisrit Jóns Helgasonar: 30. júní 1969*. Ed. Jakob Benediktsson *et al.* Reykjavik: Heimskringla, 1969, pp. 421–30; Holtsmark, Anne. "Skaldatal." *KLNM* 15 (1970), 386; Holtsmark, Anne. "Skaldediktning." *KLNM* 15 (1970), 386–90; Schottmann, Hans. *Die isländische Mariendichtung: Untersuchungen zur volkssprachigen Mariendichtung des Mittelalters*. Münchener germanistische Beiträge, 9. Munich: Fink, 1973 Almqvist, Bo. *Norrön niddiktning: Traditionshistoriske studier i versmagi. 2.1–2: Nid mot missionärer: Senmedeltida nidtraditioner*. Nordiska texter och undersökningar, 23. Stockholm: Geber, 1974; Kreutzer, Gert. *Die Dichtungslehre der Skalden: Poetologische Terminologie und Autorenkommentare als Grundlage einer Gattungspoetik*. Kronberg Taunus: Scriptor, 1974; 2nd ed. Meisenheim am Glan: Hain, 1977; "Verselære." *KLNM* 19 (1975), 662; See, Klaus von. *Skaldendichtung. Eine Einführung*. Munich and Zurich: Artemis, 1980; Lie, Hallvard. *Om sagakunst og skaldskap. Utvalgte avhandlinger*. Øvre Ervik: Alvheim & Eide, 1982; Fidjestøl, Bjarne. *Det norrøne fyrstediktet*. Øvre Ervik: Alvheim & Eide, 1982; Marold, Edith. *Kenningkunst. Ein Beitrag zu einer Poetik der Skaldendichtung*. Quellen und Forschungen zur Sprach- und Kulturgeschichte der germanischen Völker, 80. Berlin and New York: de Gruyter, 1983; Kuhn, Hans. *Das Dróttkvætt*. Heidelberg: Winter, 1983; Edwards, Diana C. "Clause Arrangement in Skaldic Poetry." *Arkiv för nordisk filologi* 98 (1983), 123–75; 99 (1984), 131–38; Perkins, Richard. "Rowing Chants and the Origins of *Dróttkvæðr Háttr*." *Saga-Book of the Viking Society* 21 (1984–85), 155–221; Lindow, John. "Addressing Thor." *Scandinavian Studies* 60 (1988), 119–36.

Bjarne Fidjestøl

[**See also:** Arnórr Þórðarson jarlaskáld; Bjarni Kolbeinsson; Bjǫrn Ásgeirsson Hítdœlakappi; Bjǫrn Breiðvíkingakappi; Bragi Boddason; Christian Poetry; Commemorative Poetry; Egill Skalla-Grímsson; Eilífr Goðrúnarson; Einarr Helgason skálaglamm; Einarr Skúlason; *Eiríksmál*; Eyvindr Finsson skáldaspillir; Gamli kanóki; Gunnlaugr ormstunga; Hallfreðr Óttarsson; *Háttalykill*; *Heiti*; *Íslendingadrápa*; Kennings; Kormákr Ǫgmundarson; *Krákumál*; *Lausavísur*; *Leiðarvísan*; *Liðsmannaflokkr*; *Lilja*; Love Poetry; *Merlínusspá*; Mythology; Óttarr svarti; Sighvatr Þórðarson; *Skáld*; *Skáldasögur*; Skaldic Meters; *Skáldkonur*, Snorra Edda; Þjóðólfr of Hvin; Þórarinn loftunga; Þórarinn svarti; Þorbjǫrn hornklofi; Þórðr Kolbeinsson; Úlfr Uggason; Víga-Glúmr Eyjólfsson]

Skáldkonur ("women skalds"). A first perusal of the standard 20th-century collections of skaldic poetry (Finnur Jónsson 1912–15, Kock 1946–50) is likely to lead the reader to conclude that the corpus of preserved poetry in Old Icelandic attributable to women poets (*skáldkonur*) is rather small. However, this first impression can be altered somewhat by tracing the verses in Finnur Jónsson's and Kock's collections back to their original saga environments. It then becomes clear, for instance, that a sizable amount of the dream verse and prophetic fragments in *Sturlunga saga* was attributed to women, or that that pithy epigram labeled "Fragment" in the modern editions was originally attributed to Bróka-Auðr in *Laxdœla saga*. Finnur Jónsson's and Kock's editions can thus be sifted to yield the following: (1) eight pre-Christian Norwegian and Icelandic *skáldkonur*, cited in the *konungasögur*, *Íslendingasögur*, and related *þættir*, (2) eight Icelandic *skáldkonur* of the Sturlung Age (13th century); (3) eleven additional early *skáldkonur* from the *Íslendingasögur* and *þættir*, but of more doubtful authenticity than those of the first group; and (4) a number of shield-maidens, witches, and troll-women cited as reciting verse in various legendary sagas. In connection with lists of this sort, however, we should bear in mind that all of the surviving skaldic poetry, whether attributed to men or women, probably represents only a small, random portion of the total amount of skaldic poetry composed during the Middle Ages.

The eight *skáldkonur* of the first group mentioned above were active in the 10th century and the first half of the 11th. The poetry of this period was dominated by the complex *dróttkvætt* ("court meter") style, and all of the compositions of these eight *skáldkonur*, with the possible exception of two *kviðlingar* (epigrams, too short to classify), were composed in that meter. The earliest three of these *skáldkonur*, Jórunn skáldmær ("skald-maid"), Hildr Hrólfsdóttir, and Gunnhildr konungamóðir ("kings' mother"), were Norwegians, tied to various kings by obligations of family, or perhaps fealty (in Jórunn's case). They were probably active in court circles, where *dróttkvætt* had become the fashionable mode of expression; accordingly, the subjects of their poetry reflected events of interest at court. The remaining five women poets in this first group were Icelanders. Their poetic commentaries on errant husbands or lovers (by Bróka-Auðr, Þórhildr skáldkona, and Steingerðr Þorkelsdóttir), satires on Christian missionaries (by Steinunn Refsdóttir), and exhortations addressed to lukewarm avengers (by Þuríðr Ólafsdóttir) may have been noncourtly in theme, but they were no less elegant as examples of the *dróttkvætt* style than the poetry of the first three.

The eight *skáldkonur* of the second group are all known from *Sturlunga saga*. One of them, Steinvǫr Sighvatsdóttir (á Keldum), is also listed elsewhere, in the *Skáldatal*, as being a professional skald in the pay of the Norwegian chieftain Gautr Jónsson (á Mel). However, the extant half-stanza (*vísuhelmingr*) by her is not a poem in praise of Gautr, but a poetic vision, as are all but one of the compositions in this group. The *skáldkona* is portrayed as having a dream or a vision, or seeing an apparition, in connection with which she experiences the poetry, which she recites upon awakening or coming out of the trance. Many of these poetic fragments are tinged with the ghostliness characteristic of Icelandic folklore down to the present day. All but one of these poetic visions are doom prophecies presaging one of the great climaxes of *Sturlunga saga*, the fall of Sturla Sighvatsson at the battle of Ǫrlygsstaðir in 1238. Their style is chant-like and simple, using eddic meters, such as *fornyrðislag* and *galdralag*, rather than *dróttkvætt*. The longest of them, eight stanzas of dream verse by the sixteen-year-old Jóreiðr Hermundardóttir (í Miðjumdal), constitutes the largest body of poetry by a single historically attestable woman that survives in Old Norse literature.

The *skáldkonur* of the final group, the women poets in the *fornaldarsögur*, are significant not so much for their own sake as for what they reveal about the attitudes toward women and poetry among the 13th-century redactors who compiled these sagas. As Guðrún Helgadóttir (1961) has noted, the saga compilers seem to have been far readier to ascribe lengthy poems to supernatural women or legendary heroines of long ago than to their own recent female ancestors.

Barði Guðmundsson (1967) has associated poetic composition by women in early Nordic society with their participation in the related fields of *seiðr* (women's sorcery) and religion (specifically the cult of the Vanir), as well as matronymic naming customs and matrilineal property ownership. He contends that *seiðr*, poetry, and cultic activities were commonly seen as female-dominated arts in early Nordic society. It is tempting to postulate a golden age for *skáldkonur*, from which we retain no poetry except for some fragments now largely embedded in the *fornaldarsögur* and in the eddic lays (*Vǫluspá*, for example). Sometime after this hypothetical golden age, and certainly sometime before the heyday of the *dróttkvætt* style, a transition seems to have occurred. Poetic composition had become disassociated from its original, female-dominated cultic or religious environment, in favor of a male-dominated court environment. Evidence for this cultural transition is admittedly sparse, but the memory of it may perhaps be preserved in the myth recounted by Snorri Sturluson in the *Prose Edda*, in which the usurper Óðinn guilefully wrests the mead of poetry from its former owners, who seem to represent earlier, female-dominated, chthonic deities (Vanir equivalents, in other words).

Ed.: Gudbrand Vigfusson, ed. *Sturlunga Saga*. 2 vols. Oxford: Clarendon, 1878, vol. 1, p. 367 [Steinvǫr]; vol. 2, pp. 219–21 [Jóreiðr]; Kahle, B., ed. *Kristnisaga*. Altnordische Saga-Bibliothek, 11. Halle: Niemeyer, 1905, pp. 27–8 [Steinunn]; Finnur Jónsson, ed. *Den norsk-islandske skaldedigtning*. Vols. 1A–2A (tekst efter håndskrifterne) and 1B–2B (rettet tekst). Copenhagen and Christiania [Oslo]: Gyldendal, 1912–15; rpt. Copenhagen: Rosenkilde & Bagger, 1967 (A) and 1973 (B), vol. 1B, p. 27 [Hildr]; 1B, pp. 53–4 [Jórunn]; 1B, p. 54 [Gunnhildr]; 1B, p. 85 [Steingerðr]; 1B, p. 95 [Þórhildr]; 1B, p. 97 [Þuríðr]; 1B, pp. 127–8 [Steinunn]; 1B, p. 172 [Auðr]; 2B, p. 154 [Steinvǫr]; 2B, p. 158 [Jóreiðr]; Sigurður Nordal and Guðni Jónsson, eds. *Borgfirðinga sǫgur*. Íslenzk fornrit, 3. Reykjavik: Hið íslenzka fornritafélag, 1938, pp. 277–8 [Þuríðr]; Einar Ól. Sveinsson, ed. *Laxdæla saga*. Íslenzk fornrit, 5. Reykjavik: Hið íslenzka fornritafélag, 1934, p. 96 [Auðr]; Bjarni Aðalbjarnarson, ed. *Heimskringla*. 3 vols. Íslenzk fornrit, 26–28. Reykjavik: Hið íslenzka fornritafélag, 1941–51, vol. 1, pp. 123–4 [Hildr]; vol. 2, pp. 426–7 [Jórunn]; Kock, Ernst A., ed. *Den norsk-isländska skaldediktningen*. 2 vols. Lund: Gleerup, 1946–50, vol. 1, p. 17 [Hildr]; vol. 1, pp. 33–4 [Jórunn]; vol. 1, p. 34 [Gunnhildr]; vol. 1, p. 50 [Steingerðr]; vol. 1, p. 55 [Þórhildr]; vol. 1, p. 71 [Steinunn]; vol. 1, p. 92 [Auðr]; vol. 1, pp. 103–4 [Þuríðr]; vol. 2, p. 82 [Steinvǫr]; vol. 2, pp. 84–5 [Jóreiðr]; Einar Ól. Sveinsson, ed. *Brennu-Njáls saga*. Íslenzk fornrit, 12. Reykjavik: Hið íslenzka fornritafélag, 1954, pp. 88–9 [Þórhildr], pp. 265–7 [Steinunn]. **Tr.**: Gudbrand Vigfusson and F. York Powell, eds. and trans. *Corpus Poeticum Boreale: The Poetry of the Old Northern Tongue from the Earliest Times to the Thirteenth Century*. 2 vols. Oxford: Clarendon, 1883; rpt. New York: Russell & Russell, 1965, vol. 2, pp. 321–2 [Jórunn]; Hollander, Lee M., trans. *The Sagas of Kormák and the Sworn Brothers*. Princeton: Princeton Univiversity Press, 1949, p. 24 [Steingerðr]; Hollander, Lee M., trans. *Heimskringla: History of the Kings of Norway*. Austin: University of Texas Press, 1964, p. 79 [Hildr]; p. 91 [Jórunn]; Magnus Magnusson and Hermann Pálsson, trans. *Njal's Saga*. Harmondsworth: Penguin, 1960, p. 96 [Þórhildr]; p. 222 [Steinunn]; Magnus Magnusson and Hermann Pálsson, trans. *Laxdæla Saga*. Harmondsworth: Penguin, 1969, p. 127 [Auðr]; McGrew, Julia, and R. George Thomas, trans. *Sturlunga saga*. 2 vols. Library of Scandinavian Literature, 9–10. New York: Twayne; American-Scandinavian Foundation, 1970–74, vol. 1, p. 327 [Steinvǫr]; vol. 1, pp. 431–4 [Jóreiðr]. **Lit.**: Olsen, Magnus. "Hild Rolvsdatters vise om Gange-Rolv og Harald Hårfagre." *Maal og* minne (1942), 1–70; Olsen, Magnus. "Har dronning Gunnhild diktet om Håkon den gode?" *Avhandlinger av Det norske Videnskaps-Akademi i Oslo 2*, Hist.-filos. kl., 1944–45, no. 1. Oslo: Dybwad, 1945, pp. 1–16; Ohlmarks, Åke. *Islands hedna skaldediktning, århundradet 878–980.* Stockholm: Almqvist & Wiksell, 1957 [Þórhildr, Auðr]; Ohlmarks, Åke. *Tors skalder och Vite-Krists: trosskiftetidens isländska furstelovskalder: 980–1013.* Stockholm: Almqvist & Wiksell, 1957 [Steinunn]; Guðrún P. Helgadóttir. *Skáldkonur fyrri alda.* 2 vols. Akureyri: Kvöldvökuútgáfan, 1961–63; Barði Guðmundsson. *The Origin of the Icelanders.* Trans. Lee M. Hollander. Lincoln: University of Nebraska Press, 1967; Kreutzer, Gert. "Jórunn skáldmær." *Skandinavistik* 2 (1972), 89–98.

Sandra Ballif Straubhaar

[See also: *Skáld*; Skaldic Meters; Skaldic Verse; *Snorra Edda*; *Sturlunga saga*]

Skarðsbók ("The Book of Skarð") is the name given by Árni Magnússon to two different MSS after the farm Skarð in Skarðsströnd, where they were housed during the 17th century.

The first, AM 350 fol., is a codex containing mainly legal texts, *e.g.*, *Jónsbók*, amendments, *Hirðskrá* (King Magnús Hákonarson's ecclesiastical law), Bishop Árni Þorláksson's ecclesiastical law, and various legal formulas, records, and ecclesiastical statutes and diplomas.

The codex comprises 157 folios, but has not been preserved entirely in its original form. Fols. 18–23 are younger and were obviously written to fill the gap left by folios of the original book that became damaged or lost. Fols. 152–157 are also younger, containing a list of the contents of the manuscript and a formula of absolution. The whole of AM 350 fol. was originally written by one person, presumably in 1363 (the date given on fol. 149r).

The codex is especially known for its beautifully illuminated initials. Selma Jónsdóttir has pointed out that one of these (fol. 2r) has a picture of the MS's donor; this detail suggests that a layman commissioned the MS and that he intended it as a gift for some ecclesiastical foundation, although it appears always to have been private property. According to Ólafur Halldórsson (1966), the codex belongs to a group of MSS (including *Codex Scardensis*) written in the Helgafell monastery, perhaps written for Lawman Ormr Snorrason (*ca.* 1320–1401 or 1402).

The second codex, *Codex Scardensis*, is a 14th-century MS containing the most complete medieval Icelandic collection of the *postola sögur, i.e.*, *Pétrs saga, Páls saga, Andreas saga, Tveggja postola saga Jóns ok Jakobs, Thómas saga, Philippus saga, Jakobs saga* (Jakobus Minor), *Bartholomeus saga, Mathias saga, Tveggja postola saga Símons ok Judas*, and *Matheus saga.*

The codex originally consisted of ninety-five folios, but one leaf is now lost (after fol. 63). It was written by two scribes, and is beautifully illuminated. On pages originally left blank at the beginning and end of the MS, two church inventories and a tithe account have since been written.

According to Ólafur Halldórsson (1966), this codex also belongs to a group of MSS written in the Helgafell monastery. It is first mentioned as being at Skarð in the Vilchin inventory of 1397, and is assumed to have been written for Lawman Ormr Snorrason, who, according to the inventory of Skarð church in the codex itself, gave it to the church. The codex presumably remained at Skarð until 1807. Around 1710, it was borrowed by Árni Magnússon and copied (AM 638 4to, AM 631 4to, and AM 636 4to). In 1807, it fell into obscurity until 1836, when it was offered

for sale in London and purchased by Sir Thomas Phillipps. In 1890, it was rediscovered by Eiríkr Magnússon and Jón Þorkelsson, and was purchased in 1965 on behalf of the banks in Iceland and presented to the Árni Magnússon Institute in Iceland.

1. AM 350 fol.: Ed.: Jakob Benediktsson, ed *Skarðsbók, Jónsbók and Other Laws and Precepts: MS No. 350 fol. in the Arna-Magnæan Collection in the University Library of Copenhagen.* Corpus Codicum Islandicorum Medii Aevi, 16. Copenhagen: Munksgaard, 1943; Jónas Kristjánsson et al., eds. *Skarðsbók. Codex Scardensis. AM 350 fol.* Manuscripta Islandica Medii Aevi, 1. Reykjavik: Lögberg, 1981. **Lit.**: Jón Helgason. "Ortografien i AM 350 fol." *Meddelelser fra norsk forening for sprogvidenskap*, 1.2. Oslo: Aschehoug, 1926, pp. 45–75; Halldór Hermannsson. *Icelandic Illuminated Manuscripts of the Middle Ages.* Corpus Codicum Islandicorum Medii Aevi, 7. Copenhagen: Levin & Munksgaard, 1935; Selma Jónsdóttir. "Gjafaramynd í íslenzku handriti." *Árbók hins íslenzka fornleifafélags 1964* (1965), 5–19; Ólafur Halldórsson. *Helgafellsbækur fornar.* Studia Islandica, 24. Reykjavik: Menningarsjóður, 1966; Stefán Karlsson, ed. *Sagas of Icelandic Bishops: Fragments of Eight Manuscripts.* Early Icelandic Manuscripts in Facsimile, 7. Copenhagen: Rosenkilde & Bagger, 1967, pp. 19–21; Wolf, Kirsten. "A Comment on the Dating of AM 226 fol." [forthcoming in *Gripla*]. **2. Codex Scardensis: Ed.**: Unger, C. R., ed. *Postola sögur: Legendariske fortællinger om apostlernes liv deres kamp for kristendommens udbredelse samt deres martyrdød.* Christiania [Oslo]: Bentzen, 1874; Slay, Desmond, ed. *Codex Scardensis.* Early Icelandic Manuscripts in Facsimile, 2. Copenhagen: Rosenkilde & Bagger, 1960; Ólafur Halldórsson, ed. *Sögur úr Skarðsbók.* Reykjavik: Almenna bókafélagið, 1967. **Lit.**: Eiríkr Magnússon. "Kodex Skardensis af postulasögur." *Arkiv för nordisk filologi* 8 (1892), 238–45; Jón Þorkelsson. "Islandske håndskrifter i England og Skotland." *Arkiv för nordisk filologi* 8 (1892), 199–237 [esp. pp. 235–6]; Ólafur Halldórsson. *Helgafellsbækur fornar.* Studia Islandica, 24. Reykjavik: Menningarsjóður, 1966; Collings, Lucy Grace. "The Codex Scardensis: Studies in Icelandic Hagiography." Diss. Cornell University, 1969.

Kirsten Wolf

[See also: Diplomatics; *Jónsbók*; Laws; *Postola sögur*]

Skírnismál ("The Lay of Skírnir"), or *Fǫr Scírnis* ("Skírnir's Journey"), as it is called in *Codex Regius* of the *Poetic Edda*, survives in three texts: the poem contained in *Codex Regius*, a fragmentary text (sts. 1–27) in AM 748 4to, and a prose summary, together with stanza 42, in ch. 23 of *Gylfaginning* in *Snorra Edda*.

Skírnismál is unique among the eddic materials as the only poem to deal exclusively with the gods known as the Vanir. The poem tells how Freyr sees the giantess Gerðr from Óðinn's high seat, is smitten by her beauty, and sends his servant Skírnir to arrange an assignation with her. Before Skírnir departs on his errand, Freyr and the other gods give him gifts. He accomplishes his mission, not by offering these objects as gifts, which she rejects, but rather by resorting to threats and a lengthy curse. The narrative portion of *Skírnismál* is composed in the *ljóðaháttr* meter, but the curse is primarily in *galdralag* meter.

Given the poem's subject matter and characters, many scholars have detected an underlying fertility myth: Freyr (the sky) loves Gerðr (the fruitful earth), and tells her that they will meet in Barri, which Olsen (1909) interprets as a kind of grain. Sahlgren (1962) took exception to this interpretation, viewing *Skírnismál* not as a fertility myth, but as a popular tale created from well-known motifs. Phillpotts (1920) builds on Olsen's views, and sees in the poem a ritual that would have been performed. Her interpretation neatly accounts for the fact that nearly every verse of the poem can be understood as dialogue, and for the fact that Skírnir, rather than the god himself, undertakes the mission. The relationship between Skírnir and Freyr has been a point of discussion, however, in that Freyr is elsewhere referred to as *skírr* ("bright, shining, pure"); some scholars have concluded that Skírnir is none other than Freyr himself. Like Olsen and Phillpotts, Dronke (1962) sees the poem as a *hieros gamos* (sacred marriage). In his structurally oriented study, Lönnroth (1977) examines the tale in terms of the marriage norms of Old Norse society, and concludes that the myth represents a legitimation and reaffirmation of the patriarchal structure of Old Norse society, and thus helps regulate human behavior. Motz (1981) sees the poem as a male-female struggle for power. Building on Lönnroth's view, Mitchell (1983) argues that the central point of the myth is to provide a matrix for resolving conflict between different families and groups through a system of exchange and intermarriage.

Skírnir's curse has commanded attention from nearly all commentators. Reichardt (1939) regards the whole curse as a later interpolation based on an indigenous tradition of Germanic magical spells. By comparing the thistle curse (st. 31.6–8) with an Old English magical charm, Harris (1975) demonstrates how the curse contrasts the brittle dryness of the weed with the fertile, phallic alternative Skírnir offers Gerðr.

Ed.: Finnur Jónsson, ed. *Edda Snorra Sturlusonar*. Copenhagen: Gyldendal, 1931, pp. 40–1; Neckel, Gustav, ed. *Edda: Die Lieder des Codex Regius nebst verwandten Denkmälern. I: Text*. 5th ed. rev. Hans Kuhn. Heidelberg: Winter, 1983, pp. 69–77. **Tr.**: Hollander, Lee M., trans. *The Poetic Edda. Translated with an Introduction and Explanatory Notes*. 2nd rev. ed. Austin: University of Texas Press, 1962; rpt. 1988, pp. 65–73 [see also other translations of the *Poetic Edda*]. **Lit.**: Olsen, Magnus. "Fra gammelnorsk myte og Kultus." *Maal og minne* (1909), 17–36; Phillpotts, Bertha S. *The Elder Edda and Ancient Scandinavian Drama*. Cambridge: Cambridge University Press, 1920; Reichardt, Konstantin. "Die Liebesbeschwörung in Fǫr Skírnis." *Journal of English and Germanic Philology* 38 (1939), 481–95; Sahlgren, Jöran. "Lunden Barre i Skírnismál." *Namn och bygd* 50 (1962), 193–203; Dronke, Ursula. "Art and Tradition in Skírnismál." In *English and Medieval Studies Presented to J. R. R. Tolkien on the Occasion of His Seventieth Birthday*. Ed. Norman Davis and C. L. Wrenn. London: Allen & Unwin, 1962, pp. 250–68; Harris, Joseph. "Cursing with the Thistle: 'Skírnismál' 31, 6–8, and OE metrical Charm 9, 16–17." *Neuphilologische Mitteilungen* 76 (1975), 26–33; Lönnroth, Lars. "Skírnismál och den fornisländska äktenskapsnormen." In *Opuscula Septentrionalia: Festskrift til Ole Widding, 10. 10. 1977*. Ed. Bent Chr. Jacobsen *et al*. Copenhagen: Reitzel, 1977, pp. 154–78; Motz, Lotte. "Gerðr: A New Interpretation of the Lay of Skírnir." *Maal og minne* (1981), 121–36; Mitchell, Stephen A. "Fǫr Scírnis as Mythological Model: fri at kaupa." *Arkiv för nordisk filologi* 98 (1983), 108–22; Harris, Joseph. "Eddic Poetry." In *Old Norse–Icelandic Literature: A Critical Guide*. Ed. Carol J. Clover and John Lindow. Islandica, 45. Ithaca and London: Cornell University Press, 1985, pp. 68–156 [esp. pp. 82–4, 152].

Stephen A. Mitchell

[**See also:** *Codex Regius*; Eddic Meters; Eddic Poetry; Mythology]

Skjǫldunga saga

Skjǫldunga saga ("The Saga of the Skjǫldungar") is a history of the prehistoric kings of Denmark, tracing some twenty generations from Skjǫldr, Óðinn's son, to Gorm the Old (d. *ca*. 940). The saga thus stands on the margin between *fornaldarsögur* (in content) and *konungasögur* (in intent). *Skjǫldunga saga* is a pioneer work in Old Norse literature. It is the earliest saga of ancient times, *i.e.*, before the settlement of Iceland, and the first Icelandic history of the kings of Denmark. After *Skjǫldunga saga*, the Icelanders began to write histories of kings other than Norwegian, and legendary history received its own genre in the *fornaldarsögur*, which in written form developed after the mid-13th century.

The original text of *Skjǫldunga saga* no longer exists. But saga authors and historians from around 1200 until 1600 used the saga as a source for their works; on the basis of these versions, it is possible to reconstruct the saga. Our primary authority is the *Rerum Danicarum fragmenta*, composed toward the end of the 16th century at the instigation of Niels Krag by Arngrímur Jónsson lærði ("the learned"; 1568–1648), who relied heavily on the saga for the section from Óðinn to Hrólfr kraki; the text known to Arngrímur contained a lacuna that extended from Hrólfr kraki as far as Sigurðr hringr. Jakob Benediktsson claimed that Arngrímur abridged the original text, but his theory was refuted by Bjarni Guðnason (1963), who argued that Arngrímur followed his source fairly closely. In addition, the *Sǫgubrot af fornkonungum* (AM 1 e β 1 fol.) is considered to be derived from the saga, although probably from a younger and expanded recension composed in the latter part of the 13th century. Snorri Sturluson relied on the saga for his *Edda* (the prologue and *Skáldskaparmál*); and in *Ynglinga saga* (ch. 29), he directly refers to it: "Frá þessi orrostu er langt sagt i Skjǫldunga sǫgu . . ." ("A long account of this battle is given in Skjǫldunga saga . . ."). From this reference, it is clear that the name of this saga is medieval, confirmed by two medieval MS catalogues, which mention MSS containing *Skjǫldunga saga*. One MS of *Skjǫldunga saga* was in the monastery of Möðruvellir in 1416. Glimpses of *Skjǫldunga saga* are also seen in Arngrímur Jónsson's *Ad catalogum regum Sveciæ annotanda*, *Upphaf allra frásagna* (AM 764 4to), *Bjarkarímur*, *Ragnarssona þáttr* (*Hauksbók*), *Óláfs saga Tryggvasonar en mesta*, *Jómsvíkinga saga*, and *Hrólfs saga kraka*.

Snorri's *Edda* (composed *ca*. 1220) forms a *terminus ante quem* for the dating of *Skjǫldunga saga*. But on the basis of the text of the *Edda*, it cannot be ascertained whether *Skjǫldunga saga* was at that time an older work, or whether it had been composed only a few years earlier. Bjarni Guðnason has attempted to demonstrate that the saga could be dated to around 1180, but the arguments are weak; stylistically, the saga is primitive, and lacks the narrative technique of the classical saga literature. And from a literary-historical point of view, *Skjǫldunga saga* must be seen as a result of the so-called 12th-century renaissance, which passed through all the countries of western and northern Europe.

By reason of its age, *Skjǫldunga saga* must have been based primarily on oral narratives, in which numerous tales about the Skjǫldungar existed, as witnessed by Saxo's *Gesta Danorum*. The author also used a great number of poems, including *Grottasǫngr*, *Rígsþula*, and the Starkad poems. The backbone of the saga, however, a written genealogy from Oddi, which may have been compiled by Sæmundr fróði ("the learned") Sigfússon (d. 1133). It is believed that the author was also acquainted with a number of foreign histories, including Geoffrey of Monmouth's *Historia regum Britanniae*, which may have inspired him, although whether he actually drew information from these works cannot be ascertained. For the account of Óðinn and his sons' migration from Asia to Scandinavia, it is possible that he relied on Frankish works.

Borrowings from Gregory the Great's *Dialogues* are also possible.

The work is anonymous, but Bishop Páll Jónsson (d. 1211) of the Oddaverjar, who claimed descent from the Skjǫldungar, may have had a hand in the composition of *Skjǫldunga saga*. The author was a learned and critical storyteller with a sense of reality, who was familiar with the etymological and historiographical methods of the Middle Ages. His goal was not only to record events directly associated with the Danish kings and Denmark, but also to give an account of the origin and history of the Norse peoples and their place in world history. Because of the genealogy, which gives the saga a framework, it must be considered well structured. When at times the work appears unbalanced, this trait can most probably be traced to the uneven information available to the medieval author.

Ed.: Jakob Benediktsson, ed. *Arngrimi Jonae Opera Latine Conscripta.* 4 vols. Bibliotheca Arnamagnæana, 9–12. Copenhagen: Munksgaard, 1950–57; Bjarni Guðnason, ed. *Sǫgur Danakonunga.* Íslenzk fornrit, 35. Reykjavik: Hið íslenzka fornritafélag, 1982. **Tr.**: Friis-Jensen, Karsten, and Claus Lund, trans. *Skjoldungernes Saga.* Copenhagen: Gad, 1984 [Danish; introduction by Claus Lund, pp. 9–42]. **Lit.**: Olrik, Axel. "Skjoldungasaga i Arngrim Jonssons Udtog." *Aarbøger for nordisk Oldkyndinghed og Historie,* Ser. 2, vol. 9 (1894), 83–164; Olrik, Axel. *Danmarks Heltedigtning. En Oldtidsstudie.* 2 vols. Copenhagen: Gad, 1903–10; Heusler, Andreas. "Die gelehrte Urgeschichte im altisländischen Schrifttum." Abh. 3. *Abhandlungen der Königlich Preussischen Akademie der Wissenschaften, philosophisch-historische Classe.* Berlin: Verlag der königlichen Akademie der Wissenschaften, 1908; Boer, R. C. "Studier over Skjoldungedigtningen." *Aarbøger for nordisk Oldkyndighed og Historie,* Ser. 3, vol. 12 (1922), 133–266; Einar Ól. Sveinsson. *Sagnaritun Oddaverja. Nokkrar athuganir.* Studia Islandica, 1. Reykjavik: Ísafold, 1937 [English summary, pp. 47–51]; Lukman, Niels Clausen. *Skjoldunge und Skilfinge. Hunnen- und Herulerkönige in ostnordischer Überlieferung.* Classica et Mediaevalia, Dissertationes, 3. Copenhagen: Gyldendal, 1943; Jakob Benediktsson. "Icelandic Traditions of the Scyldings." *Saga-Book of the Viking Society* 15 (1957–61), 48–66; Bjarni Guðnason. *Um Skjǫldungasögu.* Reykjavik: Menningarsjóður, 1963 [English summary, pp. 306–25]; Jakob Benediktsson. "Doktorsvörn." *Lingua Islandica* 4 (1963), 136–51; Einar Ól. Sveinsson. "Skjǫldungasaga. Andmælaræða við doktorsvörn Bjarna Guðnasonar 1. júní 1963." *Skírnir* 137 (1963), 163–81; Ellehøj, Svend. *Studier over den ældste norrøne historieskrivning.* Bibliotheca Arnamagnæana, 26. Copenhagen: Munksgaard, 1965; Skovgaard-Petersen, Inge. "Saxo, Historian of the Patria." *Mediaeval Scandinavia* 2 (1969), 54–77; Faulkes, Anthony. "The Genealogies and Regnal Lists in a Manuscript in Resen's Library." In *Sjötíu ritgerðir helgaðar Jakobi Benediktssyni 20. júlí 1977.* 2 vols. Ed. Einar G. Pétursson and Jónas Kristjánsson. Reykjavik: Stofnun Árna Magnússonar, 1977, vol. 1, pp. 177–90; Jónas Kristjánsson. *Eddas and Sagas: Iceland's Medieval Literature.* Trans. Peter Foote. Reykjavik: Hið íslenska bókmenntafélag, 1988.

Kirsten Wolf

[**See also:** *Fornaldarsǫgur*; Gregory, St.: *Dialogues*; *Grottasǫngr*; *Konungasǫgur*; *Rígsþula*; Saxo Grammaticus; *Snorra Edda*; Sæmundr Sigfússon inn fróði; *Ynglinga saga*]

Slavery. The thrall (Old Norse *þræll*) who appears in the medieval law codes of Norway, Iceland, Denmark, and Sweden, and in the Icelandic sagas, is a slave by any currently accepted definition of the term. Slaves appear in Finnish literature as well, but the sources for their status are much scantier.

According to *Landnámabók* and the *Íslendingasögur*, Vikings raiding in Ireland and Scotland brought slaves back with them to Iceland and Norway. Arabic accounts report that Swedes sold slaves to Islamic merchants in Russia, and they may have brought Slavic or Finnish slaves home. Since slavery was hereditary, the descendants of these captives remained slaves and may have been assimilated into an indigenous slave class. Native Scandinavians were captured in raids as well and enslaved for crime and debt. By the era of the law codes, debt servitude was temporary and distinguished from slavery, but this distinction may not always have been the case.

Under the law, slaves were property like livestock; they could be bought and sold, and tendered for payment of debts. The laws did not punish owners for harming their slaves, with a few exceptions based on Christian principles; in Iceland, for example, it was forbidden to kill one's slave during Lent. Someone who injured or killed another's slave had to pay compensation not to the slave or his kindred, as with free people, but to the owner. Except in the law of Uppland, a royal issuance that deliberately tried to ameliorate the lot of the slave, the compensation was not a *wergeld* (the price set upon a person) and had nothing to do with honor or status; it was keyed to market value, the actual damage the owner had suffered by injury to his property. The laws set standard amounts for compensation, but the level could vary depending on the value of the particular slave. Under Icelandic law, an injured slave could keep a small part of the compensation. In certain special circumstances (*e.g.*, if a slave were killed defending his master), the killer had to pay a higher price and could be outlawed.

The owner was also responsible for injuries a slave committed, unless he could prove the slave had run away. The owner might have the option of turning over the slave to the victim or his family as part of or in lieu of a compensation payment. For certain offenses, however, the law prescribed physical punishment for slaves, who owned little or no property and so could not be fined. *Landnámabók* and the sagas contain a few examples of minor slave rebellions, but flight is the only type of resistance most of the law codes consider.

In parts of Denmark and Sweden, the law recognized slave marriage. Where slaves could engage only in informal relationships, not marriage, the law either implicitly or explicitly gave a child its mother's status, a principle it may have adopted from Roman and canon law. Some of the Swedish codes provided that a child with one free parent was free, and a passage in the Uppland law implies that any child of a Christian marriage was free even if the parents were both slaves. Where the children did remain slaves, the parents had no rights over them; they belonged to the mother's owner or were split between the parents' owners. The Norwegian laws envision that slave children were a disadvantage to the owner; anyone who fathered a slave child had to pay for its upbringing. In Sweden, by contrast, ownership of children was considered an advantage. Many scholars infer that slave children were often killed by exposure in Norway and Iceland, although the evidence for this practice is scanty.

On the evidence of the sagas, slaves seem to have been members of the household labor force rather than organized in gangs on large estates. Slaves generally did the same work as free laborers or family members, though the more onerous tasks, like dunging fields, might have been reserved for them. In Denmark and Sweden, estates were larger than in Norway and Iceland, and scholars have suggested that cottagers mentioned in later documents are the descendants of slaves who worked in a plantation-like system.

Slavery was not just a legal and economic status, but also a social classification. The sagas and poetry (particularly *Rígsþula*) show contempt for slaves, depicted as cowardly, ugly, and stupid. Whether born into slavery or captured, a slave was seen as having an innately slavish character.

The laws provided mechanisms for masters to free their slaves, who then remained in a position of dependence, or for slaves or their kin to purchase their freedom. Wills from Sweden and Denmark indicate that owners freed slaves as a pious act. Although the Church may have encouraged manumission and better treatment of slaves, never in the Middle Ages did it condemn slavery itself.

Slavery was obsolescent in Iceland by the 12th century, and in Norway by the end of that century at the latest. In Denmark, slavery probably still existed into the 13th century. In Sweden, the Skara Ordinance of 1335 prohibited holding Christians as slaves in the provinces of Västergötland and Värmland, and it may be that similar ordinances that have not survived applied to the rest of Sweden.

The end of the Viking raids on western Europe has often been suggested as a reason for the ending of slavery in Iceland and Norway, but if slavery was economically advantageous, it could have continued on a hereditary basis there as it did in Sweden. As a pool of landless free laborers developed by the 11th century in Iceland (later, elsewhere), however, it may have been cheaper for landowners to hire them by the year or rent land to them than to keep slaves. In Sweden and Denmark, large estates were split up in the 13th and 14th centuries into tenant holdings, and many former slaves may have become tenants. By the later Middle Ages, the free population of Scandinavia was much more stratified socially than before, and not all free people had full political rights, but there was no longer a need for a formal category of slave.

Lit.: Wergeland, Agnes Mathilde. *Slavery in Germanic Society During the Middle Ages.* Chicago: University of Chicago Press, 1916; Henning, Sam. "Trälldomens försvinnande och de svenska landskaplagarna." *Historisk tidskrift* (Sweden) 15 (1930), 86–95; Árni Pálsson. "Um lok þrældóms á Íslandi." *Skírnir* 106 (1932), 191–203; Williams, Carl O. *Thraldom in Ancient Iceland.* Chicago: University of Chicago Press, 1937; Hasselberg, Gösta. "Den s.k. Skarastadgan och trälldomens upphörande i Sverige." *Västergötlands fornminnesförenings tidskrift* 5.3 (1944), 51–90; Finley, M. I. "Slavery." *International Encyclopedia of the Social Sciences*, 14. New York: Macmillan, 1968, pp. 307–13; Lunden, Kåre. "Om årsakene til den norske bondefridomen: Ein økonomisk-historisk forklåringsmåte." *Heimen* 15 (1971), 213–22; Nevéus, Clara. *Trälarna i landskapslagarnas samhälle. Danmark och Sverige.* Studia historica Upsaliensia, 58. Uppsala: Almqvist & Wiksell, 1974; Foote, Peter, *et al.* "Træl." *KLNM* 19 (1975), 14–28; Kristensen, Anne K. G. "Danelaw Institutions and Danish Society in the Viking Age: *Sochemanni, liberi homines* and *Königsfreie*." *Mediaeval Scandinavia* 8 (1975), 27–85; Foote, Peter. "Þrælahald á Íslandi." *Saga* 15 (1977), 41–74; Lind, Joan Dyste. "The Ending of Slavery in Sweden: Social Structure and Decision Making." *Scandinavian Studies* 50 (1978), 57–71; Wilde-Stockmeyer, Marlis. *Sklaverei auf Island. Untersuchungen zur rechtlich-sozialen Darstellung der Sklaven im skandinavischen Mittelalter.* Heidelberg: Winter, 1978; Skyum-Nielsen, Niels. "Nordic Slavery in an International Setting." *Mediaeval Scandinavia* 11 (1978–79), 126–48; Lindkvist, Thomas. *Landborna i Norden under äldre medeltid.* Studia historia Upsaliensis, 110. Uppsala: Almqvist & Wiksell,

1979; Krag, Claus. "Treller og trellehold." *Historisk tidsskrift* (Norway) 61 (1982), 209–27; Patterson, Orlando. *Slavery and Social Death: A Comparative Study.* Cambridge: Harvard University Press, 1982; Anna Agnarsdóttir and Ragnar Árnason. "Þrælahald á þjóðveldisöld." *Saga* 21 (1983), 5–26; Iversen, Tore. "Den gammelnorske trelldommen og dens avvikling." *Historisk tidskrift* (Norway) 64 (1985), 158–79; Phillips, William D., Jr. *Slavery from Roman Times to the Early Transatlantic Trade.* Minneapolis: University of Minnesota Press, 1985; Karras, Ruth Mazo. *Slavery and Society in Medieval Scandinavia.* Yale Historical Publications, 135. New Haven and London: Yale University Press, 1988; Karras, Ruth Mazo. "Concubinage and Slavery in the Viking Age." *Scandinavian Studies* 62 (1990), 141–62.

Ruth Mazo Karras

[See also: Laws; *Rígsþula*]

Sneglu-Halla þáttr ("The Tale of Shuttle-Halli"), a short Old Icelandic tale, forms part of the *konungasaga* about Haraldr harðráði ("hard-ruler"). In *Morkinskinna* and *Hulda-Hrokkinskinna*, it is found among some tales that end a section dealing with Norwegian domestic conflicts. The later part of *Flateyjarbók* places the *þáttr* after the saga proper, as the third of seven additional *þættir*. This version (designated "II" below) is considerably longer than the other two (designated "I").

Version II begins and ends in Iceland, and is set probably during the 1050s. In I as well as in II, Halli is accepted as a follower of the king, and he performs poems on several occasions. However, he comes into conflict with Haraldr, and the relationship between Halli and the court poet Þjóðólfr grows increasingly tense. In the presence of the king, they scorn each other's earlier accomplishments in Iceland. Þjóðólfr becomes so enraged that he draws his sword, and the men are forced to intervene. On a later occasion, Halli succeeds in fooling Einarr fluga ("fly") into paying fines for the assassination of a nonexistent brother. At the end, Halli embarks on a journey abroad and attracts attention in Denmark and England. Version II relates some further events in Norway and Halli's death in Iceland.

Which version is older has not been definitely settled. There are signs of expansion in II, as well as of shortening in I. And why was the *þáttr* omitted in the Haraldr saga proper in *Flateyjarbók*? Was it lacking in the original saga, or was it dismissed by the author because he knew a better version that was not available at the time? The story is very old and based on oral tradition and genuine skaldic poetry; it was probably written down around 1200. The Halli material evolved to some degree in the later tradition, and new episodes were added.

Sneglu-Halla þáttr has a looser and more paratactical construction than most other *þættir*. It consists of a series of episodes that could have been arranged otherwise just as well. Perhaps the material was too abundant to be digested into a unified work of art. The tale is characterized by a coarse, sometimes obscene comedy, and it shows a fascination with verbal talents.

Halli is mentioned in *Skáldatal*, and a half-stanza of his is cited in the *Third Grammatical Treatise*, which is included in some MSS of Snorri's *Edda*. He came from the same district in Iceland as Haraldr's court poet Þjóðólfr Arnórsson, whose preserved production is considerable. However, only in *Sneglu-Halla þáttr* does Þjóðólfr's private life shine through. Einarr fluga appears in the younger *Odds þáttr Ófeigssonar*, acting in a way similar to that in this tale.

Ed.: Jónas Kristjánsson, ed. *Eyfirðinga sögur*. Íslenzk fornrit, 9. Reykjavik: Hið íslenzka fornritafélag, 1956, pp. cix–cxiv, 263–95. **Tr.**: Hollander, Lee M., trans. *The Skalds: A Selection of Their Poems, with Introduction and Notes*. Princeton: Princeton University Press, 1945; 2nd ed. Ann Arbor: University of Michigan Press, 1968, pp. 207–13 [partial]. **Lit.**: Finnur Jónsson. *Den oldnorske og oldislandske Litteraturs Historie*. 3 vols. 2nd ed. Copenhagen: Gad, 1920–24, vol. 1, pp. 620–2; vol. 2, pp. 545–6; Vries, Jan de. *Altnordische Literaturgeschichte*. 2 vols. Grundriss der germanischen Philologie, 15–6. rpt. Berlin: de Gruyter, 1941–42; rpt. 1964–67, vol. 1, pp. 276–7; vol. 2, pp. 427–9; Gimmler, Heinrich. *Die Thættir der Morkinskinna. Ein Beitrag zur Überlieferungs - problematik und zur Typologie der altnordischen Kurzerzählung*. Berlin: Difo-Druck, 1976, pp. 57–8, 80–1; Louis-Jensen, Jonna. *Kongesagastudier: Kompilationen Hulda-Hrokkinskinna*. Bibliotheca Arnamagnæana, 32. Copenhagen: Reitzel, 1977, pp. 76–7; Danielsson, Tommy. *Om den isländska släktsagans uppbyggnad*. Skrifter utgivna av Litteraturvetenskapliga institutionen vid Uppsala universitet, 22. Uppsala: Almqvist & Wiksell, 1986, pp. 74–5.

Tommy Danielsson

[**See also:** *Flateyjarbók*; Grammatical Treatises; *Hulda-Hrokkinskinna*; *Konungasögur*; *Morkinskinna*; *Odds þáttr Ófeigssonar*; *Þáttr*]

Snorra Edda, or Snorri Sturluson's *Edda*, is sometimes called the *Prose* or *Younger Edda* to distinguish it from the *Poetic* or *Elder Edda*, which was formerly known as *Sæmundr's Edda*. A treatise in Icelandic on skaldic poetry, it has four main parts. The prologue gives a rationalistic account of the origin of heathen religions in nature worship and a euhemeristic explanation of the origin of the Norse gods as great kings descended from King Priam of Troy, who migrated to Scandinavia and came to be worshiped there. This prologue forms an introduction to *Gylfaginning* ("the tricking of Gylfi"), which takes the form of a dialogue, a contest of wisdom between three of the newly arrived Æsir (etymologized as "men of Asia," having migrated from Troy) and Gylfi, a king in Sweden, disguised as a wanderer under the name of "Gangleri." The Æsir's replies to Gylfi's questions comprise a comprehensive account of Norse mythology from the emergence of the giants and gods and the creation of the world to its end at Ragnarǫk ("doom of the gods" or, in Snorri's account, Ragnarøkkr, "twilight of the gods"). Many stories about the gods are included, among them some of Þórr's encounters with giants, the death of Baldr, and the punishment of Loki. Verses from eddic poems are freely quoted in *Gylfaginning*, chiefly from *Vǫluspá*, *Vafþrúðnismál*, and *Grímnismál*, although among the sources used were some skaldic mythological poems, such as Bragi's *Ragnarsdrápa*, and possibly some oral prose stories. At the end of *Gylfaginning*, Gylfi is cheated of his victory in the contest when he suddenly finds that the hall in which it took place has disappeared. The Æsir then decide to adopt the names of the gods they have been telling stories about so that they themselves may come to be worshiped as gods.

The third part, *Skáldskaparmál* ("the language of poetry"), is also in the form of a dialogue at first (not maintained throughout), between Bragi, god of poetry, and Ægir, personification of the sea. First, Bragi narrates some stories about the gods that lead up to the myth of the origin of poetical inspiration in the mead recovered by Óðinn from the giants. Since the 17th century, this part of the work has sometimes been referred to as *Bragaræður* ("the speeches of Bragi"). Then begins the discussion of the language of poetry, interrupted by a brief statement of the purpose of the work, which is to instruct young poets, and an excursus claiming an origin for some Norse myths in allegories of events in the Troy story, sometimes referred to as the *eptirmáli* ("epilogue"). The main part of *Skáldskaparmál* has two principal sections, the first dealing with kennings, or periphrastic descriptions, *e.g.*, "son of Óðinn" for Þórr, "tree of weapons" for warrior, "horse of the sea" for ship. The second section deals with *heiti*, or synonyms, such as steed for horse, prince for king, rhyme for poetry. The two categories are not rigorously distinguished, however, especially toward the end of this section, and various subcategories are mentioned that are not altogether clear. Both kennings and *heiti* are listed according to their meanings, beginning with those referring to heathen gods and to poetry, and including those for various natural phenomena, men and women, gold, battle, ships, and weapons, and some for Christ. The kennings and *heiti* listed are illustrated by frequent quotations from poems by numerous Norwegian and Icelandic poets of various periods, many of which are not preserved elsewhere. Some narratives are included to account for the origins of kennings, some mythological, some heroic. In connection with the myths, long passages of skaldic mythological poems not found elsewhere are quoted. As an appendix to *Skáldskaparmál*, some MSS include a series of *þulur*, or versified lists of names and synonyms, for poets to use in constructing kennings.

The last part of the work is *Háttatal* ("list of verse forms"). This section consists of a poem, or rather a series of three poems, in 102 stanzas that illustrate a variety of verse forms (although some of the variants are rhetorical rather than metrical), composed by Snorri himself, together with a prose commentary, assumed also to be by Snorri, that explains the meters and devices used, such as rhyme and alliteration. The commentary begins in dialogue form, although the speakers are anonymous. The poem offers eulogy in the conventional style of court poetry of King Hákon Hákonarson of Norway and Earl Skúli, praising both for their success in battle and generosity to their followers.

All four sections of the work show the influence both of native traditions and of the thought of the Christian Latin Middle Ages. The prologue and *Skáldskaparmál* use learned Icelandic sagas about prehistory, such as *Skjǫldunga saga* and an early version of *Vǫlsunga saga*, as well as genealogies both in verse and prose, some of the latter derived from Anglo-Saxon royal genealogies. A version of *Trójumanna saga* also seems to have been used in the prologue and "epilogue," and the author may also have known *Breta sǫgur*. The euhemeristic treatment of heathen gods in the prologue has parallels not only in Snorri's own *Ynglinga saga* and Saxo Grammaticus, but also in Latin writings dealing with classical deities. The influence of Christianity is apparent on the mythology of *Gylfaginning*, and, more specifically, patristic writings influenced the discussion of heathen religion in the prologue. Some of the native sources for myths recounted were eddic and skaldic poems now lost, but a precedent for *Háttatal* survives in the *Háttalykill* of Rǫgnvaldr Kali and Hallr Þórarinsson, although no commentary on this work has survived. *Háttatal* was also probably influenced by Latin *centimetrae*, and the use of dialogue in this part of the work is most reminiscent of Latin schoolbooks, the frame of *Gylfaginning* being more similar to that of *Vafþrúðnismál*. Snorri was probably influenced by writers on Latin grammar and rhetoric, but his classification system is not closely derivative from any that are known.

There are seven MSS or MS fragments that have independent textual value, though none of them seems to preserve the text in quite its original form. Their relationships are complex, and it is not possible to construct a traditional stemma. The oldest is probably De la Gardie 11 (early 14th century). Its text has been greatly shortened, and parts are lacking, notably the *þulur* and the latter half of *Háttatal*, as well as some passages in *Gylfaginning* and *Skáldskaparmál*. Some of the material appears in a different order from that of the other MSS. Some unconnected items are included: *Skáldatal* (a list of court poets), a genealogy of the Sturlung family, a list of Icelandic lawspeakers, and a version of the *Second Grammatical Treatise*. This MS is possibly derived from an authorial draft, since it seems to lack ordering.

Most editions are based on the *Codex Regius* (GkS 2367 4to, first half of the 14th century), which is believed to have the least altered text and is virtually complete. Although the beginning of the prologue is lacking, the missing text can be reconstructed from 17th-century copies. The eddic-type poem *Grottasǫngr* is included as part of *Skáldskaparmál*, and two unrelated poems, *Jómsvíkingadrápa* and *Málsháttakvæði*, are added at the end. This is the only MS that includes the end of *Háttatal*. Closely related to it is University Library Utrecht MS no. 1374 (*ca.* 1595), which is evidently a fairly close copy of a lost 13th-century exemplar, but lacks the end of *Háttatal* and the beginning of the prologue.

In *Codex Wormianus* (AM 242 fol., mid-14th century), the second part of *Skáldskaparmál* (dealing with *heiti*) had been extensively revised and expanded, but only fragments of this part now survive, and there are no *þulur*. Long additions containing biblical and classical material have been made to the prologue, and the MS also includes the eddic-type poem *Rígsþula* and four grammatical treatises. But some narrative passages in the first part of *Skáldskaparmál* are omitted, and the beginning and end of *Háttatal* are missing. In the 17th century, most of the missing material was added from other MSS onto paper leaves for its then-owner, Ole Worm.

Three fragmentary MSS contain parts of *Skáldskaparmál* and *þulur* only. AM 748 II 4to (*ca.* 1400) is close to the *Codex Regius*. The other two contain greatly rearranged and altered versions of the text, and both include parts of the *Third Grammatical Treatise*; AM 748 I 4to (early 14th century) also contains part of a collection of eddic poems, and AM 757a 4to (late 14th century) also contains various Christian poems. A fourth fragmentary MS (AM 756 4to, 15th century) contains parts of *Gylfaginning* and *Skáldskaparmál* derived from *Codex Wormianus*. A very large number (over 150) of other later MSS survive, most having heavily altered texts, the majority based on the version made by the priest Magnús Ólafsson of Laufás in 1609, which was also the basis of the first printed edition in 1665.

The attribution of the *Prose Edda* to Snorri Sturluson is based on a notice in De la Gardie 11, which also names him again as author of *Háttatal*. Some verses of *Háttatal* are quoted and ascribed to him in other medieval texts. He is further named in connection with references to *Skáldskaparmál* and the commentary to *Háttatal* in other MSS of the *Prose Edda*, and the work as a whole is attributed to him in the late 16th-century *Oddaverja annáll*. He most likely composed *Háttatal* shortly after his first visit to Norway in 1218–1220, and this part may have been the first written. The rest may have been compiled over a period of years, and some of the inconsistencies and illogicalities perhaps indicate that he was still revising it when he died. But the wide divergences between the contents and arrangement in the various MSS suggests that other revisers may have been at work, too. Various parts of the text have often been assumed to be additions or interpolations in Snorri's work, such as the *þulur*, the first and last chapters of *Gylfaginning*, some of the narrative parts of *Skáldskaparmál*, as well as the longer quotations from eddic and skaldic poems, the so-called epilogue, and even the prologue. On the other hand, many scholars have thought that the *Edda* is an earlier and less mature work than Snorri's *Heimskringla*. There are striking differences between the mythology of *Gylfaginning* and the treatment of heathen gods in *Ynglinga saga* (the first saga in *Heimskringla*), where, besides variations of detail, the euhemeristic doctrine is applied more consistently.

There is no universally accepted explanation of the name *Edda*. There are linguistic problems with the derivation from *óðr* 'poetry,' historical ones with connection with the place-name Oddi (where Snorri lived as a child, but not where he wrote his *Edda*), and semantic ones with identification with the word *edda* 'great-grandmother' (the sense development is unexplained). More recently, Magnús Ólafsson's suggestion has been revived, that the word was coined by Snorri as an ironical name for his book from the Latin word *edo* 'I compose' on the analogy of *kredda* 'superstition, illogically held belief,' which is derived from Latin *credo* 'I believe; creed' (Faulkes 1977). In 14th-century poems, the word is used to mean "poetics."

Snorri himself indicates, near the beginning of *Skáldskaparmál*, that the purpose of the work was to instruct young poets in the traditional techniques of skaldic verse. He was probably aware that this kind of poetry was becoming less popular and was in danger of being replaced by newer styles based on foreign models, such as ballads and romances, to which, as an aristocratic Icelander who valued the early traditions of his country, he would have been less sympathetic. But he is nevertheless a learned writer, and although he does not imitate foreign models closely, he shows acquaintance with Latin grammatical, metrical, and rhetorical treatises. Like many Latin writers, he shows more interest in the language and rhetoric of poems than in their content or overall structure. His explanations of the names of gods and of the origins of kennings are often linguistic ones, based on learned folk-etymology or on wordplay, and often seem improbable to modern scholars. This interest in language, also evidenced in the prologue, conforms with the general medieval view of grammar as embracing what we would call stylistics and literary criticism. Several MSS of *Snorra Edda* include one or more of the "Grammatical Treatises" that deal with spelling and rhetoric.

The account of mythology in *Gylfaginning* was probably included because so many skaldic kennings require a knowledge of heathen mythology. Snorri's attitude to the heathen religion is that of a historian: he shows great detachment and writes of the gods with irony and humor, distancing himself from them by the use of fictional narrators. Unlike other medieval mythographers, he shows little interest in allegorical or symbolic explanations of myths. Where he offers any interpretation at all, he presents the stories as having an etiological purpose.

Snorri's *Edda* is the only work of its kind from the Middle Ages. *Gylfaginning* provides the fullest and most systematic account of Norse mythology, and *Skáldskaparmál* and *Háttatal* offer the only comprehensive analysis of the diction and meter of poetry in a Germanic language before modern times.

Ed.: Resen, P. H., ed. *Edda Islandorum*. Copenhagen: Typis Henrici Gödiani, 1665; *Edda Snorra Sturlusonar*. 3 vols. Copenhagen: Sumptibus Legati Arnamagnæani, 1848–87 [vol. 2 contains the texts of the Uppsala MS De la Gardie 11 and the three medieval fragments]; Möbius, Th., ed. *Háttatal Snorra Sturlusonar*. Halle: Waisenhaus, 1879–81; Eeden, Willem van, Jr., ed. *De Codex Trajectinus van de Snorra Edda*. Leiden: Ijdo, 1913 [text of the Utrecht MS]; Finnur Jónsson, ed. *Edda Snorra Sturlusonar. Codex Wormianus A.M. 242, fol.* Copenhagen: Gyldendal, 1924; Snorri Sturluson. *Edda*. Ed. Finnur Jónsson. Copenhagen: Gad, 1926; Finnur Jónsson, ed. *Edda Snorra Sturlusonar*. Copenhagen: Gyldendal, 1931 [Codex Regius in original spelling with variants; unreliable on details]; Faulkes, Anthony, ed. *Two Versions of Snorra Edda from the 17th Century*. 2 vols. Reykjavik: Stofnun Árna Magnússonar, 1977–79; Snorri Sturluson. *Edda. Prologue and Gylfaginning*. Ed. Anthony Faulkes. Oxford: Clarendon, 1982. **Tr.**: Brodeur, Arthur Gilchrist, trans. *The Prose Edda by Snorri Sturluson*. New York: American-Scandinavian Foundation, 1916; rpt. 1960 [does not include *Háttatal* and omits parts of *Skáldskaparmál*]; Young, Jean I., trans. *The Prose Edda of Snorri Sturluson: Tales from Norse Mythology*. Cambridge: Bowes & Bowes, 1954; rpt. Berkeley, Los Angeles, and London: University of California Press, 1964 [includes prologue, *Gylfaginning*, narrative parts of *Skáldskaparmál* only]; Faulkes, Anthony, trans. *Snorri Sturluson: Edda*. Everyman Classics. London and Melbourne: Dent, 1987. **Bib.**: Halldór Hermannsson. *Bibliography of the Eddas*. Islandica, 13. Ithaca: Cornell University Library, 1920, pp. 74–89; Jóhann S. Hannesson. *Bibliography of the Eddas: A Supplement to Bibliography of the Eddas (Islandica XIII)*. Islandica, 37. Ithaca: Cornell University Press, 1955, pp. 93–104; Schach, Paul. "Old Norse Literature . . . The *Snorra Edda*." In *The Medieval Literature of Western Europe: A Review of Research, Mainly 1930–1960*. Ed. John H. Fisher. New York: New York University Press, 1966, pp. 266–7. **Lit.**: Baetke, Walter. *Die Götterlehre der Snorra-Edda*. Berichte über die Verhandlungen der sächsischen Akademie der Wissenschaften zu Leipzig. Philol.-hist. Klasse, 97.3. Berlin: Akademie-Verlag, 1952; Holtsmark, Anne. *Studier i Snorres mytologi*. Skrifter utg. av Det Norske Videnskaps-Akademi i Oslo. II. Hist.-filos. kl. Ny serie, 4. Oslo: Universitetsforlaget, 1964; Halldór Halldórsson. *Old Icelandic heiti in Modern Icelandic*. University of Iceland Publications in Linguistics, 3. Reykjavik: Institute of Nordic Linguistics, 1975, pp. 9–30; Hallberg, Peter. *Old Icelandic Poetry: Eddic Lay and Skaldic Verse*. Trans. Paul Schach and Sonja Lindgrenson. Lincoln and London: University of Nebraska Press, 1975, pp. 1–9; Dronke, Ursula and Peter. "The Prologue of the Prose *Edda*: Explorations of a Latin Background." In *Sjötíu ritgerðir helgaðar Jakobi Benediktssyni 20. júlí 1977*. 2 vols. Ed. Einar G. Pétursson and Jónas Kristjánsson. Reykjavik: Stofnun Árna Magnússonar, 1977, vol. 1, pp. 153–76; Faulkes, Anthony. "Edda." *Gripla* 2 (1977), 32–9; Faulkes, Anthony. "Pagan Sympathy: Attitudes to Heathendom in the Prologue to *Snorra Edda*." In *Edda: A Collection of Essays*. Ed. Robert J. Glendinning and Haraldur Bessason. University of Manitoba Icelandic Studies, 4. Winnipeg: University of Manitoba Press, 1983, pp. 283–314; Clunies Ross, Margaret. *Skáldskaparmál. Snorri Sturluson's ars poetica and Medieval Theories of Language*. Viking Collection, 4. Odense: Odense University Press, 1987.

Anthony Faulkes

[**See also:** Bragi Boddason; *Breta sǫgur*; *Codex Regius*; Eddic Meters; Eddic Poetry; *Fornafn*; Grammatical Treatises; *Grímnismál*; *Háttalykill*; *Heimskringla*; *Heiti*; Kennings; Mythology; Saxo Grammaticus; Skaldic Meters; Skaldic Verse; *Skjǫldunga saga*; Snorri Sturluson; *Trójumanna saga*; *Vafþrúðnismál*; *Vǫluspá*; *Ynglinga saga*]

Snorri Sturluson (1178/9–1241) was outstanding as a man of letters, and as a man of the world. More is known about him than about most authors of his time. He figures prominently in the major events of his day as recorded by his nephew Sturla Þórðarson in his *Íslendinga saga*, the chief item in the *Sturlunga saga* collection. We also gain glimpses of Snorri from other sagas of the *Sturlunga* collection, from Sturla Þórðarson's *Hákonar saga Hákonarsonar*, and from sagas of contemporary Icelandic bishops, especially Guðmundr Arason, as well as from annals, genealogies, letters, and verses by Snorri and his contemporaries.

Snorri's intelligence and driving ambition made him exceptional, but, at the same time, his life reflects his age and its contradictions, not least that between political turbulence and intellectual achievement.

Snorri is named in a near-contemporary source among the eight most powerful laymen in Iceland while still in his twenties. In 1215–1218 and 1222–1231/5, he held the almost presidential position of lawspeaker (*lǫgsǫgumaðr*) to the *Alþingi*, and he became the richest man in the land.

Snorri owed his worldly success to a combination of luck and shrewd management. He was born into the clan of the Sturlungar, who took their name from his father, the chieftain Sturla Þórðarson of Hvammr (d. 1183), and gave their name to one of the most tempestuous ages in Iceland's history, the "Age of the Sturlungs." Snorri's relations with his brothers Þórðr and Sighvatr and nephew Sturla Sighvatsson varied throughout their lives, but at their worst were tragically destructive. In 1227–1228, for instance, Snorri and Þórðr ousted Sturla Sighvatsson from the family chieftainship (*goðorð*) in Dalir. In 1236, Sturla attacked Snorri's farm at Reykjaholt and had his son Óraekja mutilated.

Although born into the Sturlungar, Snorri was brought up among the Oddaverjar, being fostered at Oddi, a prime center of learning, by the great chieftain Jón Loptsson (d. 1197). Partly through the agency of his foster-kinsman Sæmundr Jónsson, Snorri married Herdís, daughter of Bersi inn auðgi ("the wealthy") in 1199. He inherited Bersi's estate at Borg two years later. In 1206, Snorri moved to Reykjaholt, his main home for the rest of his life, and took over the *goðorð* there, later extending his influence (often by a shared or temporarily entrusted *goðorð*) still farther throughout the west of the country and into the northern and southern quarters. Herdís remained in Borg until her death in 1233, but before that, in 1224, Snorri had found another partner, Hallveig Ormsdóttir, a member of the Oddaverjar and the richest woman in Iceland.

Snorri also allied himself with other chieftainly families through his daughters' marriages: Hallbera's to Árni Magnússon óreiða ("the unready") of the Ámundaætt and then to Kolbeinn ungi ("the young") of the Ásbirningar; Ingibjǫrg's to Gizurr Þorvaldsson of the Haukdœlir; and Þórdís's to Þorvaldr Vatnsfirðingr. But Þorvaldr was burned to death at the instigation of Sturla Sighvatsson in 1228, and the other three marriages turned sour, and with them the alliances, which proved to be the death of Snorri, because Gizurr and Kolbeinn were leaders of the expedition that killed him.

Snorri's dealings with his fellow Icelanders, as lawspeaker, chieftain, and neighbor, and the personality that emerges from them, are far too intricate even to outline here. In essence, Snorri shunned violence and cherished an ideal of peace, which, however, could not prevail against the violence of the times or his own greed for power and ostentatious wealth. He figures variously as a reconciler, an equivocator, or a coward. His practical sense and legal expertise were often put to the service of his friends, but often used in deviously self-promoting ways; and where legal means failed, he did not flinch from inciting others to violence.

Snorri began early to court the favor of Scandinavian rulers by sending youthful praise poems to the Norwegian kings Sverrir Sigurðarson and Ingi Bárðarson, and the earl Hákon galinn ("the mad"). Hákon sent lavish gifts in return and an invitation to Norway, but died before Snorri was able to take up this offer. Snorri did, however, make the journey to see Hákon's widow, Kristín, now remarried in Gautland, during his Scandinavian visit of 1218–1220. The main focus of the visit was the Norwegian court, and Snorri spent the two winters with Earl Skúli, regent to the young King Hákon Hákonarson, becoming a royal retainer and receiving titles from them culminating in *lendr maðr* ("baron," literally "landed-man") as well as magnificent gifts. The glory and generosity of these rulers were celebrated in Snorri's grand metrical sampler *Háttatal*, and Snorri is credited with two panegyrics for Skúli alone, from which only a refrain survives. Snorri also cut a political deal in Norway, making a promise (which he kept little or not at all) to persuade the Icelanders to accept Norwegian rule, while Skúli in return gave up his intention to punish a fracas between the Oddaverjar and Norwegian traders by invading Iceland.

Snorri again sailed to Norway in 1237, thus escaping from the tightening web of hostility between Icelandic clans and within his own, and there he learned of the deaths of Sighvatr Sturluson and Sturla Sighvatsson in the battle of Ọrlygsstaðir (1238). Snorri stayed with Earl Skúli and his son Pétr, thus taking the wrong side in what became a fatal rift between Skúli and King Hákon. It was later rumored in Iceland that Skúli had secretly granted Snorri the title of "jarl," but certainly Snorri gave Hákon grounds enough for anger and a charge of treason by leaving Norway in defiance of his ban. The king's anger joined that of Gizurr Þorvaldsson, Snorri's alienated and ambitious son-in-law. Acting in delayed response to a letter from the king that had been brought to him by Árni óreiða, another former son-in-law, Gizurr, led the force of seventy men that attacked Reykjaholt on September 22, 1241. Kolbeinn ungi and one of Hallveig Ormsdóttir's sons were also in the company. A party of five warriors discovered Snorri hiding in the cellar and, despite his injunction "do not strike" (*eigi skal hǫggva*), killed him there.

To posterity, Snorri's role as a man of letters, a preserver of poetic, mythological, and historical traditions, a composer of technically ingenious verse, and a writer of at times superb prose far exceeds his importance as magnate and statesman. Yet Sturla Þórðarson only rarely refers to this side of his life, calling him a good *skáld*, and reporting spiteful comments about Snorri's poetic attempts to ingratiate himself with the Norwegian monarchy and about his tendency to compose verses rather than act. He also tells how Snorri's nephew Sturla Sighvatsson spent a winter at Reykjaholt in 1230–31, and had copies of Snorri's *sǫgubœkr* made. What saga books these were is not clear, but Snorri probably wrote his *Prose Edda*, his separate *Óláfs saga helga*, and most of *Heimskringla* in the relatively peaceful decade 1220–1230. That he also composed *Egils saga* has been argued often and persuasively, if not conclusively.

Lit.: Sigurður Nordal. *Snorri Sturluson*. Reykjavik: Þorláksson, 1920; rpt. Reykjavik: Helgafell, 1973; Paasche, Fredrik. *Snorre Sturlason og Sturlungerne*. Oslo: Aschehoug, 1922; 2nd ed. 1948; Einar Ól. Sveinsson. *The Age of the Sturlungs: Icelandic Civilization in the Thirteenth Century*. Trans. Jóhann S. Hannesson. Islandica, 36. Ithaca: Cornell University Press, 1953; rpt. New York: Kraus, 1966; Simon, John. "Snorri Sturluson: His Life and Times." *Parergon* 15 (1976), 3–15; Ciklamini, Marlene. *Snorri Sturluson*. Twayne's World Authors Series, 493. Boston: Twayne, 1978.

Diana Edwards Whaley

[**See also:** *Egils saga Skalla-Grímssonar*; *Hákonar saga gamla Hákonarsonar*; *Heimskringla*; Iceland; *Óláfs saga helga*; *Skáld*; *Snorra Edda*; Sturla Þórðarson; Sturlung Age; *Sturlunga saga*; *Ynglinga saga*]

Social Structure

1. DENMARK. In Denmark, the transition from antiquity to the Middle Ages is marked by the end of the Viking period and the breakthrough of Christianity. In spite of the great number of people who emigrated during the Viking Age, the population seems to have increased steadily, and the peoples who inhabited the Danish lands were the same as before: Jutes, Funians, Zealanders, Scanians, and so on. The rule of the chieftains in the Iron Age was in the Viking Age replaced by politically powerful kings who effectively governed the Danish realm and more; for example, Knud (Cnut) the Great ruled a North Sea empire consisting of Denmark, England, Norway, and perhaps parts of Sweden, at that time (1018–1035), the greatest empire in Europe. This empire was divided, but after King Sven Estridsen (1047–1074), Knud's nephew, the Danish territories made up a cohesive empire, whose central administration was developed thanks to the aid of the Church and to the experience the Vikings had acquired in the countries they had raided.

The earliest account of the Scandinavian lands and peoples dates from approximately 1070, when Adam of Bremen, in his *Gesta Hammaburgensis ecclesiae pontificum*, recorded what he knew about conditions in the outermost regions of missionary work, which he describes as the Nordic Isles. Besides a topographical description of the lands of the Danes, Adam provides information about the population and its conditions. In Jutland, the very large towns south of the fjords are emphasized. The oldest bishops' residences in Schleswig, Ribe, and Århus are mentioned, and in this connection the most important domestic and foreign navigational routes are cited, with the added comment that attacks from pirates constitute a danger. The king's residence is situated at Roskilde on Zealand, centrally located in the realm that included lands east of the Sound: Scania, Halland, Bornholm, and perhaps Blekinge, even though this land was hardly christianized as yet. Adam praises Scania for its beauty and wealth, both with regard to its inhabitants, and merchandise and gold collected through piracy, i.e., Viking expeditions. But now it is full of churches, 300 in all; Zealand has half as many, and Funen one third. Adam also describes peoples on the coast of the Baltic Sea.

Besides providing a topographical account, Adam relates the history of the Danes, especially based on conversations with Sven Estridsen. The memory of the time before the unification of the realm, when many kings or despots ruled at once, is still preserved.

As the text implies, the Danish realm was tied together by sea routes. During the Viking Age, the most significant technological advance was represented by the Nordic ship, which carried the Vikings throughout the world. After the Viking Age, the ship was a prerequisite for the cohesion of the realm under the rule of the king. In the Middle Ages, the coastline was in many places different from today. Toward Sweden and Germany, large expanses of forest formed natural borders.

Within these borders lived the Danish *peoples*, for one cannot yet speak of a single people. The realm consisted of countries, and countrymen were people from the same country. Not just Jutland, Funen, Zealand, and Scania, but also smaller islands were countries with their own *landsting* (parliament) and their own legal system. It is still not possible to say which or how many tribes made up the population of the realm. Skeletal remains show a homogeneous human type. But we do not know much about the physical appearance of the people. The oldest fresco paintings and sculptures in the churches date from the 12th century. They show great variation in human type, but their purpose was not to reproduce the appearance of individuals exactly.

From the Viking Age, the heathen graves betray class and sex differences, judging from the grave goods. But the custom of including grave goods ends with the rise of Christianity. It is possible only in a few cases to determine the graves of kings and noblemen in the churches by means of tomb inscriptions and written sources, and to ascertain that, for example, members of the noble family "Hvide" were very tall and powerful individuals. But other skeletons found in churches, which can be determined to be medieval, reveal an average height corresponding to that of individuals today.

The population figures of the Middle Ages are also uncertain. Various estimates, based on the number of churches and their sizes, fix the figure at approximately one million, before the plague epidemics of the 14th century reduced this number considerably.

Linguistic differences among the Danish peoples were no different than differences in dialect today. This similarity is confirmed by the laws recorded in the 13th century. Since the written language did not yet have a fixed form, linguistic variations are revealed. But Scandinavians on the whole seem to have understood each other's language much more easily during the Viking Age than now.

Earlier scholars saw the construction of buildings on farms and in towns or villages as ethnically based. The archaeological finds of the last decades, however, have shown no sharp distinction. Without doubt, the natural conditions, greater or lesser fertility, are the decisive factors. Place-name evidence indicates a wide expansion of the cultivated area during the Viking Age. The buildings and the areas of cultivation created in this way were not exceeded in the following centuries. The method of cultivation and the agricultural conditions that caused and are produced by this development form the bases for regulations concerning agrarian rights in the laws.

Nothing is certain about the mobility of the population during the early Middle Ages, except for the fact that many people moved from villages into the provincial towns that grew in the 12th and 13th centuries, not least in Denmark. In contrast to Norway and Sweden, where the towns had a common town law, each individual Danish town had its own legal system, expressed in town rights and privileges. This comprehensive mosaic of judicial rules is an important source for understanding the way of life among the urban population.

Although almost seventy Danish towns were legally organized as townships in the Middle Ages, the number of citizens constituted only a small percentage of the total population. The judicial conditions known from the agrarian laws were, to a great extent, based upon the kin as the primary social group. Inheritance rights, guardianship, and possession of land were dictated by kinship relations; and during court trials at the *ting*, the individual depended on the support of his relatives. The same was true when fines had to be paid; from ancient times, the responsibility was a collective one for the kin. By moving to the towns, the individual or family completely or partly lost the protection of relatives. Guilds were gradually established to remedy this situation.

King Valdemar's so-called *Land Register*, whose earliest sections date approximately to 1230, is found in a comprehensive, hybrid MS, because it contains some budgetary income lists to be used by the central administration of the realm. During the last century, these lists were the basis for all research on conditions and the social structure of the kingdom during the Danish Middle Ages. The detailed information contained in the *Land Register* is so contradictory, however, that an unequivocal picture cannot be formed, except for the fact that administration of the kingdom was made more efficient.

There is always a close relationship between socioeconomic development and social structure. In the later Danish Middle Ages, extensive bonded contracts were entered into, whereby the lands of the peasants were transferred to the Crown, the Church, or the nobles, who assumed the responsibility for protecting the peasants. Later, this process coincided with the widespread European phenomenon whereby great expanses of land that had been plowed earlier were left uncultivated in the Middle Ages. Since 1969 in Scandinavia, these conditions have been treated as a common subject of research, the "abandoned farm project," which has increased our knowledge about the socioeconomic problems of the medieval agrarian community in selected localities. It has been confirmed that the villages before the agrarian crisis contained farms of widely differing size, whereas it was earlier assumed, based on the rules of law, that the size and wealth of farms were more similar. Since farms were abandoned in Denmark before the plague epidemics in 1348–1350, other explanations have become necessary: demographic and climatic conditions, transition from agricultural farming to cattle raising, agrarian structural changes, or combinations of these causes that were accelerated by the plague. A reconstruction seems to have occurred in the 1380s, but the consequences were apparently not overcome until about 1500. In terms of the population figure, only a *status quo* was reached. This idea has been confirmed by the number of churches. From the 1200s up to the 1800s, very few churches were built in Denmark.

Other extensive migrations are not known in the Danish Middle Ages, with one exception: after the 1200s, a German immigration took place, consisting mainly of nobles from Holstein, who came to the kingdom via South Jutland. After the 1300s, the Danish nobles, reacting to this competition, obliged the king to employ only Danish-speaking civil servants. The German immigration was more concentrated where the Hanseatic merchants settled, thus affecting the population pattern among the citizenry. Furthermore, surnames from certain Danish provinces occur in other localities, revealing that people had moved. It was practically or legally impossible for the bonded, adscripted peasants to move.

2. NORWAY. The name *Norvegr* means "the way toward the north," *i.e.*, the navigational route along the coast. The coast more

than the inland forms the core of the country. The Norwegian population seems to have had the same basic features since the beginning of historical time. Over 2,000 skeletons dating from the advent of Christianity to the end of the Middle Ages have been found, and they indicate only small changes over the period. The population before the plague epidemic in the 14th century was possibly close to 300,000. The plague reduced it to half or less.

The common anthropological features did not, however, entail uniform cultural and occupational conditions. On the contrary, a sharp dictinction between the east and west existed, determined by differences in the living conditions and way of life. In the Middle Ages, the population in the interior was a purely peasant population to a much greater extent than it is today. Even though everywhere hunting and fishing contributed significantly to the food supply, people in the northern and southern interior were actually peasants, in contrast to the coastal inhabitants, who engaged in farming and the raising of cattle, but under such poor conditions because of climate and lack of fertile land that fishing and hunting were vital occupations. The differences between the settlements in western and eastern Norway also seem to have increased because of the close contact of the people in the west across the sea with western Europe and the islands in the Atlantic.

The settlements united early around common þing-steads, Eiðsivaþing at Eidsvold, Gulaþing near Bergen, and Frostuþing near Trondheim. The unification of the country completed by King Hálfdan svarti ("the black") Guðrøðarson and King Haraldr hárfagri ("fair-hair") Hálfdanarson was the conclusion of a development that had begun a long time before, a development that was, to a large extent, determined by improvements in the types of ships that not only served the "northern routes," but also facilitated Norwegian expansion to the islands in the Atlantic.

The natural conditions have always limited settlement in Norway to the coast and to the flat areas and valleys of the eastern region and Trøndelag. The high mountains were uninhabitable, but served as grazing and hunting lands. Deforestation was necessary for settlement, and the names of farms indicate the period in which this development took place. From the Viking Age onward, a farm usually housed an extended family, because not only married sons but also married daughters remained in the same household. However, this practice led later to the scattering, division, and creation of farms. But, because new land was not available, many people were forced to move out of the country or to the town settlements. In the early Viking Age, there were markets and commercial settlements in Norway, most of them of limited local importance, but some had connections across the sea to foreign countries and to the more remote parts of Norway, like Trondheim, Bergen, Tønsberg, and Skíringssalr.

In the 11th and 12th centuries, the social structure of the Norwegian people was similar to that of the Viking Age. The earliest recorded laws, from about the year 1100, on the whole reflect those social and legal conditions transmitted from heathen times. Where the Danish laws do not contain different penalty rates, the Norwegian penalties for manslaughter depended upon the social status of the victim, so that those social differences demonstrated by the archaeologists in the Danish villages of the later Middle Ages were developed to a higher degree in the Norwegian laws. The location of the graves in the cemetery was also determined on the basis of social status. At the lowest level were the slaves, whose number and economic importance remain uncertain.

The social structure varied from east to west of the mountains. The possibility of combining several occupations on the coast provided the opportunity for social mobility, which, in the west, was hindered by the more fixed organization of noblemen's peasants, who lived on inherited land, and tenant farmers, who lived on the land of others.

In the later Middle Ages, Norway had a new social class in the urban population. Even at its peak around the year 1300, this urban population hardly numbered more than 20,000. The largest town was Bergen, with perhaps 7,000 inhabitants, then Trondheim with 3,000, Oslo with 2,000, and Tønsberg with 1,500. The other settlements were small towns with a few hundred inhabitants. The population of the towns was almost exclusively Norwegian. Their occupations were trade, shipping, and handicrafts. The citizens were early given a certain autonomy and their own civil rights, which King Magnús lagabœtir ("law-mender") Hákonarson (1263–1280) put together into a common law book for the Norwegian towns.

In the 14th century, the North German Hanseatic merchants started to penetrate the Norwegian towns, gradually acquiring a monopoly on Norwegian foreign trade. In the same century, the number of tenant farmers increased; but the total population figure seems to have dropped from about the year 1320, when the phenomenon of the abandoned farm occurred, especially in the western and northern regions. As in Denmark, farms were abandoned before the plague spread in 1349, probably because of worsened climate and increased pressure on resources.

The second half of the 14th century is characterized by unstable conditions and by attempts at adjustments to the reduced population figure. Around the year 1450, the number of abandoned farms is estimated at more than 15,000, about 25 percent of the total. The population figure, which before the plague was possibly around 300,000, was hardly more than 180,000 as late as the Reformation. The income lists contained in the land registers often show a decline of 20 percent in the land tax before the plague. Entire settlements were depopulated, and half the cultivated land was abandoned, but not as a short-term consequence of the disasters; in large parts of the country, this condition persisted for 200 years or more, in contrast to the neighboring countries, where the consequences of the decrease in population seem to have been overcome within two or three generations. Norwegian agriculture, both grain cultivation and husbandry, was so labor-intensive that the supervisors could just barely feed themselves. In many places, the population figures continued to drop. The surplus of agricultural products carried the existing Norwegian social system and the entire political life because it supported the monarchy and the aristocracy. Now the foundation of both the central and local government disappeared. The local representatives of the monarchy were gone, and the aristocrats became peasants on a par with the other survivors. Most taxes were not paid, and if they were, they were paid in the less valuable coin minted by the king. These socioeconomic conditions form the background for the joint monarchy with the neighboring countries, which resulted from a meeting in Kalmar in 1397. The Norwegian king was now Erik of Pomerania. The joint monarchy with Denmark lasted until 1814. With the Reformation, Norway became a vassal state of Denmark.

3. SWEDEN. At the beginning of the Middle Ages, the borders between Sweden and the neighboring countries of Denmark and Norway became more fixed, while the borders with the Lapps in the north and the Finns in the east were not defined. Adam of

Bremen tells us that the Swedish population consisted of many tribes, but the skeletal remains indicate a fairly homogeneous population already in the Iron Age. Adam distinguishes between West Goths north of Scania and East Goths along the Baltic Sea, all the way up to Birka. Between Norway and Sweden lived the people of Värmland, the people of Finnveden, and others; "Now they are all Christians and belong to the church in Skara." In the north lived the Skridfinns, who surpassed the wild animals in speed. In the east, in the vast wastelands, Adam mentions the Amazons, the Dogheads, the Cyclops, who have only one eye in the middle of their foreheads, and the people who enjoy eating human flesh. The longest-lasting consequences of the original organization of the Swedish people in tribes belong to various forms of customary rights that remained valid until the last half of the 14th century.

From the late Middle Ages, the following social categories are found in Sweden: a class of nobles, peasants on inherited land (freeholder farmers), peasants on the land of others (tenant farmers) who were the descendants of relocated peasants and villagers, and casual laborers with no permanent residence. Slavery existed in Sweden, but to what extent is uncertain. Some wills have been found from the end of the 13th century containing decisions concerning the liberation of the testator's slaves. In 1296, the "law of Uppland" prohibited any purchase of Christian slaves. In 1335, slavery was abolished by law. This development has been regarded as the cause of a comprehensive effort at cultivation and the origin of a long list of villages in the 14th century, but such a connection is highly unlikely. New settlements arose, new land was plowed, and, in contrast to Norway and (in part) to Denmark, there was enough land in Sweden for anyone who took upon himself the clearing of forest and the breaking of land. Along the coast of Norland, settlement moved north toward the foreign peoples: Lapps (Samians) and West Finns, who began emigrating to Sweden early in the Middle Ages.

In certain parts of Sweden, mining had an important impact on the conditions for settlement in the Middle Ages. This development can be documented from the end of the 13th century, but may go back even farther. The population increased in the settlements where iron ore was found and processed. Many peasants became miners, and German names testify to the fact that foreign expertise was called in. A significant immigration also occurred in the growing Swedish towns.

It has been estimated that the size of the population immediately before the plague was around 650,000, and then it was greatly reduced. But at the beginning of the 16th century, the consequences of the plague had been overcome, and the earlier population figure had been reached.

The growth of the towns in the Middle Ages had an impact on the social structure, although only a small percentage of the population, living in approximately thirty-five larger or smaller townships, could be found in Sweden around the year 1500. Only two of the towns were relatively large according to the standard of the time, Visby and Stockholm, with 5,000–10,000 inhabitants. Medium-sized towns like Kalmar, Jönköping, Uppsala, and Västerås had 2,000–3,000 inhabitants at most. Except for Stockholm and Visby, the towns had an almost rural character; the chieftains were engaged in farming and kept domestic animals in addition to their urban occupations: trade or handicrafts. Despite their small size, the towns became important for the increased economic and cultural relations with foreign countries, especially Germany.

By the middle of the 12th century, German merchants appear to have settled in Visby on the island of Gotland, which quickly developed into a German township. The German element among the citizenry was so distinct at the beginning of the 13th century that immigrants from there populated the German colonial towns of Riga and Reval on the eastern coast of the Baltic Sea. German settlement not only in Visby, but also on the Swedish mainland, became such a normal event that the settlers were forced to submit to Swedish law and to become Swedish citizens on an equal footing with the Swedes. This development happened especially in Stockholm, where a powerful German citizenry actually ruled the city because of their economic superiority. This condition continued in the time of the Union. The first Union monarchs, Margrethe (1389–1412) and Erik of Pomerania (1397–1439), did nothing to restrict the influence of the Germans in Stockholm.

Outside the towns, noble families dominated throughout the Middle Ages. The oldest laws presuppose landed gentry who rented out land to peasants. In the 13th century, the noble class became more exclusive; marriage and family relations were restricted to a narrow circle. This narrowing paved the way for a feudal system in which the feudal estates and the higher offices of the country were reserved for a hereditary aristocracy. This development entailed increased social differentiation in Swedish society. The position of the tax-liable peasants worsened to the point that great numbers of them relinquished their land to squires in order to avoid paying taxes to the Crown, which then was economically weakened in comparison with the nobility. King Magnus Eriksson (1319–1363) tried to turn this development around, and an open conflict between the king and the aristocracy ensued. Both parties sought help from Germany, and anarchy was the consequence during those years when Sweden was also struck by the plague. The unity of the country was endangered. After the Kalmar Union in 1397 among Denmark, Norway, and Sweden, the Swedish noble class was weakened economically and politically. Erik of Pomerania installed Danish and German stewards and bailiffs all over the country at the expense of the Swedish nobility. Peasants and miners rebelled, supported by the clergy and the nobility. The rebellion succeeded, and the nobility regained their former powerful positions, partly by cooperating with their Danish and Norwegian equals. But the union with Denmark and Norway lasted only until 1523, when Gustav I (1523–1560) assumed the Swedish throne as the first king of the House of Vasa.

4. ICELAND. Iceland was the only Scandinavian country settled in historical times. The process of immigration and settlement (landnám) is known from medieval written sources: Íslendingabók and Landnámabók. Both emphasize that the immigrants came from Norway, even though many had lived or stayed for a shorter or longer period of time in Scotland, Ireland, or neighboring islands. The Scottish, Irish, and Celtic elements may, therefore, have been more distinct than appears from the sources mentioned.

This notion is corroborated by skeletal finds from the Viking Age; the Norwegian, Swedish, and Danish Vikings are racially identical, while the skeletons of Vikings found in the British Isles and in Iceland deviate from the Scandinavian remains. In addition to these observations, the blood-type distribution in the contemporary Icelandic population is closer to the distribution in the Scots and the Irish than to the Scandinavian distribution. These biological differences between western and eastern Vikings must, however, be cross-checked with other cultural similarities; the Icelandic language of the earlier Middle Ages, including the place-name material, and the archaeological finds of, for example, grave goods, reveal a considerable agreement with Norwegian conditions and finds.

The greatest number of immigrants presumably came to Iceland during the decades around the year 900. According to *Landnámabók*, the immigrants can be divided into three categories: the chieftains, who immigrated first and who came to possess large tracts of land; the later arrivals, who took land with the approval of the former; and those who acquired land transferred from an earlier owner, primarily as a gift or a purchase. Women also acquired land through *landnám*.

With regard to the population, the number of farms around the year 1100 is presumed to have been about 4,500. According to the estimate of archaeologists, based upon examination of farm ruins, the typical household numbered about fifteen persons, that is, about 70,000 people in all, a figure that about the year 1200 may have increased to close to 80,000, but that began to drop in the 14th century. From the beginning of the 15th century, the population was drastically reduced as a result of plagues. Around the year 1700, the population still numbered only about 50,000.

The medieval Icelandic laws and, to an even greater extent, the sagas emphasize the importance of the family and relatives for better or for worse. Relatives protected and avenged each other. In a country not threatened by external enemies, families made war on each other during destructive feuds, inhibited only with great difficulty by the Church, which was organized during the period 1030–1200. This conflict was caused by the absence of a national power executed by chieftains or kings, since the national assembly, the *Alþingi*, had no executive power.

Although there were differences within the individual family, which meant that closer relatives had precedence over more distant relatives and males over females, relatives were in fact friends; but there were great social differences among families. The Old Icelandic poem *Rígsþula* provides a poetic explanation of the origin of the various social classes. Rígr is identical to the god Heimdallr, who wanders throughout the world. He visits three families: slaves, peasants, and chieftains, who represent the three population groups made up by the Icelanders.

Farming and fishing constituted the major means of support in the Middle Ages as well as later. In a few places, barley was grown, but the damp island climate and low summer temperatures were obstacles to farming and forestry. The abundant grasslands that supplied both animal feed in the summer and hay for winter feed were decisive factors for animal husbandry. Fishing in fjords in the north and west was a necessary supplement to the sparse farming.

Iceland was politically independent from 930 to 1262. Once a year, the chieftains met at the *Alþingi* and handled laws and court cases, but there was no central government to speak of. In 1237, the Icelandic bishops' seats at Skálholt and Hólar were occupied by Norwegians, and after this date the influence of the Norwegian king increased. The Icelanders consequently submitted to the Norwegian king in 1262. In 1380, Iceland and Norway came under the rule of the Danish king, but this union did not change the living conditions of the people, which steadily deteriorated, reaching the lowest level in the 14th century as a result of major volcanic eruptions and earthquakes, and after that the plague of 1402–1404, when many families perished and many farms were abandoned. The consequences of this social and economic crisis lasted throughout the Middle Ages and far into more recent times.

Lit.: Brøndsted, Johs., ed. *Handel og samfærdsel i oldtiden*. Nordisk kultur, 16:A. Stockholm: Bonnier; Oslo: Aschehoug; Copenhagen: Schultz, 1934; Schück, Adolf. *Handel och samfärdsel under medeltiden*. Nordisk kultur, 16:B. Stockholm: Bonnier; Oslo: Aschehoug; Copenhagen: Schultz, 1934; Christensen, Aksel E. "Danmarks befolkning og bebyggelse i middelalderen." In *Befolkning i middelalderen*. Ed. Adolf Schück. Nordisk kultur, 2. Stockholm: Bonnier; Oslo: Aschehoug; Copenhagen: Schultz, 1938, pp. 1–57; Schück, Adolf. "Ur Sveriges medeltide befolkningshistoria." In *Befolkning i middelalderen*, pp. 123–66; Erixon, Sigurd, ed. *Fra træ til staal. Teknisk kultur III*. Nordisk kultur, 14. Stockholm: Bonnier; Oslo: Aschehoug; Copenhagen: Schultz, 1953; Erixon, Sigurd, ed. *Landbrug og bebyggelse*. Nordisk kultur, 13. Stockholm: Bonnier; Oslo: Aschehoug; Copenhagen: Schultz, 1956; Steensberg, Axel. "Ager." *KLNM* 1 (1956), 32–54; Skrubbeltrang, Fridlev, *et al*. "Bondi." *KLNM* 2 (1957), 84–101; Skautrup, Peter. "Dansk tunge." *KLNM* 2 (1957), 662–4; Itkonen, Erkki. "Finnar." *KLNM* 4 (1959), 276–8; Björn Þorsteinsson. "Fiske." *KLNM* 4 (1959), 302–6; Rosén, Jerker, and Kauko Pirinen. "Frälse." *KLNM* 4 (1959), 670–95; Skrubbeltrang, Fridlev. "Fæste." *KLNM* 5 (1960), 84–5; Enemark, Poul, and Björn Þorsteinsson. "Handel." *KLNM* 6 (1961), 115–19; Kumlien, Kjell, *et al*. "Hansan." *KLNM* 6 (1961), 195–216; Pirinen, Kauko. "Kyrkogods." *KLNM* 9 (1964), 694–7; Rosén, Jerjer, and Magnús Már Lárusson. "Krongods." *KLNM* 89 (1964), 434–8; Collinder, Björn. "Lapparna." *KLNM* 10 (1965), 316–20; Robberstad, Knut, *et al*. "Odelsrett." *KLNM* 12 (1967), 493–503; Møller-Christensen, Vilh., *et al*. "Pest." *KLNM* 13 (1968), 238–48; Lundman, Bertil, *et al*. "Population." *KLNM* 13 (1968), 384–95; Rosén, Jerker, and Seppo Suvanto. "Riddare." *KLNM* 545–84; Fritz, Birgitta, *et al*. "Stad." *KLNM* 16 (1971), 545–84; *Det nordiske ødegårdsprojekt*. Copenhagen: Landbohistorisk Selskab, 1972, 1977; Kumlein, Kjell, *et al*. "Tyskar." *KLNM* 19 (1975), 132–45.

Ole Fenger

[**See also:** Adam of Bremen; Agriculture; *Alþingi*; Crafts; Demography; Denmark; Family Structure; Feudal Influences and Tendencies; Fishing, Whaling, and Seal Hunting; Gotland; Guilds; Hanseatic League; Iceland; *Íslendingabók*; Land Registers; Land Tenure and Inheritance; *Landnámabók*; Landownership; Laws; Norway; Plague; *Rígsþula*; Settlement, Age of; Settlement, Rural; Slavery; Sweden; Towns; Trade]

Sólarljóð ("The Lay/Poem of the Sun") has been transmitted to us from the later Middle Ages only in paper copies of a lost original. The copies were made in the 17th century; among them, AM 166b 8vo is palaeographically the best, and AM 738 4to one of the better copies. The poem is usually dated from the second half of the 13th century because of its close proximity in style and content to the verse translation of the *Disticha Catonis*, called *Hugsvinnsmál*, and because Snorri Sturluson (1178/9–1241) seems not to have been acquainted with the poem, which he does not mention in his skaldic poetics. One verbal detail, the apocopated use of *gá* for *ganga* in stanza 25, might date *Sólarljóð* even later, to the mid-14th century, when this usage is attested elsewhere, in *Möðruvallabók*.

In form, the poem is composed in the traditional eddic meter (*ljóðaháttr*) and diction of the *Hávamál*, its artistic model in the older pagan poetry of Iceland. Some of the quasi-allegorical proper names in the poem are untraditional, *i.e.*, of the poet's invention, and therefore faultily transmitted in the paper MSS, and almost impossible to reconstruct correctly. But like the *Hávamál* and the parallel *Disticha Catonis*, *Sólarljóð* belongs to the ancient genre of wisdom literature, and in its Christian way seeks not only to instruct its readers in the perils and temptations of this life, but also to prepare their souls for the rewards and punishments in the life beyond. In its transcendent visions of heaven and hell, it surpasses its pagan models, whose wisdom does not rise much above the concerns of this life. Presumably, the author of *Sólarljóð* was a cleric who was as sensitive to the poetry of Old Norse paganism as he was devout in the Christian faith.

As we learn toward the end of the poem, from stanza 78, and again from an interpolated stanza at the very end, *Sólarljóð* was conceived as a dream-vision in which a father appears after his death to his son, and having counseled him with five warning exempla how to conduct himself in life, then proceeds to rehearse the manner of his own death and his subsequent journeys through the realms of heaven and hell, concluding with a prayer to the Trinity and a plea for eternal peace to the dead and God's mercy on the living. The poem becomes a frame story that breaks down into three roughly equal sections: the father's worldly visions (sts. 1–32), his death throes (sts. 33–45), and his otherworldly experiences, together with the closing prayers (sts. 53–82). The climactic central section, with the biblical image of Christ as "the sun of righteousness" (*cf.* Malachi 4:2), is one of the high points of expressiveness in the visionary and mystical literature of medieval Europe.

Research on the poem has so far uncovered general analogies rather than exact correspondences between *Sólarljóð* and European Latin vision literature of the Middle Ages. The image of the damned souls as singed birds or clouds of midges in stanza 53, and the punishment of the avaricious who stagger under heavy weights of lead in stanza 63 were almost certainly borrowed from continental hell visions. Despite the relative lateness of composition, the poem has no place for purgatory in its visions, and no fixed scheme of sins punishable in hell. In these respects, it fits the bipartite unschematic picture of the otherworld drawn in earlier Latin visions, before the idea of purgatory can be said to have been born (*ca.* 1200). Hence, the poem is, if not old itself, then old-fashioned in its medieval Christian perspective.

Ed.: Falk, Hjalmar, ed. and trans. *Sólarljóð* Det. Norske Videnskaps akademi, II. Hist.-filos. kl., 7. Christiania [Oslo]: Dybwad, 1914 [the fullest commentary but an uneven text]; Björn M. Ólsen, ed. *Sólarljóð. Gefin út með skíringum og athugasemdum*. Safn til sögu Íslands og íslenzkra bókmenta, 5.1. Reykjavik: Hið íslenzka bókmentafjélag, 1915 [with commentary; arbitrary emendations of text and forced interpretations]; Fidjestøl, Bjarne, ed. and trans. *Sólarljóð. Tydning og tolkningsgrunnlag*. Bergen, Oslo, and Tromsø: Universitetsforlaget, 1979 [with commentary; handy conservative version of Falk's text with helpful introductory comments on the history of the interpretation of the poem and on a number of textual cruces]; Njörður P. Njarðvík, ed. *Sólarljóð*. Íslensk rit, 10. Reykjavik: Bókmenntafræðistofnun Háskóla Íslands og Menningarsjóður, 1991 [with commentary; adds little new to Fidjestøl's edition]. **Tr.**: Baumgartner, A., S.J., trans. "Das altnordische Sonnenlied." *Stimmen aus Maria-Laach* 34 (1888), 419–43 [a careful German translation with excellent notes]; Auden, W. H., and Paul Taylor, trans. *Norse Poems*. London: Athlone, 1981. **Lit.**: Njörður P. Njarðvik. "Sólarljóð." *Gardar* 1 (1970), 11–21; Brennecke, Detlef. "Zur Strophe 78 der *Sólarljóð*." *Arkiv för nordisk filologi* 100 (1985), 97–108; Tate, George. "'Heiðar stjörnur' / 'heiðnar stjörnur.'" In *The Sixth International Saga Conference 28/7–2/8 1985. Workshop Papers*. 2

vols. Copenhagen: Det arnamagnæanske Institut, 1985, vol. 2, pp. 1021–36 [photocopies of papers distributed to participants]; Amory, Frederic. "Norse-Christian Syncretism and *interpretatio christiania* in *Sólarljóð*." *Gripla* 7 (1985), 251–66.

Frederic Amory

[**See also:** Christian Poetry; Eddic Meters; Eddic Poetry; Exempla; *Hávamál*; *Hugsvinnsmál*; Visionary Literature]

Sonatorrek *see* **Egill Skalla-Grímsson**

Stamford Bridge, Battle of. On September 25, 1066, at Stamford Bridge near York in England, the combined forces of Tostig, son of Godwine, earl of Wessex, and Haraldr harðráði ("hard-ruler") Sigurðarson of Norway suffered a defeat at the hands of Harold, Tostig's brother. That defeat brought to an end "more than two centuries of Anglo-Scandinavian conflict in a manner which brought great honour to the last Old English king" (Stenton 1943: 590). Norse accounts of the battle appear in *Morkinskinna*, *Fagrskinna*, and Snorri's *Heimskringla*, and a contemporary account in the *Anglo-Saxon Chronicle*.

The immediate events that culminated in the conflict are complex. In 1055, Tostig became earl of Northumbria; but rebellion broke out in 1065 in response to his levying heavy taxes and the murder of a number of Yorkshire thanes, for which he was held responsible. Tostig and his family were outlawed by Edward the Confessor, then king of England. Morcar, brother of Edwin, earl of Mercia, took Tostig's place. With his wife and a small band of followers, Tostig left England. One year later, Edward the Confessor died, leaving no natural heir to the throne, and Harold, the king's chief counselor, was elected to the throne. The new king had to defend England against threats from three quarters: William ("the Conquerer"), duke of Normandy, to whom Edward supposedly promised the throne; Haraldr harðráði, who saw himself as the rightful heir to Knud's (Cnut's) kingdom; and Tostig.

In early May, Tostig's forces appeared off the Isle of Wight and occupied Sandwich, supposedly with the encouragement of William. These forces, however, were defeated, and Tostig made his way to Scotland. In the north, he joined with Haraldr harðráði, and together they swiftly battled their way to Ricall, just outside York. At Fulford, two miles south of York, they defeated the English troops of Edwin and Morcar on September 20th. On September 25th, Harold Godwinsson attacked at Stamford Bridge, surprising the Scandinavian army. The invading forces were routed, and both Tostig and Haraldr harðráði were killed.

Harold Godwinsson's victory, however, was short-lived; only two days later, William invaded 250 miles to the south. On October 14th, Harold was defeated by William at Hastings in the decisive battle that opened the gateway to Norman rule.

Lit.: Brooks, F. W. *The Battle of Stamford Bridge*. York: East Yorkshire Local History Society, 1956; Blair, Peter Hunter. *An Introduction to Anglo-Saxon England*. 2nd ed. Cambridge: Cambridge University Press, 1977; Stenton, F. M. *Anglo-Saxon England*. The Oxford History of England, 2. Oxford: Clarendon, 1943; 3rd ed. 1971 [esp. pp. 576–91]; Gelsinger, Bruce E. "The Battle of Stamford Bridge and the Battle of Jaffa: A Case of Confused Identity?" *Scandinavian Studies* 60 (1988), 13–29; Hughes, Shaun F. D. "The Battle of Stamford Bridge and the Battle of Bouvines." *Scandinavian Studies* 60 (1988), 30–76.

Phillip Pulsiano

[See also: England, Norse in; Haraldr harðráði ("hard-ruler")
Sigurðarson]

Starkad *see* Divine Heroes, Native

Stave Church (*stavkirke*) is the term used for a type of wooden
church built in Norway, and to some extent Sweden, from around
1150 onward. Technically, the stave-church walls are characterized by corner posts (and sometimes intermediate posts) resting
on ground sills. The posts are joined at the top by the wall plates.
Thus, the supporting elements of the walls form frames into which
vertical planks are inserted. The planks are joined together by
tongue and groove. The building is stabilized by a developed system of bracing, using quadrant brackets to lock the parts together.
Quadrant brackets are also used for securing the structural elements of the roof, which is of a characteristically open, scissor-
braced type with principal rafters, collar beams, and purlins, but
without any tie beams at the wall-plate level.

While the majority of the medieval wooden churches in
Sweden were timber churches built of horizontal logs notched
into one another in the corners, practically all medieval churches
in Norway were stave churches. Approximately 1,000 stave
churches may have been in use at the same time in Norway during
the Middle Ages, most of them in the period 1150–1350.
Postmedieval stave churches are unknown.

Two types of stave churches occur. The more usual was a
relatively small building with a separate chancel and no aisles. A
larger type consists of a raised central part surrounded by lower
aisles on all four sides. The latter buildings have an extra set of
large-dimensioned foundation beams forming a raft that carries
both the sills of the walls and rows of freestanding, internal posts
that support the raised central part. A chancel of similar construction is joined to the east aisle. Both types are often surrounded by
pentices and may have small turrets riding over the roof ridges (*cf.*
the Borgund stave church).

The origin and development of the stave church have been
debated among Scandinavian scholars ever since serious study
began in the latter part of the 19th century. Broadly speaking, two
opinions have been set forth: (1) The basic structural features of
the stave churches are inspired by earlier domestic building traditions. According to some scholars, some sacred pagan type of
building (*hov/hof* or *horg/hǫrgr*) may have played an important
part as a model for the stave church (Boethius 1931). (2) The
design of the stave church, especially the large church with the
raised central part, is mainly the result of influence from European
stone architecture, *i.e.*, the Romanesque basilica (Dietrichson 1892,
Bugge 1935, Hauglid 1976).

The discussion has been rather hypothetical in the absence of
surviving buildings from the Viking period and the 11th century.
But archaeological evidence has to some extent contributed to
elucidating the problems. As early as in 1914, remnants of a large
wooden church from the 11th century were excavated in Lund,
Scania (Sweden). The importance of this find was not fully acknowledged until after World War II, when church excavations
started up on a large scale all over northern Europe. In Lund, two
wooden churches similar to the church found in 1914 have been
excavated, while in Denmark a whole series of wooden churches
was excavated, starting with the famous church at Jelling in 1941.
In Norway, Urnes church was excavated in 1956. This excavation
brought to light remnants of two older churches, the first of a

series of ten early wooden churches found in Norway.

Practically all early wooden churches found so far have one
thing in common: their supporting members were earth-fast. Two
types occur: (1) Buildings where the walls themselves, or parts of
them, supported the roof. Usually, this type of building seems to
have had longitudinal walls with corresponding earth-fast posts,
probably connected by transverse tie beams, thus forming a bay
system. Between the wall posts, ground sills must have been inserted, carrying upright wall planks. (2) Buildings where the weight
of the roof was carried by rows of internal posts, thus reducing the
walls to a space-limiting element. These walls seem normally to
have consisted of upright halved logs dug into the ground. There
are, however, examples of churches where roof-supporting walls
are combined with internal posts (*e.g.*, Urnes and Lom, Norway).
Examples of the latter type are found in Lund and in Greensted,
Essex, England, where the nave of a wooden church dating from
Anglo-Saxon times is still standing, although in a very rebuilt state.

Comparisons with early churches and vernacular buildings,
known through excavations in Germany (*e.g.*, Tostedt, Breberen,
Stellerburg, Husterknupp), show that the early Scandinavian
churches belong within a general North European building tradition. Thus, the forerunners of the developed stave churches do not
belong to a specifically Nordic type of building. As far as wall
construction is concerned, a continuous development can be traced
between a large group of early churches (to which all the Norwegian churches hitherto excavated belong) and the fully developed
stave church. Some churches in Gotland, Sweden (Silte, Hemse),
where the supporting elements are placed on ground sills of a
special kind, seem to form the intermediate link between the early
churches and the stave churches as we know them.

Convincing archaeological evidence of early wooden churches
with a raised central part has not yet been found. Four large
postholes found within the walls of Urnes church have been interpreted as holes for posts supporting some sort of raised structure
(Christie 1959). Based on archaeological evidence, however, it is
difficult to reconstruct the building with surrounding aisles on all
four sides. One of the churches found in Lund has been reconstructed as an aisled building with a raised central nave (Hauglid
1976). This reconstruction is conjectural and has been debated.
Thus, it is still an unsolved question from which sort of building
the stave church with a raised central part actually developed.
Some scholars still maintain that the stone basilica provided the
model. Others disagree, claiming that the stave church, which is
a central building with a chancel loosely joined to it, represents a
type of building quite different from the axial stone basilica. The
most probable answer to this question is that the stave church
with the raised central part represents a sudden leap in a domestic
evolution that took place in Norway around 1150–1200, when
the first generation of churches gradually was replaced by new
ones, either stone churches or stave churches on ground sills. The
creation of the large stave church was probably due to a challenge
from the Church to create, on a modest scale, a room that possessed some of the spatial qualities that could be experienced in
the new cathedrals built in the leading centers of Europe. The
solution, however, had to be found within the constraints imposed by a quite different building material and an established
native building tradition. The result was neither a copy of the
stone basilica nor a traditional building.

The most conspicuous difference between the early churches
and the developed stave churches lies in the field of statics. Contrary to the early churches, where the supporting members (*i.e.*,

the wall posts forming the bay system) must have formed rows of transverse units, the longitudinal walls of the stave church carry the weight of the roof, which has an "open" construction without any transverse tie beams (see above). The lifting of the whole building above the ground and putting it on sills also represents a daring experiment from a statical point of view. Such a construction also presupposes a change in the building procedure. In contrast to the early churches, developed stave churches are prefabricated structures. Thus, the stave church represents a leap to a considerably higher level of technical skill. Somehow, this skill must have emerged in Scandinavia in the years between around 1050 and 1150.

About thirty stave churches, most of them of the large type, are still standing in Norway, while only one church (Hedared) has survived in Sweden. In some respects, the Norwegian stave churches differ from district to district, Sogn in West Norway being the "classical" district, where the famous churches of Urnes and Borgund are found, while more simplified types prevail in the east valleys, such as Valdres and Numedal. In Urnes, the internal rows of freestanding posts supporting the raised central part of the building are adorned with bases and capitals to make them look like stone columns. The posts are connected by arches visually comparable to the arcading in a stone basilica. In Borgund, two sets of arches with cross braces between them form a sort of "triforium." This type of embellishment is certainly taken from stone architecture, and explains why some scholars believe that the stone basilica provided the model for the large type of stave church.

In some Valdres churches, the internal posts are reduced to four corner posts, allowing the central room and the aisles to merge into one single room at floor level. Some Numedal churches (and some of the Hallingdal churches now vanished) have only one freestanding post placed in the center of the nave and extending right up to the roof ridge. Usually, this post also supports a bell turret. These churches come close in appearance to the churches of the simple nave-and-chancel type, but they have a more complicated structural system. Large churches with rows of internal, freestanding posts carrying a raised central room are, however, also known from the eastern part of Norway, as at Lom in Gudbrandsdalen, Gol and Torpo in Hallingdal, and Heddal in Telemark.

A special type of large, cruciform, aisled stave church is known from the northwestern part of southern Norway (Møre and Romsdal) and in Iceland, where the cathedral at Skálholt, which is known from archaeological excavations, measured 39 by 12 meters, the transverse arms measuring 5 by 12 meters. These churches, all of which seem to be late medieval, were built with rows of transverse, roof-bearing units, consisting of pairs of internal posts connected by tie beams and longitudinal wall plates, probably put together in a form of construction called "reversed assembly" (Smith 1974).

The dating of the stave churches is much debated, focusing on the decorated parts, especially the magnificently carved doorways. Typological series have been established and given a chronological bearing, and influence from various European stylistic centers has been demonstrated. The route by which this influence was transmitted, and how the transformation of foreign impulses took place, are questions on which recent research concentrates (Hohler 1975).

Lit.: Dietrichson, Lorentz. *De norske stavkirker: Studier over deres system, oprindelse og historiske udvikling*. Kristiania [Oslo] and Copenhagen: Cammermeyer, 1892; rpt. Westmead: Gregg, 1971; Ekhoff, Emil. *Svenska stavkyrkor jämte iakttagelser över de norska samt redogörelse för i Danmark och England kända lämningar av stavkonstruktioner*. Stockholm: Cederquist, 1914–16; Boethius, Gerda. *Hallar, tempel och stavkyrkor*. Stockholm: Fritz, 1931; Bugge, Anders. "The Origin, Development and Decline of the Norwegian Stave Church." *Acta Archaeologica* 6 (1935), 1–15; Bugge, Anders. *Norwegian Stave Churches*. Trans. Ragnar Christophersen. Oslo: Dreyer, 1953; Christie, Haakon. "Urnes kirkes forløper belyst ved utgravning under kirken." *Fortidsminneforeningens aarbok 1958* (Oslo 1959), 49–74; Blomquist, Ragnar. "En stavkyrka från 1000–talet." *Thulegravningen 1961* (Lund 1963), 16–42; Blindheim, Martin. "The Romanesque Dragon Doorways of the Norwegian Stave Churches." *Institutum Romanum Norvegiae. Acta ad archaeologiam et artium historiam pertinentia* 11 (1965), 177–93; Lidén, Hans-Emil. "From Pagan Sanctuary to Christian Church: The Excavation of Mære Church in Trøndelag." *Norwegian Archaeological Review* 2 (1969), 3–32; Smith, John T. "The Early Development of Timber Buildings: The Passing-Brace and Reversed Assembly." *Archaeological Journal* 131 (1974), 238–63; Bjerknes, Kristian, et al. *The Stave Churches of Kaupanger: The Present Church and Its Predecessors*. Trans. Elisabeth Tschudi-Madsen. Norwegian Antiquarian Bulletin, 1. Oslo: Fabritus, 1975; Hohler, Erla Bergendahl. "The Capitals of Urnes Church and Their Background." *Acta Archaeologica* 46 (1975), 1–60; Hauglid, Roar. *Norske stavkirker. Bygningshistorisk bakgrunn og utvikling*. Oslo: Dreyer, 1976; Smith, John T. "Norwegian Stave Churches: A Review of Some Recent Publications." *Journal of the British Archaeological Association* 131 (1978), 118–25; Ahrens, Claus, ed. *Frühe Holzkirchen im nördlichen Europa*. Hamburg: Helms-Museum, 1981; Bugge, Gunnar. *Stave Churches in Norway: Introduction and Survey*. Oslo: Dreyer, 1983.

Hans-Emil Lidén

[**See also:** Architecture; Churches, Stone; Temples, Heathen; Wood Carving]

Stiklestad, Battle of. Since the year 1025, Knud (Cnut) the Great had demanded to be the king of Norway. Through gifts, he eventually managed to win most of the powerful chieftains of the country to his side. In 1028, he went to Norway and was made king. Before Knud returned to England, he appointed his nephew Earl Hákon governor of Norway. At the same time, he took hostages from all the chieftains and rich peasants in the country. King Óláfr Haraldsson fled to Sweden, and the year after to Russia.

Earl Hákon died in the winter of 1029. Norway then had no ruler, and Knud could find no one with the authority of the earl to replace him. After Hákon's death, Bjǫrn digri ("the fat"), Óláfr's former retainer (*stallari*), went to Russia and told Óláfr about the latest developments in Norway. Óláfr then decided to reclaim the throne. He left Russia for Sweden with a small group of retainers and received support from his brother-in-law, the Swedish king, and 480 men. On the way from Sweden to Norway, he gathered additional reinforcements; at the same time, some of his faithful friends in Norway, among others Haraldr Sigurðarson and King Hringr from the east, joined him on his way to Stiklestad (Stiklastaðir) in Norway. Before the beginning of the battle, Óláfr had about 3,600 men.

When the Norwegian chieftains, primarily those from Trøndelag, the west, and the north, learned of Óláfr's return, they gathered armies made up of peasants. When they heard that Óláfr was about to cross Kjølen into Verdal, they set out with the peasant army for Trondheim and Verdal. According to *Heimskringla*, they had the largest army as yet assembled in Norway, about 14,000 men.

The battle was fought at Stiklestad on July 29, 1030. Óláfr and a great number of his men fell in the battle. Snorri describes the death of Óláfr as follows: "Then Þórir hundr ["hound"] struck at him with his spear and the thrust went under the byrnie up into his maw. Kálfr then struck him, and the blow fell on the left side of his neck" (*Heimskringla* 2:385)

After the battle, Knud installed Sven Álfífuson as ruler of Norway. He soon became unpopular because of the taxes he levied upon the peasants. Two of the chieftains who had fought against Óláfr then brought his son, Magnús Óláfsson, home from Russia; he was made king of Norway in the year 1035.

Snorri tells of "miracles" just before and after the battle at Stiklestad, which were attributed to Óláfr. One year and five days after his death, he was pronounced a saint by his court bishop, Grímkell. His sainthood was soon propagated, and throughout the Middle Ages he remained Norway's national saint and eternal king, but he was never canonized by the pope.

Ed.: Bjarni Aðalbjarnarson, ed. *Heimskringla*. 3 vols. Íslenzk fornrit, 26–8. Reykjavik: Hið íslenzka fornritafélag, 1941–51. **Lit.**: Koht, Halvdan. "The Scandinavian Kingdoms Until the End of the Thirteenth Century." In *The Cambridge Medieval History* 6. Ed. J. R. Tanner *et al.* Cambridge: Cambridge University Press, 1929, pp. 362–92; Gunnes, Erik. *Rikssamling og kristning 800–1177*. Norges historie, 2. Ed. K. Mykland. Oslo: Cappelen, 1976; Andersen, Per Sveaas. *Samlingen av Norge og kristningen av landet 800–1130*. Handbok i Norges historie, 2. Bergen: Universitetsforlaget, 1977; Bagge, Sverre. *Society and Politics in Snorri Sturluson's* Heimskringla. Berkeley and Los Angeles: University of California Press, 1991; Sandnes, Jørn "Slaget på Stiklestad i lys av Frostatingslovens motstandsbestemmelser." In *Kongsmenn og krosmenn*. Ed. S. Supphellen. Trondheim: Det kongelige norske videnskabers selskab, 1992, pp. 255–63.

Jón Viðar Sigurðsson

[**See also:** *Heimskringla*; Norway; Óláfr, St.; *Óláfs saga helga*]

Stjórn is the title commonly given to a collection of material that represents the Old Testament historical literature from the Creation to the Exile. This material is found in full in one MS from the middle of the 14th century, AM 226 fol., and a number of later copies, and in part in other MSS from the same century onward, notably AM 227 fol. and 228 fol. It is not, however, a homogeneous work; rather, it comprises three different Norse versions of the historical literature that vary considerably in content and date.

In a prologue to this composite work, we are told that Hákon Magnússon, king of Norway 1299–1319, instigated the compilation of a work based on Holy Scripture that could be read aloud for the edification of those at his court who did not know Latin; and the compiler says that he used a number of other works in the compilation, notably Peter Comestor's *Historia scholastica* and the *Speculum historiale* of Vincent of Beauvais. But this statement can apply only to the first part of the work, from Genesis 1 to Exodus 18, in which the Bible story is augmented very considerably from both these works and others; indeed, the compiler does not hesitate to depart completely from the Bible on occasion. A lengthy geographical treatise from Vincent, accounts of the legendary love

affairs of Joseph and of Moses, and a couple of lenten homilies are the principal additions (Unger 1862: 3–299).

The remainder of the Pentateuch is found only in AM 226 fol. and as an addition to it; the MS gathering was cut to permit it to be inserted. A close and considerably shortened translation of the Vulgate text, it concentrates on the historical material, summarizing or omitting the legal prescriptions of Leviticus and Deuteronomy, and adds virtually nothing to the scriptural text. Although it is written in a hand from the 15th century or a little later, it is clearly a copy made from an earlier MS, presumably of the Pentateuch. Evidence based principally on error analysis suggests that the translation goes back at least to the early part of the 13th century (Unger 1862: 300–49).

The post-Pentateuchal historical material from Joshua to the Exile is found in almost complete form in the eldest of the principal MSS, AM 228 fol., which is dated to the early part of the 14th century; in AM 226 fol., the Book of Joshua follows a different translation, being based essentially not on the Vulgate but on the text of Joshua as found in Comestor's *Historia scholastica*. This version of the scriptures differs from both the others: it derives essentially from the Vulgate, but with some summarizing and omission, and some expansion and elaboration. The books of Chronicles are used to supplement the information contained in the books of Kings; Peter Comestor is used sporadically and without acknowledgment, while Honorius Augustodunensis's *Imago mundi* is among the works cited. Allegorical commentaries on Jewish heroes, representing them as types of Christ in some cases, are also included, apparently taken from Richard of St. Victor's *Liber exceptionum*. This version probably comprised a translation of the Pentateuch as well, for there is a MS fragment, AM 238 XIX fol., containing extracts from Genesis that do not correspond to the *Stjórn* text, but are very similar to this translation, notably in their use of *Imago mundi* (Unger 1862: 349–654).

Concerning authorship, nothing can be said for certain; but it is possible that the last-mentioned version was the work of Brandr Jónsson, bishop of Hólar (d. 1264), translator of the apocryphal historical material at the behest of Magnús Hákonarson, king of Norway (d. 1280). It is also possible that this version made use of an earlier, more straightforward translation, perhaps that which survives in the latter part of the Pentateuch. In turn, *Konungs skuggsjá* appears to make use of this version, for many biblical quotations in this latter work show almost exact correspondence with the Bible version.

Ed.: Unger, C. R., ed. *Stjórn: Gammelnorsk bibelhistorie fra verdens skabelse til det babyloniske fangenskab*. Christiania [Oslo]: Feilberg & Landmark, 1862; Seip, D. A., ed. *Stjórn. AM 227 fol. A Norwegian Version of the Old Testament Transcribed in Iceland*. Corpus Codicum Islandicorum Medii Ævi, 20. Copenhagen: Munksgaard, 1956 [facsimile]. **Lit.**: Guðbrandur Vigfússon. "Um Stjórn." *Ný Félagsrit* 23 (1863), 132–51; Storm, Gustav. "Om Tidsforholdet mellem Kongespeilet og Stjórn samt Barlaams og Josafats saga." *Arkiv för nordisk filologi* 3 (1886), 83–8; Einar Ól. Sveinsson. "Athugasemdir um Stjórn." *Studia Centenalia in Honorem Memoriae Benedikt S. Þórarinsson*. Ed. B. S. Benedikz. Reykjavik: Ísafold, 1961, pp. 17–32; Selma Jónsdóttir. *Illumination in a Manuscript of Stjórn*. Trans. Peter G. Foote. Reykjavik: Almenna bókafélagið, 1971; Hofmann, Dietrich. "Die Königsspiegel-Zitate in der Stiórn: Ihre Bedeutung für die Entstehungs- und Textgeschichte beider Werke." *Skandinavistik* 3 (1973), 1–40; Hallberg, Peter. "Some Observations on the Language of *Dunstanus saga*, with an Appendix on the Bible Compilation *Stjórn*." *Saga-Book of the Viking*

Society 18 (1973), 324–53; Bagge, Sverre. "Forholdet mellom Kongespeilet og Stjórn." *Arkiv för nordisk filologi* 89 (1974), 163–202; Haugen, Odd Einar. "Om tidsforholdet mellom *Stjórn og Barlaams og Josaphats saga.*" *Maal og minne* (1983), 18–28; Jakob Benediktsson. "Stjórn og Nikulás saga." *Gripla* 6 (1984), 7–11; Kirby, Ian J. *Bible Translation in Old Norse.* Université de Lausanne, Publications de la Faculté des Lettres, 27. Geneva: Droz, 1986; Astås, Reidar. *Et Bibelverk fra middelalderen: Studier i Stjórn.* 2 vols. Oslo: Novus, 1987; Wolf, Kirsten. "Brandr Jónsson and *Stjórn.*" *Scandinavian Studies* 62 (1990), 163–88; Wolf, Kirsten. "Peter Comestor's *Historia Scholastica* in Old Norse Translation." *Amsterdamer Beiträge zur älteren Germanistik* 33 (1991), 149–66.

I. J. Kirby

[See also: Bible; Christian Prose; *Gyðinga saga*; *Konungs skuggsjá*]

Strengleikar is a collection of Old Norse translations of French *lais* apparently undertaken in Norway during the reign of King Hákon Hákonarson (1217–1263). The plural of *strengleikr* means primarily "stringed instrument" and by extension "lai" or "sung story." The collection contains versions of eleven of the twelve *lais* traditionally attributed to Marie de France (*Guigemar, Equitan, Le Fresne, Bisclavret, Lanval, Deus amanz, Yonec, Laüstic, Milun, Chaitivel,* and *Chievrefoil, i.e.,* all but *Eliduc*), six anonymous *lais* found in other collections, and four *lais* for which no French source has survived.

According to the prologue, King Hákon had "the book" translated into Old Norse, but more scholarly interest has focused on trying to determine whether *Strengleikar* is the product of a single translator working for the Norwegian court or a random collection of independent translations perhaps reedited for royal purposes. The results of such an investigation have considerable consequences for the literary historian's general view of translation activity in 13th-century Norway.

Strengleikar exists primarily in one Norwegian MS from about 1270: De la Gardie 4–7 now in Uppsala University Library in Sweden. Four leaves from the end of the MS were cut out and subsequently inserted in a bishop's miter used at the cathedral church of Skálholt in Iceland; the resulting fragments are now registered as AM 666b 4to in Copenhagen. The first editors of *Strengleikar* (Keyser and Unger 1850) believed that the surviving Norwegian MS was "the first fair copy of the translator's rough draft," and it was long customary to assume that the translator was a cleric, perhaps the brother or abbot Robert associated with *Tristrams saga* and *Elis saga.*

Cook and Tveitane, who edited *Strengleikar* in 1979, were not convinced. The Norse versions of the *lais* vary considerably in the extent to which they are faithful to the extant French originals. Figures vary from an abridgment of about 15 percent (*Jonet and Tveggja elskanda ljóð*) to about 50 percent (*Milun*), and this variation seems inconsistent with the concept of a single translator. Tveitane (1973) had furthermore made a linguistic study of the MS, and noted dialect elements from different parts of the country that made original composition at one place, either at the Norwegian court or on commission in a monastery, improbable. All in all, Cook and Tveitane were more inclined to imagine two to four separate translators making drafts of their work perhaps around 1250 (1979: xxvii).

Cook and Tveitane's views have been debated. Hødnebø (1984, 1987) largely refuted Tveitane's findings concerning dia-

lect features from different parts of Norway and asserted that the two scribes who copied *Strengleikar* in De la Gardie 4–7 wrote a consistent and uninfiltrated form of Old Norwegian compatible with the dialect of the Stavanger area of West Norway; this view reduces the potential geographical spread of a disparate collection of translations. Support came in the form of the discovery of an Icelandic version of *Guiamar,* the Norse translation of *Guigemar,* that contained readings closer to the French original than those in De la Gardie 4–7 (Kalinke 1979, 1980). By conclusively demonstrating that a now-lost, earlier and better version of the Norse translation once existed, this discovery supports the idea that the text of De la Gardie 4–7 may be the result of an editorial venture to gather together in one book a number of translations of similar French material. Additional research that demonstrates knowledge of *Strengleikar* material in other Old Norse–Icelandic texts gives further indirect support (Kalinke 1981, Power 1985, Clover 1986).

Many problems remain, and some theory of a number of levels of textual development is needed to explain them. On the one hand, the deliberately rhetorical style with widespread use of parallelisms and alliteration seems consistent throughout the collection, and gives an impression of keen attention to detail. Yet scattered throughout the anthology, there are errors that distort the sense and confuse the narrative. As mentioned earlier, the Norse versions vary considerably in their faithfulness to the French originals, but it is noteworthy that despite these fluctuations authorial interventions in the first person singular and first person plural are almost always carried over from the French to the Norse, in contrast to other translations from French to Norse where this type of material is frequently omitted. The ostensible framework of a collection produced for King Hákon is only occasionally reinforced, and its didactic purpose is doubtful. Note the inconsistencies between the two parts of the prologue, the disproportionate heaviness of the didactic addition in *Equitan,* the disconcerted outburst from the translator at the end of *Chetovel:* "I have read no more about this, and I do not wish to add to it or to tell you new lies," and the precarious inclusion of the unseemly *Leikara ljóð.*

A detailed stylistic study is needed to establish whether there are significant variations in language usage among the different *lais;* similarly, key phrases that occur in many of the French texts should be checked against their Norse counterparts to see whether a theory of more than one translator can be maintained.

Ed.: Keyser, R., and C. R. Unger, eds. *Strengleikar eða Lioðabok: En Samling af romantiske Fortællinger efter bretoniske Folkesange (lais),* oversat fra Fransk paa Norsk ved Midten af trettende Aarhundrede efter Foranstaltning af Kong Haakon Haakonssön. Christiania [Oslo]: Feilberg & Landmark, 1850; Cook, Robert, and Mattias Tveitane, eds. *Strengleikar: An Old Norse Translation of Twenty-one Old French Lais. Edited from the Manuscript Uppsala De la Gardie 4–7—AM 666b, 4°.* Norsk historisk kjeldeskrift-institutt, Norrøne tekster, 3. Oslo: Kjeldeskriftfondet, 1979 [facing-page English translation]. **Bib.**: Kalinke, Marianne E., and P. M. Mitchell. *Bibliography of Old Norse–Icelandic Romances.* Islandica, 44. Ithaca and London: Cornell University Press, 1985, pp. 105–14. **Lit.**: Tveitane, Mattias. *Om språkform og forelegg i Strengleikar.* Årbok for Universitetet i Bergen, Humanistisk serie 1972, no. 3. Bergen, Oslo, and Tromsø: Universitetsforlaget, 1973; Kalinke, Marianne E. "Gvímars saga." *Opuscula* 7. Bibliotheca Arnamagnæana, 34. Copenhagen: Reitzel, 1979, pp. 106–39; Kalinke, Marianne E. "Stalking the Elusive Translator: A Prototype of *Guimars ljóð.*" *Scandinavian Studies* 52 (1980), 142–62; Kalinke, Marianne E.

"A Werewolf in Bear's Clothing." *Maal og minne* (1981), 137–44; Hødnebø, Finn. "Vokalharmonien i Strengleikar." In *Festskrift til Ludvig Holm-Olsen på hans 70-årsdag den 9. juni 1984*. Ed. Bjarne Fidjestøl *et al*. Øvre Ervik: Alvheim & Eide, 1984, pp. 162–74; Power, Rosemary. "*Le lai de Lanval* and *Helga þáttr Þórissonar*." *Opuscula* 8. Bibliotheca Arnamagnæana, 38. Copenhagen: Reitzel, 1985, pp. 158–61; Clover, Carol J. "*Vǫlsunga saga* and the Missing Lai of Marie de France." In *Sagnaskemmtun: Studies in Honour of Hermann Pálsson on His 65th Birthday, 26th May 1985*. Ed. Rudolf Simek *et al*. Vienna, Cologne, and Graz: Böhlau, 1986, pp. 79–84; Hødnebø, Finn. "De la Gardie 4–7 Folio." In *Festskrift til Alfred Jakobsen*. Ed. Jan Ragnar Hagland *et al*. Trondheim: Tapir, 1987, pp. 91–105.

Christopher Sanders

[**See also:** Hákon Hákonarson; *Ridddarasǫgur*]

Stúfs þáttr

Stúfs þáttr ("The Tale of Stúfr") is found in two versions, a shorter one in MSS of the *konungasǫgur*, including *Morkinskinna*, *Flateyjarbók*, and *Hulda-Hrokkinskinna*, and a longer one in three 15th-century paper MSS in which the text is recorded independently. The versions differ in style and in some details (*e.g.*, Stúfr is explicitly said to be blind only in the shorter version), but they tell essentially the same story. Stúfr has arrived in Norway and is staying with an unidentified farmer, when King Haraldr harðráði ("hard-ruler") Sigurðarson arrives unexpectedly. The king takes a liking to the independent-minded Icelander and asks him for entertainment late into the night. Stúfr recites unconnected verses (*flokkar*), which the king later counts at from twenty to sixty (depending on the version), but no *drápur* (laudatory poems). He promises to recite *drápur* when they next meet. Later, Stúfr asks the king for three boons, to be granted without knowing in advance what they are. He requests the king's aid in obtaining some inherited property elsewhere in Norway, permission to compose a *drápa* for the king, and admission to the king's *hirð* (the order is *drápa*, *hirð*, and inheritance in the longer version). Haraldr immediately grants aid in the matter of the inheritance, and, after some discussion about Stúfr's skaldic ancestry, allows him to compose the *drápa*. Later, after hearing the *drápa*, the king admits Stúfr to his *hirð*.

Generically, *Stúfs þáttr* falls into the *útanferð* type, in which an Icelander journeys to Norway, is tested by a king, and receives rewards from him. The usual return to Iceland is omitted.

Stúfs þáttr affords insight into medieval oral tradition. Stúfr is a *frœðimaðr* ("man of learning") because he knows many of the works of other poets; in the *þáttr*, he obtains permission to compose his own *drápa* and thus to become a skald only after the king is satisfied that Stúfr comes from a skaldic family. The *þáttr* shows the context of a performance situation: late at night, a royal audience, and a distinction between *flokkar* and *drápur*, suggesting that both would ordinarily be performed.

Most scholars date the *þáttr* to the first decades of the 13th century and regard the longer version as more original.

Ed.: Einar Ól. Sveinsson, ed. *Laxdæla saga*. Íslenzk fornrit, 5. Reykjavik: Hið íslenzka fornritafélag, 1934, pp. 279–90. **Tr.**: Leach, Henry Goddard, ed. and trans. *A Pageant of Old Scandinavia*. Princeton: Princeton University Press; New York: American-Scandinavian Foundation, 1946, pp. 195–9 [longer version]; Boucher, Alan. *A Tale of Icelanders*. Reykjavik: Iceland Review, 1980, pp. 50–5 [longer version].

John Lindow

[**See also:** *Flateyjarbók*; *Hirð*; *Hulda-Hrokkinskinna*; *Konungasǫgur*, *Morkinskinna*; *Skáld*; *Þáttr*]

Sturla Þórðarson

Sturla Þórðarson (July 29, 1214–July 30, 1284) attained eminence as a historian, poet, and legal expert. His literary fame is based on his histories: *Íslendinga saga* ("History of the Icelanders"), which covers in detail the period from 1183 to 1242, and *Hákonar saga Hákonarsonar*, a chronicle of the reign of the Norwegian king Hákon Hákonarson (1217–1263). He also composed a version of *Landnámabók* ("Book of Settlements") known as *Sturlubók*. Although much of his skaldic poetry has been lost, the surviving verses are generally considered conventional rather than exceptional in inspiration and in expression. In the last two decades of his life, he was an acknowledged authority on his native law. Following Iceland's integration into Norway (1264), the Norwegian king Magnús Hákonarson (1263–1280) appointed him a member of the commission charged with revising provincial law.

Sturla was born the illegitimate son of a major chieftain, Þórðr Sturluson, in the northwest of Iceland. Although his illegitimacy was a distinct social disadvantage, his upbringing was privileged. In his infancy, he was raised by his grandmother Guðný, a woman of remarkable intellect and energy. His father trained him early in the duties of a chieftain, which included participation in legal affairs and in armed ventures. At age thirteen, he was delegated to empower his uncle Snorri to administer his father's chieftaincy at the *Alþingi*. In his late teens, he guarded Bishop Guðmundr and his retinue of paupers during his visitation of western Iceland. Subsequently, Sturla joined his brothers in protecting their father's territory from the depredations of Snorri's son Órækja. These missions involved him in open or barely concealed enmities that would test his organizational skills and would develop his abilities as a chieftain.

In 1235, Sturla joined his uncle Snorri, the great writer and historian. A closeness developed between the two. Although Sturla would ascribe demeaning foibles to Snorri in *Íslendinga saga*, the fact remains that Snorri assigned to Sturla the administrative powers that made Sturla, at age twenty-six, one of the foremost chieftains of western Iceland (1240). Sturla acknowledged his debt by naming his oldest son after his uncle and by joining Órækja in seeking blood revenge for the slaying of Snorri (1241).

In the internecine struggles of the thirties and forties, the power of Sturla's clan, the Sturlungar, had been truncated. Increasingly, the Norwegian king manipulated the internal jockeying for power. Sturla was embroiled in these fights, both because two of the main contestants, Þórðr Kakali and Þorgils Skarði, were his cousin and nephew respectively, and because he felt compelled to protect his own territorial interests. His fortunes fluctuated as he participated, sometimes reluctantly, sometimes actively, in bitter feuds. Tragedy also touched his life. In 1253, Sturla had allied himself with Gizurr Þorvaldsson, the chieftain who had ordered Snorri's death. To strengthen the alliance, Sturla had affianced his daughter to Gizurr's son Hallr. At the end of the wedding celebration, Gizurr's manor, Flugumýrr, was put to the torch. The bride barely escaped in the attack that was futilely launched in revenge for the slaying of both Snorri and of Snorri's nephew, Sturla Sighvatsson. Moreover, Þorgils Skarði, for a brief time the major chieftain in northern Iceland and Sturla's close associate, was slain in 1258.

A period of uncertainty, dashed hopes, ill-fated alliances, and ventures ended in Sturla's exile to Norway in 1263. His stay at the court was prolonged. It was also an intellectually busy and fruitful time. Appointed court historian, he composed the official history of Magnús's father, King Hákon Hákonarson, a work based on eyewitness reports and on records in the royal chancery. Sturla was also busy with the revision of the provincial laws, including Icelandic law. He returned to Iceland with the first codification of the amended law, the so-called *Járnsíða* ("iron side"), in 1272. He then assumed the highest judiciary post. In 1277, his jurisdiction as lawman was restricted to northern and western Iceland. Concomitantly, he was summoned to Norway on charges that he was less active in discharging his duties than the newly appointed lawman for eastern and southern Iceland. Still, he was honored by the king, who appointed him a member of the court with the rank of knight (*skutilsveinn*). Again he assumed the post of royal biographer by writing the history of Magnús's reign, of which only one page survives. He resigned his post as lawman when he felt unable to cope with the question of jurisdiction over church property that pitted landowners against the bishop. He died in 1284, respected by his contemporaries for his scholarliness and integrity.

His literary work was extensive. He probably wrote, as a prologue to *Landnámabók*, an account of Iceland's christianization, *Kristni saga*, and also a lost version of *Grettis saga*. A 14th-century clerical author credits Sturla with a fantastic story about the troll-woman Selkolla. Less certain is the conjecture that he was responsible for the oldest versions of Icelandic annals and for a list of lawspeakers that has survived only in a MS of the 17th century.

The primary sources for Sturla's life are his own *Íslendinga saga*, other sagas in the collection known as *Sturlunga saga*, and *Árna saga biskups*. **Lit.**: Ker, William Paton. *Sturla the Historian*. The Romanes Lecture, 1906. Oxford: Oxford University Press, 1906; rpt. in *Collected Essays of W. P. Ker*. Ed. Charles Whibley. London: Macmillan, 1925; Einar Ól. Sveinsson. *The Age of the Sturlungs: Icelandic Civilization in the Thirteenth Century*. Trans. Jóhann S. Hannesson. Islandica, 36. Ithaca: Cornell University Press, 1953; rpt. New York: Kraus, 1966; Magerøy, Hallvard. "Sturla Tordsson." In *Norsk biografisk leksikon* 15. Oslo: Aschehoug, 1966, pp. 188–201 [contains bibliography]; Jón Jóhannesson. *A History of the Old Icelandic Commonwealth: Íslendinga saga*. Trans. Haraldur Bessason. University of Manitoba Icelandic Studies, 2. Winnipeg: University of Manitoba Press, 1974; Ciklamini, Marlene. "Biographical Reflections in *Íslendinga saga*: A Mirror of Personal Values." *Scandinavian Studies* 55 (1983), 205–21; Guðrún Ása Grímsdóttir and Jónas Kristjánsson, eds. *Sturlustefna. Ráðstefna haldin á sjö alda ártíð Sturlu Þórðarsonar sagnaritara 1984*. Reykjavik: Stofnun Árna Magnússonar, 1988.

Marlene Ciklamini

[**See also:** Conversion; *Hákonar saga gamla Hákonarsonar*; *Landnámabók*; Laws; Snorri Sturluson; Sturlung Age; *Sturlunga saga*]

Sturlaugs saga starfsama ("The Saga of Sturlaugr the Industrious"), a *fornaldarsaga* composed around 1300, is preserved in two distinct versions. The older version (A) is best represented by the vellums AM 335 4to (*ca.* 1400), AM 589f 4to (late 15th century), and AM 567 XXI 4to (fragment, late 16th century), while the later recasting (B) is found only in paper MSS, the earliest of which is AM 171a fol., from the latter part of the 17th century. A total of forty-four MSS of varying worth remains of this saga, one of which, JS 632 4to (18th century), selectively conflates the two versions.

As the saga opens, Sturlaugr, son of the chieftain Ingólfr of Naumudalr in Norway, is a *kolbítr*, or stay-at-home, who prefers games and household chores to manlier pursuits. Ingólfr suggests that he should marry Ása, daughter of Earl Hringr, but when she rejects Sturlaugr for not having distinguished himself, he angrily goes harrying in the Baltic area. Meanwhile, old King Haraldr and the sinister Kolr successively seek Ása's hand. Hringr gives pledges of betrothal to both of them. Since Haraldr is too old to battle Kolr, he calls upon Sturlaugr to take his place. Sturlaugr accepts on the condition that the king relinquish to him his betrothal claim. Reluctantly, Haraldr agrees, and Sturlaugr weds Ása. When told of the impending duel with Kolr, Ása advises Sturlaugr to see her foster-mother, the crone Véfreyja, who provides him with an extraordinary sword by means of which he slays Kolr. Subsequently, Kolr's brother, Framarr, bristling with vengefulness, challenges Sturlaugr to a duel. Although Framarr is wounded in the subsequent encounter with Sturlaugr and on the verge of death, he is healed by Véfreyja and becomes Sturlaugr's sworn brother. When Sturlaugr returns home, Haraldr gives him an arduous task to perform, recovering an aurochs horn. On the way, Sturlaugr and his men encounter three giantesses and men who yelp like dogs, with chins grown down to their chests. Eventually, they succeed in obtaining the aurochs horn and make their way back to Haraldr, into whose speechless face Sturlaugr thrusts the horn. He proceeds to his kinfolk in Sweden, where he defends the kingdom ruled by Ingifreyr. In return, Sturlaugr is made king and given territory. The remainder of the saga is largely taken up with loosely connected episodes resulting from vows made at a yule feast. Of these, those involving Framarr, who had pledged to sleep with Ingibjǫrg, are the most entertaining. After a series of frustrated attempts on the part of Framarr to win Ingibjǫrg, Sturlaugr is obliged to intervene. After a long battle in which Dagr, Ingibjǫrg's father, is killed, Sturlaugr gives Ingibjǫrg to Framarr in marriage. Thereupon, he returns to Sweden, where he performs further feats. By Ása, Sturlaugr has two sons, Hemingr and Ingólfr, each of whom becomes king after their father dies of old age.

In version B, which shows accretion from the sequel, *Gǫngu-Hrólfs saga*, as well as from *Þorsteins saga Víkingssonar*, the cast of characters is reduced, but more detailed description is offered of the main figures: Ása is described as being haughtier and mockingly eloquent; Kolr, less than human with cat-like golden eyes peering from under shaggy brows; and the giantess Hornnefja, comically grotesque when she "comes on," carrying walruses on her back and a dead bear in front. The role of Véfreyja as a helper figure is curtailed. In general, version A operates with omens, triadic groupings, and the other stocks in trade of the fairy tale, while B is more tightly knit, providing motivation often lacking in A.

Ed.: Gudmund Olofz-Son, ed. *Sagann af Sturlauge hinum Starf-sama. Eller Sturlög then Arbetsammes Historia fordom på gammal Göthiska skrifwen och nu på Swenska uthålkad* [i.e., *uttålkad*]. Uppsala, 1694 [editio princeps, poorly printed, with facing Swedish translation; text based on Holm chart. 56 fol.]; Rafn, C. C., ed. *Fornaldar sögur Nordrlanda*. 3 vols. Copenhagen: Popp, 1829–30, vol. 3, pp. 592–647 [text based on AM 173 fol.]; Zitzelsberger, Otto J., ed. *The Two Versions of Sturlaugs saga starfsama: A Decipherment, Edition, and Translation* of a *Fourteenth-Century Icelandic Mythical-Heroic Saga*. Düsseldorf: Triltsch, 1969 [diplomatic text of A based on AM 335 4to; text of B based on Nks 1228 fol.].

Otto J. Zitzelsberger

[**See also:** *Fornaldarsögur; Gǫngu-Hrólfs saga; Þorsteins saga Víkingssonar*]

Sturlu þáttr *see* Sturlunga saga

Sturlung Age (*Sturlungaöld*). The period 930–1262 is called the Commonwealth Age in Icelandic history; the end of this period is called the Sturlung Age. The name is old, but its origin is uncertain, and it is unclear what period of time it designates. However, it is connected with the dissolution that took place at the end of the Commonwealth Age, when five chieftain families were struggling for power, and the archbishop in Norway and the Norwegian king were directly involved in the power struggle.

During the last decades, scholars have placed the beginning of the Sturlung Age around 1200, 1220, or even 1235. Those who place it around 1200 emphasize, among other things, the separation of church and secular power. The Church, they point out, had come directly under foreign rule; the Icelanders no longer owned ocean-going ships and had become dependent on foreign merchants for all import and travel abroad. Furthermore, they claim that education had declined, and disputes and warfare increased around 1200.

Others place the dividing line around 1220, because then the Sturlungs had begun to assert themselves, and the royal power in Norway had become directly involved in Icelandic matters. The ancestor of the Sturlungs, Sturla Þórðarson (d. 1183) was never very powerful, but his three sons collaborated well until around 1220, and the Sturlungs were at that time the most powerful family of the country. They enjoyed the friendship of the Birkibeinar in Norway, and Snorri, Sturla's son, even tried to bring the country under Norwegian royal power in 1220, but it came to nothing.

In 1235, the son of Snorri's brother, Sturla Sighvatsson, again tried to bring Iceland under the Norwegian king. There had been a considerable power struggle between Snorri and Sturla, and Sturla now expelled his father's brother from the country. Then he turned against other chieftains and tried to chase them to the king, but fell himself in 1238. From 1235 onward, there was much unrest in the country, with many battles taking place. Some scholars claim that the Sturlung Age began at this point.

One of the two main characteristics of the Sturlung Age is the power struggle among the chieftains; the other is foreign intervention. The chieftains' controversies can be explained by the fact that five families became wealthier and more powerful than others in the 12th century, probably especially because of the church income, and then usually from the largest churches, the so-called *staðir* (sing. *staðr* 'church establishment'). They kept reasonable peace with each other until the sixth family, the Sturlungs, began to assert themselves around 1220. They had their origin in Dalir, but forced their way to power wherever they could, and conquered all the western part of Iceland and a large area in the northern part, but the Sturlungs' solidarity was eventually disrupted.

Most of the victorious chieftains of the Sturlung Age were the Norwegian king's men (*hirðmenn*), and the support of the Norwegians became increasingly important to them as the disputes also increased, both of special messengers of the king and of merchants who represented the king, but also bishops, who were all Norwegians after 1237 until the end of the Commonwealth Age. Snorri supported Earl Skúli in his rebellion in Norway and had prospects of becoming Skúli's earl in Iceland. But Skúli got the worst of it, and the king let his man, the Icelandic chieftain Gizurr Þorvaldsson, kill Snorri in 1241. The king's power was then obvious, and the chieftains who became most powerful after this time, Þórðr Kakali and Þorgils Skarði, both Sturlungs, and Gizurr, were all the king's men and dependent on him.

The primary source about the Sturlung Age is *Sturlunga saga*, a collection of sagas describing the period. Here, an account is given of the fights that took place after 1235, and the killings are described in detail. The chieftains' recruiting was large, 1,200–1,400 men at the most in each troop, but the losses were small in comparison. Around 350 men may have fallen or been killed in the period 1208–1260, and the total number of Icelanders at the time was 50,000–60,000. Mutilations were common, especially the cutting off of hands and feet, and then plundering, especially of cattle.

Þórðr Kakali and Þorgils Skarði died in 1256 and 1258, respectively. There was only one chieftain among the king's men who was likely to subject the country to the king, Gizurr Þorvaldsson. The king did not trust him for this task and tried to control him by making him his earl. Gizurr appears to have been reluctant to subjugate the country to the king, but finally was forced to do so when the king diminished his power and made it probable that he would reduce it even more. The Icelanders agreed to subjugate themselves to the king and pay taxes to him, but under certain conditions as set forth in the *Gamli sáttmáli* ("Old Covenant").

By about 1255, the farmers had tired of war, at least those in the northern part of Iceland. The king claimed that only he could secure peace, and the leaders of the Church supported him. The *Gamli sáttmáli* states that six ships should sail to Iceland over the next two years, and then according to an agreement. Many scholars interpret this statement as implying that all trade was in the hands of the Norwegians, and that the Icelanders had been forced to negotiate with the king in order to secure imports. This idea is nowhere stated explicitly, but it is possible that Norwegian merchants may have been interested in the trade. Many Icelanders may have found it unnatural not to be subject to a king; to have an Icelandic king was out of the question because of, among other reasons, the poverty and the sparse population, and then the Norwegian king may have seemed self-elected. But it is clear that the payment of taxes was a thorn in the Icelanders' side.

It was not to be expected that the Icelanders could buck the Norwegian obtrusion. With peace established in the first half of the 13th century, Norway's time as a major power had begun. The king employed a policy of expansion, and the Icelanders were no match for the Norwegians.

Most scholars consider the Sturlung Age a period of political, financial, cultural, and moral decay. There is a tendency to look at the time through modern notions of self-determination, but such ideas may have been unknown around 1250. The supposed financial decline is uncertain, and it seems that Icelandic goods were no less in demand in the 13th than in the 12th century. The role of international trade should not be overestimated. Some scholars claim that culture and education decayed after 1200, and believe that the *Íslendingasögur* and other literary genres, that came into existence in the 13th century, are a kind of swan song of the culture that had flourished especially at the end of the 12th century before the controversies began. This view is doubtful, although it is clear that the literature declined around 1300 or in the 14th century.

Tr.: McGrew, Julia, and R. George Thomas, trans. *Sturlunga Saga.* 2 vols. Library of Scandinavian Literature, 9–10. New York: Twayne; American-Scandinavian Foundation, 1970–74. **Lit.**: Einar Ól. Sveinsson. *The Age of the Sturlungs: Icelandic Civilization in the Thirteenth Century.* Trans. Jóhann S. Hannesson. Islandica, 36. Ithaca: Cornell University Press, 1953; rpt. New York: Kraus, 1966; Björn Þorsteinsson. *Íslenzka þjóðveldið.* Reykjavik: Heimskringla, 1953; Jón Jóhannesson. *A History of the Old Icelandic Commonwealth: Íslendinga saga.* Trans. Haraldur Bessason. University of Manitoba Icelandic Studies, 2. Winnipeg: University of Manitoba Press, 1974; Gunnar Karlsson. "*Goðar* and *höfðingjar* in Medieval Iceland." *Saga-Book of the Viking Society* 19 (1977), 358–70; Björn Þorsteinsson. *Íslensk miðaldasaga.* Reykjavik: Sögufélag, 1978; Jochens, Jenny. "The Church and Sexuality in Medieval Iceland." *Journal of Medieval History* 6 (1980), 377–92; Byock, Jesse L. "The Age of the Sturlungs." In *Continuity and Change: Political Institutions and Literary Monuments in the Middle Ages. A Symposium.* Proceedings of the Tenth International Symposium Organized by the Center for the Study of Vernacular Literature in the Middle Ages. Held at Odense University on 19–20 December, 1985. Ed. Elisabeth Vestergaard. Odense: Odense University Press, 1986, pp. 27–42; Byock, Jesse L. *Medieval Iceland: Society, Sagas, and Power.* Berkeley, Los Angeles, and London: University of California Press, 1988; Sigurður Nordal. *Icelandic Culture.* Trans. Vilhjálmur T. Bjarnar. Ithaca: Cornell University Library, 1990.

Helgi Þorláksson

[**See also:** Iceland; Snorri Sturluson; Sturla Þórðarson; *Sturlunga saga*]

Sturlunga saga

Sturlunga saga ("The Saga of the Sturlungar") is a huge compilation, in all some 260,000 words, from around the year 1300. It comprises a series of texts by different authors, and forms a continuous chronicle of Icelandic history during the period 1117–1264, that is, to the breakdown of the insular Free State. There are two MS versions of *Sturlunga saga*: *Króksfjarðarbók* [K] (AM 122a fol.; written 1360–1370) and *Reykjarfjarðarbók* [R] (AM 122b fol.; written somewhat later). Neither of these two MSS has preserved the text in its original form. Much has been lost, especially in R. K seems to be more faithful to the substance of the original, whereas R has incorporated some texts not found there (see below).

The designation *Sturlunga saga* does not appear until the 17th century. But the work is aptly named, because the family of the Sturlungs, with its many prominent chieftains, dominated the Icelandic scene during much of the period in question, currently referred to as the *Sturlungaöld* ("Sturlung Age").

Sturlunga saga belongs to the branch of Icelandic saga literature called *samtíðarsögur* ("contemporary sagas"). This designation distinguishes it from the *Íslendingasögur*, such as *Egils saga Skalla-Grímssonar* or *Njáls saga.* Most of the *Íslendingasögur* were written in the 13th century, but deal with Icelanders from the settlement (*landnám*), beginning in the late 9th century, up to approximately 1030, when the new community had been Christian for a generation. *Sturlunga saga* is also "contemporary" in the sense that

its authors had witnessed many of the events that they describe.

Sturlunga saga includes the following parts:

Geirmundar þáttr heljarskinns takes place in the immigration period, and ends with a chapter on Geirmundr's descendants. This short story is a kind of historical prelude, perhaps written by the compiler himself.

Þorgils saga ok Hafliða deals with the antagonism between the two chieftains named in the title in the early 12th century. There is a famous account of a wedding at Reykjahólar in 1119, where the telling of *fornaldarsögur* is of great interest for the discussion of that genre.

Ættartölur ("Genealogies") is a compressed review of the foremost families in contemporary Iceland: Oddaverjar, Sturlungar, Ásbirningar, Svínfellingar, and so on.

Haukdœla þáttr presents the main features of the famous family of Haukadalr from the immigration period up to about 1200. As a source for his narrative, the author sometimes refers to the renowned Ari Þorgilsson "inn fróði" ("the learned"; 1067–1148), who, with his *Íslendingabók*, became the pioneer in writing history in a Nordic language. From the age of seven to twenty-one, Ari spent his life at Haukadalr.

Sturlu saga is the story of Sturla Þórðarson from the farm Hvammr in western Iceland ("Hvamm-Sturla"), father of Snorri Sturluson, and his conflicts with other chieftains in the years from 1148 until his death in 1183. It gives a vivid and entertaining portrait of the man who was the founder of the Sturlung clan. Like certain other chieftains of his day, Hvamm-Sturla was an upstart. But he more than made up for his lack of pedigree through ambition, cunning, and ruthlessness. Gradually, he became the most powerful man in the western districts. In this saga, we also find the story of how his son Snorri at the age of two was adopted as foster-son by the prominent chieftain Jón Loptsson from the estate Oddi in southern Iceland. Snorri spent his youth at Oddi, a cultural center, and an important school for the future historian, mythologist, and expert in Icelandic poetry.

Formáli ("Preface") is supposed to be written by the compiler, but on the basis of an older preface by Sturla Þórðarson to his own *Íslendinga saga* (see below). The short piece is an important document on saga writing, but difficult to interpret.

Prestssaga Guðmundar Arasonar is a biography of the priest Guðmundr Arason until he became bishop in the year 1203, and afterward was heavily involved in the conflicts among the chieftains. The compiler has divided the saga into four parts and integrated them with other texts. He has shortened it considerably, and excluded passages dealing with miraculous events. It seems fairly certain that *Prestssaga* was composed by the abbot Lambkárr Þorgilsson (d. 1249), who was Guðmundr's disciple and friend.

Guðmundar saga dýra is a chronicle of feuds among chieftains in the district around Eyjafjörður in northern Iceland, especially Guðmundr Þorvaldsson (d. 1212) and Ǫnundr Þorkelsson, who fell victim to arson in 1197 ("Ǫnundarbrenna"). The compiler has divided the saga and reproduced it in two different places.

Hrafns saga Sveinbjarnarsonar is the story of a noble chieftain and renowned physician, who in 1213 was killed by his adversary Þorvaldr Snorrason (d. 1228). The saga was composed by a contemporary admirer of Hrafn, apparently shortly after Þorvaldr's death. The compiler has used only the latter part of the saga, which is elsewhere preserved entire.

Íslendinga saga is by far the weightiest single contribution to *Sturlunga saga*, both by virtue of its size (more than 100,000 words) and its central position. It was written by Sturla Þórðarson (1214–1284), a nephew of Snorri Sturluson, and is the only text in the whole compilation that can with absolute confidence be ascribed to an author. The saga begins at the death of Sturla's paternal grandfather and namesake, Hvamm-Sturla, in 1183, and follows the history of Iceland and its chieftains in the 13th century, until the Free State was forced to submit to the Norwegian king in 1262–1264. Like many of his relatives, Sturla was deeply involved in the course of events, and often refers to himself, but, with typical restraint and objectivity, always in the third person. His portraits of Snorri Sturluson and other members of his family are drawn with a steady hand by a man who knew them better than anyone else.

Þórðar saga kakala has its name from the Sturlung chieftain Þórðr Sighvatsson Kakali (1210–1256), Snorri Sturluson's nephew and cousin of the author of *Íslendinga saga*. A central episode is the naval battle between Þórðr and his competitor Kolbeinn Arnórsson (1208–1245) on the gulf Húnaflói in northern Iceland in the year 1244. The saga does not exist outside *Sturlunga saga*, where it has been merged with Sturla's *Íslendinga saga*.

Svínfellinga saga tells of strife and deceit among chieftains in southern Iceland in the years 1248–1252: the brothers Sæmundr and Guðmundr Ormsson and Ögmundr Helgason.

Þorgils saga skarða is the story of the Sturlung Þorgils Böðvarsson (1226–1258), next to *Íslendinga saga* the most volu-minous single text (45,000 words) of the compilation. It did not belong to the original composition, but was introduced in MS R, where it has been entirely integrated with *Íslendinga saga*.

Sturlu þáttr, preserved only in R and its line in the MS tradition, is a charming portrait of the main contributor to *Sturlunga saga*, Sturla Þórðarson, and of his meeting with King Magnús Hákonarson in Norway. The king at first treated Sturla with sus-picion, but ended by honoring the Icelander with the task of writ-ing his father's biography, *Hákonar saga Hákonarsonar* (ca. 1265).

Finally, one could add *Arons saga*, which is not to be found in the *Sturlunga saga* compilation itself, but which has much in common with its contents, and is thus sometimes included in modern editions of *Sturlunga saga*. *Arons saga*, supposedly com-posed around 1340, is the story of Aron Hjörleifsson (d. 1255), who is also known from Sturla's *Íslendinga saga*. Aron was a faith-ful supporter of Bishop Guðmundr Arason in his bitter quarrels with the Sturlung chieftain Sturla Sighvatsson, and was one of the most famous warriors of his time, very much in the old heroic vein. He made a pilgrimage to the Holy Land, not unusual for Icelanders in the Sturlung Age, and died in Norway as an honored member of King Hákon's *hirð*.

The political and social development in Iceland during the Sturlung Age involved a disturbance of the balance among the original thirty-six, and later forty-eight, local chieftains, the *goðar* (sg. *goði*). Each of them administered his district, his *goðorð*, and together they constituted the legislative board (*lögrétta*) of the General Assembly (*Alþingi*), meeting every summer at Þingvellir. In the 10th and 11th centuries, the power among the *goðar* had been fairly equally distributed. The *goðorð* was hereditary, but it could also be sold, temporarily transferred, or divided and held in partnership.

After the middle of the 12th century, however, individual chieftains gained control of more than one *goðorð*. Finally, the old social structure was completely disrupted. In place of many *goðar* with approximately equal power, there were a few ambitious and influential individuals and families who subjected large parts of the country to their control. Among these chieftains almost un-interrupted conflicts raged, which culminated in the 13th century, and eventually led to the submission of Iceland to the Norwegian kingdom.

The greatest interest among the feuding families centers upon the Sturlungs. Their period of power began with Hvamm-Sturla's sons, Þórðr, Sighvatr, and Snorri. Snorri gained fame not only as a learned man and historian, but also in more mundane matters, and achieved great prestige and wealth. He visited King Hákon Hákonarson (1217–1263) and Earl Skúli in Norway, and seems to have promised to work on behalf of the king and Norwegian in-terests among his countrymen. In the decades to come, the king increasingly interfered in Icelandic politics, playing off the con-tending chieftains against one another. In 1222, Snorri was elected lawspeaker for the second time, the highest office of the Icelandic Free State, and during the following years he reached the peak of his power, partly at the expense of his own kinsmen. He was rather unscrupulous in his treatment of his brother Sighvatr and his brother's son Sturla.

Sturla Sighvatsson (1199–1238) brought the political influ-ence of the Sturlungs to its first culmination. On a voyage abroad, he paid a visit to the Norwegian court. King Hákon, disappointed with Snorri's achievements, expressed the opinion that the best way to put an end to the strife in Iceland would be to introduce absolute monarchy there. Sturla undertook to work for the king's cause in return for suitable honors. When he came home again, he first turned against his uncle, Snorri Sturluson, and the latter's unruly son Órækja. In accordance with the king's instructions, Snorri was driven from his stronghold in southwestern Iceland, and finally forced into exile. But the ambitious and ruthless Sturla met his doom at the hands of two young chieftains, Gizurr Þorvaldsson (1208–1268) and Kolbeinn Arnórsson the Young (1208–1245). They joined forces, and with 1,700 men defeated Sturla and his father Sighvatr at Örlygsstaðir in the summer of 1238, the largest battle ever fought in Iceland. Both father and son were slain after a brave defense.

However, peace and quiet in Iceland were still unobtainable. After the battle at Örlygsstaðir, Snorri Sturluson returned from his exile and attempted to restore his former position. But in this situation, Gizurr and Kolbeinn had a strong trump card to play, for King Hákon had written to Gizurr and ordered him either to get Snorri out of the country or have him killed. On the authority of the king's letter, Gizurr and Kolbeinn had Snorri murdered on September 22, 1241, at his estate, Reykjaholt. It is quite consonant with the prevailing conditions of that time in Iceland that both Gizurr and Kolbeinn had formerly been married to daughters of Snorri.

In the last two decades of the Free State, other prominent men beside Gizurr and Kolbeinn played important roles. One may mention Þórðr Sighvatsson Kakali and Þorgils Böðvarsson Skarði, both of them members of the Sturlung clan, and both with their own separate sagas (see above). Þórðr was a brother of Sturla Sighvatsson but had escaped his brother's and father's fate at Örlygsstaðir, being in Norway at the time.

King Hákon's hold on Iceland became stronger and stronger. After the death of Snorri Sturluson, the king had his property and chieftaincy confiscated. Icelandic chieftains voluntarily relinquished their *goðorð* authorities to the king. In their internal disputes, they sought the support of the king and appealed to him to decide their issues. The Icelanders at last were forced into swearing loyalty and homage to the king of Norway and became tributary to the Norwegian Crown.

Sturlunga saga gives us a detailed, varied, and apparently reliable picture of the course of events, and also of the attitudes and values of the time. The Sturlung Age has a reputation for moral turbulence, because of the devastating feuds, deceit, and savagery. There are instances of chieftains who have their adversaries or their followers maimed: a hand or foot is cut off, or they were castrated. The practice of keeping a concubine was widespread, even among the clergy.

On the other hand, it has been asserted that the Sturlung Age was scarcely any worse morally than any other epoch, but has merely paid the penalty by having received such a relentless and detailed chronicle in *Sturlunga saga*. In other countries, with more complex and large-scale political conditions, the rulers, and consequently the historians, could mask their acts of violence and cruelty as a political necessity, depicting them as a more or less legal punishment. "But here in Iceland, one scarcely perceives the concept of the state among mere individuals. It is they who must shoulder the full responsibility for their deeds" (Einar Ól. Sveinsson 1953).

The tendency toward dissolution and the lack of moral focus during the Sturlung Age have been interpreted in part as a result of the tension between paganism and Christianity. Of course, paganism as a cult had been abolished long before. But the tension is revealed in the people's view of life. After men had, sometimes half-heartedly, given up the ancient values without having completely acquired the new, they could easily slide into a state of disorientation and uncertainty in the evaluation of human actions. In any case, despite its reputation, the Sturlung Age, as documented in *Sturlunga saga*, does not lack instances of heroism, of men fighting to the bitter end against odds, faithful to their fellows, and even compassionate.

Sturlunga saga is written in typical saga style, much like the *Íslendingasögur*. But there is a difference. In the *Íslendingasögur*, whatever their basis in history or tradition, the topic is remote and has been thoroughly structured according to artistic principles. In the contemporary chronicle, we still have the raw material of life in all its overwhelming fullness. It is so close to the author that it may be hard for him to see the forest for the trees; the many authentic details threaten to blur the main outlines. *Sturlunga saga* offers the reader the thrill of a more direct confrontation with historical events. This is not to say that *Sturlunga saga* is formless, neglecting narrative art and aesthetic principles. Sometimes, it reaches the heights of the best *Íslendingasögur* in dramatic composition, trenchant dialogue, and clearcut characterization.

The compiler of *Sturlunga saga* rounds off his foreword with some appreciative words about Sturla Þórðarson: "I trust completely his sound reason and honesty as a chronicler, for I knew him as the wisest and most moderate of men." Considering that Sturla was himself involved in the violent strife of his time, the balanced and objective attitude of his account is admirable. But in that respect, he was not alone among his colleagues. To be sure, we sometimes listen to clear echoes of sympathies and antipathies. But usually we meet the same discipline and calm in the rendering of facts, even when most repulsive. Nowhere else in the northern countries, and probably nowhere in all Europe, has medieval history been documented by contemporary authors with such an unbiased outlook toward men and events.

Sturlunga saga is a unique and valuable work in its own right. However, especially in later decades, it has been increasingly explored also in the study of the *Íslendingasögur*. The authors who wrote of their ancestors in the *sagaöld* ("saga age") were themselves men of the Sturlung Age. They were necessarily influenced by the time in which the lived, not just by events, but also by values and atmosphere on the whole. Obvious reflections of the Sturlung Age have been traced in the *Íslendingasögur*. For instance, an attempt has been made to interpret *Njáls saga* as a kind of *roman à clef* from the 13th century, and to identify one of the contemporary chieftains, a prominent character in *Sturlunga saga*, as its author. Whether or not this claim is valid, *Sturlunga saga* has turned out to be of great value as a background for our understanding of the *Íslendingasögur*.

Ed.: Gudbrand Vigfusson, ed. *Sturlunga saga*. 2 vols. Oxford: Clarendon, 1878; Kristian Kålund, ed. *Sturlunga saga*. 2 vols. Copenhagen: Gyldendal, 1906–11; Kristján Eldjárn et al., eds. *Sturlunga saga*. 2 vols. Reykjavik: Sturlunguútgáfan, 1946; Jakob Benediktsson, ed. *Sturlunga saga: Manuscript no. 122 A fol. in the Arnamagnæan Collection*. Early Icelandic Manuscripts in Facsimile, 1. Copenhagen: Rosenkilde & Bagger, 1958 [facsimile]. **Tr.**: McGrew, Julia, and R. George Thomas, trans. *Sturlunga Saga*. 2 vols. Library of Scandinavian Literature, 9–10. New York: Twayne; American-Scandinavian Foundation, 1970–74. **Lit.**: Björn Magnússon Ólsen. *Um Sturlungu*. In *Safn til sögu Íslands* 3. Reykjavik: Hið íslenzka bókmentafélag, 1902; Paasche, Fredrik. *Snorre Sturlason og sturlungerne*. Oslo: Aschehoug, 1922; 2nd ed. 1948; Pétur Sigurðsson. *Um Íslendinga sögu Sturlu Þórðarsonar*. In *Safn til sögu Íslands* 6.2. Reykjavik: Hið íslenzka bókmenntafélag, 1933–35; Einar Ól. Sveinsson. *The Age of the Sturlungs: Icelandic Civilization in the Thirteenth Century*. Trans. Jóhann S. Hannesson. Islandica, 36. Ithaca: Cornell University Press, 1953; rpt. New York: Kraus, 1966; Guðrún Ása Grímsdóttir and Jónas Kristjánsson, eds. *Sturlustefna. Ráðstefna haldin á sjö alda ártíð Sturlu Þórðarsonar sagnaritara 1984*. Reykjavik: Stofnun Árna Magnússonar, 1988; Úlfar Bragason. "On the Poetics of Sturlunga." Diss. University of California, Berkeley, 1986; Úlfar Bragason, "The Structure and Meaning of *Hrafns saga Sveinbjarnarsonar*." *Scandinavian Studies* 60 (1988), 277–92; Úlfar Bragason. "Sturlunga saga: Atburðir og frásögn." *Skáldskaparmál* 1 (1990), 73–88.

Peter Hallberg

[**See also:** *Arons saga Hjǫrleifssonar*; *Biskupa sögur*; *Guðmundar sögur biskups*; Iceland; Snorri Sturluson; Sturla Þórðarson; Sturlung Age]

Style

1. EAST NORSE. Medieval literature in the Swedish and Danish vernaculars varies in style as a result of three contributing influences: native oral tradition, latinized classical rhetoric, and continental romance. These three influences affect different genres, sometimes counteracting, sometimes strengthening one another. In all genres, one also finds a less easily definable, more general level of style.

According to the established view, native tradition predominates in the laws, prose chronicles, prose epics (*e.g.*, *Guta saga*), and proverbs. The Latin influence is regarded as greatest in documents and in learned or rhetorical prose, as generally in the translated, primarily religious literature. The ideals of chivalric romance characterize the style of the rhymed chronicles, ballads, and verse romances. The more general level of style is typical of the sparse attempts at a scientific, ordinary prose (*e.g.*, Henrik Harpestreng, Peder Månsson).

The laws show a very peculiar form of language. Traditionally, scholars have claimed to trace the particular law style back to a preliterary origin of the laws, as recited at the "thing" and handed down orally from father to son among the holders of the "lawspeaker" office. This background favored a linguistic form facilitating the memorization of large sequences of text, and enhancing the clarity of expression and vigor of delivery. This linguistic form has, according to the same traditional view, left very significant marks in the oldest written versions, particularly of the Swedish provincial laws. The result is an artificial spoken language, not unlike that characterizing other orally delivered literary genres. Sound effects, like alliteration, rhythm, and rhyme, are prominent features, often in combination with antithetic arrangements and pithy wordings, sometimes varied in more or less synonymous word pairs. A well-known peculiarity is the frequent habit of introducing the treatment of a case with the adverb *Nu* ("Now," as in *Nu takär mapär þiuv sin*, "Now takes man thief his," in the *Äldre Västgötalagen* ["Older Västergötland Law"]). The law style is formulaic: the rules are stated in a small number of fixed syntactic types. The syntax is simple and mainly paratactic: short sentences, few and little varied subordinate clauses. The vocabulary is, with certain exceptions for the later-added ecclesiastical sections, altogether native Norse.

Typical of the diction and the general spirit of the medieval law is the famous passage introducing the "Byggningabalkan" ("Building Section" or, more properly, the "Wiþärbo balkär" ["Neighborhood Section"]) of the Swedish *Upplandslagen* ("Uppland Law"): *Land skulu mäþ laghum byggiäs, ok äi mäþ walzwärkum. þy at þa standä land wäl, laghum fylghis* ("Lands shall with law be built, and not with violent acts. Because then stand lands well [when] law is obeyed"). The Danish *Jyske lov* ("Jutland Law") varies the familiar quotation: *Mæth logh skal land byggiæs* ("With law shall land be built").

Recent research has questioned the immediate dependence of law style upon native oral tradition, and ascribed this conception to lingering ideas born in Scandinavian 19th-century nationalist romanticism. Instead, attention has been drawn to striking similarities with continental legal writings, Roman jurisprudence as well as canon law (Foote 1977).

Originally, the language of the diplomas (charters, deeds, *etc.*) was Latin, but from the middle of the 14th century in Sweden and from the early 15th in Denmark, the vernaculars prevail. The style of Swedish and Danish diplomas is highly influenced by international Latin "officialese"; it is abstract and lengthy, with a heavy, rhetorically colored syntax, often developed in long, complicated periods. In vocabulary, Low German loans are common.

Rhetorical elements are predominant also in the religious translated literature, which was attached chiefly to the monasteries, particularly to Vadstena. In this kind of literature, rhetoric is sometimes combined with, and strengthened by, scholastic erudition and a tendency toward systematization, as in the works of mystics like Suso, in prayers, hymns, and poems to St. Mary. The result is an elaborated, sometimes overloaded, rhetorical artificial language, often with a refined, intricate syntax.

More frequently, however, the translators' rhetorical training is employed for the purpose of preaching, or even sheer entertainment. The language becomes plainer, the style more straightfor-

ward and fluent, as in sermons and edificatory writings, exegesis, and saints' legends. In certain genres, elements of realism and metaphorical language tend to bring the style closer to popular modes of expression. This style is particularly apparent in the biblical paraphrases and saints' lives, and more so in Sweden, where this kind of literature was given a more popular and less latinate shape (*e.g.*, the *Pentateuch Paraphrase*, the *Old Swedish Legendary*) than in Denmark (*Legenda aurea*, biblical translation).

All these stylistic features, rhetorical as well as "popular," occur, concentrated and in ample variation, in the sole great original religious work of medieval Scandinavia: St. Birgitta's *Revelations*.

Secular education and entertainment addressed a different public than did monastic literature, and was based on a different outlook. The ideology of chivalry was transmitted to the upper classes by chivalric verse. In the *knittelvers* of the 14th and 15th centuries (*Eufemiavisorna*, the Swedish *Erik's Chronicle* [*Erikskrönikan*], Swedish and Danish *Rhymed Chronicles*), this poetry reflects French and German originals, sometimes through West Norse intermediaries. The poets are either translators, normally very independent ones, or free imitators. In this epic poetry, one finds an East Norse language richly colored, sometimes extravagant and vivid, sometimes cultured and elegant, always fluent, adapted from spoken language, and apparently modern: inflection and syntax point toward later periods. The vocabulary is interspersed with continental, particularly German, loanwords, principally connected with the material and spiritual aspects of chivalry.

A place apart is occupied by the Swedish *Konungastyrelsen* ("De regimine principum"), the East Norse counterpart to the *Konungs skuggsjá*. The work has a peculiar style: in rhythm not unlike the austere prose of the laws, but also with a dash of chivalric refinement.

Lit.: Tigerstedt, E. N., ed. *Ny illustrerad svensk litteraturhistoria*. 1. Stockholm: Natur och Kultur, 1955; rev. ed. 1967; Foote, Peter. "Oral and Literary Tradition in Early Scandinavian Law: Aspects of a Problem." In *Oral Tradition: Literary Tradition: Proceedings of the First International Symposium Organized by the Centre for the Study of Vernacular Literature in the Middle Ages. Held at Odense University on 22–23 November, 1976*. Ed. Hans Bekker-Nielsen *et al*. Odense: Odense University Press, 1977, pp. 47–55; Kaspersen, Søren, *et al. Dansk litteraturhistorie. 1: Fra runer til ridderdigtning o. 800–1480*. Copenhagen: Gyldendal, 1984; Wollin, Lars. *Svensk latinöversättning. 1. Processen. 2. Förlagan och produkten*. 2 vols. Lundastudier i nordisk språkvetenskap, ser. A, nr. 34, 35. Lund: Blom, 1981–83; Brask, Peter, *et al. Dansk litteraturhistorie. 2: Lærdom og magi. 1480–1620*. Copenhagen: Gyldendal, 1984; *Dansk litteraturhistorie. 9: Noter og registre*. Copenhagen: Gyldendal, 1985; Lönnroth, Lars, and Sven Delblanc, eds. *Den svenska litteraturen. Från forntid till frihetstid. 800–1718*. Stockholm: Bonnier, 1987; Utterström, Gudrun. "Schwedische Provinzrechte—Ideologie und Interpretation." In *Sprachkontakt in der Hanse: Aspekte des Sprachausgleichs im Ostsee- und Nordseeraum: Akten des 7. Internationalen Symposions über Sprachkontakt in Europa, Lübeck 1986*. Linguistische Arbeiten, 191. Ed. P. Sture Ureland. Tübingen: Niemeyer, 1987, pp. 231–41.

Lars Wollin

2. WEST NORSE. Old Norse medieval literature was written or translated by well-educated persons, mostly clerics, familiar with medieval Latin style patterns and rhetoric. But these native

authors, translators, and compilers were also rooted in a tradition of vernacular language usage. Out of their handling of the mother tongue emerged different types of vernacular style. These styles existed side by side, often mixed or alternating within the same text. On the basis of salient text features and their frequency, it is convenient to distinguish among the following styles: (1) Saga Style, or Popular Style; (2) Learned Style; (3) Court Style; and (4) Florid Style, Adorned Style, or Ornate Style.

The Saga Style was developed in the first half of the 13th century. To what degree it was influenced by the spoken popular language or is to be regarded as a successful adaptation of oral narrative style is under debate. It may be considered an original Icelandic contribution to the style types of the vernaculars in the Middle Ages. Vernacular and foreign elements combine to form a distinct language tool, suited for popular narratives of native themes. The Saga Style has a cumulative, nonperiodic sentence structure. The syntactical units are brief, and subordinate clauses are few. We frequently find asyndetic collocations of sentences. A logical connective is often missing at the beginning of a sentence. The word order, however, makes up for this lack in many cases. The clauses are short, precise, and often monumental in their expressiveness. These features give the composition a bold staccato character. Subjunctive and modal auxiliaries are frequently employed. Vacillation between the preterite tense and the historical present and changes from indirect to direct speech contribute to an impression of vividness and actuality. The use of brief particles, pronouns, and adverbs of place and time have a similar effect. Understatement and litotes, reiteration of words, and deliberate use of related words and plays on words are also used effectively. Pithy discourses are used with skillful refinement. The saga writers present necessary facts, but do not anticipate. As to portrayal of persons and description of events or human reactions, the style is most often characterized by restrained, dispassionate discretion and apparent objectivity. The Saga Style predominates in the *Íslendingasögur* and the *konungasögur*, although the sagas differ somewhat from each other in the use and frequency of stylistic features.

The Learned Style grew to serve the purpose of translating religious Latin texts into the vernacular. In the late decades of the 12th century, we encounter it at an early stage in simple word-for-word translation. At the beginning of the 13th century, it develops into an artistic prose medium. It is characterized by a greater verbosity than the Saga Style. Alliterative word pairs are frequently used to render a single Latin word; parallelisms and antithetic expressions abound. Characterizing adjectives are numerous, as are superlatives and hyperbolic expressions, loanwords, and new coinages. Use of the participles and of the absolute dative is common, in contrast to the Saga Style.

In the Court Style, we have a further development of the Learned Style. This style evolved in Norway from the efforts of Hákon Hákonarson (r. 1217–1263) to raise his court to a higher level of culture and manners. He and his successors had a select library of European court literature translated, mostly from Old French (*e.g.*, *Strengleikar*). A wider range of rhetorical elements is here accepted, and well-known conventions are used more frequently and in a more sophisticated manner than in the Learned Style. The diction of the originals probably influenced the renderings into Old Norse to assume an undulating prose rhythm. Synonyms, alliterations, and assonances are common. The use of participles and antitheses is, however, more restrained than in the

Learned Style. The Court Style was obviously assessed by the contemporary public as a refined narrative art.

In the last decades of the 13th century, it became fashionable among translators into Old Norse to imitate the contemporary way of writing Latin. From their efforts in this area grew the Florid Style. The many new literary adjectives, adjective abstracts, derivates, and compounds are striking features of this style. New words are frequently formed in accordance with common Scandinavian patterns, even if they diverge from Latin. Prolix sentences and heavy genitive constructions are common. Word pairs, often synonyms, are deliberately used to obtain a higher degree of accuracy. An abundance of metaphors serves as pedagogic tools, as do digressions. The style admits of declamatory effects, and often rises to grandiloquent pathos. It was regarded as an advanced manner of writing, and Icelanders, such as the Benedictine abbot Bergr Sokkason, used the Florid Style for independent compositions from about 1300.

Lit.: Nygaard, Marius. "Den lærde stil i den norrøne prosa." In *Sproglig-historiske studier tilegnede professor C. R. Unger*. Kristiania [Oslo]: Aschehoug, 1896, pp. 153–70; Nygaard, M. *Norrøn syntax*. Kristiania [Oslo]: Aschehoug, 1905; Springer, Otto. "The Style of the Old Icelandic Family Sagas." *Journal of English and Germanic Philology* 38 (1939), 107–28; Blatt, Franz. "Latin Influence on European Syntax." *Classica et mediaevalia* 18 (1957), 133–78; Halvorsen, Eyvind Fjeld. "Høvisk stil." *KLNM* 7 (1962), 315–8; Jakobsen, Alfred. *Studier i Clarus saga. Til spørsmålet om sagaens norske proveniens*. Årbok for Universitetet i Bergen. Humanistisk Serie, 1963, No. 2. Bergen and Oslo: Universitetsforlaget, 1964; Halvorsen, Eyvind Fjeld. "Lærd og folkelig stil. Island og Norge." *KLNM* 11 (1966), 119–23; Tveitane, Mattias. *Den lærde stil. Oversetterprosa i den norrøne versjonen av Vitæ Patrum*. Årbok for Universitetet i Bergen. Humanistisk Serie, 1967, No. 2. Bergen and Oslo: Norwegian Universities Press, 1968; Hallberg, Peter. *Stilsignalement och författarskap i norrön sagalitteratur. Synpunkter och exempel*. Acta Universitatis Gothoburgensia. Nordistica Gothoburgensia, 3. Gothenburg: Almqvist & Wiksell, 1968; Halvorsen, Eyvind Fjeld. "Retorikk." *KLNM* 14 (1969), 89–95; Gardiner, Ann Broady. "Narrative Technique and Verbal Style in *Parcevals saga ok Valvers þáttr*. A Comparative Study of the Old Norse Version of Chrétien de Troyes' *Perceval*." Diss. University of Pennsylvania, 1977; Widding, Ole. "Den florissante stil i norrøn prosa (isl. skrúðstíllinn) specielt i forhold til den lærde stil." *Selskab for Nordisk Filologi. Årsberetning for 1977–78* (1979), 7–11; Jónas Kristjánsson. "Learned Style or Saga Style?" In *Specvlvm Norroenvm: Norse Studies in Memory of Gabriel Turville-Petre*. Ed. Ursula Dronke *et al.* Odense: Odense University Press, 1981, pp. 260–92; Jónas Kristjánsson. "The Court Style." In *Les Sagas de Chevaliers (Riddarasögur). Actes de la Vᵉ Conférence Internationale sur les Sagas . . . (Toulon, Juillet 1982)*. Civilisations, 10. Ed. Régis Boyer. Paris: Presses de l'Université Paris-Sorbonne, 1985, pp. 431–40; Kalinke, Marianne E. *King Arthur North-by-Northwest: The matière de Bretagne in Old Norse–Icelandic Romances*. Bibliotheca Arnamagnæana, 37. Copenhagen: Reitzel, 1981; Astås, Reidar. "Lærd stil, høvisk stil og florissant stil i norrøn prosa." *Maal og minne* (1987), 24–38; Wolf, Kirsten. "*Gyðinga saga, Alexanders saga*, and Bishop Brandr Jónsson." *Scandinavian Studies* 60 (1988), 371–400; Wolf, Kirsten. "Brandr Jónsson and *Stjórn*." *Scandinavian Studies* 62 (1990), 163–88.

Reidar Astås

[**See also:** Christian Prose; Chronicles; Chronicles,

Rhymed; Diplomatics; *Eufemiavisorna*; *Guta saga*; Harpestreng, Henrik; *Íslendingasögur*; *Knittel(vers)*; *Konungasögur*; *Konungastyrelsen*; Latin Language and Literature; Laws; *Old Swedish Legendary*; *Riddarasögur*; Saints' Lives; *Strengleikar*; Swedish Literature, Miscellaneous]

Succession. The succession pattern of Scandinavian kings reflects two opposing concepts traceable to the remotest times of the Germanic world. By their incompatibility, these two principles were destined to create havoc in society throughout the medieval period. The first, royal descent, required that a Germanic king be related by blood to a previous king, a concept that was eventually extended to automatic hereditary succession and primogeniture. The other, election by chieftains, provided a mechanism for choosing a suitable candidate, but also introduced discord and civil war.

Blending with mythology, Germanic kingship was often anchored in descent from the pagan gods. This divine descent of kings, known also as "sacral kingship," is noticeable particularly in Sweden. The connection between religion and kingship continued into the Christian era in all Scandinavian countries when after their deaths kings were occasionally designated as saints to secure stability for the current ruler and his lineage.

Royal descent and election coexisted with a modicum of harmony in the early stages of Scandinavian monarchy, when leading chieftains chose the most capable candidate from a pool of contenders claiming descent from previous kings. Warfare, Viking expeditions, division, and joint rule decimated and advanced a large number of candidates. In the 9th century, however, when single rule appeared in Norway and Denmark, other means of selection were demanded. The many civil wars in all Scandinavian countries throughout the period testify that solutions were not easy. Contenders were numerous because of the kings' sexual exploits with many women, and their number increased with the cessation of the Viking excursions. During the late 11th and early 12th century, Denmark used a horizontal system of succession that allowed five sons of Sven Estridsen to follow their father in sequence. At the same time, Norway returned to joint rule among three half-brothers, but the less-developed Sweden had not yet emerged from the stage of civil war. By the middle of the century, ecclesiastical and civil leaders developed new ideas emphasizing vertical lineage within a single dynasty. The goal was succession through primogeniture, enabling the oldest legitimate son of the royal couple to inherit his father's position. Since this system required respect for the Church's new policies of monogamy and indissolubility of marriage, it was not easily accepted, but when finally practiced it curtailed civil war and the power of the nobles significantly. Introduced in Norway in 1163, hereditary succession did not become a reality until a century later. Denmark followed the system from 1170 until 1241, when biological hazards of royal minority and childlessness again revived the control of the leaders.

Throughout the development of primogeniture, the idea of election remained. A royal candidate through hereditary right had to present himself at a local assembly, and if accepted by the chieftains, he was certified as king, the so-called *konungstekja*. Only then could he hope to receive the military support that would enable him to fight against other contenders, but the elective system continued even when single rule was established. When the hereditary succession was accepted, the magnates still formally elected the next king, often at a tender age while his father was still alive. This elective feature, testimony to the power of the nobility, resulted in the establishment of the *håndfæstning*, or coronation charter, in 14th-century Denmark, a charter to be signed by each king before being accepted. Norway became an elective monarchy in the mid-15th century, and Swedish laws stress the election of Swedish kings in the same period. The elective principle also marks the ill-fated Scandinavian Union from this period. Nevertheless, although elected, the preferred candidate was the previous ruler's oldest son, or in the absence of this normal heir, his closest biological kin.

Lit.: Schreiner, Johan. "Arvekongedømmet i Norge." *Scandia* 11 (1938), 64–92; Olivecrona, Knut. *Das Werden eines Königs nach altschwedischen Recht: Der Königsritus als magischer Akt.* Lunds Universitets Årsskrift, N. F. Avd. 1, 44.1, 1947 (1948); Hoffmann, Erich. *Die heiligen Könige bei den Angelsachsen und den skandinavischen Völkern. Köningsheiliger und Köningshaus.* Quellen und Forschungen zur Geschichte Schleswig-Holsteins, 69. Neumünster: Wachholtz, 1975; McTurk, R. W. "Sacral Kingship in Ancient Scandinavia: A Review of Some Recent Writings." *Saga-Book of the Viking Society* 19 (1975–76), 139–69; Hoffmann, Erich. *Königserhebung und Thronfolgeordnung in Dänemark bis zum Ausgang des Mittelalters.* Beiträge zur Geschichte und Quellenkunde des Mittelalters, 5. Berlin and New York: de Gruyter, 1976; Riis, Thomas. *Les institutions politiques centrales du Danemark 1100–1332.* Odense University Studies in History and Social Sciences, 46. Odense: Odense University Press, 1977; Bagge, Sverre. "Borgerkrig og statsudvikling i Norge i middelalderen." *Historisk tidsskrift* (Norway) 65 (1986), 145–97; Lönnroth, Lars. "Dómaldi's Death and the Myth of Sacral Kingship." In *Structure and Meaning in Old Norse Literature: New Approaches to Textual Analysis and Literary Criticism.* Ed. John Lindow *et al.* Viking Collection, 3. Odense: Odense University Press, 1986, pp. 73–93; Jochens, Jenny M. "The Politics of Reproduction: Medieval Norwegian Kingship." *American Historical Review* 92 (1987), 327–49.

Jenny Jochens

[See also: Kingship]

Sunesen, Anders (*ca.* 1160–1228) was archbishop of Lund from 1201/2 to 1223/4. His father, Sune Ebbesen, was a cousin of Archbishop Absalon and one of the wealthiest men in Denmark. In the 1180s, Anders studied abroad. He probably received his main training in Paris (arts and theology), but also visited Italy (for law studies in Bologna?), and England (for an unknown purpose). After becoming a master of arts perhaps by 1186, and of theology some years later, he spent some time teaching, probably theology in Paris, before becoming chancellor to King Knud VI (r. 1182–1202). His first-known job as chancellor was on an embassy in 1195 that tried to reconcile Philippe Auguste of France with his Danish queen, Ingeborg. In 1201/2, Anders succeeded Absalon as archbishop of Lund and left the chancellery to his brother Peter, bishop of Roskilde, Denmark. In 1204, Anders was named papal legate to Denmark and Sweden. During the years 1206–1222, he cooperated with King Valdemar II (r. 1202–1241) in the subjugation and christianization of pagan populations in the Baltic area, in particular Estonia. Though initially reluctant, he seems in the end to have obeyed a papal summons to attend the Fourth Lateran Council in Rome in 1215. In 1222, he petitioned the pope to be relieved of his duties as archbishop due to "an incurable bodily infirmity." His successor, Peder Saksesen, was consecrated in 1224. Anders died in 1228, leaving various possessions to Lund chapter, including a collection of books.

As archbishop, Anders was an able administrator and politician on good terms with both pope and king. A later legend, modeled on the story of Moses in Exodus 17, credits him with prayer that secured Danish victory in the decisive battle against the Estonians at Lyndanis on June 15, 1219. This legend is often combined with another, according to which the Danish flag, *Dannebrog*, was sent from heaven during the battle.

Anders produced no literary works in Danish, as far as is known. Apart from administrative documents, the following Latin works have been attributed to Anders: (1) *Hexaemeron*, a theological poem in 8,040 hexameters, extant. (2) *De vii ecclesiae sacramentis*, also in hexameters, now lost. (3) Two sequences, "Missus Gabriel de celis" and "Stella solem preter morem"; "Missus," however, seems to predate Anders, and his authorship of "Stella" is also doubtful. (4) A Latin version of the Law of Scania, extant; the attribution rests on slender evidence, but is generally accepted.

The *Hexaemeron* is preserved in one medieval MS (Copenhagen, Royal Library, E don. var. 155 4to) from the second half of the 13th century, originally in the cathedral library at Roskilde. Anders probably composed the work in Paris in the early 1190s. It consists of twelve books and combines a commentary on Genesis 1–3 (Books 1–4) with an exposition of the main points of systematic theology, excluding the sacraments (5–12 plus a digression on divine names in 2–3). Main sources include, for the commentary on Genesis, Peter Comestor's *Historia scholastica* and Richard of St. Victor's *Allegorie*, and for the remaining part of the work, Stephen Langton's *Summa* and *Quaestiones*. As a whole, the *Hexaemeron* takes the reader from the Creation (1) to the Day of Judgment (12). A second proemium in Book 10 marks off two main parts: creation and fall (1–9), recreation in Christ (10–12). Anders shows great skill as a poet of hexameters. In his handling of the Latin language and of verse technique, he dissociates himself from the classicizing school represented by Saxo. The poem seems to have had a very limited diffusion, probably because so much learning is packed into it that it makes for very difficult reading.

Ed.: *Leges Provinciales Terrae Scaniae ante annos 400 Latinæ redditae per Andream Suonis F.* Ed. Arnoldus Hvitfeldius. Copenhagen, 1590; *Andreae Sunonis filii archiepiscopi Lundensis Hexaêmeron libri duodecim.* Ed. M. Cl. Gertz. Copenhagen: Gyldendal, 1892 [includes edition of the sequences]; *Skånske lov. Anders Sunesøns parafrase.* Aakjær, S. and E. Kroman, eds. In *Danmarks gamle Landskabslove med Kirkelovene* 1.2. Ed. Johs. Brøndum-Nielsen and Poul Johs. Jørgensen. Danish Society of Language and Literature. Copenhagen: Gyldendal, 1933; *Andreae Sunonis Filii Hexaemeron Post M. Cl. Gertz.* Ed. Sten Ebbesen and L. B. Mortensen. Corpus Philosophorum Danicorum Medii Aevi, 11.1–2. Danish Society of Language and Literature. Copenhagen: Gad, 1985–88 [contains English introduction in part 1 and extensive bibliography in part 2]. **Lit.**: Kabell, Aage. "Ueber die dem dänischen Erzbischof Anders Sunesen zugeschriebenen Sequenzen." *Archivum latinitatis medii aevi* 28 (1958), 19–30; Christensen, A. E. "Sunesen, Anders." *Dansk Biografisk Leksikon* 14. Copenhagen: Gyldendal, 1983, pp. 208–11; Mortensen, Lars Boje. "The Sources of Andrew Sunesen's Hexaemeron." Université de Copenhague, *Cahiers de l'Institut du moyen âge grec et latin* 50 (1985), 113–216; Ebbesen, Sten, ed. *Anders Sunesen, stormand—teolog—administrator—digter.* Copenhagen: Gad, 1985 [contains fifteen studies on Sunesen, with English summaries and extensive bibliography]; Ebbesen, S. "Corpus Philosophorum Danicorum Medii Aevi, Archbishop Andrew (†1228), and Twelfth-Century Techniques of Argumentation." In *The Editing of Theological and Philosophical Texts from the Middle Ages.* Ed. Monika Asztalos. Acta Universitatis Stockholmiensis, Studia Latina Stockholmiensia, 30. Stockholm: Almqvist & Wiksell, 1986, pp. 267–80.

Sten Ebbesen

[**See also**: Latin Language and Literature]

Supernatural Beings

1. ELVES, DWARFS, AND GIANTS. The families of elves, dwarfs, and giants belong to Germanic folklore, myth, and literature. Of these beings, the giants (*jǫtnar, þursar, troll, risar*) are the most important. The giant Ymir of Norse mythology represents the first form of life on earth (*e.g., Vǫluspá*, st. 3, *Gylfaginning*, ch. 4), and from his body the landscape was fashioned by the gods (*Vafþrúðnismál*, st. 21, *Grímnismál*, st. 40). The world will perish in the final battle through flames kindled by the giant Surtr (*Vǫluspá*, sts. 52–57). Giants and gods engage in relentless warfare, Þórr being the defender of the gods. If all of them had escaped the force of his hammer Mjǫllnir, there would be no life left in this world, and Ásgarðr would be peopled by giants (*Hárbarðsljóð*, st. 23, *Þrymskviða*, st. 18). Heimdallr appears in a number of sources as the guardian of the gods against the giants (*Lokasenna*, st. 48). Yet the gods themselves descended from the giantess Bestla (*Gylfaginning*, ch. 5), and a giant's daughter may be sought in marriage by a god (Freyr and Gerðr; *cf. Skírnismál*, st. 41). The gods also owe important cultural possesions to the giants, such as the mead of poetry (*Skáldskaparmál*, chs. 4–6).

In sagas, especially *fornaldarsǫgur*, the giants dwell in caves and are invariably allied with the local landscape. A meeting with a giant and a love relation with a giant's daughter are standard adventures in the life of a young hero (*Hálfdanar saga Brǫnufóstra*). Giants are also depicted as hostile, man-eating monsters, who must be destroyed by the young warrior. Frequently, a giant's dwelling lies in the midst of snow and ice. Some scholars have identified the giants with the forces of chaos and destruction, with the deadly powers of wintertime, and with the primeval elements of nature. Others see them as literary creations. Recently, attention has been drawn to cultic worship offered to the race (Steinsland 1986), and there seem to be many indications that the giants were the gods of a pre-Germanic population (Motz 1984).

The family of elves (*álfar*) comprises a variety of spirits. Snorri (*Gylfaginning*, ch. 9) distinguishes between two kinds of elves: the light elves (*ljósálfar*) and dark elves (*dǫkkálfar*). The dark elves were black and lived underground; Snorri's dark elves are skilled in smithcraft like the dwarfs, and present the gods with precious gifts (*Skáldskaparmál*, ch. 1). While the closeness of the light elves to the gods is accentuated by the recurrent phrase "Æsir and elves," their form, function, or activities are never described.

In the prose narratives, elves live in mounds as spirits of great potency (*Kormáks saga*). That the elves received cultic worship is suggested by the word *álfablót* ("sacrifice to elves"; *Austrfararvísur*), most probably a sacrifice for fertility, but they are also grouped in a curse with evil spirits (*Bósa saga ok Herrauðs*). Sacrifice to a heathen king Óláfr, a petty king of southeastern Norway for a fruitful harvest, brought him his nickname *Geirstaðaálfr* ("elf of

Geirstaðir"). The Danish word *älfdans* ("elves' dance") and the Norwegian word *alfgust* ("elves' wind") indicate that belief in elves persisted in folk tradition. The elves have survived into modern times as hidden beings, and are hardly to be distinguished from the *huldufólk* ("hidden people").

Scholars consider the *álfar* either as forces of fruitlessness or of death. The family, however, shows such divergent, contradictory qualities that it is not possible to obtain a clear image of its nature. Obviously, elves are potent forces of enduring significance. The name *álfar* was extended in meaning to include spirits from many areas of faith and literature. This inclusiveness may account for the variety and forms within the group.

The dwarfs (*dvergar*) of the Norse texts are craftsmen; they brewed the mead of poetry (*Skáldskaparmál*, ch. 1) and were renowned as forgers of precious possessions, such as Óðinn's spear Gungnir, Sif's golden hair, Þórr's hammer Mjǫllnir, and Freyr's ship Skíðblaðnir (*Skáldskaparmál*, ch. 33). The dwarfs were also said to be very wise (*Alvíssmál*), and had command of esoteric knowledge, runes, and magic chants (*Hávamál*, sts. 143, 160). They lived invariably in stones and mountains.

Dwarfs are all male, and they arose asexually, molded from the earth or generated in giants' blood (*Vǫluspá*, st. 9). They do not engage in fruitful sexual encounters. Saga dwarfs show a passionate attachment to their dwelling places. They provide heroes with gifts of magical endowment and possess powers of healing and enchantment (*Gǫngu-Hrólfs saga*, ch. 23).

In both myth and literature, dwarfs serve beings of higher status than themselves to whom they offer their products willingly or under coercion. Frequently insulted and mistreated, they sometimes exact revenge (*Sigurðar saga þǫgla*, ch. 16). In spite of their generosity and skills, they are often held in low esteem. Depicted mainly in the exercise of their craft, dwarfs are the mythical representatives of a profession, counterparts of the mysterious craftsman-priests of early civilizations. They show affinity with the earth-dwelling smiths of Mediterranean tradition, such as Ptah of Egypt, Hephaistos of Lemnos, or the Daktyls of Crete.

Dwarfs in folktales show strong resemblances to their counterparts in myth and literature.

Lit.: (a) Elves: Unwerth, W. von. *Untersuchungen über Totenkult und Óðinnverehrung bei Nordgermanen und Lappen.* Germanistische Abhandlungen, 37. Breslau: Marcus, 1911; Vries, Jan de. "Van Alven en Elfen." *Nederlandsche Tijdschrift voor Volkskunde* 36 (1931), 3–30; Vries, Jan de. "Åber Sigvats Álfablót-strophen." *Acta Philologica Scandinavica* 7 (1932–33), 169–80; Vries, Jan de. *Altgermanische Religionsgeschichte.* 2 vols. Berlin: de Gruyter, 1935–37, vol. 2, pp. 373–4; Ellis Davidson, Hilda Roderick. *The Road to Hel: A Study of the Conception of the Dead in Old Norse Literature.* Cambridge: Cambridge University Press, 1943; Turville-Petre, E. O. G. *Myth and Religion of the North: The Religion of the Ancient Scandinavians.* New York: Holt, Rinehart and Winston, 1964; rpt. Westport: Greenwood, 1975, pp. 230–2; Motz, Lotte. "Of Elves and Dwarfs." *Arv* 29–30 (1973–74), 93–127. **(b) Dwarfs**: Boor, Helmut de. "Der Zwerg in Skandinavien." In *Festschrift Eugen Mogk zum 70. Geburtstag 19. Juli 1924.* Halle: Niemeyer, 1924, pp. 535–57; Gould, Nathan Chester. "Dwarf-Names: A Study in Old Icelandic Religion." *Publications of the Modern Language Association* 44 (1929), 939–67; Reichborn-Kjennerud, I. "Den gamle dvergetro." In *Studia germanica tillägnade Ernst Albin Kock den 6 December 1934.* Ed. Erik Rooth. Lunder germanistische Forschungen, 1. Lund: Gleerup, 1934, pp. 278–88; Gutenbrunner, Siegfried. "Eddastudien I. Über die Zwerge in der

Vǫluspá Str. 9–13." *Arkiv för nordisk filologi* 70 (1955), 61–75; Turville-Petre, E. O. G., *Myth and Religion of the North*, pp. 233–5; Motz, Lotte. "New Thoughts on Dwarf-Names in Old Icelandic." *Frühmittelalterliche Studien* 7 (1973), 100–17; Motz, Lotte. "The Craftsman in the Mound." *Folklore* 88 (1977), 46–60; Motz, Lotte. *The Wise One of the Mountain: Form, Function, and Significance of the Subterranean Smith: A Study in Folklore.* Göppingen Arbeiten zur Germanistik, 379. Göppingen: Kümmerle, 1983. **(c) Giants**: Sydow, Carl Wilhelm von. "Jätterna i mytologi och folktro." *Folkminnen och folktankar* 6 (1919), 52–96; Höttges, Valerie. *Die Saga vom Riesenspielzeug.* Jena: Diederich, 1931; Broderius, John R. *The Giant in Germanic Tradition.* Chicago: University of Chicago Libraries, 1932; Höttges, Valerie. *Typenverzeichnis der deutschen Riesen- und riesischen Teufelssagen.* Folklore Fellows Communications, 122. Helsinki: Academia Scientiarum Fennica, 1937; Ellis, Hilda R. "Fostering by Giants in Old Norse Saga Literature." *Medium Ævum* 10 (1941), 70–85; Chadwick, Nora K. "Þorgerðr Hölgabrúðr and the *trolla-þing*: A Note on Sources." In *The Early Cultures of North-West Europe.* H. M. Chadwick Memorial Studies. Ed. Cyrill Fox and Bruce Dickins. Cambridge: Cambridge University Press, 1950, pp. 395–417; Ciklamini, Marlene. "The Giants in Germanic Mythology." Diss. Yale University, 1961; Motz, Lotte. "The Rulers of the Mountain: A Study of the Giants of the Old Icelandic Texts." *Mankind Quarterly* 21 (1980–81), 392–416; Steinsland, Gro, and Kari Vogt. "Aukinn ertu Volse ok vpp vm tekinn." *Arkiv för nordisk filologi* 91 (1981), 87–106; Motz, Lotte. "Giantesses and Their Names." *Frümittelalterliche Studien* 15 (1981), 495–511; Motz, Lotte. "Giants in Folklore and Mythology: A New Approach." *Folklore* 93 (1982), 70–84; Motz, Lotte. "Gods and Demons of the Wilderness: A Study in Norse Tradition." *Arkiv för nordisk filologi* 99 (1984), 175–86; Gade, Kari Ellen. "Skjalf." *Arkiv för nordisk filologi* 100 (1985), 59–71; Steinsland, Gro. "Giants as Recipients of Cult in the Viking Age?" In *Words and Objects: Towards a Dialogue Between Archaeology and History of Religion.* Ed. Gro Steinsland. Institute for Comparative Research in Human Culture, Oslo, Ser. B: Skrifter, 71. Oslo: Norwegian University Press, 1986, pp. 212–22; Motz, Lotte, "Families of Giants." *Arkiv för nordisk filologi* 102 (1987), 216–36; Motz, Lotte. "Old Icelandic Giants and Their Names." *Frühmittelalterliche Studien* 21 (1987), 295–317.

Lotte Motz

2. DRAUGR AND APTRGANGA. *Draugr* (pl. *draugar* 'ghost') and *aptrganga* (pl. *aptrgöngur* 'revenant') are common Old Norse designations for deceased persons who live on after death. Usually, the terms apply to persons who had committed an evil deed during their lifetime, and who become ghosts or revenants. As such, they cause illness, insanity, and death. The idea of the dead who can find no rest in their graves and who return to harass the living is an old one, as is also the attempt to prevent their return through measures like cremation. However, it is unlikely that the burial formulae of some of the Norwegian and Swedish runic inscriptions (*e.g.*, Eggja, Högstena) can be interpreted as charms against revenants. Medieval laws contain scattered prohibitions against awakening the dead (*Norges gamle love* 1:19, 2:308). Among eddic poems, *Hervararkviða*, in which Hervǫr fetches the sword Tyrfingr from her father Angantyr's grave mound, and *Helgakviða Hundingsbana II*, where Sigrún is visited by her dead husband Helgi, offer particularly noteworthy treatments of the motif. In *Ynglinga saga* (ch. 7), Óðinn is called *draugadróttinn* ("lord of the dead").

The intervention of revenants becomes a structural narrative pattern in the saga literature of the 13th century (Boberg 1966: Mot. E 200–599, "Ghosts and Other Revenants"). Here, one finds a variety of striking episodes, such as the hauntings at Fróðá ("Fróðárundr") in *Eyrbyggja saga* (chs. 53–55), in which a group of drowned people appear, and Þórólfr bægifótr's ("twist foot's") mischief (chs. 33–34, 61); the appearance of Þorkell's ghost to Guðrún, which announces his drowning (*Laxdæla saga*, ch. 76); and, above all, Grettir's struggle with the monster Glámr (*Grettis saga*, chs. 32–35). Later texts, like *Dámusta saga*, also show familiarity with the motif of the struggle of the hero with a deceased person (Alheimr). But in these late-medieval legendary and romantic sagas, the prevailing motif is that of the deceased in a grave mound that has been opened by the hero; after a bitter wrestling match, the hero defeats the revenant and takes his treasures and weapons. *Egils saga einhenda* (ch. 7; *cf.* Saxo Grammaticus, *Gesta Danorum*, Book 5), *Hrómundar saga Gripssonar* (ch. 4), and *Hervarar saga ok Heiðreks* offer examples of such episodes, often described in great detail. In *Gǫngu-Hrólfs saga* (ch. 32), the dead king Hreggviðr voluntarily hands over his weapons to the hero.

Conceptions of the *draugar* are found in recent Icelandic folktales, where the deceased are seen as living on and intervening in people's lives in numerous ways, thus obscuring the boundary separating life and death.

The skaldic *draugr* ("tree, tree trunk," *viz.* "companion, comitatus") has nothing to do with revenants.

Lit.: Dehmer, Heinz. *Primitives Erzählungsgut in den Íslendinga-Sögur*. Leipzig: Weber, 1926; Gould, Chester Nathan. "They Who Await the Second Death: A Study in the Icelandic Romantic Sagas." *Scandinavian Studies and Notes* 9 (1926–27), 167–201; Klare, Hans-Joachim. "Die Toten in der altnordischen Literatur." *Acta Philologica Scandinavica* 8 (1933–34), 1–56; Nordén, Arthur. "Från Kivik till Eggjum, II: Runristningar med gengångarbesvärjelse." *Fornvännen* 29 (1934), 97–117; Sydow, C. W. von. "Övernaturliga väsen." In *Folketro*. Nordisk kultur, 19. Ed. Nils Lid. Stockholm: Bonnier; Oslo: Aschehoug; Copenhagen: Schultz, 1935, pp. 95–159; Nordén, Arthur. "Från Kivik till Eggjum, III: Fågel-fiskmagien och vattnet som gengångarskydd." *Fornvännen* 31 (1936), 241–8; Jungner, Hugo. "Högstena-galdern: En västgösk runbesvärjelse mot gengångare." *Fornvännen* 31 (1936), 278–304 [German summary]; Einar Ól. Sveinsson. *Um íslenzkar þjóðsögur*. Reykjavik: Margrét Lehmann-Filhés, 1940, pp. 166–71; Vries, Jan de. *Altgermanische Religionsgeschichte*. 2 vols. 2nd ed. Grundriss der germanischen Philologie, 12. Berlin: de Gruyter, 1956–57, vol. 1; Ström, Folke. "Gengångare." *KLNM* 5 (1960), 252–3; Jón Árnason. *Íslenzkar þjóðsögur og ævintýri*. 6 vols. Ed. Árni Böðvarsson and Bjarni Vilhjálmsson. Reykjavik: Þjóðsaga, 1961; Boberg, Inger M. *Motif-Index of Early Icelandic Literature*. Bibliotheca Arnamagnæana, 27. Copenhagen: Munksgaard, 1966; Lindow, John. *Comitatus, Individual and Collective Honor. Studies in North Germanic Institutional Vocabulary*. University of California Publications. Linguistics, 83. Berkeley, Los Angeles, and London: University of California Press, 1976, pp. 84–96; Kjartan G. Ottósson. *Fróðárundur í Eyrbyggju*. Studia Islandica, 42. Reykjavik: Menningarsjóður, 1983 [English summary]; Grønvik, Ottar. *Runene på Eggjasteinen. En hedensk gravinnskrift fra slutten av 600–tallet*. Oslo, Bergen, Stavanger, and Tromsø: Universitetsforlaget, 1985; Lecouteux, Claude. *Fantômes et revenants au moyen âge*. Paris: Imago, 1986; Lecouteux, Claude. *Geschichte der Gespenster und Wiedergänger im Mittelalter*. Vienna: Böhlau, 1987; Crozier, Alan. "Ørlygis draugr and ørlǫg drýgja." *Arkiv för nordisk filologi* 102 (1987), 1–12; Jón Hnefill Aðalsteinsson. "Þjóðsögur og sagnir." In *Íslensk þjóðmenning. VI. Munnmenntir ok bókmenning*. Ed. Frosti F. Jóhannsson. Reykjavik: Þjóðsaga, 1989, pp. 228–90.

Jürg Glauser

3. DÍSIR (sing. *dís*) is a collective word comprising female divine beings without individual names. Like the norns, they assist in childbirth (*Sigrdrífumál*, st. 9). As tutelary goddesses attached to an individual or a family, they offer protection against enemies (*Vǫlsunga saga*, ch. 35). Designations like "battle-*dísir*" (*Haustlǫng*, st. 17) and *Herjans dísir* (*Guðrúnarkviða*, st. 1.19), kennings for valkyries, emphasize their military aspect. As "Óðinn's *dísir*," they bring home men slain in battle (*Hamðismál*, st. 28). Óðinn announces the impending death of King Geirrøðr by reference to the anger of the *dísir* (*Grímnismál*, st. 28). *Þiðranda þáttr* in *Flateyjarbók* relates that a young Icelander, Þiðrandi, was attacked and killed by *dísir* at the "winter-nights," a time when a feast was held with customary sacrifice to the *dísir*.

In Norway and Iceland, there is evidence of a *dísir* cult, which was celebrated with a sacrifice to the *dísir* (*dísablót*) in the fall. It is probable that the *dísir* cult was primarily a private one closely associated with fertility cults: in *Gylfaginning* (ch. 35), Freyja is called Vanadís ("*dís* of the Vanir"). The name of the old market Disting near Uppsala implies that in Sweden the cult of the *dísir* was more public than in the western regions. According to Snorri, there was a great cult festival in February, during which sacrifice was made for "peace and the victory of the king." The *dísir* cult was associated with the Ynglingar clan; according to *Ynglinga saga* (chs. 19, 29), King Aðils of Uppsala was present at a sacrifice to the *dísir*, and, as he rode his horse around the hall of the *dís* (*dísarsalr*), it stumbled, and the king fell forward, striking his head on a stone, and died.

The function of the *dísir* is unclear. They appear close to norns, valkyries, and *fylgjur*, but in contrast to these supernatural beings, the *dísir* were objects of a cult, as testified by a number of Swedish-Norwegian place-names (Disåsen, Diseberg, Disevid).

Lit.: Brate, Erik. "Disen." *Zeitschrift für deutsche Wortforschung* 13 (1912), 143–52; Johansson, Karl Ferdinand. *Über die altindische Göttin Dhisána und Verwandtes: Beiträge zum Fruchtbarkeitskultus in Indien*. Skrifter utgivna af kungliga humanistiska vetenskapssamfundet i Uppsala, 20.1. Uppsala: Almqvist & Wiksell, 1918; Ström, Folke. "Tidrandes död." *Arv* 8 (1952), 77–119; Ström, Folke. *Diser, nornor, valkyrjor: Fruktbarhetskult och sakralt kungadöme i Norden*. Kungliga vitterhets, historie, och antikvitetsakademiens handlingar, filologisk-filosofiska serien, 1. Stockholm: Almqvist & Wiksell, 1954; Motz, Lotte. "Sister in the Cave: The Stature and the Function of the Female Figures of the *Eddas*." *Arkiv för nordisk filologi* 95 (1980), 168–82; Naumann, Hans-Peter. "Disen." In *Reallexikon der germanischen Altertumskunde* 5. Ed. Heinrich Beck *et al.* Berlin and New York: de Gruyter, 1982, pp. 494–7.

Hans-Peter Naumann

4. FYLGJA ("fetch, guardian spirit"; pl. *fylgjur*). The beings called *fylgjur* in Old Norse sources are of two kinds: one type has the shape of an animal, the other the shape of a woman. These two types have little in common but the name.

The *fylgja* in the shape of an animal is an alter ego, and reflects a person's character. A strong and powerful man may have a bear or a bull as a *fylgja* (*Njáls saga*, ch. 23, *Ljósvetninga saga*, chs. 11 and 16, *Vápnfirðinga saga*, ch. 13); a sly person may have a fox (*Þorsteins saga Víkingssonar*, ch. 12). The foster-father of the sons of Njáll (*Njáls saga*, ch. 41), who was a peaceful person, had a he-goat as a *fylgja*.

A *fylgja* may also indicate the social status of a person. In the nonrealistic *fornaldarsǫgur*, kings may have *fylgjur* in the shape of a lion (*Hrólfs saga Gautrekssonar*, chs. 7 and 12) or a leopard (*Sǫgubrot*, ch. 2).

A person has only one *fylgja* of the alter-ego type, which always appears in the same shape; deviations from this rule must be regarded as free use of a literary motif in conflict with the underlying folk belief. The *fylgja* follows a person throughout life, and dies with him. It is normally invisible, but may show itself to other people than its owner. When the *fylgja* shows itself to its owner, it augurs the person's death. The *fylgja* as an alter ego is also called *mannsfylgja* ("man-*fylgja*"), and when it augurs death, *dauðafylgja* ("death-*fylgja*").

The conception of a man's *fylgja* in the shape of an animal has much in common with a man's *hugr* ("mind"), a personification of a man's evil thought that always appears in the shape of a wolf. This wolf may "attack" enemies by making them sleepy or unwell, an ability that the alter-ego *fylgja* does not seem to have. In some literary works, a chieftain's *fylgja* is followed by a pack of wolves. Such a mixture in the literary motif may indicate confusion in the underlying belief.

Fylgjur, spoken of as unfriendly, harmful beings, could also result from the two conceptions having been mixed, but most likely such *ófriðarfylgjur* ("unrest-*fylgja*") and *óvinarfylgjur* ("enemy-*fylgja*") belong to the other type, the *fylgja* in the shape of a woman. This type of *fylgja* acts on its own behalf, as opposed to the alter-ego type, whose actions are solely reflections of the person's actions.

The *fylgja* in the shape of a woman is a guardian spirit, often of a whole family; but she follows the head of the family in particular, and when the old head of the family dies, she turns to the next (*Víga-Glúms saga*, ch. 9, *Hallfreðar saga*, ch. 11). A man or a family may have one *fylgja* of the guardian-spirit type, but in some sources, there may be a few more, or even a large collective of women. Normally, they are invisible, but they may also be visible both to the person they follow and, less often, to others. The *fylgja* as a guardian spirit may attack a person's enemy, or help in battle or in other critical situations. As long as she follows a person, she guarantees luck; when she leaves a person, it means that luck has gone, and the person will soon die. At the end of life, the *fylgja* riding on the grey horse of death may call for her person and bring him home to the place of the dead ancestors. The belief in the *fylgja* as a guardian spirit is most likely connected with the worship of dead ancestresses, and in some literary sources she is in fact a link between the living and the dead members of a family. In some sources (*Víga-Glúms saga*, ch. 9, *Laxdœla saga*, ch. 67), the *fylgja* is described as a woman of an unusually large size, which may indicate that she was looked upon as a semidivine character.

The *fylgja* as a guardian spirit is called by many names that focus on different aspects of her character. Besides *fylgja*, she is also spoken of as *kona* ("woman"), *fylgjukona* ("woman-*fylgja*"), and *dís*; *dís* is often used in poetry and in the nonrealistic literature. These words tell us that the guardian spirit is a woman. The names *ættarfylgja* and *kynfylgja* ("family-*fylgja*") focus on her close relationship to the whole family. The name *draumkona* ("dream-woman") tells that she often appears in a dream, and the name *spádís* ("prophecy-*dís*") that she knows the future. The names *ófriðarfylgja* and *óvinarfylgja* indicate that *fylgjur* belonging to an enemy were dangerous creatures. The name *hamingja*, which generally is a word for "luck," underlines her good and protecting nature.

Lit.: Rieger, Max. "Über den nordischen fylgienglauben." *Zeitschrift für deutsches Altertum und deutsche Literatur* 42 (1897), 277–90; Lagerheim, M. "Bidrag till kännedomen om fylgja-tron." *Svenska fornminneforeningens tidskrift* 12 (1905), 169–84; Blum, Ida. *Die Schutzgeister in der altnordischen Literatur*. Zabern: Fuchs, 1912; Oldeberg, A. "Några bidrag till kännedomen om fylgjaföreställningen hos nordborna." *Rig. Föreningens för svensk kulturhistoria tidskrift* 10 (1927), 173–8; Turville-Petre, Gabriel. "Liggja fylgjur þínar til Íslands." *Saga-Book of the Viking Society* 12 (1937–45), 119–26; rpt. in his *Nine Norse Studies*. Text Series, 5. London: Viking Society for Northern Research, 1972, pp. 52–8; Strömbäck, Dag. *Sejd: Textstudier i nordisk religionshistoria*. Nordiska texter och undersökningar, 5. Stockholm: Geber; Copenhagen: Levin & Munksgaard, 1935; Turville-Petre, Gabriel. *Myth and Religion of the North: The Religion of the Ancient Scandinavians*. New York: Holt, Rinehart and Winston, 1964; rpt. Westport: Greenwood, 1975, pp. 221–35; Mundal, Else. *Fylgjemotiva i norrøn litteratur*. Skrifter fra instituttene for nordisk språk og litteratur ved universitetene i Bergen, Oslo, Trondheim og Tromsø, 5. Oslo, Bergen, and Tromsø: Universitetsforlaget, 1974.

Else Mundal

5. NORNS (Old Norse *norn* fem., pl. *nornir*, etymology disputed). The norns in Old Norse mythology are female beings whose purpose is to determine the fate of every human being, of the gods, and probably of the whole world. The norns thus represent the highest power in the universe. Their fate-making activity is a magic act, referred to either as the spinning of a thread (*Reginsmál*, st. 13, *Helgakviða Hundingsbana* I) or as making a mark in wood (*Vǫluspá*, st. 20).

According to Snorri's *Gylfaginning*, three norns, Urðr, Verðandi, and Skuld, come from a hall by the well Urðarbrunnr, beneath the World Tree, Yggdrasill. Yggdrasill and the well below are situated in the center of Ásgarðr, the home of the gods. The *Hauksbók* version of *Vǫluspá* agrees that the norns come from a hall by the well, but the *Codex Regius* version of *Vǫluspá* says they come from the well itself, as does the norn Urðr in Kormákr's *Sigurðardrápa* (late 10th century). *Codex Regius's* and Kormákr's understanding seems to be the more genuine, since it is related to the widespread conception of female divine beings living in sacred wells.

In some sources, the norns are individualized and referred to with special names. The name Urðr (fem.) has the oldest and strongest tradition (Urðarbrunnr), derived from the verb *verða* 'to be, to become.' The masculine form, *urðr*, also has the meaning "death," and is cognate with the Old English word *wyrd* 'fate.' The norn name Verðandi (pres. part. of *verða*) is not mentioned in poems other than *Vǫluspá*. The name Skuld (the same root as in the auxiliary verb *skulu* 'shall') is mentioned in *Vǫluspá* and in the poem *Grógaldr*. But Skuld is usually the name of a *valkyrja*, a female character who chooses who is going to die. These three individualized norns are mentioned together only in *Vǫluspá* and, with reference to *Vǫluspá*, in Snorri's *Gylfaginning*, where the names probably are meant to be associated with the three aspects of time: past, present, and future. In Saxo's sixth book, in the story about Fridleivus, and in *Nornagests þáttr*, there are also three norns, but they are not named. Saxo refers to them with the Latin words *parca* and *nympha*. In *Nornagests þáttr*, the three female characters are partly referred to as norns and partly as *vǫlur*, the sibyls in Old Norse mythology.

Most often when the norns are mentioned, they are spoken of as a collective force. In *Gylfaginning*, Snorri says with reference to *Fáfnismál* that there are different norns (other than Urðr, Verðandi, and Skuld) who come to every newborn child to determine the child's life. Some of these norns are related to the gods, some to the elves, and some to the dwarfs.

In most cases, the central conception is that the norns' decision, the final outcome of which is death, can never be changed. The natural inclination to look for reasons when things go wrong burdened the norns especially with the responsibility for cruel fate. But they are also the creators of happy events, although the literary sources do not often mention this other aspect. One example of a positive attitude toward the norns is found in a stanza by Torf-Einarr Rǫgnvaldsson, earl of the Orkneys (Finnur Jónsson 1912–15: vol. 1A, p. 32, st. 2). He gives the norns credit when he has succeeded in his revenge on the killer of his father. But even a good fate, from the skald's point of view, is here linked to death, the death of an enemy.

In some late sources, we find an explanation of why happiness and length of life are so unequally divided. In Snorri's *Gylfaginning*, good fate is given by good norns, and evil fate by evil norns. In *Nornagests þáttr*, an angry norn decides to give a child a short life, and in Saxo's story about Fridleivus, an evil norn decides to give a child avarice as part of his character. These motifs are probably influenced by fairy-tale motifs of a late date, and the division between good and evil norns may be influenced by Christianity.

Fate-making is the norns' specialty. But they share some aspects with other groups of mythological female characters. The name Skuld, which is a name used both for a *valkyrja* and a norn, indicates that the two groups have been mixed, or that they have never been sharply distinguished, which is understandable since they are both associated with death. The (con)fusion of norns and *vǫlur* in *Nornagests þáttr* is probably of a late date, but the point of contact between the two groups is fate, which is created by the norns, but about which the *vǫlur* could obtain knowledge.

The norns were heathen figures, and therefore belief in them was complicated by the conversion to Christianity. The Icelandic skald Hallfreðr Óttarsson vandræðaskáld ("troublesome-poet") states in his *lausavísa*, st. 10 (from the late 10th century, if the stanza is genuine), that a Christian should reject the norns' decisions (Finnur Jónsson 1912–15: vol. 1A, p. 169). The norns' association with heathendom and malicious forces may be seen in the semantic changing of the word *norn*, which in Iceland finally acquired the meaning "witch." In Norway, the attitude toward the norns may have been more neutral. In a Norwegian church (Borgund in Sogn) from about 1200, a runic inscription says: "the norns did both good and evil; for me they decided a cruel fate." And up to modern times, the porridge that the neighboring women brought to a woman who had given birth was called *nornagrautr* ("the norns' porridge") in the Norwegian valley of Setesdal. This custom seems to be connected with the idea that norns come to every newborn child.

Ed.: Finnur Jónsson, ed. *Den norsk-islandske skjaldedigtning*. Vols. 1A-2A (tekst efter håndskrifterne) and 1B-2B (rettet tekst). Copenhagen and Christiania [Oslo]: Gyldendal, 1912–15; rpt. Copenhagen: Rosenkilde & Bagger, 1967 (A) and 1973 (B). **Lit.**: Ström, Folke. *Diser, nornor, valkyrjor: Fruktbarhetskult och sakralt kungadöme i Norden*. Kungliga vitterhets, historie, och antikvitetsakademiens handlingar,

filologisk-filosofiska serien, 1. Stockholm: Almqvist & Wiksell, 1954; Ellis Davidson, H. R. *Gods and Myths of Northern Europe*. Harmondsworth: Penguin, 1964; Weber, Gerd Wolfgang. *"Wyrd": Studien zum Schicksalsbegriff der altenglischen und altnordischen Literatur*. Frankfurter Beiträge zur Germanistik, 8. Bad Homburg v. d. H., Berlin, and Zurich: Gehlen, 1969; Bauschatz, Paul C. *The Well and the Tree: World and Time in Early Germanic Culture*. Amherst: University of Massachusetts Press, 1982.

Else Mundal

[**See also:** Mythology; *Snorra Edda*]

Susanna *see* **Drama**

Svarfdœla saga ("The Saga of the People of Svarfaðardalr") belongs to the genre of the *Íslendingasögur*. This text has a very complicated history. It is now extant in two versions: one, on paper, AM 161 fol., dating from about 1650, with one large and several small lacunae, and one parchment leaf (AM 445c 4to) from the 15th century. It has, however, proved possible to reconstruct the history of the whole text. The oldest version of *Landnámabók* contains a short tale about the settler Þorsteinn svǫrfuðr ("sweeper"?) and about the first generations of inhabitants of Svarfaðardalr, in the north of Iceland. A version of *Svarfdœla saga* had existed at that time (ca. 1250) that incorporated earlier literary models, local traditions, and folktales. This version is lost, but part of it has been preserved in the present text and in *Þorleifs þáttr jarlsskálds*. It narrated the Viking expeditions of one Þorsteinn, who married the daughter of a Swedish king. Sturla Þórðarson (d. 1284), author of the *Sturlubók* version of *Landnámabók*, knew this version (cf. *Sturlubók*, ch. 219). Then, in the 15th century, the story was recast following the taste of the time, seen in the exaggerations typical of the postclassical sagas. After the large lacuna, the saga continues in quite a different style, becoming heavy and awkward, and clearly reminiscent of local traditions. This part of the saga tells the story of settlement in Svarfaðardalr by one Þorsteinn, who may be the same as the previous character of that name. The facts, a long bloody quarrel among the inhabitants of Svarfaðardalr, are loosely connected, and the whole is very obscure. The characters are on the whole poorly depicted, with the exception of Klaufi, who marries by cunning Yngvildr fagrkinn ("fair-cheek"); he is a berserk when living and, after his death, a *draugr* who fights with his own head as a weapon. Toward the end, the saga adopts a new tone to narrate the cruel revenge that Karl, Þorsteinn's grandson, takes on Yngvildr, who has caused the death of his father: he kills her three sons and takes her into slavery abroad, until she consents, at last, to humiliate herself.

Svarfdœla saga is a baroque *Íslendingasaga*. It lacks unity in both style and narrative technique, and the characters are fairly inconsistent. It shows obvious influences from the *fornaldarsögur*, especially *Ǫrvar-Odds saga*. It incorporates popular motifs, such as the episode involving Karl, which reminds us of the history of Shakespeare's Hamlet (told also by Saxo Grammaticus in Books 3 and 4 of his *Gesta Danorum*), or the episode involving Yngvildr fagrkinn, which resembles Shakespeare's *The Taming of the Shrew*.

Ed.: Jónas Kristjánsson, ed. *Eyfirðinga sögur*. Íslenzk fornrit, 9. Reykjavik: Hið íslenska fornritafélag, 1956; Jónas Kristjánsson, ed. *Svarfdælasaga*. Reykjavik: Handritastofnun Íslands, 1966. **Lit.**: Finnur Jónsson. "Om Svarfdæla saga." *Aarbøger for nordisk Oldkyndighed og Historie*

(1884), 120–42; Björn M. Ólsen. *Um Íslendingasögur: Kaflar úr háskólafyrirlestrum. Safn til sögu Íslands* 6.3. Reykjavík: Hið Íslenzka bókmentafélag, 1937–39 [entire issue]; Turville-Petre, G. "The Author of Svarfdæla and the Reviser of Glúma." *Leeds Studies in English* 5 (1936), 74–92; Schach, Paul. "*Svarfdæla saga.*" In *Dictionary of the Middle Ages.* Ed. Joseph R. Strayer. New York: Scribner, 1982–89, vol. 11, p. 521; Schach, Paul. *Icelandic Sagas.* Twayne's World Authors Series, 717. Boston: Twayne, 1984, pp. 162–4; Boyer, R. "Saga des Gens du Svarfaðardalr." In *Sagas Islandaises.* Ed. Régis Boyer. Bibliothèque de la Pléiade, 338. Paris: Gallimard, 1987, pp. 1115–72, 1856–61.

Régis Boyer

[**See also**: *Berserkr*; *Íslendingasögur*; *Landnámabók*; *Þorleifs þáttr jarlsskálds*; *Ǫrvar-Odds saga*]

Sven Haraldsson (Forkbeard)

Sven Haraldsson (Forkbeard) was king of Denmark 987–1014. Sven seized power through a revolt against his father, Harald Gormsson (Bluetooth), who fled to the Wends and died of his wounds on November 1, 987. That Sven was captured and ransomed from the Wends following this revolt is highly dubious. According to Adam of Bremen, Sven's revolt was a pagan reaction, but its motives were more likely political; there is no other indication that Sven was a pagan. In Sven's time, Viking raids against England were resumed, and in 994 he led a raid together with Óláfr Tryggvason. He probably also took part in the raid in 991 and the battle of Maldon, but apparently not in the great raids of 997–1002 and 1009–1012. In 1003–1004, however, he conducted a raid, possibly to avenge the death of his sister Gunnhild and her husband, Pallig, in Æthelred's massacre of the Danes on November 13, 1002. In 1013, he led a raid that, in a strikingly short time, achieved the conquest of England, when Æthelred gave up resistance and left the country at Christmas, his subjects having acknowledged Sven as king. Sven's English reign was brief, however; he died on February 3, 1014, in Gainsborough and was buried first in England, then in Roskilde.

Sven also reasserted his father's claim to Norway, which had been seized, possibly with the help of Æthelred, by Óláfr Tryggvason around 995. Sven supported the sons of Earl Hákon, and, having married the widow of the Swedish king Erik Bjarnarson and thereby gaining influence in Sweden, he also supported his young stepson Olav (Skötkonung) Eriksson. Together with these allies, he won a decisive victory over Óláfr Tryggvason in the battle of Svǫlðr (Svold) and thereby restored traditional Danish overlordship over Norway.

The sources for Sven's reign are contradictory. While Thietmar and Adam of Bremen depict him as a cruel and evil ruler who was punished by the Lord with captivity, exile, and foreign conquest, and whose position was very insecure, according to the *Encomium Emmae*, he "was practically the most fortunate of all the kings of his time." Both views are obviously biased, but Sven's career to a large extent bears out the encomiast's view. To be able repeatedly to leave Denmark on prolonged campaigns, he must have enjoyed a secure position at home, suggested also by the fact that the fortifications built late in his father's reign were allowed to decay. He had remarkable political and military success in Scandinavia as well as in England.

Sven was the first Danish king to strike coins with his name on them. Only one type is known, imitating an Anglo-Saxon coin and struck by an English moneyer who apparently also worked for Óláfr Tryggvason and for Olav Eriksson. The coins of the three kings are so different, however, that they are more likely to be independent imitations than struck by the same moneyer. At the same time, imitations of English coins, but without the Danish king's name on them, began to be produced in large numbers in Lund, which developed into a town early in Sven's reign.

Ed.: Campbell, Alistair, ed. and trans. *Encomium Emmae Reginae.* Camden Society Third Series, 72. London: Royal Historical Society, 1949; Thietmar von Merseburg. *Chronik.* Ed. Werner Trillmich. Ausgewählte Quellen zur deutschen Geschichte des Mittelalters, 9. Berlin: Rütten & Loening, 1957; Adam Bremensis. *Gesta Hammaburgensis Ecclesiae Pontificum.* In *Quellen des 9. und 11. Jahrhunderts zur Geschichte der hamburgischen Kirche und des Reiches.* Ed. Werner Trillmich and Rudolf Buchner. Ausgewählte Quellen zur deutschen Geschichte des Mittelalters, 11. Berlin: Rütten & Loening, 1978. **Tr.**: Adam of Bremen. *History of the Archbishops of Hamburg-Bremen.* Trans. Francis J. Tschan. Records of Civilization: Sources and Studies. New York: Columbia University Press, 1959. **Lit.**: Skovgaard-Petersen, Inge. "Sven Tveskæg i den ældste danske historiografi. En Saxostudie." In *Middelalderstudier tilegnede Aksel E. Christensen på tresårsdagen 11. september 1966.* Ed. Tage E. Christensen et al. Copenhagen: Munksgaard, 1966, pp. 1–38; Stenton, F. M. *Anglo-Saxon England.* 3rd ed. Oxford History of England, 2. Oxford: Clarendon, 1971; Demidoff, Lene. "The Death of Sven Forkbeard—in Reality and Later Tradition." *Mediaeval Scandinavia* 11 (1978–79), 30–47; Sobel, Leopold. "Ruler and Society in Early Medieval Western Pomerania." *Antemurale* 25 (1981), 19–142; Andersson, Theodore M. "The Viking Policy of Ethelred the Unready." *Scandinavian Studies* 59 (1987), 284–95; Brown, Phyllis R. "The Viking Policy of Ethelred: A Response." *Scandinavian Studies* 59 (1987), 296–8; Sawyer, Peter. *Da Danmark blev Danmark.* Gyldendal og Politikens Danmarkshistorie, 3. Copenhagen: Gyldendal; Politiken, 1988; Sawyer, Peter. "Swein Forkbeard and the Historians." In *Church and Chronicle in the Middle Ages.* Ed. Ian Wood and G.A. Loud. London: Hambledon, 1991, pp. 27–40.

Niels Lund

[**See also**: Adam of Bremen; *Encomium Emmae reginae*; England, Norse in; Harald Gormsson (Bluetooth); Óláfr Tryggvason]

Sverrir Sigurðarson

Sverrir Sigurðarson, king of Norway 1177–1202, was a native of the Faroe Islands, where his paternal uncle held the bishopric of Kirkebø (Kirkubæur). Here, Sverrir grew up and received his education. At the age of twenty-four, he was consecrated a priest, and his Norwegian mother revealed to him that his true father was the then long-dead King Sigurðr munnr ("mouth") Haraldsson. This revelation caused Sverrir to go to Norway in 1176, quit the clergy, and fight his way to the throne in fierce opposition to the powerful Archbishop Eysteinn, who had supported Magnús Erlingsson and crowned him king in 1164. Sverrir was proclaimed king in 1177 in Trondheim, and a few years later he had succeeded in gaining control of the larger part of the country. After the battle at Fimreiti in 1184, where King Magnús fell together with the majority of the Norwegian aristocracy, Sverrir became the sole ruler of Norway, although having constantly to fight an array of pretenders to the kingdom.

Our knowledge about Sverrir comes primarily from his saga, *Sverris saga*, which presents us with a fascinating personality, seemingly embodying great contrasts. He describes himself as being fierce as the lion and mild as the lamb, both symbols found on his royal seal. His biography does indeed exhibit his wit and down-to-earth philosophy, but also the new Christian ethics of mildness and forgiveness toward one's enemies. Sverrir's complex background and subtle mind are reflected in his irony and humor, displaying great self-confidence. Sverrir was a brilliant military leader on sea as well as on land. His ingenious tactics in warfare were so untraditional that he has been called a coward despite being victorious; his guerilla attacks were often of a kind that most Norse noblemen avoided. Sverrir had a profound knowledge of the Bible. His national-church policy brought him into lasting conflict with the Norwegian bishops; eventually, the archbishop left the country. Sverrir was excommunicated by him and later by the pope.

Sverrir's struggle with the Church is set forth in a document he himself commissioned. From his *Oratio contra clerum Norvegiae* ("Speech Against the Norwegian Clergy"), as well as the contemporary *Sverris saga*, we learn about his political ideology, drawn partly from Old Testament values. At the same time that he carried out his controversies with the international Church, Sverrir introduced those theocratic traits into his dynastic policy that are so extraordinary for the 13th-century Norwegian monarchy. During his reign, Sverrir strengthened the centralization of the king's administration, and the finances of the Crown were improved by a new system of taxation.

After the Reformation, Sverrir was celebrated as the king who had the courage to speak against the authority of Rome. In the 19th-century Norwegian struggle for national independence, Sverrir became a symbolic figure for the national identity. Present-day interest in the development of the state as an institution has made Sverrir and his royal descendants much valued as the creators of a strong and highly centralized state as early as the 13th century.

Lit.: Cederschiöld, Gustaf. *Konung Sverre*. Lund: Gleerup, 1901; Paasche, Frederik. *Kong Sverre*. Oslo: Aschehoug, 1920; Koht, Halvdan. *Kong Sverre*. Oslo: Aschehoug, 1952; Gathorne-Hardy, Geoffrey M. *A Royal Impostor: King Sverre of Norway*. Oslo: Aschehoug; London: Oxford University Press, 1956; Holm-Olsen, Ludvig. "Kong Sverre i søkelyset." *Nordisk tidskrift* 34 (1958), 167–81; Helle, Knut. *Norge blir en stat, 1130–1319*. Handbok i Norges historie, 3. 2nd ed. Bergen, Oslo, and Tromsø: Universitetsforlaget, 1974; Gunnes, Erik. *Kongens ære: Kongemagt og kirke i "En tale mot biskopene."* Oslo: Gyldendal, 1971; Lunden, Kåre. *Norge under Sverreætten 1177–1319*. Oslo: Cappelen, 1976; Ólafía Einarsdóttir. "Sverrir—præst og konge." In *Middelalder, Methode og Medier. Festskrift til N. Skyum-Nielsen*. Ed. Karsten Fledelius *et al.* Copenhagen: Museum Tusculanum, 1981, pp. 67–93; rpt. in *Norske Historikere i Utvalg VI*. Oslo: Universitetsforlaget, 1983, pp. 126–41, 336–8.

Ólafía Einarsdóttir

[**See also:** Norway; *Oratio contra clerum Norvegiae; Sverris saga*]

Sverris saga, the saga of the Norwegian king Sverrir Sigurðarson (r. 1177–1202), survives in four vellum MSS, the best of which is AM 327 4to, written around 1300 probably by an Icelander in Norway. The other major vellums are *Flateyjarbók, Eirspennill*, and *Skálholtsbók yngsta*; some fragments of other medieval MSS also exist.

A Norwegian woman, Gunnhildr, married to a comb maker, gives birth to a son, Sverrir, who is sent as a child to the Faroe Islands, where he is fostered by the bishop and ordained priest. When he is twenty-four years old, his mother comes to the Faroes and tells him that she had been to Rome and confesses that his father is King Sigurðr Haraldsson (r. 1134–1155). Sverrir decides

to go to Norway to fight for his right to the throne against the rulers there, King Magnús, who had been crowned in 1164, and his father, the mighty Earl Erlingr.

In Norway, he becomes leader of the defeated army of the Birkibeinar ("birch-legs"), whose pretender had been killed in a battle against King Magnús Erlingsson. They confer on Sverrir the title of king, and in the following years he fights his way to power. Erlingr is killed in battle in 1179, and Magnús in 1184. The saga thereafter deals with Sverrir's struggle to defend his kingdom against new contenders to the throne, especially pretenders from the Baglar (Crozier) faction, his conflicts with the Church, and his death in 1202.

The prologue to *Sverris saga* states that the first part was written by Karl Jónsson (abbot of the Icelandic monastery of Þingeyrar, who was in Norway 1185–1188), while the king sat by and told him what to write. For the rest of the saga, the sources were people who remembered the events, some of whom had taken part in Sverrir's battles. Where the first part ends is not obvious; it may have extended to Erlingr's death in June 1179, but more probably it only covers Sverrir's career to the end of 1178. This problem has been much discussed, as has the question of the authorship of the continuation. The saga was most likely completed before 1210, and the fact that it has been impossible to find important stylistic differences between parts of the saga suggests that Karl Jónsson (d. 1212 or 1213) is the author of the whole work.

The first part of the saga is not primarily a historical account, but is intended chiefly to show that God had chosen Sverrir and helped him in many difficulties. Since the saga was composed while many people still remembered the events, the details are probably reliable. But the sympathy for Sverrir that characterizes the whole work makes it necessary to read it with a certain amount of skepticism. Certain facts that were embarrassing for Sverrir are omitted, especially in the account of his controversies with the Church. Here, the saga can be supplemented and modified by papal letters and other sources.

The saga includes numerous speeches, most of them given by Sverrir himself with his strange blend of gravity and humor. They contribute strongly to the vivid picture *Sverris saga* gives of one of the most outstanding medieval kings of Norway.

Ed.: Indrebø, Gustav, ed. *Sverris saga etter Cod. AM 327 4°*. Utgjevi av Den Norske Historiske Kildeskriftkommission. Kristiania [Oslo]: Dybwad, 1920; rpt. Oslo: Norsk Historisk Kjeldeskrift-Institutt, 1981. **Tr.**: Sephton, John, trans. *Sverrissaga: The Saga of King Sverri of Norway*. Northern Library, 4. London: Nutt, 1899. **Lit.**: Koht, Halvdan. "Norsk historieskriving under kong Sverre, serskilt Sverre-soga." In his *Innhogg og utsyn i norsk historie*. Kristiania [Oslo]: Aschehoug, 1921, pp. 156–96; Koht, Halvdan. *Kong Sverre*. Oslo: Aschehoug, 1952; Holm-Olsen, Ludvig. *Studier i Sverres saga*. Avhandlinger utgitt av Det norske Videnskaps-akademi. II. Hist.-filos. kl., 1952, no. 3. Oslo: Dybwad, 1953; Schreiner, Johan. "Omkring Sverres saga." *Historisk tidsskrift* (Norway) 36 (1953), 561–78; Gathorne-Hardy, Geoffrey M. *A Royal Impostor: King Sverre of Norway*. Oslo: Aschehoug; London: Oxford University Press, 1956; Brekke, Egil Nygaard. *Sverre-sagaens opphav. Tiden og forfatteren*. Skrifter utgitt av Det norske Videnskaps-akademi, II. Hist.-filos. kl., 1958, no. 1. Oslo: Aschehoug, 1958; Koht, Halvdan. "Mennene bak Sverre-soga." *Syn og segn* 65 (1959), 337–50; Holm-Olsen, Ludvig. "Sverris saga." *KLNM* 17 (1972), 551–8 [includes bibliography]; Holm-Olsen, Ludvig. "Til diskusjonen om Sverres sagas tilblivelse." In *Opuscula Septentrionalia: Festskrift til Ole Widding*. Ed.

Bent Chr. Jacobsen *et al.* Copenhagen: Reitzel, 1977, pp. 55–67 [published simultaneously in *Opuscula* 2.2. Bibliotheca Arnamagnæana, 25.2. Copenhagen: Reitzel, 1977, pp. 55–67]; Knirk, James E. *Oratory in the Kings' Sagas.* Oslo, Bergen, and Tromsø: Universitetsforlaget, 1981, pp. 99–125; Blöndal, Lárus H. *Um uppruna Sverrissögu.* Reykjavik: Stofnun Árna Magnússonar, 1982; Loescher, Gerhard. "Die religiöse Rhetorik der Sverrissaga." *Skandinavistik* 14 (1984), 1–20.

†*Ludvig Holm-Olsen*

[**See also:** *Eirspennill; Flateyjarbók; Konungasögur;* Sverrir Sigurðarson]

Svínfellinga saga *see* Sturlunga saga

Svipdagsmál ("The Lay of Svipdagr"). Two poems, *Grógaldr* ("Gróa's Spell") and *Fjǫlsvinnsmál* ("The Lay of Fjǫlsviðr"), appearing only in late paper MSS of the *Poetic Edda,* seem to form part of the same narrative and are therefore designated in modern times by one title: *Svipdagsmál.*

In *Grógaldr,* a young man approaches the grave of his mother, Gróa, to seek her protection, because a spell has been laid on him and he must proceed on a long and dangerous journey to win a bride, Menglǫð. In answer to his pleading, his mother rises from the grave and chants nine charms to protect her son. The bulk of the poem is made up of these charms.

In *Fjǫlsvinnsmál,* the young man has arrived before a stronghold, guarded by Fjǫlsviðr, a terrifying giant. The man skillfully elicits information about the castle and its owner. He is told that it belongs to a woman of great beauty, and that only one, the hero Svipdagr, will ever be allowed to rest in Menglǫð's arms. When the young man says he is Svipdagr, the doors fly open; he is welcomed by the maiden and assured of everlasting bliss within her halls. It is possible, although not stated, that through the questions, Fjǫlsviðr was tricked into pronouncing the magic name Svipdagr.

The two main motifs of Svipdagr's tale, the curse laid on him by his stepmother and his releasing a maiden from her sorrow to gain her as a bride, are frequently encountered in fairy tales. But the narrative echoes themes of Norse mythology and bears stylistic resemblances to other eddic poems. A series of charms appears in *Hávamál,* and a dialogue of questions and answers in *Alvíssmál* and *Vafþrúðnismál.* The heroine of *Skírnismál* is guarded, like Menglǫð, by dogs, a watchman, and a wall of flames. The name Fjǫlsviðr ("very wise") recalls the eddic giant's name Alsviðr ("wholly wise").

De Vries (1941–42) consequently believes that *Svipdagsmál* represents a fairy tale embellished with elements of Norse mythology to give it the semblance of a myth. Höfler (1952) detects the ritual scenario of a solar hero's entrance into the chamber of the goddess of spring. Falk (1893) points to parallels with the Celtic stories of Culhwch and Olwen, and of Parsifal. Similar themes occur in the Norse *fornaldarsögur.* Motz (1975) suggests analogies with the ritual of mystery religions in which the novice, sometimes as a bridegroom, is initiated into the sanctuary and the service of a goddess. Talbot (1976) finds a relation with the Irish harvest festival, Lugua Sadh.

Ed.: Sijmons, B., and Hugo Gering, eds. *Die Lieder der Edda.* 3 vols. Halle: Waisenhaus, 1903–31, vol. 1; Neckel, Gustav, ed. *Edda: Die Lieder des Codex Regius nebst verwandten Denkmälern. I: Text.* 5th ed. rev. Hans Kuhn. Heidelberg: Winter, 1983. **Tr.**: Hollander, Lee M.,

trans. *The Poetic Edda, Translated with an Introduction and Explanatory Notes.* 2nd rev. ed. Austin: University of Texas Press, 1962; rpt. 1988, pp. 140–52. **Lit.**: Falk, Hj. "Om Svipdagsmal." *Arkiv för nordisk filologi* 9 (1893), 311–63; Vries, Jan de. *Altnordische Literaturgeschichte.* 2 vols. Grundriss der germanischen Philologie, 15–6. Berlin: de Gruyter, 1941–42; rpt. 1964–67, vol. 2, pp. 214–7; Höfler, Otto. "Das Opfer im Semnonenhain und die Edda." In *Edda, Skalden, Saga: Festschrift für Genzmer.* Ed. H. Schneider. Heidelberg: Winter, 1952, pp. 1–67; Schröder, R. F. "Svipdagsmál." *Germanisch-romanische Monatsschrift* 16 (1966), 113–9; Motz, Lotte. "The King and the Goddess: An Interpretation of the *Svipdagsmál.*" *Arkiv för nordisk filologi* 90 (1975), 133–50; Einar Ól. Sveinsson. "Svipdag's Long Journey: Some Observations on Grógaldr and Fjǫlsvinnsmál." In *Hereditas: Essays and Studies Presented to Professor Séamus Ó Duilearga.* Ed. Bo Almqvist et al. Dublin: Folklore of Ireland Society, 1975 [= *Béaloideas* 39–41 (1971–73), 298–319]; Talbot, A. C. "The Search for the Otherworld Maiden: A Mythic Theme in Early Norse and Celtic Literature." Diss. Lancaster University, 1976.

Lotte Motz

[**See also:** *Alvíssmál;* Eddic Poetry; *Hávamál; Skírnismál; Vafþrúðnismál*]

Sweden. At the end of the Middle Ages, the Swedish realm had an almost square shape. It stretched from the Baltic city of Kalmar in the south to the large Laplandish forests in the north, and from Lödöse at the mouth of the Göta River in the west to the fortress city of Viborg at the Russian border in the east. The Swedish Crown thus reigned over a territory that in north-south direction was about 1,400 km. long and in west-east direction about 1,100 km. wide. In the west and in the south, apart from a corridor at the mouth of the Göta River, Sweden was isolated from the North Sea and the Kattegat by Norwegian and Danish coast provinces; in the east, however, the northern part of the Baltic Sea had become a Swedish inland sea. The square shape of the realm and the prevailing dominance of waterway communications gave the east-west axis the same political and economic importance as the north-south axis. At the end of the Middle Ages, Stockholm was the largest and most important city, situated in the center of the realm, not, as it is has been since the loss of Finland in 1809, at its eastern edge.

The late-medieval Swedish realm comprised about twenty provinces that in most cases formed geographically and economically independent districts. The provinces were separated from each other by large forests or lakes, and their central parts in most cases consisted of plains that, with their fertile clay soils, were fairly well suited to agriculture. The most important agricultural districts were then as now in southern and central Sweden. The northern and eastern (*i.e.,* Finnish) provinces were, on the other hand, dominated by forests. There, only the river valleys along the northern part of the gulf of Bothnia and the shores of the Finnish bay offered good conditions for farming and consequently for denser population.

The natural conditions for settlement and cultivation did not undergo any major changes during the Middle Ages, except the constant progression of the shoreline along the coast of the Baltic Sea. The progression was, and still is, a consequence of the rising of the earth's crust since the end of the latest ice age as well as of long-term changes in the water level of the world's oceans, resulting over centuries in both impairments and improvements for the coastal population. On one hand, it has made old sea routes unusable and placed earlier ports and fishing settlements far away from the coast; on the other hand, it has given the coastal villages new, productive land, which first provided fine pasture and which later, when it had dried, could be used as arable land.

The Swedish realm had developed during the end of the Viking Age and the first centuries of the Middle Ages. Exactly how it took shape and became "unified" is difficult to ascertain with precision, since the source material documenting this development is weak. At the beginning of the Swedish Middle Ages, around 1050, the provinces in middle and southern Sweden had a common king, although he apparently had difficulty in asserting royal power simultaneously in the old Svithiod (*i.e.*, the provinces around Lake Mälaren), and in the territory of the Götar around Lake Vänern and Lake Vättern (*i.e.*, Västergötland with Dalsland and Värmland and Östergötland with Småland). Sweden's first Christian king, Olav Skötkonung, had presumably been banished from the pagan Lake Mälaren region and taken refuge in Västergötland, where during his reign the first permanent Swedish bishopric was established in Skara.

The unity of the three main parts of the realm was not fully established during the early Middle Ages. Västergötland, for example, seems to have been separated from the rest of Sweden at certain periods during the 11th and 12th centuries. When the old royal family died out in the 1120s, a period of struggle for power followed lasting more than a century. The pretenders were usually drawn from two rival families, descendants of King Sverker the Elder and King Erik the Holy, respectively.

The explanation for the political instability of Sweden during the early Middle Ages lies in the varied geographical character of the realm and in the general social structure. The provinces were closed settlements, divided from each other by large forests and open lakes. They were thus not initially linked by common economic interests, and it was difficult to amass the military resources needed to bring the country under a single ruler. Regional chieftains governed the individual territories, and royal power and authority were limited to the right to lead men in combat and, when necessary, to function as the highest judicial authority.

In the 12th century, developments took place that in time would make it possible for the king to procure a stronger hold over the entire realm. The most important factor was probably that Christianity gained a strong foothold, and that, as a consequence, the country was organized into parishes and dioceses. The oldest list of Swedish episcopal towns dates from the year 1120; these can be identified as Skara, Sigtuna, Linköping, (Eskils-)Tuna, and Västerås. The list implies that the basic structure of the medieval ecclesiastical organization in Sweden already existed. The establishment of a separate archdiocese in 1164 in Uppsala, to where the see had been translated from Sigtuna, presumably indicates that the Swedish state by then had a measure of political stability that could be compared with that of other North European states. The ecclesiastical organization must have given the royal power impulses to, and, by providing able officials, resources for, developing a central but in the beginning small civil administration.

The kings of the 12th century often resided in Götland, at the centrally situated island Visingsö in Lake Vättern. The long distances and the loose organization of the realm made it necessary for the king to have a deputy, an earl, to govern that part of the realm where he did not reside. Gradually, the earl came to have certain responsibilities for commanding the *leding*, the naval military organization with roots in the Viking Age that guaranteed the king access to a certain number of warships and control over the waters along the Baltic coast. The royal power gradually became stronger, and its resources were formally organized during the late 12th and 13th centuries. A definite shift came around 1250, when the Crown, after years of internal struggles, was given to the son of Earl Birger, who in reality was a kind of Swedish *maior domus*, married to the former king's sister.

The ecclesiastical organization received its final form around 1250. Regular cathedral chapters were established; the parish subdivision received the form that, on the whole, it would retain throughout the Middle Ages; the ordinances of the Swedish Church were adjusted in all essentials to the continental model; and the Church was granted exemption from taxes for its property and the right to collect tithes from parishioners.

The administration of justice came increasingly under royal influence. At the end of the 11th century, the royal inquisition was introduced, which meant that the king or his deputy would appear every third year at the sessions of the district courts and there administer justice in cases submitted to him. Royal influence over legislation was not long in coming. To what extent the royal power, the Church, and the magnates participated in the process that led to codification of the provincial laws during the 13th century has been debated, but it is obvious that, by the middle of that century, the Crown, represented by Earl Birger, had such influence over the legislation that it could issue special laws valid for the whole realm and not just one province. Peace laws banning the use of violence in another's home, against women, in law courts, and in churches were instituted by an oath taken by the king and his men to punish infractions. Toward the end of the 13th century, the development had progressed so far that it was expressly the king who approved even new law books for the provinces, *e.g.*, the Uppland Law, which was ratified by the king in 1296.

Parallel with consolidation in the area of judicial matters came a change in taxation and administration. At the end of the 13th century, the military *leding* was converted into a fiscal *leding*, that is, a yearly tax in money and in kind imposed on all self-owning farmers instead of the duty to serve on the king's ships. This conversion of the form of the farmers' obligation to the Crown is apparently connected with changes in the art of war in Sweden as in other European countries. There are strong reasons to see the castle building that took place in Sweden in the latter half of the 13th century in connection with the introduction of permanent taxes. The new large castles, such as those in Stockholm, Nyköping, Örebo, Kalmar, Åbo, and Tavastehus (the latter two in Finland), with their bailiffs and permanent garrisons, demanded constant maintenance from the surrounding countryside, including the provisions that farmers earlier brought with them on the *leding* ships and that they now had to pay as taxes in kind. With the allocation of special maintenance districts to the castles, the realm was divided into new, extensive administrative units. The castles were certainly erected in the first place for defense against foreign enemies, but they also gave the king, at least as long as the commanders in them were loyal to him, better possibilities than before to control the different parts of the country and their often stubborn magnates.

The remodeling of the military system and the consequent need for armored horsemen instead of mobilized, sea-borne farmers and district chiefs also seem to have been the main reasons for the creation of a Swedish nobility. This development was formally regulated through a statute issued at a meeting at Alsnö in Lake Mälaren, probably in September 1280. All who served the king on horse were thereby granted exemption from royal taxes and fines, which consequently gave them the right to collect these dues from their own tenants. The new nobility came to comprise the old class of locally rooted chieftains as well as peasants who chose to continue to serve the king as warriors, but now on horseback instead of on the *leding* ship, in exchange for exemption from the new permanent taxes. It was important that all of them, aristocrats as well as the lesser nobility, became the king's men and were personally tied to him in a uniform way throughout the entire realm.

At the same time, during the last decades of the 13th century, a more permanent circle of royal counselors appeared. The royal council consisted of the bishops of the realm and a group of secular magnates, among them the three foremost public officials: the lord chief justice, who came to represent the king as supreme judge; the lord high constable, who, in the place of the king, was in command during war; and the chancellor, most often a bishop, who was in charge of the king's chancery. From the beginning, the council was probably intended to function, when necessary, as a caretaker government, but after a couple of decades it came to be considered a permanent institution, known as the Council of the Realm, charged with the task of acting as permanent counselors of the king. In addition to the council, the king could draw support from specially formed assemblies of magnates, which, even if they usually were composed *ad hoc* of locally accessible magnates, were considered to represent the whole realm.

A distinct terminal point to the development in the 11th and 12th centuries toward a stable, economically strong, and unified kingdom came in 1319 with the "Freedom Letter," sometimes called "Sweden's Magna Carta." It was issued, together with a statute dictating how a king's election should take place in Sweden, when the three-year-old Magnus Eriksson was elected to the throne after protracted internal struggles. The Freedom Letter created guarantees against arbitrary taxation and forbade alienation of the fixed income of the Crown. In addition, the king, according to the election statute, was to take an oath that no one could be imprisoned unless he had been found guilty according to the law, and that the king would not place foreigners on the council or as bailiffs in the royal castles.

Around 1300, the Swedish realm was europeanized to a much higher degree than at the beginning of the Middle Ages. It had a nationwide royal power, whose strength was based on legal claims of continental character, on taxes, and on a military organization with castles and armored horsemen of European type. The Church was fully organized and, as a member of the international Church, was an important intermediary of continental European religious, intellectual, and cultural currents. The leading class of secular magnates had achieved positions and privileges that resembled those of the continental nobility, even if the process of feudalization, in legal terms, never developed as far in Swedish society as it did, for instance, in England, France, and Germany.

Around 1300, Swedish society was europeanized also in another respect. The number of towns had then increased significantly from only one around the year 1100 (Sigtuna) to about twenty-five by 1300. The growth was especially marked at the middle of the 13th century, concentrated in central Sweden (the Mälar valley region), and connected with an increased European demand for iron and copper from the mines in that area. Sweden became closely tied to international commerce, and the resources created through this commerce must have furthered the formation of a strong Swedish kingdom. The founding of Stockholm, the future capital of Sweden, around the year 1250 must certainly be seen in this context.

The 11th and 12th centuries were also the period when Sweden's borders were established. The stabilizing process that the royal power underwent bound together the various parts of the realm. The border with Norway was regulated through several agreements made during the period 1140–1273, while the border with Denmark was determined in detail sometime during the 13th century. At the middle of the same century, Sweden was given rights to a small corridor along the Göta River into the North Sea, Sweden's only breathing space toward the west. Gotland was finally placed under the Swedish Crown around 1280. In the latter part of the 11th and the beginning of the 12th century began a mainly peaceful immigration of Swedish farmers to parts of the coast districts along the northern part of the Gulf of Bothnia and the Finnish Gulf (Österbotten, Åboland's skerries, Nyland). The immigration was followed by regular war expeditions with the joint purpose of capturing and christianizing the territory. The first "crusade" probably occurred around the middle of the 12th century and was repeated during the 13th century. At the beginning of the 14th century, an attempt was made to reach all the way to the River Neva (at the site of present-day St. Petersburg) to control the commerce heading for Novgorod. This effort was unsuccessful, and in 1323 the border between the Swedish realm and Novgorod was regulated through the peace concluded at Nöteborg. The southern part of the border established there remained in effect throughout the Middle Ages. The northern part marked spheres of interest in a no-man's land; the territories along the northeastern shore of the Gulf of Bothnia were in due time incorporated into the Swedish realm.

During the 14th and 15th centuries, Swedish society did not undergo any profound structural changes. The pattern that had developed during the early Middle Ages lasted until the introduction of the Lutheran reformation in Sweden and the reorganization of the central administration during the first decades of Gustav Vasa's rule.

In the area of foreign policy, the 14th and 15th centuries were dominated by repeated attempts to unite the Nordic realms under a single dynasty. At about the same time as he was elected king of Sweden (1319), the underage Magnus Eriksson became king of Norway through inheritance from his maternal grandfather, Håkon Magnússon. During a few decades (1332–1360), he was also lord of that part of Denmark east of the Sound (Scania, Halland, and Blekinge). Even if he never strove to create an integrated Nordic realm, his Swedish-Norwegian personal union had prepared the ground for the Nordic union created a generation later. Already in 1355, Magnus transferred the Norwegian Crown to one of his sons, Håkon, and five years later the Danish provinces were taken back by the Danish King Valdemar Atterdag ("ever-day"). In 1361, King Valdemar also incorporated Gotland into his kingdom. Magnus himself was defeated by his nephew, the German prince Albrecht of Mecklenburg, who had been summoned by the opposition Swedish magnates.

After a short while, Albrecht found himself in the same situation as King Magnus; because of poor finances, even he faced difficulties in upholding his kingdom against the Swedish magnates, who demanded greater influence over the administration of the realm. Finally, in 1388, they once more summoned a foreign monarch, Valdemar Atterdag's daughter, Margrethe, widow of Hákon Magnússon and heir of their recently deceased son, Olaf (d. 1387). Although a woman, she was recognized as regent in all three Nordic countries. In contrast to Magnus, she deliberately strove for an unlimited royal power that could unite the three realms. By playing the leading circles of the realms against each other, and by not giving her assurances legal form, she succeeded in 1397 (in Kalmar in southern Sweden) in getting her niece's son Erik, duke of Pomerania, crowned and acknowledged as king in all her Nordic realms without binding constitutional guarantees.

Even if the Union could not be maintained *de facto* during the entire 15th century, the thought of union was kept alive during more than 100 years by changing groups of magnates in the Nordic realms, who in different ways believed that they could benefit by a continued union. The Union meant certain advantages. It guaranteed peace in Scandinavia and a collective force against non-Nordic countries, especially the German powers at the Baltic Sea. Furthermore, it gave both peasants and landowners an invaluable opportunity to carry on commerce freely among themselves across the borders and with the merchants in the towns of the other realms. From the Swedish perspective, however, there remained the constant, but perhaps exaggerated, fear that the richer and more powerful Denmark would gain a dominant influence in Sweden, and in various ways exploit its resources. Finally, many of the leading Swedish aristocrats feared that they would lose, among other things, the politically important and economically profitable commissions as bailiff administrators of the Crown's castles.

Toward the end of the 15th century, after an unsuccessful attempt by King Christian 1 to subdue the Swedes with force of arms (the battle of Brunkeberg outside Stockholm in 1471), the union increasingly became a political forum without real substance. Sweden was governed by a regent, who gradually became independent in relation to the Council of the Realm, whereas the Union king, although formally acknowledged, lacked influence in Sweden. The violent attempts made by the Union king to recapture power (1497–1501, 1518–1523) finally made the Union a political impossibility.

An essential aspect of the political history of Sweden during the late Middle Ages is the question of the relationship between the Council of the Realm and royal power, whether national or union. The king tried to strengthen his grip on the administration and the finances by reducing the influence of the magnates. At the same time, the leading men of the realm strove to preserve Sweden as a real elective kingdom (which implied that they themselves chose the king within certain limits), to protect the privileges and the immunity from taxation they had obtained from the Crown, to procure guarantees that they should have the right to administer at least some of the royal castles, and to be able to induce the king to consult them in ruling the realm. During periods in which royal power was weak, such as under the latter decades of Magnus Eriksson and under the reign of King Albrecht, the influence of the Council of the Realm increased. Under stronger monarchs, such as Margrethe and King Erik in the first decades of his own reign (after 1412), royal power was strengthened.

With the uprising against King Erik, which started in 1434, the Council of the Realm took on greater importance. As the king, although formally in power, was suspended, the council developed into an independent state government with full responsibilty for the administration of the realm. An expression of this independent position was the decision of the Council of the Realm to let

a special seal of the realm, with a picture of the Swedish king St. Erik and the three crown coats of arms, replace the king's seal under important decisions.

The rebellion also led to important steps toward forming a popular Swedish representation. A formal parliament with chosen representatives for the four estates of the realm (nobility, clergy, burghers, and peasants) was certainly not established before the reign of Gustav Vasa; but it is obvious that representatives, even of the peasants, the mine owners, and the citizenry of the towns, especially around 1430, participated in meetings at which important decisions were taken on whether the union monarch was to remain in power. Earlier, peasants had been granted certain privileges in joint decision making at royal elections and in the question of taxation.

An area in which participation of the peasantry was never questioned was the administration of justice. At the local level, the district court or the thing, the jury consisted of twelve representatives for the farmers; these members of the jury could be freeholders as well as tenants of the nobility, the clerical institutions, or the Crown. According to the law, the district court at the vacancy of the district court judge had to recommend three candidates to the king, from which he should choose one as the new judge. During the reign of Magnus Eriksson, a further step was taken to unify the Swedish society by the introduction of two law books valid for the entire realm. One, the common law, which was compiled around 1350, was valid for the rural court district, that is, for the greater part of the population of the realm (*ca.* 90 percent) that lived in the countryside. The other one, the town law, which came a couple of years later, was applied to the towns of the realm and apparently based on conditions in Stockholm. A century later, a modernized version of the common law was ratified (King Christoffer's Law, 1442), but during the Middle Ages, the new version was never in general use. The common law was supplemented throughout the Middle Ages by ordinances promulgated by the reigning king and regulating particular issues.

In the ecclesiastical area, no great changes took place during the last two centuries of the Middle Ages. The subdivision into dioceses and parishes generally remained stable from the end of the 13th century, although very small parishes, particularly in southwestern Sweden, were sometimes amalgamated with a neighboring parish, and the largest parishes in Norrland and Finland were divided into two or more parishes. The monastic orders in Sweden were the same as in the rest of Europe. In the countryside, there were monasteries of the contemplative kind, in most cases belonging to the Cistercian order and founded during the 12th century. In towns, however, the mendicant orders could be found, both Dominicans and Franciscans, in most cases established during the second half of the 13th century. At the end of the 14th century, religious life in Sweden was renewed through the creation of the specifially Swedish Order of Our Savior, founded by Birgitta Birgersdotter (St. Birgitta), daughter of a Swedish magnate. The preaching of Birgitta and the founding of the monastery became very important, both spiritually and culturally. The mother monastery in Vadstena became a national concern, although during certain periods it became closely associated with the union kings and especially their consorts.

Through the bishops who were *ex officio* members of the Council of the Realm, the Church came to play a central role in the political history of the 14th and 15th centuries. As a rule, they made common cause with the leading magnates in their struggle to reduce the power of the king, since it was essential to protect the privileges of the Church (e.g., its exemption from taxes) and to defend its right to the free election of bishops. The last issue became especially important for political developments during the reign of Erik of Pomerania, since his repeated attempts to fill the Swedish sees with men, often Danes, loyal to the king led to the Church's siding with the insurgents in 1434. The struggle over the archiepiscopal see in Uppsala in 1432 and in subsequent years was an important factor in this development.

For the same reason, the Church took a cautious position when, at the end of the 15th century and the beginning of the 16th, Sten Sture and his successors as governors of the realm acquired increasingly independent power and, among other things, secured pontifical permission in 1491 to fill certain bishoprics. This situation led to the archbishops coming to play an active role against the governors when the union kings tried to take back power at the end of the Middle Ages.

A powerful contributing factor in Magnus Eriksson's and Albrecht of Mecklenburg's failure to assert their power against the magnates was endemically poor finances. The revenue of the monarchs from this vast but sparsely populated country was insufficient to support a military apparatus, where strong castles and hired horsemen were the most important ingredients. The result was that the king had to transfer a considerable number of the royal castles and their maintenance districts to individual magnates, often as pawns for loans received. This situation led in time to a weakening of the king's power.

The financial situation of the Crown declined even more as a result of the Black Death and the effects of the agrarian crisis on the economy of the realm. Even if, because of the inadequacy of the Swedish source material, we cannot follow the development very closely, it is obvious that settlement and agrarian production during the latter half of the 14th century and the beginning of the 15th decreased to such an extent that it must have had a powerful negative effect on the tax income of the Crown. Certainly, the decrease in agricultural production must have had an effect even on the secular and ecclesiastical magnates who were dependent on the income from their estates and tenants. But these magnates probably had better possibilities for compensation than the Crown, which was compelled to resort to unpopular and politically risky tax increases. An important reason for the rebellion against Erik of Pomerania in the 1430s was evidently a widespread dissatisfaction with the harsh tax increases that Margrethe and Erik put into effect a few decades earlier.

There are many indications that, after 1450, both demographic and economic development improved. The population seems to have begun slowly rising, which can be seen through the increased emigration to Norrland and the inner parts of Finland. Foreign commerce flourished, based foremost on metal products from central Sweden but also on fish and other animal products from the provinces around the Gulf of Bothnia. The modernizing of the churches, especially in central Sweden, Norrland, and Finland between 1450 and 1520, indicates that even the countryside received its share of the positive economic development.

The terminal point for the Middle Ages in Sweden is traditionally placed at 1521, with the rebellion against King Christian II, or at 1523, when the leader of the rebellion, Gustav Vasa, was elected king, or, less commonly, at 1527, when the reformation of the Swedish Church was initiated. The cited years all indicate political or ecclesiastical administrative changes, but they are not as natural if the social structure of Sweden is considered. In many respects, the new regent, Gustav Vasa (1523–1560), came to fol-

low medieval lines of development. But through his conscious organizing of resources and conditions, he laid the foundation of a modern society, structured in a new way under forceful royal leadership.

Bib.: *Svensk historisk bibliografi* [complete bibliography of publications on medieval history through 1975]. **Lit.**: Rosén, Jerker. *Svensk historia. 1: Tiden före 1718*. Stockholm: Bonnier, 1962 [still the most scholarly work; contains detailed bibliographical surveys; each section published also in a richly illustrated and expanded version: *Den svenska historien. 1: Forntid, vikingatid och tidig medeltid till 1319; 2: Medeltid 1319–1520*. Stockholm: Bonnier, 1966]; Andersson, Ingvar. *A History of Sweden*. Trans. Carolyn Hannay. Westport: Greenwood, 1975; Lindkvist, Thomas. "Swedish Medieval Society: Previous Research and Recent Developments." *Scandinavian Journal of History* 4 (1979), 253–68; Gissel, Svend, *et al. Desertion and Land Colonization in the Nordic Countries c. 1300–1600: A Comparative Report from the Scandinavian Research Project on Deserted Farms and Villages*. Stockholm: Almqvist & Wiksell, 1981; Sawyer, Peter. *Kings and Vikings: Scandinavia and Europe, A.D. 700–1100*. London and New York: Methuen, 1982; Lindkvist, Thomas, and Kurt Ågren. *Sveriges medeltid*. Stockholm: Bonnier, 1985; Dahlbäck, Göran. "Schweden und Finnland 1350–1650." In *Handbuch der europäischen Wirtschafts- und Sozialgeschichte* 3. Ed. Hermann Kellenbenz. Stuttgart: Klett-Cotta, 1986, pp. 389–437; Schück, Herman, *et al. The Riksdag: A History of the Swedish Parliament*. Ed. Michael F. Metcalf. New York: St. Martin, 1987; Dahlbäck, Göran, ed. *Svensk medeltidsforskning idag. En forskningsöversikt utarbetad på uppdrag av Humanistisk-samhällsvetenskapliga forskningsrådet*. Stockholm: Humanistisk-samhällsvetenskapliga forskningsrådet, 1987 [surveys research of the last fifteen years on all aspects of the Middle Ages; contains detailed bibliographical references]; Sjöholm, Elsa. "Sweden's Medieval Laws: European Legal Tradition—Political Change." *Scandinavian Journal of History* 15 (1990), 65–87.

Göran Dahlbäck

[**See also**: Agriculture; Birgitta, St.; Church Organization and Function; Council of the Realm; Demography; Gotland; Laws; *Leiðangr*; Monasticism; Royal Administration and Finances; Social Structure; Towns; Trade; *Þing*]

Swedish Literature, Miscellaneous.

Västgötakrönikorna are three short chronicles concerning the lives and achievements of the Swedish kings and the lawmen and bishops of Västergötland during the period from about 1000 to about 1250. They were composed about 1250. Besides *Guta saga*, these humble records are the only specimens of original Swedish historical prose, so they are also interesting from a linguistic point of view. Their historical value varies. Holm (1972, 1975) maintained that the kings' chronicle shows signs of having existed in a runic version. The lawmen's chronicle especially is rich in alliterations (e.g., *ær hans e giætit at goðþo*, "he had always been well spoken of"; *eno sinne ok aldrigh mer*, "once and never more"; *sent födes annar sliker maðær*, "not soon will be born a man like him"). The chronicles were written down around 1325 by the priest Laurentius Dyakn in an appendix to the *Äldre Västgötalagen* in Cod. Holm B 59.

Prose fiction. Namnlös och Valentin ("Nameless and Valentine") is a tale of chivalry, in which noble and courageous knights and fair virgins act against a background of evil and treachery. The principal persons belong to the royal families of France and Hungary. Familiar motifs include the hatred of the newborn Valentine's step-grandmother, who tries to kill him, but fails because a servant girl puts him in a box that she places in a river, where the boy is found and saved by his cousin Clarina. The end is happy: loving couples marry, and Valentine, Nameless, and their friend Blandamār ascend the thrones of France, Hungary, and Spain, respectively.

Apart from the stereotypes of the genre, the style has some freshness. Sometimes, it comes near to the spoken language, with doubled parts of sentences, as in *Falantin han redh effter diwrit* ("Falentine, he rode after the animal").

The immediate model for this romance is a Low German *knittel* poem; the ultimate original was an Old French poem, now lost. The romance was probably written about the middle of the 15th century. It is preserved in three MSS, Cod. Holm D 4a (from 1457 at the latest; complete), Cod. Holm D 3 (from 1476; incomplete; perhaps a copy of D 4a), and Cod. Holm K 45 (from the beginning of the 16th century; incomplete; perhaps a copy of D 3).

Satiren om abbotarna ("The Satire upon Abbots"; Old Swedish title: *Hær sigx aff abotum allum skæmptan myklæ*, literally: "Here is told about all abbots great fun"), is a funny but cruel satire on the gluttony of abbots. Allusions to the Bible are skillfully used, *e.g.*: "Then two big pots are carried in to Mr. Abbot. Mr. Abbot takes one of them in his left hand and the other in his right. He takes them both and drinks a little to find out how he likes them. Then Mr. Abbot says to the pot in his left hand, because there is bad ale in it: 'Depart from me, you cursed. . . .'" (*cf.* Matthew 25:32, 33, 41). The piece belongs to the literature of the goliards (medieval wandering students), but no real foreign model has been found, and the *Satiren om abbotarna* far surpasses its closest analogues. The satire was probably written in the first half of the 15th century, and is preserved in two MSS, Cod. Holm D 4a ("Verelianus") from 1457 and Cod. Holm D 3 ("Lady Elin's book") from 1476.

Secular narrative poetry. Beside the great *knittel* poems *Eufemiavisorna*, the *Erikskrönikan*, and other *rimkrönikor*, there survive a limited number of minor poems. To the romance genre belongs *Riddar Paris och Jungfru Vienna* ("Knight Paris and Virgin Vienna"), a very free translation-adaptation of a prose romance known in many European countries and probably written in Provence. The poem is romantic indeed; the knights are brave and gallant, the ladies beautiful and virtuous. The meter is unusual for the time: stanzas with four lines rhyming *abab*, masculine and female rhymes alternating. Unfortunately, only a fragment of the poem survives. It was probably written in the beginning of the 16th century. The MS, in Cod. Holm D 2 ("Spegelbergs bok"), was written down in 1523.

A historical event provides the theme for the *knittel* poem *Om ett gyllene år* ("About a Golden Year"), that is, the disastrous defeat that the farmers of Dithmarschen at the North Sea coast north of the River Elbe administered to the Danish (and Scandinavian Union) King Hans and his army of knights, mercenaries, and levy in the year 1500. The Swedish poem (completed in 1503) is a very free translation, made by a certain Sven Månsson, of a Low German original, *Van dem gnadenriken Gulden Jahr* ("the golden year" was an ecclesiastical jubilee year, *sanctus annus* or *annus iubilaeus*). The reason why Sven Månsson wrote his poem is obvious; he rejoices in the defeat of the Danes, the unbeloved partner of the Scandinavian Union (see *Political Verse* below). The poem is pre-

served in Cod. Holm D 8 (or "Aurivillianus") from the beginning of the 17th century.

Political verse. Sweden, Norway, and Denmark were joined in the Kalmar Union during the period 1397–1523, with many interruptions and civil wars. Denmark usually played the leading part. In Sweden, people often grumbled at the burden of taxes. It was maintained that money was brought out of the country to Denmark and that foreign bailiffs and lords of castles were tyrannical. Some poems from that time are manifestations of the discontent and of patriotic and nationalistic feelings, propaganda pamphlets from the offices of insurgents, and so on. The *Gotlandsvisan* describes how the island of Gotland was conquered in the year 1449 by the Danes, according to the author, by means of guile: *danska manna ordh / är werre än mord* ("Danish men's words / are worse than murder"). In 1456, the Swedish general Thord Bonde was murdered by a Dane, an event that was commemorated in a ballad now called *Thord Bondes mord*. In the *Brunkebergsvisan* about the battle against the Danes at Brunkeberg outside Stockholm in 1471, the author celebrates Swedish bravery and triumphantly announces the Danes' embarking on their ships. Both the *Gotlandsvisan* and the *Brunkebergsvisan* are composed in a fashionable meter of that time, the German *Minnesang* meter. Aesthetically unrivaled among the political poems is *Frihetsvisan* ("The Lay of Liberty"), written in 1439 against the union king Erik of Pomerania and in favor of the Lord High Constable Karl Knutsson Bonde. The author, Bishop Thomas of Strängnäs, chose the ecclesiastical sequence meter for his poem. He is all aflame for freedom and national steadfastness, and is able to formulate his pathos in a way that makes it still deeply affecting. The poem has been set to music, and some of the stanzas are still often sung in a slightly modernized form at national festivals. One of them runs as follows in the original version:

> Friiheeth är thet betzta thing,
> ther sökias kan all wärldin um kring
> then friheet kan wel bära.
> Wilt thw wara tik sielffuer hull,
> tw älska friiheet meer än gull
> thy friiheet fölgher ära.

> [Freedom is the best thing / that may be found anywhere / for him who can her bear. / Will you be good to yourself, / then love freedom more than gold, / for honor follows freedom.]

The political poems are found in the following MSS: the *Gotlandsvisan*, *Thord Bondes mord*, and the *Brunkebergsvisan* in "Een vijse book" (17th century), Royal Library, Stockholm; the *Frihetsvisan* in Cod. Holm B 42, *ca.* 1510, containing King Christoffer's *landslag*.

Practical (professional and technical) literature. On behalf of the monastery at Vadstena, the monk Peder Månsson resided in Rome during the years 1508–1524 as a director of St. Birgitta's house, the property of his convent. In Italy, he studied and translated into Swedish a great many books in Latin and Italian concerning various practical subjects. In some of his works, he also draws from his own experience. Especially interesting is his *Bondakonst* ("Manual on Agriculture"), for the main part modeled on *De re rustica* by Lucius J. M. Columella (written about A.D. 64 and printed in 1472), partly also on works by Petrus de Crescentiis (*Ruralia commoda*, printed several times in 1471 and later), on the "Dancus Rex" (MS), and on the "Agogo Mago" (printed 1502). The translations of Peder Månsson treat the originals freely, and his language and style are remarkably idiomatic. A great many Old Swedish words are found only in his works. He wrote charming versified prologues to the *Bondakonst* and to books about the arts of warfare (*Stridz konsth*), gem carving (*Konst grafwa stena*), mining (*Bergzbrukningh*), and educating children (now called *Barnabok*; built on Erasmus's *Institutio principis christiani*). In the *Bondakonst* prologue, he recommends bringing Finns to deserted regions of Sweden, since they are hardworking and fertile. Peder Månsson calls them "the people who say *tärffwa höffwe mees*," modern Finnish *tervä, hyvä mies*, roughly, "good morning, old chap," one of the earliest phrases ever recorded in Finnish.

Exceptionally in Old Swedish literature, nearly all of Månsson's texts are preserved in the author's autographs; they are kept in the Royal Library, Stockholm ("Liber B"), in the Diocese Library, Linköping ("Liber C"), and in the University Library, Uppsala (two nonautographs).

Läke- och Örteböcker are books about medical treatment and medicinal herbs. Advice concerning the art of healing has been written down in Europe since classical times, and exists in a great many MSS in Latin by such authors as Hippocrates, Galen, Pliny, and Albertus Magnus. Texts and extracts from them were adapted and translated into many vernacular languages, including Old Swedish, partly supplemented by the works of the Dane Henrik Harpestreng. The Old Swedish *Läkeböcker* are especially interesting because they contain words not found elsewhere. A few prescriptions seem practicable. The majority, though, are useless or even dangerous: *e.g., Tyäders hiertha hength om hals a kona som osath er wiid syn man, tha forliikas the* ("If a capercailzie [*i.e.,* grouse] heart is hung round the neck of a woman who has quarreled with her husband, then they become reconciled"). The *Läkeböcker* are scattered in a great many MSS, mostly from the 15th and 16th centuries (see Klemming 1883–86: 496–501 for MSS and locations).

Nonofficial letters. During the final decades of the Old Swedish period, a number of private persons wrote letters, which add much to our knowledge of the language of late-medieval Sweden. The letters of the prelate, diplomat, and soldier Hemming Gadh (d. 1520) are highly individual. Many of Gadh's letters were sent to his chief, Svante Sture, when Gadh was commanding the troops at Kalmar against the Danes. He conquered the town after three months in October 1506, but the Danes managed to hold the castle until the peace was signed in 1509. His epistles are characterized by oaths, colloquial and frivolous words, and elaborate metaphors and idioms, such as *Sidhan gingho the pa geta mathin*, literally "then went they on the goats' food," *i.e.,* "then they began to tackle the unpleasant task." Nearly all of Gadh's letters are housed in the "Sturearkivet" in the Swedish State Archives, Stockholm.

From Rome, the monk Peder Månsson (see above) sent letters home to his convent at Vadstena, reporting on his work and telling about life and events in Italy and elsewhere. He reveals himself as a sensible and honest man with a mastery of the Swedish language, which he used instead of Latin so as not to be understood by other readers. He was a patriot with a weakness for his countrymen and a suspicion of foreigners. He exhibits a rich store of proverbs and idioms, which he uses skillfully: *e.g.,* It is foolish to quarrel with cardinals, *thy onth är gapa moth ognxmwnnenom* ("for it is difficult to gape against the oven-mouth"). In a letter from the year 1518, he mentions that a doctor and monk in Wittenberg in Germany had written "conclusiones" against indulgence and sent them to the pope, who had them burned. Peder

Månsson comments: *Penitencia thet är tryggasthe wäghen thär wil jak döö wppa* ("Penance is the most infallible way [to salvation]; that I will believe unto my death"). The letters of Peder Månsson are housed in the Swedish State Archives, Stockholm, and in the University Library, Uppsala.

Tänkeböcker, minute books of magistrates' courts, are preserved in the cities of Arboga, Jönköping, Kalmar, and Stockholm. Most register real-estate purchases, and also give accounts of inquiries, examinations, and sentences in criminal cases (larcenies, assaults, *etc.*) and in civil actions. The stock of oaths and abusive words seems to have been very large in the late Middle Ages. Our knowledge of the store of personal names in medieval Swedish cities is to a great extent based on the information given by the *Tänkeböcker*. The *Tänkebock of Kalmar* begins in the 14th century with a few annotations in Low German; the others begin in the 15th century: Arboga in 1451, Jönköping in 1456, and Stockholm in 1474. They are kept in the University Library in Uppsala (MS E 211), the Magistrate Court's Archives in Arboga and Stockholm, respectively, and in the Landsarkiv (the Provincial Archives) in Vadstena.

Ed.: (a) The Västgötakrönikorna: Collin, H. S., and C. J. Schlyter, eds. *Incerti Auctoris Variae Adnotationes. . . .* 14, 15, 16. In *Codex Iuris Vestrogotici . . . Westgöta-Lagen.* Corpus Iuris Sueo-gotorum Antiqui. Vol. 1. Stockholm: Hæggström, 1827, pp. 295–307; new edition: Holm, Gösta, ed. *Westgöta-Lagen.* Lund: Ekstrand, 1976 [facsimile]; Beckman, Natanael. *Ur vår äldsta bok.* Stockholm: Norstedt, 1912, pp. 10–21, 29–45, 47–67; Lindquist, Ivar, ed. *Västgötalagens litterära bilagor.* Publications of the New Society of Letters in Lund, 26. Lund: Gleerup, 1941, pp. 14–8, 30–1, 40–8; Noreen, Erik, ed. "Svensk konungalängd" [The Kings' Chronicle]. In *Fornsvensk läsebok.* Lund: Gleerup, 1954, pp. 13–6. **(b) Prose fiction:** Wolf, Werner, ed. *Namnlös och Valentin. Kritische Ausgabe mit nebenstehender mittelniederdeutscher Vorlage.* Samlingar utgivna av Svenska fornskrift-sällskapet, 52. Uppsala: Almqvist & Wiksell, 1934; Klemming, G. E., ed. "Herr Abboten. Satir." In *Prosadikter från Sveriges medeltid.* Stockholm: Norstedt, 1954, pp. 103–5. **(c) Secular narrative poetry:** Klemming, G. E., ed. "Riddar Paris och Jungfri Vienna." In *Svenska medeltidsdikter och rim.* Skrifter utgifna af Svenska fornskrift-sällskapet, 25. Stockholm: Norstedt, 1881–82, pp. 443–50; Blomqvist, Gunnar, ed. *Den fornsvenska dikten om ett gyllene år.* Samlingar utgivna av Svenska fornskrift-sällskapet, 243. Uppsala: Almqvist & Wiksell, 1970 [the Old Swedish text is printed pp. 70–87, the Low German original pp. 50–8; the rest of the book contains the editor's presentation of the poems and their historical background and commentaries to certain passages and words, *etc.*]; Noreen, Erik, ed. "Början av dikten om Paris och Vienna." In *Fornsvensk läsebok*, pp. 141–4. **(d) Political verse:** Klemming, G. E., ed. "Striden om Visby 1449" [= the *Gotlandsvisan*]. In *Svenska medeltidsdikter och rim*, pp. 403–11; Klemming, G. E., ed. "Thord Bondes mord. 1456." In *Svenska medeltids dikter och rim*, pp. 412–3; Klemming, G. E., ed. "Slaget vid Brunkeberg 1471" [= *Brunkebergsvisan*]. In *Svenska medeltids dikter och rim*, pp. 414–8; Klemming, G. E., ed. "Engelbrekt och Karl Knutsson" and "Friheten" [both together = *Frihetsvisan*]. In *Svenska medeltids dikter och rim*, pp. 385–92; Noreen, Erik, ed. "'Om friheten' av biskop Thomas." In *Fornsvensk läsebok*, pp. 131–3. **(e) Practical literature:** Klemming, G. E., ed. *Läke- och örteböcker från Sveriges medeltid.* Samlingar utgifna av Svenska fornskrift-sällskapet, 26. Stockholm: Norstedt, 1883–86; Geete, Robert, ed. *Peder Månssons skrifter på svenska.* Samlingar utgifna av Svenska fornskrift-sällskapet, 43. Stockholm: Norstedt, 1913–15; Noreen, Erik. ed. "Ur Peder Månssons Bondakonst." In *Fornsvensk läsebok*, pp. 136–40. **(f) Nonofficial letters: Hemming**

Gadh: The majority is edited in: Styffe, Carl Gustaf. *Bidrag till Skandinaviens historia ur utländska arkiver samlade och utgifna* (4 and) 5. Stockholm: Norstedt, (1875) 1884 [see under "Lit." Gustafson, pp. 12–22]; **Peder Månsson**: Geete, Robert, ed. *Vadstenabrodern Peder Månssons bref på svenska från Rom till Vadstena kloster 1508–1519*. In *Småstycken på forn svenska* 2. Samlingar utgifna af Svenska fornskrift-sällskapet [unnumbered volume]. Stockholm: Norstedt, 1900–16, pp. 298–348. **(g) Tänkeböcker**: Noreen, Erik, and Torsten Wennström, eds. *Arboga stads tänkebok*. 4 vols. (with an index by Sven Ljung). Samlingar utgivna av Svenska fornskrift-sällskapet, 43.1–4. Uppsala: Almqvist & Wiksell, 1934–1950; Kjellberg, Carl M., ed. *Jönköpings stads tänkebok 1456–1548*. Meddelanden från Norra Smålands fornminnesförening. Jönköping: [s.n.], 1907–15; Modéer, Ivar, and Sten Engström, eds. *Kalmar stads tänkebok*. Samlingar utgivna av Svenska fornskrift-sällskapet, 57. Uppsala: Almqvist & Wiksell, 1945–49; *Stockholms stadsböcker från äldre tid. Andra serien. Tänkeböcker*. 5 vols. [1474–1520. Edited by Emil Hildebrand, Gottfrid Carlsson, and Johan Axel Almquist, respectively.] Stockholm: Häggström, 1917–23; Noreen, Erik, ed. "Ur Stockholms stads tänkebok 1448." In *Fornsvensk läsebok*, pp. 119–24. **Lit.**: **(a) The Västgötakrönikorna**: Holm, Gösta. *Ordhistoriska notiser*. Vol. 3. *Bore ni kiltu*. Meijerbergs arkiv för svensk ordforskning, 13. Gothenburg: Wettergren & Kerber, 1972, pp. 56–7; Holm, Gösta. "Litteratur i runskrift och ett västgötskt ortnamn." In *Nordiske studier. Festskrift til Chr. Westergård-Nielsen på 65-årsdagen den 24. november 1975*. Ed. Johs. Brøndum-Nielsen *et al*. Copenhagen: Rosenkilde & Bagger, 1975, pp. 103–21. [See also the works by Beckman and Lindquist under "Ed."]. **(b) Practical literature**: Tilander, Gunnar. *Dancus och Agogo Mago på svenska: Två obeaktade källor till Peder Månssons Bondakonst*. Acta Philologica Scandinavica, 14. Copenhagen: Munksgaard, 1939–40, pp. 83–101; Granlund, John. *Peder Månssons Bondakonst: jämte parallelltexter*. Samlingar utgivna av Svenska fornskrift-sällskapet, 254. Uppsala: [s.n.], 1983. **(c) Nonofficial letters**: Gustafson, Seth. *Hemming Gadhs språk I, II*. Lundastudier i nordisk språkvetenskap, 6. Lund: Gleerup, 1950.

Gösta Holm

[**See also:** Ballads; Chronicles; *Guta saga*; Harpestreng, Henrik; *Knittel(vers)*; Laws; Vadstena]

Sæmundr Sigfússon inn fróði ("the learned"; 1056–1133).

To his contemporaries, Sæmundr was known as a preeminent churchman and a man of great learning. To modern scholarship, he is known primarily as a founding father of historical writing in Iceland, and of the great dynasty of the Oddaverjar ("men of Oddi"). At various points in the intervening centuries, folklore accused him of sorcery, while scholarly speculation credited him with the *Eddas* and with sagas ranging from *Njáls saga* to *Jómsvíkinga saga*.

"Sæmundr (prestr) inn fróði" is mentioned several times in the *biskupa sögur* (especially *Hungrvaka*, *Kristni saga*, and the sagas of Jón Ǫgmundarson), *Íslendingabók*, annals, genealogies, and in other historical writings. But there is no coherent medieval account of his life, and virtually nothing by him survives in writing, so that much remains unknown.

Sæmundr, the son of a priest, was born into a distinguished family that had lived at Oddi, South Iceland, since about 900. He studied for some years in "Frakkland." The *Oddaverja annáll* for 1077 specifies Paris, but this may be no more than a surmise, as is the suggestion by modern scholars that Sæmundr attended the cathedral school of Notre Dame in Paris. An entertaining account of his return to Iceland in Gunnlaugr Leifsson's *Jóns saga helga*

(early 13th century) tells how Jón and Sæmundr outwitted the master astrologer who held Sæmundr in his power. This legend seems to contain the germ of later folktales in which Sæmundr, learned in the black art, uses his cleverness to foil the Devil.

After his return to Iceland in or after 1076, Sæmundr was ordained priest and became a "pillar of the church," building a new church at Oddi dedicated to St. Nicholas, increasing its endowments and clergy, and preaching and dispensing wise counsel in the neighborhood. He probably also had a school there, for he is said in *Sturlu saga* (ch. 1) to have fostered Oddi Þorgilsson, who, like Sæmundr himself, became *fróðr*, "learned (especially in native lore)." Of still greater national importance was Sæmundr's part, with the bishops, in establishing tithe laws (1096) and other ecclesiastical laws.

Little else is known of Sæmundr's life or activities as priest and secular chieftain, because the records are slight and the times relatively uneventful. However, it is known that he and his two brothers married the three daughters of Kolbeinn Flosason. With his wife, Guðrún, he had three sons and a daughter, and their descendants, who came to be known as the Oddaverjar, in many senses built on the foundations laid by Sæmundr at Oddi. Their power and wealth, augmented especially by the tithes and other revenues paid to family-owned churches, overtook those of other chieftainly families during the time of Sæmundr's distinguished grandson Jón Loptsson (1124–1197), and were maintained throughout the following decades without the viciousness found elsewhere. The intellectual tradition of Oddi also flourished. Sæmundr's son, the priest Eyjólfr, had a school there attended by the future St. Þorlákr; Jón Loptsson fostered and educated Snorri Sturluson there. Jón's son, the bishop Páll, compiled a miracle book of St. Þorlákr, and is himself the subject of one of the *biskupa sögur*. The poem *Nóregs konunga tal* was composed around 1190 to celebrate Jón Loptsson's descent through his mother from the Norwegian kings; other works, notably *Orkneyinga saga* and *Skjǫldunga saga*, may have links with Oddi.

Sæmundr is frequently named as an authority by medieval Icelandic historians, and these references provide the main clues about his learning and its transmission. That he composed a work, now lost, on the rulers of Norway from Haraldr hárfagri ("fairhair") in the late 9th century down to Magnús góði ("the good," d. 1046/7) is suggested by *Nóregs konunga tal* (st. 40), which acknowledges Sæmundr inn fróði as its model for the lives (*ævi*) of these eleven rulers. The scraps of information attributed to Sæmundr elsewhere, however, especially concern the late 10th century: the length of Hákon jarl's reign (in Oddr Snorrason's *Óláfs saga Tryggvasonar*); the number of ships in the Jómsviking fleet at Hjǫrungavágr (Liavåg) (in AM 510 4to, a late MS of *Jómsvíkinga saga*); details of Óláfr Tryggvason's christianization of Norway (in a fifty-word quotation from Sæmundr in Oddr Snorrason's saga); and the date of his death (in Ari Þorgilsson's *Íslendingabók*). Sæmundr is also named in certain versions of the Icelandic annals as authority for the ice-bound Scandinavian winter of 1047. It seems from all this evidence, and from the example of the near-contemporary *Íslendingabók*, that Sæmundr's legacy to later historiography must have been a chronological scheme, with brief narratives on each ruler, in a sober style but with Christian bias.

Sæmundr's presumed history was probably written rather than oral, especially since the long quotation from Sæmundr in Oddr Snorrason's saga (which survives only in Icelandic versions of a Latin original) is followed by "Svá hefir Sæmundr ritað um Óláf konung í sinni bók" ("Thus has Sæmundr written about King Óláfr in his book"). Storm (1873: 15) and Meissner (1902: 35ff.) nevertheless disputed that there was a written work by Sæmundr. The language seems to have been Latin, for Snorri Sturluson, in his prologue to *Óláfs saga helga* and *Heimskringla*, refers to Ari Þorgilsson as the first writer of history in Norse, although Sæmundr, an older contemporary whom Ari consulted over the writing of *Íslendingabók*, probably completed his history first. The nature of Sæmundr's writing and its influence on other histories of Norway, such as *Fagrskinna, Ágrip, Historia Norwegiae*, and even on *Knýtlinga saga*, have been much discussed by scholars such as Bjarni Aðalbjarnarson, Siegfried Beyschlag, Svend Ellehøj, and Bjarni Guðnason (see the summary in Andersson 1985).

Sæmundr is also acknowledged as an authority for certain facts about Iceland, including its discovery by the Viking Naddoddr (*Landnámabók, Sturlubók* text), but whether such matters were included in the history of Norwegian kings, whether there was a separate work on Iceland, and whether some of Sæmundr's more fragmentary pieces of learning were at first only transmitted orally cannot now be established. The "oral" theory is supported by the report in *Kristni saga*, that "in that year [1118–1119], there was such great loss of life, that the priest Sæmundr the learned said [*sagði*] at the *þing* that no fewer must have died of sickness than had come to the *þing*." It is also possible that Sæmundr simply became a model of learning, to whom miscellaneous facts could be attached. This tendency could apply to such patently clerical facts as the details about the creation of the sun and the moon (in AM 624 4to) or the body of Adam (in AM 764 4to).

The title *Sæmundar Edda* appeared on editions of the *Codex Regius* poems of the *Poetic Edda* until well into this century, and this attribution goes back to 16th- and 17th-century theories that credited Sæmundr first with the *Prose Edda* (now attributed to Snorri) and then with the *Codex Regius* poems. The connection may not be completely unfounded, for it is possible, as Halldór Hermannsson (1932) argued, that Snorri found the poetic materials for his *Edda* at Oddi, and that Sæmundr had a hand in collecting them.

Lit.: Storm, Gustav. *Snorre Sturlassöns Historieskrivning.* Copenhagen: Luno, 1873; Meissner, Rudolf. *Die Strengleikar: Ein Beitrag zur Geschichte der altnordischen Prosalitteratur.* Halle: Niemeyer, 1902; Halldór Hermannsson. *Sæmund Sigfússon and the Oddaverjar.* Islandica, 22. Ithaca: Cornell University Library, 1932; Buckhurst, Helen T. McM. "Sæmundr inn fróði in Icelandic Folklore." *Saga-Book of the Viking Society* 11 (1928–36), 84–92; Einar Ól. Sveinsson. *Sagnaritun Oddaverja. Nokkrar athuganir.* Studia Islandica, 1. Reykjavik: Ísafold, 1937 [English summary, pp. 47–51]; Turville-Petre, G. *Origins of Icelandic Literature.* Oxford: Oxford University Press, 1953; rpt. 1975 [esp. pp. 81–7]; Andersson, Theodore M. "Kings' Sagas (Konungasögur)." In *Old Norse–Icelandic Literature: A Critical Guide.* Ed. Carol J. Clover and John Lindow. Islandica, 45. Ithaca and London: Cornell University Press, 1985 [esp. pp. 197–211].

Diana Edwards Whaley

[**See also:** *Ágrip af Nóregs konunga sǫgum*; Annals; *Biskupa sögur*; *Codex Regius*; Conversion; *Fagrskinna*; *Historia Norwegiae*; *Íslendingabók*; *Jóns saga ens helga*; *Knýtlinga saga*; *Landnámabók*; *Snorra Edda*]

Sǫrla saga sterka ("The Saga of Sǫrli the Strong") relates the adventures of Sǫrli, the younger son of the Norwegian king Erlingr in Scandinavia and Africa. Central to his exploits are his killing of King Hálfdan Hringsson and the capture of his magnificent dragon-ship "Skrauti," provoking Hálfdan's sons Sigmundr and Hǫgni and his retainer Þórir to seek revenge against the saga's hero. Five main sections comprise most of the action: Sǫrli's adventures in Bláland, the battle in which Sǫrli captures Skrauti, the ensuing maneuvers of his opponents, Sǫrli's siege of their Swedish stronghold, and a final battle reconciling the warring parties. Like many *fornaldarsögur*, this saga ends with a wedding.

Sǫrli, whom King Erlingr prefers over his eldest son, Sigvaldi, decides to go abroad, taking his foster-father, Karmon, with him. Arriving by ship in Bláland, Sǫrli's shore party is destroyed, but he survives to do battle with a giant named Skrímnir, slaying him and taking his treasure after making peace with Skrímnir's giantess-wife, Mána. Back in Norway, Sǫrli is called to help King Haraldr Valdimarsson against Garðarr and his brother Tófi, from Morland; Garðarr wishes to marry Haraldr's daughter Steinvǫr, but Haraldr has refused. A pitched battle ensues in which Tófi turns into a dragon. Sǫrli slays the dragon and beheads Garðarr, ending the conflict. Sǫrli declines Haraldr's offer of Steinvǫr in marriage and goes off shortly thereafter to harry in Africa.

Returning north, Sǫrli puts in at Eyrarsund (modern Danish Øresund), where he sees Hálfdan's warship, Skrauti. Sǫrli and Hálfdan fight a long battle aboard ship. The king refuses Sǫrli's three offers of peace, whereupon Sǫrli kills him and takes the vessel; but Þórir escapes to arouse Hǫgni and Sigmundr to revenge.

Enraged, Hǫgni sails to Norway, only to find that Sǫrli, leaving Skrauti behind, has gone to Sweden to negotiate a settlement with him and his brother. Hǫgni kills the ship's overseer, takes Skrauti, and raises war against King Erlingr. Hǫgni kills Erlingr, his son Sigvaldi, and his ally King Haraldr; after this battle, Hǫgni seeks Ingibjǫrg in Erlingr's castle, but cannot find her and sails home.

Sǫrli, meanwhile, has besieged Sigmundr's and Hǫgni's walled stronghold at Litidorum. In a four-day battle, Sigmundr receives a mortal stomach wound; fresh troops from England revive the besieged Swedes, and Hǫgni arrives with Skrauti under his command. Sǫrli is challenged by Hǫgni to single combat, in which Sǫrli gains the upper hand; Hǫgni, having dropped his sword, entreats Sǫrli to let him go get it. Sǫrli does so, and Hǫgni, impressed by his opponent's honor and remembering Sǫrli's threefold offer of peace to his father, bids him make peace as friend and foster-brother. Sǫrli accepts this offer, ending the siege and the war. All parties enter the castle at Litidorum for a great feast. Hǫgni and Sǫrli marry each other's sisters, Marsibil and Ingibjǫrg, and Þórir marries Steinvǫr.

This saga is related to several *fornaldarsögur* (*Hálfdanar saga Brǫnufóstra, Hálfdanar saga Eysteinssonar*, and *Qrvar-Odds saga*) concerned either marginally or centrally with Hálfdan's great ship; it is only tangentially related to *Sǫrla þáttr eða Heðins saga ok Hǫgna*, where Sǫrli appears only in the introduction. Lukman (1977) suggested that this saga was based upon Irish annals concerning Dano-Norwegian activity in Ireland in 851–873; personal and place-name correlations between the apparent annalistic sources and elements in *Sǫrla saga* suggest creative recasting of the Irish materials.

Sǫrla saga sterka survives only in paper MSS, none earlier than the middle of the 17th century. Four of them (AM 168 fol.,

AM 171a fol., AM 560d 4to, Rask 32) are in the Arnamagnæan collection, with one (NkS 1806 4to) in the Royal Library in Copenhagen and three more in Stockholm. HB 82b 4to in the University Library in Iceland served as the basis for Björner's *editio princeps* (1737); Rafn's 1829–30 edition follows suit, supplying variants from the AM MSS.

Ed.: Björner, Erik Julius, ed. *Nordiska Kämpa Dater*. Stockholm: Horrn, 1737; Rafn, C. C., ed. *Fornaldar sögur Nordrlanda*. 3 vols. Copenhagen: Popp, 1829–30, vol. 3, pp. 408–52; Guðni Jónsson, ed. *Fornaldarsögur Norðurlanda*. 4 vols. Akureyri: Íslendingasagnaútgáfan, 1950; 2nd ed. 1954, vol. 3, pp. 367–410. **Lit.**: Lukman, Niels. "An Irish Source and Some Icelandic *fornaldarsögur*." *Mediaeval Scandinavia* 10 (1977), 41–57.

Jonathan D. M. Evans

[See also: *Fornaldarsögur*; *Hálfdanar saga Brǫnufóstra*; *Hálfdanar saga Eysteinssonar*; *Sǫrla þáttr*]

Sǫrla þáttr ("The Tale of Sǫrli"), not to be confused with *Sǫrla þáttr Brodd-Helgasonar*, is preserved only in the late 14th-century vellum *Flateyjarbók* (GkS 1005 fol., Árni Magnússon Institute in Iceland), as one of the thirty-three *þættir* inserted into *Óláfs saga Tryggvasonar en mesta*. Although the *þáttr* bears his name, Sǫrli is far from the main character, appearing in the second of the two preludes to the story of the *Hjaðningavíg* ("the battle of Heðinn and his men"), which serves as the main narrative. His life, however, is the subject of one of the *fornaldarsögur*, *Sǫrla saga sterka*. The *þáttr* combines myth, history, and legend, and is structured into two introductions, a main story, and an epilogue. The first introduction (chs. 1 and 2) tells how Freyja first obtained, lost, and regained her necklace, and sets the outline of the main story: an everlasting battle brought about by the theft of a precious treasure. The second introduction (chs. 3 and 4) functions as a transition, joining the mythological and legendary portions of the *þáttr*. It relates the adventures of Sǫrli sterki ("the strong") Erlingsson, who rose to fame as a Viking sea-king in the Baltic. It develops the theme of the "desire and theft of a precious object" and introduces both the theme of the *fóstbrœðralag* ("blood-brotherhood") and the character of Hogni. Part 3 offers a romanticized and lightly comic version of the *Hjaðningavíg*, a well-known Germanic legend recorded in the extant documents of Old English and Middle High German, in Saxo and Snorri, and in a number of Old Icelandic texts from the 10th to the 15th century. The epilogue (ch. 9) christianizes the pagan tale and appropriately recalls the close of the first introduction, by having Ívarr ljómi ("the gleam") end the cursed battle and win victory over Óðinn for Óláfr Tryggvason. There is a recent argument for an Irish source for the entire *þáttr*.

Like the other *þættir* inserted into *Óláfs saga Tryggvasonar en mesta*, *Sǫrla þáttr* includes secular, Christian, and pagan fantastical matter. Its tone is light, and its purpose, beyond offering still another example of Óláfr's (or his surrogate's) victories over

paganism, is to entertain. There is humor, both in the conjugal disenchantment of Óðinn and Freyja and in the legendary figures. Hildr, for example, who in other versions is presented as a type of demigoddess turned sorceress, the cause and perpetuator of the strife, is presented here as a reasoning and prudent young woman, a compassionate lover, and a dutiful daughter. Her charismatic qualities have been fragmented and given over to the demonic Gǫndul and the doomed queen Hervǫr. Her sole contribution to the drama of the everlasting battle is to sit in the wings and watch. Heðinn also loses his heroic veneer, and is portrayed as a kind of repentant muscleman who wishes only to slink off and hide lest men cast his "wicked deeds in his teeth."

Sǫrla þáttr has unity. Its structural simplicity is made complex by thematic repetition and balance. It begins and ends with a mythological motif. The conflict/redress configuration in each part is similar: each struggle is touched off by the obsession with a precious object belonging to another (necklace, boat, fame/love), and the redress is either a pact (Freyja's promise, the *fóstbrœðralag*) or, as in the case in the *Hjaðningavíg*, both a *fóstbrœðralag* and blood revenge. In characterization, unity is achieved by means of antithetical balancing of character, as, for example, in the figures of Óðinn and Óláfr, and of Loki (the master thief and catalyst of the everlasting battle) and Ívarr ljómi (the Christian guard who brings closure to the nightly "thefts" of watchmen and to the everlasting battle).

Ed.: Guðbrandur Vigfússon and C. R. Unger, eds. *Flateyjarbók: En Samling af norske Konge-Sagaer med indskudte mindre Fortællinger om Begivenheder i og undenfor Norge samt Annaler*. 3 vols. Christiania [Oslo]: Malling, 1860–68, vol. 1; Guðni Jónsson, ed. *Fornaldar sögur Norðurlanda*. 4 vols. Akureyri: Íslendingasagnaútgáfan, 1954, vol. 1. **Tr.**: Brodeur, Arthur Gilchrist, trans. *The Prose Edda by Snorri Sturluson*. New York: American-Scandinavian Foundation, 1916; rpt. 1967; Morris, William, and Eiríkr Magnússon, trans. "The Tale of Hogni and Hedinn." In *Three Northern Love Stories*. London: Ellis & White, 1875, pp. 189–210; Kershaw, Nora, trans. "The Tháttr of Sörli." In *Stories and Ballads of the Far Past*. Cambridge: The University Press, 1921, pp. 38–57; Garmonsway, G. N., and Jacqueline Simpson, trans. *Beowulf and Its Analogues*. London: Dent; New York: Dutton, 1968; rpt. 1971, pp. 298–300 [the Freyja episode only]. **Lit.**: Vries, Jan de. *The Problem of Loki*. Folklore Fellows Communications, 110. Helsinki: Suomalainen tiedeakatemia, Societas Scientiarum Fennica, 1933, pp. 125–41; Lukman, Niels. "The Catalaunian Battle (A.D. 451) in Medieval Epics: *Hjaðningavíg*, Kudrun, Saxo." *Classica et Mediaevalia* 10 (1949), 60–130; Malone, Kemp. "An Anglo-Latin Version of the *Hjaðningavíg*." *Speculum* 39 (1964), 35–44; Lukman, Niels. "An Irish Source and Some Icelandic *fornaldarsögur*." *Mediaeval Scandinavia* 10 (1977), 41–57; Damico, Helen. "*Sörlaþáttr* and the Hama Episode in *Beowulf*." *Scandinavian Studies* 55 (1983), 222–35.

Helen Damico

[See also: *Flateyjarbók*; Freyr and Freyja; Mythology; Óðinn; *Óláfs saga Tryggvasonar*; *Sǫrla saga sterka*; *Þáttr*]

Tale mot biskopene *see* **Oratio contra clerum Norvegiae**

Temples, Heathen. The Old Norse terms for heathen places of worship are *hof* and *hǫrgr*. The word *hof* has no sacred significance in the South Germanic areas, where it is used solely to describe secular buildings or enclosures. In Old Norse, the word indicates a building where the ritual sacrifice (the *blót*) took place. No special building seems to have been needed. The *hof* was probably identical with the largest hall or longhouse on the farm where the *blót* was held (the *veizluskáli*). In Norway, the names of twenty-two farms begin with a name of a god, followed by the word *hof*, and eighty-five farms are simply called "Hof" (Hoff, Hov). This evidence seems to indicate that *hof* could also mean a farm where cult meetings were regularly held, probably for more people than those living on the farm.

*Hof*s are mentioned in Snorri's *Heimskringla* and some of the *Íslendingasögur*. *Eyrbyggja saga* has a detailed description of a *hof*, comprising a banqueting hall where the ritual meals were eaten, and an *afhús* where the cult images were placed. Modern historical criticism, however, regards the descriptions in the sagas as learned reconstructions. Some brief notes on the erection of *hof*s in *Landnámabók* may go back to the 12th century, and are perhaps more reliable. The so-called *Úlfljótslǫg*, which occur in some versions of *Landnámabók*, reckon a number of *hof*s in each *þing* district, an organization very similar to the parish system of the Christian Church, but this again must be regarded as a learned reconstruction from around 1200.

The Old Norse word *hǫrgr* is used to describe both a natural and an artificially contrived pile of stones, usually out in the open. In the *Edda*, however, the word is used to describe the dwelling of the gods, and the *Gulaþingslǫg* penalizes anyone "making a house and calling it *hǫrgr*." Thus, the word *hǫrgr* could perhaps mean both an open place of worship and a place sheltered by some sort of roof construction. Adam of Bremen, writing around 1070, describes the heathen temple at Uppsala in Sweden, at that time still a center of pagan worship. His description is based on eyewitness accounts. According to Adam, the temple building contained the statues of Þórr, Óðinn, and Freyr ("Thor, Wodan et Fricco"). We do not know what the Swedes called their temple, but it was probably of the *hǫrgr* type, situated in the vicinity of the holy grove and spring where the votive ceremonies Adam describes took place.

Archaeological evidence. The only *hof* site that can be established with some degree of certainty was excavated at Hofstaðir in Mývatnssveit, Iceland, in 1908. On the site was a large, turf-built longhouse with a stone-built extension, interpreted as an *afhús*, added to the north gable. To the south of the building, an oval pit placed axially, filled with ashes, charcoal, pot stones, and fragments of animal bones, suggests a ritual baking pit.

In 1926, Gamla Uppsala church was excavated. Traces of earlier settlement were found in at least three different strata. Based on a number of postholes both inside and outside the oldest part of the church, Sune Lindqvist reconstructed what he believed to be the heathen temple mentioned by Adam, as an almost square building with a raised central part, not unlike the nave of a stave church. In 1967, Lindqvist reconsidered his reconstruction. On the basis of revalued documentary evidence, he maintained that the heathen temple must have been situated to the west of the church building, serving, after being "purged by fire," as a church before the present church was erected.

At Mære in North Trøndelag in Norway, mentioned in the sagas as one of the most important heathen cult centers in Trøndelag, excavation was carried out beneath the present 12th-century stone church in 1967–1968. A wooden church was found, probably dating from the second half of the 11th century, and beneath this church traces of at least two different building stages were found, the older reaching well into the Viking Age. The limited area, unaffected by Christian burials, gave no information about the form and size of the pre-Christian buildings, but around a series of postholes nineteen gold plaquettes (*gullgubber*) were found with stamped pictures of a man and a woman believed to be Freyr and Gerðr. Similar finds of gold plaquettes are known from different sites in Scandinavia, *e.g.*, Hauge, Jæren, and Borg in Lofoten, Norway; Eskilstuna, Eketorp, Öland, and Helgö in Mälaren, Sweden; and Bornholm in Denmark. The plaquettes found at Helgö form an interesting parallel to the Mære finds in that they were found around a large posthole. The excavator, Wilhelm Holmqvist, interpreted the circumstances under which the plaquettes were found as an indication of a fertility cult, which, according to him, could also explain the name of the island, Helgö (Holy Island).

Lit.: Holmqvist, W., and B. Arrhenius. *Excavations at Helgö.* 2 vols. Stockholm and Uppsala: Kungl. vitterhets historie och antikvitets akademien, 1961–64; Olsen, Olaf. "Hørg, hov og kirke." *Aarbøger for nordisk Oldkyndighed og Historie* (1966), 1–307; Stenberger, Mårten. "Eketorps borg, a fortified village on Öland, Sweden." *Acta Archaeologica* 37 (1966), 203–14; Lindqvist, Sune. "Uppsala hednatempel och första katedral. Gammal stridsfråga i nytt ljus." *Nordisk tidskrift* 42 (1967), 236–42; Lidén, Hans-Emil. "From Pagan Sanctuary to Christian Church: The Excavation of Mære Church in Trøndelag." *Norwegian Archaeological Review* 2 (1969), 3–32; Thrane, Henrik. "Das Gudme-Problem und die Gudme-Untersuchung." *Frühmittelalterliche Studien* 21 (1987), 1–48; Watt, Margrethe. "Guldageren." *Skalk* 2 (1987), 3–9.

Hans-Emil Lidén

[**See also:** Adam of Bremen; Churches, Stone; Religion, Pagan Scandinavian; Stave Church]

Textiles, Furnishing. Textile art was one of the leading arts in the Middle Ages, and beautiful textiles were as prestigious as gold and jewels. Costly silk fabrics and embroideries imported to Scandinavia have survived in surprisingly large quantities. Most of them are found in Sweden and date from the late Middle Ages. Cheaper decorative textiles in wool and linen were also imported, and it can be difficult to distinguish between such imports and domestic work. The textiles discussed here, however, are believed to be of Scandinavian origin.

Most medieval Scandinavian textiles were made as handicrafts at various levels. Male professional weavers are, with one exception (Roskilde in Denmark, 1483), unknown in Scandinavia until the 16th century, but we know the names of some professional male embroiderers from the 15th and 16th centuries. One of them is Albertus Pictor, a mural painter who headed a highly competent embroidery workshop in Stockholm from the 1470s onward. Workshops for embroidery and probably decorative weaving are also known from Scandinavian convents like Vadstena in Sweden, founded by St. Birgitta in the 14th century, and the Brigettine convent of Nådendal in Finland. Other centers of artistic skill may have been established in mansion houses and in royal courts.

Surviving embroideries from the workshops of Albertus Pictor and the convents of Vadstena and Nådendal were intended for ecclesiastical use. In fact, most of the medieval decorative textiles in Scandinavia come from churches. This origin does not necessarily mean that they were intended for a church from the start. Many of them are quite secular in character, a fact that can be explained by the custom whereby wealthy people donated valuable textiles to chuches after they had been used for secular purposes.

There were differences between the amount and kinds of textiles used for furnishing by common people and those of upper social classes. Historical records of many kinds give us information on medieval furnishing textiles, and the terminological studies of the Norwegian philologist Hjalmar Falk are important in this connection. Still, there are gaps in our knowledge.

It was customary in medieval Scandinavia on festive occasions to decorate the interior of secular houses as well as churches with long textiles hanging around the walls. The wall runners were of different types, the most important called *tjeld* (*tjald*) and *refil* (*refill*). *Tjeld* was a plain textile covering most of the wall. It was usually made of simple material like coarse woolen cloth. A narrow *refil*, with embroidered or woven decoration, was frequently hung on top of the *tjeld*. A large part of the extant medieval decorative textiles of Scandinavian origin is supposed to have been used as wall hangings.

Among the woven wall hangings, several techniques are represented. The narrow hangings from Skog and Överhogdal in Sweden are executed in a kind of soumak weave resembling the figured weaves from the Oseberg ship burial of about 850. They probably date from the 13th century, and the designs consist of hosts of people, animals, and houses. The narrative scenes in many-colored woolen yarn on a white linen ground have been the subject of various interpretations.

The hanging from the church of Baldishol in Norway is the only one in tapestry weave. It depicts two men under a low arcade, one of them riding a horse. The men represent the months April and May, and may have been part of a tapestry cycle showing the twelve months of the year. It is now generally believed that the tapestry was woven in Norway in the beginning of the 13th century.

Several hangings in pick-up doublecloth have survived; from late-medieval inventories, we know that textiles of this type were very popular. Pick-up doublecloth is not known from other parts of western Europe in the Middle Ages, and it has been suggested that the weave reached Scandinavia from the East. Four narrow *refils* from Marby, Revsund, and Överhogdal in Sweden and Rennebu in Norway are of a 13th-century type, where the pattern is formed by the interchanging of one layer in white linen and one in colored wool. The patterns include knots and interlaced motifs, and geometric human beings and animals. A later group of all-woolen doublecloths are predominantly decorated with animals. The blue and white hanging from Grödinge in Sweden, dated to the 15th century, is a splendid example with different types of beasts on a checkerboard ground as a main motif.

Three hangings from the first half of the 16th century woven in tabby brocaded on the counted thread are known from the Finnish Brigettine convent at Nådendal. One hanging, nearly 5 m. long, has ornamental borders in many-colored wool on a white linen ground. On the others, the colored woolen patterns with octagons are seen against a ground weave of red wool. Inside the octagons and surrounding them are such motifs as lions, deer, birds, human figures, and trees.

Another *refil* from Nådendal, worked in long-armed cross stitch, has a rather similar pattern with octagons. Long-armed cross stitch or simple cross stitch have also been used on Swedish *refils* like the one from the church of Fogdö from the end of the 15th century. It was probably made in the convent of Vårfruberga and depicts religious scenes under an arcade. The original length was more than 8 m. Medieval embroidered hangings, like those just mentioned, are partly worked in counted-thread embroidery, partly in free embroidery.

The unique hanging from the church of Høylandet in Norway depicting the story of the three Magi is believed to date from the first half of the 13th century. The embroidery is worked on a red woolen fabric with outlines elegantly executed in white linen yarn in stem stitch, and the figures filled in with pattern darning in colored woolen yarn and in white linen. It is skilled work, probably carried out in a workshop, and the designer might have had access to English patterns.

It is impossible to tell whether Norwegian embroidered fragments in laid and couched work, like the one from the church of

169. Hanging from Baldishol Church, Norway; probably early 13th century. Tapestry weave. Height: 118 cm. Length: 203 cm. Owner: Kunstindustrimuseet i Oslo. Photo: Teigens fotoatelier.

170. Hanging from Høylandet Church, Norway. Detail; probably first half of 13th century. Wool and linen embroidery on wool. Height: 43 cm. Owner and photo: Universitetet i Trondheim, Vitenskapsmuseet.

172. Hanging from Grödinge Church, Sweden. Detail; probably 15th century. Woven in pick-up doublecloth. Each square measures about 23.5–24.5 cm. x 22 cm. Owner: Statens Historiska Museum, Stockholm. Photo: Gabriel Hildebrand, Antikvarisk-topografiska arkivet.

171. Hanging from Skog Church, Sweden. Detail; about 1200. Soumak weave in wool and linen. Height: 35–38 cm. Owner: Statens Historiska Museum, Stockholm. Photo: Gabriel Hildebrand, Antikvarisk-topografiska arkivet.

173. Wool intarsia embroidery from Dalhem Church, Sweden. Detail; late 14th or early 15th century. Each square measures about 55 cm. x 55 cm. This ecclesiastical textile probably once belonged to the Brigettine convent of Vadstena. Similar embroideries were used for furnishing textiles like coverlets and cushions for chairs and benches. Owner: Statens Historiska Museum, Stockholm. Photo: Gabriel Hildebrand, Antikvarisk-topografiska arkivet.

Røn worked in colored woolen yarn and white linen contours on a linen ground, were part of wall hangings. Seven fallen men and a horse are seen on the fragment, which dates from the 13th century and is related to the 11th-century Bayeux Tapestry in style and technique. Textiles in laid and couched work were popular in Iceland during the Middle Ages, and several interesting examples have survived. One of them, fragmentarily preserved, is an all-woolen horizontal wall hanging from Hvammur church from the 14th century or later, with a design of interlaced circles framing animals.

Not only the walls but also the ceiling could be decorated with hangings. They were partly used to protect against soot, partly as decoration. In the Museum of National Antiquities in Stockholm, there is one such example dated to about 1527, with alternating lengths of embroidered linen and lengths of knotted silk net with loops of varying sizes.

Cushions for benches and chairs are known to have had textile covers, and bench runners of considerable length could be used for festive occasions. Swedish medieval cushions are in pattern darning, cross stitch, and gilt-membrane embroidery.

The history of table covers and tablecloths in medieval Scandinavia is unknown. However, three long linen textiles from Norway with embroidered ornamental borders in pattern darning are believed to be late-medieval examples of tablecloths. On one of the textiles, the borders are worked in blue linen thread; on the others, they are worked in many-colored woolen yarn.

Little has survived of medieval bedclothes, but some Swedish and Finnish textiles in wool intarsia embroidery with gilded leather strips are of a type known to have been used as coverlets. They are made of cloth squares with fantastic animals joined together in a chessboard manner. The animals were probably cut at the same time from two superimposed panels in contrasting colors. After the cutting, the motives were interchanged and the edges sewn together and decorated with gilt leather strips. The intarsia embroideries date approximately between 1300 and 1500.

Written sources do not reveal in detail how beds were made up, even if they mention different articles of bedclothing. People from the upper classes might have used a sheet of leather, eventually a fell, on top of the straw, or a bolster filled with feathers and down. Linen sheets are known from 14th- and 15th-century inventories. Ordinary people had one or more woolen cloths or blankets in 2/2 twill on top of the straw. Pillows of several types were used, and some of them had patterned covers. The body was covered with an upper sheet of wool or linen (known from the 14th century in the inventories of well-to-do people) with a coverlet on top. The coverlets varied from plain woolen blankets, fells, and pile rugs of the "rya" type (mentioned in sources from the 15th century onward) to decorated coverlets like the ones in intarsia embroidery. It is uncertain whether eiderdowns were used in the Middle Ages. Some beds had bed curtains and valances. Twenty-one such valances, or parts of valances, primarily worked in straight darning stitch, are preserved in Iceland. They date from the 17th and 18th centuries, but definitely show a medieval tradition.

Footcloths are frequently referred to in medieval Scandinavian sources. Most of them were fells used for protection against the cold, but Norwegian inventories show that some of them were costly woven textiles used by the upper classes for special occasions.

Lit.: Falk, Hjalmar. *Altwestnordische Kleiderkunde mit besonderer Berücksichtigung der Terminologie*. Videnskaps selskapets Skrifter. II. Hist.-filos. kl. 1918. No. 3. Kristiania [Oslo]: Dybwad, 1919; Branting, Agnes, and Andreas Lindblom. *Medieval Embroideries and Textiles in Sweden*. 2 vols. Uppsala and Stockholm: Almqvist & Wiksell, 1932; Nordman, C. A. "Klosterarbeten från Nådendal." *Finskt Museum* 50 (1943), 1–31; Engelstad, Helen. *Refil, bunad, tjeld. Middelalderens billedtepper i Norge*. Oslo: Gyldendal, 1952; Geijer, Agnes. "Det textila arbetet i Norden under forntid och medeltid." In *Lergods, ædelmetaller og væv. Teknisk kultur IV*. Ed. Sigurd Erixon. Nordisk kultur, 15:A. Stockholm: Bonnier; Oslo: Aschehoug; Copenhagen: Schultz, 1953, pp. 66–90; Geijer, Agnes. "Bildvävnad." *KLNM* 1 (1956), 536–40; Franzén, Anne Marie. "Bonad." *KLNM* 2 (1957), 76–81; Geijer, Agnes. "Broderi." *KLNM* 2 (1957), 258–65; Franzén, Anne Marie. "Drätt." *KLNM* 3 (1958), 354–55; Franzén, Anne Marie. "Dubbelvävnad." *KLNM* 3 (1958), 356–8; Franzén, Anne Marie. "Dukagång." *KLNM* 3 (1958), 360–1; Franzén, Anne Marie. "Dyna." *KLNM* 3 (1958), 395–6; Franzén, Anne Marie. "Høylandsteppet." In *Det Kgl. Norske Videnskabers Selskab. Museet. Årbok 1960*. Trondheim: Sentrum bok- og aksidenstrykkeri, 1960, pp. 87–103; Geijer, Agnes. "Matta." *KLNM* 11 (1966), 504–5; Geijer, Agnes, and Elsa E. Guðjónsson. "Rya." *KLNM* 14 (1969), 513–5; Hoffmann, Marta, *et al.* "Sengeutstyr." *KLNM* 15 (1970), 134–49; Franzén, Anne Marie. "Snärjvävnad." *KLNM* 16 (1971), 353–4; Franzén, Anne Marie. *Prydnadssömmar under medeltiden*. Kungl. vitterhets historie och antikvitets akademien. Uppsala and Stockholm: Almqvist & Wiksell, 1972; Geijer, Agnes. "Textil." *KLNM* 18 (1974), 233–8; Pylkkänen, Riitta. *The Use and Traditions of Mediaeval Rugs and Coverlets in Finland*. Helsinki: Archaeological Society of Finland, 1974; Hoffmann, Marta, *et al.* "Vever." *KLNM* 19 (1975), 679–80; Nylen, Anna-Maja. *Swedish Handicraft*. Trans. Anne-Charlotte Hanes Harvey. New York: Van Nostrand Reinhold, 1977; Guðjónsson, Elsa E. "Medieval Embroidery Terms and Techniques." In *Studies in Textile History: In Memory of Harold B. Burnham*. Ed. Veronika Gervers. Toronto: Royal Ontario Museum; Alger, 1977, pp. 133–43; Geijer, Agnes. *A History of Textile Art*. London: Wilson, 1979, pp. 240–57; Hoffmann, Marta. "Tekstil." In *Norges kunsthistorie. 2: Høymiddelalder og Hands-tid*. Oslo: Gyldendal, 1981, pp. 315–49;

Hoffmann, Marta. "Beds and Bedclothes in Medieval Norway." In *Cloth and Clothing in Medieval Europe: Essays in Memory of Professor E. M. Carus-Wilson*. Ed. N. B. Harte and K. G. Ponting. Pasold Studies in Textile History, 2. London: Heinemann, 1983, pp. 351–67; Estham, Inger. "Birgittinska broderier." In *Den ljusa medeltiden. Studier tillägnade Aron Andersson*. Museum of National Antiquities, Stockholm, Studies 4. Stockholm: Statens Historiska Museum, 1984, pp. 25–42; Guðjónsson, Elsa E. *Traditional Icelandic Embroidery*. Reykjavik: Iceland Review, 1985; Estham, Inger. "A Newly Discovered Intarsia and Gold Leather Embroidery." In *Opera Textila Variorum Temporum. To Honour Agnes Geijer on Her Ninetieth Birthday 26th October 1988*. Ed. Inger Estham and Margareta Nockert. Museum of National Antiquities, Stockholm, Studies 8. Stockholm: Statens Historiska Museum, 1988, pp. 93–110; Kjellberg, Anne, and Marta Hoffman. "Tekstiler." In *De arkeologiske utgravninger i Gamlebyen, Oslo*. Vol. 8.2: *Dagliglivets gjenstander*. Ed. Erik Schia and Petter B. Molaug. Øvre Ervik: Alvheim & Eide, 1991, pp. 13–80.

Anne Kjellberg

[**See also:** Clothmaking; Fashions; Oseberg; Tools; Vadstena]

Theodoricus: Historia de antiquitate regum Norwagiensium.

The "History of the Ancient Kings of Norway," which summarizes Norwegian history from the time of Haraldr hárfagri ("fair-hair") Hálfdanarson to the death of Sigurðr Jórsalafari ("crusader") Magnússon in 1130, was composed by the monk Theodoricus (Theodoricus monachus). The *Historia* is dedicated to Archbishop Eysteinn Erlendsson of Niðaróss (Trondheim), who died in 1188; it is thus one of the earliest Norwegian histories. Mention of a battle that took place in 1177 provides a *terminus post quem* for the completion of the work.

Nothing is known about Theodoricus beyond his authorship of the *Historia*. References to Hugh of St. Victor in the work have led scholars to believe that Theodoricus studied at the Parisian monastery of St. Victor, and a comparison of the writings he cites with the contents of the monastic library there would appear to support this assumption (Johnsen 1939). Theodoricus has been identified with Archbishop Þórir of Niðaróss (1205–1214) or Bishop Þórir of Hamarr (*ca.* 1189/90–1196), each of whom spent some time at St. Victor's, but the evidence is inconclusive.

Whether he studied at St. Victor's or elsewhere, Theodoricus received a good education; the *Historia* abounds with references to classical and medieval authors. While some of the works cited were undoubtedly available to him in Norway, others seem to have been quoted from memory or from a collection of excerpts. He is not averse to using foreign sources to correct Norwegian ones, his most notable contribution being the discovery in the *Historia Normannorum* (presumably the work of that title by William of Jumièges) that St. Óláfr was baptized not in England or Norway, as had previously been thought, but in Rouen.

Theodoricus's sources for the *Historia* included a *vita* of St. Óláfr and a "Catalogus regum Norwagiensium," presumably a regnal list giving the lengths of reign of successive Norwegian kings, a topic on which Theodoricus's information differs from Icelandic tradition (Ellehøj 1965: 195). He says that Icelanders were important informants in the introduction to his work, where he refers to traditions preserved in their "ancient songs"; this statement, as well as a number of passages in which he notes the lack of written Norwegian history, has led scholars to believe that the information obtained from Icelanders was purely oral. The question of whether

Theodoricus also had access to written Icelandic historical works, such as the writings of Sæmundr Sigfússon or Ari Þorgilsson, has been the subject of much debate. The relationships among his *Historia*, the *Historia Norwegiae*, and *Ágrip af Nóregs konunga sǫgum* are key questions for the study of early Icelandic-Norwegian historiography and *konungasǫgur*. Recent articles by Bjarni Guðnason (1977) and Theodore Andersson (1979; 1985) make strong arguments that Theodoricus did, in fact, use Icelandic writings.

Ed.: Storm, Gustav, ed. "Theodorici monachi Historia de antiquitate regum Norwagiensium." In *Monumenta historica Norvegiæ*. Oslo: Brøgger, 1880; rpt. Oslo: Norsk Historisk Kjeldeskrift-Institutt, 1973, pp. 1–68. **Lit.**: Johnsen, Arne Odd. *Om Theodoricus og hans Historia de Antiquitate Regum Norwagiensium*. Avhandlinger utgitt av Det Norske Videnskaps-Akademi i Oslo II, Hist.-filos. Kl., 1939, no. 3. Oslo: Dybwad, 1939; Hanssen, Jens. "Theodoricus monachus and European Literature." *Symbolae Osloenses* 27 (1949), 70–127; Ellehøj, Svend. *Studier over den ældste norrøne historieskrivning*. Bibliotheca Arnamagnæana, 26. Copenhagen: Munksgaard, 1965, pp. 175–276 [English summary, pp. 297–302]; Bjarni Guðnason. "Theodoricus og íslenskir sagnaritarar." In *Sjötíu ritgerðir helgaðar Jakobi Benediktssyni 20. júlí 1977*. 2 vols. Ed. Einar G. Pétursson and Jónas Kristjánsson. Reykjavik: Stofnun Árna Magnússonar, 1977, vol. 1, pp. 107–20; Andersson, Theodore M. "Ari's *konunga ævi* and the Earliest Accounts of Hákon jarl's Death." *Opuscula* 6. Bibliotheca Arnamagnæana, 33. Copenhagen: Munksgaard, 1979, pp. 1–17; Ulset, Tor. *Det genetiske forholdet mellom Ágrip, Historia Norwegiæ og Historia de antiquitate regum Norwagiensium: En analyse med utgangspunkt i oversettelsesteknikk samt en diskusjon omkring begrepet "latinisme" i samband med norrøne tekster*. Oslo: Novus, 1983; Andersson, Theodore M. "Kings' Sagas (*Konungasǫgur*)." In *Old Norse–Icelandic Literature: A Critical Guide*. Ed. Carol J. Clover and John Lindow. Islandica, 45. Ithaca and London: Cornell University Press, 1985, pp. 197–238 [esp. pp. 201–11].

Margaret Cormack

[**See also:** *Ágrip af Nóregs konunga sǫgum*; *Historia Norwegiae*; *Konungasǫgur*; Óláfr, St.; *Óláfs saga helga*; William of Jumièges: *Gesta Normannorum ducum*]

Thómas saga erkibiskups

("The Saga of Archbishop Thomas"). The life of Thomas à Becket, archbishop of Canterbury, martyred in 1170 in his struggle against the English king and canonized in 1173, became the subject of a number of contemporary biographies in Latin and also of a body of Old Norse sagas. His career furnished the ecclesiastical leadership with a forceful argument in their struggle for supremacy against the monarchy. This struggle continued throughout the Middle Ages, and no doubt was the main reason for the popularity of this saint.

Thómas saga 1 is based on the so-called *Quadrilogus prior*. Probably originating in the second half of the 13th century, the saga is preserved in MS Stock. Perg. 4to no. 17, dating from around 1300. The copy in Stock. Perg. 4to no. 17 was presumably made by a Norwegian, but certain Icelandicisms suggest Icelandic influence. Icelandic marginalia from the 14th century indicate that the MS was already in Iceland at this time. It is reasonable to assume, therefore, that the Norwegian scribe made the copy during a stay in Iceland.

The erudite translator has rendered his Latin exemplar in a free and independent manner. He adopts an ornate and flowery language, including, among other things, a number of alliterations that have no basis in the original. The style is characterized by pathos and great declamatory force.

It has customarily been taken for granted that the translator of *Thómas saga 1* was of Norwegian ancestry as well. Recently, however, some scholars have challenged this assumption. Nevertheless, investigation of the numerous alliterations in this saga shows that their linguistic basis is primarily Norwegian.

According to Icelandic tradition, two native priests composed *Thómas* sagas: Bergr Gunnsteinsson (d. 1211) and Jón Holt (d. 1312). Stefán Karlsson (1973) argued in favor of the latter's responsibility for *Thómas saga 1*. His name suggests Norwegian origin, as the use of place-names as surnames was no doubt a more common practice in Norway than in Iceland.

All the other Old Norse accounts of Thomas are Icelandic. The most complete of these (*Thómas saga 2*), dating from the first half of the 14th century, has been transcribed in *Tómasskinna* (GkS 1008 fol., *ca.* 1400) and in a few medieval fragments. The sources of this highly competent work of compilation include, among others, *Thómas saga 1*, the *Speculum historiale* by Vincent of Beauvais, and an older Icelandic translation of a now-lost life of Thomas by Robert of Cricklade from about 1173.

A third saga (*Thómas saga 3*), surviving only in fragments from the early 14th century, represents an intermediate stage between the original translation of the life by Robert of Cricklade and *Thómas saga 2*, whereas the fragmentary saga in the 14th-century Stock. Perg. fol. no. 2 (*Thómas saga 4*) seems to approximate the original translation even more closely.

There is relatively general agreement that Bergr Gunnsteinsson is responsible for the translation of the life by Robert of Cricklade, which *Thómas saga 2, 3,* and *4* have drawn on directly or indirectly. On the basis of lexical-statistical investigations, Peter Hallberg (1968) has argued that the abbot Bergr Sokkason composed *Thómas saga 2*.

Ed.: Unger, C. R., ed. *Thomas saga erkibyskups: Fortællinger om Thomas Becket Erkebiskop af Canterbury.* Christiania [Oslo]: Bentzen, 1869; Eiríkr Magnússon, ed. *Thómas saga erkibiskups: A Life of Archbishop Thomas Becket, in Icelandic.* Rolls Series, 65.2. London: Eyre & Spottiswoode, 1883 [includes translation]. **Lit.**: Foote, Peter G. "On the Fragmentary Text Concerning St. Thomas Becket in Stock. Perg. Fol. Nr. 2." *Saga-Book of the Viking Society* 15.4 (1961), 403–50; Loth, Agnete, ed. *Thomasskinna. Gl. kgl. Saml. 1008 fol. in The Royal Library, Copenhagen.* Early Icelandic Manuscripts in Facsimile, 6. Copenhagen: Rosenkilde & Bagger, 1964, pp. 8–11; Orme, Margaret. "A Reconstruction of Robert of Cricklade's Vita S. Thoma Cantuariensis." *Analecta Bollandiana* 84.3–4 (1966), 379–98; Hallberg, Peter. *Stilsignalement och författarskap i norrön sagalitteratur. Synpunkter och exempel.* Acta Universitatis Gothoburgensis. Nordistica Gothoburgensia, 3. Gothenburg: Almqvist & Wiksell, 1968, pp. 144–51, 234–6; Stefán Karlsson. "Icelandic Lives of Thomas à Becket: Questions of Authorship." *Proceedings of the First International Saga Conference. University of Edinburgh.* London: Viking Society for Northern Research, 1973, pp. 212–43; Jakobsen, Alfred. "Om bruken av aksenttegn i Sth. 17 qv. (Thomas saga erkibyskups 1)." *Maal og minne* (1977), 89–102; Jakobsen, Alfred. "Thómas saga erkibiskups 1—norsk eller islandsk oversettelse?" In *Opuscula septentrionalia. Festskrift til Ole Widding, 10.10.1977.* Ed. Bent Chr. Jacobsen *et al.* Copenhagen: Reitzel, 1977, pp. 89–99; Jakobsen, Alfred. "Et par ordformer med innskutt *a* i Thomas saga erkibiskups 1." In *Sjötíu ritgerðir helgaðar Jakobi Benediktssyni 20.*

júli 1977. 2 vols. Ed. Einar G. Pétursson and Jónas Kristjánsson. Reykjavik: Stofnun Árna Magnússonar, 1977, vol. 1, pp. 384–7.

Alfred Jakobsen

[**See also:** Christian Prose; Legenda; Saints' Lives]

Thord Bondes mord *see* Swedish Literature, Miscellaneous

Tiódels saga ("The Saga of Tiódel") is a *riddarasaga* closely related to the Old French *Lai de Bisclavret* by Marie de France and its Old Norwegian prose translation, *Bisclaretz ljóð*, the fifth story in the *Strengleikar* collection. *Bisclaretz ljóð* is a careful translation, true to its French original, but it has a few deviations. As these are also found in *Tiódels saga*, it is no doubt based on the Norwegian prose translation.

The story takes place in Syria. Tiódel is a knight endowed by God with chivalric virtues. He has the fortitude of Samson, the beauty of Absalom, the prudence of Solomon, and the kindness of Aristotle. He is respected by the king, and is the leader of 12,000 knights. The only peculiar thing about him is that he disappears a couple of days every week. His unnamed wife, who has only bad qualities and who has betrayed her husband for ten years, gets him to tell his secret: he periodically changes into a bear or some other animal. As soon as she has the opportunity, the evil wife removes Tiódel's clothes, which forces him to remain an animal. After feigning sadness, the wife marries her lover.

While the king is out hunting, he comes upon a large polar bear that acts like a human being. The animal seems to be deeply attached to the king. The king brings the bear back to his castle, and the bear follows him everywhere. At a party given by the king, the bear recognizes his rival, the present husband of his wife, and attacks him violently.

One day, the king loses his way while out hunting, and comes to the house of Tiódel's wife. She celebrates the king's arrival with a splendid party, during which she too is attacked by the furious bear, which bites off her nose.

The king intends to kill the bear, but is prevented by a poor but educated knight who is the only one capable of seeing the connection between Tiódel's disappearance and the bear's behavior. He advises the king to force the woman to tell where she has hidden the clothes. The clothes are brought to the bear, but it refuses to look at them. The king becomes angry, and condemns the knight to death for lying. The judgment is accepted by the knight, but he asks for permission to make another proposal: to allow the bear and the clothes to be left alone behind locked doors, since Tiódel may feel ashamed to show his nakedness. This notion turns out to be correct, and Tiódel changes into a man again.

The king wants Tiódel to take back his wife, but, since Tiódel refuses, she and her lover are driven away from the country. As a sign that God is angry with her, all her children are born without noses. Tiódel and his rescuer, however, end their lives in happiness and prosperity.

The name "Tiódel" is probably a Norwegian development of Old Norse *Þjóðólfr*, compounded of *þjóð* 'people' and *úlfr* 'wolf,' which would be a convenient name for a werewolf, which Tiódel may have been in the original version. Perhaps the story was adapted by a Norwegian clergyman, who wanted an example to demonstrate the reward of virtue and the punishment of evil.

Tiódels saga is preserved in twenty-three MSS dating from

about 1600 (AM 123 8vo, vellum) to the turn of the 20th century. The text is badly transmitted; there are garbled passages, and the relationship among the main MSS is not evident. An edition of the saga and of the *rímur* (three cycles) is under preparation by Ohlsson in the Editiones Arnamagnæanæ series.

Lit.: Kölbing, Eugen. "Über isländische Bearbeitungen fremder Stoffe." *Germania* 17, n.s. 5 (1872), 193–7; Meissner, Rudolf. "Die Geschichte vom Ritter Tiodel und seiner ungetreuen Frau." *Zeitschrift für deutsches Altertum und deutsche Literatur* 47 (1904), 247–76; Leach, Henry Goddard. *Angevin Britain and Scandinavia.* Harvard Studies in Comparative Literature, 6. Cambridge: Harvard University Press; London; Milford; Oxford: Oxford University Press, 1921; rpt. Millwood: Kraus, 1975, pp. 199–226; Warnke, Karl, ed. *Die Lais der Marie de France.* Halle: Niemeyer, 1925; Lagerholm, Åke, ed. *Drei Lygisǫgur. Egils saga einhenda ok Ásmundar Berserkjabana. Ála Flekks saga. Flóres saga konungs ok sona hans.* Altnordische Saga-Bibliothek, 17. Halle: Niemeyer, 1927; Richthofen, Eric von, ed. *Vier altfranzösische Lais.* Tübingen: Niemeyer, 1960; Rohlfs, Gerhard. *Vom Vulgärlatein zum Altfranzösischen.* Tübingen: Niemeyer, 1960; Jakobsen, Alfred. "En avskrivertabbe i Bisclaretz lióð." *Maal og minne* (1978), 26–9; Skårup, Povl. "Oversætter- og afskriverfejl i Strengleikar." *Maal og minne* (1979), 30–3; Cook, Robert, and Mattias Tveitane, eds. *Strengleikar: An Old Norse Translation of Twenty-one Old French Lais. Edited from the Manuscript Uppsala De la Gardie 4–7—AM 666b 4°* Norsk historisk kjeldeskrift-institutt, Norrøne tekster, 3. Oslo: Kjeldeskriftfondet, 1979; Kalinke, Marianne E. "A Werewolf in Bear's Clothing." *Maal og minne* (1981), 137–44.

Tove Hovn Ohlsson

[See also: *Riddarasǫgur; Rímur; Strengleikar*]

Tobiae Comedia *see* Drama

Tools. At the beginning of the Viking period, the city with its differentiated craftsmanship was an almost unknown phenomenon in Scandinavia. The production of crafts took place in the countryside, in the village, or on individual farms. Noblemen might employ goldsmiths and other specialized craftsmen at their farms. But most craftsmen had to master several professions. This fact is reflected in, for example, the chest of tools from Mastermyr, which contains tools for both forging and woodworking, as well as scales and other equipment used in trading. The difficult land transportation routes meant that many local variations originated with regard to manufacturing. Some of these local variations remain until today, while other rural crafts were modified under the influence of city craftsmanship.

Since the individual farm or village was self-sufficient in its daily necessities, those traces of craftsmanship found in the oldest cities are, therefore, related to whatever could not be produced locally, such as combs and other craft items in bone, amber, horn, and antler, as well as jewelry and beads made of, among other substances, glass, precious metals, and bronze. For example, in Hedeby in what was then southern Denmark, a significant amount of trade was based on imported Norwegian grindstones and soapstone jars, and the making of combs depended upon raw materials from northern Scandinavia. After the initial settlement phase, new craftsmen arrived: bakers, dyers, shoemakers, and craftsmen working with various metals. Interest turned away from remote trading, and the industrial structure was adjusted to supplying the surrounding area with a varied supply of products.

The rise of the city changed the conditions for the practice of crafts. Craftsmen joined together in organizations based on common interests. They specialized and tried to keep competitors away by requiring an education. This requirement included the rule that the apprentice who finished his apprenticeship was required to travel using his crafts for a certain period of time in order to learn his profession thoroughly before he could settle down as a master. Through these wandering journeyman, the Scandinavian craftsmen came into contact with traditional city cultures in central and southern Europe. The Scandinavian city craftsman became part of a common European culture, and his tools became those used in the rest of Europe.

With Christianity, new crafts came to Scandinavia: masonry, stonecutting, lead roofing, bell molding, new techniques in wood carving, and painting, as well as the manufacture of stained-glass windows, gold altars, illuminations and frescoes, church textiles, and so on. The baking of bricks and the manufacture of lead-glazed pottery also belong to this period. Naturally, the secular noblemen understood how to take advantage of these imported craftsmen; soon the lead-glazed pitcher, the bell molder's *aquamanile*, and bronze cooking vessels adorned the nobleman's home, which was now constructed of brick instead of wood.

By fortifying the cities and by damming to create moats, a "mill privilege" was introduced: the small hand grinders and spot mills of the individual households were replaced by the craftsmanship of the professional miller, and the weaver, the baker, and the beer brewer took over those functions that had been handled by the individual household until then.

Wood crafts. In woodworking, the change from the Viking period to the Middle Ages can be described as a transition from a "green" wood technology, where newly felled wood is processed, to a "dry" wood technology, where stored wood is used in manufacturing. The green-wood technology involved splitting the wood into boards with wedges, and squaring the timber with narrow, chisel-like side axes or adzes. Even though actual planers were known in Scandinavia from the Roman Iron Age, most of the rest of the manufacturing process was done with tools that are pulled, most often with drawing knives in various shapes and mountings, rather than with planers, which are pushed. Decorative carving was done with a knife.

In dry-wood technology, the wood is cut by sawing with a pit saw, a technique that can be observed in several Romanesque roofs. The cutting of edges is done with a felling axe, and final planing with a two-handed side axe, also called the planing axe, a special development of the medieval bearded axe. In wheel making, the T-shaped long axe was used.

All wood crafts used augers, most often spoon bits, that could be mounted as breast augers in order to transfer more power. Drills were used for making hubs and for hollowing out (where drill holes are made in both ends and the remaining wood in the middle is then removed, either with a block axe—a small, chisel-shaped side axe—or with a special hollowing adze). The medieval cooper initially used axes and drawing knives, refining the work with an adze. The process resembled those primitive rural crafts preserved in modern times, where the manufacturing of wooden shoes, the hollowing out of mugs, and the production of agricultural tools were done using traditional carpenter's techniques with the block axes or adzes, and refinements with drawing knives. At the end of the Middle Ages, the cabinet maker's profession gained ground, and the use of planes spread to related woodworking professions like the carpenter's, the cooper's, and the coach builder's. Other tools introduced in the late Middle Ages were the dished wheel, the breast auger of the coach maker, and the carpenter's twybill for cutting peg holes. The small felling axe evolved into the pointed axe, both of them having handles.

In the technique of shipbuilding, the clinker-built Scandinavian boat was replaced by the carvel-built ship, but both types of construction continued to be used by boat builders and shipwrights respectively. For the Viking ships, narrow, chisel-shaped side axes were used for preparation, and drawing knives for planing. But through mutual adjustment, both crafts started using shipwright's adzes, and planes were also introduced into the process.

In northern Germany and in the Baltic region, sawmills are known to have existed since the 1300s, but these mills and the framed pit saws connected with them seem to have been unknown in Scandinavia during the Middle Ages.

Ceramic, stone, glass, and leather crafts. The ceramic tradition of prehistoric times continued throughout the Middle Ages, and into modern times as a cottage industry. Black, unglazed earthenware was manufactured on a board that one turned on one's lap. At the end of the Middle Ages, the practice of decorating the pieces with a smoothing pattern made by a stone seems to have begun. For the initial processing, most likely those tools were used that were known from more recent times: variously shaped stones for initial processing and smoothing, plus knives, pieces of iron, and wood shavings for scraping of the charred ceramics. But in connection with the introduction of tile and brick as building material during the years after the 1150s, a new type of lead-glazed ceramics is introduced, manufactured on rotating potter's wheels. The kilns, the technology, and the tools resembled those of the rest of Europe. Painting with horn and slip-covering in special vessels is unknown before the Renaissance, which also introduced the first production of tin-glazed faience tile in the 1580s. Stoneware was not produced in Scandinavia, but was imported.

During the Viking period and the early Middle Ages, soapstone vessels and grindstones were important Norwegian exports. Like the earliest building materials of stone that came to the forefront as church building expanded, these soft stones could be processed with tools resembling those used for the processing of wood.

During the 1200s, the use of square-cut granite stones increased. For the processing of these hard stones, a hoe-shaped point hammer was used, a scabbling hammer that could also be used for the making of ornamental details; possibly the runic inscriptions were cut with a similar instrument, although this cutting was most likely done with a hammer and point chisel. Various types of chisels were used for the processing of stone.

Glass production did not exist in Scandinavia before the Renaissance, but one finds glass jewelry in the style of Roman gems from the early Viking period, most likely imported from Carolingian areas, but possibly also manufactured locally; later, one finds glass beads manufactured locally, as well as imported ones. Window framing and local production of stained glass had taken place since the Romanesque period.

The tanning and shoemaking crafts followed the common European techniques from an early period. Characteristic tools are the tanner's scraping knife and the shoemaker's crescent knife, which had one handle shaped like an awl in the Middle Ages. The kinds of axe-like tools with open handle sockets already widely in use during the Roman Iron Age were probably bark spades for debarking and for the production of tanning bark.

Metal crafts. During the Viking Age and the Middle Ages, the technique of forging was no different from that known in more recent times. A small bellows was shielded against the heat of the furnace by soapstone or, later, iron. The red-hot object was grasped by a pair of blacksmith's tongs and worked on an anvil, which could be either a block anvil or an anvil with horns. In certain cases, a stone could serve as an anvil. Objects could be swage-forged as the swage was placed in a hole in the anvil. Plates could be cut with a pair of plate scissors. Metal could be filed, and iron and steel could be welded in the furnace (blacksmith welding). For molten metal, crucibles were used.

Larger bronze objects were cast using a *cire perdue* ("lost wax") process, smaller objects in molds made of sandstone or soapstone. With the building of churches, the technique of bell molding was developed, and items like censers and bronze vessels were manufactured.

During the Viking period, gold and silver could be drawn into threads with drawing irons and tongs. Tools for the manufacture of gold and silver plate are known from the same period. It could be shaped into jewelry using a bronze matrix or a wooden mold. From the early Middle Ages, we know of soldering lamps, oblong bowls used to produce the heat necessary for soldering. The various punches, chisels, engraving cutters, and other tools of the goldsmith existed in Scandinavia prior to the Viking Age.

Boiler makers (copper smiths) are mentioned in Bergen in the year 1282. The technique of drawing copper plate is also connected with religious articles, for example, the gilded Romanesque altars in Denmark and Sweden. Pewtering, lead roofing, and lamp making (tinsmithing) are techniques imported into Scadinavia during the late Middle Ages.

Textile crafts. During the Viking period and early Middle Ages, yarn was spun on a small distaff with a weight made of stone, mortar, or clay, and later on larger distaffs made entirely of wood. The spinning wheel with a spindle was not used before the Renaissance. Yarn was manufactured using ancient techniques like plaiting, knitting (from the 1400s), tying, and piece weaving. Large pieces of cloth were woven on a standing loom with loom weights. In southern Scandinavia in the 1400s (in Hedeby perhaps much earlier by Frisian weavers), this type was replaced by the horizontal loom, which gave rise to a weaving profession that was to replace production at home.

Lit.: Sehested F. *Jydepotteindustrien.* Copenhagen: Reitzel, 1881; Nyrop, C. *Danmarks gilde- og lavsskråer fra middelalderen II.* Copenhagen: Gad, 1895–1904; Lindberg, Folke. *Medeltid och äldre Vasatid. 1: Handverkarna.* Stockholm: Tiden, 1947; Møller, Elna. "Romanske tagkonstruktioner." *Årbog for nordisk Oldkyndighed og Historie* (1953), 136–50; Olsen, Olaf, and Ole Crumlin Pedersen. "The Skuldelev Ships." *Acta Archaeologica Scandinavica* 38 (1967), 73–174; Nellemann, George, and Jan Danielsen, eds. *Gamle danske håndværk.* Copenhagen: Politiken, 1971; Clarke, Helen, ed. *Iron and Man in Prehistoric Sweden.* Stockholm: Kontoret, 1979; Christophersen, Axel. *Håndverket i forandring. Studier i horn- og beinhåndverkets utvikling i Lund c:a 100–1350.* Lund: Gleerup, 1980 [English summary]; Ambrosiani, Kristina. *Viking Age Combs, Comb Making and Comb Makers.* Studies in Archaeology, 2. Stockholm: University of Stockholm, 1981; Bender Jørgensen, Lise. *Forhistoriske textiler i Skandinavien. Prehistoric Scandinavian Textiles.* Copenhagen: Det kongelige nordiske Oldskriftselskab, 1986.

Mikael Andersen

[See also: Carving: Bone, Horn, and Walrus Tusk;
Clothmaking; Crafts; Glass; Guilds; Pottery; Textiles,
Furnishing; Wood Carving]

Towns. In Scandinavia, tendencies toward urbanization cannot
be discerned clearly until the Viking Age of the 9th and 10th
centuries. Here, as in other parts of the world, a certain level of
population and food production had to be reached to create the
"surplus" needed for aggregative living in towns. In the following
period, up to about 1300, urban life became permanently rooted
in Denmark, Norway, and Sweden. In Finland, urbanization was
mainly a late-medieval phenomenon, whereas in Iceland, early
centers did not develop into towns during the Middle Ages.

The formative development of medieval Scandinavian towns
may roughly be divided into three evolutionary stages, all influenced from abroad: early economic centers, royal and ecclesiastical centers, and more fully developed medieval towns. These stages
do not always coincide in the various regions of Scandinavia, and
they overlap to a large extent.

The first tendencies toward urbanization, that is, nucleation
of settlement with a general central function, appear along the
main trading routes of the Merovingian and Viking ages. From
continental Europe, such lines of communication led along rivers
and overland toward the Baltic and Jutland. Jutland was also reached
along the northwest continental coast. From Jutland, seaways
branched out along the southern shore of the Baltic, toward the
island of Gotland and the Lake Mälaren area of Sweden, and toward the Oslofjord region of Norway.

From the Merovingian Age and even earlier, if one takes into
consideration the excavated craft and trading center at Helgö in
Mälaren, the transshipment, exchange, and redistribution of commodities were centralized in places along the lines of communication mentioned. At the same time, the production of professional
craftsmen tended to attach itself to the early trading centers. In this
fashion, several localities acquired economically central functions.
Best known is Hedeby/Schleswig at the foot of Jutland.

In the Viking Age, economic centers of this type gained in
number and importance. It is difficult to assess to what extent the
exchange of goods and production of craftsmen in such places
were seasonal and to what extent they brought about permanent
occupation. In most cases, such activities probably had a largely
seasonal character. But permanent settlement has been proven
archaeologically in some of the early centers. In a few exceptional
cases, it is even justifiable to speak of towns. Judged by the size of
the built-up areas within their semicircular earth banks, their supposed numbers of inhabitants, and their general centrality, both
Hedeby and Birka in the Mälaren area may be termed "urban
centers" in the 10th century.

The continued development of trade and related production
led to the emergence of new, both seasonal and permanently settled,
economic centers in the centuries following the Viking Age. In the
11th and 12th centuries, the initial development of quite a few
towns in central parts of Scandinavia may be described in this
way. At the same time, such trading centers spread to more remote
areas. In Iceland, they did not develop in the Middle Ages beyond
the stages of seasonal marketplaces and fishing harbors.

Early centers did not, however, base their existence on economic activities alone. Royal protection and support were probably important for the emergence of Hedeby and Birka, and of
other Viking Age centers as well, such as that of Skíringssalr or
Kaupang at the mouth of Oslofjord. The early missionary church

established itself in Hedeby and two other Jutish trading places,
Ribe and Århus, adding a new dimension to their central function.
Thus, already in the Viking Age, there are foreshadowings of the
main forces at work in the next stage of urbanization.

From the 11th century, a broader wave of urbanization was
set in motion, probably because of a special organizing effort made
by a royal power aspiring to unite larger parts of the later Scandinavian kingdoms in close cooperation with the Christian Church.
Monarchy and Church were capable of effecting something that
had not been possible in the preceding period, when political
power was mostly local and legal-administrative and cultic functions as yet mainly of a periodic character. Governed by political,
administrative, and military considerations, the two powers started
to develop more densely populated and built-up settlements, some
of them earlier trading places. These settlements came to function
not least as fiscal centers in which were increasingly gathered royal,
ecclesiastical, and aristocratic revenues in kind. In their turn, such
centers came to act as magnets on trade and specialized crafts,
attracting such activities from a wider network of older, largely
seasonal and less-established centers.

In Denmark, royal minting places and administrative centers
were obviously important as points of departure for the development of some of the towns (*civitates*) mentioned by Adam of
Bremen in the 1070s: Viborg, Odense, Roskilde, and Lund. Adam's
other towns were also minting places: Ålborg, Hedeby, Ribe, and
Århus. The combination of royal centers and episcopal sees was
effective in creating urban settlements, as attested by the cases of
Lund and Roskilde. Urbanization picked up speed from the end of
the 10th century, when royal power had been established over the
whole of Denmark.

In the Valdemarian era from the latter half of the 12th century, Danish towns started to spread from protected situations
inland or at narrow inlets to the open coasts. This pattern partly
had to do with the sheltering functions of royal and other strongholds. The Valdemarian kings included such strongholds together
with older urban centers in their administrative system.

In Norway, there is probably a solid historical foundation for
the persistent view of later saga writers that the kings from the
11th century acted as promoters of towns. An important part of
their urbanizing record is the establishment of the first episcopal
sees. In its efforts toward political unification, Norwegian royal
power had indeed very good strategic reasons for promoting towns,
such as Trondheim, Bergen, Oslo, Borg (present Sarpsborg), and
Kongehelle (at the Göta River), all of them, together with Tønsberg,
mentioned by Odericus Vitalis as coastal *civitates* in 1135.

In Sweden, political unification and the building of a state-
like political organization came later than in Denmark and Norway, and it took longer for Christianity to become firmly established. This combination may help to explain the relatively late
urbanization of Sweden. As a combined royal and ecclesiastical
urban center, only Sigtuna in the Mälaren area goes back to the
11th century. In West Sweden, Skara may have been in the process of becoming a town-like ecclesiastical center in the same century, to be supplemented by the stronghold of Lödöse at the Göta
River as a royal center in the late 12th century. In this century, the
other episcopal sees of medieval Sweden also started to develop
into central places of urban character.

In the 13th century, the rapid urbanization of East Sweden
probably owed much to the fact that it was now also the power
base of a more state-like Swedish kingdom. Royal strongholds,
such as Kalmar and Stockholm, became focal points of urbaniza-

tion, possibly planted as parts of a more elaborate and centralized administrative system (Andersson 1985).

In the 13th century, the last and most expansive of the three formative stages of medieval Scandinavian urbanization was well on its way. The term "fully developed medieval town" implies a system of self-government based on explicit privileges and urban codes, with the town council as the leading authority from the middle of the 13th century. The monarchy could create formal towns, legally separated from the surrounding countryside, and this creation had obviously happened to a certain extent before the 13th century. From now on, towns generally functioned as legal and administrative enclaves. Throughout the rest of the Middle Ages, there was a clear tendency in royal legislation to give such enclaves a monopoly on more professional trade. In Denmark, regal rights over towns were also delegated, although in relatively few cases, to bishops and princely magnates.

There is little doubt that because of the "commercial revolution" of the High Middle Ages, economic activity from the 12th and 13th centuries became a particularly important urbanizing factor in Scandinavia. In North European commerce, the east-west axis between the Baltic and the North Sea grew into the most important one, involving Denmark and branching out toward Norway, Sweden, and Finland. The North German Hanseatic traders became the completely dominant group of merchants exploiting the new commercial possibilities. They opened up new European markets for the exports of Scandinavia, notably Swedish copper and iron, Scanian herring, and Norwegian stockfish.

Bergen, originally the royal and ecclesiastical center of West Norway, developed in the 12th century into the first international commercial town of Scandinavia. In the following century, it obtained a virtual monopoly as a staple port for foreign trade with North and West Norway and the tributary Atlantic islands. The town became the center of a satellite system of smaller towns and marketplaces farther north, including the seasonal trading places of Iceland. In the 13th century, it may also be called the first political capital of Norway.

From about 1200, the herring fisheries and connected international fairs of Scania started to expand rapidly, making a heavy impact on urban development in Scania and the neighboring areas of Blekinge and Halland, at that time a part of the Danish kingdom. In Denmark, the fairs of Scania apparently became the all-important channel of importation for most towns. Only Ribe and possibly Schleswig kept up a more independent foreign trade. Local trade was probably more decisive than long-distance trade for the emergence of most of the numerous small towns of high-medieval Denmark.

In Sweden, the commercial expansion of the 13th century led to a pronounced growth of towns, particularly in the Mälaren area and other eastern regions connected with the Baltic. The economic base of the rapid urbanization was made up of agricultural produce and, increasingly, of iron and copper mining. From the middle of the century, Stockholm rapidly achieved a dominant position as the staple port for the Mälaren area and the coastal districts of the northern Baltic. In this respect, it acquired a function comparable to that of Bergen in northwestern Scandinavia. Again like Bergen, it grew into the chief political and administrative center of its kingdom.

Few important towns expanded as purely commercial centers in high-medieval Scandinavia. Visby in Gotland is the most notable exception, because of its unique geographical position. Of

the new and mainly economic centers of the 13th century, Malmö in Scania was probably the most important. In most other cases, towns that one-sidedly based their existence on trade and specialized production tended to be relatively small. Most of the more important towns taking advantage of the great commercial changes were royal and/or ecclesiastical centers as well, as in the cases of Bergen and Stockholm.

By the mid-14th century, the medieval urbanization of the central parts of Scandinavia had largely been completed. The general decline of population and agrarian production in the following half century must have affected urban development. Some smaller towns disappeared, and contraction of settlement occurred in others. Still, a few new towns emerged even in the second half of the 14th century, and more appeared throughout the rest of the Middle Ages, not least in peripheral areas, such as Sweden north of the Mälaren area and Finland. In more central districts, old towns soon started to grow again. The increased volume of commercial shipping through the Sound gave a new impetus to the urbanization of the coastal regions on both sides and east of the Kattegat. Here, the expansion of old towns and the foundation of new ones were particularly striking in the 15th century. In 1417, Copenhagen was annexed by the Crown from the bishop of Roskilde. It grew into the largest and most important town in Denmark and obtained the position as the political capital of Denmark-Norway.

Denmark, as the most populous and densely settled medieval kingdom in Scandinavia, including the southernmost regions of present Sweden (Scania, Halland, and Blekinge), was also the most urbanized one. At the end of the Middle Ages, formal Danish towns numbered about 100. The kingdom of Sweden, including Finland, came to comprise about forty towns; the kingdom of Norway, including the present Swedish county of Bohuslän, had only fifteen. In addition, there were quite a few town-like ports and trading places without formal town status. Within the borders of the present Nordic countries, there were about seventy towns in Denmark and Sweden respectively, twelve in Norway, and six in Finland.

It is impossible to calculate the number of inhabitants in any medieval Scandinavian town. But most urban settlements were obviously quite small, numbering their populations only in hundreds and, at the most, in low thousands. Only in a handful of cases is there reason to believe that urban settlements grew into middle-sized towns by contemporary European standards, in the range of 5,000–10,000 permanent inhabitants. The international trading center of Bergen was probably the first Nordic town to reach this size, around 1300. In the late Middle Ages, it may have been followed by Stockholm, Visby, and Copenhagen. Still, as centers of royal and ecclesiastical government, administration, and specialized economic activities, the Scandinavian towns were by far more important for the surrounding territories than their number of inhabitants would seem to indicate.

By European standards, the medieval towns of Scandinavia were quite simply built. Timber was originally the dominant building material, and remained so to the end of the Middle Ages in the kingdoms of Norway and Sweden. In Denmark, half-timbering grew in importance from the 13th century and apparently came to dominate in the late Middle Ages. Building in natural stone was restricted mainly to churches, monasteries, castles, and palaces. It rarely occurred in ordinary urban tenements, and then mostly in the form of late-medieval stone cellars, used as cool and fireproof storerooms. Visby was a notable exception, because of ample supplies of chalk and good building stone. From the 13th century, brick building ousted building in natural stone in Danish and Swedish towns. Still, it had only exceptionally come into common use at the end of the Middle Ages, as in the cases of Stockholm and Malmö.

The use of urban fortifications apparently became quite widespread in Denmark, but only in the form of earth walls with palisades and ditches. In Sweden, they were rarer, and in Norway, almost nonexistent. At a later stage, stone walls with towers surrounded only a few Swedish and Danish towns, such as Visby, Stockholm, Kalmar, Kalundborg, Vordingborg, Copenhagen, and in part a few other towns.

Even if the conciliar towns of high- and late-medieval Scandinavia were allowed a measure of self-government, they were far from having the autonomy enjoyed by many European towns, notably in North Italy, in the northwest Continent, and partly in Germany. The Crown never ceased to control the towns through its urban bailiffs or other representatives. The position of royal officials may still have been somewhat stronger in Norway and Sweden than in Denmark. In this as in other respects, the Danish medieval towns were closer to European models than the towns of the neighboring Scandinavian kingdoms.

Bib.: *Bibliography of Urban History: Denmark, Finland, Norway, Sweden.* Stockholm: Stadshistoriska institutionen, 1960 [a continuation up to 1985 is being prepared]; Jansen, Henrik M., et al., eds. *A Select Bibliography of Danish Works on the History of Towns, Published 1960–1976.* Skrifter fra Institut for Historie og Samfundsvidenskab, Historie, 21. Odense: Odense Universitet, 1977; Jansen, Henrik M., et al., eds. *A Select Bibliography of Danish Works on the History of Towns Published 1979–1982.* Brede: 1983 [photocopy]; Dahlbäck, Göran. "Svensk medeltid i historiskt perspektiv." In *Svensk medeltidsforskning idag.* Ed. Göran Dahlbäck. Uppsala: Humanistisk-samhällsvetenskapliga forskningsrådet, 1987, pp. 33–40; Federspiel, Søren, and Thomas Riis. *A Select Bibliography of Danish Works on the History of Towns Published 1983–1987.* Byhistoriske hjælpemidler, 8. Odense: Dansk komité for byhistorie, 1989; Riis, Thomas, and Paul Strømsted. *A Select Bibliography of Danish Works on the History of Towns Published 1988–1989.* Byhistoriske hjælpemidler, 9. Odense: Dansk komité for byhistorie, 1990. **Lit.**: *Medeltidsstaden. Rapporter* 1–71. Stockholm: Riksantikvarieämbetet och Statens Historiska Museer, 1976– [a series of individual reports on all the formal medieval towns of present Sweden, published by the Swedish Medieval Towns Project. Most reports have already appeared; only four remain. A preliminary summary has been prepared in English: Andersson, Hans. *The Medieval Towns Project. Summary 1985. Preliminary Version for the Symposium to Be Held in Kungälv, 28–30 October 1985.* Stockholm: Riksantikvarieämbetet, 1985]; Blom, Grethe Authén, ed. *Middelaldersteder.* Urbaniseringsprosessen i Norden, 1. Oslo: Universitetsforlaget, 1977 [national reports, submitted to the Nordic conference of historians in Trondheim 1977, on the status of medieval urban research in all the present Scandinavian countries, with useful bibliographies]; Christensen, Aksel E., et al., eds. *Danmarks historie.* Vols. 1–2:1. Copenhagen: Gyldendal, 1977–80; Lund, Niels, and Kai Hørby. *Samfundet i tidlig vikingtid og tidlig middelalder.* Dansk socialhistorie, 2. Copenhagen: Gyldendal, 1980; *Medeltidsstaden. Rapporter* 1– . Helsingfors: Museiverket, 1981– [a series of individual reports being published on medieval Finnish towns, corresponding to the above-mentioned Swedish series under the same title]; Helle, Knut.

Kongssete og kjøpstad. Fra opphavet til 1536. Bergens bys historie, 1. Bergen: Universitetsforlaget, 1982 [the latest historical monograph on a Norwegian medieval town (Bergen)]; *Prosjekt Middelalderbyen* 1–. Ed. Statens Humanistiske Forskningsråd. Århus: Centrum, 1985– [a series of monographs being published on a selection of Danish medieval towns by the Danish Medieval Towns Project, with English summaries]; Andrén, Anders. *Den urbana scenen. Städer och samhälle i det medeltida Danmark.* Acta archaeologica Lundensia, Series in 8°, 13. Malmö: Gleerup, 1985 [a comprehensive treatment of Danish medieval urbanization, with English summary]. Andrén, Anders. "State and Towns in the Middle Ages: The Scandinavian Experience." *Theory and Society* 18 (1989), 585–609. In Norway there is no comprehensive medieval-towns project, but Riksantikvaren (Central Office of National Antiquity), Oslo, publishes reports on archaeological investigations in the various medieval towns.

Knut Helle

[See also: Architecture; Birka; Coins and Mints; Denmark; Fortification; Hanseatic League; Hedeby; Houses, Urban; Iceland; Kaupang; Norway; Royal Administration and Finances; Sweden; Trade]

Trade. In the Viking Age, trade in the North Sea and Baltic area seems to have been primarily over long distances with luxury products for the upper classes. Practically nothing is known of local trade, which was probably insignificant; peasants produced most of what they needed on the farm.

Scandinavian merchants carried goods between the Scandinavian and Slavonic parts of northern Europe and the more developed regions of western Europe and the Byzantine and Arab empires.

The main goods from the North were furs and slaves. Some of the furs came from northern Sweden and Norway, but most were bought in what was formerly the Soviet Union. Norwegian merchants and chieftains sailed north to Finnmark and to the White Sea and obtained furs through trade, taxation, and plunder. The largest quantities were obtained by Swedes in the eastern Baltic.

Scandinavians captured or bought slaves mainly in the former Soviet Union, and sold them both in western Europe and in the East. Viking pirates also took prisoners in western Europe and sold them as slaves in Scandinavia and probably in the East. In Hedeby, Ansgar (ca. 850) saw a group of slaves bound together by chains around the neck. Among them was a nun who had been taken prisoner somewhere in western Europe.

From western Europe, the Scandinavians bought woolen cloth, swords, pottery, and glass, from Byzantium cloth of wool and silk, and from the Arabs silver in the form of coins.

The main trade route of the Scandinavian merchants went from the river Rhine via Lake Ladoga to Constantinople. Few merchants covered all that distance; the goods could change hands several times.

In the Viking Age, the Rhine area was the most economically advanced part of northern Europe. The main city was Cologne; the main trading center toward the North Sea was Dorestad. From here, goods were brought to Hedeby near the present-day Schleswig. Eastward from Hedeby, the main route went along the Swedish coast to Birka in Lake Mälaren. This site was the central district of the Swedish kingdom, where the merchants found aristocratic customers with tastes for their goods. Those who wanted to go farther east crossed the Baltic and entered Lake Ladoga.

From there, a northern route reached the upper Volga and Bulgar, the capital of the Volga-Bulgars. Here, Scandinavians traded with Arab merchants. A few Scandinavians continued down to the Caspian Sea and even reached Baghdad. The Arab author al-Mas'ūdī (*ca.* 900–950) writes that Northmen had settled in the town of Atli, where the Volga flows into the Caspian. A southern route from Lake Ladoga followed the river Volkhov to Novgorod, then to Smolensk and along the Dnieper via Kiev to the Black Sea. The ultimate goal was Constantinople.

Denmark and Norway were attached to this great west-east trade route at Hedeby. The chieftain Óttarr (Old English Ohthere; *ca.* 880) probably lived somewhere in Troms in northern Norway. It took him one month to sail down to the trading center of Skíringssalr in Vestfold, "if he set up camp at night and the winds were favorable." From there, he sailed in five days to Hedeby.

It is often said that Óttarr traveled from Hedeby to King Alfred's court by crossing the Jutland peninsula and then crossing the North Sea to England. However, Óttarr himself does not say that he visited Hedeby and England on the same journey (*Orosius*, Book 1). In Óttarr's day, Norwegians regularly crossed the North Sea to England directly from western Norway. Danes also sailed directly to England from western Jutland, particularly the Liim Fjord area. Not all trade went via the great west-east route.

About 970, the journeys of the Swedes along the Russian rivers seem to have ended. The Scandinavians did not go further than Novgorod and the estuary ports of the great Baltic rivers. Local merchants took over the inland trade. Several explanations have been given for this change. The silver production in the Arab territories south of the Caspian Sea decreased sharply, and so did the profits of the Scandinavian merchants who traded there. But the fundamental cause must have been that the Scandinavians who had settled there intermarried with Slavs and became part of a local merchant class.

The traditional view has been that Scandinavian seafarers in the Viking Age were mainly pirates. Nobody has disputed the fact that some Scandinavian merchants traded on the route from Dorestad to Constantinople. But traders from Dorestad via Hedeby to Birka in Sweden and Skíringssalr in Norway were said to have been mainly Frisians who lived at the coast betwen the rivers Rhine and Weser. This view has been challenged by several historians, most prominent among them A. E. Christensen. The sources on this subject are scarce.

The first leg of the journey was from the Rhine to Hedeby. Rimbert (*ca.* 880) writes that many of the inhabitants of Hedeby were christened in Dorestad and Hamburg around 850. Since then, merchants from Dorestad and Sachsen had visited Hedeby, "which was earlier impossible." The last sentence should not be taken literally, but it is evident that Scandinavians as well as Frisians and Germans traveled between Hedeby and the Rhine area. Traditionally, it has been assumed that the goods went by ship from Dorestad along the Frisian coast and across Jutland to Hedeby. However, Ansgar traveled in 826 overland from Dorestad to Hedeby. The better-known trade routes of the 12th century also went by land. The Scandinavian merchants were primarily seafarers; it is therefore reasonable to assume that the Scandinavians were a minority.

The traffic from Hedeby northward and eastward, however, went by sea. We have no evidence that Frisian ships or merchants ever sailed from Hedeby or in Baltic, Danish, and Norwegian waters.

The strongest argument for Frisian presence in the Baltic has been two runic stones in Birka from around 1050–1100, which say that members of the "Frisian guild" erected the stones in memory of guild brothers. But it may just as well have been a guild of Birka merchants who traveled together to Dorestad. The evidence indicates that Scandinavians controlled the trade east and north of Hedeby.

Scandinavian trade inside Russia is equally controversial. There is general agreement that Scandinavians traveled far inside Russia to obtain furs. But traders along the Russian rivers are called "Rūs'" in the sources, and there is some controversy about how many of them were of Scandinavian and how many of Slavic origin. The Rūs' settled more or less permanently as chieftains and merchants along the main trade routes: from Lake Ladoga along the upper reaches of the Volga to Bulgar (near today's Kazan), and on the route from Ladoga to the Black Sea near the later cities of Novgorod, Smolensk, and Kiev. The Byzantine author Constantine Porphyrogenitos (*ca.* 950) tells how the Rūs' during the winter visited the local tribes whom they had subjugated and demanded taxes, which were paid mainly in furs. In spring, many of them assembled in Kiev and sailed to Constantinople. At least in the Ladoga area, the Rūs' were Scandinavians; the same identification applies to many of those settled farther north and south.

Loyn (1977) has stressed that the Scandinavian Viking Age merchants helped to start English maritime trade and urban life after the "Dark Ages."

Óttarr is the only Viking Age Scandinavian merchant whose social background is known from contemporary sources. He was no professional merchant; his main income came from agriculture and taxation. Most Scandinavian merchants must have been peasant-merchants or chieftain-merchants. The peasant-merchants of Gotland were particularly active. Up to 1951, Arab Viking Age coins were found in these quantities: around 400 in Norway, 4,000 in Denmark, but 80,000 in Sweden; of the latter, around 70 percent were found in Gotland.

In the trading centers of Hedeby, Birka, and Skíringssalr, many of the houses were probably inhabited only during the market time. But Rimbert's account and archaeological excavations show that at least some of the houses were inhabited by merchants and others who must have lived there all year. But the vast majority of Scandinavian Viking Age merchants combined commerce with other occupations.

The commercial revolution. About 1100, a commercialization of the European economies started that has continued up to the present. More people sold a larger part of what they produced, and bought more of the goods they consumed. The first stage of this development up to the Black Death (1349) has been called "the commercial revolution of the Middle Ages." In Scandinavia, it changed trade in two important ways. Goods of mass consumption entered long-distance trade for the first time, and German urban merchants took over long-distance trade from Scandinavian peasant-merchants and chieftain-merchants.

The commercial revolution in this first stage concerned only those people who had access to goods that were in demand in distant markets. From Scandinavia, mainly fish, metals, and to some degree butter and meat entered long-distance trade. The great majority of peasants were not able to produce a marketable surplus of these goods, and were little affected. Fishing in Iceland, Norway, and Scania and iron mining in Sweden mainly provided subsidiary incomes for peasants who continued to cultivate their farms. In the Swedish copper and silver mines from the 13th century and the 15th-century fishing villages of Finnmark and Iceland, however, some professional miners and fishermen were found.

The merchants first developed the resources that demanded the least capital and organization to exploit. Stockfish from the Lofoten Islands was the first Scandinavian-produced commodity sold in larger quantities on North European markets, from about 1100. The fishermen dried the fish themselves, and up to about 1350 mostly sold it to merchants at an annual market in Vågan in Lofoten. These "merchants" were partly rich peasants and landowners from the fishing districts, partly townsmen of Bergen and Trondheim. They transported the fish in small coastal cargo vessels down to Bergen, and, up to around 1310, also to Trondheim. There, they sold it to export merchants who sent the goods on larger vessels to England before 1460, and to the Rhine area and Lübeck after 1250.

Commercial stockfish production in Iceland started around 1320–1340. Up to 1412, it reached European markets via Bergen. From 1100 to 1412, the English imported all their stockfish from that town. In 1412, however, English merchants started to sail directly to Iceland and bought stockfish from Icelandic fishermen. The English built seasonal trading stations in the main fishing villages, some of which were manned also in winter. From about 1470, German merchants, mainly from Hamburg and Bremen, started to sail to Iceland in large numbers. They allied themselves with the Icelandic authorities, and in 1470–1540 chased the English from their trading stations.

Before 1200, the Scanian herring fisheries were drawn into international commerce. The fishermen were mainly Danish peasants. They sold the catch fresh to merchants when coming ashore from Lübeck and other Hansa towns along the southern shore of the Baltic, North Sea, and Zuiderzee. Most of the salting was done near the towns of Skanør and Falsterbo. Each of the larger German towns had a limited area on the shore where their merchants constructed huts, salted herring, and traded. Some towns even had their own bailiffs who passed judgments in conflicts among Hansa merchants. The Scania herring was exported to Hansa ports, such as Lübeck and Kampen, and transported to German inland cities. The fisheries declined after about 1400 because of competition from Dutch herring fisheries in the North Sea; possibly there were also fewer herring.

The start of Swedish commercial mining has been much discussed. Today, most historians assume that industrial mining for export belongs to the period after 1250. The mining districts were north and northwest of Stockholm. Miners and farmers brought the metals down to small Mälar towns like Västerås, Örebro, Köping, Enköping, and Arboga in winter on sledges, and sold them to local merchants. In spring, metals were sent in small cargo vessels to Stockholm and sold to export merchants. These buyers were almost exclusively Hansa merchants; some settled in Stockholm, some in Lübeck. The markets for Swedish metals were in the Baltic and in Flanders.

Denmark in the Middle Ages included today's southern Sweden. Apart from Scania herring, the main exports from medieval Denmark were meat, butter, and some grain produced on the manors of nobles and on peasant farms. From 1200 to 1350, most of it was probably sold at the Scanian Fair. As this fair gradually lost its importance in the later Middle Ages, more of the export went by small cargo vessels directly from the production areas to Danish and the nearest North German towns. In 1399/1400, more than 500 small vessels sailed annually from Denmark with agricultural products to Lübeck. Most of these vessels belonged to Danish noblemen, peasants, and small traders. After 1400, citizens of towns in Schleswig-Holstein, Hamburg, Lübeck, and Lüneburg bought cattle in Jutland in the autumn, and drove them to their home towns.

Scandinavian imports were dominated by three products: cloth, salt, and grain. Members of the upper classes used foreign cloth in their everyday dress, and peasants used it on special occasions. The Italian merchant Pietro Querini suffered shipwreck and came ashore at the island of Røst in Lofoten in 1432. He was surprised to discover that the peasant-fishermen wore English cloth. Up to about 1440, most of the cloth imported to Sweden and Denmark was Flemish; during the rest of the Middle Ages, Holland dominated. English cloth became important at the end of the 15th century. Norway and Iceland followed the same pattern, except that English cloth already had an important share of the market in the 12th century.

Salt was used for preservation of food. In northern Scandinavia, the climate was so dry and cold that drying in the wind and/or smoking was sufficient to preserve both fish and meat. In Norway and Iceland, salt imports were insignificant in the Middle Ages; the limited production of sea salt sufficed. Sweden and Denmark, however, needed considerable quantities for their herring fisheries. Up to 1350, the salt mines of Lüneburg, owned by Lübeck merchants, were the main suppliers. In the following period, the sea salt of Brittany and later Spain and Portugal dominated.

The need for imported grain was largest in the North. It is too cold for growing corn in normal years north of Malangen in Norway. Farther south, the growing season is so short that the crop often fails to ripen in cold summers. The scarce Icelandic crops gave the Icelanders only a small fraction of what in southern Scandinavia was considered normal consumption. By bartering stockfish for grain, Scandinavian fishermen received two to seven times more calories than they gave away. The fishermen of northern Norway took advantage of these favorable prices, and from about 1250 onward they consumed considerable quantities of rye imported from the Baltic. Before 1320, they also got regular supplies of English wheat. The Icelanders' diet included comparatively little grain; they lived mainly on meat, milk, butter, and fish. Up to 1412, grain imports were minimal, but from 1412, the English merchants and from 1470 the Germans increased the supply. Denmark, Sweden, and eastern Norway produced enough grain to satisfy the needs of the inhabitants. In normal years, the surplus of the countryside was just sufficient to supply the towns.

The commercial revolution, with greater quantities of bulkier goods, led to changes in trade routes and merchant groups. Bulky goods like grain, salt, fish, and metals had to be transported by sea rather than by land. After 1150, German merchants took over an increasing part of Scandinavian long-distance trade, and they dominated completely after about 1310.

At the close of the Viking Age, trade between western and northeastern Europe was conducted on a main route from the Rhine area to Novgorod, with a side branch up to Norway and Iceland. This structure remained to the end of the Middle Ages. As mentioned above, German and Frisian merchants probably already controlled most of the trade from the Rhine area to Hedeby during the Viking Age. Hedeby was in the domain of the Danish king, and most of its inhabitants were probably Scandinavians. In

1158, Lübeck, the first German town on the Baltic, was founded. It became the point of departure for German expansion into the Baltic and Scandinavia. In the Baltic, the main traders at the end of the Viking Age were the peasant-merchants of Gotland. In 1161, the Germans traded in Visby on Gotland; in 1165, in Novgorod. Before 1300, German merchants controlled almost all long-distance trade in the Baltic. All through the Middle Ages, Lübeck was an important distribution center for western goods to Scandinavia.

However, from 1200, the main distribution centers for West European goods to eastern Scandinavia were the towns of Skanør and Falsterbo, where the herring fisheries generated the largest market in northeastern Europe, the Scanian Fair. Merchants from Lübeck with their western goods met with merchants, landowners, and peasants from Denmark, Sweden, eastern Norway, and the rest of the Baltic.

From 1250, ships started to arrive in Scania from Kampen and other towns around the North Sea. For the first time, a direct shipping route connected the North Sea and the Baltic. Over the following 250 years, direct shipping between towns in the Baltic and the North Sea increased, while the route via Lübeck and the Scanian Fair declined. The Dutch commercial expansion into the Baltic started after 1400, and they made Gdansk their main port. Swedish metals were originally sent via Lübeck; the iron went mainly via Gdansk after 1400.

Western Norway kept up its direct trade to other North Sea ports all through the Middle Ages. After 1310, German merchants almost monopolized the export. They sold fish from Bergen to Brügge, Amsterdam, Deventer, Bremen, and Lübeck, and Boston in England.

Hansa merchants. During the last 200 years of the Middle Ages, German merchants controlled almost all long-distance trade in Scandinavian waters. How did they organize their trade, and why were they so strong?

The Hansa existed from 1161 to 1169. It was originally an organization of merchants from North German towns, which historians called "the merchant Hansa." In 1356, it was transformed into an organization of the hometowns of these merchants, "the town Hansa." The purpose was to defend the interests of merchants in foreign countries.

The Hansa had two roots. When German merchants sailed in convoy to, or traded in, a foreign market, they often elected an alderman and formed a temporary organization, often called a "Hansa." The German merchants sailing from Lübeck to Gotland formed such a Hansa called "Merchants of the Roman (*i.e.*, German) Empire visiting Gotland." Because most German merchants in the Baltic started from Lübeck and sailed via Gotland, the Gotland Hansa grew into a permanent organization that also defended merchant interests outside Gotland. The Gotland Hansa is first mentioned in 1161, three years after the founding of Lübeck. This year is usually considered the starting year of the Hansa.

These merchant Hansas had no power to oblige merchants to follow a common policy. Only the councils of their hometowns could do that. After the breakdown of imperial power in 1254, several urban leagues were formed in Germany. It was common for representatives of town councils to meet and coordinate their actions. In 1356, the German merchants in Bruges had a conflict with local authorities. Lübeck then summoned councilors of the towns sending merchants to Bruges to discuss concerted action, the first meeting of the diet of the town Hansa.

The diet did not meet every year, but was summoned by the town council of Lübeck when there were problems to be dis-

cussed. The Hansa towns were never strong enough to make war on any of the Scandinavian nations on their own. But before the Reformation, they were strong enough to be a valuable ally when Scandinavian countries clashed. By skillfully shifting alliance partners, the Hansa towns obtained favorable trade privileges in all the Scandinavian countries. Their greatest triumph was the league of Cologne in 1367, when they allied themselves with Sweden, Holstein, and Mecklenburg against Denmark and Norway. At the peace conference in 1370, they obtained control of the fortification along Øresund and at the Scania market for fifteen years.

The real strength of the Hansa merchants did not lie in military power, but in economic organization. In the Viking Age, only a small minority of Scandinavian merchants were professional. After 1100, an increasing number of them settled in towns. But as late as 1300, many of the Norwegians sending ships and goods to England, Iceland, and Greenland were churchmen, landowners, and rich peasants who lived only part of the year in town. Most Scandinavian merchants in Gotland were peasants. The Scandinavians traveled from marketplace to marketplace with their goods.

The Hansa merchants, however, were professionals, which enabled them to organize their trade in a new and more effective manner from about 1250 onward. The merchant capitalist no longer traveled with his goods, but sat in his office in his hometown and wrote letters to agents in foreign trade markets. Inside Germany, these agents were usually local merchants; Hansa merchants bought and sold goods for each other. To Scandinavia they sent servants or junior partners, who lived there for longer periods. When there were many of them in a town, they elected aldermen and formed an organization. Such Hanseatic trading stations were found in almost all the larger Scandinavian towns in the period 1300–1500.

The Hanseatic trade organization was the most effective in northern Europe 1250–1450. The Hansa merchants had wider trade contacts than other merchants and could offer their customers more and cheaper goods than their Scandinavian colleagues.

Many Hansa merchants came to Scandinavia for some weeks or months every summer. The Scanian Fair is the best example of this practice. But many stayed for years or a lifetime as representatives of merchants in Hansa towns. The largest Hanseatic colonies were found in Stockholm and Bergen. These towns also represented two opposite ways of integrating the Germans socially and politically into urban society.

The Germans in Stockholm had no special guild or organization; there was no need for it. Hansa merchants in Stockholm retained citizenship in their German hometowns. But that affiliation did not prevent many of them from also being citizens of Stockholm; double citizenship was common. Hansa merchants who owned a house in the town were given the same political rights as Swedes, paid the same taxes, and had the same duties. They were eligible for election to the ruling body of the town, the council, and the office of mayor. These Germans came to Stockholm with their families. While buying and selling on behalf of merchants in their hometowns, mostly Lübeck, they also traded on their own. Their children often stayed in Sweden and founded native Swedish merchant families. The number of Germans in Stockholm was at its highest in the years 1350–1400. At the end of the 15th century, there was an upsurge of national feeling in Sweden, and after 1471 only citizens of Swedish towns could be elected to councils and mayorships.

In Bergen, on the other hand, the Hansa merchants had a strong organization, called "the Kontor." At its maximum in 1450–1550, it organized about 1,000 Germans who lived there all year, and an additional 1,000 who came to trade there in summer. By comparison, Bergen had around 6,000 Norwegian townsmen. The resident Germans were bound by the statutes of the Kontor to remain unmarried while in Bergen, and they returned to their hometowns when they had earned enough money to establish a household of their own. They were all servants or junior partners of merchants in their hometowns. They owned houses in Bergen and were engaged in the stockfish trade. The resident Germans elected aldermen who represented them before local authorities. The aldermen were dependent on support from, and received orders from, the Hanseatic Diet and the council of Lübeck. Most of the Germans brought weapons to Bergen. During a conflict in 1455, they killed the royal bailiff, the bishop, and sixty other Norwegians. This conflict was an exception; they rarely used their actual military control of the town. Most of their houses were situated in a special quarter, Bryggen. Here, the aldermen exercised jurisdiction in cases between Germans. In practice, they did not respect Norwegian law regulating exchange of goods, duration of stay, and so on.

In other Scandinavian towns, we find elements of both patterns. Swedish towns followed Stockholm. In Oslo and Tønsberg, the Hansa merchants had their organization and sat in the council. In the Danish towns, there were fewer resident Germans because so much of the trade was done at the fair in Scania, and because the distance to the Hansa towns was so short. They were eligible for the council, but they were rarely elected. In the towns along Øresund, they had their own organizations, but not in Jutland and on Funen.

About 1100, the medieval commercial revolution started a process of economic integration in northern Europe. In the first medieval phase, it concerned limited sections of the Scandinavia economies, mainly fish and metals and to some degree butter and meat. The Hansa merchants created these economic links between Scandinavia and Europe.

Lit.: Welin, Ulla S. Linder, and Beatrice Gramberg. "Arabiska mynt." KLNM 1 (1956), 182–94; Arbman, Holger, and Ella Kivikoski. "Birkahandel." KLNM 1 (1956), 582–87; Blom, Grethe Authen, et al. Hansestæderne og Norden. Århus: Universitetsforlaget, 1957; rpt. 1972; Rafto, Thorolf, et al. "Englandshandel." KLNM 3 (1958), 658–76; Hald, Kristian. "Frisere." KLNM 4 (1959), 643–7; Kumlien, Kjell, et al. "Hansan." KLNM 6 (1961), 195–216; Blindheim, Charlotte, et al. "Handelsplasser." KLNM 6 (1961), 133–46; Yrwing, Hugo. "Handelssjöfart." KLNM 6 (1961), 158–62; Enemark, Poul. "Hedebyhandel." KLNM 6 (1961), 273–8; Hoffmann, Marta, et al. "Klede." KLNM 8 (1963), 457–74; Enemark, Poul, et al. "Kornhandel." KLNM 9 (1964), 147–62; Weibull, Curt. "Lübecks handel och sjøfart på de nordiska rikerna 1368 och 1398–1400." Scandia 31 (1966), 1–123; Yrwing, Hugo, et al. "Rysslandshandel." KLNM 14 (1969), 528–34; Yrwing, Hugo, et al. "Salthandel." KLNM 14 (1969), 700–13; Yrwing, Hugo, et al. "Smörhandel." KLNM 16 (1971), 322–36; Andersen, Per Sveaas. Vikings of the West. Oslo: Tanum, 1971; Skaare, Kolbjørn. Coins and Coinage in Viking-Age Norway: The Establishment of a National Coinage in Norway in the XI Century, with a Survey of the Preceding Currency History. Oslo, Bergen, and Tromsø: Universitetsforlaget, 1976; Enemark, Poul, et al. "Øksnehandel." KLNM 20 (1976), 674–89; Lyon, H. R. The Vikings in Britain. New York: St. Martin, 1977.

Arnved Nedkvitne

[See also: Arabic Sources for Scandinavia(ns); Birka; Gotland; Guilds; Hanseatic League; Hedeby; Kaupang; Rus'; Transport]

Transport. In the Viking Age, a marked improvement took place in Scandinavia's means of communication. This process began with the Arab expansion at the beginning of the 8th century. The European trade routes were thus shifted from the Mediterranean to the North Sea, leading to the growth in Scandinavian transit trade. The first towns were established as summer markets for the hinterland trade. Maritime conditions, such as accessibility from the sea and the possibility of further transport into the country by water, were decisive factors in this phase of establishment. When the summer markets became permanent settlements, they increasingly specialized in hinterland trade. Accordingly, a town sector came into existence, which took over part of the tool production of agriculture, and an agricultural sector, which made available possibilities for an increase in the actual agricultural production. This work division motivated improvements to the road systems. The good roads were again a prerequisite for vehicles with larger capacities and better use of the tractive force of the animals. The resident merchants in the towns had storage facilities that favored ships with more cargo-carrying capacity, which demanded fixed quays. With the town as an intermediary, the development of the means of transportation on sea and land led to the development of superior transportation systems. At the end of the Viking Age, these connected systems of transportation were established especially in southern Scandinavia and in particular in Denmark. In northern Scandinavia, natural conditions favored maritime transportation.

Carriage by sea. In addition to Scandinavian ships, foreign ships were also important. The oldest remote trade was conducted by Frisians, who made regular visits to the various trading centers. Franks and especially Saxons took over the Frisians' trade and type of ship, which developed into the Hanseatic cog. English, Frisian, and Slavic types of ships also played a role in Scandinavia in the Viking Age and the Middle Ages.

Scandinavian shipbuilding and shipping traditions can be traced back to the 7th century. At the beginning of the Viking Age, two main types were in existence, one for use in warfare and one for trade. Common characteristics were a sharp stemson and curved sterns and bows, a peculiar rib girth system, boards joined by clinker building, and a T-shaped keel.

Picture stones from Gotland show a variant of the Nordic ship with a kind of ramming stem, but otherwise it is more a troopship than a warship. They were very light and supple ships that could land on any flat beach and go deep into rivers. In the construction, great speed, maneuverability, and independence of wind power were emphasized. These requisites were managed by a relatively slim ship (the ones that have been found are between 4.5 and 7.2 times longer than broad), which was rowed by the troops themselves. Since the rowers had to sit on both sides of the vessel, with enough space to allow for rowing, the width of the frame was a decisive factor in the ship's construction. To get ashore without being seen, the mast could be laid down during the voyage through a flap in the mast partner, which was placed at deck level, and by lifting it up from the hole in the keelson in which it rested. Equipment and provisions could be stowed under the loose deck-planks.

The merchant ships were constructed to allow for maximum cargo-carrying capacity while maintaining as stable a construction as possible. This aim was managed by a broader ship with close-set ribs. The merchant ships are 2.3–4.9 times longer than broad. There was a half-deck at the stern and at the bow, and a big, open hole at midship. The cargo could be stowed under the half-decks or be secured in the hold, covered with tarpaulin. Brushwood mats, straw, or similar material was placed under the cargo in order to protect the ship against wear. The watertight bodies of a carriage of the Viking Age are possibly chests with round arches intended for transfer to the hold of the ship, employing the same principle as the modern containers (Schovsbo 1987: 34). There were, of course, no oars in the hold, and since the smaller crew, the greater width, and the heavier cargo also made rowing difficult, the sail was the most important propelling force. The sources distinguish among *knǫrr*, *búza*, and *byrðingr*.

The *knǫrr* was a large, seaworthy ship that was in use throughout the Viking Age and the Middle Ages. The *knǫrr* from Skuldelev could carry more than 30 tons, and was a rather stiff ship that, contrary to the other known Nordic ships, did not have enough elasticity to follow the movement of the waves, but plowed through them. The written sources indicate a *knǫrr* with a larger cargo-carrying capacity than that of the Skuldelev ship. Small boats of a Nordic type are known since the Viking Age. This slim, clinker-built keel-boat with thwarts strengthened by crossbeams was still in use in the 20th century for local transport and fishing in western Norway and the Faroe Islands. It could be rowed or propelled by a square sail, the only type of sail known in the Scandinavian Viking Age and the Middle Ages.

From the southern Scandinavian Nydam vessel, a warship was developed in England related to the Nordic ones. It was clinker-built and had a keel. The keel has given the ship its name (Old English *ceol*, Old Norse *kjǫll*). This type received a small sail at the same time as sails are found on the Gotland picture stones (Ellmers 1972: 47ff.). The sail seems to have spread quickly to all the northern European areas in the 7th century. In the 10th century, the term *kjǫll* was also applied to merchant ships, and this type was adopted by England's trading partners, *e.g.*, in northwestern France. Depictions on seals and other descriptions show that in the 13th century this type received fore and aft castles.

The hulk was developed from English and Frisian local shipbuilding traditions. Instead of a keel and a bow, it had a broad floor-board, which curved both in the cross-section and in the fore-and-aft direction, giving the boat the shape of a banana. The individual planks were originally pushed together and against the floor-board, and were held together by outside cappings.

The hulk is well suited for landing on a flat, sandy beach, and an example from Utrecht shows signs of wear from being pulled ashore. On this hulk, the cappings are developed into a half-round beam, which improved the stiffening of the hull and functioned as a kind of bilge keel. A mast, which for reasons of stabilization was placed rather far toward the bow, is known already in Roman times, where it was set in a hold in the frame. The hulk had only one or two pairs of oars. It used a sail, and in the 13th century received fore and aft castles as a consequence of new demands and possibilities of naval warfare. In the late Middle Ages, the hulk developed into a large ship, which ousted the cog in the Baltic.

Originally, the cog was a small fishing and merchant vessel for use in shallow tidal waters. The type is of Frisian origin, but in Denmark (the Schlei and the Liim Fjord) it was a small domestic ship before the 11th century and was still in use in the 19th century. The Danish word *kåg* thereafter came to be used as a designation for a flat-bottomed rowboat.

The early Frisian cog, such as the one found in Brügge, had a flat, carvel-built bottom, which did not allow this type of ship to go ashore. This type had reverse clinkerwork in order to stand the

pressure from the cargo when it rested on the sea floor at low tide. The mast was placed in an enlarged frame and was secured at the top with a crossbeam. Excavated remnants of quays in Viking Age towns (Hedeby and Kaupang) must most probably be seen in connection with the Frisian cog, which, outside the tidal areas, were dependent on quays, or anchoring and reloading into small boats. Since the 10th century, the cog had been used for levies, but from the 13th century onward, it was purely a sailing vessel that, like the other types of ships, received fore and aft castles, and shortly before 1250 a stern-rudder instead of a steering oar.

In the development of the seagoing cog, the T-shaped keel and the keelson construction, which was dependent on the T-shaped keel, and also the common clinkerwork were adopted from the Nordic ships. Theoretically, a new type of ship was created, which had only the name in common with the earlier cogs. By the creation of the seagoing cog, the technological prerequisite for a ship with a great cargo-carrying capacity and seaworthiness was realized, as the late-medieval cog from Bremen shows; and with the rise of the Hanseatic towns, the cog became the most important merchant ship in Scandinavia. It was, among other things, used regularly for sailing to Iceland. The great cargo-carrying capacity of the cog became such a decisive factor in the late Middle Ages that not only had new quays to be built for these ships, but also trading centers had to be moved (Ellmers 1972: 75, 164).

For a fuller survey of the various types of small boats, see the bibliography below. Here, only a few important types will be mentioned.

The dugout was common everywhere. In Scandinavia, it was still used in the 19th century or later for transportation, hunting, and fishing. Two dugouts tied together to form a barge were still used *ca.* 1900 for cattle transport in southern Denmark. The actual flat-bottomed barge was, among other things, used for fishing at Falsterbo (Ellmers 1972: 104).

Maritime transportation in the Viking Age is reflected in place-names. The name Skibby used for settlements along the rivers refers to places that could be reached by ship, and names like Draget and Skibsdræt refer to places where one had to pull the ships on rollers over land. Pulling ships over land from the North Sea to Hedeby was not uncommon.

The rafting of timber is known from all wooded areas of Scandinavia, although in Denmark it only took place sporadically as a consequence of such obstacles as mills and eel weirs. As ferries, rafts were used together with dugouts, and are mentioned in Iceland in the first half of the 12th century and in a Norwegian law by King Magnús (r. 1263–1280). Such finds are known from Sweden from the 5th to the 7th centuries and the first half of the 12th century (Ellmers 1972: 115).

Towns and quays. The summer markets, with pit houses, tents, and ships pulled up on the beach, gradually became permanent settlements. They were fortified, and roads were constructed according to the system that can be seen in Århus: one road along the inside of the fortification, and two crossroads that lead to the gates. The planked roads show traces of wear from carts, which must have placed a role in the hinterland trade. It is at this stage that the road systems to the towns are expanded and improved.

As a consequence of the growth of the towns and the expansion of the road system, a shift in trading centers took place. The open market by the beach is retained, but loses significance. Instead, large merchant's houses with storehouses, residential buildings, and possibly overnight accommodations for visiting crews were established along the rivers and fitted with landing platforms parallel to the river. The only road leads through the merchant's house to a broad public highway on the other side that paralled the river and led to the hinterland. This system is known throughout the northern European area.

Most of the visiting merchants had an established connection with a resident merchant, at whose landing they put in. He bought their goods and provided return cargo. The local farmer drove to the merchant's house with his surplus production and local homemade articles. In return, he received not only goods for private consumption, but also for resale and further purchase of goods. The resident merchant thus also stimulated increased trade in the countryside. This pattern of trade can be demonstrated in the Nordic towns well into the 20th century. In the late Middle Ages, the plots of land near the water were provided with jetties. In Bergen and Uppsala, the individual landing piers were provided with a common quay, so that one could walk along the waterside.

Road systems. In the Middle Ages, the cities' planked roads were gradually replaced by stone pavement in southern Scandinavia. In northern Scandinavia, roads were constructed with planks over a box-construction that contained drains (*e.g.*, in Trondheim). Outside the towns, the roads consisted of lanes formed by wheel tracks. In moist and wet areas, roads were strengthened with brushwood or planking, and were possibly supplied with curbstones. After the Viking Age, a predominance of paved roads is found, which were normally divided into two lanes with raised stone in between. One crossed boglands and natural fords by way of gravel causeways. Where there were no such causeways, they could be created by bringing in gravel and stones and strengthened with brushwood and planking.

Wooden bridges begin to appear in the 10th century (*e.g.*, in Varpelev, Risby, and Ravning). These may be large and long, with rammed-down poles and braces to support individual spans. A number of bridges made from carved blocks of granite are preserved from the Romanesque period (*e.g.*, in Viborg county). The need for solid stone roads in the Middle Ages is related to the increased load capacity of the carts and the military demands of the royal power. *Jyske lov* ("the Jutish Law") and *Sjællandske lov* ("the Zealand Law") attempted to secure the safety of the travelers. Concerning the maintenance of the roads, the Jutish Law says that to each town must belong four roads, those that from time immemorial have led to it. It is the duty of the plot owners to repair "the military road of the king." But if it is impassable, either because of bogland or large rivers, then all of the parish must help in the building of a bridge. In Norway, it was the duty of the local people to keep the general road in repair.

Transportation by vehicle. According to Berg (1934, 1935), carriages had been used only in Denmark, Sweden (as far as the Göteborg area and northern Uppland), Åland, Åboland, and southern Karelen, while carts were found a little farther toward the north. Although the observations are based on a limited amount of material, they draw attention to the fact that it is in the southern part of Scandinavia that the development of carriages and road construction takes place. Sporadic mention of carriages in Old Icelandic sources (*Guðrúnarkviða* and *Grágás*) may be literary loans from other parts of Scandinavia, and cannot be used as evidence for the existence of carriages. With regard to the Danish material, Schovsbo (1987) has made a complete chronology and related it to the road systems and the development of sea carriage.

The pre-Viking carriage, the Tranbær type, was relatively independent of road systems. It had four spoked wheels, resilient axles, a stiff, bifurcated long wagon, and a turning mechanism on the forecarriage. It could be drawn by horses with either a back or a neck yoke. The load capacity was 300–400 kg.

In the Viking Age, the tractive force could be increased by the use of breast-harnesses or collars instead of yokes, as in the Åstrup-Jelling carriage type. The new harnessing method meant that the load capacity could exceed 500 kg. Because of the increased weight on the wheels, this improvement took better advantage of good roads. Technological motivation had resulted in improved road systems, which was a prerequisite for the introduction of specialized wagons with markedly increased load capacities. A load capacity of 1,000 kg. was managed in the 12th or 13th century.

In the 13th century, the dished wheel was introduced for the first time in Denmark (dendrochronologically dated hub from Rønnebjerg Storgård in Vendsyssel). The idea behind the dished wheel is that the beveled wheel is mounted on an axle, the arms of which are bent down in the same angle as the camber. Thus, the spokes are loaded vertically, but the top of the wheel slopes out to such an extent that a body with sloping slides, and thus a larger load capacity, can be placed on the carriage. The idea is that these special, larger-capacity vehicles could use the wheel tracks of common vehicles; the two types of wheel design existed side by side from the 13th century until the 17th century (Schovsbo 1987: 112). In a few cases, a dished wheel was mounted onto a straight axle, but traces of wear on medieval rim flanges show that most were appropriately mounted onto sloping axle arms.

In the Viking Age, carriages appear to be the means of transportation for women of rank. Luggage was commonly transported on four-wheeled carts, while the people rode on horses. After the 15th century, the coach gained ground. In 1514, it is mentioned that the blacksmiths in Flensburg made "Wagenschenen," but it is uncertain if such wheel tires were known at that time. It may refer to tires to be nailed on. Together with inserted wear-stones, they were the precursors of wheel tires and were still known from the farmers' carriages in the middle of the 19th century. Carriage axles made of iron are mentioned in 1516 in Stockholm.

In the winter, sledges were used both for transportation of people and heavy objects, such as timber and stones. The use of oxen for carriages continued throughout the Viking Age and Middle Ages until the 20th century.

Horses. Most of the horses in the Viking Age were of the size of an Icelandic horse. The biggest horses measured 150 cm. (16 hands). The rare finds of horse bones from the Middle Ages point to these small horses.

Breast harnesses are depicted on the Oseberg textiles. Such harnesses were linked by additional harnesses or chains that transferred the draw to the pulling disks at the shafts of the forecarriage. Chains and pulling disks of iron are known from women's graves from the Viking Age.

The saddle came to Scandinavia *ca.* A.D. 400. It consisted of two saddle panels that rested on the ribs of the horse on each side of the spine, and connected with a high pommel and cantle and no horn. Mounted rings made it suitable for carrying both the rider and the load. The type was introduced in Europe by the Huns. In the second half of the 6th century and in the first half of the 7th, it was modified to become the magnificent Swedish saddle Valsgärde 7, Vallstenarum, Vendel XIV, and Vendel XII. It continued to be used throughout the Viking Age, whereas only a high pommel is known from York, and was known in the 12th–14th centuries as a craddle-saddle. During the ride, the legs were stretched forward. A special version for military use can be seen in a mural in Brejning church in Holbæk county, Denmark. As a pack saddle, this type lived a long life in northern Scandinavia, where it was in use until recent times under the name *kløvsadel*. In the 14th century, the craddle-saddle was replaced by the club-saddle, a heavier saddle with a high fork and a distinct horn. The exaggerated cantle is replaced by two side panels that are free of the saddle. A saddle pad was used, consisting of either a blanket or leather with linen sewn underneath.

A great variety of medieval stirrups show that they were made for a number of functions. The stirrup of the Viking Age often had a neck between the hole for the stirrup strap and the stirrup. The stirrup becomes shorter toward the end of the 10th century, and the neck disappears; the strap is placed around the top of the stirrup, thus making it stronger. This innovation is due to the club-saddle, which gave the horse more mobility and allowed the rider to shift his weight exclusively to the stirrups, thus requiring that the stirrups be more solid.

Among the various kinds of bits, the main types are the snaffle and the curb bit, as can be seen in depictions from throughout the Middle Ages. The snaffle is the more common type, but a few curbs have been found dating from the 13th century to the beginning of the 14th. From the Viking Age until the early Middle Ages, the snaffle with a loose guard was used. A snaffle welded together with cheek pieces appears at the latest in the middle of the 13th century, and was used throughout the Middle Ages. Simple, massive snaffles are found throughout the Middle Ages. Until the 13th century, some are consciously made sharp. Hollow, thicker, and milder bits are found at the latest around the second quarter of the 14th century, and are linked to the better control offered by the club-saddle.

From the 10th century and the beginning of the 11th, prick spurs generally follow a straight horizontal plane. In the second half of the 11th century until the mid-12th, the end of the spur tilted upward. The latest prick spur is Danish (Boringholm), and has a fan-shaped rowel.

The oldest wheeled spurs are from Lund (*ca.* 1160 and 1175). The type does not become common until the end of the 13th century. The oldest have a short shank. In the beginning of the 14th century, some spurs had a long shank.

In the Viking Age, calks rather than horseshoes were probably used. The so-called "Celtic" horseshoe is known from the end of the 11th century, and came into use possibly before the middle of the century (Thuletomten, Lund). The shoe has a wavy outer rim as a result of pressing out from the depression around the nail holes. The shoe type has calks, and the nailheads have goads that jutted down under the shoe. This feature is often seen in one-half or three-quarter shoes, and was created as a result of the interference cause by the jutting out of the rim. In the 13th century, the shoe type develops into the "triangle-shoe" with a less distinct wavy outer rim and a V-shaped inner rim. The type is known from Lund, and was probably in use until the first half of the 14th century. In France, horseshoes of the "Celtic" type were the normal ones until the last century, although fitted with common horseshoe nails.

Around 1300, we find the "Spanish" horseshoe with high calks and a raising of the hindmost part of the bars so that the calks and the front part of the bars are on the same line. Also, this type uses stud-nails. In the middle of the 14th century, the Spanish horseshoe gets a fullering: one of two small grooves on each bar. To this type belong the T-shaped nails placed alongside in the groove, but in winter the shoeing was done with the stud-nail being placed in a pair of special holes. The type of shoeing is still common.

The datable medieval oxshoes are all from the 13th century. They are made of thin iron, a couple of millimeters thick at the most, in the shape of a half-circle. Toe-clips provided added support. Like the horseshoes of he Celtic type, there was a depression around the nail holes, and the same kind of nails were used.

Other means of transportation. It was common to walk on foot with small wares and tools. Skates made from smoothed metatarsal bones of an ox were common. One poled with a piked stick, most examples of which date from the Viking Age and the early Middle Ages. Skis are mentioned in the sources, and one of the Nordic gods, Ull, was known as the ski-god. Finally, the use of woven or braided snowshoes for people and packhorses is also attested.

Perspective. The systems of transportation and trade that were established in the Middle Ages functioned unchallenged until the 20th century. Individual features could be subjected to technical innovation, but the physical frames of the town remained the same, and the trade pattern with small craft for voyages to the individual merchants and the farmers who sold their surplus production did not change.

It was the nation's military need that promoted innovation in overland and maritime transportation.

Gradually, the river harbors were abandoned, and the large docks were established along the coast. Road transport was supplied by canals. The system of transport was tied to maritime travel, but only until the railway lines were expanded, thus introducing a new epoch of town establishment, the railway towns. The physical frames of the old towns burst with the expansion of trade and increased industrialization coupled with the mass migration from the countryside. A system of transportation that had functioned for 600 years came to an end.

Lit.: Berg, Gösta. *Transporton til lands.* Nordisk kultur, 16. Stockholm: Bonnier; Oslo: Aschehoug; Copenhagen: Schultz, 1934; Berg, Gösta. *Sledges and Wheeled Vehicles.* Nordiska Museets Handlingar, 4. Stockholm: Fritz; Copenhagen: Levin & Munksgaard, 1935, Brøndsted, Johannes. *The Vikings.* Trans. Kalle Skov. Harmondsworth: Penguin, 1960, pp. 139–48; Granlund, John, et al. "Hamn." *KLNM* 6 (1961), 83–95; Enemark, Poul. "Hærvejen." *KLNM* 7 (1962), 259–63; Olsen, Olaf, and Ole Crumlin-Pedersen. "The Skuldelev Ships." *Acta archaeologica Scandinavica* 38 (1967), 73–174; Foote, Peter, and David M. Wilson. *The Viking Achievement: The Society and Culture of Early Medieval Scandinavia.* London: Sidgwick & Jackson, 1970, pp. 232–62; Crumlin-Pedersen, Ole, et al. "Skibstyper." *KLNM* 15 (1970), 482–94; Norberg, Rune, et al. "Sporre." *KLNM* 16 (1971), 530–4; Brøgger-Haakon Shetelig, A. W. *The Viking Ships: Their Ancestry and Evolution.* Oslo: Dreyer, 1971; Norberg, Rune. "Stigbygel." *KLNM* 17 (1972), 176–80; Ellmers, D. *Frühmittelalterliche Handelsschriffahrt in Mittel- und Nordeuropa.* Neumünster: Wachholz, 1972; Wittendorf, A. *Alvej og kongevej.* Copenhagen: Akademisk Forlag, 1973; Berg, Gösta, and Jakob Benediktsson. "Vagn." *KLNM* 19 (1975), 430–6; Ropeid, Andreas, et al. "Veg." *KLNM* 19 (1975), 617–27; Crumlin-Pedersen, Ole. "Danish Cog Finds." In *The Archaeology of Medieval Ships and Harbours in Northern Europe: Papers Based on those Presented to an International Symposium on Boat and Ship Archaeology at Bremerhaven in 1979.* Ed. Sean McGrail. National Maritime Museum, Greenwich

Archaeological Series No. 5; B.A.R. International Series, 66. Oxford: B.A.R, 1979, pp. 17–34; Schovsbo, P. O. *Oldtidens vogne i Norden*. Frederikshaven: Bangsbomuseet, 1987 [German summary]. The chronology of the harness is based partly on unpublished material from cand. phil. Eskil Arentoft, Århus.

Mikael Andersen

[**See also:** Navigation; Ships and Shipbuilding]

Trelleborg Fortresses *see* Fortresses, Trelleborg

Tristrams saga ok Ísoddar

Tristrams saga ok Ísoddar ("The Saga of Tristram and Ísodd") was written in Iceland, presumably in the 14th century. It survives in a vellum MS of around 1450, AM 489 4to, and in paper MSS from the 18th and 19th centuries. The probable source of the saga is *Tristrams saga ok Ísǫndar*, which was translated in Norway in 1226 for King Hákon Hákonarson by a certain Brother Robert from the *Tristan* of the 12th-century Anglo-Norman poet Thomas. However, the earliest extant MS of this translation dates from the late 15th century, postdating that of *Tristrams saga ok Ísoddar*.

The relationship between the two sagas and the literary value of the Icelandic version has been a matter for debate. The names of the characters in *Tristrams saga ok Ísoddar* do not correspond exactly with those of Brother Robert's translation; there are significant changes in the story line and significant alterations to motivation. The Icelandic version is also considerably shorter, and the style is closer to that of the *Íslendingasögur* than the Norwegian translation. In sum, the shorter Icelandic saga could be regarded as a homely retelling of the Tristram story by someone who had only an imperfect memory of Robert's *roman courtois*. This view was held by Leach (1921), and for many years it was generally accepted. But in 1960, Schach pointed out that the Icelandic saga deviated from the Norwegian source in ways that amounted to a consistent reversal of it, not least in its attempt to ennoble the characters of Tristram and Ísodd and to convince the reader of their good motives. Schach demonstrated further that the author, far from being an ignorant rustic, was well versed in the sagas, consciously imitated their style, and drew extensively upon them for many of his episodes. Kalinke (1981) argues that the saga is not merely a reply to the Norwegian translation, but a humorous commentary on Arthurian romance in general, in which the author makes fun of the tenets of the genre, exaggerating some motifs, distorting others, and generally confounding the audience's expectations. Kalinke thus places *Tristrams saga ok Ísoddar* at the zenith of the evolutionary process from translated romance to Icelandic saga.

The Icelandic and Danish Tristram ballads and the Icelandic Tristram folktale ultimately derive from the Norwegian translation, but some of the names in them may have been taken from the shorter Icelandic saga, which may also be the source for some of the motifs in the folktale.

Ed.: Gísli Brynjúlfsson, ed. "Saga af Tristram ok Ísodd, i Grundtexten med Oversættelse." *Annaler for nordisk Oldkyndighed og Historie* (1851), 3–160; Bjarni Vilhjálmsson, ed. "Tristrams saga ok Ísoddar." In *Riddarasögur*. 6 vols. Reykjavík: Íslendingasagnaútgáfan; Haukadalsútgáfan, 1949–54, vol. 6, pp. 85–145 [modern Icelandic orthography]; Blaisdell, Foster W., ed. *The Sagas of Ywain and Tristan and Other Tales: AM 489 4to*. Early Icelandic Manuscripts in Facsimile, 12. Copenhagen: Rosenkilde & Bagger, 1980. **Tr.**: Hill, Joyce, ed. *The Tristan Legend: Texts from Northern and Eastern Europe in Modern English Translation*. Leeds Medieval Studies, 2. Leeds: University of Leeds Graduate Centre for Medieval Studies, 1977, pp. 6–28. **Lit.**: Leach, Henry Goddard. *Angevin Britain and Scandinavia*. Harvard Studies in Comparative Literature, 6. Cambridge: Harvard University Press; London: Milford; Oxford: Oxford University Press, 1921; rpt. Millwood: Kraus, 1975, pp. 169–98; Schach, Paul. "The *Saga af Tristram ok Ísodd*: Summary or Satire?" *Modern Language Quarterly* 21 (1960), 336–52; Kalinke, Marianne E. *King Arthur North-by-Northwest: The* matière de Bretagne *in Old Norse–Icelandic Romances*. Bibliotheca Arnamagnæana, 37. Copenhagen: Reitzel, 1981, pp. 198–215; Schach, Paul. "*Tristrams saga ok Ýsoddar* as Burlesque." *Scandinavian Studies* 59 (1987), 86–100.

Joyce Hill

[**See also:** Old Norse–Icelandic Literature, Foreign Influence on; *Riddarasögur*; *Tristrams saga ok Ísǫndar*]

Tristrams saga ok Ísǫndar

Tristrams saga ok Ísǫndar ("The Saga of Tristram and Ísǫnd") is an Old Norse *riddarasaga* originally translated or adapted from Old French (Anglo-Norman) in 1226 by a certain Brother Robert under the auspices of the Norwegian king Hákon Hákonarson (r. 1217–1263). This piece of information is supplied by a passage preceding *Tristrams saga* in the paper MSS.

Tristrams saga is preserved in its entirety in the Icelandic paper MSS AM 543 4to (17th century), with some lacunae in ÍB 51 fol. (17th century) and in JS 8 fol., a copy of ÍB 51 fol. (18th century), which contains material not found in ÍB 51 fol. Four leaves from now-lost codices also exist (from AM 567 XXII 4to and from Library of Congress, "Reeves Fragment," in William Dudley Foulke Papers, MS Division). They contain parts of *Tristrams saga* in somewhat fuller form than the later copies. Árni Magnússon had excerpts from *Tristrams saga* made in AM 576b 4to, which also contains his notes on the text. Another résumé is found in the MS NkS 1144 fol. (18th century) and a fragment in Lbs 4816 4to (ca. 1800).

Scholars do not agree whether *Tristrams saga* should be considered a faithfully translated representative of the Tristan poem by Thomas written about 1170 and grouped with the "courtly" branch of the Tristan material, or looked upon as a conflation of both the "vulgar" and "courtly" branches. What is clear, however, is that the translator or adapter has used some sources that scholars have attributed to the "vulgar" branch.

Tristrams saga is a stylistically uneven account of the famous triangular love affair among King Mark, Ísǫnd, and Tristram. Compared with the preserved fragments of Thomas's poem, it is obvious that the translator has omitted all the explanations supplied by the poet and shortened most of the interior monologues. He has, on the other hand, tried to embellish his story with rhetorical ornamentations. Whether this translation is to be traced back to the 13th century and is, as stated in the title of the saga, a work of Brother Robert, or whether it must be looked upon as a 14th-century Icelandic adaptation, has not been investigated.

Ed.: Gísli Brynjúlfsson, ed. *Saga af Tristram ok Ísönd samt Möttuls saga*. Copenhagen: Det kongelige nordiske Oldskrift-selskap, 1878; Kölbing, Eugen, ed. *Tristrams Saga ok Ísondar. Mit einer literarhistorischen Einleitung, deutscher Uebersetzung und Anmerkungen*. Heilbronn: Henninger, 1878; rpt. Hildesheim and New York: Olm, 1978; Bjarni Vilhjálmsson, ed. "Saga af Tristram og Ísönd." In *Riddarasögur*. 6 vols.

Reykjavik: Íslendingasagnaútgáfan Haukadalsútgáfan, 1949–54, vol. 1; Schach, Paul, ed. "An Unpublished Leaf of Tristrams saga: AM 567 Quarto, XXII,2." *Research Studies* 32 (1964), 50–62; Schach, Paul, ed. "The Reeves Fragment of Tristrams saga ok Ísöndar." In *Einarsbók. Afmæliskveðja til Einars Ól. Sveinssonar. 12. desember 1969.* Ed. Bjarni Guðnason *et al.* Reykjavik: Nokkrir vinir, 1969, pp. 296–308; Vésteinn Ólason, ed. *Saga af Tristram og Ísönd.* Reykjavik: Mál og menning, 1987. **Tr.**: Schach, Paul, trans. *The Saga of Tristram and Ísönd.* Lincoln: University of Nebraska Press, 1973. **Bib.**: Kalinke, Marianne E., and P. M. Mitchell. *Bibliography of Old Norse–Icelandic Romances.* Islandica, 44. Ithaca and London: Cornell University Press, 1985, pp. 116–22. **Lit.**: Schach, Paul. "Some Observations on *Tristrams Saga.*" *Saga-Book of the Viking Society* 15 (1957–59), 102–29; Schach, Paul. "The Style and Structure of Tristrams saga." In *Scandinavian Studies: Essays Presented to Dr. Henry Goddard Leach on the Occasion of His Eighty-fifth Birthday.* Ed. Carl F. Bayerschmidt and Erik J. Friis. Seattle: University of Washington Press, 1965, pp. 63–86; Sverrir Tómasson. "Hvenær var Tristrams sögu snúið?" *Gripla* 2 (1977), 47–78; Álfrún Gunnlaugsdóttir. *Tristán en el Norte.* Reykjavik: Stofnun Árna Magnússonar, 1978; Cormier, Raymond J. "Bédier, Brother Robert and the *Roman de Tristan.*" In *Études de philologie romane et d'histoire littéraire offertes à Jules Horrent à l'occasion de son soixantième anniversaire.* Ed. Jean Marie D'Heur and Nicholetta Cherubini. Liège: [n.p.], 1980, pp. 69–75; Padel, Oliver J. "The Cornish Background of the Tristan Stories." *Cambridge Medieval Celtic Studies* 1 (1981), 53–81; Thomas, Maureen F. "The Briar and the Vine: Tristan Goes North." *Arthurian Literature* 3 (1983), 53–90;

Sverrir Tómasson

[**See also**: Old Norse–Icelandic Literature, Foreign Influence on; *Riddarasögur; Tristrams saga ok Ísoddar*]

Trójumanna saga ("The Saga of the Troy-men") survives in three redactions known as Alpha, Beta, and *Hauksbók.* The broad similarities among the redactions, taken together with their differences in detail, indicate a common origin in a lost archetype that was probably composed in the early 13th century. The Alpha redaction also seems to date back to the 13th century, although it is extant only in late paper MSS (AM 176a fol., AM 176b fol., ÍB 184 4to, and the brief fragment AM 598 IIa 4to). For the Beta redaction, a *terminus ad quem* of about 1350 has been established by the mid-14th-century vellum MS AM 573 4to and the fragment AM 598 IIb 4to. The other MSS containing the Beta redaction, in its entirety or in fragments (R 706, Ihre 76, Stock. Papp. 4to no. 29, and Stock. Papp. fol. no. 58), are late paper transcripts made in Sweden from the now-lost Icelandic vellum MS *Ormsbók,* which is dated around 1400. The *Hauksbók* redaction, as its name implies, occurs uniquely in the early 14th-century compendium made by the Icelandic scribe Haukr Erlendsson (AM 544 4to). All three redactions contain the title "Trójumanna saga."

Trójumanna saga is the Old Norse retelling of the Matter of Troy, that is, the legends of the Trojan War that pervade medieval literature in many vernaculars. The ultimate source of the medieval Matter of Troy, in general, is the late-classical Latin prose narrative *De excidio Troiae historia,* supposedly written by "Dares Phrygius"; its real author is unknown. Feigned to be the diary of a Trojan soldier named Dares, this account combats the fancifulness of the earlier Homeric tradition by excising implausible elements, such as the intervention of the Olympian gods, and by substituting a rationalized sequence of events that begins with Jason's quest for the Golden Fleece, which, according to Dares, first sparked hostilities between the Greeks and the Trojans. It ends with the fall of Troy. The various medieval works based on Dares, including *Trójumanna saga,* have enlivened this dry material with colorful details taken from Vergil, Ovid, and other sources, in addition to original touches of their own.

Of the Old Norse versions, the Alpha redaction of *Trójumanna saga* is the most faithful to Dares's account, only rarely resorting to borrowings from additional sources, such as Vergil and Ovid, and beginning and ending the narrative at the same points as Dares does; but the Alpha redaction fleshes out Dares's sketchy outline with detailed descriptions of battles and dramatic speeches by various characters, apparently inventions of the Old Norse redactor. In this sense, the Alpha redaction is the most "original" of the three, even though its adherence to the *De excidio Troiae* has earned this redaction the title of the "Dares Phrygius version" of *Trójumanna saga.*

The other two redactions show less creative flair, but they are liberal in their use of other sources to supplement Dares's narrative. The *Hauksbók* redaction contains a unique preface dealing with Greco-Roman mythology, for which the Vatican Mythographers and the *Ovide moralisé* have been suggested as the most likely sources. The Beta redaction includes extensive extracts from the *Ilias latina* (a Latin epitome of Homer's *Iliad*), as well as interpolations from Ovid's *Heroides* and *Metamorphoses.* Both the Beta and the *Hauksbók* redactions append to Dares's account an alternative Vergilian version of the fall of Troy, which counteracts Dares's rationalism by reintroducing the Trojan Horse as the means of Greek victory. Furthermore, these two redactions add a "sequel" dealing with Hector's sons and their reconquest of Troy, which would seem to derive from French sources.

The possibility of French influence on *Trójumanna saga* is, however, a controversial issue that requires further investigation. The Alpha redaction, with its fidelity to Dares and the consistently latinate names of its characters, has no part in the controversy; but for each of the other two redactions, it is still an open question to what extent the non-Daretian material results from direct consultation of classical sources or simply from use of an Old French source that had already incorporated borrowings from classical authors.

For all their reliance on foreign sources, the three redactors also strive to assimilate the story of Troy to Old Norse literary tradition. The *Hauksbók* redaction includes episodes derived from "native" sagas, such as *Vápnfirðinga saga* and *Hrólfs saga kraka,* which enhance the narrative considerably. Aside from these additions and the unique mythological preface, *Hauksbók* handles the story of Troy in a terser and more condensed style than the other two redactions. Both Alpha and Beta, but especially Alpha, impart a truly saga-like character to their foreign source material by developing dramatic scenes rich in vivid description and dialogue. The characters' speeches, full of ironic understatement and courageous resignation to fate, contribute to a distinctly Northern heroic *ethos* in these redactions of the saga.

Far more than a simple word-for-word translation of a classical account of the Trojan War, more even than an ingenious synthesis of various sources of the Troy legends, *Trójumanna saga* stands as a noteworthy achievement in Old Norse heroic narrative. It had considerable influence on subsequent literature, especially the late-medieval *riddarasögur,* which contain many names, narrative motifs, and stylistic features taken from *Trójumanna saga.*

Ed.: Jón Sigurðsson, ed. "Trójumanna saga." *Annaler for nordisk Oldkyndighed og Historie* (1848), 3–101 [*Hauksbók* redaction]; Eiríkur Jónsson and Finnur Jónsson, eds. *Hauksbók udgiven efter de Arnamagnæanske håndskrifter no. 371, 544 og 675, 4° samt forskellige papirshåndskrifter af Det kongelige nordiske Oldskrift-selskab.* Copenhagen: Thiele, 1892–96, pp. 193–226; Louis-Jensen, Jonna, ed. *Trójumanna saga.* Editiones Arnamagnæanæ, ser. A, vol. 8. Copenhagen: Munksgaard, 1963 [Beta and *Hauksbók* redactions]; Louis-Jensen, Jonna, ed. *Trójumanna saga: The Dares Phrygius Version.* Editiones Arnamagnæanæ, ser. A, vol. 9. Copenhagen: Reitzel, 1981 [Alpha redaction]. **Tr.**: Eldevik, Randi. "The Dares Phrygius Version of *Trójumanna saga*: A Case Study in the Cross-cultural Mutation of Narrative." Diss. Harvard University, 1987. **Lit.**: Greif, Wilhelm. *Die mittelalterlichen Bearbeitungen der Trojanersage.* Marburg: Elwert, 1886; Nelson, Frank G. "The Date, Sources and Analogues of *Trójumanna saga*." Diss. University of California, 1937; Lönnroth, Lars. "Det litterära porträttet i latinsk historiografi och isländsk sagaskrivning—en komparativ studie." *Acta Philologica Scandinavica* 27 (1965), 68–117; Lönnroth, Lars. *European Sources of Icelandic Saga Writing.* Stockholm: Thule, 1965; Hallberg, Peter. "Medeltidslatin och sagaprosa. Några kommentarer till Lars Lönnroths studier i den isländska sagalitteraturen." *Arkiv för nordisk filologi* 81 (1966), 258–76; Pinkernell, Gert. "Französischer Einfluss auf die altnordische Trójumanna saga?" *Archiv für das Studium der Neueren Sprachen* 208 (1971–72), 113–9; Harris, Joseph. "The Masterbuilder Tale in Snorri's *Edda* and Two Sagas." *Arkiv för nordisk filologi* 91 (1976), 66–101; Jón Helgason. "Paris i Troia, Þorsteinn på Borg och Brodd-Helgi på Hof." In *Nordiska Studier i filologi och lingvistik: Festskrift tillägnad Gösta Holm på 60-årsdagen den 8 juli 1976.* Ed. Lars Svensson *et al.* Lund: Studentlitteratur, 1976, pp. 192–4; Faulkes, Anthony. "Descent from the Gods." *Mediaeval Scandinavia* 11 (1978–79), 92–125; Glauser, Jürg. *Isländische Märchensagas: Studien zur Prosaliteratur im spätmittelalterlichen Island.* Beiträge zur nordischen Philologie, 12. Basel and Frankfurt am Main: Helbing & Lichtenhahn, 1983.

Randi Eldevik

[**See also:** *Breta sǫgur*; *Hauksbók*; *Hrólfs saga kraka*; *Riddarasǫgur*; *Snorra Edda*; *Vápnfirðinga saga*]

Tøgdrápa *see* **Þórarinn loftunga**

Þáttr (pl. *þættir*) in modern usage refers to short narratives in Old Norse–Icelandic. Scholars have yet to explain fully its etymology, but Germanic cognates mean "wick, loop, strand of rope," and the latter is the primary meaning in Old Norse. Even some of the earliest attestations, however, are metaphorical, in that they use the term to refer to members of a family (*e.g.*, Egill Skalla-Grímsson, *Lausavísa*, st. 24, *Sonatorrek*, st. 7; also the eddic *Hamðismál*, st. 4). More broadly, *þáttr* meant simply "part of a whole," a meaning attested in laws and through centuries of skaldic poetry and often used in literary contexts, meaning "part of a text." Metonymy gradually extended the meaning to more or less independent parts of larger compilations, perhaps especially MSS.

Although the meaning "part, chapter" still remains, as a literary term *þáttr* now has the special technical sense of a short independent narrative. The number of such *þættir* probably exceeds 100, but they vary greatly, and one cannot speak of a single genre. The best-known *þættir*, and the ones that best cohere to form a corpus, are those embedded in the great synoptic *konungasögur* MSS, especially *Morkinskinna* and *Fagrskinna* from the first part of the 13th century, and *Hulda-Hrokkinskinna*, whose original may date from around 1300. These *þættir* characteristically turn on an encounter between the Norwegian king, perhaps most often Haraldr harðráði ("hard-ruler") Sigurðarson, and an Icelander of relatively low social status. Through wit, luck, or pluck, the Icelander pleases the monarch after falling out with him, and receives a reward that greatly enhances his social status. A frame of the hero's journey from Iceland to Norway at the beginning of the tale and journey back out to Iceland often surrounds the central encounter and reward, and for this reason such *þættir* may be termed *útanferðar þáttir*, or "tales of a journey from Iceland to Norway." The journeys in turn may be omitted, particularly the journey back to Iceland, and some introductory and concluding material, sometimes of a genealogical nature, may begin and end the narratives. Stylistically, these *þættir* resemble the *konungasögur* in which they are embedded; that is, they employ the understated, paratactic language often called "saga style," with its seemingly neutral point of view and emphasis on showing rather than telling. Perhaps, however, because they are shorter than other kinds of texts (some fill only a few pages in the modern editions) and therefore have less time to spend on background, they rely more heavily on dialogue and indirect address than do most Old Norse prose genres, and time is relatively more telescoped. Descriptions of persons and places tend to be abbreviated.

About thirty to forty *þættir* share some of this structure, and they also exhibit thematic similarities. Friendship, hospitality, reconciliation, or religious themes operate in nearly all of them. Among the best known are *Auðunar þáttr vestfirzka*, *Hreiðars þáttr heimska*, *Halldórs þáttr Snorrasonar II*, *Brands þáttr ǫrva*, *Stúfs þáttr*, and *Ǫgmundar þáttr dytts*.

To date, most scholarship on *þættir* has focused on narratives of this sort, and indeed they clearly respond to treatment as a separate genre. Considering the original low status of the protagonist and his subsequent leap in social status in a happy ending, the telescoping of time and space, and the possibility that an *útanferðar þáttr* could be told in a single sitting, some scholars have explored the relationship of the form to folktale.

Other texts traditionally called *þættir* appear on closer examination to be nothing more than short versions of other genres. A number of *þættir* display all the structural, thematic, and stylistic features of the family sagas, and in fact no line can be drawn between some of the longer texts now called *þættir*, such as *Þorsteins þáttr stangarhǫggs* or *Ǫlkofra þáttr* (in *Mǫðruvallabók* actually called *Ǫlkofra saga*) and the short *Íslendingasögur*, such as *Þorsteins saga hvíta* or *Þorsteins saga Síðu-Hallssonar*. Similarly, a number of texts now called *þættir* are short *fornaldarsögur* in all but name. These texts exhibit the variety of *fornaldarsögur*. *Nornagests þáttr*, for example, contains snatches of eddic heroic poetry, as does *Vǫlsunga saga*; *Helga þáttr Þórissonar* and *Þorsteins þáttr bœjarmagns* offer a mixture of prehistoric fantasy and historical reality; and *Hauks þáttr Hábrókar* has fantastic elements.

Many *þættir* defy the usual taxonomy, and although scholars have resorted to such terms as "*þáttr*-like" to discuss them, it may be best to regard them simply as anecdotes that made sense to medieval authors in the contexts in which we find them recorded.

Ed.: Þorleifur Jónsson, ed. *Fjörutíu Íslendingaþættir*. Reykjavik: Sigurður Kristjánsson, 1904; Guðni Jónsson, ed. *Íslendinga þættir*. Reykjavik: Sigurður Kristjánsson, 1935; Gardiner, Edwin, ed. *Fornar* smásögur úr Noregs konunga sögum. Reykjavik: Leiftur, 1949 [notes in English]. **Bib.**: Halldór Hermannsson. *Bibliography of the Icelandic Sagas and Minor Tales.* Islandica, 1. Ithaca: Cornell University Library, 1908; rpt. New York: Kraus, 1966; Halldór Hermannsson. *The Sagas of Icelanders (Íslendinga sögur): A Supplement to Bibliography of the Icelandic Sagas and Minor Tales.* Islandica, 24. Ithaca: Cornell University Press, 1935; Jóhann S. Hannesson. *The Sagas of Icelanders (Íslendinga sögur): A Supplement to Islandica I and XXIV.* Islandica, 38. Ithaca: Cornell University Press, 1957. **Lit.**: Lange, Wolfgang. "Einige Bemerkungen zur altnordischen Novelle." *Zeitschrift für deutsches Altertum und deutsche Literatur* 88 (1957), 150–9; Harris, Joseph. "Genre and Narrative Structure in Some *Íslendinga Þættir.*" *Scandinavian Studies* 44 (1972), 1–27; Joseph, Herbert S. "The Þáttr and the Theory of Saga Origins." *Arkiv för nordisk filologi* 87 (1972), 89–96; Bjarni Guðnason. "Þættir." *KLNM* 20 (1976), 405–10; Gimmler, Herbert. "Die þættir der Morkinskinna: Ein Beitrag zur Überlieferungsproblematik und zur Typologie der altnordischen Kurzerzählung." Diss. Frankfurt am Main, 1976; Harris, Joseph. "Theme and Genre in Some *Íslendinga þættir.*" *Scandinavian Studies* 48 (1976), 1–28; Lindow, John. "Old Icelandic *þáttr*: Early Usage and Semantic History." *Scripta Islandica* 29 (1978), 3–44; Whitelaw, Elizabeth. "A Contribution to a Definition of Mediaeval Icelandic *þættir.*" Diss. University of London, 1980; Ásdís Egilsdóttir. "*Þáttr.* Einkenni og staða innan íslenskra miðaldabókmennta." Cand. mag. Diss. University of Iceland, 1982; Maack, Rodney. "*Þáttr* and Saga: Short and Long Narrative in Medieval Iceland." Diss. University of California, Berkeley, 1987.

John Lindow

[**See also:** *Ásbjarnar þáttr selsbana; Auðunar þáttr vestfirzka; Brandkrossa þáttr; Brands þáttr ǫrva; Einars þáttr Skúlasonar; Einars þáttr Sokkasonar; Fagrskinna; Gísls þáttr Illugasonar; Gull-Ásu-Þórðar þáttr; Gunnars saga Þiðrandabana; Halldórs þáttr Snorrasonar; Helga þáttr ok Úlfs; Helga þáttr Þórissonar; Hemings þáttr Áslákssonar; Hrafns þáttr Guðrúnarsonar; Hreiðars þáttr heimska; Hrómundar þáttr halta; Hulda-Hrokkinskinna; Ísleifs þáttr biskups; Jǫkuls þáttr Búasonar; Jóns þáttr biskups Halldórssonar; Konungasögur; Laxdæla saga; Möðruvallabók; Morkinskinna; Nornagests þáttr; Odds þáttr Ófeigssonar; Sneglu-Halla þáttr; Stúfs þáttr; Sturlunga saga; Sǫrla þáttr; Þinga saga; Þorgríms þáttr Hallasonar; Þorleifs þáttr jarlsskálds; Þorsteins saga hvíta; Þorsteins saga Síðu-Hallssonar; Þorsteins þáttr Austfirðings; Þorsteins þáttr bæjarmagns; Þorsteins þáttr stangarhǫggs; Þorsteins þáttr sǫgufróða; Þorvalds þáttr tasalda; Þorvarðar þáttr krákunefs; Vǫlsunga saga; Ǫgmundar þáttr dytts ok Gunnars helmings; Ǫlkofra þáttr]

Þiðreks saga af Bern ("The Saga of Þiðrekr of Bern") was compiled perhaps as late as 1250–1251, although possibly as early as the late 12th century. There are three main MSS: a Norwegian vellum (Stock. Perg. fol. no. 4) marred by several lacunae and dating from the late 13th century, and two complete Icelandic paper MSS (AM 177 fol. and AM 178 fol.), both dating from the 17th century. Other Icelandic paper MSS have no independent

textual value. There is also a Swedish translation (*Didrikskrönikan*) made in about the mid-15th century.

Þiðreks saga is usually classified with the *fornaldarsögur* or with the *riddarasögur*, although strictly speaking it has little in common with either genre with regard to motifs or structure, and is almost unique of its sort.

The saga tells of the lineage, exploits, and death of many heroes, the most famous names among them also occurring, with variant spellings, in medieval German literature, while some appear in Old English. These heroes are set in looser or closer relationship to the preeminent hero Þiðrekr af Bern (i.e., Verona). For instance, Attila (the Atli of other Old Norse works) asks Þiðrekr for help against his enemies, and later grants him asylum when he is ousted by Ermanaric (Jǫrmunrekkr in older Norse tradition), who is Þiðrek's uncle. Sigurðr the dragonslayer, of whose fortunes the saga gives a full version, is vanquished by Þiðrekr and becomes his liegeman, while Sigurðr's brothers-in-law, the Niflungs Gunnarr and Hǫgni, of whom there is also a full account in the section called "Niflunga saga," deal with Þiðrekr long before their fateful meeting at Attila's court. Velent the Smith (Vǫlundr in older Norse tradition), grandson of the Swedish king Vilkinus and son of Vaði, has a son, Viðga, who first becomes Þiðrek's liegeman and then, through marrying into Ermanaric's family, his reluctant and doomed opponent.

Such links help to give coherence to the mass of material interwoven with Þiðrek's youthful adventures, his expulsion from his city of Bern by Ermanaric, his eventual return, and his final mysterious disappearance on a black steed of satanic origin.

Þiðrekr is the legendary development of Theodoric, Ostrogothic ruler of Italy (493–526), while Ermanaric of the saga derives from the earlier Ostrogothic king Ermanaric (d. ca. 376), who in legend has taken the place of Odoacer (ca. 433–493), Theodoric's historical opponent; Odoacer, however, did not depose Theodoric but was deposed by him. Theodoric had no links with the historical Attila, who died a year or two before Theodoric was born.

The precise nature of the saga's immediate sources and its mode of composition are disputed. The prologue mentions the advantage of having lengthy (oral) stories in written form, and also mentions the saga's derivation from German sources, including lays. The saga writer, who was probably a Norwegian, although possibly an Icelander, may have collected and combined in written form various unlinked stories or poems transmitted orally. On the other hand, it is equally probable, and recent research makes it increasingly likely (Andersson 1974), that the saga writer did little more than translate an existing, written Low German version of the already integrated legends, probably compiled in Soest (Susa in the saga, Attila's capital city), although he may also have used additional orally transmitted material.

Ed.: Bertelsen, Henrik, ed. *Þiðriks saga af Bern.* Samfund til udgivelse af gammel nordisk litteratur, 34. Copenhagen: Møller, 1905–11; Guðni Jónsson, ed. *Þiðreks saga af Bern.* Reykjavik: Íslendingasagnaútgáfan, 1954. **Tr.**: Haymes, Edward R., trans. *The Saga of Thidrek of Bern.* New York and London: Garland, 1988. **Bib.**: Halvorsen, Eyvind Fjeld. "Didriks saga af Bern." *KLNM* 3 (1958), 73–6; Schier, Kurt. *Sagaliteratur.* Sammlung Metzler, M78. Stuttgart: Metzler, 1970. **Lit.**: Hempel, Heinrich. "Die Handschriftenverhältnisse der Thidrikssaga." *Beiträge zur Geschichte der deutschen Sprache und Literatur* 48 (1924), 415–

47; rpt. in *Heinrich Hempel. Kleine Schriften.* Ed. Heinrich Matthias Heinrichs. Heidelberg: Winter, 1966, pp. 111–33; Mohr, Wolfgang. "Dietrich von Bern." *Zeitschrift für deutsches Altertum und deutsche Literatur* 80 (1944), 117–55; Hempel, Heinrich. "Sächsische Nibelungendichtung und sächsischer Ursprung der Þiðrikssaga." In *Edda, Skalden, Saga: Festschrift zum 70. Geburtstag von Felix Genzmer.* Ed. Hermann Schneider. Heidelberg: Winter, 1952, pp. 138–56; rpt. in his *Kleine Schriften*, pp. 209–25; Wisniewski, Roswitha. *Die Darstellung des Niflungenunterganges in der Thidrekssaga. Eine quellenkritische Untersuchung.* Hermaea, germanistische Forschungen. Neue Folge, 9. Tübingen: Niemeyer, 1961; Vries, Jan de. "Theoderich der Grosse." *Germanisch-romanische Monatsschrift* 42 (1961), 319–30; rpt. in *Jan de Vries. Kleine Schriften.* Ed. Klaas Heeroma and Andries Kylstra. Kleinere Schriften zur Literatur und Geistesgeschichte. Berlin: de Gruyter, 1965, pp. 77–88; Hempel, Heinrich. "Niederdeutsche Heldensage." *Die Nachbarn. Jahrbuch für vergleichende Volkskunde* 3 (1962), 7–30; rpt. in his *Kleine Schriften*, pp. 134–52; Henning, Bengt. *Didrikskrönikan. Handskriftsrelationer, översättningsteknik och stildrag.* Acta Universitatis Stockholmiensis, 8. Stockholm Studies in Scandinavian Philology, n.s. 8. Stockholm: Almqvist & Wiksell, 1970; Andersson, Theodore M. "The Epic Source of Niflunga saga and the Nibelungenlied." *Arkiv för nordisk filologi* 88 (1973), 1–54; Andersson, Theodore M. "*Niflunga saga* in the Light of German and Danish Materials." *Mediaeval Scandinavia* 7 (1974), 22–30; McTurk, Rory. "The Relationship of *Ragnars saga loðbrókar* to *Þiðriks saga af Bern.*" In *Sjötíu ritgerðir helgaðar Jakobi Benediktssyni 20. Júlí 1977.* 2 vols. Ed. Einar G. Pétursson and Jónas Kristjánsson. Reykjavik: Stofnun Árna Magnússonar, 1977, vol. 2, pp. 568–85; Wagner, N. "Ich, Armer Dietrich." *Zeitschrift für deutsches Altertum und deutsche Literatur* 109 (1980), 209–28 ["Die Wandlung von Theodorichs Eroberung zu Dietrichs Flucht"]; Williams, Jennifer. *Etzel der riche.* European University Studies. Series 1, German Language and Literature, 364. Bern, Frankfurt am Main, and Las Vegas: Lang, 1981; Andersson, Theodore M. "An Interpretation of *Þiðreks saga.*" In *Structure and Meaning in Old Norse Literature: New Approaches to Textual Analysis and Literary Criticism.* Ed. John Lindow *et al.* Viking Collection, 3. Odense: Odense University Press, 1986, pp. 347–77; McLintock, David. "Dietrich und Theodrich—Sage und Geschichte." In *Geistliche und weltliche Epik des Mitteralters in Österreich.* Ed. David McLintock *et al.* Göppinger Arbeiten zur Germanistik, 446. Göppingen: Kümmerle, 1987, pp. 99–106.

†R. G. Finch

[**See also:** *Fornaldarsögur; Riddarasögur; Vǫlsung-Niflung Cycle; Vǫlsunga saga; Vǫlundarkviða*]

Þing (sing. and pl.) has no certain etymology. A Nordic word since the Middle Ages, it is still used, now especially for representative assemblies. The parliament of Iceland has been named the *Alþingi* since around 930, while the Norwegian and Danish parliaments from the 19th century were named respectively *Storting* and *Folketing.* The *Sameting* was elected in 1989, as a representative and consultative assembly of the Samis in Norway. The establishment of Finnish and Swedish *Sametings* is underway.

Þing meant a meeting of free, adult men. Slaves and children did not participate, women only occasionally (as widows) or as companions. The *þing* met at definite places at regular intervals, but might also be specifically convoked by a fellow *þingmaðr* ("*þing*-man") or by a secular or clerical authority. The *þing* might be a meeting of all men in a local community, or else a representative meeting of a larger territory or region. But only Iceland had

a national *þing* in the Middle Ages, irrespective of the occasional Estates General (*riksdag*) in Sweden since 1434.

The *þing* met or was convoked for special ends. The usual qualifying prefixes to the word *þing* indicate those ends. We shall start with the local *þing* where all men met. This starting point neither presupposes nor excludes egalitarian societies. The local communities in Denmark, western Norway, and Iceland were certainly dominated by chieftains even in prehistoric times, less so in Trøndelag or in remote Swedish villages (*byar*).

We have little positive knowledge about the *þing* on the local level. Still, we may infer that the old Nordic rural societies must have had meetings to decide questions relating to fencing, construction of bridges, clearance, pasture rights, worship, and even defense. And they must have had ways to settle conflicts.

In Norway, settlement of conflicts seems to have been arranged in the first place by a *dómr, i.e.,* six men, three nominated from either side. The *dómr* was expected to reach an agreement between the parties in matters of property as well as of, say, manslaughter. If an agreement was not reached or was eventually broken, one of the parties would call a *þing* of the community. Breaking an agreement concluded by a *dómr* was considered a robbery (*rán*). Acting as a court, this *þing* would then pronounce a judgment, eventually execute the judgment by sheer force, and confiscate for their own benefit the property of the obstinate fellow *þingmaðr.* It would appear that such *þing* were not lightly convoked, because of the potential threat of not obeying the agreement before the *dómr* and the nuisance caused to fellow *þingmenn* of the community.

Regional political units had been founded in Scandinavia well before historic times. They are the *-land* in Denmark and Sweden (Finland included), or the *-rike, -lag, -fylke* in Norway, founded within topographic settings by conquest and kept up by domination and force. The *þing* at such levels was composed of local chieftains and/or deputies picked by local or central chieftains. Tasks for such *þing* were defense, worship, and jurisdiction. Local chieftains engaged in a conflict would not easily submit to a local *þing.* They might receive more support at a regional *þing* with their peers. Or the local *þing* might not agree about a case brought before it. The outcome would then be referred to a regional *þing.* But there were no traditions of appeal in secular courts in Scandinavia in the Middle Ages.

The regional *þing* in their functions as courts may supply the background of the well-known Nordic regional codes (*landskapslover*), all lavishly published since the 19th century and even translated into modern Nordic languages. Decisions taken on the regional level had sufficient authority behind them to crystallize into regional customs and customary laws, in Sweden set forth and explained by the regional keeper of the laws (*lagmann*). German jurists in the 19th century wished to see here legal institutions from pre-Christian times, and even the famous *germanisches Urrecht,* the original Germanic law from the times of Tacitus and earlier. That supposition was an error. The Nordic regional laws stem from the latter part of the 12th until the beginning of the 14th century, the result of regional jurisprudence arranged and written by clerically trained scribes. The regional laws should be seen as evidence of the legal awakening of the high Middle Ages, in combination with the numerous regional *þing* in the Nordic countries.

As to the use of local and regional *þing* by authorities, attention should be drawn to the verb *þinga: tinge* 'negotiate, reach an agreement at a *þing*,' still in use in modern Norwegian, Icelandic, and Danish. Regional chieftains as well as the kings and the clerical authorities could use the *þing* for their own purposes.

On a local level, there were such matters to be decided as construction and equipping of the local warship (*e.g.*, in the Norwegian *skipreider* along the coast); construction and maintenance of bridges, roads, and harbors; taxes; construction and equipping of parish churches; and the provisions for parsons. The king's local steward (Norwegian *ármaðr*) might use the local *þing* to communicate royal decrees as well as to prosecute violation of the king's peace, thus by and large introducing royal jurisdiction to replace local custom.

These subjects were also negotiated in a more general way on the regional level. Negotiations at the regional *þing* explain the character of the Nordic regional laws. They were not, like the English common law, an ever-growing body of decisions *in casu*. Each regional law was general for its region, even if there were considerable differences between the regional laws. They are the main result left to us from the regional *þing*.

Royal pretenders convoked regional *þing* in order to be recognized as kings (*hyllingsþing*). The regional *þing* of Trøndelag from the 8th century onward had its meeting place at Frosta, a peninsula in the Trondheimsfjord. At the end of the 10th century, a town (*kaupang*) was founded at the delta (*eyr*) of the river Nida, with a *þing*-place. From then on, the *hyllingsþing* for royal pretenders in Trøndelag were held at the *Eyraþing* in Níðaróss. More elaborate was the Swedish *Eriksgata*. A royal pretender first designated as king at the Mora *þing* at Uppsala was required to present himself on numerous *hyllingsþing* along a fixed itinerary through all Sweden.

The regional *þing* should not be seen as something like modern legislative assemblies. The Danish regional *þing* may have been overshadowed from 1250 by the high nobility, not very interested in nationwide codes, but more in exerting direct influence through their council of nobles. Norway received the first national code in Europe in 1274, the *landslǫg* of Magnús lagabœtir ("law-mender") Hákonarson. The code was prepared in the royal chancery in Bergen, then "given" to the regional Gulaþing at midsummer 1274, the following year to the Frostuþing, and in 1276 to the two regional *þing* in eastern Norway. But in contrast with the former regional laws, these apparently regional codes are practically identical, a fact that demonstrates that the regional *þing* were not supposed to deliberate with any effect on a royal proposal. The Swedish codes (of the countryside and of the towns) from 1350 onward were uniform for the realm, prepared in common by the royal chancery and the high nobility.

The regional *þing* tended to disappear with the growth of royal power in the late Middle Ages and in the early-modern period. The local urban *þing* remained until the 18th century, the local rural *þing* well into the 19th. The local *þing* at that later stage were used for publication of contracts, for civil and criminal justice, for tax collection, and for publication of royal decrees.

Lit.: No comparative monograph on the Nordic *þing* exists. Nearest come the detailed national articles on *ting* in *KLNM* 18 (1974) 334–68, with exhaustive national bibliographies. Students should also consult university textbooks for general discussions about the role of the *þing* in medieval Nordic societies: Rosén, Jerker. *Svensk historia. 1: Tiden före 1718*. Stockholm: Bonnier, 1962; Helle, Knut. *Norge blir en stat 1130–1319*. Handbok i Norges historie, 3. Bergen, Oslo, and Tromsø: Universitetsforlaget, 1974; Andersen,

Per Sveaas. *Samlingen av Norge og kristningen av landet 800–1130*. Handbok i Norges historie, 2. Oslo, Bergen, and Tromsø: Universitetsforlaget, 1977; Skovgaard-Petersen, Inge, *et al. Danmarks historie. 1: Tiden indtil 1340*. Copenhagen: Gyldendal, 1978; Hørby, Kai, and Mikael Venge. *Danmarks historie. 2: Tiden 1340–1648*. Copenhagen: Gyldendal, 1980.

Gudmund Sandvik

[**See also:** *Alþingi*; Royal Administration and Finances]

Þinga saga ("The Saga of the Assemblies"), or *Sigurðar þáttr Hranasonar* ("The Tale of Sigurðr Hranason"), tells the story of a prolonged legal conflict supposed to have taken place 1112–1114 or 1113–1115, which arose when King Sigurðr Jórsalafari ("crusader") Magnússon accused Sigurðr Hranason of keeping for himself a part of the Lapp-tax that he was responsible for collecting. Sigurðr Hranason, however, receives legal advice from King Eysteinn, and, after a series of lawsuits, King Sigurðr's attempt to punish Sigurðr Hranason remains unsuccessful. This failure enrages King Sigurðr, who eventually threatens King Eysteinn, his brother and coregent, with civil war. To avoid such a calamity, Sigurðr Hranason places his fate in the hands of King Sigurðr, who fines him. When later it appears that Sigurðr Hranason is unable to pay the fine, King Sigurðr is convinced that Sigurðr Hranason has not been feathering his own nest as originally assumed, and they are reconciled.

Þinga saga is preserved in six MSS. There are two longer and not quite identical versions in *Hulda* (AM 66 fol.) and in *Morkinskinna* (GkS 1009 fol.); shorter versions are found in *Eirspennill* (AM 47 fol.), *Jöfraskinna*, *Gullinskinna*, and *Codex Frisianus* (AM 45 fol.; *Fríssbók*). Scholars agree that the different versions are all derived from an original **Þinga saga*, now lost, probably composed around 1200 and incorporated into the *Heimskringla* MSS during the 13th century. Storm (1877) suggested that the surviving shorter version of *Þinga saga* (which he calls *Þinga þáttr*) is an extract from the longer one, which is closest to the original. Louis-Jensen (1977), however, proposes that both versions were altered from the original saga. In her view, *Þinga saga* was composed in Norway (whereas Storm favored Iceland) and was later changed by Icelandic editors into the versions known to us today. Bjarni Einarsson (1975) suggested *Þinga saga* as a source for *Egils saga*, a theory challenged by Berger (1979).

Ed.: Storm, Gustav. *Sigurd Ranessöns Proces*. Christiania [Oslo]: Malling, 1877 [contains all the versions of *Þinga saga*]. Lit.: Bjarni Einarsson. *Litterære forudsætninger for Egils saga*. Reykjavik: Stofnun Árna Magnússonar, 1975; Louis-Jensen, Jonna. *Kongesagastudier. Kompilationen Hulda-Hrokkinskinna*. Bibliotheca Arnamagnæana, 32. Copenhagen: Reitzel, 1977; Berger, Alan J. "The Textual History of *Þinga saga*." *Arkiv för nordisk filologi* 94 (1979), 50–6.

Jannie Roed

[**See also:** *Egils saga Skalla-Grímssonar*; *Eirspennill*; *Fríssbók*; *Heimskringla*; *Hulda-Hrokkinskinna*; *Morkinskinna*; *Þáttr*]

Þjalar-Jóns saga ("The Saga of File-Jón") is an anonymous Icelandic *riddarasaga*, often known under the title *Jóns saga Svipdagssonar ok Eireks forvitna* ("The Saga of Jón Svipdagsson and Eirekr the Curious"). The saga probably came into existence in the 14th century, perhaps in Reykhólar in Breiðafjörður; its style suggests the first half of the century. *Þjalar-Jóns saga* is extant in forty MSS, of which the oldest (fragmentary) parchment MS, Stock. Perg. 4to no. 6, is dated about 1400. The *rímur* based on the material of the saga were probably composed at the end of the 16th century.

Prince Eirekr of Valland is an excellent warrior. A stranger, Gestr, spends the winter at the royal court. With him, Eirekr finds a portrait of a beautiful virgin, whom he wishes to marry. Eirekr leaves together with Gestr and sails to Kastella in Hólmgarðr (Novgorod), where Earl Róðbert rules. Gestr leads him in secret to two women, one of whom is his sister Marsilia, the woman Eirekr desires. It turns out that Gestr is in reality Jón, the son of King Svipdagr, whom Róðbert killed. After the murder, Róðbert had seized the throne while Jón was brought up by two dwarfs. Eirekr and Jón sail away with the two women. In Valland, Eirekr and Marsilia marry. The following year, they attack Róðbert with a large army and kill him after a great battle. Jón obtains the power of Holmgarðaríki, while Eirekr later becomes king of Valland.

Þjalar-Jóns saga belongs to a borderline group between *riddarasögur* and *fornaldarsögur*. On the basis of the bridal-quest plot, a popular structural device in both these genres, the text connects a large number of well-known themes and motifs to form a new and independent whole: the anonymous winter-guest, the magic gold-dripping ring (*cf.* Draupnir in the eddic mythology), the portrait of a remote beloved, the search for her as the central plot, the meeting with helpful dwarfs, the usurpation of a traitor, the murder of the hero's father, the exile of the hero in his youth, and the she-wolf who licks the honey-smeared boy and releases him. The structure of the plot in *Þjalar-Jóns saga* is noteworthy because it deals with the constellations of two heroes, as in, for example, *Viktors saga ok Blávus:* the bridal quest, the revenge, and the gaining of power are partly divided between two different plots, whereby the hero and the helper in the two parts change roles. Generally, these two texts have a number of details in common regarding motif and structure. Some MSS of *Þjalar-Jóns saga* show a late connection with *Konráðs saga keisarasonar*. *Konráðs saga* may thus serve as a *terminus post quem* for the composition of *Þjalar-Jóns saga:* in both texts, Róðbert is the main adversary and Konráðr the king of Constantinople. While analogous connections between two later sagas (*e.g.*, between *Bósa saga* and *Vilmundar saga viðutan* or between *Hálfdanar saga Brǫnufóstra* and *Ála flekks saga*) can be demonstrated on the basis of the relationship between the main characters, *Þjalar-Jóns saga* represents instead a thematic continuation of another text (*Konráðs saga*) and thus shows a tendency toward a cyclical expansion.

Ed.: Gunnlaugur Þórðarson, ed. *Sagan af Þjalar-Jóni*. Reykjavik: Egill Jónsson, 1857; 2nd ed. Reykjavik: Jón Helgason, 1907; Tan-Haverhorst, Louisa Fredrika, ed. *Þjalar Jóns saga. Dámusta saga*. Haarlem: Tjeenk Willink, 1939 [introduction in Dutch, pp. i–cxviii; edition, pp. 1–47]; Slay, Desmond, ed. *Romances: Perg. 4:o nr 6 in The Royal Library, Stockholm*. Early Icelandic Manuscripts in Facsimile, 10. Copenhagen: Rosenkilde & Bagger, 1972. **Bib.:** Kalinke, Marianne E., and P. M. Mitchell. *Bibliography of Old Norse–Icelandic Romances*. Islandica, 44. Ithaca and London: Cornell University Press, 1985, pp. 132–4. **Lit.:** Jón Þorkelsson. *Om digtningen på Island i det 15. og 16. århundrede*. Copenhagen: Høst, 1888; Kölbing, E. "Ein Beitrag zur Kritik der romantischen Sagas." *Publications of the Modern Language Association* 13 (1898), 543–59 [esp. pp. 552–3]; Leach, Henry Goddard. *Angevin Britain and Scandinavia*. Harvard Studies in Comparative Literature, 6. Cambridge: Harvard University Press; London: Milford; Oxford: Ox-

ford University Press, 1921; rpt. Millwood: Kraus, 1975; Finnur Jónsson. *Den oldnorske og oldislandske Litteraturs Historie*. 3 vols. 2nd ed. Copenhagen: Gad, 1924, vol. 3, pp. 118–9; Schlauch, Margaret. *Romance in Iceland*. Princeton: Princeton University Press; New York: American-Scandinavian Foundation; London: Allen & Unwin, 1934; rpt. New York: Russell & Russell, 1973; Björn K. Þórólfsson. *Rímur fyrir 1600*. Safn Fræðafjelagsins um Ísland og Íslendinga, 9. Copenhagen: Möller, 1934, pp. 496–8; Stefán Einarsson. *A History of Icelandic Literature*. New York: American-Scandinavian Foundation; Baltimore: Johns Hopkins University Press, 1957, pp. 163–4; Einar Ól. Sveinsson. "*Viktors saga ok Blávus:* Sources and Characteristics." In *Viktors saga ok Blávus*. Ed. Jónas Kristjánsson. Riddarasögur, 2. Reykjavik: Handritastofnun Íslands, 1964, pp. cix–ccix; Damsgaard Olsen, Thorkil. "Den høviske litteratur." In *Norrøn fortællekunst. Kapitler af den norsk-islandske middelalderlitteraturs historie*. Ed. Hans Bekker-Nielsen et al. Copenhagen: Akademisk Forlag, 1965, pp. 92–117 [esp. p. 116]; Stefán Einarsson. "Heimili (skólar) fornaldarsagna og riddarasagna." *Skírnir* 140 (1966), 272; Slay, Desmond. "The Original State of Stockholm Perg. 4:o nr 6." In *Afmælisrit Jóns Helgasonar. 30. júní 1969*. Ed. Jakob Benediktsson et al. Reykjavik: Heimskringla, 1969, pp. 270–87; Glauser, Jürg. *Isländische Märchensagas: Studien zur Prosaliteratur im spätmittelalterlichen Island*. Beiträge zur nordischen Philologie, 12. Basel and Frankfurt am Main: Helbing & Lichtenhahn, 1983; Bibire, Paul. "From riddarasaga to lygisaga: The Norse Response to Romance." In *Les Sagas de Chevaliers (Riddarasögur). Actes de la V*ᵉ *Conférence Internationale sur les Sagas . . . (Toulon. Juillet 1982)*. Ed. Régis Boyer. Civilisations, 10. Paris: Presses de l'Université de Paris-Sorbonne, 1985, p. 68; Kalinke, Marianne E. "Riddarasögur, Fornaldarsögur, and the Problem of Genre." In *Les Sagas de Chevaliers (Riddarasögur)*, pp. 77–91; Kalinke, Marianne. "Norse romance (Riddarasögur)." In *Old Norse–Icelandic Literature: A Critical Guide*. Ed. Carol J. Clover and John Lindow. Islandica, 45. Ithaca and London: Cornell University Press, 1985, pp. 316–63; Kalinke, Marianne E. *Bridal-Quest Romance in Medieval Iceland*. Islandica, 46. Ithaca and London: Cornell University Press, 1990.

Jürg Glauser

[See also: *Fornaldarsögur; Konráðs saga keisarasonar; Riddarasögur; Rímur*]

Þjóðólfr of Hvin was a poet active in southern Norway in the last decades of the 9th century and the very beginning of the 10th. *Skáldatal* (*Edda Snorra Sturlusonar* 3: 253, 261, 273) associates him with both King Haraldr Hálfdanarson and his first cousin Rǫgnvaldr heiðumhæri ("the highly honored") Ólafsson, king of Vestfold, an important kingdom on the western shore of the Oslo fjord. Another of his patrons is given as Earl Hákon Grjótgarðsson. Two major poems, *Ynglingatal* and *Haustlǫng*, are firmly ascribed to him in medieval texts, while some sources, including Snorri Sturluson in his *Edda*, attribute to Þjóðólfr hornklofi ("horn-cleaver") at least some verses of the *Haraldskvæði* (or *Hrafnsmál*), a poem in praise of Haraldr Hálfdanarson. Other MSS support Þorbjǫrn hornklofi's authorship of this work, however, and modern authorities agree with them. For a list of the MS sources and attributions of verses of *Haraldskvæði*, see Jón Helgason 1968: 105–15.

Ynglingatal ("List of the Ynglingar") is a dynastic poem that Þjóðólfr composed in honor of Rǫgnvaldr heiðumhæri. It traces his genealogy back to the legendary Ynglingar, the royal house of Uppsala, devoting one or sometimes two stanzas to each of twenty-seven ancestors. In cryptic, allusive fashion, the poet tells the manner of each king's death and records his burial place. Thus, it functions as a kind of necrology as well as a tribute to Rǫgnvaldr and an assurance of his regal credentials. *Ynglingatal* appears in the eddic measure *kviðuháttr* but makes telling use of kennings. Scholars generally believe that the poem was transmitted orally for several hundred years before it was written down in the 12th or 13th century and then incorporated by Snorri Sturluson into his *Ynglinga saga*, the mythohistorical introductory section of his history of the kings of Norway, *Heimskringla* (*ca.* 1230). An opposing view (Krag 1985) considers the poem a much more recent composition, but has to contend with the marked similarity in subject matter and ordering of material between *Ynglingatal* and the relevant parts of the 12th-century Latin *Historia Norwegiae* and Ari Þorgilsson's *Íslendingabók*.

Haustlǫng ("Autumn Long," a title thought to refer to the length of time Þjóðólfr spent composing the poem) is a shield poem like Bragi Boddason's *Ragnarsdrápa*. It is in the skaldic measure *dróttkvætt*. In the first stanza, the poet claims, his *drápa* is a repayment to a certain Þorleifr for his gift of a "well-decorated voice-cliff," a shield, on which two mythological subjects were depicted, the rape of the goddess Iðunn and her apples of immortality by the giant Þjazi (sts. 2–13) and Þórr's single combat with the giant Hrungnir (sts. 14–20). *Haustlǫng* is recorded in MSS of Snorri Sturluson's *Edda*, because Snorri or his copyists quote it in two large blocks, corresponding to the two poetic subjects, in chs. 26 (Þórr and Hrungnir; Finnur Jónsson 1931: 104–5, Faulkes 1987: 80–1) and 31 (Þjazi and Iðunn; Finnur Jónsson 1931: 110–1, Faulkes 1987: 86–8) of his *Skáldskaparmál*. He himself gives a lengthy prose retelling of both the underlying myths of *Haustlǫng* (Finnur Jónsson 1931: 78–81 and 100–5, Faulkes 1987: 59–61 and 77–81) and elsewhere in *Skáldskaparmál* uses half-stanzas from the poem to illustrate points of skaldic diction (Finnur Jónsson 1931: 113–4 [st. 14b], 166 [st. 3a], 173 [st. 2a], Faulkes 1987: 89, 133, 139). *Haustlǫng* is a poem that combines clear narrative direction with complex and effective kennings.

Ed.: *Edda Snorra Sturlusonar*. 3 vols. Copenhagen: Sumptibus Legati Arnamagnæani, 1848–87, Vol. 3 [*Skáldatal*]; Finnur Jónsson, ed. *Den norske-islandske skjaldedigtning*. Vols. 1A–2A (tekst efter håndskrifterne) and 1B–2B (rettet tekst). Copenhagen and Christiania [Oslo]: Gyldendal, 1912–15; rpt. Copenhagen: Rosenkilde & Bagger, 1967 (A) and 1973 (B), vol. 1A, pp. 7–21; vol. 1B, pp. 7–19; Noreen, Adolf, ed. and trans. *Ynglingatal: Text, Översättning och Kommentar*. Kungl. vitterhets historie och antikvitets akademiens handlingar 28.2. Stockholm: Kungl. vitterhets historie och antikvitets akademien, 1925; Finnur Jónsson, ed. *Edda Snorra Sturlusonar*. Copenhagen: Gyldendal, 1931 [for *Haustlǫng*, pp. 104–5, 110–1, 113–4, 166, 173]; Bjarni Aðalbjarnarson, ed. *Heimskringla*. 3 vols. Íslenzk fornrit, 26–8. Reykjavik: Hið íslenzka fornritafélag, 1941–51, vol. 1 [for *Ynglingatal* quoted within *Ynglinga saga*, pp. 9–83]; Jón Helgason, ed. *Skjaldevers*. Nordisk filologi. Tekster og lærebøger til universitetsbrug, A. Tekster, vol. 12. Copenhagen: Munksgaard, 1968 [selections from *Ynglingatal* and *Haustlǫng*]; Turville-Petre, E. O. G. *Scaldic Poetry*. Oxford: Clarendon, 1976, pp. 6–11 [selections from *Ynglingatal* and *Haustlǫng*]. **Tr.:** Hollander, Lee M., trans. *The Skalds: A Selection of Their Poems with Introduction and Notes*. New York: American-Scandinavian Foundation; Princeton: Princeton University Press, 1945; 2nd ed. Ann Arbor: University of Michigan Press, 1968 [*Haustlǫng* only on pp. 38–48]; Hollander, Lee M., trans. *Heimskringla: History of the Kings of Norway*. Austin: University of Texas Press, 1964; Faulkes, Anthony, trans. *Snorri Sturluson: Edda*. Everyman Classics. London and Melbourne: Dent, 1987 [*Haustlǫng* is quoted at pp. 80–1, 86–8, 89, 133, 139]. **Bib.:** Hollander, Lee M. *A Bibliography of Skaldic Studies*. Copenhagen: Munksgaard, 1958; Bekker-Nielsen, Hans. *Old Norse-Icelandic Studies: A Select Bibliography*. Toronto Medieval Bibliographies, 1 Toronto: University of Toronto Press, 1967. **Lit.:** Phillpotts, Bertha S. *The Elder Edda and Ancient Scandinavian Drama*. Cambridge: Cambridge University Press, 1920 [*Haustlǫng* as ritual drama]; Åkerlund, Walter. *Studier över Ynglingatal*. Skrifter utgivne av Vetenskaps-Societeten i Lund, 23. Lund: Gleerup, 1939; Holtsmark, Anne. "Myten om *Idun* og *Tjatse* i Tjodolvs *Haustlǫng*." *Arkiv för nordisk filologi* 64 (1949), 41–73; rpt. in her *Studier i norrøn diktning*. Oslo: Gyldendal, 1956, pp. 96–161; Beyschlag, Siegfried. *Konungasǫgur. Untersuchungen zur Königssaga bis Snorri. Die älteren Übersichtwerke samt Ynglingasaga*. Bibliotheca Arnamagnæana, 8. Copenhagen: Munksgaard, 1950; Lie, Hallvard. "Billedbeskrivende dikt." *KLNM* 1 (1956), 542–5 [on *Haustlǫng* as shield poem]; Lie, Hallvard. *"Natur" og "unatur" i skaldekunsten*. Avhandlinger utg. av Det norske Videnskaps-Akademi i Oslo. 2. Hist.-filos. kl. no. 1. Oslo: Aschehoug, 1957; rpt. in his *Om sagakunst og skaldskap. Utvalgte avhandlinger*. Øvre Ervik: Alvheim & Eide, 1982, pp. 201–315; Dumézil, Georges. *Les dieux des germains: Essai sur la formation de la religion scandinave*. Mythes et religions, 39. Paris: Presses Universitaires de France [pp. 103–13 for Þórr-Hrungnir fight; trans. as *Gods of the Ancient Northmen*. Ed. Einar Haugen. Publications of the UCLA Center for the Study of Comparative Folklore and Mythology, 3. Berkeley, Los Angeles, and London: University of California Press, 1973; Holtsmark, Anne. "Haustlǫng." *KLNM* 6 (1961), 254–5; Baetke, Walter. *Yngvi und die Ynglinger. Eine quellenkritische Untersuchung über das nordische "Sakralkönigtum."* Sitzungsberichte der sächsischen Akademie der Wissenschaften zu Leipzig, Philol.-hist. Kl., 109.3. Berlin: Adademie, 1964; Turville-Petre, Gabriel. *Myth and Religion of the North: The Religion of Ancient Scandinavia*. New York: Holt, Rinehart and Winston, 1964; rpt. Westport: Greenwood, 1975; Ciklamini, Marlene. "*Ynglinga saga*: Its Function and Its Appeal." *Mediaeval Scandinavia* 8 (1975), 86–99; Magerøy, Hallvard. "*Ynglingasaga*" and "*Ynglingatal*." *KLNM* 20 (1976), 360–4; Turville-Petre, Joan. "On Ynglingatal." *Mediaeval Scandinavia* 11 (1978–79), 48–67; Clunies Ross, Margaret. "Style and Authorial Presence in Skaldic Mythological Poetry." *Saga-Book of the Viking Society* 20 (1981), 276–304; Evans, David A. "King Agni: Myth, History or Legend?" In *Specvlvm Norroenvm: Norse Studies in Memory of Gabriel Turville-Petre*. Ed. Ursula Dronke *et al.* Odense: Odense University Press, 1981, pp. 89–105; Lindow, John. "Narrative and the Nature of Skaldic Poetry." *Arkiv för nordisk filologi* 97 (1982), 94–121; Kuhn, Hans. *Das Dróttkvætt*. Heidelberg: Winter, 1983 [esp. pp. 279–81]; Marold, Edith. *Kenningkunst. Ein Beitrag zu einer Poetik der Skaldendichtung*. Quellen und Forschungen zur Sprach- und Kulturgeschichte der germanischen Völker, N.F., 80 (204). Berlin and New York: de Gruyter, 1983 [esp. pp. 114–210]; Krag, Claus. *Ynglingatal og Ynglingasaga. En studie i historiske kilder. Første del: Ynglingatals alder*. Bø: [n.p.], 1985 [typescript]; Mitchell, Stephen A. "The Whetstone as Symbol of Authority in Old English and Old Norse." *Scandinavian Studies* 57 (1985), 1–31 [on the Þórr-Hrungnir fight]; Lönnroth, Lars. "Dómaldi's Death and the Myth of Sacral Kingship." In *Structure and Meaning in Old Norse Literature: New Approaches to Textual Analysis and Literary Criticism*. Ed. John Lindow *et al.* Viking Collection, 3. Odense: Odense University Press, 1986, pp. 73–93.

Margaret Clunies Ross

[**See also:** Borre; Bragi Boddason; Eddic Meters; *Historia Norwegiae*; Iconography; *Íslendingabók*; Kennings; Mythology; *Skáld*; Skaldic Meters; Skaldic Verse; *Snorra Edda*; Þorbjǫrn hornklofi; Viking Art; *Ynglinga saga*]

Þórarinn loftunga ("praise-tongue") is listed in *Skáldatal* as poet both to King Knud (Cnut) Svensson (d. 1035) and to Knud's son Sven Álfífuson, successor to Óláfr Haraldsson (d. 1030) in Norway.

The first of these associations is confirmed in *Fagrskinna*, *Knýtlinga saga*, and a number of extant redactions of *Óláfs saga helga*. Of Þórarinn's *Hǫfuðlausn* ("Head-ransom"), only the *stef* ("refrain"), which may represent an oral variant of one attributed to Hallvarðr Háreksblesi (11th century), remains (in MSS of Snorri's *Heimskringla* and separate sagas of St. Óláfr). We apparently have Þórarinn's verification of the considerable sum (fifty marks) he received for this composition in stanza 1 of *Tøgdrápa* (Þórarinn's eyewitness account of Knud's 1028 expedition to Norway), although this stanza is preserved in isolation, only in *Knýtlinga saga* (ca. 1260–1270). (Stanza numbers refer to Finnur Jónsson's numeration.) The six *Tøgdrápa* stanzas cited by Snorri in his separate and *Heimskringla* sagas of St. Óláfr (both early 13th century), and *Knýtlinga saga*'s single stanza, are set within narrative frameworks that combine two recurrent saga motifs: the skald's poetic ransom for his life, and the skald's reward for a well-received composition. Four of the seven and a half stanzas of *Tøgdrápa* are cited in *Fagrskinna* (1220–1240), and six in the Legendary saga of St. Óláfr (early 13th century), in each case as a historical source. The four extant *vísuorð* of stanza 8 are cited only in *Skáldskaparmál* (*Snorra Edda*; ca. 1220). Snorri describes the six full stanzas he records (in the sequence between *stef*). Whether or not the title *Tøgdrápa* (attested in st. 8, perhaps meaning "Twenty [-stanza] drápa" or "Journey-drápa") indicates the poem's original length, the extant portion seems incomplete, since the *klofastef* (divided *stef*), which apparently opens in stanza 2, is nowhere resolved.

The ten stanzas traditionally attributed to Þórarinn's *Glælognskviða* ("Sea-calm Lay") are preserved in Snorri's sagas of Óláfr, with stanza 1 (ten *vísuorð* or alliterative half-lines) also appearing in *Fagrskinna*. Stanzas 4 and (perhaps) 10 are defectively preserved, and Snorri's attribution, dating (1031–1035), and account of the significance of some or all of the stanzas may be incorrect, for the extant stanzas are primarily concerned not with Sveinn (who, according to Snorri, is the addressee of all ten) but with St. Óláfr. After what is traditionally interpreted as a description of Sveinn's settlement in Niðaróss (Trondheim), the poet describes posthumous revelations of Óláfr's sanctity. With unadorned conviction, in the *kviðuháttr* meter, Þórarinn extols Óláfr, the eternal king, mediator between man and God, to whom even his political opponent Sveinn is commended to pray.

We know little of Þórarinn other than that he was an Icelander who frequented the courts of noblemen. Although his extant corpus appears bland (*Glælognskviða* is stylistically simple, and *Tøgdrápa*, in effect, an elaborated itinerary), it is not without interest. *Glælognskviða* apparently introduces into Christian skaldic poetry the cult figure of St. Óláfr, and *Tøgdrápa* seems to represent an early example of a technical innovation, the combination of *fornyrðislag* lines and *dróttkvætt* rhyme and alliteration, which apparently gave rise to the *tøglag* meter.

Ed.: Guðbrandr Vigfússon and C. R. Unger, eds. *Flateyjarbók: En Samling af norske Konge-Sagaer med indskudte mindre Fortællinger om Begivenheder i og udenfor Norge samt Annaler*. 3 vols. Christiania [Oslo]: Malling, 1860–68 [cited in vol. 2, pp. 306–7, 369, 377]; Finnur Jónsson, ed. *Den norske-islandske skjaldedigtning*. Vols. 1A–2A (tekst efter håndskrifterne) and 1B–2B (rettet tekst). Copenhagen and Christiania [Oslo]: Gyldendal, 1912–15; rpt. Copenhagen: Rosenkilde & Bagger, 1967 (A) and 1973 (B), vol. 1A,

pp. 322–7; 1B, pp. 298–301; Guðni Jónsson, ed. *Edda Snorra Sturlusonar með Skáldatali*. Reykjavik: Sigurður Kristjánsson, 1935 [cited p. 190]; Johnsen, Oscar Albert, and Jón Helgason, eds. *Saga Olafs konungs hins helga. Den store saga om Olav den hellige efter pergamenthåndskrift i Kungliga biblioteket i Stockholm nr. 2 4to, med varianter fra andre håndskrifter*. 2 vols. Oslo: Dybwad, 1941 [stanzas cited in vol. 1, pp. 474–6, 594, 603–4]; Bjarni Aðalbjarnarson, ed. *Heimskringla*. 3 vols. Íslenzk fornrit, 26–8. Reykjavik: Hið íslenzka fornritafélag, 1941–51 [cited in vol. 2, pp. 307, 308–10, 399, 406–8]; Kock, Ernst A., ed. *Den norsk-isländska skaldediktningen*. 2 vols. Lund: Gleerup, 1946–49, vol. 1, pp. 151–3; Bjarni Guðnason, ed. *Danakonunga sǫgur*. Íslenzk fornrit, 35. Reykjavik: Hið íslenzka fornritafélag, 1982 [cited p. 125]; Heinrichs, Anne, *et al.*, eds. and trans. *Olafs saga hins helga: Die "Legendarische Saga" über Olaf den Heiligen*. Heidelberg: Winter, 1982 [cited pp. 168–71]; Bjarni Einarsson, ed. *Ágrip af Nóregskonunga sǫgum; Fagrskinna—Nóregs konunga tal*. Íslenzk fornrit, 29. Reykjavik: Hið íslenzka fornritafélag, 1984 [sts. cited pp. 191–3, 201]. **Tr.**: Gudbrand Vigfusson and F. York Powell, eds. and trans. *Corpus Poeticum Boreale: The Poetry of the Old Northern Tongue from the Earliest Times to the Thirteenth Century*. 2 vols. Oxford: Clarendon, 1883; rpt. New York: Russell & Russell, 1965, vol. 2, pp. 159–61. **Bib.**: Halldór Hermannsson. *Bibliography of the Sagas of the Kings of Norway and Related Sagas and Tales*. Islandica, 3. Ithaca: Cornell University Library, 1910; rpt. New York: Kraus, 1966; Halldór Hermannsson. *The Sagas of the Kings (Konunga sögur) and the Mythical-Heroic Sagas: Two Bibliographical Supplements*. Islandica, 26. New York: Cornell University Press, 1937; Hollander, Lee M. *A Bibliography of Skaldic Studies*. Copenhagen: Munksgaard, 1958. **Lit.**: Magerøy, Hallvard. *Glælognskviða av Toraren lovtunge. Bidrag til nordisk filologi av studerende ved Universitetet i Oslo*, 12. Oslo: Aschehoug, 1948 [text, notes, Norwegian translation, discussion]; Hofmann, Dietrich. *Nordisch-englische Lehnbeziehungen der Wikingerzeit*. Bibliotheca Arnamagnæana, 14. Copenhagen: Munksgaard, 1955, pp. 94–7; Lange, Wolfgang. *Studien zur christlichen Dichtung der Nordgermanen 1000–1200*. Palaestra, 222. Göttingen: Vandenhoeck & Ruprecht, 1958, pp. 115–20; Fidjestøl, Bjarne. *Det norrøne fyrstediktet*. Øvre Ervik: Alvheim & Eide, 1982 [see index of poems and stanzas, p. 274]; Hellberg, Staffan. "Kring tillkomsten av Glælognskviða." *Arkiv för nordisk filologi* 99 (1984), 14–48.

Mary Malcolm

[**See also:** Christian Poetry; *Fagrskinna*; *Heimskringla*; *Knýtlinga saga*; *Lausavísur*; *Óláfs saga helga*; *Skáld*; Skaldic Meters; Skaldic Verse; *Snorra Edda*]

Þórarinn svarti ("the black"), a skald of the latter half of the 10th century, lived at Mávahlíð on Snæfellsnes in western Iceland. Both *Landnámabók* and *Eyrbyggja saga* tell essentially the same story about this poet. The saga describes Þórarinn as strong and ugly, but of so peaceable a disposition that his detractors considered him effeminate. Nonetheless, when a party led by Þorbjǫrn inn digri ("the fat"), brother-in-law of Snorri goði (chieftain), attempts to accuse Þórarinn of theft, he is goaded by his mother into attacking them. In breaking up the fray, Þórarinn's wife, Auðr, loses her hand, prompting Þórarinn to pursue and attack his accusers. In the second battle, Þórarinn kills several men, including Þorbjǫrn himself. The case is taken up by Snorri, and, with the aid of his kinsmen, Þórarinn escapes Iceland in anticipation of his outlawry. Nonetheless, the enmity aroused by this incident persists, resulting in further deaths.

The saga attributes seventeen *dróttkvætt* stanzas to Þórarinn. These verses are scattered throughout the narrative after the slaying of Þorbjǫrn, although they may originally have been composed as a single poem. In tone and content, they are consistent with the saga's portrayal of events and of Þórarinn himself. They refer to Þórarinn's reputation for effeminacy and to the loss of Auðr's hand, and they express both distaste for strife as well as pride in the poet's martial triumph and the vindication of his masculinity. The verses suggest both his fear of the legal consequences of the fight and his hope of assistance from his kinsmen.

Some of the vocabulary and kennings in these verses, particularly in stanzas 11–14, suggest a date rather later than the historical Þórarinn. It is difficult to ascertain whether this anachronism is due to later interpolation of the stanzas in question or reworking of the original poetry, or whether the whole of these verses was composed by a later poet and attributed to Þórarinn. However, it is generally agreed that the verses predate the saga in its extant written form.

Most of Þórarinn's kennings are composed of two or three elements, although stanza 9 in particular includes such lengthy circumlocutions as *hjalmi hættar spámeyjar ens þunga þings vangs Þrúðar hjaldrs* ("the helm-endangering sybils of the grave meeting of the field of Þrúðr of the din") for "arrows." His kenning *líknar leiki* ("healing-play") for "peace," is unique, a reversal of the typical "battle-play" kennings, which is particularly appropriate to his peaceful nature. Stanza 4 includes some legalistic kennings and metaphors, such as *dœmisalr dóma* ("case-hall of judgments") for "mouth," suggesting the poet's preoccupation with the legal outcome of this confrontation. Þórarinn is also remarkable for his frequent references to women: his mother, his wife, Þorbjǫrn's widow, Snorri's paramour, and the woman or women to whom several of the stanzas are addressed. It is also unusual that all of this skald's surviving works were apparently composed before he had ever traveled abroad, contrary to the usual pattern of skaldic biographies.

Þórarinn's poetry was held in some esteem in medieval Iceland. The *Hauksbók* version of *Landnámabók* names his verses the *Máhlíðingavísur* ("the verses of the men of Mávahlíð"), and cites stanza 11. In *Háttatal*, Snorri Sturluson, who calls him "Þórarinn Máhlíðingr," uses two lines of stanza 3 to illustrate poetic contractions.

Ed.: Finnur Jónsson, ed. *Den norsk-islandske skjaldedigtning*. Vols. 1A–2A (tekst efter håndskrifterne) and 1B–2B (rettet tekst). Copenhagen and Christiania [Oslo]: Gyldendal, 1912–15; rpt. Copenhagen: Rosenkilde & Bagger, 1967 (A) and 1973 (B), vol. 1A, pp. 111–5; vol. 1B, pp. 105–9. **Lit.**: Kock, Ernst A. *Notationes norrœnæ: Anteckningar till Edda och skaldedigtning*. Lunds Universitets Årsskrift, n. s., sec. 1. Lund: Gleerup, 1923–44, vol. 3, pp. 45–51; vol. 14, pp. 40–2; vol. 22, pp. 17–21 [entire work published in twenty-seven parts]; Finnur Jónsson. "Skjaldekvads tolkning, Máhlíðingavísur." *Aarbøger for nordisk Oldkyndihed og Historie* (1930), 1–64; Vries, Jan de. *Altnordische Literaturgeschichte*. 2 vols. Grundriss der germanischen Philologie, 15–6. Berlin: de Gruyter, 1941–42; rpt. 1964–67, vol. 1, pp. 199–201; Einar Ól. Sveinsson. "Eyrbyggja sagas kilder." *Scripta Islandica* 19 (1968), 3–18; Poole, Russell. "The Origins of the *Máhlíðingavísur*." *Scandinavian Studies* 57 (1985), 244–85.

Jeffrey L. Singman

[**See also:** *Eyrbyggja saga*; Kennings; *Landnámabók*; *Lausavísur*; *Skáld*; Skaldic Meters; Skaldic Verse; *Snorra Edda*]

Þorbjǫrn hornklofi ("horn-cleaver"). Nothing is known of the life or family of the Norwegian skald Þorbjǫrn hornklofi (9th century), except that he was *gamall vinr konunga, er jafnan hafði í hirðum verit frá barnœsku* ("an old friend of the kings, who had been at the court constantly since his childhood"; *Fagrskinna*, ch. 2). Why he was called "horn-cleaver," a word that is used in a *þula* as a *heiti* for "raven," is not known. *Skálda saga*, preserved in *Hauksbók*, recounts an amorous adventure of Þorbjǫrn hornklofi and two other skalds, quoting a stanza by each of them, but this saga has no historical value.

The quotation from *Fagrskinna* introduces fifteen stanzas from a dialogue poem by "Hornklofi skáld," which has been called *Kvæði um hirðsiðu*, on the life at King Haraldr's court. The first part is in *málaháttr* meter, the latter part in a mixture of *málaháttr* and *ljóðaháttr*. One of these stanzas is also quoted in *Heimskringla* (*Haralds saga hárfagra*, ch. 15), and another one in *Haralds þáttr hárfagra* in *Flateyjarbók*, where it is attributed to Auðun illskælda ("poetaster").

Five stanzas in *málaháttr* about the battle in Hafrsfjǫrðr are preserved in the same sagas. In *Haralds þáttr* and *Fagrskinna* (ch. 3), they are attributed to "Þjóðólfr skáld ór Hvíni," but in *Heimskringla* (*Haralds saga ins hárfagri*, ch. 18) they are assigned to Þorbjǫrn hornklofi, as is the stanza from *Kvæði um hirðsiðu*. Half of one of them, however, is also quoted in the *Snorra Edda* under Þjóðólfr's name, as well as an additional half-stanza describing the fallen warriors lying on the sand, preserved only there.

According to the common tradition in *Fagrskinna* and *Haralds þáttr hárfagra*, the stanzas belong to poems by two or three different skalds, whereas Snorri, when he wrote *Heimskringla*, seems to have taken them as a unit. Admittedly, it is not known whether he knew more than the seven stanzas quoted in *Heimskringla* and the *Snorra Edda*.

Uniting the stanzas into one poem avoids having to explain why there are several poems about one particular king, all in the same relatively rare meter. Further, the raven's introductory announcement that he will "tell about Haraldr's war-deeds" is fulfilled only by the inclusion of the Hafrsfjǫrðr stanzas. Finally, the opening line of the first Hafrsfjǫrðr stanza, "*Heyrðir þú...,*" seems to presuppose the dialogue frame found in the *Kvæði um hirðsiðu*. Most modern scholars have therefore accepted the idea that the stanzas belong to one poem, which is commonly called *Haraldskvæði* or sometimes *Hrafnsmál*. Moreover, two additional stanzas on the king's wives, preserved in different *konungasögur*, are edited as stanzas 13–14 of the same poem. Four stanzas on King Haraldr in eddic meter preserved in *Haralds þáttr hárfagra*, and one fragment in *Fagrskinna* MS A are considered spurious, and are not included in editions of *Haraldskvæði*. Possibly, they represent an oral variant of the poem.

Although the evidence is not compelling, Þorbjǫrn hornklofi's authorship of *Haraldskvæði* is also generally accepted. Von See (1961) argued, however, that the latter part of the poem (sts. 13–23) is a later addition from the 11th–12th centuries.

Haraldskvæði, as a modern reconstruction of twenty-three stanzas of varying length, thus consists of an introductory part, containing the skald's bid for listeners and a presentation of the fictitious participants in the dialogue, a valkyrie and a raven, together with a description of the belligerent king, who prefers the Viking life at sea to sitting by the fire at home. The valkyrie is described as a beautiful woman, strangely ignorant of the king's deeds, and she lacks all numinous quality. The raven, on the other hand, has thorough knowledge of Haraldr's affairs, because the raven, like the skald himself, has "followed the young king since he came out of the egg" (cf. the quotation from *Fagrskinna* about the poet). Despite the fact that both participants in the dialogue might be considered mythological figures, their role does not in any way seem religious, but just a matter of literary devices.

The second section, which in the reconstructed *Haraldskvæði* context is taken as the raven's monologue, describes the battle in Hafrsfjǫrðr. A chief called Haklangr fell after a fierce battle, and King Kjǫtvi and his men "fled by way of Jaðar, on mead cups thinking." The beaten enemies are ridiculed by the skald in a coarse description with sexually defamatory overtones: "Then hid under benches, and let their buttocks stick up, they who were wounded, but thrust their heads keelward."

In the last section, after the stanzas on the king's marriage, which possibly are out of place in this context, the raven answers a series of questions from the valkyrie concerning the warriors, skalds, and jugglers in the king's service, and praises the generosity of the king. Whether this section is a genuine part of the original poem or not, it seems incomplete.

Haraldskvæði is the oldest of the three so-called eddic praise poems (Genzmer 1920), and it gives a historically important description of a crucial event in Norwegian history of the Viking Age, presumably from an eyewitness. Its vivid descriptions, grim irony, and terse composition make it a masterpiece of skaldic poetry.

Also preserved in *Haralds þáttr*, *Fagrskinna*, and *Heimskringla* are seven whole and two half-stanzas of a *dróttkvætt* poem by Þorbjǫrn on King Haraldr's battles, called *Glymdrápa*. The poem describes a battle "on the heath," which took place before another battle at sea, where the king defeated two other kings. Other battles took place "south of the sea" and "on the sand," where the king seems to be called "enemy of the Scots." However, as the poem mentions no place-names, the identification of the battles is hypothetical, and there is no unanimity in the sagas quoting the stanzas on this question.

Glymdrápa is the oldest praise poem in fully developed *dróttkvætt* meter, and it contains a great number of complex kennings. The description of the *Skǫglar dynr* ("the din of Skǫgur" [one of the valkyries], *i.e.*, battle) to a great extent concentrates on sound sensations, and the language is rich in (onomatopoeic?) assonances in addition to the *hendingar* required by the meter. The name *Glymdrápa* (the "clangor poem"), therefore, probably alludes to its "noisy" character. Some stanzas seem to be composed in intricate parallel patterns. In the poem's state of preservation, no *stef* can be identified. In the presumably final stanza, Haraldr is praised as the most glorious king "under the sun's old, steep chair" (heaven), a frequently recurring panegyrical formula.

Ed.: Finnur Jónsson, ed. *Den norsk-islandske skjaldedigtning*. Vols. 1A-2A (tekst efter håndskrifterne) and 1B-2B (rettet tekst). Copenhagen and Christiania [Oslo]: Gyldendal, 1912–15; rpt. Copenhagen: Rosenkilde & Bagger, 1967 (A) and 1973 (B) [basic edition]; Kershaw, Nora, ed. and trans. *Anglo-Saxon and Norse Poems*. Cambridge: Cambridge University Press, 1922 [*Haraldskvæði*]; Jón Helgason, ed.

Skjaldevers. Nordisk filologi. Tekster og lærebøger til universitetsbrug, A. Tekster, vol. 12. Copenhagen: Munksgaard, 1968 [*Haraldskvæði*]; Turville-Petre, E. O. G. *Scaldic Poetry*. Oxford: Clarendon, 1976 [text, translation and commentary of the Hafrsfjǫrðr stanzas]. **Tr.** [see also above]: Hollander, Lee M., trans. *Old Norse Poems*. New York: Columbia University Press, 1936 [*Haraldskvæði*]. **Lit.**: Genzmer, Felix. "Das eddische Preislied." *Beiträge zur Geschichte der deutschen Sprache und deutsche Literatur* (Tübingen) 44 (1920), 146–68; Holtsmark, Anne. *Þorbjǫrn hornklofes Glymdrápa*. Bidrag til nordisk filologi av studerende ved Universitetet i Oslo, 7. Oslo: Aschehoug, 1927; See, Klaus von. "Studien zum Haraldskvæði." *Arkiv för nordisk filologi* 76 (1961), 96–111; rpt. in his *Edda, Saga, Skaldendichtung: Aufsätze zur skandinavischen Literatur des Mittelalters*. Heidelberg: Winter, 1981, pp. 295–310; See, Klaus von. "Skaldenstrophe und Sagaprosa." *Mediaeval Scandinavia* 10 (1977), 58–82; rpt. in his *Edda, Saga, Skaldendichtung*, pp. 461–85; See, Klaus von. "Mündliche Prosa und Skaldendichtung." *Mediaeval Scandinavia* 11 (1978–79), 82–91; rpt. in his *Edda, Saga, Skaldendichtung*, pp. 496–505; Hofmann, Dietrich. "Sagaprosa als Partner von Skaldenstrophen." *Mediaeval Scandinavia* 11 (1978–79), 68–81; rpt. in his *Gesammelte Schriften*. 2 vols. Hamburg: Busche, 1988, vol. 1, pp. 456–69; Fidjestøl, Bjarne. *Det norrøne fyrstediktet*. Øvre Ervik: Alvheim & Eide, 1982.

Bjarne Fidjestøl

[**See also:** Eddic Meters; *Fagrskinna*; *Flateyjarbók*; *Hauksbók*; *Heimskringla*; *Heiti*; Kennings; *Lausavísur*; *Skáld*; Skaldic Meters; Skaldic Verse; *Snorra Edda*; Þjóðólfr of Hvin]

Þórðar saga kakala *see* **Sturlunga saga**

Þórðar saga hreðu ("The Saga of Quarrel-Þórðr") is one of the minor *Íslendingasögur*. It completely lacks any historical basis, although the text claims that Þórðr hreða Þórðarson was a settler in Iceland, and follows him from Norway to Iceland ostensibly during the 11th century. Most of the characters and episodes are clearly borrowed from *Landnámabók* or from other *Íslendingasögur*, many details being invented or taken from unknown sources. Consequently, this postclassical saga provides an excellent opportunity to investigate how a good *sagnamaðr* ("saga author") tells his story, draws his characters, and combines details. Oral traditions may have existed in the north of Iceland about Þórðr hreða, who built several *skálar* (sing. *skáli*, a house or small building on a farm), one of which, according to the text, still existed during the time of Bishop Egill (1332–1341). But most of the obligatory stereotypes are presented in a very conventional way, for example, in the description of fights. The saga focuses on a long family quarrel between Þórðr hreða and Miðfjarðar-Skeggi, whose son, Eiðr, has been the object of Þórðr's jeers.

Two texts concerning Þórðr hreða survive. The first is fragmentary, lacking both beginning and end; it is preserved in the *Vatnshyrna* codex (late 14th century), containing several *Íslendingasögur*. The author used themes and characters in the *konungasögur*, and he knew *Laxdœla saga*. The second version is complete: five paper MSS tell the whole story of Þórðr, including the quarrels that gave rise to his nickname. The author knew and appreciated *Njáls saga*, since episodes are borrowed from it. Arngrímur Jónsson knew this text, and provides an abstract in his *Crymogaea* (1609).

It is difficult to say whether these two versions were independent or internally related, because we lack a complete study of the MS tradition. Nonetheless, the saga is interesting because of the character Þórðr himself, who occupies an intermediate position between the heroes of *fornaldarsögur* and those in *Íslendingasögur*.

Ed.: *Nockrer Marg-Frooder Søgu-Þætter Islendinga*. Hólar, 1756; Guðbrandur Vigfússon, ed. *Bárðar saga Snæfellsáss, Víglundarsaga, Þórðarsaga, Draumvitranir, Völsaþáttr*. Nordiske Oldskrifter, 27. Copenhagen: Det nordiske Literatur-Samfund, 1860; Jóhannes Halldórsson, ed. *Kjalnesinga saga*. Íslensk fornrit, 14. Reykjavik: Hið íslenzka fornritafélag, 1959. **Tr.**: Coles, John, trans. *Summer Travelling in Iceland: Being the Narrative of Two Journeys Across the Island by Unfrequented Routes*. London: Murray, 1882, pp. 173–204. **Lit.**: Binns, Alan L. "The Story of Þorsteinn uxafót, Excursus on Ólöf Ásbjarnardóttir." *Saga-Book of the Viking Society* 14 (1953–55), 61–3; Jakob Benediktsson, ed. *Arngrimi Jonae: Opera Latine Conscripta*. 4 vols. Bibliotheca Arnamagnæana, 9–12. Copenhagen: Munksgaard, 1950–57, vol. 4, pp. 96–7, 306–7; Schach, Paul. *Icelandic Sagas*. Twayne's World Authors Series, 717. Boston: Twayne, 1984, pp. 156–7, 161.

Régis Boyer

[**See also:** *Fornaldarsögur; Íslendingasögur; Landnámabók; Laxdæla saga; Njáls saga; Vatnshyrna*]

Þórðr Kolbeinsson was an Icelandic skald born in Iceland around 974. The year of his death is not known, but he probably lived until the middle of the 11th century. Þórðr was a court poet and served as a retainer of the Norwegian Earl Eiríkr Hákonarson from 1007 to 1008. In *Skáldatal*, Þórðr Kolbeinsson is listed among the skalds of King Magnús Óláfsson of Norway (d. 1047). He is also said (doubtfully) to have composed a praise poem to the Danish Earl Sven Estridsen (d. 1076).

Þórðr Kolbeinsson is best known as the antagonist of the skald Bjǫrn Arngeirsson in *Bjarnar saga Hítdœlakappa*. The saga describes Þórðr's marriage to Bjǫrn's former fiancée Oddný eykyndill ("isle-candle") and the ensuing enmity between the two skalds (expressed in a series of *lausavísur*, twelve of which are attributed to Þórðr). The story culminates in Þórðr's killing of Bjǫrn in 1024. Þórðr lived at the farmstead Hítarnes in Iceland. He had eight children with his wife Oddný, and one of his sons was the court poet Arnórr Þórðarson jarlaskáld ("earls' skald").

Aside from the twelve *lausavísur* by Þórðr Kolbeinsson recorded in *Bjarnar saga Hítdœlakappa*, his only extant poems are seventeen *dróttkvætt* stanzas from the beginning of the 11th century: two and a half stanzas of *Belgskakadrápa* (ca. 1007), an encomiastic poem describing the death of Earl Hákon Sigurðarson and Eiríkr Hákonarson's escape to Sweden; one stanza of a *drápa* about the skald Gunnlaugr Illugason (d. 1008); and thirteen and a half stanzas of *Eiríksdrápa* (ca. 1014), a panegyric to Earl Eiríkr Hákonarson. According to *Bjarnar saga Hítdœlakappa*, Þórðr allegedly composed a poem in honor of King Óláfr Haraldsson (ca. 1016) and two satirical poems about Bjǫrn Arngeirsson and Bjǫrn's wife (*Kolluvísur, Daggeislavísur*), but none of these poems has survived.

Þórðr Kolbeinsson is referred to as "a good skald" (*Bjarnar saga Hítdœlakappa*, chs. 3 and 6; *Grettis saga*, ch. 136). His *lausavísur*, clearly superior to those of his adversary Bjǫrn Arngeirsson, show that he was indeed worthy of such distinction. His encomiastic poetry, however, shows little originality, and sev-

eral of the lines merely echo the poetry of such skalds as Hallfreðr Óttarsson (*Erfidrápa*) and Tindr Hallkelsson (*Hákonardrápa*). In Þórðr's *Eiríksdrápa* (sts. 11:5, 12:7, and 13:7), we find the first occurrences of *dróttkvætt* lines with the internal rhyme on the verb in the first position, followed by a trisyllabic compound or a similar syntactic unit whose first element carries alliteration (*e.g., brestr erfiði Austra* and *hlýð mínum brag meiðir*). This structural innovation appears to be the result of Þórðr's attempt to accommodate the place-name *Hringmaraheiðr* in *dróttkvætt* lines (*cf. Erfidrápa*, st. 12:7: *rauð Hringmaraheiði*). Lines of this type enjoyed an increasing popularity in the poetry of later skalds.

Ed.: Finnur Jónsson, ed. *Den norsk-islandske skjaldedigtning*. 2 vols. 1A-2A (tekst efter håndskrifterne) and 1B-2B (rettet tekst). Copenhagen and Christiania [Oslo]: Gyldendal, 1912–15; rpt. Copenhagen: Rosenkilde & Bagger, 1967 (A) and 1973 (B), vols. 1A, pp. 212–9; 1B, pp. 202–9; Sigurður Nordal and Guðni Jónsson, eds. *Borgfirðinga sögur*. Íslenzk fornrit, 3. Reykjavik: Hið íslenzka fornritafélag, 1938 [see also other editions of *Bjarnar saga Hítdœlakappa* and *Gunnlaugs saga ormstungu*]; Bjarni Aðalbjarnarson, ed. *Heimskringla*. 3 vols. Íslenzk fornrit, 26–8. Reykjavik: Hið íslenzka fornritafélag, 1941–51; rpt. 1979, vol. 1, pp. 275, 300, 337, 364, 371; vol. 2, pp. 31–3 [see also other editions of this work]; Kock, Ernst A., ed. *Den norsk-isländska skaldediktningen*. 2 vols. Lund: Gleerup, 1946–49, vol. 1, pp. 106–9; Bjarni Guðnason, ed. *Danakonunga sögur*. Íslenzk fornrit, 35. Reykjavik: Hið íslenzka fornritafélag, 1982, pp. 105, 114, 117–9 [see also other editions of *Knýtlinga saga*]. **Tr.**: Hollander, Lee M., trans. *Heimskringla: History of the Kings of Norway*. Austin: University of Texas Press, 1964, pp. 177, 193–4; Turville-Petre, E. O. G. *Scaldic Poetry*. Oxford: Clarendon, 1976, pp. 75–7; Bachmann, W. Bryant, Jr., trans. *Bjarnar saga Hítdœlakappa*. In *Four Old Icelandic Sagas and Other Tales*. Lanham: University Press of America, 1985, pp. 151–219. **Bib.**: Hollander, Lee M. *A Bibliography of Skaldic Studies*. Copenhagen: Munksgaard, 1958. **Lit.**: Guðmundur Þorláksson. *Udsigt over de norsk-islandske skjalde fra 9. til 14. århundrede*. Samfund til udgivelse af gammel nordisk litteratur, 8. Copenhagen: Møller, 1882, pp. 76–8; Finnur Jónsson. *Den oldnorske og oldislandske Litteraturs Historie*. 3 vols. 2nd ed. Copenhagen: Gad, 1920–24, vol. 1, pp. 560–64; Kuhn, Hans. "Die Dróttkvættverse des Typs 'brestr erfiði Austra.'" In *Afmælisrit Jóns Helgasonar 30 júní 1969*. Ed. Jakob Benediktsson *et al.* Reykjavik: Heimskringla, 1969, pp. 403–17; rpt. in his *Kleine Schriften*. 4 vols. Ed. Dietrich Hofmann *et al.* Berlin: de Gruyter, 1969–78, vol. 4, pp. 105–16; Kuhn, Hans. *Das Dróttkvætt*. Heidelberg: Winter, 1983, pp. 300–1.

Kari Ellen Gade

[**See also:** Arnórr Þórðarson jarlaskáld; *Bjarnar saga Hítdœlakappa*; Hallfreðar Óttarsson; *Lausavísur; Skáld*; Skaldic Meters; Skaldic Verse]

Þorfinnsdrápa *see* **Arnórr Þórðarson jarlaskáld**

Þorgils saga ok Hafliða *see* **Sturlunga saga**

Þorgils saga skarða *see* **Sturlunga saga**

Þorgríms þáttr Hallasonar ("The Tale of Þorgrímr Hallason"), a short Old Icelandic tale, is part of the *konungasögur* about Magnús inn góði ("the good"), in the codex *Hulda-*

Hrokkinskinna. It is found in a section dealing with the relationship between Kálfr Árnason and the king.

The story starts in Iceland, but the main events take place in Norway. In the absence of Magnús, Kálfr runs the state government. Þorgrímr, being advanced in years, is slandered by Kálfr's Icelandic poet Bjarni because of an incident in Iceland and of Þorgrímr's love for the defeated Óláfr helgi ("the holy"). Failing to incite his son Illugi to revenge, Þorgrímr himself kills Bjarni. He is outlawed and immediately killed by Bjarni's brother Þórðr. Kolgrímr, a member of Þorgrímr's retinue, kills Þórðr and is put in prison. It is now time for Magnús to return from his campaign against Denmark, as a *deus ex machina*. He liberates and rewards Kolgrímr and criticizes Kálfr for his proceedings in the conflict.

Bjarni has been identified as the court poet Bjarni gullbrárskáld ("the skald with gold brows") by Árni Magnússon, although the identification is disputable. Bjarni composed a poem entitled *Kálfsflokkr* mentioning events from as late as 1044. But, according to *Þorgríms þáttr*, he had been long dead by that time. Furthermore, the main saga text does not mention any campaign against Denmark during the time Kálfr was still living in Norway, that is, before he was pressed by Magnús to escape. These problems can be circumvented in two ways. The tale could have taken place at a later time, around 1050 in the reign of Haraldr harðráði ("hardruler") Sigurðarson, or it could be based on a corrupt or misunderstood tradition.

Þorgríms þáttr was probably composed sometime during the 13th century, with the conflict between Kálfr and Magnús as the point of departure. In spite of Þorgrímr's early death, the tale is far from tragic, as Kolgrímr immediately takes over the role as hero. He is small and subordinate, but he grows to be a leader. His friend Galti, who is big and strong, evolves in the opposite direction.

Ed.: Jónas Kristjánsson, ed. *Eyfirðinga sǫgur.* Íslenzk fornrit, 9. Reykjavik: Hið íslenzka fornritafélag, 1956, pp. cxv–cxvi, 299–303. **Lit.**: Vries, Jan de. *Altnordische Literaturgeschichte.* 2 vols. Grundriss der germanischen Philologie, 15–6. Berlin: de Gruyter, 1941–42; rpt. 1964–67, vol. 2, p. 430; Harris, Joseph. "Genre and Narrative Structure in Some *Íslendinga þættir*." *Scandinavian Studies* 44 (1972), 1–27; Harris, Joseph. "Theme and Genre in Some *Íslendinga Pættir*." *Scandinavian Studies* 48 (1976), 1–28 [esp. p. 22]; Louis-Jensen, Jonna. *Kongesagastudier. Kompilationen Hulda-Hrokkinskinna.* Bibliotheca Arnamagnæana, 32. Copenhagen: Reitzel, 1977, pp. 109–11; Danielsson, Tommy. *Om den isländska släktsagans uppbyggnad.* Skrifter utgivna av Litteraturvetenskapliga institutionen vid Uppsala universitet, 22. Uppsala: Almqvist & Wiksell, 1986, pp. 65–6.

Tommy Danielsson

[**See also**: *Hulda-Hrokkinskinna; Konungasǫgur; Skáld; Þáttr*]

Þorláks saga helga ("The Saga of St. Þorlákr") survives in ten
primary MSS and later copies of these; they represent three overlapping and sometimes incomplete medieval versions of varying length, and a fragment of a fourth. These are: (1) Stock. Perg. fol. no. 5 (mid-14th century); (2) AM 382 4to (first half of 14th century); (3) seven MSS, AM 209 fol. (17th century), AM 219 fol. (end of 14th century), AM 379–80 4to (17th century), AM 383 III-IV 4to (soon after 1400), AM 388 4to (17th century); and (4) AM 383 I 4to (mid-13th century). There also survive overlapping miracle books, and some Latin fragments, most importantly in AM 386 4to, the first half of which can be dated palaeographically to around 1200.

The saga is a life of St. Þorlákr Þórhallsson, bishop of Skálholt in Iceland (born 1133, consecrated 1178, died December 23, 1193, translated July 20, 1198). The earliest Latin fragments of his life were probably composed for Bishop Páll Jónsson's translation of St. Þorlákr's relics, and the earliest version of the vernacular saga was probably also composed at about this time, since it seems to have been reworked by the author of *Hungrvaka* and *Páls saga biskups*, perhaps at the stage when this writer assembled a cycle of sagas of the bishops of Skálholt, probably by or during the second decade of the 13th century. This revised text then formed the basis, by partly independent expansion or abridgment, of the present versions. In versions (2) and (3), a long section is added, the *Oddaverja þáttr*, dealing with the political and personal disputes between Bishop Þorlákr and the chieftain Jón Loptsson, father of Bishop Páll Jónsson. The saga is fairly strictly narrative in form, and although it is a saint's life, the conventions of this genre are accommodated happily to those of Icelandic contemporary biography. Its style is rather Latinate, and is replete with biblical quotations; further, it has both a religious passion and a homely vividness of presentation wholly lacking in *Hungrvaka*, and very largely also in *Páls saga biskups*. The miracles included in the saga and in the miracle books give correspondingly vivid glimpses of the daily life of ordinary Icelanders.

Ed.: [Jón Sigurðsson and Guðbrandur Vigfússon, eds.] *Biskupa sǫgur.* 2 vols. Copenhagen: Möller, 1858–78; Gudbrand Vigfusson and F. York Powell, eds. and trans. *Origines Islandicae: A Collection of the More Important Sagas and Other Native Writings Relating to the Settlement and Early History of Iceland.* 2 vols. Oxford: Clarendon, 1905; rpt. Millwood: Kraus, 1976, vol. 1, pp. 458–502; Guðni Jónsson, ed. *Byskupa sǫgur.* 3 vols. Reykjavik: Íslendingasagnaútgáfan; Haukadalsútgáfan, 1948, vol. 1; Jón Helgason, ed. *Byskupa sǫgur.* Editiones Arnamagnæanæ, ser. A, vol. 13:2. Copenhagen: Reitzel, 1978. **Tr.**: Gudbrand Vigfusson and F. York Powell, eds. and trans. *Origines Islandicae*, vol. 1, pp. 458–502; Wolf, Kirsten. "A Translation of the Latin Fragments Containing the Life and Miracles of St. Þorlákr along with a Collection of *Lectiones* for Recitation on His Feast-Days." *Proceedings of the PMR Conference* 14 (1989), 261–76. **Lit.**: Turville-Petre, G. *Origins of Icelandic Literature.* Oxford: Clarendon, 1967; Schach, Paul. *Icelandic Sagas.* Twayne's World Authors Series, 717. Boston: Twayne, 1984, pp. 63–6.

Paul Bibire

[**See also**: *Biskupa sǫgur; Hungrvaka;* Miracles, Collections of; *Páls saga biskups;* Saints' Lives]

Þorleifs þáttr jarlsskálds ("The Tale of Þorleifr Earl's Poet")
exists only in *Flateyjarbók* (1380–1390), except for postmedieval paper copies. Þorleifr, a young Icelander, sails to Norway during the reign of the last heathen ruler, Earl Hákon Sigurðarson, a few years before the earl's death in 995. The two quickly fall out over trading rights, and the earl confiscates the Icelander's goods, burns his ship, and hangs his crew. Þorleifr escapes to King Sven of Denmark, where he is well received. A fragment of the praise poem he recites to the Danish king is reported. But Þorleifr nurses revenge, and Sven helps him return to Norway to deliver a satirical poem (*níð*) against Hákon. Disguised as an old beggar under the name "Níðungr Gjallandason," Þorleifr contrives to come before

the earl, whom he offers to eulogize in verse. At first, Hákon thinks he is being praised, but the poem modulates into satire. As Hákon is seized by itching, he begins to recognize the poem as *níð*; challenged, Niðungr shifts into a middle portion called "Fog Verses," which conjures up a protective murk in the hall. The devastating third portion of the poem causes weapons to leap from the walls, killing many men, and rots the earl's beard and half the hair from his head. Þorleifr escapes through locked doors and returns to King Sven, who again receives him well and sends him home to Iceland with gifts. This central tale is framed on one side by a quick account of Þorleifr's early life in Iceland and the feud that motivated his journey, on the other by three further episodes. The first episode relates how Hákon, after his recovery, obtains vengeance by magic: he makes a "robot" of wood and a human heart, and sends it to assassinate Þorleifr at the Icelandic parliament. A second anecdote tells how one Hallbjǫrn hali ("tail") becomes a poet, tutored in a dream by Þorleifr's ghost. Finally, Þorleifr's brothers manage to obtain partial vengeance on Earl Hákon's property.

Þorleifs þáttr shows structural affinities with a group of short stories that tell realistically of an Icelander's relationship with a Norwegian ruler; several contrast the hero's adventures at two courts. In content and tone, however, its affinities are with later and more fantastic sagas. For example, Niðungr fastens an open bag under his false beard so that he can appear to eat huge amounts; this grotesque motif has analogues chiefly in folktales. Þorleifr also figures in *Svarfdœla saga*, which was known to the author of the story in a lost early version. He was famous as a skald and satirist. The anecdote about Hallbjǫrn hali is derived from a similar "miracle" told of the Venerable Bede and extant in an Icelandic translation (see Jónas Kristjánsson, ed. 1956: c for references). The conception of poetry there may show the influence of the *Prose Edda* of Snorri Sturluson. However, the anecdote, like the florid clerical prose prefacing the story, may be a late addition. Of the six bits of verse in the story, there is reason to believe five spurious; one fragment may well be from the famous "*Níð* Against the Earl." A cryptic alternative title, "Konu(r)vísur," perhaps because its "verses" will magically level Há-*kon* to a *kona* or woman, seems genuinely archaic. The story is generally dated to the late 13th or early 14th century.

Ed.: Jónas Kristjánsson, ed. *Eyfirðinga sǫgur*. Íslenzk fornrit, 9. Reykjavik: Hið íslenzka fornritafélag, 1956, pp. 213–29 [p. ci lists all earlier editions]. **Tr.**: Simpson, Jacqueline, trans. *The Northmen Talk: A Choice of Tales from Iceland*. London: Phoenix House; Madison: University of Wisconsin Press, 1965, pp. 141–52 ["The Scoffing Verses," a partial translation]. **Bib.**: Halldór Hermannsson. *Bibliography of the Icelandic Sagas and Minor Tales*. Islandica, 1. Ithaca: Cornell University Library, 1908, pp. 111–2; rpt. New York: Kraus, 1966; Halldór Hermannsson. *The Sagas of Icelanders (Íslendinga sögur): A Supplement to Bibliography of the Icelandic Sagas and Minor Tales*. Islandica, 24. Ithaca: Cornell University Press, 1935, p. 74; Jóhann S. Hannesson. *The Sagas of Icelanders (Íslendinga sögur): A Supplement to Islandica I and XXIV*. Islandica, 38. Ithaca: Cornell University Press, 1957, p. 85. **Lit.**: Finnur Jónsson. *Den oldnorske og oldislandske Litteraturs Historie*. 3 vols. 2nd ed. Copenhagen: Gad, 1920–24, vol. 1, pp. 538–41; vol. 2, p. 753; Vries, Jan de. *Altnordische Literaturgeschichte*. 2 vols. Grundriss der germanischen Philologie, 15–6. Berlin: de Gruyter, 1941–42; rpt. 1964–67, vol. 2, p. 429; Jónas Kristjánsson. *Eyfirðinga sǫgur*, pp. xciv–ci [most complete study]; Almqvist, Bo. *Norrön niddiktning: Traditionshistoriska studier i versmagi. 1: Nid mot furstar*. Nordiska texter och undersökningar, 21. Stockholm: Geber, 1965, pp. 35, 87, 186–205, 235–39 [English summary; important study of "satire"; rich bibliography]; Harris, Joseph. "Genre and Narrative Structure in Some *Íslendinga þættir*." *Scandinavian Studies* 44 (1972), 1–27 [esp. pp. 18–20]; Harris, Joseph. "Theme and Genre in Some *Íslendinga þættir*." *Scandinavian Studies* 48 (1976), 1–28 [esp. pp. 9–10]; Harris, Joseph. "Þættir." In *Dictionary of the Middle Ages*. Ed. Joseph R. Strayer. New York: Scribner, 1982–89, vol. 12, pp. 1–6.

Joseph Harris

[**See also**: *Flateyjarbók*; *Skáld*; *Snorra Edda*; *Svarfdœla saga*; *Þáttr*]

ÞÓRR is the god most often mentioned in Norse sources. Whereas many of the other gods are obscure as to their primary function and their position in the pantheon, most scholars agree that Þórr is a god both of war, fighting the forces of chaos, and of fertility. The relation between these functions, however, has been subject to much debate, often depending on whether or not Þórr is seen in an Indo-European framework.

Mythologically, the main stress is on Þórr's martial function. Most myths relate his battles against giants and other beings representing chaos, such as the serpent Miðgarðsormr, which he fights on more than one occasion (*Hymiskviða*, *Ragnarsdrápa*, *Húsdrápa*, *Gylfaginning*, *Vǫluspá*, and other textual and pictorial evidence; cf. Meulengracht Sørensen 1986). His battles with giants begin with different incidents, but in most cases it is obvious that he is defending Ásgarðr, the dwelling of the gods, against the dangers of Útgarðr, since these forces are constantly trying to steal something or somebody that belongs to the gods, *e.g.*, Iðunn (*Haustlǫng*, sts. 1ff.; *Skáldskaparmál*, chs. 2–3), Freyja (*Gylfaginning*, ch. 25; *Vǫluspá*, st. 25), or Þórr's hammer (*Þrymskviða*, sts. 1ff.).

In the myths, Þórr is the son of Óðinn and Jǫrð (*Skáldskaparmál*, ch. 12; *Þrymskviða*, st. 1; *Lokasenna*, st. 58). His sons are called Móði and Magni ("the angry one" and "the strong one") and his daughter Þrúðr ("power"), names that emphasize Þórr's strength and role as the killer of giants. His wife is Sif. Of the many attributes that accentuate his martial function, the most important is the hammer Mjǫllnir, which plays an important role in many myths (*e.g.*, *Haustlǫng*).

Whereas Óðinn mythologically is seen in general as the superior god, there is no doubt that Þórr was worshiped the most widely, at least during the last phase of paganism. Adam of Bremen (*Gesta Hammaburgensis ecclesiae pontificum* 4:26) states explicitly that Þórr is the mightiest of the three gods (Þórr, Óðinn, and Freyr). Whether or not this statement is correct, both personal names and place-names indicate that Þórr held the main position among the gods. The runic inscriptions also mention Þórr often, while Óðinn is mentioned only once. In the Icelandic sagas, we find the same situation: whereas Óðinn and the other gods are mentioned only occasionally, Þórr plays a major role in religious life. This discrepancy is also attested in the mythology. In the poem *Hárbarðsljóð*, where Óðinn and Þórr are quarreling, Óðinn maintains that he takes the earls when they die, whereas Þórr will get the thralls. This distinction may indicate a solution to the problem of the two gods' relationship: Þórr is associated with the farmers and other ordinary men, whereas Óðinn is associated with the warriors, the kings, and the skalds. This notion may account for the wide distribution of his cult among the Icelanders and in other parts of the North.

It is thus natural that Þórr was the god who was seen as the most direct opponent to Christ during the period of christianization. This conflict can be seen in many sagas where Þórr is portrayed as a representative of the Devil, especially in some of the *konungasǫgur*.

As stated above, it is much debated whether Þórr was primarily a god of fertility or a god of war. Adam of Bremen relates that Þórr is concerned with the fertility of the soil and with thunder and lightning. The West Norse sources, on the other hand, accentuate his role as a killer of giants. In relation to human warfare, Óðinn seems to have been the more important of the two. Dumézil has nevertheless proposed that Þórr is a god of the second function, *i.e.*, war, through comparisons with other Indo-European gods (Dumézil 1973: 66ff.). His arguments are sufficiently convincing, and most scholars today would agree that Þórr's connection with fertility has secondary importance. However, problems remain in relation to the kind of connection Þórr has with war. He seems to be mainly a defender of the cosmos, rather than an aggressive god of the berserk type. In other words, his affinity with war is not the same as that of other Scandinavian gods.

There is no doubt that Þórr is a very old deity. Some scholars think that he is pictured on the petroglyphs of the Bronze Age. Parallels with other Indo-European gods, especially the Vedic Indra, suggest the existence of a god of this type in Indo-European times.

Bib.: Lindow, John. *Scandinavian Mythology: An Annotated Bibliography*. Garland Folklore Bibliographies, 13. New York and London: Garland, 1988. **Lit.**: Turville-Petre, E. O. G. *Myth and Religion of the North: The Religion of Ancient Scandinavia*. New York: Holt, Rinehart and Winston, 1964; rpt. Westport: Greenwood, 1975, pp. 75–105; Dumézil, Georges. *Gods of the Ancient Northmen*. Ed. Einar Haugen. Publications of the UCLA Center for the Study of Comparative Folklore and Mythology, 3. Berkeley, Los Angeles, and London: University of California Press, 1973; Clunies Ross, Margaret. "An Interpretation of the Myth of Þórr's Encounter with Geirrøðr and His Daughters." In *Specvlvm Noroennvm: Norse Studies in Memory of Gabriel Turville-Petre*. Ed. Ursula Dronke *et al*. Odense: Odense University Press, 1981, pp. 370–91; Clunies Ross, Margaret, and B. K. Martin. "Narrative Structure and Intertextuality in *Snorra Edda*: The Example of Thor's Encounter with Geirrøðr." In *Structure and Meaning in Old Norse Literature: New Approaches to Textual Analysis and Literary Criticism*. Ed. John Lindow *et al*. Viking Collection, 3. Odense: Odense University Press, 1986, pp. 56–72; Meulengracht Sørensen, Preben. "Thor's Fishing Expedition." In *Words and Objects: Towards a Dialogue Between Archaeology and History of Religion*. Ed. Gro Steinsland. Institute for Comparative Research in Human Culture, Oslo. Ser. B: Skrifter, 71. Oslo: Norwegian University Press, 1986, pp. 257–78; Lindow, John. "Addressing Thor." *Scandinavian Studies* 60 (1988), 119–36.

Jens Peter Schjødt

[**See also**: Adam of Bremen; Bragi Boddason; Cosmography; *Hárbarðsljóð*; *Hymiskviða*; *Lokasenna*; Mythology; *Snorra Edda*; Þjóðólfr of Hvin; *Þrymskviða*; Úlfr Uggason; *Vǫluspá*]

Þórsdrápa *see* **Eilífr Goðrúnarson**

Þorskfirðinga saga *see* **Gull-Þóris saga**

Þorsteins draumr Síðu-Hallsonar ("The Dream of Þorsteinn Síðu-Hallsson") is probably excerpted from an *Íslendingasaga* of unknown authorship from the 13th century. *Þorsteins draumr* follows *Þorsteins saga Síðu-Hallssonar* in the paper MSS JS 435 4to and AM 142 fol., and is separately preserved in two other paper MSS, AM 564c 4to and AM 165m fol., as well as in a vellum fragment, AM 594a 4to.

Þorsteins draumr tells of the chieftain Þorsteinn Síðu-Hallsson, who, while visiting Svínafell, Iceland, dreams of three women who warn him against the treachery of one of his slaves, whom he had castrated. The first woman recites an ominous verse. When Þorsteinn wakes up, the slave cannot be found. The next night, the women reappear with the same warning, and the second one recites a verse predicting his death. Despite another search, the slave is still missing. On the third night, the women, all weeping, appear again. The third one asks Þorsteinn where they should go after his death. He replies, "To Magnús, my son." She says that they will not be there long, implying that Magnús will die an early death, and recites a third verse. The search for the slave continues on the third day, but without result. Then a storm comes up, and Þorsteinn's host is reluctant to let the guests leave. On the fourth night, the slave sneaks in and kills Þorsteinn, but is captured immediately afterward. Þorsteinn's wife tortures him by putting a red-hot wash basin on his stomach, and stops only when he threatens to put a curse on her family. He dies from the burn, and his body is sunk in a fen.

The abrupt beginning of *Þorsteins draumr* suggests that it is an excerpt from a longer saga, though not necessarily the extant *Þorsteins saga Síðu-Hallssonar*, from which it differs considerably in style. As it stands, however, *Þorsteins draumr* is a neatly structured, folktale-like episode that incorporates many motifs considered typical of the "classical" *Íslendingasaga*: the appearance of a man's *hamingjur* ("guardian spirits") before his death, ominous prophetic dreams, and a woman's vicious revenge. *Þorsteins draumr* is "classical" in its simplicity of style and in the inevitability of the events it describes, but the skaldic verses recited by the dream-women contrast with this spareness. In *dróttkvætt* meter and with the repeated last line characteristic of the utterings of supernatural creatures, the verses contain many kennings and obscure references, although their general import is clear enough.

Ed.: Jón Jóhannesson, ed. *Austfirðinga sǫgur*. Íslenzk fornrit, 11. Reykjavík: Hið íslenzka fornritafélag, 1950, pp. 321–6. **Tr.**: Kelchner, Georgia Dunham. *Dreams in Old Norse Literature and Their Affinities in Folklore*. Cambridge: Cambridge University Press, 1935; rpt. Folcroft: Folcroft Library Editions, 1976 [translates the dreams and the verses].

Elizabeth Ashman Rowe

[**See also**: *Íslendingasögur*; Kennings; Skaldic Meters; Skaldic Verse; *Þorsteins saga Síðu-Hallssonar*]

Þorsteins saga hvíta ("The Saga of Þorsteinn the White"), one of the shortest of the *Íslendingasögur*, takes as its starting point the familiar saga motif of an Icelander whose detention abroad leads to his fiancée's marrying another man. The traveler-hero is not Þorsteinn hvíti, however, but Þorsteinn fagri ("the handsome"), forced to stay an extra season in Norway because of illness. The marital poacher is his business partner and traveling companion Einarr, who not only offers the ailing Þorsteinn no help, but also mocks and lampoons him in public, and, upon returning to Iceland, spreads rumors of his death and marries Helga. When Þorsteinn fagri returns to Iceland and learns the truth, he (like Kjartan in *Laxdœla saga*) feigns indifference at first. Finally, he rides to Einarr and demands legal compensation and, when Einarr refuses, kills him. Einarr's father organizes a vengeance party; they kill Þorsteinn's brothers and get Þorsteinn himself outlawed. Þorsteinn returns to Iceland five years later and puts himself in the hands of Þorsteinn hvíti. When his grandson, Brodd-Helgi Þorgilsson, approaches maturity, Þorsteinn hvíti advises Þorsteinn fagri to return to Norway.

At first glance, the saga seems incorrectly named, for Þorsteinn hvíti's role in the story proper is minimal and for the most part indirect: his son Þorgils, married to Einarr's sister, joins the revenge action against Þorsteinn fagri's brothers and is killed in that battle. It has been proposed that the final sentence, "and here ends the saga of Þorsteinn hvíti," from which the title is taken, is either an error or a later interpolation on the part of the scribe familiar with *Vápnfirðinga saga*, in which Þorsteinn hvíti, as grandfather of Brodd-Helgi Þorgilsson, plays a larger role. Whether the title is a mistake, or whether it merely acknowledges the relative importance of the two Þorsteinns in early Icelandic history is unclear, but naming the saga after Þorsteinn hvíti does shift attention from Þorsteinn fagri's plight to Þorsteinn hvíti's grand moral gesture in taking in, and in effect, forgiving, the killer of his son.

The saga probably dates from the last quarter of the 13th century, and probably was composed as an after-the-fact prologue to *Vápnfirðinga saga*. It is preserved only in two late paper MSS (AM 156 fol. and AM 496 4to). Although it has never enjoyed great critical attention or appreciation, it is a paradigmatically structured and composed short saga.

Ed.: Jón Jóhannesson, ed. *Austfirðinga sǫgur*. Íslenzk fornrit, 11. Reykjavik: Hið íslenzka fornritafélag, 1950, pp. 1–19. **Tr.**: Jones, Gwyn, trans. *Four Icelandic Sagas*. Oxford: Oxford University Press; Princeton: Princeton University Press, 1935; Boucher, Alan, trans. *Tales from the Eastfirths*. Reykjavik: Iceland Review, 1981, pp. 20–30. **Lit.**: Andersson, Theodore M. *The Icelandic Family Saga: An Analytic Reading*. Harvard Studies in Comparative Literature, 28. Cambridge: Harvard University Press, 1967; Hume, Kathryn. "Beginnings and Endings in the Icelandic Family Sagas." *Modern Language Review* 68 (1973), 593–606; Schach, Paul. *Icelandic Sagas*. Twayne's World Authors Series, 717. Boston: Twayne, 1984.

Carol J. Clover

[**See also:** *Íslendingasögur*; *Vápnfirðinga saga*]

Þorsteins saga Síðu-Hallssonar ("The Saga of Þorsteinn Síðu-Hallsson") is an *Íslendingasaga* of unknown authorship probably from the late 13th century. The text survives in two paper MSS, AM 142 fol. and JS 435 4to (previously AM 551 4to), neither of which is complete. AM 142 fol. is the longer of the two, but it lacks the beginning of the saga, as well as a two-page section toward the end. Both are copies made by Ásgeir Jónsson of a vellum MS that Bishop Brynjólfur Sveinsson sent to Denmark in 1662. This MS remained in Copenhagen until the 18th century, but is now missing.

The chieftain Þorsteinn Síðu-Hallsson hands his chieftaincy in the East Fjords over to Þórhaddr Hafljótsson, a man with whom he has had some small conflict in the past, and leaves for the Orkneys. There, Þorsteinn becomes a highly favored retainer of Earl Sigurðr, his distant cousin. Sigurðr is killed at the battle of Clontarf (1014), but Þorsteinn survives, and becomes a retainer of King Magnús Ólafsson in Norway before returning home to Iceland. During Þorsteinn's absence, Þórhaddr quarrels with and abuses his own son-in-law, although he has been an able chieftain in all other respects. When Þorsteinn returns to Iceland, Þórhaddr yields up the chieftaincy only under the threat of force, and an irritated Þorsteinn rules that he should move off his farm. When Þórhaddr resists, Þorsteinn sets his house on fire. The removal is effected and ample restitution made to the son-in-law. Þórhaddr and his sons now begin a campaign of slander against Þorsteinn, which Þorsteinn steadfastly ignores. The provocation is less easily endured by Þorsteinn's friends, brother, and wife, all of whom urge him to take revenge. Finally, Þorsteinn's dead mother appears to him in a dream, asking when he will avenge his honor. By this time, Þórhaddr has had fourteen ominous dreams about his own fate. The next day, Þorsteinn, accompanied by a group of men, slays the sons of Þórhaddr. Despite the lacuna in the text here, we may assume that Þorsteinn goes on to slay Þórhaddr. The text resumes in the middle of Þorsteinn's genealogy, which ends the saga.

Þorsteins saga Síðu-Hallssonar is a minor work of Old Icelandic literature. Its interest for us lies chiefly in its relationship to *Njáls saga* and in its stylistic anomalies, since the defective text makes a purely literary interpretation difficult. The ultimate source of *Þorsteins saga* may be contained in stanza 23 of Haukr Valdísarson's *Íslendingadrápa*, which mentions the conflict between Þorsteinn and Þórhaddr, but this remains a conjecture. Another source of *Þorsteins saga*, both closer and more problematical, is *Njáls saga*. On one hand, there are literary echoes of *Njáls saga*; burning, slandering, and prophetic dreams occupy a prominent place in each work. *Njáls saga* apparently provided *Þorsteins saga* with still more material, and is mentioned by name at one point, although this reference could be a later interpolation. Moreover, a close relationship with *Njáls saga* could explain the curious arrangement of the saga (beginning with the protagonist, rather than with the preceding generations), since most of what would be related about Þorstein's ancestors is already told there. On the other hand, *Þorsteins saga* disagrees with *Njáls saga* on a number of genealogical points and in its description of the battle of Clontarf. Furthermore, the assumption that *Þorsteins saga* was written after *Njáls saga* (after 1280 roughly) gives us a rather late date for a text that displays a few "early" characteristics. These include the use of the preposition *of* (which gave way to *um* by about 1250, except in the East Fjords), the location of Þorsteinn's genealogy at the end of the narrative instead of at the beginning, and the less than impersonal, "nonclassical" descriptions of some of the characters. Quite possibly it is better to attribute these inconsistencies to the lack of sophistication of a late 13th-century writer from the East Fjords, and not to an early date of composition. Without the source of *Þorsteins saga*'s account of the battle of Clontarf or other evidence, we cannot say for certain.

Ed.: Jón Jóhannesson, ed. *Austfirðinga sǫgur*. Íslenzk fornrit, 11. Reykjavik: Hið íslenzka fornritafélag, 1950, pp. 297–320; Loth, Agnete, ed. *Membrana Regia Deperdita*. Editiones Arnamagnæanæ, ser. A, vol. 5. Copenhagen: Munksgaard, 1960, pp. 161–78. **Tr.**: Kelchner, Georgia Dunham. *Dreams in Old Norse Literature and Their Affinities in Folklore*. Cambridge: Cambridge University Press, 1935; rpt. Folcroft: Folcroft Library Editions, 1976 [translates some of the dreams]. **Lit.**: Schach, Paul. *Icelandic Sagas*. Twayne's World Authors Series, 717. Boston: Twayne, 1984, p. 135.

Elizabeth Ashman Rowe

[See also: *Íslendingasögur*; *Njáls saga*; *Þorsteins draumr Síðu-Hallssonar*]

Þorsteins saga Víkingssonar

Þorsteins saga Víkingssonar ("The Saga of Þorsteinn, the Son of Víkingr"), one of the more fantastic of the *fornaldarsögur*, was probably written around 1300. The hero of this saga is the father of the protagonist in *Friðþjófs saga frœkna*, which was most certainly known to the author of *Þorsteins saga*. The saga begins with a genealogical introduction that includes numerous legendary kings of Scandinavia. Despite its mythological content, this part of the saga (chs. 1–2) seems to be fairly young and was probably modeled on another pseudo-historical text, the *Upphaf allra frásagna*. The author then proceeds to tell of the adventures encountered by Þorsteinn's father, Víkingr ("the Viking"), and his blood-brother, Njǫrfi. This section spans nearly a quarter of the whole saga (chs. 3–8) and is reminiscent of some *riddarasögur* both in its motifs and exotic settings, including India and the otherwise unknown Maseraland.

Víkingr and Njǫrfi have nine sons each, who, despite the friendship of their fathers, become involved in a long and bloody feud. Only Þorsteinn and Njǫrfi's son Jǫkull survive the ensuing battles, Þorsteinn by being left for dead on the battlefield on repeated occasions. Only after the deaths of their fathers, who never gave up their friendship, do Þorsteinn and Jǫkull make a peace settlement.

The reference to Þorsteinn's son (ch. 25) leads on to *Friðþjófs saga*, to which the work may have been intended as an introduction. The structure of *Þorsteins saga*, with its genealogical introduction and plot spanning more than one generation, resembles the *Íslendingasögur* more than other *fornaldarsögur*. So does the main action of the saga, in which the heroes are driven by their desire for revenge rather than their desire and quest for a princess, which forms the plot of many other younger *fornaldarsögur* and *riddarasögur*. Nevertheless, its familiarity with *Friðþjófs saga*, and the numerous imaginative motifs included especially in the first part of the saga, betray the work as a late *fornaldarsaga* that draws on ancient heroic matter. Among the fairy-tale motifs that *Þorsteins saga* has in common with many late 14th-century Icelandic texts are magical weapons, the talking ship Elliði, shapechangers, sorcerers, and a helpful dwarf.

Ed.: Guðni Jónsson, ed. *Fornaldar sögur Norðurlanda.* 4 vols. Akureyri: Íslendingasagnaútgáfan, 1954, vol. 3. **Tr.**: Anderson, Rasmus B., and Jón Bjarnason, trans. *Viking Tales of the North: The Sagas of Thorstein, Viking's Son, and Fridthjof the Bold.* Chicago: Griggs, 1877; rpt. 1889. **Lit.**: Schlauch, Margaret. *Romance in Iceland.* Princeton: Princeton University Press; New York: American-Scandinavian Foundation; London: Allen & Unwin, 1934; rpt. New York: Russell & Russell, 1973; Nahl, Astrid van. *Originale Riddarasögur als Teil altnordischer Sagaliteratur.* Frankfurt am Main: Lang, 1981; Simek, Rudolf, and Hermann Pálsson. *Lexikon der altnordischen Literatur.* Kröners Taschenausgabe, 490. Stuttgart: Kröner, 1987, p. 362.

Rudolf Simek

[See also: *Fornaldarsögur*; *Friðþjófs saga ins frœkna*; *Íslendingasögur*; *Riddarasögur*]

Þorsteins þáttr Austfirðings

Þorsteins þáttr Austfirðings ("The Tale of Þorsteinn from the East Fjords") recounts the adventures of a young Icelander from the poor northeastern district on his pilgrimage to Rome. As Þorsteinn travels through a lonely place in Denmark, he intervenes in an unfair fight and saves a stranger, who gives his name

as "Styrbjǫrn." Later, at the court of King Magnús, Þorsteinn is mocked by the retainers but welcomed by the king, who reveals his previous identity as "Styrbjǫrn." On a later occasion, Þorsteinn again excites the laughter of the regular retainers by uncourtly table manners, but the king defends Þorsteinn in a verse. Finally, however, Þorsteinn declines preferment in Norway and returns to Iceland with rich gifts.

The historical Magnús inn góði ("the good") Óláfsson ruled Norway 1035–1047, and the story is set in the period of his Danish wars, 1042–1047. Any historical kernel is unlikely, since the *þáttr* is based on an international popular tale known as "The King in Disguise." The folktale was also used in a story attached to the Danish King Sven Estridsen and may have been transferred from the Dane to his Norwegian antagonist sometime during the 13th or 14th century. That the story was never integrated into the saga of Magnús suggests a very late date. The Icelandic *þáttr* is preserved in two paper MSS from the 17th and 18th centuries, which go back to the same vellum source.

Like a number of generically related stories, *Þorsteins þáttr* traces the relationship of an Icelander to a Norwegian king; several features of the plot seem to derive from the imposition of this pattern on the folktale. King Magnús's impromptu poem (*lausavísa*) seems to be an extraneous element, only awkwardly integrated into the tale and probably not as old as Magnús's time. A final constituent may be influence from a written story, *Auðunar þáttr vestfirzka*. The themes of *Þorsteins þáttr*, respect for strangers and the power of luck, resemble the morals of similar Icelandic tales, but *Þorsteins þáttr* is inferior to them stylistically.

Ed.: Jón Jóhannesson, ed. *Austfirðinga sǫgur.* Íslenzk fornrit, 11. Reykjavík: Hið íslenzka fornritafélag, 1950, pp. 327–32 [see pp. cxi–cxii for previous editions and MSS]. **Tr.**: Bachman, W. Bryant, Jr., trans. *Four Old Icelandic Sagas and Other Tales.* Lanham, New York, and London: University Press of America, 1985, pp. 38–42. **Bib.**: Halldór Hermannsson. *Bibliography of the Icelandic Sagas and Minor Tales.* Islandica, 1. Ithaca: Cornell University Library, 1908; rpt. New York: Kraus, 1966, p. 114; Halldór Hermannsson. *The Sagas of Icelanders (Íslendinga sögur): A Supplement to Bibliography of the Icelandic Sagas and Minor Tales.* Islandica, 24. Ithaca: Cornell University Press; London: Oxford University Press, 1935, p. 74; Jóhann S. Hannesson. *The Sagas of Icelanders (Íslendinga sögur): A Supplement to Islandica I and XXIV.* Islandica, 38. Ithaca: Cornell University Press; London: Oxford University Press, 1957, p. 87. **Lit.**: Finnur Jónsson. *Den oldnorske og oldislandske Litteraturs Historie.* 3 vols. 2nd ed. Copenhagen: Gad, 1920–24, vol. 2, p. 755; Jón Johannesson. *Austfirðinga sǫgur,* pp. cxi–cxii; Vries, Jan de. *Altnordische Literaturgeschichte.* 2 vols. Grundriss der germanischen Philologie, 15–6. Berlin: de Gruyter, 1941–42; rpt. 1964–67, vol. 2, p. 450; Harris, Joseph. "Genre and Narrative Structure in Some *Íslendinga Þættir*." *Scandinavian Studies* 44 (1972), 1–27 [esp. pp. 19–20]; Harris, Joseph. "Theme and Genre in Some *Íslendinga þættir*." *Scandinavian Studies* 48 (1976), 1–28 [esp. pp. 3–5, 15]; Harris, Joseph. "The King in Disguise: An International Popular Tale in Two Old Icelandic Adaptations." *Arkiv för nordisk filologi* 94 (1979), 57–81; Harris, Joseph. "Þættir." In *Dictionary of the Middle Ages.* Ed. Joseph R. Strayer. New York: Scribner, 1982–89, vol. 12, pp. 1–6.

Joseph Harris

[See also: *Auðunar þáttr vestfirzka*; *Lausavísur*; *Þáttr*]

Þorsteins þáttr bœjarmagns

Þorsteins þáttr bœjarmagns ("The Tale of Þorsteinn Town-strength") is a *fornaldarsaga* consisting of an introduction and four adventures. The saga dates from the late 13th century, although much of the material is considerably older. There is relatively superficial influence from romance literature.

Þorsteinn, the son of a Norwegian farmer, is a youth of great size and difficult temperament who becomes a retainer of King Óláfr Tryggvason. He undertakes a number of enterprises for the king. In the first adventure, the hero journeys to the underworld in the company of an elf. In the second, he recovers a dwarf's abducted child and is rewarded with the gift of magic objects, which prove invaluable in the third and main tale. In this adventure, he travels north on a voyage, and one day goes alone into the forest. He meets the otherworld ruler Guðmundr of Glæsisvellir, the reluctant vassal of King Geirrøðr. Guðmundr is on his way to Geirrøðargarðar to pay homage, but he fears that Geirrøðr will have him slain. Þorsteinn accompanies him, rendered invisible by the magic stone given to him by the dwarf. With the aid of other gifts from the dwarf, he thwarts the attempts by Geirrøðr and his henchmen to slay Guðmundr and his followers, and finally kills Geirrøðr and sets the hall on fire. Þorsteinn escapes, parts good friends with Guðmundr, and on the way back to his ship meets the half-human daughter of Geirrøðr's follower, Earl Agði. She accompanies him back to Óláfr, is baptized, and they marry. In the final episode, Agði retrieves two horns that Þorsteinn has stolen from the otherworld and presented to Óláfr. Þorsteinn returns to the otherworld, finds that Agði has retired to his grave mound, takes over his lands, steals the horns back from Agði's mound, and seals him in by putting a cross in the doorway. He gives the horns back to Óláfr, and then returns to his dwelling in the otherworld.

The first episode has analogues in Icelandic folktales and to some extent in the main story itself. The second is a stock episode in sagas of this kind. The final episode is based loosely on accounts of raiding the mounds of avaricious and aggressive ghosts. The main tale has attracted the most attention. It seems to be based partly on the myth of the journey of Þórr to the giant Geirrøðr and his slaying of him, and partly on Celtic tales, known through medieval Irish literature, of a delightful otherworld to which a human being journeys and settles a dispute between two otherworld rulers. After a brief sojourn in mortal lands, he may then return to the otherworld for good. Another version of the story is told by Saxo in Book 8 of his *Gesta Danorum*. In the *Gesta Danorum*, *Þorsteins þáttr*, and the closely related *Helga þáttr Þórissonar*, the author, independently in each case, stresses the values of Christianity and the defense it provides against the perilous delights of the otherworld. Guðmundr and his realm again appear in the *Hauksbók* text of *Hervarar saga*, and in *Bósa saga ok Herrauðs*, where the supernatural theme is used flippantly.

Ed.: Olrik, Jørgen, and H. Ræder, eds. *Saxonis Gesta Danorum*. Vol. 1. Copenhagen: Levin & Munksgaard, 1931, pp. 239–47; Guðni Jónsson, ed. *Fornaldar sögur Norðurlanda*. 4 vols. Akureyri: Íslendingasagnaútgáfan, 1954, vol. 4, pp. 319–44. **Tr.**: Simpson, Jacqueline, trans. *The Northmen Talk: A Choice of Tales from Iceland*. London: Phoenix House; Madison: University of Wisconsin Press, 1965, pp. 180–97; Hermann Pálsson and Paul Edwards, trans. *Gautrek's Saga and Other Medieval Tales*. London: University of London Press; New York: New York University Press, 1968, pp. 121–40; rpt. in *Seven Viking Romances*. Harmondsworth: Penguin, 1985, pp. 258–75; Ellis Davidson, Hilda, ed., and Peter Fisher, trans. *Saxo Grammaticus. The History of the Danes. Books I–IX*. 2 vols. Cambridge: Brewer; Rowman and Littlefield, 1979–80, vol. 1, pp. 262–70, vol. 2, pp. 141–7 [notes]. **Lit.**: Simpson, Jacqueline. "Grímr the Good, a Magical Drinking Horn." *Études celtiques* 10 (1962–63), 489–515; Simpson, Jacqueline.

"Otherworld Adventures in an Icelandic Saga." *Folklore* 77 (1966), 1–20; Ciklamini, Marlene. "Journeys to the Giant-Kingdom." *Scandinavian Studies* 40 (1968), 95–110; Power, Rosemary. "Journeys to the Otherworld in Icelandic *Fornaldarsögur*." *Folklore* 96 (1985), 156–75; Power, Rosemary. "Christian Influence in the *Fornaldarsögur Norðrlanda*." In *The Sixth International Saga Conference 28/7–2/8 1985. Workshop Papers*. 2 vols. Copenhagen: Det arnamagnæanske Institut, 1985, vol. 2, pp. 843–57.

Rosemary Power

[**See also**: *Bósa saga ok Herrauðs*; *Fornaldarsögur*; *Helga þáttr Þórissonar*; *Hervarar saga ok Heiðreks konungs*; *Saxo Grammaticus*; *Þáttr*]

Þorsteins þáttr stangarhøggs

Þorsteins þáttr stangarhøggs ("The Tale of Þorstein Staff-Struck") tells of a young man, Þorsteinn, who, during a horse fight, is struck on the head with a horse prod by Þórðr, a stable groom on the estate of a nearby chieftain, Bjarni. Þorsteinn pays no attention to the blow, calling it an accident instead of a deliberate injury. Later, his father Þórarinn tells him that some members of the community, especially Bjarni's housecarls Þórhallr and Þorvaldr, regard Þorsteinn's self-restraint as cowardice; he urges his son to seek vengeance. When Þórðr refuses to apologize, Þorsteinn kills him. Bjarni sends the two housecarls to kill Þorsteinn, but he slays them, too. Finally, Bjarni himself challenges Þorsteinn to a duel, in which the injuries sustained by each are offset in a complicated series of blows and counterblows. The story ends with the reconciliation of the two men, an account of Bjarni's pilgrimage to Rome, and a list of his descendants.

Þorsteins þáttr stangarhøggs is preserved in eight MSS, a parchment from the 14th century, and seven paper MSS from the 17th century or later. The early parchment, AM 162c fol., contains only the last three-fifths of the story. Of the paper MSS, the two most important for the textual tradition are AM 156c fol. and AM 496 4to; the former dates from the late 17th century, and the latter is somewhat older. Both are copies of an earlier version, not, however, the one contained in the parchment fragment, which is somewhat condensed. The main editions of *Þorsteins þáttr*, Jakobsen's (1902–03) and Jón Jóhannesson's (1950), are based on AM 156c fol.

Þorsteins þáttr stangarhøggs has a historical basis. The account of Bjarni's descendants mentions a number of Icelanders of the 13th century, from which we may conclude that the story was composed in the early 14th century. A number of passages suggest that the author was familiar with other sagas, especially *Vápnfirðinga saga*. *Þorsteins þáttr stangarhøggs* is considered one of the best examples of the *þáttr*, the short prose narrative, in medieval Icelandic literature.

Ed.: Jakobsen, Jakob, ed. *Austfirðinga sögur*. Samfund til udgivelse af gammel nordisk litteratur, 29. Copenhagen: Møller, 1902–03 [contains all of the variant readings of each MS; introduction and commentary in Danish]; Jón Jóhannesson, ed. *Austfirðinga sögur*. Íslenzk fornrit, 11. Reykjavik: Hið íslenzka fornritafélag, 1950 [useful for cultural notes; introduction and commentary in Icelandic]. **Tr.**: Wahlgren, Erik, trans. "The Saga of Thorstein Staff-Blow." *University of Kansas City Review* 11 (1945), 213–7; rpt. in Leach, Henry Goddard, ed. and trans. *A Pageant of Old Scandinavia*. Princeton: Princeton University Press; New York: American-Scandinavian Foundation, 1946, pp. 165–71; Jones, Gwyn, trans. *Eirik the Red and Other Icelandic*

Sagas. London: Oxford University Press, 1961, pp. 78–88; Hermann Pálsson, trans. *Hrafnkel's Saga and Other Icelandic Stories*. Harmondsworth: Penguin, 1971, pp. 72–81. **Lit.**: Heinrichs, Heinrich M. "Die künstlerische Gestaltung des Þorsteins þáttr stangarhöggs." In *Festschrift Walter Baetke, dargebracht zu seinem 80. Geburtstag am 28. März 1964*. Ed. Kurt Rudolph *et al*. Weimar: Böhlau, 1966, pp. 167–74; Andersson, Theodore M. *The Icelandic Family Saga: An Analytic Reading*. Harvard Studies in Comparative Literature, 28. Cambridge: Harvard University Press, 1967, pp. 3–6; Andersson, Theodore M. "The Displacement of the Heroic Ideal in the Family Sagas." *Speculum* 45 (1970), 575–93; Fichtner, Edward G. "The Calculus of Honor: Vengeance, Satisfaction and Reconciliation in the 'Story of Thorsteinn Staff-Struck.'" In *Germanic Studies in Honor of Otto Springer*. Ed. Stephen J. Kaplowitt. Pittsburgh: K & S Enterprises, 1978, pp. 103–28.

Edward G. Fichtner

[**See also:** *Þáttr*; *Vápnfirðinga saga*]

Þorsteins þáttr sǫgufróða

("The Tale of Þorstein the Saga-wise"), a short Old Icelandic tale, is part of the *konungasögur* about Haraldr harðráði ("hard-ruler") Sigurðarson. In *Morkinskinna*, it appears just before the final confrontation with King Sven of Denmark. *Hulda-Hrokkinskinna* locates it among a succession of short stories ending a section of domestic conflicts. The *þáttr* is not included in the later part of *Flateyjarbók*, but it exists independently, for example in the MS AM 496 4to. There, the main actor is called Þorsteinn, while in the *konungasögur* he performs without a name, simply as an Icelander.

Þorsteinn is accepted as a member of Haraldr's bodyguard, and entertains the men by telling sagas. Toward Christmas, he becomes anxious: he has only one saga left, and it concerns the king's own journey to Byzantium. Haraldr is willing to listen, and afterward is quite content. Þorsteinn reports having learned the saga from Halldórr Snorrason during travels to the *Alþingi*.

The versions in *Morkinskinna* and *Hulda-Hrokkinskinna* are very much alike. *Hulda* has some additional sentences in the beginning and toward the end; *Morkinskinna* has some extra passages in the middle. Moreover, the sequence of sentences varies in a short section. The independently transmitted version diverges to a greater extent. The beginning and the end are quite different. For instance, an episode where Haraldr gives a sword to Þorsteinn as a gift is presented dramatically. On the whole, the proportion of direct dialogue is larger.

The problem concerning the relationship between the versions has not been solved. Attempts have been made to judge the version in *Morkinskinna* as older than *Hulda*'s. The independent version has been looked upon as wholly independent, or as to some extent influenced by *Morkinskinna*'s. The tales are said to be early and known by the author of *Heimskringla*, or late because of the *þáttr*'s absence in *Flateyjarbók*.

Þorsteinns þáttr has been used as a proof of the existence of oral saga telling in older times at folk assemblies and among the kings' bodyguards. Attempts have even been made to estimate the length of the saga about Haraldr's travels abroad and the size of a single saga teller's repertoire. On the basis of the story, we can at least speculate how oral presentations were looked upon at the beginning of the 13th century. However, it is possible that the *þáttr* was written down to increase faith in the saga of Haraldr's journey to Byzantium.

Ed.: Jón Jóhannesson, ed. *Austfirðinga sǫgur*. Íslenzk fornrit, 11. Reykjavik: Hið Íslenzka fornritafélag, 1950, pp. cxii–cxiv, 333–6. **Tr.**: Leach, Henry Goddard, trans. *A Pageant of Old Scandinavia*. Princeton: Princeton University Press; New York: American-Scandinavian Foundation, 1946, pp. 199–201. **Lit.**: Finnur Jónsson. *Den oldnorske og oldislandske Litteraturs Historie*. 3 vols. 2nd ed. Copenhagen: Gad, 1920–24, vol. 2, pp. 199–201; Vries, Jan de. *Altnordische Literaturgeschichte*. 2 vols. Grundriss der germanischen Philologie, 15–6. Berlin: de Gruyter, 1941–42; rpt. 1964–67, vol. 1, pp. 326–8; vol. 2, pp. 449–50; Heinrichs, Heinrich Matthias. "Die Geschichte vom sagakundigen Isländer (Íslendings þáttr sǫgufróða). Ein Beitrag zur Sagaforschung." In *Literaturwissenschaft und Geschichtsphilosophie. Festschrift für Wilhelm Emrich*. Ed. Helmut Arntzen *et al*. Berlin and New York: de Gruyter, 1975, pp. 225–31; Gimmler, Heinrich. *Die Thættir der Morkinskinna. Ein Beitrag zur Überlieferungsproblematik und zur Typologie der altnordischen Kurzerzählung*. Bamburg: Difo-Druck, 1976, pp. 55–6; Danielsson, Tommy. *Om den isländska släktsagans uppbyggnad*. Skrifter utgivna av Litteraturvetenskapliga institutionen vid Uppsala universitet, 22. Uppsala: Almqvist & Wiksell, 1986, p. 72.

Tommy Danielsson

[**See also:** *Flateyjarbók*; *Halldórs þáttr Snorrasonar*; *Hulda-Hrokkinskinna*; *Konungasögur*; *Morkinskinna*; *Þáttr*]

Þorvalds þáttr tasalda

("The Tale of Þorvaldr the Tassel") is an anonymous, short *þáttr* found in *Ólafs saga Tryggvasonar* in *Flateyjarbók*. It is probable that the *þáttr* was originally independent and not incorporated into *Ólafs saga* until a later date. The *þáttr* came into existence at the end of the 13th century, or, at the very latest, at the beginning of the 14th.

The Icelander Þorvaldr goes to the Norwegian king Ólafr Tryggvason to be baptized. After a fight with one of the king's men, Þorvaldr is sent to the Upplands to conduct missionary activities, where he meets the heathen Bárðr. They come to blows when Bárðr refuses to accompany Þorvaldr to the king's court. In his distress, the Icelander appeals to God for help, but is overcome when Bárðr summons supernatural creatures to his aid. The heathen is impressed with Þorvaldr's strength, and after Þorvaldr tells Bárðr that his strength is attributed to the help of the Christian God, the heathen agrees to go with him to the Norwegian royal court, where Bárðr is baptized and dies in his baptismal gown. Þorvaldr returns to Iceland with much honor.

The *þáttr* can be grouped with other conversion narratives in *Ólafs saga Tryggvasonar*, in which the Norwegian king is shown in his function as the promulgator of Christianity, with Þorvaldr as a type of exemplary Icelander at the Norwegian royal court. The central motif of the *þáttr* reveals a close relationship with *Eindriða þáttr ilbreiðs* ("The Tale of Eindriði the Flat-footed"), also found in *Ólafs saga Tryggvasonar*, but it is difficult to determine which of the two narratives is older.

Ed.: Guðbrandur Vigfússon and C. R. Unger, eds. *Flateyjarbók: En Samling af norske Konge-Sagaer med indskudte mindre Fortællinger om Begivenheder i og udenfor Norge samt Annaler*. 3 vols. Christiania [Oslo]: Malling, 1860–68, vol. 1, pp. 378–83; Þorleifr Jónsson, ed. *Fjörutíu Íslendinga-þættir*. Reykjavik: Sigurður Kristjánsson, 1904, pp. 467–76; Guðni Jónsson, ed. *Íslendinga þættir*. Reykjavik: Sigurður Kristjánsson, 1935, pp. 405–14; Sigurður Nordal *et al.*, eds. *Flateyjarbók*. 4 vols. Akranes: Flateyjarútgáfan, 1944–45, vol. 1, pp. 420–6; Guðni

Jónsson, ed. *Íslendinga sögur.* 13 vols. 2nd ed. Akureyri: Íslendingasagnaútgáfan, 1953, vol. 8, pp. 89–100; Jónas Kristjánsson, ed. *Eyfirðinga sögur.* Íslenzk fornrit, 9. Reykjavik: Hið íslenska fornritafélag, 1956, pp. 117–26. **Tr**.: Sephton, John, trans. *The Saga of King Olaf Tryggwason Who Reigned over Norway A.D. 995 to A.D. 1000.* London: Nutt, 1895, pp. 307–12; McKinnell, John. *Viga-Glums Saga with the Tales of Ögmund Bash and Thorvald Chatterbox.* Edinburgh: Canongate, 1987. **Lit**.: Harris, Joseph. "Genre and Narrative Structure in Some *Íslendinga þættir.*" *Scandinavian Studies* 44 (1972), 1–27; Harris, Joseph. "Theme and Genre in Some *Íslendinga þættir.*" *Scandinavian Studies* 48 (1976), 1–28; Würth, Stefanie. *Elemente des Erzählens: Die þættir des Flateyjarbók.* Beiträge zur nordischen Philologie, 26. Basel and Frankfurt am Main: Helbing & Lichtenhahn, 1991.

Stefanie Würth

[**See also**: *Flateyjarbók*; *Óláfs saga Tryggvasonar*; *Þáttr*]

Þorvarðar þáttr krákunefs

Þorvarðar þáttr krákunefs ("The Tale of Þorvarðr Crow-nose"), a short Old Icelandic tale, is part of the *konungasaga* about Haraldr harðráði ("hard-ruler") Sigurðarson. In *Morkinskinna* and the later part of *Flateyjarbók*, it is located before the description of the final battle against King Sven of Denmark. It occurs somewhat later in *Hulda-Hrokkinskinna*, among a succession of short stories ending a section of domestic conflicts.

Þorvarðr intends to present a sail as a gift to Haraldr. However, the king turns it down rather curtly, because of a previous worthless gift from an Icelander. Instead, Eysteinn orri ("heathcock") receives the sail. Eysteinn invites Þorvarðr to his farm, but Þorvarðr accepts only after a renewed invitation when they meet again at sea. A feast is held, and Eysteinn detains Þorvarðr during three nights to be able to give him treasures balancing the gift of the sail. Only then does Þorvarðr leave for Iceland. Soon, Haraldr notices that Eysteinn's ship sails better than his own. Eysteinn offers his sail to the king. However, it does not function equally well on the king's vessel.

The versions of *Þorvarðar þáttr* are very much alike, even though *Hulda's* deviates to some degree in having short, irrelevant additions and some disparities in the choice of words. For instance, in *Morkinskinna* and *Flateyjarbók*, on one occasion Eysteinn comes sweeping along in his ship, while in *Hulda* he arrives rowing a beautiful barge. Further, Haraldr discovers Eysteinn's sail in different ways; in *Hulda*, this incident is discussed afterward, while in the other versions, the occasion is presented dramatically.

Eysteinn orri is the main actor of the tale, properly speaking. He is the one who is honored and who acts in a socially acceptable way. Historically, he was the son of Þorbergr, the brother of Kálfr and Finnr Árnason. Haraldr was married to his sister Þóra. Eysteinn was killed during the campaign to England in 1066. Þorvarðr, who plays a subordinate part, is not known outside the tale.

Þorvarðar þáttr was probably written down early in the 13th century and was included in *Morkinskinna* from the very start.

Ed.: Guðni Jónsson, ed. *Vestfirðinga sögur.* Íslenzk fornrit, 6. Reykjavik: Hið íslenzka fornritafélag, 1943, pp. cviii–cx, 370–4. **Lit**.: Finnur Jónsson. *Den oldnorske og oldislandske Litteraturs Historie.* 3 vols. 2nd ed. Copenhagen: Gad, 1920–24, vol. 2, p. 752; Vries, Jan de. *Altnordische Literaturgeschichte.* 2 vols. Grundriss der germanischen Philologie, 15–6. Berlin: de Gruyter, 1941–42; rpt. 1964–67, vol. 2, p. 386; Gimmler, Heinrich. *Die Thættir der Morkinskinna. Ein Beitrag zur Überlieferungsproblematik und zur Typologie der altnordischen*

Kurzerzählung. Bamburg: Difo-Druck, 1976, p. 56; Danielsson, Tommy. *Om den isländska släktsagans uppbyggnad.* Skrifter utgivna av Litteraturvetenskapliga institutionen vid Uppsala universitet, 22. Uppsala: Almqvist & Wiksell, 1986, pp. 73–4.

Tommy Danielsson

[**See also**: *Flateyjarbók*; *Hulda-Hrokkinskinna*; *Konungasögur*; *Morkinskinna*; *Þáttr*]

Þrymskviða

Þrymskviða ("The Lay of Þrymr"). Several eddic poems poke fun at the gods, Þórr in particular. *Þrymskviða* probably goes farthest in that direction. It tells of the giant Þrymr, who has stolen Þórr's hammer and will return it only if he is given Freyja as his bride. She refuses vehemently, and on Heimdallr's advice Þórr is dressed in a wedding dress and sent to Jötunheimar ("the giants' land") with Loki posing as his maid. Þórr does not play the role of a bride very convincingly, but Loki saves the situation by his clever explanations, until the hammer is carried in and placed in the lap of the "bride." Þórr then kills Þrymr and his family with the hammer

Þrymskviða is told by a skilled narrator. The plot is clear, the players are distinctly characterized through their remarks, and the language is terse and simple with few kennings. The meter is *fornyrðislag*, and the form an epic-dramatic one. *Þrymskviða* is extant only in the *Codex Regius.* Of all the eddic poems, *Þrymskviða* contains the most parallels in phraseology and contents with other eddic and skaldic poems. Examples of such parallels are found in, e.g., *Voluspá*, *Lokasenna*, *Brot af Sigurðarkviðu*, and Úlfr Uggason's *Húsdrápa*. *Þrymskviða* stanza 14 is almost identical with *Baldrs draumar* stanza 1, and between *Þrymskviða* stanza 24:5–10 and *Hymiskviða* stanza 15:5–8, there is a close connection with regard to content. Older scholars considered *Þrymskviða* very ancient and assumed, therefore, that it had played an important role as a lender of material to other eddic poems. Recent research has demonstrated, however, that the poem must be rather young, from the beginning of the 13th century. *Þrymskviða* was more likely the borrower than the lending work in most instances. The poet may have had a special purpose in alluding to older poems, intending to create a mixed effect and ironic contrasts.

Stanza 22 in *Þrymskviða* and stanza 1 in the skaldic poem *Eiríksmál* show several affinities. Jötunheimar is pitted against Valhöll, giants against fallen warriors, and the giant king Þrymr against the god Óðinn. The guest awaited by Óðinn is the fallen heroic king Eiríkr blóðøx ("blood-axe") Haraldsson; Þrymr's visitor is Þórr disguised as a bride. The allusion to *Eiríksmál* strongly heightens the comic effect of the disguise motif in *Þrymskviða*.

The myth in *Þrymskviða* has certain basic features in common with that of *Skírnismál*. Apparently, the purpose of the *Þrymskviða*-poet was to create a counterpart on a more primitive level to the love plot in *Skírnismál*. The intention was presumably to strengthen the comic and grotesque elements in *Þrymskviða*.

It has proved difficult to locate any trace of the myth of the hammer fetching outside *Þrymskviða*. No evidence of its presence is traceable in either skaldic or other eddic poetry, nor does Snorri's *Edda* make any reference to it. Hallberg (1954) hypothesizes boldly that the poem may in fact have been written by Snorri while at work on his *Edda*.

The main plot shows a certain resemblance in motif and structure to the tale of the building of Ásgarðr in Snorri's *Edda* (ch. 42). As in *Þrymskviða*, a giant demands Freyja as compensation for his services. Loki's clever tricks save the day again, and the tale ends with Þórr slaying the giant with his hammer. Hence, the possibility cannot be excluded that the *Þrymskviða*-poet to some extent drew on this tale in composing his poem.

Ed.: Bugge, Sophus, ed. *Norrœn Fornkvæði*. Kristiania [Oslo]: Malling, 1867; rpt. Oslo: Universitetsforlaget, 1965; Neckel, Gustav, ed. *Edda: Die Lieder des Codex Regius nebst verwandten Denkmälern. I: Text*. 5th ed. rev. Hans Kuhn. Heidelberg: Winter, 1983. **Tr.**: Hollander, Lee M., trans. *The Poetic Edda, Translated with an Introduction and Explanatory Notes*. 2nd rev. ed. Austin: University of Texas, 1962; rpt. 1988. **Bib.**: Harris, Joseph. "Eddic Poetry." In *Old Norse–Icelandic Literature: A Critical Guide*. Ed. Carol J. Clover and John Lindow. Islandica, 45. Ithaca and London: Cornell University Press, 1985, p. 156. **Lit.**: Vries, Jan de. "Over de Dateering der Þrymskviða." *Tijdschrift voor Nederlandsche Taal- en Letterkunde* 47 (1928), 251–322; Hallberg, Peter. "Om Þrymskviða." *Arkiv för nordisk filologi* 69 (1954), 51–77; Magerøy, Hallvard. "Þrymskviða." *Edda* 58 (1968), 256–70; Hallberg, Peter. *Old Icelandic Poetry: Eddic Lay and Skaldic Verse*. Trans. Paul Schach and Sonja Lindgrenson. Lincoln and London: University of Nebraska Press, 1976, pp. 55–8; Kvillerud, Reinert. "Några anmärkingar till Þrymskviða." *Arkiv för nordisk filologi* 80 (1965), 64–86; Jakobsen, Alfred. "Þrymskviða som allusjonsdikt." *Edda* 84 (1984), 75–80.

Alfred Jakobsen

[**See also:** *Baldrs draumar*; *Codex Regius*; Eddic Meters; Eddic Poetry; *Eiríksmál*; *Hymiskviða*; Kennings; *Lokasenna*; Loki; Mythology; *Sigurðarkviðu, Brot af*; *Skírnismál*; *Snorra Edda*; Þórr; Úlfr Uggason; *Vǫluspá*]

U

Úlfr Uggason was an Icelandic skald who flourished around the year 1000. He married Járngerðr, daughter of Þórarinn Grímkelsson and Jórunn Einarsdóttir from Stafaholt (*Landnámabók* S76, H64). His wife's family were descendants of Hrappr, son of Bjǫrn buna Veðrar-Grímsson, one of the most prominent early settlers in Iceland. His father's family is unknown.

Úlfr is represented in three sagas. *Njáls saga* portrays him as a cautious man. In ch. 60, he makes a brief appearance as the loser in an inheritance claim he contests with Ásgrímr Elliða-Grímsson. In ch. 102, he refuses to commit himself openly to physical violence in the cause of the antimissionary party in the events surrounding the conversion of Iceland to Christianity. Both here and in *Kristni saga* (ch. 9), a single verse of Úlfr's is preserved in which he responds to a poetic incitement to push the foreign evangelist Þangbrandr over a cliff. Likening himself to a wily fish, he asserts that it is not his style to swallow the fly (*esat mínligt . . . flugu at gína*)!

However, Úlfr is best known for his composition of a skaldic picture poem, *Húsdrápa* ("House-lay"), which commemorates a splendid new hall that Óláfr pái ("peacock") had built at Hjarðarholt. The *drápa* celebrates both the builder of the hall and the mythological stories depicted on its carved panels. *Laxdœla saga* (ch. 29) describes the hall and the occasion upon which Úlfr delivered his poem, the marriage feast of Óláfr's daughter Þuríðr. Excellent stories (*ágætligar sǫgur*) were carved on the wainscoting and on the hall ceiling, and these splendid carvings surpassed the wall hangings. *Laxdœla saga* does not preserve the poem, but comments only that *Húsdrápa* was well crafted (*vel ort*) and that Úlfr received a good reward for it from Óláfr. These events are usually dated, according to the saga's chronology, to about 985.

Fortunately for posterity, Snorri Sturluson preserved fifty-six lines of *Húsdrápa* in his *Edda*, mostly as half-stanzas illustrating points of skaldic diction in *Skáldskaparmál*. Out of these verses, editors have conventionally reconstructed a *drápa* of twelve stanzas or half-stanzas, which probably had the refrain *hlaut innan svá minnum* ("within have appeared these motifs").

There are three known mythological subjects Úlfr treated in *Húsdrápa*, and there may have been more. Snorri states that Úlfr composed a long passage in the poem on the story of Baldr, of which we now have five half-stanzas (7–11 in Finnur Jónsson 1912–15). They deal with the procession of supernatural beings

and their mounts riding to Baldr's funeral. In *Gylfaginning*, chs. 33–35 (Finnur Jónsson 1931: 63–8, Faulkes 1987: 48–51), Snorri gives a prose account of the funeral and other events that led up to and followed Baldr's death, for which *Húsdrápa* was probably one of his main sources.

Two other known subjects of *Húsdrápa* were Þórr's fight with the World Serpent, Miðgarðsormr, a popular choice with Viking Age skalds and sculptors (sts. 3–6), and the otherwise unrepresented myth of how the gods Heimdallr and Loki, said by Snorri to have taken the form of seals, wrestled for a "beautiful sea-kidney" (probably the necklace Brísingamen) at a place called Singasteinn. Only one stanza (2) of this section survives, although from Snorri's summary it seems likely to have been longer in the complete *drápa*.

It may be surmised that Úlfr's pictorial praise poem in honor of Óláfr pái was, in a late 10th-century Icelandic context, something of a hearkening back to the courtly, aristocratic style of skalds like Bragi Boddason and Þjóðólfr of Hvin, who lived about a century earlier than Úlfr. Judging by *Laxdœla saga*'s account of Óláfr, his splendid style of living, and Irish royal connections, he would have been flattered by an implicit comparison with Norwegian princelings and their skaldic encomiasts.

Ed.: Kahl, B. *Kristni saga. Þáttr Þorvalds ens víðfǫrla. Þáttr Ísleifs biskups Gizurarsonar. Hungrvaka.* Altnordische Saga-Bibliothek, 11. Halle: Niemeyer, 1905 [see pp. 1–57]; Finnur Jónsson, ed. *Den norske-islandske skjaldedigtning.* Vols. 1A-2A (tekst efter håndskrifterne) and 1B-2B (rettet tekst). Copenhagen and Christiania [Oslo]: Gyldendal, 1912–15; rpt. Copenhagen: Rosenkilde & Bagger, 1967 (A) and 1973 (B), vol. 1A, pp. 136–9; vol. 1B, pp. 128–30; Finnur Jónsson, ed. *Edda Snorra Sturlusonar.* Copenhagen: Gyldendal, 1931 [lines from *Húsdrápa* pp. 89, 90, 94, 96–100, 147, 152, 165, 168]; Einar Ól. Sveinsson, ed. *Laxdœla saga.* Íslenzk fornrit, 5. Reykjavik: Hið íslenzka fornritafélag, 1934; Einar Ól. Sveinsson, ed. *Brennu-Njáls saga.* Íslenzk fornrit, 12. Reykjavik: Hið íslenzka fornritafélag, 1954; Jakob Benediktsson, ed. *Íslendingabók. Landnámabók.* Íslenzk fornrit, 1. Reykjavik: Hið íslenzka fornritafélag, 1968; Turville-Petre, E. O. G. *Scaldic Poetry.* Oxford: Clarendon, 1976, pp. 67–70 [Baldr's funeral strophes from *Húsdrápa*]; Frank, Roberta. *Old Norse Court Poetry: The* Dróttkvætt *Stanza.* Islandica, 42. Ithaca and London: Cornell University Press, 1978 [texts and discussion of *Húsdrápa* pp. 104–5, 110–2, 170]. **Tr.**: Gudbrand Vigfusson and F. York Powell, eds. and trans. "Christne saga." In

Origines Islandicae: A Collection of the More Important Sagas and Other Native Writings Relating to the Settlement and Early History of Iceland. 2 vols. Oxford: Clarendon, 1905; rpt. Millwood: Kraus, 1976, vol. 1, pp. 370–406; Hollander, Lee M. *The Skalds: A Selection of Their Poems, with Introductions and Notes.* New York: American-Scandinavian Foundation, 1945; 2nd ed. Ann Arbor: University of Michigan Press, 1968, pp. 49–54; Magnús Magnússon and Hermann Pálsson, trans. *Njal's saga.* Harmondsworth: Penguin, 1960 [esp. pp. 144 and 220–1]; Magnús Magnússon and Hermann Pálsson, trans. *Laxdæla saga.* Harmondsworth: Penguin, 1960 [esp. pp. 111–3]; Faulkes, Anthony, trans. *Snorri Sturluson. Edda.* Everyman Classics. London and Melbourne: Dent, 1987 [lines from *Húsdrápa,* pp. 67–8, 71, 74–7, 116, 121, 132–3, 135]. **Bib.**: Hollander, Lee M. *A Bibliography of Skaldic Studies.* Copenhagen: Munksgaard, 1958; Bekker-Nielsen, Hans. *Old Norse–Icelandic Studies: A Select Bibliography.* Toronto Medieval Bibliographies, 1. Toronto: University of Toronto Press, 1967. **Lit.**: Lie, Hallvard. "Billedbeskrivende dikt." *KLNM* 1 (1956), 542–5; Lie, Hallvard. *"Natur"og "unatur"i skaldekunsten.* Avhandlinger utg. av Det norske Videnskaps-Akademi i Oslo. II. Hist.-filos. kl. No. 1. Oslo: Aschehoug, 1957; rpt. in his *Om sagakunst og skaldskap. Utvalgte avhandlinger.* Øvre Ervik: Alvheim & Eide, 1982, pp. 201–315; Lie, Hallvard. "Húsdrápa," *KLNM* 7 (1962), 122–4; Turville-Petre, E.O.G. *Myth and Religion of the North: The Religion of Ancient Scandinavia.* New York: Holt, Rinehart and Winston, 1964; rpt. Westport: Greenwood, 1975; Strömbäck, Dag. *The Conversion of Iceland: A Survey.* Trans. and annotated by Peter Foote. Text Series, 6. London: Viking Society for Northern Research, 1975; Schier, K. "Balder." In *Reallexikon der germanischen Altertumskunde* 2. Gen. ed. Johannes Hoops. Berlin and New York: de Gruyter, 1976, pp. 2–7; Schier, Kurt. "Die *Húsdrápa* von Úlfr Uggason und die bildliche Überlieferung altnordischer Mythen." In *Minjar og menntir: Afmælisrit helgað Kristjáni Eldjárn, 6 desember 1976.* Ed. Guðni Kolbeinsson *et al.* Reykjavik: Menningarsjóður, 1976, pp. 425–43; Schier, Kurt. "Húsdrápa, 2. Heimdall, Loki und die Meerniere." In *Festgabe für Otto Höfler zum 75. Geburtstag.* Ed. Helmut Birkhan. Philologica Germanica, 3. Vienna: Braumüller, 1976, pp. 577–88; Clover, Carol J. "Skaldic Sensibility." *Arkiv för nordisk filologi* 93 (1978), 63–81; Clunies Ross, Margaret. "Style and Authorial Presence in Skaldic Mythological Poetry." *Saga-Book of the Viking Society* 20 (1981), 276–304; Kuhn, Hans. *Das Dróttkvætt.* Heidelberg: Winter, 1983 [esp. pp. 295–6]; Meulengracht Sørensen, Preben. "Thor's Fishing Expedition." In *Words and Objects: Towards a Dialogue Between Archaeology and History of Religion.* Ed. Gro Steinsland. Institute for Comparative Research in Human Culture, Oslo. Ser. B: Skrifter, 71. Oslo: Norwegian University Press, 1986, pp. 257–78.

Margaret Clunies Ross

[**See also:** Bragi Boddason; Conversion; *Laxdœla saga*; *Njáls saga*; *Skáld*; Skaldic Meters; Skaldic Verse; Þjóðólfr of Hvin]

Vadstena is the mother house of the Brigettine Order, situated on the shores of Lake Vättern, Östergötland, Sweden. Originally the site of a castle built for Birger Jarl's son Valdemar in the mid-13th century, the land and adjoining estates were bequeathed to St. Birgitta by King Magnus Eriksson and his wife, Blanche of Namur, on May 1, 1346, for conversion to a monastery. The plans for the foundation, from the general organization down to details of the spices and herbs that were to be grown in the gardens, were conceived by Birgitta herself and recorded in her *Revelations*, in particular in the book containing the *Regula sancti salvatoris*. Construction began in 1369, and the main part of the monastery was probably ready by 1374, the year after Birgitta's death, when her remains were translated with great ceremony back to Sweden from Rome, where she had lived the latter part of her life. From 1374, Vadstena became a place of pilgrimage. The monastery was consecrated as a double foundation on October 23–24, 1384, and the Rule allowed for a maximum of sixty nuns and twenty-five priests and lay brethren, with an abbess in overall authority. A fire in 1388 destroyed the wooden chapel, two stone buildings, and part of the nuns' living quarters; but rebuilding work was quickly begun, following a large number of gifts and bequests. The great stone church was completed in 1430, to the north of which was the nuns' convent, and to the south the monastery; these buildings were joined on the west side by a *locutorium* ("conversation room") for communication between the monks and nuns. The monastery survived the first few decades of Lutheranism, but was finally dissolved in 1595. The building was used as a hospital and prison during the following centuries; in 1963, the Order was reestablished and thrives today on the original site.

The principal source of information about Vadstena is the *Diarium Vadstenense*, which survives in MS Cod. Ups. C 89. It contains entries for the years between 1344 and 1545, written in Latin by about twenty scribes, five of whom have been identified by name. Entries for the early decades of the monastery's history are sparse; apart from mentioning especially significant events (such as Birgitta's death, and that of her daughter, Katarina Ulfsdotter, the monastery's first abbess, although never consecrated, in 1381), they consist mainly of death notices for its benefactors. From the 15th and 16th centuries, there is more detailed information relating to Swedish history as well as internal events of the monastery. The foundation became embroiled in national politics and in ne-

gotiations relating to the Scandinavian Union. From 1439, events recorded are highly political in nature, and the monastery became the temporary headquarters for King Karl Knutsson and his supporters. After 1470, the recording of political events ceased, and the diarists reverted exclusively to the monastery's internal history. In the medieval period, 321 nuns and 173 monks are mentioned by name, many of them from leading Swedish noble families.

Vadstena was for a long time the most favored burial place in Sweden: Bo Jonsson Grip and Queen Philippa, wife of Erik of Pomerania and sister of Henry V of England, for instance, were buried there. The monastery became extremely prosperous through the conferment of privileges and the receipt of *Vårfrupenningen*, a tax of one penny from every adult, which was payable to the monastery. Surviving land records mention some 957 properties owned by the monastery. Relations with the twenty-seven daughter houses abroad were active throughout the medieval period, in particular Nådendal in Finland, which was an important center for devotion, and whose most famous monk, Jöns Budde, was a celebrated translator of religious texts.

Vadstena rapidly became a center for the spread of learning and the production of books. It had an important scriptorium and library, which at its height is estimated to have contained some 1,500 books. Many books were obtained abroad, or donated by daughter houses, but many were also produced and bound at the monastery. Both the monks and nuns were engaged in the production of books. Apart from copies of the *Revelations* and works relating to the Order, many devotional and liturgical texts were written, including large sermon collections, for which the Brigettine monks had a considerable reputation. There was also a significant collection of books in Swedish, which in all likelihood was kept apart from the main library and intended primarily for edificatory use by the nuns. Gradually, a distinct literary tradition evolved at the monastery and showed itself in the script and language. The script, known as *vadstenakursiv*, occurs in formal bookhands as a type of Gothic semicursive, and, for ordinary copying, as a cursive, often slightly angled hand of a more functional character. The language, known as *vadstenaspråk*, extends through several centuries and reflects many layers of linguistic change, but retains much of its distinctive character, and is acknowledged to be the foundation stone of later vernacular writing in Sweden.

Ed.: Nygren, Ernst, ed. *Liber privilegiorum monasterii Vadstenensis e codice archivi Reg. Holm. A 19 (OLIM A 23)*. Corpus Codicum Suecicorum Medii Aevi, 11. Copenhagen: Munksgaard, 1950 [facsimile]; Nygren, Ernst, ed. *Diarium Vadstenense ("Vadstena klosters minnesbok") e codice membr. Bibl. Univ. Upsal. C 89.* Corpus Codicum Suecicorum Medii Aevi, 16. Copenhagen: Munksgaard, 1963 [facsimile]; Larsson, Anna, ed. *Vadstena klosters två äldsta jordeböcker.* Samlinger utgivna av Svenska fornskrift-sällskapet, 245. Uppsala: Almqvist & Wiksell, 1971; Eklund, Sten, ed. *Den heliga Birgitta. Opera minora I. Regvla Salvatoris.* Samlinger utgivna av Svenska fornskrift-sällskapet, 2nd ser. 8.1. Lund: Berling, 1975; Gejrot, Claes, ed. *Diarium Vadstenense: The Memorial Book of Vadstena Abbey.* Acta Universitatis Stockholmiensia, 33. Stockholm: Almqvist & Wiksell, 1988. **Lit.**: Höjer, Torvald. *Studier i Vadstena klosters och Birgittinordens historia intill midten af 1400–talet.* Uppsala: Almqvist & Wiksell, 1905; Malin, Aarno. "Studier i Vadstena klosters bibliotek." *Nordisk tidskrift för bok- och biblioteksväsen* 13 (1926), 129–53; Berthelson, Bertil. *Studier i birgittinerordens byggnadsskick. I. Anläggningsplanen och dess tillämpning.* Lund: Ohlsson, 1946; Norborg, Lars-Arne. *Storföretaget Vadstena kloster. Studier i senmedeltidens godspolitik och ekonomiförvaltning.* Bibliotheca historica Lundensis, 7. Lund: Gleerup, 1958; Cnattingius, Hans. *Studies in the Order of St. Bridget of Sweden. 1: The Crisis in the 1420's.* Stockholm Studies in History, 7. Stockholm: Almqvist & Wiksell, 1963; Nyberg, Tore. *Birgittinsche Klostergründungen des Mittelalters.* Bibliotheca historica Lundensis, 15. Lund: Gleerup, 1965; Andersson, Iwar. *Vadstena gård och kloster.* 2 vols. Stockholm: Kungl. vitterhets, historie och antikvitets akademien; Almqvist & Wiksell, 1972; Lindblom, Andreas. *Vadstena klosters öden. Till 600–års minnet av Birgittas död.* Finspång: Finspång, 1973.

Bridget Morris

[**See also:** Birgitta, St.; Monasticism; Vadstena Language]

Vadstena Language

Vadstena Language (*vadstenaspråk*) is the name given to the written language that was developed, used, and taught at Vadstena Convent during the late Old Swedish period. The convent was of the "extended" sort, with a separate part for monks. We encounter this language chiefly in religious works, such as the *Revelations* of St. Birgitta, which were early translated from Latin into Swedish, but also in the relatively few secular writings emanating from the convent, among them land registers, accounts, and statutes. There are special reasons why Vadstena Convent should have come to occupy a central position for the literature and written language of late Old Swedish. Most of the nuns had little or no knowledge of Latin, so edifying literature suitable for reading aloud and for private study had to be translated or originally composed in Swedish.

One distinctive feature of Vadstena language is the occurrence of vowel balance: *i–e* and *u–o*. Thus, in a position of weak stress, *i* and *u* are used after an old short syllable, and *e* and *o* after an old long syllable. For instance, we have *giffui* but *løne*, *witu* but *kunno*. On the other hand, *a* is usually retained unchanged as a suffix vowel. Distinctive also is the treatment of the old palatal *r*: chiefly *r*-less forms of the plural in *-ar* (e.g., *dagha*, *alna*) but most often retention of the *r* in the case of plurals in *-ir*, *-er* (e.g., *winir*, *saker*) and the ones in *-ur*, *-or* (e.g., *gatur*, *gaffuor*; and similarly with regard to the definite plural: *daghane*, but usually *sakenar*, *gaffuonar*); furthermore, *r*-less forms of the genitive singular in *-ar*, and of adjectives, but for the most part retention of the *r* in the present singular (e.g., *talar*, *faar*, *trøstir*).

Many of the distinctive features of Vadstena language are in the form of orthographic phenomena that very probably had no counterpart in pronunciation. Very noticeable, for instance, is the alternation between a vowel represented by two letters before a single consonant sound in a closed syllable, and a vowel represented by one letter before the same consonant sound in an open syllable (e.g., *book–boken*). When the single consonant sound is represented by two letters (*ff*, *dh*), the vowel is more often represented by one letter than when the consonant sound is represented by one letter. This is especially noticeable in the case of a closed syllable: *book* but *bodh* (modern Swedish *bod*).

Linguistic features referred to here as characteristic of Vadstena MSS also appear in many other MSS. Peculiar to Vadstena, however, is the frequency with which such features appear, together with the fact that they appear at the same time. In sum, it can be said that Vadstena language has a generally conservative character, with written forms that would seem to be far from reflecting a contemporary pronunciation.

Despite the many important features that together render it distinctive, Vadstena language is not completely uniform. It extends over a long period. Work was begun on the convent in 1369, and the first nuns and monks were received in 1384. The same convent then remained unchanged until shortly before the Reformation, when the monks were forced to leave. It was not completely dissolved until 1595. The earliest MSS date from just before and around 1400, and the latest from around or just after 1500. It is natural that the language should change during the more than 100 years of its existence, however strong the force of tradition, and indeed there are certain differences between the earlier and the later language. Thus, for instance, the dropping of the old palatal *r* is less marked in the later than in the earlier MSS.

However, the language is not uniform even among contemporaneous MSS; the variations are, in fact, quite considerable. It is not always possible to establish why this should be so. One possibility is that the original on which a MS is based was written in a language deviating from that of Vadstena. In other cases, it may be a question of the scribe's own individual usage showing through. One well-known scribe and translator is Jöns Budde, who evidently was a Finn, but who resided and worked at the convent. His language has its own special characteristics. The same is true of another well-known Vadstena monk, Peder Månsson, who was active at the beginning of the 16th century. But one must not neglect the possibility that many styles of transcription could have been part of a written-language tradition practiced at the convent.

Complete knowledge of the oral background of Vadstena language is lacking. On the whole, however, it seems closest to dialects of the eastern part of Sweden. Most plausible, perhaps, is to see it in relation to the dialect of the county of Östergötland, and in particular the dialect of the Vadstena area, but this local connection has not been firmly established. Even if most of the nuns and monks came from the immediately surrounding area, or at least from Östergötland, it nevertheless seems that a considerable proportion came from other counties, chiefly from Västergötland and Småland, but also from Öland, Södermanland, and Västmanland. This pattern can be seen from the *Diarium Vadstenense*, a diary in Latin that covers the entire history of the convent. Among other things, it provides information concerning individual nuns and monks, their inauguration into the monastic calling, and, more regularly, their death and burial.

Vadstena language exhibits at the same time both uniformity and variation, implying both a firm tradition and different individual influences. It is clear that at Vadstena Convent there existed over the years a number of "schools of transcription" that differed from one another either to a lesser or greater extent. But it is also plausible that several such "schools" existed at the same time. Eventually, it ought to be possible to distinguish the linguistic habits of the various "schools."

Ed.: Nygren, Ernst, ed. *Diarium Vadstenense ("Vadstena klosters minnesbok") e codice membr. Bibl. Univ. Upsal. C 89*. Corpus Codicum Suecicorum Medii Aevi, 16. Copenhagen: Munksgaard, 1963 [facsimile]; Larsson, Anna, ed. *Vadstena klosters två äldsta jordeböcker*. Samlinger utgivna av Svenska fornskrift-sällskapet, 245. Uppsala: Almqvist & Wiksell, 1971; Gejrot, Claes, ed. *Diarium Vadstenense: The Memorial Book of Vadstena Abbey*. Acta Universitatis Stockholmiensia, 33. Stockholm: Almqvist & Wiksell, 1988. **Lit.**: Silfverstolpe, Carl. *Klosterfolket i Vadstena. Personhistoriska anteckningar*. Skrifter och handlingar utgifna genom Svenska autograf sällskapet, 4. Stockholm: Norstedt, 1898; Hesselman, B. "Sverige. Sprog." In *Salmonsens Konversationslexikon*. Ed. Chr. Blangstrup *et al.* Copenhagen: Schultz, 1915–30, vol. 22, pp. 729–31; Hesselman, B. *Språkformen i MB 1 eller fem Moseböcker på svenska tolkade och utlagde vid medlet av 1300-talet*. Skrifter utgivna av K. Humanistiska vetenskapssamfundet, 24.17. Uppsala: [s.n.], 1927; Lindqvist, Natan. *Bibelsvenskans medeltida ursprung*. Uppsala: Appelberg, 1929; Jansson, Valter. *Fornsvenska legendariet: Handskrifter och språk*. Nordiska texter och undersökningar, 4. Uppsala: Almqvist & Wiksell, 1934; Thorén, Ivar. *Studier över Själens tröst. Bidrag till kännedomen om den litterära verksamheten i 1400-talets Vadstena*. Nordiska texter och undersökningar utgivna i Uppsala av Bengt Hesselman, 14. Stockholm: Geber; Copenhagen: Munksgaard, 1942; Thorell, Olof. *Fem moseböcker på fornsvenska*. Nordiska texter och undersökningar utgivna i Uppsala av Bengt Hesselman, 18. Stockholm: Geber; Copenhagen: Munksgaard, 1951; Ronge, Hans H. *Konung Alexander. Filologiska studier i en fornsvensk text*. Skrifter utgivna av Institutionen för nordiska språk vid Uppsala universitet, 3. Stockholm: Almqvist & Wiksell, 1957; Henning, Samuel. *Skrivarformer och vadstenaspråk i Siælinna thrøst*. Uppsala: Almqvist & Wiksell, 1960.

Anna Larsson

[**See also:** Language; Vadstena]

Vafþrúðnismál ("The Lay of Vafþrúðnir") is one of the anonymous mythological poems of the *Poetic Edda*. Consisting of fifty-five stanzas in *ljóðaháttr* meter, it is the third poem in the *Codex Regius* MS of the *Edda* (GkS 2365 4to) after *Vǫluspá* and *Hávamál*. Stanzas 20–55 are also preserved in the MS fragment A (AM 748 I 4to). Snorri Sturluson quotes ten stanzas in whole or in part in his *Prose Edda*, and provides prose summaries of six more.

Vafþrúðnismál consists of a series of questions and answers on mythological topics. Despite the great bulk of mythological material that impedes the flow of the narrative, the poet sustains the drama through deft use of parallelism and incremental repetition. The first ten stanzas provide a frame story. Óðinn asks his consort, Frigg, for advice on his proposed journey to the hall of the giant Vafþrúðnir to engage him in a contest of wit and lore. Despite Frigg's caution, Óðinn goes in disguise to the giant's court, calling himself Gagnráðr. Vafþrúðnir challenges the god with four questions on mythological nomenclature; answering successfully, the disguised Óðinn takes his seat in the hall, and in turn challenges the giant with similar questions. Óðinn's last few questions con-

cern the fate of the world and the gods. Having obtained the information he needs, he demonstrates his mastery in lore by asking a question to which only he could know the answer: "What did Óðinn whisper in the ears of his son, before Baldr was borne to the pyre?" (st. 54). Vafþrúðnir then realizes that he has been contending with Óðinn.

The frame story in *Vafþrúðnismál* is one variant of a widespread Scandinavian mythic pattern centered on the motif of Óðinn in disguise. The core of the myth is Óðinn's mastery of sacred knowledge; this knowledge warrants his sovereignty over gods and men, and provides him with the means of protecting them from destructive and demonic forces represented by the giants. Other versions of this myth may be found in the eddic mythological wisdom poem *Grímnismál*, the "Riddles of Gestumblindi" episode in *Hervarar saga*, *Nornagests þáttr*, and the story of Óðinn's appearance to the Norwegian King Óláfr Tryggvason in the various versions of *Óláfs saga Tryggvasonar*. In *Hervarar saga*, although King Heiðrekr and the disguised Óðinn contend with secular and popular riddles rather than sacred lore, Óðinn reveals his identity and defeats the king using the same question about Baldr's death that he uses in *Vafþrúðnismál*. The eddic poem *Baldrs draumar* ("Baldr's Dreams"), which seems also to involve this catch-question motif, reflects another aspect of *Vafþrúðnismál*: the need for Óðinn not only to demonstrate his superiority in lore over the giants, but also, paradoxically, to obtain from them necessary knowledge about the fate of the world and the gods.

Ed.: Neckel, Gustav, ed. *Edda: Die Lieder des Codex Regius nebst verwandten Denkmälern. I: Text*. 5th ed. rev. Hans Kuhn. Heidelberg: Winter, 1983, pp. 45–55. **Tr.**: Hollander, Lee M., trans. *The Poetic Edda, Translated with an Introduction and Explanatory Notes*. 2nd rev. ed. Austin: University of Texas Press, 1962; rpt. 1988; Auden, W. H., and Paul B. Taylor, trans. *Norse Poems*. London: Athlone, 1981; Faber and Faber, 1983, pp. 227–33. **Lit.**: Vries, Jan de. *Altnordische Literaturgeschichte*. 2 vols. Grundriss der germanischen Philologie, 15–6. Berlin: de Gruyter, 1941–42; rpt. 1964–67, vol. 1, pp. 42–5; Haugen, Einar. "The Edda as Ritual: Odin and His Masks." In *Edda: A Collection of Essays*. Ed. Robert J. Glendinning and Haraldur Bessason. University of Manitoba Icelandic Studies, 4. Winnipeg: University of Manitoba Press, 1983, pp. 3–24; Mazo, Jeffrey Alan. "Sacred Knowledge, Kingship, and Christianity: Myth and Cultural Change in Medieval Scandinavia." In *The Sixth International Saga Conference 28/7.– 2/8. 1985. Workshop Papers*. 2 vols. Copenhagen: Det arnamagnæanske Institut, vol. 2, pp. 751–62.

Jeffrey A. Mazo

[**See also:** *Baldrs draumar*; *Codex Regius*; Eddic Meters; Eddic Poetry; *Grímnismál*; *Hervarar saga ok Heiðreks konungs*; Mythology; *Nornagests þáttr*; Óðinn; *Óláfs saga Tryggvasonar*; Riddles; *Snorra Edda*]

Valdemar, the name of several Danish kings who reigned during the heyday of the Danish medieval monarchy, the "Valdemarian Age." The kings are Valdemar I (den Store, "the great"; 1157–1182), Knud (IV) "the Sixth" (1182–1202), and Valdemar II (Sejr, "the victorious, the conqueror"; 1202–1241). The designation "Valdemarian Age" probably also comprises a number of dukes and bishops and members of the royal family bearing that name, including Duke Valdemar III of Schleswig (r. 1326–1330), King Valdemar IV (Atterdag, "ever-day"; 1340–1357), who restored kingship from its deepest crisis, and was succeeded by Queen Margrethe.

In Denmark, the early Valdemarian Age was described by the contemporary historians Saxo Grammaticus and Sven Aggesen. In Europe, the period is marked by notable developments: struggles between the imperial lines of Hohenstaufens and Welfs, German and Danish imperialism in the Baltic, crusades to the Holy Land, schismatic popes, the Magna Carta in England, and the strife surrounding Archbishop Thomas à Becket, who, incidentally, sought the advice of King Valdemar I. The intellectual renaissance of the 12th century marked the thinking of kings and archbishops alike, and the new standard of learning was attained by Danes like Archbishop Eskil, Abbot St. Vilhelm, and Archbishop Anders Sunesen. Agriculture and manufacture were characterized by technical innovation and economic growth. Trade and cities flourished to the benefit of royal revenues; and especially the herring fishery in the Sound gained in importance. Around 1167, Bishop Absalon was able to found his castle at Havn ("harbor"), later to become the city of Copenhagen ("harbor of the merchants").

Against this background, it becomes understandable how a strong kingship might emerge, most often in cooperation with the Church, once the threat of civil war had ended between the lines of the royal family. Before the sole reign of Valdemar I, at one time three kings shared the realm: Knud (son of King Niels's son Magnus, who murdered St. Knud Lavard, Canutus Dux), Sven Grathe (son of King Erik II Emune, Knud's brother), and Valdemar (son of Knud Lavard), with the country held in vassalage from the emperor. Sven attempted to murder both Knud and Valdemar at a feast, but Valdemar managed to flee and later killed Sven in a fierce battle. Many years of civil war and blood feud had exhausted the country and decisively reduced the number of candidates to the throne.

The military situation was also changing dramatically. All over the country, castles were built of the new "baked stone" (tile). Yeomen's service was increasingly replaced by payments, and the king's power to a greater extent rested on the knights or the king's permanent guard. This development did not mean that strife with magnates or descendants of kings was totally avoided, only that for the time being the king had won.

Feudalism in Denmark did not yet reach the state of dissolution known from other countries. But the feudal mode of production was gradually replacing the more undefined types of bondage and slavery. Imperialism and military victories probably also helped the kings. Partly together with, partly against the North German princes (like Heinrich Löwe, "the Lion"), Rügen and a number of other Slavonic and pagan places were won by "crusades," giving rise to the use of the cross as a regal symbol and the Danish flag, Dannebrog. For a time, Valdemar I followed Emperor Frederick Barbarossa and the schismatic Pope Victor, a stand that created strife with Archbishop Eskil, but he also strengthened the defensive wall Danevirke against Germany and eventually defied the emperor and switched papal allegiance. Then in 1170, the remains of Valdemar's recently canonized father were solemnly translated to Ringsted church, while at the same time his son Knud was acclaimed king. The saintly royal family sought to strengthen its position, and the cooperation between king and Church strengthened. The causes of the decline of this glorious age must be sought in general European developments: strengthened adversaries in Germany, feudal dissolution, the built-in problem of royal succession by hereditary rights or election, and the renewed Gregorian trends of the Church versus the idea of kingship.

Lit.: Erslev, Kr. *Valdemarernes Storhedstid. Studier og Omrids.* Copenhagen: Erslev, 1898; rpt. 1972; Christensen, Aksel E. *Kongemagt og aristokrati. Epoker i middelalderlig dansk statsopfattelse indtil unionstiden.* Copenhagen: Munksgaard, 1945; rpt: Copenhagen: Akademisk Forlag, 1976; Skyum-Nielsen, Niels. *Kvinde og Slave.* Danmarkshistorie uden retouche, 3. Copenhagen: Munksgaard, 1971 [detailed references to sources and literature]; Christensen, Aksel E. *Danmarks historie. 1: Tiden indtil 1340.* Copenhagen: Gyldendal, 1977 [extensive bibliography].

Søren Balle

[**See also:** Aggesen, Sven; Danevirke; Denmark; Knud (Cnut), St.; Margrethe I; Saxo Grammaticus; Sunesen, Anders]

Valdimars saga ("The Saga of Valdimar") is an anonymous Icelandic *riddarasaga*, probably from the 15th century. The twenty-five preserved MSS (15th–19th century) can be divided into an older (AM 557 4to, AM 589c 4to, AM 585e 4to, AM 588q 4to) and a younger redaction (*e.g.*, JS 411 8vo, ÍB 172 4to). *Valdimars saga* belongs to the group of indigenous, original *riddarasögur* composed in Iceland.

During a royal feast, Princess Marmoria of Saxony is abducted by a flying dragon. Her brother, Valdimar, sets out to search for her, and in a forest meets a dwarf, who leads him to some giants. They receive him with kindness and after two years equip him with magic charms. In Risaland ("Land of Giants"), Valdimar finds his sister and also the two royal children Blabus and Florida, whose wicked stepmother, Lúpa, had kidnaped the princess. After a terrible battle between armies of monsters, in which Lúpa, in the form of a dragon, is killed, Valdimar and Florida marry, as do Blabus and Marmoria.

In spite of its brevity, *Valdimars saga* presents in many respects a typical and ideal example of the youngest period of this late-medieval genre. A source for the whole saga will probably never be found, but the text makes considerable use of older sagas. *Valdimars saga* is probably directly influenced by *Viktors saga ok Blávus* and *Qrvar-Odds saga*, and close parallels in content are also found in *Egils saga einhenda* and *Ectors saga*. *Valdimars saga* combines widespread narrative and thematic structures, for example, from fairy tales and romances, the well-known motifs of kidnaping of a princess, journey of the hero, meeting with helpers, fights with enemies, victory, marriage, and succession to the throne. Traditional narrative patterns (feasts, battles, *etc.*) and motifs like dragon transformation, magic glass, and wicked stepmother, indicate that the text is structured in conformity with its genre.

The transmission of the MSS suggests that *Valdimars saga* had its origin in western Iceland, where several Icelandic *riddarasögur* of the 14th and 15th centuries came into existence as the literature of the landowners and owners of fishing stations. In addition to the many late paper MSS of the saga, four cycles of *Rímur af Valdimar frækna* (16th–19th century) also show the continued popularity of the story.

Ed.: H. Erlendsson and Einar Þórðarson, eds. "Sagan af Valdimar kóngi." In *Fjórar riddarasögur.* Reykjavik: E. Þórðarson, 1852, pp. 98–120; Loth, Agnete, ed. "Valdimars saga." In *Late Medieval Icelandic Romances.* 5 vols. Editiones Arnamagnæanæ, ser. B, vols. 20–4. Copenhagen: Munksgaard, 1962–65, vol. 1, pp. 51–78 [English summary]. **Bib.**: Finnur Sigmundsson. *Rímnatal.* 2 vols. Reykjavik: Rímnafélagið, 1966, vol. 1, pp. 485–7; Kalinke, Marianne E., and P. M.

Mitchell. *Bibliography of Old Norse–Icelandic Romances*. Islandica, 44. Ithaca and London: Cornell University Press, 1985. **Lit.**: Finnur Jónsson. *Den oldnorske og oldislandske Litteraturs Historie*. 3 vols. 2nd ed. Copenhagen: Gad, 1920–24, vol. 3, pp. 116–7; Björn K. Þórólfsson. *Rímur fyrir 1600*. Safn Fræðafjelagsins um Ísland og Íslendinga, 9. Copenhagen: Möller, 1934, pp. 483–5; Einar Ól. Sveinsson. "*Viktors saga ok Blávus*: Sources and Characteristics." In *Viktors saga ok Blávus*. Ed. Jónas Kristjánsson. Riddarasögur, 2. Reykjavik: Handritastofnun Íslands, 1964, p. cliv; Hugus, Frank. "Some Notes on the Sources of Blómstrvallasaga." *Opuscula* 5. Bibliotheca Arnamagnæana, 31. Copenhagen: Munksgaard, 1975, pp. 335–42 [esp. pp. 340–42]; Nahl, Astrid van. *Originale Riddarasögur als Teil altnordischer Sagaliteratur*. Texte und Untersuchungen zur Germanistik und Skandinavistik, 3. Frankfurt am Main und Bern: Lang: 1981; Glauser, Jürg. *Isländische Märchensagas: Studien zur Prosaliteratur im spätmittelalterlichen Island*. Beiträge zur nordischen Philologie, 12. Basel and Frankfurt am Main: Helbing & Lichtenhahn, 1983; Kalinke, Marianne. "Norse Romance (*Riddarasögur*)." In *Old Norse–Icelandic Literature: A Critical Guide*. Ed. Carol J. Clover and John Lindow. Islandica, 45. Ithaca and London: Cornell University Press, 1985, pp. 316–63.

Jürg Glauser

[**See also:** *Ectors saga ok kappa hans*; *Egils saga einhenda ok Ásmundar berserkjabana*; *Riddarasögur*; *Rímur*; *Viktors saga ok Blávus*; *Ǫrvar-Odds saga*]

Valkyrie *see* Maiden Warriors

Valla-Ljóts saga ("The Saga of Ljótr from Vellir") is a brief *Íslendingasaga* preserved only in postmedieval MSS, two of which have independent value as textual witnesses (AM 496 4to and AM 161 fol.). Despite the late date of these MSS, the saga is considered authentic, probably composed around 1220–1240. Indeed, in some ways *Valla-Ljóts saga* seems more classical than some of the longer, better-known *Íslendingasögur*. The saga genre, while famed for a kind of realism, often incorporates a few nonrealistic effects, such as premonitory dreams or impossibly heroic last stands. Aside from a few sensible predictions, *Valla-Ljóts saga* contains no examples of clairvoyance; nor do its protagonists loom much larger than life. The first major conflict takes place outside a pigpen, and the hero's most admired exploit consists of a resourceful retreat. The usual saga virtues of honor and loyalty prevail, but exemplified with quiet good sense, rather than apotheosized in heroic gestures.

The saga first tells of Halli Sigurðarson, an aggressive and ambitious young man with an interest in law. After his well-born father dies, Halli opposes the remarriage of his mother to Torfi, a freedman and farmer, but his elder brothers overrule him. Sent to Torfi to fetch a piglet, Halli takes umbrage when Torfi tells him to confront the sow himself. Torfi suggests that Halli is not brave enough for the task; Halli charges Torfi with punishable insult, and later ambushes and kills him. Halli then befriends his in-law Guðmundr inn ríki ("the mighty") and aggressively conducts lawsuits for him. Not content with his secondary position, however, he moves to a nearby valley presided over by the chieftain Valla-Ljótr (*i.e.*, Ljótr from the farm called Vellir). Halli charges Ljótr with working on Michaelmas; Ljótr pays him but warns Halli to behave in a more friendly fashion in the future. But Halli boasts of the deed at a feast; Ljótr dons the blue tunic that signals his

"killing mood," and kills Halli in a duel. Halli's brother Hrólfr retaliates by arranging to have Ljótr's nephew Þorvarðr killed. Þorvarðr's brother Bjǫrn and his men retaliate by killing Halli's brother Bǫðvarr and Bǫðvarr's son Bersi, who had been trading abroad while the feud developed. Ljótr negotiates the settlement, but Guðmundr is dissatisfied and later ambushes Ljótr, who escapes by sliding down a frozen glen. Skapti the lawspeaker supervises the reconciliation of the two chieftains, Ljótr and Guðmundr. But Hrólfr sails to Grímsey, where Bjǫrn has been hiding, and takes money in lieu of killing Bjǫrn. Guðmundr and Valla-Ljótr meet again and settle to their mutual satisfaction and honor.

The saga has attracted little critical discussion. Andersson (1967) outlines its narrative structure according to the model he has abstracted from the saga genre as a whole, and emphasizes the process of restoring social order. Ciklamini (1966) argues that the saga contrasts pre- and post-Christian senses of honor. Acker (1988) reviews previous opinion and discusses the motif of blue clothes and the legal issue of Sabbath breaking.

Ed.: Jónas Kristjánsson, ed. *Valla-Ljóts saga*. Samfund til udgivelse af gammel nordisk litteratur, 63. Copenhagen: Jørgensen, 1952 [diplomatic edition of AM 496 4to]; Jónas Kristjánsson, ed. *Eyfirðinga sǫgur*. Íslenzk fornrit, 9. Reykjavik: Hið íslenzka fornritafélag, 1956, pp. 231–60 [normalized; standard edition]; Jorgensen, Peter A., ed. and trans. *Valla-Ljóts saga. The Saga of Valla-Ljot. The Icelandic Text According to MS AM 161 Fol. With an English Translation, Introduction and Notes*. Bibliotheca Germanica, Series Nova, 1. Saarbücken: AQ-Verlag, 1991. **Tr.**: Bachman, W. Bryant, Jr., trans. *Four Old Icelandic Sagas and Other Tales*. Lanham: University Press of America, 1985, pp. 43–69; Acker, Paul, trans. "*Valla-Ljóts saga*: Translated with an Introduction and Notes." *Comparative Criticism* 10 (1988), 207–37; Andersson, Theodore M., and William Ian Miller, trans. *Law and Literature in Medieval Iceland*: Ljósvetninga saga *and* Valla-Ljóts saga. Stanford: Stanford University Press, 1989. **Lit.**: Ciklamini, Marlene. "The Concept of Honor in *Valla-Ljóts saga*." *Journal of English and Germanic Philology* 65 (1966), 303–17; Andersson, Theodore M. *The Icelandic Family Saga: An Analytic Reading*. Harvard Studies in Comparative Literature, 28. Cambridge: Harvard University Press, 1967; Berger, Alan John. "A Recognition Scene in *Valla-Ljóts saga*." *Germanic Notes* 8 (1977), 2–4.

Paul Acker

[**See also:** *Íslendingasögur*]

Vápnfirðinga saga ("The Saga of the People of Vápnfjǫrðr") has been preserved almost entirely in late paper MSS. Of vellums, only a single 15th-century leaf survives, now preserved in AM 162c fol. The large number of paper MSS, dating from the 17th to the 19th century, all have a lacuna beginning in ch. 13. The existing vellum leaf contains part but not all of the material that is missing in the paper MSS, as well as some material that they have. It can be deduced that all the paper MSS derive from a now-lost vellum that lacked two pages and was copied from a complete version of the MS represented by the single leaf in AM 162c fol. The editions of 1848 and 1902–1903 use AM 513 4to (*ca.* 1700) as a base text, while the edition of 1950 uses Stock. Papp. fol. no. 35, copied in Copenhagen in 1686–1687. The edition of 1987 follows that of 1902–1903 in the main and also profits from Jón Helgason's edition of the vellum fragment.

The saga was probably composed in the second quarter of

the 13th century, perhaps by a descendant of Þorkell Geitisson, whose family is mentioned in the last chapter, where no mention is made of the prominent family of Bjarni Brodd-Helgason. The author used Styrmir's version of *Landnámabók* and perhaps some other written sources, such as a version of *Droplaugarsona saga*, but his main source was oral tradition. The *Íslendingadrápa* of Haukr Valdísarson, perhaps from around 1200, mentions the principal events of the saga, the slayings of Brodd-Helgi and Geitir and the failed attempts by Þorkell to take vengeance on Bjarni, but it describes Bjarni as a more combative sort than does the saga and was probably not a source.

Vápnfirðinga saga deals with the relationships between two families in Vopnafjörður, in the northeast of Iceland, over two generations at the end of the 10th century: the Krossvíkingar, who lived on the farm Krossavík, and the Hofsverjar (from the farm Hof). The first thirteen chapters trace the decline of a friendship between Brodd-Helgi of Hof and Geitir of Krossavík, to the point where Geitir, normally a peaceful man, is provoked to attack and slay his former friend. Unfortunately, the lacuna prevents us from witnessing the fight. The friendship began to decline when each suspected the other of taking property from a Norwegian captain whose death they contrived. Things worsened when Brodd-Helgi dismissed his wife, who was Geitir's sister, and refused to return her property. Finally, when Brodd-Helgi unjustly killed oxen and cut down trees belonging to a follower of Geitir, Geitir decided to take action.

After the slaying, the second part of the saga (chs. 14–19) centers on the next generation, and contains two reversals. The first has to do with personalities: to avenge his father, Brodd-Helgi's son Bjarni kills his uncle Geitir, but he does so reluctantly and tries his best to avoid conflict for the rest of the saga, while Þorkell, son of the peaceful Geitir, aggressively seeks to lay his hands on Bjarni, but is repeatedly frustrated and out-tricked. Finally, they clash, but their fighting is ended by women who throw clothes over their weapons. The second reversal is one of plot: the saga ends with reconciliation, when Þorkell finally accepts Bjarni's offers of medical assistance and self-judgment, and in his old age he moves to Bjarni's farm at Hof. Thus, whereas the first part of the saga showed how to turn a friend into a mortal enemy, the second part shows how to make peace with an enemy.

Influences of the saga are difficult to trace. The moving scene in ch. 14, where Bjarni strikes Geitir and then in repentance supports the dying body, may have influenced the similar scene between Bolli and Kjartan in *Laxdœla saga* (ch. 49).

Ed.: Thordarson, G., ed. *Vápnfirðinga saga*. Nordiske Oldskrifter, 5. Copenhagen: Berling, 1848; Jakobsen, Jakob, ed. *Austfirðinga sǫgur*. Samfund til udgivelse af gammel nordisk litteratur, 29. Copenhagen: Møller, 1902–03, pp. 21–72; Jón Jóhannesson, ed. *Austfirðinga sǫgur*. Íslenzk fornrit, 11. Reykjavik: Hið íslenzka fornritafélag, 1950, pp. 23–65; Jón Helgason. "Syv sagablade. (AM 126 C fol., bl. 1–7)." *Opuscula* 5. Bibliotheca Arnamagnæana, 31. Copenhagen: Munksgaard, 1975, pp. 1–97 [edition of the vellum fragment]; Bragi Halldórsson *et al.*, eds. *Íslendinga sögur*. Reykjavik: Svart á hvítu, 1987, pp. 1987–2007. **Tr.**: Jones, Gwyn, trans. *Eirik the Red and Other Icelandic Sagas*. London: Oxford University Press, 1961; rpt. 1966, pp. 39–77; Boucher, Alan, trans. *Tales from the Eastfirths*. Reykjavik: Iceland Review, 1981, pp. 31–59. **Lit.**: Walter, Ernst. *Studien zur Vápnfirðinga saga*. Saga, 1. Halle: Niemeyer, 1956; Heller, Rolf. "Droplaugarsona saga—Vápnfirðinga saga—Laxdæla saga." *Arkiv för nordisk filologi* 78 (1963), 140–69; Heller, Rolf. "Studien zu Aufbau und Stil der Vápnfirðinga saga." *Arkiv för nordisk filologi* 78 (1963), 170–89; Heller, Rolf. "Über einige Anzeichen einer literarischen Beziehung zwischen der Knytlinga saga und der Vápnfirðinga saga." *Beiträge zur Geschichte der deutschen Sprache und Literatur* 90 (1968), 300–4; Jón Helgason. "Paris i Troja, Þorsteinn på Borg och Brodd-Helgi på Hof." In *Nordiska studier i filologi och lingvistik. Festskrift tillägnad Gösta Holm på 60-årsdagen den 8 juli 1976.* Ed. Lars Svensson *et al.* Lund: Studentlitteratur, 1976, pp. 192–4; Berger, Alan. "Lawyers in the Old Icelandic Family Sagas: Heroes, Villains, and Authors." *Saga-Book of the Viking Society* 20 (1978–79), 70–9; Byock, Jesse L. *Medieval Iceland: Society, Sagas, and Power.* Berkeley, Los Angeles, and London: University of California Press, 1988, pp. 203–20.

Robert Cook

[**See also:** *Droplaugarsona saga*; *Íslendingadrápa*; *Íslendingasögur*; *Landnámabók*; *Laxdœla saga*; *Þorsteins saga hvíta*]

Varangians

Varangians (Old Norse *Væringjar*, Slavic *variazi*, Greek Βάραγγοι) has slightly different meanings depending on the language in which it appears. In Slavic and Greek, it apparently meant "Scandinavians and/or Franks"; in Icelandic, as in English, it denotes a Scandinavian mercenary in the service of the Byzantine emperors, more specifically a member of the famous "Varangian Guard."

Scandinavian traders had reached Constantinople as early as the late 9th century. Some came as traders or pirates, and others joined the Byzantine army. The practice of hiring foreign troops was a legacy of the Roman Empire; such forces were used not only in the field, but also as units in the imperial guard, the *Hetairia*. The presence of Scandinavians in these groups is attested as early as the reign of Michael III (842–867). An elite corps within the *Hetairia*, the Varangian Guard was established by Basil II around 988, and survived until the fall of Constantinople in 1204. It was referred to as the "Varangians of the City" to distinguish it from other groups of Varangians of lesser importance, the "Varangians outside the city." As the name indicates, the Guard was composed primarily of Scandinavians, but included Franks, Turks, and, after the Norman Conquest in 1066, Englishmen.

Many Swedish rune stones commemorate men who died in Greece (Pritsak 1981: 374–81); however, they did not usually specify whether the deceased was a soldier, merchant, or pilgrim. Ragnvaldr, a member of a prominent family in Uppland, Sweden, raised a stone recording his service as a commanding officer (*liðs forungi*) in the imperial army (U[ppsala] 112B). One can assume that several Norsemen who died in Langbarðaland, the Byzantine catepanate of Italy, were members of the Varangian Guard; see especially the inscriptions Sö 65, Sö Lagnö, U141.

Undoubtedly, the most famous Scandinavian to enter the imperial service was the Norwegian Haraldr harðráði ("hard-ruler") Sigurðarson, half-brother of St. Óláfr, who spent the years 1034–1043 as an officer (*spatharokandidatos*) in the Byzantine army. His exploits are recounted at great length in his saga, preserved in *Morkinskinna*, *Heimskringla*, and *Fagrskinna*; he is also mentioned in a contemporary Byzantine source, the "Memoires" of Kekaumenos (trans. in Sigfús Blöndal 1978: 57–8), from which it can be seen that his position was somewhat more modest than the saga would have us believe.

Many Icelandic sagas enhance the reputations of their heroes by reporting that they served the emperor; while some of these claims may be based on fact, others are clearly fictitious (Sigfús Blöndal, ch. 9).

The following sagas contain such accounts: *Hrafnkels saga*: Þorkell Þjóstarsson and Eyvindr Bjarnason, in the mid-10th century; *Hallfreðar saga vandræðaskálds*: Gríss Sæmingsson, *ca.* 970–980; *Finnboga saga ramma*: Bersi hvíti ("the white"), a Norwegian, *ca.* 970; *Njáls saga*: Kolskeggr Hámundarson, *ca.* 989, probably one of the first members of the Varangian Guard; *Þorvalds þáttr víðfǫrla*: Þorvaldr Koðránsson and Stefnir Þorgilsson, *ca.* 995; *Heiðarvíga saga*: Gestr Þórhallason and Þorsteinn Styrsson, *ca.* 1026–1036; *Heimskringla*: Eilífr Þorgilsson, paternal uncle of the Danish king Sven Estridsen, *ca.* 1026–1036; *Laxdœla saga*: Bolli Bollason, *ca.* 1026–1030; *Grettis saga*: Þorbjǫrn Þórðarson and Þorsteinn Ásmundarson, *ca.* 1032–1033; *Heimskringla* and *Halldórs þáttr*: Halldórr Snorrason and Haraldr harðráði, *ca.* 1034–1042; and *Ljósvetninga saga*: Þormóðr Ásgeirsson, *ca.* 1064–1071.

The Varangian Guard has a special place as a kind of "hatchery" for Old Icelandic storytelling. Constantinople was the meeting place for peoples of different cultures, and the higher cultural milieu of the imperial capital stimulated the soldiers to tell stories about their adventures, in which truth and fantasy could easily be combined.

Lit.: Stender-Petersen, Adolf. *Varangica*. Århus: Luno, 1953; Sigfús Blöndal. *The Varangians of Byzantium: An Aspect of Byzantine Military History*. Rev. and trans. Benedikt Benedikz. Cambridge: Cambridge University Press, 1978; Pritsak, Omeljan. *The Origin of Rus'. 1: Old Scandinavian Sources Other than the Sagas*. Cambridge: Harvard University Press, 1981 [vol. 2 forthcoming].

Omeljan Pritsak

[See also: Russia, Norse in; Trade]

Vatnsdœla saga

Vatnsdœla saga ("The Saga of the People of Vatnsdalr") is an *Íslendingasaga* about five generations of an Icelandic chieftain family in Vatnsdalr in the north of Iceland. It begins in Norway in the 9th century, with Þorsteinn Ketilsson's rise to fame and fortune. His son, Ingimundr, a great Viking, joins Harald hárfagri ("fair-hair") Hálfdanarson before the battle in Hafrsfjǫrðr and gains his friendship. It is prophesied that he will emigrate to Iceland. He does so, and the main part of the saga recounts his fortunes and misfortunes and those of his descendants for more than a century.

The good fortune of this family is emphasized in *Vatnsdœla saga*, although not all its members are equally fortunate. In old age, Ingimundr is killed by a scoundrel he is trying to protect from his own sons' just retribution. Ingimundr himself behaves like a "noble heathen," and some of his descendants also embody the author's ideals of peacefulness and equanimity. The bravest and strongest among them, however, tend to be reckless and fall victims to misfortune. The last chieftain of the family described in the saga is said to be of the same kind as Ingimundr and his son Þorsteinn, although he has the advantage over them that "he had the right faith and loved God and prepared himself for his death in a Christian manner." Thus, he is the ideal chieftain. The saga is permeated with a mixture of Christian attitudes and traditional notions of fortune.

Vatnsdœla saga has a looser composition than most *Íslendingasögur*. Its numerous episodes are mostly connected only through the actors, and there are no prolonged feuds to bind them together. The introduction about events in Norway is fabulous, modeled on earlier sagas and legends. The continuation seems to draw on oral tradition about local feuds and skirmishes, but they have not been integrated into a convincing whole. Although minor feuds are briefly recounted, the dominant type of conflict is the cleansing of land of alien and disruptive elements: robbers, thieves, sorcerers, witches. Repeatedly, such elements "invade" the territory controlled by the Vatnsdœlir family, who succeed in driving them away or eliminating them, but often after having suffered heavy losses. Two of the leaders of the family are killed by such persons.

The style of *Vatnsdœla saga* is verbose and verges on the sentimental at times. The characterization of the heroes often seems superficial; they lack the substance that could justify the lavish praise bestowed on them. The writer makes brave attempts to glorify them as traditional heroes, but does so halfheartedly, since his values are basically Christian. In spite of the artistic shortcomings of the saga, however, it is full of material interesting for the student of folklore and folk belief.

Only a fragment of *Vatnsdœla saga* has been preserved on vellum (*ca.* 1400), but there are good paper copies of a 14th-century text. The relationship with *Landnámabók* has led scholars to conclude that it cannot have been written later than 1280. Its general character and style indicate that it is not likely to be much older than that.

Ed.: Vogt, Walther Heinrich, ed. *Vatnsdœla saga*. Altnordische Saga-Bibliothek, 16. Halle: Niemeyer, 1921; Finnur Jónsson, ed. *Vatnsdœla saga*. Samfund til udgivelse af gammel nordisk litteratur, 36. Copenhagen: Jørgensen, 1934–35; Einar Ól. Sveinsson, ed. *Vatnsdœla saga*. Íslenzk fornrit, 8. Reykjavik: Hið íslenzka fornritafélag, 1939. **Tr.**: Jones, Gwyn, trans. *The Vatnsdalers' Saga*. Princeton: Princeton University Press; New York: American-Scandinavian Foundation, 1944. **Lit.**: Bååth, Albert Ulrik. *Studier öfver kompositionen i några isländska ättsagor*. Lund: Berling, 1885; Hamel, A. G. van. "Vatnsdœlasaga and Finnbogasaga." *Journal of English and Germanic Philology* 33 (1934), 1–22; Danielsson, Tommy. *Om den isländska släktsagans uppbyggnad*. Skrifter utgivna av Litteraturvetenskapliga institutionen vid Uppsala universitet, 22. Uppsala: Almqvist & Wiksell, 1986.

Vésteinn Ólason

[See also: *Íslendingasögur*; *Landnámabók*]

Vatnshyrna

Vatnshyrna ("The Book of Vatnshorn" or "Water-logged") was a major saga codex, probably copied, like part of *Flateyjarbók*, by Magnús Þórhallsson, most likely for Jón Hákonarson of Víðidalstunga, Húnavatnssýsla, North Iceland, between 1391 and 1395; its texts of *Flóamanna saga* and *Þórðar saga hreðu* ended with genealogies down to Jón and his wife. Arngrímur Jónsson's *Crymogaea* (Hamburg, 1609) refers to its texts of *Kjalnesinga saga*, *Þórðar saga hreðu*, and *Bárðar saga Snæfellsáss*; Arngrímur presumably called it *Vatnshyrna* because it was then at Stóra Vatnshorn, Haukadalur, Dalasýsla, Northwest Iceland. A major part of it then became no. 5 in the MS collection of Peder Resen, and in 1675 passed to Copenhagen University Library. The codex then contained *Flóamanna saga*, *Laxdœla saga*, *Hœnsa-Þóris saga*, *Vatnsdœla saga*, *Eyrbyggja saga*, *Kjalnesinga saga*, *Króka-Refs saga*, *Stjǫrnu-Odda draumr*, *Bergbúa þáttr*, *Kumlbúa þáttr*, and *Þorsteins draumr Síðu-Hallssonar*. All these texts were destroyed in the great fire of Copenhagen in 1728, but reliable copies of all of them except *Króka-Refs saga*, made by Árni Magnússon and his scribe Ásgeir Jónsson, survive in the Arnamagnaean Collection.

It was formerly thought that fragments of the portion of

Vatnshyrna that did not reach Resen's collection (at least *Þórðar saga hreðu* and *Bárðar saga Snæfellsáss*) have survived in AM 564a 4to; but because these leaves include the short *þættir* that were also part of Resen's codex, this cannot be so. It now seems that there was another codex, *Pseudo-Vatnshyrna*, in part related to *Vatnshyrna*, of which fragments survive in AM 445b 4to, AM 445c 4to, and AM 564a 4to. This contained at least the *Melabók* text of *Landnámabók*, *Vatnsdœla saga*, *Flóamanna saga*, *Eyrbyggja saga*, *Bárðar saga Snæfellsáss*, *Þórðar saga hreðu*, *Bergbúa þáttr*, *Kumlbúa þáttr*, *Þorsteins draumr Síðu-Hallssonar*, *Gísla saga*, *Víga-Glúms saga*, and *Harðar saga*, the last possibly added some time after the rest of the codex. *Pseudo-Vatnshyrna* was in several hands; a minor hand in *Gísla saga* has been identified as that of Þórðr Þórðarson, priest at Skagaströnd, Húnavatnssýsla, and dated around 1390. The heading to *Harðar saga* was probably written by Hǫskuldr Hákonarson of Miklabær, Skagafjarðarsýsla, North Iceland, perhaps in the first decade of the 15th century.

Although the two codices originate in the same area and period, it appears that they were closely related only in some of their shared material. It cannot be assumed that any text for which we now have evidence from only one of them was ever present in the other.

Lit.: Stefán Karlsson. "Um Vatnshyrnu." *Opuscula* 4. Bibliotheca Arnamagnæana, 30. Copenhagen: Munksgaard, 1970, pp. 279–303 [English summary, pp. 301–3]; McKinnell, John. "The Reconstruction of Pseudo-Vatnshyrna." *Opuscula* 4, pp. 304–38; Perkins, Richard. *Flóamanna saga, Gaulverjabær and Haukr Erlendsson*. Studia Islandica, 36. Reykjavik: Menningarsjóður, 1978, pp. 14–6, 45–54.

John McKinnell

[**See also**: *Bárðar saga Snæfellsáss*; *Eyrbyggja saga*; *Flateyjarbók*; *Flóamanna saga*; *Gísla saga Súrssonar*; *Harðar saga*; *Hœnsa-Þóris saga*; *Kjalnesinga saga*; *Króka-Refs saga*; *Landnámabók*; *Laxdœla saga*; *Þórðar saga hreðu*; *Þorsteins draumr Síðu-Hallssonar*; *Vatnsdœla saga*; *Víga-Glúms saga*]

Vellekla *see* **Einarr Helgason skálaglamm**

Veraldar saga ("The Saga of the World") is an Icelandic chronicle of world history from the Creation through the 12th century. It survives in two redactions: A (AM 625 4to, beginning of the 14th century) and B (in several fragments, the oldest from *ca.* 1200, complete only in copies from *ca.* 1600 and later). The name was first assigned to the saga by Konráð Gíslason (1860) in his edition.

Veraldar saga is divided according to the Six Ages. Apart from a number of verbal variants, the redactions differ from each other in that B has allegorical explanations accompanying each of the first five ages, a pattern most likely original but omitted in A.

The core of *Veraldar saga* is probably a reworking of an unknown Latin original. The oldest part derives ultimately from Bede's and Isidore's chronicles, but is expanded with material drawn from the Bible, Bible commentaries, and other sources. Hofmann (1986) has offered convincing evidence that the author of *Veraldar saga* relied on the Icelandic *Rómverja saga* for the section on the oldest history of Rome. The history of the period after Bede is presented more concisely; the material is known from German annals and chronicles, but no definite source has been established. *Veraldar saga* closes with a list of German emperors down to Frederick Barbarossa (d. 1190). Of the last two rulers, however, it is only stated that Konrad III (r. 1138–1152) was emperor when the Icelander Gizurr Hallsson (d. 1206) was on a journey south and that Frederick Barbarossa is now emperor (thus only B). The last historical note concerns Lothar II's Roman campaign in 1137; the year of his rule is inaccurately recorded in A, while B has a lacuna. The original, therefore, probably only went as far as Lothar II, while the rest is added in the Icelandic versions along with other expansions, *e.g.*, from *Rómverja saga* and from Dares Phrygius or *Trójumanna saga*. Stefán Karlsson (1977) has pointed out on the basis of parallels in Icelandic hagiographic literature that there possibly existed a somewhat fuller redaction of *Veraldar saga*. The Icelandic reworking is obviously older than 1190; the reference to Gizurr Hallsson has led scholars to suggest that he was the author, but it is more likely that the saga was simply the product of his cultural setting in the area of the bishopric in Skálholt, Iceland. Seip's (1954) theory positing a Norwegian original of *Veraldar saga* is untenable.

Redaction A has an addition concerning the four synods in Nicea, Constantinople, Ephesus, and Chalcedon, along with a section on the patriarchs and the beginning of a list of popes. These additions are probably old; some of the them are interpolated in the B-text, and the section on the synods is found outside *Veraldar saga*, expanded with a passage on the Lateran Council of 1215. The version in A is thus older than 1215, and was probably in A's original, which can be dated to around 1200.

Ed.: Konráð Gíslason, ed. *Fire og fyrretyve for en stor Deel forhen utrykte Prøver af oldnordisk Sprog og Litteratur*. Copenhagen: Gyldendal, 1860, pp. 64–107 [A-redaction]; Morgenstern, G., ed. *Arnamagnæanische Fragmente. Ein Supplement zu den Heilagra Manna Sögur*. Leipzig and Copenhagen: Graf, 1893, pp. 35–44 [edits the oldest fragments]; Jakob Benediktsson, ed. *Veraldar saga*. Samfund til udgivelse af gammel nordisk litteratur, 61. Copenhagen: Luno, 1944; Hreinn Benediktsson, ed. *Early Icelandic Script as Illustrated in Vernacular Texts from the Twelfth and Thirteenth Centuries*. Icelandic Manuscripts, Series in Folio, 2. Reykjavik: Manuscript Institute of Iceland, 1965. **Lit.**: Seip, Didrik Arup. *Nye studier i norsk språkhistorie*. Oslo: Aschehoug, 1954, pp. 105–18; Stefán Karlsson. "Fróðleiksgreinar frá tólftu öld." In *Afmælisrit Jóns Helgasonar. 30 júní 1969*. Ed. Jakob Benediktsson *et al*. Reykjavik: Heimskringla, 1969, pp. 328–30; Marchand, James W. "The Allegories in the Old Norse *Veraldar saga*." *Michigan Germanic Studies* 1 (1975), 109–18; Stefán Karlsson. "Inventio Crucis, cap. 1, og Veraldar saga." *Opuscula* 2.2. Bibliotheca Arnamagnæana, 25. Copenhagen: Reitzel, 1977, pp. 116–33; Hofmann, Dietrich. "Accessus ad Lucanum: Zur Neubestimmung des Verhältnisses zwischen Rómveria saga und Veraldar saga." In *Sagnaskemmtun: Studies in Honour of Hermann Pálsson on His 65th Birthday 26th May 1986*. Ed. Rudolf Simek *et al*. Vienna, Cologne, and Graz: Böhlau, 1986, pp. 121–51.

Jakob Benediktsson

[**See also**: *Rómverja saga*; *Trójumanna saga*]

Vestrfararvísur *see* **Sighvatr Þórðarson**

Víga-Glúmr Eyjólfsson, the central character in *Víga-Glúms saga*, was the grandson of Ingjaldr, who established the estate at Þverá in Eyjafjörður (now Munkaþverá), and the great-grandson of Helgi inn magri ("the lean"). A number of references whose origins antedate the saga itself can help to distinguish the historical man from the literary character, but it is hard to know how far these depend on each other.

The early recensions of *Landnámabók* confirm the names of Glúmr's immediate ancestors, brothers, wife, and sons given in the saga, though there are minor differences in the names of his collateral relatives (*Landnámabók*: 253, 259, 269). They also mention his killing of Sigmundr, son of Þorkell inn hávi ("the tall"; (*Landnámabók*, ch. 1: 237, 282, and *cf. Víga-Glúms saga*, ch. 8).

The Icelandic annals record the slaying of Sigmundr under the year 944, and the battle at Hrísateigr under 983. These exact dates may be a learned guess, but the gap between them is probably based on the statement in stanza 9 in the saga that Glúmr had enjoyed power at Þverá for forty years, and this looks like an accurate tradition (trans. McKinnell, p. 14).

The saga's thirteen verses are all probably ancient; stanzas 8 and 12 are also attributed to Glúmr in Snorri's *Skáldskaparmál* (ed. Finnur Jónsson, pp. 75, 115–6, 119, 132). These verses provide support for an unjust encroachment on Glúmr's family estate (st. 1; *cf.* content of ch. 7); a battle in a meadow (st. 6; *cf.* chs. 21–23); Glúmr's loss of his estate after forty years as a result of having killed a man (sts. 8–9; *cf.* ch. 26); an inconclusive battle at an assembly whose geographical details must refer to Vaðlaþing in Eyjafjörður (sts. 10–12; *cf.* ch. 27); and his inability to avenge Grímr eyrarleggr ("bank-leg") (st. 13; *cf.* ch. 27).

Further details, found in *Þórðarbók*, are probably derived from *Melabók* and the lost **Esphælinga saga*. These details include Glúmr's relationship to King Óláfr Tryggvason (*cf.* ch. 5); the killing of Bárðr by Glúmr's son Vígfús (*cf.* ch. 19); more about the battle at Hrísateigr (*cf.* chs. 22–23); and a different and possibly more historical account of the circumstances leading up to the fight at Vaðlaþing (*cf.* ch. 27). The killing of Bárðr may also receive support from the discovery, at the place where he and Vígfús are said to have fought, of the heathen burial of a young warrior of the late 10th century (trans. McKinnell, p. 15).

Glúmr was probably born around 928, killed Sigmundr about 944, and came to power in Eyjafjörður around 946. He was a powerful chieftain until about 986, but lost the estate at Þverá as an indirect result of the battle at Hrísateigr (*ca.* 983). He was later involved in a struggle at the local assembly in which his brother-in-law Grímr eyrarleggr was killed. His son Vígfús killed Bárðr, perhaps around 976–977, and later became a retainer of Earl Hákon.

The saga attributes ten full verses and one half-verse to Glúmr; none seem to be the work of the saga writer, and only the half-verse (st. 3) need be regarded with suspicion, since it occurs in the interpolated ch. 16 and contradicts the geographical details of the episode there. Like many early skaldic poets, Glúmr (if the ten verses really are his) uses rhyme rather irregularly, except in the fourth and eighth line of each verse, although his verses are otherwise highly accomplished. He uses much mythological information, notably the names and attributes of Óðinn, *dísir*, and valkyries, and the story of Þórr and Hrungnir (st. 5). But his most noticeable traits are a fondness for "land" images, particularly concerning his own estate, and a persistent tone of egotism (none of his surviving verses praises anyone but himself; see McKinnell, pp. 22–7). His prominent and habitual portrayal of himself as a warrior also seems oddly out of keeping with a long career, which, according to his saga, included only three killings (or four, if we include the interpolated Ingólfr story) and two significant battles.

Ed.: Jónas Kristjánsson, ed. *Eyfirðinga sǫgur.* Íslenzk fornrit, 9. Reykjavik: Hið íslenzka fornritafélag, 1956, pp. 1–98; Turville-Petre, E. O. G., ed. *Víga-Glúms saga.* 2nd ed. Oxford: Clarendon, 1960; Jakob Benediktsson, ed. *Íslendingabók. Landnámabók.* Íslenzk fornrit, 1. Reykjavik: Hið íslenzka fornritafélag, 1966; Turville-Petre, E. O. G. *Scaldic Poetry.* Oxford: Clarendon, 1976, pp. 56–9. **Tr.**: Hollander, Lee M., trans. *Víga-Glúms Saga and The Story of Ögmund Dytt.* Library of Scandinavian Literature, 14. New York: Twayne; American-Scandinavian Foundation, 1972; McKinnell, John, trans. *Viga-Glums saga with the Tales of Ögmund Bash and Thorvald Chatterbox.* New Saga Library. Edinburgh: Canongate, 1987. **Bib.**: Hollander, Lee M. *A Bibliography of Skaldic Studies.* Copenhagen: Munksgaard, 1958. **Lit.**: Magerøy, Hallvard. "Viga-Glum (Draps-Glum)." *Norsk Biografisk Leksikon* 18 (1977), 7–8.

John McKinnell

[**See also:** *Landnámabók; Lausavísur; Skáld;* Skaldic Meters; Skaldic Verse; *Snorra Edda; Víga-Glúms saga*]

Víga-Glúms saga ("The Saga of Killer-Glúmr") is preserved in full in the mid-14th-century codex *Möðruvallabók* (AM 132 fol.), and in fragments of a longer version in AM 445c 4to and AM 564a 4to, two of the surviving remnants of the codex known as *Pseudo-Vatnshyrna* (*ca.* 1400). Comparison of the story of Víga-Skúta in both versions with the corresponding material in *Reykdœla saga* shows that it has been independently interpolated into both sagas from a common original, and that the *Pseudo-Vatnshyrna* text of *Víga-Glúms saga* is closer to that original than that of *Möðruvallabók*, which seems throughout to contain a condensed version of a longer original text. However, the text in *Pseudo-Vatnshyrna* already contained three major interpolations: the stories of Ingólfr (corresponding to chs. 13–15 in *Möðruvallabók*), Ǫgmundr (not in *Möðruvallabók*, but fully preserved in another version as ch. 174 of *Óláfs saga Tryggvasonar en mesta*), and Víga-Skúta (ch. 16 in *Möðruvallabók*).

The author probably lived at or near Munkaþverá in Eyjafjörður, North Iceland, of which he shows a minutely accurate knowledge; he may have been associated with the Benedictine monastery there. The date is hard to establish, but if, as seems likely, the author was bearing in mind the design of *Egils saga Skalla-Grímssonar*, *Víga-Glúms saga* must postdate that saga, which was probably written by Snorri Sturluson in the early 1220s (Sigurður Nordal 1968: 122–5). The Ingólfr story may allude to contemporary events that culminated in 1232. Although this episode is an interpolation, it uses other parts of the saga as source material, so must be later than the rest of *Víga-Glúms saga*. Together, these indications might suggest a date about 1230, although Einar Ól. Sveinsson (1969) suggests parallels between *Víga-Glúms saga* and the account in *Sturlunga saga* of the death of Snorri's brother Sighvatr in 1238. Sighvatr lived within sight of Munkaþverá at Grund, and the origins of the saga should probably be sought among his circle.

Much of the saga's source material was probably transmitted orally, including its thirteen verses, two of which are also attributed to Glúmr in *Snorra Edda*; there is probably also some quotation from memory from the legal code *Grágás*. But the genealogical details and the names of those involved in the battle at Hrísateigr in Eyjafjörður are in some ways fuller than the story requires, suggesting the use of written genealogies and annals. Jónas Kristjánsson (1956: xxvii–xxxvi) demonstrates the existence of a lost *Esphælinga saga*; this saga included a rather different account of the confrontation described in ch. 27 of *Víga-Glúms saga*, which survives in *Þórðarbók*, a late version of *Landnámabók*. Jónas Kristjánsson (1956) thinks that *Esphælinga saga* was another source of *Víga-Glúms saga*. Although the two sagas must have been related, it is hard to determine which one influenced the other. The story of Ingólfr, besides its possible allusion to contemporary events, uses an exemplary tale from the 12th-century *Disciplina clericalis* of Petrus Alphonsus, in which a young man tests his friends' loyalty by killing a calf and pretending it is a man; this episode seems to be the only use of a non-Icelandic source.

Víga-Glúms saga is essentially a biography of Víga-Glúmr Eyjólfsson, depicted as tough, self-assertive, and antiromantic. After a prologue that presents his father's youthful trip to Norway as lightly ironized folktale (chs. 1–4), Glúmr himself has adventures that function as a parody of his father's (chs. 5–6). Returning to Iceland, he is faced with oppression by Þorkell and his son Sigmundr, but kills Sigmundr and defeats Þorkell in the ensuing lawsuit, thus taking the estate at Þverá from Þorkell, but ensuring the subsequent enmity of the family at nearby Espihóll (chs. 7–10). His success leads to ambition and dishonesty among his supporters, and subsequently to killings on both sides, culminating in a battle against the Espihóll men at Hrísateigr (chs. 23–24). There, Glúmr kills Þorvaldr krókr ("crooked") Þórisson, but succeeds in getting the killing attributed to the twelve-year-old Guðbrandr, who is outlawed for it. However, a careless boast in one of Glúmr's verses leads to the reopening of the case, and although he tries to evade the consequences by means of an equivocal oath, he is eventually deprived of his estate on terms similar to those on which he gained it (chs. 25–26). He remains undaunted in old age and adversity, but is ultimately unable either to regain his former position or to obtain revenge. The tone of the saga is antiheroic and its style (in *Möðruvallabók*) terse and generally without overt value judgments, but the author's viewpoint seems to be that aggressive self-assertion is ultimately self-defeating.

Ed.: Jónas Kristjánsson, ed. *Eyfirðinga sögur*. Íslenzk fornrit, 9. Reykjavik: Hið íslenzka fornritafélag, 1956, pp. 1–98; Turville-Petre, E. O. G., ed. *Víga-Glúms saga*. 2nd ed. Oxford: Clarendon, 1960. **Tr.**: Hollander, Lee M., trans. *Víga-Glúm's Saga and The Story of Ögmund Dytt*. Library of Scandinavian Literature, 14. New York: Twayne; American-Scandinavian Foundation, 1972; McKinnell, John, trans. *Viga-Glums saga with the Tales of Ögmund Bash and Thorvald Chatterbox*. New Saga Library. Edinburgh: Canongate, 1987. **Bib.**: Jónas Kristjánsson. "Víga-Glúms saga." *KLNM* 20 (1976), 9–10. **Lit.**: Wahlgren, Erik. "Killer-Glum: A Word on Traditional Motif and Saga Portrait." In *Folklore International: Essays in Traditional Literature, Belief and Custom in Honor of Wayland Debs Hand*. Ed. D. K. Wilgus and Carol Sommer. Hatboro: Folklore Associates, 1967, pp. 221–31; Sigurður Nordal. *Um Íslenzkar fornsögur*. Trans. Árni Björnsson. Reykjavik: Mál og Menning, 1968; Einar Ól. Sveinsson. "'Ek ætla mér ekki á braut.'" In *Afmælisrit Jóns Helgasonar, 30 júní 1969*. Ed. Jakob Benediktsson et al. Reykjavik: Heimskringla, 1969, pp. 48–58; Jónas Kristjánsson. "Fóstbræðravíg." In *Einarsbók. Afmæliskveðja til Einars Ól. Sveinssonar*. Ed. Bjarni Guðnason et al. Reykjavik: Nokkrir Vinir, 1970, pp. 196–204; Heller, Rolf. "Fóstbræðra saga und Víga-Glúms saga." *Acta Philologica Scandinavica* 31 (1976), 44–57; Dronke, Ursula. "Sem jarlar forðum. The Influence of *Rígsþula* on Two Saga-Episodes." In *Specvlvm Norroenvm: Norse Studies in Memory of Gabriel Turville-Petre*. Ed. Ursula Dronke et al. Odense: Odense University Press, 1981, pp. 56–72; Davíð Erlingsson. "Eyjólfr Has the Last Laugh: A Note on *Víga-Glúms saga*, Chs. I–III." In *Specvlvm Norroenvm*, pp. 85–8.

John McKinnell

[**See also**: *Egils saga Skalla-Grímssonar*; *Grágás*; *Landnámabók*; *Lausavísur*; *Möðruvallabók*; *Óláfs saga Tryggvasonar*; *Reykdœla saga (ok Víga-Skútu)*; *Snorra Edda*; *Sturlunga saga*; *Vatnshyrna*; Víga-Glúmr Eyjólfsson]

Víglundar saga ("The Saga of Víglundr") is an *Íslendingasaga* from the end of the 14th or the beginning of the 15th century, by an anonymous author who probably lived at Snæfellsnes. The saga survives in two vellum MSS and a number of paper ones. The oldest vellum, AM 551a 4to, dates from the 15th century, and, despite the absence of one leaf, contains the best extant version of the text. The other vellum, AM 510 4to, is commonly dated to the 15th century, but may be as late as the mid-16th. It is missing two leaves, but its lacuna does not overlap with that of AM 551a 4to. The oldest paper copy, AM 160 fol., was made in the 17th century by Jón Erlendsson, and has independent value.

Víglundar saga relates the parallel adventures of successive generations of a family. Þorgrímr is a Norwegian earl's illegitimate son. He falls in love with Ólof, the beautiful daughter of Earl Þórir. Since Þórir will not consent to their marriage, they elope to Iceland at the last moment before her marriage to Ketill of Raumaríki. Þorgrímr and Ólof raise a family near Snæfellsnes and foster Ketilríðr, the daughter of their neighbors. Þorgrímr's son Víglundr falls in love with Ketilríðr. While jealousy and hostility grow between Þorgrímr's sons and Ketilríðr's brothers, Ketill sends first his daughter's suitor and then, after the suitor's death, his own sons, Sigurðr and Gunnlaugr, to kill Þorgrímr. After their ship is wrecked, Ketill's sons effect a reconciliation with Þorgrímr instead of revenge. Þorgrímr and Ketilríðr's father then conspire to save Ketilríðr from an importunate suitor; they pretend to marry her to a settler from Norway who is actually Þorgrímr's half-brother. Víglundr and the sons of Ketill return from raiding and find themselves at Ketilríðr's new home. Víglundr and Ketilríðr resist temptation, and her "husband" reveals his identity. Ketilríðr is married to Víglundr, Sigurðr marries Víglundr's sister, and Gunnlaugr marries the "husband's" daughter. The saga ends with a rhyming prayer.

Víglundar saga is usually dismissed as a late *Íslendingasaga* influenced by romance and *fornaldarsögur*, and unconnected to historical tradition. Some of the saga's characters may share names with figures known from earlier, more reputable sources, but little else. However, such a reading obscures *Víglundar saga's* many positive characteristics. Its structure, for example, compares favorably with that of classical *Íslendingasögur*; there are no marginally relevant episodes or digressions, and although the cast of characters is fairly large, all the narrative strands come together satisfyingly at the end of the story.

Víglundar saga attempts to portray Settlement Age Icelanders and Norwegians as the equals of the knights and ladies of romance in their courtesy and courtliness. The figure of Víglundr, a first-generation Icelander whose scrupulously moral pursuit of Ketilríðr does his parents' Norwegian elopement one better, is one late 14th-century Icelander's conception of an *Íslendingasaga* hero. The presumably pagan Víglundr's behavior and ethics also differ considerably from those of pagans described by 13th-century authors, since it is Christianity as a social, rather than political, force that informs the saga. Far more noticeable than battles and bloodshed are the many decisions *not* to gain one's objectives by violence. In addition, friendship and kinship function as powerful social forces, while anger and malice prove correspondingly weak. As a love story, *Víglundar saga* also contrasts with the *skáldasögur* of the 13th century. Not only does Víglundr live happily ever after with Ketilríðr, but their marriage is only one third of the triple wedding that crowns the narrative.

Víglundar saga seems to have drawn heavily on *riddarasögur* and *fornaldarsögur* for motifs and episodes. *Þorsteins saga Víkingssonar* provides the main conflict of hostility between sets of sons whose fathers are friends, and traces from *Friðþjófs saga*, *Hjálmþés saga ok Ǫlvis*, *Flóvents saga*, and other sagas have been detected. An episode of a fishing trip interrupted by a magical storm also occurs in *Bárðar saga Snæfellsáss*, but the relationship between the two sagas is unclear. *Víglundar saga* shows romance influence in its style as well as in its characterizations and plot. Burning love-flames and courtesy, groves and bowers, harp playing and chess playing ornament the narrative, but *Víglundar saga* avoids many of the empty exaggerations and stereotypes of romance.

Ed.: Jón Helgason, ed. *The Arna-Magnæan Manuscript 551 A, 4to: Bárðar saga, Víglundar saga, Grettis saga.* Manuscripta Islandica, 1. Copenhagen: Munksgaard, 1954 [facsimile]; Jóhannes Halldórsson, ed. *Kjalnesinga saga.* Íslenzk fornrit, 14. Reykjavik: Hið Íslenzka fornritafélag, 1959. **Tr.**: Eiríkr Magnússon and William Morris, trans. *Three Northern Love Stories and Other Tales.* London: Ellis & White, 1875; 4th ed. London: Longman, 1911.

Elizabeth Ashman Rowe

[See also: *Bárðar saga Snæfellsáss*; *Flóvents saga*; *Friðþjófs saga frœkna*; *Hjálmþés saga*; *Íslendingasögur*; *Skáldasögur*; *Þorsteins saga Víkingssonar*]

Viking Age.

The word "Viking" has come to be used in a general sense to describe the Scandinavian world and peoples in the period 800–1100. Contemporaries, however, used it to describe raiders and their activity. It appears in both Old English and Old Norse. Some runic inscriptions describe persons as Vikings (U 617; [cf. *Sveriges runinskrifter. Upplands runinskrifter*], DR 216 [cf. *Danmarks Runinskrifter*]); others record the death of young men "in Viking" (Vg 61 [cf. *Sveriges runinskrifter: Västergötlands runinskrifter*], DR 330, 334).

Several etymologies have been suggested; "Viking" has been derived from the region Viken in South Norway and taken to mean "people from Viken," from the substantive *vík*, and interpreted as "people lurking in a cove or fjord," from *wic* or *vicus*, giving "people attacking (or frequenting) ports of trade," and so on. The matter is unresolved.

"The Age of the Vikings began when Scandinavians first attacked western Europe and it ended when those attacks ceased" (Sawyer 1982: 6). These attacks began around 800, when a series of monasteries along the British and Irish coasts were sacked, and when Charlemagne had to strengthen the coastal defenses in northern Francia. These early raids were probably often conducted by a few men and ships, like the episode that occurred "in the days of King Beorhtric" at Portland, in which three ships were involved. Later, they grew to considerable ventures involving hundreds of ships and thousands of men, and occasional raiding gave way to

organized exploitation and even conquest. Parts of England were conquered, and Vikings settled there in the 9th century, and the whole of it was conquered once again in the 11th century, when first Sven Haraldsson (Forkbeard) and, afterward, Knud (Cnut) the Great became kings of England. Ireland, Francia, Russia, and even remoter parts like the Mediterranean and the Black and Caspian seas also suffered from Viking attacks. Many temporary lordships were created, but no permanent settlements resulted, apart from Normandy.

The Viking raids were conducted for the exaction of tribute. A whole province or even a kingdom might be held ransom and forced to buy its peace from the Vikings. A town might buy off a threatened sack with a tribute, but also individual buildings, like churches, or individuals, like bishops, abbots, or ealdormen, and even objects, like precious books, might be ransomed. The capturing of slaves may be considered from the same angle: it made little difference to the Vikings whether their prisoners were redeemed by their own family or by perfect strangers.

Viking activity also took place inside Scandinavia, and, in fact, it differed little from what was going on all over Europe in the "Dark Ages." The plundering of neighbors, the exaction of tribute from them, and their submission, to a large extent interchangeable notions, were familiar facts in western Europe as well as in Russia, but it was a new experience, and to many a shocking one when the Scandinavians began to extend their sphere of activity so far beyond their own borders. This ability depended on their superior ships.

The Vikings were organized in bands called *lið*, very much the kind of military household familiar in western Europe. A chieftain might go abroad with just his own men in a couple of ships, but more often he would join forces with greater chieftains. These were often members of royal or noble families, styling themselves kings or earls, and they often seem to have been exiles, for example, unsuccessful rivals for the throne, who were forced to seek their fortune abroad. Therefore, such men were often willing to stay abroad to serve Frankish or Byzantine rulers as mercenaries, to accept fiefs from them, and to become their vassals. They thereby became a factor in European politics, and Vikings were frequently employed by one European prince against another or against other Vikings. The clearcut clash between Christian and pagan suggested by many sources is largely false. In fact, many Viking attacks, such as those on Dorestad in the 830s, were carried out by Christian Vikings on behalf of one Christian ruler against another, in this case, on behalf of Lothar against his father, Louis the Pious.

Ed.: *Sveriges runinskrifter* 1–. Ed. Kungl. vitterhets historie och antikvitets akademien. Stockholm: [various publishers; now:] Almqvist & Wiksell, 1900– [the ongoing corpus publication, by county, e.g., vol. 5 is *Västergötlands runinskrifter*, inscriptions are cited by an abbreviation for the county plus their registration/publication number]. **Lit.**: Brøndsted, Johannes. *The Vikings.* Trans. Kalle Skov. Harmondsworth: Penguin, 1960; Foote, Peter G., and David M. Wilson. *The Viking Achievement: The Society and Culture of Early Medieval Scandinavia.* London: Sidgwick & Jackson, 1970; Sawyer, P. H. *Kings and Vikings: Scandinavia and Europe A.D. 700–1100.* London and New York: Methuen, 1982; Jones, Gwyn. *A History of the Vikings.* Rev. ed. Oxford and New York: Oxford University Press, 1984; Lund, Niels. "Allies of God or Man? The Viking Expansion in a European Perspective." *Viator* 20 (1989), 45–59; Roesdahl, Else. *The Vikings.* Harmondsworth: Penguin, 1990.

Niels Lund

[See also: America, Norse in; Arabic Sources for
Scandinavia(ns); England, Norse in; Five Boroughs; France,
Norse in; Germany, Norse in; Ireland, Norse in; Knud (Cnut)
the Great; L'Anse aux Meadows; Orkney, Norse in; Russia,
Norse in; Scotland, Norse in; Shetland, Norse in; Stamford
Bridge, Battle of; Sven Haraldsson (Forkbeard); Varangians;
Viking Art; York]

Viking Art

Animal motifs dominated Scandinavian ornament
until the 12th century, when they gradually merged with the Romanesque. But starting with the Borre style of the late 9th century
onward, ribbon and plant motifs based on European usage were
incorporated in the Scandinavian repertoire. The earliest attempts
at classification (e.g., Müller 1880) were based on the occurrence
of specific motifs, but from the time of Shetelig (1920) stylistic
criteria have gradually played a more important role. Viking style
groups are termed toponymically and much less systematically
than the classification for pre-Viking art established by Salin and
later scholars. Important Viking grave finds have given names to
the Oseberg, Borre, Jelling, and Mammen styles, while a geological
term has been abbreviated to Ringerike style, and the Urnes style
is named after a stave church. More imprecise and largely obsolete
terms may be encountered in literature: "Gripping-beast style" for
works of Salin style III:E, Oseberg, and Borre; "Great-beast style"
for monuments of Mammen, Ringerike, and Urnes; and "Runestone style" especially in Sweden for ornament of Ringerike, Urnes,
and Urnes-Romanesque. Shetelig (1920) established the relative
sequence of the Viking style groups, and pointed out that Salin
style III continued into the Viking period. Wilson laid the basis for
a modern, systematic characterization and dating (Wilson and
Klindt-Jensen 1966), and Fuglesang (1980, 1981a, 1982) worked
out a more precise and nuanced morphology especially for late
Viking ornament. In addition, a great amount of ornament that is
atypical of the stylistic categories so far established survives, especially from the early and mid-Viking periods. The most numerous
group comprises oval brooches with seminaturalistic animals of
West European extraction (Petersen 1928, Paulsen 1933, Jansson
1985).

Dating criteria. The types of evidence for artistic development and for dating changed around the middle of the 10th century. In the early and mid-Viking periods (ca. 775/800–950), the
main corpus of surviving artistic production consists of personal
ornaments and mounts found in graves. These pieces are normally
of copper alloy, and were mass-produced by casting. Consequently,
the dating criteria concern mostly the relative chronology: (1) the
typology of objects based on find associations and (2) the typology
of ornament. In addition comes the sparse evidence for absolute
dating: (3) Viking ornaments found in stratified layers, mainly
Ribe and York; (4) the fact that Scandinavian-type stone carving in
England cannot antedate the settlements that began in the late 9th
century; (5) from around 925 begin the coin-dated hoards containing ornaments, found mainly in Scandinavia and the British
Isles. In the late Viking period (ca. 950–1100), the copper ornaments were largely reproductions of types that had been developed previously. The surviving monuments that demonstrate innovative development consist of decorated memorial stones, ornaments from hoards, and carvings in wood and bone. The dating of
the late Viking style groups consequently rests mainly on evidence
for absolute chronology: (1) coin-dated hoards; (2) decorated

memorial stones that mention historically known persons or events;
(3) archaeological dating of levels in medieval towns; (4) tree-ring
dating of Danish graves; supplemented by (5) a few MSS from the
British Isles that are palaeographically datable and contain Scandinavian elements.

Neither the beginning nor the end of Viking art coincides
with the historical brackets for the the period: A.D. 793, the raid on
Lindisfarne, to 1066, the battles at Stamford Bridge and Hastings.
Early stages of what was to become the Oseberg style occur in late
8th-century associations in the workshop remains in Ribe and on
Gotlandic disc-on-bow brooches. Some Urnes-style elements continued in Romanesque ornament certainly to the mid-12th century and probably into the third quarter of that century.

Although both relative and absolute chronology begin to take
firmer shape, one must allow for normal overlaps of period fashions. Chronological assessment is today normally given in conventional quarter- and half-centuries. For early and mid-Viking
ornament, there may be additional time lags for individual objects
resulting from mass production and the practice of copying jewelry by casting from earlier pieces.

Stylistic groups: classification and dating. The continuous
tradition makes animal motifs the most important source for
morphological classification into style groups. In addition, ribbon
interlace of the mid-Viking Borre and plant motifs of the late Viking Mammen and Ringerike styles have stylistic elements diagnostic of these groups (see below).

(1) *Style III:E* corresponds to the late phase of Salin style III.
Typically, the animals are ribbon-shaped, with bodies that swell
and taper, frequently slit with wide openings, and with a marked
contraction separating the two ballooning hips. Very elongated
limbs and lappets make up open loops intertwined with the bodies. Surface patterning and frond-like terminals contribute to the
total restless effect. Contemporaneously, and in the same workshops that used style-E animals, were employed seminaturalistic
animals and birds copied from West European, probably
Frankish, models (Abraham 1937). In most cases, they were stylized with the same swelling lines, slit bodies, and intertwining
elements as the ribbon-shaped animals. Another motif introduced
at this stage is the gripping beast, always rendered as a solid entity,
juxtaposed to the style-E manner of the other motifs. The gripping
beast probably originated in the small squirrel-like animals inhabiting Anglo-Saxon scrolls (Haseloff 1951). The conglomeration of
motifs and forms of this phase is sometimes referred to as "Broa
style." This stage of eclecticism, variety, and innovation probably
reflects an increase of western European trade connections in the
second half of the 8th century, although dating evidence is tenuous. Major finds are the set of twenty-two gilt harness mounts
from Broa on Gotland, Sweden, and the typologically earliest carvings from Oseberg, Norway (the "Academician" and the "Ship
Master"). Important types of jewelry include disc-on-bow and oval
brooches. The continuation of style E into the early 9th century is
suggested by the Oseberg carvings, the occurrence of oval brooches
with style E in Birka, Sweden, and the association of disc-on-bow
brooches with metalwork looted from the British Isles in some
Norwegian graves. The evidence of the Oseberg carvings also indicates the prominent role played by style E in shaping the subsequent Oseberg style.

(2) *Style III:F* is confined to Denmark, especially Jutland and
Zealand. Distinctive is the almost abstract animal type with broad,
irregular hips, short body, and mostly profile head (Ramskou 1963,

Ørsnes 1966). Transversal striation is frequent, and outlines are incised. The compositions form carpet patterns within rectilinear panels. Only twelve pieces of characteristic style F have survived, but they represent several types of metalwork, which suggests that the style was more generally applied in Denmark. Style F is clearly adapted from Anglo-Carolingian work of the "Tassilo-chalice style," and is contemporary with Style E, *i.e.*, second half of the 8th century.

(3) The *Oseberg style* is named after the site of the famous ship burial in southern Norway that contained a rich variety of wood carving. While some of the carvings can be classified as style E, the work of the "Baroque Master" exemplified the new style (Shetelig 1920). The motifs are developed forms of the seminaturalistic and gripping-animal types introduced in style E, while ribbon-shaped animals play a subdued role. The innovations are mainly those of form. The compositions have motifs of equal size and equal compositional value, which are disposed in a carpet-pattern manner. The open loops are suppressed. Squat animal types are preferred, and the plasticity of a graded relief makes for a totally new play of light and shade. There is considerable variety within the Oseberg style, and it must have attained a pan-Scandinavian use. Especially, some types of oval brooch and the novel equal-armed brooch types reflect the personal manner of their originators, although most of the surviving specimens are attributable to copyists. For the Oseberg style proper, elements of foreign influence cannot so far be identified, but for some of the stylistically unclassifiable metalwork of the same chronological phase there are indications of Anglo-Saxon influence. Indications for the absolute dating of the Oseberg style are vague, but better than for pre-Viking ornament; and it is normally placed in the first three quarters of the 9th century.

(4) In the *Borre style*, the most common type of animal is a mixture of ribbon-shaped and gripping beast, frontally rendered, with polygonal hips, four legs, ribbon body that often forms a circular pretzel, and triangular frontal head. This animal is an indigenous innovation, while novel types of angular seminaturalistic mammals seem to have been based on European models. Almost equally important are the ribbon motifs, and especially common are the ring chain and the pretzel knot, often with animal-head terminals. The extensive use of ribbon motifs may be due to European influence, but the peculiar types of interlace and knotwork appear to be Scandinavian inventions. Plant motifs, acanthus and vine, were copied from Frankish trefoil and tongue-shaped mounts, and normally restricted to these forms of objects, which in Scandinavia were used as women's brooches. The main portion of this copying appears to have taken place around the year 900. The Borre-style form of animals and ribbons is dominated by equilateral shapes in static and repetitive compositions, with a preference for geometrical forms and use of contrasts (*e.g.*, juxtaposing circle and square, or a grooved animal body with highly polished head and legs). The Borre style is the earliest Scandinavian style to have been produced also in the Viking settlements in Iceland, England, and Russia, indicating that it had been developed in the Scandinavian homelands prior to the last quarter of the 9th century. The earliest Scandinavian coin-dated hoard with decorated metalwork was deposited around 925 at Vester Vedsted, Denmark, and contains a Borre-style animal; further hoards with late Borre-style ornaments were deposited around 940 and 950. Anglo-Scandinavian stone carving in Yorkshire apparently started around 900 and is decorated in the Borre and Jelling styles. Historical inference

suggests a dating after 910 for Anglo-Scandinavian stone carving with Borre style in Cumbria, while the Borre-style stone crosses on the Isle of Man probably postdate the Cumbrian ones. Taken together, the indications suggest dating the fully developed Borre style from the last quarter of the 9th to the mid-10th century.

(5) The *Jelling style* is a term used for a group of ribbon- and S-shaped animals. The point of departure is the engraved frieze on the small silver cup from the royal burial mound at Jelling in Jutland, Denmark: two elongated S-shaped animals in profile, intertwined in diagonal symmetry, bodies of even width and without hips. Other composition schemes continue Borre-style types, notably curving the animal body into an asymmetrical loop or a pretzel. But in contrast with Borre patterns, such Jelling-style loops are open, and animal hips are subdued. Some metalwork of the Jelling style has ribbon-shaped animals with slit bodies that suggest either a tradition or, more probably, a revival of the slit-animal types of style E. The Jelling style is the only group of ornament to have been classified by motif only, and it overlaps both the Borre and the Mammen styles. When Jelling-type animals are associated with Borre ornaments, the latter are normally attributable to an advanced stage of the Borre style, as in the hoard from Vårby in Södermanland, Sweden, deposited around 940. Other dating indications are supplied by the Jelling grave that dendrochronology has recently indicated was constructed 958–959 (Christensen 1987), and a very fine stone cross in York from a level that is archaeologically datable to the first half of the 10th century. The Jelling style is undoubtedly of Scandinavian, possibly Danish origin, but it may have been precipitated by the introduction of the sleek S-shaped animal motif that is normally used for Jelling-style designs in England.

(6) The *Mammen style* is an innovative phase of the same magnitude as style E. New motifs are the seminaturalistic lion and bird based on West European prototypes, and a revitalization of the older Scandinavian snake, which was given a novel prominence. The plant scroll was introduced from either Anglo-Saxon or continental art, and was translated into a Scandinavian style, no longer a mere copy as in the Borre phase. Characteristics of form include the use of one or two large motifs that fill a panel by abrupt twists and turns, the asymmetrical composition of scrolls, ornament lines that widen abruptly into panel-like shapes, and wavy and frequently dented outlines. The latest innovations of the mass-produced bronze ornaments took place in the Jelling style, and although such ornaments were presumably still made and worn artistic innovation seems to have passed to new groups of monuments, such as decorated memorial stones, bone carving, and engraved and filigreed silver.

The large memorial stone at Jelling in Jutland, Denmark, is a central monument. It was raised by King Harald Gormsson to commemorate his parents and himself. Its inscription dates it firmly to the period around 960–985, while plausible inference from the German annals about the conversion of the Danes narrows the dating of the monument to the 960s. The Jelling stone is unique as a ruler's monument and seems to begin the fashion of decorating runic memorials in Denmark and subsequently on the Scandinavian peninsula. The confrontation of lion and snake in battle may likewise be the earliest instance of this iconography in Scandinavia. Certainly, it has no surviving antecedent, and it came to exercise a wide influence on animal representations in the 11th century. The Crucifixion entwined by a scroll is the only Viking example of this iconography and must have had a West European vine-entwined Crucifixion as its model (Fuglesang 1981c). Further monuments include the inlaid axehead from Mammen in Jutland, Denmark, which has given the name to the style and which comes from a grave that has recently been dendrochronologically dated to the winter of 970/1 (Iversen and Vellev 1986); the famous caskets from Cammin (lost during World War II) and Bamberg with carved bone plaques and engraved mounts; as well as bone carving and metalwork of good artistic quality from undatable contexts in Scandinavia. The Mammen style flourished in the second half of the 10th century, but its geographical extent, particularly in its plant motifs, remains conjectural.

(7) In the *Ringerike style*, the animal motifs of the Mammen style were continued, although with some alterations. The main innovations lie in the handling of the plant motifs and composition schemes that indicate influence from Anglo-Saxon and Ottonian ornament. The memorial stone at Vang, Norway, exemplifies the fully developed Ringerike style: a double scroll with stems in strict axiality, asymmetrically placed groups of short and intertwined tendrils, and a rosette-shaped cross composed by alternating broad lobe with thin tendril. Above the cross, a walking lion and a small spiral with short offshoots along the outline emphasize the additive character of the full composition. The use of both Anglo-Saxon and Ottonian composition schemes (alternating tendril and lobe, and groups of short intertwined tendrils, respectively) indicates that the Ringerike style was created in Danish centers under the auspices of the nascent church organization. Its subsequent distribution followed both the Church and the traditional lines of copying and trading. It is used, for example, for the vegetal frieze on the fragments of the oldest surviving church decoration in Scandinavia, the panels from Flatatunga, Iceland. It also occurs both with and without Christian connotations on memorial stones in Norway and Sweden, on metal vanes, and on plain wooden objects recovered from the lower 11th-century levels in the medieval towns of Lund in Scania (present Sweden), and Trondheim and Oslo, Norway. The Ringerike style has a pan-Scandinavian distribution, and was also used in southern England and in Dublin. Dating is fairly dependable: in addition to the finds of the first half of the 11th century in medieval towns, there are two coin-dated hoards deposited about 1025 and 1035, and two Anglo-Saxon psalters of the second quarter of the century that contain Ringerike-style elements. The latest datable specimens are from the third quarter of the 11th century and betray influence from the Urnes style.

(8) The *Urnes style* is the latest Viking style proper. In contrast to the Mammen and Ringerike styles, animals dominate the repertoire: extremely stylized mammals (some of them lions), ribbon-shaped animals, and snakes. The winged dragon makes its first Scandinavian appearance on some Upplandic memorial stones of the second quarter of the 11th century. The cross is frequently incorporated in the decoration of the Swedish memorials: in Uppland, around 65 percent have a cross, and 25 percent a Christian invocation (Thompson 1975). Some vegetal motifs were continued from the Ringerike style, particularly the single scroll and the union knot, but are transformed into the Urnes-style idiom. Urnes-style designs are determined by an underlying aim for unity: typically, a design has only two contrasting line widths, animal heads and feet are reduced to mere elongated terminals, figure-of-eight and multiloop compositions form an open and asymmetrical network of circular shapes, and larger animals frequently exhibit a gradual swelling and tapering of body. The most impressive

monuments are the runic memorials in Sweden, with the more than 1,100 stones in Uppland forming the center of both quality and quantity. But the distribution of the style is pan-Scandinavian, and neither the area of origin nor the possible European influences have yet been determined. Some Urnes-style metalwork was manufactured in England, but by far the greater impact was made in Ireland, where the main Urnes-style elements were applied in the revitalization of Irish art in the late 11th and the 12th century. The earliest phase of the Urnes style in Scandinavia is datable to the second quarter of the 11th century, mainly on the basis of runic memorials that mention the taking of "danegeld" in England under Knud (Cnut) the Great (latest levying in 1018) and one coin-dated hoard deposited around 1050. These datings have recently been confirmed by several Urnes-style carvings from Oslo, Norway, in levels archaeologically datable to around 1050–1100. Like the Ringerike style, the Urnes style is intimately connected with church buildings and Christian monuments. Among the most important fragments of church ornament are the 11th-century doorway, post, planks, and gables incorporated in the mid-12th-century church at Urnes in Sogn, Norway, from which the name of the style has been taken. Among secular ornaments may be cited weapons, the novel type of animal-shaped brooches, and wood carving from medieval towns.

(9) The *transitional Urnes-Romanesque* style retains some of the Urnes-style motifs, notably the ribbon-shaped animal and the snake. But the main impact of the Urnes-style tradition lies in the form: contrast of two line widths, multiloop compositions, and sinuous swelling and tapering of animals and scrolls. However, most of the motifs and stylistic elements in this phase of Scandinavian art were imported from western Europe. The Romanesque types of winged dragon were introduced and became a staple, together with the full set of Romanesque animal symbols, scrolls, and leaf work. The Urnes-Romanesque phase is pan-Scandinavian, but is a much more heterogeneous style than the Urnes, with more local schools and with purely Romanesque ornament produced contemporaneously. There is a parallel development in Ireland in the first half of the 12th century, which, to judge from the donor inscriptions, has no ethnic connections with the population of the Norse towns. Similar transitional monuments in England are few in number and have restricted motifs. Dating indications in Scandinavia are few, but include the levels of around 1100–1175 in Oslo, Norway, a dating that corresponds well with those Irish monuments datable from their donor inscriptions.

Pictorial art. Narrative art must have been far more important than is commonly supposed, but is haphazardly preserved. Decorated memorial stones form the best iconographical evidence, but the fashion for such monuments had narrow chronological and geographical limitations. The stones relevant to pre-Christian iconography were raised on Gotland in the late 8th and early 9th century, and in Cumbria and on the Isle of Man in the 10th century. The iconography on the Gotlandic stones is dominated by a ship and rider, normally taken to be chthonic symbols for the journey to Valhǫll, but possibly also reflecting the social standing of the deceased. Fragments of two textiles from the early 9th century indicate that the popularity of the journey theme was not confined to memorial stones. The piece from Tune in Østfold, Norway, has a row of men and women next to a ship, while the fragments from Oseberg in Vestfold, Norway, show women, warriors, riders, and carts in what has been tentatively interpreted as a procession. The Gotlandic memorials of this period also have a high number of narrative scenes from mythology and heroic tales, but few of these pictures can be verifiably interpreted and seem only occasionally related to the haphazardly transmitted literary sources. In the first half of the 9th century, Bragi Boddason described a painted shield in the oldest surviving skaldic poem from Scandinavia. The themes of the paintings were taken from four completely unrelated sources: Sǫrli and Hamðir killing Jǫrmunrekkr, the battle of the Haddings, Gefjon ploughing Zealand from Scania, and Þórr's fishing expedition. The juxtaposition of these disparate pictures corresponds to the contemporary narrative scenes on the Gotlandic stones, but only one of Bragi's scenes, the battle of the Haddings, has with a fair amount of probability been identified on a late 8th-century Gotlandic stone (Lindqvist 1941–42).

Þórr's fishing expedition has with less credibility been identified as the boat with two men in the lower-left register on Andre VIII, although the main iconographic element of the Miðgarðsormr (World Serpent) is missing. The serpent is absent also from the Fishing Stone at Gosforth in Cumbria, of the 10th century. In fact, there survive only two renderings that are undeniably identifiable as Þórr's fishing expedition, both of the 11th century: the roughly incised picture on a stone from Hørdum in Thy, Denmark, and the well-carved memorial at Altuna in Uppland, Sweden. The fact that Þórr's fishing expedition, which is among the most frequently recurring themes in skaldic poetry throughout the Viking period, survives in only two certain, and late, pictorial versions, should give food for thought. There has been, and still exists, a philological propensity to link haphazardly surviving pictures with equally fortuitously transmitted texts, disregarding elementary rules of methodological control.

Although further scenes on the Gotlandic memorials cannot be interpreted, they are nevertheless extremely important in demonstrating a narrative art that is clearly distinct from ornament. The motifs are rendered as easily readable "pictograms" that juxtapose the highlights of several apparently unrelated themes in a figure style uninfluenced by current ornament. These scenes, although now largely undecipherable, must have been easily understood by the educated contemporaneous Scandinavian. In addition to the narrative scenes on the Gotlandic stones and the Norwegian textiles, some similarly unidentifiable figure representations survive in wood carving on the Oseberg cart, and on the memorial stone at Sparlösa in Västergötland, mainland Sweden.

But from the mid-9th to the mid-10th century, there is a hiatus for figurative representations in Scandinavia. The hiatus can to some extent be bridged by the use of skaldic poems that describe pictures, but even this material has uneven iconographical value. Hallvard Lie attributed several fragments of skaldic poems to this group (1952, 1956). A modern philological reappraisal has not been undertaken, but a critical view suggests that only those poems that specify that pictures are indeed being described should be admitted as iconographical evidence. This stipulation would limit the group to three poems: Bragi's Ragnarsdrápa mentioned above (first half of 9th century), Haustlǫng by Þjóðólfr of Hvin (10th century), and Húsdrápa by Úlfr Uggason (ca. 980). Haustlǫng purports to describe shield paintings showing the abduction of Iðunn and Þórr's fight with the giant Hrungnir, while Húsdrápa's description of the pictures in the hall of Óláfr on Iceland contains the swimming competition between Loki and Heimdallr, Þórr's fishing expedition, and the cremation of Baldr. Úlfr's description of the cremation suggests that this representation may have consisted of several units: he mentions Óðinn on Sleipnir, Heimdallr

on his horse, Freyr on his boar, and the giantess who helped the gods to push the burial ship from the beach. Erik Moltke has suggested that the giantess may be represented on one of the stones of the memorial monument from Hunnestad in Scania, although this picture coincides better with Snorri's description of her (ca. 1220) than with the contemporaneous description by Úlfr (Jacobsen and Moltke 1940–41). Narrative scenes of the 10th century survive mainly in Cumbria and on the Isle of Man, and the extent of Anglo-Saxon influence on these pictures is difficult to determine. Some of the scenes on the great cross at Gosforth church, Cumbria, have been interpreted as Ragnarǫk, the Scandinavian pagan equivalent of Judgment Day (Berg 1958). Similar scenes do not survive from Scandinavia, and on the Gosforth Cross they are combined with a Crucifixion. The Manx narratives appear to be mainly scenes from hunting and from the legend of Sigurðr, rendered within ribbon and plant ornaments. The dating of these Manx crosses is uncertain, but they are normally placed in the late 10th century (Wilson 1983). In Scandinavia, the hunting theme survives on two stones, both of the 11th century, from Alstad, Norway, and at Balingsta in Uppland, Sweden. In addition, some Upplandic Urnes-style stones show a rider and a bird, which may represent an abbreviated hunt. The iconography of the chase cannot be attributed to any surviving literary source, and seems to reflect a pan-European iconography and social ideals (Fuglesang 1980, 1986). The Sigurðr legend in Scandinavian Viking art survives in full in the memorial carving on Ramsundsberget and its derivative on the Rök Stone, both in Södermanland, Sweden. Both are attributable to the Ringerike style. In contrast to early- and mid-Viking pictures, these representations show a sequence of events from one tale. This sequencing seems to be a novel principle in Viking art, just as the hunt and the Sigurðr legend represent novel iconographical themes. Another difference from early Viking pictures lies in the ornamentation of the rendering. The older tradition of showing only the climax of a story was continued, but in the late 11th century even such scenes were incorporated in an overall ornamental scheme, as evidenced by some Upplandic Urnes-style stones and the latest group of Gotlandic memorials. In this emphasis on the ornament in narrative art, Scandinavia follows a fashion common in much contemporary European illumination. Only one outspokenly pagan monument survives from 11th-century Scandinavia, the memorial stone at Altuna church in Uppland, Sweden. But even Christian iconographic themes are rare, the main examples being the Jelling Crucifixion. The Adoration of the Magi on the memorial stones in the late 10th and the 11th centuries shows great regional and chronological variations in Scandinavia, and the use of figure representations is even more idiosyncratic (Fuglesang 1968a). What survives indicates the existence of several potential iconographical models, ranging from late offshoots of pagan themes to novel secular and Christian ones, but with an emphasis on the latter two categories. This mixture may reflect an iconographically unsettled situation during the period of conversion. But it should also be noted that the hunt represents a generally honorific category of pictures, and the Sigurðr legend was certainly used textually in the same sense when Illugi Bryndœlaskáld compared the deeds of Haraldr harðráði ("hard-ruler") Sigurðarson with those of Sigurðr in the couplets of his fragmentarily preserved poem in Haraldr's honor. In spite of many and deep-rooted differences, the manly virtues and social standing of the deceased seem to link the pictorial programs of the pagan and the Christian memorial stones.

State of research. Several studies of the last decade develop the potential of Viking art as a contemporaneous historical source capable of verification. A few examples must suffice. The excavation of stratified workshops in Ribe, Denmark, has given much new information on the manufacture of cast ornaments, and the numismatic evidence indicating a late 8th-century dating for these levels has reactivated the question of the origins of early Viking art (Bencard 1978, Bendixen 1981). Studies of mass-produced cast brooches of the early- and mid-Viking periods have given a better understanding of the economic side of the production, as well as a more reliable chronological framework (Jansson 1981, 1985, Carlsson 1983, Thunmark-Nylén 1983, Fuglesang 1987). Studies and technical analysis of filigreed ornaments have highlighted the process by which foreign techniques and models were copied and subsequently absorbed (or discarded) by the Scandinavian workshops (Duczko 1985).

The many and mutually exclusive theories on foreign influences in ornament have been critically reviewed. The present method of analyzing severally foreign influences as well as indigenous inventions, innovations, and traditions through systematic comparisons has led to an emphasis on the indigenous aspects and a better understanding of the interplay with European models (Wilson in Wilson and Klindt-Jensen 1966, Fuglesang 1980, 1981a, 1982, 1986b). The similarly broad, older claims for influence of Viking art abroad have been reduced mainly to the British Isles and the Baltic, and to specific points in time (Lang 1978, Baily 1980, Fuglesang 1986b, Graham-Campbell 1987), with the corollary that Scandinavian animal ornament played no role in the shaping of Romanesque ornament on the Continent. The claims for various ornamental motifs as peculiarly Scandinavian symbols are hardly tenable in view of the fairly quick turnover in motif repertoire, the indiscriminate use of a motif during its period of fashion, and the European origin that can be demonstrated for most of the motifs. The iconography is being reviewed in the light of several contemporaneous sources in preference to, for example, the prose texts in Snorri's *Edda* and similarly late texts (Margeson 1980, Düwel 1986, Ellmers 1986, Fuglesang 1986a, Meulengracht Sørensen 1986). Although much remains to be done, the recent, methodologically more stringent approach seems to yield results that demystify Viking art and secure it a more pedestrian but more profitable scholarly role.

Lit.: Kornerup, J. *Kongehøiene i Jellinge og deres undersøgelse efter Kong Frederik VII's befaling i 1861.* Copenhagen: Luno, 1875; Müller, S. "Dyreornamentiken i Norden. Dens oprindelse, udvikling, og forhold til samtidige stilarter. En archæologisk undersøgelse." *Aarbøger for nordisk Oldkyndighed og Historie* (1880), 185–405; Nicolaysen, N. *The Viking-Ship Discovered at Gokstad in Norway.* Trans. Thomas Krag. Christiania [Oslo]: Cammermeyer, 1882; rpt. Westmead: Gregg, 1971; Dietrichsson, Lorentz. *De norske stavkirker: Studier over deres system, oprindelse og historiske udvikling.* Kristiania [Oslo]: Cammermeyer, 1892; rpt. Westmead: Gregg, 1971; *Sveriges runinskrifter 1–.* Ed. Kungl. vitterhets historie och antikvitets akademien. Stockholm: Almqvist & Wiksell, 1900–; Salin, Berhard. *Die altgermanische Tierornamentik. Typologische Studie über germanische Metallgegenstände aus dem IV. bis IX. Jahrhundert.* Stockholm: Beckman, 1904; Kermode, P. M. C. *Manx Crosses: The Inscribed and Sculpted Monuments of the Isle of Man from About the End of the Fifth to the Beginning of the Thirteenth Century.* London: Bemrose, 1907; Friesen, Otto von. "Historiska runinskrifter I." *Fornvännen* (1909), 57–85; Friesen, Otto von. "Historiska runinskrifter II." *Fornvännen* (1911), 105–

25; Arne, T. J. *La Suède et l'Orient. Études archéologiques sur les relations de la Suède et l'Orient pendant l'âge des Vikings.* Archives d'études orientales, 8. Uppsala: Appelberg, 1914; Shetelig, Haakon. *Osebergfundet III.* Kristiana [Oslo]: Universitetets Oldsaksamling, 1920; Salin, Bernhard. "Fundet från Broa i Halla, Gotland." *Fornvännen* (1922), 189–206; Brøndsted, Johannes. *Early English Ornament: The Sources, Development and Relation to Foreign Styles of Pre-Norman Ornamental Art in England.* Copenhagen: Levin & Munksgaard, 1924; Brate, Erik. *Svenska runristare.* Stockholm: Akademiens Förlag, 1925; Petersen, Jan. *Vikingetidens smykker.* Stavanger: Dreyer, 1928; Grieg, Sigurd. *Vikingetidens skattefund.* Universitetets Oldsaksamling, Skrifter 2. Oslo: Universitetets Oldsaksamling, 1929; Nerman, Birger. *Die Verbindungen zwischen Skandinavien und dem Ostbaltikum in der jüngeren Eisenzeit.* Kungl. vitterhets-, historie- och antikvitets akademien, Handlingar. Stockholm: Akademiens Förlag, 1929; Bugge, A. "The Golden Vanes of Viking Ships: A Discussion on a Recent Find at Källunge Church, Gotland." *Acta Archaeologica* 2 (1931), 160–84; Curman, S. "Kristna gravmonument från 1000-talet funna i Vreta kloster." In *Arkeologiska studier tillägnade H. K. Kronprins Gustaf Adolf.* Stockholm: Norstedt, 1932, pp. 141–51; Paulsen, Peter. *Studien zur Wikingerkultur.* Neumünster: Wachholtz, 1933; Paulsen, Peter. *Der Goldschatz von Hiddensee.* Leipzig: Rabitsch, 1936; Arbman, Holger. *Schweden und das karolingische Reich.* Kungl. vitterhets-, historie- och antikvitets akademien, Handlingar 43. Stockholm: Wahlström & Widstrand, 1937; Brøndsted, Johannes. "Danish Inhumation Graves of the Viking Period." *Acta Archaeologica* 7 (1938), 81–228; Friesen, Otto von, and Bertil Almgren. *Sparlösastenen.* Kungl. vitterhets-, historie- och antikvitets akademien, Handlingar 46.3. Stockholm: Wahlström & Widstrand, 1940; Shetelig, Haakon, ed. *Viking Antiquities in Great Britain and Ireland.* 6 vols. Oslo: Aschehoug, 1940–54; Petersen, Jan. *British Antiquities of the Viking Period, Found in Norway.* Oslo: Aschehoug, 1940; Arbman, Holger. *Birka. 2: Die Gräber.* 2 vols. Kungl. vitterhets-, historie- och antikvitets akademien. Birka Untersuchungen und Studien, 1. Uppsala: Almqvist & Wiksell, 1940–43; Lindqvist, Sune. *Gotlands Bildsteine.* 2 vols. Stockholm: Kungl. vitterhets-, historie- och antikvitets akademien, 1941–42; *Norges Innskrifter med de yngre Runer 1–.* Oslo: Kjeldeskriftfondet, 1941–; Jacobsen, Lis, and Erik Moltke, in collaboration with Anders Bæksted and Karl Martin Nielsen. *Danmarks runeindskrifter: Text, Atlas.* 2 vols. Copenhagen: Munksgaard, 1941–42; Arwidsson, Greta. *Vendelstile, Email und Glas im 7.-8. Jahrhundert.* Uppsala: Almqvist & Wiksell, 1942; Skovmand, Roar. *De danske skattefund fra vikingetiden og den ældste middelalder indtil omkring 1150.* Aarbøger for nordisk Oldkyndighed og Historie (1942) [entire issue]; Shetelig, Haakon. *Arkeologi, historie, kunst, kultur. Mindre avhandlinger utgitt til syttiårsdagen 25. juni 1947.* Bergen: Grieg, 1947; Shetelig, Haakon. "The Norse Style of Ornamentation in the Viking Settlements." *Acta Archaeologica* 19 (1948), 69–114; Kendrick, T. D. *Late Saxon and Viking Art.* London: Methuen, 1949; Haseloff, G. "Zum Ursprung des nordischen Greiftierstils." In *Festschrift für Gustav Schwantes zum 65. Geburtstag, dargebracht von seinen Schülern und Freunden.* Neumünster: Wachholtz, 1951, pp. 202–11; Holmqvist, Wilhelm. "Viking Art in the Eleventh Century." *Acta Archaeologica* 22 (1951), 1–56; Lie, Hallvard. "Skaldestil-studier." *Maal og minne* (1952), 1–92; Kristján Eldjárn. "Carved Panels from Flatatunga, Iceland." *Acta Archaeologica* 24 (1953), 81–101; Almgren, Bertil. *Bronsnycklar och djurornamentik.* Uppsala: Appelberg, 1955; Moe, O. H. "Urnes and the British Isles." *Acta Archaeologica* 26 (1955), 1–30; Brøndsted, Johannes. "Thors fiskeri." *Fra Nationalmuseets arbejdsmark* (1955), 92–104; Kristján Eldjárn. *Kuml og haugfé.*

Reykjavik: Norðri, 1956; Lie, Hallvard. "Billedbeskrivende dikt." *KLNM* 1 (1956), 452–45; Thorvildsen, Knud. *Ladby-skibet.* Nordiske fortidsminder, 6.1. Copenhagen: Lynge, 1957; Berg, K. "The Gosforth Cross." *Journal of the Warburg and Courtauld Institutes* 21 (1958), 27–43; Christiansson, Hans. *Sydskandinavisk stil. Studier i ornamentiken på de senvikingatida runstenarna.* Uppsala: Akademisk Förlag, 1959; Wessén, Elias. *Historiska runinskrifter.* Kungl. vitterhets-, historie- och antikvitets akademien, Handlingar. Filologisk-filosofiska serien, 6. Stockholm: Almqvist & Wiksell, 1960; Zachrisson, I. "De ovala spännbucklornas tillverkningssätt." *Tor* 6 (1960), 207–38; Wilson, David M. "The Fejø cup." *Acta Archaeologica* 31 (1960), 147–73; Strömberg, Märta. *Untersuchungen zur jüngeren Eisenzeit in Schonen.* 2 vols. Bonn: Habelt, 1961; Ramskou, T. "Stil F. En skitse." *Aarbøger for nordisk Oldkyndighed og Historie* (1963), 100–18; Homqvist, Wilhelm. *Övergångstidens metallkonst.* Stockholm: Almqvist & Wiksell, 1963; Bakka, Egil. "Some English Decorated Metal Objects Found in Norwegian Viking Graves." *Universitetet i Bergen, Årbok* (1963), 3–66; Blindheim, Martin. *Norwegian Romanesque Decorative Sculpture 1090–1210.* Trans. Ada Polak. London: Tiranti, 1965; Ørsnes, Mogens. *Form og stil i Sydskandinaviens yngre germanske jernalder.* Copenhagen: Nationalmuseet, 1966; Oldeberg, Andreas. *Metallteknik under vikingatid och medeltid.* Stockholm: Seelig, 1966; Wilson, David M., and Ole Klindt-Jensen. *Viking Art.* London: Allen & Unwin, 1966; Henry, Françoise. *Irish Art During the Viking Invasions (800–1200 A.D).* London: Methuen, 1967; Forsberg, G. "Östergötlands vikingatida skattfynd." *Tor* 12 (1967–68), 12–37; Capelle, Torsten. *Der Metalsschmuck von Haithabu.* Neumünster: Wachholtz, 1968; Anker, Peter, and Aron Andersson. *L'Art scandinave.* 2 vols. La nuit des temps, 28–9. L'Abbaye Sainte-Marie de la Pierre-qui-Vire [Yonne]: Zodiaque, 1968–69 [English translation: *The Art of Scandinavia.* 2 vols. London and New York: Hamlyn, 1970]; Hägg, Inga. "Die wikingerzeitliche Frauentracht von Birka. Einige Bemerkungen zur Hemdform." *Tor* 13 (1969), 13–25; Wamers, E. "Eine Zungenfibel aus dem Hafen von Haithabu." In *Berichte über die Ausgrabungen in Haithabu.* Ed. Kurt Schietzel. 26 vols. Neumunster: Wachholtz, 1969–89, vol. 19, pp. 63–127; Henry, Françoise. *Irish Art in the Romanesque Period.* London: Methuen, 1970; Strömback, Dag. *The Epiphany in Runic Art: The Dynna and the Sika Stones.* The Dorothea Coke Memorial Lecture. London: Viking Society for Northern Research, 1970; Wilson, David M. "Manx Memorial Stones of the Viking Period." *Saga-Book of the Viking Society* 18 (1970–71), 1–18; Foote, Peter G., and David M. Wilson. *The Viking Achievement. The Society and Culture of Early Medieval Scandinavia.* London: Sidgwick & Jackson, 1970; Cubbon, A. M. *The Art of the Manx Crosses: A Selection of Photographs with Notes.* Douglas: Manx Museum and National Trust, 1971; Sjøvold, Thorleif. *The Iron Age Settlement of Arctic Norway: A Study in the Expansion of European Iron Age Culture within the Arctic Circle* 2. Tromsø Museums Skrifter, 10. Tromsø: Norwegian University Presses, 1974; Hägg, Inga. *Kvinnodräkten i Birka. Livplaggens rekonstruktion på grundval av det arkeologiska materialet.* Uppsala: Institut för arkeologi, 1974; Wilson, David M. "Men de ligger i London." *Skalk* (1974), 3–8; Moltke, E. "The Jelling Monument in the Light of the Runic Inscription." In *Jelling Problems: A Discussion. Mediaeval Scandinavia* 7 (1974), 183–208; Roesdahl, E. "The Northern Mound: Burial Chamber and Grave Goods." In *Jelling Problems,* pp. 208–23; Hohler, E. B. "The Capitals of Urnes Church and Their Background." *Acta Archaeologica* 46 (1975), 1–60; Thompson, Claiborne W. *Studies in Upplandic Runography.* Austin and London: University of Texas Press, 1975; Graham-Campbell, James. "The Viking-Age Silver and Gold Hoards of Scandinavian Character from Scotland." *Proceedings of the Society of Antiquaries of Scotland* 107 (1975–76), 114–35; Hårdh, Birgitta. *Wikingerzeitliche Depotfunde aus Südschweden: Probleme und Analysen.* 2 vols. Acta Archaeologica Lundensia, series in 4°, 9, and series in 8° minore, 6. Bonn: Habelt; Lund: Gleerup, 1976; Wilson, David M. "The Borre Style in the British Isles." In *Minjar og menntir: Afmælisrit helgað Kristjáni Eldjárn. 6. desember 1976.* Ed. Guðni Kolbeinsson. Reykjavik: Menningarsjóður, 1976, pp. 502–9; Blindheim, Martin. "A Norwegian Eleventh-Century Picture Stone: The Journey of the Magi to Bethelehem." *Journal of the British Archaeological Association* 130 (1977), 145–56; Olsen, Olaf, et al. *Fyrkat: En jysk vikingeborg.* 2 vols. Nordiske Fortidsminder, ser. B in quarto 3–4. Copenhagen: Det kgl. nordiske Oldskriftselskab, 1977, vol. 1; Lang, James, ed. *Anglo-Saxon and Viking Age Sculpture and Its Context: Papers from the Collingwood Symposium on Insular Sculpture from 800 to 1066.* British Archaeological Reports, 49. Oxford: B.A.R., 1978; Bencard, Mogens. "Wikingerzeitliches Handwerk in Ribe. Eine Übersicht." *Acta Archaeologica* 49 (1978), 113–38; Müller-Wille, M. "Frühmittelalterliche Prunkgräber im südlichen Skandinavian." *Bonner Jahrbuch* 178 (1978), 633–52; Marxen, I., and E. Moltke. "Jellingmanden. Danmarks ældste figurmaleri." *Fra Nationalmuseets Arbejdsmark* (1978), 111–8; O'Meadhra, Uaininn. *Early Christian, Viking and Romanesque Art: Motif-pieces from Ireland.* 2 vols. Stockholm: Almqvist & Wiksell, 1979–87; Bailey, Richard N. *Viking Age Sculpture in Northern England.* London: Collins, 1980; Schietzel, K., and O. Crumlin-Pedersen. "Havnen i Hedeby." *Skalk* (1980), 4–10; Graham-Campbell, James. *Viking Artefacts: A Select Catalogue.* London: British Museum, 1980; Graham-Campbell, James. *The Viking World.* London: Lincoln, 1980; Fuglesang, Signe Horn. *Some Aspects of the Ringerike Style: A Phase of 11th Century Scandinavian Art.* Mediaeval Scandinavia, Supplements 1. Odense: Odense University Press, 1980; Graham-Campbell, James, and Dafydd Kidd. *The Vikings.* London: British Museum, 1980; Margeson, S. "The Völsung Legend in Medieval Art." In *Medieval Iconography and Narrative: Proceedings of the Fourth International Symposium at Odense University 1979.* Ed. Flemming G. Andersen et al. Odense: Odense University Press, 1980, pp. 183–211; Fuglesang, Signe Horn. "Stylistic Groups in Late Viking and Early Romanesque Art." *Acta ad archaeologiam et artium historiam pertinentia. Series altera in 8°* 1 (1981), 79–125 [1981a]; Fuglesang, Signe Horn. "Woodcarvers—Professionals and Amateurs—in Eleventh-Century Trondheim." In *Economic Aspects of the Viking Age.* Ed. David M. Wilson and Marjorie L. Cayhill. British Museum Occasional Papers, 30. London: British Museum, 1981, pp. 21–31 [1981b]; Jansson, I. "Economic Aspects of Fine Metalworking in Viking Scandinavia." In *Economic Aspects of the Viking Age,* pp. 1–19; Fuglesang, Signe Horn. "Crucifixion Iconography in Viking Scandinavia." In *Proceedings of the Eighth Viking Congress, Århus, 24–31 August 1977.* Ed. Hans Bekker-Nielsen et al. Odense: Odense University Press, 1981, pp. 73–94 [1981c]; Bencard, Mogens, ed. *Ribe Excavations 1970–76.* 1– . Trans. Barbara Bluestone. Esbjerg: Sydjysk Universitetsforlag, 1981– ; Bendixen, K. "Sceattas and Other Coin Finds." In *Ribe Excavations 1970–76,* vol. 1, pp. 63–101; Roesdahl, Else, et al. *The Vikings in England.* York: Yorkshire Museum, 1981 [exhibition catalogue]; Wamers, E. "Ein karolingischer Prunkbeschlag aus dem Römisch-Germanischen Museum, Köln." *Zeitschrift für Archäologie des Mittelalters* 9 (1981), 91–128; Fuglesang, Signe Horn. "Early Viking Art." *Acta ad archaeologiam et artium historiam pertinentia. Series altera in 8°,* vol. 2. Ed. Hjalmar Torp and J. Rasmus Brandt. Rome: Bretschneider, 1982, pp. 125–73; Roesdahl, Else. *Viking Age Denmark.* Trans. Susan Margeson and Kirsten Williams. London: British Museum,

1982; Blindheim, Martin. "The Gilded Vikingship Vanes: Their Use and Technique." In *The Vikings*. Ed. R. T. Farrell. London: Phillimore, 1982, pp. 116–27; Andersson, A. *Medieval Drinking Bowls of Silver Found in Sweden*. Stockholm: Kungl. vitterhets-, historie-, och antikvitets akademien, 1983; Carlsson, Anders. *Djurhuvudforminga spännen och gotländsk vikingatid: Text och katalog*. Stockholm Studies in Archaeology, 5. Stockholm: Minabøgotab, 1983; Fell, Christine, *et al.*, eds. *The Viking Age in the Isle of Man: Select Papers from the Ninth Viking Congress, Isle of Man, 4–14 July 1981*. London: Viking Society for Northern Research, 1983; Wilson, David M. "The Art of the Manx Cross of the Viking Age." In *The Viking Age in the Isle of Man*, pp. 175–87; Thunmark-Nylén, Lena. *Vikingatida dosspännen—teknisk stratigrafi och verkstadsgruppering*. Uppsala: Institutionen för Arkeologi, 1983; Graham-Campbell, James. "Two Viking-Age Silver Fragments Believed to Be from the 1858 Skaill (Orkney) Hoard." *Proceedings of the Society of Antiquaries of Scotland* 114 (1984), 289–301; Fuglesang, Signe Horn. "Woodcarving from Oslo and Trondheim and Some Reflections on Period Styles." In *Festskrift til Thorleif Sjøvold på 70-årsdagen*. Universitetets Oldsaksamling, Skrifter, Ny rekke, nr. 5. Oslo: Universitetets Oldsaksamling, 1984, pp. 93–108; Haseloff, G. "Stand der Forschung: Stilgeschichte Völkerwanderungs- und Merowingerzeit." In *Festskrift til Thorleif Sjøvold*, pp. 109–24; Arwidsson, Greta, ed. *Systematische Analysen der Gräberfunde*. 2 vols. Stockholm: Kungl. vitterhets, historie och antikvitets akademien, 1984 [*Birka 2*]; Duczko, W. *The Filigree and Granulation Work of the Viking Period: An Analysis of the Material from Björkö*. Stockholm: Kungl. vitterhets, historie och antikvitets akademien, 1985 [*Birka 5*]; Jansson, I. *Ovala spännbucklor: En studie av vikingatida standardsmycken med utgångspunkt från Björköfynden*. Uppsala: Uppsala University, Institute of North European Archaeology, 1985; Moltke, Erik. *Runes and Their Origin: Denmark and Elsewhere*. Trans. Peter G. Foote. Copenhagen: National Museum of Denmark, 1985; Wamers, Egon. *Insularer Metallschmuck in wikingerzeitlichen Gräbern Nordeuropas: Untersuchungen zur skandinavischen Westexpansion*. Neumünster: Wachholtz, 1985; Düwel, K. "Zur Ikonographie und Ikonologie der Sigurddarstellungen." In *Zum Problem der Deutung frümittelalterlicher Bildinhalte: Akten des 1. Internationalen Kolloquiums in Marburg a.d. Lahn, 15. bis 19. Februar 1983*. Ed. Helmut Roth. Sigmaringen: Thorbecke, 1986, pp. 221–71; Fuglesang, Signe Horn. "Ikonographie der skandinavischen Runensteine der jüngeren Wikingerzeit." In *Zum Problem der Deutung frühmittelalterlicher Bildinhalte*, pp. 183–210 [*1986a*]; Ellmers, D. "Schiffdarstellungen auf skandinavischen Grabsteinen." In *Zum Problem der Deutung frühmittelalterlicher Bildinhalte*, pp. 341–72; Iversen, M., and J. Vellev. "Kammergravens alder." *Skalk* (1986), 3–8; Fuglesang, Signe Horn. "The Relationship Between Scandinavian and English Art from the Late Eighth to the Mid-Twelfth Century." In *Sources of Anglo-Saxon Culture*. Ed. Paul E. Szarmach. Studies in Medieval Culture, 20. Kalamazoo: Medieval Institute Publications, Western Michigan University, 1986, pp. 203–41 [*1986b*]; Lang, James. "The Distinctiveness of Viking Colonial Art." In *Sources of Anglo-Saxon Culture*, pp. 243–60; Sørensen, Preben Meulengracht. "Thor's Fishing Expedition." In *Words and Objects: Towards a Dialogue Between Archaeology and History of Religion*. Ed. Gro Steinsland. Institute for Comparative Research in Human Culture, Oslo. Ser. B: Skrifter 71. Oslo: Norwegian University Press, 1986, pp. 257–78; Christensen, K. "Det lykkedes!" *Nyt fra Nationalmuseet* 35 (1987), 9 [on the dendrochronological dating of the Jelling mounds]; Graham-Campbell, James. "From Scandinavia to the Irish Sea." In *Ireland and Insular Art A.D. 500–1200: Proceedings of a Conference at University College Cork, 31 October–3 November 1985*. Ed. Michael Ryan. Dublin: Royal Irish Academy, 1987, pp. 114–51 [*1987a*]; Jansson, Sven B. F. *Runes in Sweden*. 2nd rev. ed. Trans. Peter Foote. [Stockholm]: Gidlund; Royal Academy of Letters, History and Antiquities; Central Board of National Antiquities, 1987; Watt, M. "Guldageren." *Skalk* (1987), 3–9; Graham-Campbell, James. "Western Penannular Brooches and Their Viking Age Copies in Norway: A New Classification." In *Proceedings of the Tenth Viking Conference, Larkollen, Norway, 1985*. Ed. James E. Knirk. Universitetets Oldsaksamling, Skrifter, Ny rekke, nr. 9. Oslo: Universitetets Oldsaksamling, 1987, pp. 231–46; Fuglesang, Signe Horn. "The Personal Touch. On the Identification of Workshops." In *Proceedings of the Tenth Viking Conference, Larkollen, Norway, 1985*, pp. 219–20; Iversen, Mette, ed. *Mammen: Grav, kunst og samfund i vikingetid*. Viborg: Aarhus Universitetsforlag, 1991; Fuglesang, S.H. "Ornament." In *De arkeologiske utgravninger i Gamlebyen, Oslo*. Ed. E. Schia. Oslo: Alvheim & Eide, 1991, vol. 8, pp. 159–222.

Signe Horn Fuglesang

[**See also**: Borre; Bragi Boddason; Carving: Bone, Horn, and Walrus Tusk; Graves; Hoards; Iconography; Ironwork; Jelling; Jewelry; Manx Crosses; Oseberg; Painting; Pottery; Rök Stone Inscription; *Snorra Edda*; Þjóðólfr of Hvin; Úlfr Uggason; Wood Carving]

Viking Hoaxes. The so-called Vinland sagas describe the settlement of Greenland and initial exploration of the eastern coast of North America by Icelanders of Norse ancestry around the year 1000. In the early 19th century, discussion of these narratives led to efforts by laymen and scholars to find evidence of Norse landings in New England. The search gave rise to numerous misidentifications and ultimately to deliberate "Viking" hoaxes.

Among the misidentifications are Indian pictographs and various scratchings on rock, the latter produced by geological action and weathering. A prominent example of the pictograph group is the Dighton Rock at Berkley, Massachusetts. The "Viking tower" of Newport, Rhode Island, rendered famous through Longfellow's poem "The Skeleton in Armor," is pronounced by competent archaeologists to be a colonial structure that cannot antedate the early 17th century.

The most publicized Viking hoax in the 20th century is the Kensington rune stone from Douglas County, Minnesota, which may be seen as the meeting ground between ethnic patriotism in the United States and the still surviving habit in Scandinavia of carving runic inscriptions for amusement. The overwhelmingly unanimous view of authorities on Scandinavian epigraphy that the Kensington inscription is bogus has inhibited neither popular support for it nor imitations of it in other quarters.

Best known of these imitations are the Spirit Pond inscriptions, a group of four stones, the first three found in 1971 at Popham Beach, coastal Maine. The carvings include numerals, purporting to be runic, that are nevertheless anachronistically based on the Arabic system with place values. Borrowed from recent discussions of the Vinland sagas are the dates 1010 and 1011, the latter, as a triple *tour de force*, written as Roman/Arabic "M11." The runes employed have been borrowed from those of the ostensibly 350-years-younger Kensington stone. In this case, however, the language is not Swedish but a distorted pseudo-Icelandic through which shine modern thought patterns. Consistent interpretation has been obfuscated through a deliberately false segmentation of words. The poorly composed message refers to (Karlsefni's) Hóp, Vínland, *skrælingar*, a kayak, journeys, ice floe, the Canadian border, sailing ships, and a sea-serpent. There is a map of the immediate area as it appears in our day. Map and text are accompanied by drawings that illustrate the Vinland sagas: a cluster of grapes, a figure rowing a canoe, an animal pelt, a slingshot or ballista, a rattle, a human face and, as a droll substitute for the whale of Þórhallr veiðimaðr ("huntsman"), a sea-serpent. Unlike the Kensington Stone, the Spirit Pond group includes personal names: "Haakon" and "Norse folk's Ja[c]k," who may be the otherwise anonymous author. The entire concoction is a humorous satire on the Kensington stone, the Vinland sagas, the Vinland Map, the theory of runic cryptograms, and, perhaps, the Loch Ness monster. The fourth stone, not reported until 1975, is carved on the one side with a cross and on the other with what may be a "tree rune," and is pierced in its narrow end as if for a thong from which it might hang as an amulet.

Various "runic" carvings reported from Oklahoma, though not necessarily hoaxes, are manifestly of modern origin, as are "mooring holes," "battle-axes," and other asserted Norse antiquities discovered in the United States. The so-called Beardmore Finds in Ontario, Canada, are ancient, but were imported from Norway in 1923. The late 11th-century Norwegian coin from Naskeag Point in coastal Maine was probably transported from farther north by Indians. In recent years, there has been discussion of a rune-inscribed drinking horn found in 1952 at Waukegan, Illinois. Claimed as medieval, it is now known to have been inscribed in Iceland by the modern poet Hjálmar Lárusson, whose daughter has identified it. How it wound up in the United States is unknown.

Lit.: Godfrey, William S., Jr. "The Archaeology of the Old Stone Mill in Newport, Rhode Island." *American Antiquity* 17 (1951), 120–9; Wahlgren, Erik. *The Kensington Stone: A Mystery Solved*. Madison: University of Wisconsin Press, 1958; Blegen, Theodore C. *The Kensington Rune Stone: New Light on an Old Riddle*. St. Paul: Minnesota Historical Society, 1968; Whittall, James P., *et al. The Spirit Pond Runestones*. Milford and New Haven: New England Antiquities Research Association, 1972 [articles, photographs, maps, sketches]; Haugen, Einar. "The Rune Stones of Spirit Pond, Maine." *Visible Language* 8 (1974), 33–64; Holm, Gösta. "Nordbor i Amerika före Columbus. Äkta fynd och falska." *Gardar. Årsbok för Samfundet Sverige-Island i Lund-Malmö* 12 (1981), 38–47; Wallace, Birgitta. "Viking Hoaxes." In *Vikings in the West*. Ed. Eleanor Guralnick. Chicago: Archaeological Institute of America, 1982, pp. 53–76; Wahlgren, Erik. "American Runes: From Kensington to Spirit Pond." *Journal of English and Germanic Philology* 81 (1982), 157–85; Wahlgren, Erik. *The Vikings and America*. Ancient Peoples and Places, 102. London and New York: Thames & Hudson, 1986 [esp. pp. 99–120].

†Erik Wahlgren

[**See also:** America, Norse in; Kensington Stone; "Maine Coin"; Vinland Map; Vinland Sagas]

Víkingarvísur *see* Sighvatr Þórðarson

Viktors saga ok Blávus ("The Saga of Viktor and Blávus")
is a *riddarasaga* that tells how Viktor, son of the king of France, rides forth on his adventures three years after his father's death, and falls in with Blávus, a prince traveling on a magic carpet. They

form a compact of sworn brotherhood and fly for three days to Blávus's castle. They embark by ship to tackle a notorious pair of sea-kings, Qnundr and Randver. In this difficult undertaking, they are aided by their faithful guide, Kóðér, who introduces them to Skeggkarl, a poor peasant on an island. In turn, he brings them to the dwarf Dímus, a smith, who cunningly steals back the magic weapons he has earlier supplied to the sea-kings, and now provides Viktor and Blávus with invincible swords. After a severe struggle, the sea-kings are killed and buried in a mound. The sworn brothers then sail on to Cyprus, where they challenge its terrible rulers, Falr and Sóti, shape-shifters who belch venom and can sink into the ground. In the ensuing battle, Falr changes into a flying dragon, and then into a lion. Sóti becomes a mad dog, but Viktor and Blávus, with the aid of Dímus's swords and of magic venom-proof garments from Kóðér, kill and bury the berserks. Viktor now returns to France with Blávus after an absence of twelve years. The remaining third of the saga describes Viktor's suit for Fulgída, the formidable "maiden-king" of India, who has already rejected many wooers. Viktor sails to India, where he is drugged from a trick goblet, tarred, shaven, flogged, and finally rescued by Kóðér. The next year, he returns, bringing Blávus's magic carpet. He entices Fulgída onto it, but once in France she shoves him off into a tree and flies back home. Then Blávus and Kóðér sail to India, disguised as monks. Blávus wins a great reputation as a healer and, when Fulgída falls gravely ill, is persuaded to spend seven nights with her in a hall, chanting his spells. As she recovers, he invokes the name of Dímus, who then emerges from a landslide. Fulgída now recognizes Blávus as her long-lost half-brother, and agrees to go to France to marry Viktor; Dímus runs there with her on his back. Blávus remains in India, assuming the outward form of Fulgída, and consents to marry Soldan, the aging king of Serkland; after the wedding feast, he entices Soldan's beautiful daughter Rósída onto the carpet and flies off with her to France, leaving Soldan to die of anguish. Viktor marries Fulgída and reigns as king of France, while Blávus marries Rósída and becomes ruler of Serkland, and Kóðér becomes king of India.

Though much of its material and many of its personal names are ultimately of foreign inspiration, the saga has no known continental model and is presumably an original Icelandic composition. Its motifs are widely paralleled in other Icelandic romances, notably in *Gibbons saga*, *Klári saga*, and *Sigurðar saga þögla*. The theme of the misogamous maiden-king was highly developed in Icelandic romance; the part played by a magic carpet in the version here appears to derive from a tale in the popular medieval Latin collection *Gesta Romanorum*. At the beginning of the saga, the author speaks in the first person, but without providing any indication of who he was or where he lived, except that he implies that King Hákon Magnússon of Norway (almost certainly the Elder, d. 1319) is no longer alive but is well remembered. Most probably, the author worked in the second half of the 14th century.

The best MS of the saga is Stock. Perg. fol. no. 7, a vellum from about 1470, probably written in the monastery at Möðruvellir. Two other vellums survive, AM 471 4to and AM 593b 4to, both from the second half of the 15th century and evidently from northwestern Iceland. There are also numerous paper MSS, of no independent authority, from the 17th century onward. For all its lively and entertaining narrative style and its richness in romance motifs, the saga has been little known or discussed until recently, because no printed edition appeared until 1962. Three *rímur* cycles have been composed on the basis of its subject matter; the oldest, the anonymous *Viktors rímur fornu*, linguistically datable to around 1400, varies in some details of the narrative from the extant saga and perhaps reflects an earlier, now-lost, version. The highly compressed last chapter of the saga, where a more extensive account is plainly being summarized, points in the same direction.

Ed. Finnur Jónsson, ed. *Rímnasafn. Samling af de ældste islandske rimer*. 2 vols. Samfund til udgivelse af gammel nordisk litteratur, 35. Copenhagen: Møller, 1905–22 [*Viktors rímur fornu*, pp. 604–61; *Viktors rímur yngri*, pp. 661–84; the third cycle, composed in 1830, is unpublished]; Loth, Agnete, ed. "Viktors saga ok Blávus." In *Late Medieval Icelandic Romances*. 5 vols. Editiones Arnamagnæanæ, ser. B, vols. 20–4. Copenhagen: Munksgaard, 1962–65, vol. 1, pp. 1–50 [text with English plot synopsis]; Jónas Kristjánsson, ed. *Viktors saga ok Blávus*. Riddarasögur, 2. Reykjavik: Handritastofnun Íslands, 1964 [full introduction in Icelandic, with English summary, on the language and relationship of the MSS, detailed English plot synopsis, and 100-page essay by Einar Ól. Sveinsson, in English, on motifs and style]. **Lit.**: Evans, David A. H. "Observations on a New Edition of Viktors saga ok Blávus." *Arkiv för nordisk filologi* 90 (1975), 80–91; Schlauch, Margaret. "A Late Icelandic Saga as Parallel to Old French Literary Parody." *Kwartalnik Neofilologiczny* 23 (1976), 217–23; Kalinke, Marianne E. "The Misogamous Maiden Kings of Icelandic Romance." *Scripta Islandica* 37 (1986), 47–71.

D. A. H. Evans

[**See also**: *Gibbons saga*; *Klári (Clári) saga*; *Riddarasögur*; *Rímur*; *Sigurðar saga þögla*]

Vilhjálms saga sjóðs

Vilhjálms saga sjóðs ("The Saga of Vilhjálmr of Sjóðr" [?]) was composed in Iceland in the late 14th or early 15th century. It is one of the more voluminous of the original *riddarasögur* and is characterized primarily by a plethora of exotic motifs. The saga seems to have been extremely popular, and is preserved in fifty-seven MSS and fragments, the majority on paper dating from the 18th and 19th centuries. Primary MSS are AM 343a 4to (vellum, 15th century), AM 548 4to (vellum, 1543), AM 577 4to (vellum, late 15th century), AM 599 4to (vellum, *ca.* 1600), and AM 527 4to (paper, first half of the 17th century).

In a chess game with an African princess, King Ríkarðr of England wins a golden arm ring, which he gives to his son Vilhjálmr, later disappearing in a violent storm. A giant appears one day and challenges Vilhjálmr to a series of chess games with the ring as the stake. Vilhjálmr beats the giant in two successive games, winning a suit of armor, shield, and sword, but loses in the third. To redeem his head, he is obliged after three years to meet the giant in his den, where he will find ninety trolls whose names he must be able to recite. He meets the Byzantine princess Astrinomia, whose foster-mother, Ermlaug, advises him how to learn the trolls' names. With a lion he has delivered from a dragon as his companion, he sets out for the domain of the trolls in Africa, ruled over by King Herkul, where his father and a number of other kings are held captive. He recites the *Allra flagða þula* (the trolls' names in metrical form), and when the last is named, the trolls spring up and tear each other to pieces. Vilhjálmr is able to free his father and the other kings, but Herkul escapes. Next day, they meet in single combat; but neither can defeat the other, and a reconciliation is made.

Meanwhile, Astrinomia has been abducted by emissaries from Erkulus, son of King Arkistratus of Ermland, who wishes to take her as his mistress. Vilhjálmr and his father come to the rescue. A series of battles follows, in the course of which the lion is killed,

but Sjóðr, a cowardly giant, eats the lion's heart and becomes a brave hero. Vilhjálmr and Astrinomia are married and return to England. Finally, Vilhjálmr is proclaimed king of Bablyon.

The saga is a careless and sprawling work, without even a semblance of overall structure. The first part is given at least a kind of unity by the golden arm ring and the series of chess games played for it, but the second part degenerates into a repetitious series of battles with trolls and giants.

Critical commentary on the saga has been restricted for the most part to motif hunting, for which it provides ample opportunity. Schlauch (1934) lists a number of familiar motifs found in the saga, several of which, such as the unwelcome suitor, are nearly universal in the *riddarasögur*. Several motifs may be traced directly or indirectly to Chrétien de Troyes, including the dangerous bridge (*Lancelot*) and the grateful lion (*Yvain*). Einar Ól. Sveinsson (1929: lv) recognizes the motif of trolls dying when named as common to the folktale. The *Allra flagða þula* has special interest, and has been edited separately on two occasions.

Ed.: Jiriczek, Otto Luitpolt. "Zur mittelisländischen Volkskunde. Mitteilungen aus ungedruckten Arnamagnäanischen Handschriften." *Zeitschrift für deutsche Philologie* 26 (1893–94), 6–8 [*Alla flagða þula*]; *Sagan af Vilhjálmi sjóð. (Eptir gömlu handriti)*. Reykjavik: Skúli Thoroddsen, 1911; Loth, Agnete, ed. "Vilhjálms saga sjóðs." In *Late Medieval Icelandic Romances*. 5 vols. Editiones Arnamagnæanæ, ser. B, vols. 20–4. Copenhagen: Munksgaard, 1962–65, vol. 4, pp. 1–136. **Tr.**: Fellows Jensen, Gillian. In *Late Medieval Icelandic Romances*, vol. 4, pp. 3–136 [English summary]. **Bib.**: Kalinke, Marianne E., and P. M. Mitchell. *Bibliography of Old Norse–Icelandic Romances*. Islandica, 44. Ithaca and London: Cornell University Press, 1985, pp. 129–30. **Lit.**: Einar Ól. Sveinsson. *Verzeichnis isländischer Märchenvarianten. Mit einer einleitenden Untersuchung*. Folklore Fellows Communications, 83. Helsinki: Suomalainen Tiedeakatemia. Academia Scientiarum Fennica, 1929; Schlauch, Margaret. *Romance in Iceland*. Princeton: Princeton University Press; New York: American-Scandinavian Foundation; London: Allen & Unwin, 1934; rpt. New York: Russell & Russell, 1973; Harris, Richard L. "The Lion-Knight Legend in Iceland and the Valþjófsstaðir Door." *Viator* 1 (1970), 125–45; Glauser, Jürg. *Isländische Märchensagas: Studien zur Prosaliteratur im spätmittelalterlichen Island*. Beiträge zur nordischen Philologie, 12. Basel and Frankfurt am Main: Helbing & Lichtenhahn, 1983; Kalinke, Marianne. "Norse Romance (*Riddarasögur*)." In *Old Norse–Icelandic Literature: A Critical Guide*. Ed. Carol J. Clover and John Lindow. Islandica, 45. Ithaca and London: Cornell University Press, 1985, pp. 316–63.

M. J. Driscoll

[**See also**: *Riddarasögur*]

Vilmundar saga viðutan

Vilmundar saga viðutan ("The Saga of Vilmundr from Outside") is an anonymous Icelandic *riddarasaga*, probably from the 14th century. The saga is preserved in almost fifty MSS; the oldest parchment MSS are AM 586 4to, AM 343a 4to, and AM 577 4to from the 15th century. Five different *rímur* cycles came into existence in the middle of the 15th century, of which the one by Hallur Magnússon (d. 1601) formed the basis of a younger redaction of the saga (MSS Lbs. 1445 8vo, JS 411 8vo, and ÍBR 49 4to from the 18th–19th centuries). The Faroese *Vilmunds kvæði* (CCF 104) came into existence in the 19th century, based on a MS belonging to this younger redaction.

Prince Hjarandi of Garðaríki refuses to marry off his sister

Gullbrá to any man. His other sister, Sóley, agrees to marry Kolr kryppa ("hump"), but then exchanges shapes with the maid Qskubuska. While in the forest one day, Vilmundr finds a golden shoe, and later he sees three women, one of whom, Sóley, is lacking a shoe. She will marry only the man who brings it back to her. Vilmundr then goes to the royal court, where he conquers and kills a berserk and a polar bear. He becomes Hjarandi's sworn brother and offers his assistance in killing Kolr and in warding off an unwelcome suitor of Gullbrá. Finally, the courtly Prince Guðifreyr of Galicia obtains the beautiful Princess Gullbrá, while Vilmundr marries Sóley.

Vilmundar saga viðutan belongs to a borderline group between *fornaldarsögur* and original *riddarasögur*. In this regard, the genealogical connection in many MSS between *Vilmundar saga viðutan* and *Bósa saga* must also be stressed, according to which Vilmundr is Bǫgu-Bósi's grandson. Apart from *Bósa saga*, parallels in narrative structure and theme are found in a number of late *Íslendingasögur*, in *Þiðreks saga*, but primarily in *Hálfdanar saga Eysteinssonar* and in *Parcevals saga*, and perhaps also in *Erex saga*. A number of folkloristic motifs characterize the story, such as the fight with the bear and the substitution of the bride; *Vilmundar saga* has even been considered the oldest example of the Cinderella fairy tale (the shoe motif, the name Qskubuska). Scholars debate whether or not the saga illustrates the superiority of the hero coming from the farming milieu, and if this is perhaps supposed to express a certain national self-consciousness among the Icelandic audience; it is thought that the author of *Vilmundar saga viðutan* was a farmer, not a clergyman. On the other hand, the saga shows how the hero discards all rustic characteristics and fully integrates into the courtly-aristocratic society, thus arguably demonstrating the superiority of that society.

Ed.: Guðmundur Hjartarson, ed. *Sagan af Vilmundi viðutan*. Reykjavik: Einar Þórðarson, 1878; Olsson, Nils William, ed. "Vilmundar Saga Vidutan." Diss. University of Chicago, 1949 [English introduction]; Bjarni Vilhjálmsson, ed. *Riddarasögur*. 6 vols. Reykjavik: Íslendingasagnaútgáfan; Haukadalsútgáfan, 1949–54, vol. 6, pp. 1–62; Loth, Agnete, ed. "Vilmundar saga viðutan." In *Late Medieval Icelandic Romances*. 5 vols. Bibliotheca Arnamagnæanæ, ser. B, vols. 20–4. Copenhagen: Munksgaard, 1962–65, vol. 4, pp. 137–201 [English summary]; Matras, Christian, and Napoleon Djurhuus, eds. "Vilmunds kvæði." No. 104 in *Føroya kvæði: Corpus carminum færoensium* 1–. Copenhagen: Universitets-Jubilæets danske Samfund, 1941– , vol. 4, pp. 343–7; Ólafur Halldórsson, ed. *Vilmundar rímur viðutan*. Íslenzkar miðaldarímur, 4. Reykjavik: Stofnun Árna Magnússonar, 1975. **Bib.**: Finnur Sigmundsson. *Rímnatal*. 2 vols. Reykjavik: Rímnafélagið, 1966, vol. 1, pp. 501–3; Kalinke, Marianne E., and P. M. Mitchell. *Bibliography of Old Norse–Icelandic Romances*. Islandica, 44. Ithaca and London: Cornell University Press, 1985. **Lit.**: Schröder, Franz Rolf, ed. *Hálfdanar saga Eysteinssonar*. Altnordische Saga-Bibliothek, 15. Halle: Niemeyer, 1917, pp. 82–8; Finnur Jónsson. *Den oldnorske og oldislandske Litteraturs Historie*. 3 vols. 2nd ed. Copenhagen: Gad, 1920–24, vol. 3, p. 118; Schlauch, Margaret. *Romance in Iceland*. Princeton: Princeton University Press; New York: American-Scandinavian Foundation; London: Allen & Unwin, 1934; rpt. New York: Russell & Russell, 1973; Einar Sigurðsson. "Vilmundar saga viðutan." Thesis. University of Iceland, 1962; Schlauch, Margaret. "Arthurian Material in Some Late Icelandic Sagas." *Bulletin bibliographique de la Société Internationale Arthurienne* 17 (1965), 87–91 [esp. pp. 88–9]; Halvorsen, Eyvind Fjeld. "Riddersagaer." *KLNM* 14 (1969), 175–83; Togeby, Knud. "L'influence de la littérature française sur les littératures scandinaves au moyen âge." In *Généralités*. Ed. Hans Ulrich Gumbrecht. Grundriss der romanischen Literaturen des Mittelalters. Heidelberg: Winter, 1972, vol. 1, pp. 333–95 [esp. pp. 384–5]; Nahl, Astrid van. *Originale Riddarasögur als Teil altnordischer Sagaliteratur*. Texte und Untersuchungen zur Germanistik und Skandinavistik, 3. Frankfurt am Main and Bern: Lang, 1981; Glauser, Jürg. *Isländische Märchensagas: Studien zur Prosaliteratur im spätmittelalterlichen Island*. Beiträge zur nordischen Philologie, 12. Basel and Frankfurt am Main: Helbing & Lichtenhahn, 1983; Kalinke, Marianne E. "Riddarasögur, Fornaldarsögur, and the Problem of Genre." In *Les Sagas de Chevaliers (Riddarasögur)*. Actes de la Vᵉ Conférence Internationale sur les Sagas . . . (Toulon. Juillet 1982). Ed. Régis Boyer. Civilisations, 10. Paris: Presses de l'Université de Paris-Sorbonne, 1985, pp. 77–91; Kalinke, Marianne. "Norse Romance (*Riddarasögur*)." In *Old Norse–Icelandic Literature: A Critical Guide*. Ed. Carol J. Clover and John Lindow. Islandica, 45. Ithaca and London: Cornell University Press, 1985, pp. 316–63.

Jürg Glauser

[**See also**: *Berserkr*; *Bósa saga ok Herrauðs*; *Erex saga*; *Fornaldarsögur*; *Hálfdanar saga Eysteinssonar*; *Parcevals saga*; *Riddarasögur*; *Rímur*; *Þiðreks saga af Bern*]

Vinland Map is a crude map of the world, purportedly of medieval provenance, but unknown until discovered in the late 1950s in Europe by the American bookseller Lawrence Witten of New Haven. Labeled in Latin and inscribed on a worn and scraped piece of parchment, it was introduced to the world through publication by Yale University Press, with the collaboration of the British Museum, of a large volume, *The Vinland Map and the Tartar Relation*. If authentic, the Vinland portrayed on the map as a large island would be the earliest known representation of the New World. The Latin writing on the map declares among other things that "Byarnus" (Bjarni Herjólfsson) and "Leiphus" (Leifr Eiríksson) together discovered and explored "Vinilanda." That statement appears to argue that there may once have existed a third Vinland saga, for which there is no other evidence. Also mentioned in the Latin captions is a voyage in search of Vinland by an early 12th-century "Henricus . . . episcopus" (Bishop Eiríkr Gnúpsson), who is briefly mentioned in later Icelandic reports.

The earlier history of the Vinland Map has never been ascertained, Witten considering himself bound by a pledge not to reveal certain details of the map's previous ownership. This refusal and the vague circumstances surrounding its finding led to much scholarly skepticism. Cartographers have argued that the New World projections of the Vinland Map distort the representation of the world as a whole, as if added to a previous map that lacked them. There is some evidence of involvement by the late Yugoslavian cleric and historian Lukas Jelič, whose theories the map seems to confirm. In 1974, it was announced that Walter C. McCrone, a microscopist and chemist employed by Yale University's Beinecke Rare Book and Manuscript Library, had found that the ink contains large amounts of titanium dioxide, a chemical not invented until 1917. Renewed testing by Thomas A. Cahill, director of the Crocker Nuclear Laboratories of the University of California at Davis, indicates that only trace elements of the chemical can be found. The dating of the Vinland Map must accordingly be decided on other grounds.

Lit.: Skelton, R. A., *et al. The Vinland Map and the Tartar Relation.* New Haven and London: Yale University Press, 1965; Crone, G. R. "How Authentic Is the 'Vinland Map?'" *Encounter* 26.2 (February 1966), 75–8; Davies, Arthur. "The Vinland Map and the Tartar Relation: A Review." *Geography* 51 (July 1966), 259–65; Washburn, Wilcomb E., ed. *Proceedings of the Vinland Map Conference.* Chicago: University of Chicago Press, 1971 [sixteen papers read at the Smithsonian Institution in 1966; bibliography, pp. 155–81]; Wallis, Helen, *et al.* "The Strange Case of the Vinland Map: A Symposium." *Geographical Journal* (London) 140 (1974), 183–214; Cahill, T. A., *et al.* "The Vinland Map, Revisited: New Compositional Evidence on Its Ink and Parchment." *Analytical Chemistry* 59.6 (March 15, 1987), 829–33.

†Erik Wahlgren

[**See also:** America, Norse in; Viking Hoaxes; Vinland Sagas]

Vinland Sagas

Vinland Sagas describe, in varying terms, the early discovery, naming, and partial exploration of Greenland and coastal North America by Icelanders and Greenlanders of Norse extraction. The name is applied in particular to *Grœnlendinga saga* ("The Saga of the Greenlanders"), here cited as *GS*, and *Eiríks saga rauða* ("The Saga of Eiríkr the Red"), here cited as *ES*. Confusingly, *GS* is called by some writers *Grœnlendinga þáttr* ("The Tale of the Greenlanders"), a title sometimes applied as well to a short story about Einarr Sokkason. Based on Norse Greenlandic oral tradition, *GS* is believed to have been written in Iceland, possibly in Skagafjörður in about 1200. Often referred to as the *Flateyjarbók* version, it is entered in three installments in *Flateyjarbók* from about 1387. *ES* is believed to have been composed in Snæfellsnes shortly after 1264. Written in part to glorify King Óláfr Tryggvason (r. 995–1000), it has clearly been influenced by the monk Gunnlaugr Leifsson's saga about Óláfr that stresses and exaggerates the monarch's christianizing activities. *ES* has been transmitted in two closely related vellum MSS: *Skálholtsbók* (AM 557 4to) and *Hauksbók* (AM 544 4to).

Through a line-by-line examination, Jansson showed that the *Hauksbók* version, written down before 1334 by the Iceland-born Norwegian lawspeaker Haukr Erlendsson (1265–1334), was a tightened and rationalized version of the more pristine and digressive Skálholt MS. There is strong evidence (Jón Jóhannesson 1962, Wahlgren 1969) that *ES* as we now have it is in part a tendentious rewriting of the *GS* account, undertaken to magnify the exploits of Haukr's own ancestor, Þorfinnr karlsefni ("doughty man"), chief hero of *ES*. Ólafur Halldórsson (1978), tentatively supported by Jones (1986), attribute equal authority to *GS* and *ES*, whereas H. Ingstad, like Jón Jóhannesson and Wahlgren but with excellent additional arguments of his own, finds that *ES* is largely modeled on *GS*. Doubtful, however, is Ingstad's conclusion that *GS* was actually written in Greenland. Various words and phrases of *ES* reveal the author's skillful alteration to mask that saga's dependence on the earlier *GS*. That dependence is far from uniform, for *ES* reveals purposes not evident in *GS*. Better written, it is in general a more sophisticated product, with hagiographic features that demonstrably transcend the facts of history. *ES* changes both the action and the cast of characters involved in what we may call "the Vinland story."

If the *GS* were not available for comparison, we should have far fewer criteria for evaluating the general historicity of the Vinland voyages. In terms both of literature and of history, the entire picture has long been muddled through a general tendency to regard the details of the two Vinland sagas as more or less interchange-

able. The two sagas may and should be compared, but it is important to regard them as discrete, if obviously related, works. Like the *Íslendingasögur* in general, they were not intended as general histories or travel guides. Some of their details, after generations of oral transmission, were doubtless imperfectly understood by the saga writers themselves. Their confusions, together with certain obvious fictions, have led such writers as Nansen to minimize or deny the historical content of the Vinland accounts. Modern archaeological discoveries in Greenland and Canada, however, and in particular the work of H. and A. S. Ingstad at L'Anse aux Meadows in northern Newfoundland, have now vindicated the basic indications of the sagas.

Although shorter than *ES*, the *GS*, or *Flateyjarbók* tradition, identifies six Vinland voyages versus three in *ES*. The first of the six narrates the accidental discovery of some part of North America by the merchant Bjarni Herjólfsson, presumably in the year 986. Sailing from Norway to Iceland with a shipload of wares and intending to winter with his family in western Iceland, Bjarni finds that, shortly before, his kinsmen had gone off to Greenland as part of Eiríkr's project to colonize it. Rapidly changing plans, Bjarni sets sail toward Greenland. Lost for many days in the Atlantic fogs, he ultimately sights land to the west. Cautiously standing offshore, he sails northward until the sight of glaciers, presumably on Baffin Island, persuades him that he has come far enough north to make an easterly push with small risk of missing Greenland a second time. And indeed, he arrives safely at his father's estate of Herjólfsnes on the southern tip of Greenland. On a subsequent trip to Norway, he is twitted about not having explored the lands he had sighted.

The second voyage, by Eiríkr's son Leifr, was made sometime around the year 1000. Resolving to do what Bjarni had not done, he buys the latter's ship and sails to investigate the new lands to the west. Coming first to the land that Bjarni had sighted last, he sails southward, naming the areas as he goes. Three of these names have survived: *Helluland* ("Slab-rock Land"), *Markland* ("Forest Land"), and *Vínland* (long *í*) or *Vinland* (short *i*), to be interpreted as "Vine Land" or "Meadow Land." Finding grapevines and fine forest trees, they build houses for the winter. In the spring or summer, with a load of lumber, they sail back to Leifr's father's home at Brattahlíð, having rescued some shipwrecked people on the way. Leifr's voyage is followed by a third expedition captained by his brother Þorvaldr, who winters in Leifr's houses and then searchs for land for himself. Ultimately, Þorvaldr is killed by an arrow shot by one of the *skrælingar*, or natives. His companions bury him and return to Greenland. A fourth voyage, undertaken by Leifr's brother Þorsteinn, is aborted. A fifth expedition is undertaken by the wealthy trader Karlsefni, who with a crew of sixty, including five women, and several head of cattle, finds Leifr's houses, which he has agreed to lend them. They meet and trade with the *skrælingar* for furs, but the two races ultimately come to blows. The would-be colonists return to Greenland with produce of the land, including grapes, grapevines, and furs. There follows a sixth voyage, a joint-stock expedition undertaken by Leifr's illegitimate half-sister, Freydís, together with two brothers named Helgi and Finnbogi, whom, in the end, Freydís murders with their entire crew, including even the women. For a number of reasons, the historicity of this voyage is doubtful.

ES (*Skálholtsbók-Hauksbók* tradition), placing its emphasis on Karlsefni, has fewer voyages. Dispensing with Bjarni Herjólfsson, it makes Leifr discover some unnamed new lands quite by accident while returning from an adventurous and probably unhistorical voyage to the Hebrides and Norway, where King Óláfr commissions him to preach Christianity in Greenland. Leifr's brother Þorsteinn sets out on a fruitless voyage. Finally, a mighty expedition, comprising three ships and 160 men and women, sails forth under Karlsefni. They never find Vínland. Internal dissention splits the group, and strife with the *skrælingar* persuades them to abandon the venture. After three winters of growing frustration, Karlsefni, with his wife, Guðríðr, and son, Snorri, the "first white child to be born in America," returns to Greenland. *ES* adroitly makes Þorsteinn and Freydís members of Karlsefni's troupe, Freydís transformed from villainess to heroine. Leifr's follower Tyrkir in *GS*, the mellow discoverer of grapes, is replaced in *ES* by the heathen poet and curmudgeon Þórhallr veiðimaðr ("huntsman"), whose verses lament the failure to find grapes. The edible whale of *GS* becomes poisonous until Christ intervenes. Later, Karlsefni and Guðríðr found an important clan in Iceland.

Because of its economic value, Markland, source of timber for the Greenland colony, lives on for centuries in legend and in fact. Vínland/Vinland became a shadowy memory, never to be located with certainty. If the grapevines were real, the St. Lawrence Valley or New England would seem reasonable locations. For want of archaeological finds, many investigators are willing to settle for northern Newfoundland as an authentic or surrogate site for Vínland, Land of Grapes. Meanwhile, objects of medieval Norse manufacture are turning up in impressive numbers in Arctic Canada.

Ed.: Finnur Jónsson, ed. *Flateyjarbók (Codex Flateyensis) MS. No. 1005 fol. in the Old Royal Collection in the Royal Library of Copenhagen.* Corpus Codicum Islandicorum Medii Aevi, 1. Copenhagen: Levin & Munksgaard, 1930; Einar Ól. Sveinsson and Matthías Þórðarson, eds. *Eyrbyggja saga.* Íslenzk fornrit, 4. Reykjavik: Hið íslenzka fornritafélag, 1935; Strömbäck, Dag, ed. *The Arnamagnaean Manuscript 557 4to Containing inter alia the History of the First Discovery of America.* Corpus Codicum Islandicorum Medii Aevi, 13. Copenhagen: Levin & Munksgaard, 1940; Halldór Hermannsson. *The Vinland Sagas.* Islandica, 30. Ithaca, New York: Cornell University Press, 1944; Jansson, Sven B. F., ed. *Sagorna om Vinland. 1: Handskrifterna till Erik den Rödes saga.* Lund: Ohlsson, 1944 [English summary]; Guðni Jónsson, ed. *Íslendingasögur.* 13 vols. Reykjavik: Íslendingasagnaútgáfan, 1953, vol. 1; Jón Helgason, ed. *Hauksbók: The Arna-Magnæan Manuscripts 371,4°, 544,4°, and 675,4°.* Manuscripta Islandica, 5. Copenhagen: Munksgaard, 1960. **Tr.**: Reeves, Arthur Middleton, trans. *The Finding of Wineland the Good: The History of the Icelandic Discovery of America.* London: Frowde, 1890; Gathorne-Hardy, G. M., trans. *The Norse Discoverers of America: The Wineland Sagas.* Oxford: Clarendon, 1921; rpt. 1970; Haugen, Einar, trans. *Voyages to Vinland: The First American Saga.* New York: Knopf, 1942; Magnus Magnusson and Hermann Pálsson, trans. *The Vinland Sagas: The Norse Discovery of America.* Harmondsworth: Penguin, 1965; Jones, Gwyn, trans. *The Norse Atlantic Saga: Being the Norse Voyages of Discovery and Settlement to Iceland, Greenland, and North America.* Rev. ed. Oxford: Oxford University Press, 1986. **Lit.**: Fischer, Joseph. *The Discoveries of the Norsemen in America with Special Relation to Their Early Cartographical Representation.* Trans. Basil H. Soulsby. London: Stevens, Son and Stiles, 1903; Hovgaard, William. *The Voyages of the Norsemen to America.* New York: American-Scandinavian Foundation, 1914; Matthias Thórdarson. *The Vinland Voyages.* Trans. Thorstina Jackson Walters. American Geographical Society Research Series, 18. New York: American Geographical Society, 1930; Halldór Hermannsson. *The Problem of Wineland.* Islandica, 25. Ithaca: Cornell University Press, 1936; Jón Jóhannesson. "The Date of the

Composition of the Saga of the Greenlanders." Trans. Tryggvi J. Oleson. *Saga-Book of the Viking Society* 16 (1962), 54–66; Wahlgren, Erik. "Fact and Fancy in the Vinland Sagas." In *Old Norse Literature and Mythology: A Symposium.* Ed. Edgar C. Polomé. Austin and London: University of Texas Press, 1969, pp. 19–80; Ebel, Else. *Die Vínlandsagas. Ausgewählte Texte zur Entdeckung Amerikas. Mit Anmerkungen und Glossar.* Tübingen: Niemeyer, 1973; Ólafur Halldórsson. *Grænland í miðaldaritum.* Reykjavik: Sögufélag, 1978; Wahlgren, Erik. *The Vikings and America.* Ancient Peoples and Places, 102. London and New York: Thames and Hudson, 1986 [esp. pp. 139–67].

†Erik Wahlgren

[**See also:** America, Norse in; *Flateyjarbók*; Greenland, Norse in; *Hauksbók*; *Íslendingabók*; Kensington Stone; L'Anse aux Meadows; "Maine Coin"; *Ólafs saga Tryggvasonar*; Viking Hoaxes; Vinland Map]

Visio Tnugdali ("The Vision of Tundale") is a mid-12th-century account of the vision of a wicked Irish nobleman, Tundale, in a swoon during which he remained almost lifeless. After three days, he awoke and led a pious life from then on; he distributed all his possessions to the Church and the poor, and made known what he had seen and experienced in his vision. The succeeding chapters describe how his soul departed from his body and was led by an angel through the purgatorial torments of hell to the bliss of paradise until its return to Tundale's body. Because of its vivid and imaginative description of the otherworld, the story became very popular in the Middle Ages: it was translated into a number of languages and was included by Vincent of Beauvais in his *Speculum historiale* (Book 27: 88–104).

The Old Norse translation of the work, *Duggals leiðsla*, has been dated to the mid-13th century. This dating is based on the prologue, which says the translation was undertaken at the request of King Hákon (Hákonarson; r. 1217–1263). Some features of the vocabulary and syntax of *Duggals leiðsla* show an affinity with a number of translated *riddarasögur*, i.e., the Tristram group, that can be assigned on surer grounds to King Hákon's court. Hallberg (1973), who offers a statistical analysis of these works, suggests that one person was responsible for their composition, the Brother Robert mentioned in the preface to *Tristrams saga*. Cahill (1983) notes that, with regard to the vocabulary, *Tristrams saga* is more enterprising, but remarks that the author of *Duggals leiðsla* "might have felt that a more restrained style was appropriate to an explicitly religious work, even at the risk of relative dullness."

The saga is extant in AM 681a 4to (A; *ca.* 1450), AM 624 4to (B; *ca.* 1500), AM 681c 4to (C; one leaf; *ca.* 1400), and AM 681b 4to (D; two fragments, each of two leaves; *ca.* 1450). An extract from the saga is found in the primary MS of Bergr Sokkason's *Michaels saga*, AM 657a 4to (M; *ca.* 1350). A and D on the one hand and B and C on the other appear to go back to two different copies (*y and *z) of a copy (*x) of the original, whereas Bergr Sokkason seems to have drawn from a different copy (*m) of the original (Cahill 1983). A passage in Jón Guðmundsson lærði's ("the learned"; 1574–1658) *Tíjdfordríjf* appears to be derived directly from A (or a MS closely related to it), as does the text of the saga in AM 681d 4to (a[1]; early 18th century). A copy of a[1] is found in MS 1019 in Trinity College, Dublin (a[2]; 18th century), and a copy of B in NkS 1269 fol. (b; 1750–1800).

The Old Swedish translation of the *Visio Tnugdali* exists in two redactions. The so-called A-redaction (ed. Stephens and

Ahlstrand 1844) is found in the following paper MSS: SKB D 4 a (*Codex Verelianus*) from no later than 1457, SKB D 3 from 1476, StB Saml. 1a in Linköping from the end of the 15th century or the beginning of the 16th, SKB K 45 4to from the beginning of the 16th century, and SKB D 80 (a copy of SKB D 3 by Wennæsius) from around 1670; an additional MS (SKB A 58) containing a translation of the *Visio Tnugdali* is now lost (*cf.* Stephens and Ahlstrand 1844: LI). According to Kornhall (1959: 57), SKB D 4 preserves the most original text. The A-redaction presents the shorter version. Whether it is derived from a different and shorter original than the B-redaction, or whether the translator simplified or omitted certain sections of his Latin original cannot be ascertained. The B-redaction (ed. Dahlgren 1875) survives in SKB A 58 (*Jöns Buddes bok*), written 1491. It is possible that the translation was made by Jöns Budde in Nådendal monastery and that SKB A 58 represents a copy of the original translation.

No translation of the *Visio Tnugdali* into Danish has survived, but that the work was known is evident from two Danish MSS containing the Latin text (*cf.* Ronge and Gad 1975: 55–6): (1) Halle Univ.-bibl. Y c 6 4to from the 13th century; it originally belonged to the Cistercian monastery in Løgumkloster. (2) NkS 123 4to (fols. 27–36) from 1454–1462 by Peder Madsen, a priest in Ribe; the text is translated and excerpted from the *Speculum historiale* ("Istud bene est extractum compilatum et scriptum ex speculo hystoriali").

Ed.: (a) General: Wagner, Albrecht, ed. *Visio Tnugdali: Lateinisch und Altdeutsch*. Erlangen: Deichert, 1882; Means, Rodney, ed. *The Vision of Tundale ed. from B. L. MS Cotton Caligula A II*. Middle English Texts, 18. Heidelberg: Winter, 1985. **(b) Old Norse**: Unger, C. R., ed. *Heilagra manna søgur: Fortællinger og legender om hellige mænd og kvinder*. 2 vols. Christiania [Oslo]: Bentzen, 1877, vol. 1, pp. 329–58; Cahill, Peter, ed. *Duggals leiðsla*. Reykjavik: Stofnun Árna Magnússonar, 1983. **(c) Old Swedish**: Stephens, George, and J. A. Ahlstrand, eds. *S. Patriks-sagan, innehållande S. Patrik och hans järtecken, Nicolaus i S. Patriks skärseld och Tungulus*. Samlingar utgifna af Svenska fornskrift-sällskapet, 2. Stockholm: Norstedt, 1844, pp. 27–48; Dahlgren, F. A., ed. *Skrifter till läsning för klosterfolk*. Samlingar utgifna af Svenska fornskrift-sällskapet, 20. Stockholm: Norstedt, 1875, pp. 215–52. **Bib.: (a) Old Norse**: Widding, Ole, *et al.* "The Lives of the Saints in Old Norse Prose: A Handlist." *Mediaeval Studies* 25 (1963), 294–337. **Lit.: (a) General**: Gad, Tue. *Legenden i dansk middelalder*. Copenhagen: Dansk videnskabs forlag, 1961; Owen, D. D. R. *The Vision of Hell: Infernal Journeys in Medieval French Literature*. New York: Barnes & Noble, 1970; Ronge, Hans H., and Tue Gad. "Tundalus." *KLNM* 19 (1975), 53–6; Marshall, J. C. Douglas. "Three Problems in the *Vision of Tundal*." *Medium Ævum* 44 (1975), 14–22; Spilling, Herrad. *Die Visio Tnugdali. Eigenart und Stellung in der mittelalterlichen Visionsliteratur bis zum Ende des 12. Jahrhunderts*. Münchener Beiträge zur Mediävistik und Renaissance-Forschung, 21. Munich: Arbeo-Gesellschaft, 1975. **(b) Old Norse**: Fell, Christine. "Bergr Sokkason's *Michaels saga* and Its Sources." *Saga-Book of the Viking Society* 16 (1962–65), 354–71; Hallberg, Peter. "Broder Robert, Tristrams saga och Duggals leizla. Anteckningar till norska översättningar." *Arkiv för nordisk filologi* 88 (1973), 55–71; Barnes, Geraldine. "The *Riddarasögur*: A Medieval Exercise in Translation." *Saga-Book of the Viking Society* 19 (1977), 403–41; Cahill, Peter. "Three Notes on Duggals Leizla." *Saga-Book of the Viking Society* 19 (1977), 442–6. **(c) Old Swedish**: Kornhall, David. *Den fornsvenska sagan om Karl Magnus. Handskrifter och texthistoria*. Lundastudier i nordisk språkvetenskap, 15. Ed. Ivar Lindquist and Karl Gustav Ljunggren. Lund: Gleerup, 1959. **(d) Old Danish**: Jørgensen, Ellen. *Catalogus Codicum Latinorum Medii Ævi Bibliothecæ Regiæ Hafniensis*. Copenhagen: Gyldendal, 1926, p. 163; Menzel, Ottokar. "Drei Handschriften aus der ehemaligen Cisterzienserabtei Lügumkloster in der Universitätsbibliothek zu Halle." *Studien und Mitteilungen zur Geschichte der Benediktinerordens* 53 (1935), 407–11.

Kirsten Wolf

[**See also:** *Tristrams saga ok Ísǫndar*; Visionary Literature]

Visionary Literature. There may be traces of ecstatic experiences in eddic poetry, as in *Vǫluspá*, and there are many hints of shamanistic trance in diverse Scandinavian sources (Arbman 1963–70). But visionary literature as a genre of its own developed in the North only after the Conversion. The motifs employed in these texts rely heavily on Latin traditions of *revelationes*, if they are not mere translations of earlier specimens of this genre. Generally speaking, there were two types of visions during the Middle Ages. The first, ecstatic journeys of the soul to the realms of the dead, concerned the punishments of the wicked and the rewards of the just. Early examples are found in the *Dialogues* of Pope Gregory I and the *Historia Francorum* of Gregory of Tours (both late 6th century). The genre culminates in the long Latin visions of the 12th century, but declines soon afterward. The second type comprises the mystic visions, describing mostly the soul's ecstatic union with its heavenly bridegroom, Christ, as well as scenes from his passion, or allegorical themes. This type of vision is recorded from the 12th century onward.

From the large corpus of Latin journeys to the otherworld, only a small part was translated into the Scandinavian languages. The vision of St. Paul of the pains of hell, although fictitious and rejected by the Church Fathers, served as a model for the whole genre. It was translated at the end of the 12th century into Old Norse (ed. Tveitane 1964). A Danish version forms part of the legendary "Hellige Kvinder" extant in SKB K 4 from 1400–1500. An Old Norse translation (12th century) of Gregory's *Dialogues* contains the vision of the souls' bridge to paradise (ed. Unger 1877: 179–255). Dryhthelm's vision of the realm of eternal punishment first recorded by the Venerable Bede in 731 (*Historia ecclesiastica* 5:12), was repeated in Vincent of Beauvais's *Speculum historiale*, which was translated in the 14th century into Old Norse (ed. Gering 1882–84: 313). An early-medieval saint's life containing numerous dream-visions was that of Ansgar, written by Rimbert in the 9th century and translated into Old Swedish in the 14th or 15th century. The most widespread of the otherworld journeys was the *Visio Tnugdali* (mid-12th century): in his ecstasy, the Irish knight Tundale, guided by his angel, had to "taste" for himself most of the pains of the netherworld before crossing the nail-studded bridge to the regions of paradise. This fascinating if sadistic account found pious translators all over the European countries; an Old Norse translation was ordered by King Hákon Hákonarson (d. 1263) or Hákon Magnússon (ed. Cahill 1983). A Swedish version followed (ed. Stephens and Ahlstrand 1844, Dahlgren 1875). One famous record from the Irish sanctuary on an island in Lake Dergh (Ulster) treated the adventures of the knight Owein, who had to wander through the regions of purgatory and cross the slippery bridge to paradise in order to do penance for his sins. It was translated into Old Swedish (ed. Stephens and Ahlstrand 1844). Old Norse versions of Gundelin's vision (1167) were incorporated into *Maríu saga* (13th century; ed. Unger 1871: 534–41, 1162–8).

Of the mystical visions, only one translation seems to be known; it was taken from the numerous revelations of St. Elisabeth of Schönau (d. 1164), dealing with Mary's assumption (ed. Maurer 1883; Widding and Bekker-Nielsen 1961).

The Nordic countries have not produced many visions of their own; at least, not many have been preserved. There are some examples in saints' lives, especially those about King Óláfr Haraldsson, but the first and perhaps only originally independent text is *Rannveigar leizla*, incorporated into *Prestssaga Guðmundar Arasonar*. Rannveig, the concubine of several priests, was dragged through an Icelandic desert landscape and tormented by fiends, but was rescued by the Virgin and saints (ed. Stefán Karlsson 1983: 92–9). The dominating visionary of the later Middle Ages was St. Birgitta of Sweden, whose revelations, dictated in her native tongue, were immediately translated into Latin, but soon retranslated into Old Swedish (ed. Klemming 1857–84). Of her original wording, only scraps have been preserved (ed. Högman 1951, Gussgard 1961).

Sometimes, *Sólarljóð* is counted as a vision, although it is in fact a moralistic-didactic poem, as are the dialogues between the body and soul sometimes classified as visions. *Guidos Ånd* and *Arild og Ånden* are Danish translations from the Latin and Low German respectively (*cf.* Gad 1961: 356ff.), and represent examples of the many late-medieval stories in circulation about ghosts.

Ed.: Stephens, George, and J. A. Ahlstrand, eds. *S. Patriks-sagan, innehållande S. Patrik och hans järtecken, Nicolaus i S. Patriks skärseld och Tungulus*. Samlingar utgifna af Svenska fornskrift-sällskapet, 2. Stockholm: Norstedt, 1844; Klemming, G. E., ed. *Heliga Birgittas uppenbarelser*. 5 vols. Samlingar utgivna av Svenska fornskrift-sällskapet, 14. Stockholm: Norstedt, 1857–84; Brandt, C. J., ed. *De hellige Kvinder, en Legende-Samling*. Dansk Klosterlæsning, 1:2. Copenhagen: Gad, 1859; Unger, C. R., ed. *Mariu saga: Legender om Jomfru Maria og hendes jertegn*. Christiania [Oslo]: Brögger & Christie, 1871; Dahlgren, F. A., ed. *Skrifter till läsning för klosterfolk*. Samlingar utgivna af Svenska fornskrift-sällskapet, 20. Stockholm: Norstedt, 1875; Unger, C. R., ed. *Heilagra manna søgur: Fortællinger og legender om hellige mænd og kvinder*. 2 vols. Christiania [Oslo]: Bentzen, 1877; Gering, Hugo, ed. *Islendzk Æventyri*. 2 vols. Halle: Waisenhaus, 1882–84; Högman, Bertil, ed. *Heliga Birgittas originaltexter*. Samlingar utgivna av Svenska fornskrift-sällskapet, 205. Uppsala: Almqvist & Wiksell, 1951; Gussgard, Jostein. *To fragmenter på svensk av den hellige Birgittas skrifter*. Samlingar utgivna av Svenska fornskrift-sällskapet, 230. Uppsala: Almqvist & Wiksell, 1961; Widding, Ole, and Hans Bekker-Nielsen. "Elizabeth of Schönau's Visions in an Old Icelandic Manuscript, AM 764,4°." *Opuscula* 2.1. Bibliotheca Arnamagnæana, 25.1. Copenhagen: Reitzel, 1961, pp. 93–6; Tveitane, Mattias, ed. *En norrøn versjon av Visio Pauli*. Acta Universitatis Bergensis. Series Humaniorum Litterarum; Årbok for Universitetet i Bergen. Humanistisk serie 3. Bergen: Norwegian University Press, 1964; Cahill, Peter, ed. *Duggals leiðsla*. Reykjavik: Stofnun Árna Magnússonar, 1983; Stefán Karlsson, ed. *Guðmundar søgur biskups. I: Ævi Guðmundar biskups, Guðmundar saga A*. Editiones Arnamagnæanæ, ser. B, vol. 6. Copenhagen: Reitzel, 1983. **Lit.**: Maurer, Konrad. "Der Elisabeth von Schönau Visionen nach einer isländischen Quelle." *Sitzungsberichte der philosophisch-philologischen und historischen Classe der königlich bayerischen Akademie der Wissenschaften* (1883), 401–23; Gad, Tue. *Legenden i dansk middelalder*. Copenhagen: Dansk videnskabs forlag, 1961; Arbman, Ernst. *Ecstasy, or Religious Trance, in the Experience of the Ecstatics and from the Psychological Point of View*. Stockholm: Bokförlaget, 1963–70; Strömbäck, Dag. "Visiondigtning." *KLNM* 20 (1976), 171–

86; Dinzelbacher, Peter. *Vision und Visionsliteratur im Mittelalter*. Monographien zur Geschichte des Mittelalters, 23. Stuttgart: Hiersemann, 1981; Dinzelbacher, Peter. *Mittelalterliche Visionsliteratur* Darmstadt: Wissenschaftliche Buchgesellschaft, 1989; Dinzelbacher, Peter. *Revelationes*. Typologie de sources du moyen âge occidental, 57 Turnhout: Brepols, 1991.

Peter Dinzelbacher

[**See also:** Ansgar, St.; Birgitta, St.; Christian Prose; *Draumkvæde*; Gregory, St.: *Dialogues*; *Guðmundar søgur biskups*; *Maríu saga*; *Nicodemus, Gospel of*; Saints' Lives; *Sólarljóð*; *Visio Tnugdali*; *Voluspá*]

Volsung-Niflung Cycle

Volsung-Niflung Cycle comprises a wealth of literary works, both poetry and prose, that extend geographically from the Scandinavian North to the Austro-Bavarian South, and chronologically from the early lays of the *Poetic Edda*, such as *Brot af Sigurðarkviðu*, on to the early 13th-century German *Nibelungenlied*, and ending with the 16th-century *Das Lied vom Hürnen Seyfrid*.

The *Codex Regius* of the *Poetic Edda* includes eighteen lays related to the Volsung-Niflung material, some marginally, some centrally. The central group deals with (Sequence A) Sigurðr's marriage to Guðrún, daughter of King Gjúki, the resentment felt by Brynhildr, Gunnarr's wife, toward her brother-in-law Sigurðr's attitude and behavior, and Sigurðr's murder at the hands of Guðrún's brothers and their appropriation of his treasure, all this in association with (Sequence B) those lays that deal with the murder of Guðrún's brothers (termed Gjúkings, Niflungs, or Burgundians) by Atli, ruler of the Huns (the historical Attila) and Guðrún's second husband, greedy for the treasure that once was Sigurðr's, with the vengeance taken against Atli by Guðrún for the murder of her brothers, and with her own death.

Sequences A and B are in their origins two separate legends that became loosely linked through the person of Guðrún: Sigurðr's sorrowing widow is identified as Atli's vengeful queen.

The *Nibelungenlied* also falls into two sections: Part I corresponds to Sequence A of the eddic lays, and Part II to Sequence B. The forms taken by the names of the various characters are, of course, different, *e.g.*, Sigurðr is paralleled by Sifrit (*i.e.*, Siegfried), Brynhildr by Brünhilt, Gunnarr by Gunther, Hogni by Hagen, Gjúki by Gibeche, Niflungs by Nibelungs, Guðrún by Kriemhilt (Grímhildr in *Þiðreks saga af Bern*, although in the *Poetic Edda* and elsewhere in the Norse tradition, Grímhildr is Guðrún's mother), and Atli by Etzel. Kriemhilt links Parts I and II as Guðrún links Sequences A and B, but Kriemhilt, Etzel's queen, avenges not the murder of her brothers on an avaricious Etzel, but the murder of her first husband, Sifrit, on her brothers. This variant role is also found in *Þiðreks saga*, itself deriving largely from (Low) German tradition.

The older version is that of the *Poetic Edda*, because the pattern in the *Nibelungenlied* with its emphasis on the role played by the love of a wife for a beloved husband seems more modern than the theme of *Atlakviða*, because the *Nibelungenlied* presents a more sophisticated structuring of the material, and because it allows a brief glimpse of the older version to appear. Kriemhilt's joy on observing her brothers arrive at Etzel's court in full armor makes sense only if she favors their cause, as does the Norse Guðrún, and is not set on their downfall, which, in the *Nibelungenlied*, she undoubtedly is. Again, it is only if seen in the earlier context of anxiety felt for her brothers' safety that the warning of trouble ahead given to those brothers while on their way to Etzel's court by her own trusted liegeman, Eckewart, on the borders of Margrave Rüediger's domains (where, confusingly, Eckewart also functions as a sentinel for Rüediger) can be properly understood in a version in which Kriemhilt is her brothers' enemy. Kriemhilt's changed role is probably due to the need to exonerate Etzel from the murder of Hagen and Gunther in the light of a tradition developed among the Ostrogoths, and inherited by the Bavarians, that presented Attila in a favorable light.

Even in the *Poetic Edda*, there are hints of a motivation for the downfall of the Niflung brothers other than simple greed for gold. In the late *Atlamál*, belonging to Sequence B, occurs a veiled reference to their responsibility for the death by suicide of Brynhildr, Atli's sister (as she had become in the Norse tradition), while the eddic prose passage *Dráp Niflunga*, where there is no mention any more than in *Atlamál* of the Niflung treasure, implies that their doom at Atli's hands is the result of that responsibility. A clear link between Sigurðr's murder and their downfall is provided by a passage in *Vǫlsunga saga* where Atli is not only motivated by his greed for their treasure, but also by his desire to avenge Sigurðr; and in the eddic *Brot af Sigurðarkviðu*, references to the Niflungs' undoing because they broke their oaths to Sigurðr may indicate a similar if tenuous link, conceivably a spontaneous development in the North, but possibly an echo (along with the passage in *Vǫlsunga saga*) of the developed German pattern.

There are also differences between the pattern taken by the Norse legends of Brynhildr in the *Poetic Edda* and *Vǫlsunga saga* on the one hand, and the *Nibelungenlied*'s account of Brünhilt on the other. In the northern tradition represented by *Vǫlsunga saga*, Sigurðr is betrothed to Brynhildr (the "prior betrothal" theme), loses all memory of her as a result of a potion administered by Grímhildr, whose daughter, Guðrún, he is persuaded to marry. Gunnarr seeks Brynhildr's hand in marriage, but cannot pass through the flame barrier surrounding her hall. Sigurðr, however, does so, thus fulfilling the condition laid on the man Brynhildr must wed, after first magically exchanging shapes with Gunnarr, whom Brynhildr must accept as her husband, although it was Sigurðr she had expected to dare the fire. During a quarrel with Guðrún over precedence, the deception comes to light and Sigurðr is murdered at the instigation of Brynhildr, who choses to die on his funeral pyre.

In the *Nibelungenlied*, Brünhilt is the warrior-queen of Islant (presumably Iceland, although this has been disputed), and she too is won for Gunther by Sifrit, invisible in his magic cloak and Brünhilt's real opponent in three martial games, although Gunther appears to be the victor, thus fulfilling the condition for success imposed by Brünhilt on her suitors. Brünhilt will not allow consummation of her marriage to Gunther until he tells her why his sister, Kriemhilt, should enter into what seems to Brünhilt a *mésalliance* with Sifrit, who in Islant had pretended to be Gunther's liegeman and thus his feudal inferior. Sifrit, who had been given Kriemhilt's hand in marriage as a reward for his assistance in Islant, again comes to Gunther's aid. On the second night after Gunther's wedding, he seduces—chastely—the immensely strong Brünhilt, then leaves her to Gunther's embraces, her Amazon-like qualities being lost along with her virginity. Eventually, in the course of a quarrel over precedence, Kriemhilt, overstating the case, publicly calls Brünhilt Sifrit's "paramour" (in *Þiðreks saga*, Sigurðr actually deflowers Brynhildr), and Sifrit's part in the final subjugation of Gunther's wife is revealed. At Hagen's instigation (Hagen, the Burgundians' right-hand man, is not brother to Gunther, as Hǫgni

is to Gunnarr, but a distant kinsman), Sifrit's murder is plotted, and Hagen himself slays Sifrit when they are out hunting in the forest. Kriemhilt is distraught, while Brünhilt, who had also considered the need to take vengeance on Sifrit, is supremely and uncaringly arrogant.

The two fundamental differences between the two patterns are that in the *Nibelungenlied*, Brünhilt, as distinct from Brynhildr of *Vǫlsunga saga*, is not betrothed to Sifrit (Sigurðr), nor does she commit suicide, but sits "enthroned in her pride." In the *Nibelungenlied*, Brünhilt's anger and distress arise out of the deception practiced on her by Sifrit on the second night after her wedding, or for Sifrit's boasting about it to Kriemhilt, and because it has now become public knowledge.

The existence of the prior-betrothal theme in the North renders Brynhildr's feelings toward Sigurðr more complex. In *Vǫlsunga saga*, she refers to her deception by him at the same time that she shows her envy of Guðrún, who had the more eminent husband in Sigurðr; she is also in love with Sigurðr, and thus is jealous of Guðrún on that count, too. Moreover, in deceiving her, Sigurðr had made her perjure herself, for although Sigurðr braved the flames, she had to marry Gunnarr. Yet she had sworn to wed none but the man who rode through the fire, and her oath is broken. A broken oath, in pagan belief, brought doom to the perjurer, and Brynhildr's suicide may be seen as a heroic anticipation of that doom, although her self-immolation is best understood in the context of her love for Sigurðr: she is united in death to the man who in life was withheld from her, and whose downfall the code of vengeance, not invalidated by Sigurðr's enforced forgetfulness of her, impelled her to contrive. Although *Vǫlsunga saga* presents an integrated version of the eddic poems basic to the Sigurðr material, including those of the lost gathering, the treatment accorded these latter by the saga writer helps to make the precise path taken by Brynhildr's complex psychological development largely a matter of informed conjecture.

The less complex pattern of the *Nibelungenlied*, with no prior betrothal, no jealous love on Brünhilt's part, and no suicide, is very likely the narrative core of the Brynhildr/Brünhilt legend that became elaborated in Scandinavia. This core contains a further element found both in the *Nibelungenlied* and in the North. In the *Nibelungenlied*, Hagen takes action not so much to avenge the deceived and insulted Brünhilt as to get rid of Sifrit, regarded as a threat to the royal power, and to seize his immense wealth, including the Nibelung treasure. In the northern variants, it is mainly Brynhildr, although to some extent Gunnarr, who expresses this envy-fear theme, while Hǫgni is opposed to Sigurðr's murder; it is his younger brother, Guttormr, who slays Sigurðr (in the old *Brot af Sigurðarkviðu*, Hǫgni and Gunnarr together slay Sigurðr). The differences may largely be due to the changing emphasis given to Brynhildr/Brünhilt's role in the different versions of the material. In *Þiðreks saga*, she is the main instigator of Sigurðr's murder, Hǫgni simply carrying out the deed, and she voices her belief that Sigurðr poses a threat to them all, the better to ensure that action is taken for the wrong done to her. In the *Nibelungenlied*, she plays a less prominent role in this respect, where Hagen is the main instigator, as well as Sifrid's murderer, and the main propounder of the envy-fear theme. In the North, Brynhildr's role receives the fullest development, and her feelings regarding the threat posed by Sigurðr receive their most vehement expression. The envy-fear theme is a basic ingredient in a probably historically derived nucleus worked upon over the centuries by the poetic imagination.

That the more complex Brynhildr/Brünhilt pattern was known solely in the North has been disputed. Just as there are hints in Part II of the *Nibelungenlied* of an older version, so, it is suggested, there are hints in Part I of the prior-betrothal theme, for there Sifrit clearly knows about Brünhilt and is able to guide Gunther's wooing expedition to Islant. Moreover, Sifrit is recognized on the approach of the expedition, and on his arrival is the first to be greeted by Brünhilt, and without introduction. These and other so-called "hints" need be nothing of the kind; they can be accounted for by the special knowledge often attributed to heroes, by the fact that Sifrit's fame went before him, that his preeminent heroic qualities made him instantly recognizable, and by reference to the social mores of the age. *Þiðreks saga* does tell of a prior meeting, without a betrothal, between Sigurðr and Brynhildr before Sigurðr's marriage, but that meeting, along with a later retrospective reference to a betrothal, may well be due to the influence of the northern tradition on the German-based saga. It is safer to consider the prior betrothal and associated motifs as belonging together with other northern innovations in the cycle, such as the genealogical links connecting Sigurðr, his father Sigmundr, his grandfather Vǫlsungr, and his whole line with the Norse god Óðinn, and those that make Brynhildr into Atli's sister; or the lays in the *Poetic Edda* that tell of the exploits of Sigurðr's half-brother, Helgi, or yet the new theme of Guðrún's unsuccessful attempt at suicide that replaces her death on the completion of her vengeance at Atli's court, a device that links the cycle to the legends of Jǫrmunrekkr, historically the 4th-century ruler of the Ostrogoths, Ermanaric. Then there is the sudden appearance of Áslaug, unaccountably Sigurðr's daughter by Brynhildr, who provides a link with *Ragnars saga loðbrókar* and the Norwegian royal line.

A further innovation is that Hǫgni's son, Niflungr (or Hniflungr), assists Guðrún in her vengeance. It probably reflects a late development whereby Hǫgni, after being mortally wounded, begets a son who becomes his father's avenger and, according to *Þiðreks saga*, starves Attila (in a different version Grímhildr, in another both of them) to death in the Niflungs' treasure chamber.

A possible innovative link is the identification in *Vǫlsunga saga* of the sleeping valkyrie awakened by Sigurðr in the eddic *Sigrdrífumál* as Brynhildr, for in *Sigrdrífumál* her name is not Brynhildr but Sigrdrífa, and there is no betrothal. She need not have been the maiden whom Sigurðr wooed on Gunnarr's behalf. The sleeping-valkyrie adventure may have been an exploit originally independent of the central core of the legends, as are the hero's other youthful exploits, his slaying of a dragon (thought by some to be his father Sigmundr's exploit later transferred to him), and his acquisition of great wealth, the precise details and the associated themes differing from one version to another, but all supplying the victim of the murder plot with suitable heroic antecedents.

The original themes have thus undergone constant remodeling and expansion so as to embrace originally unrelated heroic legends, not least of these being those associated with Þiðrekr of Bern (in German, Dietrich), the reflex in legend of Theodoric, the 5th-century Ostrogothic ruler of Italy.

In addition to the *Poetic Edda*, *Vǫlsunga saga*, *Þiðreks saga*, and the *Nibelungenlied*, there is a brief version of the material in Snorri Sturluson's *Prose Edda*, and various aspects (not excluding further variations and accretions) are dealt with in the North by the 14th-century *Nornagests þáttr*, the late Icelandic metrical romances called *Vǫlsungsrímur*, various ballads in Norwegian,

Swedish, Danish, and Faroese, and the *Hven Chronicle*, a Danish translation made in 1603 of a lost Latin original; while in Germany there are, in addition to certain of the Dietrich poems, *Seifrid de Ardemont* (where Siegfried becomes a knight of the Round Table), the *Anhang zum Heldenbuch*, and the late *Lied vom Hürnen Seyfrid*. References to characters from the cycle are found in *Eiríksmál*, in *Flateyjarbók*, in the Old English poems *Beowulf*, the *Fight at Finnsburh*, *Widsith*, and *Waldere*, in the medieval Latin *Waltharius*, and occasionally in medieval historical chronicles, such as Simon Kezai's *Chronica Hungarorum*. Such names as Haguno, Kriemhilt, Nipulunc, Sigfrid, and Welisunc (Vǫlsungr) appear in German deeds and charters as early as the 8th century.

Although the Siegfried story is probably rooted in historical events overlaid with fairy tale and myth, both fairy tale and myth have been regarded as its primary source: Siegfried is either a heroicized fairy-tale character, or the counterpart of a mythic divine being, for instance, the redeeming god who slays in spring the dragon of winter; his death parallels that of the vegetation god, and he has been linked with the Norse god Baldr. Siegfried's historical prototype has admittedly never been positively identified, unlike those of Gunnarr/Gunther and his father, Gjúki/Gibeche, and brother Guttormr/Giselher, whose prototypes were members of the Burgundian royal house. But suggestions are not lacking: the Ostrogoth Araja, the German national hero Arminius, and Sigibert, Merovingian ruler of Austrasia, who was the husband of the Visigothic princess Brunichildis and was murdered in 575 at the behest of Fredegundis, wife of his brother, Chilperich, with whom Sigibert was at war. The doom of Gunther/Gunnarr and Hagen/Hǫgni is based on the historical destruction in 437 of the Burgundians by the Huns, not led on this occasion by Attila. Attila died from natural causes on his wedding night in 453 after marrying a Germanic maiden named Hildico. Legend rapidly made Hildico into Attila's murderer and associated his death, as an act of vengeance, with the downfall of the Burgundians, now effected by Attila himself.

The term "Niflungs/Nibelungs" may have a historical basis and perhaps derive from the city of Nivelles, an important Merovingian center, although its likely connection with Old High German *nebul*, Old Norse *nifl* 'mist' suggests a link with supernatural "mist dwellers," a term appropriate for the dwarfs often associated with the Niflungr/Niblung treasure. Hǫgni himself is said in *Þiðreks saga* to have been begotten by an "elf" (*álfr*). Vǫlsungr may contain the name Vǫlsi, a phallic fetish in *Vǫlsa þáttr*, and thus have associations with a fertility cult.

The transmission and diffusion of the early legends have been much debated. It is likely that heroic Germanic traditions were perpetuated orally not only in poetic form, but also outside it, that there existed different, parallel, versions of a given legend, and that these could influence each other. This relative lack of thematic stability does not necessarily imply the validity of the Parry-Lord Yugoslavian-based theories of improvised oral poetry for the Germanic area, and certainly not for the eddic lays.

The ancient tales are not recorded exclusively on parchment and paper, for scenes from them are found carved in wood and stone in Sweden, Norway, Denmark, England, and the Isle of Man, for example, Sigurðr slaying the dragon, Sigurðr and Gunnarr with Brynhildr, Hǫgni's heart being cut out, and Gunnarr in the snake pit. The Swedish Överhogdal tapestry also depicts Vǫlsung motifs.

There is no doubt as to the influence exerted by the central legends of the cycle on the literary imagination, both early, as revealed by the structure of the Icelandic *Laxdœla saga*, or later, as shown by Hans Sachs's 16th-century German *Der Hürnen Seyfrid*, by the 18th-century German *Volksbuch vom gehörnten Sigfrid*, by several 19th-century reworkings of the material, such as Friedrich Hebbel's, and especially Richard Wagner's, *Ring des Nibelungen*, or in our own century by Max Mell's *Der Nibelunge Not*.

Bib.: Holtsmark, Anne. "Heltediktning." *KLNM* 6 (1961), 418–9; Holtsmark, Anne. "Sigurdsdiktningen." *KLNM* 15 (1970), 230–1; Harris, Joseph. "Eddic Poetry." In *Old Norse–Icelandic Literature: A Critical Guide*. Ed. Carol J. Clover and John Lindow. Islandica, 45. Ithaca and London: Cornell University Press, 1985 [esp. pp. 133–7]. **Lit.**: Heusler, Andreas. *Nibelungensage und Nibelungenlied: Die Stoffgeschichte des deutschen Heldenepos*. Dortmund: Ruhfus, 1920; 5th ed. 1955; Tonnelat, Ernest. *La Chanson des Nibelungen. Étude sur la composition et la formation du poème épique*. Paris: Société d'Édition; Les Belles Lettres, 1926; Schütte, Gudmund. *Sigfrid und Brünhild. Ein als Mythus verkannter historischer Roman aus der Merowingerzeit*. Copenhagen: Aschehoug; Jena: Frommann, 1935; Boor, Helmut de. "Hat Siegfried gelebt?" *Beiträge zur Geschichte der deutschen Sprache und Literatur* 63 (1939), 250–71; rpt. in *Zur germanisch-deutschen Heldensage. Sechzehn Aufsätze zum neuen Forschungsstand*. Ed. Karl Hauck. Wege der Forschung, 14. Darmstadt: Wissenschaftliche Buchgesellschaft, 1961, pp. 31–51; Baesecke, Georg. *Vor- und Frühgeschichte des deutschen Schrifttums. 1: Vorgeschichte*. Halle: Niemeyer, 1940; Kralik, Dietrich von. *Die Siegfriedtrilogie im Nibelungenlied und in der Thidrekssaga*. Part 1. Halle: Niemeyer, 1941; Ellis, Hilda R. "Sigurd in the Art of the Viking Age." *Antiquity* 16 (1942), 216–36; Askeberg, Fritz. *Norden och kontinenten i gammal tid. Studier i forngermansk kulturhistoria*. Uppsala: Almqvist & Wiksell, 1944; Schneider, Hermann. *Die deutschen Lieder von Siegfrieds Tod*. Weimar: Böhlau, 1947; Kuhn, Hans. "Brünhilds und Siegfrieds Tod." *Zeitschrift für deutsches Altertum und deutsche Literatur* 82 (1948), 191–9; Ellis Davidson, Hilda R. "Gods and Heroes in Stone." In *The Early Cultures of North-West Europe*. H. H. Chadwick Memorial Studies. Ed. Cyril Fox and Bruce Dickins. Cambridge: Cambridge University Press, 1950; Panzer, Friedrich. "Das russische Brautwerbermärchen im Nibelungenlied." *Beiträge zur Geschichte der deutschen Sprache und Literatur* 72 (1950), 463–98; rpt. in *Zur germanisch-deutschen Heldensage*, pp. 138–69 [with afterword by Theodor Frings, pp. 170–2]; Beyschlag, Siegfried. "Das Motiv der Macht bei Siegfrieds Tod." *Germanisch-romanische Monatsschrift* 33 (1952), 95–108; supplemented rpt. in *Zur germanisch-deutschen Heldensage*, pp. 195–213; Kuhn, Hans. "Heldensage vor und ausserhalb der Dictung." In *Edda, Skalden, Saga: Festschrift zum 70. Geburtstag von Felix Genzmer*. Ed. Hermann Schneider. Heidelberg: Winter, 1952; rpt. in *Zur germanisch-deutschen Heldensage*, pp. 173–94; Tonnelat, Ernest. *La légende des Nibelungen en Allemagne au XIXe siècle*. Publications de la Faculté des Lettres de l'Université de Strasbourg, 119. Paris: Société d'Édition; Les Belles Lettres, 1952; Wais, Kurt. *Frühe Epik Westeuropas und die Vorgeschichte des Nibelungenliedes*. Erster Band. Mit einem Beitrag von Hugo Kuhn, *Brunhild und das Kriemheldlied*. Tübingen: Niemeyer, 1953; Beyschlag, Siegfried. "Die Erschliessung der Vorgeschichte der Nibelungen." *Germanisch-romanische Monatsschrift* 35 (1954), 257–65; Schröder, Franz Rolf. "Mythos und Heldensage." *Germanisch-romanische Monatsschrift* 36 (1955), 1–21; rpt. in *Zur germanisch-deutschen Heldensage*, pp. 285–35; See, Klaus von. "Die Werbung um Brünhild." *Zeitschrift für deutsches Altertum und deutsche Literatur* 88 (1957–58), 1–20; rpt. in his *Edda, Saga, Skaldendichtung. Aufsätze zur skandinavischen Literatur des Mittelalters*. Heidelberg: Winter, 1981, pp. 194–213; Schneider,

Hermann, and Wolfgang Mohr. "Heldendichtung." In *Reallexikon der deutschen Literaturgeschichte*. 2nd ed. Ed. Werner Kohlschmidt and Wolfgang Mohr. Berlin: de Gruyter, 1958, vol. 2, pp. 631–46; rpt. with minor changes in *Zur germanisch-deutschen Heldensage*, pp. 1–30; See, Klaus von. "Freierprobe und Königinnenzank in der Sigfridsage." *Zeitschrift für deutsches Altertum und deutsche Literatur* 89 (1959), 163–72; rpt. in his *Edda, Saga, Skaldendichtung*, pp. 214–23; Schröder, Franz Rolf. "Siegfrieds Tod." *Germanisch-romanische Monatsschrift* 41 (1960), 111–22; Höfler, Otto. *Siegfried, Arminius und die Symbolik. Mit einem historischen Anhang über die Varusschlacht*. Heidelberg: Winter, 1961; Schneider, Hermann. *Germanische Heldensage*. 2 vols. Grundriss der germanischen Philologie, 10. Berlin: de Gruyter, 1962; Wolf, Alois. *Gestaltungskerne und Gestaltungsweisen in der altgermanischen Heldendichtung*. Munich: Fink, 1965; Andersson, Theodore M. "The Textual Evidence for an Oral Family Saga." *Arkiv för nordisk filologi* 81 (1966), 1–23; Ploss, Emil. *Siegfried-Sigurd der Drachenkämpfer. Untersuchungen zur germanisch-deutschen Heldensage. Zugleich ein Beitrag zur Entwicklungsgeschichte des alteuropäischen Erzählgutes*. Beihefte der Bonner Jahrbücher, 17. Cologne and Graz: Böhlau, 1966; Finch, R. G. "Brunhild and Siegfried." *Saga-Book of the Viking Society* 17 (1967–68), 224–60; Krause, Helmut K. "Die Darstellung von Siegfrieds Tod und die Entwicklung des Hagenbildes in der Nibelungendichtung." *Germanisch-romanische Monatsschrift* 21 (1971), 369–78; Blindheim, Martin. *Sigurds saga i middelalderens billedkunst*. Oslo: Universitetets Oldsaksamling, 1972; Haymes, Edward R. *Mündliches Epos in mittelhochdeutscher Zeit*. Göppingen: Kümmerle, 1975; Beck, Heinrich. "Brynhilddichtung und Laxdœla saga." In *Festgabe für Otto Höfler zum 75. Geburtstag*. Ed. Helmut Birkhan *et al.* Philologica Germanica, 3. Vienna: Braumüller, 1976, pp. 1–14; Caples, Cynthia B. "The Man in the Snakepit and the Iconography of the Sigurd Legend." *Rice University Studies* 62.2 (1976), 1–16; Haymes, Edward R. "Oral Poetry and the Germanic Heldenlied." *Rice University Studies* 62.2 (1976), 47–54; Toman, Lore. "Der Aufstand der Frauen. Ein strukturalistischer Blick auf die Brünhild-Sage." *Literatur und Kritik* 131 (1979), 25–32; Andersson, Theodore M. *The Legend of Brynhild*. Islandica, 43. Ithaca and London: Cornell University Press, 1980; Buchholz, Peter. *Vorzeitkunde. Mündliches Erzählen und Überliefern im mittelalterlichen Skandinavien nach dem Zeugnis von Fornaldarsaga und eddischer Dichtung*. Skandinavistische Studien, 13. Neumünster: Wachholtz, 1980; Harris, Joseph. "Eddic Poetry as Oral Poetry: The Evidence of Parallel Passages in the Helgi Poems for Questions of Composition and Performance." In *Edda: A Collection of Essays*. Ed. Robert J. Glendinning and Haraldur Bessason. University of Manitoba Icelandic Studies, 4. Winnipeg: University of Manitoba Press, 1983, pp. 210–42; Vestergaard, Elisabeth. "Gudrun/Kriemhild—søster eller hustru?" *Arkiv för nordisk filologi* 99 (1984), 63–78; Harris, Joseph. "Eddic Poetry." In *Old Norse–Icelandic Literature: A Critical Guide*. Ed. Carol J. Clover and John Lindow. Islandica, 45. Ithaca and London: Cornell University Press, 1985, pp. 111–26, 138–43; Finch, Ronald G. "The Icelandic and German Sources of Wagner's *Ring of the Nibelung*." *Leeds Studies in English* 17 (1986), 1–23; Haymes, Edward R. *The Nibelungenlied: History and Interpretation*. Urbana: University of Illinois Press, 1986; Andersson, Theodore M. *A Preface to the Nibelungenlied*. Stanford: Stanford University Press, 1987.

†R. G. Finch

[**See also:** *Atlakviða*; *Atlamál*; *Codex Regius*; Eddic Poetry; *Eiríksmál*; *Flateyjarbók*; *Grípisspá*; *Guðrúnarkviða I–III*; *Guðrúnarhvǫt*; *Hamðismál in fornu*; *Helreið Brynhildar*; *Laxdœla saga*; *Nornagests þáttr*; *Oddrúnargrátr*; *Ragnars saga loðbrókar*; *Reginsmál* and

Fáfnismál; Sigrdrífumál; Sigurðarkviða in skamma; Sigurðarkviðu, Brot af; Snorra Edda; Þiðreks saga af Bern; Vǫlsunga saga; Women in Eddic Poetry]

Vǫlsunga saga ("The Saga of the Vǫlsungar"), one of the *fornaldarsǫgur*, was written not later than around 1260–1270, probably in Iceland rather than in Norway. The one vellum MS, NkS 1824b 4to, dates from around 1400; the fairly numerous paper MSS, variously located and dating from the 17th to the 19th century, derive from it.

The saga tells of Sigurðr's ancestors, descendants of Óðinn, including Vǫlsungr, Sigurðr's grandfather, and especially of Sigurðr's father, Sigmundr. It then tells of Sigurðr himself, how he slew a dragon, Fáfnir, brother of Reginn, Sigurðr's foster-father, acquired its accursed gold, and became betrothed to the valkyrie Brynhildr. A magic potion, administered by Grímhildr, King Gjúki's queen, makes Sigurðr forget Brynhildr, and he marries Grímhildr's daughter, Guðrún, sister to Gunnarr, Hǫgni, and Guttormr. Gunnarr now seeks Brynhildr's hand, but cannot ride through the flames surrounding her castle. Sigurðr and Gunnarr exchange shapes by magic, and Sigurðr/Gunnarr's wooing is successful. But Brynhildr, in the course of a quarrel with Guðrún, eventually discovers the deception and brings about Sigurðr's downfall by alleging Sigurðr's intimacy with her when he came to her as Gunnarr. Guttormr, unlike his elder brothers, is not bound to Sigurðr by oaths of blood-brotherhood; he slays Sigurðr, who avenges himself before dying. Brynhildr now declares Sigurðr's innocence, stabs herself, and dies on Sigurðr's funeral pyre. After the death of Sigurðr, Guðrún is married to Atli, Brynhildr's brother. Greedy for Sigurðr's treasure, now owned by Guðrún's brothers, Atli invites them to a feast and treacherously takes them prisoner. Gunnarr refuses to tell Atli where the gold lies hidden while Hǫgni lives. On seeing Hǫgni's bloody heart, he exults that now he alone knows the secret and that Atli never will. Gunnarr is put to death in a snake pit. Guðrún takes vengeance on Atli by giving him his sons' hearts to eat and their blood to drink. Helped by Hǫgni's son, Niflungr, she slays Atli, then sets fire to his hall. Guðrún marries a third husband, Jónakr, and incites their sons, Sǫrli, Hamðir, and Erpr, to take vengeance on Jǫrmunrekkr for the killing of Svanhildr, her daughter by Sigurðr. Jǫrmunrekkr had sent his son, Randvér, to ask for her hand on his behalf. Svanhildr was given to him, but Bikki, Jǫrmunrekkr's counselor, said she was a more fitting bride for Randvér. Jǫrmunrekkr was furious, and had his son hanged and Svanhildr trampled to death by horses.

Vǫlsunga saga forms a probably independent "prologue" to *Ragnars saga loðbrókar* and is linked to it by Áslaug, said to be daughter of Brynhildr and Sigurðr (of Óðinn's line), whom Ragnarr marries, thus providing a divine progenitor for Hákon Hákonarson, king of Norway, a descendant of the historical Ragnarr. Some assign the connecting Áslaug episode to *Vǫlsunga saga*, others to *Ragnars saga*.

Despite structural defects (*e.g.*, Brynhildr and Sigurðr are twice betrothed, and Brynhildr's residence varies between a flame-encircled castle, a "shield castle," and a normal Norse hall), this saga is at least as compelling as most of its genre.

The prose of *Vǫlsunga saga* has thirty inset stanzas; indeed, the main body of its narrative material is a retelling of certain heroic lays preserved in the *Codex Regius* MS of the *Poetic Edda*; the MS was probably not used by the saga writer. Moreover, it includes a version of the poems contained in a gathering now lost from that MS. Some argue for a prose provenance for chs. 24–28, and a postulated **Sigurðar saga* could have supplied material not deriving from the *Poetic Edda*; *Þiðreks saga* supplied at least ch. 23, probably as an addition by a later interpolator.

Ed.: Olsen, Magnus. *Vǫlsunga saga ok Ragnars saga loðbrókar.* Samfund til udgivelse af gammel nordisk litteratur, 36. Copenhagen: Møller, 1906–8; Finch, R. G., ed. and trans. *The Saga of the Volsungs.* London: Nelson, 1965. **Tr.**: Eiríkr Magnússon and William Morris. *Vǫlsunga Saga: The Story of the Volsungs and Niblungs, with Certain Songs from the Elder Edda.* London: Ellis, 1870 [various reissues, the most recent with an introduction and glossary by Robert W. Gutman (New York: Collier, 1972)]; Schlauch, Margaret, trans. *The Saga of the Vǫlsungs: The Saga of Ragnar Lodbrok, Together with the Lay of Kraka.* Scandinavian Classics, 35. New York: American-Scandinavian Foundation; Norton; London: Allen & Unwin, 1930; 2nd ed. 1949; Finch, R. G., ed. and trans. [see above]; Anderson, George K. *The Saga of the Völsungs: Together with Excerpts from the Nornagests tháttr and Three Chapters from the Prose Edda.* Newark: University of Delaware Press, 1982; Byock, Jesse L., trans. *The Saga of the Volsungs: The Norse Epic of Sigurd the Dragonslayer.* Berkeley, Los Angeles, and London: University of California Press, 1990. **Bib.**: Schier, Kurt. *Sagaliteratur.* Sammlung Metzler, M78. Stuttgart: Metzler, 1970. **Lit.**: Jackson, Jess H. "Óðinn's Meetings with Sigmundr and Sigurðr in the *Vǫlsungasaga*." *Modern Language Notes* 43 (1928), 307–8; Wieselgren, Per. *Quellenstudien zur Vǫlsungasaga.* Acta et Commentationes Universitatis Tartuensis, 34.3, 37.5, 38.2. Tartu: Mattiesen, 1935–36; Finch, R. G. "The Treatment of Poetic Sources by the Compiler of *Vǫlsunga saga*." *Saga-Book of the Viking Society* 16.4 (1965), 315–53; Halvorsen, E. F. "*Vǫlsunga saga*." *KLNM* 22 (1976), 347–49; McTurk, Rory. "The Relationship of *Ragnars saga loðbrókar* to *Þiðriks saga af Bern*." In *Sjötíu ritgerðir helgaðar Jakobi Benediktssyni 20. júlí 1977.* 2 vols. Ed. Einar G. Pétursson and Jónas Kristjánsson. Reykjavik: Stofnun Árna Magnússonar, 1977, vol. 2, pp. 568–85; Andersson, Theodore M. *The Legend of Brynhild.* Islandica, 43. Ithaca and London: Cornell University Press, 1980; Finch, Ronald G. "*Atlakviða, Atlamál* and *Vǫlsunga saga*: A Study in Combination and Integration." In *Specvlvm Norroenvm: Norse Studies in Memory of Gabriel Turville-Petre.* Ed. Ursula Dronke *et al.* Odense: Odense University Press, 1981, pp. 123–38; Clover, Carol J. "*Vǫlsunga saga* and the Missing Lai of Marie de France." In *Sagaskemmtun: Studies in Honour of Hermann Pálsson on His 65th Birthday, 26th May 1976.* Ed. Rudolf Simek *et al.* Vienna, Cologne, and Graz: Böhlau, 1986, pp. 79–84.

†R. G. Finch

[See also: *Codex Regius;* Eddic Poetry; *Fornaldarsǫgur; Ragnars saga loðbrókar; Þiðreks saga af Bern;* Vǫlsung-Niflung Cycle; Women in Eddic Poetry]

Vǫlundarkviða ("The Lay of Vǫlundr") is the tenth poem in the *Codex Regius*, known familiarly as the *Poetic Edda*. It appears between the mythological poems *Þrymskviða* and *Alvíssmál*, although standard editions of the collection, with the exception of Neckel/Kuhn, place it after *Alvíssmál* at the head of the heroic group. Vǫlundr (modern English *Wayland*, Old English *Weland*, German *Welent*, French *Galant*) is a legendary smith, but his Norse appellation "Lord of Elves" (*álfa dróttinn*) seems to have led the MS redactor into associating him with myth. Vǫlundr is probably not a native figure of Scandinavian lore. The skiing and hunting mentioned in the poem suggest a possible Finnish origin for the legend, though it is impossible to ascertain how old the figure of an archetypal smith (e.g., Ilmarinen in the *Kalevala*) actually is. The name Vǫlundr, however, is unrecorded before this poem, and figures in no early Scandinavian place-names. It may reflect the Norse root *vél* 'magic, cunning, artifice,' a sense clearly played upon in the poem (st. 20): *vél gerði hann heldr hvatt Níðuði* ("marvels he wrought, fiercely for Níðuðr"). Another possible root is Gallo-Roman *walare* 'disposed to live well.' Other names in the poem do not help, though some scholars have suspected Irish origin, since the poem's introductory prose mentions a Gaulish king Kjárr, apparently cognate with Old Irish *Ceaghall*, although Latin *Caesar* is possible. Others have sought a Gothic origin for the legend, since the Old English *Waldere* mentions Vǫlundr's son, Widia, who has been identified with the Vithigabius of Ammianus Marcellinus's 4th-century *Rerum gestarum* and with the "rex fortissimus Vidigoia" in Jordanes's 6th-century *Getica*, although neither the name nor the exploits of Vǫlundr are alluded to in these documents. The later and longer account of Vǫlundr and his son are contained in the 13th-century *Velents saga smiðs*, which forms part of the compendious *Þiðreks saga af Bern*. Here, Velent is said to be "the excellent smith whom the Varangians call Vǫlundr." Vǫlundr's brother in this account, Egill, appears early in Norse poetry, in a *vísa* by Eyvindr Finnsson skáldaspillir ("plagiarist"), and in the *Skáldskaparmál* of Snorri Sturluson, both times in a kenning for bow, *Egils vápn* ("Egill's weapon"). This scant evidence of an earlier archer legend suggests that the *Vǫlundarkviða* might well be an accretion of a native story with a continental myth.

Linguistic evidence would date the poem from the 9th century, according to both Bellows (1923) and Vigfússon and Powell (1905). The story was known to the English at this time, for the Old English poem *Deor* devotes a strophe each to the physical woes of Weland and the moral dilemma of Beaduhild, pregnant with the child of her brothers' killer. That poem's strophic form and alliterative refrain, however, have suggested to many critics a Norse origin. The 8th-century Franks Casket, now in the British Museum, depicts what appear to be scenes from the story of Vǫlundr, showing a smith at his anvil, over the bodies of two boys, receiving a cup from a woman (or giving one to her). The Old English poem *Beowulf* (l. 455) mentions Weland as the maker of the hero's mailshirt.

The poem *Vǫlundarkviða*, consisting of forty-one stanzas of two to five alliterative *fornyrðislag* lines (159 lines in all), with prose introduction and two brief prose interpolations, can be divided into four narrative units. The first five stanzas describe the capture, or embrace, of Vǫlundr and his two brothers by three swan-maidens; the prose introduction has it the other way round: the brothers capture the maidens. After a stay of eight years, the maidens depart. Vǫlundr sits fashioning jewelry, awaiting the return of Hervǫr, while his two brothers go searching for their women. The next section of twelve stanzas describes the theft of one of Vǫlundr's rings and his subsequent capture by King Níðuðr ("evil-destroyer," or "condition-of-enmity"?). A prose interpolation notes that the ring is given to the king's daughter, Bǫðvildr ("war-battle, desire-of-battle"?), while Níðuðr keeps Vǫlundr's sword for himself. The queen orders Vǫlundr to be deprived of his *sina magni* ("power of sinews"). Another prose intervention localizes the maiming in the knees before Vǫlundr is set on an island

to manufacture jewelry for the king. The third part of the poem, stanzas 18–29, comprises Vǫlundr's double revenge. First, he kills the two sons of Níðuðr and makes jeweled cups of their skulls; then, he seduces the king's daughter when she brings him her broken ring to repair. The last twelve stanzas of the poem recount Vǫlundr's boastful revelation of his acts, his flight from the island despite the king's archers by means of wings he has fashioned, and, finally, Níðuðr's lament.

Of the poem's narrative features, or motifs, the swan-maiden episode is unique to this version of the story. The capture and vengeance of Vǫlundr are alluded to in *Deor*, the Franks Casket, and *Velents saga*, while the archers are present in *Velents saga*, where it is Vǫlundr's own brother, Egill, who is ordered to shoot him down. *Vǫlundarkviða* contains at least seven distinct conventional motifs: (1) swan-maiden, or valkyries, (2) theft of a single fetish treasure, (3) a lame smith, (4) an archer (in the *Velents saga* version, Níðuðr has Egill prove his skill as an archer by shooting an apple off the head of his son, a folktale motif that must have had wide currency in Europe before being fixed popularly to the Swiss hero William Tell in the 14th century), (5) serving a child's body to the father, (6) making wings for flight from imprisonment, and (7) performance of vengeance through a sexual act. The collocation of these elements in a single poem suggests that it embodies a regeneration myth, which can be summed up as follows: a male fertility force prospers until his mate deserts him. A destructive force renders the hero powerless until he regains his powers in an act of destruction followed by conception of life. The coupling with the daughter of his oppressor replaces, or reestablishes, a sexual act of which he is deprived when his own "wife" leaves him. Regaining his ring and his power combines fetish treasure with sexual conception. The fabrication of wings offers him an efficient means of pursuing his lost maiden. Such a mythic structure is not uncommon in the mythological poems of the *Poetic Edda*. A remarkably close analogy occurs in *Þrymskviða*, which tells the story of Þórr's loss of his hammer and his recovery of it in a mock wedding ceremony that turns into a slaughter of his enemy and the saving of Freyja, goddess of fertility, for the gods. *Þrymskviða* immediately precedes *Vǫlundarkviða* in the MS.

Ed.: Gudbrand Vigfusson and F. York Powell, eds. and trans. *Origines Islandicae: A Collection of the More Important Sagas and Other Native Writings Relating to the Settlement and Early History of Iceland*. 2 vols. Oxford: Clarendon, 1905; rpt. Millwood: Kraus, 1976; Gordon, E. V. *An Introduction to Old Norse*. 2nd ed. rev. Arnold Taylor. Oxford: Clarendon, 1957; Ólafur Briem, ed. *Edduskvæði*. Íslenzk úrvalsrit, 5. Reykjavik: Skálholt, 1968 [in normalized modern Icelandic orthography]; Jón Helgason, ed. *Eddadigte*. 3 vols. Nordisk filologi, Tekster og lærebøger til universitetsbrug. A. Tekster. Oslo: Dreyer; Stockholm: Läromedelsförlagen; Copenhagen: Munksgaard, 1971, vol. 3; Neckel, Gustav, ed. *Edda: Die Lieder des Codex Regius nebst verwandten Denkmälern. I: Text*. 5th ed. rev. Hans Kuhn. Heidelberg: Winter, 1983. **Tr.**: Bellows, Henry Adams, trans. *The Poetic Edda*. New York: American-Scandinavian Foundation, 1923; rpt. Biblo & Tannen, 1969; Hollander, Lee M., trans. *The Poetic Edda, Translated with an Introduction and Explanatory Notes*. 2nd rev. ed. Austin: University of Texas Press, 1962; rpt. 1988; Taylor, Paul B., and W. H. Auden, trans. *The Elder Edda: A Selection*. London: Faber & Faber; New York: Random House, 1969; Terry, Patricia, trans. *Poems of the Vikings: The Elder Edda*. New York and Indianapolis: Bobbs-Merrill, 1969. **Lit.**: Bouman, A. C. "Vǫlundr as an Aviator." *Arkiv för nordisk filologi* 55 (1940), 27–42; Bouman, A. C. "On Vǫlundarkviða." *Neophilologus* 34

(1950), 169–73; Bouman, A. C. "Leodum is minum: Beaduhild's Lament." In his *Patterns in Old English and Old Icelandic Literature*. Leidse Germanistische en Anglistische Reeks, 1. Leiden: Leiden University Press, 1962, pp. 93–106; Taylor, Paul Beekman. "The Structure of *Vǫlundarkviða*." *Neophilologus* 47 (1963), 228–36; Burson, Anne. "Swan Maidens and Smiths: A Structural Study of *Vǫlundarkviða*." *Scandinavian Studies* 55 (1983), 1–19; Grimstad, Kaaren. "The Revenge of Vǫlundr." In *Edda: A Collection of Essays*. Ed. Robert J. Glendinning and Haraldur Bessason. University of Manitoba Icelandic Studies, 4. Winnipeg: University of Manitoba Press, 1983, pp. 187–209; Motz, Lotte. "New Thoughts on *Vǫlundarkviða*." *Saga-Book of the Viking Society* 22 (1986), 50–68; Dieterle, Richard L. "The Metallurgical Code of the *Vǫlundarkviða* and Its Theoretical Import." *History of Religions* 27 (1987), 1–31; McKinnell, John. "The Context of *Vǫlundarkiða*." *Saga-Book of the Viking Society* 23 (1990), 1–27.

Paul Beekman Taylor

[**See also:** *Codex Regius*; Eddic Meters; Eddic Poetry; Eyvindr Finnsson skáldaspillir; *Snorra Edda*; *Þiðreks saga af Bern*; *Þrymskviða*; Vǫlundr]

Vǫlundr is a craftsman of supernatural stature and endowment who appears in various areas of Germanic tradition. Named *Wieland* in German, *Wayland/Weland* in English, *Velent/Vǫlundr* in Icelandic, he partakes of folklore, myth, and literature.

His story is most fully recorded in *Vǫlundarkviða*, one of the older eddic poems, and in the Icelandic *Þiðreks saga af Bern*. In the eddic lay, Vǫlundr weds a swan-maiden who leaves him after several years of marriage. Waiting for her in sorrow, Vǫlundr forges priceless objects until he is attacked and captured by King Níðuðr. The craftsman is lamed on the queen's advice, and forced to create treasures for the king. Luring the king's sons to his workshop, Vǫlundr decapitates them, encases their skulls in silver, and sends these as drinking cups to Níðuðr. When the king's daughter breaks a ring that had been taken by the king's warriors from Vǫlundr, she goes to the smithy to have it mended. The artisan drugs her with beer, rapes and impregnates the young woman, and then rises into the air on wings he has constructed, announcing the extent of his vengeance to the king.

In *Þiðreks saga*, the craftsman's descent is traced to King Vilkinus, who begets a son, the giant Vaði, on a mermaid. Vaði fathers Velent and apprentices his son to dwarfs living in a mountain; there Velent learns his craft. His experiences of attack, mutilation, and revenge are similar to those of *Vǫlundarkviða*. But in the saga, the adventure ends in Velent's marriage to the princess and in begetting a son, the great hero Viðga, who joins the retinue of Þiðrekr.

The glorious craftsman is mentioned in the Old English poems *Deor* and *Waldere*, and Beowulf's mailshirt is designated as "Weland's creation." Wayland's Smithy is the name of a megalithic tomb in the Berkshire Downs of Wessex; here the craftsman is said to live, invisible to men, and to perform smith's work if payment is left at his door. The 8th-century Franks Casket depicts scenes from the craftsman's life. Place-names of Velent's story, as recorded in *Þiðreks saga*, indicate that it was set in northwestern Germany. The craftsman is thus encountered in English, Scandinavian, and German tradition, and partakes of Norse myth and English folklore, as well as heroic literature

Vǫlundr shares aspects with the dwarf smiths of Germanic folklore and mythology. He belongs, moreover, to a wider context;

many nations have the figure of a superhuman craftsman, such as Hephaistos of Greece or Ptah of Egypt. The act of craftsmanship in clay, stone, or metal was in archaic times apparently imbued with magical significance. We may assume that the legendary artisan originated at the time of craft specialization,

The swan-maiden episode, related in *Vǫlundarkviða*, also has worldwide diffusion, and was generated, in all likelihood, in communities of fishermen and hunters.

That a work of heroic literature should portray the triumph of an artisan over a warrior is unusual, and Vǫlundr's story has inspired many interpretations. Taylor (1963) and Grimstad (1983) believe that the eddic lay encapsules a ritual event, the ordeals and resurgence of initiation. Krappe (1930) and Ellis Davidson (1958) point to the folklore affinities. Dieterle (1987) detects themes relating to the importance of metalcraft. Burson (1983), employing a structural approach, reveals the presence of a folktale pattern; Motz (1986) indicates elements of northern hunting and fishing cultures.

Lit.: Maurus, P. *Die Wielandsage in der Literatur*. Münchener Beiträge zur romanischen und englischen Philologie, 25. Erlangen and Leipzig: Deichert, 1902; Krappe, Alexander Haggerty. "Zur Wielandsage." *Archiv für das Studium der neueren Sprachen und Literaturen* 158 (1930), 9–23; Vries, Jan de. "Bemerkungen zur Wielandsage." In *Edda, Skalden, Saga: Festschrift zum 70. Geburtstag von Felix Genzmer*. Ed. Hermann Schneider. Heidelberg: Winter, 1952, pp. 173–99; Ellis Davidson, H. R. "Weland the Smith." *Folklore* 69 (1958), 145–59; Taylor, Paul Beekman. "The Structure of *Vǫlundarkviða*." *Neophilologus* 47 (1963), 228–36; Becker, Alfred. *Franks Casket*. Regensburg: Winter, 1973; Burson, Anne. "Swan Maidens and Smiths: A Structural Study of *Vǫlundarkviða*." *Scandinavian Studies* 55 (1983), 1–19; Grimstad, Kaaren. "The Revenge of Vǫlundr." In *Edda: A Collection of Essays*. Ed. Robert J. Glendinning and Haraldur Bessason. University of Manitoba Icelandic Studies, 4. Winnipeg: University of Manitoba Press, 1983, pp. 187–209; Motz, Lotte. "New Thoughts on *Vǫlundarkviða*." *Saga-Book of the Viking Society* 22 (1986), 50–68; Dieterle, Richard L. "The Metallurgical Code of the *Vǫlundarkviða* and Its Theoretical Import." *History of Religions* 27 (1987), 1–31.

Lotte Motz

[**See also:** *Þiðreks saga af Bern*; *Vǫlundarkviða*]

Vǫluspá ("The Sybil's Prophecy") is the opening poem in the *Codex Regius* of the *Poetic Edda* (K, formerly GkS 2365 4to); another text appears in *Hauksbók* (H; *Vǫluspá* is in AM 544 4to), and Snorri uses the poem as a framework for much of *Gylfaginning*. In a series of brief flashes, it tells the story of the universe from its creation by the gods to its destruction (Ragnarǫk), and beyond.

The two main texts differ considerably: conventional stanza numbering (eds. Neckel 1983, Sigurður Nordal 1978) gives the poem sixty-six stanzas of *fornyrðislag* meter, but stanzas 34, 54, 65, and parts of 47 and 60 are not in K, while 28–33, 35:1–4, and 36–37 are not in H. Most of these stanzas are probably original, but the list of valkyries in stanza 30 may be interpolated; 34, on the punishment of Loki, looks likes an unsatisfactory alternative in H to 35:1–4 in K; and the authenticity of 65 has been much debated. The two texts of stanza 55, on Víðarr's slaying of Fenrir, are quite different; again, K seems superior. Stanzas 21–44 appear in H in a confused and illogical order; K's order of stanzas seems generally sound (see variously Sigurður Nordal ed. 1978, Schach

1983); but 37, on the halls of giants, may be misplaced (Boer 1904, McKinnell 1987). The list of dwarf names is probably interpolated: Sigurður Nordal (ed. 1978) and Schach (1983) reject stanzas 9–16, Björn M. Ólsen (1914) 11–16, Boyer (1983) 13–16. Björn M. Ólsen is probably correct not to exclude the creation of dwarfs, which could explain how the name list came to be interpolated, and dwarfs appear again at stanza 48.

Most modern interpretations of the poem's structure build on Sigurður Nordal (1970–71), although Dölvers (1969) proposes a "stream of consciousness" model with no planned structure. Three main parts, roughly corresponding to past, present, and future, are each marked by an irregularly recurring refrain, and the whole is articulated by a framework (sts. 1–2, 28–29, and probably 66). In the opening framework, the speaker demands a hearing, answers a request from Óðinn to relate the first things she remembers, and asserts her own antiquity, but without revealing the fictional situation.

She remembers the void (st. 3), before the gods made the earth and heavenly bodies, and regulated times and seasons (sts. 4–6), and created their own wealth, dwarfs, and men (sts. 7–10, 17–18). But their golden age is already troubled by three fearsome giant maidens (st. 8), and soon Yggdrasill and the norns have come into being (sts. 19–20), perhaps as patrons of change, introduced by the very act of creation. Anxiety and greed follow: the gods are visited by Gullveig ("intoxication of gold"), probably one of the Vanir and seemingly the poet's own invention. They attack and burn her, only to see her reborn as the witch Heiðr ("bright," sts. 21–22). War with the Vanir ensues, in which the Æsir lose their fortress wall (sts. 23–24), so that they must employ a giant builder and subsequently kill him because they cannot afford his price (sts. 25–26). Realizing that folly has made them oath breakers and murderers, Óðinn begins a quest for wisdom (st. 27), which motivates the framework by explaining his encounter with the prophetess who narrates the poem (sts. 28–29).

In the second section (sts. 30–44), the prophetess mocks Óðinn with the refrain: Vituð ér enn, eða hvat? ("Do you know enough yet, or what?"). Through his valkyries, Óðinn has become an agent of violent death (st. 30), and this comes to haunt the gods themselves, in the murder of Baldr and the vengeance taken for it (sts. 31–35). In an attempt to stem the rising moral chaos, the gods mete out harsh punishments to oath breakers, murderers, and seducers among men (sts. 36, 38–39), but this punishment only emphasizes their own corruption and encourages the preparations of the giants for bringing them down, until finally the bound wolf Fenrir breaks free (sts. 37, 40–44).

The third section (sts. 45–65) begins with the downfall of the gods (sts. 45–58). Moral and physical order will collapse amid universal fear (sts. 45–48); giants will converge from three directions (sts. 50–52). When battle begins, Óðinn will be killed by Fenrir but avenged by his son Víðarr (sts. 53–55); Þórr and the World Serpent will destroy each other (st. 56); the earth will sink into the sea and the heavens be consumed by fire (st. 57). But in stanzas 59–65, a new and purified earth rises, to be ruled over by the innocent gods, Baldr and Hǫðr, and inhabited in eternal happiness by trustworthy men; in stanza 65, they are joined by a supreme deity, possibly Christ. But stanza 66 reintroduces the corpse-bearing dragon Níðhǫggr; this could mean that evil, too, is reborn (Sigurður Nordal 1978–79, Turville-Petre 1964, Schach 1983), or even that time itself is seen as cyclic (Schjødt 1981), but it more probably reflects a return to the "present" of the frame-

work, with the prophetess emphasizing that Ragnarǫk is close at hand (Briem ed. 1968).

The extent of Christian influence on Vǫluspá has been debated. It seems unlikely to be directly indebted to the homilies of Wulfstan (so Butt 1969, but see Lindow 1987); but the moral framework, the idea of punishment or reward for human beings after death, the coming of inn ríki ("the mighty one"), and the obsession with the end of the world do suggest syncretic use of Christian material, notably the Book of Revelation. The poet, however, was probably not a Christian himself: the gods may be corrupt, but their fall is viewed with tragic sympathy, not with the hostility common among early Norse Christians.

Most opinion dates Vǫluspá to the late 10th or early 11th century. The valkyrie name Geirskǫgul (st. 30) may originate in a misunderstanding of Hákonarmál (st. 12), and Þorfinnsdrápa (st. 24) seems to echo Vǫluspá (st. 57); although uncertain, these points suggest a date between 961 and around 1064. Sigurður Nordal and others date the poem to the last years of West Norse heathenism and see it as colored by the millenarian fear of the imminent end of the world that swept northern Europe just before the year 1000 and again toward 1030.

Vǫluspá has been located in Norway (e.g., by Finnur Jónsson) and in the Danelaw in England (Butt 1969), but is usually considered Icelandic (Sigurður Nordal 1970–71, 1978–79, Turville-Petre 1964, Martin 1972, Schach 1983), chiefly because of imagery apparently derived from volcanic phenomena (see sts. 35, 41, 47, and notes in Sigurður Nordal ed. 1978). There are also several skaldic kennings (see, e.g., sts. 52, 57), and Sigurður Nordal (1978–79) guesses that the author may be the little-known skaldic poet Vǫlu-Steinn. Whoever composed it, Vǫluspá remains one of the most powerful and enigmatic of all Norse poems.

Ed.: Sijmons, B., and Hugo Gering, eds. *Die Lieder der Edda*. 3 vols. Halle: Waisenhaus, 1888–1931; Neckel, Gustav, ed. *Edda: Die Lieder des Codex Regius nebst verwandten Denkmälern. I: Text.* 5th ed. rev. Hans Kuhn. Heidelberg: Winter, 1983; Ólafur Briem, ed. *Eddukvæði.* Íslenzk úrvalsrit, 5. Reykjavik: Skálholt, 1968; Sigurður Nordal, ed. *Vǫluspá*. Trans. B. S. Benedikz and J. McKinnell. Durham and St. Andrews Medieval Texts, 1. Durham: Department of English Language and Medieval Literature, 1978. **Tr.**: Hollander, Lee M., trans. *The Poetic Edda, Translated with an Introduction and Explanatory Notes*. 2nd rev. ed. Austin: University of Texas Press, 1962; rpt. 1988. **Lit.**: Boer, R. C. "Kritik der Vǫluspá." *Zeitschrift für deutsche Philologie* 36 (1904), 289–370; Björn M. Ólsen. "Til Eddakvæderne. I. Til Vǫluspá." *Arkiv för nordisk filologi* 30 (1914), 129–69; Ulvestad, Bjarne. "How Old Are the Mythological Eddic Poems?" *Scandinavian Studies* 26 (1954), 49–69; Vries, Jan de. *Altnordische Literaturgeschichte*. 2 vols. Grundriss der germanischen Philologie, 15–16. Berlin: de Gruyter, 1941–42; rpt. 1964–67; Turville-Petre, E. O. G. *Myth and Religion of the North: The Religion of Ancient Scandinavia*. New York: Holt, Rinehart and Winston, 1964; rpt. Westport: Greenwood, 1975; Butt, Wolfgang. "Zur Herkunft der Vǫluspá." *Beiträge zur Geschichte der deutschen Sprache und Literatur* 91 (1969), 83–103; Dölvers, H. "Text, Gliederung und Deutung der Vǫluspá." *Zeitschrift für deutsches Altertum und deutsche Literatur* 98 (1969), 241–64; Polomé, Edgar C. "Some Comments on Vǫluspá, Stanzas 17–18." In *Old Norse Literature and Mythology: A Symposium*. Ed. Edgar C. Polomé. Austin: University of Texas Press, 1969, pp. 265–90; Sigurður Nordal. "Three Essays on Vǫluspá." Trans. B. S. Benedikz and J. S. McKinnell. *Saga-Book of the Viking Society* 18 (1970–71),

79–135; Martin, John Stanley. *Ragnarǫk: An Investigation into Old Norse Concepts of the Fate of the Gods.* Melbourne Monographs in Germanic Studies, 3. Assen: Van Gorcum, 1972; Sigurður Nordal. "The Author of *Vǫluspá.*" Trans. B. S. Benedikz. *Saga-Book of the Viking Society* 20 (1978–79), 114–30 [appeared originally as "Vǫlu-Steinn," *Iðunn* 8 (1924), 161–78]; Lönnroth, Lars. "*Iǫrð fannz æva né upphiminn*: A Formula Analysis." In *Specvlvm Norroenvm: Norse Studies in Memory of Gabriel Turville-Petre.* Ed. Ursula Dronke *et al.* Odense: Odense University Press, 1981, pp. 310–27; Schjødt, Jens Peter. "*Vǫluspá*—cyklisk tidsopfattelse i gammelnordisk religion." *Danske Studier* 76 (1981), 91–5; Boyer, Régis. "On the Composition of *Vǫlospá.*" In *Edda: A Collection of Essays.* Ed. Robert J. Glendinning and Haraldur Bessason. University of Manitoba Icelandic Studies, 4. Winnipeg: University of Manitoba Press, 1983, pp. 117–33; Schach, Paul. "Some Thoughts on *Vǫluspá.*" In *Edda: A Collection of Essays*, pp. 86–116; Harris, Joseph. "Eddic Poetry." In *Old Norse–Icelandic Literature: A Critical Guide.* Ed. Carol J. Clover and John Lindow. Islandica, 45. Ithaca and London: Cornell University Press, 1985, pp. 68–156; Lindow, John. "Norse Mythology and Northumbria: Methodological Notes." *Scandinavian Studies* 59 (1987), 308–24; McKinnell, J. "Norse Mythology and Northumbria: A Response." *Scandinavian Studies* 59 (1987), 325–37.

John McKinnell

[**See also**: *Codex Regius*; Eddic Meters; Eddic Poetry; *Hauksbók*; Mythology; *Snorra Edda*]

Warfare. The Scandinavian countries first came into the spotlight of European history in the medieval period, and therefore the preserved sources of information in Scandinavia are few for the early centuries. Nonetheless, through the Norse sagas, which were written down around the 13th century, we can gain an impression of the art of war during the early period of the Viking Age.

The primitive art of war was based on a *leiðangr* ("levy") organization in all of the Scandinavian countries, and thus the topography of the countries has great importance. Thick and large forests filled the inner part of Scandinavia as well as the Danish island realm, and made these countries difficult to traverse on land. Furthermore, for southern Denmark, the large woodlands in Holstein by Jutland's base formed a natural border toward Europe. The forests south of the Swedish lakes in what is now central Sweden protected Denmark's border toward the east. Thus, the regions of Scania, Halland, and Blekinge were naturally attached to Denmark. Also, in Norway, the mountainous areas formed an inner barrier, which meant that these mountains covered with forests were relatively impenetrable. Similarly, Sweden was enclosed by forests toward the south, west, and north, and therefore settlements gathered about the eastern lakes and outward toward the Baltic and from there along the coasts toward the north and south. Since the settlements were along the coasts, communication seldom took place over land, but instead along the coasts and by sea.

Given the topography of the countries, until the forests were cleared and routes by land made more passable, expeditions took place on sea, and attacks from enemies also took place from the seaward side. The war organization that Norway, Sweden, and Denmark could procure was therefore attached to the sea and went out from near-shore settlements. The *leiðangr* system is known in Denmark from provincial laws, which are preserved from around 1200, and reveal an organization that had its origins in the Viking Age. When exactly the *leiðangr* system arose is not known, but it seems to have been introduced almost simultaneously in all three countries. From around 1000, in the last part of the Viking Age, it is clear that the kings were able to raise themselves above the other Viking magnates with the help of the *leiðangr* organization.

The *leiðangr* system was based on a division of the country into counties (Old Norse *skipreiða*, Old Danish *skipæn*, Old Swedish *skiplagh*), which were again divided into parishes (Old Norse *manngerð, liði*, Old Danish *hafnæ*, Old Swedish *hamna*). In the county, a shipmaster (Old Norse *stýrimaðr*) was singled out, who would take care of the ship, the armament, the crew, and the provisions, and who had the command of the ship when it was at sea. The crew of the ship came from the parishes, each of which had to provide a member of the crew

In Sweden, there was a similar division of the country into *hund* and *hundare* for the armament of the ship and for providing the crew. In Norway, the division corresponds more or less to that in Denmark. When one of the countries was attacked, all men capable of bearing arms were duty-bound to defend their part of the country in a kind of militia.

The military organization was thus built up around a fleet of Viking ships. The ships were narrow, long, and light, and either used a single square sail or were rowed.

In addition, the kings' powers were based on the hird (*hirð*), with retainers (*hirðmenn*) and housecarls (*húskarlar*), who lived in the royal castle. Such a hird is known from Knud (Cnut) the Great's *Þingliði*, which he established in England in 1018. To this, a special law, the hird law (*Vederlov*) was attached. In addition, there were in the island realm of Denmark a number of circular fortifications. Such fortifications are now known in West Zealand near the Great Belt (Trelleborg), in Odense on Funen (Nonnebakken), in East Jutland near Hobro (Fyrkat), and by the Liim Fjord in North Jutland (Aggersborg). Their precise circular measurements and their regularity reveal a thorough technical knowledge and an efficient military organization, which clearly point to a strong royal power.

Leiðangr from around 1000 existed as a social duty. The historian Saxo (*ca.* 1200) tells of a reform of the *leiðangr* system around 1170, according to which only every fourth ship had to be armed and used as a watch force throughout the time of the year when navigation was possible. At the same time, the other countries, which did not provide ships, were to pay expenses and other kinds of duties. At this time, it is told that each member of the crew was to meet with a shield, sword, spear, and helmet, while the shipmaster also required a coat of mail and a crossbow. The development became more and more like the European pattern, where the shipmaster was called the "squire" and was obliged to provide a horse.

When battles in the Viking Age were fought on land, the war

forces were arranged for battle position in groups that jointly moved forward to fighting at close quarters after having first sent a volley of arrows against the enemy. The outcome of the battle was decided by man-to-man fighting. On sea, the outcome was similarly decided by an initial volley of arrows and then by an attempt to ram the enemy's ship, or an attempt to come alongside to initiate hand-to-hand combat on the enemy's deck. The best-known battles from this time took place near Svǫlðr (Svold) in 1000, where all three Scandinavian kings participated, and in 1030 at Stiklastaðir, Norway.

New strategies and tactics were gradually learned from Europe. In the beginning of the 12th century, the first horsemen appear in war in Denmark, and one of the first battles in which cavalry played an important role took place in 1134 at Fodevig in Scania, a struggle among claimants to the Danish throne.

During the 12th century, Denmark was attacked from the Baltic and the Slavonic Wends, while other Slavonic peoples directed attacks against Sweden. In the 1160s, Denmark turned attacks directly against the Slavonic countries. The island Rügen off the North German coast, a main stronghold for the Wends, was conquered, and in the beginning of the 13th century the Danish king went as far as Estland on a kind of crusade against the Slavs. The Danish flag, *Dannebrog*, dates from one of these campaigns in 1219.

Subsequently, two circumstances altered military organization. First, the kings began to levy taxes in the provinces from which *leiðangr* and war service were not demanded, and thus *leiðangr* tax came into existence, which gradually spread throughout the country, when the king needed money for armament and hired soldiers. Second, the king, to a greater extent, needed well-equipped men with horses and armament. As a result, a gulf was created between the major farmers, who could provide themselves as horsemen, and the common farmers. These increasingly powerful farmers, or nobility, who, because of their military service, were exempted from taxes, also built strongholds, which changed the forms of war even more. The squire was thus the only person who was obliged to do military service.

The cavalry, along with the archers, became a common and decisive element in battles. The first firearms, which appear at the end of the 14th century, were not a decisive factor, as the archers could shoot much faster. When the two armies joined in battle, there was only a slim possibility for tactics or strategic use of terrain, so that battles were decided by man-to-man combat, fighting between the increasingly iron-clad horsemen. It was most often horsemanship, skill in the use of arms, and physical strength that decided a battle.

In these centuries, a shift occurs. At first, hired horsemen were used together with a national infantry. Gradually, that cavalry (*i.e.*, the squires) became national, while the infantry became composed of mercenaries.

On the sea, the situation also changed. The slender and elegant Viking ships, of which the old *leiðangr* fleet had consisted, came to be replaced by completely new types. The cog, a ship broader than the longships, and set with more square sails, became predominant between 1200 and 1400, thus changing the nature of warfare. Since the cogs also rode deeply, battles were to a considerable degree decided by navigational tactics, even though action at close range and boarding constantly took place. Moreover, the introduction of cannons on the ships around 1400 meant that the maneuvering of the ships could be decisive for the outcome of the battle. Similarly, the stronger-built carvels were used increasingly, and warfare at sea then developed as in the rest of Europe.

Lit.: Ingelmark, Bo E. *Armour from the Battle of Wisby 1361*. 2 vols. Stockholm: Kungl. vitterhets historie och antikvitets akademien, 1939–40; Hafstrøm, Gerhard. *Ledung och Marlandsinddelning*. Uppsala: Almqvist & Wiksell, 1949; Harbitzs, G. P., *et al. Den norske Leidangen*. Oslo: Sjøforsvarets Overkommando, 1951; Runquist, Kjell. *Valdemarstidens hallandska ledungsflotta, dess utveckling och organisation*. Lund: Kungl. Vetenskaps Societeten i Lund, 1954; Kjersgaard, Erik. "Leding og Landeværn." In *Middelalderstudier tilegnede Aksel E. Christensen på tresårsdagen 11. september 1966*. Ed. Tage E. Christensen *et al*. Copenhagen: Munksgaard, 1966, pp. 113–40; Skovgaard-Petersen, Inge. "Vikingerne i den nyere forskning." *Historisk tidsskrift* (Denmark), ser. 12, vol. 5 (1971), 651–721; la Cour, Vilhelm. *Danske borganlæg til midten af det trettende århundrede*. 2 vols. Copenhagen: Nationalmuseet, 1972; Hedegaard, Ole A. *Leding og landeværn. Middelalderens danske forsvar*. Vedbæk: Eget, 1985; Barfod, Jørgen H. *Flådens Fødsel. Den kongelige Orlogsflåde fra Erik af Pommern til Frederik I*. Copenhagen: Marinehistorisk Selskab, 1990.

Jørgen H. P. Barfod

[**See also:** Fortification; Fortresses, Trelleborg; *Hirð*; *Leiðangr*; Weapons]

Weapons. Our knowledge of Scandinavian medieval weapons is based upon archaeological finds (*e.g.*, grave, bog, and loose finds), illustrations, and historical sources. The majority of early-medieval weapons survive from pagan graves, but a substantial number come from bogs in Denmark and South Sweden. The bog finds are interpreted as sacrifices to a war-god. The distribution of weapon graves is uneven, with few finds in Denmark and numerous finds in Sweden and especially in Norway. In Norway, the number of graves exceeds 4,000, yielding more than 2,000 swords, 1,500 spearheads, and 2,300 axes. The Swedish burial grounds at Vendel, Valsgärde, and especially Birka have yielded important material; however, the highest proportion of Swedish finds came from Gotland. When Christianity was introduced around 1000, weapons in graves became rare, and weapons from the high and late Middle Ages are usually loose finds, most often from Danish towns and fortifications.

The large majority of Migration Period (400–600) weapon graves have been found in the coastal districts of Norway. These graves contain one to four offensive weapons, such as a sword, axe, lance, and/or barbed spear, a single lance being the most common. From 600 to 1050, the Norwegian graves contain one to three offensive weapons, axes being most prevalent. In the Viking Age (800–1050), especially after 900, the weapon sets correspond to the folk weapons mentioned in the laws from the high Middle Ages, *i.e.*, swords, spears, and axes. According to the Norwegian provincial laws, and especially the *Landslǫg*, a man's armament corresponded to his wealth and status, a poor freeman being equipped with only an axe and a shield, while a wealthy man would have a shield, helmet, coat of mail, and all the folk weapons.

Swords. Depending upon the length of the blades, swords with one edge have been classified as either "saxes" or single-edged swords. Saxes had neither hilts nor knobs, and the blades varied between 25 and 70 cm. in length. The single-edged swords usually had hilts and knobs, and the blades were more than 70 cm. long. Saxes developed on the Continent around 400, and the earliest specimens were hardly more than long-bladed knives. In Scandinavia, saxes were introduced around 550 and were most prevalent in the period 600–800. Their manufacture was markedly influenced by the continental *Kurtz-*, *Schmal-*, *Breit-*, and *Langsax* (short-, narrow-, wide-, and long-bladed saxes). P. Olsén (1945) has studied the Swedish saxes, and Gudesen (1980) has divided the Norwegian specimens from East Norway into seven types according to the lengths and widths of the blades. In the Viking period, single-edged swords were particularly common in the coastal districts of Norway, but were gradually displaced by double-edged swords. The majority of the Scandinavian saxes and single-edged swords have been regarded as indigenously manufactured.

Double-edged swords with long blades reflecting Celtic traditions prevailed in the Migration and Viking periods, but were rare in the intervening centuries. In the high and late Middle Ages, when swords were used mainly by mounted knights, they changed from cutting to thrusting weapons with a long, narrow, and more rigid blade. Behmer (1939) divided the swords from 400–800 into nine types, and Petersen (1919) divided those from the Viking period into twenty-six general and twenty special types. These classifications were based mainly upon the form and decoration of the hilts and knobs. While three of Behmer's types had a characteristic Nordic distribution, one (type VI) has also been found in several other European countries. The latter type included several ring swords, *i.e.*, swords characterized by two interlocked metal rings, frequently of gold, on the upper hilt. In Germanic societies, ring swords were restricted to the highest social group. Such swords are depicted on the Torslunda plaques and have been found at the burial grounds at Vendel and Valsgärde. The Viking Age swords are more numerous and distributed over a wider area than the Migration Period specimens. Sword manufacture was a task for highly skilled smiths. However, it has remained a matter of dispute whether individual swords represent indigenous manufacture or import from the Continent. While Arbman (1937) regarded several of Petersen's types as imported, Petersen himself assumed that the large majority of the Norwegian swords represented indigenous manufacture. Scholars agree that specimens with vegetal ornamentation and inscriptions in Latin letters are imports. The most frequent inscriptions include Christian names and terms, such as "Benedictus" and "DNS" (*Dominus*), and the personal names Ulfberth, Ingelrii, and Gicelin. Swords with Ulfberth inscriptions have been dated to the period 800–1100 and Ingelrii swords to the Viking period and up to 1150, while the Gicelin swords are somewhat younger. Because of a lack of systematic investigations, little is known about the proportions and production area of swords with inscriptions. However, it has been assumed that the Rhine region represents the most likely production area. During the 14th century, swords from Passau in France, with the municipal symbol of a wolf on their blades, became common. From 1500, sword-manufacturing centers developed in Solingen in western Germany, Bréscia in northern Italy, and Toledo in Spain.

Swords were regarded as the most prestigious weapons, as attested by individual names given to them and recorded in the sagas. They also represented power and justice; kings were often depicted with swords symbolizing their rank and power. Knights pledged loyalty to their overlords by the sword, and swords were kept in city halls as symbols of justice.

Spears. Since wooden shafts are rarely preserved, early-medieval spears are represented mainly by their spearheads. Before 600, two categories of spears were used, the lance and the barbed spear, the lance being the most common. Around 600, however, the barbed spears were no longer used. Spearheads from the Merovingian or Vendel period (600–800) are characterized by wide and heavy blades. In the early Viking Age, spearheads with lugs on the socket and a high frequency of pattern-welded blades were used all over Scandinavia. Most likely, the pattern-welded specimens were imports from the Continent. In the 10th century, the spearheads had developed into slenderer weapons, with long blades and sockets with frequent silver incrustation. When cavalry was introduced in the high Middle Ages, lances with shorter blades and longer shafts were manufactured. Fett (1938) divided the Norwegian lances and barbed spears from the Migration Period into thirty-one and eight types, respectively. Gjessing (1934) and Petersen (1919) classified the Merovingian and Viking period lances into eight and eleven types.

From around 1200, pikes—*i.e.* long (5–6 m.) poles with metal spearheads—were used by foot soldiers against cavalry. The pikemen, wearing armor like knights, fought in tight formations. Pikes became the main weapon for the heavy infantry in the 16th century.

Axes. Axes were included among the weapons beginning around 500, most likely a result of Frankish influence, since special battle-axes (*fransiscs*) were used by the Franks from the latter half of the 5th century. On the Continent, battle-axes went out of use around 600. In Scandinavia, however, they were folk weapons throughout the medieval period. The earliest specimens were plain woodworker's axes, but gradually special battle-axes were manufactured. In the late Viking period, the battle-axes had thin, wide-edged blades (Danish axes). Petersen divided the Viking-period axes into twelve types, each type being less homogeneous than the sword and spearhead types. This pattern may be due to less specialized manufacture of the axes.

Pole-axes, or halberds, were combined cutting-and-thrusting weapons and represented a special development of the battle-axe. The handle was around 2.5 m. long, ending in a spear, pike, or hook, and the head had a pick or spike opposite the blade. Halberds originated in central Europe, and after being used successfully by the Swiss, they became the main infantry weapon in Europe in the 14th and 15th centuries.

Maces. Medieval maces included war clubs with metal heads; the morning-star represented a special variant: a metal ball set with spikes and chained to the handle. Maces have not been found in early-medieval graves, nor have they been recorded in the laws from the high and late Middle Ages. There are, however, indications in several of the sagas that they were used in warfare in the late Viking period and high Middle Ages. This evidence is confirmed by their depiction on the Bayeux Tapestry.

Bows. In the Stone Age, bows and arrows were used for hunting and warfare, and it may be difficult to decide which of these functions the many early-medieval iron arrowheads served. However, the numerous arrow finds in Danish bogs strongly indicate use for warfare. Until about 1100, the bow made of one piece of wood prevailed, the preferred material being European yew, ash, or elm. Later, this wooden bow was replaced by the crossbow, a powerful weapon made of laminated horn and whalebone fixed transversely on a grooved stock. Because of its superior power, the crossbow was used for shooting not slender arrows, but sturdy bolts, or "quarrels." During the 15th century, steel bows were introduced, but the introduction of firearms ended the era of bows and arrows around 1600.

Firearms. Firearms seem to have become available shortly after 1350. The earliest guns were small cannons, much like barrels in shape, generally forged or cast. Early in the 15th century, guns began to increase rapidly in size. At the same time, small arms were developed. At first, these weapons were simple forms of cannons small enough for hand use. The first projectiles were stone, but bundles or bags of stones, small balls, bits of iron, and chain were also used. Some early devices were used for shooting arrows or fire arrows. Early in the 15th century, forged iron balls became common. These projectiles were effective against castles and fortifications. Cast-iron projectiles followed, replacing stones and wrought iron.

Lit.: Falk, Hjalmar. *Altnordische Waffenkunde.* Kristiania [Oslo]: Dybwad, 1914; Petersen, Jan. *De norske vikingesverd. En typologisk-kronologisk studie over vikingetidens vaaben.* Christiania [Oslo]: Dybwad, 1919; Gjessing, Guttorm. *Studier i norsk Merovingertid.* Oslo: Dybwad, 1934 [German summary]; Nerman, Birger. *Die Völkerwanderungszeit Gotlands.* Stockholm: Verlag der Akademie, 1935; Arbman, Holger. "Zwei Ingelri-Schwerter aus Sweden." *Zeitschrift für historische Waffen- og Kostümkunde,* N. F. 5 (1936), 145–8; Brøndsted, Johannes. "Danish Inhumation Graves of the Viking Age." *Acta Archaeologica* 7 (1936), 81–228; Arbman, Holger. *Schweden und das karolingische Reich. Studien zu den Handelsverbindungen des 9. Jahrhunderts.* Stockholm: Thule, 1937; Salmo, Helmer. "Die Waffen der Merowingerzeit in Finland." *Finska Fornminnesföreningens Tidskrift* 41.1 (1938), 1–354; Behmer, Elis G. *Das zweischneidige Schwert der germanischen Völkerwanderungszeit.* Stockholm: Svea, 1939; Fett, Per. "Arms in Norway Between A.D. 400–600." *Bergens Museums Årbok* (1938), 5–89, (1938–40), 1–45; Paulsen, Peter. *Axt und Kreuz bei den Nordgermanen.* Berlin: Ahnenerbe-Stiftung-Verlag, 1939; Arbman, Holger. *Die Gräber.* 2 vols. Uppsala: Almqvist & Wiksell, 1940–43 [*Birka* 1]; Arwidsson, Greta. *Valsgärde 6. Die Gräberfunde von Valsgärde I.* Uppsala: Almqvist & Wiksell, 1942; Olsén, Pär Erik. *Die Saxe von Valsgärde I. Valsgärdestudien II.* Uppsala: Almqvist & Wiksell, 1945; Arwidsson, Greta. *Valsgärde 8. Die Gräberfunde von Valsgärde II.* Uppsala: Almqvist & Wiksell, 1954; Hoffmeyer, Ada Bruhn. *Middelalderens tveæggede sverd. En undersøgelse af dets udviklingshistorie, kronologi og nationalitet, dets stilling i den almindelige våbenhistoriske udvikling og dets krigsmæssige betydning.* 2 vols. Copenhagen: Tøjhusmuseet, 1954 [English summary]; Stenton, Frank. *The Bayeux Tapestry.* London: Phaidon, 1957; Strömberg, Märta. *Untersuchungen zur jüngeren Eisenzeit in Schonen.* 2 vols. Acta Archaeologica Lundensia. Bonn: Harbert, 1961; Stenberger, Morten. "Das Gräberfeld bei Ihre im Kirchspiel Hellevi auf Gotland. Der wikingerzeitliche Abschnitt." *Acta Archaeologica* 32 (1962), 1–134; Leppäaho, Jorma. "Späteisenzeitliche Waffen aus Finland. Schwertinschriften und Waffenverzierungen des 9.–12. Jahrhunderts. Ein Tafelwerk." *Finska Fornminnesföreningens Tidskrift* 61 (1964), 5–131; Oakeshott, R. Ewart. *The Sword in the Age of Chivalry.* London: Lutterworth, 1964; Arbman, Holger, and N. O. Nilsson. "Armes scandinaves de l'époque viking en France." *Lunds Universitets Historiska Museum. Meddelanden* (1966–68), 163–202; Nerman, Birger. *Die Vendelzeit Gotlands.* 2 vols. Stockholm: Almqvist & Wiksell, 1969–75; Müller-Wille, Michael. "Ein neues Ulfberht-Schwert aus Hamburg. Verbreitung, Formenkunde und Herkunft." *Offa* 27 (1971), 65–

88; Kivikoski, Ella. *Die Eisenzeit Finnlands. Bildwerk und Text.* Helsinki: Weilin & Göös, 1973; Gudesen, Hans Gude. "Merovingertiden i Øst-Norge. Kronologi, kulturmønstre og tradisjonsforløp." *Varia* 2 (1980) [comprises entire issue]; Solberg, Bergljot. "Spearheads in the Transition Period Between the Early and the Late Iron Age in Norway." *Acta Archaeologica* 51 (1981), 153–72; Jensen, Jørgen. *The Prehistory of Denmark.* London and New York: Methuen, 1982; Müller-Wille, Michael. "Zwei karolingische Schwerter aus Mittelnorwegen. Mit Beiträgen von K. Møllenhus, Trondheim und Birgit Arrhenius, Stockholm." *Studien zur Sachsenforschung* 3 (1982), 101–68; Solberg, Bergljot. "Social Status in the Merovingian and Viking Periods in Norway from Archaeological and Historical Sources." *Norwegian Archaeological Review* 18.1–2 (1985), 61–76.

Bergljot Solberg

[**See also:** Warfare]

Whaling *see* **Fishing, Whaling, and Seal Hunting**

William of Jumièges: Gesta Normannorum ducum.

William, monk of the monastery of Jumièges on the Seine in Normandy, wrote his *Deeds of the Dukes of Normandy* around 1060–1070. Although famous as the earliest prose account of the Norman Conquest of England in 1066, it is equally important as a source for the history of the Viking invasions and Viking settlement of Normandy in the 9th and 10th centuries. The work consists of seven books, six of which are devoted to one duke each, from the Viking Rollo (Book 2) to William the Conqueror (Book 7). The form of a serial biography, or *gesta*, was copied from his main source, Dudo of St.-Quentin, who wrote his *De moribus et actis primorum normanniæ ducum* around 994–1015. The first four books of the *Gesta* are a rewritten abbreviation of Dudo's history. The *Gesta* exists in more than fifty MSS divided into seven redactions, A–F, C being the original version written by William. The literary framework of one reign per book made it easy for later historians to interpolate the existing books or to add a new book. The most important are Orderic Vitalis (redaction E, *ca.* 1109–1113) and Robert of Torigni (redaction F, *ca.* 1139). In Book 2, on Rollo, William of Jumièges omitted many stories about the pagan Viking, which interestingly were all inserted again by the last interpolator of the *Gesta*, Robert of Torigni. William of Jumièges supplements Dudo's account of the early history of Normandy with information from annals, saints' lives, and oral tradition collected in Jumièges. In Book 5, on Duke Richard II, William's sympathy lies with the Danish occupants of England rather than with the duke's brother-in-law, the exiled Anglo-Saxon king Æthelred. However, Books 6 and 7, on Robert the Magnificent and his son William the Conqueror, reflect the loosening of Normandy's ties with Scandinavia in favor of relations with England.

Ed.: Marx, Jean, ed. *Guillaume de Jumièges, Gesta Normannorum ducum.* Rouen and Paris: Picard, 1914; Houts, Elisabeth M.C. van, ed. and trans. *The Gesta Normannorum Ducum of William of Jumièges, Orderic Vitalis, and Robert of Torigni: Vol. 1: Introduction and Books I–IV.* Oxford: Clarendon, 1992. **Tr.**: [see van Houts above]. **Lit.**: Grandsen, Antonia. *Historical Writing in England, c. 550 to c. 1307.* London: Routledge and Kegan Paul, 1974, pp. 94–7; Van Houts, E. M. C. "The Gesta Normannorum Ducum: A History Without an End." In *Proceedings of the Battle Conference on Anglo-Norman Studies 3.* Ed. R. Allen Brown. Woodbridge: Boydell & Brewer, 1981, pp. 106–18;

Van Houts, E. M. C. "The Political Relations Between Normandy and England According to the Gesta Normannorum Ducum." In *Les mutations socio-culturelles au tournant des XIe at XIIe siècles. Études Anselmiennes, ive session*. Ed. R. Foreville. Paris: CNRS, 1984, pp. 85–97.

Elisabeth M. C. van Houts

[See also: Dudo of St.-Quentin: *De moribus et actis primorum normanniæ ducum*; England, Norse in; France, Norse in]

Women in Eddic Poetry.

Women are the principal speakers in nine of the thirty-seven poems in the Neckel-Kuhn edition of the *Poetic Edda*, are central to the dramatic action in twenty-one, and appear as either minor characters or as significant referents in the remaining poems. Sexual imagery evoking the feminine is likewise pervasive. Snorri Sturluson in *Skáldskaparmál* (ch. 31) classifies female character types as *ásynjur* (goddesses), *valkyrjur* (valkyries), *nornir* (norns), and *dísir* (an untranslatable term that refers to Germanic minor female deities who appear either as friendly or hostile guardian spirits or as martial women with supernatural attributes). In addition, prominent figures include giantesses, *vǫlur* (seeresses, sibyls), and in the heroic lays, the warrior woman, a fusion of a human noblewoman and a valkyrie or a *dís*. Nonaristocratic and nonmythological women appear, but never in essential roles (but see *Rígsþula* and portions of *Hávamál*).

Eddic women are usually represented as either bright maidens or hags. Only the norns are not physically described. They are identified by name in *Hávamál* (st. 111) and in *Vǫluspá* (sts. 19–20): *Urðr* (n. 'fate'; past plural of *verða*, *urðu* 'became'), *Verðandi* (present participle of *verða* 'to become'), and *Skuld* (associated with the modal *skulu* 'shall' and *skuld*, n. 'debt'). Their names provide the sense that one's fate is composed of the inevitability of future events, the eradicability of the past, and the necessity and appropriateness of the present. In *Helgakviða Hundingsbana I* (st. 4), one norn is described as a female relative of Neri (possibly a dwarf), and, in *Fáfnismál* (sts. 11–13), Fáfnir informs Sigurðr that the norns of childbirth are of various descent, some akin to the gods, some descendants of elves, and others daughters of Dvalinn (a dwarf). They appear in action only in *Helgakviða Hundingsbana I* (sts. 1–6), where, positioned with Borghildr at Helgi's birth, they spin out the hero's fate. Elsewhere, they are referred to in passing as malevolent figures (*Guðrúnarhvǫt*, st. 13, *Helgakviða Hundingsbana II*, sts. 26–28, *Hamðismál*, st. 30, *Reginsmál*, st. 2; see also *Gylfaginning*, chs. 5, 8, *et passim*). Symbolically, the norns embody the archetypal function of women as controllers of men's destinies, an attribute that also underlies the character of heroines in the Helgi lays and of Brynhildr.

Vǫlur (seeresses, sibyls) appear infrequently in the poems, restricted to the sibyl-speaker of *Vǫluspá* (who relates her cosmological vision), to Heiðr, the evil sibyl (who is the "delight of evil women") in the same poem (*Vǫluspá*, st. 22), and to the witch-like creature who prophesies Baldr's death in *Baldrs draumar*. Whereas the norns shape men's fates, these Teiresian figures, excluding Heiðr, utter the doom of the gods. Under compulsion, usually exhibiting pain, they bring to light knowledge hidden even from Óðinn, and at his command they rise into being from the dead. The general attribute of visionary and prophetic utterance is not restricted to them, however, since it is a characteristic of the giantesses, goddesses, and the heroines of the heroic lays, although their knowledge is less than that of the *vǫlur*.

Giantesses appear as either physically beautiful and sexually desirable or as repellent. They have a number of epithets, *e.g.*, *þursa meyjar* ("maidens of the thurses"; *Helgakviða Hundingsbana I*, st. 40, *Vǫluspá*, st. 8); daughters and sisters of *iotna* ("giants"; *Þrymskviða*, st. 32, *Grímnismál*, st. 11); *gýgr* ("witch, giantess"; *Vafþrúðnismál*, st. 32, *Helreið Brynhildar*, st. 13, *Hymiskviða*, st. 14); and *fála* ("giantess"; *Helgakviða Hjǫrvarðssonar*, st. 16). These epithets probably discriminate function and status, but will be treated here under the broad category. In the heroic poems, they are haggish, malevolent creatures who strive either with the heroine (Brynhildr in *Helreið Brynhildar*) or with her surrogate (Atli in *Helgakviða Hjǫrvarðssonar*). They represent the obstacle the bright maidens Brynhildr and Sváva must overcome before being reunited with their lovers. Hrímgerðr (*Helgakviða Hjǫrvarðssonar*) is the paradigm. A sexually corrupt figure, as evidenced by her half-bestial, half-human form, she is a night raider and insatiable in her desire to avenge her father's murder (cf. Skaði). A corpse-hungry giantess with a powerful wrestling grip, she is depicted as attacking in the rush of a sea-battle. In the mythological poems, giantesses are both hostile and friendly. Giant maidens storm the Æsir, ending an idyllic world (*Vǫluspá*, st. 8). The avenging *skjaldmeyjar* ("shield-maidens") Menja and Fenja, of extraordinary physical prowess and fame in battle, grind out Fróði's gold as they prophesy his doom (*Grottasǫngr*). Except for Hyndla, who strives with Freyja (*Hyndluljóð*), giantesses are not characterized as hags in conflict with bright female figures, but themselves manifest brightness, *e.g.*, Gerðr, whose luminous arms brighten both air and water (*Fǫr Skírnis* [*Skírnismál*], st. 6); Billingr's daughter, who is *sólhvítr* ("white as the sun"; *Hávamál*, st. 97); and Skaði, *scír brúðr goða* ("shimmering bride of the gods"; *Grímnismál*, st. 11). They also show benevolence, as do Gunnlǫð (*Hávamál*, sts. 105–110) and the maids of giantland (*Vafþrúðnismál*, st. 49). The giantesses also have mythic and archetypal significance. Gerðr, for example, has been seen as a personification of the germinating elements of the earth (Olsen 1909), a sociological figure who rises to her proper status (Lönnroth 1977), and a vestige of an older dynasty of female divinities (Motz 1981). In psychological terms, the configuration of the giant hag and bright maiden may represent for the female psyche the confrontation with the Other.

Except for Freyja, the goddesses play minor roles in the poems, functioning as foils to the gods, *e.g.*, Frigg in *Vafþrúðnismál* (sts. 1–3), and in *Grímnismál* (prose before st. 1). Personified meanings of their names appear in the *Prose Edda*, and there is some fusion of function and identity among them, *e.g.*, Freyja and Frigg, Freyja and Gefjon. They appear assembled in *Lokasenna*, where Loki satirically spars with them and the gods, and where they are defamed as licentious, incestuous, adulterous, and otherwise sexually corrupt. Freyja, the most complex of the goddesses, appears as a discordant and erotic court figure (*Lokasenna*, sts. 30–32, *Þrymskviða*, *Hyndluljóð*, sts. 6, 47–48). At the same time, she is associated with battle and the realm of the dead. She and Óðinn divide the spoils of battle: she rides to the strife, chooses half the kill, and takes it back to her realm, Fólkvangr (*Grímnismál*, st. 14). She may be perceived as the Nordic Venus or Aphrodite, since she is particularly helpful and responsive to humans in matters of love (*Oddrúnargrátr*, st. 9) and possesses a necklace, the Brísingamen, an appropriate personal object for a love and fertility goddess. She owns a *hamr* (feather-coat) made of bird skin (*Þrymskviða*, st. 3), which is evocative of the goatskin *aegis* of

Athena. Her function as love- and battle-goddess and her eroticism are consistent with her representation in the *Prose Edda* (*Gylfaginning*, chs. 24, 35, 42, *Skáldskaparmál*, chs. 17, 20, 37). Freyja is the mythological exemplar for the major female figure of the heroic lays, the warrior woman.

Two other character types that bear on the characterization both of Freyja and of the warrior women in the heroic poetry are the *dísir* and the *valkyrjur* (choosers of the slain). Both terms are gender-specific, referring only to females. As noted above, the concept of the *dísir* is complex. The term has broad martial value, associated with Old High German *idisi*, the battle figures of the 10th-century *Merseburg Charm*. In eddic poetry, when used in the plural, *dísir* refers to hostile spirits who were once friendly (*Atlamál*, st. 28, *Grímnismál*, st. 53, *Hamðismál*, st. 28). When used in the singular, the term is polysemous, referring to women in a martial environment, who function as guides and protectors of the hero, and who are also called "valkyries." In the mythological lays, the valkyries are entirely supernatural with few individualizing attributes. Stripped of their religious potency, they have been reduced to serve as Óðinn's functionaries (*Grímnismál*, st. 36). In the heroic poetry, they are distinctly different in kind, characteristically appearing as brightly adorned noblewomen, metamorphosed into valkyries and *dísir* (e.g., Sigrún in *Helgakviða Hundingsbana I* and *II*, Brynhildr in *Brot af Sigurðarkviðu*). These valkyrie brides, so-called because of their erotic attachment to the hero, are composite characters. Figures of the royal court, with ties and obligations to a wordly environment (*Helgakviða Hundingsbana II*, sts. 30–38, *Sigurðarkviða in skamma*, sts. 35–41), they possess at the same time supernatural powers: they are not limited by spatial and temporal considerations (e.g., Sigrún's entrance through air, signaled by lightning in *Helgakviða Hundingsbana I*, sts. 15–16, Sváva's in *Helgakviða Hjǫrvarðssonar*, prose before sts. 6 and 10). Their major traits are boldness, profundity and resoluteness of mind, extravagance of emotion, and rhetorical brilliance (e.g., *Helgakviða Hundingsbana II*, sts. 11, 26, *Helgakviða Hundingsbana I*, st. 54, *Sigurðarkviða in skamma*, st. 34, *Helreið Brynhildar*, st. 3). They originate from the south (*Helgakviða Hundingsbana I*, st. 16, and *II*, st. 45, *Vǫlundarkviða* 1–3). They prophesy (*Helgakviða Hundingsbana I* and *II*, *Helgakviða Hjǫrvarðssonar*, *Sigrdrífumál*, *Sigurðarkviða in skamma*), and they determine the outcome of central issues that concern Germanic warrior society: the battle and the warrior's afterlife. Epithets for the valkyrie brides evoke women who are sublime, sexually active and desirable, and beneficent, offering the hero treasure, glory, and love. Radiant and nobly born, they ride into battle *hávar und hjálmom* ("sublime under helmets"). Epithets, such as *gullvarið* ("gold-adorned"), *margullin mær* ("richly decked with gold"), and *baugvarið* ("ring-adorned"), refer both to the brilliance of their warrior's dress and metaphorically to the treasure awaiting the hero at the battle's end. They are embodiments of heroic desire: gold, glory, and love. Yet, at the same time, in line with the ironic treatment of character in eddic poetry, they are objectified as the origin of the hero's destruction. The Sigrún-Sváva character of the Helgi lays best exemplifies this ambivalent figure. Scholars have allied the eddic warrior women with similar figures in Old English heroic poetry (*Elene*, *Judith*, *Juliana*).

Sigrún, Sváva, Brynhildr, and Guðrún, the major characters of eddic poetry, are complex figures, because their attributes associate them with both the temporal and the legendary. Of the four, Guðrún is the most "realistic," while Sigrún and Sváva are the

most elusive. In an attempt to give genealogical cohesion to the characters, the compiler of the *Poetic Edda* reports that Sigrún is Sváva reborn, and later, at the close of *Helgakviða Hundingsbana II*, he relates that Sigrún will be reborn into Kára, also a valkyrie. These statements may reflect remnants of a belief in ancestor worship. The critical consensus is that we are dealing with the basic story of the Skjǫldungr king Helgi (his heroic actions, his love for the valkyrie Sigrún-Sváva), and that the three poems represent a diverse treatment of original legendary material. Unlike Brynhildr and Guðrún, Sigrún and Sváva do not have clear origins in legend. Further, the characters are beset by problems brought about by the poems' being generically anomalous and fragmentary. Bugge (1899) and Höfler (1952) argue that Sigrún I represents Helgi's victory genius more than she does an actual historical personage. Harris (1983) sees Sigrún I as moving from a "human" figure toward one that is "divine." Bugge postulates Sigrún II as a merged figure, a blending of Sigrún I (5–13), Guðrún when she expresses sorrow, and Brynhildr in her single-minded drive to promote strife. Damico (1984) argues for a composite legendary and archetypal character with a counterpart in *Beowulf*.

Andersson's (1980) comprehensive and closely analyzed study of Brynhildr and the evolution of her story in the principal documents (e.g., the *Nibelungenlied*, *Þiðreks saga*, the eddic poems, and *Vǫlsungasaga*) sees her as a fusion of a historical and legendary personage and of archetypal figures, in particular the shield-maiden and the reluctant bride. In eddic poetry, she is immoderate in emotion and action, psychologically complex, erotic, and protective of her honor. As a court figure, she desires status and wealth, which leads her to succumb to Atli's blackmail and marry Gunnarr (*Sigurðarkviða in skamma*, st. 36). Her story is presented piecemeal in *Grípisspá* (which, because of its position in the MS, serves as a prologue to the succeeding lays about Sigurðr), *Sigrdrífumál*, *Brot af Sigurðarkviðu*, *Sigurðarkviða in skamma*, *Guðrúnarkviða I*, and *Helreið Brynhildar* (wherein Brynhildr justifies her action to have Sigurðr killed). Briefly, Sigurðr meets and exchanges vows with the valkyrie Brynhildr, who, as punishment from Óðinn, has been put to sleep in a hall encircled by flame, which Sigurðr has crossed. Their relationship is chaste. Subsequently, Sigurðr visits Gjúki's court. Under the effects of a drug administered by Queen Grímhildr, Sigurðr forgets Brynhildr, and instead agrees to win her for Gjúki's son Gunnarr, which he does later when disguised as Gunnarr. Sigurðr subsequently marries Gunnarr's sister, Guðrún. When Brynhildr discovers the deceit, she demands that Gunnarr kill both Sigurðr and his son as compensation for her outraged honor. Brynhildr is the central character in three poems (*Brot af Sigurðarkviðu*, *Sigurðarkviða in skamma*, *Helreið Brynhildar*) and, if one accepts her identification as Sigrdrífa, in a fourth, *Sigrdrífumál*. Her death speech in *Sigurðarkviða in skamma*, wherein she counsels Gunnarr on his actions after her death, parallels Sigrdrífa's rune lesson to Sigurðr, an act that would support the hypothesis of a Sigrdrífa-Brynhildr identification.

Guðrún, the Nordic equivalent of Kriemhilt in the *Nibelungenleid*, is the central figure in six poems and the primary speaker in four (*Guðrúnarkviða I, II, III, Guðrúnarhvǫt*), and appears as part of the dramatic action in all the poems concerning the Niflungs and Gjúkings. In line count and poetic emphasis, she overshadows her rival Brynhildr. Prior to Sigurðr's death, Guðrún is young and peerless, secure in her husband's love. After Sigurðr's murder and Brynhildr's suttee, Guðrún becomes almost demonic, unrestrained in mood and emotion, and extreme in action. Unafraid of the fates, she shapes her destiny and disdains those who do not, in particular her sons. In essence, she appropriates and develops the extravagance of character associated with Brynhildr before her death. *Guðrúnarkviða I* focuses on the boundlessness of Guðrún's grief; *Guðrúnarkviða II*, on the extremity of her alienation and despair; *Guðrúnarkviða III*, on the rigidity of her chastity; *Atlakviða* and *Atlamál*, on her single-minded drive for, and the bold monstrousness of, her revenge; and *Guðrúnarhvǫt*, on her state of frenzied exaltation informing both her incitement to her sons, which leads to their certain death, and her command to be burned on the pyre. Like Brynhildr and Sigrún-Sváva, she is a warrior woman, appearing in a byrnie with sword in hand. She shapes the battle (*Atlamál*, sts. 44–48) and abandons herself to the fight (*Atlamál*, sts. 49–53, 98–99, *Atlakviða*, sts. 35–43). Twice she is found in a Job-like situation, in inconsolable states of sadness (*Guðrúnarkviða I*) and alienation (*Guðrúnarkviða II*), surrounded by women who attempt unsuccessfully to give her comfort. In *Atlamál*, Guðrún becomes a grotesque Medea, because she has no love for the children she slays, responding to their frightened appeals with chilling satire: "Desire has long sprung up in me to cure you of old age" (*Atlamál*, st. 78).

There are numerous minor characters in the heroic poetry, and these form a unifying pattern, for they are connected to the major figures by motif. In *Frá dauða Sinfjǫtla*, for example, the motif of the scheming and deceitful queen-mother is embodied in Borghildr, Sigmundr's wife, who serves poisoned drink to her stepson, Sinfjǫtli. The motif is elaborated by Grímhildr, who offers her future son-in-law Sigurðr the drink of forgetfulness that causes him to neglect his vow to Brynhildr (*Grípisspá*), a treachery she repeats against her own child Guðrún (*Atlakviða*). The motif develops its most macabre aspect in Guðrún, who serves Atli a beaker filled with drink that has been mixed with the blood of their sons (*Atlamál*).

The women in the heroic lays have epic proportions. Characters of volition depicted at climactic moments, they instigate and control narrative action. They have unconquerable spirits, unbridled passions, and when, in line with Germanic heroic poetry, they are placed in a position where they must choose between the satisfaction of their honor or desire and the death or destruction of loved ones, they invariably choose the former. In the mythological poems, the women are less engaging. The gods dominate most of the authors' and readers' attention. Thus, in the presentation of women, one can mark a distinctive difference between the mythological and heroic poetry in the *Poetic Edda*. When the poetry becomes anthropo-centered, it turns its attention to the characterization of women.

Ed.: Dronke, Ursula, ed. *The Poetic Edda. 1: Heroic Poems.* Oxford: Clarendon, 1969; Neckel, Gustav, ed. *Edda: Die Lieder des Codex Regius nebst verwandten Denkmälern. I: Text.* 5th ed. rev. Hans Kuhn. Heidelberg: Winter, 1983. **Tr.**: Bellows, Henry Adams, trans. *The Poetic Edda.* New York: American-Scandinavian Foundation, 1923; Taylor, Paul B., and W. H. Auden, trans. *The Elder Edda: A Selection.* London: Faber & Faber; New York: Random House, 1969. **Lit.**: Bugge, Sophus. *The Home of the Eddic Poems; with Especial Reference to the Helgi-Lays.* Trans. W. H. Schófield. London: Nutt, 1899, pp. 215–25; Olsen, Magnus. "Fra gammelnorsk myte og kultus." *Maal og minne* (1909), 17–36; Vries, Jan de. *Altnordische Literaturgeschichte.* 2 vols. Grundriss der germanischen Philologie, 15–6. Berlin: de Gruyter, 1941–42; rpt. 1964–67; Höfler, Otto. "Das Opfer im Semnonenhain und die Edda." In *Edda, Skalden, Saga: Festschrift zum 70. Geburtstag von Felix Genzmer.* Ed. Hermann Schneider. Heidelberg: Winter, 1952, 1–67; Ström, Folke. *Diser, nornor, valkyrjor: Fruktbarhetskult och sakralt kungadöme i Norden.* Kungliga vitterhets historie och antikvitets akademiens handlingar, Filologisk-filosofiska serien, 1. Stockholm: Almqvist & Wiksell, 1954; Harris, Joseph. "Guðrúnarbrögð and the Saxon Lay of Grimhild's Perfidy." *Mediaeval Scandinavia* 9 (1976), 173–80; Lönnroth, Lars. "Skírnismál och den fornisländska äktenskapsnormen." In *Opuscula Septentrionalia: Festskrift til Ole Widding, 10. 10. 1977.* Ed. Bent. Chr. Jacobsen *et al.* Copenhagen: Reitzel, 1977, pp. 154–78; Andersson, Theodore M. *The Legend of Brynhild.* Islandica, 43. Ithaca and London: Cornell University Press, 1980; Motz, Lotte. "Sister in the Cave: The Stature and the Function of the Female Figures in the Eddas." *Arkiv för nordisk filologi* 95 (1980), 168–82; Motz, Lotte. "Gerðr: A New Interpretation of the Lay of Skírnir." *Maal og minne* (1981), 121–36; Præstgaard Andersen, Lise. *Skjoldmøer—en kvindemyte.* Copenhagen: Gyldendal, 1982; Glendinning, Robert J. "Guðrúnarqviða Forna: A Reconstruction and Interpretation." In *Edda: A Collection of Essays.* Ed. Robert J. Glendinning and Haraldur Bessason. University of Manitoba Icelandic Series, 4. Winnipeg: University of Manitoba Press, 1983, pp. 258–82; Harris, Joseph. "Eddic Poetry as Oral Poetry: The Evidence of Parallel Passages in the Helgi Poems for Questions of Composition and Performance." In *Edda: A Collection of Essays*, pp. 210–42; Damico, Helen. *Beowulf's Wealhtheow and the Valkyrie Tradition.* Madison: University of Wisconsin Press, 1984; Harris, Joseph. "Eddic Poetry." In *Old Norse-Icelandic Literature: A Critical Guide.* Ed. Carol J. Clover and John Lindow. Islandica, 45. Ithaca and London: Cornell University Press, 1985, pp. 68–156; Jochens, Jenny. "Old Norse Sources on Women." In *Medieval Women and the Sources of History.* Ed. Joel T. Rosenthal. Athens and London: University of Georgia Press, 1990, pp. 155–88 [useful bibliography, pp. 181–8].

Helen Damico

[See also: *Atlakviða*; *Atlamál*; *Baldrs draumar*; Eddic Poetry; Freyr and Freyja; *Grímnismál*; *Grípisspá*; *Grottasǫngr*; *Guðrúnarkviða I–III*; *Guðrúnarhvǫt*; *Hamðismál in fornu*; *Hávamál*; Helgi Poems; *Helreið Brynhildar*; *Hymiskviða*; *Hyndluljóð*; Maiden Warriors; *Oddrúnargrátr*; *Reginsmál and Fáfnismál*; *Rígsþula*; *Sigrdrífumál*; *Sigurðarkviða in skamma*; *Sigurðarkviðu, Brot af*; *Skírnismál*; *Snorra Edda*; Supernatural Beings; *Þiðreks saga af Bern*; *Þrymskviða*; *Vafþrúðnismál*; *Vǫlundarkviða*; Vǫlsung-Niflung Cycle; *Vǫlsunga saga*; *Vǫluspá*; Women in Sagas]

Women in Sagas. The picture of women, their importance, and their roles differs from genre to genre within the saga literature. The differences between the portrayal of women in the realistic and nonrealistic sagas are especially apparent. In the realistic saga genres, the picture of women must correspond to real life in a way that made the literary figures acceptable as "historical" persons, although this correspondence does not necessarily mean that the literature gives a true picture of women and their life, either within the frame of the narrative or at the time the sagas were written.

Women in the *Íslendingasögur* are regarded as strong and independent characters; this type may partly be understood against the background of the women's position in Old Norse society, which, compared with their positions in other medieval societies, was rather good. But the strong female characters in the *Íslendingasögur* are also a result of an idealizing literature. The male heroes rise considerably above ordinary men in skill, strength, and vigor, and consequently the heroines rise above ordinary women. Still, a woman is never the main character in an *Íslendingasaga*, although Guðrún in *Laxdæla saga* comes very close. She is perhaps the most interesting character in the saga, but in this genre the viewpoint follows the action, and, according to the sex roles, men are the active sex, and accordingly the main characters. The important male characters in the *Íslendingasögur* can be divided into groups of types like the light hero, the dark hero, the Christ/Baldr type, the wise man. But the characters are highly individualized within each group. The important female characters in the sagas are roughly divided into two groups only, the strong women and the weak women, most belonging to the first group. Here, we find different characters like Guðrún in *Laxdæla saga*, Bergþóra and Hallgerðr in *Njáls saga*, and Auðr and Þordís in *Gísla saga*. The weak woman is a rather rare type. Actually, she is not a weak character, but her strength and her will to live are broken by the loss of her beloved one. Hrefna in *Laxdæla saga*, Helga in *Gunnlaugs saga*, and Oddný in *Bjarnar saga Hítdælakappa* belong to this type, which is perhaps influenced by European romantic literature. Among the less central female figures, the woman skilled in magic is generally described as a wicked person, but not when she uses her skill in magic to help a hero. In some cases, a woman's skill in magic is used to explain her sex appeal, especially if the woman is elderly and the man young. Among the subordinate characters, we find female types, very little individualized, like the old foster-mother, the gossip, and the maidservant. Since the women generally play a minor part in the sagas compared with men, the picture of them is consequently less detailed, and the number of women mentioned in the sagas is considerably lower than the number of men.

The female characters act in their social roles as wives, daughters, mothers, and sisters; and their reputation depends on how well they play the roles seen from the man's point of view. The woman who urges the men to take revenge is a character found in many of the *Íslendingasögur*. She may be described as very hard, and even more eager than the men to protect the honor of the family. The women's passive role, which did not allow her to act herself, could explain such uncompromisingly hard incitement. But, in terms of narrative function, the author needs the women to speed the action. The goading scene, which to a great extent has formed our view of the saga women, is part of the author's literary technique, and must be judged in that light.

In the less idealizing contemporaneous sagas, the author seldom focuses on women. When he does, the picture of these women is much the same as in the *Íslendingasögur*, with one interesting difference: we do not have as many women bent on inciting revenge. Instead, the women on many occasions try to protect their men and prevent killing.

In the *konungasögur*, few women are mentioned, and they normally play a subordinate role. The exceptions are some queens and princesses, especially in the early period, like Queen Gunnhildr, wife of the Norwegian king Eiríkr blóðøx ("blood-axe") Haraldsson; the Swedish princess Ingibjörg, who plays an important part in the sagas of St. Óláfr; and the Swedish queen Sigríðr, who had the father of St. Óláfr killed, and who later became the deadly enemy of King Óláfr Tryggvason after he refused to marry her. The basis of these women's actions and influence resides in their high social rank.

The *konungasögur* deal with politics, which is the domain of men; consequently, women play a significant role in the story only when they are political figures or used in the political game. The king's private life and his relationship with women are normally not given much space in the *konungasögur*. But to some extent, the sagas of King Óláfr Tryggvason form an exception. The reason may be that the oldest written sagas about this king seem to be derived from a tradition that was in part shaped by women. In his saga about Óláfr Tryggvason, the monk Oddr mentions six informants, three men and three women. Whether this list of informants is Oddr's own, or was originally found in another saga about the same king (e.g., the saga by the monk Gunnlaugr), it may indicate that the women's part in shaping the tradition behind the written sagas also had some influence on the portrayal of women and on the amount of space they were accorded in the narrative.

In the nonrealistic sagas, such as the *fornaldarsögur* and the *riddarasögur*, women often take a more active part in the narrative. In these sagas, a woman may break out of the ordinary female sex role and act in the role normally reserved for men as a warrior (*skjaldmær*), commander of an army, executor of revenge, or reigning queen or princess. The importance of women and their number compared with the number of men differ considerably from saga to saga within the genres. Only one of the *fornaldarsögur*, *Hervarar saga* (*ok Heiðreks konungs*), is named after a female figure, Hervǫr, who approaches a formal main part in the saga as a person who carries out the action. Some of the Icelandic *riddarasögur* and some of the translated sagas are named both after the hero and the heroine, a fact that also reflects the importance of the female figures. In some sagas, these strong female figures not only act like men, but they also dress like men, pretend they are men, and demand to be treated as men. A common motif is that they refuse to marry. When the heroine demands to act in a male role, it underscores the fact that the male role offers possibilities that the female role does not. When women in the nonrealistic sagas act like men, it could be interpreted as the women's desire for greater freedom, although in these sagas they are not always allowed to take on a male role. The princess or queen who refuses to marry, a popular motif in the later Icelandic *riddarasögur*, is in most cases forced into marriage by her suitor, conquered militarily, and often raped, after which she marries the suitor and assumes her ordinary female role. These sagas may thus reflect different attitudes toward women, and perhaps the discussion in the late Middle Ages about women's nature and their place in society.

The female characters in all the saga genres are often praised for their beauty, but an even more constant factor is the heroine's wisdom. In fact, those traits of character that are regarded as positive in men (sense of honor, self-assertion, a strong will, courage, generosity) are also regarded as positive characteristics in women, as long as they do not use them against the men they are supposed to support. The positive assessment of the wise and strong woman is perhaps connected with the view on inheritance in Old Norse society. This society was well aware of the fact that children inherited their mother's qualities as well as their father's. And this society seems to have regarded inheritance as a much more important factor in the forming of the children's character than environmental influence. A wife with intelligence and a strong character was perhaps not easy to cope with. But these qualities are required in a desirable bride, and the explanation may be that such a bride was looked upon as an investment in the future of the unborn sons.

Lit.: Heller, Rolf. *Die literarische Darstellung der Frau in den Isländersagas.* Halle: Niemeyer, 1958 [contains bibliography]; Kress, Helga. "Ekki hǫfu vér kvennaskap. Nokkrar laustengdar athuganir um karlmennsku ok kvenhatur í Njálu." In *Sjötíu ritgerðir helgaðar Jakobi Benediktssyni 20. júlí 1977.* 2 vols. Ed. Einar G. Pétursson and Jónas Kristjánsson. Reykjavík: Stofnun Árna Magnússonar, 1977, vol. 1, pp. 293–313; Kress, Helga. "Meget samstavet må det tykkes deg. Om kvinneopprør og genretvang i Sagaen om Laksdölene." *Historisk tidskrift* (Sweden) 100 (1980), 266–80 [English summary, pp. 279–80]; Mundal, Else. "Kǫld eru kvenna råð." In *Kvinner og bøker. Festskrift til Ellisiv Steen på hennes 70-årsdag 4. februar 1978.* Ed. Edvard Beyer *et al.* Oslo: Gyldendal; Nordisk Forlag, 1978, pp. 183–93; Mundal, Else. "Kvinnebiletet i nokre mellomaldergenrar. Eit opposisjonelt kvinnesyn?" *Edda* 82 (1982), 341–71; Præstgaard Andersen, Lise. *Skjoldmøer—en kvindemyte.* Copenhagen: Gyldendal, 1982; Clover, Carol J. "Hildigunnr's Lament." In *Structure and Meaning in Old Norse Literature: New Approaches to Textual Analysis and Literary Criticism.* Ed. John Lindow *et al.* Viking Collection, 3. Odense: Odense University Press, 1986, pp. 141–83; Clover, Carol J. "Maiden Warriors and Other Sons." *Journal of English and Germanic Philology* 85 (1986), 35–49; Jochens, Jenny. "The Medieval Icelandic Heroine: Fact or Fiction?" *Viator* 17 (1986), 35–50; Heinrichs, Anne. "*Annat er vårt eðli:* the Type of the Prepatriarchal Woman in Old Norse Literature." In *Structure and Meaning in Old Norse Literature,* pp. 110–40; Jochens, Jenny. "Old Norse Sources on Women." In *Medieval Women and the Sources of History.* Ed. Joel T. Rosenthal. Athens and London: University of Georgia Press, 1990, pp. 155–88 [useful bibliography, pp. 181–8].

Else Mundal

[See also: *Bjarnar saga Hítdœlakappa; Fornaldarsǫgur; Gísla saga Súrssonar; Gunnlaugs saga ormstungu; Hervarar saga ok Heiðreks konungs; Íslendingasǫgur; Konungasǫgur; Laxdœla saga;* Maiden Warriors; *Njáls saga; Óláfs saga Tryggvasonar; Riddarasǫgur;* Women in Eddic Poetry]

Women Skalds *see* Skáldkonur

Wood Carving

1. NORWAY. Finds of wood carvings from before the Viking Age are extremely rare. On the other hand, excavations carried out in 1904 at a large burial mound on Oseberg farm in Vestfold (west of the Oslo fjord) showed that wood carving was a flourishing handicraft during the Viking Age itself. Archaeologists suddenly became aware of a rich craft dating from the first half of the 9th century, including the oldest collection of Norwegian wood carving. The burial mound contained a Viking ship where two women were buried with many valuable possessions.

The wood carving in this find bears witness to an outstanding and flourishing decorative art that must have been the result of long experience and tradition. The items decorated with wood carving include the ship, a carriage, and three sleighs with frames. The carvings cover a total of 12–15 sq. m.

The motifs are animal ornamentation and geometrical patterns, plus some narrative representations of figures. The work was done by several carvers. One can speak of a plain style and a more or less plastic style. Finds of metal objects suggest that the Oseberg styles were widespread in Scandinavia.

As early as the Oseberg find, we meet four forms of wood carving: relief, sculpture in the round or free-standing sculpture, incised, and openwork. The Oseberg carvings suggest that wood carving was a leading form of art compared with other forms of artistic expression in the Viking Age.

We also know a little about the wood carving in the period after the burial mound at Oseberg, thanks to two burial mounds from the second half of the 9th century or around 900. The mound at Nedre Gokstad in Vestfold has provided most of the wood carving in Borre style. It contained mostly incised carving and openwork, but there was also a head sculpted in the round. This style was widespread in Scandinavia, but was most common in Sweden and Norway.

Not much Norwegian wood carving has been preserved in the Jelling, Mammen, and Ringerike Viking styles from the 10th century and the first half of the 11th. They were particularly linear and plain styles. Animal ornamentation was still dominant, but plant motifs gradually appeared. Right up to the 1970s, we had no examples of Norwegian wood carving in these styles, but archaeological excavations at Trondheim have brought forth many small articles of everyday use that were made of wood with decoration in Mammen, Ringerike, and the later Urnes style.

The second half of the 11th century once again offers examples of monumental Norwegian wood carving in the last of the Viking styles, the Urnes style, which was widespread in Scandinavia and on the islands in the Atlantic, and in which animal ornamentation was again dominant. The major monument in this style comprises the older parts of the Urnes stave church in Sogn. Characteristic of its ornamentation is the interplay between thin bands (snakes) and wider animals in an open interlace pattern, where all lines are curved and figure-of-eight traceries are common. Exceptionally high relief, up to about 7 cm., alternates with very low and flat carving.

At the time when the Romanesque and Gothic styles ruled in European architecture, art, and handicraft, a large number of wooden churches (stave churches) were built in Norway, especially from about 1150 to roughly 1200. These churches were decorated with carvings, and more wood carving from the high Middle Ages has been preserved in Norway than in any other Nordic country. The Church was the foremost employer of wood carvers.

Most of the carving was on the outside of the churches, especially around the doorways. Up to 1,000 stave churches may have been in use at the same time. Only about thirty are still standing, but Norwegian museums have many carved doorways and other items from stave churches that were pulled down. In particular, the main doorway in the westernmost part of the nave could be large and magnificently decorated.

Vestiges of the Urnes style lived on for a long time in stave-church ornamentation, but gradually the decoration became colored by Romanesque style. The doorway from Ål church in Hallingdal is a good example of a large group of doorways with the same main scheme in their composition.

New decorative features were vine-like ornamentation and the winged dragon. The vine grows up from the jaws of an animal at the bottom of each plank and goes up the plank in waves to continue on the upper part of the doorway. Branches with leaves entwine to form spirals, but dragons with wings and long tails also crawl up the plank. The largest dragons are to be found at the top of the planks (the tips of their wings extend right up to the top corners) and on the upper part of the doorway. Such doorways have often been called "dragon portals."

174. Viking ship from the burial mound at Oseberg in Vestfold, Norway. Detail of the prow; 9th century. University Museum of National Antiquities, Oslo.

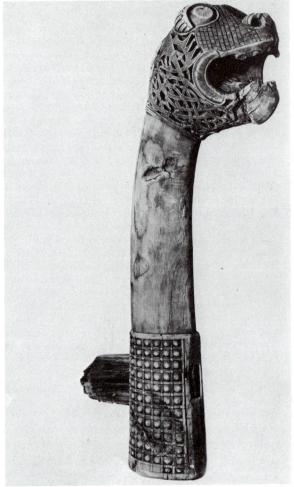

175. Animal-head post from the Oseberg find. University Museum of National Antiquities, Oslo.

176. Urnes stave church in Sogn, Norway. Part of the northern wall with carvings; second half of 11th century. Photo: University Museum of National Antiquities, Oslo.

177. Doorway from Ål stave church in Hallingdal, Norway; 12th century. University Museum of National Antiquities, Oslo.

178. Doorway planks from Hylestad stave church, Setesdal, Norway; probably from 1200–1250. University Museum of National Antiquities, Oslo.

179. Chair from Tyldal Church, Østerdalen, Norway; ca. 1150. University Museum of National Antiquities, Oslo.

180. Carved panels from Flatatunga in Skagafjör5ur, northern Iceland; second half of 11th century (?). National Museum of Iceland, Reykjavík.

181. Church door from Valþjófsstaðir in Fljótsdalur, eastern Iceland; probably *ca.* 1200. National Museum of Iceland, Reykjavík.

182. Chair from Grund in Eyjafjör5ur, northern Iceland; *ca.* 1550. National Museum of Iceland, Reykjavík.

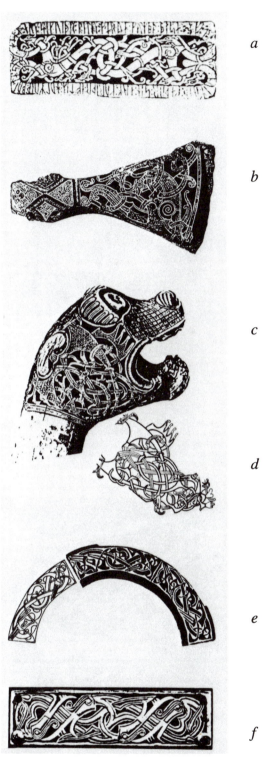

a

b

c

d

e

f

183. (a) Runic stone slab from Sundby, Södermanland, Sweden; 11th century. (b) Axe from Mammen, Jutland, Denmark; 10th century. National Museum, Copenhagen. (c) Animal-head post from Oseberg, Vestfold, Norway; 9th century. University Museum of National Antiquities, Oslo. (d) Object of unknown use from Smiss, Gotland, Sweden; 8th century. Museum of National Antiquities, Stockholm. (f) Strap mounting from Vallstena, Gotland, Sweden. Museum of National Antiquities, Stockholm.

184. Herning, Jutland, Denmark. Wall plate; late 11th century. National Museum, Copenhagen. Photo by the museum.

185. Brågarp, Scania, Denmark (now Sweden). Top piece of stave-church portal; *ca.* 1100. Lund University Historical Museum, Lund.

186. Guldrupe, Gotland, Sweden. Stave-church portal;
12th century. Gotlands Fornsal, Visby.

187. Hemse, Gotland, Sweden. Stave-church portal; 12th century.
Museum of National Antiquities, Stockholm.

188. Kungsåra, Västmanland, Sweden. Back piece of bench; 12th century. Museum of National Antiquities, Stockholm.

189. Lillhärdal, Härjedalen, Sweden (formerly Norway). Lid (of baptismal font?); 12th century. Nordiska Museet, Stockholm.

191. Rättvik, Dalarna, Sweden. Wool hamper with open-work animal ornamentation; probably post-Reformation. Nordiska Museet, Stockholm.

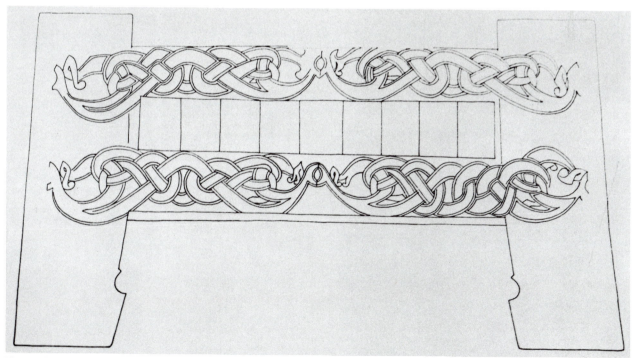

190. Bjuråker, Hälsingland, Sweden. Chest; late medieval. Nordiska Museet, Stockholm.

192. Orsa, Dalarna, Sweden. Foot of baptismal font; 16th century.

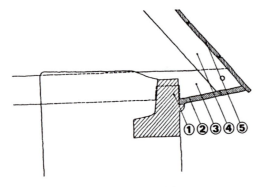

193. Top of wall of the Romanesque stone church. (1) Wall plate. (2) Eave board. (3) Tie beam. (4) Rafter. (5) Roof boarding.

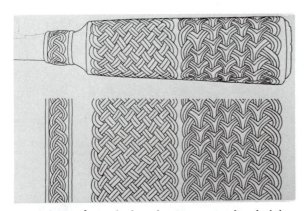

195. Söderköping, Östergötland, Sweden. Counterpoise of wooden balance with carved plait ornaments. This kind of ornamentation is found from the 10th century to the present and is impossible to date on stylistic grounds. S. Ragnhild's Guild, Söderköping.

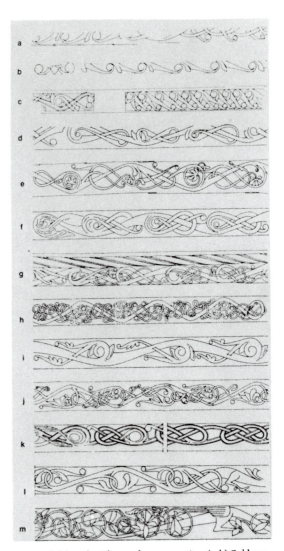

194. Swedish boards with carved ornamentation. (a, b) Guldrupe, Gotland. Eave boards; ca. 1200. Gotlands Fornsal, Visby. (c) Hablingbo, Gotland. Wall plate; 12th century. Museum of National Antiquities, Oslo. (d) Forshem, Västergötland. Wall plate; 12th century. (e) Marum, Västergötland. Eave board; 12th century. (f) Våversunda, Östergötland. Wall plate; 12th century. (g) Vrigstad, Småland. Wall plate; 12th century. Museum of National Antiquities, Stockholm. (h) Hagebyhöga, Östergötland. Eave board; 12th century. (i) Heda, Östergötland. Wall plate; 12th century. (j) Hagebyhöga, Östergötland. Eave board; 12th century. Museum of National Antiquities, Stockholm. (k) Myresjö, Småland. Eave board; 12th century. Museum of National Antiquities, Stockholm. (l) Skalunda, Västergötland. Wall plate; 12th century. (m) Dädesjö, Småland. Wall plate; middle of 13th century.

196. Nås, Jämtland, Sweden (formerly Norway). Baptismal font cut out of a thick pine log; ca. 1200. Museum of National Antiquities, Stockholm.

197. Alnö, Medelpad, Sweden. Baptismal font. Receptacle and foot were made separately. The former has been put together in the manner of a cask with ten staves; ca. 1200.

198. Gothem, Gotland, Sweden. Top pieces of choir bench; 14th century.

No completely equivalent ornamentation is found outside Norway. The Urnes style may have influenced its composition. The half-columns with a suggestion of an archivolt have been taken over from the art of building in stone. The lions, in high relief or sculptured in the round on the capitals, have relatives in the art of the Continent. The plant ornamentation is also based on foreign models. The figures of dragons are known from European Romanesque art, and no doubt come from the Orient.

The planks of a doorway from Hylestad stave church in Setesdal, probably dating from 1200–1250, provide the best example of a portal decorated with narrative scenes. They show events from the eddic poems telling of the slaying of the dragon Fáfnir by Sigurðr Fáfnisbani. Several other doorways have scenes from the same group of legends. Strangely enough, these church doorways contain motifs from heathen legends.

One group of stave-church doorways belongs to a completely different tradition and is related to stone sculpture in Niðaróss (Trondheim), from the first half and middle of the 12th century. Irrespective of the motifs, the decoration on the portals is carved mainly in relief of varying height (seldom more than 5 cm. above the lower surface).

Only a few portals show influence from the Gothic style. The late portals still have vine-like ornamentation, but the dragons are found less frequently.

The surface treatment is an important aspect of the wood carving on all groups of stave-church portals. The carvers used notches and hollows, as well as incised lines. Special tools are needed for wood carving, including knives and wood-carving chisels of various forms. Originally, the carvers probably were specialists sent from cities like Bergen and Niðaróss, but later they were local.

From the 14th century, the country suffered a general decline that was also noticeable in artistic activity, especially after the Black Death (1349–1350), which reduced the population of Norway by more than half. The planks from the doorway of Tuddal stave church in Telemark, dating from after 1369, show how the art of doorway carving had deteriorated at the time when skilled wood carvers must have been a rarity. This portal also affords an example of *Kerbschnitt* (chip-carving technique), by which the individual lobes of the leaves have been hollowed out.

Other forms of outside carved decoration on stave churches include animal heads as roof ornamentation, crosses, and openwork cappings.

Most interior carving was found in the largest churches, which might have a mask at the top of each of the inner posts supporting the roof over the nave. X-shaped cross-braces between the posts lower down were adorned with leaves. Examples also survive of carved column capitals on the lower parts of the posts. Some stave churches had carved chancel planks and rood loft fronts. On the whole, however, there was not much carving on the interior of the building. But much of the furniture was carved, although little has been preserved.

Stone churches were relatively rare in Norway. Certain parts of them could have wood carving.

The church furnishings were much the same in wooden churches and stone churches. The only preserved ciborium (canopy) over an altar is found in Hopperstad stave church in Sogn. It has been dated to roughly 1300 and has sculpted heads and openwork Romanesque plant ornamentation, somewhat influenced by the Gothic style.

As far as movable medieval church furnishings are concerned, it is mainly chairs and benches or parts of these that have been preserved. Particularly ancient is the Tyldal Chair, probably made in Niðaróss about 1150, with ribbon-like plaiting, vine ornamentation, and figures of humans and animals. Other pieces have dragon and vine-like motifs suggestive of those most commonly found on stave-church doorways, in addition to certain figurative scenes. The posts of chairs and benches usually end in gaping animal heads.

Most of the preserved furnishings are in Romanesque style, although some show features of both Romanesque and Gothic styles. It is more difficult to find church furnishings made in Norway with ornamental wood carving in pure Gothic style. When purely Gothic ornamentation is found, it is usually of late date and is used sparingly. The dragon motif has disappeared, and the plant motifs have become naturalistic. Geometrical architectural motifs seem to have been popular, particularly in late Gothic tracery. Finally, such ornamentation was "translated" into chip-carving technique.

In the latter part of the Middle Ages, most of the works of art for churches were imported from abroad, mostly from Lübeck in Germany, but to some extent from the Netherlands. Gothic reredos became very common. Nevertheless, carved furnishings of high quality were made in Norway. For example, numerous choir-stall side-members from Kirkjubø, the Faroe Islands, were probably made in Bergen in the 15th century.

Wood carving was also found on houses, furniture, and objects of everyday use, especially on large farms. On houses built of logs, the entrance in particular was emphasized by carved decoration.

The church doorways were to some extent models for the secular portals, but the latter were as a rule simpler. A good many have been preserved. Romanesque ornamentation was dominant. The secular portals, however, have more wood carving in Gothic style than the stave-church doorways.

Even fewer examples of medieval carved furniture have been preserved from the home than from the church. In addition to chests, tabletops and beds occasionally were carved, as well as smaller objects of everyday use, such as drinking vessels.

There was no Gothic flowering to compare with the rich Romanesque tradition that achieved its finest expression on the doorways of stave churches. The golden age of Norwegian wood carving was over before the Gothic succeeded in becoming common property.

From the earliest times, traces of color have been found, indicating that carvings could be painted in several colors.

The ancient, continuous tradition of wood carving appears to have become practically extinct by the end of the Middle Ages, although this applies to the representative "elite" carving. The tradition continued in folk art, however, in which the Romanesque motifs were to live on for several hundred years.

Lit.: Gjærder, Per. *Norske pryd-dører fra middelalderen.* University of Bergen. Skrifter, no. 24. Bergen: Grieg, 1952 [English summary]; Sjøvold, Thorleif. "Ornamental Wood-Carvings from a Viking Court." *The Connoisseur* 145 (February 1960), 34–7 [nine illustrations]; Fischer, Dorothea. "Tyldalstolen." *Viking. Tidsskrift for norrøn arkeologi* 26 (1963), 161–77 [English summary]; Blindheim, Martin. *Norwegian Romanesque Decorative Sculpture 1090–1210.* Trans. Ada Polak. London: Tiranti, 1965; Blindheim, Martin. "The Romanesque Dragon Doorways of the Norwegian Stave Churches: Traditions and

Influences." *Acta ad archaeologiam et artium historiam pertinentia* 2 (1965), 177–93 [sixteen plates]; Slomann, Vilhelm. *Bicorporates: Studies in Revivals and Migrations of Art Motifs. 1: Text. 2: Plates.* Trans. Eve M. Wendt. Copenhagen: Munksgaard, 1967; Anker, Peter, and Aron Andersson *L'Art scandinave.* 2 vols. La nuit des temps, 28–9. L'Abbaye Sainte-Marie de la Pierre-qui-Vire [Yonne]: Zodiaque, 1968–69 [English translation: *The Art of Scandinavia.* London and New York: Hamlyn, 1970]; Blindheim, Martin, ed. *Norge 872–1972. Norwegian Medieval Art Abroad.* Oslo: University Museum of National Antiquities, 1972 [exhibition catalogue]; Hauglid, Roar. *Norske stavkirker. Dekor og utstyr.* Oslo: Dreyer, 1973 [numerous illustrations and comprehensive bibliography. English translation: *Norwegian Stave Churches.* Trans. R. I. Christophersen. Oslo: Dreyer, 1977]; Hohler, Erla Bergendahl. "Hylestadportalen og dens forbilder." *Aust-Agder Arv.* Yearbook for Aust-Agder Museum and Aust-Agder Archives, 1971–1972 (1974), 59–81 [English summary]; Hohler, Erla Bergendahl. "The Capitals of Urnes Church and Their Background." *Acta Archaeologica* 46 (1975), 1–76 [sixteen plates]; Gjærder, Per. *Norske drikkekar av tre.* Oslo: Universitesforlaget, 1975, 1982 [English summary]; Sjøvold, Thorleif. *The Viking Ships in Oslo.* Oslo: Universitetets Oldsaksamling, 1979; Fuglesang, Signe Horn. *Some Aspects of the Ringerike Style: A Phase of 11th Century Scandinavian Art.* Mediaeval Scandinavia. Supplements, 1. Odense: Odense University Press, 1980; Wilson, David M., and Ole Klindt-Jensen. *Viking Art.* 2nd rev. ed. Minneapolis: University of Minnesota Press, 1980; Fuglesang, Signe Horn. "Woodcarvers—Professionals and Amateurs—in Eleventh-Century Trondheim." In *Economic Aspects of the Viking Age.* Ed. David M. Wilson and Marjorie L. Caghill. British Museum Occasional Paper, 30. London: British Museum, 1981, pp. 21–31; Hohler, Erla Bergendahl. "The Sogn-Valdres Design." In *The Vanishing Past: Studies of Medieval Art, Liturgy and Metrology Presented to Chrisopher Hohler.* Ed. Alan Borg and Andrew Martindale. B.A.R. International Series, 3. Oxford: British Archaeological Reports, 1981, pp. 63–88 and pls. 1–39; Fuglesang, Signe Horn. "Early Viking Art." In *Acta ad archaeologiam et artium historiam pertinentia.* Series altera 8°, vol. 2. Ed. Hjalmar Torp and J. Rasmus Brandt. Rome: Bretschneider, 1982, pp. 125–73; Magerøy, Ellen Marie. *Norsk treskurd.* Norsk kulturarv, 20. 2nd ed. Oslo: Det Norske Samlaget, 1983 [four of seven chapters discuss pre-Reformation wood carving; English summary and comprehensive bibliography]; Krogh, Knud F. *Kirkjubøstolene og Kirkjubøur. Et brudstykke af det færøske bispesædes historie.* Tórshavn: Thomsen, 1988.

Ellen Marie Magerøy

2. ICELAND. Because of the combination of wood, stone, and turf in Icelandic buildings, conditions have been especially poor for the preservation of wood carving. There are very few carved wooden objects surviving from before the Reformation. But these few pieces, mostly fragments of buildings, are of inestimable importance for our knowledge of wood carving in the Nordic countries.

Iceland has wood carvings of the late Jelling and the Ringerike styles on pieces of paneling from churches or secular houses. Probably the oldest are those from the farms of Möðrufell (thirteen pieces) and Hólar (one piece) in Eyjafjörður in northern Iceland. Each is decorated with spear-like figures in relief adorned with incised ornamentation. The decoration exhibits features of both Jelling and Ringerike styles. The four fragments of an upright panel found on the farm of Flatatunga in Skagafjörður (northern Iceland) have incised ornamentation consisting of plant motifs above a frieze of figures depicting Christ and his apostles, perhaps illus-

trating the Last Judgment. In 1973, a fragment decorated in the Ringerike style came to light when an old house was torn down on the farm of Gaulverjabær in southern Iceland. The fragment seems to be part of a chair or bench.

The remains, thirteen larger and smaller fragments, of a piece of horizontal paneling from the farm of Bjarnastaðahlið in Skagafjörður show a later style. The decoration consists entirely of incised figures, but was probably painted originally. It has been shown (by Selma Jónsdóttir 1959) that these fragments are parts of a characteristically Byzantine representation of the Last Judgment, which perhaps decorated the west wall of the nave of Hólar cathedral (Kristján Eldjárn 1960), built soon after 1106.

Six fragments of beams and of plank, carved in relief, from Hrafnagil in Eyjafjörður may be of different ages. The oldest are probably parts of a stave-church portal from the latter half of the 12th century. They seem to have been decorated with vine-like plants and winged dragons.

An important monument is the church door from Valþjófsstaðir in Fljótsdalur in eastern Iceland, probably from about 1200, with two large, circular medallions decorated in relief. The uppermost depicts a knight on horseback with helmet and shield, who saves a lion by piercing a dragon with his sword. Afterward, the lion follows him faithfully and finally dies on his grave. A runic inscription tells that the king who killed the dragon is buried there. The lower medallion contains four winged dragons intertwined in a fantastic decoration. The door was probably originally taller, with a third carved medallion. The carving has features in common with the wood carving on the portals of the Norwegian stave churches (e.g., Hylestad).

Wood carving of a more European-Romanesque type, apparently from about 1260, is found on two planks from Laufás at Eyjafjörður and two fragments of planks from Mælifell in Skagafjörður, possibly parts of church portals. The motifs are big-leaved stalks of a soft, rounded character, partly intertwined with four-legged animals. The decoration is similar on two boards from Mælifell with well-preserved wood carving.

On a doorway plank from Munkaþverá in Eyjafjörður, a long, double stalk twines up from a gaping animal mouth. The scanty leaves are decorated with chip carving. Most of the circular areas between the stalks contain figures, human beings, and animals. The plank may date from after 1300.

Although the wood carving in "Icelandic style" on a fragment from Skjaldfönn in northwestern Iceland appears to be totally Romanesque, with small-leaved spiral stalks interspersed with animals, it probably dates from the mid-15th century.

Church furnishings that have been preserved include a fragment of a chair back and two famous chairs from Grund in Eyjafjörður. A valuation document from 1551, listing the chairs as new, enables us to date these chairs roughly. They were given to the church in the chieftain's seat of Grund by the mistress of the farm, Þórunn, the daughter of Bishop Jón Arason. They represent richly carved, posted furniture with a "box" and lid. In contrast to Norwegian church furniture of a similar type, this furniture has carving only on the front of the chair back, not on the back. The carving is mainly Romanesque, with some Gothic features.

In Iceland, in spite of certain elements characteristic of later styles, the Romanesque style of wood carving lasted many centuries.

Lit.: Kristján Eldjárn. "Carved Panels from Flatatunga, Iceland." *Acta Archaeologica* 24 (1953), 81–101; Selma Jónsdóttir. *An 11th Century Byzantine Last Judgment in Iceland.* Reykjavik: Almenna Bókafélagið, 1959; Magerøy, Ellen Marie. "Flatatunga Problems." *Acta Archaeologica* 32 (1961), 153–72; Paulsen, Peter. *Drachenkämpfer, Löwenritter und die Heinrichsage. Eine Studie über die Kirchentür von Valthjofsstad auf Island.* Cologne: Böhlau, 1966; Magerøy, Ellen-Marie. *Planteornamentikken i islandsk treskurd. En stilhistorisk studie.* Bibliotheca Arnamagnæana, Supplement, 5–6. Copenhagen: Munksgaard, 1967 [two chapters deal with medieval wood carving; English and French summary, with comprehensive bibliography]; Kristján Eldjárn. "Forn útskurður frá Hólum í Eyjafirði." *Árbók hins íslenzka fornleifafélags 1967* (1968), 5–24 [English summary]; Kristján Eldjárn. "Útskurður frá Skjaldfönn." *Árbók hins íslenzka fornleifafélags 1969* (1970), 45–56 [English summary]; Þór Magnússon. "Hringaríkisútskurður frá Gaulverjabæ." *Árbók hins íslenzka fornleifafélags 1974* (1975), 63–74 [English summary]; Hörður Ágústsson. "Með dýrum kost. Athugun á viðarleifum frá Hrafnagili og skurðlist þeirra." *Árbók hins íslenzka fornleifafélags 1985* (1986), 137–65 [instructive illustrations].

Ellen Marie Magerøy

3. DENMARK AND SWEDEN. Denmark and Sweden never gloried in such eminent wood carvers as Norway's and, consequently, have nothing corresponding to the Oseberg find, the Urnes portal, or the Norwegian stave-church portals of more recent date. Vendel graves and one of the Jelling mounds, however, contain fragments of decorative wood carving, which indicates that those regions may have possessed rich carved material from the Migration and Viking periods.

The Scandinavian works of art surviving from those early periods (*ca.* 500–1050) consist mainly of metal mountings and buckles of modest dimensions. Many are cast bronze that has been gilded. They are largely of a form indicating that the motifs were originally shaped in wood, *i.e.*, in chip-carving technique. Houses, furniture, vehicles, tools, and weapons were to a large extent made of wood and were certainly richly decorated. Hardly anything remains today, but, thanks to their popular roots, patterns and motifs originating from the Migration Period survived in Swedish decorative wood carving.

During the 11th century, the overall design is balanced, sometimes symmetrical. The elongated, ribbon-shaped animal bodies, with clearly represented details, describe gentle curves and show rhythmical interaction between different kinds of ribbons, small and large, closed and open, narrow and broad, all consistently interlaced (Fig. 183a).

The finds from the two preceding centuries are less rich, rather ambiguous, and also unequally distributed. Denmark and Norway, however, retain more material than Sweden and show some interesting intermediate forms. The animal representations of the Mamen axe (Fig. 183b) are based on the same fundamental Nordic structure that is seen in Fig. 183a and that is easily recognized in the surface-covering ornamentation of one of the early 9th-century animal-head posts from the Oseberg find (Fig. 183c).

The 8th-century design is often closed and concentrated. Its zoological origin and specific anatomical details are generally subordinated to a predominant rhythmical line pattern, a distinct difference in degree but not in kind, a variation in level of abstraction inside the same complex of styles (Fig. 183d).

The origin of Scandinavian animal ornamentation lies even further back, but let us stop in the 7th century (Fig. 183e). Uppland and Gotland have grave finds from that century that answer many of the questions raised by medieval wood carving. In regard to the development of the Scandinavian style, the finds unequivocally point to its firmly rooted tradition and conservatism. There are certainly differences between Figs. 183a and 183e, but no greater than between many contemporaneous objects out of the same accepted complex of styles. More important than such divergencies of detail is that everything connects: lineation, rhythm, interlace, imagery, and the tendency of style.

This Nordic tradition of form was broken when Christianity triumphed. Missionaries and priests seem to have regarded animal ornamentation as pagan, and they resolutely worked to direct pictorial art into other paths. The artists were employed by the Church itself, and they fetched their motifs from the Christian countries from which the missions had set out.

The Christian artists who shaped the early portal reliefs, fonts, roods, mural paintings, and communion silverware were all trained and highly specialized craftsmen. This is also true of the Norwegian wood carvers, but hardly of their colleagues from Denmark and Sweden. With few exceptions, the wood carvings from the latter countries are executed in a simple scratchwork technique. They are unplastic and linear, more like drawings than sculpted reliefs. The East Scandinavian wood ornamentation has mostly been cut with a knife by local carpenters without any knowledge of the stylistic techniques in vogue.

But the most ancient material is of a different character, and belongs to the stave-church era in the 11th century and beginning of the 12th. Stylistically, it is related to the Urnes portal and to the style named after it. At the National Museum in Copenhagen, there is a fragment of a wall plate with a ribbon-shaped animal whose body forms an eight. To the right, there is its head with an eye, pointed forward, elongated jaws, and two lappets extending from the back of its neck and its upper jaw, characteristics of the pure Urnes style (Fig. 184).

From another Danish stave church comes a board that once belonged to the top piece of a portal. It is fragmentary and damaged by rot and insects, but presents several typical features of the Urnes style (Fig. 185).

Less ancient and enriched with loans out of the international Romanesque are the portal boards from the two Gotlandic stave churches at Guldrupe and Hemse (Figs. 186, 187). The same foreign influences appear in the ornamentation of the Kungsåra bench (Fig. 188). Its basic form is traditionally Nordic, like its linear rhythm, but its three winged dragons do not belong in the domestic fauna. They have thus been borrowed, but are tolerably well integrated in the Nordic pictorial language.

In the sparsely populated regions in Norrland, the animal ornamentation from the Viking Age survived for all the Middle Ages and much longer. From Lillhärdal comes a round lid that several scholars suppose belonged to a wooden font. On its upper side, there are two ribbon-shaped animals (Fig. 189). The double contours, the long lappets, and the foot that terminates each body have many Swedish forerunners as early as the Vendel period. The representation on the lid is highly retarded; the head is disintegrated and only marked by three lappets.

Closely related characteristics are found on a chest from Bjuråker (Fig. 190). The animals' bodies retain their double contours and are interlaced in the traditional way, but heads and extremities have, during the making of long series of copies, lost all their strictness. This kind of ornamentation cannot be dated on stylistic grounds. It bears a Viking Age stamp that, in extreme cases, stayed alive into the 19th century.

Sometimes, an even older tradition can be vaguely discerned. In Dalarna, one of the provinces where surviving forms have been most thoroughly investigated, patterns from the Migration Period have been repeated for over a millennium. From Rättvik comes a wool hamper, one side of which has a remarkable motif. It consists of a wavy vine that has stylized animal heads instead of leaves, whose long tongues protrude and cut across the stem of the vine (Fig. 191). Its closest parallels are found in 7th-century metal mountings. The same old-fashioned tendencies appear at Orsa, where confronting animal heads have been put together to carry the receptacle of a baptismal font (Fig. 192).

The objects in Figs. 190–192 are late-medieval or possibly even younger. Purely Romanesque, on the other hand, are a great number of beams and boards that sat under the roof pitch of our earliest stone churches (Fig. 193). The wall plate has been directly transferred from the stave church, where it occupies a key position in the construction, whereas its function in the stone church is uncertain, and where it is also most often lacking. Fig. 193 shows how the eave board sits under the projecting part of the roof truss. Both these building units were furnished with carved ornaments. Because of their exposed position, they have often been damaged by wind and weather.

In Nordic animal ornamentation, there developed very early a group of zoomorphous lappets, which in the course of the late Viking Age received a characteristic shaping. The typical lappet is long, narrow, tensely curved, with a rolled terminal and, at its base, a smaller lobe. During the missionary era, vegetative motifs began to penetrate, and the lappet was made to serve as a leaf in pure plant ornaments. In its original form, it is found in the ornamentation from Guldrupe and Hablingbo (Figs. 194b and c), with slightly modified versions of it in several other places (Figs. 194d–l). Characteristic of early Nordic vine ornamentation are symbiotic vegeto-animal forms. Sometimes, the vine extends from a dragon's body (Figs 194l and m; also Fig 188). In other cases, small animal heads burgeon from the branches (Fig. 194g).

Animal ornaments were predominant in the Scandinavian art of pre-Christian times, and a prominent feature was the use of elongated animal bodies interwoven to make intricate patterns. But besides such zoomorphous interlace, there was pure ribbon and plait ornamentation, which also survived into the popular art of more recent times. A good example of the latter type is given by a wooden balance from Söderköping (Fig. 195). Its counterpoise is covered by the kind of ring-chain pattern found on the stone crosses at Gosforth and on the Isle of Man.

East Scandinavian wood carving was thus dominated by lo- cal, stylistically retarded representations, but there were other manifestations as well. The two stave-church fragments (Figs. 184

and 185) do not belong in the predominant group, and from Norrland come two Romanesque baptismal fonts, well elaborated in the round. The one from Näs in Jämtland (Fig. 196) has been made out of one single piece probably by a skilled Norwegian sculptor; the inscribed palmettes on its foot have parallels in the Norwegian material. The font from Alnö in Medelpad (Fig. 197) is totally different and unique. The large monsters on its foot may have been borrowed from some stone font, but are very specially elaborated. The receptacle has irregular vines and abstruse figure representations, which lack parallels.

During the 14th and 15th centuries, the Danish cathedrals of Lund and Roskilde received magnificent, richly sculpted oaken choir stalls. They correspond to international models and were obviously executed by artists called in for the occasion. Also, the stalls and benches that remain in Gotlandic parish churches have been influenced by continental patterns. But they are simpler and in most cases carved by native masters. It is striking how often the Gotlandic benches are adorned with vegetative dragons (Fig. 198), i.e., the same motif that we have met before (cf. Figs. 188, 194l and 194m); the leaf shapes have been borrowed, but the basic motif has a native lineage.

To the painters, sculptors, and goldsmiths who worked for the Church, the Reformation meant a serious setback, but not to local wood carvers, who kept on tending their heritage from the Migration, oblivious of Renaissance, Baroque, and Rococo.

Lit.: Ekhoff, Emil. Svenska stavkyrkor jämte iakttagelser över de norska samt redogörelse för i Danmark och England kända lämningar av stavkonstruktioner. Stockholm: Cederquist, 1914–16; Møller, Elna. "Om danske lektiorier." Fra Nationalmuseets Arbejdsmark (1950), 129–38; Bugge, Anders. Norwegian Stave Churches. Trans. Ragnar Christophersen. Oslo: Dreyer, 1953; Anker, Peter, and Aron Andersson. L'Art scandinave. 2 vols. La nuit des temps, 28– 9. L'Abbaye Sainte-Marie de la Pierre-qui-Vire [Yonne]: Zodiaque, 1968–69 [English translation: The Art of Scandinavia. 2 vols. London and New York: Hamlyn, 1970]; Lundberg, Erik. Trä gav form. Studier över byggnadskonst vars former framgått ur trämaterial och träkonstruktion. Stockholm: Nordsted, 1971; Moltke, E. "Treskurd." KLNM 18 (1974), 619–20; Karlsson, Lennart. Romansk träornamentik i Sverige. Decorative Romanesque Woodcarving in Sweden. Stockholm Studies in History of Art, 27. Stockholm: Almqvist & Wiksell, 1976; Smith, John T. "Norwegian Stave Churches: A Review of Some Recent Publications." Journal of the British Archaeological Association 131 (1978), 118–25; Bugge, Gunnar. Stave Churches in Norway: Introduction and Survey. Oslo: Dreyer, 1983.

Lennart Karlsson

[See also: Carving: Bone, Horn, and Walrus Tusk; Iconogra- phy; Oseberg; Stave Church; Viking Art]

Ynglinga saga ("The Saga of the Ynglingar") is the first section of Snorri Sturluson's *Heimskringla*. It is a quasi-historical work, in which Snorri gives an account of the mythical and legendary ancestors of the Ynglingar, the kings of Sweden. These kings were thought to descend from the pagan Norse gods, and Snorri traces in detail their mythical ancestry, expressing the same euhemeristic views as in his *Prose Edda*, although here he carries them even further. He tells how Óðinn had led the gods from Asia to Scandinavia, where he distributed dominions among his sons and followers. After Óðinn's death, Njǫrðr became the ruler of Sweden, followed by his son, Freyr (Yngvi-Freyr), after whom the kings were called "Ynglingar." Covering a period from the end of the 3rd century to the mid-9th century, Snorri provides a systematic and concise account of events during the reigns of these kings.

In this part of *Heimskringla*, Snorri used a number of sources of various kinds. His main source was the poem *Ynglingatal*, composed in the 9th century by the Norwegian Þjóðólfr of Hvin in honor of King Rǫgnvaldr heiðumhæri ("the highly honored") to glorify the kings of southeastern Norway, demonstrating their descent from the Ynglingar. Snorri also quotes stanzas from Bragi Boddason's *Ragnarsdrápa* and Eyvindr skáldaspillir's ("plagiarist") *Háleygatal*. It appears that Snorri also borrowed from the now-lost *Skjǫldunga saga*, to which he refers in ch. 29. Influence from *Skjǫldunga saga* is particularly evident in the discussion of kings from Dyggvi to Aðils.

A list of the Ynglingar kings is found also in Ari Þorgilsson's genealogical table at the end of the existing *Íslendingabók* and in the opening section of *Historia Norwegiae*. The kings from Óláfr trételgja ("wood-cutter") are described also in the *Þáttr af Upplendinga konungum* in *Hauksbók*. The relationship between these works has been debated. Thus, an older, now-lost *Ynglinga saga has been considered the basis of both the *Historia Norwegiae* and the extant *Ynglinga saga* (Finnur Jónsson 1934). Bjarni Aðalbjarnarson (1979) suggested that *Ynglinga saga* is based on written sources derived from *Ynglingatal*, which also formed the basis of the account in *Historia Norwegiae*. Beyschlag (1950) argued that *Historia Norwegiae* and *Ynglinga saga* were both based directly on *Ynglingatal*, but that Snorri adhered more closely to the poem than the author of *Historia Norwegiae*. Ellehøj (1965) claimed that both *Ynglinga saga* and *Historia Norwegiae* were based on Ari Þorgilsson's older and now-lost *Íslendingabók*. More recent research suggests that an older version of the *Þáttr af Upplendingakonungum* forms the basis of *Ynglinga saga* and that the *Þáttr* is based on *Ynglingatal* (cf. Magerøy 1976).

Ed.: Bjarni Aðalbjarnarson, ed. *Heimskringla*. 3 vols. Íslenzk fornrit, 26–8. Reykjavik: Hið íslenzka fornritafélag, 1941–51. **Tr.**: Hollander, Lee M., trans. *Heimskringla: History of the Kings of Norway*. Austin: University of Texas Press, 1964. **Lit.**: Detter, Ferdinand. "Zur Ynglingasaga." *Beiträge zur Geschichte der deutschen Sprache und Literatur* 18 (1894), 72–105; Salin, Bernhard. "Heimskringlas tradition om asarnes invandring: Ett arkeologiskt-religionshistoriskt utkast." In *Studier tillägnade Oscar Montelius 19.9.03 af lärjungar*. Ed. Bernhard Salin *et al.* Stockholm: Norstedt, 1903, pp. 133–41; Lindqvist, Sune. "Ett 'Frös-vi' i Nerike." *Fornvännen* 5 (1910), 119–38; Nerman, Birger. "Ynglingasagan i arkeologisk belysning." *Fornvännen* 12 (1917), 226–61; Lindqvist, Sune. "Ynglingaättens gravskick." *Fornvännen* 16 (1921), 83–194; Finnur Jónsson. "Til belysning af Snorri Sturlusons behandling af hans kilder." *Arkiv för nordisk filologi* 50 (1934), 181–96; Beyschlag, Siegfried. *Konungasögur: Untersuchungen zur Königssaga bis Snorri*. Bibliotheca Arnamagnæana, 8. Copenhagen: Munksgaard, 1950; Bjarni Guðnason. *Um Skjöldungasögu*. Reykjavik: Menningarsjóður, 1963; Taylor, Paul Beekman. "*Heofon riece swealg*: A Sign of Beowulf's State of Grace." *Philological Quarterly* 42.2 (1963), 257–9; Turville-Petre, E. O. G. *Myth and Religion of the North: The Religion of Ancient Scandinavia*. New York: Holt, Rinehart and Winston, 1964; rpt. Westport: Greenwood, 1975; Nerman, Birger. "Bröt-Anunds död." *Arkiv för nordisk filologi* 79 (1964), 241–2; Ellehøj, Svend. *Studier over den ældste norrøne historieskrivning*. Bibliotheca Arnamagnæana, 26. Copenhagen: Munksgaard, 1965; Ström, Folke. "Kung Domalde i Svitjod och 'kungalyckan.'" *Saga och sed* (1967), 52–66; Schier, Kurt. "Freys und Fróðis Bestattung." In *Festschrift für Otto Höfler zum 65. Geburtstag*. 2 vols. Ed. Helmut Birkhan and Otto Gschwantler. Vienna: Notring, 1968, vol. 2, pp. 389–409; Gurevich, A. Ya. "Saga and History: The Historical Conception of Snorri Sturluson." *Mediaeval Scandinavia* 4 (1971), 42–53; Ciklamini, Marlene. "*Ynglinga saga*: Its Function and Its Appeal." *Mediaeval Scandinavia* 8 (1975), 86–99; Morgenstierne, Georg. "Áss og (J)ass (osseter)." *Maal og minne* (1975), 30–1; Magerøy, Hallvard. "Ynglingasaga." *KLNM* 20 (1976), 360–2; Kalinke, Marianne E. "*Ynglinga saga*, Chapter 21: A Case of Once Too Often." *Scandinavian Studies* 50 (1978), 72–5; Clunies Ross, Margaret. "The Myth of Gefjon and Gylfi and Its Function in Snorra Edda and Heimskringla." *Arkiv för nordisk filologi* 93 (1978), 149–65; Evans, David A. H. "King Agni: Myth, History or Legend." In *Specvlvm Norroenvm: Norse Studies in*

Memory of Gabriel Turville-Petre. Ed. Ursula Dronke *et al.* Odense: Odense University Press, 1981, pp. 89–105; Rausing, Gad. "Beowulf, Ynglingatal and the Ynglinga Saga: Fiction or History?" *Fornvännen* 80 (1985), 163–77; Lönnroth, Lars. "Dómaldi's Death and the Myth of Sacral Kingship." In *Structure and Meaning in Old Norse Literature: New Approaches to Textual Analysis and Literary Criticism.* Ed. John Lindow *et al.* Viking Collection, 3. Odense: Odense University Press, 1986, pp. 73–93.

Gad Rausing

[**See also:** Bragi Boddason; Eyvindr Finnsson skáldaspillir; *Hauksbók*; *Heimskringla*; *Historia Norwegiae*; *Íslendingabók*; *Skjǫldunga saga*; *Snorra Edda*; Snorri Sturluson; Þjóðólfr of Hvin]

Ynglingatal *see* Þjóðólfr of Hvin

Yngvars saga víðfǫrla

("The Saga of Yngvarr the Far-traveler") relates the Swedish warrior Yngvarr's famous expedition through Russia to Serkland. The saga stands on the margin between *konungasǫgur* and *fornaldarsǫgur*, but is commonly classified as belonging to the latter genre. The action takes place no earlier than the 11th century, and treats to some extent historical events and characters. Interspersed throughout the narrative are fabulous events from the *fornaldarsǫgur* and from the learned literature of the time in the tradition of Isidore.

The saga survives in two vellum MSS, AM 343a 4to (A) and GkS 2845 4to (B), both of which are defective. For his edition, Olson (1912) used also two paper MSS, AM 343c 4to (C) and Rask 31 (D) from the 17th and 18th centuries respectively; both MSS contain the complete text of the saga. Olson based his text on A with variants from B, C, and D; the lacuna in A was filled in from C. Jón Helgason (1960) has, however, demonstrated that C and D are both derived from A through a lost intermediary (*Y), and that A and B are derived from a now-lost original (*X). Apart from the fact that the MSS C and D preserve the text of the lacuna in A, they have no textual significance.

The prologue gives a survey of the history of three generations, the first two marred by personal and political conflicts. But with the third generation, represented by Yngvarr Eymundsson and his royal comrade, the son of the Swedish king Olaf Eriksson, the idea of magnaminity gains a firm ground, and the conflicts are brought to an end. Yngvarr excels as a warrior in the service of King Olaf until his refusal to bestow upon Yngvarr a royal title causes a breach in their friendship. Yngvarr gathers a force and begins his long and adventurous expedition, during which he dies "eleven years after the death of King Óláfr Haraldsson" (MS B; A has "nine years") in an epidemic that ravaged most of his force. Yngvarr's men bring his corpse to his lady-love, Queen Silkisif of Garðaríki, who instructs the men to return to Sweden and send someone to christianize the pagan country. Yngvarr's son, Sveinn, sets out on a no less perilous expedition, finalizes the conversion, marries Queen Silkisif, and has a church erected dedicated to Yngvarr.

The epilogue says that the story is based on written documents by the monk Oddr. Hofmann (1981) argues that the existing text represents an Icelandic translation from before 1200 of a now-lost Latin original composed by Oddr Snorrason at the end of the 12th century in the monastery of Þingeyrar (see, however, McDougall 1982–83).

In the entries for 1041, *Konungsannáll* and *Lǫgmannsannáll* state that "Yngvarr the Far-traveler dies" (*Islandske Annaler* 1888: 108, 250); it is, therefore, believed that in or around 1041 Yngvarr led an expedition from central Sweden, and that the expedition met with disaster somewhere southeast of Russia, in the region of the Caspian (see, however, Thulin 1975, Mel'nikova 1976, and Pritsak 1981). The approximately thirty rune stones in Sweden erected in memory of the men who fell "in the East with Yngvarr" corroborate the evidence given by the annals. In addition, Shepard (1984–85) has drawn attention to an Old Russian inscribed cross commemorating a deceased Russian. The cross stood near a land and water route from the Caspian to the Sea of Azov. Its Cyrillic inscription appears once to have borne a date corresponding to 1041, but no longer does so. The second expedition, undertaken by Sveinn, has not been historically verified.

Ed.: Storm, Gustav, ed. *Islandske Annaler indtil 1578.* Christiania [Oslo]: Grøndahl, 1888; rpt. Norsk historisk kjeldeskrift-institut, 1977; Olson, Emil. *Yngvars saga víðfǫrla jämte ett bihang om Invargsinskrifterna.* Samfund til udgivelse af gammel nordisk litteratur, 39. Copenhagen: Møller, 1912; Guðni Jónsson, ed. *Fornaldar sögur Norðurlanda.* 4 vols. Akureyri: Íslendingasagnaútgáfan, 1954, vol. 2, pp. 423–59; Jón Helgason. *The Saga Manuscript 2845, 4to in the Old Royal Collection in the Royal Library of Copenhagen.* Manuscripta Islandica, 2. Copenhagen: Munksgaard, 1955. **Tr.**: Hermann Pálsson and Paul Edwards, trans. *Vikings in Russia: Yngvar's Saga and Eymund's Saga.* Edinburgh: Edinburgh University Press, 1989 [Rev. by Robert Cook in *Saga-Book of the Viking Society* 23.2 (1990), 99–105]. **Bib.**: Halldór Hermannsson. *Bibliography of the Mythical-Heroic Sagas (Fornaldarsǫgur).* Islandica, 5. Ithaca: Cornell University Library, 1912; rpt. New York: Kraus, 1966. **Lit.**: Braun, F. "Hvem var Yngvarr enn víðfǫrla? Ett bidrag till Sveriges historia under XI århundraets första hälft." *Fornvännen* 5 (1910), 99–118; Jón Helgason. "Til Yngvars sagas overlevering." *Opuscula* 1. Bibliotheca Arnamagnæana, 20. Copenhagen: Munksgaard, 1960, pp. 176–8; Wessén, Elias. *Historiska runinskrifter.* Kungl. vitterhets historie och antikvitets akademiens, Handlingar. Filologisk-filosofiska serien, 6. Stockholm: Almqvist & Wiksell, 1960; Thulin, Alf. "Ingvarståget—en ny datering?" *Arkiv för nordisk filologi* 90 (1975), 19–29; Ellis Davidson, H. R. *The Viking Road to Byzantium.* London: Allen & Unwin, 1976; Mel'nikova, E. A. "Ekspeditsiya Ingvarra puteshestvennika na vostok i pokhod russkikh na Vizantiyu v 1043g." *Skandinavskiy Sbornik* 21 (1976), 74–87; Pritsak, Omeljan. *The Origin of Rus'. 1: Old Scandinavian Sources Other Than the Sagas.* Cambridge: Harvard University Press, 1981; Hofmann, Dietrich. "Die Yngvars saga víðfǫrla und Oddr munkr inn fróði." In *Specvlvm Norroenvm: Norse Studies in Memory of Gabriel Turville-Petre.* Ed. Ursula Dronke *et al.* Odense: Odense University Press, 1981, pp. 188–222; McDougall, David, and Ian McDougall. Rev. of Ursula Dronke *et al.*, eds. *Specvlvm Norroenvm. Saga-Book of the Viking Society* 21 (1982–83), 106–8; Larsson, Mats G. "Vart for Ingvar den vittfarne?" *Fornvännen* 78 (1983), 95–104; McGinnis, Deborah. "The Vikings in the East: *Yngvars saga víðfǫrla.*" *Scandinavian-Canadian Studies* (1983), 79–86; Hofmann, Dietrich. "Zu Oddr Snorrasons Yngvars saga víðfǫrla." *Skandinavistik* 14 (1984), 106–8; Shepard, Jonathan. "Yngvar's Expedition to the East and a Russian Inscribed Stone Cross." *Saga-Book of the Viking Society* 21 (1984–85), 222–92 [numerous bibliographical references]; Larsson, Mats G. "Ingvarstågets arkeologiska bakgrund." *Fornvännen* 81 (1986), 98–113; Larsson, Mats G. "Yngvarr's Expedition and the *Georgian Chronicle.*" *Saga-Book of the Viking Society* 22 (1987), 98–108.

Kirsten Wolf

[See also: *Fornaldarsögur*; *Konungasögur*; Runes and Runic Inscriptions; Rus'; Russia, Norse in; Varangians]

York

The Anglo-Saxon settlement of *Eoforwic* combined functions of royal site, archbishop's seat, and international trading center. It was one of just a handful of places in 7th- to 9th-century England that could be called a town, and was the first strategic target of the Viking "Great Army" that landed in England in 865. They captured York in 866, held it in face of a Northumbrian counterattack, and established a line of kings, both Danes and Norwegians, who controlled the city and its kingdom, encompassing the county of Yorkshire and lands beyond, for most of the period until 954. In that year, the last Viking king, the exiled Norwegian prince Eiríkr blóðøx ("blood-axe") Haraldsson, was expelled, but Scandinavian settlers and their descendants remained an important element in the population until the Norman Conquest and after. Their influence is demonstrated in the city's name "York," which derives from *Jórvík*, the Scandinavian version of the Old English name *Eoforwic*. Many of the street names end in the element *-gate*, also a Scandinavian derivation.

Viking Age texts, such as the *Anglo-Saxon Chronicle*, imply that Jórvík was a defended site. It was described around 1000 as full of the treasures brought from many places by merchants, particularly Danes. In William the Conqueror's *Domesday Book*, the city is shown in 1066 as divided into seven administrative areas called "shires." There were about 2,000 tenements in the city, suggesting a population of around 10,000, and various churches are named as well as one street, the Shambles or Butcher's street. This street and all of the churches still survive, in or just outside the area originally occupied by the Roman fortress and civilian town. The Anglo-Saxon commercial center focused 1 km. farther downstream, but it was abandoned at the start of the Scandinavian occupation, when the old Roman nucleus was reoccupied. Archaeological excavations at Coppergate have demonstrated clearly how an area that had been abandoned since the end of the Roman period around A.D. 400 was settled again in the mid-9th century, and divided up into tenement plots that left an enduring mark on the evolution of the neighborhood, still recognizable in the 20th century.

The Scandinavian kings revitalized the coinage of York, improving its weight and purity. Commerce was encouraged as a source of revenue, and Jórvík had links extending throughout England, to the Scandinavian colonies in Scotland and Ireland (Jórvík had close dynastic links with the rulers of Norse Dublin), to the Scandinavian homelands, to northwestern Europe, and beyond, via a series of middlemen, to the eastern Mediterranean and the Near and Middle East. Among the goods brought to the town were German wines and Byzantine silks.

Economically as important as overseas trade was Jórvík's role as a manufacturing center, supplying a wide hinterland with a range of goods and equipment. There is, for example, archaeological evidence for metalworking, including both the production of jewelry and the manufacture of such items as knives, locks, and keys; for the working of both jet and amber into jewelry; for a variety of leather working, including shoemaking and repairing; for textile production and dyeing; for the making of wooden cups and bowls; and for a wide range of bone and antler working, making combs and many other items. Sometimes, Norse taste and style can be detected, as in the evidence for making the trefoil brooches characteristic of Viking Age Scandinavia, or in the scenes from pagan Norse mythology, including the Sigurðr epic, carved on grave markers found near the Viking Age cathedral. Essentially, however, the culture of Jórvík was a hybrid, Anglo-Scandinavian one, and many of the finds would not be out of place anywhere in northwestern Europe.

With its Scandinavian links, the later 10th- and 11th-century kings were wary of the loyalty of Jórvík, and appointed earls and archbishops who were acceptable in York yet linked to the south of England, to rule it on their behalf. Just before the Norman Conquest, one of the last earls, Waltheof, built a church dedicated to St. Óláfr; a later rebuilding still stands today, and probably signals the location of the earl's palace. Similarly, the name "King's Square," first recorded as *Konungsgurtha*, probably indicates where the Viking Age royal palace lay.

The last epic battle of the Viking period took place 11 km. east-northeast of York in 1066, when Haraldr harðráði ("hard-ruler") Sigurðarson of Norway, having won an initial victory over the men of York at the battle of Fulford, was surprised, defeated, and killed by King Harold Godwinsson at Stamford Bridge. After Harold's defeat at Hastings, the Normans eventually seized control of York and built new castles and churches, but despite their interventions and those of succeeding centuries, York retains to this day the topographic framework that largely crystallized under Norse rule when Jórvík was second only to London as the largest and richest city in England.

Lit.: Hall, R. A., ed. *Viking Age York and the North*. CBA Research Report, 27. London: Council for British Archaeology, 1978; Hall, Richard. *The Viking Dig: The Excavations of York*. London: Bodley Head, 1984; several volumes in the *Archaeology of York* series, ed. P. V. Addyman (continuing), include important new material: vol. 1, *Sources for York History to AD 1000*; vol. 8, *Anglo-Scandinavian York*; vol. 14, *The Past Environment of York*; vol. 15, *The Animal Bones*; vol. 16, *The Pottery*; vol. 17, *The Small Finds*; vol. 18, *The Coins*. This series is published by the Council for British Archaeology, London, in association with the York Archaeological Trust.

R. A. Hall

[See also: England, Norse in; Stamford Bridge, Battle of]

Ǫgmundar þáttr dytts ok Gunnars helmings

("The Tale of Ǫgmundr Dint and Gunnarr Half") is an anonymous *þáttr*, written probably in the beginning of the 14th century. It is extant in its entirety only within *Óláfs saga Tryggvasonar en mesta*, although originally it was possibly an independent narrative. The *Vatnshyrna* version of *Víga-Glúms saga* tells only the first part of the story. The text is not designated as a *þáttr* in the MSS, but was classified as such by the editors of this group of texts.

On a journey from Iceland to Norway, Ǫgmundr Hrafnsson has an argument with one of Earl Hákon Sigurðarson's men. Ǫgmundr decides to take revenge, and arrives in Norway after two years. There he learns from Gunnarr that Óláfr Tryggvason is now the ruler and that his enemy, Hallvarðr, is at the court. Ǫgmundr and Gunnarr exchange cloaks, and the Icelander then goes to the king's court, kills Hallvarðr, and returns to Iceland. Because of the cloak, Gunnarr is thought to be Hallvarðr's murderer. He flees to Sweden, where he stays with a priestess of Freyr and adopts the role of the heathen deity. The inhabitants of the village do not discover the deceit, and are pleased when they discover that the priestess is expecting a child. When Óláfr Tryggvason hears of this development, he immediately suspects that Gunnarr is there, and sends his brother to take him back to Norway. Gunnarr leaves heathen Sweden, and he and his wife are baptised at the Norwegian court.

The *þáttr* can be divided into two parts, the first concerning Ǫgmundr dyttr ("dint"), and the second, Gunnarr helmingr ("half"), with the exchange of cloaks functioning as a link between the parts. Whether the two parts were originally different narratives later joined by a redactor remains an open question. The second part, in which Gunnarr plays the role of the deity Freyr, has received attention from historians of religion, although its relatively late date limits the *þáttr*'s usefulness as a source.

Ed.: Guðbrandur Vigfússon and C. R. Unger, eds. *Flateyjarbók: En Samling af norske Konge-Sagaer med indskudte mindre Fortællinger om Begivenheder i og udenfor Norge samt Annaler.* 3 vols. Christiania [Oslo]: Malling, 1860–68, vol. 1, pp. 96–9; Þorleifur Jónsson, ed. *Fjörutíu Íslendingaþættir.* Reykjavik, Sigurður Kristjánsson, 1904, pp. 509–24; Guðni Jónsson, ed. *Íslendinga þættir.* Reykjavik: Sigurður Kristjánsson, 1935, pp. 446–63; Turville-Petre, G., ed. "Ǫgmundar þáttr dytts." In *Víga-Glúms saga.* 2nd ed. Oxford: Clarendon, 1960; Sigurður Nordal et al., eds. *Flateyjarbók.* 4 vols. Akranes: Flateyjarútgáfan, 1944–45, vol. 1, pp. 368–77; Jónas Kristjánsson, ed. *Eyfirðinga sǫgur.* Íslenzk fornrit, 9. Reykjavik: Hið íslenzka fornritafélag, 1956, pp. 99–115. Tr.: Sephton, John, trans. *The Saga of King Olaf Tryggvason who Reigned over Norway A.D. 995 to A.D. 1000.* London: Nutt, 1895, pp. 251–60; Gudbrand Vigfusson and F. York Powell, eds. and trans. *Origines Islandicæ: A Collection of the More Important Sagas and Other Native Writings Relating to the Settlement and Early History of Iceland.* Oxford: Clarendon, 1905; rpt. Millwood: Kraus, 1976, vol. 2, pp. 480–6; Hollander, Lee M., trans. *Víga-Glúm's Saga and the Story of Ögmund Dytt.* Library of Scandinavian Literature, 14. New York: Twayne; American-Scandinavian Foundation, 1972, pp. 124–37; McKinnell, John, trans. *Viga-Glums Saga. With the Tales of Ögmund Bash and Thorvald Chatterbox.* Edinburgh: Canongate, 1987, pp. 132–44. Lit.: Krappe, Alexander Haggerty. "La légende de Gunnar Half. (Olafs saga Tryggvasonar, Chap. 173)." *Acta Philologica Scandinavica* 3 (1928–29), 226–33; Reuschel, Helga. "Der Göttertrug im Gunnarsþáttr Helmings." *Zeitschrift für deutsches Altertum und deutsche Literatur* 71 (1934), 155–66; Harris, Joseph. "Ǫgmundar þáttr dytts ok Gunnars helmings: Unity and Literary Relations." *Arkiv för nordisk filologi* 90 (1975), 156–82; Würth, Stefanie. *Elemente des Erzählens: Die þættir der Flateyjarbók.* Beiträge zur nordischen Philologie, 20. Basel and Frankfurt am Main: Helbing & Lichtenhahn, 1991.

Stefanie Würth

[See also: *Flateyjarbók; Óláfs saga Tryggvasonar; Þáttr; Vatnshyrna; Víga-Glúms saga*]

Ǫlkofra þáttr

("The Tale of Ǫlkofri") appears in *Möðruvallabók*, between *Droplaugarsona saga* and *Hallfreðar saga vandræðaskálds*. Following the MS title itself, as well as the content and structure of the text, *Ǫlkofra þáttr* should properly be called *Ǫlkofra saga*, because it is a truncated *Íslendingasaga*, revolving around a feud touched off by accident and culminating in a legal climax at the *Alþingi*.

Þórhallr ǫlkofri ("ale-hood"), so called because he brews and sells beer at assemblies, enjoys wealth but little social status. While making charcoal in a forest he owns, he accidentally burns down his own forest and a neighboring forest owned by six chieftains. They decide to regard the fire as intentional and sue Ǫlkofri for his property. At the *Alþingi*, Ǫlkofri is unable to gain support until Broddi Bjarnarson convinces his brother-in-law Þorsteinn Síðu-Hallsson that they should help. Counseled by Broddi, Ǫlkofri tricks the chieftains into accepting arbitration for the case and to allow him to choose the arbiters. However, Ǫlkofri chooses not the chieftains, as they had expected, but Broddi and Þorsteinn. When Þorsteinn announces the judgment, which amounts to no more than a mild fine, the chieftains' complaints are silenced by Broddi in a flyting that is the central scene of the saga. He dispatches them one by one with accusations, apparently well founded, of less than manly behavior. Later, Broddi renews ties of kinship with one of the chieftains who accompanies him safely home from the Alþingi and later visits him, cementing their relationship and, one may infer, rendering unlikely further response by the other chieftains.

Although *Ljósvetninga saga* and *Vápnfirðinga saga* touch on elements of the story, *Qlkofra þáttr* is best grouped with *Lokasenna* and *Bandamanna saga* because of the centrality of the flyting. The ridiculed chieftains of *Qlkofra þáttr* have the same high status as those of *Bandamanna saga* and the gods of *Lokasenna*, because they include the major figures Guðmundr inn ríki ("the mighty") and Snorri goði ("chieftain"); and the somewhat silly Qlkofri parallels the weak Oddr of *Bandamanna saga*. With the trickster figures of *Lokasenna* and *Bandamanna saga*, however, Broddi is less closely parallel; unlike Loki and the shabby old Ófeigr, he has only his relative youth to make him singular.

Much of the speculation on *Qlkofra þáttr* has centered on its date, conventionally set at around 1250, and its relationship to *Bandamanna saga*, which has been regarded as the borrower in more recent scholarship. Neither of these findings is secure. However, the high quality of the style and characterization of *Qlkofra þáttr* is beyond debate.

Ed.: Jón Jóhannesson, ed. *Austfirðinga sögur*. Íslenzk fornrit, 11. Reykjavik: Hið íslenzka fornritafélag, 1950, pp. 81–94. **Tr.**: Allen, Ralph B., trans. "The Icelandic Tale of Thorhall Ale-Cap." *University [of Kansas] Review* 8 (1942), 161–71; Hermann Pálsson, trans. *Hrafnkel's Saga and Other Icelandic Stories*. Harmondsworth: Penguin, 1971, pp. 82–93.

John Lindow

[**See also**: *Bandamanna saga*; *Íslendingasögur*; *Ljósvetninga saga*; *Lokasenna*; *Möðruvallabók*; *Þáttr*; *Vápnfirðinga saga*]

Qrvar-Odds saga

Qrvar-Odds saga ("The Saga of Arrow-Oddr") is a *fornaldarsaga* known in two versions. Its hero, Qrvar-Oddr, is introduced as the son of Grímr loðinkinni ("bristly-cheek") and the grandson of Ketill hœngr ("salmon"), also known from *Gríms saga loðinkinna* and *Ketils saga hœngs*, respectively. These three sagas show a remarkable likeness to each other in some of their episodes in which the heroes deal with giants. There was also a historical Ketill hœngr among the earliest Icelandic settlers, so we can surmise that originally these stories were told among his descendants.

Oddr is said to have lived to the age of 300 years. At the beginning of the story, his future is told by a prophetess, whom he scorns. The fulfillment of this prophecy, which concerns the manner of his dying, serves as a frame to the story. Soon afterward, he starts his life as a Viking, and thus shows himself to have more mettle than his predecessors, who had always been farmers. Many of the following episodes contain nothing more than a set of stereotypical Viking adventures. His nickname arose from the fact that he inherited three magical arrows from his grandfather Ketill. The singular arrow of the epithet "Arrow-Oddr" shows that in the course of time the story must have altered somewhat.

The most famous of his Viking adventures is the fight on the isle of Sámsey (Samsø, in Denmark), together with his blood-brother Hjálmarr, against a Viking band of twelve brothers. This episode is thought to be one of the oldest parts of the story. A variant appears in *Hervarar saga* and in Saxo, who also relates some other confused reminiscences of Oddr. These passages show that at one time Oddr must have been popular in the North, and that he did not originally belong to the family of Ketill hœngr, but because of his prestige was at some later point adopted into it.

The saga includes the glaring anachronism of Oddr's being a Christian during the heathen period in Scandinavia. His baptism is followed by two curious meetings with Óðinn, one of which occurs in all versions, the other only in the youngest. In both versions, Óðinn helps Oddr fight and overcome a supernatural opponent; Óðinn gives him some magical arrows, stronger than the arrows of the king of the Finns (older story), and makes him enter into blood-brotherhip with the other Vikings (younger story). One might interpret these as initiation stories, showing Oddr entering into the service of Óðinn.

But what about Oddr's baptism? The author might wish to regard him as a Christian Viking, but this identification clashes with the appearance of Óðinn. In his fight against monstrous adversaries, Oddr calls himself the inveterate enemy of both Óðinn and Freyr. We are apparently meant to think that Oddr fights against Óðinn with the help of Óðinn.

The story must be relatively young, and is usually dated from the end of the 13th or even the beginning of the 14th century.

A great number of vellum MSS and paper copies testify to the popularity of its hero. The oldest one, Stock. Perg. 4to no. 7 (S; beginning of the 14th century), lacks the episode on Sámsey. Next comes AM 344a 4to (M; second half of the 14th century), from which the paper copy AM 1793 4to derives. The 15th-century MSS AM 343 4to (A) and AM 471 4to (B) are closely related. In both of them, we find *Qrvar-Odds saga* preceded by *Ketils saga hœngs* and *Gríms saga loðinkinna*. The younger Óðinn story is preserved only in these two MSS. From A, six paper copies are derived, and from B, one paper copy with some of its poetry. M occupies an intermediary position between S and AB. The vellum fragment AM 567 4to (C) dates from the 15th century. A group of paper MSS, the best of which is AM 173 fol. (E), is assumed to have been copied from a lost MS related to AB.

Ed.: Boer, Richard Constant, ed. *Qrvar-Odds saga*. Leiden: Brill, 1888; Boer, R. C., ed. *Qrvar-Odds saga*. Altnordische Saga-Bibliothek, 2. Halle: Niemeyer, 1892; Guðni Jónsson, ed. *Fornaldar sögur Norðurlanda*. 4 vols. Akureyri: Íslendingasagnaútgáfan, 1954, vol. 2, pp. 199–363. **Tr.**: Edwards, Paul, and Hermann Pálsson, trans. *Arrow-Odd: A Medieval Novel*. New York: New York University Press; London: University of London Press, 1970; rpt. in *Seven Viking Romances*. Harmondsworth: Penguin, 1985, pp. 25–137. **Lit.**: Boer, R. C. "Über die Qrvar-Odds saga." *Arkiv för nordisk filologi* 8 (1892), 97–139; Boer, R. C. "Weiteres zur Qrvar-Odds saga." *Arkiv för nordisk filologi* 8 (1892), 246–55; Kroesen, Riti. "On the Christianization of Two Initiatory Patterns in the Qrvar-Odds Saga." *The Sixth International Saga Conference 28/7–2/8 1985. Workshop Papers*. 2 vols. Copenhagen: Det arnamagnæanske Institut, 1985, vol. 2, pp. 645–59 [photocopies of papers distributed to participants].

Riti Kroesen

[**See also**: *Fornaldarsögur*; *Gríms saga loðinkinna*; *Hervarar saga ok Heiðreks konungs*; *Ketils saga hœngs*]

INDEX

Entries are arranged alphabetically as follows: a, b, c, d, ð, e, f, g, h, i, j, k, l, m, n, o, p, q, r, s, t, þ, u, ü, v, w, x, y, z, ã, æ, ö, ø, œ, ǫ, å. Page numbers for principal entries are in boldface type.

Fjolnir, 139
Fjolsvinnsmál. See Svipdagsmál
Flateyjarannáll, 15, 198
Flateyjarbók, 21, 45, 48, 75, 105, 160,
175, 184, **197–198**, 207, 216,
222, 225, 240, 260, 262, 263, 267,
276, 278, 280, 282, 305, 306, 307,
309, 331, 340, 343, 364, 401, 419,
424, 435, 443, 449, 456, 592, 599,
613, 628, 638, 668, 671, 677, 678,
689, 704, 709
Flaxengate, 197
Fljótsdœla saga, **198–199**, 251, 334
Flóamanna saga, **199–200**, 334, 689, 690
Floire et Blancheflor, 173, 200, 498, 531,
532
Florence of Worcester, 278
Flores och Blanzeflor. See Eufemiavisorna
Flóres saga konungs ok sona hans, **200**,
529
Flóres saga ok Blankiflúr, **200–201**, 528,
531, 532, 533, 585
Flóvents saga Frakkakonungs, **201–202**,
402, 528, 531, 693
Folklore, **202–205**
Fólkvangr, 721
Food. *See* Diet and nutrition
Foreign influence on Old Norse–Icelandic
literature. *See* Old Norse–Icelandic
literature, foreign influence on
Formáli. See Sturlunga saga
Fornafn, **205–206**
Fornaldarsögur, 52, **206–208**, 398, 561
Forni annáll (Annales vetustissimi), 15
*Fornsvenska legendariet. See Old Swedish
Legendary*
Forseti, 27
Fortification, **209–216**
Fortresses, Trelleborg, 216
Fóstbrœðra saga, 198, **216–219**, 240, 263,
271, 272, 335, 368, 426, 588, 589
Fourth Grammatical Treatise, 55, 235, 237
Frá dauða Sinfjotla, 723
Frá Sigurði. See Reginsmál and *Fáfnismal*
Fragmentary Annals, 435
France, Norse in, **219–220**
Francis, St., 410
Franks Casket, 450, 546, 712, 713
Fredebern, Johan, 82
Frederick II (emperor), 260, 454
Frederik I (king), 88, 112, 384, 417
Frederik III (king), 197
Frederick Barbarossa (emperor), 108, 568,
686, 690
"Freedom Letter," 631
Freeprose theory. *See* Bookprose/freeprose
theory
Freyja, 150, 151, 309, 394, 424, 425, 503,
522, 558, 638, 672, 678, 721, 722.
See also Freyr and Freyja
Freyr, 56, 151, 301, 353, 394, 397, 406,
424, 425, 446, 503, 522, 596, 622,

623, 639, 697, 739, 743, 744. *See
also* Freyr and Freyja
Freyr and Freyja, **220–221**
Fridleivus, 625, 626
Fridthjof. See Tegnér, Esaias
Friðleifr, 245
Friðrekr (bishop), 107
Friðþjófs saga ins frœkna, 199, 206, **221**,
452, 529, 675, 693
Frigg, 27, 28, 220, 243, 394, 445, 563,
685, 721
Frihetsvisan, 634
Friis, Otto, 221
Friis, Peder Claussøn, 61, 276, 278, 306
Fríssbók (Codex Frisianus), 55, **221–222**,
260, 276, 420, 664
Frode (Fróði; Frotho) (king), 139, 151,
203, 245, 451
Fróði. See Frode
Frostuþing Law, 88, 257
Frotho. See Frode
Fulford, battle of, 741
Fulgentius of Ruspe, 290
Fundinn Nóregr, 207
Furnishing. *See* Textiles, furnishing
Fylgjur, 624–625
Fylkjatal, 225
Fyrkat, 216, 266
Færeyinga saga, 74, 184, 198, **222**, 277,
364, 448, 449
Förbindelsedikten, 82, 83
Før Skírnis. See Skírnismál

Gadh, Hemming, 635
Galdrabók, 399
Galen, 270, 635
Gallehus Horns, 521
Galterus de Castellione, 7, 147, 271, 304
Alexandreis, 7, 46, 304, 531, 567
Moralium dogma philosophorum, 271
*Gamle Sang, som haffue varit brugt i
Paffuedommet. See Thomesen,
Hans*
Gamleborg, 209
Gamli kanóki, 75, **223–224**
Harmsól, 75, 223, 505
Gamli sáttmáli, 615
*Gammeldansk digt om Christi opstandelse,
Et*, 73, 431
Garðar, 240, 241
Garnier of Rouen, 434
Gaude virgo gratiosa, 75
Gaude virgo, mater Christi, 73
Gaudet mater ecclesia, 422
*Gauks saga Trandilssonar, 426
Gausbert, 17
Gauta þáttr, 224
Gautier de Châtillon. *See* Galterus de
Castellione
Gautr Jónsson, 595
Gautreks saga, 139, 202, 203, 206, **224–
225**, 369, 444, 523

Gefjon, 55, 394, 721
Geirarðs þáttr, 402
*Geirmundar þáttr heljarskinns. See
Sturlunga saga*
Geirrøðr, 243, 423, 425
Geisli. See Einarr Skúlason
Gentilis de Cingulo, 410
Geoffrey of Monmouth
Historia regum Britanniae, 57, 58 165,
166, 271, 412, 413, 556, 567, 597
Prophetiae Merlini, 57, 244, 412
Geographical literature, **225**
George, St., 321, 322, 325, 527
Gerðr, 151, 220, 397, 406, 424, 425, 596,
622
Gereon, St., 525
Gerlandus, 111
German Hansa. *See* Hanseatic League
Germania. See Tacitus
Germany, Norse in, **225–226**
Gerpla. See Halldór Laxness
Gerson, Jean, 77
*Gesta Cnutonis regis. See Encomium
Emmae*
Gesta Danorum. See Saxo Grammaticus
*Gesta Hammaburgensis ecclesiae
pontificum. See Adam of Bremen*
*Gesta Normannorum ducum. See William
of Jumièges*
Gesta Pilati. See Nicodemus, Gospel of
*Gesta regum Anglorum. See William of
Malmesbury*
Gesta Romanorum, 173, 402, 701
Gesta salvatoris. See Nicodemus, Gospel of
*Gesta Swenomagni regis et filiorum eius et
passio gloriosissimi Canuti regis et
martyris. See Ælnoth*
Getica. See Jordanes
Gibbons saga, **226–227**, 453, 526, 529,
530, 583, 585, 701
Giraldus Cambrensis
Itinerary Through Wales, 285
Gisike (bishop), 525
Gísl Illugason, 105, 591
Gísla saga Súrssonar, 143, 203, **227–228**,
242, 289, 335, 337, 369, 460, 690
Gísli Jónsson, 421
*Gísls saga Illugasonar, 345
Gísls þáttr Illugasonar, **228**, 306
Gizurr Bjarnarson, 356
Gizurr gullbrárskáld, 588
Gizurr Hallsson, 340, 496, 690
Gizurr inn hvíti Teitsson, 107, 314, 315,
331
Gizurr Ísleifsson (bishop), 45, 46, 107,
307, 316, 332, 385, 496
Gizurr Þorvaldsson, 317, 603, 613, 615,
617
Gjafa-Refs þáttr, 207, 224, 369
Gjallarbrú, 142
Gjúki, 151, 244, 281, 420, 586, 707, 709,
711, 722

Horn carving. *See* Carving: bone, horn, and
  walrus tusk
Horologium sapientie. *See* Budde, Jöns:
  Gudeliga snilles väckare
Hortus deliciarum. *See* Herrad of Landberg
Hospitallers of St. John, 85, 86, 416, 417
Houses, **292–301**
Hovedstykket, 538
Hrabanus Maurus
  De rerum naturis, 165, 166
Hrafn Oddsson, 317
Hrafn Sveinbjarnarson, 48, 411
Hrafn Onundarson, 251, 588
Hrafnistumanna sögur, 353. *See also Áns
  saga bogsveigis; Gríms saga
  loðinkinna; Ketils saga hœngs;
  Orvar-Odds saga*
Hrafnkels saga Freysgoða, 56, 198, 199,
  220, **301**, 309, 530, 689
*Hrafns saga Sveinbjarnarsonar. See
  Sturlunga saga*
Hrafns þáttr Guðrúnarsonar, **302**, 306
Hrafnsmál. See Þorbjǫrn hornklofi:
  Haraldskvæði
Hrafnsmál. See Þormóðr Trefilsson
Hrappr (son of Bjǫrn buna Veðrar-
  Grímsson), 681
Hreiðars þáttr heimska, **302**, 661
Hreiðmarr, 520
Hringmaraheiðr (Ringmere Heath), battle
  of, 391
Hringr (king), 610
Hrings saga ok Tryggva, **302–303**, 528,
  529
*Hrímgerðarmál. See Helgakviða
  Hjǫrvarðssonar*
Hrísateigr, battle of, 691
Hrokkinskinna. See Hulda-Hrokkinskinna
*Hróks saga svarta, 207, 262
Hrókskviða, 262
Hrólfr kraki, 206, 304, 597
Hrólfs rímur Gautrekssonar, 303
Hrólfs saga Gautrekssonar, 206, 208, 224,
  303–304, 452, 453, 528, 529,
  530, 584, 625
Hrólfs saga kraka, 7, 37, 46, 47, 203, 206,
  207, 208, **304–305**, 346, 451,
  530, 597, 658
*Hrómundar saga Gripssonar, 208, 305,
  398
Hrómundar saga Gripssonar, 206, 207,
  254, **305**, 624
Hrómundar þáttr halta, **305–306**
Hrungnir, 423, 425, 691, 697
*Hryggjarstykki. See Eiríkr Oddsson
Hrynhenda. See Arnórr Þórðarson
  jarlaskáld
Hudson Bay, 13
Hugh of St. Victor
  De arrha animæ, 271
Huginn, 279, 445
Hugsvinnsmál, 272, **306**, 497, 607
Huguccio of Pisa, 128

Huitfeldt, Arild
  Danmarckis Rigis Krønike, 420
Hulda. See Hulda-Hrokkinskinna
Hulda-Hrokkinskinna, 21, 56, 199, 228,
  249, 262, 278, 282, 302, **306–
  307**, 365, 420, 443, 588, 599,
  613, 661, 664, 670–671, 677, 678
*Huldar saga, 207
Humle, 84
Hungrvaka, 45, 46, 107, **307**, 385, 496,
  636, 671
Hunting, **307–308**. *See also* Fishing,
  whaling, and seal hunting
Huon de Bordeaux, 54
Húsdrápa. See Úlfr Uggason
*Húskarlahvǫt. See *Bjarkamál in fornu
Hürnen Seyfrid, Der. See Sachs, Hans
Hvamm-Sturla (Þórðarson), 316, 616, 617
Hven Chronicle, 709
Hversu Nóregr byggðisk, 207
Hymir, 150, 308
Hymiskviða, 152, **308–309**, 395, 424, 672,
  678
Hyndla, 309, 721
Hyndluljóð, 27, 28, 198, 303, 309, 353,
  395, 522
  Vǫluspá in skamma, 309
Hälsingelagen, 386
Häme, 188, 190, 193
Högom, 58
Høyers annáll, 15
Hœnir, 520
Hœnsa Þóris saga, **309–310**, 689
Hǫðr, 27, 28, 425, 714
Hǫfuðlausn. See Egill Skalla-Grímsson
Hǫfuðlausn. See Óttarr svarti: *Óláfsdrápa
  sœnska*
Hǫfuðlausn. See Þórarinn loftunga
Hǫgni Gjúkason, 23, 24, 55, 151, 152,
  248, 443, 586, 662, 707, 708, 709,
  711
Hǫskuldr Hákonarson, 690
Hákon Borkenskegg, 356
Hákonshallen, 215
Hándfæstning, 129
Hándskriftfortegnelser. See Árni
  Magnússon

Ibn al-Qūṭīya, 18
Ibn Diḥya, 18
Ibn Faḍlān, 18, 557
Ibn Khaldūn, 18
Ibn Khurradādhbih, 18
Ibn Miskawayh, 18
Ibn Rusta, 18
Ibrāhīm ibn Ya'qūb aṭ-Ṭurṭūshī, 18
Iceland, **311–320**
Icelandic Homily Book, 37, 79, 230, 290
Iconography, **320–322**
Iðavǫllr, 150
Iðunn, 394, 423, 672
Igaliko, 240
Iliad. See Homer

Ilias latina, 271, 658
*Illuga saga eldhússgóða, 207
Illuga saga Gríðarfóstra, 206, 208, **322–323**
Illugi Bryndœlaskáld, 697
Imago mundi. See Honorius
  Augustodunensis
Indra, 673
Ing, 220
Ingadrápa. See Einarr Skúlason
Inge the Elder (king), 564
Ingeborg (wife of Philippe Auguste), 621
Ingeborg (sister of Margrethe), 406
Ingeborg (wife of Knud Lavard), 556
Ingeld. *See* Ingellus
Ingellus (Ingeld), 139
Ingemundsson, Ragvald (archdeacon), 380
Ingi I Haraldsson (king), 75, 159
Ingi II Bárðarson (king), 61, 258, 603
Ingi Magnússon (king), 61
Ingibjǫrg Snorradóttir, 602
Ingiborg (queen), 360
Ingierd Gunnarsdotter, 34
Ingigerðr (wife of Jaroslav), 556
Ingimundr Þorgeirsson (priest), 457
Ingjaldr (of Þverá), 690
Ingjaldr Geirmundarson
  Brandsflokkr, 105
Ingólfr Arnarson, 313
Ingrid of Skänninge, St., 417, 564
Ingunar-Freyr, 220. *See also* Freyr
Innocent III (pope), 128, 138
Innsteinskviða, 262
Inntak úr sǫguþætti af Jóni Upplandakóngi,
  119
Institutio principis christiani. See Erasmus,
  Desiderius
Ireland, Norse in, **323–325**
Ironwork, **325–331**
Isagoge. See Porphyry
Isidore of Seville, 110, 111, 366
  De natura rerum, 164
  Etymologiae, 14, 144, 164
Ísleifr Gizurarson (bishop), 45, 107, 307,
  331
Ísleifs þáttr biskups, 45, **331–332**
Íslendinga saga. See Sturla Þórðarson
Íslendingabók. See Ari (fróði) Þorgilsson
*Íslendingadrápa. See Eyvindr Finnsson
  skáldaspillir
Íslendingadrápa. See Haukr Valdísarson
Íslendingasögur, 52, 53, 203, **333–336**,
  561
Íslendings þáttr fróða, 262
Itinerary Through Wales. See Giraldus
  Cambrensis
Íþróttir, **337**
Ivan III, 265
Ivan, Johannes, 465
Ivan Lejonriddaren. See Eufemiavisorna
Ívarr (earl), 581
Ívarr Bárðarson, 95, 225
Ívarr Ingimundarson
  Sigurðarbǫlkr, 105